CANADA

636—6674

D1072688

MINNESOTA

St. Paul
Minneapolis

WISCONSIN

Lake Superior

Lake Huron

Lake Michigan

MICHIGAN

Lansing

Milwaukee
Madison

Detroit

Chicago

Lake Ontario

VERMONT

Mt. Washington
(6,288 ft.; 1,917 m)

Concord NEW HAMPSHIRE

Albany Manchester

Boston MASS.

NEW YORK

Buffalo

Hartford

Providence

RHODE ISLAND

CONNECTICUT

New York

Trenton

PENNSYLVANIA

Cleveland

Pittsburgh

Philadelphia

Harrisburg

NEW JERSEY

IOWA

Des Moines

ux
lls

maha

ncoln

ILLINOIS

Springfield

Indianapolis

INDIANA

Columbus

Cincinnati

OHIO

Wheeling

WEST VIRGINIA

Charleston

Dover

DELAWARE

Baltimore

Annapolis

WASHINGTON, D.C.

MARYLAND

Potomac River

Chesapeake Bay

APPALACHIAN MOUNTAINS

Kansas City

Topeka

Jefferson City

Wichita

MISSOURI

St. Louis

Frankfort

Louisville

KENTUCKY

Cumberland River

Ohio River

Missouri River

Richmond

Norfolk

VIRGINIA

Raleigh

Knoxville

Nashville

TENNESSEE

NORTH CAROLINA

Charlotte

Mt. Mitchell
(6,684 ft.; 2,037 m)

SOUTH CAROLINA

Columbia

Tulsa

OKLAHOMA

Oklahoma City

ARKANSAS

Little Rock

Memphis

Tennessee River

Mississippi River

Red River

Birmingham

Atlanta

Charleston

TIDEWATER

ATLANTIC OCEAN

MISSISSIPPI

ALABAMA

GEORGIA

Dallas
Fort Worth

LOUISIANA

Jackson

Alabama River

Montgomery

Jacksonville

Austin

Baton Rouge

Tallahassee

Houston

New Orleans

Orlando

FLORIDA

Gulf of Mexico

Lake Okeechobee

Miami

BAHAMAS

THE
UNITED STATES
OF AMERICA

Elevation

Feet	Meters
Over 13,001	Over 3,001
6,561-13,000	2,001-3,000
3,281-6,560	1,001-2,000
1,641-3,280	501-1,000
661-1,640	201-500
0-660	0-200
Below sea level	Below sea level

ATLANTIC OCEAN

VIRGIN ISLANDS

San Juan

PUERTO RICO

Caribbean Sea

0   50   100 miles

0   50   100 kilometers

CUBA

THE AMERICAN PROMISE

A HISTORY OF THE UNITED STATES

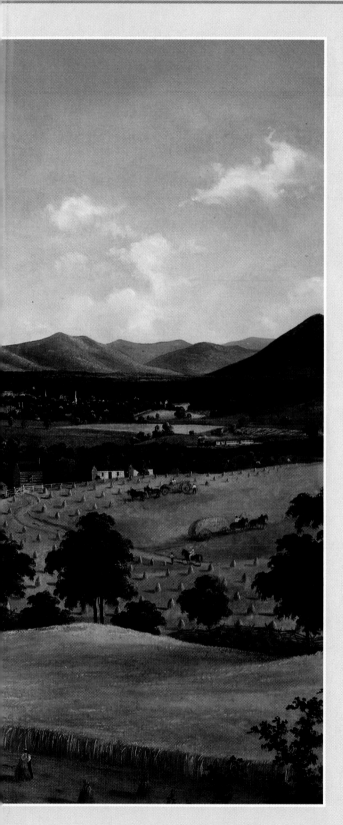

THE AMERICAN PROMISE

A HISTORY OF THE UNITED STATES

JAMES L. ROARK
Emory University

MICHAEL P. JOHNSON
Johns Hopkins University

PATRICIA CLINE COHEN
University of California at Santa Barbara

SARAH STAGE
University of Arizona, West

ALAN LAWSON
Boston College

SUSAN M. HARTMANN
The Ohio State University

BEDFORD BOOKS   Boston

For Bedford Books
President and Publisher: Charles H. Christensen
General Manager and Associate Publisher: Joan E. Feinberg
History Editor: Katherine E. Kurzman
Project Manager: Tina Samaha
Developmental Editors: Louise D. Townsend and Barbara Muller
Editorial Assistant: Thomas Pierce
Managing Editor: Elizabeth M. Schaaf
Production Assistants: Ellen C. Thibault and Deborah A. Baker
Copyeditor: Barbara G. Flanagan
Proofreaders: Mary Lou Wilshaw and Lisa Wehrle
Text Design: Wanda Kossak
Photo Researcher: Pembroke Herbert/Sandi Rygiel, Picture Research Consultants & Archives, Inc.
Cartography: Mapping Specialists Limited
Page Layout: DeNee Reiton Skipper
Indexer: Steve Csipke
Cover Design: Wanda Kossak
Cover Art: New-York State Historical Association, Cooperstown
Composition: York Graphics Services, Inc.
Printing and Binding: R. R. Donnelley & Sons

Library of Congress Catalog Card Number: 97–72376

Copyright © 1998 by Bedford Books
A Division of St. Martin's Press, Inc.

Manufactured in the United States of America.

2 1 0 9 8 7
f e d c b a

For information, write: Bedford Books, 75 Arlington Street, Boston, MA 02116 (617–426–7440)

ISBN: 0-312-09525-2 (hardcover)
ISBN: 0-312-11196-7 (paperback Vol. 1)
ISBN: 0-312-11197-5 (paperback Vol. 2)

Cover art: Trade sign above justice of the peace office, about 1800, Appleton, Ohio. This painted
wooden sculpture shows Liberty, with the sword and scales of justice, giving sustenance to the
American eagle.

BRIEF CONTENTS

CONTENTS

SPECIAL FEATURES

A NOTE FROM THE PUBLISHER
PRESENTING *THE AMERICAN PROMISE*

YOU ARE HOLDING IN YOUR HANDS an innovative new text for the American history survey course. Carefully developed with the needs of students foremost in mind, *The American Promise* deftly wraps the inherently interesting but loose strands of social history around the more formal structure of political history. It is born of two convictions: (1) faced with an overwhelming amount of information, students need help determining what's important and (2) students won't get anything out of a textbook unless it's interesting and enjoyable. The design and art program represents an attempt to rethink the "look" of a textbook, fashioning every element from running-heads to captions to serve a pedagogical function or to further the narrative.

The next few pages offer an overview of the book and introduce its student-focused features. We urge you to take a few minutes to see how we've tried to improve on what has come before us. When you're finished, we hope you'll agree with us that *The American Promise* does more for students than any other survey of American history.

EASY-TO-FOLLOW CHAPTER STRUCTURE

The authors have sought to avoid an encyclopedic approach to American history in favor of building understanding through extensive examination of only the most important events and developments. The architecture of individual chapters is carefully designed to present information in a logical and ordered fashion that emphasizes major themes in history while incorporating individual accounts to maintain students' interest. Common to each chapter is a set of features—vignette, call-outs, conclusion, chronology, and bibliography—that provide useful guides to the narrative.

Opening vignettes

Every chapter begins with an engaging anecdote that eases readers into its major themes while immersing them in a specific historical moment.

(The complete example is found on page 605.)

RECONSTRUCTION, 1863-1877

16

WHEN THE WAR WAS OVER, swarms of northern journalists and government officials rushed to the South to see what four years of fighting had accomplished. Ugly stories of stiff-necked defiance toward Yankees and brutal violence toward ex-slaves had drifted northward. Andrew Johnson, Abraham Lincoln's successor in the White House, asked General Carl Schurz to undertake a special fact-finding tour to assess conditions in the ex-Confederate states. Schurz, a leading antislavery lecturer and Union general, arrived in Charleston, South Carolina, the "Queen City of the South," in July 1865.

Charleston greeted the visitor with an empty harbor, rotting wharves, and gutted buildings. The city looked, Schurz observed, as if it had been struck with "the sudden and irresistible force of a thunderbolt." Cattle grazed in its weed-filled streets. Schurz met former cotton kings and rice barons who could not afford to buy breakfast. Ex-slaves, now Union soldiers, patrolled the city's streets. Schools overflowed with African American children whom it was formerly considered a crime to educate. The Citadel, the state's military school, where once "the chivalric youth of South Carolina was educated for the task of perpetuating slavery by force of arms," now housed the Fifty-fourth Massachusetts Colored Regiment.

Two-tiered running heads

Double bars at the top of every page let students know where they are in the book, and where they are in the chronology of American history.

606 CHAPTER 16 • RECONSTRUCTION

1863-1877

WARTIME RECONSTRUCTION **607**

1863-1877

Call-outs

While northern resolve to defend black freedom withered, southern commitment to white supremacy intensified.

Throughout each chapter, occasional brief passages have been pulled from the main text to highlight important points, focus readers' attention, and convey the liveliness of the narrative.

Conclusions

Each chapter ends with a brief conclusion that summarizes the narrative's main points, analyzes their significance, and discusses their consequences.

(The complete example is found on page 639.)

Conclusion: "A Revolution but Half-Accomplished"

In 1865, when General Carl Schurz visited the South at President Andrew Johnson's behest, he discovered "a revolution but half-accomplished." Defeat had not prepared the South for an easy transition from slavery to free labor, from white racial despotism to equal justice, and from white political monopoly to biracial democracy. The old elite wanted to get "things back as near to slavery as possible," while ex-slaves and whites who had lacked power in the slave regime were eager to exploit the revolutionary implications of defeat and emancipation.

Chronologies

A chronology at the close of each chapter provides a handy review of the most important dates and events.

(For the complete chronology, see pages 640–641.)

CHRONOLOGY

1863	**December.** Lincoln issues Proclamation of Amnesty and Reconstruction.
1864	**July.** Congress offers more stringent plan for reconstruction, Wade-Davis bill.
1865	**January.** General William T. Sherman sets aside land in South Carolina for black settlement.
	March 4. Lincoln sworn in for second term as president of United States.
	March. Congress establishes Freed-

April 14. Lin[c] 15, is succeed[ed] Andrew John[son]
Fall. Souther[n] criminatory [ ]
December. T[ ] ment abolishi[ng] of U.S. Const[ ]
1866 **April.** Congr[ess] Amendment [ ] blacks Ameri[ ]

Bibliographies

Each chapter includes an up-to-date list of recommended works of scholarship. These bibliographies begin with general references for the period with the remainder of the titles organized under subheadings that closely correspond to the chapter's major sections.

(For the complete bibliography, turn to page 641.)

BIBLIOGRAPHY

GENERAL WORKS

W. E. B. Du Bois, *Black Reconstruction in America* (1935).

Eric Foner, *Reconstruction: America's Unfinished Revolution, 1863–1877* (1988).

John Hope Franklin, *Reconstruction after the Civil War* (1961).

James M. McPherson, *Ordeal by Fire: The Civil War and Reconstruction* (1982).

Rembert W. Patrick, *The Reconstruction of the Nation* (1967).

J. G. Randall and David Donald, *The Civil War and Reconstruction* (1967).

WARTIME RECONSTR[UCTION]

Richard H. Abbott, *Th[e]* lican Party and the S[ ]

Herman Belz, *Emancip[ation]* Constitutionalism in [ ]

Ira Berlin et al., eds., [ ] Emancipation, 1861–[ ]

Louis S. Gerteis, *From [ ]* icy toward Southern [ ]

Peyton McCrary, *Abra[ham]* Louisiana Experiment[ ]

STRIKING VISUAL FEATURES

Beautifully designed and illustrated, *The American Promise* is replete with visual elements that expand upon—rather than merely decorate—the narrative. Every image has been chosen for its ability to enhance an understanding of the past.

Comprehensive illustration program with extensive captions

Hundreds of fresh images (many of them published in a survey text for the first time) dramatize and extend the story in the text. Unusually full captions—many of which include quotations, questions, or comparisons with other images—draw readers into active engagement with this visual material.

(This illustration is found on page 87.)

Chapter-opening artifacts

To emphasize the importance of material culture in studying the past, each chapter opens with a full-page reproduction of a contemporary cultural artifact, such as clothing, books, musical instruments, or political emblems. Informative captions provide background information and invite readers to consider the artifact's historical implications.

(For the complete example of a chapter-opening artifact, turn to page 688.)

TOBACCO ADVERTISEMENT
This ad for "Kositzky's Best Virginia" tobacco illustrates a colonial planter and tobacco merchant examining the quality of a sample of leaves from an open cask waiting to be shipped to London, while an onlooker samples the leaves more thoroughly by smoking. To smooth the transaction an Afr...

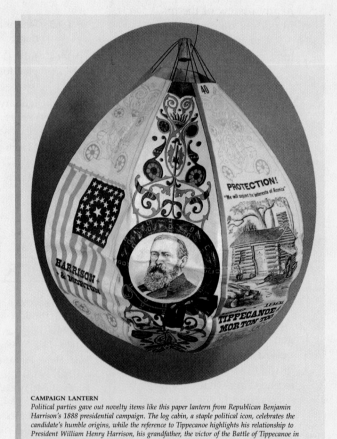

CAMPAIGN LANTERN
Political parties gave out novelty items like this paper lantern from Republican Benjamin Harrison's 1888 presidential campaign. The log cabin, a staple political icon, celebrates the candidate's humble origins, while the reference to Tippecanoe highlights his relationship to President William Henry Harrison, his grandfather, the victor of the Battle of Tippecanoe in 1811. "Protection" in bold letters underscores the Republican Party's perennial support for a ta... ...the country... from foreign co...

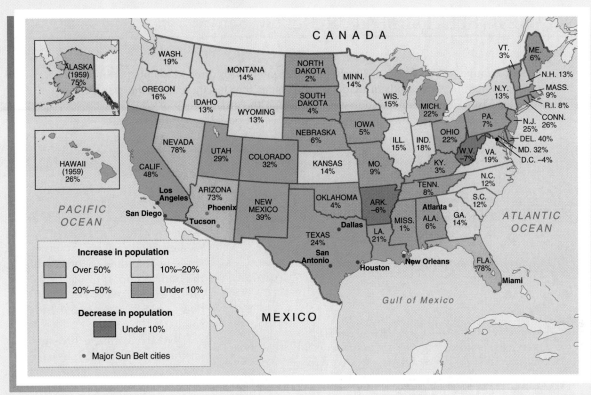

CANADA

WASH. 19%
OREGON 16%
IDAHO 13%
MONTANA 14%
WYOMING 13%
NORTH DAKOTA 2%
SOUTH DAKOTA 4%
MINN. 14%
WIS. 15%
MICH. 22%
VT. 3%
ME. 6%
N.H. 13%
MASS. 9%
R.I. 8%
N.Y. 13%
PA. 7%
CONN. 26%
N.J. 25%
ALASKA (1959) 75%
HAWAII (1959) 26%
NEVADA 78%
UTAH 29%
CALIF. 48%
COLORADO 32%
NEBRASKA 6%
IOWA 5%
ILL. 15%
IND. 18%
OHIO 22%
W.V. -7%
VA. 19%
DEL. 40%
MD. 32%
D.C. -4%
Los Angeles
San Diego
ARIZONA 73%
Phoenix
Tucson
NEW MEXICO 39%
KANSAS 14%
MO. 9%
KY. 3%
N.C. 12%
TENN. 8%
S.C. 12%
OKLAHOMA 4%
ARK. -6%
Dallas
MISS. 1%
ALA. 6%
Atlanta
GA. 14%
TEXAS 24%
San Antonio
LA. 21%
Houston
New Orleans
FLA. 78%
Miami

PACIFIC OCEAN

ATLANTIC OCEAN

Gulf of Mexico

MEXICO

Increase in population
- Over 50%
- 20%–50%
- 10%–20%
- Under 10%

Decrease in population
- Under 10%

• Major Sun Belt cities

The Rise of the Sun Belt, 1940–1960

Extensive map and graphics program

The American Promise includes numerous four-color maps that provide a visual representation of historical data. Attractively designed tables, charts, and graphs throughout the book reinforce and expand on information in the text. An accompanying workbook — available free of charge with copies of the text — provides additional opportunities to expand on themes relating to the historical significance of geography using maps from the textbook.

(This map is found on page 1079; turn to page 567 for this graph.)

Resources of the Union and the Confederacy

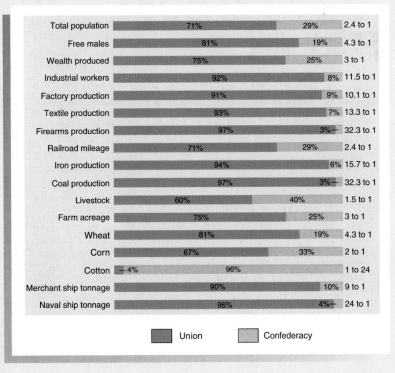

	Union	Confederacy	Ratio
Total population	71%	29%	2.4 to 1
Free males	81%	19%	4.3 to 1
Wealth produced	75%	25%	3 to 1
Industrial workers	92%	8%	11.5 to 1
Factory production	91%	9%	10.1 to 1
Textile production	93%	7%	13.3 to 1
Firearms production	97%	3%	32.3 to 1
Railroad mileage	71%	29%	2.4 to 1
Iron production	94%	6%	15.7 to 1
Coal production	97%	3%	32.3 to 1
Livestock	60%	40%	1.5 to 1
Farm acreage	75%	25%	3 to 1
Wheat	81%	19%	4.3 to 1
Corn	67%	33%	2 to 1
Cotton	4%	96%	1 to 24
Merchant ship tonnage	90%	10%	9 to 1
Naval ship tonnage	96%	4%	24 to 1

■ Union   ■ Confederacy

The narrative in *The American Promise* is augmented with three kinds of special features to highlight the kinds of evidence and issues that fascinate even the casual reader. Providing students a moment to pause in the great sweep of coverage, these documents and mini-essays allow a focus that is not possible within the main narrative.

TEXTS IN HISTORICAL CONTEXT

Japanese Internment

*A*ngrily determined that the bombing of Pearl Harbor would not be followed by more sneak attacks, military and political leaders on the West Coast targeted persons of Japanese descent—alien and citizen alike—as potential saboteurs. Early in 1942, General John DeWitt, commander of the Western Defense Command, persuaded President Franklin Roosevelt to issue an executive order authorizing the removal of the Japanese. Subsequently, some 110,000 Japanese Americans were confined to relocation camps in remote areas, surrounded by barbed wire and armed guards. DeWitt's recommendation expressed concern for military security within racist conceptions long used to curb Asian immigration.

**DOCUMENT 1. Final Recommendations
of the Commanding General,
Western Defense Command and Fourth Army,
Submitted to the Secretary of War**

February 14, 1942

Memorandum for the Secretary of War.

Subject: Evacuation of Japanese and Other Subversive Persons from the Pacific Coast.

1. In presenting a recommendation for the evacuation of Japanese and other subversive persons from the Pacific Coast, the following facts have been considered:

- Mission of the Western Defense Com-

particula

througho

Hosti
enemy ag
vicinity th
sisting er
In the
affinities
race is ar
third gen
possessed
"America
conclude
of white
affinity a
to fight a
against th
It, th
Coast ov
extraction
that thes
action at
no sabota
and conf
taken. . .

*I*mpriso
Japanes
Looking b
her confin

Texts in Historical Context

A variety of primary documents —letters, diaries, speeches, memoirs and testimony—bring students into direct contact with the human impact of major historical events and issues. Headnotes provide background and context.

(For the complete Texts in Historical Context, turn to pages 1000–1001.)

Historical Question

These interpretive essays address specific historical questions likely to be of intrinsic interest to students. Among the topics discussed are: How Could a Vice President Get Away With Murder?, and Why Did the Allies Refuse to Bomb the Death Camps? Historical Questions single out issues of ongoing interest, providing answers in greater detail than possible in the narrative.

(For this complete Historical Question, turn to pages 594–595.)

HISTORICAL QUESTION

Why Did So Many Soldiers Die?

FROM 1861 TO 1865, Americans killed Americans on a scale that had never before been seen. Not until the First World War, a half century later, would the world match (and surpass) the killing fields at Shiloh, Antietam, and Gettysburg. Why were the totals so appallingly large? Why did 260,000 rebel soldiers and 373,000 Union soldiers die in the Civil War?

The balance between the ability to kill and the ability to save lives had tipped disastrously toward death. The sheer size of the armies — some battles involved more than 200,000 soldiers — ensured that battlefields would turn red with blood. Moreover, armies fought with antiquated strategy. In the

casualty l
Confeder
with skir
had no a
the battle
liver ther
ment, w
Union h
somethin
beds." It
compel re
that the S
and South
corps, bu
and nurs
Soldi
portation
As one U
tle than t
the lines.
vanced to
in the da

Technology in America

Recognizing that the impact of technologies is of particular interest and relevance today, these brief (150–300 words) illustrated essays examine the ramifications —positive and negative—of specific technological changes.

(For this complete Technology in America, turn to page 1010.)

TECHNOLOGY IN AMERICA
Penicillin

National Archives.

The antibacterial drug, penicillin, shown being injected into a soldier, did more than any other medical advance to save lives on the battlefield during World War II. ... the culmination of

to fruition just in time to meet the de
need for drugs to fight infection. In
lish biochemist, Alexander Fleming,
discovered that mold left on laborat
plates could kill bacteria. Subsequer
using the organic form of arsenic ex
the mold, which Fleming called pen
highly effective against a wide varie
infections. These experiments succee
just as the Battle of Britain against t
bombing blitz was reaching its clim
lifesaving use of penicillin on woun
later on soldiers in North Africa, a t
researchers rushed to the United St
urge mass production of the drug. 1
came to a dramatic conclusion whe
bor bombing ended a conference on
medicine being held in Honolulu th
the British team was to present its ca
American authorities moved cautio
use of the new wonder drug. By Ap
than 500 men had received penicilli
its astonishingly successful results c
authorities early in 1944 to urge all
nel to use penicillin "without hesita
final tally of the war's damage, dea
tle were half those of World War I,
cause of penicillin, mortality

A three-part appendix serves as a convenient repository of important documents, historical data, and research resources. As with every other part of *The American Promise*, we have endeavored to enhance the usefulness of this critical material in new ways.

Documents

In addition to the complete texts of the Declaration of Independence and the Constitution, this section features unique annotations that provide appropriate background to the twenty-seven constitutional amendments—plus six that didn't make it into the final document.

(The annotated amendments are on pages A-10–A-23.)

Amendment IV

The right of the people to be secure in their persons, houses, papers, and effects, against unreasonable searches and seizures, shall not be violated, and no warrants shall issue but upon probable cause, supported by oath or affirmation, and particularly describing the place to be searched, and the persons or things to be seized.

In the years before the Revolution, the houses, barns, stores, and warehouses of American colonists were ransacked by British authorities under "writs of assistance" or general warrants. The British, thus empowered, searched for seditious material or smuggled goods that could then be used as evidence against colonists who were charged with a crime only after the items were found.

Facts and Figures

This uniquely abundant collection of political, economic, and demographic information supplements the statistical data in the text on everything from population to education. It also includes summaries of twenty-four significant Supreme Court cases.

(For Facts and Figures, see pages A-24–A-26.)

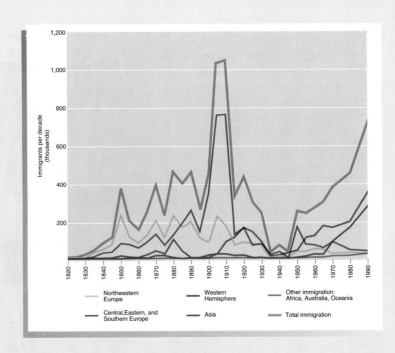

Research Resources in U.S. History

Located on pages A-67–A-69, this annotated list of reference materials and Internet offerings provides a handy starting point for research papers, with extensive suggestions for locating many kinds of primary and secondary sources.

American Memory: Historical Collection from the National Digital Library Program. <http://rs6.loc.gov/amhome.html> An Internet site that features digitized primary source materials from the Library of Congress, among them African American pamphlets, civil war photographs, documents from the Continental Congress and the Constitutional Convention of 1774–1790, materials on woman suffrage, and oral histories.

Directory of Scholarly and Professional Electronic Conferences. <http://n2h2.com/KOVAKS/>. A good place to find out what electronic conversations are going on in a scholarly discipline. Includes a good search facility and instructions on how to connect to e-mail discussion lists, newsgroups, and interactive chat sites with academic content. Once identified, these conferences are good places to raise ques-

User-friendly Index

Knowing that students use indexes primarily as study aids, the index in *The American Promise* is designed to make people, events, topics, and concepts as easy to locate as possible. Page numbers for a topic's main coverage are indicated in boldface; entries for significant people and events include dates; listings of important images, maps, and graphics are provided; and cross-references highlight related subjects.

NOTE TO INSTRUCTORS

The American Promise is accompanied by an unusually full complement of ancillaries. Available for student purchase are a documents reader, a study guide, and titles from the Bedford Series in History and Culture. For teachers, we offer an instructor's manual, a testbank, a guide for teaching assistants, and a large transparency set that includes images not found in the text and a guide with teaching suggestions. Also available to be packaged free with the textbook is a two-volume map workbook with exercises based on maps drawn from every chapter in the text. For complete descriptions of each of these ancillaries, please refer to the Preface for Instructors.

PREFACE FOR INSTRUCTORS

WE SET OUT TO WRITE *The American Promise* because, as longtime teachers of the survey course, we felt that other texts simply didn't reflect what works in our classrooms. Most survey texts emphasize either a social or a political approach to history; by focusing on one, they inevitably slight the other. In our classrooms, students need *both* the structure a political narrative provides and the insights gained from examining social and cultural experiences. In our view, the story of politics is an account not merely of parties and presidents but also of the public arena in which issues of power, interest, culture, ideology, and identity are contested. In our effort to write a comprehensive account of American history, we have focused on the public arena—as the place where politics comes together with social and cultural events—to show how Americans lived within their political culture and confronted the major issues of their times.

We have worked to keep our writing clear, direct, and interesting, never losing sight of our obligation to engage our readers and offer them guidance. Because students in the introductory course often complain that they have difficulty figuring out what they need to know and why they need to know it, we deliberately avoided unnecessary detail so that we could offer more fully developed discussions of the major political, social, cultural, and economic changes that students should understand and remember when they've completed the course.

In our view, history is the story of human agency. To show students that history was made by *people*, we have included the voices of contemporaries who confronted the issues and events of their day. Every chapter includes numerous quotations from the famous and forgotten, taken from their journals, speeches, and letters. Vignettes open every chapter, spotlighting individuals like Benjamin Franklin, Frederick Douglass, and Jane Addams who worked for change in their day and whose efforts still affect our lives. More than a dozen document features demonstrate the impact of major historical events on individuals.

The American Promise also aims to demonstrate that history is both a body of knowledge and an ongoing process of investigation. Too many beginning students believe that historians simply gather facts and string them together into a chronological narrative: that what historians write, students must memorize. To show that the story of history is a reflection of questions historians consciously pose of the past, recurring interpretive essays illustrate how contemporary curiosity shapes historical inquiry and introduce students to a more textured understanding of the discipline.

Features

The narrative in *The American Promise* is buttressed by a number of features that address the concerns most frequently voiced by teachers: that students often find history boring and difficult. Every feature has been conceived and developed with one of these two elemental problems in mind.

We have tried to make American history as accessible as possible for students. In addition to stressing the most important historical developments, each chapter is clearly structured to reinforce the essential people, events, and themes of the period. Innovative **call-outs**—attention-grabbing passages pulled from the main narrative and set in larger type—help students focus. At the close of each chapter, **conclusions** summarize the main themes and events and provide a bridge to upcoming material, **chronologies** provide a handy review of significant events and dates, and extensive **bibliographies** provide an up-to-date listing of recommended works of scholarship for additional reading and research.

Because students learn more when they're interested in the subject matter, we've made a special effort to incorporate features that bring American history to life. **Chapter-opening vignettes** invite students into the narrative with a compelling account of a person or event that embodies some of the chapter's main themes. **Historical Questions** pose and investigate specific questions of continuing interest to demonstrate to students the depth and variety of possible answers. **Texts in Historical Context** reprint primary documents that illustrate the social impact of major events and issues, and **Technology in America** highlights the ramifications that new inventions and processes—most of which we now take for granted—had when they were introduced.

Finally, we are especially proud of our art program. The publisher has provided **an impressive collection of illustrations**—many of them never published before in a survey text—that supplement the narrative, drawing students in and encouraging them to engage the visual material. Rather than leave students to make what they can from these illustrations, we offer a lot of guidance. **Comprehensive captions** unpack the layers of meaning in the pictures, supplement the information in the chapter, raise questions that challenge students to use their historical imaginations, and help students view the images analytically.

Our title, *The American Promise*, reflects our conviction that American history is an unfinished story. From the beginning, Americans have differed profoundly over the meaning of the nation's promise. Yet few doubted that unusual opportunities beckoned in America. In many ways, these potential opportunities intensified conflict over the direction of change, as Americans sought to realize a measure of the promise they sensed around them. For millions, the nation held out the promise of a better life, unfettered worship, representative government, democratic politics, and other freedoms seldom found elsewhere on the globe. But none of these promises came with guarantees. And promises fulfilled for some meant promises denied to others. As we see it, much of American history is a continuing struggle over the definition and realization of the nation's promise. Abraham Lincoln, in the midst of what he termed the "fiery trial" of the Civil War, pronounced the nation "the last best hope of Earth." That hope, kept alive by countless sacrifices, has been marred by compromises, disappointments, and denials, but it lives still. Ideally, *The American Promise* will help students become aware of the legacy of hope bequeathed to them by previous generations of Americans stretching back nearly four centuries, a legacy that is theirs to preserve and to build upon.

Supplements

A comprehensive collection of supplements, every one of them created specifically to accompany *The American Promise*, provides an integrated support system for classroom success. All of the expected el-

ements are included, but in every case we have tried to raise the bar a notch higher, adding new features to help instructors teach and students learn American history. We've also provided some new items: a guide for teaching assistants, an unusually full set of transparencies accompanied by teaching suggestions, and a map workbook that provides in-depth exercises on maps in the text.

For Students

Reading the American Past: Selected Historical Documents. This affordable two-volume collection of primary sources—selected and edited by Michael P. Johnson (Johns Hopkins University) specifically to accompany *The American Promise*—permits students to go beyond the textbook narrative and puzzle out the meanings of historical documents. Paralleling the organization of the text, each chapter includes substantial passages from several documents—including presidential speeches, court records, estate inventories, private diaries, personal letters, and oral histories. Each document is introduced by a brief headnote and followed by questions that help students understand both what the document says and what its historical significance is.

Making the Most of THE AMERICAN PROMISE: A Study Guide. This essential supplement for students, prepared by John Moretta and David Wilcox (both of Houston Community College), provides practice opportunities to reinforce the main themes and ideas from the text's narrative. For each chapter in *The American Promise*, a corresponding chapter in the study guide includes learning objectives, a brief summary, a timeline with questions on important dates, a glossary of terms, map exercises with location and analysis questions, multiple-choice questions, and essay questions. An answer key allows students to test themselves.

Mapping THE AMERICAN PROMISE: Historical Geography Workbook. Prepared by Mark Newman (University of Illinois, Chicago), this stand-alone supplement provides additional exercises using maps drawn from *The American Promise*. Because a knowledge of geography is crucial to understanding the way our country has grown over five hundred years, we make this supplement available to students free with the purchase of the text. Each exercise asks students to label landmarks on the American continent and then analyze the significance of geography in the unfolding of historical events.

Working to suggest the implications of geography for history, these exercises also reinforce basic place names in a way that helps students remember them and understand why they should.

The Bedford Series in History and Culture. Any of the volumes from this highly acclaimed series of brief, inexpensive, document-based supplements can be packaged with *The American Promise* at a reduced price. More than forty titles include *The Sovereignty and Goodness of God, The Interesting Narrative of the Life of Olaudah Equiano, The Autobiography of Benjamin Franklin, Narrative of the Life of Frederick Douglass, The Souls of Black Folk, Plunkitt of Tammany Hall,* and many more.

For Instructors

Teaching THE AMERICAN PROMISE: A Hands-On Guide for Instructors. Written by Michael Gagnon (Emory University) and Sarah E. Gardner (Mercer University), this practical two-volume guide provides myriad suggestions and resources for teaching *The American Promise.* Each of its thirty-two chapters includes an outline (in the form of questions) of the text's narrative, three lecture strategies, multiple-choice questions, a list of video and film resources, and suggestions for incorporating sources from *READING THE AMERICAN PAST* or from the Bedford Series in History and Culture. A particularly useful new feature for first-time teachers anticipates some of the most common misconceptions undergraduates have about each chapter's topics.

Testbank to Accompany THE AMERICAN PROMISE. Written by two longtime teachers of the American history survey, John Moretta and David Wilcox (both of Houston Community College), this set provides 70–80 multiple-choice, true/false, short-answer, identification, and essay questions for each of the thirty-two chapters in *The American Promise.* The testbank is available either on disk (Macintosh and Windows), with a function that allows users to customize the exams, or in booklet form.

Discussing THE AMERICAN PROMISE: A Survival Guide for First-Time Teaching Assistants. Tied directly to *The American Promise,* this unique resource provides a wealth of practical suggestions to help first-time teaching assistants develop their skills and succeed in the classroom. Written by experienced TA adviser Michael A. Bellesiles (Emory University), this brief supplement offers concrete advice on teaching from *The American Promise,* working with professors, dealing with difficult students, running discussion sections, designing assignments, grading tests and papers, relating research to classroom experience, overcoming common problems, and more.

Transparencies to Accompany THE AMERICAN PROMISE (with Teaching Suggestions). More than 150 images are available as full-color acetates to adopters of *The American Promise.* For each chapter a set of five transparencies has been assembled to highlight the chapter-opening artifacts, important maps and graphs, and striking illustrations. We have also selected additional illustrations that are not included in the text. To assist teachers in presenting these images, a guide provides background and elaborates on teaching possibilities.

Acknowledgments

We owe a great debt to the community of scholars who took time away from their own teaching and research to help us complete *The American Promise*. Many people have read chapters and offered valuable criticism; others have listened patiently and provided important advice. The authors would like to express their gratitude to:

Katherine G. Aiken, University of Idaho
Todd Beekley
Kathleen Christine Berkeley, University of North Carolina—Wilmington
John C. Burnham, The Ohio State University
Vernon Burton, University of Illinois, Urbana
Victoria Byerly
Victor Chen
Peter Coclanis, University of North Carolina at Chapel Hill
Joseph Cugini
Leonard Dinnerstein, University of Arizona, Tucson
Laura F. Edwards, University of South Florida
Joseph J. Ellis, Mount Holyoke College
Lancelot Farrar
Elizabeth Feder, Rhodes College
Dan Feller, University of New Mexico
Alan Gallay, Western Washington University
Mark Gelfand, Boston College
William Graebner, State University of New York, Buffalo at Fredonia
Michael D. Green, University of Kentucky
Jack Greene, Johns Hopkins University
Thomas Hartshorne, Cleveland State University
Ronald Howard, Mississippi College
George Juergens, Indiana University
Wilma King, Michigan State University
Barbara Loomis, San Francisco State University
George McJimsey, Iowa State University
Melinda McMahon, University of California, Santa Barbara
John Moon, Fitchburg State University
Roger L. Nichols, University of Arizona, Tucson
Donald K. Pickens, University of North Texas
John O. Pohlman
Theda Perdue, University of Kentucky
David Rankin, University of California, Irvine

Herbert Rissler, Indiana State University
Dave Roediger, University of Minnesota
Carole Srole, California State University, Los Angeles
Thomas Terrill, University of South Carolina
Daniel H. Usner, Jr., Cornell University

A project as large and as complex as this requires the talents of many individuals. The authors would like to thank Pembroke Herbert and Sandi Rygiel of Picture Research Consultants, Inc., whose research and imagination are responsible for the fine illustrations. Thanks are also due to Barbara Muller, whose accomplished editing and sage advice improved volume 1 in countless ways, and to Lynne Weiss for her extensive work on the appendix materials. Michael Gagnon of Emory University and Sarah Gardner of Mercer University drew deeply on their own experience to write the Instructor's Manual, and Michael Bellesiles of Emory University turned his talents to the TA guide. John Moretta and David Wilcox of Houston Community College combined their skills to produce the study guide and testbank. Mark Newman of the University of Illinois at Chicago developed the very useful map workbook. Thanks also to Gerry McCauley, who represents us as literary agent.

Finally, we would like to thank the many people at Bedford Books who have been crucial to this project. We are grateful to Katherine Kurzman and to Ellen Kuhl for their tireless efforts marketing the book, and to Charisse Kiino, who worked on the ancillary program. No one has carried more of the burden than our editor, Louise Townsend. Her skill, composure, and endurance brought the project from an incomplete draft to a finished work. With great skill and professionalism, Tina Samaha, our project manager, pulled all the pieces together. She kept her head when the rest of us were in danger of losing ours. Managing Editor Elizabeth Schaaf oversaw production of the book, while Ellen Thibault, Deborah Baker, and Thomas Pierce helped out on myriad editorial tasks. Copyeditor Barbara Flanagan's sharp eye improved our best efforts and made the entire book better. Charles Christensen, publisher, and Joan Feinberg, general manager, have taken a personal interest in this project from the first and have guided it through every stage of development.

THE
AMERICAN
PROMISE

A HISTORY OF THE UNITED STATES

SALADO RITUAL FIGURES

*About 1350 — more than a century before Columbus arrived in the New World — these fig-
ures were carefully wrapped in the reed mat (shown in the back, on the right) and stored in a
cave in a mountainous region of New Mexico by people of the Salado culture, descendants of
the Mimbres, who had flourished three centuries earlier. Presumably used for sacred rituals,
the effigies suggest the place of humans in the cosmos, where snakes inhabit the subterranean
world, mountain lions roam the earth, and birds soar across the sky. The haunting human figures display the high artistry of ancient Americans. Adorned with vivid pigments, cotton
string, bright feathers, and stones, the effigies hint at the objects the Salado and other ancient
Americans used and valued in their daily lives.*

The Art Institute of Chicago.

ANCIENT AMERICA
Before 1492

1

GEORGE MCJUNKIN WAS AN AFRICAN AMERICAN COWBOY who worked on a ranch near Folsom, New Mexico. Born a slave in Texas in 1851, McJunkin grew up around cowboys. The name and identity of his mother are unknown, although she must have been a slave. His father was a free black man who worked as a blacksmith; his white customers called him Shoeboy because he shoed their horses, but his real name is unknown. The younger McJunkin learned to ride wild horses as a boy and soon after he obtained his freedom in 1865 at the end of the Civil War, he worked at ranches in Colorado and New Mexico. In 1891, he became manager of the Crowfoot Ranch outside Folsom.

In August 1908, a violent storm ripped through Folsom and the surrounding countryside, causing a devastating flood. After the flood subsided, McJunkin rode out to mend fences and to look for cattle that had been killed or injured. As he rode along he noticed that the floodwaters had gouged a dry gulch named Wild Horse Arroyo eight or nine feet deeper than he had ever seen it. As he glanced around for signs of missing cattle, he noticed a deposit of stark white bones in the bank of the arroyo, about ten feet below the surface. Curious, he dismounted and chipped away at the deposit with heavy wire cutters. He continued to scrape until he had exposed an entire fossilized bone. McJunkin had seen the parched skeletons of many range cattle and buffalo in his day, but this bone fossil was far larger than those. He strapped the fossil to his saddle and took it back to his room at the ranch.

Over the next few years, McJunkin kept an eye on what he called the "Bone Pit" in Wild Horse Arroyo. He showed the huge bone he had excavated to his cowboy friends, but they had little interest in strange fossils. In 1912, McJunkin met Carl Schwachheim, a white blacksmith in Raton, New Mexico, who shared his curiosity about fossils. McJunkin told Schwachheim about the Bone Pit, but since Schwachheim had little free time and neither a horse nor a car, he could not get out to the Crowfoot Ranch to take a look for himself. When McJunkin died in 1922, Schwachheim had not yet seen the Bone Pit. A few months after McJunkin's death, Schwachheim organized an expedition to the Bone Pit. With some friends, one of whom had a car, Schwachheim went out to Wild Horse Arroyo, dug out enough bones to fill a gunnysack, and brought them back to Raton, where he and his friends examined them and argued about them. But they could not identify the animals the bones had come from.

Four years later, Schwachheim had a job delivering some cattle to the stockyards in Denver, and he carried along some of the old bones. He took them to the Denver Museum of Natural History and showed them to J. D. Figgins, a paleontologist who was an expert on fossils of ancient animals. Figgins immediately recognized the significance of the bones and a few months later began an excavation of the Folsom Bone Pit. He then hired Schwachheim to do much of the digging. In

GEORGE MCJUNKIN
This photo of McJunkin was taken a few years after he discovered the Folsom site, but about fifteen years before the significance of his discovery was understood by anyone. He appears here on horseback in his work clothes, as he probably was when he made the discovery. The fossilized bones he discovered belonged to an extinct bison species that was much larger than modern bison; the horns of the ancient animal often spanned six feet, wide enough for McJunkin's horse to have stood sideways, as it appears in the photo, between the tips of the horns.
Eastern New Mexico University, Blackwater Draw Site, Portales, New Mexico 88130.

the course of the excavation, Figgins and his associates revolutionized knowledge about the first Americans.

When Figgins began his dig at the Folsom site, archaeologists (individuals who study the artifacts of prehistoric peoples) believed that Native Americans had arrived relatively recently in the Western Hemisphere, probably no more than three or four thousand years earlier when, the experts assumed, they had crossed the icy waters of the Bering Strait from what is now Russia in small boats. Although plenty of evidence of ancient American civilizations existed in the enormous burial mounds east of the Mississippi and in the pueblos of the Southwest, few Americans saw a connection between these structures and those of contemporary Native Americans. Instead, scholars attributed the ancient ruins to people who had mysteriously vanished long before the appearance of contemporary Indians. Despite the abundant physical evidence of ancient human habitation, a general consensus existed that Indians were recent arrivals in the New World. This conventional wisdom had to be tossed on the aca-

demic trash heap once the Folsom discoveries came to light.

At Folsom, Figgins found the bones of twenty-three giant bison, a species known to have been extinct for at least 10,000 years. McJunkin had been right that these were no ordinary, modern-day buffalo bones. Far more startling were nineteen flint projectile points (Folsom points, they have since been called) associated with the bones, proof that human beings had been alive at the same time as the giant bison. Skeptics claimed that earth slides, water, or some other natural process might have accidentally pushed the man-made flint points into the vicinity of the fossils. But even skeptics were convinced by the discovery of one flint point firmly stuck between two rib bones of a giant bison, just where a Stone Age hunter had plunged it more than 10,000 years earlier. No longer could anyone doubt that human beings had inhabited the New World for at least ten millennia.

Through their curiosity and perseverance, George McJunkin, Carl Schwachheim, and J. D. Figgins rediscovered the first Americans more than four hundred years after Columbus had arrived and thousands of years after the continent was first inhabited by humans. The Folsom discovery sparked other major finds of ancient artifacts, pushing back the date of arrival of the first Americans. The artifacts make clear that 95 percent of human history in America occurred before the arrival of Columbus. Since the 1930s, scholars have tried to piece together this history, making connections between the hunters who killed giant bison with flint points, their descendants who built southwestern pueblos and eastern burial mounds, and *their* descendants among the Native Americans who live throughout the Western Hemisphere today.

Unlike Columbus and the European settlers who followed him after 1492, the first Americans did not leave written accounts of their discovery and settlement of the Western Hemisphere. Their encounters with the New World occurred long before recorded history. No documents preserve their languages or their names. No letters or poems describe their thoughts or emotions. But millions of artifacts survive that document their creativity and artistry. Clever and resourceful archaeologists have tried to reconstruct as much of the history of ancient Americans as can be gleaned from the artifacts. Instead of reading words in documents written by persons in the past—as historians normally do—archaeologists try to decipher the meaning of the ruins, garbage dumps, mummified skeletons, baskets, pots, stone blades, charred bones, and other remains left by prehistoric peoples. The story they have assembled is, of course, incomplete. Mysteries abound. Most artifacts that scholars would like to study rotted away millennia ago. Even the artifacts that have survived the millennia can be interpreted in different ways. Consequently, much of what is known about ancient America remains controversial. Nonetheless, scholars have learned enough about ancient Americans to bring into focus who they were, where they came from, and some of the most important features of their history in the thousands of years that stretched between their arrival in the New World and that moment in 1492 when Columbus stepped ashore on a small island in the Caribbean.

FOLSOM POINT AT WILD HORSE ARROYO
In 1927, paleontologist J.D. Figgins found this spear point (subsequently named a Folsom point) at the site discovered by George McJunkin. Embedded between the fossilized ribs of a bison that had been extinct for ten thousand years, this point proved that ancient Americans had inhabited the hemisphere at least that long. The importance of this find led one paleontologist to hold up several Folsom points and proclaim, "In my hand I hold the answer to the antiquity of man in America." Although he exaggerated (since Folsom was only part of the answer), the Folsom discovery stimulated archaeologists to rethink the history of ancient Americans and to uncover fresh evidence of their many cultures.

The First Americans

Human beings existed elsewhere in the world long before they reached the Western Hemisphere. The first human beings *(Homo erectus)* evolved in Africa about 1.5 million years ago. Modern humans *(Homo sapiens)* appeared later still, within the last 350,000 years. Archaeologists have found fossil remains of these ancient humans in Africa, Europe, and Asia, but not in America. For hundreds of thousands of years after human beings inhabited the rest of the

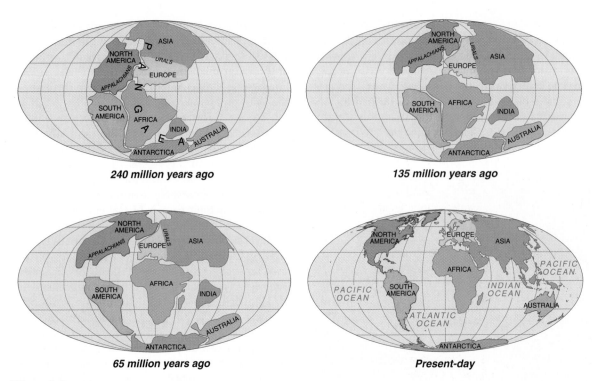

240 million years ago

135 million years ago

65 million years ago

Present-day

MAP 1.1
Continental Drift
Massive geological forces separated North and South America from other continents eons before human beings evolved in Africa in the last 1.5 million years. This continental drift explains why human life developed elsewhere on the planet for hundreds of thousands of years before the first person entered the Western Hemisphere during the last fifteen thousand years.

earth, the New World remained untouched by humankind.

The basic reason for the absence of human life from the Western Hemisphere for such a long time is that millions of years before human beings came into existence the American landmass became detached from Africa, Europe, and Asia. About 240 million years ago, North and South America were attached to Europe, Asia, and Africa in a gigantic continent scientists now call Pangaea. Slowly over the next 150 million years, powerful forces deep within the earth pushed the continents apart to approximately their present positions. This process of continental drift encircled the land of the Western Hemisphere with large oceans and isolated it from the other continents. Over 100 million years after continental drift had disrupted Pangaea, human beings evolved in Africa and eventually migrated throughout Europe and Asia. For almost 95 percent of the time *Homo sapiens* have existed on the face of the globe, no one set foot in America.

Asian Origins

Two major developments made it possible for human beings to migrate to the Western Hemisphere. The first development was humans' successful adaptation to the frigid environment near the Arctic Circle. The second was a change in the earth's climate that reconnected the land of the New World to that of the Old World.

By about 25,000 years ago, humans had learned to use bone needles to sew animal skins into warm clothing similar to that still worn by Eskimos. These snug garments permitted humans to become permanent residents of extremely cold regions like northeastern Siberia. Today the Bering Strait, a body of water about sixty miles wide, separates easternmost Siberia from westernmost Alaska. In the dead of winter the strait freezes, and a person can sometimes make the hazardous journey across the ice. Conditions now, however, are much different than they were when humans first came to America.

We live in a relatively warm period of the earth's climatic history. The last great cold spell—which scientists call the Wisconsin glaciation—endured from about 80,000 years ago to about 10,000 years ago. The colder temperatures during this era meant that snow piled up in glaciers that did not melt and release water back into the sea; the glaciers grew and the sea level dropped as much as 350 feet below its current level. When that happened, the seafloor that is now submerged 120 feet below the surface of the Bering Strait became dry land. It formed what is often called a "land bridge" between Asian Siberia and American Alaska. The word *bridge*, however, is misleading. The exposed land was not a narrow passageway. Instead, it was more like a small continent about a thousand miles wide, roughly the distance from New Orleans to Minneapolis. Scientists refer to it as Beringia.

> *There is abundant evidence that the first Americans were nomadic hunters whose primary source of food was the meat of large mammals that grazed on the tundra in the interior of Beringia. Their Asian origins seem beyond dispute.*

Periodically, Beringia sank beneath the waves when the globe experienced a warm snap for a few thousand years and the glaciers began to melt. But for most of the Wisconsin glacial period, Beringia stood above sea level. Because it received little snow, it had few glaciers. Grasses and small shrubs covered much of the land and supported herds of mammoth, bison, and horses. Smaller animals like seals, birds, and fish could also be found.

Siberian hunters presumably roamed into Beringia for thousands of years in search of game animals, especially mammoths. Some may have hopscotched along the southern coast of Beringia in small boats, establishing settlements and living off fish, waterfowl, and sea mammals until they reached the shores of Alaska, Canada, and the Pacific Northwest. No conclusive evidence has been found of such a seaborne migration of the first Americans. If it occurred, the traces of it have been submerged since the end of the Wisconsin period about 10,000 years ago when glaciers melted and Beringia once again disappeared beneath the sea, where it has remained ever since.

There is abundant evidence, however, that the first Americans were nomadic hunters whose primary source of food was the meat of large mammals that grazed on the tundra in the interior of Beringia. Archaeologists speculate that hunters trekked around Beringia in small bands of perhaps twenty-five people. How many such bands arrived in the New World before water once again covered Beringia will never be known. It may have been as few as one or two or three. When they arrived in the Western Hemisphere is hotly debated by ex-

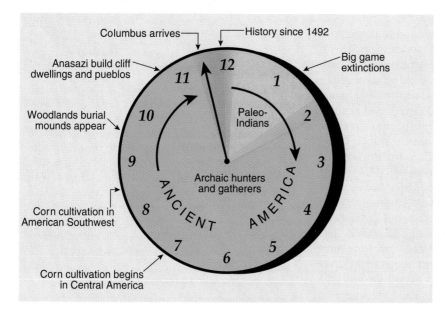

FIGURE **1.1**
Human Habitation of the Western Hemisphere
This clock face illustrates the long history of ancient Americans. If the total period of human life in the New World is converted from millenia to a twelve-hour clock, then all history since Columbus occupies only the last half-hour. Ancient American history makes up the first eleven and a half hours.

perts. It is safe to say that the first migrants arrived sometime after 15,000 years ago. Several tantalizing discoveries hint at earlier dates, but professional archaeologists strongly disagree about how to interpret these finds. None disagree that by 12,000 years ago—and possibly earlier—after human life had existed for hundreds of thousands of years, human beings had finally come to America.

The precise identity of these people can never be known. Archaeologists refer to them and their descendants for the next few millennia as Paleo-Indians. Their Asian origins seem beyond dispute. Siberians hunted large mammals such as mammoths, and Beringia provided a mammoth-hunting ground that reached all the way to the Western Hemisphere, a wide avenue that existed for no other humans at the time. Furthermore, Native Americans today still share certain obvious physical characteristics of Asians, including straight black hair, light brown skin, relatively sparse facial and body hair, and incisor teeth that often have shovel-shaped indentations on their inner surface. Detailed analyses of Native American languages and of certain blood proteins provide additional compelling evidence of Asian origins.

Paleo-Indian Mammoth Hunters

When the first humans arrived in Alaska, massive glaciers covered most of Canada. A narrow corridor not entirely obstructed by ice ran along the eastern side of the Canadian Rockies, and most archaeologists believe that Paleo-Indians filtered through it fairly quickly in pursuit of mammoths. At the southern edge of the massive glaciers, Paleo-Indians entered a hunters' paradise. The enormous territory of North, Central, and South America teemed with wildlife that had never before confronted wily two-legged predators armed with deadly, razor-sharp spears. Presumably, the abundance of big game made hunting relatively easy. Ample food permitted the Paleo-Indian population to grow in numbers, perhaps more rapidly than ever before. Good hunting also allowed Paleo-Indians to diffuse to the outermost limits of the hemisphere with remarkable speed. Within a thousand years, Paleo-Indians had reached the southern tip of South America and virtually everywhere else in the Western Hemisphere.

It may seem unlikely that after human beings had failed to migrate to the New World for hundreds of thousands of years, once they arrived they rushed from coast to coast, top to bottom, within a thousand years. Experts estimate, however, that

even if only one band of twenty-five people crossed Beringia to the Western Hemisphere, their descendants could have numbered about a million within 350 years—an assumption that an abundance of food makes feasible. Since the actual population of Paleo-Indians in the entire hemisphere probably never exceeded one million, a thousand years was plenty of time for descendants of the original migrants to be born in sufficient numbers. Likewise, the descendants did not have to sprint to spread throughout the hemisphere in a millennium; instead, they needed to migrate fewer than twenty miles a year, a speed consistent with the assumption that they moved to maintain contact with animals who had seldom or never seen a hunter.

Paleo-Indians used a distinctively shaped spearhead known as a Clovis point, named for the place in New Mexico where it was first excavated. The discovery of Clovis points throughout North

CLOVIS POINTS
These Clovis points were found in a fossilized mammoth carcass discovered at Naco, Arizona. The large number of points hints that the mammoth may have escaped from its hunters, who then failed to recover their points when the animal died. Although the points are different sizes, note the similarity in shape and workmanship, the telltale characteristics of Clovis points. Contrast these points with the smaller, more finely worked Folsom point (page 5). The size of the Clovis points also suggests the danger Paleo-Indian hunters encountered when they attacked a mammoth, using weapons tipped with these small flakes of stone against an animal almost as big as a modern African elephant.
Arizona State Museum/University of Arizona.

and Central America in sites dated between 11,500 and 11,000 years ago (9500–9000 B.C.) is powerful evidence that these nomadic hunters shared a common ancestry and way of life. Clovis hunters probably staked out a watering hole, watched for an opportunity to isolate a mammoth from a herd, and then attacked it by repeatedly stabbing their spears into the animal. The hunters probably also used a spear-thrower, called an atlatl, to hurl their spears with greater force and over a longer distance. A Clovis point probably was fastened to a tip (called a foreshaft) that detached from the spear shaft inside the animal, so that the hunter could withdraw the spear shaft and reload it with another pointed foreshaft to defend against the wounded animal and inflict another wound. Typically, an excavation of a Clovis mammoth kill uncovers one or two points, suggesting that the hunters worked in small groups of two or three. One mammoth carcass discovered in Arizona, however, has eight Clovis points, suggesting a larger hunting group and—evidently—a very tough mammoth.

The Paleo-Indians who used Clovis points to kill big animals probably also hunted smaller animals, but the artifacts that have survived the millennia indicate that they specialized in big mammals. One mammoth kill, for example, supplied meat for weeks or, if dried, for months. In addition, the hide could be used for clothing and shelter. Bones and tusks could be used to erect a framework for small, hide-covered dwellings, fashioned into a variety of useful tools, or even burned for fuel. Fatty deposits and internal organs that were not eaten could become fuel for cooking or for lamps.

About 11,000 years ago (9000 B.C.) Paleo-Indians confronted a major crisis. The big-game animals they hunted for food became extinct. Throughout the hemisphere, mammoths and other large mammals disappeared, along with certain species that preyed on them, such as saber-toothed tigers. Scientists are not completely certain why the extinction occurred, although the changing environment probably was the trigger. About this time the earth began to warm, the Wisconsin glacial period came to an end, glaciers melted, and sea levels rose. Large mammals became extinct presumably because they had difficulty adapting to the warmer climate. Many archaeologists also believe that Paleo-Indian hunters contributed to the New World extinctions by killing animals more rapidly than they could reproduce.

Paleo-Indians adapted to the extinctions by making at least two important changes in their way of life. First, throughout the hemisphere hunters focused their attention on smaller animals that did not become extinct. Second, Paleo-Indians also devoted more energy to foraging, that is, to collecting wild plant foods such as roots, seeds, nuts, berries, and fruits. When Paleo-Indians made these changes, the apparent uniformity of the mammoth-oriented Clovis culture* was replaced by great cultural diversity. Clovis points disappear from the archaeological record about the time of the extinctions. When hunters had to survive by gathering plant foods and by killing many small animals instead of a few big ones, they adapted to the natural environments throughout the hemisphere. The immense variety of natural settings—from icy tundra to steamy jungles—meant that remarkably diverse cultures came into existence. Compelling evidence of these adaptations to local environments is that after about 11,000 years ago, archaeological artifacts display great variety rather than Clovis-like uniformity.

About 11,000 years ago (9000 B.C.) Paleo-Indians confronted a major crisis. The big-game animals they hunted for food became extinct.

Post-Clovis adaptations to local environments were the origins of the astounding variety of Native American cultures that existed when Columbus arrived in 1492. By then, adaptations that had occurred for more than ten millennia caused tribes to differ from each other in languages, customs, religions, and ways of life. In 1492, more than three hundred major tribes and hundreds of lesser groups inhabited North America alone; hundreds more lived in Central and South America. Tribes spoke different languages, practiced different religions, lived in different dwellings, followed different subsistence strategies, and observed different rules of

---

*The word *culture* is used here as an all-encompassing term that connotes what is commonly called "way of life." It refers not only to how a group of people supplied themselves with food and shelter but also to their family relationships, social groupings, religious ideas, and every other feature of their way of life. In most cases—as for the Clovis people—more is known about food or shelter than other features of prehistoric cultures because of the artifacts that have survived. Ancient Americans' ideas, assumptions, hopes, dreams, and fantasies were undoubtedly important, but we know little or nothing about them.

MAP 1.2
Native North American Cultures
Environmental conditions defined the boundaries of the broad zones of cultural similarity among ancient North Americans. Using the map, try to specify the crucial environmental features that set the boundaries of each cultural region. The topography indicated on Map 1.3, "Native North Americans about 1500," may be helpful.

kinship and inheritance. During the long millennia that stretched between the end of the Wisconsin glacial period and the arrival of Columbus, hundreds of other ancient American cultures disappeared or transformed themselves as their members constantly adapted to changing environmental conditions.

A full account of those changes and the cultural diversity they created is beyond the scope of this introductory textbook of United States history. But we cannot ignore the most important changes and adaptations made by ancient Americans in the centuries between 9000 B.C. (that is, 11,000 years ago) and A.D. 1492. Any such survey necessarily oversimplifies the amazing variety of human experience in ancient America. The absence of written records makes it impossible to identify the individuals or groups responsible for the changes that occurred and makes oversimplification of complex changes unavoidable. Nonetheless, the remarkable human creativity demonstrated by the variety and longevity of ancient American cultures makes it far preferable to oversimplify their history than to overlook it.

Archaic Hunters and Gatherers

Archaeologists use the term *Archaic* to describe the many different hunting and gathering cultures that descended from Paleo-Indians. *Archaic* is a somewhat confusing term because it is used to describe both this great variety of cultures as well as the long period of time when those cultures dominated the history of ancient America, roughly from 8000 B.C. to somewhere between 2000 and 1000 B.C. Neither the cultural nor the chronological boundaries of the Archaic are sharply defined. Great Plains bison hunters, for example, did some foraging, but unlike most other Archaic peoples, they depended primarily on big-game hunting. Bison hunters and other Archaic cultures, especially those west of the Rocky Mountains, continued to thrive long after 1000 B.C. and even long after A.D. 1492. The term *Archaic* is nonetheless useful. It describes the important era in the history of ancient America that followed the Paleo-Indian mammoth hunters and preceded the development of agriculture. It also denotes a hunter-

gatherer way of life that persisted throughout most of North America during these millennia and well into the era of European settlement.

The term Archaic *describes the important era in the history of ancient America that followed the Paleo-Indian mammoth hunters and preceded the development of agriculture.*

Like their Paleo-Indian ancestors, Archaic Indians hunted with spears; but they also took smaller game with traps, nets, and hooks. Unlike Paleo-Indians, most Archaic peoples used a variety of stone tools to prepare food from wild plants; a characteristic Archaic artifact is a grinding stone used to pulverize seeds of wild plants into edible form. Most Archaic Indians migrated from place to place. The availability of plants to harvest appears to have played a larger part in their movements than access to animals to hunt. Migrating with the seasons, they usually did not establish permanent villages, although they often returned to the same river valley or fertile meadow from year to year to take advantage of abundant food resources. In certain regions where resources were especially rich—such as California and the Pacific Northwest—permanent settlements developed. Some Archaic cultures also built large mounds of earth and performed elaborate burial rituals. Many Archaic groups became highly proficient basket makers, but few made pottery. Above all, Archaic folk did not depend on agriculture for food. Instead of growing food crops, they gathered wild plants and hunted wild animals. These general traits of Archaic peoples appeared in various distinctive ways in the major environmental regions of North America.

Great Plains Bison Hunters

Big-game hunting did not end with the extinction of mammoths. Instead, Paleo-Indian hunters began to concentrate on bison. Huge herds of bison survived the post-glaciation extinctions. They grazed the grassy, arid plains that stretched for hundreds of miles east of the Rocky Mountains. For almost a thousand years after 9000 B.C., Paleo-Indians hunted bison with Folsom points (named for the site of the discoveries made by George McJunkin).

BISON KILL SITE
About eighty-five hundred years ago at this kill site near Kit Carson, Colorado, hunters stampeded a bison herd into an arroyo. By carefully studying the jumbled animal bones, archaeologists have been able to reconstruct numerous details about the hunt. Many of the carcasses lay where the animals fell, facing south, suggesting that the wind blew from the south on the day of the hunt, as the hunters stayed downwind and maneuvered the herd toward the arroyo. Cooperation among the hunters was necessary for the stampede and for the subsequent heavy labor of butchering. In all, the hunters butchered about three-fourths of these bison, feasting on bison tongues as they worked. From this hunt they obtained many valuable hides and enough meat to sustain more than one hundred people for at least a month.
Joe Ben Wheat photo, University of Colorado Museum.

Like their predecessors, Folsom hunters were nomads who moved constantly to maintain contact with their prey. Often two or three hunters from a band of several families would single out a few bison from a herd and creep up close enough to spear them. Always the hunters were on foot. The ancient horses that had once existed in the New World were extinct; from 9000 B.C. to after A.D. 1500, bison hunters walked to work. They developed techniques of trapping that made it easier to kill groups of bison. At the original Folsom site, careful study of the bones McJunkin found suggests that early one winter hunters drove bison into the arroyo and speared twenty-three of them. Most likely such kills involved cooperation by hunters from several bands. At many other sites, hunters stampeded large numbers of bison over a cliff, killing some and injuring others, which could then be readily dispatched by waiting hunters. At the well-named Head-Smashed-In site in Alberta, Canada, hunters carefully piled up stone markers to maneuver a bison herd slowly along the five-mile path toward the deadly jump-off point. Deep deposits of bison bones at the base of the Head-Smashed-In cliff demonstrate that hunters returned to the site repeatedly for more than 7,000 years.

Each band of hunters most likely included at least one shaman, who could enter a trance and communicate with the supernatural spirit world. Shamans used their powers to treat the sick, predict events, and aid hunters by appeasing or enticing animal spirits. At one kill site in Colorado, an archaeologist discovered an antler flute and other artifacts near the location of a posthole that may have held a perch for a shaman whose supernatural powers attracted bison to the kill. This interpretation is plausible because 10,000 years later Europeans observed Plains Indian shamans perched on poles and playing flutes to whistle bison toward their deaths.

Bows and arrows reached the Great Plains by A.D. 550 and largely replaced spears, which had been the hunters' weapon for more than 10,000 years. Bows permitted hunters to strike an animal from farther away, and arrows made it easy to shoot repeatedly. Also, arrow points could be crafted from stone that was more readily available than the stones required to make the larger, stronger spear points. These new weapons did not much alter the age-old techniques of bison hunting that had been developing since the Folsom era. The bison-hunting tradition continued on the Great Plains until long after the arrival of Columbus. The bison hunters were perhaps the clearest example of the continuity between the Paleo-Indians who first inhabited the continent and the numerous Native American peoples in A.D. 1492.

Great Basin Cultures

Archaic peoples in the Great Basin between the Rocky Mountains on the east and the Sierra Nevada on the west inhabited a region of great environmental diversity. During wet periods, large marshes and lakes formed in low-lying areas and many Great Basin Indians lived along the shores. Other cultures survived in the foothills of mountains, a zone between the arid, blistering heat on the desert floor and the cold, rocky, treeless mountain heights. These broadly defined zones of habitation changed constantly depending largely on the amount of rainfall. Archaic cultures in the Great Basin had to adapt to the diverse and changeable environment and be prepared for rapid and unpredictable fluctuations in the availability of food.

Much of the information about Great Basin cultures has come from cave sites, particularly in Utah, that have remained extremely dry for thousands of years. The dry conditions preserved numerous fragile artifacts that rotted away in the wetter climates prevailing elsewhere in North America. In addition,

GREAT BASIN DUCK DECOYS
These decoys were crafted about two to three thousand years ago by observant ancient Americans who resided in the Great Basin. Discovered in a cave in the arid environment of west-central Nevada, the decoys show that the ancient Great Basin environment was sometimes marshy. The decoys, skillfully constructed of shoreline plants, were presumably used to attract waterfowl toward hunters hiding among reeds in what amounted to an ancient duck blind.
Courtesy of the National Museum of the American Indian, Smithsonian Institution.

the arid climate of the caves preserved thousands of human coprolites (the dried remains of human feces), from which archaeologists can reconstruct with great accuracy what Great Basin Indians ate.

> *Despite the variety and occasional abundance of animals, plants were the most important source of food for Great Basin Archaic cultures.*

Hunters took deer, antelope, and sometimes bison, as well as smaller game like rabbits, rodents, and snakes. Some cultures used brush fires to drive animals toward a net or into a dead end where they were easily captured. They set traps and snares made from twisted plant fibers for unwary game. At sites near water, Great Basin peoples hunted waterfowl with well-crafted decoys made of reeds. When unsuspecting ducks approached a group of decoys, lurking hunters grabbed their feet underwater or tossed a net over them before they could fly away. These people also ate fish of every available size and type, taking them with bone hooks as well as with nets.

Despite the variety and occasional abundance of animals, plants were the most important source of food for Great Basin Archaic cultures. Unlike animal food, plant food could be collected in large quantities in years of abundance and then stored in baskets for long periods to protect against shortages caused by the fickle rainfall. Baskets for food gathering and storage appear in Great Basin sites well before 7000 B.C. Piñon nuts became a dietary staple for many Great Basin peoples. Great Basin sites typically include grinding stones used to pulverize wild seeds into a coarse flour. By diversifying their food sources and migrating to favorable locations, Great Basin peoples adapted to environmental challenges and maintained their basic hunter-gatherer way of life until long after A.D. 1492.

Pacific Coast Cultures

The distinctive Archaic cultures along the Pacific coast—from southern California to the Pacific Northwest—adapted to an enormously rich marine environment. The abundance of fish, shellfish, and marine mammals such as seals, sea lions, sea otters, and whales supported comparatively large and long-lived settlements.

POTLATCH BOWL AND COPPER
At Northwest coast potlatches, chiefs treated their guests royally. The huge quantities of food were sometimes served in wooden bowls as much as fourteen feet long. This smaller bowl illustrates the elaborate carving that usually decorated the fine objects chiefs displayed at potlatches. To highlight his wealth and prestige, a chief sometimes gave an especially honored guest a copper, a metal engraving more than three feet high that symbolized the chief's eminence and generosity.
Bowl: #3181(3) Courtesy Department of Library Services, American Museum of Natural History; Copper: Royal Ontario Museum, Toronto.

The richness of the California environment made the region the most densely settled in all of ancient North America. The climate permitted agriculture, but the natural environment offered such ample food that California groups remained hunters and gatherers for hundreds of years after A.D. 1492. Although anchored to the Pacific Ocean, California cultures also exploited the diverse inland environments, from the foothills of the mountains to the marshes of the great central valley, from dry canyons in the south to damp forests in the north. The diversity of California's environment encouraged corresponding diversity among the native peoples. By A.D. 1492 the complex mosaic of settlements in California included about five hundred separate tribes speaking some ninety languages, each with many local dialects. No other region of comparable size in North America exhibited such cultural variety.

Near Santa Barbara about 3000 B.C. emerged the origins of what became the Chumash culture, which lasted long after A.D. 1492. Chumash peoples hunted land animals like deer and bears, but they also preyed on sea mammals like seals, usually clubbing them while they were asleep on the shore. Chumash groups built large canoes from wooden planks and used them to fish in coastal waters and to travel along the coast and to offshore islands. They also collected plant foods, especially acorns. Over the millennia, the bounty of food evidently supported a growing population. After about 1000 B.C. the Chumash and other California cultures devoted increasing attention to gathering acorns, probably in response to the growing population and the greater need for food. Stone mortars and pestles used to grind acorns into meal have been found at sites throughout California. Since acorn meal contains toxins, Archaic Californians leached the meal with water and then boiled it to make it safe to eat. Chumash and other California cultures stored and processed acorns in finely crafted baskets rather than in pottery.

The plentiful food resources permitted Chumash peoples to establish relatively permanent villages. At the time of European contact, some villages contained a thousand people living in large dome-shaped dwellings constructed of wooden poles covered by reeds. Typically a large central village headed by a chief was surrounded by several smaller villages subordinate to the chief. After about 2000 B.C. the Chumash developed an elaborate currency system, using beads made from shells as a form of money and a status marker. Conflict frequently broke out among Chumash villages, and skeletons from prehistoric burials document a notable proportion of violent deaths. Archaeologists believe that such conflicts arose in part from efforts by Chumash villages to restrict access to their valuable acorn-gathering territory. Although few other California cultures achieved the population density and cultural complexity of the Chumash, all shared the hunter-gatherer way of life and reliance on acorns as a major source of food.

The richness of the California environment made the region the most densely settled in all of ancient North America.

Another rich natural environment lay along the Pacific Northwest coast from the California border north to Alaska. The abundance of fish and marine life permitted the ancient Americans who lived in that region to devote substantial time and energy to activities other than hunting and gathering. Especially after about 3500 B.C. they concentrated on catching large quantities of salmon, halibut, and other fish, which they dried to last throughout the year. With time free from the demands of food gathering, Northwest peoples developed sophisticated woodworking skills. They fashioned huge canoes, some big enough to hold fifty people, which they used to fish and to hunt sea mammals using artfully crafted bone harpoons. They also employed the canoes to conduct warfare against neighboring tribes. Much of the conflict among Archaic northwesterners seems to have arisen from attempts to defend good fishing sites from incursions by outsiders.

Like the Chumash, the Northwest peoples built more or less permanent villages. They constructed large, multifamily houses from cedar planks. Beginning around A.D. 500 they often adorned their houses with totems, elaborately carved images of animals, supernatural beings, or their own ancestors (it is quite possible that similar carvings were made much earlier but have simply disintegrated in the damp climate). These carvings, some of which Europeans later called "totem poles," honored the lineage of the family clan in a dwelling and displayed the clan's wealth and status. Northwest peoples enjoyed displaying their wealth; but they also liked to give it away. These cultures instituted the potlatch, a ceremony that featured a feast after which the host gave the guests as many fine things as possible. Potlatches served to redistribute wealth from the richest families to those less well off. They also reinforced the hierarchy that ascribed to certain clans the status of nobles and consigned others to lesser, common ranks. Maintaining such social distinctions was probably a principal function of the many artistic carvings that have survived to the present.

Arctic Cultures

In the Arctic environment of most of Alaska and northern Canada, the harsh, bitterly cold climate prohibited gathering plants for almost the entire year. Therefore, from Paleo-Indian times to long after A.D. 1492, Arctic peoples subsisted by hunting. They preyed on caribou that grazed on the short grasses of the Arctic tundra, and they also hunted seals, walruses, whales, and other sea mammals. Arctic hunters concentrated on these animals rather than on fish because fish contained too little of the fat that was necessary in human diets to maintain health in the polar climate. By adapting to the forbidding environment, Archaic cultures in the Arctic differed substantially from those elsewhere in North America.

Descendants of Paleo-Indians probably inhabited Alaska until around 4000 B.C. Sometime before about 2000 B.C. a new group appears to have migrated into Alaska, probably from Siberia. Although the archaeological evidence is sketchy and can be interpreted in conflicting ways, these new migrants were probably the ancestors of the Inuit (or Eskimos), whose culture came to dominate the entire Arctic. Within two or three hundred years, these newcomers had migrated east all the way to the Atlantic coast, hunting as they went. They built winter houses from blocks of hard-packed snow and obtained heat and light by burning seal fat in stone lamps. They also were the earliest ancient Americans to use bows and arrows, which are found in

Archaic Arctic sites dating to roughly 1500 B.C. Apparently they brought bows and arrows with them from Siberia; those weapons did not appear in other North American cultures until about A.D. 500, evidently the result of slow diffusion southward.

About A.D. 1000, Thule people began to spread east from Alaska to the Atlantic coast. They developed especially effective weapons for hunting sea mammals like seals, walruses, and whales far from shore: bone and ivory harpoons combined with skillfully made kayaks constructed of animal hides. Thule folk also developed dogsleds for long-distance travel across snow and ice. These Thule innovations established the basic technology used by their Inuit descendants. Thule people were probably the first ancient Americans to encounter Europeans. At a Thule site on Ellesmere Island in far northeastern Canada, archaeologists have excavated chain mail and other iron objects that demonstrate contact with Vikings who settled Greenland a few years before A.D. 1000.

Eastern Woodlands Cultures

East of the Mississippi River, the climate supported a forest environment dominated in most regions by oak and hickory trees. With the warming trend that followed the Paleo-Indian period, the deciduous forest slowly crept northward, encroaching upon the pine forests that had previously covered the northernmost regions and eventually replacing them. This Eastern Woodlands environment had numerous local variants. Among the most important were in the major river valleys, especially the Mississippi, Ohio, Tennessee, and Cumberland; the Great Lakes region; and along the Atlantic coast. Archaic peoples in these and other locales developed distinctive artifacts that demonstrated the great variety of their adaptations to the Woodlands environment. Underlying that variety, however, were certain basic similarities among all Woodlands cultures.

Deer were the most important prey of nearly all Woodlands hunters. At one Archaic dwelling site in Tennessee dating from 5000 to 3500 B.C., deer accounted for 90 percent of the excavated bones. Woodlands hunters also took bears, turkeys, opossums, raccoons, and smaller animals using spears and spear-throwers like their Archaic counterparts in other regions. If they lived near rivers, lakes, or the sea, they usually fished with bone hooks, nets, or traps and gathered shellfish. But everywhere the

deer that thrived in the Woodlands remained the hunters' primary target. In addition to food, deer supplied hides and bones that were crafted into many useful items such as clothing, weapons, needles, and other tools.

Like Archaic peoples elsewhere, Woodlands Indians gathered edible plants, seeds, and especially nuts. Hickory nuts were the most commonly gathered plant food, but pecans, walnuts, acorns, and hazelnuts were also collected. Stones for grinding nuts appear in Woodlands sites as early as 7500 B.C. and they remained a basic food processing tool until long after A.D. 1492.

Woodlands groups migrated with the seasons to favorable gathering and hunting locations. After about 4000 B.C. the Woodlands climate stabilized and, it appears, some Woodlands peoples established more or less permanent settlements in locations that offered a wide variety of plant and animal resources. These Woodlands settlements were usually near a river or lake and typically included from 25 up to about 150 people. Around 5500 B.C. Woodlands folk at a site in southern Illinois built rectangular houses roughly twenty-five feet by fifteen feet. They placed large wooden poles in the ground around the perimeter of each house and filled in the space between the poles with sticks and mud. These houses were the earliest to be constructed in all of North America, experts believe. Woodlands folk used similar building techniques for millennia afterward.

The existence of semipermanent settlements has permitted archaeologists to locate numerous Archaic burial sites that provide fascinating insights into the character of Woodlands cultures. At one burial site in Tennessee, half the women had died before the age of thirty, many of them evidently succumbing to the high risks of childbirth. In contrast, almost a fifth of the men lived to the ripe old age of sixty. At the Indian Knoll site in western Kentucky, which dates to about 2500 to 2000 B.C., archaeologists found 1,100 burials that allowed them to calculate the life expectancy at birth for these Woodlands people to be slightly over eighteen years. Some graves contained shell and copper goods that demonstrate the existence of long-distance trade, although just how the trade worked remains unknown. Some burials contain evidence of violent death; one skeleton, for example, has a spear point embedded in the rib cage. Archaeologists speculate that Woodlands groups sometimes fought over access to desirable hunting and gathering grounds.

TECHNOLOGY IN AMERICA
Weaver's Workbasket

This workbasket of a master weaver illustrates the technology of ancient American textile production. Found in a woman's grave in the Andes dating from five hundred years before the arrival of Columbus, the workbasket contains the simple tools that, when combined with the experience, skill, ingenuity, and creativity of the weaver, were used to create intricate weavings like that on page 28 of this chapter. The basket contains tools for every stage in the process of textile production. The weaver took fiber from cotton plants or animal wool (such as llama or alpaca) and spun it into thread. For colored threads, the weaver dyed the fibers before spinning, using different vegetable and mineral concoctions. The pointed sticks wrapped with thread (left center) are spindles on which the weaver spun. She used the small ceramic cup to hold one end of the spindle while she twisted the fiber through her fingers to create strong, thin thread. She used the two pieces of chalk (to the right of the ceramic cup) to make a powder that lubricated her fingers, allowing the thread to pass smoothly onto the spindle. Skeins of finished thread removed from their spindles are just to the left of the ceramic cup. This small workbasket contained more than 150 spindles for the many varieties of thread a master weaver made and used. The beadlike objects at the center are whorls the weaver placed on spindles to anchor the thread and for decoration; the designs on the whorls probably had religious meaning. On the right, above the chalk and ceramic cup are bobbins used to pass the thread through the weaving, a bone pick with fine teeth to press down on the closely woven threads and tighten the weave, and a long spine needle with a tiny hole, used for sewing and for embroidery. Mastery of this technology presumably took years of training and experience. Most likely, a master weaver passed on her skill and knowledge to her daughters or other kinswomen.

Gift of Charles H. White. Courtesy, Museum of Fine Arts, Boston.

Some experts also believe that burials were a way to stake a claim to specific territory by making it literally the land of one's ancestors.

Around 2000 B.C. two major changes occurred among Woodlands cultures. First, some groups began to cultivate plants for food. Gourds and pumpkins that originated in Mexico were grown in parts of Missouri and Kentucky before 2000 B.C. After the introduction of these Mexican crops, Woodlands peoples began to cultivate local species such as sunflowers and other seed-bearing plants. It is likely that Woodlands folk also grew tobacco, an import from South America, since stone pipes for smoking appeared by 1500 B.C. and became common by 500 B.C. Corn, the most important plant food in Mexico, did not begin to be cultivated by Woodlands groups until about 300 B.C. and did not become a significant food crop until more than a thousand years later. Cultivated crops added to the quantity, variety, and predictability of Woodlands food sources, but they did not fundamentally alter the hunter-gatherer way of life.

Around 2000 B.C. two major changes occurred among Woodlands cultures. First, some groups began to cultivate plants for food. Second, Woodlands peoples incorporated pottery in their basic hunter-gatherer cultures.

The second major change after about 2000 B.C. was the introduction of pottery. Techniques for making ceramic pots probably also originated in Mexico and may have been brought north along with Mexican seeds. Pots were used for food storage and preparation. Woodlands peoples incorporated pottery, as they did agriculture, into their basic hunter-gatherer cultures, which persisted in most areas to A.D. 1492 and beyond.

Perhaps the most spectacular Archaic Woodlands site was Poverty Point near the Mississippi River in northeastern Louisiana. The Poverty Point culture existed from about 1700 B.C. to 700 B.C. It appears to have emerged from peoples indigenous to North America rather than being a cultural outpost of Central American peoples. Poverty Point folk constructed an enormous earthworks consisting of

ANCIENT CORN POPPER
Long before movies and microwave ovens, ancient Americans munched popcorn. This corn popper comes from the Mochica culture, which thrived on the northern coast of Peru for about six hundred years after the birth of Christ. The Mochica presumably nestled the popper on a bed of coals with the opening facing up, placed corn inside, and covered the opening with a lid (not shown) while the kernels popped. The Mochica and other ancient Americans did not pop most of the corn they grew. Instead, they ground it into cornmeal, which they incorporated in a wide variety of dishes, probably including ancient counterparts of modern tortillas.
The Field Museum #A112961c, Chicago. Photographer: Diane Alexander White.

six concentric half-circles more than a half-mile in diameter; each ring was built of dirt piled nine feet high and twenty-five feet wide. The purpose of this huge earthworks is unknown. It may have been used for astronomical observations since it seems to be aligned to view the spring and fall equinoxes. The labor and organization required to build such massive earthworks suggest that important ceremonies were conducted at the site. The complex may also have served as a meeting place for traders who exchanged items that were common in one place but exotic in others. At least a thousand people and perhaps several times that many lived in dwellings near the earthworks. Nearly one hundred smaller villages clustered here and there in the surrounding countryside. The marked differences between the large central site and the smaller surrounding settlements seem to indicate a recognition of social hierarchy. Details about this and many other features of Poverty Point culture remain unknown.

Southwestern Cultures

In southwestern America—roughly including Arizona, New Mexico, and southern portions of Utah and Colorado—Archaic peoples developed distinctive cultures characterized by agriculture and eventually by multiunit dwellings called pueblos. The southwestern environment is generally arid; rainfall varies greatly from season to season and year to year. Water is more plentiful along the major rivers of the region, particularly the Colorado, Rio Grande, Pecos, and Gila. Like Archaic peoples elsewhere in North America, southwestern groups developed a wide variety of cultures adapted to local environmental circumstances. All southwestern cultures, however, confronted the challenge of a dry climate and unpredictable fluctuations in rainfall that made the supply of wild-plant food very unreliable for subsistence. These ancient Americans probably adopted agriculture in response to this basic environmental condition of the Southwest.

Corn, supplemented by squash and beans, became the staff of life of ancient southwesterners.

Until about 3000 B.C. the population of the Southwest appears to have been extremely sparse. Geographically the region lies between the Great Basin and northern Mexico, and some features of cultures from both regions exist in such artifacts as spear points and seed-grinding stones that date to the two millennia after 3000 B.C. Sometime within a few centuries of 1500 B.C. southwestern peoples began to cultivate their signature food crop, corn (as it is called in North America; elsewhere it is called maize). The date of the introduction of corn cultivation and the motivations for it are subjects of intense debate among archaeologists. The debate is important for many reasons, among them that by A.D. 1492 corn had become the basic cultivated food crop for Native American peoples throughout North America (and it remains one of the most productive food crops in the world today). It appears safe to say, however, that Southwestern peoples began to cultivate corn in a conscious attempt to provide themselves with a more predictable source of food in a highly unpredictable environment.

Corn was one of the most important developments in the history of world agriculture. Before 5000 B.C. somewhere in Central or South America, people began to cultivate seeds of the wild grass teosinte, the ancient ancestor of modern corn. Within a few centuries, selective cultivation of the bigger and more productive seeds led to progressively bigger ears of corn and progressively larger numbers of kernels harvested per kernel planted, although these prehistoric corn ears were much smaller than modern corn. Central and South American peoples grew corn for millennia before the crop made its way to southwestern America. Since ancient corn possessed enormous genetic diversity, southwestern cultures were able to select seeds and thereby develop corn varieties that would tolerate the arid, relatively short growing season of the Southwest, despite the plant's origins in wetter and warmer climates farther south.

By about 1000 B.C. southwestern folk also grew squash, and by 500 B.C. beans appeared in their gardens. Like corn, both squash and beans had traveled north from Mexico. Corn, supplemented by squash and beans, became the staff of life of ancient southwesterners. The demands of corn cultivation encouraged southwestern hunter-gatherers to restrict their migratory habits and to settle near ground that would support the growth of the crop. A vital consideration was access to water. Southwestern Indians became experts at conserving water from streams, springs, and rainfall and at distributing available water through irrigation. The adoption of agriculture and of more or less permanent settlements did not occur overnight. The process waxed and waned over the centuries depending on the availability of alternative food sources, among other considerations. The long-term trend, however, clearly pointed toward sedentary villages that depended on growing corn.

Between about A.D. 200 and 900, small settlements appeared throughout southern New Mexico marking the emergence of the Mogollon culture. Typically a Mogollon settlement included between three and fifteen pit houses made by digging out a rounded pit about fifteen feet in diameter and a foot or two deep and then erecting poles to support a roof of branches or dirt. These small clusters of pit houses probably housed members of a family. Mogollon people began to make pottery about A.D. 200, and they also engaged in trade since seashells, turquoise, and other luxuries from far away appear

MIMBRES BOWLS

Mimbres people left a vivid record of their culture on bowls like these, which were found in their graves. They punched a hole in the bottom of a decorated bowl and then placed the inverted bowl over the face of the corpse. The hole was obviously quite important in the burial ritual, but exactly what it meant is unknown. The decoration may have depicted a characteristic of the dead person. The bowls shown here, made between A.D. 1000 and 1150, illustrate the differing activities of Mimbres men and women. It is likely that Mimbres women made and decorated the bowls.

Al Ligrani Photograph, Museum of Western Colorado; Transfer, Department of Anthropology, University of Minnesota.

in these sites. Larger villages usually had one or two pit houses that were bigger than conventional dwellings and may have been used for trade or ceremonial purposes. These larger pit houses may have been the predecessors of the circular kivas, the partially underground ceremonial rooms that became a characteristic of nearly all southwestern settlements. About A.D. 1000, Mogollon culture began to decline, for reasons that remain obscure. Among their descendants were the Mimbres people in southwestern New Mexico, who produced spectacular pottery with characteristic designs that often portrayed human and animal forms. By about A.D. 1150, the Mimbres culture also disappeared.

About A.D. 500, people who appear to have emigrated from Mexico established the distinctive Hohokam culture in southern Arizona. Hohokam peoples made extensive use of irrigation to plant and harvest twice a year. The comparatively high crop yields made possible by irrigation allowed the Hohokam population to grow and seek out more land to irrigate and settle. They also built pit houses, although theirs were more rectangular than those in Mogollon villages. Hohokam culture continued to be strongly influenced by Mexican cultures. The people built sizable platform mounds and ball courts characteristic of cultures to the south. The Hohokam culture declined about A.D. 1400, for unknown reasons.

North of the Hohokam and Mogollon cultures, in a region that encompassed southern Utah and Colorado and northern Arizona and New Mexico, the Anasazi culture developed during the first century A.D. The early Anasazi built pit houses and used irrigation much like their neighbors to the south. However, since many Anasazi settlements were on mesas high above riverbeds, the people built reservoirs to capture rainwater and melted snow and then channeled the runoff to fields on the mesa and to terraces on the steep mesa walls. Beginning around A.D. 1000, for reasons that remain unclear, the Anasazi began to move their dwellings off the mesa tops. They built large, multistory cliff dwellings whose spectacular ruins can still be seen at Mesa Verde, Colorado, and Canyon de Chelly, Arizona. Other Anasazi communities, like the one whose impressive ruins can be visited at Chaco Canyon, New Mexico, erected huge, stone-walled pueblos with enough rooms to house the entire population of the settlement. Pueblo Bonito at Chaco Canyon, for example, contained more than eight hundred rooms. Anasazi pueblos and cliff dwellings typically contained one or more kivas used for secret ceremonies, restricted to men, that sought to communicate with the supernatural world.

Pueblo Bonito stood at the center of a dozen large pueblos in or near Chaco Canyon that developed between A.D. 900 and 1150. Scattered over some 25,000 square miles were scores of smaller pueblos that were linked to Chaco Canyon and to the central site of Pueblo Bonito by an amazing system of roads. Some roads were nearly thirty feet wide and extended straight from Chaco Canyon for sixty-five miles, sometimes including stairs and footholds carved in rock cliffs that threatened to interrupt a straight-line passage. Remnants of the roads are still visible today. The immense labor required to construct these roads suggests their importance, although the reason for their size remains mysterious since the Anasazi traveled exclusively on foot. The inhabitants of Chaco Canyon engaged in an extensive trade network involving turquoise, pottery, seashells, baskets, ritual items of many sorts, and even macaws—tropical birds valued for their brightly colored feathers. Around A.D. 1130, drought began to plague the region; it lasted for half a century, triggering the disappearance of the Chaco culture.

By A.D. 1200 the large Anasazi pueblos had been abandoned, for reasons that are not entirely clear. The prolonged drought may have intensified conflict among pueblos and rendered ineffective the agricultural methods that had been developed in earlier centuries. Some Anasazi migrated toward regions with more reliable rainfall and settled in Hopi, Zuñi, and Acoma pueblos that their descendants in Arizona and New Mexico have occupied ever since.

Burial Mounds and Chiefdoms

Beginning around 500 B.C., Archaic Woodlands cultures throughout the vast drainage of the Mississippi River began to build burial mounds that indicate new forms of social and political organization. The size of the mounds, the labor and organization required to erect them, and the differences in the artifacts buried with certain individuals suggest the existence of a social and political hierarchy that archaeologists term a chiefdom. Typically a chief was a man who inherited his status and who was believed to have some supernatural authority. The burial mounds suggest that a chief could command the labor and respect of many people who were not members of his immediate family.

The size of the burial mounds, the labor and organization required to erect them, and the differences in the artifacts buried with certain individuals suggest the existence of a social and political hierarchy that archaeologists term a chiefdom.

Adena and Hopewell Cultures

Between about 500 B.C. and 100 B.C., hundreds of burial mounds were built within a 150-mile radius of Chillicothe, Ohio, by the Adena peoples. The Adena were Woodlands hunter-gatherers who supplemented wild resources by cultivating some tobacco and perhaps a few local plants, but they did not grow corn. They lived in small settlements and migrated to obtain food, as did previous Woodlands cultures. But from time to time, presumably when an important person died, small groups coalesced into large gatherings that performed burial ceremonies involving the construction of mounds. Often they also built circular mounds surrounding or near the burial mound. These "sacred circles" may have been ritualistic gathering places for the deceased's clan or kin.

Normally, Adena people constructed a burial house, where the dead may have been kept until decay exposed the skeleton, permitting the bones to be coated with red pigment. The burial house was usually burned down before the body or skeleton

MOUND EXCAVATION
During the nineteenth century, long before archaeologists developed scientific methods of excava-
tion, curious Americans dug into ancient mounds. Dr. Munro Dickeson (holding a notebook at
the bottom center of the painting) excavated hundreds of mounds and gave lectures about his dis-
coveries to audiences throughout the Midwest. Dickeson used this painting of a mound he exca-
vated in Louisiana during the 1840s as a backdrop for his lectures. Part of a canvas almost 350
feet long, the painting illustrates the way mounds were constructed with alternating strata of
burials and dirt. Can you detect in the painting hints of the burial rituals enacted at this site?
Note that African Americans — presumably slaves — did the physical labor of this excavation.
The Saint Louis Art Museum. Purchase: Eliza McMillan Fund.

was covered with a mound of earth. Sometimes two or three individuals—presumably of high status—were placed in log tombs before the mound was built. With the bodies, the Adena people usually deposited a wide variety of grave goods—spear points and stone pipes as well as decorative and ritualistic items such as thin sheets of mica (a glasslike mineral) crafted into naturalistic shapes, copper ornaments like bracelets and pendants, or headdresses made from the skulls of deer. Men, evidently of high status, sometimes were buried with a skull, perhaps of an enemy or an ancestor; the surface of some such skulls is polished, suggesting that it was an important object that was handled frequently for a long time before burial. Grave goods were not restricted to the burials of important men. In fact, children's graves often included grave goods. Once the body and grave goods were in place, dirt was piled into a mound one basketful at a time. Sometimes mounds were constructed all at once, but often they were built up over many years after many burials.

About 100 B.C., Adena culture evolved into the more elaborate Hopewell culture, which lasted until about A.D. 400. It too was centered in Ohio but it extended throughout the Ohio and Mississippi valleys. Hopewell people built larger mounds and filled them with more magnificent grave goods than had their Adena predecessors. A typical Hopewell mound was 100 feet in diameter and 30 feet high. Some mounds had geometrical designs; others were shaped like animals. The immense Serpent Mound, a likeness of a snake over 1,200 feet long, can still be visited in Ohio. Like Adena people, however, Hopewell folk remained hunter-gatherers who lived in small villages and did not grow corn. Burial rituals appear to have brought many people together to honor an important personage. Some Hopewell sites contain mounds that resemble the Adena sacred circles.

Burial was probably reserved for the most important members of Hopewell groups. Most people were cremated. Careful analysis of skeletons in one Hopewell mound suggests that the more important graves contained men who were hunters; they tended to have arthritis of the elbow associated with stress to the elbow joint from using spear-throwers. Men in lesser graves showed evidence of arthritis of the wrist, perhaps associated with handwork. The men with arthritic elbows were also taller than those with arthritic wrists, suggesting that high status may have been related to stature.

Grave goods at Hopewell sites were often lavish. In one burial a young man and woman lay side by side, each wearing many items of copper jewelry, necklaces of grizzly bear teeth, and artificial copper noses; the woman was surrounded with thousands of buttons and pearl beads. Large deposits of mica, obsidian, and other valuable resources were buried with certain men; perhaps they were artisans who worked with such materials. Certainly Hopewell sites testify to the high quality of their crafts. They included objects similar to those at Adena sites, but finer, more decorative, more exquisite.

Hopewell grave goods also demonstrate the existence of a wide-ranging trade network. Sites in Ohio contain obsidian from the Yellowstone Park region of Wyoming; other stones originating in Missouri, Illinois, North Dakota, and Canada; shells and alligator teeth from the Florida and Gulf coasts; mica and minerals from North Carolina; and copper from near Lake Superior. Likewise, artifacts evidently exported from Hopewell centers appear at faraway sites in the Southeast, Northeast, and Midwest. Hopewell burial practices also spread through much of the trading area. It may be that the chiefs buried in Hopewell mounds played an important role in the vast interregional trade. Some archaeologists believe that chiefs may have used their access to trade to elevate their own status.

After about A.D. 400, Hopewell culture declined, for reasons that are obscure. Some archaeologists believe that the adoption of the bow and arrow and of increasing reliance on agriculture may have made small settlements more self-sufficient and weakened their dependence on central chiefs.

HOPEWELL EFFIGY PIPE

Hopewell burial mounds often contain effigy pipes in the shape of animals. This coyote pipe was carved from pipestone between about 200 B.C. and A.D. 100. To smoke the pipe, a Hopewell person would tamp tobacco into a bowl hollowed from the back of the coyote (not visible in the photo) and then light the pipe, perhaps with a flaming splinter. Facing the effigy, the smoker would inhale through the hole at the right end of the curved platform, under the coyote's nose. The coyote was probably more than simply an attractive decoration for a pipe, but what it signified remains unknown.

Photograph © 1996 The Detroit Institute of Arts, Dirk Bakker Collection of Ohio Historical Society, Columbus.

Mississippian Culture

About A.D. 800, another mound-building culture flourished. The Mississippian culture emerged in the floodplains of the major Southeastern river systems and lasted until about A.D. 1500. Mississippian peoples practiced agriculture, growing corn, squash, and beans. They also continued to hunt, fish, and gather wild plants. Major Mississippian sites include not only burial mounds but huge mounds with platforms on top for ceremonies and for the residences of great chiefs. The largest Mississippian site was Cahokia, Illinois, just across the Mississippi River from St. Louis, Missouri. Other important Mississippian centers were at Moundville, Alabama; Etowah, Georgia; and Spiro, Oklahoma.

At Cahokia, more than one hundred mounds of different sizes and shapes were grouped around large open plazas. Monk's Mound, the largest, covered sixteen acres at its base and was one hundred feet tall. Spreading far beyond the mounds and plazas were dwellings that at one time covered five square miles and may have housed as many as thirty thousand inhabitants, easily qualifying Cahokia as the largest settlement in North America and comparable to major centers of the era in Central America. At Cahokia and other Mississippian sites, people evidently worshiped a sun god; perhaps the mounds were a way to elevate elites nearer to the sun.

One Cahokia burial mound suggests the authority associated with a great chief. One man—presumably the chief—was buried on a platform composed of twenty thousand shell beads. Buried near him, evidently at the same time, were the dismembered bodies of several people, perhaps enemies or slaves; three men and three women of high status, perhaps relatives of the chief, accompanied by eight hundred arrowheads, numerous sheets of mica and copper, and fifteen polished stone disks used in a spear-throwing game; four men, perhaps servants or guards, whose heads and hands had been cut off; and fifty young women between the ages of eighteen and twenty-three who had evidently been strangled. Such a mass sacrifice suggests the power a Cahokian chief wielded and the obedience he commanded. However, details about how Mississippian chiefs exercised their powers remain mysterious. The sacrifices associated with the burials suggest that ordinary Mississippians may have had reason to fear their chiefs.

Cahokia and other Mississippian sites had dwindled by 1500. On the eve of European contact, most of the descendants of Mississippian cultures lived in small dispersed villages supported by agriculture, hunting, and gathering.

By 1500, all these Archaic cultures were either extinct or in decline, for reasons that are not well known. However, their monuments, dwellings, and artifacts survived, as did various remnants of their cultural practices. On the eve of European conquest, North American tribes had incorporated and adapted many of the cultural achievements of their ancestors. The rigors of the natural environment required that they continue to make cultural adaptations.

MEXICAN CEREMONIAL SKULL
This human skull, decorated by Mexican artisans with a mosaic of turquoise, jet, and shell, represented Tezcatlipoca, the supreme Mexican deity who governed human fate. Every eighteen months, a handsome young man was selected for the great honor of impersonating Tezcatlipoca for the next eighteen months. Montezuma gave the impersonator riches and privileges of all sorts, including allowing him to rule Tenochtitlán for the last five days of his life. On the last day, the impersonator climbed the steps of a temple where priests cut out his heart and decapitated him. This skull from the Tezcatlipoca ceremony presumably belonged to one of the impersonators. The skull is said to have been a gift from Montezuma to Cortés.
British Museum.

Native Americans in 1492

In the vast Eastern Woodlands region, tribes clustered into three major groups. Algonquian tribes inhabited the Atlantic seaboard from Virginia through Maine and the Great Lakes region and much of the upper Midwest. The relatively mild climate along the Atlantic permitted the coastal Algonquians to grow corn and other crops as well as to hunt and fish. Around the Great Lakes and in northern New England, however, cool summers and severe winters made agriculture impractical. Instead, the Abenaki, Penobscot, Chippewa, and other tribes hunted and fished, using canoes both for transportation and for gathering wild rice.

Inland from the Algonquians were the territories of the Iroquoian tribes, centered in Pennsylvania and upstate New York. The Iroquoian peoples also inhabited the hilly upland regions of the Carolinas and Georgia. Several features distinguished Iroquoian tribes from their neighbors. First, their success in cultivating corn and other crops allowed them to build permanent settlements, usually consisting of several bark-covered longhouses up to one hundred feet long and housing five to ten families. Second, Iroquoian societies were thoroughly matriarchal. Property of all sorts, including land, children, and inheritance, belonged to women. Women headed family clans and even selected the chiefs (normally men) who governed tribes. Third, for purposes of war and diplomacy, the Seneca, Onondaga, Mohawk, Oneida, and Cayuga tribes formed the League of Five Nations, an Iroquoian confederation that remained powerful well into the eighteenth century.

Muskogean peoples were spread throughout the Southeast, south of the Ohio River and east of the Mississippi. Including Creek, Choctaw, Chickasaw, and Natchez tribes, the Muskogean Indians inhabited a bountiful natural environment that provided abundant food both from agriculture and from hunting and gathering. Remnants of the Mississippian culture existed in the religious rites common among the Muskogean. They all practiced a form of sun worship, and the Natchez even built temple mounds modeled after those of their Mississippian ancestors.

West of the Mississippi River, Great Plains Indians straddled the boundary between the Eastern Woodlands and the western tribes. Plains Indians lived in much of the enormous region drained by the Missouri River. Many of the tribes had migrated to the Plains within the century or two before 1500, forced out of the Eastern Woodlands by Iroquoian and Algonquian tribes. They were in the process of increasing their reliance on buffalo, although some tribes—especially the Mandan and Pawnee—were successful farmers, growing both corn and sunflowers as major food crops. The Teton Sioux, Blackfeet, Comanche, Cheyenne, and Crow on the northern Plains and the Apache and other nomadic tribes on the southern plains depended on buffalo. They migrated with the huge herds that grazed the rich prairies. Lacking horses before the arrival of the Spaniards, these Indians hunted on foot with the techniques in use since human beings first came to America.

By the time Columbus arrived, the comparatively small Indian settlements in North America supported a population estimated to be about 4.5 million, slightly less than the population of the British Isles at the time and roughly half that of Spain and Portugal combined.

In the Southwest, descendants of the Anasazi, Hohokam, and Mogollon cultures lived in settled agricultural communities, many of them pueblos. However, a large number of warlike Athapascan tribes had invaded the area within the two hundred years before 1500. The Athapascans—principally Apache and Navajo—were hunters and gatherers who preyed on the sedentary pueblo Indians. They did not engage in agriculture themselves. Instead they specialized in the skills and traditions of warfare that made their raids successful and permitted them to enjoy the fruits of agriculture without the work of farming.

Tribes in the Great Basin region, such as the Comanche and Shoshone, continued to follow the subsistence practices of earlier Great Basin cultures. Likewise, Pacific coast cultures continued their distinctive hunter-gatherer ways of life.

By the time Columbus arrived, the comparatively small Indian settlements in North America supported a population estimated to be about 4.5 million, slightly less than the population of the

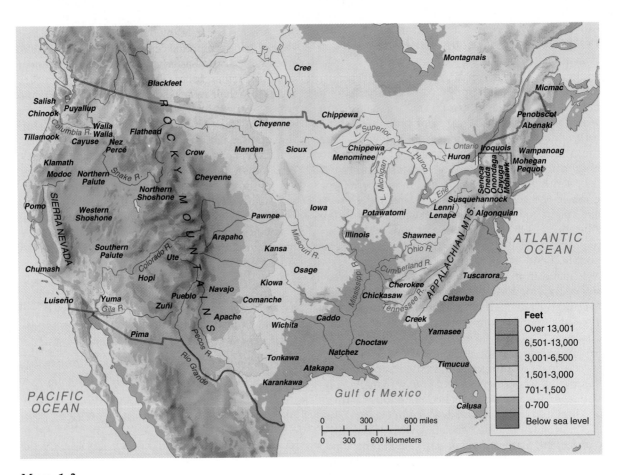

MAP 1.3
Native North Americans about 1500
*Distinctive Native American peoples resided throughout the area that, centuries later, would be-
come the United States. This map indicates the approximate location of some of the larger tribes
about 1500. In the interest of legibility, many other peoples who inhabited North America at the
time are omitted from the map.*

British Isles at the time and roughly half that of
Spain and Portugal combined. All of the Indian peoples depended on hunting wild game and gathering wild seeds, nuts, and plants for a major portion
of their food. Most of them also practiced agriculture, some far more than others. All of them used
bows and arrows, as well as other weapons, for
hunting and warfare. None of them employed writing, but they expressed themselves in many other
ways. They made drawings on stones, wood, and
animal skins; wove patterns in baskets and textiles;
painted designs on pottery; and crafted beadwork,

pipes, and other decorative items. They danced,
sang, and played music. They performed elaborate
burial ceremonies and other religious rites.

Although they had rich and varied cultural resources, they lacked certain common conveniences
found in late-fifteenth-century Europe: They did not
use wheels; sailing ships were unknown; they had
no large domesticated animals like horses, cows, or
oxen; their use of metals was restricted to copper;
and metallurgy did not exist in North America.
However, the absence of these European conveniences was profoundly irrelevant to ancient North

Americans. Their tribal cultures, in all their varieties and similarities, had developed as adaptations to the natural environment local to each tribe. That was the great similarity that underlay all the cultural diversity among native North Americans.

The Mexica: A Meso-American Culture

The ancient peoples of Central and South America were far more numerous than their North American cousins. They too lived in a natural environment of tremendous diversity. They too built impressive civilizations and great monuments. They too developed hundreds of tribal cultures, far too numerous to catalog here. But among all the Central and South American cultures the Mexica (often called Aztecs, a name they did not use) stood out. They were the most powerful Indians in the entire New World at the moment of European contact. Their empire stretched from coast to coast across central Mexico, encompassing as many as 25 million people. We know more about the fifteenth-cen-

tury Mexica than about any other Native American society of the same time. Their significance in the history of the New World after 1492, especially in the Spanish empire that shaped the expectations of other Old World colonizers, dictates a brief consideration of their culture and society.

The Mexica began their rise to prominence about A.D. 1325 when small bands settled on an unpromising marshy island in Lake Texcoco, the site of the future city of Tenochtitlán. Resourceful, courageous, cold-blooded warriors, the Mexica were often hired as mercenaries by richer, more settled tribes. The Mexica survived and prospered by making alliances with far more powerful neighboring tribes who were eager to have the fierce Mexican warriors on their side. By 1430, the Mexica succeeded in asserting their dominance over their former allies and leading their own military campaigns in an ever-widening arc of empire building. Certain tribes battled the Mexica to a standoff and managed to preserve their independence. The Tlaxcalans, the most notable of these holdouts, eventually became allies of the European conquerors. Despite these pockets of resistance, by 1500 the Mexica ruled an empire that covered more land than Spain

MEXICAN CALENDAR
The Mexican system of writing used glyphs, pictorial representations of gods, objects, and ideas. Some of the writing from before the arrival of Europeans has survived in the form of books, called codices. (Soon after the conquest, Spaniards burned all the codices they could find.) This preconquest codex is a calendar of the 260-day religious year. The central figure on each page is Tlaloc, the rain god. The glyphs along the bottom of each page represent specific days; the symbols along the top indicate the sky and rain. Tlaloc priests used the calendar for many purposes, including setting the dates of major religious rituals.
Lee Boltin.

PERUVIAN WEAVING
Ancient American women wove a dazzling variety of textiles, including this spectacular cloth made by a weaver of the Paracas people, who inhabited the southern coast of Peru from about 700 B.C. to A.D. 200. This weaving wrapped a Paracas mummy, presumably a person of high status. The jewellike quality of the cloth suggests the artistry of the weavers and the Paracas's appreciation of design, color, and exquisite workmanship in their everyday lives.
Denman Waldo Ross Collection. Courtesy, Museum of Fine Arts, Boston.

and Portugal combined and contained almost three times as many people.

The empire exemplified the central values of Mexican society. The Mexica worshiped the war god

> *Despite pockets of resistance, by 1500 the Mexica ruled an empire that covered more land than Spain and Portugal combined and contained almost three times as many people.*

Huitzilopochtli, who they believed repaid their reverence with victories. Warriors held the most exalted positions in the Mexican social hierarchy, even above the priests who performed the sacred ceremonies that won Huitzilopochtli's favor. In the almost constant battles necessary to defend and ex-

tend the empire, young Mexican men could exhibit the courage and daring that would allow them to rise in the carefully graduated ranks of warriors. The Mexica considered capturing prisoners the ultimate act of bravery. The captives were usually turned over to the priests, who sacrificed them to Huitzilopochtli by cutting out their hearts.

The empire contributed far more to Mexican society than victims for sacrifice. At the most basic level, the empire was a military and political system for collecting tribute from subject peoples. The Mexica forced conquered tribes to pay tribute in goods, not money. Tribute included everything from candidates for human sacrifice to basic food products like corn and beans as well as exotic luxury items like gold or turquoise jewelry and rare bird feathers. The total annual tribute collected by the Mexica was enormous. One scholar has estimated that it included more than 200,000 cloaks, about 650 elaborate warriors' costumes, 16,000 bales of cotton, about 5,000 large pieces of lumber (wood was scarce on the Mexica's heavily populated islands), almost 30,000 bowls made of gourds or wood, some 240 large gold disks, as well as huge quantities of corn, beans, cacao beans, chiles, tomatoes, and tropical fruits and millions of brightly colored feathers, thousands of animal skins, and other special items like wild ocelots, jaguars, snakes, and caged birds.

Tribute redistributed to the Mexica a major fraction of the goods produced by conquered tribes. Farmers and artisans in subjugated territories were required to pay in tribute as much as a third (and sometimes more) of what they produced. The Mexica employed a sizable army of tribute collectors who made certain that each conquered settlement was paid in full. On the whole, the Mexica did not

INCA MUMMY

Many ancient American peoples practiced human sacrifice as a sacred rite of communion with the gods. In the Inca ritual of capac hucha, each village sent one or two especially beautiful children between the ages of six and ten to the capital, where they were honored in religious ceremonies and then taken back to their homes in a procession of priests and villagers. After joyous festivities, the children chosen for sacrifice were given an intoxicating drink and then buried in a prepared tomb, where they died. This mummy was probably a child sacrificed in the capac hucha ritual sometime around A.D. 1500. Discovered in Chile at an altitude of about 20,000 feet, where the dry, intense cold preserved the body, the mummy was accompanied by a female votive figure wrapped in finely woven cloth and capped with a bright feather headdress, a llama figurine, a bag of coca leaves, and other objects.
Loren McIntyre.

GOLD SHAMAN FIGURE

Gold signified sacred and secular power in many Central and South American societies. The only gold artifacts to survive the plunder of the Spanish conquest — like this shaman figure — were those that had been hidden away, usually buried, often with a powerful chief. (Spaniards typically melted down any gold objects they found.) This shaman was crafted by a goldsmith of the Diquís people, who resided in Costa Rica and Colombia in the centuries just before the arrival of Europeans. The shaman's supernatural powers are suggested by the aura of crocodile heads that surround him (facing up on his shoulders and arms and down on his thighs) and by his indifference to the dangers of holding the tail of a poisonous snake in his mouth while beating a drum. Ritualistic ingestion of hallucinogens often heightened the perception that a shaman could merge human and animal forms and access the realms of cosmic mystery.
No. BCCR-963 Central Bank Museums, Costa Rica.

much interfere with the internal government of conquered regions. Instead, they usually permitted the traditional ruling elite to stay in power—so long as their tribute was paid on time. For their efforts, the conquered provinces received very little from the Mexica, except immunity from punitive raids by the dreaded Mexican warriors.

Tribute reflected the fundamental relations of power and wealth that pervaded the Mexican empire. The relatively small nobility of Mexican warriors, supported by a still smaller priesthood, possessed the military and religious power to command the obedience of thousands of nonnoble Mexica and of millions of other non-Mexica in subjugated provinces. The Mexican elite exercised their power to obtain tribute and thereby to redistribute wealth from the conquered to the conquerors, from the commoners to the nobility, from the poor to the rich. This redistribution of wealth made possible the achievements of Mexican society that eventually amazed Europeans: the temples, markets, bridges, waterworks, gardens, and zoos, not to mention the storehouses stuffed with gold and other treasures.

The empire did not permit conquered peoples to participate as full-fledged citizens of Mexican society. Instead, the empire treated the inhabitants of conquered territories as subjects. Subjugated communities felt exploited by the constant payment of tribute to the Mexica. Rather than identifying with the magnificent achievements of the empire, subject peoples felt oppressed. By depending on military conquest and constant collection of tribute, the Mexica failed to create among their subjects a belief that Mexican domination was, at some level, legitimate and equitable. The high level of discontent among subject peoples comprised the soft, vulnerable underbelly of the Mexican empire. Instead of making friends for the Mexica, the empire created many bitter and resentful opponents, a fact Spanish conquerors eventually discovered.

Conclusion: The Legacy of Ancient America

In 1492, the total indigenous population of the New World was roughly 80 to 100 million, about the same as the population of Europe. Until then, ancient Native Americans shaped the history of human beings in the New World. Much of their history remains irretrievably lost. But much can be pieced together from the artifacts they left behind over the millennia. They succeeded in establishing continuity of human habitation in the hemisphere from the time the first big-game hunters crossed Beringia until 1492 and beyond. They achieved their success through resourceful adaptation to the hemisphere's many, ever-changing natural environments. They also adapted to social and cultural changes caused by human beings—such as marriages, deaths, political struggles, and warfare—but the sparse evidence that has survived renders those adaptations almost entirely unknowable. Their creativity and artistry are unmistakably documented in the artifacts they left behind at kill sites, camps, and burial mounds. Those artifacts limn the only likenesses of ancient Americans we will ever have—blurred, shadowy images that are indisputably human but forever silent.

In the five hundred years after 1492—barely 4 percent of the time human beings have inhabited the Western Hemisphere—Europeans and their descendants began to shape and eventually to dominate American history. Native American peoples continued to influence major developments of American history from 1492 to the present. But the new wave of immigrants that at first trickled and then flooded into the New World from Europe and from Africa forever transformed the peoples and places of ancient America.

CHRONOLOGY

c. 80,000–10,000 B.C.	Wisconsin glaciation exposes Beringia, "land bridge" between Siberia and Alaska.
c. 13,000–10,000 B.C.	First humans arrive in North America.
c. 9500–9000 B.C.	Paleo-Indians in North and Central America use Clovis points to hunt big game.
c. 9000 B.C.	Mammoths and many other big-game prey of Paleo-Indians become extinct.
c. 8000–1000 B.C.	Archaic hunter-gatherer cultures dominate ancient America.
c. 7500 B.C.	Grinding stones for food processing appear in Eastern Woodlands.
c. 5000 B.C.	Corn cultivation begins in Central or South America.
c. 2000 B.C.	Some Eastern Woodlands people grow gourds and pumpkins and begin making pottery.
	Chumash in southern California develop currency based on shell beads.
c. 1700–700 B.C.	Poverty Point culture flourishes in Louisiana.
c. 1500 B.C.	Southwestern cultures begin corn cultivation.
	Bows and arrows appear among Arctic peoples.
	Stone pipes for tobacco smoking appear in Eastern Woodlands.

c. 500 B.C.	Eastern Woodlands cultures start to build burial mounds.
c. 500–100 B.C.	Adena culture develops in Ohio.
c. 300 B.C.	Some Eastern Woodlands peoples begin to cultivate corn.
c. 100 B.C.–A.D. 400	Hopewell culture emerges in Ohio and Mississippi valleys.
c. A.D. 200–900	Mogollon culture emerges in New Mexico.
c. A.D. 500	Bows and arrows appear in North America south of the Arctic.
	Pacific Northwest cultures denote wealth and status with elaborate wood carvings.
c. A.D. 500–1400	Hohokam culture develops in Arizona.
c. A.D. 800–1500	Mississippian culture flourishes in Southeast.
c. A.D. 1000	Thule people contact Vikings in northeastern Canada.
c. A.D. 1000–1150	Anasazi peoples build cliff dwellings at Mesa Verde, Colorado, and pueblos at Chaco Canyon, New Mexico.
	Mimbres culture thrives in New Mexico.
c. A.D. 1325–1500	Mexica conquer neighboring peoples and establish Mexican empire.
A.D. 1492	Columbus arrives, beginning European conquest of New World.

BIBLIOGRAPHY

GENERAL WORKS

Karen Olsen Bruhns, *Ancient South America* (1994).

Michael D. Coe, *Mexico: From the Olmecs to the Aztecs* (4th ed., 1994).

Michael Coe, Dean Snow, and Elizabeth Benson, *Atlas of Ancient America* (1986).

E. James Dixon, *Quest for the Origins of the First Americans* (1993).

Brian M. Fagan, *The Journey from Eden: The Peopling of Our World* (1990).

Brian M. Fagan, *Ancient North America: The Archaeology of a Continent* (1991).

Brian M. Fagan, *Kingdoms of Gold, Kingdoms of Jade: The Americas before Columbus* (1991).

Stuart J. Fiedel, *Prehistory of the Americas* (2nd ed., 1992).

Franklin Folsom and Mary Elting Folsom, *America's Ancient Treasures: A Guide to Archeological Sites and Museums in the United States and Canada* (4th ed., 1993).

Donald K. Grayson, *The Establishment of Human Antiquity* (1983).

Francis Jennings, *The Founders of America: How Indians Discovered the Land, Pioneered in It, and Created Great Classical Civilizations; How They Were Plunged into a Dark Age by Invasion and Conquest; and How They Are Now Reviving* (1993).

Jesse D. Jennings, *Prehistory of North America* (1974).

Jesse D. Jennings, ed., *Ancient North America* (1983).

Alvin M. Josephy Jr., *America in 1492: The World of the Indian Peoples before the Arrival of Columbus* (1992).

Richard J. Shutler Jr., ed., *Early Man in the New World* (1983).

Richard Townsend, ed., *The Ancient Americas: Art from Sacred Landscapes* (1992).

Gordon R. Willey and Jeremy A. Sabloff, *A History of American Archaeology* (2nd ed., 1980).

NORTH AMERICAN CULTURES

Mary J. Adair, *Prehistoric Agriculture in the Central Plains* (1988).

David G. Anderson, *The Savannah River Chiefdoms: Political Change in the Late Prehistoric Southeast* (1994).

Alex W. Barker and Timothy R. Pauketat, eds., *Lords of the Southwest: Social Inequality and the Native Elites of Southeastern North America* (1992).

Timothy G. Baugh and Jonathan E. Ericson, eds., *Prehistoric Exchange Systems in North America* (1994).

John Howard Blitz, *Ancient Chiefdoms of the Tombigbee* (1993).

Roy Carlson, ed., *Indian Art Traditions of the Northwest Coast* (1983).

Jefferson Chapman, *Tellico Archaeology* (1985).

Linda S. Cordell, *Prehistory of the Southwest* (1984).

Linda S. Cordell and George R. Gumerman, eds., *Dynamics of Southwest Prehistory* (1989).

David Damas, ed., *Handbook of North American Indians,* vol. 5, *Arctic* (1984).

Warren L. D'Azevedo, ed., *Handbook of North American Indians,* vol. 11, *Great Basin* (1986).

Don Dumond, *Eskimos and Aleuts* (2nd ed., 1987).

Thomas E. Emerson and R. Barry Lewis, eds., *Cahokia and the Hinterlands: Middle Mississippian Cultures of the Midwest* (1991).

Brian M. Fagan, *The Great Journey: The Peopling of Ancient America* (1987).

J. D. Figgins, "The Antiquity of Man in America," *Natural History* 27 (1927):229–39.

William Fitzhugh, ed., *Crossroads of Continents: Cultures of Siberia and Alaska* (1988).

William W. Fitzhugh and Valerie Chaussonnet, eds., *Anthropology of the North Pacific Rim* (1994).

Franklin Folsom, *Black Cowboy: The Life and Legend of George McJunkin* (1992).

Nelson Foster and Linda S. Cordell, eds., *Chilies to Chocolate: Food the Americas Gave to the World* (1992).

Kendrick Frazier, *People of Chaco: A Canyon and Its Cultures* (1986).

George C. Frison, *Prehistoric Hunters of the High Plains* (2nd ed., 1991).

George Gumerman, *A View from Black Mesa* (1984).

George Gumerman, ed., *Themes in Southwest Prehistory* (1994).

Robert F. Heizer, ed., *Handbook of North American Indians,* vol. 8, *California* (1978).

June Helm, ed., *Handbook of North American Indians,* vol. 6, *Subarctic* (1981).

R. Douglas Hurt, *Indian Agriculture in America: Prehistory to the Present* (1987).

Barry L. Isaac, ed., *Prehistoric Economies of the Pacific Northwest Coast* (1988).

Sissel Johannessen and Christine A. Hastorf, eds., *Corn and Culture in the Prehistoric New World* (1994).

Roger G. Kennedy, *Hidden Cities: The Discovery and Loss of Ancient North American Civilization* (1994).

Ruth Kirk, *Hunters of the Whale* (1975).

Theodora Kroeber, *Ishi in Two Worlds* (1965).

Steven A. LeBlanc, *The Mimbres People: Ancient Pueblo Potters of the American Southwest* (1983).

Ronald J. Mason, *Great Lakes Archaeology* (1981).

R. G. Matson, *The Origins of Southwestern Agriculture* (1991).

William E. McGoun, *Prehistoric Peoples of South Florida* (1993).

Jerald T. Milanich, *Archaeology of Precolumbian Florida* (1994).

Michael J. Moratto, *California Archaeology* (1984).

Jon Muller, *Archaeology of the Lower Ohio Valley* (1986).

Alfonso Ortiz, ed., *Handbook of North American Indians*, vol. 9, *Southwest* (1979).

Alfonso Ortiz, ed., *Handbook of North American Indians*, vol. 10, *Southwest* (1983).

Timothy R. Pauketat, *The Ascent of Chiefs: Cahokia and Mississippian Politics in Native North America* (1994).

Karl H. Schlesier, *Plains Indians, A.D. 500–1500: The Archaeological Past of Historic Groups* (1994).

Lynne Sebastian, *The Chaco Anasazi: Sociopolitical Evolution in the Prehistoric Southwest* (1992).

Lynda Shaffer, *Native Americans before 1492: The Moundbuilding Centers of the Eastern Woodlands* (1992).

Bruce D. Smith, ed., *The Mississippian Emergence* (1990).

Dean Snow, *The Archaeology of New England* (1980).

Katherine A. Spielmann, *Interdependence in the Prehistoric Southwest: An Ecological Analysis of Plains-Pueblo Interaction* (1991).

Stuart Struever and Felicia Holton, *Koster: Americans in Search of Their Prehistoric Past* (1979).

Kenneth B. Tankersley and Barry L. Isaan, eds., *Early Paleoindian Economies of Eastern North America* (1990).

Bruce G. Trigger, *The Children of Aataentsic: A History of the Huron People to 1660* (1972).

Bruce G. Trigger, *Natives and Newcomers* (1985).

Bruce G. Trigger, ed., *Handbook of North American Indians*, vol. 15, *Northeast* (1978).

J. A. Tuck, *Onondaga Iroquois Prehistory* (1971).

William Snyder Webb, *The Adena People* (1974).

Randolph J. Widmer, *The Evolution of the Calusa: A Nonagricultural Chiefdom on the Southwest Florida Coast* (1988).

THE MEXICA

Frances Berdan, *The Aztecs of Central Mexico: An Imperial Society* (1982).

David Carrasco, *Quetzalcoatl and the Irony of Empire: Myths and Prophecies in the Aztec Tradition* (1992).

Inga Clendinnen, *Aztecs: An Interpretation* (1991).

Brian M. Fagan, *The Aztecs* (1984).

Ross Hassig, *War and Society in Ancient MesoAmerica* (1992).

Richard F. Townsend, *The Aztecs* (1992).

Muriel Porter Weaver, *The Aztecs, Maya, and Their Predecessors: Archaeology of Mesoamerica* (1981).

Eric Wolf, *Sons of the Shaking Earth* (1959).

TAINO ZEMI BASKET

This basket is an example of the effigies Tainos made to represent zemis, their deities. The effigy illustrates not only the artistry of the basket maker — probably a Taino woman — but also the basket maker's incorporation of European mirrors into a sacred object. Crafted sometime between 1492 and about 1520, the effigy suggests that Tainos readily adopted goods obtained in contacts with Europeans without altering their own traditional beliefs.

Archivio Fotografico del Museo Preistorico Etnografico L. Pigorini, Roma.

EUROPEANS AND THE NEW WORLD

2

1492–1600

A HALF HOUR BEFORE SUNRISE ON AUGUST 3, 1492, Christopher Columbus commanded three ships to catch the tide out of a harbor in southern Spain and sail west. Barely two months later, in the predawn moonlight of October 12, 1492, Columbus glimpsed an island on the western horizon. At last, he believed, he had found what he had been looking for, a western route across the Atlantic Ocean to Japan, China, and India. For almost three hours—probably the longest three hours in Columbus's life—the little fleet lay offshore, awaiting daylight. To negotiate with the Muslim traders he soon expected to encounter, Columbus had brought along a translator who spoke Arabic, among other languages. At daybreak, Columbus could see people gathered on the shore of the island; they had spotted his ships. Columbus and several of his crew rowed ashore. As the curious islanders crowded around to watch, Columbus claimed possession of the land for Ferdinand and Isabella, king and queen of Spain, who had sponsored his voyage. He named the island San Salvador, in honor of the Savior, Jesus Christ.

A day or two afterward, Columbus described that first encounter with the inhabitants of San Salvador in an extensive diary he kept during his voyage. He called these people Indians (*yndios* in the original Spanish), assuming that their island, which they called Guanahani, lay somewhere in the East Indies near Japan or China. They did not seem to possess the riches Columbus expected to find in the East. "It seemed to me that they were a people very poor in everything," he wrote. He and his men gave them red caps, glass beads, small bells, and other trinkets, "in which they took so much pleasure and became so much our friends that it was a marvel," he noted. As a sign of friendship, the Indians "brought us parrots and cotton thread in balls and javelins and many other things."

The Indians were not dressed in the finery Columbus expected to see adorning people in the East. "All of them go around as naked as their mothers bore them; and the women also," he observed. Their skin color was "neither black nor white." They adorned themselves with black, white, or red pigment. He judged these people "very well formed, with handsome bodies and good faces." Their hair was "coarse—almost like the tail of a horse—and short." They were not familiar with the Spaniards' weapons. "I showed them swords," Columbus wrote, "and they took them by the edge and through ignorance cut themselves." He explained that "they have no iron. Their javelins are shafts without iron." He noted that some of the Indians had scars from wounds and he "made signs to them asking what [the scars] were; and they showed me how people from other islands nearby came there and tried to [kidnap] them." This first encounter led Columbus to conclude, "They should be good and intelligent servants, for I see that they say very quickly every-

Oceanica Classis

De Insulis inuentis

COLUMBUS'S LETTER ANNOUNCING "THE DISCOVERED ISLANDS"
Shortly after Columbus arrived back in Lisbon in 1493, he rushed a letter — written in Latin — to Ferdinand and Isabella with the good news of his discoveries across the Atlantic. His news spread quickly. In less than three months, by the time Columbus had traveled to Barcelona and reported personally to the Spanish monarchs, his letter had already been published in Spain and was soon reprinted in other countries. In the edition shown here, published in Switzerland in 1493, the ship under the Latin heading "Ocean Fleet" is the Santa María, *which had in fact run aground in the Caribbean on Christmas Eve 1492. Columbus had dismantled it and used its timbers to build a fort for the sailors he did not have room to take back to Spain on his remaining two ships.*
Special Collections, New York Public Library.

thing that is said to them; and I believe that they would become Christians very easily, for it seemed to me that they had no religion."

The people Columbus called Indians called themselves Tainos. To them, *Taino* meant "good" or "noble," and it distinguished them from the hostile Caribs who were responsible for the scars Columbus noticed. Tainos inhabited most of the islands Columbus visited on his first voyage, as had their ancestors for more than two centuries. Other ancient peoples had lived on the islands since 5000 B.C. Tainos were an agricultural people. Their principal food was cassava, a nutritious root that women grated and ground into flour. They also grew sweet potatoes, corn, cotton, tobacco, and other crops. To fish and to travel from island to island, the Tainos built canoes by hollowing out logs, some big enough to hold fifty people.

Taino villages usually contained one or two thousand people who lived in round wooden houses with thatched roofs. Each village was ruled by a chief who owed allegiance to a higher chief who governed several villages. A chief could be either a woman or a man. Tainos traced their lineage through their mothers rather than their fathers. This matrilineal system determined how property, social status, and the position of chief were inherited. Tainos worshiped gods they called zemis. Zemis included the spirits of ancestors and of natural objects like trees or stones. Tainos made effigies that represented their zemis and performed rituals to honor them. Of utmost interest to Columbus, Tainos mined gold in small quantities.

What the Tainos thought about Columbus and his men we can only surmise from what Columbus wrote. At first, Columbus believed that the Tainos thought the Spaniards came from heaven. Two days after the initial encounter, he noted that several Tainos swam out to the Spaniards' ships and called out to others on the shore, "Come see the men who came from the heavens." What these Tainos really said cannot be known. After six weeks of additional experience with Tainos, Columbus was no longer confident that he understood them. Late in November 1492, he wrote that "the people of these lands do not understand me nor do I, nor anyone else that I have with me, them. And many times I understand one thing said by these Indians . . . for another, its contrary." Clearly, the translator's knowledge of Arabic did not help communicate with these "Indians."

The confused communication between Europeans and Tainos suggests how different, how strange, each group seemed to the other. For example, Columbus's observation that the Tainos had "no religion" meant no religion that he recognized. We can only imagine what the Tainos thought about the Europeans' religion; presumably they saw it as different from their worship of zemis. Columbus's perceptions of Tainos were shaped by European ideas, attitudes, and expectations, just as Tainos' perceptions of Europeans were colored by their own culture and heritage. Yet the word that Columbus coined for the Tainos—"Indians," a word that originated in a colossal misunderstanding—hinted at the direction of the future. To Europeans, "Indians" came to mean all native inhabitants of the New World. After 1492, the perceptions and cultures of Europeans began to exert a transforming influence on the New World and its peoples.

Long before 1492, certain Europeans restlessly expanded the limits of the world known to them. Their efforts made possible Columbus's encounter with the Tainos. In turn, Columbus's landfall in the Caribbean not only changed the history of the Tainos; it also changed the history of Europe and the rest of the world. After 1492, Europeans slowly began to grasp that Columbus had located what they called a New World, a Western Hemisphere containing enormous lands separated by vast oceans from the Old World of Europe, Asia, and Africa. After 1492, neither the New World nor the Old would ever be the same.

Europe in the Age of Exploration

Europeans first encountered the New World about five hundred years before Columbus arrived on San Salvador. Around the year 1000, Norse who had ventured across the North Atlantic to Iceland and Greenland founded a small fishing settlement in North America at L'Anse aux Meadows on the tip of Newfoundland. Excavations by modern archaeologists have disclosed that the Norse occupied the fifteen or so dwellings at the site intermittently for about ten years. After 1000, the Viking expansionism that had driven the Norse to the shores of Newfoundland began to decline as the world's climate cooled, choking the North Atlantic with ice and making it impassable. Viking sagas memorialized the Norse "discovery," but it had virtually no other impact in the New World or in Europe.

Historically, the East—not the West—attracted Europeans. In 1096, Christian Crusaders set out for the Middle East to "liberate" the Holy Lands from their Muslim rulers. The Crusaders returned to the Middle East twice during the next century, but they never accomplished their religious and political goal of establishing a permanent Christian stronghold in the heart of Islamic territory. They did, however, stimulate trade in eastern goods.

Wealthy Europeans developed a taste for luxury goods from Asia and Africa, and merchants competed to satisfy that taste. The profits to be made lured ambitious Europeans to find new ways to expand trade of all kinds. As Europeans traded with the East and with one another, they developed new information about the world they inhabited. One of the things some learned was that the known world was not all there was to know. A few people —sailors, merchants, aristocrats—took the risks of venturing beyond the limits of what was known. Those risks were genuine and could be deadly. But sometimes they paid off in new information, new opportunities, and eventually in the discovery of a New World entirely unknown to Europeans.

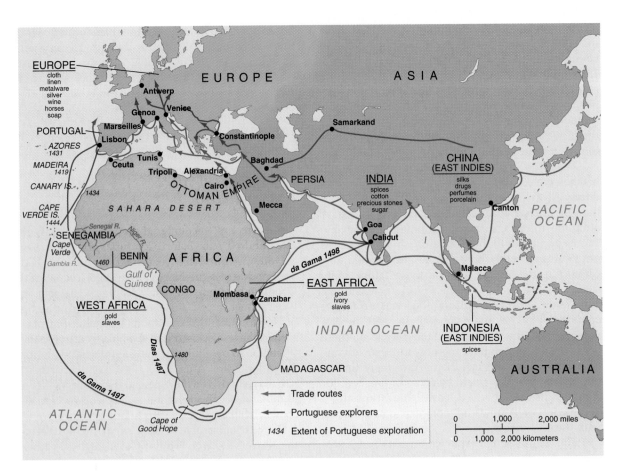

M A P 2.1
European Trade Routes and Portuguese Exploration in the Fifteenth Century
The strategic geographical position of Italian cities as a conduit for overland trade from Asia was slowly undermined during the fifteenth century by Portuguese explorers who hopscotched along the coast of Africa and eventually found a sea route that opened the rich trade of the East to Portuguese merchants.

Mediterranean Trade and European Expansion

From the twelfth century through the fifteenth century, spices, silk, carpets, ivory, gold, and other exotic goods traveled overland from Persia, Asia Minor, India, and Africa and then funneled into continental Europe through Mediterranean trade routes. Dominated primarily by the Italian cities of Venice, Genoa, and Pisa, this lucrative trade enriched Italian merchants and bankers who had been doing business with the East since the Crusades. Rival merchants and financiers in other European cities coveted a share of the Mediterranean trade.

But the Italians battled fiercely to protect their near-monopoly of access to eastern goods. Instead of trying to displace the Italians, merchants in other European countries chose the far safer alternative of trading with them.

Late in the thirteenth century a fleet of Genoese ships opened a new phase of the Mediterranean trade by venturing through the Strait of Gibraltar into the stormy waters of the North Atlantic, bringing goods from southern Europe to markets in northern Europe. Ocean-borne access to North Atlantic ports allowed Mediterranean traders to carry much larger quantities much less expensively than in the old overland trade. The vitality of the

Mediterranean trade in the fourteenth and fifteenth centuries gave merchants and governments who participated in the trade few reasons to look for fresh alternatives. New routes to the East and the discovery of new lands entirely unknown to Europeans were the stuff of fantasy.

The preconditions for turning fantasy into reality existed in fifteenth-century Europe. In the mid-fourteenth century, Europeans suffered a catastrophic epidemic of bubonic plague. The Black Death, as it was called, killed about a third of the European population, a greater disaster than anything in Europe before or since. This devastating pestilence had repercussions that lasted for more than a century. The drastic depopulation, along with other developments, disrupted the old institutions of medieval Europe. So many people died that the pressure of population on Europe's food resources was significantly eased. Survivors, many of whom had inherited property from those who died, had greater opportunities for advancement. Many peasants moved from village to village and even to cities. The experience of disruptive change undermined the traditional belief that one's place in the world was fixed and unchangeable.

Most Europeans, however, did not view these changes in positive terms. Instead, they perceived the world as a place of alarming risks where the delicate balance of health, harvests, and peace that sustained life could quickly be tipped toward disaster by epidemics, famine, and violence. A history of the world written in the late fifteenth century reflected this widespread sense of uncertainty and insecurity by referring to "the calamity of our time." Most Europeans resolved to protect themselves from what they perceived as the constant threat of calamity by worshiping the supernatural, by living amid kinfolk and friends, and by maintaining good relations with those who were richer and more powerful. Curiously, the insecurity and uncertainty of fifteenth-century life encouraged a few to take greater risks. A sailor's willingness to embark on a dangerous sea voyage through uncharted waters to points unknown was one of many European responses to the risks and opportunities of fifteenth-century life.

Some aristocrats, members of the most powerful class in European society, had reasons to hazard the risks involved in exploration. Voyages of exploration provided a convenient outlet for the military energies of lesser members of the nobility and those who aspired to noble rank. Many explorers were young sons of aristocratic families who had fallen on hard times. Others, like Columbus, were not of noble birth but hoped to gain entrance to the aristocracy as a reward for their daring achievements. By taking the risks of exploration outside Europe, explorers sought to win recognition and rewards within European society.

The insecurity and uncertainty of fifteenth-century life encouraged a few Europeans to take great risks, such as embarking on a dangerous sea voyage through uncharted waters to points unknown.

Scientific and technological advances also helped set the stage for exploration. The invention of movable type stimulated the diffusion of information among literate Europeans. In the last half of the fifteenth century, printing presses churned out thousands of books a year, accelerating the spread of fresh ideas. Columbus, like many other Europeans, bought books, read them, and grappled with them, making detailed notes in the margins of pages. Improvements in navigation made it possible for Columbus and other mariners to better determine their ship's direction, speed, and location, even when out of sight of land. By the end of the fourteenth century, the crucial navigational aids employed by explorers were already available. Compasses were in widespread use. Hourglasses allowed fairly precise determination of elapsed time, useful in estimating speed. The astrolabe and the quadrant, devices for determining latitude, were beginning to be adopted by sailors. However, the difficulty of standing on the pitching deck of a ship at sea and sighting the star Polaris while simultaneously measuring the angle it formed with the horizon often made the readings worthless. Even experienced sailors sometimes became hopelessly lost. Charts called portulanos helped them find their way if they were within sight of land. Portulanos included detailed drawings of the shoreline and compass settings for sailing from one point to another. Fifteenth-century merchant ships designed for the Mediterranean trade to the North Atlantic were built to carry heavy cargoes long distances in stormy seas—qualities as useful for exploration as for trade.

These and other technological advances were known to many people throughout fifteenth-century Europe. The Portuguese intentionally seized them to blaze a trail beyond the limits of the known world.

A Century of Portuguese Exploration

In many ways, Portugal was an unlikely candidate to take the lead in exploration. A small country, Portugal was populated by poor peasants governed by a tiny minority of noble families. Europe's richest courts and most brilliant thinkers were elsewhere, especially in Italy. Yet Portugal, with less than 2 percent of the population of Christian Europe, devoted far more energy and wealth to the geographical exploration of the world between 1415 and 1460 than all the other countries of Europe combined.

Facing the Atlantic on the Iberian peninsula, the Portuguese lived on the fringes of the thriving Mediterranean trade. During the fourteenth century, merchants and sailors in Lisbon gained valuable experience in the extensive North Atlantic trade that Italians still controlled at its eastern source. As a Christian kingdom, Portugal cooperated with Spanish monarchs in the Reconquest, the centuries-long drive to expel Muslims from their residence on the Iberian peninsula. The religious zeal that propelled the Reconquest also justified continued expansion into what the Portuguese considered heathen lands. The key victory came in 1415 when Portuguese forces conquered Ceuta, a Muslim bastion at the mouth of the Strait of Gibraltar. After 1415, Muslim enemies no longer blocked Portugal's access to the Atlantic coast of Africa.

The Portuguese government actively encouraged exploration. The most influential advocate was Prince Henry the Navigator. The third son of the Portuguese king, Henry channeled his energy and ambition into sponsoring voyages of exploration and conquest. From 1415 until his death in 1460, he stood at the forefront of Portuguese expansion, collecting the latest information about sailing techniques and geography, advocating new crusades against the Muslims, encouraging fresh sources of trade to fatten Portuguese pocketbooks, and pushing explorers to go farther and farther still.

Henry had the backing of the king and the pope to extend the Reconquest down the African coast. Missionaries were essential passengers aboard the explorers' ships. However, economic motives fueled Portuguese exploration. Conquests along the African coast promised to wrest wheat fields from their Moroccan owners and secure Portugal's food supply. Africa also supplied most of Europe's gold. Produced in mines along the headwaters of the Niger, Senegal, and Gambia Rivers, African gold passed through the hands of Mali traders, who took it by caravan across the Sahara Desert to the east-

BENIN BRONZE
This bronze was crafted in the sixteenth century by a highly skilled artist of the Benin people of western Africa. The bronze shows a Benin chief flanked by two of his warriors (lower left and right) and a Portuguese man (upper right). The Portuguese figure holds a gold spiral in his hand, presumably obtained in trade with Africans. In turn, the chief wears coral beads obtained in trade with the Portuguese on the African coast. The heavily armed chief and warriors suggest one reason why the Portuguese confined their activities to the coast. Note that the Portuguese figure does not have a weapon, clearly indicating the artist's sense of who had the upper hand.
British Museum.

ern Mediterranean. Rumors of the wealth of Mali raced through Europe after a Mali ruler made a pilgrimage to Mecca in 1324 and distributed lavish gifts transported by more than eighty camels, each of them carrying three hundred pounds of gold. Gold was the basis of currency in European trade and it was scarce in the fifteenth century. The accelerating pace of commerce increased the need for currency in Europe, while purchases in the East drained gold away from European markets.

At first, the possibility of opening a sea route to the rich trade of the East was unimaginable. It played no part in Portuguese calculations until the 1440s, about thirty years after their African explorations had begun. When the word *discovery* first entered the Portuguese language, it meant pushing back the boundaries of the Mediterranean world and penetrating the mists that had caused sailors to name the ocean off the south coast of Morocco the Sea of Darkness. Portuguese sailors slowly learned how to sail through those mists and take advantage of the winds and currents of the mid-Atlantic, laying the foundation of expertise and confidence that ultimately permitted Columbus to dream of going west.

Neither the Portuguese nor anybody else in Europe knew how big Africa was. At first, Portuguese mariners cautiously edged into the Sea of Darkness along the African coast, seldom venturing beyond sight of land. By 1434, they had reached the northern edge of the Sahara Desert, where strong westerly currents swept them far out to sea. Within the next few years they learned how to ride the powerful westerly currents far away from the coast before sailing back toward land, a technique that allowed them to reach Cape Verde by 1444.

To stow the supplies necessary for long periods at sea and to withstand the battering of ocean waves, the Portuguese developed the caravel, a sturdy ship that became the workhorse of exploration. The caravel enabled Portuguese sailors to round Cape Verde by first sailing hundreds of miles west into the Atlantic before catching favorable trade winds and currents that swung them back along the African coast. Navigating these huge westward loops into the Atlantic, Portuguese caravels sailed into and around the Gulf of Guinea and as far south as the Congo by 1480.

Portuguese explorations paid off handsomely in trade with Africans. Although fierce African resistance confined the Portuguese to coastal trading posts, Portuguese traders bartered successfully for gold, slaves, and ivory. African rulers controlled the African interior and, to a large degree, the terms of trade on the coast. The Portuguese tried to stay on good terms with the leaders of such powerful societies as the Wolof of Senegambia and the Obas of Benin. Portuguese merchants learned that relatively peaceful trading posts were far more profitable than violent conquests and attempts at colonization. In the 1460s, the Portuguese employed African slaves to develop sugar plantations on the Cape Verde Islands, inaugurating an association between African slaves and plantation labor that would flourish in the New World in the centuries to come.

About 1480, the Portuguese began a conscious search for a sea route to Asia. Sailors now had to navigate enormous westward loops, this time into the South Atlantic, to avoid the strong northerly currents streaming around the Cape of Good Hope at the southern tip of Africa. In 1488, Bartolomeu Dias sailed around the Cape far enough to discover that the African coast finally turned north. He hurried back to Lisbon with the exciting news that it appeared to be possible to sail on to India and China. In 1498, after ten years of careful preparation, Vasco da Gama commanded the first Portuguese fleet that sailed to India. Da Gama learned about the potential profits of seaborne trade with the East. Pepper, for example, could be purchased in Calicut for 96 percent less than in Venice. Portugal quickly capitalized on the obvious commercial potential of da Gama's new sea route.

Within a few years, the Portuguese established and defended trading posts in India and pushed on to Indonesia and China (collectively referred to as the East Indies). By the early sixteenth century, the Portuguese commanded a far-flung empire in the East Indies. Portuguese officials administered local governments, and Catholic missionaries baptized thousands of Asian Christians. But the lifeblood of the empire was commerce. The new sea route to the East eliminated overland travel and the numerous intermediate merchants and their markups, integral parts of the old Mediterranean trade routes. As a result, Portuguese merchants could set a much lower price on eastern goods. Lower prices allowed Europeans to purchase more eastern goods than ever before, to the great profit of Portuguese traders.

By a century of African explorations, Portugal broke the monopoly of the old Mediterranean trade with the East, dramatically expanded the known world, established a network of missions and trading posts in Africa and Asia, and developed methods of sailing the high seas that Columbus employed on his revolutionary voyage west.

A Surprising New World in the Western Atlantic

In many ways, the Portuguese were the logical candidates to discover America. They had pioneered the frontiers of seafaring, exploration, and geography for almost a century. However, the knowledge and experience that led them around the Cape of Good Hope discouraged them from trying to sail across the Atlantic. They knew better than to undertake such a risky venture. The discovery of America required someone bold enough to believe that the experts were wrong, that despite the best available scientific knowledge, it was possible to reach the East Indies by sailing west. That person was Christopher Columbus.

Born in 1451 into the family of an obscure master weaver in Genoa, Italy, Columbus received a practical education at his father's woolen looms, in the streets, and along the wharves of the city. The allure of ships from remote Mediterranean ports proved irresistible to Columbus. Like thousands of other Genoese boys, he went to sea when he was about fourteen. Crisscrossing the Mediterranean as a sailor, he learned the arts of navigation, although he continued to work as a weaver. About 1476, Columbus moved to Lisbon and two or three years later married Felipa Moniz. Felipa gave Columbus valuable connections to Portugal's royal court. Her father, Bartolomeu, had been raised in the household of Prince Henry the Navigator and had retained close ties to the prince. Bartolomeu helped conquer the Madeira Islands, where he became a prominent merchant deeply involved in the Portuguese voyages to the African coast. Although Bartolomeu died long before Felipa's marriage, Columbus inherited his maps and papers crammed with information about the currents and winds of the Atlantic gathered from innumerable Portuguese sailors. Columbus himself sailed frequently to the Madeira Islands and at least twice all the way to the coast of central Africa. He learned firsthand about the westward loops into the Atlantic that took advantage of prevailing winds and currents. By the mid-1480s, he had become obsessed with the idea of reaching Asia by continuing to sail west instead of turning back toward the African coast.

The Explorations of Columbus

Like other Europeans, Columbus believed that the earth was a sphere. Theoretically, they felt, it was possible to reach the East Indies by sailing west. Ancient scientists whose writings were revered by contemporary Renaissance scholars disagreed about the practicality of the idea. Both the philosopher Aristotle and the geographer Strabo suggested it could be done. Ptolemy, an ancient geographer whose writings were considered the final authority by most fifteenth-century Europeans, concluded that the earth was simply too big to make it feasible to sail west from Europe to Asia. Sailors would die of thirst and starvation before they reached the East Indies.

Columbus rejected this conventional Ptolemaic wisdom. He preferred the estimate of the earth's size worked out by a medieval Muslim geographer. With a series of flawed calculations converting Arabic miles to nautical equivalents, Columbus estimated the circumference of the earth at a little over 16,000 nautical miles, a good 25 percent smaller than it really is. Columbus reasoned that Asia lay about 2,500 miles from the westernmost boundary of the known world, a shorter distance than Portuguese ships routinely sailed between Lisbon and the African Congo. In fact, the shortest distance to Japan from Europe's jumping off point in the Canary Islands was almost 11,000 miles. Convinced that his misguided calculations were correct, Columbus became obsessed with a scheme to prove he was right.

Columbus tried to convince the Portuguese king to sponsor an expedition west. But his peculiar notions about geography did not divert the Portuguese monarchy from its lucrative African explorations. Disappointed by the Portuguese, Columbus moved to Spain in 1485 and sought backing from King Ferdinand and Queen Isabella. Experts on geography and navigation advised the monarchs that Columbus's plan violated the basic precepts of contemporary knowledge and had little to recommend it. He continued to lobby for his plan in Spain and even tried to interest the royal courts of England and France. He obtained only polite skepticism and a few modest but encouraging grants—until 1492, when Ferdinand and Isabella finally agreed to finance most of the journey. The monarchs saw Columbus's venture as an inexpensive gamble: If it failed, not much was lost; if it succeeded, a great deal might be gained. In addition to money and their royal blessing, the monarchs gave Columbus a letter of introduction to the Grand Khan of the Mongols, whom Columbus expected to meet soon after he arrived in China.

After barely three months of hurried preparation, Columbus and his small fleet—the *Niña* and *Pinta*, both caravels, and the *Santa María*, a larger merchant vessel—embarked for the Canary Islands along the westerly route into the Atlantic that Portuguese sailors had pioneered seventy-five years earlier. When he cast off from the Canaries, he did not head for the coast of Africa; instead he kept sailing west. Six weeks later, he landed on a tiny Caribbean island (probably Watling Island), which he named San Salvador.

MAP 2.2
European Explorations in Sixteenth-Century America
This map illustrates the approximate routes of early European explorations of the New World. Note that — with the exception of the voyage of John Cabot — English, French, and Dutch explorers were late-comers. What accounts for their tardiness?

Columbus and his men understood that they had made a momentous discovery. Yet they found it frustrating. Although the Tainos proved friendly and accommodating, they possessed little gold and none of the riches Columbus expected to find in the East. For three months Columbus cruised from island to island, looking for the king of Japan and reconnoitering these strange new lands.

In mid-January 1493, he started back, taking seven Tainos with him. Blown off course by storms, he landed first in Portugal, where he was obliged to report his exciting news to the king. The Portuguese found nothing astounding about Columbus's discovery. They believed he had simply found some new islands far out in the Atlantic. When Columbus finally managed to reach Isabella and Ferdinand in mid-March, they were overjoyed by his news. With a voyage that had lasted barely eight months, Columbus appeared to have catapulted Spain from a secondary position in the race for a sea route to Asia into that of a serious challenger to Portugal, whose explorers had not yet sailed to

India or China. Columbus and his Taino companions became the toast of the royal court. Columbus was appointed Admiral of the Ocean Sea, viceroy and governor of the islands he had discovered, and a member of the hereditary nobility, and he was permitted to use the royal insignia on his coat of arms. All seven Tainos were baptized as Christians, Ferdinand and his son serving as their godfathers.

The Spanish monarchs, following Portuguese precedent, rushed to the pope to obtain confirmation of their claim to Columbus's discoveries. Pope Alexander VI, a Spaniard, complied. In May 1493, he issued the decree *Inter caetera* granting to Spain all land discovered west of an imaginary line lying 300 miles west of the Azores. The decree alarmed the Portuguese, who believed that it violated their rights under previous papal grants. To protect their African claims, the Portuguese negotiated with Spain the Treaty of Tordesillas in 1494. The treaty shifted the imaginary line to 1,100 miles west of the Canary Islands. Land discovered west of the line belonged to Spain, while Portugal claimed land to the east. In effect, the treaty reassured Portugal and allowed Spain to follow up Columbus's discovery without being threatened by the menacing Portuguese navy.

In the fall of 1493, Isabella and Ferdinand sent Columbus back west to locate the Asian mainland. This time he commanded a fleet of seventeen ships and more than one thousand men, who planned to settle, explore, find gold, and get rich. Near the end of his first voyage, a shipwreck had forced Columbus to leave behind thirty-nine of his sailors on the island of Hispaniola. When Columbus returned in 1493, he learned that his men had terrorized the Tainos, kidnapped local women, and held them in harems; in retaliation, Taino chiefs had killed all of the Spaniards. The brief history of that first group of Spaniards to reside in the New World prefigured much of what was to happen in the years ahead.

With a voyage that had lasted barely eight months, Columbus appeared to have catapulted Spain from a secondary position in the race for a sea route to Asia into that of a serious challenger to Portugal, whose explorers had not yet sailed to India or China.

Columbus and other Spaniards sailed from island to island. Some gold turned up, but just enough to keep the Spaniards looking for more. The settlers quarreled among themselves and brutalized the Indians. Before long, prospects of beating the Portuguese to Asia began to dim along with the hope of finding vast hoards of gold. Before Columbus died in 1506, he had returned to the New World two more times (1498–1500 and 1502–1504) without relinquishing his belief that the East Indies were there, someplace. Explorers continued to search for a passage to the East or some other source of profit. But for a generation after 1492, the meager results disappointed the Spanish crown.

Nonetheless, Columbus's discoveries forced sixteenth-century Europeans to think about the world in new terms. Columbus proved that it was possible to sail from Europe to the western rim of the Atlantic in six or seven weeks and to get back to Europe. His superior navigational skills set the standard route and time of passage that prevailed for two centuries. Columbus also made clear that beyond the western shores of the Atlantic lay lands entirely unknown to Europeans. The belief that those lands must be part of Asia fired Columbus's imagination. Without this geographical fantasy he would never have undertaken his first voyage; certainly no monarch would have sponsored it. The Asian trade dangled like a tempting carrot just beyond the reach of fifteenth-century rulers and explorers. For many years after 1492, it was not clear whether Columbus had in fact discovered the Atlantic coast of Asia, as he continued to believe, or a barrier to the riches of the East, as he refused to admit.

The Geographic Revolution

Peter Martyr, a priest and humanist scholar who was Queen Isabella's chaplain, was present in 1493 when Columbus first described his discovery to the queen. Soon afterward, Peter Martyr began to use the phrase "New World" to describe what Columbus had found. He accepted Columbus's interpretation that this New World comprised the outlying islands of the East Indies. The truth slowly came into focus as explorers probed to the north and south. Within thirty years of Columbus's initial discovery, Europeans' understanding of world geography underwent a revolution. Of course most Europeans, isolated in rural villages, remained ignorant of the revolution. An elite of perhaps twenty thousand people surrounding the royal courts and trading centers of western Europe had access to information about the new geography of the world. Before 1492, they could not imagine the existence of a New World. It took a generation of additional exploration before they could comprehend the general contours of what Columbus had found.

In 1497, King Henry VII of England, who had spurned Columbus's request for sponsorship a decade earlier, sent another Genoese sailor, John Cabot, to look for a passage to the Indies across the North Atlantic. Cabot managed to reach the tip of Newfoundland, which he too believed was part of Asia. Cabot hurried back to England, assembled a small fleet to follow up his discovery, and returned in 1498. But he was never heard from again. Three thousand miles to the south, in 1498 Columbus touched the mainland of Venezuela, near the mouth of the Orinoco River. A year later, another Spanish expedition landed about six hundred miles farther south, accompanied by Amerigo Vespucci, an Italian businessman whose avocation was geography. In 1500, Pedro Álvars Cabral commanded a Por-

ORBIS TYPVS VNIVERSALIS IVXTA HYDROGRAPHORVM TRADITIONE'A

WALDSEEMÜLLER MAP

In 1507, Martin Waldseemüller prepared this map, carefully conforming to the accepted wisdom of the ancient geographer Ptolemy except, he wrote "as regards the new lands." "Hitherto [the world] has been divided into three parts, Europe, Africa, and Asia," Waldseemüller explained, following Ptolemy. "Now, a fourth part has been discovered. . . . The first three parts are continents, while the fourth is an island. . . ." The map showed that the "new lands" were not connected to Asia, but it left vague the western shores of the "island" he named America.

Courtesy of the John Carter Brown Library at Brown University.

tuguese fleet bound for the Indian Ocean; as it looped westward into the Atlantic, it made a landfall on the coast of Brazil. The next year the Portuguese sent Vespucci west to determine whether Cabral's discovery lay on their side of the Tordesillas line, as in fact it did.

By the beginning of the sixteenth century, it was clear that several large chunks of land cluttered the western Atlantic. A few cartographers speculated that these chunks were connected to one another in a continent that was not Asia. In 1507, Martin Waldseemüller, a German cartographer, published the first map that showed the New World as a continent separate from Asia; he named the continent America, in honor of Vespucci. Waldseemüller's geography did not convince everybody. Other contemporary maps continued to show a water route to Asia across the Western Hemisphere. In 1516, even Waldseemüller retreated and published a revised map that portrayed America jammed against Asia.

Two additional discoveries confirmed Waldseemüller's initial speculation. In 1513, Vasco Núñez de Balboa crossed the isthmus of Panama and reached the Pacific Ocean. Clearly, more water lay between the New World and Asia. How much water Ferdinand Magellan discovered when he set out to circumnavigate the globe in 1519. Sponsored by King Charles I of Spain, Magellan sailed first to the New World. He rounded Cape Horn at the southern tip of South America through what became known as the Straits of Magellan and entered the Pacific late in November 1520. Crossing the Pacific took almost four months. When he reached the Philippines, his crew had been decimated by extreme hunger and thirst. Magellan himself was killed by Philippine tribesmen. A remnant of his expedition continued into the Indian Ocean and managed to transport a cargo of spices back to Spain in 1522.

Magellan's voyage left no doubt that America was a continent separated from Asia by the enormous Pacific Ocean. The voyage made clear that Columbus was dead wrong about the identity of what he had discovered.

In most ways Magellan's voyage was a disaster. One ship and 18 men managed to return from an expedition that had begun with five ships and more than 250 men. But the geographic information it provided left no doubt that America was a conti-

Justifying Conquest

A few individual Spaniards raised their voices against the brutal treatment of Indians in Spanish colonial America. In 1511, a Dominican friar named Antón Montesino delivered a blistering sermon that astonished the Spaniards gathered in the church in Santo Domingo, headquarters of the Spanish Caribbean.

DOCUMENT 1. Excerpt from Montesino's 1511 Sermon

Your greed for gold is blind. Your pride, your lust, your anger, your envy, your sloth, all blind. . . . You are in mortal sin. And you are heading for damnation. . . . For you are destroying an innocent people. For they are God's people, these innocents, whom you destroyed. By what right do you make them die? Mining gold for you in your mines or working for you in your fields, by what right do you unleash enslaving wars upon them? They have lived in peace in this land before you came, in peace in their own homes. They did nothing to harm you to cause you to slaughter them wholesale. . . . Are you not under God's command to love them as you love yourselves? Are you out of your souls, out of your minds? Yes. And that will bring you to damnation.

Montesino returned to Spain to bring the Indians' plight to the king's attention. In 1512 and 1513, King Ferdinand met with philosophers, theologians, and other advisers and concluded that the only justification for conquest was to spread the Christian faith. To buttress this claim, the king had his advisers prepare the Requerimiento. *Conquistadors were commanded to read the* Requerimiento *to Indians before any act of conquest. Beginning in 1514, they routinely did so, reading aloud in Spanish while other Spaniards brandishing unsheathed swords stood nearby.*

DOCUMENT 2: Excerpt from the *Requerimiento*

On the part of the king . . . [and] queen of [Spain], subduers of the barbarous nations, we their servants notify and make known to you, as best we can, that the Lord our God, living and eternal, created the heaven and the earth, and one man and one woman, of whom you and we, and all the men of the world, were and are descendants. . . .

God our lord gave charge to one man called St. Peter, that he should be lord and superior to all the men in the world, that all should obey him, and that he should be the head of the whole human race, wherever men should live . . . and he gave him the world for his kingdom and jurisdiction.

And he commanded him to place his seat in Rome, as the spot most fitting to rule the world from. . . . This man was called Pope, as if to say, Admirable Great Father and Governor of men. The men who lived in that time obeyed that St. Peter and took him for lord, king, and superior of the universe. So also they have regarded the others who after him have been elected to the pontificate, and so has it been continued even till now, and will continue till the end of the world.

One of these pontiffs, who succeeded that St. Peter as lord of the world . . . made donation of these islands and mainland to the aforesaid king and queen [of Spain] and to their successors. . . .

---

nent separated from Asia by the enormous Pacific Ocean. The voyage made clear that Columbus was dead wrong about the identity of what he had discovered. Furthermore, while the voyage proved it was possible to sail west to reach the East Indies, it also demonstrated that that was a terrible way to go. Some sixteenth-century explorers continued to hope that a water passage across the American landmass might still be located. But most Europeans who sailed west after Magellan had their sights set on the New World, not on Asia.

Columbus's arrival in the Caribbean anchored the western end of what might be imagined as a sea bridge that spanned the Atlantic, connecting the New World to Europe. That sea bridge ended the separation of the hemispheres and opened a pathway for exploration, conquest, settlement, and commerce that has never since been disrupted. The Europeans who first ventured across that bridge carried with them the legacy of centuries of European expansion, trade, and intellectual awakening. The Native Americans they confronted on the west-

So their highnesses are kings and lords of these islands and mainland by virtue of this donation; and . . . almost all those to whom this has been notified, have received and served their highnesses, as lords and kings, in the way that subjects ought to do, with good will, without any resistance, immediately, without delay, when they were informed of the aforesaid facts. And also they received and obeyed the priests whom their highnesses sent to preach to them and to teach them our holy faith; and all these, of their own free will, without any reward or condition have become Christians, and are so, and the highnesses have joyfully and graciously received them, and they have also commanded them to be treated as their subjects and vassals; and you too are held and obliged to do the same. Wherefore, as best we can, we ask and require that you consider what we have said to you, and that you take the time that shall be necessary to understand and deliberate upon it, and that you acknowledge the Church as the ruler and superior of the whole world, and the high priest called Pope, and in his name the king and queen [of Spain] our lords, in his place, as superiors and lords and kings of these islands and this mainland by virtue of the said donation, and that you consent and permit that these religious fathers declare and preach to you. . . .

If you do so . . . we . . . shall receive you in all love and charity, and shall leave you your wives and your children and your lands free without servitude, that you may do with them and with yourselves freely what you like and think best, and they shall not compel you to turn to Christians unless you yourselves, when informed of the truth, should wish to be converted to our holy Catholic faith. . . . And besides this, their highnesses award you many privileges and exemptions and will grant you many benefits.

But if you do not do this or if you maliciously delay in doing it, I certify to you that with the help of God we shall forcefully enter into your country and shall make war against you in all ways and manners that we can, and shall subject you to the yoke and obedience of the Church and of their highnesses; we shall take you and your wives and your children and shall make slaves of them, and as such shall sell and dispose of them as their highnesses may command; and we shall take away your goods and shall do to you all the harm and damage that we can, as to vassals who do not obey and refuse to receive their lord and resist and contradict him; and we protest that the deaths and losses which shall accrue from this are your fault, and not that of their highnesses, or ours, or of these soldiers who come with us.

Indians who heard the Requerimiento *could not understand Spanish, of course. No native documents survive to record the Indians' thoughts upon hearing the Spaniards' official justification for conquest, even when it was translated into a language they understood. But one conquistador reported that when the* Requerimiento *was translated for two chiefs in Colombia, they responded that if the pope gave the king so much territory that belonged to other people, "the pope must have been drunk."*

Document 1. Zvi Dor-Ner, *Columbus and the Age of Discovery* (New York: William Morrow, 1991), 220–21. Copyright 1991 by William Morrow. Reprinted with permission.

Document 2. Adapted from A. Helps and M. Oppenheim, eds., *The Spanish Conquest in America and Its Relation to the History of Slavery and to the Government of Colonies,* 4 vols., (London and New York, 1900–1904), I, 264–67.

ern shores were biological cousins but cultural strangers. For almost a generation after 1492, Europeans straggled across the sea bridge, not quite sure what to make of these alien peoples and their world. That question was settled forever in the years just after 1519, as Spaniards pushed into the interior of Mexico. What they found there established a two-way traffic across the sea bridge that helped make Spain the most powerful country in both Europe and the New World over the course of the sixteenth century.

Spanish Exploration and Conquest

During the sixteenth century, Spain established its supremacy over the indigenous peoples of Central and South America. In the initial Caribbean phase of conquest (1492–1519), Spanish expeditions reconnoitered the islands, scouted stretches of the mainland coast, and placed settlements on the large islands of Hispaniola, Puerto Rico, Jamaica, and

Cuba. Spanish settlers subjugated island tribes, enslaved their people, and put them to work growing crops and mining gold. But the profits from these early ventures barely covered the costs required to maintain the settlers. After almost thirty years of exploration, the promise of Columbus's discovery seemed illusory.

Soon after 1519, however, that promise was fulfilled, spectacularly. The mainland phase of exploration began in 1519 with Hernán Cortés's march into Mexico and lasted until about 1545, when Spanish conquests extended from northern Mexico to southern Chile, and New World riches filled Spanish treasure chests. Cortés's expedition served as the model for all the rest.

The Conquest of Mexico

Hernán Cortés, who would become the richest and most famous conquistador (conqueror) of all, arrived in the New World in 1504, an obscure nineteen-year-old Spaniard seeking adventure and the opportunity to make a name for himself. He fought in numerous campaigns against the Caribbean Indians and participated in the conquest of Cuba. In 1519, the governor of Cuba authorized Cortés to organize an expedition to investigate rumors of a fabulously wealthy kingdom somewhere in the interior of the mainland. A charming, charismatic leader, Cortés quickly assembled a force of about six hundred men, including soldiers and assorted friars, artisans, and hangers-on. The governor of Cuba soon had second thoughts about entrusting the expedition to a magnetic and unpredictable man like Cortés, and he withdrew permission for the campaign. Characteristically, Cortés ignored the governor, loaded his ragtag army aboard eleven ships, and set out on his freelance crusade, confident that the legal niceties could be sorted out later.

Cortés's confidence that he could talk his way out of most situations and fight his way out of the rest fortified the small band of Spaniards. Landing first on the Yucatán peninsula, Cortés had the good fortune to be given a gift by a Mayan chief: a young woman named Malinali who spoke both Mayan and Nahuatl, the language of most people in Mexico and Central America. Malinali, whom the Spaniards called Marina, soon learned Spanish and became Cortés's interpreter. (She also became one of Cortés's mistresses and bore him a son.) Marina served as the essential conduit of communication between the Spaniards and the Indians. With her help, Cortés talked and fought with Indians along the Gulf coast of Mexico, trying to discover the location of the fabled kingdom.

In Tenochtitlán, the capital of the Mexican empire, the emperor Montezuma heard about some strange creatures along the coast. (Montezuma and his people are often called Aztecs, but they never used that term; they called themselves Mexica.) He feared that the strangers were led by the god Quetzalcoatl, who was returning to Tenochtitlán as predicted by the Mexican religion. Montezuma sent emissaries, carrying gifts appropriate for a god, to meet with the intruders.

When the emissaries arrived, Cortés and his men showed little interest in the dazzling featherwork and other paraphernalia suitable for Quetzalcoatl and other Mexican deities. Cortés inquired about the great emperor who had sent the emissaries, where he lived, and whether he had gold. Cortés obliged the visitors and donned the regalia they had brought, almost certain proof to the Mexica that he was indeed Quetzalcoatl. For their part, the Spaniards astounded the emissaries by blasting their cannon, showing off their iron swords and armor, and exhibiting their horses, which the Mexica had never seen and which they considered a species of supernatural deer.

The emissaries hurried back to Montezuma with their amazing news. Montezuma decided he must welcome Quetzalcoatl with food and hospitality, which he also hoped would postpone (and perhaps prevent) the god's arrival in Tenochtitlán. Montezuma arranged for large quantities of food to be brought to the coast for Cortés and his army. In addition, since Quetzalcoatl presumably hungered for blood, Montezuma sent numerous hostages for sacrifice. Before the food was served to the Spaniards, the Mexica sacrificed the hostages and soaked the food in their blood. This fare sickened the Spaniards and, alone, might have been enough to turn them back to Cuba. However, along with these divine victuals, the Mexica also brought a gift, a "disk in the shape of the sun, as big as a cartwheel and made of very fine gold," as one Mexican recalled. Here was conclusive evidence that the rumors heard by Cortés and his army had some basis in fact.

In August 1519, Cortés embarked on a march to find Montezuma. Leading about 350 men armed with swords, lances, and muskets and supported by ten cannon, four smaller guns, and sixteen horses, Cortés had to live off the land, making friends with the indigenous tribes when he could and killing them when he had to, and often when he did not

CORTÉS ENTERS TENOCHTITLÁN

This drawing by a Mexican artist illustrates Cortés entering Tenochtitlán, the capital of the Mexican empire. Montezuma (standing on the path, right center) offers the Spaniards a gift and huge quantities of food. Marina (lower center) interprets for the Spaniards. Cortés and his men appear to wait in peace, spears tilted backward. This drawing was made after the conquest; the artist almost certainly did not witness this scene. For example, the drawing shows the Spaniards wearing everday, postconquest "civilian" clothing. In fact, on the long march from the coast to Tenochtitlán, the Spaniards constantly dressed for battle, brandishing sabers, crossbows, guns, and cannon. They hoped their awe-inspiring display would intimidate the Indians, by whom they were vastly outnumbered.

Private collection.

have to. In the grueling and bloody expedition, Cortés's soldiers usually slept in their armor, their swords at their sides. Cortés never wavered in his determination to find Montezuma, and his diplomacy and leadership in battle inspired his men to continue, even though they did not know where they were going or how to get there.

On November 8, 1519, Montezuma came out to meet Cortés on a causeway leading into Tenochtitlán. After presenting Cortés with bouquets of flowers, golden necklaces, and other gifts, Montezuma welcomed Cortés and his army to the royal palace and showered them with the lavish hospitality the Mexican tribute system put at his disposal. Quickly, Cortés took Montezuma hostage and held him under house arrest, hoping thereby to make him a puppet through which the Spaniards could rule the Mexican empire. This uneasy peace existed for several months until, after a brutal massacre of many Mexican nobles by one of Cortés's subordinates, the population of Tenochtitlán revolted, murdered Montezuma, and mounted a ferocious assault on the Spaniards. On June 30, 1520, Cortés and about a hundred other Spaniards fought their way out of Tenochtitlán; the gold they had confiscated weighed them down so much they had to drop most of it in the lake and abandon it (where it remains to this day, buried somewhere in the middle of Mexico City) in order to escape with their lives. Cortés retreated to Tlaxcala, where friendly Indians allowed him to regroup, obtain reinforcements, and plan a strategy to conquer Tenochtitlán.

In the spring of 1521, Cortés mounted a complex campaign against the Mexican capital. The Spaniards and tens of thousands of Indian allies laid siege to the city. They advanced slowly along the causeways leading into the city, systematically reducing to rubble every structure in their path in order to deny the Mexica any cover when they counterattacked and forced the Spaniards to retreat, as they often did. This relentless, scorched-earth strategy, a blockade of the city's food and water supplies, and protection from sailboats the Spaniards built and launched on Lake Texcoco to defend against Mexican attacks from canoes finally succeeded in defeating the last Mexican defenders on August 13, 1521. The great capital of the Mexican empire "looked as if it had been ploughed up," one of Cortés's soldiers remembered. A few years later, one of the Mexica described the utter despair of the defeated:

> Broken spears lie in the roads;
> we have torn our hair in grief.
> The houses are roofless now, and their walls
> are red with blood.
>
> Worms are swarming in the streets and plazas,
> and the walls are splattered with gore.
> The water has turned red, as if it were dyed,
> and when we drink it,
> it has the taste of brine.
>
> We have pounded our hands in despair
> against the adobe walls,
> for our inheritance, our city, is lost and dead.
> The shields of our warriors were its defense,
> but they could not save it.
>
> We have chewed dry twigs and salt grasses;
> we have filled our mouths with dust and bits of
>   adobe;
> we have eaten lizards, rats, and worms . . .
> everything that once was precious was now
>   considered worthless.

The Search for Other Mexicos

When Cortés conquered Tenochtitlán, he and his men hoped to find more gold. Cortés was quoted as telling the Mexica, "I and my companions suffer

from a disease of the heart which can only be cured with gold." One of the Mexica who watched the Spaniards loot and pillage commented later that they "lusted for gold. Their bodies swelled with greed . . . they hungered like pigs for that gold."

Lured by their insatiable appetite for gold, conquistadors quickly fanned out from Tenochtitlán in search of other Mexicos. To the south, Guatemala, El Salvador, and Nicaragua came under Spanish control by 1524. The Mayan tribes of the Yucatán peninsula did not succumb for another twenty years. The most spectacular prize fell to Francisco Pizarro, who conquered the Inca empire in Peru. The Incas controlled a vast, complex region that contained more than nine million people and stretched along the western coast of South America for more than two thousand miles, from present-day Quito, Ecuador, to Santiago, Chile. In 1532, Pizarro and his army of fewer than two hundred men captured the Inca emperor Atahualpa and held him hostage. Pizarro demanded ransom, and the Incas responded with by far the largest treasure yet produced by the conquests: gold and silver worth 1.5 million pesos, equivalent to half a century of precious-metal production in Europe. With the ransom safely in their hands, the Spaniards executed Atahualpa. Although periodic rebellion plagued Spanish rulers in Peru until the 1570s, Inca treasure proved that at least one other Mexico did exist.

Lured by their insatiable appetite for gold, conquistadors quickly fanned out from Tenochtitlán in search of other Mexicos.

In the north, Juan Ponce de León, who had coasted around the Florida peninsula in 1513, was encouraged by Cortés's success to return to Florida in 1521, where he was killed in a battle with Calusa Indians. In 1525, Lucas Vázquez de Ayllón led an expedition that explored the Atlantic coast north of Florida to South Carolina. A year later, Ayllón established a small settlement on the Georgia coast that he named San Miguel de Gualdape, the first Spanish attempt to create a town in what is now the United States. Within a few months most of the settlers, including Ayllón, became sick and died, and the few survivors beat a retreat back to the Caribbean. In 1528, Pánfilo de Narváez surveyed the Gulf coast, moving west from Florida to Texas.

The Narváez expedition floundered badly and came to a disastrous end on the Texas coast, near Galveston, where the few survivors were enslaved by coastal Indians. After several years of enslavement, four Spaniards managed to escape and began to try to find their way back to Mexico. Led by Cabeza de Vaca, the Spaniards convinced local tribes that they were holy men who possessed the power to cure the sick. In 1536, Cabeza de Vaca and his companions, accompanied by about six hundred Indians who worshiped them, stumbled upon a group of Spanish slave hunters in northern Mexico and were finally rescued. Cabeza de Vaca's account of his amazing experiences, eventually published in Spain in 1542, stimulated additional interest in exploring the lands north of Mexico.

In 1539, Hernando de Soto, a seasoned conquistador who had taken part in the conquest of Peru, set out with nine ships and more than six hundred companions to find another Peru in North America. Landing in Florida, de Soto literally slashed his way through much of the southeastern United States for three years, employing the conquistadors' methods of brutality to find the rich, majestic civilizations he knew had to be there. After many battles and much hardship, de Soto became sick and died in 1542, and his men buried him in the Mississippi River before turning back to Mexico, disappointed.

Tales of the fabulous wealth of the mythical Seven Cities of Cíbola also lured Francisco Vásquez de Coronado to search the Southwest and Great Plains of North America. In 1540, Coronado left northern Mexico with more than three hundred Spaniards, a thousand Indians, fifteen hundred horses, and a guide named Marcos de Niza, a priest who claimed to know the way to what he called "the greatest and best of the discoveries." Cíbola turned out to be a small Zuñi pueblo of about a hundred families. When the Zuñi shot arrows at the Spaniards, Coronado attacked the pueblo and routed the defenders after a hard battle. Convinced that the rich cities must lie somewhere over the horizon, Coronado sent out scouting parties. One traveled to the edge of the Grand Canyon in northern Arizona. Coronado went east to pueblos near Albuquerque, where the residents soon rebelled against the Spaniards, who had confiscated their food, clothing, and women. Again Coronado conquered the pueblos and again he kept moving all the way to central Kansas before deciding in 1542 that the rumors he had pursued were just that, nothing more.

A SIGN OF CONQUEST
This skull was recently excavated by archaeologists from the site of a native American village in northwest Georgia visited by de Soto's expedition in 1540. The skull is that of an Indian man in his fifties who suffered a fatal sword wound above his right eye. Combined with slashed and severed arm and leg bones from the same site, the skull offers compelling proof of the brutality de Soto employed against indigenous peoples on his expedition through the Southeast. No native weapons were capable of inflicting the wounds indelibly marked on this skull and other bones.
Dr. Robert L. Blakely.

Farther west, Juan Rodríguez Cabrillo, an experienced conquistador like Hernando de Soto, led an expedition in 1542 that sailed along the coast of California. Cabrillo died on Santa Catalina Island, offshore from present-day Los Angeles, but his men sailed on to the border of Oregon, where a ferocious storm forced them to turn back toward Mexico.

Why Did Cortés Win?

By CONQUERING MEXICO, Hernán Cortés demonstrated that Columbus had in fact discovered a New World of enormous value to the Old. But why did a few hundred Spaniards so far away from home defeat millions of Indians fighting on their home turf?

First, several military factors favored the Spaniards. They possessed superior military technology. They fought with weapons of iron and steel against the Mexica's stone, wood, and copper; they charged on horseback against Mexican warriors on foot; they ignited gunpowder to fire cannon and muskets toward the attacking Mexicas, whose only source of power was human muscle. However, the Mexica's immense numerical superiority partially offset the Spaniards' weaponry.

The Spaniards also enjoyed superior military organization, although it was hardly a spit-and-polish hierarchy. Cortés's army was composed of soldiers of fortune, young men who hoped to fight for God and the king and to get rich. Far from a highly disciplined, professional fighting force, they were governed by the force of Cortés's personality, by their own desire for glory and riches, and by fear of the consequences of not following orders. The unsteady discipline among the Spaniards is suggested by Cortés's decision to beach and dismantle the ships that had brought his small army to the Mexican mainland—after that, the only way for his men to go was forward.

The Spaniards were a well-oiled military machine compared with the Mexica. The Mexica tended to attack from ambush or in waves of frontal assaults, with great courage but little organization or discipline. They seldom sustained attacks, even when they had the Spaniards on the run. In the siege of Tenochtitlán, for example, the Mexica often paused to sacrifice any Spanish soldiers they had captured, taking time to skin "their faces," one Spaniard recalled, "which they afterward prepared like leather gloves, with their beards on." Spanish tactics, in contrast, emphasized concentrating their soldiers to magnify the effect of their firepower and to maintain communication in the thick of battle.

But perhaps the Spaniards' most fundamental military advantage was their concept of war. The Mexican concept of war was shaped by the nature of their empire. They fought to impose their tribute system on others and to take captives for sacrifices. From their viewpoint, war made their adversaries realize the high cost of continuing to fight and gave them a big incentive to surrender and pay tribute. For the Spaniards, war meant destroying the enemy's ability to fight. In short, the Spaniards sought total victory; the Mexica sought surrender. All these military factors weakened the Mexica's resistance to the Spaniards, but they were insufficient to explain Cortés's victory.

Disease played a major part in the Mexica's defeat. When the Mexica confronted Cortés, they were not at full strength. An epidemic of smallpox and measles had struck the Caribbean in 1519, arrived in Mexico with Cortés and his men, and lasted through 1522. Thousands of Indians died, and many others became too sick to fight or help resist the invaders. When the Spaniards were regrouping in Tlaxcala, after their disastrous evacuation of Tenochtitlán, a great plague broke out in the Mexican capital. As one Mexica explained to a Spaniard shortly after the conquest, the plague lasted for seventy days, "striking everywhere in the city and killing a vast number of our people. Sores erupted on our faces, our breasts, our bellies; we were covered with agonizing sores from head to foot. The illness was so dreadful that no one could walk or move. The sick were so utterly helpless that they could only lie on their beds like corpses, unable to move their limbs or even their heads. A great many died from this plague, and many others died of hunger. They could not get up to search for food, and everybody else was too sick to care for them, so they starved to death in their beds."

The sickness was not confined to Tenochtitlán. It also killed and weakened people in the areas surrounding the city, spreading back along the network of trade and tribute that fed the city, reducing its food supply, and further weakening the survivors. While the Mexica were decimated by their first exposure to smallpox and measles, the Spaniards were for all practical purposes immune, having previously been exposed to the diseases. European viruses probably played at least as large a role in the conquest as weapons and military tactics.

Religion also contributed to the Mexica's defeat. Mexica religious doctrine led Montezuma to be hesitant and uncertain in confronting the Spaniards during the months when they were most vulnerable. While Cortés marched toward Tenochtitlán, it was not at all clear to the Indians that the Spaniards and their horses were mortals. Cortés worked hard

CONQUEST WARFARE

This postconquest painting by a sixteenth-century Mexican artist is one of a series illustrating crucial battles in the ultimate defeat of the Mexica. Here Mexican warriors are attacking the conquistadors shortly before the Spaniards retreated from Tenochtitlán and regrouped for the final siege. The distinctive shields and costumes of the Mexica signify their military status, which was based on their battlefield prowess. The Spaniards, in contrast, wear gray metal armor, their crossbows and guns pitted against the Mexica's spears. The Mexica won this particular battle, a point the artist suggests by making the Mexican warriors appear bigger while the massed conquistadors lean slightly backward.
Oronoz.

to maintain the illusion, hiding Spaniards who died. But by the time Cortés retreated from Tenochtitlán, the Mexica knew that the Spaniards could be killed, and their resistance stiffened accordingly.

While the Mexica's religion reduced their initial resistance to the conquistadors, Christianity strengthened the Spaniards. The Spaniards' Christianity was a confident, militant, and ruthless faith that commanded its followers to destroy idolatry, root out heresy, slay infidels, and subjugate nonbelievers. Their religious certainty had been honed for centuries in the battles of the Reconquest that recaptured the Iberian peninsula from the Muslims. Christianity was as much a part of the conquistadors' armory as chain mail and gunpowder.

Mexican military commanders often turned to their priests for military guidance. Although the Spaniards routinely celebrated mass and prayed before battles, their military and diplomatic decisions were not made by friars, but by Cortés and his subordinates, tough, practical, wily men. When the Spaniards lost battles, they did not worry that God had abandoned them. However, when the Mexica lost battles advised by their priests, they confronted the distressing question of the power of their gods. Their gods no longer seemed to listen to them. The

deadly sickness sweeping through the countryside also seemed to show that their gods had abandoned them. "Cut us loose," one Mexican pleaded, "because the gods have died."

Finally, political factors proved decisive in the Mexica's defeat. Cortés shrewdly exploited the tensions between the Mexica and their subjects. With skillful negotiation and diplomacy, Cortés obtained the cooperation of thousands of Indian soldiers, porters, and food suppliers. These Indian allies were the crucial ingredient in the Spaniards' success. Besides actually fighting alongside Cortés, the Spaniards' Indian allies provided the invaders with a fairly secure base from which to maneuver against the Mexica's stronghold. Cortés's small army fought alongside thousands of Indians who were eager to seek revenge against the Mexica. Hundreds of thousands of other Indians helped the Spaniards by not contributing to the Mexica's defense. These passive allies of the Spaniards sat on their hands, preventing the Mexica from fully capitalizing on their overwhelming numerical superiority. In the end, although many factors contributed to the conquest, Cortés won because the Mexican empire—the source of the Mexica's impressive wealth and power—was their Achilles heel.

These probes into North America by de Soto, Coronado, and Cabrillo persuaded Spaniards that, while enormous territories stretched northward, their inhabitants had little to loot or exploit. After a generation of vigorous exploration, Spaniards concluded that there was only one Mexico and one Peru.

New Spain in the Sixteenth Century

For all practical purposes, Spain dominated the New World in the sixteenth century. Portugal claimed the giant territory of Brazil under the Tordesillas treaty, but during most of the sixteenth century the Portuguese were far more concerned with exploiting their hard-won trade with the East Indies than in colonizing the New World. England and France envied the Spanish discoveries in the Western Hemisphere, especially after 1519, but they were absorbed in the affairs of Europe and largely lost interest in America until late in the century. In the decades after 1519, Spaniards created the distinctive colonial society of New Spain that gave other Europeans a striking illustration of how the New World could be made to serve the purposes of the Old.

Spaniards' economic, religious, and political dominance relegated Indians to an inferior status in New Spain, inaugurating a racial hierarchy of white supremacy that—in one way or another—was replicated endlessly in subsequent New World colonies. Spaniards forced Indians to work for them in the fields and mines that enormously enriched colonists and the Spanish monarchy. Spanish missionaries worked zealously to convert Indians to Christianity. Spanish colonial policies and European diseases had catastrophic consequences for Indians, who lost control of their world after 1492. Only on the fringes of New Spain—including the area of the present-day United States—did Native American societies elude the control of Spanish colonists. Spain established scattered outposts of settlement in North America to buttress its territorial claims, but the heartland of New Spain remained in Central and South America.

From Conquistadors to Colonists

The conquest of Mexico and the rest of New Spain had been organized and paid for by individual investors, men who hoped to find riches that would repay their investment manyfold. The soldiers who fought with Cortés, for example, purchased their own weapons, armor, and supplies. They were entrepreneurs of conquest, anticipating a high return from their high-risk venture. The Spanish monarchy, which claimed ownership of most of the land in the Western Hemisphere, gave the conquistadors permission to undertake their speculative forays. In return, the crown received the "royal fifth," that is, one-fifth of any loot confiscated by the conquerors. Virtually every expedition of conquest included a representative of the crown with the responsibility to make certain that the royal fifth was skimmed off the top of any plunder. When the conquering Spaniards captured golden artifacts made by indigenous people, they usually melted them, in part to allow the royal fifth to be assessed immediately.

In the decades after 1519, Spaniards created the distinctive colonial society of New Spain that gave other Europeans a striking illustration of how the New World could be made to serve the purposes of the Old.

Although the crown got paid first and in full, when the remaining treasure was finally divided up, the conquistadors themselves received very little, in most cases far less than they invested. For example, a horseman who accompanied Cortés and earned a share of the booty of Tenochtitlán received one hundred gold pesos, which was only about one-fifth of the man's investment in his own horse. The share of a foot soldier was even less. After almost three years of bloody, hand-to-hand combat, such token payments did not make Cortés's soldiers happy.

Luckily for Cortés and the Spanish crown, the conquistadors found something far more valuable than gold as they pillaged Tenochtitlán, room by room. The Spaniards seized the Mexica's tribute rolls, documents that pictured exactly what each town in the Mexica empire paid in tribute. They showed that 370 towns paid one-third or more of their total production in tribute to the Mexica. This knowledge, along with their lust for gold, spurred Cortés's men to split up into smaller groups and extend the conquest throughout the reaches of the Mexican empire. They found some gold, but not nearly enough to satisfy them. Cortés, aware of the

MEXICAN TRIBUTE ACCOUNT

This page from the Codex Mendoza *records the tribute paid to the Mexican capital by the Xoconochco province, a tropical region along the Pacific coast near the Guatemalan border (present-day Chiapas). Prepared by a Mexican artist around 1540 for the viceroy of New Spain, the* Codex Mendoza *provides an inventory of the tribute exacted by the Mexican empire. Most Mexican provinces paid tribute in food or textiles, but Xoconochco contributed, as this account specifies, "first, two large strings of green stones, rich stones; also one thousand four hundred bundles of rich feathers of blue, red, green, turquoise-blue, . . . which are drawn in six bundles; also eighty complete bird skins, of*

rich turquoise-blue feathers and purple breasts, of the colors drawn; also another eighty complete skins of said birds; also eight hundred bundles of rich feathers; also eight hundred bundles of rich long green feathers . . . ; also two lip plugs of clear amber decorated with gold; also two hundred loads of cacao; also forty jaguar skins . . . ; also eight hundred rich bowls for drinking cacao; also two large pieces of clear amber of the size of a brick — all of which they gave in tribute every six months." In the Mexican capital, artists crafted the exotic feathers and skins into elaborate cloaks and the stones and amber into fashionable jewelry. The cacao was brewed into a mildly intoxicating beverage.

Bodleian Library, Oxford, U.K. MS.Arch.Seld.A1.Fol.47r.

MISSIONARY CATECHISM

In the 1540s, Franciscan missionaries tried to teach basic Christian rituals by using pictures that somewhat resembled the glyphs in pre-Columbian codices (see page 27), hoping to appeal to the Mexica's respect for the power of ancient texts. Known as Testerian manuscripts, these catechisms were read from left to right across two facing pages and then back from right to left on the next line, and so on. This catechism illustrates the prayer "Salve Regina"; the words below the pictures are in the Otomi language. Can you puzzle out some of the symbols that were intended to communicate the words of the prayer? Begin with the title, "La Salve Regina," at the far left of the second line: "Hail to the Queen who reigns above / Mother of clemency and love! / Hail, thou our hope, life, sweetness! We / Eve's banished children cry to thee. / We, from this wretched vale of tears, / Send sighs and groans unto thy ears; / Oh then, sweet advocate, bestow / A pitying look on us below! / After this exile let us see / Our blessed Jesus, born of thee. / O merciful, O pious Maid / O gracious Mary, lend thy aid."
Bibliothèque Nationale, Paris/Arch. Photeb.

risks to him and the monarchy posed by poor, disgruntled, battle-hardened conquistadors, decided to compensate his men by giving them the towns the Spaniards had subdued.

The distribution of conquered towns institutionalized the system of *encomienda*, which empowered conquistadors to rule the Indians and the lands in and around one or more towns. The concept of encomienda was familiar to the Spaniards since they had employed it to govern regions recaptured from the Muslims during the Reconquest of the Iberian peninsula, and they had adopted it when they colonized the Caribbean. In New Spain, encomienda transferred to the Spanish *encomendero* (the man who "owned" the town) the tribute that the town had previously paid to the Mexica. In theory, encomienda involved a reciprocal relationship between the encomendero and "his" Indians. In return for the tribute and labor of the Indians, the encomendero was supposed to encourage the Indians to convert to Christianity, to be responsible for their material well-being, and to guarantee order and justice in the town. The theory of encomienda was an idealized version of the relationship between lord and peasant in medieval Europe. It illustrates how institutions, relationships, and ideas that were decaying in Europe were revitalized in the New World and imposed on subject peoples.

Catholic missionaries labored earnestly to convert the Indians to Christianity. Franciscan friars arrived in Mexico in 1524, and they were followed in a few years by Dominicans and Augustinians. At first, the missionaries enjoyed great success. The Indians welcomed these men who, in contrast to the despotic conquistadors, were relatively humble and kind. The friars baptized tens of thousands of Indians. "We are much busied with great and constant labor to convert the infidel," the newly appointed bishop of Mexico, Juan de Zumárraga, reported in 1531. He boasted of "five hundred [Indian] temples razed to the ground, and twenty thousand idols of the devils worshiped [by the Indians] smashed and burned." However, the missionaries soon discovered that the Indians had merely added the Christian God to their own deities, whom they continued to worship, even with human sacrifice. Some friars began to realize that authentic conversions could take place only if the Spaniards first learned exactly what the Indians did believe. A few missionaries studied Indian languages and culture; Fray Bernardino de Sahagún conducted extensive interviews with the Mexica and, over forty years, compiled a systematic firsthand account of Mexican society, *General History of the Things of New Spain*. Most friars, however, focused their efforts on instructing Indian children in the religious and other ways of the Spaniards. They did not hesitate to resort to whippings, imprisonment, and even executions to emphasize their message. They enlisted the labor of Indian converts to build numerous schools, convents, and churches. By midcentury, nearly twelve hundred missionaries toiled in Mexico and Peru. By then, most of them had come to believe that the Indians were lesser beings inherently incapable of fully understanding the mysteries of Christian faith.

The behavior of the encomenderos also departed from the assumptions of reciprocity between Indians and Spaniards. In practice, encomienda pla-

cated the conquistadors. By the 1550s, some 130 encomenderos in Mexico controlled more than 180,000 Indians. However, the encomenderos were far more interested in what the Indians could do for them than in what they could or should do for the Indians. Encomenderos subjected Indians to chronic overwork, mistreatment, and abuse. They forced them to do labor of every sort without recompense. As one Spaniard remarked, "Everything [the Indians] do is slowly done and by compulsion. They are malicious, lying, thievish. . . . They are very ungrateful. . . . They are capital enemies of the Spaniards." Encomenderos collected tribute from the Indians, then forced them to buy it back at wildly inflated prices. They confiscated Indian possessions, ravaged the women, beat them, imprisoned them, and turned dogs loose to tear at them. The encomenderos were responsible for the brutal deaths of thousands of Indians.

Economically, however, encomienda recognized a fundamental reality of New Spain. The most important treasure the Spaniards could plunder from the New World was not gold, but Indian labor. The central economic question for the rulers of New Spain was how to exploit Indian labor, the hemisphere's richest natural resource. Encomienda answered that question by giving encomenderos the right to force Indians to work when, where, and how the Spaniards pleased.

Encomienda recognized a fundamental reality of New Spain. The most important treasure the Spaniards could plunder from the New World was not gold, but Indian labor.

Encomienda engendered two groups of influential critics. A few of the missionaries were horrified at the brutal mistreatment of the Indians. The cruelty of the encomenderos made it difficult for the priests to persuade Indians of the tender mercies of the Spaniards' God. Fray Bartolomé de Las Casas pointedly criticized the treatment of the Indians. "What will [the Indians] think about the God of the Christians," he asked, when they see their friends "with their heads split, their hands amputated, their intestines torn open? . . . Would they want to come to Christ's sheepfold after their homes had been destroyed, their children imprisoned, their wives raped, their cities devastated, their maidens deflowered, and their provinces laid waste?" Las quintlahque.

EXECUTING INDIANS WHO
RESIST CHRISTIANITY
*The Spaniards did not hesitate
to execute Indians who opposed the spread of Christianity, just as the* Requerimiento
*promised (see Texts in Histori-
cal Context, page 46). This
sixteenth-century Mexican
drawing shows a woman and
five men hanging from the gallows while two Franciscan friars oversee two heretics burning at the stake under the
approving gaze of Cortés
(lower right). Indians whom
the Spaniards termed
"heretics" or "idolaters" were
guilty — in the Spaniards'
eyes — of refusing to relinquish their own religious ideas
and rituals for Christianity.
From the viewpoint of these
Indians, presumably it was the
Spaniards who were the
heretics and idolaters.*
Descriptión de Tlaxcala, fol. 242 r.

Casas vigorously defended the humanity of the Indians, arguing that they were just as much children
of God as their Spanish overlords.

Las Casas and other outspoken priests softened
few hearts among the encomenderos, but they did
win some sympathy for the Indians from the Spanish monarchy and royal bureaucracy. Brutality toward the Indians seemed excessive and somewhat
embarrassing to the government in Spain. Royal officials, however, interpreted the encomenderos'
treatment of the Indians as part of a larger general
problem: the autonomy of the encomenderos. The
Spanish monarchy sought to abolish the encomienda in an effort to undermine the authority of
the encomenderos, to take the government of New
Spain away from swashbuckling old conquistadors,
and to put it in the hands of report-writing bureaucrats who answered to the crown.

The transition from encomienda to a crown-
controlled bureaucracy was a long, slow process because of the local power of the encomenderos, the

difficulty of efficiently projecting royal authority
across the Atlantic, and the unwillingness of the
monarchy to allow reforms to interrupt the very tangible rewards that flowed from New Spain. One of
the most important blows against the encomienda
was the imposition in 1549 of a reform called the
repartimiento. The repartimiento limited the labor an
encomendero could command from his Indians to
forty-five days per year from each adult male. While
the repartimiento stripped the encomenderos of
their right to force Indians to work all the time, it
did not challenge the principle of forced labor nor
did it prevent encomenderos from continuing to
cheat, mistreat, and overwork their Indians. Enforcement was haphazard. As the old encomenderos
died, however, the crown refused to allow their
children to inherit the privileges of encomienda,
and repartimiento slowly replaced encomienda as
the basic system of exploiting Indian labor.

The central fact of the labor system of New
Spain during the sixteenth century under both en-

comienda and repartimiento was that Spaniards forced Indians to work for them. Indians did not work for wages set by a competitive labor market. They worked because their Spanish rulers forced them to, punished them if they hesitated, enslaved them if they resisted, and killed them if they proved too much of a problem. The system of coerced labor in New Spain grew directly out of the Spaniards' assumption that they were superior to the Indians. As one missionary put it, the Indians "are incapable of learning. . . . The older they get, the worse they behave. . . . The Indians are more stupid than asses and refuse to improve in anything." Therefore, most Spaniards assumed, the Indians' labor should be organized by and for their conquerors.

The Economy and Society of New Spain

In New Spain the bulk of agricultural production was consumed by the local population. Unlike the colonies that developed elsewhere in the New World in the next century, agriculture in New Spain was not devoted to production of an export crop for sale on the world market. Instead, the major crops grown throughout New Spain were the same ones grown for centuries before the Spanish arrived: corn, beans, and squash.

The Spaniards introduced a number of European crops, but only one—sugar—became an important export in the sixteenth century. The Spaniards grew sugar, mostly on islands in the Caribbean. By the end of the sixteenth century, sugar was the fourth leading export from New Spain, but it represented only the start of the sugar boom that would take place in the next century.

The Spaniards also introduced livestock to New Spain. Before the conquest, dogs and turkeys were the most important animals domesticated by the Indians. The Spaniards brought not only horses, so important in battles of conquest; but, of greater significance for the economy of New Spain, they also brought cattle. By the middle of the sixteenth century, an extensive ranching and herding economy had developed in northern Mexico. Meat from the animals was used for domestic consumption, and hides were exported to tanneries and leather shops in Spain. Hides were the second most important export from New Spain in the sixteenth century, worth twice as much as sugar. While agriculture occupied the overwhelming majority of the population of New Spain and provided a few valuable exports to Spain, crops were not what made the riches of New Spain legendary in Europe.

From the viewpoint of Spain, the single most important economic activity in New Spain was silver mining. Gold exports from the New World were

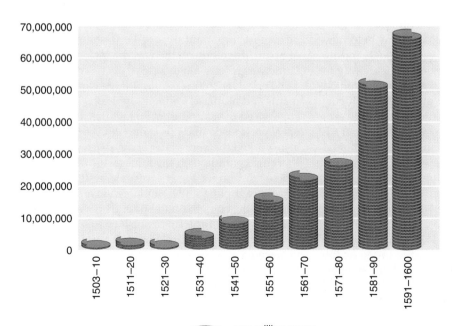

= one million pesos

FIGURE **2.1**
New World Gold and Silver Imported into Spain during the Sixteenth Century, in Pesos
Spain imported more gold than silver during the first three decades of the sixteenth century, but the total value of this treasure was quickly eclipsed during the 1530s and 1540s when rich silver mines were developed. Silver accounted for most of the enormous growth in Spain's precious metal imports from the New World.

AFRICAN SLAVES MINING GOLD

This sixteenth-century illustration provides a simplified view of African slaves mining gold in New Spain. Spaniards imported African slaves in substantial numbers after the native American population had been decimated by conquest and disease. The two slaves on the right dig ore, from which the gold is separated by the slave in the center and then washed in hot water over the fire, before the clean nuggets are given to the Spaniard, who carefully weighs them and sets them aside. How did the artist emphasize the differences between the Spaniard and the slaves? Is it possible to detect the artist's point of view about who was more "civilized"?

The Pierpont Morgan Library. MA 3900, f.100.

substantial early in the sixteenth century, as the conquistadors filled treasure chests with any gold they could find. During the 1520s, as the loot, mostly gold, from the conquest of Mexico made its way to Spain, the value of New World treasure amounted to about 1.4 million ducats (a unit of Spanish currency). During the 1530s, with the conquest of Peru, the treasure imported to Spain swelled to about 6.7 million ducats. Nonetheless, before 1533, the annual value of gold exports from New Spain did not exceed what the Portuguese brought to Europe from the west coast of Africa. The bonanza for the Spanish came from silver mines. With the discovery of the major silver deposits at Potosí, Bolivia, in 1545 and Zacatecas, Mexico, in 1546, imported bullion rose to 12.5 million ducats during the 1540s. As the mines swung into large-scale production, an ever-growing stream of silver flowed from New Spain to Old. During the 1590s, treasure fleets brought precious metals worth 83.5 million ducats to Spain, and the riches promised to continue. Overall, exports of precious metals during the sixteenth century were

worth about twenty-five times more than hides, the next most important export. From the perspective of Spain, its colony on the western shores of the Atlantic was a solid-silver asset.

The silver mines required large capital investments and numerous miners. Typically, a mine was supervised by a handful of Spaniards, and the miners were mostly Indians, although African slaves also worked the mines later in the sixteenth century. Working conditions in the mines were abominable, worse than under the encomienda system. But the mines exemplified the fundamental relationships between the colonists and Spain. The native Indian miners worked for local Spanish bosses to produce silver for export to Spain. The mines and their products were valuable principally for their contribution to the wealth of Spain, not the colony.

For Spaniards, life in New Spain was relatively easy. Only a few thousand Spaniards actually fought during the conquests. Although the riches the survivors won fell far short of their expectations, the benefits of encomienda provided a comfortable,

MIXED RACES

Residents of New Spain maintained a lively interest in each person's racial lineage. These eighteenth-century paintings illustrate three forms of racial mixture common in the sixteenth-century. In the first painting, a Spanish man and an Indian woman have a mestizo son; in the fourth, a Spanish man and a woman of African descent have a mulatto son; in the fifth, a Spanish woman and a mulatto man have a morisco daughter. The many racial permutations of parents caused residents of New Spain to develop an elaborate vocabulary of ancestry. The child of a morisco and a Spaniard was a chino; the child of a chino and an Indian was a salta abas; the child of a salta abas and a mulatto was a lobo; and so on. Can you detect hints of some of the meanings of racial categories in the clothing depicted in these paintings?

Bob Schalkwijk/INAH.

Español con India, Mestizo.

Mestizo con Española Castizo.

Castizo con Española Español.

Español con Mora Mulato.

5

6

Mulato con Española, Morisco.

Morisco con Española Chino.

7

Chino con India, Salta abas.

Salta abas con Mulata, Lobo.

leisurely existence that was the envy of many poorer noblemen in Spain. The success of the conquest and the opportunity to spend less time in a workshop or behind a plow and more time in a hammock or on a shaded patio attracted many Spaniards to the New World. As one colonist wrote his brother back in Spain, "Don't hesitate [to come]. . . . This land [of New Spain] is as good as ours [in Spain], for God has given us more here than there, and we shall be better off."

During the century after 1492, about 225,000 Spaniards came to settle in the colonies. Virtually all of them were poor young men of common (non-noble) lineage who came directly from Spain. Laborers and artisans made up the largest proportion, but soldiers and sailors were also numerous. Throughout the sixteenth century, men vastly outnumbered women among the Spanish immigrants, although the proportion of women grew from about one in twenty before 1519 to nearly one in three by the 1580s.

The gender and number of Spanish settlers shaped two fundamental features of the society of New Spain. First, despite the thousands of immigrants, Europeans never made up more than 1 or 2 percent of the total population of New Spain. Although Spaniards ruled New Spain, the population was almost wholly Indian. Second, the shortage of Spanish women meant that a great deal of concubinage and intermarriage took place between Spanish men and Indian women.

The highest social status in New Spain was reserved for natives of Spain, *peninsulares* (people born on the Iberian peninsula). Below them but still within the elite were creoles (from the Spanish word for "native," *criollo*), the children born in the New World to Spanish women. Together, peninsulares and creoles made up barely 1 or 2 percent of the population, and, unlike all the others, they were whites of European ancestry. Below them on the social pyramid was a larger group of *mestizos,* the offspring of Spanish men and Indian women, who made up 4 or 5 percent of the total population. So many of the mestizos were illegitimate that the term *mestizo* (from the Spanish word for "mixed") was almost synonymous with *bastard* during the sixteenth century. The association with illegitimacy and Indians damned mestizos in the eyes of the white elite, who scorned them and discriminated against them. However, some mestizos worked as artisans and labor overseers and managed to live well, and a few rose into the ranks of the elite, especially if their Indian ancestry was not obvious from their skin color. Most mestizos, however, were lumped with the Indians, the enormous bottom mass of the population.

The society of New Spain established the precedent for what would become a pronounced pattern in the European colonies of the New World: a society stratified sharply by social origin and race. All Europeans of whatever social origin considered themselves superior to the Native Americans. Although Europeans were only a tiny minority in New Spain, they were a dominant minority in both power and status.

In the social and political hierarchy, the Spanish monarchy was superior to all the inhabitants of New Spain. The crown administered the colony for its own purposes, mostly to provide a large and growing source of revenue for the royal treasury. The principles of royal government were simple: Tax economic transactions and retain monopolies on essential goods.

As encomienda withered, royal bureaucrats took over the administration of the Indian towns, and the crown collected the tribute that had previously gone to the encomendero. The crown also collected more than sixty other taxes. In addition, the crown enjoyed monopolies on the sale of such necessities as gunpowder, salt, liquor, and mercury (essential for refining silver). Colonists had to purchase these and other essentials at artificially inflated prices from merchants licensed by the crown. Royal regulations prohibited colonists from competing with producers in Spain. The result of royal administration in New Spain was that competition

was stifled, incentive was thwarted, and economic development was rigidly controlled for the benefit of Spain rather than the colonists.

The Toll of Spanish Conquest and Colonization

Conquest and colonization of New Spain devastated Indian cultures. The battles of conquest stripped Indian cultures of their leaders. Many were killed in combat, and the survivors were discredited by their failure to withstand the Spanish onslaught. Indian religion was called into doubt by the conquest, and on the heels of the conquistadors came Catholic priests determined to convert the Indians to Christianity. By 1560, the major centers of Indian civilization had been conquered, their leaders overthrown, their religion held in contempt, and their people forced to work for the Spaniards. Profound demoralization pervaded Indian society. As a Mexican poet wrote:

Nothing but flowers and songs of sorrow
are left in Mexico . . .
where once we saw warriors and wise men.

We wander here and there
in our desolate poverty.
We are mortal men.
We have seen bloodshed and pain
where once we saw beauty and valor.

We are crushed to the ground;
we lie in ruins.
There is nothing but grief and suffering
in Mexico.

Adding to the culture shock of conquest and colonization was the deadly toll of European diseases. As conquest spread throughout New Spain, Indians were struck by virulent epidemics of measles, smallpox, and respiratory illnesses, diseases unknown to them before the arrival of the Europeans. The epidemics decimated Indian societies. By 1570, only a half century after Cortés entered Tenochtitlán, the Indian population of New Spain had fallen to just 10 percent of what it had been when Columbus arrived. In little more than fifty years, nine out of ten Indians had succumbed to the severity of colonial policies and the even more deadly European viruses. The destruction of the Indian population was a catastrophe unequaled in human history. A Mayan Indian recalled that when the sickness struck his village, "Great was the stench of the dead. . . .

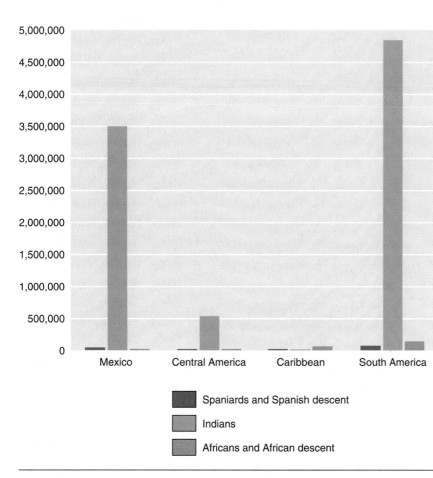

FIGURE 2.2
Estimated Population of Spanish America about 1570
This chart makes clear that Indians made up the over-whelming majority of the population in most of Spanish America by the late sixteenth century. In the Caribbean, the native population had been nearly exterminated. In all regions Spaniards and their descendants made up a tiny fraction, considerably outnumbered in South America and the Caribbean by Africans (mostly slaves) and their descendants.

The dogs and vultures devoured the bodies. The mortality was terrible. . . . So it was that we became orphans . . . all of us were thus. We were born to die!" Of course, the Spaniards did not intend to transmit their diseases and kill so many Indians. Natives of the New World had never been infected with and developed immunities to the alien viruses from Europe, Africa, and Asia that the Spaniards unwittingly carried. For most Indians, New Spain was a graveyard.

For most Indians, New Spain was a grave-yard.

For the Spaniards, the deaths meant that the most valuable resource of New Spain—Indian labor—dwindled rapidly. By the last quarter of the sixteenth century, Spanish colonists felt the pinch of a genuine labor shortage. To help redress the need

for laborers, colonists began to import African slaves. Africans had come to Mexico with the conquistadors; one Mexica recalled that among Cortés's men were "some black-skinned ones with kinky hair." In the years before 1550, while Indian labor was still ample, only 15,000 slaves were imported from Africa. Even after Indian labor began to decline, the relatively high cost of African slaves kept imports low, approximately 36,000 during the last half of the century. In later centuries, the African slave trade would supply a major portion of New World labor, but during the sixteenth century New Spain relied primarily on a diminishing number of Indians.

Northern Outposts in Florida and New Mexico

After the explorations of de Soto, Coronado, and Cabrillo, North America did not much interest officials in New Spain. The monarchy assumed that Spain owned North America as part of the grant

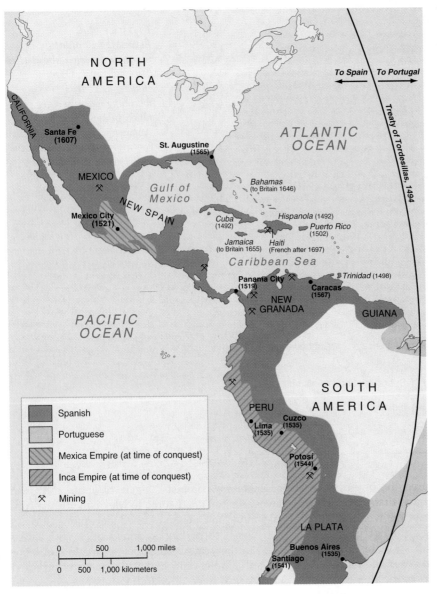

MAP 2.3
New Spain in the Sixteenth Century
Spanish control spread throughout Central and South America during the sixteenth century, with the important exception of Portuguese Brazil. North America, although claimed by Spain under the Treaty of Tordesillas, remained peripheral to Spain's New World empire.

made by the pope in 1493. By the mid-sixteenth century, however, France openly challenged Spain's claim and the papacy began to backpedal, pointing out that Spain did not have exclusive rights to North America since it had not yet been discovered in 1493. The Spanish monarchy insisted that a few settlements be established in North America to give some tangible reality to its legalistic claims. Settlements in Florida would have the additional benefit of protecting Spanish ships from pirates and privateers who lurked along the South Atlantic coast. Winds and currents in the Caribbean made the route of the Spanish treasure fleet quite predictable; the

ships rode the Gulf Stream along the east coast of Florida until they could catch favorable winds, usually off South Carolina, that propelled them toward Spain. Foreign raiders watched, waited, and attacked with great success, a practice that alarmed the monarchy.

In 1565, the Spanish king sent Pedro Menéndez de Avilés to create settlements along the Atlantic coast. In early September, Menéndez founded St. Augustine and within a few weeks mounted a deadly attack that eliminated a nearby French settlement. Menéndez established a series of small outposts along the Florida coast. In 1567 he founded the town of St. Elena, on what is now Parris Island, South Carolina.

In 1570, Menéndez sent an expedition to settle on the Chesapeake Bay, but within a few months the settlers were killed by local Indians. The Spaniards' translator, a young Algonquian whom they had captured on an earlier scouting party in the region, led the Indian attack. The young man had been sent to Mexico, where he had learned Spanish and had been given the name Luis de Velasco by his patron, the viceroy of Mexico. Among his fellow Algonquians, Luis de Velasco became known as Opechancanough, or "He Whose Soul Is White." In years to come, Opechancanough would surprise English settlers of the region, much as he did the Spaniards.

Antagonisms between Spaniards and native peoples plagued the Florida outposts. In 1576, an Indian attack forced evacuation of St. Elena. Eleven years later, the Spaniards concluded that St. Elena could not be defended from hostile Indians and marauders like the English privateer Francis Drake, who had sacked and burned St. Augustine in 1586. Spanish officials destroyed St. Elena themselves in 1587 and fell back to St. Augustine, where they dug in. St. Augustine was the first permanent European settlement within what became the United States. By 1600, the garrison town had a population of about five hundred, mostly men (although women and children lived there too), mostly soldiers, and mostly there because military orders kept them from leaving. The small town was a token Spanish presence on the vast Atlantic shoreline of North America.

More than 1,600 miles west of St. Augustine, another Spanish outpost was founded in 1598. During the 1580s, the Mexican mining frontier extended far into northern Mexico, and rumors of fabulous riches to be found just over the northern horizon still circulated, as they had in Coronado's time forty years earlier. In 1598, Juan de Oñate led an expedition of about five hundred people to settle New Mexico and develop the booty that supposedly awaited. Oñate had impeccable credentials for both conquest and mining. He came from a wealthy mining family; his father had helped discover the bonanza silver mines of Zacatecas. His wife was Isabel Tolosa Cortés Montezuma, the granddaughter of Cortés—the conqueror of Mexico—and the great-granddaughter of the Mexican emperor Montezuma. Despite the previous forays of Coronado, Oñate and other officials in New Spain had only a hazy understanding of the geography of the American Southwest. Oñate, for example, planned to supply New Mexico by sea; he requested and received permission to bring two ships a year to the new settlement.

In the spring of 1598, Oñate and his companions set out from Mexico across the Rio Grande and after two months reached a pueblo near present-day Albuquerque, where Oñate solemnly convened the pueblo's leaders in a kiva and, to his satisfaction, received their oath of loyalty to the Spanish king and the Christian God. Oñate repeated these ceremonies at additional pueblos as he made his way to a pueblo that he named San Gabriel, north of present-day Santa Fe. He soon sent out scouting parties to find the legendary treasures of the region and to locate the ocean, which he reasoned had to be nearby. Meanwhile, a large contingent of his soldiers planned to mutiny, and relations with the pueblo Indians deteriorated. When the Acoma pueblo revolted, Oñate ruthlessly suppressed the uprising, killing some eight hundred men, women, and children. Although Oñate reconfirmed the Spaniards' military superiority, he did not bring peace or stability to San Gabriel. Another pueblo revolted in 1599, and many of Oñate's settlers returned to Mexico, disillusioned. A few held on, deserting San Gabriel early in the seventeenth century for the greater security of Santa Fe. New Mexico was so marginal to New Spain that officials talked repeatedly of abandoning it, but they did not. Instead New Mexico lingered as a small, dusty token of Spanish claims to the North American Southwest.

The New World and Europe

The riches of New Spain helped make the sixteenth century Spain's Golden Age. After the death of Queen Isabella (in 1504) and King Ferdinand (in 1516), their sixteen-year-old grandson became King Charles I of Spain. Charles used the wealth of the Indies to pursue his vast ambitions in the fierce dynastic and religious battles of sixteenth-century Europe. Through the power of Spain, the New World had a major impact on Europeans.

In 1519, while Cortés made his way into Mexico, Charles I used judicious bribes to secure his selection as Holy Roman Emperor. At the age of nineteen the new Holy Roman Emperor now became Charles V (Charlemagne, who founded the Holy Roman Empire seven hundred years earlier, had prior claim to the title Charles I). His empire encompassed more than that of any other European monarch. With ambitions that matched his sprawling empire, Charles V planned to expand his empire in western Europe and defend its eastern boundary from the advances of the Ottoman Turks. Unexpectedly, Martin Luther, an obscure Catholic priest in central Germany inaugurated a new challenge that commanded the attention of the young emperor.

The Protestant Reformation and the European Order

In 1517, Martin Luther initiated the Protestant Reformation when he nailed his famous ninety-five theses on the door of the Castle Church in Wittenberg, Germany, publicizing some of his criticisms of the Catholic church. Luther's ideas, although shared by many other Catholics, were considered extremely dangerous by church officials and by many monarchs like Charles V who believed firmly that, just as the church spoke for God, they ruled for God. Although a full account of Luther's doctrines and their contribution to the complex history of the Reformation is beyond the scope of this book, it is easy to understand why the church and monarchs were alarmed.

Luther preached a doctrine known as justification by faith: Individual Christians could obtain salvation and life everlasting only by faith that God would save them; giving offerings to the church, following the orders of the priest, or participating in many church rituals did not get believers one step closer to heaven. The only true source of information about God's will, Luther argued, was not the church, but the Bible. By reading the Bible, any Christian could learn as much about God's commandments as any priest. Indeed, Luther called for a priesthood of all believers.

Martin Luther hoped his ideas would reform the Catholic church, but instead they ruptured forever the unity of Christianity in western Europe.

Nearly five centuries later, it may be difficult to appreciate the subversive implications of these ideas. In effect, Luther charged that the Catholic church, which had been the only Christian church in Europe for centuries, was in many respects fraud-

ulent: Contrary to the church's claims, priests were unnecessary for salvation and actually hindered salvation by engaging in religious practices not specifically commanded by the Bible; the church should focus not on playing a major role in the worldly realm of kings and wars and politics—as it had done for centuries—but on aiding individual Christians to understand the spiritual realm, the realm of faith revealed to them in the Bible. Although Luther hoped his ideas would reform the Catholic church, instead they ruptured forever the unity of Christianity in western Europe.

Official recognition of the rupture came in 1521 when Charles V presided over an official interrogation of Luther (who already had been excommunicated by the pope) and commanded him to recant his views. Luther refused and was banned from the empire. Witnessing Luther's intransigence, Charles V pledged to devote all his efforts to exterminate the Protestant heresies.

The wealth pouring into Spain from the New World fueled the determination of Charles V to defend against the Protestant challenge to the Catholic faith, against Muslim enemies in eastern Europe, and against any nation bold or foolhardy enough to contest Spain's supremacy. As the wealthiest and most powerful monarch in Europe, Charles V (who ruled until 1556) and his son and successor Philip II (who ruled until 1598) assumed responsibility for upholding the existing order of sixteenth-century Europe.

New World Treasure and Spanish Ambitions

During the sixteenth century, Spain received gold and silver from New Spain worth well over 1.5 trillion dollars (in 1990 terms). The value of this trade was so great that it paid for all Spanish exports to New Spain and all the costs of colonial administration in the New World and still left staggering sums for the Spanish monarchy to spend.

Both Charles V and Philip II fought wars throughout the world during the sixteenth century. The royal bureaucracy collected revenues from the New World and spent them to pay for military expeditions to defend Catholicism and Spain's empire. Mexican silver funneled through the royal treasury into the hands of military suppliers, soldiers, and sailors wherever in the world Spain's forces happened to be fighting at the time. New World treasure was dissipated in military adventures that served the goals of the monarchy but did little to benefit most Spaniards.

COLUMBIAN EXCHANGE

The arrival of Columbus in the New World initiated the transatlantic exchange of goods, people, and ideas that has continued ever since. Spaniards brought domesticated animals common in the Old World, including horses, cattle, goats, chickens, cats, and sheep. The novelty of such animals is demonstrated by the Nahua words the Mexican people initially used to refer to these strange new beasts: for horses, they used the Nahua word for deer; a cow was "one with horns"; a goat was "a bearded one with horns"; a chicken was a "Spanish turkey hen"; a cat was a "little cougar"; a sheep was referred to with the word for cotton, linking the animal with its fibrous woolen coat, which was somewhat akin to native cotton. Spaniards brought many other alien items such as cannon, which the Nahua at first termed "fat fire trumpets," and guitars, which the Nahua called "rope drums." Smuggled along unknowingly were also unseen animals, Old World microorganisms that caused devastating epidemics of smallpox, measles, and other diseases. Ancient American goods, people, and ideas made the return trip across the Atlantic. Columbus's sailors became infected with syphilis in sexual encounters with New World women and then unwittingly carried the deadly parasite from the Caribbean back to Portugal and Spain. New World tobacco, like that in the cigar smoked by the ancient Mayan lord crowned with a deer headdress, created a European rage for smoking that has yet to abate. Europeans were also introduced to such vital New World crops as corn and potatoes as well as exotic items like the pineapple, a fruit the Europeans named for its resemblance to the pinecone.

The Bancroft Library; Arxiv Mas; Francis Robicey.

In a sense, American wealth made the Spanish monarchy too rich and too powerful among the states of Europe. The ambitions of Charles V and Philip II were so great that the expenses of constant warfare far outstripped the revenues arriving from New Spain. To help maintain military expenditures, both kings continually raised taxes in Spain. Between 1527 and 1598, taxes levied on Spaniards increased more than fivefold. In accordance with the principle of privilege, the nobility—by far the wealthiest class in Spain—was completely exempt from direct taxation, so the increasing tax burden was collected mostly from the peasantry. Thus, escalating taxation, required to pursue the ambitions of the monarchy, further impoverished the vast majority of Spain's population. To the extent that New

World treasure contributed to the kings' ambitions, it indirectly resulted in making most Spaniards poorer.

New World treasure stimulated the ambition of the Spanish monarchy to exercise its great-power status on a scale that brought Spain to the brink of economic bankruptcy. Even though tax rates in Spain were ten times greater than in England, the Spanish crown did not have enough funds to fight its wars. The only alternative was to borrow, principally from Italian, German, and Flemish bankers. The drain of constant military expenditures drew the monarchy deeper and deeper into debt. By the end of the century, paying interest on debts swallowed two-thirds of the crown's annual revenues. For Spain, the riches from New Spain proved a short-term blessing but a long-term curse.

New World treasure stimulated the ambition of the Spanish monarchy to exercise its great-power status on a scale that brought Spain to the brink of economic bankruptcy.

But sixteenth-century Spaniards did not see it that way. At the beginning of the sixteenth century, Spaniards and other Europeans looked at the New World through the eyes of people who venerated the ancient authorities of classical Greece and Rome. They had trouble believing that a New World really existed, in considerable measure because ancient traditions made no mention of such a thing. By the end of the sixteenth century, Spaniards had added enormously to their knowledge. They had discovered staggering riches and built mines, cities, churches, and even universities on the other side of the Atlantic. As they looked at their accomplishments in the New World, they saw what appeared to them unmistakable signs of progress. Their own efforts were responsible for these achievements. Experience had proved a far better guide to success and progress than ancient tradition. Their military, religious, and economic achievements gave them great pride and confidence in themselves and their abilities.

Europe and the Spanish Example

The lessons of sixteenth-century Spain were not lost on Spain's European rivals. Spain proudly displayed the fruits of its New World conquests. In

1520, for instance, Charles V exhibited some of the gifts Montezuma had presented to Cortés. After seeing the objects, the German artist Albrecht Dürer wrote in his diary of his amazement at "the things which were brought to the King from the New Golden Land: a sun entirely of gold, a whole fathom [six feet] broad; likewise a moon, entirely of silver, just as big; likewise sundry curiosities from their weapons, armour, and missiles; very odd clothing, bedding and all sorts of strange articles for human use. . . . I have never seen in all my days what so rejoiced my heart, as these things. For I saw among them amazing objects, and I marvelled over the subtle ingenuity of the men in these distant lands."

Dürer's reaction illustrates the excitement the New World generated among some Europeans. But the most exciting thing about "the men in these distant lands" was that they could serve the interests of Europeans, as Spain had shown. With a few notable exceptions, Europeans saw the New World as a place for the expansion of European influence, a place where—as one Spaniard wrote—Europeans could "give to those strange lands the form of our own." Spain's success in doing just that in New Spain held irresistible allure for its European competitors.

Spain's example proved that an empire in the New World could make a major contribution to a nation's power and prestige in Europe. It also illustrated the profits that could be made in a new arena for commerce across the Atlantic. The thousands of Spaniards who emigrated to the New World found opportunities for work and comfort that far surpassed what Europe offered them, and they encouraged their friends and relatives to follow. Spain benefited, some Europeans observed, by sending to New Spain those Spaniards who would make trouble at home. But the most important lesson Europeans learned from Spain's example was that the New World was a source of fabulous riches.

France and England tried to follow Spain's example. Both nations warred with Spain in Europe, preyed on Spanish treasure fleets, and ventured to the New World, where they too hoped to find an undiscovered passageway to the East Indies or another Mexico or Peru.

In 1524, France sent Giovanni da Verrazano to scout the Atlantic coast of North America from North Carolina to Canada, looking for a northern route to the East Indies, referred to as a Northwest Passage. Eleven years later, they probed farther north with Jacques Cartier's voyage that ventured

CAROLINA ALGONQUIAN MOTHER AND DAUGHTER

When the English artist John White visited the coast of present-day North Carolina in 1585 as part of Raleigh's Roanoke expedition, he painted this watercolor portrait of the wife and daughter of a local Algonquian chief. This and White's other portraits are the only surviving likenesses of sixteenth-century North American Indians that were drawn from direct observation in the New World. The young girl holds a doll and copies her mother by suspending her right wrist from her necklace. The mother's clothing and body paint or tattoos may signify her status as a mature woman and a chief's wife. British Museum.

up the St. Lawrence River. Encouraged, Cartier returned to the region with a group of settlers in 1541, but the colony they established—like the search for a Northwest Passage—came to nothing. In 1564, a group of French Huguenots (Protestants fleeing from persecution in Catholic France) established a settlement near present-day Jacksonville, Florida, that was soon eliminated by Spaniards led by Pedro Menéndez de Avilés. French interest in North America did not revive until the seventeenth century.

English attempts to mimic Spain were slower but equally ill-fated. Not until 1576, almost eighty years after John Cabot's voyages, did the English try again to find a westward route to the East Indies. This time Martin Frobisher sailed into the frigid waters of northern Canada; his sponsor was the Cathay Company, which hoped to open trade with China. Like many other explorers who preceded and followed him, Frobisher was mesmerized by the Spanish example and was sure he had found gold. The tons of "ore" he hauled back to England proved worthless, the Cathay Company collapsed, and English interests shifted southward.

English attempts to establish North American settlements were no more fruitful than their search for a northern route to China. Sir Humphrey Gilbert, a soldier-adventurer who had won his reputation in Ireland, led an expedition in 1578 and another in 1583 that made feeble efforts to found colonies in Newfoundland, until Gilbert himself vanished at sea. In 1585, Sir Walter Raleigh organized an expedition to settle Roanoke Island off the coast of present-day North Carolina. The explorers collected valuable information about the region and its native inhabitants. The artist John White, for example, made virtually the only eyewitness drawings that exist of sixteenth-century North American Indians. Although the first group of explorers left no colonists on the island, two years later Raleigh sent a contingent of more than a hundred settlers to Roanoke under John White's leadership. White left the settlers and returned to England for supplies to keep the colony provisioned. White and the supply fleet did not return to Roanoke until 1590. By then, the Roanoke colonists had disappeared, leaving only the word "Croatoan" (whose meaning is unknown) carved on a tree. Although the fate of the Roanoke colonists remains a mystery, they most likely died from a combination of natural causes and unfriendly Indians. In any case, by the end of the sixteenth century England had failed to secure a New World beachhead.

Conclusion: The Legacy of the Sixteenth Century

The sixteenth century in the New World belonged to the Spanish, who had employed Columbus, and the Indians, who had greeted him as he stepped ashore. Spanish explorers, conquistadors, and colonists forced the Indians to serve the interests of Spanish settlers and the Spanish monarchy. Spaniards brought with them things that were novelties in the New World but were commonplace in sixteenth-century Europe, including Christianity, iron technology, sailing ships, firearms, wheeled vehicles, horses, and deadly diseases. They took back to Spain cargoes of New World silver, gold, and hides as well as crops like corn, potatoes, and tobacco that had been grown for millennia in the New World but were novelties in Europe. Historians have termed this transfer of goods, ideas, foods, and diseases the "Columbian exchange." The exchange illustrated one of the most important legacies of the sixteenth century: After millions of years, the Atlantic no longer was an impermeable barrier separating the Eastern and Western Hemispheres. After the voyages of Columbus, European sailing ships regularly bridged the Atlantic and transferred an unending stream of people, products, and ideas from one shore to the other. No European monarch could forget the seductive lesson about this transfer taught by Spain's example: The New World could vastly enrich the Old. Spain remained a New World power for almost four centuries, and its language, culture, and institutions left a permanent imprint. By the end of the sixteenth century, however, other European monarchies began to contest Spain's dominion in Europe and to make forays into the northern fringes of Spain's New World preserve. They sought to reap some of the benefits the Spaniards enjoyed from their New World domain. But to do so they had to learn a difficult lesson: how to deviate from Spain's example. That discovery lay ahead.

CHRONOLOGY

1415 Portugal conquers Ceuta at Strait of Gibraltar, gaining access to western coast of Africa.

1444 Portuguese explorers reach Cape Verde.

1451 Columbus born in Genoa, Italy.

1480 Portuguese ships reach Congo.

1488 Bartolomeu Dias rounds Cape of Good Hope.

1492 Columbus lands on Caribbean island that he names San Salvador.

1493 Columbus makes second voyage to the New World.

1494 Portugal and Spain negotiate Treaty of Tordesillas to divide New World between them.

1497 John Cabot searches for Northwest Passage.

1498 Columbus makes third voyage to New World and lands in Venezuela.

Vasco da Gama sails to India.

1500 Pedro Álvars Cabral makes landfall in Brazil.

1507 German mapmaker Waldseemüller names New World America.

1513 Vasco Nuñez de Balboa crosses isthmus of Panama.

1517 Protestant Reformation begins in Europe.

1519 Hernán Cortés leads expedition to find and conquer Mexico.

Ferdinand Magellan sets out to sail around world.

Charles I of Spain becomes Holy Roman Emperor Charles V.

1521 Cortés conquers Mexica at Tenochtitlán. Juan Ponce de León lands in Florida.	**1539** Hernando de Soto launches exploration of Southeast.
1524 Guatemala, El Salvador, and Nicaragua come under Spanish control. Franciscan missionaries arrive in Mexico.	**1540** Francisco Vásquez de Coronado starts to explore Southwest and Great Plains. **1542** Juan Rodríguez Cabrillo explores California coast.
1526 Lucas Vázquez de Ayllón establishes San Miguel de Gualdape on Georgia coast.	**1549** Repartimiento reforms begin to replace encomienda. **1565** Pedro Menéndez de Avilés establishes St. Augustine, Florida.
1528 Pánfilo de Narváez leads expedition to survey Gulf coast from Florida to Texas.	**1587** English colonists settle Roanoke Island.
1532 Francisco Pizarro begins conquest of Peru.	**1598** Juan de Oñate leads expedition into New Mexico.

BIBLIOGRAPHY

GENERAL WORKS

Alfred W. Crosby Jr., *The Columbian Exchange: Biological and Cultural Consequences of 1492* (1972).

Zvi Dor-Ner, *Columbus and the Age of Discovery* (1991).

J. H. Elliott, *The Old World and the New, 1462–1650* (1970).

Felipe Fernández-Armesto, *Before Columbus: Exploration and Colonization from the Mediterranean to the Atlantic, 1229–1492* (1987).

J. A. Levenson, *Circa 1492: Art in the Age of Exploration* (1991).

D. W. Meinig, *The Shaping of America* (1986).

Samuel E. Morison, *The European Discovery of America: The Northern Voyages, A.D. 500–1600* (1971).

Samuel E. Morison, *The European Discovery of America: The Southern Voyages, A.D. 1492–1616* (1974).

John H. Parry and Robert G. Keith, eds., *New Iberian World: A Documentary History of the Discovery and Settlement of Latin America to the Early Seventeenth Century*, 5 vols. (1984).

William D. Phillips and Carla Rahn Phillips, *The Worlds of Christopher Columbus* (1992).

David B. Quinn, *North America from Earliest Discovery to First Settlements* (1977).

David B. Quinn, ed., *New American World: A Documentary History of North America to 1612*, 5 vols. (1970).

A. J. R. Russell-Wood, *A World on the Move: The Portuguese in Africa, Asia, and America, 1415–1808* (1992).

Hugh Thomas, *Conquest: Montezuma, Cortés, and the Fall of Old Mexico* (1993).

John Thornton, *Africa and Africans in the Making of the Atlantic World, 1400–1680* (1992).

David J. Weber, *The Spanish Frontier in North America* (1992).

EXPLORERS AND EMPIRES

Charles Boxer, *The Portuguese Seaborne Empire, 1415–1825* (1969).

Lorenzo Camusso, *Travel Guide to Europe, 1492: Ten Itineraries in the Old World* (1990).

Nicholas P. Canny, *The Elizabethan Conquest of Ireland* (1976).

Philip Curtin et al., *African History* (2nd ed., 1995).

Jan De Vries, *The Economy of Europe in an Age of Crisis, 1600–1750* (1976).

William Eccles, *Canadian Frontier, 1534–1760* (1969).

Paul Hulton, *America, 1585: The Complete Drawings of John White* (1984).

Karen Ordahl Kupperman, *Roanoke: The Abandoned Colony* (1984).

Peggy K. Liss, *Isabel the Queen: Life and Times* (1992).

John Lynch, *Spain, 1516–1598: From Nation State to World Empire* (1992).

Harry A. Miskimin, *The Economy of Later Renaissance Europe, 1460–1600* (1977).

John H. Parry, *The Spanish Seaborne Empire* (1966).

David B. Quinn, *England and the Discovery of America, 1481–1620* (1974).

David B. Quinn, *Set Fair for Roanoke* (1985).

David B. Quinn, ed., *North American Discovery, 1000–1612* (1971).

Carl O. Sauer, *The Early Spanish Main* (1966).

Carl O. Sauer, *Sixteenth-Century North America: The Land and the People as Seen by the Europeans* (1971).

A. C. de C. M. Saunders, *A Social History of Black Slaves and Freedmen in Portugal, 1441–1555* (1982).

Roger C. Smith, *Vanguard of Empire: Ships of Exploration in the Age of Columbus* (1993).

Robert S. Weddle, *The Gulf of Mexico in North American Discovery, 1500–1685* (1985).

EUROPEANS ENCOUNTER THE NEW WORLD

James Axtell, *Beyond 1492: Encounters in Colonial North America* (1992).

Robert F. Berkhofer Jr., *The White Man's Indian: Images of the American Indian from Columbus to the Present* (1978).

Philip P. Boucher, *Cannibal Encounters: Europeans and Island Caribs, 1492–1763* (1992).

Nicholas Canny and Anthony Pagden, *Colonial Identity in the Atlantic World, 1500–1800* (1987).

Rebecca Catz, *Christopher Columbus and the Portuguese, 1476–1498* (1993).

Fredi Chiappelli et al., *First Images of America: The Impact of the New World on the Old*, 2 vols. (1976).

Alfred W. Crosby, *Ecological Imperialism: The Biological Expansion of Europe, 900–1900* (1986).

Alfred W. Crosby, *Germs, Seeds, and Animals: Studies in Ecological History* (1994).

Oliver Dunn and James E. Kelley Jr., trans., *The Diario of Christopher Columbus's First Voyage to America, 1492–1493* (1988).

William W. Fitzhugh, ed., *Cultures in Contact: The Impact of European Contacts on Native American Cultural Institutions, 1000–1800* (1985).

Valerie J. Flint, *The Imaginative Landscape of Christopher Columbus* (1992).

Antonello Gerbi, *Nature in the New World: From Christopher Columbus to Gonzalo Fernández de Oviedo,* trans. Jeremy Moyle (1986).

Anthony Grafton, *New Worlds, Ancient Texts: The Power of Tradition and the Shock of Discovery* (1992).

Stephen Greenblatt, *Marvelous Possessions: The Wonder of the New World* (1991).

Stephen Greenblatt, ed., *New World Encounters* (1993).

David Henige, *In Search of Columbus: The Sources for the First Voyage* (1991).

Hugh Honour, *The New Golden Land: European Images of America from the Discoveries to the Present Time* (1975).

Peter Hulme, *Colonial Encounters: Europe and the Native Caribbean, 1492–1797* (1986).

Peter Hulme and Neil L. Whitehead, eds., *Wild Majesty: Encounters with Caribs from Columbus to the Present Day* (1992).

William F. Keegan, *The People Who Discovered Columbus: An Introduction to the Prehistory of the Bahamas* (1992).

Kenneth Nebenzahl, *Atlas of Columbus and the Great Discoveries* (1990).

Anthony Pagden, *The Fall of Natural Man: The American Indian and the Origins of Comparative Ethnology* (1981).

Anthony Pagden, *European Encounters with the New World: From Renaissance to Romanticism* (1993).

Anthony Pagden, *Lords of All the World: Ideologies of Empire in Spain, Britain, and France, 1500–1800* (1995).

Irving Rouse, *The Tainos: Rise and Decline of the People Who Greeted Columbus* (1992).

David Hurst Thomas, ed., *Columbian Consequences,* 3 vols. (1991).

Samuel M. Wilson, *Hispaniola: Caribbean Chiefdoms in the Age of Columbus* (1990).

CONQUEST AND NEW SPAIN

Ida Altman, *Emigrants and Society: Extremadura and Spanish America in the Sixteenth Century* (1989).

Kenneth J. Andrien and Rolena Adorno, eds., *Transatlantic Encounters: Europeans and Andeans in the Sixteenth Century* (1991).

Frances Berdan, *The Aztecs of Central Mexico: An Imperial Society* (1982).

Frances F. Berdan and Patricia Rieff Anawalt, eds., *The Codex Mendoza*, 4 vols. (1992).

Peter J. Blackwell, *Silver Mining and Society in Colonial Mexico: Zacatecas, 1546–1700* (1971).

Peter J. Blackwell, *Miners of the Red Mountain: Indian Labor in Potosí, 1545–1650* (1984).

Frederick P. Bowser, *The African Slave in Colonial Peru, 1524–1650* (1974).

Gordon Brotherston, *Image of the New World: The American Continent Portrayed in Native Texts* (1979).

Louise M. Burkhart, *The Slippery Earth: Nahua-Christian Moral Dialogue in Sixteenth-Century Mexico* (1989).

Lawrence A. Clayton, Vernon James Knight Jr., and Edward C. Moore, eds., *The de Soto Chronicles: The Expedition of Hernando de Soto to North America in 1539–1543*, 2 vols. (1993).

Inga Clendinnen, *Aztecs: An Interpretation* (1991).

David Noel Cook, *Demographic Collapse: Indian Peru, 1520–1620* (1981).

David Noel Cook and W. George Lovell, eds., *"Secret Judgments of God": Old World Disease in Colonial Spanish America* (1991).

Cyclone Covey, trans., *Cabeza de Vaca's Adventures in the Unknown Interior of America* (1961).

Kathleen A. Deegan, ed., *America's Ancient City: Spanish St. Augustine, 1565–1763* (1991).

Bernal Díaz, *The Conquest of New Spain*, trans. J. M. Cohen (1963).

Charles Gibson, *The Aztecs under Spanish Rule* (1964).

Charles Gibson, *Spain in America* (1966).

Serge Gruzinski, *Painting the Conquest: The Mexican Indians and the European Renaissance* (1992).

Serge Gruzinski, *The Conquest of Mexico: The Incorporation of Indian Societies into the Western World, Sixteenth–Eighteenth Centuries* (1993).

Ramon A. Gutiérrez, *When Jesus Came, the Corn Mothers Went Away: Marriage, Sexuality, and Power in New Mexico, 1500–1846* (1991).

Lewis Hanke, *All Mankind Is One: A Study of the Disputation between Bartolomé de Las Casas and Juan Ginés de Sepúlveda in 1550 on the Intellectual and Religious Capacity of the American Indians* (1974).

Robert T. Himmerich, *The Encomenderos of New Spain, 1521–1555* (1991).

Paul E. Hoffman, *A New Andalucía and a Way to the Orient: The American Southeast during the Sixteenth Century* (1990).

Robert H. Jackson, ed., *Indians, Franciscans, and Spanish Colonization: The Impact of the Mission System on California Indians* (1995).

Andrew L. Knaut, *The Pueblo Revolt of 1680: Conquest and Resistance in Seventeenth-Century New Mexico* (1995).

James Lang, *Conquest and Commerce: Spain and England in the Americas* (1975).

Clark Spencer Larsen and George R. Milner, eds., *In the Wake of Contact: Biological Responses to Conquest* (1994).

Bartolomé de Las Casas, *In Defense of the Indians*, trans. Stafford Poole (1974).

Miguel Leon-Portilla, *Aztec Thought and Culture: A Study of the Ancient Nahuatl Mind* (1963).

Miguel Leon-Portilla, ed., *The Broken Spears: The Aztec Account of the Conquest of Mexico* (1962).

James Lockhart, *The Nahuas after Conquest: A Social and Cultural History of the Indians of Central Mexico, Sixteenth through Eighteenth Centuries* (1992).

James Lockhart, ed., *We People Here: Nahuatl Accounts of the Conquest of Mexico* (1993).

James Lockhart and Enrique Otte, eds., *Letters and People of the Spanish Indies: Sixteenth Century* (1976).

James Lockhart and Stuart B. Schwartz, *Early Latin America: A History of Colonial Spanish America and Brazil* (1983).

Lyle N. McAlister, *Spain and Portugal in the New World, 1492–1700* (1984).

Sabine McCormack, *Religion in the Andes: Vision and Imagination in Early Colonial Peru* (1991).

Bonnie G. McEwan, *The Spanish Missions of la Florida* (1993).

Jerald T. Milanich, *Florida Indians and the Invasion from Europe* (1995).

Jerald T. Milanich, ed., *Earliest Hispanic/Native American Interactions in the American Southeast* (1991).

Jerald T. Milanich and Charles Hudson, *Hernando de Soto and the Indians of Florida* (1993).

Jerald T. Milanich and Susan Milrath, eds., *First Encounters: Spanish Explorations in the Caribbean and the United States* (1989).

Colin A. Palmer, *Slaves of the White God: Blacks in Mexico, 1570–1650* (1976).

Carroll L. Riley, *Rio del Norte: People of the Upper Rio Grande from Earliest Times to the Pueblo Revolt* (1995).

Fray Bernardino de Sahagún, *General History of the Things of New Spain*, ed. Arthur J. O. Anderson and Charles E. Dibble, 13 vols. (1982).

Robert Silverberg, *The Pueblo Revolt* (1994).

Steve J. Stern, *Peru's Indian Peoples and the Challenge of Spanish Conquest: Huamanga to 1640* (1982).

David Hurst Thomas, *St. Catherines: An Island in Time* (1988).

David Hurst Thomas, ed., *Ethnology of the Indians of Spanish Florida* (1991).

David Hurst Thomas, ed., *The Missions of Spanish Florida* (1991).

Tzvetan Todorov, *The Conquest of America: The Question of the Other* (1984).

John W. Verano and Douglas H. Ubelaker, eds., *Disease and Demography in the Americas* (1992).

VIRGINIA ALGONQUIAN TOTEM

This object was made by one of Powhatan's people, probably a woman skilled in sewing small shell beads into intricate patterns. Soon after it appeared in England about 1630, it was called "Powhatan's mantle," a name still used for it. It is large, more than six feet long and four feet wide, constructed of four deer hides sewn together. The hides and the decorative shells used conclusively establish its Virginia Algonquian origins, although there is no firm evidence that it actually belonged to Powhatan or that it was used as a mantle or cloak. What looks like a neck opening is simply an unfinished seam between two deerskins. Furthermore, there is no record of a Virginia Algonquian wearing a cloak suspended from the neck. Cloaks worn by Powhatan, described by Captain John Smith and other settlers, evidently had fringe or animal tails dangling from them, unlike this object. A modern expert has concluded that this object was probably an image kept in a treasure house where chiefs stored their valuables. The large human figure, the deer on the right, the mountain lion on the left, and the thirty-four concentric circles probably served as totems, what Smith called "sentinels," linking the chief, the valuable objects in the treasure house, and the spirits that animated the world.

Ashmolean Museum, Oxford.

THE SOUTHERN COLONIES IN THE SEVENTEENTH CENTURY

3

1601–1700

E ARLY IN 1607, POWHATAN RULED an Algonquian chiefdom on the brink of a strange new world, a world in which white people from England would become a permanent and growing presence in North America. In Central and South America, other chiefdoms had entered this new world a century earlier when newcomers from Spain had arrived, plundering, praying, and staying. The conquistadors de Soto and Coronado made forays into North America in the 1540s. Decades later, the colonizers Menéndez and Oñate established small, struggling outposts of New Spain in Florida and New Mexico. Elsewhere in North America, no Europeans established a permanent settlement. Explorers, missionaries, fishermen, pirates, and others cruised along the Atlantic coast from time to time before 1607 and made an occasional landing. But they did not stay or, if they tried to stay —as at Roanoke—they did not survive. In 1607, all that was about to change. The Powhatan chiefdom was the first Native American group in North America to encounter the new English world that would eventually engulf them all.

Powhatan was the supreme chief—in his language, the *mamanatowick*—of about 14,000 Algonquian people who inhabited the coastal plain of present-day Virginia, near the Chesapeake Bay. Powhatan's people belonged to more than thirty subordinate chiefdoms, each headed by its own chief, called a *werowance*. Powhatan, who was probably born in the 1540s, inherited leadership of six of these subordinate chiefdoms. The others he systematically added to his chiefdom by conquest or threat. By 1607, the werowances beholden to Powhatan governed about 140 settlements scattered along the banks of the four major rivers that drained into Chesapeake Bay. Most werowances inherited their positions from female ancestors. Women sometimes served as werowances; the woman Opussunoquonuske was werowance of a town of the Appamatucks.

Hostile tribes surrounded Powhatan's chiefdom, and intertribal warfare occurred constantly. Men aspired to be courageous warriors who excelled at killing their enemies. One of Powhatan's duties as mamanatowick was to travel from village to village and listen to men boast of their heroic feats in battle. His visits energized the warrior ethic and strengthened his chiefdom. The emphasis on warfare arose partly from increased competition for access to prime deer-hunting lands caused by a growing Native American population. Another purpose of warfare was to capture women and children who could be then incorporated into Powhatan's chiefdom. Captured male children would grow into valuable warriors, and their

SECOTAN VILLAGE

This engraving, published in 1612, was copied from an original drawing John White made in 1585 when he visited the village of Secotan on the coast of North Carolina (see page 69). The drawing provides a schematic view of daily life in the village. In the lower right, men dance and sing around a circle of "posts carved on the topps lyke mens faces," White noted on the original. The fire burning behind the line of crouching men he labeled "the place of solemne prayer." The large building in the lower left was a tomb where the bodies of important leaders were kept. Dwellings similar to those illustrated on Smith's map of Virginia (see page 78) lined a central space, where men and women ate. Corn is growing in the fields along the right side of the village. The engraver has included hunters shooting deer at the upper left; hunting was probably never so convenient — no such hunters or deer appear in White's original drawing. This portrait conveys the message that Secotan was orderly, settled, religious, harmonious, and peaceful (note the absence of fortifications), and very different from English villages.

Princeton University Libraries.

mothers and sisters would give birth to still more warriors while performing valuable labor.

The arts of war were similar in many ways to the skills of hunting, the basic subsistence activity of Powhatan's men. Hunters took small game of all sorts. They hooked, netted, and trapped fish in the region's many streams and rivers. Deer were their most important prey, supplying not only meat but also hides, bones, and antlers that were crafted into clothing, tools, weapons, and decorative objects. Successful hunters who kept their families well supplied with meat were accorded high status. A young hunter who wished to marry a young woman offered gifts of meat to her as proof of his hunting skills.

Men hunted not only for food but also because Powhatan required each of his werowances to pay him an annual tribute in the form of deer hides. Powhatan collected many other forms of tribute, including turkeys, fish, shellfish, beads, copper, and especially corn. Corn was such a vital crop that Powhatan's people divided their year into five seasons: fall, winter, spring, summer, and the season when ears appeared on the corn.

Powhatan stored the hides and other goods in huge storehouses and used them to reward favorites and to provide gifts to the parents of the young women he took as wives. On his journeys from village to village, he surveyed the young virgins and selected the most desirable to be his wives. He had well over fifty wives in all; at any one time, a dozen or more lived with him. Typically, after a wife bore him a child he sent her back to her home village and kept the child to be raised in his settlement. This practice interlaced the dispersed villages in Powhatan's chiefdom with ties of kinship and loyalty to the mamanatowick. Werowances also often had more than one wife, but usually not many more since they lacked the wealth Powhatan obtained from tribute.

Women's responsibility for the essential food that came from foraging and agriculture underscored their importance and status in Powhatan's communities. Women in the chiefdom planted crops using sticks or deer bones to dig holes for seeds. They harvested, processed, stored, and cooked the produce. Cultivated crops supplied about a quarter of their families' diet. Women obtained other plant food by foraging. They also wove baskets and mats, fashioned various bone utensils, and kept the home fires burning. When an important man visited a settlement, the werowance usually assigned a woman to sleep with the visitor. If her husband consented, as many men did, a married woman could have sexual relations with other men. A man who was caught having unauthorized sex with another man's wife was killed.

By 1607, Powhatan had heard about white men who appeared from time to time. His brother Opechancanough had told him about the Spaniards' plans for a Chesapeake settlement thirty years earlier. Powhatan's warriors probably helped kill the last survivors of England's abortive Roanoke settlement. Powhatan posted scouts along the Atlantic coast to watch for white people and their "floating islands," a term one Indian coined for ships. Confident of his formidable power, Powhatan was not afraid of these white intruders. In fact, they might make useful allies against enemy tribes.

In the century after 1607, Powhatan's people were decimated by English settlers and the diseases they inadvertently brought with them. The English newcomers had different ideas about how to organize their communities, what crops to plant, what rulers to obey, what labor to perform, and why. During the seventeenth century, English notions about these matters came to dominate the coastal plain bordering the Chesapeake that had been Powhatan's chiefdom for decades before 1607. In the decades after 1607, English immigrants built a new world of permanent colonies in North America, initiating the sporadic, long-term decline of Powhatan's chiefdom and others like it. A world of Stone Age hunters and gatherers began to be replaced by a New World of farmers with tools, weapons, and ideas unknown to Powhatan.

An English Colony on the Chesapeake

By 1600, King James I of England eyed North America as a possible location for English colonies. He understood that North American colonies could extend English power across the Atlantic and might become the foundation of an English empire in the New World. Although Spain claimed all of North America under the 1494 Treaty of Tordesillas with Portugal, Spain's claim meant little if it could not be defended. In 1588, when King Philip II of Spain had sent a large fleet, the Armada, to invade England and attempt to place him on the English throne, English forces soundly defeated the Armada, demonstrating that England was capable of checking Spanish ambitions. It seemed likely that England could also prevail against Spain in North America, a distant hinterland of Spain's stoutly defended colonial heartland in Mexico and South America. Maybe England could encroach on the outskirts of Spain's New World empire, start colonies, and defend them. Maybe England could prevail against Spain's claims to North America by seizing the opportunity for colonization and daring Spain to intervene.

Colonization was an expensive undertaking. It required raising funds to purchase supplies, obtain ships and crews, and keep colonies provisioned until they became self-sufficient. Colonization was also risky. If a colony collapsed, the investments would be lost. But as the Spaniards had shown during the sixteenth century, expensive and risky as colonization was, it could also be enormously profitable. English merchants had used joint stock companies for many years to pool capital and share risks in trading voyages to Europe, Africa, and Asia. The tantalizing Spanish example lured certain Englishmen, with King James's blessing, into creating a joint stock company for the purposes of colonizing North America.

JOHN SMITH'S MAP OF VIRGINIA
In 1612, John Smith published a detailed map of early Virginia that showed not only geographical features but also the limits of exploration (indicated by small crosses), the locations of the houses of the Indian "kings" (indicated by dwellings that look like quonset huts), and "ordinary houses" of indigenous people (indicated by dots). The map shows the early settlers' intense interest in knowing where the Indians were — and were not. Note the location of Jamestown (upriver from Point Comfort) and of Powhatan's residence at the falls (just to the right of the large P outside the hut portrayed in the upper left corner). The drawing of Powhatan surrounded by some of his many wives (upper left corner) was almost certainly made by an English artist who had never been to Virginia or seen Powhatan but who tried to imagine the scene as described by John Smith.
Princeton University Libraries.

In 1606, a number of "knightes, gentlemen, merchauntes, and other adventurers of our cittie of London" organized the Virginia Company of London and petitioned King James to grant them permission to establish a colony in North America. The king gave the company a charter authorizing the group to settle a colony on the coast of Virginia and to possess "all the landes, woods, soile, groundes, havens, ports, rivers, mines, mineralls, marshes, waters, fishinges, commodities and hereditamentes [anything inheritable] whatsoever" that lay within fifty miles north and south of the coastal settlement and one hundred miles inland (later extended to the Pacific). James boldly granted the Virginia Company over six million acres and everything they might contain, in large measure because they were not his to grant. In effect, the charter was a royal license to poach on Spanish claims and on Powhatan's chiefdom.

English merchants had used joint stock companies for many years to pool capital and share risks in trading voyages to Europe, Africa, and Asia. The tantalizing Spanish example lured certain Englishmen into creating a joint stock company for the purposes of colonizing North America.

The adventurers in the Virginia Company hoped to found an empire that would strengthen England not only overseas but also at home. Richard Hakluyt, a strong proponent of colonization, argued that a colony would provide a convenient outlet for the swarms of poor "valiant youthes rusting and hurtfull by lacke of employement" in England. As colonial settlers, these jobless Englishmen would be put to work, producing goods that England currently had to import from other nations. They would also provide a ready market in the colony for English woolens. But the main reason the Virginia Company adventurers were willing to risk (or "adventure") their capital in Virginia was not to reduce unemployment in England or provide overseas markets for English textiles. Instead, they fervently hoped for quick profits.

Virginia Company investors did not know exactly how they could make money in the colony. Enthusiastic reports from the Roanoke voyages twenty years earlier claimed that in Virginia "the earth bringeth foorth all things in aboundance, as in the first creation, without toile or labour." Perhaps some valuable exotic crop could be grown in this Eden. Maybe the virtually limitless timber could be exploited to produce pitch and tar, those essentials for watertight ships. Or perhaps deposits of gold, silver, or other precious minerals awaited discovery. Another, more certain source of riches lay in Spanish treasure ships as they cruised up the North American coast to catch the trade winds that sped them home. Perhaps, the adventurers reasoned, an occasional raid on the Spanish fleet would yield quick and relatively easy returns. One way or another, Virginia promised to reward the adventurers. Or so they thought.

The Fragile Jamestown Settlement

In December 1606, the *Susan Constant, Discovery,* and *Godspeed* carried 144 Englishmen toward Virginia. Delayed by storms and a stopover in the West Indies, where they picked up plants that might prove hardy in Virginia, they arrived at the mouth of the Chesapeake Bay on April 26, 1607. That night while the colonists rested onshore, one of them later recalled that a band of Indians "creeping upon all foure, from the Hills like Beares, with their Bowes in their mouthes," attacked and dangerously wounded two men. The attack gave the colonists an early warning that the North American wilderness was not quite the paradise described by the Virginia Company's publications in England. For the next three weeks, the 105 colonists (39 had died at sea) explored the bay for a suitable place to settle. On May 14, they put ashore on a small peninsula in the James River, about sixty miles from the coast, in the midst of Powhatan's chiefdom. With the memory of their first night in America fresh in their minds, they quickly built a fort, the first building in the settlement they named Jamestown.

The fort accurately conveyed the colonists' belief that they needed to protect themselves from Indians and Spaniards. They worried that Spain might try to eliminate their fledgling colony before it got established. Spaniards did employ spies who kept them well informed about events in Virginia, and they even planned an expedition to wipe out Jamestown. But, like many other Spanish plans in the seventeenth century, this one never got beyond the planning stage. Powhatan's people, however, could not afford to be lackadaisical about defending their homeland. The Jamestown fort showed that, despite Spanish claims, English ambitions, and

the king's charter, the colonists knew that native peoples were prepared to defend Virginia as their own.

During May and June 1607, the settlers and Powhatan's warriors skirmished repeatedly. English muskets and cannon repelled Indian attacks on Jamestown, but the Indians' superior numbers and knowledge of the Virginia wilderness made it risky for the settlers to venture far beyond the Jamestown peninsula. Late in June, Powhatan sensed a stalemate and made peace overtures.

The settlers soon discovered that they confronted a far more dangerous, invisible threat: disease. For six weeks during the summer, many of the Englishmen lay "night and day groaning in every corner of the Fort most pittiful to heare," wrote George Percy, one of the settlers. By September, fifty of the colonists had died. "Our men were destroyed with [such] cruell diseases as Swellings, Fluxes, Burning Fevers, and by [Indian] warres, and some departed suddenly, but for the most part they died of meere famine," Percy recalled. "There were never Englishmen left in a forreigne Countrey in such miserie as wee were in this new discovered Virginia."

The colonists also made themselves miserable by constant bickering and plotting. While real and imaginary conspiracies occupied the attention of Jamestown's leaders, crops went unplanted and food supplies dwindled.

Powhatan's people came to the rescue of the weakened and distracted colonists. Early in September 1607, they began to bring corn to the colony for barter. When that was insufficient to keep the colonists fed, the settlers sent Captain John Smith to trade for corn with tribes upriver from Jamestown. More soldier than merchant, Smith did not hesitate to take hostages and shoot to kill when Indians were reluctant to trade away their corn. His efforts managed to keep 38 of the original settlers alive until a fresh supply of food and 120 more colonists arrived from England in January 1608.

Smith himself barely managed to survive that first year. Late in December, when he was on one of his trading forays, Powhatan's warriors captured him and brought him before the powerful chief. Smith wrote that Powhatan "feasted him after their best barbarous manner." Then, after the chief had consulted with his men, "two great stones were brought before Powhatan: then as many [Indians] as could layd hands on [Smith], dragged him to [the stones], and thereon laid his head, and being ready with their clubs, to beate out his braines." At that moment, Pocahontas, Powhatan's young daughter, rushed forward and "got [Smith's] head in her armes, and laid her owne upon his to save him from death." Powhatan spared Smith and, with a promise of friendship, released him to return to Jamestown.

Smith's famous Pocahontas story is almost too good to be true. Although Smith himself is the source of the story, it probably happened about as he claimed. Certainly he was captured and released by Powhatan; and certainly Pocahontas was friendly with the colonists—she eventually married the

SATIRICAL PLAYING CARD
Horrifying tales that filtered back to England contradicted the claims of promoters that settlers would find an idyllic land of milk and honey in Virginia. This English playing card makes fun of rich investors who "fool away A Sporting Sum in North America," getting shares of stock that will be honored only by "Asses Ears." The card hints that investing in overseas colonies made less sense than gambling — which was presumably how this card was used. What does the drawing suggest about those who became settlers rather than simply shareholders in a joint stock company?
Bodleian Library, Oxford.

Englishman John Rolfe and moved to England, where she died in 1617. Making allowances for Smith's flair for self-dramatization, the Pocahontas story emphasizes two central themes of Jamestown's first year: the colonists' dependence on the Indians and Powhatan's reluctance to drive away the struggling English settlers while he had the chance. Those themes remained central to Virginia's history for almost twenty years.

It is difficult to exaggerate the precarious state of the early Jamestown settlement. Although the Virginia Company sent hundreds of new settlers to Jamestown each year, few survived. During the "starving time" winter of 1609–10, food was so short that one or two famished settlers resorted to eating their recently deceased neighbors. When Sir Thomas Gates, the first governor of Jamestown, arrived in 1610, he found only about 60 of the 500 settlers alive. The survivors were "full of misery and misgovernment," wrote William Strachey, who accompanied Gates. They were so demoralized that, rather than "step into the Woods a stone's cast off . . . to fetch other firewood," they ripped apart the dead settlers' empty houses. When Gates announced that he would take the survivors back to England if he could not feed them from the supplies in his ship, they responded with "a general acclamation, and shoute of joy." No cheers were recorded when a shipload of fresh supplies arrived from England just in time for the survivors to prolong their flirtation with death. Although the company continued to pour new settlers into Virginia, most of them went to an early grave. In the three years from 1619 through 1621, for example, the company sent 3,570 people to Virginia to supplement the 700 settlers already there. By 1622, however, only 1,240 of the 4,270 were still alive.

Encounters between Natives and Newcomers

In retrospect, the weakened condition of the settlers raises the question of why Powhatan did not strike to eliminate them. Of course, we cannot be certain about Powhatan's motives. Since Indians relied on spoken rather than written language, they left no documents that record their ideas. All our information about them comes filtered through the distorting lenses of English eyes. However, we can be certain about what the Indians did. They vacillated. They maintained contact with the English settlers, most of the time peaceful contact. But they also kept their distance.

Becaufe many doe defire to know the manner
of their Language, I haue inferted thefe few words.

KA katorawincs yowo. What call you this.

Nemarough, a man.

Crenepo, a woman.

Marowancheffo, a boy.

Yehawkans, Houfes.

Matchcores, Skins, or garments.

Mockafins, Shooes.

Tuffan, Beds. Pokatawer, Fire.

Attawp, A bow. Attonce, Arrowes.

Monacookes, Swords.

Aumouhhowgh, A Target.

Pawcuffacks, Gunnes.

Tomahacks, Axes.

Tockahacks, Pickaxes.

Pamefacks, Kniues.

Accowprets, Sheares.

Pawpecones, Pipes. Mattaffin, Copper

Uffawaffin, Iron, Braffe, Silver, or any white mettall. Muffes, Woods.

Attaffkuff, Leaues, weeds, or graffe.

Chepfin, Land. Shacquohocan. A ftone.

Wepenter, A cookold.

Suckahanna, Water. Noughmaff, Fifh.

Copotone, Sturgeon.

Weghfhaughes, Flefh.

Sawwehone, Bloud.

Netoppew, Friends.

Marrapough, Enemies.

Maskapow, the worft of the enemies.

Mawchick chammay, The beft of friends

Cafacunnakack, peya quagh acquintan vttafantafough, In how many daies will there come hither any more Englifh Ships.
Their Numbers.
Necut, 1. Ningh, 2. Nuff, 3. Yowgh, 4. Paranske, 5. Comotinch, 6. Toppawoff, 7 Nuffwafh, 8. Kekatawgh, 9. Kaskeke 10 They count no more but by tennes as followeth.

Cafe, how many.

Ninghfapooeksku, 20.

Nuffapooeksku, 30.

Yowghapooeksku, 40.

Parankeftaffapooekfku, 50.

Comatinchtaffapooekfku, 60.

Nuffwafhtaffapooekfku, 70.

Kekataughtaffapooekfku, 90.

Necuttoughtyfinough, 100.

Necuttwevnquaough, 1000.

Rawcofowghs, Dayes.

Kefkowghes, Sunnes:

Toppquough. Nights.

Nepawwefhowghs, Moones.

Pawpaxfoughes, Yeares.

Pummahumps, Starres.

Ofies, Heavens.

Okees, Gods.

Quiyoughcofoughs, Pettie Gods, and their affinities.

Righcomoughes, Deaths.

Kekughes, Liues.

Mowchick woyawgh tawgh noeragh kaquere mecher, I am very hungry? what fhall I eate?

Yawnor nehiegh Powhatan, Where dwels Powhatan.

Mache, nehiegh yourowgh, Orapaks. Now he dwels a great way hence at Orapaks.

Vittapitchewayne anpechitchs nehawper Werowacomoco, You lie, he ftaid ever at Werowacomoco.

Kator nehiegh mattagh neer vttapitchewayne, Truely he is there I doe not lie.

Spaughtynere keragh werowance mawmarinough kekatë wawgh peyaquaugh. Run you then to the King Mawmarynough and bid him come hither.

Vtteke, e peya weyack wighwhip, Get you gone, & come againe quickly.

Kekaten Pokahontas patiaquagh ningh tanks manotyens neer mowchick rawrenock audowgh, Bid Pokahontas bring hither two little Baskets, and I will giue her white Beads to make her a Chaine. FINIS.

JOHN SMITH'S DICTIONARY OF POWHATAN'S LANGUAGE
In 1612, John Smith published this list of the English equivalents of words used by Powhatan's people, almost the only record of the coastal Algonquian language that exists. Smith probably compiled this list by pointing and listening carefully. Can you find any of Powhatan's words that made their way into common English usage? What do the words in the list suggest about Smith's encounters with Powhatan's people? What interested Smith? What compelled the interest of his informants?
Princeton University Libraries.

The Virginia Company boasted that the settlers bought from the Indians "the pearles of earth [corn] and sell to them the pearles of heaven [Christianity]." In fact, few Indians converted to Christianity, and the English devoted scant effort to encouraging them. Intermarriage between Indian women and English men was also rare, despite the acute shortage of English women in Virginia in the early years. One of the few settlers who troubled to learn the Indians' language was Captain John Smith. From Smith's notes on Indian vocabulary, we know that the settlers quickly adopted the Virginia Algonquian

Why Did English Colonists Consider Themselves Superior to Indians and Africans?

A YOUNG VIRGINIAN
In 1645, the Dutch artist Wenceslaus Hollar drew this portrait of a twenty-three-year-old Indian from Virginia. The young man had evidently been brought to London, where he posed for this likeness. Hollar portrayed his exotic adornment — the animal claw headband, shell earrings, and necklace, facial markings, Mohawk haircut, and bare-chested torso. Yet these distinctly non-European features did not cause Hollar to compromise his humane, dignified depiction of this man whose gaze seems to be fixed steadily and shamelessly upon the observer. If this young Virginian had been back in the Chesapeake rather than in London, he probably would have been engaged in the deadly warfare triggered by Opechancanough's 1644 uprising. One might imagine how this portrait would be different if it were drawn by a Virginia colonist in 1645. British Museum.

Were seeds of the racial prejudice that has been such a powerful force in American history planted in the seventeenth-century Chesapeake? To answer that question, historians have paid close attention to the words the colonists used to describe Indians, Africans, and themselves.

In the mid-1500s, the English adopted the words *Indian* and *Negro* from Spanish, where they had come to mean, respectively, an aboriginal inhabitant of the New World and a black person of African ancestry. Both terms were generic, homogenizing an enormous diversity of tribal affiliations, languages, and cultures. Neither term originated with the people to whom it referred. The New England clergyman Roger Williams, who published a book on Indian languages in 1643, reported, "They have often asked mee, why we call them *Indians*," a poignant question that reveals the European origins of the term.

After *Indians*, the word the settlers used most frequently to describe Native Americans was *savages*. The Indians were savages, in the colonists' eyes, because they lacked the traits of English civilization. As one Englishman put it in 1625, the natives of Virginia were "so bad a people, having little of humanitie but shape, ignorant of Civilitie, of Arts, of Religion; more brutish than the beasts they hunt, more wild and unmanly than that unmanned wild countrey, which they range rather than inhabite; captivated also to Satans tyranny in foolish pieties, mad impieties, wicked idlenesse, busie and bloudy wickednesse." Some English colonists counterbalanced this harsh indictment with admiration for certain features of Indian behavior. They praised Indians' calm dignity and poise, their tender love and care for family members, and their simple, independent way of life in apparent harmony with nature.

Color was not a feature of the Indians' savagery. During the seventeenth century colonists never referred to Indians as "red." Instead, they saw Indi-ans' skin color as tawny or tanned, the "Sun's livery," as one settler wrote. Many settlers held the view that Indians were innately white like the English but in every other way woefully un-English.

In effect, the English colonists defined the Indians as "them," not "us." "Us" and "them" did not

AFRICAN MAN AND WOMAN

Albrecht Dürer, the foremost German artist of the Renaissance, drew these portraits early in the sixteenth century. They are among the first portraits of Africans to be made in Europe. Dürer drew Katarina, who was the servant of a Portuguese merchant Dürer visited in the Netherlands, in the spring of 1521. The portrait of the unidentified man was done several years earlier, but exactly when is unknown; the date 1508 was added after the portrait was completed. In any case, both portraits were completed before the Atlantic slave trade had begun to boom but well after Portuguese merchants had brought thousands of African slaves to Europe. Dürer's meticulously observed portraits betray no trace of racial prejudice. Both Katarina and the man appear to wear European clothing and to be depicted with the same respect and dignity Dürer accorded his European subjects. One might imagine how these portraits would be different if they had been executed by an artist in the southern colonies of North America in the late seventeenth century.

Foto Marburg/Art Resource, NY.

merely connote the differences between colonists and Native Americans. The colonists assumed that those differences expressed a hierarchy of power and status: "We" are superior and should be dominant; "they" are inferior and should be subordinate. The English enforced that distinction ferociously. In the early years of settlement, the colonists allowed a few young men to live for a while in Indian villages to learn native languages and then serve as interpreters. However, settlers who deserted English settlements in preference for Indian ways were punished with a vengeance. (*Continued*)

The colonists identified Africans quite differently. Only a few Africans lived in the Chesapeake early in the seventeenth century. The first recorded arrival of Africans occurred in 1619, when a Dutch man-of-war brought to Virginia "20. and odd Negroes," as John Rolfe wrote. Rolfe's usage illustrates the colonists' most common term for Africans: *Negroes*. But the other word the colonists frequently used to refer to Africans was not *savage* or *heathen*, but *black*. What struck English colonists most forcefully about Africans was not their un-English ways but their un-English skin color.

Black was not a neutral color to the colonists. According to the *Oxford English Dictionary* (which catalogs the changing meaning of words), *black* meant to the English people who settled the Chesapeake "deeply stained with dirt; soiled, dirty, foul . . . having dark or deadly purposes, malignant; pertaining to or involving death, deadly; baneful, disastrous, sinister . . . foul, iniquitous, atrocious, horrible, wicked." Black was the opposite of white, which connoted purity, beauty, and goodness—attributes the colonists identified with themselves. In fact, by the middle of the seventeenth century, the colonists referred to themselves not only as English but also as free, implying that people who were not English were not free. After about 1680, the colonists stated that implication in racial terms by referring to themselves as white. By the end of the seventeenth century, blacks were "them"—un-English, unwhite, and unfree.

A few of the English dissented from such views. Thomas Phillips, a slave ship captain, declared in 1694 that he could not "imagine why they [blacks] should be despis'd for their colour, being what they cannot help, and the effect of the climate it has pleas'd God to appoint them. I can't think there is any intrinsick value in one colour more than another, nor that white is better than black, only we think it so because we are so, and are prone to judge favourably in our own case, as well as the blacks, who in odium of the colour, say, the devil is white, and so paint him."

Virginians did not legally define slavery until 1660, but the sparse surviving evidence demonstrates that they practiced slavery long before that. Although there is no way to be certain, it is likely that the "20. and odd Negroes" who arrived in 1619 were slaves. And the punishments handed out to blacks who broke the law usually took for granted that their servitude could not be extended by several years, as was the case with white servants.

The debased status of slavery strengthened the colonists' prejudice toward blacks, just as racial prejudice buttressed slavery. A Virginia law of 1662, for instance, provided that "if any christian shall committ Fornication with a negro man or woman, hee or shee soe offending" had to pay a double fine. The law also demonstrates that, despite racial prejudice, sexual relations between white and black settlers were prevalent enough to attract the attention of the legislature.

For most of the seventeenth century, possession of a black skin did not automatically and necessarily condemn one to the status of slave in the eyes of whites. Some Africans in the Chesapeake served for limited periods of time like white servants, became free like white servants, and even acquired land, reared families, and participated in local affairs like former white servants. In fact, white colonists' prejudice against blacks represented an extreme form of wealthy colonists' attitudes toward servants and other poor white people. White servants, like blacks, were often considered "the vile and brutish part of mankind" by their masters.

The colonists hardened and exaggerated English attitudes about social hierarchy, about "us" and "them." Part of the reason is that, when colonists left England, they worried that they were separating themselves from "us"—the English—and risking becoming "them"—those uncivilized people found in the colonial wilds. To temper those fears and reduce those risks, colonists defined "us" and "them" in terms that emphasized their own Englishness in both color and civilization, providing a fertile seedbed for the growth of racial prejudice.

words *tomahawk* and *moccasin*. But since Smith's writings contain almost all we know about Virginia Algonquian (the language is now extinct), we remain ignorant of English words that may have entered the Indians' vocabulary. It is safe to speculate that such words were few, given the cultural distance the Indians maintained.

Powhatan's people regarded the English with suspicion, and for good reason. While the settlers often exhibited friendship toward the Indians, they did not hesitate to use their superior weapons—muskets, swords, and cannon—to enforce English notions of proper Indian behavior. More than once the Indians refused to trade corn to the settlers, evidently hoping to starve them out. But each time, the English broke the boycott by pillaging uncooperative villages and confiscating their corn.

The Indians retaliated against English violence, but for fifteen years they did not organize an all-out assault on the European intruders. Several considerations probably caused their hesitation. Although the Indians felt no attraction to Christianity, they were impressed by the power of the settlers' God. One chief put it succinctly when he told John Smith that "he did believe that our God as much exceeded theirs as our guns did their bows and arrows." The settlers not only had guns. They had sailing ships that mysteriously arose from the eastern horizon on a regular basis. They had abundant supplies of glass beads that appeared to be crystals of divine origin. These powerful strangers would make better allies than enemies, Powhatan and his werowances probably concluded. Powhatan dealt with the settlers much as he might have done with an alien tribe, one that he could ally with and use to his own advantage, with proper diplomacy.

As allies, the English not only strengthened Powhatan's dominance over the tribes in the region. They also supplied his people with European goods, usually in exchange for corn. Although the native Virginians possessed copper before the English arrived, they immediately recognized the superiority of the settlers' iron and steel weapons and tools, and they could not get enough of them. An important reason Powhatan's people did not launch a full-scale attack against the settlers for fifteen years after 1607 was that the English possessed axes, swords, pots, and other goods that the Indians wanted.

The trade that supplied Indians with European conveniences provided the English settlers with a prime necessity: food. But why did the settlers prove unable to feed themselves for more than a decade?

First, as the staggering death rate suggests, many settlers were too sick to be productive members of the colony. They evidently succumbed to New World pathogens. Their weakened condition after their long, hazardous sea voyage increased their susceptibility to disease. Although news of the deadly conditions in Virginia filtered back to England, the Virginia Company published pamphlets that denied the worst reports, offered incentives to prospective colonists, and promoted continued settlement. A 1609 tract promised that "the general sort that shall goe to bee planters [settlers], bee they never so poore, so they be honest, and painefull [diligent], the place will make them rich." However, during the first ten years, most settlers died and the company failed to make any profit, despite huge investments. The economic failure increased the company's desire to realize some gain from the enterprise. Neither the company nor most of the settlers fully grasped that Jamestown's first priority had to be survival, not profit.

The trade that supplied Indians with European conveniences provided the English settlers with a prime necessity: food.

A second reason the colonists failed to grow sufficient food had to do with their social origins in England. Very few farmers came to Virginia in the early years. Instead, the largest group of newcomers was gentlemen and their servants, men who—in John Smith's words—"never did know what a day's work was." Except for a small number of carpenters and blacksmiths, Smith wrote, "all the rest were poor gentlemen, tradesmen, and serving men, libertines, and such like, ten times more fit to spoil a commonwealth than . . . begin one or . . . help to maintain one." In fact, the proportion of gentlemen in Virginia in the early years was six times greater than in England, a reflection of the Virginia Company's urgent need for both investors and settlers. Instead of seeing gentlemen as a liability to the colony, the company tried to attract them. In a 1610 pamphlet, the company declared that nobody should believe that Virginia "excludeth Gentlemen, whose breeding never knew what a daies labour meant; for though they cannot digge, use the square, nor practise the axe and chizell, yet [they know] . . . how to employ the force of knowledge, the exercise of counsell, the operation and power of their best breeding and qualities."

In Virginia, however, breeding and quality were worthless for growing corn, catching fish, or even hunting deer. Nevertheless, the colonists clung to English notions of hierarchy and gentle breeding. Consider the procession to Jamestown's church in 1610: Each Sunday, William Strachey observed, the governor marched from his house to church accompanied by all the captains and officers and all the gentlemen, followed by an honor guard of fifty soldiers wearing "his Lordship's Livery, faire red cloakes." The governor sat in the choir of the church, surrounded by the captains and officers, and knelt for prayer on a special velvet cushion resting on a table. After church, the worthies reassembled in the order in which they had come and marched back to the governor's home.

These weekly rituals reassured English gentlemen that they were upholding proper standards of social hierarchy in the wilderness. By those same standards, gentlemen were not supposed to work with their hands and tradesmen were not supposed to work at trades for which they had not been trained. Adherence to these English attitudes about the proper subdivision of leisure and work prevented the settlers from squarely confronting the absolute requirement for the colony's survival: labor. John Smith repeatedly pointed out that in Virginia "there is no country to pillage . . . all you [can] expect from thence must be by labor." For more than a decade, however, most of the settlers who survived clung to ideas about labor that made more sense in labor-rich England than in labor-poor Virginia. In the meantime, they depended on the Indians' corn for food.

The persistence of the Virginia colony, precarious as it was, created difficulties for Powhatan's chiefdom. As the population of the colony slowly grew, some settlers moved to farms a few miles away from Jamestown, encroaching on Indian lands. The steady contact between natives and newcomers spread European viruses among the Indians, who suffered deadly epidemics in 1608 and between 1617 and 1619. While epidemics devastated the Indian population, trade with the settlers distorted Indian culture. Virginia Indians readily incorporated English trade goods into their traditional ways, but the constant English demand for corn required Indians to produce a large surplus. If the Indians produced only enough corn for self-

sufficiency, as they had for centuries, they risked famine when the English commandeered it to feed the settlers. The need to produce a sizable corn surplus for their own survival, as well as for trade, probably introduced tensions within Powhatan's villages, increasing the significance of agriculture and women's work. But from the Indians' viewpoint, the most important fact about the Virginia colony was that it was surviving. Instead of a temporary outpost, it was proving to be a permanent settlement.

Powhatan died in 1618, and his brother Opechancanough replaced him as mamanatowick. In 1622, Opechancanough organized an all-out assault on the English settlers. Striking on March 22, the Indians killed 347 settlers, nearly a third of the English population. But the attack failed to dislodge the Virginia colonists. In the aftermath, the settlers unleashed a murderous campaign of Indian extermination that in a few years pushed Indians beyond the small circumference of white settlement. Before 1622, the settlers knew that the Indians, though dangerous, were necessary to keep the colony alive; after 1622, the settlers concluded that the life of the colony required the death of the Indians, at least in the vicinity of white settlement. After 1622, most colonists considered Indians their perpetual enemies.

From Private Company to Royal Government

The 1622 uprising came close to achieving Opechancanough's goal of pushing the colonists back into the Atlantic—so close that it prompted a royal investigation of affairs in Virginia. The investigators discovered that the appalling mortality among the colonists was caused by disease and mismanagement more than by Indian raids. In 1624, King James revoked the charter of the Virginia Company and made Virginia a royal colony, subject to the direction of the royal government rather than to the company's private investors, an arrangement that lasted until 1776.

The king now appointed the governor of Virginia, but most features of local government established under the Virginia Company remained intact. In 1619, for example, the company had inaugurated the House of Burgesses, an assembly of representatives (called burgesses) elected by the colony's inhabitants. (Historians do not know which settlers were considered inhabitants and were thus qualified to vote for burgesses.) The company authorized the burgesses to propose laws that, when approved by company officials in London, would become enforceable. Under the new royal government, proposed laws had to be approved by the king's bureaucrats in England rather than by the company. Otherwise, however, the House of Burgesses continued as before, acquiring distinction as the oldest representative legislative assembly in the British colonies. In addition, under the royal government in Virginia, all free adult men could vote for burgesses, giving the House of Burgesses a far broader and more representative constituency than the English House of Commons.

In 1624, King James revoked the charter of the Virginia Company and made Virginia a royal colony, subject to the direction of the royal government rather than to the company's private investors, an arrangement that lasted until 1776.

The demise of the Virginia Company marked the end of the first phase of colonization of the Chesapeake. From the 105 adventurers who had landed in 1607 and the hundreds more who followed, the population had grown to about 1,200 by 1624. The Indians who had first been a necessary source of support were now considered deadly enemies. Despite its promises, the Virginia Company never paid a dividend to its investors and delivered most settlers to their graves. But by 1624 it was clear that the English were in Virginia to stay. Mortality rates among newcomers continued at levels higher than those in the worst epidemics in London, but new settlers still arrived. Their arrival and King James's willingness to take over the struggling colony signaled a fundamental change under way in Virginia. After years of fruitless experimentation, it was becoming clear that English settlers could make a fortune in Virginia by growing tobacco.

TOBACCO ADVERTISEMENT

This ad for "Kositzky's Best Virginia" tobacco illustrates a colonial planter and tobacco merchant examining the quality of a sample of leaves from an open cask waiting to be shipped to London, while an onlooker samples the leaves more thoroughly, by smoking. To smooth the transaction, an African — presumably a slave — offers a glass of wine. One way the English artist emphasized the differences between the African and the other men was giving the African a skirt of leaves; it is doubtful that any slaves in the Chesapeake wore such a skirt. How else did the artist highlight differences? Kositzky must have traded in other goods; the insignia at the top features scythes used for cutting grain but useless in harvesting tobacco, perhaps a hint of ignorance common in London about how tobacco was produced in the Chesapeake.

Arents Collection, New York Public Library.

A Tobacco Society

Tobacco grew wild in the New World, and Native Americans used it for thousands of years before Europeans arrived. *Tobacco,* in fact, was a Caribbean Indian word that referred not to what we know as the tobacco plant, but to a leaf of the plant rolled into a cigarlike shape. Indians inserted the lit cigar into a nostril and inhaled, a practice Columbus observed in Cuba on his first journey of discovery. Many sixteenth-century European explorers commented on the Indians' odd habit of "drinking smoke."

By the late sixteenth century, smoking was popular enough among Europeans that the word *tobacco* first entered the English language (via Spanish) and pipes began to be commonplace in England. Before the seventeenth century, however, tobacco imported from the Spanish colonies remained an expensive luxury in the Old World.

Tobacco did not figure in the plans of the Virginia Company. In 1609, a company pamphlet listed more than twenty crops that might profitably be cultivated in Virginia, but tobacco was not among them. "As for tobacco," John Smith wrote later, "we never then dreamt of it." John Rolfe, Pocahontas's husband-to-be, began to plant West Indian tobacco seeds in 1612. His experiments demonstrated that the plant could be grown successfully in Virginia. The first commercial shipment of tobacco to England left the colony in 1617. When it sold for a handsome price, the same Virginia colonists who had difficulty growing enough corn to feed themselves quickly tried to learn how to grow as much tobacco as possible. In a sense, that first commercial cargo was a pivot on which Virginia turned from a colony of rather aimless adventurers into a society of dedicated tobacco planters.

> *The first commercial shipment of tobacco to England in 1617 was a pivot on which Virginia turned from a colony of rather aimless adventurers into a society of dedicated tobacco planters.*

Dedicated they were. In 1620, with fewer than a thousand colonists, Virginia shipped 60,000 pounds of tobacco to England. By 1630, the population had grown to 2,500 while tobacco exports mushroomed to 350,000 pounds. More than a million pounds entered English markets in 1640, and even that was only the beginning. By 1700, tobacco exports from the Chesapeake region (encompassing Virginia and Maryland) topped 35 million pounds. By then, over 98,000 colonists lived in the region, and they had learned a thing or two about growing tobacco. Per capita tobacco exports were about 70 pounds in 1620; by 1700, they exceeded 350 pounds. This fivefold growth in productivity demonstrates that Chesapeake colonists mastered the demands of growing tobacco. To a large degree, the "Stincking Weede" (a seventeenth-century Marylander's term for tobacco) also mastered the Chesapeake colonists. The routines of tobacco agriculture structured daily life on Chesapeake farms. Tobacco planters' endless need for labor attracted droves of indentured servants from England to work in tobacco fields and settle the Chesapeake.

Tobacco Agriculture

Tobacco was a demanding crop. It required close attention and a great deal of hand labor year-round. Early each spring, colonists sowed the tiny seeds in specially prepared beds for sprouting. In June, when a good rain moistened the fields, workers hurried to transplant the sprouts to mounds of earth spaced about three feet apart. Then they had to hoe the fields to eliminate weeds and to protect the roots of the plants, a routine that continued throughout the summer. As the plants grew, they had to be tended carefully to produce marketable leaves. When the leaves began to yellow in the early fall,

LEARNING TO INHALE

It took a while for Europeans to master the many refinements of smoking. This Dutch ceramic tile made early in the seventeenth century shows a smoker accomplishing the remarkable feat (at that time) of blowing smoke through his nose. Europeans rhapsodized about the many virtues of smoking. A seventeenth-century Dutch print of two men relaxing with their pipes was captioned "Vita est Fumus" — Life is Smoke.

Niemeyer Tabaksmuseum.

the stalks were cut and the plants left in the fields to wither.

Colonists then gathered the plants and strung them up in sheltered areas to dry and cure, usually for the winter. During moist weather the following spring, when the dried leaves became pliable, the workers stripped the leaves from the stalks and tightly packed them into a hogshead (a large barrel) for shipment to market. By the time one year's crop was being packed, the next year's crop was already in the ground.

Primitive tools and methods made this intensive cycle of labor even more taxing. Like the Indians, the colonists "cleared" fields not by chopping down trees but by stripping a ring of bark from each tree (known as girdling), thereby killing it. Dead trees and stumps usually studded a cleared field, making the use of plows and draft animals impractical. Instead, colonists tilled the ground with heavy hoes. To plant, a visitor noted, they "just make holes [with a stick] into which they drop the seeds," much as the Indians did. In addition to planting tobacco, the colonists grew corn and other food crops—after all, tobacco is miserable food. Work on food crops had to be done in the midst of the tobacco crop cycle, leaving little time for idleness. But in spare moments colonists enjoyed the fruits of their labor. As a traveler observed, "Everyone smokes while working or idling . . . men, women, girls, and boys from the age of seven years."

English settlers were willing to work hard because they could expect to do much better in the Chesapeake than in England. One colonist declared that "the dirt of this Province affords as great a profit to the general Inhabitant, as the Gold of Peru doth to . . . the Spaniard." Although that observation was exaggerated, it was true that a hired man would have to work two or three years in England to earn as much as he could in Chesapeake tobacco fields in just one year. Better still, in Virginia even common laborers could hope to obtain land. Land was so abundant that, by English standards, it was extremely cheap. In the mid-seventeenth century Chesapeake, a colonist could buy one hundred acres of land for less than a laborer's annual wages—an utter impossibility in England. New settlers who paid their own transportation to the Chesapeake received free land. Each such settler received a grant of fifty acres of free land (a headright), a policy begun by the Virginia Company and continued by the royal government to encourage settlement.

A Servant Labor System

Headrights, cheap land, and high wages gave poor English folk powerful incentives to immigrate to the New World. Despite the incentives, many potential immigrants could not scrape together the fare to sail across the Atlantic. Their poverty and the colonists' crying need for labor formed the basic context for the creation of a servant labor system.

Today, people tend to think of the colonial South as a slave society. The seventeenth-century Chesapeake, however, was fundamentally a servant society. Twenty Africans arrived in Virginia in 1619 and more came in subsequent years. But until the last quarter of the seventeenth century, only a small number of slaves labored in Chesapeake tobacco fields. (Large numbers of slaves came later, as chapter 5 explains.) About 80 percent of the immigrants to the Chesapeake during the seventeenth century were indentured servants. In large measure, colonists in the Chesapeake were servants, former servants, and descendants of servants. Along with tobacco, the servant labor system profoundly influenced nearly every feature of Chesapeake society.

The seventeenth-century Chesapeake was fundamentally a servant society, not a slave society. In large measure, colonists in the Chesapeake were servants, former servants, and descendants of servants.

To buy passage aboard a ship bound for the Chesapeake, an English immigrant had to come up with about £5, roughly a year's wages for an English servant or laborer. Saving a year's wages then was no easier than it is now. Many laborers, servants, and artisans did not even have steady work throughout the year. Opportunities for work were shrinking in seventeenth-century England. Many country gentlemen fenced fields they had formerly planted with crops and began to pasture sheep in the enclosures. Keeping sheep required only a few of the laborers who had previously been hired to cultivate crops; the other farmhands had to find work elsewhere, if they could. Even if they found other jobs, the purchasing power of their wages slowly deteriorated as England's population grew faster than its food supply, causing prices to rise.

A SERVANT'S INDENTURE
This document indentured the servant Richard Lowther to a Virginia master in 1627. As a written contract, an indenture specified the agreement between servant and master and could be used in court to help settle disputes. No such contract detailed the relationship between master and slaves.
Virginia Historical Society.

Unemployed servants, laborers, and tradesmen wandered from village to village looking for work. Many of them drifted to seaports like Bristol, Liverpool, and especially London. As they searched for jobs in the cities, they heard of the opportunities in the colonies, where jobs were abundant and workers were scarce.

Lacking the money to get across the Atlantic, poor immigrants entered an agreement with a local shopkeeper, mariner, or merchant. The terms of the agreement were spelled out in a contract called an indenture. The indenture specified that the local merchant would pay for the immigrant's transportation to the Chesapeake. In return, the immigrant agreed to work for a period—usually four to seven years—without pay. During this period of indentured servitude, the immigrant received food and shelter from the employer in the colonies. When the indenture expired, the employer was required to give the former

servant "freedom dues," usually three barrels of corn and a suit of clothes.

In effect, indentures allowed poor immigrants to trade their most valuable asset—their ability to work—for a trip to the New World. The English shopkeepers and merchants who signed them to indentures and paid their fare to the colonies owned the rights to their labor. When the indentured immigrants arrived in the Chesapeake, ship captains arranged to sell those rights to tobacco planters who needed some hands in the fields or rough carpenters to bang together a shed. Most planters were willing to pay about twice the cost of transportation for the right to four to seven years of an immigrant's labor. Normally, a planter literally paid with tobacco, the legal tender of the Chesapeake region. Most of the planter's payment was returned as a handsome profit to the English merchant who had indentured the immigrant and paid his or her fare.

Planters were eager to purchase as many indentured servants as they could afford. As one Virginia planter noted, "our principall wealth . . . consisteth in servants." More servants meant more hands to grow more tobacco. More servants also meant more land. For every servant purchased, a planter received from the colonial government a headright of another fifty acres of land. Even without the land, a servant was a good investment for a planter. A new servant cost about one thousand pounds of tobacco. The first year the servant worked for a planter, he or she could be expected to grow between one and two thousand pounds of tobacco plus enough corn to feed himself or herself. The servant's labor for the subsequent years of the indenture gave the planter a substantial return on his investment.

At least it did if all went well. Bad weather, crop disease, or insect pests could ruin a harvest. But the biggest risk to both the planter and the servant was that the servant would get sick and die before serving out the term of the indenture. Mortality remained at very high levels in the Chesapeake through the middle decades of the seventeenth century. About half of all children born in the Chesapeake died before they reached adulthood. A person who survived to age twenty could expect to live only twenty-five more years. Life expectancy had improved so little by 1687 that a thirty-six-year-old planter remarked, "Now I look upon myself to be in my declining age."

As immigrants to the Chesapeake, servants had a slimmer chance of surviving—the prerequisite for them to receive a payoff from their servitude. Among one group of 275 servant men who arrived in Maryland before midcentury, 40 percent died before their servitude ended. Of the survivors, another 40 percent died or moved away within ten years of obtaining their freedom. Less than a third of the original group remained in the colony for ten years after their indentures expired. Eight out of ten of these men managed to acquire small farms, and a few possessed servants of their own. For this minority, the bargain struck by signing an indenture proved hard, but real. For the vast majority of servants, the bargain was just hard.

The mayor of Bristol, England, observed that of the servants leaving for the colonies, "some are husbands that have forsaken their wives, others wives who have abandoned their husbands; some are children and apprentices run away from their parents and masters; oftentimes unwary and credulous persons have been tempted on board [ships] by men-stealers, and many [servants] . . . have been pursued by hue-and-cry for robberies, burglaries, or breaking prison." The mayor was correct that some servants came from each of these groups. For the most part, however, servants were simply poor young English men seeking work.

More than two-thirds of the servants were between the ages of fifteen and twenty-five when they came to the Chesapeake. Many of them were orphans. Typical in his desperate situation was sixteen-year-old Francis Haires, who indentured himself for seven years because "his father and mother and All friends [are] dead and he [is] a miserable wandering boy." Like Francis, most indentured servants had no special training or skills, although the majority had some experience with agricultural work. "Hunger and fear of prisons bring to us," a Virginia planter complained in 1662, "onely such servants as have been brought up to no Art or Trade." Planters were eager for skilled carpenters, blacksmiths, and coopers (barrel makers). However, only about one indentured servant in five had some training at a skilled trade, and many had apprenticed in trades with little usefulness in the Chesapeake, like button mold making or hemp dressing. With a valued skill, a servant could obtain a shorter indenture; had Francis been an experienced carpenter, he might well have served four instead of seven years. Nonetheless, few skilled craftsmen risked coming to the colonies unless they were down on their luck and, like Francis, had few prospects at home.

Women were almost as rare as skilled craftsmen in the Chesapeake and more ardently desired. In the early days of the tobacco boom, the Virginia Company tried to reduce the scarcity of women by shipping unattached young women to the colony as prospective wives for male settlers willing to pay "120 weight [pounds] of the best leaf tobacco for each of them." The company reasoned that, as one official wrote in 1622, "the plantation can never flourish till families be planted, and the respect of wives and children fix the people on the soil." The company's efforts as a marriage broker proved no more successful than its other ventures. Men continued to outnumber women by a wide margin until late in the seventeenth century.

The servant labor system perpetuated the gender imbalance. Although female servants cost about the same as males and generally served for the same length of time, only about one indentured servant in four was a woman. Planters preferred male servants for field work, although many women also hoed tobacco fields. Most women servants, however, did household chores such as cooking, washing, cleaning, gardening, and milking.

Servant life was harsh by the standards of seventeenth-century England and even by the rougher, frontier standards of the Chesapeake. In England, laborers sold their services to their masters at annual hiring fairs; in the Chesapeake, servants were bought and sold more or less like livestock. Unlike their English counterparts, Chesapeake servants had virtually no control over who purchased their labor—and thus them—for the period of the indenture. A servant might be bought and sold several times before the indenture expired. One servant wrote from Virginia in 1623 that his master "hath sold me for £150 sterling like a damnd slave." The colonial practice of treating servants as property alarmed some Englishmen. In 1625, a ship captain refused to transport servants to Virginia because "servants were sold heere upp and downe like horses, and therefore he held it not lawfull to carie any." The colonists' need for labor and the profits to be made in supplying it quickly muffled such qualms. But in England rumors persisted that, as one contemporary wrote, Chesapeake masters "abuse their servantes there with intollerable oppression and hard usage."

Some former servants argued against the scuttlebutt that indentured servitude bordered on slavery. George Alsop, who served as an indentured servant in Maryland, wrote that "the four years I served there were not to me so slavish, as a two years Servitude of a Handicraft Apprenticeship was here in London." According to Alsop, servants in the colonies had "the least cause to complain, either for strictness of Servitude, want of Provisions, or need of Apparel." Women servants, he said, "are no sooner on shoar, but they are courted into a Copulative Matrimony." Overall, Alsop argued, Chesapeake servants "live well in the time of their Service, and by their restrainment in that time, they are made capable of living much better when they come to be free."

Most servants who came to the Chesapeake probably hoped their experience would match Alsop's claims. If so, most learned otherwise. James Revel, an eighteen-year-old thief who was punished by being transported to Virginia, where he was indentured to a tobacco planter, described experiences common to most servants. In verse, Revel chronicled what happened when he arrived at his new master's plantation:

My Europian clothes were took from me,
Which never after I again could see.
    A canvas shirt and trowsers then they gave,
With a hop-sack frock in which I was to slave:
No shoes nor stockings had I for to wear,
Nor hat, nor cap, both head and feet were bare.
    Thus dress'd into the Field I next must go,
Amongst tobacco plants all day to hoe,
At day break in the morn our work began,
And so held to the setting of the Sun.
        My fellow slaves were just five Transports
            more,
With eighteen Negroes, which is twenty four:
Besides four transport women in the house,
To wait upon his daughter and his Spouse,
    We and the Negroes both alike did fare,
Of work and food we had an equal share. . . .
Six days we slave for our master's good,
The seventh day is to produce our food.
        Sometimes when that a hard days work
            we've done,
Away unto the mill we must be gone;
Til twelve or one o'clock a grinding corn,
And must be up by daylight in the morn. . . .
        And if we offer for to run away,
For every hour [away] we must serve a day;
For every day a Week, They're so severe,
For every week a month, for every month a year.
But if they murder, rob, or steal when there,
Then straightway hang'd, the Laws are so severe;
For by the Rigour of that very law
They're much kept under and to stand in awe.

Severe laws were designed to keep servants in their place in more ways than one. Punishments for petty crimes like running away or stealing a pig stretched servitude far beyond the terms of indenture. Servant Christopher Adams, for example, had to serve three extra years for running away for six months; Richard Higby received six extra years of servitude for killing three hogs. Just after midcentury, the Virginia legislature added at least three years to the servitude of most servants by requiring them to serve until they were twenty-four years old.

Women servants were subject to special restrictions and risks. They were prohibited from marrying until their servitude had expired. A servant woman, the law assumed, could not serve two masters at the same time: one who owned her indentured labor and another who was her husband.

TOBACCO PLANTATION

This print illustrates the tobacco harvest on a seventeenth-century plantation. Workers cut the mature plants and put the leaves in piles to wilt (left foreground and center background). After the leaves had dried somewhat, they were suspended from poles in a drying barn (right foreground), where they were seasoned before being packed in casks for shipping (see page 87). Sometimes they were also dried in the fields (center background). The print suggests the labor demands of tobacco by showing twenty-two individuals, all but two of them actively at work with tobacco. The one woman depicted (hand in hand with a man in the left foreground) may be on her way to work in the harvest, but it appears more likely that she and the man are overseeing the labor of their servants or employees.

From "About Tobacco" Lehman Brothers.

However, the overwhelming predominance of men in the Chesapeake population inevitably pressured women to engage in sexual relations. The pressure was strong enough that about a third of immigrant women were pregnant when they got married. Pregnancy and childbirth sapped a woman's strength, and a new child diverted her attention, reducing her usefulness to her master. Thus for a servant woman, pregnancy meant punishment: As a rule, if a woman servant gave birth to a child, she had to serve two extra years and pay a fine. When servant Ann Parke had a baby, a local court simply doubled her remaining period of servitude.

Such punishments reflected four fundamental realities of the servant labor system. First, masters' hunger for labor led them to demand as much work from their servants as possible, and they did not hesitate to devise legal ways to extend the period of servitude. Second, servants did not share masters' interest in maximum labor. Instead, servants hoped to survive their period of servitude and then use their freedom to start a family and obtain land. This conflict of interest made servants somewhat reluctant, grudging laborers. They worked as hard as they had to rather than—as their masters wanted —as hard as they could. Third, servants did not always comply meekly with their masters' demands for obedience. They saw themselves as free people in a temporary status of servitude, and they frequently resisted their masters' orders. Fourth, both servants and masters put up with this contentious arrangement because the alternatives were less desirable. Masters could not hire free men and women because few were willing to work for wages. Land was so readily available that those who were free preferred to work on their own land, for themselves. Furthermore, most masters could not depend on much labor from family members, especially sons. The skewed sex ratio among servants and in the general population meant that families were few, were started late, and thus had few children. And, until the 1680s and 1690s, slaves were expensive and hard to come by. Before then, masters who wanted to expand their labor force and grow more tobacco had few alternatives to buying indentured servants.

The Evolution of Chesapeake Society

The colonists' incessant desire to grow more tobacco propelled the evolution of Chesapeake society. The requirements of tobacco agriculture shaped patterns of settlement, making the landscape of the English colonies in the Chesapeake quite different from that of rural England. English colonists professed the Protestant and Catholic faiths, but they governed their daily lives less by the dictates of religious doctrine than by the demands of tobacco cultivation.

English colonists professed the Protestant and Catholic faiths, but they governed their daily lives less by the dictates of religious doctrine than by the demands of tobacco cultivation.

Success in the tobacco economy—whether through hard work, shrewd judgments, political favoritism, or sheer good luck—elevated some colonists far above others in wealth and status and in the capacity to grow still more tobacco. The success of some colonists was built on the indentured servitude of others, sharpening inequality in Chesapeake society by the mid-seventeenth century. Social and political polarization culminated in 1676 when Bacon's Rebellion convulsed the Chesapeake. The rebellion ultimately prompted reforms that stabilized relations between elite planters and their lesser neighbors and paved the way for a social hierarchy based less overtly on land and wealth than on race. Amidst this social and political evolution, one thing did not change: the dedication of Chesapeake colonists to growing tobacco.

Life, Faith, and Labor

Villages and small towns dotted the rural landscape of seventeenth-century England, but colonists did not reproduce that English pattern in the Chesapeake. Colonial leaders tried to promote the development of towns, but they failed, with the exception of the town surrounding the capital at Jamestown. The Chesapeake landscape was not made up of cultivated fields punctuated here and there by small villages. Instead, acres of wilderness were interrupted here and there by tobacco farms. This landscape of widely scattered farms arose from the settlers' determination to profit from tobacco, even at the expense of patterns of community life they had been accustomed to in England.

Tobacco was such a labor-intensive crop that one field worker could tend only about two acres of the plants in a year (an acre is slightly smaller than a football field). A family farmer needed to devote a few more acres to food crops, but a total of five or ten acres under cultivation sufficed to make a working tobacco farm. However, a successful farmer needed a great deal more land because tobacco quickly exhausted the fertility of the soil. Freshly cleared land produced good tobacco harvests for only three or four years. To maintain yields, farmers let depleted fields lie fallow (unplanted) and cleared new land. Although this practice appeared wasteful from the perspective of land-scarce English agriculture, land was so abundant in the Chesapeake that farmers found it easier to plant new fields than to fertilize old ones. Thus, a farmer who ran a small, family operation needed 150 to 200 acres of land. A planter who employed eight or ten indentured servants required 1,000 acres or more. Since each farmer would cultivate only 5 or 10 percent of his land at any one time, a "settled" area comprised pockets of cultivated land surrounded by virgin forest.

Arrangements for marketing tobacco also contributed to the dispersion of settlements. Ideally, tobacco planters sought land that fronted a navigable river. Oceangoing ships could then dock at the planter's doorstep, minimizing the work of transporting and loading the heavy hogsheads of tobacco leaves. To obtain these prized riverfront locations, new settlers pushed inland along watercourses, venturing as far as they dared into Indian territory. As the population grew, these riverside settlements reached the limits of navigable water. A settled region resembled a lacework of farms stitched around waterways.

On individual farmsteads, farmers built their houses from beams and planks hewn from felled timber. Although serviceable, the houses were by no means grand, imposing, or even particularly sturdy. A typical seventeenth-century tobacco farmer lived with his family and servants (if he had them) in a one- or two-room box of about four hundred square feet. A wattle and daub chimney stood at one end of the house. A few windows—without glass—let in light and air when the shutters that normally covered them were thrown open. Dried mud chinked the gaps between wall planks. Bare earth served as the floor. Of the thousands of such structures built in the seventeenth-century Chesapeake, none has survived. Such houses accurately reflected the colonists' desire for plain shelter while they tried to make a living growing tobacco.

Most Chesapeake colonists were nominally Protestants. For most of the seventeenth century, attendance at Sunday services and conformity to the doctrines of the Church of England were required of all English men and women. As much as possible, Chesapeake settlers adhered to these practices in the American wilderness. They built churches, required weekly attendance, and, when they could find a minister, heard sermons. However, clergymen were difficult to attract to the Chesapeake. Many of those who came were no more pious, righteous, or godly than their parishioners. Certainly some colonists took their religion seriously. Church courts punished fornicators, censured blasphemers, and served notice on those who spent Sundays "goeing a fishing." But on the whole, religion did not awaken the zeal of Chesapeake settlers, certainly not as it did their counterparts who settled New England in these same years (see chapter 4). Virginians went to church and enjoyed the socializing before and afterward. But what quickened the pulse of most Chesapeake folk was a close-run horse race, a bloody cock fight, a high-stakes dice game, or—most of all—an exceptionally fine tobacco crop. The religion of the Chesapeake colonists was Anglican, but their faith lay in the turbulent, grasping, competitive, high-stakes gamble of survival as tobacco planters.

The history of the Catholic colony of Maryland provides a good illustration of that faith. In 1632, King Charles I (who had succeeded James I in 1625)

INSIDE A POOR PLANTER'S HOUSE
The houses of seventeenth-century Chesapeake settlers were typically "earth-fast" — that is, the structural timbers that framed the house were simply placed in holes in the ground and the floor was packed dirt. No seventeeth-century house was substantial enough to survive today. This photo shows a carefully documented historical reconstruction of the interior of a poor planter's house at St. Mary's City, Maryland. The wall of this one-room dwelling with a loft features a window with a shutter, but no glass; when the shutter was closed, the only source of light would be a candle or a fire. Note the rustic, unfinished bench, table, and walls. These meager furnishings were usually accompanied by a storage chest and some bedding, but not a bed. If and when the planters became more prosperous, they often made a bed their first acquisition, suggesting that the lack of a good night's sleep was one of their major discomforts.
Paul Leibe, Historic St. Mary's City.

granted his Catholic friend Lord Baltimore about six and a half million acres in the Chesapeake. In return, the king specified that Lord Baltimore pay him a rent of "two Indian arrowheads" each year during Easter week. Lord Baltimore intended to use his American domain to create a refuge for Catholics,

MAP 3.1
The Chesapeake Colonies in the Seventeenth Century
The intimate association of land and water in the settlement of the Chesapeake in the seventeenth century is illustrated by this map. Why was access to navigable water so important?

who suffered severe discrimination in England. He fitted out two ships, the *Ark* and the *Dove,* gathered about 150 settlers, and sent them to the new colony, where they arrived on March 25, 1634. However, the population of Maryland grew very slowly for the next twenty years, and most settlers were Protestants rather than Catholics. While England seethed with the religious turmoil of the Puritan Revolution (discussed in chapter 4), religious tension spilled across the Atlantic, creating conflict between Maryland's few Catholics—most of them wealthy and prominent—and the Protestant majority, few of whom were either wealthy or prominent. During the 1660s, however, Maryland at last began to attract settlers as readily as Virginia, most of them

Protestants. Like the Virginians, they came to grow tobacco. Although Catholics and the Catholic faith continued to exert influence in Maryland, the colony's society, economy, politics, and culture were virtually indistinguishable from Virginia's. Both colonies shared a common devotion to tobacco, the true faith of the Chesapeake.

Tobacco was a good poor man's crop. With land, know-how, and the labor of their own hands, colonists could produce a salable commodity. Special tools or expensive equipment were unnecessary. In the early years of the tobacco boom, when the weed commanded high prices in English markets, colonists hoped to get rich. Most tobacco plantations, however, were small operations run by one planter and two or three servants. A few elite planters had larger estates and commanded ten or more servants. But mortality in the Chesapeake was so high for the first thirty or forty years that few men lived long enough to accumulate a fortune sufficient to set them much apart from their neighbors. One historian has aptly termed this the era of the yeoman planter (that is, a farmer who owned a small plot of land sufficient to support a family and tilled largely by family members and perhaps a few servants).

> *Until midcentury, the principal division in Chesapeake society was less between rich and poor planters than between free farmers and unfree servants.*

Until midcentury, the principal division in Chesapeake society was less between rich and poor planters than between free farmers and unfree servants. While these two groups contrasted sharply in their legal and economic status, their daily lives had many similarities: Most of them worked at the same tasks in the same fields, ate the same food, often at the same table, and slept in the same house. Although servants were required to be subordinate, they nonetheless looked forward to the time when their indentures would expire and they would cross the threshold of freedom. Once free, they usually had to work several more years as hired hands or tenant farmers to earn enough to buy land. Nonetheless, they readily assimilated into free society. For example, among 155 freed servants in Charles County, Maryland, in the first half of the seventeenth century, two-thirds became landowners, a third obtained servants, and almost all married, had families, and participated in the affairs of local government. On the whole, a rough, frontier equality characterized free families in the Chesapeake until about 1650.

Three major developments splintered that equality during the third quarter of the seventeenth century. First, as tobacco production increased, prices declined. In the Old World, lower prices meant that more people could afford to smoke Chesapeake tobacco. In the colonies, cheap tobacco reduced planters' profits. It became more difficult —though still not impossible—for freed servants to save enough to become landowners. While the door

to freedom remained open for servants, landownership became more difficult to attain. Second, because the mortality rate dropped, more and more servants survived their indentures and joined the swelling ranks of freemen seeking land. However, the lower prices of tobacco limited their chances of realizing their ambitions of landownership. In Northampton County, Virginia, for instance, only about a quarter of the freemen who paid taxes between 1664 and 1677 ever obtained land there. Landless freemen became more numerous and more discontent. Third, declining mortality also encouraged the formation of a planter elite. By living longer, the most successful planters compounded their success. They not only earned more from their larger tobacco crops; they also acquired more land and more servants. The wealthiest planters also began to serve as merchants, marketing crops for their less successful neighbors, importing English

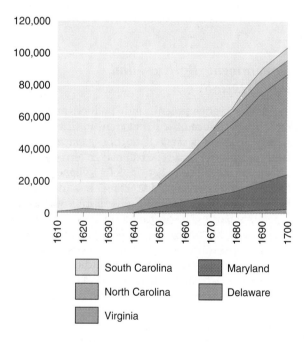

F I G U R E 3.1
Population of the Southern Colonies in the Seventeenth Century
About 1630, more than twenty years after the founding of Jamestown, the population of the southern colonies began to grow rapidly and steadily. The Chesapeake accounted for all but a tiny fraction of the population of the seventeenth-century southern colonies; for the most part, the inhabited regions of both North Carolina and Delaware were outgrowths of the Chesapeake's tobacco economy.

goods for sale, and above all giving credit to hard-pressed customers. In planter-merchant ledgers, the profits of trade added to the proceeds from tobacco.

By the 1670s, the social structure of the Chesapeake became polarized. Landowners—the planter elite and the more numerous yeoman planters—clustered around one pole. Landless colonists, mainly freed servants, gathered at the other extreme. Each group eyed the other with suspicion and mistrust. Looking down, planters saw a dangerous rabble. Looking up, landless freemen saw greedy exploiters. When a Dutch invasion threatened Virginia in 1673, the social tensions within the colony made Governor William Berkeley apprehensive about arming troops for defense. Of the men he could muster, Berkeley wrote, "at least one third are Single freemen (whose Labor will hardly maintain them) or men much in debt, both [of] which wee may reasonably expect upon any Small advantage the Enemy may gaine upon us, wold revolt to them in hopes of bettering their Condicion by Shareing the Plunder of the Country with them."

Government, Politics, and Polarization

In general, government and politics amplified rather than reduced the distinctions in Chesapeake society. The most vital distinction separated servants and masters, and the colonial government enforced it with an iron fist. In 1624, when Richard Barnes made "base and detracting" remarks about the governor of Virginia, the governor's council ordered that Barnes "be disarmed, and have his armes broken and his tongue bored through with a awl [and] . . . pass through a guard of 40 men and . . . be butted by every one of them" in addition to being banished and prohibited from ever enjoying "the priviledge of freedome of the countrey." Quick to prosecute critics, the council hesitated to censure masters who brutalized their servants. When servants Elizabeth Abbott and Elias Hinton died after beatings inflicted by their masters John and Alice Proctor, the council did not punish the Proctors, despite the testimony of witnesses that Hinton had been beaten with a rake and that Abbott had received five hundred lashes that left "her body full of sores and holes very dangerously raunckled and putrified both above her waist and uppon her hips and thighes." Members of the council believed that the government should make sure that servants obeyed their masters, no matter what. No wonder

poor men like William Tyler complained that "nether the Governor nor Counsell could or would doe any poore men right, but that they would shew favor to great men and wronge the poore."

The poor had plenty of ammunition for such views. Men from the planter elite monopolized the seats in both the governor's council and the House of Burgesses. After 1640, no former servant ever served in either body. Former servants participated in county government as jurors and in other minor offices. Members of the governor's council, however, were typically the wealthiest and most prominent planters. They were appointed by the king, usually on the recommendation of the governor, to advise the governor about colonial policies. Burgesses were chosen by popular election. Until 1670, all freemen could vote, and they routinely elected prosperous planters to the legislature. Most Chesapeake colonists, like most Europeans, assumed that the responsibilities of government were best borne by men of wealth and status.

In the 1660s and 1670s, colonial officials began to lose confidence that that assumption provided sufficient security from the growing discontent of the poor. Beginning in 1661, for example, Governor Berkeley did not call an election for the House of Burgesses for fifteen years. In 1670, the House of Burgesses limited voting rights to landowners and householders. Poor men with neither land nor homes were prohibited from voting since, the burgesses explained, "haveing little interest in the country [they] doe oftener make tumults at the election to the disturbance of his majesties peace, then by their discretions in their votes provide for the conservasion thereof."

The governor and other colonial officials did not simply administer government; they exploited their offices to make a profit. Tax agents, for example, received a slice of the revenues they collected. The secretary of the colony received fees for each document filed in official records: A land patent brought him eighty pounds of tobacco; a marriage license, forty pounds. Few governors were as brazen in their take-the-money-and-run attitude as Lord Thomas Culpepper. During his seven years as governor of Virginia, he lived in England for all but nine months, pocketed the governor's £2,000 annual salary, and hired a substitute to do the dirty work of governing the colony. Other governors spent more time in the colony, but, like Culpepper, they expected to make their office pay.

In 1660, the king himself began to collect substantial revenue from the Chesapeake. The Navigation Act passed that year required all tobacco and other colonial products (referred to in the act as "enumerated articles") to be sent only to English ports. The act supplemented laws of 1650 and 1651 that specified that colonial goods had to be transported in English ships with predominantly English crews. These regulations were designed to funnel the colonial import trade exclusively into the hands of English merchants, shippers, and seamen. A 1663 law extended that design to exports by stipulating that all goods sent to the colonies must pass through English ports and be carried in English ships by English sailors. Together, these regulations reflected the English government's assumptions about the colonies, assumptions subsequently termed "mercantilist": namely, that the colonies should benefit the mother country. What was good for England as a nation and for English people as individuals should determine policies toward the colonies.

These mercantilist assumptions underlay the import duty on tobacco inaugurated by the 1660 Navigation Act. The law assessed a duty of two pence on every pound of colonial tobacco imported into England. Two pence per pound was about the price a Chesapeake tobacco farmer received at the time; later, the price dropped lower (although of course the duty raised the price of the weed for consumers in England and on the continent). Regardless of the price planters received, the king collected his two-pence duty on imports. In fact, after 1660 a tobacco planter in Virginia earned at least as much for the king every year as he did for himself. The duty gave the king a major financial interest in the size of the tobacco crop. In the 1660s, tobacco revenues amounted to about one-quarter of all English customs duties and 5 percent of total government income, and they continued to grow.

Hierarchy permeated all levels of government and politics, from the relation between king and colonies to that between master and servant. Inequality was the organizing principle of these relationships. At every level, rulers expected to rule and to be obeyed; subjects expected to be ruled and to be punished for disobeying. To our ears, these expectations sound like a recipe for tyranny. In the seventeenth century, however, they were counterbalanced by other expectations that moderated the severity of hierarchical rule. Both rulers and subjects expected government to be administered for the good of the society as a whole. Rulers were supposed to keep in mind what was best for their subjects, and vice versa. Opinions differed—among rulers, between rulers and subjects, and among sub-

jects—about what actually was the best policy. A wise ruler steered a course that took account of conflicting opinions and that minimized the use of raw military force to crush dissenters. However, if rulers violated these precepts, the widely shared assumption that government should work for the benefit of all also provided the justification for subjects to rebel. In general, rebellions did not contest the principles of inequality and hierarchy. Instead, rebels lashed out against what they considered their rulers' failure to govern for the general good. In a sense, rebellions were directed against too much of what even the rebels conceded was a good thing: too much inequality; too much hierarchy.

In the Chesapeake after midcentury, government and politics contributed to the polarization of society and made the region ripe for rebellion. Small-scale servant rebellions broke out sporadically in the 1660s and 1670s. Sometimes the rebellious servants demanded better treatment; other times they organized plots to seize their freedom by running away. Vigilant masters, with the cooperation of the government, stifled the rebellions and conspiracies. When six servants who tried to run away from their master's plantation were captured, the court deciding on their punishment worried about "a dangerous precedent for the future time if [the servants were] left unpunished." Accordingly, the court sentenced Christopher Miller, the ringleader of the group, to "whipping . . . [with] thirty stripes and so [to] be burnt in the cheek with the letter R and to work with a shackle on his legg for one whole year and longer if said master shall see cause, and after his full time of service is Expired with his said master, to serve the colony for seven whole years." Miller's comrades received similar, though lesser, punishments. While the servant labor system continued to produce millions of pounds of tobacco that enriched the king, English traders, and colonial masters, it also produced the political crisis of the seventeenth-century Chesapeake.

Bacon's Rebellion

In 1676, Bacon's Rebellion erupted in the Chesapeake. A political upheaval that verged on civil war, the rebellion began as a dispute over Indian policy. Before it was over, however, the rebellion convulsed Chesapeake politics and society, leaving in its wake death, destruction, and a legacy of hostility between the great planters and their lesser neighbors.

Opechancanough, the old chief who had led the Indian uprising of 1622, tried again in 1644. In a surprise attack, Opechancanough's warriors killed about five hundred colonists in two days. During the next two years of bitter fighting, the colonists eventually gained the upper hand. They captured Opechancanough, jailed him, and murdered him in his cell. The peace treaty that concluded the war established policies toward the Indians that the government tried to maintain for the next thirty years. The Indians relinquished all claims to land already settled by the English. Wilderness land beyond the fringe of English settlement was supposed to be reserved exclusively for Indian use. The government's objective was to minimize contact between settlers and Indians and thereby maintain the peace.

Had the Chesapeake population remained constant, the policy might have worked. But the number of land-hungry colonists, especially poor, recently freed servants, continued to multiply. In their quest for land, they pushed beyond the treaty limits of English settlement and encroached steadily on Indian land. During the 1660s and 1670s, violence between colonists and Indians repeatedly flared along the advancing frontier. The government, headquartered in the tidewater region near the coast, far from the danger of Indian raids, took steps to calm the disputes and reestablish the peace. Frontier settlers condemned such niceties. They thirsted for revenge against what their leader, Nathaniel Bacon, termed "the protected and Darling Indians." Bacon minced no words about his intention: "Our Design [is] not only to ruine and extirpate all Indians in Generall but all Manner of Trade and Commerce with them." In 1676, Bacon and his followers demanded government support for their deadly plan.

Indians were not the only enemies Bacon and his men singled out. Bacon appealed to all colonists to consider the "nature of their Oppressions" and to investigate "by what Caball and mistery the designes of many of those whom wee call great men have been transacted and caryed on." Bacon urged the colonists to "see what spounges have suckt up the Publique Treasure and wither it hath not bin privately contrived away by unworthy Favourites and juggling Parasites whose tottering Fortunes have bin repaired and supported at the Publique chardg." In sum, Bacon charged that "Grandees," or elite planters, operated the government for their private gain, a charge that made sense to many colonists.

By most measures, Bacon himself was one of the grandees. The son of an English country gen-

tleman, Bacon came to Virginia in 1674 at the age of twenty-seven to make his fortune. A cousin of Governor Berkeley and a relative of other colonial officials, Bacon was quickly appointed to the governor's council. However, like other newcomers and most freemen, he remained outside the inner circle of established planters who ran things in Jamestown and in local government. He claimed land on the frontier near the fall line, the place where falls and rapids made Chesapeake rivers unnavigable. Within two years, he had crystallized the grievances of the lesser planters and poor farmers against both the Indians and the colonial rulers in Jamestown.

At first, Bacon simply insisted that Governor Berkeley commission him to lead a campaign against the Indians. Berkeley refused, hoping to maintain the fragile peace on the frontier. The governor expelled Bacon from the council, denounced him as a rebel, and threatened to punish him for treason. The council charged that Bacon and his supporters were a "Rabble Crue" that included "only the Rascallity and meanest of the people . . . there being hardly two amongst them that we have heard of who have Estates or are persons of Reputation and indeed very few who can either read or write." To isolate Bacon and his followers, Berkeley also called for elections for burgesses, hoping to divert the colonists' grievances into channels that he controlled.

The tactic worked better than Berkeley expected. Only five of the forty burgesses who had held office for the previous fifteen years were returned to their seats. All the other new burgesses were men who were prominent at the local level, most of them as justices of the peace. And, to Berkeley's surprise, Bacon was among the newly elected burgesses. The legislature was now in the hands of minor grandees who, like Bacon, chafed at the rule of "these men in Authority and Favour to whose hands the dispensation of the Countries wealth has been commited."

In June 1676, the new legislature passed a series of reform measures known as Bacon's Laws. Among other changes, the laws gave local settlers a voice in setting tax levies, forbade colonial officials from demanding bribes or other extra fees for carrying out their duties, placed limits on holding multiple official positions, required officials to be native-born or resident for at least three years, and restored the vote to all freemen. In late June 1676, when Bacon marched into Jamestown at the head of five hundred armed men demanding a commission to fight the Indians, Berkeley sensed that it was time to compromise. He pardoned Bacon, returned him to the council, and commissioned him to recruit additional troops for his campaign against frontier Indians.

Bacon called for and received the support of local militia units and then trekked off to the frontier in search of Indians. While he was away, several of the elite planters convinced Berkeley that it was extremely dangerous to have hundreds of armed men marauding through the countryside. What if they should decide to plunder the estates of the grandees? What if they should call for servants—who made up about half the population—to join them? They were desperate men, the secretary of the colony pointed out, "a Rabble of the basest sort of People," nearly all of them men who "were Idle and will not worke, or such whose Debaucherie or Ill Husbandry has brought [them] in Debt beyond hopes or thought of payment." Berkeley agreed. He nullified Bacon's commission and proclaimed him a rebel once again.

In late July 1676, when Bacon learned that his status as traitor had been renewed, he declared war against Berkeley and his supporters among the grandees. For three months, contingents of Bacon's forces combined fighting Indians with sacking and looting the plantations of Berkeley's men, and Berkeley's loyalists plundered the homes of Bacon's supporters in retaliation. To obtain fresh recruits, both Bacon and Berkeley promised freedom to servants and slaves who would aid their cause. In mid-September, Bacon marched on Jamestown, routed Berkeley's forces, and burned the town. The plunder continued until late in October, when Bacon unexpectedly died of a "Lousey Disease" known as "Bloody Flux," most likely dysentery. The arrival of several armed ships from England also bolstered Berkeley's forces, and Bacon's supporters dissipated. Back in power, Berkeley sent several of Bacon's allies to the gallows and revived the plunder of their plantations.

In the end, Bacon's Rebellion was not a revolt of the have-nots against the haves. Bacon's supporters included planters and small farmers as well as landless freemen. On the whole, they probably were less wealthy than Berkeley's allies. However, the crucial distinction between Bacon's rebels and Berkeley's loyalists was less between poor and rich than between outsiders and insiders. Bacon and other leading outsiders redirected the social and economic grievances of poor men toward a challenge to the rule of insider grandees. Bacon did not intend to overturn the hierarchy of Chesapeake politics and society. Instead, he challenged the ruthless and callous exploitation of the many outsiders by the few insiders.

Bacon's Rebellion did not dislodge the grandees from their seats of power. If anything, it strengthened their position. When the king learned of the turmoil in the Chesapeake and its devastating effect on tobacco exports, he ordered an investigation. The royal officials replaced Berkeley with a governor more attentive to the king's interest in increasing tobacco exports, nullified Bacon's Laws, and instituted an export tax on every hogshead of tobacco as a way of paying the expenses of government without having to obtain the consent of the tightfisted House of Burgesses. In a sense, the grandees of the Chesapeake were put in their place by still grander royal officials.

Bacon did not intend to overturn the hierarchy of Chesapeake politics and society. Instead, he challenged the ruthless and callous exploitation of the many outsiders by the few insiders.

The suppression of Bacon's Rebellion did not end turmoil in the Chesapeake. In 1682, for example, depressed tobacco prices led numerous farmers to try to reduce production by destroying the plants thriving in their neighbors' fields. Although these tobacco riots had little impact on production and petered out when prices improved, they expressed the colonists' dependence on the world market for tobacco. When prices were good, the Chesapeake prospered; when prices fell, it suffered. The tobacco riots illustrate that Chesapeake colonists in the late seventeenth century came to realize that they were not only wedded to tobacco but were shackled to it by the world market and the growing assertion of royal authority over both political and commercial affairs.

In the aftermath of Bacon's Rebellion, political stability slowly returned to the Chesapeake. Tensions between great planters and small farmers gradually lessened. By 1700, the new export duty on tobacco allowed the government to cut other taxes to just one-fourth what they had been in 1660, a move welcomed by all freemen. In the long run, however, the most important contribution to political stability was the declining importance of the servant labor system. During the 1680s and 1690s, fewer servants arrived in the Chesapeake, partly because of improving economic conditions in England. Accordingly, the number of poor, newly freed servants also declined, reducing the size of the lowest stratum of free society. In 1700, as many as one-third of the free colonists still worked as tenants on land owned by others, but the social and political distance between them and the great planters—enormous as it was—did not seem as profound as it had been in 1660. The main reason was that by 1700 the Chesapeake was in the midst of transition to a slave labor system that minimized the differences between poor farmers and rich planters and magnified the differences between whites and blacks.

Toward a Slave Labor System

The Spaniards and Portuguese engaged in an extensive African slave trade in the sixteenth century, and they established slavery as an important form of coerced labor in the New World. In the seventeenth century, British colonies in the West Indies followed the Spanish and Portuguese examples and developed sugar plantations with slave labor. In the British North American colonies, however, a slave labor system did not develop until the last quarter of the seventeenth century. During the 1670s, settlers from Barbados brought slavery to the new English mainland colony of Carolina, where the imprint of the West Indies remained strong for decades. In Chesapeake tobacco fields at about the same time, slave labor began to replace servant labor, marking the transition toward a society of freedom for whites and slavery for Africans.

The West Indies: Sugar and Slavery

The most profitable part of the British New World empire in the seventeenth century lay in the Caribbean. The tiny island of Barbados, colonized in the 1630s, was the jewel of the British West Indies. The island's economy appeared at first to be moving along the path blazed by English settlers in the Chesapeake: The early Barbadian colonists grew tobacco and cotton on small farms worked by family members and indentured servants. During the 1640s, however, the island's economy swerved away from the Chesapeake pattern and became the prototype of West Indian colonies. Barbadian planters began to grow sugarcane, with such success that a colonial official proclaimed Barbados "the most flourishing Island in all those American parts, and I verily beleive in all the world for the production of sugar." Sugar commanded high prices in England, and planters rushed to grow and sell as much as they could. By midcentury, annual sugar exports from the British Caribbean totaled about 150,000 pounds; by 1700, exports nearly reached 50 million pounds.

Sugar transformed Barbados and other West Indian islands. Starting a sugar plantation required substantial capital. Poor farmers could not afford the expensive machinery that extracted and refined the sugarcane juice; as sugar production boomed, their prospects plummeted. So many farmers left Barbados in quest of better opportunities that the white population in 1700 was only half what it had been in 1650. Planters who remained and had the necessary capital to grow sugar got rich. By 1680, a group of 175 planters owned over half the total wealth of Barbados. On the average, each of them was worth four times more than the richest tobacco grandees in the Chesapeake. The sugar grandees differed from their Chesapeake counterparts in another crucial way: The average sugar baron in Barbados in 1680 owned 115 slaves.

> *During the 1670s, settlers from Barbados brought slavery to the new English mainland colony of Carolina. In Chesapeake tobacco fields at about the same time, slave labor began to replace servant labor, marking the transition toward a society of freedom for whites and slavery for Africans.*

African slaves planted, cultivated, and harvested the sugarcane that made planters wealthy. For planters, slaves were a good buy. A planter could recover the cost of buying an African with the sugarcane the slave could be expected to grow in one year. Beginning in the 1640s, Barbadian planters purchased thousands of slaves to work their plantations, and the African population on the island mushroomed. During the 1650s, when blacks made

SUGAR MILL

This seventeenth-century drawing of a Brazilian sugar mill highlights the heavy equipment needed to extract the juice from sugarcane. A vertical waterwheel turns a large horizontal gear that exerts force on the jaws of a press, which squeezes the cane. Workers constantly remove crushed cane from the press and replenish it with freshly harvested cane as it is unloaded from an oxcart. Note that except for the overseer (just to the right of the waterwheel), all of the workers are black, presumably slaves from Africa, as suggested by their clothing. All of the mill workers appear to be men, a hint of the predominance of men among newly imported African slaves.
Musées Royaux des Beaux-Arts de Belgique.

up only 3 percent of the Chesapeake population, they had already become the majority on Barbados. By 1700, blacks, nearly all of them slaves, constituted more than three-fourths of the island's population. The island was literally a slave society that belonged to white men.

For slaves, work on a sugar plantation was a life sentence to brutal, unremitting labor. The sentence did not last long for many slaves. Planters were so eager for maximum production that they drove cane field slaves to the limits of endurance and beyond. Although precise data are lacking, it is clear that slaves' life expectancy was short and their death rate high. Furthermore, since slave men outnumbered slave women two to one, the vast majority of slaves could not form a family and have children. The unbalanced sex ratio and the high mortality rate meant that in Barbados and else-

where in the West Indies, the slave population did not grow by natural reproduction. Instead, planters had to continue to purchase slaves from Africa in order to maintain their slave force. For the most part, then, slaves on sugar plantations were African-born men and women who remembered when they had been free at home on the other side of the Atlantic. They tended to be bitter, unruly, and hostile, making sugar planters all the more ruthless in enforcing obedience.

As the sugar boom moved from island to island in the Caribbean, this distinctively West Indian colonial society was reproduced repeatedly. Although sugar plantations did not gain a foothold in North America in the seventeenth century, the West Indies nonetheless exerted a powerful influence on the development of slavery in the mainland colonies to the north.

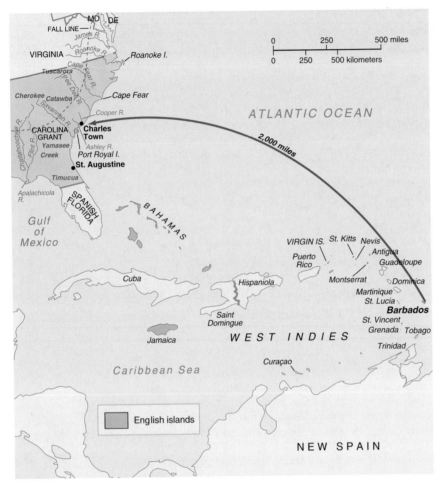

MAP 3.2
Carolina and the West Indies in the Seventeenth Century
Although Carolina was geographically closer to the Chesapeake colonies, it was culturally closer to the West Indies in the seventeenth century since its early settlers — both blacks and whites — came from Barbados. South Carolina retained close ties to the West Indies for more than a century, long after many of its subsequent settlers came from England, Ireland, France, and elsewhere.

Carolina: A West Indian Frontier

The early settlers of what became South Carolina were emigrants from Barbados. By 1680, the island was the most densely settled British colony in the New World. More colonists inhabited the island's 160 square miles than the hundreds of thousands of square miles in the Chesapeake. The governor of Barbados explained to his superiors in London that the shortage of land meant that "people no longer come to Barbados, many having departed to Carolina, Jamaica, and the Leeward Islands in hope of settling the land which they cannot obtain here."

In 1663, a Barbadian planter named John Colleton and a group of seven other men obtained a charter from King Charles II to establish a colony south of the Chesapeake. Settlers from Virginia had already begun to migrate south searching for good tobacco land around the Albemarle Sound, in what would become (in 1712) the colony of North Car-

olina. Colleton and his colleagues, known as the "proprietors," had their sights set farther south, in the vast region north of the Spanish territories in Florida. The proprietors' motives were commercial. They hoped to siphon settlers from Barbados and other colonies and encourage them to develop a profitable export crop comparable to West Indian sugar and Chesapeake tobacco.

Following the Chesapeake example, the proprietors offered headrights of up to 150 acres of land for each settler. During the 1660s, they sponsored several settlements in Carolina, but none survived. In 1670, they established the first permanent English beachhead in the colony, at a site on the west bank of the Ashley River, just across from the peninsula where the king's namesake city, Charles Towne (later spelled Charleston), was founded.

As the proprietors had planned, most of the settlers were from Barbados. In fact, Carolina was the only seventeenth-century English colony to be settled principally by colonists from other colonies rather than from England. The Barbadian immigrants brought their slaves with them. More than a fourth of the early settlers were black, and, as the colony continued to attract settlers from Barbados, the black population multiplied. By 1700, blacks made up about half of the population of Carolina.

Both economically and socially, seventeenth-century Carolina was a frontier outpost of the West Indian sugar economy.

Although few plantations existed in Carolina before 1700, the racial composition of the colony began to resemble Barbados more closely than it resembled Virginia or Maryland. English officials associated the colony so closely with Barbados that as late as 1700 they referred to "Carolina in ye West Indies."

The Carolinians experimented with tobacco, cotton, indigo, olives, and rice as potentially prof-

itable export crops. But until the end of the seventeenth century, the experiments proved disappointing. Finally, in the mid-1690s, colonists identified a hardy strain of rice and worked out successful methods of cultivation that inaugurated a flourishing rice industry in the years to come. During the first generation of settlement in the seventeenth century, however, Carolina remained an economic colony of Barbados. The king himself pointed out that "Barbados and ye rest of ye Caribee Islands . . . have not food to fill their bellies." Carolinians sniffed a market for their livestock—cattle and swine that roamed and grazed freely in Carolina's woodlands. Settlers looked after the animals and then sold them to hungry Barbadians. Since the trees on Barbados had been cut to make room for sugar plantations, Carolinians took advantage of their dense forests and exported wood, especially staves for making the barrels used to ship sugar products. Carolina settlers also exploited another "natural resource": They captured and enslaved several thousand local Indians and sold them to

LONDON COFFEEHOUSE
By the mid-seventeeth century, English merchants began to meet in coffeehouses like this one to swap gossip about colonial commerce and to make deals. Sipping coffee, puffing pipes, and comparing notes, these bewigged gentlemen may also have indulged in the amorous attention of prostitutes, as suggested by the portrait over the mantel. The female proprietor of this coffeehouse may have purveyed nothing more than coffee, tobacco, and good cheer, but her reputation may still have been sullied by the common presumption that a woman who worked in this type of male enclave must be up to no good.
E.T. Archive.

Caribbean planters. Both economically and socially, seventeenth-century Carolina was a frontier outpost of the West Indian sugar economy.

The Chesapeake: Tobacco and Slaves

By 1700, more than eight out of ten people in the southern colonies of British North America lived in the Chesapeake. Until the 1670s, almost all Chesapeake colonists were white people from England. In 1700, however, one out of eight people in the region was a black person from Africa. Although a few blacks had lived in the Chesapeake since the 1620s, the black population increased fivefold between 1670 and 1700 as tobacco planters made the transition from servant to slave labor.

At bottom, the shift to slave labor occurred simply because hundreds of individual Chesapeake planters began to purchase slaves rather than servants to work in their tobacco fields. For planters, slaves had several obvious advantages over servants. Although slaves cost three to five times more than servants, slaves did not become free after several years of servitude. They were slaves for life. By the 1680s, the mortality rate among immigrants to the Chesapeake had declined significantly, and planters could reasonably expect slaves to live far longer than a servant's period of indenture. Better yet from the planters' point of view, slaves promised to be a perpetual labor force. Children of slave mothers inherited the status of slavery. When William Fitzhugh, a wealthy Chesapeake planter, placed his order for slaves with a slave ship captain in 1682, he revealed the logic common to many other planters. Fitzhugh told the slave trader that he would "give 3000 lb. Tobo. [tobacco] for every Negro boy or girl, that shall be between the age of seven & eleven years old, . . . 4000 lb. Tobo. for every youth or girle that shall be between the age of 11 & 15 & . . . 5000 lb. Tobo. for every young man or woman that shall be above 15 years of age, & not exceed 24." Like other planters, Fitzhugh valued young slaves not simply because they would probably live and work longer than either servants or older slaves. He pointed out to a friend that his "Negroes increase being all young, & a considerable parcel of breeders, will keep that Stock [of slaves] good for ever."

For planters like Fitzhugh, slaves had another important advantage over servants: They could be controlled politically. Servants came to the Chesa-

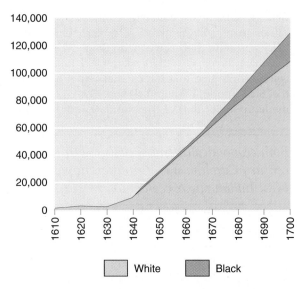

FIGURE 3.2
White and Black Populations in the Southern Colonies in the Seventeenth Century
Although the first Africans arrived in the southern colonies in 1619, Africans and their descendants remained a small fraction of the population throughout the seventeenth century. What features of this chart reflect the servant labor system, the transition to slave labor, and the settlement of Carolina?

peake expecting to become free, obtain land, and participate in colonial society. Bacon's Rebellion had demonstrated how disruptive former servants could be when their expectations were not met. Planters in the Chesapeake, like those in Barbados and Carolina, had no intention of permitting African slaves the luxuries of freedom and assimilation into free society. They determined that slaves would be a permanent laboring class excluded from the privileges of freedom expected and demanded by seventeenth-century English men and women. A slave labor system promised to avoid the political problems caused by the servant labor system. Slavery kept discontented laborers in permanent servitude, and their color was a badge of their bondage. All whites, not just the planters who owned slaves, were officially given the duty to keep blacks in their place. Slaves were even prohibited from defending themselves. A 1680 Virginia law provided that "any negroe or other slave [who] shall presume to lift up his hand in opposition against any christian" would be punished with "thirty lashes on his bare back well laid on."

The slave labor system polarized Chesapeake society along lines of race and status: All slaves were black and nearly all blacks were slaves; almost all free people were white and all whites were free or only temporarily bound in indentured servitude. Unlike Barbados, however, the Chesapeake retained a vast white majority. Among whites, huge differences of wealth and status still existed. In fact, the emerging slave labor system sharpened the economic differences among whites since only prosperous planters could afford to buy slaves. By 1700, more than three-quarters of white families had neither servants nor slaves. They grew tobacco with family labor. Nonetheless, unlike the swelling slave population, poorer white farmers enjoyed the privileges of free status. They could own property of all sorts; they could marry, have families, and bequeath their property and free status to their descendants; they could move when and where they wanted; they could associate freely with other people; they could serve on juries, vote, and even hold political office; they could work, loaf, or sleep as they chose. All these privileges and more were prohibited to slaves. These very real distinctions between slaves and free people made lesser white folk feel they had a genuine stake in the existence of slavery, even if they did not own a single slave. By emphasizing the privileges of freedom shared by all white people, the slave labor system reduced the tensions between poor folk and grandees that had plagued the Chesapeake in the 1670s.

The slaves purchased by Chesapeake planters in the seventeenth century came mostly from the West Indies. As the acting governor of Virginia wrote in 1708, "What negroes were brought to Virginia were imported generally from Barbados for it was very rare to have a Negro ship come to this Country directly from Africa." In the applications for headrights filed by masters who imported slaves, names like "Barbados Mary" appear repeatedly, an index of the link between the island and the mainland. While the demand for slaves was growing in the Chesapeake late in the seventeenth century, the market among tobacco planters was still small compared with that in the West Indies or Brazil, where African slave ships preferred to sell their human cargo. While Barbados annually imported an average of more than 1,300 slaves directly from Africa, the Chesapeake imported only about 250 to 300 slaves a year during the peak years of the 1690s. Chesapeake planters made the transition to slave labor with native-born Africans who had al-

ready been "seasoned," that is, acclimated to the natural environment of the New World and the repressive confines of slavery. Many of the slaves probably had already learned some English. The Chesapeake eased into the slave labor system at a relatively leisurely pace. The transition was still under way in 1700, but by then, although servants continued to arrive in the Chesapeake area, the majority of laborers found in Chesapeake tobacco fields were slaves.

The slave labor system polarized Chesapeake society along lines of race and status: All slaves were black and nearly all blacks were slaves; almost all free people were white and all whites were free or only temporarily bound in indentured servitude.

Slaves performed the same tasks on tobacco plantations that servants had done previously. Unlike sugar plantations, Chesapeake tobacco plantations were small operations. Often, as James Revel described in his verse (see page 92), slaves and servants worked side by side in the fields. Slave owners made up only a minority of tobacco planters, and most of them owned just a few slaves. On their farms, the white owner and his family members usually worked shoulder to shoulder with their slaves. A few wealthy planters owned twenty, thirty, or more slaves, permitting greater specialization of labor and more pronounced social distance between blacks and whites on the plantation, but nothing akin to the situation on sugar plantations, with more than a hundred slaves. In contrast to Barbados, most slaves in the seventeenth-century Chesapeake colonies had frequent and close contact with white people.

For slaves, work on a tobacco plantation was less onerous than on a sugar plantation. But the small size of tobacco farms and slaves' constant exposure to white surveillance made Chesapeake slavery especially confining. Slaves took advantage of every opportunity to slip away from white supervision and seek out the company of other slaves. Since, for the most part, few slaves lived on any one plantation, slaves who sought the companionship of the opposite sex had to "go abroad," that is, visit slaves on neighboring plantations. Planters did not like such visiting, since it loosened their control over their slaves. Nonetheless, they occasionally and grudgingly permitted slaves to spend a few hours with friends on other farms. More than once, slaves turned such seemingly innocent social pleasures to political ends, either to run away or to conspire to strike against their masters. In 1680, for example, Virginia planters uncovered a "Negro Plott, formed . . . for the Distroying and killing his Majesties Subjects . . . with a designe of Carrying it through the whole Collony of Virginia." The committee that investigated the conspiracy concluded that "the great freedome and Liberty that has beene by many Masters given to their Negro Slaves for Walking on broad on Saterdays and Sundays and permitting them to meete in great Numbers in makeing and holding of Funerals for Dead Negroes gives them the Opportunityes under pretention of such publique meetings to Consult and advise for the carrying on of their Evill and Wicked purposes and Contrivances." It became clear that slaves were no more content with their servitude than servants had been.

While slavery resolved the political unrest caused by the servant labor system, it also created new political problems. By the end of the seventeenth century, the bedrock political issue in the Chesapeake was keeping slaves in their place, at the business end of a hoe in a tobacco field. By 1700, the Chesapeake was well on its way to developing a slave labor system that stood midway —both geographically and socially—between the sugar plantations and black majority of Barbados to the south and the small farms and homogeneous villages that developed in seventeenth-century New England to the north.

Conclusion: Staple Crops, Coerced Labor, and Racial Hierarchy in the Southern Colonies

By 1700, the colonies of Virginia, Maryland, and Carolina were firmly established. The staple crops they grew for export provided a livelihood for many, a fortune for a few, and valuable revenues for shippers, merchants, and the English monarchy. Their societies differed markedly from England in most respects, yet the colonists considered themselves English people who happened to live in North America. They claimed the rights and privileges of English men and women while they denied those rights and privileges to Native Americans and African slaves. The English colonies also differed from the sixteenth-century example of New Spain. Large quantities of gold and silver never materialized in the Chesapeake. The system of encomienda was never adopted because Indians were too few and too hostile and their communities too small and decentralized, compared with those of the Mexica. Yet forms of coerced labor and racial distinction that developed in New Spain had North American counterparts, as English colonists employed servants and slaves and defined themselves as superior to Indians and Africans. By 1700, only the remnants of Powhatan's people survived. As English settlement pushed out north, west, and south of the Chesapeake, the various Indian tribes were faced with the New World that Powhatan encountered in 1607. By 1700, few doubted that the new English world in North America was there to stay.

CHRONOLOGY

1588 England defeats Spanish Armada.

1606 Virginia Company of London receives royal charter to establish colony in North America.

1607 English colonists found Jamestown settlement.

1609 Starvation plagues Jamestown.

1612 John Rolfe begins to plant tobacco in Virginia.

1617 First commercial tobacco shipment leaves Virginia for England.
Pocahontas dies in England.

1618 Powhatan dies and is replaced by Opechancanough.

1619 First Africans arrive in Virginia.
House of Burgesses begins to meet in Virginia.

1622 Opechancanough leads Indian uprising against Virginia colonists.

1624 Virginia becomes royal colony.

1632 King Charles I grants Lord Baltimore land for colony of Maryland.

1634 Colonists begin to arrive in Maryland.

1644 Opechancanough leads Indian uprising against Virginia colonists.

1660 Navigation Act requires colonial tobacco to be shipped to English ports and to be assessed customs tax.

1663 Carolina proprietors receive charter from King Charles II for Carolina colony.

1670 Charles Towne, South Carolina, is founded.
Slave labor system emerges first in Carolina and more gradually in Chesapeake colonies.

1676 Bacon's Rebellion convulses Virginia.

BIBLIOGRAPHY

GENERAL WORK

Kenneth R. Andrews, *Trade, Plunder, and Settlement: Maritime Enterprise and the Genesis of the British Empire* (1984).

Bernard Bailyn and Philip D. Morgan, eds., *Strangers within the Realm: Cultural Margins of the First British Empire* (1991).

Robert M. Bliss, *Revolution and Empire: English Politics and the American Colonies in the Seventeenth Century* (1990).

Wesley Frank Craven, *The Southern Colonies in the Seventeenth Century, 1607–1689* (1949).

K. G. Davies, *The North Atlantic World in the Seventeenth Century* (1974).

Richard Beale Davis, *Intellectual Life in the Colonial South, 1585–1763*, 3 vols. (1978).

Lewis Cecil Gray, *History of Agriculture in the Southern United States to 1860*, 2 vols. (1933).

Jack P. Greene and J. R. Pole, eds., *Colonial British America: Essays in the New History of the Early Modern Era*, (1984).

Winthrop D. Jordan, *White over Black: American Attitudes towards the Negro, 1550–1812* (1968).

John J. McCusker and Russell R. Menard, *The Economy of British America, 1607–1789* (1985).

Edmund S. Morgan, *American Slavery, American Freedom: The Ordeal of Colonial Virginia* (1975).

Gary B. Nash, *Red, White, and Black: The Peoples of Early America* (1982).

James F. Shepherd and Gary M. Walton, *The Economic Rise of Early America* (1979).

John R. Stilgoe, *Common Landscape of America, 1580–1845* (1982).

INDIANS

James Axtell, *The European and the Indian: Essays in the Ethnohistory of Colonial North America* (1981).

James Axtell, *The Invasion Within: The Contest of Cultures in Colonial North America* (1985).

Philip L. Barbour, *Pocahontas and Her World* (1970).

Kathryn E. Holland Braund, *Deerskins and Duffels: The Creek Indian Trade with Anglo-America, 1685–1815* (1993).

Wesley Frank Craven, *White, Red, and Black: The Seventeenth-Century Virginian* (1971).

Charles Hudson and Carmen Chaves Tesser, eds., *The Forgotten Centuries: Indians and Europeans in the American South, 1521–1704* (1994).

Karen Ordahl Kupperman, *Settling with the Indians: The Meeting of English and Indian Cultures in America, 1580–1640* (1981).

J. A. Leo Lemay, *Did Pocahontas Save Captain John Smith?* (1992).

James H. Merrell, *The Indians' New World: Catawbas and Their Neighbors from European Contact through the Era of Removal* (1989).

Helen C. Rountree, *The Powhatan Indians of Virginia: Their Traditional Culture* (1989).

Helen C. Rountree, *Pocahontas's People: The Powhatan Indians of Virginia through Four Centuries* (1990).

Helen C. Rountree, ed., *Powhatan Foreign Relations, 1500–1722* (1993).

Bernard W. Sheehan, *Savagism and Civility: Indians and Englishmen in Colonial Virginia* (1980).

Timothy Silver, *A New Face on the Countryside: Indians, Colonists, and Slaves in South Atlantic Forests, 1500–1800* (1990).

Peter H. Wood, Gregory A. Waselkov, and M. Thomas Hatley, eds., *Powhatan's Mantle: Indians in the Colonial Southeast* (1989).

CHESAPEAKE SOCIETY

Charles M. Andrews, ed., *Narratives of the Insurrections, 1675–1690* (1915).

Philip L. Barbour, ed., *The Complete Works of Captain John Smith*, 3 vols. (1986).

Warren M. Billings, *The Old Dominion in the Seventeenth Century: A Documentary History of Virginia, 1606–1689* (1975).

Warren M. Billings, John E. Selby, and Thad W. Tate, *Colonial Virginia: A History* (1986).

Carl Bridenbaugh, *Jamestown, 1544–1699* (1980).

Philip Alexander Bruce, *Economic History of Virginia in the Seventeenth Century*, 2 vols. (1896).

Lois Green Carr, Russell R. Menard, and Lorena S. Walsh, *Robert Cole's World: Agriculture and Society in Early Maryland* (1991).

Lois Green Carr, Philip D. Morgan, and Jean B. Russo, eds., *Colonial Chesapeake Society* (1988).

Richard Beale Davis, ed., *William Fitzhugh and His Chesapeake World, 1676–1701* (1963).

James Deetz, *Flowerdew Hundred: The Archaeology of a Virginia Plantation, 1619–1864* (1993).

Carville Earle, *The Evolution of a Tidewater Settlement System: All Hallow's Parish, Maryland, 1650–1783* (1975).

Clayton Colman Hall, ed., *Narratives of Early Maryland, 1633–1684* (1910).

James Horn, *Adapting to a New World: English Society in the Seventeenth-Century Chesapeake* (1994).

David William Jordan, *Maryland's Revolution of Government, 1689–1692* (1974).

David W. Jordan, *Foundations of Representative Government in Maryland, 1632–1715* (1987).

Aubrey C. Land, *Colonial Maryland: A History* (1981).

Aubrey C. Land, Lois Green Carr, and Edward C. Papenfuse, eds., *Law, Society, and Politics in Early Maryland* (1977).

Kenneth A. Lockridge, *The Diary, and Life, of William Byrd II of Virginia, 1674–1744* (1987).

Gloria Lund Main, *Tobacco Colony: Life in Early Maryland, 1650–1720* (1982).

Edwin J. Perkins, *The Economy of Colonial Ameria* (1980).

James Perry, *The Formation of a Society on Virginia's Eastern Shore, 1615–1655* (1990).

Jacob M. Price, *Perry of London: A Family and a Firm on the Seaborne Frontier, 1615–1753* (1992).

Darrett B. Rutman and Anita H. Rutman, *A Place in Time: Middlesex County, Virginia, 1650–1750*, 2 vols. (1984).

James F. Shepherd and Gary M. Walton, *Shipping, Maritime Trade, and the Economic Development of Colonial North America* (1972).

Thad W. Tate and David L. Ammerman, eds., *The Chesapeake in the Seventeenth Century: Essays on Anglo-American Society* (1979).

SERVANTS AND SLAVES

Philip D. Curtin, *The Atlantic Slave Trade: A Census* (1969).

David W. Galenson, *White Servitude in Colonial America: An Economic Analysis* (1981).

David W. Galenson, *Traders, Planters, and Slaves: Market Behavior in Early English America* (1986).

Henry A. Gemery and Jan S. Hogendorn, eds., *The Uncommon Market: Essays in the Economic History of the Atlantic Slave Trade* (1979).

Marcus W. Jernegan, *Laboring and Dependent Classes in Colonial America, 1607–1783* (1931).

Herbert S. Klein, *The Middle Passage: Comparative Studies of the Atlantic Slave Trade* (1978).

Paul E. Lovejoy, ed., *Africans in Bondage: Studies in Slavery and the Slave Trade* (1986).

Richard B. Morris, *Government and Labor in Early America* (1946).

James A. Rawley, *The Transatlantic Slave Trade: A History* (1981).

Abbot Emerson Smith, *Colonists in Bondage: White Servitude and Convict Labor in America, 1607–1776* (1947).

CAROLINA SOCIETY

Alan Vance Briceland, *Westward from Virginia: The Exploration of the Virginia-Carolina Frontier, 1650–1710* (1987).

Converse D. Clowse, *Economic Beginnings in Colonial South Carolina, 1670–1730* (1971).

Leland G. Ferguson, *Uncommon Ground: Archaeology and Early African America, 1650–1800* (1992).

Thomas M. Hatley, *The Dividing Paths: Cherokees and South Carolinians through the Era of the American Revolution* (1993).

Daniel C. Littlefield, *Rice and Slaves: Ethnicity and the Slave Trade in Colonial South Carolina* (1981).

Alexander S. Salley Jr., ed., *Narratives of Early Carolina, 1650–1708* (1911).

Aaron M. Shatzmann, *Servants into Planters: The Origin of an American Image: Land Acquisition and Status Mobility in Seventeenth-Century South Carolina* (1989).

Richard Waterhouse, *A New World Gentry: The Making of a Merchant and Planter Class in South Carolina, 1670–1770* (1989).

Robert M. Weir, *Colonial South Carolina: A History* (1983).

Peter H. Wood, *Black Majority: Negroes in Colonial South Carolina from 1670 through the Stono Rebellion* (1974).

THE WEST INDIES

Carl Bridenbaugh and Roberta Bridenbaugh, *No Peace beyond the Line: The English in the Caribbean, 1624–1690* (1972).

Michael Craton, *Sinews of Empire: A Short History of British Slavery* (1974).

Richard S. Dunn, *Sugar and Slaves: The Rise of the Planter Class in the English West Indies, 1624–1713* (1972).

Jerome S. Handler and Frederick W. Lange, *Plantation Slavery in Barbados* (1978).

Kenneth F. Kiple, *The Caribbean Slave: A Biological History* (1984).

Herbert S. Klein, *African Slavery in Latin America and the Caribbean* (1986).

Sidney W. Mintz, *Sweetness and Power: The Place of Sugar in Modern History* (1985).

Richard B. Sheridan, *Sugar and Slavery: An Economic History of the British West Indies, 1623–1775* (1974).

Eric Williams, *From Columbus to Castro: The History of the Caribbean, 1492–1969* (1970).

GREAT CHAIR

This thronelike chair belonged to Michael Metcalf, a teacher in seventeenth-century Dedham, Massachusetts. The oldest known piece of New England furniture inscribed with a date, 1652, the chair was made in Dedham specifically for Metcalf (note the initials flanking the date), who turned sixty-six in that year. Metcalf stored books, presumably including a well-thumbed Bible, in the enclosed compartment under the seat. No overstuffed recliner, the chair is suited less for a relaxing snooze than for alert concentration. The panels under the arms served to block chilly drafts. Otherwise, the chair shows few concessions to comfort or ease. The carved back—rigidly upright—displays motifs often found on Puritan tombstones. The grand austerity of the chair hints at the importance of serious Bible study and unflinching introspection in Puritan New England.

Dedham Historical Society/photo by Forrest Frazier.

THE NORTHERN COLONIES IN THE SEVENTEENTH CENTURY

4

1601-1700

I N 1630, AN OFFICIAL OF THE CHURCH OF ENGLAND FILED CHARGES against Reverend Charles Chauncy, a minister in the small village of Ware, a few miles north of London. Chauncy had sworn obedience to the doctrines of the Church of England, but church officials found him alarmingly disobedient.

The list of Chauncy's transgressions was long and detailed. During worship services, he refused to read aloud certain required passages from the Book of Common Prayer. He announced that "people have been deluded" by the Book of Common Prayer and the Church of England. Such speeches brought "the Book of Common Prayer and the Liturgy of the Church into contempt amongst the people," the church officials declared. But that was only the beginning of Chauncy's deviations from prescribed practices. He refused to make the sign of the cross in baptisms and marriage ceremonies. He refused to give the required lessons in church doctrine before launching into his sermon. He refused to hold worship services on the special holy days appointed by the Church of England. He preached, for example, "that there be many thousand souls damned in hell for their gaming and reveling in twelve days at Christmas time, and that the damned in hell do curse the birth of our Savior Christ and the Church for instituting the celebration thereof." Chauncy believed that the celebration of Christmas was sinful because it was not mentioned in the Bible.

That was only one of what the Church of England considered his "uncouth and strange opinion[s]." He also caused "much strife, heartburning, and dissension . . . amongst the inhabitants in Ware" by preaching constantly that "the Sabbath doth begin every Saturday at sunset." If Chauncy was correct, then innocent Saturday night pleasures were sins. Anybody in Ware who spent a few hours singing, dancing, drinking, or even working on Saturday night was violating the Sabbath—the Sabbath was for worship, not work or fun.

Chauncy "terrified the people," the Church of England asserted, by preaching that "idolatry was admitted into the Church." From the pulpit Chauncy declared "that there never [was] so much atheism, popery . . . and heresy in our Church as at this time." He said that the Church of England lacked "men of spirit and courage" who would point out the church's errors and evils. Instead, he said with "great scorn and contempt," the Church of England had too many "rotten divines and . . . pot [contemptible] ministers." Chauncy claimed that if worshipers followed the dictates of the Church of England, they sinned and would be punished in eternity.

Not surprisingly, the Church of England took the opposite view. "You have most grossly and contemptuously neglected your duty, both to God and the Church wherein you live," church officials charged Chauncy. Furthermore, they declared that "under a false pretence of zeal and purity in religion," Chauncy "would seem to be more precise than other men, and in very truth you do affect the name of Puritan."

Chauncy was indeed a Puritan, and proud of it. He warned his parishioners that "the preaching of the Gospel would be suppressed, and that some families are preparing to go for New England." Chauncy's warnings, the Church of England asserted, "caused a great distraction and fear amongst the people, . . . making them believe that there would forthwith ensue some alteration of religion."

Chauncy was correct that Puritanism was being suppressed, as the church's charges against him demonstrated. The Church of England was correct that Chauncy refused to perform his duty as defined by the church because he was a Puritan. As he saw it, his duty was defined by the Bible, the Word of God. The confusion and worry among Chauncy's parishioners are also understandable: Did they sin if they followed Chauncy or if they conformed to the Church of England? The "alteration of religion" they feared—and much more—was in fact on the historical horizon. Within a few years, Chauncy spent several months in prison in England before leaving to preach in New England.

The charges against Chauncy illustrate the religious, social, and political turmoil that pervaded England in the first decades of the seventeenth century. Puritans like Chauncy both responded to that turmoil and helped create it. Most Puritans and their followers stayed in England where, in the 1640s, they fought the battles of the Puritan Revolution. In the years before the revolution, however, thousands of other Puritans like Chauncy immigrated to New England. In the wilderness on the western shores of the Atlantic, they aspired to build a new, godly society purged of the idolatry, heresy, and corruption of England. They intended to remake England, not by revolution at home but by reconstruction abroad. The architect of their new England, they believed, was neither the king of England nor the archbishop of Canterbury, but God himself. Their blueprints for a society of saints guided their efforts to establish a new England in North America. The New England colonies reflected the rigor and discipline of their Puritan founders and the tensions within their faith.

During the seventeenth century, however, colonial experiences tempered Puritan zeal, and the goal of founding a holy new England faded. Late in the century, new colonies were founded in the mid-Atlantic region of North America. These middle colonies—New York, Pennsylvania, and New Jersey—differed sharply from the ideals and realities of New England. Despite these differences, by the end of the seventeenth century, all the North American colonies—New England as well as the middle and southern colonies—were tied more firmly to the English empire.

Puritan Origins: The English Reformation

The origins of Puritanism trace back to the English Reformation in the sixteenth century. In 1500, the church in England, like the church in other European countries, owed allegiance to the pope in Rome. The Roman church was a catholic, or universal, church. It had a monopoly on religious life in western Europe. It was also a unified church. But when the Protestant Reformation arose in Germany in 1517 and spread to other countries soon afterward, that unity shattered forever.

During the early years of the Reformation, the English church remained within the Catholic fold. King Henry VIII, who reigned from 1509 to 1547, was such a loyal Catholic that the pope bestowed on him the honorific title Defender of the Faith. Henry's faith, like that of other European monarchs, was strongly influenced by political considerations. He witnessed the bitter religious disputes and rampant popular unrest the Reformation brought to the European continent, and he hoped to prevent both from spreading to England. He also understood that in the right hands—his own—the Reformation offered a golden political opportunity. A break with the church in Rome would allow him to take control of the church in England. Taxes that English Christians paid to the pope would be redirected to Henry's treasury; the enormous landholdings of the church in England would belong to him; the power to appoint priests, bishops, and archbishops in England would be his; and the prestige and majesty of the church would be identified with the English monarchy. In short, Henry VIII realized that a rupture with the Catholic Church could make the church in England serve his purposes.

You shall be led before Princes and rulers for my names sake. *Math*, 10.

PERSECUTION OF ENGLISH PROTESTANTS
This sixteenth-century drawing shows the persecution of Protestants in England during the reign of Queen Mary, a staunch Catholic. Here Protestant prisoners are being marched to London to be tried for heresy. This pro-Protestant drawing emphasizes the severity of royal tyranny by depicting four well-armed guards, two of them mounted, escorting some fifteen prisoners, including at least five women, who are roped together, although they do not appear to be menacing or likely to run away. The guards seem to be necessary less to maintain order among the prisoners than to prevent sympathetic citizens from rushing toward the marchers and freeing them. The drawing assumes that most citizens opposed the queen's persecution of Protestants. The Bible verse from the book of Matthew underscores Protestants' fealty to Christ rather than mere "Princes and Rulers" like Queen Mary.
Folger Shakespeare Library.

The pretext for the breach with Rome was Henry's desire for a divorce from his wife, Catherine of Aragon, the daughter of Ferdinand and Isabella of Spain. Their marriage had cemented a close relationship between the kings of England and Spain, but by the mid-1520s Henry was becoming alarmed at the increasing power of the Spanish monarchy, fueled in part by New World treasure. Henry was also disappointed that Catherine had failed to give birth to a male heir; of their six children, only their daughter, Mary, survived infancy. Furthermore, Henry had become enamored of a young woman named Anne Boleyn and in 1527 he asked the pope to annul his marriage to Catherine so that he could marry Anne. The pope, who happened to be Catherine's relative, showed little inclination to grant Henry's request.

When Henry assembled Parliament in 1532, the members presented him with a long list of grievances against the Catholic Church. The grievances directly challenged the pope's supremacy by stipulating that the king must approve any religious legislation promulgated by the pope or the church hierarchy. This threat did not budge the pope from his refusal to annul Henry's marriage. In 1533, with Parliament's blessing, Henry had his marriage to Catherine annulled by his own nominee for archbishop of Canterbury, the top official in the English church, and secretly married Anne Boleyn—who was already pregnant with their daughter, Elizabeth. He was quickly excommunicated by the pope.

In 1534, Henry completed the break with Rome and formally initiated the English Reformation. At his insistence, Parliament passed the Act of Supremacy, which outlawed the Catholic Church and proclaimed the king "the only supreme head on earth of the Church of England." The vast properties of the Catholic Church in England were now the king's, as was the privilege of appointing bishops and other members of the governing hierarchy of the church. But Henry had no desire to restructure or reform the church. He wanted to control the church, not change it. Protestant doctrines advocated by Martin Luther and his followers held no attraction for him. In almost all matters of theology and religious practice, Henry remained an orthodox Catholic.

In the short run, the English Reformation allowed Henry VIII to achieve his political goal of bringing the church under the dominion of the monarchy. In the long run, however, the English Reformation brought to England the political and religious turmoil that Henry had hoped to avoid. For more than a century after 1534, English politics revolved around the question of the extent and character of the English Reformation. Henry himself sought no more than a halfway Reformation. Many English Catholics wanted no Reformation at all; they hoped to return the Church of England to the pope and to maintain Catholic doctrines and ceremonies. But many other English people insisted on a genuine, thoroughgoing Reformation; these people came to be called Puritans.

During the sixteenth century, Puritanism was less an organized movement than a set of ideas and religious principles that appealed strongly to many dissenting members of the Church of England. Puritans adhered to the doctrines of Protestantism developed by Luther and others on the European continent. They sought to purify the Church of England by eliminating what they considered the offensive features of Catholicism. For example, they demanded that the church hierarchy be abolished and that ordinary Christians be given greater control over religious life. They called for a reformed clergy composed of educated and moral men dedicated to the spiritual life of their parishioners. Many Puritans also believed that ministers should be appointed by their congregations. Puritans wanted to eliminate the ceremonies and displays of Catholic worship. They emphasized an individual's personal relationship with God developed through Bible study, prayer, and introspection. They also believed that the sermons of well-trained ministers could help them understand the Bible. They insisted that religious faith should have a powerful influ-

ence on the daily lives of individual Christians, disciplining them to think and act according to God's biblical commandments. Although there were many varieties and degrees of Puritanism, all Puritans shared a desire to carry the Reformation to its logical Protestant conclusion.

In the short run, the English Reformation allowed Henry VIII to achieve his political goal of bringing the church under the dominion of the monarchy. In the long run, however, the English Reformation brought to England the political and religious turmoil that Henry had hoped to avoid.

When Henry VIII died in 1547, the advisers of the new king, Edward VI—Henry's nine-year-old son by his third wife, Jane Seymour—initiated religious reforms that moved in a Protestant direction. The tide of reform reversed in 1553 when Edward died and was succeeded by Mary I, the daughter of Henry and Catherine of Aragon. Mary had remained a steadfast Catholic, and shortly after she became queen, she married Europe's most powerful guardian of orthodoxy, Philip II of Spain. Mary attempted to turn back the clock of the English Reformation to a pre-Reformation Catholic Church. She outlawed Protestantism and persecuted those who refused to conform, sentencing almost three hundred to burn at the stake.

The tide turned again in 1558 when Mary died and was succeeded by Elizabeth I, the daughter of Henry and Anne Boleyn. Elizabeth tried to consolidate the English Reformation midway between the extremes of Catholicism and Puritanism. She legalized Protestantism, reaffirmed the breach with Rome, and asserted her control over the Church of England. Like her father, she was less concerned with theology than with politics. Above all, she desired a church that would strengthen the monarchy and the nation. Late in the sixteenth century, the threat from Catholic Spain made Protestantism patriotic in England. By the time Elizabeth died in 1603, many people in England looked on Protestantism as a defining feature of national identity.

Shortly after Elizabeth's successor, James I, came to the throne, English Puritans petitioned for further reform of the Church of England, or Anglican-

Church. The king authorized a new translation of the Bible, known ever since as the King James version. However, neither James I nor his son Charles I, who became king in 1625, were receptive to the ideas of Puritan reformers. Increasingly hostile to both Puritans and Parliament, James and Charles moved the Church of England away from Puritanism rather than toward it. They enforced conformity to the Church of England and punished dissenters, both ordinary Christians and ministers like Charles Chauncy. The monarchy's anti-Puritan policies made many English Puritans despair that they would be permitted to live and worship in peace. A few Puritans decided to remove themselves from the political and religious repressions they suffered in England. They sought a refuge where they could build a society in harmony with their beliefs.

Puritans and the Settlement of New England

The Puritan emigration to New England resulted from the religious and political turbulence created by the Reformation during the sixteenth century. Puritans who emigrated to Plymouth colony or the much larger Massachusetts Bay settlement aspired to escape the turmoil of England and to build a new, orderly society that conformed to God's plan for humankind. Their faith shaped the colonies they established in New England in virtually every way. Some New Englanders never were Puritans, and their numbers increased during the seventeenth century. Nonetheless, Puritanism remained the paramount influence in New England not only in religion but also in politics and community life.

The Pilgrims and Plymouth Colony

One of the earliest groups to emigrate, known subsequently as Pilgrims, left their homes in Scrooby, a village in northern England, and moved to Holland in 1608. They enjoyed the Dutch republic's toleration of Protestant dissenters, but by 1620 life in exile threatened to undermine the small Pilgrim community. William Bradford, a leading member of the group, recalled that "of all the sorrows most heavy to be borne, was that many of their children, by . . . the great licentiousness of youth in that country, and the manifold temptations of the place, were

drawn away by evil examples into extravagant and dangerous courses, getting the reins off their necks and departing from their parents." The Pilgrim elders looked for a way to protect their children's piety and to preserve their community. "The place they had thoughts on," Bradford wrote, "was some of those vast and unpeopled countries of America, which are fruitful and fit for habitation, being devoid of all civil inhabitants, where there are only savage and brutish men which range up and down, little otherwise than the wild beasts." The Pilgrims had confidence that if they were the only "civil inhabitants" of someplace in America, they could preserve their vision of an uncorrupted, godly society, a society that looked like a Puritan version of England, a new England.

The Pilgrims obtained permission to settle in the extensive lands granted to the Virginia Company. To finance their journey, they formed a joint stock company with London investors. The investors provided the capital; the Pilgrims, their labor and lives. The Pilgrims agreed to share all profits with the investors for seven years. Following months of delay in Holland and England, 102 prospective settlers finally boarded the *Mayflower* in August 1620. After eleven weeks at sea, all but one of them arrived at the outermost tip of Cape Cod, in present-day Massachusetts.

The Pilgrims realized immediately that they had landed far north of the Virginia grant and had no legal authority from the king to settle in the area. However, the long, stormy voyage and the wet, bitterly cold November weather gave the Pilgrims no choice. They had to find a place to stay in what Bradford called the "hideous and desolate wilderness." To help protect themselves from the wilderness they could see and the desolation they could imagine, the Pilgrims drew up the Mayflower Compact on the day they arrived. They agreed to "covenant and combine ourselves together into a civil Body Politick, for our better Ordering and Preservation." The signers (all men) agreed to enact and obey necessary and just laws. With this pact, the Pilgrims hoped to provide order and security as well as a claim to legitimacy until the king granted them legal rights.

Early in December, the Pilgrims chose to settle at Plymouth, a site recommended by a small bay and by abandoned fields that had been cleared by Patuxet Indians, who had been decimated by an epidemic in 1617. The Pilgrims exercised their self-proclaimed political authority by electing William

PLYMOUTH FORT AND MEETINGHOUSE

This building is a careful historical reconstruction of a fort built by the Plymouth settlers in 1622, shortly after hearing of Powhatan's uprising against English colonists in Virginia (discussed in chapter 3). It is adapted from the traditional design of a seventeenth-century granary, but the ports lining the second story are not for stacking sheaves of grain but for firing on attacking Indians or on hostile Spaniards or Frenchmen. In fact, no attack ever came. The Pilgrims nonetheless made good use of the fort as a meetinghouse. Sermons, prayers, and worldly testimony—not cannon—echoed through the fort. Colonists gathered on the first floor for church services and court sessions. The building evokes the Plymouth colonists' military vulnerability and religious security.

Courtesy of Plimoth Plantation, Inc., Plymouth, MA USA/Ted Curtin.

Bradford as their governor, a position he held almost continuously until his death in 1657. That first winter "was most sad and lamentable," Bradford wrote later. "In two or three months' time half of [our] company [including Bradford's wife] died . . . being the depth of winter, and wanting houses and other comforts [and] being infected with scurvy and other diseases."

Having succeeded in founding a small Puritan haven from the religious corruptions of England and the secular temptations of Holland, the Pilgrims saw their colony as an example to the world.

In the spring, Indians rescued the floundering Plymouth settlement. First Samoset, then Squanto —both of whom had learned English from fishermen and sailors who had visited the region— befriended the settlers. Samoset arranged for the Pilgrims to meet and establish good relations with Massassoit, the chief of the Wampanoags, whose territory included Plymouth. Squanto, Bradford recalled, "was their interpreter and was a special instrument sent of God for their good beyond their expectation. He directed them how to set their corn, where to take fish, and to procure other commodities, and was also their pilot to bring them to unknown places." With Squanto's help and their own hard labor, the Pilgrims managed to store enough food to guarantee their survival through the coming winter, an occasion they celebrated in the fall of 1621 with a thanksgiving feast attended by Massassoit and many of his warriors. Despite the celebration, the colony's status remained precarious. Only seven dwellings had been erected that first year, half the original colonists were dead, and a new group of thirty-six threadbare, sickly settlers arrived in November 1621, requiring the colony to adopt stringent food rationing.

The Plymouth colony struggled to survive. The colonists quarreled with their London investors, who became frustrated and abusive when the colony failed to produce the expected profits. Additional settlers arrived periodically and the colony's population slowly grew to about four hundred. By 1630, Plymouth had become a permanent settlement, and the Pilgrims lived quietly and simply. They coexisted in relative peace with the Indians by using diplomacy and cash payments to Massassoit when settlers gradually encroached on Wampanoag territory.

Having succeeded in founding a small Puritan haven from the religious corruptions of England and the secular temptations of Holland, the Pilgrims saw their colony as an example to the world. "As one small candle may light a thousand," Bradford wrote, "so the light here kindled hath shone unto many, yea in some sort to our whole nation." But Plymouth's beacon of light did not attract many other English Puritans. The Pilgrims' desire to separate themselves from the Church of England—a heresy known as separatism and punished severely in England—destined Plymouth to become a backwater in seventeenth-century New England. That did not alarm the Pilgrims. They had given up on reforming the English church and wanted simply to live their lives as they saw fit.

The Founding of Massachusetts Bay Colony

During the 1620s, most English Puritans considered the American wilderness more ominous than the mounting religious and political unrest in England. But in 1629, King Charles I dissolved Parliament—where Puritans were well represented—and appointed the aggressive anti-Puritan William Laud as bishop of London (and later archbishop of Canterbury). Many Puritans despaired about continuing to defend their faith in England and began to make plans to emigrate. Some left for Europe, others for the West Indies. The largest number set out for New England.

In 1629, shortly before the dissolution of Parliament, a group of Puritan merchants and country gentlemen obtained a royal charter for the Massachusetts Bay Company. The charter provided the usual privileges granted to joint stock companies. It granted land for colonization from sea to sea, including the present-day states of Massachusetts, New Hampshire, Vermont, and Maine and upstate New York. The charter also bestowed the right to trade in such native commodities as furs, fish, and timber. In addition, the charter contained a unique

provision that allowed the government of the company to be located in the colony rather than in England. Exactly how the Massachusetts Bay Company slipped this innovation past the king's advisers remains unknown. But the Puritans understood its significance. With royal permission to transfer the company's government to the colony, the Puritans had a golden opportunity to put the Atlantic between themselves and the hostile rule of King Charles and Bishop Laud. They could exchange their position as a harassed minority in England for self-government in Massachusetts—which, in practice, meant Puritan government.

To lead the emigrants, the stockholders of the Massachusetts Bay Company elected John Winthrop to serve as governor. Like many other English Puritans, Winthrop came from the rural gentry. He owned Groton Manor, a handsome estate composed primarily of land that Henry VIII had confiscated from a Catholic monastery and sold for a bargain price to Winthrop's grandfather. A prosperous and respected lawyer, Winthrop had much to lose. He thought long and hard before deciding to leave the comforts of his estate and risk the perils of founding a settlement in the New World. A deliberate man, he carefully listed the reasons that persuaded him, and presumably his fellow Puritans, to take the risk.

In England, things were not as they should be. "This land grows weary of her inhabitants," Winthrop wrote, "so as man who is the most precious of all creatures is here more vile and base than the earth we tread upon, and of less price among us than a horse or a sheep." Children, servants, and neighbors, "if things were right," should "be the chiefest earthly blessing"; instead, "it is come to pass that . . . especially if they be poor, [they] are counted the greatest burden." Wealthy men, Winthrop observed, indulge in the "height of intemperance" until "no man's estate almost will suffice to keep sail with his equals, and he who fails . . . must live in scorn and contempt." Men who succeed carry on their business in a "deceitful and unrighteous" manner, while "it is almost impossible for a good and upright man to maintain his charge and live comfortably." With these examples constantly before them, "most children (even the best wits and fairest hopes) are perverted, corrupted and utterly overthrown." The wickedness of English society invited God's wrath, especially since most churches did little to set things right and much to make things worse. "Who knows," Winthrop asked, "but that God hath provided . . . [New England] to be a refuge for many whom he means to save out of the general calamity?"

Hundreds of Puritans concluded that, indeed, there was no better work than building churches in the wilderness, where, according to Winthrop, the Lord "will provide a shelter and hiding place for us and ours." They settled their affairs at home and collected the supplies necessary for starting a new life in America. Winthrop assembled the largest fleet ever to embark for an English colony. In March 1630, eleven ships crammed with seven hundred (mostly Puritan) passengers and assorted livestock, tools, and food sailed for Massachusetts; six more ships and another five hundred emigrants followed a few months later.

Winthrop's flagship, the *Arbella*, and three others arrived in Massachusetts Bay in early June, and the other ships straggled in soon afterward. A precursor of the Massachusetts Bay Company had established a small fishing and trading settlement at Salem in 1628, but the new arrivals looked elsewhere for a suitable settlement site. They did not want to be associated with the struggling separatist colony of Pilgrims at Plymouth. Instead, Winthrop and a small group moved to the peninsula that became Boston, while other settlers clustered at promising locations nearby.

In a sermon to his companions aboard the *Arbella* while they were still at sea—probably the most famous sermon in American history—Winthrop explained the cosmic significance of their journey. The Puritans had "entered into a covenant" with God to "work out our salvation under the power and purity of his holy ordinances," Winthrop proclaimed. This sanctified agreement with God meant that "the Lord will [not] bear with such failings at our hands as he doth from those among whom we have lived" in England. Having entered a covenant with the Puritans, God "looks to have it observed in every article," Winthrop warned. The Puritans had to make "extraordinary" efforts to "bring into familiar and constant practice" religious principles that most people in England merely preached. To do so, the Puritans had to subordinate their individual interests to the common good. "We must be knit together in this work as one man," Winthrop declared. "We must delight in each other, make others' conditions our own, rejoice together, mourn together, labor and suffer together, always having before our eyes . . . our community as members of the same body." To do otherwise discredited God in the eyes of humankind, jeopardized his plan for the world,

ENGLISH GENTLEMAN
This portrait of an English gentleman, painted a few years before the Puritan migration to New England, reveals the appearance considered the height of fashion among wealthy English men and women but condemned by Puritans as a vain, sinful focus on outward appearance. From head to toe, this clothing displayed intricate workmanship and artfully composed embellishment, all designed—Puritans declared—to win approving glances from other humans rather than from the Almighty.
By Courtesy of National Portrait Gallery, London.

and would surely cause him to "break out in wrath against us." The stakes could not be higher, Winthrop told the emigrants surrounding him on the deck of the *Arbella* somewhere in the North Atlantic. "We must consider that we shall be as a city upon a hill. The eyes of all people are upon us."

The whole world was not watching the settlement at Massachusetts Bay, of course. Nonetheless, that belief shaped seventeenth-century New England as profoundly as tobacco shaped the Chesapeake. The vision of a city on a hill announced the Puritans' fierce determination to keep their covenant and live according to God's laws, unlike the backsliders, trimmers, and compromisers who accommodated to the Church of England. The Puritans believed that God had one perfect plan, and they resolved to do their best to discover it through prayer, Bible study, and church attendance. Because they knew that their understanding of God's plan was imperfect, they constantly looked for evidence of God's judgment of their behavior. Surely, the Puritans reasoned, if they built a new society according to God's plan, he would be pleased and would favor them with peace, plenty, and good fortune. If, instead, the colonists experienced strife, shortage, or disaster, that might mean that God was punishing them for departing from his plan and warning them to make the necessary corrections. Or it could mean that Satan was alarmed that God's plan was being so closely followed and that he was fighting back by subjecting the Puritans to an extra dose of evil. The Puritans' determination to adhere strictly to God's plan charged nearly every feature of life in seventeenth-century New England with a distinctive, high-voltage piety.

The new colonists, as Winthrop's son John wrote later, had "all things to do, as in the beginning of the world." At first, the Puritans' high aspirations confronted the rigors of survival in the Massachusetts environment. Unlike the early Chesapeake settlers, the first Massachusetts Bay colonists encountered few Indians because the local population had been almost exterminated by an epidemic more than a decade earlier. Still, the colonists had more than enough to do building shelters, planting crops, and trying to harvest them before the bitter New England winter set in. As in the Chesapeake, the colonists fell victim to deadly ailments. More than two hundred settlers died during the first year, including one of Winthrop's sons and eleven of his servants. About the same number decided by the spring of 1631 that they had had enough and returned to England aboard the first outbound ship. But Winthrop remained confident. "I like so well to be heer," he wrote his wife, "as I doe not repent my comminge. . . . I would not have altered my course, though I had forseene all these Afflictions."

Winthrop's confidence proved more infectious than the discouraging news the returning colonists took back to England. Each year from 1630 to 1640, ship after ship followed in the wake of Winthrop's fleet. In all, more than twenty thousand new settlers came, their eyes fixed on the Puritans' city on a hill. These people differed from the thousands of other English settlers during the same years whose gaze was drawn instead to the high-risk lottery of the Chesapeake tobacco economy.

SEAL OF MASSACHUSETTS BAY COLONY
In 1629, the Massachusetts Bay Company designed this seal depicting an Indian man inviting English settlers to "Come Over and Help Us." Of course, such an invitation was never issued. Instead, the seal attempted to lend an aura of altruism to the Massachusetts Bay Company's colonization efforts. In English eyes, the Indian man obviously needed help. The only signs that he was more civilized than the pine trees flanking him were his girdle of leaves, his bow and arrow, and his miraculous use of English. In reality, colonists in Massachusetts and elsewhere were far less interested in helping Indians than in helping themselves. For the most part, that suited Indians just fine, since they did not want the colonists' "help."
Courtesy of Massachusetts Archives.

English Puritans continued to come to New England for the same reasons that had attracted Winthrop. The exact number of Puritans among the settlers cannot be determined, but there is no doubt that ships bound for Massachusetts were as full of Puritans as vessels headed toward Virginia were of indentured servants. Often, when the Anglican Church cracked down on a Puritan minister in England, he and all those in his flock who could take the risk uprooted and moved together to New England. Fragments of Puritan congregations, even of villages, moved from one side of the Atlantic to the other. By 1640, New England had one of the highest ratios of preachers to population in all of Christendom: 129 preachers had settled in New England, among them such eminences of Puritanism as John Cotton, Richard Mather, Thomas Shepard, and Thomas Hooker. But the ratio was still not high enough to provide a trained minister for every band of settlers, causing a colonist to complain that ordinary "fellowes which keepe hogges all weeke preach on the Saboth." That preachers with such unpromising credentials drew an audience indicated the colonists' hunger for religious instruction.

The vision of a city on a hill announced the Puritans' fierce determination to keep their covenant and live according to God's laws, unlike the backsliders, trimmers, and compromisers who accommodated to the Church of England.

The occupations of the New England immigrants reflected the social origins of English Puritans. On the whole, the immigrants came from the middle ranks of English society. Few representatives of the nobility or the gentry came to Massachusetts; Winthrop was an exception. Likewise, few common laborers arrived in New England. Instead, the vast majority of immigrants were either farmers or tradesmen, including carpenters, tailors, textile workers, and many others. Servants, whose numbers dominated the Chesapeake settlers, accounted for only about a fifth of those headed for New England. Most of the New England immigrants had paid their way to Massachusetts, even though the journey often took their life savings. To such people, reports like the one Winthrop sent his son must have been encouraging: "Here is as good land as I have seen there [in England], but none so bad as there. Here is sweet air, fair rivers, and plenty of springs, and the water better than in England. Here can be no want of anything to those who bring means to raise out of the earth and sea."

Family ties stitched one immigrant to another. In contrast to the Chesapeake—where immigrant women and children were nearly as rare as atheists in Boston—immigrants to New England usually arrived as part of a family. In fact, more Puritans came with family members than did any other group of immigrants in all of American history. The ship that left Weymouth, England, in 1635 carrying 106 passengers included the minister Joseph Hull and his fellow Puritans and neighbors, 98 of whom belonged to one of the 14 families aboard, typically a husband, wife, and children, sometimes accompanied by a servant or two. In Hull's group, one out of five passengers was an adult woman; two out of five were youngsters; together, women and children made up a solid majority.

These families were not democracies, of course. Fathers and husbands who headed the immigrant families expected to rule them. As Winthrop reminded the first settlers in his Arbella sermon, God "hath so disposed of the condition of mankind, as in all times some must be rich, some poor, some high and eminent in power and dignity, others mean and in subjection." All the immigrants understood that each father and husband—regardless of his wealth or status—expected to be considered "high and eminent" by his wife and children. Each family was a "little commonwealth" that mirrored the hierarchy among all God's creatures, Puritans believed. Just as humankind was subordinate to God, so young people were to be subordinate to their elders, children to their parents, and wives to their husbands. The immigrants' family ties reinforced their religious beliefs with an effective and universally understood form of government. While immigrants to the Chesapeake were disciplined mostly by the coercions of servitude and the caprices of the tobacco market, immigrants to New England entered a social order defined by the interlocking institutions of family, church, and community.

The Evolution of New England Society

The New England colonists did not scatter isolated farmsteads across the land like their counterparts in the Chesapeake. Instead, they settled in small towns

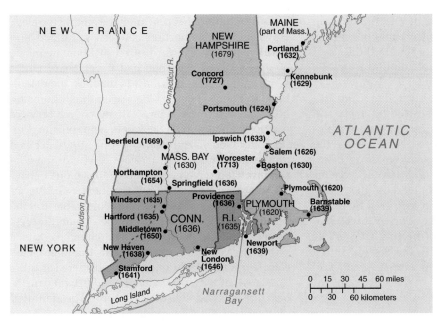

MAP 4.1
New England Colonies in the Seventeenth Century
New Englanders spread across the landscape town by town during the seventeenth century. (For the sake of legibility, only a few of the more important towns are shown on the map.) Why were towns so much more important in seventeenth-century New England than in the Chesapeake?

located either on the coast or on a river, ensuring good access to water. Massachusetts Bay colonists founded six towns in 1630 and nearly two dozen within the first decade, including several quite remote from Boston in present-day New Hampshire, Connecticut, and Rhode Island. During the entire seventeenth century, they established 133 towns. Each town had one or more churches organized by Puritan believers who had entered a covenant with God and with each other to follow God's orders. Church members' fervent piety, buttressed by the institutions of local government, enforced remarkable religious and social conformity in the small New England settlements. But the tensions within the Puritan faith and changes in New England communities during the seventeenth century splintered Puritan orthodoxy and weakened Puritan zeal. Nonetheless, by the end of the seventeenth century, Puritanism maintained a distinctive and unmistakable influence in New England.

Church, Covenant, and Conformity

At the center of each Puritan community stood the church. Often the building occupied literally the geographic center of the town; if it was not at the center, it was within walking distance of the town's residents. These buildings did not look like churches in seventeenth-century England or like the churches in New England towns today. Typically, they were unadorned wooden structures housing a simple

meeting room with wooden benches for fifty or one hundred or more. The buildings were also used for many other gatherings, such as courts and town meetings. They had no stained glass, no organs, not even any heat. At the front stood a table and a lectern or an elevated pulpit. To our eyes, the building would appear to be a plain lecture hall.

That was precisely what the Puritans intended. God's word—not music or art—was the focus of their religious services. Nothing about the meeting room should interfere with the congregation's concentration on the sermon. And it took concentration. Each Sunday, ministers preached for five or six hours, interrupted by a noontime break. A minister's prayer alone often lasted an hour. The elders (respected leaders of the congregation) sat with their backs to the preacher while they monitored the congregation's reception of his sermon. During the frigid New England winter, the people's fingers, toes, and cheeks grew numb while the communion bread and baptismal water froze solid. Whatever the weather, each town required every inhabitant to attend sermons on Sundays and usually on Thursdays too. They came, and they listened. On cold days, they could almost see God's word as the preacher's breath turned white in the icy air.

To the Puritans, however, the church was not the building where the services were held. Instead, the church was composed of men and women who had entered a solemn covenant with each other and with God. Winthrop and three other men had signed the original covenant of the first Boston church, agreeing to "Promisse, and bind our selves, to walke in all our wayes according to the Rule of the Gospell, and in all sincere Conformity to His holy Ordinaunces, and in mutuall love, and respect to each other, so neere as God shall give us grace." Church membership was restricted to men and women who entered such a covenant. A new member not only had to agree to the terms of the covenant but also had to persuade existing members that she or he had fully experienced conversion. The fervent Puritans among the early colonists, whose faith had been tempered by persecution in England and by the journey to Massachusetts, had little difficulty meeting the test of covenant membership. By 1633, the Boston church had added 132 names to the four original subscribers to the covenant; by 1635, that covenant had more than 250 members.

Church members' fervent piety, buttressed by the institutions of local government, enforced remarkable religious and social conformity in the small New England settlements.

Puritan views on church membership derived from John Calvin, the Protestant theologian of sixteenth-century Geneva, Switzerland, who insisted that Christians discipline their worldly behavior to conform strictly to their religious ideas. Calvin stressed the doctrine of predestination, which held that before the creation of the world, God chose a few human beings to receive salvation. These fortunate individuals—the "elect" or "invisible saints"—were predestined for eternal life. But only God knew who they were. Each person had no way to know for certain whether she or he was bound for heaven with the few or for Hades with the many. Nothing a person did could change God's inscrutable choice.

Puritans believed that if one were among the elect, one would surely act like it. To a certain extent, one's sainthood would become visible in one's behavior, especially if one were privileged to know God's Word as revealed in the Bible. Humans' inherent and overpowering tendency to sin made saintly behavior extremely difficult to maintain. Therefore, Puritans believed, one's ability to live a rigorously and consistently godly life—and overcome the constant temptations to sin—was proba-

bly a sign, a hint, that one might be among the elect. However, the connection between sainthood and saintly behavior was far from firm. Some members of the elect, for example, had never heard God's Word and did not know how to manifest their sainthood in their behavior. One reason the Puritans required all town residents to attend church services was to enlighten invisible saints who remained ignorant of God's Truth. Other people might act as if they were saints, yet in fact not be one of the chosen few. God gave no guarantee that pious behavior was a sign of salvation; the identity of the invisible saints remained forever unknowable. But the Puritans thought that passing the demanding test of membership in one of their churches was a promising clue that one was in fact among God's elect. Puritan church members considered it quite possible that they were visible saints, that is, members of God's invisible elect who could be identified by their highly visible godly behavior.

Members of Puritan churches ardently hoped that they were visible saints and tried to act that way. Their covenant bound them to help each other attain this lofty goal. Their covenant also required them to discipline the entire community by saintly standards. Church members kept an eye on the behavior of everybody in town. Infractions of morality, order, or propriety were reported to the elders, who summoned the wayward to a church inquiry. The Dorchester church, for example, examined Robert Spur for his offense of "giving entertainment in his house [to] loose and vain persons," Mrs. Clark for "her reproachful and slanderous tongue," and Samuel Blake for "his sin of fornication before marriage." Failure to attend sermons, drunkenness, oath swearing, disobedience to superiors, covetousness—all these and more could cause a person to be called before the elders and, if found guilty, punished. Hardly anything escaped the gaze of righteous scrutiny. When a church member chided William Hibben for "calling one of my Brethren 'sir' instead of 'brother,'" Hibben asked the Boston church to forgive him for using "an expression unsuitable for the covenant I am in." The watchfulness that set the tone of life in Puritan communities is suggested by a minister's note that "the church was satisfied with Mrs. Carlton as to the weight of her butter." By saintly surveillance of everything, including Mrs. Carlton's butter, church members enforced a remarkable degree of righteous conformity in Puritan communities.

Like churches, towns chose their residents with care and refused to accept individuals who dissented from Puritan orthodoxy. The founders of Dedham, for example, covenanted that "we shall by all means labor to keep off from us all such as are contrary minded, and receive only such unto us as may be probably of one heart with us." People who refused to conform were advised to leave town; if they did not take the advice, they were forced to leave.

THE PURITAN CHALLENGE TO THE STATUS QUO
This title page of The World Turn'd Upside Down *satirizes the Puritan notion that the contemporary world was deeply flawed. Printed in London in 1647, the pamphlet refers to the "distracted Times" of the Puritan Revolution in England. The drawing ridicules criticisms of English society that were also common among New England Puritans. The drawing shows at least a dozen examples of the conventional world of seventeenth-century England turned upside down. Can you identify them? Puritans, of course, would claim that the drawing had it wrong, that instead the conventional world turned God's order upside down. How might the drawing have been different if a devout Puritan had drawn it?*
British Library.

Despite their centrality, churches had no direct role in the civil government of New England communities. The Puritans did not want to emulate the Church of England, which they considered a puppet of the king rather than an independent church that served the Lord. They were determined to insulate New England churches from the contaminating influence of the civil state and its merely human laws. Although ministers were the most highly respected figures in New England towns, they were prohibited from holding government office. The ban guaranteed that Puritan ministers, unlike Bishop Laud, answered only to the laws of God.

Although they deplored the influence of the English government on the Anglican Church, the Puritans had no qualms whatsoever about their own churches influencing New England governments. Following Calvin, they expected the civil government to be subordinate to the church. As John Cotton said, "it is better that the commonwealth be fashioned to the setting forth of God's house, which is His church, than to accommodate the church in the civil state." Like Calvin, the Puritans believed that the government should support and reinforce God's laws.

In England, the Anglican Church had censured Charles Chauncy for his "strange opinion" that the Sabbath began at sunset on Saturday evening. In New England, Chauncy's strange opinion was the rule, except for those who believed that the Sabbath began even earlier. Winthrop, for example, presumed that the Sabbath started about three o'clock Saturday afternoon. The question was no mere theoretical concern. After the Sabbath began, townsfolk could not work, play, or travel. Fines for Sabbath breaking were issued for such transgressions as playing a flute, smoking a pipe, and visiting neighbors. When two young boys fell through the ice of a Cambridge pond and drowned, Cotton Mather, the Puritan minister, concluded that they had become victims of God's punishment for ice skating on the Sabbath.

Besides strict observance of the Sabbath, the Puritans mandated other purifications of what they considered corrupt English practices. They refused to celebrate either Christmas or Easter. They changed the names of the months from such pagan names as January and February to simple numerals. They outlawed religious wedding ceremonies; couples were married by a magistrate in a civil ceremony—the first Massachusetts wedding to be performed by a minister did not occur until 1686. They prohibited elaborate, colorful clothing, censuring such fineries as lace trim, short sleeves ("whereby the nakedness of the arm may be discovered"), and long hair. Wearing a wig was forbidden since, as one minister explained, "for a man to be discontented with his own hair which God made for him and gave to him, and to covet another's hair which God made for another and gave to another . . . is a sin of the same kind with coveting our neighbor's house or his wife." Cards, dice, shuffleboard, and other games of chance were banned, as were music and dancing. The distinguished minister Increase Mather explained that "Dancing, or Musick, or Singing are [not] in themselves sinful," but he insisted that "Mixt or Promiscuous Dancing . . . of Men and Women" could not be tolerated since "the unchaste Touches and Gesticulations used by Dancers have a palpable tendency to that which is evil." On special occasions, Puritans proclaimed days of fasting and humiliation, which, as one preacher boasted, amounted to "so many Sabbaths more." As much as possible, the Puritans brought public life into conformity with their view of God's law.

Government by Puritans for Puritanism

It is only a slight exaggeration to say that seventeenth-century New England was governed by Puritans for Puritanism. The charter of the Massachusetts Bay Company empowered the company's stockholders (known as freemen) to meet and make the laws to govern the company's affairs. The colonists transformed this arrangement for running a joint stock company into a structure for governing the colony. In 1631, the General Court expanded the small number of original stockholders by admitting almost 120 settlers to the status of freemen. At the same time, the court ruled that freemen must be male church members. Only freemen had the right to vote for governor, deputy governor, and other colonial officials. In addition, all the freemen met together as the General Court to enact laws for the colony. In the first decades of settlement, about half of the adult men in each town became freemen. When new settlers continued to be admitted as freemen, the number became too large to meet conveniently. In 1634, the freemen in each town agreed to send two deputies to the General Court to act as the colony's legislative assembly.

By restricting freemanship to male church members, the General Court hoped to assure that godly men would decide government policies. Even when church membership was not required, as in

Connecticut—which restricted freemanship to those who owned property worth £30 sterling—almost all freemen were church members anyway. Men had to apply to the General Court to gain the rights of freemen, and the court carefully weighed each man's qualifications. The court described one successful applicant for freemanship as a "settled inhabitant . . . orthodox in religion [and] of pious and laudable conversation."

New England town meetings routinely practiced a level of popular participation in political life that was unprecedented elsewhere during the seventeenth century.

Some male church members never applied for freemanship, evidently to avoid such troublesome duties as attending meetings, serving on juries, and mustering with the militia. As the decades passed, fewer men became church members and the growing population of New England made the duties of freemen more time-consuming, causing the number of freemen to shrink to roughly one in three adult men by the end of the seventeenth century.

All other men were classified as "inhabitants," and they had the right to vote, hold office, and participate fully in town government. A "town meeting," composed of all the town's inhabitants and freemen, chose the selectmen and other officials who administered local affairs. New England town meetings routinely practiced a level of popular participation in political life that was unprecedented elsewhere during the seventeenth century. Almost every adult man could speak out in town meetings and fortify his voice with a vote. However, town meetings were far from democratic. All women—even church members—were prohibited from voting, and towns did not permit "contrary-minded" men to become or remain inhabitants. New England towns were composed of people who agreed on a broad range of fundamentals, Puritan doctrine above all else. Of course, town meetings wrangled from time to time; Dorchester, for example, took steps to prevent "the disorderly jarring of our meetings, and the intemperate clashings, and hasty, undigested, and rash votes" that had "been grievous and justly offensive unto many." Despite such disagreements, widespread political participation in town meetings reinforced conformity to Puritan ideals.

Herefordshire Quarter.   *Yorkshire Quarter.*

Oystershell Field.   *Mr. Davenport's Quarter.*   *The Governor's Quarter.*

One of the most important functions of town government was distributing land among the inhabitants. Under the charter of the Massachusetts Bay Company, the General Court controlled unsettled land. Settlers who desired to establish a new town entered a covenant and petitioned the General Court for a grant of land. The court granted to suitably pious petitioners town sites that ranged from 40 up to 250 square miles. The court did not allow settlement until the Indians who inhabited a grant agreed to relinquish their claim to the land, usually in exchange for various manufactured goods, especially iron tools and utensils. In a typical transaction, William Pynchon purchased the site of Springfield, Massachusetts, from the Agawam Indians for "eighteen fathams [arm's lengths] of

Wampam, eighteen coates, 18 hatchets, 18 hoes, [and] 18 knives."

Having established their claim, the town founders would apportion the granted land among themselves and any newcomers they permitted to join them. Normally, each family received a house lot large enough for an adjacent garden as well as one or more strips of agricultural land on the perimeter of the town. Most of the house lots in a town were about the same size, between 1 and 5 acres. Agricultural land, however, was distributed according to the wealth and status of the inhabitants. Ministers and men who had contributed disproportionately to the purchase of the land from the Indians received the largest allocations, sometimes as much as 1,000 acres but usually much less. Common laborers received as little as 10 acres. Most families received more, typically 50, 100, or 150 acres. Although there was a considerable difference between the largest and smallest grants, most allocations clustered in the middle, giving New England a more homogeneous distribution of wealth than the Chesapeake. Towns usually distributed only a fraction of their total grant. They reserved some common land, which all inhabitants could use for grazing livestock and cutting wood, and saved the rest for new settlers and the descendants of the founders.

The details of land tenure and cultivation varied widely from town to town. As much as local conditions permitted, settlers adapted agricultural techniques they had used in England. Some towns enclosed fields; others used an open field system, which entailed greater cooperation in planting, cultivating, and harvesting the crops of wheat, oats, and barley.

Physically, towns were as different as the local terrain, sometimes meandering along a stream, other times rimming a bay or crisscrossing a meadow or rich valley. House lots were typically clustered in an inner core, surrounded by agricultural strips. Colonists walked from their houses to their fields and back again, with one or two trips a week to the meeting house for sermons and lectures and daily visits to neighbors. The physical layout of the towns encouraged settlers to look inward toward their neighbors, multiplying the opportunities for godly vigilance. Although the forest lay within a few hundred yards of every settler's house, most people considered it an alien environment dotted here and there with those oases of civilization, towns. The footpaths connecting one town with another were so rudimentary that even John Winthrop once got lost within a half mile of his house and spent a sleepless night in the forest, circling the light of his small campfire and singing psalms.

The Splintering of Puritanism

One voice singing psalms in the wilderness is a good metaphor for what the Puritans believed they should do in New England. And in large measure, they did it, especially for the first thirty or forty years. But almost from the beginning, Winthrop and other leaders discovered that Puritans sang with more than one voice. Puritans insisted that the Bible spelled out God's Way for humankind and that individual believers, with the guidance of an edu-

cated minister, could see that Way as clearly as they could read the lines of a psalm. In England, persecution as a dissenting minority unified Puritan voices in opposition to the Church of England. But in New England, different interpretations of the Bible, different views of God's Way, found voice and created disharmony. Puritanism's emphasis on individual Bible study led the faithful to discover not God's Way but God's Ways. Yet each Puritan remained convinced that God had only one Way. Puritan leaders interpreted dissent as an error caused either by a misguided believer or by the malevolent power of Satan. Whatever the cause, errors could not be tolerated. As one Puritan minister proclaimed, "God doth no where in his word tolerate Christian States, to give Tolerations to . . . adversaries of his Truth, if they have power in their hands to suppress them. The Scripture saith . . . there is no Truth but one." In New England, Puritan leaders had the power to suppress adversaries of their view of the Truth, even when the adversaries were themselves Puritans.

Among the immigrants who arrived in Massachusetts in 1630 was Roger Williams, a lively young minister who had trained at Cambridge University and who counted Winthrop and other Puritan elders among his friends. From the start, Williams needled the colony's leadership with his outspoken views that their church was fatally impure. He refused to accept the invitation to preach in Boston, since people who were not full church members were required to attend sermons. Such a policy "stinks in God's nostrils," Williams said. The only way to preserve the purity of the church was to exclude everyone but church members from sermons. Williams believed that the act of worship should be kept so utterly pure that even family prayers were sinful, unless all family members were visible saints (as they rarely were). Worse from the viewpoint of Winthrop and other Puritan leaders, Williams declared that the government of Massachusetts contaminated the purity of the church. He demanded that the state be kept completely separate from the church. For the church to rely in any way on the state to uphold religion—as it did, of course, in Massachusetts—defiled the church with the squalor of worldly affairs, Williams asserted. For these opinions and others, Massachusetts banished Williams in 1635. He moved to Narragansett Bay, where he established the town of Providence and helped found the colony of Rhode Island as a refuge for dissenters from Puritan orthodoxies. Williams's heresy carried one strain of Puritanism to a logical conclusion that challenged the legitimacy of the emerging Puritan order.

Another early immigrant pushed Puritan doctrines in a different direction. In 1634, Anne Hutchinson arrived in Massachusetts with her husband and their family. A brilliant woman, Hutchinson had received an excellent education from her father. The mother of fourteen children, she also served her neighbors as a skilled midwife. Most of all, she was an ardent Puritan, steeped in Scripture and absorbed by sermons, especially those of John Cotton. On board the ship to Massachusetts, Hutchinson often met with other immigrants to discuss the sermons of the minister who accompanied the group, whom Hutchinson considered second-rate. The meetings continued after the Hutchinsons settled into their home in Boston. At first, mostly women gathered at Hutchinson's home to hear her Thursday lectures on Cotton's most recent sermons. As the months passed, the meetings increased to twice a week and the crowds grew to sixty or eighty, including many of Boston's most prominent citizens, female and male.

The sermons of Hutchinson's favorite minister, John Cotton, emphasized that individuals could be saved only by God's grace in choosing them to be predestined members of the elect, a doctrine Cotton termed the "covenant of grace." Cotton contrasted this familiar Puritan tenet with the "covenant of works," the erroneous belief that one's behavior—one's works—could win God's favor and, ultimately, salvation. Belief in the covenant of works was a heresy known as Arminianism. One of the worst insults that could be leveled at a Puritan was to call her or him an Arminian; it accused the person of believing that the behavior of human beings could influence God's will. Cotton's sermons strongly hinted that many Puritans, even ministers, leaned toward Arminianism, and Anne Hutchinson agreed. It must have been easy to get that impression in the pious atmosphere of Massachusetts Bay. Hutchinson's lectures stressed that many of the leaders of the colony, under the delusion of a covenant of works, believed that their godly behavior moved them closer to heaven. Hutchinson, like Cotton, avowed that only God's gift of grace could do that. In effect, Hutchinson amplified Cotton's somewhat muted message that the leaders of the colony were repudiating the marrow of Puritan faith, and she did so without the protection of Cotton's status as a minister and a man.

The meetings at Hutchinson's alarmed her nearest neighbor, John Winthrop. He believed that Hutchinson was subverting the good order of the colony. Winthrop held conventional notions about the inferiority and necessary subordination of women: Women should stay in their place and listen to their husbands, not give lectures that both men and women find compelling. In 1637, Winthrop arranged to have formal charges brought against Hutchinson, and he confronted her in court as her chief accuser. Winthrop denounced Hutchinson's lectures as "not tolerable nor comely in the sight of God nor fitting for your sex." As the two squared off in court—Bible to Bible—he was no match for Hutchinson's learning, wit, and insight. Hutchinson gave far better than she got. She pointed to passages in the Bible that instructed women to meet and teach one another. When Winthrop claimed those Scriptures did not apply to her, she asked him, "Must I shew my name written therein?" Besides, she replied, if it is "not lawful for me to teach women . . . why do you call me to teach the court?" Outsmarted and off-balance, Winthrop pressed forward with the investigation, fishing for some heresy that he could pin on Hutchinson.

Winthrop and other elders referred to Hutchinson and her followers as "Antinomians," that is, people who opposed the law. Hutchinson's opponents charged that she believed that Christians could be saved by faith alone, that they did not need to act according to God's law in the Bible as interpreted by the colony's leaders. In her scriptural duel with Winthrop in court, Hutchinson nimbly defended herself against this accusation. Yes, she believed that men and women were saved by faith alone; but no, she did not deny the need to obey God's law. "The Lord hath let me see which was the clear ministry and which the wrong," she said. Finally, her interrogators cornered her. How could she tell which was which? "By an immediate revelation," she replied, "by the voice of [God's] own spirit to my soul." Here was the crime Winthrop had been searching for, the heresy of prophecy, the erroneous claim that God revealed his will directly to a believer instead of, as every good Puritan knew, exclusively through the Bible.

In 1638, the Boston church formally excommunicated Hutchinson. The minister decreed, "I doe cast you out and . . . deliver you up to Satan that you may learne no more to blaspheme to seduce and to lye. . . . I command you . . . as a Leper to withdraw your selfe out of the Congregation." Banished, Hutchinson and her family moved first to Rhode Island and then to Long Island, where she and her family, except for her ten-year-old daughter, were killed by Indians.

Hutchinson's admission of divine revelation was a departure from standard Puritan belief. Yet by directing believers to search for evidence of God's grace, Puritanism encouraged the faithful to listen for a whisper from God that they were among the elect. Puritanism was a volatile combination of rigid insistence on conformity to God's law and aching uncertainty about how to identify and act upon it. Despite the best efforts of Winthrop and other leaders to render God's instructions in no uncertain terms, Puritanism inspired believers to draw their own conclusions and stick to them. In this sense, Anne Hutchinson was more a product of Puritanism than a dissenter from it.

Such strains within Puritanism caused it to splinter repeatedly during the seventeenth century. The prominent minister Thomas Hooker, for example, clashed with Winthrop and Cotton over the composition of the church. Hooker argued that men and women who lived godly lives should be admitted to church membership, even if they had not experienced conversion. This question, like most others in New England, had both religious and political dimensions, since only church members could vote in Massachusetts. In 1636, Hooker led an exodus of more than eight hundred colonists from Massachusetts to the Connecticut River valley, where they founded Hartford and neighboring towns. In 1639, the towns adopted the Fundamental Orders of Connecticut, a quasi-constitution that could be altered by vote of the freemen, who did not have to be church members, although nearly all of them were.

Puritan churches divided and subdivided throughout the seventeenth century as acrimony developed over doctrine and church government. After Charles Chauncy came to New England, the colonists learned that he firmly believed that infants should be baptized by immersion rather than by mere sprinkling, a practice that—needless to say—alarmed parents; it did, however, ultimately earn him a safe appointment as president of Harvard College, which was founded in 1636. Other divisions occurred over questions of church government. Most churches followed the congregational practice, whereby individual congregations selected and dismissed ministers on their own. Some leaned toward a presbyterian structure, by which ministerial associations (or synods) set ecclesiastical policy

and influenced the selection of ministers by individual churches. Sometimes churches split over the appointment of a controversial minister. Sometimes families who had a long walk to the meeting house simply decided to form their own church nearer their houses. The schism of Puritan churches arose from the ambiguities and tensions within Puritan belief. As the colonies matured, other tensions developed as well.

Growth, Change, and Controversy

In England, Puritans led a parliamentary challenge to royal authority. King Charles I dissolved Parliament in 1629, vowing to rule without parliamentary advice. He succeeded until 1640 when, desperately in need of money to repel an invasion from Scotland, he reconvened Parliament. Members of Parliament immediately attacked the king's absolutist policies. In 1642, the political conflict escalated to civil war, known as the Puritan Revolution. The Cavaliers (the name given the king and his supporters) were defeated both politically and militarily by the parliamentary forces (known as Roundheads because of their short hair), led by the staunch Puritan Oliver Cromwell. In 1649, Cromwell's forces crowned their victories by executing Charles I and proclaiming a Puritan Republic. From 1649 to 1660, England's rulers were not monarchs who tried to suppress Puritanism but believers who tried to champion it. In a half century, English Puritans rose from a harassed group of religious dissenters to a dominant power in English government.

Such a revolutionary transformation in the fortunes of English Puritans had profound consequences in New England. In 1640, when the Puritan Revolution began, the stream of immigrants to New England dwindled to a trickle. The end of immigration brought hard times to the colonists. They could no longer consider themselves a city on a hill setting a godly example for humankind. English society was being reformed by Puritans in England, not New England. Furthermore, during the 1630s the steady current of immigrants had stimulated the New England economy. A vigorous trade developed between the latest arrivals and those who had preceded them. Newcomers brought money and English goods to exchange for the food, supplies, and services they needed to put down roots in New England. When that immigrant trade came to a halt in 1640, the colonists faced sky-high prices for scarce English goods and few customers for their plentiful colonial products. As they searched for a re-

WAMPANOAG WAR CLUB
This Wampanoag war club vividly illustrates the potency of a traditional weapon made of wood. A swing of the club generated tremendous force because of the heavy wooden ball at the end. The club could easily smash bones; even a glancing blow could knock a victim senseless. The weapon was most effective, however, only at very close range—essentially hand-to-hand combat. While these weapons were still used during King Philip's War, the Wampanoags and other native peoples inflicted far more damage with European firearms obtained in colonial trade.
Courtesy of the Fruitlands Museum, Harvard, Massachusetts.

placement for the immigrant trade, they marked out the basic patterns of the New England economy.

New England's rocky soil and short growing season ruled out cultivating the common colonial crops of tobacco, sugar, and rice that found a ready market in Atlantic ports. Instead of commercial crops for export, New England farmers planted food crops for home consumption. Towns usually granted each family enough land to grow sufficient grain, vegetables, and fruit to keep food on the table. With the labor of family members and perhaps a servant or hired hand, farmers often had a modest surplus of one thing or another—apples or eggs, milk or butter—and they eagerly sought to sell it to or barter it with their neighbors. This brisk local market linked neighbor to neighbor in a dense network of exchange, but it seldom extended much beyond town boundaries.

Exports that New Englanders could not get from the soil they took instead from the forest and the sea. During the first decade of settlement, colonists traded with Indians for animal pelts much in demand in Europe as fashionable apparel. By the 1640s, so many fur-bearing animals had been trapped that pelts became scarce unless traders ventured far beyond the frontiers of English settlement. Trees from the seemingly limitless forests of New England proved a longer-lasting resource. Masts for ships and staves for barrels of Spanish wine and West Indian sugar were crafted from New England timber. But the most important New England export was fish. During the religious and political turmoil of the 1640s, English ships withdrew from the rich North Atlantic fishing grounds and New Eng-

land fishermen quickly took their place. Dried, salted codfish found markets in southern Europe and, increasingly, in the West Indies. The fish trade also stimulated colonial shipbuilding and trained generations of fishermen, sailors, and merchants. By 1660, New England fishermen dominated the North Atlantic fishing grounds and New England merchants sailed from port to port throughout the colonies trading fish for Virginia tobacco, Carolina rice, and West Indian sugar. The commercial network they built endured for more than a century.

Under the pressures of steady population growth and integration into the Atlantic economy, New England society maintained the outward features that had been established by Winthrop's generation. But the white-hot piety of the founders cooled during the last half of the seventeenth century.

Merchants prospered in the export trade, and coastal towns catered to sailors and fishermen. But the export economy remained peripheral to most New England colonists. Their lives revolved around their farms, their churches, and their families.

Families were the source of one of the most important long-term changes in seventeenth-century New England. Although immigration came to a standstill in 1640, the population continued to boom, doubling every twenty years. In contemporary England, more than a quarter of the population never married. But in New England, nearly everybody married, men at about twenty-six, women at about twenty-three. Typically, a New England woman had eight or nine children, spaced about two years apart. Universal marriage and frequent births created an ever-growing population because New England enjoyed a healthful environment. Long, cold winters eliminated the warm-weather ailments that plagued the Chesapeake and the Carolinas. Low population density and the relative isolation of towns minimized the spread of diseases. Puritan habits of order, tidiness, and watchfulness probably helped. Men and women lived longer in New England; grandparents became relatively common in families by midcentury, though they remained rare elsewhere. Even more important to population growth, New England children survived the hazards of infancy and childhood

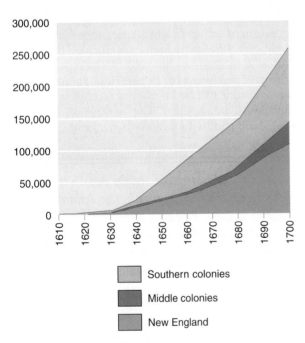

FIGURE **4.1**
Population of British North American Colonies in the Seventeenth Century
The colonial population grew at a steadily accelerating rate during the seventeenth century. On the whole, New England and the southern colonies each comprised about half the total colonial population until after 1680, when the growth in Pennsylvania and New York contributed to the surge in the population of the middle colonies.

much more frequently than children elsewhere. Although early death remained an ever-present threat, in the seventeenth century death rates in New England were much lower than in the Chesapeake. The result was that the descendants of the immigrants of the 1630s multiplied and remultiplied, quickly boosting the New England population to a rough equality with that of the southern colonies. From 1640 almost to 1700, New Englanders constituted about forty-five out of every hundred British colonists in North America, southern colonists contributed another forty-five, and the remainder inhabited the middle colonies.

Under the pressures of steady population growth and integration into the Atlantic economy, New England society maintained the outward features that had been established by Winthrop's generation. But the white-hot piety of the founders cooled during the last half of the seventeenth century. New England churches and towns continued their strict observance of God's laws, but ministers accused their congregations of a decline from the passionate faith of the founders. "The truth is," Roger Williams declared, "the great Gods of this world are God-belly, God-peace, God-wealth, God-honour, God-pleasure . . . [and] God Land."

After the 1630s, the population grew faster than church membership. All residents attended sermons on pain of fines and punishment, but many could not find seating room in the meeting houses. Boston's two churches in 1650 could house only about a third of the population. An increasing fraction of the population, men especially, practiced what one historian has called "horse-shed Christianity." They attended sermons but loitered outside (near the horse shed) as long as possible, gossiping about the weather, their corn crop, a big fish, or the scandalous behavior of Goodman Such-and-Such and Goodwife So-and-So. Their bodies came to church but their minds lingered on the profane gods described by Roger Williams. By the 1680s, women were the majority among full church members throughout New England. In some towns, only 15 percent of the adult men were church members. Puritan minister Michael Wigglesworth asked

How is it that I find
  In stead of holiness Carnality,
In stead of heavenly frames an Earthly mind,
  For burning zeal luke-warm Indifferency,
For flaming love, key-cold Dead-heartedness,
  For temperance (in meat, and drinke, and cloaths) excess?

Whence cometh it, that Pride, and Luxurie
    Debate, Deceit, Contention, and Strife,
False-dealing, Covetousness, Hypocrisie
    (With such Crimes) amongst them are so rife,
That one of them doth over-reach another?
    And that an honest man can hardly trust his
        Brother?

How is it, that Security, and Sloth,
    Amongst the best are Common to be found?
That grosser sins, instead of Graces growth,
    Amongst the many more and more abound?

Most alarming to Puritan leaders, the children of visible saints often failed to experience conversion and attain full church membership. Puritans tended to assume that sainthood was inherited—that the children of the elect were probably also among the elect. Acting on this premise, churches permitted saints to baptize their babies, symbolically cleansing the infants of their contamination with original sin. Yet during the 1640s and 1650s, children of the visible saints outwardly conformed to God's laws but seldom experienced the inward transformation that signaled conversion and qualification for church membership. The problem became urgent during the 1650s when the children of saints—people who had grown to adulthood in New England—began to have children themselves. These babies, the grandchildren of visible saints, could not receive baptism and the protection it afforded against the terrors of an early death.

Puritan churches debated what to do. To allow anyone—even the child of a saint—to become a church member without conversion was an unthinkable retreat from the most fundamental Puritan doctrine. To allow the children of the unregenerate to be baptized flung open the door of church membership to any and all—another unthinkable affront to Puritan faith. In 1662, a synod of Massachusetts ministers reached a compromise known as the Halfway Covenant. The unconverted children of saints were permitted to become halfway church members. They could baptize their infants, but they could not participate in communion or have the voting privileges of church membership. The Halfway Covenant generated a controversy that sputtered through Puritan churches for the remainder of the century. Opponents protested the "many chaffy hypocrites" the compromise brought into the covenant, if only halfway. Defenders argued that "the Lord hath not set up Churches onely that a few old Christians may keep one another warm while they live, and then carry away the Church into the

A NEW ENGLAND CHILD
Young Alice Mason, who appears to be five or six years old in this 1668 painting, shows little of the lightheartedness or endearing vulnerability we might expect in a child today. Instead, she fixes the viewer with a confident, steady gaze that suggests that she had few doubts about what she should do and that, in fact, she did it. The painting illustrates the drift away from the intense piety and plain dress of New England's founding generation. The elaborately decorated dress, especially the slashed sleeves, reflect the prosperity that some New Englanders had achieved by the 1660s, prosperity they displayed in their clothing and homes in ways the founders would have found profane. Alice stands on a floorcloth painted to resemble tile, suggesting that her family could afford to cover drab wooden floors with canvas but not with genuine tile or fine carpets that adorned the homes of a wealthy few. Adams National Historic Site.

cold grave with them when they dye." Instead, the Halfway Covenant permitted the church to "*nurse up* still successively *another Generation* of Subjects to Christ . . . so he might have a People and Kingdome successively continued to him from one Generation to another." With the Halfway Covenant, Puritan churches came to terms with the replacement of "burning zeal" by "luke-warm Indifferency," of "flaming love" by "key-cold Dead-heartedness." Nonetheless, the church survived, as did piety aplenty.

During the last half of the seventeenth century, Puritan communities continued to enforce piety with holy rigor. Beginning in 1656, small bands of Quakers began to arrive in Massachusetts determined to bear witness for their faith. Quakers—or members of the Society of Friends, as they called themselves—believed that God spoke directly to each individual through an "inner light." Neither a preacher nor the Bible was necessary to discover God's Word. Furthermore, they declared that since all human beings were equal in God's eyes, subordination to mere temporal authority should be refused unless God, speaking through each person's inner light, requested otherwise. Quakers affronted Puritan doctrines of faith and social order. They refused to observe the Sabbath, for example, because they insisted that God did not set aside any special day for worship but instead expected the faithful to worship every day.

The Quakers, the governor of Massachusetts declared, were "malignant and assiduous Promoters of Doctrines directly tending to subvert both our Churches and State." Puritan communities treated Quakers with ruthless severity. Some Quakers were branded on the face "with a red-hot iron with [an] H. for heresie." Several Quaker women were stripped to the waist, tied to the back of a cart, and whipped as they were paraded through twelve towns. When the Quakers refused to leave Massachusetts, the Boston magistrates sentenced two men and a woman to be hanged in 1659. The three Quakers walked to the gallows "Hand in Hand, all three of them, as to a Weding-day, with great cheerfulness of Heart," one colonist observed. Massachusetts authorities worried about the testimony the condemned might give to the huge crowd that gathered, so they ordered a drummer to drown out any statement they might make. The two men were executed, while the woman, Mary Dyer, was exiled—though she returned to Boston within six months and was hanged.

The punishments handed out to the Quakers demonstrate the refusal of Puritan leaders to permit deviation from Puritan doctrine. Toleration of other religions was "Sinful Toleration," Increase Mather affirmed, since "the *Toleration* of all Religions and Perswasions, is the way to have no true Religion at all left." However, the Quakers' courage and self-sacrifice awakened sympathy among the New England population. When a young Quaker mother with a nursing baby was whipped, a townswoman remarked, "Surely if she had not the spirit of the Lord she could not do this thing." Such doubts remained a barely expressed undercurrent in Puritan communities, reflecting a layperson's perspective on what Wigglesworth called "key-cold Dead-heartedness."

During the last half of the seventeenth century, an increasing number of New Englanders lost heart for the rigorous enforcement of Puritan righteousness. Beneath the surface, the zealous Puritanism of the founders of New England failed to capture the hearts of their descendants. Many of them went to church, obeyed the laws, read their Bibles, taught their children, and said their prayers. But few of them were prepared, in the name of their faith, to walk to the gallows, "with great cheerfulness of Heart."

The Puritans' success in building a godly society ultimately undermined the intense appeal of Puritanism. In the pious communities of New England, leaders did everything possible to eliminate sin. In the process, they diminished the sense of utter human depravity that was the wellspring of Puritanism. At the end of the seventeenth century, New Englanders did not doubt that human beings sinned, but they were far more concerned with the sins of others than with their own, as the Salem witch trials demonstrated. (See Historical Question, page 136.) The Brattle Street Church, founded in Boston in 1699, symbolized the change in Puritanism. Among other deviations, the Brattle Street congregation allowed any person who contributed money to the church to participate in the selection of a minister. The contrast between the financial contributors to the Brattle Street Church and the members of the covenant John Winthrop described in his *Arbella* sermon was one measure of the change in Puritanism during the seventeenth century.

The Founding of the Middle Colonies

The English colonies of New York, New Jersey, and Pennsylvania originated as proprietary colonies—that is, colonies granted by the crown to one or more proprietors, who then possessed both the land and extensive, almost monarchical, powers of government. Before the 1670s, few Europeans settled in any of these middle colonies. For the first two-thirds of the seventeenth century, the most important European outpost in the region north of the Chesapeake and south of New England was the relatively small Dutch colony New Netherland. By the end of the seventeenth century, however, the English monarchy had seized New Netherland and renamed it New York and had encouraged the creation of a Quaker colony led by William Penn.

From New Netherland to New York

In 1609, the Dutch East India Company dispatched Henry Hudson to search for a Northwest Passage to the Orient. Hudson sailed along the Atlantic coast from present-day Canada to the Chesapeake and ventured up the large river that now bears his name until it dwindled to a shallow stream that obviously did not lead to China. He discovered nothing to divert the Dutch East India Company's busy and profitable trade with Asia from its well-established eastern routes. Hudson continued to look for a shortcut to the East until 1611 when, after a brutal winter

M A P 4.2

Middle Colonies in the Seventeenth Century
For the most part, the middle colonies in the seventeenth centuries were inhabited by settlers who clustered along the Hudson or Delaware rivers. The vast geographic extent of the colonies shown in this map represented land grants authorized in England but still inhabited by Native Americans rather than settled by colonists.

locked in the ice of Hudson Bay in northern Canada, his crew mutinied and set him adrift to perish in a small boat.

The English colonies of New York, New Jersey, and Pennsylvania originated as proprietary colonies—that is, colonies granted by the crown to one or more proprietors who then possessed both the land and extensive, almost monarchical, powers of government.

A decade later, the Dutch government granted the West India Company—a group of Dutch merchants and shippers seeking to mimic the success of the East India Company—exclusive rights to trade with the Western Hemisphere. The company had less interest in Hudson's discoveries than in preying on the riches of New Spain. However, a Hudson River settlement could serve as a supply and repair stopover for ships traveling between the Netherlands and Central and South America, and it could also trade with the local Indians for furs. In 1624, the West India Company established fur trading posts on the Hudson River as well as along the Connecticut and Delaware Rivers. Two years later, Peter Minuit, the resident director of the company, purchased Manhattan Island from the Manhate Indians for trade goods worth 60 florins, the equivalent of a dozen beaver pelts. New Amsterdam, the small settlement established at the southern tip of Manhattan island, became the principal trading center in New Netherland as well as the colony's headquarters.

Unlike the English colonies, New Netherland did not attract many European immigrants. By the mid-1640s, after two decades of settlement, only about a thousand colonists lived in the town of New Amsterdam, and they made up roughly half the colony's population. The company tried to stimulate immigration by granting patroonships—allotments of eighteen miles of land along the Hudson River—to wealthy stockholders who would bring fifty families to the colony and settle them as serf-like tenants on their huge domains. Only the patroonship founded by Kiliaen van Rensselaer succeeded; the others failed to attract settlers and much of the land was sold back to the company. Like New England and the Chesapeake colonies, New Netherland never realized the profits that its sponsors dreamed of.

Why Were Some New Englanders Accused of Being Witches?

Almost everybody in seventeenth-century North America—whether Native American, slave, or colonist—believed that supernatural spirits could cause harm and misfortune. Outside New England, however, few colonists were legally accused of being witches, persons who had become possessed by evil spirits. More than 95 percent of all legal accusations of witchcraft in the North American colonies occurred in New England. In 1691 and 1692, an epidemic of witchcraft accusations broke out in Salem, Massachusetts, and more than one hundred individuals were accused. Many other New Englanders may have been called witches privately, but historians do not know about them because legal charges were never filed. After all, to charge a person with witchcraft was a serious matter. As a 1641 Massachusetts law stated, "If any man or woman be a witch . . . they shall be put to death." The other New England colonies had identical laws. During the seventeenth century, courts carried out the letter of the law: Thirty-four accused witches were executed, nineteen of them during the Salem outbreak.

To understand the peculiar New England preoccupation with witchcraft, historians have gathered a great deal of information about accused witches and the dark deeds their accusers attributed to them. Almost anyone could be accused of being a witch, but 80 percent of the accusations were leveled against women. About two-thirds of the accused women were over forty years old, past the age of childbearing. About half the men who were accused as witches were relatives of accused women. Normally one family member did not accuse another. Nor did accusers single out a stranger as a witch. Instead, accusers pointed to a neighbor they knew well, typically a woman.

Almost always the accused witch denied the charge. Occasionally, the accused confessed. A confession could sometimes win sympathy and a reduced punishment from officials. During the Salem witch-hunt, those who confessed usually saved their own skins by naming other people as witches. The testimony of the confessed witch was then used to accuse others. At Salem, authorities sought to obtain a confession from accused witch Giles Corey by piling stones on his chest until he was crushed to death.

Accusers of all descriptions stepped forward to testify against alleged witches. Witchcraft investigations often stretched over weeks, months, or even years as courts accumulated evidence against (and sometimes in favor of) the accused. About 90 percent of accusers were adults, about six out of ten of them men. Young women between the ages of sixteen and twenty-five made up almost all of the remaining 10 percent of accusers; they claimed to be tortured by the accused witches.

At Salem, for example, afflicted young girls shrieked in pain, their limbs twisted into strange, involuntary contortions. The young women pointed out the witches who tortured them. At the trial of accused witch Bridget Bishop in Salem, the court record noted that if Bishop "but cast her eyes on them [the afflicted], they were presently struck down. . . . But upon the touch of her hand upon them, when they lay in their swoons, they would immediately revive." The bewitched girls testified that "the shape of the prisoner did oftentimes very grievously pinch them, choke them, bite them, and afflict them; urging them to write their names in a book," the devil's book.

Such sensational evidence of torture by a witch was relatively rare in witch-hunts and trials. Usually, accusers attributed some inexplicable misfortune they had suffered to the evil influence of an accused witch. In Bridget Bishop's trial, for instance, one man testified that when he bought a pig from Bishop's husband, Bishop became angry because she "was hindered from fingering the money," and soon afterward the pig—obviously bewitched— "was taken with strange fits; jumping, leaping, and knocking [its] head against the fence." Another woman accused a witch whom she feared would "smite my chickens," and "quickly after [the suspected witch went away] one chicken died." One woman testified against a witch who had bewitched her cow, causing it to give discolored milk. A man was accused as a witch because his "spirit bewitched the pudding," which was inexplicably "cut lengthwise . . . as smooth as any knife could cut it." Mary Parsons testified that she suspected her hus-

WITCHES SHOW THEIR LOVE FOR SATAN
Mocking pious Christians' humble obeisance to God, witches hideously debased themselves by standing in line to kneel and kiss Satan's butt —or so it was popularly believed. This seventeenth-century print portrays Satan with hands, feet, and tail of a rodent, wings of a bat, and head of a lustful ram attached to the torso of a man. Note that women predominate among the witches eager to express their devotion to Satan and to do his bidding.
The Library and Center for Knowledge Management, University of California, San Francisco.

band, Hugh, of being a witch "because almost all that he sells to anybody does not prosper."

The list of misfortunes that accusers attributed to witches went on and on. From our perspective in the late twentieth century, the accusers seem to have been victims not of witches but of simple accidents, of overheated imaginations, or—in the case of the possessed young women—of emotional distress. But why did seventeenth-century New Englanders find the testimony of accusers persuasive?

Seventeenth-century New Englanders believed that almost nothing happened by chance. Supernatural power—whether God's or Satan's—suffused the world and influenced the smallest event, even the death of a chicken. When something bad happened, an unhappy God may have caused it to show his displeasure with the victim, who had perhaps sinned in some way. But maybe the victim was not responsible for the misfortune; maybe Satan, acting through a witch, had caused it. If misfortunes could be pinned on a witch, the accuser was absolved from responsibility; the accuser became a

helpless victim rather than a guilty party. Witches were an explanation for the disorder that continually crept into New England communities, an explanation that attributed the disorder not to chance or to the faults of the community but to the witches' evil purposes.

Accusers usually targeted a vulnerable neighbor, such as an older woman. Historians have noted that accusers often complained that accused witches were quarrelsome, grumbled about being mistreated, muttered vague threats about getting even, and seemed to be dissatisfied with their lives. Researchers have pointed out that many New Englanders had such feelings after about 1650, but most people did not express them openly or, if they did, felt guilty about doing so. Accused witches often expressed and acted on feelings that other people shared but considered inappropriate, shameful, or sinful in their zeal to lead the saintly lives prescribed by their Puritan religion. Witches made it somewhat easier for New Englanders to consider themselves saints rather than sinners.

NEW AMSTERDAM, NEW YORK
This map was made for the Duke of York, whose small fleet seized New Amsterdam in 1664. The map reflects the early transition from Dutch to English rule. Although the map still uses the Dutch name New Amsterdam, the fort at the tip of Manhattan ("the Towne of Mannados") flies an English flag, as do at least six ships in the harbor, making clear that the colony is New York in all but name. Already Manhattanites were seeking refuge in the suburbs, indicated here as the enclosures along the top of the peninsula, to the left of the city wall (the vertical line dividing city streets from the wilds of upper Manhattan).
British Library.

Although few in number, the New Netherlanders were remarkably diverse, especially compared with the homogeneous English settlers to the north and south. Religious dissenters trickled in from other North American colonies. Immigrants from Holland, Sweden, France, Germany, and elsewhere made their way to the colony. Merchants and sailors in the West Indies trade stopped over in New Amsterdam and ended up staying. In 1646, the governor of New Netherland told a visitor that the colonists spoke eighteen different languages. A few years later, a minister of the Dutch Reformed Church complained to his superiors in Holland that several groups of Jews had recently arrived, adding to the religious mixture of "Papists, Mennonites and Lutherans among the Dutch . . . [and] many Puritans . . . and many other atheists and various other servants of Baal . . . who conceal themselves under the name of Christians." Spiritually, the polyglot society of New Netherland could qualify as a New England Puritan's nightmare. One minister reported that in several New Netherland villages there were as many religious opinions as residents, while the preacher in another settlement was reported to be a "man of impious and scandalous habits, a wild, drunken, unmannerly clown, more inclined to look into the wine can than into the Bible."

The West India Company struggled to govern the motley colonists for its own purposes. Under the stern leadership of Peter Stuyvesant, who served as governor from 1647 to 1664, the population slowly grew, but it remained intractable. Stuyvesant pointed out to company officials in Holland that "the *English* and *French* colonies are continued and populated by their own nation and countrymen and consequently [are] bound together more firmly and united, while your Honors' colonies in New-Netherland are only gradually and slowly peopled by the scrapings of all sorts of nationalities (few excepted), who consequently have the least interest in the welfare and maintenance of the commonwealth." Stuyvesant tried to enforce conformity to the Dutch Reformed Church, but the company—eager for more immigrants—ordered him to "shut your eyes" to the many dissenting faiths. The company added that "the consciences of men should be free and unshackled," making a virtue of New Netherland necessity. The company never permitted the "scrapings" who settled in the colony to form a representative government. Instead, the company appointed government officials who set policies, including taxes, which many colonists deeply resented.

Spiritually, the polyglot society of New Netherland could qualify as a New England Puritan's nightmare.

In 1664, New Netherland became New York. Charles II, who became king of England after the monarchy was restored in 1660, gave his brother James, the Duke of York, an enormous grant of land that included New Netherland. Of course, the Dutch colony did not belong to the king of England and was not his to give away. But that legal technicality did not impede the king or his brother. The duke quickly organized a small fleet of warships, which soon appeared off Manhattan Island in late

summer 1664, and demanded that Stuyvesant surrender. With little choice, he did.

As the new proprietor of the colony, the Duke of York exercised almost the same unlimited authority over the colony as had the West India Company. He could appoint government officers, make laws, regulate trade, and adjudicate all matters without the bother (to him) of representative assemblies. The duke himself never set foot in New York, but his governors struggled to impose order on the unruly colonists. Like the Dutch, the duke permitted "all persons of what Religion soever, quietly to inhabit ... provided they give no disturbance to the publique peace, nor doe molest or disquiet others in the free exercise of their religion." This policy of religious toleration was more a sober recognition of reality than a farsighted affirmation of liberty of conscience. It arose from the government's grudging accommodation to the difficulties of bringing order to the most heterogeneous colony in seventeenth-century North America.

New Jersey and Pennsylvania

The creation of New York led indirectly to the founding of two other middle colonies, New Jersey and Pennsylvania. In 1664, the Duke of York subdivided his grant and gave the portion between the Hudson and Delaware Rivers to two of his friends at court. The proprietors of this new colony, New Jersey, soon discovered that Puritan and Dutch settlers already in the region stubbornly resisted paying taxes and declaring their loyalty to the new government. The continuing strife in New Jersey discouraged immigration and persuaded one of the proprietors to sell his share to two Quakers. When the two Quaker proprietors began to quarrel, they called in a prominent English Quaker, William Penn, to arbitrate their dispute. Penn eventually worked out a settlement that continued New Jersey's proprietary government but did little to end the conflict with the settlers. In the process, Penn became intensely interested in what he termed a "holy experiment" of establishing a genuinely Quaker colony in America.

Unlike most other Quakers, William Penn came from an eminent family. His father served as an admiral under both Cromwell and Charles II and had been knighted. The younger Penn trained for a military career, but the ideas of dissenters from the reestablished Anglican Church appealed to him. His father attempted to cool Penn's religious enthusiasm by sending him to Oxford University and on a tour of the continent, but by 1667—when he was twenty-three years old—Penn had become a devout Quaker.

In England, the Quakers' inner light appeared most brightly to men and women of humble origins. Tradesmen, farmers, and laborers were drawn to the Quaker teaching that God loved them and revealed his grace directly to them through the inner light. The Quakers' concept of an open, generous God who made his love equally available to all people manifested itself in unusually egalitarian religious services and social behavior that continually brought Quakers into conflict with the government.

Quaker meetings consisted of quiet meditation interrupted by spontaneous testimony from any member of the meeting who felt moved to expound on religious or moral issues. Quaker leaders were ordinary lay men and women, not specially trained preachers. More than any other seventeenth-century sect, Quakers allowed women to assume positions of religious leadership. "In souls there is no sex," they said. Since all people were equal in the spiritual realm, Quakers considered the conventional social hierarchy of their day false and evil. Like the Puritans, they condemned the ornate costumes and elegant flattery fashionable in late seventeenth-century England. Instead, they dressed in plain, somber clothing and spoke in plain, honest language. They refused to observe the prevailing etiquette that required men to remove their hats and women to curtsy when in the presence of someone of higher rank and to address their superiors in terms of respect such as "lord" or "lady," "sir" or "madam." They insisted on calling everyone "friend" and on shaking hands instead of curtsying or removing their hat—even when meeting the king. These customs enraged many non-Quakers and provoked innumerable beatings and worse. Thousands of Quakers were imprisoned and hundreds were killed during the 1660s and 1670s in England (as they were, on a smaller scale, in New England). Penn himself was jailed four times, once for nine months.

Penn was one of the most outspoken and prominent Quakers in England. By 1680, he had published fifty books and pamphlets and spoken at countless public meetings, but he appeared no closer to realizing his goal of toleration for Quakers. A Quaker colony in America held out the promise not just of toleration but of a society constructed on Quaker principles, a possibility Penn found irresistible. Despite his many run-ins with the government, Penn remained on good terms with

WILLIAM PENN
This portrait of William Penn was drawn about a decade after the founding of Pennsylvania. At a time when extravagant clothing and fancy wigs proclaimed that their wearer was an important person, Penn was portrayed informally, lacking even a coat, his natural hair neat but undressed—all a reflection of his Quaker faith. Penn's full face and double chin show that his faith did not make him a stranger to the pleasures of the table. No hollow-cheeked ascetic or wild-eyed enthusiast, Penn appears sober and observant, as if sizing up the viewer and reserving judgment. The portrait captures the calm determination, anchored in his faith, that inspired Penn's hopes for his new colony.
Historical Society of Pennsylvania.

Charles II, and he asked the king for a grant of land to found his colony. The king had begun a policy of tightening royal control of the English colonies in America, but he greeted Penn's request as an opportunity to rid England of the troublesome Quakers. In 1681, he made Penn the proprietor of 45,000 square miles for his new colony of Pennsylvania.

"The service of God first, the honor and advantage of the king, with our own profit, shall I hope be the result of all our endeavors," Penn wrote soon afterward. Penn planned to profit by selling some of his vast dominion. Although he eventually sold over 700,000 acres, profits eluded him and he remained perpetually in debt. He was far more successful in serving God by building his colony on a Quaker foundation.

Toleration and Diversity in Pennsylvania

When Penn announced the creation of his new colony, Quakers flocked to English ports in numbers exceeded only by the great Puritan migration to New England fifty years earlier. Between 1682 and 1685, nearly eight thousand immigrants came to Pennsylvania, most of them Quakers from England, Ireland, and Wales. They represented a cross section of the artisans, farmers, and laborers who predominated among English Quakers. But they also included poor men and women whose way to Pennsylvania was paid by their Quaker meetings in England. In addition, Quaker missionaries encouraged immigrants from Europe, and many came, giving Pennsylvania greater ethnic diversity than any English colony other than New York. In 1685, Penn wrote that the settlers were "a collection of Divers Nations in Europe: as, French, Dutch, Germans, Swedes, Danes, Finns, Scotch, French and English, and of the last equal to all the rest."

Despite its toleration and diversity, Pennsylvania was as much a Quaker colony as New England was a stronghold of Puritanism.

Penn was determined to live in peace with the Indians who inhabited the region he had been granted. Penn's Indian policy expressed his Quaker ideals and contrasted sharply with the hostile policies of the other English colonies. On the eve of colonization, he explained to the chief of the Lenni Lenape (or Delaware) Indians that "God has written his law in our hearts, by which we are taught and commanded to love and help and do good to one another, and not to do harm and mischief one unto another . . . [and] this great God has been pleased to make me concerned in your parts of the world, and the king of the country where I live has given unto me a great province therein, but I desire to enjoy it with your love and consent." Penn instructed his agents to obtain the Indians' consent by purchasing their land, respecting their claims, and dealing with them fairly. The Delawares readily cooperated with Penn, partly because they welcomed English allies against their own traditional enemies, the much stronger Iroquois confederation.

Penn declared that the "First Fundamental of the government of my country" was that every settler would "enjoy the free possession of his or her

faith and exercise of worship towards God." Accordingly, Pennsylvania tolerated Protestant sects of all kinds as well as Roman Catholics. Likewise, the government did not compel settlers to attend religious services or to pay taxes to maintain a state-supported church. Religious liberty was not absolute, however. It extended only to Christians "who confess and acknowledge the one almighty and eternal God to be the creator, upholder, and ruler of the world." All voters and officeholders had to be Christians.

MAKING FUN OF LAND SPECULATORS
This playing card satirizes greedy "Saints" in England who "for little" money buy "Great Tracts of Land" from the Pennsylvania Company without knowing or caring "where they lye." Don't worry, the card gibes at the gullible men lining up to purchase land from the representatives of the Pennsylvania Company, you can trust "your Quaking Friends, they're Men of Light." —The card illustrates the skepticism common in England about colonial promoters' tantalizing schemes of quick and easy wealth. Bodleian Library, Oxford.

Despite its toleration and diversity, Pennsylvania was as much a Quaker colony as New England was a stronghold of Puritanism. "Government seems to me a part of religion itself," Penn wrote, "for there is no power but of God. The powers that be, are ordained of God: whosoever therefore resists the power [of government], resists the ordinance of God." Penn believed that government had two basic purposes: "to terrify evildoers . . . [and] to cherish those that do well." He had no hesitation about using civil government to enforce religious morality. One of the colony's first laws provided that "all such offenses against God, as swearing, cursing, lying, profane talking, drunkenness, drinking of healths, obscene words, incest, sodomy, rapes, whoredom, fornication, and other uncleanness . . . all prizes, stage plays, cards, dice, May games, gamesters, masques, revels, bull-baitings, cock-fightings, bear-baitings, and the like, which excite the people to rudeness, cruelty, looseness, and irreligion, shall be . . . discouraged and severely punished." The ethnic and religious diversity of Pennsylvania prevented the strict enforcement of these prohibitions. But these Quaker expectations of godly order and sobriety nonetheless set the tone of Pennsylvania society.

Penn's Quaker principles shaped not only the colony's government and society but also its capital city, Philadelphia. Penn carefully planned the orderly grid of streets on the peninsula at the confluence of the Schuylkill and Delaware Rivers. Philadelphia soon rivaled New York—though not yet Boston—as a center of commerce. By the end of the seventeenth century, the city's five thousand inhabitants participated in a thriving trade exporting food products, especially flour, to the West Indies and importing textiles and manufactured goods. Quaker habits of industry and sobriety contributed to the prosperity of numerous merchants and tradesmen. In less than two decades, Philadelphia had become one of the most important cities in British North America.

Penn thought a great deal about how to structure the colony's government. As proprietor he had extensive power, subject only to review by the king. But he did not want a proprietary government in which "the will of one man may . . . hinder the good of an whole country." Penn proposed instead to appoint a governor who would maintain the proprietor's power to veto any laws passed by the colonial council. The members of the council were elected by property owners who possessed at least one hundred acres of land or who paid taxes. (In other colonies, the council was appointed by the governor.) The council had the power to originate laws and administer all the affairs of government. An elected assembly served as a check on the council; its members had the authority to reject or approve laws framed by the council, but otherwise it had little influence.

Penn stressed that the exact form of government mattered less than the men who served in it. "Governments, like clocks, go from the motion men give them; . . . governments rather depend upon men than men upon governments. Let men be good, and the government can't be bad. . . . But if men be bad, let the government be never so good; they will endeavor to warp and spoil it to their turn." Penn himself stayed in Pennsylvania only from 1682 to 1684 before he returned to England to defend Quakers from persecution and to lobby on behalf of his colony. But in Penn's eyes, "good men" staffed Pennsylvania's government. Despite the colony's diversity, Quakers dominated elective and appointive offices. Quakers, of course, differed among themselves. Members of the assembly struggled to win the right to debate and amend laws, especially tax laws. They finally won the battle in 1701 when a new Charter of Privileges gave the proprietor the power to appoint the council and in turn stripped the council of all its former powers and gave them to the assembly, which became the only unicameral legislature in all the British colonies.

The Colonies and the British Empire

The creation of proprietary colonies permitted the king to reward his friends with faraway lands to which he had tenuous claims and over which he exercised almost no real control. From the king's point of view, the proprietary grants were, in a sense, cheap gifts. As the colonies grew, however, the gifts became more valuable. During the last third of the seventeenth century, the crown moved, at first slowly, to exert its own proprietorship over all the English colonies. After the restoration of the monarchy in 1660, the king took initiatives to channel colonial trade through English hands and to consolidate royal authority over colonial governments. These initiatives defined the basic relationship between the colonies and England that endured until the American Revolution.

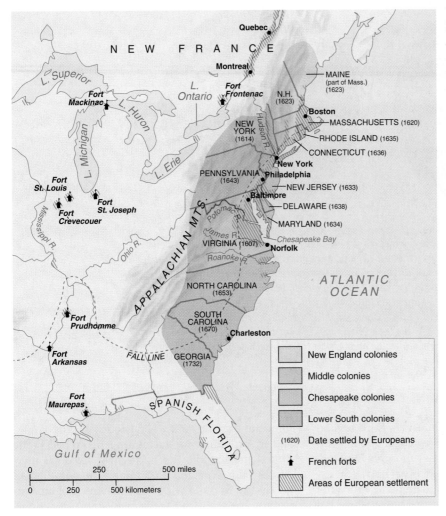

MAP 4.3
American Colonies at the End of the Seventeenth Century
By the end of the seventeenth century, settlers inhabited a narrow band of land that stretched more or less continuously from Boston to Norfolk, with pockets of settlement farther south. The colonies' claims to enormous tracts of land to the west were contested by Native Americans as well as the ambitions of France and Spain.

Royal Regulation of Colonial Trade

English economic policies toward the colonies were designed to yield customs revenues for the monarchy and profitable business for English merchants and shippers. In addition, the policies were intended to divert the colonies' trade from England's enemies, the Dutch and the French.

The Navigation Acts of 1650, 1651, and 1660 set forth two fundamental regulations governing colonial trade. First, all colonial goods imported into England had to be transported in English ships; the same held true for ships involved in the coastal trade from one colonial port to another. The law defined an English ship as one in which the captain and three-fourths of the crew were English. Since the Navigation Acts defined colonists as English, ships owned by colonial merchants and crewed by colonial sailors could continue to carry colonial products to England. No longer, however, could colonists legally ship their goods to England aboard Dutch, French, or Spanish ships.

Second, the Navigation Acts "enumerated" (listed) specific colonial products that could be shipped only to England or to other English colonies. Initially, tobacco was the only export of the British North American colonies among the enumerated products; most, like sugar, were exports of the West Indies. While enumeration prevented Chesapeake planters from shipping their tobacco directly to the European continent, it did not interfere with the commerce of New England and the middle colonies. Their principal exports—fish, lumber, and flour—were not enumerated and could still be shipped to their most important market in the West Indies.

PINE TREE SHILLING

Currency was in short supply in the colonies. Since England prohibited the export of its coins, the precious currency circulating in the North American colonies tended to be Spanish, Dutch, French, or Portuguese. In violation of English rules that forbade colonies from issuing their own currency, John Hull, a wealthy Boston merchant and shipowner, began to mint coins in 1652. Shown here is one of his pine tree shillings, boldly announcing its Massachusetts origins. A shilling was worth twelve pennies; twenty shillings equaled a pound sterling. Despite Hull's attempt to ease the currency shortage, the legal tender most colonists used consisted of such commonly available items as bushels of corn or wheat, skins of beaver or deer, or—following the Native American practice—wampum.

Courtesy of the Museum of the American Numismatic Association.

The Staple Act of 1663 imposed a third regulation on colonial trade. It required all goods imported into the colonies to pass through England. Goods manufactured in France or Italy, for example, had to be shipped first to England, unloaded and taxed, and then reloaded in English ships before they could be sent to the colonies. The Staple Act gave English merchants a monopoly on exports to the colonies and, by raising the prices of non-English goods, gave English manufacturers a competitive edge in colonial markets.

After the restoration of the monarchy in 1660, the king took initiatives to channel colonial trade through English hands and to consolidate royal authority over colonial governments. These initiatives defined the basic relationship between the colonies and England that endured until the American Revolution.

Colonial merchants found ways to evade these regulations. The Plantations Duty Act of 1673 attempted to reduce the evasions by requiring cus-

toms duties to be paid when goods left the colonies and by providing for customs agents to collect the duties and enforce the trade laws. Colonial merchants still managed to smuggle in non-English goods and to trade with other nations. Colonial juries routinely winked at the merchants' infractions. The Navigation Act of 1696 responded to such "Frauds and . . . Abuses" by creating seven vice-admiralty courts staffed by royal appointees to try violators of the trade laws. The crown also expanded the customs service, gave agents greater power to search ships and warehouses for illegal goods, and set up the Board of Trade to rigorously supervise and administer colonial commerce.

By the end of the seventeenth century, colonial commerce flowed in channels defined by the regulations of the British Empire. The regulations raised the price colonists paid for imports and subjected merchants and shippers to royal supervision. They also benefited colonists engaged in commerce by giving them access to markets throughout the British Empire on the same terms as residents of England. In addition, colonial commerce came under the protective umbrella of the British navy, the world's strongest. Commercial regulations also poured cash into the British treasury and into the pockets of British merchants. By 1700, colonial goods (including those from the West Indies) accounted for one-fifth of all British imports and for two-thirds of all goods reexported from England to the continent. In turn, the colonies absorbed more than one-tenth of British exports. The commercial regulations gave economic meaning to England's proprietorship of American colonies.

Consolidation of Royal Authority

The monarchy also took steps to exercise greater control over colonial governments. Virginia had been a royal colony since 1624; Maryland, South Carolina, and the middle colonies were proprietary colonies with close ties to the crown. The New England colonies possessed royal charters, but they had developed their own distinctively Puritan governments. Charles II, whose father, Charles I, had been executed by Puritans in England, took a particular interest in harnessing the New England colonies more firmly to the British Empire. The occasion was a royal investigation following a series of battles between colonists and Indians known as King Philip's War.

By the end of the seventeenth century, colonial commerce flowed in channels defined by the regulations of the British Empire.

In 1675, warfare between Indians and colonists erupted in the Chesapeake and in New England. Almost a half-century earlier, in 1637, Massachusetts settlers had massacred hundreds of Pequot Indians, nearly exterminating the tribe and establishing more or less peaceful relations with the more potent Wampanoags. During the subsequent decades, New Englanders encroached steadily on Indian lands and, in 1675, the Wampanoags struck back with attacks on settlements in western Massachusetts. Metacomet—whom the colonists called King Philip—was the chief of the Wampanoags and the son of Massassoit, who had befriended William Bradford and his original band of Pilgrims. Metacomet probably neither planned the attacks nor masterminded a conspiracy with the Nipmucks and the Narragansetts, as the colonists feared. But when militias from Massachusetts and other New England colonies counterattacked all three tribes, a deadly sequence of battles killed over a thousand colonists and thousands more Indians. The Indians

utterly destroyed thirteen English settlements and partially burned another half-dozen. By the spring of 1676, Indian warriors ranged freely within seventeen miles of Boston. The colonists finally forced the Indians to stop fighting, principally with a scorched-earth policy of burning their food supplies. The war left the New England colonists with an enduring hatred of Indians, a large war debt, and a devastated frontier. And in 1676, Edward Randolph, an agent of the king, arrived to investigate whether New England abided by English laws.

Not surprisingly, Randolph found all sorts of deviations from English rules, which he duly reported to the king along with the suggestion that troops be used "to reduce Massachusetts to obedience." The English government decided instead to govern New England more directly. Randolph went back to New England as a customs agent, where he met only slightly less hostility than a Narragansett

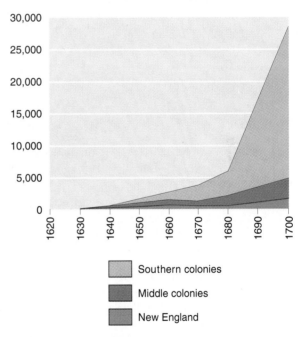

FIGURE **4.2**
African American Population in the Seventeenth Century
The African American population in the colonies grew dramatically after about 1680, especially in the southern colonies where the overwhelming majority of blacks resided after about 1660. Since slavery was legal throughout the colonies, why did the black population grow more slowly in New England and the middle colonies than it did in the South?

INDIANS VISIT JESUIT MISSION
While English colonies developed along the Atlantic coast, French explorers and missionaries established outposts on the St. Lawrence River and at strategic locations near the Great Lakes. This seventeenth-century drawing by a Jesuit priest shows three Indians trekking across the snow toward the mission at Sault St. Louis, not far from Montreal. Try to identify features of both Native American and European cultures displayed in the drawing.
Archives Departmentales de la Gironde, France.

Indian. In 1684, an English court revoked the Massachusetts charter, the foundation of the distinctive government built by the Puritan founders. Two years later, royal officials incorporated Massachusetts and the other colonies north of Maryland into the Dominion of New England.

To govern the dominion, the English sent Sir Edmund Andros to Boston. Some New England merchants cooperated with Andros, but most colonists were offended by his flagrant disregard of such Puritan traditions as keeping the Sabbath—one Sunday he held a fireworks show in honor of the king. Worst of all, the Dominion of New England invalidated all land titles held under the old

Massachusetts charter. Every landowner in New England faced the horrifying prospect of losing his or her land.

Events in England, however, permitted Massachusetts colonists to overthrow Andros and retain title to their property. When Charles II died in 1685, he was succeeded by his brother James II, a zealous Catholic. James's aggressive campaign to appoint Catholics to government posts engendered such unrest that in 1688 a group of Protestant noblemen invited the Dutch ruler William of Orange—who was married to James's daughter Mary, a Protestant—to claim the English throne. When William landed in England at the head of a large army, James fled to France and William became King William III in the bloodless Glorious Revolution. Rumors of the revolution raced across the Atlantic and emboldened colonial uprisings in Massachusetts, New York, and Maryland.

In Boston, the colonists seized Andros, Randolph, and other English officials and tossed them in jail. The rebels reestablished the government that had existed under the old Massachusetts charter, destroying the Dominion of New England. New Yorkers followed the Massachusetts example. Under the leadership of Jacob Leisler, rebels seized the royal governor and ruled the colony for more than a year. When King William's new governor arrived in 1691, Leisler relinquished control of the government without violence, but the governor executed him and one of his subordinates for treason. In Maryland, the Protestant Association, led by John Coode, overthrew the colony's pro-Catholic government in 1689, fearing it would not recognize the new Protestant king. Coode's men ruled until the new royal governor arrived in 1692 and ended both Coode's rebellion and Lord Baltimore's proprietary government.

The events that followed the Glorious Revolution proved that the colonists were capable of taking power into their own hands and that they were incapable of holding it. The trend toward consolidation of royal authority over the colonies continued during the 1690s, but the colonial governors accommodated somewhat more to the needs and sensitivities of local colonial elites. The colonists, in turn, adjusted to royal control, especially since royal protection came with it.

During the 1690s, the northern colonists valued English protection against threats from the French. Since the 1660s, French explorers and Jesuit priests had established outposts along the Great Lakes and explored the vast watershed of the Mississippi River. The French succeeded in establishing a lucrative and far-flung fur trade, draining pelts away from the mighty Iroquois, the most powerful Indians in eastern North America. In 1689, Andros encouraged the Iroquois to mount an offensive against French settlements along the Canadian border. While the colonies were distracted by the Glorious Revolution, French forces counterattacked against villages in New England and New York. Known as King William's War, the conflict with the French was a colonial outgrowth of William's war against France in Europe. The war dragged on until 1697 and ended inconclusively in both Europe and the colonies. But it made clear to many colonists that along with English royal government came a welcome measure of military security.

In Massachusetts, John Winthrop's city on a hill became another royal colony in 1691, when a new charter was issued. Under the charter, the governor was appointed by the king rather than elected by the colonists' representatives. The governor appointed judges and militia officers, but not members of the council or General Court, as in other royal colonies. Instead, colonists were permitted to elect their own representatives to the General Court, which advised the governor and served as an upper house of the legislature. But perhaps the most unsettling change was the new qualification for voting. Possession of property worth £40 sterling replaced church membership as a prerequisite for voting in colony-wide elections. Wealth replaced God's grace as the defining characteristic of Massachusetts citizenship.

Conclusion: The Seventeenth-Century Legacy of English North America

By the end of the seventeenth century, the diverse English colonies in North America had developed along lines quite different from the example New Spain had set in 1600. In the North American colonies, English immigrants and their descendants predominated, but many other settlers came from Europe, and a growing number of Africans arrived in bondage. Economically, the English colonies thrived on agriculture and trade, exporting crops of the soil and sea rather than silver and gold. Protestantism prevailed in the English colonies, relaxed in some colonies and militant in others, but religious diversity and religious indifference were growing and, in some colonies, tolerated. Politics and government differed from colony to colony, but everywhere local settlers—at least those who were free, white, adult men—had an extraordinary degree of political influence. The new world that Columbus could not imagine, that Powhatan only glimpsed, had been firmly established by 1700. During the next half-century in North America, that world would undergo surprising new developments that built upon the indelible legacies of the seventeenth-century colonies.

CHRONOLOGY

1534 Henry VIII breaks with Roman Catholic Church and initiates English Reformation.

1609 Henry Hudson searches for Northwest Passage for Dutch East India Company.

1620 English Puritans found Plymouth colony.

1626 Peter Minuit purchases Manhattan Island for Dutch West India Company and founds New Amsterdam.

1629 Massachusetts Bay Company receives royal charter for colony.

1630 John Winthrop leads Puritan settlers to Massachusetts Bay.

1635 Roger Williams, banished from Massachusetts, establishes Rhode Island colony.

1636 Thomas Hooker leaves Massachusetts and helps found Connecticut colony.
Harvard College founded.

1637 Anne Hutchinson accused of Antinomianism, excommunicated from Boston church.

1642 Civil war inflames England, pitting Puritans against royalists.

1649 English Puritans win civil war and execute King Charles I.

1656 Quakers arrive in Massachusetts, are persecuted.

1660 Monarchy restored in England; Charles II becomes king.
Navigation Act requires colonial goods to be shipped in English vessels through English ports.

1662 Many Puritan congregations adopt Halfway Covenant.

1663 Staple Act requires all colonial imports to come from England.

1664 English seize New Netherland colony from Dutch, rename it New York.
Duke of York subdivides his colony, creating new colony of New Jersey.

1673 Plantations Duty Act attempts to reduce smuggling and evasion of Navigation Acts.

1675 Indians and colonists clash in King Philip's War.

1681 King Charles II grants William Penn charter for colony of Pennsylvania.

1686 Royal officials create Dominion of New England.

1688 James II overthrown by Glorious Revolution; William III becomes king.

1691 Massachusetts becomes royal colony.

1692 Witch trials flourish at Salem.

1696 Navigation Act creates vice-admiralty courts and Board of Trade to oversee colonial commerce.

BIBLIOGRAPHY

This bibliography excludes pertinent sources listed in chapters 2 and 3. Please consult the bibliographies of those chapters for additional suggested readings.

GENERAL WORKS

Patricia U. Bonomi, *Under the Cope of Heaven: Religion, Society, and Politics in Colonial America* (1986).

Jon Butler, *Awash in a Sea of Faith: Christianizing the American People* (1990).

Lawrence A. Cremin, *American Education: The Colonial Experience, 1607–1783* (1970).

David Hackett Fischer, *Albion's Seed: Four British Folkways in America* (1989).

Stephen Foster, *The Long Argument: English Puritanism and the Shaping of New England Culture, 1570–1700* (1991).

Jack P. Greene, *Pursuits of Happiness: The Social Development of Early Modern British Colonies and the Formation of American Culture* (1988).

David D. Hall, *Worlds of Wonder, Days of Judgment: Popular Religious Belief in Early New England* (1989).

Alan Heimert and Andrew Delbanco, eds., *The Puritans in America: A Narrative Anthology* (1985).

Peter Charles Hoffer, *Law and People in Colonial America* (1992).

Stephen Innes, *Creating the Commonwealth: The Economic Culture of Puritan New England* (1995).

David S. Lovejoy, *Religious Enthusiasm in the New World: Heresy to Revolution* (1985).

Perry Miller, *The New England Mind: The Seventeenth Century* (1939).

Perry Miller, *The New England Mind: From Colony to Province* (1953).

Helena Wall, *Fierce Communalism: Family and Community in the American Colonies in the Seventeenth Century* (1990).

ENGLISH BACKGROUND

Kenneth R. Andrews, Nicholas P. Canny, and Paul E. H. Hair, eds., *The Westward Enterprise: English Activities in Ireland, the Atlantic, and America, 1480–1650* (1979).

Joyce Appleby, *Economic Thought and Ideology in Seventeenth-Century England* (1978).

Patrick Collinson, *The Religion of Protestants: The Church in English Society, 1559–1625* (1982).

Patrick Collinson, *The Birthpangs of Protestant England: Religious and Cultural Change in the Sixteenth and Seventeenth Centuries* (1988).

Jan de Vries, *The Economy of Europe in an Age of Crisis, 1600–1750* (1978).

Dewey D. Wallace Jr., *Puritans and Predistination: Grace in English Protestant Theology, 1525–1695* (1982).

Michael Walzer, *The Revolution of the Saints: A Study in the Origins of Radical Politics* (1965).

Peter O. G. White, *Predestination, Policy, and Polemic: Conflict and Consensus in the English Church from the Reformation to the Civil War* (1992).

Keith Wrightson, *English Society, 1580–1680* (1982).

INDIANS

James Axtell, *The Indian Peoples of Eastern America: A Documentary History of the Sexes* (1980).

Colin G. Calloway, *The Western Abenaki of Vermont, 1600–1800: War, Migration, and the Survival of an Indian People* (1990).

William Cronon, *Changes in the Land: Indians, Colonists, and the Ecology of New England* (1983).

Matthew Dennis, *Cultivating a Landscape of Peace: Iroquois-European Encounters in Seventeenth-Century America* (1993).

Carol Devens, *Countering Colonization: Native American Women and Great Lakes Missions, 1630–1900* (1992).

Francis Jennings, *The Ambiguous Iroquois Empire: The Covenant Chain Confederation of Indian Tribes with English Colonies from Its Beginnings to the Lancaster Treaty of 1744* (1983).

Yasughide Kawashima, *Puritan Justice and the Indian: White Man's Law in Massachusetts, 1630–1763* (1986).

James W. Mavor, *Manitou: The Sacred Landscape of New England's Native Civilization* (1989).

H. C. Porter, *The Inconstant Savage: England and the North American Indian, 1500–1660* (1979).

Daniel K. Richter, *The Ordeal of the Longhouse: The Peoples of the Iroquois League in the Era of European Colonization* (1992).

Daniel K. Richter and James H. Merrell, *Beyond the Covenant Chain: The Iroquois and Their Neighbors in Indian North America, 1600–1800* (1987).

Neal Salisbury, *Manitou and Providence: Indians, Europeans, and the Making of New England, 1500–1643* (1982).

Alden T. Vaughan, *New England Frontier: Puritans and Indians, 1620–1675* (3rd ed., 1995).

Richard White, *The Middle Ground: Indians, Empires, and Republics in the Great Lakes Region, 1650–1815* (1991).

NEW ENGLAND

David Grayson Allen, *In English Ways: The Movement of Societies and the Transferal of English Local Law and Custom to Massachusetts Bay in the Seventeenth Century* (1981).

Virginia Dejohn Anderson, *New England's Generation: The Great Migration and the Formation of Society and Culture in the Seventeenth Century* (1991).

Bernard Bailyn, *The New England Merchants in the Seventeenth Century* (1955).

Paul Boyer and Stephen Nissenbaum, *Salem Possessed: The Social Origins of Witchcraft* (1974).

Paul Boyer and Stephen Nissenbaum, eds., *Salem Village Witchcraft: A Documentary Record of Local Conflict in Colonial New England* (1972).

Theodore Dwight Bozeman, *To Live Ancient Lives: The Primitivist Dimension in Puritanism* (1988).

T. H. Breen, *Puritans and Adventurers: Change and Persistence in Early America* (1980).

Francis J. Bremer, *Shaping New Englands: Puritan Clergymen in Seventeenth-Century England and New England* (1994).

Richard Bushman, *From Puritan to Yankee: Character and the Social Order in Connecticut, 1690–1765* (1967).

Jonathan M. Chu, *Neighbors, Friends, or Madmen: The Puritan Adjustment to Quakerism in Seventeenth-Century Massachusetts Bay* (1985).

Charles Lloyd Cohen, *God's Caress: The Psychology of Puritan Religious Experience* (1986).

David Cressy, *Coming Over: Migration and Communication between England and New England in the Seventeenth Century* (1987).

Bruce C. Daniels, *The Connecticut Town: Growth and Development, 1635–1790* (1979).

Bruce Colin Daniels, *Puritans at Play: Leisure and Recreation in Colonial New England* (1995).

Andrew Delbanco, *The Puritan Ordeal* (1989).

John Demos, *A Little Commonwealth: Family Life in Plymouth Colony* (1970).

John Putnam Demos, *Entertaining Satan: Witchcraft and the Culture of Early New England* (1982).

Stephen Foster, *Their Solitary Way: The Puritan Social Ethic in the First Century of Settlement in New England* (1971).

Gordon E. Geddes, *Welcome Joy: Death in Puritan New England* (1981).

Richard P. Gildrie, *The Profane, the Civil, and the Godly: The Reformation of Manners in Orthodox New England, 1679–1749* (1994).

Richard Godbeer, *The Devil's Dominion: Magic and Religion in Early New England* (1992).

Charles S. Grant, *Democracy in the Connecticut Frontier Town of Kent* (1961).

Philip J. Greven Jr., *Four Generations: Population, Land, and Family in Colonial Andover, Massachusetts* (1970).

Philip Gura, *A Glimpse of Sion's Glory: Puritan Radicalism in Seventeenth-Century New England, 1620–1660* (1984).

David D. Hall, ed., *The Antinomian Controversy, 1636–1638* (1968).

David D. Hall, ed., *Witch-Hunting in Seventeenth-Century New England: A Documentary History, 1638–1692* (1991).

David D. Hall and David Grayson Allen, eds., *Seventeenth-Century New England* (1984).

Michael G. Hall, *The Last American Puritan: The Life of Increase Mather, 1639–1723* (1988).

Stephen Innes, *Labor in a New Land: Economy and Society in Seventeenth-Century Springfield* (1983).

Sydney V. James, *Colonial Rhode Island: A History* (1975).

Carol F. Karlsen, *The Devil in the Shape of a Woman: Witchcraft in Colonial New England* (1987).

Karen Ordahl Kupperman, *Providence Island, 1630–1641: The Other Puritan Colony* (1993).

Benjamin Labaree, *Colonial Massachusetts* (1979).

George D. Langdon, *Pilgrim Colony: A History of New Plymouth, 1620–1691* (1966).

Kenneth A. Lockridge, *A New England Town: The First Hundred Years, Dedham, Massachusetts, 1636–1736* (1970).

Kenneth A. Lockridge, *Literacy in Colonial New England: An Enquiry into the Social Context of Literacy in the Early Modern West* (1974).

Jackson Turner Main, *Society and Economy in Colonial Connecticut* (1985).

Bruce H. Mann, *Neighbors and Strangers: Law and Community in Early Connecticut* (1987).

Carolyn Merchant, *Ecological Revolutions: Nature, Gender, and Science in New England* (1989).

Perry Miller, *Errand into the Wilderness* (1956).

Perry Miller and Thomas H. Johnson, eds., *The Puritans,* 2 vols. (1963).

Edmund S. Morgan, *The Puritan Dilemma: The Story of John Winthrop* (1958).

Edmund S. Morgan, *Visible Saints: The History of a Puritan Idea* (1963).

Edmund S. Morgan, *Roger Williams: The Church and the State* (1967).

Edmund S. Morgan, ed., *The Diary of Michael Wigglesworth, 1653–1657: The Conscience of a Puritan* (1946).

James G. Mosely, *John Winthrop's World: History as a Story, the Story as History* (1992).

Carla Gardina Pestana, *Quakers and Baptists in Colonial Massachusetts* (1991).

Amanda Porterfield, *Female Piety in Puritan New England: The Emergence of Religious Humanism* (1992).

Sumner C. Powell, *Puritan Village: The Formation of a New England Town* (1963).

Michael J. Puglisi, *Puritans Besieged: The Legacies of King Philip's War in the Massachusetts Bay Colony* (1991).

Howard S. Russell, *A Long, Deep Furrow: Three Centuries of Farming in New England* (1976).

Darrett B. Rutman, *Winthrop's Boston: Portrait of a Puritan Town, 1630–1649* (1965).

Darrett B. Rutman, *The Husbandmen of Plymouth: Farms and Villages in the Old Colony, 1620–1692* (1967).

Timothy J. Sehr, *Colony and Commonwealth: Massachusetts Bay, 1649–1660* (1989).

Kenneth Silverman, *The Life and Times of Cotton Mather* (1984).

Richard C. Simmons, *Studies in the Massachusetts Franchise, 1631–1691* (1989).

David E. Stannard, *The Puritan Way of Death: A Study in Religion, Culture, and Social Change* (1977).

William K. B. Stoever, *"A Faire and Easie Way to Heaven": Covenant Theology and Antinomianism in Early Massachusetts* (1978).

Harry S. Stout, *The New England Soul: Preaching and Religious Culture in Colonial New England* (1986).

Robert J. Taylor, *Colonial Connecticut: A History* (1979).

Laurel Thatcher Ulrich, *Good Wives: Image and Reality in the Lives of Women in Northern New England, 1650–1750* (1982).

Robert E. Wall Jr., *Massachusetts Bay: The Crucial Decade, 1640–1650* (1972).

Avihu Zakai, *Exile and Kingdom: History and Apocalypse in the Puritan Migration to America* (1992).

MIDDLE COLONIES

Thomas J. Archdeacon, *New York City, 1664–1710: Conquest and Change* (1976).

Patricia U. Bonomi, *A Factious People: Politics and Society in Colonial New York* (1971).

Thomas J. Condon, *New York Beginnings: The Commercial Origins of New Netherland* (1968).

Richard S. Dunn and Mary Maples Dunn, eds., *The World of William Penn* (1986).

Joseph E. Illick, *Colonial Pennsylvania: A History* (1976).

Michael G. Kammen, *Colonial New York: A History* (1975).

Sung Bok Kim, *Landlord and Tenant in Colonial New York: Manorial Society, 1664–1775* (1978).

Donna Merwick, *Possessing Albany, 1630–1710: The Dutch and English Experiences* (1990).

David E. Narrett, *Inheritance and Family Life in Colonial New York City* (1992).

Gary B. Nash, *Quakers and Politics: Pennsylvania, 1681–1726* (1968).

Thomas Eliot Norton, *The Fur Trade in Colonial New York, 1686–1776* (1974).

John E. Pomfret, *Colonial New Jersey: A History* (1973).

Oliver A. Rink, *Holland on the Hudson: An Economic and Social History of Dutch New York* (1986).

Robert C. Ritchie, *The Duke's Province: A Study of New York Politics and Society, 1664–1691* (1977).

Jean R. Soderlund, ed., *William Penn and the Founding of Pennsylvania, 1680–1684: A Documentary History* (1983).

Allen Tully, *Forming American Politics: Ideals, Interests, and Institutions in Colonial New York and Pennsylvania* (1994).

Stephanie Grauman Wolf, *Urban Village: Population, Community, and Family Structure in Germantown, Pennsylvania, 1683–1800* (1976).

**"DUMMY BOARD" OF PHYLLIS,
A NEW ENGLAND SLAVE**

This life-size portrait of a slave woman named Phyllis, a mulatto who worked as a domestic servant for her owner, Elizabeth Hunt Wendell, was painted sometime before 1753. Known as a "dummy board," the painted wood was evidently propped against a wall or placed in a doorway. Its function is not known. Perhaps Wendell displayed the dummy board to show visitors that she possessed a servant woman. Maybe Phyllis herself moved the board from place to place in Wendell's house to indicate where she was working at the time. Or possibly the portrait was painted in recognition of some unknown special relationship between Phyllis and Wendell. Phyllis is shown as a demure, well-groomed woman whose dress and demeanor suggest that she was capable, orderly, and efficient. Although tens of thousands of slaves were brought to the British North American colonies during the eighteenth century, it does not appear that Phyllis was one of them. Instead, she was probably born in the colonies of mixed white and black parentage. Like thousands of other slave women who labored in the homes of prosperous white families, Phyllis illustrates the integration of the mundane tasks of housekeeping with the shifting currents of transatlantic commerce.

Courtesy of the Society for the Preservation of New England Antiquities/photo by David Bohl.

COLONIAL AMERICA IN THE EIGHTEENTH CENTURY

5

1701–1760

ARLY ON A SUNDAY MORNING IN OCTOBER 1723, young Benjamin Franklin stepped from a wharf along the Delaware River onto the streets of Philadelphia. As he wrote later in his autobiography, "I was dirty from my Journey; my Pockets were stuff'd out with Shirts and Stockings; I knew no Soul, nor where to look for Lodging. I was fatigu'd with Travelling, Rowing and Want of Rest. I was very hungry."

Born in 1706, Benjamin Franklin grew up in Boston, where his father, Josiah—a Puritan—had emigrated from England in 1683. Josiah Franklin worked as a tallow chandler in Boston, making soap and candles for the city's families. The father of seventeen children, he provided a modest but stable living for his large family. He made certain each of his sons served an apprenticeship to learn a trade.

When Benjamin was ten years old, Josiah put him to work in his own shop, where, Benjamin recalled, "I was employed in cutting Wick for Candles, filling the Dipping Mold, and the Molds for cast Candles, attending the Shop, going of Errands, &c." Benjamin was bored stiff. He stole time to indulge his passion for reading, even on Sunday. He admitted "evading as much as I could the common Attendance on publick Worship," for which his father scolded him. His "Bookish Inclination . . . determin'd my Father to make me a Printer." After some hesitation, the twelve-year-old Benjamin signed an indenture to serve until he was twenty-one as an apprentice to his brother James.

James Franklin, nine years older than Benjamin, had recently returned to Boston from England, where he had learned the printer's trade. He opened a shop in the city, where his young apprentice learned how to set type, compose a page, and operate the press. Benjamin also had access to the latest books and pamphlets, and he read everything he could get his hands on.

In 1721, James inaugurated the *New England Courant*, only the fourth newspaper to be published in the colonies. The articles in the *Courant*, as one of Franklin's friends said, were written "in a very easy and familiar manner, so that the meanest ploughman, the very meanest of God's people may understand them." Before long, the sixteen-year-old printer's apprentice secretly wrote fourteen essays under the pseudonym of a New England widow, Silence Dogood—a sly reference to Puritan minister Cotton Mather's work *Essays to Do Good*—and slipped them under the door of the print shop during the night.

Benjamin's responsibilities grew quickly after James aroused the ire of the government with an article that denounced men who "*dissemble* and *lie, snuffle* and

PHILADELPHIA WHARF

This early-nineteenth-century drawing of the Arch Street wharf in Philadelphia approximates the world Benjamin Franklin entered when he stepped ashore in 1723. The wharf was a center of purposeful movement, of industrious activity; almost everyone depicted appears to be working or making profitable use of their leisure (by fishing, for example). The pulse of Atlantic commerce propels casks of products from the deck of the small local sailboat (right) toward the hold of large oceangoing ships (center) bound for England and Europe. The small rowboat carrying four people (just to the right of the large ships) is probably similar to the boat Franklin rowed to the city. Coordinating the complicated comings and goings of people and goods that moved through the wharf rewarded individuals who combined intelligence, energy, and discipline with efficiency, reliability, and trustworthiness—traits Franklin and other eighteenth-century colonists sought to cultivate.

Rare Book Department, The Free Library of Philadelphia.

---

whiffle . . . [and who] will overreach and defraud all who deal with them," proclaiming that of all such knaves, "the *religious knave* is the worst." The Massachusetts government found public ridicule of religion intolerable and ordered James to submit all future issues of the *Courant* for censorship. Rather than comply, James evaded the order by making his seventeen-year-old brother the new publisher of the *Courant,* but requiring him to continue to serve out his apprenticeship.

Benjamin published the paper for several months, but he chafed under his brother's supervision. "Tho' a Brother, he [James] considered himself as my Master, and me as his Apprentice," Benjamin remembered; "and [he] accordingly expected the same Services from me as he would from another; while I thought he demean'd me too much. . . . My Brother was passionate and had often beaten me, which I took extreamly amiss." Benjamin resolved "to assert my Freedom." The young printer-author-publisher "inclin'd to leave Boston" and bought passage aboard a ship to New York, unbeknown to his brother or his father.

After three days at sea, he arrived in New York, nearly three hundred miles from anyone he knew. When he could not find work, he sailed to the New

Jersey shore and then walked fifty miles west to a town on the Delaware River upstream from Philadelphia. While strolling along the riverbank in the evening, he talked his way aboard a small boat heading down the river toward Philadelphia. After rowing half the night, Franklin and the other exhausted travelers floated up to a wharf about eight o'clock the next morning.

Franklin went straight to a bakery, ordered three cents worth of bread, and was surprised to be given "three great Puffy Rolls." He began to eat one and, "having no Room in my Pockets," which were stuffed with shirts and socks, he "walk'd off, with a Roll under each Arm." He went back to the wharf to wash down the bread with "a Draught of the River Water. . . . Thus refresh'd I walk'd again up the Street, which by this time had many clean dress'd People in it who were all walking the same Way; I join'd them, and thereby was led to the great Meeting House of the Quakers. . . . I sat down among them, and . . . I fell fast asleep, and continu'd so till the Meeting broke up."

Franklin's account of his early life in Boston and his arrival in Philadelphia is probably the most well known portrait of life in eighteenth-century colonial America. It illustrates the everyday experiences that an obscure but extraordinary printer's apprentice shared with many others in the colonies: a large family; short schooling; long hours of labor as a subordinate to the authority of a superior, whether a parent, relative, or employer; and a restless quest for something better, for escape from the ties that bound, for freedom. Franklin's account hints at other, less tangible trends: an ambition to make something of oneself in this world rather than worry too much about the hereafter; an eagerness to subvert the domination of ministers and government officials by publishing dissenting opinions expressed in simple, clear language understandable by "the meanest ploughman"; a confidence that, with a valued skill and a few coins, a young man could make his way in the world, a confidence few young women could dare assert; and a slackening of religious fervor displayed in open dissent and in Franklin's snooze during the Quaker meeting.

The simple story of Franklin's first day in Philadelphia introduces some of the major changes under way in eighteenth-century America. Those changes affected all the colonies in British North America, but they did not erase the fundamental differences among New England, the middle colonies, and the southern colonies. Instead of becoming more alike, the three regions became more

sharply differentiated. While social and economic changes tended to underscore the diversity among the colonies, important cultural and political developments tugged in the opposite direction, creating common experiences, aspirations, and identities. In 1776, when *E Pluribus Unum* (Latin meaning "From Many, One") was adopted as the motto for the Great Seal of the United States, the *Pluribus* referred to the dominant legacy from the eighteenth-century colonies. But changes in eighteenth-century America that strengthened *Pluribus* also planted the seeds of *Unum*.

A Growing Population and Expanding Economy

The most important fact about eighteenth-century colonial America was its phenomenal population growth. In 1700, colonists numbered barely more than 250,000; by 1770, they tallied well over 2 million. The eightfold growth of the population of the British North American colonies between 1700 and 1770 was unequaled in the eighteenth century. In England, by comparison, the population grew only about 40 percent in the same period, from 5 million to over 7 million. An index of the emerging significance of colonial America is that in 1700 there were 19 people in England for every American colonist, whereas by 1770 there were only 3.

The dramatic growth of the colonial population signaled the maturation of a distinctive colonial society. That society was by no means uniform or homogeneous. It encompassed the regional diversity of climate and natural environment that extended inland along the Atlantic coast from Maine to Georgia. Colonists of different ethnic groups, races, and religions lived under thirteen different colonial governments, all of them under the umbrella of the British Empire, which encouraged immigration to the colonies.

In general, the growth and diversity of the eighteenth-century colonial population derived from two sources: immigration and natural increase (that is, growth through reproduction). Natural increase contributed about three-fourths of the population growth, immigration about one-fourth. Immigration did more than boost the colonial population. New settlers from the Old World poured into the colonies in such unprecedented numbers that they changed the face of the population. They shifted the ethnic and racial balance among the colonists, making them by 1770 less English and less white than ever before. During the entire seventeenth century, about 200,000 people arrived in the mainland British colonies; 80 percent of them came from England and another 5 percent from Africa, nearly all of the latter slaves. In contrast, from 1700 to the eve of the American Revolution in 1776, almost 800,000 newcomers streamed into the colonies. Fewer than 10 percent came from England; about 36 percent were Scots-Irish, mostly from northern Ireland; 33 percent came from Africa, again almost all of them slaves; nearly 15 percent came from the many German principalities (the nation of Germany did not exist until 1871); and almost 10 percent came from Scotland. This massive influx of new colonists profoundly altered the composition of the colonial population in the century between 1670 and 1770. In 1670, more than 9 out of 10 colonists were of English ancestry, and only 1 out of 25 was of African ancestry. By 1770, only about half the colonists were of English descent, while more than 20 percent descended from Africans. By 1770, the people of the colonies had a distinctive *colonial*—rather than English—profile.

The booming population of the colonies hints at a second major feature of eighteenth-century colonial society: an expanding economy. Today, societies with rapidly growing populations often suffer from poverty and overpopulation. They have more people than they can adequately feed; or, put another way, they have a high ratio of people to land. In the eighteenth-century colonies, very different conditions prevailed.

In 1700, after almost a century of settlement, nearly all the colonists lived within 50 miles of the Atlantic coast, on the edge of a vast wilderness peopled by native Indians and a few trappers and traders. The population was overwhelmingly rural. Only about 1 colonist in 20 lived in a town of 2,500 or more, a fraction that hardly changed during the eighteenth century. The wilderness so dominated the colonies that even in the 1750s sailors approaching the American mainland could begin to smell pine trees when they were 180 miles from shore. The almost limitless wilderness gave the colonies an extremely low ratio of people to land, which had far-reaching economic consequences.

For one thing, it meant that land was cheap. Of course, it was never so cheap that every colonist owned some. But it was cheap enough that every colonist who wanted to own land had a much better chance of doing so than in eighteenth-century

M A P 5.1

Europeans and Africans in the Eighteenth Century
This map illustrates regions where Africans and certain immigrant groups clustered. It is important to avoid misreading this map. Predominantly European regions, for example, also contained colonists from other places. Likewise, regions where African slaves resided in large numbers also included many whites, their masters among them. The map suggests the polyglot diversity of eighteenth-century colonial society.

England or continental Europe. Land in the colonies commonly sold for a fraction of its price in the Old World, often for only a shilling an acre, at a time when a carpenter could earn three shillings a day. Along the frontiers of settlement, newcomers who lacked the money to buy land often lived as squatters on unoccupied land, hoping it might somehow eventually become theirs. Legally or otherwise, land was so readily available that colonial governors had difficulty recruiting soldiers during the 1740s and 1750s, since the hungry, landless men from whom armies were recruited in Europe were hard to find in large numbers in the colonies.

Without labor, land was almost worthless for agriculture. The abundance of land in the colonies made labor precious, and the colonists always needed more. The colonists' insatiable labor demand was the fundamental economic environment that sustained the mushrooming population.

The unusually low ratio of people to land in the colonies—with all that meant about access to land and demand for labor—made it possible for the colonial population to grow rapidly without producing widespread poverty. Starvation in the eighteenth-century colonies was confined to isolated catastrophes, and famine was unknown. For most colonists, food was simple but ample enough to go around. Indeed, travelers marveled that settler families often invited strangers to share the families' food and seldom asked for payment, a good sign that settlers hungered for news and companionship more than they worried about another mouth to feed.

The dramatic growth of the colonial population signaled the maturation of a distinctive colonial society. That society was by no means uniform or homogeneous.

Economic historians estimate that the standard of living of free colonists (that is, those who were not indentured servants or slaves) actually improved during the eighteenth century: The colonial economy grew fast enough not just to keep up with an eightfold increase in population, but to surpass it. By 1770, most free colonists had a higher standard of living than the majority of people elsewhere in the Atlantic world. That did not mean that most colonists were rich; far from it. Economic expansion engendered glaring inequities. Instead, it meant that the colonies' abundance of land, demand for labor, and supply of food created a rare social and economic environment that, in general, permitted free colonists to live well. Many colonists did get rich during the eighteenth century. But the unique achievement of the eighteenth-century colonial economy was less the wealth of the most success-

ful colonists (plenty of Europeans were much, much richer) than the modest economic welfare of the vast bulk of the free population. In Europe, pinnacles of wealth stood on foundations of poverty; in the eighteenth-century colonies, the pyramid of wealth was impressive not for its height but for its broad, solid base in the free population.

These general, large-scale trends in the eighteenth-century colonies evolved in distinctive patterns in New England, the middle colonies, and the southern colonies.

New England: From Puritans to Yankee Traders

The New England population grew sixfold during the eighteenth century, but it lagged behind the growth in the other colonies. The main reason New England failed to keep pace was that most immigrants steered clear of Massachusetts and Connecticut. They chose other destinations partly because Puritan orthodoxy—atrophied though it was by the eighteenth century—made these colonies comparatively inhospitable for both religious dissenters and those indifferent to theology. In 1734, for example, residents of Worcester, Massachusetts, literally demolished a new Presbyterian church built by a group of recent Scots-Irish immigrants. Rhode Island's tolerance encouraged religious heterodoxy, but its tiny land area discouraged immigrants. However, the most important reason immigrants avoided New England was that the growth of population there gave it a higher and less desirable ratio of people to land than the other colonies. As the population grew, many settlers dispersed from towns to individual farms, and Puritan communities lost much of their cohesion. Nonetheless, networks of economic exchange laced rural settlers to their neighbors, local market towns, Boston merchants, and the broad currents of Atlantic commerce. In many ways, trade became a faith that competed strongly with the traditions of Puritanism.

Natural Increase and Land Distribution

The New England population grew mostly by natural increase, much as it had during the seventeenth century. Nearly every adult woman married. The widespread expectation that women would and should marry caused unmarried adult women to be considered a little peculiar. Predictably, married women had children, and, thanks to the relatively low New England mortality rate, often many children. The perils of childbirth gave wives a shorter life expectancy than husbands, but wives often lived to have six, seven, or eight babies. When a wife died, her husband usually remarried quickly. A wife's labor and companionship were too vital for a farm family to do without. Often, a widowed husband had still more children with a second or third wife. Benjamin Franklin's father had seven children with his first wife and ten (including Benjamin) with his second. Such large families rapidly multiplied the New England population, especially since—unlike in England—most children survived to adulthood when, as husbands and wives, they made their own hearty contributions to the population.

In many ways, trade became a faith that competed strongly with the traditions of Puritanism.

The burgeoning New England population pressed against a limited amount of land. The interior of New England, bounded by the Hudson River on the west and the St. Lawrence River to the north, was smaller than that of colonies farther south. Furthermore, as the northernmost group of colonies, New England had a contested northern and western frontier. Powerful Indian tribes—especially the Iroquois and Mahicans—jealously guarded their territories. When provoked by colonial or European disputes, the French (and Catholic) colony of Quebec also menaced the English (and Protestant) colonists of New England. But the main reason New Englanders were pinched for land during the eighteenth century was what they chose to do with the land they had available.

During the seventeenth century, New England towns parceled out land to individual families. In most cases, the land allotments proved large enough to permit the original settlers to practice partible inheritance (that is, to subdivide the land more or less equally among sons). By the eighteenth century, the original land allotments had to be further subdivided to accommodate grandsons and great-grandsons, and many plots of land became too small for a family to make a living. Sons who could not hope to inherit a livable farm (like Ben-

jamin Franklin) had several options. They could find a trade or a profession in one of the scores of villages that dotted the New England countryside. Or they could try their luck in Boston, the region's one metropolis, which housed about 16,000 souls by midcentury. But if they wanted to farm, as 8 out of 10 New Englanders did, they had to move away from the town where they were born.

During the eighteenth century, colonial governments in New England abandoned the seventeenth-century policy of granting land to towns. Needing revenue, the governments of both Connecticut and Massachusetts sold land directly to individuals, including speculators. This new land policy undermined the powerful influence churches and towns had exerted over New Englanders during the seventeenth century. Now, money rather than membership in a community knit together in a church covenant determined whether a person could obtain land.

The new land policy also caused the disintegration of the seventeenth-century pattern of settlement. As New Englanders moved into western Massachusetts and Connecticut and north into New Hampshire and Maine, they tended to settle on individual farms rather than in the towns and villages that characterized the seventeenth century. New Englanders still depended on their relatives and neighbors for help in clearing land, raising a house, worshiping God, and having a good time. But far more than in the seventeenth century, they regulated their behavior in newly settled areas by their own individual dictates. A telling measure of the decline in Puritan watchfulness that accompanied the settlement on individual farms was the rising rate of premarital pregnancy. Historians have discovered that in the seventeenth century, fewer than one New England bride in ten was pregnant when she married; by the mid-eighteenth century, one-third of New England brides were pregnant, and in some communities nearly half were.

Farms, Fish, and Trade

The relative scarcity of land in New England (compared with the middle colonies and the southern colonies) encouraged agricultural diversification. New England farmers grew food for their families, but their fields did not produce a huge marketable surplus. In fact, New England farms could not grow enough wheat to feed the population, partly because of the diminished fertility of the soil and partly because a plant disease withered the wheat.

New England had to import wheat from Pennsylvania, New York, Maryland, and Virginia. Without one big crop, farmers grew many small ones and, if they had extra, sold to or traded with neighbors. Interwoven networks of local exchange reached only a few miles from each farm. Poor roads made travel difficult, time-consuming, and expensive, especially with bulky and heavy agricultural goods. The one major agricultural product the New England colonies exported—livestock—walked to market on its own four legs. A New England farm was a place to get by, not to get rich. By 1770, New Englanders had less wealth per capita than residents of the middle colonies and only one-fourth as much as free colonists in the southern colonies.

As consumers, New England farmers made up the foundation of a diversified commercial economy that linked remote farms to markets throughout the world. Although farmers had little to sell on world markets, the cash they earned in local markets they took to stores in nearby villages and towns where they could buy Chinese tea, English textiles, ceramics, tobacco, and metal goods, or possibly a newspaper, a collection of sermons, or a handy almanac. Merchants large and small stocked mostly imported goods. But farmers' needs for sturdy shoes, a warm coat, a sound cart, a tight barrel, or a solid building supported local shoemakers, tailors, wheelwrights, blacksmiths, carpenters, masons, and coopers. In the larger towns and especially in Boston, such specialized artisans as cabinetmakers and silversmiths could be found, along with tallow chandlers and printers, like Benjamin Franklin's father and brother. Skilled tradesmen made up about a third of Boston's adult men, and most of them managed to make a decent living. Shipbuilders tended to do better than other artisans because they served the most dynamic sector of the New England economy.

As consumers, New England farmers made up the foundation of a diversified commercial economy that linked remote farms to markets throughout the world.

As they had since the seventeenth century, New Englanders made their fortunes at sea. Fishermen salted and sold some of their catch to their fellow colonists, but most was exported to markets in southern Europe or, principally, the West Indies,

NATHANIEL HURD, A BOSTON ARTISAN
Like Benjamin Franklin, Nathaniel Hurd was born into an artisan family in Boston. With a tailor great-grandfather, a joiner grandfather, and an accomplished silversmith father, Hurd apprenticed with his father and became an expert engraver, designing bookplates as well as various commercial and social notices, such as loan certificates and wedding invitations. This portrait was painted in 1765 by John Singleton Copley, the most accomplished American artist of the time. Hurd's fine clothing illustrates the prosperity a highly skilled artisan in a good trade could achieve. His open collar and plain cuffs show that he was no idle gentleman; the prominence of his hands suggests their centrality in his life and work. Although Hurd's trade made him dependent on the orders of his customers, he does not appear to be obsequious; instead, he seems to be secure, even independent, though not haughty or overbearing.
© The Cleveland Museum of Art, Gift of the John Huntington Art and Polytechnic Trust, 1915.534

---

where sugar plantation slaves ate cheap New England cod. Fish accounted for more than a third of New England's exports, with livestock and timber making up another third. The West Indies absorbed two-thirds of all New England's exports, while almost all the rest went to England and continental Europe. This Atlantic commerce benefited the entire New England economy, providing jobs for la-

BOSTON COMMON IN NEEDLEWORK
This exquisite needlework was embroidered by Hannah Otis in 1750 when she was eighteen years old. Her picture illustrates the semirural character of one of the largest colonial cities. She showed the Boston Common as if the city's bustling streets and wharves were behind the viewer. Her cityscape is populated by more animals than people and covered by plants rather than paving stones. From the perspective of the late twentieth century, the scene gives few hints of a city. Try to adopt the perspective of the mid-eighteenth century and imagine how the picture might be different if it showed rural Massachusetts. Or, conversely, what features would suggest a city to an eighteenth-century viewer? The large house (center right) belonged to the Hancock family; John Hancock, who later signed the Declaration of Independence, is shown on horseback in the foreground. Does it appear that the Hancocks farmed their land? Note that Otis did not fail to show that wealthy Bostonians were familiar with slavery.
Courtesy, Museum of Fine Arts, Boston.

borers and tradesmen such as sailors, stevedores, and rope makers as well as for ship captains, clerks, and merchants of all kinds.

Merchants dominated the commercial economy of New England. Whether in inland communities like Springfield, Massachusetts, or Hartford, Connecticut, or seaports like Marblehead, Massachusetts, New London, Connecticut, or Providence, Rhode Island, merchants stood at the hub of trade between local folk and the international market. The largest and most successful merchants lived in Boston, where they not only bought and sold imported goods but also owned and insured the ships that carried the merchandise. On the whole, the New England merchants and shippers did not take part in the lucrative tobacco, sugar, and rice trade from the plantation colonies, which tended to be re-

served for British merchants. As British colonists, they benefited from the protection of the Royal Navy, but they seldom hesitated to evade imperial trade regulations when a good profit could be made. For example, although the colonists were prohibited from purchasing tea in Amsterdam—where it was much cheaper than in London, because the Dutch did not tax it as heavily as the English did—New England merchants often bought tea illegally in the Dutch West Indies and sold it back home at a lower price than English tea but with a higher margin of profit for themselves. Merchants also profited from privateering—preying on French and Spanish ships during the intermittent warfare between those nations and England during the eighteenth century.

By the 1760s, the richest Boston merchants built elegant mansions, imported ornate carriages, and had servants (often slaves) dressed in livery. When John Adams—a New England lawyer who became a leader during the American Revolution and ultimately president of the United States—was invited to a wealthy Boston merchant's home, he was stunned by its magnificence. It was a house "for a noble Man, a Prince," he wrote; "the Turkey Carpets, the painted Hangings, the Marble Tables, the rich Beds with crimson Damask Curtains and Counterpins, the beautiful Chimney Clock, the Spacious Garden, are the most magnificent of any Thing I have ever seen." The contrast Adams noted between the luxurious home of this merchant prince and the lives of other New Englanders indicates the polarization of wealth that occurred in Boston and other seaports during the eighteenth century. The thriving commercial activity concentrated wealth in the hands of the most successful merchants. In the late seventeenth century, the richest 5 percent of Bostonians owned about a third of the city's wealth; by 1770, they owned about half. At the other end of the spectrum, the share of the city's wealth possessed by the poorest two-thirds of the population declined from about one-sixth to less than one-tenth.

The rich got richer, and everybody else had a smaller share of the total wealth, but the incidence of genuine poverty did not change much. Roughly 5 or 6 percent of the New England population qualified for poor relief throughout the eighteenth century. Nonetheless, the colony's growing population increased the sheer numbers of unemployed or sick men, widows, orphans, and elderly or disabled people. Boston and other New England towns struggled to provide relief for them in families or in almshouses. To minimize the taxes required to support these relief efforts, Boston and other towns built workhouses during the eighteenth century, hoping to force able-bodied poor folk to earn something for their keep. But compared with the poverty in England, the colonists were better off. As a Connecticut traveler wrote from England in 1764, "We in New England know nothing of poverty and want, we have no idea of the thing, how much better do our poor people live than 7/8 of the people on this much famed island."

The contrast with English poverty had meaning since the overwhelming majority of New Englanders traced their ancestry to England, making the region more English and more homogeneous than any other. The population of African ancestry in the region remained small. Several merchants specialized in the African slave trade and often brought a few slaves back from their voyages to the West Indies or the southern colonies and readily sold them in New England. New Englanders had no hesitation about acquiring slaves, and many Puritan ministers, including Cotton Mather, owned one or two. But except for the Narragansett region of Rhode Island, where numerous slaves worked raising livestock, New England's family farms were unsuited for slave labor. Instead, New England's slaves concentrated in towns, especially Boston, where most of them worked as domestic servants and laborers. Although the black population of New England grew from less than 2,000 in 1700 to over 15,000 by 1770, it barely diluted the region's 97 percent white, mostly English, majority.

By 1770, the population, wealth, and commercial activity of New England differed from what they had been in 1700. Ministers still enjoyed high status in New England, but the Yankee trader had replaced the Puritan divine as the symbolic New Englander.

The Middle Colonies: Immigrants, Wheat, and Work

During the eighteenth century, the population of the middle colonies (Pennsylvania, New York, New Jersey, and Delaware) grew faster than that of New England. At the beginning of the century, almost twice as many people lived in New England as in the middle colonies. But by 1770, the population of the middle colonies had multiplied tenfold—mainly from an influx of German, Irish, Scotch, and other immigrants—and nearly equaled the population of New England. Pennsylvania received more immigrants than any other middle colony; its population grew thirteenfold between 1700 and 1770. In 1700, Pennsylvania was the sixth largest colony in British North America; by 1770, Pennsylvania's population surpassed that of every colony but Virginia.

Immigrants made the middle colonies a uniquely diverse society. The population was less English than either New England or the South. By the end of the eighteenth century, barely one-third of Pennsylvanians and less than half the total population of the middle colonies traced their ancestry to England.

NEW YORK STREET SCENE

This painting depicts John Street, a residential neighborhood of New York, in 1768, as recalled by artist Joseph B. Smith early in the nineteenth century. The painting highlights the urbane pleasures of casual encounters and friendly conversations on the street. Unlike urban streets today, noise on John Street was limited to human voices, a few yipping dogs, and the clip-clop of horses' hooves. The street appears safe and secure; the people show no sign of caution about theft or assault, nor do they appear to be in a hurry to seek refuge indoors. What do the various clusters of people suggest about patterns of sociability on John Street in the eighteenth century? Standing at the door of Wesley Chapel (the first Methodist church building in America) is Peter Williams, an African American who served as sexton of the church. Williams later earned enough money buying and selling tobacco to help build New York's first African American Methodist church.

Old John Street United Methodist Church.

German and Scots-Irish Immigrants

Germans made up the largest contingent of migrants from the European continent to the middle colonies. In 1683, a small group of Quaker and Mennonite families from Germany founded Germantown, Pennsylvania. (Like Quakers, Mennonites were sober pacifists, persecuted for their strict piety.) Not until the first decade of the eighteenth

century, however, did ships crowded with German settlers begin to dock at Philadelphia wharves. By 1770, more than 100,000 had arrived in the colonies. Their fellow colonists often referred to them as "Pennsylvania Dutch," an English corruption of the German word the immigrants used to describe themselves and their native language, *Deutsch*.

Most German immigrants came from a region along the Rhine River in southwestern Germany called the Palatinate, although some hailed from German-speaking parts of Switzerland, Austria, and the Netherlands. Families, neighbors, and sometimes whole villages uprooted to escape harsh conditions that had become intolerable. Throughout Europe, peasants suffered from exploitation by landowners and governments, and they had few opportunities to improve their lives. Palatine peasants in particular, one observer noted, were "not as well off as cattle elsewhere." Devastating French invasions of the Palatinate during Queen Anne's War (1702–1713) made ordinarily bad conditions even worse and triggered the first large-scale migration. German immigrants to the middle colonies included numerous artisans and a few merchants, but the great majority were farmers and laborers. Economically, they represented "middling" folk, neither the poorest (who could not afford the trip) nor the better off (who did not want to leave).

By the 1720s, Germans who had established themselves in the colonies wrote back to their friends and relatives, as one reported, "of the civil and religious liberties [and] privileges, and of all the goodness I have heard and seen." Such reports prompted still more Germans to pull up stakes and embark for America. Dutch shipping firms employed agents, known as "Newlanders," to amplify these messages and advertise the virtues of the colonies as they traveled the Rhine valley. Newlanders earned a small fee for every passenger they persuaded to depart for America. One disillusioned immigrant referred to Newlanders as "thieves of human beings . . . trafficking in human flesh." Others probably discounted the glowing reports from Newlanders and even the more temperate letters from those already settled in the colonies. But they left anyway, because—as several travelers told one of their stay-behind compatriots—they "preferred being slaves in America to being free townsmen" in Germany. That statement expressed the immigrants' overpowering desire to exchange the miserable certainties of their lives in Germany for the uncertain attractions of life in the colonies.

Similar motives propelled the Scots-Irish, who outnumbered German immigrants by more than two to one. The term *Scots-Irish,* like *Pennsylvania Dutch,* was a misleading label coined in the colonies. Immigrants labeled Scots-Irish actually hailed from the north of Ireland (Ulster Scots), Scotland, and northern England. Some of the Scots-Irish were Irish natives who had no personal or ancestral connection whatever with Scotland. This somewhat confusing mixture of peoples shared traits that made them recognizable to other colonists and gave rise to the umbrella term *Scots-Irish.*

Unlike the Germans, the Scots-Irish spoke English, but with a distinctive accent that set them apart. Like the Germans, the Scots-Irish were Protestants, but with a difference. Most German immigrants worshiped in Lutheran or German Reformed churches; many others belonged to dissenting sects like the Mennonites, Moravians, Dunkers, Schwenkfelders, and Amish, whose adherents sought relief in the colonies from persecution they had suffered in Europe for their refusal to bear arms and to swear oaths, beliefs they shared with Quakers. In contrast, the Scots-Irish tended to be militant Presbyterians who seldom hesitated to swear oaths or bear arms, often in that order. Also, like German settlers, Scots-Irish immigrants were clannish, residing when they could among relatives or neighbors from the old country.

Immigrants made the middle colonies a uniquely diverse society. By the end of the eighteenth century, barely one-third of Pennsylvanians and less than half the total population of the middle colonies traced their ancestry to England.

Scots-Irish immigrants trickled into the colonies during the seventeenth century. In the eighteenth century, wave after wave of Scots-Irish immigrants arrived, beginning in 1717, cresting every twelve or fifteen years thereafter, and culminating in a flood of immigration in the years just before the American Revolution. The timing of the waves was determined by deteriorating economic conditions in northern Ireland, Scotland, and England. Most of the immigrants were farm laborers or tenant farmers squeezed by landlords who sought profits by raising rents and thereby reducing tenants' income

and standard of living. Handloom weavers fled the collapsing linen industry in northern Ireland, especially after 1770. Droughts, crop failures, high food prices, and genuine famine pushed many others to depart for the colonies. An Ulster Scot remarked that "oppression has brought us" to the "deplorable state . . . [that] the very marrow is screwed out of our bones." By 1773, British officials became so concerned about the drain of people to the colonies that they began to quiz prospective settlers about why they were leaving. The answers the Scots-Irish gave echoed the motives of their predecessors in previous decades: "out of work"; "poverty"; "could not earn bread sufficient to support family"; "tyranny of landlords"; "high rents and oppression"; and to "do better in America."

Both Scots-Irish and Germans probably heard the common saying that "Pennsylvania is heaven for farmers [and] paradise for artisans," but they almost certainly did not fully understand the risks and rigors of their decision to leave their native lands. Gottfried Mittelberger, a musician who traveled from Germany to Philadelphia in 1750, described the grueling passage to America commonly experienced by eighteenth-century emigrants. Mittelberger's trip down the Rhine River from his home village to the port of Rotterdam took seven weeks because the boat had to stop at thirty-six customs houses of German principalities along the river, each of which took its time to inspect papers and baggage and to collect a fee. Mittelberger reckoned that the trip to Rotterdam cost four times more than the trip from Rotterdam to Philadelphia. Many German emigrants who set out with what they believed to be plenty of money arrived in Rotterdam with empty pockets. They still needed to maintain themselves for five or six weeks in Holland until the ship was fully loaded and ready to depart. Scots-Irish emigrants usually avoided expensive delays before sailing simply because they lived nearer the coast.

Nearly two-thirds of all German emigrants arrived at their port of departure with no money to stock up on extra provisions for the trip or even to buy a ticket. Likewise, they could not afford to go back home. Ship captains, aware of the hunger for labor in the colonies, eagerly signed up the penniless emigrants as "redemptioners," a variant of the more common arrangement for indentured servants. A captain would agreed to provide transportation to Philadelphia, where redemptioners would obtain the money to pay for their passage from a friend or relative who was already in the colonies or, as most did, by selling themselves as servants. Impoverished Scots-Irish emigrants, especially the majority who traveled alone rather than with families, typically paid for their passage by contracting to become indentured servants before they sailed from the British Isles, as English emigrants had been doing since the seventeenth century.

Mittelberger enjoyed the amenities of food and cabin service reserved for passengers who paid their way to Pennsylvania, but he witnessed the distress among the four hundred other Germans aboard his ship, most of them redemptioners. They were packed, he wrote, "as closely as herring," in bunks two feet by six feet. Seasickness compounded by exhaustion, poverty, poor food, bad water, inadequate sanitation, and tight quarters encouraged the spread of disease. Dozens died; on Mittelberger's ship, thirty-two children were buried at sea. "Groaning, crying, and lamentation go on aboard day and night," Mittelberger reported; "many people . . . become homesick at the thought that many hundreds of people must necessarily perish, die, and be thrown into the ocean in such misery. And this in turn makes their families, or those who were responsible for their undertaking the journey, oftentimes fall almost into despair—so that it soon becomes practically impossible to rouse them from their depression." The emigrants' misery continued for the seven or eight weeks usually required to sail to the colonies. Scattered evidence suggests that the dismal conditions on Mittelberger's ship were not unusual. One historian has noted that on the sixteen emigrant ships arriving in Philadelphia in 1738, over half of all passengers died en route.

When his ship finally approached land, Mittelberger explained, "everyone crawls from below to the deck . . . and people cry for joy, pray, and sing praises and thanks to God." Unfortunately, their troubles were far from over. Once the ship docked, passengers who had paid their fare could go ashore, as could redemptioners who could provide the captain some collateral while they tried to raise the funds for their passage. All the other redemptioners and indentured servants—the majority of passengers—had to stay on board until someone came to purchase them (or, more precisely, to purchase their labor). Captains advertised the sale of redemptioners and servants, and the prospects of cheap labor attracted buyers. Unlike indentured servants, redemptioners negotiated independently with their purchasers about their period of servitude. Typically, a healthy adult redemptioner agreed to four years of servitude. If a family member had died at sea, the surviving members of the family still had to pay the deceased's fare by agreeing to longer periods of servitude. Indentured servants commonly served five, six, or seven years, as did weaker, sicker, younger, and less skilled redemptioners. Children ten years old or younger usually had to become servants until they were twenty-one.

Pennsylvania: "The Best Poor [White] Man's Country"

New settlers, whether free or in servitude, poured into the middle colonies because they perceived unparalleled opportunities. Hired workers could get wages three or four times higher than in England. Pennsylvania deserved its reputation as "the best poor Man's Country in the World," indentured servant William Moraley wrote in 1743. Although Moraley reported that "the Condition of bought Servants is very hard" and masters often failed to live up to their promise to provide decent food and clothing, opportunity abounded because there was more work to be done than workers to do it.

Most servants toiled in Philadelphia, New York City, or one of the smaller towns or villages. Only a minority—roughly one-third—labored on farms. Artisans, small manufacturers, and shopkeepers prized the labor of male servants. Female servants made valuable additions to households, where nearly all of them worked cleaning, washing, cooking, and minding children. From the masters' viewpoint, servants were a bargain. A master could purchase five or six years of a servant's labor for approximately the wages a common laborer would earn in four months. Wage workers could walk away from their jobs when they pleased, and they did so often enough to be troublesome to employers. Servants, however, were legally bound to work for their masters until their terms expired. The restrictions and confinements of bondage were genuine, and they were vigorously enforced. But for servants, bondage was temporary. Much like Benjamin Franklin's service as an apprentice, it carried no lasting stigma.

A few black slaves worked in shops and homes in Philadelphia and New York City. For example, after Benjamin Franklin became prosperous, he purchased slaves named Peter, Jemima, King, Othello, and George. Since a slave cost at least three times as much as a servant, only affluent colonists could afford the long-term investment in slave labor. While the population of African ancestry (almost all

BENJAMIN FRANKLIN
This is the earliest known portrait of Benjamin Franklin. Painted by Robert Feke in about 1748 when Franklin was in his early forties, the portrait illustrates Franklin's status as an aspiring printer, merchant, and citizen of Philadelphia. To the late-twentieth-century eye, Franklin appears prim, foppish, and mannered, with an elaborately curled wig framing a composed, satisfied face. However, compare Franklin's demeanor and dress with that of Nathaniel Hurd (page 159) and of Mrs. Barnard Elliott (page 180). Franklin appears more pretentious than Hurd and less elegant than Elliott, a rough index of his in-progress social mobility from a hardworking printer to a prominent and wealthy thinker and statesman.
Courtesy of the Harvard University Portrait Collection, Bequest, Dr. John C. Warren, 1856.

slaves) in the middle colonies grew from about 3,000 in 1700 to over 30,000 in 1770, it represented only about 7 percent of the total population, and in most of the region much less. People of African ancestry made up less than 3 percent of the population of Pennsylvania for most of the eighteenth century. In New York, blacks were much more common, accounting for nearly 15 percent of the population, more than in any other colony north of the Chesapeake. This pattern had been established during the seventeenth century when New York was a Dutch colony. The Dutch, unlike the Quakers in seventeenth-century Pennsylvania, encouraged the importation of slaves because New Amsterdam had difficulty attracting white settlers and because the slave trade profited the Dutch West India Company.

During the eighteenth century, most slaves came to the middle colonies as they did to New England, in ships returning from the West Indies. Enough arrived to prompt colonial assemblies to pass slave codes that punished slaves much more severely than servants for the same transgressions. "For the least trespass," servant Moraley reported, slaves "undergo the severest Punishment." As Moraley noted, the law permitted runaway slaves to be "unmercifully whipped." In practice, both servants and slaves were governed more by their masters than by the laws. But in cases of abuse, servants had legal protections that slaves did not. Servants could and did charge masters with violating the terms of their indenture contracts. The terms of a slave's bondage were set forth in a master's commands, not in a written contract.

Small numbers of slaves managed to obtain their freedom, especially in New York City. But free African Americans did not escape whites' firm convictions about black inferiority and white supremacy. Those convictions lay at the foundation of the slave codes. Blacks worked alongside white servants and tradesmen, nursed white babies, cooked meals for white families, drank toasts with whites in taverns, and gambled with whites at horse races and fist fights. But few whites doubted that people of African ancestry should be where they were, at the bottom of the social pyramid. Whites' racism and blacks' lowly social status made African Americans scapegoats for European Americans' suspicions and anxieties. In 1741, when arson and several unexplained thefts plagued New York City, officials suspected a murderous slave conspiracy. On the basis of little more than evidence of slaves' "insolence" (that is, refusal to conform fully to whites' expectations of servile behavior), city authorities had thirteen slaves burned at the stake and eighteen others hanged. Although slaves were certifiably poor (they usually had no property whatever), they were not included among the poor for whom the middle colonies were reputed to be the best country in the world.

The reason more slaves were not brought to the middle colonies was that farmers, the vast majority of the population, had little use for them. Most farms operated with family labor. Wheat, the most

BETHLEHEM, PENNSYLVANIA

This view of the small community of Bethlehem, Pennsylvania, in 1757 dramatizes the profound transformation of the natural landscape in the eighteenth century by highly motivated human labor. Founded by Moravian immigrants in 1740, Bethlehem must have appeared at first like the dense woods on the upper left horizon. In fewer than twenty years, precisely laid-out orchards and fields had replaced forests and glades. Carefully penned livestock (lower center right) and fenced fields (lower left) kept the handiwork of farmers separate from the risks and disorders of untamed nature. Not only individual farmsteads (lower center), but impressive multistory brick town buildings (upper center) combined the bounty of the land with the delights of community life. Few eighteenth-century communities were as orderly as Bethlehem, but many effected a comparable transformation of the environment.

Miriam and Ira D. Walsh Division of Art, Prints, and Photographs, New York Public Library. Astor, Lenox, and Tilden Foundations.

widely grown crop, did not require more labor than farmers could typically muster from relatives, neighbors, and a hired hand or two.

Immigrants swarmed to the middle colonies because of the availability of land to farm. The Penn family encouraged immigration to bring in potential buyers for their enormous tracts of land in Pennsylvania. Owners of the huge estates in New York's Hudson valley preferred to rent rather than sell their land, making it more difficult for them to attract immigrants. During the seventeenth century, Pennsylvania had promoted immigration by offering a headright of fifty acres of land to servants who completed their terms. In the eighteenth century, servants' freedom dues were limited to two suits of clothing, one new and one old, and some farm tools, perhaps a hoe and a shovel, but no land. Nonetheless, the desire for farmland still tugged immigrants to Philadelphia and other seaports and then scattered them to the ever-expanding periphery of settlement, invigorating the demand for still more immigrants.

The price of farmland varied depending on soil quality, access to water, distance from a market town, and the extent of improvements. One hundred acres of improved land that had been cleared, plowed, fenced, ditched, and perhaps had a house and barn built on it might cost three or four times more than the same acreage of uncleared, unimproved land. Since the cheapest unimproved land always lay at the margin of settlement, would-be farmers tended to migrate to promising areas just beyond already improved farms. From Philadelphia, settlers moved north along the Delaware River and west along the Schuylkill and Susquehanna Rivers. By midcentury, settlement had reached the eastern slopes of the Appalachian Mountains, and newcomers spilled down the fertile valley of the Shenandoah River into western Virginia and the Carolinas. Thousands of settlers migrated from the middle colonies through this back door to the South. In 1765, for example, a young Scots-Irishman named Andrew Jackson and his wife, Elizabeth, migrated with their two young sons from northern Ireland to Pennsylvania and then trekked down the Shenandoah valley to South Carolina, where their third son, Andrew—the future president of the United States—was born in 1767.

From the beginning, Pennsylvania followed a policy of negotiating with Indian tribes to purchase additional land. This policy greatly reduced the violent clashes that flared along the frontier of settlement elsewhere in the colonies. The relative weakness of local tribes made negotiations easier for Pennsylvanians. The Susquehannocks in western Pennsylvania, for example, had been drubbed repeatedly by their powerful Iroquois enemies to the north, so it was attractive to them to sell off rights to land they could not defend very well in any case. Yet the Penn family did not shrink from pushing its agreements with Indian tribes to the limit and beyond. In a dispute with tribes on the northern Delaware in 1737, the Penn family pulled out a 1686 deed that showed that local tribes had then granted the Penns land that stretched as far as a man could walk in a day and a half. Under the terms of this infamous "Walking Purchase," the Penns sent out three runners, two of whom collapsed before the thirty-six hours expired. The third runner managed to cover sixty miles of wilderness, approximately doubling the size of the Penns' claim.

Few colonists drifted beyond the northern boundaries of Pennsylvania. The Iroquois domi-nated the lucrative fur trade of the St. Lawrence valley and eastern Great Lakes, and they had the political and military strength to defend their territory from colonial encroachment. They enforced their dominance through alliances with less mighty tribes and by clever diplomatic maneuvers that played the French colonists in Montreal, Canada, against the British colonists in Albany, New York, both of whom were eager to trade for Iroquois furs. Few settlers wanted to risk having their scalps lifted by Iroquois warriors in northern New York when they could choose to settle instead in the comparatively safe environs of Pennsylvania.

Farmers made the middle colonies the breadbasket of North America. They planted a wide variety of crops to feed their families, but they grew wheat in abundance. Flour milling was the number one industry and flour the number one export of the middle colonies. Wheat—whether as grain or flour—comprised nearly three-fourths of all exports from the middle colonies and connected Pennsylvania farmers to economic developments in the nations that rimmed the Atlantic. Pennsylvania flour fed residents in other colonies, in southern Europe, and—above all—in the West Indies. For farmers, the world grain market proved risky but profitable. Grain prices rose steadily after 1720; by 1770, a bushel of wheat was worth twice (in real terms, that is, adjusted for inflation) what it had been fifty years earlier. The ready market for surplus wheat allowed farmers to pay off debts; buy land, livestock, farm tools, and imports such as textiles, metalware, ceramics, tea, coffee, and sugar; and even to squirrel away a few shillings for a rainy day.

Prosperity and Poor Richard

The standard of living in rural Pennsylvania was probably higher than in any other agricultural region of the eighteenth-century world. Compared with their counterparts in cities, the rural South, or Europe, the wealthiest Pennsylvanians had a smaller share of the colony's total wealth. In midcentury Chester County, Pennsylvania, for example, the top 10 percent of taxpayers owned about a quarter of all wealth, the middle 40 percent possessed about half the wealth, and the bottom 50 percent had the remaining quarter. While wealth distribution in Chester County and elsewhere in the rural middle colonies was far from equitable, it contrasted sharply with such cities as Philadelphia, where the top 10 percent of the population in 1767 owned two-thirds of the wealth while the poorest half of the population had only 5 percent. The comparatively widespread prosperity of the middle colonies permitted residents to indulge in a half-century shopping spree for English imports. The middle colonies' per capita consumption of imported goods from England more than doubled between 1720 and 1770, far outstripping the per-capita consumption of English goods in New England and the southern colonies.

At the crossroads of trade in wheat exports and English imports stood Philadelphia. In the four decades after 1730, fifty-two new towns sprang up in Pennsylvania, and almost all channeled their trade through Philadelphia. The city's population grew steadily during the eighteenth century, eclipsing New York City by 1740 and Boston by 1750 to reach a population of about 40,000 by 1770. By 1776, Philadelphia had a larger population than any other city in the entire British Empire except London, which dwarfed all other cities with its 750,000 inhabitants.

Merchants occupied the top stratum of Philadelphia society. They made fortunes in trade, ship-

MAP 5.2
Atlantic Trade in the Eighteenth Century
This map illustrates the economic outlook of the colonies in the eighteenth century: that is, east toward the Atlantic world rather than west toward the interior of North America. The long distances involved in the Atlantic trade and the uncertainties of seaborne travel suggest the difficulties Britain experienced governing the colonies and regulating colonial commerce.

Plow deep, while sluggards sleep; and you shall have corn to sell and to keep.

Work to day, for you know not how much you may be hindered to morrow.

POOR RICHARD'S ALMANACK

This illustration from Poor Richard's Almanack *celebrates the virtues of work and the vices of sloth. Unlike the industrious farmers, lazy sluggards put off until tomorrow what they might do today. They will be forced to buy corn rather than growing enough to eat and to sell. However pleasant it might seem in the short run to sleep late and dillydally, in the long run lazy folk will be miserable, Poor Richard counseled. In fact, they will be like the sheep being sheared at the right: Their loss will be the gain of hard workers. One of Poor Richard's central messages was the likelihood of long-term gain in repayment for the certainty of the short-term pain of labor. Poor Richard's maxim assumed that, on the whole, workers received the fruits of their labor, an assumption that made more sense for landowning farmers or artisans like Franklin than for wage laborers, women workers, or slaves.*

Courtesy, American Antiquarian Society.

---

ping, insurance, land, and law. They dominated the wealthy oligarchy that governed the city. Only 2 percent of the city's residents owned enough property (£50) to qualify to vote. They built grand homes with elaborate formal gardens on the outskirts of Philadelphia. They sent their sons to England and the continent for education and refinement; their daughters learned enough at home, they believed. They tried their best to follow European fashions, succumbing, one observer noted, to "the evil Itch of overvaluing Foreign parts."

The ranks of merchants reached downward to aspiring tradesmen like Benjamin Franklin. After he started to print the *Pennsylvania Gazette* in 1728, Franklin opened a shop to sell stationery. Run mostly by his wife, Deborah, the shop soon branched out to sell a little bit of everything: cheese, codfish, goose feathers, sealing wax, coffee, chocolate, soap, and now and then a slave. In 1733, Franklin began to publish *Poor Richard's Almanack*, a calendar of weather predictions, astrological alignments, and pithy epigrams. The *Almanack* sold thousands of copies, quickly becoming Franklin's most profitable product. As Franklin's prosperity grew, he devoted his energies to civic improvement projects, organizing fire companies, police squads, and a subscription library. He continued to identify himself as a "leather apron man" (a tradesman), but by 1740 the ambitious, upwardly mobile printer could not resist concocting a Franklin coat of arms featuring two lions, two doves, and a dolphin, which he used for the rest of his life to mark the sealing wax on his letters.

Many of Philadelphia's wealthiest merchants were Quakers. Quaker traits of industry, thrift, honesty, and sobriety encouraged the accumulation of wealth. A colonist complained that a Quaker "prays for his neighbor on First Days [the Sabbath] and then preys on him the other six." The inner light that shone brightly for Pennsylvania's founding Quakers dimmed during the eighteenth century. As wealth piled up, the intensity of faith flickered. In 1770, a settler reported that his Quaker meeting was "disowning many for sottishness and immorality," including one man who kept gamecocks and gave "a Girl £50 to strip Stark naked before him."

The widespread conviction that good things came from work underscored the reputation of the middle colonies as the best poor man's country in the world.

"God helps them that help themselves," Poor Richard wrote, and Quakers and other colonists acted as if they agreed. The popularity of *Poor Richard's Almanack* suggests that many Pennsylvanians thought less about the pearly gates than about their pocketbooks. Where was salvation in Poor Richard's quip "Nothing but Money is sweeter than Honey"? Where was God in his slogan "In the Affairs of this World, Men are saved not by Faith but by the Want of it"? Where was divine judgment in his claim that "sin is not hurtful because it is forbidden, but it is forbidden because it's hurtful"? Where were the mysteries of divine providence in what might be considered Poor Richard's motto for the middle colonies, "God gives all Things to Industry"?

The widespread conviction that good things came from work underscored the reputation of the middle colonies as the best poor man's country in the world. Poor men and women could work. If they did, it could pay off. The promise of a worldly payoff made work a secular faith in the middle colonies. Poor Richard advised, "Work as if you were to live 100 years, Pray as if you were to die Tomorrow." Prayer might help in the hereafter, but work made all the difference in the here and now.

William Penn's Quaker utopia became a center of worldly affluence whose most famous citizen,

Franklin, was neither a Quaker nor a utopian. Quakers remained influential, but Franklin spoke for most colonists with his aphorisms of work, discipline, and thrift that echoed Quaker rules for outward behavior. Franklin's maxims did not look to the Quakers' divine inner light for guidance. They depended instead on the spark of ambition and the glow of gain.

The Southern Colonies: Land of Slavery

From 1700 to 1770, more colonists lived in the southern colonies (Virginia, Maryland, North Carolina, South Carolina, and Georgia) than in either New England or the middle colonies. During these decades the population of the southern colonies grew almost ninefold. By 1770, about twice as many people lived in the South as in either the middle colonies or New England. As elsewhere, natural increase and immigration accounted for this rapid population growth. Many Scots-Irish and German immigrants passed through Pennsylvania and funneled down the Shenandoah valley into the southern backcountry. Other immigrants were indentured servants (mostly English and Scots-Irish) who followed in the footsteps of their seventeenth-century counterparts. But involuntary immigrants —slaves—made the most striking contribution to the booming population of the southern colonies. Slaves streamed into the southern colonies during the eighteenth century, transforming the racial and ethnic composition of the population and shaping the region's economy, society, and politics.

The African Slave Trade and the Growth of Slavery

The number of southerners of African ancestry (nearly all of them slaves) rocketed from just over 20,000 in 1700 to well over 400,000 in 1770. The black population increased nearly three times faster than the South's briskly growing white population. Consequently, the proportion of southerners who were black grew from 20 percent in 1700 to 40 percent by 1770. No other region of British North America came close to having so many African-born people, so many black people of African ancestry (but not necessarily birth), or so many slaves. By 1770, the number of slaves in the South was so large that it considerably exceeded the entire population (white and black) of New England in 1750 or the middle colonies in 1760. For good reason, slavery became the defining characteristic of the southern colonies during the eighteenth century.

Southern colonists clustered into two distinct geographic and agricultural zones. The colonies in the upper South, surrounding the Chesapeake Bay, specialized in growing tobacco, as they had since the early seventeenth century. Throughout the eighteenth century, nine out of ten southern whites and eight out of ten southern blacks lived in the Chesapeake region. Virginia—the largest colony in British North America—dominated the upper South, possessing half of the region's population. The upper South retained a white majority during the eighteenth century, although it dwindled from four-fifths to two-thirds because the slave population grew so dramatically.

In the lower South, a second cluster of colonists inhabited the South Atlantic coastal region and specialized in the production of rice and indigo (a plant used to make blue dye). Lower South colonists made up a small fraction of the total population of the southern colonies, but they inched upward from 5 percent of the total in 1700 to 15 percent by 1770. South Carolina dominated the area even more than Virginia did the Chesapeake. Until 1732 when Georgia was founded, South Carolina was the sole British colony along the South Atlantic coast, and by 1770 it still accounted for 85 percent of the region's colonists. Unlike the upper South, the lower South had a distinctive black majority that reflected the dense slave populations along the tidal rivers in the South Carolina low country. In contrast to every other British mainland colony, blacks in South Carolina outnumbered whites almost two to one; in some low country districts, the ratio of blacks to whites exceeded ten to one.

The enormous growth in the South's slave population occurred through natural increase and the flourishing African slave trade to British North America. Slave ships brought almost 300,000 Africans to the British North American colonies between 1619 and 1780. Of those Africans, 95 percent arrived in the South and 96 percent arrived during the eighteenth century. The pace of the trade accelerated during the century. Unlike indentured servants or redemptioners, these Africans did not choose to come to the colonies. They came because they had no choice. They were imported. The word *imported*—a word normally used to describe the shipment of commodities, of things for sale—accu-

rately conveys their status. Most of them had been born into a free family in a village located within a few hundred miles of the West African coast. Captured in war, kidnapped, or sold into slavery by other Africans, they were brought to the coast, sold to an African trader who assembled slaves for sale, and sold again to European or colonial slave traders or ship captains who bought them for shipment to the New World. Packed aboard a slave ship with two or three hundred or more other slaves, they were subjected to the infamous Middle Passage—the crossing of the Atlantic in the hold of a slave ship—and then sold yet again by the slave ship captain either to a colonial slave merchant or to a planter in Virginia, Maryland, or South Carolina who intended to put them to work. Within months, these people had their lives utterly transformed. They had been wrenched from their homes in Africa; shackled, confined, and often beaten; transported six or seven thousand miles across the Atlantic; and sold to colonists who lived in a place they had never heard of and whose language they did not understand. And then they were expected to work efficiently and continuously as slaves for the rest of their lives.

Slaves streamed into the southern colonies during the eighteenth century, transforming the racial and ethnic composition of the population and shaping the region's economy, society, and politics.

The voices of Africans who were swept up in the slave trade have been enveloped by a deafening historical silence, with one major exception. Olaudah Equiano wrote an account of his enslavement, published in 1789, that hints at the stories that might have been told by the tens of thousands of silenced Africans.

Equiano was born in 1745 in the interior of what is now Nigeria, then part of the vast kingdom of Benin. "I had never heard of white men or Europeans, nor of the sea," he recalled. One day when Equiano was eleven years old, two men and a woman, all Africans, broke into his home, seized him and his sister, tied and gagged them, and carried them off. The kidnappers soon separated Equiano from his sister, leaving him "in a state of distraction not to be described. I cried and grieved

SECTIONS OF A SLAVE SHIP.

SLAVE SHIP

Newly enslaved Africans made the Middle Passage crammed belowdecks on a slave ship like this one, sitting upright in a space just over three feet high. Other ships installed an intermediate shelf, forcing slaves into a reclining position with barely enough vertical space to turn from side to side. Profit calculations dictated carrying as many slaves as possible to offset the fixed costs of the ship, insurance, supplies, and crew. But security precautions were the prime consideration in confining slaves to unhealthy, tight quarters belowdecks. Slaves vastly outnumbered the crew aboard the ship, and crew members justifiably feared a slave uprising. Note that the cannon on deck (pointing at one of the hatches over the slave quarters) swiveled to permit shooting at mutinous slaves as well as unfriendly ships.
British Library.

continually, and for several days did not eat anything but what they forced into my mouth."

During the next six or seven months, Equiano was sold to several different African masters, each of whom moved him closer to the coast. One evening Equiano's sister was brought to the house where he was being kept. That night, Equiano remembered, "the man to whom I supposed we belonged lay with us, he in the middle while she and I held one another by the hands across his breast all night; and thus for a while we forgot our misfortunes in the joy of being together." The next morning his sister was taken away, and he never again saw her, his parents, or any of his villagers.

When Equiano arrived at the coast, a slave ship waited offshore. The ship and its sailors terrified Equiano. He feared that he had "gotten into a world of bad spirits," that he was going to be killed and "eaten by those white men with horrible looks, red faces, and loose hair." He fainted when he was first brought on board the slave ship. Once he revived, the crew confined him belowdecks where "with the loathsomeness of the stench and crying together, I became so sick and low that I was not able to eat . . . [and] now wished for the last friend, death, to relieve me." When he refused the food the slavers offered him, they "flogged me severely. I had never experienced anything of this kind before." The beatings continued for Equiano and others who did not eat. When Equiano located other slaves aboard the ship who spoke Ibo, as he did, and heard from them that they were being taken to the whites' country, where they would be made to work, he felt somewhat relieved. But he still feared that he would be killed, since "the white people looked and acted . . . in so savage a manner" toward the slaves and each other.

Once the ship set sail, the slaves were confined to the hold, which "became absolutely pestilential." Many slaves died from sickness that swept below the deck where they were chained, crowded together in suffocating heat fouled by filth of all descriptions. "The shrieks of the women and the groans of the dying rendered the whole a scene of horror almost inconceivable," Equiano recalled. He "was soon reduced so low" that the sailors brought him on deck in hopes of keeping him alive. Others were "almost daily brought upon deck at the point of death" and died. Equiano "envied them the freedom they enjoyed, and as often wished I could change my condition for theirs."

The ship finally arrived in Barbados, and merchants and planters came on board to examine the slaves. "We thought . . . we should be eaten by these ugly men," Equiano wrote. That evening, when the slaves were confined again belowdecks, "there was much dread and trembling among us, and nothing but bitter cries to be heard all the night from these apprehensions." To calm the newly arrived slaves, "some old slaves from the land" were brought on board. They told Equiano and his shipmates that they would not be eaten but would instead work alongside "many of our country people . . . [which] eased us much." In a few days, white masters in Barbados had purchased most of Equiano's shipmates, but he and a few others "were not saleable." These leftovers "were shipped off in a sloop for North America."

The sloop sailed to Virginia and up a river some distance from the sea. There Equiano "saw few or none of our native Africans and not one soul who could talk to me." Soon, all the other slaves had been sold "and only myself was left. I was now exceedingly miserable and thought myself worse off than any of the rest of my companions, for they could talk to each other, but I had no person to speak to that I could understand. In this state I was constantly grieving and pining and wishing for death." After "some time in this miserable, forlorn, and much dejected state," Equiano was sold to a white man, the captain of a tobacco ship bound for England.

Some of the slaves brought into the southern colonies came as Equiano did, aboard ships from the West Indies. Merchants in the North American colonies often specialized in this trade; Equiano himself was owned for several years by a Quaker merchant from Philadelphia who traded exten-

OLAUDAH EQUIANO

This portrait of Olaudah Equiano was painted by an unknown English artist about 1780, when Equiano was in his mid-thirties, more than a decade after he had bought his freedom. The portrait evokes Equiano's successful acculturation to the customs of eighteenth-century England. His clothing and hairstyle reflect the fashions of respectable young Englishmen. In his Interesting Narrative, *published in 1789, Equiano explained that as a slave he had learned to speak and understand English. "I now not only felt myself quite easy with these new countrymen but relished their society and manners," he wrote. "I...looked upon them...as men superior to us [Africans], and therefore I had the stronger desire to resemble them, to imbibe their spirit and imitate their manners; I therefore embraced every occasion of improvement, and every new thing that I observed I treasured up in my memory." Equiano's embrace of English culture did not cause him to forsake his African roots. In fact, he honored his dual identity by campaigning against slavery. His* Narrative *was one of the most important and powerful antislavery documents of the time.*

Royal Albert Memorial Museum, Excter, England.

sively with the West Indies. But slaves arriving from the West Indies accounted for only about 15 percent of all the Africans brought into the southern colonies during the eighteenth century. All the rest came directly from Africa on ships that specialized in the slave trade and carried an average of two hundred slaves each. Almost all these ships (roughly 90 percent) belonged to British merchants.

Equiano accurately described the horrendous conditions aboard these ships. The slaves were wedged into only half as much space as white convicts or soldiers were assigned in eighteenth-century ships. Children under the age of fourteen, like Equiano, were relatively rare, typically no more than 10 or 15 percent of a cargo. Most slaves on board were young adults, men usually outnumbering women two to one.

Mortality during the Middle Passage varied considerably from ship to ship. On average, about 15 percent of the slaves died, but sometimes half or more perished. The average mortality among the white crew of slave ships was often nearly as bad. In general, the longer the voyage, the larger the number of deaths. Recent studies suggest that many slaves succumbed not only to virulent epidemic diseases such as smallpox and dysentery but also to acute dehydration caused by fluid loss from heavy perspiration, vomiting, and diarrhea combined with a severe shortage of drinking water to replace the lost fluids.

Although slave ship captains did not understand the dangers of dehydration, they knew about the risks of epidemics, filth, and polluted water, and they certainly wanted to keep slaves alive—a dead slave, after all, took money from their pockets. But captains tolerated the deplorable conditions aboard their ships because they feared rebellion if slaves were not kept chained belowdecks. Slave ship crews never forgot that slaves had little to lose. At bottom, the brutalities of the Middle Passage arose from the violent imperatives of slavery.

Normally an individual planter purchased at any one time a relatively small number of newly arrived Africans, or "new Negroes," as they were called. The number of slaves a planter bought reflected in part the comparatively high price of slaves. In the Chesapeake in 1735, for example, a healthy adult slave cost about the same as nineteen head of cattle. Slave prices escalated with surging demand for their labor; by 1770, a comparable slave cost as much as thirty head of cattle. Only relatively prosperous planters could afford the investment in slaves. Poor families struggling to make ends meet

TABLE 5.1	
SLAVE IMPORTS, 1451-1870	
Estimated Slave Imports to the Western Hemisphere	
1451-1600	275,000
1601-1700	1,341,000
1701-1810	6,100,000
1811-1870	1,900,000

thought twice before buying a slave. In 1735, they could buy one hundred acres of decent land for the price of one good slave. Well-off planters often bought slaves on credit, hoping to pay off their debt with the boost in production they anticipated from their new laborers.

Another reason planters preferred to purchase small groups of newly arrived Africans was to permit the newcomers to be trained by the planters' other slaves. Like Equiano, newly arrived Africans were often profoundly depressed, demoralized, and disoriented. They did not understand English. They could not know where they were or what their future held. Planters counted on their other slaves—either those who had been born into slavery in the colonies (often called "country-born" or "creole" slaves) or Africans who had arrived earlier—to help new Negroes become accustomed to their strange new surroundings on a tobacco farm in Virginia or a rice plantation in South Carolina.

Planters' preferences for slaves from specific regions of Africa aided the process of acculturation (or "seasoning," as it was called) to the routines of slave life in the southern colonies. The slaves on any given slave ship usually came from several African societies and spoke a number of different languages, partly because of the vagaries of the enslavement process in the interior of Africa and partly because slave ship captains feared the heightened prospect of slave rebellion if most of the captives aboard a vessel spoke the same language. A slave purchased by a master in the southern colonies might speak any one of the several hundred Mande, Gur, Kwa, Adamawa, Bantu, or other languages. Nonetheless, Chesapeake planters preferred slaves from Senegambia, the Gold Coast, or—like Equiano— the Bight of Biafra, the origin of 40 percent of all Africans imported to the Chesapeake. South Carolina planters favored slaves from the central African Congo and Angola regions, the origin of about 40 percent of the African slaves they im-

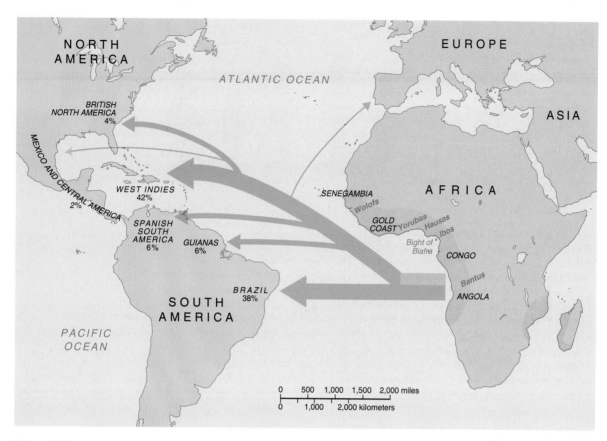

M A P 5.3

The Atlantic Slave Trade

Although the Atlantic slave trade endured for more than four centuries, the heyday of the trade occurred during the eighteenth century, when the vast majority of African slaves were imported to the New World. Only a small fraction of the African slaves imported to the Western Hemisphere were taken to British North America; most went to sugar plantations in Brazil and the Caribbean (see Table 5.1). Why were so many more African slaves sent to the West Indies and Brazil than to British North America?

ported. Although slaves within each of these regions spoke many different languages, enough linguistic and cultural similarities existed that they could communicate with other Africans from the same region. The high concentration of Africans in the slave-dense low country of South Carolina permitted the development of a distinctive pidgin language, Gullah, an amalgam of English, Hausa, Ibo, Yoruba, and other West African tongues that can still be heard among some longtime residents of the sea islands along the coast of South Carolina and Georgia. The linguistic and cultural overlap among African societies from the same region permitted slaves already in the southern colonies to ease some-

what the dehumanizing process of seasoning confronted by new arrivals.

Seasoning acclimated new Africans to the physical as well as the cultural environment of the southern colonies. Slaves who had just endured the Middle Passage were often poorly nourished, weak, and sick. In this vulnerable state of health they encountered the alien diseases of North America without having developed a biological arsenal of acquired immunities. As many as 10 or 15 percent of newly arrived Africans died during their first year in the southern colonies, and sometimes more. One Virginia planter bought thirty-two Africans in an eight-year period, and eight of them died within a year

THOMAS JEFFERSON'S CHESS SET
These pieces from Thomas Jefferson's chess set illustrate the unmistakable African presence in the eighteenth-century South, as tens of thousands of newly imported slaves flooded into the region. The origin of these chess pieces is unknown; they may have been crafted by ivory carvers in Africa and brought to Virginia with a shipment of slaves. Note that the white king has African features, unlike the other white pieces. All the dark pieces appear African, although the dark queen wears a European dress (the white queen has been lost). Imagine Jefferson and his slave-owning friends maneuvering these tiny statues of Europeans and Africans, seeking to achieve victory and avoid defeat. In many ways, the chessboard was a genteel reflection of the harsh, utterly unequal real-world contests between white masters and their black slaves.
Monticello/Thomas Jefferson Memorial Foundation.

of their purchase. Respiratory diseases proved especially deadly. New arrivals who survived for a year or two were considered seasoned. In practice, that meant they were still alive and had learned to do the work their masters commanded.

While newly enslaved Africans poured into the southern colonies, slave women made an even greater contribution to the growth of the black population. Both country-born women and seasoned Africans gave birth to slave babies, who caused the slave population to mushroom. Country-born slave women tended to have more children than seasoned Africans principally because they did not undergo the physical and emotional stresses of enslavement described by Equiano. They became mothers for the first time at a younger age and therefore had a longer period of childbearing and more children. Slaveowners profited from these births, of course. Thomas Jefferson explained, "I consider the labor of a breeding [slave] woman as no object, that a [slave] child raised every 2 years is of more profit than the crop of the best laboring [slave] man." The birth and survival of a growing number of slave babies set the southern colonies apart from other New World slave societies, which experienced natural *decrease;* that is, slave deaths exceeded births. The high

rate of natural increase in the southern colonies meant that by the 1740s the majority of southern slaves were country-born. But the large numbers of newly enslaved Africans who continued to arrive made the influence of African culture in the eighteenth-century South stronger than ever before—or since.

Slave Labor and African American Culture

Planters purchased slaves to employ them in the tobacco fields of the Chesapeake and the rice fields of South Carolina. Planters expected slaves, both men and women, to work from sunup to sundown and beyond. George Washington wrote that his slaves should "be at their work as soon as it is light, work til it is dark, and be diligent while they are at it." Masters had difficulty imposing these expectations on their slaves. The conflict between the masters' desire for maximum labor and the slaves' reluctance to do more than necessary made the threat of physical punishment a constant for eighteenth-century slaves. Eighteenth-century masters preferred black slaves over white indentured servants not just because slaves served for life rather than for a limited term and because their servitude was inherited rather than contractual, but also because colonial laws did not limit the force masters could use against slaves, as it did against servants.

Newly enslaved Africans often prompted masters on eighteenth-century plantations to reach for their whips, or worse. As a traveler observed in 1740, "A new negro . . . will require more discipline than a young spaniel . . . let a hundred men show him how to hoe, or drive a wheelbarrow; he'll still take the one by the bottom and the other by the wheel and . . . often die before [he] . . . can be conquered." Slaves, the traveler noted, were not stupid or simply obstinate; despite the inevitable punishment, they resisted their masters' demands because of their "greatness of soul," their stubborn unwillingness to conform to their masters' definition of them as merely slaves.

Some slaves escalated their acts of resistance to direct physical confrontation with the master, mistress, or an overseer. A hoe raised in anger, a punch in the face, or a desperate swipe with a knife led to swift and predictable retaliation by whites. Throughout the eighteenth-century southern colonies, the balance of physical power rested securely in the hands of whites. The likelihood of brutal retaliation made most slaves cautious about venting their hostility toward whites.

Rebellion occurred, however, at Stono, South Carolina, in 1739. Before dawn on a September Sunday, a group of about twenty slaves, mostly Angolans, attacked a country store, killed the two storekeepers, confiscated the store's guns, ammunition, and powder, and set out along the road south toward Spanish Florida after pausing to set the severed heads of the storekeepers on the store's front steps. Enticing other rebel slaves to join the march south, the group plundered and burned more than a half-dozen plantations and killed more than twenty white men, women, and children. As their numbers grew, the rebels stopped in a field to rest, to beat drums to signal still more slaves to join them, and to dance and sing in celebration. A mounted force of whites, gathered by an alarm raised by a government official who had encountered the rebels and managed to escape, attacked the exultant slaves and killed many of them. They placed rebels' heads atop mileposts along the road, grim reminders of the consequences of rebellion. At least thirty rebels fled the attack, to be hunted down by the end of the week; a few rebels remained at large for months. The Stono rebellion illustrated that eighteenth-century slaves, no matter how determined, had no

chance of overturning slavery, and very little chance of defending themselves in any bold strike for freedom. After the Stono rebellion, South Carolina legislators enacted repressive laws designed to guarantee that whites would always have the upper hand (see Texts in Historical Context, page 178). For slaves, open rebellion was a more or less rapid form of suicide. No other similar uprising occurred in South Carolina or elsewhere during the colonial period.

Day-to-day experience convinced most slaves that survival lay within the boundaries of slavery. But slaves did not readily accept their masters' definition of those boundaries. They maneuvered constantly to shift the boundaries in their favor, to protect themselves, and to gain a measure of autonomy. In the Chesapeake, close white supervision gave most slaves little autonomy at work. Most masters owned ten or fewer slaves and often worked in the tobacco fields alongside them. On larger tobacco plantations, slaves often toiled in work gangs, but almost always under the watchful eye of a white overseer. In the lower South, rice and indigo plantations were worked by groups of fifty or more slaves. Many rice planters assigned each adult slave a task, typically defined as a certain area of ground to be planted, cultivated, and harvested or a specific job to be completed. The task system reduced the need for close white supervision; planters often assigned supervisory responsibilities to slaves known as "drivers." The task system gave lower South slaves some control over the pace of their work for their master and some discretion in the use of the rest of their time. If a slave could complete the task before the end of the day, he or she could use the remainder of the day to work in a garden plot, fish, hunt, spin, weave, sew, or cook. When a master sought to increase productivity by changing the plantation's definition of tasks, slaves did their best to defend customary practices.

Eighteenth-century slaves planted the roots of African American lineages that branch out to the present.

Eighteenth-century slaves planted the roots of African American lineages that branch out to the present. Historians are only beginning to explore the kin networks eighteenth-century slaves built within the confines of bondage; much remains unknown. But it is clear that slaves valued family ties

Regulating Slavery

*T*he slave rebellion at Stono, South Carolina, in 1739 alarmed white South Carolinians. The colony's legislators responded in the spring of 1740, only a few months after the rebellion had been suppressed, by enacting new regulations governing slavery. The laws disclosed widespread perceptions among whites of the dangers posed by slaves and of the remedies that would maintain order.

DOCUMENT 1: Excerpt of an Act Requiring White Men to Serve on Patrols

Forasmuch as many late horrible and barbarous massacres have been actually committed, and many more designed, on the white inhabitants of this Province, by negro slaves, who are generally prone to such cruel practices, which makes it highly necessary that constant patrols should be established and kept in the several militia districts of this Province, for the better preventing any future insurrections or cabals of said slaves; we therefore humbly pray his most sacred Majesty that it may be enacted. . . .

That every patrol shall go to and examine the several plantations in their districts . . . at least once in a fortnight, and may take up all slaves which they shall see without the fences or cleared ground of their owners' plantations, who have not a ticket or letter to shew the reasonableness of their absence, or who have not some white person in company to give an account of his, her, or their business, and such patrol may correct every such slave or slaves by whipping with a switch or cowskin, not exceeding twenty lashes; provided no patrol man shall beat or abuse any slave quietly and peaceably being in his master's plantation. . . . And the said patrols shall have full power to search and examine all negro houses for offensive weapons and ammunition . . . [and] to enter into any disorderly tipling houses or other houses suspected of harbouring, trafficking or dealing with negroes, either of white persons, free negroes or others, and to apprehend and correct all disorderly slaves there found, by whipping.

*A*nother act sought to increase the security of the white population by imposing a tax on purchasers of African slaves which would be used to encourage white immigrants to settle in the colony.

DOCUMENT 2: Excerpt of an Act to Tax Imported Slaves

Whereas, the great importation of negroes from the coast of Africa, who are generally of a barbarous and savage disposition, may hereafter prove of very dangerous consequence to the peace and safety of this Province, and which we have now more reason to be apprehensive of from the late rising in rebellion of a great number of the negroes lately imported into this Province from the coast of Africa, in the thickest settlements of this Province, and barbarously murdering upwards of twenty persons of his Majesty's faithful subjects of this Province, within about twenty miles from the capital of this Province; and whereas, the best way to prevent those fatal mischiefs for the future, will be to establish a method by which the importation of negroes into this Province should be made a necessary means . . . for the better settling his Majesty's townships and the other frontier parts of this Province with white inhabitants, by which we may be the better enabled to suppress any future insurrection of negroes and slaves. . . . [T]here shall be imposed and paid by all and every [one of] the inhabitants of this Province . . . first purchasing any negro or other

and that kinship structured slaves' relations with each other. Slave parents often gave a child the name of a grandparent, aunt, or uncle, unmistakable evidence that they recognized and honored kinfolk. In selecting a husband or wife (when the master permitted a choice), slaves avoided first cousins or closer relatives, further evidence of their awareness of kin connections. In West African societies, kinship not only identified a person's place among living relatives. It also linked the person to ancestors among the dead and to descendants in the future. Kinship rooted people in society and in time.

slave . . . , a certain tax or sum of ten pounds current money for every such negro and other slave of the height of four feet and two inches and upwards; and for every one under that height, and above three feet two inches, the sum of five pounds like money; and for all under three feet two inches, (sucking children excepted) two pounds ten shillings like money. . . . And . . . that out of the said tax or duty on negroes and slaves . . . two-third parts . . . of the net sum arising by the tax . . . [be used] for defraying the charge of transportation or carriage of poor protestants from Charlestown to the townships or other place where they shall settle . . . and for purchasing tools necessary for planting and settling, and for provisions for one year for each of such poor protestants, (not being upwards of fifty years of age) and also for purchasing one cow and calf over and besides such provisions, for every five persons who shall actually become settlers.

The legislators also enacted a comprehensive slave code containing fifty-eight separate provisions. All the regulations indirectly acknowledged the lesson whites learned from the Stono rebels—namely, that slaves must be controlled and disciplined more rigorously.

DOCUMENT 3: Excerpt from South Carolina Slave Code

XVI. Be it . . . enacted . . . That . . . if any slave, free negro, mulattoe, Indian or mustizoe [mestizo, a person of mixed white and Indian ancestry], shall wilfully and maliciously burn or destroy any stack of rice, corn, or other grain, of the product, growth or manufacture of this Province, or shall wilfully and maliciously set fire to, burn or destroy any tar kiln, barrels of pitch, tar, turpentine or rosin, or any other [of] the goods or commodities of the growth, produce or manufacture of this Province, or shall felo-

niously steal, take or carry away any slaves, being the property of another, with intent to carry such slave out of this Province, or shall wilfully or maliciously poison or administer any poison to any person, free man, woman, servant or slave, every such slave, free negro, mulattoe, Indian . . . and mustizoe, shall suffer death as a felon. . . .

XXIV. And be it further enacted . . . That if any slave shall presume to strike any white person, such slave, upon trial and conviction . . . shall for the first and second offence, suffer such punishment as the said justice [of the peace] and freeholders . . . shall, in their discretion think fit, not extending to life or limb; and for the third offence, shall suffer death. But in case any such slave shall grievously wound, maim or bruise any white person, though it be only the first offence, such slave shall suffer death. . . .

LVI. And whereas, several negroes did lately rise in rebellion, and did commit many barbarous murders at Stono and other parts adjacent thereto; and whereas, in suppressing the said rebels, several of them were killed and others taken alive and executed; and as the exigence and danger the inhabitants at that time were in and exposed to, would not admit of the formality of a legal trial of such rebellious negroes, but for their own security, the said inhabitants were obliged to put such negroes to immediate death; to prevent, therefore, any person . . . being questioned for any matter done in the suppression or execution of the said rebellious negroes. . . . Be it enacted . . . That all and every act, matter and thing, had, done, committed and executed, in and about the suppressing and putting all and every [one of] the said . . . negroes to death, is and are hereby are declared lawful . . . as fully and amply as if such rebellious negroes had undergone a formal trial and condemnation.

Documents 1, 2, and 3. Cooper and McCord, editors, *Statutes at Large of South Carolina,* (1840s), 556–63, 568–73, 397–417.

Newly imported African slaves usually arrived alone, without kin; like Equiano, they had been snatched away from their relatives in Africa. Often slaves who had traversed the Middle Passage on the same ship adopted one another as "brothers" and "sisters." Likewise, as new Negroes were seasoned

and incorporated into existing slave communities, established families often adopted them as kin and recognized them as aunts or uncles. Through kin networks, slaves endowed their personal lives with relationships and meanings that they controlled, as much as the circumstances of slavery permitted.

Tobacco, Rice, and Prosperity

Slaves' labor bestowed prosperity on their masters, British merchants, and the monarchy. Rice exports from the lower South exploded from less than half a million pounds in 1700 to eighty million pounds in 1770, virtually all of it grown by slaves. Exports of indigo—another product of low country slaves—also boomed. Together, rice and indigo made up three-fourths of lower South exports, nearly two-thirds of them going to England and most of the rest to the West Indies, where sugar-growing slaves ate slave-grown rice. Tobacco exports from the Chesapeake did not accelerate as rapidly as rice exports, but they still leaped from about thirty million pounds in 1700 to a hundred million pounds in 1770. Many slaveless small farmers in the Chesapeake grew a little tobacco, but slaves produced the bulk of tobacco exported. Tobacco was by far the most important export from British North America; by 1770, it represented almost a third of *all* colonial exports and three-fourths of all Chesapeake exports. And under the provisions of the Navigation Acts (see chapter 4), nearly all of it went to England, where the monarchy collected a lucrative tax on each pound. British merchants then reexported over 80 percent of the tobacco to the European continent, pocketing a nice markup for their troubles. From the British viewpoint, the southern colonies were the export capital of North America: they supplied 90 percent of all North American exports to England; only about 10 percent of North American exports to England came from New England and the middle colonies combined.

These products of slave labor made the southern colonies by far the richest in North America. The per capita wealth of free whites in the South was four times greater than that in New England and three times that in the middle colonies. In the Chesapeake, about six out of ten white families owned slaves by 1770 and, of course, they reaped more profit than families without slaves. In one tobacco county, for example, white families with land and slaves had four times more wealth than families with land but no slaves and forty-five times more wealth than tenant families who owned neither land nor slaves.

At the top of the wealth pyramid stood the rice grandees of the lower South and the tobacco gentry of the Chesapeake. These elite families commonly resided on estates of a thousand or more acres adorned by handsome brick mansions and luxurious gardens, maintained and supported by

PLANTATION MISTRESS
The wife of a wealthy South Carolina rice planter, Mrs. Barnard Elliott displays the opulence made possible by the soil of plantations and the toil of untold slaves. Mrs. Elliott appears to be a discriminating consumer. Although she probably made most of her purchases in the best Charleston shops, her custom-made fashions would not have been out of place in the drawing rooms of the English gentry. Sensuous textiles, billowing lace-encrusted sleeves, a daring neckline, and dazzling jewels demonstrate Mrs. Elliott's cosmopolitan tastes despite her colonial residence. Her formal, almost regal pose evokes the enormous distance between the luxurious refinements of elite planters and the workaday plantation realities that gilded their world. Contrast the appearance of Mrs. Elliott with that of her approximate contemporary, the New England household slave Phyllis (page 152).
The Gibbes Museum of Art, Carolina Art Association.

several hundred slaves. The extravagant lifestyle of one gentry family astonished a young tutor from New Jersey who noted with amazement that during the winter months the family kept twenty-eight large fires roaring, requiring six oxen to haul in a heavy cartload of slave-cut wood four times a day. (Yeoman families—those that supported themselves on a small plot of land with no slaves—normally warmed themselves around one fire.) Slave-grown tobacco and rice were not the only sources of gentry wealth. The gentry speculated in western lands, acquiring title to huge tracts in the southern backcountry and selling off parcels as land-hungry settlers moved south from Pennsylvania or west from the coastal regions. Many wealthy planters kept stores on their plantations stocked with textiles, pots and pans, rum, and other delicacies, which they sold to their neighbors or, more often, traded for tobacco. Affluent planters also made loans to their lesser neighbors, collecting both interest payments and deference from their debtors. Land sales, store trade, and loans combined with such favors as help with marketing tobacco, sending medicine to a sick child, or sharing a toddy during a neighborly conversation laced the southern gentry to white yeomen and tenants.

The products of slave labor made the southern colonies by far the richest in North America. The per capita wealth of free whites in the South was four times greater than that in New England and three times that in the middle colonies.

The vast differences in wealth among white southerners engendered envy and occasional tension between rich and poor, but remarkably little open hostility. The gentry looked down upon the "meaner sort" and spoke of them disparagingly in private. In public, the planter elite acknowledged humble whites as their equals, at least in belonging to the superior—in their minds—white race. Looking upward, white yeomen and tenants sensed the gentry's condescension and veiled contempt. But they also appreciated the gentry for granting favors, upholding white supremacy, and keeping slaves in their place. Curiously, while racial slavery made a few whites much richer than most others, it also gave those who did not get rich a powerful reason to feel similar (in race) to those who were so different (in wealth).

The slaveholding gentry dominated politics as well as the economy of the southern colonies. In Virginia, only adult white men who owned at least one hundred acres of unimproved land or twenty-five acres of land with a house could vote. This property-holding requirement prevented about 40 percent of white men in Virginia from voting for representatives to the House of Burgesses. In South

Carolina, only fifty acres of land were required to vote, and most adult white men qualified. But in both colonies, voters elected members of the gentry to serve in the colonial legislature. And they elected them again and again and again. The gentry passed political offices from generation to generation, almost as if they were hereditary. Between 1725 and 1773, for example, nearly half of the men elected from southern Maryland to serve in the colonial legislature followed in the footsteps of their fathers, who had served in the same offices; almost as many of these men had grandfathers who had preceded them in office. Politically, the gentry built a self-perpetuating oligarchy—rule by the elite few—with the votes of their many humble neighbors.

The gentry also set the cultural standard in the southern colonies. They bought wines from France, fashions and books from London. They entertained lavishly, dancing minuets and jigs while their tables groaned under the best game and produce their slaves could prepare. They attended the Anglican Church for the twenty-minute sermon and the subsequent two hours of conversation with neighbors about crops, horses, politics, and scandals. They gambled on races, cards, cockfights, and other blood sports. Above all they cultivated a life of leisurely pursuit of happiness. They did not condone idleness; far from it. Their pleasures and their responsibilities kept them busy. Thomas Jefferson, an obsessively busy and phenomenally productive member of the gentry, recalled that his earliest childhood memory was of being carried on a pillow by a family slave—a powerful image of the slave hands beneath the gentry's leisure and achievement.

Unifying Experiences

While the societies of New England, the middle colonies, and the southern colonies became more sharply differentiated during the eighteenth century, colonists throughout British North America shared certain unifying experiences. The first was economic: The economies of all three regions had their roots in agriculture. The seasonal rhythms of plant life marked time for nearly everyone. But the tempo of commerce quickened during the eighteenth century. Colonists sold their distinctive products in markets that, in turn, offered to consumers throughout the colonies a more or less uniform array of goods. A second unifying experience was a decline in the importance of religion. Religious diversity increased dramatically during the eighteenth century, propelled by immigrants faithful to one or another of the many varieties of Protestantism. Throughout the colonies, some settlers drifted away from piety while others called for a revival of religious intensity. Yet religion mattered less, the affairs of the world more, than they did in the seventeenth century. Third, white inhabitants throughout North America in the eighteenth century became aware that they shared a distinctive identity as British colonists. Thirteen different governments presided over the North American colonies, but all of them answered to the British monarchy. Enemies the colonists perceived around them—French to the north and west, Spaniards to the south, and Indians almost everywhere—strengthened the colonists' allegiance to England. While royal officials expected loyalty from the colonists, they often had difficulty obtaining obedience to dictates from England. The North American colonists stood under the umbrella of the British Empire and asserted their prerogatives as British subjects to defend their special colonial interests.

Commerce and Consumption

Eighteenth-century commerce whetted the appetite to consume. Colonial products spurred the development of mass markets throughout the Atlantic world. A preacher in New England, a printer in Pennsylvania, a planter in South Carolina, or a merchant in London could munch a cracker made with flour from the middle colonies, sip tea from colonies in the East Indies sweetened by sugar from colonies in the West Indies, and smoke a pipe of tobacco from the Chesapeake. Massive increases in the supply of colonial products brought the price of these small luxuries within reach of nearly everyone, at least from time to time. Colonial goods brought into focus an important lesson of eighteenth-century commerce. Ordinary people, not just the wealthy elite, would buy things they desired, not only what they absolutely needed. The realm of desire, unlike the arena of need, had almost no limits. In England, for example, the per capita consumption of tea rose fifteenfold during the eighteenth century. With the appropriate stimulus to desire, markets seemed unlimited.

Eighteenth-century merchants and manufacturers catered to their customers' desires. In advertisements in the newspapers that became common-

place in the eighteenth century, in handbills distributed on street corners and posters plastered on walls, and in attractive shop window displays, merchants strove to make consumers feel that they needed what they desired, namely the items merchants had for sale. Manufacturers specialized in producing mundane goods people used daily—pots and pans, dishes, textiles, pins and needles—and in making them durable, attractive, and desirable.

Colonial goods brought into focus an important lesson of eighteenth-century commerce. Ordinary people, not just the wealthy elite, would buy things they desired, not only what they absolutely needed.

The Atlantic commerce that took colonial goods to markets in England brought these objects of consumer desire back to the colonies. English merchants and manufacturers recognized that colonists made excellent customers, and the Navigation Acts gave English exporters privileged access to the colonial market. English manufacturers boosted their output to keep up with colonial demand as the colonial market grew more rapidly than the English domestic market. By midcentury, export-oriented industries in England were growing ten times faster than firms attuned to the home market. Of course, most English exports went to the vast European market, where potential customers outnumbered those in the colonies by more than one hundred to one. But as European competition stiffened, colonial markets became even more important to English exporters. British colonies consumed about one-fifth of all English exports by 1750; twenty years later, they absorbed more than two-fifths.

North American colonists bought their share and more. British exports to North America multiplied eightfold between 1700 and 1773. For the first half of the century, exports to North America grew apace with the colonial population. After midcentury, colonists upped their purchases of English exports, and by 1760 the colonists' per capita consumption of exports had leaped 75 percent above the level of 1740. After 1750, the colonists' eagerness to consume exceeded their ability to pay, and English exporters willingly extended credit. As colonists put more of their purchases on the tab, their debts to English exporters soared.

(a) Colonial Exports by Regions
- New England
- Middle colonies
- Chesapeake
- Lower South

17% · 19% · 42% · 22%

(b) Colonial Export Destinations
- Great Britain
- Southern Europe
- West Indies

55% · 17% · 28%

(c) New England Exports
- Fish
- Livestock
- Wood products
- Whale oil
- Other

36% · 17% · 13% · 10% · 24%

(d) New England Export Destinations
- Great Britain
- Southern Europe
- West Indies

18% · 16% · 66%

(e) Middle Colonies Exports
- Grain products
- Meat and foods
- Other

77% · 7% · 16%

(f) Middle Colonies Export Destinations
- Great Britain
- Southern Europe
- West Indies

14% · 39% · 47%

(g) Chesapeake Exports
- Tobacco
- Grain products
- Other

74% · 16% · 10%

(h) Chesapeake Export Destinations
- Great Britain
- Southern Europe
- West Indies

9% · 10% · 81%

(i) Lower South Exports
- Rice
- Indigo
- Other

56% · 21% · 23%

(j) Lower South Export Destinations
- Great Britain
- Southern Europe
- West Indies

19% · 10% · 71%

FIGURE 5.1
Colonial Exports, 1768–1772
These pie charts provide an overview of the colonial export economy in the 1760s. The first two show that almost two-thirds of colonial exports came from the South and that the majority of the colonies' exports went to Great Britain. The remaining charts illustrate the distinctive patterns of exports in each colonial region. Fish, livestock, and wood products were New England's most important exports; they were sent primarily to the West Indies, only a small fraction going to Great Britain. From the colonial breadbasket in the middle colonies, grain products made up three-fourths of all exports, most of which went to the West Indies or to southern Europe. The Chesapeake also exported some grain, but tobacco accounted for three-fourths of the region's export trade, nearly all of it bound for Great Britain as mandated by the Navigation Acts. Rice and indigo comprised three-fourths of the exports from the Lower South, the bulk of which was sent to Great Britain. Taken together, these charts reveal Britain's economic interest in the exports of the North American colonies.

The flood of exports spread throughout the colonies, from Maine to Georgia, from gentry mansions to humble farmsteads. For years after he was married, Benjamin Franklin ate his breakfast of bread and milk (he considered tea too expensive) with a pewter spoon from a cheap earthenware bowl. The "first Appearance of Plate and China in our House," he recalled later, occurred one morning in the 1730s when his wife surprised him with breakfast served "in a China Bowl with a Spoon of Silver," the first of numerous purchases. Only the affluent could afford fine silver tableware, but cheaper imports were within reach of many. The German musician and traveler Gottfried Mittelberger reported from the middle colonies in the 1750s that "it is really possible to obtain all the things one can get in Europe in Pennsylvania, since so many merchant ships arrive there every year." The currents of consumption swept into the homes of backcountry farmers. In rural Massachusetts in the mid-seventeenth century, for example, knives and forks could hardly be found; most tables were set with thick wooden spoons. By the mid-eighteenth century, about one-third of New England farmers ate with knives and forks, most of them stamped out in an English factory. Farmers, like other colonists, succumbed to the seductions of desire. In the mid-seventeenth century, mirrors hardly existed in poor households; farmers and their families glimpsed their reflections in the placid surface of water in a bowl or bucket. By the mid-eighteenth century, nearly half of poor New England farmsteads possessed a mirror.

Imported mirrors, silver plate, spices, bed and table linens, clocks, tea services, wigs, books, and more infiltrated parlors, kitchens, and bedrooms throughout the colonies. Despite the many differences among the colonists, the consumption of English exports built a certain material uniformity across region, religion, class, and status. Some mirrors were small and plain, others large and ornately decorated; but all mirrors permitted colonists to scrutinize their appearance, to see themselves as others saw them. Consumption of English exports did not simply tie the colonists to the British economy. It also made the colonists look and feel more British, even though they lived at the edge of a wilderness an ocean away from England.

The rising tide of colonial consumption had other less visible but no less important consequences. Because consumption so often arose from desire rather than necessity, it presented colonists —both women and men—with a novel array of choices. In many respects the choices were small, seemingly trivial: whether to buy knives and forks, teacups, or a clock. But such small choices confronted eighteenth-century consumers with a big question: "What do you want?" That question did not simply ask about desires; it also identified who defined those desires: each person. As colonial consumers defined and expressed their desires with greater frequency during the eighteenth century, they became accustomed to thinking of themselves as individuals who had the power to make decisions that influenced the quality of their lives. Merchants worked constantly to ensure that those decisions led to still more consumption. The merchants' efforts emphasized that ordinary men and women exercised power and made important decisions—messages of considerable significance in the hierarchical world of eighteenth-century British North America.

Religion, Enlightenment, and Revival

Eighteenth-century colonists could choose from almost as many religions as consumer goods. Virtually all of the bewildering variety of religious sects represented some form of Christianity, almost all of them Protestant. Roman Catholics concentrated in Maryland as they had since the seventeenth century, but even there they were outnumbered by Protestants, whose suspicions about a conspiracy by the Roman Catholic Church kept Catholics on the defensive. Slaves made up the largest group of non-Christians. A few slaves converted to Christianity in Africa or after they arrived in North America, but for the most part, slaves did not flock to Christ's sheepfold. The haunting silence of the historical record limits our knowledge of most slaves' religious beliefs. Some professed Islam. Most, it seems clear, continued to embrace elements of indigenous African religions rather than the Christian faith of their masters.

The varieties of Protestant faith and practice ranged across an extremely broad spectrum. In such isolated communities as Ephrata, Pennsylvania, adherents of Baptist and Quaker sects tried to live a holy life untainted by profane corruptions. Throughout the plantation South and in urban centers like Charleston, New York, and Philadelphia, prominent colonists attended the Anglican Church, conforming to the rituals and relaxed worldliness of the king's faith. In New England, old-style Puritanism splintered into strands of Congregationalism that differed over fine points of theological doctrine. The thousands of immigrants in the middle colonies and the southern backcountry included militant Baptists and Presbyterians. Huguenots who had fled persecution in Catholic France peopled congregations in several cities. Some colonists ignored doctrinal distinctions and frequented several churches: If one church was good, why weren't two or more that much better?

In New England, the Congregational Church was the official established church and all residents paid taxes for its support. In the South, Anglicans enjoyed a similar status as the established state church. But in both regions, dissenting faiths grew, much as they did in colonies without a state-supported religious establishment. In New England and the South, Baptists, Quakers, Presbyterians, and others eventually won the right to worship publicly, although the established churches retained official sanction.

Rivalry and competition for converts often developed among churches. When the Anglican missionary Charles Woodmason ventured into the South Carolina backcountry in the 1760s he received a less than hearty welcome. The colonists there "wanted no D——d Black Gown Sons of Bitches [Anglican ministers] among them," he was told. Woodmason accused Presbyterians and Baptists of resorting to dirty tricks to foil his efforts: They distributed two barrels of whiskey before one service, urging the drunks to begin "firing [guns], hooping and hallowing like Indians" while Woodmason tried to administer communion; another group brought to church "57 Dogs (for I counted them) which in Time of Service they set fighting"; after communion one Sunday, some men "got into the Church and left their Excrements on the Communion Table"; others stole Woodmason's clerical robe one night and draped it over a man who slipped into the bed of a sleeping woman, "making her give out next day, that the Parson came to Bed to her."

The bickering and dissension that often tore at eighteenth-century churches grew out of the fundamental convictions of Protestantism. A faith that affirmed the priesthood of all believers (in Martin Luther's famous phrase) empowered Christians to look into their Bibles and their hearts to find God's Way. Not surprisingly, faithful and well-meaning Protestants identified different Ways, each of which had its defenders who claimed it as the one true Way while denouncing the others as misguided

heresies. The strife engendered by the core of Protestant belief led many colonists to favor toleration of religious differences and peaceful coexistence among disputing churches.

Many educated colonists became deists, looking for God's plan in nature more than in the Bible. They believed in God, but they avoided becoming mired in hair-splitting arguments about whether it was the Presbyterians' God, the Anglicans' God, the Congregationalists' God, or the Quakers' God. They commonly expressed doubts about such important Christian doctrines as original sin or Christ's divinity. But they usually had no difficulty supporting the general moral precepts of more orthodox Christians. When deist Benjamin Franklin drew up his plan "for arriving at moral Perfection" a few years after he arrived in Philadelphia, it featured a list of thirteen virtues quite compatible with Protestant morality. But a devout Protestant probably would have reordered Franklin's list. Franklin's thirteenth virtue—after temperance, silence, order, resolution, frugality, industry, sincerity, justice, moderation, cleanliness, tranquillity, and chastity—was humility, which meant to Franklin "Imitate Jesus and Socrates." Pairing Jesus with a pagan philosopher and honoring both for their meekness rather than for their message aptly illustrated deists' point of view.

Deists shared the ideas of eighteenth-century European Enlightenment thinkers, who believed that science and reason could disclose God's laws in the natural order. During the seventeenth century, Isaac Newton, the brilliant English scientist, demonstrated that all physical objects obeyed precise mathematical laws, such as the law of gravity. Newton's ideas suggested a new vision of the universe and the place of human beings in it, a vision Enlightenment thinkers found compelling. In the Newtonian universe, order was maintained not by the constant intervention of God but by basic mathematical laws. God had presumably created those laws and set the universe in motion, but then he had stepped back to observe his handiwork. God, many eighteenth-century thinkers believed, was like a watchmaker who assembled a watch from sprockets, gears, and springs and then let it run. The concept of a watchmaker God made God seem more distant from the world, less interested in the minutiae of each person's vices and virtues. In addition, a watchmaker God was not arbitrary, capricious, or vengeful, plaguing the world with floods, famine, or fires to express his displeasure. Instead, God was orderly and predictable, although still mysterious

TECHNOLOGY IN AMERICA
The Printing Press

In the eighteenth century, colonial printers began to publish newspapers. Since the 1630s, printers had used presses much like the one shown here to churn out books, pamphlets, broadsides, government announcements, legal forms, invitations, and even promissory notes. The innovation of compiling newsworthy information and publishing it on a regular schedule began in 1704 with the appearance of the *Boston News-Letter*, usually printed on both sides of a single sheet of paper smaller than conventional typing paper. Each week the *News-Letter* contained reprints of articles that had appeared in English newspapers along with a few tidbits of local news such as deaths, fires, storms, and ship arrivals. For years, the audience for such information remained small; the editor complained in 1719 that he could not sell three hundred copies of each issue. Nonetheless, a competing newspaper, the *Boston Gazette*, began publication in that year. It was printed by James Franklin on his press, shown here, which he had brought from England. Both the *Gazette* and the *News-Letter* submitted their copy to the governor for official approval before the newspapers were printed. Frustrated by this official scrutiny, Franklin started a new paper, the *New England Courant*, which set out to thumb its nose at officialdom, both governmental and religious. The *Courant* pledged "to entertain the Town with the most comical and diverting Incidents of Humane Life" and to "expose the Vice and Follies of Persons of all Ranks and Degrees." Franklin's press broadcast to the reading public dissenting opinions that previously one had to hear (or overhear) in private conversations. When the old technology of printing was used in fresh ways to publish unofficial news, all kinds of information and ideas began to diffuse more readily beyond official channels and to help form public opinion. Eighteenth-century newspapers combined old printing technology with the new currents of commerce, dissent, and enlightenment, creating a novel awareness of the problems and possibilities of public life.

Newport Historical Society.

because the deepest underlying principles of his order remained unknown.

Although human beings seemed to matter less to the Newtonian God, they had an important role to play. First, they needed to study nature to discover the basic principles of God's order. Second, they must clear away any obstacles that impeded the smooth functioning of the natural order. Some obstacles were false ideas, such as that the Bible or the church was the final authority on God's truth. Other obstacles were social or political institutions that violated natural laws. For example, in Newton's universe the same physical laws applied to all matter. The underlying concept of equality in the Newtonian universe suggested that human beings should try to eliminate social distinctions that violated the principles of the divine order.

The ideas associated with a Newtonian universe percolated through the Atlantic world during the eighteenth century, influencing devout Christians as well as skeptical deists. In the colonies as well as in Europe, Enlightenment ideas encouraged people to study the world around them, to think for themselves, and to ask whether the disorderly appearance of things masked the principles of a deeper, more profound order. Throughout the colonies, curious individuals collected specimens of odd plants and animals; experimented with seeds, grafts, and potions; and kept detailed notes on astronomy, weather patterns, topography, vegetation, and much more. From New England towns to southern drawing rooms, individuals met to discuss such matters. Philadelphia was the center of these scientific conversations, especially after the formation of the American Philosophical Society in 1769, an outgrowth of an earlier discussion group organized by Benjamin Franklin. The American Philosophical Society fostered communication among leading colonial thinkers; Benjamin Franklin was its first president, Thomas Jefferson its third. Among the purposes of these scientific discussions was to find ways to improve society. Franklin declared that the Philosophical Society would be a forum for "all philosophical experiments that let light into the nature of things, tend to increase the power of man over matter, and multiply the conveniences or pleasures of life." Franklin's interest in electricity, stoves, and eyeglasses exemplified the quest for useful knowledge. His focus on the conveniences and pleasures of life indicates the way Enlightenment ideas shifted the gaze of many eighteenth-century colonists from heaven to the here and now.

Most eighteenth-century colonists went to church seldom or not at all, although they probably vaguely considered themselves Christians. A minister in Charleston observed that on the Sabbath "the Taverns have more Visitants than the Churches." In the leading colonial cities, church members were a small minority of eligible adults, no more than 10 or 15 percent. Anglican parishes in the South rarely claimed more than one-fifth of eligible adults as members. In some regions of rural New England and the middle colonies, church membership embraced two-thirds of eligible adults, while in other areas only one-quarter of the residents belonged to a church. Women were the majority of New England church members; they tended to join in their early twenties, about the time they got married. Few unmarried New England men joined churches, and married men usually delayed joining until they were in their thirties or forties. Considering the colonies as a whole, the dominant faith was religious indifference. As a late-eighteenth-century traveler observed, "Religious indifference is imperceptibly disseminated from one end of the continent to the other." The competing varieties of Protestant faith did not persuade most colonists to lift their eyes from their worldly preoccupations.

The spread of religious indifference among most colonists, of deism among many educated leaders, of denominational rivalry, and of comfortable backsliding among the faithful profoundly concerned many ministers. A few despaired that, as one wrote, "religion . . . lay a-dying and ready to expire its last breath of life." To combat what one preacher called the "dead formality" of church services, some

ministers set out to convert the unchurched and to revive the piety of the faithful with a new style of preaching that appealed more to the heart than the head. Historians have termed this wave of revivals the "Great Awakening." In Massachusetts during the mid-1730s, the fiery Puritan minister Jonathan Edwards reaped a harvest of souls by reemphasizing traditional Puritan doctrines of humanity's utter depravity and God's vengeful omnipotence. The title of Edwards's most famous sermon, "Sinners in the Hands of an Angry God," conveys the flavor of his message. Edwards's sermons, a member of his congregation noted, caused "great moaning and crying through the whole house [church]—What shall I do to be saved—oh I am going to Hell . . . the shrieks and cries were piercing and amazing." In Pennsylvania and New Jersey, Presbyterian William Tennent and his four minister sons led revivals dramatizing conventional appeals for spiritual rebirth with accounts of God's miraculous powers—such as his raising William Tennent Jr. from the dead. Strangers flocked to the Tennents' revivals to hear about such supernatural visitations and came away, Gilbert Tennent wrote, "much affected . . . the Tears trickling down their Cheeks like Hail."

Most eighteenth-century colonists went to church seldom or not at all, although they probably vaguely considered themselves Christians.

The most famous revivalist in the eighteenth-century Atlantic world was George Whitefield. An Anglican, Whitefield preached well-worn messages of sin and salvation to large audiences in England using his spellbinding, unforgettable voice that bespoke sincerity, urgency, and utter conviction. Newspapers in England and the colonies printed reports of Whitefield's revivals, building anticipation and curiosity about him and his oratory. Whitefield visited the North American colonies seven times, staying for more than three years during the mid-1740s and attracting tens of thousands in his travels. His sermons transported many in his audience to emotion-choked states of religious ecstasy. At one revival, he wrote, "the bitter cries and groans were enough to pierce the hardest heart. Some of the people were as pale as death; others were wringing their hands; others lying on the ground; others sinking into the arms of their friends; and most lifting

GEORGE WHITEFIELD
This portrait of George White-field preaching emphasizes the power of his sermons to transport his audience to a revived awareness of divine spirituality. Light from above gleams off Whitefield's forehead. His crossed eyes and faraway gaze suggest that he spoke in a semihypnotic trance. Note the absence of a Bible at the pulpit. Rather than elaborating on God's word as revealed in Scripture, Whitefield speaks from his own inner awareness. The young woman bathed in light below his hands appears transfixed, her focus not on Whitefield but on some inner realm illuminated by his words. Her eyes and White-field's do not meet, yet the author's use of light suggests that she and Whitefield see the same core of holy Truth. The other people in Whitefield's audience appear not to have achieved this state. They remain intent on Whitefield's words, failing so far to be ignited by the divine spark.
National Portrait Gallery, London.

their eyes to heaven, and crying to God for mercy. They seemed like persons . . . coming out of their graves to judgment." Whitefield impressed even those he did not convert. The slave Olaudah Equiano attended one of Whitefield's sermons and was "much struck and impressed" by "this pious man exhorting the people with the greatest fervour and earnestness, and sweating as much as I ever did while in slavery." Equiano disclosed the source of Whitefield's magnetic appeal with his observation that "I thought it strange I had never seen divines exert themselves in this manner before, and was no longer at a loss to account for the thin congregations they preached to."

Whitefield's successful revivals spawned many lesser imitators. Itinerant preachers, many of them poorly educated, toured the colonial backcountry after midcentury, mimicking Whitefield's medium and message as best they could. Educated and established ministers often regarded them with distaste and even disgust. Charles Woodmason considered "most of those Preaching fellows . . . most notorious Thieves, Jockeys, Gamblers." Revival meetings appeared to Woodmason "a Gang of frantic Lunatics."

In fact, the revivals that Woodmason deplored attracted many to Christianity. Revivals awakened and refreshed the spiritual energies of thousands of colonists struggling with the uncertainties and anxieties of eighteenth-century America. The conversions at revivals did not substantially boost the total number of church members, however. After the revivalists moved on, the routines and pressures of everyday existence reasserted their primacy in the lives of many converts. But whether revivals were held in a well-appointed church building in New York City or a wilderness clearing in the Virginia backcountry, they imparted an important message to colonists, both converted and unconverted. The revivals communicated that every soul mattered, that men and women could choose to be saved, that individuals had the power to make a decision for everlasting life or death. Colonial revivals expressed in religious terms many of the same democratic and egalitarian values expressed in economic terms by colonists' patterns of consumption. One colonist noted the analogy by referring to itinerant revivalists as "Pedlars in divinity." Like consumption, revivals contributed to a set of common experiences that bridged colonial divides of faith, region, class, and status.

Bonds of Empire

The plurality of peoples, faiths, and communities that characterized the North American colonies arose from the somewhat haphazard policies of the eighteenth-century British Empire. Since the Puritan Revolution of the mid-seventeenth century, British monarchs had valued the colonies' contributions to trade. The propensity of colonists to enrich the mother country by exchanging colonial products for English consumer goods led royal officials to encourage the growth and development of the colonies. Unlike the French—whose policy of excluding Protestants and foreigners kept the population of its territory tiny—the British kept the door to their colonies open to anyone. The open door boosted the population of the British Empire as tens of thousands of non-British immigrants crossed the threshold of the North American colonies, settled, and raised families. The open door did not extend to trade, however, as the seventeenth-century Navigation Acts restricted colonial trade to British ships and traders. These policies did not spring from wise foresight and shrewd planning by British policymakers. Instead, British policies toward the colonies evolved during the eighteenth century because they served the interests of the monarchy and of influential groups in England and the colonies and be-

cause no group of powerful, determined opponents emerged. The policies of empire also provided the colonists a common framework of political expectations and experiences.

At a minimum, British power defended the colonists from foreign enemies. Each colony organized a militia, and privateers sailed from every port to prey on foreign ships. But the British navy and army bore responsibility for colonial defense. Royal officials warily eyed the settlements of New France and New Spain for signs of threats to British colonies, but Spanish outposts at St. Augustine and elsewhere in Florida did not significantly menace the British North American colonies. Standing on the northeastern frontier of New Spain, the Florida settlements served principally to protect Spanish treasure fleets from the depredations of other European powers, especially the British. Planters in South Carolina feared that runaway slaves would find a haven among Spanish colonists, but only a few did. Likewise, the far-flung settlements of New France scattered across the vast drainages of the St. Lawrence and Mississippi Rivers posed no imminent threat to British North America. French trappers and traders lived in Indian villages, learned native languages, and often married Indian women. In large measure, the acculturation of French settlers to Indian ways arose from the social and military weakness of New France, which was designed not to build a colonial society in the New World but principally to block British advances to the north and to divert North American furs to Paris markets. Alone, neither New France nor Spanish Florida jeopardized British North America, but with Indian allies they became a potent force that kept colonists on their guard.

The policies of the British Empire provided the colonists a common framework of political expectations and experiences.

All along the ragged edge of settlement, colonists encountered Indians. Population growth and land hunger propelled the colonists toward the Indians. Indians' impulse to defend their territory from colonial incursions warred with their desire for knives, axes, fishhooks, traps, pots, blankets, rum, guns, powder, and bullets, which tugged them toward the settlers. The fur trade was the principal medium of exchange between the two groups. To trade for goods manufactured largely by the British, Indians trapped animals throughout the interior of the continent, from north of the Great Lakes to the Gulf of Mexico, from the Appalachian slopes to the edge of the Great Plains. Colonial traders competed for Indian furs. British officials monitored the trade to prevent French, Spanish, and Dutch competitors from deflecting the flow of hides toward their own markets. Indians took advantage of this competition to improve their own prospects, playing one trader off against another. And Indian tribes and confederacies competed against each other for favored trading rights with traders from one colony or another, a competition colonists encouraged.

The shifting alliances and complex dynamics of the fur trade struck a fragile balance along the frontier of colonial settlement. The threat of violence from all sides was ever present, and the threat became reality often enough for all parties to be vigilant and prepared for the worst. Did a shot mean that a raiding party—colonial or Indian—was on its way? Was a skirmish merely the first wave of a concerted attack by British, French, or Spanish troops and their Indian allies? In the Yamasee War of 1715, for example, Yamasee and Creek Indians—with French encouragement—mounted a coordinated attack against colonial settlements in South Carolina and inflicted heavy casualties. The Cherokees, traditional enemies of the Creeks, refused to join the attack. Instead, they protected their access to British trade goods by allying with the embattled colonists and turning the tide of battle, thus triggering a murderous rampage of revenge by the colonists against the Creeks and Yamasees.

The details of relations between Indians and the colonists differed from colony to colony and from year to year. But the colonists' nagging perception of menace on the frontier kept them continually hoping for help from the British in keeping the Indians at bay and in maintaining the essential flow of trade goods. In 1754, the colonists' endemic competition with the French flared into the French and Indian War, which would inflame the frontier for years. Before the 1760s, neither the colonists nor the British developed a coherent policy toward Indians. But both colonists and British shared the view that Indians made profitable trading partners, powerful allies, and deadly enemies.

British attempts to exercise their political power in colonial governments confronted obstacles almost as implacable as those preventing peace on the frontier. British efforts to govern the colonists' trade

HURON BONNET
This dazzling bonnet illustrates the trade between Native Americans and colonists. Beads of Venetian glass were one of the many items colonists imported from Europe specifically to exchange for animal skins offered by Indian hunters and trappers. Native American women in turn incorporated these European beads into designs they had previously wrought with porcupine quills, shells, bones, and other natural objects. European needle and thread were also used to craft this bonnet. Native American artistry transformed these simple trade goods into a beautiful bonnet useful and valuable in Huron society.
Musée de l'Homme.

met with success so long as British officials were on or very near the sea. Colonists acknowledged—although they did not always readily comply with—British authority to collect customs duties, inspect cargoes, and oversee the enforcement of trade regulations. But when royal officials tried to wield their authority on land, in the internal affairs of colonies, they invariably encountered obstreperous colonial resistance. A governor appointed by the king in each of the nine royal colonies (the two royal chartered colonies of Rhode Island and Connecticut selected their own governors) or by the proprietors in each of the two proprietary colonies (Maryland and Pennsylvania) headed the government of each colony. The British tended to envision colonial governors as mini-monarchs able to exert influence in the colonies much as the king did in eighteenth-century England. But colonial governors were not kings and the colonies were not England.

Most colonial governors were appointed to their posts because of their influence with the

BEAVER HAT
European colonists, like Native Americans, adapted items obtained in trade to their own purposes. The beaver hat shown here is a careful reproduction of a seventeenth-century design. Although a colonial hatmaker pressed and molded beaver skin in the process of manufacture, the animal origins of the hat were still evident in the finished product. A good beaver hat like this one was sturdy, water-repellent, and warm. But compared to the Huron bonnet opposite, it was drab and utilitarian. Women colonists sewed garments of all kinds, but they did not create intricate designs of beadwork on hats or other items. Pilgrim Society.

British monarchy rather than with the colonists. Eight out of ten colonial governors had been born in England, not in the colonies. They lacked the knowledge about people and issues more common among native-born colonists, although American birth did not guarantee success as a colonial governor. Some governors—like the two men who served as governor of Virginia for the first half of the eighteenth century—stayed in England, close to the source of royal patronage, and delegated the grubby details of colonial affairs to subordinates. Even the best-intentioned colonial governors had difficulty developing relations of trust and respect with influential colonists because their terms of office averaged just five years and could be terminated upon the arrival of the latest instructions from London. In England, politicians cemented political alliances with the careful distribution of patronage, a clerkship here, a treasury post there. But colonial governors did not have access to many patronage positions to secure political friendships. The officials who administered the colonial customs service, for example, received their positions through patronage networks that centered in England rather than in the hands of the colonial governors. But from the standpoint of patronage, colonial governors were more like puppets than puppeteers, a situation that severely limited their ability to govern. Hamstrung by their meager resources for political persuasion, the governors received instructions from the colonial office in England detailing what must be done, now.

In obedience to their instructions, colonial governors fought incessantly with the colonists' representatives in the colonial assemblies. They battled repeatedly over the governors' veto of colonial legislation, removal of colonial judges, creation of new courts, dismissal of the representative assemblies themselves, and other local issues. Some governors developed a working relationship with the assemblies. But by the eighteenth century, the assemblies had developed the upper hand.

British policies did not clearly define the powers and responsibilities of colonial assemblies. In effect, the assemblies made many of their own rules and, by successfully defending them, established a strong tradition of representative government analogous—in their eyes—to the English Parliament. Voters often returned representatives to the assemblies year after year, building continuity in power and leadership that far exceeded that of the governor. Early in the eighteenth century, colonial assemblies won the power to initiate legislation, including tax laws and authorizations to spend public funds. Although all laws passed by the assemblies (except in Maryland, Rhode Island, and Connecticut) had to be approved by the governor and then by the Board of Trade in England, the difficulties of maintaining communication about complex subjects over long distances effectively ratified the assemblies' decisions. Years often passed before a law was repealed, and in the meantime the assemblies' law prevailed.

The heated political struggles between royal governors and colonial assemblies that occurred throughout the eighteenth century taught colonists a common set of political lessons. Colonists learned to employ traditionally British ideas of representative government to defend their own interests. They learned to resist the definition of colonial interests issued by colonial governors and other royal officials. They learned that power in the British colonies rarely belonged to the British government.

Conclusion: The Dual Identity of British North American Colonists

During the eighteenth century, a distinctive society emerged in British North America, a society that was both distinctively colonial and distinctively British. Tens of thousands of immigrants and slaves gave the colonies an unmistakably colonial complexion. People of different ethnicities and faiths sought their fortunes in the colonies, where land was cheap and labor was dear. Indentured servants and redemptioners risked a temporary period of bondage for the potential reward of better opportunities than on the Atlantic's eastern shore. Slaves endured lifetime servitude that they neither chose nor desired, and their masters benefited. Identifiably colonial products from New England, the middle colonies, and the southern colonies flowed across the Atlantic. Back came unquestionably British consumer goods along with fashions in ideas, faith, and politics. The bonds of the British Empire required colonists to think of themselves as British subjects and, at the same time, encouraged them to consider their status as colonists. By the 1750s, colonists could not imagine that their distinctively dual identity—as British and as colonists—would soon become a source of intense conflict. But by 1776, colonists in British North America had to choose whether they were British or American.

CHRONOLOGY

1702 Queen Anne's War triggers large German immigration to American colonies.	**1739** Slave insurrection occurs at Stono, South Carolina.
1717 Scots-Irish immigration to American colonies begins to increase.	**1740s** George Whitefield preaches revival of religion throughout colonies.
1733 Benjamin Franklin begins to publish *Poor Richard's Almanack*.	**1754** French and Indian War begins.
	1769 American Philosophical Society founded in Philadelphia.

BIBLIOGRAPHY

This bibliography excludes pertinent sources listed in chapters 2, 3, and 4. Please consult the bibliographies of those chapters for additional suggested readings.

GENERAL WORKS

Bernard Bailyn, *The Peopling of British North America* (1986).

Bernard Bailyn, *Voyagers to the West: A Passage in the Peopling of America on the Eve of the Revolution* (1986).

Carl Bridenbaugh, *Cities in the Wilderness: The First Century of Urban Life in America, 1625–1742* (1938).

Richard D. Brown, *Knowledge Is Power: The Diffusion of Information in Early America, 1700–1865* (1989).

R. J. Dickson, *Ulster Immigration to Colonial America, 1718–1775* (1966).

A. Roger Ekirch, *Bound for America: The Transportation of British Convicts to the Colonies, 1718–1775* (1987).

Jack P. Greene, *The Intellectual Construction of America: Exceptionalism and Identity from 1492–1800* (1993).

Richard Hofstadter, *America at 1750: A Social Portrait* (1971).

Alice Hanson Jones, *Wealth of a Nation to Be: The American Colonies on the Eve of the Revolution* (1980).

Nancy F. Koehn, *The Power of Commerce: Economy and Governance in the First British Empire* (1994).

Douglas Edward Leach, *Arms for Empire: A Military History of the British Colonies in North America, 1607–1763* (1973).

Robert D. Mitchell, *Appalachian Frontiers: Settlement, Society, and Development in the Preindustrial Era* (1991).

Gary B. Nash, *The Urban Crucible: Social Change, Political Consciousness, and the Origins of the American Revolution* (1979).

A. G. Roeber, *Palatines, Liberty, and Property: German Lutherans in Colonial British America* (1993).

Carole Shammas, *The Pre-Industrial Consumer in England and America* (1990).

NEW ENGLAND

John L. Brooke, *The Heart of the Commonwealth: Society and Political Culture in Worcester County, Massachusetts, 1713–1861* (1989).

Richard Bushman, *From Puritan to Yankee: Character and the Social Order in Connecticut, 1690–1765* (1967).

Charles E. Clark, *The Eastern Frontier: The Settlement of Northern New England, 1610–1763* (1970).

David W. Conroy, *In Public Houses: Drink and the Revolution of Authority in Colonial Massachusetts* (1995).

Edward M. Cook Jr., *Fathers of the Towns: Leadership and Community Structure in Eighteenth-Century New England* (1976).

Jay Coughtry, *The Notorious Triangle: Rhode Island and the African Slave Trade, 1700–1807* (1981).

Bruce C. Daniel, *Dissent and Conformity on Narragansett Bay: The Colonial Rhode Island Town, 1635–1790* (1979).

David E. Van Deventer, *The Emergence of Provincial New Hampshire, 1623–1741* (1976).

Toby L. Ditz, *Property and Kinship: Inheritance in Early Connecticut, 1750–1820* (1986).

Christine Leigh Heyrman, *Commerce and Culture: The Maritime Communities of Colonial Massachusetts, 1690–1750* (1984).

Christopher Jedrey, *The World of John Cleaveland: Family and Community in Eighteenth-Century New England* (1979).

Douglas Lamar Jones, *Village and Seaport: Migration and Society in Eighteenth-Century Massachusetts* (1981).

James W. Jones, *The Shattered Synthesis: New England Puritanism before the Great Awakening* (1973).

Paul R. Lucas, *Valley of Discord: Church and Society along the Connecticut River, 1636–1725* (1976).

Jackson Turner Main, *Society and Economy in Colonial Connecticut* (1985).

William E. Nelson, *Dispute and Conflict Resolution in Plymouth County, Massachusetts, 1725–1825* (1981).

Gregory H. Nobles, *Divisions throughout the Whole: Politics and Society in Hampshire County, Massachusetts, 1740–1775* (1983).

William D. Piersen, *Black Yankees: The Development of an Afro-American Subculture in Eighteenth-Century New England* (1988).

Patricia J. Tracy, *Jonathan Edwards, Pastor: Religion and Society in Eighteenth-Century Northampton* (1979).

Lynne Withey, *Urban Growth in Colonial Rhode Island: Newport and Providence in the Eighteenth Century* (1984).

Robert M. Zemsky, *Merchants, Farmers, and River Gods* (1971).

MIDDLE COLONIES

Ronald W. Clark, *Benjamin Franklin* (1983).

Thomas J. Davis, *A Rumor of Revolt: The "Great Negro Plot" in Colonial New York* (1985).

Thomas M. Doerflinger, *A Vigorous Spirit of Enterprise: Merchants and Economic Development in Revolutionary Philadelphia* (1986).

Benjamin Franklin, *The Autobiography of Benjamin Franklin,* ed. Leonard W. Labaree et al. (1964).

Douglas Greenberg, *Crime and Law Enforcement in the Colony of New York, 1691–1776* (1976).

David Freeman Hawke, *Franklin* (1976).

Arthur L. Jensen, *The Maritime Community of Colonial Philadelphia* (1963).

Sung Bok Kim, *Landlord and Tenant in Colonial New York: Manorial Society, 1664–1775* (1978).

Susan E. Klepp and Billy G. Smith, eds., *The Infortunate: The Voyage and Adventures of William Moraley, an Indentured Servant* (1992).

Jessica Kross, *The Evolution of an American Town: Newtown, New York, 1642–1775* (1983).

Ned C. Landsman, *Scotland and Its First American Colony, 1683–1765* (1985).

James T. Lemon, *The Best Poor Man's Country: A Geographical Study of Early Southeastern Pennsylvania* (1972).

James H. Levitt, *For Want of Trade: Shipping and the New Jersey Ports, 1680–1783* (1981).

Stephen L. Longenecker, *Piety and Tolerance: Pennsylvania German Religion, 1700–1850* (1994).

Edward J. McManus, *A History of Negro Slavery in New York* (1970).

Peter C. Mancall, *Valley of Opportunity: Economic Culture along the Upper Susquehanna, 1700–1800* (1991).

Gary B. Nash, *Quakers and Politics: Pennsylvania, 1681–1726* (1968).

Gary B. Nash and Jean R. Soderlund, *Freedom by Degrees: Emancipation in Pennsylvania and Its Aftermath* (1991).

Thomas Eliot Norton, *The Fur Trade in Colonial New York, 1686–1776* (1974).

Paul F. Paskoff, *Industrial Evolution: Organization, Structure, and Growth of the Pennsylvania Iron Industry, 1750–1860* (1983).

Sharon V. Salinger, *"To Serve Well and Faithfully": Labor and Indentured Servitude in Pennsylvania, 1682–1800* (1987).

Sally Schwartz, *"A Mixed Multitude": The Struggle for Toleration in Colonial Pennsylvania* (1987).

Mary M. Schweitzer, *Custom and Contract: Household, Government, and the Economy in Colonial Pennsylvania* (1987).

Beverly Prior Smaby, *The Transformation of Moravian Bethlehem: From Communal Mission to Family Economy* (1988).

Billy G. Smith, *The "Lower Sort": Philadelphia's Laboring People, 1750–1800* (1990).

Merrill D. Smith, *Breaking the Bonds: Marital Discord in Pennsylvania, 1730–1830* (1991).

Jean R. Soderlund, *Quakers and Slavery: A Divided Spirit* (1985).

Frederick B. Tolles, *Meeting House and Counting House: The Quaker Merchants of Colonial Philadelphia* (1948).

Alan Tully, *William Penn's Legacy: Politics and Social Structure in Provincial Pennsylvania, 1726–1755* (1977).

Peter O. Wacker, *Land and People: A Cultural Geography of Preindustrial New Jersey* (1975).

SOUTHERN COLONIES

Richard R. Beeman, *The Evolution of the Southern Backcountry: A Case Study of Lunenburg County, Virginia, 1746–1832* (1984).

T. H. Breen, *Tobacco Culture: The Mentality of the Great Tidewater Planters on the Eve of the Revolution* (1985).

Carl Bridenbaugh, *Myths and Realities: Societies of the Colonial South* (1952).

Edward J. Cashin, *Lachlan McGillivray, Indian Trader: The Shaping of the Southern Colonial Frontier* (1992).

Edward J. Cashin, *Governor Henry Ellis and the Transformation of British North America* (1994).

David R. Chesnutt, *South Carolina's Expansion into Colonial Georgia, 1720–1765* (1989).

Paul G. E. Clemons, *The Atlantic Economy and Colonial Maryland's Eastern Shore: From Tobacco to Grain* (1980).

Kenneth Coleman, *Colonial Georgia* (1976).

Philip D. Curtin, *The Rise and Fall of the Plantation Complex: Essays in Atlantic History* (1990).

Harold E. Davis, *The Fledgling Province: Social and Cultural Life in Colonial Georgia, 1733–1776* (1976).

A. Roger Ekirch, *Poor Carolina: Politics and Society in Colonial North Carolina, 1729–1776* (1981).

Allan Gallay, *The Formation of a Planter Elite: Jonathan Bryan and the Southern Colonial Frontier* (1989).

Jack P. Greene, *Landon Carter: An Inquiry into the Personal Values and Social Imperatives of the Eighteenth-Century Virginia Gentry* (1967).

Gwendolyn Midlo Hall, *Africans in Colonial Louisiana: The Development of Afro-Creole Culture in the Eighteenth Century* (1992).

Joseph E. Inkiori and Stanley L. Engerman, eds., *The Atlantic Slave Trade: Effects on Economies, Societies, and Peoples in Africa, the Americas, and Europe* (1992).

Rhys Isaac, *The Transformation of Virginia, 1740–1790* (1982).

Alan L. Karras, *Sojourners in the Sun: Scottish Migrants in Jamaica and the Chesapeake, 1740–1800* (1992).

Marvin L. Michael Kay, *Slavery in North Carolina, 1748–1775* (1995).

Allan Kulikoff, *Tobacco and Slaves: The Development of Southern Cultures in the Chesapeake, 1680–1800* (1986).

Robin Law, *The Slave Coast of West Africa, 1550–1750: The Impact of the Atlantic Slave Trade on an African Society* (1991).

Hugo Prosper Leaming, *Hidden Americans: Maroons of Virginia and the Carolinas* (1995).

Jan Lewis, *The Pursuit of Happiness: Family and Values in Jeffersonian Virginia* (1983).

Ronald L. Lewis, *Coal, Iron, and Slaves: Industrial Slavery in Maryland and Virginia, 1715–1865* (1979).

Paul E. Lovejoy, *Transformations in Slavery: A History of Slavery in Africa* (1983).

Gloria L. Main, *Tobacco Colony: Life in Early Maryland, 1650–1720* (1982).

Patrick Manning, *Slavery and African Life: Occidental, Oriental, and African Slave Trades* (1990).

Harry Roy Merrens, *Colonial North Carolina in the Eighteenth Century* (1964).

Joseph C. Miller, *Way of Death: Merchant Capitalism and the Angolan Slave Trade, 1730–1830* (1988).

Robert L. Mitchell, *Commercialism and Frontier: Perspectives in the Early Shenandoah Valley* (1977).

Gerald W. Mullin, *Flight and Rebellion: Slave Resistance in Eighteenth-Century Virginia* (1972).

Michael Mullin, *Africa in America: Slave Acculturation and Resistance in the American South and the British Caribbean, 1736–1831* (1992).

Paul David Nelson, *William Tryon and the Course of Empire: A Life in British Imperial Service* (1990).

Jacob M. Price, *France and the Chesapeake: A History of the French Tobacco Monopoly, 1674–1791, and of Its Relationship to the British and American Tobacco Trades* (1973).

Jacob M. Price, *Capital and Credit in the British Overseas Trade: The View from the Chesapeake, 1700–1776* (1980).

John C. Rainbolt, *From Prescription to Persuasion: Manipulation of Eighteenth-Century Virginia Economy* (1974).

Robert W. Ramsey, *Carolina Cradle: Settlement of the North Carolina Frontier, 1747–1762* (1964).

Edward Miles Riley, ed., *The Journal of John Harrower: An Indentured Servant in the Colony of Virginia, 1773–1776* (1963).

A. G. Roeber, *Faithful Magistrates and Republican Lawyers: Creators of Virginia Legal Culture, 1680–1810* (1981).

Daniel Blake Smith, *Inside the Great House: Planter Family Life in Eighteenth-Century Chesapeake Society* (1980).

Mechal Sobel, *The World They Made Together: Black and White Values in Eighteenth-Century Virginia* (1987).

Barbara L. Solow, ed., *Slavery and the Rise of the Atlantic System* (1991).

Donna Spindel, *Crime and Society in North Carolina, 1663–1776* (1989).

Gregory A. Stiverson, *Poverty in a Land of Plenty: Tenancy in Eighteenth-Century Maryland* (1977).

Charles S. Sydnor, *Gentleman Freeholders: Political Practices in Washington's Virginia* (1952).

Daniel B. Thorp, *The Moravian Community in Colonial North Carolina: Pluralism on the Southern Frontier* (1989).

Dell Upton, *Holy Things and Profane: Anglican Parish Churches in Colonial Virginia* (1986).

Betty Wood, *Slavery in Colonial Georgia, 1730–1775* (1984).

GILDED BRASS GORGET

George Washington wore this small brass gorget during the French and Indian War. It symbolized, in miniature, the throat piece of a medieval suit of armor. Eighteenth-century gorgets probably did not stop many Indian arrows, but they reminded officers of their noble loyalty to their monarch. The inscribed Latin motto, En Dat Virginia Quartam, boasts that Virginia is fourth in importance in the British Empire, after England, Scotland, and Ireland—and therefore first among the many American colonies.

Courtesy of the Massachusetts Historical Society ©.

THE BRITISH EMPIRE AND THE COLONIAL CRISIS

6

1754–1775

THOMAS HUTCHINSON WAS A FIFTH-GENERATION DIRECT DESCENDANT of Anne Hutchinson, the woman of conscience who so rattled the Puritan town of Boston in the 1630s. Thomas Hutchinson likewise was a man of conscience, but there the resemblance to his famous ancestor ended. He was a Harvard-educated member of the Massachusetts elite, from a family of successful merchants. He shared the family propensity for rigorous bookkeeping, tracking every penny and shilling in daily account books. Hutchinson was a measured and cautious man. "My temper does not incline to enthusiasm," he once wrote, in a shrewd self-assessment.

Hutchinson entered politics at a young age and in 1758 was appointed lieutenant governor after two decades of faithful service to the crown in the Massachusetts general assembly. In 1771, with Boston politics a powderkeg, he agreed to become the royal governor, knowing full well the risks. Hutchinson was one of the rare native-born royal governors, with deep roots in his home community; most of the other colonies were ruled by men British born and bred. But those deep roots did not ensure that Hutchinson would side with Americans when they began opposing British policies in the 1760s and 1770s.

Hutchinson had the misfortune to preside over the most tumultuous years in Massachusetts history. His love of order and tradition inclined him to unconditional support of the British Empire and away from the contagious enthusiasms of rebellion. Remaining loyal to England was no easy thing to do in Boston after 1765; to defend the existing order took courage and exposed Hutchinson to dangerous situations. He personally faced agitated and threatening crowds during demonstrations over the Stamp Act, the Townshend duties, the Boston Massacre, and the Boston Tea Party, all landmark events on the road to the American Revolution. Privately he lamented the stupidity of the British acts that provoked trouble, but the poker-faced, humorless administrator in him kept him from any public deviation from loyalty to the crown.

As early as anyone, Thomas Hutchinson reflected on the difficulties of maintaining full rights and privileges for Americans so far from their supreme government, the king and Parliament in England. In 1769, soon after British troops had come to occupy and pacify Boston, he wrote to a friend in England, "There must be an abridgement of what are called English liberties. . . . I doubt whether it is possible to project a system of government in which a colony three thousand miles distant from the parent state shall enjoy all the liberty of the parent state." What he could not imagine was the possibility of giving up the parent state altogether.

Others in America would draw the opposite conclusion by 1775: If the distance of governance precludes full participation in liberties, then perhaps it is time to change the government and bring it closer to home.

A sympathetic view of Hutchinson sees him as a tragic figure, a competent colonial administrator just trying to do his job, which was to defend royal policies that he knew were misguided. A less principled man would have taken the first opportunity to resign; an English-born governor would have longed to go home, to England. But Boston was Hutchinson's home, and he dug in. The more he dug in, the more his opposition flourished. Boston deserved its reputation as the leading edge of the colonial rebellion. Hutchinson gave Bostonians an immediate target, a man to vilify for defending British policies. The man not inclined to enthusiasm unleashed popular enthusiasm all around him. He never appreciated that irony.

Thomas Hutchinson was a loyalist; in the 1750s, probably most English-speaking inhabitants of the colonies would have considered themselves affectionately loyal to England. But the French and Indian War, which England and its colonies fought together as allies, shook that affection, and imperial policies in the decade following the war (1763–1773) shattered it completely. Over the course of that decade serious questions about American liberties and rights were raised insistently and repeatedly. Despite sharing a common language, the British and the colonists only slowly discovered that they sometimes meant fundamentally different things when they used words like *liberty* and *representation*. Each side in the imperial conflict was certain it was right, and that certainty limited the chances for compromise and peaceful solutions.

Many on the American side came to believe what Thomas Hutchinson could never credit, that a tyrannical Britain had embarked on a course to enslave the colonists by depriving them of their traditional English liberties. A liberty was a right, a freedom to act with independence and without coercion, and the liberty of taxation was the primary right Americans wanted to control. The opposite of liberty was slavery, a condition of unfreedom and of coercion. Political rhetoric about liberty, tyranny, and slavery heated up emotions during the many crises of the 1760s and 1770s. It was very effective as a call to arms, as a way of persuading others that very basic and significant issues were involved in the struggle with England. But this rhetoric turned out to be a two-edged sword. The call for an end to

THOMAS HUTCHINSON
The only formal portrait of Thomas Hutchinson still in existence shows an assured young man in ruffles and hair ribbons. Decades of turmoil in Boston failed to puncture his self-confidence. Doubtless he sat for other portraits, as did all the Boston leaders in the 1760s to 1780s, but no other likeness has survived. Hutchinson was hated; any portrait that fell into his enemies' hands would probably have been mutilated.
Courtesy of the Massachusetts Historical Society ©.

tyrannical slavery meant one thing when sounded by Boston merchants whose commercial shipping rights had been revoked; the same call meant something quite different when sounded by black Americans in 1775, locked in the bondage of perpetual slavery.

The French and Indian War

Whenever England was at war with France or Spain, the colonists in America also got drawn in. For twenty-two of the first fifty years of the eighteenth century, England was at war, mostly with France, and the colonists who felt it most acutely and continuously were the ones in frontier New

England, sharing an uncertain and dangerous border with the French in Quebec and Montreal and their Indian allies. A significant and costly victory in 1745—the capture by Massachusetts soldiers of the French fortress Louisbourg in Nova Scotia—held promise of cutting off all the French inland settlements to access to the Atlantic Ocean. But the Treaty of Aix-la-Chapelle in 1748 inexplicably returned the fortress to the French, a major blunder in New Englanders' eyes.

From 1754 to 1763, British and American soldiers shared the hardships of battle and the glory of victory over the French and their Indian allies.

In the 1750s, tensions returned to full force, as the French boldly extended their empire south from Canada into lands that some British colonists now eyed with desire, anticipating westward expansion. The result was the French and Indian War. From 1754 to 1763, British and American soldiers shared the hardships of battle and the glory of victory over the French and their Indian allies. But the expense of the war abruptly plunged the British and the colonists into their most serious disagreement yet.

French-English Rivalry in the Ohio Valley

The French used the period of peace after 1748 to advance south into Indian territory in the western regions of present-day New York and Pennsylvania. They also moved north and east from forts along the Mississippi River. Through strategic trade connections with Indian tribes, they planned to secure a western barrier to British-American expansion. Their goal was a solid French presence connecting New Orleans with its Canadian outposts.

But the French had competition. A well-organized group of Virginians had designs on what was called the Ohio valley. Virginia had long had an exaggerated idea of its territory, claiming its original charter included all lands west to the Mississippi River and far north to Lake Superior. In 1747 some wealthy Virginians, including the brothers Lawrence and Augustine Washington, formed the Ohio Company and obtained a grant from the king to some 200,000 acres of forests in the region of the Monongahela, Allegheny, and Ohio Rivers. The Vir-

ginians were interested in profits from the eventual resale of the land; the British government was more interested in blocking the advances of the French. The crown promised even more free acreage if the Ohio Company could launch a settlement of one hundred families and a fort. By 1753, the enterprising Virginians had blazed an eighty-mile road into their land grant and set up a trading post near present-day Pittsburgh. The French, meanwhile, were moving troops south from Lake Erie, strewing their path with iron tablets that announced French ownership of the land. The Virginia governor, Robert Dinwiddie, himself a major shareholder in the Ohio Company, sent a messenger to warn the French that they were trespassing on Virginia land.

The man who volunteered to be the messenger on this dangerous mission was George Washington, younger half-brother of the Ohio Company leaders.

WASHINGTON'S MAP OF FRENCH FORTS
Washington's surveying skill was essential to his 1753–1754 journey to the French forts. His map combines an artistic perspective of the Allegheny Mountains as seen from the Virginia tidewater with a roughly accurate aerial map showing French troop encampments in western Pennsylvania.
British Library.

TABLE 6.1

EUROPEAN WARS OF EMPIRE

European Name	American Name	Years	Summary
War of the League of Augsburg	King William's War	1689–1697	Treaty of Ryswick signed. France and England surrender all American territory gained during war. Colonial possessions remain almost unchanged.
War of Spanish Succession	Queen Anne's War	1702–1713	Treaty of Utrecht signed. France surrenders to England the Hudson Bay region, Newfoundland, and Nova Scotia region of Acadia. France returns two major colonies of New France; Canada and Louisiana.
War of Austrian Succession	King George's War	1744–1748	Treaty of Aix-la-Chapelle signed. England and France give back territory won in the war, including return of fortress of Louisbourg to French.
Seven Years' War	French and Indian War	1754–1763	Treaty of Paris signed. England gains Canada, Spanish Florida, and most French possessions east of Mississippi River. Spain receives all French territory west of the Mississippi and New Orleans. France's empire in North America reduced to West Indian islands of Martinique, Guadeloupe, St. Domingue, and tiny islands of St. Pierre and Miquelon off Newfoundland.

Although he was only twenty-one, Washington was an ambitious youth whose imposing height (six foot three) and air of silent competence convinced the governor he could do the job. And Washington was eager to volunteer. As the middle child in a family of eight, he could not count on inheriting wealth. When George was eleven, his father had died, and his landholdings had been fragmented among his sons. George's mother could not afford to send him to England for classical schooling, as his half-brothers had enjoyed. Instead George learned geometry and trigonometry and with this relatively uncommon skill had found steady employment as a surveyor. But his path upward, he knew, required that he cultivate the Virginia elite. Leading a mission to the French would give him the kind of visibility he craved.

Washington took Governor Dinwiddie's letter to the French commander's headquarters near Lake Erie. While he waited for the official response, he counted the French soldiers, made sketches of their forts, and picked up boasts from French soldiers of their goal to capture all the land west of the Appalachians and drive out the few English traders and settlers already there. This information led the Virginia governor to appoint Washington to raise troops against the French. In the spring of 1754, a small military force numbering less than a hundred men moved west searching for nine hundred French troops said to be encamped along the Ohio River. Washington recruited Indian support as well, and a small group of Mingos, fewer than two dozen, joined him. But after an initial skirmish with about forty French soldiers—in the opening battle of what came to be called the French and Indian War—in May 1754, the Indians dropped out, realizing the Virginians would be greatly outnumbered. The Virginians built a flimsy fortification, called Fort Necessity, and in early July the nine hundred French troops stormed and took it. Washington was captured and then sent back to his governor carrying a new message: The French had no intention of departing from the disputed territory.

Thus began the French and Indian War, just six years after the end of the last war. Unlike earlier French-British conflicts, this one started in America, and its battles would be centered there. By 1756, the war had escalated to include a half dozen European countries, and battles had occurred in the Caribbean and in Europe. To the Europeans, the war was known as the Seven Years' War, once it concluded in 1763. But for Americans, with their two-year head start, it actually lasted nine years.

The Albany Congress and Intercolonial Defense

To succeed in even a limited war, the British needed coordinated support from the American colonists as well as some way to woo Indians at least into neutrality. Requisitioning soldiers and supplies from each individual colonial government was time-consuming and also difficult, since not every colony cared about French movements into the Ohio valley. So London officials instructed the colonies from Virginia north to send delegates to a meeting in Albany, New York. One goal of the Albany Congress was to construct an intercolonial agency to provide for the mutual defense of the colonies. A second and perhaps more crucial goal was to attempt to persuade some of the key Indian tribes of the powerful Iroquois Nation of western New York to support the English, or at least to promise neutrality in the war with the French.

PORTRAIT OF GEORGE WASHINGTON, BY CHARLES WILLSON PEALE
In 1772, George Washington posed for the artist Charles Willson Peale in his splendid uniform from the French and Indian War. Note the ornamental gorget (see page 196), the graceful sash, and the brass vest buttons that still meet buttonholes over the Virginian's forty-year-old girth. Washington's pocket contains an "Order of March," implying that military duty still lies ahead. Peale captured Washington's grandeur in his clothes but not his face, which appears plain and simple. Washington wrote a friend that he was "in so grave—so sullen a mood" and often so sleepy "that I fancy the skill of this gentleman's pencil will be hard put to it, in describing to the world what manner of man I am."
Washington and Lee University

In June 1754, twenty-four delegates from seven colonies met in Albany, among them Benjamin Franklin of Pennsylvania and Thomas Hutchinson of Massachusetts, two men in their mid-forties who were rising political stars in their home colonies. For several years Franklin had urged closer connections among the colonies because he feared the military alliance of the French and Native American peoples in the west. Hutchinson was more generally in favor of restructuring and streamlining imperial authority. At Albany, the two men drew up the Albany

Plan of Union. No radical desire for increased colonial power motivated them; the Plan of Union humbly reaffirmed Parliament's authority over the colonies. The plan proposed a new top layer of colonial government consisting of a president general, appointed by the crown, and a grand council, with members selected by the colonial assemblies. The president and the council would have powers only in the areas of defense and Indian affairs.

Despite Franklin's best efforts to publicize the Albany Plan, not a single colony ever approved it. The Massachusetts assembly feared it was nothing but "a Design of gaining power over the Colonies," especially the power of taxation. Others suspected that the colonies could never agree on policies toward hundreds of quite different Indian tribes. Oddly enough, the British government never backed the Albany Plan either, which perplexed both Franklin and Hutchinson, who were earnestly trying to solidify British authority. England in 1754 was not yet ready to press for more control. Some forty years later, long after the Revolution, Franklin almost wistfully reflected that if the Albany Plan "had been adopted and carried into Execution, the subsequent Separation of the Colonies from the Mother Country might not so soon have happened." The irony was, said Franklin, that "the Crown disapprov'd it, as having plac'd too much Weight in the democratic Part; and every Assembly as having allow'd too much to Prerogative," that is, to the king's rights.

Representatives of the Iroquois League, embracing the Seneca, Mohawk, Onondaga, Cayuga, Oneida, and Tuscarora tribes, also attended the Albany Congress. They collected thirty wagon loads of gifts and made ambiguous promises to the colonists but then left without actually pledging to fight the French. The Iroquois preferred to stall and play off the English against the French, for their best interests were served by being on the winning side, which in 1754 looked as if it might well be the French. Not until 1759, when the tide turned in the war, would the Iroquois deliver on their vague promise of support for the British colonies.

The War Heats Up

By 1755, Washington's frontier skirmish had turned into a major mobilization of British and American troops against the French. At first the British government hoped for quick victory by throwing armies at the French in three strategic places. General Edward Braddock from England was sent to at-

tack the French at Fort Duquesne at the confluence of the Ohio, Allegheny, and Monongahela Rivers. In Massachusetts, Governor William Shirley raised a force of colonial militiamen to take Fort Niagara, critically located at the narrow land neck between Lakes Erie and Ontario. And finally, William Johnson of New York, a wealthy and influential Indian trader, was charged with leading troops to unseat the French at Lake Champlain and push them back to Canada.

Unfortunately for the British, a French spy in England learned details of the plans, so the French were ready. In July 1755, General Braddock set out from Virginia with more than two thousand regular army troops to clear the French out of Fort Duquesne. Washington and several hundred Virginia militiamen accompanied him. But a day short of their objective, they were ambushed by a combined French and Indian force, and 976 British were killed or wounded. The British redcoats, said Washington, "broke and ran as sheep pursued by dogs." Washington was unhurt, though two horses in succession were shot from under him; Braddock was killed. For the second time in the young man's short military career, Washington returned to Virginia to report defeat. But this time, the news of his valor on the field of battle caused the governor to promote him to commander of the Virginia army. At age twenty-two, Washington was beginning to realize his ambitions.

News of Braddock's defeat alarmed the other two armies, then hacking their way through dense New York forests. Shirley's forces simply turned back and did not try to capture Niagara. William Johnson's troops were attacked and put on the run by the French before they ever got to Lake Champlain. For the next two years, the British stumbled badly on the American front of a war that was quickly expanding to sites in Europe and the Caribbean. British political leaders were initially unwilling to commit large reserves of troops to the

MAP 6.1
European Areas of Influence and the French and Indian War, 1754–1763
In the mid-eighteenth century, France, England, and Spain claimed vast areas of North America, many of them already inhabited by various Indian peoples. The early flash points of the French and Indian War occurred in regions of disputed claims where the French had allied with powerful native groups — the Iroquois and the Algonquin — to put pressure on the westward-moving English.

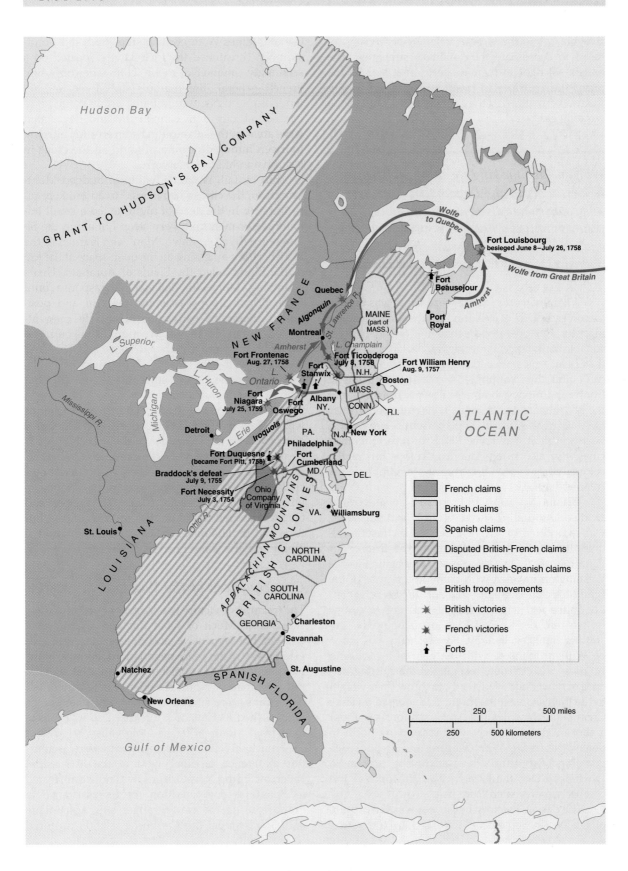

Hudson Bay

GRANT TO HUDSON'S BAY COMPANY

Wolfe to Quebec

Fort Louisbourg
besieged June 8–July 26, 1758

Wolfe from Great Britain

Amherst

NEW FRANCE

Fort Beauséjour

Quebec

Algonquin

MAINE
(part of
MASS.)

Port Royal

Montreal

St. Lawrence R.

Amherst

L. Champlain

L. Superior

Fort Frontenac
Aug. 27, 1758

Fort Ticonderoga
July 8, 1758

Fort William Henry
Aug. 9, 1757

L. Huron

L. Ontario

Fort Stanwix

N.H.

Boston

L. Michigan

Fort Niagara
July 25, 1759

Fort Oswego

Albany
NY.

MASS.

CONN.

R.I.

Mississippi R.

Iroquois

L. Erie

PA.

N.J.

New York

ATLANTIC OCEAN

Detroit

Philadelphia

Fort Duquesne
(became Fort Pitt, 1758)

Fort Cumberland

Braddock's defeat
July 9, 1755

MD.

DEL.

Fort Necessity
July 3, 1754

Ohio
Company
of Virginia

APPALACHIAN MOUNTAINS

St. Louis

Ohio R.

VA.

Williamsburg

LOUISIANA

BRITISH COLONIES

NORTH
CAROLINA

SOUTH
CAROLINA

GEORGIA

Charleston

Savannah

Natchez

St. Augustine

New Orleans

SPANISH FLORIDA

Gulf of Mexico

	French claims
	British claims
	Spanish claims
	Disputed British-French claims
	Disputed British-Spanish claims
→	British troop movements
✸	British victories
✸	French victories
⚑	Forts

0   250   500 miles

0   250   500 kilometers

struggle, while the various colonies perversely refused to coordinate their military strategies. The French sat tight in their western forts, and all the major Indian tribes in the frontier rushed to ally themselves with what they anticipated would be the winning side.

William Pitt, the king's leading minister, recklessly declared, "I know that I can save this country and that no one else can," and then committed a massive infusion of troops and money to an all-out war effort.

What finally turned the war around was the rise to power in 1757 of William Pitt, the king's leading minister. Pitt operated beyond the bounds of reasonable confidence; he recklessly declared, "I know that I can save this country and that no one else can," and then committed a massive infusion of troops and money to an all-out war effort. He sent the best generals with large, well-equipped armies to America in 1757. In 1758, he sent a large naval fleet up the St. Lawrence River to threaten French cities. Pitt also pried American troops out of the colonial assemblies with promises to reimburse the colonies later.

Within two years, Pitt's strategy resulted in a string of resounding successes. In 1758, Louisbourg was recaptured by English and Massachusetts soldiers led by Sir Jeffrey Amherst. The British advanced on Fort Duquesne again, and again George Washington traveled with them, in a reprise of the Braddock campaign. But this time the French abandoned the fort without a fight, and the victorious British renamed it Fort Pitt, in honor of the unstinting minister. In 1759, Fort Niagara was taken by William Johnson, with the help of a thousand Iroquois, who by now recognized the shifting balance of power and were ready to throw their weight to the English. Next the fort at Ticonderoga on Lake Champlain was taken by Amherst's forces without a shot fired; the French were scrambling north to defend Montreal. With Niagara and Ticonderoga gone, and the British navy advancing up the St. Lawrence River, the French cities of Montreal and Quebec were isolated from help.

The decisive victory in the war was the capture of Quebec in September 1759. Led by the young

General James Wolfe, British ships had, since midsummer, threatened the fortress city, located on a seemingly invincible rocky cliff. The opposing French general, the marquis de Montcalm, defended it with his outnumbered army. Wolfe bombarded the city with cannon fire and devastated large areas of the surrounding countryside, burning fourteen hundred farmhouses and all the crops in a campaign of sustained terror.

But by fall, Wolfe had still not budged Montcalm from the city, so he resorted to an unlikely direct attack. In the dead of night he led a small initial force of men up a very steep hill along the St. Lawrence River. At dawn, Montcalm learned of the British troops amassing on the open space at the top of the bluff, called the Plains of Abraham. Unaccountably, Montcalm delayed his response until more British troops ascended the cliff and positioned themselves advantageously. He then attacked, but in less than thirty minutes his outnumbered troops were a mangled mess, and he—and Wolfe as well—lay dying on the field of battle. Montcalm signed a full surrender of the city and died several minutes later.

The backbone of the French in North America was broken by the fall of Quebec. The victory was completed by the surrender of the French at Montreal to Amherst in late 1760. American colonists rejoiced, but the French and Indian War was not officially over yet. Battles continued in the Caribbean, where the French sugar islands Martinique and Guadeloupe fell to the English in 1762, and in Europe and India. France finally capitulated, and the Treaty of Paris was signed in 1763.

Consequences of the War

The triumph of victory was sweet but unfortunately short-lived. Much of what England should have won in this expensive and spectacular war was given away at the peace negotiations, because of the inexperience of the minister who replaced William Pitt. The map of North America was redrawn, but Americans were surprised at the outcome. France relinquished its Canadian territory and its claim to forts from Montreal to the Ohio valley, so at least the French threat from the north and west was gone. But all French territory west of the Mississippi River, including New Orleans, was now transferred to Spain, as compensation for its assistance to France during the war. Stranger still, Martinique and Guadeloupe, the Caribbean islands captured

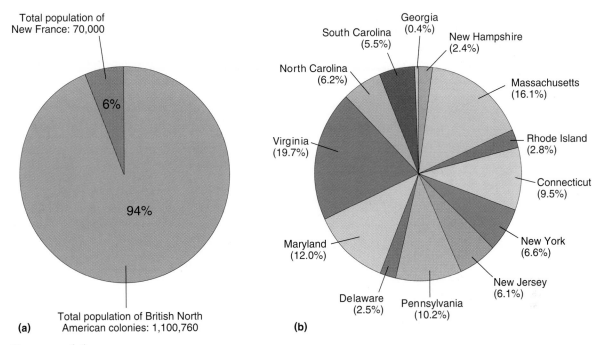

FIGURE 6.1
Population of British and French North American Colonies, circa 1750
British colonies from New Hampshire south to Georgia had a total population far larger than the
number of French settlers in New France (Quebec and Montreal). In fact, more than half of the
colonies each had a larger population than New France. However, the French army in the French
and Indian War had unnumbered Indian allies to draw upon for aid: war with England was
therefore not a foolish enterprise for them.

late in the war, were returned to France. Older
Americans who remembered the Aix-la-Chapelle
treaty of 1748, which ended the last war, bitterly
wondered whether Louisbourg and perhaps all of
Canada might be returned again to the enemy. Some
shrewd colonists deduced an indirect advantage
to England in allowing France to keep its sugar
islands: A French presence might worry Americans and keep them dependent on England for
protection.

In truth, the French islands in the Caribbean
were hardly a threat to Americans, for they provided a brisk and profitable trade in smuggled molasses. The main threat to the safety of colonists
came instead from Indians disheartened by England's victory. The Treaty of Paris dictated terms for
the European powers but completely ignored the
Indians. Indian lands were "won" and assigned to
English rule on the map, but of course there was no
way to compel the native inhabitants to vacate. With
the French gone, the Indians had lost the advantage

of having two opponents to play off against each
other, and they now had to cope with the westward-
moving Americans. Indian policy would soon become a serious bone of contention between the
British government and the colonists.

England's version of the victory of 1763
awarded all credit to the redcoats of the British
army. In this version, ungrateful colonists had
dragged their feet in providing troops for a war
fought to save them from the French. More worrisome still, reliable reports reached England about
business-as-usual smuggling. An illegal trade in
beaver pelts, conducted by Albany merchants with
French fur traders, was not dented in the least by
the war, and neither was the illegal molasses trade
in the Caribbean. An informant counted more than
a hundred American ships anchored at one of the
French islands, no doubt picking up cargoes of
cheap molasses. American traders, grumbled the
British leaders, were really traitors. William Pitt was
convinced that the illegal trade "principally, if not

MAP 6.2
North America before and after the French and Indian War, 1750–1763.
In the peace treaty of 1763, France ceded its interior lands but retained fishing rights and tiny islands in the far north, and, more important, several sugar islands in the Caribbean. A large part of France's claim —to land called Louisiana west of the Mississippi River —went not to England but to Spain.

alone, enabled France to sustain and protract this long and expensive war."

Colonists, of course, read the lessons of the war differently. What they remembered were the British redcoats under Braddock, a professional army incompetent to fight Indians. American militia units turned out in force, but the troops had been relegated to second-rate status by arrogant British military leaders, who assigned them arduous trench-digging duties and made them haul the cannons. General Braddock had confidently predicted to Benjamin Franklin that "these savages may, indeed, be a formidable enemy to your raw American militia, but upon the king's regular and disciplined troops, sir, it is impossible they should make any impression." Braddock's defeat "gave us Americans," Franklin wrote, "the first suspicion that our exalted ideas of the prowess of British regulars had not been well founded." Yet four years later in the war, the British still had not altered their negative impressions. The impetuous General Wolfe had been heard to remark that the Americans were nothing but "contemptible dogs," and Americans believed that his prejudice was widely shared yet completely undeserved.

The human costs of the war were also etched sharply in the minds of New England colonists, who had contributed most of the colonial troops. About one-third of all Massachusetts men between age fifteen and thirty had seen service. Many families had suffered death and disease, the ultimate sacrifices of war, and this cost would not soon be forgotten.

The enormous expense of the war cast another huge shadow over the victory. Pitt's no-holds-barred military strategy was effective but costly. By 1763, England's national debt, double what it had been when Pitt took office, posed a formidable challenge to the next decade of leadership in England. At the heart of the matter was disagreement about the relative responsibility the colonists should bear in helping to pay off that debt.

From 1754 to 1763, power alignments had sharply shifted in America. The French-Indian alliance had posed a serious threat to a rapidly expanding British-American population, but with defeat came the virtual disappearance of the French. For the winners, mutual misgivings and suspicions immediately marred the satisfactions of the victory and set England and its colonies on a collision course. The Indians would soon find they had new allies, the British, to help them dam the flow of westward-moving settlers.

Tightening the Bonds of Empire

Throughout the 1760s, inconsistent leadership in England pursued a hodgepodge of policies toward the colonies. A new and inexperienced king had gained the throne in 1760, and he spent the next ten years searching for a prime minister he could trust. Nearly half a dozen ministers in succession took their turns formulating policies designed to address one basic, underlying British reality: A huge war debt needed to be serviced, and the colonists, as British subjects, should expect to have to pay. From the American side, however, these policies deeply violated what colonists perceived to be their rights and liberties as British subjects.

British Leadership and the Indian Question

In 1760, in the middle of the French and Indian War, George III, age twenty-two, came to the British throne, quite underprepared for his monarchical duties. The grandson of the previous king, George II, he had not been trained for leadership because it was assumed that his father would inherit the crown first. But the father unexpectedly died when George was thirteen, and the new heir-apparent emerged quickly from an unhappy childhood to undergo a crash course in kingship. When he assumed power nine years later, he was timid and insecure; he trusted only his tutor, John Stuart, earl of Bute, a Scotsman who was an outsider to power circles in London. George III therefore installed Bute in his cabinet of ministers.

Bute opposed Pitt's strategy on the war in America as "too bloody and expensive." He next squandered England's war victory by negotiating the unfavorable Treaty of Paris. Within two years the best talents in the cabinet had resigned, leaving Bute isolated. In his short remaining time in office, Bute made one other significant decision—to keep a standing army in the colonies. In terms of money and political tension, this was a costly move.

The ostensible reason for keeping ten thousand British troops in America was to maintain the peace between the colonists and the Indians. This was not a misplaced concern. Three months after the Treaty of Paris was signed, Pontiac, chief of the Ottawa tribe in the northern Ohio region, seized the moment to attack the westernmost settlers. A British trader in the region called Pontiac "a shrewd, sensible Indian of few words, who commands more re-spect amongst these nations than any Indian I ever saw could do amongst his own tribes." From spring until fall 1763, Pontiac's uprising visited destruction on isolated settlements in far western Pennsylvania, the Ohio country, and north into the Great Lakes re-gion. Pontiac mobilized the Chippewa, Huron, Delaware, and Seneca tribes and captured all but three British forts in the region. More than two thou-sand colonists were killed or taken captive. Scots-Irish men in the town of Paxton, in western Lan-caster County, decided that the Pennsylvania assembly was shirking its responsibility to defend against Pontiac's warriors, and they descended on two nearby Indian settlements—inhabited by friendly Conestoga Indians, as it happened—and murdered twenty of them. Several hundred men from Paxton then marched on Philadelphia to de-mand better protection and a larger voice in the state assembly; they were never punished for their murderous vigilante injustice to the Conestoga. Pontiac's uprising was quelled in December 1763 by the combined efforts of British and colonial sol-diers, plus the news that French aid to the Indians would not materialize. Pontiac later wrote to the British, "All my young men have buried their hatchets."

The potential for continued and costly wars with the Indians, so well illustrated by Pontiac's up-rising, caused the British government to issue an order, called the Proclamation of 1763, which for-bade colonists to settle west of a line drawn from Canada to Georgia along the crest of the Appa-lachian Mountains. The ten thousand British troops were to police this line. Meant as a temporary ex-pedient rather than a permanent boundary, the line promised to provide a reserve to protect in the short run not only the Indians but also the lucrative fur trade, now in British rather than French hands. But the pressure of frontier population meant that the proclamation line would be very difficult to enforce. Settlers had already moved into the western regions of Pennsylvania and Virginia, and they were now instructed to return east of the mountains. During Pontiac's uprising, many of these settlers had fled east, but they had no intention of permanently abandoning their farmlands and were swiftly mov-ing back in 1764. The proclamation line had also been breached by land speculators, such as those of Virginia's Ohio Company. For them, a restriction on westward movement would severely limit their op-portunities for profitable resale of their claims.

MOHAWK WARRIOR
This rear view of a Mohawk warrior highlights clothes and body decoration: arm and ankle bracelets, earrings, a hair ornament, and body paint. An important element of frontal display is included by the English watercolor artist — the warrior's tomahawk.
Ville de la Rochelle.

Bute's decision to leave a standing army in the colonies was thus cause for concern for western set-tlers and speculators alike.

Growing Resentment of British Authority

The mission of George Grenville, the king's next chief minister, was to tackle the problem of the war debt, which in 1763 amounted to £123 million, a shockingly high figure that grew larger every day because of the continued expenses of maintaining the standing army. The annual interest alone on the debt was nearly £5 million, owed to edgy London bankers.

Grenville's attention first alighted on the customs service, a division of the government that stationed customs officers in British and American ports. Their job was to monitor the flow of ships and goods and to collect the customs duties on specified items. But the customs service was in a sorry state. Grenville found that the total sum paid as salary to the officers was four times larger than the total revenue collected in duties. One reason for this imbalance was that some customs officers in effect sold their jobs: An officer would stay in England and hire someone at a lesser salary to work in his place in the distant colonies. The replacement person on the smaller stipend was thus a susceptible target for bribes to augment his income, and some shippers found it more convenient to pay the officer directly in bribe money than to pay duties. Grenville ordered absentee customs officers to stop this practice, and he demanded rigorous attention to paperwork and a strict accounting of collected duties.

For the most part, American shippers did abide by the various navigation acts and customs duties regulating trade. But one trade law in particular, the Molasses Act of 1733, presented a hardship for Americans in the Caribbean trade, so through long tradition they simply ignored it and smuggled molasses into the country. The Molasses Act imposed a stiff duty on any molasses purchased from non-British sources. The idea was to encourage trade with the British islands by making French molasses more expensive. Without the tax, French molasses was cheap. A by-product of sugar production, molasses was a key ingredient in making rum, a drink the French scorned. So French planters on Martinique and Guadeloupe were willing to sell it to the rum-loving Americans on extremely favorable terms.

American shippers had long flouted the Molasses Act, even during the French and Indian War. Grenville's goal was to capture the revenue lost to smuggling, and his ingenious solution was to lower the duty on French molasses, to make it more attractive to obey the law, at the same time raising penalties for smuggling. Whereas the Molasses Act required a duty of six pence per gallon on non-British molasses, the new Revenue Act of 1764 (popularly dubbed the Sugar Act) lowered the tax to three pence. It passed Parliament with no opposition, for it seemed to be a clear example of navigation legislation designed to regulate trade. But Grenville had added a new twist: His actual intent was to raise a revenue, not redirect trade. He was using an established form of law for new ends, and he was doing it by the novel means of lowering a duty.

The Sugar Act set out tougher enforcement policies. From now on, Grenville announced, British naval crews could act as impromptu customs officers, boarding ships suspected of smuggling and seizing cargoes found to be in violation. (The enthusiasm of the captains and crews of the naval ships was secured by a provision that they all earned a share of the profits in seized cargoes.) American smugglers caught without proper paperwork would be prosecuted for their offense, not in a friendly civil court with a local jury, but in a vice-admiralty court located in Halifax, Nova Scotia, where a single judge presided without a jury. The implication was that justice would be more sure and severe.

Grenville hoped that his tightening of the customs service and the lowered duties of the Sugar Act would reform American smugglers into law-abiding shippers and in turn generate income for the empire. Unfortunately, the decrease in duty was not sufficient to offset the attractions of smuggling, and the new vigilance in enforcing the act annoyed American shippers and created ill feeling. The presence of new personnel in the customs service made it harder for shippers to rely on the old smooth-working system of bribery, and several ugly confrontations occurred in key port cities such as Newport, Rhode Island, and New York City. But in general, larger political questions about the power of taxation lay hidden in the Sugar Act, and they stayed hidden. Americans who objected to the law came from the seacoast cities, and their objections were based on the financial damage the act caused them personally. Mainly, they tried to evade the law by carrying forged papers or by unloading cargoes at night in small harbors.

One other new act engineered by Grenville added to the growing resentment of British authority. The Currency Act of 1764 flatly prohibited the colonies from issuing any more paper money. Paper money had been issued frequently in the colonies during the emergency of the French and Indian War. Assemblies used it to finance war-related expenses, allowing it to circulate briefly as a medium of exchange and then be retired as payment for taxes. In

PAPER CURRENCY OF THE 1750S TO 1770S
Colonial paper currencies contained text that stipulated the legality and value of the money, accompanied by elaborate designs that discouraged counterfeiting. Handwritten numbers and signatures authenticated each paper. Parliament's Currency Act of 1764 prohibited paper money, but some colonies continued to print it, and it returned with force in 1775 when the Continental Congress began printing dollars (lower left).
Courtesy of the Decorative & Industrial Arts Collection of the Chicago Historical Society.

the short run, paper money in modest issues lubricated the economy by increasing the volume of money in a society that was always short of adequate silver and gold coins. But London merchants squawked about not getting full value for their goods, and Grenville persuaded Parliament to ban new paper money, a dire solution indeed because it left the colonial governments with no short-term financing flexibility and a reduced flow of money.

From the British point of view, the 1763 Proclamation Act, the Sugar Act, and the Currency Act all seemed to be reasonable efforts to administer the colonies. British leaders were looking for ways to consolidate their empire and bring the colonies under closer economic supervision. From the American point of view, however, the British supervision appeared to be a disturbing intrusion into colonial practices.

The Stamp Act Crisis

By his second year in office, Grenville had made almost no dent in the national debt. Continued evasion prevented the Sugar Act from becoming the moneymaker he had hoped it would be. So in February 1765, he significantly escalated his revenue program by securing passage of the Stamp Act in Parliament. He thus precipitated the first major, open conflict between England and the colonies over Parliament's right to tax. The crisis generated a second and much more surprising result: It politicized many colonists who had not before participated in politics in the eighteenth century.

Taxation and Consent

The Stamp Act imposed a tax on various colonial documents—newspapers, pamphlets, contracts, court documents, licenses, deeds, wills, ships' bills of lading—and required that a special stamp be embossed on the documents proving that the tax had been paid. Unlike the Sugar Act, which was part of a trade regulation system, the Stamp Act broke new ground. It instituted a tax whose purpose was plainly and simply to raise money. Grenville was not trying to encourage or discourage the use of paper. He was out to raise cash, and, what is more, the tax had to be paid in sterling silver, a condition that made the Stamp Act even more unpopular, because hard money was in short supply.

Grenville was no fool, and he anticipated that some Americans might be leery of the stamp tax. He therefore decided that the administration of the act should be delegated to Americans themselves, to avoid the problem of hostility to British enforcers, an unfortunate feature of the Sugar Act. He let it be known that in each colony, native stamp distributors would be hired at a handsome salary of 8 percent of the revenue collected.

The passage of the Stamp Act in 1765 precipitated the first major, open conflict between England and the colonies over Parliament's right to tax.

Benjamin Franklin was working in London that winter as the official agent (or lobbyist) of the Pennsylvania government. Franklin was not enthusiastic about the Stamp Act, and he and three other colonial agents met with Grenville personally to warn him that Americans favored taxing themselves. But Franklin nonetheless nominated a friend of his to be the Philadelphia stamp distributor, and the Connecticut agent who accompanied Franklin put forth his own name. Obviously they underestimated just how unpopular the Stamp Act would prove to be.

Grenville had other warnings that this tax might be extremely unpopular. Thomas Hutchinson, lieutenant governor of Massachusetts, wrote to

his colony's London agent to urge him to lobby against the tax. Hutchinson immediately appreciated the key legal issue at stake. Aside from the navigation acts, which were intended to regulate trade and not make money, Parliament had levied no taxes on the colonists before this. Hutchinson warned that the colonies could reasonably conclude that Parliament had conceded to them the right to tax themselves, after all these years of no taxation by Parliament. On practical grounds, Hutchinson also urged the British officials to consider potential disruptions to trade if the colonists tried to evade the use of stamped customs documents. The disruptions might well cost more than the revenue the act generated, Hutchinson noted. But Hutchinson's warnings went unheeded.

The colonists, of course, paid taxes to support their local governments, but the taxing bodies were always the colonial assemblies, composed of elected representatives. A long English tradition held that taxation was a gift of the people to the king offered by the people's representatives. This view of taxes, as a freely given gift, preserved an essential concept of English political theory, the idea that citizens have the liberty to enjoy and use their property without fear of confiscation. The king could not simply demand money; only the House of Commons could grant it. Grenville himself completely agreed

TAX ASSESSMENT BOOK
American colonists routinely paid property taxes to local authorities. This 1772 tax book from Rowley, Massachusetts, records amounts due in pounds, shillings, and pence. The several entries for each name indicate assessments on real estate, personal property, and a poll (per head) tax. Notice that two women owe taxes. Since married women by law owned no property, we can conclude that these were widows. Several numbers are frequently repeated; what might that suggest?
Chicago Historical Society.

with this concept. He openly supported the colonists' privilege "of being taxed only with their own Consent." But, he argued, they were already "virtually" represented in Parliament, just as citizens in the new factory towns of Birmingham and Leeds in England were virtually represented, electing no member to Parliament on their own. All members of the House of Commons represented all British subjects, wherever they were. This British view of representation was emphatically rejected by colonial leaders. A Maryland lawyer named Daniel Dulany wrote a best-selling pamphlet explaining that virtual representation, while it might perhaps work within England, could not withstand the stretch across the Atlantic to the colonial dependencies. The flaw consisted in the fact that Parliament might well levy special taxes on the colonies —like, for example, the Stamp Act—whereas taxes within England were likely to be more uniform. Voters in Anne Arundel County, Maryland, denounced Grenville's reasoning as illusory: "The MINISTER'S *virtual Representation* in Support of the TAX on us is fantastical and frivolous."

Resistance Strategies

The Stamp Act passed Parliament with a November 1, 1765, start-up date. News of the act first reached the colonies in April 1765, so the colonists had a space of seven months to contemplate a response. Colonial governors might have argued for repeal, but since most of them owed their office to the king, they were unwilling to challenge the law. The colonial assemblies were another potential source of leadership on the issue, and eight of them did discuss objections to the Stamp Act. The assembly in Massachusetts met to denounce it, but Lieutenant Governor Hutchinson persuaded the legislators to moderate their outrage and humbly petition Parliament to indulge them in the privilege —not the right—of taxing themselves. Hutchinson privately thought the Stamp Act was bad policy— "happy would it have been for us if it had not passed"—but he was simply by nature incapable of publicly defying a British law. (Hutchinson also knew that his brother-in-law Andrew Oliver had been appointed stamp distributor for Massachusetts.) As in Massachusetts, all of the other colonial assemblies had a hard time grappling with the logical consequences of objecting to the Stamp Act, for any consideration of Parliament's right to tax Americans soon led to the question of Parliament's general authority over the colonies.

Virginia's assembly, the House of Burgesses, waded into the implications of objecting to the Stamp Act and learned where that road led. The burgesses were at first not willing to object very loudly, but at the very end of their May 1765 sitting, when two-thirds of the members had already left town to go home, a twenty-nine-year-old lawyer named Patrick Henry, a newly elected member, presented a series of resolutions on the Stamp Act that were debated and passed, one by one. They came to be called the Virginia Resolves.

The drift of Henry's successive resolutions inched the assembly toward radical opposition to the Stamp Act. The first two resolutions merely affirmed that Virginians were British citizens with all the same rights and privileges they would have in England. The third resolution identified self-taxation as one of those rights, and the fourth stated the simple fact that Virginians had always taxed themselves, via their representatives in the House of Burgesses. The fifth resolution took the radical leap, by pushing the other four unexceptional statements to one logical conclusion—that the Virginia assembly alone had the sole right to tax Virginians. Henry persuaded the small group of burgesses present to endorse this declaration, but the ebbing numbers of positive votes indicated shrinking support for the implications of these resolutions.

Two more fiery resolutions were debated, but majority support eroded as Henry pressed the logic of his case to the extreme. The sixth resolution denied any legitimacy to a tax law originating outside Virginia, and a seventh boldly called anyone who disagreed with these propositions an enemy of Virginia. Such rhetoric was inflammatory, but Henry's logic, through the sixth resolution, was controlled and persuasive. However, it was too much for the burgesses. They backed away from resolutions six and seven and the following day, after Henry had left, retreated on number five as well, voting to rescind it.

Their caution hardly mattered, however, because newspapers in other colonies printed the whole set of seven Virginia Resolves, yielding the impression that a daring first challenge to the Stamp Act had taken place in Virginia. This made it easier for other assemblies to adopt more radical positions.

By fall 1765, the colonial assemblies were sufficiently emboldened to take a step together. In October, nine assemblies sent delegates to a meeting in New York City called the Stamp Act Congress. The delegates were extremely cautious about the larger issue of Parliament's power over the colonies and instead focused narrowly on the Stamp Act. The outcome of the congress was a polite petition sent to Grenville that affirmed the colonies' subordination to Parliament and asked for repeal of the Stamp Act.

Individual colonial assemblies beyond Virginia and Massachusetts debated the Stamp Act, and several finally confronted the larger question at stake: By what authority could Parliament legislate for the colonies without taxing them? No one disagreed, in 1765, that Parliament was the supreme body ruling the colonists, who were, after all, British subjects. But several assemblies developed the argument that there was a distinction between *external* taxes, those imposed on foreign trade to regulate it, and *internal* taxes, such as a stamp tax or a property tax, that in the long English tradition could only be self-imposed. So long as Americans were not represented in Parliament, internal taxes had to be managed by the colonial assemblies, they argued.

Crowd Politics

Besides the governors and the assemblies, there was a third arena for response to the Stamp Act: the local community. Every person whose livelihood required the use of official paper had to decide whether to comply with the act. Noncompliance could come in three forms. First, each individual could avoid using any stamped paper. But the cost of avoidance might be prohibitively large; if enough people ceased using stamped paper, the information network of newspapers, the legal system, and the world of trade might grind to a halt. A second option was to continue business as usual and ignore the required stamp. The risk here was that such an action was plainly illegal, and violators, if few in number, might be identified and fined or jailed. A third option thus seemed all the more attractive: to destroy the stamped paper or prevent its distribution at the source, before the law took effect; this tactic would ensure universal noncompliance.

The capital of Massachusetts was Boston, a port city of about seventeen thousand people packed into a square-mile peninsula jutting into a large bay. Virtually all of Boston's major occupational groups —lawyers and politicians, merchants and shipowners, tradesmen and artisans, dockworkers and sailors—depended on official papers to conduct business. In June 1765, the *Boston Gazette* denounced the response of the Massachusetts assembly to the Stamp Act as "tame" and "insipid." In contrast, it offered its readers the Virginia Resolves, all seven

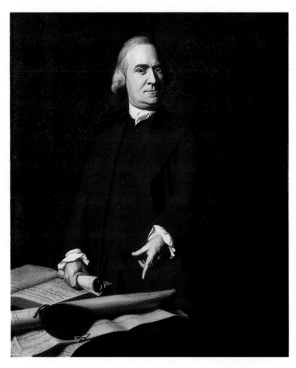

SAMUEL ADAMS
Samuel Adams consented to pose for Boston artist John Singleton Copley in 1770. The portrait highlights Adams's face, which projects a dramatic intensity and dominates the bulky body, subdued by dark clothes. Adams stares thoughtfully and silently at the viewer and points to important legal documents before him, including the Massachusetts charter of 1689. Wealthy merchant John Hancock commissioned the portrait, which hung in his house. Copley painted scores of Boston's leaders in the 1760s, both loyalists and patriots. He maintained neutrality until 1773, when his father-in-law became an official East India tea distributor. Copley's home was threatened by a crowd, and he left for England in 1774.
Deposited by the City of Boston, Museum of Fine Arts, Boston.

of them, as an example of a "spirited" response. The *Gazette* did not shy away from appropriating the language of the seventh resolution and calling anyone who agreed that Parliament could tax Massachusetts "AN ENEMY TO THIS HIS MAJESTY'S COLONY." Left unreported in the *Gazette* was the news of the Virginia burgesses' own timidity in rejecting the sixth and seventh resolutions and rescinding their approval of the fifth. The royal governor of Massachusetts, Francis Bernard, feared that the Virginia Resolves were "an Alarm bell to the disaffected."

Over the summer a plan took shape to head off the Boston stamp distribution at its source. The leadership behind the plan came from a small group of shopkeepers, master craftsmen, distillers, and the printer of the *Boston Gazette*, Benjamin Edes, working closely with Samuel Adams, a forty-three-year-old town politician. Together they formed the core of the Boston Sons of Liberty. Adams, the son of a prosperous brewer, attended Harvard College in his youth and from an early age showed an interest in politics. His graduating thesis at Harvard was an essay on the question "Whether it be lawful to resist the Supreme Magistrate if the Commonwealth cannot otherwise be preserved?" Adams's carefully reasoned reply was yes. In the 1760s, Adams had settled into an unrewarding occupation, that of town tax collector. In distinct contrast to Thomas Hutchinson, Adams cared nothing for status, exalted office, or fine material goods. He was oblivious to his daily clothing, a matter that occasionally distressed his friends. Adams devoted himself not to appearances but to politics in the town meeting, Boston's arena of local government, and in the Massachusetts assembly. He had shrewd political instincts and a gift for organizing.

Both his contemporaries and later historians have portrayed Adams in a multitude of ways. Critics (like Hutchinson) viewed him as a troublemaker, the devil incarnate, or a puppeteer who craftily manipulated ordinary men into doing his bidding. Others have seen him as a man of the people or a man of vision who was among the first to favor independence from England. A distant and much younger cousin, John Adams, later wrote that Samuel Adams's character "will never be accurately known to posterity, as it was never sufficiently known to its own age." The consummate politician ensured that he would be a mystery man by burning or shredding much of his correspondence over his long lifetime. "None of my friends shall ever suffer by my negligence," he wrote.

The plan hatched by Samuel Adams and others in August 1765 called for a street demonstration to convince Andrew Oliver, the stamp distributor, that his personal safety would best be served by resigning. With no stamp distributor, there could be no stamps sold. Adams enlisted as demonstrators men from craft and artisan groups, as well as a shoemaker named Ebenezer MacIntosh, the leader of a South End gang of laborers, apprentices, and sailors, who forged their identity in opposition to the rival North End gang. The two groups staged ritual mock battles every year on Guy Fawkes Day,

a century-old British anti-Catholic celebration falling in early November. They were already experienced in the ways of symbolic action and costumed street theater, just the sort of behaviors that might throw a scare into Andrew Oliver.

On the morning of August 14, an effigy (stuffed dummy) of Oliver was found hanging from a tree. Governor Bernard met with Hutchinson and the governor's council and decided to take no action, in an effort to keep tensions under control. In the evening, a large crowd of two to three thousand people paraded the effigy around town, using it as a prop in short plays demonstrating the dangers of selling the stamps. The crowd then pulled down a small building on Oliver's dock, reported to be the future stamp office. Next, at Oliver's house, they beheaded and burned the effigy and broke some windows. The flesh-and-blood Oliver was in hiding; the next day he resigned his office in a well-publicized announcement.

There were lessons from the August 14 demonstration for everyone. Oliver learned that stamp distributors would be very unpopular people. Bernard and Hutchinson learned the limitations of their own powers to govern, with no police to call on. Hutchinson had attempted to confront the crowd at Oliver's house at eleven at night and learned that his personal authority meant nothing. The demonstration's leaders learned that street action was very effective. And hundreds of laborers, sailors, and apprentices learned what the Stamp Act was all about and, what is more, learned that some of their customary behaviors could have political significance.

Twelve days later a second crowd action, more properly termed a riot, showed just how well some of these lessons had been learned. On August 26, a crowd assembled and visited the houses of four detested officials. One was a customs officer, and two others were officers of the admiralty courts, where smugglers were tried; windows were broken and wine cellars raided. The fourth house was the finest dwelling in Massachusetts, owned by the stiff-necked Thomas Hutchinson. Rumors abounded that Hutchinson had urged Grenville to adopt the Stamp Act. In fact, he had done the opposite, but he refused to set the record straight, saying curtly, "I am not obliged to give an answer to all the questions that may be put me by every lawless person." His family fled the house, but Hutchinson stood his ground until his daughter returned and begged him to leave. Shortly after, the crowd attacked and worked all night to destroy his house, leaving only the exterior walls standing.

The destruction of Hutchinson's house brought a halt to crowd activities in Boston for a while. The Boston town meeting issued a statement of sympathy; but a reward of £300 for the arrest and conviction of riot organizers failed to produce a single lead. The emerging Sons of Liberty denied planning the event.

Essentially, the opponents of the Stamp Act in Boston had won the day; no one volunteered to replace Oliver as distributor. When November 1 arrived, the day the Stamp Act took effect, the customs officers in Boston allowed ships to pass through the harbor without properly stamped clearance papers. They had little choice; they simply did not have the staff to force the ships to halt. Hutchinson in his role as chief justice of the Massachusetts court could not tolerate this defiance of the law, nor could he bring the lawbreakers to justice in his court. So he did the only thing he could do as a principled man: He resigned his judgeship. Hutchinson was far from out of hot water, however. He was still the lieutenant governor, and within five years he would agree to become the royal governor.

Liberty and Property

Boston's crowd actions of August sparked similar eruptions by groups calling themselves the Sons of Liberty in virtually every colony. In New York City, the stamp distributor quit on August 22, as soon as he heard the details of Oliver's humiliation. In September, October, and into November, stamp distributors in nearly every colony hastened to resign. By the end of the year, fifty towns had witnessed demonstrations. The New Hampshire distributor resigned three times in public places, to make sure that the word got out. The Connecticut colonial agent in England who had snapped up a distributor's office even as he told Grenville how unwise the tax was, returned to his colony from England to face an angry crowd for whom simple resignation was not enough. The people were not satisfied until he also threw his hat and powdered wig in the air and shouted a cheer of "Liberty and property!" But this man fared much better than another Connecticut stamp agent, who was nailed in a coffin and lowered in the ground by the Sons of Liberty. Only when the thuds of dirt sounded on the box did he have a sudden change of heart and shout out his resignation to the crowd above. Luckily he was heard. In the South too, Sons of Liberty emerged. In Charleston, South Carolina, the stamp distributor resigned in late October after crowds burned effi-

SEAL OF ANDREW OLIVER
This amethyst seal suggests that important business was a routine event for its owner, Bostonian Andrew Oliver. Long before he became the unfortunate stamp distributor in 1765, Oliver held a succession of offices—overseer of the poor, collector of taxes, member of the provincial council, and secretary of Massachusetts. He thus had many occasions to press the unique seal into melted wax to authenticate documents. The stone bears the tough-minded motto Pax Quaeritur Bello *(Peace Is Obtained by War), an appropriate maxim for the man willing to become the royal lieutenant governor of Massachusetts in 1770.*
Collection of the Oliver Family, photo by Clive Russ.

gies and chanted "Liberty! Liberty!" But when a crowd of Charleston blacks paraded with similar shouts of "Liberty!" a few months later, the town militia turned out in a hurry to break up the demonstration.

The rallying cry of "Liberty and property" made perfect sense to many white Americans of all social ranks who feared that their traditional rights as English subjects were threatened by the Stamp Act. Englishmen claimed liberty as a birthright, meaning that they had a right to be free from interference by other people. The opposite of liberty was slavery, the condition of being under the total control of someone else. Civil society required some interference to perfect freedom in the form of laws, but Englishmen preserved liberty by making sure that only representative governments passed the laws. Up to 1765, Americans consented to accept Parliament as a body that in some way represented them, at least for purposes of legislation. But the right to own property was a special kind of liberty, requiring even stricter safeguards, given the likelihood that powerful rulers might become greedy and try to deprive citizens of their property. It was for this reason that the tradition arose that only a directly representative body could tax British subjects, so that taxation could be said to be truly self-imposed.

One Pennsylvania pamphlet writer asserted that the Stamp Act threatened to plunge the colonies into "a state of slavery." A Maryland writer warned that if the colonies lost "the right of exemption from all taxes without their consent," that loss would "deprive them of every privilege distinguishing freemen from slaves."

To Americans, the Stamp Act violated this principle of liberty and property, and some Americans began to speak and write about a plot by British leaders to enslave them. One Pennsylvania pamphlet writer asserted that the Stamp Act threatened to plunge the colonies into "a state of slavery." A Maryland writer warned that if the colonies lost "the right of exemption from all taxes without their consent," that loss would "deprive them of every privilege distinguishing freemen from slaves." The oppositional meanings of *liberty* and *slavery* were utterly clear to white Americans' minds; but they stopped short of applying similar logic to the one million black Americans they held in bondage.

The Declaratory Act

It was not colonial demonstrations and noncompliance alone that undermined the Stamp Act; the merry-go-round of British ministers contributed as well. In the summer of 1765, Grenville fell out of favor with George III and was dismissed. The new prime minister, Charles Watson-Wentworth, the marquess of Rockingham, was much less determined to force the Stamp Act on Americans. London merchants had besieged the government for repeal of the measure, in fear of disastrous disruptions in trade. Rockingham's dilemma was to find a way out of the Stamp Act, without conceding the Americans' claim that Parliament could not tax them.

Rockingham's strategy was to secure the repeal of the Stamp Act by emphasizing the economic hardships suffered by British merchants. Unluckily for Rockingham, both William Pitt and George Grenville sat in Parliament, and neither one could let go of the larger principle. Pitt electrified—and confused—the other members by essentially agreeing with the American view of taxation. "It is my opinion that this kingdom has no right to lay a tax upon the colonies," he said. "At the same time, I assert the authority of this kingdom over the colonies, to be sovereign and supreme, in every circumstance of government and legislation whatsoever." In other words, Parliament ruled the colonies, but it could not tax them. Pitt clung to the ancient presumption that the gift of taxation could be granted only by a people's representatives, and Americans had no such representatives in Parliament. One member who was very impressed with Pitt's argument struggled to reconstruct it for a friend and gave up: "If you understand the difference between representative and legislative capacity it is more than I do, but I assure you it was very fine when I heard it."

Grenville was angered by Pitt's speech and responded with a stirring condemnation of American ingratitude. Grenville offered his listeners the example of the familiar arrangements of patriarchal power to help them understand the colonial relationship: "Protection and obedience are reciprocal. Great Britain protects America; America is bound to yield obedience." Grenville then challenged the defiance of the colonies: "When they want the protection of this kingdom, they are always ready to ask for it. . . . The nation has run itself into an immense debt to give them their protection; and now [when] they are called upon to contribute a small share towards the public expence, an expence arising from themselves, they renounce your authority, insult your officers, and break out, I might almost say, into open rebellion."

Ultimately Rockingham succeeded in sidestepping these two elder statesmen. In March 1766, the Stamp Act was repealed, but Parliament at the same time passed the Declaratory Act, which asserted the principle that Parliament had the right to legislate for the colonies "in all cases whatsoever." Perhaps the stamp tax had been inexpedient, but the power to tax—one prime case of a legislative power—was stoutly upheld.

Over the year-long period of the Stamp Act crisis, Americans had confronted a fundamentally new assertion of British control, the power to tax. They had challenged that control, through statements of defiance from the Virginia House of Burgesses followed by milder requests from an unprecedented body, a colony-wide Stamp Act Congress. As the crisis deepened, many thousands of ordinary Americans, unused to any regular political role, demonstrated a newfound competence to ponder questions of political authority and to protest grievances. News of the repeal of the Stamp Act set off celebrations in America, some restrained and others more carnival-like, with firecrackers and public drinking. But the general sense of celebration could not erase the growing uneasiness that the Declaratory Act marked the beginning, not the end, of trouble.

The Townshend Acts and Economic Retaliation

Rockingham did not last long as prime minister. By the summer of 1766, George III had persuaded William Pitt to return to office. Pitt appointed other new ministers, among them Charles Townshend, who served as chancellor of the exchequer, the chief financial minister in the government. Townshend assumed the upper hand in formulating colonial policy when Pitt became ill and incapacitated in the spring of 1767. As the chief financial minister, Townshend was still struggling to solve the old war debt problem. The continuing costs of the British army in America suggested again the idea of deriving revenue in some way from the colonies. Townshend's knowledge of the developing political climate in the colonies was unfortunately limited; his simple idea to raise revenue turned quickly into a major blunder.

The Townshend Duties

Townshend proposed new taxes in the old form of a navigation act. Officially called the Revenue Act of 1767, it established new duties on tea, glass, lead, paper, and painters' colors imported into the colonies, to be paid by the importer but surely passed on to consumers in the retail price. A year before, the duty on French molasses had been re-

duced from three pence down to one pence per gallon, and finally the Sugar Act was pulling in a tidy revenue of about £45,000 annually, so it was not unreasonable to suppose that new duties might also improve the cash flow. Townshend and others in the ministry were proceeding on the assumption that external taxes—that is, duties levied on the transatlantic trade—would be more acceptable to Americans than internal taxes, such as the stamp tax. During the turmoil of 1765, several American essayists and politicians had drawn this distinction, and in a calculating fashion Townshend was seizing on it to smooth the path for his new tax scheme. At the same time, he also beefed up the customs service to improve the collection of the duties. Townshend established a five-man American Board of Customs Commissioners whose members would now reside in the colonies, the better to oversee the customs service. Townshend picked Boston for the board's home base, a decision that yet again showed he was not very shrewd about colonial protest politics.

"We are taxed without our consent . . . We are therefore—SLAVES," wrote Philadelphia lawyer John Dickinson, calling for "a total denial of the power of Parliament to lay upon these colonies any 'tax' whatever."

The Townshend duties by themselves were not especially burdensome, but the principle they embodied—taxation extracted through trade duties—looked different to the colonists now, when seen against the backdrop of the Stamp Act crisis. If there had ever been a clear distinction between external taxes and internal taxes, that distinction was wiped out by the realization that the Townshend duties were flatly intended to raise money. John Dickinson, a Philadelphia lawyer, articulated this view in a series of articles titled *Letters from a Farmer in Pennsylvania,* widely reprinted in colonial newspapers and pamphlets in the winter of 1767–68. To pretend that the new taxes were merely a form of trade regulation, he wrote, would permit "a new servitude" to be slipped upon unwary Americans. "We are taxed without our consent. . . . We are therefore—SLAVES." Dickinson called for "a total denial of the power of Parliament to lay upon these colonies any 'tax' whatever."

Unlike the Stamp Act, the Townshend duties directly affected few people. Sleepy country villages woke up for the Stamp Act, but they were lulled back to local affairs in the wake of the Stamp Act's repeal and were unlikely to recognize a tax on painters' colors and lead as a momentous outrage. What made the duties a red flag for the colonies was a second key provision, which directed that some of the income generated would be used to pay the salaries of the royal governors and judges. The prevailing practice had been for each local assembly to set and pay the salaries of its own officials, which in effect gave the assemblies a measure of influence over crown-appointed officeholders. But the assemblies seemed to Townshend to be getting out of hand, and he wanted to strengthen the independence of the governors.

In New York, for example, the assembly had refused to enforce a rule of 1765 called the Quartering Act, which directed the colonies to provide shelter and firewood, drink, salt, and candles for the British army, and the royal governor seemed unable to make them comply. Part of the army had been stationed in the west near the Proclamation Line since 1763, but in 1766 units were being moved to New York City in the wake of the crowd actions protesting the Stamp Act. The New York assembly, deeply unhappy about the arrival of the troops, argued that the Quartering Act was really a tax measure since it required New Yorkers to pay money by order of Parliament. Townshend came down hard on the New York assembly: He orchestrated a parliamentary order, the New York Suspending Act, which declared all of the assembly's acts null and void until it met its obligations to the army.

Both these measures—the new way to pay royal officials' salaries and the suspension of the governance functions of the New York assembly—struck a chill throughout the colonies. Many Americans wondered if their legislative government was at all secure.

The Massachusetts assembly quickly took the lead in protesting the Townshend duties by issuing a circular letter (so called because it was widely circulated) to all the other assemblies in early 1768. Samuel Adams, a member from Boston, drafted the letter, which argued that any form of parliamentary taxation was unjust because Americans were not represented in Parliament and that the new way to pay the royal officials' salaries subverted the proper relationship between the people and the rulers. Adams urged the other assemblies to officially endorse the circular letter. Not since the Stamp Act

Congress of 1765 had there been any similar attempt to coordinate the response of the colonies to British measures.

When the circular letter reached the British ministry, there was yet again a new man in charge of colonial affairs, Wills Hill, Lord Hillsborough, appointed to a newly created post, secretary of colonial affairs. Hillsborough fired back his own circular letter to the assemblies, telling them to treat the Massachusetts document, which he termed seditious, "with the contempt it deserves." He instructed the Massachusetts governor, Francis Bernard, to dissolve the assembly if it refused to rescind its statement. The assembly refused to rescind, by a vote of 92 to 17, and Governor Bernard carried out his instruction. In the summer of 1768, Boston was in an uproar.

Nonconsumption and the Daughters of Liberty

The Boston town meeting had already passed resolutions, termed "nonconsumption agreements," calling for the boycott of British-made goods. Nearly three dozen other New England towns passed similar resolutions in 1767, and by 1768 nonconsumption as a tactic against the Townshend duties was widespread. The town of New Haven, Connecticut, for example, listed prohibited purchases, which included carriages, house furniture, hats, clothing, shoes, gold, silver, lace, iron plate, clocks, jewelry, textiles, furs, toys, velvets, linseed oil, malt liquors, and cheese. The idea was to encourage home manufacture of such items and to hurt trade with Britain, causing London merchants to pressure Parliament for repeal of the duties.

The trouble with nonconsumption agreements as a strategy was that they were very hard to enforce. With the Stamp Act, there was one hated item, a stamp, and a limited number of official distributors. Choking off the supply of stamps was a straightforward strategy. But an agreement to boycott British goods was extremely diffuse, and it also required serious personal sacrifice. Many merchants were wary of nonconsumption because it hurt their pocketbooks. Many continued to import British goods, to be ready for the day nonconsumption ended, or indeed to sell to people choosing to ignore nonconsumption. In Boston, such merchants found themselves blacklisted in newspapers and broadsides.

A more direct blow to trade came from nonimportation agreements, but it proved even more dif-

EDENTON TEA LADIES

American women in many communities renounced British apparel and tea during the early 1770s. Women in Edenton, North Carolina, publicized their pledge and drew hostile fire in the form of a British cartoon. The cartoon's message is that brazen women who meddle in politics will undermine their femininity. Neglected babies, urinating dogs, wanton sexuality, and mean-looking women are some of the dire consequences, according to the artist. The cartoon works as humor for the British because of the gender inversions it predicts and because of the insult it poses to American men.

Library of Congress.

ficult to get merchants to agree to these. There was always the risk that merchants in other colonies might continue to trade and thus receive handsome profits if neighboring colonies prohibited trade. Not until late 1768 could Boston merchants agree to suspend trade through nonimportation agreements. Sixty men signed the agreement, to be in effect exactly one year—from January 1, 1769, to January 1, 1770. New York merchants soon followed suit, as did Philadelphia and Charleston merchants in 1769.

Planters in Virginia were more eager than merchants to join the boycott. George Washington and George Mason spearheaded the formation of the As-

sociation for Non-Importation in 1769. When the royal governor dissolved the Virginia House of Burgesses because it issued a strong condemnation of the Townshend duties, eighty-nine burgesses walked down the street from the capitol to the Raleigh Tavern in Williamsburg and drew up the nonimportation agreement. Washington hoped for a second major benefit from nonimportation, beyond the pressure on British merchants. Extravagant living had brought some Virginia planters to the brink of ruin because they owed large debts to British merchants for luxury purchases. Nonimportation would provide "a pretext to live within bounds," Washington felt.

Doing without British products, whether they were luxury goods or basics such as tea or textiles, no doubt was a hardship for the American population. But it also presented an opportunity, for many of the British goods specified in nonconsumption agreements were household items and goods traditionally under the control of women. By 1769, male leaders in the patriot cause clearly understood that women's cooperation in nonconsumption and home manufacture was essential. The Townshend duties thus provided an unparalleled opportunity for developing and showcasing female patriotism. During the Stamp Act crisis, Sons of Liberty took to the streets in protest. During the difficulties of 1768–1769, the phrase "Daughters of Liberty" emerged and gave shape to a new idea—that women could play a role in public affairs.

Any individual woman could express affiliation with the colonial protest by complying with the nonconsumption agreements and by taking up home manufacture of items previously imported from England. One young Philadelphia woman inscribed some "patriotic poesy" in her commonplace book in 1768, the gist of which was that women can take up the patriotic cause even if men falter and stumble: "If the Sons (so degenerate) the Blessing despise, / Let the Daughters of Liberty nobly arise, / And tho' we've no Voice, but a negative here, / The use of the Taxables, let us forbear, / (Then Merchants import till yr. Stores are all full / May the Buyers be few and yr. Traffick be dull.) / Stand firmly resolved and bid Grenville to see / That rather than Freedom, we'll part with our Tea." On a more organized level, women in some towns met to sign nonconsumption agreements. Three hundred women in Boston drew up a petition agreeing to abstain from tea, "sickness excepted," to protest the duty on tea. A similar group in Edenton, North Carolina, agreed to forgo tea and found themselves

THE BLOODY MASSACRE PERPETRATED IN KING STREET, BOSTON, ON MARCH 5, 1770
This mass-produced engraving by Paul Revere sold for six pence per copy. In this patriot version, the soldiers fire on an unarmed crowd under orders of their captain. The tranquil dog is an artistic device to signal the crowd's peaceful intent; not even a deaf dog could actually hold that pose during the melee. Among the five killed was Crispus Attucks, a black dock worker, but Revere shows only whites among the casualties.
Anne S. K. Brown Military Collection, Providence, R.I.

ridiculed in an English political cartoon that depicted bad women—sexually loose, neglectful of children—signing a boycott petition.

Homespun cloth became a prominent badge of patriotism. In the latter half of 1769, dozens of towns organized public spinning "frolicks" or bees— women dusted off their spinning wheels and looms (dusty with disuse over the previous two decades of textile importation) and gathered for daylong competitions in spinning and weaving. Local newspapers publicized the "frolicks" and reported on the yards of cloth produced, thus further encouraging participation in the boycotts. Cloth making was no longer simply a chore of family service, but a task invested with political content. A Connecticut girl who spun ten knots of wool in one day proclaimed in her diary that her work made her feel "Nationly." Said the editor of the Boston *Evening Post*, "The industry and frugality of American ladies must exalt their character in the Eyes of the World and serve to show how greatly they are contributing to bring about the political salvation of a whole Continent."

On the whole, the year of boycotts was a success. British imports fell by more than 40 percent, and British merchants felt the pinch.

Military Occupation and "Massacre" in Boston

By the summer of 1768, the turmoil in Boston thoroughly alarmed Governor Bernard. Townshend's new customs commissioners had been forced to flee to an island in Boston harbor for safety. After Bernard dissolved the assembly, men from ninety-six Massachusetts towns staged a convention (a gathering closely resembling the dissolved assembly) to appeal—unsuccessfully—for reinstatement. On August 15, a rollicking anniversary celebration of the Stamp Act demonstration of 1765 put crowds in the street and apprehension in the hearts of Governor Bernard and Lieutenant Governor Hutchinson. With no police force and no reasonable hope of controlling the town militia, Bernard concluded that he needed British soldiers to help keep the peace.

Four regiments of troops from a garrison at Halifax, Nova Scotia, arrived in the fall of 1768, packing a total of three thousand uniformed soldiers into Boston. They camped out on the Boston Common and in rented warehouses, turning Boston into an occupied city. The soldiers conspicuously drilled on the Common, played loud band music on the Sabbath, set up a sentry point at the narrow Boston neck (the only entry to the city by land), and in general grated on the nerves of Bostonians. To occupy their spare time, some soldiers took casual day-labor work, putting themselves in direct competition with the laboring men of the town for low-wage jobs.

Although the situation was frequently tense, there were no major troubles during that winter and into the spring of 1769. In May, two of the four regiments departed, and in July Governor Bernard himself left for England, having been recalled by the king. Wild celebrations in Boston marked his departure, including massive bonfires and ceremonial bell ringing, no compliment to his years of rule. Thomas Hutchinson, the lieutenant governor, assumed the acting governorship.

At the very end of 1769, Boston's year-long nonimportation agreement drew to a close. The ban on British goods had been enforced by public pressure, but as January 1 approached, it was clear that some merchants could no longer be kept in line. Hutchinson's two sons, for example, were both importers hostile to the boycott, and they had already ordered new goods from England, anticipating a return to business as usual. The early months of 1770 were thus bound to be an eventful and conflict-ridden period in Boston.

Serious troubles began in January. The Hutchinson sons prepared to sell imported tea, and their shop was visited by a crowd that smeared "Hillsborough paint," a potent mixture of human excrement and urine, on the door. In mid-February another shopowner, who had complained that the nonimportation movement was akin to coercive lawmaking without his consent, found tar and feathers slapped on his storefront. The next day, a crowd surrounded the house of Ebenezer Richardson, a cranky, low-level customs official. Richardson panicked and pulled out his musket to defend his house and family. But when he fired it, the shot struck an eleven-year-old boy on the fringes of the crowd; he died within hours. The Sons of Liberty orchestrated an impressive funeral procession, with two lines of five hundred schoolboys accompanying the coffin and two thousand men and women trailing through Boston streets. This was the first instance of violent death in the struggle with England.

For the next week the mood was especially tense in Boston. Soldiers and young laborers engaged in brawls, typically over the odd-job employment sought by moonlighting soldiers. The climax came on Monday evening, March 5, 1770. Townsmen roved the streets, taunting soldiers on guard duty. One sentry guarding the entrance to the customs house on King Street was subject to verbal abuse from a growing crowd. Among other things, he was called a "damned rascally Scoundrel Lobster Son of a Bitch." (The red uniforms of the British were often likened to lobsters.) The sentry threatened to respond with force, but being vastly outnumbered, he hesitated to act. About 8:30 P.M., the town bells mysteriously began to ring, drawing more citizens into the streets. British Captain Thomas Preston decided to send a seven-man guard to join the lone sentry. The soldiers fended off the hostile crowd with loaded and raised muskets. Onlookers threw snowballs and chunks of ice, daring the soldiers to fire. Preston restrained his men, but finally one of the soldiers, hit by a piece of ice, slipped to the ground and rose up with a blast from his gun. After a second's pause, the other soldiers fired as well. Eleven men in the crowd were hit, five of them fatally. The victims had funerals befitting martyrs, with elaborate orations by leaders of the Sons of Liberty about the threat to all Americans posed by the British army.

The Boston Massacre, as it quickly became called, was over in minutes, but its repercussions were serious and long-lasting. In the immediate aftermath, Acting Governor Hutchinson showed courage in confronting the crowd personally, from the balcony of the customs house. By daybreak of March 6, he accepted the necessity of removing the full two regiments to an island in the harbor to prevent further bloodshed. Hutchinson also jailed Preston and the eight soldiers, as much for their own protection as to appease the townspeople, and promised they would be held accountable for their actions. But he also postponed their trial for nearly eight months, in the hope that angry tempers would subside.

Preston and the soldiers came to trial in the fall of 1770, defended by two young attorneys, John Adams and Josiah Quincy. Because Adams and Quincy had direct ties to the leadership of the Boston Sons of Liberty, their decision to defend the British soldiers at first seems odd. The thirty-five-year-old John Adams had recently become a member of the Massachusetts assembly, in an election engineered by his distant cousin and ally Samuel Adams. John Adams had a thriving legal practice in Boston, and, in his view, Preston sought out his services because he was simply the best lawyer in town. Adams was deeply committed to the idea that even unpopular defendants deserve a fair trial. Throughout his long public life, he was never shy

Who Got Tarred and Feathered, and Why?

TARRING AND FEATHERING as a form of vigilante brutality has long been associated with the American Revolution. British political cartoons gave wide currency to images of befeathered victims in humiliating postures. Boston loyalist Peter Oliver (brother-in-law of Thomas Hutchinson) claimed that tarring and feathering was an American invention and supplied shocked British friends with the "recipe," as he termed it:

> First, strip a Person naked, then heat the Tar untill it is thin, & pour it upon the naked Flesh, or rub it over with a Tar Brush, *quantum sufficit*. After which, sprinkle decently upon the Tar, whilst it is yet warm, as many Feathers as will stick to it. Then hold a lighted Candle to the Feathers, & try to set it all on Fire; if it will burn so much the better.

Both the cartoon depictions and Oliver's recipe for this messy ritual must be taken cautiously, however, for they were promulgated by pro-British men who had a stake in portraying Americans as barbarians. How often did tarring and feathering really occur? Who were the victims? Was actual harm done? Answers to such questions allow historians to evaluate the role of violence and terrorism as tactics of revolutionary struggle.

Recorded incidents of tarring and feathering do not support Oliver's assertion that the practice was frequent. Probably fewer than a dozen instances occurred between 1765 and the outbreak of war in April 1775. The practice peaked in popularity in the turbulent year 1775, making a total of perhaps two to three dozen cases in all the colonies.

Tarred and feathered victims were *not* British officials. For a person openly identified with British authority, the ritual of choice was hanging or burning an effigy of their body or conducting a mock funeral. Such dramatic representations of crowd dis-

pleasure made a chilling point without doing any physical harm. Ceremonies with effigies released anger, tempered by a measure of restraint.

Tarring and feathering pushed the boundaries of restraint, for the act involved considerable bodily discomfort. Victims of the sticky, feathery assault were usually community members suspected of being informers, violators of agreements to spurn British goods, or men conspicuous for their animosity toward the revolutionary point of view. They were men *of* the community who had to be rit-

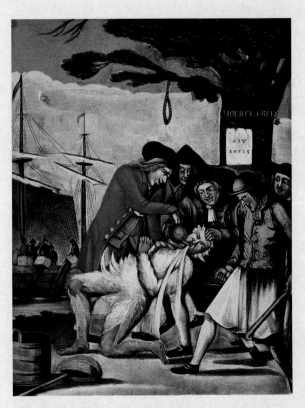

TAR AND FEATHERING CARTOON
John Malcolm, a customs official in Boston, becomes a feathery chicken forced to drink tea. A tar bucket and brush are in the left foreground; the Boston Tea Party— in reality ten months before the cartoon was published— proceeds in the rear. The Liberty Tree has become a gallows; posted to it is the Stamp Act, upside down.
Courtesy of John Carter Brown at Brown University.

ually distanced from the community for breaking a moral code, not a law. The standard treatment for lawbreakers was a flogging, fine, or jail, imposed by a judge. Moral code transgressors, in contrast, got symbolic punishments from their neighbors on the local committee of public safety, without benefit of legal procedures.

Tarring and feathering was a severe variant in a long tradition of ritual humiliations for transgressive people. Typical humiliations imposed on fornicators, adulterers, or other deceivers included dressing victims in clothes of the opposite sex, riding them around town backward on an ass, or making them stand in public wrapped in white sheets. The object was to shame them into apologizing for their bad behavior as a condition of acceptance back into the community. Tarring and feathering introduced a new variation on the theme: A person was rendered into an animal—a fowl or chicken—and paraded around in a state of near nakedness, the better to garner public shame.

For example, in 1771 a Providence, Rhode Island, man suspected of informing on smugglers was stripped, tied up, painted with warm tar, and feathered, after which dirt was thrown in his face. A man in Charleston, South Carolina, snarled, "Damnation to the Committee and their proceedings" and was soon tarred and feathered for his outburst. A New Jersey artisan who reviled the Continental Congress in late 1775 was set upon by townsmen, stripped, tarred and feathered, and paraded in a wagon for a half hour until he begged pardon. Probably the most famous case occurred in 1774, involving the Bostonian John Malcolm, a dishonest customs collector who extorted extra money from shippers. Malcolm's horrid fate was immortalized in a London cartoon showing five cruelly gleeful Americans forcing tea into his mouth, yanking his hair, and terrorizing him with a noose about his neck.

Peter Oliver's assertion that feathers were set on fire was a serious exaggeration. Hot tar of course hurt, and the eventual removal of the suit of feathers posed the risk of additional pain. It mattered what feathers were used. Soft goose down was an expensive household item in the eighteenth century; few revolutionary women would relinquish treasured quilts and pillows easily. A more prevalent source of feathers, scratchy ones at that, was the chicken coop. Powerful humiliation, not serious injury, was the goal. In one of the few known instances of a female-inspired sticky assault, girls at a quilting frolic in a small Hudson River village in fall 1775 reportedly stripped to the waist a young man of loyalist sympathies and adorned him with molasses and weeds.

In one unusual case, British soldiers in Boston in March 1775 turned the tables and attacked a rural man who had tried to buy a gun from a soldier. The man was stripped, tarred, feathered, and hauled around on a cart, with a sign affixed to his back proclaiming "American Liberty, or a Specimen of Democracy"—meaning, a sorry specimen. A fife and drum accompanied him, playing "Yankee Doodle" to irritate the Bostonian onlookers, and twenty bayonet-bearing British soldiers surrounded him, to prevent a rescue attempt. The soldiers' inversion fundamentally changed the ritual: No longer community-confirming, the event became in their hands a mockery of the civilian population.

Tarring and feathering was not practiced often. Other tactics involving less personal violence were more frequently used: publishing offenders' names in the newspaper, boycotting businesses, intimidating their families, and breaking windows. Sometimes just the threat of a tar and feather treatment was sufficient, as when a Pennsylvania loyalist had his nose pushed up to a barrel of tar or when a warning directed at an individual mysteriously appeared in a newspaper, signed by a fictional "Committee for Tarring and Feathering."

Peter Oliver did not think so, but historians generally agree that the years of revolutionary turmoil from 1765 to the 1770s were remarkably free of serious personal violence, aside from organized warfare. The Boston Massacre of five people hardly qualifies as a massacre by twentieth-century war zone standards. Tarring and feathering was rough stuff, but it did not cause death. The American Revolution, even in its aspects that resemble a civil war, stopped short of the kind of massive bloodshed and torture of civilians against civilians that would characterize revolutions from the 1789 French Revolution onward.

of taking on unpopular causes, although he was continually sensitive about the wounds and imagined insults his advocacy cost him. Samuel Adams respected his cousin's decision to take the case, for there was a tactical benefit as well: It showed that the Boston leadership was not lawless but could be seen as defenders of British liberty and law.

Preston was fully acquitted of all responsibility for the Boston Massacre, as were all but two of the soldiers, who were convicted of manslaughter and then branded on the thumbs and released. John Adams was very satisfied with the outcome. It was, he wrote, "one of the most gallant, generous, manly, and disinterested Actions of my whole Life, and one of the best Pieces of Service I ever rendered my Country. Judgment of Death against those Soldiers would have been as foul a Stain upon this Country as the Executions of the Quakers or Witches, anciently." Samuel Adams was not displeased with the trial outcome either. Nothing materialized in the trial testimony to fix blame for the massacre on anyone at all—not on the soldiers, or on any crowd participants, or on the leaders of the Sons of Liberty. The defense lawyers were no doubt men of integrity, but they were at the same time very sympathetic to the patriot side. They astutely chose to defend without pointing the finger of blame elsewhere. To this day, the question of who was responsible for the Boston Massacre remains obscure.

The years from 1767 to 1770 propelled the growing crisis into deeper and murkier channels. The nebulous Townshend duties lacked the symbolic punch of the Stamp Act, and the decision to try the tactics of nonimportation and nonconsumption created serious divisions in the American population. A military occupation of Boston brought the first fatalities in the coming Revolution, but, electrifying as that was to Bostonians, colonists distant from that city could still indulge the luxury of thinking that the crisis was perhaps not all that serious.

The Tea Party and the Coercive Acts

In the same week as the Boston Massacre, the new British prime minister, Frederick North, contemplated the decrease in trade caused by the Townshend duties and recommended repeal. A skillful politician, Lord North took office in 1770 and kept it for twelve years; at last George III had stability at the helm. Lord North sought peace with the colonies and prosperity for British merchants, so all the Townshend duties were removed, except the tax on tea, which served as a pointed reminder of Parliament's ultimate power. Leniency in repealing the Stamp Act, North believed, had invited Americans "to insult our authority, to dispute our rights, and to aim at independent government." North hoped to cool tensions without sacrificing principles.

Those few Americans who could not abide the symbolism of the tea tax turned to smuggled Dutch tea. The renewal of trade and the return of cooperation between England and the colonies gave men like Thomas Hutchinson hope that the worst of the crisis was behind them. For nearly two years, it looked as though Hutchinson's hope might be realized.

The Calm before the Storm

With the repeal of the Townshend duties, there was little desire to continue nonimportation agreements. Artisans in cities and planters in the Chesapeake tried to extend the boycott, to protest the remaining duty on tea, but the lure of trade and profits was too strong for the merchants to withstand. By fall 1770, nonimportation was a dead issue in Boston, Philadelphia, New York, and Baltimore. What was more, the leaders of the popular movement seemed to be losing their power. Samuel Adams, for example, ran for a minor local office in Boston and lost to a conservative merchant. And trade boomed in 1770 and 1771.

In 1772, however, several incidents brought the conflict with England into focus again. One was the burning of a Royal Navy ship off the coast of Rhode Island. The *Gaspée* had been harassing local vessels for some time in a search for customs violators. Local newspapers unkindly characterized the British commander as a pirate, a hog stealer, and a chicken thief. In June 1772, the ship was chasing down suspected smugglers when it ran aground in shallow waters. Some irate Rhode Islanders seized the opportunity to board the *Gaspée*. They wrecked the interior and then burned the hull, allowing the crew to leave first—not unharmed, however, for the despised commander was shot in the groin. A royal investigating commission could not identify any suspects to arrest (even though one young man had been seen the next day sporting the commander's lace-trimmed beaver hat). But the commission announced it would send suspects, if it found any, back to England for trial for high treason; burning the *Gaspée* was an act of war against the king.

This decision seemed to fly in the face of the traditional English right to a trial by a jury of one's peers. When the news of the *Gaspée* investigation spread, it was greeted with disbelief in other colonies. Patrick Henry, Thomas Jefferson, and Richard Henry Lee from the Virginia House of Burgesses proposed that a network of standing committees be established to link the colonies and pass along alarming news. By mid-1773, every colony except Pennsylvania had a "committee of correspondence." The British handling of the *Gaspée* incident had backfired, for it provoked the first serious effort to create semiofficial links among the American colonial governments.

Another British action in 1772 led to a second important communications network. Just as Charles Townshend had tried to free royal governors from colonial control by paying their salaries, now Lord North proposed to do the same for the superior court justices, paying their salaries out of the tea duty instead of allowing colonial assemblies to set the stipends. The Boston town meeting took particular exception to this idea, which threatened to subvert justice itself by putting judges in the pockets of their new paymasters. Samuel Adams tried to persuade Thomas Hutchinson to call a meeting of the Massachusetts assembly to respond to the salary issue, and Hutchinson predictably refused. So Adams proposed that each Massachusetts town set up a committee of correspondence to exchange vital information about unfolding political events. In December 1772, the Boston committee of correspondence sent out a letter to other towns describing the judges' salary policy as the latest move in a British plot to undermine traditional English "liberties" in the colonies. First there was unjust taxation, followed by a military occupation and massacre. This latest policy would "compleat our Slavery," claimed the Boston committee.

By spring 1773, half of the towns in Massachusetts had set up their own committees of correspondence and were busily doing exactly what Samuel Adams had envisioned: debating issues, voting on resolutions, and responding to circular letters from the more radical Boston group. The institution of such committees thus provided a forum for politicizing ordinary townspeople and served as a substitute for the usual flow of political power and information through the colony's royal government.

The third and final incident that irrevocably shattered the relative calm of the early 1770s was the Tea Act of 1773. Lord North had thus far avoided conflict by ignoring the colonies. In the spring of 1773, his attention was turned to a major but seriously troubled English joint stock company, the East India Company; many members of Parliament were among its stockholders, as was Thomas Hutchinson. Americans had been drinking moderate amounts of English tea and paying the tea duty without objection, but they were also smuggling large quantities of Dutch tea, and the East India Company was experiencing sagging sales. So Lord North proposed special legislation giving favored status to the East India Company, allowing it to sell its tea through special agents, appointed by the government, rather than through public auction to independent merchants. The hope was that the price of the East India tea, even with the duty, would then fall below that of the smuggled Dutch tea, creating an incentive for Americans to obey the law as well as boosting sales for the East India Company.

The Boston Tea Party

In the fall of 1773, news of the Tea Act reached the colonies. Parliamentary legislation to make tea inexpensive struck many colonists as a subtle and therefore evil plot to trick Americans into buying large quantities of the dutied tea. The real goal, some argued, was the increased revenue, which would then be used to pay the royal governors and judges. The Tea Act was thus a sudden and painful reminder of Parliament's claim to the power to tax and legislate for the colonies.

As with the Stamp Act and the Townshend duties, the colonists' strategy was crucial. Nonimportation was not a viable option, because the trade was too lucrative to expect colonial merchants to give it up willingly. Consumer boycotts of tea had proved ineffective since 1770, chiefly because it was extremely hard to distinguish between dutied tea (the object of the boycott) and smuggled tea (illegal but politically clean) once it was in the teapot. Like the Stamp Act, the Tea Act mandated special agents to handle the tea sales, and that requirement provided one convenient target for colonists' actions. A revived patriot group in New York City publicly identified the tea agents and pressured them to resign. In Philadelphia, the Sons of Liberty held a mass meeting and resolved that any merchant who handled East India tea was "an enemy to his country." They also issued threats to tar and feather anyone who assisted the landing of the tea ships; the first captain who arrived with tea took that warning to heart and turned his ship around. In

Charleston, South Carolina, tea ships did arrive and unload in December 1773, but the tea agents had resigned their positions, under pressure from the local Sons of Liberty, so there was no way to sell the cargo. After twenty days, the governor impounded the tea for nonpayment of duty, and it rotted in storage cellars.

The Boston Sons of Liberty were slower to act than their compatriots in other cities, but their action—more direct and illegal than anywhere else—ultimately provoked the most alarming reprisals from England. The first ship bearing 114 chests of tea arrived in Boston in late November 1773, and the next day the city was showered with notices calling for "manly opposition to the machinations of tyranny." As mass meetings engaging up to six thousand people debated the fate of the tea, two more ships arrived. They cleared customs and unloaded their other cargoes, but the tea remained on board. The owner of one ship, a Quaker from the island of Nantucket, off the Massachusetts coast, readily agreed to return the tea to England. But he found he was stuck in a legalistic nightmare of the sort that only a Thomas Hutchinson would scrupulously enforce: Because the ship had already entered the harbor, it could not get clearance to leave without first paying the tea duty. And there was a twenty-day limit on the stay allowed in the harbor, by which time either the duty had to be paid or the tea would be confiscated and sold by the authorities. The ever stiff-necked Governor Hutchinson would not bend the rules.

It took three hours to dump 342 chests of tea into Boston harbor. Bostonians quickly dubbed the event the Boston Tea Party, a jolly name that blunted the massive illegal destruction of property.

For the full twenty days, pressure built in Boston. Daily mass meetings energized the citizenry not only from Boston but from surrounding towns, alerted by the committees of correspondence. On the final day, December 16, the Quaker shipowner made one last effort to obtain a pass to leave the harbor and reported his failure to a large gathering at the Old South Church in Boston, presided over by Samuel Adams. At that point, Adams declared to the crowd, "This meeting can do nothing more to save the country." Perhaps the meeting could not,

but some people at the meeting had already concocted a plan to end the stalemate. At Adams's words, whoops rang out, and a large part of the crowd moved to Griffin's Wharf, where the three ships were anchored. Some five dozen men dressed as Indians destroyed the tea while a crowd of two thousand watched. It took three hours to dump 342 chests of tea into Boston harbor; the total weight was ninety thousand pounds, and it was worth £10,000 sterling. Bostonians quickly dubbed the event the Boston Tea Party, a jolly name that blunted the massive illegal destruction of property.

TEA DESTROYED BY INDIANS
A broadside was a one-page printed notice that could be tacked up on walls. This broadside of 1773 relates lively verses about the Boston Tea Party, useful for episodes of planned or spontaneous public singing. Notice the use of racial and gender stereotypes in the first verse in the references to manliness, fair Liberty, foreign Indians, and savage Moors.
Courtesy of the Massachusetts Historical Society ©.

BOSTONIANS IN DISTRESS
This British cartoon portrays the effects of the closure of the port of Boston in 1774. Men in a cage, surrounded by cannons and British soldiers, act like animals eating raw fish. The three fishermen get a bundle labeled "promises" in return. Is this cartoon sympathetic to the distress of Boston, or is it scornful?
Courtesy of the John Carter Brown Library at Brown University.

The Coercive Acts

Lord North's response was swift and stern. Within three months he persuaded Parliament to issue the first of the Coercive Acts, a series of four laws meant to punish Massachusetts for the Tea Party. The laws were soon known as the Intolerable Acts in America, along with a fifth one not aimed at Massachusetts alone, the Quebec Act.

The first, the Boston Port Act, closed Boston harbor to all shipping traffic as of June 1, 1774, for as long as the destroyed tea was not paid for. In effect, England was obliterating the commercial life of the city.

The second, called the Massachusetts Government Act, altered the colony's charter (in itself an unprecedented step, underscoring Parliament's claim to supremacy over Massachusetts): The royal governor's powers were greatly augmented; the council became an appointive, not elective, body; and no town meeting beyond the annual spring election of town selectmen could be held unless the governor expressly permitted it. Not only Boston but every Massachusetts town felt the punitive sting. The act was meant to undermine local control of politics.

The third of the Coercive Acts, the Impartial Administration of Justice Act, stipulated that any royal official accused of a capital crime—for example, Captain Preston and his soldiers at the Boston Massacre—would now be tried in a court in England. It did not matter that Preston in fact got a fair trial in Boston. What this act ominously suggested was that down the road, there might be more Captain Prestons and soldiers firing into crowds.

The fourth of the Coercive Acts was a new amendment to the 1765 Quartering Act, permitting military commanders to lodge soldiers wherever necessary, even in private households. For Boston this was no idle gesture, for in a related move, Lord North appointed General Thomas Gage, commander of the Royal Army in New York, to be the new governor of Massachusetts. Thomas Hutchinson was out, relieved at long last of his duties, and military rule, including soldiers, returned once more to Boston.

The fifth Intolerable Act, the Quebec Act, had little to do with the first four but, ill-timed, it greatly fed the alarm of Americans. It confirmed the continuation of French civil law, government form, and Catholicism for Quebec, all an affront to Protestant New Englanders denied their own representative government. The act also gave Quebec control of disputed lands (and hence control of the lucrative fur trade) throughout the Ohio River valley, lands claimed variously by Virginia, Pennsylvania, and Connecticut.

If England could step on Massachusetts and change its charter, suspend government, inaugurate military rule, and on top of that give Ohio to Catholic Quebec, then what liberties were possibly secure?

When the Boston Port Act was passed, many merchants in Boston and other cities favored simply paying reparations for the tea. But with the rapid issuance of further punitive acts, alarm spread. If England could step on Massachusetts and change its charter, suspend government, inaugurate military rule, and on top of that give Ohio to Catholic Quebec, then what liberties were possibly secure?

In Virginia, the House of Burgesses proposed a day of fasting and prayer in sympathy with Massachusetts for the Port Act. Despite the moderate nature of this proposal, the governor, John Murray, Lord Dunmore, dissolved the house for its gesture of solidarity with rebellious Massachusetts. If the burgesses were complacent about their liberties before that moment, they could not be now. Eighty-nine of them met in the Raleigh Tavern in Williamsburg, just as they had done in 1769 in the Townshend duties crisis, and in this unauthorized form passed resolutions on parliamentary and colonial rights. Via the committees of correspondence, they urged all the other colonial assemblies to meet in Philadelphia in the fall of 1774 to respond to the crisis.

The First Continental Congress

Every colony except Georgia sent delegates to Philadelphia for the meeting of the First Continental Congress in September 1774. In six colonies, specially reconstituted assemblies made the delegate selections, for, as in Virginia, the royal governors were dissolving the official bodies as fast as they could. The gathering in Philadelphia included the leading patriots, such as Samuel and John Adams from Massachusetts and George Washington and Patrick Henry from Virginia. A few colonies sent men who were cool to provoking a crisis with England, like Pennsylvania's Joseph Galloway, whose mission was to slow down the revolutionary momentum. Whatever their views, most of the delegates were the leading statesmen of their localities. John Adams wrote to his wife, Abigail, that "the magnanimity and public spirit which I see here make me blush for the sordid, venal herd which I have seen in my own Province."

Two difficult tasks confronted the congress: The delegates wanted to agree on exactly what liberties they claimed as English subjects and what rights Parliament held over them, and they needed to make a unified response to the Coercive Acts. Some delegates wanted a total ban on trade with England, to force a repeal of the Coercive Acts, but others—especially from the southern colonies heavily dependent on the export of tobacco and rice—could not afford such a comprehensive stoppage. Samuel Adams and Patrick Henry were more than eager for a ringing denunciation of all parliamentary control, whereas the conservative Joseph Galloway proposed a plan (quickly defeated) to create a colonial miniparliament in America to assist the British Parliament in ruling the colonies.

The congress met for seven weeks in Carpenter's Hall, Philadelphia, and eventually hammered out a declaration of rights, couched in traditional language: "We ask only for peace, liberty and security. We wish no diminution of royal prerogatives, we demand no new rights." Yet the rights assumed already to exist were in fact radical, from England's point of view. Chief among them was the claim that Americans were not represented in Parliament and so each colonial government had the sole right to legislate for and tax its own people. The one slight concession to England was a carefully worded agreement that the colonists would "cheerfully consent" to trade regulations, for the larger good of the empire—so long as trade regulation was not a covert means of raising revenue. By consenting to this one power, however, the patriots were implying their right to revoke consent at any time. To express their displeasure with the Boston Port Act, the delegates also agreed to a staggered and limited ban on trade—imports prohibited this year, exports the following year, and rice totally exempted, to keep South Carolinians happy. As with previous attempts to curtail trade, they developed an enforcement strategy for the boycott, in the form of a Continental Association, which would have chapters in each town. Local associations, variously called committees of public safety or of inspection, would monitor all commerce and confront suspected violators of the boycott. Its work done, the congress disbanded on October 26, 1774, with a vote to reconvene the following May in a Second Continental Congress.

The committees of public safety, the committees of correspondence, the regrouped colonial assemblies, and the Continental Congresses were all functioning political bodies without any formal constitutional authority. British officials did not recognize them as legitimate, but many Americans who supported the patriot cause instantly accepted them. A key reason for the stability of such unauthorized bodies throughout the Revolutionary period was that they were composed of the same men, by and large, who had composed the official bodies now disbanded.

England's severe reaction to the Boston Tea Party finally succeeded in making many colonists from New Hampshire to Georgia realize that the problems of British rule went far beyond questions of taxation. The Coercive Acts infringed on liberty and denied self-government; they could not be ignored. With one colony subordinated to military rule now, and a British army at the ready in Boston, the threat of a general war was at the doorstep.

Domestic Insurrections

Before the Second Continental Congress could meet, war began in Massachusetts. General Thomas Gage, military commander and new governor, thought he had a domestic insurrection on his hands that needed only a show of force to quiet it. The Americans saw things differently: They were defending their homes and liberties against an intrusive power that was trying to enslave them. To the south, a different and inverted version of the same story began to unfold, as thousands of enslaved black men and women seized an unprecedented opportunity to mount a different kind of domestic insurrection, against planter-patriots who looked over their shoulders uneasily whenever they called out for liberty from the British.

Lexington and Concord

Over the winter of 1774–1775 the Continental Association enforced the import ban with enthusiasm. Some hoped the collapse of the Coercive Acts was just around the corner. Others, more pessimistic, started accumulating arms and ammunition. Militiamen started to drill and train. In Massachusetts, gunpowder and shot were stored in strategic places, and special militia units calling themselves "minutemen" prepared to be ready on a minute's notice to respond to unusual movements of the British soldiers now occupying Boston.

Thomas Gage felt the increased tensions and experienced something close to panic. He knew that a single aggressive show of force on his part would plunge the country into war, and so he wrote to Lord North asking for twenty thousand reinforcements. The people, he informed North, were "numerous, worked up to a fury, and not a Boston rabble but the freeholders and farmers of the country." The "disease" of rebellion is now "so universal there is no knowing where to apply a remedy." With the men he had, he had secured Boston's port and closed it to traffic, but his force was inadequate to stop smuggling at nearby peninsulas and islands in Boston harbor. Gage had set up cannon on the narrow neck of land connecting Boston to the mainland, and he was attempting to acquire maps of the countryside by sending out scouts disguised as civilians. To the king, Gage strongly suggested that the Coercive Acts should be repealed, simply to defuse a very tense situation. But his advice was

BRITISH TROOPS IN CONCORD CENTER

*In this contemporary engraving by Amos Doolittle, two British officers seek the high ground of
the cemetery in Concord, Massachusetts, to orient themselves to the unfamiliar town at around
9 A.M. on April 19, 1775. Their troops march in formation, fresh from the skirmish at Lexington.
American militiamen had amassed at the Old North Bridge, off to the right about a mile from the
town center. The officer with the telescope is undoubtedly scanning for them.*

Miriam and Ira D. Walsh Division of Art, Prints and Photographs, The New York Public Library. Astor, Lenox and
Tilden Foundations.

spurned as an unacceptable admission of failure. Instead, on April 14, 1775, Gage got orders from England: Arrest troublemaking leaders and stop things
before the Americans got better organized.

For four days, Gage worked quickly to orchestrate a surprise attack on an ammunition storage
site at Concord, a village about eighteen miles west
of Boston. Boats along the Charles River were
quickly pulled ashore in Boston and caulked, in
preparation for troop movement across the water.
On the evening of April 18, just before midnight,
British soldiers in the small boats crossed the wide
expanse of river in the direction of Concord. Boston
silversmith Paul Revere and another close observer,
William Dawes, raced ahead to wake the minutemen. At 4:30 A.M., about 70 sleepy American men
assembled on the village green at Lexington, about
five miles east of Concord, unsure of what awaited
them. When the British soldiers arrived, their commander barked out, "Lay down your arms, you
damned rebels, and disperse." The militiamen hesitated and then began to comply, turning to leave
the green, but then someone fired—who it was has
never been clear. In the next two minutes, more firing left eight Americans dead and ten wounded.
Only one British soldier was slightly wounded.

The British units then moved on to Concord,
along a narrow wooded road, no longer under cover
of dark or with any pretense of surprise. Three companies of minutemen nervously occupied the center of Concord but offered no challenge to the British
troops as they wheeled into town and moved north,
away from the center, toward a particular house
thought to hold the ammunition supply. But no
weapons were in fact located there. The British
turned back to the town but encountered several
hundred minutemen at the Old North Bridge over
the Concord River. Again some shots were exchanged, resulting in the deaths of two Americans
and three British soldiers.

By now both sides were very apprehensive. The
British had failed to find the expected powder magazine, and the Americans had failed to thwart the
British incursion. As the British retreated to Boston
along the narrow road, militia units attacked from
the sides in the bloodiest fighting of the day. In the
end, 273 British soldiers were wounded or dead; the
toll for the Americans stood at about 95.

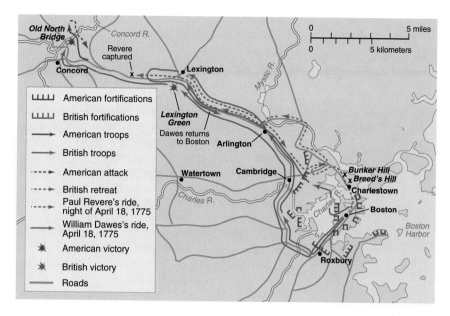

M A P 6.3
*Lexington and Concord,
April 1775*
*Under pressure from England,
British forces at Boston staged
a raid on a suspected rebel arms
supply in Concord, Massachusetts, starting the first battle of
the Revolutionary War.*

Another Rebellion against Slavery

News of the battles of Lexington and Concord
spread rapidly. Within eight days, Virginians had
heard of the fighting, and, as Thomas Jefferson reflected, "A phrenzy of revenge seems to have seized
all ranks of people." The royal governor of Virginia,
Lord Dunmore, had just removed a large quantity
of gunpowder from the Williamsburg powder
house, and in the dead of night he had it placed on
a ship, out of reach of any frenzied Virginians. Next,
Dunmore threatened to arm the slaves, if necessary,
to ward off any attacks by colonists. To the British
ministry he wrote, "My declaration that I would
arm and set free such slaves as should assist me
if I was attacked has stirred up fears in them [the
colonists] which cannot easily subside as they know
how vulnerable they are in that particular."

This was clearly Dunmore's ace card, for he understood full well how to produce panic among the
planters. Yet he did not play the card until November 1775, when he issued an official proclamation
promising freedom to defecting, able-bodied slaves
who would fight for the British. Dunmore's
dilemma was that while he wanted to scare the
planters, he had no intention of liberating all slaves
or of starting a real slave rebellion. So his offer was
limited to able-bodied men. Female, young, and elderly slaves were not welcome behind British lines,
and many were sent back to face irate masters. Astute blacks noticed that Dunmore neglected to free
his own slaves. A Virginia barber named Caesar de-

clared that "he did not know any one foolish
enough to believe him [Dunmore], for if he intended
to do so, he ought first to set his own free."

In the northern colonies as well, slaves clearly
recognized the evolving political struggle with England as an ideal moment to bid for freedom. A
twenty-one-year-old Boston domestic slave employed sarcasm in a 1774 newspaper essay to call
attention to the hypocrisy of local slave owners:
"How well the Cry for Liberty, and the reverse Disposition for exercise of oppressive Power over others agree,—I humbly think it does not require the
Penetration of a Philosopher to Determine." This assertive young woman, Phillis Wheatley, had already
gained international fame through a book of poems
published in London in 1773. Kidnapped from
Africa at age eight, sold to a Boston merchant
named John Wheatley in 1761, fully literate in English within sixteen months and Latin by age twelve,
Phillis Wheatley became an accomplished poet by
age sixteen. She earned the regard of both Governor Thomas Hutchinson and merchant John Hancock, whose testimonials endorsed her book and affirmed her remarkable life story. Possibly neither
Hutchinson nor Hancock fully appreciated the
irony of their endorsement, however, for Wheatley's
poems spoke of "Fair Freedom" as the "Goddess
long desir'd" by Africans enslaved in America. At
the urging of his wife, John Wheatley freed the
young poet in 1775.

Wheatley's poetic ideas about freedom found
concrete expression among other discontented

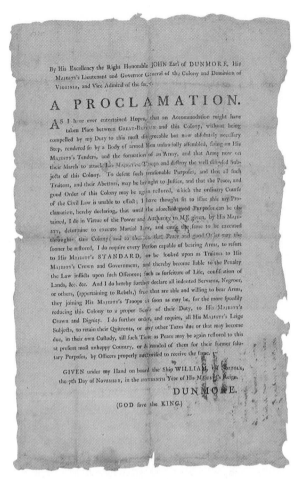

LORD DUNMORE'S PROCLAMATION
In November 1775, Lord Dunmore of Virginia offered freedom to "all indented Servants, Negroes, or others (appertaining to Rebels)" who would help put down the rebellion. Dunmore issued multiple printed copies in broadside form from the safety of a ship anchored at Norfolk, Virginia.
Special Collections. University of Virginia Library.

groups. Some slaves in Boston petitioned Thomas Gage, promising to fight for the British if he would liberate them. Gage turned them down. In Ulster County, New York, along the Hudson River, two blacks were overheard discussing gunpowder, and thus unraveled a plot that involved at least twenty slaves in four villages, discovered to have gunpowder and shot stashed away.

The numerical preponderance of black slaves in the southern colonies deepened white fears of rebellion. In Maryland, soon after the news of the Lexington battle arrived, slaves exhibited impatience with their status, in light of the revolutionary movement unfolding around them. One Maryland

planter reported that "the insolence of the Negroes in this county is come to such a height, that we are under a necessity of disarming them. . . . We took about eighty guns, some bayonets, swords, etc." In North Carolina, whites mounted night patrols to enforce a 9 P.M. curfew for all slaves. In July, a planned uprising was uncovered, and scores of slaves were arrested. No one seemed to see any irony in the fact that it was the revolutionary committee of public safety that dealt severely with this quest for liberty: Each conspiring slave suffered eighty lashes on the back and had both ears cropped.

In Orange County, Virginia, a twenty-four-year-old member of the committee of public safety named James Madison worried about the implications of a recently uncovered slave plot: "Lately a few of those unhappy wretches met together and chose a leader who was to conduct them when the English troops should arrive—which they thought would be very soon and that by revolting to them they should be rewarded with their freedom. Their intentions were soon discovered and the proper precautions taken to prevent the Infection." Madison well understood the contagion of ideas about liberty and slavery, so potent to blacks and whites as well: "It is prudent such attempts should be concealed as well as suppressed."

Probably for that reason, Lord Dunmore's proclamation to encourage slave defection was not reported in many southern newspapers, for fear it would spread the news to slaves. Blacks, however, did not depend on newspapers for their information. John Adams was assured by southern delegates to the Continental Congress that a proclamation like Dunmore's would quickly draw twenty thousand slaves in South Carolina because "the Negroes have a wonderful art of communicating Intelligence among themselves; it will run several hundreds of miles in a week or fortnight." The contagion of liberty spread quickly by newspaper, by word of mouth, and even by drumbeat.

In 1775, probably several thousand slaves in Virginia took Lord Dunmore up on his offer. The numbers grew in 1776 and 1777, and by 1778 as many as thirty thousand black Virginians had defected from slavery. Possibly as many as eighty thousand southern blacks over the course of the Revolutionary War voted against slavery with their feet. Many of them did not find the liberation they were seeking. The British army used them for menial labor and failed to feed or clothe them adequately. Disease, especially smallpox, devastated encampments of runaways, and the British offered no medical help. More than five hundred blacks died of smallpox on an island off the Virginia coast in 1776. Twenty years later the skeletons were still there, where the refugees had been abandoned.

In South Carolina, Sullivan's Island became a refugee camp for escaped slaves. Located near Charleston, the island was one of the few secure places held by the British in 1775, and it became a magnet for fleeing slaves. One black man went there after delivering to his white master a grand speech. The master reported, "Though he is my Property, he has the audacity to tell me, he will be free, that he will serve no Man, and that he will be conquered or governed by no Man." But the Charleston committee of public safety decided otherwise. The encampment held an estimated five hundred slaves and in the committee's view its existence undermined public order. In December 1775, the Charleston revolutionaries organized a surprise raid on the island. About fifty blacks were killed, their tents were burned, and hundreds were sent back to slavery.

Without self-government, some argued, Americans would be reduced to slavery. Thousands of actual slaves grasped the implications of these ideas and seized the moment.

Lexington and Concord marked the military beginnings of the American Revolution. The minutemen fought to protect their towns from invasion and to protest the undermining of traditional English rights to liberty and property, which had ceased to exist in Massachusetts. Without self-government, some argued, Americans would be reduced to slavery. Thousands of actual slaves grasped the implications of these ideas and seized the moment offered by Lord Dunmore in Virginia. Far fewer of the white population of the colonies could extend their own revolutionary rhetoric that far.

Conclusion: How Far Does Liberty Go?

The French and Indian War set the stage for the imperial crisis of the 1760s and 1770s by driving a wedge of suspicion between England and its colonies and by creating a huge deficit in the British

treasury. The years from 1763 to 1775 brought repeated attempts by the British government to rein in the colonies and make them subordinate, paying partners in the larger scheme of empire.

American resistance grew slowly over those years. In 1765, at the time of the Stamp Act, the issue for men like Samuel Adams and Patrick Henry was unjust taxation, by a government body—Parliament—that did not adequately represent American interests. For a few years, American and British leaders talked past each other, with different understandings of what constituted adequate representation and of the different forms taxation could take. But as the misunderstandings escalated, so did the level of tension and, eventually, violence. British troops originally intended to protect the colonists from Indians were drafted into police duties in the cities. British efforts to make Americans pay for their own protection looked to the Americans like confiscation of their property, an infringement of a basic liberty.

By 1775, events propelled Adams, Henry, and a host of American leaders to the conclusion that a concerted effort was afoot to deprive Americans of all their liberties. The first liberty threatened was the right to self-taxation, the next was their right to live free of an occupying army, and finally came their right to self-rule. It appeared to them that England was trying to enslave them, and they used the term "abject slavery" very often to describe the ultimate and most horrible stage of being unfree, deprived of all liberty and property, the status to be avoided at all costs. Thousands of minutemen amassed around Concord in the spring of 1775, prepared to fight to the death to assert these American liberties. April 19 marked the start of their rebellion.

Another rebellion under way in 1775 was doomed to be short-circuited. This uprising involved black Americans who had experienced over the course of a century and a half the condition of being abject slaves deprived of all liberties and rights. They now listened to shouts of "Liberty!" in the Stamp Act crowds and appropriated the language of revolution swirling around them that spoke to their deepest needs and hopes. Defiance of authority was indeed contagious.

The emerging leaders of the patriot cause were mindful of a delicate balance they felt they had to strike. To energize the American public about the crisis with England, they had to politicize masses of men—and eventually women too—and infuse them with a keen sense of their rights and liberties, now presumably threatened by British policies. But in so doing, they became fearful of the unintended consequences of teaching a vocabulary of rights and liberties. They worried that the rhetoric of enslavement might go too far.

The question of how far the crisis could be stretched before something snapped was largely unexamined in 1765. Patriot leaders in the year of the Stamp Act were amazed to find Parliament passing unprecedented tax laws that seemed to strike at the heart of the ancient liberties of English subjects. What they wanted was a correction, a return to the status quo ante. But the course of actions in the decade up to 1775 convinced many that no return to the old ways was possible. A challenge to Parliament's right to tax had led, step by step, to a challenge to Parliament's right to legislate over the colonies in any matter. If Parliament's sovereignty was set aside, then who actually had authority over the American colonies? By 1775, with the outbreak of fighting and the specter of slave rebellions, American leaders turned to the king for the answer to that question.

CHRONOLOGY

1745 Massachusetts and British soldiers capture French fortress Louisbourg in Nova Scotia.

1747 Ohio Company of Virginia formed.

1748 Treaty of Aix-la-Chapelle.

1754 French and Indian War begins in America.
Albany Congress proposes Plan of Union and courts Iroquois support.

1755 General Braddock defeated by French and Indians in Pennsylvania.

1757 William Pitt, prime minister in Britain, fully commits to war effort.

1758 Louisbourg recaptured by British and American forces.

1759 Quebec falls to British.

1760 George III becomes king.

1763 Treaty of Paris ends French and Indian War.
Pontiac's uprising provokes fear and destruction in western frontier settlements.
Proclamation of 1763 prohibits settlement west of Appalachians.

1764 The Revenue (Sugar) Act lowers tax on foreign molasses to promote compliance with trade duty.

1764 Currency Act prohibits issuance of colonial paper money.

1765 Stamp Act imposes tax on documents.
May. Patrick Henry sponsors Virginia Resolves.
August. Crowd actions in Boston inaugurate Sons of Liberty.
October. Stamp Act Congress meets in New York City.

1766 Stamp Act repealed; Declaratory Act asserts Parliament's control over colonies.

1767 Townshend duties reinstate revenue-raising taxes.

1768 **Fall.** British troops stationed in Boston.

1769 Year of nonimportation agreements; Daughters of Liberty appear.

1770 **March 5.** Boston Massacre.
Townshend duties repealed; Lord North comes to power.

1772 **June.** *Gaspée* attacked off Rhode Island.
Committees of Correspondence formed.

1773 Tea Act lowers price of tea to tempt American boycotters.
December 16. Boston Tea Party.

1774 Parliament passes Coercive Acts (Intolerable Acts): Boston Port Act, Massachusetts Government Act, Impartial Administration of Justice Act, Quartering Act, Quebec Act.

September. First Continental Congress meets. Continental Association formed.

1775 **April 19.** Battles of Lexington and Concord.
Virginia's Lord Dunmore promises freedom to defecting slaves.

BIBLIOGRAPHY

GENERAL WORKS

Edward Countryman, *The American Revolution* (1985).

Marc Egnal, *A Mighty Empire: The Origins of the American Revolution* (1988).

Lawrence H. Gipson, *The Coming of the Revolution, 1763–1775* (1954).

Jack P. Greene, ed., *The American Revolution: Its Character and Limits* (1987).

Merrill Jensen, *The Founding of a Nation: A History of the American Revolution, 1763–1776* (1968).

Bernhard Knollenberg, *Origin of the American Revolution, 1759–1766* (1960).

Bernhard Knollenberg, *Growth of the American Revolution, 1766–1775* (1975).

James Kirby Martin, *In the Course of Human Events: An Interpretive Exploration of the American Revolution* (1979).

Robert Middlekauff, *The Glorious Cause: The American Revolution, 1763–1789* (1982).

Edmund S. Morgan, *The Challenge of the American Revolution* (1976).

Gordon Wood, *The Radicalism of the American Revolution* (1992).

Esmond Wright, *The Causes and Consequences of the American Revolution* (1966).

Alfred F. Young, *The American Revolution: Explorations in the History of American Radicalism* (1976).

NATIVE AMERICANS AND THE FRENCH AND INDIAN WAR

Fred Anderson, *A People's Army: Massachusetts Soldiers and Society in the Seven Years' War* (1984).

Francis Jennings, *Empire of Fortune: Crowns, Colonies, and Tribes in the Seven Years War in America* (1988).

Douglas E. Leach, *Roots of Conflict: British Armed Forces and Colonial Americans, 1677–1763* (1986).

Michael N. McConnell, *A Country Between: The Upper Ohio Valley and Its Peoples, 1724–1774* (1992).

Richard Middleton, *The Bells of Victory: The Pitt-Newcastle Ministry and the Conduct of the Seven Years' War, 1757–1762* (1985).

Howard H. Peckham, *Pontiac and the Indian Uprising* (1947).

Jack M. Sosin, *Whitehall and the Wilderness: The Middle West in British Colonial Policy, 1760–1775* (1961).

Richard White, *The Middle Ground: Indians, Empires, and Republics in the Great Lakes Region, 1650–1815* (1991).

THE BRITISH VIEW OF EMPIRE

Bernard Bailyn, *The Origins of American Politics* (1968).

Thomas C. Barrow, *Trade and Empire: The British Customs Service in America, 1660–1775* (1967).

John Brewer, *Party Ideology and Popular Politics at the Accession of George III* (1976).

John Brooke, *King George III* (1972).

John L. Bullion, *A Great and Necessary Measure: George Grenville and the Genesis of the Stamp Act, 1763–1765* (1983).

Ian R. Christie, *Crisis of Empire: Great Britain and the American Colonies, 1754–1783* (1966).

Bernard Donoughue, *British Politics and the American Revolution: The Path to War, 1773–1775* (1964).

Jack P. Greene, *Peripheries and Center: Constitutional Development in the Extended Politics of the British Empire and the United States, 1607–1788* (1986).

James A. Henretta, *"Salutary Neglect": Colonial Administration under the Duke of Newcastle* (1972).

Michael Kammen, *A Rope of Sand: Colonial Agents, British Politics, and the American Revolution* (1968).

Michael Kammen, *Empire and Interest: The American Colonies and the Politics of Mercantilism* (1970).

Philip Lawson, *George Grenville: A Political Life* (1984).

James L. McKelvey, *George III and Lord Bute* (1973).

Alison Gilbert Olson, *Making the Empire Work: London and American Interest Groups, 1690–1790* (1992).

Alan Rogers, *Empire and Liberty: American Resistance to British Authority, 1755–1763* (1974).

John Sainsbury, *Disaffected Patriots: London Supporters of Revolutionary America, 1769–1782* (1987).

Carl Ubbelohde, *The Vice-Admiralty Courts and the American Revolution* (1960).

THE REVOLUTIONARY CRISIS OF THE 1760S–1770S

David Ammerman, *In the Common Cause: American Response to the Coercive Acts of 1774* (1975).

Bernard Bailyn, *The Ideological Origins of the American Revolution* (1967).

Bernard Bailyn, *The Ordeal of Thomas Hutchinson* (1974).

Bernard Bailyn, *Faces of Revolution: Personalities and Themes in the Struggle for American Independence* (1990).

Richard R. Beeman, *Patrick Henry* (1974).

Ruth H. Bloch, *Visionary Republic: Millennial Themes in American Thought, 1750–1800* (1985).

John L. Brooke, *The Heart of the Commonwealth: Society and Political Culture in Worcester County, Massachusetts, 1713–1861* (1989).

Joseph A. Ernst, *Money and Politics in America, 1755–1775* (1973).

John E. Ferling, *The First of Men: A Life of George Washington* (1988).

David Hackett Fischer, *Paul Revere's Ride* (1994).

Jay Fliegelman, *Prodigals and Pilgrims: The American Revolution against Patriarchal Authority, 1750–1800* (1982).

Dirk Hoerder, *Crowd Action in Revolutionary Massachusetts, 1765–1780* (1977).

Thomas A. Lewis, *For King and Country: The Maturing of George Washington, 1748–1760* (1993).

Paul K. Longmore, *The Invention of George Washington* (1988).

Pauline Maier, *From Resistance to Revolution: Colonial Radicals and the Development of American Opposition to Britain, 1765–1776* (1972).

Pauline Maier, *The Old Revolutionaries: Political Lives in the Age of Samuel Adams* (1980).

Edmund S. Morgan, *The Genius of George Washington* (1980).

Edmund S. Morgan, *Inventing the People: The Rise of Popular Sovereignty in England and America* (1988).

Edmund S. Morgan and Helen M. Morgan, *The Stamp Act Crisis: Prologue to Revolution* (1962).

Gary B. Nash, *The Urban Crucible: Social Change, Political Consciousness, and the Origins of the American Revolution* (1979).

Peter Shaw, *American Patriots and the Rituals of Revolution* (1981).

Peter D. G. Thomas, *The Townshend Duties Crisis: The Second Phase of the American Revolution, 1767–1773* (1987).

Peter D. G. Thomas, *Tea Party to Independence: The Third Phase of the American Revolution, 1773–1776* (1991).

Peter D. G. Thomas, *The Revolution in America: Britain and Her Colonies, 1763–1776* (1992).

John W. Tyler, *Smugglers and Patriots: Boston Merchants and the Advent of the American Revolution* (1986).

Ann Fairfax Withington, *Toward a More Perfect Union: Virtue and the Formation of American Republics* (1991).

Hiller B. Zobel, *The Boston Massacre* (1970).

WOMEN

Richard Buel and Joy Day Buel, *The Way of Duty: A Woman and Her Family in Revolutionary America* (1984).

Ronald Hoffman and Peter J. Albert, eds., *Women in the Age of the American Revolution* (1989).

Linda Kerber, *Women of the Republic: Intellect and Ideology in Revolutionary America* (1980).

Mary Beth Norton, *Liberty's Daughters: The Revolutionary Experience of American Women, 1750–1800* (1980).

SLAVERY

Ira Berlin and Ronald Hoffman, *Slavery and Freedom in the Age of the American Revolution* (1983).

Jeffrey Crow, *The Black Experience in Revolutionary North Carolina* (1977).

David Brion Davis, *The Problem of Slavery in the Age of Revolution, 1770–1823* (1975).

Sylvia Frey, *Water from the Rock: Black Resistance in a Revolutionary Age* (1991).

Winthrop D. Jordan, *White over Black: American Attitudes toward the Negro, 1550–1812* (1968).

Sidney Kaplan and Emma Nogrady Kaplan, *The Black Presence in the Era of the American Revolution* (1973; rev. ed., 1989).

Duncan J. Macleod, *Slavery, Race, and the American Revolution* (1974).

Benjamin Quarles, *The Negro in the American Revolution* (1961).

Donald L. Robinson, *Slavery in the Structure of American Politics, 1765–1820* (1971).

REGIONAL STUDIES

Richard R. Beeman, *The Evolution of the Southern Backcountry: A Case Study of Lunenburg County, Virginia, 1746–1832* (1984).

T. H. Breen, *Tobacco Culture: The Mentality of the Great Tidewater Planters on the Eve of the American Revolution* (1985).

Richard D. Brown, *Revolutionary Politics in Massachusetts: The Boston Committee of Correspondence and the Towns, 1772–1774* (1970).

Richard Bushman, *King and People in Provincial Massachusetts* (1985).

Edward Countryman, *A People in Revolution: The American Revolution and Political Society in New York, 1760–1790* (1981).

Jere R. Daniell, *Experiment in Republicanism: New Hampshire Politics and the Revolution, 1741–1794* (1970).

A. Roger Ekirch, *"Poor Carolina": Politics and Society in North Carolina, 1729–1776* (1981).

Larry R. Gerlach, *Prologue to Independence: New Jersey in the Coming of the Revolution* (1976).

Paul Gilje, *Road to Mobocracy: Popular Disorder in New York City, 1763–1834* (1987).

Jack P. Greene, *The Quest for Power: The Lower Houses of Assembly of the Southern Royal Colonies, 1689–1776* (1963).

Robert A. Gross, *The Minutemen and Their World* (1976).

Ronald Hoffman, *A Spirit of Dissension: Economics, Politics, and the Revolution in Maryland* (1973).

Rhys Isaac, *The Transformation of Virginia, 1740–1790* (1982).

Richard M. Jellison, ed., *Society, Freedom, and Conscience: The Coming of the Revolution in Virginia, Massachusetts, and New York* (1976).

Davis S. Lovejoy, *Rhode Island Politics and the Revolution, 1760–1776* (1958).

Stephen E. Lucas, *Portents of Rebellion: Rhetoric and Revolution in Philadelphia, 1765–1776* (1976).

Bernard Mason, *The Road to Independence: The Revolutionary Movement in New York, 1773–1777* (1966).

John A. Neuenschwander, *The Middle Colonies and the Coming of the American Revolution* (1973).

William Pencak, *Politics and Revolution in Provincial Massachusetts* (1981).

Steven Rossman, *Arms, Country, and Class: The Philadelphia Militia and the "Lower Sort" during the American Revolution* (1987).

Richard A. Ryerson, *The Revolution Is Now Begun: The Radical Committees of Philadelphia, 1765–1776* (1978).

Albert H. Tillson, *Gentry and Common Folk: Political Culture on a Virginia Frontier, 1740–1789* (1991).

Richard Walsh, *Charleston's Sons of Liberty: A Study of the Artisans, 1763–1789* (1959).

PAINTED DRUM

Drums were essential military equipment in eighteenth-century wars. Small to carry but loud in use, they provided a percussive beat that penetrated the din of the battlefield to signal troop advances, retreats, or other field movements. Drummers often stood right behind soldiers in firing formation, regulating the timing of each volley of shots. The eagle painted on this Revolutionary-era drum from Fort Ticonderoga in New York holds a banner inscribed "Sons of Liberty," a name adopted in 1765 to distinguish protesters of British policies toward the colonies.

Fort Ticonderoga Museum.

THE WAR FOR AMERICA
1775–1783

7

ABIGAIL ADAMS WAS IMPATIENT for American independence. While her husband, John, was away in Philadelphia as a member of the Second Continental Congress, Abigail tended house and farm in Braintree, Massachusetts, just south of British-occupied Boston. She had four children to look after, aged three to eleven, and in addition to her female duties, such as cooking, sewing, and making soap, she also had to shoulder male duties in her husband's absence—hiring farm help, managing rental property, selling the crop. John wrote to her often, approving of the fine "Farmeress" who was conducting his business so well. She wrote him often in return, conveying not only news of the family but shrewd commentary on the brewing war and revolutionary politics. In December 1775, she chastised the congress for being too timid and urged that independence be declared. "Let us separate, they are unworthy to be our Brethren," she wrote angrily. In January, John sent her a copy, hot off the press, of *Common Sense*, an electrifying pamphlet by the recently arrived Englishman Thomas Paine who made a strong case for independence. Abigail passed the pamphlet around Braintree, hoping its "Weighty truths" would help convince reluctant friends and neighbors.

While Abigail was impatient for independence, many other Americans were reluctant to contemplate such a move. In the months after the battles of Lexington and Concord, the colonies moved deeper into war, yet still many Americans feared that independence was a rash move. What kind of civilized country had no king? Who, if not mother Britain, would protect Americans from the French and Spanish? How could the colonies possibly win a war against the most powerful military machine on the globe? Such arguments against independence surfaced in newspapers, in pamphlets, and in outdoor speeches, by people who favored reconciliation with England. Abigail thought of another reason, not much publicly mentioned, why some Americans, namely slave owners, might be reluctant to fight a war in the name of liberty: "I have sometimes been ready to think," she wrote John at the end of March 1776, "that the passion for Liberty cannot be Equally strong in the Breasts of those who have been accustomed to deprive their fellow Creatures of theirs."

"I long to hear that you have declared an independency," she continued in this same March letter. "And by the way in the new Code of Laws which I suppose it will be necessary for you to make I desire you would Remember the Ladies, and be more generous and favourable to them than your ancestors." If Abigail was politically precocious for being in favor of independence and for being suspicious of slave owners' devotion to liberty, she showed herself to be positively visionary in this extraordinary plea to her husband to "Remember the Ladies." "Do not put such unlimited power into the hands of the Husbands," she advised. "Remember all Men would be tyrants if they could." Abigail had put her finger on another form of tyranny that was rarely remarked on in her society: that of men over women.

But to soften her criticism of men (whom she characterized as "Naturally Tyrannical"), she slipped into a humorous tone, borrowing the language of the male revolutionaries to dress up a pretended threat: "If particular care and attention is not paid to the Ladies we are determined to foment a Rebellion, and will not hold ourselves bound by any Laws in which we have no voice, or Representation."

Abigail assumed that the Continental Congress would be drawing up a new code of laws, but she was directing her advice to the wrong political body. Criminal and civil law (including family law, which dictated the legal subservience of wives to husbands) was the concern of the men founding state governments in 1775 and 1776, and they simply adopted traditional British family law. John Adams, of course, did respond to his wife's provocative idea, but he dismissed it as a "saucy" suggestion: "As to your extraordinary Code of Laws, I cannot but Laugh." The Revolution had perhaps unleashed discontent among other dependent groups, he allowed; children, apprentices, students, Indians, and blacks had grown "disobedient" and "insolent." "But your Letter was the first Intimation that another Tribe more numerous and powerful than all the rest were grown discontented." Men were too smart to repeal their "Masculine Systems," John assured her, for otherwise they would find themselves living under a "despotism of the petticoat."

This clever exchange between husband and wife in 1776 says much about the cautious, limited radicalism of the American Revolution. Both John and Abigail Adams understood (Abigail probably far more than John) that ungluing the hierarchical bond between the king and his subjects potentially unglued other kinds of social inequalities. John was surely joking in listing the groups made unruly in the spirit of a challenge to authority, for children, apprentices, and students were hardly rebellious in the 1770s. But it would soon prove to be an uncomfortable joke, because Indians and blacks did take up the cause of their own liberty during the Revolution, and the great majority of them saw their liberty best served by joining the British side in the war.

The Continental Congress did not concern itself with codes of laws or with the rights and privileges of citizens. Its members were much too busy with more immediate tasks: raising an army, financing a war, putting together a pro-independence coalition, and exploring diplomatic alliances with foreign countries. For the next six years, the war for

ABIGAIL ADAMS
Abigail Smith Adams was twenty-two when she sat for this pastel portrait in 1766. A wife for two years and a mother for one, Adams exhibits a steady, intelligent gaze. Pearls and a lace collar anchor her femininity, while her facial expression projects a confidence and maturity not often credited to young women of the 1760s.
Courtesy of the Massachusetts Historical Society ©.

America engrossed everyone's attention. In part, it was a classic war with professional armies and textbook battles. But it was also a civil war in America, at times even a brutal guerrilla war, of committed rebels versus those who stayed loyal to England.

Only in one glorious moment did the congress issue a ringing statement about social hierarchy and how it would be rearranged in America after submission to the king was undone. That was on July 4, 1776, when the Declaration of Independence asserted in its preamble that "all men are created equal." This striking phrase went completely unremarked in the two days of congressional debate spent tinkering with the language of the Declaration. The solvent to dissolve social inequalities in America was created at that moment, but none of the men at the congress, or even Abigail Adams up in Braintree, fully realized it at the time.

The Second Continental Congress

On May 10, 1775, nearly one month after the onset of fighting at Lexington and Concord, the Second Continental Congress assembled in Philadelphia. The congress immediately set to work on two crucial and seemingly contradictory tasks: to raise and supply an army and to negotiate a reconciliation with England. But as the war progressed and hopes of reconciliation faded, delegates at the congress began to ponder the treasonous act of declaring independence.

Assuming Political Authority

Like the First Continental Congress, the second had no legal authority for existing. Neither did most of the legislatures that had selected the delegates to go to Philadelphia. Like the Virginia House of Burgesses, which by late 1775 had reconstituted itself as the Virginia Convention, the political leadership of one colony after another subverted British authority by simply assuming power on its own.

The same pattern was replicated in town after town as well: Men who had once been the selectmen or town councillors now called themselves the committee of public safety, of inspection, or of correspondence and took it upon themselves to be the ruling body of the town. The inspiration for such creative government came initially from the Coercive Acts that had crippled town government in Massachusetts in 1774. Government by committee spread to other colonies when the First Continental Congress implemented the Continental Association and recommended that local committees of public safety form to enforce economic boycotts of British goods.

Royal administrators found there was little they could do to stop such actions, with no police force and a militia of, at best, uncertain loyalty. For their own protection, governors packed their bags and headed for British naval vessels in the coastal harbors. The governor of New York tried to run his office from shipboard for several months. Other governors gave up and sailed for England, and by the end of 1775 no royal governor commanded any political authority whatsoever. On the colonial level, royal authority was virtually dead, a feat accomplished with hardly a single act of violence.

The new holders of political authority were not really new to politics, for they had run the colonial assemblies before 1775. To the British, these men looked like rebels and revolutionaries, but to the other colonists, they looked like the customary legislative leaders.

The delegates to the Second Continental Congress likewise were well-established political figures likely to command respect and authority, even though the body they served in existed beyond the bounds of legitimate power. John Hancock, a wealthy Boston merchant and an active member of the Massachusetts assembly, presided over the deliberations of the congress. Some of the delegates had attended the First Continental Congress in 1774 and already knew each other. But that did not mean that they were of similar minds about the political issues facing them; nor was each man consistent over time in his views. The Adams cousins, John and Samuel, would soon diverge sharply in political beliefs, but in 1775 they sat together at the radical end of the political spectrum, favoring independence from England. John Dickinson, a returning delegate from Pennsylvania, was no longer the same eager revolutionary who had dashed off *Letters from a Farmer* back in 1767. He was now a moderate, prepared to block any radical action that would interfere with a reconciliation with England.

George Washington and Benjamin Franklin cut sharply contrasting figures among the delegates. Washington daily wore his old military uniform from the French and Indian War, a conspicuous nonverbal statement about his views on the coming conflict. Franklin, in contrast, was feared by some to be a British spy. He had returned from an eleven-year residence in England just five days before the congress met. His long sojourn abroad, plus his long silences in the congress in the first months, made his loyalty suspect. James Madison, a young Virginian just making his entry into political life, heard the gossip about Franklin and jumped to a hasty conclusion: "The least suspicion of his guilt amounts very nearly to a proof of its reality." The men of the Second Continental Congress were still in the process of getting to trust each other. Mutual suspicions flourished easily when the undertaking was so dangerous, opinions were so varied, and a misstep could spell disaster.

Despite their prior experience in the First Continental Congress, most of the delegates were not yet prepared to break with England. Total independence was an alarming idea to many, and some legislatures, chiefly those in the middle colonies such as New York and Pennsylvania, had instructed their delegates to oppose any such move. Some felt that government without a monarchical element was surely unworkable and that continued allegiance to the king was essential. Others feared that the colonies would always need the protection of England against their traditional enemies, France and Spain, and that independence would therefore be suicidal. Colonies that traded actively with England feared undermining their economies. Nor were the vast majority of ordinary Americans ready or able to envision independence from the British monarchy. From the Stamp Act to the Coercive Acts, the decade-long constitutional struggle with England had turned on the issue of parliamentary power. During that decade almost no one questioned the legitimacy of the monarchy.

The few men at the Continental Congress who did think that independence was desirable were, not surprisingly, the Massachusetts delegates. Their colony had been stripped of civil government under the Coercive Acts and their capital was occupied by the British army. Even so, these men knew that it was premature to push for a decisive break with England before others were ready. John Adams wrote to Abigail in June 1775: "America is a great, unwieldy body. Its progress must be slow. It is like a large fleet sailing under convoy. The fleetest sailors must wait for the dullest and slowest."

Raising an Army

As slow as the American colonies were in sailing toward political independence, they needed to take swift action to coordinate a military defense, for the Massachusetts countryside was under the threat of further attack. The congress feared that New England militia units were inadequate to defend against the British army in Boston, thought to be over ten thousand strong. (In truth, the contingent of redcoats numbered only five thousand in late spring 1775.) All the delegates in the congress, even the hesitant moderates, agreed that a military buildup was necessary, a feeling shared widely in the colonies. Voluntary militia units from New York to Georgia collected arms and were drilling on village greens in anticipation.

The next military encounter after Lexington and Concord was hardly a defensive maneuver, however. In May 1775, Connecticut militiamen (led by Captain Benedict Arnold) and riflemen from the Green Mountains in what is now Vermont (led by Ethan Allen) attacked Fort Ticonderoga in northern New York, situated along the water route to Que-

bec. The British had held the fort as a military storage depot since the French and Indian War; the fifty soldiers who manned it surrendered with little resistance. The capture of the fort netted sixty cannons, which were relocated south of Boston and trained on the occupied city. Fort Ticonderoga gave the Americans control of the major water link between New York and Canada; it was thus destined to be a contested spot in short order, for the British wanted it back.

In June, the congress took further steps to prepare for war. Needing money to purchase gunpowder and other military supplies, the congress authorized a currency issue of $2 million. The Continental dollars were merely paper; they did not represent gold or silver, for the congress owned no precious metals. The delegates somewhat naively expected that the currency would be accepted as valuable on trust as it spread in the population through the hands of soldiers, farmers, munitions suppliers, and beyond. They assumed it would eventually be retired from circulation through local taxation.

On June 14, the congress voted to create an army, which mainly meant proclaiming that the New England soldiers dug in around Boston *were* the American army, henceforth called the Continental army and directed and paid by the congress. The congress also called for ten companies of riflemen from Virginia, Maryland, and Pennsylvania to join the New England troops. Rifles were the weapon of choice in frontier regions, for their long, specially grooved barrels allowed marksmen to hit small targets at 150 or 200 yards. In contrast, the militias and the British regular army fought with muskets, which were straight-bore weapons and hence much less accurate, with a range of only about 50 yards. To maximize firepower, musketmen worked as a unit in rows three deep. Men in the front row knelt and fired simultaneously in the direction of the target; in the hail of shots surely some would hit. The second row of men readied themselves to fire, and the men in the third row, who had been in the front row moments before, regrouped and reloaded on signal. Musketmen had to move like a well-oiled machine, and their precision required weeks of drill. But it was the riflemen who were most feared by the British soldiers, at least at first. A joke circulated that the entire Continental army should be outfitted in western hunting shirts, to make the redcoats think they were all riflemen. However, the riflemen's propensity for solitary, freelance shooting and their frontier distaste for the discipline of army life did not mesh well with eighteenth-century military styles. The Continental army made relatively little use of them after the first two years of the war.

Choosing a commander in chief to lead the army presented the congress with an opportunity to demonstrate yet again that this was no local war of a single rebellious colony. The most obvious candidate for the job was Artemus Ward, a Connecticut man with leadership experience from the French and Indian War who was already commanding the soldiers massed around Boston. But John Adams, working closely with southern delegates, argued that the commander ought to be from a distant colony to demonstrate widespread commitment to the war beyond New England. Virginia planter George Washington actually had far less experience commanding soldiers than did Ward, and he was not much known beyond his native region. But the forty-three-year-old Washington, who looked every bit the part of commander in his old military uniform, was unanimously chosen to lead the Continental army.

In just two months, the Second Continental Congress had taken on the major functions of a legitimate government, both military and financial, without any legal basis for its authority.

Next, a committee of the congress drew up a document called "A Declaration of the Causes and Necessity of Taking Up Arms," which rehearsed familiar arguments about the tyranny of Parliament and the need to defend traditional English liberties. This document was first drafted by a young Virginia planter, Thomas Jefferson, a newcomer to the congress and a radical on the question of independence. The moderate John Dickinson complained that the declaration was offensive to England and would shut the door to reconciliation. Jefferson later wrote that Dickinson "was so honest a man, and so able a one, that he was greatly indulged even by those who could not feel his scruples. We therefore requested him to take the paper, and put it into a form he could approve." Dickinson toned it down; however, he still left much of Jefferson's highly charged language about choosing "to die freemen rather than to live slaves." Even a man as reluctant

for independence as Dickinson acknowledged the necessity of military defense against an invading army.

In just two months, the Second Continental Congress had created an army, declared war, and issued its own currency. It had taken on the major functions of a legitimate government, both military and financial, without any legal basis for its authority, for it had not—and would not for a full year yet—declare independence from the legitimate authority of the king. Equally unnoticed, the congress's assumption of governance lacked any real power to compel compliance by Americans. Enthusiasm for the cause drew recruits to the army, and optimism kept the newly printed Continental dollars afloat at full value for a time. But when that initial enthusiasm waned, the congress and the war effort fell on hard times.

Pursuing Both War and Peace

Three days after the congress voted to raise the Continental army, the bloodiest battle of the entire Revolution occurred. The British commander in Boston, Thomas Gage, had recently received troop reinforcements, three talented major generals (William Howe, John Burgoyne, and Henry Clinton), and new instructions to root out the rebels around Boston. But before Gage could take the offensive, Massachusetts and Connecticut militias fortified the hilly terrain of Charlestown, a peninsula just north of Boston, on the night of June 16, 1775.

The British generals could have nipped off the peninsula where it met the mainland, to box in the Americans. But General Howe insisted on a bold frontal assault, across the water and up the hill, more intimidating but potentially costly. Howe's forces numbered about 2,500 men, and he loaded them with equipment and food weighing more than seventy-five pounds each. They crossed from Boston to the Charlestown shore, protected by eight artillery pieces aimed at the American lines. (See Map 6.3, page 231.)

The Americans had perhaps 1,400 men atop Breed's Hill in hastily dug trenches. In close rank, the British soldiers, burdened with their heavy packs, moved up the hill. The Americans held their fire until the British were about twenty yards away; their commander, Colonel William Prescott, a veteran of the Louisbourg campaign in the French and Indian War, had instructed them to wait until the redcoats were close enough to "see the whites of their eyes." At that distance the musket volley was

MAP OF BOSTON, CHARLESTOWN, SHOWING THE BUNKER HILL BATTLE

A contemporary map refers to significant Boston landmarks ("Government House," Old South Meeting House, Faneuil Hall) and then shifts to a representation of Charlestown, north across the Charles River, to portray the Battle of Bunker Hill in the thick of fighting.
Courtesy of The Bostonian Society, Old State House.

sure and deadly, and the British turned back. Twice more General Howe sent his men up the hill to receive the same blast of firepower; the third time he permitted them to remove their packs, but the men encountered another obstacle—the bodies felled in the two previous attempts. The eight artillery pieces proved worthless; the British had ferried across the wrong size cannon balls.

On the third assault, the British took the hill, mainly because the American ammunition supply gave out, and the defenders quickly retreated across the Charlestown neck. The Battle of Bunker Hill (it was named for another Charlestown hill) was thus a British victory, but an expensive one. The dead numbered 226 on the British side, with more than 800 wounded; the Americans suffered 140 dead, 271 wounded, and 30 captured. As General Clinton later remarked, "It was a dear bought victory; another such would have ruined us."

Clinton wanted to pursue the fleeing Americans to their headquarters at Cambridge, a few miles away, but Howe overruled him and pulled the army back to Boston. There they sat, penned up, unwilling to risk more forays into the countryside. Their food had to be shipped in by British naval vessels. Gage bewailed his position. "I wish this place was burned," he wrote to a friend, "the only use is its harbour, which may be said to be material; but in all other respects it's the worst place either to act offensively from, or defensively." If Gage had had any grasp of the basic instability of the American units gathered at Cambridge, he might have pushed westward and perhaps decisively defeated the core of the Continental army in its infancy. Instead the British lingered in Boston, abandoning it without a fight nine months later.

A week after Bunker Hill, General Washington hurried to Cambridge to take charge of the new Continental army. He found enthusiastic but undisciplined troops. Sanitation was an unknown concept, with inadequate numbers of latrines fouling the campground and posing severe risk of disease. Drunkenness on duty was common. Washington was amazed to find that a large number of the soldiers were on furlough, their leaders oddly lax about comings and goings. Washington attributed the disarray to the New England custom of letting militia units elect their own officers, a custom he felt undermined deference and respect. A captain from a Connecticut regiment was spotted shaving one of his own men, an inappropriate gesture of personal service on the part of a superior officer. But in civilian life the captain was a barber; he had been chosen as an officer by the men of his town, who saw nothing strange in his practicing his trade in the camp. Washington moved quickly to establish military discipline and respect for hierarchy, staging whippings and frequent courts-martial to impress on the soldiers the importance of his policy. "Discipline is the soul of the army," he stated; officers must be zealous, the men properly obedient.

Another immediate problem was getting men to sign up for longer enlistments. Militia units expected only three-month obligations, but Washington knew that no extended campaign could work with three-month soldiers. The Continental army required one-year enlistments, but by December 1775 only four thousand additional men had signed up. Washington wanted an army of twenty thousand, but he had fewer than half that number.

While military plans moved into high gear, the Second Continental Congress pursued its second, contradictory objective, reconciliation with England. Delegates from the middle colonies, especially Pennsylvania, Delaware, and New York, whose merchants depended on trade with England, urged that channels for negotiation remain open. Congressional moderates led by John Dickinson engineered an appeal to the king, called the Olive Branch Petition, in July 1775. The petition affirmed loyalty to the monarchy and resorted to a convenient fiction of blaming all the troubles on bad advice from the king's ministers and on Parliament. It proposed that the American colonial assemblies be recognized as individual parliaments, all under the umbrella of the monarchy. That Dickinson himself could write both the "Declaration on the Causes and Necessity of Taking Up Arms" and the Olive Branch Petition within a few days of each other shows how ambivalent the American position was in the summer of 1775.

By late fall 1775, however, reconciliation was out of the question. King George rejected the Olive Branch Petition and heatedly condemned the Americans, calling them rebels, traitors, and enemies. It was thereafter hard to maintain the illusion that ministers and not the king himself were to blame for the conflict. But still the Continental Congress shied away from an official declaration of independence. In January 1776, Dickinson and other moderates convinced the congress to issue a statement "respecting Independency," to reassure the king that independence was not the goal of the Americans. This document, rambling and overlong, justified resistance to England while denying independence, a tricky position to maintain. Dickinson ended the statement with what he probably imagined was a desperate plea for indulgence from England: "Though an independent empire is not our wish . . . it may be the fate of our countrymen and ourselves." Far from interpreting this statement as a plea, British officials read it accurately as a sign of resignation: Moderates like Dickinson could no longer keep a lid on revolutionary sentiments.

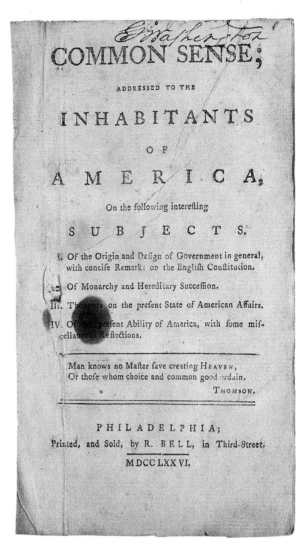

WASHINGTON'S INSCRIBED COPY OF *COMMON SENSE*
Thomas Paine's incendiary pamphlet Common Sense *was widely read after its publication in Philadelphia in January 1776. Copies were passed from hand to hand and read aloud in public. Virginian George Washington, a member of the Second Continental Congress, inscribed his name on the title page to declare his ownership of Paine's booklet.* Boston Athenaeum.

Thomas Paine and the Case for Independence

One day after Dickinson tried to reassure himself and whoever else would listen that independence was not the goal of the congress, a pamphlet titled *Common Sense* appeared in Philadelphia. Thomas Paine, its author, was an English artisan and coffeehouse intellectual who had befriended Benjamin Franklin in London. Paine came to America in the fall of 1774 with letters of introduction from Franklin to some of Philadelphia's printers. He landed a job with the *Pennsylvania Magazine* and soon met delegates from the Second Continental Congress. With their encouragement, he wrote *Common Sense* to lay out a lively and compelling case for complete independence.

"One of the strongest natural proofs of the folly of hereditary right in kings," Thomas Paine wrote, *"is that nature disapproves it; otherwise she would not so frequently turn it into ridicule by giving mankind an* ass for a lion.*"*

In simple yet forceful language, Paine elaborated on the absurdities of the British monarchy. Why should one man, by accident of birth, claim extensive power over others? he asked. A king might be foolish or wicked. "One of the strongest natural proofs of the folly of hereditary right in kings," Paine wrote, "is that nature disapproves it; otherwise she would not so frequently turn it into ridicule by giving mankind an *ass for a lion*." The king was nothing but a "brute," a "crowned ruffian," and the descendant of a French bastard.

Calling the king of England an ass broke through the automatic deference most Americans still had for the monarchy. And by moving the focus from Parliament to the king, Paine succeeded in making a case for independence. To replace monarchy, he advocated republican government, based on the consent of the people. Rulers, according to Paine, were only representatives of the people, and the best form of government relied on frequent elections to achieve the most direct democracy possible.

Paine's pamphlet sold more than 150,000 copies in a matter of weeks. Newspapers reprinted it, men read it aloud in taverns and coffeehouses, Abigail Adams passed it around to neighbors. Another of John Adams's correspondents wrote him in late February that ninety-nine out of a hundred New Englanders desired an official declaration of independence. But then New England had two armies on its doorstep. The middle and southern colonies remained uncertain; their hesitation prompted Samuel Adams to suggest that one military engagement to the south of New England would do the trick.

One factor hastening official independence was the advantage of an alliance with France. France could provide military supplies as well as naval power, but not without firm assurance that the Americans would separate from England. News that the British were negotiating for German mercenary soldiers further solidified support for independence. By May, all but four colonies were agitating for a declaration. The exceptions were Pennsylvania, Maryland, New York, and South Carolina, the latter two containing large loyalist populations.

Finally on June 7, 1776, the Virginia delegation introduced a resolution calling for independence: "Resolved, That these United Colonies are, and of right ought to be, free and independent States, that they are absolved from all allegiance to the British Crown, and that all political connection between them and the State of Great Britain is, and ought to be, totally dissolved." Here was the assertion everyone had been anticipating, some with impatience, others with dread. (See Texts in Historical Context, page 248.) The moderates still commanded enough support to postpone a vote on the measure until July. Thomas Jefferson and others formed a committee to draft a longer document explaining the justification for independence. In the meantime, the abstaining delegations went home to consult with their assemblies. Probably no one doubted that once a vote was taken, the measure would pass. But political sense dictated that the positive vote should be nearly unanimous, to present a united front to England.

On July 1, the first vote was taken on the resolution of June 7. Pennsylvania and South Carolina voted against it, while the two-man Delaware delegation was split and the New Yorkers abstained. On July 2, after a night of politicking, a second vote shifted South Carolina and Pennsylvania into the pro-independence camp, and a newly elected delegate from Delaware rode all night to cast the deciding pro-independence vote. The New Yorkers still abstained, as required by their assembly's instructions, but since they had not voted negatively, the congress could truthfully claim that the resolution for independence had passed without a negative vote. John Adams predicted that "the second day of July, 1776, will be the most memorable

DECLARATION OF INDEPENDENCE READ TO A CROWD
Printed copies of the Declaration of Independence were read aloud in public places throughout America in the weeks after July 4, 1776, often accompanied by carefully orchestrated celebrations.
Historical Society of Pennsylvania.

epocha in the history of America. I am apt to believe that it will be celebrated, by succeeding generations, as the great anniversary festival. . . . It ought to be solemnized with pomp and parade, with shows, games, sports, guns, bells, bonfires and illuminations, from one end of this continent to the other, from this time forward, forevermore." He was right about the celebration, if wrong about the date.

On July 2 and 3, the congress turned to the document drafted by Thomas Jefferson. Jefferson began with a preamble that articulated philosophical principles about natural rights, equality, the right of revolution, and the consent of the governed as the only true basis for government. He then listed more than two dozen specific grievances against King George.

The congress merely glanced at the political philosophy, finding nothing exceptional in it; the ideas about natural rights and the consent of the governed were seen as "self-evident truths," just as the document claimed. In itself, this absence of comment showed a remarkable transformation in political thinking since the end of the French and Indian War. The single phrase declaring the natural equality of "all men" was also passed over without comment; no one elaborated on its radical implications.

What the congress did wrangle over were the specific grievances. Jefferson included an impassioned statement blaming the king for slavery, which delegates from Georgia and South Carolina struck out. They had no intention of denouncing their labor system as an evil practice. Northern delegates were also relieved to drop it, for influential merchants from Boston and Newport, Rhode Island, were deeply implicated in the overseas trade of Africans. But the congress let stand another of Jefferson's grievances, blaming the king for mobilizing "the merciless Indian Savages" into bloody frontier warfare. Following the same strategy as that of Paine's *Common Sense,* Jefferson intended to fix blame on the king himself for everything wrong in America.

On July 4, the corrections to Jefferson's text were complete and the delegates formally affixed their signatures to it. Four men, including John Dickinson, declined to sign; several others "signed with regret . . . and with many doubts," according to John Adams. The document was then printed and distributed by the thousands. It was read aloud in cities and towns. In New York, a crowd listened and then toppled a lead statue of George III on horseback to melt it down for bullets. On July 15, the New York delegation switched from abstention to endorsement, making the vote on independence truly unanimous.

Printed copies of the Declaration of Independence did not include the signers' names, for they had committed treason, a crime punishable by death. At the moment of signing, they had indulged in gallows humor. When Benjamin Franklin paused before signing to look over the Declaration, John Hancock teased him, "Come, come, sir. We must be unanimous. No pulling different ways. We must all hang together." Franklin replied, "Indeed we must all hang together. Otherwise we shall most assuredly hang separately." The overweight Benjamin Harrison from Virginia remarked to the extremely slight Elbridge Gerry of Massachusetts, "When the

The Issue of Independence

In May and June 1776, talk of independence gripped Americans everywhere. When would it come? What would it mean? Why was the congress so slow to declare it? Town meetings all over Massachusetts were voting for immediate action; with war already on their doorstep, they saw no reason to delay. In contrast, political leaders in New York City were ambivalent and divided, and they did their best to avert calls for action. Independence-minded planters in Virginia worried that the common people might take a completely different meaning from the rush for independence. And merchants everywhere expressed anxiety that a declaration would kill all chances at reconciliation. While congress no doubt hoped that the July 4 Declaration of Independence would help unite the country, the reality was that disunity was fearfully evident.

Men of Scituate debated independence on June 4, 1776, and conveyed their remarks to their town representative.

DOCUMENT 1. The Town Meeting of Scituate, Massachusetts, Pledges to Fight for Independence

The Inhabitants of this Town being called together on the recommendation of our General Assembly to Signify our minds on the great point of Independence on Great-Britain, think fit to Instruct you on that head.

The Ministry of that Kingdom, having formed a design of Subjecting the Colonies to a distant, external and absolute power in all Cases whatsoever, wherein the Colonies have not, nor in the nature of things can have any share by Representation, have, for a course of years past, exerted their utmost Art and Endeavours to put the same plan, so destructive to both Countries, into Execution. But finding it, through the noble and virtuous opposition of the Sons of Freedom, impracticable by means of mere political Artifice and Corruption, they have at

length had a fatal Recourse to a Standing Army, so repugnant to the nature of a free Government, to fire and Sword, to Bloodshed and Devastation, calling in the aid of foreign Troops, as well as endeavouring to stir up the Savages of the wilderness to exercise their barbarities upon us, being determined, by all appearances, if practicable, to extirpate the Americans from the face of the Earth, unless they tamely resign the Rights of humanity, and to repeople this once happy Country with the ready Sons of Vassalage, if such can be found.

We therefor, Apprehending such a subjection utterly inconsistent with the just rights and blessings of Society, unanimously Instruct you to endeavour that our Delegates in Congress be informed, in case that Representative Body of the Continent should think fit to declare the Colonies Independant of Great Britain, of our readiness and determination to assist with the our Lives and Fortunes in Support of that, we apprehend, necessary Measure.

In New York, a group of craftsmen drafted their own document justifying independence. They delivered it to the assembly and encountered a chilly reception.

DOCUMENT 2. Minutes of the New York Assembly, June 3, 1776

A number of citizens, who style themselves a Committee of Mechanicks, having come into the Congress-Chamber . . . and delivered at the Chair a paper which they style an Address, the House was ordered to be cleared, in order that the said paper may be inspected, to discover whether it is proper for this Congress to receive the same. . . . The door was opened, and the said citizens were desired to come into the Chamber, . . . the said paper being read by Lewis Thibou.

They therein set forth that they are devoted friends to their bleeding country; that they are afflicted by beholding her struggling under heavy loads of oppression and tyranny; . . . that their Prince is deaf to petitions for redressing our grievances; that one year has not sufficed to satisfy the rage of a cruel Ministry in their bloody pursuits, designed to reduce us to be slaves, and to be taxed by them without our consent; that, therefore, they rather wish to separate from such oppressors; and declare that, if this Congress should think proper to instruct their Delegates in Continental Congress to cause these United Colonies to become independent of Great Britain, it would give them the highest satisfaction.

We are of opinion that the Continental Congress alone have that enlarged view of our political circumstances which will enable them to decide upon those measures which are necessary for the general welfare. We cannot presume . . . to make or declare any resolutions upon so momentous a concern; but are determined patiently to await and firmly to abide by whatever a majority of that august body shall think needful.

In Virginia, ordinary citizens circulated petitions pressing for a Declaration of Independence in May 1776. Landon Carter, a wealthy and worried planter, feared that what they meant by independence might be far more radical than he could accept. In a letter to George Washington on May 9, Carter expressed his concerns.

Document 3. Virginian Landon Carter Warns Fellow Planter George Washington

I need only tell you of one definition that I heard of Independency: It was expected to be a form of Government that, by being independent of the rich men, every man would then be able to do as he pleased. . . . One of the Delegates [to the Virginia assembly] I heard exclaim against the Patrolling law, because a poor man was made to pay for keeping a rich man's slaves in order. I shamed the fool so much for it that he slunk away; but he got elected by it. . . . I know who I am writing to, and therefore I am not quite so confined in my expressions. . . . And from hence it is that our independency is to arise! Papers, it seems, are everywhere circulating about for poor ignorant creatures to sign, as directions to their Delegates to endeavour at an independency. In vain do we ask to let it be explained what is designed by it!

Even after July 4, many merchants remained dubious about the wisdom of independence. The Philadelphia merchant Joseph Reed wrote to Robert Morris on July 18.

Document 4. Merchants Joseph Reed and Robert Morris Exchange Fading Hopes for Reconciliation

I fear the die is irrevocably cast, and that we must play out the game, however doubtful and desperate. . . . My private judgment led me to think that if the two great cardinal points of exemption from British taxation and charge of internal government could have been secured, our happiness and prosperity would have been best promoted by preserving the dependence. The Declaration of Independence is a new and very strong objection to entering into any negotiation. . . . But I fancy there are numbers, and some of them firm in the interests of America, who would think an overture ought not to be rejected.

Robert Morris replied to Reed on July 21.

I am sorry to say there are some amongst us that cannot bear the thought of Reconciliation on any terms. I cannot help Condemning this disposition as it must be founded in keen Resentment or on interested Views. . . . I have uniformly voted against & opposed the declaration of Independence because in my poor oppinion it was an improper time and will neither promote the interest or redound to the honor of America, for it has caused division when we wanted Union.

Document 1. Henry S. Commager and Richard B. Morris, eds., *The Spirit of Seventy-Six* (1958; reprint, 1975), 298–99. Original in the Massachusetts Archives, CLVI, 103.

Document 2. Peter Force, *American Archives,* Fourth Series, vol. 6 (1846), 1362–63.

Document 3. Peter Force, *American Archives,* Fourth Series, vol. 6 (1846), 389–92.

Document 4. John H. Hazelton, *The Declaration of Independence: Its History* (1906), 226–28.

hanging scene comes to be exhibited, my friend, I shall have all the advantage over you. With me it will be over in a minute. But you, you'll be dancing on air an hour after I'm gone!" Independence had finally been launched, but the outcome was far from certain; a small dose of caution was perfectly in order.

The First Two Years of War

Both sides had cause to approach the war for America with caution and trepidation. The Americans faced the mightiest military power in the world, and many thought it was foolhardy to expect victory. Further, pockets of loyalism remained strong; the country was not united. But the British faced serious obstacles as well. Their utter disdain for the fighting abilities of the Americans had to be reevaluated in light of their costly Bunker Hill victory. The logistics of supplying an army across three thousand miles of water were daunting. Each soldier required a minimum of two pounds of food per day, consisting of salted meat and grains, which amounted to a third of a ton per year per man—plus oats for the many horses. Since the British goal was to regain allegiance, not to destroy and conquer, the army was often constrained in its actions.

The American Military Forces

Americans claimed that the initial months of war were purely defensive, triggered by the British army's invasion. But quickly the war also became a rebellion, an overthrowing of long-established authority. As both defenders and rebels, Americans were generally highly motivated to fight, and the potential manpower that could be mobilized was in theory very great.

The recruitment pool, able-bodied men aged sixteen to sixty, already had some military training arising out of the American tradition of militia service. From the earliest decades of settlement, local defense rested with a militia requiring service from nearly every man. There were some exceptions: Apprentices and servants (including blacks in many colonies) were generally exempted, as were friendly Indians, vagabonds, ministers, important politicians, and, in New England, Harvard and Yale students. All other men were required to assemble regularly, usually several times a year, to practice the complicated and deft maneuvers of mass musket firing with their own guns. In many communities, muster day was a holiday, the hours of parading capped off with hearty drinking and picnicking.

The militia style of warfare was well suited to American defensive needs; for two centuries the main threat to public safety came from occasional Indian attacks. In the mid-eighteenth century, southern militias trained with potential slave rebellions in mind (and hence the general rule that friendly Indians and blacks could not serve). In cities, militias became a police force in rare times of civil disorder. Americans prided themselves on their citizen defense units, which they liked to contrast with the expensive and potentially repressive standing professional armies in Europe.

But now an army was necessary. Militias worked well in limited circumstances, and they continued to function in local theaters of war, but they were not appropriate for extended wars and military campaigns far from home. The congress formed the Continental army and set enlistment at one year, but army leaders soon learned that that was not enough time to train soldiers and carry out campaigns. A three-year enlistment earned a new soldier a twenty-dollar bonus, paid up front, while men who committed for the duration—however long the war took—were promised a postwar land grant of one hundred acres. To make this inducement effective, of course, recruits had to believe that the Americans would win. By early 1777, the army was the largest it would ever be—29,000 troops; it was still not enough.

The Continental Congress assigned troop quotas to each state, and state assemblies directed communities to produce certain numbers. The local committees of public safety began to function like draft boards. From 1778 to the end of the war, draftees tended to be the marginal men in a community, such as servants or the unemployed; thus the army had a very different look from the state militias. In some towns, suspected loyalists were drafted first, either as an effective way to smoke them out or as a way to punish them for their British sympathies. Although it proved hard to get adequate numbers of men to enlist, the total number of individual enlistments over the course of the war totaled 231,950 men, or roughly one-quarter of the white male population over age sixteen.

Women also served in the Continental army. They were needed to do the everyday cooking and washing, and after battle they nursed wounded men. The professional British army established a

TECHNOLOGY IN AMERICA
The Committee of Safety Musket and Standardized Firearms

In the early months of war, soldiers had fought with hunting guns or antiquated firearms from the French and Indian War. These guns were often in ill repair and also required many different sizes of ammunition, a highly inconvenient state of affairs. In April 1775, Committees of Safety were directed by the Continental Congress to order standardized muskets from the five hundred gunsmiths operating from the Carolinas to New England. Each state authorized one main Committee of Safety to oversee arms acquisition and to swap and trade guns or parts with other states' committees; the plan was the earliest American example of systematic weapons procurement. The Congress insisted on precise specifications: 3/4-inch bore, a 44-inch barrel, and an 18-inch bayonet. Each musket, made of brass, iron, and wood parts, weighed around 10 pounds; soldiers also carried a powder horn of gunpowder and enough bullets for 20 or 30 rounds of fire.

Despite this effort to acquire standardized muskets, a perpetual shortage of firearms meant that American soldiers often fought with whatever weapon was available. A Prussian general, who volunteered his expertise to the Continental army, arrived at Valley Forge in 1778 and was shocked to find "muskets, carbines, fowling pieces, and rifles" all in the same company of troops. Not until the first two decades of the nineteenth century would the United States begin to manufacture firearms whose components were machine-tooled rather than hand-crafted under a system known as interchangeable parts. Firearms in the field — in Indian wars and the War of 1812 — could be fully uniform and easily repaired with standardized parts. The concept of machine-tooled parts that grew out of the need for standardized firearms would ultimately revolutionize manufacturing techniques in many industries.

The Historical Society of York County, Pennsylvania.

---

ratio of one woman to every ten men; in the Continental army, the ratio was set at one woman to fifteen men. Close to twenty thousand women served during the war, probably most of them wives of men in service. Children tagged along as well, and babies were born in the camps and on the road.

Black Americans were at first excluded from the Continental army, a rule that slave owner George Washington made on his fifth day as commander in chief. (Blacks had already fought at Concord and Bunker Hill, in the militias; they were allowed to continue their service when their units became the foundation of the Continental army.) But as manpower needs increased, the northern states began to welcome free blacks into service; even slaves could serve in some states, with their masters' permission. About five thousand black men served in the Revolutionary War on the rebel side, mostly from the northern states. (At least ten times that number of enslaved southern blacks disobeyed their owners and ran off to join the British.) Black Continental

soldiers sometimes were segregated into separate units; two battalions from Rhode Island were entirely black. Just under three hundred blacks joined regiments from Connecticut. While some of these were draftees, others were clearly men inspired by the ideals of freedom being voiced in a war against tyranny. For example, five Connecticut blacks gave "Liberty" as their surname at the time of enlistment, and another eighteen said their name was "Freedom" or "Freeman." The assumption that blacks in uniform were freemen must have encouraged enslaved blacks to join, in the hopes they could slip over the line to real freedom after the war. A white doctor in Westfield, Massachusetts, volunteered his slave Gilliam to go in his place when he was drafted, but then he discovered that Gilliam had already enlisted on his own. The doctor appealed to recover his human property but was turned down. Northern states as well as Maryland and Virginia allowed masters to send slaves as substitutes for themselves, but South Carolina and Georgia understood all too

The American army was at times raw and inexperienced, and much of the time woefully undermanned. It never had the precision and discipline of European professional armies. But it was never as bad as the British continually assumed. Early intelligence reports confidently informed the British high command that the Continental army was relying heavily on Irishmen (who were presumed to be little more than savages) and was basically "a contemptible body of vagrants, deserters, and thieves." The British were to learn that it was a serious mistake to underrate the enemy.

The British Strategy

The American strategy was relatively straightforward—to repulse and defeat an invading army. The British strategy was not nearly so clear. England wanted to put down a rebellion and restore monarchical power in the colonies, but the question was how to accomplish this. A decisive defeat of the Continental army was essential but not sufficient to end the rebellion, for there were all those militiamen around the countryside to contend with. An armed and highly motivated insurgent population promised to be a tough enemy for England.

Furthermore, there was no single political nerve center whose capture would spell certain victory. The Continental Congress floated from place to place, staying just out of reach of the British. During the course of the war, the British captured and for a time occupied every major port city—Boston, New York, Newport, Philadelphia, and Charleston—but with no significant gain. The British needed these harbor cities for their constant caravan of supply ships, but capturing them brought no real loss to the Americans, 95 percent of whom lived in the countryside.

England's delicate task was to restore the old governments, not to destroy an enemy country. Hence, the British generals were usually reluctant to ravage the countryside, confiscate food, or burn villages and towns. There were thirteen distinct political entities to capture, pacify, and then restore to the crown, and they were spread out in a very long line from New Hampshire to Georgia. Clearly a large land army was required for the job. Without the willingness to seize food from the locals, such an army needed hundreds of supply ships that could keep several months' worth of food in storage.

Another ingredient of the British strategy was the assumption (quite untested) that large numbers

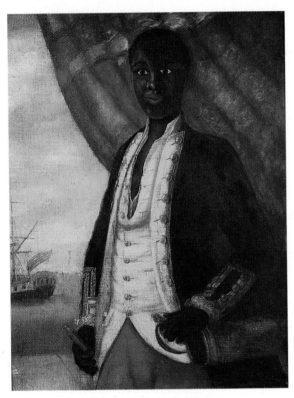

BLACK REVOLUTIONARY WAR SAILOR
Thousands of black men served on the patriot side as soldiers and sailors, usually at the rank of private or ordinary seaman. Their names are preserved in regiment records and crew lists; rarely, however, were their faces preserved. This 1780 portrait by an unknown artist shows an unnamed man, sword and scabbard at hand, dressed in military finery with a ship in view to establish his naval connection. His clothing suggests he was an officer.
Collection of A. A. McBurney.

well the contradiction, and the risk, of forcing or allowing enslaved blacks to fight for the cause of white people's liberty. Blacks from the Deep South were thus prohibited from becoming Continentals.

Military service helped to politicize Americans during the early stages of the war. In early 1776, independence was a new and risky idea, treasonous from the British point of view. But as the war heated up and leaders and recruiters demanded commitment, some apathetic Americans discovered that apathy had its dangers as well. Anyone who refused to serve ran the risk of being called a traitor to the cause. Military service established one's credentials as a patriot; it became a prime way of defining and demonstrating political allegiance.

of Americans remained loyal to the king and would come to the aid of the British army. Without substantial numbers of loyal subjects, the plan to restore old royal governments made no sense.

The British plan focused on New York, the state judged to harbor the greatest number of loyal subjects—perhaps as much as half the population—and therefore presumably the easiest to subdue and restore. New York offered a geographic advantage as well: Control of the Hudson River would allow the British to isolate the most troublesome states, those in New England. Armies could descend from Canada and move up from New York City along the Hudson River into western Massachusetts. Between a naval blockade on the eastern coast and army raids in the west, Massachusetts would be driven to surrender. Or so the British hoped.

England's delicate task was to restore the old governments, not to destroy an enemy country.

South of New York, in New Jersey and Pennsylvania, the British expected to find large pockets of loyalist strength to secure their advances. Rebellious citizens were to be convinced to sign loyalty oaths to the crown. Virginia was a problem, like Massachusetts, but the British were confident that the Carolinas contained many loyalists and that they could thus isolate and subdue Virginia. The overall plan was a divide-and-conquer approach to recapturing the thirteen colonies.

There were some in England who bravely questioned the wisdom of going to war to win back America. Why hold on to the colonies if they were so troublesome? Quite likely the established commercial ties would remain intact even without political control; the financial advantages of the colonial trade relationship, these critics argued, did not outweigh the costs of war. But this economic analysis did not factor in a key preoccupation of King George and his ministers: Losing the colonies was a severe blow to the glorious dreams of a British empire to rival those of France and Spain.

Quebec, New York, and New Jersey

While Washington disciplined his troops in Massachusetts, an American expedition was launched in late 1775 to capture the British cities Montreal and Quebec, a clear sign that the war was not merely a defensive reaction to the invasion of Massachusetts. The two cities were symbolic as well as strategic goals, having been sites of contest in the French-British wars of the 1740s and 1750s. Some Americans even mistakenly expected that the French at Quebec would welcome them as a liberating army. American commanders moved swiftly north to attack before British reinforcements could arrive. A force of New York Continentals commanded by General Richard Montgomery took Montreal easily in September 1775 and then advanced on Quebec. Meanwhile, a second contingent of Continentals led by Colonel Benedict Arnold moved through Maine on the Kennebec River to Quebec, a punishing trek through rain and snow with woefully inadequate food and boats; many men died. Arnold's fierce determination to get to Quebec was heroic, but in human costs the campaign was a tragedy. Arnold and Montgomery jointly attacked Quebec in December but suffered heavy losses. Montgomery was killed, and for months afterward the "Ghost of Montgomery" became a favorite pseudonym for anyone who penned an article pressing for independence. Arnold sustained a wound in his leg and, despite the failure to take Quebec, was hailed a hero because of his courage in the face of terrible odds.

The main action of the first year of war came not in Canada, however, but in New York, the state deemed crucial to England. In August 1776, some 20,000 fresh British troops (including 8,000 German mercenary soldiers, called Hessians) landed on Staten Island, south of New York City. They were joined by regiments withdrawn from Boston by General Howe and shipped down from Nova Scotia, bringing the total to nearly 45,000 soldiers. General Washington had anticipated that New York would be Howe's target and had moved his army, numbering about 20,000, from Massachusetts to an area of heightened, fortified ground on Long Island.

The Battle of Long Island, in late August 1776, pitted the well-trained British redcoats against a very green Continental army. Howe advanced 15,000 men from three directions on the American fortifications. The American troops panicked and ran off to a second line of fortifications on Brooklyn Heights, leaving behind their blankets, guns, ammunition, and packs. Washington was furious. In one day, August 27, the Continental army sustained 1,500 casualties (dead and wounded), while the British suffered only 370. It was a terrible defeat and a severe blow to morale. More such blows would follow in the days and weeks ahead.

BRITISH NORTH AMERICA

Battle of Quebec
Dec. 31, 1775

Siege of Quebec
Nov. 1775–Mar. 1776

Trois Rivières
June 7, 1776

Arnold 1775

Montgomery 1775

MAINE
(part of MASS.)

Montreal

St. Leger

St. Lawrence R.

L. Champlain

Burgoyne

Kennebec R.

VERMONT
(Claimed by
N.Y. & N.H.)

NEW
HAMPSHIRE

Fort Ticonderoga
Captured by British
July, 1777

Fort Stanwix
Held by Americans
under Benedict Arnold,
Aug., 1777

L. George

Arnold 1775

L. Ontario

Saratoga
Burgoyne surrenders,
Oct. 17, 1777

Bemis Heights
Oct. 7, 1777

Bennington
Aug. 16, 1777

Newburyport

Bunker Hill
June 17, 1775

Howe, 1776

British leave Boston
March 17, 1776

Fort
Oswego

Oriskany
Aug. 6, 1777

Mohawk R.

Gates

Albany

Concord
April 19, 1775

Lexington
April 19, 1775

Siege of Boston
July 1775–March 1776

NEW YORK

MASSACHUSETTS

Hudson R.

CONNECTICUT

R.I.

Delaware R.

Morristown
American winter quarters
1776–77

Fort
Lee

Fort Washington

Long Island

PENNSYLVANIA

N.J.

Brooklyn
Aug. 27, 1776

Howe, 1776

Germantown
Oct. 4, 1777

Princeton
Jan. 3, 1777

Manhattan

Staten Island

Valley Forge
American winter quarters
1777–78

Washington

Clinton

Monmouth Court House
June 28, 1778

Brandywine Creek
Sept. 11, 1777

Trenton
Dec. 26, 1776

ATLANTIC
OCEAN

Philadelphia
captured by British
under Howe,
Sept. 26, 1777

MARYLAND

DEL.

VIRGINIA

Chesapeake Bay

Howe, 1777

→ American forces

→ British forces

✳ American victories

✳ British victories

0   25   50   75   100 miles

0   50   100 kilometers

If General Howe had pressed a direct frontal attack on the Continentals at Brooklyn Heights, he probably would have wiped out the army altogether. Instead Howe, perhaps remembering the costly victory of Bunker Hill, waited for ships with artillery. Washington meanwhile evacuated his troops to Manhattan Island in the dead of night, under cover of an unusually thick fog. Hundreds of small, unlighted boats ferried silently across the East River, and in the morning an amazed Howe discovered that Brooklyn Heights had been abandoned.

Washington knew it would be hard to hold Manhattan against a British attack. One of his generals recommended burning the city; two-thirds of the buildings belonged to loyalists anyway, and burning it would prevent the British from housing troops there. Washington vetoed this idea, preferring instead to strip it of ammunition and supplies and leave quickly.

But the British advanced before Washington could leave. They sailed up the East River with booming cannons. Connecticut troops had been stationed at Kip's Bay, a probable landing spot, but these soldiers were no match for the sound of cannons. They had been in the army less than a week; when the British arrived, they ran, scrambling over fields and fences to get away. One of them, a youth named Joseph Plumb Martin, later recalled running off with two other men to a house "in which were two women and some small children, all crying most bitterly." They asked the women for some "spirits" and after imbibing a glass of rum each, they "bid them goodbye, [and] betook ourselves to the highway again."

Meanwhile, four thousand British troops landed on Manhattan and started moving inland, looking for an enemy to engage. Washington rode up and commanded the fleeing men to assume defensive positions, but no one obeyed him. The disheartened Virginian lingered on the field of nonbattle, muttering about the "scum" in his army;

his aides swooped in and led him to safety. Howe had again failed to press his advantage, for the capture of General Washington would have been a significant victory for the British. Instead Howe stopped to take cake and wine with the wife of a Quaker merchant named Robert Murray, an avowed pacifist and presumed loyalist. The gracious Mrs. Murray invited the British officers in and detained them more than two hours while the American army was making its hasty exit up the west side of Manhattan Island.

Another woman demonstrated more extreme means to make Manhattan inhospitable to the British. As the redcoats rolled in, fire broke out and raged for two days, burning a quarter of the city. Washington had vetoed arson as an official strategy, but a private citizen carried it out anyway. The British traced the fire to a soot-covered woman in a cellar full of incendiary devices. A member of Parliament pointed to the violent act of this "miserable woman" to illustrate the stubborn tenacity the British could expect to encounter in subduing America: "Knowing that she would be condemned to die, upon being asked her purpose, [she] said, 'to fire the city!' and was determined to omit no opportunity of doing what her country called for."

From September to November, the two armies juggled for position and engaged in limited fighting. In November, Howe finally attacked and captured two critical forts on either side of the Hudson River, Fort Washington and Fort Lee, taking thousands of prisoners. Washington retreated quickly across New Jersey into Pennsylvania. The British army followed him; at one point, Howe was only one hour behind Washington, but he rested his men for a day and widened the gap. As Howe moved through New Jersey, the Continental Congress, meeting in Philadelphia, fled to Baltimore.

Yet again, Howe unaccountably failed to take advantage of the situation. He could have attacked Washington's army at Philadelphia and probably would have taken the city. Instead he parked his German troops in winter quarters along the Delaware River and returned himself to New York City, to be close to his supply ships. Perhaps he knew that many of the Continental soldiers' enlistment periods ended on December 31, so he felt confident that the Americans would not attack him. But he was wrong. On Christmas—a holiday Germans celebrated with much more spirit (and spirits) than did Americans—Washington recrossed the Delaware River at night with 2,400 men and made a quick capture of the unsuspecting (and largely hungover)

German soldiers at Trenton. The victory was impressively executed, and it did much to restore the sagging morale of the patriot side. For the next two weeks, Washington remained on the offensive, dancing just ahead of the British army, capturing supplies in a clever attack on British units at Princeton on January 3. Soon he was safe in Morristown, in northern New Jersey, settled in for the winter.

All in all, in the first year of declared war, the rebellious Americans had a few isolated moments to feel proud of but also much to worry about. The very inexperienced Continental army had barely hung on in the New York campaign. Washington had shown exceptional daring as well as admirable restraint, but what really saved the American army may have been the repeated reluctance of the British to follow through militarily when they had the advantage.

The Home Front

Battlefields alone did not determine the outcome of the war. Struggles on the home front were equally important. Many years later, John Adams insisted that "the revolution was in the minds and hearts of the people" long before "hostilities commenced," but that was wishful misremembering on his part. In 1776, each community contained small numbers of highly committed people on both sides, and far larger numbers who were either apolitical or uncertain about whether independence was worth a war. The contest for the "minds and hearts" of the many neutrals thus figured as a major factor, and both persuasion and force were used. Revolutionaries who took control of local government often used it to punish loyalists and intimidate neutrals. On their side, loyalists worked to reestablish British authority. The struggle to secure political allegiance was complicated greatly by the wartime instability of the economy. The creative financing of the fledgling government brought hardships as well as opportunities, forcing Americans to confront new manifestations of virtue and corruption.

Patriotism at the Local Level

Committees of correspondence, of public safety, and of inspection dominated the political landscape in patriot communities. These committees took on more than customary local governance; they enforced boycotts, picked army draftees, and policed suspected traitors. Committees of inspection visited homes to search for contraband goods and auctioned off confiscated property. In some places, committees even regulated public amusements deemed inappropriate to the revolutionary mood, banning horse racing, gaming, cockfighting, plays, and other entertainments.

Some citizens, loyalists especially, were dismayed by what seemed to them to be excessive or arbitrary power taken on by committees. On occasion, secret and resourceful loyalists managed to get elected to these committees in order to subvert them. Others were open with their denunciations. A man in Westchester, New York, described his response to intrusions by committees: "Do as you please; if you like it better, choose your committee or suffer it to be chosen by a half dozen fools in your neighborhood—open your doors to them—let them examine your tea-cannisters and molasses-jugs, and your wives' and daughters' petty coats—bow and cringe and tremble and quake—fall down and worship our sovereign lord the mob. . . . Should any pragmatical committee-gentleman come to my house and give himself airs, I shall show him the door, and if he does not soon take himself away, a good hickory cudgel shall teach him better manners." Excessive or not, the powers of the local committees were rarely challenged. Committees of safety and of correspondence became the local governing agencies, and their persuasive powers convinced many middle-of-the-road citizens that neutrality was not a comfortable option.

Another group new to political life—white women—increasingly demonstrated a capacity for patriotism at the local level as wartime hardships dramatically altered their own work routines. Like Abigail Adams on her Braintree farm, many wives with husbands away on military or political service found themselves taking on masculine duties. Their increased competence to tend farms and make business decisions appears to have encouraged some to assert competence in political matters as well. Eliza Wilkinson managed a plantation on the South Carolina coast and talked revolutionary politics with her women friends. "None were greater politicians than the several knots of ladies who met together," she remarked, alert to the unusual turn female conversations had taken. "We commenced perfect statesmen."

Women from prominent Philadelphia families went a step beyond political talk to action. In 1780, they formed the Ladies Association, going door to door collecting a substantial sum of money, which

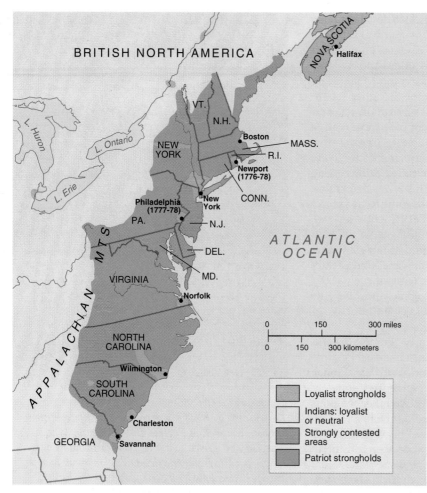

MAP 7.2
Loyalist Strength and Rebel Support
The exact number of loyalists can never be known. No one could have made an honest count at the time; in addition, political allegiance often shifted with the winds. This map shows the pockets of loyalist strength that the British relied on—the lower Hudson valley, the Carolina piedmont, and the areas most hotly contested by both sides: New Jersey and the Mohawk River Valley, regions repeatedly torn by battles and skirmishes.

they planned to distribute directly to Continental soldiers in the field as a gift of appreciation. A published broadside, "The Sentiments of an American Woman," defended their female patriotism against anticipated male criticism by recalling heroic biblical women and famous female monarchs of the past. "The time is arrived to display the same sentiments which animated us at the beginning of the Revolution, when we renounced the use of teas . . . [and] when our republican and laborious hands spun the flax." The Philadelphia women were right to expect criticism. General Washington rejected their monetary gift and instead requested that the women buy material and sew shirts for the soldiers, an offering he deemed more appropriately feminine.

The Loyalists

Between 20 and 30 percent of the American population remained openly loyal to the British monarchy in 1776, and another 20 to 40 percent could be described as neutral. Such a large population base could have sustained the British Empire in America, if only the British army leaders had known how to use it.

In general, loyalists were people who still found the idea of the British Empire, with all its historical, cultural, and economic ties, an appealing vision. They were convinced that American prosperity and stability depended on British rule and on a government anchored by monarchy and aristocracy. Perhaps most of all, they feared democratic tyranny. Like Abigail Adams, they understood that dissolving the automatic respect that submissive subjects had for their king could potentially lead to a society where all deference and hierarchy came unglued. Adams welcomed this chance to identify tyranny in unequal power relations, as between men and women; loyalists feared it. Patriots seemed to them to be unscrupulous, violent, self-interested men, men of ambition and malice who simply wanted power for themselves.

The most visible and dedicated loyalists (also called Tories by their enemies) were royal officials, not only top officeholders like Thomas Hutchinson in Massachusetts, but also local judges and customs officers. Wealthy merchants with commercial ties to England were made uneasy by the thought of abandoning the trade protections of navigation acts and the British navy. Urban lawyers of a conservative temperament found it impossible to imagine forgoing the stability of British law and order. New Yorker Peter Van Schaack committed a long essay to his private journal justifying his loyalism on those grounds: "If it be asked how we come to be subject to the authority of the British Parliament, I answer, by the same compact which entitles us to the benefits of the British constitution and its laws; and that we derive advantage even from some kind of subordination, is evident, because, without such a controlling common umpire, the colonies must become independent states, which would be introductive of anarchy and confusion among ourselves."

The early-eighteenth-century grants of religious liberty to grateful groups like the Palatine Germans in upstate New York and the French Huguenots in the Carolinas influenced some of them to remain loyal to Britain. Two other religious enclaves, the Quakers and the Moravians, located in Pennsylvania and North Carolina, were pacifists by religious conviction and were therefore often treated as though they were loyalists. Very recent immigrants, notably the Scots who had settled the North Carolina piedmont in the early 1770s, felt gratitude to the crown for providing royal land grants.

Some were loyalists merely as a product of oppositional politics with leading patriot men. For example, backcountry farmers in the Carolinas gravitated toward loyalism out of resentment over the political and economic power of the lowlands gentry. Southern slaves had their own resentments against the white slave-owning class. Many thousands in Virginia responded to Lord Dunmore's promise of eventual freedom if they would defect and aid the British, and more still in South Carolina ran off to Charleston to seek refuge with the British army when it occupied the city.

Many, indeed most, Indians eventually supported the British side. Some tribes, like the powerful Iroquois Nation in New York, had strong economic ties to the empire. One young Mohawk leader, Thayendanegea (known to Americans as Joseph Brant), traveled to England in 1775 to complain to King George about how the king's subjects

JOSEPH BRANT
The Mohawk leader Thayendanegea, called Joseph Brant, had been educated in English ways at Eleazar Wheelock's New England school (which became Dartmouth College in 1769). In 1776, Brant traveled to England with another warrior to negotiate Mohawk support for the British. There he had his portrait painted by George Romney. The thirty-four-year-old Brant wears a feudal gorget around his neck over his English shirt (compare with Washington, page 201), along with Indian armbands and headdress.
National Gallery of Canada, Ottawa.

repeatedly deceived the Mohawks. "It is very hard when we have let the King's subjects have so much of our lands for so little value," he wrote, "they should want to cheat us in this manner of the small spots we have left for our women and children to live on. We are tired out in making complaints & getting no redress." Thayendanegea negotiated his people's support for the king in exchange for protection from encroaching settlers, under a revived implementation of the Proclamation Act of 1763. On his return, Thayendanegea toured the western portions of New York and Pennsylvania, building Indian support for the British on the grounds that the Americans were a serious threat to the Indians' "own Country and Liberty." Another rationale for extensive Indian loyalism was the widespread assumption that England would surely win the war, and it was always better to side with the winners.

Pockets of loyalism thus existed everywhere. The largest pockets were in the middle colonies and the backcountry of the South. But even New England towns at the heart of turmoil, like Concord, Massachusetts, had a small and increasingly silenced core of loyalists who refused to countenance armed revolution.

The loyalists were most vocal between 1774 and 1776, when the possibility of a full-scale rebellion from England was still uncertain. Loyalists challenged the emerging patriot side using pamphlets, broadsides (single-sheet flyers designed to be publicly posted), and newspapers; every major city had one or sometimes two loyalist printers. In New York City in 1776, some loyalists circulated a broadside titled "A Declaration of Dependence," a direct answer to the Continental Congress's July 4 manifesto. "So far from having given the least countenance or encouragement, to the most unnatural, unprovoked Rebellion that ever disgraced the annals of Time," they wrote, "we have on the contrary, steadily and uniformly opposed it, in every Stage of its rise and progress at the risque of our Lives and Fortunes."

Speeches and rallies amplified the spread of loyalism in backcountry areas where print culture had not fully penetrated. Loyalist ministers used their pulpits, while other defenders of the empire staged rallies or disrupted patriot gatherings. At an open-air rally in backcountry South Carolina in 1775, a loyalist elbowed his way to the platform to remind the audience of the superior might of the British army and of the damage to trade that would surely follow any attempt at independence. But his winning argument was to invoke the backcountry's fears and resentments of the coastal planters' wealth and political power: It is ironic, he said, that "the charge of our intending to enslave you should come oftenest from the mouths of those lawyers who in your southern provinces, at least, have long made you slaves to themselves."

Who Is a Traitor?

The rough treatment that loyalists experienced at the hands of the revolutionaries seemed to substantiate their worst fears. In June 1775, the First Continental Congress passed a resolution declaring loyalists to be traitors. Over the next year, state after state wrote laws defining treasonable acts and their punishments. Anyone who joined the British army or supplied it with food or ammunition was said to have committed treason. In some states, it was treason to discourage men from enlisting in the Continental army or to say or print anything that could undermine patriot morale. New Hampshire actually made it treasonable to maintain a personal belief in the legitimacy of British authority. Punishments ranged from house arrest and suspension of voting privileges to dire penalties such as confiscation of property and deportation. And sometimes self-appointed committees of Tory hunters bypassed the judicial niceties and terrorized loyalists, raiding their houses or tarring and feathering them.

"They call me a brainless Tory, but tell me . . . which is better—to be ruled by one tyrant three thousand miles away, or by three thousand tyrants not a mile away?"

A question rarely asked in the heat of the revolutionary moment was whether the wives of loyalists were traitors as well. When loyalist families fled the country, they usually fled together, and property held in the name of the family patriarch was then confiscated. But what if the wife stayed? One Connecticut woman brought witnesses before a justice of the peace to testify that she was "a steady and true and faithful friend to the American states in opposition to her husband, who has been of quite a different character." In such cases, the court typically allowed the woman to keep her dower rights (one-third of the property, the amount she was due if widowed) and confiscated the rest. But even when the wife fled with her husband, was she necessarily a traitor? Could she have independent political beliefs apart from her husband's? If he ordered her to flee with him, was she not obligated to go? (The centuries-old English legal doctrine of *feme covert*, specifying the rights and duties of married women, held that a wife was a nonperson under law and that her husband was responsible for her actions.) Such questions came up in several lawsuits after the Revolution, where descendants of refugee loyalists sued to regain property that had entered the family through the mother's line of inheritance. In one well-publicized case in Massachusetts in 1805, the issue of female responsibility for political acts was debated by some of the best legal minds of the time. The outcome confirmed the traditional view of women as political blank slates; the son of loyalist

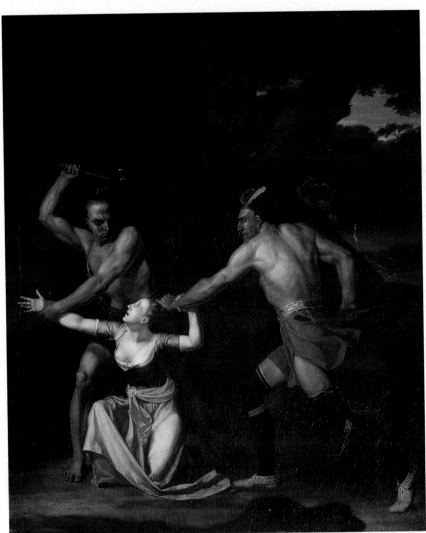

DEATH OF JANE MCCREA
This 1804 painting by John Vanderlyn memorializes the martyr legend of Jane McCrea. McCrea lived with her patriot family in upstate New York, but in July 1777 she fled to join her fiancé, a loyalist fighting with Burgoyne's army. She was murdered en route, allegedly by Iroquois allies of the British. The American General Horatio Gates sent Burgoyne an accusatory letter. "The miserable fate of Miss McCrea was particularly aggravated by her being dressed to meet her promised husband," Gates wrote, "but she met her murderers employed by you." Gates skillfully used the story of the vulnerable, innocent maiden dressed in alluring clothes as propaganda to inspire his soldiers' drive for victory at Saratoga. Vanderlyn's painting, and a half dozen similar pictorial representations, emphasized McCrea's helplessness and sexuality. Yet had McCrea been a man, her flight would have been traitorous. What explains this different treatment of a woman? Wadsworth Atheneum, Hartford.

refugee Anna Martin recovered her property on the grounds that she had no independent will to be a loyalist.

Tarring and feathering, property confiscation, deportation, terrorism—to the loyalists, such denials of liberty of conscience and of freedom to own private property proved that democratic tyranny was more to be feared than the monarchical variety. A Boston loyalist, Mather Byles, aptly expressed this point: "They call me a brainless Tory, but tell me . . . which is better—to be ruled by one tyrant three thousand miles away, or by three thousand tyrants not a mile away?" Byles, a minister, was later sentenced to deportation. "Discord and tyranny, in the guise of liberty, stalk forth among us," complained an embittered New York loyalist in 1775.

Throughout the war, probably seven to eight thousand loyalists fled to England, while twenty-eight thousand found closer haven in Canada. But many chose to remain in the new United States and tried to manage to swing with the changing political fortunes of their communities as best they could. In some places, that proved extremely hard to manage. In New Jersey, for example, three thousand Jerseyites felt protected enough by the occupying British army in 1776 to swear an oath of allegiance to the king. Even a man who just months before had signed the Declaration of Independence, Richard Stockton, came forward to beg pardon for his action. What those three thousand publicly sworn loyalists could not foresee was that General Howe would draw back to New York City and leave them at the mercy of local patriot committees. British strategy depended on using loyalists to hold occupied territory, but the New Jersey experience showed just how poorly that strategy was put into practice.

Financial Instability and Corruption

Wars cost money—to pay soldiers; to pay suppliers for food, clothing, and housing; to pay manufacturers for muskets, cannon, and gunpowder. The Continental Congress printed money, but within a few short years its value had deteriorated, since there were no reserves of gold or silver held by the congress to back the currency. In practice, the currency was worth only what a buyer and seller agreed it was worth. The dollar eventually bottomed out at one-fortieth of its face value; a loaf of bread that once sold for two and a half cents now sold for a dollar. States too were printing their own paper money to pay for wartime expenses, further complicating the economy.

Soon the congress had to resort to other means to procure needed supplies and labor. One method was to borrow hard money (not paper) from wealthy men, who in return would get certificates of debt (also called public securities) promising repayment with interest. In effect, the wealthy men had bought government bonds. To pay soldiers, the Congress offered land bounties, which amounted to a promise of a tangible form of wealth. In short order, public securities and land bounties became a form of negotiable currency too. For example, a soldier with no paycheck or cash might sell his land bounty certificate to get food for his family. These certificates also fluctuated in value, mainly depreciating.

Depreciating currency inevitably led to rising prices, as sellers compensated for the falling value of the money. The wartime economy of the late 1770s, with its unreliable currency and inflation in prices, was unprecedented and extremely demoralizing to Americans everywhere. Prices of goods and labor in the prewar decades had generally been stable and predictable. So local committees of public safety in 1778 began to fix prices. A committee would decree the price of flour, bread, and other essentials for one month in an effort to impose some brief stability. Such short-run expectations for holding down prices testifies to the wild character of the economy.

Inevitably, some Americans turned this roller-coaster situation to their advantage. Money that fell fast in value needed to be spent quickly; being in debt was suddenly advantageous because the debt could be repaid weeks later in devalued currency. A brisk black market sprang up in prohibited luxury imports, such as tea, sugar, textiles, and wines. No matter that these items came from Britain. As one Virginia lawyer said, "Such is the Spirit to trade, that if Beelzebub [the devil] was to appear with a Cargoe—the people would deal with him." The governor of New Jersey sarcastically observed that the best way to get good wine imported to America might be to declare war on Portugal. A New Hampshire delegate to the congress denounced the extravagance that flew in the face of the virtuous homespun association agreements of just a few years before: "We are a crooked and perverse generation, longing for the fineries and follies of those Egyptian task masters from whom we have so lately freed ourselves."

The Campaigns of 1777: Highs and Lows

In early 1777, the Continental army had a bleak road ahead. Washington had shown considerable skill in avoiding outright military defeat, but the small victories in New Jersey lent only faint optimism to the American side. The British still intended to pursue their plan to isolate New England by controlling the waterway between Canada and New York City. The large numbers of British regular soldiers who arrived to reinforce Quebec in May 1776 gave the British the manpower they needed to start the northern squeeze on the Hudson River valley.

Burgoyne's Army

General John Burgoyne commanded the British troops in Canada in 1777. Familiar with America, he had served in the French and Indian War and again under General Thomas Gage in Boston in 1775. Between war stints, Burgoyne wrote treatises on the use of artillery and occupied a seat in Parliament; he also dabbled in playwriting and acquired a reputation for being a high-living gambler.

Burgoyne had an army of 7,800 uniformed soldiers, plus another 1,000 assorted "camp followers" such as wives, cooks, laundresses, and musicians, and 400 Indians to serve as scouts. This very large army did not travel light. In addition to food supplies for more than 9,000 people, Burgoyne the cannon expert insisted on bringing lots of heavy artillery. The artillery required more than 400 horses to haul it, and the horses in turn required hay. Burgoyne also traveled with more than thirty personal trunks of such useful wilderness amenities as elegant clothing and fine wines. Not for nothing was his nickname "Gentleman Johnny."

Burgoyne's instructions were to capture Albany, a town 150 miles north of New York City near the intersection of the Hudson and Mohawk Rivers. But his first goal was Fort Ticonderoga. About 3,000 American troops held the fort, but they had not anticipated a major invasion from Canada so soon, and they were low on food and supplies. After spying the approaching artillery power, the Americans crept away one dark early morning, without offering a fight. Fort Ticonderoga was back in British hands.

The British gave immediate chase, moving south toward Albany. But Burgoyne lost ground quickly because he insisted on moving his entire army, camp followers and all, taking a land route instead of traveling on Lake George. Local farmers created obstacles by felling trees in his path. Burgoyne lost a critical month hacking his way down the road, and meanwhile his supply lines back to Canada were severely stretched. Soldiers sent out to forage food were beaten back by militia units from New Hampshire and Vermont. The general's opinion, that "the great bulk of the country is undoubtedly with the Congress in principle and zeal," could not have been welcome news to the British government.

Saratoga

The logical second step in isolating New England should have been to advance troops up the Hudson from New York City. General Howe still held Manhattan, and American surveillance indicated that he was readying his men for a major troop movement. George Washington, in New Jersey, was sure Howe would go north to meet Burgoyne. With disbelief he watched while Howe loaded his men on ships in August 1777 and sailed south. Howe had decided to try to capture Philadelphia. Not until Howe's ships had entered the mouth of the Chesapeake Bay did Washington fully accept that Howe was not going to help Burgoyne. Another British general in New York, Henry Clinton, was dismayed by

Howe's decision and later flatly called it a mistake. Clinton promised to send reinforcements to Burgoyne, but he could not get them to Albany in time.

In addition, British troops were supposed to move east from the Great Lakes down the Mohawk River, joined by Indians of Joseph Brant's Iroquois League. The British believed that the Palatine Germans of the Mohawk valley were heavily loyalist, so they expected little trouble moving forward. Fort Stanwix, left over from the French and Indian War, marked the western gateway to the Mohawk valley, and it was guarded by 750 Continental soldiers. Local militias hastily assembled to reinforce the small garrison of Continentals; despite widespread Palatine loyalism, many Germans were fiercely devoted to the rebel cause. The Mohawk valley was a particularly bloody example of the Revolution as civil war, as neighbors fought neighbors over the course of several years, even when the British army was not around. The rebel militia unit moving toward Stanwix met with ambushing Indians in a narrow ravine and suffered great losses (200 killed and another 200 taken prisoner). Fort Stanwix was spared a similar fate only because General Benedict Arnold, still highly esteemed for his heroism in Quebec, arrived with reinforcements (bolstered by a well-circulated but false rumor of even more reinforcements to come), and this scared the British into retreating. Burgoyne, camped forty miles north of Albany, thus did not have the expected help. He was isolated and stuck; his food supplies were dwindling, and his men were deserting.

The Continentals at Albany, now under the new command of General Horatio Gates, advanced to Saratoga, a small farming community on the Hudson River north of Albany. Gates had 7,000 men, including Arnold's division, several New York militia units and some Virginia riflemen, whose hunting shirts and wild turkey calls intimidated the British.

Burgoyne decided to attack first, since every day his army weakened, and retreat was unthinkable and humiliating. The first Battle of Saratoga joined both armies in a classic military engagement, with the two sides facing each other and pressing forward. By day's end, Burgoyne's army claimed the victory, but the loss of men (600 dead and wounded) made it costly; the relative unimportance of the battle location made it a dubious victory.

Three weeks later, a repeat engagement at Saratoga cost Burgoyne another 600 men and most of his cannon as well. Burgoyne tried to retreat, but Gates's army blocked his path. With food running out and many wounded and demoralized men, Bur-

WASHINGTON'S TENT
When in the field, General Washington traveled with three tents, one each for sleeping, eating, and storage. Pictured here is his sleeping tent, containing a cot and a folding table.
Collection of the New York Historical Society.

goyne finally officially surrendered to the Americans on October 17, 1777.

Americans on the side of the rebellion were jubilant. This was the first decisive victory for the Continental army. Almost overnight, a popular dance called "General Burgoyne's Surrender" swept through the country, and bookies in the major cities set odds at five to one that the war would be won in just six months. Both the American leaders, Gates and Arnold, were lauded as the heroes of Saratoga.

General Howe, meanwhile, had succeeded in taking Philadelphia in September 1777. Washington had moved his army south of the city to defend it, but he lost a crucial battle at Brandywine Creek. The Continental Congress had departed nine days earlier for Lancaster, sixty miles west. The British government figured that Burgoyne's surrender was evenly balanced by the capture of Philadelphia and thus proposed a negotiated settlement—not including independence—to end the war. But the Americans refused; they danced "Burgoyne's Surrender" and remained optimistic about eventual victory.

The optimism was not well founded, however, in the winter of 1777–1778; spirits ran high, but finances and supplies ran precariously low. Washington moved his troops into winter quarters at Val-

ley Forge, a day's march west of occupied Philadelphia. Quartered in drafty sheds, the men lacked blankets, boots, and stockings. Washington complained to the congress that nearly three thousand of his men were "unfit for duty because they are bare foot and otherwise naked"; without blankets, large numbers were forced to "set up all Night by fires, instead of taking comfortable rest in a natural way." Food was also scarce. Standard rations dwindled for a time to "firecake," a tasteless pancake made with plain flour and water only, and in one week in February there were no food rations at all. Local farms had produced adequate food that year, but Washington was sure that the farmers were selling their grain to the British, who could pay with the king's silver. Washington claimed that such Americans were worse than the enemy and expressed a grim desire to hang the whole lot. His young aide-de-camp Alexander Hamilton openly wondered if the country was even worth fighting for, so corrupt did it seem.

The evidence of corruption indeed appeared abundant. Army suppliers too often provided defective food, clothing, and gunpowder. Washington's men unfolded a shipment of blankets only to discover that they were a quarter of their customary size. Barrels of flour arrived short-weighted, with "the Center Scooped out and the sides standing." Teamsters who hauled barrels of preserved salted meat might drain out the brine to lighten their load and then refill the barrels later, allowing the meat to rot in transit. Selfishness and greed seemed to infect the American side. A new slang vocabulary identified this new breed of war enthusiasts: "Sharpers," "cheats," and "mushroom gentlemen" were war profiteers, wheeling and dealing in an unstable economy. As one Continental officer said, "The people at home are destroying the Army by their conduct much faster than Howe and all his army can possibly do by fighting us."

The French Alliance

On their own, the Americans could not have defeated England. Essential help arrived as a result of the victory at Saratoga, which convinced the French to enter the war. Two days after news reached the French court, the Americans and French drafted a formal alliance against England and signed it in February 1778. France recognized the United States as an independent nation and promised full military and commercial support throughout the war. The most crucial support was the French navy,

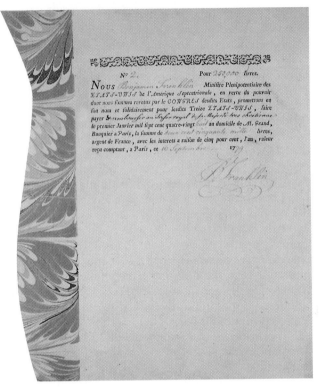

PROMISSORY NOTES NEGOTIATED BY FRANKLIN
Benjamin Franklin, in France in 1778, negotiated loans from the French government to the United States. The preprinted loan form calls Franklin a "Minister Plenipotentiary" with authority to act on behalf of the thirteen (united states); the fact that the form is printed suggests that the French anticipated making several, or many, such loans; this one is numbered 2. It called for repayment in 1779 at five percent interest.
American Philosophical Society Library.

which now could challenge England's transatlantic pipeline of supplies and troops.

France had been waiting for a promising American victory to justify a formal declaration of war, for it was foolish as well as dangerous to ally openly with a loser. Yet since 1776, France had aided the Americans in every way short of becoming official partners in war. It had provided military goods— cannons, muskets, gunpowder—funneled through a dummy private firm secretly financed by the French government. Highly trained French military experts had "volunteered" to help the American army in the field with technical advice and military strategy. The marquis de Lafayette, a young nobleman, was one of several French officers advising Washington in 1777. France had opened its ports to

American shipping without restriction, a favor that was most useful in the French West Indies. Most important, France anticipated participation in the war by gearing up its navy in the two years prior to 1778, building new and repairing old warships, so that when the treaty was finally signed, France could be an instant combatant.

Even defeat was not a full disaster for France, if the war took many years and drained England of men, money, and psychological energy.

French sympathies for the Americans were secured through the artful diplomacy of Benjamin Franklin, who lived in Paris for several years as the agent of the Continental Congress. Franklin's deft social skills, impressive scientific knowledge, and rustic charm smoothed his way at court and kept French interest in the American cause high.

Yet monarchical France was understandably cautious about endorsing a democratic revolution that attacked the principles of kingship. The main attraction of an alliance for France was simply the opportunity to defeat England, its archrival. A victory would also open pathways to trade. A French minister, the count of Vergennes, predicted that "the power that will first recognize the independence of the Americans will be the one that will reap the fruits of this war." France coveted the British West Indies, which might fall to them in a victory. And even defeat was not a full disaster for France, if the war took many years and drained England of men, money, and psychological energy. The French alliance proved to be essential for American victory, but it by no means meant that the parties to the alliance shared close goals.

The French navy arrived off the coast of Virginia in July 1778, bearing arms and supplies, and then moved north to threaten (but not attack) the British in New York, occupying the harbor for a week. In August, the allied ships went farther north to Newport, Rhode Island, also held by the British, and engaged in limited battle before heading on to Boston, now returned to American rule. By 1781, the French proved indispensable to the American victory, but the first months of the alliance brought no dramatic victories, inducing grumbling from some Americans that the partnership would prove worthless. "These murmurings the governing powers

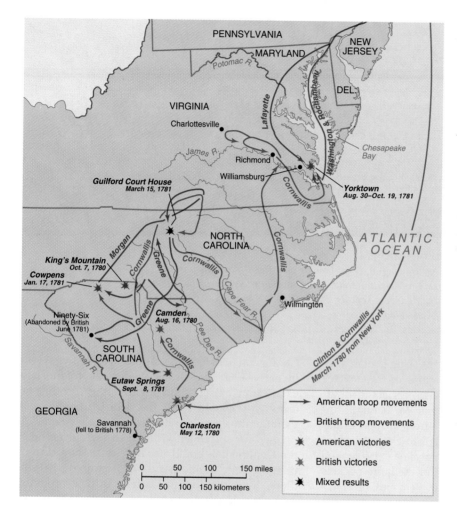

MAP 7.3
*The War in the South,
1780–1781*
*After taking Charleston in
1780, the British advanced
into South Carolina and the
foothill region of North Carolina, leaving a bloody civil
war in their wake. Cornwallis
next invaded Virginia but was
overpowered by American and
French forces at Yorktown in
1781 in the final battle of the
Revolutionary War.*

prudently endeavored to suppress, that they might not give offence to their new allies," observed a British captain. Indeed, by late fall of 1778, the French fleet had sailed off for the West Indies.

The Southern Strategy: 1778–1781

When France joined the war, some British officials paused to consider whether the fight was worth continuing. A troop commander, arguing for an immediate negotiated settlement, shrewdly observed that "we are far from an anticipated peace, because the bitterness of the rebels is too widespread, and in regions where we are masters the rebellious spirit is still in them. The land is too large, and there are too many people. The more land we win, the weaker our army gets in the field." The commander of the British navy argued for abandoning the war, and even Lord North, the prime minister of King George's cabinet, was believed to be in favor of ending it quickly. But the king was determined to crush the rebellion, the French notwithstanding, and he encouraged the development of a new strategy for victory. It was a brilliant but desperate plan.

Georgia and South Carolina

The new strategy shelved the plan to isolate New England and instead focused on the South, thought to be easier to recapture for the crown. The entry of the French navy into the war pulled the center of gravity southward, because of France's interest in the British West Indies. Some British strategists even argued that the thirteen rebel colonies should be written off entirely, in favor of defending the much more valuable sugar islands. But the southern colonies, with their tobacco, rice, and indigo crops,

AMERICAN LIGHT CAVALRY AND DRAGOONS
An artist inked and watercolored this drawing in 1775 showing American cavalrymen in uniform poses. A shortage of horses in fact kept cavalry units minimal; probably fewer than a thousand served in the war. The expense of feeding horses kept British cavalry to a minimum as well.
Anne S. K. Brown Military Collection, Providence, R.I.

were also very valuable, so the king's plan prevailed. The high slave populations of these states were also a factor. White southerners could ill afford the instability of all-out war, for it might unleash violence from two sides—from the British and from slaves seizing the moment to claim freedom themselves. Georgia and the Carolinas also looked promising for victory because of the large pockets of loyalism presumed to be prevalent and, most important, militant. The British hoped to recapture the southern colonies one by one, restore the loyalists to power, leave them in control, and then move north to the more problematic middle colonies, leaving prickly New England for last.

Georgia, the first target, fell easily at the end of December 1778. A small army of British and German soldiers occupied Savannah and Augusta, and a new royal governor and loyalist assembly were quickly installed. Taking Georgia was easy because the bulk of the Continental army was in New York and New Jersey, keeping an eye on General Clinton, Howe's replacement as commander in chief, and the French were in the West Indies. The British in Georgia quickly organized twenty loyal militia units, and 1,400 Georgians swore an oath of allegiance to the king. So far, the plan looked as if it might work.

The next target was South Carolina. General Clinton moved British troops south from New York, while the Continental army put ten regiments into Charleston to defend the capital city. For five weeks in early 1780, the British laid siege to the city. Charleston citizens had assured the Continental army they would resist the British mightily, but their enthusiasm dissipated and they quickly pressed for surrender. Without strong citizen help, the Continentals could not hold out. They surrendered the city in mid-May 1780, sending 3,300 soldiers, a tremendous loss, into British captivity. Again, the king's new strategy seemed to be working as planned.

Clinton returned to New York, leaving the task of pacifying South Carolina to General Charles Cornwallis and 4,000 troops. Of all the British generals in the war for America, Lord Cornwallis was the boldest in his willingness to send his men into action. Clinton and Howe, in contrast, were extremely cautious about risks; Burgoyne, gambler that he was, loved risks but was not very prudent about them. Cornwallis moved into action. He chased out the remaining Continental army units and established military control of the state by midsummer 1780. He purged rebels from government office and disarmed potential rebel militias. The export of South Carolina's main crop, rice, resumed, suggesting an easy normalization of relations between England and the colony. Pardons were offered to Carolinians who swore loyalty oaths to the crown, as in Georgia, but there was one severe requirement in the Carolina pledge: Oath takers were required to join the fight against the rebels or face arrest. In effect, Cornwallis forced men into taking the loyalty oath, since punishment followed refusal.

In August 1780, the Continental army was ready to strike back at Cornwallis. General Gates, the hero of the Battle of Saratoga, arrived in South Carolina with more than 3,000 troops, some of them experienced army units and others untried militiamen. They met Cornwallis's army of 2,000 British regular soldiers at Camden, South Carolina, on August 16. Gates put the militiamen into the center of the battle, and despite the fact that they outnumbered the British, a contagious panic gripped them at the sight of the approaching enemy cavalry. Men threw down unfired muskets and ran from the field of battle. When regiment leaders tried to regroup the next day, only 700 showed up. The rest were either dead, captured, or still in flight—including Gates, who traversed a speedy 180 miles in three days before he stopped to file a report on the battle. Camden was a devastating defeat; prospects now seemed very grim for the Americans.

Benedict Arnold's Treason

The new British strategy succeeded in 1780 partly as a product of improved information about American troop movements and supplies that was secretly furnished to General Clinton in New York by Benedict Arnold, the erstwhile hero of Ticonderoga, Quebec, and Saratoga. Arnold, thirty-nine and a native of Connecticut, had enjoyed a remarkable army career and the confidence of George Washington, who valued his brilliant military talents. But Arnold was also a deeply insecure man who craved approval from superiors and never felt he got his due. He was argumentative, uncooperative, uncharitable, and often grasping. He bickered with other military leaders, he insulted civilian leaders, he filed exaggerated expense accounts, and he made secret pacts with war profiteers. For Arnold, the war mainly represented an opportunity to gain fame and reputation and to line his pockets.

After being wounded at Saratoga, Arnold was appointed to an inactive command, as military commandant of Philadelphia in June 1778 soon after the British had vacated it. During his months there, he used his power to continue his private financial speculations, for example, issuing passes to loyalist trading ships in which he owned interests and using army wagons to transport his own commerce. He also married an eighteen-year-old woman, Peggy

Shippen, from a wealthy, loyalist-leaning family, and threw lavish parties for her social set. At one point, his coach was mobbed in the street by a pro-revolutionary crowd angered by his hobnobbing with rich men of suspicious loyalty. Soon some (but not all) of his business irregularities came to light, and he found himself on the defensive in a court-martial that challenged his integrity and led to an official rebuke. Probably the final straw for Arnold came when he failed to earn promotion to higher rank, while men he considered inferior were promoted over him. Through his wife's contacts, he let

PEGGY SHIPPEN ARNOLD
The British Major John André met the pert, flirtatious Peggy Shippen in 1778, when the British occupied Philadelphia. He frequently escorted the seventeen-year-old to social events and the theater. He sketched Peggy, showing her in a beribboned dress with an even more extravagant, gravity-defying hairstyle. If the two were romantically involved, it was not serious on André's part. The gallant officer socialized with several other young women as well. In 1779, Peggy married the American General Benedict Arnold. Through Peggy, Arnold gained access to André's superiors.
Yale University Art Gallery.

BENEDICT ARNOLD
Benedict Arnold in 1776, when he was the hero of the Quebec campaign.
Anne S. K. Brown Military Collection, Providence, R.I.

the British commander in New York, Henry Clinton, know that with sufficient reward—say, £8,000—he would deliver a major prize that would tip victory England's way.

The ever-hesitant General Clinton remained cautious about Arnold for more than a year. Arnold had named an enormous sum for his reward, and it was not at all clear what he could deliver from his inactive duty in Philadelphia. Meanwhile, to show good faith, Arnold passed along whatever he learned from Washington—about the arrival of the French fleet, about the weak state of Charleston's defenses, even about a planned invasion of Canada that was actually disinformation on Washington's part. Arnold's main task throughout 1779 and early 1780 was to acquire an active command that would be worth something to the British, in addition to quietly closing out his property holdings in Connecticut and Philadelphia in anticipation of flight.

Arnold lobbied Washington for the command of West Point, a fortress guarding a critical narrows in the Hudson River about sixty miles north of New York City. West Point was being fortified to protect against the original and still ultimate British goal, controlling the Hudson and isolating New England. Its easy seizure would be worth a lot to the British; it might well mean instant victory. Arnold's plan was to invite the British to attack and to make their victory effortless by giving them full information on the Americans' defense plans.

Granted command in the spring of 1780, Arnold proceeded to slow down the fortification efforts while entering into serious negotiations with the British about the exact terms of his payoff. He demanded to meet an emissary from Clinton in person, to argue the terms; Clinton hesitated for weeks, knowing the danger. Finally Clinton sent a trusted aide, Major John André, behind enemy lines at night, and Arnold, ever true to character, detained him until daybreak haggling over the payment. Arnold then sent him back unescorted and burdened with drawings and plans for the fort's defense. Near the British line, André was halted by three Americans, and when he offered to bribe them for his release with his gold watch, his horse, and a large sum of money, they quickly became suspicious. The discovery of the fortress plans on his person sealed his doom, and word of his arrest went upriver, to Arnold and to General Washington nearby. Arnold escaped to the British in New York only minutes ahead of the arrival of a consternated Washington. Major André was tried as a spy and hanged ten days later, in October 1780, much lamented by his British friends and by American officers as well, who were moved by his honorable acceptance of the gallows. Arnold was safe but not sound in New York City, surrounded by British officers who now despised him for luring their esteemed young aide into the danger that caused his death and, equally, for failing to deliver West Point, the prize that would have made Clinton victorious.

News of the Arnold treason spread quickly throughout America. Arnold represented all of the patriots' worst fears: greedy self-interest like that of the war profiteers, unprincipled abandonment of the war aims like that of the turncoat Tories of the South, a final fleeing panic like that of the terrified soldiers with Gates at the Battle of Camden. But instead of symbolizing and magnifying all that was troubling about the American side of the war, the treachery of Arnold became celebrated in a kind of displacement of the anxieties of the moment. Vilifying Arnold allowed Americans to stake out a wide distance between themselves and this truly evil man. Parades and effigy burnings in many cities equated Arnold with the devil, and his opponents as therefore men of virtue. It inspired a renewal of patriotism at what had been a particularly low moment. Smoking out Arnold worked to cleanse the American war effort.

The Other Southern War: Guerrillas

Both Gates's defeat at Camden and the treason of Benedict Arnold revitalized rebel support in western South Carolina, an area that Cornwallis had believed to be pacified and loyal. The backcountry of the South soon became the site of a guerrilla war. In hit-and-run attacks, both sides burned and ravaged not only enemy property but the property of anyone claiming to be neutral. The loyalist militia units organized by the British were met by fierce rebel militia units who now figured they had little to lose. It did not help matters that Cornwallis had hanged several men captured at Camden who had signed loyalty oaths but had gone over to the rebel militia. Bloody, extreme tactics only escalated the violence. Guerrilla warfare soon spread to Georgia and North Carolina. In South Carolina, some 6,000 men became active partisan fighters, and they entered into at least twenty-six engagements with loyalist units. Some of these were classic battles; but on other occasions the fighters were more like bandits than soldiers. Both sides murdered enemies, committed atrocities, and plundered property, clear deviations from standard military practice.

The British southern strategy counted on sufficient loyalist strength—in terms of both numbers of people and the respect and authority they could command—to hold reconquered territory as the army moved north. The backcountry civil war proved this assumption false. The Americans won few major battles in the South, but they ultimately succeeded by dogging the British forces, nipping at their heels, harassing them, preventing them from foraging for food. Cornwallis boldly moved the war into North Carolina in late 1780, not because he thought South Carolina was secure—it was not—but because the North Carolinians were supplying the South Carolina rebels with arms and men. As he wrote to Clinton (who was safely resting in New York City), "It may be doubted by some whether the invasion of North Carolina may be a prudent measure; but I am convinced it is a necessary one, and that if we do not attack that province, we must give up both South Carolina and Georgia, and retire within the walls of Charleston." Cornwallis headed north, but news of a brutal defeat—a massacre, actually—of loyalist units in western South

Carolina at Kings Mountain, at the hands of 1,400 frontier riflemen, sent him hurrying back. The British were stretched too thin to hold even two of their onetime colonies.

Surrender at Yorktown

In the early months of 1781, Cornwallis set out to try his North Carolina plan again; if successful, it would isolate South Carolina and Georgia. For months, he moved his army around the state, taking land but not holding it. In February 1781, Cornwallis proclaimed, prematurely, that North Carolina was reconquered, a move calculated to increase loyalist support. But few loyalists could be found who were willing to take up arms against the energized rebel forces.

Cornwallis decided to push the war further north, into Virginia. He captured Williamsburg, which had been the capital until the previous year. Then he raided Charlottesville, where Virginia's revolutionary government was meeting, and seized members of the assembly; Governor Thomas Jefferson narrowly avoided capture. (More than a dozen of Jefferson's slaves ran off to seek refuge with the British army.) As late as the start of September, Cornwallis was not wrong to think he had the upper hand in Virginia.

What changed the picture dramatically was an infusion of French military support. A large French army under the command of the comte de Rochambeau had joined Washington in Rhode Island in mid-1780. News that a large fleet had sailed from France in the spring of 1781 set in motion Washington's plan to defeat the British. The fleet was bound for the Chesapeake Bay, so Washington and Rochambeau fixed their attention on Cornwallis's campaign in Virginia. Bypassing New York (where Clinton had been expecting an attack), thousands of American and French soldiers headed south in the last week of August 1781, traveling on four separate roads to confuse the British.

British intelligence about the French fleet movement had been delayed, and by the time British ships arrived at the mouth of the Chesapeake, the French had already taken control of it. A five-day naval battle in early September sent the British ships limping away and left the French in clear command of the bay and the Virginia and North Carolina coasts. This proved to be the decisive factor in ending the war, because it eliminated a water escape route for Cornwallis's land army, encamped at Yorktown, Virginia.

THOMAS NELSON HOUSE

The finest house in Yorktown belonged to Thomas Nelson, the American governor of Virginia in 1781. During the British occupation of Yorktown, Nelson recommended that American guns be trained directly on his home, on the presumption that Cornwallis had made it his headquarters. Fifteen years later an artist sketched the damaged house, still unrepaired and surrounded by British defensive earthworks.

The Library of Virginia.

General Cornwallis and his 7,500 troops now faced a combined French and American army numbering over 16,000. Thousands of civilian sightseers also flocked around, attracted to the scene by the army's long parade south. For twelve days, the Americans and French laid siege to the British fortifications at Yorktown, bombarding the British with cannon and shells. Quickly Cornwallis ran low on food and ammunition. An American observer keeping a diary noted that "the enemy, from want of forage, are killing off their horses in great numbers. Six or seven hundred of these valuable animals have been killed, and their carcasses are almost continually floating down the river." Realizing escape was impossible, Cornwallis signaled his intention to surrender.

On October 19, 1781, the British leaders formally capitulated. Cornwallis claimed "indisposition" and sent a subordinate as substitute. The defeated troops marched through a double line of American and French soldiers to relinquish their weapons; an American diarist reported that "their mortification could not be concealed. . . . Many of the soldiers manifested a sullen temper, throwing their arms on the pile with violence as if determined to render them useless." Washington allowed Cornwallis his personal liberty, and he sailed off to New York City with as many loyalists as could fit on one ship. The remaining British soldiers were packed off to prison camps in Virginia and Maryland.

What had begun as a promising southern strategy by the British in 1778 had turned into a discouraging defeat by 1781. British attacks in the South energized American resistance, as did the timely exposure of Benedict Arnold's treason. The arrival of the French fleet sealed the fate of Cornwallis at Yorktown, and the military war quickly came to a halt.

The Losers and the Winners

The surrender at Yorktown proved to be the end of the war, but it took some time for the principals to realize that. The peace treaty was nearly two years in the making, and in the meantime both the American and the British armies remained in the field, in case the treaty fell through.

Peace Slowly Dawns

Cornwallis had surrendered his army at Yorktown, but he had no authority to end the war. Clinton continued to hold New York City with many thousands of soldiers; Charleston and Savannah, too, stayed under British control, although the British had been chased out of the rest of the South. King George tenaciously clung to the idea of pursuing the war, but the sentiment for peace was growing in Parliament. A vote taken soon after Cornwallis's surrender showed that only a bare majority favored continuing the war. A resolution to end the war a few months later lost by only a single vote, and five days later the necessary majority was rounded up. The war had become unpopular among the British citizenry in general, and support for it dwindled until finally the king had to realize it was over.

The Continental Congress appointed three commissioners, Benjamin Franklin, John Adams, and John Jay of New York, to negotiate the settlement. It took more than six months to come to preliminary agreement. The Americans met with the British negotiator in Paris, ostensibly so that they could consult with their ally France. But France had different and conflicting interests from the Americans, and the British tried playing the two allies off against each other. The French would have been quite content to divide up the colonies, awarding New York, the Carolinas, and Georgia to the British; the Americans wanted not only all thirteen colonies but Canada as well.

In late November 1782, eighty-two articles of peace were agreed to. The first article went to the heart of the matter: "His Britannic Majesty acknowledges the said United States to be free Sovereign and independent States." Other articles described the boundaries of the new country: a northern line separating Canada, which remained British, a western line along the Mississippi River, and a southern line sectioning off Florida, which England soon handed over to Spain in a separate treaty. Creditors on both sides were entitled to col-

lect debts owed them, in sterling money; this was an important provision for British merchants, especially those in the southern trade, who claimed that commercial debts owed them had gone uncollected during the war. A legalistic provision dealt with loyalist property: The Continental Congress agreed to recommend that state legislatures restore confiscated property to the loyalists. But since the congress had no power to compel the states to return property, no property was returned under this provision. England agreed to withdraw its troops in a timely fashion; more than a decade later, this article would still not be fully satisfied.

The final, official peace treaty—the Treaty of Paris—was signed nearly a year later, on September 2, 1783. The Americans were waiting for a separate peace agreement between the British and the French. Meanwhile, the British army continued to occupy three cities (New York, Charleston, and Savannah) and a string of forts in western New York, Pennsylvania, and the Ohio country. The logistical problems of evacuating the army from the cities proved to be nearly as difficult as sending and supplying the army during the war. There simply were not enough ships to remove all the soldiers, artillery, and stores of food, let alone the thousands of loyalists who rightly feared for their safety once the British were gone.

The final evacuation proceeded in stages. It took 129 ships to do the job from Charleston; small boats and even canoes had to be pressed into service to take loyalists—whites and blacks—from upriver settlements down the coast to St. Augustine, Florida. In the fall of 1783, hundreds of ships converged on New York City to load the headquarters of the British after their seven-year occupation. More than 27,000 soldiers and 30,000 loyalists left New York for Nova Scotia, where a second convoy took many on to England. In a final act of mischief, on the November day when the last ships left, the losing side raised the British flag at the southern tip of Manhattan, cut away the ropes used to hoist it, and greased the flagpole.

Why the British Lost

England began the war for America with a conviction that it could not lose. What a later century termed "the arrogance of power" afflicted British officials and caused them to underestimate their task. But they had some grounds for confidence. They had the strongest and best-trained army and navy in the world; they were familiar with the

American landscape from the French and Indian War; and they outnumbered their opponents in uniform. They easily captured the capital and every other port city of consequence in America. Probably one-fifth of the population was loyalist, and another two-fifths were undecided. Why, then, did they lose?

One continuing problem the British faced was the practical one of food and supplies. Instead of the six-month food supply the generals wanted, reserves typically hovered at the level of a thirty-to-sixty-day supply; at one grim moment in 1780, General Clinton was down to only six days of food before a resupply arrived. Uncertainty about food helps explain the repeated reluctance of Howe and Clinton to push aggressively into the interior in pursuit of the Continental army. Yet it does not fully explain other moments when British commanders refused to coordinate their operations and come to one another's aid, as when Burgoyne at Saratoga was left to his fate, and likewise Cornwallis at Yorktown. Personal jealousies among the commanders appear to have interfered with the larger goal of winning the war.

A second obstacle to British success was their continual misuse of loyalist energies. Any plan to repacify the colonies required the cooperation of the loyalists as well as new support from the many neutrals. But again and again, the British failed to back the loyalists, leaving them to the mercy of vengeful rebels. In the South, they allowed loyalist militias to engage in vicious guerrilla warfare that drove away potential converts among the rest of the population. There was no real program to court the neutrals and to show them that the stability of British rule was preferable to the rebel government. If the British had been more lenient and forgiving, they might have succeeded in retaking the South. But perhaps the central problem was that there simply were not enough loyalists, and the British did nothing to augment their numbers.

The French alliance looms large in any explanation of the British defeat. The artillery and ammunition they supplied throughout the war, even before 1778, were critical necessities for the Continental army. In 1780, the French army brought a fresh infusion of troops to a war-weary America, and the French navy made the Yorktown victory possible. The symbolic impact of the major naval defeat in the Chesapeake, just before the Yorktown siege, dissolved the pro-war spirit in England and forced the king to admit defeat.

Finally, the British abdicated civil power in the colonies in 1775 and 1776, when royal officials were forced to flee to safety, and they never really regained it. For nearly seven years, the Americans of necessity created their own government structures, from the Continental Congress to local committees and militias. Staffed by many who before 1775 had been the political elites, these new government agencies had remarkably little trouble establishing their credentials and authority to rule. The single effort in Georgia to appoint a new royal governor was not successful, and the British did not try to repeat the experiment. The basic British goal in the war—to turn back the clock to imperial rule—receded into impossibility as the war dragged on.

Conclusion: The Dynamic of Equality and Liberty

The war for America had taken five and a half years to fight, from Lexington to Yorktown; negotiations and the evacuation took two more. It remains the second longest war in American history, second only to the Vietnam War. It profoundly disrupted the lives of Americans everywhere, from Canada to Georgia. It was a war for independence from England, but it was also much more. It was a war that required men and women to think about politics and the legitimacy of authority. New government structures had to be forged to replace the vacuum left by the departing British. The precise disagreement with England about representation and political participation had profound implications for the kinds of governance the Americans would choose to adopt, both in the short-run moment of emergency, as extralegal committees and bodies took charge, and in the longer run of the late 1770s and early 1780s when state constitutions began to be written and the Continental Congress pondered its own legitimacy. The rhetoric employed to justify the revolution against England put words like *liberty, tyranny, slavery, independence,* and *equality* into common usage. But these words carried deeper meanings than a mere complaint over taxation without representation, meanings that came to the surface as Americans struggled to articulate what kind of new government they should institute. As Abigail Adams and others saw, the Revolution unleashed a dynamic of equality and liberty. That it was largely unintended and unwanted by the revolutionary leaders of 1776 made it all the more potent a force in American life in the decades to come.

CHRONOLOGY

1775 **May 10.** Second Continental Congress convenes in Philadelphia.

May. Fort Ticonderoga falls to American forces.

June 14. Continental Congress creates Continental army.

June 17. Battle of Bunker Hill.

July. Congress offers the Olive Branch Petition in attempt at reconciliation with king.

American armies march on Montreal and Quebec.

1776 **January 1.** Americans lose assault on Quebec.

January. Thomas Paine's *Common Sense* published.

March. British evacuate Boston.

July 4. Declaration of Independence adopted.

August 27. Battle of Long Island.

September 15. British take Manhattan.

September 21. Part of New York City burned.

November. Americans retreat to Philadelphia.

December 26. Washington surprises British and Hessians at Trenton.

1777 **January.** Washington winters at Morristown, New Jersey.

July. Burgoyne takes Fort Ticonderoga for British.

August 6. Fort Stanwix ambush.

September. British occupy Philadelphia.

October 17. Burgoyne surrenders at Saratoga.

December. Washington goes into winter quarters at Valley Forge, Pennsylvania.

1778 **February.** France enters war on American side.

July–August. French fleet threatens New York and Newport, Rhode Island.

December. Savannah, Georgia, falls to British.

1779 **January–June.** Skirmishes in South Carolina and Georgia.

October. British evacuate Newport.

1780 Philadelphia Ladies Association raises money for soldiers.

March–May. British lay siege to Charleston, South Carolina.

July. Rochambeau and French army arrive at Newport.

August 16. Battle of Camden, South Carolina, dims hopes for Americans.

September–October. Benedict Arnold's treason exposed.

September–December. Guerrilla warfare in South.

October 7. Battle of Kings Mountain, South Carolina.

1781 **January 17.** Battle of Cowpens, South Carolina.

May–August. Cornwallis in Virginia.

August. Cornwallis occupies Yorktown, Virginia.

September 5. French fleet takes Chesapeake Bay.

September 28–October 19. Siege of Yorktown.

October 19. Cornwallis surrenders.

1783 Treaty of Paris ends war.

BIBLIOGRAPHY

GENERAL WORKS

John R. Alden, *The American Revolution, 1775–1783* (1954).

Edward Countryman, *The American Revolution* (1985).

Don Higginbotham, *The War of Independence: Military Attitudes, Policies, and Practices, 1763–1789* (1983).

Don Higginbotham, *George Washington and the American Military Tradition* (1985).

Don Higginbotham, *War and Society in Revolutionary America: The Wider Dimensions of Conflict* (1988).

Ronald Hoffman and Peter J. Albert, *Arms and Independence: The Military Character of the American Revolution* (1984).

Piers Mackesy, *The War for America, 1775–1783* (1964).

James Kirby Martin, *In the Course of Human Events: An Interpretive Exploration of the Revolution* (1979).

Robert Middlekauff, *The Glorious Cause: The American Revolution, 1763–1789* (1982).

Charles Royster, *A Revolutionary People at War: The Continental Army and American Character, 1775–1783* (1979).

John Shy, *A People Numerous and Armed: Reflections on the Military Struggle for American Independence* (rev. ed., 1990).

James L. Stokesbury, *A Short History of the American Revolution* (1991).

THE WARTIME CONFEDERATION

John Alden, *George Washington* (1984).

Joseph J. Ellis, *Passionate Sage: The Character and Legacy of John Adams* (1993).

E. James Ferguson, *The Power of the Purse: A History of American Public Finance: 1776–1790* (1961).

John Ferling, *John Adams: A Life* (1992).

Jay Fliegelman, *Declaring Independence: Jefferson, Natural Language, and the Culture of Performance* (1993).

Eric Foner, *Tom Paine and Revolutionary America* (1976).

Edith Gelles, *Portia: The World of Abigail Adams* (1992).

James H. Hutson, *John Adams and the Diplomacy of the American Revolution* (1980).

Jackson Turner Main, *The Sovereign States, 1775–1783* (1973).

Jerrilyn Greene Marston, *King and Congress: The Transfer of Political Legitimacy, 1774–1776* (1987).

Jack N. Rakove, *The Beginnings of National Politics: An Interpretive History of the Continental Congress* (1979).

John Phillip Reid, *A Constitutional History of the American Revolution: The Authority of Rights* (1986).

Peter Shaw, *The Character of John Adams* (1976).

William C. Stinchcombe, *The American Revolution and the French Alliance* (1969).

Garry Wills, *Inventing America: Jefferson's Declaration of Independence* (1978).

Lynne Withey, *Dearest Friend: A Life of Abigail Adams* (1981).

THE LOYALISTS

Bernard Bailyn, *The Ordeal of Thomas Hutchinson* (1974).

Wallace Brown, *The Good Americans: The Loyalists in the American Revolution* (1969).

Robert M. Calhoon, *The Loyalists of Revolutionary America, 1760–1781* (1973).

Robert M. Calhoon, *The Loyalist Perception and Other Essays* (1989).

John Ferling, *The Loyalist Mind: Joseph Galloway and the American Revolution* (1977).

Malcolm Frieberg, *Prelude to Purgatory: Thomas Hutchinson in Provincial Massachusetts Politics, 1760–1770* (1990).

Adele Hast, *Loyalism in Revolutionary Virginia* (1982).

Neil MacKinnon, *This Unfriendly Soil: The Loyalist Experience in Nova Scotia, 1783–1791* (1986).

William N. Nelson, *The American Tory* (1961).

Mary Beth Norton, *The British-Americans: The Loyalist Exiles in England, 1774–1789* (1972).

William Pencak, *American's Burke: The Mind of Thomas Hutchinson* (1982).

Janice Potter, *The Liberty We Seek: Loyalist Ideology in Colonial New York and Massachusetts* (1983).

James W. St. G. Walker, *The Black Loyalists: The Search for a Promised Land in Nova Scotia and Sierra Leone, 1783–1870* (1976).

THE WAR IN THE NORTH

Rodney Atwood, *The Hessians* (1980).

Michael A. Bellesiles, *Revolutionary Outlaws: Ethan Allen and the Struggle for Independence on the Early American Frontier* (1993).

Clare Brandt, *The Man in the Mirror: A Life of Benedict Arnold* (1994).

Richard Buel Jr., *Dear Liberty: Connecticut's Mobilization for the Revolutionary War* (1980).

E. Wayne Carp, *To Starve the Army at Pleasure: Continental Army Administration and American Political Culture, 1775–1783* (1984).

Edward Countryman, *A People in Revolution: The American Revolution and Political Society in New York, 1760–1790* (1981).

John C. Dann, ed., *The Revolution Remembered: Eyewitness Accounts of the War for Independence* (1980).

Gregory E. Dowd, *A Spirited Resistance: The North American Indian Struggle for Unity, 1745–1815* (1992).

William M. Fowler Jr., *Rebels under Sail: The American Navy during the Revolution* (1976).

Sylvia Frey, *The British Soldier in America: A Social History of Military Life in the Revolutionary Period* (1965).

Barbara Graymont, *The Iroquois in the American Revolution* (1972).

Robert Gross, *The Minutemen and Their World* (1976).

Ira D. Gruber, *The Howe Brothers and the American Revolution* (1972).

Richard J. Hargrove Jr., *General John Burgoyne* (1983).

Sidney Kaplan and Emma Nogrady Kaplan, *The Black Presence in the Era of the American Revolution* (1989).

Isabel T. Kelsay, *Joseph Brant, 1743–1807* (1984).

Richard M. Ketchum, *The Winter Soldiers* (1973).

Donald R. Lennon and Charles E. Bennett, *A Quest for Glory: Robert Howe and the American Revolution* (1991).

James Kirby Martin and Edward Mark Lender, *A Respectable Army: The Military Origins of the Republic, 1763–1789* (1982).

Paul David Nelson, *General Horatio Gates* (1976).

Dave R. Palmer, *The Way of the Fox: American Strategy in the War for America, 1775–1783* (1975).

Gary A. Puckrein, *The Black Regiment in the American Revolution* (1978).

Willard Sterne Randall, *Benedict Arnold: Patriot and Traitor* (1990).

John Shy, *Toward Lexington: The Role of the British Army in the Coming of the American Revolution* (1965).

John A. Tilley, *The British Navy and the American Revolution* (1987).

Anthony F. C. Wallace, *The Death and Rebirth of the Seneca* (1969).

Donald Wallace White, *A Village at War: Chatham, New Jersey, and the American Revolution* (1979).

Robert K. Wright Jr., *The Continental Army* (1983).

DIPLOMACY

Jonathan R. Dull, *A Diplomatic History of the American Revolution* (1985).

R. Ernest Dupuy et al., *The American Revolution: A Global War* (1977).

Ronald Hoffman and Peter Albert, eds., *Peace and the Peacemakers: The Treaty of 1783* (1986).

Reginald Horsman, *The Diplomacy of the New Republic, 1776–1815* (1985).

James H. Hutson, *John Adams and the Diplomacy of the American Revolution* (1980).

Lee Kennett, *The French Forces in America, 1780–1783* (1977).

Richard Morris, *The Peacemakers: The Great Powers and American Independence* (1965).

THE SOUTHERN STRATEGY

R. Arthur Bowler, *Logistics and the Failure of the British Army in America, 1775–1783* (1975).

Jeffrey J. Crow and Larry Tise, eds., *The Southern Experience in the American Revolution* (1978).

John Ferling, ed., *The World Turned Upside Down: The American Victory in the War of Independence* (1988).

M. Thomas Hatley, *The Dividing Paths: Cherokees and South Carolinians through the Era of Revolution* (1993).

W. Robert Higgins, ed., *The Revolutionary War in the South* (1979).

Ronald Hoffman, Thad W. Tate, and Peter J. Albert, eds., *An Uncivil War: The Southern Backcountry during the American Revolution* (1985).

Henry Lumpkin, *From Savannah to Yorktown* (1981).

Jerome J. Nadelhaft, *The Disorders of War: The Revolution in South Carolina* (1981).

James H. O'Donnell III, *Southern Indians in the American Revolution* (1973).

John S. Pancake, *This Destructive War: The British Campaign in the Carolinas, 1780–1782* (1985).

Hugh Rankin, *The North Carolina Continentals* (1971).

John E. Selby, *The Revolution in Virginia, 1775–1783* (1988).

Timothy Silver, *A New Face on the Countryside: Indians, Colonists, and Slaves in South Atlantic Forests, 1500–1800* (1990).

Russell F. Weigley, *The Partisan War: The South Carolina Campaign of 1780–1782* (1970).

REVOLUTIONARY WAR FLAG FROM NEW HAMPSHIRE

This cotton and linen flag from the early 1780s shows the final, official version of the Stars and Stripes. The earliest forms of the flag simply reconfigured the British Union Jack symbol of double red and white crosses on a field of blue. Washington's army in Massachusetts adopted a banner called the Grand Union Flag in January 1776, which embedded the Union Jack symbol in a flag with thirteen red and white stripes representing the thirteen colonies. Such a flag reflected genuine ambivalence about independence and a symbolic allegiance to British sovereignty. Worse still, it ran the risk of signaling capitulation in battle. In June 1777, the Continental Congress decreed a new American flag, carrying thirteen red and white stripes and a blue corner embellished with thirteen stars in no prescribed pattern.

David A. Schorsch, NYC.

BUILDING A REPUBLIC
1775–1789

8

I N 1781, MERCY OTIS WARREN AND HER HUSBAND, JAMES, purchased an elegant residence that had once belonged to Thomas Hutchinson in Milton, Massachusetts, six miles south of Boston. The ex-royal governor would not have been pleased to know that his archenemies the Otis and Warren families entertained in his parlor and slept in his bedroom. Hutchinson, however, was in exile in England, the war was finally over, and James and Mercy were ready to contribute their energies to the work of fashioning the new republic. The move from Plymouth, their home for twenty-seven years, to Milton, much closer to the Boston capital, was designed to facilitate that work. James happily terminated his wartime duties on the navy board of the Continental Congress and in the Massachusetts militia and resumed his seat in the state's assembly, where he had served repeatedly in the 1760s and 1770s. Mercy turned to her ambitious task of the 1780s, the writing of a substantial history of the American Revolution.

Mercy Otis Warren, then fifty-three, was the foremost female political commentator and intellectual of her day. She had grown up in a household that lived and breathed politics. Her father, the lawyer James Otis, represented his town of Barnstable for fifteen years in the Massachusetts House, serving as speaker. He provided his sons with the extensive tutoring required for entrance to Harvard College: The local minister, a Yale man, was engaged to teach them the Greek and Latin classics, history, and English literature. In an extraordinary move, Mercy, a bright and confident girl, was fully included in these private lessons. That decision of James Otis's, to educate his daughter on a par with college-bound sons, was virtually unprecedented in mid-eighteenth-century America.

Mercy married James Warren, a Harvard classmate of her brother James's, and the three men in her life—father, brother, and husband—immersed themselves in the tumultuous events of the 1760s in Boston that slowly led to the Revolution. Through her relatives, Mercy met other rising leaders, such as the Adams cousins Samuel and John; her house in Plymouth became a meeting place where strategies were debated and tactical ideas like the committees of correspondence were forged. Soon, in the early 1770s, Mercy took up her pen in the cause of American liberty, producing poems and satirical plays with thinly disguised characters that made the royal officials look like corrupt buffoons. The plays were published in Boston, New York, and Philadelphia newspapers, anonymously of course. As antigovernment satires, they required protection for the author. But just as important, Mercy Warren needed to conceal her authorship to protect her identity as a woman. A woman writing about politics violated a well-established gender boundary of the eighteenth century. Even in her letters to John Adams, a close personal friend in the 1770s, Mercy carefully prefaced her political opinions with apologies for stepping "so far beyond the line of my sex."

By the 1780s, Mercy Warren's confidence in her political judgment had grown. So had her anxiety about the direction of the newly independent Republic, which "resembled the conduct of a restless, vigorous youth, prematurely emancipated from the authority of a parent, but without the experience necessary to direct him to act with dignity or discretion." First came years of disagreement among the states over the ownership of western lands, followed by bickering over taxation and the war debt. At times it seemed to Mercy and James that the country was on the brink of total disaster.

To make matters worse, severe economic chaos clouded much of the 1780s. No currency could keep value for long; prices fluctuated wildly, and speculators grew rich while other people grew poor. Mercy Warren worried that the simplicity, virtue, and self-sacrifice cherished by the sturdy American patriots of 1776 had vanished overnight, replaced by a greed to profit from the uncertain economy and a selfish desire to indulge in luxury. A bewildered Warren wrote, "Such a total change of manners in so short a period, I believe was never known in the history of man. Rapacity and profusion, pride and servility, and almost every vice is contrasted in the same heart."

By the mid-1780s, the Massachusetts state government embarked on a course the Warrens disapproved of, taxing inhabitants at high rates to retire the state debt. But they equally disapproved of citizens' armed protests against taxes. Mercy Warren considered such protesters "incendiary and turbulent" and "too ignorant to distinguish between an opposition to regal despotism and a resistance to a government recently established by themselves."

When a group of American leaders responded to such protests by drafting a new constitution for the Republic, Mercy Warren, now thoroughly alarmed, took up her pen again to denounce the "many-headed monster" that threatened individual liberties. Her unsigned nineteen-page pamphlet gained wide circulation.

By 1788, Mercy Warren's views had lost out and the Constitution had been ratified. The Warrens also lost their own little indulgence, their new house; the financial instability of the 1780s forced them to sell it. They returned to Plymouth, where Mercy spent the next fifteen years polishing her three-volume *History of the Rise, Progress, and Termination of the American Revolution*. Finally published in 1805, the work credited its author, "Mrs. Mercy Warren," on the title page. Here she was finally at liberty to claim her political views as her own, backed up by quo-

MERCY OTIS WARREN
The Boston artist John Singleton Copley painted Mercy Warren when she was thirty-six. The blue satin gown adorned with point lace sleeves and silk braid conveys a message of proper—and prosperous—femininity. Mercy Warren's warm and intelligent face bears a gentle yet appraising expression.
Bequest of Winslow Warren, Courtesy, Museum of Fine Arts, Boston.

tations from leading participants and footnotes from documents of record. The work's public reception, however, fell far short of its genuine merit. Her onetime friend and mentor John Adams objected strongly to her treatment of him and the other proponents of the Constitution. "History is not the Province of the Ladies," he fumed. But Mercy Otis Warren's own life proved him wrong.

The Articles of Confederation

For five years, from independence in 1776 until 1781, the Second Continental Congress continued to meet in Philadelphia and other cities. It existed as an extralegal body, without any formal constitutional basis, while its members groped to establish a government on principles congruent with the themes of the Revolution. With monarchy gone, where did sovereignty lie? If people could not be taxed except by their representatives, where did the power of taxation lie? What was the nature of representation? If distant governments inevitably lost sight of the interests of the people, what was the proper size for a political entity? And just who were "the people" anyway?

The initial answers to these questions took the form of a plan called the Articles of Confederation. The plan, however, proved to be controversial and difficult to implement. By the time the Articles were finally ratified, in 1781, they were virtually obsolete.

Congress and Confederation

The Second Continental Congress had assumed power in May 1775, when the British attack on Lexington and Concord required a unified colonial response. Only as they fashioned the Declaration of Independence a year later did the delegates consider the need for a written document that would specify what powers the congress had, by what authority it existed, and how it was to be constituted. Several men briefly tried drafting such a document; but finally it was John Dickinson, the moderate conciliator from Pennsylvania, who chaired the committee entrusted with this important task. Dubious as he was about the prospects of independence, Dickinson was intrigued by the assignment of setting forth the powers and structure of the congress.

Dickinson's draft of the Articles of Confederation reveals the wide scope of agreement that existed about how the congress should function. The delegates thought of themselves as a harmonious body, fairly well unified by their opposition to England. Most agreed that the congress should handle functions such as pursuing war and peace, conducting foreign relations, regulating trade, and running a postal service.

Dickinson's draft called for a congress with those powers plus the authority to issue bills of credit and to borrow money, to settle all disputes between states, and to administer the unsettled western lands. It was these final two points—the preeminent authority of the congress over the states and over western lands—that proved to be the major sources of disagreement over the draft. Some states, such as Virginia and Connecticut, had very old colonial charters that located their western boundaries many hundreds of miles to the west. States without extensive land grants could not abide

such grandiose claims. Dickinson's Articles granted the congress final authority on this and many other matters.

Off and on over the next sixteen months, the congress tinkered with the Articles; its immediate attention, however, was focused on the war. When the possibility of a French alliance began to materialize in 1777, the delegates returned to the task of hammering out the Articles. They reasoned that some sort of government, however imperfect, was better than no official government at all; they wanted to look like a serious country to the French. And there were growing problems, too, that called for a constitution. As things stood, the congress could tell the states to raise men, money, and supplies for the war, but no one had any clear idea what to do if a state ignored the request.

A final version of the Articles of Confederation emerged in November 1777. Dickinson had resigned from the congress many months before and was not there to argue for his expansive version of the congress's powers. What resulted, after amendment, was a document that clearly identified the union as a loose confederation of states. Gone was the provision giving the congress control of state boundaries and western lands. Also absent was the statement of congress's superior authority. Instead, the Articles opened with two carefully crafted declarations about state powers and the nature of the union. Each state retained all powers and rights not expressly delegated to the congress, and the union was characterized as "a firm league of friendship" existing mainly to foster a common defense. There was no national executive office (that is, no president) and no national judiciary.

The structure of the government closely paralleled that of the existing Continental Congress. The confederation was embodied in a congress, composed of two to seven delegates from each state. The actual number was not critical, since each state delegation cast a single vote; in a confederation of thirteen equal states, Rhode Island's vote was the equal of Virginia's. The Articles specified that the delegates be selected annually by the state legislature, with only two limitations: No one could serve more than three years out of any six, and no one could hold another government office at the same time. Thus was established the principle of rotation in office and an end to the practice of plural office-holding.

Routine decisions in congress required a simple majority of seven states; for momentous powers, such as declaring war, nine states needed to agree. But to approve or amend the Articles required the unanimous consent of the thirteen states —not just of the thirteen delegations in the congress, but of the thirteen state legislatures. The congressional delegates undoubtedly thought they were guaranteeing that no individual state could be railroaded by the other twelve in fundamental constitutional matters. But what this requirement really did was to hamstring the government. One renegade state could—and did—hold the rest of the country hostage to its demands.

In general, the lack of centralized authority in the confederation government was exactly what many state leaders wanted in the late 1770s.

On the delicate question of deriving revenue to run the government, specifically to finance the war, the Articles provided an ingenious but ultimately troublesome solution. Each state was to contribute to the common treasury in proportion to the current property value of the state's land. Large and populous states would contribute more than small or sparsely populated states whose land was not settled and improved. The actual taxes would be levied by the state legislatures, not by the congress, to preserve the Revolution's principle of taxation only by direct representatives. However, no mechanism was created to compel states to contribute their fair share.

In general, the lack of centralized authority in the confederation government was exactly what many state leaders wanted in the late 1770s. A league of states with rotating personnel, no executive branch, no power of taxation, and a requirement of unanimity for any major change seemed to be a good way to avoid the potential tyranny of government. But soon the inherent weaknesses of these features became apparent.

The Problem of Western Lands

Once approved by the congress, the Articles of Confederation had to be approved unanimously by the state legislatures. Newspapers published the plan, but there was little public debate because the war monopolized the news. No pamphlets appeared debating the pros and cons of the Articles, and hardly any politicking went on in state legislatures. The congress scheduled only five days for the final debate and promptly dismissed all but one of the thirty-six amendments proposed by the various state legislatures.

The one proposed change that took time to debate was a plea by five states to give the congress administrative control of the western lands up to the Mississippi River as a national domain that could eventually constitute new states. Not surprisingly, these five states were small, with charters granting them boundaries at most a few hundred miles from the coast: Maryland, Delaware, New Jersey, Rhode Island, and Pennsylvania. Though Pennsylvania was much larger than the others, about one-fifth of its area was simultaneously claimed by Connecticut, whose charter set its western boundary unimaginably far west. Connecticut's claim was not an empty threat. By the late 1770s, Connecticut families were moving into the area of the upper Susquehanna River in Pennsylvania, leading to violent skirmishes with the Pennsylvanians also staking out land claims there.

By contrast, the charters of the states with more land specified ambitious but vague western boundaries. Virginia's charter dated from 1624, a time when the royal grantors lacked realistic knowledge of the geography and demography of the American continent. Consequently, Virginia could claim, on paper anyway, to own territory west to the Mississippi River and north to Lake Superior, taking in present-day West Virginia, Kentucky, Ohio, Indiana, Illinois, Michigan, and Wisconsin. Connecticut was sure that its territory cut through Virginia's domain, and Massachusetts claimed a strip of present-day New York, Michigan, and Wisconsin. The Carolinas and Georgia drew their western boundaries at the Mississippi River. A great portion of the contested western lands actually fell under the control of another group not party to the disputes in the Continental Congress: the many thousands of Indians who inhabited that region, who would have been very surprised to learn that they lived in Virginia or Connecticut territory.

The five smaller states were not entirely without western claims of their own. Ambitious individual investors from Maryland, New Jersey, and Pennsylvania had purchased large tracts of land in the Ohio valley from Indians in the 1760s, and they wanted the confederated government to confirm their ownership and make the rest into a national domain. Many of these speculators were also leading politicians in their state governments. While wearing their political hats, they tried to make their arguments as principled as possible. Maryland leg-

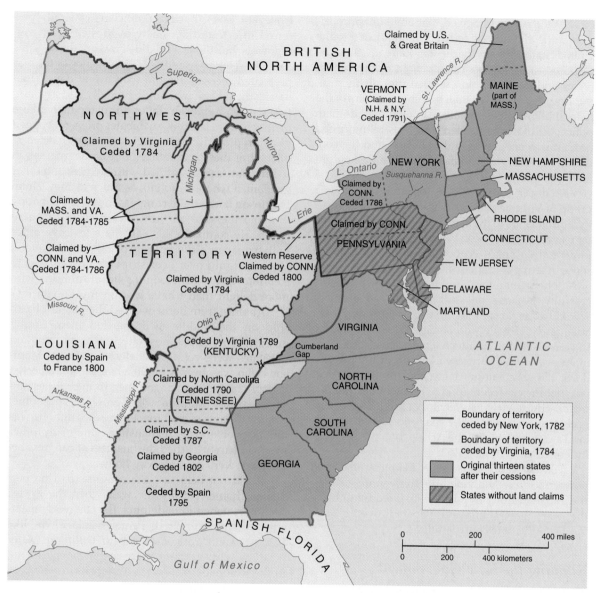

M A P 8.1

Cession of Western Lands, 1782–1802

The thirteen new states found it hard to ratify the Articles of Confederation without settling their conflicting land claims in the west, an area larger than the original states and occupied by Indian tribes.

islators, for example, protested the unfairness of allowing Virginia a wealth of unsettled land. With it, Virginia would easily meet its financial obligations to the confederated government through land sales, while states like Maryland had no alternative to painful taxation of its citizens.

The other eight states were ready to sign the Articles of Confederation as approved by the congress. Rhode Island, Pennsylvania, and New Jersey finally capitulated and signed, "not from a Conviction of the Equality and Justness of it," said a New Jersey delegate, "but merely from an absolute Necessity there was of complying to save the Continent." But Delaware and Maryland continued to hold out for many months, insisting on a national domain policy. In a compromise move, near the end of 1779 the congress agreed that any "unappropriated lands that may be ceded or relinquished to the United States, by any particular state, . . . shall be disposed of for the common benefit of the United States and be settled and formed into distinct Republican States, which shall become members of the federal union." Here finally was a national domain policy; all that was needed now was relinquished land. It was enough to pull Delaware into the confederation; Maryland remained the single holdout for more than a year.

Finally, in early 1781, the logjam broke when a group of Virginians led by Thomas Jefferson agreed to cede all lands to the confederation except the area that later became West Virginia. The compromise undercut Virginia's economic interests but made sense in terms of republican principles. Such a large area, Jefferson argued, could not be governed successfully because the seat of state government would be too far from its citizens to represent them adequately. Not all Marylanders were pleased, for the offer failed to acknowledge the claims of speculators who had purchased land from Indians. Indeed, the speculators' claims took so long to sort out that the confederation government did not formally acquire Virginia's territory until 1784. But Virginia's offer removed the main obstacle to Maryland's ratification, and the Articles at long last went into effect in February 1781.

The western lands issue demonstrated that powerful interests divided the thirteen new states; the apparent unity of purpose inspired by fighting the war against England papered over sizable cracks in the new confederation.

Running the New Government

No fanfare greeted the long-awaited inauguration of the new government. The congress continued to sputter along, its problems far from solved by the signing of the Articles. Day-to-day activities were often hampered by the lack of a quorum. The Articles required representation from seven states to conduct business, with a minimum of two men for each state's delegation. But some days fewer than fourteen men showed up.

State legislatures were slow to select delegates; those appointed were often reluctant to attend. (James Warren of Massachusetts, Mercy's husband, was chosen twice by his state to be a delegate, yet he failed to show up for even one session.) The confederation congress at times seemed deadlocked or

irrelevant, and so active politicians generally preferred to devote their energies to their state governments. For those who did show up, the sessions could be seemingly endless. The urgency of the war prevented recess for more than a few days; what breaks there were came unexpectedly and involuntarily, when a quorum failed to materialize. Many members were lawyers, so debates often got bogged down in procedural intricacies. One delegate complained of the "time it takes to transact matters in so large an Assembly filled with lawyers and other gentlemen who love to talk as much as they." John Dickinson had left the congress in July 1776, happy to avoid the vote on the Declaration of Independence. He compared his eagerness to leave office with the eagerness of a groom on his wedding night: "No youthful Lover ever stript off his Cloathes to step into Bed to his blooming beautiful bride with more delight than I have cast off my Popularity."

Absence from home worked the greatest hardship on the middle-aged married men. Consequently, some of the most effective and committed delegates were young bachelors like James Madison, who was twenty-eight when he was selected to serve from Virginia, and men in their fifties and sixties whose families were grown, like Samuel Adams. Adams served for seven years until he was finally overcome by exhaustion. But many other men had barely learned the business of congress before they were on their way home.

It did not help that the congress had no permanent home. During the war, when the British army threatened Philadelphia, the congress repeatedly relocated, to small Pennsylvania towns like Lancaster and York and then to Baltimore. After hostilities ceased, the congress still moved about, from Trenton to Princeton to Annapolis to New York City, seeking a congenial home base.

To address the inherent difficulties of an inefficient congress with long-winded delegates and rapid turnover, some members advanced the idea of a standing committee system. Executive boards of war, finance, and foreign affairs were created to handle the purely administrative functions of government, but still the congress got bogged down in tedious details. A major reorganization in 1781 created executive departments run by secretaries. When the secretaries were ambitious—as was Robert Morris, a wealthy Philadelphia merchant who served as superintendent of finance—they could exercise considerable executive power. The Articles of Confederation had deliberately refrained from setting up an executive branch, but a modest one was being invented by necessity.

Because of the pressing needs of running a war machine, the confederation government got a slow start on writing its justifying document, the Articles. Then the difficulties over the ownership of western lands slowed down ratification for years. By the time the Articles were fully functioning, yet another problem emerged. Much more exciting political work was going on at the state level, especially during the creative burst of state constitution–writing in the late 1770s. Before 1776, the cream of political talent in the country was attracted to the Continental Congress, but between 1776 and 1780 the talent flowed to the state governments.

The Sovereign States

In the first decade of independence, the states were sovereign and all-powerful. Only a few functions, like that of declaring war and peace, had been transferred to the confederation government. Familiar and close to home, state governments claimed the allegiance of their citizens. As Americans discarded their English identity, they thought of themselves instead as Virginians or New Yorkers or Pennsylvanians. Few people, even among the wealthy, traveled far from home, so their primary affiliation was local. State government was thus the arena where the Revolution's innovations would first be tried.

The State Constitutions

Unlike the Continental Congress, almost every state legislature made it a top priority to pass a written constitution without delay. In May 1776, the congress in Philadelphia recommended that all the states draw up constitutions based on "the authority of the people." By 1778, ten of the thirteen states had produced documents spelling out the liberties, rights, and obligations of citizens and rulers. Two more states, Connecticut and Rhode Island, simply adopted and updated their original colonial charters.

The idea of a written constitution laying out the powers and duties of government was essentially new. When the British invoked their own ancient and venerable constitution, they were referring to a collection of traditions, customs, and privileges, nowhere written down. Americans felt they had

been injured by the unwritten nature of British traditions; liberties they had assumed they were entitled to had been denied them. They wanted a written contract whose basic principles could not be easily altered by the particular government in power at the moment.

A shared feature of all the state constitutions was the conviction that government ultimately rests on the consent of the governed. Political writers in the late 1770s embraced the concept of republicanism as the underpinning of the new governments. Republicanism meant more than just the practice of popular elections and representative institutions. For some, it invoked a way of thinking about who leaders should be—ideally autonomous, virtuous, public-minded citizens who placed civic values above private interests. For others, it suggested direct democracy, delivered best by a political structure that put the fewest obstacles before the will of the people. For all, it meant that the primary end of government was to promote the people's welfare. "The word *republic*," wrote Thomas Paine, "means the *public good,* or the good of the whole, in contradistinction to the despotic form, which makes the good of the sovereign, or of one man, the only object of the government."

Widespread agreement about the virtues of republican government went hand in hand with another axiom of political theory, the idea that republics could succeed only in relatively small units. A government run for and by the people had to be near at hand, so the people could make sure their interests were being served. If a republic was too large, the people's representatives would be out of touch with their constituents—perhaps even unknown to them. It was on these grounds that Virginia was willing to give up its western land claim. Distant governments could easily become tyrannical governments; that was the lesson of the 1760s.

It followed, then, that the best form of government was the one that allowed maximum voice to the people. Nearly every state continued the colonial practice of a two-chamber assembly. Under British rule, the upper chamber had consisted of a small council of handpicked elites who helped the royal governor rule over an elected lower assembly; in contrast, the newly formed states greatly augmented the powers of the lower house. Two states, Pennsylvania and Georgia, established a unicameral, or one-house, legislature; why even bother with an upper house if its main function was to curb the lower house elected by the people?

Virtually all of the state constitutions went to great lengths to restrain and subdivide power. They severely limited the powers of the governor, identified in most people's minds with the royal governors of colonial days. Governors could no longer convene or dismiss legislatures at will, and they were stripped of veto power over legislation. They were also deprived of informal means of influence. No longer could governors make land grants, once a surefire way of buying loyalty. State constitutions devised elaborate mechanisms—such as New York's Council of Appointments—to take job patronage away from the executive. Most states also restricted the governor to a short term of office, usually one year, with limited eligibility for reelection. In fact, legislatures usually chose the governor; his very job security depended on close cooperation with that body. Little wonder that the two unicameral states, Pennsylvania and Georgia, decided to abolish the office of governor altogether.

The legislatures' lower houses were the centerpieces of the new republican governments, and most states made them very responsive to popular majorities. Annual elections and guaranteed rotation in office prevented anyone from monopolizing power; if a representative displeased his constituents, he could be out of office in a matter of months. Daily governance of the state rested with the lower house, whose most important decisions were economic. Each state was trying to finance its war effort, and each legislature had to make crucial decisions about printing, borrowing, taxing, and spending money.

Six of the state constitutions included bills of rights. These were lists of basic individual rights that governments could not abridge, not even democratic governments that expressed the voice of the majority. Virginia debated and passed the first bill of rights in June 1776, and many of the other states borrowed from it, with alterations. Its language also bears a close resemblance to the wording of the Declaration of Independence that Thomas Jefferson was composing that same June in Philadelphia: "That all men are by nature equally free and independent, and have certain inherent rights, of which, when they enter into a state of society, they cannot by any compact deprive or divest their posterity; namely, the enjoyment of life and liberty, with the means of acquiring and possessing property, and pursuing and obtaining happiness and safety." Thus life, liberty, property, and the pursuit of happiness and safety were defined as inherent rights,

along with more specific rights to freedom of speech, freedom of the press, and trial by jury.

Who Are "the People"?

When the Continental Congress called for state constitutions based on "the authority of the people," and when the Virginia bill of rights granted "all men" certain rights, who was meant by "the people"? Who exactly were the citizens of this new country, and how far did the principle of democratic government extend? Different people answered this question differently, but in the 1770s certain limits to full political participation by all Americans were widely agreed upon among the lawmakers and constitution writers.

Every state set property qualifications for voters and candidates alike. Although the precise threshold for qualifying varied from state to state, the idea prevailed everywhere that the propertied classes were the only legitimate participants in government. In nearly every state, property qualifications for public office were structured so that the highest offices—the governorship and membership in the upper house—would draw only on the richest segment of the population. In Maryland, for example, a candidate for the lower house had to own real or personal property worth £500; candidates for governor had to be worth £5,000; these were very large sums of money, restricting candidacy to the very upper stratum. Voters in Maryland had to own fifty acres of land or £30, a sum that would screen out perhaps a third of adult white males. In the most democratic state, Pennsylvania, voters and candidates alike needed only to be taxpayers—that is, to own enough property to owe taxes.

The justification for restricting political participation to property owners was so widely accepted that it rarely needed to be explained. Only property owners were presumed to possess the necessary independence of mind to make wise political choices. Are not propertyless men, asked John Adams, "too little acquainted with public affairs to form a right judgment, and too dependent upon other men to have a will of their own?" Like women and children, he reasoned, such men were dependent on others and would "talk and vote as they are directed by some man of property, who has attached their minds to his interest." Adams and others assumed that only property owners would feel a keen sense of community and thus be able to think clearly about the common interest. Besides, it did not seem right to give a propertyless man a voice in decisions to levy taxes if he was not going to be paying taxes himself.

Probably one-quarter to one-half of all adult white males were disfranchised by property qualifications, depending on the state. Not all of them took their nonvoter status quietly. One Maryland man wondered what was so special about being worth £30: "Every poor man has a life, a personal liberty, and a right to his earnings; and is in danger of being injured by government in a variety of ways." Why then restrict such a man from voting for his representatives? Others pointed out that propertyless men were fighting and dying in the Revolutionary War; surely they were expressing an active concern about politics that did not spring solely from property ownership. A company of Maryland militiamen dramatized their demand for the vote by marching on a polling place in 1776; all of them together owned less than £40, but they felt they had a right to the vote. Finally, a very few radical voices challenged the notion that owning property automatically transformed men into good citizens. Perhaps it did the opposite: The richest men might well be greedy and selfish, the worst kind of citizen. A writer in a Rhode Island newspaper in 1775 even advanced the idea that there should be an absolute legal limit on property holding, to prevent unhealthy concentrations of power, influence, and wealth.

If suffrage is brought up for debate, John Adams warned, "there will be no end of it. New claims will arise; women will demand a vote . . . and every man who has not a farthing, will demand an equal voice with any other."

But ideas like this were clearly outside the mainstream. The men who wrote the new constitutions were themselves men of property and material substance, and they viewed the Revolution as an effort to guarantee people the right to own property and to prevent unjust governments from appropriating it through taxation. John Adams urged the framers of the Massachusetts constitution not even to discuss the scope of suffrage but simply to adopt the traditional colonial property qualifications. If it is brought up for debate, he warned, "there will be

no end of it. New claims will arise; women will demand a vote; lads from twelve to twenty-one will think their rights not enough attended to; and every man who has not a farthing, will demand an equal voice with any other." Adams was astute enough to anticipate complaints about excluding women, youth, and poor men from political life, but it did not even occur to him to worry about another excluded group: slaves.

Equality and Slavery

Restrictions on political participation did not mean that propertyless people enjoyed no civil rights and liberties. The inalienable rights enumerated in the various state bills of rights were meant to apply to all individuals who had, as the Virginia bill so carefully phrased it, "enter[ed] into a state of society." No matter how poor, a free person was entitled to life, liberty, property, and freedom of conscience. Unfree people, however, were another matter.

The author of the Virginia bill of rights was George Mason, a plantation owner with 118 slaves. When he penned the sentence "all men are by nature equally free and independent," he did not have his slaves in mind. He was doubtless invoking this principle of equality to argue that Americans were the equals of the British and could not be denied the liberties of British citizens. Other members of the Virginia legislature who debated his proposed bill were less sure of the meaning of the phrase. The discussion lengthened and became heated, and one impatient member reported that "a number of absurd or unmeaning alterations have been proposed" for that one line. The difficulty, specifically, was that some feared that the words could be construed to apply to slaves. These aristocratic slaveholders were finally put at ease by the addition of the phrase specifying that rights belonged only to people who had entered civil society. As one wrote, with relief, "Slaves, not being constituent members of our society, could never pretend to any benefit from such a maxim." They let Mason's sentence remain in the Virginia constitution, smug in their faith that it could not upset their slave-based society and economy.

One month later, the Declaration of Independence used essentially the same phrase about equality in its preamble, this time without the modifying clause about entering society. Most white people probably assumed, like Mason, that it referred to a comparison of American and British citizens. Two state constitutions also included the inspiring language about equality, again without modifying or limiting it as in Virginia. One was Pennsylvania, whose constitution drafters embraced some of the most radical thoughts about democracy and politics. The other was Massachusetts, whose framers were more cautious and ambivalent. In Massachusetts, debate on the meaning of equality filtered down to the level of town meetings; Massachusetts alone had decided that, to be a truly democratic document, the state constitution needed to be ratified town by town. So ordinary citizens had the opportunity to comment on the meaning of the sentence "All men are born free and equal." One town, Hardwick, sent back the suggestion that the sentence be reworded to read "All men, whites and blacks, are born free and equal." The suggestion fell on deaf ears.

The only other state to include language about equality in its constitution was Vermont, whose 1777 constitution explicitly made slavery illegal and based its logic on the equality phrase. (Vermont had almost no slaves within its borders. Its statehood was not recognized until 1791 because New York and New Hampshire, each of whom claimed the Vermont land as its own, had many friends in the Continental Congress.) This reluctance to adopt the phrase in state bills of rights and constitutions probably means that after 1776, its radical implications for domestic institutions, however unanticipated and unwelcomed, were being recognized.

Nevertheless, the ideals of the Revolution— natural equality, rights to life and liberty, republicanism—began to eat away at the institution of slavery. In some cases, enslaved blacks themselves challenged their legal status. In 1777, some Massachusetts slaves petitioned the state legislature, claiming a "natural & unalienable right to that freedom which the great Parent of the Universe hath bestowed equally on all mankind." They modestly asked for freedom for their children at age twenty-one and were turned down. In 1779, similar petitions in Connecticut and New Hampshire met with no success. Seven Massachusetts freemen, including the mariner brothers Paul and John Cuffe, refused to pay taxes for three years on the grounds that they could not vote and so were not represented. The Cuffe brothers landed in jail in 1780 for tax evasion, but their petition to the state legislature spurred the extension of suffrage to taxpaying free blacks in that state.

Another way to bring the issue before the lawmakers was to sue in court. In 1781, a Massachu-

PAUL CUFFE'S SILHOUETTE
Captain Paul Cuffe of Martha's Vineyard, off the Massachusetts coast, was the son of a Wampanoag Indian woman and an African father who had purchased his own freedom from a Quaker owner. Cuffe studied navigation and went to sea at age sixteen during the American Revolution (enduring several months of capture by the British). After the war, he and his brother petitioned for tax relief, a move that foreshadowed Cuffe's life of dedication to racial questions. In his thirty-year career as shipbuilder and master mariner, Captain Cuffe traveled extensively. By 1812, when this engraving with silhouette was made, Cuffe had explored the African country of Sierra Leone as a possible site for resettlement of American blacks and had met with African kings, English dukes, and an American president.
Library of Congress.

setts black man named Quok Walker ran away from his master, who pursued and beat him. Walker pressed charges for assault and battery, and his lawyers argued in court that he was in fact a free man, given the assertion in the Massachusetts constitution that "all men are born free and equal." Walker won the assault case and was set free, a decision confirmed in an appeal to the state's superior court in 1783. Several similar court cases followed, and by 1789 judges agreed that slavery had indeed been abolished by judicial decision in Massachusetts.

Pennsylvania was the first state to prohibit slavery by statute, in 1780. Gradual emancipation laws were passed in Rhode Island and Connecticut, in 1784; New York and New Jersey passed such laws in 1785 and 1786, respectively. Gradual emancipation illustrates the tension between radical and conservative implications of republican ideology. Republican government was designed to protect

people's liberties and property; yet slaves were both people and property. Gradual emancipation balanced the civil rights of blacks and the property rights of their owners by delaying the promise of freedom. Most such laws declared that children born after a certain date would be free at a particular age, usually twenty-one or twenty-eight.

In the Upper South—Maryland and Virginia—general emancipation bills were debated and defeated. Slavery was too deeply entrenched and too important to the economy to abolish. However, legal restrictions were eased on individual acts of emancipation, under new manumission laws that governed private grants of freedom. Virginia's law passed in 1782, and two years later the number of free blacks in the state had doubled. Clearly, a significant number of white Virginians were struggling to square their consciences with revolutionary ideals. By 1790, close to ten thousand Virginia slaves had been freed under this law. Most remained in Virginia and formed free black communities complete with schools and churches, a visible alternative to the system of slavery.

Every state from Pennsylvania northward acknowledged that the enslavement of blacks was fundamentally inconsistent with revolutionary ideology; "all men are created equal" was beginning to acquire real force as a basic principle.

Lawmakers in the Carolinas and Georgia never discussed liberalizing manumission, let alone emancipation. Freedom for slaves was unthinkable for Deep South whites. Yet more than ten thousand slaves from South Carolina—more than in all the northern states combined—achieved immediate freedom in 1783 by leaving with the British army from Charleston, and another six thousand set sail under the British flag from Savannah, Georgia. In sheer numbers alone, this was by far the largest emancipation of blacks in the entire country. Some went to Canada, some to England, and a small number relocated in the 1790s to Sierra Leone, on the west coast of Africa. Another three thousand made a similar escape with the British from New York. In both Charleston and New York, the British were extremely legalistic about who was entitled to go. Slaves belonging to loyalists were refused passage, as were slaves who had escaped from a master who happened to live within the British lines. The British intent in promising freedom during the war to some blacks was to inconvenience the enemy, not to liberate black men and women. This distinction tripped up a woman named Mercy, who fled her patriot owner in Westchester County, New York, only to be denied passage out of Manhattan with the British because her county had been held by the British since 1776.

Legal emancipation affected fewer blacks in the North, simply because there were fewer of them to begin with. Nevertheless, the symbolic importance of the North's gradual emancipation was enormous. Every state from Pennsylvania northward acknowledged that the enslavement of blacks was fundamentally inconsistent with revolutionary ideology; "all men are created equal" was beginning to acquire real force as a basic principle. On some level, southerners also understood this, but their inability to imagine a free biracial society prevented them from taking action. George Washington owned 390 slaves and freed not one of them in the 1780s, even when his friend the French general Lafayette urged him to do so as a model for others. (When Washington lived in Philadelphia as president in the 1790s, he brought house slaves with him, but he carefully rotated them back to Virginia to prevent any from remaining long enough to qualify as legal residents of a free state.) In his will, Washington provided for the eventual freedom of his slaves —but only after his wife, Martha, died. From the 1780s on, the North was associated with freedom and the South with slavery. This geographical pattern would have profound consequences for the next two centuries of American history.

All the states individually created constitutions and had them in place before the confederation ratified its Articles. Citizens looked primarily to their states for the blessings of liberty, for the right to self-rule, and for most government functions that affected their lives. The sharp variations that emerged in the state constitutions reflected a wide range of interpretations of republicanism. The differences—in voting rights, in slavery—did not cause much difficulty under the loose confederation government.

The Critical Period

Historians often refer to the years from 1781 to 1788 as "the critical period." A sense of crisis indeed gripped some—but not all—of the revolutionary leaders when they contemplated the inadequacies of the Articles of Confederation. The confederation government had been purposely constructed to be weak and secondary to state governments, but there were dangers in such weakness. Other leaders defended the weak Articles as the best guarantee of individual liberty, because the real issues of governance then were dealt with at the state level, closer to the people's inspection. Political theorizing about the proper relation among citizen, state, and confederation remained active and controversial throughout the decade as the new government confronted questions of finance, territorial expansion, and civil disorder.

Financial Chaos and Paper Money

Seven years of war produced a booming but chaotic economy in the 1780s. The confederation and the individual states had run up huge war debts, financed by printing paper money and borrowing from private sources. Some $400 to $500 million in paper currency had been injected into the economy, and prices and wages fluctuated wildly. Private debt and rapid expenditure flourished; why save money when it is plunging in value? Newspapers of the era bemoaned the rampant spending on imported luxury items—hats, silks, laces, china, rum, tea—indulged in even by ordinary people. Instead of celebrating a rising standard of living, some political economists of the 1780s warned that the economy was headed for a disastrous fall. Ordinary families knew that trouble was on the horizon too. Private debt actions quadrupled in many localities over the prewar levels, and debtors' prisons became crowded. Twenty-eight men in the Worcester, Massachusetts, county debtors' jail complained to the court one December of their "Suffering Condition Occasioned by the Rapid Augmentation of their Number, the Smallness of the Gaol,—and the Coldness of the Weather." A serious postwar depression settled in by the mid-1780s and did not lift until the 1790s.

Capable minds disagreed about the source of the depression. Some people blamed paper money for undermining the economy through turbulent inflation. By 1781, Continental dollars had lost almost all value: It took 146 of them to buy what a dollar had bought in 1775. Several state legislatures continued to print their own currency well into the 1780s. Rhode Island, where supporters of paper money gained control of the government in 1786, passed strict legal-tender laws requiring that the state currency be accepted at full face value, which was a real boon for debtors, who were mostly farmers. Creditors, who were most often big merchants, suffered; they called the state "Rogues' Island."

The confederation government was itself in a terrible financial fix in 1781, and desperate times required desperate measures. Six years earlier, a financial wizard from Philadelphia named Robert Morris had been a delegate to the Continental Congress. Morris had single-handedly bought huge amounts of supplies and equipment for the army

RHODE ISLAND MONEY
Rhode Island's paper money in 1786 stated directly on each bill that an act passed in May by the state assembly required the acceptance of such paper for all payments at face value.
Rhode Island Historical Society.

from overseas sources, fronting the money himself out of his considerable fortune and shipping in much-needed arms from the French (still nominally neutral in the war) disguised in crates addressed to his private Philadelphia firm. Morris resigned from the congress in 1778 under a cloud of suspicion that he had unfairly profited from his public service efforts; indeed, he left public life several million dollars richer than he had entered it, and the stark contrast between his riches—advertised by his fancy carriage, opulent clothes, and swank dinner parties—and the starving troops a few miles away at Valley Forge that winter was more than some could stomach.

But in 1781, the congress needed his financial services again, and Pennsylvania obliged by select-

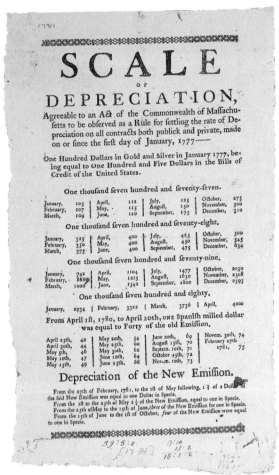

SCALE OF DEPRECIATION

This complicated chart shows the monthly value of United States Continental dollars from 1777 to February 1781, as stipulated by the government of Massachusetts. For example, in March 1780, it took $3,736 Continental dollars to equal the buying power of $100 in gold or silver, up from $3,322 the month before. Such a chart was needed when debtors and creditors settled accounts contracted at one point in time and paid off later in greatly depreciated dollars.

Courtesy, American Antiquarian Society.

ing him as a delegate to the congress. Morris accepted but made it a condition that he be allowed to pursue his private business simultaneously. From 1781 to 1784, Morris served as superintendent of finance for the confederation, applying his considerable talents to the confederation's economic problems. Not everyone was pleased. Mercy's husband, James Warren, wrote to John Adams: "Morris is a King, and more than a King. He has the Keys of the Treasury at his Command, Appropriates Money as

he pleases, and every Body must look up to him for Justice and for Favour."

Morris first sought a way to augment the revenue of the confederation government. He proposed a 5 percent impost—that is, a tax imposed on goods imported into the country. There was no authority in the Articles of Confederation for any such tax. States lucky enough to have port cities already collected their own impost, paid by the merchants who bought the duties cargoes; the merchants then passed the tax on to consumers in the form of higher prices for the goods. (Consumers in portless New Jersey, whose imported goods came through Philadelphia or New York, were thus involuntarily helping those neighbors to retire their state debt.) Morris's impost plan required a constitutional amendment to the Articles reached unanimously by the thirteen states. Despite general agreement that the financial situation of the central government was desperate, unanimous agreement proved impossible. In 1781, Morris came close, but not close enough. The states with bustling ports were reluctant to give up the right to impose their own taxes; Rhode Island, with its active wharves at Newport and Providence, absolutely refused to agree. When Morris pushed the impost amendment again in 1783, it was New York (whose premier port had just been newly freed from British occupation) that now refused.

Morris's next idea for shoring up the economy was the creation of a private bank, the Bank of North America, which would enjoy a special relationship with the confederation government. It would hold the government's hard-money deposits (insofar as there were any deposits to make) as well as private deposits, and it would make short-term loans to the government. Private investors owned the bank; specifically, Morris and three close friends bought 40 percent of the bank stock, and Morris also controlled the sizable chunk of stock held by the confederation government. The bank's contribution to economic stability came in the form of banknotes, pieces of paper inscribed with a dollar value. The fundamental difference between banknotes and paper money was that the banknotes were to be backed by hard money in the bank's vaults; thus, they would not depreciate. Morris invited any holder of a banknote to visit the bank and claim the hard money. In fact, however, more banknotes were issued than there was hard money; Morris was counting on the probability that relatively few people would test his claim—it was enough that people had confidence it was true. Morris hoped that the new circulating medium of banknotes would perform the functions of paper money without any of its drawbacks. Congress agreed and voted to approve the bank in 1781.

The Bank of North America, located in Philadelphia, had limited success curing the confederation's economic woes. In the short run, the bank supplied the government with a currency that held its value, but it issued so little that the impact remained very small. The bank enriched Morris and his associates and made enemies among other financial interests in Philadelphia; when its charter expired in 1786, the state of Pennsylvania refused to renew it. By that time, Morris was out of the Continental Congress because of a three-year limit for holding office. Morris continued to be active in politics well into the 1790s, but he lost all his wealth in a complete financial reversal and ended his career in debtors' prison.

If Morris could not resuscitate the economy in the 1780s, probably no one could have. Because the Articles of Confederation reserved most economic functions to the states, congress was helpless to tax trade, control inflation, curb the flow of state-issued paper money, or pay the mounting public debt. But the confederation had acquired one source of potential enormous wealth: the huge territory ceded by Virginia, which in 1784 became the national domain.

Land Ordinances and the Northwest Territory

The Continental Congress appointed Thomas Jefferson to draft a policy for handling the national domain. Jefferson embraced this task as an unparalleled opportunity to embed an extravagant version of revolutionary ideals, highlighting rationalism and economic democracy, into the permanent landscape of America. He proposed dividing the territory north of the Ohio River and east of the Mississippi—called the Northwest Territory—into ten new states. Each state would be subdivided into townships ten miles square, and each township would consist of one hundred sections one mile square. Jefferson became so enamored of his decimal-based brainchild that he even proposed to lengthen the mile to make one square mile equal to 1,000 acres; the traditional square mile contains 640 acres.

Three other features of Jefferson's proposal illustrate how innovative this precision-minded, scientific intellectual from Virginia could be. First, he

THOMAS JEFFERSON
This miniature shows Thomas Jefferson at age forty-five, during his years as a diplomat in Paris. The American artist John Trumbull visited France in 1788 and painted Jefferson's likeness in this five-by-four-inch format so he could later copy it into his planned large canvas depicting the signing of the Declaration of Independence. Jefferson requested three replicas of the miniature to bestow as gifts, a common and intimate item of exchange. One went to his daughter Martha, another to an American woman in London, and the third to Maria Cosway, a British artist of whom the widower Jefferson had grown very fond during his stay in France.
Monticello.

advocated giving the land to settlers, rather than selling it, on the grounds that the improved lands would so enrich the country through property taxes over the years that there was no need to make the settlers contribute to the government's coffers twice. His aim was to encourage rapid and democratic settlement of the land, to build a nation of freeholders (as opposed to renters), and to avoid speculative frenzy. Second, Jefferson insisted that the new states have representative governments enjoying equal

JEFFERSON'S MAP OF THE NORTHWEST TERRITORY
Thomas Jefferson sketched out borders for ten new states in his initial plan for the Northwest Territory in 1784. Straight lines and right angles held a strong appeal for him. But such regularity ignored inconvenient geographical features like rivers and even more inconvenient political features like Indian territorial claims, most unlikely to be ceded by treaty in orderly blocks of land. Jefferson also submitted ten distinctive names for the states. Number 9, for example, was Polypotamia, or "land of many rivers" in Greek.
William L. Clements Library.

status with the original states once they reached a certain minimum population. The United States had freed itself from a colonial empire, and Jefferson did not want the new nation to become a colonial power itself. Finally, Jefferson's draft prohibited slavery and involuntary servitude from all of the ten new states.

The congress cheerfully adopted parts of Jefferson's plan in the Ordinance of 1784: the rectangular grid, the decimal mile, and the ten states, which Jefferson proposed naming Sylvania, Michi-

gania, Cherronesus, Assenisipia, Metropotamia, Illinoia, Washington, Saratoga, Polypotamia, and Pelisipia. (The congress's 1784 legislation simply ignored the names, a telling reminder that Thomas Jefferson's suggestions were sometimes rejected.) The congress accepted the guarantee of self-government and equality with the original states, although there was some grumbling about wild frontiersmen who perhaps were not worthy of self-government. What the congress found too radical to swallow was the proposal to give away the land;

MAP 8.2

The Northwest Territory and Ordinance of 1785

Surveyors mapping the eastern edge of the Northwest Territory followed the Land Ordinance of 1785, using the stars as well as polls and chains (standard surveying equipment) to run long boundary lines. The result was a blanket of six-mile square townships, further subdivided into one-mile squares containing sixteen forty-acre farms.

the national domain was the confederated government's only source of independent wealth. And the slavery prohibition failed to be included by only one state's vote.

A year later, the congress reconsidered the land act and passed a new version, called the Ordinance

of 1785. The decimal theme and the stretched-out mile, though intellectually elegant, were too impractical. The new plan called for walkable townships six miles square, each containing thirty-six sections; a one-mile section was once again 640 acres, and a quarter section offered an adequate-sized farm of 160 acres. One lot in each township was set aside for educational purposes. The 1785 ordinance also revised Jefferson's plan for ten neatly rectangular states, after it was noticed that some would have no river access at all, a disastrous disadvantage. The new ordinance called for three to five states whose boundaries would conform to natural geographical features like the Great Lakes and major rivers instead of abstractly drawn survey lines.

Imposing a relentlessly regular township grid on the irregular hills, valleys, rivers, and lakes of the Northwest Territory created more solvable problems. Though even in size, the land squares were not all equally valuable. How should they be priced for sale? The 1785 ordinance established land offices to sell the land at public auction; the minimum price was $1 an acre, but the auction mechanism allowed for market forces to drive up the prices of the most desirable land. Two further restrictions applied: Land was sold in minimum parcels of 640 acres each, and payment had to be in hard money or in certificates of debt issued by the confederation government.

To join in the land boom, a purchaser thus had to have at least 640 hard dollars or an equivalent amount in debt certificates. These certificates had largely passed out of the hands of the original holders, such as farmers who had sold food to the Continental army in exchange for the IOUs. Like every other currency substitute in the war years, debt certificates had been circulated, depreciated, and purchased by speculators at a small fraction of their face value. The speculators tended to be wealthy easterners who could afford to tie up a modest sum of money in the depreciated certificates, taking the risk that they would plummet to worthlessness — or somehow suddenly be worth a handsome amount. The Land Ordinance of 1785 made good their bet.

Even before the land was surveyed, the congress, gravely in need of revenue, sold one and a half million acres to a group of investors called the Ohio Company. Speculators who rushed to purchase usually had no intention of settling on the land themselves but were holding it for subsequent resale. They could thus avoid direct contact with the most serious obstacle to speedy settlement of the Northwest Territory: the dozens of Indian tribes that occupied the land. Treaties signed at Fort Stanwix in 1784 and Fort McIntosh in 1785 coerced partial cessions of land from Iroquois, Delaware, Huron, and Miami tribes, but a united Indian meeting near

Detroit in 1786 issued an ultimatum: No cession would be valid without unanimous consent. The Indians advised the United States to "prevent your surveyors and other people from coming upon our side of the Ohio river" — precisely the land claimed as the new national domain. For two more decades, violent and terrible Indian wars in Ohio and Indiana would continue to impede settlement, as the nation struggled to find an Indian policy consistent with the drive to cash in on the wealth of the national domain.

In 1787, a third land act, called the Northwest Ordinance, confirmed the promise of eventual self-government when the white male population reached five thousand, but it devised an interim plan for sparsely settled territories with a congressionally appointed governor. The other landmark feature of the 1787 act was a prohibition on slavery in the entire region, which this time passed without any debate. For the first time, the confederation government presumed to dictate the domestic institutions of a part of the United States. The congress would not have dreamed of applying a similar prohibition to an existing state, but nothing in the Articles restricted the congress's power over new territories not yet states. Something less than a fervent antislavery sentiment was at work in the passage of this provision, as shown by an accompanying warning that fugitive slaves escaping into the Northwest Territory could be caught and returned to their lawful owners. And the prohibition applied only to the area north of the Ohio River; plenty of territory south of the river and west of Georgia was still available for the spread of slavery. The congress was evidently less interested in curbing slavery than in discouraging blacks from coming to the Northwest Territory. Still, the prohibition on slavery in the Northwest Territory perpetuated the dynamic of gradual emancipation in the North: A North-South sectionalism, based on slavery, was slowly taking shape.

Shays's Rebellion

Without an impost amendment, the confederation turned to the states to contribute revenue voluntarily. The states were struggling with their own war debts; since heavy taxation tends to create disgruntled constituents, some legislatures were hesitant to push too hard. There were some who favored heavy taxation: The holders of the public debt certificates wanted to be paid, and wealthy people in general hoped taxation would counteract the alarming depreciation of paper money that was eroding their net worth. But the vast majority of ordinary Americans preferred low taxes, cheap money, easy credit, and stay laws (laws restraining creditors from foreclosing on debtors). And popularly elected representatives, facing annual elections, liked to give people what they wanted.

Western farmers had learned from their experience in the American Revolution how to respond to oppressive taxation.

Massachusetts, however, had a tough-minded, fiscally conservative upper house with veto power over its lower house. The upper house, dominated by the commercial centers of eastern Massachusetts, vetoed the cheap-money legislation the lower house tried to pass. Its goal was to retire the state debt by raising taxes; to make matters worse, the upper house insisted that taxes be paid in hard money, not cheap paper. Farmers in the western half of the state found such taxes nearly impossible to pay, and by 1786 sheriffs routinely descended on tax delinquents to confiscate their salable property (such as livestock), foreclose on their real estate, and ultimately throw them in jail.

However, the western farmers had learned from their experience in the American Revolution how to respond to oppressive taxation. They called conventions to discuss their grievances and circulated petitions demanding tax reductions and debt relief legislation. At least eight towns called for the abolition of the profession of law, since sharp lawyers seemed to be lurking everywhere, handling foreclosure and jailing proceedings as well as dominating the legislature. As more and more defaulting taxpayers were hauled into court for nonpayment, groups of men marched on the county courthouses to shut them down. In the fall of 1786, armed men threatened the courts in three western Massachusetts counties. The leader of this tax revolt was a farmer and onetime captain in the Continental army, Daniel Shays; about 2,500 other men joined him in arms, while many more attended the town conventions and cheered the Shaysites from the sidelines.

The governor of Massachusetts, James Bowdoin, who had once organized protests against British taxes, did not hesitate now to characterize the Shaysites as illegal rebels and to call out the militia. Another former rebel, Samuel Adams, took the

lead in defining the protest movement as a treasonous rebellion: "County conventions and popular committees served an excellent purpose when they were first in practice," he wrote. "But as we now have constitutional and regular governments and all our men in authority depend upon the annual and free elections of the people, we are safe without them." Safe without them—and apparently unsafe with them, for Adams took the extreme position that "the man who dares rebel against the laws of a republic ought to suffer death."

Why did the protesting farmers so upset the aging tax protesters of an earlier era? The Shaysites were a threat to men like Adams and Bowdoin because their very existence challenged the idea that popularly elected governments would always be fair and just. The revolutionary generation, and particularly its most democratically inclined members, had given little thought to the possibility that popular majorities, embodied in a state legislature, could be oppressive, just as monarchs could. The farmers now felt they were an oppressed minority in Massachusetts with no hope of altering the composition of the state legislature (especially given its dominance by the eastern seaboard population cen-

SILVER BOWL FOR ANTI-SHAYS GENERAL
The militia of Springfield in western Massachusetts presented its leader, General William Shepard, with this silver bowl to honor his victory over the insurgents in Shays's Rebellion. Presentational silver conveyed a double message. It announced gratitude and praise in engraved words, and it transmitted considerable monetary value in the silver itself. General Shepard could display his trophy on a shelf, use it as a punch bowl, will it to descendants to keep his famous moment alive in memory, or melt it down in hard times. Not only is Shepard's name commemorated on the silver; SHAYS too appears in the last line, there for the ages to remember.
Yale University Art Gallery, Mabel Brady Garvan Collection.

ters). Adams's advice that they wait patiently until the next election did not begin to give them hope.

Bowdoin sent more than four thousand soldiers to quell the rebellion, paying them with money raised quickly and privately among worried eastern seaboard merchants. The militia met the protesters at Springfield in January 1787 and dispersed the ragtag dissidents back to their homes. The leaders fled the state, but more than a thousand men were rounded up and thrown in jail. The legislature passed the Disqualifying Act prohibiting the rebels from ever again voting, holding public office, working as schoolmasters, or operating taverns. The first two prohibitions denied the men a political voice, and the second two denied them occupations in which they could instruct or influence others.

Samuel Adams's absolute faith in republican institutions made him recoil from the Shaysites; men from the opposite and more conservative side of the political spectrum recoiled for very different reasons. The men of wealth who chipped in to pay for the militia worried that a dangerous leveling influence was at work. In Massachusetts and throughout the country, men who were already worried that the confederation might fail to hold together speculated about what Shays's Rebellion portended. Perhaps there were similar "combustibles" in other states, awaiting the spark that would set off a dreadful political conflagration. Lawyer and diplomat John Jay in New York wrote to George Washington, "Our affairs seem to lead to some crisis, some revolution—something I cannot foresee or conjecture. I am uneasy and apprehensive; more so than during the war." Planter Charles Pinckney of South Carolina characterized the threat as one of "anarchy—or what's worse, pure democracy." For such men, it was entirely possible to be a supporter of republican government and still disdain a democracy based on majority rule. Benjamin Franklin, in his eighties, shrewdly observed that in 1776 Americans had feared "an excess of power in the rulers," whereas now the problem was "a defect of obedience" in the subjects. A merchant in Philadelphia saw more ominous implications in the fears inspired by domestic insurrection: "A Convulsion of some kind seems to be desirable," he wrote, for it is "the only chance we have of restoration to political health."

The years of unstable finances were of course directly related to the cause of Shays's Rebellion. Rigid efforts to pay off a state debt, in an economy already hit with the burdens of a precarious currency, had ignited a spark of tax rebellion again, producing an ironic predicament for old rebels now taking a hard line against civil disorder. To some, the sense of crisis in the confederation had greatly deepened.

The Federal Constitution

Events in the fall of 1786 provoked an odd mixture of fear and hope that the government under the Articles of Confederation was losing its grip on power. Efforts to augment the financial powers of the government had nearly ground to a halt, and some people worried that the country would have to hit bottom before fully realizing the crisis it was in. A small circle of Virginians decided to try one last time to augment the powers of the Articles. Their call for a meeting to discuss trade regulation led, more quickly than they could have imagined in 1786, to a total reworking of the national government.

From Annapolis to Philadelphia

The Virginians took their lead from James Madison, now thirty-five years old and still a bachelor with time on his hands. Madison was the eldest son of a wealthy planter from the Piedmont region of Virginia. A Princeton graduate, bookish and solitary by nature, Madison was a bright and avid student of politics. He entered active political life as a member of Virginia's extralegal assembly in 1776 and found that it suited him; by 1779, he had been chosen to represent his state at the Continental Congress. His father's money and his lack of dependents freed him from the obligations that made other delegates yearn to get back to private life. After four diligent years in the congress, he returned to the Virginia assembly, where he tried hard to secure his state's cooperation in keeping the Confederation afloat.

Madison's strategy was to prompt the states to consider a relatively modest modification of the Articles, giving the congress power to regulate trade. He persuaded the Virginia legislature to call for a meeting of the states, bypassing the confederation's congress. Even if unsuccessful, such a meeting would establish a precedent for new pathways to alter the Articles. State legislatures were invited to send representatives to the meeting, set for Annapolis, Maryland, in September 1786.

JAMES MADISON,
PORTRAIT BY CHARLES WILLSON PEALE
This miniature portrait was made of James Madison in
1783 when he was in his early thirties. The natural hair
and smooth face emphasized his youthful looks.
Library of Congress.

New Jersey and then King's College (soon renamed Columbia College) in New York City. Hamilton was nineteen when the Continental army swept through in 1776, and the youth joined General Washington's staff and served at the great man's side through much of the Revolution. After the war, Hamilton studied law, married into a wealthy New York mercantile family, and sat in the Continental Congress for two years. Despite his stigmatized childhood, he identified fully with the elite classes and their fear of democratic disorder.

Support for Hamilton's expanded agenda for the Philadelphia meeting was augmented by the urgent crisis unfolding that fall in Massachusetts, Shays's Rebellion. Some states worried that the confederated government lacked authority to quell domestic rebellions and so welcomed major revisions to the Articles. Others worried about the dangers of major revisions and so sent representatives to scuttle revisionist efforts. The ambitious scope of the Hamilton agenda thus ensured a good turnout of delegates. States that could ignore a pesky proposal on trade regulation could not afford to ignore this meeting. After five months, the congress of the confederation government reluctantly endorsed the Philadelphia meeting, limiting the agenda to "the sole and express purpose of revising the Articles of Confederation."

It took more than a week for a quorum to assemble in Philadelphia. Meanwhile, Madison and the other Virginians settled into lodging houses and used the time to draw up a fifteen-point plan for a completely restructured federal government. They intended to seize the initiative at the convention and keep it.

The fifty-five men who assembled at Philadelphia that spring to consider the shortcomings of the Articles of Confederation were by no means a representative cross section of Americans, or even of the political leadership of the states. They were generally those most concerned about weaknesses in the present government. Alexander Hamilton, for example, lobbied to be a delegate to Philadelphia; the New York legislature warily sent him, but in the company of two firm opponents of fundamental revisions to the Articles, so that his vote would not carry the delegation. In general, however, few attended who were unalterably opposed to revising the Articles. Patrick Henry, author of the Virginia Resolves in 1765 and more recently the governor of his state, refused to go, saying he "smelled a rat." Rhode Island, ever the odd state out in the 1780s,

Only five of the nine states that agreed to participate actually sent representatives. Like Madison, the dozen men who attended were deeply troubled by a sense of impending crisis. They decided to reschedule the meeting for Philadelphia in May 1787, again inviting the state legislatures to reappoint representatives. One representative, lawyer Alexander Hamilton of New York, defined the agenda of the meeting much more ambitiously: "to devise such further provisions as shall appear to them necessary to render the constitution of the Federal Government adequate to the exigencies of the Union."

Alexander Hamilton by character was suited for such bold steps. Only thirty years old, he had risen far and fast through a series of bold undertakings. The bright son of a struggling single mother on a small West Indies island, Hamilton at age sixteen impressed an American trader, who rescued him from obscurity and sent him to school first in

THE PENNSYLVANIA STATEHOUSE
The Constitutional Convention assembled at the Pennsylvania statehouse to sweat out the summer of 1787 with the windows tightly closed. Built in the 1740s to house the colony's assembly, the statehouse accommodated the Continental Congress at various times in the 1770s and 1780s. The building is now called Independence Hall, in honor of the signing of the Declaration of Independence within its walls in 1776.
Free Library of Philadelphia.

refused to send any delegates at all. The two New Yorkers sent to neutralize Hamilton went home in the middle of the convention because they did not like what was happening. The men who stayed to work over the summer of 1787 shared a sense of crisis about weaknesses in the confederation government and a willingness to take bold steps.

There were no artisans or day laborers at this gathering of white men, or even farmers of middling wealth. Two-thirds of the delegates were lawyers. The majority had served in the Continental Congress and were intimately familiar with the workings and deficiencies of that government. Fully half had been officers in the Continental army during the war, and their experiences gave them a practical perspective on the financial difficulties faced by the confederation government. Seven men had

been governors of their states and knew firsthand the frustrations of thwarted executive power. A few august elder statesmen like Benjamin Franklin attended; but on the whole, the delegates were young, like Madison. George Washington, sent by Virginia to lend solidity, respectability, and integrity to its delegation, was promptly elected to preside over the convention, but the venerable general rarely participated in the debates.

The Virginia and New Jersey Plans

The convention pursued its work under a cloak of secrecy, so the men could freely explore alternatives without fear that their honest opinions could come back to haunt them. They even nailed the windows of the State House shut, to eliminate the chance of being heard by eavesdroppers. With quiet understatement, Mercy Otis Warren evaluated the public reaction to the news blackout: "It was thought by some, that the greatest happiness of the greatest number was not the principal object of their contemplations, when they ordered their doors to be locked, their members inhibited from all communications abroad, and when proposals were made that their journals should be burnt, lest their consultations and debates be viewed by the scrutinizing eye of a free people."

The Virginia delegation seized the initiative and laid out the Virginia Plan, a radical departure from the Articles and a total repudiation of the principle of a confederation of states. Although it was largely the work of Madison, a taller and more prepossessing Virginian, Edmund Randolph, made the presentation. The plan set out a three-branch government composed of a two-chamber legislature, a powerful executive, and a judiciary. It virtually eliminated the voices of the smaller states by pegging representation in both houses of the congress to population. The theory was that government operated directly on people, not on states. Further bad news for state governments lay in the breathtaking powers assigned to the congress, including the rights to veto state legislation, to coerce states militarily to obey national laws, and to legislate "in all cases to which the separate States are incompetent," however that might be defined. The congress would not be absolutely powerful in Madison's proposal; the executive and judiciary could jointly veto the actions of the congress.

It took time for the opponents of the Virginia Plan to discover their alliances and coordinate their efforts. Each night for two weeks, delegates from New Jersey, Connecticut, Delaware, and New Hampshire, all small states, met in their lodging rooms to share alarm over the eclipse of state power and to fashion an alternative proposal. By mid-June, they were ready to unveil it, and they chose William Paterson of New Jersey—at four foot eleven someone even the five foot one Madison could look down on—to present it.

The New Jersey Plan resembled the existing Articles of Confederation structure in that it set out a single-house congress in which each state would have one vote. Acknowledging the need for an executive, it created a plural presidency to be shared by three men elected by the congress from among its membership. Where it sharply departed from the existing government was in the sweeping powers it gave to the congress: the right to tax (using impost

and stamp taxes), to regulate trade, and to use force on unruly state governments. In favoring national power over states' rights, it aligned itself with the Virginia Plan. But the New Jersey Plan retained the confederation principle: The national government was to be an assembly of states, not of people.

For two weeks, the convention debated the two plans, focusing on the key issue of representation. The small-state delegates were willing to concede that one house in a two-house legislature could be apportioned by population, but they clearly would never agree that both houses could be. Madison was equally vehement about bypassing representation by state, which he viewed as the fundamental flaw in the Articles. He was convinced that the new government had to act directly on the people.

Each night for two weeks, delegates from small states met in their lodging rooms to share alarm over the eclipse of state power and to fashion an alternative proposal for a government.

The debate seemed deadlocked, and for a while the convention was "on the verge of dissolution, scarce held together by the strength of a hair," according to one delegate. Benjamin Franklin suggested the need for divine guidance and moved that clergymen be recruited to offer prayers, an idea rejected by others, who feared that such an action would unduly alarm the public.

Next, Alexander Hamilton took the floor for the better part of a day to present his own plan: a two-house legislature with upper-house members serving for life; a lifetime president who could unconditionally veto the legislature; and congressional appointment of state governors, who would have absolute veto power over state legislatures. The other delegates listened politely while Hamilton expressed deep admiration for monarchy and hinted that abolishing state governments altogether would save money. When he finished, there was no discussion of his plan whatsoever. It is unclear whether Hamilton intended what he in fact accomplished: His long-winded diversion on the splendors of regal power made the Virginia Plan look moderate and reasonable.

It took weeks, into mid-July, until the so-called Great Compromise broke the logjam and produced the basic structural features of the emerging United

States Constitution. Proponents of the competing plans pooled the plans' common features—a government with three branches and supreme power over the states—and agreed on a bicameral legislature in which the lower house, the House of Representatives, would be apportioned by population and the upper house, called the Senate, would represent each state. But instead of one vote per state in the upper house, as the New Jersey Plan favored, the compromise plan provided two senators who voted independently of each other.

Representation by population turned out to be an ambiguous concept once it was subjected to rigorous discussion. Who counted? Were slaves, for example, people or property? As people, they added weight to the southern delegations in the House of Representatives, but as property they added to the tax burdens of those states. What emerged was the remarkable compromise known as the three-fifths clause: All free persons plus "three-fifths of all other Persons" constituted the numerical base for the apportionment of representatives.

Using "all other persons" as a euphemism for slaves indicates the discomfort delegates felt in acknowledging the existence of slavery in a republican document. The words *slave* and *slavery* appear nowhere in the Constitution, but the slave labor system figured in two other places in addition to the three-fifths clause. Trade regulation, for example, a power of the new Congress, naturally included regulation of the slave trade. South Carolina and Georgia delegates wanted assurance that the slave trade would not be curbed by a coalition of northern free states combining with Maryland and Virginia, two slave states with an abundance of native-born slaves. The result was another compromise, again in euphemistic language: "The Migration or Importation of such Persons as any of the States now shall think proper to admit, shall not be prohibited by the Congress prior to the Year one thousand eight hundred and eight." A third provision on slavery guaranteed the return of fugitive slaves: "No person, held to Service or Labour in one State, under the Laws thereof, escaping into another, shall, in Consequence of any Law or Regulation therein, be discharged from such Service or Labour but shall be delivered up on Claim of the party to whom such Service or Labour may be due." Slavery was nowhere named, but it was recognized, guaranteed, and thereby perpetuated by the U.S. Constitution.

Plenty of fine-tuning followed the Great Compromise of mid-July, but the most difficult problem—that of representation—had been solved. The small states worked to consolidate power in the Senate, where their weight would be proportionately greater than in the lower house, and Madison slowly recovered from the crushing sense of defeat he experienced at first. He had entered the convention convinced that the major flaw in the old government was that it had relied on unreliable states, and he feared that the Great Compromise perpetuated that flaw. But as the respective powers of the House and Senate were hammered out, he lent his support to the package as the most reasonable of political outcomes. After the convention, he would become one of the most prominent defenders of the Constitution, Senate and all.

Democracy versus Republicanism

In deciding the crucial details of the Constitution, the delegates made a distinction between democracy and republicanism that had been absent from the political vocabulary a decade earlier. When state constitutions were written, the two words were often used interchangeably to refer to a government that rested ultimately on popular consent. At the Philadelphia convention, however, pure democracy was taken to be a dangerous thing. As a Connecticut delegate put it, "The people . . . should have as little to do as may be about the Government. They want [lack] information and are constantly liable to be misled." A Massachusetts delegate declared that "the evils we experience flow from the excess of democracy." Edmund Randolph of Virginia similarly criticized "the turbulence and follies of democracy." The delegates still claimed to favor republican institutions, but they created a government that gave direct voice to the people only in the House and that granted a check on that voice to the Senate, which would be composed of men more removed from the control of the people.

In the final document, senators held office for six years and had the privilege of unlimited reelection. They were to be elected not by direct popular vote but by the state legislatures. In a country that was itself only eleven years old, a guaranteed six years in office was a very long time. Senators were thus protected from the whims of democratic majorities; the men at Philadelphia assumed that tumultuous, fickle passion characterized democracies. Long terms also fostered experience and maturity in office. Madison and the other men who had served in the confederation congress had seen the ineptitude and inconvenience caused by the revolving door concept of public service.

Similarly, the presidency evolved during the Philadelphia convention into a powerful office out of the reach of direct democracy. The delegates devised an elaborate mechanism, called the electoral college, whose only function was to elect the president and vice president. Each state's legislature chose the electors, amounting in number to the sum of representatives and senators for each state, an interesting melding of the two principles of representation. What resulted was a president who owed his office not to the Congress, the states, or the people, but to an ephemeral body of distinguished citizens who could vote their own judgment on the candidates.

Madison's proposal to grant the new government sweeping powers in all areas where the states were incompetent was too vague to survive debate. Instead, the convention carefully listed the powers of Congress and of the president. The president could initiate policy and propose legislation; he could veto acts of Congress; he could command the military and direct the foreign policy of the country; and he could make appointments to numerous lesser executive offices and to the entire judiciary, subject only to the approval of the Senate. Congress held the purse strings: the power to levy taxes, to regulate trade, and to coin money and control the currency. States were expressly forbidden to issue paper money. Two further powers of Congress—to "provide for the common defence and general Welfare" of the country and "to make all laws which shall be necessary and proper" for carrying out the enumerated powers—provided elastic language that came closest to Madison's wish to grant sweeping powers to the new government.

The framers had developed a far more complex form of a federal government than that provided by the Articles of Confederation. In curbing the excesses of democracy, they did not assume that states and their leaders would always be virtuous and wise. They devised a government with limits and checks on all branches. They set forth a powerful president who could veto Congress, but then gave Congress power to override his vetoes. They set up a national judiciary to settle disputes between states and citizens of different states. They made each branch of government as independent from every other branch as they could, by basing election on different universes of voters—voting citizens, state legislators, the electoral college.

The Constitution was a product of lengthy debate and compromise; no one was entirely satisfied with every line. Madison himself, who was later

called the Father of the Constitution, remained unsure that the most serious flaws of the Articles had been expunged. But when the final vote was taken at the Philadelphia convention in September 1787, only three dissenters refused to endorse the Constitution. The thirty-nine who signed it (thirteen others had gone home early) no doubt wondered how to sell this plan, with its powerful executive and Congress and its deliberate limits on pure democracy, to the American public. The Constitution specified a mechanism for ratification that avoided the dilemma faced earlier by the confederation government: Nine states, not all thirteen, had to ratify it, and special ratifying conventions instead of state legislatures would make the crucial decision. The innovation of debating the Constitution in special bodies elected only for that purpose had been used once before, for the Massachusetts state constitution. It drew attention to a major theme of the proposed plan: that the national government was no longer a league of states, but a government for all the people. Equally important practical considerations motivated the choice of popular ratifying conventions: No one could expect state legislatures to cede their powers willingly to the new government, so it was convenient to bypass them entirely. But who could predict how the people, acting through the ratifying conventions, would react?

Ratification of the Constitution

Had a popular vote been taken on the Constitution in the late fall of 1787, it would probably have been rejected. In the three most populous states—Virginia, Massachusetts, and New York—substantial majorities opposed a powerful new national government. North Carolina and Rhode Island refused to call conventions. In only a few of the eight remaining states could the proponents of the Constitution count on an easy victory. To secure the agreement of nine states, they faced a formidable task.

The Federalists

The proponents of the Constitution plotted their course carefully and moved into action swiftly. To silence the charge that they had illegally bypassed the confederation government (which indeed they had, by failing to adhere to the legal procedure for

Was the New United States a Christian Country?

REBECCA SAMUEL, a Jewish resident of Virginia, conveyed her excitement about the new U.S. Constitution when she wrote her German parents in 1791 that finally "Jew and Gentile are as one" in the realm of politics and citizenship. Other voices were distinctly less favorable. An Antifederalist pamphlet warned that the pope could become president; another feared that "a Turk, a Jew, a Roman Catholic, and what is worse than all, a Universalist, may be President."

The document that produced such wildly different readings was indeed remarkable in its handling of religion. The Constitution did not invoke Christianity as a state religion. It made no reference to an almighty being, and it specifically promised, in Article 6, section 3, that "no religious test shall ever be required as a qualification to any office or public trust under the United States." The six largest congregations of Jews—numbering about two thousand and located in Newport, New York, Philadelphia, Baltimore, Charleston, and Savannah—were delighted with this nearly unprecedented statement of political equality and wrote George Washington to express their hearty thanks.

But more than a few Christian leaders were stunned at the Constitution's near silence on religion. It seemed to represent a complete turnabout from the state constitutions of the 1770s and 1780s. A New Yorker warned that, "should the Citizens of America be as irreligious as her Constitution, we will have reason to tremble, lest the Governor of the universe . . . crush us to atoms." A delegate to North Carolina's ratifying convention played on anti-immigrant fears by predicting that the Constitution was "an invitation for Jews and pagans of every kind to come among us." A concerned Presbyterian minister asked Alexander Hamilton why God was not in the Constitution, and Hamilton reportedly quipped, "Indeed, Doctor, we forgot it."

Measured against the practices of state governments, Hamilton's observation is hardly credible. The men who wrote and debated the state and federal constitutions from 1775 to 1787 actively thought about principles of inclusion and exclusion when they defined citizenship, voting rights, and office-holding. They carefully considered property ownership, race, gender, and age in formulating rules about who could participate. And they also thought about religious qualifications.

Most leaders of the 1780s took for granted that Christianity was the one true faith and the essential foundation of morality. All but two state constitutions assumed the primacy of Protestantism, and a third of them collected public taxes to support Christian churches. Every state but New York required a Christian oath as a condition for office-holding. For example, every member of Pennsylvania's legislature swore to "acknowledge the Scripture of the Old and New Testament to be given by divine inspiration." North Carolina's rule was even more restrictive, since it omitted Catholics: "No person who shall deny the being of God or the truth of the Protestant religion, or the divine authority of the Old or New Testaments" could hold office. In South Carolina all *voters* had to be Protestants.

Other common political practices affirmed that the United States was a Christian country. Governors proclaimed days of public thanksgiving in the name of the Holy Trinity; chaplains led legislatures in Christian prayer. Jurors and witnesses in court swore to Christian oaths. New England states passed Sabbath laws prohibiting all work or travel on Sunday. Blasphemy laws punished people who cursed the Christian God or Jesus.

These laws and customs continued, even though close to half the state constitutions included the right to freedom of religion as an explicit guarantee. But freedom of religion meant only that difference would be tolerated; it did not guarantee political equality.

How then did the U.S. Constitution come to be such a break from the immediate past? Had the framers really just forgotten about religion?

Not James Madison of Virginia. Madison arrived at the 1787 convention fresh from a hard-won victory in Virginia to establish religious liberty. At the end of 1786, he had finally secured passage of a bill written by Thomas Jefferson seven years earlier, called the Virginia Statute of Religious Freedom. "All men shall be free to profess, and by argument to maintain, their opinions in matters of religion, and that the same shall in no wise diminish, enlarge, or affect their civil capacities," the bill read. Madison had convinced both the Episcopalians and the Baptist dissenters, at war with each other over state support, that to grant either or even both churches tax money would be to concede to the state forever the authority to endorse one religion—and by implication to crush another. The statute separated church from state to protect religion. Further, it went beyond mere toleration to guarantee that religious choice was independent of civil rights. Jefferson was proud that his law protected "the Jew and the Gentile, the Christian and Mahometan, the Hindoo, and infidel of every denomination."

In Madison's judgment, it was best for the U.S. Constitution to say as little as possible about religion, especially since state laws reflected a variety of positions. When Antifederalists demanded a bill of rights, Madison drew up a list for the First Congress to consider. Two items dealt with religion, but only one was approved. One became part of the First Amendment: "Congress shall make no law respecting an establishment of religion, or prohibiting the free exercise thereof." In a stroke, Madison set

religious worship and the privileging of any one church beyond Congress's power. Significantly, his second proposal failed to pass: "No State shall violate the equal rights of conscience." Evidently, the states wanted to be able to keep their Christian-only rules without federal interference. Different faiths would be tolerated—but not guaranteed equal standing. And the very same session of Congress proceeded to hire Christian chaplains and proclaim days of thanksgiving.

Gradually, states deleted restrictive laws, but as late as 1840, Jews still could not hold public office in four states. Into the twentieth century, some states maintained Sunday laws that forced business closings on the Christian Sabbath, working enormous hardship on those whose religion required Saturday closings. The guarantee of freedom of religion was embedded in state and federal founding documents in the 1770s and 1780s, but it has taken many years to fulfill Jefferson's vision of what true religious liberty meant: the freedom for religious belief to be independent of civil status.

amending the government and overstepping their charge to revise only the Articles), they sent the new document to the Continental Congress for approval. The congress, at first reluctant, finally resolved to send the Constitution to the states for their consideration. It helped that James Madison was then a member of the congress and was able to speak persuasively for the plan.

Had a popular vote been taken on the Constitution in the late fall of 1787, it would probably have been rejected.

The pro-Constitution forces shrewdly secured another advantage by calling themselves Federalists. By all logic, this label was more suitable for the backers of the confederation concept, since the Latin root of the word *federal* means "league." The new Federalists, however, preempted the term and its positive Revolutionary-era associations and applied it to a comparatively nonfederalist plan to diminish the power of the states in a national government. Their opponents cast around for a label to identify themselves; Republican Federalist was tried, but that was too close to their opponents' name. In the end, they became known as Antifederalists, a label that made them sound defensive and negative, lacking a program of their own.

The Federalists identified the states most likely to ratify quickly, and they immediately scheduled special local elections to select delegates to ratifying conventions in those states. Delaware managed to push through elections, convention, and unanimous ratification by early December, before the Antifederalists had barely begun a campaign. Pennsylvania, New Jersey, and Georgia quickly followed. In the latter two states, voter turnout was extremely low; apathy favored the Federalists. These early victories established a Federalist momentum that enhanced their chances for further success.

Delaware and New Jersey were small and relatively weak states that lived in the shadows of more powerful neighbors; a government that would regulate trade and set taxes according to population was an attractive proposition to them. Georgia had a different reason for favoring a powerful national government: It sat at the southernmost end of the country, bordered by hostile Indians and Spanish Florida. "If a weak State with the Indians on its back and the Spaniards on its flank does not see the ne-

cessity of a General Government there must I think be wickedness or insanity in the way," said Federalist George Washington.

Another three states to ratify with relative ease were Connecticut, Maryland, and South Carolina. As in Pennsylvania, merchants, lawyers, and urban artisans in general favored the new Constitution, as did large landowners and slaveholders. This tendency for the established political elite to be Federalist enhanced the prospects of Federalist victory, for they already had power disproportionate to their numbers. Antifederalists in these states tended to be rural, western and noncommercial, men whose access to news was limited and whose participation in state government was tenuous.

Massachusetts was the only early state to ratify in which the Federalists encountered difficulty. The popular vote gave a twenty-delegate advantage to the Antifederalists, whose strength came mainly from the western areas, home to Shays's Rebellion. Easterners opposed it too: Mercy Otis Warren weighed in with her Antifederalist pamphlet, authored by "a Columbian Patriot," a sustained analysis of the dangers of corruption invited by the proposed government. One rural delegate from the town of Sutton voiced widely shared suspicions: "These lawyers and men of learning and money men that talk so finely, and gloss over matters so smoothly, to make us poor illiterate people swallow down the pill, expect to get into Congress themselves; they expect to be the managers of the Constitution and get all the power and all the money into their own hands, and then they will swallow up all us little folks." But another delegate from Berkshire County, in the western part of the state, showed signs of compromise: "I am a plain man . . . not used to speak in public," he began. But he had read the Constitution "over and over. I had been a member of the convention to form our own state constitution, and had learnt something of the checks and balances of power, and I found them all here. . . . These men of learning are all embarked on the same cause with us, and we must all sink or swim together, and shall we throw the Constitution overboard because it does not please us alike?" The Antifederalist lead was slowly eroded by a vigorous newspaper campaign. The final vote in the early 1788 ratifying convention was 187 to 168; it was the closest squeak yet for the Federalists. The victory was accomplished only with promises that amendments to the Constitution suggested by the Massachusetts Antifederalists would be taken up at the first Congress.

THE TENSIONS OF 1787

A New Haven engraver named Amos Doolittle captured the tensions of 1787. A wagon named Connecticut *sinks in the mud. To the left, under sunshine, men spouting nationalist ideas try to pull it out: "Pay Commutation" (pensions to veteran officers), "Comply with Congress." To the right, under severe weather, localist men call out "Tax Luxury," "Success to Shays," and "The People Are Opres'd."*

The Connecticut Historical Society, Hartford.

By May 1788, eight states had ratified; only one more was needed. The Federalists knew that North Carolina and Rhode Island were hopeless, and New Hampshire looked nearly as bleak. More worrisome was their failure to win over the largest and most important states. Because Virginia and New York both had articulate and prominent Antifederalist leaders, the goal in those states was to move slowly and overcome the opposition by forceful debate. It was in those states that the Antifederalists emerged distinctly and coherently as opponents of the Constitution.

The Antifederalists

Antifederalists were a composite group, united mainly in their desire to block the Constitution. A good part of Antifederalist strength came from rural and backcountry sources, in areas with a long tradition of suspicion of the motives of the eastern elites. Yet clearly many Antifederalist leaders came from the same social background as Federalist leaders; economic class alone did not differentiate them. Antifederalism drew strength in states already on a sure economic footing, like New York, that could afford to remain independent entities. Probably the biggest appeal of antifederalism lay in the long-nurtured fear of the danger that distant power might infringe on people's liberties. The language of the

1760s and 1770s revolutionary movement was not easily forgotten or set aside.

But by the time eight states had ratified, the Antifederalists faced a far harder task than they had at first imagined. First, they were no longer defending the status quo, now that the momentum lay with the Federalists. Second, it was difficult to defend the confederation government with its admitted flaws. Even so, they remained genuinely fearful that the new plan of government would lead to disaster. The innovation of superimposing a republican government on thirteen states was unprecedented in history. According to prevailing political philosophy, such an experiment must fail: Republican governments had to stay close to the people, to reflect their needs and interests. A distant government whose workings could not be observed and checked might easily become corrupt or tyrannical.

The new government was indeed distant. The House of Representatives was the only directly democratic element of the government, yet one member represented some thirty thousand people. How could such a representative really know or communicate with his constituency, the Antifederalists wanted to know? And how could the constituents judge his service to them? The status quo was preferable, as one Antifederalist explained: "The members of our state legislatures are annually elected—they are subject to instructions—they are

MAP 8.3
Ratification of the Constitution, 1788–1790
Populated areas cast votes for delegates to state ratification conventions. This map shows Anti-federalist strength generally concentrated in backcounty, noncoastal and nonurban areas, but with significant exceptions (for example, Rhode Island).

chosen within small circles—they are sent but a small distance from their respective homes. Their conduct is constantly known to their constituents. They frequently see, and are seen, by the men whose servants they are."

Under the new system, the Antifederalists were convinced, the elected representatives would always turn out to be members of the elite—that is, prominent members of the gentry with name recognition among voters. Such men "will be ignorant of the sentiments of the middling and much more of the lower class of citizens, strangers to their ability, unacquainted with their wants, difficulties, and distress," worried a Maryland man. None of this would be a problem under a confederation system,

according to the Antifederalists, because real power would continue to reside in the closely watched state governments. But the new Constitution eclipsed state power.

The Federalists generally agreed with the Antifederalist assumption that the elite would be favored for election to Congress, not to mention the Senate and the presidency. That was precisely what they hoped. The Federalists wanted power to flow to intelligent, virtuous, public-spirited leaders, like themselves. They did not envision a government constituted of every class of people. "Fools and knaves have voice enough in government already," according to a New York Federalist, without being guaranteed representation in proportion to the total population of fools. Alexander Hamilton claimed that mechanics and laborers preferred to have their social betters represent them. The Federalists were sure that a natural aristocracy of talented, educated, virtuous statesmen stood ready to take up the reins of government. The Antifederalists challenged the notion that any class of men could be free of selfish interests. Society was too heterogeneous; it was foolish to expect that "lawyers and planters" could be "adequate judges of tradesmen's concerns." They feared that the Federalists were merely resurrecting rule by an aristocracy of wealth.

Antifederalists also fretted over other features of the Constitution besides its undermining of state governments and its undemocratic principles. Proponents of paper money understood well that the Constitution would prohibit further issues of currency by the states. A particularly mistrustful objection was the fear that authorizing Congress to regulate the time, place, and manner of congressional elections would lead to such abuses as allowing only one polling place per state and thus deliberately inconveniencing distant western voters. The most widespread and quite reasonable objection to the Constitution was its lack of any guarantees of individual liberties. Unlike nearly half of the state constitutions, the proposed Constitution did not contain a bill of rights.

The decisive ninth vote for ratification was delivered by tiny New Hampshire, once assumed to be securely Antifederalist. Federalists there succeeded in getting the convention postponed from February to June and in the interim conducted an intense lobbying effort on specific delegates. The Constitution passed in New Hampshire with a ten-vote margin.

The Big Holdouts: Virginia and New York

Four states still remained outside the new union, and a glance at a map demonstrated the necessity of pressing the Federalist case in Virginia and New York. Though Virginia was home to Madison and Washington, an influential Antifederalist group led by Patrick Henry and George Mason made the outcome uncertain. Mason had been present throughout the Philadelphia convention and was one of the three delegates who refused to sign the Constitution; this made him an especially effective opponent. The Federalists finally won his support with

a carefully worded resolution declaring certain individual rights and republican principles inviolate in the new government and listing twenty specific amendments that Antifederalist Virginians desired. But the vote to ratify was not explicitly contingent on those amendments. The Antifederalists' escape clause was an assertion that, when a government derives its power from the people, the people can always take back any power the federal government uses to injure them. By a 10-vote margin, out of 168 votes cast, the Federalists got their ratification.

The New York ratifying convention was in session when news of the Virginia vote arrived, carried by express couriers traveling day and night. As in Virginia, powerful New York politicians opposed the Constitution. George Clinton, governor of the state, represented agrarian interests in upstate New York, but more central to his antifederalism was a sense that a state as large and powerful as New York did not need to relinquish so much authority to the new federal government.

New York was also home to some of the most persuasive and resourceful Federalists, such as Alexander Hamilton. Hamilton collaborated with James Madison and New York lawyer John Jay on a series of essays on the political philosophy of the new Constitution, starting in October 1787. Ultimately numbering eighty-five, the essays were published in New York newspapers and later republished as *The Federalist Papers.* The essays brilliantly set out the failures of the Articles of Confederation and offered an analysis of the complex nature of federalism. In one of the most compelling essays in *The Federalist Papers,* Madison argued for successful large-scale republican government, a direct challenge to one of the Antifederalists' most heartfelt convictions. Whereas the Antifederalists assumed that a true republic could succeed only in a small, homogeneous area, Madison argued that a large and diverse population was itself a guarantee of liberty. In such a state, no single faction or self-interested group could ever be large enough to subvert the freedom of other groups. "The smaller the society, the fewer will probably be the distinct parties and interests, the more frequently will a majority be found of the same party; and the smaller the compass within which they are placed, the more easily will they . . . execute their plans of oppression. Extend the sphere, and you take in a greater variety of parties and interests; you make it less probable that a majority of the whole will have a common motive to invade the rights of other citizens." Madison called this a "republican remedy for the diseases most incident to republican government."

New York's ratifying convention met at Poughkeepsie, halfway between New York City and Albany, deep in the heart of Antifederalist country. A clear majority of the delegates were Antifederalist, but newspaper debate and heavy lobbying produced some switches in votes. At one point, Hamilton threatened that New York City would secede from the state and join the union by itself if upstate farmers held out. The last-minute arrival of news from Virginia finally tipped the balance in favor of ratification.

New York's ratification assured the solidity and legitimacy of the new government. It took another year and a half for the Antifederalists in North Carolina to come around, and fiercely independent Rhode Island, still full of "rogues" to the Federalists, held out until May 1790, and even then barely ratified, by a two-vote margin.

In less than twelve months, the U.S. Constitution was both written and ratified. An amazingly short time by twentieth-century standards, it is equally remarkable for the late eighteenth century with its horsepowered transportation and handprinted communications. The Federalists had faced a formidable task, but by building momentum and assuring a bill of rights, they carried the day.

Conclusion: Decade of Decision

Thus ended one of the most intellectually tumultuous and creative decades in American history. Americans experimented with ideas and drew up plans to embody their evolving and conflicting notions of how a society and a government ought to be formulated. Widespread agreement supported the concept of a republican government, one in which the people are sovereign and government leaders derive their power and authority from the people. State constitutions, the Articles of Confederation, and finally the federal Constitution wrestled with different conceptions of the degree of democracy—of the amount of direct control of government by the people—that was workable in American society and consistent with the ideal of republicanism.

The decade began in 1776 with a confederation government that could barely be ratified, so cumbersome were its procedures to ensure unanimity. Unanimity was thought desirable, so that no state could be squeezed or stepped on by others. But it also proved to be unworkable. As the decade progressed, Americans came to see that diversity of opinion was not only an unavoidable reality; it was a hidden strength of the new society beginning to take shape.

The Federalists still hoped for a society in which men of exceptional wisdom would rule and would intuitively discern the best path for public policy. In their vision of leadership they looked backward, to a society of hierarchy, rank, and benevolent rule by an aristocracy of talent. Meanwhile, however, they created a government with thoroughly forward-looking checks and balances as a guard against corruption, which they figured would most likely emanate from the people. The Antifederalists, by contrast, looked backward to an old order of small-scale direct democracy and local control, based on the virtue of people who could hold their potentially corruptible rulers to account. They envisioned a larger world of contentious, heterogeneous, self-interested leaders who needed to be held in check. In the 1790s, these two conceptions of republicanism and of leadership would be tested in real life.

CHRONOLOGY

1775	**May.** Second Continental Congress begins.
1778	State constitutions completed.
1776	Virginia adopts bill of rights.
	John Dickinson of Pennsylvania drafts Articles of Confederation.
1777	**November.** Final draft of Articles of Confederation approved by congress and sent to states.
1780	Pennsylvania abolishes slavery.
1781	Articles of Confederation finally ratified.
	Creation of executive departments; Robert Morris appointed superintendent of finance.
	Bank of North America formed.
	Quok Walker, a slave, sues for his freedom in Massachusetts.
1782	Virginia relaxes state manumission law.
1783	Treaty of Paris signed.
1784	Gradual emancipation laws passed in Rhode Island and Connecticut.
	Treaty of Fort Stanwix with Iroquois.
1785	Gradual emancipation in New York.
1786	Gradual emancipation in New Jersey.
	Bank of North America expires.
	Virginia adopts Statute of Religious Freedom.
	Shays's Rebellion in western Massachusetts.
	Annapolis meeting proposes convention to revise Articles of Confederation.
1787	Northwest Ordinance allows self-government and prohibits slavery in Northwest Territory.
	May–September. Constitutional convention meets in Philadelphia.
1788	United States Constitution is ratified.

BIBLIOGRAPHY

GENERAL WORKS

John P. Diggins, *The Lost Soul of American Politics: Virtue, Self-Interest, and the Foundations of Liberalism* (1984).

Joseph J. Ellis, *After the Revolution: Profiles of Early American Culture* (1979).

Merrill Jensen, *The New Nation: A History of the United States During the Confederation, 1781–1789* (1950).

James Kirby Martin, *Men in Rebellion: Higher Governmental Leaders and the Coming of the Revolution* (1973).

Forrest McDonald, *E Pluribus Unum: The Formation of the American Republic, 1776–1790* (1965).

Edmund S. Morgan, *Inventing the People: The Rise of Popular Sovereignty in England and America* (1988).

Richard B. Morris, *Witnesses at the Creation: Hamilton, Madison, Jay, and the Constitution* (1985).

Richard B. Morris, *The Forging of the Union, 1781–1789* (1987).

John Phillip Reid, *The Concept of Liberty in the Age of the American Revolution* (1988).

Robert E. Shalhope, *The Roots of Democracy: American Thought and Culture, 1760–1800* (1990).

Richard Sinopoli, *The Foundations of American Citizenship: Liberalism, the Constitution, and Civic Virtue* (1992).

Gerald Stourzh, *Alexander Hamilton and the Idea of Republican Government* (1970).

Gordon Wood, *The Creation of the American Republic, 1776–1787* (1969).

Alfred F. Young, ed., *Beyond the American Revolution: Explorations in the History of American Radicalism* (1993).

Rosemarie Zagarri, *The Politics of Size: Representation in the United States, 1776–1850* (1987).

Rosemarie Zagarri, *A Woman's Dilemma: Mercy Otis Warren and the American Revolution* (1995).

THE CONFEDERATION GOVERNMENT
Joseph L. Davis, *Sectionalism in American Politics, 1774–1787* (1977).

Daniel M. Friedenberg, *Life, Liberty, and the Pursuit of Land: The Plunder of Early America* (1992).

J. James Henderson, *Party Politics in the Continental Congress* (1974).

Reginald Horsman, *The Frontier in the Formative Years, 1783–1815* (1970).

Merrill Jensen, *The Articles of Confederation: An Interpretation of the Social-Constitutional History of the American Revolution, 1774–1781* (1940).

Jackson Turner Main, *Political Parties before the Constitution* (1973).

Peter S. Onuf, *The Origins of the Federal Republic: Jurisdictional Controversies in the United States, 1775–1787* (1983).

Peter S. Onuf, *Statehood and Union: A History of the Northwest Ordinance* (1987).

Peter S. Onuf and Cathy D. Matson, *A Union of Interests: Political and Economic Thought in Revolutionary America* (1990).

Jack N. Rakove, *The Beginnings of National Politics: An Interpretive History of the Continental Congress* (1979).

THE SOVEREIGN STATES AND CITIZENSHIP
Willi Paul Adams, *The First American Constitutions: Republican Ideology and the Making of the State Constitutions in the Revolutionary Era* (1980).

Edward Countryman, *A People in Revolution: The American Revolution and Political Society in New York, 1760–1790* (1981).

Robert Dinkin, *Voting in Revolutionary America* (1982).

Elisha P. Douglass, *Rebels and Democrats* (1965).

Eric Foner, *Tom Paine and Revolutionary America* (1976).

Van Beck Hall, *Politics without Parties: Massachusetts, 1780–1791* (1972).

Ronald Hoffman and Peter J. Albert, eds., *Sovereign States in an Age of Uncertainty* (1981).

Linda Kerber, *Women of the Republic: Intellect and Ideology in Revolutionary America* (1980).

James H. Kettner, *The Development of American Citizenship, 1608–1870* (1978).

Donald Lutz, *Popular Consent and Popular Control: Whig Political Theory in the Early State Constitutions* (1980).

Jackson Turner Main, *The Sovereign States, 1775–1783* (1973).

Richard P. McCormick, *Experiment in Independence: New Jersey in the Critical Period, 1781–1789* (1950).

Gary B. Nash and Jean R. Sonderlund, *Freedom by Degrees: Emancipation in Pennsylvania and Its Aftermath* (1991).

Steven E. Patterson, *Political Parties in Revolutionary Massachusetts* (1973).

Irwin H. Polishook, *Rhode Island and the Union, 1774–1795* (1969).

Marylynn Salmon, *Women and the Law of Property in Early America* (1986).

Robert J. Taylor, *Western Massachusetts in the Revolution* (1954).

Patricia Watlington, *The Partisan Spirit: Kentucky Politics, 1779–1792* (1972).

Chilton Williamson, *American Suffrage: From Property to Democracy, 1760–1860* (1960).

Alfred Young, *The Democratic-Republicans of New York: The Origins, 1763–1797* (1967).

Arthur Zilversmit, *The First Emancipation* (1967).

THE CRITICAL PERIOD
William G. Anderson, *The Price of Liberty: The Public Debt of the American Revolution* (1983).

Robert A. Becker, *Revolution, Reform, and the Politics of American Taxation, 1763–1783* (1980).

Thomas M. Doerflinger, *A Vigorous Spirit of Enterprise: Merchants and Economic Development in Revolutionary Philadelphia* (1986).

E. James Ferguson, *The Power of the Purse: A History of American Public Finance, 1776–1790* (1961).

Dall W. Forsythe, *Taxation and Political Change in the Young Nation, 1781–1833* (1977).

Robert A. Gross, ed., *In Debt to Shays: The Bicentennial of an Agrarian Rebellion* (1993).

David P. Szatmary, *Shays' Rebellion: The Making of an Agrarian Insurrection* (1980).

THE CONSTITUTION AND RATIFICATION
John K. Alexander, *The Selling of the Constitutional Convention: A History of News Coverage* (1990).

Charles Beard, *An Economic Interpretation of the Constitution* (1913).

Richard Beeman, Stephen Botein, and Edward C. Carter II, eds., *Beyond Confederation: Origins of the Constitution and American National Identity* (1987).

Herman Belz, Ronald Hoffman, and Peter J. Albert, eds., *To Form a More Perfect Union: The Critical Ideas of the Constitution* (1992).

Richard B. Bernstein and Kym S. Rice, *Are We to Be a Nation? The Making of the Constitution* (1987).

Steven R. Boyd, *The Politics of Opposition: Antifederalists and the Acceptance of the Constitution* (1979).

M. E. Bradford, *Original Intentions: On the Making and Ratification of the United States Constitution* (1993).

Irving Brant, *James Madison: The Nationalist, 1780–1787* (1948).

Robert E. Brown, *Charles Beard and the Constitution* (1956).

Roger H. Brown, *Redeeming the Republic: Federalists, Taxation, and the Origins of the Constitution* (1993).

Patrick T. Conley and John P. Kaminski, eds., *The Bill of Rights and the States: The Colonial and Revolutionary Origins of American Liberties* (1992).

Linda Grant DePauw, *The Eleventh Pillar: New York State and the Federal Constitution* (1966).

Michael Allen Gillespie and Michael Lienesch, eds., *Ratifying the Constitution* (1989).

A. E. Dick Howard, ed., *The United States Constitution: Roots, Rights, and Responsibilities* (1992).

Calvin C. Jillson, *Constitution Making: Conflict and Consensus in the Federal Convention of 1787* (1988).

Michael Kammen, *A Machine That Would Go of Itself: The Constitution in American Culture* (1986).

Ralph Ketcham, *James Madison* (1971).

Ralph Ketcham, *Framed for Posterity: The Enduring Philosophy of the Constitution* (1993).

Peter B. Knupfer, *The Union As It Is: Constitutional Unionism and Sectional Compromise, 1787–1861* (1991).

Donald S. Lutz, *Origins of American Constitutionalism* (1988).

Staughton Lynd, *Class Conflict, Slavery, and the United States Constitution* (1967).

Jackson Turner Main, *The Anti-Federalists: Critics of the Constitution* (1961).

Forrest McDonald, *We the People: The Economic Origins of the Constitution* (1958).

Forrest McDonald, *Novus Ordo Seclorum: The Intellectual Origins of the Constitution* (1985).

William Lee Miller, *The Business of May Next: James Madison and the Founding* (1992).

Ellen Franken Paul and Howard Dickman, eds., *Liberty, Property, and the Foundations of the American Constitution* (1989).

Jack N. Rakove, *James Madison and the Creation of the American Republic* (1990).

Jack N. Rakove, *Original Meanings: Politics and Ideas in the Making of the Constitution* (1996).

John Phillip Reid, *Constitutional History of the American Revolution: The Authority of Rights* (1986).

John Phillip Reid, *Constitutional History of the American Revolution: The Authority to Tax* (1987).

Robert A. Rutland, *The Ordeal of the Constitution: The Antifederalists and the Ratification Struggle of 1787–1788* (1966).

Stephen L. Schechter, *The Reluctant Pillar: New York and the Adoption of the Federal Constitution* (1985).

Garry Wills, *Explaining America: The Federalist* (1981).

RELIGION

Ruth H. Bloch, *Visionary Republic: Millennial Themes in American Thought, 1756–1800* (1985).

Morton Borden, *Jews, Turks, and Infidels* (1984).

Naomi W. Cohen, *Jews in Christian America: The Pursuit of Religious Equality* (1992).

Nathan O. Hatch, *The Sacred Cause of Liberty: Republican Thought and the Millennium in Revolutionary New England* (1977).

Jacob Marcus, *The American Colonial Jew: A Study in Acculturation* (1967).

Jacob Marcus, *United States Jewry, 1776–1985* (1989).

MISS LIBERTY NEEDLEWORK

An unknown artist skillfully rendered Miss Liberty offering drink to an eagle, executed in a combination of needlework and watercolor. Liberty's cap — the symbol that always accompanied a female figure representing liberty — sits atop a flagpole. The pose of woman, eagle, and flagpole is borrowed exactly from a popular 1796 engraving by the American artist Edward Savage and was copied many times in needlework and watercolor by amateurs, many of them young women. Where Savage put Boston harbor in the background of his picture, this needleworker (perhaps a New Jersey resident) chose to paint the decorative arches at Trenton, New Jersey, erected to honor George Washington on his inaugural journey to New York City to assume the presidency.

The Daughters of the American Revolution Museum, Washington, D.C. (Gift of New Jersey State Society).

THE NEW NATION TAKES FORM

9

1789–1800

THE ELECTION OF GEORGE WASHINGTON in February 1789 was quick work. Seven months earlier, right after Virginia and New Hampshire ratified the Constitution, many July 4 orators and newspaper editors considered the Virginia planter as good as president, and the tallying of the unanimous votes by the electoral college became a mere formality. Washington was everyone's first choice. He perfectly embodied the republican ideal of disinterested, virtuous, public-spirited leadership; indeed, he worked strenuously to cultivate precisely that perception. His self-sacrificing leadership during the Revolutionary War had earned him the gratitude of many Americans. Here was a general who had refused all salary for his war service and who had chosen to winter with his army in the field, instead of retiring to more privileged housing. The general had brilliantly inspired disheartened subordinates and even once defused a potential military coup. At the war's end, he dramatically surrendered his sword to the Continental Congress in a gesture symbolizing the subservience of military power to the law.

Washington professed a reluctance to accept the presidency, which only added to his popularity; no one could accuse him of lusting for power. He wrote in his diary that his impending inauguration made him feel like "a culprit who is going to the place of his execution, so unwilling am I, in the evening of a life nearly consumed in public cares, to quit a peaceful abode for an Ocean of difficulties." His diary, of course, was not really a private document, as Washington knew full well; his sense of his place in history already controlled his pen in his daily chronicling of events. Instead, he entrusted his confidences to Alexander Hamilton, the young New Yorker who had served at his side in the army. Could he really profess reluctance and then accept the presidency, he wondered, and still avoid the charge of excessive ambition? Hamilton replied that he in fact must accept the office: "The necessity of your filling the station in question is so universal that you can run no risk of any uncandid imputation, by submitting to it."

Washington accepted, and in April he made the journey from Virginia to the capital, New York City, in six days. Cheering crowds, banquets, large triumphal arches, military parades, and cannon salutes greeted him at many towns and villages en route. In Philadelphia, a crowd of twenty thousand lined the streets to glimpse him. In Trenton, New Jersey, the site of his 1776 Christmas Day victory over the British, scores of women and girls spread flowers in his path and held a banner proclaiming "The Defender of the Mothers Will Also Defend the Daughters." Newly elected representatives and senators joined him in the barge that conveyed him across the Hudson River, escorted by a fleet of decorated vessels firing cannons. Once in New York City, Washington, on a white horse, headed a procession down Broadway while a crowd of thirty thousand applauded wildly. A week later, he took the oath of office on a balcony of the newly built Federal Hall overlooking Broad and Wall Streets. A festive red-and-white striped canopy framed the scene and directed the crowd's visual attention. His voice could not be heard, of course, but guns fired in the harbor minutes later announced his inauguration to the world.

The clear meaning of the inaugural pageantry was something very like hero worship for Washington as an individual. But the question, as yet unresolved, was whether the office of the presidency itself would be grandly heroic. The arches, the crowds, the gun salutes, the grand entry on a white horse—all this was an uneasy reminder of the trappings of monarchy.

In its first month, Congress debated the proper form of address for the president, raising explicitly the issue of how kingly this new presidency was to be. Vice President John Adams insisted on the dignity of a regal title. He preferred "His Highness, the President of the United States of America and Protector of Their Liberties," but he was willing to compromise on "His Majesty, the President." Virginia representative James Madison soundly ridiculed Adams. "His Highness" was as distasteful and unnecessary as "splendid tinsel and gorgeous robes," Madison complained. A few other representatives joked that the plump vice president should be called "His Rotundity." (Adams did not enjoy universal support; he had won the vice presidency by only thirty-four of the possible sixty-nine electoral votes.)

Yet Washington himself was known to favor being addressed as "His High Mightiness," so Adams was not altogether out of step. Significantly, the representatives targeted the vice president for ridicule, not the great man himself. Several former Antifederalists sitting in Congress held out for a less exalted title. The final version was simply "President of the United States of America," and the established form of address became "Mr. President," a subdued yet dignified title in a society where only independent, property-owning adult white males could presume to be called "Mister."

Washington's genius in establishing the presidency lay in his capacity for implanting his own reputation for integrity into the office itself. He was not a particularly brilliant thinker, nor was he a shrewd political strategist. He was not even a very congenial man. In the political language of the day,

GEORGE WASHINGTON BY JOSEPH WRIGHT
George Washington wears a laurel wreath, the traditional mark of honor in ancient times. Carved in beeswax in 1784, the work elevates Washington to the status of a Greek or Roman hero.
Courtesy of the Mount Vernon Ladies Association.

he was virtuous. Washington cultivated a personal style that was aloof, resolute, and dignified, to the point of appearing wooden at times. He encouraged pomp and ceremony to create respect for the authority of his office, traveling with no fewer than six horses drawing his coach, hosting formal balls, and surrounding himself with servants in livery. He even held weekly levees, as European monarchs did, hour-long audiences granted to a group of distinguished visitors. At these events, Washington, attired in black velvet, a feathered hat, and polished sword, accepted formal bows and avoided the egalitarian familiarity of handshakes. But he always managed, perhaps just barely, to avoid the extreme of royal splendor.

The thirteen American states had just come through a difficult decade, swinging between a distrust of executive power on the one hand and a fear of the turbulent effects of party politics on the other. Washington's reputation for integrity boosted confidence that executive power could be compatible with the public good. And his strong pronouncements about the evils of divisive factions and "party animosities" raised hopes that at last America was on a steady course.

National harmony proved to be elusive, however. Political parties developed in the 1790s, despite the best intentions of the decade's statesmen. The surprise was that factions emerged within the camp of the 1788 Federalists. Men who had worked together to ratify the Constitution found that the process of implementing it exposed serious disagreement. Economic policy and foreign affairs proved to be the two most significant fissures that split the political leadership of the 1790s. The disagreements were articulated around particular events and particular policies, but at heart they arose out of fundamentally opposing ideological stances about the value of democracy, the nature of leadership, and the limits of federal power. By 1800, these divisions had crystallized into full-fledged political parties, the Federalists and the Republicans.

The Search for Stability

Conventional wisdom today praises the development of a two-party system: Parties organize conflict, legitimize disagreement, and mediate among competing political strategies. Yet they were entirely unanticipated by the writers of the Constitution. James Madison had argued in *The Federalist Papers* in 1788 that a superior feature of the national government was precisely that its extensive size would prevent small, selfish factions from becoming dangerously dominant. No one was prepared for the intense and passionate polarization of the 1790s.

Instead, leaders in the early 1790s sought stability to heal divisions of the 1780s. Veneration for the president provided one powerful source of unity, and George Washington commanded near-universal respect. People trusted him to initiate the untested and perhaps elastic powers of the presidency. But a sterling leader alone was not enough to bring stability to the country. Schemes to promote national harmony and public virtue abounded in the 1790s. Passage of the Bill of Rights in 1791 lessened the scars of the battle over ratification of the Constitution. The private virtue of women was mobilized to bolster the public virtue of male citizens; republicanism was forcing a rethinking of women's relation to the state. Finally, politicians and writers took up numbers and statistics to chart the progress of the nation and confer legitimacy on republican institutions. The economic growth revealed by the numbers offered assurance that the hard times and political instability of the 1780s were now in the past.

SUIT WORN BY WASHINGTON AT SECOND INAUGURAL

At his first inauguration, Washington wore a suit of plain brown cloth woven in Connecticut to symbolize the independence of America from European manufacturers. Four years later at his second inauguration, in 1793, the president chose this suit of French black velvet. Possibly he felt that American independence was now adequately established, whereas presidential authority required the boost of a luxury fabric. The suit is elegant and dignified yet simple, avoiding all but a hint of monarchical opulence.

Courtesy of the Chicago Historical Society, Hope B. McCormick Costume Center. Gift of Virginia Lewis Mitchell, Laura Landon Mitchell, and Neville Mitchell Smith.

Washington's Cabinet

At first President Washington had relatively little to do. Major decisions, like establishing the executive departments and the federal court system, fell to the initiative of Congress. Washington fretted about his competency—"I feel an insuperable diffidence in my own abilities," he wrote to a South Carolina friend in May—and fended off the dozens of job seekers who sought his approval and appointment. He set up a fixed social schedule; in addition to his Tuesday levees for male guests, he established a Friday night tea party and a Wednesday dinner at 4 P.M. for selected guests of both sexes. He also made it a rule never to accept a dinner invitation to someone else's table.

Within four months, Congress had created the departments of war, treasury, and state, and now Washington could begin his work. His antiparty assumptions guided his choices; he did not require any political test for office. Instead he picked talented and experienced individuals, not lackeys, to head the departments. Their deep philosophical differences did not trouble him. For the Department of War, he chose Henry Knox, who had headed the same department in the confederation government. For the Treasury, he quickly turned to Alexander Hamilton of New York, known for his general brilliance as well as financial genius. Washington knew that this post, the most important one in the government, would require the adept political skills Hamilton clearly had. Revenue problems excited discontent and division and had largely been the cause of the failure of the confederation government. To lead the Department of State, the foreign policy arm of the executive branch, Washington chose Thomas Jefferson, who had just returned from a four-year stint as minister to France. The Franco-American alliance that had won the Revolutionary War was complicated now by the early stages of a democratic revolution sweeping France in the summer of 1789. No one understood the immediate intricacy of diplomatic relations better than Jefferson.

Beyond the three executive departments, Washington had legal appointments at his disposal. He turned to Virginian Edmund Randolph to be the first attorney general. In 1787, Randolph had presented the Virginia Plan on Madison's behalf at the Philadelphia convention, so clearly he was friendly to the idea of a powerful government. Yet Randolph had turned Antifederalist for a time; he was one of only three at the convention who had refused to sign the final Constitution, largely because he preferred a ratification process that gave more voice to the voters to advocate for change. John Jay, the New York lawyer who vigorously defended the Constitution along with Madison and Hamilton in the *Federalist Papers*, became the first chief justice of the Supreme Court, a job with slight duties in the first few years.

> *No one anticipated that fundamental disagreements leading to two decades of party turbulence would emerge from the brilliant but explosive mix of Washington's first cabinet.*

Washington liked and trusted all these men, and by 1793, in his second term, he was meeting regularly with them, thereby establishing the precedent of a presidential cabinet. (Vice President Adams did not join these meetings; his only official duty was to preside over the Senate, a job he found "a punishment" because he could not actually participate in legislative debates. He complained to his wife, Abigail, "My country has in its wisdom contrived for me the most insignificant office.") No one anticipated that fundamental disagreements leading to two decades of party turbulence would emerge from the brilliant but explosive mix of Washington's first cabinet.

The Bill of Rights

Most members of the First Congress, which convened in April 1789, had been ardent supporters of ratification, so for a time harmony prevailed. In a spirit of conciliation, they turned to the work of constructing a bill of rights. Many Antifederalists had complained about the absence of guarantees of individual liberties and limitations to federal power, and seven states had ratified the Constitution on the express condition that a bill of rights be swiftly incorporated. Many state constitutions protected freedom of speech, press, religion, peaceable assembly, and the right to petition and to have jury trials, so it seemed to Antifederalists that the federal government could do no less.

In the final days of the 1787 Philadelphia convention, only one voice at the meeting (the Virginian George Mason's) had called for a bill of rights. James Madison and the other delegates decided that an enumeration of rights was unnecessary. Perhaps a general fatigue after the four months of wrangling contributed to their hasty dismissal. But the complaint surfaced continually in the ratification process. Alexander Hamilton tried to answer it in one of the *Federalist Papers*. Enumerating individual rights was actually dangerous, he claimed: "Why declare that things shall not be done which there is no power to do?" This was little comfort to uneasy Antifederalists, who saw it as circular reasoning.

By 1789, James Madison had reversed himself and prepared a set of amendments to satisfy the Antifederalists. He still did not think that the lack of a bill of rights was a serious flaw in the Constitution; in his view, the real threat to individual liberties came not so much from government as from popular majorities acting with the sanction of law. He hoped that a clear, solemn statement of fundamental rights would help fix these truths in the public mind and would contribute to public virtue.

Members of the First Congress had little quarrel with any of the particular rights Madison specified in his first draft. No one wanted a government that could force citizens to incriminate themselves or to quarter soldiers in peacetime. But with more pressing items on the congressional agenda, such as how best to raise money for the new government, Congress sidelined Madison's proposals for five months. And even then, the eventual debate was lackluster and indifferent. Some of the members quibbled over details, and one provided a moment of humor by asking, in exasperation, if every possible right had been listed, pointing out one somehow overlooked: that "a man should have a right to wear his hat."

Final agreement from both House and Senate on the first ten amendments to the Constitution came in September 1789. Numbers one through eight dealt with individual liberties, and nine and ten concerned the boundary between federal and state authority. The amendments did have the immediate effect of cementing a sense of national unity. The process of ratifying the amendments in the states took another two years, but there was no serious doubt about the outcome. North Carolina and Rhode Island, the two holdout states, came into the Union in large part because the most credible argument against joining had now been deflated.

But not everyone was entirely satisfied. Amendments that would change the structural details of the new government, ardently desired by some Antifederalists, were never considered by Congress. Madison had no intention of reopening debates settled at the Philadelphia convention,

about the length of term for the president or the power to levy excise taxes or the power of Congress to maintain a peacetime army.

The Right to Vote

Significantly, no one complained about another striking omission in the Bill of Rights: the right to vote. Only much later did voting come to be seen as a fundamental liberty requiring protection by constitutional amendment—indeed, by four additional amendments. The 1788 Constitution deliberately left all decisions about defining voters to individual states, precisely to promote stability in the new federal government. Any uniform federal voting law would run the double risk of excluding some who could already vote in state elections or including too many new voters somehow deemed undesirable in the more restrictive states.

Most states maintained property qualifications of varying degree. The assumption held that only property owners would be independent enough to vote in perfect freedom. Slaves, servants, apprentices, tenants, children, wives, and a new and growing class of propertyless wage laborers at the lower end of the social scale were thought to lack the necessary independence of mind, being subject to pressure from masters, husbands, and bosses. And, since a major purpose of government was to secure private property, as many leaders of the revolutionary generation thought, then it made sense to them to restrict participation to those who actually owned property. Or so they reasoned. Widening the circle of voters could lead to major disruptions, if, for instance, the many have-nots decided to tax the rich heavily.

The Constitution counted on the states to set limits on voters. Only one state expanded its pool of voters beyond the customary bounds, and that was at first unintentional. The New Jersey constitution of 1776 enfranchised "all free inhabitants" worth "over 50 pounds." The lawmakers simply forgot to specify the words *white* and *male,* so deeply was it implanted in their minds that voters would of course be white men. But in the 1780s, unmarried women and free blacks who met the property qualification quietly began to participate in elections in a few towns. (Married women owned no property, for by law their husbands held title to everything, so they were still excluded under this law.) What began as an oversight soon became acceptable: A revised election law of 1790 used the words *he or she* in reference to voters, thus making woman suffrage explicitly legitimate. As one legislator boasted, "Our Constitution gives this right to maids or widows *black or white.*"

This highly unusual state of affairs lasted until 1807, when a new law specifically disfranchised both blacks and women in New Jersey. Heated local elections in the decade preceding 1807 had brought attention to voter qualifications. In one election in particular, in Newark, fraudulent voting boosted the returns to more than three times the usual number of voters. Stories circulated about voters in petticoats herded to the polls by men who cared deeply about the outcome of the election and nothing about political rights for women. No matter that by far the largest chunk of illegal votes came from men, not women: A fifty-pound banknote hidden in a shoe allowed any young man to swear honestly that he was "over fifty pounds" and therefore entitled to vote. The response of the New Jersey legislature to such corrupt election practices was to redefine voting rights to include propertyless white males and to exclude women and blacks. In other words, independence of mind, that essential precondition of voting, was now redefined to be sex- and race-specific. After 1807, free black men could not vote again in New Jersey until 1870, with the passage of the Fifteenth Amendment to the U.S. Constitution; for women, white and black, it took until 1920, when the Nineteenth Amendment became law.

The Republican Wife and Mother

The exclusion of women from politics did not mean that they had no civic role or responsibility. Federal and state constitutions may not have remembered "the ladies," as Abigail Adams had hoped in 1776, but a flood of periodical articles of the 1790s certainly did. The writers, both male and female, reevaluated courtship, marriage, and motherhood in light of republican ideals. Unlimited, tyrannical power in the ruler, whether king or husband, was now declared a thing of the past. Affection, not duty, bound wives to their husbands and citizens to their government. The power relations of republican marriage were supposed to mirror the power relations of civil society. Specifically, the writers claimed that women had the capacity to reform the morals and manners of men. One male author, in a 1795 article titled "Female Influence," promised women that "the solidity and stability of the liberties of your country rest with you; since Liberty is never sure, 'till Virtue reigns triumphant." By upholding public virtue, women bolstered political liberty.

REPUBLICAN WOMANHOOD: MRS. REUBEN HUMPHREY OF CONNECTICUT
This late-eighteenth-century American mother displayed her gentility by the objects she chose to grace her portrait: an intricate wood frame mirror, a silver tea service, a plumed hat incongruously worn indoors while tending the baby. Mrs. Reuben Humphrey of East Granby, Connecticut, was married to the superintendent of a state prison; this painting was done by a prisoner.
The Connecticut Historical Society, Hartford.

Until the 1790s, public virtue was strictly a masculine quality. The Latin root *vir* literally meant "man," and *virtue* in a political context suggested manliness, just as *virile* means "manly potency." But another sort of virtue loomed in importance in the late eighteenth century: sexual chastity, a private asset prized as a feminine quality. Essayists of the 1790s explicitly linked these qualities in advising young women to use sexual virtue to produce more public virtue in men. "Love and courtship . . . invest a lady with more authority than in any other situation that falls to the lot of human beings," one writer proclaimed. If women spurned selfish suitors, they could promote good morals more than any social institution could, the essayists promised.

Republican ideals cast motherhood in a new light as well, centering on the importance of mothers as the teachers of virtuous sons. Benjamin Rush, a Pennsylvania physician and trustee of the Philadelphia Young Ladies Academy, founded in

1787, justified female education because "our ladies should be qualified to a certain degree, by a peculiar and suitable education, to concur in instructing their sons in the principles of liberty and government." Throughout the 1790s, advocates legitimized female education, still a controversial proposition, through the claim of the significant influence of republican motherhood on sons, the future male citizenry. A series of essays published under the pseudonym "Constantia" took the idea to its most advanced level. The author, Judith Sargent Murray of Massachusetts, favored education that would remake women into self-confident, competent, rational beings, poised to become the equals of men. But even Murray had to dress her advanced ideas in the cloak of the republican motherhood argument, justifying female education in the context of family duty.

This shift in understanding about women's relation to the state was subtle but profoundly important. Citizenship was still a masculine preserve, but now women's domestic obligations as lovers, wives, and mothers were infused with political meaning, and a few women became so bold as to claim an expanded scope for women's intellectual development as well. But nothing about this shift altered traditional gender relations. The analogy between marriage and civil society worked precisely because of the self-subordination inherent in the term *virtue*. Men should put the public good first, before selfish desires, just as women must put their husbands and families first, before themselves. Women might gain literacy and knowledge, but only in the service of improved maternal duty. Many of the essayists troubled to caution wives that they must still always defer to their husbands. In Federalist America, wives and citizens alike should feel affection for and trust in their rulers and should never rebel.

Counting on Progress

Even with a virtuous president, a harmonious (for the moment) Congress, and a dutiful set of republican wives and mothers, Federalists still worried that large-scale republican government, at heart still an untried experiment, might simply fail. This concern led some to adopt empirical reasoning to prove the progress of the new nation. Dozens of gazetteers published in the 1790s and early 1800s brimmed with numerical boasts about population growth, land values, prices, wages, imports and exports, and the lengths of roads and rivers. The popularity of

data collection was grounded in assumptions that progress was measurable and that bigger meant better.

Numbers suddenly mattered in a representative democracy. The Constitution established a regular census, a straightforward head count of free and unfree persons every ten years to determine each state's representation in Congress. But even before the first one was taken, in 1790, James Madison and Thomas Jefferson proposed enlarging it to include information on age, sex, race, and occupation. Every decade thereafter, the census was enlisted to collect more data of use to the government.

"Our ladies should be qualified to a certain degree, by a peculiar and suitable education, to concur in instructing their sons in the principles of liberty and government," wrote Benjamin Rush in 1787.

By the end of the 1790s, the data collectors and legislators found a word, recently coined in Scotland, that perfectly captured their project: *statisticks*. It originally meant descriptive facts about the state, but within a decade, *statisticks* came to refer to quantitative facts. As quantities, statistics presented the appearance of being certain, objective, indisputable. Some even argued that incontestable facts were the answer to party politics. "Whence arises the diversity of opinion?" asked an editor in 1804. His answer was "a want of certain data," or insufficient facts: "Did all men know alike, though imperfectly, their opinions must be the same."

The enthusiasm for statistics elevated arithmetic to a new importance. By long tradition, arithmetic had been taught primarily as a commercial subject, in connection with a mercantile career. Now arithmetic texts were rewritten and simplified, so that every schoolchild could become adept at elementary calculation. Like literacy, numeracy became valued for the thinking skill it conferred on students.

The most important simplification of arithmetic came with the reform of the country's monetary system. Before the 1790s, English pounds, shillings (twenty to a pound), and pence (twelve to a shilling) mixed freely with thirteen individual state currencies, most of them based on the English system, and Continental dollars. Calculating prices, figuring currency exchanges, and factoring in rapid depreciation during the 1780s were more than most ordinary people with rudimentary arithmetic skills could handle. But under the Constitution, the federal government alone had the power to coin money, and other currencies were phased out. Thomas Jefferson drew up a plan basing federal money for the first time on the decimal system. Dollars, dimes, cents, and half-cents were far easier to reckon with than pence and shillings. "The policy of tyrants," said one author of a new arithmetic text, is "to keep their accounts in as intricate and perplexing a method as possible," so that no one could figure out taxes and public debts. "But Republican money ought to be simple, and adapted to the meanest capacity." Decimal money enabled the average farmer or mechanic to participate more fully in the widening world of commerce.

Sources of Economic Change

Following a decade of severe economic instability, the 1790s ushered in a period of prosperity and sustained economic growth. New agricultural opportunities, transportation improvements, and innovations in finance were beginning to transform not only the economy but the way ordinary men and women thought about their work and their chances for bettering their lives. The simplified monetary system and serious attention to arithmetic training allowed many more people to participate confidently in the world of commercial exchange.

Commercial Agriculture

From at least the mid-eighteenth century, most farmers had participated in market transactions at local stores and in nearby towns. Self-sufficiency was simply not possible in a society where a taste for some of the luxuries of life had taken hold. For example, a store in the village of Brookfield, in central Massachusetts, stocked fine cloth—velvets and silks—from England and India; watch chains and shoe buckles; teapots and dishware; raisins, allspice, salt, sugar, and tea. Rarely was cash actually exchanged at the moment of purchase. Instead, the store owner recorded transactions in his account book, keeping a running total of each customer's debt, which was periodically paid off in either cash or, more likely, "country goods," meaning a surplus of cheese, butter, or grain from the farmer's own production.

This pattern of local market exchange was altered in the 1790s, when dramatic increases in the international price of grain motivated farmers to step up their grain production. Food prices were generally rising in Europe in the late eighteenth century, driven up by demand caused by marked population growth. After 1793, prices rose even more sharply, when France and England entered into two decades of conflict known as the Napoleonic Wars. Soon all the major European powers were embroiled in war, leaving the United States, the only neutral shipper, with a monopoly on the Atlantic trade. Thomas Paine in his 1776 pamphlet *Common Sense* had predicted that America could count on prosperity as long as "eating is the custom of Europe," and his prediction was borne out in the 1790s. American grain farmers from the Connecticut River valley in the North to the Chesapeake region in the South responded to the attractive European market by putting more acres under cultivation. In Virginia and Maryland, soil worn out by tobacco cultivation could be renewed by a switch to wheat production. The increase in overseas grain trade generated a host of new jobs in related areas as the number of millers, coopers, and ship and wagon builders expanded. The grain trade generated moral pride as well: American production was concentrated on food, a basic human need, not on luxury items.

A second type of commercial agriculture also embarked on a new course after 1793. Limited amounts of smooth-seed cotton had long been grown in the low-lying coastal areas of the southern states, but this variety of cotton did not prosper in the drier, inland regions. Green-seed cotton, in contrast, grew well inland throughout the South but contained many rough seeds that adhered tenaciously to the cotton fibers. Typically, it took an entire day to clean a pound of cotton by hand. Southern cotton growers were thus intent on finding a way to diminish the laborious task; some states even offered bounties for the invention of an efficient mechanical way to separate the rough seeds from the cotton.

In 1793, a clever young Yale graduate named Eli Whitney, visiting friends at a Georgia plantation, turned his mechanical talents to the task. His invention, the cotton gin, could clean fifty pounds of cotton per day. Whitney improved and patented his machine in 1794, but not before imitators eagerly leaped into the business of making cotton gins. The English textile industry provided a ready market for all cotton grown; the demand was high, and now supply could meet it. The figures of cotton production tell the whole story: 138,228 pounds of cotton were grown in the South in 1792; two years later, the number was 1,601,000, eleven times as much. In 1795, production amounted to 6,272,000 pounds, a fourfold increase over just the year before; and by 1800, the figure was 35 million pounds of cotton. Cotton fever had gripped the South, with momentous and chilling consequences for the one million enslaved black Americans living there.

Transportation

The prosperous cash economy made possible by grain exports and cotton culture was initially confined to areas within easy reach of the port cities—farming regions usually within thirty miles of navigable waterways or the coast. Poor roads presented the single biggest obstacle to the spread of commercial farming, because of the high cost of transporting goods over muddy or rutted paths barely wide enough for a wagon. The only major continuous road existing at the beginning of the 1790s was the Post Road, running near the East Coast for 1,600 miles from Maine to Georgia. It consisted of local country roads, linked together in the 1780s, and it carried an ever-increasing load of passenger traffic in stagecoaches as well as freight and the U.S. mail.

In the 1790s, east-to-west road building commenced. In 1794, the Lancaster Turnpike, the first private toll road in the nation, connected Philadelphia with Lancaster, sixty-five miles west, and, later, with Pittsburgh in western Pennsylvania. Soon another turnpike connected Boston with Albany, New York. Private companies under charter by state governments financed these projects; the company built the roadbed, often made of solid stone covered by gravel, and collected fees from all vehicles. Some surfaces were made of planks or felled logs placed side by side, which prevented mudhole problems but shook up passengers frightfully. From Albany, a new highway moved along the Mohawk River valley, pushing west into land once held by the powerful Iroquois until the Revolutionary War forced them farther west. In the Upper South, a major road extended southwest down the Shenandoah Valley between the crest of the Blue Ridge Mountains and the Appalachians. In the west, a road named Zane's Trace moved across southern Ohio in 1796; and another road linked Richmond, Virginia, with the Tennessee towns of Knoxville and Nashville in the interior. An early Ohio law reveals the primitive character of these western roads compared with state-of-the-art gravel turnpikes in the

STAGE COACH ADVERTISEMENT

Stagecoach lines advertised their schedules and terms in newspapers. This is from the New York Journal and Patriotic Register *for August 21, 1793. It promises to accommodate passengers in the most agreeable manner and to reach Philadelphia in "about" twenty-four hours.*

Courtesy, American Antiquarian Society.

East: The law prohibited stumps in the roadway higher than one foot. Western roads greatly facilitated the migration of settlers, but they were too slow to allow an economical movement of heavy, bulky agricultural products like grain. Consequently, western farmers usually opted to distill their surplus farm produce into a much more compact form—wheat and rye whiskeys—for transport to eastern markets.

By 1800, a dense network of dirt, gravel, or plank roadways connected cities and towns in southern New England and the Middle Atlantic states, while isolated roadways and old Indian trails fanned out to the west. Commercial stage lines connected major eastern cities, offering four-day travel time between Boston and New York and an exhausting but speedy thirty-six-hour trip between New York and Philadelphia. Whereas in 1790 only three stagecoach companies operated out of Boston, in 1800 there were twenty-four. On the roads far-

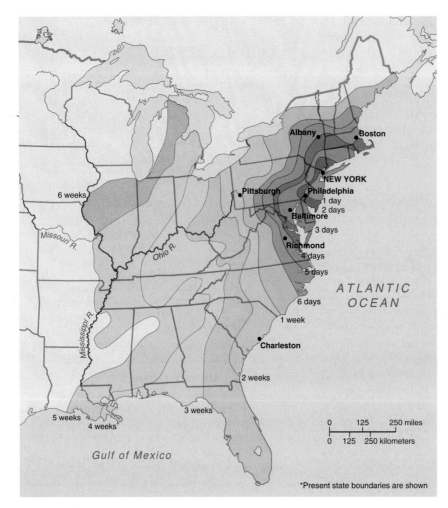

MAP 9.1
Travel Times from New York City in 1800
Notice that the first week of travel out of New York extends over a much greater distance than subsequent weeks because of poor or nonexistent roads in the west, mountain barriers, and Indian dangers. River corridors in either west or east speeded up travel — if one were going downriver. Also note that travel by sea (north and south along the coast) was much faster than land travel.

ther west, the sons and daughters of eastern farm families trekked by the thousands in search of fresh homesteads, and four new states—Vermont, Kentucky, Tennessee, and Ohio—became sufficiently populated to join the Union by 1800. In that year, Kentucky had more settlers than did five of the original thirteen states.

South of the Potomac River, road building and commercial stagecoach travel remained in a primitive state, chiefly because of low passenger demand. Two-thirds of the southern population—the enslaved blacks and the poorer whites—could not travel, and the elite of the planter class generally owned their own coaches and wagons. Growers of cotton and tobacco continued to rely on the many southern rivers to move produce to market, which reinforced the economic dominance of property owners fronting on the eastern waterways.

Merchants and Capital

The surge in the overseas grain and cotton trades stimulated the growth of the commercial classes in the seacoast cities of the new nation. At the pinnacle of the business community were the merchants, often men with multiple financial dealings. The word *merchant* had a more specific meaning in the late eighteenth century than now, for it designated a person involved in both wholesale and retail operations. Someone who merely retailed goods to the public was a shopkeeper. The richest merchants had lines of trade stretching across the Atlantic. Not only did they buy and sell foreign goods, they typically owned some fraction of the ships that carried the goods. With each ship owned by four to six merchants, the risk of financial catastrophe from the loss of a ship was thus spread out over several firms.

In the 1780s, states could and did erect trade barriers, but the creation of the new federal government finally removed all obstacles to interstate business alliances and guaranteed the free movement of goods across state borders. The horizons of the business community widened, and the volume of trade mushroomed. New investment opportunities beckoned, not only in mercantile trades but also in such areas as the chartering of turnpike companies and stagecoach lines or the development of spinning factories or woolen mills in New England.

These opportunities required a larger and longer commitment of capital than did a joint venture for a single cargo in a ship. The need for investment capital was met by the development of commercial banking, a financial innovation that had not existed in America before the Revolution. During the 1790s, the number of banks multiplied nearly tenfold, from three at the beginning of the decade to twenty-nine in 1800. (By 1810, there were more than one hundred banks.) Banks drew in money chiefly through the sale of stock. They then made loans in the form of banknotes, paper currency issued by the bank and backed by the gold and silver paid in by stockholders. Because they issued two or three times as much money in banknotes as they held in hard money, banks were really creating new money for the economy.

Rich merchants in particular embraced banking schemes with enthusiasm. In one feverish week in New York City in 1792, three rival banks were proposed, with aimed-for stock subscriptions totaling about $4 million. Isaac Roosevelt, the president of the Bank of New York, typified the multiventure involvement of this new breed of merchants who were developing innovative and complex financial dealings. Roosevelt owned a sugar refinery, financed overseas shipping, and speculated heavily in confiscated loyalist real estate. As president of the leading New York bank, he had ready access to investments (buying stock in the bank) as well as access to credit. Not everyone in New York was appreciative of the virtues of commercial banking, however. When Roosevelt and his fellow merchants applied for a state charter for their bank, one New York newspaper condemned the bank for being "an odious combination of wealthy men."

Hamilton's Political Economy

In late 1790, the government moved from New York to Philadelphia, a more centrally located city with a merchant class no less enterprising than that in New York. This too was a temporary home; the long-range plan entailed construction of the capital on the Potomac River between Maryland and Virginia, independent of any state. (See Historical Question, page 324.) Many Philadelphians, hoping to derail the Potomac plan, welcomed the government officials with lavish displays of the social attractions of their city. A whirl of entertainments caused Abigail Adams, the vice president's wife, to complain about the "continued scene of parties upon parties," but the outward friendliness could not mask the growing political rifts over economic policy. A different sort of party scene, even more upsetting than the social whirl, was in the making. At the center of growing controversy was the head of the Treasury, Alexander Hamilton.

TABLE 9.1

GROWTH OF THE U.S. POSTAL SERVICE, **1790-1820**

Year	Number of Post Offices	Miles of Post Road	Letters (millions)	Newspapers Mailed (millions)
1790	75	1,875	.3	.5
1800	903	20,817	2.0	1.9
1810	2,300	36,406	3.9	n.a.
1820	4,500	72,492	8.9	6.0

Postal rates set in 1792 favored newspapers over letters to promote the spread of information: letters cost 6 cents to a dollar, newspapers cost either 1 or 1.5 cents. The number of newspapers posted at first exceeded that of letters, and never fell far behind.

Source: Richard R. John, *Spreading the News: The American Postal System from Franklin to Morse* (1995).

How Did Washington, D.C., Become the Federal Capital?

WHY DIDN'T BOSTON, Philadelphia, or New York City become the capital of the United States? The great cities of London and Paris were great precisely because political power was situated at the heart of commerce and culture in those European countries. Although much smaller in scale, the several American cities boasted elegant houses, cultural institutions, lively economies, newspapers, food markets, taverns, coffeehouses, and stagecoach and shipping lines—nearly everything necessary to accommodate the political elites who would be running the new government. Instead, the infant United States chose marshy, vacant acreage along the Maryland shore of the Potomac River for its permanent capital.

While the choice of that particular site was by no means inevitable, the country's leaders agreed that there should be only one site. During the war years, the Continental Congress had jumped around many times, from Philadelphia, Lancaster, and York in Pennsylvania to Princeton and Trenton in New Jersey, and down to Baltimore, often on the run from the British army. Even after the war, the congress continued to circulate, meeting at Trenton, at Annapolis and Georgetown in Maryland, and finally in New York City. When the confederation government commissioned an equestrian statue of George Washington to inspire and dignify its meetings, a humorist suggested that the marble horse be fitted with wheels so it could be towed from place to place.

For some, a floating capital symbolized the precarious status of the confederation. But the alternative, a fixed location, put the federal government at the mercy of the particular state it sat in. If irate citizens stormed the congress, as had happened once in Philadelphia in 1783, could the local state's militia always be counted on to protect it? The writers of the Constitution thus came up with a novel solution. They decided to locate the capital on land not controlled by any state. The 1788 Constitution specified a square district, not exceeding ten miles on a side, where Congress would have sole jurisdiction; but they deferred the complicated choice of the exact site to the First Congress.

In 1790, more than forty cities and towns clamored for consideration, from Kingston and Newburgh in New York's Hudson River valley, down to Richmond and Williamsburg in Virginia. Eleven contenders clustered along the Delaware River between New Jersey and Pennsylvania, roughly the demographic center of the country. Six more sites fell in the interior of Pennsylvania, along the Susquehanna River, each claiming to be the future geographic center as the country grew westward. Another eleven locations dotted the Potomac River from Chesapeake Bay to the Appalachian Mountains. Clearly, river transportation figured heavily in all these plans, and investors in canal and river navigation companies took special notice. Local property prices as well as the value of water transport services would skyrocket once a capital city was established.

The First Congress struggled to reconcile private interests, regional jealousies, and genuine dilemmas of citizen access. A Pennsylvania proposal naming a Susquehanna River site finally passed the House but not the Senate. Virginians held out for the Potomac, drawing objections from New Englanders fearful of disease-laden southern swamps. Philadelphians insisted that their city, the premier cultural and economic center of America, was the only logical choice. In short, the situation was at a stalemate.

Another, unrelated stalemate obstructed Congress in early 1790. Alexander Hamilton presented Congress with his controversial plan to fund the public debt, including assumption, the proposal for the federal government to assume all the states' debts as well. James Madison objected and led the opposition against assumption, leaving Hamilton without the necessary votes—at first.

Hamilton approached Robert Morris of Pennsylvania to propose a deal: If Morris would deliver votes for assumption, the influential Hamilton would back a capital site in Pennsylvania. But Morris could not command enough congressional votes, so Hamilton next approached Thomas Jefferson, secretary of state, who invited him to dinner with James Madison. There the three reached agreement:

PLAN FOR WASHINGTON, D.C., ON A HANDKERCHIEF
In 1791 and 1792, the pressure was high to get a detailed map of the proposed capital city into circulation so that prospective land buyers could be lined up. Finally a Philadelphia engraving firm produced this plan of the future city with each block numbered. It was reproduced on large handkerchiefs in an early marketing strategy to entice buyers. The actual site in 1792 consisted of fields and marshes.
Library of Congress.

principal investor—stood to benefit, but this was not considered a conflict of interest in the 1790s. What made the Potomac advantageous both for a capital site and for investment in navigation was the fact that it penetrated the farthest inland of any East Coast river, traversing the lowest point in the Appalachian Mountains. Washington's scouting trips convinced him that with short portages, water routes could connect the Chesapeake Bay to western Pennsylvania and beyond to the Ohio and Mississippi Rivers.

Next, the rural site had to be purchased from the Maryland farmers who owned it. Washington and Jefferson purposely deployed surveyors in widely scattered locations up and down the river, to keep local owners from guessing where the government center would finally rest within the district —and thus to keep a lid on land prices. The president also deputized friends to purchase the land, "as if for yourselves, and to conduct your propositions so as to excite no suspicion that they are on behalf of the public."

Washington then hired a French-born master designer to plan the capital. Pierre L'Enfant, an architect living in New York City, mapped out a grid of streets slashed dramatically by wide diagonal boulevards. L'Enfant envisioned a mall surrounded by grand government buildings. The rest of his map showed small lots intended for private buyers, who, it was hoped, would provide housing and services for the government population. The proceeds of the land sales would fund the government construction, so that a city could be built without having to draw on the U.S. Treasury at all.

In the end, the capital landed in the South because a major east–west river was there and because the South had crucial votes to trade on the assumption bill. Washington, D.C., represented the geographic but not the demographic center of the thirteen states. Its placement exerted a southern tug on the federal government, augmented by the fact that five of the first seven presidents were also southerners. The capital of the republic sat in the heart of a slave society; in all the political horse-trading over choosing the site, nobody thought that fact was worthy of remark. But it would turn out to be of major significance some sixty years later, when the capital of President Abraham Lincoln's Union sat surrounded by slavery, with many of its inhabitants of doubtful loyalty to the Union.

enough southern votes for assumption in exchange for a Potomac River site. Madison could not bring himself to vote for assumption, but he rounded up the necessary votes from men representing districts along the river. In the final bill, Philadelphia was named the interim capital until 1800, by which time a site on the Potomac River, to be selected by President Washington, would be constructed and open for business. Robert Morris gloated that the Virginians had been tricked; he felt sure that Philadelphia's charms would ensnare the government permanently. Assumption quickly passed, by six votes.

Washington, drawing on his surveying expertise, took another year to select the hill-banked plain east of Georgetown, after scouting far up the river. For any location he chose, the Potomac Company —of which Washington himself was president and

The Public Debt and Taxes

The youthful Hamilton was clearly something of a prodigy. At age twenty, he had been indispensable to George Washington during the Revolutionary War; at age twenty-six, he had gained admission to the bar after only three months of study. At age thirty, he had had enough credibility in New York to be chosen for the Philadelphia convention. His vigorous defense of the Constitution's political philosophy in the *Federalist Papers* and his tactical maneuvering in the ratification process made it clear that he had a brilliant political future. At age thirty-four, he joined President Washington's first cabinet as "First Lord of the Treasury," as he once styled himself. To rectify the instabilities of the 1780s economy, Hamilton proposed a three-part plan.

He first turned his attention to the very large public debt, a sum amounting to $52 million. About $11.7 million was owed to foreign creditors, while a tangled web of IOUs and interest-bearing public securities amounted to a further $40.4 million of domestic indebtedness. The debt dated from the difficult war years, when the government needed supplies and manpower but had no independent source of revenue. In the 1780s, the actual paper IOUs and certificates of debt had fallen in value, in some states to as little as one-twentieth of the original value; this drop reflected the widespread belief that the confederation government could never make good on them. In recent years, wealthy speculators were buying the IOUs cheaply and quietly, betting that they might rise in value in the long run.

Even though the 1787 Constitution contained a clause specifically guaranteeing that all debts contracted under the previous government "shall be as valid against the United States under this Constitution, as under the Confederation," a close reading of those words reveals an ambiguity. The public debt of the confederation government may have been valid, but it was not being honored before the Constitution; that document therefore made no new promises. But neither did it repudiate the debt, for that would have been a blow to the country's integrity. The question now was open: What exactly should be done about the debt?

Hamilton's answer, elaborated in his *Report on Public Credit* in January 1790, was that the debt, both foreign and domestic, be funded at full value. This meant that an old IOU or a certificate of debt would be rolled over into a new bond, at the same value, with a schedule of regular interest payments from government to holder and a promise to retire the

ALEXANDER HAMILTON
Alexander Hamilton in 1792 at age thirty-seven, painted by John Trumbull.
Yale University Art Gallery.

debt in forty years, using government income from import taxes. Thus there would still be a public debt, but it would be secure, supported by the confidence of Americans in their new government. The old fluctuating certificates would be retired, traded in for the new bonds, which would circulate as a stable medium of exchange, injecting new and more valuable money into the economy. "A national debt if not excessive will be to us a national blessing; it will be a powerfull cement of our union," Hamilton wrote to another financier.

Probably about 2 percent of the white population held the largest portions of the debt. Now these influential men would have a direct stake in the new government, support that Hamilton regarded as essential to the country's stability. He was also providing those same few men with more than $40 million released for new investment, a distinct improvement over the old depreciated bonds, which had circulated in daily transactions at only a small fraction of their face value.

If the *Report on Public Credit* had only gone this far, it would have been somewhat controversial. But

Hamilton took a much bolder step by adding into the federal debt another $25 million still owed by some state governments to individuals. All the states had obtained supplies during the war by issuing IOUs to farmers, merchants, and moneylenders. Some states, such as Virginia and New York, had paid off these debts entirely, while others, like Massachusetts, had accomplished partial success through heavy and painful taxation of the inhabitants; about half the states had made little headway. Hamilton called for the federal government to assume these state debts and add them to the federal debt. Hamilton's "assumption plan" in effect consolidated federal power over the states.

The assumption of state debts required the federal government to exercise even stronger powers of taxation. To meet the interest payments on a national debt swollen to some $77 million, Hamilton did not propose raising import duties, for that would have been unacceptable to the merchant class whose support he was seeking. Instead, he convinced Congress in 1791 to pass a hefty excise tax on distilled spirits, amounting to 25 percent of the eventual market value of the whiskey, to be paid by the farmer when he brought his grain to the distillery. Members of Congress favored the tax, especially those from New England where the favorite drink was rum, an imported beverage already taxed under the import duty laws. A New Hampshire representative pointed out that the country would be "drinking down the national debt," an idea he evidently thought was good.

> "A national debt if not excessive will be to us a national blessing; it will be a powerful cement of our union," Hamilton wrote.

Congress passed Hamilton's funding and assumption plans, but not without first considering a serious objection. Congressman James Madison agreed on paying full value to an original holder of the debt, but he objected to the windfall profits that would go to speculators. He also strenuously objected to assumption of all the states' debts. A large debt is dangerous, Madison warned, especially because the government must tax heavily to service the interest on the debt, and so money flows out of the pockets of ordinary people and moves to the purses of the few rich creditors. Madison's plan to differentiate between original and new holders of the debt was too complex and probably unworkable because the government lacked records of the original transactions. Other representatives complained that even original holders could be like speculators, if they had made their loans to the government in the form of the virtually worthless Continental dollars. Madison's amendments were voted down, and the debt was funded Hamilton's way. Madison and Hamilton, so recently allies in writing the *Federalist Papers,* were very quickly becoming opponents.

Secretary of State Jefferson, too, was fearful of Hamilton's schemes. Cabinet meetings had become disagreeable and uncomfortable, a situation that prompted President Washington to rebuke them both. Hamilton misread the motives of Madison and Jefferson, thinking they were rivals for his power. Jefferson had a clearer picture of the problem: "No man is more ardently intent to see the public debt soon and sacredly paid off than I am. This exactly marks the difference between Colonel Hamilton's views and mine, that I would wish the debt paid tomorrow; he wishes it never to be paid, but always to be a thing where with to corrupt and manage the legislature." Jefferson feared that rich speculators with a financial stake in the government would meddle with the Congress, just as he suspected that Hamilton was already corrupted. In a letter to the president in 1792, Jefferson characterized Hamilton as "the man who has the shuffling of millions backwards & forwards from paper into money & money into paper, from Europe to America, & America to Europe, the dealing out of Treasury-secrets among his friends in what time & measure he pleases, and who never slips an occasion of making friends with his means."

The First Bank of the United States

A second major element of Hamilton's economic plan was his proposal for a national Bank of the United States, which he presented to the Congress in December 1790. Believing that banks were the "nurseries of national wealth," Hamilton modeled his plan on the Bank of England: a private corporation that worked primarily for the public good. In Hamilton's plan, 20 percent of the bank's stock would be bought by the federal government. In effect, the bank would become the fiscal agent of the new government, holding and handling its revenue money derived from import duties, land sales, and the whiskey excise tax. The other 80 percent of the bank's capital would come from private investors, who could buy stock in the bank with either hard money (silver or gold) or federal securities. By its size and privilege of being the only national bank, the bank would help stabilize the economy by exerting prudent control over credit, interest rates, and the value of the currency. Five of the twenty-five directors of the bank would be appointed by the government, to look out for the public interest. Hamilton had extraordinarily good faith in the virtue of the other twenty directors, who would be chosen from among the private stockholders and thus be merchants drawn from the world of commerce and high finance.

Madison tried to stop the bank plan in Congress, but he could not muster the necessary support. Again he complained that the rich would have undue influence in the government's finances and in setting economic policy. Jefferson advised Washington that creating a national bank was unconstitutional, because there was nothing about chartering banks in the list of specified powers granted to Congress by the Constitution. Hamilton, however, argued that the same list specified many powers to regulate commerce and ended with a broad grant of the right "to make all Laws which shall be necessary and proper for carrying into execution the foregoing Powers." Washington considered both arguments for two weeks and then agreed with Hamilton. He scrapped a statement vetoing the bank, which he had asked Madison to draft, and signed the bank bill in February 1791, chartering the bank for twenty years.

When the bank's stock—the 80 percent that was to be privately held—went on sale in New York City in July, it sold out in a few hours, touching off an immediate mania of speculation in the resale of stock shares. A discouraged Madison reported that "the Coffee House is an eternal buzz with the gamblers" meeting over hot drinks to trade stock shares. Two months later, the gamblers had moved their game to an office and formally organized as the New York Stock Exchange, for the more efficient buying and selling of bank stock.

The **Report on Manufactures**

The third component of Hamilton's plan was set out in December 1791 in the *Report on Manufactures,* a proposal to encourage the production of American-made goods. Manufacturing was in its infancy in 1790, the result of years of dependence on British imports. Hamilton recognized that a balanced and self-reliant economy required the United States to produce its own cloth and iron products. His plan mobilized the new powers of the federal government to impose tariffs and grant subsidies to encourage the growth of local manufacturing. Tariffs were a tricky business, however, for Hamilton had to be careful not to undercut his important merchant allies who made their money trading with England and whose trade, in turn, generated over half the government's income. A high tariff would either seriously dampen that trade or would force merchants into smuggling, a practice well known from the days of British rule. So Hamilton favored a moderate tariff, with extra bounties paid to American manufacturers to encourage production.

The *Report on Manufactures* was the one Hamiltonian plan that was not approved by Congress. Hamilton himself was somewhat indifferent and did not push hard for its adoption. Much of the work of drafting the report had been done by his assistant Tench Coxe, a Pennsylvanian who had headed a group called the Manufacturing Society of Philadelphia. Hamilton was far more interested in a financial investment he helped set up earlier in 1791, the Society to Encourage Useful Manufactures, which funneled capital from merchant investors into stock purchases in new textile factories being built in Paterson, New Jersey. The plan was friendly primarily to investors and secondarily to manufacturers, and then only large-scale manufacturers. In the late 1790s, the small manufacturers of America—the cotton spinners, the cloth weavers, the gun makers, and paper manufacturers—favored Hamilton's opponent, the emerging Republican Party of Jefferson and Madison, as the more likely source of protective trade tariffs.

The Whiskey Rebellion

Hamilton may have been a financial genius, but he still could make serious political mistakes, as his excise tax on whiskey showed. Many more voters were grain farmers and whiskey drinkers than were merchants. Western farmers with an abundance of wheat and rye suddenly faced high taxes at the distillery when they presented their grains for processing. The tax was up-front money that could not be recovered until the product was transported to market and sold. Cash-short farmers deeply resented their assigned role in Hamilton's plan for economic recovery.

In 1791, angry grain farmers in the western parts of Pennsylvania, Virginia, Maryland, and the Carolinas and throughout Kentucky conveyed to

WHISKEY REBELLION "FIRE COPPER"
This forty-gallon "fire copper" produced Monongahela rye whiskey in the 1790s in western Pennsylvania. Mashed rye grain was mixed and heated with mash from a previously distilled brew. The distiller next added yeast and water and let the mixture ferment for several days. The mixture was then heated to 175 degrees, the boiling point of alcohol, in this three-foot copper vessel (called a still, as in distilling). Alcohol-laden vapor from the boiling brew cooled and condensed in a spiral copper tubing that dripped whiskey into a jug. High-proof, expensive whiskey required a second processing in the still to concentrate the vapors. The owner of this fire copper was James Miller, whose nephew Oliver Miller Jr. was an early fatality in the Whiskey Rebellion.
Oliver Miller Homestead/Photo by Andrew Wagner; Courtesy of American History Magazine.

Congress their resentment of Hamilton's tax. Marginal farmers stood to lose the most under the law; one man who petitioned Congress explained that he already had handed over half his grain as payment to the local distillery for distilling his rye, and now the distiller was paying the tax on the whole quantity of whiskey out of the farmer's remaining half alone. This "reduces the balance to less than one-third of the original quantity. If this is not an oppressive tax, I am at a loss to describe what is so." Many such petitions of protest arrived at Congress, which produced modest modifications in the tax in 1792; but even so, discontent was rampant.

Simple evasion of the law was the most common response. And indeed, the tax proved hard to collect. Federally appointed tax inspectors soon learned the unpleasant consequences, as crowds threatened to tar and feather them. A congressional representative from Pennsylvania, William Findley, observed that "it is well known that in some counties, as well of Virginia as of Pennsylvania, men have not, and cannot be induced by any consider-

ation to accept of the excise offices." With no tax collectors, by late 1792 the tax was dead in northwest Virginia, western North Carolina, and all of Kentucky. Even in Philadelphia, the nation's capital, major distilleries right under Hamilton's nose were evading the tax by underreporting their production by nearly half. With embarrassment, Hamilton admitted to Congress that the revenue yield from the tax was far less than anticipated. But rather than abandon the law, he tightened up on the prosecution of tax evaders.

In western Pennsylvania, Hamilton had one ally, a stubborn tax collector who had refused to quit even after a group of spirited farmers had burned an effigy of him and after his deputies had received ominous midnight visits from men wearing disguises. In late May 1794, this tax collector filed charges against seventy-five farmers and distillers for tax evasion. In mid-July, the collector and a federal marshal were ambushed in Allegheny County by a group of forty men, and during the next two days the tax collector's house was burned to the ground by a crowd estimated at five hundred. At the end of July, seven thousand farmers staged a march on Pittsburgh to express their hostility to the hated tax.

An angry Hamilton convinced President Washington to respond with a show of force. Washington nationalized the Pennsylvania militia, and the aged ex-general donned his old military garb and set out, with Hamilton at his side urging him on, at the head of fifteen thousand soldiers. This was as large a force as had served in any single campaign of the Continental army, when the enemy was the British army. Their goal now was to quell the "rebellion," as Hamilton called it, in the counties around Pittsburgh. Since a one-day demonstration of seven thousand farmers is not exactly a full-scale rebellion, it was undoubtedly Hamilton's plan to make an example of western Pennsylvania that would send a message to other noncomplying regions.

By the time the military force arrived, in late September, the demonstrators had all gone home. No battles were fought, and no fire was exchanged. Twenty men were rounded up as rebels and charged with high treason, but only two were convicted, and both were soon pardoned by President Washington, with the faint excuse that one was insane and the other dimwitted.

> *At the core of the Whiskey Rebellion lay the question of what citizens can and cannot do when they think a law is unjust and what governments can and cannot do when groups of citizens resort to extralegal and even violent means to express their grievances.*

Had the government overreacted? Or was Hamilton right to think that the whiskey rioters posed a serious threat to the stability of the federal government? At issue was more than the hardships of western farmers short on money and resentful of taxes, and more than Hamilton's need to get the debt funded and to restore confidence in the nation's economy. At the core of the Whiskey Rebellion lay the question of what citizens can and cannot do when they think a law is unjust and what governments can and cannot do when groups of citizens resort to extralegal and even violent means to express their grievances.

The long colonial tradition of crowd action to protest unfair practices or to express public opinion had worked comfortably in a political culture where ordinary people had limited formal access to power. But in a republic, laws were passed by the supposed representatives of the people, not by tyrannical kings or distant parliaments. Burning effigies of stamp tax collectors in 1765 made sense as an effective contribution to the political process. In contrast, burning effigies of whiskey tax collectors in 1792 appeared to many to be an unlawful rejection of the will of the people as expressed through Congress. Hamilton thought so, and that is why he convinced the president to lead an army west. This was his chance to replay Shays's Rebellion of 1786, this time with a federal government empowered to raise armies and put down rebellions.

The whiskey rebels, however, recognized oppressive taxes for what they were and felt entitled to resort to protest and demonstration. Representative government had not worked to their benefit. The Whiskey Rebellion was an early example of what would prove to be a long-term conflict, the tension between minority rights and majority rule.

Conflicts West and East

Washington's second term began in 1793, after a smooth and again unanimous reelection. But as the Whiskey Rebellion demonstrated, the widespread admiration for the individual man did not translate to complete domestic tranquillity. While the whiskey rebels challenged federal leadership from within the country, considerable disorder threatened the United States from external sources as well. To the west, a powerful confederation of Indian tribes in the Ohio country resisted white encroachment as thousands of settlers moved onto their tribal lands. The result was a brutal war. At the same time, conflicts between the major European powers forced Americans to take sides and nearly thrust the country into another war, this time across the Atlantic.

To the West: The Indians

By the Treaty of Paris of 1783, England had given up all land east of the Mississippi River to the United States. But unfortunately this land was not entirely England's to give; the English neglected to consult their allies in the Revolutionary War, the In-

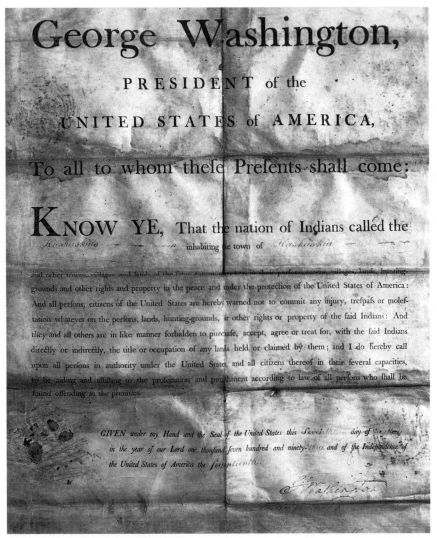

George Washington,

PRESIDENT of the

UNITED STATES of AMERICA,

To all to whom thefe Prefents shall come:

KNOW YE, That the nation of Indians called the *Kaskaskia* inhabiting the town of *Kaskaskia*

and other towns, villages, and lands of that fame nation in their feveral towns, villages, lands, hunting grounds and other rights and property in the peace and under the protection of the United States of America: And all perfons, citizens of the United States are hereby warned not to commit any injury, trefpafs or molef- tation whatever on the perfons, lands, hunting-grounds, or other rights or property of the faid Indians: And they and all others are in like manner forbidden to purchafe, accept, agree or treat for, with the faid Indians directly or indirectly, the title or occupation of any lands held or claimed by them; and I do hereby call upon all perfons in authority under the United States, and all citizens thereof in their feveral capacities, to be aiding and affifting to the profecution and punifhment according to law of all perfons who fhall be found offending in the premifes.

GIVEN under my Hand and the Seal of the United States this Seventh day of May in the year of our Lord one thoufand feven hundred and ninety-three and of the Independence of the United States of America the fourteenth.

G. Washington

WASHINGTON'S PROCLAMATION ABOUT THE KASKASKIA INDIANS' LAND
The president's name, in bold print, prefaces a warning that American citizens were forbidden to injure Indians or trespass their lands in the Northwest Territory. When the federal government signed treaties with tribes ceding land, it often guaranteed protections for land not ceded. This poster of 1793 announced federal protection for the Kaskaskia Indians in central Illinois Territory. The warnings were not very effective, however. Washington wrote in 1796, "I believe scarcely any thing short of a Chinese Wall, or line of Troops will restrain Land Jobbers, and the Incroachment of Settlers, upon Indian Territory."
Chicago Historical Society.

dian tribes who inhabited 25,000 square miles of that very land. As recently as 1768, England had formally guaranteed the Indians their rights to all land north of the Ohio River, but the Treaty of Paris simply ignored that obligation.

British commanders at forts in the Great Lakes region at first concealed the terms of the 1783 treaty from local natives, the Chippewas, Potawatomis, and Ottawas. They perhaps hoped that the thirteen unsteady states would fail to create a viable country, and then the British forts could simply continue with the fur trade as before. When the commander at Fort Niagara finally told the Iroquois neighbors about the treaty terms, the Indians expressed astonishment. They "look upon our conduct to them as treacherous and cruel. They told me they never

could believe that our king could pretend to cede to America what was not his own to give." In southern Ohio, British Indian agents assured the Shawnees and Delawares that England had relinquished only political control to the United States but that Indians still had the right to occupy the land over the claims of American settlers. Such confusion and misrepresentation only aggravated an already volatile situation.

A doubled American population, from 2.5 million in 1770 to 5 million in 1790, created an insistent pressure for western land. Several thousand settlers a year moved down the Ohio River in the mid-1780s, some bound for tranquil Kentucky but many others eyeing the fresh forests and fields north of the Ohio River. For seven months in the fall and

TREATY OF GREENVILLE
*General Anthony Wayne meets with Chief Little Turtle of the Miamis and Chief Tarhe the Crane
of the Wyandots to negotiate the Treaty of Greenville in 1795.*
Chicago Historical Society.

winter of 1786–87, an officer at an American garrison counted 177 boats, 2,689 people, 1,333 horses, 766 cattle, and 102 wagons moving west; the increasing flow of traffic was also observed by wary Indians. By the late 1780s, government land sales in eastern Ohio commenced.

Even western Ohio was not safe from American incursions. Downriver, at the site of present-day Cincinnati, an outpost named Fort Washington was constructed in 1789 and put under the command of General Arthur St. Clair, a military man who was also named governor of the entire Northwest Territory. If the Indians had any initial hope that American military outposts would function as the British forts had, as tiny way stations in the fur trade, they soon realized their mistake. St. Clair's mission was to displace the Indians and clear the way for permanent American settlement in Ohio. He first tried peaceful tactics: He got an assortment of Indians to sign a treaty yielding land near the Muskingum River, in eastern Ohio. But the signing Indians were not chiefs authorized to undertake negotiations, so the dubious treaty did nothing to improve the chances for peace in the region.

Bloody frontier raids and skirmishes between settlers and Indians led the United States to expand its military force. Finally, St. Clair took direct action. In the fall of 1791, more than two thousand men (and two hundred women camp followers) marched north from Fort Washington to engage in battle with Miami and Shawnee Indians. The Miami chief Little Turtle and the Shawnee chief Blue Jacket anticipated the army and attacked first, at daybreak on November 4, at the headwaters of the Wabash River in western Ohio. The ferocious battle was a total disaster for the Americans. The dead and wounded amounted to 55 percent of the force before noon; only three of the women escaped alive. It was the worst defeat in the entire history of the U.S.-Indian wars. The Indians captured valuable guns and artillery and scalped and dismembered the bodies of the dead and dying. They pursued fleeing survivors for miles into the forest. The grisly tales of St. Clair's Defeat—the battle has no other official name—became instantly infamous, increasing, if this were possible, the level of sheer terror that Americans brought to their confrontation with the Indians.

President Washington responded by doubling the American military presence in Ohio, attracting the new recruits by significant pay raises for all soldiers. He appointed a new commander, General Anthony Wayne of Pennsylvania. Wayne, an officer in the Continental army during the Revolution, had earned the nickname "Mad Anthony" for his headstrong and rambunctious style of leadership. He was a heavy drinker, inclined to incautious decisions, and intolerant of disobedient soldiers. About the Indians he wrote, "I have always been of the opinion that we never should have a permanent peace with those Indians until they were made to experience our superiority."

The hasty Wayne was persuaded to delay the full thrust of his campaign for a year, while federal negotiators resumed talks with some tribes. The victory over St. Clair had given the Indians a momentary sense of bargaining strength, so they held out in peace talks for the removal of all American settlers in western Ohio. But the main function served by the delay was to allow time for the U.S. forces to train and rearm. With some 3,500 men, Wayne established two new military camps, Fort Greenville and Fort Recovery, deep in Indian territory in western Ohio.

Finally, in December 1793, Wayne was ready to seize the initiative. Moving north from Fort

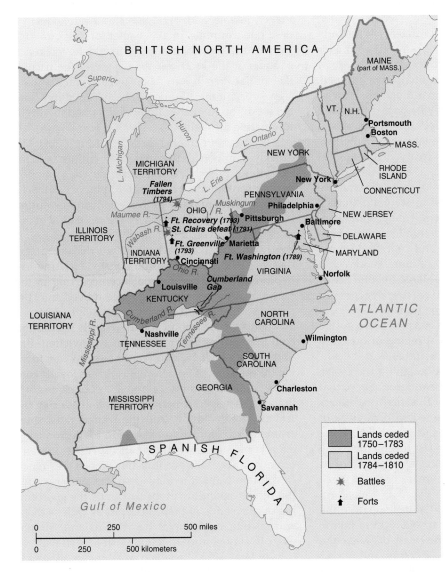

M A P 9.2
Western Expansion and Indian Land Cessions to 1810
By the first decade of the nineteenth century, the period of intense Indian wars had resulted in significant cessions of land to the U.S. government by treaty. The battles of the 1790s concentrated in Ohio, and in 1803 the region was pacified sufficiently to become the seventeenth state in the Union.

Greenville, Wayne's army camped on the very site of St. Clair's defeat in 1791. His troops faced a chilling task: They had to pile up the hundreds of skeletons and broken muskets littering the ground in order to pitch their tents. By spring, Wayne's army had engaged in several skirmishes with the Shawnees and Delawares. The decisive action came in August 1794 at the Battle of Fallen Timbers, near the Maumee River at a spot where a recent severe rainstorm had felled many trees. The confederated Indians—mainly Ottawas, Potawatomis, and Delawares, numbering around 800—first ambushed the Americans, but they were underarmed, many having only tomahawks. Wayne's well-disciplined troops made effective use of their guns and bayonets, and in just over an hour the Indians had retreated and scattered.

Fallen Timbers was a major defeat for the Indians. The Americans had also destroyed cornfields and villages on the march north, and with winter approaching, the Indians' confidence was sapped. They reentered negotiations in a much less powerful bargaining position. In 1795, about a thousand Indians representing a confederacy of nearly a dozen tribes met with Wayne and other American emissaries to work out the Treaty of Greenville. Wayne flourished a copy of the 1783 treaty with the British to prove the Americans' right to the land. He then offered $25,000 worth of treaty goods (calico shirts, yard goods, axes, knives, baling wire, blankets, kettles, mirrors, ribbons, thimbles, and abundant wine and liquor casks) and promised an annual shipment worth $10,000 of more goods—but always first deducting a rather large freight charge. The government's idea was to create a dependency on American goods to keep the Indians friendly. In exchange, the Indians ceded most of Ohio to the Americans; only the northwest region of the territory was reserved solely to the Indians.

One Indian leader held off signing the treaty. Little Turtle of the Miami tribe did not believe that the British had any right to give his tribal lands away in the first place. He argued with Wayne, but to no avail. Finally he signed the document, saying with a heavy heart that as the last to sign the treaty he would be the last to break it, even though he did not agree with its terms. The treaty brought peace to the region, but it did not bring back a peaceful life to the Miamis. The annual allowance from the United States too often came in the form of liquor. "More of us have died since the Treaty of Greenville than we lost by the years of war before, and it is all owing to the introduction of liquor among us," said

Little Turtle in 1800. "This liquor that they introduce into our country is more to be feared than the gun and tomahawk."

Across the Atlantic: France and England

In 1793 and 1794, while the nation battled Indians in Ohio, other conflicts stirred far to the east, across the Atlantic. Since 1789, a violent revolution had been raging in France. At first, the general American reaction was positive, for it was flattering to think that the American Revolution had inspired imitation in France. Monarchy and privilege were overthrown in the name of republicanism; towns throughout America celebrated the victory of the French people with civic feasts and public festivities. For example, in the winter of 1793, townspeople in Augusta, Maine, gathered for a French banquet at the local courthouse under the tricolor flag of the French Republic. Citizens stuck a giant sign proclaiming "France, Liberty, Equality" into the ice of the Kennebec River and bathed it with illumination all night.

But news of the beheading of King Louis XVI quickly dampened the uncritical enthusiasm for everything French. Now Americans were divided in their sentiments. Those who fondly remembered the excitement and risk of the American Revolution were apt to regard France with the same kind of optimism. However, the reluctant revolutionaries of the 1770s and 1780s, who had worried about excessive democracy and social upheaval in America, deplored the far greater violence occurring in the name of republicanism as France moved into the revolutionary period known as the Reign of Terror.

Until 1793, support for the French Revolution could remain a matter of personal conviction. But in that year, England and France went to war, turning the question of French versus British loyalty into a very delicate and critical foreign policy question. France had helped America substantially during the American Revolution, and the confederated government had signed an alliance in 1778 promising aid if France were ever under attack. Americans still optimistic about the eventual outcome of the French Revolution wanted to deliver on that promise now. But others, including those shaken by the guillotining of thousands of French people, as well as those with strong commercial ties to England, sought ways to stay neutral in the English-French war.

In May 1793, President Washington issued a Neutrality Proclamation, with friendly assurances to both sides. His aim was to cool the tensions abroad and protect American interests in both countries. But tensions at home flared in response to official neutrality. "The cause of France is the cause of man, and neutrality is desertion," wrote H. H. Brackenridge, a western Pennsylvanian, to the president, voicing the sentiments of thousands who were still partial to France. Dozens of popular, pro-French political clubs sprang up around the country, called Democratic or Republican Societies. The societies mobilized farmers and mechanics, issued circular letters, injected pro-French and anti-British feelings into local elections, and in general heightened the degree of popular participation and public interest in foreign policy. The activities of these societies also made Washington and Hamilton intensely uncomfortable, for they vented opposition to the policies of the president. The evils of party spirit seemed to be gaining momentum.

The Neutrality Proclamation was in theory a fine idea, in view of Washington's goal of staying out of European wars. Yet American ships continued to trade between the French West Indies and France, carrying primarily grains, sugar, and other foodstuffs. In late 1793 and early 1794, England expressed displeasure with the limited American interpretation of neutrality by capturing more than three hundred of these ships in the vicinity of the West Indies. A crisis was provoked, and even pro-British politicians like Hamilton agreed that it was necessary to make a formal agreement with England. Washington sent John Jay, the chief justice of the Supreme Court and a man known to have very strong pro-British sentiments, to negotiate a treaty.

The Jay Treaty

John Jay's assignment was to secure agreement about general commercial ties between the two countries and to negotiate compensation for the seizure of American ships. In addition, he was supposed to resolve several long-standing problems dating from the end of the Revolutionary War. Southern planters wanted reimbursement for the slaves lured away by the British army during the war, and western settlers wanted England to vacate the western forts still occupied for their strategic proximity to the Indian fur trade.

Jay returned from his diplomatic mission with a treaty that almost no one liked because of several major concessions to the British. First, the treaty made no direct provision for the captured ships or the lost property in slaves. Instead, it set up com-

missions and complicated, lengthy procedures to settle liability charges. Second, although the Jay Treaty arranged for the evacuation of the western forts, it granted the British eighteen more months to withdraw while guaranteeing them continued rights in the fur trade. Many Americans felt that the British had already retained the forts for twelve years too long; a continued British presence in the Great Lakes region would only offer their Indian allies hope of making Michigan into the next territory of terror, as Ohio had been. Finally, the Jay Treaty called for repayment with interest of the debts some American planters still owed to British firms dating from the Revolutionary War years. In exchange for granting such generous terms to England, Jay secured some favorable commercial agreements for the United States, but even there the results were mixed. The Jay Treaty was widely regarded by many as exchanging the country's strong moral bargaining power (the outrage over the seized ships) for an improved trading status beneficial to only a handful of merchants in the overseas trade. The treaty did stave off war with England, which had been a distinct possibility in view of the hundreds of ships the British had captured. However, peace was bought at a high price, according to pro-French Americans.

John Jay returned from his diplomatic mission with a treaty that almost no one liked.

Washington sent the Jay Treaty to the Senate for approval. (Under the Constitution, only the Senate has treaty-making powers.) He tried to keep its terms secret, but a newspaper editor got hold of it and printed it, with damning commentary. In short order, powerful opposition to the treaty emerged from Maine to Georgia. In Massachusetts, graffiti appeared on a wall: "Damn John Jay! Damn everyone who won't damn John Jay! Damn everyone who won't stay up all night damning John Jay!" A newspaper in New Jersey used accessible gender imagery to explain to its readers the implications of the Jay Treaty: "The nation has been secretly, I will not say treacherously, divorced from France, and most clandestinely married to Great Britain: we are taken from the embraces of a loving wife, and find ourselves in the arms of a detestable and abandoned whore, covered with crimes, rottenness, and corruption."

The Jay Treaty passed the Senate in 1795 by a vote of twenty to ten. Some representatives in the House, led by Madison, tried to undermine the Senate's approval by insisting on a chance to vote on the funding provisions of the treaty, on the grounds that the House controlled all money bills. Finally in 1796, the House approved funds to implement the various commissions mandated by the treaty, but the vote was close, with approval squeaking by with just a three-vote margin. The cleavage of votes in both houses of Congress divided along the same lines as the Hamilton-Jefferson split on economic policy.

Federalists and Republicans

The assumption that a division into political parties was a sign of failure was soon put to a severe test. In Washington's second term, consistent voting blocs first appeared in Congress on economic issues. By the time of the Jay Treaty, party labels—Federalist and Republican—had come into use, and rival newspapers were beginning to identify with one or the other label. Washington's decision not to run for a third term opened the floodgates to serious partisan electioneering. Both the Federalists and Republicans scurried to win the highest executive office for one of their own.

The Election of 1796

Washington struggled to appear to be above party politics, and in his farewell address of September 1796, he stressed the need to maintain a "unity of government" reflecting a unified body politic. He also urged the country to "steer clear of permanent alliances with any portion of the foreign world." The leading contenders for his position, John Adams of Massachusetts and Thomas Jefferson of Virginia, in theory both agreed with him: Political parties were deplorable, and neutrality toward England and France was essential. But around them raged a party contest split along pro-English versus pro-French lines.

Adams and Jefferson were not adept politicians in the modern sense. They were men of intellect and integrity rather than of persuasion and intrigue. Jefferson had resigned as secretary of state in 1793, partly to escape conflict with Alexander Hamilton. He retired to Monticello, his home in the Virginia foothills, and claimed to be devoting himself to

JOHN ADAMS BY JOHN TRUMBULL
John Adams in 1793 at age fifty-eight.
National Portrait Gallery, Smithsonian Institution/Art Resources, N.Y.

farming, even to the extent of shunning newspapers. Adams's job as vice president kept him closer to the political action, but his personality often kept people at a distance. He was temperamental, thin-skinned, and quick to take offense. A friend once listed his shortcomings as a politician: "He can't dance, drink, game, flatter, promise, dress, swear with gentlemen, and small talk and flirt with the ladies."

While the two principal contestants sat above the fray, the leading Federalists and Republicans met to choose candidates. To run with Adams, the Federalists picked Thomas Pinckney of South Carolina; the Republicans agreed on Aaron Burr of New York to pair with Jefferson. The Constitution did not anticipate parties and tickets. Instead, each electoral college voter could cast two votes, on only one ballot; the top vote-getter became president and the next highest assumed the vice presidency. (This procedural flaw was corrected by the Eleventh Amendment to the Constitution, adopted in 1804.) With only one ballot, careful maneuvering was required to make sure the chief rivals for the presidency did not land in the top two spots.

Into that maneuverable moment stepped Alexander Hamilton. Hamilton had resigned from the Treasury in 1795 to return to his law practice, but he still exercised great influence over Washington. Hamilton did not trust Adams, who was too independent to take orders directly from Hamilton and who had committed the sin of not warmly embracing Hamilton's various economic plans. Hamilton's preferred candidate was Pinckney, and he tried to influence electors to throw their support to the South Carolinian. But his plan backfired: Adams was elected president with seventy-one votes, and Jefferson came in second with sixty-eight votes and thus became vice president. Pinckney got fifty-nine votes, while Burr trailed with thirty.

John Adams's Presidency

Adams's inaugural speech before Congress echoed the themes of Washington's farewell address. Adams emphasized his determination to rise above party strife and put the interests of all the people ahead of party loyalty. He promised to be neutral in foreign affairs and lifted Republican hopes by noting his great respect for the French people based on seven years' residence there. As he began the speech, Adams watched the aging George Washington in the audience. Later he told his wife, Abigail, that he imagined that the old man was taunting him: "I am fairly out and you fairly in! See which of us will be happiest!" Adams had desperately wanted to be president, but now he was uneasy about managing the job.

President Adams's first mistake was to retain the same cabinet members in office at the end of Washington's administration. Adams probably thought that continuity would help some of the Washington magic rub off on him. But as it happened, the three cabinet officers—Secretary of State Timothy Pickering, Secretary of the Treasury Oliver Wolcott, and Secretary of War James McHenry—had no magic to lend him. They were mediocre appointments, in office mainly because Hamilton had recommended them to Washington. Even worse, all three were in Hamilton's pocket, writing him frequently for advice and passing that advice on to the unwitting Adams as their own. Thus, private citizen Hamilton exercised a great deal of power in the Adams presidency.

Vice President Jefferson, a gracious loser to Adams after the electoral college balloting, extended a conciliatory arm when the two old friends met in Philadelphia, still the capital. They had not seen each other in four years, and they took temporary lodging in the same boarding house as if expecting to work closely together. But quickly the Hamiltonian cabinet ruined the honeymoon. Jefferson's advice was spurned, and he withdrew from active counsel of the president, not wishing to be associated with what he regarded as bad policies.

The XYZ Affair

Foreign policy lay at the heart of the rift between Adams and Jefferson and between Federalists and Republicans. If the Jay Treaty heated tempers in 1795 and 1796, the French response to the treaty in 1797 was like oil added to the fire.

France read the Jay Treaty as the Republicans did: as a document giving so many concessions to the British that it made America a British satellite. In retaliation, France abandoned the terms of the 1778 wartime alliance with the United States and allowed privateers—armed private vessels—to seize American ships carrying British goods. The old principle of "free ships, free goods" (meaning that if the ship was not an enemy's and hence was free to pass, the goods on it were also free to pass) was disregarded. By March 1797, when Adams's inaugural address promised evenhanded neutrality, French privateers had already detained more than three hundred American vessels and seized the goods on board. In a related move, in the winter of 1796–97, France refused to recognize a new minister sent by President Washington, Charles Cotesworth Pinckney (brother of Thomas Pinckney, the defeated Federalist candidate for vice president). French authorities rudely chased him out of Paris, claiming his credentials and papers were not in order. In fact, Pinckney did have the right papers, but he was of the wrong political persuasion to suit the French, being a staunch Federalist.

To avenge these insults, Federalists started murmuring openly about war with France. President Adams wanted to try further negotiations, and he appointed a three-man commission to approach the French government. Two of the three appointees were Federalist hard-liners: Charles Pinckney and John Marshall, a lawyer from Virginia. The third man on the commission was a Republican-leaning moderate, Elbridge Gerry, a Massachusetts friend of John Adams. Adams dramatically called a special session of Congress in May 1797 to announce the mission to France and to recommend new expenditures for military defense. Negotiations, it appeared, would be backed by the muscle of military preparedness. Congress approved money for building three new naval frigates, for adding arms to some merchant vessels, and for improving defenses in coastal cities.

In the fall of 1797, the three Americans arrived in Paris to a cool welcome. But at least they were not chased out; instead, they waited several weeks to gain an official meeting with someone in power. Finally the French minister of foreign affairs, Talleyrand, sent three agents, unnamed and later known to the American public as X, Y, and Z, to the American commissioners with the suggestion that $250,000 might grease the wheels of diplomacy and obtain an official interview with Talleyrand. The French agents also insisted that the price of a peace treaty would be a $12 million loan to the French government. The three Americans were incensed by the suggestion of a bribe, and they departed to inform the president.

The American reaction to the XYZ affair was shock and anger. Even staunch pro-French Republicans began to reevaluate their allegiance. The Federalists' demand for military action became more insistent. Congress voted to expand both the army and the navy and repealed all prior treaties with France. In 1798, some twenty naval warships launched the United States into its first undeclared war, called the Quasi War by historians to underscore its uncertain legal status. The main scene of action was the Caribbean, where more than one hundred French privateers were captured; closer to home, a French ship was also captured off the New Jersey coast.

Adams was beginning to suspect that his cabinet was more loyal to Hamilton than to the presidency.

Abigail Adams wrote her sister, "Why, when we have the thing, should we boggle at the Name?" She was perplexed at Congress's reluctance to vote an outright declaration of war. Yet her husband the president was equally reluctant to take the offensive in war, because of the opposition it would generate among the Republicans. Better to "wage war and call it self-defence," said a Federalist senator from Massachusetts.

An enhanced navy presence was a military plan with broad support, but Hamilton, working through his puppets in the cabinet and his friends

in Congress, was equally interested in beefing up the army. The Federalist-dominated Congress obliged him by appropriating money to recruit ten thousand men immediately and a provisional army of another fifty thousand. Republicans feared—with justification—that the Federalists' real aim was to use the army against domestic dissenters. There was little chance of a land invasion by France, yet Hamilton convinced ex-president Washington (none too active a man now, only a year away from his death) to command the army and then insisted that the retired leader appoint Hamilton as second in command. President Adams was mistrustful, but his cabinet pressured for Hamilton, and Adams was too weak politically to prevail. He was, however, beginning to suspect that his cabinet was more loyal to Hamilton than to the presidency.

Even without a declaration, war fever remained strong among the Federalists, and intense antagonism grew between Federalists and Republicans. Republican newspapers launched heated attacks on Adams: One denounced him as "a person without patriotism, without philosophy, and a mock monarch." Another declared that he was "old, querulous, bald, blind, crippled, and toothless" and accused him of appointing relatives to office and of misusing public monies. On July 4, 1798, a pro-French mob roamed the streets in Philadelphia wearing hats with cockades, small ribbon florets that indicated solidarity with the radical revolutionaries of France. An alarmed Adams smuggled guns and ammunition into his house, fearing attack by a Republican mob.

Federalists too were taking offensive action. In Newburyport, Massachusetts, they staged a huge bonfire, burning issues of the state's Republican newspapers. The Virginia militia began drilling in the streets of Williamsburg. Officers in a New York militia unit drank a menacing toast on July 4, 1798: "One and but one party in the United States." A leading Federalist newspaper declared that "he who is not for us is against us." Jefferson wrote to a friend, "Men who have been intimate all their lives cross the streets to avoid meeting, and turn their heads another way, lest they should be obliged to touch their hats."

The Alien and Sedition Acts

If the United States had actually declared war on France, the pro-French Republicans could have been labeled traitors, subject to laws of treason. In-

CARTOON OF MATTHEW LYON FIGHT IN CONGRESS
The political tensions of 1798 were not merely intellectual. A February session in Congress degenerated from name-calling to a brawl. Roger Griswold, a Connecticut Federalist, called Matthew Lyon, a Vermont Republican, a coward. Lyon responded with some well-aimed spit, the first departure from the gentleman's code of honor. Griswold responded by raising his cane to Lyon, whereupon Lyon grabbed nearby fire tongs to beat back his assailant. Madison wrote to Jefferson that the two should have dueled: "No man ought to reproach another with cowardice, who is not ready to give proof of his own courage" by negotiating a duel, the honorable way to avenge insults.
Library of Congress.

deed, some Republicans suspected that the main impetus for a declaration of war was precisely the opportunity to treat dissenters as traitors. But without a declared war, Federalists had to invent another law to muffle opposition. In June and July 1798, Congress hammered out a two-part Sedition Act that mandated a heavy fine or a jail sentence for anyone engaged in conspiracies or revolts against the government. Further, it set penalties (up to $2,000) for anyone convicted of "speaking, writing, or publishing any false, scandalous, or malicious statement, with the intent to defame or bring into contempt or disrepute the President, the Congress, or the Government." In other words, spoken or written words that falsely criticized government leaders were now criminal utterances. The trick, of course, was to be able to distinguish between malicious opposition on the one hand and legitimate criticism on the other. Federalists in 1798 had a hard time with that distinction.

Along with the Sedition Act, Congress passed two Alien Acts. The first extended the waiting period required for an alien to achieve status as a naturalized citizen from five to fourteen years and required all aliens to register with the federal government. The second, called the Alien Enemies Act, empowered the president in time of war to deport or to imprison without trial any foreigner suspected of being a danger to the United States. The clear intent of the alien laws was to harass French immigrants in the United States and discourage others from coming.

One of the first persons prosecuted under the Sedition Act was an unfortunate man named Luther Baldwin, who was idling away a morning in a tavern in Newark, New Jersey, in July 1798. President

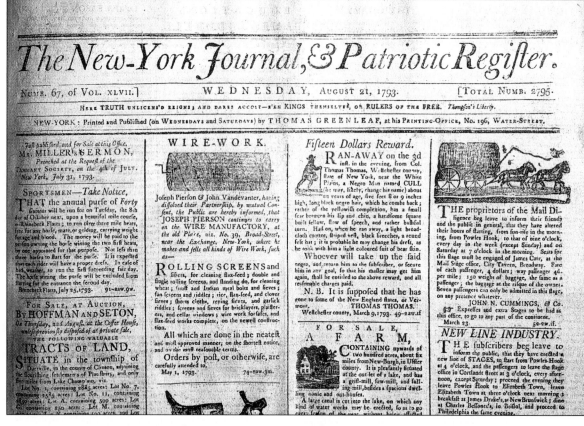

THE NEW YORK JOURNAL MASTHEAD
Newspapers proliferated in the 1790s. The New York Journal and Patriotic Register *supported the Republicans; it was issued twice a week. Like all newspapers until the mid-nineteenth century, it devoted page 1 to ads and routine notices. Current news came on page 2, spilling over to page 3. Page 4, the final sheet, again consisted of ads that continued in successive issues. All type was hand-set; the most efficient format allowed blocks of type to stay in place over many issues.*
Courtesy, American Antiquarian Society.

Adams was passing nearby that day, traveling from Philadelphia to his home in Massachusetts, and Newark had honored him with a display of flags, the ringing of church bells, and a sixteen-gun salute. When the guns fired, a drinking companion joked, "There goes the President, and they are firing at his ass." The truculent Baldwin replied, "I do not care if they fire through his ass." He probably roused a laugh from drinking companions, but the tavern owner reported the remark to Federalist leaders, who agreed that Baldwin had violated the law on sedition by expressing malicious contempt for the president. Baldwin was convicted in a federal court, fined $150, and sent to prison until he could pay it.

Baldwin's arrest was something of a fluke, for the real targets of the Sedition Act were the Republican newspaper editors who were free and abusive in their criticism of the Adams administration. One Federalist in Congress justified his vote for the law with reference to the Republican press: "Let gentlemen look at certain papers printed in this city and elsewhere, and ask themselves whether an unwarrantable and dangerous combination does not exist to overturn and ruin the government by publishing the most shameless falsehoods against the representatives of the people." In all, twenty-five men, almost all newspaper editors, were charged with sedition; twelve were convicted by juries.

The First Amendment in the Constitution's Bill of Rights guarantees freedom of speech and freedom of the press, and it is likely that a court today would strike down the 1798 Sedition Act as an unconstitutional abridgment of those liberties. Yet complete freedom to say or write anything has always been curtailed by considerations of truth versus falsity, malicious intent, and public safety. The Federalists truly thought that calling the president nasty names endangered the security of the government, just as shouting "Fire!" in a crowded theater endangers public safety. Today's laws distinguish between libelous speech about public figures and about private citizens, allowing greater freedom for hostile or inflammatory speech against public officials. The defendants charged with sedition in 1798 generally argued that their writings were legitimate political opinion protected by the First Amendment, and some of them won their cases on those grounds. Slowly the concept of legitimate opposition in politics was taking shape.

Jefferson and Madison strongly opposed the Alien and Sedition Acts on the grounds that they were in conflict with the Bill of Rights. The Sedition Act in particular was a direct blow to the Republican Party. The Republicans did not have the votes to revoke the acts in Congress, nor could the federal judiciary, dominated by Federalist judges, be counted on to challenge them. So Jefferson and Madison turned to the state legislatures, the only other competing political arena, to mount their opposition. They each drafted a set of resolutions condemning the Alien and Sedition Acts and had the legislatures of Virginia and Kentucky present them to the federal government in late fall 1798. The Virginia and Kentucky Resolutions tested the novel argument that state legislatures have the right to judge the constitutionality of federal laws and to nullify laws that infringe on the liberties of the people as defined in the Bill of Rights. No other legislatures joined the Virginia and Kentucky protest, and the resolutions made little dent in the application of the Alien and Sedition Acts. But the idea of a state's right to nullify federal law did not disappear; it surfaced again some thirty years later and played a role in the coming of the Civil War.

Amidst all the war hysteria, sedition fears, and party conflict in 1798, President Adams somehow managed to regain a measure of caution. Though his character tended toward the temperamental and vain and he generally stewed over personal insults, he was remarkably restrained in pursuing opponents under the Sedition Act. And he finally refused to be pushed into a hasty declaration of war by the extreme Federalists to avenge American honor. No doubt he was beginning to realize how much he had been the dupe of Hamilton. He also shrewdly realized that France was in fact not eager for war and that a peaceful settlement might be close at hand. In January 1799, a peace initiative from France

WASHINGTON'S DEATH

The death of George Washington in 1799 occasioned many memorial souvenirs. This painting on glass represents Washington as the Pater Patriae, *the father of his country. A soldier weeps, while Columbia with her shield and spear looks stunned with grief. Minerva, the goddess of war, holds the great man's portrait, and an angel trumpets his famous military victories. Nothing in the memorial notes his service as president, except the oblique statement that he was "Great in the Senate," a reference to ancient Roman government service. Curiously, the amateur artist failed to capture Washington's actual likeness.*

The Metropolitan Museum of Art, Gift of Edgar William and Bernice Chrysler Garblach, 1964 (64.309.6).

arrived, in the form of a letter assuring Adams that diplomatic channels were open again and that new commissioners would be welcomed in France. Adams accepted this overture and appointed a new negotiator; by late 1799, the Quasi War with France had subsided. But in responding to the French initiative, Adams lost the support of a significant part of his own party, thus sealing his fate as the first one-term president of the United States.

In responding to the French initiative, Adams lost the support of a significant part of his own party, thus sealing his fate as the first one-term president of the United States.

The election of 1800 was openly organized along party lines, with the self-designated national leaders of each group meeting to handpick their candidates for president and vice president. Adams ran again but was doomed to lose. When the election was over, the new president, Thomas Jefferson, mounted the inaugural platform to announce, "We are all republicans, we are all federalists." He meant that everyone was both at once, an appealing rhetoric of harmony appropriate to an inaugural address. But his formulation perpetuated a denial of the validity of party politics, a denial that ran deep in the founding generation of political leaders.

Conclusion: Parties Nonetheless

During the crisis of 1798–1799, a strong sense of peril gripped the nation, and out of that arose the initial acknowledgment of the existence of political parties. The Federalists grew out of the main core of supporters for the Constitution in 1788, and they dominated Congress and the presidency throughout the 1790s. They persisted in thinking of themselves as the legitimate, disinterested rulers who could give the country enlightened leadership; they did not like their leadership challenged. Under Hamilton's urgings, they supported economic plans to develop commerce and enhance the strength of the federal government.

But those economic plans quickly engendered opposition, initially among onetime Federalists in Congress like Madison. As opposition widened—to the whiskey tax, to the Jay Treaty, and finally to the Alien and Sedition Acts—it drew in larger numbers of citizens beyond the elected members of the federal government and began to coalesce into a widespread and still diverse group that took the name Republican. The Federalists were pro-British, pro-commerce, and ever alarmed about the potential excesses of democracy, while the Republicans celebrated, up to a point, the radical republicanism of France. Grafted into the Republican group was the 1780s Antifederalist suspicion of a powerful federal government; the Sedition Act seemed an especially clear example of what the Republicans feared.

When Jefferson offered his conciliatory assurance that the political citizens of the United States were at the same time "all republicans" and "all federalists," he was possibly thinking of widely shared ideas that undergirded political institutions in the new nation. Certainly his listeners favored republican government, where power derived from the people, and likewise they favored the unique federal system of shared governance structured by the Constitution. But by 1800, these same two words, adapted to be the proper names of parties, had come to signify competing philosophies of government. Federalists and Republicans had strong disagreements that had developed over a decade of decision making. Jefferson's speech was spoken aloud; his listeners could not hear the presence or absence of capital letters. For at least some of his listeners, Jefferson's assertion of harmony across party lines could only have seemed bizarre.

CHRONOLOGY

1789	Washington inaugurated president. French revolution begins. First Congress meets in New York City.		**1793**	Washington issues Neutrality Proclamation. Battle of Fallen Timbers; U.S. victory over Indians in Ohio.

1789 Washington inaugurated president.
French revolution begins.
First Congress meets in New York City.

1790 Hamilton's funding and assumption plans approved.
Government moves from New York to Philadelphia.
First federal census conducted.

1791 Bill of Rights ratified by states.
Bank of the United States chartered by Congress.
St. Clair's defeat by Ohio Indians.
Congress passes whiskey tax.

1793 Washington's second term begins.
War breaks out between France and England.

1793 Washington issues Neutrality Proclamation.
Battle of Fallen Timbers; U.S. victory over Indians in Ohio.

1794 Whiskey Rebellion in western Pennsylvania.

1795 Treaty of Greenville with Indians.
Jay Treaty with England.

1796 John Adams elected president, Thomas Jefferson vice president.

1797 XYZ affair with France.

1798 Quasi War with France.
Alien and Sedition Acts.
Virginia and Kentucky Resolutions.

1800 Election campaign between Adams and Jefferson.

1801 Jefferson elected president.

BIBLIOGRAPHY

GENERAL WORKS

Rudolph M. Bell, *Party and Faction in American Politics: The House of Representatives, 1789–1801* (1973).

Richard Buel, *Securing the Revolution: Ideology in American Politics, 1789–1815* (1972).

William Nisbet Chambers, *Political Parties in a New Nation: The American Experience, 1776–1809* (1963).

Stanley Elkins and Eric McKitrick, *The Age of Federalism: The Early American Republic, 1788–1800* (1993).

John F. Hoadley, *Origins of American Political Parties, 1789–1803* (1986).

Ralph Ketcham, *Presidents above Party: The First American Presidency, 1789–1829* (1984).

John C. Miller, *The Federalist Era, 1789–1800* (1960).

John R. Nelson, *Liberty and Property: Political Economy and Policymaking in the New Nation, 1789–1812* (1987).

James Rogers Sharp, *American Politics in the Early Republic: The New Nation in Crisis* (1993).

WASHINGTON'S ADMINISTRATION

Bob Arnebeck, *Through a Fiery Trial: Building Washington, 1790–1800* (1991).

Kenneth R. Bowling, *Politics in the First Congress, 1789–1791* (1990).

Kenneth R. Bowling, *The Creation of Washington, D.C.: The Idea and Location of the American Capital* (1991).

Steven R. Boyd, ed., *The Whiskey Rebellion: Past and Present Perspectives* (1985).

Alexander DeConde, *Entangling Alliance: Politics and Diplomacy under George Washington* (1958).

James T. Flexner, *George Washington and the New Nation, 1783–1793* (1970).

James T. Flexner, *George Washington: Anguish and Farewell, 1793–1799* (1972).

Constance McLaughlin Green, *Washington: Village and Capital, 1800–1878,* vol. 1 (1962).

Forrest McDonald, *The Presidency of George Washington* (1974).

John Reps, *Washington on View: The Nation's Capital since 1790* (1991).

Robert A. Rutland, *The Birth of the Bill of Rights, 1776–1791* (1991).

Bernard Schwartz, *The Great Rights of Mankind* (1977).

Thomas P. Slaughter, *The Whiskey Rebellion: Frontier Epilogue to the American Revolution* (1986).

Leonard White, *The Federalists: A Study in Administrative History* (1948).

SOCIETY AND CULTURE

Richard D. Brown, *Knowledge Is Power: The Diffusion of Information in Early America, 1700–1865* (1989).

Patricia Cline Cohen, *A Calculating People: The Spread of Numeracy in Early America* (1983).

Nancy Cott, *The Bonds of Womanhood: Women's Sphere in New England, 1780–1835* (1977).

Cathy N. Davidson, *Revolution and the Word: The Rise of the Novel in America* (1986).

Emory Elliott, *Revolutionary Writers: Literature and Authority in the New Republic, 1725–1810* (1982).

Richard B. Kielbowicz, *News in the Mail: The Press, the Post Office, and Public Information, 1700–1860* (1989).

Laurel T. Ulrich, *A Midwife's Tale: The Life of Martha Ballard, Based on Her Diary, 1785–1812* (1990).

THE ECONOMY AND HAMILTON'S PROGRAM

Joyce Appleby, *Capitalism and a New Social Order: The Republican Vision of the 1790s* (1984).

Christopher Clark, *The Roots of Rural Capitalism: Western Massachusetts, 1780–1860* (1990).

Jacob E. Cooke, *Tench Coxe and the Early Republic* (1978).

Jacob E. Cooke, *Alexander Hamilton* (1982).

Clarence Danhof, *Change in Agriculture: The Northern United States, 1820–1870* (1969).

Robert A. Hendrickson, *The Rise and Fall of Alexander Hamilton* (1981).

James A. Henretta, *The Origins of American Capitalism: Collected Essays* (1991).

Joan Jensen, *Loosening the Bonds: Mid-Atlantic Farm Women, 1750–1850* (1986).

Allan Kulikoff, *The Agrarian Origins of American Capitalism* (1992).

James Lemon, *The Best Poor Man's Country: A Geographical Study of Early Southeastern Pennsylvania* (1972).

Winifred Rothenberg, *From Market-Places to a Market Economy: The Transformation of Rural Massachusetts, 1750–1850* (1992).

Gerald Stourzh, *Alexander Hamilton and the Idea of Republican Government* (1970).

NATIVE AMERICANS AND THE FRONTIER

Robert F. Berkhofer Jr., *Salvation and the Savage: An Analysis of Protestant Missions and American Indian Response, 1787–1862* (1965).

Colin G. Calloway, *Crown and Calumet: British-Indian Relations, 1783–1815* (1987).

Gregory E. Dowd, *A Spirited Resistance: The North American Indian Struggle for Unity, 1745–1815* (1992).

Dorothy Jones, *License for Empire: Colonialism by Treaty in Early America* (1982).

Francis Paul Prucha, *American Indian Policy in the Formative Years: The Indian Trade and Intercourse Acts, 1780–1834* (1962).

Malcolm J. Rohrbough, *The Transappalachian Frontier: People, Societies, and Institutions, 1775–1850* (1978).

Wiley Sword, *President Washington's Indian War: The Struggle for the Old Northwest, 1790–1795* (1985).

Richard White, *The Middle Ground: Indians, Empires, and Republics in the Great Lakes Region, 1650–1815* (1991).

J. Leitch Wright, *Britain and the American Frontier, 1783–1815* (1975).

FOREIGN RELATIONS

Henry Ammon, *The Genet Mission* (1973).

Albert H. Bowman, *The Struggle for Neutrality: Franco-American Diplomacy during the Federalist Era* (1974).

Jerald A. Combs, *The Jay Treaty: Political Battleground of the Founding Fathers* (1970).

Lawrence D. Cress, *Citizens in Arms: The Army and the Militia in American Society to the War of 1812* (1982).

Alexander DeConde, *The Quasi-War: The Politics and Diplomacy of the Undeclared War with France, 1797–1801* (1966).

Peter P. Hill, *French Perceptions of the Early American Republic, 1783–1793* (1988).

Daniel G. Lang, *Foreign Policy in the Early Republic* (1985).

Charles R. Ritcheson, *Aftermath of Revolution: British Policy toward the United States, 1783–1795* (1969).

William Stinchcombe, *The XYZ Affair* (1981).

Richard J. Twomey, *Jacobins and Jeffersonians: Anglo-American Radicalism in the United States, 1790–1820* (1989).

FEDERALISTS AND REPUBLICANS

Ralph A. Brown, *The Presidency of John Adams* (1975).

Joseph Charles, *The Origins of the American Party System* (1956).

Noble Cunningham, *The Jeffersonian Republicans: The Formation of Party Organization, 1789–1801* (1957).

Larry D. Eldridge, *A Distant Heritage: The Growth of Free Speech in Early America* (1994).

Joseph J. Ellis, *Passionate Sage: The Character and Legacy of John Adams* (1993).

John Ferling, *John Adams: A Life* (1992).

Richard Hofstadter, *The Idea of a Party System: The Rise of Legitimate Opposition in the United States, 1780–1840* (1969).

John R. Howe, *The Changing Political Thought of John Adams* (1966).

Richard H. Kohn, *Eagle and Sword: The Federalists and the Creation of the Military Establishment in America, 1783–1802* (1975).

Stephen G. Kurtz, *The Presidency of John Adams: The Collapse of Federalism, 1795–1800* (1957).

Leonard Levy, *Jefferson and Civil Liberties: The Darker Side* (1963).

Leonard Levy, *The Emergence of a Free Press* (1985).

Drew McCoy, *The Elusive Republic: Political Economy in Jeffersonian America* (1980).

Drew McCoy, *The Last of the Fathers: James Madison and the Republican Legacy* (1989).

Peter Shaw, *The Character of John Adams* (1976).

James Morton Smith, *Freedom's Fetters: The Alien and Sedition Laws and American Civil Liberties* (1966).

Donald H. Stewart, *The Opposition Press of the Federalist Period* (1969).

John Zvesper, *Political Philosophy and Rhetoric: A Study of the Origins of American Party Politics* (1977).

STATE HISTORIES

Richard R. Beeman, *The Old Dominion and the New Nation, 1788–1801* (1972).

Paul Goodman, *The Democratic-Republicans of Massachusetts* (1964).

Norman Risjord, *Chesapeake Politics, 1781–1800* (1978).

Charles Steffen, *The Mechanics of Baltimore: Workers and Politics in the Age of Revolution, 1763–1812* (1984).

Alan Taylor, *Liberty Men and Great Proprietors: The Revolutionary Settlement on the Maine Frontier, 1760–1820* (1990).

Alfred Young, *The Democratic-Republicans of New York: The Origins, 1763–1797* (1967).

A JEFFERSON FAN

Ladies' fans became increasingly popular fashion accessories in the late eighteenth and early nineteenth centuries. This folding fan of vellum and carved ivory, made in the early 1800s, features a medallion portrait of President Thomas Jefferson. Carried by the ribbon on a woman's wrist, the fan could be flicked open to announce a partisan political statement. Fans and other hand-held articles such as parasols and handkerchiefs expanded the repertoire of nonverbal expression for women, who by the custom and training of the time were expected to be less assertive than men in mixed conversation. Many emotions and messages — including modesty, coyness, and flirtatiousness, as well as anger, irritability, and boredom could be communicated by the expert deployment of this delicate emblem of femininity.

Collection of David J. and Janice L. Frent.

REPUBLICAN ASCENDANCY 10

1800–1824

MERIWETHER LEWIS CAME UPON three Shoshone women near the Continental Divide in mid-August 1805; one ran off and the other two sank to their knees to await their fate. Lewis and three other white men were an advance party of the Lewis and Clark expedition, sent by President Thomas Jefferson to explore the vast continent from the Mississippi River to the Pacific Ocean. On that August day, Lewis was anxiously searching for the Shoshone tribe to acquire horses and guides to get his expedition over the Rocky Mountains before the fall. Lewis had written in his journal that week, "If we do not find them or some other nation who have horses I fear the successfull issue of our voyage will be very doubtfull."

Lewis approached the women, pulled them up with his hand, and gave them beads and leather-making tools to show his friendly intentions. He also rolled up his sleeve to make a show of his whiteness, to demonstrate the "truth of the ascertion that I was a white man for my face and hands which have been constantly exposed to the sun were quite as dark as their own." He assumed that being white was less threatening to the women than being an Indian from an unknown tribe.

Meriwether Lewis was a twenty-eight-year-old Virginian and a close friend of President Jefferson's. Jefferson had hired him as his personal secretary, and for two years the men shared quarters at the presidential residence (later known as the White House) where the older man schooled the younger in natural history and habits of scientific observation. For some time, Jefferson eyed the trans-Mississippi west with intense curiosity; in early 1803, he arranged congressional funding for a secret exploration into Spanish and Indian territory and appointed Lewis to head it. Although he had already opened negotiations with the French to obtain New Orleans, Jefferson did not know that within the year much of the region Lewis was sent to explore would be transferred from Spain to France and then to the United States, in a stupendous land deal known as the Louisiana Purchase.

Lewis sought out William Clark as his co-leader. Clark, thirty-two, lived in Kentucky; the two men knew each other from shared military service in the 1790s Indian wars. In a letter to Clark, Lewis outlined the requirements for their recruits: He wanted "good hunters, stout, healthy, unmarried men, accustomed to the woods, and capable of bearing bodily fatigue in a pretty considerable degree." They rejected more than a hundred applicants, finally choosing a crew of forty-five, including expert rivermen, gunsmiths, carpenters, fishermen, hunters, some soldiers, and a cook. Two men of mixed Indian and French parentage served as interpreters, and a man named York, a slave in his thirties belonging to William Clark, rounded out the group.

Jefferson's intentions were scientific. He instructed Lewis to investigate Indian languages and kinship systems, to collect plant and animal specimens, and to chart the geography of the rivers and mountains of the West. The explorers were equipped with measuring devices—a quadrant, a microscope, thermometers—and an authoritative treatise on animal classification. Nine of the men kept journals. Congress had more traditional goals in mind: The expedition was to scout out possible locations for military posts, open commercial agreements for the fur trade, and seek out that centuries-old goal, a water pathway between the East and West Coasts.

The explorers left St. Louis in the spring of 1804, working their way northwest up the Missouri River on a large barge. Abandoned Indian villages, their onetime residents victims to smallpox, dotted the river's shores, grim evidence that European contact was not new in 1804. By the time the chill of October came, the men had passed through Sioux territory and arrived at what is now the central part of North Dakota, where they camped for the winter at a Mandan village. The Mandan Indians were familiar with British and French traders from Canada, but the black man York created a sensation. As happened repeatedly on the trip, Indians rubbed moistened fingers over the man's skin to see if the color was painted on. York was of imposing size and strength, yet he danced with agility and amazed the Indians that "so large a man should be active," according to Lewis.

Early next spring, they turned west, now aided by a hired guide, a French trapper accompanied by his wife, a sixteen-year-old Indian woman named Sacajawea, who had just had a baby. What first seemed to be a burden to Lewis and Clark—a mother and infant—was to prove unexpectedly helpful. Indian tribes encountered en route withdrew their suspicion that the Americans were hostile because, as Lewis wrote in his journal, "no woman ever accompanies a war party of Indians in this quarter."

When Lewis met the three Shoshone women in August, Sacajawea was not with him. Yet his friendly overtures were accepted, and the women led him to their tribe. Soon Lewis was sharing a pipe with Cameahwait, the Shoshone chief, who removed his moccasins to smoke as a gesture of trust —and insisted that a reluctant Lewis do likewise. The Indian leaders delivered many cheek-to-cheek embraces to Lewis; "we wer all carresed and be-

SACAJAWEA

Sacajawea and baby, as imagined by mid-nineteenth-century artist Edgar S. Paxson, who produced a series of paintings of grand moments on the Lewis and Clark expedition. The young Shoshone mother was also called "Janey" by the explorers, who admired her courage and fortitude. Her baby, Jean Baptiste Charbonneau, was nicknamed Pompey. William Clark brought the boy to St. Louis when he was six to educate him. In the 1820s, the youth was taken to Germany by the prince of Württemberg; he returned six years later, fluent in German, French, Spanish, and English. Half Shoshone and half French, Charbonneau became a guide and interpreter for many trading expeditions throughout the West until his death in the 1860s.

Sacajawea oil painting by Edgar S. Paxson. The University of Montana Museum of Fine Arts Collection.

smeared with their grease and paint till I was heartily tired of the national hug," Lewis recorded in his journal.

When the rest of the expedition caught up, they were surprised to discover that Cameahwait was in fact Sacajawea's brother. The young mother had been kidnapped from her tribe some years before and taken captive by the Hidatsas near the Mandan village before being traded to her French husband. The Shoshone provided the needed horses and guides, and the expedition continued west, Sacajawea and infant choosing to accompany them.

The Lewis and Clark expedition reached the Pacific at the mouth of the Columbia River, in what is now Oregon, in November 1805. The party wintered there and then returned home by the same route. Upon their return they were greeted as national heroes. They had established favorable relations with dozens of Indian tribes. They had collected information on the people, soils, and geography of the West that was invaluable to later travelers. Their scientific observations of plants and animals extended the frontiers of knowledge in botany and biology. And they inspired a nation of restless explorers and solitary imitators.

The success of the Lewis and Clark expedition created a high point in Jefferson's early presidency. Other undertakings proved far more problematic. A difficult election had marred Jefferson's glory in winning the high office. Serious Indian troubles in the Northwest Territory continued to plague his administration, and soon those Indians allied with the British, mounting pressures for war. Jefferson adopted experimental economic policies to forestall war, but the War of 1812 came anyway and perilously split the United States. Jefferson's successors in office, James Madison and James Monroe, continued his policies, only to find that the combination of slavery and westward movement created the first great constitutional crisis, over Missouri statehood in 1820.

The Lewis and Clark expedition turned out to be the high point in the explorers' lives as well. Sacajawea died of a fever about ten years later in the Dakota region. Meriwether Lewis met a violent end in 1809 under mysterious circumstances, ruled a suicide at the time. Clark became governor of the Missouri Territory and struggled through the 1820 Missouri crisis. And York, who had carried a gun, danced with Indians, and attracted favorable attention, to the great benefit of his white companions on the trip, returned to slavery in Kentucky.

Jefferson's Presidency

Thomas Jefferson later called his election the "revolution of 1800." Certainly the years 1799–1800, marked by conflict and instability, had many classic ingredients of a revolutionary moment. Pervasive discontent engulfed the country, touched off by the Alien and Sedition Acts and the Quasi War with France. Newspaper invective intensified, making it seem that the very survival of the United States was at stake.

At the same time, a different and truly deadly "revolution of 1800" crystallized. A literate slave named Gabriel who worked in Richmond, Virginia's capital, followed the abusive rhetoric of the presidential campaign and figured that when white men were so badly divided, the time was right to strike for freedom. Rebellion perhaps seemed logical to Gabriel, but it took Federalists and Republicans alike by surprise.

What Jefferson probably really meant when he recalled 1800 as a moment of revolution was the new vision of republican simplicity he brought to bear on the federal government. Throughout his years in office, he aimed for a limited government, and yet he also found that circumstances sometimes required him to draw on the expansive powers of the presidency.

The "Revolution of 1800"

Although John Adams had ensured his own defeat in 1800 by reopening diplomatic channels with France, it was by no means assured that Thomas Jefferson—both Adams's vice president and his Republican opponent—would therefore win the presidency. It took seven months in 1800 for the states to select electoral college voters. Then the electoral college produced a tie vote—surprisingly, between Jefferson and his running mate, Senator Aaron Burr of New York, both with seventy-three votes. (Adams got sixty-five votes and Charles Cotesworth Pinckney of South Carolina, sixty-four.) The election was thus thrown to the House of Representatives, where a Federalist-dominated chamber would make the final choice.

Into this uncertain moment stepped Gabriel, a twenty-four-year-old blacksmith owned by Virginian Thomas Prosser. From spring to midsummer of 1800, Gabriel recruited hundreds of coconspirators from five Virginia counties to a plot to end slavery.

They planned to march on Richmond, set diversionary fires, capture a major arsenal, and then take the governor, James Monroe, hostage. Gabriel ordered his followers to spare Methodists and Quakers, known to hold antislavery views, and he also expected Indians and "the poor white people" of Richmond and Norfolk to join him. Knowing that Governor Monroe was a pro-French (and thus liberty-loving) Republican, Gabriel assumed he might prove sympathetic to their cause. Gabriel, it appears, took the Federalist rhetoric about Republican Francophiles too seriously.

Gabriel's Revolt never actually materialized. A massive thunderstorm scuttled it on the appointed day, and a few nervous slaves spilled the secret. Within days, scores of implicated conspirators were locked in jail and brought to trial. One of the accused, Jack Ditcher, declared in court, "We have as much right to fight for our liberty as any men," and another compared himself to the most venerated icon of the early Republic: "I have nothing more to offer than what General Washington would have had to offer, had he been taken by the British and put to trial by them."

Such talk invoking the specter of a black George Washington made Governor Monroe and Vice President Jefferson exceedingly uneasy. Persistent rumors implicated two white Frenchmen in the plot as well; if that connection had been established, it would have strengthened the Federalists' claim that slave insurrections were a logical outcome of Republican slogans about liberty and equality. Meanwhile, Virginia judges were keeping the Richmond gallows busy. Eventually, twenty-seven black men were hanged for contemplating rebellion, really for taking to heart the language of revolutionary rights. A troubled Jefferson advised Governor Monroe that the killings had gone far enough and that perhaps deportation was a better alternative.

In the end, Gabriel's Revolt terrified the South but had little real impact on the election of 1800, despite Federalist hopes. The country as a whole took a sharp turn for the Republicans, as seen in the congressional elections, which gave Jefferson's party sixty-five seats in the House, compared with the Federalists' forty-one. But it was the existing House, not the new one, that would choose the new president.

In February 1801, the House met to consider its options. The choice was not at all obvious; for example, some wished to elect neither of the candidates who had tied in the electoral college, but instead preferred Adams or even Pinckney. Jefferson had been the intended Republican presidential candidate, but Burr, driven by ambition and vanity, had declined to withdraw. Burr was smart; he was also high-strung, arrogant, and subject to manipulation by clever flatterers. It took thirty-six separate ballots and six days for Jefferson to secure the presidency. What finally determined the outcome was Alexander Hamilton's support of his enemy Jefferson. Hamilton recognized that Burr's unstable character would be more dangerous in the presidency than Jefferson's hated but steady habits of republicanism.

The Jefferson Vision of Republican Simplicity

Jefferson was the first president inaugurated in Washington, D.C. In 1801, the capital city consisted of a set of fine street plans scarcely realized. Only three thousand people inhabited the swampy site along the Potomac River. "Being told that we were entering Washington city," one visitor recalled, "I continued looking for the houses for some little time; but seeing none, I thought I had misunder-

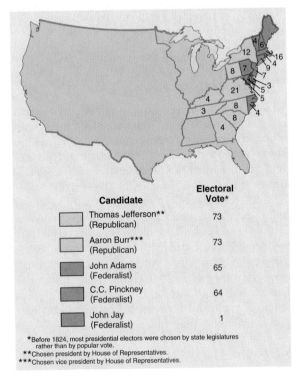

Candidate	Electoral Vote*
Thomas Jefferson** (Republican)	73
Aaron Burr*** (Republican)	73
John Adams (Federalist)	65
C.C. Pinckney (Federalist)	64
John Jay (Federalist)	1

*Before 1824, most presidential electors were chosen by state legislatures rather than by popular vote.
**Chosen president by House of Representatives.
***Chosen vice president by House of Representatives.

MAP 10.1
The Election of 1800

stood the gentleman, who . . . told me, laughing that we were almost in the very middle of it." The typical residential structure was the boardinghouse, providing temporary quarters for members of Congress who lived in town for a few months at a time. Jefferson stayed in a humble boardinghouse while he waited out the many House ballots on his candidacy. On inauguration day, he dressed in everyday wear, to strike the tone of republican simplicity, and walked to the Senate chamber in the Capitol for the modest swearing-in ceremony.

> *Hamilton recognized that Burr's unstable character would be more dangerous in the presidency than Jefferson's hated but steady habits of republicanism.*

Once in office, Jefferson continued to emphasize simplicity and frugality. He scaled back on Federalist building plans for Washington and cut the government budget. He continued to wear plain clothes and presented an appearance that was "neglected but not slovenly," according to one appraising onlooker. He cultivated a casual approach, wearing slippers to greet important guests and seating them haphazardly at his table, avoiding the formality of state dinner parties or majestic levees like Washington's. Jefferson's studied carelessness was very deliberate.

Jefferson was no Antifederalist. At a distance, he had supported the Constitution in 1788 from his diplomatic post in France, although he had some qualms about the unrestricted reelection allowed to the president. But his political service of the 1790s, first as Washington's secretary of state and then as Adams's vice president, caused him to fear what he considered an inappropriate stretching of governmental powers in the executive branch.

Jefferson watched with mounting distrust as Hamilton led the Federalists to fund the public debt, establish a national bank, and secure commercial ties with England. The Hamiltonian program seemed to Jefferson to be wrongly promoting the interests of a small circle of money-hungry speculators, at the expense of the rest of the country. Jefferson was not at all anticommerce. As he liked to put it, he very much valued commerce as the "handmaiden" of agriculture. But financial schemes that seemed merely to allow rich men to become richer, without enhancing the vast and natural productiv-

JEFFERSON'S RED WAISTCOAT
During his presidency, Jefferson often wore this red silk waistcoat as informal daywear. The garment had a velvet collar, woolen sleeves, and a thick lining made from recycled cotton and wool stockings. The thrifty Jefferson preferred to conserve firewood by wearing layers of warm clothes. A New Hampshire senator visited in December 1802 and reported in dismay that the president was "dressed, or rather undressed, with an old brown coat, red waistcoat, old corduroy small clothes, much soiled, woolen hose, and slippers without heels." Another guest in 1804 found him in the red waistcoat, green velveteen breeches with pearl buttons, and "slippers down at the heels" and concluded he looked like an ordinary farmer. Such colorful clothing in silk and velveteen carries dressy or feminine connotations in the twentieth century, but not in 1800. Jefferson did dress up in silken hose and clean linen for fancy dinner parties; and when he lived in Paris in the 1780s, he wore an elaborately embroidered silk waistcoat under a greatcoat trimmed with gold lace. But in the 1800s, he used his simple, colorful clothes to make a point about republican manners. Not until the 1830s did black suits become standard wear for men.
Courtesy Monticello, photo by Colonial Williamsburg.

ity of America, were corrupt and worthless, he believed, and their promotion had no authority under the Constitution.

In Jefferson's vision, the source of true freedom in America was the independent farmer, someone who owned and worked his land, producing agricultural products both for himself and for the market. Widespread landownership, which would support unsubservient and therefore virtuous citizens, was Jefferson's cornerstone of liberty. The dependence of tenancy, on the other hand, "begets subservience and venality, suffocates the germ of virtue, and prepares fit tools for the designs of ambition." He embedded the idea of easy access to land in the various land ordinances he designed in the 1780s for the Northwest Territory. Once, he even went so far as to suggest that Virginia use its vast western domain to hand fifty acres of land, free of charge, to every landless white man. Members of the Virginia legislature, substantial landowners who had gotten their land the old-fashioned way (inheritance, shrewd marriage, or outright purchase) found his idea much too radical—free land devalued existing private property—and his idea was quickly dismissed. But Jefferson remained committed to the idea of cheaply available land; abundant, unsettled western land seemed to him to be the insurance policy that guaranteed American freedom.

> *In Jefferson's vision, the source of true freedom in America was the independent farmer, someone who owned and worked his land, producing agricultural products both for himself and for the market.*

Fresh with distrust of Hamiltonian plans, Jefferson as president set about to dismantle as many as he could of the Federalist governmental powers. He reduced the size of the army by a third, leaving only three thousand soldiers, and cut back the navy from twenty-five to seven ships. Peacetime defense, he felt, should rest with "a well-disciplined militia," not a standing army. With the consent of Congress, he abolished all federal internal taxes, including both those based on population and the hated whiskey tax; government revenue would now derive solely from customs duties and from the sale of western lands. (This maneuver was of particular benefit to the South, where the three-fifths clause of the Constitution counted slaves for both representation and taxation. Now the South enjoyed its extra weight in the House of Representatives without having to pay any extra monies in taxes.) Jefferson's goal aimed at republican simplicity in government, and by the end of his first term he had deeply reduced Hamilton's cherished national debt.

A properly limited federal government, according to Jefferson, really had little cause to be expensive in times of peace. It was responsible for running a postal system, maintaining the federal courts, staffing lighthouses, collecting customs duties, and conducting a census once every ten years. There were a few salaries to be paid, but those were kept to a minimum. The president had just one private secretary to help him with his correspondence, and Jefferson paid him out of his own pocket. (Another 14 servants performed domestic and valet chores for the president, and they were also paid—or owned—by Jefferson.) The Department of State employed only 8 people: Secretary James Madison, 6 clerks, and a messenger. The Treasury Department was by far the largest unit, with 73 revenue commissioners, auditors, clerks, and two watchmen. The entire payroll of the executive branch of the government amounted to a mere 130 people in 1801. In the hot summer months, it shrank to just a few dozen men.

And they were all men. Albert Gallatin, who headed the Treasury, once suggested to Jefferson that they consider remedying a shortage of qualified candidates by appointing talented women, to which Jefferson brusquely replied, "The appointment of a woman to office is an innovation for which the public is not prepared, nor am I." The shortage of willing and able male employees resulted from the temporary nature of the work and the severe interruption it posed to family life and to more lucrative careers that would suffer if let go. Lawyer John Marshall, for example, served in President Adams's cabinet, traveled to France as a diplomat to negotiate the XYZ affair, and then reluctantly allowed himself to be nominated as chief justice of the Supreme Court in 1801, all the while fearing that his profitable law practice was ebbing away. He wrote his ailing wife, back home in Richmond, Virginia, "Oh God, how much time and how much happiness have I thrown away?"

The Judiciary and the Midnight Judges

Marshall was in fact genuinely surprised to be nominated for the Supreme Court, but he took the job to help out the Federalist Party. John Adams's re-

**JEFFERSON'S
INDEPENDENT FARMER**
*A Jeffersonian vision of rustic
virtue: a farmer plows his
field on the outskirts of Salem,
North Carolina. The farmer
wears a hat, coat, and long
trousers to protect his legs;
he also appears to be barefoot.*
Collection of the Wachovia Historical
Society.

sponse to the sweeping Republican victory in the 1800 election was to quickly appoint Federalists to the one branch of government he still controlled: the judiciary.

The federal court system took its shape from the Judiciary Act of 1789, built on the skeleton provided by the Constitution, which said only that there would be a Supreme Court and "such inferior courts as the Congress may from time to time ordain and establish." The 1789 act established six Supreme Court justices who would simultaneously preside over six circuit courts, which traveled to hear cases over a large territory. No one imagined that the Supreme Court would need to meet often, or even together, so it seemed natural to design other duties for the justices. But the travel required by circuit-riding was grueling, and the best legal minds of the day were reluctant to accept appointment to the Supreme Court. In the 1790s, the Court met infrequently, and justices issued decisions separately.

One of the last acts of the Federalist presidency and Congress was to pass the Judiciary Act of 1801, which Adams signed into law in February, his final month in office. The new act set up sixteen circuit courts, an increase of ten districts, and separated them from the Supreme Court justices. The ratio-

nale for the change was sound: More courts were in fact needed, and releasing Supreme Court justices from circuit-riding duties was a blessing for the experienced (and usually aged) judges best suited to the highest court. Under the new plan, the Supreme Court would take cases on appeal from circuit courts run not by themselves but by different judges. All of these changes were reasonable, but they had a huge drawback to the Republicans: The act produced a political windfall of new appointments for the Federalists. If he could act quickly, President Adams suddenly could appoint sixteen new judges who would hold lifetime tenure in the job, plus dozens more state attorneys, marshals, and clerks to go with each court. The Judiciary Act of 1801 also reduced the size of the Supreme Court, from six to five justices. Adams had recently appointed John Marshall, a solid Federalist, to a vacant sixth seat, but once the Judiciary Act became law, the Republican president would not be able to fill the next resigned seat.

Adams and Marshall worked feverishly in the last weeks of February. They secured agreements from 217 men to serve in judicial, diplomatic, and military posts—an astonishing number, in view of the slowness of mail and travel and an expectation of considerable refusals. The two men were still at

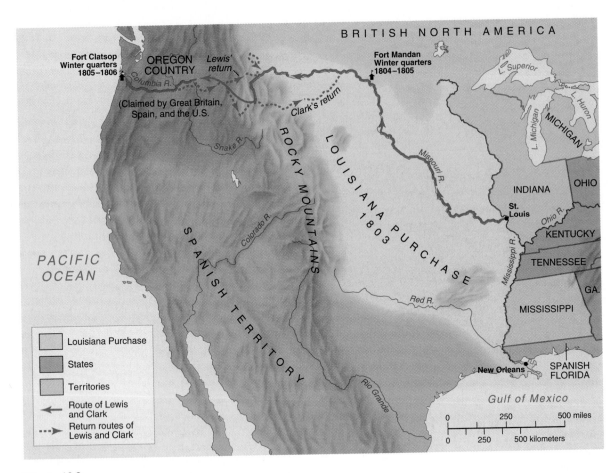

MAP 10.2
Lewis and Clark and the Louisiana Purchase
Lewis and Clark's expedition in 1804–1806 brought the Indians of the far Northwest their first look at Anglo American and African American men. The huge dimensions of the Louisiana Purchase of 1803 were scarcely imaginable to East Coast Americans. Federalists of New England, worried that their own geographically based power in the federal government would someday be eclipsed by the West, voted against the purchase.

work until 9 P.M. on the last night Adams was president, signing and delivering commissions to the new appointees.

The appointment of "midnight judges" greatly infuriated the Republicans. Jefferson, upon taking office, immediately canceled the appointments of the non-life-tenured men. A few commissions had not yet been delivered, by Marshall's oversight, and Jefferson refused to send them out. One of them was addressed to William Marbury, who soon decided to sue the new secretary of state, James Madison, for failure to make good on the appointment. This action gave rise to a landmark Supreme Court case, *Marbury v. Madison*, decided in 1803. The Court, presided over by John Marshall, ruled that although Marbury's commission was valid and the new president should have delivered it, the Court could not compel him to do so. That much sounded splendid to the Republicans, and they celebrated the wisdom and impartiality of the Marshall Court decision. What made the case significant was little noted at the time: The Court based its reasoning on a finding that the grounds of Marbury's suit, resting in the Judiciary Act of 1789, were in conflict with the Constitution. For the first time, the Court had acted to disallow a law (part of the 1789 act) on the grounds that it was unconstitutional. John Marshall had quietly established the concept of judicial review; the Supreme Court in effect had assumed the legal authority to nullify acts of the other branches of the federal government.

The reach of the *Marbury* decision went largely unnoticed in 1803 because the president and Congress were completely preoccupied with other major issues. One was a concerted effort to repeal via Congress the Judiciary Act of 1801. Republicans argued that so many new courts were expensive. Federalists argued that they were necessary and, furthermore, that removing judgeships in effect removed judges, an unconstitutional act because they had been guaranteed lifetime tenure during good behavior, and nothing but a criminal trial could unseat them. At issue was the power relation between Congress and the judiciary. It seemed to the Federalists that the Republicans had found a devious way to unseat politically unpopular judges, by phasing out their jobs. The Republicans claimed that if Congress could create courts, it could abolish them. The Judiciary Act was finally repealed in 1802.

John Marshall and the other justices on the Supreme Court agreed with the Federalists that the repeal was unconstitutional, but no case was brought to test it. But just the fact that the justices could agree signaled a departure in itself. Marshall had transformed and solidified the Court into a unitary body. Instead of rendering their diverse opinions in isolation, the justices now all came to Washington for several months of the year and lived and worked together. Cases, precedents, and opinions were chewed over and debated during meals at the boardinghouse table. Marshall, who remained chief justice until 1835, had succeeded in creating an institution whose authority was now commensurate with the legislative and executive branches of the government.

The Louisiana Purchase

Jefferson's vision of a limited federal government could be sustained as long as international affairs remained peaceful. The rise of Napoleon to power in France in 1799 soon brought France and England into open warfare again. And renewed European tensions created an unexpected opportunity for Jefferson's administration.

In 1800, the Mississippi River formed the western boundary of the United States; the expanse of land west of the river was under the flag of Spain. For a century before the French and Indian War, France had claimed and partly settled the territory,

only to lose it to Spain in 1763 under the terms of the Treaty of Paris. Spain never sent adequate forces to control or settle the land, however; Spanish power remained precarious everywhere outside New Orleans.

Meanwhile, American farming families were advancing west, to Kentucky and Tennessee, in the 1790s. They settled along rivers emptying into the upper Mississippi, on which they depended for shipping their agricultural produce. For a while the Spanish governor of New Orleans allowed free navigational rights on the lower Mississippi, and American farmers supplied the city with flour, whiskey, and other foodstuffs. The Spanish crown even encouraged Americans to settle across the river, in an effort to augment the population. Settlers had to take oaths of allegiance to the Spanish king in exchange for legal title to free land, proportional to the number of workers they brought with them, a system much like the headright system of the British Chesapeake colonies. Americans took the oath and took the land, but they proved to be unruly subjects.

By 1801, Americans made up a sizable minority of the sparse population of present-day Louisiana. The American government was secretly very pleased with Spain's attractive policy. Jefferson lodged formal complaints against Spain for luring United States citizens into foreign lands, but that was a deception crafted to keep Spain ignorant of the shortsightedness of its policy. Privately, Jefferson wrote, "I wish a hundred thousand of our inhabitants would accept the invitation; it will be the means of delivering to us peaceably, what may otherwise cost us a war." Jefferson's fears of war were not unrealistic. In 1802, the Spanish governor of New Orleans revoked American shipping privileges through or past his city. Congressional representatives in Washington began muttering about taking the city by force; talk of war, especially in Federalist newspapers, became commonplace.

In the same year, rumors reached Jefferson that Spain had struck a secret bargain with France to hand over Louisiana to Napoleon, in exchange for a duchy in Italy. Spain had proved a weak western neighbor, but France was another story. Jefferson was sufficiently alarmed that he dispatched trusted diplomats Robert R. Livingston and James Monroe to Europe with instructions to try to buy New Orleans. At first the French denied they owned the city, but Livingston politely exposed that evasion by announcing that he had seen the treaty with Spain.

The Americans suggested that the United States might simply seize New Orleans, if buying it was not an option, hinting that a military alliance with the British might also be part of the plan. Finally, the French negotiator suddenly asked Livingston to name his price for the entire Louisiana Territory, stretching north to Canada. Livingston stalled, and the Frenchman floated prices ranging from $125 million to $60 million. Livingston, sensing a French eagerness to sell, shrewdly stalled some more. He pointed out that if the price was too high, "it would render the present Government [Jefferson's] unpopular, and have a tendency, at the next election, to throw the power into the hands of men who were most hostile to a connection with France. I asked him," Livingston wrote to Jefferson just hours after the meeting, "whether the few millions acquired at this expense would not be too dearly bought?" Within a few days, the French sold the entire territory for the bargain price of $15 million.

Jefferson and most of the Congress were delighted with the outcome of the diplomatic mission. Congress quickly approved the purchase and voted for a bond issue to raise money for the price. However, all but one of New England's representatives voted against it. (The one affirmative vote was that of John Quincy Adams.) Federalist-dominated New England had been willing to consider war to seize New Orleans and control navigation rights on the river. But the huge territory that came along with the city raised sudden anxiety about the ultimate geographic balance of power in the United States. So much land, sure to be carved into states one day, made some fear the eventual marginalization of New England.

Jefferson had his own reason to be reluctant about the Louisiana Purchase. The price was right, and the enormous expansion of territory fulfilled Jefferson's dream of abundant farmland for generations of Americans to come. But by what authority in the Constitution could he justify the purchase? His frequent criticism of the Hamiltonian stretching of the Constitution came back to haunt him. His legal reasoning told him he needed a constitutional amendment to fully authorize the addition of territory; more expedient minds told him the treaty-making powers of the president could be invoked to cover his action. Expediency won out. In late 1803, the American army took formal control of the Louisiana Territory, and the United States was now 828,000 square miles larger than it had been before.

Republicans in a Dangerous World

The election of 1804 proved an easy triumph for the Republican Party. Jefferson's Federalist opponent, Charles Cotesworth Pinckney of South Carolina, garnered only 14 votes in the electoral college, in contrast to 162 for the president. New England, the stronghold of federalism, was lukewarm for Jefferson, but only Connecticut's electoral votes went for Pinckney. Just months before the election, the Federalists had lost their shrewdest statesman: Alexander Hamilton, called by some "the brains of the Federalist Party," was tragically killed in a duel, gunned down by Aaron Burr. (See Historical Question, page 358.) Republicans would hold the presidency for another twenty years.

In his second term, Jefferson turned his attention to serious troubles arising out of the ongoing war between France and England, which gravely imperiled the United States. As a peaceful alternative to war, the president experimented with economic sanctions and trade embargoes. Jefferson and his successors in office faced war threats not only across the Atlantic but also in the new states of the old Northwest Territory, where a powerful new Indian confederacy challenged the westward press of American settlement.

Troubles at Sea

In the 1790s, American shipping had prospered when the two leading European powers, France and England, were at war, for they left trade routes and markets wide open for American ships to fill. England and France determined not to make that mistake again. When war broke out between them in 1803, the two powerful countries established restrictions on American trade with the enemy. England declared a vast array of goods, far beyond war materials, to be forbidden and announced a blockade of the French coast to stop American ships and to search for illegal goods. France too, starting in 1807, declared it would seize any American ship caught trading with England.

When the British started enforcing their threats in 1806, the costs were felt by many hundreds of Americans. In addition to searching for prohibited goods, British naval patrols claimed the right to seize (and impress into service) sailors whom they accused of being deserters from the British navy. In

TWO CAPTAINS AT SEA
The captains of two sailing ships confer at sea, using horns to amplify their voices, in this water-color by Benjamin Latrobe (also the architect of the Capitol). New England coastal towns like Salem, Newburyport, Portsmouth, and Portland played a major role in the shipping trade and extended their routes to China and India in the early nineteenth century, in addition to the West Indies–Europe circuit. Some schooners really were as small as these depicted, measuring fifteen to eighteen feet wide and as little as forty feet long. Jefferson's embargo worked a great hardship on the New England industry.
Maryland Historical Society, Baltimore.

fact, some deserters had fled and taken new jobs in the American merchant marine. Some had even become naturalized U.S. citizens. The impressment sweeps captured those men but also caught up hundreds of native-born Americans as well. Between 1807 and 1812, about 2,500 men were taken captive by imperious British commanders and were impressed into royal naval service. Jefferson and the American public were outraged.

One incident in particular made the usually cautious Jefferson nearly belligerent. In June 1807, an American ship, the *Chesapeake*, had picked up some British deserters, and a short time later a British frigate ordered the *Chesapeake* to stop for inspection. The *Chesapeake* refused, and the British opened fire, killing three Americans. The attackers

then boarded the ship and forcibly removed four British subjects. Provocative as the incident was, what made it even more insulting was the location: The attack occurred in Chesapeake Bay, well within U.S. territory. President Jefferson assembled his cabinet to read his draft of a heated manifesto he wanted to issue to Great Britain, demanding an end to impressment. One cabinet member described the high tension of the moment: The incident, he wrote, "has excited the spirit of '76 and the whole country is literally in arms." But the country was not actually prepared for war—the much reduced army and navy presented a serious problem—and so Jefferson's cabinet toned down his challenge to England. Instead, Jefferson banned British warships from all travel in American waters. Plans were put in

How Could a Vice President Get Away with Murder?

ON JULY 11, 1804, the vice president of the United States, Aaron Burr, shot Alexander Hamilton, the architect of the Federalist Party, in a duel on a narrow ledge below the cliffs of Weehawken, New Jersey, across the Hudson River from New York City. The pistol blast tore through a rib, demolished Hamilton's liver, and splintered his spine. The forty-seven-year-old Hamilton died the next day, in agonizing pain.

How could it happen that a sitting vice president and a prominent political leader could put themselves at such risk? Why did men who made their living by the legal system go outside of the law and turn to the ancient ritual of the duel? Here were two eminent attorneys, skilled in the legalistic negotiations meant to substitute for violent dispute resolution, firing .54-caliber hair-trigger weapons at ten paces. Did anyone try to stop them? How did the public react? Was Hamilton's death a criminal act? How could Burr continue to fulfill his federal office, presiding over the U.S. Senate?

Burr challenged Hamilton in late June after learning about a newspaper report that Hamilton "looked upon Mr. Burr to be a dangerous man, and one who ought not be trusted with the reins of government." As Burr well knew, Hamilton had long held a very low opinion of the vice president and had never hesitated to say so in private, but now his private disparagement had inadvertently made its way into print. Compounding the insult were political consequences Burr now suffered: He was sure that Hamilton's remark flat-out cost him election to the governorship of New York.

Quite possibly he was right about that. Knowing that Jefferson planned to dump him from the federal ticket in the fall 1804 election, Burr had chosen to run for New York's highest office. His opponent was an obscure Republican judge; Burr's strong edge for victory depended on the support of the old Federalist leadership in the state. Up to the eve of the election, he appeared to have it—until Hamilton's remark was circulated.

So on June 18, Burr challenged Hamilton to a duel if he did not disavow his comment. Over the next three weeks, the men exchanged several letters clarifying the nature of the insult that aggrieved Burr. Hamilton the lawyer evasively quibbled over words, causing Burr finally to rail against his focus on syntax and grammar. At heart, Hamilton could not deny the insult, nor could he spurn the challenge without injury to his reputation for integrity and bravery. Both Burr and Hamilton were locked in a highly ritualized procedure meant to uphold a code of honor deemed essential by all gentlemen.

Each man had a trusted "second," in accord with the code of dueling, who helped frame and deliver the letters and finally assisted the two men at the duel site. Only a handful of close friends knew of the challenge, and no one tried to stop it. Hamilton did not tell his wife. He wrote her a tender farewell letter the night before, to be opened in event of his death. He knew full well the pain dueling brought to loved ones, for his nineteen-year-old son Philip had been killed in a duel three years earlier, at the same ledge at Weehawken, as a result of hotheaded words exchanged at a New York the-

AARON BURR BY JOHN VANDERLYN
Aaron Burr was forty-six years old and vice president of the United States at the time of this portrait, painted in 1809 by the New York artist John Vanderlyn.
Collection of The New-York Historical Society.

ater. Even when Hamilton's wife was called to her husband's deathbed, she was first told he had terrible spasms from an illness. Women were completely shut out of the masculine world of dueling.

News of Hamilton's death spread quickly in New York and then throughout the nation. On the day of the funeral, church bells tolled continuously and New York merchants shut down all business. Thousands joined the procession, and the city council declared a six-week mourning period. Burr fled to Philadelphia, fearing retribution by the crowd.

Northern newspapers expressed indignation over the illegal duel and the tragic death of so prominent a man. (Response in the South was more subdued. Dueling was fully accepted there as an extralegal remedy for insult, and Burr's grievance fit perfectly the sense of violated honor that legitimated duels. In addition, Southerners had never been particularly fond of the Federalist Hamilton.) Many northern states had criminalized dueling under recent statute law, treating a challenge as a misdemeanor and a dueling death as a homicide. Even after death the loser of an illegal duel could endure one final penalty—being buried without a coffin, having a stake driven through the body, being strung up in public until the body rotted, or, more horrible still for the time, being donated to medical students for dissection. Such prescribed mutilation of the dead showed that northern lawmakers themselves participated in the code of honor by using threats of postmortem humiliation to discourage dueling. Hamilton's body was spared such a fate. But two ministers in succession refused to administer holy communion to him in his dying hours because he was a duelist; finally, one relented.

The public demanded to know the reasons for the duel, so the seconds prepared the correspondence between the principals for publication. A coroner's jury in New York soon indicted Burr on misdemeanor charges for issuing a challenge; a grand jury in New Jersey indicted him for murder. By that time, Burr was a fugitive from justice hiding out with sympathetic friends in South Carolina.

But not for long. Amazingly, he returned to Washington, D.C., in November 1804 to resume presiding over sessions of the Senate, a role he continued to assume until his term ended in February 1805. Federalists snubbed him, but eleven Republican senators petitioned New Jersey to drop its indictment, on the grounds that "civilized nations" do not treat dueling deaths as "common murders." New Jersey did not pursue the murder charge. Burr freely vis-

DUELING PISTOLS
FROM THE BURR-HAMILTON DUEL
Hamilton's brother-in-law John B. Church purchased this pair of dueling pistols in London in 1797. He used them once in a duel with Aaron Burr, occasioned by Church's calling Burr a scoundrel in public; neither man was hurt. Hamilton's son Philip borrowed them for his duel, fought at Weehawken; Philip died. When Burr challenged Hamilton, the latter turned to John Church for the weapons. The guns stayed in the Church family until 1930, when they were given to the Chase Manhattan Bank in New York City, chartered in 1799 as the Manhattan Company. (Burr, Church, and Hamilton all served on the bank's board of directors.) When the pistols were cleaned in 1874, a hidden hair trigger came to light, which could be cocked by moving the trigger forward one-eighth inch. It then required only a half-pound pull, instead of ten pounds, to fire the gun. Hamilton gained no advantage from the hair trigger, if he knew of it.
Courtesy of Chase Manhattan Archives.

ited New Jersey and New York for three more decades, paying no penalty for killing Hamilton.

Few would doubt that Burr was a scoundrel, albeit a brilliant one. A few years later, he was indicted for treason against the U.S. government in a presumed plot to break off part of the United States and start his own country in the Southwest. (He dodged that bullet too, in a spectacular trial presided over by John Marshall, chief justice of the Supreme Court.) Hamilton certainly thought Burr a scoundrel, and when that opinion reached print, Burr had cause to defend his honor under the etiquette of dueling. The accuracy of Hamilton's charge was of absolutely no account. Dueling redressed questions of honor, not questions of fact.

Dueling continued to be a feature of southern society for many more decades, but in the North, the custom became extremely rare by the 1820s, helped along by the disrepute of Hamilton's death and by the rise of a legalistic society that now preferred evidence, interrogation, and monetary judgments to avenge injury.

motion to increase the armed forces substantially, but still Jefferson preferred diplomacy as the instrument of foreign policy. He instructed James Monroe, the American ambassador in England, to pressure the government there to repudiate the policy of impressment. Monroe's efforts were unsuccessful.

The Embargo and Its Aftermath

Jefferson's initial response to the British threat against American shipping in 1806 had been to push nonimportation laws in Congress. A select list of British-made goods was declared off limits for trade. But the *Chesapeake* incident triggered much stronger measures. Jefferson and his secretary of state, James Madison, developed the idea of a total embargo on all trade.

In December 1807, Congress passed the Embargo Act, which forbade any American ships from engaging in any trade with any foreign port. It was a drastic measure, but it was intended as economic coercion substituting for a far more drastic possibility, a declaration of war. The immediate goal was to make England suffer, and all foreign ports were included in the ban so as to discourage illegal trading through secondary ports. The two Republican leaders were convinced that England needed America's trade goods, mainly agricultural products, far more than America needed British goods. Jefferson's long-standing anti-English prejudice had by now rubbed off on Madison, who belittled British imports as "superfluities or poisons," things Americans would be better off without. At his peak of personal influence, the president secured swift agreement from a Republican-dominated Congress bent on sending a signal to England.

The Embargo Act of 1807 was a total disaster. From 1790 to 1807, U.S. exports had increased fivefold, and in an instant the Embargo Act wiped out all commerce. Worse, it was ineffective as a penalty to the enemy. England did not suffer much at all; it simply turned to South American countries for agricultural supplies, unhindered now by American vessels, which were no longer on the seas. New England, the heart of the shipping industry, complained the loudest. Trade was at a standstill, and unemployment began to rise. Emergency town meetings convened to plan a course of action; protest petitions flooded Washington. Federalists in Barre, Massachusetts, pointed out that the damage to trade also hurt farmers: "We consider the interest of Agriculture and Commerce as inseparable"; the "belief that the farmer can flourish, while [the merchant] is

neglected and depressed" was a serious error, they warned. Connecticut Federalists dredged up Jefferson's own words from the 1798 Kentucky Resolutions, suggesting that state nullification of the federal embargo might be in order. States could "interpose their protecting shield between the rights and liberties of the people and the assumed power of the general government," said Connecticut's governor, Jonathan Trumbull. The South hurt mightily as well; tobacco rotted on the docks and cotton went unpicked. The wheat crop of the central and western states plummeted in value, and river traffic came to a halt. The federal government itself suffered too, for import duties were the chief source of national revenue.

> *The Embargo Act was a drastic measure, but it was intended as economic coercion substituting for a far more drastic possibility, a declaration of war.*

The Embargo Act proved difficult to police, and inevitably American shippers reacquainted themselves with their Revolutionary-era traditions of illegal smuggling. Despite the evasions, the U.S. economy was severely affected. Prices of basic agricultural products like corn fell by a third from the boom year of 1804. The Federalist Party, in danger of fading away after its very weak showing in the election of 1804, began to pick up considerable strength from the anti-Jefferson protest.

The embargo stayed in place until the last day of Jefferson's presidency, in March 1809, but it created a very rocky and bewildering final year for the administration. Congress finally repealed it and replaced it with the Non-Intercourse Act of 1809, which prohibited trade only with the two belligerent nations, England and France, and their colonial possessions. In effect, the new law opened the way for a legal, indirect trade, so the economic anguish of New England shippers and southern planters in the export trade was greatly diminished, for the moment.

Madison Gets Entangled

In mid-1808, Jefferson made it clear that he planned to follow George Washington's lead and limit his presidency to two terms. James Madison, the secretary of state for eight years and Jefferson's closest ally in the government, was the clear heir apparent.

Disgruntled Republicans from hurting tobacco regions of the South made a move to support James Monroe, another Virginia planter with wide experience as a diplomat to England, but Madison was the clear front-runner choice of the various state caucuses of Republicans. At this point, party politics, still held to be a bad thing by leading statesmen, operated through informal coalition building and statewide caucuses that orchestrated state and local elections. The Federalist caucuses, thinking they would gain strength from the unpopular Embargo Act, chose Charles Cotesworth Pinckney again. Pinckney did much better than in 1804; he received forty-seven electoral votes, nearly half the number that the winner, James Madison, got. Support for the Federalists remained centered in the New England states, where they regained a number of seats in both the House and the Senate, but Republicans still held the balance of power.

The depredations of England on American ships continued. Sailors still faced captivity and impressment, while cargoes were subject to inspection. The British claimed that their actions could be construed as enforcement of the American Non-Intercourse Act. But Madison took as insult the notion that England should presume to enforce American laws at all. He insisted that Americans were neutral in the British-French conflict and that a neutral ship must by definition be carrying a neutral cargo.

In 1810, the Non-Intercourse Act expired, and Congress replaced it with a complicated law called Macon's Bill Number 2, named for a North Carolina congressman. This law now permitted direct trade with either France or England, the lucky country being the one to first give assurance that it had lifted restrictions on American shipping. The French ruler Napoleon seized the initiative and declared that France would revoke its restrictions, on condition that the United States reinstate its embargo against England. Madison too hastily accepted Napoleon's offer without waiting to see if the French leader backed up his pledge with action. With trade to France reopened, Madison notified England that he intended to reinstate the embargo in the spring of 1811, unless England rescinded its search and seizure policy.

Unfortunately for Madison, the duplicitous French leaders continued to seize American ships. Furthermore, the British made no move to stop impressments or to repeal trade restrictions, and Madison was forced to reactivate the embargo, much to the great displeasure of the New England shipping industry. In 1811, the country was seriously divided

and in a deep quandary about what to do. To some, it seemed the United States must be on the verge of war; but it was hard to decide if the enemy should be France or England. To others, war meant disaster, for it would surely finish off the grievously hurting shipping industry. Madison knew he had been duped by France, but he persisted in treating England as the bigger threat to American security.

A new Congress, elected in the fall of 1810, arrived in Washington in March 1811 just as Madison's threatened embargo was to take effect. Some of the new and much younger members were eager to avenge the insults from abroad. In particular, Henry Clay, thirty-four, from Kentucky, and John C. Calhoun, twenty-nine, from South Carolina, became the center of a group informally called the War Hawks. Though calling themselves Republicans, like Madison, these younger men had much more expansive ideas of the way the United States should meet the challenge of enemies abroad.

Indian Troubles in the West

In the atmosphere of indecision about war with European powers, news filtered east about renewed difficulties with Indian tribes in the old Northwest Territory. Since the mid-1790s, after the Battle of Fallen Timbers, a general peace had been obtained in the Ohio valley. The Treaty of Greenville had established a boundary to Indian territory that had held until recent years. But by 1810, white settlement was again encroaching north and west, through the boundary in some cases; more than 230,000 Americans now lived in the Ohio Territory. Concerned Indians were renewing their alliances with supportive British Indian agents and fur traders in Canada, who were a potential source of food and weapons. While Madison contemplated war with England, he could be certain that part of the sting of that war would be felt on the frontier, as Indians and the British reinvigorated the alliance they had shared since the 1760s.

But this time a new element emerged in the Indian strategy. A powerful and charismatic Shawnee war chief named Tecumseh was successfully building a confederacy among the many Indian tribes in the Indiana, Ohio, and Michigan region. Tecumseh's remarkable political talents were enhanced by the reputation of his visionary brother Tenskwatawa, known throughout the region as the "Prophet." Tecumseh and Tenskwatawa had lost their father and two brothers in various battles with whites in the late eighteenth century. Their widowed mother, a Creek woman who had married a Shawnee chief, had moved south when Tecumseh was ten and left him and his younger siblings in the care of an aunt. Tecumseh trained for the warrior role, while his younger brother followed a much more sedentary and embittered life of idleness and excessive drinking. But in 1805, Tenskwatawa fell into a state of near death. His wife prepared him for burial, but then the man revived and recounted a startling vision, a meeting with the Master of Life. Tenskwatawa now claimed to have prophetic powers. He urged Indians everywhere to return to the customs of their ancestors and to give up borrowed practices —using European dress, plows, firearms, bread, and alcohol—learned from the white invaders. The Prophet's teachings sparked a religious revival throughout the Ohio valley and beyond, as far as the Mississippi.

From 1805 to 1807, the Prophet's popularity spread. He preached that the Americans were children of the Evil Spirit, scum and pollution destined in the end to be destroyed. The Master of Life wished the Indians to stay forever where they were, he said, and so the Prophet led his people to a site where Tippecanoe Creek joined the Wabash River in northern Indiana and established a village called Prophetstown. Tecumseh, too, inspired followers and denounced white Americans. "Once," he said, "there was not a white man in all this country. Then it all belonged to the redmen . . . now made miserable by the white people, who are never satisfied but always encroaching on our land. . . . The only way to stop this evil, is for all the redmen to unite in claiming a common right in the soil, as it was at first, and should be now." The brothers together pledged a potent blend of spiritual regeneration and political unity that proved very attractive to tribes such as the Chippewa, Potawatomi, Delaware, Miami, Kickapoo, Wyandot, and Winnebago.

The Shawnee chief Tecumseh advised that "the only way to stop this evil, is for all the red-men to unite in claiming a common right in the soil, as it was at first, and should be now."

The American governor of the Indiana Territory, William Henry Harrison, became alarmed by the two brothers' growing power. In early 1806, he issued a challenge to the Indians near him in Indi-

TENSKWATAWA

Tenskwatawa, the Shawnee Prophet, and his brother Tecumseh led the spiritual and political efforts of a number of Indian tribes to resist land-hungry Americans moving west in the decade before the War of 1812. The Prophet is shown in a portrait by George Catlin with necklaces, metal arm- and wristbands, earrings, and a necklace that looks very similar to George Washington's gorget (see page 201).

National Museum of American Art, Washington, D.C./Art Resource, New York.

---

ana: Who is this man the Prophet, and why do you believe he has divine powers? Harrison proposed that the test for divinity be an ability to perform miracles, and he named a few which he was certain would be impossible. "Ask of him to make the sun stand still, or the moon to alter its course—or the dead to rise from their graves." But as it happened, an eclipse of the sun was near at hand, in June 1806, and somehow the Prophet knew that in advance. He invited doubters to come to Prophetstown on the appointed day to see the sun stand still. His apparent miracle magnified his reputation enormously.

Harrison was skeptical about the Prophet's powers, but he understood that with Tecumseh he was up against a worthy opponent. He described the Indian leader as "one of those uncommon geniuses which spring up occasionally to produce rev-olutions." Harrison was not about to concede de-feat, however. If Tecumseh's goal was to build an Indian confederacy based on the concept that all In-dian lands were held in common by all the tribes, so that no individuals or even single tribes could sell land to U.S. agents, Harrison would undermine it. In 1809, he arranged with the leaders of three tribes to cede tribal lands in a document called the Treaty of Fort Wayne, in exchange for annual pay-ments of money. Tecumseh, discouraged and angry, began to extend his confederacy and to prepare for war.

In 1811, while Tecumseh was on a trip to Al-abama to forge alliances with the Creek and Chick-asaw tribes, Governor Harrison decided to march on Prophetstown, to disperse the Shawnees with the Prophet and burn their settlement. With one thou-sand armed men he approached Tippecanoe Creek, but the Indians attacked first. The two-hour battle resulted in about a hundred deaths—sixty-two Americans and forty Indians—before the Prophet's forces fled the area. Harrison burned the town and its food supplies. The November 1811 Battle of Tippecanoe was heralded as a glorious victory for the Americans; Harrison acquired the nickname "Tippecanoe" and used it as a patriotic rallying cry nearly thirty years later when he ran for and won the presidency in 1840. The Indians' faith in the Prophet's magical powers diminished sharply; Tenskwatawa never again enjoyed such influence.

The War of 1812

The Indian conflicts in the Northwest Territory in 1811 soon merged into the wider conflict with Eng-land known as the War of 1812. The defeat at Tippecanoe pushed Tecumseh into a renewal of the old alliance with British military commanders sta-tioned at outposts in lower Canada. If there had been doubt before about who should be the target of a declaration of war, France or England, it was now abundantly clear, especially to westerners liv-ing near the frontier, that the British should get the honor.

The War Begins

The several dozen young War Hawks new to Con-gress saluted Harrison's Tippecanoe victory and continued to urge the country on to war. Mostly lawyers by profession, they came from the West and South, and they welcomed a war with England both to legitimize war with Indians and to bring an end to impressment. Many were expansionists, looking to occupy Florida and threaten Canada. Represen-tative Felix Grundy from Tennessee, for example, rejected British maritime plundering, asserting, "I prefer war to submission." The Indian troubles in Indiana could be explained by Grundy "in one way only: Some powerful nation must have intrigued with them, and turned their peaceful disposition to-wards us into hostilities. . . . We shall drive the British from our Continent . . . [and] receive the Canadians as adopted brethren."

Kentuckian Henry Clay was elected Speaker of the House, an extraordinary honor in view of his youthful age and his lack of prior experience in Congress. John C. Calhoun from South Carolina got a seat on the Foreign Relations Committee. The War Hawks urged major defense expenditures; the army, for example, was quadrupled in size. Through all these war preparations, New England Federalists in Congress staunchly refused to endorse any of them, just as they had opposed the embargo in 1807.

In early 1812, President Madison called for a re-newed embargo on all American shipping. Unlike the first embargo, designed to be economic coercion, this version was a two-month embargo designed to clear merchant ships off the ocean in preparation for war. (While Congress debated the embargo in se-cret session, Federalists leaked word of the trade stoppage to mercantile friends. The wharves of Bal-timore, Philadelphia, New York City, and Boston in-stantly filled to capacity with ships shoving off with one last cargo. In the space of a few days, hundreds of ships set sail.) When the embargo expired in June 1812, Congress declared war on Great Britain. The vote divided on sectional lines: New England and some of the Middle Atlantic states opposed the war, while the South and West were strongly for it.

Ironically, Great Britain had just decided to re-peal its authorization for British ships to search and seize American ships. News of that diplomatic breakthrough arrived too late, however; the war machine was in motion and would not be stopped. The Foreign Relations Committee issued an elabo-rate document titled *Report on the Causes and Rea-sons for War*, written mainly by Calhoun. The report went far beyond a condemnation of Britain's search and seizure policy. War was necessary, the docu-ment said, to avenge the insults of Great Britain in treating the United States as though it was a third-rate power. Extravagant language about Britain's "lust for power," "unbounded tyranny," and "mad ambition" suggested that America was actually engaged in a second revolution for independence; failure to resist and fight Great Britain would lead to a "shameful degradation" of the United States. These were fighting words, in a war that was in large measure about insult and honor.

The War Hawks proposed an invasion of Canada, Britain's colony to the north, confidently predicting victory in four weeks, before the fall elections. Instead, the war lasted thirty months, and Canada never fell. The northern invasion turned out to be a series of strategic blunders that revealed the grave unpreparedness of the country for war. The combined strength of British soldiers and Indian allies was unexpectedly powerful, and, in addition, the United States made no attempt at the outset to create a naval presence on the Great Lakes. Detroit quickly fell to the British and Indian forces, as did Fort Dearborn (site of the future Chicago). The American plan called for a three-pronged attack by land moving toward Montreal. But all three attack routes failed, and by the fall of 1812, the war was in a dismal state.

The northern invasion of Canada turned out to be a series of strategic blunders that revealed the grave unpreparedness of the country for war.

Worse, the New England states dragged their feet in raising troops, and New England merchants continued to carry on an illegal trade with Great Britain. Later in the war, Britain as a war measure blockaded the United States coastline to prevent trade—everywhere except New England. The British understood full well the potential for friendly alliance with the New England states and were pursuing a divide and conquer strategy. New Englanders drank India tea in Liverpool cups, while President Madison fumed in Washington about Federalist disloyalty.

The presidential election in fall 1812 solidified Federalist discontent with the war. Madison stood for a second term, opposed by DeWitt Clinton of New York. Clinton was only marginally identified with the Federalists; his uncle George Clinton, a venerable New York Republican, had served Madison as vice president in 1808–1812. The younger Clinton called himself a Republican, but one of a different stripe from Madison. The Federalist strongholds fell naturally into his camp. Clinton picked up all of New England's electoral votes, with the exception of Vermont's, and also took New York, New Jersey, and part of Maryland, states with significant antiwar feeling. Madison won in the electoral college, 128 to 89, but his margin of victory was considerably smaller than in the 1808 election.

In late 1812 and early 1813, Americans began to turn the tide in the war for a time. First came some reassuring victories at sea, by the navy ships *Con-*

MAP 10.3
The War of 1812
Battles in this war were fought along the border of Canada and in the Chesapeake region. The most important American victory came in New Orleans, two weeks after peace had been agreed to in England.

A BOXING MATCH, or Another Bloody Nose for JOHN BULL.

Courtesy, American Antiquarian Society.

WAR OF 1812: BOXING MATCH
A battle between the American ship Enterprise *and the British ship* Boxer *off the Maine coast sparked this wishful-thinking cartoon. A bare-knuckled James Madison has just punched King George III, blackened his eye, and made his nose bleed. The king begs "Mercy, mercy on me," and acknowledges "your [Madison's] superior skill." Madison asserts "we are an Enterpriseing Nation" capable of "equal force any day." This Madison clearly does not anticipate the humiliating burning of Washington in 1814.*

stitution, *Wasp,* and *Hornet;* but little lasting gain came with these successes. Americans attacked York (now Toronto), the capital of Upper Canada, and burned it in April 1813. A few months later, Commodore Oliver Hazard Perry defeated the British fleet at the western end of Lake Erie. Emboldened by these successes, General William Henry Harrison drove an army into Lower Canada from Detroit and in October 1813 defeated British and Indian fighters at the Battle of the Thames, where the Shawnee chief Tecumseh met his death.

Another battle with Indians proved successful, yet vicious. A lanky and eccentric Tennessee general named Andrew Jackson led 2,500 Tennessee militiamen south in an attack on Creek Indians who had shown signs of allying with the Indian confederacy of the Northwest Territory. At the Battle of Horseshoe Bend in March 1814, Jackson defeated the Creeks, leaving more than 550 Indians dead, including women and children along with the warriors. A subsequent treaty with surviving Creeks opened the rich lands of northern Alabama to American settlement. Jackson next marched to Pensacola, Florida, directly against the president's orders to leave the Spanish settlers alone. (War Hawks were enthusiastic, however.) Jackson's excuse was that the Spanish had been supplying Creeks with arms. His men captured a Spanish fort in November and then withdrew.

The British Offensives of 1814

In August 1814, British ships sailed into Chesapeake Bay toward Washington, D.C. For three days, Washington dwellers were thrown into a panic, wondering what to expect. Families evacuated their children and valuables, banks removed their money, and government clerks packed up boxes of important papers to be carted away. One clerk in the State Department quickly located the Declaration of Independence and removed it to safety.

When five thousand British troops landed and marched toward the city, the only defense came from inexperienced militia units from Maryland. President Madison and his cabinet had been planning to dine together; instead they mounted horses and vainly tried to inspire the militia, who fled in disorder as the British advanced. The president's wife waited at home until she could hear the enemy troops, at which point she left hurriedly with a black servant named Sukey and a canvas portrait of George Washington quickly removed from its frame. When the British commanders entered the president's residence, they helped themselves to the meal roasting in the kitchen, toasted the king with the president's wines, and then set fire to the house. They also burned the Capitol, a newspaper office, some dockyards, and a well-stocked arsenal of weapons. Only a violent thunderstorm that night brought an end to the conflagration. August 24 was a low moment for the American side.

Instead of trying to hold the city, the British left swiftly and headed north for Baltimore. Baltimore, however, was ready, with road barricades and old boat hulks sunk in the harbor to prevent the entry of the larger British warships. Some thirteen thousand Maryland militiamen guarded the city resolutely. The British attacked on September 11, 1814, but the fierce defense by the militia and a steady barrage of gunfire from Fort McHenry in the harbor kept them at bay. The firing continued until midnight, motivating Francis Scott Key to compose a poem he called "The Star-Spangled Banner" the next day. The nighttime firing also motivated the British to give up. The British had not lost much in the assault, but it was equally clear that it would cost a lot to take the city.

September 1814 marked another powerful offensive by the British. From Canada an army of eighteen thousand advanced into New York State, down the route by Lake Champlain that had been used in the Revolutionary War. The British had every advantage—trained soldiers, superior artillery, cavalry, professional leaders. But a series of blunders cost them a minor naval engagement at Plattsburgh on the northern end of Lake Champlain. It also cost them their nerve, for, without ever engaging the by now astonished American troops, the British general turned his huge army around and retreated to Canada.

This nonbattle was in fact a decisive military event, for British leaders in England, when they heard the news of the retreat, concluded that incursions by land into the United States would be costly, difficult, and perhaps ineffective. Sudden retreat happened again in Maine, after the British invaded Bangor and took it without any resistance. Maine militia units flew into a state of readiness. This was New England's only moment of direct participation in the war. Earlier some New Englanders had actually celebrated British victories, but now the wolf was at their door. Oddly, however, the British shipped out.

The final British assault on America came when a large army landed in lower Louisiana in December 1814. General Andrew Jackson hurried to New Orleans from Florida with his militiamen. In early January, on a plain along the Mississippi River five miles outside New Orleans, the British attacked, and Jackson's forces dramatically carried the day. The British suffered between two and three thousand casualties, the Americans less than eighty.

General Jackson became an instant hero in America. The Battle of New Orleans was the most glorious and decisive victory the Americans had experienced.

The War Ends

The irony, of course, was that the celebrated victory counted for nothing, because peace negotiations, in progress since the summer of 1814, had succeeded in ending the war two weeks earlier. The Treaty of Ghent, signed in December 1814, settled few of the surface issues that had led to the war. Neither country could claim the role of victor, and no land traded hands. Instead, the treaty reflected a mutual agreement to give up certain goals. The Americans yielded on impressment and conceded their claim to Canada; and the British agreed to evacuate western forts and relinquished their plan to create a buffer state reserved for Indians in the Northwest Territory. Nothing was said about neutral rights, but both sides agreed to submit lingering trade disputes to arbitration at a future time. The most concrete result was an agreement to set up a commission to determine the exact boundary between the United States and Canada. Mainly, both governments were simply anxious for the war to end.

New England Federalists, united in opposition to the war, did not enjoy a sense of triumph over its ambiguous conclusion. Instead they felt a sting of disgrace, because of a serious miscalculation they made in December 1814. The British offensive of that fall spurred New England politicians to call an antiwar meeting in Hartford, Connecticut. Some of the delegates to the Hartford Convention, as it came to be called, proposed secession from the Union, but they were in the minority. Eventually, the convention settled on a plan to protect New England's sectional interests; the plan included seven new amendments to the U.S. Constitution. One amendment called for an end to the three-fifths clause, which granted southern states representation in the House based on a total of the free population plus three-fifths of all "others," meaning slaves. Several other amendments proposed that congressional powers to pass embargoes, admit states, or declare war require a two-thirds vote instead of the simple majority specified in the Constitution. Another proposal called for a limit to the presidency of one term only and a further limit that no single state could send two presidents in a row to Washington. The cumulative effect of these proposed changes was to remove political power from the South and break the lock of the Virginia dynasty on national office. New England wanted to make sure that no sectional party or group could again lead the country into war against the clear interests of some other section.

Just as the Hartford Convention broke up, news came first of the splendid victory of Jackson at New Orleans and then of the formal peace treaty signed at Ghent. The combative list of amendments suddenly looked very unpatriotic and were dismissed out of hand by the U.S. Congress. The Federalist Party never recovered its grip after that, and within a few years its hold even in New England was reduced to a shadow.

No one really won the War of 1812. Americans celebrated as though they had, however, with candlelight parades, bonfires and fireworks, artillery salutes, and public prayer. The war succeeded in distilling a new spirit of nationalism in the country, which even the foot-dragging New England states embraced after the war. The humiliation of the burning of the capital was quickly forgotten, and the paranoia over British tyranny evident in the 1812 declaration of war was laid to rest. Americans could feel pride in their new and more equal relationship with the old mother country.

Perhaps the biggest winners in the War of 1812 were the young men, once called War Hawks, who took up the banner of the Republican Party and carried it in new, expansive directions. These younger politicians secured a hold in national and state politics. They favored trade, western expansion, internal improvements, and the energetic development of new economic markets after the war. The biggest losers of the war were the Indians. Tecumseh was dead, the Prophet discredited, the prospects of an Indian confederacy dashed, and the British protectors now no longer nearby to hold out hope and supplies against the onrushing American settlers.

Women's Legal Status in the Early Republic

Unlike the American Revolution, the War of 1812 had little impact on the status of women. Relatively few localities were directly affected by troop movements and battles. Campaigns and militia enlistments were short, minimizing the inconvenience caused by absentee husbands and sons. Furthermore, the patriotic ideology supporting the war— rights at sea, shipping and trade, and honor— sprang from masculine concerns and endeavors.

The war barely disturbed feminine duties on the home front.

Even on the war front, many women remained uninvolved. As was customary, women traveled with the army, both as officers' wives and as cooks and laundresses. Mrs. Lydia Bacon, a twenty-five-year-old quartermaster's wife captured by the British at Detroit in 1812, ate tea and cake with the wife of a British officer and secured safe passage back to the American side, assured by the British command that "we have not made war upon the Ladies."

Developments in women's status in the early Republic came not as a result of wartime emergency but instead in incremental steps. State legislatures and court systems grappled with questions of the legal dependency of married white women in a country where independence was the defining characteristic of citizenship. In a parallel development, a number of religious organizations struggled to redefine the role of women in church governance.

Women and the Law

Mrs. Bacon's tea and safe passage in a war zone in 1812 signified a larger Anglo-American view of women, implanted in British common law, that wives had no independent legal or political personhood and were therefore not accountable for political allegiances. This was the decisive argument in the 1805 suit brought by the heirs of Anna Martin, a loyalist wife who fled the country with her husband during the Revolutionary War (see chapter 7). The legal doctrine, *feme covert*, held that a wife's civic life was completely subsumed, or covered, by her husband's. The winning lawyer in the Martin case drove that point home: "If he commanded it [fleeing the country], she was bound to obey him, by a law paramount to all other laws— the law of God"; the *feme covert*, he expanded, "has no *political* relation to the *state* any more than an alien." A wife was obligated to obey her husband and follow where he went. Her property was his, her domestic and sexual services were his, even their children were legally his. In the event of a father's death, the local orphans' court assigned children to a guardian, usually a near male relative, who then assumed financial responsibility (often in return for the children's services). Women under coverture had no right to their own wages, to make contracts, or to sue or be sued. Any crime committed by a wife in the presence of her husband was chargeable to him, with two exceptions: treason

CURIOSITY

Curiosity *is the playful title of this 1833 painting, done in New York City by a young German-born artist, Christian Mayr. Three women, possibly a mother and two daughters, have apparently just shown a gentleman caller into a room behind a large wooden door. Is it a business call on the man of the house? A courtship call on an older sister? The women, ears and eyes pressed to the door, are keen to know what is going on. Information networks often had important gender dimensions built into them in the 1830s.*

against the state and keeping a brothel. The fundamental assumption of the law of coverture was that husbands did—and ought to—control their wives.

State legislatures, when codifying their laws, generally passed up the opportunity to rewrite the laws of domestic relations, even though they were redrafting so much other law in light of republican principles. For Federalists and Republicans alike, the British common law governing women and marriage seemed fully adequate and in no need of change. As the practice of law expanded and more young men gained legal training to meet the growing needs of the population, legal treatises appeared in print offering handy compilations articulating common law principles and practices of current courts. One influential treatise on family law, published in 1816 by Tapping Reeve, founder of one of the country's leading law schools, at Litchfield, Connecticut, was titled *The Law of Baron and Feme* ("lord and woman"). Reeve's terminology was exactly the common legal usage. Lawyers never paused even to defend, much less to challenge, the assumption that unequal power relations lay at the heart of marriage.

Marriage in the early Republic was a legal event that joined two consenting persons for life under a binding contract whose terms were specified by the state. The laws of coverture defined the restrictions and duties of wives; in exchange, wives were entitled to economic support and protection by husbands. The early Republic's conception of the "republican wife and mother" (see chapter 9) in no way altered this legal framework. The virtuous wife whose obedience was earned by affection and the enlightened mother who acquired intellectual skills to transmit to her citizen sons still operated well within the boundaries of the expected female subservience and obligation to men.

The one aspect of family law that changed in the early Republic was divorce. Before the Revolution, only New England jurisdictions had recognized a right to divorce; by 1820, every state except South Carolina had set up divorce procedures. Divorce was uncommon and difficult, however, for it was obtainable only under carefully circumscribed conditions that found substantial fault with one partner, such as desertion or adultery. In many states, divorces could be obtained only by petition to the state's legislature, probably a daunting obstacle for many ordinary people. In some instances, divorcing couples were denied legal dissolution on the grounds that they had conspired to deceive authorities about their marital problems; a mutual wish to terminate a marriage was by itself insufficient grounds for divorce. A New York judge affirmed that "it would be aiming a deadly blow at public morals to decree a dissolution of the marriage contract merely because the parties requested it. Divorces should never be allowed, except for the protection of the innocent party, and for the punishment of the guilty." States were clearly invested in upholding the institution of marriage, both to protect persons they thought of as naturally dependent (women and children) and to regulate the use and inherited transmission of property. And certainly the state's enforcement of marriage as an unequal relationship played a major role in maintaining gender inequality in the nineteenth century.

Single adult women could own and convey property, make contracts, initiate suits, and pay taxes. They could not vote (except in New Jersey until 1807; see chapter 9), serve on juries, or practice law, so their civil status was limited. Single women's economic status was often limited as well: Unless a woman had inherited adequate property, being a single adult woman in Jeffersonian America was highly correlated with poverty.

> *Lawyers never paused even to defend, much less to challenge, the assumption that unequal power relations lay at the heart of marriage.*

One form of legal action involving single women that became more prevalent in the early decades of the nineteenth century was the seduction suit. Its increased usage as a legal remedy points to a heightened social value attached to female virginity. When unmarried women lost their virginity (with pregnancy being a closely related, highly visible, and yet not legally necessary symptom of the condition), they and their relatives increasingly concluded they had lost value in the marriage market. The legal remedy to recover damages was a seduction suit, brought against the accused man—not by the woman, but by her father or master. The law squarely reflected the traditional assumption that women were a form of property owned by fathers or masters, whose injury resulted from the loss of services they suffered when girls were seduced. Seduction suits were therefore a part of property law, not family law. And yet judges and juries typically awarded successful plaintiffs large damage judgments, on the order of $800 to $1,200, figures far in excess of the annual market value of any young woman's labor. A Pennsylvania judge in 1822 observed that loss of service was merely a "technical form of action" and that the real loss being compensated was "the destruction of the family's honor." Apparently the value of a woman's sexual honor was very high. From seduction suits to coverture, the evolving American legal system expressed the nineteenth century's commonsense notions about the status, capacity, and expected behavior of men and women in society.

Free men and women, that is. None of the legal institutions that structured white gender relations applied to blacks enslaved in the South. Slaves were denied the opportunity of marriage sanctioned by the state. As property themselves, they could not

freely consent to any contractual obligations, including marriage. The protective features of state-sponsored unions were thus denied to black men and women. Husbands could not guarantee support, nor could wives guarantee exclusive services, because both were controlled by a more powerful authority, the slave owner. But this also meant that slave unions did not establish unequal power relations backed by the force of law, as did free marriages.

Still, one prevalent cultural assumption about wives' incapacity apparently could apply to slave women as well as free women under coverture: the assumption that only husbands and not wives were responsible for political actions and decisions. Just as Anna Martin was not held accountable for being a loyalist in her own right, so too Nanny, the wife of Gabriel who plotted revolution in Virginia in 1800, was not arrested by Richmond authorities. Indeed, she was not even questioned about her husband's planned insurrection, nor was any other woman.

Women and Church Governance

In most Protestant denominations around 1800, white women made up the majority of congregants, as they had for some time. Although they usually outnumbered men at prayer meetings and services, the church hierarchy, consisting of ordained ministers and elders, was exclusively male, and the governance of most denominations rested in men's hands.

There were some exceptions, however. In several small evangelical groups, notably Baptist congregations in New England that had been strongly affected by the Great Awakening of the mid-eighteenth century, women served along with men on church governance committees, deciding admission of new members, voting on the hiring of ministers, participating in disciplinary proceedings, and even debating doctrinal points. The Awakening's emphasis on more egalitarian social relations worked to elevate women's authority in these Baptist congregations.

Quakers, too, another nonhierarchical religious group, had a history of recognizing that women's spiritual talents could equal men's. Quaker women who felt a special call were accorded the status of ministers, which among Quakers meant persons capable of leading and speaking in a religious meeting. Quaker governance, however, proceeded along sex-segregated lines: Separate men's and women's committees heard disciplinary cases and formulated church policy.

Between 1790 and 1820, a small and highly unusual set of women emerged who actually engaged in open preaching. Most were from the Freewill Baptist groups centered in Maine, New Hampshire, and Vermont, with a group in upstate New York via migration. Others were from small Methodist sects, and yet others rejected any formal religious affiliation. Probably fewer than a hundred such women existed, most of them single or widowed, but several dozen became known beyond their local communities because they traveled (some of them hundreds of miles), creating converts and controversy wherever they went. They spoke from the heart, without prepared speeches, often exhibiting trances and emotional religious states. Some denied they were infringing on the male domain of preaching and instead were exhorting and praying in public. But exhorting—that is, counseling or warning—was in practice sometimes hard to distinguish from preaching. Fanny Newell, a Methodist woman in Maine, described in 1809 her compulsion to speak out: "I felt such an impression to speak, that I did not dare to neglect it; but rose and exhorted the people, and had great liberty in so doing." But none of these women were ordained ministers, with official credentials to preach or perform baptisms.

Perhaps the most unusual and well known exhorting woman was Jemima Wilkinson, who called herself the "Publick Universal Friend." After a near-death experience from high fever in 1776, Wilkinson awoke to proclaim that her body was no longer female *or* male, but the incarnation of the "Spirit of Light." She dressed in men's clothes, wore her hair in a masculine style, shunned gender-specific pronouns, and preached openly in Rhode Island and Philadelphia, drawing some committed followers but also many hecklers. In the early nineteenth century, Wilkinson withdrew to a settlement called New Jerusalem in western New York with more than 250 followers, her fame sustained by periodic newspaper articles that fed a public curiosity about her lifelong transvestism and her unfeminine forcefulness.

As more women exhorters cropped up, their behavior came under increasing fire. A Baptist periodical in Massachusetts printed frequent reminders of the biblical prohibition "Let your women learn to keep silence in the churches" (1 Corinthians 14:34). An 1810 article elaborated on the logic of this prohibition: It arises "from the relation [women] bear to men, as being the weaker vessel, the derived,

WOMEN AND THE CHURCH: JEMIMA WILKINSON
Jemima Wilkinson, the Public Universal Friend, in an early woodcut, wears a clerical collar and body-obscuring robe, in keeping with the claim that the former Jemima was now a person without sex or gender. Her hair is pulled back tight on her head and curled at the neck in a masculine style of the 1790s.
Rhode Island Historical Society.

the dependent part." Therefore, for women to speak their faith in church "is not only in opposition to scripture, but to nature itself." Female preachers well knew the scriptural passages that dictated women's subordination, and they were ready with biblical interpretations of their own, as in Deborah Pierce's 1817 book *A Scriptural Vindication of Female Preaching, Prophesying, and Exhortation.*

Even though women on the radical fringes of a few denominations carved out some sort of role as exhorters, in the more mainstream religious societies women's leadership status was in decline. Even the New England Baptist communities that for a half century had allowed women to participate in church governance steadily withdrew that privilege. Between 1790 and 1810, women disappeared from church committees, their disfranchisement rarely commented on in the records. One glimpse of the tension over the issue emerges in an 1823 grievance lodged by a woman in Warren, Rhode Island, against her Baptist brethren, commenting that "the Sisters were formerly capable of executing the business of Committees, and if they were not now, they had better be cutt off from the church." Apparently the men agreed; this woman was excommunicated five months later for "disorderly conduct."

The decades from 1790 to the 1820s marked a period of unusual confusion, ferment, and creativity in American religion. New denominations blossomed, new styles of religiosity gripped adherents, and an extensive periodical press devoted to religion popularized all manner of theological and institutional innovations. In such a climate, even the age-old tradition of gender subordination came into question here and there among the most radically democratic of the churches. Yet on balance, the presumption of male authority over women was deeply entrenched in American culture. Individual churches established their respectability by reinstating patterns of dominance and subordination along gender lines.

Madison's Successors

Through the elections of 1812, 1816, and 1820, Republican Virginians extended their lock on the presidency to twenty-four years. The Federalists never recovered from the taint of disloyalty after the Hartford Convention, and the party moved into its twilight days, dying a surprisingly graceful death. In 1816, James Monroe beat Federalist Rufus King of Massachusetts for the presidency by an electoral vote of 183 to 34. When Monroe stood for reelection in 1820, the national presence of the Federalists was fully eclipsed. All but one electoral vote went to Monroe, the sole dissenting vote cast for John Quincy Adams, the son of Federalist John Adams, who wasn't even running. The unanimity of the 1820 election did not reflect voter satisfaction with the status quo, however, for barely a quarter of eligible voters bothered to vote. Apathy in federal elections was at an all-time high.

Monroe's two terms were dubbed the "Era of Good Feelings" by a contemporary newspaper.

Americans congratulated themselves on finally having achieved the perfection of the one-party state. Yet Monroe's presidency was not at all placid. A major constitutional crisis emerged over the admission of Missouri to the Union, pitting the North against the South. Foreign policy questions animated sharp disagreements as well. The election of 1824 brought forth an abundance of candidates, all claiming to be Republicans. A one-party political system was put to the test of practical circumstances; it failed and then fractured.

The Missouri Compromise

The faith that good and wise statesmen could find broad areas of agreement was put to the test in 1819 and 1820 over the question of admitting Missouri to the Union. The origins of the crisis lay in a seemingly routine event: Missouri applied for statehood. In the years since 1815, four other states had joined the Union (Indiana, Mississippi, Illinois, and Alabama), reflecting the fast westward flow of population now unimpeded by any Indian confederacy. Generally the constitutional pathway from territory to statehood operated smoothly, as it had since the 1790s.

What was different about Missouri was that while it shared a northern geography with the lower portions of Illinois, Indiana, Ohio, and Pennsylvania, it already contained a significant number of slaves. Many southern whites had been migrating across the Mississippi River from Virginia, Kentucky, and Tennessee, bringing their slaves with them to stake claim to the rich soil of this part of the Louisiana Purchase. The ten thousand slaves taken there by owners amounted to about one-sixth of the territory's population.

The first sign that Missouri's unusual combination of geography and demography would cause trouble arose in February 1819, when white Missourians petitioned Congress for statehood. On that occasion, a New York representative named James Tallmadge Jr. proposed two amendments to the Missouri statehood bill: that slaves thereafter born in Missouri would be free at age twenty-five and that no new slaves could be imported into the state. The combined effect of the two conditions, if federally imposed, was to abolish slavery in Missouri. Tallmadge's plan would mean that by 1844 the only slaves in Missouri would be the survivors of the existing ten thousand now in residence; in another generation, when they died out, Missouri would be entirely a free state. The gradual emancipation fea-

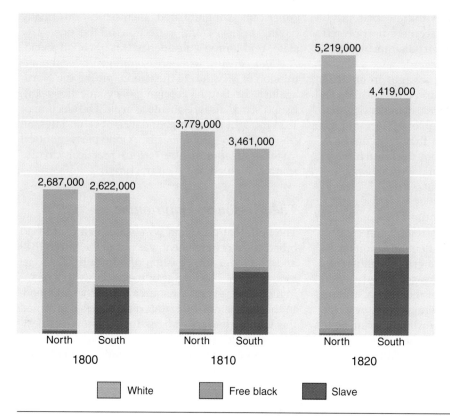

FIGURE **10.1**
Population Trends,
1800–1820
Population in the northern
states grew more rapidly than
in the South, increasing the
North's representation in Con-
gress. Slaves remained a sub-
stantial part of the South's
population. By the Constitu-
tion's three-fifths clause, slaves
augmented southern political
power, even though they
lacked all rights of citizenship.

ture very much resembled the plan New York had adopted in 1785. It did not strip slave owners of their current property, even giving them full use of the labor of newborn slaves well into their prime productive years, at which point a profit-minded owner could simply sell his property in the South rather than let twenty-fifth birthdays rob him of his investment. In the short run, this was hardly a radical plan to eradicate slavery and deprive individual owners of their property.

Nevertheless, southerners in Congress loudly protested Tallmadge's amendments. Under gradual emancipation, owners would not lose their shirts, but they would, in losing slaves and thus slavery, lose their distinctive manner of livelihood. Even larger loomed the question of Missouri as an eventual free state, a prospect gravely alarming to the South. Just as southern economic power rested on slave labor, southern political power also drew extra strength from enumerated slave bodies: The Constitution's three-fifths clause ordained that representation in Congress was based on the total population, with each slave counting as three-fifths of a white person. In 1820, the South as a region had seventeen more representatives in Congress than it would have had if only whites had figured in the population basis. Without slaves, the South's political power would be much diminished. Hence, southerners argued that the federal government had no authority to alter social systems in new states.

In 1820, the South as a region had seventeen more representatives in Congress than it would have had if only whites had figured in the population basis. Without slaves, the South's political power would be much diminished.

Both of Tallmadge's amendments passed in the House of Representatives, but with a close and sharply sectional vote of North against South (with a few northern Republicans taking the side of the South). The debate was ferocious and explosive, nearly a complete dress rehearsal of all the main ar-

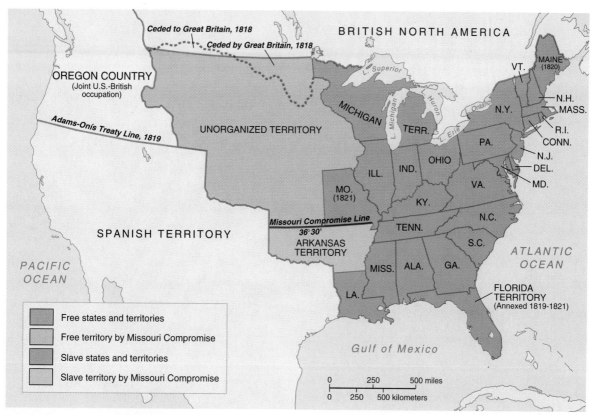

M A P 10.4
The Missouri Compromise, 1820
After a difficult battle in Congress, Missouri entered the Union in 1821 as part of a package of compromises. Maine was admitted as a free state to balance slavery in Missouri; and a line drawn at latitude 36°30' put most of the rest of the Louisiana Territory off limits to slavery in the future.

guments that would surface a generation later in the 1850s struggle leading to civil war. A Georgia representative predicted that the Missouri slavery question had started "a fire which all the waters of the ocean could not extinguish. It can be extinguished only in blood."

The Senate, with an even number of slave and free states, voted down the amendments, with some border states joining the proslavery line. The deadlock of House versus Senate meant that the total package of Missouri statehood was set aside for the next congressional term.

When it came up again in 1820, it was clear that the passions ignited in 1819 had not cooled in the least. It took a northern senator of southern origins (Jesse Thomas, formerly of Maryland, who now lived in Illinois with his five black "apprentices") to

come up with the pieces of a compromise, a plan with something for everyone. One new element was that Maine now wanted statehood. Thomas proposed a dual admission, Maine as a free state and Missouri as a slave state, to maintain the balance of power in the Senate. To make the North feel less alarmed about such a northern-reaching state being part of the slave South, Thomas proposed that the southern latitude of Missouri, 36'30", become a permanent line dividing slave from free. All of the Louisiana Territory north of that line—except Missouri—would be closed to slavery. Senator Thomas's plan passed in the Senate.

The northern-dominated House was not so easily persuaded, but in the end the compromise passed. The North secured a large area where federal prohibition of slavery was guaranteed and got

A VIEW OF ST. LOUIS FROM AN ILLINOIS TOWN
*Just fifteen years after the Missouri Compromise, St. Louis was already a booming city, having
gotten its start in the eighteenth century as a French fur trading village. It was incorporated as a
town in 1809 and chartered as a city in 1822. In this 1835 view, commercial buildings and
steamships line the riverfront; a ferry on the Illinois shore prepares to transport travelers across
the Mississippi River. Black laborers (in the foreground) handle loading tasks. The Illinois side is
a free state; Missouri, where their ferry lands, is a slave state.*
The Saint Louis Art Museum.
Private Collection of Dorothy Ziern Hanon and Joseph B. Hanon.

Maine as an immediate counterbalance to Missouri. The South got Missouri without any interference with slavery. The whole package passed only because seventeen northern representatives decided that minimizing sectional conflict was in the best interests of the United States and so voted with the South for the unrestricted entry of Missouri.

President Monroe and Thomas Jefferson, retired to his home in Charlottesville, Virginia, worried that the schism over admitting Missouri meant that a Federalist Party was regrouping to challenge the Republicans, and that a new party division would fracture along sectional lines, the free North versus the slave South. But even ex-Federalists agreed that this was too dangerous a fault line to let shape national politics. When new parties did develop in the 1830s, they took pains to bridge geography, each party developing a presence in both North and South. Monroe and Jefferson also worried about the future of slavery. Each understood slavery to be deeply problematic, but, as Jefferson said, "We have the wolf by the ears, and we can neither hold him, nor safely let him go. Justice is in one scale, and self-preservation in the other."

A HOUSE IN MAGNOLIA, FLORIDA
The artist who completed this 1829 watercolor of a balconied home was a thirteen-year-old boy named George Washington Sully, whose family moved to the Florida Panhandle in the first decade of U.S. ownership of the territory. Many frontier settlements were springing up and real estate speculation flourished. Magnolia, along the St. Marks River, attracted three hundred settlers in less than a decade, lured by four brothers from Maine who had originally purchased the land. In 1835, Magnolia was bypassed by an early Florida railroad, and within two years it was a virtual ghost town. George Sully's watercolor suggests the grand intentions so quickly abandoned by the early settlers. His family moved to New Orleans.
Collection of Samuel H. and Roberta Vickers/The Florida Collection.

The Monroe Doctrine

While the Congress struggled to compromise on north-south divisions internal to the country, President Monroe was challenged by external issues of foreign policy. In 1816, American troops led by General Andrew Jackson invaded the northern part of Spanish Florida in pursuit of hostile Seminole Indians, who had been welcoming escaped slaves across the border into territory owned by Spain. Jackson declared himself the commander of northern Florida in 1817, and he demonstrated his power in

1818 by executing two British men who he claimed were dangerous enemies.

In asserting rule over the territory, and surely in executing the two British subjects on Spanish land, Jackson had gone too far. Privately, President Monroe was grievously distressed and considered court-martialing Jackson. But Jackson's immense popularity as a war hero dissuaded Monroe. Instead, John Quincy Adams, the secretary of state, opened negotiations with Spain to acquire the territory. The result was a treaty that delivered Florida to the United States in 1819. In exchange, the Amer-

376 CHAPTER 10 • REPUBLICAN ASCENDANCY

1800-1824

icans agreed to abandon any claim to Texas or Cuba, which was taken in the South as a considerable concession, since southerners had eyed both places as potential slave states. Adams's treaty also established a boundary between New Spain to the west and the Louisiana Territory.

Spain at that moment was preoccupied with its other colonies in South America, several of which were on the verge of breaking away. One after another—Chile, Colombia, Peru, and finally Mexico—declared themselves independent in the early 1820s. For a time, it appeared that Spain, perhaps joined by allies France and Prussia, might try to regain the lost colonies. Britain proposed an alliance with the United States to block any such effort, but Monroe was wary of an alliance with the adversary of the War of 1812.

Instead, Monroe formulated his own declaration of principles on South America. In December 1823, he incorporated into his annual message to Congress several passages enunciating what would come to be known, decades later, as the Monroe Doctrine. Basically, his message had two parts: noncolonization and nonintervention. He asserted that "the American Continents, by the free and independent condition which they have assumed and maintain, are henceforth not to be considered as subjects for future colonization by any European power." Any new attempt to interfere in the Western Hemisphere or to control or subvert the newly independent countries would be regarded as "the manifestation of an unfriendly disposition towards the United States."

Monroe articulated these policy goals without any real force to back them up in 1823. The American navy was not up to the task of defending Chile or Peru against Spain or France. Monroe did not even have the backing of Congress for his statement; it was merely his idea of a sound policy laid out in a public message. It is doubtful that Monroe saw his message as an implied promise or threat to make the United States the policeman of the Western Hemisphere or to assert U.S. dominance over South America, both usages to which the Monroe Doctrine was put many years later. In exchange for noninterference by Europeans, Monroe pledged that the United States would stay out of European struggles.

The Election of 1824

Monroe was the last president to wear a powdered wig and knee breeches. In late-eighteenth-century style, he had assembled a cabinet that contained

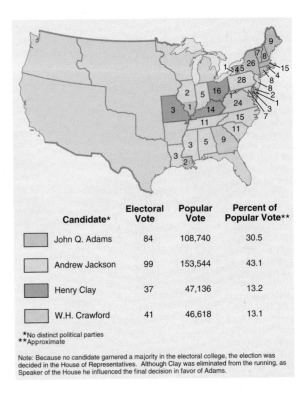

Candidate*	Electoral Vote	Popular Vote	Percent of Popular Vote**
John Q. Adams	84	108,740	30.5
Andrew Jackson	99	153,544	43.1
Henry Clay	37	47,136	13.2
W.H. Crawford	41	46,618	13.1

*No distinct political parties
**Approximate

Note: Because no candidate garnered a majority in the electoral college, the election was decided in the House of Representatives. Although Clay was eliminated from the running, as Speaker of the House he influenced the final decision in favor of Adams.

MAP 10.5
The Election of 1824

men of sharply different philosophies. Secretary of State John Quincy Adams represented the urban Northeast, South Carolinian John C. Calhoun spoke for the commercial planter aristocracy as secretary of war, and William H. Crawford of Georgia, secretary of the treasury, was a throwback to early Jeffersonian states' rights and limited federal power.

Well before the end of Monroe's second term, this group of rather different Republicans began to maneuver for the presidency. Since Jefferson's term, the secretary of state had always been the successor. Adams thus thought he had some presumptive right to run, after his eight years heading the State Department. But four other men vied for the office, and the prolonged politicking created bitter feelings.

Since 1800, the congressional caucuses of each party had met to identify and lend their considerable but still informal authority to the leading candidate from each party. In 1824, with only one party, the caucus system splintered. Some New York and Virginia representatives met and endorsed Crawford, for eight years the secretary of the treasury. Crawford perhaps best represented Monroe's old

Republican views of a limited government. Unfortunately, Crawford, then fifty-one, had just suffered a serious stroke, which left him partially paralyzed and barely able to speak.

Henry Clay, Speaker of the House, also was a declared candidate. The Kentuckian was forty-seven but had vast experience in the workings of Congress. He had also engaged in high-level diplomacy, having accompanied John Quincy Adams to Ghent to negotiate the 1814 peace treaty with Britain. Clay put forth a set of policies he called the American System, a package of protective tariffs to promote manufacturing and federal expenditures for extensive internal improvements, many of them roads and canals in the western states. John C. Calhoun, secretary of war, was another serious contender. At

forty-two, he was the youngest candidate, but he had worked in Washington since 1811, in the House and in several cabinets. A product of Yale College and then Tapping Reeve's law school in Connecticut, Calhoun combined the riches of a well-off Carolina planter with the agile mind of a bright lawyer. Like Clay, he favored internal improvements, protective tariffs, and banking measures, which he figured would earn him standing in northern urban areas.

The final candidate battling for office was an outsider: General Andrew Jackson of Tennessee. Unlike the others, Jackson had only the mere wisp of actual experience in political office, having served brief terms of service in Congress. Monroe had appointed him to be governor of the territory

THE ELECTION OF 1824: THREAD BOX FOR JOHN QUINCY ADAMS
Purchasers of this thread box confirmed their loyalty to John Quincy Adams, presidential candidate in 1824. The inside cover carried a picture of Adams, made by a lithographic process just coming into wide use in the 1820s that made possible the production of thousands of pictures from a single master stone plate. (Wood and copper plates, the earlier technology, produced prints numbering only in the hundreds before deteriorating under pressure.) The velvet pincushion on the outside cover is printed with the slogan "BE FIRM FOR ADAMS."
Collection of Janice L. and David J. Frent.

THE ELECTION OF 1824: JACKSON CUP PLATE
A ceramic saucer of 1824 doubles as an object of veneration for General Andrew Jackson in his first bid for the presidency. It shows Jackson in civilian clothes, even though his reputation was largely military. This particular image of Jackson was mass-produced on housewares, using a newly developed transfer process. Even the English pottery industry made articles for the specialized election market, attaching Jackson's face to expensive pitchers imported to America. Both the saucer and the thread box were household implements associated with women's daily lives. The thread box was, then, no longer just a thread box; it was a commodity that allowed its purchaser to imagine a partisan identity for herself, even though the rules of politics formally excluded her.
Collection of Janice L. and David J. Frent.

of Florida in 1821, a post Jackson held for only three months. His considerable fame rested completely on his reputation as a military leader.

Jackson's launch into the national election arena was not meant to be a serious bid at the beginning. Some Tennessee politicians entered his name as a candidate for that state's electoral votes to buy time for Henry Clay, their real candidate from neighboring Kentucky. The idea was that Jackson's name would keep Crawford or Calhoun from tying up Tennessee. But almost immediately there was a surge of popular interest in Jackson, not just in Tennessee but in other states as well. Experienced politicians in divergent places such as Pennsylvania, Ohio, Alabama, and New Jersey wrote each other worried letters about a "Jackson contagion" sweeping their districts. Calhoun was sufficiently impressed with Jackson's grip on Philadelphia voters that he dropped out of the race and shifted his attention to winning the vice presidency.

The 1824 election was the first presidential contest in which popularity with ordinary voters really mattered. Recent changes in state constitutions now gave voters in all but six states the power to choose electors for the electoral college. (Before, state legislators had held this power.) Jackson was by far the most popular candidate with voters. He won more than 153,000 votes, while Adams was second with 109,000; Clay won 47,000 votes and the incapacitated Crawford managed to garner 46,600. This was not a large voter turnout, probably amounting to only a quarter of adult white males. Many more voters participated regularly in local and state elections, where the real political action generally lay. But it was the first election where a vote tally across states could indicate the people's preference for president.

Translated to the electoral college, Jackson had 99 votes, Adams 84, Clay 37, and Crawford 41. Jackson did not have a majority, so the election was thrown to the House of Representatives, for the second (and last) time in American history. Each state delegation voted as one vote, and only the top three candidates could enter the runoff, under the terms of the Eleventh Amendment to the Constitution, passed in 1804, which had reconfigured the election procedure. Thus Henry Clay, Speaker of the House, was out of the race and in a position now to throw his considerable support to one of the remaining candidates.

The election of 1824 came to be characterized as the "corrupt bargain" in the eyes of Jackson supporters. Clay backed Adams, finally, and six states voted for Adams that had been in another candidate's column in the electoral vote. (Five of those six states were in the West or Southwest: Ohio, Illinois, Kentucky, Missouri, and Louisiana.) Adams was the winner—by one vote in the House. Clay's support for Adams made sense on many levels: He and Adams were close on the issues, particularly on the convergence between Clay's American System and Adams's backing of internal improvements. Clay was uneasy with Jackson's volatile temperament, military ways, and unstated political views and with Crawford's diminished capacity. But Clay's choice still was not easy, because of his strong personal animosity for Adams.

What made Clay's decision look unseemly was that three days after the election, Adams offered to appoint Clay secretary of state—and Clay accepted. In the weeks before the vote in the House, rumors of exactly such a deal were whispered about and breezily dismissed by Adams and Clay supporters, confident that two such archenemies could never cooperate. There probably was no actual bargain; Adams's subsequent cabinet appointments abundantly demonstrate that he was incapable of making appointments to office for purely political reasons. But the Clay appointment looked bad, and a storm of public protest greeted it. Andrew Jackson felt that the election had been stolen from him and wrote bitterly that "the Judas of the West has closed the contract and will receive the thirty pieces of silver." The new vice president, John Calhoun, astutely noted that his own state, South Carolina, had gone solidly for Jackson and began distancing himself from the new administration immediately.

The Adams Administration

John Quincy Adams, like his father before him, was a one-term president. His career had been built on diplomacy, not electoral politics, and, as the "corrupt bargain" incident indicated, his political horse sense was not well developed. His choice of the other cabinet posts was governed by a Monroe-like desire to draw the opposition into his inner circle. He asked three of Monroe's secretaries to stay on, including Crawford at Treasury (which included as well all the dozens of men loyal to Crawford who filled lower positions in the revenue office). He retained the postmaster general, an openly pro-Jackson man, even though that position controlled thousands of patronage appointments in post of-

TECHNOLOGY IN AMERICA
Eli Terry's Clock

Eli Terry of Connecticut apprenticed to learn the high art of clockmaking in the late eighteenth century, crafting tall case clocks one at a time. In 1806, he invented a new design and system of manufacture, called interchangeable parts, that soon enabled him to produce thousands of small shelf clocks annually at a very low price. Instead of building each clock individually, using custom-cut metal parts laboriously fitted together, Terry patterned and machine-cut inexpensive wooden cogs and wheels that fit interchangeably into any of his clocks. By the 1820s, Terry's clocks were sold all over the United States. They revolutionized timekeeping by bringing fairly accurate measurement of time — within a few minutes — into the reach of many householders, enabling factory workers to coordinate with the factory bell, bankers and businessmen to set meetings on a brisk schedule, and travelers to make stagecoach and canal boat departure times. In its peak year, 1836, Terry's company made eighty thousand clocks that sold for about ten dollars each.

Courtesy of The Time Museum, Rockford, Illinois.

fices all over the country. Most amazingly, he decided to ask Andrew Jackson to join his cabinet as secretary of war. With Calhoun as vice president and Clay at State, the whole argumentative crew was thrust into the executive branch. Crawford and Jackson had the good sense to decline these appointments—but legions of Crawford and Jackson men stayed on, in the Treasury and Post Office.

Adams had lofty ideas for federal action during his presidency. He quickly presented a national improvement plan to Congress so sweeping in its scope that it took Henry Clay aback. Adams called for federally sponsored roads, canals, and harbors. He endorsed the idea of a national university in Washington as well as government-sponsored scientific research, modeled on the Lewis and Clark expedition. He called for the building of observatories, to advance astronomical knowledge and to promote precision in earthly timekeeping. He proposed that the United States formally adopt a decimal-based system of weights and measures to benefit both science and commerce, putting forward a massive report on the subject he had written when he was secretary of state. In all these en-

deavors, Adams believed he was picking up where both Jefferson and Madison had left off, using the powers of government to advance knowledge. But his opponents feared he was taking too much from Hamilton's legacy, using federal power inappropriately to advance commercial interests.

Whether he was more truly Federalist or Republican was a moot point, however. Lacking political skills, Adams was unable to implement much of his program. He scorned the idea of courting voters to gain support. He also scorned the use of the patronage system to enhance his power. He often used his appointive powers (to posts like customs house collectors) to placate enemies rather than reward friends. Mostly he left appointments to others, and Jackson supporters were not shy about stepping forward. A story of a toast offered to the president may well have been strictly mythical, but as humorous folklore it made the rounds during his term and came to summarize Adams's precarious hold on leadership. Some dignitary raised a glass and pledged, "May he strike confusion to his foes . . . ," to which another voice scornfully chimed in, "as he has already done to his friends."

Conclusion: From Jefferson to Adams

The nineteenth century opened with the Jeffersonian Republicans in power, trying to undo much of the Federalist structure created in the 1790s. Jefferson's desire for a more limited government, in size, scope, and power, finally had to give way to the realities of an increasing interaction with foreign powers. Jefferson's diplomats steered between France and Spain and unexpectedly acquired the huge Louisiana Territory as a result. Jefferson and Madison struggled to steer a course between France and England, trying to avoid war with high-minded but costly trade embargoes, but eventually the country's sense of honor required a declaration of war. The War of 1812 thus had more meaning as a symbolic event than as a concrete economic or political struggle. Its conclusion at the Battle of New Orleans allowed Americans to feel they had fought a second war of independence against the mother country.

The war elevated to national prominence General Andrew Jackson, whose sudden popularity with voters in the 1824 election surprised the traditional politicians and threw the one-party rule of Republicans into a tailspin. John Quincy Adams barely secured the presidency in the early months of 1825 before the election campaign of 1828 was off and running. Appeals to the people—the mass of white male voters—would be the hallmark of all elections after 1824. It was a game at which Adams was at quite a disadvantage.

Women of course did not vote. But in the years from 1800 to 1828, subtle changes in family law, divorce law, and litigation over sexual injuries expanded by a tiny fraction their possibilities for gaining some personal autonomy. Religious societies of the early Republic offered the greatest opportunity for women to move beyond their appointed and limited sphere, but critics aplenty attacked women exhorters and developed a defense of women's natural and scriptural subservience to men.

The War of 1812 started in motion another chain of events of momentous importance in the decades to come. Jefferson's long embargo and Madison's wartime trade stoppages gave strong encouragement to American manufacturing, momentarily protected from competition with English factories. When peace resumed in 1815, the years of independent development burst forth into a period of sustained economic growth that continued nearly unabated into the mid-nineteenth century. Economic growth brought about a vast reorganization of production, consumption, and market relations, all of which built an essential foundation for the coming revolution in politics during the years of Andrew Jackson's presidency.

CHRONOLOGY

1789 Judiciary Act establishes six Supreme Court justices who preside over circuit courts.

1800 Thomas Jefferson and Aaron Burr tie in electoral college.

Gabriel's Rebellion fails in Virginia.

1801 Judiciary Act reduces Supreme Court justices to five and allows for sixteen circuit judges.

Jefferson elected president by House of Representatives.

1802 Judiciary Act of 1801 repealed.

1803 *Marbury vs. Madison* declares part of Judiciary Act of 1789 unconstitutional.

Embargoes on American shipping by both England and France.

Louisiana Purchase from France.

1804 Jefferson reelected president.

Burr-Hamilton duel.

1804–1806 Lewis and Clark expedition.

1807 **June.** *Chesapeake* attacked and searched by British in Chesapeake Bay.

December. Embargo Act forbids all American trade with England and France and their colonies.

1808 James Madison elected president.

1809 Treaty of Fort Wayne with Indians in Indiana Territory.

Non-Intercourse Act.

1810 Macon's Bill Number 2.

1811 Battle of Tippecanoe won by William Henry Harrison's troops.

1812 **June.** War declared on Great Britain.

Madison reelected president.

1814 British attack Washington, D.C., burning several buildings.

Treaty of Ghent ends War of 1812.

Hartford Convention.

1815 Battle of New Orleans won by Andrew Jackson's forces.

1816 James Monroe elected president.

1819 Adams-Onís Treaty with Spain cedes Florida to United States.

1820 Missouri Compromise admits Missouri as slave state and Maine as free state.

Monroe reelected president.

1823 Monroe Doctrine asserts independence of Western Hemisphere from European intervention.

1824 "Corrupt bargain" election of John Quincy Adams.

BIBLIOGRAPHY

GENERAL WORKS

Joyce Appleby, *Capitalism and a New Social Order: The Republican Vision of the 1790s* (1984).

Lance Banning, *The Jeffersonian Persuasion: Evolution of a Party Ideology* (1978).

James Broussard, *The Southern Federalists, 1800–1816* (1978).

Noble E. Cunningham, *In Pursuit of Reason: The Life of Thomas Jefferson* (1987).

John R. Howe, *From the Revolution through the Age of Jackson* (1973).

Ralph Ketcham, *Presidents above Party: The First American Presidency, 1789–1829* (1984).

Marshall Smelser, *The Democratic Republic, 1801–1815* (1968).

Stephen Watts, *The Republic Reborn: War and the Making of Liberal America, 1790–1820* (1987).

James Sterling Young, *The Washington Community, 1800–1828* (1966).

JEFFERSON AND REPUBLICANS

Thomas Abernethy, *The Burr Conspiracy* (1954).

Leonard Baker, *John Marshall: A Life in Law* (1974).

Doron S. Ben-Atar, *The Origins of Jeffersonian Commercial Policy and Diplomacy* (1993).

Noble E. Cunningham, *The Jeffersonian Republicans in Power: Party Operations, 1801–1809* (1963).

Noble E. Cunningham, *The United States in 1800: Henry Adams Revisited* (1988).

Alexander DeConde, *This Affair of Louisiana* (1976).

Richard E. Ellis, *The Jeffersonian Crisis: Courts and Politics in the Young Republic* (1971).

David Hackett Fischer, *The Revolution of American Conservatism: The Federalist Party in the Era of Jeffersonian Democracy* (1965).

Morton J. Horwitz, *The Transformation of American Law, 1780–1860* (1977).

Robert M. Johnstone Jr., *Jefferson and the Presidency: Leadership in the Young Republic* (1978).

Lawrence S. Kaplan, *"Entangling Alliances with None": American Foreign Policy in the Age of Jefferson* (1987).

Ralph Ketcham, *James Madison: A Biography* (1971).

Milton Lomask, *Aaron Burr* (1982).

Dumas Malone, *Jefferson the President: First Term, 1801–1805* (1970).

Dumas Malone, *Jefferson the President: Second Term, 1805–1809* (1974).

Richard K. Matthews, *The Radical Politics of Thomas Jefferson: A Revisionist View* (1984).

Drew R. McCoy, *The Elusive Republic: Political Economy in Jeffersonian America* (1980).

Drew R. McCoy, *The Last of the Fathers: James Madison and the Republican Legacy* (1989).

R. Kent Newmyer, *The Supreme Court under Marshall and Taney* (1986).

Peter Onuf, ed., *Jeffersonian Legacies* (1993).

Merrill Peterson, *Thomas Jefferson and the New Nation: A Biography* (1970).

Willard Sterne Randall, *Thomas Jefferson: A Life* (1993).

Norman K. Risjord, *The Old Republicans: Southern Conservatism in the Age of Jefferson* (1965).

Robert A. Rutland, *The Presidency of James Madison* (1990).

Thomas C. Shevory, ed., *John Marshall's Achievement: Law, Politics, and Constitutional Interpretations* (1989).

Jack M. Sosin, *The Aristocracy of the Long Robe: The Origins of Judicial Review in America* (1989).

Francis N. Stites, *John Marshall: Defender of the Constitution* (1981).

Robert W. Tucker, *Empire of Liberty: The Statecraft of Thomas Jefferson* (1990).

G. E. White, *The Marshall Court and Cultural Change, 1815–1835* (1988).

Sean Wilentz, *Chants Democratic: New York City and the Rise of the American Working Class, 1788–1850* (1984).

LEWIS AND CLARK AND THE WEST

John Logan Allen, *Passage through the Garden: Lewis and Clark and the Image of the American Northwest* (1975).

Stephen E. Ambrose, *Undaunted Courage: Meriwether Lewis, Thomas Jefferson, and the Opening of the American West* (1996).

Andrew Cayton, *The Frontier Republic: Ideology and Politics in the Ohio Country, 1780–1825* (1986).

Paul Russell Cutright, *Lewis and Clark: Pioneering Naturalists* (1969).

Albert Furtwangler, *Acts of Discovery: Visions of America in the Lewis and Clark Journals* (1993).

David Freeman Hawke, *Those Tremendous Mountains: The Story of the Lewis and Clark Expedition* (1980).

Donald Jackson, *Thomas Jefferson and the Stony Mountains: Exploring the West from Monticello* (1981).

Robert Mitchell, ed., *Appalachian Frontiers: Settlement, Society, and Development in the Preindustrial Era* (1991).

James P. Ronda, *Lewis and Clark among the Indians* (1984).

FOREIGN POLICY AND WAR OF 1812

James M. Banner, *To the Hartford Convention: The Federalists and the Origins of Party Politics in Massachusetts, 1789–1815* (1969).

Pierre Berton, *The Invasion of Canada* (1980).

Harry L. Coles, *The War of 1812* (1965).

Clifford L. Egan, *Neither Peace nor War: Franco-American Relations, 1803–1812* (1983).

Ronald L. Hatzenbuehler and Robert L. Ivie, *Congress Declares War: Rhetoric, Leadership, and Partisanship in the Early Republic* (1983).

Donald R. Hickey, *The War of 1812: A Forgotten Conflict* (1989).

Reginald Horsman, *The Causes of the War of 1812* (1962).

Linda K. Kerber, *Federalists in Dissent: Imagery and Ideology in Jeffersonian America* (1970).

Alan Lloyd, *The Scorching of Washington: The War of 1812* (1974).

Bradford Perkins, *Prologue to War: England and the United States, 1805–1812* (1961).

Burton Spivak, *Jefferson's English Crisis: Commerce, Embargo, and the Republican Revolution* (1979).

J. C. A. Stagg, *Mr. Madison's War: Politics, Diplomacy, and Warfare in the Early American Republic, 1783–1830* (1983).

SLAVERY

David Brion Davis, *The Problem of Slavery in the Age of Revolution, 1770–1823* (1975).

Douglas Egerton, *Gabriel's Rebellion* (1993).

Sylvia Frey, *Water from the Rock* (1991).

Robert McColley, *Slavery and Jeffersonian Virginia* (1964).

Gary B. Nash, *Forging Freedom: The Formation of Philadelphia's Black Community, 1720–1840* (1988).

Albert J. Raboteau, *Slave Religion: The "Invisible Institution" in the Antebellum South* (1978).

Donald L. Robinson, *Slavery in the Structure of American Politics, 1765–1820* (1971).

Shane White, *Somewhat More Independent: The End of Slavery in New York City, 1710–1810* (1991).

NATIVE AMERICANS

Henry Warner Bowden, *American Indians and Christian Missions: Studies in Cultural Conflict* (1981).

Gregory E. Dowd, *A Spirited Resistance: The North American Indian Struggle for Unity, 1745–1815* (1992).

R. David Edmunds, *The Shawnee Prophet* (1983).

R. David Edmunds, *Tecumseh and the Quest for Indian Leadership* (1984).

Bil Gilbert, *God Gave Us This Country: Tekamthi and the First American Civil War* (1989).

H. S. Halbert and T. H. Ball, *The Creek War of 1813 and 1814* (1969).

Reginald Horsman, *Expansion and American Indian Policy, 1783–1812* (1967).

William G. McLoughlin, *Cherokees and Missionaries, 1789–1839* (1984).

James Merrell, *The Indians' New World: Catawbas and Their Neighbors from European Contact through the Era of Removal* (1989).

Paul Francis Prucha, *The Great Father: The United States Government and the American Indians* (1984).

Bernard W. Sheehan, *Seeds of Extinction: Jeffersonian Philanthropy and the American Indians* (1973).

John Sugden, *Tecumseh's Last Stand* (1985).

Anthony F. C. Wallace, *The Death and Rebirth of the Seneca* (1969).

Richard White, *The Middle Ground: Indians, Empires, and Republics in the Great Lakes Region, 1650–1815* (1991).

WOMEN AND RELIGION

Norma Basch, *In the Eyes of the Law: Women, Marriage, and Property in Nineteenth-Century New York* (1982).

John Boles, *The Great Revival, 1787–1805* (1972).

Jon Butler, *Awash in a Sea of Faith: Christianizing the American People* (1990).

Nancy Cott, *The Bonds of Womanhood* (1977).

Philip Greven, *The Protestant Temperament: Patterns of Childrearing, Religious Experience, and the Self in Early America* (1977).

Michael Grossberg, *Governing the Hearth: Law and the Family in Nineteenth-Century America* (1985).

Nathan Hatch, *The Democratization of American Christianity* (1989).

Janet Wilson James, *Changing Ideas about Women in the United States, 1776–1825* (1981).

Joan Jensen, *Loosening the Bonds: Mid-Atlantic Farm Women, 1750–1850* (1986).

Susan Juster, *Disorderly Women: Sexual Politics and Evangelicalism in Revolutionary New England* (1994).

Linda Kerber, *Women of the Republic* (1980).

Jan Lewis, *The Pursuit of Happiness: Family and Values in Jefferson's Virginia* (1983).

Carla Pestana, *Quakers and Baptists in Colonial Massachusetts* (1991).

Marylynn Salmon, *Women and the Law of Property in Early America* (1986).

Laurel Thatcher Ulrich, *A Midwife's Tale: The Life of Martha Ballard, Based on Her Diary, 1786–1812* (1990).

MONROE AND ADAMS PRESIDENCIES

Harry Ammon, *James Monroe: The Quest for National Identity* (1971).

George Dangerfield, *The Era of Good Feelings* (1952).

George Dangerfield, *The Awakening of American Nationalism, 1815–1828* (1965).

Don E. Fehrenbacher, *The South and Three Sectional Crises* (1980).

Mary W. M. Hargreaves, *The Presidency of John Quincy Adams* (1986).

Walter LaFeber, ed., *John Quincy Adams and American Continental Empire* (1965).

Shaw Livermore, *The Twilight of Federalism: The Disintegration of the Federalist Party, 1815–1830* (1962).

Ernest R. May, *The Making of the Monroe Doctrine* (1975).

Glover Moore, *The Missouri Controversy, 1819–1821* (1953).

Dexter Perkins, *Hands Off: A History of the Monroe Doctrine* (1941).

Robert V. Remini, *Andrew Jackson and the Course of American Empire, 1767–1821* (1977).

**SHIP'S FIGUREHEAD OF
ANDREW JACKSON**

*Carved in 1834 and affixed to the bow
of the revered navy frigate* Constitution, *this figurehead of Andrew Jackson
symbolized national pride by putting
"the image of the most popular man of the
West upon the favorite ship of the East," according
to the commodore who commissioned it. But when
Jackson introduced a new, strict banking policy,
his popularity in the urban East quickly evapo-
rated. In Boston, where the* Constitution *was docked, protesters
complained that the figurehead of a tyrant corrupted their ship. On the night of July 3, 1834,
the eve of the national holiday, an eighteen-year-old youth stole on board at night and decapitated the figurehead, sawing it through just below the ears. The commodore, himself alert to
symbolic statements, wrapped the headless statue in a flag and sent it to New York City
where woodworkers fashioned a new head in 1835. It was reattached to the ship in another
port: Jackson's banking policies still rankled in urban financial centers, and naval authorities
did not want to risk a second mutilation of the president's image.*
Museum of the City of New York.

ANDREW JACKSON'S AMERICA

11

1815–1840

P RESIDENT ANDREW JACKSON WAS THE DOMINANT FIGURE of his age, as even his enemies conceded. Yet his precarious and unhappy childhood little foretold the fame, fortune, and influence he would enjoy in the years from 1815 to 1840. Jackson was born to a poor Scots-Irish family in the Carolina backcountry in 1767. His father died before he was born, and his mother struggled to support three small boys. During the Revolution, young Andrew, at age thirteen, accompanied one of his brothers into battle against the British, but both were taken prisoner and caught smallpox; the brother died. His oldest brother died of a camp fever in the militia, and within the year cholera took his mother. Alone at fourteen, Jackson drifted around, drinking, gambling, brawling, and indifferently trying to find a trade.

But at seventeen he started to study law with a North Carolina lawyer, and his prospects bettered. In three years he was licensed to practice law, and he went west to Nashville, a small frontier settlement, where he immediately was appointed public prosecutor. The urban frontier provided great opportunities for a young man of Jackson's legal training and aggressive temperament. He married into a leading local family, began to acquire land and slaves, and became active in politics. When Tennessee became a state in 1796, Jackson served a term as its first representative to the U.S. Congress.

Jackson captured national attention in 1815 when he led the victorious American forces at the Battle of New Orleans. With little else to celebrate about the War of 1812, many Americans seized on the Tennessee general as the champion of the day. Songs, broadsides, and an admiring biography commemorated his heroism and cast him in a new light: His early orphanhood framed Jackson as the original self-made man, the parentless child fully responsible for his own destiny. He had little formal education and no inherited advantages, but these deficits were now transformed into virtues. Jackson seemed to have created himself, a gritty, forceful personality extracting opportunities from the dynamic, turbulent frontier.

Jackson enhanced his national reputation by fighting Creek and Seminole Indians. His unauthorized adventure into Spanish Florida in 1817–1818 angered President Monroe and triggered a congressional investigation for insubordination. But even Congress would not censure him, for, as one member said, Jackson was a Hercules, an immortal hero, and "the American people will not be pleased to see their great defender, their great avenger, sacrificed."

The New Orleans and Florida episodes proved that Jackson was a man of action. He was also strong-willed, reckless, and quick to anger. When a slave ran away from him in 1804, he advertised a fifty-dollar reward "and ten dollars extra for every hundred lashes any person will give to the amount of three hundred." He impulsively challenged men to duels on slight pretexts. His best-known fight, an 1806 pistol duel, acquired legendary status as an example of Jackson's obstinacy. His opponent was an expert marksman who could hit a silver dollar at twenty-four feet (as he demonstrated on the way to the duel site, to unnerve Jackson). Jackson deliberately let the marksman shoot first. The bullet hit him in a rib, but he masked all sign of injury under a loose cloak and immobile face. He then took careful aim at the astonished man and killed him. Such steely courage chilled his political opponents.

Jackson's image as a frontier man of action and force set him apart from the learned and privileged gentlemen from Virginia and Massachusetts who had monopolized the presidency up to 1828. When he lost the 1824 election to John Quincy Adams, an infuriated Jackson vowed to fight a rematch and started running for the office immediately. He won, in 1828 and again in 1832, capturing large majorities of voters. His appeal stretched across the urban working classes of the East, frontier voters of the West, and slaveholders in the South, who all saw something of themselves in Jackson. Once elected, he brought a combative style to politics and enlarged the powers of the presidency.

The confidence and even recklessness of Jackson's personality mirrored the new confidence of American society in the years after 1815. An entrepreneurial spirit gripped the country, producing a market revolution of unprecedented scale. Old social hierarchies appeared to be eroding; the most ordinary of men could dream of moving high on the wheel of fortune, just as Jackson had done. Stunning advances in transportation and economic productivity fueled such dreams and propelled thousands to move west and many thousands more to move to cities. Urban growth and technological change fostered the diffusion of a distinctive and vibrant public culture, spread through newspapers and the spoken word. The development of rapid print allowed popular opinions to coalesce and intensify; Jackson's sudden nationwide celebrity was a case in point.

Expanded communication transformed politics dramatically. Sharp disagreements over the best way to promote individual liberty, economic opportunity, and national prosperity in the new market economy defined salient differences between Jackson and Adams and the parties they gave rise to in the 1830s. The process of party formation brought new habits of political participation and party loyalty to many thousands more adult white males. Religion became democratized as well: An evangelical revival of national proportions brought its adherents the confidence that salvation and perfection were now available to all. For those less than perfect, the evangelicals set out to reform their unhappy ways.

As president from 1828 to 1836, Jackson presided over all these changes, fighting some and supporting others in his vigorous and volatile way. And, as with his own stubborn personality, there was a dark underside to the confidence and expansiveness of American society. Steamboats blew up, banks and businesses periodically collapsed, alcoholism rates soared, Indians were killed or relocated far west, and slavery continued to expand. The brash confidence that turned some people into Jackson-like, rugged, self-promoting individuals inspired others to think about the human costs of rapid economic expansion and thus about reforming society in dramatic ways. The common denominator was a faith that people and societies can shape their own destinies.

The Market Revolution

The return of peace in 1815 unleashed powerful economic and social forces that revolutionized the organization of the market. Said one Philadelphia editor, the war "emancipated us from our former slavish dependence on the looms and the anvils of Great Britain." Spectacular changes in transportation (termed by contemporaries "internal improvements") facilitated the movement of commodities, information, and people. Textile mills and other factories created many new jobs, especially for young unmarried women, for whom the chief opportunity in wage labor had been domestic service. Innovations in banking functions, legal practices, and tariff policies promoted swift economic growth.

This was not yet an industrial revolution, but a market revolution. The old standbys, water, wood, beasts of burden, and human muscle, still constituted the energy supply; factories were limited to sites near rapid rivers, mostly in New England. What distinguished the changes as a market revolution was the accelerated pace of economic activity, which made a new variety and volume of consumption goods available in national markets. Men and women were drawn out of old patterns of rural

MAP 11.1
*Routes of Transportation
in 1840*
Transportation advances by the
1830s had cut travel times significantly. Goods and people
could move from New York City
to Buffalo, New York, in four
days via the Erie Canal, a trip
that took two weeks by road in
1800. A four-week trip from
New York to New Orleans in
1800 could now be accomplished
in less than half that time, due
to steamboats on the western
rivers.

self-sufficiency and into the wider realm of market
relations; labor once used for home production was
now released for industrial employment. At the
same time, the nation's money supply enlarged considerably, leading to speculative investments in
commerce, manufacturing, transportation, and
land. The changed nature and scale of production
and consumption changed behavior, attitudes, and
expectations.

Confidence in the commercial market was
sharply punctured by the panic of 1819, but within
a few years strong growth resumed for another two
decades, until the panic of 1837. By the 1830s, observers noted that this boom and bust economy distributed its rewards unevenly. Disagreement about
the causes and consequences of inequalities in
wealth came to define a major difference between
the political parties emerging in the 1830s.

Improvements in Transportation

Before 1815, transportation in the United States was
so slow and difficult that it cost as much to ship
freight over 30 miles of domestic roads as it did to
send the same weight of cargo across the Atlantic
Ocean. Mailing a one-ounce letter via the U. S. mail
for a distance of 150 to 400 miles cost seventy-four
cents (when, in comparison, a pound of bread cost
six and a half cents). A stagecoach trip from Boston
to New York took an uncomfortable four days. But
between 1815 and 1840, networks of roads, canals,
steamboats, and finally railroads dramatically
raised the speed and lowered the cost of travel. Migrants like Andrew Jackson got to Nashville in the
1790s by walking or riding horseback for weeks
along old Indian trails. But when the newly elected
President Jackson went to Washington, D.C., in 1829

for his inauguration, he traveled by steamboat down the Cumberland River and up the Ohio to Pittsburgh and thence by turnpike to the capital city in a matter of days.

The benefits of improved transportation to economic development were abundantly clear: Products could be sold more cheaply in a wider market. Equally important, transportation facilitated the flow of political information; traffic in newspapers had profound consequences for Jacksonian-era elections. Travel encouraged cultural change as well. Easily accessible passenger travel lifted men and women out of their local communities, brought country merchants and their wives the excitement of a visit to urban amusements, and allowed adolescents of both sexes to obtain new forms of employment in cities or factory towns, where they lived away from home. Commercial passenger travel provided opportunities for family visits, an important counterweight to the isolating effects of the massive westward migration of settlers. These forms of travel required new rules for class and gender behavior in public, to balance the adventure and freedom inherent in escape from hometown moorings with the potential dangers such freedom entailed. Public coaches mixed respectable citizens with con artists, thieves, and seducers who were riding the roads in search of their own opportunities for gain.

The economic, political, and cultural attractions of enhanced public transport did not alone cause the building of thoroughfares. Such undertakings were very expensive, and benefits were not uniform. A canal in New York or a road in Kentucky produced no benefit for South Carolina. Transportation routes directed economic traffic in certain grooves—and of necessity bypassed others. The key questions involved the issues of who would plan, pay for, and profit from improved transportation.

Both Congress and the early Republican presidents hesitated to undertake federally sponsored road projects. Thomas Jefferson and James Madison valued improved transportation but held that federal funding for it was unconstitutional. During Jefferson's presidency, Congress approved start-up funding for the National Road, to connect Baltimore with the heart of Ohio, provided that the money came directly from the sale of Ohio public lands, the area that would benefit. By 1818, the gravel roadbed of the National Road crossed the Cumberland Gap and extended to Wheeling, West Virginia, reaching

its terminus in the 1830s at Columbus, Ohio. In the 1820s, President John Quincy Adams departed from his cautious predecessors and proposed that transportation improvements be undertaken at government expense. Essentially he adopted the pro-development view of Henry Clay's American System, a multifaceted plan to promote banking, manufacturing, and transportation. But Congress would not oblige Adams. Hence it fell largely to private investors to undertake transportation improvements. They pooled resources and chartered stagecoach, canal, and railroad companies, with significant aid from the states in the form of subsidies and guarantees of monopolistic rights.

Turnpike and roadway mileage dramatically increased after 1815, reducing the cost of land shipment of goods. Stagecoach lines proliferated in an extensive network of passenger corridors dense in the populated East and fanning out to the Mississippi River. Travel time on main routes was cut in half; Boston to New York now took two days. Not only did people, mail, and newspapers move across space, the coach itself became a site of vital information exchange with its dozen strangers locked in close contact. Foreign travelers often noted with amazement that American men relished controversial conversation topics about politics, religion, and slavery. Equally amazing to foreigners was the presence of American women traveling on public stagecoaches, often without male escorts. The English writer Harriet Martineau toured America for many months in 1834 and found the "liberty" of women on the road "highly amusing." But she also condemned women travelers in general for being "spoiled children. Screaming and trembling at the apprehension of danger are not uncommon." Martineau herself once experienced an overturned coach in New Hampshire and later a burst steam-boiler on a railway in Virginia, but presumably she kept a firm grip on her fears.

Steamboats signaled an important advance in the technology of transportation. In 1807, Robert Fulton adapted a steam engine to propel a 133-foot boat, the *Clermont*. Its first voyage, up the Hudson River from New York City to Albany, took thirty-two hours against a head wind, compared with two days for the land route. Onlookers at Poughkeepsie stared in astonishment, according to one eyewitness: "Some imagined it to be a sea-monster, whilst others did not hesitate to express their belief that it was a sign of the approaching judgement," the heavy black smoke and huge flames suggesting the

TECHNOLOGY IN AMERICA
Early Steamboats

Steamboats revolutionized travel in the 1820s and 1830s. The basic technology consisted of a steam engine, powered by the steam from a furnace-heated boiler, that propelled a boat by turning a wooden paddlewheel. In concept, steam-powered travel was ingenious, but it took years of trial-and-error to reduce risks. Between 1811 and 1851, accidents destroyed nearly a thousand boats, a third of all steam vessels built in that period. More than half the accidents resulted from snags — tree trunks or other debris — which penetrated hulls and sank boats. Fires, too, were fearsome hazards in wooden boats that commonly carried highly combustible cargoes, such as raw cotton in burlap bags. The development of sheet metal, which strengthened hulls and protected wooden surfaces near the smokestacks from sparks, was a major safety advance.

But the traveling public focused its greatest apprehension on the terror of boiler explosions. As so powerfully shown in the lithograph of the steamboat Lexington, whose boiler blew up in Long Island Sound in January 1840, by far the greatest loss of life on steamboats came from scalding steam, fly-ing wreckage, and the predictable fire that would engulf a boat in a matter of minutes. In the 1830s alone, eighty-nine boiler explosions caused 861 deaths and many more injuries. The cause of explosion was often mysterious: Was it excessive steam pressure or weak metal? Exactly how much pressure could plate iron fastened with rivets really withstand? Did a dangerous or explosive gas develop in the boiler when the water level fell too low? Or was it principally human error — reckless or drunk engineers (none of them licensed) or captains bent on breaking speed records or bowing to the economics of competition?

The first federal grant for scientific research was awarded in 1830 during John Quincy Adams's term, when the Franklin Institute of Philadelphia undertook to explain the causes of boiler explosions. In 1852, the U.S. Congress mandated steamboat inspection regulations to ensure public safety. After the Civil War, affordable sheet steel and the development of new welding techniques produced boilers that were much stronger.

Library of Congress.

LANDSCAPE WITH FREIGHT TRAIN AND TOW BOAT
A canal boat and train pass through a village, each transporting goods, not passengers. Three horses on a tow path power the boat; a coal-burning locomotive steam engine drives the train. The utility poles along the train tracks (probably telegraph wires) indicate that this anonymous watercolor dates no earlier than the late 1840s.
Gift of Maxim Karolik. Courtesy, Museum of Fine Arts, Boston.

possible end of the world. Fulton's *Clermont* was not the first steamboat ever—there had been prototypes back to the early 1790s, both in Europe and in the United States. But Fulton linked his technology to the business and legal know-how of Robert R. Livingston, whose precocious interest in steam technology had led him to acquire from New York in 1798 a twenty-year monopoly on all steam transportation on the Hudson, if he could create a steamboat that traveled four miles per hour.

Steamboat transportation arrived in the popular consciousness in 1807 with the *Clermont*; after 1815, a steamboat craze was in full swing. By 1820, a dozen steamboats left New York City daily, churning up the Hudson to Albany in half a day or moving east on the Long Island Sound. Captains of rival companies sometimes staged impromptu races at wide sections of the Hudson, thrilling (and sometimes killing) the passengers as the boilers were pushed to their limits. Traffic soon spread to the western rivers and the Great Lakes. A voyager on one of the first steamboats to go down the Mississippi reported that the Chickasaw Indians called the vessel a "fire canoe" and considered it "an omen of evil . . . the sparks from the chimney of the boat being likened to the train of the celestial visitant"—that is, a comet, also feared as an omen of evil. By the early 1830s, more than seven hundred steamboats had been swiftly launched into operation on the Ohio and Mississippi Rivers. A journey from New

Orleans to Louisville, Kentucky, took one week, in contrast to the three months a keelboat required.

Repeatedly, boiler explosions revealed the risks of steam transport; by 1830, close to eighty vessels had been blasted out of the water. Such accidents brought terrible loss of life, since each boat carried several hundred passengers and swimming was an uncommon skill (assuming one could escape the flaming wreckage). One newspaper called for a citizens' investigation to be conducted by a committee of twenty disinterested men with mechanical genius: "The Steam Boat Oliver Evans lately exploded and scattered such abundance of boiling water, that eleven persons were scalded to death and many others dangerously wounded. Must we wait for the sacrifice of many valuable lives before one single precaution is taken to guard our wives, children, and friends, from so dreadful a calamity?" But newspaper reports of the horrors of accidents made little dent in the traveling public's excitement over fast travel.

The early practice of states granting monopolies to encourage investment in steam transportation came to seem restrictive and unfair to newcomers in the business by the 1820s. In a landmark decision of 1824, *Gibbons v. Ogden,* the Supreme Court under John Marshall ruled that navigation on the Hudson River was actually a form of interstate commerce and thus was under the jurisdiction of the federal government; state-granted monopolies were therefore declared invalid on rivers that traversed two or more states.

Canals were another major innovation of the revolution in transportation. Before 1815, a few states licensed private investors to dig canals, usually modest undertakings just a few miles in length to connect existing riverways. The virtues of entire highways made of water soon became apparent. Canals did not have to be very deep; usually four feet of water sufficed for a flat-bottomed barge. At a width of thirty to forty feet, the placid canals could accommodate two-way traffic. The barges were powered by horses or mules that trudged the towpaths along the embankment pulling the barges. The animals produced speeds of under two miles per hour, but the economy came from increased loads: The low-friction water allowed one horse to pull a fifty-ton barge. In winter, canals froze over and became smooth, stump- and rock-free highways for sleighs.

Pennsylvania in 1815 and New York in 1817 commenced major state-sponsored canal enter-

prises intended to create large regional markets for goods. Pennsylvania's Schuylkill Canal stretched 108 miles when it was completed in 1826. It was overshadowed by the impressive Erie Canal in New York, begun in 1817 and finished in 1825, which connected the 350 miles between Albany on the Hudson River with Buffalo on Lake Erie. In effect, the Erie Canal linked the port of New York City with the inland region of New York State and, via the Great Lakes, the entire Northwest Territory. Wheat and flour moved east, textiles and books moved west; by the 1830s, the cost of shipping by canal fell to less than a tenth of the cost of overland transport, and New York City developed in short order into the premier city of trade and commerce in the United States.

The Erie Canal also quickly became the principal passenger route west. As many as forty people crowded on each tiny barge and practiced the novel custom of ducking or lying down several times an hour as they passed under low bridges. The canal's well-maintained towpaths made overnight travel possible, and canal boats, like steamboats, generally provided an interior ladies' cabin where women could retreat from men and sleep undisturbed (except by the ever-present bedbugs). Such cabins had to be extremely low in height, given the shallow water; the Englishwoman Harriet Martineau found the "compressed crowd, lying packed like herrings in a barrel" so repulsive that sleeping with the men on the open decks seemed preferable—until it started to rain.

In the 1830s, private railroad companies began to give canals stiff competition, and by the mid-1840s the canal-building era was over. (Use of the canals for freight continued well into the twentieth century.) The nation's first railroad, the Baltimore and Ohio, boasted thirteen miles of track in 1829, laid out west from Baltimore grandly gesturing in the direction of Ohio. During the 1830s, three thousand more miles of track materialized nationwide, the result of a speculative fever in railroad construction masterminded by bankers, locomotive and iron manufacturers, and state legislators, who provided subsidies, charters, and land rights-of-way. Lines in the 1830s were generally short, on the order of twenty to one hundred miles; they were not yet an efficient distribution system for goods. But passengers flocked to experience the marvelous travel speeds of fifteen to twenty miles per hour, despite the frightful noise and cascades of ashes and cinders that rained on them.

Factories, Workingwomen, and Wage Labor

Transportation advances promoted a rapid expansion of manufacturing after 1815. Teamsters, wagoners, and bargemen hauled products like shoes, textiles, clocks, guns, and books into nationwide distribution. Some of the gain in manufacturing, especially in the textile industry, came from the development of water-driven machinery, built near fast-coursing rivers. (The steam power harnessed for steamboats and railroads had limited application in industry until the 1840s.) But much of the new manufacturing involved only a reorganization of production, still using the power and skill of human hands. Both mechanized and manual manufacturing pulled young women into the labor market for the first time and greatly enlarged the segment of the population earning a living by selling labor for hourly wages.

The earliest factory appeared in Pawtucket, Rhode Island, in the 1790s. British immigrant Samuel Slater designed a mechanical spinning machine that produced thread and yarn. By 1815, 169 spinning mills dotted the lower New England countryside.

Slater followed the British model of hiring whole families, including children, but the male portion of his labor force tended to disappear inconveniently at harvest time, responding to the seasonal need for increased agricultural labor. As early as 1791, Treasury Secretary Alexander Hamilton in his *Report on Manufactures* had argued that women made the ideal factory labor force. Young farm women in particular, said Hamilton, were idle and underemployed; female labor would allow American manufacturing to develop without undermining the agricultural sector, where men worked. (Hamilton's assumption that young women were idle made sense only in the context of the developing market revolution that defined productive labor as labor that generates wages. Only in a wage economy could wives' and daughters' arduous but unpaid household tasks of cooking, cleaning, sewing, and childrearing be rendered invisible.) A division of labor by sex was also attractive because it promised to save America from the worst feature of English manufacturing cities, the permanent impoverishment of whole families who worked in health-threatening, low-wage factories. Young American women, the theory ran, would gladly work for minimal wages, so long as the pay was higher than domestic service wages. After a few years they would then happily retire to marriage, their places taken by fresh recruits from the New England countryside earning a beginner's wage. There would thus be no permanent poor clustered around factories, and factory labor would stay cheap for employers.

A female labor force came to be called the "Waltham system" after 1814, when a group of Boston entrepreneurs headed by Francis Cabot Lowell consolidated and mechanized all aspects of cloth production—carding, fulling, spinning, weaving, and dyeing—in one location, in Waltham, Massachusetts, and hired young women. A decade later, the Waltham system was improved on at Lowell, Massachusetts, a new manufacturing town built along the Merrimack River at Lowell and his business group, the Boston Associates. Short canals captured the river's power enough to drive eight separate mills, which by 1830 employed more than six thousand young women. A key innovation in Lowell was the close moral supervision of the female workers, who lived in company-owned boardinghouses run by middle-aged women. Parents back on the farms were assured that their daughters would be watched and guarded. Mill owners too profited from having "an industrious, sober, orderly, and moral class of operatives," according to a local clergyman who took pride in the new city's technique for combining factory employment with high moral standards. "No persons are employed on the corporations who are addicted to intemperance, or who are known to be guilty of any immoralities of conduct," he wrote; girls dismissed for bad conduct were blacklisted. Soon the Waltham system was replicated in many towns in New Hampshire and Maine.

The mill workers welcomed the unprecedented if still limited personal freedom of living in an all-female social space, away from parents, excused from all domestic tasks, and with the exhilarating bonus of a little pocket money.

The vast majority of mill workers were women aged sixteen to twenty-three; they signed on for a minimum of a year and often worked a total of three or four, usually broken up into several periods. Pay averaged about two dollars a week plus another dollar in value for room and board. While this was

BEDROOM OF A BOARDING-HOUSE IN LOWELL, MASSACHUSETTS
Lowell mill girls of the 1830s lived in closely supervised boardinghouses, four to six persons per room (that is, two to three per double bed, as in this photograph of a restored bedroom). Trunks took the place of closets or chests of drawers; and the roommates took turns using the writing table and water stand.
Courtesy Lowell National Historical Park.

more than what a seamstress or domestic servant could earn, it was less than young men's wages. Many of the workers contributed earnings to their families, while managing to keep a little for themselves. The work was not pleasant or easy: The women tended noisy machines like spinning jennies and power looms, quickly repairing sudden breaks in the yarn, in rooms kept hot and humid (ideal for yarn, not so comfortable for people). The hours were long, typically twelve to thirteen hours a day, six days a week, with mandatory Sunday church attendance. The boardinghouses were often crowded, sometimes with six girls to a bedroom.

Despite the discomforts, young women flocked to obtain textile jobs. Animated by the same energy that moved Andrew Jackson westward, the faith that people can shape their own destinies, the mill workers left rural farms behind and traveled to new factory towns in the hope of becoming more autonomous individuals. They welcomed the unprecedented if still limited personal freedom of living in an all-female social space, away from parents, excused from all domestic tasks, and with the exhilarating bonus of a little pocket money. In Lowell, the women workers could engage in evening self-improvement activities, like lectures, and the company established a newspaper, *The Lowell Offering,* written and edited by some of the working-women.

In the mid-1830s, worldwide changes in the cotton market impelled the mill owners to try to get more productivity from their labor force by adding more machines per worker and by lowering wages.

The workers, emboldened by their communal living arrangements and by their relative independence from the job, protested. In 1834 and again in 1836, many hundreds of them went out on strike, or "turnouts" as they termed their action. Their sense of independence derived from the fact that they were temporary, not lifelong, employees, so they could afford to challenge the owners; male workers dependent on long-term employment could take fewer risks. At mill sites all around New England, young women were the leaders in planning strikes and forming labor unions. Women strikers at a turnout in Dover, New Hampshire, in 1834 denounced their owners for trying to turn them into "slaves": "However freely the epithet of 'factory slaves' may be bestowed upon us, we will never deserve it by a base and cringing submission to proud wealth or haughty insolence." Their assertiveness surprised many; but ultimately their easy replaceability undermined their bargaining power. Still, the owners realized that an all-female labor force could not be counted on to be compliant and submissive. A decade later, while the mill women concentrated their efforts on state legislatures to get a ten-hour workday law passed, mill owners began to shift to immigrant families as their labor source. By midcentury, American factory towns came to resemble European industrial sites with their permanent working class.

Other manufacturing enterprises of the 1820s and 1830s, such as shoemaking, employed women in ever larger numbers. No new machinery transformed the actual work, but new modes of organizing the work allowed the manufacturers to step up production, control wastage and quality, and lower wages by subdividing the tasks and by hiring women. No longer did a cobbler make an entire pair of shoes. Now leather would be cut by male workers at a central shop under the shoe boss's careful eye. Men made the soles, usually in work groups of fewer than twenty. The stitching of the upper part of the shoe, called shoebinding, became women's work, performed at home as outwork so that it could mesh with women's domestic chores. Women shoebinders earned piecework wages, that is, a pay-

FANCY WEDDING SHOES MADE IN LYNN, MASSACHUSETTS

These shoes from Lynn, Massachusetts, were part of the wedding outfit of Emily Lucinda Alden when she married Addison Davis in 1840. The soles are flat, with no heel, and the upper shoe is hand-stitched of white satin. Nothing except the ankle lacing distinguishes right from left shoe. (All footwear from the period was made with identical rights and lefts; only usage over time differentiated each shoe.) An extraordinary clue about women and marriage is revealed in this picture. The bride affixed her name-to-be to the shoe box. Etiquette books of the 1840s, however, uniformly decreed that her correct public name should be Mrs. Addison Davis. We might surmise that Emily, on the verge of marriage, had not entirely internalized the eclipse of her own public and legal personage that marriage would soon impose on her. Another bride of 1840, Elizabeth Cady, married Henry Stanton, and had to do battle to be called Mrs. Elizabeth Cady Stanton when she became a leader of the emerging women's rights movement in 1848 (see chapter 13, pages 488–489).
Lynn Historical Society/photo by Lightstream.

ment per item completed. Women's wages were much smaller than men's, but their contribution to family income was now tangible, in cash. By 1830, there were more women shoebinders in Massachusetts than mill girls.

The new shoe entrepreneurs who had reorganized the industry moved to cut shoebinder wages in the economically turbulent 1830s. Unlike the mill workers, women shoebinders worked in relative isolation, a serious hindrance to organized protest. In Lynn, Massachusetts, a major shoemaking center, women turned to other female networks, mainly churches as sites of meetings and religious newspapers as forums for communication. The Lynn shoebinders who demanded higher wages in 1834 built on a collective sense of themselves as women even though they did not share daily work lives. "Equal rights should be extended to all—to the weaker sex as well as the stronger," they wrote in a document forming the Female Society of Lynn. Even so, they proceeded cautiously in blaming men: The women binders "would reluctantly impute to their employers of the other sex, any unworthy motives, or any willingness to oppress them; but there appears to be somewhere a manifest *error*, a want of justice, and reasonable compensations to the females; which calls imperiously for redress. While the prices of their labour have been reduced, the business of their employers has appeared to be improving and prosperous, enabling them to increase in wealth. *These things ought not so to be!*" The women affirmed their rights of petition and assembly and defined "freedom from want" as a natural right as well.

Yet ultimately, the Lynn shoebinders' protests of the 1830s failed to achieve wage increases for women in the industry. Isolated workers all over New England continued to accept low wages, undercutting attempts to establish a minimum rate. And even within the town of Lynn, many shoebinders shied away from organized protest, preferring to situate their work in the context of family duty instead of market relations. Such women felt they stitched uppers to help their menfolk in finishing each shoe; for them, wages represented compensation for undone domestic chores rather than calculable fractions of the market value of the shoes. The isolation and family context of shoebinding allowed shoe manufacturers to count on a pliant female labor force for several decades to come, until sewing machines and factory work sites dramatically altered the women workers' views in the 1850s.

Bankers and Lawyers

Entrepreneurs like the Boston Associates who built the Lowell factories relied on innovations in the banking system to finance their ventures. The number of state-chartered banks in the country more than doubled in the boom years 1814–1816, from fewer than 90 to 208; by 1830, there were 330, and hundreds more by 1840. Banks stimulated the economy both by making loans to businessmen, manufacturers, and real estate purchasers and by enlarging the country's money supply. Borrowers were issued loans in the form of banknotes, certificates unique to each bank. The borrowers then used the notes exactly like money, good for all transactions. Neither federal nor state governments issued paper money, so banknotes became the currency of the country.

In theory, a note could always be traded in at the bank for its equivalent in gold or silver (in a transaction known as "specie payment"). A note from a solid local bank might be worth exactly what it was written for; a ten-dollar note could purchase ten dollars' worth of goods. But if the note came from a distant or questionable bank, its value would be discounted by some fraction. The money market of Jacksonian America definitely required knowledge, caution, and trust. Many city newspapers of the 1820s and 1830s devoted considerable space to regional banking news and prevailing discount rates. But even scrupulous caution sometimes failed to detect counterfeiters, many in number, who found it inviting and rewarding to forge banknotes. Entrepreneurial skills took many forms in this era.

Bankers exercised great power over the economy in their decisions about who would get loans and what the discount rates would be. The most powerful bankers sat on the board of directors for the second Bank of the United States, chartered in 1816. The charter of the first Bank of the United States, granted by Congress in 1791 for twenty years, had expired in 1811; at the time, Madison's administration was confident that state banks could provide all needed services. But difficulties financing the War of 1812 forced the administration to change its stance. In 1816, the second bank, located again in Philadelphia, opened for business under a twenty-year charter, with eighteen branches throughout the country. The rechartering of this second bank would prove to be a major issue in Andrew Jackson's reelection campaign in 1832.

Accompanying the market revolution was a revolution in commercial law. In the decades after

OFFICE SAFE
Financial records, banknotes, and stock certificates required safekeeping in the stepped-up commercial world of the 1830s. This small office safe opened by key.
Eric Long/Smithsonian Institution.

1815, lawyers both inside and outside of state governments fashioned a legal system that advanced the interests of commercial activity and enhanced the prospects of private investment.

Of particular significance was the changing practice of legal incorporation, the chartering of businesses by states. Up to now, states chartered businesses formed to meet the public good, such as to build a bridge. Under new state laws, corporations could be formed for any reasonable purpose. New York passed the first such state incorporation law in 1811. The new laws limited the liability of the investors to the value of their original investment. Thus, if a corporation failed, the private fortunes of its investors were spared any risk. In 1800, there were perhaps twenty corporations in the United States; by 1817, there were eighteen hundred.

The legal revolution of these decades reformulated older concepts of contract to reflect the burgeoning entrepreneurial marketplace. Courts had enforced business contracts in the eighteenth century in light of notions of fairness. If a seller foolishly contracted to sell a barrel of wheat for half its true or accepted value and then had regrets, he could rely on the courts to declare the agreement void. In the nineteenth century, courts moved toward an interpretation of contracts as freely negotiated, legally binding agreements, regardless of the fairness of the outcome; the law now presumed that a price was, simply, what a buyer and seller agreed it should be.

Several landmark Supreme Court decisions clarified these concepts as they were being shaped by state courts and legislatures. One early case before the Marshall Court was *Fletcher v. Peck* (1810), a conflict involving corrupt land deals in the Yazoo land tract of western Georgia. The Georgia state legislature, under the heavy influence of bribes, had sold this land in 1795 to several land companies for the amazingly low price of one and a half cents per acre. An angry voting public unseated the corrupt state officials in the next election, and the new legislature overturned the land sales the following year —but not before the land companies had managed to sell much of the Yazoo lands for ten cents an acre to speculators in New England. The complicated situation gave rise to complicated interstate lawsuits, finally put to the Supreme Court. The Court held the inviolability of contracts: No matter how corrupt, the original state land grant constituted a binding contract. The *Fletcher* decision was one of the first in which the Supreme Court in effect invalidated a state law, the law rescinding the land sale.

A second landmark Supreme Court case on contracts and corporations was *Dartmouth College v. Woodward* (1819). The New Hampshire college was founded in 1769 by a charter granted by King George III. In 1816, the state government annulled the charter and made Dartmouth a public university; it expanded the board of trustees and fired the existing college president. The original trustees, abundantly alarmed, entered the courts to reclaim control of their institution. The Supreme Court ruled in favor of the trustees on the grounds that the original charter constituted a contract and that, once the charter was granted, the state had no right to interfere in the running of the corporation. Again, the Supreme Court had overruled a state legislative action.

In all these disputes, lawyers predominated. After the War of 1812, the majority of representatives in the U.S. Congress were lawyers, and a similar wave of legal professionals moved into state politics. Articulate, trained in legal reasoning, and able to advocate all sides of a question in the interest of winning for a client, lawyers brought formidable skills to the job of writing and enforcing the new laws governing commerce. More rustic and ordinary citizens who stood for election and entered government service found themselves at a clear disadvantage.

Working through legislatures and courts, lawyers established rights to contract without state interference and designed the model of the business corporation that would carry the United States through the commercial and industrial transformation of the nineteenth century. Lawyers outlawed the use of strikes by aggrieved employees, on the grounds that strikes constituted illegal conspiracies. They wrote the laws of eminent domain, empowering states to buy land for roads and canals, even from unwilling sellers. They drafted legislation on contributory negligence, relieving employers from responsibility for workplace injuries if it could be shown that the employees exercised inadequate caution and thus contributed to the injuries. In these ways and many others, entrepreneurial lawyers of the 1820s and 1830s created the legal foundation for an economy that gave priority to ambitious individuals interested in maximizing their own wealth.

Not everyone applauded these developments. Andrew Jackson, himself a skillful lawyer-turned-politician, spoke for a large and mistrustful segment of the population when he warned about the abuses of power "which the moneyed interest derives from a paper currency which they are able to control, from the multitude of corporations with exclusive privileges which they have succeeded in obtaining in the different states, and which are employed altogether for their benefit." Jacksonians believed that ending government-granted privileges was the way to maximize individual liberty and economic opportunity.

Booms and Busts

One aspect of the economy that the lawyer-politicians could not control was the threat of financial collapse. The boom years from 1815 to 1818 exhibited an energy and volatility that resulted in the first large-scale economic panic in U.S. history; the pattern was repeated in the 1830s. Rapidly rising consumer demand stimulated rising prices for goods, and speculative investment opportunities with high payoffs abounded—in bank stocks, western land sales, urban real estate, and commodities markets. Steep inflation made some people wealthy but created hardships for workers on fixed incomes.

When the bubble first burst in 1819, the overnight rich suddenly became the overnight poor. Some suspected that a precipitating cause of the panic of 1819 was the second Bank of the United States. For too long, the bank had neglected to exercise control over state banks, many of which had suspended specie payments—the exchange of gold or silver for banknotes—in their eagerness to make loans and expand the economic bubble. Then, in mid-1818, the Bank of the United States started to call in its loans and insisted that state banks do likewise. The contraction of the money supply created tremors throughout the economy, a foretaste of the catastrophe to come.

What made the crunch worse was a parallel financial crisis in Europe in the spring of 1819. Overseas prices of agricultural products plummeted; cotton, tobacco, and wheat suddenly fell in value by more than 50 percent. Now when the Bank of the United States and state banks tried to call in their outstanding loans, debtors involved in the commodities trade could not pay. The number of business and personal bankruptcies skyrocketed.

The intricate web of credit and debt relationships meant that almost everyone with even a toe in the new commercial economy was affected by the panic of 1819. Thousands of Americans lost their savings and property. Estimates of unemployment suggest that a half million people lost their livelihoods nationwide.

The intricate web of credit and debt relationships meant that almost everyone with even a toe in the new commercial economy was affected by the panic of 1819.

It took several years for the country to recover from the panic of 1819. Prices continued to fall and bottomed out only in 1821 and 1822. Unemployment rates slowly improved, but the emotional shock and bitterness lasted for many years. A powerful resentment against banks lingered, ready to be mobilized by politicians in the decades to come. The dangers of a system that depended on extensive credit were now clear: In one memorable, folksy formulation that gained circulation around 1820, a farmer was said to compare credit to "a man pissing in his breeches on a cold day to keep his arse

warm—very comfortable at first but I dare say. . . you know how it feels afterwards."

By the mid-1820s, the booming economy was back on track, driven by high productivity, a resumed consumer demand for goods, a greatly accelerating volume of international trade, and a restless and calculating people moving goods, human labor, and investment capital in ever larger and expanding circles of commerce. But an undercurrent of fear and anxiety about rapid economic change continued to shape the political views of many Americans.

The Tariff of 1828

The federal government promoted the booming economy—and fattened itself as well—by passing tariffs on imported goods. The first significant federal tariff had passed easily in 1816, winning support in both the North and the South. It levied an import duty of about 25 percent on cotton cloth from abroad, to shelter the new American textile mills from foreign competition. In 1824, Congress passed a much expanded tariff bill, covering iron, iron products, glass, hemp, wool, and woolen goods, at levels significantly higher than in 1816, about 33 percent on average.

This measure was opposed by some southern congressional leaders, who feared that steep tariffs would decrease overseas shipping and hurt the South's export of raw cotton. Concerns also were raised about the uneven benefits of the tariff. A high tax on imported iron might be of great financial advantage to iron-rich central Pennsylvania, but anyone who wanted to make or buy machinery, stoves, guns, or nails in Massachusetts or Georgia, places without a natural supply of iron, had to pay an extra 33 percent for imported iron. During John Quincy Adams's administration (1825–1829), tariffs began to generate heated debate.

The final and most controversial tariff of the 1820s passed in 1828. Pieces of it were added by members of Congress from every section of the country and every type of industry; in the main, it was pro-Jackson men in Congress who assembled the package and engineered support for it, loading it with duties on raw materials needed by New England. In return, protectionist New Englanders heaped on other duties. One wealthy cotton mill owner laughed that the tariff would "keep the South and West in debt to New England the next hundred years." The final bill was a strange agglomeration of dozens of tariffs, many as high as 50 percent and some in conflict with each other as economic policy. Southerners quickly dubbed it the "Tariff of Abominations" and loudly protested its passage.

The significance of the tariff of 1828 was twofold. It represented an impressive source of income for the federal government, perhaps ten times as great as income from the sale of western lands. In the 1830s, the federal government would retire all its debts and be flush with surplus money, for the first and last time in American history. But that happy eventuality was seriously undercut by the second result of the high tariff, the development of very grave sectional divisions. The traditional American lament over unjust taxation surfaced; the tariff—the only tax now collected by the federal government—was unevenly paid, and its benefits (protection for industries) were unevenly distributed. The tariff of 1828 precipitated a major constitutional crisis in 1832–1833 over one southern state's attempt to nullify it (see p. 417). Like the Missouri Compromise debates of 1819–1820, nullification of the tariff of 1828 became another dress rehearsal for the conflict that led to the Civil War.

The Spread of Democracy

Just as the market revolution held out the promise, if not the reality, of economic opportunity for anyone who worked hard, the political transformation of the 1830s held out the promise of political opportunity for hundreds of thousands of new voters. Between 1828 and 1836, the years of Andrew Jackson's presidency, the second American party system took shape, although not until 1836 would the parties have distinct names and consistent programs that transcended the particular personalities running for office. Over those years, more men could and did vote, and new methods of arousing public interest developed. In 1828, Jackson's charismatic personality defined his party. By 1836, both parties had institutionalized one of his most successful themes: that politicians had to appear to have the common touch in an era when popularity with voters drove the electoral process.

Popular Politics and Partisan Identity

The election of 1828 was the first presidential contest in which popular votes determined the outcome; in twenty-two out of twenty-four states, voters now designated electors committed to a particular candidate. More than a million voters participated, nearly three times the number in 1824, reflecting the high stakes voters perceived in the Adams-Jackson rematch. Throughout the 1830s, the number of voters rose to all-time highs. Partly this increase resulted from relaxed voting qualifications; by the mid-1830s, all but three states allowed universal white male suffrage, without property qualifications. But the higher turnout also indicated increased interest in elections. In contrast to the sleepy Monroe elections of 1816 and 1820, more than half the electorate voted in 1828, and in some states the turnout ran as high as 70 percent. By 1840, the presidential election pulled in 78 percent of the adult white male vote nationwide.

The 1828 election inaugurated new campaign styles as well. State-level candidates routinely gave speeches to woo the voters, appearing at picnics and public banquets. (Adams and Jackson still declined such activities in 1828 as too undignified; but Henry Clay of Kentucky, campaigning for Adams, earned the nicknames the "Barbecue Orator" and the "Gastronomic Cicero.") Campaign rhetoric began to change under the necessity to create popular appeal, becoming more informal and often blunt.

As party rivalry evolved, political leaders in the 1830s orchestrated public events such as rallies and parades. The Jackson camp established many Hickory Clubs, trading on Jackson's popular nickname, "Old Hickory," a common Tennessee tree suggesting resilience and toughness. (Jackson was the first presidential candidate to have an affectionate and widely used nickname.) Published compilations of voting statistics made their first appearance in statistical almanacs, allowing party leaders to calculate and strategize their party's strength. Political committees made sure their supporters got to the polls, which could be a day's ride or more away from some voters.

Beginning with the 1828 election, partisan newspapers defined issues and publicized political personalities as never before. Party leaders cultivated editors and judiciously dispensed subsidies and other favors to secure the loyalties of papers, even in remote towns and villages. In New York State, where party development was most advanced, a pro-Jackson group called the Bucktails had fifty weekly publications under its control. Papers were unabashedly open about their political affiliation, often declaring it right on the masthead. Bargain postal rates for newspapers allowed party leaders to create networks of sympathetic editors. Stories from the leading Jacksonian paper in Washington, D.C., would be reprinted two days later in a Boston or Cincinnati paper, as fast as the mail stage could carry them. Presidential campaigns now took place with accountability to a public arena that encompassed the whole nation.

Parties declined to adopt official names in 1828, still honoring the fiction of Republican Party unity. Instead, they called themselves the Jackson party or the Adams party. By the 1832 election, labels began to appear; Adams's political heir, Henry Clay, represented the National Republicans, while Jackson's supporters opted for Democratic Republicans. Both parties were still claiming the mantle of the Jefferson-to-Monroe heritage by keeping "Republican" in the name, but Clay's National Republicans looked to a large arena of national action to promote commercial development, while Jackson's Democratic Republicans confirmed by their name their promise to be responsive to the will of the majority. By 1834, a few state-level National Republicans shortened their name to the Whig Party, a term that was gradually accepted and in common use by 1836, the same year that Jackson's party became simply the Democrats. Thus, Whig and Democrat crystallized as names only at the end of an eight-year evolutionary process.

The Election of 1828 and the Character Issue

The campaign of 1828 was modern in more ways than just the drawn-out politicking and the importance of majority rule. It was also the first national election in which scandal and character questions reigned supreme in the campaign coverage, a feature of electioneering made possible by the insistent voice of partisan newspapers.

John Quincy Adams was vilified by his opponents as a hopeless elitist, a bookish academic, and perhaps a monarchist, a man out of touch with the common American, a man who looked to European culture for refinement. Much was made of the fact that Adams had a billiard table and an ivory chess set installed in the White House, widely taken to be symbols of aristocratic degeneracy. The "corrupt bargain" of 1824, alleging an election deal between Adams and Henry Clay, was publicized endlessly. Jackson men were especially happy to malign Clay because they considered him the chief architect of anti-Jackson propaganda as well as the most credible threat in future elections.

The Adams men returned fire with fire. They portrayed Jackson as the bastard son of a prostitute,

a story made remotely plausible by his fatherless childhood. Worse, the cloudy, undocumented circumstances around his marriage to Rachel Donelson Robards gave rise to the story that Jackson was a seducer and an adulterer. Jackson claimed he had married Robards in 1791, but at that time her divorce from her first husband was not yet final, necessitating a remarriage in 1794. Adams papers howled that Jackson was a sinful and impulsive man, while Adams was portrayed as a man of restraint, piety, learning, and virtue.

Editors for Adams played up Jackson's notorious violent temper, evidenced by the many duels, brawls, and canings they could recount. Jackson men, of course, used the same stories to prove the old man's strength and resolve. Critics complained of his impetuous style of military justice that resulted in his execution of six Tennessee militiamen for insubordination during the war with the Creek Indians in 1814. One ardent Jackson editor shrewdly trounced that complaint: "Pshaw! Why don't you tell the whole truth? On the 8th of January, 1815, he murdered in the coldest blood 1,500 British soldiers!" Jackson's supporters preferred to project him as a tough frontier hero who knew how to command obedience and who stood up to abusive men (like Rachel Robard's first husband) who dishonored women. In this version of events, his capacity for violence became the muscle that gave force to

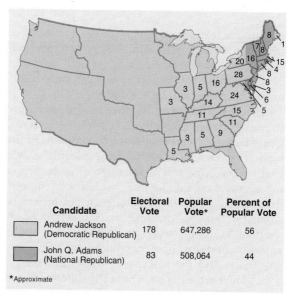

Candidate	Electoral Vote	Popular Vote*	Percent of Popular Vote
Andrew Jackson (Democratic Republican)	178	647,286	56
John Q. Adams (National Republican)	83	508,064	44

*Approximate

MAP 11.2
The Election of 1828

COFFIN HANDBILL
This 1828 campaign broadside memorialized the six soldiers Andrew Jackson ordered to be shot in 1815 for desertion. John Binns, editor of the anti-Jackson Democratic Press in Philadelphia, wanted to horrify readers by turning Jackson into the murderer of six martyred men, each of whose name and story graced a coffin. Binn printed thousands of copies, but his "coffin handbill" soon backfired and made him the target of pro-Jackson crowds that threatened to clap him in a coffin and carry him around town.
Louisiana State Museum.

his admirable sense of honor. And as for learning, Jackson's rough frontier education gave him a "natural sense," wrote a Boston editor, which "can never be acquired by reading books—it can only be acquired, in perfection, by reading men."

These stories were not smoke screens to obscure the "real" issues in the election. They became real issues because voters used them to comprehend the kind of public officer each man would make. Not every voter could follow the nuances of tariff policy or cared to ponder the wisdom of federally funded astronomical laboratories, a pet project of Adams's. But the character issues, conveyed in shorthand through stories about masculinity, spoke to larger questions about morality, honor, discipline, obedience, and the sanctity of contracts. Jackson and Adams presented two radically different styles of masculinity, and the voters, all men of course, concluded that the gendered behavior of these candidates foreshadowed their presidential styles and policies.

Throughout the campaign, Jackson deliberately kept his stand on economic and political issues vague; he was famous for his willingness to support a "judicious tariff," taken by different groups to mean quite different things. Adams stood by his record, mainly his promise to promote commerce through federal action, which brought him strength in New England and parts of New York. His stewardship over the passage of the 1828 tariff won him some friends in the manufacturing Northeast and among grateful hemp growers in Kentucky and sugar planters in Louisiana. Jackson's near-silence on issues like the tariff, banking, public land sales, and government patronage gave him a diffuse combination of backers, who could be sure only that he would favor western expansion and more limited federal powers than Adams.

Jackson won a sweeping victory, with 56 percent of the popular vote and 178 electoral votes (compared to Adams's 83). The general took most of the South and West and carried Pennsylvania and

New York as well. His vice president was John C. Calhoun, who had just been vice president under Adams but had broken with Adams's policies. Here was a clue that the firm lines dividing Jackson and Adams men were still fluid when it came to all offices below the presidency.

After 1828, national politicians no longer deplored the existence of political parties, as they had since the days of George Washington.

After 1828, national politicians no longer deplored the existence of political parties, as they had since the days of George Washington. They were coming to see that parties mobilized and delivered voters, sharpened the focus of differences in candidacies, and created party loyalty that surpassed individual candidates and elections. Jackson was an especially charismatic man, and his election did much to solidify voter loyalty to what would soon be called the Democratic Party. An election over personalities went far to create a party system that could withstand and override personality contests. What sounds like a contradiction makes sense because the personalities of Jackson and Adams so perfectly symbolized and defined for voters the competing ideas of the emerging parties: a moralistic, top-down party ready to make major decisions to promote economic growth competing against a contentious, energetic party ready to embrace liberty-loving individualism.

Jackson's Democratic Agenda

Between the November election and the inauguration in March 1829, Rachel Jackson died. An embittered Andrew Jackson, certain that the ugly campaign had hastened her death, went into deep mourning. His depression was worsened by constant pain from the 1806 bullet still lodged in his chest and by lead and mercury poisoning unwittingly caused by the medicines he took constantly. Sixty-two years old, he carried only 140 pounds on his six-foot-one frame. His adversaries doubted he would make it to a second term.

His supporters, however, went wild at the inauguration. Thousands cheered his ten-minute inaugural address, the shortest in history. Senator Daniel Webster of Massachusetts, allied with the emerging National Republican Party, wrote, "A monstrous crowd of people is in the City. I never saw anything like it before. Persons have come 500 miles to see Genl Jackson & they really seem to think that the country is rescued from some dreadful danger." An open reception at the White House turned into a near-riot as well-wishers jammed the premises, used windows as doors, stood on furniture for a better view of the great man, and broke thousands of dollars' worth of china and glasses.

One of Jackson's first tasks was to repair the damage to the White House. In addition to new upholstery, the president added east and west wings and installed twenty spittoons in the East Room. This extraordinary capacity for accommodating spit met the needs of the throngs that continued to arrive daily to see the president. Some came without invitation to seek jobs in the new administration. Others were tourists just calling on the old man to chat. The courteous Jackson, committed to his image as the president of the "common man," held audience with unannounced tourists throughout his two terms.

Jackson's cabinet appointments marked a departure. Whereas past presidents had tried to lessen party conflict by including men of different factions in their cabinets, Jackson would have only Jackson loyalists, a reasonable tactic followed by most later presidents. The most important position, secretary of state, he offered to Martin Van Buren, one of the shrewdest politicians of the day and newly elected governor of New York. Jackson barely knew him, but they quickly developed great mutual respect. The other principal candidate for leadership was South Carolina's John C. Calhoun, but he was installed in the ornamental post of vice president, where he impatiently chafed at the bit. The rest of Jackson's cabinet consisted of a loyal but undistinguished group of men. For advice, Jackson relied mainly on Van Buren and on a group of old Tennessee and Kentucky friends who were dubbed by the press "the kitchen cabinet."

Jackson's general agenda quickly came into focus once he was in office. He favored a Jeffersonian limited federal government, fearing that intervention in the economy inevitably favored some groups at the expense of others. He therefore opposed federal internal improvements and grants of monopolies and charters that privileged wealthy investors. In theory, he opposed protective tariffs, too, but he let stand the high tariff of 1828 since it generated revenue that reduced the federal debt. Like Jefferson, he anticipated rapid settlement of the interior of the country, where land sales would spread economic democracy to settlers. Establishing a federal Indian policy would thus have high priority.

Unlike Jefferson, however, Jackson exercised full presidential powers over Congress. Early in his first term, in 1830, he vetoed the Maysville Road bill, a highway project in Kentucky that Congress voted to support with federal dollars. In addition to his principled objection that it was unconstitutional, Jackson took satisfaction from the fact that the project he was killing was centered in Henry Clay's home state. (Clay was fast becoming the center of the opposition party.) Jackson used the veto twelve times during his tenure in office; all previous presidents, taken together, had exercised that right a total of nine times.

Cultural Shifts

Despite differences about the best or fairest way to enhance commercial development, Jackson's Democratic Republicans and Henry Clay's National Republicans shared enthusiasm for the outcome—a growing, booming economy. For increasing numbers of families, especially in the highly commercialized Northeast, the standard of living rose, consumption patterns changed, and the nature and location of work altered. All of these changes had a direct impact on the roles and duties of men and women in families and on the training of youth for the economy of the future. New ideas about gender relations appropriate to the new economy surfaced in books, periodicals, newspapers, and public behavior. In Jacksonian America, a widely shared public culture came into being, spread easily through rising levels of literacy, an explosion of print, and an increase in performance arts, both theatrical and oratorical.

The Family and Separate Spheres

The centerpiece of a new set of ideas about gender relations held that husbands found their status and authority in the new world of work, leaving wives to tend the hearth and home. Sermons, advice books, periodical articles, and novels reinforced the idea that men and women inhabited separate spheres with separate duties. "To woman it belongs . . . to elevate the intellectual character of her household [and] to kindle the fires of mental activity in childhood," wrote Mrs. A. J. Graves in a popular book titled *Advice to American Women.* For men,

in contrast, "the absorbing passion for gain, and the pressing demands of business, engross their whole attention" so that thay can converse only about bank discounts, stock jobbing, and tariffs. In particular, the private home, now the exclusive domain of women, was sentimentalized as the source of intimacy, love, and safety, an island of refuge from the cruel and competitive world of market relations. An 1830 magazine article pronounced that "it is at home, where man seeks a refuge from the vexations and embarrassments of business, . . . where is [found] the treasury of pure, disinterested love, such as is seldom found in the busy walks of a selfish and calculating world."

Some new aspects of society gave substance to this formulation of separate spheres. Men's work, especially in the manufacturing and urban North-

CELESTIA BULL'S DOMESTIC SCENE, CONNECTICUT
Celestia Bull of Winchester, Connecticut, painted this domestic scene as part of a "friendship book" for her friend Sarah Sawyer in 1826. The garlanded inscription at the top notes that "Lord Charles is fiddling . . . Lady Sarah is sewing." The billing doves make clear that this is a scene of marital bliss. Charles has the leisure to play music to his lady while she intently sews; sheet music and books lie open on the table.

Private collection. Photograph courtesy Walters-Benisek Art & Antiques, Northampton, Mass. David Stanbury Photography, Springfield, Mass.

east (not coincidentally the site of most book production), was undergoing profound change in the years after 1815. Increasingly, men's jobs brought cash to the household. Farmers and tradesmen sold products in a market, and bankers, bookkeepers, shoemakers, and canal diggers got pay envelopes. Even ministers, who used to get their allowance in country goods and cords of wood, now got cash instead. Furthermore, many men's jobs were performed outside the home, at an office or store. For nonfarm men, work indeed seemed newly disconnected from the home.

The home end of this dichotomy, however, was more complicated than the cultural prescriptions indicated. The vast majority of married white women did not hold paying jobs, but they certainly continued to find the home a site of time-consuming labor. The advice books treated household tasks as loving familial duties performed as a demonstration of feminine nurturance. Housework as *work* was thereby rendered invisible in an economy that evaluated work by its cash-generating potential.

In reality, wives directly contributed to family income in many ways. Some took in boarders, while others engaged in outwork, earning pay for shoebinding, hatmaking, or needlework done at home. Women stretched men's dollars through thrift and recycling. Even among the most comfortable classes, the market intruded whenever wives hired domestic servants to perform the heavy household tasks no true lady would consider doing, like laundry. Most middle- and upper-income families hired servants; households striving to meet a respectable level of class display simply could not be run on the labor of one woman. A wife was therefore also an employer, facing tensions similar to those of her husband in supervising unruly, underpaid workers in the competitive world of market relations.

Why then did ideas about the sentimental, non-commercial, feminine home and the masculine world of work gain a wide acceptance in the 1830s (and well beyond)? In part, the cultural dominance of the middle and upper classes of the Northeast allowed them to assert their own experience as a universal characteristic of all society. In part, the doctrine of separate spheres functioned as all divisions of labor by gender function, to provide clear messages for how to be masculine and feminine. Men achieved a sense of manhood through work and pay; women established a sense of femininity through proper subordination to duty and service to others. The convenient fiction of this partic-

ular formulation of gender difference helped smooth the path for the first generation of Americans experiencing the market revolution. The doctrine of separate spheres ordained that men would absorb and display the values appropriate to the market economy—competition, acquisitiveness—while women would exemplify and foster older noncommercial values of loving service to family and community. Both men and women of the middle classes benefited from this bargain; men were set free to pursue wealth, while women gained moral authority within the home.

The Education and Training of Youth

The market economy and the new division of labor by sex required fresh methods of training the rising youth of both sexes. The generation that came of age in the 1820s and 1830s had opportunities for education and work unparalleled in previous generations. Northern states adopted public schooling between 1790 and the 1820s, and within another decade southern states began to provide "common schools" for white children. Most schools were one-room affairs, sometimes providing two entry doors to admit the sexes separately, another small but daily reminder of gender difference. The curriculum produced pupils able, by age twelve or fourteen, to read and to participate in marketplace calculations. Remarkably, girls received the same basic education as boys. Literacy rates for white females climbed dramatically, nearly catching up to male rates for the first time.

The fact that taxpayers paid for children's education created an incentive to seek an inexpensive teaching force. By the 1830s, northeastern school districts had replaced male teachers with young females. Like mill workers, teachers were in their late teens and regarded the work as temporary. In Massachusetts, one-fifth of all women taught school during their unmarried years. Some had acquired education in private girls' academies that were springing up to meet the middle-class ambition for polished daughters. In the 1840s, several states opened teacher training schools ("normal" schools) for women students. Only one college in the 1830s admitted women: Oberlin College in Ohio in 1837 opened a Ladies Department. The school also admitted black male students, so clearly it was unusually progressive. No other regular colleges admitted women until after the Civil War, but a handful of private "female seminaries" established

MARY JANE PATTERSON,
OBERLIN'S FIRST BLACK WOMAN GRADUATE
Mary Jane Patterson was the first black woman to earn a bachelor's degree in the United States. Oberlin College in Ohio was founded by evangelical and abolitionist activists in the 1830s; it admitted white and black, men and women to its collegiate program — although in the early years the black students were all male and the women students were all white. Patterson, the daughter of slaves, earned her degree in 1862. She taught school in Philadelphia and Washington for the next three decades, until her death in 1894.
Oberlin College Archives, Oberlin, Ohio.

a rigorous curriculum that rivaled that of the best men's colleges. The three most prominent were the Troy Seminary in New York, founded by Emma Willard in 1821; the Hartford Seminary in Connecticut, founded by Catharine Beecher in 1822; and Mount Holyoke in Massachusetts, founded by Mary Lyon in 1837. These women educators argued that women made better teachers than men: "If men have more knowledge, they have less talent at communicating it. Nor have they the patience, the long-

suffering, and gentleness necessary to superintend the formation of character," said the author Harriet Beecher Stowe, who taught at her sister's Hartford school.

Male youths leaving the common school faced two paths. A small percentage continued at private boys' academies (numbering in the several hundreds nationwide), and a far smaller number matriculated at the country's two dozen colleges. More typically, boys left school at fourteen to train for an occupation. Some apprenticed to learn specific trades, while many others flooded to old cities like Boston and Baltimore or new towns like Rochester and Cincinnati, seeking business careers in entry-level clerkships. The new practice of separating home and work among the commercial classes meant that these employees, as young as fourteen, were unlikely to live under the direct supervision of their employers. A new form of urban housing materialized in the 1830s: the male boardinghouse.

Changes in patterns of youth employment and training meant that large numbers of youngsters in the 1830s and later had escaped the watchful eyes of their families.

Young girls also headed for the cities in unprecedented numbers, seeking work in the expanding service sectors as seamstresses and domestic servants. The female migrants generally resided with their employers; a boardinghouse for women too much resembled a brothel.

Changes in patterns of youth employment and training meant that large numbers of youngsters in the 1830s and later had escaped the watchful eyes of their families. Moralists fretted about the dangers of the situation. In the wake of a serious criminal case, a Newburyport, Massachusetts, newspaper urged parents to "inquire about the morals of the business supervisor of your child" because "a want of suitable companions and advisers for his leisure hours" could lead to the downfall of any young boy. Worthy organizations set up apprentice's libraries and lecture series to keep young people uplifted — and off the streets. An outpouring of advice books numbering in the hundreds rose to the challenge of instructing youth in the virtues of hard work and delayed gratification. Other forms of inexpensive reading matter came their way, however, not so easily screened for correct moral values. And, at loose in the city with evenings free, boys and young men turned to the attractions of urban amusements like the theater.

The Penny Press of the 1830s

Cultural ideals about gender and youth spread rapidly in a climate increasingly saturated with the printed word. In the 1790s, fewer than ninety newspapers, each printing a few thousand copies per issue, provided the knowledge base of current events; by 1830, there were eight hundred papers, sixty-five of them urban dailies, and the number continued to expand.

Innovations in printing technology, as well as rising literacy rates, helped spur this rapid expansion. New steam-driven rotary presses with an automatic feed device made possible a much higher output of copies than the old-style handpresses were capable of. Circulation figures for the most successful urban newspapers of the 1830s jumped to twenty thousand. But neither literacy rates nor technology changes fully account for this revolution. It took a new style of journalism, called the penny press, published in small format with lively human interest stories, to draw thousands of new readers into the information networks of Jacksonian America.

The traditional political and commercial papers of the 1830s cost six cents and were large, often two by three feet, a size that required a table or counter for reading. They targeted the business classes with coverage of banking, shipping, and complete transcripts of political speeches. In contrast, the penny papers were cheap and small, on the order of twelve by eighteen inches, and hence convenient to read anywhere—in a crowded tenement, in a saloon, even in a privy. They featured breezy political coverage, irreverent editorializing on current events, local news and exposés, drama reviews, racetrack

LURID COVER OF A CRIME PAMPHLET, NEW YORK

Cheap and easy printing in the early nineteenth century gave rise to new genres of popular reading matter, including a large pamphlet literature detailing horrific murder stories that invited readers to contemplate the nature of evil. This woodcut cover from 1836 promises to reveal the "interesting particulars" of the murder of Ellen Jewett, a New York City prostitute axed to death in her brothel bed. The pamphlet claims to constitute "an impressive warning" to youth about the tragedies of "Dens of Infamy." But the crude picture of the female corpse, with bare legs and breasts fully exposed, suggests that alternative, less moralistic readings of the same material were certainly possible for the purchasers.
William L. Clements Library.

TABLE 11.1				
THE GROWTH OF NEWSPAPERS, 1820–1840				
	1820	*1830*	*1835*	*1840*
U.S. Population (in millions)	9.6	12.8	15.0	17.1
Number of newspapers published	500	800	1200	1400
Daily newspapers	42	65	—	138

results, and crime reporting. Before long, the traditional papers also began to attend to such forms of news.

New York was home to the first penny paper in 1833, and by 1835 there were three. By 1836, Philadelphia, Boston, and Baltimore each had penny papers selling thousands of copies. Their influence was felt far beyond the urban centers, facilitated by a regular system of newspaper exchange via the postal system. Town and village papers far from the East Coast reprinted the snappy political editorials and sensationalized crime stories, putting very undeferential ideas into the heads of readers new to politics.

Public Life and Popular Amusements

Newspapers were not the only new medium for spreading a shared American culture. Starting in the 1830s, traveling lecturers crisscrossed the country, bringing entertainment and instruction to small-town audiences. Some were organized through a central agency called the Lyceum, while others were independent operators who booked local halls and collected admissions of about twenty-five cents. Speakers gave dramatic readings of plays or poetry or lectured on history, current events, or controversial topics like advanced female education. Some speakers specialized in medical knowledge and came equipped with wax models of body parts to illustrate physiology and anatomy.

Theater blossomed in the 1830s, providing Americans with their most common form of shared entertainment. The number and size of theaters greatly increased and ticket prices dropped, putting theatergoing within the reach of many ordinary Americans. The major cities each had a half dozen or more theaters, with as many as three thousand seats apiece. With performances six nights a week, they could accommodate a large segment of the urban population (and urban visitors). Audiences mostly comprised white men of all classes, but women and blacks attended as well, in smaller numbers. The highest level of the gallery in most theaters was by custom reserved for blacks, prostitutes, and men seeking prostitutes.

Shakespeare's plays were an all-round favorite. In 1835 in Philadelphia, sixty-five separate Shakespeare productions were held. Other English and American productions of tragedies, comedies, and melodramas rotated nightly. Before and after plays, theaters provided short acts of singers, dancers, and, increasingly, minstrelsy, a blackface musical comedy first performed in New York City in 1831. White performers with blackened faces parodied everything from romance to Shakespeare, trading on (and thereby reinforcing) racist stereotypes about African Americans' speech, dress, and conduct.

Playgoing audiences were responsive and interactive. Applause was joined by hisses, jeers, whistling, and stomping; actors expected interruptions or even projectiles thrown at them. Audience response helped to shape the content of the productions. An actor in 1822 in New Orleans tried out a new song on a theater audience made up of keelboat men: "The Hunters of Kentucky," a sprightly ditty praising Jackson's militiamen for legendary (and largely mythical) heroics at the Battle of New Orleans. The rivermen made him sing it three times that night; he was immediately forced to make it a regular part of any show he appeared in. Within a few years it was a wildly popular tune, sung all over the country, a happy circumstance for Jackson's electoral fortunes.

The public culture of the theater demonstrates a fluidity of cultural styles in the 1830s. In the era of the "common man," ordinary men and women had a surprisingly well-honed acquaintance with Shakespeare, knowing the scripts so well that they could hoot and stomp when actors muffed their lines or laugh uproariously at clever satires of the Bard. Not until the 1840s and beyond would a kind of market segmentation appear in public amusements, with different theaters aiming at different audiences—some targeting the cultural elite and others the working classes.

The theater world also promoted a new vision of what a public woman could be. Traditionally, a "public woman" was a prostitute, and actresses suffered from the association; there had been no way for a woman to have a public persona without calling her sexual respectability into question. The spectacular success of theaters beginning in the 1830s made some women stars of the stage, drawing admiration, fans, and respectability around them in well-tended publicity campaigns. Women on the stage could speak commanding words in loud voices. In Shakespeare's day, boys had played the female roles precisely to prevent that undesired display of female power. But now actresses could routinely perform roles that enlarged the scope of possibilities for female behavior; some, indeed, dressed in breeches and played male parts. The trade-off, of course, was that theaters also offered actresses's bodies to the largely male audience for viewing.

Finally, the popularity of theaters exemplified a general cultural turn toward the celebration of brilliant public speech. In this golden age of oration, actors, lawyers, politicians, and ministers could hold crowds spellbound with their flawless elocution and elegant turns of phrase. Criminal trials, for example, were astonishingly short by modern standards, but the lawyers' closing arguments might continue for many hours, with crowds of spectators hanging on every word. Senator Daniel Webster of Massachusetts was the acknowledged genius of political oration, putting grown men into raptures. At a Webster speech commemorating the Pilgrims' arrival, one man in a crowd of fifteen hundred recalled that "three or four times I thought my temples would burst with the gush of blood." Ministers with gifted tongues could in the space of hours transform crowds of sinners into deeply moved believers. Skillful speakers demanded and generally got skillful, attentive listeners. Catchy slogans had little place in this oratorical style.

A widely shared national culture became possible in the 1830s as movement of books, newspapers, and people spread ideas and values. This culture was not universal, of course; it originated with the new commercial classes whose superior access to publication and transportation helped ensure the dominance of their ideas. They pioneered new ways of organizing private life, ordering gender relations, and educating the young that affirmed values appropriate to the market revolution. The culture was not monolithic either; simply getting ideas in circulation does not ensure that everyone will agree. Indeed, the proliferation of print in many instances promoted disagreement and debate. Democrats and Whigs, for example, made conflict a natural part of the political culture, and a parallel divergence in religious styles rocked the spiritual life of the country.

Democracy and Religion

An unprecedented revival of evangelical religion peaked in the early 1830s, after gathering three decades of momentum in states across the North and the upper South. Known as the Second Great Awakening, the outpouring of religious fervor changed the shape of American Protestantism. The heart of the evangelical message was that salvation was available to anyone willing to eradicate individual sin and accept faith in God's grace. Just as

universal male suffrage allowed all white men to vote, democratized religion offered salvation to all who chose to embrace it.

Among the most serious adherents of evangelical Protestantism were men and women of the new mercantile classes whose self-discipline in pursuing market ambitions meshed well with the message of self-discipline in pursuit of spiritual perfection. Not content with individual perfection, many of these men and women sought to perfect society as well.

> Just as universal male suffrage allowed all white men to vote, democratized religion offered salvation to all who chose to embrace it.

They provided the moral and intellectual drive behind reform movements devoted to eradicating general sins and social ills in the 1830s.

The Second Great Awakening

The earliest manifestations of an unusual outbreak of fervent piety appeared in 1801 in Kentucky. A crowd estimated from ten to twenty thousand people camped out on a hillside at Cane Ridge for a revival meeting that lasted several weeks. By the 1810s and 1820s, camp meetings had spread to the Atlantic seaboard states, finding especially enthusiastic audiences in western New York and Pennsylvania. By the 1830s, frequent regional meetings flourished in places easy to reach by public transport.

The gatherings attracted women and men hungry for a more immediate access to spiritual peace —no need to engage in years of Bible reading and soul-searching preparation. Ministers adopted an emotional style and invited audience members to an immediate experience of conversion and salvation. One eyewitness at a revival reported that "some of the people were singing, others praying, some crying for mercy in the most piteous accents. . . . At one time I saw at least 500 swept down in a moment as if a battery of a thousand guns had been opened upon them, and then immediately followed shrieks and shouts that rent the very heavens." Self-selected individuals put themselves in the line of fire by choosing to occupy the "sinners' bench" or "anxious seat" at the front of the audience.

THE BROADWAY TABERNACLE.

CHARLES G. FINNEY'S BROADWAY TABERNACLE
The Reverend Charles G. Finney took his evangelical movement to New York City in the early 1830s, operating out of existing Presbyterian churches. In 1836, the Broadway Tabernacle was built for his pastorate. In its use of space the Tabernacle resembled a theater more than a traditional church, but in one respect it departed radically from one very theaterlike tradition of churches, — the custom of charging pew rents. In effect, most churches required worshipers to purchase their seats. In contrast, Finney insisted that all seats in his house were free, unreserved, and open to all.
Oberlin College Archives, Oberlin, Ohio.

From 1800 to 1820, church membership doubled in the United States, much of it among the evangelical groups. Methodists, Baptists, and Presbyterians formed the core of the new movement, while Episcopalians, Congregationalists, Unitarians, Dutch Reformed, Lutherans, and Catholics maintained strong skepticism about the emotional enthusiasm. Women more than men were attracted to the evangelical movement, and the pattern of recruitment typically involved wives and mothers who then were able to persuade husbands and sons to join them.

The leading exemplar of the Second Great Awakening was a lawyer-turned-minister named Charles Grandison Finney. Up to his late twenties, Finney showed no religious inclinations; he had never read the Bible until shortly before his own awakening in 1821. Finney lived in western New York, where the completion of the Erie Canal in 1825 fundamentally altered the social and economic landscape overnight. Towns swelled with new inhabitants, who brought in remarkable prosperity along with other, less admirable aspects of urban growth, namely prostitution, drinking, and gaming.

Finney's genius was to see New York canal towns like Utica, Rome, and Buffalo as ripe for evangelical awakening. In Rochester, New York, Finney sustained a six-month revival through the long winter of 1830–31, generating thousands of new converts.

The message that Finney preached was directed primarily at women and men of the business classes, and, true to his training, Finney couched his message in legal metaphors. "The world is divided into two great political parties," he announced in a sermon, the party of Satan and the party of Jehovah. "Ministers should labor with sinners, as a lawyer does with a jury . . . ; and the sinner should weigh his arguments, and make up his mind as upon oath and for his life, and give a verdict upon the spot." Finney urged his listeners to take control of their own salvation, arguing that a reign of Christian perfection loomed. The promise of perfection required a public-spirited outreach to the less than perfect, to foster their salvation; Christian benevolence, or do-good action, was demanded of all believers. Evangelicals promoted Sunday schools to bring piety to children; they battled to end mail delivery, stop public transport, and close shops on Sundays to honor the Sabbath. Many women formed Missionary Societies, which printed and distributed millions of Bibles and religious tracts, taking the message of the Sunday sermon out of the pulpit and into individual parlors. Maternal Associations sprang up to promote a new style of moral mothering. Through such avenues, evangelical religion offered women expanded spheres of influence.

In 1832, Finney moved to New York City and renovated a disreputable theater on Chatham Street into a Free Presbyterian church. His dynamic, theatrical performances suited the location perfectly. A scribe took down his sermons, and the New York *Evangelist* carried his message weekly to a national readership. Finney adopted tactics of Jacksonian-era politicians to sell his cause: publicity, argumentation, rallies, and dramatic speeches. His object, he said, was to get Americans to "vote in the Lord Jesus Christ as the governor of the Universe."

The Temperance Movement

The evangelical disposition—a combination of righteousness, energy, self-discipline, and faith—animated a vigorous campaign to define alcohol as an unacceptable and dangerous self-indulgence. Millions of Americans took the pledge to abstain from strong drink, and temperance in the 1830s became a middle-class fixation.

Alcohol consumption had steadily risen in the decades before the 1830s. On the supply side, increased acreage planted in wheat, corn, and rye resulted in abundant whiskey, for it was far cheaper to transport distilled grains than to ship bulky and less valuable flour products. On the demand side, alcohol consumption rose in direct correlation to urban growth and the expansion of the wage-earning classes. Where master artisans had once handed out beverages (in moderate quantities) to their apprentices and journeymen, the reorganized wage labor force of the new market put social distance between workers and employers, who now frowned on alcohol as counterproductive to good work habits. Drinking off the job, as a leisure activity, accordingly increased.

Historians estimate that by 1830 the per capita annual consumption of alcohol for the entire population over age thirteen amounted to an astonishing 9.5 gallons of hard liquor plus 30.3 gallons of hard cider, beer, and wine. Since a substantial portion of that population abstained, the actual consumption level for serious drinkers was higher still.

Leisure-time drinking flourished in urban streets with their multitudes of saloons, barbershops, and groceries selling liquor by the glass. A lively saloon culture fostered mutual aid, job contacts, and masculine camaraderie among laborers. It also fostered excessive alcohol consumption and a new style of binge drinking that alarmed older proponents of moderate drinking.

Alcoholism was not limited to the working classes. In elite homes, sociable customs separated men and women after dinner gatherings, the men to imbibe whiskey and smoke cigars, the women to chat and sip sherry. Colleges before 1820 routinely served students a pint of ale with meals, and the army and navy made a pint of rum a standard daily ration. Middle-class sons working away from home fell under the spell of oyster bars and the port served there. The attraction of bottled, fermented drinks among all classes made a certain amount of sense, given the uncertain availability of safe drinking water and the lack of reliable refrigeration.

Organized opposition to drinking first surfaced in the 1810s among groups in New England concerned about health issues. In 1826, Lyman Beecher, the father of Catharine Beecher and Harriet Beecher Stowe and the Connecticut minister of an "awakened" church, founded the American Temperance Society, stamped with the moral condemnation of indulgent behavior. Moderate drinking was not sufficiently virtuous, Beecher preached: "The daily use

TEMPERANCE WOMEN SERVING TEA
The woodcut artist titled this picture Women Enjoying a Seated Tea While Making a Strong Stand in Favor of Temperance. *No actual tea is in sight in the drawing; the menu seems to consist of fruit and pie. The guests look on with approval as the hostess empties a wine bottle out the window; wineglasses on the table are turned upside down. The drawing, dating from 1840, symbolizes women's rejection of alcohol; it seems highly unlikely that such a scene was actually played out.*
Courtesy, American Antiquarian Society.

of ardent spirits, in any form, or in any degree" was a grievous sin leading to poverty, idleness, crime, and family violence. Adopting the methods of evangelical ministers, temperance lecturers traveled the country expounding the damage of drink and encouraging converts to the cause. By 1833, more than six thousand local affiliates of the American Temperance Society had a membership of more than a million people.

Annual conventions in New York City and a national newspaper called the *Temperance Recorder* helped bind members together and publicized the statistics of excessive drink and its detrimental effect on productivity. Manufacturers and business owners began to require temperance pledges from all employees. The American Temperance Society

reached a mass audience and achieved a respectable dent in alcohol consumption, which diminished by 1845 to one-quarter of the per capita consumption of 1830. Using evangelical arguments, the society succeeded in changing individual behavior, both by free will and by coercion (in the case of the pledge as a condition of employment). But mostly it was the middle classes that quit drinking. Workingmen, no longer able to drink on the job, withdrew to saloons in their own neighborhoods.

In 1836, the temperance leaders regrouped into a new society, the American Temperance Union, which required total abstinence of its adherents; even sacramental wine was condemned. The intensified war against alcohol moved beyond individual moral suasion into the realm of politics, as reformers sought to deny taverns liquor licenses and to wipe out the dram shops where purchase by the glass kept liquor affordable. Reformers urged the passage of state laws governing the quantities of liquor that could be sold. Several states prohibited sales in quantities less than fifteen gallons; the clear effect of such laws was to restrict legal purchase to those who could afford to buy in bulk. Temperance advocates would have preferred total bans on liquor, but they were willing to settle for a halfway measure that allowed only people of means to purchase it. Not until 1851 did a state go entirely dry: Maine banned the sale or manufacture of all alcoholic beverages. Other states followed suit in the second half of the century.

The Campaign for Moral Reform

More controversial than evangelical temperance was a social movement called "moral reform," which first aimed at public morals in general but quickly narrowed to a campaign to eradicate sexual sin. A group of Finneyite women (including Charles Finney's wife) started the New York Female Moral Reform Society in 1833. In the previous decade, concern over increasing prostitution had sparked the formation of small Magdalen Societies (named for the biblical Mary Magdalene) in New York and Philadelphia. Those groups were run by benevolent men who hoped to reform prostitutes into respectable if humble domestics and seamstresses. In contrast, the Female Moral Reform Society targeted men as the ones in need of reformation. Its members insisted that male sexual expression, the ultimate in lack of self-control, posed a serious threat to society in general and to women in particular.

The women reformers published a newspaper, *The Advocate of Moral Reform*, that quickly established a national circulation. It was the first major woman-edited, woman-written, and woman-typeset paper in the country. Columns were devoted to lurid admonitions, to first-person tales of woe, and to ideas for what local women's groups could do about sexual sin. One typical article praised a quick-thinking moral reform advocate for rescuing an inexperienced girl on a Hudson River steamboat. The reformer spotted "one of those birds of prey that hover over all the routes of travel, a moral vulture," a well-dressed man whispering offers of employment in the girl's ear. The female reformer intervened and saved the girl, with the captain's help. "All ladies, (and gentlemen too) [should] watch in all their tours and travels, to protect female virtue

and youthful innocence and inexperience, from the crafty wiles of those who lay in wait to destroy." The reformers condemned clerks who visited brothels and country merchants who befriended and then seduced girls on public transport; they even named names of particularly noteworthy villains. Within five years, more than four thousand auxiliary groups had sprung up, mostly in New England, New York, Pennsylvania, and Ohio, all in areas where evangelical religion was strong. Not content merely to publicize sin, the New York group engaged in direct action, stationing women outside brothels to intimidate the patrons. They urged chaste women to sign pledges (like the pledges of the temperance movement) promising to accept only virtuous men in courtship.

> Sexual excess was presented as a powerful drain on the bodily economy: A robust man who hoped to retain his vital energies for the world of getting and spending had best not waste his powers in selfish indulgence.

Some men worried about moral reform as well, but their analysis was less related to gender than to age. Male reformers tended to see sexual sin as the affliction of undisciplined youth of both sexes. One leading author of an advice book, Sylvester Graham, linked stimulating foods, liquor, and excessive "amativeness" as the downfall of an overindulgent civilization. Graham and others painted dark pictures of the urban hellholes that lured young people to fates worse than death. Sexual excess was presented as a powerful drain on the bodily economy: A robust man who hoped to retain his vital energies for the world of getting and spending had best not waste his powers in selfish indulgence.

The Female Moral Reform Society drew on the evangelicals' familiar themes of self-control and suppression of sin. But in its analysis of the causes of licentiousness and its conviction that women had a duty to speak out about unspeakable things, it pushed the limits of what even the men in the evangelical movement could tolerate. Yet the moral reformers did not consider themselves to be radicals of any kind. They were simply pursuing the logic of a gender system that defined home protection and morality as their special sphere and a religious conviction that called for the eradication of sin. By the 1840s, in response to criticism, they toned down their tactics and concentrated on rescue work among downtrodden girls.

Organizing against Slavery

Even more radical than moral reform was the effort to eradicate slavery in the 1830s, which evangelicals saw as a national sin of injustice. The abolition movement, as it was called, excited fierce resistance from white Americans, North and South. The debate leading to the Missouri Compromise of 1820 showed how divisive and irreconcilable the issue was. A group of Maryland and Virginia planters had founded the American Colonization Society in 1817 to promote gradual emancipation, by which slave owners voluntarily released slaves and had them transported to Africa. By the early 1820s, several thousand African Americans were living on the West African coast in a new colony (later a country) called Liberia, created for freed slaves. (Liberia's capital was named Monrovia in honor of President James Monroe, who advocated colonization.) Not surprisingly, newly freed men and women were often not eager to move to Liberia; their African roots were three or more generations in the past. Migration across the Atlantic proved to be so gradual (and expensive) as to have a negligible impact on American slavery.

A more insistent attention to the evils of slavery emerged in 1831, dictated by the perfectionist impulse of the Second Great Awakening. Charles Finney's religious campaigns in Rochester and New York City identified slavery as a major obstacle to America's progress toward perfection. Both of those cities quickly became centers of antislavery agitation.

In Boston, an antislavery movement developed around William Lloyd Garrison, who started publishing a weekly newspaper called the *Liberator* in 1831. Garrison was then twenty-six; raised in Massachusetts, he had spent some time in Baltimore, where he absorbed a firsthand knowledge of both slavery and Quaker antislavery sentiment. Back in the North, he launched his drive for immediate abolition, promising that his paper would be "as harsh as truth, and as uncompromising as justice. On this subject, I do not wish to think, or speak, or write, with moderation. No! No! Tell a man whose house is on fire to give a moderate alarm; tell him to moderately rescue his wife from the hands of the ravisher; tell the mother to gradually extricate her

babe from the fire into which it has fallen;—but urge me not to use moderation in a cause like the present." No gradualist plan could ever be acceptable to Garrison.

Garrison's visibility in Boston built on several years of growing local antislavery sentiment. In 1829, a black Bostonian named David Walker published *An Appeal to the Colored Citizens of the World*. Walker, a forty-four-year-old freedman born in North Carolina, was a printer and an active member of the recently formed Massachusetts Colored Association. His pamphlet condemned racism, invoked the egalitarian language of the Declaration of Independence, and hinted at racial violence if whites did not change their prejudiced ways. "Wo, wo, will be to you if we have to obtain our freedom by fighting. Throw way your fears and prejudices then, and enlighten us and treat us like men, and we will like you more than we do now hate you, and tell us now no more about colonization, for America is as much our country, as it is yours." Walker's fervent *Appeal* electrified Garrison, pushing him into a more radical stance on slavery. It electrified the South as well, and several southern states prohibited its circulation.

From 1831 to 1833, a young black woman, Maria Stewart, newly widowed, staged a series of public lectures in Boston on slavery and racial prejudice. She spoke to black audiences, and while her arguments against slavery were welcomed, her voice—that of a woman—created problems. Few American-born women had yet engaged in public speaking beyond ceremonial or theatrical performance; Stewart was breaking a social taboo. Compounding her audience's discomfort was the fact that Stewart also criticized members of her own race for contributing to their oppressed condition. She faulted black women for accepting deadening domestic jobs instead of pursuing an education, while black men lacked "ambition and force" to combat racial prejudice. Boston's elite black men in the audience discouraged her career, and she retired from the platform in 1833. Garrison published her lectures, giving them wider circulation. A cresting wave of antislavery sentiment was about to break over many northeastern cities.

Southerners feared Garrison's cresting wave. Eight months after the *Liberator* started, a charismatic slave named Nat Turner led the largest and most deadly of all slave insurrections, in Southampton County, Virginia (see chapter 12). The event left the South reeling with palpable paranoia about future slave revolts. As they had with Walker's *Ap-*

ABOLITIONIST CRIB QUILT

This crib quilt (left) was sewn by women of the Boston Female Anti-Slavery Society in 1836. Many abolitionist women produced handcrafted items for sale at antislavery fairs to raise money to support antislavery agents in the field and publication costs of abolitionist literature. The central square of this quilt (detail) reminds mothers hugging their own free babies to "Think of the negro mother, when Her child is torn away; Sold for a little slave — oh then, For that poor mother pray!"

Courtesy of Society for Preservation of New England Antiquities/photo by David Bohl.

peal, several southern states ordered local postmasters to refuse delivery of the *Liberator.*

In 1832 and 1833, the antislavery movement got organized. The New England Anti-Slavery Society coalesced in 1832 around Garrison, with a women's auxiliary run by Maria Weston Chapman, an assistant editor of the *Liberator.* The New York Anti-Slavery Society became active in 1833, as did another in Philadelphia. Within five years, there would be 1,350 local antislavery societies pocketed all over the North, with a membership totaling a quarter of a million men and women. This was a significant number, but by no means a large one in relation to the North's population.

Abolitionists borrowed revivalist techniques. Conventions drew like-minded people together, as camp meetings did, to hear speeches and debate strategy. The print media were fully enlisted, with a dozen antislavery newspapers as well as pamphlets and books in profusion. Effective public speakers were hired as agents to travel on speaking tours, like itinerant ministers. Antislavery agents inspired the formation of new local societies, but they also drew hecklers and worse in many towns.

Many northerners were not prepared to embrace the abolitionist call for emancipation, immediate or gradual. They might oppose slavery as a blot on the country's ideals or as a rival to the free labor system of the North, but at the same time most white northerners remained antiblack and therefore antiabolition. From 1834 to 1838, there were several dozen eruptions of serious mob violence against abolitionists; sometimes the violence was also viciously directed against black neighborhoods, as in New York in 1834. Garrison once grappled with a lynch mob in Boston. Antislavery headquarters in Philadelphia burned to the ground in 1838, after which the mob burned a black church and the Shelter for Colored Orphans. The depth of negative feeling for abolition sprang from deep wells of northern racism; abolitionists were called "amalgamationists," a potent label suggesting that abolitionists favored racial intermixing, both social and sexual.

Women played a prominent role in abolition, just as they had in moral reform and evangelical religion. They formed women's auxiliaries and engaged in fundraising to support agents in the field and the expenses of pamphlet publication. In the political realm, women circulated antislavery petitions, which they presented to the U.S. Congress with tens of thousands of signatures.

Garrison particularly welcomed women's activity. The *Liberator* had a women's department, featuring appeals to northern women to extend their protective feminine sympathies to their black sisters of the South. When a southern plantation daughter named Angelina Grimké wrote him about her personal repugnance for slavery, Garrison published the letter in the *Liberator* and brought her overnight fame. Grimké and her older sister Sarah, now living in Philadelphia, quickly became agents with the antislavery movement and started a speaking tour of Massachusetts in 1837 to offer personal testimony about slavery to women's groups. Grimké's powerful eyewitness speeches attracted men as well, causing the Congregational church leadership of Massachusetts to issue a warning to all its ministers not to let the Grimké sisters use their podiums. As with Maria Stewart, the Grimkés had violated a gender norm by presuming to instruct men. It certainly did not help that their message involved the most controversial political topic of the 1830s.

In the late 1830s, the cause of abolition divided the nation as no other subject did. It had its martyr: An antislavery editor in Illinois, Elijah Lovejoy, was killed by a rioting crowd that tried to destroy his printing press. Even among the abolitionists there emerged significant divisions. The Grimké sisters, radicalized by the public reaction to their speaking tour, began to write and speak about women's rights. Moderate abolitionists unwilling to push the woman question retreated from the implications of their own egalitarian rhetoric employed in their race speeches. Some radical men, like Garrison, embraced women's rights fully, working to get women leadership positions in the national antislavery group. Out of the New England antislavery movement came the first organized women's rights movement in U.S. history, in the 1840s. The more moderate New York group stayed with antislavery as a single issue and in the 1840s moved more directly into politics, founding first the Liberty Party and then the Free-Soil Party, precursors to the Republican Party of the 1850s.

The many men and women active in reform movements in the 1830s found their initial inspiration in evangelical Protestantism's dual message: Salvation was open to all and society needed to be perfected. Their activist mentality squared well with the interventionist tendencies of the party forming in opposition to Andrew Jackson's Democrats. On the whole, reformers gravitated to the Whig Party.

Jackson Defines the Democratic Party

In his eight years in office, Jackson worked to implement his vision of a politics of opportunity for all white men. He also greatly enhanced the power of the presidency. He favored rapid western land settlement, which required him to disrupt certain Indian tribes and to face down the Supreme Court when it backed some of their claims. He had a dramatic confrontation with John C. Calhoun and South Carolina when that state tried to nullify the tariff of 1828. Disapproving of all government-granted privilege, Jackson challenged what he called the "monster" Bank of the United States and took it down to defeat, along with the National Republican leadership who tried to pin the 1832 campaign to it. Jackson's legacy to his successor, Martin Van Buren, was a Democratic Party strong enough to withstand the passing of the powerful old man.

Indian Policy and the Trail of Tears

For forty years, white Americans moving west had encountered strong resistance from Indian tribes east of the Mississippi River. After 1815, improved transportation greatly accelerated the westward flow of white settlers, and states containing Indian enclaves rapidly joined the Union. When Jackson took office, fundamental questions remained unresolved: What was the legal status of the quarter of a million Indians now resident in the United States? Were they subject to state and federal law?

From the 1790s to the 1820s, the federal government negotiated treaties with tribes, just as colonies had done in the pre-independence period, on the assumption that Indians were foreign nations. The Indians asserted their own sovereignty and communal rights to their land, even though they now lived within state borders. Treaty making, however, proved a precarious practice. American negotiators found it hard to strike workable terms that whole tribes would accept when trading money or promises of security in exchange for Indian land. All too often, a few Indians with no legitimacy to speak for their tribes were persuaded to sign treaties ceding vast acreage.

After the War of 1812, Andrew Jackson as an army general negotiated many such treaties, but he

CHEROKEE PHOENIX

Around 1820, Sequoyah, about forty-five years old and nephew of a Cherokee chief, invented written symbols to convey the Cherokee language. Each symbol represented a syllable of sound. In 1828, the Cherokee in New Echota, Georgia, ordered custom-made type embodying the new symbols and began printing a newspaper, the Cherokee Phoenix, *the first newspaper published by Native Americans, printed in both English and Cherokee.*

Special Collections Division, Georgetown University Library, Washington, D.C.

privately thought it was "absurd" to assume that the Indians were foreigners. In his view, the Indians were now subjects of the United States, perhaps entitled to keep their villages and improved land but not their large hunting grounds. When he became president in 1829, he moved to implement his idea.

Others in the period from 1790 to the 1820s proposed assimilation as a more peaceable solution. Nationally organized missionary associations tried to "civilize" native peoples by converting them to Christianity. In 1819, Congress authorized $10,000 a year for interdenominational missions to instruct Indians in religion, reading and writing, and agricultural practices. Missionaries were also eager to institute their own notions of private property and correct gender relations, assumed by them to be essential features of a civilized society. They hoped to persuade Indian tribes to limit women to domestic

tasks, forcing men to do agricultural tasks usually done by women. But assimilation proved to be slow going. Indian women were particularly reluctant to adopt a gender system that accorded them less power than their tribal system. The general failure of assimilation moved Jackson to a more drastic policy.

In his first message to Congress in 1829, President Jackson declared that Indians within the United States borders could not remain independent and in sovereign control of tribal lands. Congress agreed and passed the Removal Act of 1830, appropriating $500,000 to relocate tribes west of the Mississippi River.

For northern tribes, their numbers greatly diminished by years of war, gradual removal was well under way. But not all the Indians went quietly. In 1832 in western Illinois, Black Hawk, a leader of the Sac and Fox Indians, convinced his people to refuse to leave their Indian lodges when whites claimed them under a dubious treaty signed by four unauthorized Sac Indians. Federal troops sent by Jackson attacked and chased the Indians into southern Wisconsin, where, after several skirmishes and battles, Black Hawk was captured and many of his two thousand people massacred.

The southern tribes proved to be even more resistant to removal. The powerful Creek, Chickasaw, Choctaw, and Cherokee, whose lands encompassed parts of North Carolina, Tennessee, and northern Georgia, Alabama, and Mississippi, at first refused to relocate. But their land attracted cotton-hungry white settlers, and a rumor of gold on Cherokee land in Georgia in 1829 only intensified the pressure.

Ironically, the seventeen thousand members of the Cherokee tribe had "assimilated" most success-

fully, spurred by dedicated missionaries living with them. Starting in 1808, they adopted written laws, culminating in 1827 in a constitution with a bicameral legislature, an executive office, and a court system modeled on those of the United States government. The constitution defined the boundaries of their nation, which they claimed was independent of Georgia. More than two hundred of the wealthiest Cherokee had intermarried with whites and had adopted white styles of housing, dress, and cotton agriculture, including the ownership of over a thousand African American slaves. They had developed a written alphabet and published a newspaper as well as Christian prayerbooks in their language. The missionaries supported them fully in their battle first with Georgia and then with Jackson.

In 1826, Georgia asserted the dependent status of the Cherokee: "The Indians are tenants at Geor-

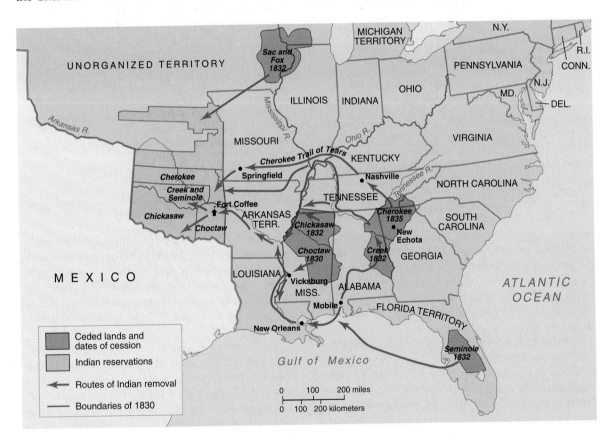

MAP 11.3

Indian Removal and the Trail of Tears, 1830s

The federal government under President Andrew Jackson pursued a vigorous policy of Indian removal in the 1830s. Southern tribes were forcibly moved west to land known as the Indian Territory, to the west of Arkansas (in present-day Oklahoma). As many as a quarter of the Cherokee Indians died in 1838 on their route, known as the Trail of Tears.

gia's will, and Georgia may at any time she pleases determine that tenancy by taking possession of the premises." President Jackson sided with Georgia, so the legal-minded Cherokee resorted to the U.S. government's weapon of choice: a team of first-rate lawyers who brought suit before the Supreme Court.

In 1831 in *Cherokee Nation v. Georgia*, the Cherokee sued to prohibit Georgia from subjecting them to state laws. Chief Justice John Marshall set aside the case on technicalities but encouraged the Cherokee to seek further legal redress. When Georgia jailed two missionaries, Samuel Worcester and Elizur Butler, under an 1830 law forbidding missionary aid to Indians without state permission, the Cherokee brought suit again. In the 1832 case, *Worcester v. Georgia*, the Supreme Court found for the missionaries and made the larger point for the Cherokee, recognizing their existence as "a distinct community, occupying its own territory, in which the laws of Georgia can have no force."

An angry President Jackson announced that he would ignore the Court's decision. "John Marshall has made his opinion, now let him enforce it," he reportedly declared. Jackson instead proceeded with the Removal Act. "If they [the Cherokee] now refuse to accept the liberal terms offered, they can only be liable for whatever evils and difficulties may arise. I feel conscious of having done my duty to my red children."

Still, the Cherokee remained in Georgia for two more years without significant violence. Then, in 1835, a small, unauthorized part of the tribe signed a treaty ceding all the tribal lands to the state, and Georgia rapidly sold off the land to whites through a state lottery. Several thousand Cherokee petitioned the U.S. Congress to ignore the bogus treaty, but their pleas went unheard.

The disputed treaty relinquished a large piece of northern Georgia in exchange for $5 million and equal acreage west of Arkansas, in present-day Oklahoma. But most of the Cherokee refused to move, and in May 1838, the deadline for voluntary evacuation, federal troops arrived to deport them. Moving in groups of a thousand each, under armed guard, the Cherokee embarked on a twelve-hundred-mile journey that came to be called the Trail of Tears. A Maine newspaperman traveling in Kentucky encountered the migration stream, some in wagons but others walking barefoot. "Even aged females, apparently, nearly ready to drop into the grave, were travelling with heavy burdens attached to the back—on the sometimes frozen ground. . . .

We learned from the inhabitants on the road where the Indians passed that they buried fourteen to fifteen at every stopping place, and they make a journey of ten miles per day only on an average." Nearly a quarter of the Cherokee died en route, from hardship and starvation. They joined fifteen thousand Creek, twelve thousand Choctaw, and five thousand Chickasaw Indians also forcibly relocated to what is now Oklahoma. In the early 1840s, the small surviving remnant of the Florida Seminole tribe was moved west, after a seven-year war that killed nearly half of them and fifteen hundred federal soldiers as well. Jackson's Indian policy proved to be costly in human life.

> *Jackson genuinely believed that exile to the west was necessary to save Indian culture from destruction.*

In his farewell address to the nation in 1837, Jackson justified Indian removal with high-minded language about the benefit of the policy to the forlorn natives: "This unhappy race . . . are now placed in a situation where we may well hope that they will share in the blessings of civilization and be saved from the degradation and destruction to which they were rapidly hastening while they remained in the states." Jackson genuinely believed that exile to the west was necessary to save Indian culture from destruction.

Nullification: Federal Power versus States' Rights

Jackson's Indian policy happened to harmonize with the principle of states' rights: The president supported Georgia's right to ignore the Supreme Court decision in *Worcester v. Georgia*. But in another pressing question of states' rights, Jackson trounced on South Carolina's claim to ignore federal tariff policy.

South Carolina had been smarting since the "Tariff of Abominations" passed in 1828. Worldwide prices for cotton were already in sharp decline in the late 1820s and early 1830s, and the further depression of shipping caused by high tariffs hurt the South's export of agricultural products. In 1828, a group of South Carolina politicians headed by John C. Calhoun drew up a statement outlining a doctrine of nullification. The Union, they argued, was a confederation of states that had yielded some but not all power to the federal government. When Congress overstepped its powers, states had the right to nullify its acts, and as precedents they pointed to the Virginia and Kentucky Resolutions of 1798, which had attempted to invalidate the Alien and Sedition Acts. Congress had erred in using tariff policy as an instrument to benefit specific industries, the South Carolinians claimed; tariffs should be used only to raise revenue.

The 1828 statement was an assertion of principles, not a declaration of action, and it was not officially endorsed by the South Carolina legislature. Jackson ignored it, except to avoid appointing South Carolinians to high administrative office. He was stuck with Calhoun in the vice presidency, but he effectively deprived him of influence or power. Sensing futility, Calhoun resigned from the vice presidency in 1832 and accepted election by the South Carolina legislature to a seat in the U.S. Senate, where he could better protect his state's anti-tariff stance.

Tariff revisions in early 1832 had brought little relief to the South. Strained to their limit, the South Carolina leaders called a special convention on tariff law, and in November 1832 they implemented nullification by declaring the federal tariffs to be null and void in their state as of February 1, 1833.

Finally, the constitutional crisis was out in the open. Jackson opted for a dramatic confrontation. He sent armed ships to Charleston's harbor and threatened to invade the state. He pushed through Congress a bill, called the Force Bill, defining the Carolina stance as treason and authorizing military action to collect federal tariffs.

At the same time, Congress was busy patching together a revised tariff more acceptable to the South. The astute Senator Henry Clay rallied support for a moderate bill that gradually lowered tariffs by half, back to the level prevailing in 1816. Both the new tariff and the Force Bill were passed on the same day in Congress, March 1, 1833. South Carolina responded by withdrawing its nullification of the old tariff—and then nullifying the Force Bill. It was a symbolic gesture, since Jackson's show of muscle was no longer necessary. Both sides took a measure of satisfaction in the immediate outcome. Federal power had prevailed over a dangerous assertion of states' rights; and South Carolina got the lower tariff it wanted.

In the long run, however, the question of federal power versus states' rights was far from settled. The implied threat behind nullification was se-

cession, a position articulated in 1832 by some South Carolinians whose concerns went beyond tariff policy. The growing voice of antislavery activism in the North threatened the South's economic system. If and when a northern-dominated federal government decided to end slavery, the South Carolinians thought, the South must have the right to remove itself from the Union.

The Bank War and the Panic of 1837

Along with the tariff and nullification, President Jackson had another political battle on his hands over the Bank of the United States. After riding out the panic of 1819, the bank had prospered under the leadership of Philadelphian Nicholas Biddle. It handled the federal government's deposits, extended credit and loans, and issued banknotes—by 1830 the most secure and steady circulating currency in the country. With twenty-nine branches, it spread its stabilizing benefits to the whole nation. Jackson, however, did not find the bank's temperate functions sufficiently valuable to offset his criticism of the concept of a national bank. In his first and second messages to Congress, in 1829 and 1830, Jackson claimed that the bank concentrated undue economic power in the hands of a few. His Democratic allies privately hoped he would be content with anti-bank rhetoric, without taking concrete action.

Senators Henry Clay and Daniel Webster, leaders of the National Republicans, decided to force the issue. They convinced Biddle to apply for renewal of the bank's federal charter in 1832, well before the fall election, even though the twenty-year charter ran until 1836. They fully expected that Congress's renewal would force Jackson to follow through on his rhetoric with a veto. The unpopular veto would then cause Jackson to lose the election, while the bank would survive on an override vote from a new Congress swept into power in the anti-Jackson tide.

At first the plan seemed to work. Biddle applied for recharter, Congress voted to renew, and Jackson, angry over being manipulated, issued his veto. But it was a brilliantly written veto, full of fierce language about privileges of the moneyed elite who oppress the liberties of the democratic masses in order to concentrate wealth in their own hands. "Many of our rich men have not been content with equal protection and equal benefits, but have besought us to make them richer by act of Congress," Jackson wrote.

Biddle and Clay thought that Jackson's economic ideas were so absurd and his language so shocking that they distributed thousands of copies of the bank veto as campaign material for the National Republicans. A confident Henry Clay headed the ticket for the presidency. But they miscalculated. Jackson had translated the bank controversy into a language of class antagonism and egalitarian ideals that strongly resonated with many Americans. Old Hickory won the election easily, with 55 percent of the popular vote and a lopsided electoral college vote of 219 to only 49 for Clay. The Jackson party still controlled Congress, so no override was possible. The bank's fate was sealed; it would cease to exist after 1836.

But Jackson took his reelection as a mandate to destroy the bank sooner. Calling the bank a "monster," he ordered the secretary of the treasury to remove the federal deposits from Biddle's vaults, despite the fact that nearly his entire cabinet disagreed with the action. The money was redeposited into "pet banks," Democratic-leaning institutions throughout the country; because of the high tariffs and high-volume sales of public lands, this government nest egg was quite sizable. In retaliation, Biddle showed he still had formidable powers by tightening credit in the economy. He accomplished this by raising interest rates and calling in loans, which he claimed he had to do since the bank's deposits were now dangerously low. This action caused a minor recession in 1833 and actually enhanced Jackson's claim that the bank was too powerful for the good of the country.

Unleashed and unregulated, the economy went into high gear, to Jackson's dismay. Perhaps only a small part of the problem arose from irresponsible banking practices; just at this moment, an excess of silver from Mexican mines had made its way into American banks' deposits, giving bankers license to print ever more banknotes. Inflation soared from 1834 to 1837; prices of basic goods rose more than 50 percent. Real estate in hot markets like Manhattan inflated 500 percent. Southern planters bought land and slaves fast, paying as much as 30 percent interest on bank loans for their purchases. Many hundreds of new private banks were quickly chartered by the states, each bank issuing its own banknotes and setting interest rates as high as the market would bear. Entrepreneurs borrowed and invested money, much of it funneled into privately financed railroads and canals.

The market in western land sales heated up. In 1834, about 4.5 million acres of the public domain

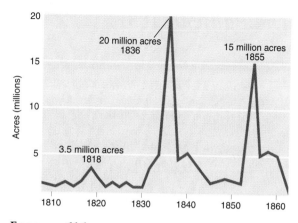

FIGURE 11.1

Western Land Sales, 1810–1860
Land sales peaked in the 1810s, 1830s, and 1850s as Americans rushed to speculate in western lands sold by the federal government. In particular the surges in 1818 and 1836 demonstrate the volatile, speculative economy that suddenly collapsed in the panics of 1819 and 1837.

had been sold, the highest annual volume since the peak year 1819. A year later, the figure rose to more than 13 million acres, and in 1836, the total reached an astonishing 20 million acres. What was most disturbing to the Jackson administration was that the purchasers were overwhelmingly eastern capitalists, not individual yeoman farmers who intended to settle on the land.

In one respect, the economy attained an admirable goal: The national debt disappeared, and, for the first and only time in American history, from 1835 to 1837 the government had a surplus of money. But much of it consisted of questionable bank currencies—bloated, diseased currencies, in Jackson's vivid terminology.

Jackson decided to restrain the economy. In 1836, the Treasury Department issued the Specie Circular, ordering that public land could be purchased only with hard money, federally coined gold and silver. In response, bankers started to reduce their loans, fearing a general contraction of the economy. Compounding the difficulty, the Bank of England also now insisted on hard-money payments for American loans, which had grown fat in the years since 1831 because of a trade imbalance. Some short-run failures in various crop markets, a downturn in the price of cotton on the international market, and the silver glut, all unrelated to Jackson's fiscal policies, fed the growing economic crisis.

The Panic of 1837

The panic of 1837 brought fright and hysteria to city after city. Crowds of hundreds thronged the banks during the spring to get their money out. Business came to a standstill and many merchants appeared to be ruined overnight. Whig leaders were certain that the crisis could be traced to President Jackson's antibank and hard money policies, but others blamed it on what they saw as an immoral frenzy of greed and speculation that had gripped the nation for the preceding few years.

Harriet Martineau traveled throughout the United States and described booming land sales in the infant city of Chicago in 1836.

DOCUMENT 1. An English Visitor Describes the "Mania" for Speculation

I never saw a busier place than Chicago was at the time of our arrival. The streets were crowded with land speculators, hurrying from one sale to another. A negro, dressed up in scarlet, bearing a scarlet flag, and riding a white horse with housings of scarlet, announced the times of sale. At every street-corner where he stopped, the crowd flocked round him; and it seemed as if some prevalent mania infected the whole people. The rage for speculation might fairly be so regarded. As the gentlemen of our party walked the streets, store-keepers hailed them from their doors, with offers of farms, and all manner of land-lots, advising them to speculate before the price of land rose higher. A young lawyer of my acquaintance there, had realised five hundred dollars per day, the five preceding days, by merely making out titles to land. . . . Of course, this rapid money-making is a merely temporary evil. A bursting of the bubble must come soon. The absurdity of the speculation is so striking, that the wonder is that the fever should have attained such a height as I witnessed. The immediate occasion of the bustle which prevailed, the week we were at Chicago, was the sale of lots . . . along the course of a projected canal. . . . Persons not intending to game, and not infected with mania, would endeavour to form some reasonable conjecture as to the ultimate value of the lots, by calculating the cost of the canal, the risks from accident, from the possible competition from other places, &c., and finally, the possible profits, under the most favourable circumstances, within so many years' purchase. Such a calculation would serve as some sort of guide as to the amount of purchase-money to be risked. Whereas, wild land on the banks of a canal, not yet even marked out, was selling at Chicago for more than rich land, well improved, in the finest part of the valley of the Mohawk, on the banks of a canal [the Erie] which is already the medium of an almost inestimable amount of traffic. If sharpers and gamblers were to be the sufferers by the impending crash at Chicago, no one would feel much concerned: but they, unfortunately, are the people who encourage the delusion, in order to profit by it. Many a high-spirited, but inexperienced, young man; many a simple settler, will be ruined for the advantage of knaves.

Philip Hone, a wealthy New York Whig, had an early taste of the crash to come when his son's business failed in March, on the last day of President Jackson's term.

DOCUMENT 2. The Diary of Philip Hone, 1837.

Saturday, March 4.—This is the end of Gen. Jackson's administration—the most disastrous in the annals of the country. . . .

This is a dark and melancholy day in the annals of my family. Brown & Hone stopped payment to-day, and called a meeting of their creditors. My eldest son has lost the capital I gave him, and I am implicated as endorser for them to a fearful amount. The pressure of the times, the immense amount they have paid of extra interest, and the almost total failure of remittances have been the causes of their ruin. . . .

Friday, March 17.—The great crisis is near at hand, if it has not already arrived. The banking house of I. and L. Joseph . . . stopped payment to-day, and occasioned great consternation in Wall Street, for their business has been enormous. . . . The immediate cause of this disaster was the intelligence received from New Orleans by this day's mail of the stoppage of the House of Hermann & Co. and others connected with them, for whom the Josephs are under acceptances to the amount of two millions of dollars. This is another evidence of the reckless manner in which business has been conducted, or rather, to speak more charitably, of the straits to which men have been driven by the wicked interference of the government with the currency of the country. . . .

Wednesday, May 10.— . . . The volcano has burst and overwhelmed New York; the glory of her merchants is departed. After a day of unexampled excitement, and a ruthless run upon all the banks, which drew from their vaults $600,000 in specie yesterday, nearly as much having been drawn on Monday, the officers held a meeting last evening and resolved to *suspend specie payments.* . . .

Thursday, May 11.—A dead calm has succeeded the stormy weather of Wall Street and the other places of active business. All is still as death. No business is transacted, no bargains made, no negotiations entered into; men's spirits are better because the danger of universal ruin is thought to be less imminent. A slight ray of hope is to be seen in countenances where despair only dwelt for the last fortnight, but all is wrapped up in uncertainty. Nobody can foretell the course matters will take. The fever is broken, but the patient lies in a sort of syncope, exhausted by the violence of the disease and the severity of the remedies.

The July 1837 issue of the Christian Examiner, *a Boston monthly, counseled that some good would come from the catastrophe.*

DOCUMENT 3. A Religious View of "Existing Commercial Embarrassments"

There will be then much individual improvement of character. . . . One of the first and most valuable . . . will be a check upon that extravagant estimate and overstrained pursuit of wealth, which are marked features in the character of the nation and the times. That such a check was needed and will be a blessing to the social and moral condition of the community, cannot be doubted. We were getting to be almost insane upon the subject of wealth. The lust of accumulation has ever been the root of much evil among men, but in this country several causes have naturally operated to give a strong impulse to this passion. Our political organization is that which offers the widest scope to enterprise, and applies the strongest stimulus to ambition and exertion, while, at the same time, it produces a state of society in which wealth is necessarily the principal distinction, the surest and readiest of attainment, and therefore the first and most eagerly sought. . . . A new country like ours, of almost unbounded extent, rich beyond comparison in resources, . . . naturally awakens in its inhabitants earnest and insatiable desires. . . .

. . . Great benefits have . . . flowed from . . . enterprise. . . . Towns have been built and cities reared, mountains levelled, and valleys filled, and distant places brought near, and the wide wilderness of nature changed to a garden of human civilization, comfort, and luxury. . . .

But the moral influence of these causes has not all been good. They were making us proud, presumptuous, extravagant, luxurious, visionary. We were getting to think that there was no end to the wealth, and could be no check to the progress of our country; that economy was not needed, that prudence was weakness, that moderation was a sinful neglect of the golden chances by which many were winning fortunes. The tardy gains of honorable enterprise were spurned, that the lucky speculation of an hour might bestow a fortune. We needed a check, a restraint, a rebuke. Many felt that it was needed and foresaw that it must come, and he who ruleth over the nations has at length sent it. As in other general calamities, the evil in many individual cases falls on those who may not themselves have been guilty, but the benefit will be reaped by all. The fever which has raged in society will abate.

Document 1. Harriet Martineau, *Society in America* (London, 1837), 350–52, reprinted in David Brion Davis, *Antebellum American Culture: An Interpretive Anthology* (Lexington, Mass., D. C. Heath, 1979), 121–22.

Document 2. Allan Nevins, ed., *The Diary of Philip Hone, 1828–1851* (New York: Dodd Mead, 1936), 244, 248–49, 257, 259.

Document 3. "Existing Commercial Embarrassments," *Christian Examiner and General Review,* 22, 3rd series, vol. 4 (1837): 395–96.

FISTFIGHT BETWEEN OLD HICKORY AND BULLY NICK
This 1834 cartoon represents President Andrew Jackson squaring off to fight Nicholas Biddle, the director of the Bank of the United States. Pugilism as a semiprofessional sport gained great popularity in the 1830s; the joke here is that the aged Jackson and the aristocratic Biddle would strip to such revealing tight pants and engage in open combat. To Biddle's left are his seconds, Daniel Webster and Henry Clay; behind the president is his vice-president, Martin Van Buren. Whiskey and port lubricate the action.
The Library Company of Philadelphia.

Suddenly, the familiar events of the panic of 1819 unfolded again, with terrifying rapidity. In April 1837, a wave of banks and businesses failed, and the credit market tumbled like a house of cards. (See Texts in Historical Context, page 420.) The Specie Circular was only one precipitating cause, but the Whig Party held it and Jackson responsible for the depression. For more than five years after the panic of 1837, the United States suffered from economic hard times.

Van Buren's One-Term Presidency

The election of 1836, which preceded the panic by six months, demonstrated the transformation of the Democrats from coalition to party. The personality of Jackson had stamped the elections of 1824, 1828, and 1832, but now party apparatus was sufficiently developed to support itself. Local and state committees existed throughout the country. Democratic candidates ran in every state election, gaining success even in old Federalist states like Maine and New Hampshire. More than four hundred newspapers were affiliated as Democratic. In 1836, the Democrats repeated an innovation begun in 1832, holding a national convention that nominated Martin Van Buren of New York for president, balanced by

vice presidential candidate Richard M. Johnson of Kentucky. (Johnson was a slave owner from the West who insistently championed Sunday mail delivery and boasted that he was the actual killer of Shawnee chief Tecumseh back in 1813.)

Sophisticated party organization was Martin Van Buren's specialty. Friends nicknamed him the "Little Magician" for his consummate political skills. Another nickname, the "Red Fox of Kinderhook," honored his once red hair, his Dutch heritage, and his shrewd and calculated maneuvers. From humble origins in a Dutch village of New York's Hudson River valley, Van Buren overcame an inadequate early education and with the help of influential patrons became a lawyer. As a youth, he learned politics with Jeffersonian Republicans in New York City, and two decades later he was the acknowledged leader of a statewide coalition, the Bucktails, which pioneered many of the loyalty-enhancing techniques the Democrats used in the 1830s. After engineering a rewriting of his state's constitution in 1821, which implemented dramatic democratic reforms, Van Buren served as senator and then was elected governor just as Jackson tapped him to be secretary of state in 1828. From the State Department he moved to the vice presidency in 1832. His eight years in the volatile Jackson administration required the full measure of his political deftness, as he sought repeatedly to save Jackson both from his enemies and from his own obstinacy.

Van Buren was a backroom politician, not a popular public figure, and his candidacy gave hope to the Whigs that he might be defeatable. In many states Whigs had captured high office in 1834, shedding the awkward National Republican label and developing statewide organizations to rival those of the Democrats. However, no figure at the national level could command support in all regions; Massachusetts Senator Daniel Webster, for example, had absolutely no following in the South, a heavily pro-Jackson region. The result was that three candidates opposed Van Buren in 1836, each with a solid popular regional base. Webster could deliver New England; Tennessee Senator Hugh Lawson White attracted proslavery, pro-Jackson, but anti–Van Buren voters in the South; and the aging General William Henry Harrison of Indiana, memorable for his Indian war heroics in 1811, pulled in the western, anti-Indian vote. Only Webster and Harrison actually identified themselves as Whigs, while White, a banker, kept his affiliation ambiguous. Not one of the three candidates could have won the presidency, but together they came close to denying Van Buren a majority vote. Their combined strength pulled many Whigs into office at the state level and laid the groundwork for an alternative to the Democrats in the South, an area that had been a solid pro-Jackson block until 1836. In the end, Van Buren had 170 electoral votes, while the other three received a total of 113.

Van Buren took office in March 1837, and a month later the panic hit. The new president called a special session of Congress to consider creating an independent treasury system to fulfill some of the functions of the defunct Bank of the United States. Such a treasury system, funded by the government's deposits, would deal only in hard money, and gold and silver would thus flow out of commercial banks, restricting their issuance of paper currency. Equally important, the new system would not make loans, thus avoiding the danger of speculative meddling in the economy. In short, an independent treasury system could exert a powerful moderating influence on inflation and the credit market without itself being directly involved in the market. But Van Buren encountered strong resistance in Congress to the independent treasury, even from Democrats. It finally won approval in 1840,

but by then Van Buren's chances of a second term in office were virtually at an end. The four years had proved to be tumultuous for the economy, with federal bank policy at a stalemate while twenty-six separate state legislatures battled over controversial bank regulation.

In 1840, the Whigs settled on William Henry Harrison, aged sixty-seven, as their single candidate to oppose Van Buren. The campaign drew on voter involvement as no other presidential campaign ever had. The Whigs took tricks out of the Democrats' book: Harrison was touted as a common man, born in a log cabin, although a Virginia plantation was the real site. His Indian-fighting days, now thirty years behind him, were played up to give him an aura like that of Jackson. Whigs staged festive rallies all over the country, drumming up mass appeal with candlelight parades and song shows. (One spirited campaign tune recited "Van, Van, Van's a used up man.") Women participated in campaign rallies as they never had before. Some 78 percent of eligible voters cast ballots—the highest percentage ever in American history. Even so, the campaign was not really close. Harrison took 53 percent of the popular vote and won a resounding 234 electoral college votes, to Van Buren's 60. A Democratic editor lamented, "We have taught them how to conquer us!"

Conclusion: Democrats and Whigs

From 1828 to 1840, the Democrats put together and then held together an unlikely, tenuous, but ultimately workable coalition of rural western farmers, urban laborers, pro–state bank commercial men, and wealthy southern slave owners. What united these groups was a common vision of an America where the highest value was placed on personal liberty, free competition, and egalitarian opportunity open to all white men. Jacksonian Democrats accepted drinking and tolerated Sabbath violations, preferring not to legislate morality. Democrats of the 1830s never debated the wisdom of slavery, if they could help it.

In contrast, the Whigs were the party of activist moralism and state-sponsored entrepreneurship. Wealthy northerners and merchants from Boston to Savannah, with their appreciation for institutions like the Bank of the United States and for legislated protective tariffs, tended to be Whigs. So did the evangelical middle classes, enthused with the hope that salvation could be brought within the reach of all. Personal liberty was a fine thing, Whigs thought, but it had to be tempered by responsibility, self-discipline, and internal controls, helped along by state-sponsored controls that, for example, prohibited liquor sales or stagecoach travel on Sundays. Abolitionists tended to vote for Whigs, even though most Whig politicians shied away from antislavery ideas.

National politics in the 1830s were more heated and divisive than at any time since the 1790s, when Federalists and Republicans had defined competing visions of government. The second party system of Democrats and Whigs cut far deeper into the electorate than had the first. Partly this was a function of technological changes that brought political information to the backwoods. More generally, the mass politicization reflected the involvement of voters in an expansive economy where they stood to

gain or lose, depending on the government's economic policy. Politics acquired immediacy and excitement, and four out of five white men cast a ballot in 1840.

Yet one of the deepest divisions in American society was almost completely ignored by the political parties of the 1830s, that of slavery. Indeed, the practice of coalition politics required that silence be maintained on this taboo subject, so that each party could build strength in the South. Whigs found this silence harder to maintain than Democrats, since their party contained wider divergence on the issue, stretching from ex-president John Quincy Adams, now sponsoring antislavery petitions from his Whig seat in the House of Representatives, to John C. Calhoun, nullifier, slaveholder, and Whig cabinet member in Harrison's new administration.

Slavery, however, was the defining difference in American social, economic, and political life in the nineteenth century. It could not be ignored for long by either Whigs or Democrats.

CHRONOLOGY

1807 Robert Fulton develops first commercially successful steamboat, the *Clermont.*

1810 In the case of *Fletcher v. Peck,* Supreme Court overturns a state law for first time.

1816 Second Bank of the United States chartered for twenty years.
Import tariff imposed on foreign cotton cloth.

1817 American Colonization Society founded to promote gradual emancipation and removal of African Americans to Liberia.

1818 National Road links Baltimore and Wheeling, West Virginia.
In *Dartmouth College v. Woodward,* Supreme Court overturns state action and reinstates Dartmouth College as private institution.

1819 Economic collapse and panic nationwide.

1824 Congress passes expanded tariff bill on variety of products—iron, glass, wool, and others.

1825 Erie Canal spans 350 miles in New York State.

1826 Schuylkill Canal—108 miles long—opens in Pennsylvania.

1828 Tariff of Abominations passed.
Andrew Jackson elected president.

1829 First railroad, Baltimore and Ohio, consists of thirteen miles of track.
David Walker's *Appeal* published.

1830 Indian Removal Act appropriates money to relocate Indian tribes west of Mississippi River.

1831 William Lloyd Garrison begins publishing abolitionist newspaper the *Liberator.*
Nat Turner's rebellion in Virginia.
Charles G. Finney stages revival in Rochester, New York.

1831	*Cherokee Nation v. Georgia* set aside by the Supreme Court, allowing Georgia to continue to subject Indians to state laws.	**1833**	Nullification crisis: South Carolina declares federal tariffs void in the state.
			New York and Philadelphia Anti-Slavery Societies founded.
1832	Supreme Court in *Worcester v. Georgia* recognizes Cherokee as distinct community outside legal jurisdiction of Georgia.	**1834, 1836**	Female mill workers strike in Lowell, Massachusetts.
		1836	Jackson issues Specie Circular.
	Jackson vetoes Bank of United States charter.		Martin Van Buren elected president.
		1837	Economic panic.
	New England Anti-Slavery Society founded.	**1838**	Trail of Tears—Cherokee forced to relocate west.
	Andrew Jackson reelected president.	**1840**	Independent Treasury Act.

BIBLIOGRAPHY

GENERAL WORKS

Jean H. Baker, *Affairs of Party: The Political Culture of Northern Democrats in the Mid-Nineteenth Century* (1983).

Michael F. Holt, *Political Parties and American Political Development from the Age of Jackson to the Age of Lincoln* (1992).

Richard P. McCormick, *The Second American Party System: Party Formation in the Jacksonian Era* (1966).

Merrill D. Peterson, *The Great Triumvirate: Webster, Clay, and Calhoun* (1987).

Charles G. Sellers, *The Market Revolution: Jacksonian American, 1815–1846* (1991).

Peter Temin, *The Jacksonian Economy* (1969).

Ronald Walters, *American Reformers, 1815–1860* (1978).

Harry L. Watson, *Liberty and Power: The Politics of Jacksonian America* (1990).

Robert H. Wiebe, *The Opening of American Society: From the Adoption of the Constitution to the Eve of Disunion* (1984).

THE MARKET REVOLUTION

Eugene Alvarez, *Travel on Southern Antebellum Railroads, 1828–1860* (1974).

Elizabeth Blackmar, *Manhattan for Rent, 1785–1850* (1989).

Mary H. Blewett, *Men, Women, and Work: Class, Gender, and Protest in the New England Shoe Industry, 1780–1910* (1988).

Jeanne Boydston, *Home and Work: Housework, Wages, and the Ideology of Labor in the Early Republic* (1990).

Stuart Bruchey, *The Roots of American Economic Growth, 1607–1861* (1965).

Christopher Clark, *The Roots of Rural Capitalism: Worcester, Massachusetts, 1780–1860* (1990).

Thomas C. Cochran, *Frontiers of Change: Early Industrialism in America* (1981).

Clarence H. Danhof, *Change in Agriculture: The Northern United States, 1820–1870* (1969).

Alan Dawley, *Class and Community: The Industrial Revolution in Lynn* (1976).

Thomas Dublin, *Women at Work: The Transformation of Work and Community in Lowell, Massachusetts, 1826–1860* (1979).

Thomas Dublin, *Transforming Women's Work: New England Lives in the Industrial Revolution* (1994).

Albert Fishlow, *American Railroads and the Transformation of the Ante-Bellum Economy* (1965).

Tony A. Freyer, *Producers versus Capitalists: Constitutional Conflict in Antebellum America* (1994).

Erik F. Haites, James Mak, and Gary M. Walton, *Western River Transportation: The Era of Early Internal Development, 1800–1860* (1975).

Bray Hammond, *Banks and Politics in America from the Revolution to the Civil War* (1957).

Brooke Hindle, *Emulation and Invention* (1981).

Morton J. Horwitz, *The Transformation of American Law, 1780–1860* (1977).

David J. Jeremy, *Transatlantic Industrial Revolution: The Diffusion of Textile Technologies between Britain and America, 1790–1830s* (1981).

Bruce Laurie, *Artisans into Workers: Labor in Nineteenth-Century America* (1989).

Otto Mayr and Robert C. Post, eds., *Yankee Enterprise: The Rise of the American System of Manufactures* (1981).

Judith A. McGaw, *Most Wonderful Machine: Mechanization and Social Change in Berkshire Paper Making, 1815–1885* (1987).

Richard B. Stott, *Workers in the Metropolis: Class, Ethnicity, and Youth in Antebellum New York City* (1990).

George R. Taylor, *The Transportation Revolution, 1815–1860* (1951).

Peter Temin, *The Jacksonian Economy* (1969).

Christopher L. Tomlins, *Law, Labor, and Ideology in the Early American Republic* (1993).

Barbara Tucker, *Samuel Slater and the Origins of the American Textile Industry, 1790–1860* (1984).

THE SPREAD OF DEMOCRACY

Ronald P. Formisano, *The Birth of Mass Political Parties: Michigan, 1827–1861* (1971).

Paul Goodman, *Towards a Christian Republic: Antimasonry and the Great Transition in New England, 1826–1836* (1988).

Daniel W. Howe, *The Political Culture of the American Whigs* (1980).

Lawrence Frederick Kohl, *The Politics of Individualism: Parties and the American Character in the Jacksonian Era* (1989).

Robert V. Remini, *The Election of Andrew Jackson* (1963).

Robert V. Remini, *Andrew Jackson and the Course of American Freedom, 1822–1832* (1981).

Alexander Saxton, *The Rise and Fall of the White Republic: Class Politics and Mass Culture in Nineteenth-Century America* (1990).

Sean Wilentz, *Chants Democratic: New York City and the Rise of the American Working Class, 1788–1850* (1984).

CULTURE AND SOCIETY

Gerald J. Baldasty, *The Commercialization of News in the Nineteenth Century* (1992).

Stuart M. Blumin, *The Emergence of the Middle Class: Social Experience in the American City, 1760–1900* (1989).

Richard L. Bushman, *The Refinement of America: Persons, Houses, Cities* (1992).

Kenneth Cmiel, *Democratic Eloquence: The Fight over Popular Speech in Nineteenth-Century America* (1990).

Daniel A. Cohen, *Pillars of Salt, Monuments of Grace: New England Crime Literature and the Origins of American Popular Culture, 1674–1860* (1993).

Faye E. Dudden, *Women in the American Theatre: Actresses and Audiences, 1790–1870* (1994).

Ann Fabian, *Card-Sharps, Dream Books, and Bucket Shops: Gambling in Nineteenth-Century America* (1990).

Timothy J. Gilfoyle, *City of Eros: New York City, Prostitution, and the Commercialization of Sex, 1790–1920* (1992).

Karen Halttunen, *Confidence Men and Painted Women: A Study of Middle-Class Culture in America, 1830–1870* (1982).

Carl F. Kaestle, *Pillars of the Republic: Common Schools and American Society, 1780–1860* (1983).

John F. Kasson, *Rudeness and Civility: Manners in Nineteenth-Century America* (1990).

Michael P. Kramer, *Imagining Language in America: From the Revolution to the Civil War* (1991).

Lawrence W. Levine, *Highbrow/Lowbrow: The Emergence of Cultural Hierarchy in America* (1988).

Lewis Perry, *Boats against the Current: American Culture between Revolution and Modernity, 1820–1860* (1993).

Ellen K. Rothman, *Hands and Hearts: A History of Courtship in America* (1984).

E. Anthony Rotundo, *American Manhood: Transformations in Masculinity from the Revolution to the Modern Era* (1993).

Mary P. Ryan, *Women in Public: Between Banners and Ballots, 1825–1880* (1990).

Michael Schudson, *Discovering the News: A Social History of American Newspapers* (1978).

Stanley K. Schultz, *The Culture Factory: Boston Public Schools, 1789–1860* (1973).

Carroll Smith-Rosenberg, *Disorderly Conduct: Visions of Gender in Victorian America* (1985).

Christine Stansell, *City of Women: Sex and Class in New York, 1789–1860* (1986).

Ronald J. Zboray, *A Fictive People: Antebellum Development and the American Reading Public* (1993).

REFORM AND RELIGION

Robert Abzug, *Passionate Liberator: Theodore Dwight Weld and the Dilemma of Reform* (1980).

Robert Abzug, *Cosmos Crumbling: American Reform and the Religious Imagination* (1994).

R. J. M. Blackett, *Building an Antislavery Wall: Black Americans in the Atlantic Abolitionist Movement, 1830–1860* (1983).

Lawrence J. Friedman, *Gregarious Saints: Self and Community in American Abolitionism, 1830–1870* (1982).

Lori D. Ginzberg, *Women and the Work of Benevolence: Morality, Politics, and Class in the Nineteenth-Century United States* (1990).

Nathan O. Hatch, *The Democratization of American Christianity* (1989).

Blanche Glassman Hersh, *The Slavery of Sex: Feminist-Abolitionists in America* (1978).

Nancy A. Hewitt, *Women's Activism and Social Change: Rochester, New York, 1822–1872* (1984).

Barbara Meil Hobson, *Uneasy Virtue: The Politics of Prostitution and the American Reform Tradition* (1987).

Donald M. Jacobs, ed., *Courage and Conscience: Black and White Abolitionists in Boston* (1993).

Paul Johnson, *A Shopkeeper's Millennium: Society and Revivals in Rochester, New York, 1815–1837* (1978).

Gerda Lerner, *The Grimké Sisters from South Carolina: Pioneers for Woman's Rights and Abolition* (1967).

Katharine Du Pré Lumpkin, *The Emancipation of Angelina Grimké* (1974).

Donald Mathews, *Religion in the Old South* (1977).

Keith Melder, *Beginnings of Sisterhood: The American Woman's Rights Movement, 1800–1850* (1977).

Lewis Perry and Michael Fellman, eds., *Anti-Slavery Reconsidered: New Perspectives on the Abolitionists* (1979).

Mary P. Ryan, *Cradle of the Middle Class: The Family in Oneida County, New York, 1790–1865* (1981).

Carroll Smith-Rosenberg, *Religion and the Rise of the American City: The New York City Mission Movement, 1812–1870* (1971).

Dorothy Sterling, *Ahead of Her Time: Abby Kelley and the Politics of Antislavery* (1991).

Ian Tyrrell, *Sobering Up: From Temperance to Prohibition in Antebellum America, 1800–1860* (1979).

Ronald Walters, *The Antislavery Appeal: Abolitionism after 1830* (1976).

Jean Fagan Yellin and John C. Van Horne, eds., *The Abolitionist Sisterhood: Women's Political Culture in Antebellum America* (1994).

JACKSONIAN POLITICS

Irving H. Bartlett, *John C. Calhoun: A Biography* (1993).

Donald B. Cole, *The Presidency of Andrew Jackson* (1993).

Richard E. Ellis, *The Union at Risk: Jacksonian Democracy, States' Rights, and the Nullification Crisis* (1987).

Daniel Feller, *The Public Lands in Jacksonian Politics* (1984).

William W. Freehling, *Prelude to Civil War: The Nullification Controversy in South Carolina, 1816–1836* (1965).

William W. Freehling, *The Road to Disunion: Secessionists at Bay, 1776–1854* (1990).

Peter B. Knupfer, *The Union As It Is: Constitutional Unionism and Sectional Compromise, 1787–1861* (1991).

Richard B. Latner, *The Presidency of Andrew Jackson: White House Politics, 1829–1837* (1979).

John M. McFaul, *The Politics of Jacksonian Finance* (1972).

John Niven, *Martin Van Buren: The Romantic Age of American Politics* (1983).

John Niven, *John C. Calhoun and the Price of Union: A Biography* (1988).

Robert V. Remini, *Henry Clay: Statesman for the Union* (1991).

Leonard Richards, *The Life and Times of Congressman John Quincy Adams* (1986).

Arthur M. Schlesinger Jr., *The Age of Jackson* (1945).

James Roger Sharp, *The Jacksonians versus the Banks: Politics in the States after the Panic of 1837* (1970).

Glyndon G. Van Deusen, *The Jacksonian Era, 1828–1848* (1959).

Major L. Wilson, *The Presidency of Martin Van Buren* (1984).

NATIVE AMERICANS

John A. Andrew, *From Revivals to Removal: Jeremiah Evarts, the Cherokee Nation, and the Search for the Soul of America* (1992).

John R. Finger, *The Eastern Band of Cherokees, 1819–1900* (1984).

William G. McLoughlin, *Cherokees and Missionaries, 1789–1839* (1984).

Theda Perdue, *The Cherokee* (1989).

Michael Paul Rogin, *Fathers and Children: Andrew Jackson and the Subjugation of the American Indian* (1975).

Anthony F. C. Wallace, *The Long, Bitter Trail: Andrew Jackson and the Indians* (1993).

Philip Weeks, *Farewell, My Nation: The American Indian and the United States, 1820–1890* (1990).

J. Leitch Wright, *The Only Land They Knew: The Tragic Story of the American Indians in the Old South* (1981).

GOURD FIDDLE

Found in St. Mary's County, Maryland, this slave-made gourd fiddle is an example of the many musical instruments that African Americans crafted and played throughout the South. Henry Wright, an ex-slave from Georgia, remembered: "I made a fiddle out of a large sized gourd — a long wooden handle was used as a neck, and the hair from a horse's tail was used for the bow. The strings were made of catgut." A hybrid of African and European elements, this fiddle offers material evidence of the cultural transformation of African slaves. While Africans lost much in their forced journey to the Americas, Africa remained in their cultural memory. Black men and women drew on the traditions of their homeland and the cultures they encountered as slaves in the South to create something new, an African American culture. Music, a crucial component of that sustaining culture, provided slaves with a creative outlet and relief from the rigors of slavery.

Smithsonian Institution/Aldo Tutino/Folio.

THE SLAVE SOUTH
1820–1860

12

I N 1822, IN THE BEAUTIFUL CITY OF CHARLESTON, SOUTH CAROLINA, with its white steeples, shaded gardens, and lovely mansions, a free black man named Denmark Vesey plotted a bloody slave rebellion. Until the year 1800, Vesey had been a slave, as were more than nine of every ten African Americans in the South. He had worked as a seaman in the Caribbean trade on the ship of his master, Captain Joseph Vesey.

In 1800, in Captain Vesey's home port of Charleston, Denmark Vesey won $1,500 in a lottery, bought his freedom, and set up a carpentry shop. Vesey prospered, and in time he owned a home on Bull Street and became a respected leader of the African Church of Charleston. But despite his own free status and considerable wealth, he continued to identify with the humiliation and oppression of slaves. At the age of fifty-five, he decided to take his people out of the land of bondage or die trying.

The historical evidence is too sparse to be entirely certain about what propelled Vesey down the path of revolution, but there are clues. A literate man, he regularly followed national politics through the pages of Charleston newspapers. In 1820, the papers bristled with news about the debate over slavery in Missouri, and the crisis convinced Vesey that whites were badly divided on the issue of human bondage. He was also acquainted with the Declaration of Independence, with its ringing assertions of the natural rights of freedom and equality. More specifically, he knew about the way those ideals had become a reality on the Caribbean island of Santo Domingo, where slaves had risen up, overthrown slavery, and established the black republic of Haiti in 1804.

Denmark Vesey was also an avid reader of the Bible. To him, the Scriptures proved that slavery was contrary to God's will. In 1821, moreover, Charleston's white authorities had closed Vesey's beloved church. Founded in 1818, when thousands of the city's black Methodists withdrew from the white-led Methodist Church, the African Church had provoked anxiety among whites who feared black independence. Finally, Vesey had a slave wife and children. Taken together, Vesey's beliefs and circumstances bred a discontent so powerful that he risked everything to bring slavery down.

He quietly began gathering his lieutenants. All were slaves, most belonged to the banned African Church, and some were African-born, as Vesey himself might have been. Gullah Jack Pritchard, an Angolan, was a conjurer, a sorcerer who drew upon African traditions and distributed crab claws he claimed would protect anyone who joined the insurrection. The conspirators' plan was evidently quite simple. At midnight on July 14, 1822, they would storm Charleston's arsenal, capture its weapons, kill any white who stood in their way, and set fire to the city. The flames would signal rebels in the countryside to rush in and complete the victory. Vesey may have planned to crowd as many slaves as he could on a ship and sail away to Haiti.

But the revolt never occurred. Before the conspiracy could become full-blown insurrection, it was betrayed by other blacks, both slave and free. The first arrests came in May. One arrest led to another as suspects, prodded by torture and the threat of death, implicated others. Shaken badly by the disclosures, whites feverishly tracked down every conspirator. After three months, the authorities had arrested 131 blacks. In the end, whites banished more than two dozen blacks from the state and executed 37 others, including Denmark Vesey.

The Vesey affair not only reveals the complex calculation of blacks about how best to defend themselves—join Vesey or betray him—but also illustrates the determination of whites to beat back any challenge to their supremacy. Slave revolts were whites' worst nightmare. The Vesey affair was doubly terrifying because it occurred in the wake of the Missouri controversy of 1819–1820, with its display of powerful antislavery, antisouthern political forces. By the 1820s, the northern states had either abolished slavery or put it on the road to extinction while the southern states aggressively built the largest slave society in the New World. The division of the nation generally coincided with the "Mason-Dixon line"—the line drawn in 1763 by the English surveyors Charles Mason and Jeremiah Dixon to decide the boundary between the bickering colonies of Maryland and Pennsylvania. A half century later, the English surveyors' mark divided the free North and slave South.

Black slavery dominated southern society and shaped the South into a distinctive region. Slavery molded the experiences of all of the region's inhabitants, those who had direct personal experience with slavery and those who did not. Still, the South was too vast and sprawling to form a solid block with a uniform viewpoint. Antebellum (pre–Civil War) Southerners included diverse peoples who at times found themselves at odds with one another —not only slaves and free people, but also women and men; Indians, Africans, and Europeans; aristocrats and common folk; merchants and mule drivers; and politicians and thinkers. Nevertheless, beneath this diversity of Southerners there was also "a South," with features that arose from slavery and that distinguished it from the North. Increasingly, a sectional self-consciousness spread among most white Southerners. The South was a slave society, and most white Southerners were proud of it.

In the decades after 1820, Southerners raced westward, spreading slavery, cotton, and plantations halfway to the Pacific. Geographic expansion meant that slavery became more vigorous and profitable than ever, embraced more people, and increased the South's political power. In the end, the South's identification with slavery and insistence on its preservation culminated in the creation of a separate Confederacy that ultimately brought about what Denmark Vesey had tried in vain to achieve in 1822: the end of slavery. Curiously, some of the white Charlestonians who witnessed Vesey's execution lived to see slavery's death in 1865. But from 1820 through 1860, most white Southerners simply assumed that slavery was a permanent and valuable feature of their society, as it had been for nearly two centuries before 1820. In their eyes, slavery made the South the South—and always would.

The Southern Difference

When the Frenchman Alexis de Tocqueville visited the United States in the early 1830s, he observed that the inhabitants "constitute a single people . . . more truly a united society than some nations of Europe which lived under the same legislation and the same prince." Tocqueville identified an important truth about the young nation. Southerners and Northerners were all Americans.

The Mason-Dixon line was a surveyor's mark on a map, not a physical barrier dividing North and South. No impenetrable jungle, insurmountable mountain range, or impassable desert separated the sections. From the earliest settlements, inhabitants of southern colonies had shared a great deal with northern colonists. Much of the white population of both sections was British in origin, although non-British Europeans migrated in large numbers to the colonies in the 1700s. Most settlers were Protestants. They spoke a common language,

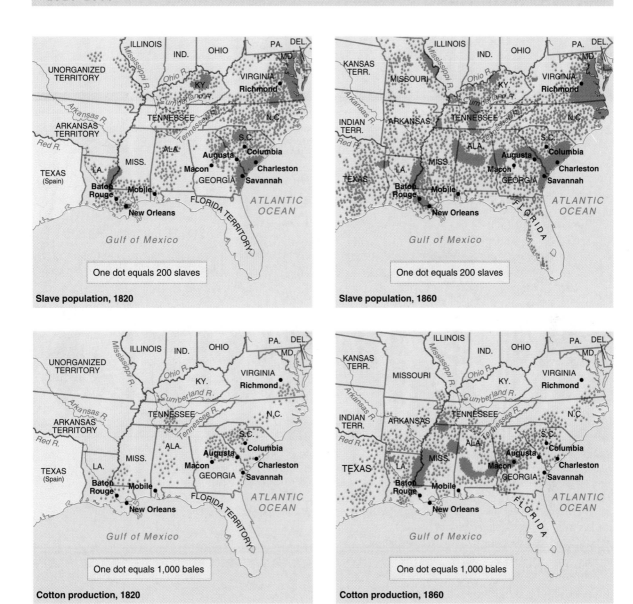

MAP 12.1
Cotton Kingdom, Slave Empire: 1820 and 1860
As the production of cotton soared, the slave population increased dramatically. Slaves continued to toil in tobacco and rice fields along the Atlantic seaboard, but increasingly they worked on cotton plantations in Alabama, Mississippi, and Louisiana.

even if a regional twang or drawl flavored their speech. They shared an exuberant pride in their victorious revolution against British rule. The creation of the new nation under the Constitution in 1789 forged strong political ties that bound all Americans. And by the mid-nineteenth century, an incip-

ient national economy was fostering economic interdependence and communication across sectional boundaries. White Americans everywhere celebrated the achievements of the prosperous, powerful young nation, and they looked forward to its seemingly boundless future.

SLAVE TRADERS: SOLD TO TENNESSEE
Slave trading, or "Negro speculation" as it was called by contemporaries, was a booming business in the antebellum South. This color drawing by Lewis Miller portrays slaves on their way from Virginia to Tennessee under the watchful eyes of professional slave traders. A few children accompany the adults, some of whom presumably are their parents, but forced migrations almost always resulted in separation of black families.
Abby Aldrich Rockefeller Folk Art Center, Williamsburg, Va.

Despite these national similarities, Southerners and Northerners were different. Tocqueville believed he knew why. "I could easily prove," he asserted in 1831, "that almost all the differences which may be noticed between the character of the Americans in the Southern and Northern states have originated in slavery." A quarter century later, most Americans agreed with the Frenchman. And neither Northerners nor Southerners liked what they saw on the other side of the Mason-Dixon line. "On the subject of slavery," the Charleston *Mercury* declared, "the North and South . . . are not only two Peoples, but they are rival, hostile Peoples." Slavery made the South different, and it was the differences between the sections, not the similarities, that came to shape antebellum American history.

Cotton Kingdom, Slave Empire

In the first half of the nineteenth century, legions of Northerners and Southerners migrated west, but the southern surge westward was propelled by an insatiable hunger for more and better cotton land. The stampede began in 1815, with the end of the War of 1812 against Great Britain and with the start of Indian removal east of the Mississippi River. Eager slaveholders seeking virgin acreage for new plantations, struggling yeomen looking for patches of good land for small farms, herders and drovers pushing their hogs and cattle toward fresh pastures —anyone who was restless and ambitious felt the pull. Southern farmers pushed into the territories of Alabama, Mississippi, Louisiana, Arkansas, and elsewhere, until by midcentury the South encompassed nearly a million square miles, much of it planted in cotton.

The South's climate and geography were ideally suited for the cultivation of cotton. That fact is remarkable because as Southerners advanced a thousand miles west from the Atlantic, they encountered a variety of terrain, soil, and weather. But the short-staple (or green-seed) cotton seeds they carried with them were very adaptable. They grew in the sandy plains of the tidewater, the red clay of the Piedmont, and especially the rich soils of the black belt (named for the dark color of the soil) and the alluvial deltas. Cotton requires two hundred frost-free days from planting to picking and prefers rains that are plentiful in spring and lighter in fall, conditions found in much of the South. In less than a half century, cotton fields stretched from southern Virginia to central Texas. Production soared, and by 1860 the South produced three-fourths of the world supply. The South—especially that tier of states from South Carolina west to Texas known as the lower South—had become the cotton kingdom.

The cotton kingdom was also a slave empire. The South's cotton boom rested on the backs of slaves, who grew 75 percent of the crop on plantations, toiling in gangs in broad fields under the direct supervision of whites. As cotton agriculture expanded westward, slavery's center of gravity shifted away from the old seaboard states. Hundreds of thousands of slaves were driven toward the Southwest. Some accompanied masters who were leaving behind worn-out, eroded plantations in the East. Most, however, were victims of a brutal but thriving domestic slave trade. Traders advertised for slaves who were "hearty and well made" and marched black men, women, and children hundreds of miles to the new plantation regions of the Lower South. Cotton, slaves, and plantations moved west together.

Slavery made the South different, and it was the differences between the sections, not the similarities, that came to shape antebellum American history.

The slave population also grew enormously. Southern slaves numbered fewer than 700,000 in 1790, about 2 million in 1830, and by 1860 about 4 million, an increase of almost 600 percent in seven decades. By 1860, slavery spread from Delaware to Texas and from Missouri to Florida. The South contained more slaves than all the other slave societies in the New World combined. The extraordinary growth was not the result of huge purchases in the international slave trade. The United States outlawed the importation of slaves in 1808. Afterward, only about 50,000 slaves were smuggled into the South illegally. The main reason for the growth in the slave population was natural reproduction. By the nineteenth century, most slaves were southern-born. They were black Southerners.

The South in Black and White

In 1860, the South contained 95 percent of the nation's African American population. One in every three Southerners was black (about 4 million blacks and 8 million whites). In the Lower South, the proportion was higher, for whites and blacks lived there in almost equal numbers. In Mississippi and South Carolina blacks were the majority. In certain areas within those two states—the sea islands of South Carolina and the plantation district surrounding Vicksburg, Mississippi—blacks constituted 90 percent of the population. The contrast with the North was striking. In 1860, only one Northerner in seventy-six was black (about 250,000 blacks to 19 million whites).

The presence of large numbers of African Americans had profound consequences for the South. Southern culture—language, food, music, religion, and even accents—was shaped by blacks. But the most direct consequence of the South's biracialism was the response it stimulated in the region's white majority. Southern whites were dedicated to white supremacy. Northern whites were, too, but they lived in a society in which blacks made up only 1 percent of the population. Their commitment to white supremacy lacked the intensity and urgency felt by white Southerners, who were preoccupied with racial hierarchy. After all, white Southerners lived among millions of blacks whom they simultaneously despised and feared. They despised blacks because they considered them members of an inferior race, further degraded by their status as slaves. They feared blacks because they realized that slaves had every reason to hate their oppressors and to seek to end their oppression, as Denmark Vesey had, by any means necessary.

Attacks on slavery—from blacks within and from abolitionists without—jolted southern slaveholders into a distressing awareness that they lived in a dangerous world. In response, in the 1820s and

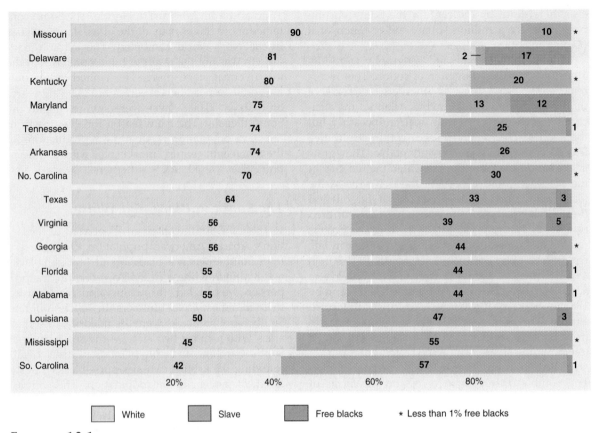

FIGURE 12.1
Proportion of Black and White Population in the South, 1860
Despite considerable variation from state to state, blacks represented a much larger fraction of the
population in the South than in the North.

1830s, southern leaders initiated fresh efforts to strengthen slavery and ward off threats. State legislatures constructed elaborate slave codes that required the total submission of slaves to their masters and to white society in general. As the Louisiana code stated, a slave "owes his master . . . a respect without bounds, and an absolute obedience." The laws underlined the authority of all whites, not just masters. Any white could stop a slave on a road and demand to see the slave's written permission to be away from his home. Any white could expect a slave to step aside to let him or her pass. Any white could "correct" slaves who did not stay "in their place" and show the proper deference.

Intellectuals joined legislators in the campaign to strengthen slavery. The South's academics, writers, and clergy constructed a proslavery argument that sought to unify the region's whites around slavery, smother any doubts that disturbed tender consciences, and provide ammunition for the emerging war of words with northern abolitionists. Under the intellectuals' tutelage, the white South gradually moved away from defending slavery as a "necessary evil"—the halfhearted argument popular in Jefferson's day—and toward a full-throated, aggressive defense of slavery as a "positive good."

The presence of large numbers of African Americans had profound consequences for the South. Southern culture—language, food, music, religion, and even accents—was shaped by blacks.

Slavery's champions employed every imaginable defense. The law protected slavery, they observed, for slaves were legal property. And wasn't the security of property the bedrock of American

ATTENTION PAID A POOR SICK WHITE MAN.

ATTENTION PAID A POOR SICK NEGRO.

PROSLAVERY WOODCUTS

As antislavery critics accelerated their verbal attacks, white Southerners fought back. These 1853 woodcuts contrast the callousness of free labor with the benefits of slavery. The message was clear: While free laborers ("wage slaves") were carted directly from the factory to the poorhouse, aged and infirm slaves were made comfortable by their masters and mistresses. Proslavery polemicists asked: Which society was brutally exploitative and which cared for its laborers from cradle to grave?

Josiah Priest's *In Defense of Slavery*, Rare Book and Manuscript Department, Boston Public Library.

liberty? History also endorsed slavery. Weren't the great civilizations—those of the Hebrews, Greeks, and Romans—slave societies? In addition, the Bible, properly interpreted, sanctioned slavery. Didn't the Old Testament patriarchs own slaves? Didn't Paul in the New Testament return the runaway slave Onesimus to his master? Some proslavery spokesmen went on the offensive and attacked the economy and society of the North. The Virginian George Fitzhugh argued that behind the North's grand slogans—individualism and egalitarianism—lay a heartless philosophy: "Every man for himself, and the devil take the hindmost." Gouging capitalists exploited wage workers unmercifully, Fitzhugh said, and he contrasted the vicious capitalist-laborer relationship with the humane relations he believed prevailed between masters and slaves because slaves were valuable capital that masters sought to protect.

Since slavery was a condition Southerners reserved exclusively for African Americans, at bottom the white defense of slavery rested on claims of black inferiority. Black enslavement was both necessary and proper, defenders argued, because Africans were inferior beings. Rather than exploitative, slavery was a mass civilizing effort that lifted lowly blacks from barbarism and savagery, taught them disciplined work, and converted them to soul-saving Christianity. According to Virginian Thomas R. Dew, "the slaves of a good master are his warmest, most constant, and most devoted friends." Freeing blacks, the Charleston *Mercury* declared, would mean their destruction, as well as the destruction of southern "civilization, society, and government."

Black slavery encouraged whites to unify around race rather than to divide by class. The South Carolinian James H. Hammond argued that every society had its "mudsill" class, the poor, degraded workers who did the dirty work. Black slaves filled that niche in the South, and every white man stood above them looking down. The grubbiest, most tobacco-stained white man could proudly proclaim his superiority to blacks and his equality with the most refined southern patrician. Because slaves were not recognized as citizens in the South, Georgia attorney Thomas R. R. Cobb observed, everyone who was a citizen "feels that he belongs to an elevated class. It matters not that he is no slaveholder; he is not of the inferior race; he is a freeborn citizen." Consequently, the "poorest meets the richest as an equal; sits at his table with him; salutes him as a neighbor; meets him in every pub-

lic assembly, and stands on the same social platform." In the South, Cobb boasted, "there is no war of classes."

In reality, slavery did not create perfect harmony among whites or ease every strain along class lines. But by providing every white symbolic membership in the ruling class, racial slavery helped whites bridge differences in class, wealth, education, and culture. Slavery meant white dominance, white superiority, and white equality. Slaveless whites united with slave masters in opposition to black freedom and equality.

The Plantation Economy

Race was important in unifying white Southerners because most whites did not own slaves. The majority of the South's whites worked small farms with just the help of family members. Only about one-quarter of the white population lived in families that owned slaves. A majority of masters owned fewer than five. Small slaveholders often worked their fields shoulder to shoulder with their sons and their slaves. About 12 percent of the slave owners (about 46,000 individuals) owned twenty or more slaves, the number historians consider necessary to distinguish a planter from a farmer. Fewer than 1 percent of slaveholders (about 2,300) owned one hundred or more slaves and thus could be considered "great planters." Wade Hampton III was one of the greatest. In the 1850s, he held about three thousand slaves on plantations in South Carolina and Mississippi. Although greatly outnumbered by nonslaveholders and small slaveholders, planters dominated the southern economy. A majority (52 percent) of the South's slaves lived and worked on plantations. Plantation slaves produced more than 75 percent of the South's export crops, the backbone of the region's economy.

The majority of the South's whites worked small farms with just the help of family members. Only about one-quarter of the white population lived in families that owned slaves.

Patterns of plantation slavery established along the Atlantic seaboard persisted as Southerners raced westward in the nineteenth century. A new crop, new climates and soils, new and more primitive

TECHNOLOGY IN AMERICA
The Cotton Gin

By the 1790s, the English had succeeded in mechanizing the manufacture of cotton cloth, but they were unable to get enough raw cotton. The South could grow cotton in unimaginable quantities, but cotton that was stuck to seeds was useless in English textile mills. In 1793, Eli Whitney, a Northerner who was serving as a tutor on a Savannah River plantation, built a simple little device for separating the cotton from the seed — just wire teeth set in a wooden cylinder that, when rotated, reached through narrow slats to pull cotton fibers away from seeds, while the brush swept the fibers from the revolving teeth. Widespread use of the cotton gin (the word *gin* is simply short for *engine*) broke the bottleneck in the commercial production of cotton and eventually bound millions of African Americans to slavery.

Smithsonian Institution.

---

frontier conditions did not sever the South's deeply rooted connection with plantation slavery. Indeed, fresh land reinvigorated plantation slavery by providing an escape hatch for slaveholders in the Southeast who limped along on exhausted acreage and by creating a vigorous market for the East's surplus slaves. Although slavery was slowly dying elsewhere in the New World, slave plantations increased their domination of southern agriculture with each antebellum decade. And agriculture, in turn, remained the central feature of the southern economy.

Staple Agriculture

The dominant crops of southern agriculture were the five major staples grown on plantations: tobacco, hemp, sugar, rice, and cotton. All plantations had similar features, but they differed depending on the staple crop they produced.

Tobacco was the original plantation crop in North America. By the nineteenth century, however, most planters around the Chesapeake had shifted to wheat and other crops, and tobacco had moved to western Virginia and to Tennessee and Kentucky. Samuel Hairston, a Virginia tobacco planter, owned at midcentury fifteen hundred slaves and was worth more than $3 million. Work in the tobacco fields was labor-intensive. Most phases of the process—planting, transplanting, thinning, picking off caterpillars, cutting, drying, packing—required field hands to stoop or bend down in painful labor over the tobacco plants.

Hemp, grown to make into bale rope and bagging for cotton, was the least important plantation crop and was found only in portions of Kentucky, Tennessee, and Missouri. Planters hoped to produce rope that was acceptable to the American navy, but American hemp was really not competitive in price or quality with imported hemp. It survived only because a steep tariff protected it from foreign competition. The American navy, which wanted the best, bought its rope abroad.

Large-scale sugar production began in 1795, when Étienne de Boré built a modern sugar mill in what is today New Orleans. Like hemp, sugar owed its existence to a tariff. Without protection, American sugar would have been driven from the market by cheaper sugar from tropical Latin America, especially Cuba. Labor on sugarcane plantations was reputed to be the most physically demanding in the antebellum South. Masters elsewhere would attempt to frighten obstinate slaves with the threat of selling them "down the river"—down the Mississippi River to sugar planters. During the fall, slaves worked eighteen hours a day to cut the cane and haul it to the sugar mill, where they would grind and boil it. Sugar plantations, which were confined almost entirely to Louisiana, required large sums for expensive refining equipment to turn cane juice into sugar and for large gangs of slaves. Magnolia Plantation in Plaquemines Parish contained 2,200

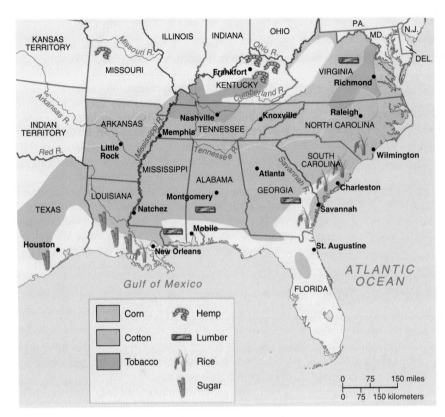

MAP 12.2
The Agricultural Economy of the South, 1860
Cotton dominated the South's agricultural economy, but the region grew a diversity of crops and was largely self-sufficient in foodstuffs.

acres and in 1861 produced sugar valued at nearly $150,000. Southerners understood the truth in the adage that "a man has to be a rich cotton planter before he can start as a poor sugar planter."

Commercial rice production began in seventeenth-century South Carolina. Like sugar, rice was confined to a small geographical area, a narrow strip of the tidewater stretching from the Carolinas into northern Georgia. Because of the need for canals, dikes, and gates to flood rice fields with water and then drain them and to protect the ripening plant from salt water, rice planting was an expensive undertaking. Like sugar planters, rice planters were one of the wealthiest groups in America. When rice planter Nathaniel Heyward died in 1851, he left two thousand slaves and five thousand acres of prime rice land, worth a total of more than $2 million. Since rice plantations required huge numbers of slaves, blacks accounted for 90 percent of the population in the coastal rice districts. For slaves, rice meant danger and extreme discomfort. Working in water and mud in the heat of a Carolina summer regularly threatened slaves with malaria, yellow fever, and other diseases.

If tobacco, hemp, sugar, and rice were princes of plantation agriculture, cotton was king. Cotton became commercially significant after the invention of the cotton gin by Eli Whitney in 1793. By the early years of the nineteenth century, cotton had displaced tobacco and had begun to dominate the southern economy. The white fluffy stuff was grown almost everywhere in the South and by almost everyone, small farmer and planter alike. It was relatively easy to grow and took little capital to get started—just enough for land, seed, and simple tools. Nonetheless, plantations produced three-quarters of the South's cotton, and planters received a disproportionate slice of the region's income. While hardscrabble farmer Jessup Snopes grew half a bale, Mississippian Frederick Stanton, who owned more than fifteen thousand prime acres, produced 3,054 bales of cotton worth $122,000 in 1859. With a record-breaking crop of 4,861,000 bales in 1859, the South's planters were, as they liked to put it, in "high cotton."

Plantations grew more than staples. Even the largest, most commercial plantations usually produced enough corn, beans, sweet potatoes, and pork to become self-sufficient in food. Two crops—cotton and corn—dovetailed particularly well. The amount of labor required to cultivate cotton varied with the growing season. In late summer, just when the pace slackened in the cotton fields, when the slaves had finished the last plowing, corn demanded their attention. In the fall, when every hand was needed to pick cotton, corn was usually already harvested. Because cultivating corn did not take time away from cultivating cotton, slaves were able to grow their own food (at almost no additional cost to the planter) and at the same time produce the South's major cash crop. Corn fed not only the slaves and the millions of white farmers who grew it, but also the South's livestock. The livestock industry was no minor affair. In 1860, the value of the animals (particularly hogs) butchered in the South exceeded that in the North.

Economic Vulnerability

Northerners claimed that slavery was a backward, inefficient form of labor, one that had been superseded by the more modern, more productive freelabor system. A whip could not stimulate continuous hard work the way individual self-interest did, economists argued. When Northerners cast their eyes southward, they seemed to find evidence that confirmed their theory. By standards that equated economic progress with diversification, industrialization, and urbanization, the Old South's economy was backward.

Judged by other criteria, however, it was productive and profitable. For those who owned slaves, slavery paid off handsomely. The rate of return for investments in cotton plantations was about 8 percent annually, a profit equal to that in most other businesses in which planters could have invested. The South was fortunate to have nearly a monopoly on the hottest commodity in the international marketplace. Because the world demand for cotton increased about 5 percent annually between 1820 and 1860, the South could extend the cotton kingdom westward a thousand miles and vastly increase production, without (in most years) glutting the market and driving down cotton prices. Not only did planters earn money from the sale of cotton and other staple crops, but they also gained from the rising values of land and slaves, from the hiring out of slaves, and, most important, from the birth of

COTTON LEVEE, NEW ORLEANS
This 1860 view of the New Orleans levee attempts to capture the magnitude of the cotton trade in the South's largest city and major port. Twelve years earlier, visitor Solon Robinson expressed his awe in words: "It must be seen to be believed; and even then, it will require an active mind to comprehend acres of cotton bales standing upon the levee, while miles of drays [carts] are constantly taking it off to the cotton presses. . . . Boats are constantly arriving, so piled up with cotton, that the lower tier of bales on deck are in the water." Amidst the mountains of cotton and forests of smokestacks, few doubted that cotton was king.
Chicago Historical Society.

slave children. Slaves were a rare kind of capital that reproduced itself. Judged by the size of planters' profits, then, the plantation economy flourished in the Old South.

Plantation slavery also benefited the national economy. Throughout the antebellum years, the products of southern plantations made up the greatest part of America's exports. By 1840, cotton alone accounted for more than 60 percent of the nation's sales abroad. Much of the profit from sales of cotton overseas returned to planters, but some did not. Cotton had to be bought, sold, insured, warehoused, and shipped before it reached the mills in Great Britain and elsewhere. Increasingly, these services were in the hands of northern middlemen, each of whom made a profit from slave-grown southern crops. As these profits were invested in the burgeoning northern economy, industrial development there received much-needed capital. Furthermore, planters provided an important market for northern textiles, shoes, agricultural tools, and other manufactured goods. Without cotton, one economist has estimated, American industrial development would have been retarded a generation.

In part because of the vitality of plantation agriculture, the economies of North and South steadily diverged. While the North developed a mixed economy—agriculture, commerce, and manufacturing—the South remained overwhelmingly agricultural. Since planters were earning healthy profits, they saw little reason to diversify. Moreover, economic change could conceivably threaten plantation slavery, the key to the social and economic order that planters dominated. Planters knew that if southern economic development followed the path blazed by the North, then manufacturing in the South would mean the rise of an urban, industrial working class without direct ties to slavery and the plantation. Would city-living factory workers accept rural planter rule and give their hearty support to slavery, or would they favor free labor, as northern workers did? Planters did not want to find out. Year after year, they funneled the profits they earned from land and slaves back into more land and slaves.

With its capital flowing into agriculture, the Old South did not develop many factories. By 1860, only 10 percent of the nation's industrial workers were in the South. Overwhelmingly, Southerners worked the land, where they produced 100 percent of the country's sugar, rice, and cotton, about 90 percent of the hemp and tobacco, and significant fractions of the nation's food crops and livestock. By 1860,

Indiana and Illinois—two midwestern states known for agriculture—had more capital invested in industry than the seven Lower South states, including Louisiana with its sugar mills.

The South was not entirely without factories, of course. They usually processed agricultural products and raw materials produced in the region. In terms of the value of the products, flour and corn milling were the most important southern manufacturing activities. Lumbering employed the most manufacturing workers. In the Upper South (that tier of slave states north and west of North Carolina), the manufacture of tobacco products grew in importance. By 1860, more than ten thousand workers in Richmond, Virginia, made snuff, cigars, and plugs of chewing tobacco. Cotton mills developed where there were cotton, water power, and cheap labor. The most famous was William Gregg's South Carolina factory, which employed three hundred workers, mostly white women and children. Still, in 1860 the region that produced 100 percent of the nation's cotton manufactured less than 7 percent of its cotton textiles.

Without significant economic diversification, the South developed fewer cities than the North. In 1860, it was the least urban region in the country. While nearly 37 percent of New England's population lived in towns, less than 12 percent of Southerners were urban dwellers. That figure would have been dramatically smaller without Maryland's 34 percent urban population (because of Baltimore) and Louisiana's 26 percent (because of New Orleans). In fact, nine southern states had 5 percent or fewer of their people in towns. Only one town in Arkansas numbered more than 2,500; rural Iowa had nine that large.

Not only were cities less common in the South, but they were also different from those in the North. They were mostly port cities on the periphery of the region and busy principally with exporting the agricultural products of plantations in the interior. The region's energetic, enterprising urban merchants provided agriculture with indispensable economic services, such as hauling, insuring, and selling the South's cotton, rice, and sugar. But as the tail of the plantation dog, southern cities did not become significant manufacturing centers or important independent centers of social and economic innovation.

Because the South had so few cities and industrial jobs, it attracted relatively small numbers of European immigrants. Seeking economic opportunity, not competition with slaves, immigrants steered well north of the South's slave-dominated, agricul-

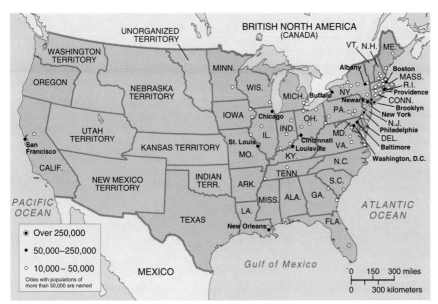

M A P 12.3
Major Cities in 1860
By 1860, northern cities were both more numerous and larger than southern cities. In the slave states, cities were usually seaports or river ports that served the needs of agriculture, especially cotton.

tural economy. Thus in 1860, more than 3,580,000 people of foreign birth lived in the nonslave states, whereas only a little more than 550,000 lived in the slave states. Nationally, 13 percent of Americans were foreign-born. But in nine of the fifteen slave states, only 2 percent or fewer were born abroad. Immigrants who did venture below the Mason-Dixon line concentrated in cities, as they did in the North. In 1850, more than one-fifth of the inhabitants of Charleston and more than one-third of those of Mobile, Alabama, were foreign-born. But nearly nine of every ten Southerners lived in rural areas, and there foreign-born whites remained rare.

Not every Southerner celebrated the region's plantation economy. Critics railed against the excessive commitment to cotton and slaves and bemoaned the "deplorable scarcity" of factories. In his widely circulated journal *De Bow's Review*, James D. B. De Bow of New Orleans challenged southern farmers to produce more grain crops and livestock and implored southern manufacturers to make more of nearly everything. Reformers complained that Southerners were rocked in cradles manufactured in the North, were dressed in northern-made clothes, used northern plows and agricultural tools, and were buried in northern coffins. Diversification, they promised, would make the South not only economically independent but more prosperous and healthy as well.

Economic reformers attracted some attention, especially when profits in the plantation economy sagged, as they did when cotton prices temporarily

fell following the panics of 1819 and 1837. State governments encouraged economic development by helping to create banking systems that supplied credit for a wide range of projects, industrial as well as agricultural. State and local governments joined private investors in building an extensive railroad network. Alabama constructed its first railroad in 1830, just five years after the first modern railroad in the world was constructed in England and only three years after the inauguration of the first railroad in America. Thirty years later, 9,280 miles of track spanned the South.

But encouragement of a diversified economy had clear limits. State governments failed to create some of the essential services modern economies require. By midcentury, for example, no southern legislature had created a statewide public school system. Consequently, the South's illiteracy rate for whites topped 20 percent. Dominant slaveholders failed to see any benefit in educating the region's labor force. Railroads also illustrate the limits of the South's commitment to modernization. Despite the flurry of railroad building, the South's mileage in 1860 was less than half that of the North. Moreover, northern railroads crisscrossed the region connecting towns and cities and carrying manufactured goods as well as agricultural products. In the South, most rail lines ran from port cities back into farming areas and were built to export staple crops.

Northerners claimed that slavery was outmoded and doomed, but few Southerners perceived economic weakness in their region. Indeed, the planters' pockets were never fuller than at the end of the antebellum period. But planters' individual profits did not automatically translate into long-term regional economic health. When the South bet on plantation agriculture, especially cotton, it not only committed itself to slavery but also left itself vulnerable to the fickle world market. The super-heated international demand for cotton would not last forever. Compared with antebellum Northern-ers, Southerners committed less of their capital to investment in industry, transportation, and public education. Planters' decisions to reinvest in staple agriculture ensured the continuity and inertia of the plantation economy and the social and political re-lationships that were rooted in it.

Masters, Mistresses, and the Big House

Nowhere was the contrast between northern and southern life more vivid than in the plantations of the South. Located on a patchwork of cleared fields and dense forests, a plantation typically included a "big house" and slave quarters. Scattered about were numerous outbuildings, each with a special function. Near the big house were the kitchen, store-house, smokehouse (for curing and preserving meat), and hen coop. More distant were the stables, barns, toolsheds, artisans' workshops, and over-seer's house. Large plantations sometimes had sep-arate buildings for an infirmary, nursery, and chapel for the slaves. Depending on the crop, there was a tobacco shed, a rice mill, a sugar refinery, or a cot-ton gin house. Lavish or plain, plantations every-where had an underlying similarity.

The plantation was the home of masters, mis-tresses, and slaves. Slavery shaped the lives of all the plantation's inhabitants but affected each dif-ferently. Relationships were governed by a hierar-chy of rigid roles and duties. Presiding was the mas-ter, who according to both law and convention ruled his wife, children, and slaves, none of whom had many legal rights and all of whom were designated by the state as dependents under his dominion and protection.

Plantation Masters

Because planters lived off the toil of their slaves, it is not surprising that masters devoted considerable energy to plantation management. Plantations were

FIGURE 12.2
A Southern Plantation
Slavery determined how masters laid out their planta-tions, where they situated their mansions and the quar-ters, and what kinds of buildings they constructed.

Adapted from *Back of the Big House: The Architecture of Plantation Slavery* by John Michael Vlach. Copyright © 1993 by the University of North Carolina Press. Original illustration property of the Historic American Buildings Survey, a division of the National Park Service.

usually organized quite simply. Smaller planters su-pervised the labor of their slaves themselves. Larger planters usually hired an overseer. Overseers were either ambitious young white men—perhaps rela-tives of the planter or poor men from the neigh-borhood—or professionals who made a career of supervising slaves. Because overseers went to the fields with the slaves, planters could limit themselves to only occasional inspections and concentrated instead on marketing, finance, and general plantation affairs.

The plantation was the home of masters, mistresses, and slaves. Presiding was the master, who according to both law and convention ruled his wife, children, and slaves.

Increasingly in the nineteenth century, planters characterized the master-slave relationship in terms of what historians have called "paternalism." The concept of paternalism denied that the form of slavery practiced in the South was brutal and exploitative. Instead, it defined slavery as a set of reciprocal obligations between masters and slaves. In exchange for the slaves' labor and obedience, masters provided slaves with basic care and necessary guidance. To northern claims that they were tyrants and exploiters, slaveholders responded that they were stewards and guardians. As owners of blacks, masters argued, they had the heavy responsibility of caring for a childlike, dependent people. If slav-

ery was a burden, they said, whites shouldered it, not blacks. In 1814, Thomas Jefferson captured the essence of the. ideal: "We should endeavor, with those whom fortune has thrown on our hands, to feed & clothe them well, protect them from ill usage, require such reasonable labor only as is performed voluntarily by freemen, and be led by no repugnancies to abdicate them, and our duties to them."

Paternalism was part propaganda and part self-delusion. But it was more. Indeed, there was some truth in the assertion that master-slave relationships in the South were unique. Unlike planters elsewhere in the New World, southern planters usually owned a single plantation, on which they lived. Absentee owners were not unknown, but most planters lived year-round where their slaves worked, which meant that slave management was an everyday affair and the relationship between master and slave was face to face, direct, and personal. In addition, slavery in the South reached its prime in the nineteenth century, after the nation had closed its external slave trade in 1808. Masters realized that the expansion of the slave labor force could come only from natural reproduction. Thus, masters had to provide slaves with a certain minimum level of physical welfare if they wanted more slaves, and they certainly did want more slaves.

SOUTHERN MAN WITH CHILDREN AND THEIR MAMMY *Obviously prosperous and projecting the aura of a man accustomed to giving orders and to being obeyed, this patriarch poses around 1848 with his young daughters and their nurse for a family portrait. The absent mother may have been dead, which might in part explain the inclusion of the slave woman in the family circle. But her presence also confirms her importance in the household. Fathers devoted little attention to domestic matters and left the raising of children to mothers and nurses. However important, the black woman is clearly a servant, a status indicated by both her race and her attire.* Collection of the J. Paul Getty Museum, Malibu, Calif.

How Often Were Slaves Whipped?

As IMPORTANT AS THIS QUESTION IS to historians (and obviously was to slaves), we have very little reliable evidence on the frequency of whipping. We know from white sources that whipping was the prescribed method of physical punishment on most antebellum plantations. Masters' instructions to overseers authorized whippings and often set limits on the number of strokes an overseer could administer. Some planters allowed fifteen lashes, some fifty, and some one hundred. But slave owners' instructions, as revealing as they are, tell us more about the severity of beatings than their frequency.

Remembrances of former slaves confirm that whipping was widespread and frequent. In the 1930s, more than 2,300 African Americans were interviewed about their experiences as slaves. Their accounts offered grisly evidence of the cruelty of slavery. "You say how did our Master treat his slaves?" asked one woman. "Scandalous, they treated them just like dogs." She was herself whipped "till the blood dripped to the ground." A few slaves remembered kind masters and never personally felt the sting of the lash. Bert Strong was one such slave, but he also recalled hearing slaves on other farms "hollering when they get beat." He said, "They beat them till it a pity." Beatings occurred often, but how often?

A remarkably systematic record of whippings over a sustained period of time comes from the diary of Bennet H. Barrow, the master of Highland plantation in West Feliciana Parish, Louisiana. For a twenty-three-month period in 1840–1841, Barrow meticulously recorded every whipping he administered or ordered. On most large plantations, overseers handled the business of day-to-day management, but in 1838, Barrow concluded that overseers were "good for nothing" and "a perfect nuisance." He dismissed his white overseer and, assisted only by a black driver, began managing his own plantation.

What does the Barrow evidence show? In 1840, according to the federal census, Barrow owned 129 slaves. In the twenty-three-month period, Barrow recorded 160 whippings. That means that, on the average, a slave was whipped every four and one-half days. Sixty of the 77 slaves who worked in the fields were whipped at least once. Most of the 17 field slaves who escaped being beaten were children and pregnant women. Eighty percent of male cotton pickers and 70 percent of the female cotton pickers were whipped at least once in this period. Dave Barley received eight floggings, more than any other Barrow slave, and Patience received six whippings, more than any other female slave.

In most instances, Barrow recorded not only the fact of a whipping but also its cause. All sorts of "misconduct," "rascality," and "disorderly acts" made Barrow reach for his whip. The provocations included family quarrels in the slave quarters, impudence, running away, and failure to keep curfew. But nearly 80 percent of the acts recorded related to poor work. Barrow gave beatings for "not picking as well as he can," for picking "very trashy cotton," and for failing to pick the prescribed weight of cotton. One slave claimed to have lost his eyesight and for months refused to work until Barrow "gave him 25 cuts yesterday morning & ordered him to work Blind or not."

Whippings should not be mistaken for spankings. Some planters used whips that raised welts, caused blisters, and bruised. Others resorted to rawhide and cowhide whips that broke the skin, caused scarring, and sometimes permanently maimed. Occasionally, slaves were beaten to death. Whipping was not Barrow's only means of inflicting pain. He was inventive. His diary mentions confining slaves to a plantation jail, putting them in chains, shooting them, breaking a "sword cane" over one slave's head, having slaves mauled by dogs, placing them in stocks, "staking down" slaves for hours, "hand sawing" them, holding their heads under water, and a variety of punishments intending to ridicule and to shame, including making men wear women's clothing and do "women's work," such as the laundry. Still, Barrow's preferred instrument of punishment was the whip.

GORDON

This photograph of Gordon, a runaway slave from Baton Rouge, Louisiana, was taken on April 2, 1863, and sent home from the Civil War by Frederick W. Mercer, an assistant surgeon with the Forty-seventh Massachusetts Regiment. Mercer examined four hundred other runaways and found many "to be as badly lacerated." Masters claimed that they whipped only when they had to and only as hard as they had to, but slave testimony and photographic evidence refute their defense of slavery as a benign institution. Courtesy of the Massachusetts Historical Society.

On the Barrow plantation, as on many others, whipping was public. Victims were often tied to a stake in the quarters, and the other slaves were made to watch. In a real sense the entire slave population on the plantation experienced a whipping every four and one-half days. Even though some never felt the lash personally, all were familiar with its terror and agony.

Was whipping effective? Did it produce a hardworking, efficient, and conscientious labor force? Not according to Barrow's own record. No evidence indicates that whipping changed the slaves' behavior. What Barrow considered bad work continued. Unabated whipping is itself evidence of the failure of punishment to achieve the master's will. Slaves knew the rules. Yet they continued to act "badly." And they continued to suffer. It was a gruesome drama—the master seeking from his slaves hard labor and slaves denying their master what he most wanted—day after day.

Did Barrow whip with the same frequency as other planters? We simply do not know. Because of the lack of quantifiable evidence, we will never know precisely how often whippings occurred. We do know that Barrow did not consider himself a cruel man. He bitterly denounced his neighbor as "the most cruel Master i ever knew of" for castrating three of his slaves. Moreover, Barrow had dispensed with the overseers in part because of their "brutal feelings" toward slaves. Like most whites, he believed that the lash was essential to get work done. He used it no more than he believed necessary.

Most masters, including Barrow, tried to encourage work with promises of small gifts and brief holidays, but punishment was their most important motivator. We will never know if the typical slave was beaten once a year as on the Barrow plantation, but the admittedly scanty evidence suggests that on large plantations the whip fell on someone's back every few days.

And former slaves remembered. More than half a century after emancipation, their sharpest recollections usually involved punishment. They remembered the pain, the injustice, and their bitter resentment. They evaluated their former masters according to how frequently they reached for the whip. According to one former slave, "some was good and some was bad, and about the most of them was bad."

One consequence was a relative improvement in slaves' material welfare. The nineteenth-century slaves' diet still consisted mainly of fatty pork and cornmeal. The cabins still had cracks large enough, slaves said, for cats to slip through. Slaves' clothing seldom amounted to much more than two crude outfits a year. Nevertheless, conditions in the quarters got better. In the fields, workdays remained sunup to sundown, but planters often provided a rest period in the heat of the day. And most owners ceased the eighteenth-century practices of punishing slaves by branding, castrating, and other forms of mutilation.

Paternalism should not be mistaken for "Ol' Massa's" kindness and goodwill. It had nothing to do with gentleness and niceness. It encouraged better treatment, but it was essentially self-interested and self-serving. Planters who accepted paternalism (and not all did) certainly did not suffer financially. Paternalism and profits went hand in hand. It made economic sense to provide at least minimal care for scarce and valuable slaves. Nor did paternalism require that planters put aside their whips. They could lay on the leather and claim that they were only fulfilling their responsibilities as guardians of their childlike, yet at times insubordinate, dependents. Paternalism gave slaves some protection against the most brutal punishments, but whipping remained the planters' essential coercion. (See Historical Question, page 444.)

Southern planters took plantation management seriously, but they did not tend to business all the time. Quite often they escaped to town to discuss the weather, to the courthouse and legislature to debate politics, and to the woods to hunt and fish. Planters had reputations as accomplished drinkers and gamblers. They enjoyed horse racing and cockfighting. Southern boys were expected to master the "manly" arts.

The Virginian Edmund Randolph argued that slavery created in white southern men a "quick and acute sense of personal liberty" and a "disdain for every abridgement of personal independence." Indeed, prickly individualism and aggressive independence became crucial features of the southern concept of honor. Social standing, political advancement, and even self-esteem rested on a reputation of honor. Defending honor became a male passion. Andrew Jackson's mother reportedly told her son, "Never tell a lie, nor take what is not your own, nor sue anybody for slander or assault and battery. *Always settle them cases yourself.*" Among planters, such advice sometimes led to duels. Dueling arrived from Europe in the eighteenth century. It died out in the North, but in the South, even after legislatures banned it, gentlemen continued to defend their honor with pistols at ten paces. Honor was a tender thing, and duels were fought by Andrew Jackson, whose wife one foolish man slandered, as well as by two college students who happened at dinner to reach simultaneously for the last piece of trout.

Southerners also expected an honorable gentleman to be a proper patriarch. Nowhere in America was patriarchy more accentuated. In the South, slavery buttressed the power of husbands and fathers. Planters described the plantation as a single social unit, incorporating their "white and black families"—their personal households and the slave quarters. Reputation required that the husband possess absolute authority. Attempts by family members to assert themselves against the patriarch—the head of the family, the master of slaves—threatened slavery itself. Slaves were experts at exploiting divisions among whites, whether among masters and overseers or planters and their wives and children. Slavery simply did not allow democracy in the big house. Planters liked to think of themselves as firm but fair, strong, and ready with a pistol if necessary, the defenders of all those in their custody.

Individualistic impulses were strong among planters, but duty to family was paramount. In time, as the children of one elite family married the children of another, planters were linked to one another by ties of blood and kinship as well as ideology and economic interest. Conscious of what they shared as slaveholders, planters worked together to defend their common interests. The values of the big house—slavery, honor, male domination—washed over the boundaries of plantations and flooded all of southern life.

Plantation Mistresses

Like their northern counterparts, southern ladies were expected to possess feminine virtues of piety, purity, chastity, and obedience within the context of marriage, motherhood, and domesticity. Southerners also expected ladies to exemplify all that was best in plantation society. Countless toasts praised her as the perfect complement to her husband, the patriarch. She was physically weak, "formed only for the less laborious occupations," and thus dependent on male protection. To gain this protection, she was modest and delicate, beautiful and graceful, cultured and charming. Freed from physical labor, she cultivated fashion, polished her French, and performed magically at the piano and in the ballroom. The lady, southern men said proudly, was an "ornament."

Southern men put elite women atop a very high pedestal. But for women, the image of the lady, which rigidly prescribed proper character and behavior, was no blessing. Chivalry—the South's romantic ideal of male-female relationships—glorified the lady but simultaneously subordinated her. Chivalry's underlying assumptions about the weakness of women and the protective authority of men resembled the assumptions that underlay the paternalistic defense of slavery. Indeed, the most articulate proslavery advocates also eloquently defended the subordination of women. Just as the slaveholder's mastery was written into law, so too were the paramount rights of husbands. Once married, antebellum southern women found divorce almost impossible.

Daughters of planters confronted chivalry's demands at an early age. Their educations aimed at fitting them to take their ordained places as southern ladies. At their private boarding schools they read literature, learned languages, and struggled to master the requisite drawing-room arts. Elite women married early, usually before they were twenty. Kate Carney exaggerated only slightly when she wrote in her diary: "Today, I am seventeen, getting quite old, and am not married." Elizabeth Ruffin, who was about the same age, complained of being pushed into a wedding. Everyone, she said, seemed determined to "deter me from all the anticipated horrors of *old-maidenhood.*" When they married, elite women made enormous efforts to live up to their region's lofty ideal. Caroline Merrick of Louisiana told a friend in 1859, "We owe it to our husbands, children, and friends to represent as nearly as possible the ideal which they hold so dear."

In fact, they faced an impossible task. The ideal of southern lady clashed with the daily reality of the plantation mistress. Rather than being freed from labor by servants, she discovered that having servants required her to work long hours. Like her husband, the mistress had managerial responsibilities. She managed the big house, often supervising anywhere from two or three to more than a dozen servants. One slaveholder remembered that the house he grew up in had "two cooks, two washerwomen, one dining room servant, two seamstresses, one house girl, one house boy, one carriage driver, one hostler [stableman], one gardener, [and] one er-

SOUTHERN BELLE
Lucy Petway Holcombe, a legendary Texas beauty, was twenty-six when she married twice-widowed Francis W. Pickens, a wealthy South Carolina planter, congressman, and governor. Lucy believed that she had made "a sacrifice" in marrying a man twice her age. She told her mother that she had married Pickens to pay off her father's debts and to obtain a plantation for herself. But there may have been more to her decision. She married Pickens only after her true love had been killed on a private military adventure in Cuba. Lucy had a Confederate company named after her, and her picture appeared on the Confederate hundred-dollar bill.
Orville Vernon Burton, *In My Father's House Are Many Mansions.*

rand boy." And, he added, they were "all under the supervision of my mother."

But unlike her husband, who was often insulated from the aggravations of direct supervision of slaves, the mistress had no overseer. All the house servants answered to her. She assigned them tasks each morning, directed their work throughout the day, and punished them when she found fault. In addition to supervising a complex household, she had responsibility for the henhouse and dairy. And on some plantations, she directed the slave hospi-

THE PRICE OF BLOOD
This 1868 painting by T. S. Noble depicts a transaction between a slave trader and a rich planter. The trader nervously pretends to study the contract, while the planter waits impatiently for the completion of the sale. The planter's mulatto son, who is being sold, looks away. The children of white men and slave women were property and could be sold by the father/master. But the tragedy of miscegenation extended beyond the son shown here. Who is absent from the painting? Who else's son is being sold away?
Morris Museum of Art, Augusta, Ga.

tal and nursery and rationed supplies for the slave quarters. Although she did little manual labor herself, she spent a long day engaged in decidedly unromantic chores. In addition, she bore the burdens of childbearing and child rearing. Southern ladies did not lead lives of leisure.

The mistress's life was circumscribed by the plantation, as was the slave's life. Masters used their status as slaveholders as a springboard into public affairs, but their wives served the family, not the community. Masters left the plantation when business demanded or just when they pleased, but plantation mistresses could not leave. Up to their elbows with responsibilities in the big house, they could not readily take off. Besides, white women needed

chaperones to travel. When they could, they went to church, for their faith was important to them. But women spent most days on the plantation, where they often became lonely. In 1853, Mary Kendall wrote how much she enjoyed her sister's letter: "For about three weeks I did not have the pleasure of seeing *one white female face*, there being no white family except our own upon the plantation." But sometimes a parade of family, friends, and strangers broke the isolation. Visitors were welcome, but the burden of hospitality fell on the mistress and the house slaves, not the master.

As members of slaveholding families, mistresses lived privileged lives. But they also had significant grounds for discontent, and a few independent-minded women protested. Some complained of their exhausting burdens as mistresses. Others protested their tiring and dangerous cycle of childbearing. Two decades of childbearing could mean ten or eleven children. And some women denounced slavery itself. In the early 1820s, Sarah and Angelina Grimké, daughters of a Charleston planter, fled their home for the North, where they wrote blistering attacks on slavery. Sarah's *Letters on the Equality of the Sexes* also protested the South's "image of women."

No feature of plantation life generated more rage and anguish among mistresses than miscegenation, the sexual mixing of the races. Laws prohibited interracial sex. Some masters condemned sex with slaves as immoral and practiced self-restraint. Others merely urged discretion. How many trips masters and their sons made to slave cabins is impossible to tell, but as long as slavery gave white men extraordinary power over black women, liaisons occurred. No white woman denounced the practice more scathingly than Mary Boykin Chesnut of Camden, South Carolina. She wrote in her diary: "God forgive us, but ours is a monstrous system, a wrong and iniquity. Like the patriarchs of old, our men live all in one house with their wives and their concubines; and the mulattos one sees in every family partly resemble the white children. Any lady is ready to tell you who is the father of all the mulatto children in everybody's household but her own. Those, she seems to think drop from the clouds."

But the mistress's world rested on slavery, just as the master's did. Most planters' wives—including Mary Boykin Chesnut—found ways to accept slavery. Mistresses worked hard and made enormous contributions to their husbands' estates. They raised their children, instructing, disciplining, and loving them. And when they had time, they read literature and their Bibles. They lived busy and responsible lives, but they were not considered equal to menfolk. According to the southern ideal, the white man ruled over all in his household—wife, children, and slaves.

Slaves and the Quarters

On most plantations, only a few hundred yards separated the big house and the slave quarters. The distance was short enough to assure whites easy access to the labor of blacks. Yet the distance was great enough to provide slaves with some privacy, despite increased paternalistic intrusion. Out of eyesight and earshot of the big house, slaves drew together and built lives of their own.

The rise of plantations still left a substantial minority of slaves living and working elsewhere. Most worked on small farms, where they wielded a hoe alongside another slave or two and perhaps their master. But by the mid-nineteenth century, as many as half a million slaves (one in eight) did not work in agriculture at all. They were employed in towns and cities as domestics, stevedores, day laborers, bakers, barbers, tailors, and more. Other slaves, far from urban centers, toiled as fishermen, lumbermen, railroad workers, and deckhands and stokers on riverboats. Slavery was a flexible labor system, and slaves could be found in virtually every skilled and unskilled occupation throughout the South, including the region's few factories. Nevertheless, a majority of slaves counted plantations as their homes and workplaces.

Work

Above all, what masters wanted from slaves was work. The desire for exploitable labor was the chief explanation of slavery's origin in the New World and the principal reason it persisted into the nineteenth century. Slaves understood clearly the motive for their enslavement. As ex-slave Albert Todd recalled, "Work was a religion we was taught."

Masters thought they knew what it took to make slaves work. Without close supervision and coercion, whites believed, black men and women would not labor. Whites reasoned that blacks were naturally lazy, a trait that they believed was the racial inheritance of a tropical people. On most plantations, a white man on horseback patrolled the fields to make sure slave laborers were bent over their hoes. A flick of his whip painfully reminded slackers that he believed that slaves were put on this earth to labor.

All slaves who were capable of productive labor worked. Young children were introduced to the world of work as early as age five or six. Ex-slave Carrie Hudson recalled that children who were "knee high to a duck" had to work. Some were sent to the fields to carry water to thirsty workers or to protect ripening crops from hungry birds. Others helped in the slave nursery, caring for children even younger than themselves, or in the big house, where they did simple chores, such as sweeping floors or shooing flies in the dining room. When slave boys and girls reached the age of eleven or twelve, masters sent most of them to the fields, where they learned farmwork by laboring alongside their parents. After a lifetime of labor, old women left the fields to care for the small children and spin yarn and old men to mind livestock and clean stables.

Slaves understood clearly the motive for their enslavement. As ex-slave Albert Todd recalled, "Work was a religion we was taught."

The overwhelming majority of slaves in 1860 were field hands. Planters sometimes assigned men and women to separate gangs, the women working at lighter tasks and the men doing the heavy work of clearing and breaking the land. But women also did heavy work. "I had to work hard," Nancy Boudry remembered, "plow and go and split wood just like a man." Sally Neely recalled that her owner "used the slave negro woman just like he did the slave man. He never did let the slave girl do one kind of work and the slave boy another, he worked us right on together." Although the daily tasks of slaves working in tobacco, rice, and sugar fields differed from those of slaves laboring in cotton fields, the backbreaking labor and the monotonous year-round routines made for grim similarity. As one ex-slave observed, on the plantation the "history of one day is the history of every day."

A few slaves became house servants. But only one or two in every ten worked in the big house, and virtually all of those who did (nine of ten) were women. There, under the critical eye of the white mistress, they cooked the white family's food, cleaned their house, babysat their infants, washed their clothes, and did the dozens of other tasks the master and mistress required. House servants enjoyed certain advantages, such as somewhat less physically demanding work, better food, and more comfortable quarters. But working in the big house had significant drawbacks. House servants were constantly on call. They had no time that was entirely their own. They worked in the incessant presence of whites. Since no servant could please constantly, most bore the brunt of white frustration and rage. Ex-slave Jacob Branch of Texas remembered, "My poor mama! Every washday old Missy give her a beating." No wonder some house servants wished they could trade places with field hands.

Even rarer than house servants were skilled artisans. In the cotton South, no more than one slave in twenty (almost all men) worked in a skilled trade. Most were blacksmiths and carpenters, but slaves also worked as masons, mechanics, cotton gin makers, millers, and shoemakers. Slave craftsmen took pride in their skills and often exhibited an independence of spirit that caused slaveholder James H. Hammond of South Carolina to declare in disgust that when a slave became a skilled artisan, "he is more than half freed." Skilled slave fathers often taught their crafts to their sons. "My pappy was one of the black smiths and worked in the shop," John Mathews remembered. "I had to help my pappy in the shop when I was a child and I learnt how to beat out the iron and make wagon tires, and make plows."

Rarest of all slave occupations was that of driver. Probably no more than one slave in a hundred —all men—worked in this capacity. These men were well named, for their primary task was driving other slaves to greater efforts in the fields. In some drivers' hands, the whip never rested. Ex-slave Jane Johnson of South Carolina called her driver the "meanest man, white or black, I ever see." But other drivers showed all the restraint they could. "Ole Gabe didn't like that whippin' business," West Turner of Virginia remembered, "but he couldn't help hisself. When Marsa was there, he would lay it on 'cause he had to. But when old Marsa wasn't lookin', he never would beat them slaves."

Work dominated the slaves' daylight hours. Normally, slaves worked from what they called "can to can't," from "can see" in the morning to "can't see" at night. Even with a break at noon for a meal and rest, it made for a long day. And nightfall did not necessarily mean an end of labor. After women had worked all day in the cotton patch, Pinkie Kelley remembered, we "had to shell a bushel of corn before we could go to bed, and then we was so tired we didn't have no time for nothin' and was glad to get to bed." One ex-slave remembered that no slave suffered from that "disease known as 'mattress fever.'" For slaves, Lewis Young recalled, "work, work, work, 'twas all they do."

Family, Religion, and Community

Despite the grind of exhausting labor, there was life after slaves left the fields. From dawn to dusk, slaves worked for the master. But from dusk to dawn, when the labor was done, and all day Sun-

NANCY FORT, HOUSE SERVANT

This rare portrait of a slave woman at the turn of the nineteenth century depicts a strong and dignified person. Some who worked in domestic service took pride in their superior status and identified more with the master than with the slaves. "Honey, I wan't no common eve'day slave," one former servant recalled proudly. "I [helped] de white folks in de big house." But intense interaction with whites did not necessarily breed affection. Most domestic servants remained bound by ties of kinship and friendship, as well as by common oppression, to the slave quarters.

Courtesy of Georgia Department of Archives and History.

SLAVE CARPENTER

Haywood Dixon (1826–c. 1889) was a slave carpenter who worked in Greene County, North Carolina. In this 1854 daguerreotype, he is posed with a symbol of his profession, the carpenter's square. When work was slow on the home plantation, masters could hire out their skilled craftsmen to neighbors who needed a carpenter, blacksmith, or mason.

Collection of William L. Murphy.

days and usually Saturday afternoons, slaves were left largely to themselves. Bone tired perhaps, they nonetheless used the time and space to develop and enjoy what mattered most: family, religion, and community.

In the quarters, slaves lived lives that their masters were hardly aware of. Temporarily leaving the master-slave relationship at their cabin doors, slaves became husbands and wives, mothers and fathers, sons and daughters, preachers and singers, fiddlers and hunters, storytellers and conjurers. Over the generations, they created a community and a culture of their own that buoyed them up during long hours in the fields and brought them joy and hope in the few hours they had to themselves.

One of the most important consequences of the slaves' limited autonomy was the preservation and persistence of the family. Perhaps the most serious charge abolitionists leveled against slavery was that it wrecked black family life, a telling indictment in a society that put family at the heart of decent society. Slaveholders sometimes agreed that blacks had no family life, but they placed the blame on the slaves themselves, claiming that blacks chose to lead licentious, promiscuous lives.

Contrary to both abolitionists' and slaveholders' claims, the black family survived slavery. Indeed, family was the chief fact of life in the quarters. Several factors account for the durability of the slave family. First, owners sometimes encouraged the cre-

SLAVE CABIN
Other than the well-built brick chimney, this one-room, dirt-floored cabin on a small Georgia plantation had little to recommend it. Still, it no doubt housed a family. The six children in the photograph probably lived there with their mother and perhaps with their father. It may be Sunday — the oldest children are working about the cabin rather than in the fields, while the youngest children are playing in the bare yard. "The first seven or eight years of the slave-boy's life are about as full of sweet content as those of the most favored and petted white children," recalled Frederick Douglass. The two boys in straw hats are about the age when childhood ended and "light" chores began, chores that would grow increasingly heavy over the slave's lifetime.
Collection of the New-York Historical Society.

ation and maintenance of families. Some masters wanted slaves to live morally upright lives and rewarded those who married with small presents and punished those who divorced with whippings. Others encouraged slave families because of their financial interest in slave reproduction. And some masters realized that families made the quarters more stable and orderly places. It is not surprising that most runaways were young, unmarried men.

Despite occasional white encouragement, marriage and family in the quarters were primarily the result of black commitment. Masters were often indifferent to the living arrangements of their slaves, as long as the quarters were quiet. Moreover, no slave marriage was recognized by law, and therefore no master or slave was legally obligated to honor the bond. Still, plantation records show that slave marriages were often long-lasting. Young men and women in the slave quarters fell in love, married, and set up housekeeping in cabins of their own. The primary cause of the ending of slave marriages was death, just as it was in white families. An elderly widow remembered fondly the slave husband to whom she had been married most of her life: "He was the first one and the best one and the last one." But the second most frequent cause of the end of slave marriages was sale of the husband or wife, something no white family ever had to fear. Precise figures are unavailable, but one scholar estimates that in the years 1820–1860, sales destroyed 300,000 slave marriages. Years after Moses Grandy was parted from his slave wife, he said, "I have never seen or heard of her from that day to this." And he added, "I loved her as I love my life."

Plantation records also reveal that a majority of children grew up in two-parent households, one family to a cabin. Not all fathers could live with their children—some men had been sold away and others had married women on neighboring plantations—but most fathers were present. And contrary to common belief, they were significant figures. Naming practices reveal fathers' importance. Despite slave fathers' inability to fulfill the traditional roles of provider and protector, slave parents often named their sons after their fathers. Slave fathers gained status by doing what they could to provide for their families: hunting, raising hogs, cultivating a garden, making furniture. In the eyes of slaves, an ex-bondsman recalled, "the man who does this is a great man amongst them." Still, masters sharply circumscribed the authority of slave husbands. Unlike white men, slave husbands could not exercise patriarchal dominion over their wives and children. Nevertheless, ex-slaves held both their mothers and fathers in high esteem, grateful for the refuge they had provided from the rigors of slavery.

Families were an important feature of a distinctive African American culture that flourished in the quarters. And families became the principal means of passing the slaves' culture on from generation to generation. But families were only one of the quarters' vital institutions. A second was religion. Like families, religion provided slaves with a refuge and a reason for living.

Christianity arrived late in the quarters. In the seventeenth century and for most of the eighteenth, masters cared little about the spiritual lives of their slaves, and most blacks clung to their African beliefs. Beginning about the time of the American Revolution, however, Protestant evangelical sects, particularly the Baptists and Methodists, began trying to convert slaves. Evangelicals offered an emotional "religion of the heart" to which blacks (and many whites as well) responded enthusiastically. By the mid-nineteenth century, perhaps as many as one-quarter of all slaves claimed church membership, and many of the rest would not have objected to being called Christians.

Planters began promoting Christianity in the quarters because they came to see the slaves' salvation as part of their obligation and to believe that religion made slaves more obedient. Certainly, the Christianity that masters broadcast to slaves emphasized the meeker virtues. White preachers admonished their black congregants to love God and to obey their owners. Many slaves laughed up their

BRASS ORNAMENT
Artifacts recovered by archaeologists excavating plantation sites help us understand how an African heritage was transplanted, reinterpreted, or replaced in America. This small brass ornament decorated with a clenched hand was recovered from a slave cabin at the Hermitage, the home of Andrew Jackson outside Nashville, Tennessee. Such a charm, one former slave recalled, is "what will keep de witches away."
The Hermitage: Home of President Andrew Jackson, Nashville, Tenn.

sleeves at the message. "That old white preacher just was telling us slaves to be good to our masters," a Virginia ex-slave chuckled. "We ain't cared a bit about that stuff he was telling us 'cause we wanted to sing, pray, and serve God in our own way."

Meeting in their cabins or secretly in the woods, slaves created a hidden African American Christianity that served their needs, not the masters'. Although it was illegal in the South after the 1830s to teach slaves to read, some slaves could read enough to struggle with the Bible. With the help of black preachers, they interpreted the Christian message themselves. Rather than obedience, their faith emphasized justice. God kept score, and accounts of this world would be settled in the next. "God is punishing some of them old suckers and their children right now for the way they use to treat us poor colored folks," an ex-slave declared contentedly. But the slaves' faith involved more than retribution. It also spoke to their experiences in this world. In the Old Testament they discovered Moses, who delivered his people from slavery, and in the New Testament they found Jesus, who offered salvation to all and thereby established the equality of all people. Jesus' message of equality provided a potent antidote to the planters' claim that blacks were an inferior people whom God condemned to slavery and a crucial buttress to the slaves' self-esteem.

Christianity did not entirely drive out traditional African beliefs. Some slaves saw no contradiction between their belief in Christianity and in conjurers, witches, and spirits. Depending on whether he or she was a friend or an enemy, the conjurer could make one lucky in love or give one boils. "They can take your garter or your stocking top and drop it in running water and make you run the rest of you life—you'll be in a hurry all the time," ex-slave Nancy Bradford claimed. Christian music, preaching, and rituals showed the influence of Africa, as did much of the slaves' secular activities, such as wood carving, quilt making, and storytelling.

Resistance and Rebellion

Slaves did not suffer slavery passively. They were, as whites said, "troublesome property." Slaves understood that accommodation to what they could not change was the price of survival, but in a hundred ways they protested their bondage. Theoretically, the master was all-powerful and the slave powerless. Indeed, masters had available powerful instruments of coercion. But oppressed, seemingly powerless people have always found ways to resist their oppressors. Slaves were no different. Sustained by their culture and emboldened by the slave community, slaves engaged in day-to-day resistance against their enslavers.

The spectrum of slave resistance ranged from mild to extreme. Telling a pointed story by the fireside in a slave cabin was probably the mildest form of protest. But when the weak got the better of the strong, as they did in tales of Brer Rabbit and Brer Fox ("Brer" is a contraction of "Brother"), listeners could enjoy the thrill of a vicarious victory over their masters. Trickster tales distilled the folk wisdom of Africa. The American versions taught slaves, especially young ones, how to survive the plantation regime. The tales did not always have happy endings, and slaves learned that dull-witted resisters got punished for their bungling.

Protest in the fields was more active than that around firesides. Slaves were particularly inventive in resisting their master's demand that they work. They dragged their feet getting to the fields, hoed excruciatingly slowly, put rocks in their cotton bags before putting them on the scale to be weighed, feigned illness, terribly mistreated the master's work animals, and pretended to be so thickheaded that they could not understand the simplest instruction. Slaves broke so many hoe handles that owners outfitted the hoes with oversized handles. Slaves so mistreated the work animals that masters switched from horses to mules, which could absorb more abuse. While slaves worked hard in the master's fields, they also sabotaged his interests.

One widespread form of protest that was particularly aggravating to masters was slaves attempting to escape from the plantation. Runaway slaves denied masters what they wanted most from their slaves—work. Sometimes runaways sought the ultimate prize: freedom in the North or in Canada. Over the decades, thousands of slaves, mostly from the Upper South, made it. But from the Lower South, escape to freedom was almost impossible. At most, the average runaway could hope to escape for a few weeks. Runaways usually stayed close to the plantation, keeping to the deep woods or swamps and slipping back into the quarters at night to get food. "Lying out," as it was known, usually ended when the runaway, worn out and ragged, gave up or was finally chased down by slave-hunting dogs.

Standing up to whites was an even bolder protest, and it occurred more often than we might expect. Direct confrontation rarely ended in a slave's triumph, however. An ex-slave from North Carolina remembered the night when patrollers broke up an unauthorized dance in the quarters. "Uncle Joe's son he decide they was one time to die and he started to fight," she recalled. "He say he tired standing so many beatings, he just can't stand no more." After the whites had overpowered the young man and had whipped him "for a long time, then one of them take a stick and hit him over the head, and just bust his head wide open."

While resistance was common, outright rebellion—a violent assault on slavery by large numbers of slaves—was rare. The scarcity of revolts in the antebellum South is not evidence of the slaves' contentedness. Rather, existing conditions gave rebels virtually no chance of success. Whites outnumbered blacks two to one and were heavily armed. Moreover, slaves were spread relatively thinly in the South, communication between plantations was difficult, and, with the partial exceptions of the Dismal Swamp (in Virginia and North Carolina), the Okefenokee (in Georgia and Florida), and the Everglades (in Florida), the South provided little protective wilderness into which rebels could retreat and defend themselves. Organized rebellion in the American South was virtual suicide.

Given the odds, it is perhaps surprising to find any organized rebellion. But slaves in the antebellum South did rise up. The best-known slave revolt, led by Nat Turner, occurred in 1831 in Southampton County, Virginia. All of his life, Turner believed that he "was ordained for some great purpose in the hands of the Almighty." He worked as a field hand, but he also preached to the slaves. "Ol' Prophet Nat," the slaves called him. In time, Turner became convinced that God had appointed him an instrument of divine vengeance. He set out to punish sinful white slaveholders and free their suffering slaves. Following an eclipse of the sun, which he took as a sign from the Lord, Turner and a few disciples murdered his master and his family. By the next day, some 60 other slaves, armed with axes, had joined the insurrection. White militiamen crushed the revolt in less than two days, but by then the rebels had killed about 60 white men, women, and children. In retaliation, whites killed about 120 blacks, many of them innocent bystanders. Turner managed to escape to the woods, but the authorities captured him nine weeks later. By then, 20 of his followers had been executed and 10 others exiled. Tried on November 5, 1831, Nat Turner was hanged six days later.

Antebellum southern history is also punctuated with slave conspiracies, rebellions that were suppressed before they exploded. Some so-called conspiracies were simply the product of overheated white imaginations. But in 1800, Gabriel Prosser, a slave in Richmond, planned a real rebellion that whites foiled at the last minute. And there was Denmark Vesey, the free black man in Charleston who was thwarted in 1822 in his effort to become a black Moses.

Although masters often boasted that their slaves were "instinctively contented," steady resistance and occasional rebellion proved otherwise. Slaves found challenging white authority a risky but invigorating business. By asserting themselves, they affirmed their humanity and worth. By resisting their masters' will, slaves also helped shape

their own destiny. They became actors in the plantation drama, helping to establish limits beyond which planters and overseers hesitated to go. Slaves did not have the power to end their bondage, but they remained thorns in their masters' sides.

It would be false to the historical record to minimize what the lack of freedom meant to slaves. Because the essence of slavery was the inability to shape one's own life, slavery blunted and thwarted African Americans' hopes and aspirations. Slavery broke some and crippled others. But slavery's destructive power had to contend with the resiliency of the human spirit. Slaves fought back physically, culturally, and spiritually. They not only survived bondage but created in the slave quarters a vibrant African American culture and community that would sustain them through more than two centuries of bondage and after.

Black and Free: On the Middle Ground

Not every black Southerner was a slave. In 1860, some 260,000 (approximately 6 percent) of the region's 4.1 million African Americans were free. What is surprising is not that their numbers were small but that they existed at all. "Free black" seemed a contradiction to most white Southerners. According to the dominant racial thinking, blacks were supposed to be slaves; free people were supposed to be white. Nature had decreed it and a decent society required it, proslavery theorists declared. Blacks who were free did not fit neatly into the South's idealized social order. They stood out, and whites made them objects of special scrutiny. Free blacks realized that they stood precariously between slavery and full freedom, on what a young free black artisan in Charleston characterized in 1848 as "a middle ground."

White Response to Free Blacks

Free blacks were rare in the colonial era, but their numbers swelled after the Revolution, when the natural rights philosophy of the Declaration of Independence and the egalitarian message of evangelical Protestantism joined to challenge slavery. Although probably not more than one slaveholder in a hundred freed his slaves, a brief flurry of emancipation visited the Upper South, where the ideological assault on slavery coincided with a deep depression in the tobacco economy. Other planters permitted favorite slaves to work after hours to accumulate money with which to buy their freedom. By 1810, free blacks numbered more than 100,000 and had become the fastest-growing element of the southern population. Burgeoning numbers of free blacks worried white Southerners, who, because of the cotton boom, wanted desperately to see more slaves, not more free blacks.

In the 1820s and 1830s, state legislatures acted to stem the growth of the free black population and to shrink the liberty of those blacks who had already gained their freedom. To cut down access to freedom, laws denied masters the right to free their slaves. Additional laws humiliated and restricted the South's existing free blacks by subjecting them to special taxes, requiring them to register annually with the state or to choose a white guardian, prohibiting them from interstate travel, denying them the right to have schools and to participate in politics, and requiring them to carry "freedom papers" to prove they were not slaves. Increasingly, whites subjected free blacks to many of the same laws as slaves. They could not testify under oath in a court of law or serve on juries. They were liable to punishment meted out to slaves such as whipping and the treadmill. Like slaves, free blacks were forbidden to strike whites, even to defend themselves. "Free negroes belong to a degraded caste of society," a South Carolina judge summed up in 1848. "They are in no respect on a perfect equality with the white man. . . . They ought, by law, to be compelled to demean themselves as inferiors."

The elaborate system of regulations confined most free African Americans to a constricted life of poverty and dependence, which led most whites to despise them as degraded parasites.

The elaborate system of regulations confined most free African Americans to a constricted life of poverty and dependence, which led most whites to despise them as degraded parasites. Whites pushed the majority of free blacks to the bottom of the southern social hierarchy. Typically, free blacks were rural, uneducated, unskilled agricultural laborers and domestic servants, scrambling to find work and eke out a living. Opportunities of all kinds—for work, education, community—were slim. Planters looked upon free blacks as worthless rascals, likely to set a bad example for slaves. They believed that free blacks subverted the racial subordination that was the essence of slavery.

Achievement despite Restrictions

Despite increasingly harsh and constricting laws and stepped-up harassment and persecution, free African Americans made the most of the advantages their status offered. Unlike slaves, free blacks could legally marry. They could protect their families from arbitrary disruption by whites and pass on their heritage of freedom to their children. Freedom also meant that, unlike slaves, free blacks could choose occupations and own property. For most, however, these proved only theoretical rights, for whites allowed most free blacks few economic opportunities. Unlike whites, a majority of the antebellum South's free blacks remained propertyless.

Still, some free blacks escaped the poverty and degradation whites thrust upon them. Particularly in urban areas—especially in the cities of Charleston, Mobile, and New Orleans—a small elite of free blacks developed and even flourished. Urban whites enforced many of the restrictive laws only sporadically, allowing free blacks room to maneuver. The elite consisted overwhelmingly of light-skinned African Americans who worked at skilled trades, as tailors, carpenters, mechanics, and the like. Their customers were prominent whites—planters, merchants, judges—who appreciated their able, respectful service. The small white working class, however, resented their competition and their profitable connections with white aristocrats. The free black elite illegally operated schools for their children, illegally traveled in and out of their states, worshiped with whites (in separate seating) in the finest churches, and lived scattered about in white neighborhoods, not in separate ghettos. Though this small elite lived in proximity to dark-skinned free blacks and to slaves, they put distance between themselves and other African Americans.

Yet in one important way, the free black elite was not remote from slaves. In 1860, about 3,200 blacks owned slaves. Blacks could own blacks because, despite all of the restrictions whites placed on free African Americans, whites did not deny them the right to own property, which in the South included human property. Most owned only a few, who were sometimes family members whom they could not legally free. But others owned slaves in

MADDEN'S TAVERN
Completed in about 1840, the tavern was built, owned, and oper-
ated by Willis Madden (1799–1879), a free black. One of the best-
known taverns in Culpeper County, Virginia, it numbered among
its patrons, who were all white, the area's most prominent citizens.
Employment for free blacks was hard to come by in the slave South,
and Madden also operated a general store and a blacksmith shop,
which provided work for his sons and relatives. Heavily damaged by
Union troops, the tavern ceased operations after the Civil War.
Department of Historic Resources, Virginia.

large numbers, none of whom were family and all of whom were exploited for labor.

One such free black slave owner was William Ellison of South Carolina. Ellison was himself born a slave in 1790, but by 1860 he was the wealthiest free black in his state and owned more slaves than any other free black in the South outside Louisiana. In 1816, Ellison bought his freedom from his white master (who may have been his father) and moved to a booming plantation district about one hundred miles north of Charleston. He set up business as a cotton gin maker, a trade he had learned as a slave. Ellison's gin business grew with the cotton boom until by 1835 he was prosperous enough to purchase the home of a former governor of the state. Ellison lived in the house until his death in 1861. By then, he had become a big planter, making a hundred bales of cotton a year with sixty-three slaves on an eight-hundred-acre plantation.

Not every free black was willing to accommodate to whites and enslave and exploit other blacks. At the very time Ellison was building his slave empire, Denmark Vesey was plotting slavery's destruction. Most free blacks followed a middle course. They neither became slaveholders nor sought to raise a slave rebellion. They simply tried to preserve their freedom, to deny whites what they most wanted—a society in which all whites were free and all blacks were slaves. Increasingly under attack from planters who wanted to eliminate or enslave them and from white artisans who coveted their jobs, they sought to impress whites with their reliability, their economic progress, and their good behavior.

The Plain Folk

Most whites in the South did not own slaves, not even one. In 1860, more than 6 million of the South's 8 million whites lived in slaveless families. Some slaveless Southerners—artisans, traders, and mechanics, for example—were urban dwellers, but their numbers were relatively small because the South had few cities. Others—storekeepers, parsons, and schoolteachers, for example—lived in the country but worked outside agriculture. But most "plain folk" were small farmers. Perhaps three out of four were yeomen, small farmers who owned their own land. As in the North, farm ownership provided a family with an economic foundation, social respectability, and political standing. Unlike their northern counterparts, however, southern yeomen lived in a region whose economy and society were dominated by unfree labor. Not even the nonslaveholding white majority escaped the influence of slavery.

In an important sense, the South had more than one white yeomanry. The huge southern landscape provided space enough for two yeoman societies, separated roughly along geographical lines. Yeomen throughout the South had a good deal in common, but the life of a small farm family in the upcountry—the area of hills and mountains—differed from the life of one in the plantation belt—the flatlands that included the black belt and delta regions.

Plantation Belt Yeomen

Plantation belt yeomen lived within the orbit of the planter class. Small landholdings actually outnumbered the larger plantations, but they were dwarfed in importance. Although only small fry, yeomen participated in the dominant cotton economy. They

GATHERING CORN
In this 1865 drawing, two white men, perhaps kinfolk or neighbors, join in harvesting corn. While one cuts and gathers the stalks, the other shucks the corn. A black man, who was probably a slave either owned or hired by one of the white men, loads the corn into a wagon. Corn was a primary crop of most antebellum yeoman farmers, even those who grew considerable cotton. Yeomen usually grew about twice the corn needed for their families and livestock and marketed the rest.
Library of Congress.

devoted a significant portion of their land to growing cotton and with family labor produced perhaps five or six 400-pound bales each year. (Large planters measured their crop in hundreds of bales.) Small farmers also grew food crops. Both their cotton and their corn tied them to planters. Unable to afford cotton gins or baling presses of their own, they relied on helpful neighborhood slave owners to gin and bale their small crops. With no link to merchants in the port cities, yeomen turned to better-connected planters to ship and sell their cotton. If a yeoman had surplus corn one season, he might find a local planter who had run short and would pay a fair price. More likely, the farmer himself would run short and would receive from the neighborly planter a few bushels to tide him over.

A dense network of personal relationships laced small farmers and planters together in patterns of reciprocity and mutual obligation. A planter sometimes sent his slaves to help a newcomer build a house or a sick farmer get in his crop. He hired out surplus slaves to ambitious yeomen who wanted to expand cotton production. He sometimes chose his overseers from among the sons of farm families in the community. Plantation mistresses sometimes nursed ailing neighbors. Family ties often spanned class lines, making rich and poor kin as well as neighbors. Yeomen shared the planters' commitment to white supremacy and actively defended black subordination. Rural counties required adult white males to ride in slave patrols, which nightly scoured country roads to make certain that no slaves were moving about without permission. On Sundays, plantation dwellers and plain folk came together in church to worship and afterward lingered to gossip and to transact small business.

Yeomen throughout the South had a good deal in common, but the life of a small farm family in the upcountry—the area of hills and mountains—differed from the life of one in the plantation belt—the flatlands that included the black belt and delta regions.

Yeomen may have envied, and at times even resented, wealthy slaveholders, but in general small farmers learned to accommodate. Planters made accommodation easier by going out of their way to provide necessary services, behave as good neigh-

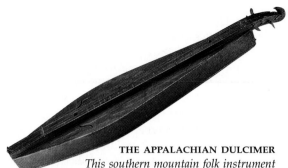

THE APPALACHIAN DULCIMER
This southern mountain folk instrument has its origins in Germany, Sweden, and Norway and may have been introduced to the Appalachians by Pennsylvania Germans. As pleasing to the eye as to the ear, dulcimers were usually crafted in "teardrop" or "figure-eight" shapes. When plucked, dulcimers emit a soft and gentle, somewhat melancholy, sound. Mountain people fashioned these instruments to accompany doleful Scottish and English ballads as well as to play lively instrumental tunes.
Collection of the Blue Ridge Institute and Museum/Ferrum College.

bors, and avoid direct exploitation of slaveless whites in their community. As a consequence, rather than raging at the oppression of the planter regime, the typical plantation belt yeoman sought entry into it. He dreamed of adding acreage to his farm, buying a few slaves of his own, retiring from field work, and perhaps even joining his prosperous neighbors on their shady verandas for a cool drink.

Upcountry Yeomen

The hills and mountains in the interior of the South resisted the penetration of slavery and plantations. While increasing participation in the market was a trend everywhere in the South, the western parts of Virginia, North Carolina, and South Carolina, northern Georgia and Alabama, and eastern Tennessee and Kentucky retained a quite different economy and society. The higher elevation, colder climate, rugged terrain, and poor transportation made it difficult for commercial agriculture to make headway. These regions were characterized by small farms, few slaves, food crops, and production for home consumption. For yeomen who lived in the hills and mountains, planters and slaves were not everyday acquaintances. Geographically isolated, the upcountry was a yeoman stronghold.

At the core of the distinctive upcountry culture was the independent farm family working its own patch of land; raising a considerable number of hogs, cattle, and sheep; and seeking self-sufficiency and independence. Toward that end, all members of the family worked, their tasks depending on their sex and age. Husbands labored in the fields, and with their sons they cleared, plowed, planted, and cultivated primarily food crops—corn, wheat, sweet potatoes, and perhaps some fruit. Although pressed into field labor at picking or harvest time, wives and daughters worked in and about the cabin most of the year. One upcountry farmer remembered that his mother "worked in the house cooking, spinning, weaving [and doing] patchwork." In addition, the women tended the vegetable garden, kept a cow and some chickens, preserved foods, cleaned their homes, fed their families, and cared for the infants and toddlers. Male and female tasks were equally crucial to the farm's success, but as in other white southern households, the female domestic sphere was subordinated to the will of the male patriarch.

The typical upcountry yeoman also grew a little cotton or tobacco, but production for home consumption was more important than production for the market. Not much currency changed hands in the upcountry. Credit was common, as was direct barter. A yeoman might trade his small commercial crop to a country store owner for a little salt, lead shot, needles, and nails. Or he might swap extra sweet potatoes with the blacksmith for a plow or with the tanner for leather. Networks of exchange and mutual assistance tied individual homesteads to the larger community. Farm families swapped goods and work and joined together in logrolling, house- or barn-raising, and cornhusking. Strong ties to a cooperative community made the yeoman's goal of maintaining his family's independence realistic.

Plain folk did not usually associate "book learning" with the basic needs of life. In any case, the children of yeomen had limited opportunity for schooling. A northern woman visiting the South in the 1850s observed, "Education is not extended to the masses here as at the North." Private academies charged fees that yeomen could not afford, and public schools were scarce. Even where schools existed, terms were short, only about 50 or 60 days a year in the South compared with 100 to 150 days in the North. Although most people managed to pick up a basic knowledge of the "three R's," approximately one southern white man in five was illiterate in 1860, and the rate for white women was even

higher. "People here prefer talking to reading," a Virginian remarked. Telling stories, reciting ballads, and singing hymns were important activities in yeoman folk culture.

Many plain folk spent more hours in revival tents than in classrooms. By no means were all rural whites religious, but many were, and the most characteristic feature of their evangelical Christian faith was the revival. The greatest of the early-nineteenth-century revivals occurred in 1801 at Cane Ridge, Kentucky, where some twenty thousand people gathered to listen to a host of preachers who spoke day and night for a week. Ministers sought to convert and save souls by bringing individuals to a personal conviction of sin. Revivalism crossed denominational lines, but Baptists and Methodists adopted it wholeheartedly and by midcentury had become the South's largest religious groups. By emphasizing free choice and individual worth, the plain folk's religion was hopeful and affirming. Hymns and spirituals provided guides to right and wrong—praising modesty and steadfastness, condemning drinking and devilish activity like dancing. Above all, hymns spoke of eventual release from worldly sorrows and the assurance of eternal salvation:

> A few more struggles here,
> A few more partings o'er,
> A few more toils, a few more tears,
> And we shall weep no more,
> And we shall weep no more,
>   Happy thought to die no more,
> No, never, never more.

Yeomen did not have the upcountry entirely to themselves. Even the hills had some plantations and slaves. But they existed in much smaller numbers than in the plantation belt. Many upcountry counties were less than a quarter black, whereas counties in the plantation belt were more than half black. Only a small fraction of upcountry folks owned slaves, and those who did usually had only two or three. As a result, slaveholders had much less direct social and economic power, and yeomen had more. Farmers and farms, not planters and plantations, dominated upcountry culture. Yeoman domination did not mean that the upcountry opposed slavery. As long as they were free to lead their own lives, upcountry plain folk defended slavery and white supremacy just as staunchly as did other white Southerners.

Poor Whites

Northerners denied the claim that the South's white majority constituted a sturdy yeomanry—hardworking, landholding, small farmers. Instead, they charged that the institution of slavery had pushed slaveless whites to the bottom of the social and economic ladder, where they had lost heart, ambition, and energy. The majority of the South's whites, according to northern critics, were landless, shiftless, and degraded. Contemporaries called these Southerners a variety of derogatory names: snuff dippers, clay eaters, hillbillies, crackers, rednecks, and poor white trash. Even slaves were known to chant: "I'd rather be a nigger an' plow ol' Beck, / Than a white hill-billy with a long red neck." Poor whites were not just whites who were poor. The label carried a moral as well as a material meaning. It suggested not only poverty but cultural degeneracy as well. Poor whites were supposedly ignorant and inbred, sick in body and culture. According to the South's critics, slavery meant riches, esteem, and power for the few and deprivation, degradation, and impotence for the white majority.

Significant numbers of Southerners were poor, as the critics claimed. Perhaps one in four farmers was landless. Landless farm families lived as tenants, renting rather than owning land. Other poor rural Southerners worked as unskilled day laborers, hunters, herders, and fishermen. Living on the periphery of the southern economy, some barely made a go of it. Wits could declare that "poor whites were born lazy and had a relapse." In fact, poor whites subsisted on unhealthy diets, lived in miserable housing, spent summers going barefooted around animals, and, consequently, suffered high incidences of hookworm, pellagra, and other severely debilitating diseases that thrived in the South's warm, wet climate. Although impoverished, most of these Southerners were not degenerate. Instead, they were ambitious people kicking and scratching to survive and aspiring to climb into the yeomanry.

Poor whites were sometimes poor only temporarily. The Lipscomb family illustrates the possibility of upward mobility. In 1845, Smith and Sally Lipscomb and their children abandoned tired land in South Carolina for Benton County, Alabama. "Benton is a mountainous country but ther is a heep of good levil land to tend in it," Smith wrote back to his brother. Alabama, Smith declared, "will be better for the rising generation if not for ourselves

but I think it will be the best for us all that live any length of time." Indeed, primitive conditions made survival uncertain. All of the Lipscombs fell ill, but all recovered, and the entire family went to work. Because they had no money to buy land, they squatted on seven acres. With the help of neighbors, they built a twenty-two-foot-by-twenty-four-foot cabin, a detached kitchen sixteen feet square, and two stables. Each day, from daylight to dark, Smith and his sons worked the land. Nature cooperated, and they produced plenty of food and several bales of cotton. The women worked just as hard in the cabin, and Sally managed to contribute to the family's income by sewing shirts, which she sold for seventy-five cents, and knitting socks, selling for thirty-seven cents a pair. In time, the Lipscombs bought land of their own. Eventually, they joined Hebron Baptist Church and completed their transformation from landless poor whites to respectable yeomen.

The upward mobility demonstrated by the Lipscombs became rarer in the 1850s. The prosperity of the cotton economy encouraged planters to expand their operations, driving the price of land beyond the reach of poor families. Squeezed by competition with plantation slavery and pushed to the least fertile regions of the South, such as the pine barrens along the Atlantic coast, poor whites were likely to remain poor.

The Politics of Slavery

Like every other significant feature of southern society, politics showed the impress of slavery. Even after the South's politics became democratic in form for the white male population, political power remained less than evenly distributed. The nonslaveholding white majority wielded less political power than their numbers indicated. The slaveholding white minority wielded more. Self-conscious, cohesive, and with a well-developed sense of class interest, slaveholders busied themselves with party politics, campaigns, and officeholding and made demands of state governments. As a result, they received significant benefits. But most nonslaveholding whites were more concerned with preserving their liberties and keeping their taxes low. Collectively, they asked government for little of an economic nature, and they received little.

Slaveholders worried about nonslaveholders' political loyalty to slavery. Ultimately, they need not have fretted. Since the eighteenth century, the mass of whites had accepted the planters' argument that the existing social order served *all* Southerners' interests. Slavery gave the planter class enormous advantages, but the slaveless white majority gained as well. Slavery compensated every white man—no matter how poor—with membership in the South's white ruling class. It also provided the means by which nonslaveholders might someday advance into the ranks of the planters. White men in the South fought furiously about many things, but they agreed that they should take land from Indians, promote agriculture, uphold white supremacy, and defend slavery from its enemies.

The Democratization of the Political Arena

The political reforms that swept the nation in the first half of the nineteenth century reached deeply into the South. Southern politics became democratic politics—for white men. State by state, Southerners eliminated the wealth and property requirements that had restricted political participation. By the early 1850s, every state had extended suffrage to all white males who were at least twenty-one years of age. Most southern states also removed the property requirements for holding state offices. In addition, increasing numbers of local and state officials were chosen by the voters. Justices of the peace, judges, militia officers, and others had to win elections rather than the favor of the governor or legislature. To be sure, undemocratic features lingered. In several states, the plantation districts still wielded disproportionate power in the legislatures. Nevertheless, with certain exceptions, southern politics increasingly took place within a democratic political structure.

> *The nonslaveholding white majority wielded less political power than their numbers indicated. The slaveholding white minority wielded more.*

White male suffrage ushered in an era of vigorous electoral competition. Eager voters rushed to the polls to exercise their new rights. In South Carolina, for example, in the 1810 election—the last election with voting restrictions in place—only 43 percent of white men cast ballots. But in the first election held after the state dropped its property requirement, nearly 64 percent of white men voted. And by 1824, the number of white men voting had climbed to a remarkable 76 percent. High turnouts became hallmarks of southern electoral politics. Elections in this democratic arena were spirited, even raucous. Governor John A. Wise claimed that in Virginia, "everybody talked politics everywhere." Candidates crisscrossed their electoral districts, speaking to groups several times a day for weeks on end. Voters displayed considerable political savvy and expected solid argument as well as stirring oratory. They also demanded good entertainment—barbecues and bands, rum and races. Candidates competed in producing extravaganzas, hoping to attract attention and votes.

As politics became aggressively democratic, it also grew fiercely partisan. From the 1830s to the 1850s, Whigs and Democrats battled for the electorate's favor. In most southern states, the two parties competed fairly equally. Whigs and Democrats both presented themselves as the plain white folks' best friend. All candidates declared their fervent commitment to republican equality and pledged themselves to defend the people's liberty. Each party sought to sour the other party's relationship with voters by portraying it as a collection of rich, snobbish, selfish men who had antidemocratic designs up their silk sleeves. Each, in turn, claimed for itself the mantle of humble "servant of the people."

The Whig and Democratic Parties sought to serve the people differently, however. Southern Whigs tended, as Whigs did elsewhere in the nation, to favor government intervention in the economy, and Democrats tended to oppose it. Whigs generally backed state support of banks, railroads, and corporations, arguing that government aid would stimulate the economy, enlarge opportunity, and thus increase the general welfare. Democrats emphasized the threat to individual liberty that government intervention posed, claiming that granting favors to special economic interests would result in concentrated power, which would jeopardize the common man's opportunity and equality. Beginning with the panic of 1837, the parties clashed repeatedly on concrete economic and financial issues.

No simple formula explains who was likely to become a Whig or a Democrat. Many factors came into play, but in the South, party conflict often reflected geography. Different regions within states had different economic needs, which encouraged them to tilt toward one party or the other. In North Carolina, for example, farmers in the eastern coastal plain (a region that was intersected by navigable rivers) had little need for better transportation facilities for their crops and thus displayed little interest in the Whig Party's program of expensive, government-backed internal improvements. But ambitious farmers in the western Piedmont and mountains (regions without good natural transportation) looked more favorably on state aid to internal improvements and thus on the Whig Party. Other southern states revealed similar relationships among geography, economic need, and party loyalty. Inevitably, however, party allegiance also reflected intangibles such as friendships, family histories, and neighborhood traditions.

Planter Power

Whether Whig or Democrat, southern officeholders were likely to be slave owners. The power slaveholders exerted over slaves did not translate directly into political authority over whites, however. In the nineteenth century, political power could be won only at the ballot box, and almost everywhere, nonslaveholders were in the majority. Yet year after year, proud and noisily egalitarian common men elected wealthy slaveholders.

In 1850, the percentage of slave owners in state legislatures ranged from 39 percent in Texas to more than 81 percent in North Carolina. Legislators not only tended to own slaves—they often owned large numbers. The percentage of planters (individuals with twenty or more slaves) in southern legislatures in 1850 ranged from 5.5 percent in Texas to 53.5 percent in South Carolina. In North Carolina, where only 3 percent of the state's white families belonged to the planter class, 36 percent of the legislature were planters. In Georgia's legislature, the president of the Senate owned 65 slaves and the speaker of the House of Representatives owned 122 slaves. The democratization of politics in the nineteenth century meant that more ordinary citizens served in government than in the eighteenth century, but yeomen and artisans remained rare sights in the halls of southern legislatures.

Upper-class dominance of southern politics represented, in part, the persistence of old patterns. It reflected the strength of the rural folk culture, which valued tradition, continuity, and stability. In the colonial era, yeomen had looked to the upper class for political leadership. Large planters pos-

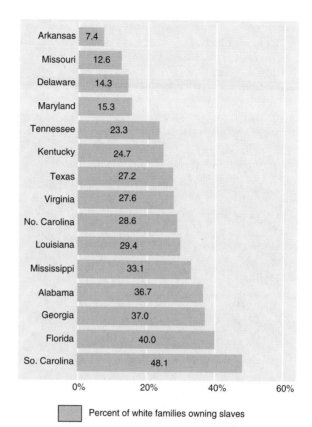

FIGURE 12.3
Slave Ownership, 1860
Whites in the Lower South were much more likely to own slaves than whites in the Upper South.

sessed great wealth, education, oratorical gifts, leisure, experience in public affairs, the habit of command, and eagerness to serve. Notions of hierarchy and habits of deference declined in the nineteenth century as egalitarianism and democracy rose, but planter status remained important in the South and the surest ticket to political advancement.

But tradition was not enough to ensure planter rule. Slaveholders had to persuade the white majority that what was good for slaveholders was also good for them. Slaveless whites proved to be receptive to the planters' argument. The South had, on the whole, done well by them. Most had farms of their own. They participated as equals in a democratic political system. As white men, they enjoyed an elevated social status, above all blacks and in theory equal to all other whites. As long as slavery existed, they could dream of joining the planter class, of rising above the drudgery of field labor.

TABLE 12.1

SLAVEHOLDERS AND PLANTERS IN LEGISLATURES, 1850 AND 1860

Percent of Slaveholders		
Legislature	1850	1860
Virginia	67.1	67.3
Maryland	56.3	53.4
North Carolina	51.5	85.8
Kentucky	66.4	60.6
Tennessee	41.0	66.0
Missouri	35.9	41.2
Arkansas	53.6	42.0
South Carolina	80.5	81.7
Georgia	69.7	71.6
Florida	N/D*	55.4
Alabama	66.4	76.3
Mississippi	61.5	73.4
Louisiana	42.6	63.8
Texas	38.8	54.1

Percent of Planters†		
Legislature	1850	1860
Virginia	22.9	24.2
Maryland	12.6	19.3
North Carolina	22.8	36.6
Kentucky	14.9	8.4
Tennessee	7.0	14.0
Missouri	1.3	5.3
Arkansas	10.3	13.0
South Carolina	53.5	55.4
Georgia	29.8	29.0
Florida	N/D	20.0
Alabama	33.6	40.8
Mississippi	30.3	49.5
Louisiana	19.8	23.5
Texas	5.5	18.1

*N/D: not determined.
†Planters: owned 20 or more slaves.

Source: Adapted from Ralph A. Wooster, *The People in Power: Courthouse and Statehouse in the Lower South, 1850–1860* (1969), 41; *Politicians, Planters, and Plain Folks: Courthouse and Statehouse in the Upper South* (1975), 40. Courtesy of the University of Tennessee Press.

And they were as certain as any slave owner that emancipation would be catastrophic. Slaveless men found much to celebrate in the slave South and saw their slaveholding neighbors as men to respect, emulate, and elect to public office.

Slaveholders took pains to win the plain folk's trust and to nurture their respect. In the plantation districts especially, where slaveholders and non-slaveholders lived side by side, planters had to act sensitively. Planters were powerful neighbors, and economic advantage lay heavily on their side. But the gentry learned that flexing their economic muscle was a poor way to win the political allegiance of common men. Instead, they developed a lighter touch, fully attentive to their own interests but aware of the personal feelings of poorer whites. One South Carolinian told his wealthy neighbor that he had a bright political future because he never thought himself "too good to sit down & talk to a poor man."

Not all of the gentry behaved astutely, however. Plain folk still encountered strutting slave owners. A slaveless farmer in Tennessee declared that in his neighborhood, "all who owned as much as one negro seemed to feel that they were in a separate and higher class than the common people." Another claimed that "Negroes and white men did the work" while slaveholders spent their time "hunting and fishing and riding around." But no slave master with political ambitions could afford to play the aristocrat. Even if he believed that the hierarchical social relations of plantations should extend to the broader community, he could not treat white men like slaves. Open elitism was political suicide.

Smart candidates found ways to convince wary yeomen of their democratic convictions and egalitarian sentiments, whether they were genuine or not. When Walter L. Steele ran for a seat in the North Carolina legislature in 1846, he commented sarcastically to a friend that he was "busily engaged in proving to the people, the soundness of my political faith, and the purity of my personal character & playing the fool to a considerable extent, as you know, all candidates are obliged to do." He detested pandering to the electorate, but he had learned to speak with a "candied tongue."

Young John A. Quitman understood what it took to win a seat in the Mississippi legislature. At one campaign stop, he amazed a boisterous crowd of small farmers by not only entering but winning contests in jumping, boxing, wrestling, and sprinting. For his finale he outshot the area's champion marksman. Then, demonstrating his deft political touch, he gave his prize, a fat ox, to the defeated rifleman. The electorate showed its approval by sending Quitman to the state capital.

The massive representation of slaveholders ensured that southern legislatures would make every effort to preserve slavery. Georgia politics show how well the planters protected themselves in the political struggle. In 1850, about half of the state's revenues came from taxes on slave property, the characteristic form of planter wealth. However, the tax rate on slaves was trifling, only about one-fifth the rate on land. Moreover, planters benefited far more than other social groups from public spending, for financing railroads—which carried cotton to market—was the largest state expenditure in the late antebellum period. The legislature established low tax rates on land, the characteristic form of yeoman wealth, which meant that the typical yeomen's annual tax bill was small. Still, relative to their wealth, large slaveholders paid less than did other whites. Relative to their numbers, they got more. A sympathetic slaveholding legislature protected planters' interests and gave the impression of protecting the small farmers' interest as well.

In the 1830s, white Southerners decided that slavery was too important to debate, especially with the specter of abolitionism in the North. "So interwoven is [slavery] with our interest, our manners, our climate and our very being," one man declared in 1833, "that no change can ever possibly be effected without a civil commotion from which the heart of a patriot must turn with horror." A "cotton curtain" descended along the Mason-Dixon line that ended free speech on the slavery question. Slavery's critics were dismissed from college faculties, driven from pulpits, and hounded from political life. Sometimes they fell victim to vigilantes and mob violence. One could defend slavery; one could even delicately suggest mild reforms. But no Southerner could safely call slavery evil or sinful or advocate its destruction.

By gagging slavery's critics, slaveholders gained real advantages. In 1857, for example, Hinton Rowan Helper, a North Carolinian who moved north, published *The Impending Crisis of the South*, in which he argued that slavery denied nonslaveholding whites the opportunities for economic advancement that free-labor societies offered. Slaveholders found *The Impending Crisis* deeply disquieting, but rather than confront the book's arguments, they simply banned it. The South's small farmers, whose economic advancement had stalled in the 1850s, remained unaware of Helper's economic broadside against slavery. Instead, they heard the South's politicians, academics, and clergy celebrate slavery's benefits.

In the antebellum South, therefore, the rise of the common man occurred alongside the continuing, even growing, power of the planter class. Rather than pitting slaveholders against nonslaveholders, elections remained an effective means of binding the region's whites together. Elections affirmed the sovereignty of white men, whether genteel planter or plain folk, and the subordination of African Americans. Those twin themes played well among white women as well. Although unable to vote, white women supported equality for whites and slavery for blacks.

Conclusion: A Slave Society

Southerners and Northerners came to see the South as fundamentally different from the rest of the nation. It was a rural region with a biracial population that reflected the dominance of plantation slavery. Regional differences generally increased over time, not merely because the South became more and more dominated by slavery, but also because developments in the North rapidly propelled it in a very different direction.

Much more than racial slavery contributed to the South's distinctiveness and to the loyalty and regional identification of its whites. Southerners felt strong attachments to local communities, to extended families, to personal, face-to-face relationships, to rural life, to evangelical Protestantism, and to codes of honor and chivalry, among other things. But slavery was crucial to the South's economy, society, and culture, as well as to its developing sectional consciousness. After the 1830s, little disturbed the white consensus south of the Mason-Dixon line that racial slavery was necessary and just. By making all blacks a pariah class, all whites gained a measure of equality and harmony.

Racism did not erase all stress along class lines. Nor did the other features of southern life that helped confine class tensions: the wide availability of land, rapid economic mobility, the democratic nature of political life, the shrewd behavior of slaveholders toward poorer whites, common kinship, and rural folkways. Anxious slaveholders continued to worry that yeomen would defect from the proslavery consensus, but during the 1850s a far more ominous division emerged between the "slave states" and the "free states."

CHRONOLOGY

1808	External slave trade outlawed.
1810s–1850s	Suffrage gradually extended throughout South to white males over twenty-one years of age.
1820s–1830s	Southern legislatures enact slave codes to strengthen slavery.
	Southern legislatures enact laws to restrict growth of free black population and to hem in freedom of free blacks.
	Southern intellectuals begin to fashion systematic defense of slavery.
1820–1860	Cotton production soars from about 300,000 bales to nearly 5 million bales.
1822	Denmark Vesey's slave rebellion thwarted in South Carolina.
1831	Nat Turner's slave rebellion occurs in Virginia.
1860	The slave population of the South exceeds 4 million, an increase of 600 percent in seven decades.

BIBLIOGRAPHY

GENERAL WORKS

John B. Boles, *The South through Time: A History of an American Region* (1995).

W. J. Cash, *The Mind of the South* (1941).

William J. Cooper Jr. and Thomas E. Terrill, *The American South: A History* (1991).

Carl N. Degler, *Place over Time* (1977).

James McPherson, "Antebellum Southern Exceptionalism: A New Look at an Old Question," *Civil War History* (September 1983), 230–44.

I. A. Newby, *The South: A History* (1978).

James Oakes, *Slavery and Freedom: An Interpretation of the Old South* (1990).

David C. Roller and Robert W. Twyman, eds., *The Encyclopedia of Southern History* (1979).

Charles R. Wilson and William Ferris, eds., *Encyclopedia of Southern Culture* (1989).

C. Vann Woodward, *The Burden of Southern History* (rev. ed., 1968).

THE ECONOMY

Fred Bateman and Thomas Weiss, *A Deplorable Scarcity: The Failure of Industrialization in the Slave Economy* (1981).

Peter A. Coclanis, *The Shadow of a Dream: Economic Life and Death in the South Carolina Low Country, 1670–1920* (1989).

Henry C. Dethloff, *A History of the American Rice Industry, 1685-1985* (1988).

Charles B. Dew, *Ironmaker to the Confederacy: Joseph R. Anderson and the Tredegar Iron Works* (1966).

Robert W. Fogel, *Without Consent or Contract* (1988).

Robert W. Fogel and Stanley Engerman, *Time on the Cross* (1974).

Eugene D. Genovese, *The Political Economy of Slavery* (1965).

Lewis C. Gray, *History of Agriculture in the Southern United States*, 2 vols. (1933).

Herbert G. Gutman, *Slavery and the Numbers Game* (1975).

Sam B. Hilliard, *Atlas of Antebellum Southern Agriculture* (1984).

Richard G. Lowe and Randolph B. Campbell, *Planters and Plain Folk: Agriculture in Antebellum Texas* (1987).

John H. Moore, *The Emergence of the Cotton Kingdom in the Old Southwest* (1988).

Joseph P. Reidy, *From Slavery to Agrarian Capitalism in the Cotton Plantation South* (1993).

Larry Schweikart, *Banking in the American South from the Age of Jackson to Reconstruction* (1987).

Harold D. Woodman, *King Cotton and His Retainers* (1968).

Gavin Wright, *The Political Economy of the Cotton South* (1978).

Gavin Wright, *Old South, New South* (1986).

SLAVEHOLDERS

Carol Bleser, ed., *The Hammonds of Redcliff* (1981).

Carol Bleser, ed., *Secret and Sacred: The Diaries of James Henry Hammond, a Southern Slaveholder* (1988).

Jane T. Censer, *North Carolina Planters and Their Children, 1800–1860* (1984).

Catherine Clinton, *The Plantation Mistress* (1982).

Drew G. Faust, *James Henry Hammond and the Old South* (1982).

Drew G. Faust, ed., *The Ideology of Slavery* (1981).

Elizabeth Fox-Genovese, *Within the Plantation Household* (1988).

Jean Friedman, *The Enclosed Garden* (1985).

Eugene D. Genovese, *The World the Slaveholders Made* (1969).

Jan Lewis, *The Pursuit of Happiness: Family and Values in Jefferson's Virginia* (1983).

James Oakes, *The Ruling Race* (1982).

Michael O'Brien, *A Character of Hugh Legare* (1985).

Theodore Rosengarten, *Tombee: Portrait of a Cotton Planter* (1986).

Anne F. Scott, *The Southern Lady* (1970).

Steven M. Stowe, *Intimacy and Power in the Old South* (1987).

Michael Tadman, *Speculators and Slaves: Masters, Traders, and Slaves in the Old South* (1989).

Larry Tise, *Proslavery* (1987).

C. Vann Woodward, ed., *Mary Chesnut's Civil War* (1981).

SLAVES, SLAVERY, AND RACE RELATIONS

For general works, see:

John W. Blassingame, *The Slave Community* (1972).

John W. Blassingame, ed., *Slave Testimony* (1977).

John B. Boles, *Black Southerners, 1619–1869* (1983).

Carl N. Degler, *Neither Black nor White: Slavery and Race Relations in Brazil and the United States* (1971).

Paul D. Escott, *Slavery Remembered* (1979).

George M. Fredrickson, *The Black Image in the White Mind* (1971).

George M. Fredrickson, *The Arrogance of Race* (1988).

Eugene D. Genovese, *Roll, Jordan, Roll* (1974).

Vincent Harding, *There Is a River* (1981).

Peter Kolchin, *Unfree Labor* (1987).

Peter Kolchin, *American Slavery, 1619–1877* (1993).

Lawrence W. Levine, *Black Culture and Black Consciousness* (1977).

Randall M. Miller and John David Smith, eds., *Dictionary of Afro-American Slavery* (1988).

Leslie H. Owens, *This Species of Property* (1976).

George P. Rawick, ed., *The American Slave: A Composite Autobiography*, 41 vols. (1972–1979).

George P. Rawick, *From Sundown to Sunup* (1972).

Willie Lee Rose, *Slavery and Freedom* (1982).

Willie Lee Rose, ed., *A Documentary History of Slavery in North America* (1976).

Kenneth M. Stampp, *The Peculiar Institution* (1956).

Sterling Stuckey, *Slave Culture* (1987).

For important aspects of slavery, see:

Eugene D. Genovese, *From Rebellion to Revolution* (1979).

Herbert G. Gutman, *The Black Family in Slavery and Freedom, 1750–1925* (1976).

Michael P. Johnson, "Work, Culture, and the Slave Community," *Labor History* (Summer 1986), 325–55.

Jacqueline Jones, *Labor of Love, Labor of Sorrow* (1985).

Ann Patton Malone, *Sweet Chariot: Slavery, Family, and Household Structure in Nineteenth-Century Louisiana* (1992).

Albert Raboteau, *Slave Religion* (1978).

Todd Savitt, *Medicine and Slavery* (1978).

William K. Scarborough, *The Overseer* (1966).

Robert S. Starobin, *Industrial Slavery in the Old South* (1970).

Brenda E. Stevenson, *Life in Black and White: Family and Community in the Slave South* (1996).

William L. Van Deburg, *The Slave Driver* (1979).

Richard C. Wade, *Slavery in the Cities* (1964).

Thomas L. Webber, *Deep like the Rivers: Education in the Slave Quarter Community* (1978).

Deborah G. White, *Ar'nt I a Woman? Female Slaves in the Plantation South* (1985).

For state and local studies:

Randolph B. Campbell, *An Empire for Slavery: The Peculiar Institution in Texas, 1821–1865* (1989).

Margaret W. Creel, *"A Peculiar People": Slave Religion and Community-Culture among the Gullahs* (1988).

Charles B. Dew, *Bond of Iron: Master and Slave at Buffalo Forge* (1994).

Douglas R. Egerton, *Gabriel's Rebellion: The Virginia Slave Conspiracies of 1800 and 1802* (1993).

Charles Joyner, *Down by the Riverside: A South Carolina Slave Community* (1984).

John Lofton, *Denmark Vesey's Revolt* (1983).

Melton A. McLaurin, *Celia, a Slave* (1991).

Stephen B. Oates, *The Fires of Jubilee: Nat Turner's Fierce Rebellion* (1975).

SOCIETY AND CULTURE

Adele Logan Alexander, *Ambiguous Lives: Free Women of Color in Rural Georgia* (1991).

Harriet E. Amos, *Cotton City: Urban Development in Antebellum Mobile* (1985).

Edward L. Ayers, *Vengeance and Justice* (1984).

David Bailey, *Shadow on the Church: Southwestern Evangelical Religion and the Issue of Slavery, 1783–1860* (1985).

Fred Arthur Bailey, *Class and Tennessee's Confederate Generation* (1987).

Peter Bardaglio, *Reconstructing the Household: Families, Sex, and the Law in the Nineteenth-Century South* (1995).

Ira Berlin, *Slaves without Masters* (1974).

John B. Boles, *The Great Revival, 1787–1805* (1972).

Dickson D. Bruce Jr., *And They All Sang Hallelujah* (1974).

Dickson D. Bruce Jr., *Violence and Culture in the Antebellum South* (1979).

Orville Vernon Burton, *In My Father's House Are Many Mansions: Family and Community in Edgefield, South Carolina* (1985).

Orville Vernon Burton and Robert C. McMath Jr., eds., *Class, Conflict, and Consensus: Antebellum Southern Community Studies* (1982).

Victoria Bynum, *Unruly Women: The Politics of Social and Sexual Control in the Old South* (1992).

Randolph B. Campbell and Richard G. Lowe, *Wealth and Power in Antebellum Texas* (1977).

Bruce Collins, *White Society in the Antebellum South* (1985).

Leonard P. Curry, *The Free Black in Urban America, 1800–1850* (1981).

Carl N. Degler, *The Other South* (1974).

Paul Escott, *Power and Privilege in North Carolina, 1850–1900* (1985).

James O. Farmer Jr., *The Metaphysical Confederacy: James Henley Thornwell and the Synthesis of Southern Values* (1986).

Drew G. Faust, *A Sacred Circle: The Dilemma of the Intellectual in the Old South* (1977).

Barbara J. Fields, *Slavery and Freedom on the Middle Ground: Maryland during the Nineteenth Century* (1985).

J. Wayne Flint, *Dixie's Forgotten People* (1979).

Walter J. Fraser et al., eds., *The Web of Southern Social Relations* (1985).

David R. Goldfield, *Urban Growth in the Age of Sectionalism: Virginia, 1774–1861* (1977).

David R. Goldfield, *Cotton Fields and Skyscrapers* (rev. ed., 1989).

Stephen Hahn, *The Roots of Southern Populism* (1983).

J. William Harris, *Plain Folk and Gentry in a Slave Society* (1985).

John C. Inscoe, *Mountain Masters, Slavery, and the Sectional Crisis in Western North Carolina* (1989).

Michael P. Johnson and James L. Roark, *Black Masters* (1984).

Robert C. Kenser, *Kinship and Neighborhood in a Southern Community: Orange County, North Carolina, 1849–1881* (1987).

Lawrence H. Larsen, *The Rise of the Urban South* (1985).

Suzanne Lebsock, *The Free Women of Petersburg* (1984).

Anne C. Loveland, *Southern Evangelicals and the Social Order, 1820–1860* (1980).

Donald G. Mathews, *Religion in the Old South* (1977).

John M. McCardell, *Idea of a Southern Nation* (1979).

Stephanie McCurry, *Masters of Small Worlds: Yeoman Households, Gender Relations, and the Political Culture of the Antebellum South Carolina Low Country* (1995).

Sally G. McMillen, *Motherhood in the Old South* (1990).

Grady McWhiney, *Cracker Culture* (1988).

Gary B. Mills, *The Forgotten People: Cane River's Creoles of Color* (1984).

Thomas D. Morris, *Southern Slavery and the Law, 1619–1860* (1996).

John Solomon Otto, *The Southern Frontiers, 1607–1860* (1989).

Loren Schweninger, *Black Property Owners in the South, 1790–1915* (1990).

Bertram Wyatt-Brown, *Southern Honor* (1982).

POLITICS AND POLITICAL CULTURE

Paul H. Bergeron, *Antebellum Politics in Tennessee* (1982).

William J. Cooper Jr., *The South and the Politics of Slavery, 1828–1856* (1978).

William J. Cooper Jr., *Liberty and Slavery: Southern Politics to 1860* (1983).

Lacy K. Ford Jr., *Origins of Southern Radicalism: The South Carolina Upcountry, 1800–1860* (1988).

William M. Freehling, *Prelude to Civil War: The Nullification Controversy in South Carolina, 1816–1836* (1966).

William M. Freehling, *The Road to Disunion* (1990).

Kenneth S. Greenberg, *Masters and Statesmen: The Political Culture of American Slavery* (1985).

Thomas E. Jeffrey, *State Parties and National Politics: North Carolina, 1815–1861* (1989).

Marc W. Kruman, *Parties and Politics in North Carolina, 1836–1865* (1983).

Robert E. May, *John A. Quitman* (1985).

Craig M. Simpson, *A Good Southerner: The Life of Henry A. Wise of Virginia* (1985).

J. Mills Thornton III, *Politics and Power in a Slave Society: Alabama, 1800–1860* (1978).

Peter Wallenstein, *From Slave South to New South: Public Policy in Nineteenth-Century Georgia* (1987).

Harry L. Watson, *Jacksonian Politics and Community Conflict: The Emergence of the Second Party System in Cumberland County, North Carolina* (1981).

Ralph A. Wooster, *The People in Power: Courthouse and Statehouse in the Lower South, 1850–1860* (1969).

Ralph A. Wooster, *Politicians, Planters, and Plain Folks: Courthouse and Statehouse in the Upper South, 1850–1860* (1975).

**HOME INDUSTRIES
POLITICAL EMBLEM**

Common trades practiced by American workers are represented on this political emblem designed in Pennsylvania to be carried in political parades in 1840 by supporters of presidential candidate William Henry Harrison. Like most northern Whigs, Harrison favored a tariff to protect home industries. Carpenters, tanners, shoemakers, blacksmiths, masons, butchers, bakers, tailors, and farmers were represented by their tools. Try to identify the tool each might use. Note that the emblem identifies industries with hand tools rather than with complex machinery, illustrating that the transition to industrial production was still at an early stage in the 1840s and 1850s. The emblem also engages in a kind of political misrepresentation. Tariffs mostly protected domestic manufacturers of machine-made goods like textiles that already were produced in factories. Whigs used the symbols of handwork in this emblem to provide an appealing apple-pie image for the manufacturing industries that were protected by the tariffs. One cannot imagine, for example, a Whig enthusiast parading around with an emblem of a textile mill. Also notice that the emblem does not illustrate the skilled work done by women in homes throughout the nation such as cooking, dairying, and cleaning. What tools might be portrayed if the emblem featured women's work?

Chester County Historical Society, West Chester, Pa; George J. Fistrovich, Photographer.

ABRAHAM LINCOLN'S AMERICA

13

1800-1860

I
N DECEMBER 1816, Thomas Lincoln uprooted his young family—his wife, Nancy, and their children Sarah and Abraham—from their small Kentucky farm and moved across the Ohio River to south central Indiana. At that time Indiana "was a wild region," Abraham Lincoln remembered later; "the panther's scream filled the night with fear and bears preyed on the swine." For more than two months in the dead of winter, the Lincolns lived in a crude lean-to enclosed on three sides by limbs and brush, warmed somewhat by a fire just beyond the open side. Thomas built a log cabin nearby, and the family moved in shortly before Abraham's eighth birthday. The cabin stood "in an unbroken forest," Abraham recalled, and was so rough-hewn that when "a flock of wild turkeys approached the new log-cabin . . . [he] with a rifle gun, standing inside, shot through a crack, and killed one of them." Thomas did not own the land on which he built the cabin; instead, he squatted on land that belonged to the government. Months later, he filed papers and made a down payment to buy 160 acres from the government for two dollars an acre.

Thomas Lincoln had not been blessed with an easy life. Orphaned in 1782 after his father was killed by an Indian, Thomas became "a wandering laboring boy and grew up literally without education," his son Abraham explained. Thomas never learned to read and, Abraham wrote, he "never did more in the way of writing than to bunglingly sign his own name."

Hired out to neighbors and relatives in Kentucky, Thomas learned carpentry and, by the time he was twenty-five, had saved enough to buy a small farm, where he married Nancy Hanks in 1806. Like her husband, Nancy could not read; unlike him, she could not even sign her name. While he farmed, Thomas continued to work as a carpenter and used the income to buy more land. By the time Abraham was born in 1809, Thomas had purchased more than 500 acres of land in Kentucky. But by 1816, poor surveys and conflicting legal claims called into question Thomas's ownership of his land. Demoralized, he decided to start over in Indiana.

At the family's new homestead in the Indiana forest, Abraham Lincoln recalled later, "the clearing away of surplus wood was the great task ahead." Although Abraham was only eight years old, he "was large of his age, and had an axe put into his hands at once; and from that til within his twenty-third year, he was almost constantly handling that most useful instrument—less of course in plowing and harvesting seasons." While clearing land to farm, the Lincolns suffered another setback. Nancy Lincoln died in 1818. The next year, Thomas married Sarah Bush Johnston, a widow with three children. Including Thomas's own two children and a cousin who had come to stay with them, eight now lived in Lincoln's cabin.

And they made a go of it. "I was raised to farm work," Abraham wrote in 1859. He worked for neighbors for twenty-five cents a day and gave the money to his father. When he could be spared from work, the boy attended school, less than a year in all. "There was absolutely nothing to excite ambition for education," Lincoln recollected. Abraham hungered for learning. He borrowed every book he could find and read voraciously. At nineteen, he took his first trip away from home. He and a friend were hired to build a flatboat, load it with local produce, and float it down the Ohio and Mississippi to New Orleans. Lincoln earned $24 on the trip and gave the money to his father. But even with Thomas's earnings as a carpenter, that was not enough to keep the family afloat.

In 1830, Thomas decided once again to start over. For $125, considerably less than he had paid for it, he sold the Indiana farm where he and his family had labored for fourteen years. With his twenty-one-year-old son straddling one of the oxen pulling the family's three wagons, they moved two hundred miles west to the Sangamon River in central Illinois. Abraham's sister Sarah did not accompany them; in 1828, a year after her marriage to a young Indiana farmer, she had died in childbirth. Once again the Lincolns built a log cabin and moved in; once again Abraham pitched in to make "sufficient of rails to fence ten acres of ground, [then] fenced and broke the ground, and raised a crop of sown corn upon it the same year." When the spring thaw came, Thomas Lincoln picked up stakes again and moved about thirty miles east to Coles County, Illinois. But this time his son Abraham did not go along. This time Abraham set out on his own, a "friendless, uneducated, penniless boy," he wrote later, who had "separated from his father."

In 1851, after Abraham Lincoln had become a prosperous lawyer and ambitious politician who had represented his district in the Illinois legislature and the United States House of Representatives, Thomas Lincoln lay dying on his Coles County farm. Lincoln ignored letters from his step-brother, John D. Johnston, asking him to write to his father. When Thomas died, Abraham did not attend the funeral. When Lincoln heard that Johnston planned to sell out and move to Missouri, Lincoln wrote him a stinging letter that spelled out shortcomings Lincoln may also have glimpsed in his father, Thomas:

> What can you do in Missouri, better than here? Is the land any richer? Can you there, any more than here, raise corn, & wheat & oats, without work? Will any body there, any more than here, do your work for you? If you intend to go to work, there is no better place than right where you are; if you do not intend to go to work, you can not get along any where. Squirming & crawling about from place to place can

ABRAHAM LINCOLN'S HAT
Abraham Lincoln wore this stovepipe hat, made of beaver pelt, during his years as president of the United States. Stovepipe hats were worn by established, respectable, middle-class men in the 1850s. Workingmen and farmers would have felt out of place wearing such a hat, except perhaps on special occasions like weddings or funerals. Growing up in Kentucky, Indiana, and Illinois, Lincoln may have seen stovepipe hats on the leading men of his community, but he probably never owned one until he became an aspiring Illinois lawyer and politician. Wearing such a hat was a mark that one had achieved a certain success in life, in Lincoln's case the enormous social distance he had traveled from his backwoods origins to the White House. But even as president he continued a backwoods practice he began as a young postmaster in New Salem, Illinois, using his hat as a place to store letters and papers. Lincoln's law partner, William Herndon, termed Lincoln's hat "an extraordinary receptacle [that] served as his desk and memorandum book." Smithsonian Institution.

do no good. You have raised no crop this year, and what you really want is to sell the land, get the money and spend it . . . . [The] truth is, you are destitute because you have *idled* away all your time . . . . *Go to work* is the only cure for your case.

With relentless effort, Abraham Lincoln rose to the White House in 1861 from that three-sided lean-to in the Indiana wilderness in 1816. Like Lincoln, millions of Americans believed that with work they could make something of themselves, whatever their origins. From their point of view, individuals like John D. Johnston who did not work—who were improvident, foolish, or waiting for somebody else to help them—had only themselves to blame if they did not succeed. Work was a prerequisite, not a guarantee. As Thomas Lincoln's experience illustrated, the difficulties and risks were great. But as Abraham Lincoln's career showed, the possibilities were enormous. Such calculations spurred mid-nineteenth-century Americans to efforts that shaped the economic, cultural, and political contours of Lincoln's America and pushed the boundaries of the nation to the Rio Grande in the Southwest and the shores of the Pacific Ocean in the Far West. That expansion—economic, political, and geographical—also raised anew the question of slavery, a question Lincoln ultimately confronted when he became commander in chief.

Economic and Industrial Evolution

In 1801, news that Thomas Jefferson had been elected president of the United States spread as fast as a man could ride on horseback. When Jefferson traveled the hundred miles to Washington from his home at Monticello in Virginia, he had to swim his horse across the five rivers that lacked a ferry. Sixty years later, when the electoral college confirmed Abraham Lincoln's election to the White House, the news raced almost instantaneously along telegraph lines that connected Washington to the far corners of the nation. Lincoln journeyed to Washington from his home in Springfield, Illinois, by railroad. When Jefferson became president, Springfield did not exist. In 1801, the geographical center of the U.S. population lay *east* of Washington, D.C. By 1861, the geographical center of the nation's population had moved more than five hundred miles west, near Chillicothe, Ohio. The changes that occurred between the elections of Jefferson and Lincoln—changes that happened mostly within Lincoln's lifetime—signaled the economic growth that transformed the nation into a bustling transcontinental colossus.

Economic Growth, 1800–1860: An Overview

In 1800, the United States faced daunting obstacles to economic growth. Unlike England—the world leader in mechanization, factory production, and steam power—the United States produced nearly all manufactured goods by hand in small shops or at home rather than by machines in factories. Wind, water, and muscle powered production, as they had

for centuries. Nearly all of the nation's 5 million people lived east of the Appalachian Mountains. Unbroken forest stretched from the Appalachians almost to the Mississippi River. Long-distance transportation was difficult, time-consuming, and unpredictable. Travelers from New York City could book better, more comfortable passage to London, England, than to Albany, New York.

Despite these obstacles to economic change, a profound economic transformation occurred during the first six decades of the nineteenth century. (Economic changes in the early nineteenth century are discussed in chapter 11.) By 1860, Americans' per capita income was twice what it had been in 1800. At first glance that does not seem impressive evidence of economic growth. But consider that during those same years the nation's population grew sixfold, to over 31 million. Therefore, the total output of the American economy multiplied twelve times in sixty years. Fundamental changes in American society fueled this phenomenal economic growth.

> *The changes that occurred between the elections of Jefferson and Lincoln—changes that happened mostly within Lincoln's lifetime—signaled the economic growth that transformed the nation into a bustling transcontinental colossus.*

First, the American population began a long-term shift from farms to cities that would continue well into the twentieth century. As the nation's population grew, the number of rural Americans increased from about 5 million in 1800 to more than 25 million in 1860. Farmers still made up 80 percent of the nation's population in 1860. But like Abraham Lincoln, millions of Americans left the farm to make a life in the city. The fraction of Americans who lived in urban areas grew from 6 percent in 1800 to 20 percent in 1860. In 1800, the nation had only 7 cities roughly the size of Lincoln's hometown of Springfield, Illinois (9,500 people in 1860); by 1860, there were 186 such cities. Large cities also grew. In 1800, only Philadelphia had a population over 50,000; by 1860, there were 16 such cities. People in these large cities made up 10 percent of the nation's population in 1860, compared with only 1 percent in 1800.

A second major change, closely related to the shift of population from farms to cities, was that a growing number of Americans worked in factories. In 1800, only about 3 percent of American workers were engaged in manufacturing outside the home; by 1860, almost 20 percent of the labor force worked in factories. This trend made an important contribution to the nation's economic growth because, in general, factory workers were twice as productive (in output per unit of labor input) as agricultural workers.

A third fundamental change—a change in the source of energy—permitted factories to be brought to the labor force in cities. The first American factories had to be situated on streams that supplied water power, and workers had to be attracted to the factory site. But steam power freed business owners to locate their factories anywhere workers and materials could be readily brought together. Since manufacturers needed a steady supply of cheap labor, they tended to locate factories in cities and ship in the materials of production. Steam power had other important advantages over water power. It could be generated year-round regardless of the weather, and it could be produced in greater or lesser quantities as needed for the job at hand.

Beginning around 1840, steam became harnessed to manufacturing, but the transition was slow, delayed by the continued effectiveness of water-powered factories. By 1850, steam supplied just 10 percent of the total inanimate power used in manufacturing; animal and human muscles still provided 33 times more energy for manufacturing than steam. The trend toward steam accelerated during the 1850s. By 1860, for example, Massachusetts manufacturers used steam to produce most of their wood and metal products.

The shortage of cheap, plentiful fuel was the chief obstacle to earlier use of steam in factories. During the 1830s, extensive mining began in the Pennsylvania coal fields and massive quantities of coal became available for industrial fuel. Heat from coal not only powered steam engines in factories. It also permitted new methods of iron production and metalworking required for the full-scale mechanization of production. In addition, those methods made it possible to couple steam power to land transportation in the building of railroads.

This cascade of interrelated developments—steam, coal, iron, mechanization, railroads—had begun to transform the character of the American economy by the 1850s. Historians have often referred to this transformation as an industrial revolution.

Certainly the profound changes in the American economy between 1800 and 1860 pushed the nation toward industrialization. Yet those changes did not cause a revolutionary discontinuity in the economy or society during these years. The United States remained overwhelmingly agricultural. Old methods of production continued alongside the new. Changes in production tended to be evolutionary and cumulative. In the long term—by the early twentieth century—the consequences of these and other changes were indeed revolutionary. Between 1800 and 1860, however, the American economy underwent a process that might best be termed "industrial evolution."

That process was made possible by a fourth fundamental development that propelled American economic growth. Between 1800 and 1860, the declining fraction of the population engaged in agriculture managed to grow enough food to feed themselves and the growing population in cities. Clearly, agricultural productivity (defined as crop output per unit of labor input) increased. Economic historians estimate that agricultural productivity nearly doubled during the sixty-year period. This dramatic increase contributed more than any other single factor to the economic growth of Lincoln's America. While cities, factories, and steam engines blossomed throughout the nation—especially outside the South—the roots of American economic growth lay in agriculture.

Agriculture and Land Policy

It may seem odd to consider an ax a basic agricultural tool, like a hoe or shovel. Yet farmers in Lincoln's America needed axes. Lincoln wrote that he had "an axe put into his hands" when he was eight years old and he "was almost constantly handling that most useful instrument." A French traveler observed in 1831 that "country-dwelling Americans spend half their lives cutting trees, and their children learn . . . at an early age to use the axe against the trees, their enemies." Americans had "a general feeling of hatred against trees," the Frenchman reported. Although the traveler exaggerated, his observation contained an important truth. Forests impeded agriculture. With their "most useful instrument," farmers leveled trees, cleared land for planting, and built cabins, fences, and barns.

The sheer physical labor required to convert forest to field limited agricultural productivity. Energy that might have gone to growing crops went instead to felling trees. But as farmers like Thomas

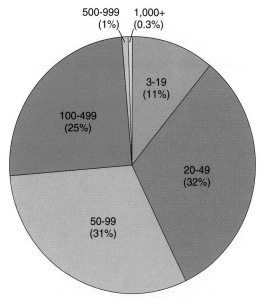

500-999
(1%)   1,000+
(0.3%)

3-19
(11%)

100-499
(25%)

20-49
(32%)

50-99
(31%)

Farm sizes (in acres) as a percent of all farms

FIGURE 13.1
Farm Sizes in 1860
The United States was a nation of small farms; almost
three out of four farms were under 100 acres. All but
a few of the farms over 1,000 acres were located in
the South.

Lincoln pushed the frontier of farming westward, they encountered thinner forests and eventually the Midwest's comparatively treeless prairie. Rich prairie soils produced somewhat higher crop yields than eastern farms, and farmers migrated to the Midwest by the tens of thousands between 1830 and 1860. The population of Indiana, Illinois, Michigan, Wisconsin, and Iowa exploded tenfold, growing from 500,000 in 1830 to more than 5 million by 1860, four times faster than the growth of the nation as a whole. During the 1850s, Illinois added more people than any other state in the Union. On the midwestern prairie, farmers could spend less time with an ax and more time at the plow or hoe. The diminished need for axes on midwestern farms significantly boosted agricultural productivity by markedly reducing the labor required to grow a bushel of corn or wheat.

Labor-saving improvements in other farm implements also hiked agricultural productivity. Abraham Lincoln pointed out that as a youngster he used his ax "less of course in plowing and harvesting seasons," when every farmer's labor needs peaked. Early in the nineteenth century, most farmers used

wooden plows, if they plowed at all. Frontier farmers commonly planted their first crop simply by dropping kernels of corn into holes chopped in the ground with an ax or a hoe. Wooden plows required strenuous efforts from the animals who pulled them and the farmers who guided them because they tended to stick to the soil rather than cut through it. They also broke easily. In 1819, Jethro Wood patented a plow that used replaceable cast-iron parts to cut and scour the soil. Wood's cast-iron plow required only half as much labor as a wooden plow, and farmers throughout the Northeast quickly adopted it or one of the many variations crafted by local blacksmiths.

But cast-iron plows proved too weak and sticky for the thick turf and dense soil of the midwestern prairie. In 1837, John Deere patented a strong, smooth steel plow that sliced through prairie soil so cleanly that farmers called it the "singing plow." Deere's steel plow underwent many improvements that made plowing less work, prairie farmers more productive, and Deere's company the leading plow manufacturer in the Midwest, turning out more than ten thousand plows a year by the late 1850s. Farmers, blacksmiths, and mechanics continually tinkered to make plows stronger, easier to use, and cheaper. In 1860 alone, the federal government issued 109 patents for plow improvements. By 1860, the energy for plowing still came from animal and human muscles, but better plows permitted that energy to break more ground and plant more crops.

Improvements in grain harvesting also multiplied farmers' productivity. Nearly all American farmers grew corn as a basic dietary staple for themselves and their animals. Corn pone, corn fritters, corn bread, corn mush, and other corn delicacies appeared on plates throughout rural America. Farmers harvested hundreds of millions of bushels of corn every year, all by hand. Labor-saving devices developed instead for the wheat harvest. Outside the South, most farmers planted wheat, and in the Midwest—where soil and climate conditions were nearly ideal—many planted mostly wheat. Wheat was more difficult than corn to grow and harvest, but it was also more desirable. More dense and less bulky than corn, wheat was more readily transported to market and sold for a much higher price.

The crucial point in wheat production came at harvest time. Once ripe, wheat had to be cut quickly before rain or wind ruined the crop or overripe grains dropped from the stalk and scattered uselessly on the ground. Early in the nineteenth century, farmers harvested wheat by cutting the stalks

HARVESTING GRAIN WITH CRADLES
This late-nineteenth-century painting shows the grain harvest during the mid-nineteenth century at Bishop Hill, Illinois, a Swedish community where the artist, Olof Krans, and his parents settled in 1850. The men swing cradles, slowly cutting a swath through the grain; the women gather the cut grain into sheaves to be hauled away later for threshing. As a well-organized community, Bishop Hill could call upon the labor of a large number of men and women at harvest time. Most farmers had only a few family members and a hired hand or two to help with the harvest. Note that although the grain field appears level enough to be ideal for a mechanical reaper, all the work is done by hand; no machine is in sight.
Bishop Hill State Historic Site, Illinois Historic Preservation Agency.

with a sharp-bladed scythe. Working hard, a farmer could scythe three-fourths of an acre of wheat a day. By 1850, most farmers had adopted scythes with cradles (a frame that projected above the scythe). Their long wooden fingers were able to gather more grain stalks to be cut by each stroke of the attached blade. A cradle allowed a farmer to harvest two or three acres of wheat a day—a considerable advance over the old-fashioned scythe—but it was heavy, backbreaking work.

Tinkerers throughout the nation tried to fashion a mechanical reaper that would make the wheat harvest easier and quicker. In 1830, Cyrus McCormick cobbled together a prototype reaper that indicated both the possibilities and the problems.

McCormick and others experimented with designs, parts, and methods of manufacturing until the late 1840s, when more than a few mechanical reapers were at work in American wheat fields. McCormick went from farm to farm touting his reaper, trying to talk farmers into buying one for $100 to $150. A mechanical reaper allowed a farmer to harvest twelve acres a day, at least when it worked. As design and manufacturing improved, reapers became more reliable and more readily repaired, and thousands of farmers decided to buy them. By 1860, about 80,000 reapers had been sold, making it possible for the new owners to harvest three or four times more wheat than with a cradle. Although reapers represented the cutting edge of agricultural technology, they still had to be powered by the muscles of a horse or an ox. Most farmers had not yet shifted their wheat harvest to animal power, so they continued to muscle the heavy cradle through their grain.

Mechanical reapers and better plows permitted farmers to produce more corn or wheat only because the labor farmers saved could be used to plow and plant more land. Neither the reapers nor the plows increased the yield of a given acre of cultivated land. Instead, they allowed more land to be brought into cultivation. Without access to fresh, uncultivated land, farmers could not have doubled the corn and wheat harvests between 1840 and 1860, as they in fact did. In the end, the agricultural productivity that fueled the nation's economy was an outgrowth of federal land policy.

From 1800 to 1860, the United States continued to be land rich and labor poor. During these years the nation became a great deal richer in land, acquiring more than a billion acres with the Louisiana Purchase and the annexation of Florida, Oregon, and vast territories following the Mexican War (discussed later in this chapter). The federal government made the land available for purchase to attract settlers and to generate revenues.

In 1800, federal land cost $2 an acre and a buyer was required to purchase at least 320 acres (half a square mile). Over the next six decades, the price of federal land dropped and the size of the minimum purchase shrank, bringing more land within reach of more farmers more readily. From 1820 to 1854, federal land cost $1.25 an acre. The minimum purchase shrank to 160 acres in 1804, to 80 acres in 1820, and to 40 acres in 1832.

Despite these reductions in price and minimum purchase requirements, millions of farmers could not afford federal land. Like Thomas Lincoln, they squatted on unclaimed federal land and carved out a farm they neither rented nor owned. These squatters sought the right (called "preemption") to buy the land they had made into a farm before the government sold it to some other buyer. In 1830, Congress passed a law guaranteeing such preemption and renewed the law until it became permanent in 1841. Although many poor farmers never accumulated enough money to purchase the land on which they squatted, they still benefited from the preemption laws. Poor squatters often sold their preemption right to somebody else who, in effect, paid them for the labor they had invested in clearing land and building a farm. That person could then exercise the squatters' right of preemption and purchase

the land at the government price while the squatters moved elsewhere, often to unclaimed federal land where they renewed the cycle of squatting and preemption.

Government land policy not only aided small farmers. It also enriched wily speculators who found ways to claim large tracts of the most desirable plots and sell them to settlers at a generous markup. Nonetheless, by making land available to millions of ordinary people, the federal government achieved the goal of attracting settlers to the new territories, which in due course joined the Union as new states. Above all, federal land policy created the basic precondition for the increase in agricultural productivity that underlay the nation's impressive economic growth.

Manufacturing and Mechanization

Changes in manufacturing arose in the context of the nation's land-rich, labor-poor economy. Manufacturers in England and other European countries worked in land-poor, labor-rich economies; there, meager opportunities in agriculture kept factory laborers plentiful and wages low. In the United States, geographical expansion and government land policies buoyed agriculture, keeping millions of people on the farm and thereby limiting the supply of workers for manufacturing and elevating wages. Because of this shortage of workers, manufacturers searched constantly for ways to save labor. Mechanization offered the best prospects. But it was easier to say "mechanize" than it was actually to build a machine to do a task previously done by human hands—and to do it better, faster, cheaper, and with tireless repetition.

Because of the shortage of workers, manufacturers searched constantly for ways to save labor. Mechanization offered the best prospects.

Consider the seemingly simple process of making axes. The ax market was a manufacturer's dream since Americans needed as many axes as they could get. In the early 1830s, however, each ax still had to be crafted by a skilled metalworker who welded a steel bit (the cutting edge) to a cast-iron poll (the head), pounded the metal into a wedge shape, made a hole for the handle, and then heated, hammered, ground, and polished the ax until it was ready to be sold. Between 1836 and 1849, Elisha K. Root, a machinist who worked at the Collins ax factory in Connecticut, invented a series of sophisticated machines that carried out these steps more quickly, safely, and cheaply and that did not require skilled operators. Root's machines allowed fewer workers with less skill to turn out twenty-five times as many axes as skilled craftsmen, and the machine-made axes were of better quality.

Manufacturers had such a strong incentive to save labor that mechanization marched forward as quickly as innovative ideas like Root's could be fashioned into workable combinations of gears, levers, screws, and pulleys. Outside the textile industry (see chapter 11), homegrown machines set the pace. Early in the nineteenth century, the manufacture of firearms was mechanized, led by gun makers at the federal armories who had to keep the army supplied with rifles and pistols. The desire to make each gun as much as possible like every other encouraged gun makers to devise uniform parts that could be interchanged from one gun to another. Although the parts often were not uniform enough to be literally interchangeable, with some filing here and jimmying there they were close enough to establish the principle of interchangeable parts as a distinctive feature of American manufacturing. The practice of manufacturing and then assembling interchangeable parts spread from industry to industry and became known as the "American system." Clock makers used it; sewing machine makers used it; even ax makers used it.

Mechanization became so integral to American manufacturing by the 1830s that some machinists specialized in what came to be called the machine tool industry. That is, they built machines that made parts for other machines that, in turn, produced goods for general consumption. Nothing better illustrated the transformation in American manufacturing than this mechanization of machine making.

New England led the nation in manufacturing. Manufacturing and agriculture meshed into a dynamic national economy. New England products like clocks, guns, and axes were shipped west and south, while commodities like wheat, pork, whiskey, tobacco, and cotton flowed north and east. Manufacturers specialized in producing for the gigantic domestic market rather than for export. British goods dominated the international market and, on the whole, they were cheaper and better than American-made products. U.S. manufacturers, however, supported tariffs to minimize British competition. But their best protection from British competitors

was to be more sensitive to, more responsive to, and more eager to please their American customers, the vast majority of whom were farmers. From their side, farmers were only too happy to buy manufactured goods, if they were affordable and especially if they saved labor that could be redirected to plow more furrows and plant more seeds.

Manufacturers not only produced old things like axes in new ways; they also built entirely new labor-saving devices, like mechanical reapers and sewing machines. Both reapers and sewing machines promised far-reaching social and economic changes, the former in the field, the latter by the fireside. But neither machine began to be manufactured in considerable numbers until the 1850s. Through 1855, Cyrus McCormick had built a total of only 12,000 reapers, and the Singer Sewing Machine Company had produced just 2,500 machines. During the last half of the decade, production and sales accelerated; McCormick turned out 22,000 reapers and Singer built 33,000 sewing machines. The machines, however, had barely made a dent in the traditional methods of hand reaping and hand sewing that prevailed on most farms and in most households in 1860.

Throughout American manufacturing, hand labor continued to be an essential component of production, despite the advances in mechanization. Even in heavily mechanized industries, factories remained fairly small, few having more than twenty or thirty employees. A measure of the distinctive character of manufacturing in this predominantly agricultural economy is that by 1860 iron manufacturing—so important in virtually all phases of mechanization—was only the sixth largest industry (in value), following cotton goods, lumber, boots and shoes, flour and meal, and men's clothing, in that order. The industrial evolution under way from 1800 to 1860 would quicken later in the nineteenth century; railroads were a harbinger of that future.

Railroads: Breaking the Bonds of Nature

To a degree unequaled by any other industry, railroads incorporated the most advanced developments of the age: steam energy; massive, powerful, complicated locomotives; mile after mile of iron rails ribboned across plains, through valleys, up hills, over passes; boldly engineered bridges that vaulted rivers and chasms; unprecedented sums of money to undertake these tasks; and large, complex organizations to keep the trains running efficiently,

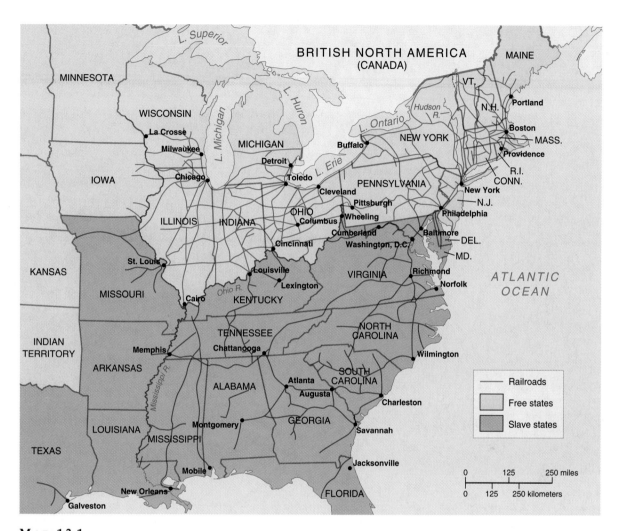

MAP 13.1
Railroads in 1860
Railroads were a crucial component of the revolutions in transportation and communications that transformed nineteenth-century America. The railroad system reflected the differences that had developed in the economies of the North and South.

safely, and on time. No wonder a Swedish visitor in 1849 noticed that American schoolboys constantly doodled sketches of locomotives, always smoking, always in motion.

Railroads captured Americans' imaginations in part because they seemed to break the bonds of nature. When canals and rivers froze in winter or became impassable during summer droughts, trains steamed ahead. When becalmed sailing ships went nowhere, locomotives kept on chugging. Heavy barges cruised along canals at two or three miles an hour, the pace of the mules that pulled them; horse-drawn stagecoaches could go a bit faster; but steam-powered trains left both in the dust, averaging over twenty miles an hour during the 1850s. Above all, railroads offered cities not blessed with canals or navigable rivers a way to compete for the trade of the countryside. A railroad was akin to a river of iron designed not by the ancient geological whims of nature but by the contemporary commercial desires of human beings.

On July 4, 1828, Charles Carroll, the last surviving signer of the Declaration of Independence, broke ground for the Baltimore and Ohio Railroad.

RAILROAD TRAVEL

In addition to carrying people and goods more quickly and reliably than ever before, railroads also brought many Americans face to face for the first time with machinery that was much larger and more powerful than any human being. (Compare, for example, the locomotives in this paint-ing with the handtools in the illustration on page 470.) This painting of a train leaving Rochester, New York, in 1852 contrasts the size and power of human beings and machines. The huge, lov-ingly portrayed, steam-belching locomotive is barely held back by some unseen brake against which the massive engine strains, ready to pull the long train through the columns of the station, out of the past and into the future. The people, in contrast, appear indistinct, passive, and depen-dent. They are waiting for the train rather than vice versa. Except for the two women and child in the foreground, the people face backward, and all of them avoid looking directly at the locomo-tive. The painting evokes the way the almost incomprehensible power of the railroads dwarfed human effort.

Rochester Historical Society.

Baltimore merchants and bankers feared that with-out the B&O, they would lose access to western commerce that would drain down the Ohio and Mississippi Rivers to New Orleans or float from the Great Lakes to the Hudson River along the recently completed Erie Canal. By connecting Baltimore to the Ohio River, the B&O promised to short-circuit western trade away from New Orleans, Philadel-phia, and New York. Building the roadbed and lay-ing track went slowly; by 1830, the B&O had 13 miles of track; by 1834, it had 84 miles; by 1842, the route consisted of 125 miles; and finally, by 1852, the 379 miles that connected Baltimore to Ohio were completed.

Despite the slow pace of construction, the B&O motivated leading citizens in other American cities to undertake railroad projects to bring western commerce to their own shops, markets, and wharves. In 1830, the entire nation had fewer than 100 miles of railroad track. By 1850, trains steamed along 9,000 miles of track, almost two-thirds of it in New England and the Middle Atlantic states. During the 1850s, construction exploded, especially in the Midwest. In 1856 alone, construction gangs laid more than 3,600 miles of new track. By 1860, several railroads had crossed the Mississippi River to link frontier farmers to the nation's 30,000 miles of track, approximately as much as all the rest of the world combined. (In 1857, for example, France had 3,700 miles of track; England and Wales had a total of 6,400 miles.) Chicago stood at the hub of eleven railroads, including the Illinois Central, the longest railroad in the world.

By 1860, the visions of railroad promoters that had once seemed fantastic had become commonplace realities. In 1800, a traveler needed six weeks to get from New York City to Chicago; in 1860, the trip by railroad took two days. By 1860, the volume of freight carried on railroads surpassed that shipped by canals, and railroads emerged as the iron skeleton of the nation's economy. The massive expansion of railroads in Lincoln's America helped the United States catapult into position as the world's second leading industrial power, behind Great Britain.

In addition to speeding transportation, railroads also fostered the growth of other industries. Locomotive manufacturers hardly existed in 1830, but by the 1850s they annually produced about 500 of the twenty-five-ton behemoths; by 1860, some 8,500 locomotives were in operation. Iron production grew five times faster than the population during the decades up to 1860, in part to meet the demand for rails, wheels, axles, and locomotives. Likewise, coal production more than doubled during the 1850s to provide fuel for iron furnaces and locomotive boilers. Heavy, gravity-defying iron bridges were built to carry trains across rivers; a spectacular example completed in 1855 was the suspension bridge across the Niagara River designed and built by John Roebling.

Railroads also stimulated the fledgling telegraph industry. In 1844, Samuel F. B. Morse persuasively demonstrated the potential of his telegraph by transmitting a series of dots and dashes that instantly conveyed an electronic message along forty miles of wire between Washington and Balti-

more. By 1852, more than 23,000 miles of telegraph wire hummed with messages while construction crews strung out more. By 1861, in excess of 50,000 miles of wire stretched across the continent to the Pacific. Many telegraph lines were strung alongside railroad tracks, and railroad managers soon discovered the advantages of instantaneous communication. Most railroads consisted of only one set of tracks, so careful scheduling was required to avoid disastrous head-on collisions. Telegraph messages permitted railroad managers to speed trains on their way when a track was clear and hold them when it was not. By 1860, nearly every railroad station had a clattering telegraph.

Almost all railroads were built and owned by private corporations rather than by local, state, or federal governments. In contrast, three-fourths of the total capital invested in canals by 1860 had come from government sources. By selling stocks and bonds, railroad companies had attracted well over a billion dollars in investments by 1860, more than five times the total capital invested in canals. Undergirding these private investments was massive government aid, especially federal land grants. Up to 1850, the federal government had granted a total of seven million acres of federal land to various turnpike, highway, and canal projects. In that year, Illinois senator Stephen A. Douglas obtained congressional approval for a precedent-setting grant of federal land to railroads, including the Illinois Central. The 1850 law provided a grant of six square miles of federal land for each mile of track constructed. Railroad companies quickly lined up congressional support for other lucrative land deals. By 1860, Congress had granted railroads more than twenty million acres of federal lands, establishing a generous policy that would last for decades.

The railroad boom of the 1850s was a signal of the growing industrial might of the American economy. But railroads, like other industries, succeeded because they served farms as well as cities. Passengers and freight routinely sped along tracks by 1860. But the continued significance of more traditional forms of transportation is suggested by the operation of the federal postal system, which reached into virtually every village and hamlet. By 1857, trains carried about one-third of the mail; most of the rest still went by stagecoach or horseback. In 1860, most Americans were still far more familiar with horses than with iron horses.

The economy of Lincoln's America linked axes, muscles, animals, and farms to machines, steam, railroads, and cities. Abraham Lincoln split rails as a young man and defended railroad corporations as a successful attorney. His legendary upward mobility illustrated the direction of economic change and the opportunities that change offered to enterprising individuals.

Free Labor: Promise and Reality

The impressive performance of the antebellum economy did not reward all Americans equally. Some, like Abraham Lincoln, moved far beyond their roots on hardscrabble farms to success in law, medicine, the ministry, journalism, or politics. A few, like Cyrus McCormick, became fabulously wealthy manufacturers or financiers. Many others strove to make a decent living as farmers, tradesmen, or laborers. While many prospered, many others barely kept their heads above water, and still others sank. With few exceptions, women were excluded from the opportunities open to men. Although tens of thousands of women worked as seamstresses, laundresses, domestic servants, factory hands, and teachers, both men and women tended to think of the economy of Lincoln's America as a man's world, and in particular a white man's world. Outside the South, slavery was slowly eliminated in the half century after the American Revolution, but free African Americans in the North found themselves relegated, on the whole, to dead-end jobs as laborers and servants. This discrimination against women and free blacks did not trouble most white men; with certain notable exceptions, they considered it proper and just. Instead, the varied experiences of white men—the presence of poverty in the midst of prosperity, of failure alongside success, of the bust that seemed to follow every boom—caught the attention of influential spokesmen.

The Free-Labor Ideal: Freedom plus Labor

During the decades before the Civil War, leaders throughout the North emphasized a set of ideas that seemed to explain why the changes under way in their society benefited some more than others. They referred again and again to the advantages of what they termed "free labor." (The word "free" referred to laborers who were not slaves; it did not mean laborers who worked for nothing.) By the 1850s, "free labor" identified the basic character of the economy and society taking shape in the North. Free-labor ideas contrasted northern society with the South, whose slave economy also prospered during these years. Free-labor ideas proposed a social and economic ideal that accounted for both the successes and the shortcomings of northern society.

Free-labor spokesmen celebrated hard work, self-reliance, and independence. They proclaimed that the door to success was open not just to those who inherited wealth or status but also to self-made men like Abraham Lincoln. Lincoln himself declared, "Free labor—the just and generous, and prosperous system, which opens the way for all—gives hope to all, and energy, and progress, and improvement of condition to all." Most Americans, Lincoln explained, were "men, with their families—wives, sons and daughters—[who] work for themselves, on their farms, in their houses and in their shops, taking the whole product to themselves." The free-labor system permitted these independent producers to reap what they sowed, to keep the products of their own labor. The free-labor system also benefited individuals who worked for wages, Lincoln and others pointed out. Unlike slaves, wage laborers were not fixed in perpetual bondage. Also unlike slaves, they received a wage that compensated them for their labor.

> By the 1850s, "free labor" identified the basic character of the economy and society taking shape in the North.

Ultimately, the free-labor system made it possible for hired laborers to become independent property owners, proponents argued. A laborer worked for wages only temporarily. "The prudent, penniless beginner in the world," Lincoln asserted, "labors for wages awhile, saves a surplus with which to buy tools or land, for himself; then labors on his own account another while, and at length hires another new beginner to help him." Wage labor was the first rung on the ladder that reached upward toward self-employment and, eventually, to hiring others. Lincoln acknowledged that some laborers did not manage to climb the ladder of success. "If any continue through life in the condition of the hired laborer, it is not the fault of the system [of free labor]," he said, "but because of either a dependent nature which prefers it, or improvidence, folly, or singular misfortune."

A YOUNG MECHANIC
This 1848 painting shows a young boy, a mechanic or tradesman, sitting behind the counter of a cluttered and worn woodworking shop. The painting hints that the young boy is an apprentice or perhaps the son of the mechanic who owns the shop. The better-dressed boys on the opposite side of the counter appear to be talking with the young mechanic about whittling a new mast for their toy boat. The barefoot young girl in the foreground appears to be the sister of the young mechanic; her attention is focused on the customers. The painting evokes the physical setting of a none-too-prosperous tradesman's workshop and the social differences that separated an open-faced young artisan and his better-off, shadowed customers. The image suggests that such routine encounters of the free-labor system were so commonplace that children reenacted them in play.
Los Angeles County Museum of Art, Gift of the American Art Council and Mr. and Mrs. J. Douglas Pardee.

The free-labor ideal affirmed an egalitarian vision of human potential. Lincoln and other spokesmen stressed the importance of universal education to permit "heads and hands . . . [to] cooperate as friends." Throughout the North, communities supported public schools to make the rudiments of learning available to young children. By 1860, many cities and towns boasted that up to 80 percent of children aged seven to thirteen attended school, at least for a few days each year. In rural areas, where the labor of children was more difficult to spare, schools typically enrolled no more than half the school-age children. Lessons included not just arithmetic, penmanship, and a smattering of other subjects. Textbooks and teachers—most of whom were young women—drummed into students the virtues of the free-labor system: self-reliance, discipline, and above all hard work. "Remember that all the ignorance, degradation, and misery in the world is the result of indolence and vice," one textbook intoned. Free-labor ideology, whether in school or out, emphasized labor as much as freedom.

Economic Inequality

The free-labor ideal made sense to many Americans, especially in the North, because it seemed to describe their own experience. Lincoln frequently referred to his humble beginnings as a hired laborer and silently invited his listeners to consider how far he had come. In 1860, his wealth of $17,000 easily placed him in the top 5 percent of the population. The opportunities presented by the expanding economy made a few men much, much richer. In 1860, the nation had about forty millionaires, including Cyrus McCormick, whose wealth exceeded $2 million. Most Americans, however, measured success in far more modest terms. The average wealth (defined as real and personal property) of adult white men in the North in 1860 barely topped $2,000. Only about a quarter of American men possessed that much. Nearly one-half had no wealth at all; almost 60 percent owned no land. It is difficult to estimate the wealth of adult white women since property possessed by married women was normally considered to belong to their husbands, but certainly women had less wealth than men. Free African Americans had still less; 90 percent were propertyless.

Free-labor spokesmen considered these economic inequalities a natural outgrowth of freedom, the inevitable result of some individuals being more able, more willing to work, and luckier. These inequalities suggest, however, the gap between the promise and the performance of the free-labor ideal in Lincoln's America. Thomas Lincoln, who had become a landowner by the time he died, was far more characteristic of the free-labor system than his more famous son. By 1860, a majority of American men had yet to obtain their own land and match Thomas Lincoln's achievement. The economic growth of Lincoln's America permitted many men to move from landless squatters to landowning farmers and from hired laborers to independent, self-employed producers. But many more Americans remained behind, landless and working for wages. The expanding economy, especially the availability of federal land, kept alive the aspirations at the heart of the free labor ideal. By 1860, however, those aspirations were much more widespread than the achievements promised by free-labor proponents. Even most of those who had realized their aspirations had a precarious hold on their independence; bad debts, crop failure, sickness, or death could quickly eliminate a family's gains.

Since the free-labor ideal pointed to individuals as the source of both success and failure, many Americans felt anxious about their prospects. The ambition and striving that led to high achievements could also engender a gnawing dissatisfaction with one's place in life. Seeking out new opportunities in pursuit of free-labor ideals created restless geographic mobility. Commonly up to two-thirds of the residents of a rural area moved every decade, and the population turnover in cities was even greater. Such constant coming and going weakened community ties to neighbors and friends and threw individuals even more upon their own resources for help in times of trouble. The stress on individual achievement encouraged personal introspection that often turned into intense self-doubt. The social and geographic mobility the free-labor system fostered permitted many, like Abraham Lincoln, to become quite different persons from what they had been. But such individuals, including Lincoln, sometimes suffered from a lack of confidence that they had genuinely transformed themselves. Lincoln managed to get out of the log cabin he grew up in; but that log cabin—with its economic insecurities, educational deficiencies, an illiterate mother, and a semiliterate father—remained with him, reminding him how far he had come and how few had come so far.

Immigrants and the Free-Labor Ladder

The risks and uncertainties of free labor did not deter millions of immigrants from entering the United States, especially during the 1840s and 1850s. Almost four and a half million immigrants arrived between 1840 and 1860, six times more than had come during the previous two decades. The

half million immigrants who came in 1854 accounted for nearly 2 percent of the entire population, a higher proportion than in any other single year of the nation's history. By 1860, foreign-born residents made up about one-eighth of the American population, a fraction that held steady well into the twentieth century.

Nearly three out of four of the immigrants who arrived between 1840 and 1860 came from either Germany or Ireland. The vast majority of the 1.4 million Germans who entered the United States during these years were skilled tradesmen and their families. They left Germany to escape deteriorating economic conditions and to seize opportunities offered by the expanding economy of Lincoln's America, where skilled artisans had little difficulty finding work. German butchers, bakers, beer makers, carpenters, shopkeepers, machinists, and others tended to congregate in cities, particularly in the Midwest. In St. Louis, Cincinnati, and Milwaukee, German immigrants made up as much as one-third of the population; Chicago, Cleveland, Detroit, and other cities had almost as many. Roughly a quarter of German immigrants were farmers, most of whom scattered throughout the Midwest, although some settled in Texas. German immigrants did not have a common religion; some were Protestants, others Catholics, and others Jews. They did, however, share the German language and cultural roots in the Old World. That ethnic heritage spawned dozens of Little Germanies, urban neighborhoods with a distinctly middle European flavor where, for example, families relaxed in beer gardens and sang or listened to band music, even on Sundays. On the whole, German Americans settled into that middle stratum of sturdy independent producers celebrated by free-labor spokesmen; relatively few Germans occupied the bottom rung of the free-labor ladder as wage laborers or domestic servants.

Irish immigrants, in contrast, entered at the bottom of the free-labor ladder and had difficulty climbing up. Nearly 1.7 million Irish immigrants arrived between 1840 and 1860, nearly all of them desperately poor and often weakened by hunger and disease. Potato blight struck Ireland in 1845 and returned repeatedly in subsequent years, spreading a catastrophic famine throughout the island. Millions of poor farmers and hired hands depended on potatoes as their principal source of food. When the blight ruined the potatoes, tens of thousands literally starved to death; hundreds of thousands fell sick and died. The lucky ones, half-starved,

EVICTION OF IRISH TENANT
An Irish tenant (the seated man with crossed arms) and his family (two barefoot boys are shown) are evicted; their few pieces of furniture have been piled outside the cottage. The landlord or his agent (the man near the doorway) has brought four armed police to force the tenant to leave. Evictions like this were common in Ireland in the mid-nineteenth century, an example of the poverty and human suffering that pushed many Irish immigrants to the United States.
Lawrence Collection, National Library of Ireland.

crowded into the holds of ships and set out for America. As one immigrant group declared, "All we want is to get out of Ireland; we must be better anywhere than here." Death trailed after them. So many died crossing the Atlantic that ships from Ireland were often termed "coffin ships." Many more died soon after arrival. But enough survived to make the Irish the largest single immigrant group in Lincoln's America.

Roughly three out of four Irish immigrants worked as laborers or domestic servants. Irish men dug canals, loaded ships, built railroad tracks, and took what other work they could find. Irish women hired out to cook, wash and iron, mind children, and clean house. Slaveholders often preferred to hire Irish laborers for heavy, dangerous jobs rather than risk injury to their valuable slaves. Most Irish immigrants, however, congregated in cities. By 1860, Irish immigrants made up one-fourth of the population of Boston and New York City and almost one-fifth of Pittsburgh, St. Louis, and Chicago. Almost all Irish immigrants were Catholics, a fact that set them apart from the overwhelmingly Protestant native-born residents. Many natives regarded the Irish as hard-drinking, obstreperous, half-civilized folk. Such views lay behind the discrimination that often excluded Irish immigrants from better jobs; job announcements commonly stated, "No Irish need apply." Despite these preju-

dices, native residents hired Irish immigrants because they accepted low pay and worked hard.

In the labor-poor economy of Lincoln's America, Irish laborers could earn in one day wages that would require several weeks' work in Ireland, if work could be found there. In America, one immigrant explained in 1853, there was "plenty of work and plenty of wages plenty to eat and no land lords thats enough what more does a man want." But some immigrants wanted more, especially respect and decent working conditions. One immigrant recalled that Irish laborers were thought of as "nothing . . . more than dogs . . . despised and kicked about." Another immigrant who dug cellars prayed, "May heaven save me from ever again being compelled to labour so severely . . . driven like horses . . . a slave for the Americans as the generality of the Irish . . . are."

Such testimony illustrates that the realities of the free-labor system, whether for immigrants or native-born laborers, often did not match the optimistic vision outlined by Abraham Lincoln and others. If wage laborers could not realistically aspire to become independent, self-sufficient property holders—if wage laborers became a permanent rather than a temporary working class—what would become of the free-labor ideal? By 1860, a few workingmen asked such questions, but the continuing economic expansion muted their voices.

Reforming Self and Society

The emphasis on self-discipline and individual effort at the core of the free-labor ideal pervaded Lincoln's America. Many Americans believed that insufficient self-control caused the most important social problems of the era. Evangelical Protestants struggled to control individuals' propensity to sin, and temperance advocates exhorted drinkers to control their urge for alcohol. In the midst of the worldly disruptions of geographic expansion and economic change, evangelicals brought more Americans than ever before into churches. Historians estimate that church members accounted for about one-third of the American population by midcentury. Most Americans remained outside churches, as did Abraham Lincoln. But the influence of evangelical religion reached far beyond those who belonged to churches.

Church members' zeal and organization gave them considerable power. In 1851, for example, they helped push a law through the Maine legislature to prohibit the sale or manufacture of alcoholic beverages. Within four years, thirteen other states had enacted what were known as Maine laws; New England, New York, and parts of the Midwest were officially dry. In part, the Maine laws targeted the habits of German and Irish immigrants, who enjoyed tipping a glass, even on Sundays. Although the prohibition laws were eventually repealed, they illustrated the ability of the vocal evangelical minority to define propriety and Americanism. The evangelical temperament—a conviction of righteousness coupled with energy, self-discipline, and faith that the world could be improved—animated most reformers to one degree or another.

The emphasis on self-discipline and individual effort at the core of the free-labor ideal pervaded Lincoln's America.

A few activists pointed out that certain fundamental injustices lay beyond the reach of self-control. Transcendentalists and utopians believed that perfection could be attained only by rejecting the values of the larger society. Women's rights activists and abolitionists sought to reverse the subordination of women and to eliminate the enslavement of blacks by changing society. They confronted the daunting challenge of repudiating widespread assumptions about male supremacy and white supremacy and somehow subverting the entrenched institutions that reinforced those assumptions: the family and slavery.

The Pursuit of Perfection: Transcendentalists and Utopians

A group of New England writers that came to be known as transcendentalists believed that individuals should not conform to the competitive, materialistic world or to some abstract notion of religion. Instead, people should look within themselves for truth and guidance. In 1836, the leading transcendentalist, Ralph Waldo Emerson—an essayist, poet, and lecturer—proclaimed that "man has access to the entire mind of the Creator, [and] is himself the creator in the finite. This view . . . animates me to create my own world through the purification of my soul." Emerson and other transcendentalists, such as the writers Henry David Thoreau and Margaret Fuller, had supreme confidence in the powers of individual human beings to know God. Emerson declared that "the currents of the Universal Being circulate through me; I am part or particle of God." Through introspection, each person could communicate with the divine order and conduct himself or herself accordingly. Most Americans failed to lift their eyes from the mundane task of making a living. "We hear . . . too much of the results of machinery, commerce, and the useful arts," Emerson wrote. "Avarice, hesitation, and following are our diseases." The remedy for these diseases, transcendentalists believed, was not to join a reform society, or circulate petitions, or even to vote. "Every thing that tends to insulate the individual . . . tends to true . . . greatness," Emerson proclaimed. The power of the solitary individual was nearly limitless. Emerson explained that "if the single man plant himself indomitably on his instincts, and there abide, the huge world will come round to him."

Transcendentalists influenced many writers in the northern states, but they had a limited appeal to the broader society. Emerson gave lectures throughout the North during the 1840s and 1850s, spreading the infectious gospel of self-reliance more than the abstruse doctrines of transcendentalism, which novelist Herman Melville ridiculed as "oracular gibberish." In many ways, transcendentalism represented less an alternative to the values of mainstream society than an exaggerated form of the rampant individualism of the age. Melville called it "self-conceit."

Unlike transcendentalists, a few reformers tried to change the world by organizing utopian communities. Although these communities never involved more than a few thousand people, their activities demonstrated both their dissatisfactions with the larger society and their efforts to realize their visions of perfection. Like their members, the utopian communities varied considerably.

Some communities functioned essentially as retreats for those who did not want to sever their ties with the larger society. Reformers active in the peace, women's rights, antislavery, educational, and temperance movements founded Hopedale in 1842 in Milford, Massachusetts. They used the community as a home base from which they frequently traveled to spread their reform messages. Brook Farm, organized in 1841 in West Roxbury, Massachusetts, provided a haven for individual development apart from the constraints of conventional society. Brook Farm attracted literary and artistic New Englanders who agreed to balance bookish pursuits with manual labor; novelists and essayists often weeded the garden while others read poetry to them. Emerson, who declined to join, described Brook Farm as "a perpetual picnic." Despite their attractions, both Brook Farm and Hopedale had financial difficulties and collapsed within a few years.

Other communities set out to become models of perfection that they hoped would ultimately point the way toward a better life for everyone. During the 1840s, more than two dozen communities—principally in New York, New Jersey, Pennsylvania, and Ohio—organized around the ideas of Charles Fourier, a French critic of contemporary society. Members of these Fourierist communities (or phalanxes, as they were called) believed that individualism and competition were evils that denied the basic truth that "men . . . are brothers and not competitors." Fourierist phalanxes tried to replace competition with harmonious cooperation based on communal ownership of property through a system of shareholding by individual members. In addition, members were supposed to work not because they had to but because their work was satisfying and fulfilling. One former member complained that in his phalanx "there was plenty of discussion, and an abundance of variety, which is called the spice of life. This spice however constituted the greater part of the fare, as we sometimes had scarcely anything to eat." Such complaints signaled the failure of the Fourierist communities to achieve their ambitious goals. Few of the phalanxes survived more than two or three years.

MARY CRAGIN, ONEIDA WOMAN
Mary Cragin, one of the founding members of the Oneida community, had a passionate sexual relationship with John Humphrey Noyes even before the community was organized. Within the bounds of complex marriage as practiced by the Oneidans, Cragin's magnetic sexuality made her a favorite partner of many men. In her journal Cragin confessed that "every evil passion was very strong in me from my childhood, sexual desire, love of dress and admiration, deceit, anger, pride." Oneida, however, transformed evil passion to holy piety. Cragin wrote, "In view of [God's] goodness to me and of his desire that I should let him fill me with himself, I yield and offer myself, to be penetrated by his spirit, and desire that love and gratitude may inspire my heart so that I shall sympathize with his pleasure in the thing, before my personal pleasure begins, knowing that it will increase my capability for happiness." After she accidentally drowned in 1851, a eulogist proclaimed that, "Her only ambition was to be the servant of love and she was beautifully and wonderfully made for the office." Oneida's sexual practices were considered outrageous and sinful by almost all other Americans. Even Oneidans did not agree with all of Noyes's ideas about sex. "There is no reason why [sex] should not be done in public as much as music and dancing," he declared. It would display the art of sex, he explained, and watching "would give pleasure to a great many of the older people who now have nothing to do with the matter." Nonetheless, public sex never caught on among Oneidans.
Oneida Community Mansion House/James Demarest.

The Oneida community went beyond the Fourierist notion of communalism. John Humphrey Noyes, the charismatic leader of Oneida, believed that individuals who had achieved salvation were literally without sin. The larger society's commitment to private property, however, made even saints greedy and selfish. Noyes believed that the root of the evil of private property lay in marriage, in men's conviction that their wives were their exclusive property. With a substantial inheritance, Noyes organized the Oneida community in New York in 1848 to permit himself and others to live according to his ideas. Oneidans practiced what Noyes called "complex marriage," which meant that sexual intercourse was permissible between any man and woman in the community who had been saved; in effect, every saved man in the community was married to every saved woman. Noyes usually reserved for himself the duties of "first husband," namely introducing sanctified young virgins to complex marriage. In time, Oneidans developed a formal procedure for the day-by-day operation of complex marriage: A member who desired intercourse with another member of the opposite sex approached a third member, who brokered the arrangement and registered it in a public community ledger. To prevent a population explosion and to promote health and self-control, Noyes insisted that Oneida men practice "male continence," that is, sexual intercourse without ejaculation. Noyes also required all members to relinquish their economic property to the community, which developed a lucrative business manufacturing animal traps. Oneida's sexual and economic communalism attracted several hundred members, but most of their neighbors considered Oneidans eccentric, heretical free lovers, adulterers, blasphemers, and worse. Yet the practices that set Oneida apart from its mainstream neighbors also strengthened the community, and it survived long after the Civil War.

Women's Rights Activists

Women participated in the many reform activities that grew out of evangelical churches. Women church members outnumbered men two to one, and they worked to put their religious ideas into practice by joining peace, temperance, antislavery, and other societies. Although women supplied much energy and membership in these societies, men normally headed the groups. Assumptions of male supremacy were so strong and pervasive that even women's rights activists feared the consequences of openly confronting them. Involvement in reform organizations gave a few women activists practical experience in such political arts as speaking in public, running a meeting, drafting resolutions, and circulating petitions. Along with such experience came confidence. Abolitionist Lydia Maria Child pointed out in 1841 that "those who urged women to become missionaries and form tract societies . . . have changed the household utensil to a living energetic being and they have no spell to turn it into a broom again." (See Texts in Historical Context, pages 490–491.)

In 1848, about one hundred living energetic beings, led by reformers Elizabeth Cady Stanton and Lucretia Mott, gathered at Seneca Falls, New York, for the first women's rights convention in the United States. None of the boldest women's rights activists in the nation was willing to chair the meeting; instead, they asked James Mott, Lucretia's husband, to assume that duty. The Seneca Falls women did not shrink, however, from proclaiming in their Declaration of Sentiments, "The history of mankind is a history of repeated injuries and usurpations on the part of man toward woman, having in direct object the establishment of an absolute tyranny over her." The Declaration of Sentiments declared that male tyranny caused women to "feel themselves aggrieved, oppressed, and fraudulently deprived of their most sacred rights." In the style of the Declaration of Independence, the Seneca Falls Declaration listed the ways women had been discriminated against. Through the tyranny of male supremacy, men "endeavored in every way that [they] could to destroy her confidence in her own powers, to lessen her self-respect, and to make her willing to lead a dependent and abject life." The Seneca Falls Declaration insisted that women "have immediate admission to all the rights and privileges which belong to them as citizens of the United States," particularly the "inalienable right to the elective franchise."

After the Seneca Falls meeting adjourned, Stanton, Mott, and others worked to gain support for woman suffrage. They wrote tracts, gave speeches, and tried to recruit other women to campaign for the cause. But it was tough going. Nearly two dozen women's rights conventions assembled in the years before the Civil War (1861–1865), repeatedly calling for suffrage. But they had difficulty receiving a respectful hearing, much less obtaining legislative action. No state came close to permitting women to vote. Politicians and editorialists hooted at the idea. Everyone knew, they sneered, that a woman's place

ABOLITIONIST MEETING
This rare daguerreotype was made by Ezra Greenleaf Weld in August 1850 at an abolitionist meeting in Cazenovia, New York. Frederick Douglass, who had escaped from slavery in Maryland twelve years earlier, is seated on the platform next to the woman at the table. One of the nation's most brilliant and eloquent abolitionists, Douglass also supported equal rights for women. The man immediately behind Douglass gesturing with his outstretched arm is Gerrit Smith, a wealthy New Yorker and militant abolitionist whose funds supported many reform activities. Note the two black women in similar clothing on either side of Smith and the white woman next to Douglass. Most mid-nineteenth-century white Americans considered such voluntary racial proximity scandalous and promiscuous. Clearly, what scandalized these respectable-appearing Americans was slavery, not biracial protest meetings.
Collection of the J. Paul Getty Museum, Malibu, Calif.

was in the home, rearing her children and civilizing her man. Nonetheless, the Seneca Falls Declaration served as a path-breaking manifesto of dissent against male supremacy and of support for women's suffrage, which would become the focus of the women's rights movement during the next seventy years.

Abolitionists and the American Ideal

During the 1840s and 1850s, abolitionists continued to struggle to draw the nation's attention to the plight of slaves and the need for emancipation. Former slaves like Frederick Douglass, Henry Bibb, and Sojourner Truth lectured to reform audiences throughout the North about the cruelties, horrors,

and indignities of slavery. Abolitionists published newspapers, held conventions, and petitioned Congress. But they never attracted a mass following among white Americans. Leading white abolitionists criticized the pervasive assumptions of black inferiority and white supremacy and affirmed their belief in human equality.

Many white Northerners became convinced that slavery was wrong, but they still believed that blacks were inferior. Many other white Northerners shared the common view of white Southerners that because blacks were inferior, slavery was necessary and even desirable. The pervasive racism among most whites in the North limited the reach of the abolitionist appeal. The geographical expansion of the nation during the 1840s (discussed later in the chapter) offered abolitionists an opportunity to link

Women's Politics

Although women failed to gain the right to vote before the Civil War, many women nonetheless participated in public political activities. They not only attended women's rights conventions but also signed petitions asking legislators to change laws that discriminated against women and worked to put the ideas of women's equality into practice in their personal lives.

In 1852, for example, Harriot K. Hunt protested having to pay taxes when she was prohibited from voting. A physician who had practiced medicine in Boston since 1835, Hunt had been refused admission to Harvard Medical School before she finally received her medical degree in 1853 from the Female Medical College of Philadelphia.

DOCUMENT 1. Harriot K. Hunt's Letter "to . . . [the] Treasurer, and the Assessors, and other Authorities of the city of Boston, and the Citizens generally"

Harriot K. Hunt, physician, a native and permanent resident of the city of Boston, and for many years a taxpayer therein, in making payment of her city taxes for the coming year, begs leave to protest against the injustice and inequality of levying taxes upon women, and at the same time refusing them any voice or vote in the imposition and expenditure of the same. The only classes of male persons required to pay taxes, and not at the same time allowed the privilege of voting, are aliens and minors. The objection in the case of aliens is their supposed want of interest in our institutions and knowledge of them. The objection in the case of minors, is the want of sufficient understanding. These objections can not apply to women, natives of the city, all of whose property interests are here, and who have accumulated, by their own sagacity and industry, the very property on which they are taxed. But this is not all; the alien, by going through the forms of naturalization, the minor on coming of age, obtain the right of voting; and so long as they continue to pay a mere poll-tax of a dollar and a half, they may continue to exercise it, though so ignorant as not to be able to sign their names, or read the very votes they put into the ballot-boxes. Even drunkards, felons, idiots, and lunatics, if men, may still enjoy that right of voting to which no woman, however large the amount of taxes she pays, however respectable her character, or useful her life, can ever attain. Wherein, your remonstrant would inquire, is the justice, equality, or wisdom of this?

Stymied by male politicians' indifference to petitions like Hunt's, women's rights activists pondered how to translate their dedication to equality into arenas of life more directly under their personal control. In an 1855 letter to a friend, suffragist leader Elizabeth Cady Stanton explained how women's fashions could be tailored to promote equality.

DOCUMENT 2. Elizabeth Cady Stanton's Letter on Women's Fashions

I fully agree with you that woman is terribly cramped and crippled in her present style of dress. I have not one word to utter in its defense; but to me, it seems that if she would enjoy entire freedom, she should dress just like a man. Why proclaim our sex on the house-tops, seeing that it is a badge of degradation, and deprives us of so many rights and privileges wherever we go? . . . In male attire, we

their rather unpopular ideal to a goal that many white Northerners found much more attractive—limiting the geographical expansion of slavery. That issue moved to the center of national politics after the Mexican War (and it is discussed in detail in chapter 14).

Black leaders rose to prominence in the abolitionist movement during the 1840s and 1850s. African Americans had actively opposed slavery for decades, but a new generation of leaders came to the forefront in these years. Men like Douglass, Henry Highland Garnet, William Wells Brown, and Martin R. Delany became impatient with white abolitionists' appeals to the conscience of the white majority. For example, Garnet proclaimed in 1843 that slaves should rise in insurrection against their mas-could travel by land or sea; go through all the streets and lanes of our cities and towns by night and day, without a protector; get seven hundred dollars a year for teaching, instead of three, and ten dollars for making a coat, instead of two or three, as we now do. All this we could do without fear of insult, or the least sacrifice of decency or virtue. If nature has not made the sex so clearly defined as to be seen through any disguise, why should we make the difference so striking? Depend upon it, when men and women in their every-day life see and think less of sex and more of mind, we shall all lead far purer and higher lives.

Marriage typically consigned women to a legal status inferior to their husbands, but women's rights activists refashioned marriage vows to honor equality rather than subordination. When women's rights leader Lucy Stone married Henry B. Blackwell in 1855, both signed the following statement.

DOCUMENT 3. Lucy Stone–Henry B. Blackwell Marriage Agreement

While acknowledging our mutual affection by publicly assuming the relationship of husband and wife, yet in justice to ourselves and a great principle, we deem it a duty to declare that this act on our part implies no sanction of, nor promise of voluntary obedience to such of the present laws of marriage, as refuse to recognize the wife as an independent, rational being, while they confer upon the husband an injurious and unnatural superiority, investing him with legal powers which no honorable man would exercise, and which no man should possess. We protest especially against the laws which give to the husband:

1. The custody of the wife's person.
2. The exclusive control and guardianship of their children.
3. The sole ownership of her personal [property], and use of her real estate. . . .
4. The absolute right to the product of her industry.
5. Also against laws which give to the widower so much larger and more permanent an interest in the property of his deceased wife, than they give to the widow in that of the deceased husband.
6. Finally, against the whole system by which "the legal existence of the wife is suspended during marriage," so that in most States, she neither has a legal part in the choice of her residence, nor can she make a will, nor sue or be sued in her own name, nor inherit property.

We believe that personal independence and equal human rights can never be forfeited, except for crime; that marriage should be an equal and permanent partnership, and so recognized by law; that until it is so recognized, married partners should provide against the radical injustice of present laws, by every means in their power. . . .

Thus reverencing law, we enter our protest against rules and customs which are unworthy of the name, since they violate justice, the essence of law.

(signed) Henry B. Blackwell
Lucy Stone

Document 1. Elizabeth Cady Stanton, Susan B. Anthony, and Matilda Josyln Gage, eds., *History of Woman Suffrage* (New York: Fowler & Wells, 1881), 1:259.
Document 2. Ibid., 841.
Document 3. Ibid., 260–61.

ters; "there is not much hope of Redemption without the shedding of blood," he declared. Calls for slaves to slay their masters alienated some black abolitionists and most white abolitionists, and they were anathema to the larger white majority. Such views reflected, however, the emerging independence of black abolitionists. Although they still cooperated with white abolitionists, black abolitionists founded their own newspapers, held their own antislavery conventions, and expressed their own uncompromising ideas.

The commitment of black abolitionists to battling slavery grew out of their own experiences with white supremacy. The 250,000 free African Americans in the North constituted less than 2 percent of the total population. They confronted the humiliations of racial discrimination in virtually every arena of daily life: at work, at school, at church, in shops, in the streets, on trains, in hotels, and elsewhere. Only four New England states (Maine, Massachusetts, New Hampshire, and Vermont) permitted black men to vote; New York imposed a special property-holding requirement on black—but not white—voters, effectively excluding most black men from the franchise. All other states prohibited black voting. The pervasive racial discrimination in the North both handicapped and energized black abolitionists. Garnet said, as if he were speaking to slaves, "While you have been oppressed, we have also been partakers; nor can we be free while you are enslaved. We . . . [are] bound with you." African American leaders organized campaigns against segregation in northern communities, particularly in transportation and education. Their most notable success came in 1855 when Massachusetts integrated public schools. Elsewhere, despite their protests, white supremacy continued unabated.

Outside the public spotlight, many free African Americans in the North contributed to the antislavery cause by quietly aiding fugitive slaves. Harriet Tubman escaped from slavery in Maryland in 1849 and repeatedly risked her freedom and her life to return to the South and escort scores of slaves to freedom. Few matched Tubman's heroic courage, but when the opportunity arose, many free blacks in the North provided fugitive slaves with food, a safe place to rest, and a helping hand. A few whites also participated in this "underground railroad"

from slavery to freedom. Mainly, however, the underground railroad ran through black neighborhoods, black churches, and black homes. The underground railroad transported only a few thousand slaves to freedom. But it did illustrate the substratum of antislavery sentiment and opposition to white supremacy that unified virtually all African Americans in the North.

The ideas and activities of reformers challenged mainstream institutions and assumptions of Lincoln's America. While reformers appealed to widespread ideals of justice, equality, democracy, and freedom, they also confronted equally widespread impediments of sin, male supremacy, white supremacy, and slavery. Although reformers had limited influence in national politics, the continued geographic expansion of the nation pushed the issue of slavery to the center of national politics and confronted all Americans with the question reformers had debated for many years: What steps should be taken to bring American society into harmony with American ideals?

The Westward Movement

The 1840s ushered in an era of rapid westward movement. Until then, the overwhelming majority of Americans lived east of the Mississippi River. To the west, Native Americans inhabited the plains, prairies, and deserts to the rugged coasts of the Pa-

NORTHERN SLOPES OF THE SIERRA NEVADA BY C. S. SCHUMANN AFTER EGLOFFSTEIN, 1854.

cific. The British claimed the Oregon Country, and the Mexican flag flew over the vast expanse of the Southwest. But by 1850, the boundaries of the United States stretched to the Pacific, and the nation had more than doubled its size. By 1860, the great migration had carried four million Americans west of the Mississippi River.

Thomas Jefferson, John Quincy Adams, and other government officials had helped clear the way for the march across the continent. The nation's revolution in transportation and communication, its swelling population, and its booming economy propelled the westward surge. But the emigrants themselves pushed to conquer the continent. Farmer-settlers craved land and stubbornly shoved ahead. Unimpressed with the claims of native people, Mexicans, and British, they simply asserted their "right" to the land. Shock troops of American empire, frontier settlers took the soil and then lobbied their government to follow them with the flag. The human cost of westward expansion was high. Two centuries of Indian wars east of the Mississippi ended during the 1830s, but the old, fierce struggle between native inhabitant and invader continued for another half century in the West.

Manifest Destiny

Most Americans believed that the superiority of their institutions and white culture bestowed on them a God-given right to spread their civilization across the continent. They imagined the West as a howling wilderness, empty and undeveloped. If they recognized Indians and Mexicans at all, they dismissed them as primitive drags on progress who would have to be redeemed, shoved aside and isolated, or exterminated. The sense of uniqueness and mission was as old as the Puritans, but by the 1840s the conviction of superiority had been bolstered by the young nation's amazing success. What right had Americans, they asked, to keep the blessings of liberty, democracy, and prosperity to themselves? The West needed the civilizing power of the hammer and plow, the ballot box and pulpit, that had transformed the East.

As important as national pride and racial arrogance were to Manifest Destiny, economic gain made up its core. Land hunger drew hundreds of thousands of average Americans westward.

In the summer of 1845, New York journalist John L. O'Sullivan coined the term "Manifest Destiny" as the latest justification for white settlers to take the land they coveted. Slight of build, pale complexioned, with thick glasses, O'Sullivan was an armchair expansionist, but he took second place to no one in his passion for conquest of the West. O'Sullivan called on Americans to resist any foreign power—British, French, or Mexican—that

Courtesy the Center for American History, the University of Texas at Austin.

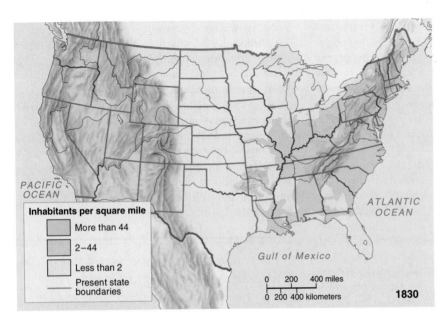

MAP 13.2
Population Advances Westward, 1830–1850
Millions of Americans moved westward in the middle decades of the nineteenth-century, crowding into the cities of the Northwest and hacking out farms and plantations in the great Mississippi River valley.

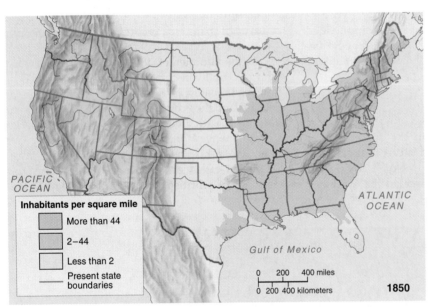

attempted to thwart "the fulfillment of our manifest destiny to overspread the continent allotted by Providence for the free development of our yearly multiplying millions." He dismissed those who raised the law as an objection to American expansion. What justified America's continental march, he said, was "the right of our manifest destiny to . . . possess the whole of the continent which Providence has given us for the development of the great experiment of liberty and federative self-government entrusted to us." Almost overnight, the magic phrase "Manifest Destiny" swept the nation and provided an ideological shield for conquering the West.

As important as national pride and racial arrogance were to Manifest Destiny, economic gain made up its core. Land hunger drew hundreds of thousands of average Americans westward. Some politicians, moreover, had become convinced that national prosperity depended on capturing the rich trade of the Far East. To trade with Asia, the United States needed the Pacific ports that stretched from

San Francisco to Puget Sound. No one was more eager to extend American trade in the Pacific than Missouri senator Thomas Hart Benton. Since the 1820s, he had beat the drum for western expansion, all the way to China and India. "The sun of civilization must shine across the sea: socially and commercially," he declared. The United States and Asia must "talk together, and trade together. Commerce is a great civilizer." In the 1840s, American economic expansion came wrapped in the rhetoric of uplift and civilization.

The concept of Manifest Destiny captured the temper of the nation. It gave a spine-tingling name to Americans' conviction and desire. Self-righteous and self-serving, Manifest Destiny also spoke of sincere belief. The nation looked forward to a time, contemporaries said, when the American eagle would have its beak in Canada, its talons in Mexico, and its wings flapping in the Atlantic and Pacific Oceans.

"Oregon Fever" and the Overland Trail

Oregon Country, that vast region bounded on the west by the Pacific, on the east by the Rockies, on the south by the forty-second parallel, and on the north by Russian Alaska, caused the pulse of American expansionists to race. But Americans were not alone in hungrily eyeing the Pacific Northwest. The British traced their interest (and their rights) to the voyage of Sir Francis Drake, who, they argued, discovered the Oregon coast in 1579. Americans matched the British assertion with historic claims of their own. Unable to agree on ownership, the United States and Great Britain decided in 1818 on a "joint occupation" that would leave Oregon "free and open" to settlement by both countries. A handful of American fur traders and "mountain men" roamed the region in the 1820s, but in the 1830s and 1840s, expansionists made Oregon Country an early target of Manifest Destiny.

"Oregon fever" broke out in 1833 when a Methodist journal published a fictitious letter from an Indian in the Northwest begging for the Bible. Pulpits across the East broadcast the plea, and soon earnest missionaries raced west. The Indians they encountered displayed a decided lack of enthusiasm for Christianity, but the missionaries' letters home glowed with astonishment at the bounty nature had bestowed on Oregon. By the late 1830s, settlers began to trickle along the Oregon Trail, following a path blazed by "mountain men." The first Oregon

wagon trains hit the trail in 1841, and by 1843 about 1,000 emigrants a year set out from Independence, Missouri. By 1869, when the first transcontinental railroad was completed, something like 350,000 migrants had traveled west to the Pacific over the Oregon Trail.

When they traversed the vast reaches of the West, the emigrants encountered Plains Indians, whose cultures differed markedly from those of the Eastern Woodlands tribes. The quarter of a million Native Americans who populated the area between the Rocky Mountains and the Mississippi River defy easy generalization. Some were farmers who lived peaceful, sedentary lives, but a majority of Plains Indians—the Sioux, Cheyenne, Shoshoni, and Arapaho of the Central Plains and the Kiowa, Wichita, Apache, and Comanche in the Southwest—were horse-mounted, nomadic, nonagricultural peoples whose warriors symbolized the "savage Indian" in the minds of whites.

Horses, which had been brought to the continent by Spaniards in the sixteenth century, permitted the Plains tribes to become highly mobile hunters of buffalo. In time they came to depend on buffalo for most of their food, clothing, shelter, and fuel. As they followed the huge herds over the Plains, the people bumped into one another. Rival tribes learned from these encounters, but they also fought. Warfare became a crucial component of their way of life. Young men were introduced to the art of war early, learning to ride ponies at breakneck speed while firing off arrows and, later, rifles with astounding accuracy.

Plains Indians struck fear in the hearts of whites who rode on the wagon trains. But Native Americans had far more to fear from whites. Indians killed fewer than 400 emigrants on the trail between 1840 and 1860, while whites proved to be deadly to the Indians. Even though they were usually just passing through on their way to the Pacific slope, whites brought alcohol and disease, especially destructive epidemics of smallpox, measles, cholera, and scarlet fever. Moreover, whites killed the buffalo, slaughtering hundreds of thousands for fun and leaving their carcasses to rot in the sun. Buffalo still numbered some twelve million in 1860, but the herds were shrinking rapidly, intensifying conflict among the Plains Indians. Intertribal warfare weakened the Indians and made them more vulnerable to conquest.

As white migration increased, overland emigrants insisted that the federal government provide them more protection. The government responded by constructing a chain of forts along the trail. More important, the United States adopted a new Indian policy of "concentration." To clear the way, the government rescinded the "permanent" frontier it had granted the Indians west of the ninety-fifth meridian, which was only a few miles west of the Mississippi River. Then, in 1851, it called the Plains tribes to a conference at Fort Laramie, Wyoming. Some ten thousand Dakota, Sioux, Arapaho, Cheyenne, Crow, and other Indians showed up, hopeful that something could be done to protect them from the ravages of the wagon trains. Instead, government negotiators persuaded the chiefs to sign agreements restricting their people to specific areas that whites promised they would never vio-

late. This policy of isolation became the seedbed for the subsequent policy of reservations. But whites would not keep out of Indian territory, and Indians would not easily give up their traditional way of life. Competition meant warfare for decades to come.

Still, Indians threatened emigrants less than life on the trail did. The men, women, and children who headed west each spring could count on four to six months of grueling travel through often inhospitable country. Until 1860, maps labeled the vast area between the Rockies and the Mississippi River as the "Great American Desert." With nearly two thousand miles to go and traveling no more than fifteen miles a day, the pioneers endured parching

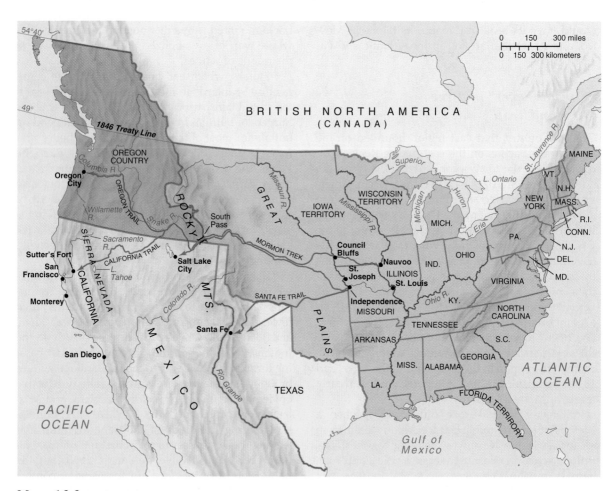

MAP 13.3
Trails to the West
In the 1830s, wagon trains began snaking their way to the Southwest and the Pacific coast. Deep ruts soon marked the most popular routes.

WI-JUN-JON, AN ASSINIBOIN CHIEF
Pennsylvania-born artist George Catlin, the painter of this 1845 dual portrait, was present in the Assiniboin village when Wi-Jun-Jon returned from Washington, D.C., wearing the military uniform that President Andrew Jackson had presented to him. His uniform and ceaseless boasting bred so much dislike and distrust that a young warrior from a nearby tribe murdered him. Catlin was convinced that the western Indian cultures that he had begun observing in the 1830s would soon disappear, and he sought to document Indian life through hundreds of paintings and prints.
Library of Congress.

heat, drought, treacherous rivers, disease, rattlesnakes, bad water, accidents, physical and emotional exhaustion, and, if the snows closed the mountain passes before they got through, freezing and starvation. Women sometimes faced the dangers of trailside childbirth. It was said that one could walk from Missouri to the Pacific stepping only on the graves of those who had failed to make it.

Everyone experienced hardships on the trail, but no one felt the burden quite as much as the women who made the trip. Since husbands usually decided to pull up stakes and go west, many wives went involuntarily. One miserable woman, trying to keep her children dry in a rainstorm and to calm them as they listened to Indian shouts, wondered "what had possessed my husband, anyway, that he should have thought of bringing us away out through this God forsaken country." Men viewed the privation as a necessary step to a new, better life; women tended to judge it by the homes, kin, and friends they had left behind to take up what one called "this wild goose chase."

Consumed with the tasks of surviving and getting to the coast, men and women abandoned eastern notions of "men's work" and "women's work." Women performed new chores, such as gathering buffalo dung for fuel. As gender boundaries faded, women also took on traditionally male work. One woman remembered learning to drive a team of oxen on the trail along the Platte River, while another told how she had managed to "crack that big whip." Some shouldered rifles to hunt or to guard their families. While women took on male tasks, men rarely reciprocated. Every emigrant woman knew the truth expressed by one young wife who found "as I was told before I started that there is no rest in such a journey."

The men who trekked westward usually sought land and, with it, the independence and economic opportunity that had eluded them in the East. But not all emigrants who reached Oregon celebrated what they found. Hezekiah Packingham, writing from the Willamette Valley in March 1847, claimed that Oregon was "a mean, dried up, and drowned country." He gave it credit for "only one or two things, and these are, good health and plenty of salmon, and Indians." Most disturbing to this single man, he found that Oregon was "rapidly filling up with young men, (but no girls)." Richard R. Howard saw things differently, in part no doubt because he was married. While he agreed that one-third of the men "are without wives," he believed that Oregon was "one of the greatest countries in the world." From "the Cascade mountains to the Pacific," he declared, "the whole country can be cultivated." His wife, he added, "was never more satisfied with a move in her life." But, he added guardedly, "she is fast recovering her health."

When women reached Oregon, they confronted a wilderness, not new homes. "I had all I could do to keep from asking George to turn around and bring me back home," one woman wrote to her mother in Missouri. Oregon, another noted, "was a hard country for a woman." Neighbors were few and far between, and the isolation weighed heavily. Moreover, things were in a "primitive state." One young wife set up housekeeping with her new husband with only one stew kettle and three knives. Necessity continued to blur the division between men's and women's work. "I am maid of all traids," one busy woman remarked in 1853. Work seemed unending. "I am a very old woman," remarked

twenty-nine-year-old Sarah Everett. "My face is thin sunken and wrinkled, my hands bony withered and hard." Pioneer life left little room for leisure or refinement. As one wife observed, "A woman that can not endure almost as much as a horse has no business here."

Despite the ordeal of the trail and the difficulties of starting from scratch, emigrants kept coming. By 1845, Oregon counted five thousand American settlers. And from the beginning, they clamored for the protection of the U.S. government.

The Mormon Migration

Not every wagon train heading west had the Pacific slope as its destination. One remarkable group of religious emigrants chose to settle in the heart of the arid West. Halting near the Great Salt Lake in what was then Mexican territory, the Mormons deliberately chose the remote site as a refuge. After years of persecution in the East, they sought religious freedom and communal security in the West. Protected by mountains and deserts, Deseret, as they called their kingdom, lay a thousand miles from the Kansas frontier.

In 1830, Joseph Smith Jr., who was only twenty-four, published *The Book of Mormon* and founded the Church of Jesus Christ of Latter-Day Saints (the Mormons). A decade earlier, the upstate New York farm boy had begun to have uncommon religious experiences. His visions and revelations were followed, he said, by a visit from an angel who led him to golden tablets buried near his home. With the aid of magic stones, he translated the mysterious language on the tablets. What was revealed was *The Book of Mormon*. It told the story of an ancient Christian civilization in the New World and predicted the appearance of an American prophet who would reestablish Jesus Christ's undefiled kingdom in America. Converts, attracted to the promise of a pure faith in the midst of antebellum America's social turmoil and rampant materialism, flocked to the new church.

"Gentile" neighbors branded Mormons heretics and resented their close-knit community, what they considered the Mormons' religious self-righteousness, and their sympathy toward abolitionists and Indians. Persecution drove Smith and his followers from New York to Ohio, then to Missouri, and finally in 1839 to Nauvoo, Illinois. Over the next five years, they built Nauvoo into a prosperous community of fifteen thousand. Visitors marveled at

GREAT SALT LAKE CITY IN 1853, LOOKING SOUTH
This 1853 sketch by Englishman Frederick Piercy reveals that only six years after its founding
Salt Lake City was already on its way to becoming a monumental city. For plans, the Mormons
looked to the ideas of their martyred prophet Joseph Smith. The city was laid out with very broad
streets—132 feet wide, said to be broad enough to allow ox-drawn wagons to turn around. It
had huge blocks—660 feet on a side—and sidewalks 20 feet wide. This would be a grand city,
the temple city, the religious capital of the Latter-Day Saints.
Library of Congress.

Nauvoo's broad streets, neat squares, and spectacular temple, but the Mormons had not outrun trouble. Dissenters within the church accused Smith of advocating plural marriage (polygamy) and published an exposé of the practice. Non-Mormons caught wind of the controversy and eventually arrested Smith and his brother. On June 27, 1844, a mob stormed the jail and shot both men dead.

The embattled church turned to an extraordinary new leader, Brigham Young, who immediately began to plan the exodus of his people. In 1846, the Mormons evacuated Nauvoo. Traveling in 3,700 wagons, twelve thousand Mormons made their way to eastern Iowa, where they established refugee camps. In 1847, Young led an advance party to their new home beside the Great Salt Lake. Young described it as a barren waste, "the paradise of the lizard, the cricket and the rattlesnake." Within ten years, however, the Mormons developed an efficient irrigation system and made the desert bloom. They accomplished the feat through cooperative labor, not the individualistic and competitive enterprise common among most emigrants. Under the stern leadership of Young and other church leaders, the Mormons built a thriving community.

In 1850, only three years after its founding, Deseret became annexed to the United States as Utah Territory. Although the Mormons professed loyalty to the Constitution, they paid little attention to distant Washington. What focused the nation's attention on the Latter-Day Saints was the announcement by Brigham Young in 1852 that many Mormons practiced polygamy. Although only one Mormon man in five had more than one wife (Young had twenty-three), Young's public statement caused an outcry that forced the government to establish its authority in Utah. In 1857, twenty-five hundred U.S. troops invaded Salt Lake City in what was known as the Mormon War. The bloodless occupation illustrates that most Americans viewed the Mormons as a threat to American morality, law, and institutions. The invasion did not dislodge the Mormon Church from its central place in Utah, however, and for years to come, most Americans perceived the Mormon settlement as a strange, and suitably isolated, place.

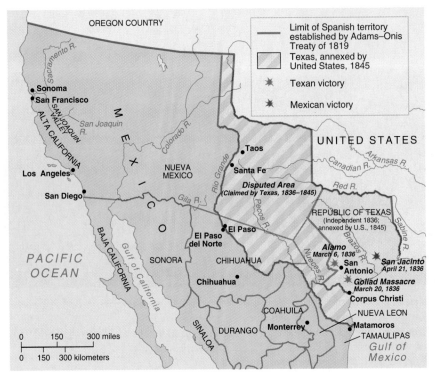

MAP 13.4
Texas and Mexico in the 1830s

As Americans spilled into lightly populated and loosely governed northern Mexico, Texas and then other Mexican provinces became contested territory.

The Mexican Borderlands

In the Mexican Southwest, westward-moving Anglo-American pioneers confronted northern-moving Spanish-speaking frontiersmen. On this frontier as elsewhere, cultures, interests, and aspirations collided. Since 1821, when Mexico won its independence from Spain, the Mexican flag had flown over the vast expanse that stretched from the Gulf of Mexico to the Pacific and from Oregon Country to Guatemala. Mexico's borders remained ill-defined, and its northern provinces were sparsely populated. Moreover, severe problems plagued the young nation: civil wars, economic crises, quarrels between the Roman Catholic Church and the state, and devastating raids by the Comanche, Apache, and Kiowa. Between 1833 and 1855, the presidency of Mexico changed hands thirty-six times. The central government found it increasingly difficult to defend its borderlands, especially when faced with a northern neighbor that was convinced of its superiority and bent on territorial acquisition.

The American assault began quietly. In the 1820s, Anglo-American trappers, traders, and settlers began drifting into the far northern provinces of Mexico. Santa Fe, a remote outpost in the province of New Mexico, became a magnet for

American enterprise. In 1821, a band of American traders stumbled into Santa Fe and discovered that newly independent Mexico was eager for American business. Each spring thereafter, American traders gathered at Independence, Missouri, for the long trek southwest along the Santa Fe Trail. Traders crammed their wagons with inexpensive American manufactured goods and returned with Mexican silver, furs, and mules. Trade between Mexico and the United States gradually pulled Mexico's far northern frontier into the American economic orbit.

The Mexican province of Texas attracted a flood of Americans who had settlement, not long-distance trade, on their minds. The Mexican government, which wanted to populate and develop its northern territory, granted the American Stephen F. Austin a huge tract of land, and in the 1820s he established a thriving settlement along the Brazos River. Land was cheap—only ten cents an acre—and thousands of farmers poured over the border. Most of the migrants were Southerners, who brought cotton and slaves with them. By 1835, the number of settlers—free and slave—in Texas had reached 30,000, while the Mexican population was barely 7,800. By and large, Anglo-American settlers were not Roman Catholic, did not speak Spanish, and cared little about assimilating into a culture that was so different from their own. The Mexican government realized that it had a problem on its hands; in 1829 it sought to arrest further immigration with an emancipation proclamation, which it hoped would make Texas less attractive. The settlers sidestepped the decree by calling their slaves servants, but they had other grievances, most significantly the puny voice they had in local government. General Antonio López de Santa Anna all but extinguished that voice when he seized political power and concentrated authority in Mexico City.

Faced with what they considered tyranny, the Texan settlers rebelled and declared the independent Republic of Texas. Santa Anna took the field and in March 1836 arrived at the outskirts of San Antonio with 6,000 troops. The rebels, who included the Tennessee frontiersman Davy Crocket, and the Louisiana adventurer Jim Bowie, took refuge in the old Franciscan mission the Alamo. Wave after wave of Mexicans crashed against the walls until the attackers finally broke through and killed all 186 defenders. A few weeks later in the small town of

SURVEYING TEXAS LAND
Land has always bred conflict in Texas. The new republic (1836–1845) wrestled with a confusing variety of Spanish, Mexican, and Texas claims, surveys, and titles. This painting by Theodore Gentilz in about 1844 documents the efforts of surveyor John James to settle the thorny issues. Five years later, however, Texas Governor P. H. Bell could still observe: "There is no subject which addresses itself more forcibly . . . than that of settling upon a secure and permanent basis the land titles of the country."
Courtesy, Mr. Larry Sheerin.

Goliad, Mexican forces surrounded and captured a garrison of 365 Texans. Following orders from Santa Anna, Mexican firing squads executed the men as pirates. But in April at San Jacinto, Santa Anna suffered a crushing defeat at the hands of forces under General Sam Houston. Mexico made no further military effort to bring Texas back into the fold. Texans elected Sam Houston president of their Lone Star Republic, and in 1837 the United States recognized the independence of Texas from Mexico.

The distant Mexican province of California also caught the eye of a few Americans. Spain had first extended its influence into California in 1769, when it sent a naval expedition north from Mexico to the San Francisco Bay in an effort to block Russian fur traders who were moving south along the Pacific coast from their base in Alaska. The Spanish built garrisoned towns (*presidios*), but, more important, they constructed a string of twenty-one missions, spaced a day's journey apart, along the coast from San Diego to Sonoma. Junípero Serra and other Franciscan friars converted the Indians to Christianity and drew them into the life and often hard agricultural labor of the missions. In 1824, in an effort to increase Mexican migration to thinly settled California, the Mexican government granted *ranchos*—huge estates devoted to cattle raising—to new settlers. *Rancheros* ruled over near-feudal empires worked by Indians whose condition sometimes approached that of slaves. Not satisfied, Mexican *rancheros* coveted the vast lands controlled by the Franciscan missions. In 1834, they persuaded the government to confiscate the missions and make their lands available to new settlement. Some seven hundred new *ranchos* followed, a development that accelerated the decline of California Indians. Devastated by disease, the Indians, who numbered approximately 300,000 when the Spanish arrived in California, declined by mid-nineteenth century to barely 150,000.

Despite the efforts of the Mexican government, California counted a population of only 7,000 Mexican settlers in 1840. Non-Mexican settlers numbered only 380, but among them were Americans who championed Manifest Destiny. Thomas O. Larkin, a prosperous merchant, John Marsh, a successful *ranchero* in the San Joaquin Valley, and others became boosters who sought to attract Americans from Oregon Country to California. The first overland party arrived in California in 1841. Thereafter, wagon after wagon followed the California Trail, which forked off from the Oregon Trail near the Snake River and led through the Sierra Nevada

at Lake Tahoe. As the trickle of Americans became a river, Mexican officials grew alarmed. California, they feared, would go the way of Texas. As a New York newspaper put it in 1845, "Let the tide of emigration flow toward California and the American population will soon be sufficiently numerous to play the Texas game." Indeed, many Americans in California continued to live apart, unassimilated, and to view themselves as superior to their Mexican neighbors. Not all Americans in California wanted to play the "Texas game," but many dreamed of living again under the American flag.

The U.S. government made no secret of its desire to acquire California. In 1835, President Andrew Jackson tried to purchase it. In 1842, Commodore Thomas Catesby Jones, hearing a rumor that the United States and Mexico were at war, seized the port of Monterey and ran up the American flag. The red-faced officer promptly ran it down again when he learned of his error. But his actions left no doubt about Washington's intentions. In 1846, American settlers in the Sacramento Valley took matters into their own hands. Prodded by John C. Frémont, a former army captain and explorer who had arrived in December 1845 with a party of sixty buckskinclad frontiersmen spoiling for a fight, the Californians raised an independence movement known as the Bear Flag Revolt. By then, James K. Polk, a champion of expansion, sat in the White House.

The Politics of Expansion

Although emigrants were the advance guard of American empire, there was nothing automatic about the U.S. annexation of territory in the West. Acquiring territory required political action, and in the 1840s the difficult problems of Texas, Oregon, and the Mexican borderlands intruded into national politics. The politics of expansion thrust the United States into dangerous diplomatic crises with Great Britain and Mexico. Even more ominous, expansion became hopelessly entangled with sectionalism and the slavery question.

Tyler and the Whig Fiasco

The complicated issues of westward expansion and the nation's boundaries ended up on the desk of John Tyler when he became president in April 1841. William Henry Harrison, a Whig, had been elected president in 1840, but one month after he took of-

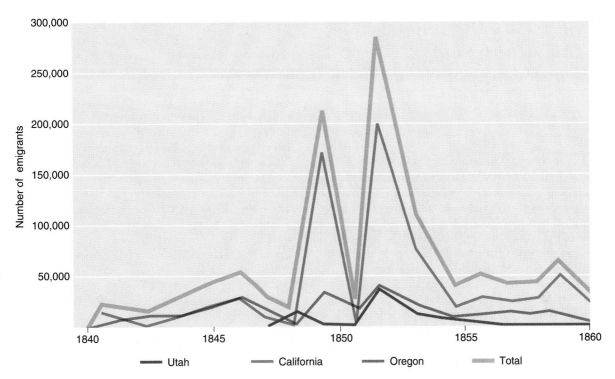

FIGURE **13.2**
Emigration to the West, 1840–1860
Land drew a steady stream of emigrants westward, but gold attracted torrents of emigrants to California.

fice, he died, the victim of pneumonia caught as he delivered his long inaugural address. For the first time in American history, a president had died in office, and it was not clear whether Vice President Tyler—"His Accidency," as his opponents called him—could legally exercise the full powers of an elected president.

The politics of expansion thrust the United States into dangerous diplomatic crises with Great Britain and Mexico.

Worse for the Whigs, Tyler was really a Democrat in Whig clothing. The fifty-one-year-old Virginian was a Whig only because he had fallen out with Andrew Jackson over Jackson's strong-armed tactics during the South Carolina nullification crisis. Whigs had placed Tyler on the ballot to balance the ticket and to appeal to Southerners. Tyler had consistently opposed all the measures of the Whig Henry Clay's American System: protective tariffs,

the national bank, and internal improvements at federal expense. Tyler favored strict construction and states' rights, positions closer to John C. Calhoun and the Democrats than to Clay and the Whigs. But the Whigs never expected that Tyler would wield power. Even after Tyler moved into the White House, they assumed that he would bow to the party's leader, Kentucky senator Henry Clay.

Clay viewed the Whig victory in 1840 as "a great civil revolution." After twelve years of Democratic rule, he could hardly wait to translate Whig programs and principles into law. He knew Tyler's views but remained optimistic because, as a reporter wrote, "If [Clay] was to intimate a wish that the majority of the Senate should go to [hell] . . . , they would immediately raise a committee to ascertain the most direct and eligible route." Clay guided a raft of legislation through Congress. Tyler accepted the repeal of the Democrat's independent treasury and grudgingly approved a slightly higher tariff, but he vetoed a bill for internal improvements. Clay pressed on, emerging from Congress with a bill for a new national bank. The president

What Was the Impact of the California Gold Rush?

ON A COLD JANUARY MORNING in 1848, while James Marshall was walking along the American River in the foothills of the Sierra Nevada, he detected the glint of yellow metal in the stream. The nuggets he found set off the California gold rush, one of the wildest mining stampedes in the world's history. Between 1849 and 1852, more than 250,000 forty-niners, as the would-be miners were known, descended on the Golden State.

Marshall discovered gold in the same year that the Treaty of Guadalupe Hidalgo transferred California and other northern provinces of Mexico to the United States. Americans did not find it surprising that the discovery coincided with American acquisition. "God kept that coast for a people of the Pilgrim blood," one minister intoned. "He would not permit any other to be fully developed there." Most Americans were determined that the West would be an enclave for Anglo-American enterprise and culture.

Gold proved irresistible to easterners. Newspapers went crazy with stories about prospectors who extracted half a pan of gold from every pan of gravel they scooped from western streams. Soon, cities reverberated with men singing:

Oh Susannah, don't you cry for me;
I'm gone to California with my wash-bowl on
my knee.

Scores of ships sailed from East Coast ports, headed either around South America to San Francisco or to Panama, where the passengers made their way by foot and canoe to the Pacific and waited for a ship to carry them north. Even larger numbers of gold seekers took riverboats to the Missouri River and then set out in wagons, on horseback, or by foot for the West.

But young men everywhere contracted gold fever. As stories of California gold circled the globe, Chinese and Germans, Mexicans and Irish, Australians and French, Chileans and Italians, and dozens of other nationalities set out to strike it rich. Louisa Knapp Clappe, wife of a minister and one of the few women in gold country, remarked that when she walked through Indian Bar, the little mining town where she lived, she heard English, French, Spanish, German, Italian, Kanaka (Hawaiian), Asian Indian, and American Indian languages. Hangtown, Hell's Delight, Gouge Eye, and a hundred other crude mining camps became temporary home to a diverse throng of nationalities and peoples.

One of the largest groups of new arrivals was the Chinese. Between 1848 and 1854, Chinese men numbering 45,000 (but almost no Chinese women) arrived in California. Most considered themselves sojourners, temporary residents who planned to return home as soon as their savings allowed. The majority came under a Chinese-controlled contract labor system in which the immigrant worked out the cost of his transportation. In the early years, most worked as wage laborers in mining. By the 1860s, they dominated railroad construction in the West. Ninety percent of the Central Pacific Railroad's 10,000 workers were Chinese. The Chinese also made up nearly one-half of San Francisco's labor force, working in the shoe, tobacco, woolen, laundry, and sewing trades. By 1870, the Chinese population had grown to 63,200, including 4,500 women. They constituted nearly 10 percent of the state's people and 25 percent of its wage-earning force.

The presence of peoples from around the world shattered the Anglo-American dream of a racially and ethnically homogeneous West, but ethnic diversity did nothing to increase the tolerance of Anglo-American prospectors. In their eyes, no "foreigner" had a right to dig gold. In 1850, the California legislature passed the Foreign Miners' Tax Law, which levied high taxes on non-Americans to drive them from the gold fields, except as hired laborers working on claims owned by Americans. Stubborn foreign miners were sometimes hauled before "Judge Lynch." One of the earliest lynchings in the gold fields was of a Frenchman and a Chilean.

Anglo-Americans considered the Chinese devious and unassimilable. They also feared that hardworking, self-denying Chinese labor would undercut white labor and drive it from the country. As a consequence, the Chinese were segregated residentially and occupationally and made ineligible for citizenship. Along with blacks and Indians, Chinese were denied public education and the right to testify in court. In addition to exclusion, they suffered from violence. Mobs drove them from Eureka, Truckee, and other mining towns.

American prospectors swamped the *Californios*, the Spanish and Mexican settlers who had lived in California for generations. On the eve of the American takeover, *Californios* included *rancheros*, professionals, merchants, artisans, and laborers. Raging prejudice and discriminatory laws increasingly pushed Hispanics into the ranks of unskilled labor. Americans took their land, even though the federal government had pledged to protect Mexican and Spanish land titles after the cession of 1848. Anglo forty-niners branded Spanish-speaking miners, even native-born *Californios*, "foreigners" and drove them from the diggings. Mariano Vallejo, a leading *Californio*, said of the forty-niners: "The good ones were few and the wicked many."

For Native Americans, the gold rush was a catastrophe. Numbering about 150,000 in 1848, the Indian population fell to 25,000 in 1856. *Californios* had exploited the native peoples, but the forty-niners wanted to eradicate them. Starvation, disease, and a declining birthrate took a heavy toll. Indians also fell victim to wholesale murder. "That a war of extermination will continue to be waged between the two races until the Indian race becomes extinct must be expected," declared California governor Peter W. Burnett in 1851. Nineteenth-century historian Hubert Howe Bancroft described white behavior toward Indians during the gold rush as "one of the last human hunts of civilization, and the basest and most brutal of them all." To survive, Indians moved to the most remote areas of the state and tried to stay out of the way.

The forty-niners created dazzling wealth—in 1852, eighty-one million ounces of gold, nearly one-half of the world's production. But because Anglo-Americans made the rules, not everyone shared equally. Of course, only a few prospectors—of whatever race and nationality—struck it rich. The era of the individual prospector panning in streams quickly gave way to corporate-owned deep-shaft mining. Most forty-niners eventually took up farming or other lines of work. But because of gold, an avalanche of people had roared across California. Anglo-Americans were most numerous, and Anglo dominance developed early. But the gold rush also brought a rainbow of nationalities. Anglo-American dominance and ethnic and racial diversity in the West both count among the most significant legacies of the gold rush.

promptly rejected it with a Jackson-like argument that it was "unconstitutional."

With his second veto, Tyler forfeited all claim to Whig leadership. His views on economic policy flew in the face of his party and left Clay's plan in shambles. The Whigs formally expelled Tyler from the party, and, in an unprecedented move, most of the cabinet resigned. Secretary of State Daniel Webster, however, stayed on to settle the boundary between Canada and the United States, still undetermined after fifty-six years. Britain sent Lord Ashburton to Washington, where he renewed the friendly relationship he and Webster had established in England. Observers dubbed the negotiations the "battle of the maps," but the cooperative mood led in 1842 to the Webster-Ashburton Treaty, which settled all border issues with Canada, except Oregon.

Even Webster's success could not redeem the Tyler administration. Tyler betrayed the economic principles of his supposed party, and the Whigs suffered near-complete domestic stalemate. Clay did not hesitate to compare John Tyler to Benedict Arnold. "Tyler is on his way to the Democratic camp," Clay declared. "They will give him lodgings in some outhouse, but they will never trust him. He will stand here, like Arnold in England, a monument of his own perfidy and disgrace." Writing off Tyler, Clay's followers hoisted his banner for the presidency in 1844. Clay resigned from the Senate to prepare for the race. Tyler dove into a quest for the Democratic nomination, but he needed an issue that could provide a bridge back to his former party.

Texas, Oregon, and the Election of 1844

Fending off Clay's economic program demanded most of John Tyler's energy, but the issue that stirred his blood, and that of much of the nation, was Texas. Texans had sought admission to the Union almost since their independence from Mexico in 1836, and Tyler, an ardent expansionist, knew that the acquisition of Texas would appeal strongly to southern and western Democrats. He also understood that Texas was a dangerous issue. Any suggestion of adding another slave state to the Union brought many Northerners to a boil. Andrew Jackson and his successor, Martin Van Buren, had cautiously avoided annexation because they doubted it was worth the price. Annexing Texas also risked precipitating war because Mexico had never relinquished its claim to its lost province.

Inhabitants of the Lone Star Republic lived a precarious existence. They often exchanged shots with Mexicans along the border, and they worried that Mexico would launch a new invasion. Cold-shouldered by the United States, Texans explored Great Britain's interest in recognition and trade. They discovered that the British were eager to keep Texas independent. In Britain's eyes, Texas provided a buffer against American expansion and a new market for English manufactured goods. Moreover, Britain hoped to persuade Texas to adopt gradual emancipation. Southern slaveholders accused the British of plotting to end slavery in Texas and to seal off the South's expansion to the west. Other Americans worried that Britain's real object was adding Texas to the British Empire. This fluid mix of threat, fear, and opportunity convinced Tyler to risk negotiations with Texas, and he worked vigorously to annex the republic before his term expired. His efforts pushed Texas and the slavery issue to the center of national politics.

In April 1844, after months of secret negotiations between Texas and the Tyler administration, the new secretary of state, South Carolinian John C. Calhoun, laid an annexation treaty before the Senate. But when Calhoun publicly linked annexation to the defense of slavery, he doomed the treaty. His statement strengthened the abolitionist claim that annexation was merely a proslavery plot, and howls of protest against annexation erupted everywhere north of the Mason-Dixon line. When the Senate soundly rejected the treaty, it appeared that Tyler had succeeded only in inflaming sectional conflict.

The issue of Texas had not died down by the 1844 elections. Henry Clay expected to win the Whig Party's presidential nomination and looked forward to waging his campaign on the old Whig economic issues in his American System that Tyler had frustrated. But everywhere he spoke, he confronted a barrage of questions about Texas. Finally, to appeal to northern voters, he came out against the immediate annexation of Texas. "Annexation and war with Mexico are identical," Clay declared. When news of Clay's statement reached Andrew Jackson at his plantation in Tennessee, he chuckled, "Clay [is] a dead political Duck." In Jackson's shrewd judgment, no man who opposed annexation could be elected president. But the Whig Party paid no attention, nominated Clay, and adopted a platform that proclaimed the principles of Clay's American System while remaining silent on Texas.

Among Democrats, Martin Van Buren expected to receive the party's nomination, but when he an-

TECHNOLOGY IN AMERICA
Hydraulic Mining

Individual prospectors who made the first gold strikes used a simple process known as placer mining, requiring only a decent claim and basic tools. As one awed visitor to the gold fields in 1848 observed: "No capital is required to obtain this gold, as the laboring man wants nothing but his pick and shovel and tin pan with which to dig and wash the gravel." But when these easy pickings along the rivers and streams gave out, a good deal of gold still remained trapped in quartz or buried deep in the earth, extractable only by methods far beyond the means and capacity of the average prospector.

Soon capital and technology invaded the diggings. Corporations initiated hydraulic operations to pursue the hidden veins of gold. These high-pressure streams of water blasted the ore loose and, later, other equipment was used to break down the rock and extract the precious gold. Eager to make a quick profit, the purveyors of this new technology gave little thought to its impact on the environment. The hydraulic jets demolished entire mountains, devastating stream beds and creating heaps of rubble. As big business gradually took over mining, corporations found laborers among the disillusioned forty-niners, who could earn more as wageworkers than as independent miners using pans. This scene probably shows the Timbuctoo operation near the Yuba River.
Collection of Matthew Isenburg.

A POLK SNUFFBOX
*The use of political paraphernalia to appeal to the elec-
torate is not a new phenomenon. James K. Polk, the Democratic presidential candidate in 1844, was portrayed on
this fine snuffbox. In a time when almost every adult male
used tobacco in one form or another, this handsome political object was sure to attract attention.*
Collection of Janice L. and David J. Frent.

nounced his opposition to Texas annexation, his
candidacy collapsed in the South. Van Buren's
demise opened the door at the Democratic convention. After John Tyler generated little support, James
K. Polk of Tennessee gained his party's presidential
nomination. Fourteen years in Congress had
brought Polk modest fame, but Texas lifted him into
the national spotlight. Polk was as strong for annexation as Clay was against it.

In the 1844 election, Democrats sought to champion Texas annexation without splitting their party
or the nation. They succeeded by yoking Texas to
Oregon, thus tapping the desire for expansion in the
free states of the North as well as in the slave states
of the South. The Democratic platform pulled out
all the stops on behalf of Manifest Destiny. It called
for the "reannexation of Texas" and the "reoccupa-
tion of Oregon." The suggestion that the United
States was merely reasserting its existing rights was
poor history but good politics. And by "Oregon"
the Democrats meant all of Oregon Country, from
the northern border of Mexican California to the
southern border of Russian Alaska, a huge coun-

terweight to balance massive Texas. According to
the Democratic formula, Texas annexation did not
give an advantage to slavery and the South. Linked
to Oregon, Texas expanded America to the advantage of the entire nation.

Much to Henry Clay's discomfort, Texas, not
the tariff, emerged as the dominant issue of the 1844
campaign. When Clay finally recognized the
groundswell for expansion, he lost his nerve. He
waffled on Texas, hinting that he might accept annexation under certain circumstances. His retreat
won little support in the South and only succeeded
in alienating antislavery opinion in the North. The
fledgling Liberty Party, which stood firmly against
annexation, denounced him as "rotten as a stagnant
fish pond." The Liberty Party candidate, James G.
Birney, picked up the votes of thousands of disillusioned Clay supporters. In the November election,
Polk received 2,698,609 votes and Clay got only
38,180 votes fewer. But Polk's electoral majority was
wider, 170 to 105. New York's 35 electoral votes
proved critical to Clay's defeat. Birney received
15,000 votes in New York, but since Clay lost the
state by only 5,000, a shift of just one-third of Birney's votes to Clay would have given him the state
and the presidency.

The nation did not have to wait for Polk's inauguration to see results from his victory. One
month after the election, President Tyler announced
that the Democratic triumph provided a mandate for
the annexation of Texas "promptly and immediately." After a fierce debate between antislavery and
proslavery forces, Congress approved a joint resolution offering the Republic of Texas admission to
the United States. On March 1, 1845, three days before Polk took office, Texas entered the Union as a
slave state. Nine years after its independence, Texas
achieved statehood. Almost four years after taking
office, Tyler had an achievement to crow about.

Tyler had seen to Texas, but James Polk had
promised Oregon, too. Settlers in the West and
expansionists elsewhere demanded that the new
president make good on the Democrats' campaign
slogan—"Fifty-four Forty or Fight"—that is, all of
Oregon, right up to Alaska ("fifty-four forty" being
the southern latitude of Russian Alaska). But Polk
never coveted the Northwest as he did the Southwest. Moreover, he was close to war with Mexico
and could not afford a simultaneous war with
Britain over its claims to Canada. After the initial
bluster, therefore, Polk buried the Democrats' campaign promise and renewed an old offer to divide
Oregon along the forty-ninth parallel. After some

hesitation, the British accepted the compromise. Westerners cried betrayal, but most Americans celebrated the agreement that gave the nation an enormous territory peacefully. Besides, when the Senate finally approved the treaty in June 1846, the United States and Mexico were already at war.

The Mexican War

From its independence in 1821, Mexico realized that its security and success in nation building depended on harmonious relations with its northern neighbor. The United States, however, exhibited expansionist tendencies from the beginning. Aggravation between the two nations escalated to open antagonism in 1845 when the United States annexed Texas. Absorbing territory still claimed by Mexico ruptured diplomatic relations between the United States and Mexico and set the stage for war. But it was President James K. Polk's insistence on having Mexico's other northern provinces that made war certain. Polk and the expansionist crowd never doubted the justice of their quest. Justice looked very different in Mexico City. The war was not as easy as Polk anticipated, but it ended in American victory and acquisition of a new American West. Mexicans could only lament, "Poor Mexico, so far from God, so near the United States."

"Mr. Polk's War"

From the day he entered the White House, Polk craved Mexico's remaining northern provinces: California and New Mexico, land that today makes up California, Nevada, and Utah, most of New Mexico and Arizona, and parts of Wyoming and Colorado. Polk hoped to buy the territory. If the Mexicans refused to sell, however, he was willing to take what he wanted. Polk made a last-ditch effort to gain the territory peacefully by sending an envoy, John Slidell, to Mexico City to negotiate the purchase of New Mexico and California. But the Mexicans refused to sell off their country, and in March 1846 they sent Slidell packing. A furious Polk concluded that it would take military force to realize the United States' Manifest Destiny.

Polk had already ordered General Zachary Taylor to march his 4,000-man Army of Occupation of Texas from its position on the Nueces River, the southern boundary of Texas according to the Mexicans, to the banks of the Rio Grande 150 miles

south, the boundary claimed by Texans. Excitement ran high as the raw, young troops entered the disputed territory. Lieutenant George G. Meade, who would command troops at Gettysburg a few years later, admitted, "I hope for a war and a speedy battle, and I think one good fight will settle the business; and really, after coming so far . . . it would hardly be the thing to come back without some laurels." Action came quickly enough. The Mexican general in Matamoros viewed the American advance as aggression and ordered Taylor back to the Nueces. Taylor refused, and on April 25, Mexican cavalry attacked a party of American soldiers, killing or wounding 16 and capturing the rest. Even before news of the battle arrived in Washington, Polk had already obtained his cabinet's approval of a war message.

Polk and the expansionist crowd never doubted the justice of their quest. Justice looked very different in Mexico City.

On May 11, 1846, the president told Congress, "Mexico has passed the boundary of the United States, has invaded our territory, and shed American blood upon American soil." Thus "war exists, and, notwithstanding all our efforts to avoid it, exists by the act of Mexico herself." Two days later, Congress passed a declaration of war and began raising an army. Despite years of saber rattling toward Mexico and Britain, the American army was pitifully small, only 7,400 soldiers. Faced with the nation's first foreign war, up against a Mexican army that numbered more than 30,000, Polk called for volunteers who would serve for six to twelve months. Men everywhere rushed to the colors. The city of Baltimore met its quota in thirty-six hours. More than 30,000 Tennesseans competed for the state's 3,000 allotted positions. Even Massachusetts, where many citizens denounced the war as a plot to extend slavery, filled its quota within a month. Eventually, more than 112,000 white Americans (blacks were banned) joined the army to fight in Mexico.

Despite the outpouring of support, the war divided the nation. Whigs displayed considerably less enthusiasm for the Mexican adventure than did Democrats. Northerners were not nearly as hot-blooded about the war as Southerners. Although some Northerners kept their opposition to themselves because they did not want to appear unpa-

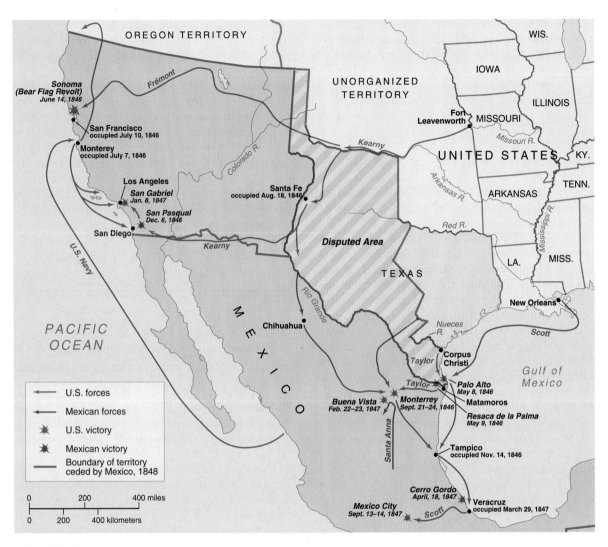

MAP **13.5**
The Mexican War, 1846–1848
*American and Mexican soldiers skirmished across much of northern Mexico, but the major
battles took place between the Rio Grande and Mexico City.*

triotic or unwilling to support American soldiers in the field, a hard core of northern Whigs loudly condemned the war as the unwarranted bullying of a weak nation by its greedy expansionist neighbor.

In January 1848, a gangly freshman representative from Illinois rose from his back-row seat in the House of Representatives to deliver his first important speech in Congress. Abraham Lincoln took direct aim at the president and his war. Polk's defense of the war, Lincoln declared, was from beginning to end the "sheerest deception." He challenged the president's version of the incident that precipitated

war and sought to disprove Polk's claim that the territory between the Nueces and the Rio Grande was indisputably American soil. He likened the president's views to "the half-insane mumbling of a fever dream" and proclaimed Polk "a bewildered, confounded, and miserably perplexed man." Before he sat down, Lincoln had questioned the president's intelligence, honesty, and sanity. President Polk simply ignored the upstart representative, but antislavery, antiwar Whigs kept up the attack throughout the conflict. In their effort to undercut national support, they labeled it "Mr. Polk's War."

Since most Americans backed the war, it was not really Polk's war, but the president acted as if it were. Although he had no military experience, he directed the war personally. Working eighteen hours a day, Polk established overall strategy and oversaw the details of military campaigns. He planned a short war in which American armies would occupy Mexico's northern provinces and defeat the Mexican army in a decisive battle or two, after which Mexico would sue for peace and the United States would keep the territory its armies occupied. But Mexico surprised Polk. Although its government was in disarray and its army poorly led, trained, and equipped, Mexico fought stubbornly rather than surrender its territory.

Taking the Borderlands

In May 1846, Zachary Taylor's troops drove south from the Rio Grande and routed the Mexican army, first on the plain of Palo Alto and then in a palm-filled ravine known as Resaca de la Palma. Taylor became an instant war hero. Sixty-two years old, "Old Rough and Ready," as he was affectionately known, had an undistinguished career behind him. But his simplicity and informality, as well as his cool behavior under fire, endeared him to his men. Polk rewarded Taylor for his victories by making him commander for the conquest of Mexico.

A second prong of the campaign to occupy Mexico's northern provinces centered on Colonel Stephen Watts Kearny, who led a 1,700-man army from Missouri into New Mexico. Without firing a shot, American forces took Santa Fe in August 1846. Kearny promptly proclaimed New Mexico American territory and with 300 troops headed for California. On the trail, incredibly, he met Kit Carson, part of John C. Frémont's buckskin army, who was hurrying east with the news of the American seizure of California. Thinking the contest already won, Kearny sent two-thirds of his men back to Santa Fe and pushed westward, with Carson as his scout. After nearly three months on the trail, Kearny's small band marched into San Diego and into a major Mexican rebellion against American rule. In January 1847, after several clashes, the American forces occupied Los Angeles. California and New Mexico were in American hands.

By then, Taylor had driven deep into the interior of Mexico. In September 1846, after a five-day siege and house-to-house fighting, he took the fortified city of Monterrey. With reinforcements and fresh supplies, Taylor pushed his 5,000 troops southwest, where the Mexican hero of the Alamo, General Antonio López de Santa Anna, was concentrating a huge army of 21,000, which he hoped would strike a decisive blow against the invaders from the north.

MEXICAN FAMILY
Mexican civilians, like this family in 1847, were vulnerable to atrocities committed by an invading army. Volunteers, a large portion of American troops, received little training and resisted military discipline. The "lawless Volunteers stop at no outrage," Brigadier General William Worth declared. "Innocent blood has been basely, cowardly, and barbarously shed in cold blood." Generals Zachary Taylor and Winfield Scott gradually tamed the "wild volunteers" by employing stern military justice.
Courtesy Amon Carter Museum, Fort Worth.

On Washington's birthday 1847, Taylor's troops met Santa Anna's at Buena Vista. Superior American artillery and accurate musket fire won the day, but the Americans suffered heavy casualties, including Henry Clay Jr., the son of the man who had opposed Texas annexation for fear it would precipitate war. But the Mexicans suffered even greater losses, and during the night Santa Anna removed his battered army from the battlefield, much to the "profound disgust of the troops," one Mexican officer remembered. "They are filled with grief that they were going to lose the benefit of all the sacrifices that they had made; that the conquered field would be abandoned, and that the victory would be given to the enemy; and finally, to affirm the idea already general in the army—that it was impossible to conquer the Americans."

The series of uninterrupted victories in northern Mexico fed the American troops' sense of superiority and very nearly led to a feeling of invincibility. "No American force has ever thought of being defeated by any amount of Mexican troops," one soldier declared. The Americans worried about other hazards, however. "I can assure you that fighting is the least dangerous & arduous part of a soldier's life," one young man said. Letters home told of torturous marches across burning, arid wastes alive with tarantulas, scorpions, and rattlesnakes. Others recounted clouds of flies, mosquitoes, and fleas. One soldier complained to his sister that "if [we] dont soon get a ship load of blood brought over we [will] be in a bad fix for the fleas and gnats have sucked all the blood out of us and eat our hides up." Dysentery, malaria, smallpox, cholera, and yellow fever were not joking matters. Of the 13,000 American soldiers who died in Mexico, only 2,000 fell to Mexican bullets and shells. Disease killed most of the others. Medicine was so primitive and conditions so harsh that army doctors could do little. As a Tennessee man observed, "nearly all who take sick die."

Victory in Mexico

Although Americans won battle after battle, President Polk's strategy misfired. Despite its loss of territory and men, Mexico determinedly refused to trade land for peace. One American soldier captured the Mexican mood: "They cannot submit to be deprived of California after the loss of Texas, and nothing but the conquest of their Capital will force them to such a humiliation." Polk had arrived at the same conclusion. Zachary Taylor had not proven

decisive enough for Polk, and the president tapped another general to carry the war to Mexico City. While Taylor occupied the north, General Winfield Scott would land his army on the Gulf coast of Mexico and march 250 miles inland to the capital. Polk's plan entailed enormous risk; it meant that Scott would have to cut himself off from supplies on the coast and lead his men deep into enemy country against a numerically superior foe.

After months of careful planning and the skillful coordination of army and navy, an amphibious landing near Veracruz put 8,600 American troops ashore in five hours without the loss of a single life. The Americans encircled the city, and after eighty-eight hours of furious shelling, Veracruz surrendered. Scott immediately began preparations for the march west. Transportation alone posed enormous problems. His army required 9,300 wagons and 17,000 pack mules, 500,000 bushels of oats and corn, and 100 pounds of blister ointment before it could begin the mountainous journey. In early April 1847, the army moved out, following the path that had been trodden more than three centuries earlier by Hernán Cortés.

Meanwhile, after the frightful defeat at Buena Vista, Santa Anna had returned to Mexico City. He rallied his ragged troops and marched them east to set a trap for Scott in the mountain pass at Cerro Gordo. But the Americans knifed through Mexican lines, almost capturing Santa Anna, who fled the field on foot. So complete was the victory that Scott gloated to Taylor, "Mexico no longer has an army." But Scott barely had one either. One-third of his troops—some 3,000 men—were volunteers whose year's service had expired. Scott had no choice but to release them and wait for reinforcements. In July 1847, with the army topping 14,000 soldiers, Scott resumed his march. Ever resilient, Santa Anna again rallied the Mexican army. Some 30,000 troops took up defensive positions on the outskirts of Mexico City, where they hurriedly began melting down church bells to cast new cannon.

In August, Scott began his assault on the Mexican capital. The fighting proved the most brutal of the war. Santa Anna backed his army into the city, fighting each step of the way. At the battle of Churubusco, the Mexicans took 4,000 casualties in a single day and the Americans more than 1,000. At Chapultepec, a castle that stood two hundred feet above the marsh that surrounded it, American troops scaled the walls and fought the Mexican defenders hand to hand. Santa Anna lost 1,800 men that day, and Scott lost more than 400. After Cha-

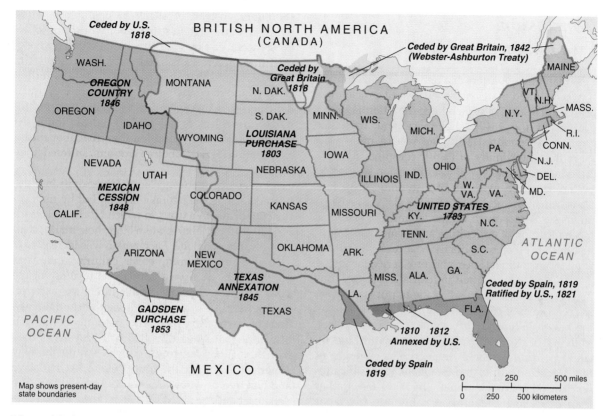

M A P 13.6
Territorial Expansion by 1860
*Less than a century after its founding, the United States had spread from the Atlantic seaboard
to the Pacific Ocean. War, purchase, and diplomacy had gained a continent.*

pultepec, Mexico City lay open. But during the night, Santa Anna evacuated the capital, and on September 14, 1847, General Winfield Scott rode in triumphantly. The ancient capital of the Aztecs had fallen once again to an invading army.

With Mexico City in American hands, Polk sent Nicholas P. Trist, the chief clerk in the State Department, to Mexico to negotiate the peace. When Trist arrived, he found that Santa Anna had resigned as president and had fled the country. But Trist began talks with commissioners appointed by a new Mexican president and on February 2, 1848, signed the Treaty of Guadalupe Hidalgo. Mexico agreed to give up all claims to Texas above the Rio Grande and to cede the huge provinces of New Mexico and California to the United States. The United States agreed to pay Mexico $15 million and to assume $3.25 million in claims that American citizens had against Mexico. Some Americans clamored for all of Mexico, but the treaty gave the pres-

ident what he wanted. Polk sent the treaty to the Senate, which ratified it by a vote of thirty-eight to fourteen in March 1848. The last American soldiers left Mexico a few months later.

The American triumph in the Mexican War had enormous consequences. With the northern half of Mexico in American hands, for example, California gold would never make Mexicans rich or bankroll Mexico's economic development. The war also reinforced the worst stereotypes Mexicans and Americans had of each other. A virulent anti-Yankee sentiment took root in Mexico, while deeply prejudiced views of Mexicans and Mexican culture flourished in the fertile soil of American victory. For Mexico, defeat meant national humiliation, but it also had a positive effect. It generated for the first time a genuine nationalism, no small thing in a country still trying to build a nation. In America, victory increased the sense of superiority that was already deeply ingrained.

Conclusion:
Free Labor, Free Men

Less than three-quarters of a century after its founding, the United States achieved its self-proclaimed Manifest Destiny to stretch from the Atlantic to the Pacific. In the 1840s, diplomacy and war had handed the nation 1.2 million square miles and more than 1,000 miles of Pacific coastline. To most Americans, vast geographical expansion seemed to be the natural companion of a stunning economic transformation. A cluster of interrelated developments—steam power, railroads, and the growing mechanization of agriculture and manufacturing—resulted in greater productivity, a burst of output from farms and factories, and prosperity for many.

To Northerners, their industrial evolution confirmed the choice they had made to put slavery on the road to extinction and to promote free labor as the key to independence, equality, and prosperity. Millions of Northerners, like Abraham Lincoln, could point to personal experience as evidence of the practical truth of the free-labor ideal. But millions of others had different stories to tell. Rather than producing economic equality, the free-labor system saw wealth and poverty continue to rub

shoulders. Instead of social independence, more than half of the nation's free-labor workforce toiled for someone else by 1860. Free-labor enthusiasts denied that the problems were built into the system. They argued that most social ills—including poverty and dependency—sprang from individual deficiencies. Consequently, reformers usually focused on the lack of self-control and discipline, on sin and alcohol. They denied that free labor meant exploitation. Slaves, not free workers, suffered, they argued.

Differences between North and South had appeared early in the nation's history, but by midcentury the distinctive ways in which North and South organized their labor systems left their mark on all aspects of regional life. Each region was increasingly animated by economic interests, cultural values, and political aims that were antithetical to those of the other. In the midst of deepening differences between the regions, Mexican land thrust the fundamental issue of slave or free labor into the center of national life. Now that Americans had half of Mexico, they had to decide what to do with it. Would the new American West, like the United States, be half slave and half free, or would it be all one or the other? The debate about the territory taken from Mexico became a struggle over the nation's future.

CHRONOLOGY

1828 America's first railroad, the Baltimore and Ohio, breaks ground.	William Henry Harrison dies in office after one month.
1836 Texas declares independence from Mexico.	**1842** Webster-Ashburton Treaty settles all border issues with British Canada except Oregon.
1837 John Deere patents his steel plow.	
1840s Americans begin harnessing steam power to manufacturing. Cyrus McCormick and others create practical mechanical reapers.	**1844** Democrat James K. Polk elected president on platform calling for annexation of Texas and Oregon. Samuel F. B. Morse invents telegraph.
1841 Congress approves permanent pre-emption law. First wagon trains set out for West on Oregon Trail. Vice President John Tyler becomes president of the United States when	**1845** Term "Manifest Destiny" coined by New York journalist John L. O'Sullivan; used as justification for Anglo-American settlers to take land in West. United States annexes Texas, which enters Union as slave state.

1846 Bear Flag Revolt, independence movement to secede from Mexico, takes place in California. **May 13.** Congress declares war on Mexico. United States and Great Britain agree to divide Oregon Country at forty-ninth parallel. **1847** Brigham Young leads advance party of Mormons to Great Salt Lake in Utah. **1848** Treaty of Guadalupe Hidalgo ends Mexican War. Mexico gives up all claims to Texas north of Rio Grande and cedes provinces of New Mexico and California to United States. Oneida community organized in New York.	First women's rights convention in United States takes place at Seneca Falls, New York. **1849** California gold rush begins. Harriet Tubman escapes from slavery in Maryland. **1850** Mormon community of Deseret annexed to United States as Utah Territory. **1851** Conference in Laramie, Wyoming, between U.S. government and Plains tribes marks beginning of government policy of forcing Indians onto reservations. Maine prohibits sale or manufacture of alcoholic beverages. **1855** Massachusetts integrates public schools as result of campaigns led by African American leaders.

BIBLIOGRAPHY

GENERAL WORKS

Roy P. Basler, ed., *The Collected Works of Abraham Lincoln,* 8 vols. (1953).

Stuart Bruchey, *Enterprise: The Dynamic Economy of a Free People* (1990).

Lawrence A. Cremin, *American Education: The National Experience, 1783–1876* (1980).

David B. Danbom, *Born in the Country: A History of Rural America* (1995).

David Brion Davis, ed., *Antebellum American Culture: An Interpretive Anthology* (1979).

David Herbert Donald, *Lincoln* (1995).

John Mack Faragher, *Sugar Creek: Life on the Illinois Frontier* (1986).

Lori D. Ginzberg, *Women and the Work of Benevolence: Morality, Politics, and Class in the Nineteenth-Century United States* (1990).

Nathan O. Hatch, *The Democratization of American Christianity* (1991).

John F. Kasson, *Rudeness and Civility: Manners in Nineteenth-Century Urban America* (1990).

Bruce Laurie, *Artisans into Workers: Labor in Nineteenth-Century America* (1989).

Bruce Levine, *Half Slave and Half Free: The Roots of the Civil War* (1992).

Patricia Nelson Limerick, Clyde A. Milner II, and Charles E. Rankin, eds., *Trails: Toward a New Western History* (1991).

Clyde A. Milner II, Carol A. O'Conner, and Martha A. Sandweiss, eds., *The Oxford History of the American West* (1994).

Richard White, *"It's Your Misfortune and None of My Own": A New History of the American West* (1991).

THE ECONOMY AND FREE LABOR

James R. Beniger, *The Control Revolution: Technological and Economic Origins of the Information Society* (1986).

Allan G. Bogue, *From Prairie to Corn Belt* (1963).

Alfred D. Chandler Jr., *The Visible Hand: The Managerial Revolution in American Business* (1977).

Thomas C. Cochran, *Frontiers of Change: Early Industrialism in America* (1981).

Lee Craig, *To Sow One Acre More: Childbearing and Farm Productivity in the Antebellum North* (1993).

Stanley L. Engerman and Robert E. Gallman, eds., *Long-Term Factors in American Economic Growth* (1986).

Paul Faler, *Mechanics and Manufacturers in the Early Industrial Revolution: Lynn, Massachusetts, 1780–1860* (1981).

Albert Fishlow, *American Railroads and the Transformation of the Ante-Bellum Economy* (1965).

Robert E. Gallman and John J. Wallis, eds., *American Economic Growth and Standards of Living before the Civil War* (1992).

Paul W. Gates, *The Farmer's Age: Agriculture, 1815–1860* (1960).

Jonathan A. Glickstein, *Concepts of Free Labor in Antebellum America* (1991).

Brooke Hindle, *Emulation and Invention* (1981).

Brooke Hindle and Steven Lubar, *Engines of Change: The American Industrial Revolution, 1790–1860* (1986).

Susan E. Hirsch, *Roots of the American Working Class: The Industrialization of Crafts in Newark, 1800–1860* (1978).

Donald R. Hoke, *Ingenious Yankees: The Rise of the American System of Manufactures in the Private Sector* (1990).

David A. Hounshell, *From the American System to Mass Production, 1800–1932* (1984).

Louis C. Hunter, *A History of Industrial Power in the United States, 1780–1930*, vol. 1, *Water Power in the Century of the Steam Engine* (1979), vol. 2, *Steam Power* (1985), vol. 3, *The Transmission of Power* (1991).

Paul Israel, *From Machine Shop to Industrial Laboratory: Telegraphy and the Changing Context of American Invention, 1830–1920* (1992).

Allan Kulikoff, *The Agrarian Origins of American Capitalism* (1992).

Bruce Laurie, *Working People of Philadelphia, 1800–1850* (1980).

Judith A. McGaw, *Most Wonderful Machine: Mechanization and Social Change in Berkshire Paper Making, 1801–1885* (1987).

Jonathan Prude, *The Coming of Industrial Order: Town and Factory Life in Rural Massachusetts, 1810–1860* (1983).

Daniel T. Rodgers, *The Work Ethic in Industrial America, 1850–1920* (1978).

W. J. Rorabaugh, *The Craft Apprentice: From Franklin to the Machine Age in America* (1986).

Merritt Roe Smith, *Harpers Ferry Armory and the New Technology* (1977).

John F. Stover, *The Life and Decline of the American Railroad* (1970).

John F. Stover, *Iron Road to the West: American Railraods in the 1850s* (1978).

George Rogers Taylor, *The Transportation Revolution, 1815–1860* (1951).

ANTEBELLUM CULTURE AND REFORM

Norman Basch, *In the Eyes of the Law: Women, Marriage, and Property in Nineteenth-Century New York* (1982).

Thomas Bender, ed., *The Antislavery Debate: Capitalism and Abolition as a Problem in Historical Interpretation* (1992).

Stuart Blumin, *The Emergence of the Middle Class: Social Experience in the American City, 1790–1900* (1989).

Jeanne Boydston, *Home and Housework: Housework, Wages, and the Ideology of Labor in the Early Republic* (1990).

Christopher Clark, *The Communitarian Moment: The Radical Challenge of the Northhampton Association* (1995).

Ellen Carol DuBois, *Feminism and Suffrage: The Emergence of an Independent Women's Suffrage Movement in America, 1848–1869* (1978).

Barbara Leslie Epstein, *The Politics of Domesticity: Women, Evangelism, and Temperance in Nineteenth-Century America* (1981).

Michael Fellman, *The Unbounded Frame: Freedom and Community in Nineteenth Century American Utopianism* (1973).

George Forgie, *Patricide in the House Divided: A Psychological Interpretation of Lincoln and His Age* (1979).

Lawrence Foster, *Religion and Sexuality: Three American Communal Experiments of the Nineteenth Century* (1981).

Lawrence Foster, *Women, Family, and Utopia: Communal Experiments of the Shakers, the Oneida Community, and the Mormons* (1991).

Rhoda Golden Freeman, *The Free Negro in New York City in the Era before the Civil War* (1994).

Peter Dobkin Hall, *The Organization of American Culture, 1700–1900* (1982).

Karen Halttunen, *Confidence Men and Painted Women: A Study of Middle-Class Culture in America, 1830–1870* (1982).

Blanche Glassman Hersh, *The Slavery of Sex: Feminist Abolitionists in America* (1978).

Nancy A. Hewitt, *Women's Activism and Social Change: Rochester, New York, 1822–1872* (1984).

Sylvia D. Hoffert, *When Hens Crow: The Women's Rights Movement in Antebellum America* (1995).

Joan M. Jensen, *Loosening the Bonds: Mid-Atlantic Farm Women, 1750–1850* (1986).

Carl F. Kaestle, *Pillars of the Republic: Common Schools and American Society, 1780–1860* (1983).

John F. Kasson, *Civilizing the Machine: Technology and Republican Values in America, 1776–1900* (1976).

Mary Kelley, *Private Women, Public Stage: Literary Domesticity in Nineteenth-Century America* (1984).

Spencer Klaw, *Without Sin: The Life and Death of the Oneida Community* (1993).

Jack Larkin, *The Reshaping of Everyday Life, 1790–1840* (1988).

William J. McFeely, *Frederick Douglass* (1991).

Keith E. Melder, *Beginnings of Sisterhood: The American Women's Rights Movement, 1800–1850* (1977).

Kerby A. Miller, *Emigrants and Exiles: Ireland and the Irish Exodus to North America* (1985).

Steven Mintz, *Moralists and Modernizers: America's Pre-Civil War Reformers* (1995).

Steven Mintz and Susan Kellogg, *Domestic Revolutions: A Social History of American Family Life* (1988).

C. Peter Ripley et al., eds., *Witness for Freedom: African American Voices on Race, Slavery, and Emancipation* (1993).

W. J. Rorabaugh, *The Alcoholic Republic: An American Tradition* (1979).

John R. Stilgoe, *Borderland: Origins of the American Suburb, 1820–1939* (1988).

Shirley Yee, *Black Women Abolitionists: A Study in Activism, 1828–1860* (1992).

Jean Fagan Yellin, *Women and Sisters: The Antislavery Feminists in American Culture* (1989).

Jean Fagan Yellin and John C. Van Horne, eds., *The Abolitionist Sisterhood: Women's Political Culture in Antebellum America* (1994).

POLITICS AND EXPANSION

Nels Anderson, *Desert Saints: The Mormon Frontier in Utah* (2nd ed., 1966).

Leonard J. Arrington and Davis Bitton, *The Mormon Experience* (1979).

Irving H. Bartlett, *John C. Calhoun: A Biography* (1993).

Richard A. Bartlett, *The New Country: A Social History of the American Frontier, 1776–1890* (1974).

William A. Bowen, *The Willamette Valley: Migration and Settlement on the Oregon Frontier* (1978).

Gene M. Brack, *Mexico Views Manifest Destiny, 1821–1846* (1975).

John Faragher, *Women and Men on the Overland Trail* (1979).

William H. Goetzmann, *New Lands, New Men: America and the Second Great Age of Discovery* (1986).

Norman A. Graebner, *The Foundation of American Foreign Policy* (1985).

William Greever, *Bonanza West: The Story of the Western Mining Rushes, 1848–1900* (1963).

Thomas R. Hietala, *Manifest Design: Anxious Aggrandizement in Late Jacksonian America* (1985).

Albert L. Hurtado, *Indian Survival on the California Frontier* (1988).

Reginald Horseman, *Race and Manifest Destiny: The Origins of American Racial Anglo-Saxonism* (1981).

Robert H. Jackson and Edward Castillo, *Indians, Franciscans, and Spanish Colonization: The Impact of the Mission System on California Indians* (1995).

Julie Roy Jeffrey, *Frontier Women: The Trans-Mississippi West, 1840–1880* (1979).

Rudolph M. Lapp, *Blacks in Goldrush California* (1977).

Patricia Nelson Limerick, *The Legacy of Conquest: The Unbroken Past of the American West* (1987).

Ward McAfee and J. Cordell Robinson, eds., *Origins of the Mexican War: A Documentary Source Book*, 2 vols. (1982).

Charles J. McClain, *In Search of Equality: The Chinese Struggle against Discrimination in Nineteenth-Century America* (1994).

D. W. Meinig, *The Shaping of America: A Geographical Perspective on Five Hundred Years of History*, vol. 2, *Continental America, 1800–1867* (1993).

Frederick Merk, *Manifest Destiny and Mission in American History* (1963).

Michael C. Meyer and William L. Sherman, *The Course of Mexican History* (4th ed., 1991).

Rodman W. Paul, *Mining Frontiers of the Far West, 1848–1880* (1963).

David M. Pletcher, *The Diplomacy of Annexation: Texas, Oregon, and the Mexican War* (1973).

Glenda Riley, *The Female Frontier: A Comparative View of Women on the Prairie and the Plains* (1988).

Malcolm J. Rohrbough, *The Trans-Appalachian Frontier* (1978).

Charles Sellers, *The Market Revolution: Jacksonian America, 1815–1846* (1991).

Joel H. Silbey, *The American Political Nation, 1838–1893* (1991).

Kevin Starr, *Americans and the California Dream, 1850–1915* (1973).

Ronald Takaki, *Iron Cages: Race and Culture in Nineteenth-Century America* (1979).

John D. Unruh, *The Plains Across: The Overland Emigrants and the Trans-Mississippi West, 1840–1860* (1979).

Robert M. Utley, *The Indian Frontier of the American West, 1846–1890* (1984).

David J. Weber, *The Mexican Frontier, 1821–1846* (1982).

Sanford Wexler, ed., *Westward Expansion: An Eyewitness History* (1991).

THE MEXICAN WAR

K. Jack Bauer, *The Mexican War, 1846–1848* (1974).

Seymour V. Conner and Odie B. Faulk, *North America Divided: The Mexican War, 1846–1848* (1971).

John S. C. Eisenhower, *So Far from God: The U.S. War with Mexico, 1846–1848* (1989).

Robert W. Johannsen, *To the Halls of the Montezumas: The Mexican War in the American Imagination* (1985).

Ernest M. Lander Jr., *Reluctant Imperialists: Calhoun, the South Carolinians, and the Mexican War* (1980).

James M. McCaffrey, *Army of Manifest Destiny: The American Soldiers in the Mexican War, 1846–1848* (1992).

Ramon Eduardo Ruiz, ed., *The Mexican War: Was It Manifest Destiny?* (1963).

John H. Schroeder, *Mr. Polk's War* (1973).

Otis A. Singletary, *The Mexican War* (1960).

FREDERICK DOUGLASS DOLLS
These dolls were made in the late 1850s by Cynthia Hill of New Bedford, Massachusetts, where Frederick Douglass had first settled after he escaped from slavery. They celebrate Douglass's transformation from barefoot, tattered slave to dignified, respectable man of substance. They also announce more generally that African Americans were held back by their enslavement, not by their race.
Old Dartmouth Historical Society, New Bedford Whaling Museum.

THE HOUSE DIVIDED

1846–1861

14

ALREADY KNOWN AS THE "GATEWAY TO THE WEST," St. Louis, Missouri, in 1830 was a thriving river port. Among the newcomers arriving that year was Dred Scott, a slave. Scott had been born in Virginia at the turn of the century and in 1818 had moved with his master Peter Blow to a cotton plantation in Alabama. Twelve years later, the Blow family and their six slaves moved to St. Louis. St. Louis's population of six thousand included some twelve hundred African Americans, both slave and free. Free blacks lived hard lives—crammed into rotten shacks in dismal alleys, employed in the meanest jobs, excluded from much of the city's activities, harassed on account of their race. Because details of Dred Scott's life are scarce, we can't be certain of his circumstances, but we know that freedom —even the severely restricted freedom of St. Louis's free blacks—became Dred Scott's dream.

In 1833, Scott was sold to Dr. John Emerson, an army doctor who took Scott with him as his personal servant when he was posted to Fort Armstrong in Illinois. Two years later, Scott accompanied Emerson when he was transferred to Fort Snelling on the Minnesota River in Wisconsin Territory. In 1836 or 1837, while living at Fort Snelling, Scott met and married Harriet Robinson, the slave of an Indian agent stationed nearby. Her owner either gave her or sold her to Emerson. In 1838, Dred and Harriet Scott followed Emerson to Fort Jessup in Louisiana, but a few months later all three returned to Fort Snelling. New orders sent Emerson to Florida, but this time he left the Scotts with his wife in St. Louis. In 1842, Emerson quit the army and died a year later. On April 6, 1846, Dred and Harriet Scott sued to prove that they and their two daughters, Eliza and Lizzie, were legally entitled to their freedom.

Dred Scott's claim was based on his travels and residences. He argued that living in Illinois, a free state, had made him free. Moreover, living in Wisconsin Territory (twice) made him free because the Missouri Compromise of 1820 had prohibited slavery in this portion of the Louisiana Purchase. His years in these free areas, Scott argued, had made him and his family free; and once free they remained free, even after returning to Missouri, a slave state.

The Scotts had a strong claim. Missouri had freed a dozen slaves on similar grounds, and in January 1850, a jury of twelve white men sided with the Scotts. But Dr. Emerson's widow was determined to keep them as her slaves. On appeal, the Missouri Supreme Court overturned three decades of precedents and reversed the lower court. The decision was clearly political. "Times are not now as they were when the former decisions on this subject were made," Chief Justice William Scott declared. "Since then, not only individuals but States have been possessed with a dark and fell spirit in relation to slavery. . . . It does not behoove the State of Missouri to show the least countenance to any measure which might gratify this spirit."

In other words, rather than judging the case on its merits, the justices had retaliated against the abolitionists.

But Dred and Harriet Scott and their supporters (white friends, several sympathetic lawyers, and probably some of St. Louis's free blacks) were not easily discouraged. In 1854, Dred Scott turned to the federal courts in Missouri, but lost. He and his family remained slaves. Scott then appealed to the highest court of the land—the U.S. Supreme Court. Although proslavery and antislavery forces had begun to see the potential opportunity (and danger) in the *Dred Scott* case, no one could have anticipated the sweeping decision that came down from the Supreme Court in 1857. It left the Scotts slaves, and it brought the nation closer to civil war.

What had begun as the straightforward effort of one black family to gain freedom had become entangled in the national debate over slavery. One month after the Scotts filed their first lawsuits for freedom in 1846, the United States went to war with Mexico. Three months later, Representative David Wilmot introduced a bill to prohibit slavery from any territory that might be acquired as a result of the war. After that, the nation was bitterly divided by the problem of slavery in the territories. The principle of excluding slavery from the territories set the course of national politics for the next decade and a half. South Carolina Senator John C. Calhoun saw the sad truth of Mexican land earlier than most. "Mexico is to us the forbidden fruit," he declared in May 1846. "The penalty of eating it [is] to subject our institutions to political death."

Once Mexican land thrust the issue of the expansion of slavery into national politics, no one could get it out. For a decade and a half, slavery poisoned national political debate and contaminated issues that were only distantly related. Slavery proved powerful enough to transform party politics into sectional politics. Rather than Whigs and Democrats confronting one another across party lines, Northerners and Southerners eyed one another with hostility across the Mason-Dixon line. Sectional politics worked like a blacksmith's hammer on the South's separatist impulses. A fitful tendency before the Mexican War, southern separatism gained strength with each blow. As the nation lurched from crisis to crisis, southern disaffection and alienation mounted. Year by year, the constituency for conciliation and compromise wore away. The era ended as it began—with a crisis of the Union. By 1861, men who had fought side by side at Buena Vista and Cerro Gordo trained their cannon on one another. As Abraham Lincoln predicted, "a house divided against itself cannot stand."

Fruits of War

Congress had faced the question of slavery in the national territories before the Mexican War. But history provided contradictory precedents. In 1787, Congress passed the Northwest Ordinance, which banned slavery north of the Ohio River. In 1803, when the United States acquired the Louisiana Territory, where slavery was already legal, Congress allowed slavery to remain. As part of the Missouri Compromise of 1820, Congress voted to prohibit slavery in part of the territory and allow it in the rest.

In 1846, when it appeared that the war with Mexico would mean new U.S. territories, politicians put on the table a variety of very different plans. David Wilmot proposed totally excluding slavery from the territories. President James K. Polk and others called for extending the Missouri Compromise line of 36°30' all the way to the Pacific. Southerners often advocated the uninhibited spread of slavery to all the territories. Some Northerners and Southerners joined to advocate letting the people of each territory themselves decide whether to allow slavery. When the Mexican War ended in 1848, Congress had made no headway in solving the great issue before it. Nor did the presidential election that year produce an answer. Instead, the territorial issue ripped apart the Whig and Democratic Parties, spawned a third party, and raised the political temperature of the nation to a boil. In 1850, after four years of strife, Congress patched together a settlement, one that promised to be permanent but actually proved transient.

The Wilmot Proviso and the Expansion of Slavery

Curiously, between 1846 and 1861, Americans did not focus on slavery where it existed but on the possibility that it might expand into areas where it did not exist. The Constitution confined the sectional controversy to these narrow limits. Except for a few abolitionists who strove to uproot slavery wherever they found it, most of the nation agreed that the Constitution had left the issue of slavery to the in-

PINE FOREST, OREGON
This 1844 engraving by William E. Tucker illustrates the gargantuan size of the Northwest's timber.
Some Easterners were awed by the size of nature's bounty; others calculated the board feet in a single
tree. Images such as this inspired hundreds of thousands of white men to dream of land in the West.
Library of Congress.

dividual states to decide. One by one, northern states had done away with slavery, while southern states had retained it. But what about slavery in the nation's territories? The Constitution stated that "Congress shall have Power to . . . make all needful Rules and Regulations respecting the Territory . . . belonging to the United States." The debate between the North and South about slavery, then, turned toward Congress and the definition of its authority over western lands.

The spark for the national debate was provided in August 1846 by a young Democratic representative from Pennsylvania, David Wilmot, who proposed that Congress bar slavery from all lands acquired in the war with Mexico. He modeled his proposal, which became known as the Wilmot Proviso, after the Northwest Ordinance of 1787, which banned slavery in territory north of the Ohio River.

Wilmot explained that the Mexicans had already abolished slavery in all of their territory. "God forbid," he declared, "that we should be the means of planting this institution upon it."

Although a newcomer to Congress, Wilmot had his finger on the pulse of northern sentiment. Regardless of party affiliation, Northerners wanted to stop the spread of slavery. The Wilmot Proviso rallied an interesting assortment of antislavery Northerners. Abolitionists, of course, supported "free soil," that is, territory from which slavery was prohibited. They saw slavery as a moral disaster and wanted Congress not only to deny slavery room to expand but also to destroy it where it existed. Many Whigs also stepped forward on the basis of principle. They often denounced slavery as a sin and emphasized Congress's authority to ban it from the territories.

But not all Northerners who opposed slavery's extension did so out of sympathy for slaves. Support for the Wilmot Proviso did not stem entirely, or even primarily, from humanitarian concern. The proviso also found support among Democratic politicians who feared that the Whigs would pick up voters by claiming that the Mexican War was a landgrab for slaveholders. By denying slavery a place in the territory the United States took from Mexico, Democrats could support expansion without offending antislavery constituents. A Connecticut representative declared that it was time "when the Northern democracy should make a stand. . . . We must satisfy the northern people . . . that we are not to extend the institution of slavery as a result of this war." Another Northerner declared that the "adoption of the principle of the 'Wilmot proviso' is the only way to *save* the Democratic party in the free states." Without coming out against slavery's expansion, Democrats "are destined to defeat and doomed . . . from Iowa to Maine."

Support for blocking slavery's expansion also came from Northerners—Whigs as well as Democrats—who were not so much antislavery as they were anti-South. New slave territories would eventually mean new slave states, and they wanted nothing to do with magnifying the power of Southerners in national politics. From experience they knew that proslavery Southerners often brought to Congress economic policies radically different from their own, especially in banking, internal improvements, and the tariff.

Further support came from Northerners who were hostile to slavery's expansion because they were hostile to African Americans. They wanted to reserve new lands for whites. Wilmot himself had blatantly encouraged racist support when he declared, "I would preserve for free white labor a fair country, a rich inheritance, where the sons of toil, of my own race and own color, can live without the disgrace which association with negro slavery brings upon free labor." Hundreds of thousands of white men dreamed of land in the West, and few wanted to work shoulder to shoulder with slaves or with free African Americans. It's no wonder that some called the Wilmot Proviso the White Man's Proviso.

While the specter of new slave territory alarmed diverse Northerners, the thought that slavery might be excluded outraged diverse Southerners. From the colonial era, yeoman and planter alike regarded the West as a ladder for economic and social opportunity. Southern whites never thought of expansion apart from slavery. Southerners who recognized that the arid West was less than ideal plantation country still agreed that the exclusion of slavery was a slap in the face. From Virginia to Texas, whites denounced the proviso as grossly unfair and insulting. "If by your legislation you seek to drive us from the territories of California and New Mexico . . . thereby attempting to fix a national degradation upon half the States of this Confederacy," Robert Toombs of Georgia fumed, "*I am for disunion.*" An Alabaman pointed out that at least half of the American soldiers in Mexico were Southerners. "When the war-worn soldier returns home," he asked, "is he to be told that he cannot carry his property to the country won by his blood?"

But to Southerners, territorial expansion involved even more than economic opportunity, social mobility, and honor. Southern leaders had always understood the need for political parity with the North to protect the South's interests, especially slavery. The need never seemed more urgent than in the 1840s, when the North's population and wealth was booming. James Henry Hammond of South Carolina predicted that ten new states would be carved from the acquired Mexican land. If free soil won, the North would "ride over us rough shod" in Congress, he claimed. "Our only safety is in *equality* of POWER."

In the nation's capital, foes of slavery's expansion squared off against foes of slavery's exclusion. Because Northerners had a majority in the House, they easily passed the Wilmot Proviso over the united opposition of Southerners. In the Senate, John C. Calhoun denied that Congress had constitutional authority to exclude slavery from the nation's territories. In a series of closely reasoned resolutions, he declared that the territories were the "joint and common property" of all the states, that Congress could not justly deprive any state of equal rights in the territories, and that Congress therefore could not bar citizens of one state from migrating with their property (including slaves) to the territories. Where Wilmot demanded that Congress slam shut the door to slavery, Calhoun required that Congress hold the door wide open. Because slave states outnumbered free states fifteen to fourteen, southern senators stopped the proviso.

Between these extremes there appeared to be little middle ground. One plan—to extend the Missouri Compromise line to the Pacific—generated no significant enthusiasm. But Senator Lewis Cass of

Michigan offered a compromise that he hoped would find support among moderates everywhere. He proposed the doctrine of "popular sovereignty": letting the people who actually settled the territories decide for themselves slavery's fate. This solution, Cass argued, sat squarely in the American tradition of democracy and local self-government. It had the added attraction of removing the incendiary issue of the expansion of slavery from Congress and lodging it in distant, sleepy territorial legislatures, where it would excite fewer passions.

Northerners who demanded no new slave territory anywhere, ever, and Southerners who demanded free entry for their slave property into all territories, or else, staked out their extreme positions.

The most attractive feature of Cass's popular sovereignty plan was its ambiguity about the precise moment when settlers could determine slavery's fate. That imprecision made possible different predictions about the plan's consequences. Northern advocates told their constituents that the decision on slavery could be made as soon as the first territorial legislature assembled. With free-soil majorities likely, they would shut the door to slavery almost before the first slave arrived. Southern supporters, for their part, declared that popular sovereignty guaranteed that slavery would be unrestricted throughout the entire territorial period. Only at the very end, when settlers drew up a constitution and applied for statehood, could they decide the issue of slavery or freedom. By then, slavery would have sunk deep roots. The southern interpretation made popular sovereignty almost indistinguishable from Calhoun's doctrine. As long as the matter of timing remained vague, popular sovereignty provided some Northerners and some Southerners common ground.

When Congress ground to a halt in 1848, no plan had won a majority in both houses. Northerners who demanded no new slave territory anywhere, ever, and Southerners who demanded free entry for their slave property into all territories, or else, staked out their extreme positions, further polarizing the issue. Unresolved in Congress, the territorial question naturally intruded into the presidential election of 1848.

The Election of 1848

The Democratic and Whig Parties were both hurting in 1848. The territorial debate revealed free-soil factions in both parties. Antislavery northern Democrats challenged Democratic President Polk and the dominant southern element of their party. Northern Whigs split between an antislavery faction called Conscience Whigs and a more conservative group, Cotton Whigs (because many of them were textile mill owners) who sought to compromise the territorial issue to hold the party together. Conscience Whigs denounced the evil alliance of northern "lords of the loom" and southern "lords of the lash" and threatened to bolt the party.

Polk—worn out, ailing, and unable to unite the Democratic Party—chose not to seek reelection. The Democratic convention nominated Senator Lewis Cass of Michigan, the man most closely associated with the doctrine of popular sovereignty, but the party platform avoided a firm position on slavery in the territories. One angry antislavery Democratic faction, dubbed the Barnburners, nominated their own candidate, former president Martin Van Buren, on a free-soil platform.

The Whigs followed a different strategy in their effort to patch the fissures within the party over slavery. They passed over "Mr. Whig" himself—

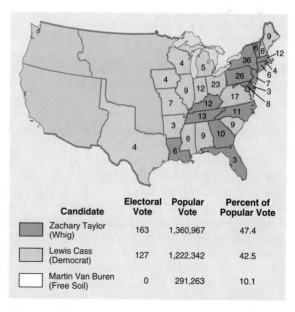

Candidate	Electoral Vote	Popular Vote	Percent of Popular Vote
Zachary Taylor (Whig)	163	1,360,967	47.4
Lewis Cass (Democrat)	127	1,222,342	42.5
Martin Van Buren (Free Soil)	0	291,263	10.1

MAP 14.1
The Election of 1848

GENERAL TAYLOR CIGAR CASE
This papier-mâché cigar case portrays General Zachary Taylor, Whig presidential candidate in 1848, in a colorful scene from the Mexican War. Shown as a dashing, elegant officer, Taylor was in fact a short, thickset, and roughly dressed Indian fighter who had spent his career commanding small frontier garrisons. The inscription reminds voters that Taylor was a victor in the first four battles fought in the war and directs attention away from the fact that in politics he was a rank amateur.
Collection of Janice L. and David J. Frent.

Henry Clay, the seventy-one-year-old founder of the party and chief spokesman for its American System. Clay carried the burden of being a three-time loser in presidential campaigns as well as the additional liability of having opposed the successful war with Mexico. Instead, the Whigs nominated the hero of Buena Vista, "Old Rough and Ready," General Zachary Taylor, and they declined to adopt any party platform, no matter how vague. The Whigs bet that a military hero who had never voted and who had no known political opinions, combined with total silence on the central issue before the country, would carry the day.

Taylor, who owned more than one hundred slaves on plantations in Mississippi and Louisiana, was hailed by Georgian Robert Toombs as a "Southern man, a slaveholder, a cotton planter." Conscience Whigs balked and looked for an alternative. As old party allegiances unraveled, the time seemed ripe for a major political realignment. Senator Charles Sumner called for "one grand Northern party of Freedom," and in the summer of 1848 antislavery Democrats and antislavery Whigs founded the Free-Soil Party. Nearly 15,000 noisy Free-Soilers gathered in Buffalo, New York, where they welded the factions together by nominating a dissident

Democrat, Martin Van Buren, for president and a Conscience Whig, Charles Francis Adams, for vice president. The platform boldly proclaimed, "Free soil, free speech, free labor, and free men."

The November election dashed the hopes of the Free-Soilers. Although they succeeded in making slavery the campaign's central issue, they could not lure enough Whigs and Democrats out of the old parties to win. The Free-Soil Party gained 291,000 votes but did not carry a single state. The major parties went through contortions to present their candidates favorably in both the North and the South, and their evasions succeeded. The Whigs' Taylor polled 1,360,000 votes to 1,222,000 for the Democrats' Cass. Taylor won the all-important electoral vote 163 to 127, carrying eight of the fifteen slave states and seven of fifteen free states. (Wisconsin had entered the Union earlier in 1848, making fifteen slave states and fifteen free states.) Northern voters proved they were not yet ready for Sumner's "one grand Northern party of Freedom," but the struggle between freedom and slavery in the territories had shaken the major parties badly.

The "Great Debate"

Zachary Taylor was very much a mystery when he entered the White House in March 1849. He had purposefully remained vague on the slavery issue throughout the campaign, and no one could claim to know what this political novice would do in office. He surprised almost everyone—and he infuriated Southerners. Who among them had imagined that the slaveholding father-in-law of Mississippi Senator Jefferson Davis would champion a free-soil solution to the problem of western land? But he did. The discovery of gold in California and the rush of 1849 made the existing military rule of California and New Mexico pitifully inadequate and the need for competent civil government urgent. Taylor sent agents west to urge settlers to frame constitutions and apply immediately for admission to the Union as states. The settlers acted quickly. Predominantly antislavery, they began writing free-state constitutions and anticipated knocking on Congress's door for admission. "For the first time," Jefferson Davis declared, "we are about permanently to destroy the balance of power between the sections."

When Congress convened in December 1849, anxious citizens packed the galleries. Latecomers spilled over into the halls and lobbies, happy even for standing room at the "Great Debate." They witnessed what proved to be one of the longest, most contentious, and most significant sessions in the history of Congress. For seven months, politicians orated, debated, buttonholed, cajoled, and threatened in efforts to fashion a solution to the problems that divided the nation.

The previous Congress had left a raft of unfinished business, and foremost was the territorial issue. In January 1850, President Taylor urged Congress to admit California as a state immediately and to admit New Mexico, which lagged behind by a few months, as soon as it applied. Southerners exploded. In their eyes, Taylor had betrayed his region. Southerners who would "consent to be thus degraded and enslaved," a North Carolinian declared, "ought to be whipped through their fields by their own negroes." Calhoun almost lost heart. "As things now stand," he said in February, the South "cannot with safety remain in the Union." The sense of emergency strengthened the movement toward southern unity that Calhoun had pushed for years. From Mississippi came a menacing call for a convention of southern states "to devise and adopt some mode of resistance to northern aggression." It would meet in Nashville on the first Monday in June 1850.

Into this rancorous scene stepped Henry Clay, recently returned to the Senate by his home state of Kentucky. His reputation preceded him: the "Great Pacificator," master of accommodation, architect of Union-saving compromises in the Missouri and nullification crises. At seventy-two, Clay remained a powerful public speaker, and he had no doubt that the South's desperate mood threatened the survival of the Union.

"Mr. President," Clay declared when he took the floor on January 29, 1850, "I hold in my hand a series of resolutions which I desire to submit to the consideration of this body. Taken together, in combination, they propose an amicable arrangement of all questions in controversy between the free and slave states, growing out of the subject of slavery." His comprehensive plan consisted of a series of proposals that sought to balance the interests of the slave and free states. Admit California as a free state, he proposed, but organize the rest of the Southwest without restrictions on slavery. Abolish the slave trade in Washington, D.C., but confirm slavery itself in the nation's capital. Require Texas to abandon its claim to parts of New Mexico, but compensate it by assuming its preannexation debt. Reassert Congress's lack of authority to interfere with the in-

JOHN C. CALHOUN
Hollow-cheeked and dark-eyed in this 1850 daguerreotype by Mathew Brady, Calhoun had only months to live. Still, his passion and indomitable will come through. British writer Harriet Martineau once described the champion of southern rights as "the cast-iron man who looks as if he had never been born and could never be extinguished."
National Portrait Gallery, Smithsonian Institution/Art Resource, N.Y.

terstate slave trade. And enact a more effective fugitive slave law. The Peacemaker offered concessions to both sections in the hope of finding a balance that would preserve the imperiled Union.

Abolitionists and "fire-eaters" (as radical southern secessionists were called) stumbled over one another in their rush to condemn Clay's plan. Senator Salmon Chase of Ohio ridiculed it as "sentiment for the North, substance for the South." Senator Henry S. Foote of Mississippi denounced it as more offensive to the South than the speeches of abolitionists William Lloyd Garrison, Wendell Phillips, and Frederick Douglass combined.

The most ominous response came from the mighty Calhoun. Too weakened by consumption to deliver his own speech, he slumped in his Senate chair, wrapped his black cloak around him, and listened as a colleague read for him his gloomy words concluding that the time for compromise had passed. Unending northern agitation on the slavery question, Calhoun said, had "snapped" many of the "cords which bind these states together in one common Union . . . and has greatly weakened all the others." The fragile political equilibrium between North and South depended on continued equal representation in the Senate, which Clay's plan for a free California destroyed. Without equality, Calhoun declared, Southerners were defenseless and could not remain in the Union. The Senate had never witnessed a more somber diagnosis of the Union's health.

After Clay and Calhoun had spoken, it was time for the third member of the "great triumvirate," Daniel Webster of Massachusetts. The Senate debate of 1850 proved to be the final scene for these three statesmen, whose careers had dominated national politics for decades. All were born during the American Revolution. Calhoun would be gone in less than a month, Clay and Webster in two years. They gave virtuoso performances, with Calhoun prophesying darkly that all was lost and Clay and Webster eloquently championing conciliation.

"Mr. President," Webster began his March 7 address, "I wish to speak today, not as a Massachusetts man, nor as a Northern man, but as an American. . . . I speak today for the preservation of the Union. 'Hear me for my cause.'" Admitting that the South had grievances that required redress, he argued forcefully that secession from the Union would mean civil war. He also appealed for an end to reckless proposals, and, to the dismay of many Northerners, he mentioned by name the Wilmot Proviso. A legal ban on slavery in the territories was unnecessary, he said, because nature prohibited the expansion of cotton and slaves into the Southwest. Why, then, "taunt" or "reproach" Southerners with the proviso? "I would not take pains to reaffirm an ordinance of nature nor to reenact the will of God," he said. Like Clay, Webster sought to balance the grievances of the North and South and build a constituency for compromise among moderates.

Free-soil forces recoiled from Webster's desertion. Theodore Parker, a Boston clergyman and abolitionist, could only conclude that "the Southern men" must have offered Webster the presidency. Senator William H. Seward of New York responded that Webster's and Clay's compromise with slavery was "radically wrong and essentially vicious." He flatly rejected Calhoun's argument that Congress lacked constitutional authority to exclude slavery from the territories. In any case, Seward said, in the most sensational moment in his address, there was a "higher law than the Constitution"—the law of God—to ensure freedom in all the public domain. Claiming that God was a Free-Soiler did nothing to cool the superheated atmosphere of Washington.

Still, other politicians feverishly sought a solution. In May, a Senate committee (with the tireless Clay at its head) reported a bill that joined Clay's resolutions into a single comprehensive package, known as the Omnibus Bill because it was a vehicle on which "every sort of passenger" could ride. Clay bet that a majority of Congress wanted compromise and that while the omnibus contained items individuals disliked, each would vote for the package to gain an overall settlement of sectional issues. Clay's bundle of resolutions helped to take the wind out of the sails of the fire-eaters at the Nashville convention, which met in early June 1850. With the omnibus before the Senate, secessionists found it impossible to persuade delegates from nine southern states that there was no hope for the South in the Union. The convention adjourned after doing nothing more threatening than agreeing to a vague resolution in favor of southern rights.

Zachary Taylor came out against Clay's omnibus and reaffirmed his own plan for California and New Mexico. The president's opposition threatened to sink Clay's bill, but on July 9, 1850, Taylor suddenly died. Prospects for compromise soared when his successor, Vice President Millard Fillmore of New York, gave his support to Clay. Still, as critics had predicted, the omnibus strategy backfired. Clay had barely released his bill—his "dove of peace," he said—when congressional sharpshooters took aim. Free-Soilers, Conscience Whigs, and proslavery Southerners would support separate parts of Clay's bill, but they would not endorse the whole. After seventy speeches defending his plan, Clay saw it go down to defeat.

Fortunately for those who favored a settlement, Senator Stephen A. Douglas, a rising Democratic star from Illinois, stepped into Clay's shoes. He had never believed in the omnibus strategy. Instead, he broke the bill into its various parts and skillfully ushered each through Congress by fashioning a different coalition for the support of each bill. The agreement Douglas won in September 1850 was very much the one Clay had proposed in February.

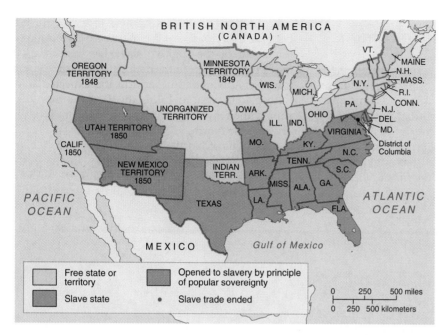

MAP 14.2
The Compromise of 1850
The patched-together sectional agreement was both clumsy and unstable. Few Americans — in either the North or the South — supported all five parts of the compromise.

California entered the Union as a free state. New Mexico and Utah became territories in which the question of slavery would be decided by popular sovereignty. Congress enacted a more stringent fugitive slave law. It ended the slave trade in the District of Columbia. Texas accepted its present-day boundary with New Mexico and received $10 million from the federal government. In September, President Fillmore signed each bill into law.

The "Compromise" of 1850

After seven months of some of the most majestic oratory and roughest infighting in Senate history, Congress completed its patchwork settlement of the sectional problem. Collectively known as the Compromise of 1850, it was hailed by President Fillmore as "the final settlement."

Unionists everywhere breathed a sigh of relief and then broke out in raucous celebration. The Union had teetered at the edge of an abyss, and Americans had snatched it back. Free-soil and southern rights forces, however, saw little to cheer about and much to regret. From 1846 to 1850, anti-slavery Northerners had demanded that Congress prohibit slavery's expansion into the territories. Now Congress had abandoned the Wilmot Proviso and promised noninterference with slavery in New Mexico and Utah. Similarly, proslavery Southerners steadfastly demanded equality in the Senate, and

now California's statehood ended the old balance of slave and free states.

Actually, the Compromise of 1850 was not a true compromise at all. Douglas's parliamentary skill, not a spirit of conciliation, led to legislative success. Douglas understood that true compromisers—individuals who were willing to make mutual concessions—were a decided minority. But compromisers held the balance of power between the larger blocs of Northerners and Southerners who voted along sectional lines. Only by nimbly allying the compromisers and Southerners on one bill, then the compromisers and Northerners on another, did Douglas gain the majority for each separate measure.

Nor, we now know, was the settlement "final." Congress had managed to fashion only a truce, an armistice. The settlement resolved certain pesky conflicts, and it preserved the Union and peace for the moment, no small feat given the severity of the threats. But it scarcely touched the deeper conflict over slavery. Free-Soiler Salmon Chase was correct when he told Congress, "The question of slavery in the territories has been avoided. It has not been settled."

Still, the settlement broke the deadlock between the North and the South that had paralyzed the national government for four years. Now, most Americans hoped, Congress could do business without confronting the eternal slavery question.

The Sectional Balance Undone

The words "final settlement" echoed through the halls of Congress like a magical phrase, but, in reality, the Compromise of 1850 began to come apart almost immediately. The thread that unraveled the Compromise was not slavery in the Southwest, the crux of the disagreement, but runaway slaves in New England, a component of the settlement that had received relatively little attention. Southerners made it clear from the beginning that sectional peace depended on Northerners living up to the bargain, every part of it. But Northerners found enforcement of the fugitive slave law repulsive. It made them players in the national drama, and some found it impossible to perform the expected role. Rather than restore calm, the Compromise disrupted their lives by bringing the horrors of slavery into the North.

Millions of Northerners who never saw a runaway slave also discovered slavery in the early 1850s. Harriet Beecher Stowe's *Uncle Tom's Cabin*, a novel that vividly depicted the brutality and heart-

PRACTICAL ILLUSTRATION OF THE FUGITIVE SLAVE LAW.

FUGITIVE SLAVE CARTOON
In this scathing attack on the Fugitive Slave Act of 1850, a brutal southern slave catcher rides Daniel Webster, who counseled compliance with the act. With a chain in one hand and a rope in the other, the slave catcher attempts to capture a woman and take her south. The slave catchers parade the fact that they have the law on their side, but the woman's black and white defenders take up arms nevertheless. "Every slave-hunter," Frederick Douglass declared, "who meets a bloody death in this infernal business, is an argument in favor of the manhood of our race."
Library of Congress.

lessness of the South's "peculiar institution," swept the North. It aroused passions so deep that many found goodwill toward white Southerners nearly impossible. But no popular uprising forced Congress to reopen the slavery controversy. Politicians did it themselves. Four years after Congress delicately stitched the sectional compromise together, it ripped the threads out. It reopened the question of slavery in the territories, the most deadly of all sectional issues.

The Fugitive Slave Act

When Henry Clay and Daniel Webster died within four months of each other in 1852, eulogies for the statesmen emphasized a single theme: the preservation of the Union. Yet one week after Webster's death, Theodore Parker, a preacher and abolitionist, sounded a very different note. Yes, Parker said, Webster was a great man, his boyhood hero, but the truth was that Webster was a fallen angel. Among his sins, none was blacker than his March 7 speech in the Senate in 1850. "Think of him!" Parker shouted. "The Daniel Webster of Plymouth Rock advocating the 'Compromise Measures.' . . . Think of Daniel Webster become the assassin of Liberty in the Capitol! Think of him . . . scoffing at the Higher Law of God." Indeed, as Parker noted, Webster had spoken vigorously during his last two years of life for the enforcement of the Compromise, including its Fugitive Slave Act. "No man is at liberty to set up . . . his own conscience as above the law," Webster had reminded New Englanders. But Theodore Parker denounced the law as "a hateful statute of kidnappers" and headed a Boston vigilance committee that openly violated it.

The Fugitive Slave Act proved the most explosive of the Compromise measures. The issue of runaways was as old as the Constitution, which contained a provision for the return of any "person held to service or labor in one state" who escaped to another. In 1793, a federal law gave muscle to the provision by authorizing slave owners to enter other states to recapture their slave property. It also denied runaways jury trials and the right to testify in their own defense. Proclaiming the 1793 law a license to kidnap free blacks, northern states in the 1830s began passing "personal liberty laws" that provided fugitives with some protection. Many northern communities also formed vigilance committees to help runaways and to obstruct white Southerners who came north to reclaim them. Each year, a few hundred slaves escaped into free states

and found friendly northern "conductors" who put them aboard the "underground railroad," which was not a railroad at all but a series of secret "stations" (hideouts) on the way to Canada.

Furious about northern interference, Southerners in 1850 insisted that any comprehensive settlement of sectional differences include an effective fugitive slave law. They got what they wanted in the stricter law passed as part of the Compromise. To seize an alleged slave, a slaveholder or his agent simply had to appear before a commissioner appointed by the court and swear that the runaway was his. The commissioner earned ten dollars for every black returned to slavery but only five dollars for those set free. Most galling to Northerners, the law stipulated that all citizens were expected to assist officials in apprehending runaways. That required Northerners to become slave catchers. Sickened by the prospect, thousands vowed never to track down people who had risked their lives fleeing slavery.

The words "final settlement" echoed through the halls of Congress like a magical phrase, but in reality the Compromise of 1850 began to come apart almost immediately.

Within a month, slaveholders claimed runaways from the East Coast to the Great Lakes. Storms of resistance sprang up. On October 8, 1850, a slave owner claimed a black man in Detroit and had him arrested. Several hundred armed African Americans surrounded the jail. Instead of attacking, they raised five hundred dollars and offered to buy the runaway's freedom. The owner pocketed the money and quickly got out of town. An angry crowd in Boston showed less restraint. In February 1851, they overpowered federal marshals and snatched a runaway named Shadrach from a courtroom, put him on the underground railroad, and whisked him off to Montreal, Canada. Many communities, however, lost longtime African American residents. In Indiana, agents ripped one man away from his wife and children and returned him to a slave owner who claimed the man had run away nineteen years earlier.

Southerners viewed the Fugitive Slave Act as the one true concession they received in the Compromise. Now it seemed that the "fanatics of the 'higher law' creed" had whipped Northerners into a frenzy of massive resistance. Actually, the overwhelming majority of fugitives claimed before federal commissioners were reenslaved and shipped South peacefully. Spectacular rescues such as the one that saved Shadrach were rare. Still, brutal enforcement of the unpopular law had a radicalizing effect in the North, particularly in New England. Textile owner Amos A. Lawrence, a Cotton Whig eager for good relations with the South, said that "we went to bed one night old fashioned, conservative, Compromise Union Whigs & waked up stark mad Abolitionists." He exaggerated, but it did seem to Southerners that Northerners had betrayed the Compromise and the Constitution. And as a Tennessee man warned in November 1850, "If the fugitive slave bill is not enforced in the north, the moderate men of the South . . . will be overwhelmed by the 'fire-eaters.'"

Uncle Tom's Cabin

The spectacle of shackled African Americans being herded south seared the conscience of every Northerner who witnessed such a scene. But, curiously, even more Northerners were turned against slavery by a fictional account, a novel. Harriet Beecher Stowe, a Northerner who had never seen a plantation, made the South's slaves into flesh-and-blood human beings, more real than life.

The daughter of evangelist Lyman Beecher and a member of the famous clan of preachers, teachers, and reformers, Stowe despised the slave catchers. She had done a bit of writing in moments snatched from her domestic responsibilities as wife of Calvin Stowe and mother of seven children, and she decided to do something that would expose the sin of slavery. Beginning in June 1851 as a serial in an antislavery weekly, *Uncle Tom's Cabin, or Life among the Lowly* made the author famous before the final installment was printed ten months later. Published as a book in March 1852, it kept the presses running night and day. After a year, it had sold 300,000 copies and had become America's first literary blockbuster. By the end of the decade, more than three million copies had been sold at home and overseas.

Stowe's characters leaped from the page. Here was the gentle slave Uncle Tom, a Christian saint who forgave those who beat him to death; the courageous slave Eliza, who fled with her child across the frozen Ohio River; and the fiendish Simon Legree, whose Louisiana plantation was a nightmare of torture and death. Stowe aimed her most powerful blows at slavery's destructive impact on the family. Deeply committed to the values of motherhood and domesticity, Stowe said later that her loss of a baby to cholera had taught her "what a poor slave mother may feel when her child is torn away from her." *Uncle Tom's Cabin* is especially sensitive to the anguish of slave mothers. Eliza succeeds in keeping her son from being sold away, but other mothers are not so fortunate. When told that her infant has been sold, Lucy drowns herself. Driven half mad by the sale of a son and daughter, Cassy decides "never again [to] let a child live to grow up!" She gives her third child an opiate and watches as "he slept to death." Rivers of tears flowed when Northerners read the novel aloud around their family hearths.

Responses to the novel depended on geography. In the North, common people and literary giants alike sang its praises. The poet John Greenleaf Whittier sent "ten thousand thanks for thy immortal book," and poet Henry Wadsworth Longfellow judged it "one of the greatest triumphs recorded in literary history." What northern readers accepted as truth, southern ones denounced as slander. The New Orleans *Crescent* called Stowe "part quack and part cutthroat," a fake physician who came with arsenic in one hand and a pistol in the other to treat diseases she had "never witnessed." Virginian George F. Holmes proclaimed Stowe a member of the "Woman's Rights" and "Higher Law" schools and dismissed the novel as a work of "intense fanaticism." Unfortunately, he said, this "maze of misinterpretation" had filled those who knew nothing about slavery "with hatred for that institution and those who uphold it." Holmes found only one character convincing: Simon Legree. Stowe had made Legree a transplanted Yankee.

As Legree's northern origins suggest, the novel did not indict just the South. Stowe rebuked the entire nation for tolerating the scourge of slavery. Although it is impossible to measure precisely the impact of a novel on public opinion, *Uncle Tom's Cabin* clearly helped to crystallize northern sentiment against slavery and to confirm Southerners' suspicion that they no longer had any sympathy in the free states. Other writers—ex-slaves who knew life in slave cabins firsthand—also produced stinging indictments of slavery that attacked the ignorance and moral indifference of whites. Solomon Northup's compelling *Twelve Years a Slave* (1853) sold 27,000 copies in two years, and Frederick Douglass's powerful *Narrative of the Life of Frederick Douglass, as Told by Himself* (1845) eventually sold more

THEATER POSTER

During the 1850s, at least ten individuals, including Harriet Beecher Stowe herself, dramatized the novel Uncle Tom's Cabin. *These plays, known as "Tom Shows," drew crowds in America and Britain. Stowe's moral indictment of slavery translated well to the stage. Scenes of Eliza crossing the ice with bloodhounds in pursuit, the cruelty of Legree, and Little Eva borne to heaven on puffy clouds gripped the imagination of audiences and fueled the growing antislavery crusade.*
Smithsonian Institution.

than 30,000 copies. But no work touched the North's conscience like the novel by the woman who had never set foot on a plantation. A decade later, when Stowe visited Abraham Lincoln at the White House, he reportedly said, "So this is the little lady who made this big war."

The Election of 1852

The fugitive slave law and *Uncle Tom's Cabin* added new recruits to militant antislavery forces in the North. Heightened criticism from the free states stung white Southerners into increasingly belligerent defenses of slavery and southern society. Still, the arguments across the Mason-Dixon line failed to destroy popular support for the Compromise of 1850. Majorities in both sections continued to defend it as the "final settlement," a bulwark against

dangerous sectional forces. Evidence that allegiance was sincere and widespread came in the summer of 1852, when both the Whig and Democratic Parties adopted platforms accepting the Compromise as the settlement of the slavery question.

As national elections approached in 1852, Democrats and Whigs sought to close the rifts that had opened along sectional lines within their parties. The Democrats were more successful. As their presidential nominee, they turned to Franklin Pierce of New Hampshire. Pierce was an amiable veteran of the Mexican War and a former senator, but his most valuable asset was his well-known sympathy with southern views on public issues. His leanings caused northern critics to include him among those they contemptuously called "doughfaces," northern men with principles that were malleable enough to champion southern causes. The Whigs were less

TABLE 14.1
THE ELECTION OF 1852

Candidate	Electoral Vote	Popular Vote	Percent of Popular Vote
Franklin Pierce (Democrat)	254	1,601,000	50.9
Winfield Scott (Whig)	42	1,385,000	44.1
John P. Hale (Free Soil)	0	156,000	5.0

successful in compromising differences. They agreed to reject the incumbent, Millard Fillmore, but disagreed for fifty-two ballots on someone else. Finally, adopting the formula that had proved successful in 1848, they chose another Mexican War hero, General Winfield Scott of Virginia.

Hopelessly divided between Conscience and Cotton factions, the Whigs suffered a humiliating defeat in 1852. The Democrat Pierce carried twenty-seven states to the Whig Scott's four, 254 electoral votes to 42. In the afterglow of the Compromise, the Free-Soil Party lost almost half of the voters who had turned to it in the tumultuous atmosphere of 1848.

Eager to leave the sectional controversy behind, the new president turned swiftly to foreign expansion. The spread-eagle nationalism that had propelled Manifest Destiny during the Polk administration remained robust. In his inaugural address, Franklin Pierce promised that his administration would not be inhibited "by any timid forebodings of evil for expansion." He filled his cabinet with expansionists and even found a minor office for John L. O'Sullivan, the journalist who had coined the term "Manifest Destiny." Pierce's major objective was Cuba, which was owned by Spain and in which slavery flourished. Earlier efforts by Polk to purchase the island had failed. Private efforts by southern slaveholders to take it by force met disaster. In 1851, Southerners bankrolled a Latin American adventurer, Narciso López, who invaded the island with an army of five hundred American volunteers, several hundred of whom died in the aborted effort. Pierce's own clumsy diplomatic efforts to acquire Cuba galvanized antislavery Northerners, who denounced the administration for promoting expansion on behalf of slavery and blocked Cuba's acquisition.

Although Pierce's foray in Cuba ended badly, his fortunes improved in Mexico. In 1853, he sent an envoy, James Gadsden, who negotiated a $15 million purchase of some 45,000 square miles of territory south of the Gila River in present-day Arizona and New Mexico. The Gadsden Purchase stemmed from the dream of a transcontinental railroad to California. The burgeoning population of the Pacific coast made it obvious that the vast, loose-jointed republic needed a railroad to bind it together. Talk of a railroad ignited rivalries in cities from New Orleans to Chicago as they maneuvered to become the eastern terminus. Gadsden's real estate transaction served the needs of a proposed southern route. A victory in the railroad contest assured the winning city's economic future and also promised to stimulate growth in its region. Thus the railroad became a sectional contest, which by the 1850s inevitably involved slavery.

The Kansas-Nebraska Act

No one played the railroad game more enthusiastically than Senator Stephen A. Douglas. The "Little Giant," as he was called, was a "steam engine in britches," an energetic spokesman for western economic development. He also badly wanted the transcontinental railroad for Chicago and his home state, Illinois. His chairmanship of the Senate Committee on Territories provided him with an opportunity. Any railroad that ran west from Chicago would pass through a region that Congress in 1830 had designated a "permanent" Indian reserve. Douglas proposed giving this vast area between the Missouri River and the Rocky Mountains an Indian name, Nebraska, and then nullifying Indian titles and throwing the Indians out. Once the region achieved territorial status, whites could survey and sell the land, establish civil government, and build a railroad.

Congress's promise to the Indians did not cause Douglas to hesitate, but another of its promises did. Nebraska lay within the Louisiana Purchase north of 36°30', which, according to the Missouri Compromise of 1820, closed it to slavery. Since Douglas could not count on New England to back western economic development, he needed southern votes to pass his Nebraska legislation. But Southerners had no incentive to create another free territory or to assist a northern city win the Pacific railroad. Douglas learned, however, that Southerners might agree to organize Nebraska—for a price.

The price was steep: nothing less than the repeal of the Missouri Compromise. Southerners insisted that Congress organize Nebraska according to popular sovereignty, the formula it had used in 1850 in New Mexico and Utah. It meant giving slavery a chance in the Nebraska Territory and reopening the terribly dangerous issue of slavery expansion that Douglas himself had so ably helped to resolve only four years earlier. A politician with presidential ambitions, a champion of his state's economic interests, a defender of western development, and a believer in popular sovereignty, Douglas persuaded himself that Nebraska was worth the price.

In January 1854, Douglas introduced his bill to organize the Nebraska Territory, leaving to the settlers themselves the decision about slavery. At southern insistence, and even though he knew it would "raise a hell of a storm," Douglas added an explicit repeal of the Missouri Compromise. He attempted to make his plan more acceptable by sheltering it under the Compromise of 1850. He claimed that Congress had established a new federal policy of settler democracy when it adopted the formula for the territories of New Mexico and Utah. His plan, he argued, only extended that policy to the unorganized portions of the Louisiana Purchase. Douglas claimed, moreover, that climate barred slavery's expansion into the plains. He pleaded with free-soilers to be reasonable, not to stand on empty principle, but to accept "squatter sovereignty" as a practical solution that would permit the nation to get on with building badly needed railroads.

The Nebraska bill raised a storm of controversy. Antislavery Northerners wanted no part of a proposal that failed to condemn slavery as a moral disaster and instead offered it a chance to expand. The truth was that Douglas's bill reopened to slavery a region that the nation had reserved for freedom.

PAPAGO INDIANS
Major William Emory's Mexican boundary survey of the early 1850s provided Americans with glimpses of a little-known southwestern frontier. In this drawing, Papago Indian women in Arizona Territory use sticks to knock down cactus fruit.
The Center for American History, the University of Texas at Austin.

Free-soil forces rightly denied that Congress in 1850 had intended popular sovereignty to apply to territories other than Utah and New Mexico. They branded Douglas's plan "a gross violation of a sacred pledge" and an "atrocious plot" to transform free land into a "dreary region of despotism, inhabited by masters and slaves." Such reactions became the opening shots of a ferocious debate that lasted nearly four months.

As Douglas said later, he could have traveled from Washington back to Chicago by the light of his own burning effigies. But, coolest under fire, he marshaled all his political skills and shepherded the

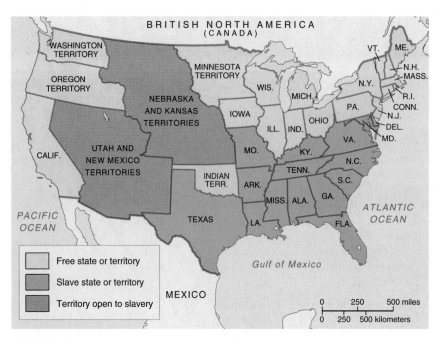

MAP 14.3
The Kansas-Nebraska Act, 1854
Americans hardly thought twice about dispossessing the Indians of lands guaranteed them by treaty, but many worried about the outcome of repealing the Missouri Compromise and opening up lands to slavery.

bill through Congress in May 1854. It passed because nine-tenths of all southern members (Whigs and Democrats) and half of the northern Democrats cast votes in favor. Still, ominously, half of the northern Democrats broke with their party and opposed it. In its final form, the Kansas-Nebraska Act divided the territory into two parts: Nebraska west of Iowa and Kansas west of the slave state of Missouri.

The Realignment of the Party System

The Kansas-Nebraska Act marked a fateful escalation of the sectional conflict. Douglas's ill-advised measure had several consequences, none more crucial than the realignment of the nation's political parties. Since the rise of the Whigs as an opposition party to Andrew Jackson's Democrats in the early 1830s, Whigs and Democrats had organized and channeled political conflict in the nation. This party system dampened sectionalism and strengthened the Union. To achieve national political power, Whigs and Democrats had to retain strength in both the North and the South. Strong northern and southern wings required that the party compromise and find positions acceptable to both.

The Kansas-Nebraska controversy shattered this conservative political system. In place of two national parties with bisectional strength, the mid-1850s witnessed the development of one party heavily dominated by one section and another party entirely limited to the other section. Rather than "national" parties, the country had what one critic disdainfully called "geographical" parties. Not

> *In place of two national parties with bisectional strength, the mid-1850s witnessed the development of one party heavily dominated by one section and another party that was entirely limited to the other section.*

everyone opposed the new political system, however. Parties now had the advantage of sharpening ideological and policy differences between the sections and no longer muffling moral issues, like slavery. But the new party system also thwarted political compromise. Instead, it promoted political polarization. The breakup of the old party system of the 1830s and 1840s snapped one of what John C. Calhoun called the "cords of Union." The new party system of the 1850s reflected the sectional division between North and South and offered little encouragement to sectional reconciliation.

WHIG PARTY MEMBERS
On February 18, 1853, George Howe made this daguerreotype of the Log Cabin and Hard Cider Club of Portland, Maine. This Whig organization took its name and its emblem from William Henry Harrison's 1840 presidential campaign, a rousing effort to depict the tony Virginian as a man of the people. Well-heeled and respectable, these Maine shopkeepers, bankers, and farmers made up the spine of the Whig Party. Before long, these solid citizens would be looking for a new party.
Collections of the Maine Historical Society.

The breakup of the old parties had personal meaning as well as national significance. In the political universe of antebellum America, most citizens had far stronger attachments to their parties than most Americans do today. "Unflinching adherence to party is principle with them," a visiting Englishman observed in the 1850s, and "to forsake a party is regarded as an act of greatest dishonor." But many Americans had no choice but to find new parties. The parties they found had much clearer sectional profiles.

The Old Parties: Whigs and Democrats

Distress signals could be heard from the Whig camp as early as the Mexican War, when members clashed over the future of slavery in annexed Mexican lands. But the disintegration of the party dated from 1849–1850, when proslavery Southerners watched in stunned amazement as Whig President Zachary Taylor sponsored a plan for a free California. Southern Whigs felt betrayed and began to question their party affiliation. Above the Mason-Dixon line, the strains of the slavery issue split northern Whigs. The Conscience Whigs, who responded to slavery as a moral blight, gained a majority by 1852. The party could please the southern wing or the northern

wing but not both. The Whigs' miserable showing in the election of 1852 made clear that they were no longer a strong national party. By 1856, after more than two decades of contesting the Democrats, they were hardly a party at all.

The decline and eventual collapse of the Whig Party left the Democrats as the country's only national party. But the Democrats were not immune to the disruptive pressures of the territorial question. David Wilmot, after all, was a Democrat. However, Democrats discovered in popular sovereignty a doctrine that many of its members could support. Popular sovereignty very nearly undid the party as well. When Stephen Douglas applied the doctrine to that part of the Louisiana Purchase where slavery had been barred, he destroyed the dominance of the Democratic Party in the free states. Most of the northern Democrats in the House who had cast ballots in support of Douglas's Kansas-Nebraska bill were not reelected the following year. As a result, northern Democratic representation in the House fell sharply, and after 1854, the Democrats became a southern-dominated party.

Nevertheless, Democrats remained the dominant party throughout the 1850s. Gains in the South more than balanced losses in the North. During the decade, Democrats elected two presidents and won majorities in Congress in almost every election. But national power required that they maintain a north-

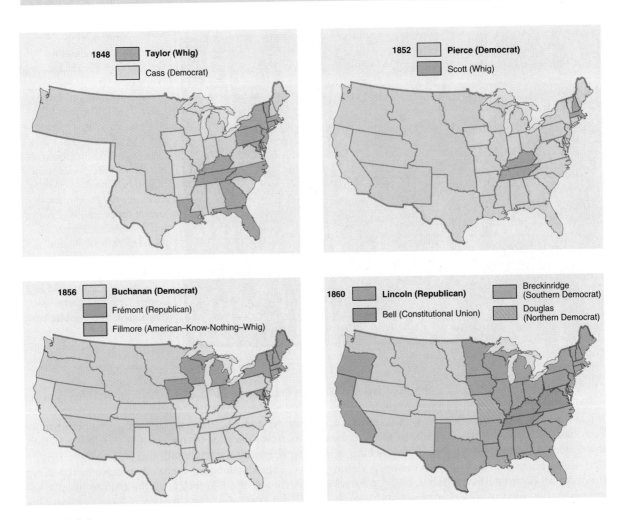

M A P 14.4
Political Realignment, 1848–1860
In 1848, slavery and sectionalism began hammering the country's party system. The Whig party
was an early casualty. By 1860, national parties — those that contended for votes in both the
North and the South — had been replaced by regional parties.

ern and a southern wing, which in turn required that they avoid the issue of the expansion of slavery. The fate of the Whigs constantly reminded Democrats that slavery was neither easily avoided nor compromised.

The breakup of the Whigs and the disaffection of significant numbers of northern Democrats set many Americans politically adrift. As they searched for new political harbors, they discovered that they had plenty of choices. The death of the old party system created a kaleidoscope of fresh political alternatives. The question was, Who would attract the drifters?

The New Parties: Know-Nothings and Republicans

Among the new organizations that vied to replace the Whigs as the second party in the national two-party system were splinter groups with such odd names as Anti-Nebraskaites, Fusionists, Maine Lawites, Temperance men, Rum Democrats, Hard Shell Democrats, Half Shells, Soft Shells, and others. Out of this confusion, two organizations emerged as true contenders. One grew out of the slavery controversy, a spontaneous coalition of indignant antislavery Northerners. The other major new party arose from an entirely different split in American society, that between Roman Catholic immigrants and native Protestants.

The tidal wave of immigrants that broke over America in the decade from 1845 to 1855 produced a nasty backlash among Protestant Americans, who believed they were about to drown in a sea of Irish and German Roman Catholics. The new arrivals encountered economic prejudice, ethnic hostility, and religious antagonism. Because some of them displayed a taste for whiskey and beer, they also drew the wrath of the temperance movement. When the immigrants entered American politics, largely as Democrats because they perceived that party as more tolerant of newcomers than were the Whigs, they met sharp political opposition. In the early 1850s, nativists (individuals who were anti-immigrant) began to organize, first into secret fraternal societies such as the Order of the Star-Spangled Banner, then into a political party. Recruits swore never to vote for either foreign-born or Roman Catholic candidates. The party retained its secret rit-

uals, and members promised not to reveal any information about the organization. When questioned, they said: "I know nothing." Officially, they were the American Party, but most Americans called them Know-Nothings.

Pledged to reducing the political power of immigrants, the Know-Nothings exploded onto the political stage in 1854 and 1855 with a series of dazzling successes. They captured state legislatures in the Northeast, West, and South and claimed dozens of seats in Congress. Their greatest triumph came in Massachusetts, a favorite destination for the Irish. Know-Nothings elected the Massachusetts governor, all of the state senators, all but two of the state representatives, and all of the congressmen. Know-Nothings attracted both Democrats and Whigs, but with their party crumbling, more Whigs responded to the attraction. In 1855, an individual might reasonably have concluded that the American Party had emerged as the successor to the Whigs.

But Know-Nothings were not the only new party making noise. Among the new antislavery or-

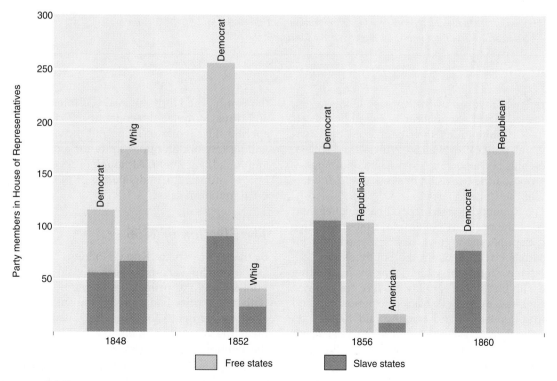

FIGURE 14.1
Changing Political Landscape, 1848–1860
The polarization of American politics between the free states and slave states occurred in little more than a decade.

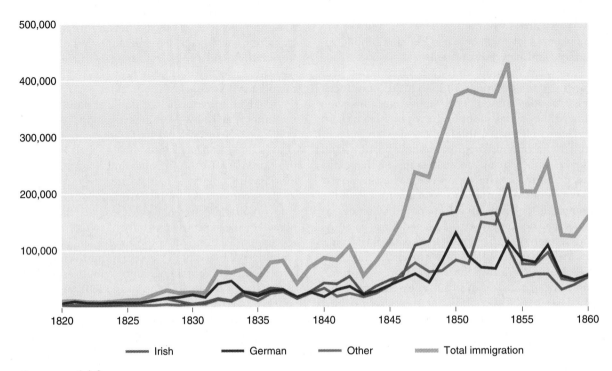

FIGURE 14.2
Antebellum Immigration, 1820–1860
After increasing gradually for several decades, immigration shot up in the mid-1840s. Between
1848–1860, nearly 3.5 million immigrants entered the United States.

ganizations provoked by the Kansas-Nebraska Act, one called itself Republicans. Republicans attempted to unite under their banner all the dissidents and political orphans—Whigs, Free-Soilers, anti-Nebraska Democrats, even Know-Nothings—who opposed the extension of slavery into any territory of the United States.

The Republican creed tapped basic beliefs and values of the northern public. Slave labor and free labor, Republicans argued, had spawned two incompatible civilizations. In the South, slavery degraded the dignity of white labor by associating work with blacks and servility. Slavery condemned most whites, as well as blacks, to ignorance and poverty. Repression and tyranny laid heavily on every Southerner, except planter aristocrats. Those insatiable slave lords, whom antislavery Northerners called the Slave Power, now conspired to expand slavery, subvert liberty, and undermine the Constitution through the Democratic Party. Only by restricting slavery to the South, Republicans believed, could free labor flourish elsewhere. Free labor created in the North a society that was the opposite of

the South. The North hitched self-interest to effort and thus stimulated economic efficiency. It respected the dignity of labor and provided anyone willing to work an opportunity for a decent living and for advancement. Although exaggerated, these images attracted a hodgepodge of Northerners to the Republican cause.

The Election of 1856

By the mid-1850s, the Know-Nothings had emerged as the principal champion of nativism and the Republicans as the primary advocate of antislavery. Both new parties had scored astonishing successes almost overnight. Together, they had helped to break the Whigs and to bloody the Democrats. But the Republicans emerged as the Democrats' main challenger. The election of 1856 revealed that their political star was rising sharply, whereas that of the Know-Nothings was dead.

Slavery in the territories became the election's only issue. The Know-Nothings came apart when party leaders insisted on a platform that endorsed the Kansas-Nebraska Act, and most Northerners walked out. The Know-Nothings who remained nominated ex-President Millard Fillmore. The Republicans, in contrast, adopted a platform that focused almost exclusively on "making every territory free." When they labeled slavery a "relic of barbarism," Republicans announced that they had written off the South. For president, they nominated the dashing soldier and California adventurer John C. Frémont, "Pathfinder of the West." Though a celebrated explorer, he lacked political credentials. Political know-how resided in his wife, Jessie Frémont, who, as a daughter of Senator Thomas Hart Benton of Missouri, knew the political map as well as her husband knew western trails.

The Democrats, successful in 1852 in bridging sectional differences by nominating a northern man with southern principles, chose another "doughface," James Buchanan of Pennsylvania. Regarding slavery, the Democrats took refuge in the ambiguity of popular sovereignty. They portrayed Republicans as extremists whose support for the Wilmot Proviso risked pushing the South out of the Union.

The Democratic strategy helped carry the day for Buchanan, but Frémont did astonishingly well. Buchanan won 174 electoral votes against Frémont's 114 and Fillmore's 8. Frémont carried all but five of the states north of the Mason-Dixon line. The election made clear that the Whigs had disintegrated, that the Know-Nothings would not ride nativism to national power, and that the Democrats were badly strained. But the big news was the "glorious defeat" of the Republicans. Despite being a brand-new party and purely sectional, they challenged other parties for national power. Sectionalism had fashioned a third party system, one that spelled danger for the Republic.

JOHN C. AND JESSIE BENTON FRÉMONT
The election of 1856 was the first time a candidate's wife appeared on campaign items. Appropriately, the woman who made the breakthrough was Jessie Benton Frémont, as seen here on a silk ribbon with her husband, John C. Frémont, Republican Party presidential nominee. Jessie proved a valuable asset, helping to plan her husband's campaign, coauthoring his election biography, and drawing northern women into political activity as never before. Jessie Frémont was, as Abraham Lincoln observed ambivalently, "quite a female politician."
Collection of Janice L. and David J. Frent.

TABLE 14.2
THE ELECTION OF 1856

Candidate	Electoral Vote	Popular Vote	Percent of Popular Vote
James Buchanan (Democrat)	174	1,833,000	45.3
John C. Frémont (Republican)	114	1,339,000	33.1
Millard Fillmore (American)	8	872,000	21.6

Freedom under Siege

The "triumph" of the Republicans meant that the second party in the new two-party system was entirely sectional. It felt no compelling need to compromise, to conciliate, to keep a southern wing happy. Indeed, the Republican Party organized around the premise that the slaveholding South provided a profound threat to "free soil, free labor, and free men." It declared northern society healthy and upright while condemning the South as rotten and depraved. Republicans kept up a steady drumbeat of charges against the Slave Power, the most important of which was that proslavery southern Democrats threatened free men's liberties.

> *The Republican Party organized around the premise that the slaveholding South provided a profound threat to "free soil, free labor, and free men." It declared northern society healthy and upright while condemning the South as rotten and depraved.*

Northerners who resisted the Republican message encountered disturbing new evidence in the four years following the passage of the Kansas-Nebraska Act in 1854. Events in distant Kansas Territory provided the young Republican organization with an enormous boost. Kansas reeled with violence between proslavery and antislavery settlers, which Republicans argued was southern in origin. Kansas offered a window onto southern values and intentions, they claimed. Nor was the southern fondness for the club, knife, and revolver evident only on the Kansas frontier, Republicans argued. They pointed to the brutal beating by a Southerner of a respected northern senator on the floor of Congress. Even the Supreme Court, in the Republicans' view, reflected the South's drive toward tyranny and minority rule. In 1858, the issues dividing North and South received an extraordinary airing in a senatorial contest in Illinois, when the nation's foremost Democrat debated a resourceful Republican.

"Bleeding Kansas"

Three days after the House of Representatives approved the Kansas-Nebraska Act, Senator William H. Seward of New York boldly challenged the South. "Come on then, Gentlemen of the Slave States," he cried, "since there is no escaping your challenge, I accept it in behalf of the cause of freedom. We will engage in competition for the virgin soil of Kansas, and God give the victory to the side which is stronger in numbers as it is in right." Because of Stephen Douglas, popular sovereignty would determine whether Kansas became slave or free. No one really expected New Mexico and Utah to become slave states when Congress instituted popular sovereignty there in 1850. By 1860, only twenty-nine slaves lived in arid Utah and none in New Mexico. But Kansas was different. Kansas sat on the borderline, and everyone believed it could go either way. In reality a majority of settlers sought the traditional goals of getting a farm, building a town, or speculating in real estate. But Kansas was hardly a typical frontier. Free-state and slave-state settlers each sought majorities at the ballot box, claimed God's blessing, and kept their rifles ready.

In the North, emigrant aid societies sprang up to promote settlement from the free states. The most famous, the New England Emigrant Aid Company, sponsored some 1,240 settlers in 1854 and 1855. In the South, proslavery expansionists eagerly took up Seward's challenge. Tiny rural communities from Virginia to Texas raised money to support proslavery settlers. Missourians especially thought it important to secure Kansas for slavery. Already bordered on the east by the free state of Illinois and on the north by the free state of Iowa, they did not relish another free state to the west. Plenty of western Missourians, hell-for-leather frontier types, prepared to do whatever it took to prevent abolitionists from seizing Kansas.

In theory, popular sovereignty meant an orderly tallying of ballots. In Kansas, however, elections became circuses. Thousands of Missourians, egged on by Missouri Senator David Rice Atchison, invaded Kansas. "There are eleven hundred coming over from Platte County to vote," Atchison reported, "and if that ain't enough we can send five thousand—enough to kill every God-damned abolitionist in the Territory." Not surprisingly, proslavery candidates swept the early elections. When the first territorial legislature met, it enacted laws that made the Missouri slave law look tame. It became a felony merely to argue that slavery did not legally exist in Kansas. The law prohibited antislavery men from holding office or serving on juries. Assisting a runaway slave became a capital offense. Ever-pliant President Pierce endorsed the work of the fraudulently elected proslavery legislature. Free-state men

**FRAUDULENT VOTING
IN KANSAS**

*In this northern indictment of
the corruption of popular sovereignty by Missourians,
rough frontier types, with pistols and knives tucked into
their belts, rush to get free
whiskey and then line up at
the polling place, where next
to a sign, "*DOWN WITH THE
ABOLITIONISTS,*" they doubt-
lessly voted the proslavery
ticket.*

The Kansas State Historical Society,
Topeka, Kansas.

did not. They elected their own legislature, which promptly banned both slaves *and* free blacks from the territory and applied for admission to the Union as a free state. Organized into two rival governments and armed to the teeth, Kansans verged on civil war.

Fighting broke out on the morning of May 21, 1856. Under banners inscribed "Southern Rights" and "South Carolina," a mob of several hundred entered the town of Lawrence, the center of free-state settlement. They wrecked the offices of antislavery newspapers and, after failing to destroy the Free State Hotel with cannon fire, burned it to the ground. Only one man died—a proslavery raider who was killed when a burning wall collapsed—but the Sack of Lawrence, as free-soil forces called it, inflamed northern opinion. The press reported dozens of bodies strewn over the town, crumpled beside hundreds of charred chimneys. In Kansas, news of Lawrence provoked one free-soil settler, John Brown, to "fight fire with fire." Announcing that "it was better that a score of bad men should die than that one man who came here to make

Kansas a Free State should be driven out," he led a posse that massacred five allegedly proslavery settlers along the Pottawatomie Creek. After that, guerrilla war engulfed the territory. (See Texts in Historical Context, pages 542–543.)

By providing graphic evidence of a dangerously aggressive Slave Power, "Bleeding Kansas" gave the fledgling Republican Party an enormous boost. The Republicans received additional encouragement from an event that occurred in the national capital. On May 19 and 20, 1856, Senator Charles Sumner of Massachusetts delivered a scathing speech entitled "The Crime against Kansas." He damned the administration, the South, and proslavery Kansans. He also indulged in a scalding personal attack on South Carolina's elderly Senator Andrew P. Butler, whom Sumner described as a "Don Quixote" who had taken as his mistress "the harlot, slavery."

Preston Brooks, a young South Carolina member of the House and a kinsman of Butler, felt compelled to defend the honor of his aged relative and of his state. For his instrument of chastisement,

Kansas: Contested Ground

I llinois Senator Stephen A. Douglas, author of the Kansas-Nebraska Act, promised that squatter sovereignty offered a peaceful means of settling the fate of slavery in the Kansas and Nebraska Territories. In a speech in Peoria, Illinois, Abraham Lincoln denounced opening territory that was previously free to the possibility of slavery and predicted that bloodshed, not tranquility, would result.

Document 1. Abraham Lincoln Warns of the Consequences of Squatter Sovereignty, October 16, 1854

Some yankees, in the east, are sending emigrants to Nebraska, to exclude slavery from it; and, so far as I can judge, they expect the question to be decided by voting, in some way or other. But the Missourians are awake too. They are within a stone's throw of the contested ground. They hold meetings, and pass resolutions, in which not the slightest allusion to voting is made. They resolve that slavery already exists in the territory; that more shall go there; that they, remaining in Missouri will protect it; and that abolitionists shall be hung, or driven away. Through all this, bowie-knives and six-shooters are seen plainly enough; but never a glimpse of the ballot-box. And, really, what is to be the result of this? Each party WITHIN, having numerous and determined backers WITHOUT, is it not probable that the contest will come to blows, and bloodshed? Could there be a more apt invention to bring about collision and violence, on the slavery question, than this Ne-

braska project is? I do not charge, or believe, that such was intended by Congress; but if they had literally formed a ring, and placed champions within it to fight out the controversy, the fight could be no more likely to come off, than it is. And if this fight should begin, is it likely to take a very peaceful, Union-saving turn? Will not the first drop of blood so shed, be the real knell of the Union?

A s Lincoln predicted, elections became circuses, and worse. Missourians believed that they were defending home territory against an invasion of Northerners. In 1856, a congressional committee gathered evidence of intimidation and violence at Kansas polls.

Document 2. Samuel N. Wood Recounts His Experience on Election Day, March 30, 1855

I first came into the Territory in June, 1854, from the State of Ohio. . . . I was here on the day of election of the 30th of March, 1855; it was a Friday. On the Wednesday evening before, I saw some two or three hundred men encamped on the ravine bottom near the ford, who said they were from Missouri, and were going above to some place to vote, and there would be about 1,000 more to vote at this place. The next day, Thursday, they commenced coming in here to Lawrence on horseback, on mules, in wagons and carriages. . . .

It was found pretty difficult, when the polls were opened, for any one to get to the window to vote. . . . They formed two lines of them near from the window out on the prairie . . . standing some six feet apart, and those who voted had to enter in at the outer end of these two lines, walk up to the window, and vote. . . . Soon after the voting commenced

Brooks chose something he believed appropriate for a social inferior. On May 22, armed with a walking cane, Brooks entered the Senate, where he found Sumner working at his desk. After accusing him of libel, Brooks began beating Sumner over the head with his cane. After about a minute, Sumner lay bleeding and unconscious on the Senate floor. Brooks resigned his seat in the House, only to be promptly reelected. In the North, the southern hero became the archvillain. Like Bleeding Kansas,

"Bleeding Sumner" provided the Republican Party with a potent symbol of the South's twisted and violent "civilization."

The Dred Scott Decision

As the French visitor Alexis de Tocqueville observed in the 1830s, "Scarcely any question arises in the United States that is not resolved, sooner or later, into a judicial question." Because the Constitution

I heard quite an excitement a little to the left of where I was standing. . . . I saw a man running from the house towards the river, and as many as a hundred running after him. I started after them . . . and I saw it was a Mr. Bond, of this place. There were some two or three pistol-shots fired after him. There was considerable excitement on the bank. Several of them said they must drive all the damned abolitionists off the ground. . . .

These Missourians had almost exclusive control of the polls until late in the afternoon. . . . I recollect that a man named Willis, who lived in this place at that time, came up about the middle of the afternoon to vote, when about half of these Missourians had left. When he came up they raised a cry that he was a damned abolitionist, a negro thief, &c., and hallooed "Kill him!" "Shoot him!" &c. There were several of our men on the ground, and they told them if they wanted to commence that game they could do so, and that they would find the matter would not end here in Kansas Territory; and they quieted down very much. I think Willis voted.

*T*he Committee also received testimony from Mahala Doyle, the widow of a man who was slaughtered by John Brown's antislavery "army."

DOCUMENT 3. Mahala Doyle Testifies

I am the widow of the late James P. Doyle . . . my husband, myself, and children moved into the Territory of Kansas some time in November, A.D. 1855, and settled on Mosquito creek . . . where it empties into Pottawatomie creek . . . on Saturday, the 24th day of May, A.D. 1856, about 11 o'clock at night, after we had all retired, my husband, . . . myself, and five

children . . . were all in bed, when we heard some persons come into the yard and rap at the door. . . . My husband got up and went to the door. Those outside inquired for Mr. Wilkson, and where he lived. My husband told them that he would tell them. Mr. Doyle, my husband, opened the door, and several came into the house, and said that they were from the army. My husband was a pro-slavery man. They told my husband that he and the boys must surrender, they were their prisoners. These men were armed with pistols and large knives. They first took my husband out of the house, then they took two of my sons—the two oldest ones, William and Drury. . . . My son John was spared, because I asked them in tears to spare him. In a short time afterwards I heard the report of pistols. I heard two reports, after which I heard moaning, as if a person was dying; then I heard a wild whoop. They had asked before they went away for our horses. We told them that the horses were out on the prairie. My husband and two boys, my sons, did not come back any more. I went out next morning in search of them, and found my husband and William, my son, lying dead in the road near together, about two hundred yards from the house. My other son I did not see any more until the day he was buried. . . . Fear of myself and the remaining children induced me to leave the home where we had been living. We had improved our claim a little. I left all and went to the State of Missouri.

Document 1. Roy P. Basler, ed., *The Collected Works of Abraham Lincoln* (New Brunswick, N.J.: Rutgers University Press, 1953), 2:271–72.

Document 2. *Report of the Special Committee Appointed to Investigate the Troubles in the Territory of Kansas*, 34th Cong., 1st sess., 1856, H. Doc. 200, serial 869, 140–41.

Document 3. Ibid., 1175–76.

lacked precision on the issue of slavery in the territories, political debate reflected sectional interests and party politics. Only the Supreme Court spoke definitively about the meaning of the Constitution. In 1857, in the *Dred Scott* case, the Court proved that it enjoyed no special immunity from the sectional and partisan passions that convulsed the land.

Eleven years after Dred and Harriet Scott first sued for freedom, the Supreme Court ruled in the case. The justices could have settled the immediate

issue of Scott's status as a free man or slave on narrow grounds, but they saw the case as an opportunity to settle once and for all the vexing question of slavery in the territories. The justices believed that their ruling would finally remove this divisive issue from the political arena. Many Americans wanted the Supreme Court to settle the troubling territorial question. No one was more eager than Southerners, for five of the nine justices were from the South and seven were Democrats.

THE DRED SCOTT FAMILY

The Dred Scott *case in 1857 produced a fierce political storm, but it also fueled an enormous curiosity about the family suing for freedom. Popular magazines rushed to supply the demand with images and interviews. The correspondent for the popular* Frank Leslie's Illustrated *met Dred Scott in St. Louis and reported: "We found him on examination to be a pure-blooded African, perhaps fifty years of age, with a shrewd, intelligent, good-natured face, of rather light frame, being not more than five feet six inches high."*

Library of Congress.

On the morning of March 6, 1857, seventy-nine-year-old Chief Justice Roger B. Taney read the majority decision of the Court. Taney hated Republicans and detested racial equality, and the Court's decision reflected those prejudices. First, the Court ruled that Dred Scott could not legally claim that his constitutional rights had been violated because he was not a citizen of the United States. At the time of the Constitution, Taney said, blacks "had for more than a century before been regarded as beings of an inferior order . . . so far inferior, that they had no rights which the white man was bound to respect." Second, the laws of Missouri determined Dred Scott's status, and his travels in free areas did not make him free. Third, Congress's power to make "all needful rules and regulations" for the territories did not include the right to exclude slavery. The Court then explicitly declared the Missouri Compromise unconstitutional, even though it had already been voided by the Kansas-Nebraska Act.

Republicans exploded in outrage. Taney's extreme proslavery decision ranged far beyond a determination of Dred Scott's freedom. By declaring unconstitutional the Republican program of federal exclusion of slavery in the territories, the Court had cut the ground from beneath the party. Moreover, as the *New York Tribune* lamented, the decision seemed to mean that "all our Territories are henceforth Slave Territories on the way to be ripened into Slave States." Particularly frightening to African Americans in the North was the Court's declaration that blacks were not citizens and have "no rights which the white man was bound to respect." It's no wonder that black abolitionist Frederick Douglass denounced the Dred Scott decision as "a most scandalous and devilish perversion of the Constitution."

The Republican rebuttal to Taney's decision relied heavily on the brilliant dissenting opinion of Justice Benjamin R. Curtis. Scott *was* a citizen of the United States, Curtis argued. At the time of the writing of the Constitution, free black men could vote in five states and participated in the ratification process. Scott *was* free. Because slavery was prohibited in Wisconsin, the "involuntary servitude of a slave, coming into the Territory with his master, should cease to exist." And the Missouri Compromise *was* constitutional. The Founders meant exactly what they said: Congress had the power to make "*all* needful rules and regulations" for the territories, including barring slavery.

Unswayed by Curtis's dissent, the Court's seven-to-two majority had validated the most extreme statement of the South's territorial rights.

John C. Calhoun's claim that Congress had no authority to exclude slavery now became the law of the land. One Southerner gloated that the *Dred Scott* decision was "the funeral sermon of Black Republicanism . . . crushing and annihilating the anti-slavery platform." But what southern Democrats cheered, northern Democrats found profoundly disturbing. They feared that the *Dred Scott* decision annihilated not just the Wilmot Proviso but popular sovereignty as well. If Congress did not have the authority to exclude slavery, how could Congress's creation, a territorial government, assume that right? No one was in a tighter bind than Stephen A. Douglas. Civil war raged in Kansas at that very moment because Douglas's Kansas-Nebraska Act had opened the territory to popular sovereignty. Now, contrary to Douglas's promise, it appeared that a free-soil majority could not keep slavery out. No one could exclude slavery until the moment of statehood. By draining the last drop of ambiguity out of popular sovereignty, the *Dred Scott* decision jeopardized not only Douglas's presidential ambition but the ability of the Democratic Party to hold its northern and southern wings together.

Ironically, the *Dred Scott* decision strengthened the young Republican Party by giving credence to its claim that a hostile Slave Power conspired against northern liberties. Only the capture of the Supreme Court by the "slavocracy," Republicans argued, could explain the tortured and historically inaccurate *Dred Scott* decision. Although President Buchanan praised the decision as the "final settlement . . . of the question of slavery in the Territories," the decision inflamed sectional tensions and further polarized positions. The justices' efforts had failed as dismally as the politicians' efforts. As for Dred Scott, although the Court rejected his suit, he did in the end gain his freedom. White friends, the sons of his first owner, Peter Blow, purchased and freed Scott and his family. Dred Scott died less than a year later.

Prairie Republican: Abraham Lincoln

The reigniting of sectional flames provided Republican politicians with fresh challenges and fresh opportunities. None proved more eager for them than Abraham Lincoln of Illinois. Lincoln had long since put behind him his hardscrabble, log cabin beginnings in Kentucky and Indiana. At the time of the *Dred Scott* decision, he lived in a fine two-story house in Springfield, had enough business from the

Illinois Central Railroad to be known as the "railroad lawyer," and by virtue of his marriage and successful practice associated with men of reputation and standing.

The law provided Lincoln's living, but politics was his life. "His ambition was a little engine that knew no rest," observed his law partner William Herndon. At age twenty-six, he served his first term in the Illinois state legislature. Between 1847 and 1849, he enjoyed his only term in the House of Representatives, where he fired away at "Mr. Polk's War" and cast dozens of votes for free soil but otherwise served inconspicuously. When he returned to Springfield, he pitched into his law practice but kept his eye fixed on public office. As a young man, he had chosen as his political hero the Whig Henry Clay. He deeply admired the man, his principles, and his program. On the vexing issues of Union, slavery, and race, Clay exemplified for Lincoln the reasonable moderate, the realistic pragmatist, and the effective compromiser.

But, like Whigs everywhere in the mid-1850s, Lincoln had no political home. With their party in shambles, a good many Illinois Whigs gravitated to the Know-Nothings. Mary Todd Lincoln, Lincoln's Kentucky-born wife, sympathized with the nativists, for she knew, she said, the burdens of "wild Irish" servants. But Lincoln was not a Know-Nothing. "How could I be?" he asked. "How can any one who abhors the oppression of negroes be in favor of degrading classes of white people?" Lincoln's credo—opposition to "the *extension* of slavery"— made the Democrats an impossible choice. But the Republicans made free soil their principal tenet, and in 1856 Lincoln joined the party.

The Kansas-Nebraska Act of 1854 had pushed Lincoln into new levels of political awareness and engagement. Its repeal of the Missouri Compromise —that "sacred compact"—left him "thunderstruck and stunned." Convinced that slavery was a "monstrous injustice," a "great moral wrong," and an "unqualified evil to the negro, the white man, and the State," he was certain that Douglas had jeopardized the Founders' plan to contain the spread of slavery. He admitted that the Constitution sanctioned slavery in those states where it existed; but penned in, plantation slavery would exhaust southern soil at the same time the number of slaves increased. Slaveholders would have no choice but to end slavery themselves. By providing fresh, life-giving lands, however, Douglas put slavery "on the high road to extension and perpetuity." Lincoln conveniently forgot those moments when the Founders

permitted slavery to spread westward, but he remained convinced that the "spirit of seventy-six and the spirit of Nebraska are utter antagonisms."

Lincoln realized that slavery was yoked with race. Just as he staked out the middle ground on antislavery, he also held what were, for his times, moderate racial views. Like a majority of Republicans, he defended black humanity without challenging white supremacy. He denounced slavery as immoral and believed that it should end, but he also viewed black equality as impractical and unachievable. "Negroes have natural rights . . . as other men have," he said, "although they cannot enjoy them here." Insurmountable white prejudice made it impossible to extend full citizenship and equality to blacks in America. Freeing blacks and allowing them to remain in this country would lead to race war. In Lincoln's mind, social stability and black progress required that slavery end and that blacks leave the country.

Lincoln realized that because most Northerners lacked sympathy for blacks, humanitarian concern would not mobilize them to fight for free soil. Instead, he linked northern labor's self-interest to halting slavery's advance. He described the territories as "places for poor people to go to, and better their conditions." If slavery expanded, white men would compete with slave labor. He spoke to those millions of Americans who were in lowly stations and wanted to make something of themselves: farmhands who wanted to become farm owners, clerks who aspired to be merchants, rail-splitters who dreamed of being lawyers. "The *free* labor system," he said, "opens the way for all—gives hope to all, and energy, and progress, and improvement of condition to all." In Lincoln's view, slavery's expansion threatened this freedom to succeed.

Lincoln became persuaded that slaveholders formed an aggressive and dangerous conspiracy to nationalize slavery. Evidence abounded. The Kansas-Nebraska Act repealed the restriction on slavery's advance in the territories. The *Dred Scott* decision denied Congress the right to impose fresh restrictions. The next step, Lincoln warned, would be "another Supreme Court decision, declaring that the Constitution of the United States does not permit a *State* to exclude slavery from its limits." Unless its citizens woke up, he warned, the Supreme Court would make "Illinois a slave State."

In his memorable 1858 "House Divided" speech, Lincoln declared provocatively that the nation could not "endure, permanently half slave and half free." Either opponents of slavery would arrest

DISCUSSING THE NEWS

Newspapers permitted Midwesterners to keep up-to-date. Here a farmer takes a break from his task of cutting firewood to debate the latest news with his friends. He is so engrossed that he ignores the little girl tugging at his pants leg and trying to get him to notice the woman waving in the doorway. Men like these increasingly accepted Lincoln's portrait of the Republican Party as the guardian of the common people's liberty and economic opportunity. When Lincoln claimed that southern slaveholders threatened free labor and democracy, they listened.

its spread and place it on the "course of ultimate extinction" or its advocates would push it forward until it became legal in "*all* the States, *old* as well as *new*—*North* as well as *South.*" Lincoln identified Illinois's own son Stephen A. Douglas as a chief conspirator. Douglas's philosophy of not caring whether slavery was "voted down or voted up" in the territories fed a complacency that eased the way for new advances by the Slave Power.

As Lincoln developed and honed his ideas about slavery and freedom, he tried them out on audiences across the North. His words stirred many of his listeners, touching their deepest hopes and anxieties. In time, his convictions that slavery was wrong, that Congress must stop its spread, and that it must be put on the road to extinction formed the core of the Republican ideology. By 1858, he had so impressed his fellow Republicans in Illinois that they put him forward to challenge the nation's premier Democrat who was seeking reelection to the Senate.

The Lincoln-Douglas Debates

When Stephen Douglas learned that Abraham Lincoln would be his opponent for the Senate, he confided in a fellow Democrat: "I shall have my hands full. He is the strong man of the party—full of wit, facts, dates—and the best stump speaker, with his droll ways and dry jokes, in the West. He is as honest as he is shrewd, and if I beat him my victory will be hardly won."

Not only did Douglas have to contend with a formidable foe, but he also carried the weight of a burden not of his own making. The previous year, the nation's economy experienced a sharp downturn, a depression that antebellum Americans called a "panic." Prices plummeted, thousands of businesses failed, and unemployment rose. The causes of the panic of 1857 lay in the international economy, but Americans reflexively interpreted the panic in sectional terms. Northeastern businesses and industries suffered most, and Northerners blamed the southern-dominated Congress, which had just months before reduced tariff duties to their lowest levels in the nineteenth century. Given this invitation, Northerners believed, foreign competition ravaged the northern economy. Southerners, who had largely escaped hardship because cotton prices remained high, saw the panic as proof of the feebleness of a free-labor economy and the hardiness of their own system of plantation slavery. Although Illinois suffered less than the Northeast, Douglas had to go before the voters in 1858 as a member of the freshly accused, southern-dominated Democratic Party.

Douglas's response to another crisis in 1857, however, helped shore up his standing with his constituents. During the previous winter, proslavery forces in Kansas met in Lecompton, drafted a proslavery constitution, and applied for statehood. President Buchanan blessed the Lecompton constitution and instructed Congress to admit Kansas as the sixteenth slave state. Everyone knew that free-soilers outnumbered proslavery settlers two or three to one, and Republicans denounced the "Lecompton swindle." Douglas broke with the Democratic administration and came out against the proslavery constitution, not because it accepted slavery but because it violated the democratic requirement of popular sovereignty.

In choosing to defend political principle, Douglas also practiced political self-preservation. He knew that a vote for the bogus Lecompton constitution would have handed over Kansas to slavery and marked him as a southern flunky in the eyes of Illinois voters. Coming out against the constitution declared his independence from the South and, he hoped, made him acceptable at home. True, his anti-Lecompton stance cost him dearly with white Southerners, who mounted a vicious attack on him. But he had first to secure his political base in Illinois. In March 1858, despite Douglas's vigorous opposition, the Senate passed the Kansas statehood bill, but the northern majority in the House killed it. (When Kansans would reconsider the Lecompton constitution in an honest election, they would reject it six to one, and Kansas would enter the Union in 1861 as a free state.)

A relative unknown and a decided underdog in the Illinois election, Lincoln challenged the incumbent Douglas to debate him face to face. Douglas agreed, and the two met in seven communities for a legendary series of debates. To the thousands who stood straining to see and hear, they must have seemed an odd pair. Douglas was five feet four inches tall, broad, and stocky; Lincoln was six feet four inches tall, angular, and lean. Douglas was in perpetual motion, darting across the platform, shouting, and jabbing the air. Lincoln was almost lethargic, speaking deliberately, sincerely. Douglas wore the latest fashion and dazzled audiences with his flashy vests. Lincoln wore good suits but managed to look rumpled anyway. But their differences in physical appearance and style were of least importance. They showed the citizens of Illinois (and much of the nation because of national press coverage) the difference between an anti-Lecompton Democrat and a true Republican. They debated, often brilliantly, the central issue before the country: slavery and freedom.

Lincoln badgered Douglas with the question of whether he favored the spread of slavery. If not, how did he expect to stop it, since the *Dred Scott* decision declared that citizens had a right to carry their slaves into the national territories? Lincoln tried to force Douglas into the damaging admission that the Supreme Court had repudiated his territorial solution, popular sovereignty. In the debate at Freeport, Illinois, Douglas answered Lincoln's challenge by declaring that popular sovereignty still had plenty of life. Settlers could not now pass legislation barring slavery, he admitted, but they could ban slavery just as effectively by not passing protective laws.

Without "appropriate police regulations and local legislation," such as those found in slave states, he explained, slavery could not live a day, an hour. Southerners condemned Douglas's "Freeport Doctrine" and charged him with trying to steal the victory they had gained with the *Dred Scott* decision. Lincoln chastised his opponent for his "don't care" attitude, for "blowing out the moral lights around us," and for treating the great issue of slavery like just another election question.

For his part, Douglas worked the racial issue. He called Lincoln an abolitionist, a miscegenationist (one who favored marriage between the races), and a color-blind egalitarian enamored with "our colored brethren." Lincoln denied every charge. Put on the defensive, he came close to staking out positions on abolition and race that were as conservative as Douglas's. Lincoln reiterated his belief that slavery enjoyed constitutional protection where it existed. He also reaffirmed his faith in white rule. "I will say, then, that I am not, nor ever have been, in favor of bringing about in any way the social and political equality of the white and black race." But Lincoln was no negrophobe like Douglas, who told racist jokes and spit out racial epithets. Lincoln always tried to steer the debate back to what he considered the true issue: the morality and future of slavery. "Slavery is wrong," he repeated, because "a man has the right to the fruits of his own labor."

As Douglas predicted, the election was hard-fought. It was also closely contested. In the nineteenth century, citizens voted for state legislators, who in turn selected the U.S. senator. Republicans gained a slight plurality of the votes, but because of the way Illinois was apportioned, the Democrats won a majority in the legislature. The new legislature chose to return Douglas to the Senate. But the debates thrust Lincoln into the national spotlight. No one expressed Republican principles more compellingly.

The Union Collapses

Lincoln's thesis that the "slavocracy" conspired to make slavery a national institution now seems exaggerated and fantastical. But from the northern perspective, the Kansas-Nebraska Act, the Brooks-Sumner affair, the *Dred Scott* decision, the panic of 1857, and the Lecompton constitution seemed irrefutable evidence of the South's aggressiveness. Lincoln was surely right that the house was divided.

If he was also right that it must become all one thing or the other, then the tilt, Northerners increasingly agreed, was clear and frightening.

Southerners, of course, saw things differently. They were the ones who were under siege and had grievances, they declared. Which was the minority section? they asked. In a democracy, how could a minority hope to control the government? Signs were everywhere, they argued, that the North planned to use its numerical advantage to attack slavery, and not just in the territories. Republicans had already proved themselves unwilling to be bound by the Constitution as interpreted by the Supreme Court in the *Dred Scott* case. After a Northerner attempted to incite a slave insurrection in Virginia in 1859, Southerners argued that Republicans had also proven themselves unwilling to be bound by Christian decency and reverence for life.

The 1850s delivered powerful blows to Southerners' confidence that they could remain Americans and protect slavery and their way of life.

Threats of secession increasingly laced the sectional debate. Talk of leaving the Union had been heard for years, of course. In 1827, Thomas Cooper of South Carolina warned that "we shall 'ere long be compelled to calculate the value of the union; and to enquire of what use to us is this most unequal alliance." Until the final crisis, however, Southerners used secession as a ploy to gain concessions within the Union, not to destroy the Union. But the 1850s delivered powerful blows to Southerners' confidence that they could remain Americans *and* protect slavery and their way of life. When the Republican Party defeated the Democrats in 1860, many Southerners concluded that national power had shifted permanently. Still, Southerners fell short of unity. Within states and among states, they responded to the crisis differently. At the same time, generations of slavery had also created among southern whites shared values and deep commitments.

John Brown's Raid

Three years after the 1856 Pottawatomie massacre in Kansas, John Brown reemerged. Time had not dampened his zeal for abolition. More than ever, he

JOHN BROWN

Was John Brown crazy? The debate about Brown's mental state began with his contemporaries and has raged ever since. Those who argue that he was a madman have asked: Would a sane man have butchered innocent victims at Pottawatomie Creek and set out for Harpers Ferry to overthrow slavery with fewer than two dozen men? But others see a resolute and selfless hero, not a psychotic. They have asked, would New England's Secret Six (four of them Harvard men) have sworn allegiance to a lunatic? Boston Athenaeum.

was a man on fire. He had spent thirty months begging money from New England abolitionists to support his vague plan for military operations against slavery, perhaps in Kansas, perhaps in the South itself. The rough-hewn but hypnotic Kansas fighting man captivated the genteel Easterners, particularly the Boston elite. Although he won more hearts than pocketbooks, Brown received enough in gifts to gather a small band of antislavery warriors.

On the night of October 16, 1859, John Brown took his war against slavery into the South. With only twenty-two men, including five African Americans, he crossed the Potomac River and occupied a federal arsenal at Harpers Ferry, Virginia. The invaders were quickly surrounded, first by local militia and then by Colonel Robert E. Lee, who com-

manded the U.S. marines in the area. When Brown refused to surrender, federal troops charged with bayonets. It was all over in less than thirty-six hours. Seventeen men, including two slaves, lost their lives. Ten of Brown's raiders, including two of his sons, died. Although a few of Brown's troops escaped, federal forces captured seven men, among them Brown himself, who suffered a painful but not serious sword wound.

John Brown's precise objective remains somewhat hazy, but he apparently wanted to initiate a slave insurrection. "When I strike, the bees will begin to swarm," Brown told Frederick Douglass a few months before the raid. As slaves rushed to Harpers Ferry, Brown would arm them with the pikes (long spears) that he carried with him and with weapons stolen from the arsenal. They would then fight a war of liberation. In fact, Brown neglected to inform the slaves that he had arrived, and the few who knew wanted nothing to do with the suicidal enterprise. "It was not a slave insurrection," Abraham Lincoln observed later. "It was an attempt by white men to get up a revolt among slaves, in which the slaves refused to participate. In fact, it was so absurd that the slaves, with all their ignorance, saw plainly enough it could not succeed."

If Brown had been killed during his raid, his impact on history would probably have been minor. As it was, he lived, was tried by the state of Virginia for treason and conspiracy to incite insurrection, and on December 2, 1859, was hanged. In life, "Old Brown" was a ne'er-do-well who failed at nearly everything he tried. He died, however, with courage, dignity, and composure. With his "piercing eyes" and "resolute countenance," he uttered some of the most stirring words ever to issue from a courtroom: "If it is deemed necessary that I should forfeit my life for the furtherance of the ends of justice, and mingle my blood further with the blood of my children and with the blood of millions in this slave country whose rights are disregarded by wicked, cruel, and unjust enactments, I say, let it be done."

Some Northerners grieved for John Brown. One abolitionist proclaimed Brown the "bravest and humanest man in all the country." In Boston, the essayist Ralph Waldo Emerson dubbed him "that new saint" who "will make the gallows glorious like the cross." Writer Henry David Thoreau compared him to Christ and called him "an angel of light." Some abolitionists went beyond canonizing Brown to explicitly endorsing his cause of slave rebellion. Even the abolitionist William Lloyd Garrison, who professed pacifism, announced, "I am prepared to say 'success to every slave insurrection at the South and in every slave country.'" Generally, however, abolitionists did not condone violence, and northern opinion did not celebrate bloody slave insurrection. Lincoln spoke for the majority when he endorsed Brown's antislavery stance but concluded that noble ideals could not "excuse violence, bloodshed, and treason."

In the South, the din of eulogies drowned out Lincoln's sober voice. Mississippians denounced the bloodthirsty fiend whose mission was "to incite slaves to murder helpless women and children." Especially after it came out that Brown had received financial aid from leading New England citizens (known as the Secret Six), white Southerners felt a cold fury. They contemplated what they had in common with people who "regard John Brown as a martyr and a Christian hero, rather than a murderer and robber." Many Southerners lost the capacity to distinguish between Northerners who opposed slavery, like Lincoln, and those who were willing to see it washed away in a river of blood, like Brown. Robert Toombs of Georgia announced solemnly that Southerners must "never permit this Federal government to pass into the traitorous hands of the black Republican party." At that moment, the presidential election was only months away.

Republican Victory in 1860

Calm did not follow John Brown's storm. Anxieties provoked by his raid flared for months as southern whites feverishly searched for abolitionists and tarred and feathered (or treated even worse) those they suspected. Moreover, other events in the eleven months between Brown's hanging and the presidential election heightened sectional hostility, incrimination, and estrangement.

First, a small southern business convention meeting in Nashville shocked the country (including many Southerners) by calling for the reopening of the African slave trade, closed since 1808 and considered an abomination everywhere in the Western world. Next, Chief Justice Taney whipped up new indignation when the Supreme Court ruled northern personal liberty laws unconstitutional and reaffirmed the Fugitive Slave Act. Then, in February 1860, the normally routine business of electing a Speaker of the House of Representatives turned into one of the ugliest moments in the history of Congress. When Republicans and Democrats deadlocked, it looked for a while as if they would simply shoot it out. "The only persons who do not have a revolver and a knife are those who have two revolvers," observed a South Carolinian. Congress averted bloodshed when a few Know-Nothings pitched in with the Republicans to elect an old Whig. Finally, Jefferson Davis demanded that the Senate adopt a federal slave code for the territories, a goal of extreme proslavery Southerners for several years. Not only could Congress not block slavery's spread, he argued, but it must offer it all "needful protection."

The demand for a federal slave code gave notice that Southerners intended to make their extreme position binding doctrine when Democrats converged on Charleston for their convention in April 1860. Meeting only blocks from the grave of John C. Calhoun, the party immediately split along sectional lines. On home turf, encouraged by cheering galleries, southern fire-eaters denounced Stephen Douglas and demanded a platform that included federal protection of slavery in the territories. "Ours are the institutions which are at stake; ours is the property that is to be destroyed; ours is the honor at stake," shouted the Alabama extremist William Lowndes Yancey. But northern Democrats needed a platform that they could take home, and northern voters would not stomach a federal slave code. When two platforms—one with a federal slave code and one with popular sovereignty—came before the delegates, popular sovereignty won. Representatives from the entire lower South and Arkansas stomped out of the convention. The remaining delegates adjourned to meet a few weeks later in Baltimore, where they nominated Douglas for president and adopted a platform that required nothing more than congressional noninterference in the territories.

When southern Democrats met, they nominated Vice President John C. Breckinridge of Tennessee for president and approved a platform with a federal slave code. But southern moderates refused to hand over their section to Breckinridge and the fire-eaters. Senator John J. Crittenden of Kentucky and others formed a new party that would provide voters a Unionist choice. Instead of adopting a platform—which inevitably fanned controversy—the new Constitutional Union Party merely approved a vague resolution pledging "to recognize no political principle other than *the Constitution . . . the Union . . . and the Enforcement of the Laws.*"

For president they picked former Senator John Bell of Tennessee. Republicans gently mocked the new party as the "Old Gentleman's Party." Southern Democrats accused it of "insulting the intelligence of the American people" when it ignored "the slavery question. That issue must be met and settled."

The Republicans smelled victory. Four years earlier they had enjoyed a "glorious defeat." Now the Democratic Party had broken up. Still, Republicans estimated that they needed to carry nearly all the free states to win. That required that they remedy deficiencies in both their candidate and their platform. In 1856, the party had suffered from following Frémont, a "pathfinder" who got lost in the political woods, and from the perception that it was a one-idea party. Antislavery sentiment had stiffened in the North in the previous four years, but Republicans decided to broaden their appeal. This time they built a platform with more than a single plank. Free homesteads, a protective tariff, a Pacific railroad, and a guarantee of immigrant political rights defined an economic and social agenda broad enough to unify the North. Republicans did not back away from antislavery, but they did soften its expression. While recommitting themselves to stop-

ping the spread of slavery, they also denounced John Brown's raid as "among the gravest of crimes" and confirmed the security of slavery in the South. Republicans hoped that by denying that they were abolitionists they would blunt charges that a vote for the Republican Party was a vote for northern extremism and thus southern secession.

Republicans cast about for a moderate candidate to go with their evenhanded platform. The foremost Republican, William H. Seward, had enemies. His famous "higher law" doctrine and "irrepressible conflict" speech made conservatives shiver. Moreover, charges of corruption during his term as governor of New York jeopardized Republican plans to exploit the recent evidence of graft and bribery in the Buchanan administration. Several lesser-known Republicans, including Abraham Lincoln, set their sights on the nomination. Lincoln had not sat on his hands since bursting onto the national scene in 1858. A speaking tour through the Midwest and East demonstrated his clear purpose, good judgment, and solid Republican credentials. That, combined with his rock-solid reputation for integrity and his residence in Illinois, a crucial state, made him attractive to the party. Masterful maneuvering by Lincoln's managers converted his status as the second choice of many delegates into a majority on the third ballot. Defeated by Douglas in a state contest less than two years earlier, Lincoln now stood ready to take Douglas on for the presidency.

The election of 1860 was like none other in American politics. It took place in the midst of the nation's severest crisis. Moreover, four major candidates crowded the presidential field. Rather than a four-cornered contest, however, the election broke into two contests, each with two candidates. In the North, Lincoln faced Douglas, and in the South, Breckinridge confronted Bell. Southerners did not even permit Lincoln's name to appear on the ballot in ten of the fifteen slave states, so outrageous did they consider the Republican Party. After John Brown, the name "Republican" conjured up well poisoners, arsonists, and men who passed out pikes to slaves. Northerners were wrapped in myths of their own. They dismissed the threats of secession as so much bluster, "the old game of scaring and bullying the North into submission to Southern demands and Southern tyranny." Like the boy who cried wolf, fire-eaters had lost their credibility.

An unprecedented number of voters cast ballots on November 6, 1860. Approximately 82 per-

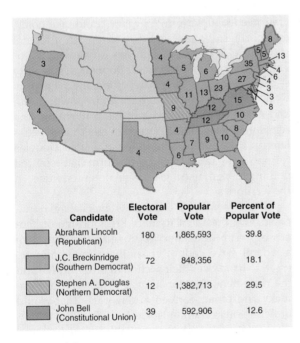

Candidate	Electoral Vote	Popular Vote	Percent of Popular Vote
Abraham Lincoln (Republican)	180	1,865,593	39.8
J.C. Breckinridge (Southern Democrat)	72	848,356	18.1
Stephen A. Douglas (Northern Democrat)	12	1,382,713	29.5
John Bell (Constitutional Union)	39	592,906	12.6

MAP 14.5
The Election of 1860

ABRAHAM LINCOLN

Lincoln actively sought the Republican presidential nomination in 1860. When in New York City to give a political address, he had his photograph taken by Mathew Brady. "While I was there I was taken to one of the places where they get up such things," Lincoln explained, sounding more innocent than he was, "and I suppose they got my shaddow, and can multiply copies indefinitely." Multiply they did. Copies of the dignified photograph of Lincoln soon replaced the less flattering drawings. Later, Lincoln credited his victory to his New York speech and to Mathew Brady.

The Lincoln Museum, Fort Wayne, Indiana. Photo: #0-17; drawing: #2024.

cent of eligible northern men and nearly 70 percent of eligible southern men went to the polls. The Republican platform succeeded in attracting a broad coalition of northern interests, and Lincoln swept all of the eighteen free states except New Jersey, which split its votes between him and Douglas. While Lincoln received only 39 percent of the popular vote, he won easily in the electoral balloting, gaining 180 votes, 28 more than he needed for victory. Douglas came in second in the popular voting, but carried only Missouri. Breckinridge was third and Bell fourth in the popular voting. Lincoln did not win simply because his opposition was splintered. Even if the votes of his three opponents were combined, Lincoln would still have won. Ominously, however, Breckinridge, running on a southern-rights platform, won the entire Lower South plus Delaware, Maryland, and North Carolina. Two fully sectionalized parties swept their regions, but the northern one won the presidency.

Lincoln did not receive a single electoral vote south of the Mason-Dixon line and had sought none. The Republican platform did not reflect the give-and-take that characterized bisectional parties.

Now, Southerners reasoned, one party, hostile to the South's interests, could make decisions about slavery. A vote for Breckinridge was definitely a vote for southern rights, but what precisely did that mean now that the Republicans had won? Not much, answered most Northerners. "The people of the South have too much sense," Lincoln said, "to attempt the ruin of the government." A different answer was emerging in the South. Polarization was almost complete.

Secession Winter

The telegraphs had barely stopped tapping out the news of Lincoln's victory when anxious Southerners began reappraising the value of the Union. Although Breckinridge had carried the South, a vote for "southern rights" was not necessarily a vote for secession. In fact, Breckinridge steadfastly denied that he was a secession candidate. Besides, slightly more than half of the Southerners who voted cast ballots for Douglas and Bell, two stout defenders of the Union. During the winter of 1860–61, Southerners debated what to do.

Southern Unionists tried to calm the fears that Lincoln's election triggered. Let the dust settle, they pleaded, and then proceed deliberately. Extremists in both sections, they argued, had created the crisis. "Abolitionists and the Nullifiers were uniting to destroy the Union," a Louisiana planter shouted. "Webster and Clay are gone," another complained, "and God has given us over to fools and mad men." Former Congressman Alexander Stephens of Georgia eloquently defended the Union. He asked what Lincoln had done to justify something as extreme as secession. Hadn't he promised to respect slavery where it existed? In Stephens's judgment, the fire-eaters' cure would be worse than the Republican disease. Secession jeopardized the very society it intended to preserve. It might lead to war, he said, which would loosen the hinges of southern society, possibly even open the door to slave insurrection or a revolt by nonslaveholding whites. "Revolutions are much easier started than controlled," Stephens warned. "I consider slavery much more secure in the Union than out of it."

Secessionists emphasized the urgency of the moment and the dangers of delay. No Southerner should mistake Republican intentions, they argued. "Mr. Lincoln and his party assert that this doctrine of equality applies to the negro," Howell Cobb of Georgia asserted, "and necessarily there can exist no such thing as property in our equals." The South's minority status made it helpless to defend slavery within the Union. Why wait for Lincoln to appoint Republican judges, marshals, customs collectors, and postmasters everywhere in the South? Each one would become an abolitionist emissary spreading dangerous ideas among blacks and attempting to turn nonslaveholding whites against slaveholders. As for war, there would be none. The Union was a voluntary compact, and coerced patriotism was alien to America. If Northerners did resist secession with force, the conflict would be brief, for one southern woodsman could whip five of Lincoln's greasy mechanics.

For all their differences, southern whites were generally united in their determination to defend slavery, to take slave property into the territories, and to squeeze from Northerners an admission that they were good and decent people. They disagreed about whether the mere presence of a Republican in the White House made it necessary to exercise what they considered a legitimate right to secede.

> *For all their differences, southern whites were generally united in their determination to defend slavery, to take slave property into the territories, and to squeeze from Northerners an admission that they were good and decent people.*

The debate about what to do was briefest in South Carolina. Always on the front lines of southern radicalism, it seceded from the Union on December 20, 1860. By February, the six other Deep South states marched in South Carolina's footsteps. Only South Carolinians voted overwhelmingly in favor of secession, however. Elsewhere, the vote was close; in Georgia it was so close that the anti-secessionists may actually have won. In general, the South's plain folks, the nonslaveholding inhabitants of the pine barrens and mountain counties, displayed the greatest attachment to the Union. Slaveholders spearheaded secession. On February 4, 1861, representatives from South Carolina, Georgia, Florida, Alabama, Mississippi, Louisiana, and Texas met in Montgomery, Alabama, where three days later they celebrated the birth of the Confederate States of America. Jefferson Davis became president

"THE UNION IS DISSOLVED!"
On December 20, 1860, the Charleston Mercury *put out this special edition of the paper to celebrate South Carolina's secession from the Union. Six weeks earlier, upon hearing the news that Lincoln had won the presidency, it had predicted as much. "The tea has been thrown overboard," the* Mercury *announced. "The revolution of 1860 has been initiated."*
Chicago Historical Society.

and Alexander Stephens, who had spoken so eloquently about the dangers of revolution, became vice president.

Lincoln's election had split the Union. Now secession split the South. Seven slave states seceded during the winter, but eight did not. Citizens of the

Upper South debated just as furiously whether the South could defend itself better inside or outside the Union, but they came down on the other side, at least for the moment. The fact was that the Upper South had a smaller stake in slavery. Only about half as many white families in the Upper South held slaves (21 percent) as did those in the Lower South (37 percent). Slaves represented twice as large a fraction of the population in the Lower South (48 percent) as in the Upper South (23 percent). Consequently, whites in the Upper South had fewer fears that Republican ascendancy meant economic catastrophe, racial war, and social chaos. Lincoln would have to do more than just be elected to provoke them into disunion.

The nation had to wait until March 4, 1861, to see what Lincoln would do. ("Lame duck" presidents survived for four months before the Twentieth Amendment to the Constitution shifted the inauguration forward to January 20.) Throughout the winter, while Southerners debated the fate of the Union, President-elect Lincoln watched from Springfield. President James Buchanan watched from Washington. Buchanan took a position that was quite at odds with the one that President Andrew Jackson had adopted when he had faced down a secession crisis a generation earlier. Buchanan firmly denied the constitutionality of secession but also denied that he had power to resist it. William H. Seward lampooned the president's strange reasoning. Buchanan demonstrated, Seward declared, that "no state has the right to secede unless it wishes to" and that "it is the President's duty to enforce the laws, unless somebody opposes him." Without leadership from the White House, the search for a peace-saving compromise shifted to Congress.

Appropriately, the task fell to Henry Clay's successor as senator from Kentucky, John J. Crittenden. To allay southern fears, his Senate committee hastily recommended a series of constitutional amendments, the most important of which revived the Missouri Compromise. Slavery would be prohibited in territories north of 36°30' and protected south of it. Northern responses ranged from enthusiasm to ridicule. Lincoln, in private communications, counseled standing firm on Republican principles. The Crittenden compromise, he said, "acknowledges that slavery has equal rights with liberty" in the territories and thus "surrenders all we have contended for." Republicans blocked the measure, but the Confederate states showed little interest in the proposal in any case. People in those states no longer focused on the territorial issue. Since the election of a Republican president, they had independence on their minds.

Finally, Lincoln arrived in Washington, forced to sneak in at night because of an assassination plot. His entrance did nothing to build confidence in a nation that doubted that this odd-looking man with almost no national political experience would be up to the task before him. The frantic search for a sectional compromise had failed. Virginia's last-minute effort to call a peace conference in Washington had not seemed promising enough to the Lower South to send delegates. The Confederate States of America acted as if it were independent and assumed that the price of secession would be censure, nothing more.

In his inaugural address, Lincoln sought to enunciate his policy. He began with reassurances to the South. He had "no lawful right" to interfere with slavery where it existed, he said again and, for emphasis, added that he had "no inclination to do so." There would be "no invasion—no using of force against or among the people anywhere." In filling federal posts, he would not "force obnoxious strangers" on the South. Conciliatory toward Southerners, he proved inflexible about the Union. The Union, he declared, is "perpetual." Secession was "anarchy" and "legally void." The Constitution required him to execute the law "in all the States." He would hold federal property, collect federal duties, and deliver the mails.

The decision for civil war or peace rested in the South's hands, he said. "You can have no conflict, without being yourselves the aggressors. *You* have no oath registered in Heaven to destroy the government, while *I* shall have the most solemn one to 'preserve, protect, and defend' it." What Southerners in Charleston held in their hands at that very moment were the cords for firing the cannons that they aimed at the federal garrison at Fort Sumter.

Conclusion: The Failure of Compromise

Northerners and Southerners had clashed as early as the writing of the Constitution. As their economies, societies, and cultures diverged in the nineteenth century, friction increased. But sectionalism shifted into a new gear in 1846 when David Wilmot proposed banning slavery in any Mexican territory won in the war. "As if by magic," a Boston newspaper observed, "it brought to a head the great question that is about to divide the American people." During the extended crisis of the Union that stretched from 1846 to 1861, the nation's attention fixed on the expansion of slavery. But from the beginning, both Northerners and Southerners recognized that the controversy had less to do with the expansion of slavery than with the future of slavery in America. The territories, then, were "merely the skirmish line of a larger and more fundamental conflict."

Lincoln doubted that the nation could endure "permanently half slave and half free." But for more than seventy years, imaginative statesmen had found compromises that, while making no improvement in the condition of millions of slaves in the South, did preserve the Union. Citizens on both sides of the Mason-Dixon line took enormous pride in the national experiment in republican democracy, and few gave up the experiment easily. But accommodation and adjustment had limits. Whites in the Deep South took Lincoln's election in 1860 as a signal that slavery and the society they had built on it were at risk in the Union, and they left. In his inaugural, Lincoln pleaded, "We are not enemies but friends. We must not be enemies." But by then, the Deep South had ceased to sing what he called "the chorus of the Union." It remained to be seen whether disunion would mean war.

CHRONOLOGY

1846 Wilmot Proviso proposes barring slavery from all lands acquired in Mexican War.

1847 John C. Calhoun challenges Wilmot Proviso on constitutional grounds, stating that Congress has no power to exclude slavery from the nation's territories.

Senator Lewis Cass offers compromise of "popular sovereignty," allowing people of territories to determine the fate of slavery.

1848 Opponents of expansion of slavery found Free-Soil Party.

General Zachary Taylor, Whig, elected president of United States, defeating Democrat Lewis Cass and Free-Soil candidate Martin Van Buren.

1850s Vigilance committees in North challenge and sometimes thwart Fugitive Slave Act.

1850 **July 9.** President Zachary Taylor dies; succeeded by Vice President Millard Fillmore.

Senator Henry Clay proposes Omnibus Bill to avert territorial crisis over slavery; bill ultimately defeated.

Senator Stephen Douglas's compromise bills (Compromise of 1850) pass Congress, signed into law by President Fillmore.

1852 Harriet Beecher Stowe's *Uncle Tom's Cabin* published.

Democrat Franklin Pierce elected president of United States, defeating Whig Winfield Scott.

1853 Gadsden Purchase adds 45,000 square miles of territory in present-day Arizona and New Mexico.

1854 American Party (Know-Nothings) emerges, advocating nativist positions.

Kansas-Nebraska Act opens the Kansas and Nebraska Territories to popular sovereignty.

Republican Party emerges on platform opposing extension of slavery in territories.

1856 Armed conflict between proslavery and antislavery forces erupts in Kansas.

Preston Brooks of South Carolina brutally assaults Charles Sumner of Massachusetts on Senate floor.

Democrat James Buchanan elected president of United States, defeating Republican John C. Frémont.

1857 *Dred Scott* decision declares that African Americans have no constitutional rights, that Congress cannot exclude slavery in the territories, and that the Missouri Compromise is unconstitutional.

Nation experiences economic downturn, panic of 1857.

1858 In Illinois senatorial campaign, Abraham Lincoln and Stephen A. Douglas debate slavery; Douglas defeats Lincoln for the Senate seat.

1859 **October 16.** John Brown's attempt to foment slave uprising in Harpers Ferry, Virginia, further alienates South and moves nation toward war.

1860 Republican Abraham Lincoln elected president in four-way race that divides electorate along sectional lines.

December 20. South Carolina secedes from Union.

1861 Representatives of seven southern states, meeting in Montgomery, Alabama, form Confederate States of America.

BIBLIOGRAPHY

GENERAL WORKS

Eric Foner, *Politics and Ideology in the Age of the Civil War* (1980).

William W. Freehling, *The Road to Disunion* (1990).

Bruce Levine, *Half Slave and Half Free: The Roots of Civil War* (1992).

James M. McPherson, *Ordeal by Fire: The Civil War and Reconstruction* (1982).

James M. McPherson, *Battle Cry of Freedom: The Civil War Era* (1988).

Allan Nevins, *Ordeal of the Union*, 2 vols. (1947).

Allan Nevins, *The Emergence of Lincoln*, 2 vols. (1950).

Roy F. Nichols, *Disruption of American Democracy* (1949).

David M. Potter, *The Impending Crisis, 1848–1861* (1976).

Richard H. Sewell, *A House Divided: Sectionalism and Civil War, 1848–1865* (1988).

Kenneth M. Stampp, *The Imperiled Union: Essays on the Background of the Civil War* (1980).

Kenneth M. Stampp, ed., *The Causes of the Civil War* (rev. ed., 1991).

Mark W. Summers, *The Plundering Generation: Corruption and the Crisis of the Union, 1849–1861* (1987).

SLAVERY IN THE TERRITORIES

Irving H. Bartlett, *Daniel Webster and the Trial of American Nationalism, 1843–1852* (1972).

Paul B. Bergeron, *The Presidency of James K. Polk* (1987).

Eugene H. Berwanger, *The Frontier against Slavery: Western Anti-Negro Prejudice and the Slavery Extension Controversy* (1967).

Charles H. Brown, *Agents for Manifest Destiny: The Lives and Times of the Filibusterers* (1979).

Don E. Fehrenbacher, *The Dred Scott Case: Its Significance in American Law and Politics* (1978).

Paul Finkelman, *An Imperfect Union: Slavery, Federalism, and Comity* (1981).

Holman Hamilton, *Prologue to Conflict: The Crisis and Compromise of 1850* (1964).

Michael F. Holt, *The Political Crisis of the 1850s* (1978).

Robert W. Johannsen, *Stephen A. Douglas* (1973).

Frederick Merk, *Slavery and the Annexation of Texas* (1972).

Chaplain W. Morrison, *Democratic Politics and Sectionalism: The Wilmot Proviso Controversy* (1967).

James Oakes, *Slavery and Freedom: An Interpretation of the Old South* (1990).

James A. Rawley, *Race and Politics: "Bleeding Kansas" and the Coming of the Civil War* (1969).

Joseph G. Rayback, *Free Soil: The Election of 1848* (1970).

Kenneth Stampp, *America in 1857: A Nation on the Brink* (1990).

Gerald W. Wolff, *The Kansas-Nebraska Bill: Party, Section, and the Coming of the Civil War* (1977).

NORTHERN SECTIONALISM

Richard H. Abbott, *Cotton and Capital: Boston Businessmen and Antislavery Reform, 1854–1868* (1991).

Tyler Anbinder, *Nativism and Slavery: The Northern Know Nothings and the Politics of the 1850s* (1992).

R. J. M. Blackett, *Building an Antislavery Wall: Black Americans in the Atlantic Abolitionist Movement, 1830–1860* (1983).

Frederick Blue, *The Free Soilers: Third Party Politics, 1848–1854* (1973).

Stanley W. Campbell, *The Slave Catchers: Enforcement of the Fugitive Slave Law, 1850–1860* (1970).

Merton L. Dillon, *The Abolitionists: The Growth of a Dissenting Minority* (1974).

David H. Donald, *Charles Sumner and the Coming of the Civil War* (1960).

Robert R. Dykstra, *Bright Radical Star: Black Freedom and White Supremacy on the Hawkeye Frontier* (1993).

Don E. Fehrenbacher, *Prelude to Greatness: Lincoln in the 1850s* (1962).

Eric Foner, *Free Soil, Free Labor, Free Men: The Ideology of the Republican Party before the Civil War* (1970).

Ronald P. Formisano, *The Birth of Mass Political Parties: Michigan, 1827–1861* (1971).

William E. Gienapp, *The Origins of the Republican Party, 1852–1856* (1987).

Len Gougeon, *Virtue's Hero: Emerson, Antislavery, and Reform* (1990).

Michael F. Holt, *Forging a Majority: The Formation of the Republican Party in Pittsburgh, 1848–1860* (1969).

Harry V. Jaffa, *Crisis of the House Divided: An Interpretation of the Lincoln-Douglas Debates* (1959).

Robert W. Johannsen, *Lincoln, the South, and Slavery: The Political Dimension* (1991).

Bruce Levine, *The Spirit of 1848: German Immigrants, Labor Conflict, and the Coming of the Civil War* (1992).

William S. McFeely, *Frederick Douglass* (1991).

Thomas D. Morris, *Free Men All: The Personal Liberty Laws of the North, 1780–1861* (1974).

Stephen B. Oates, *To Purge This Land with Blood: A Biography of John Brown* (1970).

Thomas H. O'Connor, *Lords of the Loom: The Cotton Whigs and the Coming of the Civil War* (1968).

Lewis Perry and Michael Fellman, eds., *Antislavery Reconsidered: New Perspectives on the Abolitionists* (1979).

Benjamin Quarles, *Allies for Freedom: Blacks and John Brown* (1974).

James P. Rawley, *Race and Politics: "Bleeding Kansas" and the Coming of the Civil War* (1969).

Anne C. Rose, *Victorian America and the Civil War* (1992).

Louis Ruchames, ed., *John Brown: The Making of a Revolutionary* (1959).

Richard H. Sewell, *Ballots for Freedom: Antislavery Politics in the United States, 1837–1860* (1976).

Thomas P. Slaughter, *Bloody Dawn: The Christiana Riot and Racial Violence in the Antebellum North* (1991).

James Brewer Stewart, *Joshua R. Giddings and the Tactics of Radical Politics* (1970).

James Brewer Stewart, *Holy Warriors: The Abolitionists and American Slavery* (1976).

James Brewer Stewart, *Wendell Phillips: Liberty's Hero* (1986).

Hans L. Trefousse, *The Radical Republicans: Lincoln's Vanguard for Racial Justice* (1969).

Wendy Hamand Venet, *Neither Ballots nor Bullets: Women Abolitionists and the Civil War* (1991).

Ronald G. Walters, *The Antislavery Appeal: American Abolitionism after 1830* (1976).

David Zarefsky, *Lincoln, Douglas, and Slavery: In the Crucible of Public Debate* (1990).

SOUTHERN SECTIONALISM

William L. Barney, *The Road to Secession: A New Perspective on the Old South* (1972).

John Barnwell, *Love of Order: South Carolina's First Secession Crisis* (1982).

Irving H. Bartlett, *John C. Calhoun: A Biography* (1993).

William J. Cooper Jr., *The South and the Politics of Slavery, 1828–1856* (1978).

Avery O. Craven, *The Growth of Southern Nationalism, 1848–1861* (1953).

Drew G. Faust, *James Henry Hammond and the Old South: A Design for Mastery* (1982).

Don E. Fehrenbacher, *The South and Three Sectional Crises* (1980).

Lacy K. Ford Jr., *Origins of Southern Radicalism: The South Carolina Upcountry, 1800–1860* (1988).

Thelma Jennings, *The Nashville Convention: Southern Movement for Unity, 1848–1851* (1980).

Vicki Vaughn Johnson, *The Men and the Vision of the Southern Commercial Conventions, 1845–1871* (1992).

John McCardell, *The Idea of a Southern Nation: Southern Nationalists and Southern Nationalism, 1830–1860* (1979).

John Niven, *John C. Calhoun and the Price of Union* (1988).

David M. Potter, *The South and the Sectional Conflict* (1969).

Ronald T. Takaki, *A Pro-Slavery Crusade: The Agitation to Reopen the African Slave Trade* (1971).

J. Mills Thornton III, *Politics and Power in a Slave Society: Alabama, 1800–1860* (1978).

Eric E. Walther, *The Fire-Eaters* (1992).

John M. Wiltse, *John C. Calhoun: Sectionalist, 1840–1850* (1951).

SECESSION

William L. Barney, *The Secessionist Impulse: Alabama and Mississippi in 1860* (1974).

Walter L. Buenger, *Secession and the Union in Texas* (1984).

Steven A. Channing, *Crisis of Fear: Secession in South Carolina* (1970).

Daniel W. Crofts, *Reluctant Confederates: Upper South Unionists in the Secession Crisis* (1989).

Dwight L. Dumond, *The Secession Movement, 1860–1861* (1931).

William J. Evitts, *A Matter of Allegiances: Maryland from 1850 to 1861* (1962).

John Hope Franklin, *The Militant South* (1956).

James L. Huston, *The Panic of 1857 and the Coming of the Civil War* (1987).

Michael P. Johnson, *Toward a Patriarchal Republic: The Secession of Georgia* (1977).

David M. Potter, *Lincoln and His Party in the Secession Crisis* (1942).

Kenneth M. Stampp, *And the War Came: The North and the Secession Crisis, 1860–61* (1960).

James M. Woods, *Rebellion and Realignment: Arkansas's Road to Secession* (1987).

Ralph A. Wooster, *The Secession Conventions of the South* (1962).

DAGUERREOTYPE OF DRUMMER BOY OF SHILOH

The Civil War is often called a "brother's war." Families sometimes split and offered up sol-
diers for both the Union and the Confederate armies. But the war was also a children's war, as
this daguerreotype of the twelve-year-old John Clem, a drummer boy at the battle of Shiloh,
reminds us. Beneath the lofty rhetoric of God and glory lay the heartbreak of youth destroyed
and innocence lost.

Library of Congress.

THE CRUCIBLE OF WAR

15

1861–1865

I N 1838, A TWENTY-YEAR-OLD MARYLAND SLAVE by the name of Frederick Bailey fled north to freedom. The young runaway took a new name, Frederick Douglass, and might understandably have settled into obscurity, content just to avoid the slave catchers and to live quietly as a free man. Instead, he chose to wage war against slavery. An agent for the Massachusetts Anti-Slavery Society observed in 1841 that "the public have itching ears to hear a colored man speak, and particularly a *slave*." Dozens of fugitive slaves brought to northern audiences the authority of hard personal experience. None stripped away the myth of the contented slave more eloquently than Frederick Douglass. In 1845, he published his immensely popular autobiography. In 1847, he began the *North Star*, an antislavery newspaper that reached thousands. Douglass's powerful denunciations of slavery and moving pleas for emancipation made him the most famous African American in the English-speaking world.

Publicly, Douglass remained optimistic. Throughout the 1840s and 1850s, he declared repeatedly that the nation was in the "seed time" of abolition and promised that the "harvest" would soon follow. Privately, however, Douglass thought that he labored in vain. In his eyes, his two decades of speaking and writing had brought the country no closer to ending slavery. In some ways the situation had grown worse. When Douglass fled slavery in 1838, two million Americans were slaves. By 1860, the number had grown to four million. Every step forward—the birth of the Republican Party, for instance—was followed by a giant step back—such as the *Dred Scott* decision. To Douglass, the 1850s ended as they began, no closer to the eradication of slavery. "How long! How long! O Lord God of Sabbath!" he cried, "shall the crushed and bleeding bondsman wait?"

During the secession winter of 1860–1861, Douglass found himself torn between hope and despair. Abraham Lincoln's election in November had revived his optimism. "The slaveholders know that the day of their power is over," Douglass exulted. But he realized that the Republican Party's free-soil principles fell short of abolition. Republicans opposed slavery's right to expand into the national territories, not slavery's right to exist in the South. Indeed, Douglass feared that the Republicans would become "the best protectors of slavery where it now is."

When news came from Charleston in April 1861 that Southerners had fired on the American flag, Douglass celebrated the outbreak of fighting. He cheered Lincoln's vow to maintain the Union. He realized, however, that in going to war "the North only strikes for government . . . against anarchy . . . for loyalty . . . against treason and rebellion." But much earlier than most, he understood that a war to save the Union would inevitably affect slavery. The South had initiated a "war for slavery," Douglass said, and it followed that a war to crush southern independence must become a war *against* slavery. Even though "the Government is not yet on the side of the oppressed, events mightier than the Government are bringing about that result," Douglass declared. *"Friends of freedom!"* he cried, *"be up and doing;—now is your time."*

Few Northerners, certainly not Abraham Lincoln, agreed that the outbreak of fighting marked the beginning of the end of slavery. For eighteen months, Northerners fought solely to uphold the Constitution and preserve the nation. The framers of the Constitution had dodged the question of whether sovereignty lay with the federal government or with the states. Incredibly, the nation existed for nearly three-quarters of a century without agreement about its fundamental nature. Although the nation achieved dazzling material success and physical growth, it fell short of unity and harmony. The political collision over slavery made it impossible to avoid the Constitution's ambiguity about the nature of the Union.

Even if the Civil War had not touched slavery, the war would still have transformed America. The carnage lasted four years and cost the nation 633,000 lives, nearly as many as in all of its other wars before and after. The war became a crucible that molded the modern American nation-state. The federal government emerged with new power and responsibility over national life. War furthered the emergence of a modern industrializing nation. But because the war to preserve the Union also became a war to destroy slavery, the northern victory had truly revolutionary meaning. Defeat and emancipation destroyed the slave society of the Old South and gave birth to a different society.

Years later, remembering the Civil War years, Douglass said, "It is something to couple one's name with great occasions." It *was* something—for millions of Americans. Great and terrible public events overtook private lives. Whether they battled or defended the Confederacy, whether they labored behind the lines to produce goods for northern or southern soldiers, whether they kept the home fires burning for Yankees or rebels, all Americans experienced the crucible of war. But the war affected no group more than the four million African Americans who began the war in 1861 as slaves and emerged in 1865 as free people.

FREDERICK DOUGLASS
The North's antebellum black community was avidly abolitionist. Like Frederick Douglass, however, black crusaders sometimes lost heart. "The time has gone by for colored people to talk of patriotism," Charles L. Remond said in the wake of the 1857 Dred Scott decision. "We owe no allegiance to a country which grinds us under its iron heel and treats us like dogs." Yet, like Douglass, the black community stayed the course and helped transform a war against rebellion into a war for freedom. This photograph taken about 1847 was given by Douglass to Susan B. Anthony.
Chester County Historical Society, West Chester, Pa.

"And the War Came"

For Abraham Lincoln the first few weeks in office were a nightmare. New to high office, he faced the worst crisis in the history of the nation. But what drove him nearly to distraction were the hordes of callers who besieged the White House. Diplomats, delegates, lobbyists, and most especially office seekers greedy for a share of the spoils of the Republican victory jammed Washington. In one hotel, three hundred men camped in the dining room, eager for a chance to see the president. It took weeks for Lincoln to dispense with the "vultures," as he called them, and to give himself fully to the grave national issue of disunion.

Lincoln revealed his strategy on March 4, 1861, in his inaugural address, which was carefully crafted to combine firmness with patience and conciliation. First, he would try to stop the contagion of secession. Eight slave states had said no to disunion, but they remained suspicious and skittish. Lincoln was determined to do nothing that would push the Upper South (North Carolina, Virginia, Maryland, Delaware, Kentucky, Tennessee, Missouri, and Arkansas) into leaving. Second, he would buy time so that emotions could cool. By reassuring the Deep South (South Carolina, Georgia, Florida, Alabama, Mississippi, Louisiana, and Texas) about the safety of slavery, he would provide Unionists there the opportunity to reassert themselves and to overturn the secession decision. Always, Lincoln expressed his uncompromising will to oppose secession and to uphold the Union.

His counterpart, Jefferson Davis, fully intended to establish the Confederate States of America as a permanent independent republic. To achieve permanence, he had to sustain the secession fever that had carried the Deep South out of the Union and to dampen reunion sentiment among antisecession elements. Even if the Deep South held firm, however, the Confederacy remained weak without additional states from the Upper South. Davis watched for opportunities to add new stars to the Confederate flag.

Neither man sought war. Both wanted to achieve their objectives peacefully. But as Lincoln later observed, "Both parties deprecated war, but one of them would *make* war rather than let the nation survive, and the other would *accept* war rather than let it perish. And the war came."

The Surrender of Fort Sumter

Fort Sumter's thick brick walls rose forty feet above the tiny island on which it perched at the entrance to Charleston harbor. Only four miles from the city, the fortress could easily be seen by strollers who took the air at the water's edge each evening. The sight infuriated good Confederates. Major Robert Anderson and some eighty U.S. soldiers occupied what Charlestonians claimed as Confederate property. The fort became a hateful symbol of the nation they had abandoned, and Southerners wanted federal troops out. But Sumter was also a symbol to Northerners, a beacon affirming federal sovereignty in the seceded states. Even President James Buchanan had understood its value. In January

1861, with uncharacteristic energy and firmness, he dispatched an unarmed merchant vessel, the *Star of the West*, to carry two hundred additional troops and provisions to the undermanned and ill-supplied federal garrison. Shots from South Carolina artillery drove the ship away before it could deliver its cargo. When Lincoln entered the White House in March, the soldiers in the fort were running dangerously short of food.

Always, Lincoln expressed his uncompromising will to oppose secession and to uphold the Union.

The situation at Fort Sumter presented Lincoln with hard choices. Without fresh supplies, Anderson would soon be starved out. Lincoln could order the fort's evacuation. That would play well in the Upper South, whose edgy slave states threatened to bolt to the Confederacy if Lincoln resorted to military force. But yielding the fort would make it appear that Lincoln accepted the Confederacy's existence. Abandonment would divide the North, batter the new Republican administration, and magnify the rebel nation's status in the eyes of the world. Lincoln decided to hold Fort Sumter. In the first week in April, he authorized a peaceful expedition to bring supplies, but not military reinforcements, to the fort. Lincoln understood that in seeking to relieve the fort he risked war. But his plan honored his inaugural promises to defend federal property and to avoid using military force unless first attacked. Masterfully, Lincoln had shifted the fateful decision of war or peace to Jefferson Davis.

On April 9, 1861, Jefferson Davis and his cabinet met to consider the situation in Charleston harbor. The territorial integrity of the Confederacy demanded the end of the federal presence, Davis argued. But his secretary of state, Robert Toombs of Georgia, pleaded against military action. "Mr. President," he declared, "at this time it is suicide, murder, and will lose us every friend at the North. You will wantonly strike a hornet's nest which extends from mountain to ocean, and legions now quiet will swarm out and sting us to death." President Davis rejected Toombs's prophecy and sent word to General Pierre Gustave T. Beauregard, the Louisianan commanding Confederate troops in Charleston, to take the fort before the relief expedition arrived. When Anderson refused Beauregard's demand to evacuate, southern cannon commenced firing.

Thirty-three hours of bombardment reduced the fort to rubble, but, miraculously, the four thousand Confederate artillery rounds did not take the life of a single Union soldier. On April 14, with the fort ablaze, Anderson offered his surrender. The Confederates had Fort Sumter, but they also had a war.

The response of the free states was thunderous. When Lincoln called for 75,000 troops to put down the rebellion, several times that many rushed to defend the flag. Lincoln asked Indiana for six regiments, and the governor wired that "without seriously repressing the ardor of the people, I can hardly stop short of twenty." A Harvard professor observed that the "whole population, men, women, and children, seem to be in the streets with Union favors and flags." Democrats responded as fervently as Republicans. Stephen A. Douglas, the recently defeated Democratic candidate for president, hurried to the White House to pledge his support. "There are only two sides to the question," he told a massive crowd in Chicago. "Every man must be for the United States or against it. There can be no neutrals in this war, *only patriots—or traitors.*" No one faced more acutely the issue of loyalty than the men and women of the Upper South.

The Upper South Chooses Sides

Lincoln's election in November 1860 had not dislodged a single one of the eight slave states in the Upper South from the Union. Throughout the winter, whites there denied that the seven seceding cotton states had sufficient cause to leave. A Tennessee man believed that secession would boomerang. It was both "unwise and impolitic," he said, and would likely bring about the "ruin and overthrow of negro slavery" and jeopardize the "freedom and liberty of the white men." But Unionism in the Upper South often came with conditions. Many antisecessionists made it clear that if the federal government resorted to military force to hold the Lower South in the Union, they would jump to the Confederate camp. In his inaugural, Lincoln had promised to maintain the Union without "bloodshed or violence . . . unless it be forced upon the national authority." Now, even though the Confederates fired first, Lincoln's call for troops confronted the Upper South with a horrendous choice: either to fight against the Lower South or to fight against the North.

Many who had only months earlier rejected secession now embraced the Confederacy. To oppose southern independence was one thing, to fight fellow Southerners was another. Thousands felt betrayed, believing that Lincoln had promised to achieve reunion peacefully by waiting patiently for Unionists to reassert themselves in the seceding states. One man furiously denounced the conflict as a "politician's war" but conceded that "this is no time now to discuss the causes, but it is the duty of all who regard Southern institutions of value to side with the South, make common cause with the Confederate States and sink or swim with them."

Some found the choice excruciating. Robert E. Lee, a career military officer and the son of one of Virginia's oldest families, observed the crisis with accelerating horror. Neither a defender of slavery nor a supporter of secession, he denounced separation as the work of cotton state hotheads. "I can anticipate no greater calamity for the country than a dissolution of the Union," he told his son in January 1861. Still, he said, "a Union that can only be maintained by swords and bayonets . . . has no charm for me." Following the bombardment of Fort Sumter, Lee was summoned from his white-columned mansion in Arlington, Virginia, to the nation's capital, where he was offered command of federal military forces. But Lee could not fight against the South. When he returned home, he learned that Virginia had left the Union. He quickly penned his resignation from the United States army and declared, "Save in defense of my native State, I never desire again to draw my sword." His beloved Virginia offered no sanctuary for his tortured allegiances. Richmond would soon be the capital of the Confederacy, Virginia would be a battleground, and Lee would again command military forces.

One by one the other states of the Upper South jumped off the fence. Within weeks, Arkansas, North Carolina, and Tennessee followed Virginia's lead. But in the border states of Delaware, Maryland, Kentucky, and Missouri, Unionism triumphed. Only in Delaware, where slaves accounted for less than 2 percent of the population, was the victory easy. In Maryland, Unionism needed a helping hand. Rather than allow the state to secede (and make Washington, D.C., a federal island in a Confederate sea), Lincoln suspended the writ of habeas corpus, essentially establishing martial law and setting aside normal constitutional guarantees such as trial before a jury of peers, and marched troops into Baltimore. Maryland's legislature, frightened by the federal invasion and aware of the strength of Union sentiment in the western counties, rejected secession.

The struggle turned violent in the West. In Missouri, the proslavery Democratic governor and the

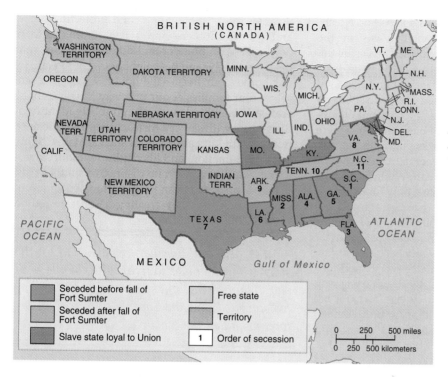

MAP 15.1
Secession
After Lincoln's election, the fifteen slave states debated what to do. Seven states quickly left the Union, four left after the firing on Fort Sumter, and four refused to go.

state legislature attempted to deliver their state to Jefferson Davis, only to be blocked by a state convention that rejected secession. Even though Unionists won, southern-sympathizing guerrilla bands roamed the state for the duration of the conflict, waging bloody war on civilians and soldiers alike. In Kentucky, Unionists narrowly defeated secession, but, as in Missouri, a prosouthern minority claimed that the state had severed its ties with the Union. The Richmond government, not particularly fastidious in counting votes, eagerly made Missouri and Kentucky the twelfth and thirteenth Confederate states. Throughout the border states, but especially in Kentucky, the Civil War was truly a "brother's war." Seven of Henry Clay's grandsons fought in the Civil War: four for the Confederacy and three for the Union.

Lincoln understood that the border states—particularly Kentucky—contained indispensable resources, population, and wealth, and they controlled major rivers and railroads. "I think to lose Kentucky is nearly the same as to lose the whole game," Lincoln said. "Kentucky gone, we can not hold Missouri, nor, as I think, Maryland. These all against us, and the job on our hands is too large for us. We would as well consent to separation at once." Although Kentucky and Missouri rejected secession, they were not securely in the Union fold. The

North could lose them through military defeat or by adopting policies that people in those states considered injurious to their interests. No interest was touchier than slavery, and skeptical inhabitants of the border states adopted a wait-and-see attitude.

Neither Lincoln's election nor the bombardment of Fort Sumter united the South. In the end, only eleven of the fifteen slave states joined the Confederate States of America. Moreover, the four seceding Upper South states contained significant populations that felt little affection for the Confederacy. Dissatisfaction was so rife in the western counties of Virginia that citizens there voted to create the separate state of West Virginia in 1863 and to remain loyal to the Union. Still, the acquisition of four new Confederate states greatly strengthened the cause of southern independence.

The Combatants

The outbreak of fighting ended drift and indecision. Although fierce struggle continued in the border states and in some areas within the seceding states of the Upper South, most whites in the South chose to defend the Confederacy. For them, Yankee "aggression" was no longer a secessionist's abstraction;

it was real, and it was at their doors. For Northerners, rebel "treason" threatened to destroy the noble experiment of republican self-government. Men rallied behind their separate battle flags, fully convinced that they were in the right and that God was on their side. Passion often overrode sober reflection in the early months of the war, but all citizens had to answer for themselves what they were fighting for and what they were fighting against.

Northerners and Southerners also had to consider what they had to fight with. While both sides claimed the lion's share of virtue, only fools argued that the South's resources and forces equaled the North's. The briefest glance at the census figures contradicted such a notion. Yankees took heart at their superior power, but the rebels believed they had advantages that nullified every northern strength. Both sides mobilized swiftly in the spring and summer of 1861, and each devised what it believed would be a winning military and diplomatic strategy.

What They Fought For

Across the South, planters, yeomen, and artisans raced to enlist and to fight Yankees. Contemporary Northerners were puzzled by the willingness of ordinary whites to fight to preserve slavery, which Alexander Stephens, vice president of the Confederacy, identified as the new nation's "cornerstone." Why should poor men who owned no slaves be willing to die to ensure that rich men could keep theirs?

Only slaveholders, of course, had a direct economic stake (estimated at some $3 billion in 1860) in preserving slavery. But all white Southerners—slaveholders and nonslaveholders alike—united in the defense of slavery. Slavery controlled blacks, whom they thought an inferior and potentially dangerous race. Moreover, the degraded and subjugated status of blacks was the basis of an elevated status for even the most humble whites. "It matters not whether slaves be actually owned by many or by few," one observer declared. "It is enough that one simply belongs to the superior and ruling race, to secure consideration and respect." Ordinary and elite whites understood the Mississippian who announced that he would rather "be exterminated" than be forced to live in the same society "with the slaves if freed."

Ordinary whites, however, did not explicitly name slavery as their reason for fighting. Instead, they emphasized defending a special southern civilization from "subjugation" and protecting hearth and home, mothers and wives, from northern hordes bent on plunder and domination. One man declared that he and his neighbors went to war "for our homes, our lives—the honor & safety of ourselves, our families & our property." Even Confederate officials shied away from publicly identifying their cause with slavery. Instead, their rhetoric overflowed with lofty abstractions such as states' rights, self-determination, and liberty. But without slavery there would have been no distinctive southern civilization, no Republican Party to threaten it, and no reason to ensure it by creating a separate nation.

> *Northerners and Southerners also had to consider what they had to fight with. While both sides claimed the lion's share of virtue, only fools argued that the South's resources and forces equaled the North's.*

In 1861, white Southerners equated their position with that of American patriots in 1776. In both cases, they argued, a freedom-loving minority waged war to protect its liberty against the encroachments of a tyrannical central government. As one Georgia woman observed, Southerners wanted "nothing from the North but—*to be let alone*—and *they*, a people like ourselves whose republican independence was won by a rebellion, whose liberty was achieved by a secession, to think that they should attempt to coerce us—the idea is preposterous."

Northerners saw secession as an unconscionable attack on the best government on the face of the earth. The South's failure to accept the lawful election of a president and its firing on the nation's flag challenged the rule of law, the authority of the Constitution, and the ability of the people to govern themselves. Northerners believed that the South's effort to wreck the Republic threatened them in a very personal way. As an Indiana soldier told his wife, a "good government is the best thing on earth. Property is nothing without it, because it is not protected; a family is nothing without it, because they cannot be educated."

Lincoln captured the Union's special magnetism. "This is essentially a People's contest," he declared on the first Fourth of July after the war began. The Union's cause, he said, was the preservation of the government "whose leading object is, to elevate the condition of man—to lift artificial weights from all shoulders—to clear the paths of laudable pursuit for all—to afford all, an unfettered start, and a fair chance, in the race of life." In short, secession menaced the life chances of millions of eager and aspiring individuals. That is why Northerners were not willing to allow the South to go in peace. Too much was at stake. In villages, towns, and cities across the North, self-interest, as well as patriotic fervor, welded individuals to the preservation of the nation. That steel-like bond sustained men and women through four years of war.

How They Expected to Win

The balance sheet of northern and southern resources reveals enormous advantages for the Union. The twenty-three states remaining in the Union had a population of 22,300,000, while the eleven Confederate states had a population of only 9,100,000, of whom 3,670,000 (40 percent) were slaves. The North had 22,000 miles of railroads; the South had only 9,280. The states in the Union manufactured more than 90 percent of the nation's industrial goods. The North had 1,300,000 industrial workers,

the South only 110,000. The North produced 17 times as much textiles; 21 times as much coal; 24 times as many locomotives; 5 times as much tonnage in ships; and 32 times as many firearms. The list is nearly endless.

As lopsided as the inventory is, statistics do not tell the full story of the North's advantage. Not only did it have superiority in people and equipment, but it could replace both more readily than could the South. Most of the South's stockpile of war-making materiel—locomotives, rails, arms, munitions, textiles, and more—had been imported from outside the region. When an item was used up, destroyed, or captured, Southerners would have no easy way to replace it. The North's vast, expanding manufacturing and industrial economy could produce and deliver all that northern soldiers needed.

So overwhelming were the North's advantages that the question becomes why did the South make war at all? Was not the outcome written in the statistics? Was not the South's cause lost before Confederates lobbed the first rounds at Fort Sumter? The answer quite simply is no. Southerners expected to win—and for some good reasons. They came very close to doing it.

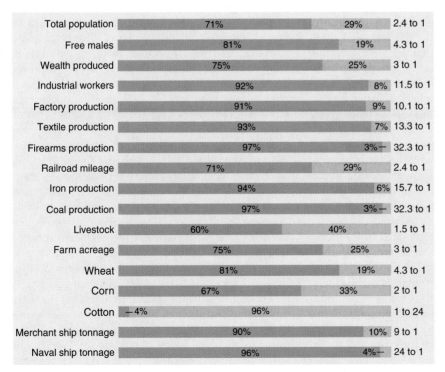

Total population	71% / 29%	2.4 to 1
Free males	81% / 19%	4.3 to 1
Wealth produced	75% / 25%	3 to 1
Industrial workers	92% / 8%	11.5 to 1
Factory production	91% / 9%	10.1 to 1
Textile production	93% / 7%	13.3 to 1
Firearms production	97% / 3%	32.3 to 1
Railroad mileage	71% / 29%	2.4 to 1
Iron production	94% / 6%	15.7 to 1
Coal production	97% / 3%	32.3 to 1
Livestock	60% / 40%	1.5 to 1
Farm acreage	75% / 25%	3 to 1
Wheat	81% / 19%	4.3 to 1
Corn	67% / 33%	2 to 1
Cotton	4% / 96%	1 to 24
Merchant ship tonnage	90% / 10%	9 to 1
Naval ship tonnage	96% / 4%	24 to 1

Union   Confederacy

FIGURE **15.1**
Resources of the Union and Confederacy
The Union's enormous statistical advantages failed to convince Confederates that their cause was doomed.

During the secession crisis, Southerners equated their cause with that of liberty-loving American colonists, and they hugged the example of 1776 even closer when they contemplated the similarity in military situations. Southerners bucked the military odds, but hadn't the colonists, too? "Britain could not conquer three million," a Louisianan proclaimed, and "the world cannot conquer the South." David had beaten Goliath, and history brimmed with examples of smaller, weaker peoples defeating larger, stronger adversaries.

Southerners believed that they would triumph because of their region's lofty cause, superior civilization, and unsurpassed character. They genuinely thought that the South produced better men. How could anyone doubt the outcome of a contest between lean, hard, country-born rebel warriors, defending family, property, and liberty, and soft, flabby, citified Yankee mechanics waging an unconstitutional war of aggression and subjugation? No wonder Southerners would claim after the war that they had not been "whipped" but had "worn themselves out whipping Yankees."

The South's confidence also rested on its estimation of the economic clout of cotton. A war correspondent for the London *Times* found that "King Cotton" was "the fixed idea everywhere." For years, Southerners had argued that northern prosperity depended on the South's cotton. It followed then that without southern cotton, New England textile mills would stand idle. Without southern markets, northern factories would drown in their own surpluses. Without the foreign exchange earned by the overseas sales of cotton, the financial structure of the entire Yankee nation would collapse. One Virginian spoke for most Confederates when he declared that in the South's ability to "withhold the benefits of our trade, we hold a power over the North more powerful than a powerful army in the field."

King Cotton not only could decree the destruction of the North's economy but could also command European intervention on behalf of the Confederacy. After all, England's economy depended almost as much on cotton as did the North's. Indeed, some four million British subjects earned their livings from the textile industry. Of the 900 million pounds of cotton England imported annually, more than 700 million came from the South. Southerners figured that if the supply were interrupted, "sheer necessity" would make England a Confederate ally. And because the British navy ruled the seas, the North would find Britain a formidable, indeed overwhelming, foe.

Southerners' faith in the superiority of their fighting men and in the power of cotton seems naive today because that faith turned out to have been misplaced. But even hard-eyed European military observers picked the South to win. Offsetting the North's power was the South's expanse. Its huge area (750,000 square miles), with its rugged terrain and bad roads, made Lincoln's task enormous. The North, Europeans predicted, could not conquer the vast territory from the Potomac to the Rio Grande. It would require raising a massive invading army, supplying it with huge quantities of provisions and arms, and protecting supply lines that would stretch farther than any in modern history.

Indeed, the South enjoyed major advantages, and the Confederacy devised a military strategy to take advantage of them. Jefferson Davis called it an "offensive-defensive" strategy. It recognized that a victory by the North required the North to defeat and subjugate the South. A victory by the South, in contrast, required only that it stay at home, blunt northern invasions, avoid battles that risked annihilating its army, and outlast the northern will to fight. When an opportunity presented itself, the South would strike the invaders. Like the American colonists, the South could win independence by not losing the war.

If the North did nothing, the South would by default establish its independence. The Lincoln administration therefore adopted an offensive strategy. Four days after the president issued the proclamation calling for 75,000 volunteers to put down the rebellion, he issued another proclamation declaring a naval blockade of the Confederacy. He sought to pen cotton inside the Confederacy, thus denying the Confederacy use of its most valuable commodity. Without the sale of cotton abroad, the South would have far fewer dollars to pay for war goods. Even before the North could mount an effective blockade, however, Jefferson Davis decided voluntarily to cease exporting cotton. He wanted to create a cotton "famine" that would enfeeble the northern economy and precipitate European intervention.

Southerners were not the only ones with illusions. Lincoln's call for only 75,000 men for only ninety days illustrates his failure to predict the magnitude and duration of the war. He was not alone. Most Americans thought of war in terms of their most recent experience, the Mexican War in the 1840s. In Mexico, fighting had taken place between relatively small armies, had taken relatively small numbers of lives, and had inflicted only light damage on the economy.

THE ORANGE AND ALEXANDRIA RAILROAD BRIDGE
Confederate forces would burn southern railroads and bridges to slow Union advances, interdict federal supply lines, and protect Confederate retreats. West Point-trained Herman Haupt, seen here inspecting a rebuilt bridge, was in charge of the Union's efforts at railroad construction and repair. While the railroad had been used as an instrument of war in the Crimea in the 1850s, it was during the Civil War that the railroad took on revolutionary importance. Railroads helped set new standards of overland mobility, rapid maneuver, and concentration of forces.
Library of Congress.

The American Civil War, however, proved to be the first modern war, a "total war" that mobilized entire populations, harnessed the productive capacities of entire economies, and enlisted millions of troops, with single battles pitting more than 200,000 soldiers and casualties mounting into the tens of thousands. Individual bravery would play a role in the outcome, but the morale of the people, the quality of political leadership, and the ability to utilize to the fullest the industrial economy would prove critical.

Americans on the eve of the Civil War had no crystal ball with which to peer into the future. They could not know that four ghastly years of bloodletting lay just over the horizon. On the contrary, both sides anticipated relatively clean victories. Early theories and strategies, however, like the expectations of military glory and fame, quickly confronted harsh reality.

Lincoln and Davis Mobilize

Mobilization required effective political leadership, and at first glance it appeared that the South had the decided advantage. An aristocrat from a Mississippi planter family, Jefferson Davis brought to the office of Confederate president a distinguished political career, including a stint in the U.S. Senate. He was also a West Point graduate, a combat veteran of the Mexican War, and a former secretary of war. Dignified and erect, with "a jaw sawed in *steel*," Davis appeared to be everything a nation could want in a wartime leader.

In contrast, an Illinois lawyer-politician occupied the White House. He brought with him one undistinguished term in the House of Representatives, where he had opposed the Mexican War in which Davis had served gallantly. He had almost no administrative experience, and his sole brush with anything military was as a captain in the militia in the Black Hawk War, a brief struggle in Illinois in 1832 in which whites expelled the last Indians from the state. Lincoln later joked about his service in the Black Hawk War as the time when he survived bloody encounters with mosquitoes and led raids on wild onion patches. The lanky, disheveled Westerner looked anything but military or presidential in his bearing, and even his friends feared that he was in over his head.

Davis, however, proved to be less than he appeared. Even in military matters, he disappointed. Possessing little capacity for broad military strategy and yet vain about what he considered his own superior judgment, he intervened constantly in military affairs. He was an even less able political leader. Quarrelsome and proud, he had an acid tongue that made enemies the Confederacy could ill afford. Davis had a better side, but he kept it hidden from all but his family and close friends. It is true that Davis faced a daunting task. For example, state sovereignty, which was enshrined in the Confederate constitution, made Davis's task of organizing a new nation and fighting a war difficult in the extreme. His wife, Varina, reported that her husband "hardly takes time to eat his meals and works late at night," but his best efforts proved inadequate. An even more talented man might have been defeated by the Confederacy's intimidating problems.

In Lincoln, however, the North got far more than met the eye. He proved himself a master politician and a superb leader. He never allowed personal feelings to get in the way of his objectives. He shrugged off insults such as those offered by the arrogant young Union general George McClellan, who called Lincoln the "original Gorilla." When he formed his cabinet, Lincoln shrewdly appointed representatives of every Republican faction, men who were often his chief rivals and critics. He made Salmon P. Chase secretary of the treasury, knowing that Chase intended to replace him on the Republican ticket at the next election. As secretary of state, he chose his chief opponent for the Republican nomination in 1860, William Seward, who expected to twist Lincoln around his little finger and formulate policy himself. Despite his civilian background, Lincoln displayed an innate understanding of military strategy. In time, no one proved more crucial in mapping the Union war plan. Moreover, Lincoln was an enormously eloquent man who reached out to the North's people, galvanizing them in defense of the nation he called "the last best hope of earth."

Guided by Lincoln and Davis, the North and South began gathering their armies. Southerners had the task of building almost everything from scratch, and Northerners had to mobilize their superior numbers and industrial resources for war. The puny federal army numbered only 16,000 men in 1861, most of whom were scattered over the West subjugating Indians. One-third of the officers followed Robert E. Lee's example, resigned their commissions, and headed south. The navy was in better shape. Forty-two ships were in service, and a large merchant marine would in time provide more ships and sailors. Most of the officers and men were Northerners and loyal to the Union.

The Confederacy had no navy and few shipyards for building one. But it had strong leadership in its secretary of the navy, Stephen R. Mallory, who immediately commissioned shipyards in Britain to produce several fast commerce raiders, which roamed the Atlantic preying on northern shipping. Still, the Confederate navy was never a match for the Union fleet, and the South pinned its hopes on its armies. Military companies sprang up everywhere. Since soldiers at first supplied their own uniforms, Confederate gray was just one of a rainbow of colors. Moreover, volunteers brought their own weapons, as often Bowie knives and shotguns as rifles and pistols.

From the beginning, the South exhibited more enthusiasm than ability to provide its soldiers with supplies and transportation. The Confederacy made prodigious efforts to build new factories to produce tents, shoes, blankets, and uniforms, but many soldiers spent nights with stars for a roof, huddled together for warmth, without proper clothes and sometimes without shoes. Even when factories managed to produce what soldiers needed, southern railroads—constructed to connect plantations with ports—often could not deliver what the factories made. And before long, most railroads were captured, destroyed, or in disrepair. Food production proved less of a problem, but food sometimes rotted before it reached the soldiers. The one bright spot was the Confederacy's Ordnance Bureau, headed by Josiah Gorgas, a near miracle worker when it came to manufacturing gunpowder, cannons, and rifles. In April 1864, Gorgas observed with justifiable pride: "Where three years ago we were not making a gun, a pistol nor a sabre, no shot nor shell . . .—a pound of powder—we now make all these in quantities to meet the demands of our large armies."

Recruiting and supplying huge armies required enormous public spending. Before the war, the federal government's tiny income had come primarily from tariff duties and the sale of public lands. Massive wartime expenditures made new revenues imperative. At first, both the North and the South resorted to selling war bonds, which essentially were loans from patriotic citizens. In time, both North and South began printing paper money. Inflation soared, but the South suffered more because it financed a greater part of its wartime costs through the printing press. Prices in the North rose about 80 percent during the war, while in the South inflation topped 9,000 percent. Eventually, the Union and the Confederacy turned to taxes, but the North raised one-fifth of its wartime revenue from this source, while the South raised only one-twentieth. The North proved far more able to adapt its system of public finance to extraordinary wartime conditions than did the South, and its success translated into greater economic and military might.

Within months, both sides had found men to fight and people to supply and support them. But the underlying strength of the northern economy gave the Union the decided advantage. With their military and industrial muscles beginning to ripple, Northerners became itchy for action. Northerners wanted an invasion that would once and for all smash the rebellion. Horace Greeley's *New York Tribune* began the chant: "Forward to Richmond! Forward to Richmond!"

The Battlefields, 1861–1862

During the first year and a half of the war, armies fought major campaigns in two theaters: in Virginia-Maryland in the East and in Tennessee-Kentucky in the West. With rival capitals of Richmond and Washington, D.C., only ninety miles apart and each

threatened more than once with capture, the eastern campaign was more dramatic and naturally attracted public attention. But the battles in the West proved more decisive. And while Yankee and rebel armies pounded each other on land, their navies fought it out on the seas and their diplomats sought advantage in the corridors of power in Europe. All the while, casualty lists reached appalling lengths.

Stalemate in the Eastern Theater

As one of his first important acts as commander in chief, Lincoln appointed Irvin McDowell commanding general of the army assembling outside Washington. An officer in the regular army, McDowell had no thought of taking his raw recruits into battle during the summer of 1861. But Lincoln ordered McDowell to prepare his 30,000 men for an attack on the Confederate army gathered at Manassas, a railroad junction in Virginia about thirty miles southwest of Washington. McDowell complained bitterly, but Lincoln replied, "You are green, it is true, but they are green, also; you are all green."

Repeating to the last that he did not want to go, McDowell moved his greenhorn troops out on July 16. Five days later, the Union army forded Bull Run, a branch of the Potomac, and engaged the southern forces effectively. But when federal troops failed to pin down Confederates in the Shenandoah Valley, fast-moving southern reinforcements blunted the Union attack and then counterattacked. What began as an orderly retreat turned into a panicky stampede. Demoralized soldiers ran over shocked civilians as they raced back to Washington. Thousands of dirty, disheveled, wild-eyed young soldiers served as evidence of the magnitude of the Union defeat.

By Civil War standards, casualties at Manassas (or Bull Run, as Northerners called the battle) were light, but the significance of the battle lay in the lessons Northerners and Southerners drew from it. For Southerners, it confirmed the superiority of rebel fighting men and the inevitability of Confederate nationhood. Manassas was *"one of the decisive battles of the world,"* a Georgian proclaimed. It *"has secured our independence."* While victory lifted southern conceit to new levels, defeat sobered Northerners and made them even more resolute. It was a major reversal, admitted the *New York Tribune*, but, the writer added, "Let us go to work, then, with a will." For Lincoln, Manassas was a slap in the face that awakened him to the realization that victory would be neither quick nor easy. Within four days of the disaster, the president signed bills authorizing the enlistment of one million men.

Lincoln also found a new general, replacing McDowell with the vain young George B. McClellan. Born in Philadelphia of well-to-do parents, educated in the best schools before graduating from West Point second in his class, the thirty-four-year-old McClellan believed that he was a great soldier and that Lincoln was a moron. A superb administrator and organizer, McClellan was brought to Washington as commander of the newly named Army of the Potomac. In the months following his appointment, McClellan energetically whipped his army into shape. Dispirited veterans and fresh recruits gained confidence and discipline and developed into a powerful fighting machine. The troops cheered their boyish general when he rode among them, in part no doubt because of his reluctance to send them into battle. Lincoln said McClellan had a bad case of "the slows," and, indeed, McClellan lacked decisiveness and the will to act. He defended his inactivity by claiming that his troops needed more drill or that the enemy outnumbered him—three or four to one. In actuality, McClellan commanded 120,000 troops in October 1861, while the Confederates facing him numbered only 45,000. Lincoln wanted a general who would advance, take risks, and fight, but McClellan went into winter quarters without budging from the Potomac. "If General McClellan does not want to use the army I would like to *borrow* it," Lincoln declared in frustration.

Finally, in the spring of 1862, McClellan launched his long-awaited offensive. He transported his highly polished army, now 130,000 strong, down the Chesapeake Bay to the mouth of the James River and began moving up the peninsula toward Richmond. McClellan took two and a half months to advance sixty-five miles. When he was within six miles of the Confederate capital, Confederate General Joseph Johnston hit him like a hammer. In the assault, Johnston was wounded and was replaced by Robert E. Lee, the reluctant Confederate who would become the Confederacy's most celebrated general. Lee named his command the Army of Northern Virginia.

The contrast between Lee and McClellan could hardly have been greater. McClellan overflowed with conceit and braggadocio, while Lee was courteous and reserved. But on the battlefield, where McClellan became timid and irresolute, Lee became audaciously, even recklessly, aggressive. McClellan's natural impulse was to dig in; Lee's was to attack. Lee had at his side in the peninsula campaign military men of real talent: General Thomas J. ("Stonewall") Jackson, so nicknamed for holding the line at Manassas, and James E. B. ("Jeb") Stuart, the twenty-nine-year-old cavalry commander who wore a red-lined cape, yellow sash, and hat with ostrich feather plume and rode circles around Yankee troops. Lee's assault initiated the Battle of Seven Days and began McClellan's backward march down the peninsula. By the time McClellan reached the water and the safety of the Union navy, 30,000 men had died or been wounded. Although Southerners suffered twice the casualties of Northerners, Lee had saved Richmond and achieved a strategic success. Lincoln wired McClellan to abandon the peninsula campaign and replaced him with General John Pope.

In August, just north of Richmond, Pope had his own rendezvous with Lee. At the Second Battle of Bull Run, Lee's smaller army battered Pope's forces and sent them scurrying back to Washington. Lincoln ordered Pope to Minnesota to pacify Indians and again put McClellan in command. Lincoln had not changed his mind about McClellan's capacity as a warrior. Instead, he reluctantly concluded, "There is no man in the Army who can lick these troops of ours into shape half as well as he. . . . If he can't fight himself, he excels in making others ready to fight."

Lee could fight. Sensing that he had his enemy on the ropes, he sought to land the knockout punch. Lee pushed the Army of Northern Virginia across the Potomac and invaded Maryland. A victory on northern soil would dislodge Maryland from the Union, Lee reasoned, and might even cause Lincoln to sue for peace. On September 17, 1862, McClellan's forces finally engaged Lee's army at Antietam Creek. Earlier, a Union soldier had found a copy of Lee's orders to his army wrapped around some cigars, dropped by a careless Confederate officer. McClellan had a clear picture of Lee's position, but his characteristic slowness meant that he missed a great opportunity to destroy the opposing army. Still, he did it great damage. In some of the most frenzied fighting of the war, with "solid shot . . . cracking skulls like egg-shells," the armies threw everything they had at one another. By nightfall the battlefield lay littered with 6,000 men dead or dying and 17,000 more wounded, making the Battle of Antietam the bloodiest day of the war. Badly damaged and deeply disappointed, Lee headed back to Virginia.

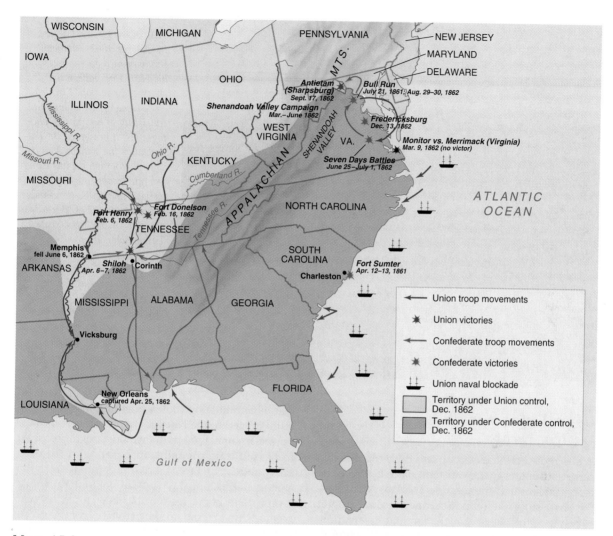

MAP 15.2
The Civil War, 1861–1862
*While eyes focused on the eastern theater, especially the tiny geography between the two
capitals of Washington and Richmond, strategic victories were being won by Union troops
in the West.*

But Lee remained alert for an opportunity to punish his enemy. In December, General Ambrose Burnside, yet another replacement for the ineffectual McClellan, provided the Virginian a fresh chance. At Fredericksburg, Virginia, Burnside's 122,000 Union troops faced 78,500 Confederates dug in behind a stone wall on the heights above the Rappahannock River. Half a mile of open ground lay between the armies. A Confederate artillery officer predicted that "a chicken could not live on that field when we open on it." Yet Burnside ordered a frontal assault. Wave after wave of bluecoats crashed against impregnable defenses. When the guns finally ceased, the federals counted nearly 13,000 casualties while the Confederates suffered fewer than 5,000. It was one of the Union's worst defeats.

At the end of 1862, the North seemed no nearer to taking Richmond, to whipping Lee, or to ending the rebellion than it had been when the war began. Rather than checkmate, military struggle in the East had reached a stalemate.

THE DEAD OF ANTIETAM
In October 1862, Mathew Brady opened an exhibition at his New York gallery that shocked the nation. Entitled "The Dead of Antietam" and consisting of ninety-five photographs, it presented the battlefield as the soldiers saw it. This photograph depicts Confederate troops lined up for burial. Among the thousands of visitors to the exhibit was a reporter for the New York Times, *who observed: "Mr. Brady has done something to bring to us the terrible reality and earnestness of the war. If he has not brought bodies and laid them in our door-yards and along [our] streets, he has done something very like it."*
Library of Congress.

Union Victories in the Western Theater

While most eyes focused on the East, the decisive early encounters of the war took place between the Appalachians and the Ozarks. The West's rivers—the Mississippi, the Tennessee, and the Cumberland—became the keys to the military situation. Whether they were arrows into the midsection of the Union or the heart of the Confederacy depended on who drew the bow. Southerners looked northward along the rivers and spied Missouri and Kentucky, states they claimed but did not control. Looking southward, Northerners knew that by taking the Mississippi they would split Arkansas, Louisiana, and Texas from the Confederacy. And the Cumberland and Tennessee penetrated one of the Confederacy's main producers of food, mules, and iron—all vital resources.

Ulysses S. Grant became the key northern figure on the western battlefields. Although Grant had graduated from West Point, when war broke out he was a thirty-nine-year-old dry goods clerk in Galena, Illinois. Gentle at home, he became pugnacious on the battlefield. "The art of war is simple," he said. "Find out where your enemy is, get at him as soon as you can and strike him as hard as you can, and keep moving on." Grant's philosophy of war as annihilation took a huge toll in human life, but it played to the North's strength: superior manpower. In time, the North fashioned victory from it. In his old uniform and slouch hat, with his tired, sad, nondescript face, Grant did not look much like a general. But Lincoln, who did not look much like a president, knew his worth. Later, to critics who wanted him to remove Grant from his command because of his fondness for the bottle, Lincoln would reply: "*I can't spare this man. He fights.*"

Manassas disabused Lincoln of the illusion of a short war, and, after Shiloh, Grant "gave up all idea of saving the Union except by complete conquest."

In February 1862, operating in tandem with navy gunboats, Grant captured Fort Henry on the Tennessee and Fort Donelson on the Cumberland. Defeat forced the Confederates to withdraw from all of Kentucky and most of Tennessee. Without pausing to savor his victories, Grant pushed after the retreating rebels until, on April 6, General Albert Sidney Johnston's army surprised him at Shiloh Church in Tennessee. Although his troops were badly mauled the first day, Grant remained cool and brought up reinforcements throughout the night. The next morning, the Union army counterattacked, driving the Confederates before it. The battle was terribly costly; there were 20,000 casualties, including the death of Johnston. Manassas disabused Lincoln of the illusion of a short war, and, after Shiloh, Grant "gave up all idea of saving the Union except by complete conquest."

Although no one knew it at the time, Shiloh inflicted a mortal wound to the Confederacy's bid to control the Mississippi valley. Rebel armies in the West still had plenty of fight in them, but from then on it was a downhill slide. In short order, the Yankees captured the strategic town of Corinth, Mississippi, the river city of Memphis, and New Orleans, the South's largest city. By the end of 1862, most—but not all—of the Mississippi valley lay in Union hands.

War and Diplomacy in the Atlantic Theater

With a blockade fleet of only about three dozen ships at the beginning of the war and more than 3,500 miles of southern coastline to patrol, the U.S. navy faced an impossible task. At first, rebel ships slipped in and out of port nearly at will. Yankees probably nabbed no more than one in ten. Taking on cargoes in the Caribbean, the sleek, fast blockade runners brought in vital supplies—guns and medicine—and also small quantities of luxury goods such as tea and liquor. But with the U.S. navy commissioning a new blockader almost weekly, the fleet eventually reached 150 ships on duty, and the Union navy dramatically improved its score.

Unable to build a conventional navy equal to the expanding federal fleet, the Confederates experimented with a radical new maritime design: the ironclad warship. At Norfolk, Virginia, they layered the wooden hull of the frigate _Merrimack_ with two-inch-thick armor plate and armed the saltwater marvel with ten guns. Rechristened _Virginia_, it steamed out in March 1862 to engage the federal blockade fleet off Hampton Roads, Virginia. Within a few hours, it sank two large federal ships, killing at least 240 sailors. But when the _Virginia_ returned the following morning to finish its work, it found the _Monitor_, a federal ironclad that had arrived from Brooklyn during the night. Alerted months earlier by rumors of the rebel invention, the federal government had built its own ironclad, a ship of even more radical design, including a revolving turret containing two eleven-inch guns. The _Monitor_ and the _Virginia_ hurled shells at one another for two hours, but because neither could penetrate the other's armor, the duel ended in a draw.

Both sides built other ironclads, but the Confederacy never found a way to break the blockade. Each month the blockade grew tighter until by 1865 the Union fleet intercepted about one of every two southern ships that attempted to break through. Even more significant than the ships the Union fleet captured (about 1,500 in total) were the ships that never sailed for fear of being captured. By 1863, the South had abandoned its embargo policy and desperately wanted to ship cotton to pay for imports needed to fight the war. But the growing effectiveness of the blockade meant that the South's seaborne trade declined by more than two-thirds. The federal blockade, a southern naval officer observed, "shut the Confederacy out from the world, deprived it of supplies, weakened its military and naval strength."

What they could not achieve on saltwater, Confederates sought to gain through foreign policy. According to the theory of King Cotton, however, Southerners should not have had to lift a diplomatic finger, for cotton-starved European nations supposedly had no choice but to break the blockade and recognize the Confederacy. The British and French briefly discussed joint action to lift the blockade, but it came to nothing. Although European nations granted the Confederacy "belligerent" status, which enabled it to buy goods and build ships in European ports, none recognized Confederate nationhood.

King Cotton diplomacy failed for several reasons. A bumper cotton crop in 1860 meant that the warehouses of British textile manufacturers bulged with surplus cotton throughout 1861. In 1862, when Europe began to feel the pinch of the cotton famine, manufacturers found new sources of cotton in Egypt and India. In addition, a brisk trade developed between the Union and Britain—British war materiel for American grain and flour—which helped offset the decline in textiles and encouraged Britain to remain neutral. Moreover, U.S. Secretary of State William Seward warned Europe sternly against meddling in America's civil war, which he defined as strictly an internal affair. British Foreign Minister Lord Russell agreed, observing, "They who in quarrels interpose, will often get a bloody nose." Even when the Union stepped hard on tender British toes, the British remained tolerant. In November 1861, a Union warship intercepted a British mail packet, the *Trent*, and illegally removed James Mason and John Slidell, Confederate diplomats on their way to Europe. Sentiment for war flared briefly in Britain, but when Lincoln ordered the Southerners' release, the British allowed the affair to end peacefully.

Europe's temptation to intervene withered in 1862. Union military successes, especially on the rivers of the West, made Britain and France think twice about linking their fates to the Confederacy. And in the fall of 1862, Lincoln announced a new policy that made an alliance with the Confederacy an alliance with slavery. The president finally acknowledged what Frederick Douglass had predicted—that it was impossible to fight for union without fighting against slavery.

Union and Freedom

Slavery and freedom had coexisted in North America for more than two centuries when the Civil War erupted. In his inaugural address in March 1861, Abraham Lincoln solemnly announced to the nation that the war would not disturb that ancient relationship. He had "no legal right" and "no inclination" to interfere with slavery, he said. For a year and a half Lincoln insisted that emancipation was not a goal; the war was strictly to save the Union.

> In the field among military commanders, in the halls of Congress, and in the White House, the truth gradually came into focus: To defeat the Confederacy, the North would have to destroy slavery.

Despite Lincoln's pronouncements, the war for union became a war for African American freedom. The transformation of northern purpose took place in fits and starts. The Lincoln administration sought to avoid the slavery issue, but rapidly evolving events made it impossible to maintain its conservative policy. Each month the war dragged on, it became clearer that the Confederate war machine depended heavily on slavery. Rebel armies used slaves to build fortifications, haul materiel, tend horses, and perform camp chores. On the home front, slaves labored in ironworks and shipyards, and they grew the food that fed both soldiers and civilians. Slavery undergirded the Confederacy as certainly as it had the Old South. In the field among military com-

**SLAVE WITH
CONFEDERATE SOLDIERS**
*The slave Scott poses in 1863
with members of a Georgia regiment. Many slaveholders took
"body servants" with them to
war. These slaves cooked, washed,
and cleaned for the white soldiers.
In 1861, James H. Langhorne
reported to his sister: "Peter . . .
is charmed with being with me &
'being a soldier.' I gave him my
old uniform overcoat & he says
he is going to have his picture
taken . . . to send to the servants."
Peter may have been "puttin'
on ol' massa" or just glad to be
free of plantation labor.*
From *Milledgeville* by James C. Bonner,
University of Georgia Press, 1978.

manders, in the halls of Congress, and in the White House, the truth gradually came into focus: To defeat the Confederacy, the North would have to destroy slavery. "I am a slow walker," Lincoln said, "but I never walk back."

From Slaves to Contraband

Personally, Lincoln detested human bondage, but as president he felt compelled to act prudently. He doubted his right under the Constitution to tamper with the "domestic institutions" of any state, even those in rebellion. He clung to the hope that if he avoided the slavery issue, Unionists in the South would reassert themselves and topple the Confederacy from within. Probably most important, he feared the consequences for the Union war effort. An astute politician, he worked within the limits of public opinion, and in 1861 Lincoln believed those limits were tight. The issue of black freedom was particularly explosive in the loyal border states, where slaveholders threatened to jump into the arms of the Confederacy at even the hint of emancipation. Black freedom also attracted attention in the free states. The Democratic Party gave notice that emancipation would kill the bipartisan alliance and make the war strictly a Republican affair. Democrats were as ardent for union as Republicans, but they fought against treason—period. They marched under the banner "The Constitution As It Is, the Union As It Was."

Moreover, while most white Northerners had no love of slavery, they were not about to risk their lives to satisfy abolitionist "fanaticism." "We Won't Fight to Free the Nigger," one popular banner read. They feared that emancipation would propel "two or three million semi-savages" northward, where they would crowd into white neighborhoods, compete for white jobs, and mix with white "sons and daughters." An anti-emancipation backlash, then, threatened to dislodge the loyal slave states from the Union, alienate the Democratic Party, deplete the armies, and perhaps even spark race warfare. Lincoln believed that he could not afford to jeopardize the Union coalition and proceeded cautiously.

Proponents of emancipation pressed Lincoln as relentlessly as the anti-emancipation forces. Black and white abolitionists argued that by seceding, Southerners had forfeited their right to the protection of the Constitution. Lincoln could now—as the price of treason—legally confiscate their property in slaves. When Lincoln stubbornly refused, abolitionists scalded him. Frederick Douglass labeled Lincoln "the miserable tool of traitors and rebels." Abolitionists won increasing numbers of converts during the war, especially among the radical faction of the Republican Party, which came to believe that restoring the Union with the moral evil of slavery intact would make a mockery of the sacrifices of Union soldiers.

The Republican-dominated Congress refused to leave slavery policy entirely in Lincoln's hands.

CONTRABANDS

These refugees from slavery crossed the Rappahannock River in Virginia in August 1862 to seek the sanctuary of a federal army. Most slaves fled with little more than the clothes on their backs, but not all escaped slavery empty-handed. The oxen, wagon, and goods seen here could have been procured by a number of means—purchased during slavery, "borrowed" from the former master, or gathered during flight. Refugees who possessed draft animals and a wagon had much more economic opportunity than those who had only their labor to sell.
Library of Congress.

Even the moderate majority advanced more rapidly on the slavery issue than the cautious president. In August 1861, Congress approved the First Confiscation Act, which allowed the seizure of any slave who was employed directly by the Confederate military. It also fulfilled the free-soil dream of prohibiting slavery in the territories and abolished slavery in Washington, D.C. Democrats and border state representatives voted against even these mild measures, but little by little, Congress displayed a stiffening of attitude as it cast about for a just and practical slavery policy.

Slaves, not politicians, became the most insistent force for emancipation. By escaping their masters by the tens of thousands and running away to Union lines, they placed slavery on the North's wartime agenda. Union officials could not ignore the flood of fugitives, and runaways precipitated a series of momentous decisions on the part of the military, Congress, and the president. Were the run-

aways now free, or were they still slaves who, according to the fugitive slave law, had to be returned to their masters? At first, most Yankee military commanders believed that administration policy required them to send the fugitives back. But Union armies needed laborers, and some officers accepted the runaways and put them to work. At Fort Monroe, Virginia, General Benjamin F. Butler not only refused to turn them over to their owners but provided them with a new status. He called them "contraband of war," meaning "confiscated property." Congress established national policy in March 1862 when it forbade the practice of returning fugitive slaves to their masters. Slaves were still not legally free, but there was a tilt toward emancipation.

Lincoln's policy of noninterference with slavery gradually crumbled. To maintain control of federal action, he proposed alternatives of his own. Lincoln assumed that the hemorrhaging of slavery in the border states, where runaways found Union lines easiest to reach, had weakened slaveholder resistance to emancipation. Consequently, he proposed a scheme that would both end slavery in the border states and honor his promise not to attack the institution. In April 1862, Congress (at Lincoln's urging) approved a voluntary emancipation program that paid slaveholders to give up their slaves. Lincoln asked masters to recognize that the war itself would kill off slavery "by mere friction and abrasion," and they would then not collect a dollar for their losses. But Lincoln badly misread border state slaveholders. They rejected the plan outright, proving that they were as stubborn about keeping their slaves as any master in the Confederacy was.

To calm Northerners' racial fears, which he considered the chief obstacle to Union acceptance of emancipation, Lincoln offered colonization, the deportation of African Americans from the United States and resettlement in Haiti, Panama, or elsewhere. In the summer of 1862, he defended colonization to a delegation of black visitors to the White House. He told them that the deep-seated racial prejudice of whites made it impossible for blacks to achieve equality in this country. For blacks to be truly free, he said, they had to emigrate to countries where opportunities existed. An African American from Philadelphia spoke for the group when he told the president, "This is our country as much as it is yours, and we will not leave it." Con-

gress did vote a small amount of money to underwrite colonization, but after one miserable experiment on a Caribbean island, practical limitations and black opposition sank further efforts.

At the same time that he developed his own initiatives, Lincoln snuffed out actions he believed jeopardized northern unity. He was particularly alert to Union commanders who tried to dictate slavery policy from the field. In August 1861, for example, when John C. Frémont, commander of federal troops in Missouri, impetuously freed the slaves belonging to Missouri rebels, Lincoln forced the general to revoke his edict and then removed him from command. The following May, when General David Hunter issued a proclamation freeing the slaves in Georgia, Florida, and South Carolina, Lincoln countermanded his order. Events moved so rapidly, however, that Lincoln found it impossible to control federal policy on slavery. He had to hurry just to keep up.

From Contraband to Free People

On August 22, 1862, Lincoln replied to another angry abolitionist who demanded that he go after slavery. "My paramount objective in this struggle *is* to save the Union," Lincoln said deliberately, "and is *not* either to save or destroy slavery. If I could save the Union without freeing *any* slave I would

FORMER SLAVES LISTEN TO LABOR CONTRACT
In November 1861, federal forces occupied the Sea Islands near Beaufort, South Carolina. Some ten thousand slaves came under federal authority. Emancipated workers gather in 1863 to hear a white man, probably a northern labor superintendent named Josiah Fairfield, read the terms of a free-labor contract. Little was settled about their future, and these former slaves appear to listen attentively, ready to defend their interests. One freedman accused Fairfield of having a "ractified mind," meaning that he was obstinate and hot-tempered.
The South Carolina Historical Society.

do it, and if I could save it by freeing *all* the slaves I would do it; and if I could save it by freeing some and leaving others alone I would also do that." At first glance, it seemed a restatement of his old position: that union was the North's sole objective. But what marked it as a radical departure was Lincoln's refusal to say that slavery was safe. Instead, he said that he would emancipate every slave if it would preserve the nation.

By the summer of 1862, events were tumbling rapidly toward emancipation. On July 17, Congress adopted a second Confiscation Act. The first had freed slaves employed by the Confederate military, the second declared all slaves of rebel masters "forever free of their servitude." In theory, this breathtaking measure freed most of the slaves in the Confederacy, for slaveholders formed the backbone of the rebellion. Congress had traveled far since the war began. Lincoln had too, but he wanted to blaze his own path. On July 21, the president informed his cabinet that he was ready "to take some definitive steps in respect to military action and slavery." The next day, he read a draft of a preliminary emancipation proclamation that promised to free *all* slaves in the seceding states on January 1, 1863.

Lincoln described emancipation as an "act of justice," but it was not the abolitionists' appeal to conscience that finally brought him around. It was the lengthening casualty lists. The duration and difficulty of the war eroded and then ended Lincoln's policy of noninterference. Emancipation, he declared, was "a military necessity, absolutely essential to the preservation of the Union." Only freeing the slaves would "strike at the heart of the rebellion." His cabinet approved Lincoln's plan but advised him to wait for a military victory before announcing it so that critics would not call it an act of desperation. On September 22, five days after the battle at Antietam, Lincoln served notice that if the rebel states did not lay down their arms and return to the Union by January 1, 1863, their slaves "shall be then, thenceforward, and forever free."

Lincoln had taken a risk, and he had good cause to be concerned about reaction in the North. Abolitionists generally approved, but the limitations of the proclamation—it exempted the loyal border states and the Union-occupied areas of the Confederacy—caused some to ridicule the act. The London *Times* observed cynically, "Where he has no power Mr. Lincoln will set the negroes free, where he retains power he will consider them as slaves." But Lincoln had no power to free slaves in loyal states, and invading Union armies would liberate slaves in the Confederacy as they advanced.

But it was conservative reaction Lincoln feared. By presenting emancipation as a "military necessity," he hoped he had disarmed his critics. Emancipation would shorten the war and thus save lives. Still, Democrats exploded with rage. They charged that the "shrieking and howling abolitionist faction" had captured the White House and made it "a nigger war." The fall elections were only weeks away, and Democrats sought to make political hay out of Lincoln's action. War-weariness probably had as much to do with the results as emancipation, but Democrats gained thirty-four congressional seats in 1862. When House Democrats proposed a resolution branding emancipation "a high crime against the Constitution," the Republicans, who maintained narrow majorities in both houses, beat it back. As promised, on New Year's Day, Lincoln issued the final Emancipation Proclamation. In addition to freeing the slaves in the states that were in rebellion, the edict also committed the federal government to the fullest use of African Americans to defeat the Confederate enemy.

War of Black Liberation

Even before Lincoln proclaimed freedom a Union war aim, African Americans in the North had volunteered to fight. But the War Department, doubtful of their abilities and fearful of white reaction to serving shoulder to shoulder with them, refused to make black men soldiers. Instead, the army employed black men as manual laborers; black women sometimes found employment—usually as laundresses and cooks—but less often. The navy, however, from the outset accepted blacks as sailors. They usually served in noncombatant roles, but within months a few blacks served on gun crews.

As the Union experienced manpower shortages, Northerners gradually and reluctantly turned to African Americans to fill blue uniforms. With the Militia Act of July 1862, Congress authorized enrolling blacks in "any military or naval service for which they may be found competent." Lingering resistance to black military service largely disappeared in 1863. After the Emancipation Proclamation, whites—like it or not—were fighting and dying for black freedom, and few were likely to insist that blacks remain out of harm's way behind the lines. Indeed, rather than resist black military participation, whites insisted that blacks share the

DRESS PARADE FOR THE FIRST SOUTH CAROLINA INFANTRY
The First South Carolina was the first official black regiment organized by the federal government. Made up overwhelmingly of ex-slaves, it was led by Colonel Thomas W. Higginson, a white Massachusetts clergyman and abolitionist. After the regiment's first skirmish with Confederate soliders, Higginson celebrated his men's courage: "No officer in this regiment now doubts that the key to the successful prosecution of this war lies in the unlimited employment of black troops. . . . Instead of leaving their homes and families to fight they are fighting for their homes and families."
National Archives.

danger, especially after March 1863, when Congress resorted to the draft to fill the Union army.

Black soldiers discovered that the military was far from color blind. The Union army established segregated black regiments, paid black soldiers $10 per month rather than the $13 it paid to whites, refused blacks the opportunity to become commissioned officers, punished blacks as if they were slaves, and assigned blacks to labor battalions rather than to combat units. But nothing deterred black recruits. When the war ended, 179,000 African American men had served in the Union army, approximately 10 percent of the army total. An astounding 71 percent of black men age eighteen to forty-five in the free states wore blue, a participation rate that was substantially higher than that of white men. More than 130,000 black soldiers came from the slave states, perhaps 100,000 of them ex-slaves. In time, whites allowed blacks to put down

their shovels and to shoulder rifles. At the battles of Port Hudson and Milliken's Bend on the Mississippi and at Fort Wagner in Charleston harbor, black courage under fire finally dispelled notions that African Americans could not fight. More than 38,000 black soldiers died in the Civil War (a mortality rate that was higher than that of white troops). Blacks played a crucial role in the triumph of the Union and the destruction of slavery.

From the beginning, African Americans viewed the Civil War as a revolutionary struggle for black liberation. They fought to overthrow slavery and to gain equality for their entire race. "Once let the black man get upon his person the brass letters, U.S.; let him get an eagle on his button, and a musket on his shoulder and bullets in his pocket," Frederick Douglass predicted, "and there is no power on earth which can deny that he has earned the right of citizenship." Whether or not the war changed white attitudes about black rights, it changed black Americans. When black men became liberators, they and their families gained new confidence, pride, and self-esteem. Military service taught them new skills, showed them more of the world, and introduced them to political struggle as they battled for their rights within the army. War's experiences and lessons stood African Americans in good stead when the war of liberation was over and the battle for equality began. But first, there was the matter of the rebellion. Victory depended as much on what happened behind the lines as on the battlefields.

The South at War

During the secession winter of 1860–61, a Louisiana planter had declared confidently that the creation of the Confederate States of America would "guarantee order, security, tranquility, as well as liberty." The irony was staggering. By seceding, Southerners brought on themselves a firestorm of unimaginable fury. Monstrous losses on the battlefields nearly bled the Confederacy to death. But white Southerners also perceived themselves as under attack on the home front.

The most surprising thrust came from their own government in Richmond. Its efforts to centralize power to fight the war more effectively convinced a majority that the Confederacy had proven false to them and to the South's cause. Jefferson Davis became the South's most hated politician after Lincoln. Southerners also endured severe deprivation. Wartime economic changes hurt everyone, but some hurt more than others. Unequal suffering meant that by 1863, planters and yeomen no longer stood shoulder to shoulder. Instead of promoting solidarity among whites, war produced fissures. Most disturbing of all, slaves became open participants in the destruction of slavery and the Confederacy.

Revolution from Above

When Jefferson Davis arrived in Richmond in 1861, he faced the gargantuan task of building an army and navy from scratch, supplying them from factories that were scarce and anemic, and paying for it all from a treasury that did not exist. The president agreed with one of his generals who observed that Southerners were engaged in a total war "in which the whole population and the whole produc-

REBEL SOLDIER
Treasvant "Tris" D. Childers was twenty-seven years old in March 1862 when he enlisted as a private in Phelan's Battery, Alabama Light Artillery. He fought at Chickamauga, Missionary Ridge, Franklin, and Nashville, and survived. His older brothers William and Thomas died while fighting in Virginia. After the war, Childers moved to Arkansas and became a farmer. When he died in 1910, his widow, Emma McShan Childers, collected a state pension for her husband's service in the Civil War.
Private Collection.

tion . . . are to be put on a war footing, where every institution is to be made auxiliary to war." Davis and his administration met the challenge head on. Building the army proved easiest. Hundreds of officers defected from the federal army, and hundreds of thousands of eager young rebels volunteered to follow them into battle. Very quickly, the Confederacy developed formidable striking power.

The Confederacy's economy and finances proved tougher. Because of the Union blockade, the government had no choice but to build an industrial sector itself. Government-owned clothing and shoe factories, mines, arsenals, ordnance plants, and powder works "sprung up almost like magic," according to one wide-eyed Mississippian. In addition, the government gave contracts to private companies, such as the huge Tredegar Iron Works in

Richmond, spurring a frenzy of production. The Davis administration attacked its financial task just as briskly. But Southerners had invested most of their capital in land and slaves, which were not easily tapped for the war. Richmond experimented and came up with a mix of bonds, taxes, and paper money to finance the war effort.

With ferocious energy, the Davis administration sought to revolutionize and redirect the southern economy. Despite its boldness, however, it failed to transform the slave-labor, staple-producing agricultural economy into a modern industrial one. The Confederacy manufactured much more than many people imagined possible, but it never produced all that the South needed. Each month, the gap between the North's and the South's production widened. Richmond's financial plan proved to be a complete fiasco. The flood of paper money ("shinplasters" Southerners called it) caused debilitating inflation. By 1863, Charlestonians paid ten times more for food and twenty times more for clothing and boots than they had at the start of the war. By Christmas 1864, a Confederate soldier's monthly pay no longer bought a pair of socks.

The economic revolution from above failed, but not from a lack of effort. Richmond intruded in unprecedented ways into the private lives of Confederate citizens. In one of his first moves, Davis embargoed cotton, the lifeblood of the plantation economy. In April 1862, the Confederate Congress passed the first conscription (draft) law in American history. All able-bodied white males between the ages of eighteen and thirty-five (later seventeen and fifty) were liable to serve in the rebel army for three years. When Union forces threatened Richmond in 1862, Davis proclaimed martial law. The Confederate government adopted a policy of impressment, which allowed officials to confiscate food, horses, wagons, or whatever they wanted from private citizens and to pay for them at below-market rates. After March 1863, they also legally impressed slaves, employing them as government military laborers. In addition, Richmond took control of the South's railroads and shipping. The war necessitated much of the government's unprecedented behavior, but citizens found it arbitrary and inequitable. In time, many grew as disaffected with Richmond as with Washington.

Resistance from Below

Richmond's centralizing efforts ran head-on into the South's traditional values of states' rights and unfettered individualism. The states lashed out at

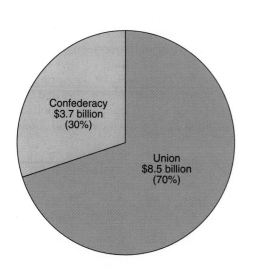

a) Overall cost of the war
(1967 constant dollars)

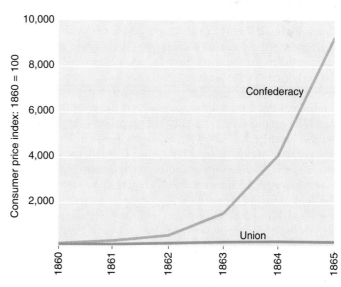

b) Cumulative wartime inflation
(1860=100)

FIGURE 15.2
The Economics of the Civil War
The Union outspent the Confederacy and avoided debilitating inflation. The Union's economic strength translated into military strength.

TECHNOLOGY IN AMERICA
Confederate Artillery

When it came to big-gun warfare, the South was at a decided disadvantage. When the war broke out, it suffered from an almost total lack of modern field guns. The government quickly established foundries in Georgia, Mississippi, Alabama, and South Carolina, but the Confederacy's largest supplier was Richmond's Tredegar Iron Works, which had been casting cannons since 1842. Tredegar's mainstay was the powerful twelve-pounder bronze Napoleon gun. It could be fired rapidly, and at close range it was like a giant shotgun, which made it an excellent infantry killer. So reliable was it that General Lee urged that other bronze cannon be melted down to build more Napoleons. Tredegar cast an impressive 1,099 cannon — nearly half of all the artillery pieces manufactured in the Confederacy. By comparison, federal production surpassed 6,000 guns, which were consistently better in quality. The South's lack of industrial capacity, skilled labor, and strategic raw materials severely handicapped its efforts to manufacture cannon.

High Impact/Larry Sherer.

what Georgia Governor Joseph E. Brown denounced as the "dangerous usurpation by Congress of the reserved right of the States." A tug-of-war between Richmond and the states ensued for control of money, supplies, and soldiers, with damaging consequences for the war effort. Individual citizens also objected to the government's radical departures. They were accustomed to government that rarely intruded in what they considered private affairs. They remembered that Davis had promised to defend southern "liberty" against Republican "despotism." Luckily for Davis, the Confederate constitution provided for a single, six-year term for the president, which meant he did not have to face the voters during the war.

Hardships were widespread, but they fell most heavily on the poor, who were least able to bear them. Inflation, for example, spared no one, but it threatened the poor with starvation. Salt—necessary for preserving meat—shot up from $2 to $60 a bag during the first year of the war. Flour that cost three or four cents a pound in 1861 cost thirty-five cents in 1863. Food prices became critical when the draft depopulated yeomen farms of men, leaving the women and children to grow what they ate. A rampaging army, a drought, a sickness, a lame mule —any one calamity could cost a family a crop.

When farm wives succeeded in bringing in a harvest, government agents took 10 percent of it as a "tax-in-kind" on agriculture. Shortages, like inflation, also afflicted the entire population, but the rich lost luxuries while the poor lost necessities. Before long, some poor women and children were eating berries and boiled potato vines. In the spring of 1863, bread riots broke out in a dozen cities and villages across the South. In Richmond, a mob of nearly a thousand hungry women broke into shops and took what they needed.

Yeomen saw a profound inequality of sacrifice. They called it "a rich man's war and a poor man's fight," and they had evidence.

Severe deprivation had powerful consequences. As one southern leader observed in November 1862, "men cannot be expected to fight for the Government that permits their wives & children to starve." As things grew worse at home, women sometimes told men to choose between country and family. A Mississippi deserter explained, "We are poor men and are willing to defend our country but our families [come] first." Some wealthy individuals shared their bounty, the Confederacy made some efforts at social welfare, and the states did even more, but every effort fell short. As a result, the army leaked badly. By some estimates, when the war ended, one-third of the soldiers had already gone home.

The Confederacy also failed to persuade the suffering white majority that the war's burdens were being shared equally. Instead, yeomen saw a profound inequality of sacrifice. They called it "a rich man's war and a poor man's fight," and they had evidence. The original draft law permitted a man who had money to hire a substitute to take his place. Moreover, the "twenty-Negro law" exempted one white man on every plantation with twenty or more slaves. The government intended to provide protection for white women and to see that slaves tended the crops. But yeomen perceived rich men evading military service. A slaveless Mississippian complained to his governor about stay-at-home planters who sent their slaves into the fields to grow cotton while, in plain view, "poor soldiers' wives are plowing with *their own* hands to make a subsistence for themselves and children—while their husbands are suffering, bleeding and dying for their country." In fact, most slaveholders went off to war, but the extreme suffering of common folk fueled class animosity.

In such a long, grueling war, social strain was inevitable, but government policy aggravated stress. Officials hoped that the crucible of war would mold a region into a nation. Confederate nationalism, they believed, would provide a powerful emotional bond for southern unity. Instead, war increased discord among whites and widened divisions. War also threatened to rip the southern social fabric along its racial seam.

The Disintegration of Slavery

The legal destruction of slavery was the product of presidential proclamation, congressional legislation, and eventually constitutional amendment, but the practical destruction of slavery was the product of war, what Lincoln called war's "friction and abrasion." When the war ended in 1865, the institution had taken a heavy pounding, especially from within. More than 100,000 men fled bondage, took up arms, and attacked slavery directly. Other men and women stayed in the slave quarters, but they were not content to wait passively for blue-coated liberators. Well schooled in the slave's ways of survival, they watched and waited, alert for opportunities. Over the four years of war, they found plenty.

In dozens of ways, the war disrupted the routine, organization, and discipline of bondage. Almost immediately, it called the master away, leaving white women to assume managerial responsibilities, which they found "a new and strange business." Plantation mistresses success-

SOUTHERN WOMEN
Women such as these North Carolinians were expected to shift their energies from family to the southern cause. Most served by sewing uniforms, knitting socks, and rolling bandages at home. Some founded hospitals, others worked in them nursing the sick and wounded. Sally Tompkins, twenty-eight and unmarried in 1861, ran Richmond's Robertson Hospital, which treated more than twelve hundred sick and wounded over four years. As the war ground on, southern women had their hands full trying to keep their families fed and safe. Museum of the Confederacy.

fully oversaw the transition of the plantation from cotton to food production. As one woman wrote to a newspaper, "Do impress upon the soldiers, that they are constantly in our thoughts, that we are *working* for them, while they are *fighting* for us— and that their wants shall be supplied, as long as there is a *woman* or a *dollar* in the 'Southern Confederacy.'" But plantation mistresses could not maintain traditional standards of slave discipline. No one could. War had stifled the production of cotton, divorcing slaves from their principal work. War also meant the impressment of slaves, severing the personal relationship between masters and slaves. Moreover, military action increasingly sliced through the South's farms and plantations. Sometimes slaveholders fled, leaving behind their slaves. More often, they took their slaves with them, "refugeeing" out of the path of the Yankee invaders. But flight meant additional chaos and offered slaves more opportunities to resist bondage.

At night, slaves shared the scraps of war news and debated what it meant for their lives. From the beginning, they anticipated that a Union victory would mean freedom, but they proceeded cautiously. As the slaveholders' grip loosened, they staked claim to more freedom. Increasingly, masters complained about the slaves' "demoralization," a term that covered every sort of misbehavior—in the masters' eyes—from rudeness to rebellion. Running away to Union lines became so common that whites kept lists of their slaves' names and crossed out those who fled to "Lincoln land." Those who stayed on the plantations got to the fields late, worked more casually, and quit early. They grew less deferential to whites and more assertive.

The balance of power between master and slave gradually shifted toward the slave quarters. Some slaveholders responded violently, but most saw no alternative but to strike bargains to keep slaves at home and at work. Slaveholders offered "gifts" at harvest time, but slaves demanded more, perhaps a portion of the crop or even wages. When planters balked, slaves grew food just for their own tables. An Alabama woman reported that she had to rely on "moral suasion" to "get them to do their duty." She "begged . . . what little is done." The changes in slave behavior shocked slaveholders. They had prided themselves on "knowing" their slaves, and they learned that they did not know them at all. When the war began, a North Carolina woman praised her slaves as "diligent and respectful." When it ended, she said, "As to the idea of a *faithful servant, it is all a fiction.*"

Throughout the war, rumors of "servile insurrection" raced across the South, especially after the Emancipation Proclamation. Whites claimed that Lincoln wanted to "convert the quiet, ignorant, dependent black son of toil into a savage incendiary and brutal murderer." In fact, Lincoln worried that his proclamation might provoke black violence, but no explosion occurred. Blacks rarely took revenge for more than two centuries of slavery. Instead, they undermined white mastery and expanded control over their own lives.

The North at War

Because rebel armies generally remained within the Confederate borders, northern farms, factories, towns, and cities remained untouched by fighting. But Northerners could not avoid being touched by war. Almost every family had a son, a husband, a brother in uniform. Moreover, this war—a total war —blurred the distinction between home front and war front. As in the South, men marched off to fight, but preserving the country, either Union or Confederacy, was also women's work. During the war, traditional definitions of "manly" and "womanly" behavior tended to break down. For civilians as well as soldiers, for women as well as men, war was transforming.

The need to build and fuel the Union war machine caused the northern economy to boom. The North sent nearly two million men into the military and still increased production in almost every area. It supplied the largest army in the world with the food, weapons, munitions, clothing, and transportation it needed to crush a powerful rebellion. The boom produced impressive private wealth. But because the rewards and burdens of patriotism were not evenly distributed, the North experienced sharp, even violent, divisions. Workers confronted employers, whites confronted blacks, and Republicans confronted Democrats. Still, Northerners on the home front remained fervently attached to the ideals of their free-labor society.

The Government and the Economy

Democrats and Republicans traditionally disagreed about the best way to encourage economic growth. Democrats generally argued that in economic matters, the less government intrusion the better, while

UNION ORDNANCE, YORKTOWN, VIRGINIA
As the North successfully harnessed its enormous industrial capacity to the needs of war, cannon, mortars, and shells poured out of its factories. A fraction of that abundance is seen here in 1862 at Yorktown, ready for transportation to Union troops in the field. Two years later, Abraham Lincoln observed that the Union was "gaining strength, and may if need be maintain the contest indefinitely. . . . Material resources are now more complete and abundant than ever. . . . The national resources are unexhausted, and, as we believe, inexhaustible." Library of Congress.

Republicans advocated government support to advance enterprise and develop economic resources. Democratic domination of national politics for two decades before the war meant that the Republicans inherited a financial and economic structure that reflected the Democrats' belief in feeble government direction of the economy. There were no national banking system, no national currency, and no federal income or excise taxes.

> *For civilians as well as soldiers, for women as well as men, war was transforming.*

The secession of eleven slave states cut the Democrats' strength in Congress in half and destroyed their capacity to resist the Republican steamroller. The Republican platform of 1860 advocated an array of federal programs to encourage economic growth, and during the war Republicans had little trouble enacting their philosophy into law. In May 1862, Congress approved the Homestead Act, which offered 160 acres of public land to settlers who would live and labor on it. In time, the Homestead Act resulted in more than a million new farms in the West. Two months later, Congress passed the Pacific Railroad Act, which provided massive federal assistance for the building of a transcontinental railroad. When completed in 1869, the railroad ran from Omaha to San Francisco. Congress also enacted a higher tariff. Republicans defended their program by pointing to the relationship between additional economic muscle and increased Union military might.

The escalating demands of the war compelled additional changes in government's role in the economy. The Legal Tender Act of February 1862 created a national currency, paper money that Northerners called "greenbacks." With passage of the National Banking Act in February 1863, Congress created a system of national banks. Republicans sought to overturn the antebellum system of decentralized state banks (each with its own banknotes) and to replace it with a national banking system with a more stable currency. It took several years, but by 1873 state banknotes had largely disappeared. Congress also enacted a series of sweeping tax laws that taxed everything from incomes to liquor to billiard tables. The Internal Revenue Act created the Bureau of Internal Revenue, the government's tax collection agency, which has become a permanent fixture. Although Salmon Chase of Ohio had no financial experience when he became secretary of the treasury, he learned quickly and built solidly. By revolutionizing the country's banking, monetary, and tax structures, the Republicans generated enormous economic and military power.

In northern agriculture and industry, the war accelerated antebellum trends. The North's 1,300,000 farms were no strangers to commercialization, mechanization, specialization, and integration into national and international markets. Still, war made a deep imprint. Two new initiatives from Washington had significant and long-term consequences. Congress created a Department of Agriculture and passed the Land-Grant College Act (also known as the Morrill Act after its sponsor, Representative Justin Morrill of Vermont), which set aside public lands to support universities that emphasized "agriculture and mechanical arts." The first task of Lincoln's administration was winning the war, but initiatives from Washington were permanently changing the nation.

Women and Work on the Home Front

With more than a million farm men called to the military, farm women stepped into new roles. In addition to their traditional labor within the farm house (and in gardens, henhouses, and cow barns), they added men's chores to their own. "I met more women driving teams on the road and saw more at work in the fields than men," a visitor to Iowa reported in the fall of 1862. Rising production figures testified to their success in plowing, planting, and harvesting. Rapid mechanization assisted farm women in their new roles. Cyrus McCormick sold 165,000 of his reapers during the war years. The combination of high prices and increased production ensured that war and prosperity walked hand in hand in the rural North.

While a few industries, such as textiles (which depended on southern cotton), declined during the war, many more grew. Huge profits prompted one Pennsylvania ironmaster to remark, "I am in no hurry for peace." The boom proved friendlier to owners than to workers, however. In industry, as in agriculture, prewar trends continued to accelerate: concentration, mechanization, growth in the size of the workplace, impersonalization, and loss of control over the pace and nature of the work. Yet with orders pouring in and a million workers siphoned off into the military, the number of jobs expanded and unemployment declined. Wages often rose, but inflation and taxes cut so deeply that workers' standard of living actually fell. Some urban laborers suffered severe hardship.

As on the farm, women in cities rushed into manufacturing jobs vacated by men and also into essentially new occupations, such as government civil service. Often, they had no choice because they could not make ends meet on their husbands' army pay. Women already made up about one-quarter of the manufacturing workforce when the war began. The fraction had increased to one-third when it ended. But as more women entered the wartime workforce, employers cut wages. By 1864, fourteen-hour days earned New York seamstresses only an average of $1.54 per week. As Cincinnati seamstresses explained to Abraham Lincoln, their wages were not enough "to sustain life." Urban workers resorted increasingly to strikes to wrench decent salaries from their employers, but protest rarely succeeded. However, tough times failed to undermine the patriotism of most workers. They remained loyal to the Union cause and took pride in their contribution to northern victory.

In everything but the actual fighting, women participated and contributed. Middle-class white women were supposed to be homebodies, nurturing families and supporting husbands, and hundreds of thousands contributed mightily to the war effort in traditional ways. Like many southern white women, they labored long hours in sewing circles, wrapped bandages, and sold homemade goods at local fairs to raise money to aid the soldiers. Unpaid labor by "lady volunteers" proved crucial in supplying the opposing war machines.

But some women expressed their patriotism in an untraditional way—as wartime nurses. Thousands of women on both sides defied prejudices about female delicacy and volunteered to nurse the wounded. Many of the northern female volunteers worked through the U.S. Sanitary Commission, a civilian organization that bought and distributed clothing, food, and medicine and recruited doctors and nurses. Nursing meant working in the midst of unspeakable sights, sounds, and smells, but it brought the profound satisfaction of displaying competence and serving well. Katherine Wormeley of Rhode Island, who served three months as a volunteer nurse on a hospital ship in 1862, recorded in her diary, "We all know in our hearts that it is thorough enjoyment to be here,—it is life."

Some volunteer nurses went on to become paid military nurses. In April 1861, Dorothea Dix, well known for her efforts to reform insane asylums, was named "Superintendent of Female Nurses," and eventually some three thousand women served under her. Most nurses worked in hospitals behind the battle lines, but some, like Clara Barton, who later founded the American Red Cross, worked in several battlefield units. At Antietam, as Barton was giving a wounded man a drink, a bullet ripped through her sleeve and struck him in the chest, killing him instantly. Several of the women who served in the war went on to lead the postwar movement to establish training schools for female nurses.

Politics and Dissent

For a moment in 1861 it looked as if the outbreak of war had silenced politics. Democrats gave the Union as full-throated a roar of allegiance as Republicans. But bipartisan unity did not last. The war and the way in which Lincoln chose to fight it set the political agenda. Within a year, Democrats were labeling the Republican administration a "reign of terror," and Republicans were calling Democrats the party of "Dixie, Davis, and the Devil." As bruising as the political struggle became, the North's two-party system actually strengthened government. In the Confederacy, which had no well-organized parties, political disagreement spiraled down into fruitless bickering, but in the Union, rival parties helped to discipline and legitimize political debate. Fear of being driven from office by their rival's victory helped to unify each party and to strengthen the political structure.

Nevertheless, Republican policy pushed the Democrats toward a dangerous alienation. Under Lincoln, the Republicans emancipated the slaves, subsidized private business, and expanded federal power at every turn. And Democrats, traditionally the party of limited government, resisted at every step. "Shall we sink down as serfs to the heartless, speculative Yankee for all time," one Democrat inquired, "swindled by his tariff, robbed by his taxes,

skinned by his railroad monopolies?" The Lincoln administration argued that the war required a loose interpretation of the Constitution, to which the Democrats countered, "The Constitution is as binding in war as in peace."

Democrats had good evidence that Lincoln did not always reach first for a copy of the Constitution when he confronted a problem. He could be very practical, especially in the realm of civil rights. In September 1862, in an effort to stifle opposition to the war, Lincoln placed under martial law any person who discouraged enlistments, resisted the draft, or engaged in "disloyal" practices. Before the war ended, his administration had imprisoned nearly fourteen thousand individuals, most in the border states. The campaign fell short of a reign of terror, for most were not northern Democratic opponents but Confederate citizens, blockade runners, and foreign nationals, and most of the arrested gained quick release. But the administration's heavy-handed tactics and habit of branding Democratic dissent as disloyal did suppress free speech.

One Democratic dissenter, ex-Congressman Clement L. Vallandigham of Ohio, proved indefatigable. "It is the desire of my heart," he announced just after the war began, "to restore the Union, the Federal Union as it was forty years ago." Consistent with that desire, he lambasted every Republican innovation, which meant most of Lincoln's conduct of the war. After the Emancipation Proclamation, which he considered abolitionist fanaticism, Vallandigham came out against the war itself. He denounced this "wicked, cruel and unnecessary war" waged "for the purpose of crushing out liberty and erecting a despotism . . . a war for the freedom of the blacks and the enslavement of the whites."

Was such talk protected by the right of free speech, or was it treason? In April 1863, General Ambrose Burnside decided that "the habit of declaring sympathy for the enemy will not be allowed" and arrested Vallandigham for treason. Lincoln had not ordered the arrest but decided to back his general, arguing that the Constitution permitted the military arrest of civilians during rebellions. "Must I shoot a simple-minded soldier boy who deserts, while I must not touch a hair of a wily agitator who induces him to desert?" Lincoln asked. Vallandigham's arrest and conviction in a military court sparked Democratic protest throughout the North. Hoping to avoid creating a martyr, Lincoln ordered Vallandigham banished to the Confederacy. In 1866, a year after the war ended, the Supreme

Court in *Ex parte Milligan* declared unconstitutional military trials of civilians where civil courts were still able to operate.

When the Republican-dominated Congress enacted the draft law in March 1863, Democrats had another grievance. As in the South, grim news from the battlefields had dried up the stream of volunteers. The North, like the South a year earlier, turned to military conscription to fill the ranks. The act required that all men between the ages of twenty and forty-five enroll and make themselves available for a lottery, which would decide who went to war. What poor men found particularly galling were provisions that allowed a draftee to hire a substitute or simply to pay a $300 fee and get out of his military obligation. As in the South, common folk could be heard chanting, "A rich man's war and a poor man's fight."

Democrats linked the draft and emancipation, arguing that Republicans employed an unconstitutional means (the draft) to achieve an unconstitutional end (emancipation). In the summer of 1863, antidraft, antiblack mobs went on rampages in northern cities. New York experienced an explosion of unprecedented proportions. Solidly Democratic Irish workingmen, crowded into stinking, disease-ridden tenements, gouged by inflation, enraged by the inequities of the draft, and dead set against fighting to free blacks, erupted in four days of rioting. Mobs attacked federal draft offices, sacked Republican newspapers, and waylaid any well-dressed man ("a $300 man") they caught on the streets. But their principal victims were blacks, whom they chased down and murdered and whose property, including the Colored Orphan Asylum, they burned. By the time police and soldiers restored order, at least 105 people lay dead.

The riots stunned black Northerners, but the racist mobs failed to achieve their purpose: the subordination of African Americans. Free black leaders had lobbied aggressively for emancipation, and after Lincoln's proclamation they fanned out over the North agitating for equality. They won small wartime successes against discrimination. Illinois and Iowa overturned laws that excluded blacks from entering the states. Illinois and Ohio began permitting blacks to testify in court. Streetcars in Washington, D.C., began allowing blacks to ride. But defeat was more common. Indiana, for example, continued to forbid blacks to vote, testify, and attend public schools, and additional blacks were not allowed to enter the state.

Grinding out Victory, 1863–1865

In the early months of 1863, the Union's prospects looked bleak, while the Confederate cause stood at high tide. But in July 1863, the tide receded. The military man who was most responsible for seeing that it never rose again was Ulysses S. Grant. Lifted up from obscurity by brilliant successes in the West in 1862 and 1863, Grant became the darling of the North. Grant was "*the* great man of the day," one man observed in July 1864, "perhaps of the age." Elevated to supreme command, Grant knit together a powerful war machine that integrated a sophisticated command structure, modern technology, and complex logistics and supply systems. But the plain arithmetic of this plain man remained unchanged: Killing more of the enemy than he kills of you equals "the complete overthrow of the rebellion." In William T. Sherman and Philip H. Sheridan he found like-minded men. The three generals set out to teach the South that war was hell. Grant instructed Sheridan "to push the enemy to the very death."

The North ground out the victory, bloody battle by bloody battle. The balance tipped in the Union's favor in 1863, but if the Confederacy was beaten, Southerners clearly did not know it.

The North ground out the victory, bloody battle by bloody battle. The balance tipped in the Union's favor in 1863, but if the Confederacy was beaten, Southerners clearly did not know it. The fighting reached new levels of ferocity in the last two years of the war. As national elections approached in the fall of 1864, a discouraged Lincoln expected a war-weary North to make him a one-term president. Instead, northern voters declared their willingness to continue the war in the defense of the ideals of union and freedom.

Vicksburg and Gettysburg

Perched on the bluffs above the eastern bank of the Mississippi River, Vicksburg, Mississippi, bristled with cannon and dared Yankee ships to try to pass.

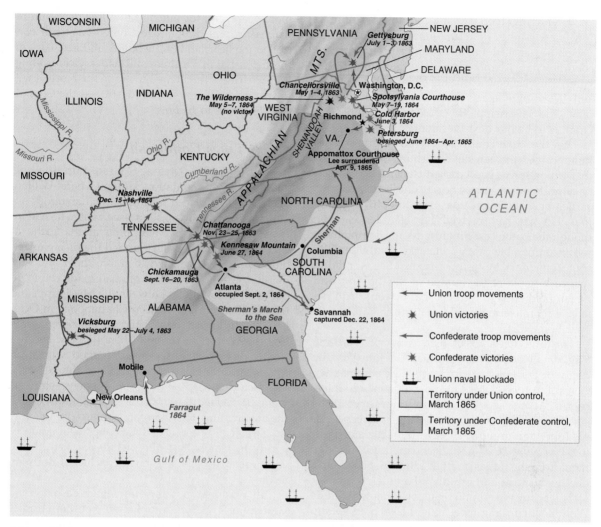

M AP 15.3
The Civil War, 1863–1865
Ulysses S. Grant's victory at Vicksburg divided the Confederacy at the Mississippi River.
William T. Sherman's march from Chattanooga to Savannah divided it again. In northern
Virginia, Robert E. Lee fought fiercely, but Grant's larger, better-supplied armies prevailed.

This Confederate stronghold stood between Union forces and complete control of the river. Since impenetrable terrain made it impossible to take the city from the north, Grant gambled on an attack from the south and east. To get his army south of Vicksburg, he marched it down the western bank of the Mississippi. After four water-logged failures, the troops made it through the swamps, but their supply wagons remained behind, up to their axles in the muck. Grant readied supply barges and several gunboats north of Vicksburg, and on the night of April 16, 1863, they ran the Confederate gauntlet. Rebel fire destroyed two ships, but the rest rendezvoused with Grant's army below the city. Union forces crossed the Mississippi River, marched northeast more than one hundred miles, wheeled sharply left, and attacked the city from the rear. When the Confederates beat back the assault, Grant began siege operations to starve out the enemy. Civilian inhabitants took to living in caves to escape incessant Union cannon bombardment and soon began eating mules and rats to survive.

Eventually, the siege took its toll. On July 4, 1863, nearly thirty thousand rebels marched out of Vicksburg, stacked their arms, and surrendered unconditionally. A Yankee captain wrote home to his wife: "The backbone of the Rebellion is this day broken. The Confederacy is divided . . . Vicksburg is ours. The Mississippi River is opened, and Gen. Grant is to be our next President."

On the same Fourth of July that a grateful nation received the news of Vicksburg, word arrived that Union forces had crushed General Lee at Gettysburg, Pennsylvania. Lee's triumph two months earlier at Chancellorsville over Joseph "Fighting Joe" Hooker had revived his confidence, even though the battle cost him his favorite commander, the incomparable Stonewall Jackson, accidentally shot in the dark by his own troops. Lee wanted to relieve Virginia of the burden of the fighting, and he felt bold enough to think that he could still deliver a morale-crunching defeat to the Yankees on their home turf.

In June, Lee's 75,000-man Army of Northern Virginia invaded Pennsylvania. On June 28, the Army of the Potomac, under its new commander, General George G. Meade, moved quickly to intercept it. Advanced units of both armies met at the small town of Gettysburg, and Union forces occupied the high ground. Three days of furious fighting, involving 165,000 soldiers, could not dislodge them from the ridges and hills. But Lee ached for a decisive victory, and on July 3 he ordered a major assault against the Union center on Cemetery Ridge. With bloodcurdling rebel yells, 12,000 men sprang forward in what became known as Pickett's Charge. The open, rolling fields provided the dug-in Yankees with three-quarters of a mile of clear vision, and they raked the mile-wide line of Confederates with cannon and rifle fire. Time and again, the rebels closed ranks and raced on, until finally their momentum failed. Gettysburg cost Lee more than one-third of his army—28,000 casualties. "It's all my fault," he said. In a drenching rain on the night of July 4, 1863, he marched his battered army back to Virginia.

The twin disasters at Vicksburg and Gettysburg proved to be the turning point of the war. The Confederacy could not replace the nearly 60,000 soldiers who were captured, wounded, or killed. Lee never launched another major offensive north of the Mason-Dixon line. No European power ever again considered intervening on behalf of the rebellion. But it is hindsight that permits us to see the pair of battles as decisive. The war dragged on nearly two more years, and for much of the time the result remained in real doubt. The Confederacy still controlled the heartland of the South, and Lee, back on the defensive in Virginia, still had a vicious sting. War-weariness threatened to erode the North's will to win before Union armies destroyed the Confederacy's ability to go on.

Grant Takes Command

In the fall of 1863, Ulysses S. Grant burnished his already shining reputation. Union General William Rosecrans had placed his army in a dangerous situation in Chattanooga, Tennessee, where he had retreated after taking a whipping at the battle of Chickamauga. Rebels surrounded the disorganized bluecoats and threatened to starve them into submission. Grant, whom Lincoln had made commander of all Union forces between the Mississippi and the Appalachians, arrived in Chattanooga in October. Within weeks, he opened an effective supply line, broke the siege, and then (largely because troops disobeyed orders and charged wildly up Missionary Ridge) routed the Confederate army. The victory at Chattanooga had immense strategic value. It opened the door to Georgia and became the staging area for Sherman's "march to the sea" in 1864. It also confirmed Lincoln's estimation of Grant. In March 1864, the president asked him to come east to become the general in chief of all Union armies.

In Washington, Grant implemented his grand strategy of a war of annihilation. Southern armies were already worn to less than half the size of their enemy's, and Grant pressed even harder. He ordered a series of simultaneous assaults from Virginia to Louisiana. Two actions proved more significant than the others. In one, Sherman, whom Grant appointed his successor to command the western armies, plunged southeast toward Atlanta. In the other, Grant, who took control of the Army of the Potomac, went head to head with Lee for almost four straight weeks in Virginia.

Grant and Lee met in early May 1864 at the Wilderness, a dense tangle of scrub oaks and small pines that proved to be Lee's ally, for it helped offset the Yankees' numerical superiority. Often unable to see more than ten paces, the armies pounded away at each other until 18,000 Yankees and 11,000 rebels had fallen. But the savagery of the Wilderness did not compare with that at Spotsylvania Court House a few days later. Frenzied men fought hand to hand for eighteen hours in the rain. One

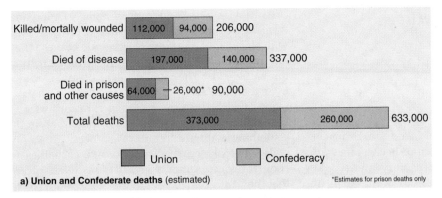

a) Union and Confederate deaths (estimated)

*Estimates for prison deaths only

	Union	Confederacy	Total
Killed/mortally wounded	112,000	94,000	206,000
Died of disease	197,000	140,000	337,000
Died in prison and other causes	64,000	26,000*	90,000
Total deaths	373,000	260,000	633,000

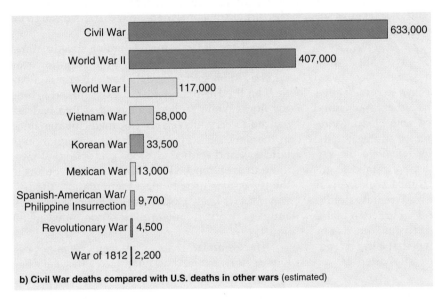

b) Civil War deaths compared with U.S. deaths in other wars (estimated)

War	Deaths
Civil War	633,000
World War II	407,000
World War I	117,000
Vietnam War	58,000
Korean War	33,500
Mexican War	13,000
Spanish-American War/ Philippine Insurrection	9,700
Revolutionary War	4,500
War of 1812	2,200

FIGURE 15.3
Civil War Deaths
The loss of life in the Civil War was almost equal to the losses in all other American wars.

veteran remembered men "piled upon each other in some places four layers deep, exhibiting every ghastly phase of mutilation. Below the mass of fast-decaying corpses, the convulsive twitching of limbs and the writhing of bodies showed that there were wounded men still alive and struggling to extricate themselves from their horrible entombment." Spotsylvania cost Grant another 18,000 casualties and Lee 10,000. But the Yankee bulldog would not let go. Rather than disengage and lick his wounds, Grant kept moving and caught Lee again at Cold Harbor, where he lost 13,000 additional troops to Lee's 5,000.

Twice as many Northerners as Southerners died in the four weeks of fighting in Virginia in the spring of 1864. Yet Grant did not consider himself defeated. Since Lee had only half the number of troops, he lost proportionally as many men as Grant. And the Union commander, ever the mathematician of war, knew that the South could not replace its losses.

Moreover, the campaign had carried Grant to the outskirts of Petersburg, just south of the Confederate capital. Since most of the major railroad lines supplying Richmond ran through Petersburg, Lee had little choice but to defend the city. Grant abandoned the costly tactic of the frontal assault and began a siege, one that immobilized both armies and dragged on for nine months.

There was no pause in "Uncle Billy" Sherman's invasion of Georgia. Grant had ordered his friend to smash Confederate General Joseph E. Johnston's army and to "get into the interior of the enemy's country as far as you can, inflicting all the damage you can against their War resources." In early May, while Grant thrashed in the Wilderness, Sherman moved 100,000 men south against the 65,000 rebels in the rugged mountains of northern Georgia. Skillful maneuvering, constant skirmishing, and one pitched battle (Kennesaw Mountain) brought Sherman to Atlanta, which fell on September 1.

Why Did So Many Soldiers Die?

From 1861 to 1865, Americans killed Americans on a scale that had never before been seen. Not until the First World War, a half century later, would the world match (and surpass) the killing fields at Shiloh, Antietam, and Gettysburg. Why were the totals so appallingly large? Why did 260,000 rebel soldiers and 373,000 Union soldiers die in the Civil War?

The balance between the ability to kill and the ability to save lives had tipped disastrously toward death. The sheer size of the armies — some battles involved more than 200,000 soldiers — ensured that battlefields would turn red with blood. Moreover, armies fought with antiquated strategy. In the generals' eyes, the ideal soldier remained the veteran of Napoleonic warfare, a man trained to advance with his comrades in a compact, close-order formation. Theory also emphasized frontal assaults. In classrooms at West Point and on the high plains of Mexico in the 1840s, men who would one day be officers in rival armies learned that infantry advancing shoulder to shoulder, supported by artillery, carried the day.

But by the 1860s, modern technology had made such strategy obsolete. Weapons with rifled barrels were replacing old smoothbore muskets. Whereas muskets had an effective range of only about eighty yards, rifles propelled spinning bullets four times as far. The rifle's greater range and accuracy, along with cannons firing canisters filled with flesh-ripping, bone-breaking steel shot, made sitting ducks of charging infantry units and gave enormous advantage to entrenched defensive forces. As a result, battles took thousands of lives on a single afternoon. On July 2, 1862, the morning after the battle at Malvern Hill in eastern Virginia, a Union officer surveyed the scene: "Over five thousand dead and wounded men were on the ground . . . enough were alive and moving to give to the field a singular crawling effect."

Soldiers who littered the battlefields often lay for hours, sometimes days, without water or care of any kind. When the war began, no one anticipated casualty lists with thousands of names. Union and Confederate medical departments could not cope with skirmishes, much less large-scale battles. They had no ambulance corps to lift the wounded from the battlefields. They had no field hospitals to deliver them to. At first, the Quartermaster Department, which was responsible for constructing Union hospitals, answered demands that it do something with the retort "Men need guns, not beds." It took the shock of massive casualties to compel reform. Although a lack of resources meant that the South lagged behind the North, both North and South gradually organized effective ambulance corps, built hospitals, and hired trained surgeons and nurses.

Soldiers did not always count speedy transportation to a field hospital as a blessing, however. As one Union soldier said, "I had rather risk a battle than the Hospitals." Real danger lurked behind the lines. While the technology of killing had advanced to very high standards, medicine remained in the dark ages. Physicians had the reputation of butchers, and soldiers dreaded the operating table more than entrenched riflemen. Serious wounds to the leg or arm usually meant amputation, the best way doctors knew to save lives. After major battles, surgeons worked among piles of wounded men's limbs.

The wounded man's real enemy was not callous doctors, but medical ignorance. Physicians had almost no knowledge of the cause and transmission of disease or the use of antiseptics. Lacking knowledge of basic germ theory, they spread infection almost every time they operated. Doctors wore the same bloody smock for days and washed their hands and their scalpels and saws in buckets of dirty water. When they had difficulty threading their needles, they wet the thread with their own saliva. Soldiers often did not survive amputations, not because of the operation but because of the infection that inevitably followed. More than half of the Union soldiers whose legs were amputated above the knee died. A Union doctor discovered in 1864 that bromine arrested gangrene, but the best most amputees could hope for was maggots, which ate dead flesh on the stump and thus inhibited the spread of infection. During the Civil War, nearly one wounded rebel soldier died for every five wounded and one in every six Yankees. A century later, in Vietnam, the proportion was one wounded American soldier in four hundred.

WOUNDED MEN AT SAVAGE'S STATION
Misery did not end when the cannon ceased firing. This heap of mangled humanity strewn on the ground was but a fraction of the cost of General George McClellan's campaign on the Virginia peninsula in 1862.
Library of Congress.

Soldiers who avoided battlefield wounds and hospital infections still faced disease. Killer diseases swept through crowded army camps, where latrines were often in dangerous proximity to water supplies. The principal killers were dysentery and typhoid, but pneumonia and malaria also cut down thousands of men. Doctors did what they could, but their treatments often only added to the misery. They prescribed doses of turpentine for patients with typhoid, fought respiratory problems with mustard plasters, and attacked intestinal disorders with blisters and sulfuric acid.

Dorothea Dix, Clara Barton, Juliet Ann Opie Hopkins, and thousands of other female nurses in the North and South improved the wounded men's odds and alleviated their misery. Civilian relief agencies, such as the U.S. Sanitary Commission and the Women's Relief Society of the Confederacy, promoted hygiene in army camps and made some headway. Nevertheless, disease killed approximately twice as many soldiers as did combat. Many who died of disease were prisoners of war. Approximately 30,000 Northerners died in Confederate prisons, and approximately 26,000 Southerners died in Union prisons. No northern prison, however, could equal the horror of Andersonville in southern Georgia, where 33,000 men lived in unspeakable conditions and 13,000 of them perished.

In the end, 633,000 northern and southern soldiers died, a staggering death toll.

GRANT AT COLD HARBOR
Seated next to his chief of staff, John A. Rawlins, at his Cold Harbor, Virginia, headquarters, Ulysses S. Grant plots his next move against Robert E. Lee. On June 3, 1864, Grant ordered frontal assaults against entrenched Confederate forces, resulting in enormous losses. "I am disgusted with the generalship displayed," young Brigadier General Emory Upton exclaimed. "Our men have, in many cases, been foolishly and wantonly slaughtered." Grant always regretted Cold Harbor, but he kept pushing toward Richmond.
Chicago Historical Society.

Sherman was only warming up. Intending to "make Georgia howl," he marched out of Atlanta on November 15 with 62,000 battle-hardened veterans, heading for Savannah, 285 miles away. "We are not only fighting hostile armies," he said before torching Atlanta, "but a hostile people, and must make old and young, rich and poor, feel the hard hand of war." They felt it, for Sherman's troops cut a swath from 25 to 60 miles wide, and, as one veteran remembered, the Yankees "destroyed all we could not eat, stole their niggers, burned their cotton & gins, spilled their sorghum, burned & twisted their R. Roads and raised Hell generally." Sherman sought to destroy the will of the southern people to make war. A few weeks earlier, General Philip Sheridan had tried as much in the Shenandoah Valley, complying with Grant's order to turn the valley into "a barren waste . . . so that crows flying over it for the balance of this season will have to carry their provender [food] with them." When Sherman's troops entered an undefended Savannah in the third week of December, the general telegraphed Lincoln that he had "a Christmas gift" for him.

The Election of 1864

In the fall, white men in the Union states turned to the election of a president. Never before had a nation held general elections in the midst of war. "We can not have free government without elections," Lincoln explained, "and if the rebellion could force us to forgo, or postpone a national election, it might fairly claim to have already conquered and ruined us."

Lincoln's determination to hold elections is especially noteworthy because the Democratic Party smelled victory. The Union war effort had stalled during the summer. With Sherman temporarily checked outside Atlanta and Grant bogged down in the siege of Petersburg, frustration had settled over the North. Moreover, rankled by inflation, the draft, the attack on civil liberties, and the commitment to blacks, Northerners appeared ready for a change. Even Lincoln concluded in the gloomy summer of 1864, "It seems exceedingly probable that this administration will not be re-elected."

Democrats were badly divided, however. "Peace" Democrats insisted on an armistice, while "war" Democrats supported the conflict but opposed Republican means of fighting it. They tried to paper over the chasm by nominating a war candidate, General George McClellan, but adopting a peace platform that demanded that "immediate efforts be made for a cessation of hostilities." The platform also attacked emancipation and arbitrary government power, but the Republicans directed their fire at the Democrats' peace plank. Republicans labeled it a conspiracy of "Copperheads" (after a deadly, easily concealed snake) to sell out the Union and claimed that it "virtually proposed to surrender the country to the rebels in arms against us."

Lincoln was no shoo-in for renomination, much less reelection. The president had found it difficult to gain the respect of his own party. Conservatives believed he had acted precipitously in emancipating the slaves. Radicals criticized him for moving too slowly to free them and for failing to champion black equality. Members of both factions skewered him for being an inept military leader. But frightened by the strength of the peace Democrats, the Republican Party renominated Lincoln. In an effort to reach out to the largest number of voters, however, the Republicans made two changes. First, they chose a new name. As the Union Party, they made it easier for prowar Democrats to embrace Lincoln. Second, they chose a new vice presidential candidate. Dumping Hannibal Hamlin of Maine, the incumbent vice president, they turned to Andrew Johnson of Tennessee, the only southern senator to remain in Congress when his colleagues fled south in the winter of 1860–61. As a Southerner, a former slaveholder, and a former Democrat, Johnson personified the message that the party of Lincoln was broad enough to include any uncompromising Unionist.

Lincoln's pessimism about being reelected proved to be unfounded. After the fall of Atlanta in September, the political tide turned in favor of the Republicans. Lincoln received 55 percent of the popular vote, but his electoral margin was a whopping 212 to McClellan's 21. The Republicans also stormed back in the congressional elections, gaining large margins over the Democrats in the Senate and the House. The Union Party bristled with factions, but they united for a resounding victory. The victory gave Lincoln a mandate to continue the war until slavery was gone and the South had surrendered.

The Confederacy Collapses

Jefferson Davis found little to celebrate as the new year of 1865 dawned in Richmond. Military disaster littered the Confederate landscape. With the destruction of John B. Hood's army at Nashville in

RUINS OF RICHMOND
A Union soldier and a small boy in a Union cap contemplate the silence and devastation of Richmond, the Confederacy's capital. On their way out of the city on the evening of April 2, 1865, Confederate demolition squads set fire to tobacco warehouses and ammunition dumps. Huge explosions tore holes in the city, and windswept fires destroyed much of what was left standing. As one Confederate observed, "The old war-scarred city seemed to prefer annihilation to conquest."
Library of Congress.

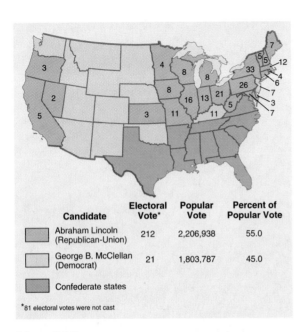

Candidate	Electoral Vote*	Popular Vote	Percent of Popular Vote
Abraham Lincoln (Republican-Union)	212	2,206,938	55.0
George B. McClellan (Democrat)	21	1,803,787	45.0
Confederate states			

*81 electoral votes were not cast

MAP 15.4
The Election of 1864

November, the interior of the Confederacy lay in Yankee hands. Sherman's troops, resting momentarily in Savannah, eyed South Carolina hungrily. Only Lee's army remained, and Grant had it pinned down in Petersburg just a few miles from Richmond. The home front grew more desperate every day. Officials reported actual starvation. Deprivation and exhaustion generated major peace movements in North Carolina, Georgia, and elsewhere. Yeomen grew surly and cursed both the planters and the government, and slaves seemed to work only when they wanted to. Southerners took out their frustration and bitterness on their president. Kinder than most, Alexander Stephens, vice president of the Confederacy, likened Davis to "my poor old blind and deaf dog."

But Davis would not accept defeat. He vowed to fight until the rebels won. And he concluded that there was one unused arrow in the Confederate quiver. Slaves would become soldiers. The Confederacy had impressed both slaves and free blacks in noncombatant military roles, but now Davis proposed arming slaves and, with a vague promise of freedom as an incentive, sending them to fight the Yankees. This bizarre notion indicates Davis's desperation, but Lee approved, and in March 1865, so did the Confederate Congress. Slaveholders in the countryside, however, refused to sacrifice slavery to

win southern nationhood. A South Carolina planter asked who gave Richmond the right "to destroy that which it was created to protect and perpetuate." "No!" cried a plantation mistress, "freedom for whites, slavery for negroes, God has so ordained it!" But before Southerners could attempt the experiment, time ran out for the Confederacy.

At the end, events came with a rush. On February 1, 1865, Sherman's troops stormed out of Savannah into South Carolina, the "cradle of the Confederacy." They twisted train rails and lit fires with even more enthusiasm than they had in Georgia. But before Sherman could push through North Carolina and arrive at the rear of Lee's army at Petersburg, where he expected to crush the Confederates between his hammer and Grant's anvil, Lee abandoned the city. Jefferson Davis fled Richmond, and the capital city fell a few days later. Grant pursued Lee for one hundred miles, until he surrendered on April 9, 1865, in a farmhouse near Appomattox Courthouse, Virginia. The beaten man arrived in an immaculate full-dress uniform, complete with sash and sword; the victor came in his usual mud-splattered private's outfit. Grant offered a generous peace. He allowed Lee's men to return home and to take their horses to help "put in a crop to carry themselves and their families through the next winter." With Lee gone, the remaining ragtag Confederate armies lost hope and gave up. After four years, the war was over.

The day after Lee's surrender, a brass band led a happy crowd of three thousand up to the White House, where they pleaded with Lincoln for a speech. He begged off and asked the band to strike up "Dixie." He knew that the rebels had claimed the tune as their own, he said, but it was one of his favorites, and now he was taking it back. The crowd roared its approval, and the band played "Dixie," following it with "Yankee Doodle." No one was more relieved than Lincoln that the war was over, but his celebration was restrained. He told his cabinet that his postwar burdens would weigh almost as heavily as those of wartime. But Lincoln had other things on his mind when he attended the theater on the evening of Good Friday, April 14, 1865. While he and his wife, Mary, enjoyed *Our American Cousin*, a British comedy, John Wilkes Booth, an actor with southern sympathies, slipped into the president's box and mortally wounded Lincoln with a single shot to his head. The man who had led the nation through the war would not lead it in its postwar search for a just peace.

Conclusion: The Second American Revolution

The Civil War had a profound effect on the nation and its people. The northern victory permanently discredited the idea of secession. It laid waste to the South. Three-fourths of southern white men of military age served in the army, and at least half of them were captured, wounded, or killed or died of disease. War raked the countryside. It destroyed two-fifths of the South's livestock, wrecked half of the farm machinery, obliterated two-thirds of the region's assessed wealth, smashed thousands of farms and plantations, blackened dozens of cities and towns, and ended slavery, the linchpin of southern society and economy. The immediate impact of the war on the North was more paradoxical. Putting down the slaveholders' rebellion cost the North a heavy price: 373,000 lives. But rather than devastating the land, the war set the countryside and cities humming with business activity.

The task of fighting the rebellion transformed the nation. Antebellum America was decentralized politically and loosely integrated economically. To bend the resources of the country to a Union victory, Congress enacted legislation that altered the nation's political and economic character. It adopted policies that established the sovereignty of the federal government and the dominance of industrial capitalism. With the South out of the Union, the Republicans laid the foundations for modern America. Moreover, the common sacrifice of northern people to save the nation created an even more fierce national loyalty. The shift in power from South to North and the creation of a national government, a national economy, and a national spirit led one historian to call the American Civil War the "Second American Revolution."

Most revolutionary of all, the war would end slavery. Because that ancient labor and racial system was entangled in almost every aspect of southern life, slavery's uprooting would mean fundamental change. But the full meaning of abolition remained unclear in 1865. The task of determining the new economic, political, and social status of four million ex-slaves would be the principal task of Reconstruction.

CHRONOLOGY

1861 **March 4.** Abraham Lincoln sworn in as sixteenth president of the United States.

April 12–13. Confederate forces attack Fort Sumter, South Carolina, in opening engagement of Civil War.

April. Dorothea Dix named superintendent of female nurses.

April–May. Four Upper South states secede and join Confederacy.

July. Union forces routed at Manassas, Virginia, in first major clash of war.

August. Congress approves First Confiscation Act, which allows seizure of any slave employed by Confederate military.

1862 **February.** Legal Tender Act creates first national currency, called "greenbacks."

February. Union forces in West under General Ulysses S. Grant capture Fort Henry and Fort Donelson and drive Confederates from Kentucky and most of Tennessee.

April. Battle of Shiloh in Tennessee results in huge casualties and ends Confederate bid to control Mississippi valley.

April. Confederate Congress passes first draft law in American history.

May. Homestead Act offers western land to those who would live and labor on it.

1862   **May–July.** General George McClellan's Union forces defeated during peninsula campaign in Virginia.

July. Congress approves second Confiscation Act, freeing all slaves of rebel masters.

July. Congress passes Militia Act, authorizing enrollment of blacks in Union military.

September 17. Battle of Antietam stops Lee's advance into Maryland, but Confederate forces escape back into Virginia.

September 22. Lincoln announces preliminary emancipation proclamation.

December. Battle of Fredericksburg results in huge Union casualties.

1863   **January 1.** Emancipation Proclamation becomes law, freeing slaves in areas still in rebellion.

February. National Banking Act creates system of national banks.

March. Congress authorizes draft.

July. Vicksburg falls to Union forces under Grant, effectively cutting Confederacy in two along Mississippi River.

July. Battle of Gettysburg results in Confederate defeat and Lee's last offensive into North.

1864   **March.** Grant appointed general in chief of all Union forces.

May–June. Grant's forces engage Confederates in Virginia in bloodiest fighting of war, from Wilderness campaign to beginnings of siege of Petersburg.

September. Atlanta falls to Union forces under General William T. Sherman.

November. Lincoln reelected president.

December. Sherman occupies Savannah after scorched-earth campaign in Georgia.

1865   **April 9.** Lee surrenders to Grant at Appomattox Courthouse, Virginia, essentially ending Confederate resistance.

April 14. Lincoln shot by John Wilkes Booth at Ford's Theatre in Washington. He dies on April 15, succeeded by Vice President Andrew Johnson.

BIBLIOGRAPHY

GENERAL WORKS

Shelby Foote, *The Civil War: A Narrative,* 3 vols. (1958–1974).

James M. McPherson, *Battle Cry of Freedom: The Civil War Era* (1988).

Allan Nevins, *The War for the Union,* 4 vols. (1971).

Peter J. Parish, *The American Civil War* (1975).

J. G. Randall and David Donald, *The Civil War and Reconstruction* (1969).

Charles P. Roland, *An American Iliad: The Story of the Civil War* (1991).

Frank E. Vandiver, *Blood Brothers: A Short History of the Civil War* (1992).

Edmund Wilson, *Patriotic Gore: Studies in the Literature of the American Civil War* (1962).

THE COMBATANTS

Michael Barton, *Goodmen: The Character of Civil War Soldiers* (1981).

Ira Berlin et al., eds., *Freedom: A Documentary History of Emancipation, 1861–1867* (1982–).

David W. Blight, *Frederick Douglass's Civil War: Keeping Faith in Jubilee* (1989).

Gabor S. Boritt, ed., *Lincoln's Generals* (1994).

Catherine Clinton and Nina Silber, eds., *Divided Houses: Gender and the Civil War* (1992).

Thomas L. Connelly, *The Marble Man: Robert E. Lee and His Image in American Society* (1977).

Dudley Cornish, *The Sable Arm: Black Troops in the Union Army, 1861–1865* (1966).

Marilyn Mayer Culpepper, *Trials and Triumphs: Women of the American Civil War* (1991).

Richard Nelson Current, *Lincoln's Loyalists: Union Soldiers from the Confederacy* (1992).

Charles B. Dew, *Ironmaker to the Confederacy: Joseph R. Anderson and the Tredegar Iron Works* (1966).

David Donald, *Lincoln* (1995).

Russell Duncan, ed., *Blue-Eyed Child of Fortune: The Civil War Letters of Colonel Robert Gould Shaw* (1992).

Byron Farwell, *Stonewall: A Biography of General Thomas J. Jackson* (1992).

Douglas Southall Freeman, *R. E. Lee,* 4 vols. (1934, 1935).

Joseph T. Glatthaar, *Forged in Battle: The Civil War Alliance of Black Soldiers and White Officers* (1990).

Frank H. Heck, *Proud Kentuckian: John C. Breckinridge, 1821–1875* (1976).

Randall C. Jimerson, *The Private Civil War: Popular Thought during the Sectional Conflict* (1988).

Gerald F. Linderman, *Embattled Courage* (1987).

John F. Marszalek, *Sherman: A Soldier's Passion for Order* (1993).

Waldo Martin, *The Mind of Frederick Douglass* (1985).

William S. McFeely, *Grant* (1981).

William S. McFeely, *Frederick Douglass* (1991).

Richard M. McMurry, *John Bell Hood and the War for Southern Independence* (1982).

James M. McPherson, *Abraham Lincoln and the Second American Revolution* (1990).

Reid Mitchell, *Civil War Soldiers: Their Expectations and Their Experiences* (1988).

Robert Manson Myers, ed., *The Children of Pride: A True Story of Georgia and the Civil War* (1972).

Mark E. Neely Jr., *The Last Best Hope of Earth: Abraham Lincoln and the Promise of America* (1993).

Stephen B. Oates, *With Malice toward None: The Life of Abraham Lincoln* (1977).

Stephen B. Oates, *A Woman of Valor: Clara Barton and the Civil War* (1994).

Benjamin M. Quarles, *The Negro in the Civil War* (1953).

Edwin S. Redkey, ed., *A Grand Army of Black Men: Letters from African-American Soldiers in the Union Army, 1861–1865* (1992).

C. Peter Ripley, ed., *Witness for Freedom: African American Voices on Race, Slavery, and Emancipation* (1993).

James I. Robertson, *Soldiers Blue and Grey* (1988).

Charles P. Roland, *Albert Sidney Johnston: Soldier of Three Republics* (1964).

William Kauffman Scarborough, ed., *The Diary of Edmund Ruffin,* 3 vols. (1972, 1976, 1989).

Stephen W. Sears, *George B. McClellan: The Young Napoleon* (1988).

Robert E. Shalhope, *Sterling Price: Portrait of a Southerner* (1971).

Craig L. Symonds, *Joseph E. Johnston: A Civil War Biography* (1992).

Emory Thomas, *Lee* (1995).

Bell I. Wiley, *The Life of Johnny Reb: The Common Soldier of the Confederacy* (1943).

Bell I. Wiley, *The Life of Billy Yank: The Common Soldier of the Union* (1952).

C. Vann Woodward, ed., *Mary Chesnut's Civil War* (1981).

MILITARY HISTORY

Richard E. Beringer et al., *Why the South Lost the Civil War* (1986).

Gabor S. Boritt, ed., *Why the Confederacy Lost* (1992).

Albert Castel, *Decision in the West: The Atlanta Campaign of 1864* (1992).

Bruce Catton, *The Centennial History of the Civil War,* 3 vols. (1961–1965).

Joseph P. Cullen, *The Peninsula Campaign, 1862: McClellan and Lee Struggle for Richmond* (1973).

Joseph P. Burke Davis, *Sherman's March* (1980).

William C. Davis, *Battle at Bull Run: A History of the First Major Campaign of the Civil War* (1977).

David H. Donald, ed., *Why the North Won the Civil War* (1961).

Michael Fellman, *Inside War: The Guerrilla Conflict in Missouri during the American Civil War* (1989).

William A. Frassanito, *Gettysburg: A Journey in Time* (1975).

Joseph T. Glatthaar, *The March to the Sea and Beyond: Sherman's Troops in the Savannah and Carolinas Campaigns* (1985).

Herman Hattaway and Archer Jones, *How the North Won* (1983).

John T. Hubbell, ed., *Battles Lost and Won: Essays from Civil War History* (1975).

Archer Jones, *Civil War Command and Strategy: The Process of Victory and Defeat* (1992).

James Pickett Jones, *Yankee Blitzkrieg: Wilson's Raid through Alabama and Georgia* (1976).

Alvin M. Josephy Jr., *The Civil War in the American West* (1991).

James Lee McDonough, *Shiloh: In Hell before Night* (1977).

James Lee McDonough, *Stones River: Bloody Winter in Tennessee* (1980).

Richard M. McMurry, *The Road Past Kennesaw: The Atlanta Campaign of 1864* (1972).

Richard M. McMurry, *John Bell Hood and the War for Southern Independence* (1982).

James M. McPherson, ed., *The Atlas of the Civil War* (1994).

Grady McWhiney and Perry D. Jamieson, *Attack and Die: Civil War Military Tactics and the Southern Heritage* (1982).

James V. Murfin, *The Gleam of Bayonets: The Battle of Antietam and the Maryland Campaign of 1862* (1965).

Howard P. Nash, *A Naval History of the Civil War* (1972).

Charles Royster, *The Destructive War: William Tecumseh Sherman, Stonewall Jackson, and the Americans* (1991).

Stephen W. Sears, *Landscape Turned Red: The Battle of Antietam* (1983).

Richard J. Sommers, *Richmond Redeemed: The Siege at Petersburg* (1981).

Wiley Sword, *Shiloh: Bloody April* (1974).

Richard Wheeler, ed., *The Siege of Vicksburg* (1978).

Steven Woodworth, *Jefferson Davis and His Generals* (1990).

Steven Woodworth, *Davis and Lee at War* (1995).

UNION AND FREEDOM

Herman Belz, *Emancipation and Equal Rights: Politics and Constitutionalism in the Civil War Era* (1978).

Ira Berlin et al., eds., *Freedom: A Documentary History of Emancipation, 1861–1867* (1982–).

Gabor S. Boritt, ed., *Lincoln, The War President* (1992).

LaWanda Cox, *Lincoln and Black Freedom: A Study in Presidential Leadership* (1981).

Robert F. Durden, *The Gray and the Black: The Confederate Debate on Emancipation* (1972).

Barbara Jean Fields, *Slavery and Freedom on the Middle Ground: Maryland during the Nineteenth Century* (1985).

John Hope Franklin, *The Emancipation Proclamation* (1963).

George M. Fredrickson, *White Supremacy: A Comparative Study in American and South African History* (1981).

Louis S. Gerteis, *From Contraband to Freedman: Federal Policy toward Southern Blacks, 1861–1865* (1973).

Janet Hermann, *The Pursuit of a Dream* (1981).

Victor B. Howard, *Black Liberation in Kentucky: Emancipation and Freedom, 1861–1884* (1983).

Peter Kolchin, *First Freedom: The Response of Alabama's Blacks to Emancipation and Reconstruction* (1972).

Leon F. Litwack, *Been in the Storm So Long: The Aftermath of Slavery* (1979).

James M. McPherson, *The Negro's Civil War: How American Negroes Felt and Acted during the War for the Union* (1965).

William F. Messner, *Freedmen and the Ideology of Free Labor: Louisiana, 1862–1865* (1978).

Clarence L. Mohr, *On the Threshold of Freedom: Masters and Slaves in Civil War Georgia* (1986).

Benjamin M. Quarles, *Lincoln and the Negro* (1962).

C. Peter Ripley, *Slaves and Freedmen in Civil War Louisiana* (1976).

Willie Lee Rose, *Rehearsal for Reconstruction: The Port Royal Experiment* (1964).

Hans L. Trefousse, *The Radical Republicans: Lincoln's Vanguard for Racial Justice* (1968).

Bell I. Wiley, *Southern Negroes, 1861–1865* (1938).

THE SOUTH AT WAR

Stephen V. Ash, *When the Yankees Came: Conflict and Chaos* (1995).

Douglas B. Ball, *Financial Failure and Confederate Defeat* (1991).

Richard E. Beringer et al., *The Elements of Confederate Defeat: Nationalism, War Aims, and Religion* (1989).

E. Merton Coulter, *The Confederate States of America, 1861–1865* (1950).

William C. Davis, *Jefferson Davis: The Man and His Hour* (1991).

Mary A. DeCredico, *Patriotism for Profit: Georgia's Urban Entrepreneurs and the Confederate War Effort* (1990).

Marshall L. DeRosa, *The Confederate Constitution of 1861: An Inquiry into American Constitutionalism* (1991).

Wayne K. Durrill, *War of Another Kind: A Southern Community in the Great Rebellion* (1990).

Clement Eaton, *A History of the Southern Confederacy* (1954).

Paul D. Escott, *After Secession: Jefferson Davis and the Failure of Confederate Nationalism* (1978).

Drew Gilpin Faust, *The Creation of Confederate Nationalism: Ideology and Identity in the Civil War South* (1988).

Drew Gilpin Faust, *Mothers of Invention: Women of the Slaveholding South in the American Civil War* (1996).

Ervin L. Jordan Jr., *Black Confederates and Afro-Yankees in Civil War Virginia* (1994).

Frank L. Owsley, *King Cotton Diplomacy: Foreign Relations of the Confederate States of America* (2nd ed. rev., 1959).

George C. Rable, *Civil Wars: Women and the Crisis of Southern Nationalism* (1989).

George C. Rable, *The Confederate Republic: A Revolution against Politics* (1994).

James L. Roark, *Masters without Slaves: Southern Planters in the Civil War and Reconstruction* (1977).

Emory M. Thomas, *The Confederacy as a Revolutionary Experience* (1971).

Emory M. Thomas, *The Confederate Nation, 1861–1865* (1979).

Bell I. Wiley, *The Plain People of the Confederacy* (1943).

THE NORTH AT WAR

Iver Bernstein, *The New York City Draft Riots* (1990).

Allan C. Bogue, *The Earnest Men: Republicans of the Civil War Senate* (1981).

Arthur C. Cole, *The Irrepressible Conflict, 1850–1865* (1934).

Emerson D. Fite, *Social and Industrial Conditions in the North during the Civil War* (1910).

George Fredrickson, *The Inner Civil War: Northern Intellectuals and the Crisis of the Union* (1965).

Paul W. Gates, *Agriculture and the Civil War* (1965).

Wood Gray, *The Hidden Civil War: The Story of the Copperheads* (1942).

Earl J. Hess, *Liberty, Virtue, and Progress: Northerners and Their War for the Union* (1988).

Alvin M. Josephy Jr., *The Civil War in the American West* (1991).

Theodore J. Karamanski, *Rally 'round the Flag: Chicago and the Civil War* (1993).

Frank L. Klement, *The Copperheads in the Middle West* (1960).

Frank L. Klement, *Dark Lanterns: Secret Political Societies, Conspiracies, and Treason Trials in the Civil War* (1984).

Ernest A. McKay, *The Civil War and New York City* (1990).

David Montgomery, *Beyond Equality: Labor and the Radical Republicans, 1862–1872* (1967).

James M. Moorhead, *American Apocalypse: Yankee Protestants and the Civil War, 1860–1869* (1978).

Eugene C. Murdock, *One Million Men: The Civil War Draft in the North* (1971).

Mark E. Neely Jr., *The Fate of Liberty: Abraham Lincoln and Civil Liberties* (1991).

Jacquelyn S. Nelson, *Indiana Quakers Confront the Civil War* (1991).

Grace Palladino, *Another Civil War: Labor, Capital, and the State in the Anthracite Regions of Pennsylvania, 1840–1868* (1990).

Philip S. Paludan, *"A People's Contest": The Union and Civil War, 1861–1865* (1988).

Philip S. Paludan, *The Presidency of Abraham Lincoln* (1994).

James A. Rawley, *The Politics of Union: Northern Politics during the Civil War* (1974).

Joel Silby, *A Respectable Minority: The Democratic Party in the Civil War Era, 1860–1868* (1977).

George W. Smith and Charles Judah, eds., *Life in the North during the Civil War* (1966).

Damon Wells, *Stephen Douglas: The Last Years, 1857–1861* (1971).

ba be bi bo bu | **ra re ri ro ru**
da de di do du | **sa se si so su**
fa fe fi fo fu | **ta te ti to tu**
ka ke ki ko ku | **va ve vi vo vu**

Top. | Hen and chickens. | Drum.

la le li lo lu | **ya ye yi yo yu**
na ne ni no nu | ***ca ce ci co cu**
pa pe pi po pu | **ga ge gi go gu**

Bugle.

ab eb ib
ab ed id
af ef if
ag eg i

Zebra. | Hobby-horse.
Fire Engine. | Snake.
Turkey. | Hoopoe
| Squirrel.

AMERICAN
ONE CENT
PRIMER.

NEW YORK:
KIGGINS & KELLOGG, PUBLISHERS,
Nos. 123 & 125 WILLIAM STREET,
Between John & Fulton.

ONE-CENT PRIMER

"The people are hungry and thirsty after knowledge," a former slave from South Carolina observed after the Civil War. Future African American leader Booker T. Washington remembered "a whole race trying to go to school. Few were too young, and none too old, to make the attempt to learn." Inexpensive elementary textbooks (this humble eight-page primer cost a penny) offered poor ex-slaves the basic elements of literacy — the letters of the alphabet and the sounds they make. For people who had been forbidden to learn to read and write as slaves, literacy symbolized freedom. It also meant that deeply religious people could experience the joy of reading the Bible. Literacy provided a crucial tool for negotiating the hostile world of the postwar South. Reading and writing permitted African Americans to understand labor agreements, sign contracts, and participate knowledgeably in politics.

The William Gladstone Collection.

RECONSTRUCTION, 1863-1877

16

WHEN THE WAR WAS OVER, swarms of northern journalists and government officials rushed to the South to see what four years of fighting had accomplished. Ugly stories of stiff-necked defiance toward Yankees and brutal violence toward ex-slaves had drifted northward. Andrew Johnson, Abraham Lincoln's successor in the White House, asked General Carl Schurz to undertake a special fact-finding tour to assess conditions in the ex-Confederate states. Schurz, a leading antislavery lecturer and Union general, arrived in Charleston, South Carolina, the "Queen City of the South," in July 1865.

Charleston greeted the visitor with an empty harbor, rotting wharves, and gutted buildings. The city looked, Schurz observed, as if it had been struck with "the sudden and irresistible force of a thunderbolt." Cattle grazed in its weed-filled streets. Schurz met former cotton kings and rice barons who could not afford to buy breakfast. Ex-slaves, now Union soldiers, patrolled the city's streets. Schools overflowed with African American children whom it was formerly considered a crime to educate. The Citadel, the state's military school, where once "the chivalric youth of South Carolina was educated for the task of perpetuating slavery by force of arms," now housed the Fifty-fourth Massachusetts Colored Regiment.

Some whites openly expressed their hatred for the new order. Schurz came across defiant young men still "in a swearing mood" who wanted to "fight the war over again." Women in particular, he discovered, remained as "vindictive and defiant as ever." Schurz witnessed one incident in a hotel. "A day or two ago a Union officer, yielding to an impulse of politeness, handed a dish of pickles to a Southern lady at the dinner-table," he said. "A look of unspeakable scorn and indignation met him. 'So you think,' said the lady, 'a Southern woman will take a dish of pickles from a hand that is dripping with the blood of her countrymen?'"

As Schurz slowly made his way across the South to New Orleans, he concluded that most whites "accept things as they are," but he meant only that they recognized that the Confederacy was dead and legal slavery was gone. More than that, they refused to grant. When they professed loyalty to the Union, they did so with a scowl. Moreover, they had not changed their minds about slavery. "The nigger is free, to be sure," ex-slaveholders told him repeatedly, "but he will not work unless compelled to work; we must make him work somehow." Former masters "study not how to build up and develop a true system of free labor," Schurz observed, "but how to avoid it." Where there were no federal troops to stop them, they resorted to the "bowie-knife and revolver, to keep the negroes in their former subjection."

But Schurz found little evidence of black-initiated violence. "Another race . . . would probably have proceeded to cut the throats of those who were in the habit

RUINS OF PINCKNEY HOUSE, CHARLESTON, SOUTH CAROLINA
Northerners had a special hatred for Charleston. According to one inhabitant, Northerners promised: "The rebellion commenced where Charleston is, and shall end, where Charleston was." A devastating fire and three years of Yankee bombardment had almost fulfilled the promise. But in 1865, other consequences of the war alarmed white Charlestonians even more than the physical destruction. Henry Middleton told his sister in Philadelphia that no one could imagine "the utter topsy-turveying of all our institutions."
Library of Congress.

of whipping wives and mothers," he thought, but freedmen simply stood up "a little more independently before their former owners." As for former slaves' performance as free laborers, Schurz deemed it only "middling-fair." He believed he knew why. "The idea has got into the heads of the negroes that the land belongs to them," he declared. They were in no hurry, consequently, to work for whites who claimed to be landlords. Still, he concluded, "the colored man will learn sooner what he has to do as a free laborer than the white man in these parts will learn how to treat a free laborer."

Two months in the South convinced Schurz that withdrawing federal troops and restoring self-government would be a fatal error. He called the Civil War a "revolution but half accomplished." Military victory had destroyed slavery, but it had not erased proslavery ideas. Left to themselves, ex-Confederates would "introduce some new system of forced labor, not perhaps exactly slavery in its old form but something similar to it." To defend themselves, blacks would need land of their own and voting rights, Schurz concluded. Until whites "cut loose

from the past," he declared, "it will be a dangerous experiment to put Southern society upon its own legs."

As Schurz discovered, the end of the war did not mean the beginning of peace. Instead, the nation entered one of its most chaotic and conflicted eras—Reconstruction. It was not that the Civil War failed to resolve anything. Northern victory had determined once and for all the fates of secession and slavery, but out of the war emerged two new divisive questions. First, what was the status of the defeated South within the Union? Would the eleven ex-Confederate states be quickly and forgivingly welcomed back, or would they be held at arm's length and required to reform before resuming their former places? Second, what would freedom mean for ex-slaves? Would they be left to make their place in the South on their own, or would the federal government guarantee full citizenship, free labor, and equality?

Throughout Reconstruction, little was fixed, and the pace of change was swift. What seemed an unlikely possibility at one moment found majority support the next. In the months after the war, calls to extend the ballot and full citizenship to freedmen generated hysteria, but the proposals quickly became standard Republican policy and the law of the land. "These are no times of ordinary politics," Boston lawyer and reformer Wendell Phillips declared in 1867. "These are formative hours; the national purpose and thought grows and ripens in thirty days as much as ordinary years bring it forward."

In one way or another, everyone agreed that the central issue in reconstruction was the place of African Americans in American society. North and South divided over the issue, but neither region spoke with a single voice. Still, a majority of southern whites rejected black rights. Southern intransigence in turn helped northern Republicans to close ranks and shifted the party's center toward more radical definitions of black freedom. It was never simply a debate between whites, however. Blacks emerged from slavery with their own ideas, and they became active agents in the struggle to define freedom.

The political part of that struggle took place in the nation's capital and in the state legislatures and county seats of the South. But the struggle also engaged the economic and social consequences of emancipation. In masters' kitchens and in plantation fields, ex-slaves strove to leave slavery behind and to become free laborers and free people. Many whites, as Carl Schurz learned, resisted letting go of the Old South. Nevertheless, emancipation and the developments of Reconstruction had profound consequences for blacks and whites in the South and for the nation as a whole.

Wartime Reconstruction

Reconstruction did not wait for the end of war. As the odds of a northern victory increased, thinking about reunification quickened. Immediately, a question arose: Who had authority to devise a plan of reconstruction? The Founders had not anticipated such a problem, and so the Constitution stood silent. Lincoln believed firmly that reconstruction was a matter of executive responsibility. Congress just as firmly asserted its jurisdiction. Fueling the argument about who had authority to set the terms of reconstruction were significant differences about the terms themselves. Lincoln's primary aim was the restoration of national unity, which he sought through a program of speedy, forgiving political

reconciliation. Congress feared that the president's lenient program amounted to restoring the old southern ruling class to power. It wanted greater assurances of white loyalty and greater guarantees of black rights. Rival plans emerged during the war, but Lincoln and Congress managed to bridge their differences. Only continued cooperation would achieve victory over the South and abolition of slavery.

In their eagerness to formulate a plan for political reunification, neither Lincoln nor Congress gave much attention to the South's land and labor problems. But war was rapidly eroding slavery and traditional plantation agriculture, and Yankee military commanders in the Union-occupied areas of the Confederacy had no choice but to oversee the emergence of a new labor system. With little guidance from Washington, northern officials felt their way along, bumping heads with both planters and freedmen. Although hastily assembled and improvised, their labor system ultimately had more staying power than any reconstruction policy formulated in wartime Washington.

"To Bind Up the Nation's Wounds"

On March 4, 1865, President Abraham Lincoln delivered his second inaugural address. His words blazed with religious imagery as he surveyed the history of the long, deadly war and then looked ahead to peace. "With malice toward none; with charity for all; with firmness in the right, as God gives us to see the right," Lincoln said, "let us strive on to finish the work we are in; to bind up the nation's wounds . . . to do all which may achieve and cherish a just, and a lasting peace." Lincoln had contemplated reunion for nearly two years. Deep compassion for the enemy guided his thinking about peace. But kindness is not the key to understanding Lincoln's program. His reconstruction plan aimed primarily at shortening the war and ending slavery.

Lincoln believed firmly that reconstruction was a matter of executive responsibility. Congress just as firmly asserted its jurisdiction.

In his Proclamation of Amnesty and Reconstruction, issued in December 1863, when Union forces had finally gained the upper hand on the battlefield, Lincoln offered a full pardon to rebels willing to renounce secession and to accept the abolition of slavery. (Pardons were valuable because they restored all property, except slaves, and full political rights.) His offer excluded several groups of Confederates, such as high-ranking civilian and military officers, but the plan called for no mass arrests, no trials for treason, and no executions. Instead, when only 10 percent of men who had been qualified voters in 1860 had taken an oath of allegiance, they could organize a new state government. Lincoln hoped that war-sick rebels would embrace the easy terms of reunification, renew their allegiance to the Union, and abandon both slavery and secession. His plan did not require that ex-rebels extend social or political rights to ex-slaves, nor did it anticipate a program of long-term federal assistance to freedmen. Clearly, the president sought to restore the broken Union, not to reform it.

Lincoln's easy terms enraged abolitionists like Wendell Phillips, who charged that the president "makes the negro's freedom a mere sham." He "is willing that the negro should be free but seeks nothing else for him," Phillips declared. He compared Lincoln unfavorably to the most passive of the Civil War generals: "What McClellan was on the battlefield—'Do as little hurt as possible!'—Lincoln is in civil affairs—'Make as little change as possible!'" Phillips and other radicals called instead for revolutionary change, for a thoroughgoing overhaul of southern society. Their ideas proved to be too drastic for most Republicans during the war years, but Congress agreed that Lincoln's plan was inadequate. In July 1864, Congress put forward a plan of its own.

As General William T. Sherman was marching on Atlanta, Congressman Henry Winter Davis of Maryland and Senator Benjamin Wade of Ohio jointly sponsored a bill that threw out Lincoln's "10 percent plan" and demanded that a majority of voters in a conquered rebel state take the oath of allegiance before reconstruction could begin. Moreover, the Wade-Davis bill banned ex-Confederates from participating in the drafting of new state constitutions. Finally, the bill guaranteed the equality of freedmen before the law. Congress's reconstruction would be neither as quick nor as forgiving as Lincoln's. Still, the Wade-Davis bill angered radicals because it did not include a provision for black suffrage. When Lincoln exercised his right not to sign the bill and let it die instead, Wade and Davis published a manifesto charging the president with usurpation of power. They warned Lincoln to confine himself to "his executive duties—to obey and

execute, not make the laws—to suppress by arms armed rebellion, and leave political organization to Congress."

Undeterred, Lincoln continued to nurture the formation of loyal state governments under his own plan. Four states—Louisiana, Arkansas, Tennessee, and Virginia—fulfilled the president's requirements. Lincoln acknowledged that a government based on only 10 percent was not ideal, but he argued that it would be a "rallying point" for lukewarm rebels. "We shall sooner have the fowl by hatching the egg than by smashing it," Lincoln told Charles Sumner. "The eggs of crocodiles can produce only crocodiles," the Massachusetts senator retorted. Congress refused to seat representatives from the "Lincoln states." In his last public address in April 1865, Lincoln defended his plan but stressed his willingness to be flexible. For the first time he expressed publicly his endorsement of suffrage for southern blacks, at least "the very intelligent, and . . . those who serve our cause as soldiers." The announcement demonstrated that Lincoln's thinking about reconstruction was still evolving. Four days later, he was dead.

Land and Labor

Of all the problems raised by emancipation, none proved more critical than the transition from slave to free labor. Slavery had been, at bottom, a labor system, and while Republicans agreed that free labor would replace forced labor, they disagreed about what free labor would mean in the South. As Yankee armies proceeded to invade and occupy the Confederacy during the war, hundreds of thousands of slaves became free workers. Moreover, Yankee occupation meant that Union armies controlled vast territories where legal title to land had become unclear. The wartime Confiscation Acts punished "traitors" by confiscating their property. What to do with federally occupied land and how to organize labor on it engaged former slaves, former slaveholders, Union military commanders, and federal government officials long before the war ended.

From Virginia's tidewater to Louisiana's bayous, a variety of wartime labor experiments arose. The system that developed in the Mississippi valley proved to be a preview of postwar southern labor relations. Up and down the Mississippi, occupying federal troops ended slavery, which had already begun to fall apart because of slaves' resistance, and announced a new labor code. It required

THE EXECUTION OF BOOTH'S CO-CONSPIRATORS
Union troops tracked down and killed Lincoln's assassin, John Wilkes Booth, on April 26, 1865. Eight others were convicted of conspiring in the murder. On July 7, four were hanged, including Mary Surratt. Although Surratt knew Booth and had clearly been a Confederate sympathizer, there was no concrete evidence that she had participated in the murder plot.
Meserve-Kunhardt Collection.

planters to sign contracts with their laborers and to pay wages. The code also obligated employers to provide food, housing, and medical care. It outlawed whipping and other forms of physical punishment, but it reserved to the army the right to discipline blacks who refused to work. The code required black laborers to enter into contracts, work diligently, and remain subordinate and obedient. While the military took aim at slavery, it clearly had no intention of fomenting a social or economic revolution. Instead, it sought to restore plantation agriculture with wage labor. The effort resulted in a hybrid system of "compulsory free labor" that satisfied no one. Depending on one's point of view, it either provided too little or too much of a break with the past.

Planters complained because the new system fell short of slavery. A Louisiana sugar planter predicted that the military's plan would fail because Northerners did "not understand the Negro." Ex-slaves could not be "transformed by proclamation," he warned. Yet under the new system, blacks "are expected to perform their new obligations without coercion, & without the fear of punishment which is essential to stimulate the idle and correct the vicious." Without the right to whip, he concluded, the new labor system did not have a chance.

African Americans also criticized the new regime. They found it too reminiscent of slavery to be called "free labor." Of its many shortcomings, none disappointed ex-slaves more than the failure to provide them land of their own. "What's the use of being free if you don't own land enough to be buried in?" one man asked. "Might just as well stay a slave all your days." Freedmen were determined to become independent, and that required land. They believed they had a moral right to land because they and their ancestors had worked it without compensation for more than two centuries. Moreover, several wartime developments seemed to indicate that the federal government planned to link black freedom and landownership.

In January 1865, General Sherman had set aside for black settlement the Sea Islands off the South Carolina coast and part of the coast south of Charleston. He devised the plan to relieve himself of the burden of thousands of impoverished blacks who trailed desperately after his army. By June 1865, some 40,000 freedmen sat on 400,000 acres of "Sherman land." In addition, in March 1865, Congress established the Bureau of Refugees, Freedmen, and Abandoned Lands. The Freedmen's Bureau, as it was called, distributed food and clothing to destitute Southerners and eased the transition of blacks from slaves to free persons. But Congress also authorized the agency to divide abandoned and confiscated land into forty-acre plots, to rent them to freedmen, and eventually to sell them "with such title as the United States can convey." By June 1865, the bureau had situated nearly 10,000 black families on a half million acres that had been abandoned by fleeing South Carolina and Georgia planters. Hundreds of thousands of other ex-slaves eagerly anticipated getting farms of their own.

Despite the flurry of activity, wartime reconstruction had settled nothing. Two years of controversy had failed to produce agreement about whether the president or Congress had the authority to devise and direct policy or what proper policy should be. Lincoln had organized several new state governments, but Congress had not readmitted a single "reconstructed" state into the Union. There were hints that the price of defeat for the South would be a revolution in landholding, but the "compulsory free labor" system that emerged on plantations in the Mississippi valley suggested more continuity with antebellum traditions. Clearly, the nation faced dilemmas and difficulties almost as burdensome as those of the war.

The African American Quest for Autonomy

Although white politicians had difficulty agreeing, ex-slaves never had any doubt about what they wanted freedom to mean. They had only to contemplate what they had been denied as slaves. Slaves had to remain on their plantations; freedom

AN INDEPENDENT BLACK CHURCH
Poor freedmen found that one of the sweetest fruits of emancipation was the opportunity to worship in churches of their own. White observers characterized black worship as nothing but "visions and trances," but independent black churches did more than permit members to dance and shout if they wanted. They also promoted black education, extended relief to freedmen who could not provide for themselves, and engaged in Republican politics.
South Carolina Historical Society.

allowed blacks to go wherever they pleased. Thus, in the first heady weeks after emancipation, freedmen often abandoned their plantations just to see what was on the other side of the hill and to feel freedom under their feet. Slaves had to be at work in the fields by dawn; freedom permitted blacks to taste the forbidden pleasure of sleeping through a sunrise. Slaves had to defer to whites; freedom saw them test the etiquette of racial subordination. "Lizzie's maid passed me today when I was coming from church *without speaking to me*," huffed one plantation mistress. When she asked her own house servant to scour some kettles, the black woman snapped, "You better do it yourself. Ain't you smarter than me? You think you is—why don't you scour them yourself."

To whites, it looked like pure anarchy. Without the discipline of slavery, they said, blacks had reverted to their natural condition: lazy, irresponsible, and wild. Actually, former slaves were experimenting with freedom, in both trivial and profound ways. But poor black people could not long afford to roam the countryside, neglect work, and casually provoke whites. Soon, most were back on plantations, at work in the fields and kitchens.

But other items on ex-slaves' agenda of freedom endured. Freedmen did not easily give up their quest for economic independence. In addition, slavery had deliberately kept blacks illiterate, and freedmen emerged from bondage eager to read and write. Moreover, bondage had denied slaves secure family lives and the ability to worship openly as they saw fit. Consequently, families and religion became areas of persistent black aspiration.

Although slave marriages and family relations had existed only at the master's whim, slaves had nevertheless managed to create deep, enduring family bonds. Still, slave sales had often severed family ties. As a consequence, thousands of black men and women took to the roads in 1865 to look for relations who had been sold away. One northern newspaperman encountered a ragged freedman who had walked six hundred miles to North Carolina, where he had *heard* that his wife and children had been sold. Couples who emerged from slavery with their marriages intact often rushed to northern military chaplains to legalize their unions. (See Texts in Historical Context, page 612.)

The end of slavery saw families abandon the slave quarters and scatter over plantations, building separate cabins on the patches of land they rented. In independent households, far from whites, black families escaped white intrusion. Parents no

MARRIAGE CERTIFICATE
During the Civil War, blacks serving in the Union army married under military authority. Henry M. Turner, a black chaplain, officiated at the wedding of Elisabeth Turner and Rufus Wright. After the war, thousands of ex-slaves whose marriages had no legal standing under slavery rushed to formalize their unions.
National Archives.

longer had to endure interference in the raising of their children. Women were less vulnerable to violation by masters and their sons. Some wives were able to exchange field labor for housework. Whites claimed that they were "acting the lady," but what whites meant was that black women were not acting like slaves. Instead, they behaved like mothers and housewives, occupied with the same arduous domestic chores as poor white women. Extreme poverty eventually forced most black women back into the cotton fields (at least at picking time) or into white kitchens. Nevertheless, safe and secure families came high on every ex-slave's list of freedom's blessings.

Another hunger that freedom permitted African Americans to satisfy was independent worship. Under slavery, blacks had often, like it or not,

The Meaning of Freedom

On New Year's Day 1863, President Abraham Lincoln issued the Emancipation Proclamation. It stated that "all persons held as slaves" within the states still in rebellion "are, and henceforward shall be, free." Although it did not in and of itself free any slaves, it transformed the character of the war. Despite often intolerable conditions, black people focused on the possibilities of freedom.

John Q. A. Dennis, formerly a slave in Maryland, wrote to Secretary of War Edwin M. Stanton to ask his help in reuniting his family.

DOCUMENT 1. Letter from John Q. A. Dennis to Edwin M. Stanton

Boston July 26th 1864

Dear Sir I am Glad that I have the Honour to Write you afew line I have been in troble for about four yars my Dear wife was taken from me Nov 19th 1859 and left me with three Children and I being a Slave At the time Could Not do Anny thing for the poor little Children for my master it was took me Carry me some forty mile from them So I Could Not do for them and the man that they live with half feed them and half Cloth them & beat them like dogs & when I was admitted to go to see them it use to brake my heart & Now I say agian I am Glad to have the honour to write to you to see if you Can Do Anny thing for me or for my poor little Children I was keap in Slavy untell last Novr 1863. then the Good lord sent the Cornel borne [William Birney?] Down their in Marland in worsester Co So as I have been recently freed I have but letle to live on but I am Striveing Dear Sir but what I went too know of you Sir is is it possible for me to go & take my Children from those men that keep them in Savery if it is possible will you pleas give me a permit from your hand then I think they would let them go. . . .

Hon sir will you please excuse my Miserable writeing & answer me as soon as you can I want get the little Children out of Slavery, I being Criple would like to know of you also if I Cant be permited to rase a Shool Down there & on what turm I Could be admited to Do so No more At present Dear Hon Sir

Freedom also prompted ex-slaves to seek legal marriages, which under slavery had been impossible. On February 28, 1865, in Little Rock, Arkansas, A. B. Randall, the white chaplain of a black regiment, in a report to the adjutant general of the Union army, confirmed the importance of marriage to freed slaves and emphasized their conviction that emancipation was just the first step toward full freedom.

DOCUMENT 2. Report from Reverend A. B. Randall

Weddings, just now, are very popular, and abundant among the Colored People. They have just learned, of the Special Order No' 15. of Gen Thomas [Adjutant General Lorenzo Thomas] by which, they may not only be lawfully married, but have their Marriage Certificates, *Recorded*; in a *book furnished by the Government*. This is most desirable. . . . Those who were captured . . . at Ivy's Ford, on the 17th of January, by Col Brooks, had their Marriage Certificates, taken from them; and destroyed; and then were roundly cursed, for having such papers in their posession. I have married, during the month, at this Post; Twenty five couples; mostly, those, who have families; & have been living together for years. I try to dissuade single men, who are soldiers, from marrying, till their time of enlistment is out: as that course seems to me, to be most judicious.

The Colord People here, generally consider, this war not only; their *exodus*, from bondage; but the road, to Responsibility; Competency; and an honorable Citizenship—God grant that their hopes and expectations may be fully realized.

Early efforts at political reconstruction prompted petitions from former slaves demanding civil and political rights. In January 1865, black Tennesseans petitioned a convention of white unionists debating the reorganization of state government.

DOCUMENT 3. Petition "to the Union Convention of Tennessee Assembled in the Capitol at Nashville, January 9th, 1865"

We the undersigned petitioners, American citizens of African descent, natives and residents of Tennessee, and devoted friends of the great National cause, do most respectfully ask a patient hearing of your honorable body in regard to matters deeply affecting the future condition of our unfortunate and long suffering race.

First of all, however, we would say that words are too weak to tell how profoundly grateful we are to the Federal Government for the good work of freedom which it is gradually carrying forward; and for the Emancipation Proclamation which has set free all the slaves in some of the rebellious States, as well as many of the slaves in Tennessee. . . .

We claim freedom, as our natural right, and ask that in harmony and co-operation with the nation at large, you should cut up by the roots the system of slavery, which is not only a wrong to us, but the source of all the evil which at present afflicts the State. For slavery, corrupt itself, corrupted nearly all, also, around it, so that it has influenced nearly all the slave States to rebel against the Federal Government, in order to set up a government of pirates under which slavery might be perpetrated.

In the contest between the nation and slavery, our unfortunate people have sided, by instinct, with the former. We have little fortune to devote to the national cause, for a hard fate has hitherto forced us to live in poverty, but we do devote to its success, our hopes, our toils, our whole heart, our sacred honor, and our lives. We will work, pray, live, and, if need be, die for the Union, as cheerfully as ever a white patriot died for his country. The color of our skin does not lessen in the least degree, our love either for God or for the land of our birth. . . .

We know the burdens of citizenship, and are ready to bear them. We know the duties of the good citizen, and are ready to perform them cheerfully, and would ask to be put in a position in which we can discharge them more effectually. We do not ask for the privilege of citizenship, wishing to shun the obligations imposed by it. . . .

This is a democracy—a government of the people. It should aim to make every man, without regard to the color of his skin, the amount of his wealth, or the character of his religious faith, feel personally interested in its welfare. Every man who lives under the Government should feel that it is his property, his treasure, the bulwark and defence of himself and his family, his pearl of great price, which he must preserve, protect, and defend faithfully at all times, on all occasions, in every possible manner.

This is not a Democratic Government if a numerous, law-abiding, industrious, and useful class of citizens, born and bred on the soil, are to be treated as aliens and enemies, as an inferior degraded class, who must have no voice in the Government which they support, protect and defend, with all their heart, soul, mind, and body, both in peace and war. . . .

. . . The nation is fighting for its life, and cannot afford to be controlled by prejudice. Had prejudice prevailed instead of principle, not a single colored soldier would have been in the Union army to-day. But principle and justice triumphed, and now near 200,000 colored patriots stand under the folds of the national flag, and brave their breasts to the bullets of the rebels. As we are in the battlefield, so we swear before heaven, by all that is dear to men, to be at the ballot-box faithful and true to the Union.

The possibility that the negro suffrage proposition may shock popular prejudice at first sight, is not a conclusive argument against its wisdom and policy. No proposition ever met with more furious or general opposition than the one to enlist colored soldiers in the United States army. The opponents of the measure exclaimed on all hands that the negro was a coward; that he would not fight; that one white man, with a whip in his hand could put to flight a regiment of them; that the experiment would end in the utter rout and ruin of the Federal army. Yet the colored man has fought so well, on almost every occasion, that the rebel government is prevented, only by its fears and distrust of being able to force him to fight for slavery as well as he fights against it, from putting half a million of negroes into its ranks.

The Government has asked the colored man to fight for its preservation and gladly has he done it. It can afford to trust him with a vote as safely as it trusted him with a bayonet.

Document 1. Ira Berlin, Joseph P. Reidy, and Leslie S. Rowland, eds., *Freedom: A Documentary History of Emancipation, 1861–1867. Series I, Volume I, The Destruction of Slavery* (Cambridge University Press, 1985), 386.

Document 2. Ira Berlin, Joseph P. Reidy, and Leslie S. Rowland, eds., *Freedom: A Documentary History of Emancipation, 1861–1867. Series II, The Black Military Experience* (Cambridge University Press, 1982), 712.

Document 3. Ibid., 811–816.

prayed with whites in biracial churches. Full expression of black spirituality could be found only in the dead of night in secret religious services. Intent on religious independence, blacks greeted freedom with a mass exodus from white churches. Some joined the newly established southern branches of all-black northern churches, such as the African Methodist Episcopal Church. Others formed black versions of the major southern denominations, Baptists and Methodists. On the eve of the war, 42,000 blacks had worshiped in biracial Methodist churches in South Carolina; by 1870, all but 600 had left. Slaves had viewed their tribulations through the lens of their deeply felt Christian faith, and freedmen comprehended the events of the Civil War and Reconstruction as people of faith. It was not surprising that ex-slaves claimed Abraham Lincoln as their Moses.

Presidential Reconstruction

Abraham Lincoln died on April 15, 1865, just hours after John Wilkes Booth had shot him at a Washington, D.C., theater. Chief Justice Salmon P. Chase immediately administered the oath of office to Vice President Andrew Johnson. Lincoln's assassination thrust the Tennessean into responsibility at a time of grave national crisis. Moreover, Congress had adjourned in March, which meant that legislators were away from Washington when Lincoln was killed. They would not reconvene until December unless the new president called Congress back into special session. But Johnson preferred to have Washington to himself while he made critical decisions about the future of the South. Like Lincoln, he believed that responsibility for restoring the Union lay with the president. Throughout the summer and fall, therefore, the "accidental president" presided over the nation without a sitting Congress. With dizzying speed, Johnson drew up and executed a plan of reconstruction.

Congress returned to the capital in December to find that, as far as the president and former Confederates were concerned, Reconstruction was over. Appalled by what they saw, members of Congress challenged the president's prerogative and policies. To most Republicans, Johnson's modest demands of ex-rebels made a mockery of the sacrifice of Union soldiers. In an 1863 speech dedicating the cemetery at Gettysburg, Lincoln had spoken of the "great task remaining before us . . . that we here highly resolve

that these dead shall not have died in vain—that this nation, under God, shall have a new birth of freedom." Instead, Johnson had acted as midwife to the rebirth of the Old South. He had achieved political reunification at the cost of black liberty. To let his program stand, Republican legislators said, would mean that the North's dead had indeed died in vain.

Johnson's Program of Reconciliation

Born in 1808 in Raleigh, North Carolina, Andrew Johnson was the son of very poor, illiterate parents. Unable to afford to send her son to school, Johnson's widowed mother apprenticed him to a tailor. Self-educated and ambitious, the young man ran away before completing his indenture and headed for Tennessee. There he worked as a tailor, accumulated a fortune in land, acquired five slaves, and built a career in politics championing the South's common white people and assailing its "illegitimate, swaggering, bastard, scrub aristocracy." According to an old political foe, "If Johnson were a snake, he would lie in the grass to bite the heels of rich men's children." The only senator from a Confederate state to remain loyal to the Union, Johnson held no grudge against the South's rebel yeomen. He believed that they had been hoodwinked by slaveholding secessionists. Less than two weeks before he became president, he made it clear what he would do to the rascals if he ever had the chance: "I would arrest them—I would try them—I would convict them and I would hang them."

Throughout the summer and fall, the "accidental president" presided over the nation without a sitting Congress. With dizzying speed, Johnson drew up and executed a plan of reconstruction.

No wonder the South's elite trembled when Lincoln died. Republicans who looked forward to drastic changes in the South celebrated their powerful new ally in the White House. In reality, however, Johnson was no friend. Indeed, he was no Republican. A Democrat all his life, Johnson occupied the White House only because the Republican Party in 1864 had needed to broaden its appeal to loyal, Union-supporting Democrats. As a Tennessee congressman and senator, Johnson had championed traditional Democratic causes, vigorously defending states' rights (but not secession) and opposing Republican efforts to expand the power of the federal government, especially in the economic realm. He had voted against almost every federal appropriation, including a bill to pave the streets of Washington.

Moreover, Johnson had been a steadfast defender of slavery. He had owned slaves until 1862, when Tennessee rebels, angry at his Unionism, confiscated them. He only grudgingly accepted emancipation. When he did, it was more because of his hatred for slaveholders than sympathy for slaves. "Damn the negroes," he said. "I am fighting those traitorous aristocrats, their masters." At a time when the nation faced its moment of truth regarding black Americans, the new president harbored unshakable racist convictions. Africans, he said, were "inferior to the white man in point of intellect —better calculated in physical structure to undergo drudgery and hardship." On the eve of his inauguration as vice president, he had reiterated his belief in a white man's government.

One month after becoming president, Johnson announced his plan of reconstruction. He presented it as a continuation of Lincoln's plan, and in some ways it was. Like Lincoln, he stressed reconciliation between the Union and the defeated Confederacy and rapid restoration of civil government in the South. He offered to pardon most ex-rebels who promised future loyalty to the Union. Like Lincoln, Johnson excluded high-ranking ex-Confederates, but he also excluded all ex-rebels with property worth more than $20,000. The Tennessee tailor was apparently taking aim at his old enemy, the planter aristocrats. Wealthy individuals would have to apply directly to the president for pardons. Johnson recognized the state governments created by Lincoln and set out his own requirements for restoring the rebel states to the Union. All that the citizens of a state had to do was to renounce the right of secession, deny that the debts of the Confederacy were legal and binding, and ratify the Thirteenth Amendment abolishing slavery, which had become part of the Constitution in December 1865. Johnson's plan ignored Lincoln's acceptance near the end of his life of some form of limited black voting.

Johnson's eagerness to normalize relations with southern states and his lack of sympathy for blacks also led him to instruct military and government officials to return to pardoned ex-Confederates all confiscated and abandoned land, even if it was in the hands of freedmen. Reformers were shocked.

They had expected the president's vendetta against planters to mean the permanent confiscation of the South's plantations and the distribution of the land to loyal freedmen. Instead, his instructions canceled the promising beginnings made by General Sherman and the Freedmen's Bureau to settle blacks on land of their own. As one freedman observed, "things was hurt by Mr. Lincoln getting killed."

Johnson's reconstruction envisioned a quick and easy political reconciliation between North and South and demonstrated almost no concern for freedmen. Predictably, Republicans who sought a drastic overhaul of southern society denounced the plan. "Is there no way to arrest the insane course of the President?" asked Congressman Thaddeus Stevens. It appeared that the president was committed to surrendering blacks and the Republican Party to the "tender mercies of the rebels."

Southern Resistance and Black Codes

In the summer of 1865, delegates across the South gathered to draw up the new state constitutions required by Johnson's plan of reconstruction. They revealed that while they had been defeated, they had not been subdued. Rather than take their medicine, they choked on even the president's mild requirements. Refusing to declare their secession ordinances null and void, the South Carolina and Georgia conventions merely "repudiated" their ordinances, preserving in principle their right to secede. In addition, every state convention wrangled over the precise wording of the constitutional amendment ending slavery. In the end, Mississippi rejected the Thirteenth Amendment outright, and Alabama rejected it in part. Finally, South Carolina and Mississippi refused to repudiate their Confederate war debts. These defiant acts provoked only mild responses from Andrew Johnson. He recommended, suggested, and even pleaded, but he did not demand that Southerners comply with his lenient terms.

White Southerners learned dangerous lessons from this initial experience. By failing to draw a hard line, Johnson rekindled southern resistance. White Southerners began to think that, by standing up for themselves, they—not victorious Northerners—would shape the transition from slavery to freedom. In the fall of 1865, newly elected southern legislators set out to reverse the "retreat into barbarism" that followed emancipation.

Under the mantle of protectors of the freedmen, state governments across the South adopted a se-

THE BLACK CODES
Entitled Selling a Freeman to Pay His Fine at Monticello, Florida, *this 1867 drawing from a northern magazine equates the black codes with the reinstitution of slavery. The laws stopped short of reenslavement, but they did sharply restrict blacks' freedom. In Florida, as in other southern states, certain acts, such as breaking a labor contract, were made criminal offenses, the penalty for which could be involuntary plantation labor for a year.*
Library of Congress.

ries of laws known as the black codes. Rejecting the principle of legal equality, legislators argued that ex-slaves required special laws. While emancipation had brought freedmen important rights that they had lacked as slaves—to own property, to make contracts, to marry legally, and to sue and be sued in court—the black codes made a travesty of freedom. They sought to keep blacks subordinate to whites. Scores of laws subjected blacks to every sort of discrimination. Mississippi made insulting gestures and language a criminal offense. Several states made it illegal for blacks to own a gun. Blacks were barred from jury duty. Not a single southern state granted any black—no matter how educated, wealthy, or refined—the right to vote.

At the core of the black codes, however, lay the matter of labor. Faced with the death of slavery and the disintegration of plantations, legislators sought to channel freedmen back into traditional tasks. South Carolina attempted to limit blacks to either farmwork or domestic service by requiring them to pay annual taxes of $10 to $100 to work in any other occupation. Mississippi demanded that by January of each year blacks possess written evidence of employment. An offender could be declared a vagrant and be subject to fine or involuntary plantation labor. Most states allowed judges to bind black children—orphans and others whose parents they

deemed unable to support them—to white employers. Under these so-called apprenticeship laws, courts bound out thousands of black children to planter "guardians," often over the protests of their parents. Legislators bent every effort to resuscitate the traditional plantation economy and resurrect as nearly as possible the old regime.

Johnson refused to intervene decisively. A staunch defender of states' rights, he believed that the citizens of every state—even those citizens who had attempted to destroy the Union—should be free to write their own constitutions and laws. Moreover, since he shared other white Southerners' eagerness to restore white supremacy and black subordination, the black codes did not particularly offend him or seem excessive. Besides, he could point proudly to the fact that by December 1865, enough states had approved the Thirteenth Amendment to make it a part of the Constitution.

But Johnson also followed the path he believed offered him the greatest political return. A conservative Tennessee Democrat at the head of a northern Republican Party, he began to look southwards for political allies. Despite tough talk about punishing traitors, he issued more than 14,000 special pardons to wealthy or high-ranking ex-Confederates. He no doubt enjoyed the sight of former aristocrats lining up humbly to beg his pardon, but

Johnson recognized that these supplicants could also be useful politically. By pardoning planters and Confederate officials, by acquiescing in the South's black codes, and by accepting the new southern governments even when they failed to satisfy his minimal demands, he won useful allies.

If Northerners had any doubts about the mood of the South, they evaporated in the elections of 1865. To represent them in Congress, white Southerners chose former Confederates, not loyal Unionists. Of the eighty senators and representatives they sent to Washington, fifteen had served in the Confederate army, ten of them as generals. Another sixteen had served in civil and judicial posts in the Confederacy. Nine others had served in the Confederate Congress. One—Alexander Stephens—had been vice president of the Confederacy. Some had not yet even received pardons, but Johnson granted immediate clemency so that they could take office. In December, this remarkable group arrived on the steps of the nation's Capitol to be seated in Congress. As one Georgian later remarked: "It looked as though Richmond had moved to Washington."

Expansion of Black Rights and Federal Authority

Southerners had blundered monumentally. They had assumed that what Andrew Johnson was willing to accept, the northern public and Congress would accept as well. But southern intransigence compelled even moderate Republicans to conclude that ex-rebels were a "generation of vipers," still dangerous, still untrustworthy. Northerners sought evidence of a change of heart, but they searched in vain for remorse for slavery, secession, or waging a devastating war. Since white Southerners denied that they were sinners, they refused to repent. Without repentance, Northerners could not forgive.

The black codes in particular soured moderate Republicans on the South's efforts at reconstruction. The codes became a symbol of southern intentions not to accept the verdict of the battlefields, but instead to "restore all of slavery but its name." Northerners were hardly saints when it came to racial justice, but black freedom had become a hallowed war aim. The deaths of Union soldiers had sanctified it. "We tell the white men of Mississippi," the *Chicago Tribune* roared, "that the men of the North will convert the State of Mississippi into a frog pond before they will allow such laws to disgrace one foot of the soil in which the bones of our soldiers sleep and

THE LOST CAUSE
While politicians in Washington, D.C., debated the future of the South, white Southerners were coming to grips with their emotions and history. They began to refer to their failure to secede from the Union as the "Lost Cause." They enshrined the memory of certain former Confederates, especially Robert E. Lee. Lee's nobility and courage represented the white South's image of itself. This quilt from about 1870, with Lee stitched in the center, illustrates how common whites incorporated the symbols of the Lost Cause into their daily lives. The unknown maker of the quilt also included miniature Confederate flags and memorial ribbons.
Valentine Museum, Cook Collection.

over which the flag of freedom waves." Moderate Republicans generally agreed that the "first fruits of reconstruction promise a most deplorable harvest, and the sooner we gather the tares [weeds], plow the ground again and sow new seed, the better."

Moderates represented the mainstream of the Republican Party and wanted only assurance that slavery and treason were dead. They did not seek a revolution of the entire southern social order. They did not champion black equality or the confiscation of plantations or black voting, as did the Radicals, a minority faction within the Republican Party. In December 1865, however, when Congress convened in Washington, it became clear that events in the

South had succeeded in forging unity (at least temporarily) among Republican factions. Exercising Congress's right to determine the qualifications of its members, the moderate majority and the Radical minority came together to refuse to seat the southern representatives. Rather than accept Johnson's claim that the "work of restoration" was done, Congress countered his executive power. Congressional Republicans enjoyed a three-to-one majority over the Democrats, and if they could agree on a program of reconstruction, they could easily pass legislation and even override presidential vetoes.

The moderates took the initiative. Senator Lyman Trumbull of Illinois declared that the president's policy of trusting southern whites proved that the ex-slave would "be tyrannized over, abused, and virtually reenslaved without some legislation by the nation for his protection." Early in 1866, the moderates produced two bills that strengthened the federal shield. The first, the Freedmen's Bureau bill, prolonged the life of the agency established by the previous Congress. Since the end of the war, it had distributed food, supervised labor contracts, and sponsored schools for freedmen. To the cheers of southern whites and the dismay of Republican moderates, President Johnson vetoed the Freedmen's Bureau bill. The Constitution, he argued, never contemplated a "system for the support of indigent persons." Congress failed by a narrow margin to override the president's veto.

Johnson's shocking veto galvanized nearly unanimous Republican support for the moderates' second measure, the Civil Rights Act. Designed to nullify the black codes, it affirmed the rights of blacks to enjoy "full and equal benefit of all laws and proceedings for the security of person and property as is enjoyed by white citizens." Modest on its surface, the act boldly required the end of legal discrimination in state laws and represented an extraordinary expansion of black rights and federal authority. The president argued that the civil rights bill amounted to an "unconstitutional invasion of states' rights" and vetoed it. In essence, he denied that the federal government possessed authority to protect the civil rights of blacks. Had Johnson's veto stood, reconstruction would have been over, and the president would have had the final word. But in April 1866, a thoroughly aroused Republican Party again pushed a civil rights bill through Congress and overrode another presidential veto. Then in July, it sustained another Freedmen's Bureau Act. For the first time in American

history, Congress had overridden presidential vetoes of major legislation.

Johnson's vetoes represented a decisive moment in reconstruction. Even moderate Republicans who wanted to avoid a break with the president concluded that he had declared war on the freedmen and the Republican Party. Jettisoning his moderate Republican political allies, he had snuggled up to conservative Democrats. Moreover, he had compounded the harm with vulgar racist statements (suggesting that a logical consequence of congressional policy would be interracial marriage), with inflammatory personal attacks (comparing certain Republicans to Judas and himself to Christ), and in general exhibiting a pugnacious, nasty temperament that made compromise and cooperation impossible. As a worried South Carolinian observed in the spring of 1866, Johnson had succeeded in uniting the Republicans and probably touched off "a fight this fall such as has never been seen."

Congressional Reconstruction

By the summer of 1866, President Andrew Johnson and Congress had dropped their gloves and stood toe to toe in a bare-knuckled contest unprecedented in American history. Johnson had made it clear that he would not budge on either constitutional questions or policy. Moderate Republicans made a major effort to resolve the dilemma of reconstruction by amending the Constitution, but the obstinacy of Johnson and white Southerners pushed Republican moderates steadily closer to the Radicals and to acceptance of additional federal intervention in the South. Each escalation of federal power brought forth new charges of congressional tyranny from the White House. Each new law produced fresh obstruction. Finally, Congress sought to end presidential interference with its prerogatives by impeaching Andrew Johnson.

Congressional reconstruction evolved haltingly and unevenly, but through it all black suffrage acted like a powerful magnet that steadily drew discussion its way. In time, white men in Congress debated whether to give the ballot to black men. Outside of Congress, blacks raised their voices on behalf of color-blind voting rights, while women argued that it was time to make voting sex-blind as well as color-blind.

The Fourteenth Amendment and Escalating Violence

In April 1866, Republican moderates introduced the Fourteenth Amendment to the Constitution, which both houses of Congress approved in June by the necessary two-thirds majority. The amendment then went to the states for ratification. Although it took two years to gather approval from the required three-fourths of the states, the Fourteenth Amendment had immediate consequences.

The most important provisions of this complex amendment made all native-born or naturalized persons American citizens and prohibited states from abridging the "privileges and immunities" of citizens, depriving them of "life, liberty, or property without due process of law," and denying them "equal protection of the laws." Lawyers have battled ever since about the meaning of this broad language, but by making blacks national citizens the amendment nullified the *Dred Scott* decision of 1857 and provided a national guarantee of equality before the law. In essence, it protected the rights of citizens against violation by their own state governments.

The Fourteenth Amendment also dealt with voting rights. Republicans revealed that while genuinely committed to black freedom, they were also alert to partisan advantage. Rather than explicitly granting the vote to blacks, as Radicals wanted, the amendment gave Congress the right to reduce the congressional representation of states that withheld suffrage from some of its adult male population. In other words, white Southerners could either allow their former slaves to vote or see their representation in Washington slashed.

Moderate Republicans soft-pedaled the voting issue because they feared that Northerners would reject any amendment that forced them to enfranchise northern blacks. At that time, only five New England states permitted black men to vote. But without the extension of voting rights to blacks, the return of the southern states to Congress would mean renewed ascendancy for the Democratic Party in the South (most southern whites were Democrats, while southern blacks could be counted on to support the party of Lincoln) and perhaps in the nation as a whole. Ironically, abolition had increased the South's representation in Congress because it had effectively ended the three-fifths compromise (a constitutional provision that had based representation on all free persons and three-fifths of all slaves). Now African Americans were free and thus whole persons in the eyes of the Constitution. Understandably, Republicans refused to sit idle while ex-rebels denied freedmen the vote and simultaneously increased by some twenty seats their power in the House of Representatives.

The Republicans drafted the Fourteenth Amendment in such a way that they could not lose. If southern whites caved in and granted voting rights to freedmen, the Republican Party, entirely a northern party since its birth, would gain valuable black votes, establish a wing in the South, and secure its national power. But if whites refused, southern representation in Congress would plunge, and Republicans would still gain immunity from southern Democratic political power. Of course, the Fourteenth Amendment's voting provision included northern states, where whites were largely hostile to black suffrage. But northern states could continue to withhold suffrage and not suffer in Washington, for their black populations were too small to count in figuring representation. Radicals labeled the Fourteenth Amendment's voting provision "hypocritical" and a "swindle," but they understood that it was the best they could get at the time.

By the summer of 1866, President Andrew Johnson and Congress had dropped their gloves and stood toe to toe in a bare-knuckled contest unprecedented in American history.

Tennessee approved the Fourteenth Amendment in July, and Congress promptly welcomed its representatives and senators back. Had Johnson counseled other southern states to ratify this relatively mild amendment and warned them that they faced the fury of an outraged Republican Party if they refused, they might have listened. Instead, Johnson advised Southerners to reject the Fourteenth Amendment and to rely on him to trounce the Republicans in the fall congressional elections.

Johnson had decided to make the Fourteenth Amendment the overriding issue of the 1866 congressional elections and to gather its white opponents into a new conservative party, the National Union Party. In August, his supporters met in Philadelphia. Democrats came, but the poor Republican turnout made it clear that rather than drawing disgruntled party members to him, Johnson had united nearly the entire Republican Party against him.

The president's strategy had already suffered a setback two weeks earlier when whites in several southern cities went on rampages against blacks. It was less an outbreak of violence than an escalation of the violence that had never ceased. In New Orleans, a mob assaulted delegates to a black suffrage convention, and thirty-four blacks died. In Memphis, white mobs hurtled through the black sections of town and killed at least forty-six people. The slaughter shocked Northerners and renewed skepticism about Johnson's claim that southern whites could be trusted. "Who doubts that the Freedmen's Bureau ought to be abolished forthwith," a New York observer declared sarcastically, "and the blacks remitted to the paternal care of their old masters, who 'understand the nigger, you know, a great deal better than the Yankees can.'"

In a last-ditch effort, Johnson took his case directly to the people. In August, he made an ill-fated "swing around the circle," which took him from Washington to Chicago and St. Louis and back to Washington. However, the president embarrassed himself and his office. When hostile crowds hurled insults, he gave as good as he got. It was Johnson at his worst—intemperate, crude, undignified. Even a friend agreed that he had "made an ass of himself." Johnson's reception on the campaign trail foretold the fate of the National Union movement in the elections. Rather than witnessing the birth of a new conservative party, the elections pitted traditional rivals: Democrats (who lined up with Johnson) against Republicans (who lined up against him). The result was an overwhelming Republican victory in which the party retained its three to one congressional majority.

Johnson had bet that Northerners would not support federal protection of black rights. He expected a racist backlash to defeat the Fourteenth Amendment and blast the Republican Party. But the cautious (and ingenious) amendment was not radical enough to drive Republican voters into Johnson's camp. Besides, the war was still fresh in northern minds. As one Republican explained, southern whites "with all their intelligence were traitors, the blacks with all their ignorance were loyal."

Radical Reconstruction and Military Rule

The elections of 1866 should have taught southern whites the folly of relying on Andrew Johnson as a guide through the thicket of reconstruction. But when Johnson continued to urge Southerners toward rejection of the Fourteenth Amendment, one by one every southern state except Tennessee voted it down. "The last one of the sinful ten," thundered Representative James A. Garfield of Ohio, "has flung back into our teeth the magnanimous offer of a generous nation." In the void created by the South's rejection of the moderates' program, the Radicals seized the initiative.

Each act of defiance by southern whites had boosted the standing of the Radicals within the Republican Party. At the core was a small group of men who had cut their political teeth on the antebellum campaign against slavery, who had goaded Lincoln toward making the war a crusade for freedom, and who had carried into the postwar period the conviction that only federal power could protect the rights of the freedmen. Except for freedmen themselves, no one did more to make freedom the "mighty moral question of the age." Men like Senator Charles Sumner, that pompous but sincere Massachusetts crusader, and Thaddeus Stevens, the caustic, cadaverous representative from Pennsylvania, did not speak with a single voice, but they united in calling for civil and political equality. They insisted on extending to ex-slaves the same opportunities that northern working people enjoyed under the free-labor system. The southern states were "like clay in the hands of the potter," Stevens declared in January 1867, and he called on Congress to have "the courage to do its duty." Stevens urged that reconstruction begin all over again, that the nation return to "the point where Grant left off the work, at Appomattox Court-House."

In March 1867, after exhaustive debate, moderates joined the Radicals to overturn the Johnson state governments and initiate military rule of the South. The Military Reconstruction Act (and three subsequent acts) divided the ten unreconstructed Confederate states into five military districts. Congress placed a Union general in charge of each district and instructed him to "suppress insurrection, disorder, and violence" and to begin political reform. After the military had completed voter registration, which would include black men and exclude all those barred by the Fourteenth Amendment from holding public office, voters would elect delegates to conventions that would draw up new state constitutions. Each constitution would guarantee black suffrage. When the voters of each state had approved the constitution and the first legislature had ratified the Fourteenth Amendment, the state could submit its work to Congress. If Congress approved, the state's senators and representatives could be seated and political reunification would be accomplished.

Radicals proclaimed the provision for black suffrage "a prodigious triumph." The doggedness of the Radicals and of African Americans, along with the pigheadedness of Johnson and the white South, had swept the Republican Party far beyond the timid suffrage provisions of the Fourteenth Amendment. Republicans finally agreed with Sumner that only the voting power of ex-slaves could bring about a permanent revolution in the South. Indeed, suffrage provided blacks with a powerful instrument of change and self-protection. When combined with the disfranchisement of thousands of ex-rebels, it promised to cripple any neo-Confederate resurgence and guarantee Republican governments in the South.

Despite its bold suffrage provision, the Military Reconstruction Act of 1867 disappointed those who advocated the confiscation and redistribution of southern plantations. No one in Washington was more distressed than Thaddeus Stevens. Unlike Sumner, who conceived of Reconstruction primarily in political terms, Stevens believed it was at bottom an economic problem. He agreed wholeheartedly with the ex-slave who said, "Give us our own land and we take care of ourselves, but without land, the old masters can hire us or starve us, as they please." Stevens envisioned confiscating the estates of traitors, breaking them up into small farms, and distributing them widely to create a loyal black yeomanry. But Johnson's offers of amnesty and pardon had reversed the small program of land transfer begun during the war. By early 1867, nearly all of the land had been returned to its ex-Confederate owners.

Congress steadfastly refused to put land into the hands of ex-slaves. Most Republicans believed

BLACK POLITICS

The Reconstruction Act of 1867 revolutionized southern politics. It also galvanized the region's African American population. One black minister remembered, "Politics got in our midst and our revival or religious work for a while began to wane." While Congress enfranchised only black men, black women participated in the debates that sprang up everywhere. Political rights meant that freedmen had access to the power of the state to advance their interests, and women, as well as men, recognized the unprecedented opportunity.
Library of Congress.

that they had already provided blacks with the critical tools: equal legal rights and the ballot. Besides, confiscation was too radical, even for some Radicals. Confiscating private property in the South, declared the *New York Times*, "strikes at the root of all property rights in both sections. It concerns Massachusetts quite as much as Mississippi." Moreover, giving land to blacks amounted to "government paternalism," most Republicans argued. In the end, it would undermine, not strengthen, black independence. Civil and political equality, a majority of Republicans believed, gave blacks "a perfectly fair chance." If they were to get forty acres, they would have to gain it themselves.

Declaring that he would rather sever his right arm than sign such a formula for "anarchy and chaos," Andrew Johnson vetoed the Military Reconstruction Act. Congress overrode his veto the very same day, dramatizing the shift in power from the executive to the legislative branch of government. With the passage of the Reconstruction Acts of 1867, congressional reconstruction was virtually completed. Congress had left white folks owning most of the South's land, but in a radical departure it had given black folks the ballot. More than any other provision, black suffrage justifies the term "radical reconstruction." In 1867, the nation began an unprecedented experiment in interracial democracy—at least in the South, for Congress's plan did not touch the North. Soon the former Confederate states would become the primary theater for political struggle. But before the spotlight swung away from Washington, the president and Congress had one more scene to play.

Impeaching a President

Although Johnson had lost the support of the northern people and faced a hostile Republican majority in Congress, he had no intention of yielding control of reconstruction. Ever defiant, he fought a guerrilla campaign to obstruct and delay implementation of Republican policies in the South. As president, he was responsible for enforcing the laws that Congress enacted. As commander in chief, he oversaw the military rule of the South that Congress instituted. Yet in a dozen ways he sabotaged Congress's will and encouraged white belligerence and resistance. He issued a flood of pardons to undermine efforts at political and economic change. He waged war against the Freedmen's Bureau by removing officers who sympathized too fully with ex-slaves. And he replaced Union generals eager to enforce

ANDREW JOHNSON, WITH ADDITIONS
This dignified 1868 portrait by Currier and Ives of President Andrew Johnson was apparently amended by a disgruntled citizen. Johnson's vetoes of several reconstruction measures passed by Congress caused his opponents to charge him with arrogant monarchical behavior.
Museum of American Political Life.

Congress's Reconstruction Acts with conservative men who were eager to defeat them. Johnson believed that Congress had exceeded its authority when it launched military rule and imposed black suffrage, and he claimed that he was merely defending the "violated Constitution." At bottom, however, he subverted congressional reconstruction to protect southern whites from what he considered the horrors of "Negro domination."

When Congress learned that overriding Johnson's vetoes did not assure victory, it attempted to tie the president's hands. Congress required that all orders to field commanders pass through the General of the Army, Ulysses S. Grant, who Congress believed was sympathetic to southern freedmen, Unionists, and Republicans. It also enacted the

Tenure of Office Act, which required the approval of the Senate for the removal of any government official who had been appointed with Senate consent. Republicans were seeking to protect Secretary of War Edwin M. Stanton, the lone cabinet officer who supported congressional policies. Some Republicans, however, claimed that efforts to subdue Johnson were useless. Nothing less than removing him from office could save reconstruction, they claimed, and they initiated a crusade to impeach the president. According to the Constitution, the House of Representatives can impeach and the Senate can try any federal official for "Treason, Bribery, or other high Crimes and Misdemeanors."

As long as Johnson refrained from breaking a law, however, impeachment languished. Moderates interpreted "high Crimes and Misdemeanors" to mean violation of criminal statutes, and they did not believe that the president had committed an actual crime. Radicals denounced the moderates' interpretation as excessively narrow and argued that Johnson's abuse of constitutional powers and his failure to fulfill constitutional obligations were impeachable offenses. But in August 1867, Johnson suspended Secretary of War Stanton from office. As required by the Tenure of Office Act, he requested the Senate to consent to dismissal. When the Senate balked, the president removed Stanton anyway. "Is the President crazy, or only drunk?" asked a dumbfounded Republican moderate. "I'm afraid his doings will make us all favor impeachment."

News of Johnson's open defiance of the law did indeed convince every Republican in the House to vote for a resolution impeaching the president. Chief Justice Salmon Chase presided over the Senate trial, which lasted from March until May 1868. Chase refused to allow Johnson's opponents to raise the broad issues of misuse of power, his "great crimes," and forced them to argue their case exclusively on the narrow legal grounds of Johnson's removal of Stanton. Johnson's lawyers argued that he had not committed a criminal offense, that the Tenure of Office Act was unconstitutional, and that in any case it did not apply to Stanton, who had been appointed by Lincoln. When the critical vote came, seven moderate Republicans broke with their party and joined the Democrats in voting "not guilty." With thirty-five in favor and nineteen opposed, the impeachment forces fell one vote short of the two-thirds needed to convict.

Republicans had put Johnson on trial because he threatened their efforts to remake the South. But some, including Chief Justice Chase, feared that impeachment for insufficient cause would permanently weaken the office of president. Others shied away from conviction because they feared Benjamin Wade, president pro tem of the Senate, the man who would take Johnson's place in the White House. A crusty old Ohio Radical, Wade professed ideas about monetary policy, the rights of workingmen, and female suffrage that frightened moderates. So Johnson survived, but he did not come through the ordeal unscathed. After his trial he called a truce, and for the remaining ten months of his term reconstruction proceeded unhindered by presidential interference.

The Fifteenth Amendment and Women's Demands

In February 1869, Republicans passed their last major piece of reconstruction legislation: the Fifteenth Amendment to the Constitution. The amendment prohibited states from depriving any citizen of the right to vote because of "race, color, or previous condition of servitude." The Reconstruction Acts of 1867 had already required black suffrage in the South, but the Fifteenth Amendment extended black voting to the entire nation. Some Republicans felt morally obligated to do away with the double standard between North and South. (Eleven northern states and five border states had stubbornly resisted enfranchising blacks.) Others believed that the freedman's ballot required the extra armor of a constitutional amendment to protect it from white counterattack. But partisan advantage also played an important role in the amendment's passage. Gains by northern Democrats in the 1868 elections worried Republicans, and black voters now represented the balance of power in several northern states. By giving ballots to northern blacks, Republicans could lessen their political vulnerability. As one Republican congressman observed, "party expediency and exact justice coincide for once."

Some Republicans, however, found the final wording of the Fifteenth Amendment "lame and halting." Rather than absolutely guaranteeing the right to vote, the amendment merely prohibited exclusion on grounds of race. The distinction would prove to be significant. In time, inventive white Southerners would devise tests of literacy and property and other apparently nonracial measures that would effectively disfranchise blacks and yet not violate the Fifteenth Amendment. But an amendment that guaranteed the right to vote courted defeat in the North. Rising antiforeign sentiment—against the Chinese in California and against European immigrants in the Northeast—caused states to resist giving up control of suffrage requirements. In March 1870, after three-fourths of the states had ratified it, the Fifteenth Amendment became part of the Constitution. Republicans generally breathed a sigh of relief, confident that black suffrage had been "the last great point that remained to be settled of the issues of the war."

But the Republican Party's reappraisal of suffrage had ignored completely the band of politicized and energized women who had emerged from the war demanding "the ballot for the two disenfranchised classes, negroes and women." Founding the Equal Rights Association in 1866, Susan B. Anthony and Elizabeth Cady Stanton lobbied for "a government by the people, and the whole people; for the people and the whole people." They felt betrayed when their old antislavery allies, who now occupied positions of national power, proved to be fickle and would not work for their goals. "It was the Negro's hour," Frederick Douglass later explained. The Republican Party had to avoid anything that might jeopardize black gains, Charles Sumner declared. He suggested that woman suffrage could be "the great question of the future."

It was not the first time women's expectations had been dashed. The Fourteenth Amendment had provided for punishment of any state that excluded voters on the basis of race but not on the basis of sex. It had also introduced the word *male* into the Constitution when it referred to a citizen's right to vote. Stanton had predicted that "if that word 'male' be inserted, it will take us a century at least to get it out." The Fifteenth Amendment proved to be no less disappointing. Although women fought hard to include the word *sex*, the amendment denied states the right to forbid suffrage only on the basis of race. Stanton and Anthony condemned the Republicans' "negro first" strategy and concluded that woman "must not put her trust in man."

On the eve of the Civil War, individuals who had advocated black suffrage risked ridicule in the North and their lives in the South. A decade later, in William Lloyd Garrison's words, blacks had progressed from "the auction-block to the ballot-box." Most Republicans believed that the Fifteenth Amendment completed reconstruction. "The Fifteenth Amendment," Congressman James A. Garfield of Ohio proclaimed, "confers upon the African race the care of its own destiny. It places their fortunes in their own hands." Even Wendell Phillips, that uncompromising crusader for equal-

SUSAN B. ANTHONY
Like many outspoken suffragists, Anthony, depicted here around 1850, had begun her public career in the temperance and abolitionist movements. Her continuing passions for other causes — improving working conditions for labor, for example — caused some conservatives to oppose women's political rights because they equated the suffragist cause with radicalism in general. Women could not easily overcome such views, and the long struggle for suffrage eventually drew millions of women into public life.
Meserve-Kunhardt Collection.

ity, argued that the black man held "his sufficient shield in his own hands. . . . Whatever he suffers will be largely now, and in future, wholly, his own fault." In essence, northern Republicans declared victory and scratched the "Negro question" from the agenda of national politics.

The Struggle in the South

While Northerners believed they had discharged their responsibilities with the Reconstruction Acts and the amendments to the Constitution, Southerners knew that the battle had just begun. Black suffrage and large-scale rebel disfranchisement that came with congressional reconstruction had destroyed traditional southern politics and established the foundation for the rise of the Republican Party. Gathering together outsiders and outcasts from traditional society, the Republicans in the South won elections, wrote new state constitutions, and formed new state governments.

Challenging the established class for political control was dangerous business. Equally dangerous were the confrontations that took place on farms and plantations from Virginia to Texas. In the countryside, blacks sought to give practical, everyday meaning to their newly won legal and political equality. But ex-masters and other whites had their own ideas about the social and economic arrangements that should replace slavery. Freedom, then, remained contested territory, and Southerners fought pitched battles with each other to determine the boundaries of their postemancipation world.

Freedmen, Yankees, and Yeomen

African Americans made up the majority of southern Republicans. Freedmen emerged from bondage illiterate and politically inexperienced, but they understood their own interests. They realized that without the ballot they were almost powerless, and they threw themselves into the suffrage campaign. Southern blacks gained voting rights in 1867, and within months virtually every eligible black man had registered to vote. While almost all voted Republican, blacks (like whites) did not have identical political priorities. Free-born, light-skinned southern blacks were often educated, property-holding artisans who tended to be economically conservative but socially radical. Concentrated in the South's towns and cities, they showed little enthusiasm for land reform, but they ached to tear down racial barriers that inhibited their everyday lives. Ex–field hands, in contrast, showed less concern about "whites only" signs in hotels and restaurants than they did about land of their own. Blacks united, however, in their desire for education and equal treatment before the laws.

Northern whites who decided to make the South their home after the war were a second element of the South's Republican Party. Conservative white Southerners called any northern migrant a "carpetbagger," a man so poor that he could pack all his earthly belongings in a single carpet-sided suitcase and swoop southward like a buzzard to "fatten on our misfortunes." Some Northerners who moved south were scavengers, but most were restless, relatively well-educated young men, often former Union officers and Freedmen's Bureau agents who looked upon the South as they did the West—as a promising place to make a living. Only a few chose politics, but in the early years of Reconstruction carpetbaggers exercised leadership in the fledgling Republican Party far beyond their limited numbers. Illinois-born Henry C. Warmoth, for example, arrived in Louisiana with the army in 1864 and within months became the state's first Republican governor. Northerners in the southern Republican Party consistently supported programs that encouraged vigorous economic development along the lines of the northern free-labor model.

Black suffrage and large-scale rebel disfranchisement that came with congressional reconstruction had destroyed traditional southern politics and established the foundation for the rise of the Republican Party.

The Republican Party gained even more recruits among white Southerners. Some businessmen found Republican economic policies attractive and hoped that an infusion of northern capital, know-how, and bustle would cure the sick southern economy. But yeoman farmers in the Piedmont accounted for the vast majority of white Republicans in the South. Many were Unionists who emerged from the war with bitter memories of Confederate persecution. Some small farmers also nursed long-standing grievances against planter domination and welcomed the Republican Party because it promised to end favoritism toward plantation interests. Yeomen usually supported initiatives for public schools and for expanding economic opportunity within a reinvigorated southern economy. Approximately one out of four white Southerners voted Republican. The other three never considered joining the party of Lincoln and cursed those who did. They condemned southern-born white Republicans as traitors to their region and their race and called them "scalawags," a term for runty horses and low-down, good-for-nothing rascals.

The Republican Party in the South, then, was made up of freedmen, Yankees, and yeomen—an improbable coalition. The mix of races, regions, and classes inevitably meant friction as each group maneuvered to define the party. Despite the stress and strain, Reconstruction represents an extraordinary moment in American politics: Blacks and whites joined together to pursue political change. The Republican Party defended the political and civil equality of black Southerners and struggled to bring the South into the mainstream of American social and economic development. Formally, of course, only men participated in politics—casting ballots and holding offices—but women also played parts in the political struggle. Women joined in parades and rallies, attended stump speeches, and even campaigned. In 1868, black maids in Yazoo, Mississippi, shocked their white employers when they showed up for work boldly wearing buttons depicting the Republican candidate for president: Ulysses S. Grant.

Reconstruction politics was not for cowards. Any political act, even wearing a political button, took courage. Congress had introduced hundreds of thousands of ex-slaves into the southern electorate against the will of the white majority. Then, according to one Democrat, the Republican Party herded them to the polls like "senseless cattle." Most whites in the South condemned the entire political process as illegitimate and felt justified in doing whatever it took to stamp out Republicanism. Violence against blacks—the "white terror"—took brutal institutional form in 1866 with the formation of the Ku Klux Klan. The Klan went on a rampage of whipping, hanging, shooting, burning, and throat-cutting to defeat reconstruction and restore white supremacy. (See Historical Question, page 628.) Rapid demobilization of the Union army after the war left only twenty thousand troops to patrol the entire South, a vast territory. Without effective military protection, southern Republicans had to take care of themselves.

Democratic Equality and the General Welfare

The Reconstruction Acts required southern states to draw up new constitutions before they could be readmitted to Congress. Beginning in the fall of 1867, states held elections for delegates to constitutional conventions. About 40 percent of the white electorate stayed home, either because they had been disfranchised or because they were boycotting politics. Republicans won three-fourths of the seats. About 15 percent of the Republican delegates were Northerners who had moved south, 25 percent were African Americans, and 60 percent were white Southerners. As a British visitor observed, the elec-

tions reflected "the mighty revolution that had taken place in America." But Democrats described the conventions as zoos of "baboons, monkeys, mules . . . and other jackasses." In fact, the gatherings brought together serious, purposeful men who hammered out the legal framework for a new order.

The reconstruction constitutions introduced extensive changes into southern life. In general, changes fell into two categories: those that reduced aristocratic privilege and increased democratic equality and those that expanded the state's responsibility for the general welfare. In the first category, the constitutions adopted universal male suffrage, abolished property qualifications for holding office, and made more offices elective and fewer appointive. In the second category, they enacted prison reform; made the state responsible for caring for orphans, the insane, and the deaf and mute; and aided debtors by exempting their homes from seizure.

These forward-looking constitutions provided blueprints for a New South. But they stopped short of the specific reforms advocated by particular groups within southern Republicanism. Despite the wishes of virtually every former slave, no southern constitution confiscated and redistributed land. Despite the prediction of Unionists that unless all former Confederates were banned from politics they

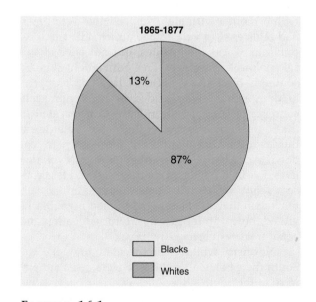

FIGURE 16.1
Southern Congressional Delegations
The statistics contradict the myth of black domination of Congressional representation.

THE STATE CONVENTION AT RICHMOND, VIRGINIA
*Between 1867 and 1869, every southern state except Tennessee held a convention to draft a
new constitution. For the first time in American history, black delegates joined whites in making laws. In Virginia, where blacks were more than 40 percent of the population, they made
up about 20 percent of the convention.*
Valentine Museum, Cook Collection.

would storm back and wreck reconstruction, no
constitution disfranchised ex-rebels wholesale. And
despite the desires of free-born blacks and others,
no constitution outlawed all forms of racial segregation.

But Democrats were blind to the limits of the
Republican program. In their eyes, they stared at
wild revolution. According to Democrats, Republican victories initiated "black and tan" (ex-slave and
mulatto) governments. But the claims of "Negro
domination" had almost no validity. Four out of five
Republican voters were black men, but more than
four out of five Republican officeholders were
white. Southerners sent fourteen black congressmen
and two black senators to Washington, but only 6
percent of Southerners in Congress during Reconstruction were black. With the exception of South
Carolina, where blacks briefly held a majority in one
house of the legislature, no state experienced
"Negro rule," despite black majorities in the populations of three states.

Democrats mocked black officeholders as ignorant field hands. Although many had only "agri-

cultural degrees" and "brick yard diplomas," most
were literate. One of Mississippi's two black U.S.
senators, free-born Hiram R. Revels, had attended
Knox College, and the other, ex-slave Blanche K.
Bruce, had learned to read while in bondage, run
away, and opened a school in Missouri. Francis Car-
dozo, South Carolina's secretary of state and secretary of the treasury, had studied at universities in
England and Scotland. But whatever their educational achievements, blacks were decidedly junior
partners in white-dominated Republican governments. Republicans sought to counter the racist attack by portraying themselves as "the poor man's
party" that promised to end the rule of the back-
ward-looking, arrogant planter aristocracy.

In almost every state, voters ratified the new
constitutions and swept Republicans into power.
After they ratified the Fourteenth Amendment, the
former Confederate states were readmitted to Congress. Southern Republicans then turned to the critical task of governing. They faced a staggering array
of problems. Wartime destruction still littered the
landscape. The war had destroyed one-third of all

What Did the Ku Klux Klan Really Want?

IN THE SUMMER OF 1866, six Confederate veterans in Pulaski, Tennessee, founded the Ku Klux Klan. Borrowing oaths and rituals from a college fraternity, the young men innocently sought fun and fellowship in a social club. But they quickly tired of playing pranks on one another and shifted to more serious matters. By the spring of 1868, when congressional Reconstruction went into effect, new groups or "dens" of the Ku Klux Klan had sprouted throughout the South.

According to former Confederate general and Georgia Democratic politician John B. Gordon, the Klan owed its popularity to the "instinct of self-preservation . . . the sense of insecurity and danger, particularly in those neighborhoods where the Negro population largely predominated." Everywhere whites looked, he said, they saw "great crime." Republican politicians organized ignorant freedmen and marched them to the polls, where they blighted honest government. Blacks drove overseers from plantations and claimed the land for themselves. Black robbers and rapists made white women cower behind barred doors. It was necessary, Gordon declared, "in order to protect our families from outrage and preserve our own lives, to have something that we could regard as a brotherhood—a combination of the best men of the country, to act purely in self-defense." According to Gordon and other conservative white Southerners, then, Klansmen were good men who stepped forward to do their duty, men who wanted nothing more than to guard their families and defend decent society from the assaults of degraded ex-slaves and a vindictive Republican Party.

Behind the Klan's high-minded and self-justifying rhetoric, however, lay another agenda. It was revealed in their actions, not their words. Klansmen embarked on a campaign to reverse history. Garbed in robes and hoods, Klansmen engaged in hit-and-run guerrilla warfare against free labor, civil equality, and political democracy. They aimed to terrorize their enemies—ex-slaves and white Republicans—into submission. As the South's chief terrorist organization between 1868 and 1871, the Klan whipped, burned, and shot in the name of white supremacy. Changes in four particular areas of southern life proved flash points for Klan violence: racial etiquette, education, labor, and politics.

The Klan punished those blacks and whites guilty of breaking the Old South's racial code. The Klan considered "impudence" a punishable offense. Asked to define "impudence" before a congressional investigating committee, one white opponent of the Klan responded: "Well, it is considered impudence for a negro not to be polite to a white man—not to pull off his hat and bow and scrape to a white man, as was done formerly." Klansmen whipped blacks for crimes that ranged from speaking disrespectfully to refusing to yield the sidewalk to raising a good crop to dressing well. Black women who "dress up and fix up like ladies" risked a midnight visit from the Klan. The Ku Klux Klan sought to restore racial subordination in every aspect of private and public life.

Klansmen also took aim at black education. White men, especially those with little schooling, found the sight of blacks in classrooms hard to stomach. Schools were easy targets, and scores of them went up in flames. Teachers, male and female, were flogged, or worse. Klansmen drove northern-born teacher Alonzo B. Corliss from North Carolina for "teaching niggers and making them like white men." In Cross Plains, Alabama, the Klan hanged an Irish-born teacher along with four black men. But not just ill-educated whites opposed black education. Planters wanted ex-slaves back in the fields, not at desks. Each student meant one less laborer. In 1869, an Alabama newspaper reported the burning of a black school and observed that it should be "a warning for them to stick hereafter to 'de shovel and de hoe,' and let their dirty-backed primers go."

Planters turned to the Klan as part of their effort to preserve plantation agriculture and restore labor discipline. An Alabama white admitted that in his area, the Klan was "intended principally for the negroes who failed to work." Masked bands

KU KLUX KLAN ROBE AND HOOD
The white robes that we associate with the Ku Klux Klan are a twentieth-century phenomenon. During Reconstruction, Klansmen donned robes of various designs and colors. It is unlikely that the man who wore this robe about 1866 — with its eye holes carefully trimmed with blue fabric — sewed it himself. Women did not participate in midnight raids, but mothers, wives, and daughters of Klansmen often shared their reactionary vision and did what they could to bring about the triumph of white supremacy.
Chicago Historical Society, Hope B. McCormick Center. Worn by Joseph Boyce Stewart, Lincoln County, Tenn., c.1866. Gift of W. G. Dithmer.

"punished Negroes whose landlords had complained of them." Sharecroppers who disputed their share at "settling up time" risked a visit from the night riders. Klansmen murdered a Georgia blacksmith who refused to do additional work for a white man until he was paid for a previous job. It was dangerous for freedmen to consider changing employers. "If we got out looking for some other place to go," an ex-slave from Texas remembered, "them KKK they would tend to Mister negro good and plenty." In Marengo County, Alabama, when the Klan heard that some local blacks were planning to leave, "the disguised men went to them and told them if they undertook it they would be killed on their way." Whites had decided that they would not be "deprived of their labor."

Above all, the Klan terrorized Republican leaders and voters. Klansmen became the military arm of the Democratic Party. They drove blacks from the polls on election day and terrorized black officeholders. Klansmen gave Andrew Flowers, a black politician in Chattanooga, a brutal beating and told him that they "did not intend any nigger to hold office in the United States." Jack Dupree, president of the Republican Club in Monroe County, Mississippi, a man known to "speak his mind," had his throat cut and was disemboweled while his wife was forced to watch.

Between 1868 and 1871, political violence reached astounding levels. Arkansas experienced nearly three hundred political killings in the three months before the fall elections in 1868, including Little Rock's U.S. congressman, J. M. Hinds. Louisiana was even bloodier. Between the local elections in the spring of 1868 and the presidential election in the fall, Louisiana experienced more than one thousand killings. Political violence often proved effective. In Georgia, Republican presidential candidate Ulysses S. Grant received no votes at all in 1868 in eleven counties, despite black majorities. The Klan murdered three scalawag members of the Georgia legislature and drove ten others from their homes. As one Georgia Republican commented after a Klan attack: "We don't call them democrats, we call them southern murderers."

It proved hard to arrest Klansmen and harder still to convict them. "If a white man kills a colored man in any of the counties of this State," observed a Florida sheriff, "you cannot convict him." By 1871, the death toll had reached thousands. Federal intervention—in the Ku Klux Klan Acts of 1870 and 1871—signaled an end to much of the Klan's power but not to counterrevolutionary violence in the South. Other groups continued the terror.

the South's livestock, and the $3 billion that was invested in slaves was gone. The South's share of the nation's wealth had fallen from 30 percent to only 12 percent. Manufacturing limped along at a fraction of prewar levels, agricultural production remained anemic, and the region's railroads had hardly advanced from the devastated condition in which Sherman had left them. Without the efforts of the Freedmen's Bureau, people would have starved. Moreover, reactionary violence and racial harassment dogged the steps of Southerners who sought reform. In this desperate context, Republicans struggled to breathe life into their new state governments.

Activity focused on three major areas. First, every state inaugurated a system of public education and began furiously building schools and training teachers. Before the Civil War, whites had deliberately kept slaves illiterate, and planter-dominated governments rarely spent tax money to educate the children of yeomen. By 1875, half of Mississippi's and South Carolina's eligible children (the majority of whom were black) attended school. Persistent underfunding meant too few schools, dilapidated facilities, and poorly trained teachers, but literacy rates rose sharply nevertheless. Although public schools were racially segregated, education remained for blacks a tangible, deeply satisfying benefit of freedom and Republican rule.

Second, states attacked racial discrimination and defended civil rights. Republicans especially resisted efforts by whites to establish separate facilities for blacks in public transportation. Texas replaced its law requiring segregation in its railroads with one that outlawed seating by race. Mississippi went further, levying fines of up to $1,000 and three years in jail for railroads, steamboats, hotels, and theaters that denied "full and equal rights" to all citizens. But passing color-blind laws was one thing; enforcing them was another. Fiercely determined that the South remain a white man's preserve, white Southerners sought to demonstrate the continued mastery of whites and the social inferiority of blacks. Segregation—the separation of blacks and whites in public places—developed at white insistence despite the law and became a feature of southern life long before the end of Reconstruction.

Third, Republican governments launched ambitious programs of economic development. They envisioned a South of diversified agriculture, roaring factories, and booming towns. Republican legislatures chartered scores of banks and industrial companies, appropriated funds to fix ruined levees and to drain swamps, and initiated a vigorous program of internal improvements. The South went on a railroad-building binge, repairing old lines and adding some seven thousand miles of track during Reconstruction. The mania for railroads and state-sponsored economic development fell far short of solving the South's economic troubles, however. Republican spending to stimulate economic growth meant rising taxes and enormous debt that drained funds from schools and other programs.

The southern Republicans' record, then, was mixed. None of the initiatives in education, civil rights, or economic growth was an unqualified success. To their credit, the biracial Republican coalition had taken up an ambitious agenda to change the South. Success would have been difficult under the best of circumstances. As it was, money was scarce. In addition, Democrats kept up a constant drumbeat of harassment, while factionalism threatened the party from within. Moreover, corruption infected Republican governments in the South. Public morality reached new lows everywhere in the nation after the Civil War, and the chaos and disruption of the postwar South proved fertile soil for bribery, fraud, and influence peddling. Despite all of its problems and shortcomings, however, the Republican Party had made headway in its early efforts to purge the South of aristocratic privilege and racist oppression.

White Landlords, Black Sharecroppers

Reconstruction politics did not arise within a vacuum. Sharp dissatisfaction with conditions in the southern countryside politicized blacks and fueled political upheaval. On farms and plantations, freedmen confronted ex-masters who persisted in believing that blacks were unfit for free labor. A Tennessee man declared two years after the end of the war that blacks were "a trifling set of lazy devils who will never make a living without Masters." Blacks responded that if any class was lazy, it was the masters, "who lived in idleness all of their lives on stolen labor." Clashes occurred daily between ex-slaves who wished to take control of the conditions of their own labor and ex-masters who wanted to reinstitute old ways.

The system of agricultural labor that emerged in 1865 grew out of the labor program begun during the war by the federal military. When the war ended, supervision shifted to the Freedmen's Bureau, which renewed the army's campaign to restore production by binding black laborers and

M A P 16.1

A Southern Plantation in 1861 and 1881

The maps of the Barrow plantation in Georgia illustrate some of the ways that ex-slaves expressed their freedom. Former slaves deserted the clustered living quarters behind the Big House, scattered over the plantation, built new family cabins, and farmed rented land. These ex-slaves also worked together to build a school and a church.

planters with wage contracts. Except for having to put down the whip and pay subsistence wages, planters were not required to offer many concessions to emancipation. Instead, they moved quickly to restore the antebellum world of work gangs, white overseers, field labor for black women and children, clustered cabins, minimal personal freedom, and even corporal punishment whenever they could get away with it.

Ex-slaves resisted every effort to roll back the clock. "The fact is, the colored people are very anxious to get land of their own to live upon independently," one black man remarked, "and they want money to buy stock [mules] to make crops." Disgusted planters confirmed that freedmen wanted to become "landholders" and not "hirelings." Blacks were equally determined to end planters' involvement in their personal lives. They wanted, for ex-

ample, to make their own decisions about whether women and children would labor in the fields. Indeed, within months after the war, black women (perhaps one-third of them) abandoned field labor and began working full time within their own households. Moreover, hundreds of thousands of black children enrolled in school.

The freedmen's dream of landownership never came true. Despite the ex-slaves' political agitation, Congress and southern legislatures refused to confiscate the planters' land. And without political intervention, landownership proved to be beyond the reach of all but a small fraction of blacks. Poverty-stricken freedmen were lucky to have two nickels to rub together, and few white people would offer them credit to purchase real estate. Even blacks who had money discovered that planters resisted selling them land. Whites who contemplated selling land

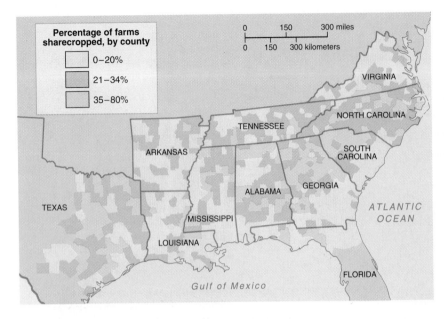

MAP 16.2
The Sharecropping System in the South, 1880
Fifteen years after the end of the Civil War, sharecropping dominated southern agriculture. White and black farmers found themselves enmeshed in a system that left them landless and impoverished.

to blacks knew they risked midnight raids from unhappy neighbors. Without land, ex-slaves would have little choice but to work on plantations.

Although blacks were forced to return to the planters' fields, freedmen resisted efforts to restore slavelike conditions. By working fewer days and shorter hours, by boycotting annual contracts, by striking, and by abandoning the most reactionary employers, they sought to force concessions. A tug-of-war between white landlords and black laborers took place on thousands of farms and plantations and out of it emerged sharecropping, a new system of southern agriculture.

Sharecropping was a compromise that offered both ex-masters and ex-slaves something but satisfied neither. Under the new system, planters divided their cotton plantations into small farms of twenty-five to thirty acres that freedmen rented, paying with a share of each year's crop, usually half. Sharecropping gave blacks more freedom than labor gangs and released them from the day-to-day supervision of whites. It meant that black families could now decide who would work, for how long, and how hard. Moreover, even half a crop seemed to promise a princely income after the subsistence of slavery and the puny wages of the Freedmen's Bureau's contract system. Still, most blacks remained dependent on the white landlord, who retained the power to expel them at the end of each season. For planters, sharecropping offered a way to resume agricultural production, but it did not allow them to reinstitute the unified plantation sys-

tem or to administer what they considered necessary discipline. An experiment at first, sharecropping spread quickly throughout the cotton South. By 1870, the old gang system, direct white supervision, and clustered black living quarters were fading memories. As increasing numbers of white yeomen lost their land in the downward spiral of postwar southern agriculture, moreover, sharecropping ensnared small white farmers as well as black farmers.

Reconstruction Collapses

By 1870, Northerners looked forward to putting "the southern problem" behind them. They had written guarantees of civil and political rights for blacks into the Constitution and enacted a program of political reunification that had restored ex-Confederate states to the Union. Now, after a decade of engagement with the public issues of war and reconstruction, they wanted to turn to their own affairs. In Washington, matters that had taken a back-seat to the southern problem—economic development, foreign policy, scandal and corruption—clamored for attention. Increasingly, practical business-minded men came to the forefront of the Republican Party, replacing the band of reformers and idealists who had been prominent in the 1860s. Civil War hero Ulysses S. Grant succeeded Andrew Johnson as president in 1869 and quickly became an issue himself, proving that brilliance on the battle-field does not necessarily translate into competence in the White House.

Each year, events in the South received less of the North's attention. Reconstruction slipped further into the background, and Northerners signaled growing unwillingness to intervene in southern affairs. While northern resolve to defend black freedom withered, southern commitment to white supremacy intensified. Throughout the South, Democrats redoubled their attack on Republican rule. Without northern protection, southern Republicans were no match for the Democrats' economic coercion, political corruption, and violence. One by one, Republican state governments fell. The election of 1876 both confirmed and completed the collapse of reconstruction.

The Grant Regime: Cronies, Corruption, and Economic Collapse

When the Civil War ended, Ulysses S. Grant was easily the most popular man in the nation, at least north of the Mason-Dixon line. But the return of peace meant that the general risked slipping back into his former obscurity. Determined to avoid that fate, he settled in Washington and plunged into reconstruction politics, playing the political game on the dangerous middle ground between President Andrew Johnson and Congress. Lesser men might not have survived the crossfire, but Grant shrewdly maneuvered between the warring factions. At first he appeared to be Johnson's man, but during the impeachment crisis he broke with the president and linked arms with Congress.

While northern resolve to defend black freedom withered, southern commitment to white supremacy intensified.

Grant was the obvious choice for the Republican Party's presidential nomination in 1868. Radicals preferred someone with a deeper moral commitment to black equality, but Grant supported congressional reconstruction and that was enough for the Republican convention. The Democrats chose Horatio Seymour, former governor of New York. Their platform blasted congressional reconstruction as "a flagrant usurpation of power . . . unconstitutional, revolutionary, and void." Republi-

cans answered by "waving the bloody shirt," that is, they reminded the voters that the Democrats were "the party of rebellion," the party that stubbornly resisted a just peace. During the campaign, the Ku Klux Klan erupted in another reign of terror, murdering hundreds of southern Republicans. Terrorist tactics cut into Grant's tally, but he gained a narrow 300,000-vote margin in the popular vote and a substantial victory (214 votes to 80) in the electoral college.

Grant understood that most Northerners had grown weary of reconstruction. Conservative business-minded Northerners had become convinced that recurrent federal intrusion was itself a major cause of instability. Eager to invest in the South and especially to resume the profitable cotton trade, they sought order, not disruption. A growing number of northern Republican leaders began to question the wisdom of their party's alliance with the South's lower classes—its small farmers and share-croppers. Grant's secretary of the interior, Jacob D. Cox of Ohio, proposed allying with the "thinking and influential native southerners . . . the intelligent, well-to-do, and controlling class."

The talents Grant had demonstrated on the battlefield—decisiveness, clarity, and resolution—deserted him in the White House. Unclear about his objectives, he grew tentative, unsure of himself, and bewildered. He gave the impression of a good man who was in over his head. Able advisers might have helped, but Grant surrounded himself with fumbling kinfolk and old cronies from his army days. He increasingly hobnobbed with the rich and powerful, even frequenting their expensive tailors. Grant was slow to realize that it was the desire for personal gain, not loyalty to him, that caused bankers and businessmen to cozy up to him. He also made a string of dubious appointments that led to a series of damaging scandals. Charges of corruption tainted his vice president, Schuyler Colfax, and brought down his secretary of war and secretary of the navy as well as his private secretary. Grant's dogged loyalty to liars and cheats only compounded the damage. While never personally implicated in any scandal, Grant was guilty of extreme gullibility. Before long, his administration was synonymous in many people's minds with greed, graft, and corruption.

Grant could not fairly be held responsible for the low moral tone that characterized the entire nation after the Civil War. New inventions, new technology, and new forms of business organization fed feverish growth throughout the economy. The head-

I BEG TO REPEAT THAT THESE FRAUDS ON THE GOVERNMENT SHALL BE PROBED TO THE VERY BOTTOM.

TAMMANY RING. CANAL RING. WHISKEY RING. INDIAN RING. PRESS RING. STATE RING. COUNTY RING. TOWN RING. WARD RING.

BELKNAP · FRAUD CLAIMS · BACK PAY GRAB · EMMA MINE · WHISKEY FRAUDS · BRIBERY

GRANT AND SCANDAL
This anti-Grant cartoon by the nation's most celebrated political cartoonist, Thomas Nast, shows the president falling headfirst into the barrel of fraud and corruption that tainted his administration. During Grant's eight years in the White House, many in his administration failed him. Sometimes duped, sometimes merely loyal, Grant stubbornly defended wrongdoers, even to the point of perjuring himself to keep an aide out of jail.
Library of Congress.

long advance provided enormous opportunity for graft and corruption. Democrats stole at least as brazenly as Republicans. The Tweed Ring, the Democratic political machine in New York City, pocketed some $200 million of the citizens' money. The buying and selling of politicians at the state level dwarfed federal corruption. It was said that the Standard Oil Company could do anything it wanted with the Pennsylvania legislature except refine it. The spoils system, by which victorious parties rewarded loyal workers with public office, had become a fixture of public life before Grant moved into the White House. Still, Grant was aggravatingly naive and his administration filled with rot.

In 1872, disgusted anti-Grant Republicans bolted and launched a third party, the Liberal Republicans. The Liberals promised to create a government "which the best people of this country will be proud of." They condemned the Grant regime as a riot of vulgarity—crude graft, tasteless materialism, and blatant anti-intellectualism. To clean up the mess, they proposed ending the spoils system and

replacing it with a nonpartisan civil service commission that would oversee competitive examinations for appointment to office. Moreover, they demanded that the government remove federal troops from the South and restore "home rule." Democrats especially liked the Liberal's southern policy, and the Democratic Party endorsed the Liberal presidential candidate, Horace Greeley, the longtime editor of the *New York Tribune*. Despite Grant's problems, however, the nation still felt enormous affection for the man who had saved the Union. In the 1872 election, voters gave him 56 percent of the popular vote, the most lopsided victory since Andrew Jackson swept into the White House forty-four years earlier.

Grant was not without accomplishments during his eight years as president. Ironically, he scored his greatest triumph on an issue he cared little about: the settlement of the U.S. claim against Great Britain for wartime damages caused by British-built Confederate ships. When Britain denied any wrongdoing, tempers flared. But in 1872, Hamilton Fish,

Grant's able secretary of state, skillfully orchestrated a peaceful settlement that paid the United States $15.5 million in damages.

Grant's great passion in foreign affairs—annexation of Santo Domingo in the Caribbean—ended in utter failure. Grant argued that the acquisition of this tropical land would permit the United States to expand its trade in the Caribbean and simultaneously provide a new home for the South's blacks, who were so desperately harassed by the Klan. Aggressive foreign policy had not originated with the Grant administration. Lincoln and Johnson's secretary of state, William H. Seward, had thwarted French efforts to set up a puppet empire under Maximilian in Mexico, and his purchase of Alaska ("Seward's Ice Box") from Russia in 1867 for only $7 million had fired Grant's imperial ambitions. But the Republican Party split over the president's scheme to acquire Santo Domingo, and in the end Grant could not marshal the votes needed to approve the treaty of annexation.

The Grant administration was caught up in a tangle of complicated economic problems, but by far Grant's most difficult was the depression that began in 1873. Railroads, which had fueled the postwar boom, led directly to the bust. Jay Cooke, head of a major Philadelphia bank, had poured enormous sums into railroads, became overextended with debt, and went under, initiating the panic of 1873. Like dominoes, other companies failed, and soon the nation sank into its most severe depression to that time. More than 18,000 businesses collapsed in two years, and more than one million workers lost their jobs. Urban dwellers who were lucky enough to avoid unemployment saw their wages shrivel by 25 percent while food costs declined only 5 percent. Government relief did not exist, and private charities were swamped. Desperate times arrived at the doorsteps of most working people. Industrial violence kept pace with economic hardship. The violence subsided as men and women returned to work, but only at the end of the decade did the depression lift. By then, southern Republican governments had fallen, and the experiment of reconstruction had ended.

Northern Resolve Withers

Although Northerners wanted desperately to shift their attention to the new issues, the old ones would not go away. When southern Republicans pleaded for federal protection from Klan violence, Congress enacted three laws in 1870 and 1871 that were intended to break the back of white terrorism. The severest of the three, the Ku Klux Klan Act, made interference with voting rights a felony and authorized the use of the army to enforce it. Intrepid federal marshals arrested thousands of suspected Klansmen. While the government came close to destroying the Klan, it did not end terrorism against blacks. Congress also passed the Civil Rights Act of 1875, which boldly outlawed racial discrimination in transportation, public accommodations, and juries. But federal authorities did little to enforce the law, and segregated facilities remained the rule throughout the South.

In reality, the retreat from reconstruction had begun in 1868 with Grant's election. Grant genuinely wanted to see blacks' civil and political rights protected, but he felt uneasy about an open-ended commitment that seemed to ignore constitutional limitations on federal power. Like his predecessor, he distributed pardons liberally and encouraged the passage of a general amnesty. In May 1872, Congress obliged and restored the right of officeholding to all but three hundred ex-rebels. Radicals did what they could to stiffen the North's resolve, but reform had lost its principal spokesmen. By 1874, Charles Sumner, Thaddeus Stevens, and Salmon Chase were all dead. Others, such as Benjamin Wade of Pennsylvania, had lost their seats in Congress. Still others had washed their hands of reconstruction, concluding that the quest for black equality was mistaken or hopelessly naive. Republicans who bolted to the Liberal Republican Party, for example, welcomed the South's "best people" back to power. Traditional white leaders, it seemed to them, offered the best hope for honesty, order, and prosperity.

The North's abandonment of reconstruction rested on more than weariness, greed, and disillusionment. Underlying everything was unyielding racial prejudice. Emancipation failed to uproot racism in either the South or the North. During the war, Northerners had learned to accept black freedom, but deep-seated prejudice prevented many from equating freedom with equality. Even the actions that they took on behalf of blacks often served partisan political advantage. Whether they expressed it quietly or boisterously, Northerners generally supported Indiana Senator Thomas A. Hendricks's declaration that "this is a white man's Government, made by the white man for the white man." Increasingly, when Radicals asked Northerners to remember reconstruction's victims, northern sympathy went out to white Southerners.

The U.S. Supreme Court also did its part to undermine reconstruction. From the first, Republicans had feared that the conservative Court would declare their southern policies unconstitutional. Indeed, at times the Court gave the impression of seeking to dismantle reconstruction. In the 1870s, a series of Court decisions significantly weakened the federal government's ability to protect black Southerners under the Fourteenth and Fifteenth Amendments. In the *Slaughterhouse* cases (1873), the Court distinguished between national and state citizenship and ruled that the Fourteenth Amendment protected only those rights that stemmed from the federal government. Since the Court decided that most rights derived from the states, it sharply curtailed the federal government's authority to protect black citizens. Even more devastating, the *United States v. Cruikshank* (1876) ruling said that the reconstruction amendments gave Congress power to legislate only against discrimination by states, not by individuals. The "suppression of ordinary crime," such as assault, remained a state responsibility. The Supreme Court did not declare reconstruction unconstitutional, but it gradually undermined its legal foundation.

The mood of the North found political expression in the election of 1874, when for the first time in eighteen years the Democrats gained control of the House of Representatives. Voters blamed the Grant administration for the economic hard times that had begun the previous year, but they also sent a message about reconstruction. As one Republican observed, the people had grown tired of the "negro question, with all its complications, and the reconstruction of the Southern States, with all its interminable embroilments." Voters turned to the Democrats, who had from the beginning attacked reconstruction as unconstitutional, unnatural, and unwise. After 1874, even the most stubborn Republicans knew that perpetuating reconstruction was political suicide.

Reconstruction had come apart in the North. Congress gradually abandoned it. President Grant grew increasingly unwilling to enforce it. The Supreme Court busily denied the constitutionality of significant parts of it. And the people sent unmistakable messages that they were tired of it. Rather than defend reconstruction from its southern enemies, Northerners backed away from the challenge. After the early 1870s, southern blacks faced the forces of reaction largely on their own.

White Supremacy Triumphs

Republican governments in the South attracted more bitterness and hatred than any other political regimes in American history. In the eyes of the majority of whites, each day of Republican rule produced fresh insults: Black militia patrolled town streets, black laborers negotiated contracts with former masters, black maids stood up to former mistresses, black voters cast ballots, and black legislators enacted laws. The northern retreat from reconstruction permitted southern Democrats to harness this white rage to politics. Taking the name "Redeemers," they promised to replace "bayonet

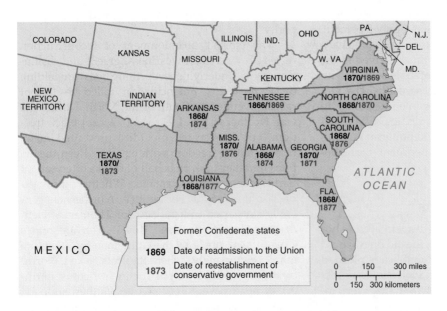

MAP 16.3
The Reconstruction of the South
Myth has it that Republican rule of the former Confederacy was not only harsh but long. In most states, however, conservative southern whites stormed back into power in only a matter of a couple of months or a very few years. By the election of 1876, Republican governments could be found in only three states. And they soon fell.

rule" (federal troops continued to be stationed in the South) with "home rule" (white southern control). They branded Republican governments a carnival of extravagance, waste, and fraud and promised that honest, thrifty Democrats would supplant the irresponsible tax-and-spend Republicans. Above all, they swore to save civilization from a descent into African "barbarism" and "negro rule." As one Redeemer put it, "We must render this either a white man's government, or convert the land into a Negro man's cemetery."

The Republican governments bore little resemblance to the Redeemer stereotypes. Nevertheless, numerous problems plagued their experiment in biracial democracy and made them vulnerable to attack. Republicans often promised more than they could deliver. Efforts to solve the massive economic problems of the devastated South often misfired. And while Democrats exaggerated in charging that "greed was unchecked and roguery unabashed," kickbacks, payoffs, and scams were common. But southern Republicans had no monopoly on corruption. During the Grant era, political dishonesty knew no particular party, region, or race.

By the early 1870s, however, Democrats understood that race was their most potent weapon. They adopted a two-pronged racial strategy to overthrow Republican governments. First, they sought to polarize the parties around color, and, second, they relentlessly intimidated black voters. They went about gathering all the South's white voters into the Democratic Party, leaving the Republicans to depend on blacks. The "straight-out" appeal to whites promised great advantage because whites made up a majority of the population in every southern state except Mississippi, South Carolina, and Louisiana.

Republican governments in the South attracted more bitterness and hatred than any other political regimes in American history.

Democrats employed several devices to dislodge whites from the Republican Party. First and foremost, they fanned the flames of racial prejudice. In South Carolina, a Democrat crowed that his party appealed to the "proud Caucasian race, whose sovereignty on earth God has proclaimed." Ostracism also proved effective. Local newspapers published the names of whites who kept company with blacks. So complete was the ostracism that one of its victims said, "No white man can live in the South in

IS THIS A REPUBLICAN FORM OF GOVERNMENT?
This powerful 1876 drawing by Thomas Nast depicts the end of Reconstruction as the tragedy it was. As white supremacists in the South piled up more and more bodies, supporters of civil rights accused the Grant administration of failing to protect black Southerners and legitimately elected governments. They pointed specifically to the constitutional requirement that "[t]he United States shall guarantee to every State in this Union a Republican Form of Government, and shall protect each of them . . . against domestic violence" (Article IV, section 4).
Library of Congress.

the future and act with any other than the Democratic party unless he is willing and prepared to live a life of social isolation."

In addition, Democrats exploited the small white farmer's severe economic plight by blaming it on Republican financial policy. Government spending soared during Reconstruction, and small farmers saw their tax burden skyrocket. Farms in Mississippi were taxed at four times the prewar level. When cotton prices fell by nearly 50 percent in the 1870s, yeomen farmers found cash in short supply. To pay their taxes, one man observed, "people are selling every egg and chicken they can get."

Those unable to pay lost their land. In 1871, Mississippi reported that one-seventh of the state's land —3,300,000 acres—had been forfeited for the non-payment of taxes. The small farmer's economic distress had a racial dimension. Because few freedmen succeeded in acquiring land, they rarely paid taxes. In Georgia in 1874, blacks made up 46 percent of the population but paid only 2 percent of the taxes. From the perspective of the small white farmer, Republican rule meant not only that he was paying more taxes but that he was paying them to aid blacks. Democrats asked whether it was not time for hard-pressed yeomen to join the white man's party.

If racial pride, social isolation, and Republican financial policies proved insufficient to drive yeomen from the Republican Party, Democrats turned to terrorism. "Night riders" targeted scalawags as well as blacks for murder and assassination. By the early 1870s, then, only a fraction of southern whites any longer claimed allegiance to the party of Lincoln. White yeomen were willing for a time (as they would be again late in the century) to rise above racism and link arms with blacks to improve their common welfare, but the Republicans could not hold their allegiance. Racial polarization became a reality, and rich and poor whites united in opposition to reconstruction. Yeoman defection to the Redeemers proved a heavy blow to southern Republicanism.

The second prong of Democratic strategy—intimidation of black voters—proved equally devastating. Antiblack political violence escalated to unprecedented levels. In 1873 in Louisiana, a clash between black militiamen and gun-toting whites killed two white men and an estimated seventy black men. Half of the latter were slaughtered after they had surrendered. Although the federal government indicted more than one hundred white men, local juries failed to convict a single one.

Even before adopting the all-out white supremacist tactics of the 1870s, Democrats had already captured Virginia, Tennessee, and North Carolina. The new campaign brought fresh gains. The Redeemers regained Georgia in 1872, Texas in 1873, and Arkansas and Alabama in 1874. In 1875, Mississippi fell. The story in Mississippi was one of open, unrelenting, and often savage intimidation of black voters and their few remaining white allies. Planters warned the black sharecroppers who rented land from them: Vote Republican and find yourselves on the road. Whites used the flimsiest pretext to hunt down and shoot blacks who kept the Republican faith. In a "riot" in Vicksburg, Mississippi, thirty-five blacks and two whites lost their lives. As the state election approached in 1875, Republican Governor Adelbert Ames appealed to Washington for federal troops to control the violence, only to hear from the attorney general that the "whole public are tired of these annual autumnal outbreaks in the South." Abandoned, Mississippi Republicans succumbed to the Democratic onslaught in the fall elections. By 1876, only three Republican state governments—in Florida, Louisiana, and South Carolina—survived.

An Election and a Compromise

The centennial year of 1876 witnessed one of the most tumultuous elections in American history. Its chaos and confusion provided a fitting conclusion to the experiment known as reconstruction. The election took place in November, but not until March 2 of the following year, at 4 A.M., did the nation know who would be inaugurated president on March 4. For four months the country suffered through a constitutional and political crisis that jeopardized the peaceful transfer of power from one administration to the next. Sixteen years after Lincoln's election, Americans feared that a presidential contest would again precipitate civil war.

The Democrats had nominated New York's reform governor, Samuel J. Tilden, who immediately targeted the corruption of the Grant administration and the despotism of Republican reconstruction. The Republicans put forward a reformer of their own, Rutherford B. Hayes, governor of Ohio. Privately, Hayes considered "bayonet rule" a mistake, but he concluded that waving the bloody shirt, as threadbare as it was, remained the Republicans' best political strategy. "It leads people away from 'hard times,' which is our deadliest foe," Hayes said lamely.

On election day, Tilden tallied 4,284,000 votes to Hayes's 4,036,000. Yet in the all-important electoral college, Tilden fell one vote short of the majority required for victory. However, the electoral votes of three states remained in doubt and thus were uncounted. Both Democrats and Republicans claimed the nineteen votes of South Carolina, Louisiana, and Florida, the only remaining Republican strongholds in the South. To win, Tilden needed only one of the contested votes. Hayes had to have all of them to take the election. The two par-

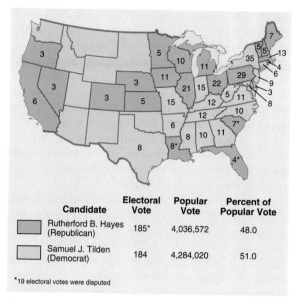

Candidate	Electoral Vote	Popular Vote	Percent of Popular Vote
Rutherford B. Hayes (Republican)	185*	4,036,572	48.0
Samuel J. Tilden (Democrat)	184	4,284,020	51.0

*19 electoral votes were disputed

MAP 16.4
The Election of 1876

ties traded charges of fraud and intimidation. To be sure, Republicans had stuffed some ballot boxes, but stepped-up violence by the Democrats had kept hundreds of thousands of southern Republicans from the polls.

Congress had to decide who had actually won the elections in the three southern states and thus who would be president. The Constitution provided little guidance. Moreover, Democrats controlled the House, and Republicans the Senate. To break the deadlock, Congress created a special electoral commission to arbitrate the disputed returns. An odd and cumbersome compromise, the commission was made up of five representatives (two Republicans, three Democrats), five senators (two Democrats, three Republicans), and five justices of the Supreme Court (two Republicans, two Democrats, and David Davis, considered to be an independent). But before the commission could meet, the Illinois legislature elected Justice Davis to the Senate. The other four justices filled his place with Justice Joseph Bradley, a fair-minded man but decidedly a Republican. The commissioners all voted the straight party line, giving every state to Hayes and putting him over the top in electoral votes.

Some outraged Democrats vowed to resist Hayes's victory. But the impasse was broken when negotiations behind the scenes between Hayes's lieutenants and some moderate southern Demo-

crats resulted in an informal understanding, known as the Compromise of 1877. In exchange for a Democratic promise not to block Hayes's inauguration and to deal fairly with the freedmen, Hayes vowed not to use the army to uphold the remaining Republican regimes. The South would also gain substantial federal subsidies for internal improvements. Less than two days later, the nation observed Hayes's peaceful inauguration.

Stubborn Tilden supporters bemoaned the "stolen election" and damned "His Fraudulency," Rutherford B. Hayes. Old-guard radicals such as William Lloyd Garrison denounced Hayes's bargain as a "policy of compromise, of credulity, of weakness, of subserviency, of surrender." But the nation as a whole celebrated. The Republic had weathered a grave crisis, and it had ended reconstruction. The last three Republican state governments fell quickly once Hayes abandoned them. The Compromise of 1877 confirmed the conservatism that had been growing in the North for years. New priorities meant that Northerners no longer wanted to intervene in the South, and, even without a deal, Hayes would probably have withdrawn the troops.

The nation's solution to this last sectional crisis marked a return to the antebellum tradition of sectional compromise. As in previous crises, whites had found a way to bridge their differences and retain the peace, and again blacks had paid the price. In 1877, Republicans followed a path of expediency and gained the presidency. Southern Democrats got home rule and a free hand in racial matters. When reconstruction ended, black Southerners were not completely subordinated to whites, but their prospects in the New South looked bleak.

Conclusion: "A Revolution but Half-Accomplished"

In 1865, when General Carl Schurz visited the South at President Andrew Johnson's behest, he discovered "a revolution but half-accomplished." Defeat had not prepared the South for an easy transition from slavery to free labor, from white racial despotism to equal justice, and from white political monopoly to biracial democracy. The old elite wanted to get "things back as near to slavery as possible," while ex-slaves and whites who had lacked power in the slave regime were eager to exploit the revolutionary implications of defeat and emancipation.

Congress pushed the revolution along. Although it refused to provide an economic underpinning to black freedom, it required defeated Confederates to accept legal equality and share political power. But conservative whites fought ferociously to recover their power and privilege. When they regained control of politics, they used the power of the state, along with private violence, to wipe out many of the gains of reconstruction. A visitor to the South in the late 1870s would have seen a landscape reminiscent of antebellum days. Blacks were back in the fields and kitchens, cotton had resumed its throne, and white Southerners again controlled the courthouses and state houses. So successful were the reactionaries that one observer concluded that the North had won the war but the South had won the peace.

But the Redeemer counterrevolution did not mean a return to slavery. Freedom meant something, and blacks knew it best. Abolition destroyed the old plantation of slavery days, and ex-slaves gained the freedom not to be whipped or sold, to send their children to school, to worship in their own churches, and to work independently on their own rented farms. The lives of impoverished sharecroppers overflowed with miseries and hardships, but even sharecropping provided more autonomy and economic welfare than bondage had. It was limited freedom, to be sure, but it was not slavery.

Emancipation set in motion the most profound upheaval in the nation's history, and nothing whites could do could entirely erase its revolutionary effects. War destroyed the richest and largest slave society in the New World. It cost masters $3 billion in lost property and destroyed the foundation of planter wealth. Slavery had defined the antebellum South, and abolition overturned the social and economic order that had dominated the region for nearly two centuries. The world of masters and slaves succumbed to that of landlords and sharecroppers. Even today, some Southerners divide history into "before the war" and "after the war."

The Civil War and emancipation mark a watershed not just in the South's history but in that of the entire nation. The scope of the revolution was not fully apparent in the 1870s, but already it was clear that the country had embarked on a new course. War had served as midwife for the birth of a modern nation-state, and for the first time sovereignty rested uncontested in the federal government. National unification was accompanied by a massive shift of power away from the landed classes to the new industrialists. The South returned to the Union, but as a junior partner. The victorious North possessed the power to establish the nation's direction, and it set its compass toward the expansion of corporate capitalism. War had laid the foundation for the power of big business and its captains in postwar America.

Still, the Civil War remained only a "half-accomplished" revolution. As such, Reconstruction represents a tragedy of enormous proportions. The nation did not fulfill the promises that it seemed to hold out to black Americans at war's end. The revolution raced forward, halted, and then slipped back, coming to rest far short of equality and justice. The failure had enduring consequences. Almost a century after reconstruction, the nation would embark on what one observer called a "second reconstruction," another effort to fulfill nineteenth-century promises. Many of the gains of the earlier reform effort had been negated, but the solid achievements of the Thirteenth, Fourteenth, and Fifteenth Amendments to the Constitution would provide a legal foundation for the renewed commitment. It is worth remembering, though, that it was only the failure of the first Reconstruction that made a modern civil rights movement necessary.

CHRONOLOGY

1863 **December.** Lincoln issues Proclamation of Amnesty and Reconstruction.

1864 **July.** Congress offers more stringent plan for reconstruction, Wade-Davis bill.

1865 **January.** General William T. Sherman sets aside land in South Carolina for black settlement.

March 4. Lincoln sworn in for second term as president of United States.

March. Congress establishes Freedmen's Bureau.

April 14. Lincoln shot, dies on April 15, is succeeded by Vice President Andrew Johnson.

Fall. Southern legislatures enact discriminatory black codes.

December. The Thirteenth Amendment abolishing slavery becomes part of U.S. Constitution.

1866 **April.** Congress approves Fourteenth Amendment making native-born blacks American citizens and guaranteeing all American citizens "equal protection under the laws." Amendment becomes part of Constitution in 1868.

April. Congress passes Civil Rights Act over President Johnson's veto.

May. Susan B. Anthony and Elizabeth Cady Stanton found Equal Rights Association to lobby for vote for women.

July. Congress extends Freedmen's Bureau over President Johnson's veto.

Summer. Ku Klux Klan founded in Tennessee.

November. Republicans triumph over Johnson in congressional elections.

1867 **March.** Congress passes Military Reconstruction Act imposing military rule on South and requiring states to guarantee vote to black men.

1868 **March–May.** Senate impeachment trial of President Johnson results in acquittal.

November. Ulysses S. Grant elected president of the United States.

1869 **February.** Congress approves Fifteenth Amendment prohibiting racial discrimination in voting rights. Amendment becomes part of Constitution in 1870.

1871 **April.** Congress enacts Ku Klux Klan Act in effort to end white terrorism in South.

1872 **November.** President Grant reelected.

1873 Economic depression sets in for remainder of decade.

1874 **November.** Elections return Democratic majority to House of Representatives.

1875 **February.** Civil Rights Act of 1875 outlaws racial discrimination, but federal authorities do little to enforce law.

1877 **March.** Special congressional committee awards disputed electoral votes to Republican Rutherford B. Hayes, making him president of United States; Hayes agrees to pull military out of South.

BIBLIOGRAPHY

GENERAL WORKS

W. E. B. Du Bois, *Black Reconstruction in America* (1935).

Eric Foner, *Reconstruction: America's Unfinished Revolution, 1863–1877* (1988).

John Hope Franklin, *Reconstruction after the Civil War* (1961).

James M. McPherson, *Ordeal by Fire: The Civil War and Reconstruction* (1982).

Rembert W. Patrick, *The Reconstruction of the Nation* (1967).

J. G. Randall and David Donald, *The Civil War and Reconstruction* (1967).

Kenneth M. Stampp, *The Era of Reconstruction, 1865–1877* (1965).

WARTIME RECONSTRUCTION

Richard H. Abbott, *The First Southern Strategy: The Republican Party and the South, 1855–1877* (1986).

Herman Belz, *Emancipation and Equal Rights: Politics and Constitutionalism in the Civil War Era* (1978).

Ira Berlin et al., eds., *Freedom: A Documentary History of Emancipation, 1861–1867* (1982–).

Louis S. Gerteis, *From Contraband to Freedman: Federal Policy toward Southern Blacks, 1861–1865* (1973).

Peyton McCrary, *Abraham Lincoln and Reconstruction: The Louisiana Experiment* (1978).

William S. McFeely, *Yankee Stepfather: General O. O. Howard and the Freedmen* (1968).

James M. McPherson, *The Struggle for Equality: Abolitionists and the Negro in the Civil War and Reconstruction* (1964).

Willie Lee Rose, *Rehearsal for Reconstruction: The Port Royal Experiment* (1964).

Brooks D. Simpson, *Let Us Have Peace: Ulysses S. Grant and the Politics of War and Reconstruction, 1861–1868* (1991).

Hans L. Trefousse, *The Radical Republicans: Lincoln's Vanguard for Racial Justice* (1969).

PRESIDENTIAL RECONSTRUCTION

W. R. Brock, *An American Crisis: Congress and Reconstruction, 1865–1867* (1963).

Albert Castel, *The Presidency of Andrew Johnson* (1979).

LaWanda F. Cox and John H. Cox, *Politics, Principles, and Prejudice, 1865–1866* (1963).

David H. Donald, *The Politics of Reconstruction, 1863–1867* (1965).

Edward L. Gambill, *Conservative Ordeal: Northern Democrats and Reconstruction, 1865–1868* (1981).

Martin E. Mantell, *Johnson, Grant, and the Politics of Reconstruction* (1973).

Eric L. McKitrick, *Andrew Johnson and Reconstruction* (1966).

Donald G. Nieman, *To Set the Law in Motion: The Freedmen's Bureau and the Legal Rights of Blacks, 1865–1868* (1979).

J. Michael Quill, *Prelude to the Radicals: The North and Reconstruction during 1865* (1980).

Patrick W. Riddleberger, *1866: The Critical Year Revisited* (1979).

Robert D. Sawrey, *Dubious Victory: The Reconstruction Debate in Ohio* (1992).

James E. Sefton, *Andrew Johnson and the Uses of Constitutional Power* (1980).

Hans L. Trefousse, *Impeachment of a President: Andrew Johnson, the Blacks and Reconstruction* (1975).

Hans L. Trefousse, *Andrew Johnson: A Biography* (1989).

CONGRESSIONAL RECONSTRUCTION

Eric Anderson and Alfred A. Moss Jr., eds., *The Facts of Reconstruction: Essays in Honor of John Hope Franklin* (1991).

Michael Les Benedict, *The Impeachment and Trial of Andrew Johnson* (1973).

Michael Les Benedict, *A Compromise of Principle: Congressional Republicans and Reconstruction* (1974).

Richard F. Bensel, *Yankee Leviathan: The Origins of Central State Authority in America, 1859–1877* (1990).

Fawn M. Brodie, *Thaddeus Stevens: Scourge of the South* (1959).

David H. Donald, *Charles Sumner and the Rights of Man* (1970).

William Gillette, *The Right to Vote: Politics and the Passage of the Fifteenth Amendment* (1965).

Victor B. Howard, *Religion and the Radical Republican Movement, 1860–1870* (1990).

Harold M. Hyman, *A More Perfect Union: The Impact of the Civil War and Reconstruction on the Constitution* (1973).

Stanley Kutler, *The Judicial Power and Reconstruction Politics* (1968).

Michael L. Lanza, *Agrarianism and Reconstruction Politics: The Southern Homestead Act* (1990).

William S. McFeely, *Grant* (1981).

James C. Mohr, *The Radical Republicans and Reform in New York during Reconstruction* (1973).

David Montgomery, *Beyond Equality: Labor and the Radical Republicans, 1862–1872* (1967).

William E. Nelson, *The Fourteenth Amendment: From Political Principle to Judicial Doctrine* (1988).

Patrick W. Riddleberger, *George Washington Julian: Radical Republican* (1966).

Joel H. Silbey, *A Respectable Minority: The Democratic Party in the Civil War Era, 1860–1868* (1977).

Mark W. Summers, *Railroads, Reconstruction, and the Gospel of Prosperity* (1984).

Margaret S. Thompson, *The "Spider Web": Congress and Lobbying in the Age of Grant* (1985).

Hans L. Trefousse, *The Radical Republicans* (1963).

THE STRUGGLE IN THE SOUTH

James D. Anderson, *The Education of Blacks in the South, 1860–1935* (1988).

Stephen V. Ash, *Middle Tennessee Society Transformed, 1860–1870: War and Peace in the Upper South* (1988).

Dwight B. Billings Jr., *Planters and the Making of a "New South"* (1979).

Randolph B. Campbell, *A Southern Community in Crisis: Harrison County, Texas, 1850–1880* (1983).

Dan T. Carter, *When the War Was Over: The Failure of Self-Reconstruction in the South, 1865–1867* (1985).

Barry A. Crouch, *The Freedmen's Bureau and Black Texans* (1992).

Richard N. Current, *Those Terrible Carpetbaggers: A Reinterpretation* (1988).

Joseph G. Dawson III, *Army Generals and Reconstruction: Louisiana, 1862–1877* (1982).

Edmund L. Drago, *Black Politicians and Reconstruction in Georgia* (1982).

Barbara J. Fields, *Slavery and Freedom on the Middle Ground: Maryland during the Nineteenth Century* (1985).

Michael W. Fitzgerald, *The Union League Movement in the Deep South: Politics and Agricultural Change during Reconstruction* (1989).

Eric Foner, *Nothing but Freedom: Emancipation and Its Legacy* (1983).

Steven Hahn, *The Roots of Southern Populism: Yeoman Farmers and the Transformation of the Georgia Upcountry, 1850–1890* (1983).

William C. Harris, *Day of the Carpetbagger: Republican Reconstruction in Mississippi* (1979).

Janet Sharp Hermann, *The Pursuit of a Dream* (1981).

Thomas Holt, *Black over White: Negro Political Leadership in South Carolina during Reconstruction* (1977).

Elizabeth Jacoway, *Yankee Missionaries in the South* (1979).

Jacqueline Jones, *Soldiers of Light and Love: Northern Teachers and Georgia Blacks, 1865–1873* (1980).

Peter Kolchin, *First Freedom: The Responses of Alabama's Blacks to Emancipation and Reconstruction* (1972).

Leon F. Litwack, *Been in the Storm So Long: The Aftermath of Slavery* (1979).

Richard Lowe, *Republicans and Reconstruction in Virginia, 1865–1870* (1991).

Jay R. Mandle, *Not Slave, Not Free: The African American Economic Experience since the Civil War* (1992).

Donald Nieman, *To Set the Law in Motion: The Freedmen's Bureau and the Legal Rights of Blacks, 1865–1868* (1979).

Michael Perman, *Reunion without Compromise: The South and Reconstruction, 1865–1868* (1973).

Michael Perman, *The Road to Redemption: Southern Politics, 1869–1879* (1984).

Lawrence N. Powell, *New Masters: Northern Planters during the Civil War and Reconstruction* (1984).

Howard Rabinowitz, ed., *Southern Black Leaders of the Reconstruction Era* (1982).

George C. Rable, *But There Was No Peace: The Role of Violence in the Politics of Reconstruction* (1984).

Roger L. Ransom and Richard Sutch, *One Kind of Freedom: The Economic Consequences of Emancipation* (1977).

William L. Richter, *Overreached on All Sides: The Freedmen's Bureau Administrators in Texas, 1865–1868* (1991).

C. Peter Ripley, *Slaves and Freedmen in Civil War Louisiana* (1976).

James L. Roark, *Masters without Slaves: Southern Planters in the Civil War and Reconstruction* (1977).

James E. Sefton, *The United States Army and Reconstruction, 1865–1877* (1967).

Crandall A. Shifflett, *Patronage and Poverty in the Tobacco South: Louisa County, Virginia, 1860–1900* (1982).

Joe G. Taylor, *Louisiana Reconstructed* (1974).

Allen Trelease, *White Terror: The Ku Klux Klan Conspiracy and Southern Reconstruction* (1967).

Ted Tunnell, *Crucible of Reconstruction: War, Radicalism, and Race in Louisiana, 1862–1877* (1974).

Clarence E. Walker, *A Rock in a Weary Land: The African Methodist Episcopal Church during the Civil War and Reconstruction* (1982).

Peter Wallenstein, *From Slave South to New South: Public Policy in Nineteenth-Century Georgia* (1987).

Michael Wayne, *The Reshaping of Plantation Society: The Natchez District, 1860–1880* (1983).

Jonathan M. Wiener, *Social Origins of the New South, 1860–1885* (1978).

Joel Williamson, *After Slavery: The Negro in South Carolina during Reconstruction* (1966).

Sarah Woolfolk Wiggins, *The Scalawag in Alabama Politics, 1865–1881* (1977).

Gavin Wright, *Old South, New South: Revolutions in the Southern Economy since the Civil War* (1986).

COLLAPSE OF RECONSTRUCTION

William Gillette, *Retreat from Reconstruction, 1869–1879* (1979).

Otto H. Olsen, ed., *Reconstruction and Redemption in the South* (1980).

Ian Polakoff, *The Politics of Inertia: The Election of 1876 and the End of Reconstruction* (1973).

Terry L. Seip, *The South Returns to Congress: Men, Economic Measures, and Intersectional Relationships, 1868–1879* (1983).

John G. Sproat, *"The Best Men"* (1968).

C. Vann Woodward, *Reunion and Reaction: The Compromise of 1877 and the End of Reconstruction* (1951).

KENTUCKY SUN QUILT

This carefully hand-stitched quilt, made from pieces of leftover wool clothing and blankets, shows how a woman named Nancy Miller Grider responded creatively to the challenges of her life in Russell County, Kansas, in the 1880s. Historically, women have produced quilts as a visual language, to tell something about themselves by using materials at hand. The circular pattern in Grider's quilt may represent the spokes of a wheel — a fitting symbol not only of her own migration west but of the mass migrations taking place after the Civil War when restless Americans on the move peopled the West and fed the growth of the big cities.

Collection of the Kentucky Quilt Project, Photograph courtesy of the Kentucky Quilt Project, Inc., Louisville, Ky.

AMERICANS ON THE MOVE: THE SETTLEMENT OF THE WEST AND THE RISE OF THE CITY

17

1860–1900

A MISSOURI HOMESTEADER REMEMBERED packing as the family pulled up stakes and headed west to Oklahoma:

> We were going to God's Country. Eighteen hundred and 90. . . . It was pretty hard to part with some of our things. We didn't have much but we had worked hard for everything we had. You had to work hard in that rocky country in Missouri. I was glad to be leaving it. We were going to God's Country. . . . We were going to a new land and get rich.

In the Dakotas an Oglala Sioux recalled moving with his family as a child:

> The snow was deep and it was very cold, and I remember sitting in another pony drag beside my father and mother, all wrapped up in fur. We were going away from where the soldiers were, and I do not know where we went, but it was west.

In the Midwest a young man turned his face to the city, leaving his hometown behind:

> He saw again in his mind's eye, as he tramped the road, a picture of the map on the wall of the railway station—the map with a picture of iron roads from all over the Middle West centering in a dark blotch in the corner. . . .
> "Chicago!" he said to himself.

And in Russia a young girl on her way to America bid good-bye to her village:

> I remember how the women crowded around mother . . . how, finally, the ringing of the signal bell set them all talking faster and louder than ever, in desperate efforts to give the last bits of advice, deliver the last messages, and, to their credit let it be said, to give the final, hearty, unfeigned good-bye kisses, hugs, and good wishes.

Americans in the nineteenth century were a people on the move, in search of jobs, land, and opportunity. In the last three decades of the century, their movement took many forms and went in many directions. The trek to the West continued apace as homesteaders, ranchers, miners, and settlers sought their fortunes. They in turn pushed Native Americans off the land and farther toward the sunset.

At the same time, the pull of the great industrial centers in the Northeast counterbalanced the westward migration. Farmers left the country to seek jobs in industrial centers like Chicago, New York, Pittsburgh, and Detroit. African Americans from the South began a migration to the northern cities, and Canadians crossed the border to work in the factories and mill towns of New England.

Fourteen million immigrants braved the Atlantic to come to America from Europe, creating the great migration that we think of as part of a worldwide westward movement. But the movement of peoples was by no means limited to one direction. Immigrants from Mexico and Latin America journeyed to "El Norte." Canadians headed south. Asians voyaged east across the Pacific to work on the "gold mountain" of California. It is not an exaggeration to say that the decades surrounding the turn of the twentieth century witnessed a migration unmatched in the history of the world.

Within the country, restless, footloose Americans joined the churning masses in motion. The typical urban American in the late nineteenth century moved, on the average, as much as or more than we commonly move today. An industrial worker might hold as many as thirty different jobs in perhaps a dozen cities during a lifetime.

By the end of the century, Americans on the move had peopled a continent and created the outlines of modern America. As industrial capitalism transformed the nation from a rural agrarian economy into an increasingly urban industrial society, it touched and transformed life not just in the burgeoning cities but also on the plains of the Dakotas, in the mines of Colorado, and on the farms of Texas and California. Iron rails and a national market economy inextricably linked the country and the city.

Land Fever

Americans by the hundreds of thousands packed up and moved, pinning their hopes and ambitions on the American West. In the three decades following 1870, this westward stream of migration swelled into a torrent, spilling across the remainder of the prairies, moving on to the Pacific coast, and even-

tually flooding back onto the Great Plains. During this brief span of time, more land was settled than in all the previous history of the country. Between 1876 and 1900, eight new states entered the Union—Colorado, Montana, North and South Dakota, Washington, Idaho, Wyoming, and Utah—leaving only three territories—Oklahoma, New Mexico, and Arizona—in the continental United States.

Two factors stimulated the rapid settlement of the trans-Mississippi West. The Homestead Act of 1862 promised 160 acres free to any citizen or prospective citizen, male or female, who settled on the land for five years. And railroads opened up new areas for settlement and actively recruited settlers. Those who took advantage of the government's offer of free land were called homesteaders, as distinguished from settlers, who purchased their land from private parties. Often they bought from speculators who took up land with an eye to profit, never intending to live on it. In the 1870s, the promise of land lured thousands west across the plains in covered wagons, a hard journey that took many months and cost many lives. With the completion of a transcontinental railroad system in the 1880s, settlers could choose from four competing rail lines and often made the trip in less than a week.

While the country was rich in land and resources, not all who wanted to own their own land were able to do so. Land prices soared to giddy heights as speculating drove prices up. At the same time, large landowners, often foreign investors, gobbled up huge ranches in California and the Southwest. The South, still reeling from the economic impact of the Civil War, saw the old plantation system give way to tenancy and peonage. A growing number of Americans found themselves dispossessed, forced to work for wages on land they would never own.

Moving West: Farmers, Homesteaders, and Speculators

Families who ventured west searching for "God's country" faced hardship, loneliness, and deprivation. To carve a farm from the raw prairie of Iowa, the plains of Nebraska, or the forests of the Pacific Northwest took more than fortitude and backbreaking toil. It took luck. Farming, as one historian acknowledged, was "a risky, uncertain, and often heartbreaking business." Blizzards, tornadoes, grasshoppers, hailstorms, drought, prairie fires, accidental death, and disease were only a few of the catastrophes that could befall even the best farmer.

RAILROAD LOCOMOTIVE
In the years following the Civil War, the locomotive replaced the covered wagon, enabling settlers to travel from Chicago or St. Louis to the West Coast in two days. By the 1890s, more than 72,000 miles of track stretched west of the Mississippi River. In this photograph, men and women hop aboard a locomotive to celebrate the completion of a section of track.
Library of Congress.

Debt was a constant nightmare. Homesteaders on "free" land needed as much as a thousand dollars for a house, a team of farm animals, a well, fencing, and seed. Poor sodbusters did without even these basics, living in dugouts carved in the land and using muscle instead of machinery.

Americans in the nineteenth century were a people on the move, in search of jobs, land, and opportunity.

"Father made a dugout and covered it with willows and grass," one Kansas girl recounted. When it rained, water flooded the dugout and "we carried the water out in buckets, then waded around in the mud until it dried." Rain wasn't the only problem. "Sometimes the bull snakes would get in the roof and now and then one would lose his hold and fall down on the bed, then off on the floor. Mother would grab the hoe . . . and after the fight was over Mr. Bull Snake was dragged outside."

For women on the frontier, simple daily necessities like obtaining water and fuel meant back-breaking labor. Women lugged bucketfuls of water from wells. Out on the plains, where water was scarce, women often had to trudge to the nearest creek or spring. "A yoke was made to place across the shoulders, so as to carry at each end a bucket of water," one daughter recollected, "and then water was brought a half mile from spring to house." Fifteen years of such unremitting hard labor, the daughter sadly observed, "brought her [mother] worn-out to the grave at the age of 58 years." Gathering fuel was another heavy chore. Without ready sources of coal or firewood, settlers on the prairies and plains turned to what substitutes they could scavenge. Anything burnable—twigs, tufts of grass, old corncobs, sunflower stalks—was used for fuel. But by far the most prevalent fuel used for cooking and heating were "chips", which were chunks of dried cattle and buffalo dung found in abundance on the plains and grasslands.

Food preparation provided another challenge to the farm wife. Cookstoves were virtually unknown in the territories. Settlers cooked in kettles suspended over the fireplace and boiled most of their food. Baking was accomplished using footed iron kettles set in the coals. Simplicity and monotony characterized the settlers' regular diet, which was heavy on corn, wheat, and potatoes. "Our living at first was very scanty," recalled one Kansas woman, "mostly corn coarsely ground and made into hominy." But things improved. The family raised a crop of wheat and ground it into flour. "We would invite the neighbors proudly telling them we

have 'flour doings.'" When the farm wife began to raise chickens, the family added "chicken fixings" to its diet, "and when we could have 'flour doings and chicken fixings' at the same meal we felt we were on the road to prosperity."

The costs and expenses of farming made farmers habitual debtors. The first years were critical. If the farm did not fare well, if the crop failed, the farmer faced a downward spiral into a mire of debt. Dependent on the weather, the bank, the railroad, and the market, the so-called independent farmer

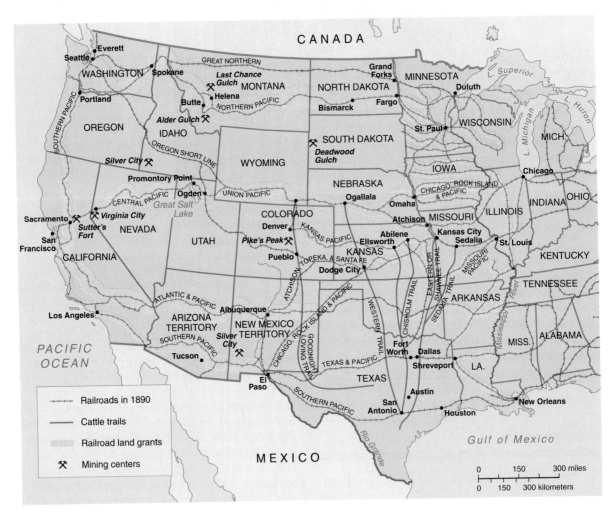

MAP 17.1
Federal Land Grants to Railroads and the Development of the West, 1850–1900
Generous federal land grants meant that railroads could sell the desirable land next to the track at a profit or hold it for speculation. Railroads received over 180 million acres, an area equal to the size of Texas. Note how the cattle trails connect with major railheads in Dodge City, Abilene, and Kansas City and to mines in Montana, Nevada, Colorado, and New Mexico.

OUR HOME

A mother and her children pose in front of their dugout near McCook, Nebraska, in the 1890s. With its real roof, glass windowpanes, and solid door, their dugout is more substantial than most.

Nebraska State Historical Society.

labored against heavy odds. No wonder some settlers didn't bother to farm at all. The West had more than its share of small-time speculators, who took up land in the hope of selling it for a profit.

Many homesteaders and settlers succeeded in building comfortable lives. But for others the opportunities of the West failed to materialize. Already by the 1870s, much of the best land had been taken, given to the railroads as land grants or to the states to finance education. Too often, the homesteaders found that only the least desirable tracts were left —poorer lands, far from markets, transportation, and society. Land speculators took the lion's share. "There is plenty of land for sale in California," one migrant complained in 1870, but "the majority of the available lands are held by speculators, at prices far beyond the reach of a poor man."

The railroads were by far the biggest single winners in the scramble for western land. To encourage railroad building in the decades after the Civil War, the federal government and the states gave public lands to the railroads. Together the land grants totaled approximately 180 million acres—an area almost one-tenth the size of the United States.

In California alone the railroads held some 20 million acres by 1870. Farmers who went west to homestead often ended up buying land from the railroads or from the speculators and land companies that quickly followed the railroads into the new territories. The value of Nebraska railroad land went from $8 an acre in 1870 to $25 an acre by 1890. Of the 2.5 million farms established on public lands between 1860 and 1900, homesteading accounted for only one in five; the vast majority of farmland sold for a profit.

As land for homesteading grew scarce on the prairie in the 1870s, farmers began to push farther westward, moving into western Kansas, Nebraska, and eastern Colorado—the land called the Great American Desert by settlers who had passed over it on their way to California and Oregon. The Homestead Act tempted settlers out onto the Great Plains, where 160 acres of plains land was too dry to support a farm. Although many agricultural experts warned that the semiarid land (where less than twenty inches of rain fell annually) should be reserved for grazing, their words of caution were drowned out by the extravagant claims of western promoters. Railroad companies pictured the plains as an agricultural paradise where settlers would "all become prosperous, and many will acquire fortunes in a short period." "Rain follows the plow" became the slogan of western boosters, who insisted that cultivation would alter the climate of the region and bring more rainfall.

It would have been more accurate to say that drought followed the plow. Periodic droughts at roughly twenty-year intervals were a fact of life on the Great Plains. Plowed up, the dry topsoil blew away in the wind. A period of relatively good rainfall in the early 1880s encouraged settlement, but a protracted drought in the late 1880s and early 1890s sent starving farmers reeling back from the plains. Hundreds of thousands retreated from western Kansas and Nebraska, some in wagons carrying the slogan "In God we trusted, in Kansas we busted." A popular ballad bitterly summed up the plight of the worst off, those too poor to leave:

> How happy I am on my government claim,
> Where I've nothing to lose and nothing to gain,
> Nothing to eat and nothing to wear,
> Nothing from nothing is honest and square.
> But here I am stuck and here I must stay,
> My money's all gone and I can't get away;
> There's nothing will make a man hard and profane
> Like starving to death on a government claim.

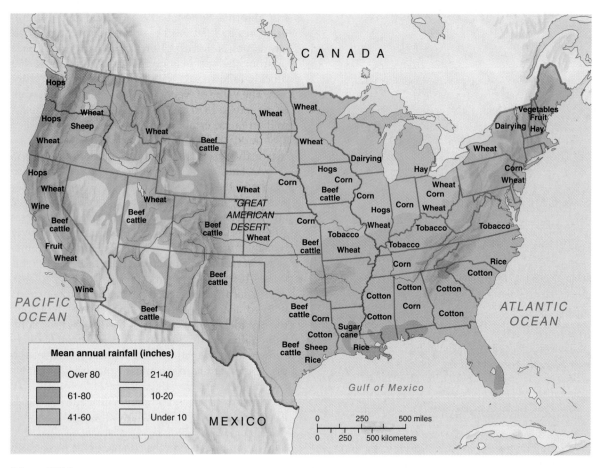

MAP 17.2
Rainfall and Agricultural Regions, around 1890
Early travelers called the grasslands of the Great Plains "The Great American Desert" as they hurried over this flat, semi-arid land on their way to California or Oregon. But by the 1870s much of the best far western land was taken and land fever tempted farmers onto the plains in western Kansas, Nebraska, and eastern Colorado. Many would go bust in the great droughts of the late 1880s.

The fever for fertile land set off a series of spectacular land runs in Oklahoma. When the government opened two million acres in former Indian territory to settlement in 1889, thousands rushed to grab a piece. Federal troops kept order as the homesteaders massed on the border. On April 22 at noon, pistol shots signaled the opening, and they were off. "Along the line as far as the eye could reach, with a shout and a yell the swift riders shot out, then followed the light buggies or wagons and last the lumbering prairie schooners and freighters' wagons," a reporter wrote. "Above all a great cloud of dust hover[ed] like smoke over a battlefield." It was a wild scramble, the reporter confessed, "a rough and tumble contest filled with excitement and real peril." By the end of the day, hundreds of homesteaders had staked claims, and Oklahoma boasted two tent cities with more than 10,000 residents.

In later years, other portions of Indian territory opened for settlement. In a frenzied land rush on the Cherokee strip in Oklahoma Territory in 1893, more than 100,000 homesteaders competed for 40,000 claims. Several settlers were killed in the stampede, and nervous men guarded their claims with rifles. Some simply moved onto Indian lands. Called "boomers" or "sooners," they had to be removed by force. As public lands grew smaller, the hunger for land grew even fiercer.

The Dispossessed: Tenants, Sharecroppers, and Migrants

Landownership, the symbol of the American dream in the nineteenth century, remained an elusive goal for many Americans—newly freed slaves, immigrants arriving from Europe and Asia, and Mexicans on the Texas border. In the post–Civil War period, as agriculture became a big business tied to national and global markets, an increasing number of dispossessed laborers worked land that they would never own.

In the southern United States, the farmer labored under particularly heavy burdens. The Civil War wiped out much of the region's capital, which had been invested in slaves, and crippled the plantation economy. The newly freed slaves rarely managed to obtain land of their own. Instead, they soon found themselves reduced to propertyless farm laborers. "The colored folks stayed with the old boss man and farmed and worked on the plantations," a black Alabama sharecropper observed bitterly. "They were still slaves, but they were free slaves."

Tenancy and sharecropping became a way of life for poor blacks and whites alike. The tenant rented land; the sharecropper worked someone else's land for a share of the proceeds. Even those who owned their own land faced enormous difficulties. In the states of the old Confederacy, both money and credit were in short supply. Southern farmers in desperation turned to the country merchant for credit. Before the war, tiny rural stores had dotted the South, serving the modest needs of small white farmers. After the war, thousands of small stores mushroomed across the landscape to provide food, clothing, and necessary supplies to the increased numbers of tenant and sharecropper farmers, both white and black. Some of the merchants were ex-masters who opened stores on their plantations. Under an arrangement called crop lien, local merchants supplied goods to the farmers on credit; in return, the farmers put up their next year's crop as collateral. The merchants charged exorbitant interest, up to 60 percent, on the goods they sold—from seed to a slab of bacon. At "settling up time," after the landlord took half the farmer's yield, the merchant consulted the debt ledger. Invariably, the farmer's expenses exceeded the income from his half of the cotton crop, and the cropper went home empty-handed, only to begin the cycle all over again.

There was no escape. Indebtedness bound the sharecropper to the landlord and to the merchant by prohibiting him from moving or buying from another store. Even small farmers who owned their own land suffered under the crop lien system. After seven years, farmers who did not "pay out" lost their land. Across the South the merchant became known as the "furnishing man." Black farmers called him simply "the man." The crop lien system over which he presided led generations of farmers, white and black, into a mire of debt and dependency. By the beginning of the twentieth century, a majority of white farmers had become landless share-

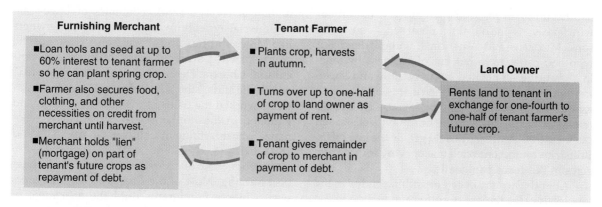

Furnishing Merchant

- Loan tools and seed at up to 60% interest to tenant farmer so he can plant spring crop.
- Farmer also secures food, clothing, and other necessities on credit from merchant until harvest.
- Merchant holds "lien" (mortgage) on part of tenant's future crops as repayment of debt.

Tenant Farmer

- Plants crop, harvests in autumn.
- Turns over up to one-half of crop to land owner as payment of rent.
- Tenant gives remainder of crop to merchant in payment of debt.

Land Owner

Rents land to tenant in exchange for one-fourth to one-half of tenant farmer's future crop.

FIGURE 17.1
Tenancy and the Crop Lien System
The crop lien system was designed to deal with the shortage of money and credit in the post-Reconstruction South. The local furnishing merchant provided seed and supplies to farmers who pledged their crop as collateral. A complex skein of relationships developed between merchant, landowner, and tenant farmer.

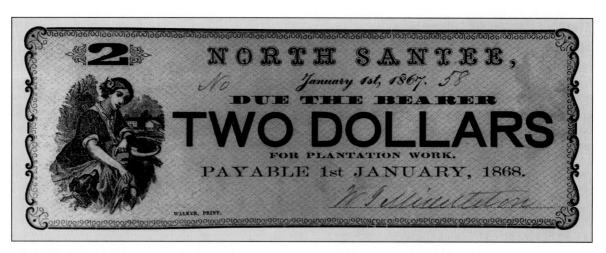

SHARECROPPER SCRIP

Both money and credit were in short supply in the South after the Civil War. To get around the problem, landowners issued scrip in lieu of cash to the landless sharecroppers who worked their fields. Redeemable only at the plantation store, the scrip locked the sharecroppers into an insidious system. The sharecroppers, forced to buy food and other goods at high prices from their creditors/employers, often fell into a cycle of debt and dependency. This note circulated in South Carolina in 1868.

The South Carolina Historical Society.

croppers, outnumbering even the freedpeople caught in the system.

In Texas, the coming of the railroads at the turn of the century undermined ranch culture and led to the rise of a segregated farm society in which a growing number of Mexican wageworkers labored on huge spreads owned by Anglos or by European syndicates. As early as the 1860s, the large ranchers had begun to enclose the open range with barbed-wire fences. As one old-timer observed, "Those persons, Mexicans and Americans, without land but who had cattle were put out of business by fencing." Fencing eliminated landless cattle and sheep ranchers, who had grazed their herds on the open range, and forced small-time landowners who could not afford to buy barbed wire or to sink wells to sell out for the best price they could get. By the late 1880s, British investors controlled one of every four or five acres in the Texas panhandle.

After the heyday of cattle ranching ended in the late 1880s came the rise of cotton production in the southeastern regions of Texas. Ranchers turned their pastures into sharecroppers' plots and hired displaced cowboys, most of them Mexican, as seasonal laborers for as little as seventy-five cents a day. Within the space of ten years, ranch life in southern Texas gave way to a growing army of agricultural wageworkers.

In California, a pattern of land monopoly and large-scale farming fostered tenancy and migratory labor. By the 1870s, less than one percent of the population owned half of the state's available agricultural land. A German, Henry Miller, in partnership with an Alsatian immigrant, Charles Lux, acquired thousands of acres in the rich San Joaquin valley. By 1900, the Miller-Lux empire constituted over a million acres. The rigid economics of large-scale commercial agriculture as practiced by rich owners like Miller and Lux and the seasonal nature of the crops spawned a ragged army of migratory agricultural laborers. Derisively labeled "blanket men" or "bindle stiffs," these homeless and landless transients worked the fields in the growing season and wintered in the flophouses of San Francisco. Bonanza wheat farming in California in the 1870s and 1880s exhausted the land and was replaced, with the introduction of irrigation, by fruit and sugar beet farming. Most of the California farm laborers were Chinese immigrants until the enactment of Chinese exclusion in 1882 forced big growers to tap other groups, including Mexicans, Filipinos, and Japanese, for farm labor.

The dispossessed—those with no land and no hope of owning their own land—became a growing part of the workforce in the United States by the end of the century.

The Changing Face of Rural America

In the late nineteenth century, America's population remained overwhelmingly rural. The 1870 census showed that nearly 80 percent of the nation's people lived in areas of less than eight thousand inhabitants. In 1900, the figure had dropped to 66 percent. But while the percentage of rural inhabitants fell, the number of farms grew—from 2 million in 1860 to more than 5.7 million in 1900. Rapid growth in the West accounted for the rise in the number of farms, but not all the nation's farmers lived in the West. The rural population spread evenly across the country, with rural inhabitants outnumbering city dwellers even in industrial states like Pennsylvania and New York as late as 1880. Like all aspects of American life, farm life changed rapidly in the last decades of the century. With the rise of industrialization and the growth of big cities, many farmers gave up their farms and moved to towns and cities. Those who stayed behind increasingly adopted new technologies, making farming less a way of life and more a business venture. In the states of the old

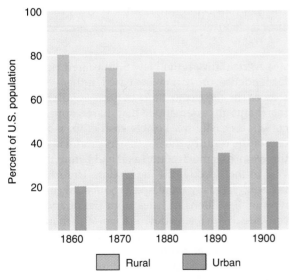

FIGURE 17.2
Changes in Rural and Urban Populations, 1860–1900
Between 1860–1900 not only did the number of urban dwellers increase, but the number of rural inhabitants fell. Mechanization made it possible to farm with fewer hands and fueled the exodus from farm to city throughout the second half of the nineteenth century.

Confederacy, enthusiastic advocates of industrial development trumpeted the New South as the region scrambled to build blast furnaces and mills alongside its cotton fields. Nevertheless cotton remained king in the New South, and the region's emphasis on a cash-crop economy signaled a nationwide trend away from family farming and toward agribusiness.

The Colonial Economy of the New South

In the decades following the Civil War, the South struggled to regain its economic footing. The region's economy, devastated by war and altered forever by the abolition of slavery, foundered at the same time the North experienced an unprecedented industrial boom. No wonder some Southerners called for a New South modeled on the industrial North. Henry Grady, the ebullient young editor of the *Atlanta Constitution*, used his paper's substantial influence (it boasted the largest circulation of any weekly in the country) to extol the virtues of a new industrial South. Part bully, part booster, Grady exhorted the South to use its natural advantages—cheap labor and abundant natural resources—to go head to head in competition with northern industry.

Grady's message fell on receptive ears. Many Southerners, men and women, black and white, joined the national migration from farm to city, leaving the old plantations to molder and decay. Between 1870 and 1890, villages and towns in the South experienced unprecedented growth. With the end of military rule in 1877, southern Democrats, calling themselves "Redeemers," regained political power in the southern states. But whatever their plantation pedigrees, they readily cast their lot with the corporate North. The sons of the old planter class enthusiastically embraced northern promoters who promised prosperity and profits. Northern capital rushed south in the waning years of the 1870s as the country recovered from the hard times precipitated by the panic of 1873. The railroads came first, opening up the region for industrial development. Railroad mileage grew fourfold from 1865 to 1890. So too did the number of cotton spindles soar as textile mill owners abandoned New England en masse in search of the cheap labor, low taxes, and proximity to raw materials promised in the South. By 1900, the South had become the nation's leading producer of cloth, and more than 100,000 Southerners, many of them women and children, had traded agricultural labor for work in textile mills.

In only one industry did the South truly dominate—tobacco. Soon after the Civil War, Julian Carr of North Carolina began to build Bull Durham tobacco with a massive advertising campaign that made the bull on the trademark an international symbol for smoking tobacco. Capitalizing on the invention of a machine for rolling cigarettes, the Duke family of Virginia challenged Bull Durham in the 1880s and boosted their fortunes, eventually dominating the industry with their American Tobacco Company. The new popularity of cigarettes, which replaced chewing tobacco among America's growing urban population, provided a booming market for Duke's "ready-made" cigarettes. James "Buck" Duke boosted sales by launching clever advertising campaigns that featured risqué pictures of "cigarette girls." Within four years, the company was selling 400,000 cigarettes a day.

The extractive industries, mining and lumber, also experienced a boom in the New South, but with devastating results. Coal from Appalachia could now be transported by rail to fuel the blast furnaces and factories of the nation. In the race to exploit the South's coal reserves, whole mountains were eaten up, often with catastrophic environmental and human costs. Fortunes were made, but few of them by Southerners. Investors in the North and abroad reaped the lion's share. The miners themselves violently protested their poor wages and dangerous working conditions in a series of strikes that gave one county in Kentucky the name Bloody Harlan. In the lumber industry, the demand for southern wood led to untrammeled growth. Northern lumber syndicates cut a wide swath through the virgin forests of the South, stripping them of timber and leaving the soil to erode. Warnings that such a course would lead to ecological disaster fell on deaf ears. Twenty years of milling led to what one contemporary forestry expert called "probably the most rapid and reckless destruction of forests known to history."

Of all its industries the New South was proudest of its iron and steel industry, which grew up in the area surrounding Birmingham, Alabama. Soon the smokestack replaced the white-pillared plantation as the symbol of the South. Would-be iron barons built twenty-five blast furnaces in Alabama alone. Pennsylvania iron magnate Andrew Carnegie toured the region in 1889 and observed, "The South is Pennsylvania's most formidable industrial enemy." But as long as control of southern industry remained in the hands of northern investors, Pennsylvania had nothing to fear. Whatever the South's natural advantages, northern bankers and investors had no intention of letting the South beat the North at its own game. Elaborate mechanisms rigged the price of southern steel, inflating it, as one northern insider confessed, "for the purpose of protecting the Pittsburgh mills and in turn the Pittsburgh steel users."

In practical terms the industrialized New South proved a chimera. While a handful of owners and managers prospered, the vast majority of Southerners, black and white, toiled for low wages in poor or dangerous conditions. Instead of thriving, the South found itself reduced virtually to the status of an economic colony of the North. Just as colonial economies the world over feature cheap labor, extractive industries, and exported raw materials, so too did the New South. Similarly, the region experienced low wages, absentee ownership, and little control over policy or pricing—key determinants of colonial status.

In practical terms the industrialized New South proved a chimera. Instead of thriving, the region found itself reduced virtually to the status of an economic colony of the North.

Agriculture in the New South fared no better. Dependence on cotton increased rather than decreased in the postbellum period. Landlords and merchants alike demanded that sharecroppers grow cotton, an easily marketable cash crop. Before the end of the century, the South was producing nearly three times as much cotton as it had before the Civil War in the heyday of King Cotton. Unfortunately, the South's vastly increased production, combined now with millions of bales from Egypt and India, coincided with a slowdown in world demand. Cotton prices plummeted. Even worse, relentless cotton cultivation exhausted the soil and eroded the countryside. It seemed that in agriculture, as in industry, Southerners had hitched their economic futures to a falling star. Although a few merchants and landowners managed to hold on and even profit, the majority of Southerners succumbed to the numbing poverty that settled over the rural South. Dissatisfaction with this state of affairs would fuel the Populist movement in the 1890s.

From the Family Farm toward Agribusiness

The promise of cheap land lured many settlers west at the same time the growing cities acted as a powerful magnet, particularly to young people, pulling them off the farm. By the 1890s, depopulation caused a growing chorus of alarm. Many feared that a way of life was dying. In the pages of popular periodicals, writers voiced the growing concern. "One by one, family by family, [the] inhabitants slip away in search of other homes," a New England writer lamented. "The young, the hopeful, the ambitious" left, while "the superannuated, the feeble, the dull" stayed. Although enough workers remained to carry on the common business of life, the writer noted sadly that "the world's real work is done elsewhere." Contrary to popular prejudice, however, it was not just the aged and dimwitted who chose to stay. Those who stayed behind increasingly adapted to changing conditions by adopting new technologies and moving toward commercial farming.

The loss of population was by no means limited to New England. More than half the rural townships of Ohio, Indiana, and Illinois lost population between 1880 and 1890, and the rate in Iowa was not far behind. Alarmed observers wondered who would be left to feed the growing city population if all the farmers left the fields. They needn't have

worried. The countryside in the late nineteenth century actually experienced surplus population. The birthrate in the country exceeded that in the city, while rural mortality rates ran significantly lower than urban rates. At the same time, scientific farming and mechanization enabled one farmer to do the work of several hands. New plows and reapers halved the time and labor cost of production. With fewer farmers producing more food, the drift from the countryside to the city was a healthy economic adjustment. The changes in rural America resulted as much from the push of a successful revolution in agriculture as from the failure of the farm to compete with the pull of urban economic opportunities.

To say that the farmer suffered from too much success, however, only obscures the economic realities as well as the social and cultural implications of the shift from the country to the city. In the 1870s and 1890s, crop failures and economic depression forced many farmers into foreclosure and off the land. For them the move from the farm represented a personal and economic defeat. That defeat came to be mirrored in the popular culture, where the farmer, who had once been the symbol of America, was increasingly ridiculed and caricatured. Derogatory terms like "hayseed" and "hick" entered the American vocabulary.

By the end of the century, a growing number of writers, influenced by the new trend toward literary realism, took a grim look at rural life. Hamlin Gar-

IOWA FARMHOUSE
This farmhouse in Clay County, Iowa, was built in the 1870s to replace the log cabin at the left where the homesteaders had lived when they first migrated from Kentucky. The rocking chair on the porch hints at the leisure the family could now occasionally enjoy. As some farmers prospered, they were able to construct white clapboard houses like this one, replicating the homes they had known back East.
Collection of Julia Booth.

land, a son of the Midwest who went east to school, revisited Iowa, Wisconsin, and North Dakota in the late 1880s. Garland's first collection of short stories, *Main Traveled Roads*, published in 1891, recounted his growing bitterness as he encountered "the ugliness, the endless drudgery, and the loneliness of the farmer's lot." Writers like Garland and Frederic Howe, who had themselves abandoned the farm for the city, acknowledged the farmer's diminished stature. "The farmer," wrote one novelist, "is as far out of it as if he lived in Alaska. Perhaps there was a time when a man could live in what the poet calls a daily communication with nature and not starve his mind and dwarf his soul, but this isn't the century."

However much the image of the farmer suffered in the popular culture of the time, in the late nineteenth century farming itself was thriving as an agricultural revolution transformed American farm life. The diversified family farm of the past began to give way to specialized, commercial farming. By the turn of the century, American agriculture had already entered the era of what would come to be called "agribusiness"—farming as a big business.

Industrialization and urbanization provided farmers with expanding markets for their produce, and railroads carried farmers' crops to markets thousands of miles away. At the same time, mechanization made it possible to farm vast tracts of land. Farming was on its way to becoming a business enterprise, not simply a way of life or a means of existence.

Business became the order of the day. Instead of extolling the virtues of the self-sufficient farmer, farm journals, agricultural societies, and educators pushed farmers to act more like businessmen, to specialize and to consolidate. Together they helped to create a striking new image of what constituted successful farming. "Farming for business, not for a living—this is the motif of the New Farmer," announced an agricultural writer at the turn of the century. The message was clear: The job of the up-to-date farmer was to produce money, not just crops.

East of the Mississippi, new farming techniques led to greater output and increased specialization. New Englanders gave up trying to compete with the Midwest in meat, grain, and wool and concentrated their energies instead on dairy farming, vegetables, and fruit. In the Midwest, Illinois and Iowa farmers turned the region into the nation's corn belt and feedlot. In the West, specialization led to huge bonanza wheat farms, some comprising over 100,000 acres, in California and the Red River valley

of North Dakota and Minnesota. In Washington, Oregon, and California, growers plunged headlong into the production of hops. In Oklahoma and the South, cotton remained king. Although general farming continued to prevail in large sections of the country, agricultural specialization marked the growing trend in late-nineteenth-century farming.

Farmers soon discovered that cash-crop farming had its hazards, subjecting the farmer to the twin risks of crop failure and soil depletion. Farmers who did not raise their own food had trouble surviving the periodic droughts and depressions that were common in the 1870s, 1880s, and 1890s. And in their determination to turn a profit, farmers used up the soil with as little regard for the depletion of its resources as the western miners, notorious for their rape of the land.

As farming moved onto the prairies and plains, mechanization took command. Steel plows, reapers, mowers, harrows, seed drills, combines, and threshers replaced human muscle on the farm. Horse-drawn implements gave way to steam-powered machinery. By 1880, a new harvester could reap and shock twenty acres of wheat in a day, and a single combine could do the work of twenty men. Farmers rushed to take advantage of the new technology, mortgaging their farms to pay for the expensive new machinery. Between 1860 and 1900, the value of farm machinery produced annually in the United States rose from $21 million to $101 million. Machines enabled farmers to vastly increase their acreage. Two men with one machine could cultivate 250 acres of wheat. Production soared. The agricultural revolution meant that by the second half of the nineteenth century, Americans raised more than four times the corn, five times the hay, and seven times the wheat and oats than they had before the Civil War.

The new farmer existed in a web of dependence, not only on weather and credit but increasingly on a world market.

The new farmer existed in a web of dependence, not only on weather and credit but increasingly on a world market. American foodstuffs fed people as far away as England and Germany. Farmers exported 217 million bushels of wheat by 1897 and 212 million bushels of corn. Like the cotton farmer in the South, northern grain and livestock

TECHNOLOGY IN AMERICA
The Combine

The mechanization of the farm helps explain how a declining farm population could greatly increase the output of farm products. The combine, pictured here, was so named because it combined the work of both a harvester and a thresher. Drawn by twenty-four horses, it reaped the grain, threshed it, and bagged it, all in one simultaneous operation. Benjamin Holt invented the combine in the early 1880s and founded what eventually became the Caterpillar Company.

The superiority of the new technology was not lost on contemporary observers. In the words of an early enthusiast, "If the total time required to build a combine is 300 man-days and the combine, doing the work of 1,000 men, is used 30 days per years for 10 years, the ratio of labor efficiency is 1,000 man-days saved for each day expended."

The effect of labor-saving machinery on the scale of agricultural operations can best be seen in the rise of huge wheat farms, like the one pictured here in Walla Walla, Washington. By the 1890s two men with the aid of machinery could farm well over 250 acres. John Deere Museum.

farmers increasingly depended on foreign markets for their livelihood. A fall in commodity prices meant that a farmer's entire crop went to pay off debts. In periods of depression, great numbers of heavily mortgaged farmers lost their land to creditors.

The protective tariff, endorsed by every Republican president from Abraham Lincoln to William Howard Taft, further hurt the farmer. The tariff, designed to protect "infant industries," prevented foreign competition and effectively raised the price of manufactured goods. Almost everything the farmer purchased, from plows and reapers to kerosene and calico, cost more because of the tariff. Habitual debtors, farmers also suffered from the government's deflationary monetary policy. The gold standard caused a steady deflation, which forced debtors to repay loans with money worth much more than the money they had originally borrowed. Or put in terms of labor, a farmer who had borrowed a thousand dollars in 1868 had to grow twice as much wheat in 1888 than he would have had to grow twenty years earlier to pay back the loan. Farmers also resented the profits made by bankers and mort-

gage lenders and by the owners of grain elevators, who often made more money storing the farmers' grain than the farmers made when they sold it. "Every agent, pedlar, and Every profession of men is Fleecing the Farmer," a Texas cotton farmer complained in the 1890s. "By the time the World Gets their Liveing *out* of the *Farmer* as we have to Feed the World," he went on, his eloquence not blunted by his crude grammar and poor spelling, "we the Farmer has nothing Left but a Bear Hard Liveing."

Since the days of Thomas Jefferson, farming had been linked with the highest ideals of a democratic society. Now agrarianism itself had been transformed. The farmer was no longer the self-sufficient yeoman, but a businessman on the one hand or a dispossessed wage laborer on the other, both tied to a global market. And even as farm production soared, industrial production outstripped it. More and more farmers left the fields for the factories. Now that the future lay with the cities, was democracy itself at risk? This question would ignite a farmers' revolt in the 1880s and dominate political debate in the 1890s.

The American West: A Clash of Cultures

In the movies, the American West is portrayed in mythic terms as a picturesque landscape where strong-jawed heroes square off against villains. The good guys are always white, even their hats. Often the bad guys are red—Indians, the name Columbus mistakenly gave to Native Americans. In this masculine tableau the setting is so timeless that it is easy to forget that the action takes place at roughly the same time that waves of new immigrants sailed past the Statue of Liberty, engineers built the Brooklyn Bridge, and men like John D. Rockefeller consolidated their empires in emerging industrial America. The mythical West exists away from all of this, out of time.

Once the West is situated within its historical context, however, once it is seen as a particular place at a particular time, reality supersedes myth, and the West appears to be not so different from the rest of the country. The problems and issues facing the nation at the beginning of the twentieth century— the growing power of corporations, ethnic and racial animosity, the exploitation of labor and of natural resources—all played themselves out under western skies.

The Peoples of the Great Plains and the Far West

"West" has always been a relative term. Until the gold rush of 1849 focused attention on California, the West for settlers lay beyond the Appalachians and east of the Mississippi in the lands drained by the Ohio River, a part of the country that we now call the Old Northwest. But by the last three decades of the nineteenth century, the West increasingly referred to the land across the Mississippi, from the Great Plains to the Pacific Ocean.

The West of the late nineteenth century was a polyglot place, as much so as the big cities of the East. An illustrator on his way to the California goldfields deftly depicted the mix:

> The stranger, as he ascends the mountains towards the mining towns . . . notices the contrast in the scenes around him to anything he ever saw before. Indians are met in groups. . . . Strings of Chinamen pass, and greet you in broken English. . . . Next comes a Negro, with polite 'good morning, sar'; or Chileno, Mexican, or Kanaka.

The parade of peoples who came to the West included immigrants from England, Ireland, Wales, Germany, Greece, Scandinavia, Portugal, China, Japan, and Canada, not to mention New Englanders, Mormons, African Americans, Mexicans, Latinos, numerous Indians, and a sprinkling of European nobles. Prejudice and racial hostility erupted into violence on the frontier, just as they did in the cities. The Chinese suffered brutal treatment at the hands of employers and other laborers. Fearful of competition, workingmen rioted in the 1870s and fought to keep the Chinese out of the United States. Hispanic peoples, who had lived in Texas and the Southwest since Juan de Oñate led his pioneer settlers up the Rio Grande in 1598 and who had occupied the Pacific coast since San Diego was founded in 1769, overnight were reduced to a "minority" after the United States annexed Texas and took California in the Mexican War of the 1840s. African Americans who ventured out to the territories faced hostile settlers determined to keep the West "for whites only." And Native Americans, who once warred with one another, increasingly united to fight off white encroachment.

The sheer number of races that came together and mingled in the West produced a complex racism. One historian has noted, not entirely facetiously, that there were at least eight oppressed races in the West—Indians, Latinos, Chinese, Japanese, blacks, Mormons, strikers, and radicals.

The Mormons, followers of Joseph Smith, the founder and prophet of the Church of Jesus Christ of Latter-day Saints, fled west to avoid religious persecution. They believed that they had a divine right to the land, and their messianic militancy, as well as their favorable view of Indians and other pioneers' suspicions that they were abolitionists, contributed to making them outcasts. Although they were not the only religious sect of this period to practice plural marriage, the Mormons' polygamy became a convenient point of attack for those who hated and feared the group. After Smith was killed by an Illinois mob in 1844, Brigham Young led the flock, which numbered more than twenty thousand, over the Rockies to the valley of the Great Salt Lake in Utah. Often the pioneers pulled their carts by hand, dragging their children and belongings across the plains. The Utah land that they settled was a virtual desert, but the Mormons quickly set to work irrigating it. Lacking foreign or eastern capital to back them, they relied on cooperation and communalism. The church established and controlled water supplies, stores, insurance companies, and later factories and mining smelters. By 1882, the Mormons had built a thriving city of more than 150,000 souls with a grand tabernacle in Salt Lake City. Congress refused to grant Utah statehood until the church discontinued the practice of polygamy. Utah did not enter the Union until 1896.

One historian has noted, not entirely facetiously, that there were at least eight oppressed races in the West—Indians, Latinos, Chinese, Japanese, blacks, Mormons, strikers, and radicals.

Prospectors and cowboys have a special place in the lore of the West. The wide-open boomtowns of Nevada's Comstock Lode and the cattle towns on the Chisholm Trail—along with names like Virginia City, Tombstone, and Deadwood—conjure up visions familiar from American folklore. Yet by the

1870s, both mining and cattle had become big business. The colorful prospector, with his pan and his burro, gave way to huge underground operations and quartz mines in which rock was crushed to extract gold and base metals. Corporate control replaced individual prospecting, and New York replaced San Francisco as the center of speculation in mining stock.

The story of mining in the West is a tale of one rush after another in western lands rich with gold, silver, lead, zinc, and copper. Boomtown to ghost town in a matter of years was a pattern common in western mining, a pattern that left an ominous legacy of reckless exploitation. Labor as well as land was harshly treated. Miners in the West, like their counterparts in Kentucky, worked for low wages in dangerous conditions. In a scenario familiar in the East, desperate miners in Coeur d'Alene, Idaho, struck for union recognition in 1892, only to be put down by state troops.

COPPER MINE
This 1887 photograph of the Phelps-Dodge copper mining operation in Morenci, Arizona, indicates the development of western mining. In 1881, a westerner named William Church, who had bought out the original prospector, traveled to New York to persuade the giant Phelps-Dodge mining corporation to lend him $50,000 to develop a copper mine at Morenci. Phelps-Dodge agreed. Six years later Church sold out, leaving the corporation the sole owner of the mine. In a story told over and over again, mechanized mining replaced the prospector and his burro, and mining became a big business with western mines owned by large eastern conglomerates. Note the pollution attendant on copper mining evidenced by the slag heaps in the foreground.
Courtesy of the Arizona Historical Society, Tucson, #26,720.

Like mining, cattle ranching became a big business in the 1870s. On the range, the cowboy gave way to the cattle king. Cattle ranchers followed the railroads onto the plains, establishing in the years between 1865 and 1885 a cattle kingdom from Texas to Wyoming. Texas longhorns pushed the bison off the range, overgrazing the once abundant grasses. In three years the buffalo all but disappeared in Montana. Cattle ranching in the West, much of it financed by foreign capital, was characterized by speculation and absentee ownership. Wealthy Europeans and Americans occasionally tried their hand at ranching. The Marquis of Mores, complaining that he was "weary of civilization," came to ranch in the Dakotas. Not far away lived Theodore Roosevelt, a New Yorker who, in his typical fashion, sought to overcome his grief over the death of his wife by throwing himself headlong into the physical exertion of cowboy life.

By 1886, cattle overcrowded the range. Severe blizzards during the next two winters decimated the herds. "A whole generation of cowmen," wrote one chronicler, "went dead broke." As the heyday of the cattle kingdom came to an end, Roosevelt and the Marquis packed up and went home. Cattle ranching, like mining, became largely a corporate business with distant boards of directors in the East and wage-earning workers on the range.

The cowboy, that symbol of American independence, became, like the miner, a wage laborer. Though the cowboy was more colorful than his eastern counterparts in the factory, his life was no easier. "No class is harder worked or so poorly paid," observed Karl Marx's daughter on a trip to America. Many cowboys were African Americans and Mexicans (although western literature chose to ignore that fact and transformed the black cowboy Deadwood Dick into a white man). Like many other dissatisfied workers, cowboys organized labor unions in the 1880s and mounted strikes in both Texas and Wyoming.

The American West in the nineteenth century witnessed more than its share of bloodshed. Violence broke out between cattle ranchers and sheep ranchers, between ranchers and farmers, between strikers and bosses, between rival Indian groups, and between whites and those whom they judged "lesser breeds." At issue was who would control the vast resources of the emerging region. Each group claimed the public domain as its own, and each group was prepared to fight for it. In the ensuing struggle for preeminence, the biggest losers were those with the best claim to the land, the Americans who had been living on it since before Columbus or Coronado or de Soto arrived.

The Final Removal of the Indians

In the 1830s, President Andrew Jackson initiated the policy of Indian removal by pushing the Cherokee, Choctaw, Chickasaw, Creek, and Seminole tribes off their lands in the southern United States. Jackson's Indian removal forced thousands of men, women, and children to leave their homes in Georgia and Tennessee and walk hundreds of miles to lands across the Mississippi River. So many died of hunger, exhaustion, and disease along the way that the Cherokees called their path "the trail on which we cried." At the end of this trail of tears stood the Great Plains. Here, the government promised the Indians, they could remain "as long as grass shall grow."

But in the 1840s, the gold rush in California, the Mexican War, and Oregon land fever put an end to the promise. Settlers repeatedly trespassed onto Indian land and then were surprised when they encountered hostility. Indignantly, they demanded protection from the U.S. army. The result was thirty years of Indian wars that culminated in a final removal of the Indians.

The Indian wars on the plains lasted from 1861 until 1890. By the time they ended, only 250,000 Native Americans remained of the estimated 2.5 million who had lived on the continent when Columbus landed. To Americans filled with theories of racial superiority, the Indian constituted, in the words of a Colorado militia major, "an obstacle to civilization." Testifying before a congressional commission in 1864, the major concluded that they "should be exterminated." The federal government, acting through the army, adopted a different policy, succinctly summed up by General William T. Sherman: "Rather remove all to a safe place and then reduce them to a helpless condition." The government herded the Indians into ever dwindling reservations where the U.S. Bureau of Indian Affairs, a pitifully weak, badly managed agency, often acting through corrupt agents, supposedly ministered to their needs.

On the plains, the Sioux, Cheyenne, Arapaho, Nez Perce, Comanche, Kiowa, Ute, Apache, and Navajo nations put up a determined resistance. The Indian wars involved violence and atrocities on both sides. In 1864 at Sand Creek, Colonel John M. Chivington, leader of the local Colorado militia, slaughtered an entire village of Cheyenne. An up-

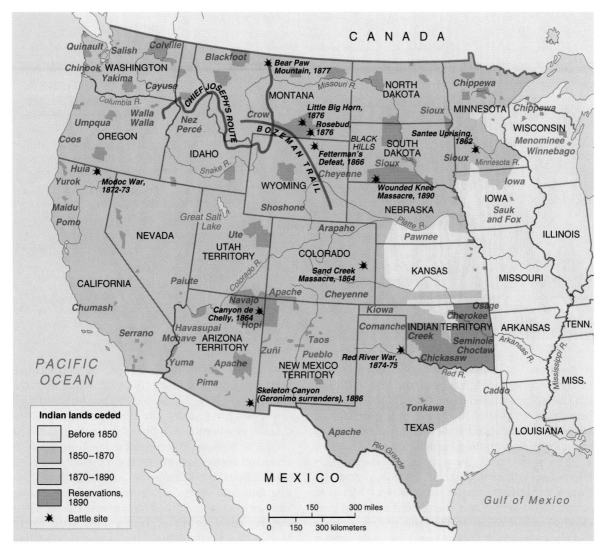

MAP 17.3
The Loss of Indian Lands, 1850–1890
By 1890, western Indians were isolated on small, scattered reservations. Native Americans strug-
gled to retain their land in major battles, from the Santee Uprising in Minnesota in 1862 to the
massacre at Wounded Knee, South Dakota, in 1890.

right Methodist elder, Chivington watched as his
men mutilated their hapless victims and later justified the killing of Indian children with the terse remark "Nits make lice." The city of Denver treated
Chivington and his men as heroes, but after a congressional inquiry he was forced to resign his commission to avoid court-martial.

Two years later, the Cheyenne united with the
Sioux and retaliated on the Bozeman Trail. Captain

William Fetterman, who had boasted that with
eighty men he could ride through the Sioux nation,
was killed, along with all eighty-one of his troops.
The Sioux's impressive victories led to a treaty in
1868, under which the government promised to give
the Indians lands stretching from the Missouri River
to the Black Hills in western South Dakota in return
for their promise to stop fighting. The great chief
Red Cloud led many of his people onto the new

INDIANS

Sevara, identified as a Ute chieftain, poses with three generations of his family in this photograph. Pictures like this one depict a way of life that by the end of the nineteenth century was already becoming extinct. Only in posed photographs carefully crafted for public consumption did the proud history of Native Americans seem able to survive.

From *Birth of a Century*, KEA Publishing Services, Ltd.

reservation. But several young chiefs, among them Crazy Horse of the Oglala band and Sitting Bull of the Hunkpapa, refused to go. Crazy Horse said that he wanted no part of the "piecemeal penning" of his people. Renegade bands of Sioux continued to roam the plains, hunting buffalo.

The buffalo had a more dangerous enemy than the Indian—the railroad. To the Sioux and the Kiowa the buffalo constituted a way of life—the source of food, fuel, and shelter and a central part of religion and ritual. To the railroads the buffalo were a nuisance, at best a target for sport and a source of cheap meat for the workers. Buffalo hunters hired by the railroads decimated the great herds; sport hunters fired at random from railroad cars just for the thrill of it. In the heyday of buffalo hunting in the 1880s, hunters sold as many as fifty thousand hides at a time to tanneries in the East. General Philip Sheridan applauded the hunters for "destroying the Indians' commissary." In thirty years, more than sixty million animals were slaughtered. The army took credit for subduing the Indians, but their defeat came about more as a result of the decimation of the buffalo herds.

In 1876, rumors of gold in the Black Hills effectively nullified the government's promise to Red Cloud. Miners began pouring into the area, and the Northern Pacific Railroad made plans to build tracks. Lieutenant Colonel George Armstrong Custer fed the gold fever by trumpeting news of the first strikes. Under the leadership of Crazy Horse and Sitting Bull, the Sioux tribes massed to resist the incursion. In June, Custer led the two hundred men of the Seventh Cavalry into the largest group of Indians ever assembled in one place on the plains. At the Little Bighorn River in Montana Territory, four thousand Sioux warriors set upon them. No federal soldier lived to tell the story, but Crazy Horse, Sitting Bull, and others recounted the killing of Long Hair, as the Indians called the dashing Custer. Their victory was short-lived. In the next year, Crazy Horse was killed and Sitting Bull surrendered. Chief Joseph of the Nez Percé resisted removal and fled toward Canada. Just forty miles from freedom, federal troops caught up with his band. With his people cold and starving, the chief surrendered. His speech stands as an eloquent statement of the plight of the Indians:

> Tell Captain Howard I know his heart. What he told me before I have in my heart. I am tired of fighting. Our chiefs are killed. . . . It is cold and we have no blankets. The little children are freezing to death. My people, some of them, have run away to the hills, and have no blankets, no food; no one knows where they are—perhaps freezing to death. I want to have time to look for my children and see how many I can find. Maybe I shall find them among the dead. Hear me, my chiefs, I am tired; my heart is sick and sad. From where the sun now stands, I will fight no more forever.

The policy of rounding up Indians and herding them onto reservations gained momentum. After Custer's Last Stand, as the battle in 1876 came to be called, policy toward the Indians toughened. Even the most philanthropic Americans seemed convinced that the Indian way of life must go. Instead of remaining American Indians, they had to become Indian Americans. When Indians resisted, their children were taken off the reservations and sent to special schools to learn white ways—to play the piano, to farm, to act like white Americans.

In 1887, Congress passed the Dawes Act, breaking up the reservations and giving each Indian an allotment of land. The act effectively reduced Indian lands from 138 million acres to a scant 48 million, making it, in the words of one critic, "a bill to despoil the Indians of their lands and to make them vagabonds on the face of the earth." The surplus land was then opened to white settlement, setting off the great land rushes in Oklahoma. Well-meaning philanthropists viewed the Dawes Act as a way to foster individualism among the Indians and to extend to them the rights of citizenship. The result of this legislation, however, was the further destruction of Indian culture.

Faced with the extinction of their entire way of life and means of livelihood, the Indians turned to a compelling religious cult. The Paiute shaman Wovoka, drawing on a cult that had developed in the 1870s, combined elements of Christianity and traditional Indian religion to found the Ghost Dance religion in 1889. Wovoka claimed that he had received a vision in which the Great Spirit spoke through him to all Indians, urging them to unite and promising that whites would be destroyed in an apocalypse. The Indian warriors slain in battle would return to life, and buffalo once again would roam the land unimpeded. Followers of the Ghost Dance religion developed a ritual that involved five days of worship by dancing and meditation. Wearing white ghost shirts that were supposedly impervious to bullets, Indians danced until they dropped from exhaustion. This religion of despair with its message of hope spread like wildfire over the plains, alarming the whites, who feared that it would spark an uprising. "Indians are dancing in the snow and are wild and crazy," wrote the Bureau of Indian Affairs agent at the Pine Ridge reservation in South Dakota. Frantic, he pleaded for reinforcements. "We are at the mercy of these dancers. We need protection, and we need it now." President Benjamin Harrison dispatched several thousand federal troops to Sioux country to handle any outbreak.

In December 1889, when Sitting Bull sought permission to go to the Pine Ridge reservation to meet with Wovoka, the local Indian agent laid a trap for him, and Sitting Bull was shot. His people, fleeing the scene, were apprehended by the Seventh Cavalry, Custer's old regiment, near Wounded Knee Creek, South Dakota. As the Indians laid down their arms, a shot rang out and the army opened fire. In the ensuing melee, Indian warriors stormed the troops, killing more than thirty soldiers. But they were badly outgunned. Men, women, and children were mowed down in minutes by the army's brutally efficient Hotchkiss machine guns. More than two hundred Sioux lay dead or dying in the snow. Settler Jules Sandoz surveyed the scene the day after the massacre. "Here in ten minutes an entire community was as the buffalo that bleached on the plains," he wrote. "There was something loose in the world that hated joy and happiness as it hated brightness and color, reducing everything to drab agony and gray."

Although the massacre at Wounded Knee did not end the story of Native Americans, it ended a way of life. The Indian population would gradually recover; the 1990 census showed 1.9 million Native Americans. But their culture sustained a crushing blow. In the words of the visionary Black Elk, "The nation's hoop is broken and scattered. There is no center any longer, and the sacred tree is dead."

The West of the Imagination

Even as the Old West was dying, the myth of the West was being created. The dime novel, a precursor of today's paperback, capitalized on western heroes like Kit Carson, Wild Bill Hickok, Calamity Jane, and Deadwood Dick to entertain eastern readers seeking escapist fare. Published in the East and sometimes written by tenderfeet who had never ventured beyond the Hudson River, dime novels sold at a prodigious rate. The firm of Beadle and Adams pioneered the genre and published over a million copies a year.

The prince of the dime novel heroes was Buffalo Bill, featured in more than two hundred titles. A masterful showman, the real-life Buffalo Bill capitalized on his success and formed a touring Wild West company in 1883. Unlike the cowboy actors of the twentieth century, Buffalo Bill was the authentic article. Born William F. Cody, he had panned for gold, ridden for the Pony Express, scouted for the army, and earned his nickname hunting buffalo for the railroad. A ham actor and impresario, he turned

Did Whites Teach Indians to Scalp?

IN 1879, JUST THREE YEARS AFTER Custer and his troops were massacred at the Little Bighorn, Susette La Flesche, a member of the Omaha tribe, made a national tour to promote justice for Native Americans. Using her Indian name, Bright Eyes, La Flesche made a fascinating spokesperson for Indian rights. Her father, one of the best known of the Omaha chiefs, was of mixed blood, as was his wife. The La Flesche family embraced Christianity and advocated "progressive" Indian policy. Working closely with Presbyterian missionaries, they attacked the use of alcohol and urged Indians to take up farming. Susette grew up in the first frame house on the reservation in Nebraska. All the La Flesche children attended Presbyterian mission school at the Omaha agency. Later Susette and her sisters were sent to boarding school in New Jersey. Susette's sister Susan La Flesche Picotte became the first Indian woman to receive a medical degree, and her brother Francis became the first Indian anthropologist employed by the Smithsonian Institution. To Victorian society, the remarkable La Flesche family offered an inspiring example of the transition from "savagery" to civilization.

Susette La Flesche's East Coast tour was intended to publicize the plight of the Ponca Indians, who had lost their land in one of the many swindles perpetrated by the federal government. Boston audiences expecting an Indian "princess" dressed in deerskin encountered instead an educated young woman in a black velvet bonnet. But for all her modest demeanor, Susette did not hesitate in pointing out the routine barbarity of the U.S. army in its treatment of the Plains tribes. In Chicago, she was accosted by a reporter who chided her, pointing to the Indians' "barbarous . . . acts of atrocity upon captives and the bodies of the dead." La Flesche shot back, "Scalping, you mean, I suppose. Don't you know that the white man taught Indians that?" She insisted that "scalping was first practiced in New England on the Penobscot Indians." The General Court of the province of Massachusetts, she informed the reporter, "offered a bounty of forty pounds for every scalp of a male Indian brought in as evidence of his being killed, and for every scalp of a female or male Indian under twelve years, twenty pounds."

A hundred years later, La Flesche's charge that European colonists in New England had taught the Indians to scalp was well on its way to becoming accepted wisdom. Native American author Vine Deloria, in his widely read manifesto *Custer Died for Your Sins* (1969), echoed the belief that eighteenth-century European settlers with their bounty laws had introduced the practice of scalping among the eastern tribes.

Certainly scalping became synonymous with Indian barbarity. Europeans might draw and quarter, burn at the stake, and introduce the tortures of the iron maiden, but Indian mutilation of the dead remained the quintessential symbol of "savagery." Not surprisingly, La Flesche's effort to rehabilitate the popular image of the Indian in 1879 and Deloria's similar effort a century later began by calling into question the Indian origin of scalping. If whites had taught Indians to scalp, who, then, was the "savage"? As scholars became more sympathetic to the dispossession of American Indians and sought to rehabilitate the stereotype of the "fiendish savage," the charge that scalping was a white invention gained wide acceptance. But was it factual? Had the European settlers, with their bounties on scalps, introduced the practice?

Historian James Axtell set out to find the answer. But what sources would provide "proof"? Axtell drew on the records of early explorers and set-

SUSETTE LA FLESCHE
Susette La Flesche toured the country in 1879 using her Indian name, Bright Eyes, to publicize the plight of the Ponca Indians. It was La Flesche who alleged that whites had taught the Indians to scalp.
Nebraska State Historical Society.

tlers and on the work of ethnohistorians and archaeologists. All of the evidence seemed to point in the opposite direction from Susette La Flesche's confident assertion. Among the earliest visitors to American shores, Jacques Cartier in 1535 described "skins of five men's heads, stretched on hoops, like parchment." The practice was widespread, noted by Cartier in the North and by Hernando De Soto's men in Florida and the Southeast. As Axtell carefully demonstrated, "the list of Europeans who found scalping among the eastern Indians in the earliest stages of contact could be extended almost indefinitely."

Furthermore, although Europeans practiced many barbarities during the sixteenth and seventeenth centuries, nowhere was there evidence that they ever scalped their victims. The European languages did not even have a word to describe the practice. Archaeological evidence, too, pointed away from La Flesche's claim. Pre-Columbian skulls collected by early anthropologists showed distinct evidence of scalping.

What role, then, did scalping play in Indian culture? According to ethnohistorians and their Indian subjects, the practice, while widespread, varied markedly from tribe to tribe. Often the scalp served as more than physical proof of valor. The Iroquois believed that after death the soul hovered by the body. To take the scalp, they believed, was to take the spiritual life of the enemy. However, the practice of scalping took on a different character during the French and Indian War when both sides offered their Indian allies bounties for scalps, sometimes as

much as one hundred pounds (roughly two hundred dollars) for every scalp of an adult male. Soon the trading of scalps became part of the complex web that bound Indians and whites in colonial commerce. In Salem, Massachusetts, scalps that had been redeemed for bounties decorated the walls of the town courthouse until it was torn down in 1785.

By the nineteenth century, bounties had long been outlawed, and scalping existed among the Plains Indians in the context of tribal practice. Black Elk, an Oglala Sioux, recounted how he took his first scalp and proudly presented the trophy to his mother for her approval.

One final intriguing piece of the puzzle is the question of how Custer escaped scalping. Well known for his flowing locks, Custer, by all accounts, was not scalped after the battle, as were many of his men. Although no soldier lived to describe the battle scene, Indian accounts are unanimous in their assertion that Custer's body was not mutilated, except for one fingertip. Why did the Indians not take his scalp for a trophy? In large part the answer has changed as Custer's fortunes with historians and the public have waxed and waned. At the time of his death, when Custer was viewed as a brave martyr, writers conjectured that his Indian foes respected his bravery and refused to mutilate the man they called Pahuska, or Long Hair. As Custer's reputation sank to low ebb in the mid-twentieth century, writers became more skeptical. One author guessed that Custer, who was balding by 1879 and had cut his hair, was spared because from a warrior's point of view his scalp made a poor trophy.

BUFFALO BILL POSTER
Buffalo Bill Cody used colorful posters to publicize his Wild West show during the 1880s and
1890s. One of his most popular features was the reenactment of Custer's Last Stand, which he
performed for Queen Victoria in London and at the World Columbian Exposition in Chicago.
Buffalo Bill Historical Center, Cody, Wyoming.

to melodrama in the 1870s and a decade later hit his stride with the Wild West Show. Part circus, part theater, the Wild West extravaganza featured exhibitions of riding, shooting, and roping and presented dramatic reenactments of great moments in western U.S. history. The star of the show was Annie Oakley, a crack shot who delighted the crowd by shooting a dime out of her husband's hand. A herd of buffalo, bucking broncos, and a sizable contingent of authentic cowboys and Indians trouped with the show. During the 1885 season, Sitting Bull toured with Buffalo Bill.

Cody performed in Europe for Queen Victoria, in Paris under the Eiffel Tower, in New York's Madison Square Garden, and on the road in hundreds of towns across the United States from 1883 until he went bankrupt in 1913. The centerpiece of his Wild West Show was the reenactment of Custer's Last

Stand, in which Indians in war paint and bonnets massacred the hapless Custer and his men. At the end, Buffalo Bill galloped in with a cloud of dust and dramatically mouthed the words "Too late!"

The Wild West that Buffalo Bill presented to the American people indiscriminately mixed the authentic with the romantic until reality itself was blurred in the popular mind. Cody had not arrived too late at the Little Bighorn. But some of the Indians in his troupe had been there and knew their parts firsthand. The rapid demise of the Wild West that Buffalo Bill enshrined in his show may perhaps best be comprehended if we juxtapose Cody with historian Frederick Jackson Turner. At the 1893 Columbian Exposition in Chicago, Turner addressed the American Historical Association on the significance of the frontier in American history. Turner noted that the frontier had vanished, that by 1890

American settlers had filled the map of the West so that no clear frontier line could be discerned. What Turner theorized—that the frontier which he claimed made America unique was now a part of the past—was perhaps nowhere better demonstrated than across the fairground in the spectacle of Buffalo Bill Cody's Wild West Show performing the "Battle of the Little Bighorn" to sellout crowds in the bleachers. After the show, fans sought out Indian "chiefs" and paid a dollar for the autograph of "the Indian who had killed Custer." The high drama of the struggle for the West in the years from 1876 to 1890 had become no more than a thrilling but harmless entertainment.

The images of the daring cowboy hero and the Indian (fiendish in victory but noble in defeat) that became so enshrined in the national imagination obscured the complex realities of the history of the American West.

The West of the imagination, the West of Buffalo Bill, of artists Frederic Remington and Albert Bierstadt, of novelists Owen Wister and Zane Grey, endured longer than its reality and was responsible for shrouding the region in myth. The images of the daring cowboy hero and the Indian (fiendish in victory but noble in defeat) that became so enshrined in the national imagination obscured the complex realities of the history of the American West, as much as the myth of moonlight and magnolias distorted the truth of the Old South.

The historical reality is every bit as dramatic as the fictions it sparked. But from the vantage point of the late twentieth century, it is no longer the simple morality tale of the triumph of good guys over bad guys, progress over primitivism, and civilization over the frontier that it once seemed. Whatever the moral ambiguities occasioned by the change, one thing was certain: By the 1890s, the American West had been transformed. More than seven-tenths of the farmland west of the Mississippi River was owned by investors who neither farmed nor ranched the land themselves. The shift from farming and ranching to agribusiness, not the disappearance of some magical frontier line, marked the end of an era in America. Far from being a mythic landscape out of place and time, the West was linked inextricably to the urban East by capital investment and iron rails that carried western goods to world markets.

The Rise of the City

"We cannot all live in cities, yet nearly all seem determined to do so," New York editor Horace Greeley complained. Greeley, who had urged young men to go West in the 1850s, lamented the growth of America's cities. Although much of the nation remained heavily rural, the last decades of the nineteenth century witnessed an urban explosion. Cities and towns grew more than twice as rapidly as the total population, far outstripping rural growth. Despite regional variations, the population of cities everywhere pushed upward, the greatest growth occurring in the industrial centers of New England, the Middle Atlantic states, and the Great Lakes states. Patterns of global migration contributed to the ascendancy of urban America. In the port cities, new immigrants from southern and eastern Europe lived in dense ghettos where the English language was rarely heard. The word *slum* entered the American vocabulary during these years and with it a growing concern over the gap between the rich and the poor, a gap only widened by the changing social geography of the cities. First horsecars, then trolleys and subways made it possible for those who could afford it to work downtown and flee after work to the "cool green rim" of the cities where residential tracts and suburbs catered to the middle class and well-to-do.

The Urban Explosion

The percentage of Americans living in towns and cities leaped from 20 percent in 1870 to 33 percent by 1900. In actual numbers, the urban population tripled, from nearly 10 million to over 30 million. The Census Bureau deemed any village of more than 8,000 inhabitants an urban place, lumping together Dubuque and Detroit, Kankakee and Cleveland. Growth in the urban population actually divided about evenly between large and small cities. But the emergence of the modern metropolis marked the most dramatic demographic development of the period. The number of cities with more than 100,000 inhabitants jumped from eighteen in 1870 to thirty-eight by 1900. Chicago grew at a meteoric rate, from 100,000 in 1860 to over a million in 1890, doubling its population each decade despite the ravages of the Great Fire of 1871, which destroyed three square miles and left 18,000 homeless. In the West, Los Angeles capitalized on its climate to explode from a sleepy village of 5,000 in 1870 to a metropolis of more than 100,000 by 1900. At the turn of the century, the United States could boast three cities with more than a million inhabitants— New York, Chicago, and Philadelphia.

Railroad growth stimulated urban development. In the West, the railroads moved in advance of settlement. Cities like Reno, Butte, and Cheyenne sprang up along the tracks long before the surrounding countryside was settled. The generous land grants given to promote railroad building made the railroads the largest private landholders in the country. Railroads encouraged settlement by selling the lands they had been granted in alternate sections along their right of way. Towns that the railroads bypassed failed to grow, while the transcontinental lines set off booms in Kansas City, Omaha, and Salt Lake City.

The astonishing growth of American cities that occurred from 1870 to 1900 came about not from the natural increase of the city population but from the internal and international movement of people.

Industrialization and urbanization went hand in hand. The continued growth of the urban population fueled a constantly expanding market. In a process that economists call the multiplier effect, the growing market in turn stimulated greater and greater production, creating more jobs in an expanding spiral. The emergence of a mass consumer market enabled cities to become centers for wholesaling and retailing, not just manufacturing and industry. Chicago, with its mail order houses like Montgomery Ward and Sears, Roebuck, along with its great department stores, Marshall Field and Carson Pirie Scott, led the country as an urban marketing center.

The astonishing growth of American cities that occurred from 1870 to 1900 came about not from the natural increase of the city population but from the internal and international movement of people.

From the Farm to the City: A Global Migration

The United States grew up in the country and moved to the city, or so it seemed by the late nineteenth century. Hundreds of thousands of farm boys and girls ran away to the city looking for jobs in the burgeoning industrial centers and hoping to make their fortunes. The lure of the bright lights and the promise of wages, coupled with the theaters, the dance halls, the great amusement resorts like Coney Island in New York, and the cultural and educational advantages offered by the city, served as a powerful magnet for many young women and men.

For at least one group of migrants, the move to the city promised something more. African Americans came north looking not just for economic opportunity. Demeaning laws that segregated blacks, called Jim Crow laws, became common throughout the South in the decades following Reconstruction. Further, the 1890s witnessed the systematic disfranchisement of black voters in state after state in the Old South. The South's efforts to segregate and subordinate African Americans gained federal endorsement when in 1896 the United States Supreme Court in the landmark case *Plessy v. Ferguson* upheld the legality of segregated facilities under the doctrine of "separate but equal." Intimidation and lynching, justified by white Southerners as necessary to "keep the Negro in his place," also became increasingly common throughout the South. These indignities combined with the lack of economic choices to move African Americans out of the South. "To die from the bite of frost is far more glorious than at the hands of a mob," proclaimed the *Defender*, Chicago's largest African American newspaper. As early as the 1890s, many blacks agreed. The African American migrants, nearly all of them rural, headed to the cities, settling in the great urban centers of the Northeast and the Midwest. There they found jobs, usually at the bottom of the occupational ladder as janitors, cooks, common laborers, or domestic servants. Racial discrimination and poverty limited blacks' options in the North, just as they had in the South. Yet the urban North continued to attract African Americans. By 1900, New York, Philadelphia, and Chicago contained the largest black communities in the nation. Although the greatest African American migration out of the South would occur during and after the end of World War I, 185,000 African Americans had already moved north by 1890. The great exodus was under way.

Rural migrants to the cities were by no means limited to American farmers and southern blacks. Worldwide in scope, the movement from rural areas to industrial centers attracted to the United States more than fourteen million Europeans in the waning decades of the nineteenth century. That migration came in two distinct waves that have been called

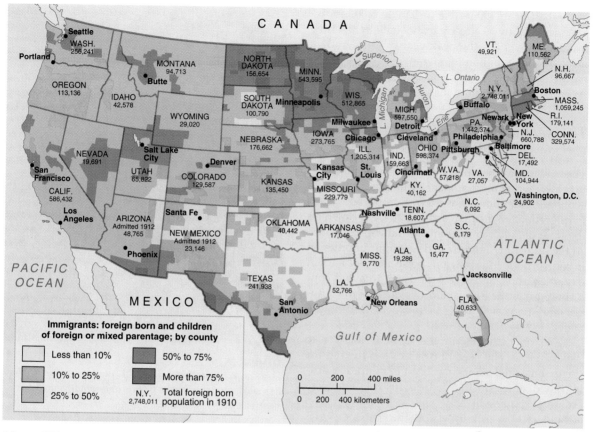

MAP 17.4

The Impact of Immigration to 1910

By 1910 the immigrant population was spread throughout the country, with the notable exception of the southern states. In some areas — along the Canadian border and the Rio Grande and in the nation's burgeoning cities — the foreign born and their children totaled more than 75 percent of the population.

the old and the new immigration. Before 1880, the bulk of the new arrivals came from northern and western Europe, with the Germans, Irish, English, and Scandinavians making up approximately 85 percent of the newcomers.

After 1880, the pattern shifted, with more and more immigrant ships carrying passengers from southern and eastern Europe. Italians, Hungarians, eastern European Jews, Turks, Armenians, and Poles, Russians and other Slavic peoples accounted for more than 80 percent of all the immigrants by 1896. Alongside the tide of new European immigrants streamed Japanese coming east from Asia, French Canadians flowing south to work in New England's mill towns, and Mexicans and other Latin Americans heading north to settle in California and the Southwest.

In sheer numbers, the new immigration was unprecedented. In 1888 alone, more than half a million Europeans came to America, 75 percent landing in New York City. The Statue of Liberty, a gift from the people of France erected in 1886, stood sentinel in the harbor. An immigrant girl named Emma Lazarus penned the verse at Liberty's base:

Give me your tired, your poor,
Your huddled masses yearning to breathe free,
The wretched refuse of your teeming shore,
Send these, the homeless, tempest-tost to me,
I lift my lamp beside the golden door!

The tide of immigrants soon swamped the immigrant office at Castle Garden in New York harbor. An imposing new brick facility opened on Ellis Island in the harbor in 1900. Able to handle 5,000 immigrants a day, it was already inadequate by the time it opened. By 1907, the peak year of immigration, more than one million immigrants passed through the gates at Ellis Island, and on a record day inspectors processed more than 11,700.

The New Immigrants and the Call for Immigration Restriction

The new wave of immigration at the turn of the century resulted from a number of factors. Improved economic conditions in western Europe, as well as immigration to Australia and Canada, cut down on the flow of "old" immigrants to the United States. At the same time, a protracted economic depression in southern Italy, the religious persecution of Jews in eastern Europe, and a general desire to avoid conscription into the Russian army led many in southern and eastern Europe to move to the United States.

Economic factors in the United States also played a role. The need of America's industries for cheap, unskilled labor stimulated immigration during good times. In the depressions following the economic panics in 1873 and 1893, immigration slowed, only to pick up again when prosperity returned. Although the U.S. government did not offer direct inducements to immigrate, the steamship companies courted immigrants, who provided a highly profitable, self-loading cargo. Agents from the large lines traveled throughout Europe drumming up business. Colorful pamphlets and posters mingled fact with fantasy to advertise America as the land of promise.

Large economic and social forces affected immigration, but the decision to come to America remained an individual or a family choice. Immigrants were neither the passive "huddled masses" commemorated in Emma Lazarus's inscription on the Statue of Liberty nor bold adventurers determined at any cost to enter "the golden door." Increasingly, historians have rejected simplistic and monolithic views that treat immigrants collectively, instead acknowledging that each single individual or family decided to go or stay.

Nevertheless, immigration fever affected whole villages, as Mary Antin, writing of her Russian village in 1891, recounted:

"America" was in everybody's mouth. Businessmen talked of it over their accounts; the market women made up their quarrels that they might discuss it

IMMIGRANTS
Dressed in the clothing of the old country (cap and collarless shirt, apron and shawl), this immigrant couple carry their meager possessions, bedding in his bundle, food and utensils in her basket, and two umbrellas tied together. Note how the man gazes confidently, almost defiantly, into the camera, while the woman, looking miserable, averts her eyes. What do their postures tell about whose decision it was to come to America and about their hopes and apprehensions?
Wide World Photos, Inc.

from stall to stall; people who had relatives in the famous land went around reading their letters for the enlightenment of less fortunate folks; . . . children played at emigrating; old folks shook their sage heads over the evening fire, and prophesied no good for those who braved the terrors of the sea and the foreign goal beyond it;—all talked of it, but scarcely anybody knew one true fact about this magic land.

Would-be immigrants eager for information about America relied on letters, advertisements, and word of mouth—sources that were not always reliable or truthful. Promotional pamphlets exaggerated America's economic opportunities until Europeans dreamed of a land "where the streets were paved with gold." Glowing letters from immigrants to friends and relatives left behind boasted of life in America. Even photographs proved deceptive—

American workers dressed in their Sunday best looked more prosperous than they actually were to the eyes of relatives in the old country, where only the very wealthy wore white collars or silk dresses. As one Italian immigrant recalled, "Everything emanating from America reached [Italy] as a distortion. . . . News was colored, success magnified, comforts and advantages exaggerated beyond all proportions." No wonder immigrants left for America believing "that if they were ever fortunate enough to reach America, they would fall into a pile of manure and get up brushing the diamonds out of their hair."

In at least one respect, life in the new world differed markedly from that in the old. In their countries of origin, most of the newcomers had been rural peasants, farmers, and villagers. In America they became urbanites, both out of inclination and out of necessity. They were drawn by the availability of jobs in the nation's industrial centers at the same time poverty limited their ability to buy land in the West.

The concentration of immigrants in the nation's industrial cities was a characteristic of the age. By 1900, almost two-thirds of the country's immigrant population resided in cities. Although nowhere did the foreign-born population outnumber established inhabitants, the foreign-born and their American-born children did constitute a majority in many of the nation's largest cities. Fifty percent of Philadelphia's population was foreign-born or born of foreign parents, and the percentages were even higher in other cities: 66 percent in Boston, 75 percent in Chicago, and an amazing 80 percent in New York City.

Not all the newcomers came to stay. Perhaps eight million, mostly young men, worked for a year or a season and then returned to their homelands. American immigration officers referred to these young male immigrants as "birds of passage" because they followed a regular pattern of migration to and from the United States. By 1900, almost 75 percent of the new immigrants were single young men. Intent on making money as quickly as possible, they were willing to accept conditions that other workers regarded as intolerable. They showed little interest in labor unions and organized only when the dream of returning home faded, as it did for millions who ultimately remained in the United States.

Jews from eastern Europe most often came with their families and came to stay. In the 1880s, a wave of violent persecutions, or pogroms, in Russia and Poland led to the departure of more than a million Jews in the next two decades. They settled mostly in the port cities of the East. New York City's Lower East Side replicated the Jewish ghettos of eastern

**STUDIO PORTRAIT
OF IMMIGRANTS**
Studio portraits of immigrant families, like this one of a Russian Jewish family taken at the turn of the century, showed everyone dressed in their finest clothes — the men in starched shirts and collars, the women in silk dresses or lacy shirtwaists. Mailed back to relatives in Europe, these pictures provided a tantalizing but not always entirely accurate picture of the promise of America.
Collection of Sharon Salinger.

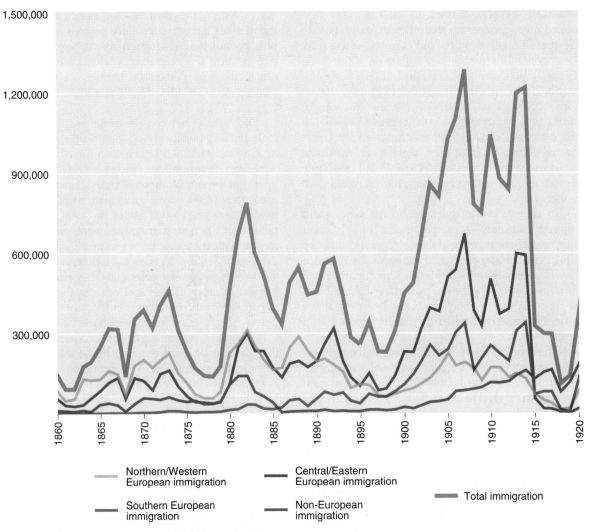

FIGURE **17.3**

The Old and the New Immigration, 1860–1920

The immigration of the 1880s was dominated by southern and eastern Europeans. Before 1880, over 85 percent of immigrants had come from Western Europe — Germany, Ireland, England, and the Scandinavian countries. After 1880, 80 percent of the new arrivals came from Italy, Turkey, Hungary, Armenia, and Poland, Russia, and other Slavic countries.

Europe, teeming with street peddlers and pushcarts. Hester Street, at the heart of New York's Jewish section, rang with the calls of vendors hawking their wares, from pickles to feather beds.

The new immigration raised a chorus of criticism. The Italians, Russian Jews, and Slavs who formed the bulk of the new immigrants were compared unfavorably to the Germans, the Irish, the British, and the Scandinavians who had led the procession before the 1880s. To many older-stock Amer-

icans, the new immigrants from southern and eastern Europe seemed impossible to assimilate. "These people are not Americans," editorialized the popular journal *Public Opinion*, "they are the very scum and offal of Europe." The new immigrants were castigated for being uneducated, backward, and outlandish in appearance. Terence Powderly, head of the labor organization the Knights of Labor, complained that the newcomers "herded together like animals and lived like beasts."

Old-stock aristocrats such as Senator Henry Cabot Lodge of Massachusetts formed an unlikely alliance with organized labor to press for immigration restriction. A precedent for keeping out "undesirable" immigrants had been established in 1882, when labor agitation and racism in California led to passage of the Chinese Exclusion Act, which put a stop to the legal immigration of Chinese nationals. On the East Coast, Lodge and his followers championed a literacy test, a device designed to limit immigration from Italy and eastern Europe by requiring immigrants to demonstrate the ability to read and write in their native language. Since the vast majority of Italian and Slavic peasants had no schooling, it was assumed that few would be able to pass the test. In 1906, Congress approved a literacy test for immigrants, but President Grover Cleveland promptly vetoed it. "It is said," the president reminded Congress, "that the quality of recent immigration is undesirable. The time is quite within recent memory when the same thing was said of immigrants, who, with their descendants, are now numbered among our best citizens." Cleveland's veto forestalled immigration restriction but did not stop the forces seeking to close the gates. They would continue to press for restriction until they achieved their goal in the 1920s.

How Both Halves Lived

Much of what worried comfortable Americans about the new immigrants was the poverty and squalor of the immigrant ghettos in the big cities. In 1890, a young police reporter named Jacob Riis took his notebook and his camera into the tenements of New York's Lower East Side; the result was the best-selling book *How the Other Half Lives*. Riis invited his audience into a Cherry Street tenement:

> Be careful please! The hall is dark and you might stumble over the children pitching pennies back there. . . . Close? Yes! What would you have? All the fresh air that ever enters these stairs comes from the hall door and is forever slamming, and from the windows of dark bedrooms that in turn receive from the stairs their sole supply of the elements God meant to be free, but man deals out with such niggardly hand. . . .
>
> Here is a door. Listen! That short hacking cough, that tiny, helpless wail—what do they mean? They mean that the soiled bow of white you saw on the door downstairs will have another story to

tell—Oh! a sadly familiar story—before the day is at an end. The child is dying with measles. With half a chance it might have lived; but it had none. That dark bedroom killed it.

As Riis discovered, poverty, crowding, dirt, and disease constituted the daily reality of New York's poor. Riis's book, like his photographs, presented a world of black and white. He oversimplified the life of New York's working class by lumping together the day laborer, the unionized craftsman, the small-time artisan, the shop girl, and the pushcart peddler. There were many layers to the population Riis labeled "the other half" and distinctions furthered by ethnicity, religion, race, and gender. *How the Other Half Lives* must be read more as a call to action than as an accurate portrayal. Like many other middle-class Americans, Riis worried that the tenements would spawn not only disease and ignorance, but social unrest. In a chapter entitled "The Man with the Knife," Riis mused that a man driven by hunger to steal a loaf of bread for his family might also, driven by rage at injustice, rise in vengeance to strike at the comfortable middle class. Unlike the rest of his book, which sought to document the reality of immigrant life, the "man with the knife" was purely a figment of Riis's imagination. In reality, the underclass man with the knife more often turned it on his poor neighbors, for despite fears of social uprising, crime and violence rarely touched the well-off. Nevertheless, Riis's "man with the knife" was a potent symbol of the growing concern over the widening gap between the rich and the poor.

Jacob Riis's audience shivered at his revelations about the "other half." But middle-class Americans worried equally about the excesses of the wealthy. The chasm between the rich and the poor grew more visible in cities such as New York, where the mansions on Fifth Avenue stood only blocks from the tenements in Hell's Kitchen. Many middle-class Americans shared Jacob Riis's view that "the real danger to society comes not only from the tenements, but from the illspent wealth which reared them."

The excesses of newly minted millionaires in the decades following the Civil War were nowhere more visible than in the lifestyle of the Vanderbilts. "Commodore" Cornelius Vanderbilt, the uncouth ferryman who built the New York Central Railroad, died in 1877, leaving his son $90 million. William Vanderbilt doubled that sum and his two sons proceeded to spend it on French mansions and on "cottages" in Newport, Rhode Island, which, with their marble and gold leaf, rivaled the palaces of Europe.

MULBERRY STREET AND FIFTH AVENUE
These New York City streetscapes tell a tale of two cities. At the left is Mulberry Street, a crowded tenement district on the Lower East Side. Vendors hawk their wares, wash hangs out to dry, and children throng the street. Compare the teeming life of Mulberry Street with the fashionable crowd on Fifth Avenue. Here men and women promenade to see and be seen. Their dress is elaborate and formal — the women with sweeping skirts and large-brimmed hats, the men with canes and silk top hats. While Fifth Avenue seems as crowded as Mulberry Street, looks can be deceiving. The actual population density on the Lower East Side in 1894 rivaled that of Calcutta, India, with nearly ten thousand men, women, and children per acre.
Gift of John Worth Edmonds, Museum of the City of New York; Collection of the New York Historical Society.

Caroline (Mrs. William) Astor, who reigned as queen of established New York society, determined to act as gatekeeper and keep out the nouveau riche (newly rich). So Astor, whose husband had inherited old wealth and increased it by investments in slum property, spurned Alva Vanderbilt (Mrs. William K. Vanderbilt I), whose husband's railroad money was of more recent origin. In 1883, Alva Vanderbilt threw a costume party that promised to be so lavish and publicized that the Astor daughters forced their mother to relent and leave her calling card at the Vanderbilts, acknowledging them as social equals. The Vanderbilt ball became a legend in the annals of social excess. Dressed as a Venetian princess, Alva Vanderbilt greeted her 1,200 guests. But her sister-in-law capped the evening, appearing in costume as that miraculous new invention the electric light, resplendent in a white satin evening dress studded with diamonds. Many costumes cost as much as $1,500 apiece, three times the average yearly wage of a worker. The New York *World* speculated that the party as a whole had cost over a quarter of a million dollars. Alva got her money's worth. One guest observed that the ball had placed the Vanderbilts "at the top of the heap in what is recognized as good society in New York."

Such ostentatious displays of wealth became even more alarming when they were coupled with disdain for the general welfare of the people. When a reporter in 1882 asked William Vanderbilt whether he considered the public good in running his railroads, he shot back, "The public be damned." The fear that America had become a plutocracy—a society ruled by the rich—gained credence from the fact that the wealthiest one percent of the population owned more than half the real and personal property in the country (compare that with a century later, when the top one percent controlled less than a quarter).

Jacob Riis's audience shivered at his revelations about the "other half." But middle-class Americans worried equally about the excesses of the wealthy.

Although images of the Vanderbilt ball and the impoverished "other half" oversimplified the social reality of the city, the distortions highlighted a growing apprehension. In editorials, speeches, and conversations, well-to-do Americans uneasily evoked the image of the Paris Commune of 1871, when for seventy-three days the workers of Paris seized control of the city, burning and destroying monuments of the empire and attacking and murdering the clergy. The specter of revolution haunted America in the 1880s and 1890s. Uneasy politicians and judges were quick to call for repression whenever it looked as though angry workers might "threaten property." At the same time, urban growth fostered the very social fragmentation and division that fueled the flames of class antagonism.

The Social Geography of the City

In the 1870s, Cleveland, Ohio, was a small city, in both population and geographical area. Oil magnate John D. Rockefeller could, and often did, walk from his large brick townhouse on Euclid Avenue to his office downtown. On his way he passed the small homes of his clerks and other middle-class families. Behind these homes ran miles of alleys crowded with the dwellings of Cleveland's working class. Farther out, on the shores of Lake Erie, close to the factories and foundries, clustered the shanties of the city's poorest laborers.

Within two decades, the Cleveland that Rockefeller knew no longer existed. With the coming of mass transit, the walking city was transformed. In

CLEVELAND STREET SCENE
Horse-drawn carriages, pedestrians, and pushcarts vie with the new electric trolley line in Public Square, Cleveland, Ohio. The development of mass transit at the turn of the century, signaled here by the trolley lines, marked the end of the walking city and the development of a new urban and social geography.
Library of Congress.

its place emerged a central business district surrounded by concentric rings of residences graded by ethnicity and income. This pattern of development was repeated throughout the country as urban congestion and suburban sprawl forever altered the social geography of the city.

Mass transit drastically changed the American city. First the horsecar in the 1870s and then the electric streetcar in the 1880s made it possible to commute to work. City workers could enjoy single-family homes with lawns, gardens, and trees and still travel to work downtown for as little as five cents a day. By the early twentieth century, over half of Cleveland's residents rode the streetcars to work.

The central business district grew increasingly congested as banks, offices, department stores, wholesalers, theaters, restaurants, and clubs jostled one another for space on the city's main streets. Consumerism became a chief function of the central business district, and "going downtown to shop" constituted a typical outing. Some industries, like the garment trade and small manufacturers, competed with the commercial establishments for downtown space. Soaring real estate values in the central business district pushed many other manufacturers to the city's edge, along the railroad lines. Chicago's stockyards and the Homestead steel mills outside of Pittsburgh provide examples of this centrifugal movement.

The city's poor, unable to afford even the few cents for trolley fare, crowded into the inner city or lived "back of the yards" near the factories where they worked. There they lived in filthy, overcrowded, and overpriced dwellings: in dilapidated houses cut up into tenements, in shanties and cellars, and sometimes in alleyways and under bridges. The term *slum* came into common use by the mid-nineteenth century, coinciding with the increased social segregation of the poor in the least desirable areas of the city. This social segregation—rich and poor, ethnic and old-stock Americans—was one of the major social changes engendered by the rise of the industrial metropolis, and it occurred not only in Cleveland but in cities across the nation.

Race and ethnicity also affected the way in which cities evolved. Newcomers to the burgeoning cities, whether Jews and Italians "just off the boat" or African Americans up from the South, sought out their kin and countryfolk and struggled to maintain their culture in distinct neighborhoods that often formed around the synagogue or church. Blacks typically experienced the greatest residential segregation. Every large city had its ethnic neighborhoods, its Little Italy, Chinatown, Bohemia Flats, or Germantown, where one could walk for blocks without hearing a word of English. Jacob Riis observed, "A map of [New York] city, colored to designate nationalities, would show more stripes than on the skin of a zebra, and more colors than any rainbow."

City Life and City Images

In America, private enterprise built the cities. Boosters, builders, businessmen, planners, and politicians all had a hand in creating the modern city. With a few notable exceptions, such as Washington, D.C., there was no such thing as a comprehensive city plan. Cities simply mushroomed, formed by the dictates of private enterprise and the exigencies of local politics.

With the rise of the city came the need for public facilities, transportation, and services that would tax the imaginations of America's architects and engineers and provide the backdrop for the rough and tumble story of big-city politics and politicians.

Big-City Government

The physical growth of the cities required the expansion of public services and the creation of entirely new facilities: streets, subways, elevated trains, bridges, docks, parks, sewers, and public utilities. There was work to be done and money to be made. The professional politician—the colorful big-city boss—became a phenomenon of nineteenth-century urban growth. Although corrupt and often criminal, the boss saw to the building of the city and provided needed social services for the new residents. But not even the big-city boss could be said to rule the unruly city. The governing of America's cities resembled more a tug-of-war than boss rule.

The most notorious of all the city bosses was William Marcy Tweed of New York. At midcentury, Boss Tweed's Democratic Party machine held sway. A machine was really no more than a political party organized on the grassroots level. It existed to win elections and rewarded its followers with jobs on the city's payroll. New York's citywide Democratic organization, Tammany Hall, consisted of an army of party functionaries. At the bottom were the district captains. In return for votes, they provided services for their constituents, everything from a scuttle of coal in the winter to housing for an evicted family.

TAMMANY BANK

This cast-iron bank, a campaign novelty, is named after the New York City Democratic machine. It tells its political reform message graphically: When you put a penny into the politician's hand, he puts it in his pocket. Tammany Hall dominated city politics for more than a century, dispensing contracts and franchises worth millions of dollars. Some of those dollars invariably found their way into the pockets of Tammany politicians.
Collection of Janice L. and David J. Frent.

At the top were the powerful ward bosses who distributed lucrative franchises for subways and streetcars. They formed a shadow government, more powerful than the city's elected officials. Boss Tweed held the official title of alderman. But as a ward boss and chairman of the Tammany general committee, he wielded more power than the mayor. Through the use of bribery and graft he held the Democratic Party together and ran the city.

The cost of Tweed's rule was staggering. The construction of New York City's courthouse, budgeted at $250,000, ended up costing the taxpayers $14 million. The inflated sum represented bribery, kickbacks, and the greasing of many palms. The excesses of the Tweed ring soon led to a clamor for reform and cries of "Throw the rascals out." Cartoonist Thomas Nast pilloried Tweed in the pages of *Harper's Weekly*. His cartoons, easily understood even by those who couldn't read, did the boss more

harm than hundreds of outraged editorials. Tweed fled to Europe in 1871 to avoid prosecution, but eventually he was tried and convicted and died in jail.

The sheer extent and pervasiveness of corruption in Tweed's New York have led some historians to question whether the boss in fact "ruled" or whether he resorted to graft and bribery in a struggle to exercise a tenuous control over his followers. As Tweed himself complained, "This population is too hopelessly split up into races and factions to govern it under universal suffrage, except by the bribery of patronage and corruption."

New York was not the only city to be charged with bossism and corruption. The British visitor James Bryce concluded in 1888, "There is no denying that the government of cities is the one conspicuous failure of the United States." More than 80 percent of the nation's thirty largest cities experienced some form of boss rule in the decades around the turn of the century. Cincinnati's boss George B. Cox reigned undisputed over that city's Republican machine for a decade. Alexander R. Shepherd bossed Washington, D.C., and, to his credit (as well as his personal gain), helped to transform the city from a "swampy mudhole" into the beautiful capital envisioned by its architect, Pierre L'Enfant. Bossism did not stop at the Mississippi. Denver had its boss Robert Speer. Saloonkeeper Jim Pendergast dominated Kansas City politics. And "Blind Boss" Christopher Buckley ran San Francisco in the 1880s.

Infighting among powerful ward bosses was more typical in municipal government than domination by one big-city boss. "Czar" Martin Lomasney in Boston, "Big Tim" Sullivan in New York, and Chicago's "Bathhouse" John Coughlin and Michael "Hinky Dink" Kenna exemplified the breed. Their colorful nicknames signaled their distance from respectable society and hinted at unsavory connections with an underworld of crime and vice. The power they wielded belied the charge that any single boss enjoyed hegemony in the big cities.

Occasionally, a political strategist of more than ordinary skill emerged to become a bona fide boss. Less notorious but more powerful than Boss Tweed was Richard Croker of New York. Croker, who ruled Tammany Hall beginning in 1886, relied more on bureaucracy than boodle (bribery). He directed the distribution of lucrative construction contracts, he controlled franchises for street railways and public utilities, and he made sure these plums went to men who supported the party machine. Like Tweed, Croker held no elective office. As boss, he did not want to govern, he simply wanted to ensure that he and his supporters benefited from government. Unlike Tweed, who died in jail, Croker retired in 1901 to Wantage, his country estate in Ireland, a move that led one of his critics to quip, "New York's wastage is Croker's Wantage."

In the late nineteenth century, urban reformers and proponents of good government (derisively called "goo goos" by their rivals) challenged machine rule and sometimes succeeded in electing reform mayors. But the reformers rarely managed to stay in office for long. Their detractors called them "mornin' glories," observing that they "looked lovely in the mornin' and withered up in a short time." New York's William Strong is a fair example of the breed. A businessman, he won office in 1894 on the basis of his reputation for honesty and integrity. But Strong lacked the political skills needed to win reelection. However sporadic, the victories of urban reform signaled that the city boss was not without powerful rivals whom he had to counter or appease.

The bosses enjoyed continued success over the reformers for one main reason: the help the urban political machine handed out to the cities' immigrants and poor. In return for votes the machine provided legal aid, jobs, fuel, temporary shelter, and a host of small favors. In the words of Boston's Czar Lomasney, the immigrant poor needed "none of your law and justice, but help." The ability to combine philanthropy and politics was a hallmark of the urban boss. "What tells in holding your district is to go right down among the poor and help them in the different ways they need help," a Tammany ward boss observed. "It's philanthropy, but it's politics, too—mighty good politics." For the social services they received (and not because they were ignorant or undemocratic, as critics charged) the urban poor remained the bosses' staunchest allies.

Some reform mayors achieved success and longevity, however. In cities where they sponsored public services and championed the working class, reformers proved as unbeatable as any boss. Hazen S. Pingree of Detroit exemplified the successful reform mayor. A businessman who went into politics in the 1890s, Pingree, like most good-government candidates, promised to root out dishonesty and inefficiency. He did, but he also tangled with business interests when he tried to lower streetcar fares and utility rates. When the depression of 1893 struck, Pingree emerged as a champion of the working class and the poor. He hired the unemployed to build schools, parks, and public baths. And he fought for and got public ownership of electric utilities. By

providing needed services, he built a powerful political organization based on working-class support. Detroit's voters kept him in the mayor's office for four terms and then helped elect him governor twice.

Later reform mayors such as Toledo's Samuel "Golden Rule" Jones and Cleveland's Tom Johnson learned from Pingree. All three of these wealthy Yankee reform mayors won the support of ethnic voters by championing social services and avoiding so-called purity issues that might alienate working-class constituents. For example, while most good-government candidates harped on the Sunday closing of saloons and attacked vice and crime, Pingree demurred. "The most dangerous enemies to good government are not the saloons, the dives, the dens of iniquity and the criminals," he insisted. Detroit's problems could be "traced to the temptations which are offered to city officials when franchises are sought by wealthy corporations, or contracts are to be let for public works."

For all the color and flamboyance of the big-city boss, he was simply one of many actors in the drama of municipal government.

Not only the urban poor but the business class benefited from bossism and corruption, as Pingree shrewdly observed. The boss could juggle tax assessments for property owners and provide lucrative franchises. Through the skillful orchestration of rewards, an astute political operator like Croker exerted powerful leverage and lined up support for his party from a broad range of constituents, from the urban poor to wealthy industrialists. When journalist Lincoln Steffens wrote *The Shame of the Cities* in 1904, a series of articles exposing city corruption, he found that business leaders who fastidiously refused to mingle socially with the bosses nevertheless struck deals with them. "He is a self-righteous fraud, this big businessman," Steffens concluded. "I found him buying boodlers in St. Louis, defending grafters in Minneapolis, originating corruption in Pittsburgh, sharing with bosses in Philadelphia, deploring reform in Chicago, and beating good government with corruption funds in New York."

The complexity of big-city government, apparent in the levels of corruption Steffens uncovered, pointed to one conclusion: For all the color and flamboyance of the big-city boss, he was simply one of many actors in the drama of municipal government. The successful boss was not an autocratic ruler but

a power broker. Businesspeople, old-stock aristocrats, new professionals, saloonkeepers, pushcart
peddlers, and politicians all fought for their
interests in the hurly-burly of city government. They
didn't much like each other and they sometimes
fought savagely. But they learned to live with one
another. Compromise and accommodation—not
boss rule—best characterized big-city government
by the turn of the century.

Building Cities of Stone and Steel

"A town that crawled now stands erect," boasted
an ironworker. "And we whose backs were bent
above the [open] hearths know how it got its spine."
Technology transformed the urban landscape in
the late nineteenth and early twentieth centuries.
Where once wooden buildings had stood rooted in
the mire of unpaved streets, new cities of stone and
steel sprang up. The skyscrapers and mighty
bridges dominated the imagination and the urban
landscape at the turn of the century. Less imposing,
but no less significant, were the paved streets, the
parks and public libraries, and the subways and
sewers. In the late nineteenth century, Americans
rushed to embrace new technology, making their
cities the most modern in the world.

The Brooklyn Bridge opened in May 1883 and
was quickly proclaimed "one of the wonders of the
world." The world's longest suspension bridge
soared over the East River in a single mile-long span
connecting Brooklyn and Manhattan. Begun in 1869
during the days of Boss Tweed, the great bridge was
the dream of John Roebling. Roebling never lived
to see it completed. He died of an infection after he
injured his foot while surveying the waterfront site.
His son, Washington Roebling, carried on the great
work.

The building of the Brooklyn Bridge called forth
heroic effort. It took fourteen years and cost the lives
of twenty men. To sink the foundation deep into the
riverbed, laborers tunneled down through the mud
and debris, working in reinforced wooden boxes
called caissons, which were open at the bottom and
pressurized to keep the water from flooding in.
When the men emerged after a hard day's work,
they often came up too quickly and suffered from
the crippling effects of the bends. Washington Roebling himself fell victim to this disorder and ended
up an invalid. He directed the completion of the
bridge from his window in Brooklyn Heights
through a telescope while his wife, Emily Warren
Roebling, acted as site superintendent and general

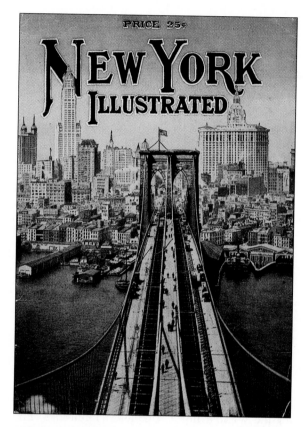

BROOKLYN BRIDGE
*Completion of the Brooklyn Bridge in 1883 made possible
the creation of Greater New York two years later by linking previously independent Brooklyn with Manhattan.
Roebling's bridge has proven not only aesthetically pleasing, but remarkably functional for more than a century.
The raised walkway allows pedestrians to enjoy their view
above the traffic.*
Picture Research Consultants & Archives.

engineer of the project. When the bridge was dedicated in 1883, Roebling turned to his wife and said,
"I want the world to know that you, too, are one of
the Builders of the Bridge."

Arching 130 feet above the East River, the
bridge carried two roadways, one for vehicles and
above it a pedestrian walkway. Together they
pierced massive granite towers through two huge
Gothic arches. John Roebling intended the bridge to
stand as "a great work of art" as well as "a successful specimen of advanced Bridge engineering."
Generations of artists and poets have testified to his
success.

A decade after the Brooklyn Bridge opened, the
growing city needed another bridge. This time en-

gineers utilized the new technology of structural steel. The Williamsburg Bridge opened in 1903. More prosaic than its southern neighbor, it was longer by four feet and was completed in half the time. It became the model for future building as the age of steel supplanted the age of stone and iron.

Skyscrapers as well as bridges changed the cityscape. Competition for space in Manhattan pushed the city up into the air even before the use of steel. The invention of Elisha Otis's elevator (called a "safety hoister") in the 1850s led to the construction of cast-iron buildings with elevators that carried passengers as high as ten stories. In 1890, the Pulitzer Building climbed to 349 feet, the tallest office building in the world. But until the advent of structural steel, no building in Manhattan topped the spire of Wall Street's Trinity Church.

Chicago, not New York, gave birth to the modern skyscraper. Rising from the ashes of the Great Fire of 1871, Chicago offered a generation of skilled architects and engineers the chance to experiment with new technologies. Commercial architecture reached an art form at the hands of a skilled group of architects who together constituted the "Chicago school." Men of genius such as Louis Sullivan and John Wellborn Root gave Chicago some of the world's finest commercial buildings. Employing the dictum "form follows function," they built startlingly modern structures. The massive commercial buildings, in Root's words, "carried out the ideas of modern business life, simplicity, breadth, dignity." A fitting symbol of modern America, the skyscraper expressed and exalted the domination of corporate power.

Alongside the skyscrapers rose new residential apartments for the rich and middle class. The "French flat" gained popularity in the 1880s as city dwellers overcame their distaste for multifamily housing (which carried the stigma of the tenement) and gave in to "flat fever." Fashionable new apartments, built for affluent tenants, boasted such modern luxuries as electricity, telephones, central heating, elevators, and modern plumbing. The convenience of apartment living appealed particularly to women. "Housekeeping isn't fun," cried one New York woman. "Give us flats!" In 1883 alone, more than one thousand new apartments went up in Chicago.

The flush toilets, bathtubs, and lavatories of the new apartments would not have been possible without major improvements in city sewers and water mains. Under the direction of enlightened city engineers, municipalities enlarged and expanded their sewers and devised ingenious ways to bring

BANDSTAND AT CENTRAL PARK
Landscape architect Frederick Law Olmsted designed his great urban parks as places where city dwellers could retreat for solitude and silence. But New Yorkers had other ideas, using Olmsted's Central Park for entertainment and amusement as well. Here a crowd jostles shoulder to shoulder at a concert at the bandstand.
Lake County (Illinois) Museum, Curt Teich Postcard Archives.

clean water to the urban population. City engineer Ellis S. Chesborough tunneled two miles out into Lake Michigan to assure Chicagoans that the water they drank would not be tainted by sewage. Rudolph Herring earned the title Dean of Sanitary Engineering by planning the sewer systems for Philadelphia, New York City, Chicago, Los Angeles, Baltimore, Washington, D.C., Minneapolis, Montreal, Toronto, and Mexico City. By the 1890s, the residents of American cities demanded and received, at the twist of a faucet, water for their bathtubs, toilets, and even their lawn sprinklers. Those who could afford it enjoyed a standard of living that was the envy of European capitals.

Throughout the United States, municipal governments undertook public works on a scale unknown in European cities. They paved streets with asphalt, replaced gas lamps with electric lights, ran trolley tracks on the old horsecar lines, and dug underground to build subways and then tore down the unsightly elevated tracks that clogged the city streets. In San Francisco, Andrew Smith Hallidie mastered the city's hills, building a system of cable cars in 1873. Montgomery, Alabama, became the first city in the country to install a fully electrified streetcar system in 1886. Boston completed the nation's first subway system in 1897, and New York and Philadelphia soon followed.

To fight disease and dirt, cities enlisted an army of public health inspectors. European scientists may have discovered the microbe in the 1870s, but Americans led the fight against germs. Using the latest methods, they battled cholera, smallpox, and diphtheria. In 1874–1875 alone, New York vaccinated more than 126,000 people against smallpox. Municipal health departments, with the help of urban boosters, worked to make American cities among the healthiest in the world.

Cities became not only healthier, but also more beautiful. American cities created public parks that were unrivaled in their scope and execution. Much of the credit goes to one man—landscape architect Frederick Law Olmsted. Olmsted designed parks in Atlanta, Brooklyn, Buffalo, Boston, Rochester, Detroit, Chicago, Milwaukee, Bridgeport, Hartford, and Louisville. The indefatigable Olmsted also laid out the grounds for the U.S. Capitol, designed the campuses of Stanford University and Gallaudet College, and planned an entire city, Riverside, Illinois. The Boston park system, a seven-mile ring of green that Olmsted called the city's "emerald necklace," was his most ambitious and successful project. But he is best remembered for the creation of New York's Central Park. He and his partner Calvert Vaux directed the planting of more than five million trees, shrubs, and vines to transform the eight hundred acres between 59th Street and 110th Street into an oasis for urban dwellers. "We want a ground to which people may easily go after their day's work is done," he wrote, "where they may stroll for an hour, seeing, hearing, and feeling nothing of the bustle and jar of the streets."

Olmsted intended his parks for contemplation, but in the 1880s and 1890s, parks became playgrounds for the people. Lincoln Park in Chicago offered baseball diamonds, tennis courts, a zoo, bicycle and bridle paths, and a band shell. San Francisco's Golden Gate Park, built on a sandy waste, by 1900 stood as a magnificent recreational area complete with a Japanese tea garden and a herd of grazing buffalo.

American cities did not overlook the mind in their efforts at improvement. They created a comprehensive free public school system that educated everyone from the children of urban professionals to the sons and daughters of immigrants. The exploding urban population strained the system and led to crowded and inadequate facilities, but no one was

turned away. In 1899, more than 544,000 pupils attended school in New York's five boroughs. Schools in Boston, New York, Chicago, and Detroit as well as other cities and towns provided the only classrooms in the world where students could attend secondary school free of charge.

In addition to schools, the cities built libraries to educate their citizens. American cities in the late nineteenth century created the most extensive free public library system in the world. In 1895, the Boston Public Library opened its bronze doors under the inscription "Free to All." More than 700,000 volumes stood on the shelves, ready to be checked out. Designed in the style of a Renaissance palazzo, replete with a grand marble staircase and murals by John Singer Sargent, the library earned the description "a palace of the people." Across the United States, other cities participated in the public library movement. Cincinnati, Detroit, St. Louis, Chicago, and Cleveland sponsored libraries in the 1870s. And in New York, Philadelphia, and Buffalo, the city stepped in with support when private libraries faltered in the 1890s.

The enduring monuments of America's cities —the bridges, skyscrapers, apartments, parks, and libraries—stood as the undeniable achievements of the same system of municipal government that Lord Bryce dismissed as a "conspicuous failure."

Despite the Boston Public Library's legend "Free to All," the poor did not share equally in the advantages of city life. The parks, the libraries, and even the subways and sewers benefited some city dwellers more than others. Few library cards were held by Boston's laborers, who worked six days a week and found the library closed on Sunday. And in the 1890s there was nothing central about New York's Central Park. It was a four-mile walk from the tenements of Hester Street to the park's entrance at 59th Street and Fifth Avenue. Cities spent more money on plumbing improvements for affluent apartment dwellers than on public baths and lodging houses for the down and out. Even the uniform subway fare, which enabled Boston and New York riders to travel anywhere in the system for five cents, worked to the advantage of the middle-class commuter and not the downtown poor. Then, as now, the comfortable majority and not the indigent minority reaped a disproportionate share of the benefits in the nation's big cities.

Any story of the American city, it seems, must be a tale of two cities—or, more correctly, given the great diversity, a tale of many cities within each metropolis. At the turn of the century a central paradox emerged: The enduring monuments of America's cities—the bridges, skyscrapers, apartments, parks, and libraries—stood as the undeniable achievements of the same system of municipal government that Lord Bryce dismissed as a "conspicuous failure."

White City or City of Sin?

Americans have always been of two minds about the city. They boast of its skyscrapers and bridges, its culture and sophistication, and they pride themselves on its bigness and bustle. At the same time they fear it as the city of sin, the home of immigrant slums, the center of vice and crime. Americans in the late nineteenth century experienced the same ambivalence. Nowhere did the divided view of the American city take form more graphically than in Chicago in 1893.

In that year, Chicago hosted the Columbian Exposition, the grandest world's fair in the nation's history. The fairground, nicknamed the White City and built on the shores of Lake Michigan to honor the four hundredth anniversary of Columbus's discovery of America, offered a lesson in what Americans on the eve of the twentieth century imagined

a city might be. Only five miles down the shore of Lake Michigan from Chicago, the White City seemed light-years away. Its very name celebrated a harmony, a uniformity, and a cleanliness unknown in Chicago, with its stockyards, slums, and bustling terminals. "Formal," "academic," and "monumental" are words that best describe the city built for the Columbian Exposition. Frederick Law Olmsted and architect Daniel Burnham supervised the transformation of a wasteland on the shores of Lake Michigan into a pristine paradise of lagoons, fountains, wooded islands, gardens, and imposing white buildings. "Here," wrote the novelist Theodore Dreiser, "hungry men, raw from the shops and fields, idylls and romances in their minds, builded them an empire crying glory in the mud."

What did it mean, this harmony, this White City, juxtaposed against big-shouldered, brash Chicago? To Louis Sullivan, whose Transportation Building was judged the most innovative of the main buildings, the very harmony of the White City marked a triumph of uniformity over invention. Sullivan branded the fair a blight, a "virus." Its celebration of the neoclassical and Renaissance styles, he argued, set back modern architecture a generation.

But the average American delighted in the classical beauty of the White City. "Sell the cookstove and come," the novelist Hamlin Garland wrote to his parents on the farm. "You *must* see this fair." And come they did, in spite of the panic and depression that broke out only weeks after the fair opened in May 1893. More than 27 million people

FIRE AT THE WHITE CITY, CHICAGO
Spectators watch as the White City goes up in smoke in July 1894. After the World Columbian Exposition closed in 1893, the grounds became home to growing numbers of homeless unemployed thrown out of work following the panic of 1893. Unsure of what to do with the buildings, city officials may have been relieved by the fire, which broke out in a clash between federal troops and striking railway workers.
Chicago Historical Society.

attended the Columbian Exposition. They marveled at the art and architecture, strolled the elaborate grounds, visited the exhibits—everything from an eleven-ton cheese to the gigantic Yerkes telescope —and were by turns educated and entertained. Half carnival, half culture, the great fair offered something for everyone. On the Midway Plaisance, a separate concession away from the White City proper, crowds thrilled to the massive wheel built by Mr. Ferris and watched agog as Little Egypt danced the hootchy kootchy.

William Dean Howells, an influential author and the unofficial dean of American letters, judged the fair an expression of America's utopian vision, "a glorious dream of universal brotherhood." For historian Henry Adams, one of the more astute observers of his era, the fair offered not so much a lesson as a riddle. "Chicago," Adams wrote, "asked in 1893 for the first time the question whether the American people knew where they were driving."

The White City's appeal seemed to lie in its distance from everyday life. But that distance could be disconcerting. Hamlin Garland treated his parents to a trip to the fair during the summer of 1893. His mother had grown old, worn down by the work and troubles of farm life. He fancied that the trip could somehow make it up to her. Eagerly he led his parents from one exhibit to another, from one grand vista to the next. The result was not what he anticipated.

> Stunned by the majesty of the vision, my mother sat in her chair, visioning it all yet comprehending little of its meaning. . . . These gorgeous scenes dazzled her, overwhelmed her. . . .
>
> At last, utterly overcome, she leaned her head against my arm, closed her eyes, and said, "Take me home. I can't stand any more of it."

In October the fair closed its doors in the midst of the worst depression the country had seen. The depression turned the decaying White City into a city of the poor and unemployed. During the winter of 1894, Chicago's homeless took over the grounds, vandalized the buildings, and frightened the respectable population. When Daniel Burnham was asked what should be done with the moldering remains of the White City, he responded, "It should be torched." And it was. In July 1894, in a clash between federal troops and striking railway workers, incendiaries set fire to the great buildings. In a matter of hours, nothing remained but a mass of rubble and twisted girders.

In the end, the White City remained what it had always been, a dreamscape. Buildings that looked like marble from a distance began to crumble even before fire destroyed the fairgrounds. Some had talked of preserving the vision, of building a permanent landmark for the city. But times were hard, and money was scarce. With the exception of the Arts Building, erected to house the Museum of Science and Industry, the White City remained a fantasy, never destined to endure. Perhaps it was not so strange, after all, that the legacy of the White City was felt most directly on Coney Island, where two new amusement parks, Luna and Dreamland, sought to combine, in a cheapened form, the beauty of the White City with the thrill of the Midway Plaisance.

Conclusion: The City and the Country

Those like Henry Adams who pondered the riddle of where the country was heading as the nineteenth century gave way to the twentieth would have been better advised to leave the White City and look to Chicago. There in the young metropolis, with its stockyards and skyscrapers, its terminals and rail yards, the answer could be found. Americans on the move had populated a continent and, along with a host of newcomers from around the world, filled the cities, doubling Chicago's population each decade. A vast spider web of railway tracks radiating out from Chicago linked burgeoning urban America with the orange groves of California, the cotton fields of Texas, and the cattle ranches of Montana, collapsing distance and difference. Increasingly, the city and the country were two parts of one whole, tied together by iron rails in an intricate web of dependence.

The story of Chicago was the story of America, where it had been and where it was heading. In the three decades between 1870 and 1900, the United States had filled out the map of the continent all the way to the Pacific Ocean. Iron rails crisscrossed the nation, carrying American goods and products to seaports for the world market. Settlers pushed into the trans-Mississippi West, forcing the Native Americans onto reservations and establishing eight new states and territories. A massive migration of peoples on the move, global in its scope, transformed the geography of the country, populating the West and leading to an urban explosion. No longer a set of isolated entities, the farms, the villages and towns, and the cities of the United States were by the twentieth century part of a vast network, linked to a global market by rails of steel.

CHRONOLOGY

1860– 2.5 million farms established on public
1900 lands.

1862 Homestead Act promises 160 acres of western land to anyone who settles on land for five years.

1870s Cattle ranching and mining become big business in the West.

1870 80 percent of the population lives in rural areas, according to U.S. census.

1871 William Marcy Tweed's rule in New York ends in ignominy.

Fire ravages Chicago and leads to new boom in architectural innovation as city rebuilds.

1873 Panic on Wall Street leads to nation-wide economic depression.

1876 George Armstrong Custer and cavalry force of two hundred are killed by four thousand Indians near Little Bighorn River in Montana Territory.

Statehood granted to Colorado.

1880– Rural areas of New England and Mid-
1890 west suffer depopulation.

1880s Immigration patterns shift as more people arrive from southern and eastern Europe.

Heyday of buffalo hunting in the West leads to slaughter of 60 million animals.

1882 Chinese Exclusion Act prohibits immigration of Chinese nationals to U.S.

1883 Buffalo Bill Cody begins to tour with his Wild West company.

Brooklyn Bridge opens over New York City's East River.

1886 Statue of Liberty, a gift from France, dedicated in New York harbor.

1886– Severe blizzards in Dakotas devastate
1887 cattle ranching.

1887 Congress passes Dawes Act, breaking up Indian lands.

1887– Massive droughts defeat homesteaders
1890s on Great Plains.

1889 Rise of Ghost Dance religion among Native Americans in the West.

Sitting Bull killed by U.S. soldiers at Pine Ridge reservation.

Government opens two million acres of former Indian territory in Oklahoma to settlement.

Statehood granted to Montana, North Dakota, South Dakota, and Washington.

1890 Last remnant of Sioux surrender, and army troops kill 200 Indians at Wounded Knee, South Dakota. Only 250,000 Indians remain from an estimated 25 million living when Christopher Columbus landed.

Jacob Riis's *How the Other Half Lives* documents harsh poverty in New York City tenements.

Statehood granted to Idaho and Wyoming.

1890s First wave of African American migration from South to North begins.

1891 Author Hamlin Garland publishes *Main Traveled Roads,* his first collection of short stories about farm life in Midwest.

1893 Panic on Wall Street touches off major economic depression.

Columbian Exposition opens in Chicago.

Frenzied land rush takes place on Cherokee strip in Oklahoma Territory.

1895 Boston Public Library opens under the slogan "Free to All."

1896 Statehood granted to Utah.

1900 Ellis Island, in New York harbor, opens to process newly arrived immigrants.

Census finds that 66 percent of population live in rural areas, compared with 80 percent in 1870.

Three cities—New York, Chicago, and Philadelphia—top one million inhabitants.

BIBLIOGRAPHY

GENERAL WORKS

William Cronin, *Nature's Metropolis: Chicago and the Great West* (1991).

Allan Dawley, *Struggles for Justice: Social Responsibility and the Liberal State* (1991).

John Higham, *Strangers in the Land* (1955).

Nell Irvin Painter, *Standing at Armageddon: The United States, 1877–1919* (1987).

Jon C. Teaford, *Unheralded Triumph: City Government in America, 1870–1920* (1984).

Alan Trachtenberg, *Incorporation of America: Culture and Society, 1865–1893* (1982).

Richard White, *"It's Your Misfortune and None of My Own": A History of the American West* (1991).

Robert Wiebe, *The Search for Order, 1877–1920* (1967).

C. Vann Woodward, *The Origins of the New South, 1877–1913* (1951).

RURAL AMERICA

Jane Adams, *The Transformation of Rural Life, Southern Illinois, 1880–1990* (1994).

Edward L. Ayers, *The Promise of the New South: Life after Reconstruction* (1992).

Hal S. Barron, *Those Who Stayed Behind: Rural Society in Nineteenth-Century New England* (1984).

John B. Boles, *The South through Time* (1995).

Sucheng Chan, *This Bittersweet Soil: The Chinese in California Agriculture, 1860–1910* (1986).

Maisie Conrat and Richard Conrat, *The American Farm: A Photographic History* (1977).

Cletus E. Daniel, *Bitter Harvest: A History of Farmworkers, 1870–1941* (1981).

Everett Dick, *Sod-House Frontier* (1954).

Deborah Fink, *Agrarian Women, Wives and Mothers in Rural Nebraska, 1880–1940* (1992).

Gilbert C. Fite, *The Farmers' Frontier, 1865–1900* (1966).

Ian Frazier, *Great Plains* (1989).

John Brinckerhoff Jackson, *American Space: The Centennial Years, 1865–1876* (1972).

Julie Roy Jeffrey, *Frontier Women: The Trans-Mississippi West, 1840–1880* (1979).

Katherine Jellison, *Entitled to Power: Farm Women and Technology, 1913–1963* (1993).

Gerald McFarland, *A Scattered People: An American Family Moves West* (1985).

Sally McMurry, *Families and Farmhouses in Nineteenth-Century America: Vernacular Design and Social Change* (1988).

Carey McWilliams, *North from Mexico: The Spanish-Speaking People of the United States* (1948).

Carey McWilliams, *Factories in the Fields* (1971).

Eric H. Monkkonen, ed., *Walking to Work: Tramps in America, 1790–1935* (1984).

Sandra L. Myres, *Westering Women and the Frontier Experience, 1800–1915* (1982).

Nell Irvin Painter, *Exodusters: Black Migration to Kansas after Reconstruction* (1976).

Rodman W. Paul, *The Far West and the Great Plains in Transition, 1859–1900* (1988).

Paula Petrik, *No Step Backward: Women and Family on the Rocky Mountain Mining Frontier* (1987).

Glenda Gates Riley, *The Female Frontier: A Comparative View of the Prairie and the Plains* (1988).

Lillian Schlissel, Byrd Gibbens, and Elizabeth Hampsten, *Far from Home: Families of the Westward Journey* (1989).

Fred A. Shannon, *The Farmer's Last Frontier: Agriculture, 1860–1897* (1945).

Richard Slotkin, *Gunfighter Nation: The Myth of the Frontier in Twentieth-Century America* (1992).

Mary L. Smith, *Going to God's Country* (1941).

Joanna L. Stratton, *Pioneer Women: Voices from the Kansas Frontier* (1981).

Gregory R. Woirol, *In the Floating Army: F. C. Mills on Itinerant Life in California, 1914* (1988).

THE WEST

Rudolfo Acuna, *Occupied America: A History of Chicanos* (1981).

Stephen E. Ambrose, *Crazy Horse and Custer: The Parallel Lives of Two American Warriors* (1975).

Ralph K. Andrist, *Long Death: Last Days of the Plains Indians* (1964).

Lewis Atherton, *The Cattle Kings* (1961).

Gunther Barth, *Bitter Strength: A History of the Chinese in the United States, 1850–1870* (1964).

Monroe Lee Billington, *New Mexico's Buffalo Soldiers, 1866–1900* (1991).

Dee Brown, *Bury My Heart at Wounded Knee* (1970).

David Dary, *Cowboy Culture* (1981).

Sarah Deutsch, *No Separate Refuge* (1987).

Richard Drinnon, *Facing West: The Metaphysics of Indian-Hating and Empire-Building* (1980).

Robert R. Dykstra, *Cattle Towns* (1968).

C. Robert Haywood, *Victorian West: Class and Culture in Kansas Cattle Towns* (1991).

Robert V. Hine, *The American West: An Interpretive History* (2nd ed., 1984).

Richard Hogan, *Class and Community in Frontier Colorado* (1990).

Frederick E. Hoxie, *A Final Promise: The Campaign to Assimilate the Indians* (1984).

Howard R. Lamar, *The Far Southwest, 1846–1912* (1966).

Patricia Nelson Limerick, *The Legacy of Conquest: The Unbroken Past of the American West* (1987).

H. Elaine Lindgren, *Land in Her Own Name: Women as Homesteaders in North Dakota* (1991).

K. Tsiana Lowawaima, *They Called it Prairie Light: The Story of Chilocco Indian School* (1994).

Janet A. McDonnell, *The Dispossession of the American Indian, 1887–1934* (1991).

Devon A. Mihesuah, *Cultivating Rosebuds: The Education of Women at the Cherokee Female Seminary* (1993).

David Montejano, *Anglos and Mexicans in the Making of Texas, 1836–1986* (1989).

Donald J. Pisani, *From the Family Farm to Agribusiness: The Irrigation Crusade in California, 1850–1930* (1984).

Jules David Prown et al., *Discovered Lands, Invented Pasts* (1992).

Lillian Schlissel, Vicki Ruiz, and Janice Monk, eds., *Western Women, Their Land, Their Lives* (1988).

Richard Slatta, *Cowboys of the Americas* (1990).

Russell Thornton, *American Indian Holocaust and Survival: A Population History since 1492* (1987).

Robert A. Trennert Jr., *The Phoenix Indian School* (1988).

Kathleen Underwood, *Town Building on the Colorado Frontier* (1987).

Francis Utley, *The Last Days of the Sioux Nation* (1963).

Robert M. Utley, *The Indian Frontier of the American West, 1846–1890* (1984).

Robert M. Utley, *Cavalier in Buckskin: George Armstrong Custer and the Western Military Frontier* (1988).

Wilcomb Washburn, *The Indian in America* (1975).

Walter Webb, *The Great Plains* (1931).

Elliott West, *Growing Up with the Country: Childhood on the Far Western Frontier* (1989).

Donald Worster, *Rivers of Empire* (1985).

Donald Worster, *Under Western Skies* (1992).

THE CITY

Reid Badger, *The Great American Fair: The World's Columbian Exposition and American Culture* (1979).

Gunther Barth, *Instant Cities: Urbanization and the Rise of San Francisco and Denver* (1975).

Gunther Barth, *City People: The Rise of Modern City Culture in Nineteenth-Century America* (1980).

Josef J. Barton, *Peasants and Strangers: Italians, Rumanians, and Slovaks in an American City, 1890–1915* (1975).

Amy Bridges, *A City in the Republic: Antebellum New York and the Origins of Machine Politics* (1984).

David F. Burg, *Chicago's White City of 1893* (1976).

Edmund Chapman, *Cleveland: Village to Metropolis* (1964).

Charles W. Cheape, *Moving the Masses: Urban Public Transport in New York, Boston, and Philadelphia, 1880–1912* (1980).

Elizabeth Collins Cromley, *Alone Together: A History of New York's Early Apartments* (1990).

Mona Domosh, *Invented Cities, The Creation of Landscape in Nineteenth-Century New York and Boston* (1996).

Robert Fishman, *Bourgeois Utopias: The Rise and Fall of Suburbia* (1987).

James Gilbert, *Perfect Cities: Chicago's Utopias of 1893* (1991).

Thomas J. Gilfoyle, *City of Eros: New York City, Prostitution, and the Commercialization of Sex, 1790–1920* (1992).

Ray Ginger, *Altgeld's America* (1973).

Charles N. Glabb, ed., *The American City: A Documentary History* (1963).

Charles N. Glabb and A. Theodore Brown, *A History of Urban America* (1967).

David R. Goldfield and Blain A. Brownell, *Urban America: A History* (2nd ed., 1990).

Constance McLaughlin Green, *The Rise of Urban America* (1965).

William D. Griffin, *The Book of Irish Americans* (1990).

Peter B. Hales, *Constructing the Fair: Platinum Photographs by C. D. Arnold of the World's Columbian Exposition* (1993).

David C. Hammack, *Power and Society: Greater New York at the Turn of the Century* (1982).

Elizabeth Hawes, *New York, New York: How the Apartment House Transformed Life in the City, 1869–1930* (1993).

Leo Hershkowitz, *Tweed's New York: Another Look* (1977).

Melvin Holli, *Reform in Detroit: Hazen S. Pingree and Urban Politics* (1969).

Helen Lefkowitz Horowitz, *Culture and the City: Cultural Philanthropy in Chicago from the 1880s to 1917* (1976).

Kenneth T. Jackson, *Crabgrass Frontier: The Suburbanization of the United States* (1985).

Frederic C. Jaher, *The Urban Establishment: Upper Strata in Boston, New York, Charleston, Chicago, and Los Angeles* (1982).

Lawrence Karsen, *The Rise of the Urban South* (1985).

Ann Durkin Keating, *Building Chicago: Suburban Developers and the Creation of a Divided Metropolis* (1988).

Kenneth L. Kusmer, *A Ghetto Takes Shape: Black Cleveland, 1870–1930* (1976).

Donald A. Mackay, *The Building of Manhattan* (1987).

Seymour M. Mandelbaum, *Boss Tweed's New York* (1965).

Margaret Marsh, *Suburban Lives* (1990).

Carolyn Marvin, *When Old Technologies Were New: Thinking about Electric Communication in the Late Nineteenth Century* (1988).

Blake McKelvey, *The Urbanization of America, 1860–1915* (1963).

Ross Miller, *American Apocalypse: The Great Fire and the Myth of Chicago* (1990).

Zane L. Miller, *Boss Cox's Cincinnati* (1968).

Zane L. Miller and Patricia M. Melvin, *The Urbanization of Modern America: A Brief History* (2nd ed., 1987).

Raymond A. Mohl, *The New City: Urban America in the Industrial Age, 1860–1920* (1985).

Eric H. Monkkonen, *America Becomes Urban* (1988).

Humbert S. Nelli, *The Italians in Chicago, 1860–1920* (1970).

David E. Nye, *Electrifying America: Social Meanings of a New Technology, 1880–1940* (1990).

Maureen Ogle, *All the Modern Conveniences: American Household Plumbing, 1840–1890* (1996).

Gilbert Osofsky, *Harlem: The Making of a Ghetto, 1890–1930* (1966).

Kathy Peiss, *Cheap Amusements: Working Women and Leisure in Turn-of-the-Century New York* (1986).

Henry Petroski, *Engineers of Dreams* (1994).

Harold L. Platt, *The Electric City: Energy and Growth of the Chicago Area, 1880–1930* (1991).

Allan Pred, *Spatial Dynamics of U.S. Urban Growth, 1800–1914* (1971).

Samuel H. Preston and Michael R. Haines, *Fatal Years: Child Mortality in Late Nineteenth Century America* (1991).

William L. Riordan, *Plunkitt of Tammany Hall* (1905; reprint, 1963).

Moses Rischin, *The Promised City* (1962).

Roy Rosenzweig and Elizabeth Blackmar, *The Park and the People: A History of Central Park* (1992).

Luc Sante, *Low Life: Lures and Snares of Old New York* (1991).

David Schuyler, *The New Urban Landscape: The Redefinition of City Form in Nineteenth-Century America* (1986).

Richard Sennett, *Families against the City: Middle-Class Homes of Industrial Chicago, 1872–1890* (1970).

Joseph Siry, *Carson Pirie Scott: Louis Sullivan and the Chicago Department Store* (1988).

Carl Smith, *Urban Disorder and the Shape of Belief* (1995).

Allan H. Spear, *Black Chicago, 1860–1920* (1966).

Elizabeth Stevenson, *Park Maker: A Life of Frederick Law Olmsted* (1977).

John R. Stilgoe, *Borderland: Origins of the American Suburb, 1820–1939* (1988).

William R. Taylor, *In Pursuit of Gotham: Culture and Commerce in New York* (1992).

Jon C. Teaford, *City and Suburb: The Political Fragmentation of Metropolitan America, 1850–1970* (1979).

Stephan Thernstrom, *The Other Bostonians: Poverty and Progress in the American Metropolis* (1973).

Stephan Thernstrom and Richard Sennett, eds., *Nineteenth-Century Cities: Essays in the New Urban History* (1969).

John Emerson Todd, *Frederick Law Olmsted* (1982).

Alan Trachtenberg, *Brooklyn Bridge: Fact and Symbol* (1965).

David B. Tyack, *The One Best System: A History of American Urban Education* (1974).

Sam Bass Warner Jr., *Streetcar Suburbs* (1962).

Sam Bass Warner Jr., *The Urban Wilderness* (1972).

Gwendolyn Wright, *Moralism and the Model Home: Domestic Architecture and Cultural Conflict in Chicago, 1873–1913* (1980).

Oliver Zunz, *The Changing Face of Inequality* (1982).

IMMIGRANTS

Glenn C. Altschuler, *Race, Ethnicity, and Class in American Social Thought, 1865–1919* (1982).

Mary Antin, *From Plotzk to Boston* (1986).

John Bodnar, *Immigration and Industrialization: Ethnicity in an American Mill Town* (1977).

John Bodnar, *The Transplanted: A History of Immigration in Urban America* (1985).

Richard Ehrlich, ed., *Immigrants in Industrial America* (1977).

Steven Erie, *Rainbow's End: Irish-Americans and the Dilemmas of Urban Machine Politics, 1840–1985* (1988).

Donna Gabaccia, *From the Other Side, Women, Gender and Immigrant Life in the U.S., 1820–1990* (1995).

Oscar Handlin, *The Uprooted* (1951).

Thomas Kessner, *The Golden Door: Italian and Jewish Immigrant Mobility in New York City, 1880–1915* (1977).

Alan M. Kraut, *The Huddled Masses: The Immigrant in American Society, 1880–1921* (1982).

Robert Anthony Orsi, *The Madonna of 115th Street: Faith and Community in Italian Harlem, 1880–1950* (1985).

Gilbert Osofsky, *Harlem, the Making of a Ghetto: Negro New York, 1890–1930* (1971).

Thomas M. Pitkin, *Keepers of the Gate: A History of Ellis Island* (1975).

George Sanchez, *Becoming Mexican American: Ethnicity, Culture, and Identity in Chicano Los Angeles, 1900–1945* (1993).

CAMPAIGN LANTERN

Political parties gave out novelty items like this paper lantern from Republican Benjamin Harrison's 1888 presidential campaign. The log cabin, a staple political icon, celebrates the candidate's humble origins, while the reference to Tippecanoe highlights his relationship to President William Henry Harrison, his grandfather, the victor of the Battle of Tippecanoe in 1811. "Protection" in bold letters underscores the Republican Party's perennial support for a tariff designed to protect the country's industries from foreign competition.

Collection of Janice L. and David J. Frent.

BUSINESS AND POLITICS IN THE GILDED AGE

18

1877–1895

THROUGHOUT THE WINTER OF 1894–95, in the midst of the worst depression the country had yet seen, President Grover Cleveland walked the floor of the White House, sleepless over the prospect that the United States might go bankrupt. The Treasury's gold reserves had dipped so low that unless gold could be purchased abroad, the unthinkable might happen—the U.S. Treasury might not be able to meet its obligations.

Cleveland, like many honest and upright men of his era, believed that the only sound money was gold. Although other forms of currency circulated, notably paper money like banknotes and greenbacks, the government's support of the gold standard meant that all currency could be redeemed for gold. A major Wall Street panic in 1893 precipitated financial uncertainty, and in its wake banks and individuals rushed to cash in their banknotes and demand gold.

In late January 1895, with the Treasury's gold reserves sinking dangerously low, New York financiers August Belmont and John Pierpont Morgan suggested a plan whereby a private group of bankers would purchase gold abroad and supply it to the Treasury. Cleveland knew only too well that the scheme might give the financial community confidence, but it would bring a thunder of protest from people and politicians suspicious of the power the influential bankers wielded. Cleveland vacillated, hesitant to strike a deal.

Early in February 1895, J. P. Morgan traveled by private railway car to Washington to meet with the president. Cleveland, still brooding over his dilemma, refused to see Morgan. The great banker appeared unruffled by the snub. "I have come down to see the president," he told the crowd of reporters, "and I am going to stay here until I see him."

The next day, Cleveland summoned Morgan to the White House. When a phone call informed the president that only $9 million in gold remained in the New York branch of the Treasury, Morgan responded ominously that he knew of a $10 million debt outstanding. "What suggestion have you to make, Mr. Morgan?" Cleveland asked. To save the gold standard, the president had no choice but to turn to Morgan for help.

A storm of controversy erupted over the deal between Cleveland and Morgan. The press claimed that the president had lined his own pockets in the transaction and rumored that Morgan had made $8.9 million in profits. With the convenience of hindsight, it is difficult to see what all the fuss was about. The historical record has shown that Cleveland was an honest though stubborn man and that Morgan acted more from patriotism than for profit. (His share, far from the millions his critics claimed, amounted to $295,652.) Today, having survived as a nation for over half a century since President Franklin D. Roosevelt took the country off the gold standard, we find it hard to believe that a time existed when Americans expected to go to the bank and cash in dollar bills for real gold.

Yet the passions stirred by Cleveland's action in 1895 cannot be dismissed lightly. Undoubtedly, Morgan saved the gold reserves. But if President Cleveland managed to salvage the gold standard, his action did not save the country. The winter of 1894–95 was one of the hardest in American history. People faced unemployment, cold, and hunger. It never occurred to Cleveland that his great faith in gold prolonged the depression, favored creditors over debtors, and caused immense hardship for millions of Americans.

Perhaps the real meaning of the crisis of 1895 was what bothered the more thoughtful commentators of the time, who recognized that the issue was not gold but power. Cleveland's actions made it clear that J. P. Morgan, and not the president, had it in his power to save the Treasury. How had such enormous power accrued to businessmen? And what did it mean for the future of American democracy? Historian Henry Adams, the great-grandson of President John Adams and the grandson of President John Quincy Adams, voiced many Americans' fears about the growing power of the new business titans. Democracy itself, he feared, was threatened by what he called a "new caesarism"—a dictatorship of corporate power. The increasing emphasis on money and moneymaking stimulated by industrial development also worried the writer Mark Twain, who used the label "the Gilded Age" to highlight the crass materialism of the era.

In the years following the Confederate surrender at Appomattox, the country experienced a profound shift. President Rutherford B. Hayes observed, "We are in a period when the old questions are settled, and the new ones are not yet brought forward." Slavery and sectionalism, the twin forces fueling antebellum politics, yielded to new concerns as industry and the industrialists took center stage. After the end of the Civil War, industrial development in the United States speeded to a fever pitch. By the end of the century, the United States led the world in manufacturing, far surpassing Great Britain. America's manufacturing economy had its roots in the early nineteenth century, but in the years between 1865 and the 1890s the country was transformed, moving slowly but surely from a nation of farms to a nation of factories. Industrial progress, however, did not march forward smoothly at an even pace.

Economic growth was uneven, marred by cycles of boom and bust. Panics, sharp economic downturns usually precipitated by a stock market plunge and accompanied by bank failures and unemployment, occurred routinely and touched off two major depressions, one following the panic of 1873 and a more profound depression after the panic of 1893. Nor was industrial growth uniform across the country. Large areas of the United States, particularly in the South and the West, remained predominantly rural and agricultural. Industries developed more quickly in the Northeast and the areas touching the Great Lakes, where busy ports witnessed an influx of cheap labor and a correspondingly impressive outflow of American industrial goods.

The rise of industrialism in the United States and the interplay of business and politics strike the key themes in the Gilded Age, the period from the 1870s to the 1890s. Bound closer by a network of railroads and telegraphs, with the fate of small towns linked as never before to the fortunes of big cities, America in the late nineteenth century became united in fact as well as in name. Industrial development transformed the lives of all Americans, from factory workers to farmers. In the United States, the transition from a rural, agricultural economy to urban industrialism proved a deeply unsettling experience. The hopes and fears that industrialism inspired can be seen in the public's attitude toward the great business moguls of the day, men like Jay Gould, Andrew Carnegie, John D. Rockefeller, and J. P. Morgan. These larger-than-life figures dominated not only business but the popular imagination as the heroes and villains in the high drama of industrialization. At no other period in U.S. history would the industrial giants and the businesses they built (and sometimes wrecked) loom so large in American life.

Old Industries Transformed, New Industries Born

In the years following the Civil War, the scale and scope of American industry expanded dramatically. Old industries became modern big businesses, while discovery and invention stimulated new industries such as oil and electric power. A number of factors contributed to the prodigious growth of American industry. The country boasted an abundance of raw materials and energy sources—coal, iron, timber, oil, and water power. Human resources, too, seemed almost unlimited as record numbers of immigrants came to the United States and farmers migrated to industrial centers. American inventiveness also contributed to the growth of industry. The telephone, typewriter, electric light, sewing machine, refrigeration, and the automobile—all invented between the 1870s and 1890s—became integral parts of American life. Just as technological ingenuity created the machinery for industrial growth, a revolution in the management of industry enabled expanding businesses to organize their far-flung industrial networks.

The rise of the railroad played the key role in the transformation of the American economy in the post–Civil War period. The railroads created a national market that enabled businesses to expand from a local to a nationwide scale. Needing more and better rails to carry freight, the railroad radically changed the iron industry by speeding the transition from iron to steel. Railroads also made possible innovations in meatpacking and food processing. The railroad had what economists call a multiplier effect, speeding the pace of growth in many segments of the economy.

The Railroads, America's First Big Business

In the decades following the Civil War, the United States built the greatest railroad network in the world and in the process created America's first big business. The railroad in turn stimulated the development of many more businesses as the United States experienced an unprecedented industrial boom. Well before the Civil War, the railroad had replaced canals and turnpikes as a cheaper, more direct, and faster way to move goods and passengers. By 1857, the traveler who had once spent three weeks going from New York to Chicago could make the trip by rail in three days. And, more important for shippers, the railroads, unlike the canals, remained operable through the winter months. The steam locomotive ushered in a new era in American economic life as businesses grew in scale and scope. Given the central importance of the railroad to America's economic life, it is surprising to note that it was built with no central plan or vision. Instead it grew up piecemeal, built by speculators, promoters, boosters, merchants, manufacturers, capitalists, and outright crooks. Nevertheless, in less than twenty years, iron rails spanned the continent, and by the 1880s the enormous task of railroad building was virtually complete. To under-

stand how the railroads developed and came to dominate American life, there is no better study than the career of Jay Gould, a man who came to personify the Gilded Age.

The rise of the railroad played the key role in the transformation of the American economy in the post–Civil War period.

Jason "Jay" Gould bought his first railroad before he was twenty-five years old. It was only sixty-two miles long, in bad repair, and on the brink of failure. But within two years, he had sold it at a profit of $130,000. Thus began the career of the man who would pioneer the development of America's railway system and become the era's most notorious speculator. Gould, the sickly, frail son of a farmer, decided early to run away to the city to make his fortune. Like many Americans in the 1850s, he saw the railroad as the key to the future.

Gould, by his own account, knew little about railroads and cared less about their operation. Nevertheless, he became a master of corporate expansion, the architect of the vast railway systems that developed in the 1870s. The secretive Gould operated like a shark in the stock market, looking for vulnerable railroads, buying enough of their stock to take control, and threatening to undercut his competitors until they bought him out at a high profit. The railroads that fell into his hands, like the Erie, fared badly and often went bankrupt. But Gould's genius lay in cleverly buying and selling railroad stock, not in providing transportation.

Jay Gould's power and success underscored the haphazard development of the American railway system. To encourage railroad building, the federal and state governments provided the railroads with generous cash subsidies and grants of land. States and local communities clamored to offer inducements to railroad builders, knowing that towns and villages along the tracks would grow and flourish. Since the federal government held vast tracts of public land in the West, Congress did not hesitate to give it away to promote railroad building. The railroads not only received land for rights-of-way but were granted liberal sections on alternating sides of the track to do with as they pleased, most often to sell to the settlers who followed the railroads into the West. Over the years, the federal government alone granted the railroad builders a total of 175 million acres, an area larger than the state of Texas.

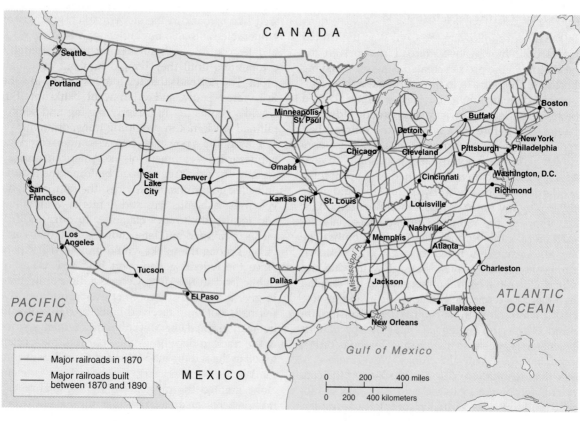

MAP 18.1

Railroad Expansion, 1870–1890

Railroad mileage nearly quadrupled between 1870 and 1890, with the greatest growth coming in the trans-Mississippi west. New transcontinental lines — the Great Northern, the Northern Pacific, the Southern Pacific, and the Atlantic and Pacific — were completed in the 1880s. Small feeder lines like the Oregon Short Line and the Atchison, Topeka & Santa Fe fed into the great transcontinental systems, knitting the nation together.

But the lion's share of capital for the railroads came from investors in the United States and abroad.

After a brief lull during the Civil War, a frenzy of railroad building took place. America's first transcontinental railroad system was completed in 1869 when the Union Pacific and Central Pacific tracks came together in Promontory Point, Utah, and a golden spike was driven to commemorate the occasion. Between 1870 and 1880, the amount of track laid in the country doubled, and it nearly doubled again in the following decade. By 1900, the country boasted over 193,000 miles of track, more than all of Europe and Russia combined. Despite the great leaps in growth, the railroads were in no sense well organized or integrated. Early rail lines, with the exception of the first transcontinental, did not connect with one another, and trains ran on tracks that had not yet been standardized to the same size and width. More than one thousand separate lines sprang up, often built more for financial speculation than for transportation. Speculators profited from "watered stock"—that is, stock issued in excess of the actual assets of the railroads. As long as investors remained optimistic about the future, a boom mentality prevailed. Buyers could be found for the overvalued stock, and speculators turned huge profits.

Lack of planning soon led to overbuilding. Already by the 1870s, the railroads competed fiercely with one another for business on the eastern seaboard. A manufacturer who needed to get goods to the market and who was fortunate enough to be in an area served by a number of competing railroads could get a substantially reduced shipping rate in return for promising the railroad steady business. Because this kind of competition caused the railroad owners to lose money, they tried to set up agreements or "pools" to divide up territory and set rates. But these informal combinations invariably failed because they had no legal standing and be-

cause men like Jay Gould could not resist undermining their competitors.

In the 1880s, Gould moved to put together a second transcontinental railroad to compete with the Union Pacific and Central Pacific. His decision meant that other railroads had no choice but to defend their interests by adopting his strategy of expansion and consolidation. By the 1890s, large railway systems, including the Southern Pacific, the Northern Pacific, and the Atchison, Topeka, and Santa Fe railroads, dominated American rail travel.

The unsung heroes of the railroad business were the managers, accountants, and financial officers—men like Daniel L. McCallum of the Erie and J. Edgar Thomson of the Pennsylvania. They developed new cost accounting methods and business structures that enabled the railroads to run at a profit and gave new meaning to the term "big business." In the 1850s, even the largest textile mill employed only 800 workers, most often working in one town or even one factory. The Pennsylvania Railroad in 1874, by contrast, employed more than 55,000 workers and managers and controlled more than six thousand miles of track spanning half the continent. Capitalized at over $400 million, the Pennsylvania could boast that it was the largest private enterprise in the world. The challenges to business posed by such size contributed to the creation of new systems of organization and operation that transformed American business as firms grew from small partnerships to huge corporations.

A similar revolution in communications accompanied and supported the growth of the railroads. In the 1840s, Samuel F. B. Morse developed a code to send messages across electrical wire. Morse's intricate series of dots and dashes, tapped out on a single key, enabled telegraphers to send messages virtually instantaneously over the wires, thus giving the country its first national communication system. The telegraph marched across the continent with the railroad, on rights-of-way furnished by the rail lines themselves. Telegraph wires formed the nervous system of the new industrial order. They provided the instantaneous communication the railroads needed to control their far-flung networks in order to avoid accidents and improve efficiency. Here again, Jay Gould had a hand. By 1878, through stock manipulation he had gained control of Western Union, the company that monopolized the telegraph industry.

Not all the early railroad builders were as unscrupulous as Jay Gould. James J. Hill built the Great Northern and built it well. Without benefit of

LET THEM HAVE IT ALL, AND BE DONE WITH IT!

RAILROAD TYCOONS
This political cartoon appeared in Puck, *a magazine with a partisan Democratic bent. Here the railroad barons, notably Jay Gould and William Vanderbilt, are caricatured carving up the country with long knives. The power wielded by these railroad tycoons worried many who feared that their machinations were detrimental to small business, farmers, and labor.*
Culver Pictures.

land grants or subsidies, Hill had to plan carefully and calculate which areas would best be served by the railroad in order to maximize returns to his investors. As a result, the Great Northern was one of the few major railroads able to weather the hard times of the 1890s. In contrast, speculators like Daniel Drew and James Fisk, Gould's partners at the Erie, could more accurately be described as wreckers than as builders. They ruined the Erie Railroad, gambling with its stock to line their own pockets. In the West, the Big Four railroad builders—Collis P. Huntington, Richard Crocker, Leland Stanford, and Mark Hopkins—became so powerful that critics charged that the Southern Pacific held California in the grip of an "octopus."

The public's alarm at the control wielded by the new railroads provided a barometer of attitudes toward big business itself. When Jay Gould died in 1892, the press described him as "the world's richest man," estimating his fortune at over $100 million. His competitor, "Commodore" Cornelius Vanderbilt, who built the New York Central Railroad, judged Gould "the smartest man in America." But to the American public, who found in Gould a symbol of all that most troubled them about the rise of big business, he was, as he himself admitted shortly before his death, "the most hated man in America." Why? Many no doubt remembered Gould's arrogant attempt to corner the gold market in 1869. Anti-Semitism also played a role since many mistakenly believed Gould to be Jewish. And a dislike of men who made their money by speculation rather than by producing goods further clouded Gould's reputation. Yet by the time Gould died, more than 150,000 miles of railroad track stretched across the continent and no one could claim to have had a greater hand in its building than Jay Gould.

Andrew Carnegie and Vertical Integration

Railroad building led directly to the development of a second major industry—steel. The first railroads ran on iron rails, which cracked and broke with alarming frequency. Steel, stronger and more flexible than iron, remained too expensive for use in rails until an Englishman named Henry Bessemer developed a way to make steel from pig iron. After the Civil War, with the discovery of rich iron ore deposits near the Great Lakes, the Bessemer process came into use in America. Andrew Carnegie was among the first to champion the new "King Steel," and he came to dominate the emerging steel industry.

If Jay Gould was the man Americans loved to hate, Andrew Carnegie was one of America's heroes. The hatred toward the one man and the popularity of the other testified to the country's divided reaction to industrialism. Carnegie, a Scots immigrant, landed in New York in 1848 at the age of twelve. He rose from a job cleaning bobbins in a textile factory at $1.20 a week to become one of the richest men in America. Before he died, he gave away more than $300 million of his fortune, most notably to public libraries. His generosity, combined with his own rise from poverty, gave him a positive image with the public. But he had another side—that of a shrewd businessman capable of making harsh demands on those who worked for him.

Carnegie's swift rise seemed to support the popular myth promoted by author Horatio Alger, who maintained that in America any boy could become a millionaire. Readers devoured novels with titles like *Ragged Dick, Mark the Matchboy,* and *Pluck and Luck* in which intrepid young men rose, if not from rags to riches, at least from rags to respectability. Carnegie, like Alger's fictional heroes, owed his success to both pluck and luck. When he was still a teenager, his skill as a telegraph operator caught the attention of Tom Scott, then superintendent of the Pennsylvania Railroad. Scott hired the young Carnegie, soon promoted him, and lent him the money for his first investments. Carnegie's

ANDREW CARNEGIE
Andrew Carnegie, shown here in 1861, made a small fortune as a young man. In 1868, he totaled his assets. "Thirty three and an income of $50,000 per annum," he recorded. "Beyond this never earn — make no effort to increase fortune, but spend the surplus each year for benovelent [sic] purposes." Carnegie didn't stick to his plan. In 1872, he founded Carnegie Steel and went on to become one of the richest men in America, giving away an estimated $300 million to charitable causes before his death in 1919. Carnegie Library.

twelve years with the railroad furnished him with an unequaled education in business management, which he put to good use when he struck out on his own to reshape the iron and steel industries.

After making a small fortune in the stock market, he plunged into the steel business in 1872. "My preference was always manufacturing," he wrote at the age of twenty-seven. "I wished to make something tangible." By applying the lessons of cost accounting and efficiency that he had learned at the Pennsylvania Railroad, Carnegie turned steel into the nation's first manufacturing big business. In Braddock, on the outskirts of Pittsburgh, Pennsylvania, in 1872 he built the most up-to-date Bessemer steel plant in the world and began turning out steel at a furious rate. At that time, steelmakers were able to produce about seventy tons a week. Within two decades, Carnegie's blast furnaces poured out an incredible ten thousand tons a week. Using railroad accounting methods, he cut the cost of making rails in half, from $58 to $25 a ton. Carnegie's formula for success was simple: "Cut the prices, scoop the market, run the mills full; watch the costs and profits will take care of themselves." And they did. By 1900, Carnegie Steel earned $40 million in a single year.

To guarantee the lowest costs and the maximum output, Carnegie pioneered a system of business organization called vertical integration. All aspects of the business were under Carnegie's control. Vertical integration in steel meant, in the words of one observer, that "from the moment these crude stuffs were dug out of the earth until they flowed in a stream of liquid steel in the ladles, there was never a price, profit, or royalty paid to any outsider." Between 1875 and 1900, Carnegie sought to control every aspect of the steelmaking process, from the mining of iron ore to its transport on the Great Lakes to the production of crude steel and rails.

Always, Carnegie kept his eyes on the account books, looking for ways to cut costs and increase production. The great productivity that he encouraged came at a high price. He deliberately pitted his employees against one another, rewarding the winners with a small share in the company and firing the losers. His workers achieved the high productivity Carnegie demanded by enduring long hours, low wages, and dangerous working conditions. Steel workers toiled twelve hours a day in his Homestead plant, and when the shift changed every other week, they worked twenty-four hours at a stretch in the hazardous steel mills. Carnegie held an absolute majority of stock in his company and rarely paid dividends to his stockholders. Instead, he poured the profits back into new plants and new machinery. Even Carnegie's partners found his rule harsh.

Andrew Carnegie dominated the steel industry for three decades, building Carnegie Steel into an industrial giant, the largest steel producer in the world. Carnegie's steel built the first skyscraper in America, formed the skeleton of the Washington Monument, supported the elevated trains in Chicago and New York, and provided the superstructure for the Brooklyn Bridge. By the turn of the century, Andrew Carnegie had become the best-known manufacturer in the world and steel had replaced iron.

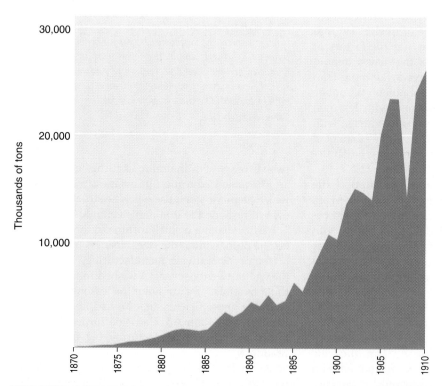

FIGURE 18.1
Iron and Steel Production in the U.S. 1870–1910
Iron and steel production in the U.S. grew from virtually nonexistent to ten million tons a year by 1900. In terms of steel production, the secret to the great increase was the use of the Bessemer process and the vertical integration pioneered by Andrew Carnegie. By 1900 Carnegie's mills alone produced more steel than all of Great Britain. With corporate consolidation after 1900, the rate of growth in iron and steel production was even more spectacular.

ADVERTISING IN THE GILDED AGE
Trade cards were an important form of early advertising. Agents handed them out to retailers and customers. In this early card advertising the H. J. Heinz Company, women bottle pickles wearing aprons and caps and looking clean, happy, and attractive. How accurately do you think the ad portrays the Heinz plant?
Collection of Sally Fox.

The Emergence of Mass Marketing

By the 1880s, the railroads made possible a national mass market for consumer goods. Manufacturers integrated methods of mass production with those of mass distribution to achieve the first big consumer businesses in America. These enterprises came to dominate many of the nation's most vital industries. Successful organizational changes in the meatpacking and food processing industries enabled manufacturers to reap huge profits from products like hot dogs and ketchup.

What Carnegie did for steel, Gustavus Swift did for meatpacking. Until well after the Civil War, cattle were transported out of the West on the hoof to be slaughtered by local butchers. Swift, who first visited Chicago in 1875 to buy beef for a Boston company, realized that it would be more efficient to slaughter cattle in the Midwest and transport the meat to the East in refrigerated railway cars. He put together a vertically integrated meatpacking business that controlled the entire process—from the purchase of cattle for slaughter to the mass distribution of meat to retailers and consumers. Swift pioneered the use of the refrigerated railroad car and warehouse, and, through high quality, low prices, and effective advertising, he won over consumers who at first worried about purchasing meat that had not been butchered locally. The success of Swift and Company led the older meatpackers, such as Philip Armour, to build similarly integrated businesses to compete with Swift, selling processed meat in the form of bologna and hot dogs.

Just as Swift combined mass production with mass distribution to revolutionize meatpacking, Henry John Heinz transformed the processed food industry. In 1880, Heinz was a local producer of pickles, sauces, and condiments. Operating outside of Pittsburgh, Heinz was still recovering from a bankruptcy brought on by the depression of the 1870s. In the 1880s, he adopted new, more efficient methods of canning and bottling and built a network of sales offices to advertise his fifty-seven varieties of condiments and sell them across the nation. To ensure a steady flow of vegetables and other foodstuffs into his factories, he created a large buying and storing organization to contract with local farmers. By 1888, Heinz had become one of Pittsburgh's wealthiest citizens, and ketchup had become an American staple. Using similar methods, other food processors, including Quaker Oats, Campbell Soup, and Borden Condensed Milk, coordinated mass production with mass distribution to produce low-priced, packaged consumer goods for the national market. Businesses in other industries, including tobacco, grain, matches, soap, and photography, integrated manufacturing and distribution to dominate their markets. Companies such as American Tobacco, Procter & Gamble, Quaker Oats, Pillsbury Flour, and Eastman Kodak are still a part of the American economy today.

Advertising played a vital role in helping new companies win a national audience. Just as the railroads made possible a national market, newspapers made possible advertising on a national scale. In its infancy, advertising bore little resemblance to the slick, sophisticated industry of today. Yesterday's ad agent neither wrote the copy nor selected the illustrative materials. All of that was done by the advertiser, the "client" in today's parlance. What the agent did was to buy and sell space in the newspapers. With more than eight thousand papers printed in the United States by 1876, few advertisers could afford the time away from their own businesses to learn the names and locations of the papers, let alone check the circulation figures and bargain for advertising space. The agent took on those tasks, accepting the advertiser's prepared copy and placing it in specified papers. The advertising agent was paid not by the advertiser directly but by the newspapers' publishers in the form of a commission, usually 15 to 25 percent of the cost of the space purchased. Given this anomalous position, an agent was hard put to say precisely whether he worked for the advertiser who hired him or the publisher who paid him. In practice most agents gave in to the temptation to increase their profits by getting from the advertisers all they could and paying the publishers as little as possible. The agents then pocketed the difference in addition to collecting their commissions.

Advertising in the Gilded Age suffered from its association with patent medicines, cure-alls for complaints ranging from dandruff to pneumonia. Products like Lydia E. Pinkham's Vegetable Compound, a "sure cure for female complaints," pioneered early advertising and made Lydia Pinkham a household name. Reputable firms scorned advertising because of its dubious claims. Professional ethics crafted by organizations like the American Medical Association prohibited members from plying their trade in print. But by the turn of the century, advertising and attitudes toward it had begun to change. As companies sought a larger share of the emerging national market, they turned to advertising to stimulate sales by extolling the virtues of their products. Ivory soap ("99.44% pure", "It floats"), Quaker oats ("The easy food"), and Coca-Cola ("The ideal brain tonic") cashed in on the growing trend toward national advertising. For their part, advertising agents became more reputable and responsible, increasingly writing ads as well as placing them. By the twentieth century, advertising had become an important part of the product package.

Rockefeller, Standard Oil, and the Trust

Edwin Drake's discovery of oil in Pennsylvania in 1859 sent thousands rushing to the oil fields in search of "black gold." In the days before the automobile and gasoline, crude oil was refined into lubricating oil for machinery and kerosene for lamps, a major source of lighting for nineteenth-century Americans in the age before electricity. Observing the difference between the price of the crude oil gushing from wells at fifty cents a barrel (forty-two gallons) and the kerosene sold in the East at fifty cents a gallon, smart investors turned to oil refining. The amount of capital needed to buy or build an oil refinery in the 1860s and 1870s remained relatively low, less than $25,000, or roughly what it cost to lay one mile of railroad track. Since investment cost was low, the story of the new petroleum industry was one of riotous competition among many small refineries. Ultimately, one man came to dominate oil refining through the use of a new organizational strategy called the trust. That man, John D. Rockefeller, eventually succeeded in controlling nine-tenths of the oil refining business through his Standard Oil Company.

John D. Rockefeller grew up the son of a shrewd Yankee doctor who peddled quack cures for cancer. Under his father's rough tutelage, he learned early how to drive a hard bargain. "I cheat my boys every time I get a chance," Big Bill Rockefeller boasted. "I want to make 'em sharp." John D. started as a book-

JOHN D. ROCKEFELLER
Like Andrew Carnegie, John D. Rockefeller made his fortune at a young age. Shown here in 1884, the year he moved his Standard Oil offices from Cleveland to New York City, Rockefeller was already a millionaire many times over. Nevertheless, as a newcomer to the big city, he looks at once wary and diffident.
Courtesy Rockefeller Archive Center.

keeper in Cleveland and owned his own business by the time he turned twenty-one. One of the secrets of his success lay in his ability to obtain loans. He borrowed and borrowed to build up his profits, making other people's money work for him. A taciturn young man with a devouring passion for business, Rockefeller hired a substitute to fight for him during the Civil War, as did Gould, Carnegie, and J. P. Morgan. By the time the fighting ended, Rockefeller had become a moderately wealthy man. In 1865, he bought out his partner with borrowed money and took control of the largest oil refinery in Cleveland. Like a growing number of businessmen, Rockefeller abandoned partnership or single pro-

prietorship to embrace the corporation as a business structure best suited to maximizing profit and minimizing personal liability. In 1870, he incorporated his oil business, founding the Standard Oil Company, the precursor of today's Exxon Corporation.

As the largest refiner in Cleveland, Rockefeller demanded rebates, or secret refunds, from the railroads. These rebates enabled him to undercut his competitors. The railroads wanted his business so badly that they not only gave him the rebates on his shipping fares but also granted him a share of the rates paid by his competitors. This devil's bargain meant that not only did Rockefeller ship his oil at fully a dollar a barrel cheaper on the average than his competitors, but he also received fully a dollar a barrel "rake-off" on every barrel his competitors shipped. Using this kind of leverage, Rockefeller soon pressured competing refiners to sell out to him or face ruin. By 1871, Standard Oil had conquered the petroleum business in Cleveland, and Rockefeller set his sights on the national market.

Cleveland, Pittsburgh, Philadelphia, New York City, and the oil region in Pennsylvania competed for top place in the petroleum business. By combining railroad rebates with efficient production, Standard Oil strengthened its position. Major refiners began to sell out. In a series of secret mergers, or combinations, they received stock in Standard Oil and continued to run their refineries as before under their own names. Often stubborn independents who refused to sell to Rockefeller unwittingly sold to companies that were secretly controlled by Standard Oil. Not until 1879, when a legislative committee in New York investigated railroad practices in the state, did the American people learn the extent of Standard Oil's hidden empire.

John D. Rockefeller served as a lightning rod for the nation's fear of industrial consolidation. Americans vilified him because they feared the vast power of the Standard Oil trust.

Secrecy was necessary because at first such combinations were illegal. Laws forbade one corporation from controlling another. But Standard Oil developed an organizational structure called the trust, which had the advantage of being legal. Several trustees held stock in the various refineries "in trust" for Standard's stockholders. The trust was a form of horizontal integration, which differed

VOL. XXIII. | All the News. Four Editions Daily. | NEW YORK, MONDAY, JULY 19, 1880. | $12 Per Year in Advance. Single Copies, Five Cents. | NO. 2280.

A HORRIBLE MONSTER,
WHOSE TENTACLES SPREAD POVERTY, DISEASE AND DEATH, AND WHICH IS THE PRIMAL CAUSE OF THE NUISANCES AT HUNTER'S POINT.

THE STANDARD OIL OCTOPUS
This 1880 cartoon from the New York Times *portrays the Standard Oil Company as an octopus, not for its monopolistic practices but for the dangerous pollution caused by its Hunter's Point, New York refinery. The environmental damage caused by burgeoning American industry rarely received the same attention the press and public focused on the trusts. Yet here is a graphic portrayal of the problems of pollution — houses rendered uninhabitable, boat passengers and diners forced to cover their faces to ward off noxious fumes, and a woman with an infant threatened by windborne "disease and death." Note the smokestacks spewing black clouds in the upper corners.*
Corbis-Bettmann.

markedly from Carnegie's vertical approach in steel. At first, Rockefeller did not attempt to control every aspect of the oil business from the crude oil at the well to the final product. Rather, he moved horizontally to control only the refining process by taking over virtually all the refineries. He used the trust to increase profits by controlling output, thus raising the price to the consumer. Because Standard Oil controlled so much of the market, it made a good target for people who argued that the trusts constituted a conspiracy against the public to extract private profit.

When the government threatened to outlaw the trust as a violation of free trade, Standard changed its tactics and in 1889 organized into a holding company. Holding companies operated in much the same way as trusts, but they were legal. Instead of competing companies entering into agreements to set prices and determine territories, the holding company simply combined competing companies under one central administration. New Jersey facilitated the development of the holding company by passing a law in 1889 that allowed corporations chartered in the state to hold stock in out-of-state ventures. Other businesses, such as Diamond Matches and the American Sugar Refining Company soon imitated Standard Oil's tactics, creating first trusts and later holding companies. By the 1890s, New Jersey had become the home of a number of holding companies, the largest of which was Standard Oil.

IDA TARBELL AND *MCCLURE'S*
Ida Tarbell's History of the Standard
Oil Company *ran in* McClure's
magazine for three years. Her revelations of the ruthless practices Rockefeller used to seize control of the oil industry convinced many readers that it was time for economic and political reforms to curb the power of big business. Tarbell grew up in the oil region and knew firsthand how Standard Oil forced out its competitors.
Culver Pictures; Corbis-Bettmann.

As Rockefeller's empire grew, central control became essential. Rockefeller moved to New York City in 1884. From his office at 26 Broadway he began to integrate Standard Oil vertically, even as he expanded horizontally. Through centralized control, Standard Oil ended the independence of the refinery operators and closed inefficient plants. Next Rockefeller moved to control sources of crude oil and took charge of the transportation and marketing of petroleum products. By the 1890s, Standard Oil controlled a vast, vertically integrated organization that was involved in every aspect of the petroleum business.

John D. Rockefeller enjoyed unequaled business success. Before he died in 1937, at the age of ninety-eight, he had become the country's first billionaire. For most of his adult life, he was unquestionably the richest man in America. But despite his modest habits, his pious Baptist faith, and his many charitable gifts, he never shared in the public affection that Carnegie enjoyed.

Journalist Ida M. Tarbell, whose *History of the Standard Oil Company* ran for three years (1902–1905) in serial form in *McClure's Magazine,* largely shaped the public's harsh view of Rockefeller. She had grown up in the Pennsylvania oil region, and her father had owned one of the small refineries gobbled up by Standard Oil. Her devastatingly thorough history chronicled the methods Rockefeller had used to gain control of the oil industry.

By the time she finished her story, Rockefeller slept with a loaded revolver by his bed to ward off would-be assassins. Standard Oil and the man who created it had become the symbol of heartless monopoly.

Rockefeller served as a lightning rod for the nation's fear of industrial consolidation. Americans vilified him because they feared the vast power of the Standard Oil trust. With its iron control of the market, its own secret codes and spy system, and its ruthless suppression of competition, the company Rockefeller created earned the title "the sovereign state of Standard Oil."

Electricity and the Telephone

Although Americans frequently disliked industrial giants like Rockefeller, they admired inventors. At the turn of the century, Thomas Alva Edison and Alexander Graham Bell became folk heroes. But no matter how dramatic the inventors or the inventions themselves were, the new electric and telephone industries they pioneered soon eclipsed their inventors and fell under the control of the bankers and the industrialists.

Alexander Graham Bell, a Scot with a passion to find a way to teach the deaf to speak, instead developed a way to transmit voice over wires—the telephone. The emperor of Brazil, dumbfounded by the telephone on display at the Philadelphia Centennial Exposition in 1876, cried out, "My God, it talks!" Bell's demonstration of the telephone immediately caught the attention of Western Union. But the telegraph company, momentarily distracted by a battle with Jay Gould, missed the opportunity to buy Bell's patent. Instead, American Bell, a company formed by the inventor in 1880, marketed the telephone under the skilled direction of a professional manager named Theodore N. Vail. Vail pioneered long lines, or long-distance telephone service, creating American Telephone and Telegraph (AT&T) to build the lines as a subsidiary of American Bell. In 1900, AT&T became the parent company of the system as a whole, controlling Western Electric, which manufactured and installed the equipment, and coordinating the Bell regional divisions. In practical terms, this complicated organizational structure meant that men and women could communicate not only locally in their towns and cities but across the country. And unlike a telegraph message, which had to be written out and taken to a telegraph station, sent over the wire, and then delivered by hand to

THE TELEPHONE IN THE HOME
The telephone achieved spectacular success, despite the daunting technical and marketing problems posed by a new technology that called for linking towns and cities by electrical wires to transmit voice. The number of phones soared from 310,000 in 1895 to over 1.5 million by 1900.
Corbis-Bettmann.

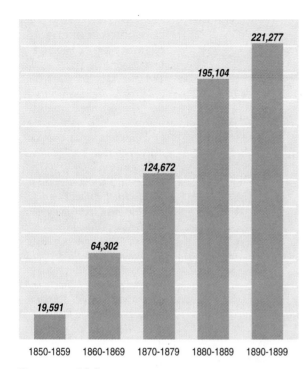

FIGURE 18.2
Patents Issued by Decade, 1850–1900
The second half of the nineteenth century was an age of invention, as witnessed by the striking increase each decade in the number of patents issued.

the recipient, the telephone connected both parties immediately and privately. Bell's invention proved a boon to business, contributing greatly to speed and efficiency.

Thomas Alva Edison embodied the old-fashioned virtues of Yankee ingenuity and rugged individualism that Americans most admired. A self-educated dynamo, he worked twenty hours a day in his laboratory in Menlo Park, New Jersey, vowing to turn out "a minor invention every ten days and a big thing every six months or so." He almost made good on his promise. At the height of his career, he averaged a patent every eleven days and invented such "big things" as the phonograph, the motion picture camera, and the electric lightbulb.

No industry that developed in the years following the Civil War faced a more difficult set of problems than electric light and power. Edison's development of a filament for the electric lightbulb in 1879 ushered in the age of electricity. But how was he to sell his wonderful invention? Before he could

begin marketing electric light and power, the inventor faced an enormous task. He had to develop an integrated system of conductors, power stations, generators, lamps, and electrical machines. And because electricity was so technically complex and so potentially dangerous, it demanded an entirely new system of marketing, one that relied on skilled engineers. At first the new industry depended on private generators. J. P. Morgan had electricity installed in his New York City mansion at 219 Madison Avenue in 1882, making it the first private home with electric lighting. An engineer visited the house daily to start the generator. When the lamp in Morgan's library short-circuited and set his desk on fire, the engineer promptly fixed the problem. Morgan, his faith in electricity restored, invested heavily in the Edison General Electric Company.

TABLE 18.1
NOTABLE AMERICAN INVENTIONS, **1850–1900**

Year	Invention
1851	Ice-making machine
1852	Elevator brake
1855	Gas burner
1857	Sewing machine
1860	Repeating rifle
1865	Web printing press
1865	Railroad sleeping car
1867	Typewriter
1867	Barbed wire
1868	Railroad refrigerator car
1869	Oleomargarine
1870	Stock ticker
1876	Telephone
1877	Phonograph
1879	Cash register
1882	Electric fan
1885	Adding machine
1886	Coca Cola
1888	Kodak camera
1889	Kinetoscope
1890	Electric chair
1891	Zipper
1895	Kellogg's Corn Flakes
1895	Safety razor
1896	Electric stove
1896	Ice cream cone
1899	Tape recorder
1900	Alkaline storage cells

AN UNRESTRAINED DEMON.

FEARS OF ELECTRICITY
Electricity was by no means a technology easy to sell, as this 1889 cartoon shows. Innocent pedestrians are electrocuted by the wires, a woman swoons, presumably as a result of the buzzing current, a horse and driver have collapsed, and a policeman runs for help. The skull in the wires attached to the electric lightbulb warns that this new technology is deadly. Ironically, inventor Thomas Alva Edison fueled the public's fears. In his battle with George Westinghouse over the virtues of direct versus alternating current, Edison repeatedly pointed to the dangers of electricity. Yet the gaslights it replaced posed risks of their own — gas leaks could cause explosions and fire.
The Granger Collection.

Edison worked steadily to build power stations and provide electric current. But his system had one major flaw—it relied on direct current, which could reach only two miles from a power station. Soon George Westinghouse, the inventor and manufacturer of the air brake for trains, experimented with alternating current, which could travel much greater distances. Westinghouse soon challenged Edison General Electric. Both companies created large, complex, vertically integrated enterprises to meet their unique marketing and distribution needs. They staffed sales offices with engineers trained to advise potential customers, safely install and operate equipment, and provide repair services. And they created research laboratories to find new uses for electricity. Despite Edison's protests, Westinghouse's superior alternating current became the accepted standard for electric power.

By 1900, electricity had become a part of American urban life. It powered trolley cars, subways, and factory machinery. It lighted homes, apartments, factories, and office buildings. Indeed, electricity became so prevalent in urban life that it became synonymous with the city, whose "bright lights" contrasted with a rural America, left largely in the dark. As late as the 1930s, only 10 percent of the nation's farms had electricity.

While Americans thrilled to the new electric cities, the day of the inventor quietly yielded to the heyday of the corporation. In 1892, J. P. Morgan consolidated the electric industry, selling Edison General Electric out from under its inventor and dropping Edison's name from the corporate title. The new General Electric Company, which was four times the size of Westinghouse, soon dominated the market.

TECHNOLOGY IN AMERICA
Vertical Transport: The Elevator

In 1890, for the first time a building in New York City exceeded the height of the steeple of Trinity Church in lower Manhattan. The Pulitzer Building gave New York its first skyscraper, a feat that would have been impossible without the development of vertical transport — the invention of the elevator.

The concept of the elevator was not new. As early as the Renaissance, Leonardo da Vinci had plans for one among his drawings, and by the mid-nineteenth century power elevators, often operated by steam, were used to convey materials in factories, mines, and warehouses. But not until Elisha Graves Otis perfected the "safety hoister" and patented it in the 1860s did the elevator become safe enough for people to use. Otis, a master mechanic in a bed factory, was an ambitious inventor who pioneered the safety elevator in a warehouse in Yonkers, New York. Otis devised an ingenious mechanism consisting of two metal pieces fastened to the elevator platform. If the rope or cable supporting the elevator broke, the metal pieces would spring out and stop the downward motion. In a dramatic demonstration at the Crystal Palace Exposition in New York in 1854, Otis cut the cable and proved the safety of his elevator.

Otis designed his first elevator to carry freight, but it was as a people mover that the elevator came into its own. The safety elevator transformed the value of urban real estate, making it possible to build into the air. As his son Charles later wrote, "I do not suppose that my father had the slightest conception at the time of what the outcome of this invention would be." Otis died in 1861 before his invention made him a fortune. His sons, who proved to be astute businessmen as well as skilled mechanics, founded the Otis Elevator Company and contin- ued to pioneer vertical transportation, developing the escalator in 1900. In 1898, Otis Elevator, capitalized at $11 million, was formed through the merger of eight other elevator companies. The company went on to become one of the greatest industrial enterprises in America as well as one of the first multinational companies. Otis Elevator, currently a subsidiary of United Technologies, continues to be the world leader in elevator sales and service with a revenue of $2 billion a year.

Archive United Technologies Corporation, Hartford, Conn., 06101.

From Competition to Consolidation

Even as industrial giants like Rockefeller and Carnegie built their empires, their days were numbered. Business increasingly developed into the anonymous corporate world of the twentieth century as as the corporation became the dominant form of business organization and as corporate mergers restructured American industry, replacing the great business titans with faceless boards of directors.

Already by the end of the nineteenth century, the corporation had begun to eclipse the partnership and sole proprietorship as the major form of American business. Corporations had the advantage of limited liability, which protected investors from losing their own assets should the company fail. A corporation could outlive its owners and was not prey to the vagaries that plagued family businesses where one generation could ruin a business painstakingly built by its predecessors. Corporations had the added advantage of separating ownership and management, placing the actual day-to-day running of the company in the hands of professional managers. Since the corporation could raise money by issuing stocks and bonds, the owners in most

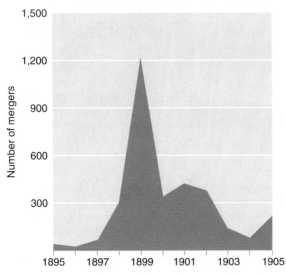

FIGURE 18.3
Merger Mania, 1890–1905
The depression of the 1890s fueled a "merger mania," as businesses consolidated and reorganized, often at the prompting of finance capitalists like J.P. Morgan. The number of mergers peaked in 1899 but continued into the first decade of the twentieth century.

cases were individual investors intent on making a profit and more than willing to leave management to elected boards of directors and operations to trained professionals. Also, because the law recognized the corporation as a "person" and granted it protection under the due process clause of the Fourteenth Amendment, it was difficult to regulate corporations through legislation. Last, corporations could buy out and control other corporate entities, and it was this power that came to dominate in the early twentieth century as businesses consolidated into ever larger corporate giants.

The merger mania that was apparent in the formation of Standard Oil and General Electric speeded up in the years between 1890 and 1903. When trusts came under fire, businesses consolidated into holding companies, as Standard Oil had done, to avoid prosecution. And as businesses foundered during the depression of the 1890s, many corporations went into bankruptcy courts where they were restructured, reorganized, and consolidated by court-appointed receivers. Banks and financiers played a key role in this consolidation, so much so that the era of the individual entrepreneur yielded to a new era of finance capitalism — investment sponsored by banks and bankers. The great banker J. P. Morgan took the lead in reshaping American business at the turn of the century, consolidating several major industries, including the railroads and steel. During these years, a new social philosophy based on the theories of Charles Darwin helped to justify consolidation and to inhibit state or federal regulation and control of business. The Supreme Court, a bastion of conservatism during this period, further proscribed attempts to control business by consistently declaring unconstitutional legislation designed to regulate railroad rates and to outlaw trusts and monopolies.

J. P. Morgan and Finance Capitalism

The great business leaders of the era loathed competition and sought whenever possible to substitute consolidation and central control. None had a greater passion for order, predictability, and profit than J. P. Morgan, the banker who became the architect of business consolidation. John Pierpont Morgan dominated the financial world of Wall Street. Aloof and silent, he looked down on the climbers and the speculators with a haughtiness that led his rivals to call him "Jupiter," after the Roman god. Physically, Morgan stood six feet tall, towering over Andrew Carnegie and Jay Gould, both of whom

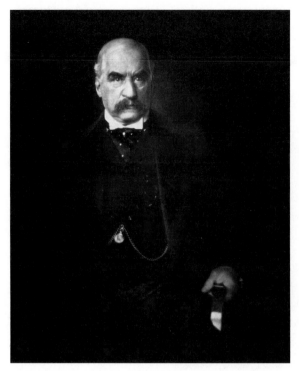

J. P. MORGAN, PHOTOGRAPH BY EDWARD STEICHEN
*Journalist Mark Sullivan wrote of financier J. P. Morgan,
"One thought of Morgan as of the bank buildings in
which he had his several thrones — structures impressing
the public (and designed to impress it), solid granite and
gold, marble and mahogany in every detail. He presented
no false facade to the public." Until the passage of the
Federal Reserve Act in 1913, Morgan functioned for all
intents and purposes as the bank of the United States. In
times of panic, two presidents would turn to him to intervene in order to avert financial disaster.*
Courtesy of George Eastman House, reprinted with permission of
Joanna T. Steichen.

were well under five feet five, the average height of
men at the time. Throughout his life, Morgan suffered from acne rosacea, which left him with a mis-
shapen strawberry of a nose. But it was his eyes that
people remembered—eyes so piercing that the
great photographer Edward Steichen observed that
"meeting his gaze was a little like confronting the
headlights of an express train." For three decades,
Morgan dominated American banking and finance,
exerting an influence so powerful that his critics
charged that he controlled a vast "money trust."

The son of a prominent banker, J. P. Morgan inherited along with his wealth the stern business
code of the old-fashioned merchant bankers, men
who valued character and reputation. From his own

age, Morgan absorbed some of the thrust and push
of enterprise. He moved investment banking into
the modern era, reaching out to reorganize business
and transform the stock market.

Morgan acted as a power broker in the reorganization of the railroads and the creation of industrial giants like General Electric and U.S. Steel.
When the railroads fell on hard times in the 1890s,
Morgan, with his passion for order and his access
to capital, took them in hand. He had already restructured the Baltimore and Ohio, the Reading,
and the Chesapeake and Ohio Railroads in the
1880s. After 1893, he added the Santa Fe, the Erie,
the Northern Pacific, and the Southern Railroads to
his list. In 1901, he crowned his achievement by
helping to create the Northern Securities Company,
a supersystem designed to bring peace between the
warring Great Northern and Northern Pacific Railroads. Other investment bankers managed similar
railroad reorganization, but none on the scale of
J. P. Morgan.

Morgan eliminated competition between the
railroads by creating a "community of interest"
among the managers, men he handpicked. Often,
Morgan partners sat on the boards of competing
firms, forming interlocking directorates. By the time
Morgan was finished, seven major groups controlled two-thirds of the nation's railroad mileage.

Banker control of the railroads rationalized, or
coordinated, the industry. But peace came at a high
price. Morgan heavily "watered" the stock of the
railroads, issuing new stock lavishly to keep old
investors happy and to guarantee huge profits.
Morgan's firm made millions of dollars from commissions and from blocks of stock acquired through
reorganization. The flagrant overcapitalization created by the watered stock hurt the railroads in the
long run, saddling them with enormous debts.
Equally harmful was the management style of the
Morgan directors who ran the railroads. They were
not railroad men. They looked at the railroads from
a banker's viewpoint, "as a group of men and a set
of books." Their conservatism discouraged the continued technological and organizational innovation
needed to run the railroads effectively.

In 1898, Morgan moved into the steel industry.
The story of his acquisition of Carnegie Steel is the
story of the passing of one age and the coming of a
new one. The era of the individual entrepreneur was
ending, and in its place came the rise of the huge
corporation. Carnegie represented the old order,
Morgan the new. As he began to challenge Carnegie's
control, Morgan supervised the mergers of several

THE HOMESTEAD STEEL MILL
The Homestead steel works outside of Pittsburgh, Pennsylvania, was just one of the mills J. P. Morgan purchased from Andrew Carnegie in 1900 for $480 million. Morgan's acquisition led to the creation of the country's first billion-dollar corporation, U.S. Steel, known today as USX.
Hagley Museum and Library.

smaller steel companies, which soon began to integrate vertically by moving from the manufacture of finished goods into steel production. Carnegie, who for decades had controlled the production of crude steel, countered by creating a new plant for the manufacture of finished products such as tubing, nails, wire, and hoops. A pugnacious Carnegie cabled his partners in the summer of 1900: "Action essential: crisis has arrived . . . have no fear as to the result; victory certain."

The era of the individual entrepreneur was ending, and in its place came the rise of the huge corporation. Carnegie represented the old order, Morgan the new.

The press trumpeted news of the impending fight between the feisty little Scot and the haughty Wall Street banker, but the "battle of the giants" in the end proved little more than the wily maneuvering of two businessmen so adept that even today it is difficult to say who won. The sixty-six-year-old Carnegie, for all his belligerence, yearned to retire to Skibo Castle, his home in Scotland, and may well have invited Morgan's bid for power. Surely

Carnegie knew that Morgan was probably the only individual who commanded the capital to buy him out. When a go-between sought out Carnegie on the golf course and asked him to name his price, Carnegie scrawled a number in pencil on his scorecard. Hurrying to Morgan's office, the intermediary handed him the scrap of paper. Morgan, who disdained haggling, glanced at it and said, "I accept this price." Without blinking an eye, Morgan had agreed to pay $480 million for Carnegie Steel. Carnegie's personal share alone amounted to more than $250 million. According to legend, when Carnegie later teased Morgan, saying that he should have asked $100 million more, Morgan had the last word: "You would have got it if you had."

Morgan quickly moved to pull together Carnegie's chief competitors to form a huge new steel corporation, United States Steel, known today as USX. U.S. Steel, created in March 1901, became America's first billion-dollar corporation. Capitalized (some said grossly overcapitalized) at $1.4 billion, U.S. Steel was the largest corporation in the world. Yet for all its size, it did not hold a monopoly in the steel industry. Significant small competitors such as Bethlehem Steel remained independent, creating a competitive system called an oligopoly, in which several large combinations, not one alone, controlled production. Other industries, such as electricity and meatpacking, were also oligopolies. Businesses in the new oligopolies seldom competed by cutting prices, as older businesses had done. Instead, the smaller firms simply followed the lead of giants like U.S. Steel in setting prices and dividing the market so that each business held a comfortable share. Although oligopoly did not entirely eliminate competition, it did effectively blunt it.

When J. P. Morgan died in 1913, his estate totaled $68 million, not counting an estimated $50 million in art treasures. Andrew Carnegie, who gave away more than $300 million before his death six years later, is said to have quipped, "And to think he was not a rich man!" But Carnegie's gibe missed the mark. The quest for power, not wealth, characterized J. P. Morgan, and his power could best be measured not in the millions he owned, but in the billions he controlled. Morgan, even more than Carnegie or Rockefeller, left his stamp on twentieth-century America. When the country faced bankruptcy in 1895, it was Morgan to whom the president turned. And as the reorganizer of America's railroads and the creator of U.S. Steel, General Electric, and other large combinations, Morgan ushered in the era of oligopoly that has continued to characterize twentieth-century American business.

Social Darwinism and the Gospel of Wealth

John D. Rockefeller Jr., the son of the founder of Standard Oil, once told his Baptist Bible class that the Standard Oil Company, like the American Beauty rose, resulted from "pruning the early buds that grew up around it." The elimination of smaller, inefficient units was, he said, "merely the working out of a law of nature and a law of God."

The comparison of the business world to the natural world formed the backbone of a new theory of society based on the "law of evolution" formulated by British scientist Charles Darwin. In his monumental work *On the Origin of Species,* published in 1859, Darwin theorized that in the struggle for survival, the process of adaptation to environment triggered a natural selection process among species that led to evolutionary progress. In the late nineteenth century, Herbert Spencer in Britain and William Graham Sumner in the United States developed a theory called social Darwinism. Applying Darwin's teachings to human society, they concluded that progress came about as a result of relentless competition in which the strong survived and the weak died out.

In social terms, the doctrine of "survival of the fittest" had profound significance, as Sumner, a professor of political economy at Yale University, made clear in his 1883 book *What Social Classes Owe to Each Other.* "The drunkard in the gutter is just where he ought to be, according to the fitness and tendency of things," Sumner insisted. Any efforts by one class to aid another only tampered with the rigid laws of nature and slowed down evolution.

In an age when men like Rockefeller and Carnegie amassed hundreds of millions of dollars while the average worker earned $500 a year, social Darwinism justified economic inequality.

Social Darwinism's insistence that human interference hampered evolutionary progress acted as a strong curb to reform at the same time that it glorified great wealth. In an age when men like Rockefeller, Carnegie, Morgan, and Vanderbilt amassed hundreds of millions of dollars while the average worker earned $500 a year, social Darwinism justified economic inequality.

Andrew Carnegie, like most businessmen, never fully grasped social Darwinism, but he welcomed a philosophical system that placed money-making beyond good and evil and gave it scientific backing. In 1889 in his book *The Gospel of Wealth,* Carnegie offered his own American adaptation of social Darwinism. The millionaire, Carnegie insisted, acted as a "mere trustee and agent for his poorer brethren, bringing to their service his superior wisdom, experience, and ability to administer, doing for them better than they could or would do for themselves." Carnegie broke with rigid social Darwinists like Sumner, who rejected philanthropy as harmful to evolutionary progress. Instead, Carnegie preached the duty of the rich to "live unostentatious lives" and "administer surplus wealth for the good of the people." For Carnegie, whose vanity was nearly as big as his pocketbook, an element of self-promotion colored his charities; the public libraries he so generously endowed each contained a portrait of the donor. His Gospel of Wealth earned him much praise but converted few followers. J. P. Morgan, for example, though he gave to worthy causes, preferred to hoard private treasures in his marble library rather than to distribute his wealth as Carnegie counseled.

Social Darwinism and the Gospel of Wealth nicely suited an age in which the baffling changes accompanying industrialization seemed to cry out for some rational explanation. According to social Darwinism, the success of huge industries and great industrialists was a sign of their superiority and therefore inevitable. Social Darwinism claimed that to interfere with natural law would only slow evolutionary progress. This inflexible "law" assuaged the individual's conscience and made it possible to neglect the poor in the name of "race progress." When the poor were different—new immigrants, poor blacks—as they so often were, social Darwinism smacked of racism. This ugly aspect was never far from social Darwinist ideology, which judged Anglo-Saxons superior to all other groups. Carnegie's Gospel of Wealth, by stressing the responsibilities of the rich, replaced the pitiless social laws of Spencer with a doctrine that was more acceptable to American tastes. But either way, social Darwinism provided a comfortable system of belief that justified wealth and success.

Laissez-faire and the Courts

At first glance it seems ironic that William Graham Sumner, who so often sounded like an apologist for the rich, incurred the wrath of wealthy Yale alumni. But in 1890, they almost succeeded in getting him fired. The problem was that strict social Darwinists like Sumner insisted absolutely that the government ought not to meddle in the economy, subscribing to a doctrine called laissez-faire (literally, "let it alone"). In practice, Sumner opposed protective tariffs, which levied duties on imported goods to raise their prices so that they could not compete effectively with American products. Sumner rightly judged tariffs as government intervention in the market. His sharp attacks on the high tariffs angered Yale's alumni, who were not troubled by the discrepancy between theory and practice. While in theory laissez-faire constrained the government from playing an active role in business affairs, in practice businessmen fought for government favors—whether tariffs, land grants, or subsidies—that helped business. Only when it came to taxes or regulation were they quick to cry laissez-faire.

Business found a strong ally in the U.S. Supreme Court. During the 1880s and 1890s, the Court increasingly reinterpreted the Constitution to protect business from taxation, regulation, labor organization, and antitrust legislation. In a series of landmark decisions, the Court used the Fourteenth Amendment, originally intended to protect freed slaves from state laws violating their rights, to protect corporations. The Fourteenth Amendment declares that no state can "deprive any person of life, liberty, or property, without due process of law." By defining corporations as "persons" under the law, the Court determined that legislation designed to regulate corporations deprived them of "due process." Using this reasoning, the Court struck down state laws regulating railroad rates, declared income tax unconstitutional, and judged labor unions a "conspiracy in restraint of trade." In the face of the host of economic and social dislocations caused by industrialism, the Court insisted on elevating the rights of property over the rights of people. According to Justice Stephen J. Field, the Constitution "allows no impediments to the acquisition of property." Field, born to a wealthy family and educated at the best schools of his day, spoke with the bias of the privileged class to whom property rights were sacrosanct. Imbued with this ideology, the Court refused to impede corporate consolidation and did nothing to curb the excesses of corporate capitalism.

Party Politics in an Age of Enterprise

Writing of the late-nineteenth-century presidents, the novelist Thomas Wolfe observed, "Garfield, Arthur, Harrison, and Hayes, for me they were the lost Americans: Their gravely vacant and be-whiskered faces mixed, melted, swam together in the sea depths of a past intangible, immeasurable, and unknowable." Why do the great industrialists like Rockefeller, Morgan, and Carnegie jump vividly from the pages of the past while the presidents of that period remain so pallid? The answer rests in the relative weakness of the presidency and the federal government in the administrations between Abraham Lincoln (1861–1865) and Theodore Roosevelt (1901–1909). After the Civil War, power shifted from the government in Washington to leaders in business and industry. This waning of federal power in peacetime became a persistent pattern in American government interrupted only by the activism that accompanied the progressive movement in the first decade of the twentieth century and that emerged later in the Great Depression of the 1930s.

The presidents from Rutherford B. Hayes (1877–1881) to Grover Cleveland (1885–1889, 1893–1897) are indeed forgotten men, largely because so little was expected of them. Until the 1890s, few Americans seemed to think the president or the national government had any role in addressing the problems accompanying the industrial transformation of the nation. The dominant creed of laissez-faire, coupled with the dictates of social Darwinism, warned government to leave business alone: Intervention to soften even the most evil effects of industrialization would only slow evolutionary progress. This crippling view of the rights and responsibilities of the federal government in the economy and in society reduced it to something of a sideshow. The real action took place elsewhere—in party politics on the local and state levels and in the centers of business and industry.

Nevertheless, important changes transformed American political life in the decades following the Civil War, as industrialism replaced sectionalism as the driving force in national politics. The corruption and abuses associated with party politics produced civil service reform. By the 1880s, important economic issues such as the protective tariff, the currency, and federal regulation of the trusts and the railroads moved to the forefront. The presidents, for their part, were competent though not charismatic men who worked to bring the nation together after decades of sectional strife and to create one nation with a unified political life.

Politics and Culture

There is some irony when we observe that the voters of the day swarmed to the polls in record numbers to elect presidents who today seem so colorless. Voter turnout in the three decades following the Civil War averaged a hefty 80 percent, compared with a turnout of 49 percent in 1996. Why were voters then so eager to cast their ballots?

The answer lies in the role politics played in the culture of the late nineteenth century. Political parties used state, local, and federal jobs to reward voters for their support. Many voters owed their livelihood to party bosses. Political affiliation also provided a sense of group identity for many participants proud of their loyalty to the Democrats or the Republicans. Moreover, politics constituted one of the chief forms of entertainment for voters and nonvoters alike in an age before mass recreation and amusement. Political parties sponsored parades, rallies, speeches, picnics, torchlight processions, and Fourth of July fireworks, attracting millions of Americans. Outside the big cities, only religious revivals and traveling shows could compete.

Electoral politics, like tobacco, remained exclusively a male pursuit. Women did not vote until the 1890s and then in only four western states: Wyoming (1890), Colorado (1893), and Utah and Idaho (1896). Elsewhere, they continued to fight for suffrage by campaigning for state referenda across the nation. And, increasingly in the 1890s, politics became limited to white males only. Although black men gained the vote during Reconstruction, the withdrawal of federal troops from the South in 1877 led to a massive deterioration in black voters' power.

> *Until the 1890s, few Americans seemed to think the president or the national government had any role in addressing the problems accompanying the industrial transformation of the nation. . . . The real action took place elsewhere—in party politics on the local and state levels and in the centers of business and industry.*

The Democratic Party, which traced its roots to Thomas Jefferson and Andrew Jackson, and the Republican Party of Abraham Lincoln remained the two dominant political forces after the Civil War. The parties vied vigorously for voter support, and most voters showed a strong party identification. Party loyalty in industrial America, however, had little to do with economic issues. Rather, it served to reinforce the cultural identity formed by allegiance to a region or to an ethnic or religious group.

After the end of Reconstruction, the old Confederate South voted Democratic in every election for the next seventy years. Labeling the Republican Party the agent of "Negro rule," Democrats urged white Southerners to "vote the way you shot." Opposing the "solid South" was the Republican Northeast, with nearly enough electoral votes to guarantee control of the presidency. To preserve Republican rule, the party had to carry key states such as Ohio, Indiana, and New York and had to prevent an alliance from developing between the agricultural South and the West. Republican politicians, like their Democratic rivals, encouraged sectional divisions by emotional appeals to the Civil War, a tactic known as "waving the bloody shirt," which had been used effectively in the election of 1868 and continued to rouse voters. Strong Unionist states in the Midwest responded by voting consistently Re-

*Decrease because of expansion of eligibility with the enfranchisement of 18- to 21-year olds.

FIGURE 18.4
Voter Turnout 1868–1900 and 1968–1996
Despite the weakness of the presidency and the largely undistinguished men who filled the office, voters turned out in record numbers to vote in the late 19th century elections. Compare the robust rate of participation to the anemic turnout in the late 20th century elections. What factors do you think account for the change?

publican. "Iowa will go Democratic," one observer joked, "when Hell goes Methodist." Veterans of the Grand Army of the Republic formed an important base for the Republican Party, which rewarded their loyalty with generous pensions. By 1886, an astounding one-quarter of the federal budget went to pensions, not a penny of that to ex-Confederates.

Religion and ethnicity also played a significant role in politics. In the North, Protestants from the old-line denominations, particularly Presbyterians and Methodists, were drawn to the Republican Party, which championed a series of moral reforms such as temperance, the campaign against alcoholic beverages. The Democratic Party courted immigrants and attracted Catholic and Jewish voters by consistently opposing laws to close taverns and other businesses on Sunday and by charging that crusades against liquor only masked attacks on immigrant culture.

The power of the two major parties remained about equally divided throughout the 1870s and 1880s and into the 1890s. Although the Republicans captured the White House in four out of five elections, they rarely controlled the Congress. The Dem-

ocrats, noted more for their local appeal than for their national unity, for the most part dominated the U.S. House of Representatives.

During this period, senators were not directly elected by the voters but were selected by state legislatures. In an era noted for its tolerance of all but the most flagrant bribery and corruption, state legislatures frequently came under the influence of powerful business interests. In *Wealth against Commonwealth* (1894), his book on the Standard Oil Company, journalist Henry Demarest Lloyd wrote, "The Standard has done everything with the Pennsylvania legislature except to refine it." Senators were often closely identified with business interests, as in the case of Nelson Aldrich, the powerful Republican from Rhode Island. Aldrich, whose daughter married John D. Rockefeller Jr., did not object to being called "the senator from Standard Oil."

Corruption and Party Strife

The political corruption and party factionalism that were characteristic of the administration of Ulysses S. Grant (1869–1877) continued to trouble the nation in the 1880s. The spoils system—the awarding of jobs for political purposes—remained the driving force of party politics. The concept of ethics in government, precluding private individuals from getting rich from public office, remained an issue raised only by a small band of reformers during this period. Most respectable Americans viewed politics as a sordid business; corruption at the ballot box and in public office came to be taken for granted.

President Rutherford B. Hayes, whose disputed election in 1876 marked the end of Reconstruction in the South, proved to be a hardworking, well-informed executive who wanted peace, prosperity, and an end to party strife. Although he was ridiculed by the Democratic press as "Rutherfraud" and "His Fraudulency," Hayes was a figure of honesty and integrity who seemed well suited to his role as a national leader. But it was not an easy task. The Republican Party remained divided into factions led by strong party bosses who boasted that they could make or break a president.

The three Republican factions bore the colorful names Stalwarts, Half-Breeds, and Mugwumps. The Stalwarts, led by Senator Roscoe Conkling of New York, remained loyal to Grant and consequently carried with them the taint of corruption from the scandals of his administration. Opposing them were the Half-Breeds, led by Senator James G. Blaine of Maine, a group that was only slightly less corrupt in its pursuit of spoils. Standing against both factions was a small but prominent group of liberal Republican reformers, mostly from Massachusetts and New York, whose critics later dubbed them Mugwumps. The name came from an Indian chief of the Algonquian but was used derisively by those who insisted that the Mugwumps straddled the fence on issues of party loyalty, "with their mug on one side and wump on the other." Often Mugwumps were men of influence like former abolitionist and Union general Carl Schurz and E. L. Goodkin, editor of the *Nation*. They were eager to reform government and put it in the hands of competent, honest men like themselves. In their pursuit of reform, they largely evaded the complex and divisive economic issues of the day and called instead for the purification of the government through civil service reforms designed to set standards for officeholders and put an end to the spoils system.

President Hayes, despite his virtues, soon managed to alienate his party. A realist, he used federal patronage to build Republican strength by selecting for government jobs if not the best men, the best Republicans he could find. To the Stalwarts, who wanted more positions, his action constituted betrayal; to the Mugwumps, it smacked too much of the spoils system. Hayes soon found himself a man without a party and announced that he would not seek reelection in 1880.

The power of party bosses like Blaine and Conkling more than matched the limited power of the president. Fiery and dynamic leaders, they dominated national politics. The imperious Conkling combined in equal mixture vanity, brilliance, and petulance. Known for his biting insults and his close association with corporate interests, he had nothing but contempt for the Mugwumps. He ridiculed "snivel service" reform. "Parties," he lectured, "are not built up by deportment, or by ladies' magazines, or gush!" His archrival Blaine was a magnetic Irish American politician whose followers dubbed him the "Plumed Knight," and supported him so enthusiastically that they were called "Blainiacs." Blaine opposed the flagrant corruption of the Stalwarts but was himself tarnished by certain shady dealings in railroad bonds. They had come to light with the publication of a set of incriminating letters bearing the ominous but ignored warning "Burn this letter." More careless than criminal in his business dealings, Blaine, like so many in his era, drew no fine distinction between public service and private gain. The shadow of corruption would cost him the Republican nomination in 1880 and the presidency in 1884.

In 1880, the Republicans resisted Stalwart attempts to bring Grant back and passed over Blaine to nominate a dark horse candidate, Representative James A. Garfield from Ohio. To appease Conkling, they chose a Stalwart, Chester A. Arthur of New York, as vice presidential candidate. The Democrats made an attempt to break down sectionalism and establish a national party by selecting as their presidential standard-bearer the old Union general Winfield Scott Hancock. But as one observer noted, "It is a peculiarly constituted party which sends rebel brigadiers to Congress because of their rebellion, and which nominated a Union General as its candidate for president because of his loyalty." Although the popular vote was close, Garfield won 214 electoral votes to Hancock's 155.

Garfield, Guiteau, and Civil Service Reform

Government bureaucracy grew in the years following the Civil War until nearly 150,000 jobs existed on the federal payroll. The spoils system proved a poor way to select qualified individuals to serve as the clerks, civil engineers, and trained professionals needed in the new government posts. Politicians from the president down were tormented by a steady stream of office seekers. Critics soon called for civil service reform designed to mandate examinations and establish a merit system to screen applicants for government jobs. The cry for qualified employees was both an earnest attempt to be sure the "best men" served the government as well as a veiled attack on the increasing ethnic diversity in American politics. The struggle for civil service reform would come to a head with the assassination of President James Garfield.

"My God," President Garfield swore after only a few months in office, "what is there in this place that a man should ever want to get into it?" Garfield, like Hayes, faced the difficult task of remaining independent while pacifying the bosses and placating the reformers. To an indecisive man like Garfield, the presidency was a torment. He found the task of dispensing federal patronage grueling and distasteful. More than 140,000 federal jobs, not counting those in the military, needed filling. Thousands of office seekers swarmed to the nation's capital, each clamoring for a place. In an era before presidents received Secret Service protection, the White House door stood open to all comers. Garfield took a fatalistic view. "Assassination," he told a friend, "can no more be guarded against than death by lightning, and it is best not to worry about either."

On July 2, 1881, less than four months after taking office, Garfield was shot in the back at a Washington, D.C., railroad station while catching a train. His assassin, Charles Guiteau, though clearly insane, was a disappointed office seeker who claimed to be motivated by political partisanship. He told the police officer who arrested him, "I did it; I will go to jail for it; Arthur is president, and I am a Stalwart." Garfield lingered on through the hot summer while the nation held a long deathbed vigil. He died on September 19, 1881.

The press almost universally condemned the Stalwarts, if not for inspiring Guiteau, then for creating the political climate that produced him. Ironically, Guiteau's bullets led to the downfall of the very faction that he claimed to support. Stalwart leader Roscoe Conkling, who came under heavy attack for his partisanship in the wake of the assassination, had to give up his presidential ambitions and retire to a career in corporate law. Attacks on

the spoils system increased, as did a rising public demand for civil service reform. But though Garfield's death crystallized the desire for civil service reform, the debate was long and hard. Many of those who opposed reform recognized that civil service had built-in class and ethnic biases. They knew that when Mugwumps spoke of government run by the "best men," they meant men of their own class. Just as Irish Americans were beginning to carve out a place for themselves in local and state politics, civil service threatened to turn government back over to an educated Yankee elite. At a time when few men had more than a grammar school education, office seekers did not relish the prospect of written civil service examinations. One opponent argued, "George Washington could not have passed examination for a clerkship," noting that "in his will written by his own hand, he spells clothes, cloathes."

The legislation that established civil service reform—the Pendleton Act—passed in 1883, after more than a year of congressional debate and compromise. Both parties claimed credit for the act, which established a permanent Civil Service Commission of three members, appointed by the president. Some 14,000 jobs were placed under a merit system that required examinations for office and made it impossible to remove jobholders for political reasons. Half of the postal jobs and most of the customhouse jobs, the lion's share of the spoils system's bounty, passed to the control of the Civil Service Commission. The new law sought to prohibit federal jobholders from contributing to political campaigns, thus drying up a major source of the party bosses' revenue. Soon business interests replaced officeholders as the nation's chief political contributors. Ironically, civil service reform thus gave business an even greater influence in political life than it already had.

"Chet Arthur, president of the United States! Good God!" incredulous men exclaimed on hearing of Garfield's death. Surely little in his background made Chester A. Arthur seem like a man suited for the highest office in the country. Only four years earlier, he had been dismissed from his position in the customhouse in New York because of his close association with corrupt politicians. But as president, he quickly dispelled the nation's fears and acted independently, signing the Pendleton Act that his fellow Stalwarts had so long opposed. Arthur himself had little "faith in reform" but knew enough of politics not to stand in the path of public sentiment. Beyond civil service he did little, other than to refurbish the White House at his own expense and in keeping with his bachelor taste (he added a billiard room in the basement). As Carl Schurz observed, "whenever Arthur did a creditable thing, people would say, 'He is after all a better man than we thought he was.'" Arthur surprised his critics by turning out to be a competent president, but his was a lackluster administration. The Republicans quickly looked to Blaine to bear the party standard in 1884.

The Political Circus: The Campaign of 1884

With the downfall of Conkling and the Stalwarts, Blaine assumed leadership of the Republican Party and at long last captured the presidential nomination in 1884. But to many reformers, the Plumed Knight personified corruption. Led by Carl Schurz, who insisted that Blaine "wallowed in spoils like a rhinoceros in an African pool," the Mugwumps bolted the party and embraced the Democratic presidential candidate, the stolid Grover Cleveland, reform governor of New York. The burly, beer-drinking Cleveland distinguished himself from an entire generation of politicians by the simple motto "A public office is a public trust." First as mayor of Buffalo and later as governor of New York, he built a solid reputation for honesty, economy, and administrative efficiency. He soon alienated the Tammany Hall political machine; but with reform in the air, the enemies he made only added to his appeal. The Democrats, who had not won the presidency since 1856, rushed to nominate him. As was expected, Cleveland received the enthusiastic endorsement of the Mugwumps, who announced that "the paramount issue this year is moral rather than political."

They would soon regret their words. The 1884 contest degenerated into nasty mudslinging. One disgusted journalist styled it "the vilest campaign ever waged." Grover Cleveland, whatever his reform virtues, made an easy target. In July, his hometown paper, the Buffalo *Telegraph*, dropped the bombshell that the bachelor candidate had fathered an illegitimate child in an affair with a widow named Maria Halpin. The crestfallen Mugwumps tried to argue the difference between public and private morality. But robbed of their moral righteousness, they lost much of their enthusiasm. "Now I

fear it has resolved itself into a choice of two evils," one weary reformer confessed.

At public rallies, Blaine's partisans taunted Cleveland, chanting:

> Ma, ma, where's my pa?
> Going to the White House
> ha! ha! ha!

Cleveland supporters roared back:

> Blaine, Blaine, James G. Blaine
> Continental liar from the State of Maine
> Burn this letter!

The stoic Cleveland admitted responsibility for his illegitimate child. Silent but fuming, he waged his campaign in the traditional fashion by staying home. Blaine broke precedent by making a national tour. On a last-minute stop in New York, the exhausted candidate overlooked a remark by a local clergyman—and he may have lost the election as a result. The Reverend Samuel Burchard, while introducing Blaine, blasted the Democrats as the party of "Rum, Romanism, and Rebellion." An Associated Press correspondent hurriedly filed his story, crying, "If anything will elect Cleveland, these words will do it." By linking drinking and Catholicism, Burchard's unfortunate remark cast a slur on Irish Catholic voters, who had been counted on to desert the Democratic Party and support Blaine because of his Irish background.

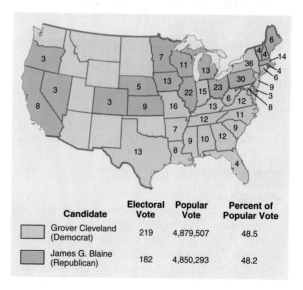

Candidate	Electoral Vote	Popular Vote	Percent of Popular Vote
Grover Cleveland (Democrat)	219	4,879,507	48.5
James G. Blaine (Republican)	182	4,850,293	48.2

MAP 18.2
The Election of 1884

With less than a week to go until the election, Blaine had no chance to recover from the negative publicity. He lost New York State by less than 1,200 votes and with it the election, although the vote was so close that the outcome remained uncertain for several days. In the final tally, the Democrats ended twenty-five years of Republican rule, defeating Blaine by a scant 30,000 votes nationwide, but winning 219 electoral votes to 182. Cleveland's followers had the last word:

> Hurrah for Maria! Hurrah for the kid!
> I voted for Cleveland,
> And Damned glad I did!

ANTI-CLEVELAND POSTER, 1888

In this early example of negative campaign advertising, Republicans pillory Democratic President Grover Cleveland as an advocate of free trade, while dredging up the image of his illegitimate child, which had proved such a scandal in the 1884 campaign. The bottom lines echo the earlier campaign ditty "Ma Ma, Where's My Pa?" In this election the tariff became a potent issue, winning support from business and labor and helping to elect Republican Benjamin Harrison.
Collection of David J. and Janice L. Frent.

Economic Issues and Party Realignment

Four years later, in the election of 1888, fickle voters would turn Cleveland out, electing Republican Benjamin Harrison, the grandson of President William Henry Harrison. Then, in the only instance in America's history when a president who had been defeated at the polls was returned to office, the voters brought Cleveland back in the election of 1892. What factors account for such a surprising turnaround? The strengths and weaknesses of the men themselves partially determined the outcome. The stubborn Cleveland, newly married to Frances Folsom in 1886, resented demands on his time and refused to campaign in 1888. Although he won more votes than Harrison, he lost the electoral college. Once in office, Harrison proved to be a cold and distant leader. His critics called him "the human iceberg." But issues as well as personalities increasingly swayed the voters. The 1880s witnessed a remarkable political realignment as a new set of economic concerns replaced the Civil War rhetoric of carpetbaggers, rebels, and the bloody shirt. The tariff, federal regulation of the railroads and trusts, and the campaign for free silver restructured American politics.

The Tariff and the Politics of Protection

The concept of a protective tariff to raise the price of imported goods and stimulate American industry dated back to Alexander Hamilton in the founding days of the Republic. Congress enacted the first tariff following the War of 1812. The Republicans turned the tariff to political ends by enacting a measure in 1861 that rewarded their industrial supporters who wanted protection from foreign competition at the same time that it raised revenues for the Civil War. After the war, the Republicans continued to revise and enlarge the tariff at the prompting of northeastern industrialists. By the 1880s, the tariff posed a threat to prosperity—it generated too much money! Ironic as it may seem, the government found its enormous surplus revenue more embarrassing than today's huge deficits. The surplus sat in the Treasury's vaults, depriving the country of money that might otherwise have been invested to create jobs and products, while the government argued about how (or even whether) to spend it.

To many Americans, particularly southern and midwestern farmers who sold their crops in a world market yet had to buy high-priced protected goods, the answer was simple: Reduce the tariff. Advocates of free trade and moderates agitated for tariff reform. But those who benefited from the tariff—industrialists like Andrew Carnegie who insisted that America's "infant industries" needed protection and westerners producing protected raw materials such as wool, hides, and lumber—firmly opposed lowering the tariff. Many workers, too, believed that the tariff protected American wage levels by giving American products a competitive edge over goods imported from other countries.

The 1880s witnessed a remarkable political realignment as a new set of economic concerns replaced the Civil War rhetoric of carpetbaggers, rebels, and the bloody shirt. The tariff, federal regulation of the railroads and trusts, and the campaign for free silver restructured American politics.

The Republican Party seized on the tariff issue to forge a new national alliance. James G. Blaine shrewdly recognized its potent political uses. "Fold up the bloody shirt and lay it away," he advised a colleague in 1880. "It's of no use to us. You want to shift the main issue to protection." By encouraging an alliance among industrialists, labor, and western producers of raw materials, Blaine hoped to solidify the North and West against the solidly Democratic South.

Although his tactic failed in the election of 1884, it worked four years later. Cleveland, who straddled the tariff issue in the election of 1884, startled the nation in 1887 by calling for tariff reform. The Republicans countered by arguing that "tariff tinkering" would only unsettle prosperous industries, drive down wages, and shrink the farmers' home market. Benjamin Harrison, who supported the tariff, captured the White House in 1888. Cleveland won the popular vote by less than 1 percent, but Harrison carried all the northern and western states except Connecticut and New Jersey, winning 233 electoral votes to Cleveland's 168.

Back in office, the Republicans demonstrated their new commitment to economics over ideology by abandoning their support for freed slaves at the same time that they curried favor with the new industrialists. Senator Henry Cabot Lodge's Force Bill, a federal election law to restore the vote to African Americans in the South, died in the same Republican Congress that passed the highest tariff in the nation's history in 1890. The new tariff sponsored by representative William McKinley of Ohio stirred a hornet's nest of protest. The American people had elected Harrison to preserve protection, not to enact a higher tariff. The McKinley tariff set about solving the vexing problem of too much revenue by raising duties so high that foreign producers no longer wanted to sell their goods to Americans. Democrats condemned the McKinley tariff and labeled the Republican Congress that passed it the "Billion Dollar Congress" for its carnival of spending. The Fifty-first Congress earned its title by spending the nation's surplus on a series of "pork barrel" programs—legislation shamelessly designed to bring federal money to their constituents. In their haste to spend the federal surplus, members of Congress passed a series of giveaways, from veterans' pensions to public works. In the congressional election of 1890, angry voters swept the hapless Republicans, including tariff sponsor McKinley, out of office. Two years later, Harrison himself was defeated as Grover Cleveland, whose call for tariff revision had lost him the election in 1888, triumphantly returned to the White House vowing to lower the tariff. Such were the changes in the political winds whipped up by the tariff issue.

The Railroads, the Trusts, and the Federal Government

American voters may have divided on the tariff, but increasingly they agreed on the need for federal regulation of the railroads and federal legislation against the trusts. As early as the 1870s, angry farmers had organized to attack the railroads. The Patrons of Husbandry, or the Grange, founded in 1867 as a social and educational organization for farmers, soon became politicized. Grangers launched an independent political movement to do something about the high rates and unfair practices of the railroads. By electing Grangers to state office, farmers made it possible for several midwestern states to pass laws regulating the railroads. At first the Supreme Court upheld their right to do so. In *Munn v. Illinois* (1877), the Court ruled in favor of regulation. But in 1886, the Supreme Court reversed itself in the *Wabash* case (*Wabash, St. Louis, and Pacific Railway Co. v. Illinois*) and ruled that because railroads

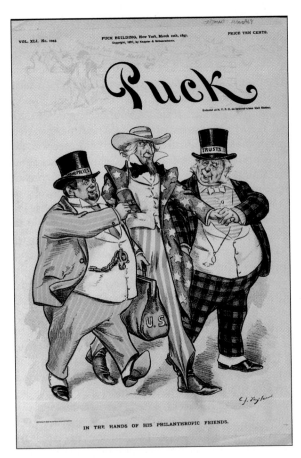

VOL. XLI. No. 1044.   PUCK BUILDING, New York, March 10th, 1897.   PRICE TEN CENTS.

Puck

IN THE HANDS OF HIS PHILANTHROPIC FRIENDS.

**THE CORRUPTION OF GOVERNMENT
BY BIG BUSINESS**

In this Puck *cartoon, a gullible Uncle Sam is being led by
trusts and monopolies, satirically styled as "his philanthropic friends." Concern over the power of big business
led in 1890 to the passage of the Sherman Antitrust Act,
the first attempt to regulate business by making it illegal
to restrict competition.*

Picture Research Consultants & Archives.

crossed state boundaries, they fell outside state jurisdiction. With more than three-fourths of railroads
crossing state lines, the Supreme Court's decision
effectively quashed railroad regulation.

Anger over the Supreme Court decision finally
led to the passage of the first federal law to regulate the railroads, the Interstate Commerce Act,
passed in 1887 during Cleveland's first administration. The act established the nation's first federal
regulatory agency, the Interstate Commerce Commission (ICC). Belatedly, the federal government
used powers granted under the Constitution's interstate commerce clause to bring about railroad

regulation. In its early years, the ICC was never
strong enough or sure enough of what it should do
to pose a serious threat to the railroads. It proved
more important as a precedent than effective as a
watchdog.

Concern over the growing power of the trusts
led the federal government to pass the Sherman Antitrust Act in 1890. By then a consensus had emerged
favoring the regulation of business if it could be accomplished without hurting the economy. The Sherman Act allowed bigness but struck at the trusts.
Businesses could no longer enter into agreements to
restrict competition. The law outlawed pools and
trusts but did nothing to prohibit huge holding
companies like Standard Oil, since a holding company, no matter how big, was one entity and not an
agreement among separate businesses to set prices
or restrict trade.

The Sherman Act proved to be a weak sword
against the trusts. In the decade after its passage,
the government successfully struck down only six
trusts. However, the law was used four times
against labor by outlawing unions as a "conspiracy
in restraint of trade." In 1895, the Supreme Court
dealt the law a crippling blow in the *E. C. Knight*
case. The Court drastically narrowed the law by allowing the American Sugar Refining Company,
which controlled 98 percent of the production of
sugar, to continue its virtual monopoly on the
grounds that *manufacture* did not constitute *trade*.

Both the Interstate Commerce Commission and
the Sherman Antitrust Act testified to the nation's
concern about the abuses of big business and to a
growing willingness to use federal power to intervene on behalf of the public interest. Not until the
twentieth century would more active presidents
sharpen and use these weapons against the large
corporations.

The Fight for Free Silver

Although the trusts stirred up a good deal of public outrage, the most potent political issue to emerge
in the 1880s had to do with the currency. During the
Civil War, the Union printed greenbacks (paper
money), which provided funds for the war effort
and incidentally contributed to inflation since the
dollars were not backed with gold or silver. Debtors,
who could pay back their loans with the devalued
dollars, liked inflation; creditors of course opposed
it. Because many debtors were farmers in the West
and South and many creditors were investors and

bankers in the Northeast, the issue of inflation versus deflation in its many forms—greenbacks versus hard money and later gold versus silver—fostered a new sectionalism, this time with the West joining forces with the South to challenge the dominance of the Northeast.

In the 1870s, supporters of cheap money launched the Greenback Labor Party, arguing that the nation needed an expanding monetary system to keep up with population growth and commercial expansion. Greenbacks, their supporters insisted, were "the people's currency, elastic, cheap, and exportable, based on the entire wealth of the country." But in 1879, Congress supported creditors over debtors by voting to resume the gold standard, tying the nation's currency to its gold reserves. The Greenback Labor Party responded by running General James B. Weaver for president in 1880. Despite the broad appeal of inflation among southern and midwestern farmers, voters below the Mason-Dixon line could not bring themselves to cast their ballots for a former Union general, and the party fell apart.

In the 1880s, the currency problem refused to go away. After the nation returned to the gold standard in 1879, money became even tighter. By the 1890s, the call for easier money and credit resurfaced, this time in the demand not for greenbacks but for silver.

The silver issue stirred passions like no other issue of the day. On one side stood those who believed that gold constituted the only honest money. Many, but not all, were eastern creditors who did not wish to be paid in devalued dollars. On the opposite side stood the silver mining interests, whose stake in the battle was clear. The silver bonanza in the West in the 1860s and 1870s led to a flood of metal on the market, which drove down the price of silver. Mining states such as Nevada and Colorado wanted the government to buy silver and mint silver dollars to help jack up the price.

The appeal of silver extended well beyond the Rocky Mountain states. Allied with the silver interests for very different reasons were farmers from the West and South who had suffered economically during the 1870s and 1880s and who saw in silver an all-purpose solution to their problems. A grinding cycle of debt and deflation had left the farmers in desperate need of relief. "The farmer pays his debts with his labor," observed a Kansas newspaper editor in 1891. "His crops cost him as much labor now as in 1870, but he receives only from one-

fourth to one-half as much for them." The farmers hoped that increasing the money supply with silver dollars would give them some relief.

Advocates of silver pointed out that until 1873 the country had enjoyed a system of bimetallism, with both silver and gold minted into coins. In that year, Congress had demonetized (stopped buying and minting) silver, an act advocates of bimetallism denounced as the "crime of '73." They later branded it a conspiracy to limit the money in circulation and place the West and South at the mercy of eastern financiers. In 1878, Congress took steps to appease advocates of silver by passing the Bland-Allison Act over President Hayes's veto. The measure required the government to buy silver and issue silver certificates. The Bland-Allison Act helped mine owners, who now had a buyer for their ore, but it had little inflationary impact.

Pressures for inflation continued, but the silver advocates were unable to make any headway until 1890, when in return for their support of the McKinley tariff, Congress passed the Sherman Silver Purchase Act, increasing the amount of silver the government bought. Once again, the measure failed to produce the desired inflationary effect, and advocates began to call for "the free and unlimited coinage of silver," a plan whereby virtually all the silver that was mined would be minted into silver coins circulated at the rate of sixteen ounces of silver to one ounce of gold.

The silver issue crossed party lines, but the Democrats hoped to use it to achieve a union between western and southern voters. Unfortunately, Democratic President Grover Cleveland, a conservative in money matters, sat in the White House, where he supported the gold standard with his usual stubbornness. Overlooking the crying need for depression relief, he called a special session of Congress in August 1893 and bullied the legislature into repealing the Sherman Silver Purchase Act. Repeal did not produce recovery or save the gold reserves. But it did divide the country, making the Mississippi River for a time as potent a political boundary as the Mason-Dixon line. Angry farmers warned Cleveland not to travel west of the river if he valued his life.

As their economic plight worsened after the panic of 1893 touched off a deep economic depression, farmers increasingly talked of a conspiracy of eastern financial interests, or "gold bugs." A Nebraska newspaper adopted the rhetoric of class warfare, charging, "The conflict between the common people and the overbearing, despotic, insulting monied aristocracy, who have set themselves up as our dictators, is inevitable."

In the winter of 1894–95, Cleveland aggravated the already highly charged political climate by his deal with J. P. Morgan to save the country's gold reserves. The Morgan bond sale underscored the government's ties to the great money men. By the 1890s, the United States faced a crisis. Agrarian discontent, labor unrest, depression, unemployment—problems that were not only economic but also social and political—cried out for solutions. In the grim darkness of the winter of 1894–95, men and women talked of revolution, some of them in fear and some of them in anger.

Conclusion: Mark Twain and the Gilded Age

Mark Twain, humorist, author, and one of the shrewdist critics of his era, called the period following Reconstruction the "Gilded Age." He chose this title to ridicule the ugliness, crass materialism, and sham of a time when glitter on the outside masked what lay beneath.

The Gilded Age seemed to tarnish all who touched it. No one knew that better than Twain, who, even as he attacked it as an "era of incredible rottenness," fell prey to its enticements. Born Samuel Langhorne Clemens in a rough Mississippi river town, he first became a riverboat pilot. Taking the pen name Mark Twain, he gained fame as the chronicler of California's gold rush. Twain came east in 1866 to launch a career as an author and itinerant humorist. He played to packed houses, but his work was judged too vulgar for the genteel tastes of the time because he wrote about common people and used common language. *The Adventures of Huckleberry Finn*, his masterpiece of American realistic fiction, was banned in Boston when it appeared in 1884.

Huck Finn's creator eventually stormed the citadels of polite society, hobnobbing with the wealthy and living in increasingly expensive and elegant style. He built an ornate Victorian mansion in Hartford, Connecticut, and maintained a townhouse off Fifth Avenue in New York City. Succumbing without much struggle to the money fever of his age, Twain plunged into one scheme after an-

MARK TWAIN
Popular author Mark Twain (Samuel Langhorne Clemens) wrote acerbically about the excesses of the Gilded Age. No one knew the meretricious lure of the era better than Twain, who succumbed to a get-rich-quick scheme that left him virtually bankrupt.
Beinecke Rare Book and Manuscript Library, Yale University.

other in the hope of making millions. The Paige typesetting machine proved his downfall. This elaborate invention (it had more than eighteen thousand parts) promised to mechanize typesetting, replacing human labor with machine. The idea was a good one—Ottmar Mergenthaler soon patented the Linotype and made a fortune. But Paige's elaborate invention proved much too complicated and temperamental to be practical. By the 1890s, Twain faced bankruptcy. Only the help of Standard Oil millionaire Henry H. Rogers enabled him to begin his dogged climb out of debt. Twain's fall from fortune constituted a tale told over and over again in an age when the promise of wealth led as many to ruin as to riches.

A child of his age, Twain knew intimately the

allure of money and power and the giddy rise and fall of fortune. His indictment of his times was not the detached disdain of an observer, but the bitter recognition of a man deeply mired in the gaudy, meretricious lure of the era he named the "Gilded Age."

Mark Twain's label the "Gilded Age" has stood for more than a century as a fair representation of an era when political corruption strutted with the haughty arrogance of a Conkling and industrialists like William Vanderbilt cried, "The public be damned!" But if the age spawned greed, corruption, and vulgarity on a grand scale, it was not without its share of solid achievements. In these years, America made the leap into the industrial age. Factories and mills poured out American goods in unprecedented numbers. Where dusty roads and cattle trails once sprawled across the continent, steel rails now bound together a nation. Cities grew from the ground into the sky. In New York City, the Brooklyn Bridge spanned the East River with steel and stone, more strikingly beautiful than all the showy mansions on Fifth Avenue. In the offices and boardrooms of business, men like Rockefeller, Carnegie, and Morgan consolidated American industry. By the end of the century, the country had achieved industrial maturity. No other era in the nation's history witnessed such a transformation.

It remained to be seen whether the nation could curb the vast power of the industrialists and work to solve the social and economic problems accompanying industrialization.

CHRONOLOGY

1869	Completion of first transcontinental railroad.
1870	John D. Rockefeller incorporates Standard Oil Company in Cleveland.
1872	Andrew Carnegie builds largest Bessemer process steel plant near Pittsburgh.
1873	U.S. government decides to stop minting silver dollars.
	Panic on Wall Street leads to major economic depression.
1874	Pennsylvania Railroad capitalized at $400 and employing 55,000; largest private enterprise in the world.
1876	Alexander Graham Bell demonstrates telephone at Philadelphia Centennial Exposition.
1877	Rutherford B. Hayes sworn in as president of United States after disputed election.
	U.S. Supreme Court upholds right of states to regulate railroads in *Munn v. Illinois*.
1879	Congress votes to resume the gold standard.

	Thomas Alva Edison perfects filament for incandescent lightbulb.
1880s	Jay Gould becomes architect of a transcontinental railway system.
	Gustavus Swift revolutionizes meatpacking with refrigerated railway cars to transport meat east.
	H. J. Heinz pioneers mass production and distribution of his fifty-seven varieties of condiments.
1880	Greenback Labor Party runs General James B. Weaver for president.
	Dark horse Republican candidate James A. Garfield elected president of United States.
1881	President Garfield assassinated by Charles Guiteau; Vice President Chester A. Arthur becomes president.
1882	Standard Oil develops the trust.
1883	Congress passes Pendleton Act establishing civil service reform.
1884	Grover Cleveland wins presidency, first Democrat to serve since before the Civil War.

Mark Twain's *Huckleberry Finn* published and subsequently banned in Boston.

1886   In *Wabash* case, U.S. Supreme Court reverses itself and disallows state regulation of railroads that cross state lines.

1887   Congress passes Interstate Commerce Act, first federal law to regulate railroads.

1888   Benjamin Harrison elected president of United States.

1889   Standard Oil reorganizes into holding company.

1890   Congress passes McKinley tariff and Sherman Siver Purchase Act.

Congress passes Sherman Antitrust Act.

1892   Grover Cleveland elected to second term as president.

J. P. Morgan consolidates electric industry, creating the General Electric Company.

1893   Panic devastates financial markets and touches off national depression.

1895   J. P. Morgan bails out U.S. Treasury and saves country's gold reserves.

1901   J. P. Morgan buys out Carnegie Steel and creates U.S. Steel, first billion-dollar corporation in United States.

BIBLIOGRAPHY

GENERAL WORKS

Sean Dennis Cashman, *America in the Gilded Age* (1984).

Alfred Chandler Jr., *The Visible Hand: The Managerial Revolution in American Business* (1977).

Alan Dawley, *Struggles for Justice: Social Responsibility and the Liberal State* (1991).

Vincent P. DeSantis, *The Shaping of Modern America, 1877–1920* (2nd ed., 1989).

Sidney Fine, *Laissez Faire and the General Welfare State: A Study of Conflict in American Thought, 1865–1914* (1956).

John A. Garraty, *The New Commonwealth, 1877–1890* (1968).

Ray Ginger, *The Age of Excess* (1963).

Samuel P. Hays, *The Response to Industrialism, 1885–1914* (1957).

Edward C. Kirkland, *Industry Comes of Age: Business, Labor, and Public Policy, 1860–1897* (1967).

Nell Irwin Painter, *Standing at Armageddon: The United States, 1877–1919* (1987).

Alan Trachtenberg, *The Incorporation of America: Culture and Society in the Gilded Age* (1982).

Robert Wiebe, *The Search for Order, 1877–1920* (1967).

BUSINESS

Robert Bannister, *Social Darwinism* (1979).

John Brooks, *Telephone: The First Hundred Years* (1976).

Travis Brown, *Historical First Patents* (1994).

W. Elliott Brownlee, *Dynamics of Ascent: A History of the American Economy* (rev. ed., 1979).

Robert V. Bruce, *Alexander Graham Bell and the Conquest of Solitude* (1973).

Stuart Bruchey, *Growth of the Modern American Economy* (1975).

Vincent P. Carosso, *The Morgans: Private International Bankers, 1854–1913* (1987).

John G. Cawelti, *Apostles of the Self-Made Man: Changing Concepts of Success in America* (1965).

Alfred D. Chandler Jr., *The Railroads, the Nation's First Big Business: Sources and Readings* (1965).

Alfred D. Chandler Jr., *Scale and Scope: The Dynamics of Industrial Capitalism* (1990).

Ron Chernow, *The House of Morgan* (1990).

Peter Collier and David Horowitz, *The Rockefellers: An American Dynasty* (1976).

Robert Fogel, *Railroads in American Economic Growth* (1964).

Edwin Gabler, *The American Telegrapher: A Social History, 1860–1900* (1988).

Louis Galambos, *The Public Image of Big Business in America, 1880–1940: A Quantitative Study in Social Change* (1974).

Robert W. Garnet, *The Telephone Enterprise* (1985).

Ellen Gruber Garvey, *The Adman in the Parlor, Magazines and the Gendering of American Culture* (1996).

Robert B. Gordon, *American Iron, 1607–1900* (1996).

Julius Grodinsky, *Jay Gould, 1867–1892* (1957).

David Freeman Hawke, *John D.: The Founding Father of the Rockefellers* (1980).

Robert L. Heilbroner, with Aaron Singer, *The Economic Transformation of America* (1977).

Morton J. Horowitz, *The Transformation of American Law, 1870–1960* (1992).

David H. Howard, *People, Pride, and Progress: 125 Years of the Grange in America* (1992).

Jonathan Hughes, *The Vital Few: The Entrepreneur and American Economic Progress* (1965; expanded ed., 1986).

John Ingham, *Making Iron and Steel: Independent Mills in Pittsburgh, 1820–1920* (1991).

Matthew Josephson, *The Robber Barons: The Great American Capitalists, 1861–1901* (1934).

Matthew Josephson, *Edison* (1959).

Justin Kaplan, *Mr. Clemens and Mark Twain* (1966).

John F. Kasson, *Civilizing the Machine* (1976).

Edward Chase Kirkland, *Dream and Thought in the Business Community, 1860–1900* (1956).

Maury Klein, *The Life and Legend of Jay Gould* (1987).

Maury Klein, *Union Pacific* (1987).

James T. Kloppenberg, *Uncertain Victory: Social Democracy and Progressivism in European and American Thought, 1870–1920* (1986).

Harold C. Livesay, *Andrew Carnegie and the Rise of Big Business* (1975).

Albro Martin, *Railroads Triumphant: The Growth, Rejection, and Rebirth of a Vital American Force* (1992).

Carolyn Marvin, *When Old Technologies Were New* (1988).

Andre Millard, *Edison and the Business of Innovation* (1990).

Ralph L. Nelson, *Merger Movements in American Industry, 1895–1956* (1959).

Allan Nevins, *Grover Cleveland: A Study in Courage* (1933).

Allan Nevins, *John D. Rockefeller: The Heroic Age of American Enterprise*, vol. 1 (1940); vol. 2 (1941).

James D. Norris, *Advertising and the Transformation of American Society, 1865–1920* (1990).

Douglass C. North, *Growth and Welfare in the American Past* (1966).

Richard O'Connor, *Gould's Millions* (1962).

Glenn Porter, *The Rise of Big Business, 1860–1910* (1973).

Andrew Sinclair, *Corsair: The Life of J. Pierpont Morgan* (1980).

William Graham Sumner, *What Social Classes Owe to Each Other* (1883; reprint, 1973).

George Rogers Taylor and Irene D. Neu, *The American Railroad Network, 1861–1890* (1956).

Peter Temin, *Iron and Steel in Nineteenth-Century America* (1964).

Joseph Frazier Wall, *Andrew Carnegie* (1970).

James A. Ward, *Railroads and the Character of America, 1820–1887* (1986).

John Hoyt Williams, *The Great and Shining Road: The Epic Story of the Transcontinental Railroad* (1988).

Oliver Zunz, *Making America Corporate, 1870–1920* (1990).

POLITICS

Paula Baker, *The Moral Frameworks of Public Life: Gender, Politics, and the State in Rural New York, 1870 – 1930* (1991).

Geoffrey Blodgett, *The Gentle Reformers* (1966).

Kenneth Davison, *The Presidency of Rutherford B. Hayes* (1972).

John M. Dobson, *Politics in the Gilded Age: A New Perspective on Reform* (1972).

Justus D. Doenecke, *The Presidencies of James A. Garfield and Chester A. Arthur* (1981).

Richard J. Ellis, *American Political Cultures* (1993).

Lewis L. Gould, *William McKinley: A Biography* (1988).

Ari Hoogenboom, *Outlawing the Spoils: The Civil Service Reform Movement, 1865 – 1883* (1961).

Ari Hoogenboom, *The Presidency of Rutherford B. Hayes* (1988).

Matthew Josephson, *The Politicos, 1865 – 1896* (1938).

Paul Kleppner, *The Cross of Culture: A Social Analysis of Midwestern Politics, 1850 – 1900* (1970).

Robert D. Marcus, *Grand Old Party: Political Structure in the Gilded Age* (1971).

Robert Green McCloskey, *American Conservatism in the Age of Enterprise, 1865 – 1910* (1951).

Gerald W. McFarland, *Mugwumps, Morals, and Politics, 1884 – 1920* (1975).

Michael E. McGerr, *The Decline of Popular Politics: The American North, 1865 – 1928* (1986).

H. Wayne Morgan, *From Hayes to McKinley: National Party Politics, 1877 – 1896* (1969).

D. Sven Nordin, *Rich Harvest: A History of the Grange, 1867 – 1900* (1974).

Arnold M. Paul, *Conservative Crisis and the Rule of Law: Attitudes of Bar and Bench, 1887 to 1895* (1969).

David J. Rothman, *Politics and Power: The United States Senate, 1869 – 1901* (1966).

Mary Ryan, *Women in Public: Between Banners and Ballots, 1825 – 1880* (1990).

Homer E. Socolofsky and Allan B. Spetter, *The Presidency of Benjamin Harrison* (1987).

John Sproat, *The Best Men: Liberal Reformers in the Gilded Age* (1968).

John Tomsich, *A Genteel Endeavor: American Culture and Politics in the Gilded Age* (1971).

Rexford Tugwell, *Grover Cleveland* (1968).

Irwin Unger, *The Greenback Era: A Social and Political History of American Finance* (1964).

Allen Weinstein, *Prelude to Populism: Origins of the Silver Issue, 1867–1878* (1970).

Richard E. Welch, *The Presidencies of Grover Cleveland* (1988).

MINER'S SAFETY LAMP AND CANVAS CAP WITH OIL LAMP

This lamp and cap were used by coal miners in Pennsylvania in the mid to late nineteenth century. The oil-wick lamp, attached to the cap by a hook, was introduced by immigrant miners from Great Britain. The wick was soaked in oil stored inside the lamp and lit the miner's path with a smoky flame. Although these lamps were cheaper and burned longer than the candles they replaced, any open flame presented a serious danger: explosions and fires often resulted when flame came in contact with methane and other underground gases. Falling rock and cave-ins were also common occurrences, but the canvas hat offered little protection. Improvements in safety were implemented gradually. British inventors developed a lamp that enclosed the flame in steel netting to prevent reaction with gases. Because the flame grew higher when exposed to certain gases, the safety lamp (left) did double duty in lighting the miners' way and detecting dangerous gases. After World War I, cloth caps were replaced by hard hats with electric lights.

Pennsylvania Historical and Museum Commission, Bureau of Historic Sites and Museums, Anthracite Museum Complex.

AMERICA THROUGH THE EYES OF THE WORKERS

19

1870–1890

FOR TWO WEEKS DURING THE SUMMER OF 1877, President Rutherford B. Hayes faced an insurrection that was greater than any since the Civil War. Hayes met daily with his cabinet to plan military strategy and sat up late into the night receiving reports from his generals. He dispatched federal troops to nine states, ordered warships to protect the nation's capital, and threatened to declare martial law. Not since the Confederates fired on Fort Sumter had the nation witnessed such an alarm. Who posed this threat to the Republic? Not former rebels or foreign armies, but American workers engaged in the first nationwide labor strike in the country's history.

The summer of 1877 witnessed a spontaneous labor uprising known as the Great Railroad Strike. Economic depression following the panic of 1873 had thrown as many as three million people out of work. Those who were lucky enough to keep their jobs watched as pay cuts eroded their wages until they could no longer feed their families. When a Cincinnati cigar worker with a wife and three children was asked how he lived on $5 a week, he replied, "I don't live. I am literally starving. We get meat once a week, the rest of the week we have dry bread and black coffee."

The burden of the depression fell disproportionately on the backs of the country's working class. Corporations tried to economize by laying off workers and cutting wages so that the corporations could continue to pay dividends to their investors. When the Baltimore and Ohio (B&O) Railroad announced a 10 percent wage reduction in the same week that the company declared a 10 percent dividend to its stockholders, the brakemen in West Virginia, whose wages had already fallen from $70 to $30 a month, walked out on strike. One B&O worker described the hardship that had driven him to take such desperate action: "We eat our hard bread and tainted meat two days old on the sooty cars up the road, and when we come home, find our children gnawing bones and our wives complaining that they cannot even buy hominy and molasses for food."

The strike by brakemen in West Virginia touched off a nationwide uprising that spread rapidly, to Chicago and St. Louis, Kansas City and San Francisco. Within a few days, nearly 100,000 railroad workers went out on strike. The spark of rebellion soon fired other workers to action. An estimated 500,000 joined the striking train workers. Violence erupted as the strikers clashed with state militia. President Hayes, after hesitating briefly, called up federal troops. In three weeks it was over.

"The strikes have been put down by *force*," Hayes noted in his diary on August 5. "But now for the real remedy. Can't something be done by education of the strikers, by judicious control of the capitalists, by wise general policy to end or diminish the evil? The railroad strikers, as a rule, are good men, sober, intelligent, and industrious."

The uprising of the workers in 1877 underscored the tensions produced by rapid industrialization and pointed to many legitimate grievances on the part of labor. The explosion of industrial growth that occurred after the Civil War came about as a result of the labor of millions of men, women, and children who toiled in workshops and factories, in sweatshops and mines, on the railroads and on construction sites across America. Their stories provide a different perspective from that of the great industrialists and the politicians. Through their eyes it is possible to gauge how corporate capitalism transformed old work patterns and affected the social as well as the economic and political life of the United States.

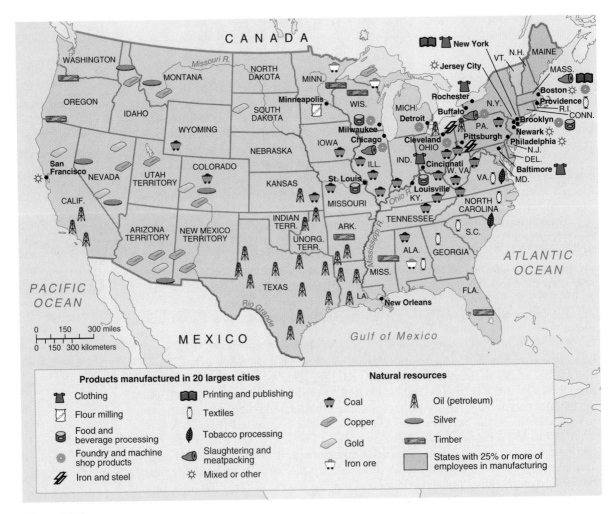

MAP 19.1

Industrialization, 1865–1900

Industrial development between 1865 and 1900 shows the clustering of industry in the Northeast and Great Lakes states. Only in these regions did industry employ 25 percent or more of the region's labor force. The West supplied raw materials — oil, minerals, and timber, while in the South and the Midwest agriculture and attendant industries such as tobacco processing and meatpacking dominated. Note, however, the movement of textile manufacturing from the Northeast to the South.

What were the lives of America's workers—white collar as well as blue collar—like? Who were they, and where did they come from? What did they do to earn their bread? Increasing business consolidation in the late nineteenth century had a significant impact on workers' lives. American society was profoundly reshaped by new corporate structures. As businesses consolidated and large corporations replaced partnerships and small proprietorships, work took on an increasingly impersonal quality. Traditional ideas about equal competition and the independence of employees broke down when the boss became a faceless corporation. Increasingly, workers tried to better their bargaining position by taking collective action. President Hayes's "sober, intelligent, and industrious" workers not only precipitated the uprising in 1877 but also stimulated the organization of nationwide labor unions to fight for the right to bargain collectively for better working conditions, shorter hours, and higher pay. Concern about the growing labor unrest led many comfortable, middle-class Americans to ask what could be done to curb the worst excesses of exploitation and inequity that accompanied corporate capitalism.

America's New Industrial Workers

America's industrial growth in the years following the Civil War brought about a massive redistribution of the country's population as agricultural workers moved to the city and became recruits in the industrial labor force. Burgeoning industrial centers such as Pittsburgh, Chicago, New York, and Detroit acted like giant magnets, attracting workers from the countryside.

The movement from the rural periphery to industrial centers was not just American in its scope. Farm boys and girls from western Pennsylvania who left for the mills of Pittsburgh were part of a global migration that included rural immigrants from Ireland, southern Italy, Russia, Japan, and China. As labor historian David Montgomery has pointed out, "the rural periphery of the nineteenth century industrial world became the primary source of supply for 'human machines.'"

The great diversity of American workers made it difficult for them to achieve solidarity. Differences in language, religion, ethnicity, and race raised powerful barriers that workers had to struggle to overcome if they wished to act collectively. Often forced

to put their children in the mines and factories, to take in boarders, or to rely on women's paid work when one paycheck did not spell survival, the working class by the end of the century increasingly took action, whether through strikes, politics, or union organizing, to achieve a better life.

Workers from the Rural Periphery

By the 1870s, the world could be viewed as being divided into three interlocking geographic regions forming roughly concentric circles. At the center stood an industrial core bounded by Chicago and St. Louis in the West; Toronto, Glasgow, and Berlin in the North; Warsaw in the East; and Milan, Barcelona, Richmond, and Louisville in the South.

> *The ability to draw on cheap labor on a global scale helps explain why, in spite of the soaring demand for laborers after the Civil War, the wages of unskilled workers in the United States remained relatively stagnant.*

Surrounding the industrial core and its urban outposts lay a vast agricultural domain encompassing Canada, much of Scandinavia, Russia and Poland, Hungary, Greece, Italy and Sicily, southern Spain, the defeated Confederate States and the Great Plains of America, central and northern Mexico, the hinterlands of Canton, China, and later the southern islands of Japan. (See Map 19.2, page 728.) Capitalist development in the late nineteenth century shattered traditional patterns of economic activity in this rural periphery. As old patterns broke down, the rural areas exported, along with other raw materials, new recruits for the industrial labor force.

Beyond this second circle lay an even larger "third world" including the Caribbean, Central and South America, the Middle East, Africa, India, and most of Asia. This area too became increasingly tied to the industrial core in the late nineteenth century, but its peoples largely stayed put. They worked on the plantations and railroads, in the mines and ports as part of a huge export network managed by foreign powers that staked out spheres of influence and colonies, often with gunboats and soldiers.

Beginning in the 1870s, railroad building and low steamship fares gave the world's peoples a newfound mobility that enabled industrialists to draw on a worldwide population for cheap labor.

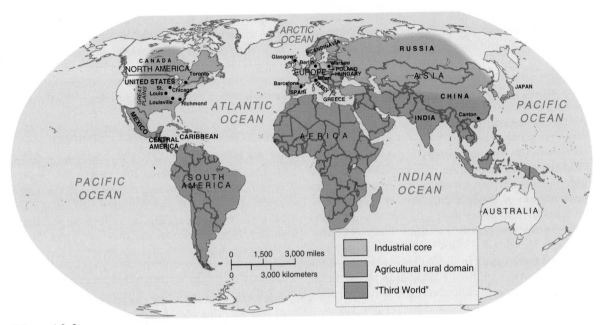

MAP 19.2
Economic Regions of the World
The global nature of the world economy at the turn of the century is indicated by three interlocking geographic regions. At the center was the industrial core—Western Europe and the northeastern United States; the agricultural rural periphery (rural domain) supplied immigrant laborers to the industries in the core. Beyond these regions lay a "Third World" tied economically to the industrial core by colonialism.

The Carnegie steel mills outside of Pittsburgh provide a good example. When Andrew Carnegie opened his first mill in 1872, Captain Billy Jones, his superintendent, hired workers for the blast furnaces from the Pennsylvania countryside. Jones's favorite workers were what he called "buckwheats"—young American boys just off the farm. By the 1890s, however, Carnegie's workforce was liberally sprinkled with other rural boys—Hungarians and Slavs who had migrated to the United States, willing to work for low wages.

The ability to draw on cheap labor on a global scale helps explain why, in spite of the soaring demand for laborers after the Civil War, the wages of unskilled workers in the United States remained relatively stagnant. Their pay fell dramatically during the depressions of 1873–1878 and 1893–1896 and did not regain 1872 levels before the end of the century.

Immigration, Ethnic Rivalry, and Racism

Ethnic diversity played a role in dividing skilled workers (those with a craft or specialized ability) from the unskilled (those who supplied muscle and brawn). As managers increasingly mechanized to replace skilled craftsworkers with lower-paid, unskilled labor, they played on ethnic prejudices to pit workers against each other. Carnegie's manager Henry Clay Frick hired Hungarians and Slavs as strikebreakers in the Pennsylvania coal fields in 1884, and when they went on strike six years later, he brought in Italians. With the bulk of the new, unskilled industrial laborers coming from southern and eastern Europe after 1880, the skilled workers, most of whom came from northern or western Europe, found it easy to criticize the newcomers. As one Irish worker complained, "There should be a law . . . to keep all the I-talians from comin' in and takin' the bread out of the mouths of honest people."

The Irish worker's resentment of the new Italian immigrants brings into focus the importance of the ideology and practice of racism in the experience of America's immigrant laborers. Throughout the nineteenth century, ethnic and even religious differences were perceived as *racial* characteristics. Members of the educated elite as well as workers spoke of the Polish "race" or the Jewish "race" in uncomplimentary terms. Each wave of newcomers was perceived as being somehow inferior to the

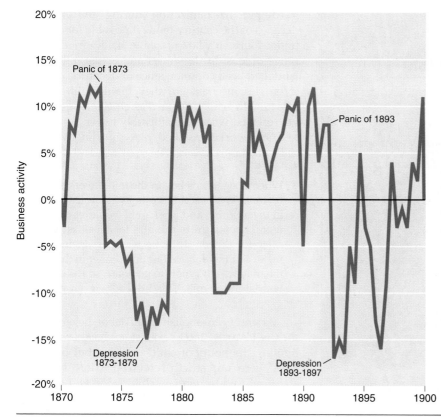

FIGURE **19.1**
*The U.S. Business Cycle,
1870–1890*
The overall economy grew between 1865 and 1900, but the growth was not steady. The business cycle resembles a wild roller coaster ride; deep troughs represent major depressions — one following the panic of 1873 and another following the panic of 1893. The period from 1882–1885 witnessed a drop nearly as severe. During these downward spirals tens of thousands of Americans faced unemployment and economic hardship.

established residents. The Irish who judged the Italians so harshly had themselves been seen as a subhuman species just a generation before. But it is not surprising that immigrants, who brought their own religious and racial prejudices to this country, also absorbed the popular prejudices of American culture. Social Darwinism, with its strongly racist overtones, decreed that whites stood at the top of the evolutionary ladder. But who was "white"? The social construction of race is nowhere more apparent than in the testimony of an Irish dockworker, who boasted that he hired only "white men" to load cargo, a category that he insisted excluded "Poles and Italians."

Racism took its most blatant form in the treatment of African Americans and Asians. Like other migrants from the rural periphery, African American men in the South, former slaves and the children of slaves, found work as human machines. The labor gang system that was used in many industries reached its most extreme and brutal form in the South. There the convict lease system allowed private employers to contract prison labor, mostly African Americans jailed for such minor "crimes" as vagrancy. Shackled together by chains as they

worked under the watchful eyes of armed guards, these workers formed the bottom rung on labor's ladder. A Georgia man who escaped the brutal chain gang system remarked, "Call it slavery, peonage, or what not, the truth is we lived in a hell on earth."

The racism encountered by Asian immigrants in the western United States took a somewhat different form from that experienced by either European immigrants or black laborers. The Chinese and later the Japanese were vigorously attacked as the "tools of corporate interest" recruited by the bosses to undercut wages and threaten "white society." On the West Coast especially, Asian immigrants became the scapegoats of the changing economy. Politicians, newspaper publishers, preachers, labor leaders, and the general populace attacked Asians as "heathens," claiming that they jeopardized the whole fabric of economic opportunity and small enterprise. The labor movement itself played a key role in the struggle to exclude Asians from American life. Labor unions practiced exclusionary policies against both Chinese and Japanese workers and championed the 1882 Chinese Exclusion Act, which prohibited the immigration of Chinese nationals to the United States.

THE COMPETITION OF CHEAP LABOR

Big business looks on approvingly as cheap immigrant labor outweighs American workers in this political cartoon published in the weekly Judge *in 1888. "As long as I am plentifully supplied with immigrant labor," says the portly manufacturer, "I shall be deaf to the demands of the native workingmen." Cartoons like this one underscored organized labor's concern with the number of foreign workers entering the country in the 1880s — nearly eight million, twice the number of the previous decade. Not only did the seemingly unlimited supply of immigrant laborers keep wages low, but the new recruits, who knew nothing of labor's struggles, often took work as strikebreakers.*
Judge, *February 11, 1888.*

The Family Economy: Women and Children

Many working-class families, whether native-born or immigrant, lived in poverty or near poverty. Family economic survival depended on the contributions of all, regardless of sex or age. In a wage economy, the paid and unpaid work of women and children became essential for family survival and economic advancement.

Rapid mechanization during the last two decades of the century made it possible for children under fourteen years of age to hold a much wider range of jobs. In the mines and textile mills, child labor had been common since midcentury. As other industries mechanized, they hired children, who often could tend machines as efficiently as adults, yet received wages considerably lower.

One worker recalled his youth in the textile mills of Massachusetts:

> When I began as a boy in the mill, I worked fifteen hours a day. I used to go in at a quarter past four in the morning and work until a quarter to eight at night, having thirty minutes for breakfast and the same for dinner, drinking tea after ringing out at night. But I took breakfast and dinner in the mill as the time was too short to go home, so I was sixteen hour[s] in the mill. This I did for eleven years. . . .

Attempts to abolish child labor began before the Civil War. By 1863, seven states had passed laws limiting the hours of child workers, but often the laws were not strictly enforced. Most southern states refused to regulate child labor, and children continued to be widely employed in southern mills, some as young as six or seven years old. In the nation's mines, particularly in Appalachia, young boys were recruited to pick out the slate and waste from coal as it passed along chutes. Suspended on wooden boards over the moving coal, these breaker boys engaged in backbreaking, dangerous work. A boy who slipped into the coal had little chance of surviving without serious injury. When a child labor committee investigated conditions in Pennsylvania, it found that more than 10,000 children were illegally employed in the coal fields. Coal mining was not the only dangerous industry that employed children. At the turn of the century, over 98 percent of the 7,000 boys under sixteen years of age employed in America's glass factories worked in the intense heat of the furnace rooms where mortality figures ran high.

Child labor increased decade by decade, with the percentage of children under fifteen engaged in paid labor not dropping until after World War I. The 1900 census showed that 1,750,178 children age ten to fifteen were employed, an increase of more than one million since 1870. Children from ten to fifteen years old constituted over 18 percent of the labor force and 7 percent of all nonagricultural workers in 1900, compared with 1880, when ten-to-fifteen-year-olds constituted 16.8 percent of the total labor force and 6 percent of those employed in nonagricultural work.

Even children who didn't work for wages contributed to the family economy by scavenging firewood and coal for fuel. Gangs of children patrolled the railroad tracks, picking up the coal that fell from the coal cars that fueled the locomotives. Bands of street children roamed the towns and cities, sometimes stealing and breaking windows. Other children worked as street vendors, newsboys, and bootblacks. Although laws in many states mandated school attendance, enforcement proved difficult. Harried truant officers found it hard to collar children whose parents insisted it was their prerogative to put them to work rather than send them to school.

At the turn of the century, women entered the workforce in greater and greater numbers, although they were paid less than men. In the late nineteenth century, the number of women workers rose sharply, with their most common occupation changing slowly from domestic service to factory work and then to office work. The 1870 census listed 1.5 million women working in nonagricultural occupations. By 1900, more than 4.9 million women

earned wages, and women constituted 18.8 percent of those employed in manufacturing.

Women's working patterns varied considerably according to race and ethnicity. White married women, even among the working class, rarely worked outside the home. In 1890, only 3 percent of white married women were employed. Nevertheless, many married women found ways to contribute money to the family economy. Families often took in boarders to supplement the family income. In many Italian families, homework, such as artificial flower making, allowed married women to contribute a wage to the family economy without leaving their homes and disrupting the cultural code that dictated that husbands guard the reputations of their wives. Black women, however, married and unmarried, worked for wages outside their homes at a much higher rate than white women. The 1890 census showed that 25 percent of African American married women worked outside the home, often in the houses of white families, where they did cooking and cleaning and child care.

Whatever activity wives and children performed, their contributions were often essential to the family's living. One statistician estimated that

"BREAKER BOYS"
Child labor in America's mines and mills was common at the turn of the century, despite state laws that attempted to restrict it. Here "breaker boys" in the 1890s take a rest from their twelve-hour day in the coal mines of Appalachia. Their unsmiling faces bear testimony to their hard and dangerous work. A committee investigating child labor found more than 10,000 children illegally employed in the Pennsylvania coal fields.
Brown Brothers.

in 1900, as many as 64 percent of working-class families relied on income other than the husbands' wages to make ends meet.

At Work

Throughout the nineteenth century, America's industrial workers toiled in a variety of settings. There were still skilled craftsmen and artisans who worked in small workshops or alone. But with the rise of corporate capitalism, large factories, mills, and mines increasingly dotted the landscape. Sweatshops and outwork, the contracting of piecework performed in the home, provided a different sort of work experience from that of the factory operative (machine tender) or the industrial worker who labored in the mines. Pick and shovel labor, whether on the railroads or in the building trades, constituted another kind of work. The best way to get a sense of the diversity of workers and workplaces is to look at several distinct types of industrial work: common labor, skilled work, factory work, sweatshop labor, and mining.

A Common Laborer

In her book *China Men,* Maxine Hong Kingston tells the story of Ah Goong, one of the *gam saan haak* (travelers to the gold mountain) who came to California in 1863 and went to work for the Central Pacific Railroad building the nation's first transcontinental railroad. Chinese work gangs laid the roadbed from San Francisco over the Sierra Nevada and across the Mojave Desert to Utah. For less than a dollar a day, Ah Goong hung in a basket on the cliffs above the American River, setting black powder in the crevices and firing the fuses to blast a path through the mountains. When the track came to a stop against a difficult stretch in the mountains, he tunneled through the granite with pick and shovel. The railroad experimented with the dangerous explosive nitroglycerine, and Ah Goong set the charges. To earn an extra dollar, he sometimes risked his life to go back into the tunnel to investigate when the highly volatile nitro had not exploded.

Working in the dark tunnel, Ah Goong toiled on eight-hour shifts seven days a week. When the railroad tried to increase the shift to ten hours, Ah Goong and ten thousand of his fellow workers went on strike in 1867. They demanded the same wages paid to the white, mostly Irish gangs, who earned

$40 a month compared with Ah Goong's $30. Construction superintendent Charles Crocker broke the strike, but in the end he raised the wages of the Chinese workers to $35 a month.

Common laborers built the railroads and subways, tunneled under the East River to anchor the Brooklyn Bridge, and helped to lay the foundation of industrial America.

Life was cheap on the Central Pacific. Men died on the cliffs when the ropes to the baskets broke or when the men failed to scramble out of the way before the blast. Men died in the tunnels when the nitroglycerine exploded without warning. The railroad received a subsidy for each mile of track laid, and Crocker worked the men throughout the win-

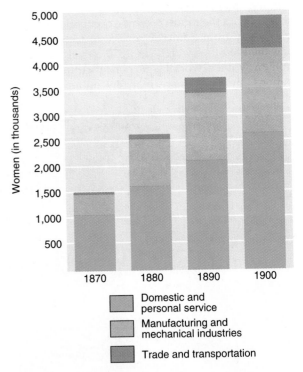

FIGURE 19.2
Women and Work, 1870–1900
In 1870 close to 1.5 million women worked in nonagricultural occupations. By 1900 that number had more than tripled to 4.9 million, with women constituting 18.8 percent of those employed in manufacturing. The total number of women workers rose sharply while the most common occupation changed from domestic work to industry and later to office work.

CHINESE RAILROAD WORKERS
Chinese workers like this section gang pictured at Promontory Point, Utah, in 1869 made up more than 80 percent of the workforce that built America's first transcontinental railroad. Charles Crocker of the Central Pacific hired them, reasoning that the race that built the Great Wall could build his road across the treacherous Sierra Nevada. Besides, the Chinese workers were a bargain: Crocker paid them $10 dollars a month less than he paid his Irish section gangs.
Denver Public Library, Western History Collection, photo by J. B. Silvis.

ters of 1866 and 1867, digging a tunnel through the Donner Summit, that infamous spot where, twenty years earlier, a party of settlers trapped in the snow had resorted to cannibalism to survive. More than forty-four feet of snow fell during the winter of 1867. In the freezing cold, the workers' fingers stuck to the iron rails and snow-blind men stumbled about with bandannas over their eyes. Blasting loosened walls of snow and buried workers alive. In the spring, when the snow melted, the crew uncovered the corpse of one worker, his tools still frozen in his hand.

Ah Goong was one of the lucky ones; he lived to see the Central Pacific reach Promontory Point, Utah, where it joined the Union Pacific to form the first transcontinental railroad in 1869. In the celebration that followed, orators basked in the accom-

plishment of the "greatest monument of human labor" and congratulated themselves that Californians had proved themselves "capable of any achievement." They made no mention of the Chinese although over 80 percent of the workers on the Central Pacific were Chinese. When the photographer took the famous picture of the driving of the golden spike to commemorate the meeting of the two railroads, the Chinese workers, whose prodigious labor had built the railroad, were nowhere in sight.

Common laborers like Ah Goong formed the backbone of the American labor force throughout the century. Although their pick and shovel work had changed little over the centuries, they nevertheless constituted an important part of such major modern industries as steel, railroads, and mining.

Common laborers built the railroads and subways, tunneled under the East River to anchor the Brooklyn Bridge, and helped to lay the foundation of industrial America.

A Skilled Ironworker

At the opposite end of the ladder from common laborers were skilled craftsmen like iron puddler James J. Davis. Davis, a Welsh immigrant boy, went into the iron mills in Sharon, Pennsylvania, at the age of eleven and won the title master puddler by sixteen. He later became a labor organizer and served in Congress and as secretary of labor in the 1920s.

Iron puddlers were an elite among skilled craftsmen. Using brains along with brawn, they took the melted pig iron in the heat of the furnace and, with long poles, formed the cooling metal into two-hundred-pound balls, relying on eye and intuition to make each ball uniform. Davis compared the task to baking bread: "I am like some frantic baker in the inferno kneading a batch of iron bread for the devil's breakfast. My spoon weighs twenty-five pounds, my porridge is pasty iron, and the heat of my kitchen is so great that if my body was not hardened to it, the ordeal would drop me in my tracks."

Possessing such a skill meant earning good wages, up to $7 a day, when there was work. But often no work could be found. Much industry and manufacturing in the nineteenth century remained seasonal; it was a rare worker who could count on year-round pay. In addition, the business cycle, those alternating periods of boom and bust regarded as inevitable by economists, produced two major depressions only twenty years apart, in 1873 and 1893, with accompanying unemployment and hardship. Davis, along with many other skilled workers, tramped the countryside looking for work in the 1890s.

Davis's experience demonstrated that even fiercely independent craftsmen like puddlers had no cushion against catastrophe. Once they could no longer work, whether because of unemployment, illness, or industrial accident, they faced impoverishment. In an era before unemployment insurance, workers' compensation, or old-age pensions, even the best worker could not guarantee security for his family. "The fear of ending in the poor-house is one of the terrors that dog a man through life," Davis confessed.

To protect their livelihood, highly skilled workers like iron puddlers jealously guarded their skill, passing it from one generation to the next. Davis had to leave the mill at eighteen because his father was not yet ready to retire and turn his furnace over to his son. In the iron industry, puddlers ruled the furnace absolutely, controlling the pace of work, the organization of the job, and the rate of pay. Such worker control posed a challenge to employers, who, as the century wore on, tried as much as possible to limit the workers' autonomy by replacing men with machinery, breaking down skilled work into ever smaller parts, and replacing skilled workers with unskilled operatives who worked for less money at piece rates.

A Factory Operative

The textile mills provide a classic example of mechanized factory labor in the nineteenth century. Mary, a weaver at the mills in Fall River, Massachusetts, told her story to the *Independent* magazine in 1903. She had gone to work in the 1880s at the age of twelve and had begun weaving at fourteen. Mechanization of the looms had reduced the job of the weaver to watching for breaks in the thread. "At first the noise is fierce, and you have to breathe the cotton all the time, but you get used to it," Mary told her interviewer. "When the bobbin flies out and a girl gets hurt, you can't hear her shout—not if she just screams, you can't. She's got to wait, 'till you see her. . . . Lots of us is deaf," she confessed.

The majority of factory operatives were young, unmarried women like Mary. The gendered nature of the work kept pay low and limited chances for advancement.

Because their jobs as machine tenders were easily defined and measured, weavers increasingly received their pay by the piece rather than by the day or hour. Mary worked from six in the morning to six at night, six days a week, and took home about a dollar a day. To increase productivity, managers assigned workers to more looms. Mary complained, "You got so tired drivin' at eight looms, and when they gave us twelve looms I didn't see that we could make out to live at all. It makes you crazy watchin' 'em." The majority of factory operatives were young, unmarried women like Mary. The gendered nature of the work kept pay low and limited chances for advancement. Mary resented the gender division of labor in the mills that made female

TEXTILE MILL WORKER
This woman weaver is typical of factory operatives who worked in New England's textile mills. Young, unmarried women formed the majority of mill workers. The weaver's job was to watch the looms to be sure the threads did not break. The work was both nerve-racking and unhealthy — note the lint on the floor. What can't be seen is the tremendous racket made by the huge machines — so loud that many women lost their hearing.
Courtesy George Eastman House.

workers subject to sexual harassment from male supervisors. "Good lookin' girls get the best chance," Mary acknowledged. "Now there's French Charlie, he's one of the 'supers'—he will take only pretty girls; he takes mostly French girls, too, of course."

During the 1880s, the number of foreign-born mill workers almost doubled. At the Amoskeag mill in New Hampshire, foreign-born workers, many French Canadian, constituted over half the workforce. Ethnic rivalries between the old-stock English and Scots immigrants, like Mary and her family, and the newcomers made organizing difficult. "There's plenty waitin' at the gates for our jobs," Mary complained, using a common derogatory term to identify a rival group. "The Polaks learn weavin' quick, and they just as soon live on nothin' and work like that. But it won't do 'em much good for all they'll make out of it."

The seasonal nature of the work also drove wages down. "Like as not your mill will 'shut down' three months," and "some weeks you only get two or three days' work, when they're curtailin'," Mary recounted. After twenty years of working in the mill, Mary's family had not been able to scrape together enough money to buy a house. "We saved some, but something always comes."

With the growing move toward industry in the South, textile mills spread from New England into states like the Carolinas and Georgia. There, whole families went to work in the mills. But southern mill work remained largely for whites only; black men were hired only for the dirtiest, lowest-paid jobs. Because southern workers would work for less money, many of the textile mills in New England relocated in the twentieth century, often abandoning mills in New England to set up south of the Mason-Dixon line.

A Sweatshop Garment Maker

In the garment industry, the impact of mechanization transformed independent tailors into factory workers. The introduction of the foot-pedaled sewing machine in the 1850s and the use of mechanical cloth-cutting knives in the 1870s mechanized hand tailoring, but, paradoxically, mechanization at the same time revived primitive forms of homework. Particularly in the 1880s, specialization led manufacturers to distribute cut cloth in bundles to contractors, who bid against one another for the work and then hired other workers to help sew together the pieces. Working in sweatshops, small rooms hired for the season or even in the contractor's own tenement, women and children formed an important segment of garment workers.

Sadie Frowne, a sixteen-year-old Polish Jew, went to work in a Brooklyn sweatshop in the 1890s making underskirts. In a room twenty feet long and fourteen feet wide containing fourteen machines, Frowne sewed for eleven hours a day. "The machines go like mad all day, because the faster you work the more money you get," she recalled. She earned about $4.50 a week and, by rigid economy, tried to save $2. As a young, single woman with no family, a "woman adrift" in the common parlance of the time, she had to struggle to support herself. Like many other young women, she relied on her steady boyfriend to treat her to trips to Coney Island and other entertainment. Frowne enjoyed dancing and going out on the town and liked to buy stylish clothes. She justified her extravagance, observing, "A girl who does not dress well is stuck in a corner, even if she is pretty."

The typical woman wage earner in the late nineteenth century was young and single. The largest percentage worked in the needle trades, like Frowne, but factory work ranked a close second. In 1890, the average workingwoman had started to work at age fifteen and was now twenty-two, working twelve hours a day, six days a week, and earning less than $6 a week. These young workingwomen formed a unique subculture, seeking pleasure and autonomy in the "cheap amusements" of their day—dance halls, social clubs, and amusement parks. Their wage earning generally lasted eight to ten years at the most, until they married. Discrimination against women in the marketplace, where they earned less than men, served to reinforce their dependence and make them vulnerable economically and sexually.

An Underground Miner

Metal and coal mining, along with extractive industries such as lumbering, constituted the most hazardous work in the nation. To look closely at conditions in the mines, mills, and forests, in the words of one historian, is to enter a "chamber of horrors." Ross Moudy, a miner in Cripple Creek, Colorado, recounted the dangers he faced, first in a chlorination mill. For nine or ten hours a day, he worked for $1.50 to $2 a day, breathing sulfur dioxide or chlorine fumes and working in dust so thick that "one cannot see an object two feet away." On the advice of the company surgeon (who swore him

to secrecy lest the managers find out), he quit the chlorination mill and went to work in a Cripple Creek gold mine.

The mine, according to Moudy, was "safe," as mines went. The "dangers do not seem so great to a practiced miner, who is used to climbing hundreds of feet on . . . braces put about six feet apart . . . and then walking the same distance on a couple of poles sometimes not larger than fence rails, where a misstep would mean a long drop." When a group of stockholders came to tour the mine, Moudy recounted how one man, white as a ghost after a near fall, told the miner beside him "that instead of being paid $3.00 per day they ought to have all the gold they could take out."

Miners died in explosions, cave-ins, and fires. New technology eliminated some dangers but often added others. Machinery could maim and kill. Dust from machine-powered drills got into miners' lungs and led to serious respiratory illnesses. In the hard-rock mines of the West in the 1870s, accidents annually disabled one out of every thirty miners and killed one in eighty. Those who avoided accidents still breathed air so dangerous that respiratory diseases eventually disabled them.

After a year on the job, Moudy joined the union "because I saw it would help me to keep in work and for protection in case of accident or sickness." The union provided good sick benefits and hired nurses, "so if one is alone and sick he is sure to be taken care of." Moudy acknowledged that there were some "hotheads" in the union, the militant Western Federation of Miners. But he insisted that most union men "believe the change will come about gradually and not by revolution."

Moudy's biggest worry was the "mine gas" (carbon dioxide) that often filled the tunnels because of poor ventilation. "Many times," he confessed, "I have been carried out unconscious and not able to work for two or three days after." When asked how such conditions could exist, he replied, "The mining laws of Colorado are not enforced at all and it is on account of this that so many lives are lost." Moudy counted himself among the lucky ones. "Outside of getting a couple of toes smashed from falling rocks and a crack on the head from a bolt which fell about two hundred feet down the shaft . . . knocking me out for over a week, I got out of the district rather luckily." While still a young man, he quit mining and found work as assistant state chemist for Wyoming.

The conditions that Moudy described were no worse and probably a good deal better than those in other mines. An Appalachian anthracite coal miner, who had gone into the mine at twelve and worked for twenty-three years, confessed, "We get old quickly. Powder, smoke, after-damp, bad air— all combine to bring furrows to our faces and asthma to our lungs." In the 1890s, the miner earned $33 a month, barely enough to cover rent and groceries. Observing that the mine's mules were better fed than the miners, he concluded, "The luxuries of the rich we do not want; we do want butter for our bread and meat for our soup."

American workers lived close to the bone in the late nineteenth century. Although real wages (pay measured in terms of buying power) rose 15 percent between 1873 and 1893, workers did not share equally in the improvement. African American men and women, for example, continued to be paid at a much lower rate than white men, as did immigrant laborers and white women. And the protracted depressions following the panics of 1873 and 1893 undercut many of labor's gains. What most distin-

guished American wages by 1900 from those in industrialized Europe was not simply the higher average wage but rather the striking differential between workers.

Managers and White Collars

The late nineteenth century witnessed the growth of a new managerial class and a burgeoning army of new white-collar workers—those in sales, clerical, and service work. Business expansion and consolidation led to a managerial revolution, creating a need for a new class of managers and for a growing number of clerical and secretarial workers. As skilled workers saw their crafts erode, some moved into management positions as foremen or supervisors. At the same time, new white-collar jobs in department stores and offices attracted a growing number of women workers.

COAL MINERS
Coal miners come up out of the shaft in the "cage" in Scranton, Pennsylvania. As one observer commented, "Although the mines are always cold and wet, yet the labor of drilling and handling the coal is so great that the miner, stripped to his shirt, soon becomes wet with sweat while the dust from the coal is at times almost stifling. The work is thirst-provoking and each miner carries with him a bottle or can, often a quart or more of strong, black coffee for the purpose of washing the dust from his throat."
Picture Research Consultants & Archives.

The New Managerial Class

"The middle class is becoming a salaried class," the *Independent* magazine observed in 1903, "and is rapidly losing the economic and moral independence of former days." For better or for worse, the *Independent* articulated a trend that had begun decades earlier. As large business organizations consolidated and created national markets, they sought to control and rationalize business, replacing what economist Adam Smith had called "the invisible hand" of market forces with the "visible hand" of management. At the same time, corporate development separated management from ownership, and the job of directing the firm became the province of salaried managers and executives. The new managerial class drew its recruits primarily from the ranks of the white middle class; a group of workers who in the past might have started their own businesses now found employment working on salary for big business.

Bureaucracy was invented not by government, but by business. Business consolidation and expansion in the decades after the Civil War, led by the railroads, produced elaborate organizational hierarchies that were designed to bring order to operations and to maximize profits. A new rank of middle managers stood between the executives of a company and its workers. These salaried bureaucrats often regarded labor unions with hostility, seeing in unions a challenge to their right to manage.

The majority of these new middle managers were white men drawn from the 8 percent of the American population who held high school diplomas. In 1880, the middle managers at the Chicago, Burlington, and Quincy Railroad earned between $1,500 and $4,000 a year, while senior executives, generally recruited from the college-educated elite, took home $4,000 or more, and the company's general manager made $15,000 a year.

Not all managers came from the middle class. Some were skilled workers who were able to move into management at the very moment mechanization was eroding the independence of skilled craftsmen. Until late in the century, when engineering schools began to supply recruits, corporations drew on skilled workers trained on the job to provide expertise. As a result, many technical executives rose from the shop floor to positions of considerable responsibility.

The career of Captain William "Billy" Jones provides a glimpse of a skilled ironworker turned manager. Jones, the son of a Welsh immigrant, grew up in the heat of the blast furnaces, where he started working as an apprentice at the age of ten. During the Civil War, he served in the Union army and gained the rank of captain, a title he used for the rest of his life. When Andrew Carnegie opened his steelworks on the outskirts of Pittsburgh in 1872, he hired Jones as his plant superintendent. By all accounts, Jones was the best steel man in the industry. He loved his work and drove himself and his men. "Good wages and good workmen" was his motto. Carnegie constantly tried to force down wages, but Jones fought for his men. In 1881, he succeeded in shortening the shift from twelve to eight hours a day by convincing Carnegie that good labor policy could also mean good business because it would reduce absenteeism and accidents. Jones himself demanded and received a "hell of a big salary." Carnegie paid him $25,000—the same salary as the president of the United States—a stupendous sum in 1881 and one that testified to the value the tightfisted Carnegie placed on his superintendent. Captain Jones did not have long to enjoy his newfound wealth. He died in 1889 when a blast furnace exploded, adding his name to the estimated 35,000 killed each year in industrial accidents.

Office Work and Women "Typewriters"

The expansion and consolidation of business in the decades after the Civil War brought more and more workers into the office. As businesses became larger and more far-flung, the greater volume of correspondence and the need for more elaborate and exact records led to the hiring of more office workers. Mechanization soon transformed business as it had industry and manufacturing. The adding machine, the cash register, and the typewriter came into general use in the 1880s. Employers seeking literate workers soon turned to women, who not only worked for lower wages than men but tended to be better educated than the males available for clerical work. Men had too many other career choices. But for women, secretarial work constituted one of the few areas where they could put their literacy to use for wages. By 1900, they outnumbered men as stenographers and typists.

Sylvie Thygeson was typical of the young women who went to work as secretaries in the 1880s. Thygeson grew up in an Illinois prairie town in a middle-class family that valued education. Her father was a small-town lawyer, and her mother was

CLERICAL WORKER
A stenographer takes dictation in an 1890s office. Note that the apron, a symbol of feminine domesticity, has accompanied the woman into the workplace. In the 1880s, with the invention of the typewriter, many women were able to put their literacy skills to use for wages in the nation's offices.
Brown Brothers.

a woman who took pride in the fact that all eight of her children graduated from high school. When her father died in 1884, Thygeson went to work at the age of sixteen. After a brief stint as a country schoolteacher, she learned typing and stenography and found work as a secretary to help support her family. According to her account, she made "a fabulous sum of money." Nevertheless, she gave up her job after a few years when she met and married her husband.

Thygeson's story demonstrates the growing importance of clerical work for women workers, particularly those from the white middle class. Called "typewriters," these women workers were quite literally identified as indistinguishable from the machines they operated. But far from seeing their work as dehumanizing, young middle-class women like Sylvie Thygeson viewed it with pride and relished the economic independence it afforded them. By the 1890s, secretarial work was the overwhelming choice of white, native-born women, who constituted over 90 percent of the female clerical force. Not only was it considered more genteel than factory work or domestic labor, but office work meant more money for shorter hours. Boston's clerical workers made more than $6 a week in 1883, compared with less than $5 for women working in manufacturing. For Sylvie Thygeson and thousands of women like her, the office provided a welcome alternative to the limited options available to women workers.

The Department Store

The department store provides another good setting in which to examine the working life of the new white-collar class. With the rise of industrial capitalism, a new consumer culture came to dominate American life. Men and women increasingly sought security, comfort, material well-being, and pleasure. Indeed, the emphasis on acquisition and consumption gave the Gilded Age its name. Department stores became the symbol of this new consumer culture.

The department stores that emerged in the nineteenth century created a unique new urban environment. Shoppers learned the modern art of consumption in palaces designed to lend magic and glamour to even the most everyday things of life—such as men's trousers or bedsheets. Boasting ornate facades, large plate-glass display windows, marble and brass fixtures, and elegant skylights and galleries, department stores like Macy's in New York, Wanamaker's in Philadelphia, Filene's in

CONSUMER CULTURE

With the rise of consumer culture in urban America came huge new department and specialty stores. Johnson's Broadway store in New York advertised as "the largest millinery house in the world." In an era when no woman left her home without a hat, millinery stores sold the laces, flowers, ribbons, and feathers used to trim ladies' hats. The insatiable demand for fancy feathers led a group of prominent Boston women in 1896 to found the Massachusetts Audubon Society. Named for naturalist and painter John James Audubon, the group protested the indiscriminate slaughter of birds to provide feathers for the millinery trade.
Library of Congress.

Boston, and Marshall Field in Chicago stood as monuments to the material promise of the era and to the new culture of consumption.

With a vast array of personnel—stock boys, cashiers, salesclerks, elevator operators, bookkeepers, stenographers, telephone operators, buyers, and floorwalkers—the modern department store signaled the beginning of the shift in employment from production to services and heralded the rise of a new white-collar class. By the late 1890s, Macy's employed more than three thousand people, and Marshall Field more than doubled that figure within a few years.

Within these palaces of consumption, one could find cash girls, stock clerks, and wrappers who earned as little as $3 a week. At the top of the scale, buyers like Belle Cushman of the fancy goods department at Macy's earned $25 a week in 1871, an unusually high salary for a woman. But ordinarily, the gender segregation that kept women's wages low operated in the white-collar world of the department store just as it did in the office and the factory. Male supervisors, called floorwalkers, commanded salaries from $10 to $16 per week at a time when the typical Macy's saleswoman received $5 to $6. In all stores, saleswomen were subject to harsh and arbitrary discipline. Sitting was forbidden, and conversation with other clerks led to instant dismissal. The imperious Marshall Field fired any employee with ties to a labor union. Fines for tardiness or gum chewing pared down already meager wages. Yet white-collar workers counted themselves a cut above factory workers, even when their pay envelopes were thinner and did not justify the sense of superiority.

At Home and at Play

The growth of American industrial capitalism not only dramatically altered the workplace but indirectly transformed home and family life and gave rise to new forms of commercialized leisure. One of the major changes was the separation of work and home. In preindustrial society, trade and manufacturing generally took place in or close to the home. Industrialization redefined the very concepts of work and home. Increasingly, men went out to work for wages, while most white married women stayed home, either working in the home without pay—cleaning, cooking, and raising children—or supervising paid domestic servants who did the housework. The growing separation of workplace and home led to a new ideology, one that sentimentalized the home and women's role in it.

Domesticity and "Domestics"

The separation of the workplace and the home that marked the shift to industrial society in the early nineteenth century redefined the home as a "haven in the heartless world," presided over by a wife and mother who made the household her "separate sphere." The cultural ideology that dictated that woman's place was in the home has been called the "cult of domesticity," a phrase used to describe an ideal of womanhood that dominated the period from 1820 to the end of the nineteenth century.

The cult of domesticity purveyed an image of womanhood that was more appropriate for women of the middle and upper classes than for their working-class counterparts. With its insistence that the "true" woman confine her activities exclusively to the home, the cult soon fostered an invidious distinction between the "lady" and the working-woman. Since a lady, by definition, remained at home, women who worked for wages suffered a social stigma. In common slang, prostitutes were referred to as "working girls." Respectable working-class daughters who suffered by association struggled hard to transform the epithet into a term of dignity, but their task was complicated by the class

implications inherent in the nineteenth-century notion of true womanhood, which decreed that ladies remain in the home.

The cult of domesticity and the elaboration of the middle-class home in the nineteenth century led to a major change in patterns of hiring household help in the North (the South continued to rely on black female labor, first slave and later free). Domestic labor changed over the course of the nineteenth century from the "hired girl," who worked beside the housewife/employer, to the live-in servant, or "domestic." This transition reflected both economic and ideological change and was indirectly but distinctly tied to the maturing industrial capitalist economy, with its labor market, rising standard of living, system of unequal rewards, and created consumer "needs."

As the cult of domesticity and growing consumerism raised the expectations of the urban middle and upper classes, they relied more and more on paid domestic labor to perform menial household tasks. Domestics no longer "helped"; increasingly they carried the main burden of housework alone. In American cities by 1870, from 15 to 30 percent of all households included live-in domestic servants, more than 90 percent of whom were women.

> *The growth of American industrial capitalism not only dramatically altered the workplace but indirectly transformed home and family life and gave rise to new forms of commercialized leisure.*

The life of the domestic was far from enviable. During the nineteenth century, native-born women took up other work and left domestic service to immigrants. By midcentury, the maid was so often Irish that "Bridget" became a generic term for female domestics. Investigators found that domestic servants not only worked longer hours than any other women workers but also spent the remainder of their time on call. "She is liable to be rung up at all hours," one study reported. "Her very meals are not secure from interruption, and even her sleep is not sacred."

Domestic servants by all accounts resented their lack of privacy and their limited opportunities for socializing. Furthermore, going into service carried a social stigma. As one young woman observed, "If a girl goes into the kitchen she is sneered at and called 'the Bridget,' but if she goes behind the counter she is escorted by gentlemen." No wonder domestic service was the occupation of last resort, a "hard and lonely life" in the words of one servant girl. With the opening of factory and office positions for women, only those with very limited skills chose service. "I would change my occupation if I knew enough to do anything else," confided one woman.

As workingwomen developed other options, the so-called servant problem became chronic, and white middle-class women lamented their inability to find "good help." For women of this class, domestics were a boon, freeing them from household drudgery and giving them more time to spend with their children or to pursue club work, reform, or woman suffrage. Thus, domestic service, while it supported the association of women with domesticity, created for those women who could afford it opportunities for activities that expanded women's horizons outside the home and worked to subvert accepted notions of "woman's place."

The House and the Home

As if to emphasize the new role of the home as a refuge and a haven in the decades after the Civil War, the typical middle-class dwelling itself became more embellished architecturally and its interiors more cluttered. Possession of such a home, indeed of any home at all, marked the gulf between the working poor and the middle class. Homeowners constituted only 36 percent of the housing population in 1900, compared with 64 percent today.

By 1890, the middle-class, urban home could boast such technological and sanitary improvements as central heating, hot and cold running water, and bathrooms. Electricity, which became available to city dwellers early in the twentieth century, expanded the hours of the day in a literal sense and also changed housework. As one architect noted, electricity "is used in operating telephones, call bells [for servants], for driving laundry, kitchen ventilating and pumping apparatus, and in some cases for refrigerating machinery."

Although few white women worked after marriage, the inequality of the incomes of their husbands created a yawning gulf between working-class wives and the wives of middle- and upper-class men. Wealthy and middle-class homemakers enjoyed sufficient income to purchase commodities women had previously produced at home and to avoid the drudgery of housework by hiring servants. This freedom enabled them to realize the cult of domesticity as a distinct and important social vocation.

The polarization between working-class austerity and the trappings associated with middle-class respectability becomes apparent in the comparison

SUNDAY DINNER
Sunday dinner at the home of the S.H. Fairfield family of Topeka, Kansas, is served by their African American domestic servant. Middle-class families as well as the wealthy relied on domestic help in the nineteenth century. Unlike white women, who rarely worked after marriage, more than 25 percent of African American married women worked for wages outside their homes, many as domestics. Often they had to leave their own homes and children and live in the homes of their white employers.
The Kansas State Historical Society, Topeka, Kansas.

of two households. Margaret Byington, a reformer who undertook a scientific survey of Homestead, the Carnegie mill town outside of Pittsburgh, recounted her visit to the family of a Slavic worker. The family lived in a two-room tenement, and she found the young mother doing the family laundry in a big washtub set on a chair in the middle of the room, struggling to keep her two babies from tumbling into the scalding water. Byington noted the sparse furnishings:

> On one side of the room was a huge puffy bed, with one feather tick to sleep on and another for covering; near the window stood a sewing machine; in the corner, an organ,—all these, besides the inevitable cook stove upon which in the place of honor was simmering the evening's soup. Upstairs in a second room, a boarder and the man of the house were asleep. Soon they would get up and turn their beds over to two more boarders, who were out at work.

Compare the Slavic family's household with the description of a middle-class home taken from *The Gilded Age,* the 1876 novel by Mark Twain and Charles Dudley Warner:

> Every room had its book-cases or book-shelves, and was more or less a library; upon every table was liable to be a litter of new books, fresh periodicals and daily newspapers. There were plants in the sunny windows and some choice engravings on the walls, with bits of color in oil or watercolors; the piano was sure to be open and strewn with music; and there were photographs and little souvenirs here and there of foreign travels.

In the eyes of Byington and many middle-class reformers, the Slavs' crowded tenement, with its boarders and its lack of privacy, could scarcely be dignified by the term "home." Yet for all the obvious differences between the households described, one can see in the workers' two feather ticks, sewing machine, and organ the same urge for sociability and impulse toward respectability that was apparent in the middle-class home.

Mill Towns and Company Towns

Mill towns like the one Byington studied became a feature of the industrial landscape in the nineteenth century. Many, like Homestead, grew up haphazardly. By 1892, eight thousand people lived in

Homestead, transforming a rural village into a bustling mill town that belied its pastoral name. As the Carnegie steelworks expanded, they encroached on the residential area, pushing the homes out of the flatlands along the Monongahela River. Workers moved into the hills and ravines. In an area called the Hollow, shanties hung precariously on the hillsides. These small, boxlike dwellings—many no larger than two rooms—housed the unskilled laborers from the mills.

Elsewhere, particularly in New England and the South, the company itself planned and built the town. The Amoskeag textile mill in Manchester, New Hampshire, was a self-contained world laid out according to a master plan conceived in the 1830s. Such planned communities rested on the notion of benevolent corporate paternalism. Viewing the workers as the "corporation's children," Amoskeag's owners sought to socialize their increasingly immigrant workforce to the patterns of industrial work and to instill loyalty to the company, curb labor unrest, and prevent unionization.

By the 1880s, Amoskeag employed tens of thousands of workers, housing many of them in corporation tenements. "The corporations," as workers called them, were three-to-five-story attached brick houses strung along the streets leading down from the center of the city to the mill yard. Workers paid the equivalent of $1 per room a month for company housing. To qualify, more than one family member had to work in the mill, a requirement that encouraged child labor. The substantial brick row houses with high ceilings and hardwood floors offered a striking comparison to the ramshackle shanties of Homestead. Only a third of Amoskeag's workers lived in company housing, however, making Manchester different from a classic company town. The majority of Amoskeag's workers rented houses in the city, and a significant number owned their own homes. The mill nevertheless exerted a powerful hold over the lives of its workers. "If you told the boss to go to hell, you might as well move out of the city," one mill worker acknowledged.

Perhaps the most famous company town in the United States was built by sleeping car king George M. Pullman nine miles south of Chicago on the shores of Lake Calumet. In the wake of the Great Railroad Strike of 1877, Pullman determined to remove his plant and workers from the "evil influences" of the city. In 1880, Pullman purchased 4,300 acres of bare prairie away from the "snares of the great city." On this isolated site he built his model town according to the principle on which he built the Pullman Palace cars that made his fortune—to be orderly, clean, and with the appearance of luxury. It was "to the employer's interest," he determined, "to see that his men are clean, contented, sober, educated, and happy." Pullman believed firmly that his practical philanthropy would guarantee larger profits by eliminating "loss of time and money consequent upon intemperance, labor strikes, and dissatisfaction," which, he insisted, "generally result from poverty and uncongenial home surroundings."

When the first family moved in on January 1, 1881, the model town of Pullman boasted parks, artificial lakes, fountains, playgrounds, an auditorium, a library, a hotel, shops and markets, a men's club, and 1,800 units of housing. Noticeably absent was a saloon. One worker lamented that he frequently walked by and "looked at but dared not enter Pullman's hotel with its private bar." The worker's intimidation underscored a major flaw in Pullman's plan. In his eagerness to inculcate what he referred to as the "habits of respectability," Pullman consulted his own wishes and tastes, never those of his workers.

With its clean, wide streets, its parks, and its model tenements, Pullman's town offered housing that was clearly superior to that in neighboring towns. But workers paid for the eye appeal. Pullman intended the town to support itself and expected a 6 percent return on his investment. As a result, Pullman's rents ran 10 to 20 percent higher than working-class accommodations in nearby communities. And a family could not own its own home in Pullman. George Pullman refused to "sell an acre under any circumstances." As long as he controlled the town absolutely, he held the powerful whip of eviction over his employees and could quickly get rid of troublemakers.

Although observers were at first dazzled by its beauty and order, it was not long before critics compared Pullman's model town to a "gilded cage" for workers. "The company owns everything," complained one critic, "and it exercises a surveillance over the movement and habits of the people." When labor organizers attempted to meet in Pullman, the company paid spies, or spotters, to report those who attended. The young economist Richard T. Ely went to the heart of what most concerned workers and critics alike when he concluded in 1884: "The idea of Pullman is un-American. . . . It is benevolent, well wishing feudalism, which desires the happiness of the people, but in such way as shall please the authorities."

The autocracy that many feared in Pullman was realized south of the Mason-Dixon line in the southern textile mill towns. "Practically speaking," a federal investigator observed, "the company owns everything and controls everything, and to a large extent controls everybody in the mill village." These largely nameless company towns, with their company-controlled stores, churches, schools, and houses, are a classic example of social control over workers. Paid in company currency, or scrip, workers had no choice but to patronize the company store, where high prices led to a mounting spiral of debt that reduced the workers to virtual captives of the company. At the turn of the century, 92 percent of southern textile workers' families lived in company towns.

The mill towns and company towns of America provide only the most dramatic examples of the ways in which industrialization and the rise of corporate capitalism changed the landscape of the United States and altered traditional patterns of work and home life. After the Civil War, communities where men and women of different classes knew and dealt with one another on a personal basis became more and more rare. In the face of increasing business consolidation and impersonality, traditional ideas about equal competition in the marketplace and the relative independence of employers and employees lost much of their hold.

Cheap Amusements

The poor and members of the working class took their leisure, when they had it, in the streets, the dance halls, the music houses, the ballparks, and the amusement arcades, which by the 1890s formed a familiar part of the landscape. For the most part the social divisions that marked American life existed in recreation. Poor and working-class people played largely apart from the retreats of the better-off. The tavern was the poor man's club. Saloons played a central role in workers' lives, often serving informally as political headquarters, employment agencies, or union halls. Not all the working class thronged to the saloons. Recreation varied according to ethnicity, religion, gender, and age. For many new immigrants, social life revolved around the family; weddings, baptisms, birthdays, and bar mitzvahs constituted the chief celebrations. Generally, older-stock American men spent more time away from home in neighborhood clubs, saloons, and fraternal orders than did their immigrant counterparts. German beer gardens, for example, were

TECHNOLOGY IN AMERICA
Moving Pictures at the Nickelodeon

The advent of projected motion pictures marked the culmination of the efforts of many inventors to present lifelike moving pictures on the screen. During the second half of the nineteenth century, a host of inventions, including the kinematoscope, the choreutoscope, the phasmatrope, and the zoopraxiscope, were designed to make pictures move. But it was Thomas Alva Edison's inventions in 1889 of the motion picture camera (kinetograph) and a peephole device to display the moving pictures (kinetoscope) that led to the commercial development of the cinema and the rise of the first moving picture theaters, the nickelodeons.

Edison launched the first exhibition of his motion pictures in a New York music hall in 1896. The result was an overnight sensation. Viewers marveled at the moving images — horses, dancers, waves on a beach. But the novelty soon wore off and audiences wanted a story. In 1903, *The Great Train Robbery*, an eleven-minute movie with a simple cops-and-robbers plot, proved such a hit that silent movies soon challenged the popularity of music halls, vaudeville houses, and penny arcades.

The years 1900 to 1907 were the heyday of the nickelodeons, the first motion picture theaters. The name came from combining *nickel*, the price of admission, with *melodeon*, the old reed organ sometimes played to accompany the silent films. Audiences flocked to these storefront theaters; by 1907, there were some five thousand nickelodeons across the United States. A viewer described the early shows: "A picture about 2×4 feet was projected from an Edison machine and a reel of film 300 to 400 feet in length was a complete show, lasting for four or five minutes. After each show the house was cleared and filled again."

It is not too much to say that modern cinema began with the nickelodeons, for their sudden growth stimulated the demand for movies, and the first studios quickly formed to feed the public's growing appetite for feature films. By the late 1920s, the film industry had taken root in Hollywood, California, and motion pictures had become one of the country's fastest-growing industries.

Corbis-Bettmann.

---

designed for the whole family. But more often, men and women took their leisure separately, except during the period of youth and courtship.

The growing anonymity of urban industrial society posed a challenge to traditional rituals of courtship. Adolescent working girls, immigrant and old stock, no longer met prospective husbands only

through their families. Fleeing crowded tenements, the young sought each other's company in dance halls and other commercialized retreats. Reformers worried that the commercial dance halls served as a breeding ground for drunkenness and prostitution. In 1884, millionaire heiress Grace Dodge, determined to help young working women find re-

CONEY ISLAND
Coney Island became a pleasure resort in the 1870s, but at the turn of the century, with the development of elaborate amusement parks like Steeplechase, Luna, and Dreamland, Coney Island came into its own as the capital of commercialized leisure. This offical guide highlighted the beach, vaudeville hall, and the midway with its rides and its risqué harem dancers. In the foreground a barker gesticulates and a hawker urges a young man in a straw hat to buy souvenir photographs for his companion.
Brooklyn Historical Society.

Baseball became a national pastime in the 1870s —then, as now, one force in urban life that was capable of uniting a city across class lines. Cincinnati mounted the first professional team, the Red Stockings, in 1869. Teams proliferated in cities across the nation in the next decade. By 1888, as many as thirteen thousand fans regularly packed the Polo Grounds for weekend games of the New York Giants. Mark Twain hailed baseball as "the very symbol, the outward and visible expression, of the drive and push and rush and struggle of the raging, tearing, booming nineteenth century."

The increasing commercialization of entertainment in the last decades of the nineteenth century can best be seen at Coney Island. A two-mile stretch of beach that was close to Manhattan by trolley or steamship, Coney Island in the 1870s and 1880s attracted visitors to its beaches, its boardwalk, and its dance pavilions and penny arcades. In the 1890s, Coney Island was transformed into the site of some of the largest and most elaborate amusement parks in the country. Promoter George Tilyou built Steeplechase Park in 1897, advertising "10 hours of fun for 10 cents." With its mechanical thrills and funhouse laughs, the amusement park encouraged behavior that one schoolteacher aptly described as "everyone with the brakes off." By 1900, as many as half a million New Yorkers flocked to Coney Island on a weekend for fun. Other cities rushed to build their own playgrounds—Boston's Paragon Park and Revere Beach, Philadelphia's Willow Grove, Cleveland's Euclid Beach—but none rivaled Coney Island. The popularity of the amusement park signaled the rise of mass entertainment, making Coney Island the unofficial capital of a new mass culture.

The Labor Movement

Labor organization was not new in American society. Since colonial times, skilled workers had formed craft unions. And in the 1860s, William H. Sylvis, a Pennsylvania iron molder, briefly put together a National Labor Union to unite the skilled trades. With increased mechanization, craftsmen found their skills undermined as managers attempted to take control away from skilled workers through the use of machinery. Many of the old craft unions were broken up or badly weakened in the 1860s.

spectability, set up a Working Girl's Club in New York City. Members contributed twenty-five cents a month to rent and furnish a comfortable club room where young women could relax and entertain. Designed as an alternative to commercial dance halls and amusement resorts, the Working Girl's Club sought to replicate patterns of middle-class courtship, where the young met under the watchful eye of older adults. By 1885, branches had sprung up in Brooklyn, Philadelphia, and Boston. But by far the majority of young workingwomen seemed to prefer the pleasure (and danger) of the dance halls.

By the late nineteenth century, workers were losing control in the workplace. At the same time, the growing anonymity of corporate capitalism pitted the individual worker against huge corporations determined to cut costs. As labor became viewed less in human terms and more as a commodity, workers sought to act collectively to better their condition through politics and reform movements and also increasingly through labor unions.

Mechanization and the Erosion of Skilled Work

In 1883, a machinist described to a U.S. Senate committee the changes taking place in his shop:

> The trade has been subdivided and those subdivisions have been again subdivided, so that a man never learns the machinist's trade now. Ten years ago he learned, not the whole trade, but a fair portion of it. Also, there is more machinery used in the business, which again makes machinery.... It is merely laborers' work.

The machinist clearly recognized the way in which industrial capitalism was transforming the world of work. Jobs done by skilled craftsmen had increasingly been mechanized until the bulk of industrial workers were unskilled machine tenders or factory operatives by the end of the century. In the fierce competition to lower prices, industrialists like Andrew Carnegie invested heavily in new machinery that enabled them to replace skilled workers with unskilled workers. Wages fell accordingly, and workers found that they had less and less control over the workplace. The destruction of skill and the redefinition of labor as machine tending left the worker with a loss of independence and a growing sense of individual helplessness.

Along with the loss of independence came a threat to Americans' belief in individualism. The idea that a man could one day own his own business stood at the heart of the nineteenth-century ideology of the self-made man. Yet with the rise of large business combinations, the amount of capital that was required placed entrepreneurship out of reach for most Americans. The machinist testifying before the Senate committee expressed his growing disillusionment when asked whether his fellow workers ever hoped to become bosses or manufacturers:

> There is no chance. They have lost all desire to become bosses now ... because the trade has become

demoralized. First they earn so small wages; and, next, it takes so much capital to become a boss now that they cannot think of it, because it takes all they can earn to live.

The ranks of wage laborers, those who worked by piece rates or by the hour, grew hand in hand with the rise of big business. In 1870, wage laborers represented more than half of those counted by the census as gainfully employed. The number of nonagricultural wage laborers increased after 1870 more than twice as rapidly as the country's population, and the number of male industrial wage laborers rose from 35.9 percent in 1870 to 48.3 percent in 1900. America, which prided itself on its small businesses and skilled craftsworkers, was rapidly becoming a nation of corporations and unskilled industrial laborers.

Alone, the worker might be helpless in the face of the anonymous corporation, but together, workers could challenge the bosses and reassert their power in the workplace.

For skilled workers, who prided themselves on their working-class identity, the loss of skilled positions meant a loss of control in the workplace. This erosion of individual power served as a spur to collective action. Alone, the worker might be helpless in the face of the anonymous corporation, but together, workers could challenge the bosses and reassert their power in the workplace.

The Great Railroad Strike of 1877

Labor flexed its muscle and showed its combined might with notable results during the summer of 1877 in the Great Railroad Strike. The strike, which began on the Baltimore and Ohio Railroad in West Virginia on July 16, quickly swept across the nation's rails until it involved 100,000 railroad workers on the B&O, the Pennsylvania Railroad, and the New York Central in cities from Baltimore to San Francisco. The strikers, whose wages had been repeatedly cut, aroused a good deal of public sympathy, even among the militia sent to put them down. In Reading, Pennsylvania, militiamen refused to fire on the strikers, saying, "We may be militiamen, but we are workmen first." Rail traffic ground to a halt, and for a brief period the nation lay paralyzed by the strike.

Violence erupted as the strike spread. In Pittsburgh, striking Pennsylvania Railroad workers were joined in the streets by steel rollers, mechanics, the unemployed, and women and children who were determined to "make a common fight against the corporations." Militiamen recruited from Philadelphia arrogantly boasted that they would clean up the "workingmen's town." Opening fire on the crowd, they killed twenty people. Angry workers retaliated, and the resulting conflagration destroyed 39 buildings, 104 engines, 46 passenger cars, and more than 1,200 freight cars and reduced an area of two miles along the track to smoldering rubble. Before the day ended, twenty more workers had been shot and the railroad had sustained property damage totaling $2 million.

Railroad officials stubbornly refused to arbitrate, hoping that federal and state authorities would step in to break the strike. Within the space of eight days, the governors of nine states, acting at

the prompting of the railroad owners and managers, defined the strike as an "insurrection" and called for federal troops. President Rutherford B. Hayes (who, according to the New York *World,* owed his contested election in 1876 to the influence of Pennsylvania Railroad president Tom Scott) hesitated briefly, then called up the troops. By the time federal troops arrived, the violence had run its course. The army did not shoot a single striker in 1877. Its primary task consisted of acting as strikebreaker—opening rail traffic, protecting nonstriking "scab" train crews, and maintaining peace along the line.

Although the Great Strike was spontaneous and unorganized, it frightened the authorities and upper classes like nothing before in U.S. history. They quickly tried to blame the tiny radical Workingman's Party and predicted a bloody uprising. "Any hour the mob chooses it can destroy any city in the country—that is the simple truth," wrote future Secretary of State John Hay to his wealthy father-in-law. The *New York Times* editorialized about

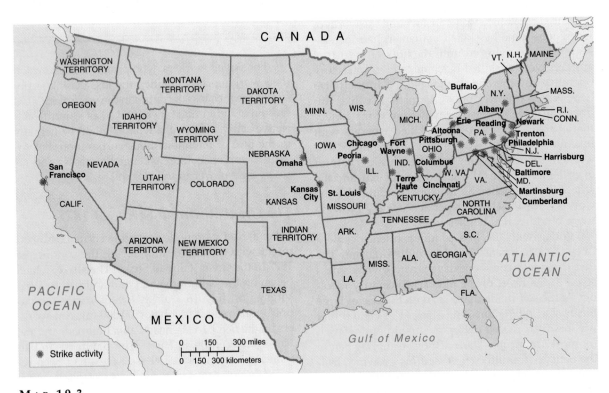

M A P 19.3
The Great Railroad Strike of 1877
Starting in West Virginia and Pennsylvania, the Great Railway Strike of 1877 spread as far north as Buffalo, and as far west as San Francisco, bringing rail traffic to a standstill.

PITTSBURGH AFTER THE GREAT RAILROAD STRIKE
The Great Railroad Strike of 1877 left two miles of downtown Pittsburgh a mass of twisted rails and rubble. When the militia fired on the crowds, angry workers fought back. More than forty people were shot, and damage to property amounted to two million dollars. The middle class, which had initially sympathized with strikers, grew fearful of the violence and destruction. The shift in public opinion helped the railroad owners put down the strike.
Carnegie Library, Pittsburgh.

the "dangerous classes," and the *Independent* magazine offered the following advice on how to deal with "rioters":

> If the club of a policeman, knocking out the brains of the rioter, will answer, then well and good; but if it does not promptly meet the exigency, then bullets and bayonets, canister and grape . . . constitutes the one remedy and one duty of the hour.

Although many middle-class Americans had initially sympathized with the conditions that led the workers to strike, they blamed the strikers for the violence and property damage that occurred.

In the end, the strikers, whose united action had raised the specter of revolution, won few concrete gains. On most railroads, wage cuts remained in force, and hundreds of strikers were fired and their names circulated on a blacklist to prevent them from ever being rehired. But the workers were far from demoralized. They had learned the power of concerted action and would use it in the future. As labor leader Samuel Gompers acknowledged fifty years later, "The railroad strike of 1877 was the tocsin [alarm bell] that sounded a ringing message of hope to us all."

The Knights of Labor and the American Federation of Labor

The Great Strike served as a stimulus to labor organizing. The Knights of Labor, the first mass organization of America's working class, proved the chief beneficiary of labor's newfound consciousness. The Noble and Holy Order of the Knights of Labor had been founded in 1869 by Uriah Stephens, a Philadelphia garment cutter. A secret but peaceable society of workers, the Knights envisioned a "universal brotherhood" of all laborers, from the common laborer to the master craftsman. Although the Knights had played no active role in the 1877 strike, its membership swelled as a result of the growing interest in unionism. In 1878, the organization dropped the trappings of secrecy and launched an ambitious campaign to organize workers regardless of skill, sex, race, or nationality.

Under the direction of General Master Workman Terence V. Powderly, the Knights became the dominant force in labor during the 1880s. The union grew from 50,000 to a membership of over 700,000 by 1885. The Knights advocated a kind of workers' democracy that embraced a wide spectrum of reforms including free land, income tax, public ownership of the railroads, equal pay for work performed by women, and the abolition of child labor. The union sought to remove class distinctions and encouraged its local assemblies to welcome all comers, employees and employers alike. "I hate the word 'class' and would drive it from the English language if I could," Powderly stated. Only the "parasitic" members of society—gamblers, stockbrokers, lawyers, bankers, and liquor dealers— were denied membership.

In theory, the Knights of Labor opposed strikes. Powderly considered the strike "a relic of barbarism." He championed arbitration and preferred to use boycotts. But in practice, much of the organization's appeal came from the successful strike the Knights mounted in 1885 against three railroads controlled by Jay Gould. The Knights won a sweeping victory, including the revocation of a 15 percent pay cut. Despite the reservations of its leadership, the Knights of Labor was quickly becoming a militant labor organization that excited passionate support from working people with the slogan "An injury to one is the concern of all."

The Knights of Labor was not without rivals. Other trade unionists disliked the broad reform goals of the Knights and sought to focus on issues in the workplace. Samuel Gompers, a cigar maker born in London of Dutch Jewish ancestry, promoted what he called "pure and simple" unionism. Gompers founded the Organized Trades and Labor Unions in 1881 and reorganized it in 1886 into the American Federation of Labor (AFL), an organization to coordinate the activities of craft unions throughout the United States. His plan was simple: Organize skilled workers, those with the most bargaining power, and use strikes to gain immediate objectives such as higher pay and better working conditions. Gompers's "bread and butter" unionism at first drew few converts. The AFL had only 138,000 members in 1886, compared with 730,000 for the Knights of Labor. But events soon brought down the Knights and enabled Gompers to take control of the labor movement.

Haymarket and the Specter of Labor Radicalism

While the AFL and the Knights of Labor competed for members, more radical socialists and anarchists offered competing visions of labor's true path. The radicals, many of whom were immigrants steeped

SAMUEL GOMPERS
Samuel Gompers, pictured here in 1895, founded the American Federation of Labor in 1886 and served as its president continuously (except for 1895) until his death in 1924. Unlike the Knights of Labor, who supported the Populist Party in the 1890s, the AFL advocated "pure and simple unionism." Gompers, convinced that workers could gain little from politics, organized only skilled workers and focused on bread-and-butter issues.
The George Meany Memorial Archives.

in the tradition of European socialism, believed that reform was futile; they called for social revolution, in theory if not in practice. Anarchists also wanted revolutionary change but envisioned a smaller role for the state than the socialists did. Both groups, sensitive to criticism that they preferred revolution in theory to improvements here and now, rallied around the popular issue of the eight-hour day.

Ever since the 1840s, labor had sought to end the twelve-hour workday, which was standard in industry and manufacturing. To Ira Steward, who devoted his life to the struggle, the shorter workday meant not only greater leisure but also an opportunity for the workers to study politics and "escape from slavery and ignorance." By the mid-1880s, it seemed clear that labor shared too little in the new prosperity of the decade. Once again, pressure mounted for the eight-hour day. The radicals seized on the popular issue and launched major rallies in cities across the nation. Supporters of the movement set May 1, 1886, as the date for a nationwide general strike in support of the eight-hour day.

All factions of the nascent labor movement came together in Chicago on May Day, for what was billed as the largest demonstration in history in support of the eight-hour day. Chicago's Knights of Labor rallied to the cause even though Powderly and the union's leadership, worried by the increasing activism of the rank and file, refused to champion the movement for shorter hours. A group of radicals led by anarchist Albert Parsons, a *Mayflower* descendant, and August Spies, a German immigrant, spearheaded the eight-hour movement in Chicago. Combining passionate conviction with the fiery rhetoric of class warfare, they sent shivers of fear through the propertied classes with slogans like "Death to the foes of the human race."

Samuel Gompers was on hand, too, to rally the city's trade unionists, although he privately urged the AFL assemblies not to participate in a general strike. Gompers's skilled workers were labor's elite. Many still worked in small shops where negotiations between workers and employers took place in an environment tempered by personal relationships. In their Prince Albert coats and starched shirts, they stood in sharp contrast to the dispossessed strikers across town at Chicago's huge McCormick reaper works. There, strikers watched helplessly as the company brought in strikebreakers, or scabs, to take their jobs and marched them to work under the protection of the Chicago police and security guards supplied by the Pinkerton Detective Agency. Cyrus McCormick Jr., son of the inventor of the mechanical reaper, viewed labor organization as a threat to his power as well as to his profits; he was determined to smash the union.

On May Day, 45,000 workers paraded peacefully down Michigan Avenue in support of the eight-hour day, many singing the song that had become the movement's anthem:

> We mean to make things over;
>   we're tired of toil for naught
> But bare enough to live on: never
>   an hour for thought.
> We want to feel the sunshine; we
>   want to smell the flowers;
> We're sure that God has willed it,
>   and we mean to have eight hours.
> We're summoning our forces from
>   shipyard, shop, and mill:
> Eight hours for work, eight hours for rest,
>   eight hours for what we will!

Trouble came two days later, when strikers attacked scabs outside the McCormick works and police opened fire, killing or wounding six men. Angry radicals rushed out a circular urging workingmen to "arm yourselves and appear in full force" at a rally in Haymarket Square.

At Haymarket on the evening of May 4, the turnout was disappointing. No more than 2,000 to 3,000 gathered in the drizzle to hear Spies, Parsons, and the other anarchist speakers. Mayor Carter Harrison, known as a friend of labor, mingled conspicuously in the crowd, pronounced the meeting peaceable, and went home to bed. A short time later, police Captain John "Blackjack" Bonfield, a man who had made his reputation by cracking skulls, marched his men into the crowd (by now no more than 300 people) and demanded that they disperse.

Suddenly, someone threw a bomb into the police ranks, and the street echoed with the fiery blast. After a moment of stunned silence, the police drew their revolvers. "Fire and kill all you can," shouted a police lieutenant. Cries and curses mingled with the groans of the wounded as people took cover in doorways and behind walls and empty barrels, leaving the streets littered with bodies. When it was over, seven policemen and an unknown number of civilians lay fatally wounded. An additional sixty policemen and some thirty or forty civilians suffered injuries from the blast and the ensuing melee.

News of the "Haymarket riot" provoked a nationwide convulsion of fear, followed by blind rage directed not only at the bomb thrower, whose identity was never discovered, but also against anarchists, labor unions, strikers, immigrants, and the working class in general. The hysteria ran deepest in Chicago. The police rounded up Spies and the other Haymarket speakers and jailed hundreds of radicals. Although none of these men had thrown the bomb, seven of them, all German immigrants, were put on trial for conspiracy to commit murder. Parsons, who had managed to escape capture, turned himself in to stand trial with his fellows.

"Convict these men," cried State's Attorney Julius S. Grinnell, "make examples of them, hang them, and you save our institutions." The men were on trial for their ideas, not their actions. Although the state could not link any of the defendants with the bomb throwing, the jury nevertheless found all eight men guilty. Four were executed, one committed suicide, and three received prison sentences. On the gallows, August Spies spoke for the Haymarket martyrs: "The time will come when our silence will be more powerful than the voices you throttle today."

In 1893, Governor John Peter Altgeld, after a thorough investigation, pardoned the three remaining Haymarket anarchists. He denounced the trial as a shameless travesty of justice and concluded that Captain Bonfield was "the man really responsible for the death of the police officers." The governor's action brought on a storm of protest and cost him his political career. But through the entire process, Altgeld never wavered. "If I decide they are innocent, I will pardon them," he promised, "even if I never hold office another day." He did, and he didn't.

The bomb blast at Haymarket had lasting repercussions. For years, the memory of Haymarket and the dread of anarchy haunted the American consciousness and heightened the country's deep distrust of labor militancy. By the association of labor organization with terrorism and foreign radicals, the Haymarket bomb, in the eyes of one observer, proved "a godsend to all enemies of the labor movement." It effectively scotched the eight-hour movement and dealt a fatal blow to the Knights of Labor. On the same day as the Haymarket affair, Jay Gould, who had retaliated against the Knights of Labor in another strike, the Great Southwestern Railroad Strike of 1886, this time forced the union to come to terms. The Knights never recovered.

With the labor movement everywhere under attack, many workers severed their radical connections, and many skilled workers turned to the American Federation of Labor (AFL). Under the leadership of Samuel Gompers, the AFL soon became the dominant voice of American labor. Until his death in 1924, Gompers worked to shape skilled workers into a disciplined force able to exert bargaining leverage against employers.

Gompers developed a pragmatic philosophy concerning labor, a strategy forged in the aftermath of Haymarket. Disillusioned with broad reform goals, disappointed in politics as a route to change, and angry at radicals who jeopardized the future of labor, Gompers urged workers to focus on concrete gains. The AFL would push for changes here and now—higher wages, shorter hours—and use strikes and boycotts judiciously to win its demands. Gompers expected no help from the government, pointing out that the courts, the lawmakers, and the executive branch sided with property owners in every instance. Given the times, Gompers's narrow economic strategy made sense and enabled one segment of the workforce—the skilled—to organize effectively and achieve tangible gains. But the vast majority of unskilled workers remained largely untouched by the AFL's brand of "pure and simple" trade unionism.

Visions of a Better Life

Fear of social upheaval generated by the uprisings of workers in the 1870s and 1880s led to a search for social solutions. Liberal reformers, sympathetic to labor's plight but fearful of violence, sought schemes that would mitigate economic injustice without threatening bloodshed or class warfare. Two journalists, Henry George and Edward Bellamy, put forward visions of a better life that captured the imagination of their times. The utopian plans of George and Bellamy expressed both their fears about the present and their hopes for a better future.

Henry George and the Single Tax

The Great Railroad Strike of 1877 inspired San Francisco journalist Henry George to write a book that soon became a classic of American political economy. George knew poverty firsthand and harbored a deep sympathy for the underdog. In this spirit, he published *Progress and Poverty* in 1879, dedicating it "to those who, seeing the vice and misery that spring from the unequal distribution of wealth and privilege, feel the possibility of a higher social state and would strive for its attainment."

Liberal reformers, sympathetic to labor's plight but fearful of violence, sought schemes that would mitigate economic injustice without threatening bloodshed or class warfare.

In *Progress and Poverty*, George explored the paradox central to American life: Why, in a land so rich, was there such inequality? He had watched in frustration how the growth of monopoly went hand in hand with land speculation in California. In *Progress and Poverty*, he elaborated a theory that tied increasing inequality and growing monopoly to the scarcity of land caused by speculation (the practice of buying land and holding it till the price went up). Land speculators, he charged, contributed nothing to the economy yet made huge profits in "unearned increment."

As a cure for the nation's industrial problems, he championed a single tax on unimproved land. Once speculators could no longer turn large profits on the land they held, the way lay open to utopia, in George's view. Land would become available for farming. Industrial workers would leave the factories for the farms. Wages would naturally increase, and the life of industrial laborers would become more secure. Government, and with it the political corruption of the Gilded Age, would virtually disappear. George devoted an entire section of his book to a picture of the future that awaited the enactment of his simple law.

To underscore the urgent need for change, he ended his book with an apocalyptic vision of what would befall the United States if action were not taken: disease, pauperism, and an atmosphere of "brooding revolution." His single tax offered a way out, an alternative to class warfare. In George's view, venturesome capitalists and honest laboring people were not class enemies. The real villain was the grasping land speculator. The single tax, then, promised to bring America back from the brink of disaster and usher in a golden age.

George's message found many ready adherents who made the single tax a rallying cry for reform. George moved east after the publication of *Progress and Poverty* and became interested in politics. In 1886, in the aftermath of the Haymarket affair, he ran for mayor of New York City on the United Labor Party ticket. George appealed to labor, which saw him as one of its own. A printer, a unionist, and a member of the Knights of Labor, George believed that labor should take a more active role in politics, particularly on the municipal level. Tammany Hall attempted to buy him off, promising to run him for Congress on the Democratic ticket. "You cannot be elected," a Tammany pol told George, "but your running will raise hell." To which George responded, "I do not want the responsibility and the work of the Mayor of New York, but I do want to raise hell."

At first, George's opponents dismissed him as a "humbug" and a "busybody" with no real chance. But when 34,000 laborers signed a petition endorsing him, Democrats and Republicans began to take him seriously. Samuel Gompers himself became the chair of George's city organization and headed the speakers' bureau. Staunch Republican liberals, fearful of class war, threw their support to the Demo-

crats and tarred George as a "revolutionist" and "an apostle of anarchy and destruction." At the prompting of Tammany Hall, the Catholic archbishop of New York warned his flock not to "be deluded by men who advocate revolutionary doctrines." In what George accurately described as "one of the fiercest contests that ever took place in this or any other city," he lost the election by 20,000 votes, despite strong working-class support. The Democratic candidate beat George, who in turn nosed out his Republican rival, a political newcomer named Theodore Roosevelt.

Looking Backward from the Year 2000

While Henry George campaigned for mayor of New York and the country awaited the execution of the Haymarket anarchists, Edward Bellamy took up his pen to write one of the most influential novels in American history, a political work that ranks with Harriet Beecher Stowe's antislavery novel *Uncle Tom's Cabin* in terms of sales and influence. Bellamy, a Massachusetts newspaper writer forced by tuberculosis to give up his editorial career, had turned to writing novels. In 1888, he published *Looking Backward: 2000–1887*, a combination of utopian fantasy and genteel romance that spoke to the concerns of millions in the United States who were looking for a peaceful solution to the labor problem.

In *Looking Backward*, Edward Bellamy's hero, Julian West, falls asleep in Boston in 1887 and wakes in the year 2000 to find the world transformed. No labor strife, no class antagonism, no extremes of poverty and wealth exist in the twenty-first century. Instead, the people are organized into an efficient industrial army in which all men and women between the ages of twenty-one and forty-five work for the same guaranteed annual income. In Bellamy's highly centralized state, the disharmony, corruption, and party strife of the Gilded Age have vanished, replaced by benevolent bureaucracy.

Bellamy's utopia comes complete with visions of technological marvels that were unheard of in the 1880s—the radio and moving sidewalks. But although the material conditions of the people have improved, Bellamy makes it clear that the new world came about from a spiritual and not a material transformation. The Religion of Solidarity, or "nationalism," as it is called, transformed society. The Nationalist Party, Julian learns, grew almost overnight from a tiny band of evangelists to a force

From Rags to Riches: How Do Historians Measure Success?

T HE RAGS TO RICHES FABLES of novelists like Horatio Alger fueled the dreams of countless young people at the turn of the century. Alger's formulaic novels feature fatherless young men who through the right combination of "pluck and luck" move ahead in the world. Yet despite the myth, few Americans rose from rags to riches. Even Alger's heroes, like his popular *Ragged Dick* (1866), more often traded rags for respectability.

Without exception, Alger's characters came from old stock and were not the new immigrants who poured through the "golden door" into the United States at the turn of the century. What were their chances of success? Literature written by the new immigrants themselves tells different stories. Abraham Cahan's *The Rise of David Levinsky* (1917) describes the experience of an eastern European Jewish immigrant who, as the title indicates, rises to gain material success. But the author laments that Levinsky's "rise" is paralleled by a spiritual loss. Mike Gold tells a darker story of immigrant life in *Jews without Money* (1930), an autobiographical tale of the implacable economic forces that devastated Gold's fictional family and turned its young protagonist to communism. Gold's characters inhabit a world of grinding poverty and ignorance, a landscape so bleak that one character comes to doubt the existence of a benevolent God, asking plaintively, "Did God make bedbugs?" Yet Gold's own success belied the grim economic determinism of his fiction. He made it out of the ghetto and into the world of literature and social activism.

Historians have been fascinated by the question of "making it" in America. Repeatedly they have attempted to measure economic and social mobility, from colonial times to the twentieth century. Looking at the lives of common folk, scholars have struggled to determine who made it and who didn't and why. Was America a land of boundless opportunity where the poor could rise? Or did the rich stay rich and the poor stay poor-to-middling, as pioneering studies of social mobility in the 1950s indicated?

By the 1960s, quantitative methods made possible by advances in computer technology promised to move history away from the "impressionistic," anecdotal evidence of fiction and memoirs and provide a statistical framework in which to measure success. But just what could historians measure with their new tools? Comparing Jewish and Italian immigrants in New York City at the turn of the century, one historian concluded that the Jews had done a better job of making it. By employing a table that categorized occupations, ranking them from professional, white-collar jobs to unskilled labor, the historian duly noted the movement from one category to another, concluding from his data that Jews moved more quickly into the white-collar class.

Studies of occupational mobility, however, contained major flaws. In a country where money has been and continues to be the common measure of success, historians' decision to use occupational categories and not income as the yardstick of mobility and success seemed to beg the question. Yet the choice was not surprising, given that census data, the staple of quantitative studies, provide information on occupation but not on income. Even occupational mobility proved difficult to measure accurately. For example, in the study cited, peddlers somewhat arbitrarily ranked at low white-collar status because they were self-employed. Yet the pushcart peddler and the Italian street vendor could hardly be said to have enjoyed white-collar status in the larger society in which they moved. Students must look carefully at what historians are measuring, recognizing that occupational mobility may not equate with social mobility or economic success.

The larger question remains: What is "making it" in America and how best can it be measured—in dollars and cents, in job satisfaction, occupational status, in comparison with the lives of one's parents or neighbors? And what of the immigrants them-

RAGS TO RICHES

Horatio Alger's novels like Ragged Dick *(1867), pictured here, invariably end with the young hero on the road to success. Contrast Alger's cheerful message with the bathos of the 1900 song "No One Cares for Me," in which the young newsboy in his rags replicates Alger's hero. But instead of getting ahead, his lot is portrayed as one of cruel neglect. Which portrait is more accurate? Historians for decades have wrestled with the question of social mobility and success.*

Picture Research Consultants & Archives; Culver Pictures.

selves? How did they define it? If becoming a bricklayer spelled success to the Italian immigrant and his family, do studies of occupational mobility based on statisticians' categories and job rankings distort his lived reality? In dealing with the issue of "making it" in America, historians have increasingly come to recognize that each immigrant group had its own unique definition of success. Not all immigrants sought upward mobility, whether economic or occupational. Cultural factors, such as the value Italians placed on loyalty to the family, also played a key role. Ultimately, questions of success and mobility cannot easily be quantified, and they demand attention to the larger cultural context that shaped individual economic and occupational choices.

that succeeded in eliminating the destructive energies of both capitalist greed and proletarian envy and hatred. All society had to do was recognize and cooperate in the inevitable evolutionary process from competition to cooperation.

Julian himself experiences a conversion and, by the book's end, overcomes the smug selfishness that was the hallmark of his class. Looking back at his old life, he compares society in the late nineteenth century to "a prodigious coach which the masses of humanity were harnessed to and dragged toilsomely along a very hilly and sandy road." The driver of the coach is hunger, and his whips cut deep into the backs of the struggling team below. On top of the coach, "well up out of the dust," perch the passengers, who occasionally call down encouragement to the toilers below, "exhorting them to patience, and holding out hopes of possible compensation in another world for the hardness of their lot." Such inhumanity, Julian patiently explains to his twenty-first-century audience, could be explained by the conviction that "there was no other way in which Society could get along, except that the many pulled at the rope and the few rode." Besides, the riders suffer from the hallucination that "they [are] not exactly like their brothers and sisters" but are made "of finer clay." "This seems unaccountable," Julian confesses, "but, as I once rode this very coach and shared that very hallucination, I ought to be believed."

In the parable of the stagecoach, Bellamy offered a scathing critique of social Darwinism and a call to action. The book caused a sensation. Within three years, over a million copies had been sold, and enthusiastic readers launched 165 Bellamy Clubs devoted to discussing nationalism and implementing the social goals expressed in *Looking Backward*. While neither George's single tax nor Bellamy's nationalist utopia produced the kind of massive social change envisioned by the two authors, the enthusiastic response to both books indicated that many Americans feared social cataclysm and were ready to take action.

Conclusion: The Workers' Own Struggle

The late nineteenth century witnessed many competing visions of a better life as Americans sought solutions to the problems attending urban industrialism and corporate capitalism. Henry George's single tax won supporters across the country and rallied New York's laborers to support him for mayor. Bellamy's nationalist utopia attracted followers drawn largely from the "sensible middle class." President Hayes called for "education" and a "wise judicious policy" to avoid labor upheavals like the Great Railroad Strike of 1877. American workers themselves had their own vision of what a better life might be—a life in which the independence eroded by industrialization could be countered by collective action, workers could regain some control of the workplace, and a shorter day and a higher wage promised escape from a brutal life of toil. Their vision and their willingness to fight for it made them active agents of social change, willing to risk their livelihood and sometimes their lives in the struggle.

Looking at the impact on his life occasioned by industrialization, a Massachusetts machinist declared in the 1890s:

> The workers of Massachusetts have always been law and order men. We loved our country and respected the laws. For the last five years the times have been growing worse every year, until we have been brought down so far that we have not much farther to go. What do the Mechanics of Massachusetts say to each other? I will tell you: "We must have a change. Any thing is better than this. We cannot be worse off, no matter what the change is."

Mounting anger and frustration would lead American workers and farmers to join forces in the 1890s and create a grassroots movement to fight for change under the banner of a new People's Party.

CHRONOLOGY

1869 Uriah Stephens founds Knights of Labor.

Cincinnati mounts first professional baseball team, the Red Stockings.

1870 Wage earners account for over half of those employed in 1870 census.

1872 Andrew Carnegie opens his steelworks outside Pittsburgh.

1877 Great Railroad Strike paralyzes nation's transportation system.

1878 Knights of Labor campaign to organize workers regardless of skill, sex, or race.

1879 Henry George publishes *Progress and Poverty.*

1880 George M. Pullman builds model town on 4,300 acres near Chicago.

1881 Samuel Gompers founds Organized Trades and Labor Unions.

1883 Andrew Carnegie acquires the Homestead Steel Mill outside Pittsburgh after labor strikes force owners to sell.

1884 Grace Dodge organizes first Working Girl's Club in New York City.

1886 Organized Trades and Labor Unions reorganized as the American Federation of Labor (AFL).

May 1. Massive rally in support of eight-hour workday takes place in Chicago.

Haymarket bombing in Chicago results in widening fear of anarchy and a blow to the labor movement.

Henry George campaigns for mayor of New York City on United Labor Party ticket and loses to Tammany Hall Democrat in close election.

1888 Edward Bellamy publishes *Looking Backward.*

1890 Average worker earns $500 per year.

1893 Governor John Peter Altgeld pardons three remaining Haymarket anarchists.

1897 Steeplechase amusement park opens on Coney Island.

BIBLIOGRAPHY

GENERAL WORKS

Alan Dawley, *Struggles for Justice: Social Responsibility and the Liberal State* (1991).

Melvyn Dubofsky, *Industrialism and the American Worker, 1865–1920* (1975).

Ray Ginger, *Altgeld's America* (1973).

Herbert C. Gutman, *Work, Culture, and Society in Industrializing America: Essays in American Working-Class and Social History* (1976).

David M. Katzman and William M. Tuttle Jr., *Plain Folk: The Life Stories of Undistinguished Americans* (1982).

David Montgomery, *The Fall of the House of Labor: The Workplace, the State, and American Labor Activism, 1865–1925* (1987).

Nell Irvin Painter, *Standing at Armageddon: The United States, 1877–1919* (1987).

Leon Stein and Philip Taft, eds., *Workers Speak* (1971).

WORKERS

Karen Anderson, *Changing Woman: A History of Racial Ethnic Women in America* (1996).

Eric Arnesen, *Waterfront Workers in New Orleans: Race, Class, and Politics, 1863–1923* (1991).

Cindy Sondik Aron, *Ladies and Gentlemen of the Civil Service: Middle-Class Workers in Victorian America* (1987).

Gunther Barth, *Bitter Strength: The History of the Chinese in the United States, 1850–1870* (1964).

Mary H. Blewett, *Men, Women, and Work: Class, Gender, and Protest in the New England Shoe Industry, 1780–1910* (1988).

John Bodnar, *Workers' World* (1982).

David Brody, *Steelworkers in America: The Nonunion Era* (1960).

David Brody, *Workers in Industrial America: Essays on the Twentieth-Century Struggle* (1980).

Milton Cantor and Bruce Laurie, eds., *Class, Sex, and the Woman Worker* (1977).

Ping Chiu, *Chinese Labor in California: An Economic Study* (1967).

Patricia A. Cooper, *Once a Cigar Maker: Men, Women, and Work Culture in American Cigar Factories* (1987).

Margery W. Davies, *Woman's Place Is at the Typewriter: Office Work and Office Workers, 1870–1930* (1982).

James J. Davis, *The Iron Puddler: My Life in the Rolling Mills and What Became of It* (1922).

Alan Derickson, *Workers' Health, Workers' Democracy: The Western Miners' Struggle, 1891–1925* (1988).

Sigmund Diamond, ed., *The Nation Transformed: The Creation of an Industrial Society* (1963).

Faye E. Dudden, *Serving Women: Household Service in Nineteenth-Century America* (1983).

Philip S. Foner, *Women and the American Labor Movement: From the First Trade Unions to the Present* (1979).

Michael H. Frisch and Daniel J. Walkowitz, eds., *Working-Class America: Essays on Labor, Community, and American Society* (1983).

John Debo Galloway, *The First Transcontinental Railroad* (1950).

Sherna Gluck, *From Parlor to Prison: Five American Suffragists Talk about Their Lives* (1976).

David M. Gordon, Richard Edwards, and Michael Reich, eds., *Segmented Work, Divided Workers: The Historical Transformation of Labor in the United States* (1982).

William H. Harris, *The Harder We Run: Black Workers since the Civil War* (1982).

Elizabeth Hasanovitz, *One of Them: Chapters from a Passionate Autobiography* (1918).

Jacqueline Jones, *The Dispossessed: America's Underclasses from the Civil War to the Present* (1992).

David M. Katzman, *Seven Days a Week: Women and Domestic Service in Industrializing America* (1978).

Susan E. Kennedy, *If All We Did Was to Weep at Home* (1979).

Alice Kessler-Harris, *Out to Work: The History of Wage-Earning Women in the United States* (1982).

Alexander Keyssar, *Out of Work* (1986).

Maxine Hong Kingston, *China Men* (1977).

S. J. Kleinberg, *The Shadow of the Mills: Workingclass Families in Pittsburgh, 1870–1907* (1989).

George Kraus, *High Road to Promontory: Building the Central Pacific across the High Sierra* (1969).

A. T. Lane, *Solidarity or Survival? American Labor and European Immigrants, 1830–1924* (1987).

Larry Lankton, *Cradle to Grave: Life, Work, and Death at Lake Superior Copper Mines* (1991).

Janet Lecompte, ed., *Emily [French]: The Diary of a Hard-Worked Woman* (1987).

Susan Levine, *Labor's True Women: Carpet Weavers, Industrialization, and Labor Reform in the Gilded Age* (1984).

Julie A. Matthaei, *An Economic History of Women in America: Women's Work, the Sexual Division of Labor, and the Development of Capitalism* (1982).

Cathy L. McHugh, *Mill Family: The Labor System in the Southern Cotton Textile Industry, 1880–1915* (1988).

Joanne J. Meyerowitz, *Women Adrift: Independent Wage Earners in Chicago, 1880–1930* (1988).

Gwendolyn Mink, *Old Labor and New Immigrants in American Political Development* (1986).

David Montgomery, *Workers' Control in America* (1979).

Victor G. Nee and Brett de Bary Nee, *Longtime Californ': A Documentary Study of an American Chinatown* (1972).

William L. O'Neill, ed., *Women at Work* (1972).

Cornelia Stratton Parker, *Working with the Working Women* (1922).

Samuel H. Preston and Michael R. Haines, *Fatal Years: Child Mortality in Late Nineteenth Century America* (1991).

Marilyn D. Rhinehart, *A Way of Work and a Way of Life* (1992).

Richard B. Rice, William A. Bullough, and Richard J. Orsi, *The Elusive Eden: A New History of California* (1988).

M. B. Schnapper, *Women at Work: The Autobiography of Mary Anderson as Told to Mary N. Winslow* (1951).

Dorothy Schweider, *Black Diamonds: Life and Work in Iowa's Coal Mining Communities, 1895–1925* (1983).

Carl Smith, *Urban Disorder and the Shape of Belief* (1995).

Daphne Spain, *Gendered Spaces* (1992).

Frank Hatch Streightoff, *The Standard of Living among the Industrial People of America* (1911).

Sharon Hartman Strom, *Beyond the Typewriter: Gender, Class, and Origins of Modern American Office Work, 1900–1930* (1992).

Ronald Takaki, *Strangers from a Different Shore: A History of Asian Americans* (1989).

Leslie Woodcock Tentler, *Wage-Earning Women: Industrial Work and Family Life in the United States, 1900–1930* (1979).

Carole Turbin, *Working Women of Collar City: Gender, Class, and Community in Troy, New York, 1864–1886* (1992).

Jules Tygiel, *Workingmen in San Francisco, 1880–1901* (1992).

Lynn Y. Weiner, *From Working Girl to Working Mother: The Female Labor Force in the United States, 1920–1980* (1985).

Robert E. Weir, *Beyond Labor's Veil: The Culture of the Knights of Labor* (1996).

Barbara Wertheimer, *We Were There: The Story of Working Women in America* (1977).

Richard White, *"It's Your Misfortune and None of My Own": A New History of the American West* (1991).

Mark Wyman, *Round-Trip to America: The Immigrants Return to Europe, 1880–1930* (1993).

Virginia Yans-McLaughlin, *Family and Community: Italian Immigrants in Buffalo, 1880–1930* (1977).

MILL TOWNS AND COMPANY TOWNS

William Adelman, *Touring Pullman: A Study in Company Paternalism* (1977).

Stanley Buder, *Pullman: An Experiment in Industrial Order and Community Planning, 1880–1930* (1967).

John S. Garner, *The Company Town: Architecture and Society in the Early Industrial Age* (1992).

Jacquelyn Dowd Hall, James Leloudis, Robert Korstad, Mary Murphy, Lu Ann Jones, and Christopher B. Daly, *Like a Family: The Making of a Southern Mill World* (1987).

Tamara K. Hareven, *Family Life and Industrial Time: The Relationship between the Family and Work in a New England Industrial Community* (1982).

Tamara K. Hareven and Randolph Langenbach, *Amoskeag: Life and Work in an American Factory-City* (1978).

LIFE AND LEISURE

Elaine Abelson, *When Ladies Go A'Thieving: Middle-Class Shoplifters in the Victorian Department Store* (1989).

Judith Adams, *The American Amusement Park Industry: A History of Technology and Thrills* (1991).

Gunther Barth, *City People: The Rise of Modern City Culture in Nineteenth-Century America* (1980).

Susan Porter Benson, *Counter Cultures: Saleswomen, Managers, and Customers in American Department Stores, 1890–1940* (1986).

George Chauncey, *Gay New York* (1994).

Warren Goldstein, *Playing for Keeps: A History of Early Baseball* (1989).

John F. Kasson, *Amusing the Million: Coney Island at the Turn of the Century* (1978).

William Leach, *Land of Desire: Merchants, Power, and the Rise of a New American Culture* (1993).

John Lucas and Ronald Smith, *The Saga of American Sport* (1978).

Karen Lystra, *Searching the Heart: Women, Men, and Romantic Love in Nineteenth Century America* (1989).

Steven Mintz, *A Prison of Expectations: The Family in Victorian Culture* (1983).

Steven Mintz and Susan Kellogg, *Domestic Revolutions: A Social History of American Family Life* (1988).

David Nasaw, *Going Out: The Rise and Fall of Public Amusements* (1993).

Kathy Peiss, *Cheap Amusements: Working Women and Leisure in Turn of the Century New York* (1986).

Steven Pope, *Patriotic Games: Sporting Traditions in the American Imagination, 1876–1926* (1996).

Steven A. Riess, *Touching Base: Professional Baseball and American Culture in the Progressive Era* (1980).

Roy Rosenzweig, *Eight Hours for What We Will: Workers and Leisure in an Industrial City, 1870–1920* (1983).

Sheila M. Rothman, *Woman's Proper Place: A History of Changing Ideals and Practices, 1870 to the Present* (1979).

Carol Smith-Rosenberg, *Disorderly Conduct: Visions of Gender in Victorian America* (1986).

LABOR STRIFE AND ORGANIZED LABOR

Paul Avrich, *The Haymarket Tragedy* (1984).

Robert V. Bruce, *1877: Year of Violence* (1959).

Henry David, *The History of the Haymarket Affair* (1963).

Melvyn Dubofsky, *When Workers Organize: New York City in the Progressive Era* (1968).

Leon Fink, *Workingman's Democracy: The Knights of Labor and American Politics* (1983).

Philip S. Foner, *The Great Labor Uprising of 1877* (1977).

William E. Forbath, *Law and the Shaping of the American Labor Movement* (1991).

Dee Garrison, *Mary Heaton Vorse: The Life of an American Insurgent* (1989).

Stuart B. Kaufman, *Samuel Gompers and the Origins of the American Federation of Labor* (1973).

John Laslett, *Labor and the Left: A Study of Socialist and Radical Influences in the American Labor Movement, 1881–1924* (1970).

Sidney Lens, *The Labor Wars: From the Molly Maguires to the Sitdowns* (1974).

Harold C. Livesay, *Samuel Gompers and Organized Labor in America* (1978).

Milton Meltzer, *Bread and Roses: The Struggle of American Labor, 1865–1915* (1967).

Henry Pelling, *American Labor* (1960).

Christopher L. Tomlins, *The State and the Unions: Labor Relations, Law, and the Organized Labor Movement in America, 1880–1960* (1985).

Robert E. Weir, *Beyond Labor's Veil: The Culture of the Knights of Labor* (1996).

Samuel Yellen, *American Labor Struggles* (1936).

Irwin Yellowitz, *Industrialization and the American Labor Movement, 1850–1900* (1977).

REFORMERS

Charles Albro Barker, *Henry George* (1955).

Edward Bellamy, *Looking Backward: 2000–1887* (1888).

Henry George, *Progress and Poverty* (1954).

Edward J. Rose, *Henry George* (1968).

John L. Thomas, *Alternative America: Henry George, Edward Bellamy, Henry Demarest Lloyd, and the Adversary Tradition* (1983).

FARMERS' ALLIANCE SONGBOOK

In the 1800s, the Farmers' Alliance recruited followers in the South and Midwest at the rate of twenty thousand a month, using lecturers, camp meetings, and even songs to educate and organize. This Farmers' Alliance songbook was offered for sale, by the copy and by the hundred — testimony to the growing movement. In the picture an Alliance farmer shakes the hand of a blacksmith, who bears a not coincidental resemblance to Abraham Lincoln. The handshake symbolizes the willingness of the alliance to make common cause with laborers of every stripe, a message reiterated in the four corners with images of school, farm, factory, and ship.

East Carolina Manuscript Collection, J. Y. Joyner Library, East Carolina University, Greenville, N. C.
Photo by Dewan Frentger.

FIGHTING FOR CHANGE IN THE TURBULENT NINETIES

20

1890–1900

S T. LOUIS IN FEBRUARY 1892 played host to one of the most striking political gatherings of the century. Thousands of farmers, laborers, reformers, orators, and common people flocked to Missouri to attend a meeting that was, in the words of one observer, "different from any other political meeting ever witnessed in St. Louis." The cigar-smoking professional politicians who generally worked the convention circuit were nowhere to be found. In their place, a reporter noted, were "mostly gray-haired, sunburned and roughly clothed men" assembled under a banner that proclaimed, "We do not ask for sympathy or pity. We ask for justice."

Exposition Music Hall presented a colorful spectacle. "The banners of the different states rose above the delegates throughout the hall, fluttering like the flags over an army encamped," wrote one reporter. Ignatius Donnelly, the crowd's favorite orator, attacked the money kings of Wall Street. Mary Elizabeth Lease, a veteran campaigner from Kansas known for exhorting farmers to "raise less corn and more hell," lent her powerful voice to the cause. Terence V. Powderly, head of the Knights of Labor, called on workers to join hands with farmers against the "nonproducing classes." And Frances Willard of the Woman's Christian Temperance Union argued for temperance and woman suffrage. Between speeches the crowd sang songs like "Hurrah for the Toiler," "All Hail the Power of Laboring Men," and "Justice for the Farmer."

In the course of the next few days, delegates hammered out a series of demands that were breathtaking in their scope. They tackled the tough questions of the day—the regulation of business, the need for banking and currency reform, the rights of labor, and the role of the federal government in guaranteeing democracy. The convention, noted a reporter, ended its work amid a din of cheers. "As if by magic, everyone was upon his feet in an instant. Thundering cheers from 10,000 throats greeted these demands as the road to liberty. Hats, paper, handkerchiefs, etc., were thrown into the air; wraps, umbrellas and parasols waved; cheer after cheer thundered and reverberated through the vast hall reaching the outside of the building where thousands who had been waiting the outcome, joined in the applause till for blocks in every direction the exultation made the din indescribable."

What was all the shouting about? People were building a new political party, the People's, or Populist, Party. Dissatisfied with the Democrats and Republicans, a broad coalition of groups came together in St. Louis to fight for change. They determined to reconvene in Omaha in July to nominate candidates for the upcoming presidential election.

The 1890s witnessed one of the most turbulent decades in U.S. history. Unrest, agitation, agrarian revolt, labor strikes, and a severe financial panic and depression marked the decade. While the major parties continued to do business as usual, Americans flocked to organizations like the Knights of Labor, the Farmers' Alliance, and the Woman's Christian Temperance Union and worked together to create new political alliances. The St. Louis gathering marked just one milestone on the road to a new politics. The People's Party challenged laissez-faire by insisting that the federal government play a more active role to ensure greater economic equity in industrial America. This challenge to the status quo would culminate in 1896 in one of the most hotly contested presidential elections in the nation's history. At the close of this tumultuous decade, America entered the twentieth century after a war for expansion that healed the nation's wounds even as it raised new questions about the direction in which the United States was heading.

Militant Women

"Do everything," Frances Willard urged her followers in 1881. The new president of the Woman's Christian Temperance Union (WCTU) meant what she said. She soon led the organization into politics and reform. The path of the WCTU followed a trajectory that was common in the late nineteenth century. As women organized to deal with issues that touched their homes and families, they moved almost inevitably into politics, lending a new urgency to the cause of woman suffrage (the vote for women). Women's activism and reform were by no means limited to the white middle class, as Ida B. Wells's antilynching campaign forcefully demonstrated.

Frances Willard and the Woman's Christian Temperance Union

Frances Willard, the visionary leader of the WCTU, spoke for a group that was left almost entirely out of the electoral process—women. In 1881, only two territories, Utah and Wyoming, allowed women to vote. Elsewhere, woman suffrage was either nonexistent or severely limited. Michigan women voted in school elections, as did women in Minnesota and Kansas. But lack of the franchise did not mean that women were apolitical. The WCTU demonstrates

WCTU FLYER
This Woman's Christian Temperance Union flyer shows the wife pitted against the saloon keeper for her husband's pay. The economic consequences to the family of a drinker were a serious matter. At a time when the average worker made only $500 a year, the money spent on alcohol meant less to eat for the family. As the poster indicates, thirty cents a day for a year paid for a substantial amount of family staples. Beer and liquor lobbyists worked hard not only to counter the WCTU but to fight woman suffrage because they feared when women got the vote they would enact prohibition.
Culver Pictures.

the breadth of women's political activity in the late nineteenth century.

The WCTU was created in 1874 following a spectacular uprising in the Midwest known as the Woman's Crusade. During the winter of 1873–74, women, armed with Bibles and singing hymns, marched on taverns and saloons and refused to leave until the proprietors signed a pledge to quit selling liquor. The crusade spread like a prairie fire through small towns in Ohio, Indiana, Michigan, and Illinois and soon moved east into New York, New England, and Pennsylvania. Before it was over, more than 100,000 women marched in over 450 cities and towns. The crusade marked the first time since the days of the antislavery movement that middle-class, respectable churchwomen had taken to the streets.

The women's tactics were new, but temperance (the movement to ban the sale of alcoholic beverages and eliminate drunkenness) dated back to the 1820s. It had won significant victories in the 1850s when states, starting with Maine, passed laws to prohibit the sale of liquor (the laws became known as "Maine laws"). But by the late 1860s and 1870s, the liquor business was on the rise, with about one saloon for every fifty males over the age of fifteen. Willing to spend as much money as it took, the liquor interests mounted a powerful lobby to fight temperance.

Temperance was an especially explosive issue that divided communities, pitting middle class against working class, native-born against immigrant, Protestant against Catholic, and women against men. In 1869, a national Prohibition Party formed, but it attracted little support. In the North, most "drys," as the temperance advocates were called, stayed in the Republican Party, while the Democrats, with their strength in urban immigrant areas, won the support of the "wets." In practice, both major political parties avoided the divisive issue by leaving it up to counties and towns to decide whether to ban the sale of liquor.

After a decade of quiescence, the Woman's Crusade dramatically brought the issue of temperance back into the national spotlight. In 1874, women built on the success of the crusade to mount a new national organization, the Woman's Christian Temperance Union. Composed entirely of women, the new organization advocated total abstinence from alcohol. In its first five years, under the leadership of Annie Wittenmyer, the WCTU relied on education and moral suasion to achieve its goal. When Frances Willard became president in 1879, she radically changed the direction of the organization. Using "home protection" as her watchword, she capitalized on the cult of domesticity to move women into public life, arguing that they needed to attack the saloon to protect the home and family.

Women supported the temperance movement because they felt particularly vulnerable. The drunken, abusive husband epitomized the evils of

a society in which women remained second-class citizens. Temperance provided women with a respectable outlet for their increasing resentment of women's inferior status and their growing recognition of women's capabilities. Seeing all women's interests as essentially the same, crossing class, ethnic, and racial lines, women reformers like the leaders of the Woman's Christian Temperance Union did not hesitate to use the singular *woman* to emphasize gender solidarity. Although largely white and middle class, the women of the WCTU resolved to speak for their entire sex.

As women organized to deal with issues that touched their homes and families, they moved almost inevitably into politics, lending new urgency to the cause of woman suffrage.

As the second president of the WCTU, Frances Willard greatly expanded the activities of the union. In its pursuit of temperance, the organization soon moved toward advocacy of woman suffrage (again the singular, "woman"), which Willard supported as early as 1875 and which the WCTU formally embraced in 1884 by calling for the "home protection ballot." A grassroots organization, the WCTU recruited members in every state and territory. By the 1890s, the WCTU network of local unions had penetrated all but the most isolated rural areas of the country. Strong and rich, with 150,000 dues-paying members, the WCTU was a force to be reckoned with.

Willard's "Do Everything" slogan accurately described the breathtaking sweep of the WCTU's concerns. Under her leadership, the WCTU moved closer to the view that alcoholism was a disease and not a sin and that poverty could be as much a cause as a result of drink. Accordingly, social action replaced prayer as women's answer to the threat of drunkenness. By 1896, twenty-five of the WCTU's departments dealt with nontemperance issues. The organization worked to establish women's reformatories and promoted the hiring of female police officers. The Chicago branch sponsored day nurseries, Sunday schools, an industrial training school, a mission for homeless women, a free medical dispensary, and a lodging house for men.

At the same time, the WCTU turned its attention to labor issues, joining with the Knights of Labor to press for better working conditions. One WCTU worker described the condition of factory operatives in a textile mill. "It is dreadful to see those girls stripped almost to the skin, wearing only a kind of loose wrapper, and running like race-horses from the beginning to the end of the day," she wrote in the *Union Signal,* the WCTU's monthly magazine. "The hard slavish work," she concluded, "is drawing the girls into the saloon."

Willard attempted to create a broad reform coalition in the 1890s, embracing the Knights of Labor, the People's Party, and the Prohibition Party. Until her death in 1898, Willard led, if not a women's rights movement, then the first organized mass movement of women united around a women's issue. As she herself observed, "All this work has tended more toward the liberation of women than it has toward the extinction of the saloon."

The WCTU under Willard's leadership secularized, politicized, and legitimized women's concerns. Frances Willard and the organization that she led championed a new kind of womanhood. Before 1873, most WCTU women had worked only in their churches. By 1900, women could claim a generation of experience in political action—speaking, lobbying, organizing, drafting legislation, and running private charitable institutions. Willard's death left a legacy of political activism.

The Suffrage Movement

Unlike the WCTU, the organized movement for woman suffrage was small and relatively weak in the late nineteenth century. But militant suffragists, like the temperance women, fought aggressively for change. The women's rights movement that had begun at Seneca Falls in 1848 had split over the issue of the Fourteenth Amendment, which had granted voting rights to African American men. Women's rights activists like Elizabeth Cady Stanton and Susan B. Anthony had wanted the Fourteenth Amendment to apply to women as well as to African Americans newly freed from slavery. "I will cut off this right arm of mine before I will ever work for or demand the ballot for the Negro and not the woman," Stanton had declared. But advocates of black suffrage such as Lucy Stone and Frederick Douglass urged women to wait, insisting that it was "the Negro's hour."

Stanton fought the Fourteenth Amendment because it did not include woman suffrage. Her strong stance led to a split among women's rights activists that produced two rival woman suffrage organizations. Stanton and Anthony formed the National Woman Suffrage Association (NWSA) in 1869,

launching the first independent women's rights movement in the United States. The more conservative American Woman Suffrage Association formed the same year. Unlike the NWSA, this group included men as well as women and welcomed many members who believed that women should vote in local but not national elections.

In 1890, the two groups united under the rubric of the National American Woman Suffrage Association (NAWSA). Twenty years had made a great change. Woman suffrage was not yet generally supported, but it was no longer considered a crackpot idea. Thanks to the WCTU's support of the "home protection ballot," suffrage had become accepted as a means to an end even when it was not embraced as woman's natural right. The NAWSA honored Elizabeth Cady Stanton by electing her its first president, but Susan B. Anthony, who took the helm in 1892, emerged as the leading figure in the new united organization.

In the 1890s, the NAWSA launched campaigns on the state level to gain the vote for women. The group won a victory in Colorado in 1893 and another in Idaho in 1896. In addition, two states joined the suffrage column when the territories of Wyoming and Utah entered the union in 1890 and 1896, respectively. But women suffered a bitter defeat in a California referendum in 1896.

Although it would take almost three decades for all women to gain the vote with the ratification of the Nineteenth Amendment in 1920, the unification of the two woman suffrage groups in 1890 signaled a new era in women's fight for the vote. And Frances Willard's place on the platform in 1892 at the founding of the People's Party in St. Louis symbolized women's growing role in politics and reform.

Ida B. Wells and the Antilynching Campaign

While most white women focused on reforms designed to counter the impact of urban industrialism in the North, black women followed a different path. The majority of African Americans were neither urban nor industrial. As late as 1890, more than 90 percent of the black population remained in the South, and those who migrated north found that discrimination blocked their employment in industry. As a result, African American women activists formed clubs and voluntary associations for self- and community improvement and organized around issues that affected life in the rural South. Foremost among their activities was the antilynch-

IDA B. WELLS
Ida B. Wells led the movement to end lynching, traveling the country to raise the nation's consciousness about this heinous and illegal practice. In 1895, Wells married Ferdinand L. Barnett, a black attorney, editor, and founder of the Chicago Conservator. *Shown here with Charles, the first of the couple's four children, Wells remained active in African American leadership, helping to found the National Association of Colored Women in 1896.*
Courtesy of University of Chicago, Department of Special Collections.

my eyes to what lynching really was." For the three men had been killed not for some offense, real or imagined, against white womanhood—the common excuse for the murder or "lynching" of black men in the South. Instead their deaths could be traced to purely economic causes. The three men owned and operated the People's Grocery, a store that competed with a white-owned establishment just across the street. When the white owner instigated an attack on his black rivals, a shoot-out resulted that left three white men wounded. Despite the fact that they had acted in defense of their property, the three black grocers were arrested and jailed. In the dead of night, a lynch mob seized the men in their cells, dragged them to a waiting railroad car, carried them north of the city, and brutally shot them to death.

For Wells the crime underscored how lynching served "as an excuse to get rid of Negroes who were acquiring wealth and property and thus keep the race terrorized." Determined to do something, Wells began systematically to collect data on lynching. During 1892, she found, 241 people were lynched in twenty-six states. Of that number, 160 were identified as African Americans, and 152 of the 160 lynchings occurred in former slaveholding states. In the decade between 1882 and 1892, lynching in the South increased by an overwhelming 200 percent. The increase testified to the retreat of the federal government following Reconstruction and to Southerners' determination to maintain white supremacy through terrorism and intimidation.

At the time Wells began her antilynching campaign in 1892, she had already earned a reputation as a militant activist for African American rights. Born a slave in Holly Springs, Mississippi, in 1862, Wells grew up during Reconstruction. Her parents were active in the struggle for Negro rights and provided their daughter with strong role models. Their deaths from yellow fever left Wells an orphan at the age of sixteen. She took over as head of the family, leaving Rust College to support her five siblings. Wells found work in the Memphis city schools and became an active member in the local African Methodist Episcopal church. She also joined a local lyceum, or literary group. It was there that she began her career as a journalist, writing for the lyceum's newspaper. In 1889, she became the co-owner of the *Free Speech and Headlight,* later shortened to *Free Speech.*

Wells did not shrink from controversy. In 1884, after being forcibly removed from a seat in the ladies' car on the train, she had sued the Chesa-

ing campaign mounted by Ida B. Wells. Wells mobilized black women throughout the country and stimulated the organization of the National Association of Colored Women.

In March of 1892, Ida B. Wells, editor of the African American newspaper *Free Speech,* learned of the murder of her friend Thomas Moss. Moss had been found in a field north of Memphis, his body riddled with bullets. Two other men, Calvin McDowell and Wil Stewart, had also been killed. The appalling crime, as Wells later recounted, "opened peake, Ohio, and Southwestern Railroad and had won, only to see the decision overturned by the Tennessee Supreme Court. And in 1891, an editorial pressing for better school facilities for black children had cost her her teaching position in the Memphis schools. By the time she took up the antilynching cause, Wells had earned a reputation for her bold stand on race relations and for her work as a journalist whose syndicated columns appeared in African American papers across the country.

As the first salvo in her attack on lynching, Wells put to rest the "old threadbare lie that Negro men assault white women." As she pointed out, violations of black women by white men, which were much more frequent than black attacks on white women, went unnoticed and unpunished. Wells articulated lynching as a problem of race and gender, with the myth of black attacks on "white Southern womanhood" masking the reality that mob violence had more to do with economics and the shifting social structure of the South than with rape. She demonstrated in a sophisticated way how the southern patriarchal system, having lost its control over blacks with the end of slavery, used its control over women to circumscribe the liberty of black men.

Wells's strong stance immediately resulted in reprisal. While she was traveling in the North, her office was ransacked and her printing equipment destroyed. The warning that she would be killed on sight if she ever returned to Memphis only stiffened her resolve. As she wrote in her autobiography, *Crusade for Justice*, "Having lost my paper, had a price put on my life and been made an exile . . . , I felt that I owed it to myself and to my race to tell the whole truth now that I was where I could do so freely."

Antilynching became a lifelong commitment that took Wells twice to Britain, where she placed lynching on the international agenda. As a reporter, first for the *New York Age* and later for the *Chicago Inter-Ocean*, she used every opportunity to hammer home her message. After her marriage in 1895 to Ferdinand Barnett, she shifted the focus of her activities to Chicago, where she raised a family.

Wells's activities mobilized other black women, including Victoria Earle Matthews and Maritcha Lyons, who were already engaged in social reform and self-improvement. They hosted a testimonial dinner for Wells in New York in 1892 that led to the organization of a black women's club, the Women's Loyal Union. The club became a spearhead for the creation of the National Association of Colored Women (NACW) in 1896. The organization's first president, Mary Church Terrell of Washington, D.C., urged her followers to "promote the welfare of our race, along all the lines that tend to its development and advancement." Taking as their motto "Lifting As We Climb," the women of the NACW shouldered the double burden of self-improvement and social reform. They attacked myriad issues, including health care, housing, education, and the promotion of a positive image of the Negro race. (In their efforts, African American club women enjoyed little help from white women's clubs. The General Federation of Women's Clubs remained largely segregated at the insistence of its southern constituency.) The NACW played a critical role in Wells's antilynching campaign by lobbying for legislation that would make lynching a federal crime. Beginning in 1894 and continuing for decades after, antilynching bills were introduced in Congress only to be defeated by southern opposition.

Lynching did not end during Ida B. Wells's lifetime, nor did antilynching legislation gain passage in Congress; but Wells's forceful voice brought the issue to national prominence. At her funeral, black leader W. E. B. DuBois eulogized Wells as the woman who "began the awakening of the conscience of the nation."

The Farmers' Revolt

Hard times in the 1880s and 1890s created a groundswell of agrarian revolt. A bitter farmer wrote from Minnesota, "I settled on this Land in good Faith Built House and Barn Broken up Part of the Land. Spent years of hard Labor in grubing fencing and Improving." About to lose his land to foreclosure, he lamented, "Are they going to drive us out like tresspassers . . . and give us away to the Corporations?"

Farm prices fell, decade after decade. Wheat that sold for a dollar a bushel in 1870 dropped to eighty cents in 1885 and to sixty cents in the 1890s. The farmer actually got less, closer to thirty-five cents a bushel. Cotton plummeted from fifteen cents to five cents a pound. Corn started at forty-five cents and fell to thirty cents a bushel by the 1890s. In parts of Kansas, it sold for as little as ten cents a bushel, and angry farmers burned their crop for fuel rather than market it at that price. By 1894, almost half the farms in Kansas had fallen into the hands of the banks through foreclosure because poor farmers could not make enough money to pay their mortgages.

NEBRASKA FARM COUPLE
*Many hardworking farmers like this Custer County, Nebraska, couple, photographed in 1888,
joined the Farmers' Alliance and later the Populist Party to give voice to their political, economic,
and social concerns about the direction in which America was heading.*
Nebraska State Historical Society, Solomon D. Butcher Collection.

In the West, farmers rankled under a system in which railroads charged exorbitant freight rates while granting discounts to large shippers. Also, the railroads' policy of charging higher rates for a short haul than for a long haul meant that large grain elevator companies could ship their wheat from Chicago to New York and across the ocean to England for less money than it cost a Dakota farmer to send a crop to mills in nearby Minneapolis. In the South, the lack of currency and credit had driven farmers to the stopgap credit system of the crop lien, turning the entire region into a "vast pawn shop." The combined southern states actually had

less money in circulation than did the state of Massachusetts.

During the depression of the 1890s, the human cost was staggering. "I Take my pen in hand to let you know that we are Starving to death," a Kansas farm woman wrote to the governor in 1894. Everywhere, the farmer seemed to be the victim of rules, such as the tariff, that worked to the advantage of big business. At the heart of the problem stood a banking system that was rooted in the gold standard and dominated by eastern commercial banks. In the face of their grievances, angry farmers across the United States raised a chorus of protest.

The Farmers' Alliance

Farm protest was not new. In the 1870s, farmers had supported the Grange and the Greenback Labor Party. But with the farmers' situation growing more desperate, the 1880s witnessed a spontaneous outbreak as farmers from Texas to Louisiana, from Kansas through the Dakotas organized into alliances. The first group of farmers gathered at a Lampasas County farm in Texas and banded together into the Farmers' Alliance to fight "landsharks and horse thieves." In frontier farmhouses in Texas, in log cabins in backwoods Arkansas, in the rural parishes of Louisiana, separate groups formed similar alliances for self-help.

As the movement grew, the farmers consolidated into two regional alliances, the Northwestern Farmers' Alliance, which included the old Granger states of the Midwest, and the more radical Southern Farmers' Alliance, which began in Texas but soon spread into Georgia and united with groups in Louisiana and Arkansas. Determined to reach black farmers as well as whites, the Southern Alliance sponsored a separate National Colored Farmers' Alliance that recruited more than a quarter of a million members.

In the 1880s, traveling lecturers such as S. O. Daws and William Lamb in Texas spread the alliance message. Daws traveled far and wide, denouncing credit merchants, railroads, trusts, and the money power. Worn-out men and barefoot women reduced to extreme poverty by the crop lien system did not need to be convinced that something was wrong. The alliance lecturers articulated the indignation already felt by farmers. Overnight, scores of local alliances sprang up, each with its own lecturer, who in turn carried the word to every crossroads in the South. The Southern Alliance recruited at the amazing rate of 20,000 a month in the autumn of 1886. By 1887, the alliance had grown to more than 200,000 members, and by 1890 it counted more than three million members in the South alone.

At the same time, the Farmers' Alliance broadened its base by reaching out to workers during the Great Southwestern Strike against Jay Gould's Texas and Pacific Railroad in 1886. The Southern Farmers' Alliance issued a proclamation in support of the Knights of Labor, calling on farmers to boycott Gould's railroad, and rushed food and supplies to the strikers. William Lamb sponsored the boycott, observing simply that it was "a good time to help the Knights of Labor in order to secure their help in the near future." The alliance insisted that the farmer, too, was a worker and that the labor question was a crucial issue for both the farmer and the wage laborer. United as producers against those

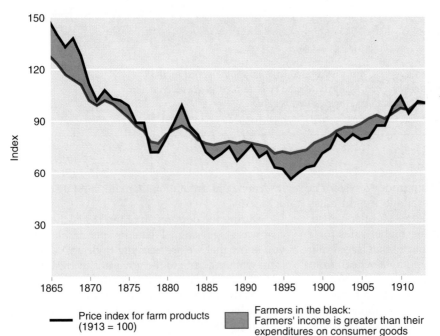

FIGURE 20.1
Consumer Prices and Farm Income, 1865 – 1913
In 1865 consumer prices and farm income were about equal. During the 1880s and 1890s, however, farmers suffered great hardships as prices for their crops declined steadily and the cost of consumer goods continued to rise.

Price index for farm products (1913 = 100)

Consumer Price Index (1913 = 100)

Farmers in the black: Farmers' income is greater than their expenditures on consumer goods

Farmers in the red: Farmers' income is less than their expenditures on consumer goods

ON THE WAY TO A POPULIST MEETING IN KANSAS
Populism was more than a political movement; it was a culture unto itself. For farmers in sparsely set-tled regions, the movement assured them that they were not alone, that others shared their problems, and that solutions could be found. When the Populists called a meeting, wagons came from miles around as in this gathering in Dickinson County, Kansas. Men, women, and children were embraced by the Pop-ulist movement, which recognized that a strong economic and political movement could be a social force.
Kansas State Historical Society, Topeka, Kansas.

who profited from their labor, the Farmers' Alliance and the Knights of Labor joined hands.

"The farmers seem like unto ripe fruit—you can gather them by a gentle shake of the bush," an alliance lecturer gloated in 1887. But ripe for what? Although its leadership insisted that the alliance was not political, it became increasingly politicized in the late 1880s. At the heart of the alliance move-ment was a series of farmers' cooperatives. By "bulking" their cotton, that is, selling it together, farmers could negotiate a better price. And by set-ting up trade stores and exchanges, they sought to escape the grasp of the merchant/creditor. Soon al-liances in a dozen states competed to pioneer new purchasing cooperatives. Through the cooperatives, the Farmers' Alliance promised to change the way farmers lived. "We are going to get out of debt and be free and independent people once more," exulted one farmer. "We Georgia people are in earnest about this thing."

Cooperatives flowered throughout the South and West. In 1888, farmers scored a major victory when they defeated the jute-bagging trust in its scheme to double the price of the bags used to bale cotton. But the alliance failed in its attempt to re-place the furnishing merchant in the South with co-operative stores. Opposition by merchants, bankers, wholesalers, and manufacturers made it impossible for the cooperatives to get credit. The Texas ex-change survived only one season. Farmers soon re-alized that the alliance cooperatives stood little chance of working unless fundamental changes were made in the American money and credit system.

As the cooperative movement died, a new cul-ture of politics was born. Cooperatives served as a recruitment vehicle through which huge numbers of farmers in the South and West became politicized. What had begun as an organization for self-help moved toward direct political action. Texas farmers drafted a set of demands in 1886 and pressured po-litical candidates to endorse them. These demands became the basis of a platform proposed by the Southern Alliance in 1890 that called for railroad regulation and control, laws against land specula-tion, and currency and credit reform.

The alliance urged farmers to use the platform as a "yardstick," warning that candidates must "stand up and be measured." But it proved easier to get politicians to make promises than to get them to enact reform legislation. Confounded by the fail-

---

TABLE 20.1
THE 1892 POPULIST PARTY PLATFORM AND RESOLUTIONS

- Adoption of the sub-treasury plan
- Free and unlimited coinage of silver
- A graduated income tax
- Establishment of postal savings banks for safe deposit of earnings
- Government ownership and operation of railroads, telephone, telegraph, and postal system
- Return of land held by railroads and corporations (in excess of their "actual needs"); return of land owned by the foreign-born to native-born settlers
- Tariff reduction
- Payment of "fair and liberal" pensions to ex-Union soldiers and sailors
- Immigration restriction to prevent newcomers from undercutting and crowding out native-born wage-earners
- A shorter work day
- Prohibition of the use of Pinkerton agents to suppress strikers
- Electoral reforms including: direct popular election of senators, direct primaries, the initiative, the referendum, the secret ballot, and limiting the office of the president and vice president each to one term

---

ure of the Democrats and Republicans to break with commercial interests and support the farmer, the alliance moved, often reluctantly, in the direction of a third party.

At its start in 1877, alliance leader C. W. Macune had insisted, "The Alliance is a strictly white man's nonpolitical, secret business association." But by 1892, after more than a decade of organization, education, and politicization, the alliance was none of those things. Although some southern leaders, like Macune, made it clear that they would never threaten the unity of the white vote in the South by leaving the Democratic Party, advocates of a third party carried the day at the convention of laborers, farmers, and common folk in St. Louis. There, the Farmers' Alliance gave birth to the People's Party and launched the Populist movement.

The Populist Movement

"There is something at the back of all this turmoil more than the failure of crops or the scarcity of ready cash," a journalist observed in 1892. Populism was more than a set of demands and a list of economic grievances. At its heart were the emotion and the spirit of a religious revival. Wagon trains of ten thousand farmers gathered at camp meetings to listen to speeches by the angry prophets of the

movement. Populism, growing out of the Farmers' Alliance, was a mass movement with its own political language and its own slogan: "The alliance is the people and the people are together."

Henry Demarest Lloyd observed, "The People's Party . . . is the organized aspiration of the people for a fuller, nobler, richer, kindlier life for every man, woman, and child . . ."

The Populists mounted a critique of industrial society and a call for action. Convinced that the money and banking systems of the day worked to the advantage of the few and not the many, they demanded economic democracy. To solve the farmers' credit problem, C. W. Macune hit on the ingenious idea of the subtreasury, a plan that would allow farmers to store nonperishable crops in government storehouses until the market was advantageous. At the same time, they would receive commodity credit from the federal government that would enable them to buy needed supplies and seed. The subtreasury became an article of faith in the South, where it promised to eliminate the crop lien system once and for all. Although Macune's idea would be enacted piecemeal in Progressive and New Deal legislation after the turn of the century, at the time he proposed it in the 1890s it was dismissed by conservatives as far-fetched and communistic.

For the western farmer, whose enemy was not the merchant but the mortgage, Populism promised land reform. The Populists called for a plan that would reclaim excessive lands granted or sold to railroads and foreign investors. The Populists' boldest plan called for government ownership of the railroads and telegraphs to put an end to discriminatory rate practices. With the powerful railroads dominating politics and effectively nullifying the Interstate Commerce Act, which had passed in 1887 to regulate the railroads, Populists saw no solution short of government ownership. They did not shrink from advocating what their opponents called state socialism.

Money joined credit and land as the third major thrust of the Populist movement. Farmers in all sections rallied to the cry for cheaper currency, endorsing platform planks calling for free silver and greenbacks. To show their support for labor, Populists supported the eight-hour day and an end to contract labor. And to empower the common people, the platform called for the direct election of senators and electoral reforms including the secret ballot and the right to initiate legislation, to recall elected officials, and to submit issues to the people via referendum. More than just a response to hard times, Populism presented an alternative vision of what America could become. As Henry Demarest Lloyd, an enthusiastic supporter of Populism, observed, "The People's Party is more than the organized discontent of the people. It is the organized aspiration of the people for a fuller, nobler, richer, kindlier life for every man, woman, and child in the ranks of humanity." It represented, in Lloyd's words, "an uprising of principle."

The Labor Wars

While the farmers united to fight for change, industrial laborers fought their own battles in a series of bloody strikes so fiercely waged on both sides that one historian has called them the "labor wars." Coal miners struck to fight the use of convict labor in the mines of eastern Tennessee. Miners in Coeur d'Alene, Idaho, and Cripple Creek, Colorado, joined the militant Western Federation of Miners and battled the bosses. Railroad switchmen went on strike in Buffalo, New York, and a general strike

closed down the port of New Orleans. At issue was the right of labor to organize and speak through unions and to fight for better conditions and more control in the workplace.

The two major conflicts of the period, the Homestead lockout of 1892 and the Pullman strike of 1894, raised fundamental questions about the rights of laborers and the sanctity of private property.

Skilled workers had watched as management undermined their autonomy, replacing men with machines and systematically reducing skilled jobs to unskilled work. The proportion of craftsworkers had shrunk, and their control over the workplace diminished at the same time that a growing number of common laborers, many of them immigrants from southern and eastern Europe, came into the mills. Workers felt increasingly threatened. In the 1890s, they made a stand. The two major conflicts of the period, the Homestead lockout and strike of 1892 and the Pullman strike of 1894, raised fundamental questions about the rights of laborers and the sanctity of private property.

The Homestead Lockout and Strike

At first glance it seemed ironic that Carnegie steel's Homestead mill became the storm center of labor's fight for the right to unionize. Andrew Carnegie was unique among industrialists as a self-styled friend of labor. In 1886 he had written, "The right of the workingmen to combine and to form trades unions is no less sacred than the right of the manufacturer to enter into associations and conferences with his fellows, and it must sooner or later be conceded." Yet six years later at Homestead, Carnegie set out to crush a union in one of labor's legendary confrontations.

As much as he cherished his liberal beliefs, Carnegie cherished his profits more. Labor unions had worked well for him during the years when he was building his empire. Labor strife at Homestead during the 1870s had enabled Carnegie to buy the plant from his competitors at cost and take control of the steel industry. And during the 1880s, strong national craft unions ensured that competing mills could not undercut his labor costs. But by the 1890s, Carnegie held a dictatorial grasp on the steelmaking business, and the benefits of unionism were no longer so evident to the great steelmaker. Carnegie wanted complete control.

Standing in his way was the Amalgamated Association of Iron and Steel Workers, one of the largest and richest of the craft unions that made up the American Federation of Labor. In 1892, when the Amalgamated attempted to renew its contract at Carnegie's Homestead mill, its leaders were told that since "the vast majority of our employees are Non union, the Firm has decided that the minority must give place to the majority." While it was true that only eight hundred skilled workers belonged to the elite Amalgamated, the union had long enjoyed the support of the plant's three thousand nonunion workers. Slavs who did much of the unskilled work made common cause with the Welsh, Scots, and Irish who belonged to the union. Never before had the Amalgamated been denied a contract.

As the situation built toward a showdown, Carnegie sailed to Scotland. No doubt aware of his hypocrisy, he preferred not to be directly involved. He left Henry Clay Frick, the toughest antilabor man in the industry, in charge of the Homestead plant.

By summer a strike looked inevitable. Frick prepared for the showdown by erecting a fifteen-foot fence around the plant and topping it with barbed wire. With platforms for searchlights and holes for rifles, the fence gave the mill a distinctly military look. Workers aptly dubbed it "Fort Frick." To defend his fort, Frick hired three hundred mercenaries from the Pinkerton Detective Agency at the rate of five dollars per day, more than double the wage of the average Homestead worker.

The Pinkerton National Detective Agency, founded before the Civil War, came into its own in the 1880s as businessmen like Frick used Pinkerton agents as a private security force. Largely recruited from the ranks of the unemployed, the Pinkertons included some criminals and hoodlums as well as college boys on vacation. The "Pinks" earned the hatred of workers by protecting strikebreakers and acting as company spies.

On June 28, Frick locked the workers out of the mills. They immediately rallied to the support of the Amalgamated and declared a strike. Hugh O'Donnell, the young Irishman who led the union, vowed to prevent strikebreakers from entering the plant. On July 6 at four in the morning, a lookout spotted two barges moving up the Monongahela River in the fog. Frick was attempting to smuggle his Pinkertons into Homestead. Workers sounded the alarm, and within minutes a crowd of more than one thousand, hastily armed with rifles, hoes, and fence posts, rushed to the riverbank to meet the enemy. When the Pinkertons attempted to come ashore, gunfire broke out, and more than a dozen Pinkertons and some thirty strikers fell, killed or wounded. The Pinkertons retreated back onto the barges.

In the twelve hours that followed, the strikers threw everything they had at the barges, but they could not blow them out of the water. Finally, the Pinkertons hoisted a white flag and arranged with O'Donnell to surrender. With eight strikers dead or dying and scores wounded, the crowd, now numbering perhaps ten thousand, was in no mood for conciliation. As the Pinkertons came up the hill, they were forced to run a gauntlet of screaming, cursing men, women, and children. One woman used her umbrella to poke out the eye of a hated "Pink." When a young guard dropped to his knees, weeping for mercy, he was clubbed unconscious. Only one Pinkerton had been killed in the siege on the barges, but in the grim rout that followed their surrender, three men died as a result of the beatings, and not one of the three hundred avoided injury.

The "battle of Fort Frick" ended in a dubious victory for the workers. They took control of the plant and elected a council to run the community. At first, public opinion favored their cause. Newspapers urged Frick to negotiate or submit to arbitration. The Populists, meeting in St. Louis, condemned the use of "hireling armies." A congressman castigated Carnegie for "skulking in his castle in Scotland."

But the action of the strikers struck at the heart of the capitalist system, pitting the workers' right to their jobs against the rights of private property. Four days after the confrontation, the Pennsylvania governor, who sympathized with the workers, nonetheless yielded to pressure and ordered eight thousand National Guard troops into Homestead to protect Carnegie's mills.

At first the strikers welcomed the guard, but they soon became disillusioned. The guard's ninety-five-day occupation not only protected Carnegie's property but also enabled Frick to reopen the mills using strikebreakers. "We have been deceived," workers bitterly complained. "We have stood idly by and let the town be occupied by soldiers who come here, not as our protectors, but as the protectors of non-union men. . . . If we undertake to resist the seizure of our jobs, we will be shot down like dogs."

Then, in a bizarre episode accompanying the Homestead lockout, Alexander Berkman, a Russian immigrant and anarchist, attempted to assassinate

THE BATTLE AT THE HOMESTEAD STEEL MILL
This contemporary lithograph portrays scenes from the battle between workers and strikebreakers in July 1892: workers attacking the barges, cannonading of the barges, surrender of the Pinkertons, captives being led to prison, and, finally, arrival of the militia and the soldiers in camp. The lithograph also shows (lower right) the revenge the strikers took on the hated "Pinks." Of the 316 Pinkertons, not one escaped injury as the angry crowd, armed with clubs, hoes, and brickbats, forced them to run a bloody gauntlet.
Carnegie Library, Pittsburgh.

Henry Clay Frick. Berkman's ally in his undertaking was the noted anarchist Emma Goldman, a Russian Jewish immigrant who had won a national reputation for her fiery speeches against capitalism and in favor of birth control. Together Berkman and Goldman planned the assassination of Frick in the belief that it would ignite a general uprising. But they badly miscalculated. Berkman bungled his attempt. Frick, shot twice, survived and showed considerable courage, allowing doctors to remove the bullets from his neck but refusing to leave his desk until the day's work was completed. "I do not think that I shall die," Frick remarked coolly, "but whether I do or not, the Company will pursue the same policy and it will win." Overnight, the man castigated for hiring Pinkertons won the nation's sympathy.

After the assassination attempt, in August, public opinion turned against the workers. Berkman was quickly tried and sentenced to prison. Although the Amalgamated and the AFL denounced his action, the incident served to couple anarchism and unionism, already associated in the public mind as a result of the Haymarket bombing in 1886. Hugh O'Donnell later wrote that "the bullet from Berkman's pistol, failing in its foul intent, went straight through the heart of the Homestead strike."

In the end, the workers' resistance was crushed. The strike collapsed after four and a half months. The Homestead mill reopened and the men returned to work, except for the union leaders, who were blacklisted in every steel and iron mill in the country. In the drama and melodrama of events surrounding Homestead, the ideological and political significance of what occurred often remained obscured: The workers at Homestead had been taught a lesson. They would never again, in the words of the National Guard commander, "believe the works are their's [sic] quite as much as Carnegie's."

"Our victory is now complete and most gratifying," Frick wired Carnegie. "Do not think we will ever have serious labor trouble again. . . . We had to teach our employees a lesson and we have taught them one that they will never forget." With the owners firmly in the saddle, the mills reopened. The company slashed wages, reinstated the twelve-hour day, and eliminated five hundred jobs. The workers lapsed into a demoralized and hopeless state. It would take another forty-five years before steelworkers successfully unionized. In the meantime, Carnegie's production tripled, even in the midst of a depression. "Ashamed to tell you profits these days," Carnegie wrote a friend in 1899. And no wonder; his profits had grown from $4 million in the year of the lockout to $40 million in 1900.

Eugene V. Debs and the Pullman Strike

A year after the Homestead lockout, a major panic and depression hit the nation. A stock market crash on Wall Street in the spring of 1893 led to bitter hard times. The ranks of the unemployed swelled to three million, almost half of the working population. Nowhere were workers more demoralized than in the model town of Pullman on the outskirts of Chicago. George M. Pullman, who made his millions by building Pullman Palace cars and leasing them to the railroads, prided himself on his enlightened approach to labor. But in 1893, Pullman's workers saw their pay sliced five times between May and December. Altogether, they sustained cuts of at least 28 percent.

At the same time, Pullman refused to lower the rents in his model town, insisting that "the renting of the dwellings and the employment of workmen at Pullman are in no way tied together." When workers went to the bank to cash their checks, the rent was taken out. One worker found that he had only forty-seven cents to live on for two weeks. When the bank teller asked him whether he wanted to apply it to his back rent, he retorted, "If Mr. Pullman needs that forty-seven cents worse than I do, let him have it." In the meantime, Pullman continued to pay his stockholders an 8 percent dividend, and the company accumulated a $25 million surplus.

At the heart of the labor problems at Pullman was not only economic inequity but the company's attempt to take control of the work process, substituting piecework for day wages and narrowing the difference between the skilled work performed by craftsworkers and the work of operatives. During the depression, Pullman's supervisors repeatedly imposed lower piece rates, forcing workers to make the same parts for less money and undermining the work of skilled craftsworkers. A woman complained of the "tyrannical and abusive treatment" meted out at Pullman. When workers protested, management instituted new forms of shop discipline, forbidding the workers to talk or assemble in a futile attempt to keep them from unionizing. Workers like painter Theodore Rhodie resented not only the drop in wages but also the loss of autonomy. Rhodie argued that it was his "right as an American citizen" to speak to whomever he chose.

The Pullman workers rebelled. During the spring of 1894, they flocked to the ranks of the American Railway Union (ARU), a new union led by Eugene Victor Debs. The ARU, unlike the skilled craft unions of the AFL, pledged to organize all railway workers from the elite engineers down to the lowliest engine wipers and section hands. Its belief in industrial democracy, however, was not matched by a commitment to racial equality; by a narrow margin, union members voted to exclude black workers.

Eugene V. Debs was a homegrown Hoosier labor leader with strong compassion for the unskilled workers at the bottom of labor's hierarchy. "It has been my life's desire," he wrote, "to unify railroad employees and to eliminate the aristocracy of labor, which unfortunately exists, and organize them so all will be on an equality." Workers who had long been excluded from the railroad's elite craft unions joined the new union at the rate of 200 to 400 a day in the fall of 1893. Within a year, the ARU had grown to 150,000.

George Pullman responded to his workers' grievances by firing three of the union's leaders the day after they led a delegation to protest wage cuts. Angry men and women walked off the job in disgust. What began as a spontaneous protest in May 1894 blossomed into a strike that involved more than 90 percent of Pullman's 3,300 workers. "We do not know what the outcome will be, and in fact we do not much care," one worker confessed. "We do know that we are working for less wages than will maintain ourselves and families in the necessaries of life, and on that proposition we refuse to work any longer." Pullman countered by shutting down the plant.

In June, the Pullman strikers appealed to the ARU to come to their aid. Debs sympathized with the strikers, but he hesitated to commit his fledgling union to a major strike in the midst of a depression. He pleaded with the workers to find another solution. When Pullman adamantly refused to arbitrate, the ARU, brushing aside Debs's call for caution, voted to boycott all Pullman cars. Beginning on June 29, switchmen refused to handle any train that carried Pullman cars.

The conflict escalated quickly. The General Managers Association (GMA), a combination of managers from twenty-four different railroads, acted in concert to quash the boycott. Determined to kill the ARU, they quickly retaliated by recruiting strikebreakers and firing all the switchmen who refused to handle Pullman cars. Their tactics set off a chain reaction. Disgusted with long hours, arbitrary treatment, and wage cuts, entire train crews walked off the job in a show of solidarity with the Pullman workers. In a matter of days the boycott/strike spread to more than fifteen railroads and affected twenty-seven states and territories. On day one, 18,000 workers walked out; on day three, the number grew to 40,000; and by the fourth day, more than 125,000 railroad workers were out on strike, despite the opposition of the conservative railroad unions in the AFL. By July 2, rail lines from New York to California lay paralyzed. Even the GMA was forced to concede that the railroads had been "fought to a standstill."

The strike remained surprisingly peaceful. Mobs stopped trains carrying Pullman cars and forced their crews to uncouple the cars and leave them on the sidings. But no major riots broke out, and no serious damage was done to railroad property. Debs, a whirlwind of activity, fired off telegrams to all parts of the country advising his followers to avoid violence, to use no force to stop trains, and to respect law and order. But the nation's newspapers, fed press releases by the GMA, distorted and misrepresented the strike. Across the country, papers ran headlines like "Wild Riot in Chicago," "Mob Is in Control," and "Law Is Trampled On." Editors rushed to denounce "Dictator Debs."

In Washington, Attorney General Richard B. Olney, a lawyer with strong ties to the railroads, determined to put down the strike. Acting in concert with the GMA, he sought to convince President Grover Cleveland that federal troops should intervene on the pretext of protecting the mails. When Cleveland balked, Olney advised the federal attorney in Chicago to obtain an injunction from a federal court requiring the workers to stop the boycott. Two Chicago judges quickly complied, issuing an order so sweeping that it prohibited Debs from even speaking in public. Through the use of the injunction, the court in effect made striking a crime punishable by a jail sentence for contempt of court, a civil process that did not require trial by jury. The injunction had the effect of outlawing the boycott and the strike. Even the conservative *Chicago Tribune* judged the injunction "a menace to liberty . . . a weapon ever ready for the capitalist." Furious, Debs risked jail by refusing to honor it.

Olney's strategy worked. With the strikers acting in violation of a federal injunction and with the mails in jeopardy (the GMA made sure that Pullman cars were put on every mail train), Cleveland called out the army. But he did so over the heated objections of the governor of Illinois, John Peter Altgeld. Altgeld, with his keen sense of fair play, had refused to use state militia to stop the strike. "At present some of our railroads are paralyzed," he had written the president calmly, "not by reason of obstruction, but because they cannot get men to operate their trains." When Cleveland called up federal troops, Altgeld protested that he had neither asked for nor desired the intervention of the army. He pointedly reminded Cleveland that "local self-government is a fundamental principle of our Constitution." Cleveland brushed aside Altgeld's objections, noting briefly that he thought it his duty to "restore obedience to law and to protect life and property."

On July 5, the army marched into Chicago, nearly two thousand strong, along with five thousand special federal deputy marshals, many reputedly recruited from the "dregs of the city." The GMA was jubilant. "It has now become a fight between the United States Government and the American Railway Union," a spokesman observed, "and we shall leave them to fight it out."

Violence immediately erupted. Crowds blocked railroad cars and set them on fire. In one day, more than $340,000 worth of property was destroyed, twenty-five workers were shot, and more than sixty were wounded. In the face of bullets and bayonets, the strikers held firm. "Troops cannot move trains," Debs reminded the striking ARU locals, a fact that was borne out as the railroads remained paralyzed despite military intervention. But if the army could not put down the strike, the injunction could and did. Debs was arrested and imprisoned for contempt of court. In a matter of days, the strike collapsed. With its leader in jail, its headquarters raided and ransacked, and its members demoralized, the ARU was defeated along with the strike. The Pullman factory reopened, hiring new workers to replace many of the strikers and leaving sixteen hundred workers without jobs and without the means to relocate. In August, Governor Altgeld toured Pullman, where he found widespread misery and starvation. The ARU and labor had suffered an overwhelming defeat.

In the aftermath of the strike, a special commission investigated the events at Pullman, taking testimony from 107 witnesses, from workers at the car company to George M. Pullman himself. Stubborn and self-righteous, Pullman spoke for the business orthodoxy of his era, steadfastly affirming the right of business to safeguard its interests through confederacies like the General Managers Association and, at the same time, denying labor's right to organize. In response to questioning, Pullman defended his actions. "If we were to receive these men as representatives of the union," he candidly confessed, "they could probably force us to pay any wages which they saw fit." Arguing that "no prudent employer would submit to arbitration," he insisted that there was a principle at stake: the company's "control of its own business."

In his Woodstock jail cell, Eugene Debs reviewed the events of the Pullman strike. With the army and the courts ready to come to the aid of property, labor had little recourse, Debs realized. Strikes seemed futile, and unions remained helpless; workers must take control of the state itself. Debs went into jail a trade unionist and came out six months later a socialist. After a brief flirtation with Populism, he would go on to form the Socialist Party in 1900 and run for president on its ticket five times, once from jail, where he again found himself in 1920 for opposing America's entry into World War I.

The Pullman strike revealed the evils of industrial paternalism, but it also demonstrated the power of organized management and the willingness of the government to come to the aid of the employers by wielding the court's power of injunction and by dispatching federal troops. When push came to shove at Pullman, as at Homestead, the federal government's police function of protecting property took precedence over labor's right to organize and to strike.

From Homestead to Coeur d'Alene, from Pullman to Cripple Creek, workers in the 1890s struggled to organize and to gain legitimacy for their right to bargain collectively and to have some say on the shop floor. Against them they found arrayed the might of the state, the power of the courts, and the influence of the press. In the end it was no contest. Although labor would make many gains in the coming decades, it would take the passage of the Wagner Act in 1935 before unions gained, once and for all, the right to bargain collectively. The labor wars of the 1890s rarely ended successfully for the strikers, but they dramatized the willingness of workers to fight for their rights and forced the nation to confront the issue of industrial strife.

Depression Politics

"A fearful crisis is upon us," wrote a labor publication in the winter of 1893. "Countless thousands of our fellow men are unemployed; men, women and children are suffering the pangs of hunger!" Railroad magnate Chauncey Depew concurred. "I have been through all the panics of the last thirty years," he wrote, "but I have never seen one in which the distress was so widespread and reached so many people."

The burden of feeding and sheltering the unemployed and their families fell to private charity, city government, and some of the stronger trade unions. The states and the federal government appropriated not a cent for aid.

The depression that began in the spring of 1893 and lasted for more than four years put nearly half of the labor force out of work. The country swarmed with people looking for jobs. They road the rails, slept in barns, begged for work, and, when they couldn't get work, begged for food. Dismissed as tramps or hoboes by the press, this army of the unemployed sought jobs, not handouts. Populist Governor Lorenzo Lewelling of Kansas, one of the few to sympathize with their plight, issued his "tramp circular" in December 1893. In it he lashed out at vagrancy laws that imprisoned "thousands of men, guilty of no crime but poverty," and promised that the poor would not be harassed in Kansas.

The burden of feeding and sheltering the unemployed and their families fell to private charity, city government, and some of the stronger trade unions. The states and the federal government appropriated not a cent for aid. Following the harsh dictates of social Darwinism and laissez-faire, the majority of Americans believed that it was inappropriate for the government to intervene. When Cincinnati set up a public works program for the unemployed, the business community complained that it "demoralized" the poor and attacked the program as "communistic" and a "waste of taxpayers' money."

The scope of the depression made it impossible for local agencies to supply relief, although they set up soup kitchens across the land to feed the hungry. Increasingly, voices called on the federal government to take action. The American Federation of Labor declared that the "right to work is the right

to life" and argued that "when the private employer cannot or will not give work, the municipality, state or nation must." Calls for government intervention mounted throughout the decade as poverty created its own politics.

Coxey's "Army"

Masses of unemployed Americans marched to Washington, D.C., in the spring of 1894 to call attention to their plight and to urge Congress to take action. From Seattle, from San Francisco, from Los Angeles, and from Denver, hundreds joined the trek to Washington. Jacob S. Coxey of Massilon, Ohio, led the most publicized contingent. Coxey, a wealthy manufacturer, had a plan to end unemployment. "What I am after," he told the press, "is to try to put this country in a condition so that no man who wants work shall be obliged to remain idle." He proposed to put the jobless to work building badly needed roads. Coxey had been an ardent

COXEY'S ARMY
Coxey's army called itself a "petition in boots." Here a group of Coxeyites in coats, ties, and bowler hats march behind the American flag as women and children join a curious crowd to greet the marchers as they pass. These well-dressed marchers hardly seem like a menacing army. But many feared Coxey and his followers, and the military rhetoric of the press only fueled their fears. Coxey dramatized the plight of hundreds of thousands of workers left unemployed in the wake of the panic of 1893.
Library of Congress.

Greenbacker (he named his son Legal Tender), and he planned to finance his program of public works by an issue of paper currency (greenbacks) and no-interest bonds. His plan won the support of the American Federation of Labor and the Populists.

Starting out from Ohio with one hundred men, Coxey's "army" swelled as it marched east through the spring snows of the Alleghenies. In Homestead, Coxey recruited several hundred from the ranks of those left unemployed in the wake of the lockout. Called by Coxey the "Commonweal of Christ," the army marched to the tune of "Marching through Georgia":

> We are marching to the Capitol,
>   three hundred thousand strong,
> With live petitions in our boots
>   to urge our cause along.
> And when we kick our congressmen,
>   they'll feel there's something wrong,
> As we go marching with Coxey.
>
> We are not tramps nor vagabonds,
>   that's shirking honest toil,
> But miners, clerks, skilled artisans,
>   and tillers of the soil
> Now forced to beg our brother worms
>   to give us leave to toil,
> While we are marching with Coxey.
>
> Hurrah! hurrah! for the unemployed's appeal
> Hurrah! hurrah! for the marching commonweal!
> Stop the trust and combine steal,
> For we are marching with Coxey.

On May 1, Coxey's army arrived in Washington. Given permission to parade but forbidden to speak from the Capitol, Coxey defiantly marched his men onto the Capitol grounds. Police set upon the band, cracking heads and arresting Coxey and his lieutenants. Coxey went to jail for twenty days and was fined five dollars for "walking on the grass."

Mass demonstrations of the unemployed served only to frighten comfortable Americans, who saw the specter of insurrection and rebellion everywhere in 1894. Those who had trembled for the safety of the Republic heaved a sigh of relief after Coxey's arrest, hoping that it would halt the march on Washington. But other armies of the unemployed, possibly as many as five thousand, were still on their way. Too poor to pay for railway tickets, they rode the rails as "freeloaders." The more daring contingents commandeered entire trains, stirring fears of revolution. Nervous midwestern

governors put trains at the marchers' disposal to speed them quickly out of the state. Journalists who covered the march did little to quiet the nation's fears. They delighted in military terminology, dubbing the marchers "armies" and describing themselves as "war correspondents." Their writing gave to the episode a tone of urgency and heightened the sense of a nation imperiled.

By August, the tattered armies dissolved. Although the "On to Washington" movement proved ineffective in forcing federal legislation, Coxey's army dramatized the plight of the unemployed and acted, in the words of one participant, as a "living, moving object lesson." Coxey's tattered "soldiers of misfortune" roused compassion among some they met along the way and stimulated discussion of what should be done. Although much of the eastern press heaped ridicule on Coxey and his motley crew of commonwealers, their uneasy laughter did not disguise the stark fact that something was seriously wrong. Like the Populist revolt, Coxey's army called into question the underlying values of the new industrial order and demonstrated how ordinary citizens turned to means outside the regular party system to influence politics in the 1890s.

The People's Party

"We meet in midst of a nation brought to the verge of moral, political, and material ruin," the Populists declared when they met in Omaha in July 1892 to nominate a national ticket. In the lengthy preamble to their platform, they cataloged their discontent:

> Corruption dominates the ballot-box, the legislatures, the Congress, and touches even the ermine of the bench. The people are demoralized. . . . The fruits of the toil of millions are boldly stolen to build up colossal fortunes for a few. . . . From the same prolific womb of governmental injustice we breed the two great classes—tramps and millionaires.

A sense of the world gone wrong, lurching toward catastrophe, fueled the Omaha convention. Ignatius Donnelly, author of the fiery preamble, spoke of a "vast conspiracy against mankind" and warned of "terrible social convulsions, the destruction of civilization." To answer this threat, he called on the Populists "to restore the government of the Republic to the hands of 'the plain people.'"

The Populists who arrived in Omaha on the Fourth of July to nominate a national slate for "the new party of the industrial millions" came by

CAMPAIGN RIBBONS

Political paraphernalia from the election of 1892 tells a good deal about each party's candidates and beliefs. The People's Party standard-bearer, General James B. Weaver, and his running mate are pictured under a banner promising "Homes for the Toilers, Equal Rights to All, Special Privileges to None." Populist issues are clearly spelled out — "Money, Land, and Transportation." The Populists' hope that these economic issues would replace sectional loyalties is evident in the symbolism of the blue Union and gray Confederate hands shaking. The beliefs of Democratic candidate Grover Cleveland are summed up in the phrase that became his motto, "Public Office Is a Public Trust." Republican Benjamin Harrison, who enjoyed the support of the business community, is aptly portrayed as sponsored by the Bankers and Brokers Republican Club.
Collection of Janice L. and David J. Frent.

wagon, by oxcart, and on foot. Few could afford train fare. The railroad chiefs had evidently read the St. Louis platform, with its call for government ownership of railroads. The Populists did not receive the reduced rates usually given to political delegates.

The Farmers' Alliance, remnants of the Grange, the Knights of Labor, and the WCTU were all on hand. Conspicuously absent was Leonidas L. Polk, the new party's first choice as its standard-bearer. He had died suddenly and the Populists scrambled to find a replacement. They nominated as their presidential candidate General James B. Weaver of Iowa,

a former Union general who had headed the Greenback Labor ticket in 1880. To balance the slate, they selected an ex-Confederate general as his running mate. The legacy of the Civil War cast its long shadow over Populist Party politics. Many southern Democrats, such as C. W. Macune, could not bring themselves to break with the Democratic "party of the fathers" and stayed away from the convention.

As befitted a party of principle, the longest ovation came not for the candidate but for the platform. When the chairman read the list of demands hammered out in St. Louis in February, the crowd went wild. To the eyes of a frightened eastern journalist, the enthusiasm evoked the spirit of the French Revolution. "Cheers and yells," he wrote, "rose like a tornado from four thousand throats and raged without cessation for thirty-four minutes, during which women shrieked and wept, men embraced and kissed their neighbors, locked arms . . . leaped upon tables and chairs in the ecstasy of their delirium."

The eastern press magnified the journalist's fears, rushing to denounce the Populists as "cranks, lunatics, and idiots." Righteous editors dismissed the Populists as "calamity howlers." Branding the Populist leaders with derogatory nicknames such as "Sockless" Jerry Simpson, Davis "Bloody Bridles" Waite, and James H. "Cyclone" Davis, the press denounced them as crackpots and dangerous radicals. The Populists shot back. "They say that I am a 'calamity howler,'" Lorenzo Lewelling of Kansas retorted. "If that is so I want to continue to howl until those conditions are improved." And Mary Elizabeth Lease, accused of being a communist, responded unperturbed, "You may call me an anarchist, a socialist or a communist, I care not, but I hold to the theory that if one man has not enough to eat three times a day and another man has $25 million, that last man has something that belongs to the first."

The Populists garnered more than a million votes in the election of 1892, a respectable showing for a new party. They won three governorships and ten seats in Congress, and they captured twenty-two electoral votes. On the local level, they won fifty state posts and put into office more than fifteen hundred county officials and state legislators. By working with the party out of power, usually the Democrats in the West and the Republicans in the South, they tipped the balance in the national election. This kind of fusion worked best in the West, where it took enough votes away from the incumbent Republican President Benjamin Harrison to allow Democrat Grover Cleveland to return to the White House. Viewing the election as a successful test of strength for a new party, Eugene Debs predicted, "The People's Party will come into power with a resistless rush as did the Republican party a little more than 30 years ago."

The fusion tactic worked in the West, but in the South the Populists made a disappointing showing. It was hard for southern Democrats to fuse with Republicans, especially to vote for a former Union general. Weaver proved an unpopular candidate south of the Mason-Dixon line. He had to cut short his

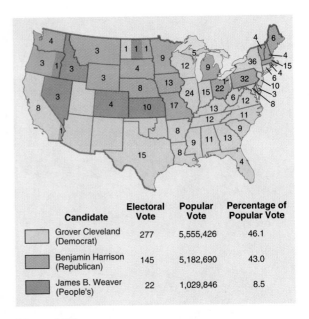

Candidate	Electoral Vote	Popular Vote	Percentage of Popular Vote
Grover Cleveland (Democrat)	277	5,555,426	46.1
Benjamin Harrison (Republican)	145	5,182,690	43.0
James B. Weaver (People's)	22	1,029,846	8.5

MAP 20.1
The Election of 1892

speaking tour in the South after Georgia crowds pelted him with rotten eggs until he looked like "a walking omelet." The People's Party fared better in the 1894 congressional elections, when, unencumbered by a Yankee general, the Populists added half a million voters to their column.

But more than their alliance with the Yankee North, it was the Populists' willingness to form common cause with black farmers that made them anathema in the South. Tom Watson of Georgia tackled the "Negro question" head on in 1892. Realizing that race prejudice obscured the common interests of black and white farmers, Watson campaigned as a Populist for Congress, promising "to wipe out the color line." He openly courted African Americans, appearing on platforms with black speakers. When angry Georgia whites threatened to lynch a black Populist preacher, Watson rallied two thousand gun-toting Populists to the man's defense. "We are determined," said the Populist sheriff of McDuffie County, "in this free country that the humblest white or black man that wants to talk our doctrine shall do it, and the man doesn't live who shall touch a hair of his head, without fighting every man in the people's party." The spectacle of white Georgians protecting a black man from lynching was symptomatic of the enormous changes Populism promised in the South.

McKinley, Bryan, and the Election of 1896

As the election of 1896 approached, depression intensified the need for currency reform. Once again, cries for free silver (the coinage of silver in addition to gold) stirred rebellion in the ranks of both the Democratic and Republican Parties. When the Republicans nominated Governor William McKinley of Ohio on a platform pledging the preservation of the gold standard, western advocates of free silver walked out of the convention. Open rebellion also split the Democratic Party as vast segments in the West and South repudiated President Grover Cleveland because of his support for the gold standard. In South Carolina, Benjamin Tillman won his race for Congress by promising, "Send me to Washington and I'll stick my pitchfork into [Cleveland's] old ribs!"

The spirit of revolt animated the Democratic convention in Chicago in the summer of 1896. "Pitchfork" Ben Tillman set the tone by attacking the party's president, denouncing the Cleveland administration as "undemocratic and tyrannical." But the man of the hour was William Jennings Bryan of Nebraska, the thirty-six-year-old "boy orator from the Platte," who whipped the convention to a frenzy with his passionate call for free silver. In his keynote address, Bryan masterfully cataloged the grievances of farmers and laborers, closing his dramatic speech with the ringing exhortation "Do not crucify mankind upon a cross of gold." Pandemonium broke loose. The delegates seized Bryan and hoisted him to their shoulders. In the demonstration that followed, delegates stampeded to support Bryan. Overnight, the young Nebraskan found himself propelled into the national spotlight, the youngest candidate ever to win a presidential nomination.

The juggernaut of free silver rolled out of Chicago and on to St. Louis, where the People's Party met a week after the Democrats adjourned. Smelling victory, many western Populists urged the party to endorse Bryan. In their haste, they were willing to jettison the Omaha platform and run on the issue of silver alone. "I care not for party names," declared Jerry Simpson, "it is the substance we are after, and we have it in William J. Bryan." A note of warning came from Populists like Tom Watson of Georgia. Watson denounced the Bryanites as opportunists and urged the Populists to steer clear of both major parties and stick to "the middle of the road." In the South, where Democrats had resorted to fraud and violence to steal elections from the Pop-

ulists in 1892 and 1894, support for a Democratic ticket proved especially hard for Populists to swallow. Another obstacle in the path of fusion was Arthur M. Sewall, Bryan's running mate. A Maine shipbuilder, railway director, and bank president, Sewall had been placed on the ticket to appease more conservative Democrats. But to the Populists, Sewall symbolized everything they opposed.

Populist delegates tried to remain true to their principles and their platform in St. Louis. They voted to support all the planks of the old Omaha platform, added to it a call for public works projects for the unemployed, and narrowly defeated a plank for woman suffrage. Only deceit and trickery enabled the fusionists to carry the day. In an unorthodox turn of events, the convention selected the vice presidential candidate first. By nominating Tom Watson to replace Sewall, the party undercut opposition to fusing with the Democrats. Bryan quickly wired the chairman of the convention, protesting that he would not drop Sewall as his running mate or run on a Populist ticket with Watson. Mysteriously, his message never reached the convention floor. Watson's nomination paved the way for the selection of Bryan by a lopsided vote. The Populists did not know it, but their cheers for Bryan in St. Louis signaled not a chorus of victory, but the death knell of the People's Party.

Few contests in the nation's history have been as fiercely fought and as full of emotion as the presidential election of 1896. On the one side stood Republican William McKinley, backed by the wealthy industrialist and party boss Marcus Alonzo Hanna. Hanna played on business fears of free silver to raise more than $4 million for the Republican war chest, double that of any previous campaign. J. P. Morgan and John D. Rockefeller reputedly contributed $174,000 each. McKinley, best known for the high protective tariff that he had sponsored while in Congress, styled himself the "advance agent of prosperity." Ironically, the advance agent had nearly gone bankrupt in the panic of 1893. Only the generous contributions of Hanna and his friends kept McKinley afloat and able to run in 1896. Following the time-honored tradition, McKinley waged a "front porch" campaign from his home in Canton, Ohio. But despite McKinley's low profile, the Republicans, with unlimited funds at their disposal, mounted an impressive campaign. The party relied on speakers, posters, buttons, and printed circulars —over 250 million of them. With so much literature and campaign paraphernalia, Theodore Roosevelt,

MECHANICAL REPUBLICAN CAMPAIGN CARD
In the fiercely contested election of 1896, Republicans, with a war chest of four million dollars, spent lavishly to get their message across. A colorful rotating campaign card promises "political object lessons." The candidates appear to receive even-handed treatment, but the message is clearly Republican. McKinley supports the gold standard with the positive slogans "Honest Payment of Honest Debts" and "Gold Is the Universal Standard of the World," while Bryan's free silver policy "Means Repudiation [of debts], Bankruptcy, and Dishonor." Idle workers outside a closed factory, an abandoned farm, and empty docks decorate the Bryan part of the card in contrast to the prosperity in the McKinley sections. Collection of Janice L. and David J. Frent.

who harbored his own presidential ambitions, complained that Mark Hanna "advertised McKinley as if he were a patent medicine."

William Jennings Bryan had few assets beyond his silver tongue. The Democrats raised less than a tenth of what the Republicans spent, even with the support of silver barons such as the publisher William Randolph Hearst. Bryan struggled to make up in energy and eloquence what his party lacked in campaign funds. He set a new style for presidential campaigning, actively going to the voters. Crossing and recrossing the country in a whirlwind tour, he traveled more than eighteen thousand miles, visited twenty-seven states, and delivered more than six hundred speeches in three months. According to his own reckoning, he spoke to more than five million Americans. The poet Vachel Lindsay, growing up in Illinois during the race, likened Bryan's campaign to a cyclone:

> Prairie avenger, mountain lion,
> Bryan, Bryan, Bryan, Bryan,
> Gigantic troubadour, speaking like a siege gun,
> Smashing Plymouth Rock with his boulders from the West,
> And just a hundred miles behind, tornadoes piled across the sky,
> Blotting out the sun and moon,
> A sign on high.

While throngs in the West stirred to Bryan's "cross of gold" speech, editors in the East grew nearly hysterical in their condemnation of Bryan as a "dangerous revolutionary." Theodore Roosevelt, caught up in the fervor, compared the Democrats to French revolutionaries. In his typical bellicose fashion, he proposed "taking ten or a dozen of their leaders out, standing . . . them against a wall, and shooting them dead."

As election day approached, the silver states of the Rocky Mountains lined up for Bryan. The Northeast stood solidly for McKinley. Much of the South, with the exception of the border states, came back to the Democratic fold, leaving Tom Watson to lament that in the politics of fusion, "we play Jonah while they play the whale." The Midwest was in the balance. Bryan intensified his campaign in Illinois, Michigan, Ohio, and Indiana. But midwestern farmers could smell economic recovery and were less receptive to the blandishments of free silver than were voters farther west. In the cities, Democrats charged the Republicans with mass intimidation. "Men, vote as you please," the head of the Steinway Piano

Company reportedly announced on the eve of the election, "but if Bryan is elected tomorrow the whistle will not blow Wednesday morning."

Intimidation alone did not explain the failure of urban labor to rally to Bryan. In an effective campaign ploy, Republicans handed out wooden coins carrying Bryan's picture on one side and on the other side the inscription "In God We Trust . . . for the other 47 cents." Republicans repeatedly warned workers that if the Democrats won, the inflated silver dollar would be worth only fifty cents. However much farmers and laborers might insist that they were united as producers against the nonproducing plutocrats, it was equally true that inflation did not promise the boon to urban laborers that it did to western debtors.

On election day, four out of every five voters went to the polls in an unprecedented turnout. In the critical midwestern states, as many as 95 percent of the eligible voters cast their ballots. While some charged that the Republicans "voted the cemeteries" (stuffed the ballot boxes) for McKinley, fraud alone did not account for the high voter participation. To the voters in 1896, something momentous seemed to be at stake. Anxious crowds milled outside the newspaper offices and gathered on courthouse steps, waiting for news of the outcome. Bryan piled up a staggering total. He polled more than 6.5 million votes, double the number of any previous presidential candidate. McKinley bested him with 7.1 million. In the end the election outcome hinged on as few as one hundred to one thousand votes in several key states. Although McKinley won twenty-three states to Bryan's twenty-two, the electoral vote showed a lopsided 271–176. Despite his reputation in the East as a revolutionary firebrand, Bryan yielded with grace and cabled his congratulations to McKinley. Among the many telegrams that poured into McKinley's home in Canton came one from the jubilant Mark Hanna that said simply, "God's in his Heaven, All's right with the World!"

The biggest losers in 1896 turned out to be the Populists. On the national level, they polled less than 300,000 votes, over a million less than in 1894. In the clamor to support Bryan, Populists in the South drifted back into the Democratic Party. The People's Party was crushed, and with it died the agrarian revolt.

By the time William McKinley took the oath of office in March 1897, the political storms that had lashed the 1890s had died down. The decade had witnessed bold new political initiatives on the part of women, farmers, and laborers. For a time it looked as though they might forge a lasting alliance in the People's Party. In the end, although Populism proved unsuccessful, it set the political agenda for the United States in the next decades, highlighting issues such as banking and currency reform, electoral reforms such as the direct election of senators, and an enlarged role for the federal government in the nation's economic life. As the decade ended, the bugle call to arms drowned out the trumpet of reform as a "splendid little war" whipped up patriotic fervor, uniting the country and announcing the emergence of the United States as a major world power.

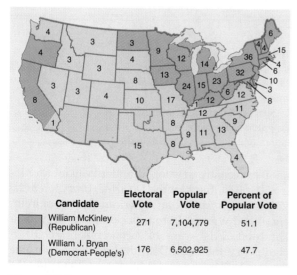

Candidate	Electoral Vote	Popular Vote	Percent of Popular Vote
William McKinley (Republican)	271	7,104,779	51.1
William J. Bryan (Democrat-People's)	176	6,502,925	47.7

MAP 20.2
The Election of 1896

American Expansionism and the "White Man's Burden"

As the United States stood on the brink of the twentieth century, the European powers—Great Britain, France, Germany, Spain, and Belgium—as well as an increasingly powerful Japan competed for empires abroad, gobbling up what they liked to call the great "empty spaces" on the globe in Asia, Africa, Latin America, and the Pacific. Between 1870 and 1900, European nations gained control of more than 20 percent of the land and 10 percent of the earth's population. The United States, intent on con-

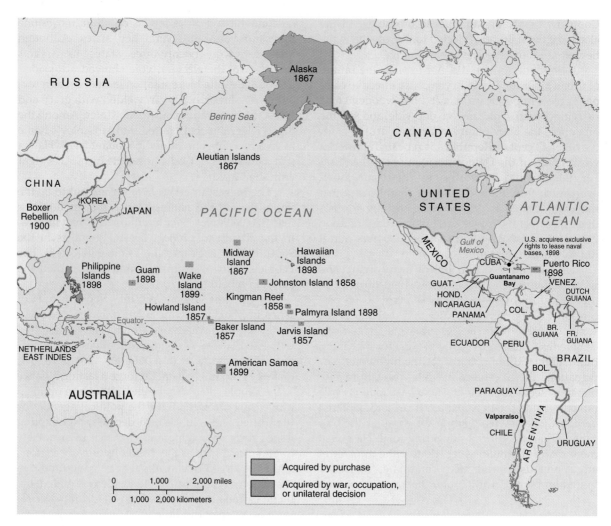

MAP 20.3
U. S. Territorial Expansion through 1900
The United States extended its interests abroad with a series of territorial acquisitions. Alaska was purchased in 1867; the Philippines and other Spanish island possessions, including Puerto Rico and Guam, were won in the Spanish-American War of 1898. Although Cuba was granted independence, the Platt amendment kept the new nation firmly under U.S. control. For good measure, President McKinley annexed Hawaii. In the wake of the Spanish-American War, the United States woke up to find it held an empire extending half way around the globe.

quering its own western frontier, had remained largely aloof from the scramble for colonies but not uninterested in the riches to be found abroad.

The Monroe Doctrine and the Open Door Policy

American foreign policy at the dawn of the twentieth century rested on two pillars, one that dated back to President James Monroe in the 1820s and

another recently developed under William McKinley. The first, the Monroe Doctrine, proclaimed the Western Hemisphere an American "sphere of influence" and warned European powers to keep their hands off or risk war. The second pillar of U.S. foreign policy, the Open Door dealt with Asia, an area coveted by American merchants since the 1840s, the days of the clipper ships and the China trade. In the 1890s, China, weakened by years of warfare, looked as if it might be partitioned into spheres of influ-

THE OPEN DOOR
The trade advantage gained by the United States through the Open Door policy enunciated by Secretary of State John Hay in 1900 is portrayed graphically in this political cartoon. Uncle Sam stands prominently in the "open door" while representatives of the other Great Powers seek admittance to the "Flowery Kingdom" of China. Great Britain is symbolized by the stocky figure of John Bull; czarist Russia is portrayed by the bearded figure with the hat sporting the imperial double eagle. Other imperialist powers variously represented have yielded to Uncle Sam, who holds the golden key of "American Diplomacy" while the Chinese beam with pleasure. In fact, the Open Door policy promised only equal access for all powers to the China trade, not United States preeminence as the cartoon implies.
Culver Pictures.

ence by the imperial powers—England, Japan, Germany, France, and Russia. Concerned about American trade and, coincident to it, the integrity of China, Secretary of State John Hay in 1899–1900 hastily wrote a series of notes calling for an "open door" policy that would ensure trade access to all and maintain the semblance of Chinese sovereignty. The notes—sent to Britain, Germany, and Russia and later to France, Japan, and Italy—were greeted with polite evasions. Nevertheless, Hay boldly an-

nounced in 1900 that the Open Door was international policy.

American foreign policy reflected a curious paradox. Just as the United States wished to keep the Western Hemisphere (particularly Latin America and the Caribbean) closed to foreign influences, it wished to keep the Eastern Hemisphere (especially Asia) open for its own purposes. The twin pillars of U.S. foreign policy may not have been consistent, but they worked well to further America's economic interests. By insisting on its Open Door policy in Asia, the United States largely avoided the problems of maintaining a far-flung colonial empire while at the same time exerting its economic power.

Throughout much of the last half of the nineteenth century, the interests of the American public —and the American government—in foreign policy took a backseat to domestic developments. "Foreign relations," one historian has written, "were composed of incidents, not policies." One of these incidents occurred in 1889, when Germany threatened war with the United States. Eleven years after a treaty gave the United States the right to the harbor at the Pacific port of Pago Pago in the Samoan Islands, Germany, seeking dominance over the islands, sent warships to support its honor and its claims. But before any fighting broke out, a great typhoon destroyed the German and American ships. Acceding to the will of nature, the potential combatants divided the islands amicably between themselves.

American foreign policy reflected a curious paradox. Just as the United States wished to keep the Western Hemisphere closed to foreign influences, it wished to keep the Eastern Hemisphere open for its own purposes.

Elsewhere, America's foreign adventures appeared little more than a sidelight to business development. In Hawaii, American sugar interests fomented a rebellion in 1893, toppling the increasingly anti-American Queen Liliuokalani. They then proceeded to press President Cleveland to annex the islands, a move that would allow the planters to avoid the high duties on sugar recently imposed by the McKinley tariff. Cleveland balked. When he learned that the Hawaiian population opposed annexation, he withdrew the treaty from Senate consideration.

Closer to home, the United States actively worked to buttress the Monroe Doctrine, with its assertion of American hegemony (domination) in the Western Hemisphere. In the 1880s, Republican Secretary of State James G. Blaine promoted hemispheric peace and trade through Pan-American cooperation at the same time that he used American troops to intervene in Latin American border disputes. In 1891, war with Chile almost erupted after two American sailors were killed and several were injured in a barroom brawl in Valparaíso. President Benjamin Harrison threatened war but backed down after Chile apologized—he was wise to do so, for Chile had a better equipped navy than the United States. Late in the century, the United States began to strengthen its navy, but its army remained little more than a token force of 25,000, barely large enough to handle disturbances at home, let alone fight abroad.

Nevertheless, in 1895, Americans risked war with Great Britain to enforce the Monroe Doctrine. When a border dispute arose between Venezuela and British Guiana over lands where gold had been discovered, President Cleveland asserted the U.S. prerogative to step in and mediate, reducing Venezuela to the role of mere onlooker. Secretary of State Richard Olney boldly informed the British, "Today, the United States is practically sovereign on this continent," insisting that "its fiat is law." Unpersuaded, Britain refused to accept the United States as mediator. Conflict seemed imminent. "Let the fight come if it must," wrote Theodore Roosevelt. "I don't care whether our sea coast cities are bombarded or not; we would take Canada." Cleveland, less bellicose than Roosevelt, wished only to see America's presence in the hemisphere respected and its solution for peace accepted. He was relieved when the British, who also wished to avoid war, accepted the terms of U.S. mediation. The Venezuelan crisis signaled the willingness of the United States to play an active role beyond its borders, especially to preserve the Monroe Doctrine.

Markets and Missionaries

The depression of the 1890s provided a powerful impetus to American commercial expansion. As markets weakened at home, American businesses looked abroad for profits. Captain Alfred Thayer Mahan, leader of a growing group of American expansionists that included Henry Cabot Lodge, John Hay, and Theodore Roosevelt, prophesied as early as 1890, "Whether they will or not, Americans must now begin to look outward. The growing production of the country requires it." Although not all U.S. business leaders thought it advantageous to undertake adventures abroad, the logic of acquiring new markets to absorb the nation's growing capacity for production proved convincing to many. As the depression deepened, one diplomat warned that Americans "must turn [their] eyes abroad, or they will soon look inward upon discontent." Enthusiasts of expansion spoke glowingly of Asian markets: "Four hundred million Chinese without shoes!" American exports of cloth, kerosene, flour, and steel already constituted a small but significant percentage of the profits of American business. And where American interests led, businessmen expected American power and influence to follow to protect their investments. Companies like Standard Oil actively sought to use the government as their agent, often putting foreign service employees on the payroll. "Our ambassadors and ministers and consuls," wrote John D. Rockefeller appreciatively, "have aided to push our way into new markets to the utmost corners of the world." Whether by "our" he meant the United States or Standard Oil remained ambiguous; in practice, the distinction was of little importance in late-nineteenth-century foreign policy.

However compelling the economic arguments about markets and overproduction proved, material interest alone did not account for the new expansionism that seized the nation during the 1890s. As Mahan confessed, "Even when material interests are the original exciting cause, it is the sentiment to which they give rise, the moral tone which emotion takes that constitutes the greater force." Much of that moral tone was set by American missionaries intent on spreading the gospel of Christianity to the "heathen." No area on the globe constituted a greater challenge than China. In 1858, the Tientsin

treaty admitted foreign missionaries — Roman Catholics from France, Protestants from Britain, Germany, and the United States — to spread the gospel to the hinterlands. Young women particularly were attracted to the independence and excitement promised by mission work. Missions accepted single women over twenty-six years of age. By 1890, women constituted more than 60 percent of the mission force. Young women from the rural Midwest who would not have ventured into Chicago alone set off for China. Foreign mission work promised adventure and autonomy few other callings for women could match.

Although they never lost their optimism, the missionaries' success proved limited and their converts few. By the turn of the century, an estimated 100,000 converts existed in a total population of 400 million Chinese. Nevertheless, as the missionaries pointed out, the number marked a significant increase over the 8,000 Christian converts counted in 1870.

Increased missionary activity and Western enterprise touched off a series of antiforeign uprisings in China that culminated in the Boxer Rebellion of 1900–1901. The Chinese particularly resented the interference of missionaries in village life and the preference and protection they afforded their Christian converts. Opposition to foreigners took the form of antiforeign secret societies, most notably the

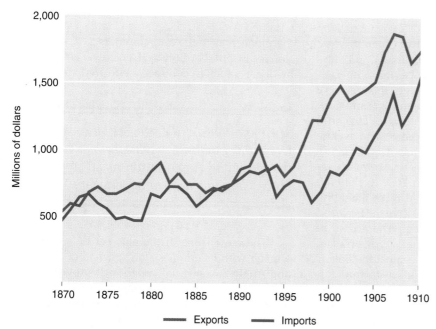

FIGURE 20.2
Expansion in U.S. Trade, 1870 – 1910

Between 1870 and 1910 American exports nearly tripled. Although imports rose, they were held in check by the high protective tariff championed by Republican presidents from Ulysses Grant to William Howard Taft. A decline in imports is particularly noticeable after passage of the prohibitive McKinley tariff in 1890.

WOMEN MISSIONARIES IN CHINA
Methodist women missionaries in the Szechuan province of China rely on traditional means of transportation, in this case "back chairs." The independence enjoyed by women missionaries, who made up more than 69 percent of the foreign mission force by 1890, stood in marked contrast to the restrictions placed on young women of their class at home.
Courtesy of the Yale Divinity School Library.

Boxers, whose Chinese name translated literally into "Righteous Harmonious Fist." No simple pugilists, the Boxers believed that through ritual they could induce a trance that would make them invincible to Western weapons. Under the slogan "Uphold the Ch'ing Dynasty, Exterminate the Foreigners," they began to terrorize Chinese Christians and later missionaries in the north of China. As they became bolder, they attacked railroads and telegraph lines, the twin symbols of Western imperialism. Their rampage eventually led to the massacre of some 2,000 Chinese converts and 250 missionaries and their families. The missionaries clamored for the American government to protect and avenge them. Fearing for their lives, they showed little toleration for the cautious diplomatic approach favored by Secretary of State John Hay. In the end, 2,500 U.S. troops joined an Allied force including British and German troops sent to save the besieged foreigners in Peking (now Beijing). The arrival of foreign troops chastened the imperial government, which adopted a tougher stance against the Boxers and a more accommodationist policy toward foreign missionaries.

In their fight against the Boxers, the missionaries saw no paradox in bringing Christianity to China at gunpoint. "It is worth any cost in money, worth any cost in bloodshed," argued one bishop, "if we can make millions of Chinese true and intelligent Christians." In truth, expansionists and missionaries worked hand in hand; trade and Christianity marched into China together. "Missionaries," admitted American clergyman Charles Denby, "are the pioneers of trade and commerce. . . . The missionary, inspired by holy zeal, goes everywhere, and by degrees foreign commerce and trade follow."

The moral tone of the age, set by social Darwinism with its emphasis on survival of the fittest and Anglo-Saxon racial superiority, proved ideally suited to imperialism.

The moral tone of the age, set by social Darwinism with its emphasis on survival of the fittest and Anglo-Saxon racial superiority, proved ideally suited to imperialism. Congregational minister Josiah Strong revealed the mix of racism and missionary zeal that fueled American adventurism abroad when he remarked, "It seems to me that God, with infinite wisdom and skill, is training the Anglo Saxon race for an hour sure to come in the world's future." British poet Rudyard Kipling put it better in verse.

> Take up the white man's burden
>   Send forth the best ye breed—
> Go bind your sons to exile
>   To serve your captive's need;
> To wait, in heavy harness,
>   On fluttered folk and wild—
> Your new-caught sullen people,
>   Half devil and half child.

The irony that is apparent in Kipling's poem evidently escaped those Americans who rushed to champion U.S. expansion. Jingoism, extreme nationalism tinged with belligerency, became the style. No one exemplified the new chauvinism more than Theodore Roosevelt, the rising young Republican from New York. Always more concerned with manliness than money, Roosevelt believed that nations and individuals needed the test of combat to maintain their virility. "This country needs a war," Roosevelt asserted in 1895. Power, not profits, motivated expansionists of Roosevelt's stripe. Intent on asserting the United States' place in the world of nations, they pressed for a more expansionist policy, judging imperialism "a fine expression of the American spirit."

Missionary zeal, patriotism, profit, and power all fueled American expansionism. The volatile mix reached the combustion point in 1898, propelling the United States into war and leading to the country's foray into colonialism.

The United States Becomes a World Power

As the leading industrial nation in the world, the United States was destined to play a significant role in world politics. Yet not until the end of the century did the country take its place on the world stage by confronting and easily defeating a European power. On the surface the Spanish-American War seemed a giant contradiction: A war begun as a humanitarian effort to free Cuba from Spain's colonial grasp ended with the United States itself becoming a colonial power. And in the jungles of

the Pacific, American troops fought a dirty guerrilla war with Filipino nationalists, who, like the Cubans, sought independence. Yet behind the contradiction stood the twin pillars of American foreign policy. The Monroe Doctrine's insistence on American control in the Western Hemisphere made Spain's presence in Cuba unacceptable, while the determination to keep an open door in Asia rendered the Philippines a convenient stepping-stone to China.

"A Splendid Little War"

Looking back on the Spanish-American War of 1898, Secretary of State John Hay judged it "a splendid little war; begun with the highest motives, carried on with magnificent intelligence and spirit, favored by that fortune which loves the brave." At the close of a decade marred by bitter depression, social unrest, and political upheaval, the war offered Americans a chance to wave the flag and march in unison. War fever proved as infectious as the tune of a John Philip Sousa march. Few argued the merits of the war until it was over and the time came to divide the spoils.

At the close of a decade marred by bitter depression, social unrest, and political upheaval, the Spanish-American War offered Americans a chance to wave the flag and march in unison.

The war began with moral outrage over the treatment of Cuban revolutionaries, who had launched a fight for independence against the Spanish colonial regime in 1895. In an attempt to isolate the guerrillas, Spanish General Valeriano Weyler y Nicolau herded Cubans into crowded and unsanitary concentration camps, where thousands died of hunger, disease, and exposure. Starvation soon spread to the cities. Tens of thousands of Cubans died, and countless others were left without food, clothing, or shelter. By 1898, fully a quarter of the island's population had perished in the revolution.

As the Cuban war dragged on, pressure for American intervention mounted. Public outrage at Spain was whipped to a frenzy by American newspapers. A fierce circulation war raged in New York City between William Randolph Hearst's *Evening*

THE BIG TYPE WAR OF THE YELLOW KIDS.

YELLOW JOURNALISM

Newspaper publishers Joseph Pulitzer and William Randolph Hearst square off in "The Big Type War."
As the cartoon indicates, Hearst insisted he had the better right to cover the Spanish-American War be-
cause he "bought and paid for it." In their 1890s circulation war, Hearst and Pulitzer not only used big
type in sensational headlines, but employed color in new comic sections. Hearst's Sunday American
promised "eight pages of polychromatic effulgence that make the rainbow look like a lead pipe." Hearst
also stole the era's most famous cartoon character, the "Yellow Kid," from Pulitzer after a bidding war
for the cartoonist's talents. Soon all forms of sensational writing were labeled "yellow journalism."
Library of Congress.

Journal and Joseph Pulitzer's *World*. Their competition provoked what came to be called "yellow journalism," which pandered to the public's appetite for violence and sensationalism. The Cuban war provided Hearst with a wealth of sensational copy. His papers fed the nation a daily diet of "Butcher" Weyler and alleged Spanish atrocities. He sent artist Frederic Remington to document the horror, and when Remington wired home, "Everything is quiet. There is no trouble here. There will be no war," Hearst shot back, "You furnish the pictures and I'll furnish the war."

But other factors accounted for U.S. intervention. American interests, in the words of the U.S. minister to Spain, were more than "merely theoretical or sentimental." American business had more than $50 million invested in Cuban sugar, and American trade with Cuba, a brisk $100 million a year before the war, had dropped to near zero as a result of the revolution. Nevertheless, the business community balked, wary of a war with Spain. When industrialist Mark Hanna, Republican kingmaker and senator from Ohio, ever the barometer of business opinion, urged restraint, a hot-headed Theodore

Roosevelt exploded, "We will have this war for the freedom of Cuba, Senator Hanna, in spite of the timidity of commercial interests."

To expansionists like Roosevelt, more than Cuban independence was at stake. War with Spain opened up the prospect of expansion into Asia as well since Spain controlled not only Cuba but Puerto Rico, Guam, and the Philippine Islands. As assistant secretary of the navy, Roosevelt worked for preparedness whenever his boss's back was turned. While Secretary John D. Long was vacationing, Roosevelt audaciously ordered the U.S. fleet to Manila, in the Philippines. In the event of conflict with Spain, he put the navy in a position to capture the islands and gain an important stepping-stone to China.

President McKinley slowly and reluctantly moved toward intervention. In a show of American force, he dispatched the armored cruiser *Maine* to Cuba. On the night of February 15, 1898, a mysterious explosion destroyed the *Maine,* killing 266 crew members. Enraged Americans immediately blamed the Spanish government. Rallying to the cry "Remember the *Maine,*" Congress declared war in April. In the surge of patriotism that followed, more than 235,000 men enlisted. War brought with it a unity of purpose and national harmony that ended a decade of internal strife. "In April, everywhere over this good fair land, flags were flying," wrote the Kansas editor William Allen White. "Little children on fences greeted the soldiers with flapping scarfs and handkerchiefs and flags; at the stations, crowds gathered to hurrah for the soldiers, and to throw hats into the air, and to unfurl flags."

They soon had something to cheer about. Five days after McKinley signed the war resolution, the U.S. navy under Admiral George Dewey destroyed the Spanish fleet in Manila Bay. Dewey's stunning

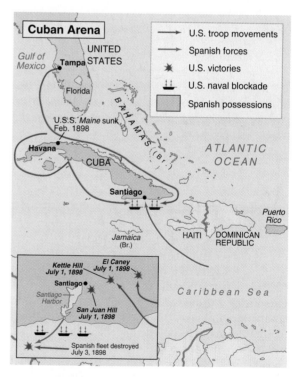

MAP 20.4

The Spanish-American War, 1898

The Spanish-American War was fought in two theaters, the Philippine Islands and Cuba. Admiral George Dewey captured Manila without the loss of a single American sailor five days after President William McKinley called for a declaration of war. The war lasted only a matter of months. U.S. troops landed in Cuba in mid-June and by mid-July they had taken Santiago and Havana and the Spanish fleet had been destroyed off Santiago.

The Spanish-American War: Eyewitness Accounts

*T*he Spanish-American War received more eyewitness news coverage than any previous war in American history. Hearst's papers had fanned the flames of war and, once it started in earnest, reporters fed a public hungry for news about the conflict. In addition to daily newspapers, weekly illustrated papers like Collier's, Leslie's, and Harper's covered the war, using dispatches wired from the front and illustrations by some of the leading artists of the day.

The press shared the country's enthusiasm for battle. Richard Harding Davis, a star foreign correspondent, observed on the eve of the troops' departure from Tampa, "It was a most happy-go-lucky expedition, run with real American optimism and readiness to take big chances, and with the spirit of a people who recklessly trust that it will come out all right in the end. . . . As one of the generals on board said, 'This is God Almighty's war, and we are only His agents.' "

*M*en's letters home spoke to more mundane aspects of army life.

Document 1. Rough Rider Arthur Fortunatus Cosby, Letter to a friend, June 1898

Personally I expected anything and I have no complaints to make, but a lot of the "boys" don't like it. Our food on board ship is the same; coffee, hardtack, with canned beef (that must have been cooked it is so stringy and tasteless), canned tomatoes and beans. These are travel rations and we have now had ten days of them with 5 days more on the road. We get the coffee hot, but the other things are usually cold unless an enterprising fellow will make a mess of the whole thing which he calls a stew.

We have all gone expert in "rustling" food, begging it, buying it from the ship's cook who is supposed not to sell, smuggling it in from shore etc. . . .

All the boys have lost flesh at the most astonishing rate. . . . Then too although our passage has been remarkably quiet many of the boys have been sea-sick. This with the confinement and heat to which they are not accustomed, and poor food has weakened them. I am very much afraid that we shan't do much.

*W*hen the troops put ashore, General William Shafter attempted to hold the reporters on the ship until after the troops had landed. An irate Richard Harding Davis confronted the general, explaining that he was a "descriptive writer" and needed to be at the scene. Shafter retorted, "I do not care a damn what you are, I'll treat all of you alike." Davis managed to catch up to the troops and dispatch the following account of the landing.

Document 2. Richard Harding Davis Reports on the Cuban Landing, June 1898

No one slept that night, for until two o'clock in the morning troops were still being disembarked in the surf, and two ships of war had their searchlights turned on the landingplace, and made Siboney as light as a ball-room. Back of the searchlights was an ocean white with moonlight, and on the shore red camp-fires, at which the half-drowned troops were drying their uniforms, and the Rough Riders, who had just marched in from Daiquiri, were cooking their coffee and bacon. . . .

It was one of the most weird and remarkable scenes of the war, probably of any war. An army was being landed on an enemy's coast at the dead of night, but with somewhat more of cheers and shrieks of laughter than rise from the bathers in the surf at Coney Island on a hot Sunday. . . . The men still to be landed from the "prison hulks," as they called the transports, were singing in chorus, the men already on shore were dancing naked around the camp-fires on the beach, or shouting with delight as they plunged into the first bath that had offered in seven days, and those in the launches as they were pitched headfirst at the soil of Cuba, signalized their arrival by howls of triumph.

Once on shore, Davis traveled with Theodore Roosevelt and General Leonard Wood, so close as to be almost a third commander. He was the first to spot Spanish troops and point them out to Wood. At one point, Davis picked up a rifle and fired a few shots at the enemy. No wonder his dispatches contain such a spontaneous account of the action, as in this description of the decisive charge up San Juan Hill, which took place on July 1, 1898.

Document 3. Richard Harding Davis at San Juan Hill

They had no glittering bayonets, they were not massed in regular array. There were a few men in advance, bunched together, and creeping up a steep, sunny hill, the tops of which roared and flashed with flame. The men held their guns pressed across their breasts and stepped heavily as they climbed. Behind these first few, spreading out like a fan, were single lines of men, slipping and scrambling in the smooth grass, moving forward with difficulty, as though they were wading waist high through water, moving slowly carefully, with strenuous effort. It was much more wonderful than any swinging charge could have been. They walked to greet death at every step, many of them, as they advanced, sinking suddenly or pitching forward and disappearing in the high grass, but the others waded on, stubbornly, forming a thin blue line that kept creeping higher and higher up the hill. It was inevitable as the rising tide. It was a miracle of self-sacrifice, a triumph of bull-dog courage, which one watched breathless with wonder.

[The journalist later recollected:]

I have seen many illustrations and pictures of this charge on the San Juan hills, but none of them seem to show it just as I remember it. In the picture-papers the men are running up a hill swiftly and gallantly, in regular formation, rank after rank, with flags flying, their eyes aflame, and their hair streaming, their bayonets fixed, in long, brilliant lines, and invincible overpowering weight of numbers.

Instead of which I think the thing which impressed one the most, when our men started from cover, was they were so few. It seemed as if someone had made an awful and terrible mistake. One's instinct was to call to them to come back.

Colonel Theodore Roosevelt himself kept diaries and later published his own account of the battle. He recalled that after his troops had taken nearby Kettle Hill, he called the Rough Riders to charge the line of Spanish trenches on San Juan Hill.

Document 4. TR Charges San Juan Hill

Thinking that the men would all come, I jumped over the wire fence in front of us and started at the double; but, as a matter of fact, the troopers were so excited, what with shooting and being shot, and shouting and cheering, that they did not hear, or did not heed me; and after running about a hundred yards I found I had only five men along with me.

[Going back to gather his forces, Roosevelt ordered them to charge.]

The men of the various regiments which were already on the hill came with a rush, and we started across the wide valley which lay between us and the Spanish intrenchments. . . . Long before we got near them the Spaniards ran, save a few here and there, who either surrendered or were shot down. When we reached the trenches we found them filled with dead bodies in the light blue and white uniform of the Spanish regular army. . . .

I was with Henry Bardshar [his aide-de-camp], running up at the double, and two Spaniards leaped from the trenches and fired at us, not ten yards away. As they turned to run I closed in and fired twice, missing the first and killing the second. My revolver was from the sunken battleship *Maine*.

There was very great confusion at this time, the different regiments being completely intermingled —white regulars, colored regulars [African American soldiers in the 21st Infantry], and Rough Riders. . . . We were still under heavy fire, and I got together a mixed lot of men and pushed on from the trenches and ranch-houses which we had just taken driving the Spaniards through a line of palm trees, and over the crest of a chain of hills. When we reached these crests we found ourselves overlooking Santiago.

Document 1. Frank Freidel, *The Splendid Little War* (Little, Brown, 1958), 75–76.
Document 2. Ibid., 95–97.
Document 3. Ibid., 162.
Document 4. Ibid., 167, 170.

THE BATTLE OF SAN JUAN HILL
*This idealized 1898 lithograph portrays a highly romantic version of the Battle of San Juan Hill,
far from the truth. The famous charge was much less glamorous than pictured here. Theodore
Roosevelt, whose Rough Riders had taken nearby Kettle Hill, called to his men to charge the next
line of Spanish trenches in the San Juan hills. But in the excitement of the battle, they didn't
hear him and Roosevelt found himself charging virtually alone. He had to go back and rally the
Rough Riders, who then charged the hill on foot. The illustration does get one thing right.
Theodore Roosevelt led the charge wearing his spectacles. Roosevelt was so myopic he feared he
might lose his glasses in battle and had Brooks Brothers, who custom-made his uniform, include
a dozen pockets for extra eyeglasses.*
Library of Congress.

victory caught the nation by surprise. Although
naval strategists like Roosevelt had been orches-
trating the move for some time, few Americans had
ever heard of the Philippines. Even McKinley confessed that he could not immediately locate the
archipelago on the map. He nevertheless dispatched
U.S. troops to secure the islands.

The war in Cuba ended almost as quickly as it
had begun. The first troops landed on June 22, and
after a handful of battles the Spanish surrendered
on July 17. (See Texts in Historical Context, page 792.)

The war lasted just long enough to elevate Theodore
Roosevelt to the status of bona fide war hero. Roosevelt, sensitive to charges that he and his friends
were no more than "armchair or parlor jingoes," resigned his post to lead a regiment. His Rough Riders, composed about equally of Ivy League polo
players and cowboys Roosevelt had met during his
sojourn in the Dakotas, made excellent copy for the
journalists and photographers hungry for stories
while the troops languished in Tampa awaiting
their orders. Roosevelt and his men staged daily

rodeos for the press, with the likes of New York blueblood William Tiffany busting broncs in competition with Dakota cowboy "Dead Shot" Jim Simpson. When the Rough Riders shipped out to Cuba, journalists fought for a berth with the colorful regiment. Roosevelt's charge up Kettle Hill and his role in the decisive battle of San Juan made front-page news. Overnight, Roosevelt became the most famous man in America. By the time he sailed home from Cuba, a coalition of independent Republicans was already busy making plans to nominate him for governor of New York. Tom Platt, nicknamed New York's "Easy Boss," voiced the only reservation. "If he becomes governor," Platt remarked, "sooner or later, with his personality, he will have to be President." Platt confessed that he was "afraid to start that thing going."

The Debate over American Imperialism

After a few brief campaigns in Cuba and Puerto Rico and Dewey's stunning naval victory in the Philippines, the American people woke up with an empire that stretched halfway around the globe. Cuba had been promised independence, but while it escaped Spanish colonialism, the United States stopped short of granting the island full autonomy. The Platt Amendment, tacked onto the peace treaty with Spain, gave the United States the right to intervene in Cuba whenever it pleased. The treaty ceded to the United States control of Puerto Rico and Guam, former Spanish colonies. McKinley added Hawaii for good measure, annexing the islands in July 1898. But what to do with the Philippines? After much prayer, the president resolved to keep this former Spanish colony. As Finley Peter Dunne, a popular humorist of the era, wryly observed through his mouthpieces, the barroom philosophers Hennessy and Mr. Dooley: "I know what I'd do if I was Mack," Hennessy insisted. "I'd hist a flag over th' Ph'lippeens, and I'd take in th' whole lot iv them." "An yet," his foil Mr. Dooley mused, "tis not more thin two months since ye larned whether they were islands or canned goods."

America would soon feel the weight of the "white man's burden" in the Philippines. Empire did not come cheap. When Spain balked, the United States agreed to pay an indemnity of $20 million for the islands. Nor was the cost measured in money alone. Filipino insurrectionaries under Emilio

Aguinaldo, who had greeted U.S. troops as liberators, bitterly fought the new masters. It would take seven years and four thousand American dead—almost ten times the number killed in Cuba—not to mention an estimated twenty thousand Filipino casualties, to defeat Aguinaldo and secure American control of the Philippines.

At home a vocal minority, composed largely of former Populists and Democrats, resisted the country's foray into empire, judging it unwise, immoral, and unconstitutional. William Jennings Bryan, who had enlisted in the army along with Roosevelt but contracted typhoid fever and never saw action, came to the conclusion that American expansionism served only to distract the nation from its real problems at home. What did imperialism offer the ordinary American? Bryan asked. His answer: "Heavier taxes, Asiatic emigration and an opportunity to furnish more sons for the army." Mark Twain, lending his bitter eloquence to the cause of anti-imperialism, lamented that the United States had become "yet another Civilized Power, with its banner of the Prince of Peace in one hand and its loot-basket and its butcher-knife in the other."

In the end the anti-imperialists would prove prophetic, and Hay's Open Door notes would demonstrate the principle that it was more effective for the United States to spread its influence abroad through economic power than by conquest. But in 1898, as the *Washington Post* trumpeted, "The taste of empire is in the mouth of the people," and Americans thrilled at the prospect of "an imperial policy, the Republic renascent, taking her place with the armed nations."

Conclusion: The End of a Tumultuous Decade

As the nineteenth century came to a close, the Spanish-American War symbolized America's entry onto the world stage as a significant player in global politics. A decade of domestic strife ended amid the blare of martial music and the waving of flags. During the 1890s, Americans, poised on the brink of the twentieth century, not only searched for order but fought for competing visions of who should manage the new industrial society. Women fought drunkenness and the conditions that fostered it and mounted a suffrage movement to secure their basic political rights. Ida B. Wells brought the brutality of lynching into the public spotlight. Laborers staged bloody strikes to determine once and for all who controlled the workplace, the workers who toiled there or the bosses who owned the machines and made the profits. The Homestead lockout and the Pullman strike demonstrated the power of property and the conservatism of the laissez-faire state. Like the striking workers, farmers in the 1890s demanded a greater voice and forged the People's Party to fight for a vision of economic democracy. Their willingness to increase the power of the federal government challenged the notion of laissez-faire and laid the foundation for a new liberal state capable of countering the power of large corporations. This shift away from laissez-faire and toward a more active role for the federal government marked the major political development of the period.

While none of the movements of the 1890s succeeded in that decade, they laid the groundwork for what was to come. Militant women, strikers, and farmers all fought for change and, in doing so, contributed to the forging of a new politics. In their struggles, the 1890s witnessed a decade of strife the likes of which the country would not see again for another seventy years.

CHRONOLOGY

1884 The Woman's Christian Temperance Union (WCTU), under leadership of Frances Willard, calls for "home protection ballot" (suffrage for women).

1887 Farmers' Alliance organized.

1890 National American Woman Suffrage Association (NAWSA) formed, elects Elizabeth Cady Stanton as president.

Wyoming enters Union with woman suffrage.

1892 Ida B. Wells begins her antilynching crusade.

People's Party (also known as Populist Party) founded in St. Louis.

Homestead lockout pits Carnegie steelworkers against hired Pinkertons.

Anarchist Alexander Berkman's attempt to assassinate Henry Clay Frick turns public opinion against Homestead workers.

People's Party wins more than one million votes for its presidential candidate, James B. Weaver.

Susan B. Anthony becomes president of NAWSA.

1893 Severe economic depression touched off by panic on Wall Street.

Referendum grants women right to vote in Colorado.

1894 Coxey's "army" marches from Ohio to Washington, D.C., to dramatize plight of unemployed.

Federal troops crush Pullman strike; union leader Eugene V. Debs jailed for violating court injunction.

1896 Democrats nominate William Jennings Bryan for president and adopt platform of free silver.

Republican William McKinley defeats Democrat William Jennings Bryan for presidency.

California voters defeat referendum granting women right to vote.

Women gain vote in Idaho. Utah enters Union with woman suffrage.

National Association of Colored Women formed, with Mary Church Terrell as president.

1898 Spanish-American War: United States intervenes in Cuba, defeating Spanish.

1898 United States acquires Puerto Rico, Guam, and Philippines in wake of war with Spain and annexes Hawaii.

Frances Willard, president of Woman's Christian Temperance Union, dies.

1899– Secretary of State John Hay enunciates
1900 Open Door policy in China to guarantee U.S. trade access.

1900– Boxer Rebellion in China leads to
1901 deaths of more than 250 missionaries and their families.

BIBLIOGRAPHY

GENERAL

Alan Dawley, *Struggles for Justice: Social Responsibility and the Liberal State* (1991).

David Montgomery, *The Fall of the House of Labor: The Workplace, the State, and American Labor Activism, 1865–1925* (1987).

Nell Irvin Painter, *Standing at Armageddon: The United States, 1877–1919* (1987).

Alan Trachtenberg, *The Incorporation of America: Culture and Society in the Gilded Age* (1982).

Robert Wiebe, *The Search for Order, 1877–1920* (1967).

MILITANT WOMEN

Karen J. Blair, *The Clubwoman as Feminist: True Womanhood Redefined, 1868–1914* (1980).

Jack S. Blocker Jr., *"Give to the Winds Thy Fears": The Women's Temperance Crusade, 1873–74* (1985).

Ruth Bordin, *Women and Temperance: The Quest for Power and Liberty, 1873–1900* (1981).

Ruth Bordin, *Frances Willard: A Biography* (1986).

Ellen Carol DuBois, *Feminism and Suffrage: The Emergence of an Independent Women's Movement in America, 1848–1869* (1978).

Barbara Leslie Epstein, *The Politics of Domesticity: Women, Evangelism, and Temperance in Nineteenth Century America* (1981).

Sara M. Evans, *Born for Liberty: A History of Women in America* (1989).

Eleanor Flexner, *Century of Struggle: The Women's Rights Movement in the United States* (1973).

Glenda Elizabeth Gilmore, *Gender and Jim Crow: Women and the Politics of White Supremacy in North Carolina, 1896–1920* (1996).

Darlene Clark Hine, ed., *Black Women in America* (1993).

Beverly Washington Jones, *Quest for Equality: The Life and Writings of Mary Eliza Church Terrell* (1990).

Glenna Matthews, *The Rise of Public Woman: Woman's Power and Woman's Place in the United States, 1630–1970* (1992).

Glenda Riley, *Inventing the American Woman: A Perspective on Women's History, 1865 to the Present* (1986).

Jacqueline Jones Royster, *Southern Horrors and Other Writings: The Anti-Lynching Campaign of Ida B. Wells, 1892–1900* (1996).

Dorothy Salem, *To Better Our World: Black Women in Organized Reform, 1890–1920* (1990).

Anne Firor Scott, *Natural Allies: Women's Associations in American History* (1991).

Kathryn Kish Sklar, *Florence Kelley and the Nation's Work: The Rise of Women's Political Culture, 1830–1900* (1995).

Ian Tyrell, *Woman's World, Woman's Empire: The Woman's Christian Temperance Union in International Perspective, 1880–1930* (1991).

Charles Harris Wesley, *The History of the National Association of Colored Women's Clubs: A Legacy of Service* (1984).

THE FARMERS' REVOLT

Peter Argersinger, *Populism and Politics: William Alfred Peffer and the People's Party* (1974).

Edward L. Ayers, *The Promise of the New South: Life after Reconstruction* (1992).

Lawrence Goodwyn, *The Populist Moment: A Short History of the Agrarian Revolt in America* (1978).

Sheldon Hackney, *Populism and Progressivism in Alabama* (1969).

Steven Hahn, *The Roots of Southern Populism: Yeoman Farmers and the Transformation of the Georgia Upcountry, 1850–1890* (1983).

John D. Hicks, *The Populist Revolt: A History of the Farmers' Alliance and the People's Party* (1961).

Matthew Josephson, *The Politicos, 1865–1896* (1938).

Robert McMath, *Populist Vanguard* (1975).

Scott G. McNall, *The Road to Rebellion: Class Formation and Kansas Populism, 1865–1900* (1988).

Theodore R. Mitchell, *Political Education in the Southern Farmers' Alliance, 1887–1900* (1987).

Norman Pollack, *The Populist Response to Industrial America: Midwestern Populist Thought* (1962).

Norman Pollack, *The Just Polity: Populism, Law, and Human Welfare* (1987).

Norman Pollack, ed., *The Populist Mind* (1967).

Theodore Saloutos, *Farmer Movements in the South, 1865–1933* (1960).

Barton Shaw, *The Wool-Hat Boys: Georgia's Populist Party* (1984).

Lala Carr Steelman, *The North Carolina Farmers' Alliance* (1985).

George Brown Tindall, ed., *A Populist Reader: Selections from the Works of American Populist Leaders* (1966).

Urwin Unger, *The Greenback Era: A Social and Political History of American Finance, 1865–1879* (1964).

C. Vann Woodward, *Tom Watson: Agrarian Rebel* (1963).

THE LABOR WARS

Stanley Buder, *Pullman: An Experiment in Industrial Order and Community Planning* (1976).

Arthur G. Burgoyne, with afterword by David P. Demarest Jr., *The Homestead Strike of 1892* (1979).

Leon Fink, *Workingman's Democracy: The Knights of Labor and American Politics* (1983).

Philip S. Foner, *History of the Labor Movement in the United States*, vol. 2, *From the Founding of the American Federation of Labor to the Emergence of American Imperialism* (1955).

Edward C. Kirkland, ed., *Andrew Carnegie: The Gospel of Wealth and Other Essays* (1962).

Sidney Lens, *The Labor Wars: From the Molly Maguires to the Sitdowns* (1974).

Thomas G. Manning, ed., *The Chicago Strike of 1894: Industrial Labor in the Nineteenth Century* (1960).

Milton Meltzer, *Bread and Roses: The Struggle of American Labor, 1865–1915* (1967).

Nick Salvatore, *Eugene V. Debs: Citizen and Socialist* (1982).

William Serrin, *Homestead: The Glory and Tragedy of an American Steel Town* (1992).

Carl Smith, *Urban Disorder and the Shape of Belief: The Great Chicago Fire, the Haymarket Bomb, and the Model Town of Pullman* (1995).

Leon Stein, ed., *The Pullman Strike* (1969).

U.S. Strike Commission, *Report on the Chicago Strike of June–July 1894*, U.S. Congress, 53rd Cong., 3rd sess., Senate Executive Document no. 7 (1894).

Joseph Frazier Wall, *Andrew Carnegie* (1970).

Alice Wexler, *Emma Goldman: An Intimate Life* (1984).

Leon Wolff, *Lockout: The Story of the Homestead Strike of 1892* (1965).

Samuel Yellen, *American Labor Struggles* (1936).

DEPRESSION POLITICS

Robert A. Allen, *Reluctant Reformers: Racism and Social Reform Movements in the United States* (1974).

Robert W. Cherny, *A Righteous Cause: The Life of William Jennings Bryan* (1985).

Paolo Coletta, *William Jennings Bryan*, 3 vols. (1964–1969).

Robert F. Durden, *The Climax of Populism: The Election of 1896* (1969).

Paul W. Glad, *McKinley, Bryan, and the People* (1964).

Matthew Josephson, *The Politicos, 1865–1896* (1938).

Louis W. Koenig, *Bryan: A Political Biography of William Jennings Bryan* (1971).

Donald L. McMurry, *Coxey's Army: A Study of the Industrial Army Movement of 1894* (1968).

Samuel McSeveney, *The Politics of Depression* (1972).

Carol A. Schwantes, *Coxey's Army: An American Odyssey* (1985).

AMERICA ON THE WORLD STAGE

David Anderson, *Imperialism and Idealism: American Diplomacy in China, 1861–1898* (1985).

William Becker, *The Dynamics of Business-Government Relations* (1982).

Robert Beisner, *From the Old Diplomacy to the New, 1865–1900* (1975).

Charles Campbell, *The Transformation of American Foreign Relations, 1865–1900* (1976).

John Dobson, *America's Ascent: The United States Becomes a Great Power, 1880–1914* (1978).

Harold U. Faulkner, *Politics, Reform, and Expansionism, 1890–1900* (1959).

Philip S. Foner, *The Spanish-Cuban-American War and the Birth of American Imperialism*, 2 vols. (1972).

Frank Friedel, *The Splendid Little War* (1958).

Willard Gatewood Jr., *Black Americans and the White Man's Burden* (1975).

Kenneth Hagen, *American Gun-Boat Diplomacy* (1973).

Louis J. Halle, *The United States Acquires the Philippines: Consensus vs. Reality* (1985).

Jane Hunter, *The Gospel of Gentility: American Women Missionaries in Turn-of-the-Century China* (1984).

Walter LaFeber, *The New Empire: An Interpretation of American Expansion, 1860–1898* (1963).

Gerald F. Linderman, *The Mirror of War: American Society and the Spanish-American War* (1974).

H. Wayne Morgan, *America's Road to Empire: The War with Spain and Overseas Expansion* (1965).

Edmund Morris, *The Rise of Theodore Roosevelt* (1979).

Ivan Musicant, *The Banana Wars: A History of U.S. Military Intervention from the Spanish-American War to the Invasion of Panama* (1990).

Thomas Patterson, ed., *Imperialism and Anti-Imperialism* (1973).

Emily S. Rosenberg, *Spreading the American Dream: American Economic and Cultural Expansion, 1890–1945* (1982).

Mark Sullivan, *Our Times*, vol. 2, *America Finding Herself* (1927).

James C. Thompson Jr., Peter W. Stanley, and John Curtis Perry, *Sentimental Imperialists: The American Experience in East Asia* (1981).

Richard Turk, *The Ambiguous Relationship: Theodore Roosevelt and Alfred Thayer Mahan* (1987).

Albert K. Weinberg, *Manifest Destiny: A Study of Nationalist Expansion in American History* (1935).

William Appleman Williams, *The Tragedy of American Diplomacy*, rev. ed. (1962).

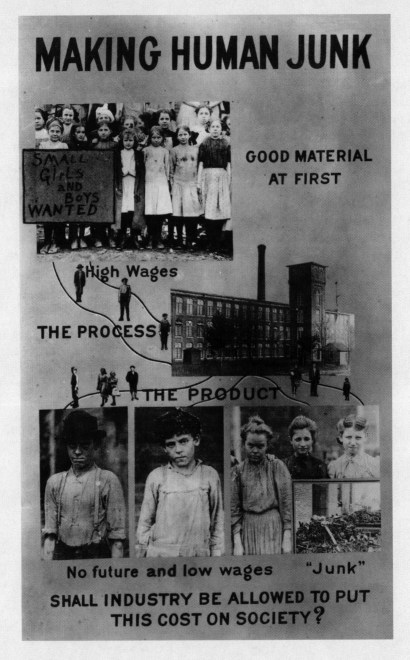

PROGRESSIVE POSTER CONDEMNING CHILD LABOR

This poster attacks child labor, borrowing the convention of the business flow chart to portray graphically how industries employing children are "making human junk." Progressives' concern for the plight of poor children won them the label "the child savers." Although activists worked hard to enact federal legislation prohibiting child labor in 1916, the Supreme Court declared the law unconstitutional two years later on the grounds that Congress had no right to regulate manufacturing within states.

Library of Congress.

PROGRESSIVE REFORM FROM THE GRASS ROOTS TO THE WHITE HOUSE

21

1890–1916

I N THE SUMMER OF 1889, a young woman leased the upper floor of a dilapidated mansion on Chicago's West Side in the heart of a burgeoning immigrant population of Italians, Russian Jews, and Greeks. Watching the preparations at number 335, the neighbors scratched their heads, wondering why the well-dressed woman, who surely could afford a better house in a better neighborhood, chose to live on South Halsted Street. For Jane Addams, the house built by Charles Hull precisely suited her needs. In September, she and her college friend Ellen Gates Starr moved in. "Probably no young matron ever placed her own things in her own house with more pleasure," she wrote. But Addams was no traditional matron. Her plan was to throw open the doors of Hull House to her immigrant neighbors in an attempt to bridge the gap between the rich and the poor.

For Jane Addams, personal action marked the first step in the search for solutions to the social problems fostered by urban industrialism. Her object was twofold: She wanted to help her neighbors and she wanted to offer an opportunity for educated women like herself to find meaningful work. As she later wrote in her autobiography, *Twenty Years at Hull-House* (1910), "I gradually became convinced that it would be a good thing to rent a house in a part of the city where many primitive and actual needs are found, in which young women who had been given over too exclusively to study might restore a balance of activity along traditional lines and learn of life from life itself." Addams's emphasis on the reciprocal relationship between the classes made Hull House different from other philanthropic enterprises. She wished to do things with, not just for, Chicago's poor.

By 1907, Hull House had expanded from one rented floor in the old brick mansion to some thirteen buildings that housed a remarkable variety of activities. The bathrooms in the basement had been converted into public baths; a coffee shop and restaurant sold take-out food to workingwomen too tired to cook after their long shifts; and a nursery and kindergarten provided care for neighborhood children. Clubs of every description and for every age met in the rooms. Hull House offered classes, lectures, art exhibits, musical instruction, and college extension courses. It boasted a gymnasium, a theater, a manual training workshop, a labor museum, and the first public playground in Chicago.

But Hull House was more than a group of buildings. From the first, it attracted a remarkable set of inhabitants. Some stayed for decades, as did Julia Lathrop before she went to Washington, D.C., in 1912 to head the Children's Bureau. Others, like Gerard Swope, who later became president of the General Electric Company, came for only a short while. Almost all had jobs, paid room and board, and devoted time to research and reform. The women and men who lived at Hull House were among the first to investigate the problems of the city with scientific precision. They surveyed housing conditions, investigated child labor and the sweatshop, documented the cocaine traffic in the neighborhood, studied the problems of juvenile delinquency, and conducted investigations into every aspect of urban life. Armed with statistics, they launched campaigns to improve housing, end child labor, fund playgrounds, mediate between labor and management, and lobby for protective legislation.

Although Addams had not intended to go into politics, Hull House soon became a political force. The evolution can best be dramatized in Addams's attempt to clean up Halsted Street. Piles of decaying garbage overflowed the street's wooden trash bins, breeding flies and disease. Investigation revealed that a contractor received a fat fee from the city to remove the garbage. The contract was a political plum awarded by the local ward boss, and the contractor felt under no obligation to provide adequate service. To end the graft, Addams herself applied for the contract. Instead, the mayor appointed her garbage inspector for the nineteenth ward. Out on the streets at six in the morning, Addams rode atop the garbage wagon as it made its rounds to be sure that the men did their work. Her diligence greatly annoyed the ward boss, who managed to have her removed after a year. What had begun as an attempt to clean up Halsted Street developed into a call for municipal reform as Addams squared off against the boss and his hirelings. In her attempt to oust the boss, she came to understand his role in city life. After backing several unsuccessful electoral campaigns to unseat him, Addams learned just how the machine worked among its poor constituency to provide jobs and favors. Judging the boss a symptom and not a cause of urban poverty, Addams moved on to press for state and national legislation designed to better the living conditions of the urban poor.

Addams had learned an important lesson. It was impossible to deal with urban problems without getting into politics. Her path led her not only to city hall but to the state capitol and on to Washington, D.C. A strong advocate of woman suffrage, she argued that city women needed the ballot, not the broom, to keep their neighborhoods clean.

JANE ADDAMS

Jane Addams was twenty-nine years old when she founded Hull House on Halsted Street in Chicago. Her desire to live among the poor, her insistence that settlement house work provide benefits for educated women like herself, as well as for the poor neighborhood residents, separated her from the charity workers who had come before her and marked the distance from philanthropy to progressive reform.
University of Illinois at Chicago, The University Library, Jane Addams Memorial Collection.

Under Jane Addams's leadership, Hull House became not only the premier social settlement in the United States but a "spearhead for reform," part of a broader movement that contemporaries called the progressive movement. The transition from personal action to political activism that Addams personified became one of the hallmarks of this reform period which lasted for almost three decades, from the 1890s to World War I.

What motivated comfortable, middle-class women and men to undertake the series of reforms that together constituted one of the major movements for social and political reform in U.S. history? There is no one answer because there is no single progressive profile. The "progressives," as they called themselves, were a diverse group with a variety of goals. A sense of Christian mission inspired some progressives. Others, frightened by the political tensions of the 1890s, feared social upheaval unless conditions were improved. Progressives shared a growing concern about the power of wealthy individuals and corporations and a strong dislike of the trusts. But often they feared the new immigrants as well and sought to control and Americanize them. Along with moral fervor, a belief in expertise and scientific principles informed progressivism and made the cult of efficiency part and parcel of the progressive movement. All of these elements—uplift and efficiency, social justice and social control—came together in the Progressive Era.

Grassroots Progressivism

Progressive reform began at the grassroots level and percolated upward into local, state, and eventually national politics as progressive reformers attacked the social problems fostered by industrialism. While reform flourished in many different settings across the country, the problems of urban America called forth the greatest efforts of the women and men who styled themselves progressives. A sense of moral outrage over conditions in the cities, coupled with a fear of growing class division, fueled progressive reform. In their zeal to "civilize the city," reformers founded settlement houses, professed a new Christian social gospel, and campaigned against vice and crime in the name of "social purity." Allying with the working class, they sought to better the lot of sweatshop garment workers and end child labor. (See Texts in Historical Context, page 804.) While their reform efforts often began on the local level, they just as often ended up being debated in state legislatures, in Congress, and in the Oval Office. From Hull House to the White House, progressivism became a major political force in the first decade of the twentieth century.

Civilizing the City

Progressive reform efforts were multifaceted, and reformers of many stripes participated in the campaign to civilize the city. Typically, progressives attacked the problems of the city on many fronts: The settlement house movement attempted to bridge the distance between the classes; the social gospel called for the churches to play a new role in social reformation; and the social purity movement campaigned to clean up vice, particularly prostitution.

The settlement house movement, which originated in England, was imported to America in 1886 with the opening of the University Settlement House in New York City. In 1889, in the same month that Jane Addams moved into Hull House, a group of graduates from Smith College founded the College Settlement in Brooklyn. Americans modified the settlement significantly, abandoning the strong religious overtones of the English movement. Settlement house workers quickly recognized that it would be divisive and counterproductive to promote Protestantism among their largely Catholic and Jewish neighbors.

Another significant change from the English model was the substantial role that women, particularly college-educated women, played in American settlement houses. Women formed the backbone of the settlement house movement and helped it to grow in the decades between 1891 and 1911 from six settlements to more than four hundred. Eager to use their knowledge, educated women found themselves blocked by sex discrimination from medicine, law, and the clergy. Fewer than fifteen hundred women practiced law in 1900, and women constituted only 6 percent of the medical profession. College women like Jane Addams found settlements a way to put their talents to use in the service of society. In the process they created the new profession of social work. Florence Kelley, Julia Lathrop, Alice Hamilton, and Grace and Edith Abbott are only a few of the best known of these influential settlement house residents.

Progressive reform began at the grassroots level and percolated upward into local, state, and eventually national politics as progressive reformers attacked the social problems fostered by urban industrialism.

For their part, the churches confronted the social problems raised in the cities by enunciating a new "social gospel," one that saw its mission as being not simply to reform individuals but to reform society. On the simplest level, the social gospel offered a powerful corrective to the Gospel of Wealth, with its belief that riches somehow signaled divine favor. Washington Gladden, a prominent social gospel minister, challenged that view when he urged Congregationalists to turn down a gift from John D. Rockefeller, arguing that it was "tainted money." In place of the Gospel of Wealth, the clergy urged their congregations to put Christ's teachings to work in their daily lives. The Reverend William Stead made the point in the best-seller *If Christ Came to Chicago* (1894), and Charles L. Seldon's popular book *In His Steps* (1898) called on men and women to Christianize capitalism by asking the question "What would Jesus do?"

Women formed the backbone of the settlement house movement and helped it to grow in the decades between 1891 and 1911 from six settlements to more than four hundred. In the process they created the new profession of social work.

For Walter Rauschenbusch, a Baptist minister working in New York's Hell's Kitchen (a poor neighborhood in Manhattan), the social gospel grew out of the harrowing experience of the depression of the 1890s that left hundreds of thousands of people unemployed. "They wore down our threshold and they wore away our hearts," he later wrote. "One could hear human virtue cracking and crumbling all around." In *Christianity and the Social Crisis* (1907), Rauschenbusch called for the church to play a new role in promoting social justice.

Under the influence of the social gospel, churches began to provide social services. The Reverend George Rainsford of St. George's Episcopal Church in New York risked offending his most generous parishioner, J. P. Morgan, by inaugurating a gymnasium, a school for industrial training, and a boys' club to serve his immigrant neighborhood. Although the social gospel had its greatest effect among Protestant denominations, liberal Catholics like New York City's Father Edmund McGlynn also engaged in social action. McGlynn's strong support of the Irish working class, coupled with his attacks on capitalism, almost led to his excommunication. Like McGlynn, a radical fringe of social gospel ministers including Congregationalist George D. Herron called for Christian socialism—the nonviolent overthrow of capitalism and the creation of a cooperative society.

Ministers also played an active role in the social purity movement, the campaign to attack vice. The Reverend Charles Parkhurst shocked his New York congregation in the 1890s by donning a disguise and touring the city's brothels, asking at each dive, "Show me something worse." As Parkhurst discovered, the brothel was a common feature of urban life. Progressives insisted that poverty bred prostitution and argued for higher wages. "Is it any wonder," asked the Chicago vice commission, "that a tempted girl who receives only six dollars per week working with her hands sells her body for twenty-five dollars per week when she learns there is a demand for it and men are willing to pay the price?"

To end the "social evil," as reformers euphemistically called prostitution, the social purity movement brought together doctors who were concerned about the spread of venereal disease, ministers like Parkhurst who wished to stamp out sin, and women reformers who were determined to fight the double standard that made it acceptable for men to engage in premarital and extramarital sex but punished women who strayed. Together, they attempted to shut down dance halls, saloons, and the dubious "employment agencies" that recruited women into prostitution. They waged campaigns to close "red-light districts" in cities across the country and lobbied for the Mann Act, passed in 1910, which made it illegal to transport women across state lines for immoral purposes. On the state level, they struck at venereal disease by securing legislation making it compulsory to have a blood test for syphilis before marriage.

Attacks on alcohol went hand in hand with the push for social purity. The temperance campaign launched by the Woman's Christian Temperance Union (WCTU) heated up in the early twentieth century. The Anti-Saloon League, formed in 1895 under the leadership of Protestant clergy, campaigned for an end to the sale of liquor. The clergy were joined by reformers who saw alcoholism as a threat to health, the family, and society. Reformers pointed to the links connecting drink with prostitution, wife and child abuse, unemployment, and industrial accidents. The powerful liquor lobby fought back, spending liberally in elections to defeat not only prohibition but woman suffrage and, in the process, fueling the charge that liquor corrupted the political process.

An element of nativism (dislike of foreigners) ran through the move for prohibition. Progressives failed to see the important role the tavern played in many ethnic communities. They sought to enforce Sunday closings of taverns and other forms of social control to deny the working class access to alcohol. By 1912, seven states had outlawed the liquor traffic.

Progressives' efforts to civilize the city, whether by launching social settlements or campaigning against prostitution and alcohol, demonstrated their willingness to take action, their belief that environment, not heredity alone, determined human potential, and their optimism that conditions could be corrected without radically altering America's economy or institutions. All of these attitudes characterized the progressive movement.

Progressives and the Working Class

Day-to-day contact with their neighbors made settlement house workers particularly sympathetic to labor unions. As Florence Kelley observed, "At Hull-House one got into the labor movement as a matter of course, without realizing how or when." When Mary Kenney O'Sullivan told Jane Addams that her bookbinders' union met in a dirty, noisy saloon, Addams invited the union to meet at Hull House. And during the Pullman strike in 1894, Hull House residents organized strike relief and lent their prestige and financial resources to the strike. "Hull-House has been so unionized," grumbled one Chicago businessman, "that it has lost its usefulness and become a detriment and harm to the community." But to the working class, the support of middle-class reformers marked a significant gain.

Attempts to forge a cross-class alliance became institutionalized in 1903 with the creation of the Women's Trade Union League (WTUL). The WTUL brought together middle-class "allies" and women workers. Its goal was to organize workingwomen into unions under the auspices of the American Federation of Labor (AFL). However, the AFL provided little more than lip service to the organization of women workers. From the leadership to the rank and file, the AFL men shared traditional notions of women's place. As one workingwoman confided, "The men think that the girls should not get as good work as the men and should not make half as much money as a man." When it came to women, the AFL's main concern seemed to be to protect men from female competition. Samuel Gompers, president of the AFL, endorsed the principle of equal pay for equal work, shrewdly observing that it would help male workers more than women, since many employers hired women precisely because they could be paid less. Given the AFL's attitude, it was not surprising that the money and leadership to organize women came largely from wealthy allies in the WTUL.

Two remarkable sisters provided the financial backing and leadership for the WTUL: Mary Dreier, who headed the New York branch, and Margaret Dreier Robins, president of the national league from

WOMEN STRIKERS
The "uprising of twenty thousand" pitted garment workers against their employers in a strike that lasted throughout the bitter winter of 1909–1910. The strikers, primarily young women from the Jewish and Italian immigrant communities, joined the International Ladies' Garment Workers Union and showed that women could be unionized and mount an effective strike. Labor-Management Documentation Center, Cornell University.

What Do Early Documentary Texts Tell Us about the Men and Women Who Called Themselves Progressives?

I N THE 1880s, Jacob Riis took his camera into the tenements of New York City to document the living conditions of the poor. The result was the runaway best-seller *How the Other Half Lives* (1890). Riis, a Danish immigrant who covered the crime beat for the *New York Tribune,* had a keen eye for telling details and a colorful prose style. Through dozens of individual vignettes, piled one upon another, Riis built for his readers the concept of a slum.

Along with his descriptive text, he included his pictures. The first edition of *How the Other Half Lives* contained 39 images taken from Riis's photographs. The pictures are remarkable, both for the story they tell and for their place in the history of photography. The invention of flash powder made Riis's work possible by enabling him, literally, to shed light on his subjects. Lugging his bulky box camera and tripod into the dark alleys and dingy tenements of lower Manhattan, Riis pioneered photographic journalism. In Riis's day, photography was a dangerous business. He had to ignite magnesium flash powder in the close quarters of firetrap tenements.

Once he nearly blinded himself. Another time, when he was photographing the residents of a tenement on "Blind Man's Alley," he set the place on fire. He later claimed the tenement, nicknamed the "Dirty Spoon," was so filthy it wouldn't burn. He was able to douse the flames without his blind subjects ever realizing their danger.

Over a century after the book's publication, *How the Other Half Lives* is still a valuable tool for historians, as much for what it tells us about the progressive reformers who set out to document the evils of urban industrialism as for what it reveals about the conditions they brought to light.

Riis's ethnocentrism is immediately apparent. His pages are filled with racial and ethnic stereotypes—stealthy and secretive Chinese; colorful but murderous Italians; greedy, quarrelsome Jews; happy, fun-loving Negroes; dirty Arabs; orderly, thrifty Germans. The degree of his opprobrium rises in direct proportion to the distance his subjects are from Riis's native Denmark, a reminder that racism and prejudice were by no means native to American soil. Another troubling aspect of Riis's book is its voyeurism. Riis unabashedly invites his readers to go "slumming."

Riis's impressionistic view of the life of the urban poor was soon followed by more scientific studies. The gathering of information and the publicizing of urban conditions became staples of settlement house work. Jane Addams and Florence Kelley undertook a statistical survey of economic conditions in their Chicago neighborhood; they published the results in 1895 as *Hull-House Maps and Papers.* This passion for information was an important part of the progressive ethos. Sociology, a new field in the emerging "social sciences," was predicated on the need for accurate and precise infor-

1907 to 1922. The two sisters, daughters of a wealthy German-born merchant, grew up in Brooklyn, where they became interested in working girls' clubs and joined the fledgling WTUL. In 1906, Margaret married social activist Raymond Robins and moved to Chicago, where the couple lived among the working class in a cold-water flat not far from Hull House.

Although the alliance between the workingwomen, primarily immigrants and the daughters of immigrants, and their middle-class allies was not without tension, the WTUL helped workingwomen

achieve significant gains. The most notable success came in 1909 in the "uprising of twenty thousand."

In November 1909, hundreds of women employees of the Triangle Shirtwaist Company in New York City went on strike to protest low wages, dangerous and demeaning working conditions, and management's refusal to recognize their union, the International Ladies' Garment Workers Union (ILGWU). In support of the walkout, the ILGWU called for a general strike of all garment workers. An estimated twenty thousand workers, most of mation to stimulate reform. Soon sociologists attempted to supplant "storytellers" like Jacob Riis.

Their most ambitious project was the famous Pittsburgh survey undertaken under the auspices of the Russell Sage Foundation. Among the best-known volumes produced by the survey was Margaret Byington's study *Homestead: The Households of a Mill Town*, published in 1910. Byington lived in Homestead, Pennsylvania, for six months studying ninety families during the economic downturn of 1907–1908. Like Riis, she documented in text and photographs the lives of the workers in U.S. Steel's mills. And like Addams and Kelley, she provided a statistical analysis of her findings. Yet despite her rigorous claims to scientific method, the assumptions underlying Byington's study repeat the same ethnocentric patterns observed in Riis. Byington's treatment of Homestead's families is filtered through the nativist lens of her era. In dealing with family life, she can't hide her disapproval of the "Slavs," a catchall term for various nationalities of eastern and southern Europe. These poorest of the Homestead families supplemented their wages by taking in boarders. The practice appalled Byington, who subscribed to the middle-class notion that the home should remain inviolate. As a result, her study of Homestead's households defined family as she wished it to be, not as it was.

Historians seeking to uncover details about the daily lives of the urban poor turn to these documentary sources with the caveat that the cultural assumptions of the authors need to be looked at as closely as their photographs and text. The documentary evidence collected by early reformers reveals not only the everyday lives of the working poor but also a great deal about the men and women who called themselves "progressives"—their attitudes, their cultural beliefs, and their biases. Their greatest strength was their resolve for action, their determination to right the worst wrongs brought about by urban industrialism. They refused to believe the tenets of social Darwinism with its negation of human agency. Instead, they resolved to act. But often their actions aimed at the symptoms and not the causes of urban poverty. In Riis's case, he damned the tenement and not the economic system that produced it. Nor did Riis have a clear idea of the consequences of his battle against the tenement. He wanted to abolish substandard housing, but he never questioned what would happen to the people turned out on the street. In *How the Other Half Lives*, he noted with surprise that after he managed to get a building condemned, its pitiful inhabitants crept back in.

Riis, who had landed in New York in 1870 at the age of twenty-one and spent three years looking for work, knew firsthand the flophouses and the dirty alleys of New York. But he never lost faith in the promise of America. Riis never saw the slum as part of the burgeoning industrial economy just as he never subscribed to the growing criticism of capitalism.

Like Riis, most progressives rarely questioned the economic system or wished to tinker with it. Instead, they believed that publicity alone could solve problems. "The power of the fact is the mightiest lever of this or any day," Riis wrote with conviction. Too often, progressive reformers saw their role as simply to place the "facts" before the public. (For a Riis photo see page 810.)

These early documentary texts, then, profile not only the lives of the urban poor but present a progressive profile, pointing to the reformers' strengths and to their limitations.

them teenage girls and many of them Jewish and Italian immigrants, went out on strike and stayed out through the winter, picketing in the bitter cold. More than six hundred were arrested, and many were sent to jail for "streetwalking," a move by the authorities to try to break the spirit and impugn the morals of the striking women. By the time the strike ended in February 1910, the workers had won some important demands in many shops. But they lost their bid to gain recognition for their union, the ILGWU. The solidarity shown by the women workers proved to be the strike's greatest achievement. As Clara Lemlich, one of the strike's leaders, exclaimed, "They used to say that you couldn't even organize women. They wouldn't come to union meetings. They were 'temporary' workers. Well we showed them!"

The WTUL made enormous contributions to the success of the strike. The league provided volunteers for the picket lines, posted more than $29,000 in bail, protested police brutality, organized almost overnight a massive parade of ten thousand

TRIANGLE SHIRTWAIST FACTORY FIRE
A grim newspaper photo shows the broken bodies of garment workers who jumped to their death when fire broke out in the Triangle Shirtwaist Factory on Saturday, March 25, 1911. Nearly five hundred women and girls worked in the firetrap and many were unable to escape because the doors had been locked to prevent employees from taking breaks. Firefighters rushed to the scene, but their ladders reached only to the sixth floor, leaving those on the seventh, eighth, and ninth floors with little choice but to jump.
The New York Herald, March 26, 1911.

strikers, took part in the arbitration conference, arranged mass meetings, appealed for funds, and generated publicity for the strike. Mary Dreier herself marched on the picket line and was arrested. Under the leadership of the WTUL, women from every class of society, from J. P. Morgan's daughter Anne to socialists on the Lower East Side, joined the strikers in a dramatic demonstration of cross-class alliance.

But for all its success, the uprising of the twenty thousand failed fundamentally to change conditions for women workers, as the tragic Triangle fire dramatized in 1911. A little over a year after the shirtwaist makers' strike ended, fire alarms sounded at the Triangle factory. The ramshackle building, full of lint and combustible cloth, went up in flames in minutes. A WTUL member described

the scene below on the street. "I was coming down Fifth Avenue on the Saturday afternoon, when a great, swirling, billowing cloud of smoke swept like a giant streamer out of Washington Square," she recounted. "Two young girls whom I knew to be working in the vicinity came rushing toward me, tears were running from their eyes and they were white and shaking as they caught me by the arm. 'Oh,' shrieked one of them, 'they are jumping. Jumping from ten stories up! They are going through the air like bundles of clothes, and the firemen can't stop them and the policemen can't stop them and nobody can help them at all.'"

The terrified Triangle workers had little choice but to jump. One door was blocked by flames, and the door to the fire escape had been locked to prevent the girls from sneaking out on breaks. The lucky ones made their way to the roof and escaped. Of 500 workers, 146 died and scores of others were injured. The owners of the Triangle firm were later tried for negligence, but they escaped conviction when authorities determined that the fire had been started by a careless smoker. The Triangle Shirtwaist Company reopened in another firetrap within a matter of weeks.

Outrage and a sense of futility overwhelmed Rose Schneiderman, a leading WTUL organizer, who made a bitter speech at the memorial service for the dead Triangle workers. "I would be a traitor to those poor burned bodies if I came here to talk good fellowship," she told her audience. "We have tried you good people of the public and we have found you wanting. . . . I know from my experience it is up to the working people to save themselves . . . by a strong working class movement."

The Triangle fire tested severely the bonds of the cross-class alliance. Along with Rose Schneiderman, WTUL leaders experienced a growing sense of futility. It seemed not enough to organize and to strike, particularly when the AFL paid so little attention to women workers. Increasingly, the WTUL turned its efforts to lobbying for protective legislation—laws that would limit hours and regulate working conditions.

The principle of protective legislation won a major victory in 1908 when the U.S. Supreme Court, in the landmark case *Muller v. Oregon*, reversed its previous rulings and upheld an Oregon law that limited the hours women could work to ten a day. A mass of sociological evidence put together by Florence Kelley of the National Consumers League and Josephine Goldmark of the WTUL and presented by Goldmark's brother-in-law, lawyer Louis Brandeis, demonstrated the ill effects of long hours on the health and safety of women. The "Brandeis brief" convinced the Court that long hours endangered women and therefore the entire race. The Court's ruling set a precedent, but one that separated the well-being of women from that of the rest of the workforce by arguing that women's reproductive role justified special treatment. Later generations of women fighting for equality would question the effectiveness of such a strategy and argue that it ultimately closed good jobs to women workers. But for the WTUL, protective legislation was greeted as a first stage in the attempt to ensure the safety not just of women but of all workers.

The National Consumers League, like the WTUL, fostered cross-class alliance. Formed in 1899 and led by Florence Kelley, the Consumers League

urged middle-class women to boycott stores and exert pressure for decent wages and working conditions for women employees, primarily saleswomen. The league published a "white list" of stores that met its standards. But, like the WTUL, the Consumers League turned increasingly to protective legislation to achieve its goals in the first decade of the twentieth century. The tendency to seek legislative solutions to social problems was another hallmark of progressivism. Frustrated by the reluctance of the private sector to respond to the need for reform, progressives turned to the government at all levels. Critics would later charge that the progressives assumed too easily that government regulation could best solve social problems.

Reform also fueled the fight for woman suffrage. For women like Jane Addams and Florence Kelley, involvement in social reform led inevitably to support for woman suffrage. These new suffragists spoke less of natural rights than their predecessors Elizabeth Cady Stanton and Susan B. Anthony had done. Instead they emphasized the reforms that could be accomplished if women had the vote. When they talked of the need for the ballot, they often compared it to the broom. Jane Addams insisted that in an urban, industrial society a good housekeeper could not be sure the food she fed her family or the water and milk they drank were pure unless she became involved in politics and wielded the ballot instead of the broom to protect her family.

Progressivism: Theory and Practice

Progressive reformers developed a theoretical basis for their activist approach by countering social Darwinism with a dynamic new reform Darwinism and by championing the uniquely American philosophy of pragmatism. The progressives emphasized action and experimentation. No longer was the universe seen as a massive, slow-moving machine, but as a system amenable to tinkering by human intelligence. An unchecked admiration for speed and efficiency also characterized a significant component of progressive thought and led to enthusiasm for scientific management and a new cult of efficiency. These varied strands of progressive theory found practical application in state and local politics. Political progressivism originated at the local level and percolated upward to the state and national governments. The politicians who became premier progressives

PICTURING CHILD LABOR

Each of the photographs of children pictured here was designed consciously to carry a message. Jacob Riis intended his photograph of homeless newsboys sleeping in an alley to be emblematic of the plight of the city's poor children. The boy miner, photographed by the mining company he worked for, was intended to counter criticism of child labor. Entitled A Youthful Gold Digger, the photograph carried the caption "Eight-year-old Bill Scott of [Clarksburg, West Virginia] is all set to go to work in the mines. He's fully outfitted for his day's labor — with pipe, headlight, pick axe, lunch can, high shoes, overall coat and bandanna." Ironically, the pictures evoke in a modern audience the opposite responses from those the photographers intended. The staged aestheticism of Riis's photo works against the grim reality Riis intended it to convey, while the mine's blatant promotion of child labor is shocking, and the plucky eight-year-old evokes our pity and horror.

Homeless boys: The Jacob A. Riis Collection, #121, Museum of the City of New York; miner: Library of Congress.

were generally the followers, not the leaders, in a movement that was already well advanced at the grassroots level. Yet they left their stamp on the movement. Among the preeminent progressive politicians were Tom Johnson, the mayor of Cleveland, Ohio, and Robert La Follette, who as governor and later a senator, determined to make the state of Wisconsin a laboratory for progressivism.

Reform Darwinism and Pragmatism

The active, interventionist approach of the progressives directly challenged social Darwinism, with its insistence that the world operated on the principle of survival of the fittest and that human beings were powerless in the face of the law of natural selection. Without abandoning the evolutionary framework of Darwinism, a new group of sociologists argued that evolution could be advanced more rapidly if men and women used their intellects to alter the environment. Sociologist Lester Frank Ward put it clearly in his book *Dynamic Sociology* (1883), which emphasized an activist approach to the problems of urban industrialism. "I insist the time must soon come," he wrote, "when the control of blind natural forces in society must give way to human foresight." Dubbed "reform Darwinism," the new sociological theory condemned laissez-faire, insisting that the liberal state should play a more active role in solving social problems. Reform Darwinism provided a rationale for attacking social ills and became the ideological basis for progressive reform.

Although progressivism drew support from many people, much of its leadership came from the new urban middle class, a group composed of physicians, businesspeople, scientists, engineers, and social workers. These men and women put their skills and intellects to work to solve the problems caused by industrialization and to impose order on what many perceived as a dangerously chaotic society. This group of progressives championed the scientific method and promoted efficiency, seeking scientific solutions to social problems.

In their pursuit of reform, they were influenced by the work of two philosophers, William James and John Dewey. James and Dewey argued for a new test for truth, insisting that there were no eternal verities and that the real worth of any idea was in its consequences. They called their pluralistic, relativistic philosophy "pragmatism." Dewey put his theories to the test in the classroom of his laboratory school at the University of Chicago. A pioneer in American education, he emphasized process rather than content and encouraged more child-centered schools where students learned by doing. By championing social experimentation, the American pragmatists provided an important impetus for progressive reform.

Scientific Management and the Cult of Efficiency

Increased emphasis on means as well as ends marked progressive reform. Efficiency and expertise became watchwords in the progressive vocabulary. The journalist and critic Walter Lippmann, in *Drift and Mastery* (1914), a classic statement of the progressive agenda, called for skilled technocrats who would use scientific techniques to control social change, substituting mastery for aimless drift. A fascination with "social engineering" was a characteristic of progressive reform. Ellen Richards, the first woman graduate and instructor at the Massachusetts Institute of Technology, urged college women and men to act as "social engineers." This emphasis on expertise inevitably fostered a kind of elitism. Whereas Populism had called for a greater voice for the masses, progressivism, for all its emphasis on social justice, insisted that experts be put in charge.

Although progressivism drew support from many people, much of its leadership came from the new urban middle class, a group composed of physicians, businesspeople, scientists, engineers, and social workers.

At its extreme, the application of expertise and social engineering took the form of scientific management, which alienated the working class while elevating productivity and efficiency above all other considerations. Frederick Winslow Taylor, who after a nervous breakdown left Harvard to become a machinist, pioneered "systematized shop management." Taylor was obsessed with making humans and machines produce more and faster. After he earned a master of engineering degree in 1885, he went back to work at Midvale Steel, restructuring the workplace, taking control away from individual workers, and placing it in the hands of managers. With his stopwatch he carefully timed workers and then attempted to break their work down into its simplest components, one repetitious action after another, on the theory that productivity would increase if tasks were reduced to their simplest parts. Employees at Midvale cursed him and called him a slave driver. When he died in 1915, with his stop-watch in his hand, workers bitterly pointed to the speedup—pushing workers to produce more in less time and for less pay—as his legacy. But Taylor's many advocates included progressives like Louis Brandeis who applauded the increased productivity and efficiency brought about under Taylor's system.

The progressive reformers who championed scientific management and social engineering as methods to solve social problems never faced the contradiction between the means they advocated and the ends they desired. The central paradox of progressivism was its insistence that social justice could be brought about by social engineering—that a just society could be achieved by applying scientific principles.

Progressivism in Action: Cleveland and Wisconsin

Progressivism burst forth at every level in 1901, but nowhere more forcefully than in Cleveland, Ohio, where the voters elected Thomas Lofton Johnson mayor. Johnson, a self-made millionaire by the age of forty, turned his back on business and entered politics after reading Henry George's *Progress and Poverty*. A Democrat and an advocate of free trade and Henry George's single tax, Johnson pledged during the campaign to reduce the streetcar fare to three cents. His election touched off a seven-year war between advocates of the lower fare and the entrenched interests who ran Cleveland's streetcars. Johnson believed that workingmen and -women paid a disproportionate share of their meager earnings for transportation. When the streetcar industry and its supporters argued that they couldn't meet costs with the lower fare, Johnson fought them. Arrayed against him were powerful adversaries, including Ohio Senator Marcus Alonzo Hanna, the Republican kingmaker who had managed William McKinley's successful campaign for president in 1896. When Johnson responded by building his own streetcar line, his foes tore up the tracks or blocked him with court injunctions and legal delays. At the prompting of his opponents, the state legislature sought to limit Johnson's mayoral power by revoking the charters of every city in the state, replacing home rule with central control from the state capital at Columbus.

During his tenure as mayor, Johnson fought for home rule, fair taxation, and municipal ownership

and championed greater democracy through the use of the initiative, referendum, and recall, devices that allowed the voters to have a direct say in legislative and judicial matters. Frustrated in his attempt to bring the streetcar industry to heel, he pushed for municipal ownership of street railways and public utilities, a tactic that progressives called "gas and water socialism." The city bought the streetcar system and instituted the three-cent fare. Under Johnson's administration, Cleveland became, in the words of journalist Lincoln Steffens, the "best governed city in America."

In Wisconsin, Robert M. La Follette, who as a young congressional representative had supported William McKinley, abandoned Republican conservatism and converted to the progressive cause early in the 1900s. An astute politician, La Follette capitalized on the grassroots movement for reform to launch his long political career, first as governor (1901–1905) and later as senator (1906–1925). A graduate of the University of Wisconsin, La Follette

THREE-CENT STREETCAR TOKEN
Tom Johnson, the reform mayor of Cleveland, Ohio, from 1901 to 1909, fought for a three-cent streetcar fare for more than seven years, winning the support of the working class at the same time he angered the business interests who ran the city's streetcars. To get his cheaper fare, Johnson finally called for municipal ownership of the transit system. Here Johnson uses a three-cent token in his re-election campaign in 1907.
The Western Reserve Historical Society, Cleveland, Ohio.

brought scientists and professors into his administration and used the university, only a few blocks from the state house in Madison, as a resource to help in drafting legislation. La Follette advocated railroad regulation, tax reform, and direct democracy. As governor, he lowered railroad rates, raised railroad taxes, improved education, championed conservation, established factory regulation and workers' compensation, instituted the first direct primary in the country, and inaugurated the first state income tax. Under his leadership, Wisconsin earned the title "laboratory of democracy."

A fiery orator, "Fighting Bob" La Follette united his supporters around issues that transcended old party loyalties. He successfully formed a coalition of farmers and laborers who reelected him many times. This emphasis on reforms rather than party identification became a characteristic of progressivism, which attracted followers from both major parties. Democrats like Tom Johnson and Republicans like Robert La Follette could lay equal claim to the label "progressive." When La Follette moved to the U.S. Senate in 1906, he joined a coalition of insurgent progressives, Democrats and Republicans alike, who crossed party lines to work together for reform.

Progressivism Finds a President: Theodore Roosevelt

On September 6, 1901, President William McKinley was shot and gravely wounded while attending the Pan American Exposition in Buffalo, New York. After lingering for a week, he died on September 14. When news of McKinley's assassination reached his friend and political mentor Marcus Alonzo Hanna, Hanna is said to have growled, "Now that damned cowboy is president." Hanna was speaking of Vice President Theodore Roosevelt, the colorful hero of San Juan Hill, who had indeed punched cattle in the Dakotas in the 1880s.

Roosevelt's status as a Spanish-American war hero had propelled him to the governorship of New York in 1898. A moderate reformer, he clashed with New York's Republican "Easy Boss," Tom Platt. To get rid of Roosevelt, the party bosses "kicked him upstairs" to the vice presidency in 1900, where he added luster to the ticket and helped reelect McKinley to a second term. As vice president, Platt and the party leaders reasoned, Roosevelt could do

little harm. But one bullet proved the error of their logic. Overnight, Roosevelt was president, and Mark Hanna was not alone in his concern that the world of conservative politics that McKinley personified had died with him. A skillful politician, Roosevelt would ride the wave of progressive reform, a wave that would swamp his successor, William Howard Taft.

An activist and a moralist, imbued with progressive spirit, Roosevelt would turn the White House into a "bully pulpit" and, in the process, shift the nation's center of power from Wall Street to Washington.

In the first days of his presidency, Roosevelt reassured the shocked nation that he intended "to continue absolutely unbroken" the policies of McKinley. But anyone who knew Roosevelt knew that that was impossible. McKinley had been Mark Hanna's man, taking his cue from the Ohio senator and the ruling clique of conservatives in Congress. Roosevelt was as different from McKinley as the twentieth century was from the nineteenth. An activist and a moralist, imbued with progressive spirit, he would turn the White House into a "bully pulpit" and, in the process, shift the nation's center of power from Wall Street to Washington.

The Square Deal

At the age of forty-two, Roosevelt was the youngest man ever to move into the White House. A patrician by birth and an activist by temperament, Roosevelt brought to the job enormous talent and energy. By the time he graduated from Harvard, he was already an accomplished naturalist, an enthusiastic historian, and a naval strategist. He could have picked from any of these promising careers. Instead, he chose politics, not a bad choice for a man who wanted power and relished competition.

Roosevelt was shrewd enough to realize that the path to power did not lie in the good-government leagues formed by his well-bred friends. Instead, he apprenticed himself to the local ward boss, who held court in a grimy, smoke-filled Republican club above a Manhattan saloon. Roosevelt's rise in politics was nothing less than meteoric. He went from the New York state assembly at the age of twenty-three to the presidency in twenty years, with time out to be a cowboy in the Dakotas, police commissioner of New York City, and colonel of the Rough Riders.

The "absolutely vital question" facing the country, Roosevelt wrote to a friend in 1901, was "whether or not the government has the power to control the trusts." The Sherman Antitrust Act of 1890 had been badly weakened by a conservative Supreme Court and by attorneys general more willing to use it against unions than against monopolies. To determine if the law had any teeth left, Roosevelt, in one of his first acts as president, ordered his attorney general to begin a secret antitrust investigation of the Northern Securities Company.

Roosevelt trained his sights on a good target. Northern Securities resulted from one of the most controversial mergers in American history. When Edward C. Harriman, who controlled the Union Pacific and the Southern Pacific Railroads, attempted to add the Northern Pacific to his holdings, James J. Hill of the Great Northern squared off against him. The result was a ruinous railroad war that precipitated a panic on Wall Street, bankrupting thousands of small investors. To bring peace, financier J. P. Morgan created the Northern Securities Company in 1901, linking under one management three competing railroads. This new behemoth monopolized railroad traffic in the Northwest. Small investors still smarting from their losses, farmers worried about freight rates, and the public in general saw in Northern Securities the symbol of corporate high-handedness.

In February 1902, Wall Street rocked with the news that the government had filed suit against Northern Securities. As one editor sarcastically observed, "Wall Street is paralyzed at the thought that a President of the United States would sink so low as to try to enforce the law." An indignant J. P. Morgan demanded to know why he had not been consulted. "If we have done anything wrong," he told the attorney general, "send your man to my man and they can fix it up." Roosevelt, amused, later noted that Morgan "could not help regarding me as a big rival operator." In a sense, that was just what Roosevelt intended. Roosevelt's thunderbolt put Wall Street on notice that the money men were dealing with a president who demanded to be treated as an equal and who was willing to use government as an instrument to control business. Perhaps sensing the new mood, the Supreme Court, in a significant turnaround, upheld the Sherman Act and called for the dissolution of Northern Securities in 1904.

"Hurrah for Teddy the Trustbuster," cheered the papers. Roosevelt went on to use the Sherman Act against forty-three trusts, including such giants as the American Tobacco Company, Swift and Company, Du Pont, and Standard Oil. But despite the reputation he earned, Roosevelt never believed in trust-busting alone. He was no foe of big business. Like Morgan, he recognized that combination was inevitable and not necessarily a bad thing. Always a moralist, he insisted on a "rule of reason." He would punish the "bad" trusts (those that broke the law) and leave the "good" ones alone. In practice, he preferred regulation to antitrust suits. In 1903, he pressured Congress to pass the Elkins Act, a law outlawing railroad rebates (money returned to a shipper to guarantee his business). And he created the new cabinet department of Commerce and Labor with a subsidiary Bureau of Corporations to act as a corporate watchdog.

Observing Roosevelt in action, journalist Joseph Pulitzer remarked, "He has subjugated Wall Street." Pulitzer exaggerated, but Roosevelt had masterfully asserted the moral and political authority of the executive, underscoring, in his words, the "duty of the President to act upon the theory that he is the steward of the people."

Roosevelt's handling of the anthracite coal strike in 1902 provided the country with another example of his willingness to use the power of the presidency, this time to mediate between labor and management. In May, more than fifty thousand coal miners in Pennsylvania went out on strike, demanding higher wages, shorter hours, and recognition of the United Mine Workers (UMW) union. "The miners don't suffer," scoffed George Baer, the operator's spokesman, "why they can't even speak English." Six eastern railroads owned over 70 percent of the anthracite mines. With the power of the railroads behind them, the mine owners refused to budge.

The strike dragged on through the summer and into the fall. Hoarding and profiteering drove the price of coal up from $2.50 to $6 a ton. Most homes were heated with coal, and, with winter approaching, near riots broke out in big cities. Labor's sympathizers called for national ownership of the coal mines. Business leaders urged Roosevelt to follow President Cleveland's example in 1894 and call out federal troops to break the strike. In the face of mounting tension, Roosevelt kept his balance and steered a middle course. In October, he issued a personal invitation to representatives from both sides to meet in Washington. His unprecedented intervention served notice that government counted itself an independent force in business and labor disputes. At the same time, it gave unionism a boost

THEODORE ROOSEVELT
At forty-two, Theodore Roosevelt was the youngest president to occupy the White House. He brought to the office energy, intellect, and activism in equal measure, moving the presidency into the twentieth century. Described aptly as a "steam engine in trousers," Roosevelt enjoyed the presidency and worked tirelessly to make the office a "bully pulpit" from which he advocated an astounding series of reforms, from conservation to simplified spelling.
Collection of the New-York Historical Society.

by granting the UMW a place at the table. At the meeting, Baer and the mine owners arrogantly refused to talk to the union representatives, managing to insult both the president and the attorney general. By comparison, John Mitchell of the UMW impressed Roosevelt as both honest and sincere. The meeting ended in impasse.

Beside himself at the "wooden-headed obstinacy and stupidity" of management, Roosevelt threatened to seize the mines and run them with federal troops. It was a powerful bluff, one that called into question not only the supremacy of private property but the rule of law. The specter of federal troops being used to operate the mines quickly brought management around. At the prompting of J. P. Morgan, the mine owners agreed to arbitration. In the end, the miners won a reduction in hours and a wage increase, and the owners succeeded in preventing formal recognition of the UMW.

Taken together, Roosevelt's actions in the Northern Securities case and the anthracite coal strike marked a dramatic departure from the tradition of William McKinley. Roosevelt's actions demonstrated conclusively that government intended to act independently to provide a countervailing force to the power of the big corporations. Pleased with his role in the anthracite strike, Roosevelt announced that all he had tried to do was give labor and capital a "square deal."

The phrase became his slogan in the 1904 election campaign. To win the presidency in his own right, Roosevelt had to wrest control of the Republican Party from Mark Hanna, the only man who stood between him and the nomination. By the time Hanna died of typhoid fever in 1904, Roosevelt was the undisputed leader of the party.

In the presidential election of 1904, Roosevelt easily defeated the Democrats, who abandoned William Jennings Bryan, their candidate in the previous two elections, to support Judge Alton B. Parker. Parker was a "safe" candidate who they hoped would win business votes away from Roosevelt. In the months before the election, the president prudently toned down his criticism of big business. Wealthy Republicans like J. P. Morgan, while they privately branded Roosevelt a class traitor, remained loyal to the party and gave it their money and their votes. In November 1904, Roosevelt swept into office with the largest popular majority any candidate had polled to that time.

Roosevelt and Regulation

"Tomorrow I shall come into my office in my own right," Roosevelt is said to have remarked on the eve of his election. "Then watch out for me!" The conservative Republicans who had helped to elect him intended to do just that. No longer under the illusion that Roosevelt would continue McKinley's role as a silent partner to business interests, they reassured themselves that Congress remained firmly in the grip of conservative, standpat Republicans. The old guard in the Senate was led by Nelson Aldrich of Rhode Island, who was called "the senator from Standard Oil" (an alliance cemented when his daughter married John D. Rockefeller Jr.). In an era when state legislatures still chose U.S. senators, many like Aldrich openly served special business interests. The old guard stood squarely in the path of Roosevelt and reform.

Roosevelt needed all the popularity and political savvy he could muster to guide the reform measures that he championed through the conservative Congress. His ability to compromise led more idealistic progressives like La Follette to judge him a "trimmer." Others, however, have been more impressed by his flexibility, concurring with the judgment that Roosevelt was a "skillful broker of the possible."

Roosevelt's pet project remained railroad regulation. The Elkins Act prohibiting rebates had not worked. No one could stop big shippers from wresting concessions from the railroads. The Interstate Commerce Commission (ICC), created in 1887 to regulate the railroads, had been stripped of its powers by the Supreme Court. In the face of a widespread call for railroad reform, Roosevelt determined that the only solution lay in giving the ICC real power to set rates and prevent discriminatory practices. A strengthened ICC, in Roosevelt's words, would enable "the corporation that wishes to do well from being driven into doing ill, in order to compete with its rival, which prefers to do ill." But for all Roosevelt's lectures on what was legally and morally right, business remained adamant in its opposition

to federal rate setting. The right to determine the price of goods or services was an age-old prerogative of private enterprise and one that business had no intention of yielding to government without a fight.

To ensure passage of the Hepburn Railway Act, a bill increasing the power of the ICC, Roosevelt worked skillfully behind the scenes. Once again, he showed his power to bluff. By threatening to call for tariff reform, a volatile issue that might split the party, he succeeded in getting a recalcitrant House of Representatives to pass the Hepburn Act. But the bill bogged down in the Senate, where the old guard, led by Aldrich, attempted to amend it to death. One amendment, intended to cripple the ICC's rate-making power, gave the railroads the right to appeal to the courts. To get the best bill possible, Roosevelt first worked with insurgent progressives and then, when they could not muster the needed votes, switched sides and succeeded in getting Aldrich and the Republican regulars to accept a compromise. In its final form, the Hepburn Act, passed in May 1906, gave the ICC power to set rates subject to court review. Progressives like La Follette judged the bill a defeat for reform. Die-hard conservatives branded it a "piece of populism." Both exaggerated. The bill was by no means perfect. It left the courts too much power, and it failed to provide adequate means for the ICC to determine rates realistically. But its passage marked a landmark in the evolution of federal control of private industry. For the first time, a government commission had the power to investigate private business records and to set rates. The Hepburn Act signaled a victory for President Roosevelt and stood as testimony to his stature as a political leader and a practical idealist.

Roosevelt as "Lame Duck"

Passage of the Hepburn Act in 1906 marked the high point of Roosevelt's presidency. In the years that followed, his power eroded, although he continued to be an active and resourceful president. In a serious political blunder, Roosevelt brought some of his problems on himself by announcing on the eve of his election in 1904 that he would not run again. By 1906, his term was starting to run out, and his influence on Congress and his party was waning. Ironically, he had become a "lame duck" at the very moment when he was enjoying his greatest public popularity and when he needed and wanted to press for more reform.

Roosevelt, always an apt reader of the public temper, witnessed a growing appetite for reform fed by the revelations of corporate and political wrongdoing that filled the papers and boosted the sales of popular periodicals. In October 1902, Lincoln Steffens's "Tweed Days in St. Louis" appeared in *McClure's Magazine*, the first part of a series entitled "The Shame of the Cities" (later published as a book). The next month, Ida Tarbell, a schoolteacher turned journalist, began her sharply critical series on Standard Oil in *McClure's*. S. S. McClure, the magazine's publisher, watched circulation skyrocket to more than 370,000. Soon other journalists such as Ray Stannard Baker and Robert Hunter tried their hand at the new brand of investigative reporting. Their hard-hitting exposés swelled magazine circulation and touched off a public clamor for reform.

Roosevelt, a man who brandished publicity like a weapon in reform and who assiduously cultivated the press, counted many of these new journalists, notably Jacob Riis and Lincoln Steffens, as his friends. But when David Graham Phillips attacked the Republican old guard in 1906 in a series of articles entitled "The Treason of the Senate," the character assassination of his fellow Republicans offended the president. Roosevelt cautioned restraint and warned journalists that they should not be like the allegorical character in *Pilgrim's Progress* who was so busy raking up muck that he took no notice of higher things. Roosevelt's criticism gave the American vocabulary a new word: *muckraker*. Journalists soon appropriated the term and turned it into a badge of honor.

Muckraking, as Roosevelt was keenly aware, had been of enormous help in securing progressive legislation. The passage of the Pure Food and Drug Act and the Meat Inspection Act were powerful examples of the role of the muckrakers. In 1905, the president had belatedly thrown his support behind legislation to outlaw misbranded and adulterated foods, drinks, and drugs. For years, Dr. Harvey Washington Wiley, chief chemist in the Department of Agriculture, had agitated for a federal law requiring accurate labeling of foods and drugs. "Let the Label Tell" became the slogan of reformers intent on stopping the trade in dangerous and adulterated products. Mark Sullivan's exposés of patent medicines in the *Ladies' Home Journal* and Samuel Hopkins Adams's "Great American Fraud" series in *Collier's* kept the issue before the public. "Gullible America," Adams announced in 1905, "will spend this year some 75 millions of dollars in the purchase of patent medicines . . . it will swallow huge quantities of al-

cohol, an appalling amount of opiates and narcotics, a wide assortment of varied drugs . . . and far in excess of all other ingredients, undiluted fraud."

In the spring of 1906, the publicity generated by the muckrakers goaded Congress into action. With Roosevelt's backing and the support of the American Medical Association, the General Federation of Women's Clubs, and the National Consumers League, a pure food and drug bill passed the Senate and went to the House, where its opponents hoped to keep it locked up in committee. There it would have died, had not Upton Sinclair's novel *The Jungle*, with its sensational account of the filthy conditions in the meatpacking industry, sparked a massive public outcry that revived the pure food and drug debate. Public outrage led to the passage in 1906 of a tough Pure Food and Drug Act requiring medicine makers to list dangerous ingredients on their labels.

In the meantime, Roosevelt was so revolted by Sinclair's depiction of the meatpacking industry

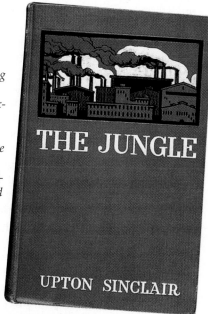

THE JUNGLE *Novelist Upton Sinclair, a lifelong socialist, wrote* The Jungle *to expose the evils of capitalism. But readers were more horrified by the unsanitary conditions he described in the meatpacking industry, where Sinclair's hapless hero encountered rats, filth, and diseased animals processed into potted beef. It was rumored that after reading the book, President Theodore Roosevelt could no longer stomach sausage for breakfast. The president immediately ordered a thorough study of conditions in the meatpacking industry. The public outcry surrounding* The Jungle *contributed to the enactment of pure food and drug legislation and federal meat inspection. Sinclair ruefully remarked, "I aimed at the public's heart, but I hit them in the stomach."* By permission of the Houghton Library, Harvard University.

that he launched his own investigation. Under public pressure, Congress hastily framed a meat inspection measure that passed the Senate. In the House, the bill languished until Roosevelt threatened to publish his "sickening report," which supported Sinclair's depiction of filthy conditions. In the glare of publicity, foreign markets moved to block exports of American meat. Knowing that they were beaten, the packers closed ranks to secure legislation "strong enough to still the public clamor, while not so drastic as to inconvenience them too greatly," in the words of one insider. The result was the passage in 1906 of a meat inspection provision that promised packers a government stamp of approval in return for meeting federal inspection standards.

As his term expired, Roosevelt moved to the left, allying with the more progressive elements of the Republican Party. In speech after speech he attacked the "malefactors of great wealth." Styling himself a "radical," he claimed credit for leading the "ultra conservative" party of McKinley to a position of "progressive conservatism and conservative radicalism." His rhetoric led John D. Rockefeller to predict early in 1907 that Roosevelt's attacks on big business would precipitate a depression.

When a sharp business panic developed in the fall of 1907, business interests quickly blamed the president. The panic of 1907 proved to be severe but short. Once again J. P. Morgan stepped in to avert disaster, switching funds from one bank to another to prop up weak institutions and keep them from failing. For his services, he claimed as a prize the Tennessee Coal and Iron Company, an independent steel business that had long been coveted by his U.S. Steel. Morgan dispatched his lieutenants to Washington, where they told Roosevelt that the sale of the company would aid the economy "but little benefit" U.S. Steel. Roosevelt, willing to take the word of a gentleman, tacitly agreed not to institute antitrust proceedings against U.S. Steel. As Roosevelt later learned, Morgan and his men had been less than candid. The acquisition of Tennessee Coal and Iron for a price under market value greatly strengthened U.S. Steel and undercut the economy of the Southeast. The episode would come back to haunt Roosevelt, as it gave rise to the charge that he acted as a tool of the Morgan interests.

The charge of collusion between business and government underscored the extent to which enlightened business leaders like Morgan and his partner George W. Perkins found federal regulation preferable to unbridled competition or harsher state measures. During the Progressive Era, advanced

business leaders participated in the creation of regulatory legislation and worked to develop a détente with government. Through a series of "gentlemen's agreements," like the one Morgan obtained in the Tennessee Coal and Iron merger, they sought the advice of the president and cooperated with government in the hope of avoiding antitrust prosecution. As much as Roosevelt attempted to make business subordinate to government, in practice Morgan still enjoyed equality with the chief executive and continued to operate on the principle of sending "my man to your man" that had so amused Roosevelt in 1902. Convinced that regulation was the best way to deal with big business, Roosevelt never acknowledged the extent to which his regulatory policies worked to further business interests and bring about business stability. As Roosevelt's actions in the panic of 1907 demonstrated, for all his harsh attacks on the "malefactors of great wealth," the president remained indebted to Morgan, who still functioned as the national bank and would continue to do so until the passage of the Federal Reserve Act six years later.

During the Progressive Era, advanced business leaders participated in the creation of regulatory legislation and worked to create a détente with government.

In at least one area, Roosevelt was well ahead of his time. Robert La Follette, who found much to criticize in Roosevelt's presidency, called his efforts in conservation of natural resources the progressive president's "greatest work." When Roosevelt took office, some 45 million acres of land remained as government reserves. He tripled that number to 150 million acres, buying land and creating national parks and wildlife preserves by executive order. To conserve natural resources, he fought not only the western cattle barons, lumber kings, and mining interests but powerful leaders in Congress, including Speaker of the House Joseph Cannon, who was determined to spend "not one cent for scenery." (See Map 21.1, page 819).

Roosevelt had no sooner entered the White House than he launched his conservation campaign, naming the able and enlightened Gifford Pinchot his chief forester. Together, the two worked zealously to put a stop to a century of exploitation. In one of their more effective ploys, they fought pri-

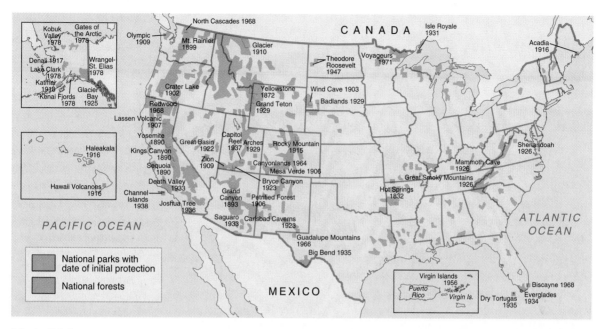

MAP 21.1

National Parks and Forests

The national park system in the West began with Yellowstone in 1872, followed in 1890 by Grand Canyon, Yosemite, King's Canyon, and Sequoia. During his presidency Theodore Roosevelt added six new parks — Crater Lake, Wind Cave, Petrified Forest, Lassen Volcano, Mesa Verde, and Zion.

vate utilities that were intent on gobbling up water-power sites and creating a monopoly of hydroelectric power. Pinchot withdrew 2,565 sites, often on the pretext that he planned to establish ranger stations on the lands. "Public rights come first and private interest second," Roosevelt insisted.

By 1907, Roosevelt had stepped on the toes of every major interest in the West. Timber, cattle, and mining kings, as well as eastern conservatives, were determined to stop him. Congress added a rider to an appropriations bill that barred the creation of any new reserves in six western states. The president could not veto the bill, but he worked feverishly in the ten days before it became law to establish twenty-one new reserves and save 16 million acres for posterity. Once again, he had outwitted his adversaries. "Opponents of the forest service turned handsprings in their wrath," he wrote gleefully, "but the threats . . . were really only a tribute to the efficiency of our action." Today, six national parks, sixteen national monuments, and fifty-one wildlife refuges stand as witness to Roosevelt's substantial accomplishments as a conservationist.

Roosevelt the Diplomat

Roosevelt took a keen interest in shaping foreign policy and hoped to see the United States take its place among world leaders. An active proponent of America's interest abroad, he was convinced that Congress was inept in foreign affairs, and he relied on executive power to effect a vigorous foreign policy, sometimes stretching those powers beyond legal limits in his pursuit of American interests.

A man who relished military discipline and viewed life as a constant conflict for supremacy, Roosevelt believed that the "civilized nations" should police the world and hold the "backward" countries in line. In his relations with the great European powers, he relied on military strength and diplomacy, a combination he aptly described with the aphorism "Speak softly but carry a big stick."

In the Caribbean, Roosevelt jealously guarded the Monroe Doctrine's American sphere of influence closed to rival European powers. In the Venezuelan dispute of 1902, he risked war with Germany to preserve the United States' prerogative in

ROOSEVELT AND MUIR
In this famous photograph, Theodore Roosevelt poses at Glacier Peak in Yosemite National Park in 1903 with John Muir, naturalist and founder of the Sierra Club. Roosevelt's years as a rancher in the Dakotas made him the first president to have experienced firsthand the American West. As president, he acted vigorously to protect the beauty and resources of the West for posterity, using executive power to set aside more than a hundred million acres in government reserves and to create six national parks.
Yosemite Museum/Leroy Radanovich.

the Western Hemisphere. Venezuela had borrowed money in Europe, and the country's dictator (whom Roosevelt dismissed as "a villainous little monkey") could not pay it back. When Germany threatened to intervene, Roosevelt issued an ultimatum to the kaiser, warning him to stay out of Latin American affairs or face war with the United States. The matter was eventually settled by arbitration.

Roosevelt's proprietary and paternalistic attitude toward the hemisphere became evident in the infamous case of the Panama Canal. A firm advocate of naval power and an astute naval strategist, Roosevelt had long been a strong supporter of an isthmian canal connecting the Caribbean and the Pacific. By enabling the navy to move quickly from the Atlantic to the Pacific, the canal would, in effect, double the nation's naval power. The United States began a joint venture with England to build a canal but in 1901 abandoned the partnership and moved forward alone. Two sites were possible, one in Nicaragua, which had the advantage of being at sea level, and another in Panama, where the rough and hilly terrain demanded a system of locks. In the end, the choice was made not by logic but by politics. Private investors who held rights to build a Panamanian route lobbied Congress shamelessly until they won approval for the route.

A man who relished military discipline and viewed life as a constant conflict for supremacy, Roosevelt believed that the "civilized nations" should police the world and hold the "backward" countries in line.

The Panamanian isthmus was at this time part of Colombia, so in 1902, Roosevelt began negotiations to gain access to the land. He offered the Colombian government $10 million and an annual rent of $250,000. When the government in Bogotá

"THE NEWS REACHES BOGOTÁ"

Like a modern Gulliver, President Theodore Roosevelt straddles the isthmus and begins digging the Panama Canal. "I took Panama," Roosevelt boasted. This contemporary political cartoon evidently views Roosevelt's action in a favorable light, mocking the Colombian government with the caption "The News Reaches Bogotá." Few raised objections at the time, but Roosevelt's successors would eventually apologize to Colombia and pay a $25 million indemnity; in 1978, the United States signed a treaty to turn the canal over to the Panamanians.
Theodore Roosevelt Collection, Harvard College Library.

refused to accept the offer, Roosevelt became incensed at what he called the "homicidal corruptionists" in Colombia for trying to "blackmail" the United States. The result was an uprising in Panama in 1903 arranged by investors in New York and staged with Roosevelt's implicit backing. The U.S. government aided and protected the "revolution" by placing the warship *Nashville* off the isthmus, and the State Department recognized the new government of Panama within twenty-four hours after the uprising. The new Panamanian government promptly accepted the $10 million, and the building of the canal got under way. Roosevelt later boasted that he "took Panama"; although most Americans applauded his action, the episode became a national disgrace. President Woodrow Wilson would later insist on

paying the Colombian government $25 million, much to Roosevelt's disgust and mortification.

In the wake of the Panama affair and the confrontation with Germany over Venezuela, Roosevelt announced what became known as the Roosevelt Corollary to the Monroe Doctrine. The United States would not intervene in Latin America as long as nations conducted their affairs with "decency." But Roosevelt warned that if any Latin American nation proved guilty of "brutal wrongdoing," as in the case of Venezuela's default on its debt to Germany, the United States would insist on stepping in. The Roosevelt Corollary in effect made the United States the policeman of the hemisphere and served notice to the European powers to keep out. Critics called Roosevelt's policy "gunboat diplomacy," and with good reason. In the administrations of Roosevelt and his successor, William Howard Taft, U.S. marines were frequently dispatched to the Caribbean to take over customhouses or to show U.S. force. The legacy of gunboat diplomacy was a bitter anti-American sentiment that would last throughout the century.

In the Far East, Roosevelt inherited the Open Door policy initiated by Secretary of State John Hay in 1899, which was designed to ensure U.S. commercial entry into China. And as a result of victory in the Spanish-American War, the United States now enjoyed a foothold in the region with its pos-session of the Philippines. As Britain, France, Russia, Japan, and Germany raced to secure Chinese trade and territory, Roosevelt was tempted to use force to enter the fray and gain economic or possibly territorial concessions. Sensibly, he held back. He realized that the American people would not support an aggressive Asian policy. In the end, he fell back on Hay's Open Door policy, which sought to maintain Chinese territorial integrity and guarantee the United States an equal share with the European powers in trade and investment.

In his relations with Europe, Roosevelt sought to establish the United States, fresh from its victory

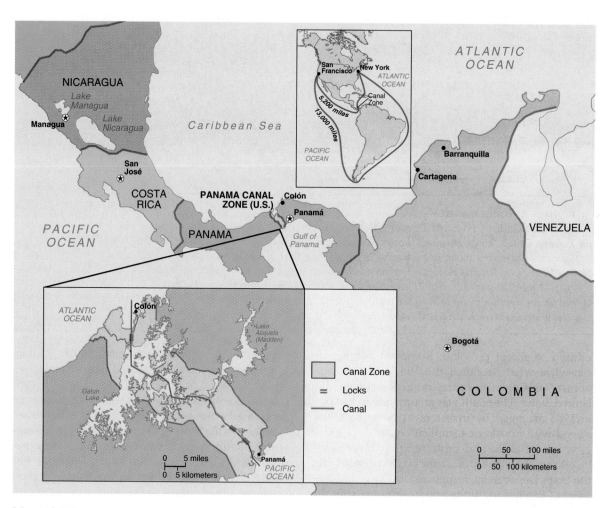

MAP 21.2
The Panama Canal, 1914
The Panama Canal, completed in 1914, bisected the isthmus in a series of massive locks and dams. As Theodore Roosevelt had planned, the canal greatly strengthened the navy by allowing ships to move from the Atlantic to the Pacific in a matter of days.

over Spain, as a rising force in world affairs. He proved himself a consummate diplomat when he succeeded in preserving peace after tensions flared between France and Germany in Morocco in 1905. Roosevelt set up a conference in Algeciras, Spain, where he worked to maintain a balance of power to help neutralize German ambitions. His skillful mediation of the dispute gained him a reputation as an astute player on the world stage and demonstrated the United States' new presence in world affairs.

In 1906, Roosevelt earned the Nobel Peace Prize for his role in negotiating an end to the Russo-Japanese War, which had broken out when the Japanese invaded Chinese Manchuria, threatening Russia's sphere of influence in the area. Again, Roosevelt sought to maintain a balance of power, in this case working to curb Japanese expansionism. Roosevelt admired the Japanese, judging them "the most dashing fighters in the world." But he did not wish Japan to become too strong in Asia. He offered to mediate and presided over the peace conference at Portsmouth, New Hampshire. At the peace conference, he was able to prevent Japan from dominating Manchuria, but he had no qualms about granting the Japanese control of Korea, a sovereign country.

Roosevelt fumed when the United States' good relations with Japan were jeopardized in 1906 by discriminatory legislation in California that called for segregated public schools for "Orientals." The Japanese government, sensitive to the racial slur, responded indignantly. Roosevelt castigated the "idiots" in California and managed to smooth over the incident by negotiating a "gentlemen's agreement" in 1907. He offered to reverse the segregation order in exchange for certain restrictions on Japanese immigration to the United States. This informal arrangement allowed the Japanese to save face, while at the same time placating nativist sentiment in California.

To counter Japan's growing bellicosity, Roosevelt dispatched the Great White Fleet, the navy's most up-to-date battleships, on a "goodwill" mission around the world. This show of American force constituted a classic example of his dictum "Speak softly but carry a big stick."

The Troubled Presidency of William Howard Taft

When Roosevelt retired from the presidency in 1909 at the age of fifty to go on safari and shoot big game in Africa, he turned the White House over to his handpicked successor, William Howard Taft. Any

man would have found it difficult to follow in Roosevelt's footsteps, but Taft proved hopelessly ill suited to the task. A genial man with a talent for law, Taft had little experience in elective office, having served as governor of the Philippines and as Roosevelt's secretary of war. Taft had no talent or instinct for politics, no ability to compromise, and no nerve for controversy. His ambitious wife coveted the office and urged him to take it. He would have been better off listening to his mother, who warned, "Roosevelt is a good fighter and enjoys it, but the malice of politics would make you miserable."

Taft ran in 1908 with Roosevelt never far in the background. He soundly defeated the perennial Democratic candidate, the "Great Commoner," William Jennings Bryan, but his popular majority was only half of Roosevelt's record in 1904. On the eve of his inauguration, Taft showed little enthusiasm about his triumph and little zest for the future. In fact, the presidency for Taft proved an ordeal to be endured. As a symptom of his discomfort in office, his weight ballooned from an already hefty 297 pounds to over 350 pounds.

Taft proved a perfect tool in the hands of Republicans who yearned for a return to the days of McKinley. Whereas Roosevelt had moved in advance of his party, Taft was by nature cautious and was easily led. He saw his role as being to conserve the gains made by Roosevelt and not to press for additional reforms. With the country riding the crest of progressive reform, he was badly out of tune with his times.

Taft's greatest strength proved to be his greatest weakness. A lawyer by training and instinct, he believed that it was up to the courts, not the president, to arbitrate social issues. Roosevelt had carried presidential power to a new level, often castigating the judiciary and flouting the separation of powers. Taft the legalist found it difficult to condone such actions. Wary of the progressive insurgents in his own party and without Roosevelt to guide him, Taft relied increasingly on conservatives in the Republican Party. As a progressive senator lamented, "Taft is a ponderous and amiable man completely surrounded by men who know exactly what they want."

Taft's troubles began on the eve of his inaugural when he called a special session of Congress to deal with the tariff. Roosevelt had been too politically astute to tackle the troublesome tariff issue, even though he knew that rates needed to be lowered. Taft, with his stubborn courage, blundered into the fray. The House of Representatives passed a modest downward revision and, to make up for lost

WILLIAM HOWARD TAFT
William Howard Taft had little aptitude or stomach for politics. When Theodore Roosevelt tapped him as his successor in 1908, Taft had never held an elected office. A legalist by training and temperament, Taft moved congenially in the conservative circles of the Republican Party. His actions dismayed progressives and eventually led Roosevelt to challenge him for the presidency in 1912. The break with Roosevelt saddened and embittered Taft, who heartily disliked the presidency and was glad to leave it.
Library of Congress.

revenue, imposed a small inheritance tax. Led by Senator Aldrich, the conservative Senate struck down the tax and added more than eight hundred crippling amendments to the tariff. The Payne-Aldrich bill that emerged actually raised the tariff. Taft, as if paralyzed, neither fought for changes nor vetoed the measure.

Progressives and Democrats attacked the swollen tariff as a triumph for big business over consumers. Perhaps flummoxed by his conservative friends, Taft insisted that the tariff was "really a good bill" and that it represented a downward revision in tariff duties. On a tour of the Midwest in 1909, he was greeted with jeers when he claimed,

"I think the Payne bill is the best bill that the Republican party ever passed." In the eyes of a growing number of critics, his praise of the tariff made him either a fool or a liar.

Taft's legalism got him into hot water again in the controversy over conservation. Roosevelt, in his zeal to protect the wilderness, had not hesitated to bend the law. Taft refused to endorse his predecessor's methods. He undid Roosevelt's work to preserve water power sites when he learned that they had been improperly designated as ranger stations. Chief forester Gifford Pinchot, angry at what he perceived as a rollback of Roosevelt's conservation policies, publicly denounced Taft's secretary of the interior, Richard Ballinger, as a tool of western land-grabbers. Taft fired Pinchot, touching off a storm of controversy that hurt Taft and alienated Roosevelt.

Talk of substituting Roosevelt on the ticket in 1912 grew as Republican progressives became increasingly dissatisfied with Taft's policies. In June 1910, Roosevelt returned to New York, where he received a hero's welcome. Back at Sagamore Hill, his home in Oyster Bay, New York, the ex-president attracted a stream of visitors and reporters seeking his advice and opinions. Hurt, Taft kept his distance. By late summer, Roosevelt had taken sides with the progressive insurgents in his party. "Taft is utterly hopeless as a leader," Roosevelt confided to his son as he set out on a speaking tour of the West. Reading the mood of the country, Roosevelt began to sound more and more like a candidate.

With the Republican Party divided, the Democrats swept the congressional elections of 1910. Branding the Payne-Aldrich tariff "the mother of trusts," they captured a majority in the House of Representatives and won several key governorships. The revitalized Democratic Party could look to new leaders, among them the progressive governor of New Jersey, Woodrow Wilson.

With a Democratic majority in the House and progressive Republicans holding the balance of power in the Senate, Congress enacted a number of key reforms. Legislation to regulate mine and railroad safety, to create a Children's Bureau, and to establish an eight-hour day for federal workers passed. Two significant constitutional amendments —the Sixteenth Amendment, which provided for a modest graduated income tax, and the Seventeenth Amendment, which called for the direct election of senators (who had formerly been chosen by their state legislatures)—went to the states for ratification. While Congress rode the high tide of progressive reform, Taft sat on the sidelines.

In foreign policy as well as in the domestic arena, Taft had a difficult time following in Roosevelt's footsteps. In the Caribbean he pursued a policy of "dollar diplomacy," championing commercial goals rather than the strategic aims that Roosevelt had advocated. He provoked anti-American feeling by attempting to force commercial treaties on Nicaragua and Honduras and by dispatching the U.S. marines to Nicaragua and Santo Domingo in 1912.

In the Far East, Taft's foreign policy proved even more disastrous. He openly avowed his intent to promote in China "active intervention to secure for . . . our capitalists opportunity for profitable investment." Lacking Roosevelt's understanding of power politics, Taft naively believed that he could substitute "dollars for bullets." He never recognized that an aggressive commercial policy could not exist without military might. As a result, dollar diplomacy was doomed to failure. Even Taft was forced to recognize its limits when revolution broke out in Mexico in 1911. Under pressure to protect American investment, which amounted to more than $4 billion, he mobilized troops along the border. But in the end, he had to rely on diplomatic pressure to salvage American interests.

Always a legalist at heart, Taft hoped to encourage world peace through the use of a world court and arbitration. He unsuccessfully sponsored a series of arbitration treaties that Roosevelt, who prized national honor more than international law, vehemently opposed. By 1910, Roosevelt had become a vocal critic of Taft's foreign policy, which he dismissed as "maudlin folly."

The final breech between Taft and Roosevelt came in 1911, when Taft's attorney general filed an antitrust suit against U.S. Steel. In its brief against the steel giant, the government cited Roosevelt's agreement with the Morgan interests in the 1907 acquisition of Tennessee Coal and Iron by U.S. Steel. The incident greatly embarrassed Roosevelt by making it clear he had either been hoodwinked or had acted as a tool of Wall Street. Thoroughly enraged, Roosevelt lambasted Taft's "archaic" antitrust policy and began to hint that he might be persuaded to run for president again.

The Election of 1912

In February 1912, Roosevelt announced, "My hat is in the ring." Convinced that he was the only progressive who had a chance to win nomination and carry the election, he shoved aside Robert La Follette

and prepared to take on Taft. But for all his popularity, Roosevelt no longer controlled the party machinery. Taft, with uncharacteristic strength, refused to step aside. As he bitterly told a journalist, "Even a rat in a corner will fight." Roosevelt took advantage of newly passed primary election laws and ran in thirteen states, winning 278 delegates to Taft's 48. But at the Chicago convention, Taft's bosses refused to seat the Roosevelt delegates. Fights broke out on the convention floor as Taft won renomination on the first ballot. Crying robbery, Roosevelt's supporters marched out and bolted the party.

Seven weeks later, in the same Chicago auditorium, a hastily organized Progressive Party met to nominate Roosevelt. Few Republican officeholders joined the new party, but the advance guard of progressivism turned out in full force. Amid a thunder of applause, Jane Addams seconded Roosevelt's nomination. The convention resembled a religious revival with delegates singing "Onward Christian Soldiers" and "The Battle Hymn of the Republic." Full of reforming zeal, the delegates approved the most advanced platform since the Populists' in 1892. Planks called for woman suffrage, the direct election of senators, presidential primaries, electoral reforms, the recall of judges, conservation of natural resources, minimum wages for women, an end to child labor, workers' compensation, social security, and a federal income tax.

But for all the excitement and the cheering, the new Progressive Party was doomed, and the candidate knew it. The people may have supported the new party, but the politicians, even insurgents like La Follette, stayed within the Republican fold. The Progressive Party had only two assets: Roosevelt's personality and the money supplied by his many backers.

Roosevelt arrived in Chicago to accept the nomination and announced that he felt as "strong as a bull moose," giving the new party a nickname and a mascot. "I am under no illusion about it," he confessed to a friend. "It is a forlorn hope." But he had gone too far to turn back. He led the Bull Moose Party into the fray, exhorting his followers in ringing biblical tones, "We shall not falter, we stand at Armageddon and do battle for the Lord."

The Democrats, delighted at the split in the Republican ranks, smelled victory for the first time since 1892. Their convention turned into a bitter fight for the nomination. After forty-six ballots, William Jennings Bryan threw his support to Woodrow Wilson, and the party nominated the governor of New Jersey. Wilson's career in politics had proved even more astounding than Roosevelt's. After only eighteen months in office, the former professor and president of Princeton University found himself running for president of the United States.

Wilson ran on a platform hammered out by Democrats over the past fifteen years and designed to appeal to the constituent groups of the Democratic Party. To the farmers, the platform promised a lower tariff and cheaper agricultural loans; to labor unions, it promised to limit the use of injunctions and antitrust laws against labor; and to small business owners, it vowed to return to competition through the breakup of the trusts. As if that were not enough, Wilson's vice presidential candidate, Thomas R. Marshall, went on record avowing, "What America needs is a good five-cent cigar."

Voters in 1912 could choose from three candidates, each of whom claimed to be a progressive. That the term could stretch to cover all three underscored some major disagreements in progressive thinking about the relationship between business and government. Taft, for all his trust-busting, never succeeded in convincing the public of his progressivism and was generally conceded to be the candidate of the old guard. The real contest was between Roosevelt and Wilson and the two political philosophies summed up in their campaign slogans: "The New Nationalism" and "The New Freedom."

Roosevelt's New Nationalism enunciated his belief in federal planning and regulation. He accepted big business as inevitable but demanded that big government supervise it and act as a steward for labor and the consumer. Roosevelt called for an increase in the power of the federal government, a decrease in the power of the courts, and an active role for the president. He urged legislation creating a commission able to regulate manufacturing and trade along the lines of the ICC. As Herbert Croly pointed out in *The Promise of American Life* (1909), Roosevelt hoped to use the Hamiltonian means of greater centralization to further the Jeffersonian ends of greater democracy.

Voters in 1912 could choose from three candidates, each of whom claimed to be a progressive.

Woodrow Wilson, a Virginia-born Democrat schooled in the principle of limited government and states' rights, set a markedly different course with his New Freedom. He saw no benefit in bigness in

PASS PROSPERITY AROUND

BULL MOOSE POSTER
Accepting the nomination of the Progressive Party in 1912, Theodore Roosevelt exclaimed, "I feel as strong as a bull moose." Instantly the new party had a mascot and a nickname. The Bull Moose soon decorated party emblems, as in this poster where the animal is featured more prominently than Roosevelt or his vice presidential candidate, Hiram Johnson. The slogan "Pass Prosperity Around" may refer to the party's platform, which pledged to tax the great fortunes of the day by enacting the country's first graduated income tax.
Collection of Janice L. and David J. Frent.

business or government. Tutored in economics by *Muller v. Oregon* lawyer Louis Brandeis, who railed against the "curse of bigness," Wilson promised to use antitrust legislation to get rid of big corporations. He advocated strong antitrust laws that, he argued, would give small businesses and farmers better opportunities in the marketplace.

Throughout the campaign, Wilson and Roosevelt fought it out, each pointing to the weakness of his rival's program. Wilson labeled Roosevelt's New Nationalism a plan to "regulate monopoly," a thinly disguised partnership between government and business. Roosevelt castigated Wilson for being backward looking, for advocating a kind of "rural toryism." Each candidate's criticisms contained some truth. Roosevelt, in practice, did advocate détente between government and business. As Wilson never tired of pointing out, George Perkins, Morgan's ex-partner, was Roosevelt's campaign manager and chief financial backer. But it was equally true that Wilson's New Freedom was a rural program that affirmed the hopes and desires of the farmers and small business owners who formed the backbone of the Democratic Party.

In the end, only the energy and emotional enthusiasm of the Bull Moosers obscured the inevitable outcome of a race in which the Republican vote was split while the Democrats remained united. No candidate could claim a majority in the three-way race. Wilson captured a bare 42 percent of the popular vote, polling fewer votes than Bryan had received when he lost to Taft in 1908. Roosevelt and his Bull Moose Progressive Party won 27 percent of the vote, an unprecedented vote for a new party. The incumbent Taft ran third with 23 percent. But in the electoral college, Wilson won a decisive 435, with 88 going to Roosevelt and only 8 to Taft.

The election marked a triumph for the forces of reform. Clearly, Americans wanted a change from the policies of Taft. In the excitement for change, Eu-

gene V. Debs, the Socialist Party candidate, captured nearly a million votes. Wilson carried the traditional Democratic strongholds in the cities and the farmlands. But without the split in the Republican Party, the Democrats could not have won the White House. The real loser in 1912 was not Taft but the Bull Moose Party, which essentially collapsed after Roosevelt's defeat. It had always been, in the words of one observer, "a house divided against itself and already mortgaged."

Woodrow Wilson and Progressivism at High Tide

Born in Virginia and raised in Georgia, Woodrow Wilson was the first Southerner to be elected president since James K. Polk (in 1844) and only the second Democrat to occupy the White House since Reconstruction. Democrats who anticipated a wild celebration when Wilson took office soon had their hopes dashed. The son of a Presbyterian minister, Wilson was a teetotaler more given to Scripture than to celebration. He canceled the inaugural ball and called instead for a day of prayer.

This lean, ascetic man with an otherworldly gaze had come to politics by a strange route. A scholar and an academician, he had earned his doctorate at Johns Hopkins University and had taught at Bryn Mawr, Wesleyan, and Princeton, serving as president of the latter for eight years. In 1910, the New Jersey Democratic machine, looking for a respectable candidate, tapped him for governor. Once in office, he quickly cut his ties with the bosses and went over to the progressive camp. He was a man, his biographer conceded, whose "political convictions were never as fixed as his ambition."

As governor, Wilson put New Jersey in the vanguard of progressivism by signing laws to reform the election process, to provide workers' compensation, to end corrupt practices in state government, and to regulate railroads and public utilities. A year into his term, Wilson already had his eye on the presidency. Even though he loathed William Jennings Bryan, he courted him until he won Bryan's political blessing; afterward he rewarded the Great Commoner by naming him secretary of state. Always able to equivocate, Wilson was rarely able to compromise. At Princeton, he had split the university community in a bitter fight over the location of the graduate school. From an early age, Wilson believed that he was destined to lead and dreamed of

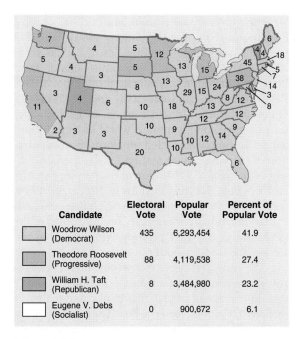

Candidate	Electoral Vote	Popular Vote	Percent of Popular Vote
Woodrow Wilson (Democrat)	435	6,293,454	41.9
Theodore Roosevelt (Progressive)	88	4,119,538	27.4
William H. Taft (Republican)	8	3,484,980	23.2
Eugene V. Debs (Socialist)	0	900,672	6.1

MAP 21.3
The Election of 1912

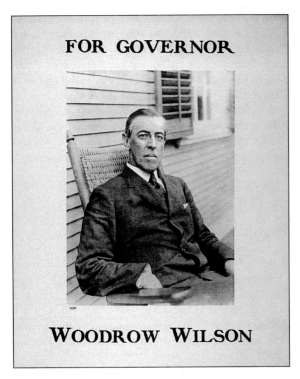

WOODROW WILSON
Woodrow Wilson's political career was meteoric, propelling him from the presidency of Princeton University to the presidency of the United States in three years. As governor of New Jersey from 1910 to 1912, Wilson turned his back on the Democratic machine that had backed him and made a reputation as a champion of progressive reform. Elected to the White House in 1912, he presided over the high tide of progressive reform.
Collection of Janice L. and David J. Frent.

moving the masses with great speeches. He brought to the White House a gift for oratory, a stern will, and a set of fixed beliefs. His tendency to turn differences of opinion into personal hatreds would impair his leadership and damage his presidency. Fortunately for Wilson, he came to power with a Democratic Congress ready to do his bidding.

Although he opposed big government in his campaign, Wilson viewed himself as the only leader who could speak for the country. He was prepared to work on the base built by Roosevelt to strengthen presidential power, exerting leadership and working through his party in Congress to accomplish the Democratic agenda. Before he was finished, Wilson would preside over progressivism at high tide and see enacted not only the platform of the Democratic Party but the humanitarian reforms championed by Roosevelt's Progressive Party as well.

Tariff and Banking Reform

In March 1913, Wilson, proud of his ability as an orator, became the first president since John Adams to go to Capitol Hill and speak directly to Congress, calling for tariff reform. "The object of the tariff," Wilson told his audience, "must be effective competition." Eager to topple the high tariff, the Democratic House of Representatives hastily passed the Underwood tariff, which lowered rates by 15 percent. To compensate for lost revenue, Congress added a provision for a moderate income tax made possible by the ratification of the Sixteenth Amendment a month earlier. In the Senate, lobbyists for industries quietly went to work to get the tariff raised, but Wilson rallied public opinion by attacking the "industrious and insidious lobby." Robert La Follette went further and demanded an investigation of the ties between business and the legislature. When senators for the first time had to disclose their finances, the public learned that more than a few were on the payrolls of big corporations. In the harsh glare of publicity, the Senate passed the Underwood tariff, which earned praise as "the most honest tariff since the Civil War."

Wilson turned his attention next to banking. The panic of 1907 had dramatically testified to the failure of the banking system. Once again, a president had had to turn to J. P. Morgan. But Morgan's legendary power was coming under close scrutiny. Pressure for federal intervention mounted in 1913 with the sensational findings of the Pujo committee. Arsène Pujo, a Democratic senator from Louisiana, set out to investigate the "money trust." Pujo's committee summoned the great lords of Wall Street, including Morgan himself, to testify about the powerful and mysterious world of New York finance. Testimony revealed an alarming concentration of banking power that had developed as a result of mergers. J. P. Morgan and Company and its affiliates held 341 directorships in 112 corporations, controlling assets of more than $22 billion. By casting the harsh light of publicity on the doings of the financial moguls, the Pujo committee helped to create a mandate for banking reform.

The Federal Reserve Act, passed in 1913 as a result of the outcry, established a national banking system composed of regional banks under the direction of a Federal Reserve Board appointed by the president. The bill was a compromise measure. Bankers initially fought for a central bank under banker control, while Bryan and the progressives insisted that government control the system and issue the currency. Influenced by his adviser Louis Brandeis, who sided with the progressives, Wilson backed public control of a central bank and stood firm against a howl of protest from the bankers. Progressives, who had wanted public control of regional banks as well, were disappointed. But southern agrarians did succeed in getting the regional reserve banks to issue short-term loans, the "corn tassel currency" that they had sought since the days of the Populists. To get his measure through the Senate, Wilson once again borrowed a tactic from Roosevelt and issued a public statement claiming that Wall Street was attempting to defeat his bill by creating fears of an impending panic.

Before he was finished, Wilson would preside over progressivism at high tide and see enacted not only the platform of the Democratic Party but the humanitarian reforms championed by Roosevelt's Progressive Party as well.

The Federal Reserve Act of 1913 was the most significant piece of domestic legislation in Wilson's presidency. It provided for twelve Federal Reserve banks, privately controlled but regulated and supervised by a Federal Reserve Board appointed by the president. It gave the United States its first efficient banking and currency system and, at the same time, provided for a larger degree of government control over banking than had ever existed before. The new system made currency more elastic and credit adequate for the needs of business and agriculture. It did not, however, attempt to take control of the boom and bust cycles in the U.S. economy that would produce another major depression in the 1930s.

Wilson and the Trusts

Flushed with success, Wilson tackled the trust issue. When Congress reconvened in January 1914, Wilson supported the Clayton bill to outlaw interlocking directorates (directors from one corporation sitting on the board of another) and unfair practices. By spelling out which practices were unfair, Wilson hoped to guide business activity back to healthy competition without resorting to regulation.

An anemic Clayton Antitrust Act finally passed in 1914. Its preamble declared, "The labor of human beings is not a commodity or article of commerce."

But the Clayton Act did not succeed in breaking the alliance of business and the judiciary. Despite the fact that AFL President Samuel Gompers hailed the Clayton Act as the "Magna Carta of labor," the conservative courts continued to issue injunctions and to use antitrust legislation against labor unions.

In the midst of the fight for the Clayton Act, Wilson, at the prompting of Louis Brandeis, changed his tactics. In a dramatic turnaround, he threw his support behind the creation of the Federal Trade Commission (FTC), precisely the kind of federal regulatory agency that Roosevelt had advocated under his New Nationalism and that Wilson had denounced. The FTC, created in 1913, had not only wide investigatory powers but the authority to prosecute corporations for "unfair trade practices" and to enforce its judgments by issuing "cease and desist" orders. Along with the Clayton Act, which outlawed "unfair competition"—practices such as price discrimination and interlocking directorates —Wilson's antitrust program worked to regulate rather than to break up big business.

With the enactment of antitrust laws, Wilson had exhausted the stock of ideas that made up the New Freedom. In the autumn of 1914, he alarmed progressives by declaring that the progressive movement had fulfilled its mission and that the country needed "a time of healing." During the next two years, Wilson consistently wooed bankers and businessmen. Having fought provisions in the Federal Reserve Act that would give bankers control, Wilson promptly named a banker, Paul Warburg, as the first chief of the Federal Reserve Board. Appointments to the new Federal Trade Commission also went to conservative businessmen. Disgruntled progressives charged that Wilson was attempting to nullify progressive legislation with his conservative appointments. But the progressive penchant for expertise helps explain Wilson's choices. Believing that experts in the field could best understand the complex issues at stake, Wilson appointed bankers to oversee the banks and businessmen to regulate business.

Wilson, Reluctant Progressive

Progressives watched in dismay as Wilson repeatedly obstructed or obstinately refused to encourage further progressive reforms. He failed to support labor's demand for an end to injunctions and for a promise to exempt unions from prosecution under antitrust laws as conspiracies "in restraint of trade." He twice threatened to veto legislation providing for farm credits on nonperishable crops. He refused to support child labor legislation or woman suffrage, and he vetoed legislation sponsored by labor to curb immigration. Wilson justified his actions in the rhetoric of the New Freedom by claiming that his administration would condone "special privileges to none." Virtually the only progressive measure that passed was the Seaman's Bill, a long overdue measure to improve the working conditions of sailors.

In the face of Wilson's obstinacy, reform might have ended in 1913 had not political motives forced the president to adopt the progressive agenda. In the congressional elections of 1914, the Republican Party, no longer split by Roosevelt's moribund Bull Moose faction, won substantial gains. Democratic strategists, with their eyes on the 1916 presidential race, recognized that Wilson needed to pick up support in the Midwest and the West by capturing votes from former Bull Moose progressives.

Wilson responded belatedly to this political pressure by championing reform in 1916. In a sharp about-face, he cultivated social reformers, farmers, and union labor. To please labor, he appointed Louis Brandeis to the Supreme Court. To woo farmers, he threw his support behind legislation to obtain rural credits. And he won support from advanced progressives such as Jane Addams by supporting workers' compensation and the Keating-Owen child labor law. When a railroad strike threatened in the months before the election, Wilson virtually ordered Congress to establish an eight-hour day at ten-hour pay on the railroads. He had moved a long way from his position in 1912 to embrace many of the social reforms championed by Theodore Roosevelt. As Wilson boasted, the Democrats had "opened their hearts to the demands of social justice" and had "come very near to carrying out the platform of the Progressive Party."

The Limits of Reform

Progressivism, no matter how much it challenged standpat conservatism, was never a radical movement. Its goal remained the preservation of the existing system, by government intervention if necessary, but without uprooting any of the traditional American political, economic, or social institutions. As Theodore Roosevelt, the bellwether of the movement, insisted, "The only true conservative is the man who resolutely sets his face toward the future." Roosevelt was such a man, and progressivism was such a movement. Its basic conservatism can be seen by comparing it to more radical movements of the era and by looking at the groups that were left out of progressive reform.

Radical Alternatives

It was inevitable, given the turbulence of the times, that the progressivism of Roosevelt and Wilson would be challenged by more radical voices. Some came from within the movement. Robert La Follette, always an implacable idealist, repeatedly called for stronger measures to curb corporate power and democratize the tax system. But the most cogent criticism of progressivism came from American socialists.

The year 1900 witnessed the birth of the Social Democratic Party in America, later called simply the Socialist Party. Like the progressives, the socialists were surprisingly middle class and native-born. They had broken with the older, more militant Socialist Labor Party precisely because of its dogmatic approach and immigrant constituency. (The party refused to allow the use of English at its meetings.) The new group of socialists, men such as Upton Sinclair, Walter Lippmann, and John Reed, were eager to appeal to a broad mass of Americans.

The socialists chose as their standard-bearer Eugene V. Debs, whose experience in the Pullman strike of 1894 convinced him that "there is no hope for the toiling masses of my countrymen, except by the pathways mapped out by Socialism." Debs's brand of socialism, which owed as much to the social gospel as to the theories of Karl Marx advocated cooperation to replace competition and urged men and women to liberate themselves from "the barbarism of private ownership and wage slavery." Described by his followers as "a poet, a saint, a sweetly strong man," Debs declared, "While there is a lower class I am of it, while there is a criminal class I am of it, while there is a soul in prison I am not free."

Roosevelt immediately labeled Debs a "mere inciter to murder and preacher of applied anarchy." Debs, for his part, pointed to the conservatism that underlay Roosevelt's fiery rhetoric. He urged workers not to be fooled by Roosevelt. In the 1912 election, Debs indicted both parties as Tweedledee and Tweedledum, each dedicated to the preservation of capitalism and the continuation of the wage system. The Socialist Party alone, he argued, was the "revolutionary party of the working class." Debs would

EUGENE DEBS CAMPAIGNING
Socialist candidate Eugene Victor Debs ran for president five times, in 1900, 1904, 1908, 1912, and 1920. Here he campaigns by cross-country train, the "Socialist Presidential Special." Debs, in the back row holding a baby, argued in 1912 that Roosevelt and Wilson were as alike as Tweedledee and Tweedledum and that only the Socialist Party spoke for the working class. He polled almost a million votes.
Indiana State University.

run for president five times, in every election (except 1916) from 1900 to 1920, when he ran from jail for opposing U.S. entry into World War I. But his biggest victory came in 1912, when he polled 6 percent of the popular vote, capturing almost a million votes.

Farther to the left of the socialists stood the Industrial Workers of the World (IWW), nicknamed the Wobblies. In 1905, Debs, along with Big Bill Haywood, created the IWW, "one big union" dedicated to organizing the most destitute segment of the workforce. The IWW preached syndicalism, the French doctrine that held that workers' unions or syndicates would lead the people to socialism. In practice, the IWW set out to organize the poorest and worst treated workers—western miners, migrant farmworkers, lumbermen, and immigrant textile workers. These unskilled workers were disdained by the craft unions of Samuel Gompers's AFL. Haywood, a craggy-faced miner with one eye

(he had lost the other in an industrial accident), was a charismatic leader and an authentic proletarian intellectual. While Debs insisted that change could come from ballots, not bullets, the IWW unhesitatingly advocated direct action, sabotage, and the general strike—tactics designed to trigger a workers' uprising. In the intolerant atmosphere of World War I, the IWW made a conspicuous target and was persecuted and prosecuted until it all but disappeared.

In contrast to political radicals like Debs and Haywood, who championed unionism and socialism, Margaret Sanger, a nurse and social activist, promoted birth control as a movement for radical change. Sanger coined the term *birth control* in 1915 and launched a movement with broad social implications. She and her followers saw birth control not only as a sexual and medical reform but also as a means to alter social and political power relationships and to alleviate human misery.

The movement for birth control during the Progressive Era was another example of a cross-class alliance, in which middle-class women like Sanger made common cause with the working class. The leading advocates of birth control from 1914 to 1920 came from the ranks of feminists and socialists. Radicals such as the anarchist Emma Goldman were the first to publicly advocate birth control. They saw it as a way to improve the plight of the workers and urged working-class women to quit producing recruits for the factory and the army.

In contrast to political radicals like Eugene Debs and Big Bill Haywood, who championed unionism and socialism, Margaret Sanger, a nurse and social activist, promoted birth control as a movement for radical change.

Sanger, the daughter of a radical Irish father and a mother who died at fifty after bearing eleven children, became the birth control movement's strongest advocate. As a nurse, she saw firsthand the desperation of poor women who sought to limit the size of their families. After watching one woman die from a botched abortion, Sanger vowed to do something.

Although birth control became a public issue only in the early twentieth century, the birthrate in the United States had been falling consistently throughout the nineteenth century, with the average number of children born to white women falling from 7 in 1800 to 3.6 by 1900. The desire for family limitation was widespread, and, in this sense, birth control was nothing new. But the open advocacy of contraception, the use of artificial means to prevent pregnancy, seemed to many people both new and shocking. Theodore Roosevelt fulminated against birth control as "race suicide" and castigated white middle-class couples for having small families, warning that the "white" population was declining while immigrants and "undesirables" continued to breed. Purity laws passed in the 1870s made it illegal to distribute information on birth control or contraceptive devices. Although there was a brisk underground trade in such items, limited access meant that many couples had to rely on methods such as withdrawal, abstinence, or abortion to reduce the size of their families.

Convinced that women needed to be able to control their pregnancies but unsure of the best methods for doing so, Sanger traveled to Europe in 1913 to learn more about contraceptive techniques. On her return in 1914, she promoted birth control in her newspaper, the *Woman Rebel*. When the post office declared the publication obscene and brought charges against Sanger, she responded defiantly by drafting a detailed pamphlet called "Family Limitation" and getting the IWW to distribute 100,000 copies. Facing arrest, she fled to Europe, where she worked with advanced sexual theorist Havelock Ellis. Sanger returned to the United States in 1916 something of a national celebrity. In her absence, birth control had become linked with free speech and had been taken up as a liberal cause. Under pressure from public opinion, the government dropped charges against her and Sanger undertook a nationwide tour to publicize the birth control cause.

Impatient with propaganda, Sanger turned to direct action in 1916, opening the first birth control clinic, in the Brownsville section of Brooklyn, New York. Located in the heart of a Jewish and Italian immigrant neighborhood, the clinic attracted 464 clients in the nine days it was open. On the tenth day, police shut down the clinic and put Sanger in jail. By then she had become a national figure, and the cause she championed had gained legitimacy if not legality. After World War I, the birth control movement would become much less radical as Sanger turned to doctors for support. But in its infancy, the movement that she led was part of a radical vision for reforming the world that made common cause with the socialists and the IWW in challenging the limits of progressive reform.

Progressivism for White Men Only

The day before President Woodrow Wilson's inauguration in March 1913, more than five thousand demonstrators marched in Washington to demand the vote for women. Inez Milholland, on a white horse, led the parade of women and men wearing the yellow suffragist emblem. A rowdy crowd on hand to celebrate the Democrats' triumph heckled the marchers, as did the police. "If my wife were where you are," a burly cop told one suffragist, "I'd break her head." But for all the marching, Wilson, who didn't believe that a "lady" should vote, pointedly ignored woman suffrage in his inaugural address the next day.

The march served as a reminder that the political gains of progressivism were not spread equally in the population. When the twentieth century

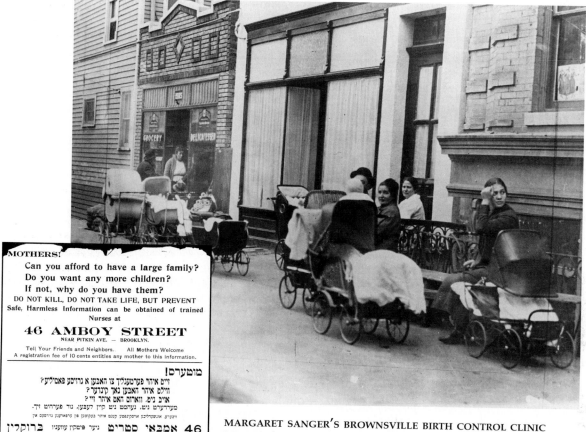

MARGARET SANGER'S BROWNSVILLE BIRTH CONTROL CLINIC
Margaret Sanger opened the first birth control clinic in the United States in the Brownsville section of Brooklyn in 1916. During the nine days it operated before police shut it down, more than four hundred women visited the clinic. Here they are shown waiting patiently in line with their baby carriages. Sanger published her flyers in English, Yiddish, and Italian, and her clinic attracted immigrant women, proving that Italian Catholics and Russian Jews wanted birth control information as much as their middle- and upper-class Protestant counterparts.
Sophia Smith Collection.

dawned, women still could not vote in most states. Increasingly, however, woman suffrage had become an international movement. In Great Britain, Emmeline Pankhurst and her daughters Cristabel and Sylvia promoted a militant new suffragism. They seized the spotlight in a series of marches, mass meetings, and acts of civil disobedience, which sometimes escalated to include violence, riots, and arson. The activism of the British suffragists sparked new action in the United States, where progress toward full suffrage had moved slowly. After a victory in Washington state in 1910, suffragists experienced a stinging defeat in California in 1911. Kansas, Oregon, and Arizona joined the suf-

frage column in 1912, evidence that suffragists were perfecting their lobbying techniques. Yet some suffragists, attracted to the flamboyance of the British movement, urged more direct action. Alice Paul, a Quaker social worker who had visited England and participated in suffrage activism there, returned to the United States in 1910 at a time when suffrage was in the doldrums. Paul infused new life into the movement, planning the mass march on the eve of Wilson's inauguration and lobbying for a federal amendment to give women the vote. But Paul's dramatic tactics alienated many in the National American Woman Suffrage Association. In 1914, she broke with the group and continued her work

The Issue of Child Labor

*B*y the early years of the twentieth century, as many as four million children between the ages of ten and fifteen toiled long hours at low pay. They could be found in the depths of coal mines, in the searing heat of glass factories, in canneries and textile mills, in cotton fields —wherever employers coveted small size and nimble fingers. Progressive reformers, often called the "child savers," attempted to curb exploitation of children under the age of fourteen in sweatshops, mines, and mills across America. But they ran into solid opposition not only from employers, who had a vested interest in the cheap labor children performed, but also from parents, who counted on the meager wages of their children. For them the issue was at once economic and cultural. In rural America, no one had questioned a parent's right to put children to hard tasks in the fields and on the farm. Similarly, immigrants from rural Italy, Germany, or Russia could see no harm in putting children to work in factories or sweatshops in America's industrial cities and viewed it as the parents' prerogative to command their children's wages. Progressives found themselves up against stiff opposition.

Not just immigrants but old-stock Americans relied on child labor, particularly in the South, where entire families of poor whites left the land to work side by side in the textile mills. On May 22, 1914, a South Carolina mill owner testified before the House of Representatives Committee on Labor on why child labor was necessary in the South.

Document 1. Testimony from Lewis W. Parker

It is not possible for a man who has been working on a farm who is an adult—after the age of 21 years, for instance—to become a skilled employee in a cotton mill. His fingers are knotted and gnarled; he is slow in action, whereas activity is required in working in the cotton mills. Therefore, as a matter of necessity, the adult of the family had to come to the cotton mill as an unskilled employee, and it was the children of the family who became the skilled employees in the cotton mills. For that reason it was the children who had to support the families for the time being. I have seen instances in which a child of 12 years of age, working in the cotton mills, is earning one and one-half times as much as his father of 40 or 50 years of age.

*P*rogressives countered these arguments with poignant testimony about the plight of young workers and the failure of the states to enforce the law. At the same 1914 committee hearings, reformer Florence Kelley described her experiences investigating child labor practices in Illinois.

Document 2. Florence Kelley Testimony before the Congressional Committee on Labor, 1914

. . . I was at one time chief inspector of factories and workshops in the State of Illinois. I found great numbers of children working at night—working illegally. The superintendent of a glass-bottle company told me himself that this occurred once when he was rushed with work: A widow had come to him bringing two little boys, one still in kilts [baby skirts worn by small boys] and one in knee breeches. She told him that their father had just been killed on the railroad, and that they were penniless; and she wanted the older little boy to go to work in the glassworks, where he would get 40 cents a day. The superintendent was pressed for boys, and said, "I won't take the bigger fellow alone, but if you will take the baby back home and put him into knee pants, and then bring them both back in trousers, I will take them both." She did so, and those two little fellows, aged 9 and 7 years, began their work on the night shift.

*D*espite heavy odds against them, progressives achieved victory in 1916 when the National Child Labor Committee finally convinced Congress and President Woodrow Wilson to enact the Keating-Owen Bill forbidding the regular employment of children under sixteen.

The child savers' victory proved short-lived, however. Powerful business interests and a Supreme Court sympathetic to their views took advantage of the waning fervor for reform and in 1918 in Hammer v. Dagenhart struck down the child labor law on the grounds that Congress could not regulate manufacturing within states. This decision made it legal for the chief plaintiff in the case, Roland Dagenhart, to continue having his young sons work in a North Carolina cotton mill. It also protected the boys' "constitutional right" to continue to work at the mill, where they put in twelve-hour days and sometimes worked night shifts as well.

Ironically, one of the plaintiffs in the Dagenhart case had a very negative view of its outcome. In 1923, reporter Lowell Mellett tracked down Reuben Dagenhart, one of the boys in whose favor the Supreme Court had ruled six years earlier. In an article published in Labor in November 1923, Mellett recounted his meeting with Dagenhart.

DOCUMENT 3. Lowell Mellett Interview with Reuben Dagenhart.

I found him at his home in Charlotte. He is about the size of the office boy—weighs 105 pounds, he told me. But he is a married man with a child. He is 20 years old.

"What benefit," I asked him, "did you get out of the suit which you won in the United States Supreme Court?"

"You mean the suit the Fidelity Manufacturing Company won? (It was the Fidelity Company for which the Dagenharts were working.) I don't see that I got any benefit. I guess I'd been alot better off if they hadn't won it. . . .

"Look at me! A hundred and five pounds, a grown man and no education. I may be mistaken, but I think the years I've put in in the cotton mills have stunted my growth. They kept me from getting any schooling. I had to stop school after the third

grade and now I need the education I didn't get."

"How was your growth stunted?"

"I don't know—the dust and the lint, maybe. But from 12 years old on, I was working 12 hours a day—from 6 in the morning till 7 at night, with time out for meals. And sometimes I worked nights besides. Lifting a hundred pounds and I only weighed 65 pounds myself."

He explained that he and his sister worked together, "on section," spinning. They each made about a dollar a day, though later he worked up to where he could make $2. His father made $15 a week and infant John, at the time the suit was brought, was making close to $1 a day.

"Just what did you and John get out of that suit, then?"

"Why, we got some automobile rides when them big lawyers from the North was down here. Oh, yes, and they brought both of us a coca-cola! That's all we got out of it."

"What did you tell the judge when you were in court?"

"Oh, John and me never was in court! Just Paw was there. John and me was just little kids in short pants. I guess we wouldn't have looked like much in court. We were working in the mill while the case was going on. But Paw went up to Washington."

Reuben hasn't been to school, but his mind has not been idle.

"It would have been a good thing for all the kids in this state if that law they passed had been kept. . . . I know one thing. I ain't going to let them put my kid sister in the mill. . . . She's only 15 and she's crippled and I bet I stop that!"

Despite the efforts of committed reformers, child labor persisted into the 1920s, immune from federal law and condoned by states reluctant to exercise their authority against the force of private money and growing public indifference.

Documents 1 and 2. House of Representatives Hearings before the Committee on Labor (1914), 93, 35-36.

Document 3. *Labor* (November 17, 1923).

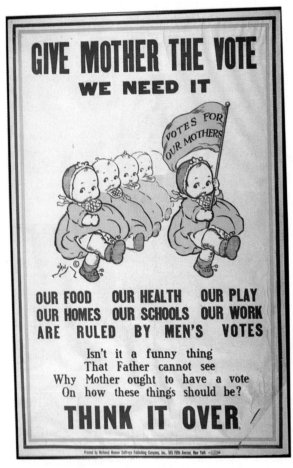

WOMAN SUFFRAGE

The campaign for woman suffrage in its final phase in the 1910s argued that women needed the vote to fulfill their domestic duties. This 1916 poster echoed this sentiment, arguing that women as mothers needed the vote to protect their children. The more militant National Woman's Party, led by Alice Paul, insisted that women as women, not simply as housewives or mothers, deserved the vote.

Collection of Janice L. and David J. Frent.

through the Congressional Union for Woman Suffrage, which provided a base from which to press for a national strategy to achieve the vote. In 1916, she founded the militant National Woman's Party (NWP), which became the radical voice of the suffrage movement, advocating direct action and civil disobedience. Paul and her followers rejected the state-by-state strategy of the NAWSA and continued to press for a constitutional suffrage amendment, called by its supporters the Susan B. Anthony amendment, to provide woman suffrage.

The NAWSA, spurred by the actions of Paul and her followers, gained new direction when Carrie Chapman Catt became president in 1915. Catt revitalized the organization with a carefully crafted "winning plan" designed to achieve suffrage in six years. While Paul and her Woman's Party held a six-month vigil outside the White House with banners that read "Mr. Wilson, What Will You Do for Woman Suffrage?" Catt led a carefully disciplined and centrally directed effort that worked on several levels. In states where women already voted, Catt lobbied for a federal amendment. Where state referenda could be won, she launched campaigns to maintain the suffrage momentum. Catt's strategy was to "keep so much 'suffrage noise' going all over the country that neither the enemy [n]or friends [of suffrage] will discover where the real battle is." Catt's "winning plan" worked effectively, taking only four years instead of the six Catt had predicted.

World War I would provide the final impetus for woman suffrage. Paul and the NWP refused to work for the war and insisted that "democracy should begin at home." Arrested and jailed, they used hunger strikes to publicize their cause. For her part, Catt seized the mantle of patriotism, insisting that there was no conflict between fighting for suffrage and aiding the war effort. It would take several more years before the Nineteenth Amendment became part of the U.S. Constitution, but when it was ratified in August 1920, the victory belonged both to Catt and to Paul, for without the militancy of the Woman's Party, the NAWSA would not have seemed so moderate and respectable.

Women were not alone in being left out of progressive advances. African Americans fared even worse. The Progressive Era witnessed the systematic disfranchisement of black voters and the enactment of statutes, known as "Jim Crow" laws, to segregate public facilities. (The name "Jim Crow" derived from a character in a popular minstrel song.) It was one of the great ironies of progressivism that, as it was practiced south of the Mason-Dixon line, it preached disfranchisement of black voters as a "reform." During the bitter electoral fights that had pitted Populists against Democrats in the 1890s, the charge was often made that the party of white supremacy held its power only by the votes of the black belt. To guard against electoral fraud, where, it was alleged, African American votes were purchased by money or threats of coercion, southern progressives proposed to "reform" the electoral system by eliminating the black vote entirely. Southern states, beginning in 1890 with Mississippi, sought to curtail the African American vote through devices like the poll tax (a fee required to vote) and the literacy test. Not coincidentally, these measures also denied access to poor, illiterate whites likely to vote against the reigning Democrats and for the Populist Party. But the racist intention of southern voting legislation became clear when states resorted to such transparent ruses as the "grandfather clause," a legal device that allowed anyone to vote whose grandparent had cast a ballot, thus including virtually any southern white and excluding every black voter, whose grandparent had most likely been a slave.

It was one of the great ironies of progressivism that, as it was practiced south of the Mason-Dixon line, it preached the disfranchisement of black voters as a "reform."

The rise of the railroad precipitated segregation in the South where it had rarely existed, at least on paper, before. Blacks found themselves increasingly relegated to separate "Jim Crow" train coaches, even when they paid a first-class fare. Soon separate waiting rooms, separate bathrooms, and separate dining facilities sprang up across the South. In courtrooms in the state of Mississippi, blacks were even required to swear on a separate Bible.

In the face of this growing repression, Booker T. Washington, the preeminent black leader of the day, urged caution and restraint. A former slave, Washington founded the Tuskegee Institute in Alabama to teach vocational skills to African Americans. Washington emphasized education and economic progress for his race and urged African Americans to put aside issues of political and social equality. In an 1895 speech in Atlanta, which came to be known as the "Atlanta Compromise," he stated, "In all things that are purely social we can be as separate as the fingers, yet one as the hand in all things essential to mutual progress." Washington presided over an alliance of northern philanthropists and white leaders of the New South in which blacks agreed to segregation and disfranchisement in return for the promise of a share in economic growth. His accommodationist policy appealed to whites in all sections, who elevated Washington to the role of national spokesman for African Americans.

The year after Washington proclaimed the Atlanta Compromise, the Supreme Court upheld the legality of racial segregation, affirming in *Plessy v. Ferguson* the constitutionality of the doctrine of "separate but equal." Blacks could be segregated in separate facilities, from schools to rest rooms, as long as the facilities were "equal." In actuality, facilities rarely were equal. In the North, where the growing tide of new immigrants led to a clamor for restrictive legislation, support for African American rights found few advocates. Increasingly, the doctrine of "white supremacy" found support in all sections of the country.

When Theodore Roosevelt invited Booker T. Washington to dine at the White House in 1901, a storm of racist criticism erupted. One southern editor fumed that the White House "had been painted black." But Roosevelt's racist detractors missed the point. Roosevelt summoned Washington to talk politics and patronage, not African American rights. Busy tearing apart Mark Hanna's Republican machine and creating his own, Roosevelt wanted Washington's counsel in selecting black Republicans for party posts in the South. The president remained more interested in his own political fortunes than in those of African Americans. His attitude was obvious in the Brownsville incident in 1906, when he dishonorably discharged three companies of black soldiers because he believed that they were shielding the murderer of a white saloonkeeper who had been killed in a shoot-out in the Texas town.

When Woodrow Wilson came to power, he brought with him southern attitudes toward race and racial segregation. Despite the support of prominent African American intellectuals such as William Monroe Trotter and W. E. B. Du Bois, Wilson showed no compunction in allowing his postmaster general to segregate facilities, including drinking fountains and rest rooms, in the nation's capital. When critics attacked the policy, Wilson insisted that segregation was "in the interest of the Negro."

Faced with intolerance and open persecution, educated blacks in the North rebelled against the conservative leadership of Booker T. Washington. Harvard graduate W. E. B. Du Bois challenged Washington's political power. In *The Souls of Black Folk* (1903), he attacked the "Tuskegee Machine," comparing Washington to a political boss and charging that he used his influence to silence his critics and reward his followers. Du Bois founded the Niagara movement in 1905, calling for univer-

EQUALITY

DINNER GIVEN AT THE WHITE HOUSE BY PRESIDENT ROOSEVELT TO BOOKER T. WASHINGTON, OCTOBER 17th, 1901

BOOKER T. WASHINGTON AND THEODORE ROOSEVELT DINE AT THE WHITE HOUSE
When Theodore Roosevelt invited Booker T. Washington to the White House in 1901, he stirred up a hornet's nest of controversy that continued into the election of 1904. Here in a Republican campaign piece, the meeting is portrayed positively, with TR and Washington pictured under a portrait of Abraham Lincoln, signaling the party's historic commitment to African Americans. Democrats portrayed the meeting in a very different light, their campaign buttons pictured Washington with darker skin and implied that Roosevelt favored "race mingling."
Collection of Janice L. and David J. Frent.

sal suffrage, civil rights, and leadership by a black intellectual elite. In 1909, the Niagara movement helped found the National Association for the Advancement of Colored People (NAACP), a coalition of blacks and whites that sought legal and political rights for African Americans. Like many progressive reform coalitions, the NAACP contained a diverse group—social workers, socialists, and black intellectuals. In the decades that followed, the NAACP came to represent the future for African Americans, while Booker T. Washington, who died in 1915, represented the past.

Conclusion: Progressivism in Perspective

The limitations of progressive reform should not obscure its very real achievements. The progressive movement brought significant gains as government moved away from laissez-faire and social Darwinism to embrace a more active role designed to bring about social justice and to achieve a better balance between business and government. Progressivism contained many paradoxes. A diverse coalition of individuals and interests, the progressive movement began at the grass roots but left as its legacy a stronger presidency and unprecedented federal involvement in the economy and social welfare. A movement that believed in social justice, progressivism often promoted social control. And while progressives called for greater democracy, they worshiped experts and efficiency. Many threads made up this complex reform movement. But whatever

its inconsistencies, progressivism attempted to deal with the problems posed by urban industrialism and, by increasing the power of the presidency and expanding the power of the government, helped to launch the liberal state into the twentieth century. War on a global scale would provide progressivism with yet another challenge even before it had completed its ambitious agenda.

CHRONOLOGY

1889 Jane Addams opens Hull House in Chicago.

1895 Booker T. Washington enunciates "Atlanta Compromise," accepting segregation in return for economic opportunity.

Anti-Saloon League founded by Protestant clergy.

1896 U.S. Supreme Court upholds doctrine of "separate but equal" in *Plessy v. Ferguson*.

1900 Socialist Party founded with Eugene V. Debs as standard-bearer.

1901 Thomas Lofton Johnson elected mayor of Cleveland, Ohio.

Robert M. La Follette elected governor of Wisconsin.

Theodore Roosevelt succeeds to presidency following assassination of William McKinley.

Roosevelt intervenes in anthracite coal strike to bring labor and management to bargaining table.

Roosevelt initiates investigation of Northern Securities Company for antitrust violations.

1902 Dispute between United States and Germany over Venezuelan debt ends in arbitration.

Lincoln Steffens's muckraking series "The Shame of the Cities" begins to run in *McClure's Magazine*.

U.S. government files antitrust suit against Northern Securities Company.

1903 U.S.-backed uprising in Panama leads to Panamanian independence and to U.S. acquisition of rights to build canal.

In *The Souls of Black Folk*, W. E. B. Du Bois challenges Booker T. Washington.

Women's Trade Union League (WTUL) founded.

1904 Theodore Roosevelt wins presidential election in landslide.

1905 Industrial Workers of the World (IWW) founded by Big Bill Haywood.

1906 Pure Food and Drug Act and Meat Inspection legislation passed after publicity generated by Upton Sinclair's muckraking novel *The Jungle*.

Robert M. La Follette elected U.S. senator.

Congress passes Hepburn Act to regulate railroads and strengthen Interstate Commerce Commission.

Roosevelt receives Nobel Peace Prize for his role in mediating Russo-Japanese War.

1907 Social gospel minister Walter Rauschenbusch publishes *Christianity and the Social Crisis*.

Panic on Wall Street. J. P. Morgan's U.S. Steel acquires Tennessee Coal and Iron Company.

Roosevelt dispatches navy's Great White Fleet on world cruise to display U.S. naval power.

1908 U.S. Supreme Court upholds Oregon state law limiting women's working hours to ten a day (*Muller v. Oregon*).

William Howard Taft elected president to succeed Theodore Roosevelt.

1909 "Uprising of twenty thousand" occurs in New York City, a shirtwaist makers' strike backed by WTUL.

National Association for the Advancement of Colored People (NAACP) formed.

President Taft defends Payne-Aldrich tariff.

1911 Triangle fire in New York City kills 146 workers.

1912 President Taft sends marines into Nicaragua and Santo Domingo.

Theodore Roosevelt runs for president on Progressive Bull Moose Party ticket after losing Republican nomination to incumbent President William Howard Taft.

Democrat Woodrow Wilson elected president, defeating Taft and Theodore Roosevelt.

1913 Federal Reserve Act reforms nation's banking system by providing twelve regional banks supervised by a Federal Reserve Board.

Woodrow Wilson signs legislation establishing Federal Trade Commission (FTC).

1914 Congress passes Clayton Antitrust Act.

Walter Lippmann publishes *Drift and Mastery*, a statement of the progressive philosophy.

1915 Carrie Chapman Catt takes over leadership of national woman suffrage movement.

1916 Alice Paul launches National Woman's Party.

Margaret Sanger opens first birth control clinic, in Brooklyn, New York.

BIBLIOGRAPHY

GENERAL WORKS

John Whiteclay Chambers II, *The Tyranny of Change: America in the Progressive Era, 1900–1917* (2nd ed., 1992).

Allen F. Davis, *Spearheads for Reform: The Social Settlements and the Progressive Movement, 1890–1914* (1967).

Alan Dawley, *Struggles for Justice: Social Responsibility and the Liberal State* (1991).

Vincent P. DeSantis, *The Shaping of Modern America, 1877–1920* (2nd ed., 1989).

Arthur Ekrich, *Progressivism in America* (1974).

Sara M. Evans, *Born for Liberty: A History of Women in America* (1989).

Harold U. Faulkner, *Politics, Reform, and Expansion, 1890–1900* (1959).

Samuel P. Hays, *The Response to Industrialism, 1885–1914* (1957).

Richard Hofstadter, *The Age of Reform* (1955).

Linda K. Kerber, Alice Kessler-Harris, and Katherine Kish Sklar, *U.S. History as Women's History* (1995).

Gabriel Kolko, *The Triumph of Conservatism* (1963).

Bruce Kuklick, *The Rise of American Philosophy* (1977).

Arthur Mann, ed., *The Progressive Era* (1975).

George Mowry, *The Era of Theodore Roosevelt* (1958).

William L. O'Neill, *The Progressive Years: America Comes of Age* (1975).

Nell Irvin Painter, *Standing at Armageddon: The United States, 1877–1919* (1987).

Alan Trachtenberg, *The Incorporation of America: Culture and Society in the Gilded Age* (1982).

James Weinstein, *The Corporate Ideal in the Liberal State, 1900–1918* (1969).

Robert H. Wiebe, *The Search for Order, 1877–1920* (1967).

GRASSROOTS PROGRESSIVISM

Jane Addams, *Twenty Years at Hull-House* (1910).

Joyce Antler, *Lucy Sprague Mitchell* (1987).

Karen J. Blair, *The Clubwoman as Feminist: True Womanhood Redefined, 1868–1914* (1980).

Steven Boyer, *Urban Masses and Moral Order in America, 1820–1920* (1978).

Kathleen Brady, *Ida Tarbell: Portrait of a Muckraker* (1984).

Robert Bremmer, *From the Depths: The Discovery of Poverty in the United States* (1956).

John D. Buenker, *Urban Liberalism and Progressive Reform* (1973).

Mina Carson, *Settlement Folk: Social Thought and the American Settlement Movement, 1885–1930* (1990).

Robert Cross, *The Church in the City* (1958).

Robert M. Crunden, *Ministers of Reform: The Progressive Achievement in American Civilization, 1889–1920* (1982).

Allen F. Davis, *American Heroine: The Life and Legend of Jane Addams* (1973).

Allen F. Davis and Mary Lynn McCree, *Eighty Years at Hull-House* (1969).

Nancy Schrom Dye, *As Equals and as Sisters: Feminism, Unionism, and the Women's Trade Union League of New York* (1980).

John H. Ehrenreich, *The Altruistic Imagination: A History of Social Work and Social Policy in the United States* (1985).

Ellen Fitzpatrick, *Endless Crusade: Women, Social Scientists, and Progressive Reform* (1990).

Philip S. Foner, *Women and the American Labor Movement.* vol. 1, *From Colonial Times to the Eve of World War I* (1979).

Lynn D. Gordon, *Gender and Higher Education in the Progressive Era* (1989).

Samuel Haber, *Efficiency and Uplift: Scientific Management in the Progressive Era, 1899–1920* (1964).

Alice Kessler Harris, *Out to Work: A History of Wage Earning Women in the United States* (1982).

Helen Lefkowitz Horowitz, *Culture and City: Cultural Philanthropy in Chicago from the 1880s to 1917* (1976).

Hull-House Maps and Papers (1895; reprint, 1970).

Michael B. Katz, *In the Shadow of the Poorhouse: A Social History of Welfare in America* (1986).

Seth Koven and Sonya Michel, eds., *Mothers of a New World: Maternalist Politics and the Origins of the Welfare State* (1993).

Christopher Lasch, *The Social Thought of Jane Addams* (1965).

William Leach, *True Love and Perfect Union: The Feminist Reform of Sex and Society* (1980).

James Lieby, *A History of Social Work in the United States* (1978).

Walter Lippmann, *Drift and Mastery* (1914).

Rivka Lissak, *Pluralism and Progressives: Hull House and the New Immigrants, 1890–1919* (1989).

Roy M. Lubove, *The Progressives and the Slums* (1962).

Henry F. May, *Protestant Churches and Industrial America* (1949).

Kathleen McCarth, ed., *Lady Bountiful Revisited: Women, Philanthropy, and Power* (1990).

David Montgomery, *Workers' Control in America* (1979).

Robyn Muncy, *Creating a Female Dominion in American Reform* (1991).

David Musto, *American Disease: Origins of Narcotic Control* (expanded ed., 1987).

Donald Nelson, *Frederick W. Taylor and the Rise of Scientific Management* (1980).

Charles Parkhurst, *Our Fight with Tammany* (1895).

Peggy Pascoe, *Relations of Rescue: The Search for Female Moral Authority in the American West* (1990).

Elizabeth Payne, *Reform, Labor, and Feminism: Margaret Dreier Robins and the Women's Trade Union League* (1988).

David Pivar, *The Purity Crusade: Sexual Morality and Social Control* (1973).

Jean B. Quandt, *The Social Thought of Progressive Intellectuals* (1970).

Ruth Rosen, *The Lost Sisterhood: Prostitutes in America* (1984).

Rosalind Rosenberg, *Beyond Separate Spheres: The Intellectual Roots of Modern Feminism* (1982).

John Rury, *The Cultural Moment: The New Politics, the New Woman, the New Psychology, the New Art, and the New Theatre in America* (1991).

Anne Firor Scott, *Natural Allies: Women's Associations in American History* (1991).

Peter R. Shergold, *Working Class Life: The "American Standard" in Comparative Perspective, 1899–1913* (1982).

Kathryn Kish Sklar, *Florence Kelley and the Nation's Work: The Rise of Women's Political Culture, 1830–1900* (1995).

Theda Skocpol, *Protecting Soldiers and Mothers* (1992).

Barbara Miller Solomon, *In the Company of Educated Women* (1985).

Sharon Hartman Strom, *Beyond the Typewriter: Gender, Class, and the Origins of Modern American Office Work, 1900–1930* (1992).

Meredith Tax, *The Rising of the Women* (1980).

Barbara Mayer Wertheimer, *We Were There: The Story of Working Women in America* (1977).

Harold S. Wilson, *McClure's Magazine and the Muckrakers* (1970).

R. Jackson Wilson, *Reform, Crisis, and Confusion, 1900–1929* (1970).

LOCAL AND STATE REFORM

Melvin Holli, *Reform in Detroit: Hazen S. Pingree and Urban Politics* (1969).

William A. Link, *The Paradox of Southern Progressivism, 1880–1930* (1992).

Carl Lorenz, *Tom L. Johnson, Mayor of Cleveland* (1911).

Richard L. McCormick, *From Realignment to Reform: Political Change in New York State* (1981).

George Mowry, *The California Progressives* (1951).

Spencer Olin Jr., *California's Prodigal Sons: Hiram Johnson and the Progressives, 1911–1917* (1968).

Judith Sealander, *Grand Plans: Business Progressivism and Social Change in Ohio's Miami Valley, 1890–1919* (1988).

David P. Thelen, *The New Citizenship: Origins of Progressivism in Wisconsin, 1885–1900* (1972).

David P. Thelen, *Robert M. La Follette and the Insurgent Spirit* (1985).

C. Vann Woodward, *The Origins of the New South* (1951).

James Wright, *The Progressive Yankees* (1987).

PROGRESSIVISM AND NATIONAL POLITICS

Donald E. Anderson, *William Howard Taft* (1973).

Judith Icke Anderson, *William Howard Taft: An Intimate History* (1981).

Howard K. Beale, *Theodore Roosevelt and the Rise of America to World Power* (1956).

John Morton Blum, *Woodrow Wilson and the Politics of Morality* (1956).

John Morton Blum, *The Republican Roosevelt* (2nd ed., 1977).

John D. Buenker, *Urban Liberalism and Progressive Reform* (1973).

Ron Chernow, *The House of Morgan* (1990).

Ron Chernow, *The Warburgs: The Twentieth Century Odyssey of a Remarkable Jewish Family* (1993).

Lewis L. Gould, *Reform and Regulation: American Politics from Roosevelt to Wilson* (2nd ed., 1986).

Lewis L. Gould, *The Presidency of Theodore Roosevelt* (1991).

Otis Graham Jr., *The Great Campaigns: Reform and War in America, 1900–1929* (1971).

William H. Harbaugh, *The Life and Times of Theodore Roosevelt* (rev. ed., 1982).

Samuel P. Hays, *Conservation and the Gospel of Efficiency* (1959).

James Kloppenberg, *Uncertain Victory: Social Democracy and Progressivism in European and American Thought, 1870–1920* (1986).

Arthur S. Link, *Woodrow Wilson*, 5 vols. (1947–1965).

Arthur S. Link, *Woodrow Wilson: Revolution, War, and Power* (1979).

Richard L. McCormick, *The Party Period and Public Policy* (1986).

James L. Penick Jr., *Progressive Politics and Conservation: The Ballinger-Pinchot Affair* (1968).

Emily S. Rosenberg, *Spreading the American Dream: American Economic and Cultural Expansion, 1890–1945* (1982).

Lincoln Steffens, *The Autobiography of Lincoln Steffens*, vols. 1 and 2 (1931).

Phillipa Strum, *Louis D. Brandeis* (1984).

David P. Thelen, *Robert M. La Follette and the Insurgent Spirit* (2nd ed., 1985).

Craig West, *Banking Reform and the Federal Reserve* (1977).

William Appleman Williams, *The Tragedy of American Diplomacy* (1959).

Clarence E. Wunderlin Jr., *Visions of a New Industrial Order: Social Science and Labor Theory in America's Progressive Era* (1992).

James Harvey Young, *Securing the Federal Food and Drug Act of 1906* (1989).

RADICAL ALTERNATIVES

Mary Jo Buhl, *Women and American Socialism, 1870–1920* (1981).

Ellen Chesler, *Woman of Valor: Margaret Sanger and the Birth Control Movement in America* (1993).

John Diggins, *The American Left in the Twentieth Century* (1973).

Melvyn Dubofsky, *"Big Bill" Haywood* (1987).

Melvyn Dubofsky, *We Shall Be All: A History of the Industrial Workers of the World* (2nd ed., 1988).

Leslie Fishbein, *Rebels in Bohemia: The Radicals of the Masses, 1911–1917* (1982).

David J. Goldberg, *A Tale of Three Cities: Labor Organization and Protest in Paterson, Passaic, and Lawrence, 1916–1921* (1988).

Linda Gordon, *Woman's Body, Woman's Right* (1977).

J. Morgan Kousser, *The Shaping of Southern Politics* (1974).

Neil R. McMillen, *Dark Journey: Black Mississippians in the Age of Jim Crow* (1989).

Bruno Ramirez, *When Workers Fight: The Politics of Industrial Relations in the Progressive Era, 1898–1916* (1978).

Salvatore Salerno, *Red November, Black November: Culture and Community in the Industrial Workers of the World* (1989).

Nick Salvatore, *Eugene V. Debs: Citizen and Socialist* (1982).

L. Glen Seretan, *Daniel DeLeon: The Odyssey of an American Marxist* (1979).

David Shannon, *The Socialist Party* (1955).

Elliott Shore, *Talkin' Socialism* (1988).

Ann Huber Tripp, *The IWW and the Paterson Silk Strike of 1913* (1987).

Alice Wexler, *Emma Goldman: An Intimate Life* (1984).

RACE RELATIONS AND WOMAN SUFFRAGE

Eleanor Flexner, *Century of Struggle: The Women's Rights Movement in the United States* (1959).

Kevin K. Gaines, *Uplifting the Race, Black Leadership, Politics, and Culture in the Twentieth Century* (1996).

Louis R. Harlan, *Separate and Unequal: Public School Campaigns and Racism in the Southern Seaboard States, 1900–1915* (1968).

Louis R. Harlan, *Booker T. Washington: The Making of a Black Leader, 1856–1901* (1972).

Louis R. Harlan, *Booker T. Washington: The Wizard of Tuskegee, 1901–1915* (1983).

Charles F. Kellogg, *NAACP: A History of the National Association for the Advancement of Colored People, 1909–1920* (1967).

Jack Temple Kirby, *Darkness at the Dawning: Race and Reform in the Progressive South* (1972).

Ann J. Lane, *The Brownsville Affair: National Crisis and Black Reaction* (1971).

Christine Lunardini, *From Equal Suffrage to Equal Rights: Alice Paul and the National Woman's Party, 1910–1928* (1986).

Mary E. Odem, *Delinquent Daughters, Protecting and Policing Adolescent Sexuality in the United States, 1885–1920* (1995).

Elliot M. Rudwick, *W. E. B. Du Bois* (1968).

Donald Spivey, *Schooling for the New Slavery: Black Industrial Education, 1868–1915* (1978).

Cheryl A. Wall, *Women of the Harlem Renaissance* (1995).

Booker T. Washington, *Up from Slavery* (1901).

John D. Weaver, *The Brownsville Raid* (1970).

Joel Williamson, *The Crucible of Race* (1984).

C. Vann Woodward, *The Strange Career of Jim Crow* (1955).

WAR

Which Bird?

As viewed by Life

LIFE MAGAZINE COVER

This 1914 magazine cover provides a vivid visual demonstration of the American press's very early tendency to support U.S. entry into World War I. The image makes no bones about the way a viewer should answer the question posed below it. The American eagle in the center, wings spread and screaming for action, dominates the picture and makes the dove holding an olive branch appear pathetically weak. Considering the stereotyped knife, gun, and bomb-wielding foreigners lurking in the background, the sailor has understandably turned toward the eagle for inspiration to intervene in the British lion's battle against the enemies of democracy.

Picture Research Archives and Consultants.

THE UNITED STATES AND THE "GREAT WAR"

22

1914–1920

IN AUGUST 1914, after more than forty years of peace, Europe exploded in war. The booming of the great guns could be heard in Paris and even in London when conditions were right. Washington, D.C., was three thousand miles from the tragedy, but President Woodrow Wilson felt it deeply nevertheless. When the news arrived that war had broken out, the American progressive president cried: "What a pathetic thing to have this come just as we were so full of hope!" Dazed by the suddenness of events and weighed down by the thought of the renewal of barbarism, he paced the corridors of the White House. Wilson also shouldered a crushing personal burden. His beloved wife, Ellen, lay dying. He received war reports while sitting at her bedside, holding her hand. When she died on August 6, 1914, Wilson was devastated. According to the White House physician, he was a "man with his heart torn out."

Although nearly numb with grief, Wilson formulated a national policy regarding the war in Europe. He never had any doubt that the only possible course was absolute neutrality. There were compelling reasons for not intervening. Even though his sympathies lay with Great Britain and France, Wilson concluded that blame for the war did not lie entirely with Germany. Moreover, he believed that the United States had no vital stake in the outcome of the war. It was a remote European contest, and nothing required that the United States give up its safety and security. Wilson agreed with the American ambassador in London, who declared, "Again and ever I thank heaven for the Atlantic Ocean." In addition, the United States was a nation of immigrants, millions of whom had only recently come from countries that were now at war. As Wilson told the German ambassador, "We definitely have to be neutral, since otherwise our mixed populations would wage war on each other."

There was another reason to stay out of the European struggle. On August 19, 1914, Wilson explained to the American people the international good that could come from strict neutrality. As a great neutral power, he said, the United States could offer "impartial mediation" and show the world the way to reconciliation and a healing peace. Because support for one side or the other would wreck this opportunity for service, Wilson told the American people that they must remain "impartial in thought as well as action." If they could curb their emotions and show the "true spirit of neutrality, which is the spirit of impartiality and fairness and friendliness to all concerned," then, Wilson declared, Americans could help him persuade the warring nations to lay down their arms in exchange for a just peace.

Like Wilson, the great majority of the American people were pro-peace and antiwar. They showed almost no sympathy for intervention. The nation wrapped itself in the concept of neutrality and tried to go about its business. If attention strayed outside the country, it fixed on the grand opening of the Panama Canal on August 15, 1914. By the beginning of 1915, newspaper coverage of the war had shrunk to a few columns. Few Americans felt the least worry over any prospect of involvement in the war in Europe. So secure and distant did Congress feel that in 1915 the House came within a few votes of slashing the Navy Department's moderate program for battleship construction.

But U.S. citizens learned that the Atlantic was no moat. Trade and travel webbed the modern world. After nearly three years of trying to steer a neutral course, Woodrow Wilson went before Congress on April 2, 1917, to ask for a declaration of war against Germany. He attempted to square America's entrance with his original progressive hopes for neutrality. America's military might would end the carnage of war, he said. And America's goodness and disinterestedness would ensure a just peace. The country's participation would make the First World War the war to end wars, the war "to make the world safe for democracy."

Called the "Great War," the First World War was great in its destructive power and in its transformative influence. It defined an era of revolutionary upheaval, cataclysmic conflict, and shifts in the balance of power that threatened the very foundations of the international order. The fighting that raged in Europe was the most savage the world had ever witnessed. War stretched across continents, and nations measured their casualties in the millions. When peace arrived in 1919, both the victors and the vanquished were decimated and exhausted.

America's experience was different, however. At home, war and prosperity went hand in hand. But America paid a price as citizens and the government cracked down on dissent and demanded conformity. "Over There," as Americans called the war theater in Europe, the nation lost 112,000 soldiers, but their performance on the battlefields affected the outcome of the war. In the peace negotiations that followed the armistice, Woodrow Wilson played a principal role, but the results did not confirm Wilson's impossible vision of himself as personal savior of the world. He had promised more than anyone could deliver, and the nation turned bitter and disillusioned.

In December 1919, Wilson's personal friend and chief foreign policy adviser, Colonel Edward House, summarized the nation's ordeal: "We came near doing a great thing in a great way, but Fate ordained otherwise and while something may still be done, it will be done in a small way and in a way full of humiliation for those who wished to see the United States lead in a new world movement."

Woodrow Wilson and the World

Shortly after winning election to the presidency in 1912, Woodrow Wilson confided to a friend: "It would be an irony of fate if my administration had to deal chiefly with foreign affairs." Indeed, Wilson had based his life and career on local attachments. He had never shown an interest in venturing far from where he was born and worked and had traveled abroad only on brief vacations. As president of Princeton University and then governor of New Jersey, his career kept him rooted in domestic concerns. During his campaign for the presidency, Wilson had argued passionately for domestic reform, referring only rarely to foreign affairs.

But Wilson could not avoid the world. The Wilsonian foreign policy that emerged in 1913–1914 reflected his conviction that the United States should be a moral example in international affairs. He championed the principles of liberal democracy. Those principles included respect for human rights and the rule of law, the right of self-determination to ensure that people could choose their own governments and leaders, and the reduction of tariffs that would impede trade and cause international conflict. Support for these principles meant opposing imperialism, large armed forces, and trade barriers. "We dare not turn from the principle that morality and not expediency is the thing that must guide us," Wilson announced loftily, "and that we will never condone iniquity because it is most convenient to do so."

A rising tide of militarism, nationalism, and violence severely tested Wilson's liberal principles. His first challenge arose in the Western Hemisphere, where according to the Monroe Doctrine the United States had special responsibilities and power. Reflecting that perspective, Wilson found the urge to intervene irresistible. When war broke out in Europe in 1914, however, Wilson claimed no such right to intervene. Instead, he offered his services as a peace broker. Fervently, Wilson sought acceptance of a "peace without victory," but the prevailing conviction among the warring nations that honor required defeat of the enemy ruled out compromise.

It was only a matter of time before the escalating fight caused incidents that wounded America's own interests and sense of honor and drew the nation into the tragic conflict.

Taming the Americas

When Wilson came to office, he sought to distinguish his foreign policy from that of his Republican predecessors. To Wilson, Theodore Roosevelt's "big stick" smacked of the blatant use of military force. William Howard Taft's "dollar diplomacy" appeared to be a crude flexing of economic muscle. Wilson sought a morally superior alternative. He underlined the new direction in foreign policy by appointing William Jennings Bryan to be Secretary of State. A pacifist on religious grounds, Bryan immediately turned his attention to making agreements with thirty nations for the peaceful settlement of disputes.

But Wilson and Bryan, like Roosevelt and Taft, also believed that the Monroe Doctrine bestowed on the United States special rights and responsibilities in the Western Hemisphere. The Wilson administration wanted to encourage justice and democracy and also to protect and expand American investments. Both principle and economic aspiration promoted American intervention as vigorous as that of the Roosevelt and Taft administrations. Wilson accepted the 1912 occupation of Nicaragua by U.S.

marines to thwart a radical revolution that threatened order and American property. In 1915, he sent marines into Haiti to quell lawlessness and to protect American interests. In 1916, Wilson followed a similar course in the Dominican Republic. So firm was his view of American dominance in the hemisphere that when the Central American court of justice issued a ruling against the American military presence as a violation of traditional rights of national sovereignty, Wilson simply ignored it.

The Wilson administration wanted to encourage justice and democracy in the Western Hemisphere and also to protect and expand American investments there.

Wilson's most serious and controversial involvement in Latin America came in Mexico. Just weeks before Wilson was elected, Francisco Madero, who had become president of Mexico after the democratic revolution of 1911, was assassinated by henchmen of the reactionary General Victoriano Huerta. Most European nations promptly recognized Huerta, but Wilson balked, declaring that he would not support a "government of butchers." In April 1914, Huerta's refusal to apologize for briefly detaining American sailors in Tampico prompted

"PANCHO" VILLA AND GENERAL PERSHING
Here in 1914 Mexican revolutionary Francisco "Pancho" Villa and American general John J. Pershing (right) pose genially as allies in the struggle to overthrow the dictatorial ruler of Mexico, Victoriano Huerta. Soon afterward Villa and Pershing would be adversaries. After a raid by "Villistas" across the New Mexico border in 1915 to punish Americans for aiding Villa's revolutionary rivals, Pershing pursued Villa into Mexico.
Corbis-Bettmann.

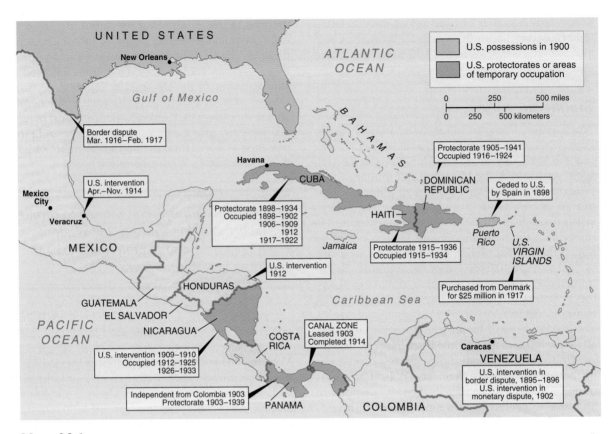

M A P 22.1
U.S. Involvement in the Caribbean and Latin America, 1895–1941
Victory against Spain in 1898 made Puerto Rico an American possession and Cuba a protec-
torate. America also gained control over the Panama Canal and was quick to protect expanding
economic interests with military force to make sure that stable, if not necessarily democratic,
governments prevailed.

Wilson to declare that it was time "to teach the South American republics to elect good men!" The president ordered eight hundred marines to seize the port of Veracruz and prevent the unloading of a large shipment of arms for Huerta, who was by then involved in a civil war of his own. In the fighting that followed, 19 Americans and 126 Mexicans died. Huerta, seeing the handwriting on the wall, fled to Spain, and the United States recognized a new government in Mexico.

Wilson was not able to escape from Mexico that easily, however. A rebellion erupted among desperately poor farmers who believed that the new government, aided by American business interests, had betrayed the revolution's promise to help the common people. Their leader, Francisco "Pancho" Villa, had instilled in his followers a brutal willingness to strike back at their oppressors. In January 1916, a

band of Villistas seized a trainload of gold from an American-owned mine deep within Mexico and killed the seventeen American engineers who were carrying it to Texas. Emboldened by that profitable act of revenge, another Villista band crossed the border on March 9 for a predawn raid on the town of Columbus, New Mexico, that cost several lives and left the town in flames. Wilson promptly dispatched twelve thousand troops led by General John J. Pershing, who years earlier had chased the Apache chief Geronimo through the same Mexican desert and who would soon command American forces in France. The American cavalry never managed to catch and punish Villa's raiders. In January 1917, Pershing finally led his weary troops back across the border, ending Woodrow Wilson's heavy-handed intervention into Mexican affairs. The cataclysmic revolution raged on in Mexico until 1920, however, and ended in the death of about two million people, one out of every eight Mexicans. Well before then, American attention had shifted to the situation in Europe.

The European Crisis

Early in the twentieth century, European leaders often proclaimed proudly that they had done away with war. But the many years of peace enjoyed by the great powers before 1914 masked profound tensions caused by imperial rivalries and nationalist desires. The consolidation of the German and Italian states into unified nations and the similar ambition of Russia to create some sort of "Pan-Slavic" union initiated new rivalries throughout Europe. As the conviction spread that colonial possessions were a mark of national greatness, competition expanded onto the world stage. In particular, Germany, under the leadership of Kaiser Wilhelm II, sought national greatness by creating an empire abroad and building industrial muscle at home. Its desire for colonies and economic might, together with its obsession with building a navy to overcome Britain's traditional domination of the sea, threatened Europe's balance of power and stimulated anxious competition among other nations.

Within this explosive atmosphere, a complex web of military and diplomatic alliances grew. By 1914, Germany, Austria-Hungary, and Italy (the Triple Alliance) stood opposed to Great Britain, France, and Russia (the Triple Entente). In their effort to avoid war, the nations of Europe had actually magnified the possibility of conflict by creating national borders that were in effect trip wires between two heavily armed power blocs. With rising dismay, those who had hoped for safety through a balance of power came to realize that the system gave a lone assassin the power to set off a catastrophe.

The fuse to the European powder keg was lit in southeastern Europe, in the Balkans. On June 28, 1914, a Bosnian Serb terrorist fatally shot Archduke Franz Ferdinand of Austria as he toured the city of Sarajevo, then part of the Austro-Hungarian Empire. The assassin sought to dramatize Serbia's persistent desire to extend its territory all the way to the Adriatic Sea. The nations of Europe mobilized their armies. Austria-Hungary, holding Serbia to account for the assassination, declared war on that nation on July 28. The alliance system locked into place, and in swift sequence the nations of Europe plunged into war. Russia, determined to protect its Slavic kin, announced that it would back the Serbs.

Germany felt compelled to support Austria-Hungary as a kindred Germanic state and declared war on Russia and on Russia's ally France. In response, Great Britain, upholding its treaty with France, declared war on Germany. Halfway around the globe, Japan saw an opportunity to rid itself of competition in China and went to war against Germany, making the conflict the First World War.

It became the most devastating and most hideous war the world had ever known. England's foreign secretary, Edward Grey, sighed his epitaph for the civilization he had known: "The lamps are going out all over Europe. We shall not see them lit again in our lifetime." But the foreign secretary and other national leaders who had been charged with tending the lamps faced the task of explaining why they had snuffed them out. With his usual grave dignity, Grey assured Parliament that Great Britain would rally to the cause of war when it "realizes what is at stake, what the real issues are." The next day on the other side of the barricades, the German imperial chancellor, Theobald von Bethmann Hollweg, insisted that Germany had grown strong "in the works of peace" and that "only in defense of a just cause shall our sword fly from its scabbard." But beyond vague assertions from each side that aggression must be halted and honor upheld, little was done to define "just cause."

Across the Atlantic, Woodrow Wilson perceived no just cause and labored to keep the United States neutral and its progressive mission intact.

The Ordeal of Neutrality

When the United States declared its neutrality, it also claimed neutral rights. The concept of neutrality was fuzzy in international law, but the United States had traditionally insisted on the broadest possible definition. In the American view, "free ships made free goods," that is, neutral nations had the right to trade freely with all nations at war, to send their ships safely through the open seas, and to demand the safe passage of their citizens on the merchant and passenger ships of all belligerents. More was involved in upholding neutral rights than principle. The year before Europe went to war, the American economy had started to slide into a recession that threatened to rival the depression of the 1890s. American trade with Europe offered hope of ending unemployment and hardship at home; a disruption of European trade would add greatly to the distress.

It was inevitable that the United States would run into trouble if it insisted on continuing to ship

MAP 22.2
European Alliances after the Outbreak of World War I
With Germany and the Austro-Hungarian Empire wedged between their Entente rivals, and all parties fully armed, Europe was poised for war when the Archduke Franz Ferdinand of Austria was assassinated in Sarajevo in July 1914.

goods to Europe. Great Britain was the first to step on tender neutral rights. Britain's powerful fleet controlled the seas, and it quickly threw up a blockade around Germany. By denying Germany maritime imports, Britain hoped to bring its enemy to its knees. The United States vigorously protested British action, but Britain refused to give up its naval advantage. In the fall of 1914, the Wilson administration reluctantly accepted the British blockade, thus indicating the widespread sympathy for Britain within the State Department and beginning the fateful process of alienation from Germany. American anger about the violation of its neutral rights was undercut by the huge volume of war-related trade that sprang up between the United States and Britain. So great was the demand for American agricultural and industrial goods to break the German blockade that wartime orders succeeded in pulling the American economy out of its prewar slump.

The debate over the definition of neutrality also involved American loans to belligerents. In August 1914, Secretary of State William Jennings Bryan outlawed loans to nations at war on the grounds that for bankers to continue business as usual would be "inconsistent with the true spirit of neutrality." But

in 1915, when lack of funds threatened Britain's ability to continue its trade with the United States, Secretary of the Treasury William G. McAdoo warned Wilson: "To maintain our prosperity, we must finance it." Neutrality would henceforth be defined not by restrictions on the United States but in terms of the country's right to trade freely and to lend money. Although some continued to argue that vast loans to Britain would tie the United States to Britain and draw it into war, between 1914 and the spring of 1917 the United States advanced almost $2.5 billion in loans to the Allies and only $27 million to Germany. Trade showed an even greater imbalance. Driven by war-related goods, exports to Britain escalated some 300 percent, while British sea power reduced trade with Germany and its allies to the vanishing point.

Faced with the almost totally effective British blockade, Germany retaliated with a blockade of its own. But there was a difference. The British fleet was a surface fleet, and the German navy consisted primarily of deadly, torpedo-firing submarines. The German *Unterseebooten*, or U-boats, could not operate according to traditional rules. Surface ships could halt American freighters. Submarines could only sink them. Subs were effective only when they surprised their quarry. And once they sank a ship, the tiny, cramped U-boats could not possibly pick up the survivors. To much of the world, submarine warfare violated notions of how a "civilized" nation waged war. Nevertheless, in February 1915, the German high command declared the waters around Britain a war zone and warned that any ship in the area would be subject without notice to attack.

Woodrow Wilson responded harshly, branding the sinking of a merchant ship "a wanton act." He declared that the United States would regard the loss of an American ship or the loss of American lives on a belligerent ship as "a flagrant violation of neutral rights" and would hold Germany to "strict accountability." What "strict accountability" meant was still unclear when Wilson received the shocking news of the sinking of the British liner *Lusitania*

on May 7, 1915, off the coast of Ireland. The *Lusitania* was one of the great passenger ships of its day, the "Queen of the Atlantic." Journalist Mark Sullivan later recounted that for years afterward people could "remember the surroundings in which they read [the news of the sinking], the emotions they had, their actions the rest of the day." The sinking caused the loss of 1,198 lives, including 128 Americans.

American newspapers appeared with drawings of drowning women and children and cries for war. The majority of Americans, however, did not want to break relations with Germany. Some pointed out that the German embassy had warned prospective passengers that they would be entering a war zone where the ship would be subject to attack. Others observed that the *Lusitania* carried millions of rounds of ammunition as well as passengers.

SINKING OF THE LUSITANIA *Military prowess and civilian tragedy came together with shocking effect in the sinking of the British passenger liner* Lusitania, *on May 7, 1915. Captain Walter Schwieger, commander of the German submarine U-20, who spotted the ship off the coast of Ireland, skillfully sank the great liner with a single torpedo. After watching the chaos that ensued in which more than 1,200 people lost their lives, he remembered the scene as the most awful one he had ever witnessed. For Americans, the fate of the* Lusitania *was crucial in turning public sentiment against Germany. This poster by Fred Spear captured the outrage felt at the loss of many women and almost 100 children. Nearly two years before America entered the war, posters like this urged Americans to enlist as preparation for the day when they must surely save civilization from German barbarism.*
UPI/Bettmann Archive; Library of Congress.

Woodrow Wilson maintained his commitment to peace and neutrality, declaring on May 10 that "there is such a thing as a man being too proud to fight." Former president Theodore Roosevelt, a leading advocate of arming the nation against German aggression, never forgave Wilson for being such a "flub dub and mollycoddle," for not realizing he should be too proud *not* to fight. Yet Wilson's policy was not passive. He sent strongly worded notes to Germany condemning the sinking as an "illegal and inhuman act" and demanding payment for damages. Any further destruction of ships, Wilson warned, would be regarded as "deliberately unfriendly" and might lead the United States to break diplomatic relations with Germany.

Although the sinking of the *Lusitania* did not result in war, it turned Wilson against the peace movement within his administration. Secretary of State Bryan, the leading pacifist voice in the cabinet, argued that Germany had a right to protect itself from British importation of armaments. A ship carrying war materials, he said, "should not rely on passengers to protect her from attack—it would be like putting women and children in front of an army." He asked Wilson to warn American citizens using ships of belligerent countries that they traveled at their own risk. Instead, Wilson branded the sinking as a brutal attack on innocent people and reasserted the rights of American citizens to travel unharmed across the oceans. Bryan realized that Wilson had left Germany little choice but to cease submarine warfare and abandon its blockade of Britain or to risk war with the United States. In protest, Bryan resigned as secretary of state, and Robert Lansing, a veteran State Department officer and a strong advocate of the Allied cause, took his place.

Then the tension subsided. Germany, anxious not to provoke the United States into joining the Allied cause, apologized for the *Lusitania* deaths and offered an indemnity. After the sinking of the English steamer *Sussex* in 1916, at the cost of two more American lives, the German government quickly acted to head off war by promising that there would be no more submarine attacks without warning and without provisions for the safety of civilians. Observers hailed the pledge as a victory for Wilson's policy of careful negotiation between the poles of Bryan's pacifism and Roosevelt's bellicosity.

The lull stirred hope that a peaceful end to the war might be found. Colonel Edward House, Wilson's trusted adviser on foreign affairs, set off for London, Paris, and Berlin in January 1916. His hope was to get the belligerents to the conference table. How the bitterly hostile sides could reconcile their differences remained a mystery, but at least there would be a chance if they agreed to meet. On the basis of that slender thread of hope, Wilson appealed for a "peace without victory," speaking eloquently about the need to establish a new world order after the fighting ceased. He called for a peace settlement that would guarantee freedom of the seas, a reduction in military arms, free and open trade, and national self-determination. To provide the means for peaceful resolution of disputes in the future, he endorsed British Foreign Secretary Grey's suggestion to create a "league of nations" that would "insure peace and justice throughout the world."

Although the sinking of the Lusitania *did not result in war, it turned Wilson against the peace movement within his administration.*

Wilson's efforts for peace served him well in his bid for reelection in 1916. Still, controversies over neutrality, intervention in Mexico, and the government's role in regulating the economy made Wilson's chances uncertain. Unlike the situation in 1912, Wilson faced a united Republican challenge after Theodore Roosevelt declined to run for the Progressive Party. Wilson's opponent was the able associate justice of the Supreme Court Charles Evans Hughes, who had formerly been governor of New York. The Democratic Party ran Wilson under the slogan "He kept us out of war," but Wilson shied away from the claim, protesting that "they talk of me as though I were a god. Any little German lieutenant can push us into the war at any time by some calculated outrage." But Wilson said nothing when the Democrats also argued that the Republican candidate was more likely to lead the nation into war. Ultimately, Wilson's case for neutrality appealed to the majority in favor of peace. Wilson won, but the Democratic incumbent squeaked through by only 600,000 popular votes and only 23 electoral votes. The narrowness of his victory left in doubt whether Wilson spoke for the nation in foreign policy.

The United States Enters the War

In the end, the determination by the warring sides to achieve peace on their own terms scuttled any chance for a negotiated peace. The Germans refused to specify their war aims as a condition for mediation. The Allies made mediation difficult in any event by announcing aims that would have broken up the Austro-Hungarian Empire and required the Germans to pay damages for the war. In early January 1917, the German military high command forced the issue by persuading the kaiser that the country could no longer afford to allow neutral shipping to reach Great Britain while the enemy blockade threatened to starve Germany. Instead, Germany would resume unrestricted submarine warfare at the end of the month and sink without warning any ship found in the waters off Great Britain. The German military understood that it risked war with the United States but gambled that Germany would achieve a quick military victory before the United States could bring its armed might to bear.

Most of Wilson's advisers joined Theodore Roosevelt in demanding a declaration of war as soon as Germany announced its unrestricted submarine policy, but Wilson, still hoping for a peaceful way out, would only go so far as to sever diplomatic relations with Germany. Then on February 25, 1917, British authorities informed Wilson of a secret telegram sent by the German foreign secretary, Arthur Zimmermann, to the German minister in Mexico. It promised that in the event of war between Germany and the United States, Germany would see that Mexico regained the territories it lost in the Southwest in the Mexican-American War in exchange for a declaration of war against the United States. Wilson angrily responded to the Zimmermann telegram by asking Congress to approve a policy of "armed neutrality" that would equip merchant ships to fight back against any attackers. On a deeper plane, as the newspapers played up the Zimmermann note to sensational effect, the president moved to the conclusion that the war was, indeed, a defense of democracy against autocratic German aggression.

In mid-March, German submarines sank five American vessels in the sea lanes to Britain. After agonizing over the probable consequences, the president prevailed on Congress to issue a declaration of war on April 6. No longer too proud to fight, Wilson accused Germany of "warfare against mankind." But he insisted that the destruction of Germany was not the U.S. goal. Instead, the United States fought to make the world "safe for democracy" and to "vindicate the principles of peace and justice" in which a reconstructed Germany would find a democratic place.

Wilson did not overlook the tragic difference between those lofty aims and the brutal means chosen to achieve them. He spoke despairingly to a friend just before his appearance before Congress. "Once lead this people into war, and they'll forget there ever was such a thing as tolerance. To fight you must be brutal and ruthless, and the spirit of ruthless brutality will infect Congress, the courts, the policeman on the beat, the man in the street." Wilson then set out to lead the fight for American ideals.

The Crusade for Democracy

Wilson embraced the war as a mission to rescue a troubled world. His high-minded and idealistic goals for American participation rallied leading progressives to his side. Progressives hoped that war would improve the quality of American life as well as free Europe from its bondage to tyranny and militarism. The American Expeditionary Force (AEF) that eventually carried two million troops to Europe, by far the largest military venture the United States had ever undertaken on foreign soil, was trained to be morally straight and knowledgeable about the civilization they were to save. Progressive enthusiasm also powered the mobilization of industrial and agricultural production. Unfinished items on the progressive agenda achieved success. Moreover, labor shortages provided new opportunities in the booming wartime economy. African Americans and women found work where once they had been excluded, and women also gained new respect and recognition for their wartime endeavors.

The crusade strove for loyalty from a general public whose ancestry was rooted in all the belligerent nations. Wilson favored democratic persuasion, and to instill loyalty he supported indoctrination in the schools, set up a government agency to promote official propaganda, and sponsored parades, rallies, films, and other forms of patriotic expression. But with commitment to patriotism also went suppression of dissent. The government launched a harsh assault on civil liberties. In addition, mobs assaulted those whom they considered disloyal. Increasingly, attachment to the war stressed emotion rather than reason. In the end, as Wilson predicted, the progressive ideal of rational progress and free expression suffered grievous loss as the nation undertook its crusade for democracy.

The Call to Arms

When the United States entered the war in April 1917, the nation was woefully unprepared. It was clear, however, that the Allies could win only with massive and swift American involvement in Europe. War-weary Britain and France were virtually exhausted after almost three years of conflict. Hundreds of thousands of British and French soldiers had perished in the trenches. Morale in the French army was so bad that troops in the rear were firing on troops who deserted the front. Food supplies were dangerously short. Russia was in turmoil: A democratic revolution had forced Czar Nicholas II's abdication in March 1917, and eight months later the Bolshevik Revolution removed Russia from the war. To meet the demand for fighting men, food, and war materiel, the United States would have to mobilize not only an army but its economy as well.

On May 18, 1917, Wilson signed a sweeping Selective Service Act, which transformed a tiny volunteer armed force of 80,000 men, spread thinly around the United States and outposts from the Caribbean to China, into a vast army and navy. In 1917, about half of the standing military forces manned coastal artillery batteries. The rest were tactical units bearing light weaponry. There were no heavy field artillery, tanks, or modern planes. But in just two months, more than 9 million men had registered for the draft. Although almost 350,000 inductees either failed to report or claimed conscientious objector status, the draft boards eventually inducted 2.8 million men into the armed services. Another 2 million volunteered. Almost half of the 4.8 million American military eventually served in Europe.

But first, training camps had to transform raw recruits into fighting men. Progressive reformers viewed the camps as laboratories where medical examinations, along with recently developed sociological and psychological techniques, could take the measure of American youth. The shocking news that almost 30 percent of those drafted were rejected on physical grounds acted as a crucial stimulus to the public health and physical education movements. Intelligence tests given to recruits yielded even more disheartening results. According to the data (which later proved flawed), 47 percent of all whites and 89 percent of all blacks were below the mental age of thirteen. Some analysts used these results as proof that the lower classes had little interest in education. Others concluded that they proved genetic differences between the races. So

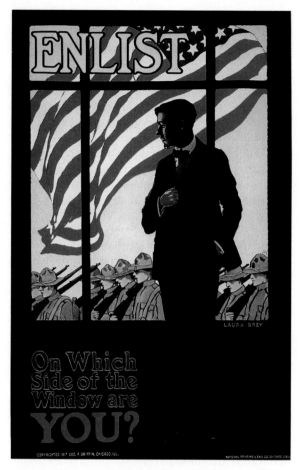

WORLD WAR I RECRUITING POSTER
Recruiting posters often appealed to young men's concerns about chivalry and manhood. One navy poster showed a uniform draped over a chair, with the words "It takes a man to fill it." In another, a provocative woman beckoned saying, "I want you . . . for the navy." In this poster, anxiety is the key. The fastidious appearance and somewhat languid pose of the worried civilian in his darkened interior contrasts with the bright, flag-filled outdoors of the marching troops. Of course, anyone with an ounce of spunk would go out and fall in line.
Library of Congress.

deep-seated was the cultural bias toward native-born middle-class white standards that it did not occur to the experts that farmers, factory workers, and recent immigrants might not be expected to notice that a net was missing from the picture of a tennis court or to know that mauve is a color.

Progressives in characteristically optimistic fashion accepted the dismal physical and mental data as an opportunity for improvement. Secretary of War Newton D. Baker, whose outlook had been shaped by reform crusades as mayor of Cleveland, created a Commission on Training Camp Activities staffed by YMCA workers and veterans of the settlement house and playground movements. They saw to it that military training merged with games, singing, and college extension courses. To further ensure a healthy environment, the Military Draft Act of 1917 prohibited prostitution and alcohol near training camps. Never before had there been such armed encampments, which Baker described in full progressive fervor as "national universities—training schools to which the flower of American youth is being sent." These "universities" taught recruits how to sing as well as to fight. They sought to provide the youthful crusaders with an "invisible armor" of education, comradeship, and moral fitness.

Wilson's selection of General John J. Pershing to command the new American Expeditionary Force recognized the need for hard professionalism in the lead, not the sort of romantic patriotism that had given amateurs like Theodore Roosevelt the chance to command combat troops in the Spanish-American War. Pershing had graduated from West Point in the 1880s and had seen combat in the Indian wars on the plains and against the Spanish in Cuba, where his command of black troops had earned him the nickname "Black Jack." Pershing's impeccable military bearing—erect, dignified, unflappable—enhanced his professional standing and gave promise that he would carry out his duties in the cool, efficient way required of modern war on a vast scale. Pershing's stoic fortitude had hardened to steel in 1915 when he learned that his wife and daughters had perished in San Francisco in a fire.

When Pershing and the wide-eyed troops of the AEF marched through Paris on the Fourth of July 1917, just a week after the first troopship landed, a grateful populace showered them with flowers. Even the impassive general was moved by the parade. "With wreaths about their necks and bouquets in their hats and rifles," Pershing recalled, "the column looked like a moving flower garden." At the statue of the hero who symbolized France's aid to the American Revolution, an officer stepped out and proclaimed in an inspired phrase that summed up the spirit of the occasion, "Lafayette, we are here!"

The Progressive Stake in the War

The idea of the war as an agent of social improvement fanned the old zeal and earnestness of the progressive movement. In particular, the war

captivated progressives who were believers in strong government and who had been lukewarm about Wilson's cautious New Freedom. The Wilson administration realized that Washington would have to assert greater control to mobilize the nation's resources and to avoid chaos. To oversee the transformation of the economy, the administration established a multitude of new federal war agencies to deal with specific war needs.

The War Industries Board (WIB), created to direct and stimulate industrial production, was fortunate in the choice of Bernard Baruch to head it. Because he was at once a wealthy southern gentleman, a Jewish Wall Street stockbroker, and a reform Democrat, Baruch could speak to many constituencies. Shrewdly bullying and wheedling, he managed to weld scientists, industrialists, public administrators, and public relations experts into units that maximized production, limited waste, and delivered according to tight schedules. Efficient production of everything from boots to bullets made the American soldier the most fully equipped in the world, though it took time for the quality of his weaponry to catch up with that of the Europeans who had long fielded large armies.

Alongside Baruch's coordination of industry, Herbert Hoover, self-made millionaire engineer, headed the Food Administration. Sober and tireless, he led remarkably successful "Hooverizing" campaigns for conservation, with "wheatless" Mondays and "meatless" Tuesdays. By guaranteeing high prices for wheat, the Food Administration caused a dramatic increase in production. The American heartland not only supplied the needs of the American people and its armed forces but also became the breadbasket of America's allies, France and Britain. By planting fallow land, farmers provided feed to boost meat production from 640,000 tons to almost 3.5 million tons. The First Family, including Wilson's new wife, Edith Galt, joined countless others in answering the call to do their part. During the growing season, sightseers could gawk at the White House "victory garden" and the sheep munching the White House lawn in place of the gardeners, who had moved on to new work in the war effort.

Washington soon bristled with other hastily created agencies charged with managing the war effort. The Railroads' War Board directed railroad traffic, the Fuel Administration coordinated the coal industry and other fuel suppliers, the Shipping Board organized the merchant marine, and the National War Labor Policies Board resolved labor disputes. The administration gave progressives reason to believe that the new federal agencies would serve as mediating forces between business and government and encourage harmony in the public interest. Adding to the enthusiasm of industrial leaders was the fact that, while agencies often achieved greater production and efficiency, they also presided over the tripling of corporate profits, despite higher wartime taxes. Buoyed by these developments, influential voices like those of philosopher-educator John Dewey and journalist-critic Walter Lippmann argued for public support of the war as a means of progressive reform at home as well as abroad.

Reformers brought high expectations to the war and had cause to celebrate the way the less advantaged shared in some of the benefits. Full mobilization meant high prices for farmers and plentiful jobs in the new war industries.

The Wilson administration also devised shrewd and rousing strategies of raising the funds to pay for the war. No one could have guessed that the war would eventually cost the nation $33 billion (more than the federal government's total expenses from 1789 to 1917), but Secretary of the Treasury McAdoo, a witty and outgoing political operator

who also happened to be Wilson's son-in-law, deftly appealed to Americans to sacrifice through higher taxes. He also became the principal cheerleader for the purchase of war bonds, called Liberty Bonds. McAdoo's fund-raising, which included parades, posters, celebrity endorsements, and musical salutes, often left the line between patriotism and showmanship hard to discern, but it was wildly successful.

Reformers brought high expectations to the war and had cause to celebrate the way the less advantaged shared in some of the benefits. Full mobilization meant high prices for farmers and plentiful jobs in the new war industries. Reformers who had battled for workers' rights celebrated labor's gains. Increased industrial production required peaceful labor relations and the avoidance of strikes. The National War Labor Policies Board and other agencies, therefore, accepted the eight-hour day, a living minimum wage, and collective bargaining rights in industries that had long resisted them. Even merchant sailors, one of the most notoriously ill-treated groups throughout the nation's history, finally gained enough sympathy because of the submarine menace for Congress to legislate seamen's insurance and better working conditions. Wages rose sharply during the war, and the American Federation of Labor saw its membership soar from 2.7 million to over 5 million. Mobilization also aided the struggle to provide workers with insurance against injury on the job. After long resisting all efforts in this free en-

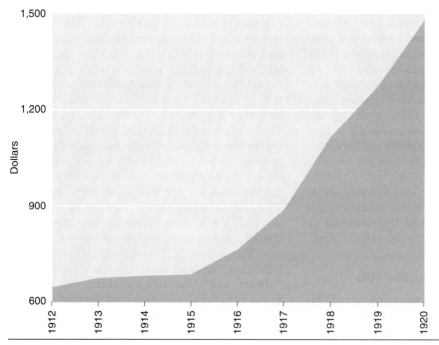

FIGURE 22.1
Industrial Wages, 1912–1920
With help from unions and Progressive reformers, wage workers gradually improved their economic condition. The entry of millions of young men into the armed forces caused labor shortages and led to a rapid surge in wages.

terprise area, Congress bowed to the patriotic cause of providing death and disability insurance for the armed forces.

The war also presented new opportunities for women. More than twenty thousand women served with the armed forces, a large number of them as nurses in France. In the private sector, long-standing barriers against hiring women fell when millions of workingmen became soldiers and few new immigrant workers succeeded in finding safe passage across the Atlantic. The growing presence of women in the war effort moved the government to create the Women's Bureau of the Department of Labor. This agency, along with the Women's Trade Union League (WTUL), helped open jobs to women, often against the opposition of the major trade organization, the American Federation of Labor (AFL). For the first time, women in sizable numbers found work with the railroads and in defense plants as welders and heavy machine operators. Some gained entry to labor unions, whose members usually earned far higher wages than nonunion workers. The future for women looked bright. "This is the women's age," exulted Margaret Dreier Robins, president of the Women's Trade Union League. "At last . . . women are coming into the labor and festival of life on equal terms with men."

In addition to gains in the workplace, women claimed victory in another arena. The struggle for woman suffrage dated back to the Seneca Falls con-

vention of 1848, where women voiced their first formal demand for the ballot. But on the eve of the First World War, decades of grueling effort had produced only a few local victories. Using a state-by-state approach, suffragists had achieved success in Wyoming in 1890 and in several other western states in the following years, but elsewhere in the nation they met tremendous resistance and defeat. In New York, for example, suffragists waged a massive referendum campaign in 1915 for an amendment to the state constitution. In an attempt to canvass all of New York City's 661,000 registered voters, hundreds of women trudged up and down tenement stairs, visited shops and factories, and called at huge office buildings with their thousands of workers. Still, New York voters rejected woman suffrage resoundingly. Two years later in Ohio, suffragists succeeded in convincing the legislature to approve a bill that allowed women to vote in presidential elections, only to have opponents mount a petition drive that put the issue on the ballot, where a majority voted in favor of taking the vote away from women.

But riding a wave of wartime idealism and energized by increasingly militant tactics, the crusade for woman suffrage finally triumphed. Suffragists continued to struggle state by state, but they increasingly focused on the national level and on an amendment to the Constitution. Women's wartime service as nurses, factory workers, and patriotic vol-

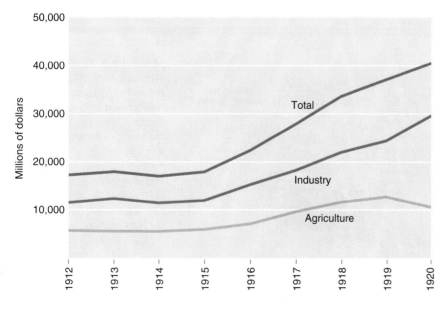

Agriculture: cash receipts.
Industry: includes mining, electric power, manufacturing, construction, and communications.

FIGURE 22.2
Manufacturing and Agricultural Income, 1912–1920
Following the postwar decline in demand for food and materiel, agriculture quickly fell into recession. Industry, spurred by new inventions and technologies, maintained a steady upward momentum.

unteers convinced many American men that women could shoulder public responsibilities. It would be wrong, Woodrow Wilson conceded, not to reward the "partnership of suffering and sacrifice" with a "partnership of privilege and right." Militant suffragists, such as Alice Paul, head of the new National Woman's Party, made it impossible for the nation to dodge the suffrage issue. Radical women picketed the White House. When they refused police orders to disperse, they were sent to jail, where they went on hunger strikes. In 1919, Congress passed the Nineteenth Amendment, granting woman suffrage, and by 1920 it had been ratified by the required two-thirds of the states and had become law. Looking back on the struggle, two suffrage leaders remarked: "How much of time and patience, how much work, energy and aspiration, how much faith, how much hope, how much despair went into it." To the women involved, "its success became a monumental thing."

Progressives found that the war provided a huge boost to another stalled campaign for a constitutional amendment. Before the war, progressives had campaigned widely against alcoholic beverages, and by 1917, nineteen states had gone dry. Liquor's opponents now claimed that America's success in the war rested on the national prohibition of liquor. Outlawing strong drink would make the cause of democracy powerful and pure, they claimed. Shutting down the distilleries would save millions of bushels of grain that could feed the United States and its allies. And taking aim at the nation's breweries, especially those with German names like Schlitz, Pabst, and Anheuser-Busch, would be a patriotic blow at Kaiser Wilhelm and the German cause. In December 1917, the Eighteenth Amendment, which banned the manufacture, transportation, and sale of alcohol, passed Congress. After ratification, the amendment went into effect on January 1, 1920.

The "Great Migration" of African Americans

In 1900, thirty-five years after emancipation, African Americans had made little progress toward achieving full citizenship. Nine of every ten African Americans were Southerners, and disfranchisement, segregation, and violence dominated their lives. The majority of black men still toiled in agriculture, either mired in the new servitude of tenancy or working for wages of sixty cents a day. Black women worked in the homes of whites as domestics for two dollars or less a week. Vicious racial violence descended on anyone whites considered "uppity." As the Vicksburg *Commercial Appeal* warned: "Don't monkey with white supremacy; it is loaded with determination, gun-powder, and dynamite." If blacks somehow managed to climb off the bottom, whites pushed them back down. "If we own a good farm or horse, or cow, or bird-dog, or yoke of oxen," a black Mississippian observed in 1913, "we are harassed until we are bound to sell, give away, or run away, before we can have any

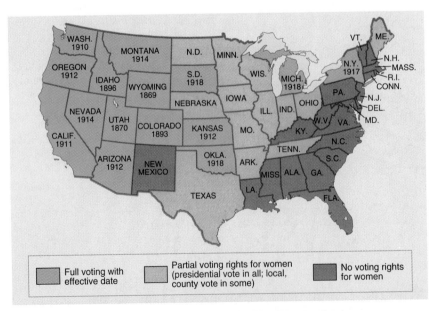

MAP 22.3
Women's Voting Rights before the Nineteenth Amendment
The long campaign for women's voting rights reversed the pioneer epic — rolling eastward from its first successes in the new democratic openness of the West toward the entrenched male-dominated public life of the Northeast and South.

| Full voting with effective date | Partial voting rights for women (presidential vote in all; local, county vote in some) | No voting rights for women |

WOMAN SUFFRAGE
This cartoon sought to help the cause of woman suffrage by linking tradition with prejudice. Against the old-guard claim that the moral influence of women would decline if they became involved in the rough and tumble of politics, the woman racing toward the light escapes the spooky oppression of those who had claimed to be women's guardians.
Collection of Grunwald Center for the Graphic Arts, UCLA. Gift of Mr. and Mrs. Kenneth Chamberlain.

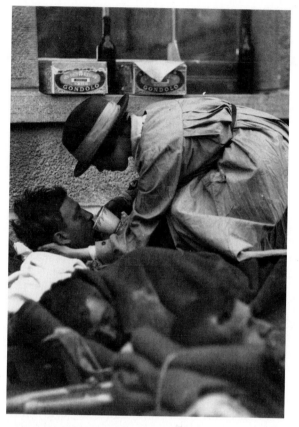

WORLD WAR I RED CROSS WORKER
An American Red Cross worker gives water to a badly wounded British soldier on a French railway platform in May 1918. More than twenty thousand women served with the armed forces, many of them as nurses in France.
National Archives.

peace in our lives." Southern blacks accommodated to what they could not change, but they looked for a way out.

The First World War provided African Americans with the opportunity to escape the South's cotton fields and kitchens. The labor shortage in northern industries during the war meant that blacks who were once welcome in the urban North only in personal service occupations now found work as unskilled and semiskilled industrial workers. Job opportunities were trumpeted by black newspapers like the militant Chicago *Defender* and by industrial recruiters who flooded the South looking for black workers. Young black men, who made up the bulk

of the migrants, found jobs in steel mills, shipyards, munitions plants, railroad yards, and mines. From 1915 to 1920, half a million blacks (approximately 10 percent of the South's black population) boarded trains bound for Philadelphia, Detroit, Cleveland, Chicago, St. Louis, and other industrial cities.

Blacks who joined the "great migration" were not just moving north. They were fleeing the South. In addition to jobs, they sought human dignity and personal freedom. The émigrés wrote letters that were read aloud in their home churches. One man announced proudly that he had recently been elevated to "first assistant to the head carpenter." "What's the news generally around Hattiesburg?"

What Did the War Mean to African Americans?

WHEN THE UNITED STATES ENTERED the First World War, some black leaders remembered the crucial role of African American soldiers in the Civil War. They rejoiced that military service would again offer blacks a chance to prove their worth. Robert Moton, president of the nation's foremost black college, Tuskegee Institute, recollected clearly when that thought had come to him. He was sitting in the midst of "dignified bankers [and] merchants" gathered in the Waldorf-Astoria hotel in New York City to promote the sale of Liberty Bonds. At that moment of patriotic inclusion, Moton "could not but feel that my people by their contribution, their loyalty, and their spirit . . . realized fully that they are heirs of America, and that as such they must be sharers of her struggles as well as partakers of her glory."

More surprising was the support for the war voiced by W. E. B. Du Bois. Known for his bold dissent against the white power structure, Du Bois shocked many readers with his editorial in the NAACP's journal the *Crisis*, urging blacks to "close ranks" and "forget our special grievances" until after a unified nation had won the war. The enemy of the moment, Du Bois insisted, was German "military despotism." Unchecked, that despotism "spells death to the aspirations of Negroes and all darker races for equality, freedom, and democracy."

Although critics bitterly assailed Du Bois for not demanding equal treatment for blacks who fought for their country, African Americans generally followed his advice and closed ranks. On the first day of registration for military service, July 5, 1917, more than 700,000 black men signed in at their draft boards. By war's end, 370,000 blacks had been inducted, some 31 percent of the total registered. The figure for whites was 26 percent.

During training, black recruits suffered the same prejudices that they had encountered in civilian life. Rigidly segregated, they were usually assigned to labor battalions. They faced crude abuse and miserable conditions. One base in Virginia that trained blacks as cargo handlers quartered troops in tents without floors or stoves and provided no changes of clothes, no blankets for the winter, or even facilities for bathing. Only several deaths from disease and exposure moved the authorities to make conditions barely tolerable.

When black soldiers began arriving in Europe, white commanders made a point of maintaining racial distinctions. A special report from the headquarters of the American commander, General John J. Pershing, advised the French that their failure to draw the color line threatened Franco-American relations. They should resist the urge, the report declared, to accept blacks as equals or to thank them for their efforts, for fear of "spoiling the Negroes."

Under such circumstances, German propagandists raised some painful questions. One leaflet distributed by the Germans to black troops reminded them that they lacked the rights that whites enjoyed and that they were segregated and were often lynched. "Why, then, fight the Germans," the leaflet asked, "only for the benefit of the Wall Street robbers and to protect the millions they have loaned to the British, French, and Italians?" Why, indeed?

Black soldiers hoped to prove a point. While they worked at first mainly as laborers and stevedores, before long they had their chance to fight. In February 1918, General Pershing received an urgent call from the French for help in the Meuse-Argonne sector. Reluctant to lose command over the white troops he valued the most, he sent black soldiers— the 369th, 370th, 371st, and 372nd Regiments of the 92nd Division—to the front, where they were integrated into units of the French army. In the 191 days spent in battle—longer than that spent by any other American outfit — the 369th Regiment won the most medals of any American combat unit, more than one hundred Croix de Guerre alone, and had no prisoners taken. In June 1918, the French high command paid its highest respect by asking the Americans to send all the black troops they could spare.

When the battle-scarred survivors of the 92nd Division returned home, they marched proudly past cheering crowds in Manhattan and Chicago. Black spokesmen proclaimed a new era for black Americans. In May 1919, Du Bois argued that it was time for African Americans to collect what was due them. "We return from fighting," Du Bois declared. "We return fighting. Make way for Democracy. We saved it in France, and by the Great Jehovah, we will save it in the U.S.A., or know the reason why."

Reasons soon presented themselves. Segregation remained entrenched, and its defenders con-

AFRICAN AMERICAN MACHINE GUN COMPANY
*This company from the 370th Regiment of the Illinois National Guard, shown early in their train-
ing, exemplifies the proud determination of black soldiers to prove their worth in battle. Once in
France, the 370th encountered resistance from American commanders reluctant to use combat-
ready black troops for anything but hard labor behind the lines. When desperation in the face of a
German offensive in the spring of 1918 gave them the chance to fight with French units, the
370th showed its mettle and received the Croix de Guerre. Adding to the irony of black soldiers
having to gain respect as Americans by serving with the French was the fact that the first black
soldier from Lincoln's state of Illinois to fall in battle was a private named Robert E. Lee.*
Picture Research Consultants and Archives.

tinued to hold power in Congress and in the White House. Postwar recession left blacks worse off economically than before their wartime glory and also made them scapegoats for white resentments. Whites launched race riots against blacks in two dozen cities. The willingness of blacks to stand their ground showed a more determined self-esteem, but it also meant more suffering from escalating violence. Nor did the armed services permanently offer new opportunities. Until the late 1940s, after the next world war, the American military remained segregated and almost devoid of black officers. Discrimination extended even beyond the ultimate sacrifice. When the organizers of a trip to France for parents of soldiers lost in the First World War announced that the boat would be segregated, black mothers felt honor-bound to decline the offer to visit the cemeteries where their sons lay.

It took decades for the nation to recognize the sacrifice and heroism of black soldiers in France. As one critic observed about the 92nd Regiment, "the example [they set] was so bright that most eyes closed against it." But in 1991, as the nation cheered American success in the Persian Gulf War, Americans began to see the light. A Defense Department investigating team, though insisting it had found no evidence of discrimination in the fact that none of the 127 Medals of Honor awarded during World War I had gone to blacks, declared that the time had come to correct an "administrative oversight." For leading a charge on September 28, 1918, up a German-held hill that cost him and 40 percent of his company their lives, Corporal Freddie Stowers would receive the Medal of Honor—until then the only one attained by an African American in the world wars. The slain soldier's elderly sister, who had survived seventy-three years to accept the award for her hero brother, could take solace that recognition came under the command of General Colin Powell, the first black chairman of the Joint Chiefs of Staff.

AFRICAN AMERICANS MIGRATE NORTH

This group of newcomers to a northern city in 1912 poses in its best dress on the threshold of a changed life. Several factors combined to prompt almost four and a half million African Americans to leave the South by midcentury. To the burden of racism was added the steady erosion of opportunities to make a living. In the 1920s many rural blacks lost work when a boll weevil invasion reduced the cotton crop drastically. Subsequently, mechanization and government programs to support crop prices by reducing acreage drove many more people off the land.

Schomburg Center for Research in Black Culture, New York Public Library.

he asked. "I should have been here 20 years ago. I just begin to feel like a man. It's a great deal of pleasure in knowing that you got some privileges. My children are going to the same school with the whites and I don't have to [h]umble to no one. I have registered—will vote the next election and there ain't any 'yes sir'—it's all yes and no and Sam and Bill." Whole churches, almost entire communities, sometimes transplanted themselves to northern cities. By 1930, for example, Chicago claimed nearly forty thousand black Mississippians, almost as many as Jackson, Meridian, and Greenville combined.

But blacks discovered that the North was not all milk and honey. As poor southern blacks poured into blighted northern slums looking for work and housing, they encountered a white backlash. To whites, fearful of losing jobs and status, the "great migration" looked more like a great invasion. They lashed out against the latest immigrants. In 1918, the nation witnessed ninety-six lynchings of blacks, some of them veterans still wearing their military uniforms. Race riots ripped two dozen northern cities. One of the worst occurred on a hot July night in 1917 in East St. Louis, Illinois. A mob of whites invaded a section of the city crowded with blacks who had been recruited to help break a strike. The white attackers killed at least thirty-nine people and set a series of fires that left most of the black district in flames.

African Americans in the military also experienced racial violence. The most disastrous episode occurred in August 1917 when a group of armed black soldiers went to Houston, Texas, to avenge incidents of harassment by the police. In the clash that followed, thirteen whites, including several policemen, and one black soldier were killed. With vengeful swiftness that denied any appeal to the War Department, thirteen of the black soldiers were hanged and forty-one others sentenced to life imprisonment. Black leaders responded grimly that the incident demonstrated the tragic shortcomings of America's crusade for democracy.

Through it all, the hope for a better life kept the great black migration flowing northward. Although often disappointed with what they found, black émigrés rarely went back. As one man said in 1919: "When a man's home is sacred; when he can protect the virtue of his wife and daughter against the brutal lust of his alleged superiors; when he can sleep at night without the fear of being visited by the Ku Klux Klan . . . then I will be willing to return to Mississippi."

The Struggle over National Purpose

From the moment war broke out in Europe in 1914, Wilson's foreign policy had become a lightning rod for critics. Interventionists like Theodore Roosevelt hounded Wilson to abandon his announced policy of neutrality and to enter the war on the side of the British. Noninterventionists like William Jennings Bryan declared that Wilson's insistence on protecting American passengers on ships carrying war materials to England failed the neutrality test and could lead to war against Germany. When Wilson finally did commit the nation to war, most peace advocates rallied around the flag. The Carnegie Endowment for International Peace, for example, issued a resolution that "the most effectual means of promoting peace is to prosecute the war against the Imperial German Government" and adopted new stationery with the heading "Peace through Victory."

As prewar peace societies converted from pacifism to patriotism, a handful of new groups took up the cause of peace. As early as 1914, a group of professional women, led by settlement house leader Jane Addams and economics professor Emily Greene Balch, convened a group to resist what Addams described as "the pathetic belief in the regenerative results of war." The Women's Peace Party that emerged in 1915 and its foreign affiliates in the Women's International League for Peace and Freedom (WILPF) led the struggle to persuade governments to negotiate peace and spare dissenters from harsh punishment. It was discouraging, unpopular work. Participants were routinely labeled cowards and Communists, their efforts crushed by the steamroller of war enthusiasm. (See Texts in Historical Context, pages 870–872.)

Wilson's major strategy for fending off criticism of the war was to whip up patriotism with fervent flag-waving. To promote the cause and his leadership, in 1917 the president created the Committee on Public Information (CPI) under the direction of a progressive journalist, George Creel. Handsome and dynamic, Creel thumped for the war like an enthusiastic cheerleader at the big game. He sent "Four-Minute Men," a squad of 75,000 volunteers, around the country to give brief pep talks on the need to "make the world safe for democracy." His energetic team distributed millions of press releases that described successes on the battlefields and in the factories. But information and education slid easily into propaganda. The CPI created a stream of posters and cartoons that depicted brave American soldiers and sailors defending freedom and democracy against the evil Hun.

To help Creel's campaign, the film industry, then primarily a medium for working-class entertainment, sent movie stars to appear at fund-raising rallies. Hollywood cranked out reels of melodrama about battle-line and home-front heroes and gave audiences the chance to hiss at the German kaiser,

THE LIBERTY LOAN CHOIR
In promoting the war as a moral crusade, religion and patriotism often fused in the spirit of the popular hymn "Onward Christian Soldiers." On the steps of New York's City Hall in April 1918, the Liberty Loan Choir add their voices to the chorus of opera singers, movie stars, and political celebrities who were used throughout the war to rally the public to buy bonds to finance the war.
NA, US Army Signal Corps, AU, 1651, Paul Thompson.

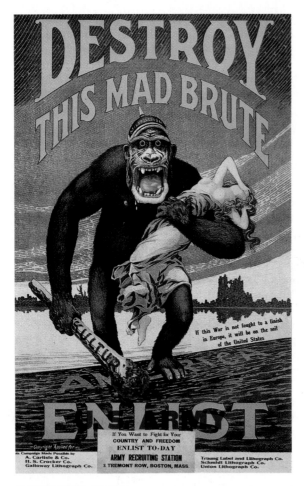

PROPAGANDA POSTER

All the primal fears of rape, invasion, and violence at the hands of a monster wielding the weapon of "Kultur" are brought together in this 1916 scare poster. Germans so resented the dehumanizing portrait of themselves that in World War II, Nazi propagandists reproduced the poster with the warning that the poster had really been telling the American people to "destroy the German people." Library of Congress.

otherwise known as "the Beast of Berlin" and "the Leper of Potsdam." For the more privileged, colleges and universities churned out war propaganda in the guise of scholarship and added courses designed to show the war as a culmination of the age-old struggle for civilization. Professor Samuel Harding of Indiana University declared that "if the teacher cannot conscientiously and wholeheartedly lend his influence to supporting the war with Germany, . . . he ought at least to keep silent." When Professor James McKeen Cattell of Columbia decided not to be quiet about his view that America should seek peace with

Germany short of victory, university president Nicholas Murray Butler arranged to get him fired. In a blunt summation of the campaign for patriotic conformity, Butler declared in his 1917 commencement address that "what had been folly is now treason." The university would not hesitate to purge "all who are not with whole heart and mind and strength committed to fight with us to make the world safe for democracy."

Encouraged thus by schools and government, a firestorm of anti-German passion swept the nation. Campaigns with the slogan "100% American" enlisted ordinary people eager to act as vigilantes sniffing out disloyalty and treason. German, the most widely taught foreign language in 1914, virtually disappeared from the high school and college curriculum. German-born Americans were ostracized, including Karl Muck, conductor of the Boston Symphony Orchestra, and the renowned violinist, Fritz Kreisler, who were driven from the concert stage. The rabid attempt to punish the enemy reached its extreme, however, with the lynching of Robert Prager in Collinsville, Illinois. In the atmosphere of mob rule, it was enough that Prager was German-born and had socialist leanings, even though he had not opposed American participation in the war. The defense lawyer for the drunken men who had beaten Prager and dragged him through the streets praised what he called a "patriotic murder." The local jury took only twenty-five minutes to acquit.

As hysteria increased, absurdity mingled with cruelty. In Montana, a school board barred a history text that had good things to say about medieval Germany. Menus across the nation changed German toast to French toast and sauerkraut to liberty cabbage. The fearful saw evidence of the enemy everywhere. One vigilant citizen claimed to see a periscope in the Great Lakes, and on the dunes of Cape Cod the fiancée of one of the war's leading critics was caught dancing and was held on suspicion of signaling to German submarines.

The Wilson administration took up the task of suppressing dissent with an eagerness that stood in ironic contrast to the army's commitment to defend democracy. The administration guided through Congress reckless legislation that went far beyond the legitimate goal of protecting the nation from espionage and sabotage. The Espionage Act (June 1917), the Trading with the Enemy Act (October 1917), and the Sedition Act (May 1918) gave the government sweeping powers to crush dissent. Among other things, the government could punish any opinion it considered "disloyal, profane, scurrilous, or abusive" of the American flag or uniform.

Two members of Wilson's cabinet, Attorney General Thomas Gregory and Postmaster General Albert Burleson, spearheaded the frenzy of repression. Both Texans, they had been active before the war in efforts to improve the lot of farmers, but after 1917 their antiforeign perspective and tendency to divide the world into friends and enemies moved them to crack down on dissent. Eventually, the government charged some fifteen hundred individuals with sedition. All but a dozen of them had merely spoken words the government found objectionable. Gregory also sponsored the American Protective League, made up of zealous private citizens, to carry out "slacker raids" against those thought to have avoided service or to have doubted official war aims. The league's net caught a carelessly accused mix of young men out of uniform and foreigners thought to be radical opponents of war. The vigilante spirit fomented several violent assaults against the Industrial Workers of the World (IWW), a radical union opposed to the war on grounds that it was capitalist exploitation of the workers who were forced to fight it.

Postmaster General Burleson, a zealot of such self-importance that Wilson dubbed him "the Cardinal," blocked mailing privileges for journals and books he personally considered disloyal. Burleson's suppression eventually hounded one of the leading literary journals, *Seven Arts*, out of business and intimidated another, the *Dial*, into removing Randolph Bourne, the most articulate voice against the war, from his editorial post. The Socialist Party, favored by Bourne and other rebellious young intellectuals, also came under attack for opposing the war. In a mortal blow, the party's leader, Eugene V. Debs, who had received almost a million votes for president in 1912, was convicted under the Espionage Act for speeches condemning the war as a capitalist plot and was sent to the Atlanta penitentiary.

Encouraged by schools and government, a firestorm of anti-German passion swept the nation.

At the center of the mounting hysteria, Wilson vacillated between backing repression, sometimes in strong language, and mildly protesting when his subordinates went to extremes. Though he had dreaded such a twist of fate, Wilson allowed his administration to evolve from the celebration of free expression characteristic of progressive reform to authoritarian insistence on loyalty to wartime goals.

ANTI-GERMAN SENTIMENT
Patriotic fervor during World War I condemned all things German — even in Cincinnati, long a center of German "Kultur." The photograph shows Dr. Ernst Kunwald, who had been driven from his post as conductor of the Cincinnati Symphony Orchestra in 1917, being escorted into custody as a prisoner of war.
War Department.

Even chief propagandist George Creel noted the sad disparity between the "great crusade" he promoted and some of the means being employed to force it on the nation.

Wilson hoped that national commitment to the war would subdue partisan politics. He could not legitimately repress his Republican rivals, however, and they found many opportunities to use the war as a weapon against the Democrats. The trick was to oppose Wilson's conduct of the war but not the war itself. For example, Republicans outshouted Wilson on the nation's need to mobilize for war but then complained that Wilson's War Industries Board was a tyrannical agency that crushed free enterprise. Republican attacks appealed to widely diverse business, labor, and patriotic groups. With each month of the war, Republicans gathered power against the coalition of Democrats and progressives that had narrowly reelected Wilson in 1916.

Wilson erred when he attempted to make the off-year congressional elections of 1918 a referendum on his leadership. His effort backfired, and he was roundly denounced for playing politics with the war. The Republicans gained a narrow majority in both houses of Congress. The end of Democratic control of Congress not only halted any possibility of further domestic reform but also meant that the United States would advance toward victory with authority divided between a Democratic presidency and a Republican Congress.

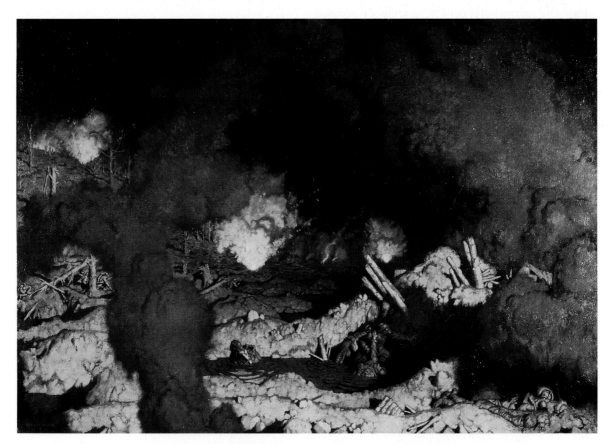

HELL

As the war dragged on, artistic visions of combat as a means to promote the war effort gave way to angry and despairing images of suffering. Georges Leroux was moved to paint this picture after seeing soldiers — alive and dead — illuminated by shell bursts at night in giant shell craters half full of water. He called the painting Hell *both because the landscape was horrifying, and because the scene resembled so closely traditional religious images of the inferno.*

L'Enfer (Hell), 1916 by Georges Paul Leroux (1877–1957), Imperial War Museum, London/Bridgeman Art.

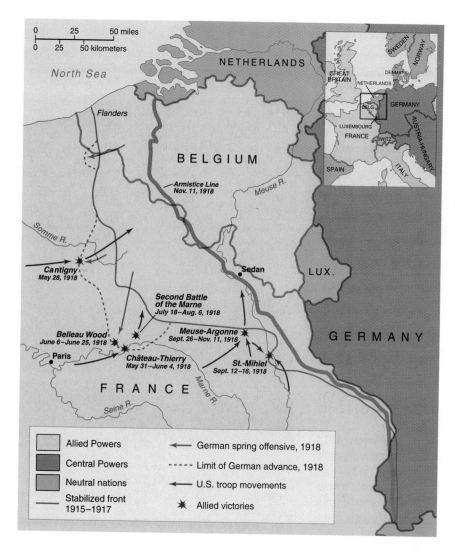

MAP 22.4
*The American
Expeditionary Force,
1917–1918*

*In the last year of the war, the
American Expeditionary Force
joined the French army on the
western front to counterattack
the final German offensive and
pursue the retreating enemy
until surrender.*

Over There

As the struggle over leadership and aims unfolded
at home, the American Expeditionary Force gathered strength in Europe. At the front, however, the
AEF discovered a desperate situation. The three-
year-old war had degenerated into a stalemate of
armies dug defensively into mile upon mile of
trenches snaking across France. Miserable, hollow-
eyed soldiers huddled in the stinking mud, separated from the enemy only by a few hundred yards
of "no-man's-land." When ordered "over the top,"
troops raced furiously toward the enemy's trenches,
only to be entangled in vicious barbed wire and
mowed down by machine guns and artillery. In
1915, Germany added poison chlorine gas to its
lethal arsenal. Enormous casualties did not lead to
decisive victories. At the Battle of the Somme in

1916, French and British forces lost 600,000 dead and
wounded, while German losses reached 500,000. As
a result, the French and British advanced their
trenches a few muddy miles across devastated land.

General John J. Pershing, leader of the AEF, was
appalled by what he saw. He was not about to commit his fresh new army of crusaders to the tactics
of stalemate. The lessons that Civil War veterans
had given him at West Point and his service in swift,
mobile warfare on the plains and in Cuba left him
permanently committed to what has been termed
the "American way of war"—heavy frontal pressure through weight of numbers combined with
swift surprise attacks on the flanks by infantry and
cavalry. Pershing refused to allow his troops to
merge with French and British units, despite the
warning of the Allied commander in chief, General
Ferdinand Foch, that a separate American com-

mand would leave the Allies dangerously uncoordinated. Pershing would, instead, save his soldiers for the moment when a series of lightning strikes might prove decisive.

In the best army fashion, then, American troops had hurried to France, only to wait. They saw almost no combat in 1917. But they were not exactly idle either. Young men who had never been far from home thought of going to France as a great adventure and carried with them all sorts of rumors about "Gay Paree." American officials did not object to some tourism, provided that it was high-minded and enlightened. Flustered officials quickly declined French Premier Georges Clemenceau's offer to supply American troops with licensed prostitutes. In only partly mock horror, Secretary of War Baker warned his deputy not to tell the president, "or he'll stop the war." Instead, the YMCA gave cultural tours, and servicemen used their unorganized moments to sightsee. Soldiers filled diaries and letters with serious attempts to explain what they had seen and done. Most often they expressed their awe at the antiquity of European society and the groomed landscapes they had seen before only in paintings. In contrast, their hosts, after three exhausting years of war, were most impressed by how the Yanks laughed and sang.

Sightseeing ended abruptly in March 1918 when the Germans launched a massive offensive aimed at French ports on the Atlantic. After six thousand cannons had let loose the heaviest barrage in history, a million German soldiers smashed a hole forty miles deep into the French and British lines west of the Somme River at a cost of a quarter of a million casualties on each side. Paris became gripped with the greatest terror of the war when shells fired eighty miles away by "Big Bertha" cannons began falling on the city. More than a thousand civilians died, and a mood of defeatism began to rise. Pershing, who had waited impatiently for months for a call to the front, visited Commander in Chief Foch to ask for the "great honor" of becoming "engaged in the greatest battle in history." Overcome, Foch agreed to Pershing's terms of a separate American command and in May assigned a combined army and marine force to the central sector.

Once committed, the Americans remained true to their way of war. At Cantigny and then at Château-Thierry, the fresh but green Americans checked the German advance with a series of dashing assaults. Then they headed toward the forest stronghold of Belleau Wood. The American force,

AVENUE OF THE ALLIES
Childe Hassam, the impressionist painter famous for his colorful portrayals of New York City, expressed his strong support of World War I through a series of paintings of flags draped along the "Avenue of the Allies" section of Fifth Avenue. This 1918 painting featuring French flags had great emotional impact on its viewers as American troops were fighting in France, helping to bring the war to a close. A French critic praised Hassam's uniquely American character: "No one had ever painted flags before; so now when one thinks of flags one thinks of Hassam's flag pictures. . . . He made the flags symbols of his heritage."
Musée National de la Cooperation Franco-Americaine © photo RMN-Jean.

with the Fifth and Sixth Marine Regiments in the lead, made their way against streams of refugees and retreating Allied soldiers who cried to them that the Germans had won: *"La guerre est finie!—*(The war is over)!" But when a French officer commanded the marines to turn and retreat with them, the Amer-

THE WORLD VICTORIOUS
This 1919 painting by Arthur Crisp was the center panel behind the speaker's platform on the "Victory Way" parade route in New York City. The bold array of flags identifies the victorious nations and projects a vision of postwar international unity of the sort the League of Nations sought to establish.

Photography Collection, Miriam and Ira D. Wallach Division of Art, Prints and Photographs. The New York Public Library.

ican commander replied sharply, "Retreat, hell. We just got here." After charging through a wheat field against withering machine gun fire, the marines plunged into a hand-to-hand forest battle of stalking and ambush. Victory came hard. On the single day of June 6, 1918, the marine spearhead lost 1,087 men, more than had been killed in the previous 143 years of Marine Corps history. In praise of the enemy's spirit, a German report noted that "the Americans' nerves are not yet worn out." Indeed, it was German morale that was on the verge of cracking.

In July 1918, the Allies launched a massive counteroffensive that would end the war. A quarter of a million American troops joined in the rout of German forces along the Marne River. In September, more than a million Americans joined the assault that threw the Germans back from positions along the Meuse River. American forces drove toward the town of Sedan, where the French had lost a war to Germany in 1870 and whose capture was thus of great symbolic importance. In early November, the Allies overran stubborn German resistance

around Sedan and sent the survivors trudging northward. Soon after, a revolt against the German government sent Kaiser Wilhelm fleeing to Holland. On November 11, 1918, a delegation from the newly established German republic met with the French high command in a railroad car in Compiègne to sign an armistice that brought the fighting to an end.

The adventure of the AEF was brief, bloody, and victorious—just the right combination to fix vivid memories of a successful crusade. When Germany resumed unrestricted U-boat warfare in 1917, it had gambled that it could defeat Britain and France before the Americans could raise and train an army and ship it to France. The German military had miscalculated. Of the 2 million American troops in Europe, 1.3 million saw at least some action. Some 112,000 soldiers of the AEF perished, their deaths divided equally between wounds and disease. Another 230,000 Americans suffered casualties but survived, many of them with permanent physical and psychological disabilities. Only the Civil War, lasting for a much longer period, had been

For and Against World War I

*W*orld War I became a battleground of loyalties as well as of guns. Through the Committee on Public Information (CPI), the Wilson administration developed the art of propaganda far beyond anything known before. The CPI promoted the war by organizing rallies and parades, blanketing the country with posters and cartoons, publishing a daily Official Bulletin, and mobilizing 75,000 volunteers to give speeches to hometown audiences. Only a few conscientious objectors, socialists, and disillusioned idealists were left to argue that war could not produce democracy but would instead destroy many lives and perhaps cherished values of progress and reform as well.

The Committee on Public Information recruited volunteers in local communities to carry the official version of the war directly to their neighbors. Called "Four-Minute Men" because their speeches were supposed to be only four minutes long, these enthusiasts spoke from carefully crafted scripts. The following example indicates how audiences were encouraged to buy war bonds by rousing their indignation against the Germans.

DOCUMENT 1.
A "Four-Minute Man" Speech

While we are sitting here tonight enjoying a picture show, do you realize that thousands and thousands of Belgians, people just like ourselves, are *languishing in slavery* under Prussian masters? . . .

Prussian "Schrecklichkeit" (the deliberate policy of terrorism) leads to almost unbelievable besotten brutality. The German soldiers—their letters are reprinted—were often forced against their wills, they themselves weeping, to carry out unspeakable orders against defenseless old men, women, and children, so that *"respect"* might grow for German "efficiency." For instance, at Dinant the wives and children of 40 men were forced to witness the execution of their husbands and fathers.

Now, then, do you want to take the *slightest* chance of meeting Prussianism here in America?

If not, then you'll have to help in summoning all the resources of this country for the giant struggle. For resources will win the war.

Here's the way you can help save our resources. Instead of throwing money away on unnecessary things, buy Thrift Stamps, 25 cents, and War-Savings-Stamps, $4.12, worth $5 in five years, 4 percent compound interest. They're good as government money; like a mortgage on the U.S.A.

*T*o influence public opinion, the War Department enlisted journalists and professors to write a series of "war information pamphlets." In the following example, history professor John S. P. Tatlock of Stanford University describes the sort of invasion that could be expected if the German hordes were not checked.

DOCUMENT 2. John S. P. Tatlock,
"Why America Fights Germany," 1918

Now let us picture what a sudden invasion of the United States by these Germans would mean; sudden, because their settled way is always to attack suddenly. First they set themselves to capture New York City. While their fleet blockades the harbor and shells the city and the forts from far at sea, their troops land somewhere near and advance toward the city in order to cut its rail communications, starve it into surrender and then plunder it. One body of from 50,000 to 100,000 men lands, let us suppose, at Barnegat Bay, New Jersey, and advances without meeting resistance, for the brave but small American army is scattered elsewhere. They pass through Lakewood, a station on the Central Railroad of New Jersey. They first demand wine for the officers and beer for the men. Angered to find that an American town does not contain large quantities of either, they pillage and burn the post office and most of the hotels and stores. Then they demand $1,000,000 from the residents. One feeble old woman tries to conceal $20 which she has been hoarding in her desk drawer; she is taken out and hanged (to save a cartridge). Some of the teachers in two district schools meet a fate which makes them envy her. The Catholic priest and Methodist minister are thrown into a pig-sty, while the German soldiers look on and laugh. Some of the officers quarter themselves in a handsome house on the edge of the town, insult the ladies of the family, and destroy and defile the contents of the house. By this time some of the soldiers have managed to get drunk . . . and then hell breaks loose. Robbery, murder and outrage run riot. Fifty leading citizens are lined up against the First National Bank building, and shot. Most of the town and the beautiful pinewoods are burned, and then the troops move on to treat New Brunswick in the same way—if they get there.

This is not just a snappy story. It is not fancy. The general plan of campaign against America has been announced repeatedly by German military men. And every horrible detail is just what the German troops have done in Belgium and France.

True to her belief in reason, not force, the leader of the settlement house movement, Jane Addams, helped form the Women's Peace Party in 1915. Soon afterward Addams participated in the Hague Conference of Women in Holland and then, with a group of the delegates, visited the capitals of six warring nations to urge the leaders to those countries to seek peaceful resolution of the conflict. On July 9, 1915, Addams spoke to a New York City audience about the conclusions she had drawn from her tour of Europe.

Document 3. Jane Addams, Address at Carnegie Hall, New York City, July 9, 1915

The first thing which was striking is this, that the same causes and reasons for the war were heard everywhere. Each warring nation solemnly assured you it is fighting under the impulse of self-defense. . . .

In each of the warring nations there is this other point of similarity. Generally speaking, we heard everywhere that this war was an old man's war; that the young men who were dying, the young men who were doing the fighting, were not the men who wanted the war, and were not the men who believed in the war; that somewhere in church and state, somewhere in the high places of society, the elderly people, the middle-aged people, had established themselves and had convinced themselves that this was a righteous war. . . .

I quote a letter published in the *Cambridge Magazine* at Cambridge University and written by a young man who had gone to the front. . . .

" . . . Just when the younger generation was beginning to take its share in the affairs of the world, and was hoping to counteract the Victorian influences of the older generation, this war has come to silence us,—permanently or temporarily as the case may be. Meanwhile, the old men are having field days on their own. In our name, and for our sakes as they pathetically imagine, they are doing their very utmost, it would seem, to perpetuate, by their appeals to hate, intolerance and revenge, those very follies which have produced the present conflagration." . . .

It seemed to me . . . that the older men believed more in abstractions, shall I say; that when they talked of patriotism, when they used certain theological or nationalistic words, these meant more to them than they did to the young men; that the young men had come to take life much more from the point of view of experience . . . and when they went to the trenches and tested it out, they concluded that it did not pay, that it was not what they wanted to do with their lives.

Perhaps the most shocking impression left upon one's mind is this, that in the various countries the temper necessary for continuing the war is worked up and fed largely by the things which have occurred in the war itself. . . .

Let us say that there are two groups of boys in a boys' club, and I have much experience of that sort in boys' clubs to draw upon. If one says, "We did this because the other fellows did that," you will simply have to say, "I won't go into the rights and wrongs of this, but this thing must stop, because it leads nowhere and gets nowhere." . . .

. . . And what it needs, it seems to me, and to many of us, is a certain touch of human nature. . . . When you find that you can't talk to a woman on any subject, however remote from the war, without finding at once that she is in the deepest perplexity, —that while she is carrying herself bravely and going on with her accustomed activities because she thinks thereby that she is serving her country, her heart is being torn all the time,—it is borne in upon you that at last human nature must revolt. . . . Then men must see the horrible things which have happened; they will have to soberly count up the loss of life, and the debt they have settled upon themselves for years to come. . . .

Continued

Encouraged by civilian and military officials to make their crusade in Europe an enlightening experience, many soldiers recorded their impressions in diaries and letters. In the case of one anonymous soldier, the task became so absorbing that it eventually found its way into print as Wine, Women, and War: A Diary of Disillusionment *(1926). As time in combat dragged on, the diary changed its tone and looked critically at war aims and their probable outcome.*

DOCUMENT 4. Diary of an Anonymous American Soldier

25 August 1918: Base Hospital at Neuilly: Has the Lord ordained that from hideous mangling of flesh beautiful things should come? . . . Can't evade it— there is sublimity in war. Man made in mold of divinity, and more than a flavor of his origin still clinging to his soul. The cheer of these lads, their quiet grave resignation, too beautiful for marring touch of praise. . . .

One comes away from this eddy of human wreckage, a little sick at heart. But one presently forgets the bodies shattered, the faces marred, the freshness of lives become stale and useless, and remembers only that "God fulfills himself in many ways." The singular evangelism of blood. . . .

18 October 1918: Three hundredth day from Hoboken! Damned cold. Shivering, fingers numb as lead, and not even November yet. . . . Race between Kaiser and my pants still on. Vital interest in early termination of conflict! Each day another seam opens or another button drops from fatigue—and can't keep pants up by merely gritting teeth. Each morning, scan communiques first—then breeches. Strain beginning to tell.

After the war problems of readjustment, hitherto kept in background, going to make all sorts of trouble. League of Nations, not mere imaginative sentimental Utopia, but only practicable solution of world in chaos. . . . The real victors in this war will be determined 10 or 20 years afterwards, and they will be the nation who will be the best able to face the growing discontent of a disillusioned people, to ward off impending famine, and to save their people from the appalling consequences of the universal bankruptcy to which Europe is speeding every day with increasing pace.

Vast amount of nonsense about Germany. Silly idea of demanding huge indemnities, and in same breath refusing to allow access to raw material, i.e., ask tree to give fruit, but shut off sun and air. . . . Either slaughter entire Teutonic race, or take them back and try to make something of them. No middle ground. No sense hating Germans. Only proper object for hate, to anyone with brains God gave little snails, is an idea. And can't destroy ideas, or crush them, or punish them. Can only substitute good ideas for bad ones.

This life hard on illusions. Not many left. A hell of a way from best of all possible worlds, and man certainly a son-of-a-bitch when he puts his mind to it. But hope not to travel too far along road on which so many realists stub their silly toes, of believing there is no angel worth mentioning in poor, complex human heart. Heaven and hell both there.

Document 1. James R. Mock and Cedric Larson, *Words That Won the War* (Princeton, 1939), 123-124.

Document 2. John S. P. Tatlock, "Why America Fights Germany," War Information Series pamphlet no. 15, War Department, 1918.

Document 3. Jane Addams, "The Revolt against War" *Survey,* July 17, 1915.

Document 4. Anonymous, *Wine, Women, and War: A Diary of Disillusionment* (New York, 1926).

more costly in American lives. European nations suffered much greater losses, however: 2.2 million Germans, 1.9 million Russians, 1.4 million French, and 900,000 Britons died in the war. Where they had fought and died, the landscape was as blasted and barren as the moon. One grim jest made the telling point that the war would last one hundred years— four years of fighting and ninety-six more to roll up the barbed wire.

A Compromised Peace

Wilson decided to reaffirm his noble war aims by announcing his peace aims even before the end of hostilities was in sight. He hoped that America's allies would rally around his generous ideas. He soon discovered, however, that the worldwide popular appeal he enjoyed as the savior of Europe did not translate into ready acceptance of his plan for international democracy. The leaders of England, France, and Italy understood that Wilson's principles jeopardized their own postwar plans for the acquisition of enemy territory, new colonial empires, and reparations. In his effort to draw public opinion to his side, Wilson had to confront bitter political opposition at home as well as abroad. In the end, Wilson failed to convince the world's leaders to create a new world order based on democratic ideals, and he stood repudiated.

Wilson's Fourteen Points

On January 8, 1918, ten months before the armistice in Europe, President Woodrow Wilson delivered before Congress a speech that summarized U.S. war aims and provided his vision of a liberal peace. In his famous "Fourteen Points," Wilson provided a

THE BIG FOUR
Cynics who sought a glimpse behind the flags and victory parades suspected that the world war had been orchestrated by leading politicians, bankers, and industrialists for their own advantage. This cartoon was typical of the view that deals struck behind closed doors made a mockery of Wilson's profession that "open covenants of peace, openly arrived at" would "make the world safe for democracy."
Catherine LeRoy/AP, print courtesy Time Inc. Picture Collection.

blueprint for a new democratic world order. Echoes of his New Freedom and progressive thought reverberated as he eloquently spoke of a generous peace, a peace without vengeance, a peace that would transform the sordid, self-interested war into something permanently good and uplifting. Only if the war resulted in a peaceful and stable world could the American sacrifices be justified, he insisted.

Wilson's Fourteen Points provided a blueprint for a new democratic world order, affirmed basic liberal ideals, and supported the right of European peoples to self-determination.

Wilson's Fourteen Points dealt with broad principle as well as practical matters. The first five points affirmed basic liberal ideals: "open covenants of peace, openly arrived at," that is, an end to secret treaties; freedom of the seas in war and peace; removal of economic barriers to free trade; reduction of weapons of war; and recognition of the rights of colonized peoples. The next eight points supported the right to self-determination of European peoples dominated by Germany or its allies. Wilson's final point called for a "general association of nations"—a League of Nations—to provide "mutual guarantees of political independence and territorial integrity to great and small states alike." Wilson's insistence on a League of Nations reflected his lifelong dream of a "parliament of man." Only such an organization, he believed, could resolve and justify the war. Wilson concluded his speech by assuring Germany that the United States did not seek its destruction or humiliation. Instead, if it would renounce its militarism and imperialism, the United States would welcome Germany into the family of "peace-loving nations."

The Fourteen Points roused popular enthusiasm in the United States and every Allied country. Armed with such public support, Wilson felt confident that he could prevail against undemocratic forces at the peace table. During the final year of war, he pressured the Allies to accept the Fourteen Points as the basis of the settlement. Through a barrage of speeches and leaflets, Wilson conveyed his willingness, if necessary, to speak over the heads of government leaders directly to the people and so expand his presidential role as spokesman for American citizens to the grand role of champion of all the world's people. The Allies had won the war; Wilson would win the peace.

The Paris Peace Conference

Buoyed by his sense of mission, Wilson decided to attend the Paris peace conference in 1919 as head of the American delegation himself. The decision to leave the country at a time when his opponents were sharply contesting his leadership was risky in itself. But his stubborn refusal to include prominent Republicans in the delegation proved foolhardy. The ranking Republican on the Senate Foreign Relations Committee, the formidable Henry Cabot Lodge of Massachusetts, had never cared much for Wilson. Now he began to despise him. Ignoring his critics, Wilson set sail for Europe on the liner *George Washington*. He sought the great feat of converting skeptical, even cynical, Allies to his idealistic vision without having his own nation firmly behind him.

Still, the peace venture began well. As Wilson's motorcade made its way from the port of Le Havre to Paris, huge crowds cheered the American president. After four terrible years of war, men and women in Europe looked upon Wilson as a kind of savior, someone who would create a safer, more decent world.

When the peace conference convened at Louis XIV's magnificent palace at Versailles, however, Wilson encountered a very different reception. Representing the Allies were the decidedly unidealistic David Lloyd George of Britain, Georges Clemenceau of France, and Vittorio Orlando of Italy. To them, Wilson was a naive and impractical man who understood little about hard European realities. The Allies wanted to fasten blame for the war on Germany, totally disarm it, and make it pay so dearly for the destruction it had wrought that it would never be able to threaten its neighbors again. The French, in particular, upon whose soil most of the fighting was waged and who suffered an enormous loss of young manhood, demanded retribution in the form of territory and assurances that the German attack of 1914 would never be repeated.

Wilson was forced to measure success in inches, each small victory the product of tough negotiations and often unsavory compromise. He persuaded the Allies to agree that Germany would not be dismembered. Although France recovered Alsace-Lorraine, which Germany had won in the Franco-Prussian War of 1871, it did not gain additional German territory. Still, Germany's Rhineland was demilitarized and the mineral-rich Saar region was placed under international control, with France having the right to work the coal mines until an election after fifteen years would determine which nation the people of the region would join. In return for French moderation of their territorial claims, Wilson agreed to support Article 231 of the peace treaty, assigning war guilt to Germany, and to endorse the concept of German repayment for damage to civilian property. Germany was outraged at being singled out as the instigator of the war and saddled with more than $33 billion in damages. Although the United States decided to waive its share of the reparations, the Germans felt betrayed by Wilson, who they believed had falsely promised that the peace terms would be based on his generous Fourteen Points.

Among the most pressing questions was where to draw national boundaries. Wilson proposed that dependent emerging nations, called mandates, would develop into democratic states under the guidance of the League of Nations, which would assign the mandates to small nations that had retained their virtue by not creating colonial empires. He gained considerable agreement on the principle of self-determination, though Italian ambitions to acquire coastal regions of the Balkans along the Adriatic Sea and French demands for Alsace-Lorraine had to be appeased. In applying democratic principles of self-determination, the conference redrew the map of Europe. Portions of the Austro-Hungarian Empire were ceded to Italy, Poland, and Romania, and the remainder reassembled into Austria, Hungary, Czechloslovakia, and Yugoslavia—independent republics with boundaries determined according to concentrations of ethnic groups. More arbitrarily, the Ottoman Empire was carved up into small mandates (including Palestine) under the control of France and Great Britain, partly to meet Allied concerns about stability in the Middle East and partly in accord with historical patterns of national sovereignty. Thus, with varying degrees of danger from ethnic and nationalist rivalries, each reconstructed nation faced the challenge of trying to make a new democratic government work.

Wilson hoped that Germany's colonies in Asia and Africa would be turned over to the League of Nations as mandates and either granted independence or ruled temporarily by smaller, nonimperialist nations. The Allies had other ideas. They had taken control of the colonies during the war, and they planned to keep them. A compromise left the colonies in the major powers' hands, but they agreed that the League of Nations would help administer them through the mandate system. Technically, the mandate system rejected imperialism. Yet it smacked of the old imperialist ways and drew

MAP 22.5
Europe after World War I
The post–World War I settlement redrew boundaries to create new nations based on ethnic groupings. This left bitter peoples within defeated Germany and Russia who resolved to recover territory that the new arrangements took from their homelands.

criticism from reformers and those who had suffered domination by the Western powers.

Adding to the taint was the refusal of the peace conference to endorse the proposal of Japan, an Allied nation during the war, for a clause proclaiming the principle of racial equality. Wilson's belief in the superiority of whites, as well as his apprehension about how Americans would respond to such a declaration, led him to oppose the clause. To soothe hurt feelings, Wilson agreed to grant Japan a mandate over the Shantung Peninsula in northern China, which had formerly been controlled by Germany. The gesture mollified Japan's moderate leaders, but the military faction getting ready to take over the country remained bitter about Western colonialism and racial prejudice.

Revolutionary changes that had taken place in Russia during the war intensified and confused certain key issues. In March 1917, after terrible defeats in the war, Czar Nicholas II was forced to abdicate, and reformers announced a new democratic era. To Wilson, who was just then leading his country into war, the Russian Revolution seemed to confirm his hopes that democracy would rise from the ashes of destruction. In reckless enthusiasm, Wilson declared that Russia had always been "democratic at

heart." With the autocracy gone, he continued, "the great, generous Russian people have been added in all their naive majesty and might to the forces that are fighting for freedom." A very different reality soon emerged, however. Appealing to a widespread desperation in Russia to leave the war, a group of Marxist radicals calling themselves Bolsheviks seized control of the nation in November 1917 and made their leader, Vladimir Ilyich Lenin, total ruler of the revolutionary state that came to be known as the Soviet Union. On December 15, 1917, Lenin concluded an armistice with Germany. To make matters worse for Wilsonian idealists, Lenin insisted that the war was being fought not for democracy but to extend the power of capitalist nations. Outraged by what he considered the Bolsheviks' betrayal of the Russian Revolution, Wilson reacted as he had to the Mexican revolution by refusing to recognize the new Russian government.

Respect for self-determination kept Wilson from agreeing with his British ally Winston Churchill that "the Bolshevik infant should be strangled in its cradle" by direct military action. The president did agree, nonetheless, to send fourteen thousand troops in September 1918 to join British and French forces in Siberia. Officially, the military mission was only to safeguard the movement of British materiel and a contingent of Czech soldiers to the western front; but in addition, Allied troops assisted the so-called White Army, loyal to the deposed czar, in trying to overthrow Lenin and annul the Bolshevik Revolution. Wilson finally withdrew the expedition in April 1920 but continued to oppose Lenin's regime. Public opinion divided significantly in the face of these momentous events. A few observers were inspired by the Russian Revolution to believe that the war had created possibilities for suffering millions throughout the world to overthrow the tyrants who had oppressed them. Most Americans, however, saw the outcome as evidence that the cause of democracy had fallen short and left the world full of radical menace. The decision of subsequent American administrations to continue withholding recognition of the Soviet Union until 1933 indicated how deeply Americans disapproved of communism and everything that seemed tainted with its radical, alien mark.

Despite his many frustrations, however, Wilson gained what he most wanted at Versailles—acceptance of the League of Nations. He considered the league, an international organization designed to promote peace, as the cornerstone of international order, a forum for the nations of the world to solve their common problems. Wilson envisioned the league actively stopping aggression, pursuing disarmament, and protecting freedom of the seas and free trade. If necessary, it could invoke economic and even military sanctions against aggressor nations. Wilson realized the shortcomings of the treaty that the Allies were hammering out at Versailles, but he hoped that the league could remedy the imperfections born of compromise. Moreover, he knew that the postwar world was a precarious place, beset with national and ethnic rivalries, psychological wounds, and shattered economies and societies. The league, Wilson believed fervently, would provide peace its strongest ally.

To many Europeans and Americans whose hopes had been stirred by Wilson's lofty aims, the Versailles treaty came as a bitter disappointment. Wilson's admirers were shocked that the president dealt in compromise, like any other politician. But compromise and concession were inevitable. And without Wilson's presence, the treaty that was signed in the Hall of Mirrors at Versailles on June 28, 1919, would surely have been more vindictive. Wilson returned home in July 1919 convinced that the treaty he carried was the best obtainable.

The Fight for the Treaty

The tumultuous reception Wilson received when he arrived home persuaded him that the American people supported the treaty as well as American membership in the League of Nations. But the people would not vote on the treaty. The United States Senate would. Exhausted by six months of wrangling at Versailles, Wilson returned to Washington grimly determined to win the two-thirds vote needed for Senate approval.

On July 10, 1919, Wilson submitted the treaty to the Senate, warning that failure to ratify it would "break the heart of the world." But by then, news of the treaty's provisions had spread, and criticism was mounting. The most raucous voices raised against it were those of Americans still concerned about their countries of ethnic origin. German Americans complained that forcing Germany to pay heavy reparations and lose territory meant that the Fatherland was being blamed for a war that was really caused by many national rivalries. Italian Americans protested Wilson's refusal to cede more territory on the Adriatic coast to Italy. Irish Americans deplored Wilson's failure to follow his principle of self-determination by supporting the independence of Ireland from British rule. Even Wilson's liberal supporters worried that the president's concessions at Versailles had jeopardized the treaty's capacity to provide a generous plan for rebuilding Europe and guarantee the peace.

The treaty's most potent critics were found in the U.S. Senate. After the election of 1918 had given Republicans a slight edge over Democrats, forty-nine to forty-seven, a group of Republican "irreconcilables," which included such powerful senators as Hiram Johnson of California and William Borah of Idaho, condemned the treaty for entangling the United States in world affairs. They favored a return to the tradition of noninvolvement. A larger group of Republicans did not object to U.S. participation in world politics but feared that membership in the League of Nations would jeopardize the nation's independence in foreign affairs. No Republican, moreover, was eager to hand Wilson and the Democrats a foreign policy victory with the 1920 presidential election little more than a year away.

At the center of Republican opposition was Wilson's archenemy Senator Henry Cabot Lodge of Massachusetts. A spare man of sixty-nine whose piercing eyes and pointed beard gave him a slightly satanic look, Lodge found many reasons to loathe

WOODROW WILSON
An exhausted Wilson shows the flag in San Francisco during his 1919 cross-country tour to rouse support for the Versailles treaty. Reaction on the West Coast was mixed. Bitter labor unrest brought hecklers into the San Francisco crowds; before that, in Seattle, where a general strike had recently been crushed, the IWW lined the streets with protesters who stood in stony silence as the rattled president drove by. A week after this photograph was taken, a stroke felled Wilson and brought this mission to an end.
UPI/Bettmann Archive.

Wilson, personal pride prominent among them. Before Wilson had entered politics, Lodge, with his Ph.D. and historical publications, had become known as "the Scholar of the Senate." It rankled Lodge to be eclipsed by a rival of greater intellectual eminence who had also risen above him politically to become president. In the midst of one argument with the administration, Lodge exclaimed: "I never expected to hate anyone in politics with the hatred I feel toward Wilson." The enmity between the two men was especially acute over foreign policy. Lodge was no isolationist. Like his friend Theodore Roosevelt, who had died in January 1919, Lodge expected the United States' economic might and strong army and navy to propel the nation into a major role in world affairs. But Lodge insisted that mem-

bership in the League of Nations, which would require collective action to maintain the peace, threatened the nation's freedom of choice in foreign relations.

To undermine public support of the treaty, Lodge used his position as chairman of the Senate Foreign Relations Committee to air every sort of complaint. Out of the committee hearings came several "reservations," or amendments, that sought to limit the consequences of American membership in the league. For example, several reservations required approval of both the House and the Senate before the United States could participate in league-sponsored economic sanctions or military action. Eventually, it became clear that ratification of the treaty depended on acceptance of the Lodge reservations. Democratic senators, who overwhelmingly supported the treaty, urged Wilson to accept the reservations, arguing that they left the essentials of the treaty intact. Wilson, however, insisted that the reservations amounted to a "nullification" of the treaty. "*Lodge* reservations?" he thundered. "Never! I'll never consent to adopt any policy with which that impossible name is so prominently identified."

Whether American membership could have prevented another war in Europe in 1939 is debatable, but America's failure to join the League of Nations certainly left it a much weaker institution.

With the treaty about to be reported from the Foreign Relations Committee to the full Senate with reservations attached, Wilson decided to take his case directly to the people. On September 3, 1919, he set out by train on the most ambitious speaking tour ever undertaken by a president. Always uncomfortable with stump speaking and warned by his doctors that his health would not stand the strain, Wilson nevertheless became more eloquent, more forceful each week. But in Pueblo, Colorado, on September 25, just as his appeal seemed to be gaining momentum, Wilson collapsed and had to return to Washington. There he suffered a massive stroke that partially paralyzed him. From his bedroom, Wilson sent messages through his wife and cabinet instructing Democrats in the Senate to hold firm against any and all reservations. In the end, Wilson commanded enough loyalty to ensure a vote against the Lodge reservations. But his victory in that battle cost him the war. When the treaty came up for a vote in the Senate in March 1920, the combined opposition of the Republican irreconcilables and Republican reservationists left Wilson six votes short of the two-thirds majority needed for passage.

The nations of Europe went about organizing the league at Geneva, Switzerland, but the United States never became a member. Whether American membership could have prevented another war in Europe in 1939 is debatable, but America's failure to join certainly left the league a much weaker institution. Brought low by their feud, Woodrow Wilson and Henry Cabot Lodge both died in 1924, never seeing international order or security, never knowing the whirlwind that would eventually follow the failure to make the world safe for democracy.

Postwar Change

The defeat of Wilson's idealistic hopes for international democracy was the crowning blow to progressives at home who had hoped that the war could serve as a vehicle for reform. The reaction against idealism included an urge to demobilize swiftly. In the process, servicemen, defense workers, and farmers lost their connection to national purpose and much of their economic security. The combination of displaced veterans returning home, a stalled economy, and leftover wartime patriotism looking for a new cause was so volatile that it could hardly fail to explode. The American people moved toward the view that the main benefit of victory in the war had been to protect the nation against alien menace. It followed that postwar policy should strive to root out similar enemies at home, especially supporters of the Bolshevik Revolution in Russia. Then the country could move from wartime sacrifice to the normal pursuits of wealth and happiness.

Economic Hardship and Labor Upheaval

With news of the armistice came the need to convert the United States back to a peacetime economy. The impulse to end the wartime experiment in government-business cooperation, dismantle the federal agencies responsible for war production, and return to the hallowed traditions of free enterprise proved irresistible to economic and political leaders. Deconversion of the economy and demobilization of the armed forces came swiftly and was largely unplanned. The government simply abandoned its wartime controls on the economy and almost overnight canceled millions of dollars in orders for war materiel. In a matter of months, more than three million soldiers were mustered out of the military with only sixty dollars and a one-way ticket home. When war production ceased and veterans flooded the job market, unemployment rose sharply. At the same time consumers went on a postwar spending spree, and inflation soared. In 1919, prices rose an astonishing 75 percent over prewar levels, and in 1920, while inflation slowed, prices rose another 28 percent.

Labor had enjoyed a share of wartime prosperity, but most of the gains for workers evaporated in the postwar period. Business, freed from control and eager to restore the more favorable position it

**After the Welcome Home –
a JOB!**
U.S. EMPLOYMENT SERVICE *Dep't of Labor*

RETURNING VETERANS AND WORK

After the triumphal parades passed by, attention turned to the question of what the heroes would do at home. The Department of Labor poster tries to convey a strong image of purposefulness and prosperity by framing a soldier in a victory arch in front of a booming industrial landscape. Under the circumstances, though, the soldier can best be regarded as a displaced person, teetering on a windowsill, dangerously high in the air. The U.S. Employment Service had little to offer veterans beyond posters such as this; and unions were unprepared to cope with the massive numbers of former soldiers who needed retraining. As workplace conditions deteriorated, the largest number of strikes in the nation's history broke out in 1919. The Chicago steel strikers in the photograph look very different from the returning soldier in the poster. Their fate was to lose the strike and return to harsh conditions. No record was kept of ex-servicemen, left to find their own way in the postwar world.

Library of Congress; UPI/Bettmann Archive.

held before the war, turned against the eight-hour day and declared war on labor unions. Rather than sit back and watch inflation eat up their paychecks and bosses destroy their unions, labor fought back. The year 1919 witnessed nearly 3,600 strikes involving four million workers.

In February 1919, a spectacular strike in the Northwest vividly demonstrated the depth of workers' discontent. In Seattle, large numbers of metalworkers and shipbuilders had been put out of work by demobilization. A coalition of two labor organizations—the radical Industrial Workers of the World (IWW) and the moderate American Federation of Labor (AFL)—called a general strike. The strike, the largest in American history, shut down the city for several days. Nationwide, elected officials and newspaper editorials echoed claims in the Seattle *Times* that the walkout was "a Bolshevik effort to start a revolution" engineered by "Seattle labor criminals." An effort to deport strike leaders failed because they were citizens, not aliens, but the suppression of the general strike by Seattle's anti-union mayor, Ole Hanson, and widespread alarm about radicalism cost the AFL much of the support it had gained through its wartime service and contributed to the destruction of the IWW soon afterward.

The ominous linkage of labor unrest and radical subversion reflected the Wilson administration's encounter with revolutionary socialism. Since the late nineteenth century, refugees from autocratic regimes in Europe had flocked to America, often bringing with them radical ideas about replacing private ownership of the means of production with a welfare state controlled by the working class. Socialists had played only a minor part in the progressive debate about how the United States should be reformed, but they had irked Wilson by challenging his New Freedom ideal of decentralized democracy. Under the pressures of socialist and Bolshevik denunciation of the war, Wilson's antagonism slid easily into the conviction that his radical critics were a subversive menace.

The outcome of a strike for higher pay by Boston policemen in the fall of 1919 also demonstrated rising postwar hostility toward labor militancy. Without police walking their beats, looters sacked the city. After two days of near anarchy, Boston's mayor fired the police force and began hiring new officers. The mayor had the approval of the Massachusetts governor, Calvin Coolidge, who gained national fame by calling out the National Guard to restore order. The public, frightened by news of radicalism abroad and yearning for peace and quiet at home, was grateful for Coolidge's reassurance that "there is no right to strike against the public safety by anybody, anywhere, any time."

Labor suffered an even more serious blow in the defeat of a widespread steel strike in 1919. Steelworkers had serious grievances, but for decades the steel industry had succeeded in beating back all their efforts to unionize. In 1919, however, the AFL, still led by its founding father, Samuel Gompers, caught wind of the steel industry's plan to renew the oppressive prewar system of seven-day weeks and twelve-hour days for weekly wages of about twenty dollars. Having loyally supported the government's war effort, the AFL expected federal support for its effort to unionize steelworkers. When Gompers began to recruit union members, however, he learned that he faced the steel barons alone. Elbert Gary, director of U.S. Steel, and Charles Schwab, his counterpart at Bethlehem Steel, announced that they would not negotiate a contract with the AFL. Gompers called for a strike, and 350,000 workers in fifteen states responded by walking out in September 1919.

Denying that the workers had legitimate complaints, the steel industry hired 30,000 strikebreakers (many of them African Americans) and turned public opinion against the strikers by portraying them as Bolsheviks bent on subverting the Republic. State and federal troops blocked an effective response by the union by keeping striking members from getting close to the steel mills and discouraging scabs from crossing their picket line. In January 1920, after 18 workers had been killed, the strike collapsed. The failure in the steel industry initiated a sharp decline in the fortunes of the labor movement, a trend that would last throughout the 1920s.

The steel strike offered dramatic testimony to the continuation of a nasty wartime development. To whip up popular enthusiasm for the defense of the American heritage, government and private propagandists had demonized the nation's enemies, transforming, for example, Germans into evil Huns. The steel barons took advantage of Americans' suspicion and hatred of foreigners by pinning the label Red, or Communist, on the strikers, many of whom were recent immigrants from the much hated Austro-Hungarian Empire. The leader of the steelworkers' union within the AFL, William Z. Foster, though born in the slums of Philadelphia, had once been a member of the IWW. As such, and for having uttered the conviction that the government represented capitalist oppression, he was lumped in with "dangerous" foreign radicals.

A new organization for veterans of the war, the American Legion, played an important role in the controversy over bolshevism, patriotism, and security. The organization provided a peacetime identity for veterans, with a name that harked back to the Roman ideal of a vigilant citizenry permanently ready to defend against the enemies of the state. Initially, the American Legion responded to the fact that, after the parades had ended for the two million American troops who returned from Europe, the veterans were left to make their way in an uncertain world. To assist them, the Legion persuaded Congress to award veterans' bonuses and create a Veterans' Bureau to provide medical care and other benefits. But the Legion's sense of patriotic service, expressed by its motto, "For God and Country," also included taking action against individuals and groups that showed disloyalty toward established institutions. In the struggle to maintain order and quell radical dissent, the Legion proved to be a potent weapon.

The Red Scare

In 1919–1920, fear of internal subversion swept the nation. The "Red scare" of that time far outstripped the hysteria, violence, and systematic denial of civil liberties during the war. This sad episode stemmed in part from the severe stresses and strains in American society, including the postwar recession, labor unrest, and the return of millions of veterans. But unsettling events abroad also added to Americans' anxieties. The victory of the Bolsheviks in Russia, itself disturbing, became even more menacing in March 1919 when the new Soviet leaders created the Third International to foment revolution in capitalist countries. The chance of a Communist revolution in the United States was zero, but a flurry of isolated terrorist acts in 1919 made it seem to edgy Americans that revolutionaries were at the door. Thirty-eight mail bombs were sent to prominent Americans, including Supreme Court Justice Oliver Wendell Holmes and financier J. P. Morgan Jr. The post office intercepted all but one of the bombs, but that one blew off the hand of the maid of a Georgia senator.

Fear and anger, mingled with bafflement over how to understand the motives of terrorists, led swiftly to a hunt for scapegoats. Middle-class Americans had long stigmatized immigrants as radicals. Business had stereotyped labor organizers as subversives. And most Americans identified socialists and others on the political left as dangerous to the

Republic. In 1919 and 1920, Attorney General Thomas Gregory and his successor, A. Mitchell Palmer, helped galvanize the nation's prejudices into an all-out assault on alleged conspirators. To protect the country from "Bolshevik tyranny," Mitchell decided that "there could be no nice distinctions drawn between the theoretical ideals of the radicals and their actual violations of our national laws." Targeting men and women who had broken no laws but who harbored what Mitchell considered dangerous thoughts, the Justice Department unleashed a witch-hunt against the supposed enemies of America.

> *The chance of a Communist revolution in the United States was zero, but a flurry of isolated terrorist acts in 1919 made it seem to edgy Americans that revolutionaries were at the door.*

In January 1920, Palmer ordered a series of raids that netted six thousand suspected subversives. He expected to discover plans for revolution and caches of weapons. Three pistols did not constitute a revolutionary armory, but Palmer nevertheless ordered five hundred of the suspects deported. Catching the spirit of the occasion, one Protestant minister suggested that the "Reds" should be sent away on ships of stone, with sails of lead, the wrath of God at their backs for a breeze and the port of hell for their destination. Government officials had already deported the country's most notorious radical, the Russian immigrant Emma Goldman. Before the war, Goldman's passionate support of labor strikes (including the Homestead lockout), women's rights, and birth control had made her a leading symbol of subversion and outspoken disrespect for mainstream opinion. During the war, she attacked conscription and earned a stay in prison. Her activities caught the eye of the fervent young director of the Radical Division of the Justice Department, J. Edgar Hoover, who targeted her for deportation. In December 1919, officials loaded Goldman and 250 other unwanted alien radicals on a ship for exile in the Soviet Union. When a jeering bystander yelled "Merry Christmas, Emma!," the unchastened rebel turned, thumbed her nose, and disappeared from the deck. A lawyer, commenting on her departure, noted, "With Prohibition coming in and Emma Goldman goin' out, 'twill be a dull country."

The effort to rid the country of alien radicals was matched by efforts to crush those entitled to remain. The climax was reached on Armistice Day, November 11, 1919, in Centralia, Washington. A rugged lumber town, Centralia contained one of only two IWW halls left in the state. Rumors circulated that the hall would be raided on the first anniversary of the end of the war. When members of the local American Legion post gathered in front of the hall, nervous IWW members fired into their ranks, killing three Legionnaires. Several union members were captured and later convicted of murder, but one, Wesley Everest, an ex-soldier, was tortured, castrated, and hung from a bridge, where his body was riddled with bullets. The coroner ruled the death a suicide, his report stating that Everest "jumped off [the bridge] with a rope around his neck and then shot himself full of holes." The incident roused other law enforcement officials to conduct raids to rid their cities and towns of "Reds."

Public institutions of all kinds joined the attack on civil liberties. Local libraries removed dissenting books. Schools and colleges fired unorthodox teachers. Police shut down radical newspapers. State legislatures refused to seat duly elected representatives who professed socialist ideas. In 1919, Congress removed its lone Socialist representative, Victor Berger, on the grounds that he was a threat to national safety. And that same year, the Supreme Court provided a formula for restricting the exercise of free speech. In upholding the conviction of Socialist Charles Schenck for publishing a pamphlet urging resistance to the draft during wartime (*Schenck v. United States*), Justice Oliver Wendell Holmes for the Court established a "clear and present danger" test. Such utterances as Schenck's during a time of national peril, Holmes wrote, could be considered the equivalent of shouting "Fire!" in a crowded theater. Congress had the right to protect the public against such an incitement to panic, the Court ruled. But the analogy was a false one. Schenck's pamphlet echoed faintly in the open air, not in a crowded theater, and had little power to provoke a public firmly opposed to its message.

In time, the relentless cries of Attorney General Palmer and other government leaders that the Communists were coming lost credibility. The lack of any real radical menace became clear after newspaper headlines carried Palmer's warning that radicals were planning to celebrate the Bolshevik Revolution with a nationwide wave of violence on May 1, 1920. Palmer supplied all federal buildings with armed guards. Throughout the nation, officials responded by calling out state militia, fortifying public buildings and churches, mobilizing bomb squads, even putting machine gun nests at major city intersections. When May 1 came and went without a single disturbance, the public mood turned from fear to scorn, and Palmer, who had taken to calling himself the "Fighting Quaker," was jeered as the "Quaking Fighter."

Conclusion: Troubled Crusade

At home and abroad, the First World War was a traumatic experience for the American people. Woodrow Wilson sought to keep the nation out of war, but when war arrived in 1917, he promised that American intervention would further the noble cause of worldwide democracy. Serving under idealistic banners, American soldiers and sailors encountered unprecedented horrors—submarines, poison gas, machine guns—and more than 100,000 died. Rather than redeem their sacrifice, the peace that followed the armistice tarnished it. Few found consolation in the fact that the war thrust the nation into a position of international preeminence. At home, war brought prosperity, but rather than permanently improve working conditions, advance public health, and spread educational opportunity as progressives had hoped, the war threatened to undermine the achievements of the previous two decades. The immediate postwar years witnessed unemployment, inflation, racial conflict, labor unrest, and a ruthless crackdown on dissent.

In 1920, a bruised and disillusioned society stumbled into a new decade. The era coming to an end had called on Americans to crusade and sacrifice. Now whoever could promise them peace, prosperity, and a good time would have the best chance to win their hearts.

CHRONOLOGY

1914 In an attempt to impose democracy on Mexico, President Woodrow Wilson sends marines to occupy port of Veracruz.

August 6. All-out conflict when Germany declares war on Russia.

1915 German submarine sinks British liner *Lusitania,* with loss of almost 1,200 lives, including 128 Americans.

Settlement House reformer Jane Addams helps form Women's Peace Party to seek peaceful resolution of war.

1916 General Pershing leads military expedition into Mexico in pursuit of rebel leader "Pancho" Villa.

1917 British authorities inform Wilson of Zimmermann telegram.

April 6. Submarine attacks on American vessels convince Wilson to declare war on Germany.

Wilson creates Committee on Public Information, to promote U.S. war aims.

Selective Service Act authorizes military draft that brings 2.8 million men into armed services.

Espionage Act passed, limiting First Amendment rights.

Resentment against blacks migrating northward in search of work ignites violent race riot in East St. Louis, Illinois.

Armed action by black soldiers against racial discrimination in Houston results in execution of thirteen of the soldiers and life sentences for forty-one more.

Bolshevik Revolution ends Russian participation in the war.

1918– American forces deployed in Russia
1920 to protect Allied supplies and ports from Germany and then to support White Russian efforts to undo Bolshevik Revolution.

1918 **January 8.** President Wilson outlines his fourteen-point plan for peace.

May – June. American marines succeed in their first major combat with the Germans at Cantigny and Château-Thierry.

November 11. Armistice signed ending World War I.

1919 **January 18.** Paris peace conference begins, with President Wilson as head of U.S. delegation.

June 28. Versailles peace treaty signed.

Wilson undertakes speaking tour to rally support for ratification of Versailles treaty and League of Nations.

Postwar recession and ending of wartime support for labor unions lead to wave of strikes.

1919– Attorney General A. Mitchell Palmer
1920 leads effort, known as Red scare, to rid country of anarchists and aliens.

1920 **January 1.** Prohibition goes into effect, following ratification of Eighteenth Amendment.

Organized labor suffers its greatest defeat by ending the steel strike without a settlement.

Senate votes against ratification of Versailles peace treaty.

August 18. Nineteenth Amendment, granting women the vote, ratified by states.

BIBLIOGRAPHY

GENERAL WORKS

John Milton Cooper Jr., *Pivotal Decades: The United States, 1900–1920* (1990).

Robert H. Ferrell, *Woodrow Wilson and World War I, 1917–1921* (1985).

Ellis W. Hawley, *The Great War and the Search for a Modern Order: A History of the American People and Their Institutions, 1917–1933* (1979).

Derek Heater, *National Self-Determination: Woodrow Wilson and His Legacy* (1994).

David Kennedy, *Over Here: The First World War and American Society* (1980).

Nell Irwin Painter, *Standing at Armageddon: The United States, 1877–1919* (1987).

Robert D. Schulzinger, *American Diplomacy in the Twentieth Century* (1984).

David Steigerwald, *Wilsonian Idealism in America* (1994).

David Stevenson, *The First World War and International Politics* (1988).

J. M. Winter, *The Experience of World War I* (1989).

Neil A. Wynn, *From Progressivism to Prosperity: World War I and American Society* (1986).

EUROPEAN CONTEXT

Modris Ecksteins, *Rites of Spring: The Great War and the Birth of the Modern Age* (1990).

James Joll, *The Origins of the First World War* (1992).

Dwight Lee, *Europe's Crucial Years: The Diplomatic Background of World War I, 1902–1914* (1974).

George L. Mosse, *Fallen Soldiers: Reshaping the Memory of the World Wars* (1990).

Roland Stromberg, *Redemption by War: The Intellectuals and 1914* (1982).

Barbara W. Tuchman, *The Guns of August* (1962).

WOODROW WILSON AND THE WORLD

Kendrick A. Clement, *William Jennings Bryan, Missionary Isolationist* (1982).

Kendrick A. Clement, *Woodrow Wilson, World Statesman* (1987).

Patrick Devlin, *Too Proud to Fight: Woodrow Wilson's Neutrality* (1974).

John S. D. Eisenhower, *Intervention! The United States and the Mexican Revolution, 1913–1917* (1993).

Lloyd C. Gardner, *Safe for Democracy: The Anglo-American Response to Revolution, 1913–1923* (1987).

Burton I. Kaufman, *Efficiency and Expansion: Foreign Trade Organization in the Wilson Administration, 1913–1921* (1974).

Thomas Knock, *To End All Wars: Woodrow Wilson and the Quest for a New World Order* (1992).

Gordon N. Levin, *Woodrow Wilson and World Politics: America's Response to War and Revolution* (1970).

Arthur S. Link, *Wilson*, 5 vols. (1947–1965).

Manuel A. Machado Jr., *Centaur of the North: Francisco Villa, the Mexican Revolution, and Northern Mexico* (1988).

THE CRUSADE FOR DEMOCRACY

Daniel Beaver, *Newton D. Baker and the American War Effort, 1917–1919* (1966).

William T. Breen, *Uncle Sam at Home: Civilian Mobilization, Wartime Federalism, and the Council of National Defense, 1917–1919* (1984).

Jean Conner, *The National War Labor Board: Stability, Social Justice, and the Voluntary State in World War I* (1983).

Robert D. Cuff, *The War Industries Board: Business-Government Relations during World War I* (1973).

Carol S. Gruber, *Mars and Minerva* (1975).

John F. McClymer, *War and Welfare: Social Engineering in America, 1890–1925* (1980).

Ronald Schaffer, *America in the Great War: The Rise of the War Welfare State* (1991).

Stephen Vaughn, *Holding Fast the Inner Lines: Democracy, Nationalism, and the Committee for Public Information* (1980).

PACIFISM AND DISSENT

Charles Chatfield, *For Peace and Justice: Pacifism in America, 1914–1941* (1971).

Emma Goldman, *Living My Life* (1931).

Frederick C. Griffin, *Six Who Protested: Radical Opposition to the First World War* (1977).

C. Roland Marchand, *The American Peace Movement and Social Reform* (1973).

Marian J. Morton, *Emma Goldman and the American Left* (1992).

Paul L. Murphy, *World War I and the Origin of Civil Liberties in the United States* (1979).

Cass Sunstein, *Democracy and the Problem of Free Speech* (1993).

THE WAR IN MEMORY AND IMAGINATION

Peter Aichinger, *The American Soldier in Fiction, 1880–1963: A History of Attitudes towards Warfare and the Military Establishment* (1975).

Stanley Cooperman, *World War I and the American Novel* (1970).

Richard Cork, *The Bitter Truth: Avant-Garde Art and the Great War* (1994).

Paul Fussell, *The Great War and Modern Memory* (1975).

Jon Glover and Jon Silkin, eds., *The Penguin Book of First World War Prose* (1989).

Ernest Hemingway, *A Farewell to Arms* (1929).

Michael T. Isenberg, *War on Film* (1981).

Lyn Macdonald, *1914–1918: Voices and Images of the Great War* (1988).

BLACK AMERICA

Arthur E. Barbeau and Florette Henri, *The Unknown Soldiers: Black American Troops in World War I* (1974).

Carole Marks, *Farewell—We're Good and Gone: The Great Black Migration* (1989).

Bernard C. Nalty, *Strength for the Fight: A History of Black Americans in the Military* (1986).

Gerald Wilson Patton, *War and Race: The Black Officer in the American Military, 1915–1941* (1981).

Joe William Trotter Jr., ed., *The Great Migration in Historical Perspective* (1991).

GENDER AND SOCIETY

Nancy F. Cott, *The Grounding of American Feminism* (1987).

Sara Evans, *Born for Liberty: A History of Women in America* (1989).

Maurine Weiner Greenwald, *Women, War, and Work: The Impact of World War I on Women Workers in the United States* (1980).

Margaret Randolph Higonnet, Jane Jenson, Sonya Michel, and Margaret Collins Weitz, eds., *Behind the Lines: Gender and the Two World Wars* (1987).

Barbara J. Steinson, *American Women's Activism in World War I* (1982).

MILITARY ORGANIZATION AND EXPERIENCE

Michael C. Adams, *The Great Adventure: Male Desire and the Coming of World War I* (1990).

John Whiteclay Chambers II, *To Raise an Army: The Draft Comes to Modern America* (1987).

J. Garry Clifford, *The Citizen Soldiers* (1972).

Edward M. Coffman, *The War to End All Wars: The American Military Experience in World War I* (1968).

Kenneth J. Hagan, *This People's Navy: The Making of American Sea Power* (1990).

Lee Kennett, *The First Air War, 1914–1918* (1990).

Allan R. Millett and Peter Maslowski, *For the Common Defense: A Military History of the United States of America* (1984).

G. Kurt Piehler, *Remembering War the American Way* (1995).

Dominick A. Pisano, Thomas J. Dietz, Joanne M. Gernstein, and Karl S. Schneide, *Legend, Memory, and the Great War in the Air* (1992).

Daniel M. Smith, *The Great Departure: The United States and World War I* (1965).

Donald Smythe, *Pershing* (1986).

David F. Trask, *The AEF and Coalition War-Making, 1917–1918* (1993).

Russell F. Weigley, *The American Way of War: A History of United States Military Strategy and Policy* (1977).

Stanley Weintraub, *A Stillness Heard Round the World: The End of the Great War, November 1918* (1985).

PEACE AND POSTWAR CHANGE

David Brody, *Labor in Crisis: The Steel Strike of 1919* (1965).

Melvyn Dubofsky, *We Shall Be All: A History of the Industrial Workers of the World* (1969; reprint, 1988).

Melvyn Dubofsky, *The State and Labor in Modern America* (1994).

David S. Fogelsong, *America's Secret War against Bolshevism: U.S. Intervention in the Russian Civil War, 1917–1920* (1995).

John L. Gaddis, *Russia, the Soviet Union, and the United States* (1978).

John Maynard Keynes, *The Economic Consequences of the Peace* (1920).

Charles L. May Jr., *The End of Order: Versailles, 1919* (1980).

Robert K. Murray, *Red Scare: A Study in National Hysteria, 1919–1920* (1955).

William Pencak, *For God and Country* (1989).

Richard Polenberg, *Fighting Faiths: The Abrams Case, the Supreme Court, and Free Speech* (1987).

William G. Ross, *Forging New Freedoms: Nativism, Education, and the Constitution, 1917–1927* (1994).

Francis Russell, *A City in Terror: 1919, the Boston Police Strike* (1975).

Richard Severo and Lewis Milford, *The Wages of War: When America's Soldiers Came Home—from Valley Forge to Vietnam* (1989).

Ralph A. Stone, *The Irreconcilables: The Fight against the League of Nations* (1970).

William Tuttle Jr., *Race Riot: Chicago and the Red Summer of 1919* (1970).

Arthur Walworth, *Wilson and His Peacemakers: American Diplomacy at the Paris Peace Conference, 1919* (1986).

William C. Widenor, *Henry Cabot Lodge and the Search for an American Foreign Policy* (1980).

PANORAMIC HATBOX

Illustrated hatboxes, like the hats within them, were a favorite symbol of affluent style in the 1920s. This hatbox displays the extravagance of life on Fifth Avenue, the most fashionable milieu of all. Americans looked to New York wit and sophistication as a guide to how to transform the nation into an urban society.

Picture Research Consultants & Archives.

FROM "NORMALCY" TO THE GREAT DEPRESSION

23

1920–1932

O N A GRAY CHRISTMAS MORNING IN 1922, Federal Prisoner #9653 began his last day at the Atlanta penitentiary. The frail old man glanced at the crucifix on his cell wall before exchanging his jailhouse fatigues for the cheap new suit the guard had brought. Then he gathered his few belongings and prepared to leave. For Eugene Victor Debs, the leader and five-time presidential candidate of the Socialist Party, a long ordeal was over. President Warren G. Harding had granted him the pardon Woodrow Wilson had so bitterly refused. After three long years in prison for opposition to World War I, Debs was at last a free man.

As he neared the main prison gate, Debs remembered, he heard behind him "what seemed a rumbling of the earth as if shaken by some violent explosion." He turned back to face the stark walls and watched as a cry of farewell thundered from the other prisoners. Against every rule, the warden had allowed all 2,300 inmates out of their cells to witness this unprecedented departure. They responded with cheers for the man they had come to know as a sympathetic friend. Debs had an uncanny hold on their hopes and feelings. His cell mate, Sam Moore, recalled many years later the vivid impression that Debs made. "As miserable as I was I would defy fate with all its cruelty as long as Debs held my hand, and I was the most miserably happiest man on earth when I knew he was going home Christmas."

Debs's first stop was the White House, where his benefactor, President Harding, curious to meet America's most famous political prisoner, had invited him for a visit. The genial Harding bounded from behind his desk to shake Debs's hand, exclaiming, "Well, I have heard so damned much about you, Mr. Debs, that I am now very glad to meet you personally."

At the end of his journey, in Terre Haute, Indiana, a crowd estimated at 25,000 met Debs at the station. They lifted the old warrior into the same horse-drawn wagon that had carried him back from his imprisonment in 1895, when he had gone to jail for defying a federal injunction during the Pullman strike. When the parade arrived at the family home near the railroad tracks, Debs gave an impromptu speech from the porch, urging his cheering supporters to view his release as a step toward the ultimate victory of socialism and the working class.

It was a touching moment, but despite Debs's show of the old revolutionary fire, he faced a society very different from the one he envisioned. By pardoning America's leading antiwar martyr, the Harding administration shrewdly eased opposition to the "normalcy" it was putting in place to prevent the success of any new radical champions. The old radicals and reformers, bitterly disillusioned with the outcome of World War I, no longer thrilled to the Christian moralism or idealism that had fueled the crusades of the socialists and progressives. Although Debs's stature as a jailed martyr had won him 919,000 votes (the most ever for a Socialist candidate) when he ran for president from his cell in 1920, the Socialist Party itself was in drastic decline. By the time Debs left prison, Socialist membership had fallen to 120,000. The party had to sell its headquarters in Chicago and move into an attic to stave off bankruptcy.

The nation had turned a corner. The failure of the war to make the world safe for democracy and the tawdriness of the Versailles treaty had ended the craving for reform that had characterized the Progressive Era. The lack of strong leadership once Wilson fell ill left a vacuum at the center of American life that the energy released by the war and the subsequent development of America's economy rushed to fill. The nation enjoyed a spectacular burst of economic prosperity. The freewheeling economy mirrored a new sense of freedom in popular culture. The war seemed to accelerate the pace of American life, so much so that Secretary of Commerce Herbert Hoover declared that Americans had entered a "new era."

The 1920s were not without contradictions, however. The nation was enduring the final stages of the transition from a rural, agricultural nation to a modern, urban, machine-oriented one. Signs of tension and stress were clearly visible. Cities and industry grew enormously, yet nostalgia idealized the farm and the small town. The nation prospered, but the new wealth widened the gap between rich and poor. City life and diversity flourished, but they met renewed intolerance and demands for conformity. While millions admired the new, sophisticated style, millions of others condemned the vulgarity of postwar society. And in one of the most significant outpourings of creative talent in the nation's history, artists of all types indicted the United States for being artistically barren.

Competing myths and legends about the 1920s found expression in the labels attached to the age. Some labels express the era's high-spirited energy: "Roaring Twenties," "Jazz Age," "Flaming Youth," and "Age of the Flapper." Others echo the rising importance of money—"Dollar Decade," "Golden Twenties," "Prosperity Decade"—or reflect the sinister side of gangster profiteering—"Lawless Decade." Still other terms emphasize fragile dreams and loneliness: "the Lost Generation," "the Beautiful and the Damned." Ultimately, perhaps, it was an age best summed up by President Calvin Coolidge, who declared, "The business of America is business." During the 1920s, the values and ideology of the business community reigned supreme, only to be toppled abruptly with the stock market crash and subsequent depression.

Normalcy

In a speech during his campaign for the presidency in 1920, Republican candidate Warren G. Harding told the people that "America's present need is not heroics, but healing; not nostrums [questionable remedies] but normalcy; not revolution but restoration; . . . not surgery but serenity." But what was "normalcy"? Harding explained: "By 'normalcy' I don't mean the old order but a regular steady order of things. I mean normal procedure, the natural way, without excess." So defined, "normalcy" (Harding's speechwriter had written the more familiar "normality"), captured the electorate and made its way into the dictionary. The urbane *New York Times* understood its appeal, observing, "Mr. Harding is not writing for the super-fine weighers of verbs and adjectives but for the men and women who see in his expressions their own ideas." In the 1920s, it was Harding and the Republican Party that spoke the people's language. From 1921 to 1933, power rested securely in business-minded and conservative Republican hands.

Postwar Politics and the Election of 1920

The economic chaos that accompanied the return to a peacetime economy after World War I spelled serious trouble for the Wilson administration. As inflation soared, people on fixed salaries—teachers, ministers, social service workers, store clerks, and others of the middle class who had formed the backbone of progressive support for Wilson—watched inflation shrink their purchasing power. Organized labor, having lost its great effort to strike for better conditions in 1919, faced grim prospects. By the winter of 1920–21, the national unemployment rate hit 20 percent, the highest ever suffered up to that time. For those still working, inflation and the fear of unemployment ruined any hope of enjoying a higher standard of living. Farmers fared worst, as their bankruptcy rate increased tenfold and real farm income fell far below wartime levels. For a decade that would become known for its economic miracles, the twenties began with a thud.

President Woodrow Wilson, bedridden and partially paralyzed from the stroke he had suffered in 1919, squandered his party's chances by refusing to allow anyone within his administration to construct a program for the new postwar era. Instead, Wilson insisted that the 1920 election would be a "solemn referendum" on the League of Nations. The Democratic nominee for president, James M. Cox, three-time governor of Ohio, and for vice president, the New York aristocrat Franklin Delano Roosevelt, bearer of his uncle Teddy's famous name, dutifully campaigned on Wilson's international ideals.

The Republican Party chose a presidential candidate who embodied the change in national sentiment from global crusade to peaceful prosperity. Handsome and gregarious, with a pleasing, resonant voice, Senator Warren Gamaliel Harding of Ohio stood as an accurate representative of his age. A jovial joiner who belonged to a host of fraternal orders, Harding epitomized the essence of conventional small-town life.

Unlike the increasing number of young men from small towns who headed for the city to make their fortunes, Harding had stayed home in Marion, Ohio, to edit the town newspaper. At a Repub-

lican gathering, Harding attracted notice from a shrewd local lawyer, Harry Daugherty. Watching Harding make his way with casual charm through a throng of politicians, Daugherty thought immediately, "What a president he'd make!" Under Daugherty's guidance, Harding's rise in party politics was more a tribute to charm and amiability than to any political commitment. He vaguely opposed the prevailing progressive policies of economic regulation, agricultural subsidies, and graduated income taxes. Harding repeatedly demonstrated an ability to land on the winning side of an issue without having to grapple with conscience or complexity. On the two most heated domestic issues of the day—woman suffrage and prohibition—Harding showed little knowledge or conviction. He remarked that he saw no good reason for the reforms, but eventually he voted for them in a nod to public opinion.

The keys to Harding's success in 1920 lay in his image—it was generally agreed that he looked like a president—and in his appeal to harmony and good fellowship. Eager to put the poisonous atmosphere of the Red scare and the labor strife of 1919 behind them, the voters responded to Harding's call for normalcy by giving him the largest margin of victory any presidential candidate had ever received. The contrast between Harding's determinedly optimistic administration and the moribund one he replaced became immediately evident to the nation. In early March, as the Washington weather started to thaw, the Hardings arrived at the White House, threw open the barred gates, which had been closed since the declaration of war in 1917, and raised the window blinds. Bright flowers, birdhouses on the lawn, and, above all, a welcome to the public, who came by the thousands to see the Harding White House, lifted the national pall and signified a new era of easygoing good cheer.

The Republican Party chose a presidential candidate who embodied the change in national sentiment from global crusade to peaceful prosperity. Handsome and gregarious, with a pleasing, resonant voice, Harding stood as an accurate representative of his age.

Harding managed to choose some talented people for his cabinet, including Charles Evans Hughes, former associate justice of the Supreme Court, for secretary of state. Herbert Hoover, the self-made millionaire and former head of the wartime Food Administration, was tapped for secretary of commerce. The new president picked the leading champion of scientific agriculture, Henry C. Wallace, as secretary of agriculture. But wealth also counted. Conservative Republicans pressed Harding to name Andrew Mellon, one of the richest men in America (and a heavy contributor to the party), as secretary of the treasury. Harding also remembered his friends. "God, I can't be an ingrate," he is said to have remarked. Regardless of their experience, friends found themselves in high office. This curious combination of merit and cronyism would typify Harding's administration and set the stage for both a few "best minds" to argue over national needs and for lesser men to tarnish themselves and the Harding administration in scandal.

The "Noble Experiment" and Woman Suffrage

The shift from reform earnestness to normalcy showed in the public reaction to the last two great progressive achievements passed prior to Harding's inauguration—prohibition and woman suffrage. In January 1920, the Eighteenth Amendment prohibiting the sale of alcohol took effect. Thus began what advocates of the measure referred to as "the noble experiment." While it succeeded in lowering the consumption of alcohol, at least in rural America, the ultimate result of prohibition was widespread disregard for the law. Federal enforcement of prohibition was lax, and any citizen who wanted a drink could find one. The "speakeasy," a place where men (and, increasingly, women) drank publicly, became a common feature of the urban landscape. Liquor dealers, called "bootleggers" because they hid bottles in their tall boots, provided the thirsty with their drink of choice. Liquor was smuggled in from Canada or concocted in makeshift stills, giving rise to the term "bathtub gin." Mort Mortimer, who operated in Washington, D.C., boasted a card that styled him as the "President's Bootlegger."

But, eventually, serious criminals took over most of the liquor trade. Al Capone became the era's most notorious gang lord by establishing a bootlegging empire in Chicago that reputedly grossed more than $60 million in a single year. Gangsters employed hundreds of gunmen, and gang wars raged in several American cities, most notably Chicago, where Al Capone held sway. The violence that marked the struggle for control of the lucrative market encouraged public cynicism about the

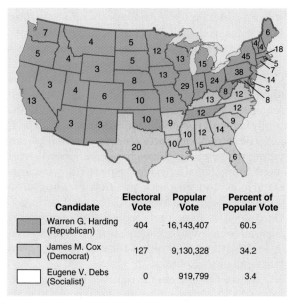

Candidate	Electoral Vote	Popular Vote	Percent of Popular Vote
Warren G. Harding (Republican)	404	16,143,407	60.5
James M. Cox (Democrat)	127	9,130,328	34.2
Eugene V. Debs (Socialist)	0	919,799	3.4

MAP 23.1
The Election of 1920

SATURDAY NIGHT

With a sly wink, the young dandy dips for movie money, while his date looks dubious about what will go on in the dark of that dry night. With this title, Harry Ruby, the popular songwriter, capitalizes on the expectation that resourceful Americans out for a good time will find ways around the prohibition amendment's attempt to enforce sober morality.

Picture Research Consultants & Archives.

WOMEN VOTING IN NEW YORK CITY

Sharply attired New York City officials look wearily resigned or bemused as one of them hands ballots to two women voting for the first time in 1920. The contrast in appearance and demeanor of the two groups facing each other is strikingly reminiscent of photographs of apprehensive new immigrants applying for entry.

UPI/Bettmann Archive.

"noble experiment." Each year, the constituency supporting prohibition shrank, until in 1933 opponents succeeded in repealing the Eighteenth Amendment.

The Nineteenth Amendment, ratified in 1920, granted women the vote, ending nearly a century of struggle to achieve political rights for women. But how would women vote? Alice Paul, head of the militant National Woman's Party, wanted them to vote as a bloc and fight for an Equal Rights Amendment (ERA) that she put before Congress in 1923. The more moderate National American Woman Suffrage Association pursued a different course. The organization disbanded, forming the nonpartisan League of Women Voters (LWV) to educate the new electorate on the issues. Most activists in both groups, as well as many political observers

outside, looked to woman suffrage, the greatest single change ever made in voting eligibility, to reshape the political landscape. Female activists hoped to have decisive influence in enacting protective legislation for women and children that had long been high on their reform agenda.

As with prohibition, however, reality did not bear out utopian expectations. Ignorance of their right to vote and male domination, especially among immigrant groups and Southerners, kept many women away from the polls. Partly for that reason, in 1920 and 1924, for the first time in American history, less than a majority of eligible voters cast ballots in the presidential elections. Those women who did vote showed no unified commitment to the goals of suffrage leaders. Conservatives had wrested control of the Republican Party from

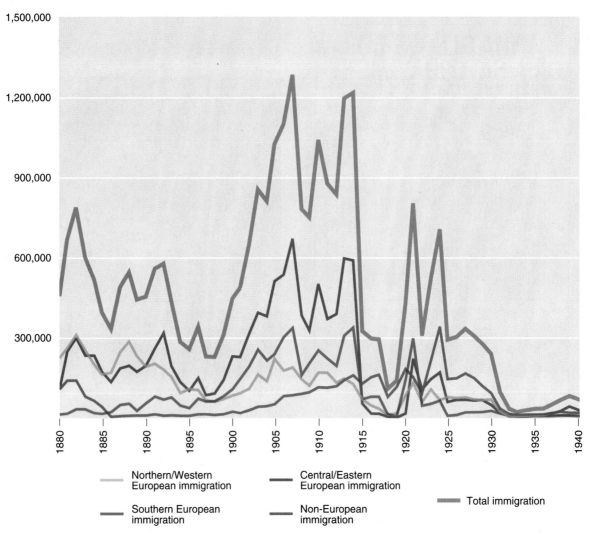

FIGURE 23.1
Immigration, 1880–1940
Reflecting harsh and unstable conditions in many foreign countries, emigration to the United States increased sharply in the early twentieth century. After World War I, Americans reacted to failed hopes and fear of outsiders by imposing stringent immigration quotas.

the progressives and were in charge of the White House and the congressional majority. In the Democratic Party, conservatives had also routed Wilsonian liberals, and antifeminist, segregationist Southerners took charge. Ruefully, Abe Martin, the cracker-barrel philosopher of the Indianapolis *News*, lamented in 1926: "Wouldn't the way things are goin' these days make a fine argymint in favor of woman's suffrage if we didn't already have it!"

But it took a while for politicians to realize that they need not fear any female voting bloc. Assuming that women would have considerable political leverage, the new Congress passed the Sheppard-Towner bill in 1921, providing federal funds for maternal and infant health care. As the weakness of the new voters' influence sank in, however, and doctors protested "socialist" interference, Congress reduced funds for the program and in 1928 eliminated it altogether. Those women who stuck with a progressive agenda had to join others seeking change outside the mainstream. Within a network of private agencies and reform associations, they continued to press the causes of birth control, protective legislation for the work place, legal equality for minorities, and the end of child labor. They looked toward the day when their efforts would be supported by those in power.

The United States Retreats from the World

Harding's desire for harmony equipped him well to preside over the country's retreat from international leadership. He began by shedding some responsibilities that stemmed from the world war. Only four months after his inauguration, he concluded peace treaties with Germany, Austria, and Hungary that removed the United States from supervision over their affairs. To lessen tensions closer to home, he handed over $25 million to Colombia as compensation for the loss of territory that nation had suffered when President Theodore Roosevelt "took Panama" to build the canal. Harding's most ambitious effort, however, was the Washington Disarmament Conference he convened in 1921 to establish a global balance of naval power. By gaining agreement on the proportional reduction of naval might among the major powers—Britain, France, Japan, Italy, and the United States—Harding hoped to provide a measure of security for the nation without the trouble of joining the League of Nations. A grateful citizenry breathed a sigh of relief that the threat of war seemed so easily removed at a conference noted for its international goodwill and optimism.

The campaign to limit immigration, however, was more ominous. Its barely veiled intent was to keep the nation's destiny in the hands of people of Anglo-Saxon stock. Though the Red scare had petered out before Harding's election, the specter of bomb-throwing radicals from revolutionary countries of eastern and southern Europe continued to haunt the American imagination.

The trial of Italian anarchists Nicola Sacco and Bartolomeo Vanzetti testified to a new wave of hysteria. Arrested in 1920 for robbery and murder in South Braintree, Massachusetts, the two were sentenced to death by a judge who openly referred to them as "anarchist bastards." Mounting public opinion called the verdict into question: It appeared to many that the men had been convicted because of their ideas and nationality. The governor of Massachusetts named a blue ribbon committee of establishment notables, including the presidents of Harvard and MIT, who found the trial judge guilty of a "grave breach of official decorum." Nevertheless, they closed ranks and refused to recommend a motion for retrial.

Supporters tried for six years to save Sacco and Vanzetti. Instead, on August 23, 1927, the two men were sent to the electric chair. More than fifty thousand protesters marching beside the coffins at the funeral seemed to bear out Vanzetti's defiant martyr's statement just before he died: "Never in our full life could we hope to do such work for tolerance, for justice, for man's understanding of man, as now we do by accident. . . . This agony is our triumph!" But

AGITATING FOR SACCO AND VANZETTI
This image appeared in the anarchist journal that Bartolomeo Vanzetti's friend and fellow immigrant Aldino Felicani created to raise support for pardoning Sacco and Vanzetti. By writing in English under an Italian masthead, Felicani sought to make the two accused men symbols of both immigrant and working-class suffering. In the cartoon's dramatic version of events, capitalism's executioner, leaning on the electric chair like a sinister barber, summons working-class victims to their doom. In fact, deportation and mob violence were the typical weapons used against alien radicals and others deemed dangerously un-American.
L'Agitazione, August 20, 1921.

many of the mourners saw things differently. One of them, the writer John Dos Passos, spoke for those who viewed the incident as proof that America was in the grip of a ruling class that would act viciously to suppress dissent and immigrant minorities. In *The Big Money* (1936), Dos Passos's panoramic novel about how the culture of wealth and privilege works, one of the mourners standing in the rain sums up the executions as a death blow to the idea of inclusive democracy. "All right," he declares with grim resignation, "all right, we are two nations."

By the time Harding took office, tensions about ethnic class differences had convinced public opinion that the time had come for drastic immigration restriction. Alongside the "100 percenters"—native-born Americans totally opposed to immigration on racist and patriotic grounds—stood union members, who feared immigrant competition for jobs, and traditionalists, who felt that the nation had completed its destined growth. In full accord, Harding made it one of his first acts to sign a quota law. The law limited the number of immigrants to no more than 357,000 per year and gave each European nation a quota, based on 3 percent of the number of people from that country listed in the U.S. census of 1910. The law effectively reversed the trend toward immigration from southern and eastern Europe, which by 1914 had amounted to 75 percent of the total. From an open welcome to millions of "huddled masses yearning to breathe free," the United States built high walls. In 1923, Congress cut the quota in half. The following year it specifically excluded Asians and increased the advantage for northern Europeans by shifting the census standard back from 1910 to 1890, before the great influx of southern and eastern Europeans.

Scandal

Having pulled back from international responsibilities and shut the door to undesirable immigrants, the Harding administration concentrated on prosperity at home. Harding sought to strengthen the power of American business but cast his policies in terms of benevolence and the general welfare. Profit making and public service, he declared, joined to form the core of the American way. He supported high tariffs, price supports for agriculture, and the complete dismantling of wartime government control over industry in favor of unregulated private direction. Passage of the Fordney-McCumber tariff in 1922 raised duties on imports to unprecedented heights. Ironically, by making it more difficult for foreign countries to sell goods in the United States, the tariff prevented European nations from paying off their wartime debts to the U.S. treasury.

Eventually Harding's small-town congeniality and trusting ways became a liability. Wheeler-dealers, including many of his old friends from Ohio, descended on Washington, lured by visions of easy pickings. This "Ohio gang" held forth at what became known as the "little green house on K Street," a hideaway where whiskey and poker mixed with business, some of it illegal. The affable Harding resisted for as long as he could the recognition that some of his friends were involved in lawbreaking more serious than drinking bootlegged gin.

The scandals began when Charles Forbes, an army colonel Harding had met playing poker and offhandedly appointed director of the Veterans' Bureau, was caught defrauding the government. Forbes and a collaborator had found a number of ways to line their pockets, including selling off hospital equipment. Together they stole an estimated $200 million. Enraged by the betrayal of trust, Harding called Forbes into his office and, as the president told it, "shook him as a dog would a rat." Harding nevertheless allowed Forbes to flee to Europe and tried to write off the scandal. But the suicide of Forbes's henchman brought on a congressional hearing and with it a tide of trouble for Harding.

Before the investigations concluded, three of Harding's appointees would go to jail and others would come under indictment. Secretary of the Interior Albert Fall was convicted of accepting bribes of more than $400,000 from oil magnates Harry Sinclair and Edward L. Doheny. Fall had received the money at the taxpayers' expense by leasing Sinclair and Doheny oil reserves on public land in Teapot Dome, Wyoming, and Elk Hills, California. Doheney and Sinclair escaped conviction, but Fall went to jail, and "Teapot Dome" became a term synonymous with political corruption. Later, Attorney General Daugherty, the president's oldest crony, was indicted for selling political influence. Early inklings of these wrongdoings shattered Harding's confidence and, with it, his health.

Harding set off on a trip to Alaska in the summer of 1923 to escape his troubles. Baffled about how to deal with "my God-damned friends," the president found no rest and his health continued to decline. On August 2, 1923, a shocked nation learned of President Harding's sudden death at the age of fifty-eight from a stroke. Subsequent scandals revealed the extent of the rot in the Harding administration. Harding himself was not involved in any financial wrongdoing, but only his death saved him from further embarrassment. As president, he was a man in over his head and he knew it. When Nicholas Murray Butler, his friend and the president of Columbia University, found him up late one night doggedly answering routine mail and protested that the president should not waste time on such matters, Harding responded, "I suppose so, but I am not fit for this office and should never have been here."

The Business of America

By 1922, the American economy had pulled out of the nosedive that followed the war and began a long period of vigorous growth. Despite the conservatism of the Republican administrations of the 1920s and their claims that the best government was one that did the least, the federal government worked closely with business to sustain and extend the business prosperity of the decade. Henry Ford, the man who put America on wheels, broadcast a compelling vision of the new age, complete with new terms of production, promotion, and distribution. The key to abundance, he preached, was modern mass production. Ford liked to say that his business principles "are all summed up in the single word 'service.'" Others liked to frame the "New Era" in terms of advanced technology, business efficiency, and scientific management. Others simply said that the age was caught up in "money madness." According to the caustic Baltimore journalist H. L. Mencken, the businessman "is the only one who always seeks to make it appear, when he attains the object of his labor, i.e., the making of a great deal of money, that it was not the object of his labors." And for every product manufacturers produced, someone had to buy.

A Business Government

Vice-president Calvin Coolidge was vacationing at his family's farmhouse in Plymouth Notch, Vermont, when he was wakened during the night with the news of Harding's death. The family gathered in the parlor where, by the flickering light of an oil lamp, Coolidge's father, a justice of the peace, swore his son in as president. This rustic drama had a calming effect on the nation. Americans welcomed as Harding's successor a man seemingly steeped in the country ways of the Yankee past.

A spare, solemn man—one critic thought he must have been "weaned on a pickle"—Coolidge had won national publicity in 1919 when as governor of Massachusetts he had called out the National Guard to maintain order during the Boston police strike. In 1920, the Republican convention chose him as a man of decisiveness to stand behind the more pliable Harding. When he became president in 1923, the nation soon recognized differences between the Coolidge administration and its discredited predecessor—a more formal and proper White House, a close-mouthed presidential style, and absolute uprightness. But these differences obscured the basic similarities in their policies, particularly regarding business.

Despite the conservatism of the Republican administrations of the 1920s and their claims that the best government was one that did the least, the federal government worked closely with business to sustain and extend the business prosperity of the decade.

Coolidge, who once remarked, "The man who builds a factory builds a temple, the man who works there worships there," shared the era's infatuation with businessmen. As president, he proved an even stronger ally of business than Harding had been. He said baldly: "The business of America is business. . . . This is a business country, and it wants a business government." While Coolidge himself rarely stirred in the White House (he took a nap every afternoon), his administration made every effort to help businesses operate efficiently and profitably. Secretary of the Treasury Andrew Mellon, millionaire aluminum magnate, focused on getting tax cuts for corporations and the rich. Under his prodding, Congress cut taxes by about half. Secretary of Commerce Herbert Hoover devoted his efforts to building trade associations. He believed that cooperation, rather than cutthroat competition, among rival firms within a particular industry would reduce waste and increase stability.

The Supreme Court played its part in the pro-business thrust. After a period of validating a series of advanced social and economic legislation during the Progressive Era, the Court joined the nation in attempting to roll back the reform tide, launching a powerful attack on the rights of state and federal governments to regulate business. The Court op-

COOLIDGE POSING AS A FARMER
After the labor wars subsided, the idea of Coolidge as the enforcer of law and order gave way to the more placid image of "Silent Cal." Though he knew the ways of farming from his youth, the hay and pitchfork of this image are mere props for playing a political game Coolidge does not manage to disguise. His gleaming dress shoes and the official car with Secret Service men in the background show how the old rural imagery had become window dressing for the New Era of wealth and power.
Brown Brothers.

posed any federal regulation of hours, wages, and working conditions. In 1916, the Court had struck down the Child Labor Act, making it clear that its prohibition of federal labor regulation included the work done by children. Taking aim at state regulation in 1923, the Court declared unconstitutional the District of Columbia's minimum-wage law for women, asserting that the law interfered with the freedom of employer and employee to make labor contracts. In addition, the Court limited the rights of labor unions to organize, while confirming the rights of businesses to form trade associations.

The election of 1924 underscored the defeat of progressive principles. Coolidge easily won the Republican presidential nomination, while the Democrats nominated John W. Davis, a corporate lawyer whose conservative views differed little from Republican principles. In a last-gasp attempt to offer a reform alternative, the feisty Progressive Party made Senator Robert La Follette of Wisconsin its presidential nominee. Though ailing, La Follette remained fiercely loyal to progressive reform principles favoring strong labor unions, regulation of business, and civil liberties. In the showdown, for which Republicans coined the slogan "Coolidge or Chaos," the mostly silent president managed to capture more votes than both his opponents put

together, and the Republicans strengthened their majorities in both houses of Congress.

American business expressed its appreciation for the Coolidge administration's pro-business activity. "The American businessman is the most influential person in the nation," the United States Chamber of Commerce said proudly. "Never before, here or anywhere else, has a government been so completely fused with business." A close connection was not new, of course. During World War I, government and business had forged a partnership to produce war materiel to defeat the Germans. In the 1920s, the relationship no longer needed the stimulation of war. To many Americans, it seemed entirely natural.

Henry Ford and the Automobile

According to several surveys in the 1920s, the most admired man in America was Henry Ford. Ford and the automobiles he created stood at the center of the New Era. He began life in 1863 on a farm in Dearborn, Michigan, just outside Detroit. From the first, Ford hated the drudgery and animal messiness of farmwork and turned instead to tinkering with machines. In 1893, he built one of the first successful gasoline-driven carriages in the United States. In

1903, equipped with $28,000 from a few backers impressed by his mechanical skills, Ford left for Detroit to create the Ford Motor Company with twelve workers in a 250-by-50-foot plant.

Ford's timing and location could not have been better. The growing country had moved to its outer limits, leaving Americans, especially those west of the Mississippi, distant from neighbors and community services. With fewer than ten people to a square mile, the Midwest needed machinery to help its farmers make a living and to escape isolation on the vast tracts they called home. Ford's Detroit was well situated. The mining and manufacture of key materials for the automobile and the tractor—steel, oil, glass, and rubber—were concentrated in nearby cities in Pennsylvania, Ohio, Indiana, and Illinois. The waterways of the Great Lakes and the railroads stretching across the flat midwestern landscape made it easy to supply Detroit with what it needed. The automobile industry's demands for lead, nickel, plate glass, rubber, and especially steel proved so great that by 1929 an estimated one American in four found employment directly or indirectly in the industry. It was no wonder that one commentator quipped that "Give us our daily bread" was no longer addressed to the Almighty, but to Detroit. Henry Ford's reward was dominance over the market. The Fordson tractor and Model T automobile set the standards before World War I and stayed out front for many years after that. Despite the vast expansion of the automotive industry in the 1920s, the Ford Motor Company remained the industry leader throughout the decade, peaking in 1925 when it outsold all its rivals combined.

When Ford began his rise, progressive critics were vilifying the industrial giants of the nineteenth century as "robber barons." While the industrialists lived in luxury, progressives charged, laboring people lived in rags. In contrast, Ford styled himself as a poor farm boy trying to get ahead and offered lacerating comments of his own about the modern-day robber barons who stood in his way. Expressing sympathy for the common folk he hoped to enlist as employees, Ford was able to claim his place as benefactor of a nation yearning to be free and mobile.

The key to Ford's success in the factory was mass production. By installing a continuous conveyor belt or assembly line in his plant in 1913, Ford was able to produce a car every ninety-three minutes, in contrast to the fourteen hours it had taken before. Mass production enabled Ford to drop the price of his cars from $845 to less than $300. Soon the working class joined the wealthy on the roads. The Model T—homely and available only in black, but rugged and cheap—became a prime symbol of the New Era. Aided by a new federal road-building program, cars, trucks, and buses surged past the railroads by the end of the 1920s as the primary haulers of passengers and freight.

At the start of the decade there were about 9 million vehicles on the road—one for every 11 citizens. With the Ford Motor Company leading the

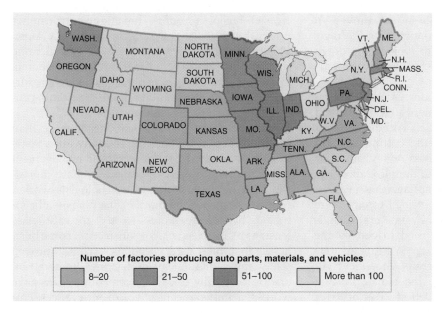

M A P   2 3 . 2
Auto Manufacturing
By the mid-1920s, the massive coal and steel industries of the Midwest had made the region the center of the new automobile industry. A major road-building program by the federal government carried the thousands of new cars produced each day to every corner of the country.

Number of factories producing auto parts, materials, and vehicles
8–20   21–50   51–100   More than 100

way, some ten thousand Model T engine blocks rolled off the assembly line every day by mid-decade, and the total number of buses, trucks, autos, and motorcycles on the road in 1929 rose to twenty-seven million—one for every 4.5 citizens.

The automobile changed the face of America. It blurred the distinction between country and city. At first rural folk greeted the horseless carriage as a "devil wagon" associated with rich city people who frightened the horses they so often needed to pull their cars out of the mud. But Ford's cheap, durable autos soon became, as Ford intended them to be, invaluable to rural dwellers. In 1920, about 30 percent of farmers owned a car; by 1930, the figure was 60 percent.

Hundreds of small towns and villages declined or died within the decade, largely because the automobile could connect people in rural communities with distant cities and thus bypass the small towns that had formerly provided services in simpler, duller ways. The one-room schoolhouse and the crossroads church began to vanish from the landscape. At the same time, some larger towns prospered by catering to the new auto trade. Country "guest cottages" were thrown up for auto tourists, and the word *motel* was coined to describe roadside accommodations. More prosperous towns paved and widened city streets, cutting down the trees on Main Street to make way for parking spaces —all in the name of the automobile age.

Americans took to the wheel in surprising numbers. That men drove came as no surprise, but even before women voted they demanded and got the right to drive. The automobile, in fact, proved an important asset in the long campaign for suffrage. And for young people, the car won hands down over the horse-drawn carriage for the privacy it accorded a courting couple.

Nobody entertained grander or more contradictory visions of the new America he had helped to create than Henry Ford himself. Although his automobile plants represented the cutting edge of modern technology and business organization, he also liked to look backward and moralize about the country's rural values. To memorialize such values, he created Greenfield Village outside Detroit, where he relocated buildings from a bygone era, such as his parents' farmhouse, and tried to convey the rural simplicity of his childhood. With its exhibits of homespun family life and crafts, Greenfield Village contrasted sharply with the roaring, racing Ford plant farther along the Detroit River at River Rouge. In the factory toiled the African American

and immigrant workers left out of Ford's village idyll. All would be well, Ford insisted, if Americans somehow remained loyal to the virtues of an agrarian past and yet were modern and scientific at the same time.

Specialization and Scientific Management

With reform in eclipse and the government promoting the unbridled interests of business, those interested in progress turned to technology and science. After the First World War, planners and efficiency experts shifted their talents to the private sector to help make industries and corporations more productive. Scientific management, which Frederick Winslow Taylor had pioneered at the end of the nineteenth century at Midvale Steel Company in Pennsylvania, reached its heyday during the 1920s, when industrial engineers fanned out across the nation searching for greater efficiencies in machines and labor. No one did more to advance Taylor's principles and the cult of productivity than Henry Ford. Ford's staggering success with the assembly line broadcast modern production techniques throughout American industry. Radios, refrigerators, washing machines, vacuum cleaners, and other mass-produced goods flooded the nation. Productivity—the efficiency of production—increased about 75 percent during the decade. Although the number of workers remained approximately the same, the workforce produced almost twice as many goods. Mass production resulted in vastly increased business profits, much lower consumer prices, but only slightly higher wages for labor. Moreover, as the moving assembly line became standard in almost every American factory, laborers lost whatever skills they had managed to retain during the industrial revolution of the nineteenth century and much of the fulfillment of work.

But scientific management meant more than time-and-motion studies and assembly lines. Some industries adopted new paternalistic management techniques that came to be called "welfare capitalism." Owners used industrial psychologists, worker councils, and contributory pension plans—all controlled by management—to try to ease class tensions by increasing labor satisfaction. Some businesses instituted paid vacations; others improved safety and sanitation inside factories. In some industries, carefully controlled company unions gave workers a limited means of voicing grievances. This "welfare capitalism" promoted by business in the

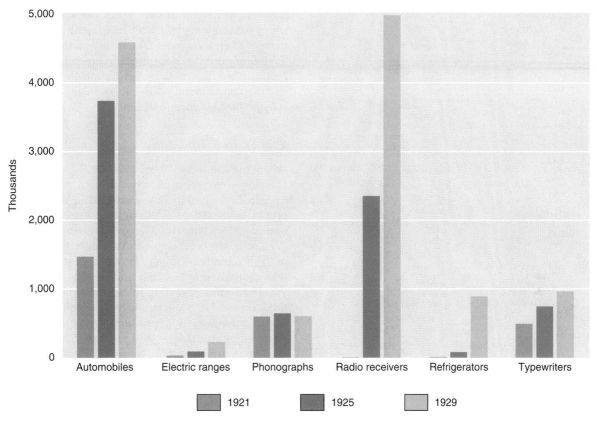

FIGURE **23.2**
Production of Consumer Goods, 1920–1930
Transportation, communications, and entertainment changed the lives of consumers in the 1920s.
While labor-saving devices for the home were popular, vastly greater sales of automobiles, and radios
showed that consumerism was more powerful in moving people's attention beyond their homes.

economic boom of the 1920s would wither in the bust of the 1930s, but it had lasting effects, promoting new expectations among workers who came to see job security, high wages, and health benefits as achievable goals.

Scientific management in the 1920s also meant the culmination of the revolution in business organization that had been under way for decades. In an effort to become more streamlined and efficient, corporations established increasingly bureaucratic management structures. Businesses created specialized divisions—procurement, production, marketing, employee relations—each with its own team of managers who were increasingly professionally trained.

Belief in scientific management also helped advance the cause of higher education and the pro-

fessions: Corporations needed educated managers. By the end of the decade, enrollment in colleges and universities had more than tripled since the turn of the century. During the 1920s, graduate education expanded at an even faster rate. Funding agencies such as the Rockefeller Foundation, the John Simon Guggenheim Foundation, and the Social Science Research Council were established to support scientific research and channel it into useful applications. Private business kept pace by increasing the number of industrial research laboratories from around three hundred in 1920 to more than a thousand by the end of the decade.

These trends were not limited to business and research science. Welfare service also underwent professional change, especially in the growing new field of social work. Trained social workers often

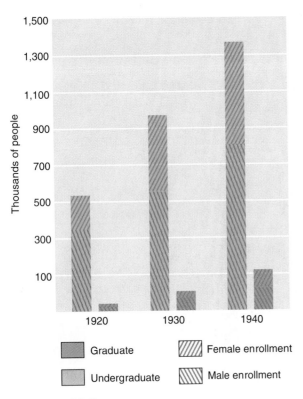

FIGURE 23.3
Higher Education Enrollments, 1920–1940
Both the prosperity of the twenties and the anxious striving for improvement of the thirties drew rising numbers of people to college. The steady ratios of men to women and undergraduate enrollment to graduate showed that the distribution of opportunity in higher education remained much the same in good times and bad.

discarded as amateur the social justice concerns of the settlement house founders in favor of a hard-headed casework method that increasingly focused on individual psychology as the main cause of problems. In the process, understanding of human behavior became more precise, but also more detached and fragmented. The aim was to adjust clients to the new, highly organized, tensely hurried business civilization all around them, not to nurture an independent sense of community and identity.

During the 1920s, as American economic dominance increased, scientific management cast a lengthening shadow over the thinking of industrial nations. In France, Germany, and Great Britain, Henry Ford's autobiography, *My Life and Work* (1922), inspired a wave of critical interest among intellectuals, artists, and manufacturers alike. Enthusiasts concentrated on the promise that efficiency in the new industrial system would combine maximum economic benefit with functionally beautiful design. Even the Soviet Union turned to Ford and Taylor for guidance. Joseph Stalin predicted that the "essence" of his country's revolutionary future lay in "the combination of the Russian revolutionary sweep with American efficiency."

The New Consumers

Following the recession of 1921–1922, the nation's economy grew spectacularly during the rest of the decade. Per capita income increased by a third, the cost of living stayed the same, and unemployment remained low. Americans enjoyed the highest standard of living on the globe. Although the rewards of the economic boom were not evenly distributed, white, urban, middle-class, and upper-class Americans had more spending money and more leisure time to spend it. Mass production meant an explosion of affordable new products—especially those powered by electricity—and produced a consumer-goods revolution. In this new era of abundance, millions of Americans sought the American dream, the good life, through consumption.

No better guide exists to how the business boom and business values of the 1920s affected average American life than the sociological classic *Middletown* (1929). The authors, Robert Lynd, trained as a Protestant minister, and his wife, Helen, a professional sociologist, visited the small city of Muncie, Indiana, to compile data on secular and spiritual life. The almost entirely native-born, white population of Muncie (referred to as "Middletown" in the study) closely approximated the national ideal in the age of normalcy. At the end of five years of study, the Lynds determined that Muncie was, above all, "a culture in which everything hinges on money."

Mass production meant an explosion of affordable new products—especially those powered by electricity—and produced a consumer-goods revolution.

To the Lynds, Middletowners had been caught in what the fashionable term of the day called a "cultural lag." Technological and organizational change had become too complex for the average citizen to comprehend. Mystified and feeling increasingly powerless, many Middletowners had

INDIAN DETOUR TOUR GUIDES
Entrepreneurs in the 1920s found ways to draw restless, monied people to new and exotic places. The wealthy often went to Paris and the French Riviera. Others settled for less dazzling destinations. These four tour guides advertise an "Indian detour" — off the beaten track — for the Santa Fe Railroad in 1926. For several years, the Indian cultures of the Southwest had attracted writers and artists in search of peace and the mystical wisdom of Native American pueblo dwellers. The "detourists" were more interested in bargain prices for native crafts and jewelry. Resourcefully, Pueblo Indians and Hispanics mass-produced trinkets and even invented "traditional" dances to entertain the new consumers.
Hunter Publishing Company.

lost confidence in their ability to play an effective role in town meetings and civic organizations. Instead, they deferred to the supposed expertise of leaders in politics and economics and even in the domestic sphere of child raising. The new passivity had a spiritual cost as well, the Lynds lamented. Religion, once a "spontaneous and pervasive part of the life of the city," had been reduced to a social ritual.

The pied piper of these disturbing changes, according to the Lynds, was the rapidly expanding business of advertising, which "pounded away" to convert an independent community into a homogenized consumer aggregate. Indeed, a mature industrial society required radical adjustments by the American people. The values and habits that had built the economy of the 1920s seemed hopelessly inadequate to cope with new realities. The New Era required new truths. Independence and self-suffi-

ciency were out of place in a modern, integrated society where most people lived and worked in complex bureaucracies and organizations. America had solved the age-old problem of production—its factories could produce unimaginable quantities of goods. The question became: How could people be persuaded to buy?

Advertising attacked the old notions of thrift, frugality, and savings, replacing them with a buy-now, pay-later mentality that kept the goods moving, whether consumers had cash or not. Advertising, which became a massive business in the 1920s, touted products and titillated consumers. Newspapers, magazines, radios, and billboards told Americans what they had to have in order to be popular, secure, and successful. And installment buying—a little down, a payment each month—allowed them to buy expensive items before they had saved the

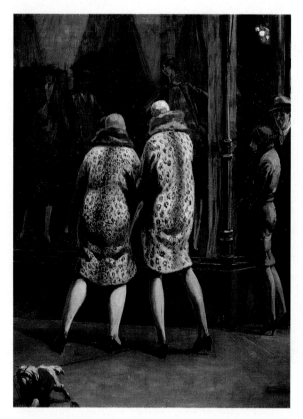

THE SHOPPERS
In this satirical painting, New York City scenic artist Martin Lewis shows two shoppers of the 1920s so attuned to fashion that they are wearing identical outfits and standing as if dancing the Charleston. Shown from the back to accent their anonymity, the pair look at store dummies who outdo them in style and grace, while a man nearby glances at the shoppers dully. The composition captures a certain awkward, comic yearning within the consumption boom of the 1920s for ways of purchasing elusive qualities of elegance and class.
Collection of John P. Axelrod.

cessful advertising agent, Bruce Barton, in 1925. The man nobody knew turned out to be Jesus Christ, who, according to Barton, had been mistakenly portrayed as spiritual and effeminate. The real Jesus, Barton argued, had been a salesman and businessman whose parables were "the most powerful advertisements of all time." Jesus, Barton explained, was a genius at management, a man who "picked up twelve men from the bottom ranks of business and forged them into an organization that conquered the world."

New Era Culture and Its Discontents

When Sigmund Freud visited the United States in 1908, his pioneering work in the psychology of the unconscious remained relatively unknown. But by the 1920s, Freud had become a household name. Most Americans, who didn't bother to read Freud, knew nothing of the complexity and pessimism of his works. They learned about Freud in the popular magazines, which simplified and distorted him. Still, people knew enough to realize that Freud offered a new way of looking at the world that was as radically different and important to the twentieth century as Charles Darwin's theory of evolution had been to the century before.

Freudian psychology, with its probing of the unconscious and its emphasis on the sexual origins of neurotic behavior, sought to break through the resistance of Victorian morality and to deal openly and honestly with sexuality. Freud's aim was to help people face problems and control their destructive impulses. Americans in the 1920s turned Freud on his head. If it is wrong to deny that we are sexual beings, they reasoned, then the key to health and happiness must lie in following impulse freely. Those who doubted this reasoning were simply "repressed." "I'm hipped on Freud," one of F. Scott Fitzgerald's fictional flappers announced, demonstrating her commitment to sexual freedom.

That new ethic excited a significant number of Americans to seek pleasure without guilt in a frenzy of activity that earned the decade the name "the Roaring Twenties." Others, held back by conscience or concern for appearances, enjoyed the spectacle through the miracles of modern technology and new means of mass communication.

money. Radios, vacuum cleaners, washing machines, and automobiles were bought by people who, according to the old values, could not afford them. But to keep the new economy humming, it appeared that people had to spend all they had, and more. As one newspaper announced, "The first responsibility of an American to his country is no longer that of a citizen, but of a consumer."

The extent to which the new values overwhelmed the old became apparent in the runaway best-seller *The Man Nobody Knows*, written by a suc-

TECHNOLOGY IN AMERICA
Frozen Foods

In this 1939 picture a grocer in Springfield, Massachusetts, stands beside a freezer that the Birdseye company had provided him, ready to be one of the first to introduce frozen foods to the nation. This sweeping advance in making food available in all seasons began accidentally during a government-sponsored survey of wildlife in Labrador in the early 1920s. Biologist Clarence Birdseye noted that fish rapidly frozen in that drastically cold climate retained freshness far better than did food frozen in slow-acting food lockers. Back at his seaport home in Gloucester, Massachusetts, Birdseye determined that quick freezing preserved food better because it produced smaller ice crystals that did not damage food cells or dry them out. With a patented process, Birdseye set up his own tiny General Foods Company in 1924 and began marketing locally caught frozen haddock. Five years later, when the large C. W. Post Company bought out the Birdseye name and patents, observers predicted that the Birdseye company would soon have sales of $1 billion per year. But it was not for another decade, when redesign had lowered the cost of freezers by 75 percent, that Birdseye moved beyond supplying steamships and hotels with special long-range storage needs and introduced frozen food to the general public. Typical of the rosy expectations that followed was a 1944 prediction in *Science Digest* that

"high frequency radio waves" would make feasts prepared "under the direction of world-famous chefs" ready for dinner tables. Beyond the imagination of the time was the actual exodus from the dining room altogether, led by the well-named TV-dinner.

BIRDSEYE is a registered trademark of Kraft General Foods, Inc. Reproduced with permission.

At the Movies

Americans seeking pleasure and escape increasingly went to the movies. Starting with the construction of the Regent Theatre in New York City in 1913, thousands of movie palaces, some of them larger and more ornate than European opera houses, sprang up in cities across the country. Uniformed ushers escorted patrons through cavernous foyers lined with mirrors that let plain people see themselves in classy surroundings. Admission was inexpensive for everyone, and the ideal of the good life for common folk and the privileged alike could be savored in the dark.

Little did Thomas Edison realize when he invented the kinetoscope in 1896 that his device for projecting moving images would form the technological base for one of the country's greatest indus-

tries. Soon, "nickelodeons," so named for the five cents admission, flourished throughout the country. These early peep shows treated people to little more than scenes of disconnected actions, usually some form of chase. But narrative sophistication came swiftly. *The Great Train Robbery*, made in 1903, became the first action film with a plot. Before World War I, audiences for the new motion pictures came mostly from the working class, while the more well-to-do retained their attachment to the live theater. But by 1910, the phenomenal success of the movies had produced ten thousand movie houses nationwide.

The center of the new industry moved in the 1920s from makeshift sound stages in New York City to Hollywood, California, where producers found open space to film any sort of epic and, more important for camera work, endless sunshine. Like

Ford's River Rouge plant, the Hollywood dream factory mass-produced enough pictures to satisfy Americans' growing appetite for vicarious experience. By 1929, as many people went to the movies in a single week as lived in the entire country.

In the 1920s, significant numbers of Americans sought pleasure without guilt in a frenzy of activities that earned the decade the name "the Roaring Twenties."

In Hollywood, a new breed of industrial entrepreneur, the movie mogul, soon hit upon the successful formula of combining images of opulence, sex, and adventure in thrillers, westerns, and Bible epics. Actors with exotic names like Pola Negri, Rudolph Valentino, and Vilma Banky drew audiences into films of romance in foreign lands where passion was allegedly freer. For settings closer to home, "America's Sweetheart," Mary Pickford, and her real-life husband, Douglas Fairbanks, offered more wholesome adventure. Comedy made the closest connection with audiences, however. Buster Keaton and Harold Lloyd were especially innovative in calling sympathetic attention to the pitfalls and absurdity ordinary people faced. Through slapstick and daring stunts they poked fun at the regimentation and stuffy social custom that made it hard for the average person to be secure and successful. Most versatile of all the comics was Charlie Chaplin, whose famous character the wistful tramp showed an endearing inability to cope with the rules and complexities of modern life.

Moralists who worried that the alluring images on the screen might subvert propriety soon pressed for government regulation. To head off censorship, in 1922 the Motion Picture Producers and Directors of America hired former Postmaster General Will Hays to monitor films for "decency and taste." Hays screened films and tried to balance the interests of public morality, creativity, and commerce without eliminating the raciness that made the movies so popular.

To match the grand surroundings of the theater palaces, Hollywood created the "movie star." Actors and actresses, with their furs, tuxedos, and perfect forms and faces, attended world premieres at the leading theaters, while searchlights broadcast the event beyond the horizon and humble ticket-paying admirers stood mesmerized by the circle of

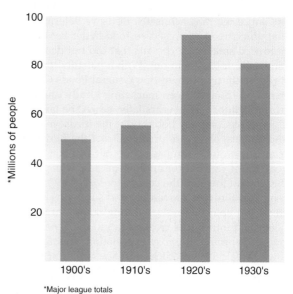

FIGURE 23.4
Movie and Baseball Attendance
America's favorite pastimes, movies and baseball, served as a fever chart for the economy. The percentage of national income spent by spectators of movies and major league baseball remained nearly constant during the interwar years; the rise and fall of weekly movie attendance and seasonal baseball attendance mirrored the rise and fall of prosperity.

---

light. Like a magnet, the movie industry drew its leading figures from all points of the compass. Many studio owners and producers came from eastern European immigrant communities, while directors were often refugees from the stage or European film studios. Actors came from all over. People of color were still largely excluded (except when they were used for comic relief or as villains). But among the white majority, anyone who looked

HEROES AND HEROINES
Within popular lore of the 1920s, two kinds of women looked up adoringly at two kinds of heroes.
A wholesome image is seen on this 1927 cover of the Popular Monthly Homecraft Magazine.
Here the healthy outdoor girl type, smartly turned out in her raccoon coat and pennant, seems in
flattering control of a naive college football hero. The pale, sensitive damsel Vilma Banky kneels
imploringly before the hypnotic gaze of the movies' greatest heartthrob, Rudolph Valentino. The
1926 ad titillates with ambivalence. Is the pale heroine beseeching her kidnapper to release her?
Or is she swooning with desire as the sheik begins to disrobe?
Picture Research Consultant & Archives; Billy Rose Theatre Collection, The New York Public Library at Lincoln
Center

good on screen and could invent an elegant or rugged-sounding name could hope to become a star. Hollywood turned out to be entertainment's best contribution to the melting pot ideal. In the 1920s, the movies' focus on fun and happiness, vicarious thrills and romance, held American audiences spellbound.

Sports and Hero Worship

Along with celluloid heroes, Americans found their heroes in sports. Baseball, professionalized since 1871, became the national pastime. Early in the century, New York and Philadelphia built large stadiums, signaling the arrival of the sport into a new age of big money and influence. Still, by the 1920s, baseball remained essentially a game played by and for the working class, an outlet for raw energy and even a tinge of rebelliousness. Babe Ruth was the most cherished free spirit of the time. An orphan who never really grew up, Ruth mixed his record-setting home runs with rowdy escapades, satisfying the general view that sports offered a way to break out of the ordinariness of everyday life.

The public also fell in love with a young boxer from the grim mining districts of Colorado. As a teenager, Jack Dempsey had made his living hanging around saloons betting he could beat anyone in the house. When he took the heavyweight crown just after World War I from the giant champion Jess Willard in a spectacular slugfest, he was revered as America's equalizer, a stand-in for the average American who felt increasingly detached from natural impulses and hemmed in by complex bureaucracies and a machine-made culture.

The greatest football player of the decade, Red Grange of the University of Illinois, was a quiet, straitlaced son of the prairies whose steady attention to the business side of football proved crucial to the development of the professional game. The most celebrated college coach, Knute Rockne of Notre Dame, was beloved for his earnest advocacy of football as a parable of the good life of hard work and teamwork. Let the professors make learning as interesting as football, Rockne advised, and the problem of getting youth to learn would disappear.

The decade's hero worship reached its zenith in the celebration of a young pilot, Charles Lindbergh. On May 20, 1927, Lindbergh took off in his monoplane and became the first person to fly solo across the Atlantic. It took thirty-three hours, and as far as the lanky, painfully shy young man was concerned, the feat ended when he landed in Paris. But the American people would not let the adventure end. Lindbergh became the idol of the nation. His return home was a triumphant entry, unmatched in the nation's history.

Newspapers tagged Lindbergh the "Lone Eagle." One magazine declared: "Charles Lindbergh is the heir of all that we like to think is best in America. He is the stuff out of which have been made the pioneers that opened up the wilderness. His are the qualities which we, as a people, must nourish." Americans who celebrated Lindbergh lived in a world in which solitary, courageous achievement was rapidly becoming almost impossible. The United States was rapidly becoming a modern, urban, machine-oriented civilization, a world of bureaucracies and institutions, a place in which men and women did not act independently but found themselves cogs in large corporate or government organizations. It was painful for some to accept that success had become more a matter of cooperation, winning friends, and influencing people than courageous independent achievement.

But "Lucky Lindy," as he was known, referred to himself and his plane as "we," and he cautioned cheering crowds not to forget the wonderful engine that made it all possible. Man and machine (the most advanced piece of technology America's modern industrial economy had produced) were partners, not enemies, Lindbergh said. He sought to reassure Americans that possibilities for adventure remained in the modern, technological, and bureaucratic world. In the end, the celebration embraced both the heroic individual and the complex machine. It was a fitting response from a people who were enduring the final stages of the transition from a rural, agricultural nation to an urban, industrial one.

Women and Men of the Jazz Age

The first licensed radio station, KDKA in Pittsburgh, began broadcasting in 1920, and soon American airwaves buzzed with news, sermons, market information, police calls, soap operas, labor reports, sporting events, comedy shows, music, and advertisements. Americans in the most isolated outposts of the high plains laughed at the latest jokes from New York or Chicago. For the first time, citizens were able to listen to the voices of political candidates without leaving home. And, most important, radio allowed advertisers to reach prospective customers in the intimacy of their own living rooms. Door-to-door salesmen, traditionally rebuffed at the door, now came into the nation's parlors via the airwaves to pitch their products. Between 1922 and 1929, the number of radio stations increased from 30 to 606. In those seven short years, the number of homes with radios jumped from 60,000 to a staggering 10,250,000.

Jazz challenged its audience to be—or seem to be—young and carefree. For the first time, in the 1920s youth became a social class distinct in itself.

Along with advertising and consumer goods, radio added to the growth of popular music, especially jazz. Jazz, with its energetic style and its suggestion of youthful freedom and sexual openness, was the product of African American artists. But in the 1920s, although a radio broadcast might occasionally feature the headlong, ragged rhythms of the King Oliver Creole Jazz Band or the "walking bass" stride piano style of James P. Johnson, white audiences for the most part embraced a classically trained musician aptly named Paul Whiteman. Although Whiteman's "symphonic jazz," with its strict tempos and avoidance of improvisation, left most black jazz fans cold, Whiteman helped make jazz the national favorite with white audiences. George Gershwin composed his jazz-classical hybrid *Rhapsody in Blue* for Whiteman's orchestra, and it was Whiteman on the radio who spread Jazz Age dances like the shimmy, the black bottom, and, most popular of all, the Charleston.

Jazz, even white jazz, challenged its audience to be—or seem to be—young and carefree. For the first time, in the 1920s youth became a social class distinct in itself, much idolized and fretted over. As the traditional bonds of community and religion eroded, family constraints loosened and the young felt less pressure to imitate their elders. Instead, they developed their own culture. An increasing number of college students helped the "rah-rah" style of college life become a fad, promoted in movies, songs, and advertisements. The collegiate set was the vanguard of the decade's "flaming youth."

Most stunning were the changes in the behavior of young women. In the 1920s, the typical urban woman shed up to twelve yards of clothing, "parked" her corset in the cloakroom (if she wore one at all), bared her knees, smoked cigarettes, drank in speakeasies, and generally played havoc with traditionally conservative notions of female behavior. The daring "flapper," as she was called, became the symbol of youthful revolt. As her contemporary and chronicler F. Scott Fitzgerald described her in his novel *This Side of Paradise* (1920), she was "lovely and expensive and about nineteen."

For all their spirit, the youth of the 1920s managed to disappoint reformers by their lack of interest in politics as much as they angered traditionalists with their unconventional morality. For the most part, young people remained apathetic about social issues and eager to participate in the new consumer culture. Rarely did they pose a threat to the status quo. "Flaming youth" rapidly cooled in office jobs and suburbs, and high-spirited flappers eventually settled down to become wives and mothers and employees.

Yet, even at home women's lives reflected the changes of the new era. Thanks to the greater availability of birth control devices, married people could remain passionate and yet have fewer children to take care of. New home appliances also lightened the load. While men are judged by how successfully they delegate work, one advertisement declared, "the wise woman delegates to electricity all that electricity can do." Advertisers went too far, however, in claiming that electricity had made

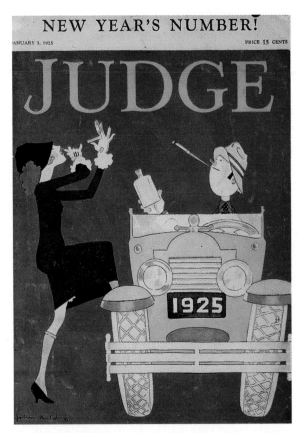

HELD MAGAZINE COVER
Artist John Held drew and lived the extravagant life of the flaming youth of the Roaring Twenties. Raised in Mormon, Utah, Held followed his artistic and journalistic skills to New York City and there found endless subjects to amuse himself. His caricatures of the Jazz Age came to typify it and made him a fortune. Like the high-living sorts he satirized, Held married and divorced a couple of times, dividing his time among his New York penthouse, Palm Beach cabana, and estate in Connecticut. Then, following the curve, he went broke in the Great Crash of 1929. Held gave up cartooning for landscape painting and sculpture and settled down on a small farm. Shown here is Held's inimitable style on the cover of the 1920s leading humor magazine: sporty convertible, the flapper, and Held's signature caricature of the round-headed, almost puppetlike young man.
Culver Pictures.

housewives ladies of leisure. Most rural homes were beyond the reach of power lines; and urban middle class women who had appliances, still spent a lot of hours cooking, mending, and cleaning.

For women who worked outside the home, the changing economy of the 1920s offered fresh, but still limited, opportunity. Many factory jobs, such as those in the booming automobile industry, and most management positions remained male domains, but "pink-collar" jobs (in poorly paying service occupations) became readily available. Women continued to become teachers and nurses, but even more found work as secretaries, typists, and file clerks, keeping the modern corporation afloat while receiving few of its rewards. Women also worked as salesclerks, playing a crucial role in the new consumer society. By 1930, nearly eleven million women were employed, constituting 24 percent of the workforce, compared with 18 percent in 1900.

Black Assertion and the Harlem Renaissance

Cheers for the black soldiers who marched up Broadway after the First World War soon faded, and grim days of race riots and hardship followed. Still, a sense of optimism remained strong among African Americans. It was in New York City that the key elements of hope and talent came together to form an exceptionally dynamic moment in black history. In the years before the war, black people in New York had moved uptown from their cramped confinement in Hell's Kitchen to the spacious heights of Harlem. A highly cosmopolitan population soon filled the new area, including poor migrants from the South responding to the economic opportunities offered by the war and a more sophisticated wave of immigrants from the West Indies. On the crest of the new wave were black artists and writers who made Harlem a special place. There the "New Negro," as critic and historian Alain Locke put it in a book by that name, could rise from the ashes of a subjugated past and discover the race's true, creative identity.

That quest for autonomy would prove more aggressive than it had been before the war. The military service of black troops raised expectations of higher status in American society. Disillusioned with mainstream politics, African Americans looked for new leadership, and many poor urban blacks turned to a forceful Jamaican visionary named Marcus Garvey. Garvey urged African Americans to rediscover the heritage of Africa and to take pride in their own culture and achievements. In 1917, Garvey launched the Universal Negro Improvement Association (UNIA) to help African Americans gain economic and political independence entirely outside of white society. Through their own shipping company, the Black Star Line, Garvey's followers aimed to finance their Back to Africa movement. The dream of returning to a "promised land" in Africa linked anticolonialist fervor with pride in race. UNIA proposed a return to Africa for the Africans so that the true beauty and nobility of blacks could emerge from beneath the mask of servility forced upon them by white oppression in the United States.

Garvey excelled in stirring support for his vision. In parades, he cut a fine figure, riding in an open car in a feather-plumed uniform while his African Legion marched behind. His black nationalist message drew enthusiastic crowds in Harlem and brought delegates from many countries to the UNIA convention of 1920. But Garvey was a naive businessman and was unprepared for the rough opposition he encountered. Sharp operators sold bad ships to the Black Star Line, and the federal government, opposed to minority movements that challenged the status quo, jailed Garvey briefly on dubious mail fraud charges and then in 1927 deported him to Jamaica. But Garvey's black nationalist vision survived and continued to find spokesmen in the African American community. Moreover, other black people pondered the questions Garvey raised about black identity, racial pride, and the search for equality and security.

Black writers and artists who explored the African American experience unleashed an artistic explosion in the 1920s called the Harlem Renaissance. They embraced a cultural tradition far removed from the world of the white elite. The poet Langston Hughes summed up the central thrust of the movement when he shouted: "I am a Negro— and beautiful." Probing the black cultural tradition, African American intellectuals celebrated the rich achievement within harsh conditions.

In his music and writing, James Weldon Johnson focused on the migrants from the South, the gritty working people and churchgoers of Harlem. In 1903, he had written the "Negro national anthem," "Lift Every Voice," and in 1927, in "God's Trombones," he offered an interpretation of black folktales. Zora Neale Hurston came to Harlem from Florida, and as a scholarship student at Barnard College she studied anthropology and later collected black folktales. Her masterpiece, *Their Eyes Were Watching God* (1937), explores the indomitable spirit of poor, uneducated black people. Langston Hughes, Claude McKay, Countee Cullen, Nella Lar-

NOAH'S ARK

The Harlem Renaissance gained its principal visual expression at the hands of Kansas-born painter Aaron Douglas. When Douglas arrived in New York City in 1925, he quickly attracted the attention of W. E. B. DuBois, who placed great importance on the arts as a carrier of the African American soul. At Du Bois's urging, Douglas sought ways of integrating the African cultural heritage with American experience. This depiction of an African Noah commanding the loading of the ark displays a technique that became closely associated with African American art: strong silhouetted figures awash in misty color, indicating a connection between Christian faith and the vital, colorful origins of black Americans in a distant, mythologized African past.

Fisk University Art Galleries, Nashville, Tennessee.

sen, and other writers eloquently expressed both the plight of black Americans and their vital culture. Artist Aaron Douglas tried to capture slave and African folklore on canvas. His bold symbolic figures were a striking example of the Harlem Renaissance's clear assertion of self-esteem.

Whites who finally became aware of Harlem usually chose to go to the area at night and hardly noticed its serious side. For them Harlem was an exotic dark continent just up the street. They sought a modern version of the old-time minstrel show, and Harlem nightclubs sprang up to provide black performers for whites-only audiences. The most famous white outpost in Harlem, the Cotton Club, was a gangster-owned outlet for the bootleggers who made fortunes out of the prohibitionist society that club patrons were fleeing. As for the black performers, they had to enter by the delivery doors and make careful preparations not to need the restrooms, which were for whites only.

Garvey's Back to Africa movement and the Harlem Renaissance signified a new awareness among African Americans. The Great Migration that had carried a million blacks out of the South and their subsequent northern urban experiences altered black ideas and attitudes. Urban blacks, not just in Harlem, were showing a stronger racial consciousness and a willingness to act on it.

The Lost Generation

Observing the collection of American writers and artists who flocked to her salon in Paris during the 1920s, the writer Gertrude Stein remarked, "They are the lost generation." Out of step with American society, despising its business mentality, its consumer culture, and its small-town hypocrisy, a number of artists and critics renounced America altogether. Rather than try to reform it as the progressives had done before the war, they chose to leave it. The writer Harold Stearns announced the secession most conspicuously when he gathered a group of some thirty authors to publish a book of essays scornfully entitled *Civilization in the United States* (1922). Relentlessly, their essays condemned the way sexual prudery and greed blighted virtually every aspect of the America they knew. Then, amid much public fanfare, Stearns and other alienated critics set sail for France.

Young, and mostly college-educated men, these expatriates, as they were called, were profoundly embittered by World War I. The devastation wrought by the war had left them feeling betrayed and deceived by the older generation. The poet Ezra Pound asked what so many young men had died for. His answer:

For an old bitch gone in the teeth
For a botched civilization.

Fed up with Wilsonian rhetoric, skeptical of the possibility of progress, and appalled by the vulgarity and materialism of the New Era, the young exiles scattered throughout Germany, Spain, and France. Mostly, however, they favored Paris, where the cost of living was low and the culture receptive to their hopes and struggles. Far from the complications of home and steady work, they helped launch the most creative period in American art and literature in the twentieth century.

The novelist whose sparse, clean style best exemplified the expatriate writers' efforts to strip writing of its cant and make language into the exact mirror of things was Ernest Hemingway. Born in suburban Chicago, Hemingway had served in a volunteer ambulance corps during the war. In his novel *The Sun Also Rises* (1926), Hemingway's main character is impotent, the result of a war wound. Void of conventional beliefs, he and his friends set out on an aimless journey through France and Spain, discovering little in the world to sustain them. In Hemingway's view, paring words and images down to basics showed life as a struggle with brute forces. His own stern personal code of honor dismissed creeds, ideologies, and patriotism as pious attempts to cover up the fact that life is a losing battle with death. His ideal of macho courage, "grace under pressure," guided a lonely, doomed struggle with the inevitable.

Writers who remained in America were exiles in spirit who hoped that freedom from claims of duty and convention would help them in exploring the limits of creativity. One prominent critic boosted his reputation for good judgment by proclaiming that "the great problems of the world — social, political, economic, and theological — do not concern me in the slightest." Within that atmosphere novelist Sinclair Lewis in *Main Street* (1920) and *Babbitt* (1922) devastatingly satirized his native Midwest as a cultural wasteland. Humorists like James Thurber and Don Marquis created outlandish forms and characters to poke fun at taboos and inhibitions. And southern writers, led by William Faulkner, rallied against the South's reputation as a literary Sahara by exploring the dark undercurrents of that region's class and race heritage. But doubts about the new freedom surfaced as well. From the vantage of his own fame and wealth as chronicler of flaming youth, F. Scott Fitzgerald spoke with guilty brilliance in *This Side of Paradise* (1920) of a disillusioned generation "grown up to find all Gods dead, all wars fought, all faiths in man shaken."

Rural America and Resistance to Change

Rural America and urban America had eyed each other warily since the nineteenth century. But suspicion turned to outright hostility in the 1920s. Though the number of people in small towns and rural areas continued to increase, country people saw the center of gravity of American life shift from farm to city. The 1920 census established that for the first time more Americans lived in towns and cities than in the country. The rapid growth of cities and suburbs cost rural America its dominance over the nation's political and cultural life.

It also put economic distance between city and country. The prosperity of the 1920s was very much an urban phenomenon. Between 1918 and 1921, the value of farmland and farm incomes fell by 30 to 50 percent. Technological advances benefited large-scale farming, but the average farm family had to incur huge and risky debts to buy the new machinery it needed to compete. Most farmers held fast to the agrarian ideal of self-reliant individualism, but by the end of the decade, 40 percent of the nation's farmers had become landless tenants. Moreover, despite the flood of new technology, 90 percent of rural homes in 1930 were still without indoor plumbing, gas, or electricity.

In the eyes of many country folk, the cities stood for everything that rural areas stood against. Rural Americans saw themselves as Anglo-Saxon (conveniently forgetting that most blacks still lived in the rural South), while the cities filled with strangers from around the world. Rural America was the home of traditional Protestant values, and the cities were the home of Catholics, Jews, liberal Protestants, and atheists. Rural America championed old-fashioned Puritan moral standards of abstinence and self-denial, and the cities seemed to be places of unbounded hedonism and sexual vice. Rural youth were not children of the Jazz Age, running around with raccoon coats and hip flasks or with stockings rolled daringly at the knee.

Increasingly, the nation divided along the line drawn between the country and the city. At the end of the previous decade, rural Americans had helped enact prohibition and in the 1920s they defended it while urban dwellers lined up at speakeasies. The defense mechanisms of rural America began working overtime in the 1920s. Country people joined with other frightened Americans to push through immigration restrictions, cutting off the foreign flood that they feared was going to engulf them. Religious fundamentalism challenged modern values. And in 1928, the clash of cultures reached national politics, as city and country squared off in a presidential election.

The Rebirth of the Ku Klux Klan

Some of those who felt slighted or offended by the modern world channeled their desperation into a revived version of the Ku Klux Klan that first appeared in 1915. Although the new Klan rose once again in the South, where its predecessor had been created to curb the rights of blacks during Reconstruction, it swiftly moved beyond the region. Imperial Grand Wizard Hiram Wesley Evans, a Texas dentist who styled himself as "the most average man in America," employed modern sales techniques to organize a network of klaverns (local societies) across the country. The nation, Evans argued, stood in need of a thorough cleansing. He promised that Klansmen would stoutly defend family, morality, and traditional values against the threat offered by blacks, immigrants, and radicals. In 1926, Evans complained that "the sacredness of our Sabbath, of our homes, of chastity, and finally even of our right to teach our children in our own schools fundamental facts and truths were torn away from us." This potent argument of a lost birthright brought into the Klan at its peak some three to four million members, a substantial fraction of whom lived in towns and cities.

The Klan's brand of narrow-mindedness and intolerance offered a certain counterfeit dignity for those who felt passed over by a changing society. It played on the decade's love of fraternal societies with their secrecy, uniforms, and rituals. Like the Elks or the Odd Fellows, the Klan also promised the practical advantage of forging business contacts. At the same time, it appealed to the vengeful and brutal, enabling its cloaked and hooded members to intimidate and punish anonymously and with little fear of consequences. The brotherhood and camaraderie of the Klan served also as a pathetic substitute for the fading village community. Nostalgia and violence came together in the KKK.

Like the original Klan, the new Klan terrorized blacks, but it also took aim at other people. Any group that threatened traditional values, as the Klan defined them, ran the risk of vigilante action. Klansmen threatened, roughed up, and even murdered

bootleggers, drunks, wife beaters, advocates of birth control, and teachers who contradicted the Bible. They sought to drive Catholics, Jews, and foreigners from their communities. Economic insecurity underlay Klansmen's sense of a world out of control. Long-term economic changes had marooned white farmers and small merchants between corporate giants on the one hand and the growing army of wage laborers on the other. Economic inequality grew during the 1920s, and prosperity remained a stranger in the American countryside. Their old world was unraveling, and Klansmen sought reactionary means to knit it back together. By the mid-1920s, the Klan had gained considerable political power, virtually controlling Indiana and influencing politics in Illinois, California, Oregon, Texas, Louisiana, Oklahoma, and Kansas.

THE LAW IS TOO SLOW
This stark depiction of a lynching by George Bellows in 1923 appeared just as the revived Ku Klux Klan was proclaiming itself the defender of traditional virtue in a sinful modern world. Bellows, an athlete as well as an artist, had gained fame as a realist and tough-minded radical before World War I and continued until his death in 1925 to spur social conscience even after doing so had gone out of fashion.

By the late 1920s, the Klan had withered away, partly because immigration restrictions removed the threat of invading foreigners and partly out of public disgust. Grand Dragon David Stephenson of Indiana, for example, went to jail after a sensational trial that found him guilty of the kidnap and rape of a woman who subsequently committed suicide. Yet the social grievances and hard economic problems that had produced such alienation and attracted recruits to the Klan remained.

The Scopes Trial

The clash between the old-time religion and the new spirit of science reached a dramatic climax in the Scopes trial in 1925. The confrontation occurred after several southern and border states passed legislation in the early 1920s against the teaching of Charles Darwin's theory of evolution in the public schools. Fundamentalist Protestants insisted that the Bible's creation story be taught as the literal truth. In answer to a clamor from scientists and civil liberties organizations for a challenge to the law, John Scopes, a young schoolteacher in Dayton, Tennessee, offered to test his state's ban on teaching evolution. When Scopes was brought to trial in the summer of 1925, Clarence Darrow, a brilliant defense lawyer from Chicago, volunteered to defend him. Darrow, an avowed agnostic, took on the state's attorney William Jennings Bryan, the old war horse of the Democratic Party and symbol of rural America. Bryan, now aging and ill, styled himself as the defender of Christian opposition to the idea that humans had evolved from apes.

> *The Ku Klux Klan and the Scopes trial dramatized and inflamed divisions between city and country, intellectuals and the unlettered, the privileged and the outcasts, the scoffers and the faithful.*

The Scopes trial quickly degenerated into a freakish media circus, despite the serious religious and philosophical issues underlying it. As the first trial to be covered live on the radio, it attracted an avid nationwide audience. The reporters from big-city papers who converged on Dayton were for the most part hostile to Bryan, none more so than the incomparably cynical H. L. Mencken. Mencken gleefully painted Bryan as a sort of Darwinian miss-

ing link ("a sweating anthropoid," a "gaping primate"). When, under relentless questioning by Darrow, Bryan declared on the witness stand that he did, indeed, believe the world was created in six days and that Jonah had lived in the belly of a whale, his humiliation in the eyes of most urban observers was complete. Although the Tennessee court upheld the law in defiance of modern intellectual consensus and punished Scopes with a $100 fine, Mencken had the last word in a merciless obituary for Bryan, who died just weeks after the trial ended. Portraying the "monkey trial" as a battle between the country and the city, Mencken flayed Bryan as a "charlatan, a mountebank, a zany without shame or dignity," motivated solely by "hatred of the city men who had laughed at him for so long."

As Mencken's acid prose indicated, Bryan's humiliation was not purely a victory of reason and science. It also served to reduce the esteem in which country people and their old values were held. The Ku Klux Klan and the Scopes trial dramatized and inflamed divisions between city and country, intellectuals and the unlettered, the privileged and the outcasts, the scoffers and the faithful.

Al Smith and the Election of 1928

The shock of Calvin Coolidge's announcement in the summer of 1927 that "I do not choose to run for President in 1928" caught the country off guard and evened the playing field for the Democrats. But in the election of 1928, issues splitting the nation—prohibition, religious bigotry, and the clash between rural and urban values—emerged with a vengeance.

Among Republicans, the logical choice as Coolidge's successor seemed to be Herbert Hoover. Hoover enjoyed a great reputation as the wonder-working dynamo of the Commerce Department during the Harding and Coolidge administrations. Some uneasiness surfaced during the primaries about Hoover's lack of a common touch and a feel for electoral politics, but the powerful insiders who ran the party believed that Hoover was best able to continue Coolidge's pro-business programs and secured him the nomination.

The Democrats nominated Governor Alfred E. Smith of New York. Smith epitomized big-city values. Born to Irish Catholic immigrant parents, Smith had grown up on the sidewalks of New York. The Democrats balanced the ticket with a southern conservative, Senator Joseph Robinson of Arkansas, and sought to woo farmers with the promise of lower tariffs and labor with calls for reforms including collective bargaining. The platform advocated an active government, and Smith, an outspoken "wet" (an opponent of prohibition), actively championed repeal of the Eighteenth Amendment.

Very quickly the contest boiled down to controversy over the urban and religious values Smith represented. As the first Catholic to run for president, Smith made an easy target. An editorial in the *Baptist and Commoner* declared that the election of Smith "would be granting the Pope the right to dictate to this government what it should do." There would be edicts from the White House saying "to hell with our public schools" and "Protestants are now living in adultery because they were not married by a priest." Are you willing, the editorial asked, to accept a president who would tell us "our offspring are bastards"? Smith's connections with the Tammany Hall political machine cost him additional support in the countryside. Radio broadcasts also damaged Smith among listeners who found his New York City accent alien and offputting.

Smith supporters attacked Hoover as a heartless tool of big-money interests, but with little effect. It is doubtful anyone could have beaten Hoover, who neatly combined the image of morality, efficiency, service, and prosperity. But in 1928, a Catholic had very little chance. Hoover won the election by a landslide. He received 58 percent of the vote, taking all but eight states, and gained 444 electoral votes to Smith's 87. The Republicans managed to retain support of blacks in the South at the same time they made a calculated appeal to southern whites in the fundamentalist Bible belt. Hoover wrenched five states loose from the formerly solid Democratic South. But Republican strength in the cities and among discontented farmers suffered an ominous erosion. The nation's largest cities voted Democratic in a striking reversal from 1924, indicating the rising strength of ethnic minorities, including Smith's fellow Catholics.

From the New Era to the Great Crash

At his inauguration in 1929, Herbert Hoover told the American people, "We in America today are nearer to the final triumph over poverty than ever before in the history of any land. The poorhouse is vanishing from among us." The nation had not yet reached that goal, he said, "but, given a chance to go forward with the policies of the last eight years,

we shall soon with the help of God be in sight of the day when poverty will be banished from this nation." Those words came back to haunt Hoover, for in eight short months the Roaring Twenties came to a crashing halt. The prosperity Hoover touted collapsed with the stock market crash, and the nation fell into the most serious economic depression of all time. Hoover and his reputation were among the first casualties, along with the reverence for business that had been the hallmark of Hoover's New Era.

Herbert Hoover: The Great Engineer

It is ironic, and a little unfair, that the Great Depression struck during Hoover's presidency. Coming into office in 1929, Hoover seemed to have the credentials to be a great president. He was undoubtedly a vast improvement over his immediate predecessors. Born in 1874 into a poor Iowa farm family and orphaned at twelve, Hoover was raised by hardworking Quaker relatives who had braved the pioneer trail to Oregon. In 1896, he graduated with Stanford University's first class with a degree in geology and forty dollars in his pocket. By the time he was thirty, he was one of the world's top mining engineers. By the time he was forty, he had become a millionaire with offices in London, New York, San Francisco, Petrograd (St. Petersburg), and Paris. Hoover and his wife and Stanford classmate, Lou Henry Hoover, lived lives of high adventure in mining camps around the world, surviving primitive conditions, labor wars, and even bombardment during China's Boxer Rebellion.

The prosperity Hoover touted collapsed with the 1929 stock market crash, and the nation fell into the most serious economic depression of all time.

In 1914, Hoover's renown as an organizational genius and tireless worker won him the directorship of the task force set up to feed the Belgians, who had been devastated by the German attack through their country at the beginning of World War I. Hoover's success in heading the greatest relief effort in history won him the title "the Great Humanitarian" and led Woodrow Wilson to choose him for head of the Food Administration when the United States entered the war. In the 1920s, he

HOOVER CAMPAIGN POSTER
Herbert Hoover's 1928 campaign poster neatly framed his major positions: middle-class prosperity in a house in the suburbs, complete with a car in every garage and, presumably, a chicken in every pot. To complete the display, smoking chimneys at a discreet distance remind voters that Hoover as secretary of commerce had promoted industry that made the suburban idyll possible.
Collection of Janice L. and David J. Frent.

served in the Harding and Coolidge cabinets as secretary of commerce, where he put into practice the things he believed in—material welfare, efficiency, voluntary cooperative enterprise, and individual initiative in the context of government-business partnership.

In 1922, Hoover had formulated his political philosophy in a slender book titled *American Individualism*. He extolled rugged individualism—"a quality of the individual alone"—and assumed that the United States offered opportunity to everyone. He measured a person's stature and achievement by wealth. As he summed it up, a man who had not made a million dollars by the time he was forty didn't amount to much. Hoover thought of himself as a progressive, but his reluctance to use the government to force change and equalize conditions distanced him from the reform spirit of prewar progressives. Government's task, Hoover felt, was simply to promote private initiative and enforce rules of fair play. While government could encourage cooperation among businesses, a vibrant economy and free society required that businesses participate voluntarily.

For all his strengths, hindsight reveals that Hoover had significant liabilities when he became

president. The only elective office he had ever held was treasurer of his class at Stanford. Having spent most of his adult life abroad, he had never voted in a presidential election. He had very little political know-how. He had no network of political contacts. He had a poor political touch. He was too stiff and too thin-skinned. And he also suffered the liability of being oversold. Before he took office, Hoover told a friend: "I have no dread of the ordinary work of the presidency. What I do fear is the . . . exaggerated idea . . . I am a sort of superman, that no problem is beyond my capacity." And he added prophetically, "If some unprecedented calamity should come upon the nation . . . I would be sacrificed to the unreasoning disappointment of a people who expected too much."

Hoover's greatest liability, however, was his stubborn integrity. He knew what he believed, and he would not be shaken. He had developed precise ideas that to him spelled out the proper workings of an economy and the correct relationship between citizen and government. Those ideas were popular and at least partially successful during the 1920s. But the world changed in the 1930s, and Hoover became a victim of his own beliefs. He doggedly stuck to his principles, even as the nation slipped deeper and deeper into depression. In the end, the man who had fed Europe became a symbol of hunger, the brilliant administrator a symbol of disaster. He carried the shame of the depression on his shoulders until he died in 1964. To some, his name remains linked with reactionary conservatism. In reality, the depression was inevitable by the time he entered the White House. What he did to combat it once it struck is another matter.

The Unstable Economy

In the spring of 1929, when Hoover moved into the White House, the United States basked in the sunshine of economic prosperity. Most Americans saw no more than a few wispy clouds on the horizon. In fact, thunderheads loomed.

Abroad, an unstable international economy spelled trouble. Massive expenditures during the First World War had nearly bankrupted the European powers. The United States, new to its role as the world's dominant economic power, failed to step in and help rebuild Europe's shattered economy. Instead, it demanded that European nations repay their war loans. Unable to pay, the European countries asked for and received new loans to pay off the old ones. In addition, the United States erected tariff barriers that kept other nations from selling their goods to Americans. As a consequence, foreign nations had less money to buy American goods, which were pouring out in record abundance. To keep trade with other nations alive, the United States extended more credit. Debt piled onto debt in an absurd pyramid. By the end of the decade, the United States accounted for 40 percent of the world's economic production and acquired most of the world's gold in return for its exports.

At home, too, prosperity rested on shaky foundations. Behind the glittering facade of affluence, poverty was rampant. Farmers continued to suffer from low prices for their crops and chronic indebtedness. The average income of families on the land amounted to only $240 per year, and 54 percent earned less than $1,000. Labor's wages rose slightly in the 1920s, but they failed to keep up with productivity and corporate profits. Nearly two-thirds of all American families lived on less than the $2,000 per year that was needed to "supply only basic necessities." The 1920s produced fabulous wealth, but most of it settled in the corporate sector. By the end of the decade, the top 1 percent of the population received 15 percent of the nation's income, an amount equal to that received by the bottom 42 percent of the population.

The imbalance of wealth produced a serious problem in consumption. Money rushing to the top prompted extravagant behavior—the acquisition of opulent houses, cars, and polo ponies. The rich, brilliantly portrayed in F. Scott Fitzgerald's *The Great Gatsby* (1925), gave the era much of its mythical glitter with their careless spending. But they could absorb only a tiny fraction of the nation's output. Ordinary folk, on whom the system ultimately depended, did their best, but they were too poor to buy all that American industry produced. At first, Americans thought that credit would handle the problem of consumer demand. Installment buying became a standard practice. At the end of the decade, four out of five automobiles and two out of three radios were bought on credit. Personal indebtedness swelled, but credit had its limits.

Signs of the economic slowdown began at mid-decade. Between 1921 and 1928, during the heyday of the New Era, some five thousand banks had failed. Two crucial industries began to totter. After 1925, the boom in the construction industry subsided, and the automobile industry also faltered. With nearly thirty million cars already on the road, demand had been met and producers began to cut back and lay off workers. The warning signs went largely unnoticed, however. Confidence in fundamental soundness and eagerness to profit from it created a blindness to underlying flaws in the economy.

The Great Crash of 1929

The most spectacular example of the credit binge of the 1920s occurred in the stock market—the nerve center and symbol of the boom. Even after the economy began weakening in the mid-1920s, a get-rich-quick mania hit Wall Street. There, buying stocks on margin—that is, putting up only part of the money at the time of purchase—became rampant. The lure of vast returns for very little investment lured tens of thousands of speculators into the market. And many got rich in paper profits. But those who bought on credit could finance their loans only if their stock increased in value. Thus, the stock market became dependent on continued expansion. Many naively believed that the market would continue to go up forever. There was some reason to think so. Between 1924 and 1929, the values of stocks listed on the New York Stock Exchange increased more than 400 percent. From that height it was hard to imagine what would happen were the market to fall and speculators forced to meet their margin loans with cash they never had.

When stock purchased on margin rose to about 20 percent of the total by the summer of 1929, Hoover summoned Richard Whitney, the head of the New York Stock Exchange, to urge him to tighten requirements. But Whitney, who later went to Sing Sing prison for stealing money from trust funds to cover his own bad investments, gave only empty promises of cooperation. Other representatives from prestigious banks and investment houses assured Hoover that all was well. Former President Coolidge stated tersely that at current prices, stocks were a bargain. The prudent Hoover, however, decided to sell some of his own stocks. In rejecting the optimistic advice of the boosters, Hoover took to a saying he kept repeating for the rest of his battle-scarred life: "The only trouble with capitalism is capitalists. They're too damned greedy."

Finally, in the fall of 1929, the market hesitated. Like rabbits sniffing danger, investors nervously began to sell their overvalued stock. The dip quickly became a rush, building to panic on October 24, the day that came to be known as Black Thursday. Brokers jammed the stock exchange and overflowed into the street. Stirred by the cries of "Sell! Sell!" just outside their windows, the giants of finance gathered in the offices of J. P. Morgan Jr., son of the nineteenth century Wall Street lion, to plot ways of restoring confidence. They injected $100 million of their assets to bolster the market and issued brave declarations of faith. But more panic selling came on Black Tuesday, October 29, the day the market suffered the greatest drop in history.

During the month of October alone, the listings on the New York Stock Exchange lost more than one-third of their value and continued steadily downward until 1932. During that slide, stocks worth $87 billion at the crest of the boom dropped to only $18 billion. In one of the few jaunty quips the panic produced, the weekly theatrical trade journal *Variety* headlined, "Wall Street Lays an Egg."

It was a very large egg out of which hatched the deepest, longest-lasting depression in the nation's history. It was once thought that the Great Crash *caused* the Great Depression. It did not. In 1929, the national and international economies were riddled with severe problems, but the collapse of Wall Street was significant nevertheless. The dramatic loss of 10 percent of Americans' total personal wealth and the fear of risking what was left acted

BLACK FRIDAY
Edward Laning, a mural painter who lost his personal fortune in the stock market crash, gained a measure of revenge in this melodramatic version of panic on the Stock Exchange floor. The painting shows Stock Exchange president Richard Whitney standing firm in the center as prices and brokers collapse around him. A few years later, however, Whitney went to prison for stealing from other people's accounts to cover his own losses. Laning, on the other hand, went on to fame for the murals he painted to adorn Ellis Island and the New York Public Library.
Collection of John P. Axelrod.

as a great brake on economic activity. With the collapse of the stock market went the aggressive confidence in America's future as a land of perpetually expanding prosperity. That faith had been crucial to the New Era.

Hoover and the Limits of Individualism

Admirers of American capitalism at first shrugged off the Great Crash with the explanation that human nature and bad judgment accounted for recurring cycles of boom and bust. They insisted that holding resolutely to free market principles would bring things right again. "Prosperity," the boosters insisted, "is just around the corner"—close at hand, though out of sight. President Herbert Hoover stubbornly maintained that the American economic system was "fundamentally sound."

Hoover's first act in the aftermath of the crash was characteristic. He called a White House conference of business and labor leaders and urged them to join in a voluntary plan for recovery. The president asked businesses to forge ahead with their pre-crash investment plans, maintain production, and keep their workers on the job. He asked labor to accept the status quo and relinquish demands for improvements in wages, hours, or conditions. Within a few months, however, the bargain had fallen apart. As demand for their products declined, industrialists cut production, sliced wages, and laid off workers. Poorly paid or unemployed workers could not buy much, and decreased buying led to further cuts in production and further loss of jobs. And thus began the terrible spiral of economic decline.

Hoover did not just sit back and watch the depression cut its swath through American society. He worked long hours, wracked his brain for solutions, and, despite what people thought, felt the suffering of the American people. But he confronted the unprecedented problems of the depression within the constraints of the ideology he brought to the White House. He remained wedded to the notion of voluntary compliance and resisted plans that called for the federal government to intervene in the private sector. But he was not a do-nothing president. He did not agree with his secretary of the treasury, Andrew Mellon, who counseled that there was nothing the administration could do but let the depression run its course and eventually right itself. The people, Mellon said, would simply have to endure.

Hoover called on Congress to use its legitimate power to combat the depression. In 1930, he got Congress to authorize $420 million for public works projects to give the unemployed something useful to do and create greater purchasing power. Congress also agreed to cut taxes by $140 million to stimulate investment. To deal with the problems of rural America, Congress in 1930 passed the Agricultural Marketing Act. It created the Farm Board, which used its budget of $500 million to buy up agricultural surpluses and thus, it was hoped, raise prices. Although the Farm Board bought one-third of the nation's wheat supply, conditions worsened. Hoover also thought that American farmers would benefit from protective tariffs on agricultural goods. The Hawley-Smoot tariff of 1930 established the highest rates in history. None of Hoover's initiatives halted the downward slide of the economy, however. Each year of his administration, conditions grew more desperate. Some of his programs were well conceived but too puny to do much good. Others, such as the new tariff, ran contrary to what was needed. Dismayed foreign nations retaliated with increased tariffs of their own that further crippled American farmers' ability to sell abroad.

The nation's most pressing problem, however, was the relief of the unemployed. Each month, hundreds of thousands of additional workers lost their jobs. By 1932, one-quarter of the American workforce—more than 12 million men and women—were unemployed. There was no federal relief, and state services and private charities were swamped. Cries grew louder for the federal government to give hurting people relief. But Hoover absolutely refused. He believed that relief of suffering was a local responsibility. Federal aid, which he called a "dole," would destroy an individual's "moral fiber," he declared again and again. Hoover's fidelity to "rugged individualism" caused immeasurable suffering. In time, he fudged his principles a little. In 1931, he began to allow the Red Cross to distribute federal agricultural surpluses to the hungry. And in 1932, he allowed states to receive small federal loans, not gifts, to help them in their relief efforts. But Hoover's concessions were no more than Band-Aids on deep wounds.

By 1932, however, Hoover was forced to step up federal action. He reluctantly sponsored the Reconstruction Finance Corporation (RFC), a federal agency empowered to lend government funds to endangered banks, insurance companies, and railroads. The idea was that the RFC would lend money to these large enterprises so that they could keep going and continue to provide their employees with paychecks. It was a "trickle-down" theory: Pump money into the economy at the top, and in the long run the people at the bottom would benefit. Critics called the RFC a "millionaires' dole." Others charged that Hoover "tried to feed the sparrows by feeding the horses." In the most notorious instance, the RFC refused money to the city of Chicago to provide welfare for suffering victims of the crash but allocated $90 million to the Central Republic Bank in that city, headed by Charles Dawes, former head of the RFC.

None of Hoover's initiatives, including the RFC, turned the economy around. The great need

PRIVATE CAR
In the mid-1930s, LeConte Stewart, an artist who spent most of his life painting the landscapes
of his native Utah, noticed a new sight. From his remote hillside above the Union Pacific railroad
tracks, he witnessed a stream of tramps heading west. The sight of one young man jauntily
braced in the doorway of a boxcar made Stewart think of the elegant private cars of millionaires
that used to travel along those same tracks. Stewart entitled this painting Private Car *and*
achieved fame for his beautifully ironic depiction of a new wave of pioneers fleeing trouble.
Private Car *by Le Conte Stewart. © The Church of Latter-Day Saints. Used by permission.*

was to increase consumer demand and in the process create jobs. Hoover's insistence on individual self-reliance severely limited the role that the federal government could play in fighting the depression and helped guarantee that the economy would continue to slump.

Life in the Great Depression

In 1930, the nation woke up to the realization that prosperity was not "just around the corner." The trouble was too deep, the engine too cold to restart. Suffering and trial on a massive scale began, and a mood of cold despair settled over the land. Americans were wracked with want and fear. It was not just a matter of hunkering down and waiting for

bad times to pass. Each year of the Hoover administration, times got harder. Hollow-eyed men and women were bewildered. They saw agricultural surpluses in the countryside and knew that their children were going to bed hungry. They saw factories standing idle and knew that they and millions of others were willing to work. The gap between Herbert Hoover and the American people widened as the depression deepened. By 1932, America's economic problems had become a dangerous social crisis.

The Human Toll

Statistics provide a scaffolding for understanding the human dimension of the Great Depression. When Herbert Hoover took office in 1929, the American economy stood at its peak. When he left in 1933, it had reached its twentieth-century low. More than nine thousand banks had shut their doors, and depositors had lost more than $2.5 billion. In 1929, national income was $88 billion. By 1933, it had declined to $40 billion. In 1929, unemployment was 3.1 percent, one and a half million workers. By 1933, unemployment stood at 25 percent, twelve and a half million workers. One by one, the nation's great steel mills and foundries, once the noisy centers of industrial might, had fallen quiet. U.S. Steel, the country's largest producer, operated at only 12 percent capacity in 1932. The reduction reflected in part the huge cutback of automobile and railroad manufacture, which also made the streets emptier and added to the stillness. After having produced an average of six hundred locomotives a year during the 1920s, the American Locomotive Company turned out only one in 1932. "Once I built a railroad," lamented one of the popular songs of the year, "now it's done. Brother, can you spare a dime?"

Jobless, homeless victims wandered in search of work, and the tramp, or hobo, became one of the most visible figures of the decade. Young men and women unable to land their first job, made up about half of the million-strong army of hoboes. Many hit the road so that their younger brothers and sisters at home could have more to eat and a bed to sleep in. Riding the rails or hitchhiking, the vagabonds tended to move southward and westward, toward the sun and warmth and opportunities, they hoped, for seasonal agricultural work.

In addition to provoking industrial workers and farmers into militant protest, hard times also revived the left in America.

Other unemployed men and women, less hopeful or sick, huddled in doorways—human "junk," as one writer put it. Scavengers haunted alleys behind restaurants and picked over garbage dumps in search of food. In describing what he called the "American Earthquake," the writer Edmund Wilson told of an elderly woman who always took off her glasses to avoid seeing the maggots crawling over the garbage she ate. Starvation claimed more than a few victims. Four New York City hospitals reported 95 deaths from hunger in 1931. But enervating, rampant malnutrition posed the greater threat. The Children's Bureau announced that one of five schoolchildren did not get enough to eat.

The worst hardships hit the jobless and their families, estimated by *Fortune* magazine to include 34 million persons. But those at work also felt the

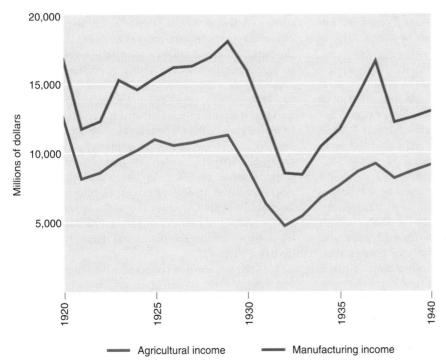

FIGURE 23.5
Manufacturing and Agricultural Income, 1920–1940
After economic collapse, recovery in the 1930s began under New Deal auspices. Sharp declines in 1937–1938, when federal spending was reduced, indicated that restoring manufacturing and agricultural income still needed New Deal stimuli.

pinch. The average weekly wage in 1932 was only $16.21. Some paychecks dwindled away to virtually nothing. In Chicago, the majority of workingwomen received less than 25 cents an hour. In the lumber industry, hourly rates fell to 10 cents, in general contracting to $7\frac{1}{2}$ cents, and in the sawmills to a nickel. Having a job, then, did not necessarily mean avoiding hunger or destitution.

Rural poverty was most acute. Landless tenant farmers and sharecroppers, mainly in the South, came to symbolize the ways poverty crushed the human spirit. In 1930, eight and a half million people, three million of them black, lived in tenant and sharecropping families—amounting to one-quarter of the total southern population. Often illiterate, usually without cash incomes, they crowded into two- and three-room cabins lacking screens or even doors, without plumbing, electricity, running water, or sanitary wells. They subsisted—just barely—on salt pork, cornmeal, molasses, beans, peas, and whatever they could hunt or fish. All the diseases of dietary and vitamin deficiencies wracked them. When the English economist John Maynard Keynes was asked whether anything like this degradation had existed before, he replied, "Yes, it was called the Dark Ages and it lasted four hundred years."

To meet this human catastrophe, the nation was equipped with the most limited welfare system in the Western world. There was no federal assistance, only a patchwork of voluntary institutions and pinchpenny state and local agencies. For a family of four without any income, the best the city of Philadelphia could do was provide $5.50 per week. That was not enough to live on, but still comparatively generous. New York City, where the greatest number of welfare cases gathered, provided only $2.39 per week. In Mississippi, the figure was $1.50. And Detroit, devastated when the bottom fell out of the auto industry, allotted 60 cents a week before the city ran out of money entirely.

The deepening crisis roused old fears and caused some Americans to cast about for scapegoats. Mexican Americans quickly became victims. During the prosperous years of the 1920s, cheap agricultural labor from Mexico flowed legally and unrestricted across the United States border, welcomed by the large farmers and growers. In the 1930s, however, public opinion turned on the newcomers, styling them as dangerous aliens who took jobs from Americans. Government officials, most prominently those in Los Angeles County, targeted all Mexican residents for deportation, without regard to citizenship status. With support from the Department of Labor, as many as half a million Mexicans and Mexican Americans were deported or fled to Mexico. Among them were children born in the United States, American citizens who had never lived outside the country.

The depression deeply affected the American family. Young people postponed marriage, and when they did marry, they produced so few children that demographers warned that, for the first time, the United States was on the verge of losing population. White women, who generally worked in low-paying service areas—cooks, salesclerks, and secretaries—did not lose their jobs as often as men who worked in industry. Even as hostility to women workers increased during the depression, economic necessity drove unmarried women as well as married women, who usually stayed in the home before the depression, into the marketplace. Married women's employment actually rose during the decade from about 12 percent to 15 percent. Overall, some 25 percent more women were employed for wages in 1940 than in 1930.

As more women became breadwinners and men sat at home unemployed, families experienced enormous stress. After a decade of exuberant consumption, smaller incomes led to significant belt tightening. Working women became increasingly decisive and self-reliant at the same time idle men fell prey to guilt and loss of self-esteem. Family violence escalated, as did rates of alcoholism and suicide. The divorce rate, however, went down; the desperately poor could not afford the legal expense. Instead, in dramatically rising numbers, men resorted to desertion.

Increasingly, the down-and-out huddled in makeshift shantytowns that sprang up on the edges of America's cities. The clusters of shacks were known as "Hoovervilles." So many people were using newspapers as blankets that newspapers became known as "Hoover blankets." An empty pocket turned inside out was a "Hoover flag." Jackrabbits were "Hoover hogs." In times of trouble, people have a tendency to personify their problems. In the 1930s, the blame fell squarely on Herbert Hoover.

As the economy sank, so too did Hoover's personal reputation. When men and women weren't cursing him, they were busy making him the butt of a thousand bitter jokes. One asserted that there was no question about Hoover being the world's greatest engineer: "In a little more than two years, he has drained, ditched, and damned the United States." Another told of Hoover's request to Andrew Mellon for a nickel to call up a friend. Mellon replied, "Here's a dime, call up all your friends."

Denial and Escape

In the midst of the mounting crisis, J. P. Morgan Jr., the living symbol of American capitalism, testified before a congressional committee where he defended the importance of preserving an economic elite. "If you destroy the leisure class," he declared, "you destroy civilization." When pressed to define the "leisure class," Morgan responded that it included all those who could afford a maid—about twenty-five or thirty million people, he reckoned, until informed that there were only about two million servants in the entire country. Morgan's ignorance was typical of many from his class who appeared before the committee. Under scrutiny, those who had presided over the economic collapse and now sought to lead the nation back to prosperity showed how little they had troubled to learn about the society that had made them rich. Morgan had learned enough, it turned out, to avoid paying income tax from 1929 to 1932. This revelation did little to win him support among the rising chorus of critics who, only a short time ago, had worshiped wealth and those who had it.

Although Herbert Hoover was no J. P. Morgan, he too was perceived as uncaring. His steadfast refusal to provide federal aid for the victims of the depression encouraged the image of the heartless millionaire in the White House. Hoover's personal habits did not help. Throughout the ordeal, the president sought to provide a personal example by keeping up appearances. Like his favorite comic strip hero, Daddy Warbucks in "Little Orphan Annie," he favored formal dress and manners. For dinner, with or without guests, he appeared in tuxedo, attended by a retinue of valets and waiters. No one was starving, he calmly assured the American people.

Not that his administration considered it the business of the federal government to find out. Walter Gifford, president of the American Telephone and Telegraph Company, appointed by Hoover to coordinate private relief efforts, acknowledged to a Senate subcommittee that he had made no attempt to get figures on how many people were out of work or on relief. Exasperated, Senator Robert La Follette asked if Gifford had any impulse to find out the facts of the situation. Gifford's response reflected the serene way the nation's business leadership distanced itself from the problems of failure and poverty. "Well," said Gifford genially, "I will not say that I did not make any estimate for my own interest and amusement."

While the wealthy practiced denial, other Americans sought refuge from reality at the movies. Throughout the depression, between sixty and seventy-five million people (nearly two-thirds of the nation) managed to scrounge up enough dimes to fill the movie palaces every week. People sought diversion and escape in the plush darkness. They momentarily forgot their troubles as the silver screen filled with wild comedies by the Marx Brothers or lavish musicals. Hollywood excelled at producing musical extravaganzas. Box office successes typically blended nostalgia for the lost Golden Twenties with the hope that renewed prosperity lay just around the corner. The leading musicals in 1933, *Forty-Second Street* and *Gold Diggers*, each offered a variation on the old rags-to-riches story of the chorus girl who makes the most of her big break. In *Gold Diggers*, as the sheriff arrives to foreclose on a bankrupt Broadway show, a wealthy banker suddenly realizes the value of entertainment and his love for a chorus girl. He breaks with his stuffy family to underwrite the show, and everyone dances off toward the dawn of a new day.

But as conditions in the country worsened, filmmakers also turned to grittier material. Films such as King Vidor's *Our Daily Bread* (1932) and John Ford's *The Grapes of Wrath* (1940) were razor-sharp social commentaries. Gangster films taught grim lessons about ill-gotten gains. Indeed, under the new production code of 1930, designed to protect public morals, all movies had to find some way to show that crime did not pay. In *Little Caesar* (1930), the main character is gunned down when he tries to get too much of what belongs to the big boys. *Public Enemy* (1931), a classic story of a hoodlum with a saintly mother, presents a cautionary tale about the doom that awaits those who succumb to easy money and reject virtue.

Despite Hollywood's efforts to keep Americans on the right side of the law, crime increased in the 1930s. Away from the movie palaces, out in the countryside, the plight of people who had lost their farms to bank foreclosures cut so deep that lawlessness gained a romantic popular appeal. In the wake of bank-robbing sprees across the Midwest and Southwest, a legend took shape that the thieves

Was Samuel Insull a Villain or a Victim?

HENRY FORD BECAME the most famous American of his time for his production-line success in putting America on wheels. But most of the rest of the technological marvels that transformed society during the 1920s — the bright lights on Main Street, the movie palaces, radios, phonographs, labor-saving appliances, and gadgets of all kinds — depended on the way Samuel Insull organized the mass production of electricity.

Born the son of a poor dairyman in England, Insull showed an aptitude for business from the time he left school at fourteen and hired on with an auction firm in London. His quickness with numbers attracted the attention of Thomas Edison's representative in England and led to Insull's coming to America in 1881 as the great inventor's private secretary. Impressed by his assistant's shrewd attention to detail—as "tireless as the tides" and "always thinking of the dollar angle"—Edison rewarded Insull in 1893 by making him president of the Chicago Edison Company.

Within fifteen years, Insull had gained control of the electric industry in Chicago. From there his rise to vast wealth and international prominence was swift. He served as president of 11 companies and board chairman or member of 150 more. His Edison Commonwealth empire, which included six thousand power plants in thirty-nine states, manufactured more than 10 percent of the nation's power and sold to twenty million customers. Honors showered down on Insull, and he responded by becoming a patron of culture. In 1929, Insull made his grandest gesture by building Chicago a new opera house that dazzled the eye with its gilt and murals. To a proud city, Insull seemed the perfect model of success, a strong moral contrast to the notorious criminal wealth flaunted by Al Capone and other Chicago gangsters.

Insull had no doubt that he deserved Chicago's adulation. When one of his opera singers gushed that he was like another Napoleon, Insull reminded her that Napoleon was only a soldier. Yet, like Napoleon, Insull overreached himself. Much of his empire had been bought on credit through the use of investors' money. To cover his tracks, Insull used his accounting genius to construct a network of holding companies. As the dominant shareholder— usually with about 25 percent of the total stock— Insull could run the companies' boards of directors and thus decide how to use their entire assets. The higher Insull's pyramid of holding companies rose, the wider the gap between Insull's actual cash assets and the paper value of his empire. By the end of the 1920s, Insull's inner circle, including his brother and his son, held assets with a market value of about $2.5 billion, for which they had invested only $100 million, most of it other people's money.

The stock market crash in October 1929 brought down Insull's paper empire. Besieged by debt and unable to borrow more money, Insull resorted to the tactic of declaring bankruptcy for his holding companies. As more and more investors learned that they had lost everything in the bankruptcy maneuvers and the nation lurched into the depression, the conviction grew that Insull personified those whose fake prosperity had brought on the Great Crash. They laughed bitterly at cowboy comedian Will Rogers's definition of a holding company as "a thing where you hand an accomplice the goods while the policeman searches you." The Union League Club, a Chicago watering hole for conservative investors, expressed its contempt for Insull by papering its dining room with Insull's worthless stock certificates. But the bottom was not reached until October 1932, when a grand jury indicted Insull and his brother on charges of embezzlement, larceny, and use of the mails to defraud. *Who's Who* rendered its own verdict by dropping the former first citizen of Chicago from its roster.

Insull read about the indictment in Paris, where he had fled after signing over all his bankrupt assets. Yet even with a trail of ruined lives behind him and ample time to reflect on his career, Insull still could not understand why he had lost favor. "Why am I not more popular in the United States?" he asked. "What have I done that every banker and business magnate has not done in the course of busi-

SAMUEL INSULL

This May 1934 Time *magazine cover shows Samuel Insull hiding his face as he enters the courtroom to face criminal charges. The quotation underneath reminds readers that Insull had a key role both in building up and in tearing down the country. Journalists and moralists were eager to use Insull, America's most famous fugitive from justice, as the main symbol in a morality tale of how ruthlessly greedy tycoons had brought on the Great Depression.*

ness?" When extradition orders for income tax evasion arrived, Insull fled to Italy and then eastward through Athens until he was finally cornered in a dank jail cell in Istanbul, where he was being held as a vagrant.

The captive's return to depression-wracked America in the spring of 1934 had the usual melodramatic touches of courtroom drama and disgrace. Insull appeared on the cover of *Time* magazine in the typical fugitive pose, hat pulled down over his face as he was hustled up the courthouse steps, while all around the country pundits declaimed that he had betrayed the public trust.

In the end, however, the incredible complexity of the financial empire that led to Insull's ruin also saved him. With checks, bonds, and stock certificates moving swiftly from one Insull subsidiary to another, who could tell what belonged to whom at any particular moment? No sleuth could match Insull's ingenuity in devising what one headline called the "Insull Daze-Maze." Even the U.S. Senate Banking and Currency Committee, which was investigating the stock market collapse, was stymied. One expert witness, Owen D. Young, a distinguished banker, confessed to "a feeling of complete helplessness when I began to examine the complicated structure of the Insull group. . . . It was impossible to get an accounting system that would not have misled even the officers themselves."

While the state attorney thrashed about for incriminating evidence, Insull pleaded his case directly to the jurors. Abandoning his pose as a Napoleonic commander of industry, Insull presented himself as just another seeker of the American dream, who like other Americans, from office boys to tycoons, had been caught in a terrible historical accident. For hours, he told the jury of his struggle to overcome meager origins and his bewilderment now, as just a poor old man, over how disaster had befallen the era of prosperity. In his summation to the jury, Insull's lawyer drove the point home. "You have had a description here of an age in American history which we hope will never be repeated. I say that we are trying that age." The jury agreed and found the age guilty, but Insull innocent.

Free but unwilling to remain in America as a nobody, Insull returned to anonymity in Paris, where he died in 1938. According to the police report, Insull collapsed and died of a heart attack in the Paris subway with only about 85 cents of loose change on him. But that was not quite right. Insull had ample resources stashed away and always carried a considerable amount of cash. Someone else from humble origins and similarly committed to the advancement of self-interest must have found the body first. Then Samuel Insull, the artful dodger of American finance, had his own pocket picked, and the police never noticed.

stole to get back what the banks had taken from the poor. Woody Guthrie, the populist folk singer from Oklahoma, captured the public's inclination to see criminals as modern Robin Hoods in his widely admired tribute to a murderous bank robber with a choirboy face, "The Ballad of Pretty Boy Floyd":

Yes, as through this world I ramble,
I see lots of funny men,
Some will rob you with a six-gun,
Some will rob you with a pen.
But as through your life you'll travel,
Wherever you may roam,
You won't never see an outlaw drive
A family from their home.

The Rise of Working-Class Militancy

Although the nation's working people bore the brunt of the economic collapse, the labor movement, including the dominant American Federation of Labor (AFL), was slow to respond. Organized labor had been hobbled during the 1920s by the willingness of the courts to issue injunctions curtailing the right of unions to organize and strike. Early in the depression, William Green, head of the AFL, sounded like Hoover's twin when he argued that a dole would turn the worker into "a ward of the state." But by 1931, the normally benign Green had turned ferocious. "I warn the people who are exploiting the workers," he shouted at the AFL's annual convention, "that they can drive them only so far before they will turn on them and destroy them. They are taking no account of the history of nations in which governments have been overturned. Revolutions grow out of the depths of hunger." Green's lieutenant, Edward F. McGrady, told a Senate subcommittee that, if the government did not act to create work for the unemployed, "as far as I am personally concerned, I would do nothing to close the doors of revolt if it starts."

Like the labor leaders, the American people were slow to anger. At first, they were too numb to raise protests about the depression. More likely, they turned the blame inward, wondering what they had done to lose their jobs, feeling ashamed when they could not find new ones. As the shock wore off and they realized that millions were in the same circumstances, people began to get angry. On the morning of March 7, 1932, several thousand unemployed autoworkers massed at the gates of the

Ford Company's River Rouge factory in Dearborn, Michigan, to demand work. Henry Ford sent out his private security forces, who told the demonstrators to disperse. The workers refused and began hurling rocks. The Ford army responded with tear gas and freezing water but quickly escalated to gunfire. When they stopped, four demonstrators were dead and dozens more wounded. An outraged public— forty thousand strong—turned out for the unemployed men's funerals. People from coast to coast denounced Ford's callous and brutal resort to violence.

Farmers, who desperately needed relief, mounted the broadest protest. Their spokesmen in Washington asked the government to guarantee farm prices that would at least equal the cost of production, but Congress would not budge. On May 7, 1932, some three thousand farmers, led by the flamboyant Milo Reno, created the National Farmers' Holiday Association. Invoking the Boston Tea Party, they promised vigilante action to keep farm produce from reaching the markets until prices improved. Although the rebellion was short-lived, Reno and his followers barricaded roads around Sioux City, Iowa, turned back farmers heading for market, and dumped thousands of gallons of milk in the ditches.

Farm militants had more success with their "penny sales." With so many farms falling under the auctioneer's hammer, farm dissidents packed auctions with members pledged to pay only a few cents to buy the foreclosed property and return it to the bankrupt owners. Under this kind of pressure, some states suspended debts or reduced mortgages. Where evictions continued, farmers stepped up their protests. In early 1933, some Iowa farmers hauled Judge Charles Bradley out of his courtroom in midtrial. Taking him to a remote place, they beat him, smeared him with grease, and finally released him when he lost consciousness with a noose around his neck. That same year in California, where landowners cut their already substandard wages, more than fifty thousand farmworkers, most of them Mexicans, went on strike. In 1933, John Simpson, president of the National Farmers Union, observed that "the biggest and finest crop of revolutions you ever saw is sprouting all over the country right now."

In addition to provoking industrial workers and farmers into militant protest, hard times also revived the left in America. When the crash struck, Eugene Debs was dead and so, for all purposes, was the Socialist Party. But the Great Depression—the massive failure of Western capitalism—provided a hothouse environment that brought socialism back to life and the American Communist Party to its greatest size and influence in American history. Eventually, some 100,000 disillusioned Americans —workers, intellectuals, college students—joined the Communist Party and sought radical change in the United States. Party leader William Z. Foster sketched the future in his book *Toward a Soviet America* (1932).

Although the American Communist Party declared that it was homegrown, purely American, and beholden to no one, it clearly followed the party line laid down by the Soviet Union. By the late 1930s, Moscow's demands for conformity had driven most Americans out of the party, but in the early years of the depression, members engaged in protest on a broad front. In 1931, the party entered the labor wars. In Harlan County, Kentucky, Communists fearlessly faced the mine owners' thugs and increased membership in the National Miners Union from one hundred to twenty-five thousand. Newspapers and newsreels graphically portrayed the violence unleashed against the strikers. Eventually, the miners lost, but the Communist Party emerged from the coal fields stronger than before.

Jobless, homeless victims wandered in search of work, and the tramp, or hobo, became one of the most visible figures of the decade.

Almost alone among American organizations, the Communist Party attacked racism and spoke out on behalf of African Americans. When nine young black men in Scottsboro, Alabama, were arrested on trumped-up rape charges, the party rushed to their defense. The Communists managed to save the defendants from the electric chair and thereby gained wide publicity as crusaders against racism. The party also gained publicity by organizing black sharecroppers in Alabama who faced expulsion by white landlords. Efforts on behalf of African Americans attracted new recruits to the party. From only about fifty black members in 1930, the Party counted ten thousand by the end of the decade.

It was not only Communists who believed that capitalism meant poverty and unemployment. Protest by workers and farmers who never had a radical thought in their lives dwarfed the effort of

the left. Breadlines, soup kitchens, foreclosures, unemployment, and cold despair drove patriotic men and women to question American capitalism. "I am as conservative as any man could be," a Wisconsin farmer explained, "but any economic system that has in its power to set me and my wife in the streets, at my age—what can I see but red?"

Conclusion: The Era of Boom and Bust

The decade of the 1920s has persistently defied generalization. To many observers, it looked like the New Business Epoch and the New Era. Living standards rose, economic opportunity increased, and the flow of consumer goods appeared endless. Others focused on the thrill of cultural liberation and called the decade the Great Spree, the Roaring Twenties, and the Jazz Age. But the dominant images of the decade had little meaning for many Americans. They experienced neither the glitter nor the jazz and lacked the power to offer labels of their own. Instead of plunging into speculation on Wall Street or shimmying at the Cotton Club, the nation's farmers and industrial laborers struggled to make ends meet.

Almost overnight, the 1920s ended. In just a little over ten years following the triumph of World War I, the United States veered dizzily from its steepest rise in power and wealth to a free fall into its deepest depression. Smug urbanites were humbled, but men and women already living on the margins suffered more. The 1930s found new symbols: glut without buyers; empty apartments and homes alongside rude cardboard shantytowns; mountains of oranges rotting in the California sun while guards with shotguns chased away the hungry. As government stubbornly refused to alleviate the suffering and some of the rich seemed immune, sullen apathy increasingly turned to angry revolt.

On a night in June 1931, on the outskirts of Gary, Indiana, a man driving a large car slammed on the brakes when a brick crashed through the windshield. "What's the big idea?" he shouted out. Out of the darkness came the reply: "All rich guys ought to be strung up." "Who are you?" the driver asked. "We're the fellows that'll do the stringing." Later that night a hotel clerk tried to explain: "Their patience is at an end. . . . Another four years of Hoover and . . . ."

CHRONOLOGY

1920   Eighteenth Amendment, prohibiting the sale of liquor, goes into effect.

Nineteenth Amendment, granting women the vote, ratified.

Station KDKA in Pittsburgh begins first regular commercial radio broadcasts.

Marcus Garvey hosts Universal Negro Improvement Association conference in Harlem.

Republican Warren G. Harding elected president.

1921   Sheppard-Towner Act, providing infant health care, passes in Congress.

1922   Fordney-McCumber Act sets protective tariffs at record heights.

Principles of new business-minded era expressed in publication of Henry Ford's *My Life and Work* and Herbert Hoover's *American Individualism*.

About thirty artists and intellectuals renounce American society in *Civilization in the United States*.

1922, 1924   New laws imposing quotas according to nationality end historical tradition of open immigration.

1923   Equal Rights Amendment introduced in Congress.

August. Harding dies in office and is succeeded by Calvin Coolidge.

1924   Calvin Coolidge elected president.

1925   John Scopes convicted for violating Tennessee statute forbidding teaching of evolution.

Alain Locke expresses cultural aspirations of Harlem Renaissance in *The New Negro*.

1926   Ernest Hemingway's novel of expatriate Paris, *The Sun Also Rises*, published.

1927   Charles Lindbergh becomes America's most famous hero by flying alone across Atlantic.

Italian anarchist immigrants Sacco and Vanzetti executed.

1928   Herbert Hoover defeats Alfred E. Smith.

1929   Robert and Helen Lynd publish their study of an average American small city, *Middletown*.

October 24. Stock market collapses on Black Thursday.

1931   Nine black men arrested in Scottsboro case.

1932   Several thousand demonstrators at Ford plant protest unemployment; security forces fire on crowd, killing four.

Farmers' Holiday movement blocks roads and pours milk on ground to protest falling prices.

BIBLIOGRAPHY

GENERAL WORKS

Frederick Lewis Allen, *Only Yesterday: An Informal History of the Nineteen-Twenties* (1930).

Dorothy Brown, *Setting a Course: American Women in the 1920s* (1987).

Norman Cantor, *Twentieth Century Culture: Modernism to Deconstruction* (1988).

Paul A. Carter, *Another Part of the Twenties* (1977).

Stanley Coben, *Rebellion against Victorianism: The Impetus for Cultural Change in 1920s America* (1991).

Lynn Dumeril, *The Modern Temper: American Culture and Society in the 1920s* (1995).

Ellis W. Hawley, *The Great War and the Search for a Modern Order: A History of the American People and Their Institutions, 1917–1933* (1979).

William E. Leuchtenburg, *The Perils of Prosperity, 1914–1932* (1958).

Robert S. Lynd and Helen M. Lynd, *Middletown: A Study in Modern American Culture* (1929).

Michael Parrish, *Anxious Decades: America in Prosperity and Depression, 1920–1941* (1992).

Geoffrey Perrett, *America in the Twenties: A History* (1982).

MAINSTREAM POLITICS

David Burner, *Herbert Hoover: A Public Life* (1979).

Warren I. Cohen, *Empire without Tears: America's Foreign Relations, 1921–1933* (1987).

Frank Costigliola, *Awkward Dominion: American Political, Economic, and Cultural Relations with Europe, 1919–1933* (1984).

Paula Elder, *Governor Alfred E. Smith: The Politician as Reformer* (1983).

Lewis Ethan Ellis, *Republican Foreign Policy, 1921–1933* (1968).

Christine A. Lunardini, *From Equal Suffrage to Equal Rights: Alice Paul and the National Woman's Party, 1912–1928* (1986).

Donald R. McCoy, *Calvin Coolidge* (1967).

Michael E. McGerr, *The Decline of Popular Politics: The American North, 1865–1928* (1986).

Robert K. Murray, *The Harding Era: Warren G. Harding and His Administration* (1969).

Francis Fox Piven and Richard A. Cloward, *Why Americans Don't Vote* (1988).

William Appleman Williams, *The Tragedy of American Diplomacy* (1959).

Joan Hoff Wilson, *Herbert Hoover: Forgotten Progressive* (1975).

THE NEW ERA OF SCIENCE AND CONSUMPTION

Susan Porter Benson, *Counter Cultures* (1986).

James J. Flink, *The Automobile Age* (1988).

Louis Galambos and Joseph Pratt, *The Rise of Corporate Commonwealth: U.S. Business and Public Policy in the Twentieth Century* (1988).

Kenneth T. Jackson, *Crabgrass Frontier: The Suburbanization of the United States* (1985).

Robert E. Kohler, *Partners in Science: Foundations and Natural Scientists, 1900–1945* (1991).

T. J. Jackson Lears, *Fables of Abundance: A Cultural History of Advertising in America* (1994).

Roland Marchand, *Advertising the American Dream: Making Way for Modernity, 1920–1940* (1985).

David F. Noble, *America by Design: Science, Technology, and the Rise of Corporate Capitalism* (1977).

Ronald C. Tobey, *The American Ideology of National Science, 1919–1930* (1971).

Reynold M. Wik, *Henry Ford and Grass-Roots America* (1972).

LABOR

American Social History Project, *Who Built America? Working People and the Nation's Economy, Politics, Culture, and Society*, vol. 2, *From the Gilded Age to the Present* (1992).

Irving Bernstein, *The Lean Years: A History of the American Worker, 1920–1933* (1960).

Colin Gordon, *New Deals: Business, Labor, and Politics in America, 1920–1935* (1994).

Sanford M. Jacoby, *Employing Bureaucracy: Managers, Unions, and the Transformation of Work in American Industry, 1900–1945* (1985).

John A. Salmond, *Gastonia 1929: The Story of the Loray Mill Strike* (1995).

Winifred Wandersee, *Women's Work and Family Values, 1920–1940* (1981).

Robert H. Zeiger, *Republicans and Labor, 1919–1929* (1969).

RURAL AND SMALL-TOWN LIFE

Michael L. Berger, *The Devil Wagon in God's Country: The Automobile and Social Change in Rural America, 1893–1929* (1979).

James N. Gregory, *American Exodus: The Dust Bowl Migration and Okie Culture in California* (1989).

Jack Temple Kirby, *Rural Worlds Lost: The American South, 1920–1960* (1987).

Donald Worster, *Dust Bowl: The Southern Plains in the 1930s* (1979).

POPULAR CULTURE

Ann Douglas, *Mongrel Manhattan in the 1920s* (1994).

Ronald Edsforth, *Popular Culture and Political Change in Modern America* (1991).

Lewis Erenberg, *Steppin' Out: New York City Nightlife and the Transformation of American Culture, 1890–1930* (1981).

Paula S. Fass, *The Damned and the Beautiful: American Youth in the 1920s* (1977).

Larry May, *Screening out the Past: The Birth of Mass Culture and the Motion Picture Industry* (1980).

Kathy H. Ogren, *The Jazz Revolution: Twenties America and the Meaning of Jazz* (1989).

Kathy Peiss, *Cheap Amusements* (1986).

Arnold Shaw, *The Jazz Age: Popular Music in the 1920s* (1987).

Robert Sklar, *Movie-Made America* (1975).

Robert Smith, *Babe Ruth's America* (1974).

Susan Smulyan, *Selling Radio: The Commercialization of American Broadcasting, 1920–1934* (1994).

Ted Vincent, *Mudville's Revenge: The Rise and Fall of American Sport* (1981).

EDUCATION AND ART

Charles C. Alexander, *Here the Country Lies: Nationalism and the Arts in Twentieth-Century America* (1980).

Malcolm Cowley, *Exile's Return* (1934).

Malcolm Cowley, *The Dream of the Golden Mountains: Remembering the 1930s* (1980).

Helen Lefkowitz Horowitz, *Campus Life: Undergraduate Cultures from the End of the Eighteenth Century to the Present* (1987).

Lary May, *Outside In: Minorities and the Transformation of American Education* (1989).

Maren Stange, *Symbols of Ideal Life: Social Documentary Photography in America, 1890–1950* (1989).

William Stott, *Documentary Expression and Thirties America* (1973).

Elizabeth Hutton Turner, *American Artists in Paris, 1919–1929* (1988).

RESISTANCE TO CHANGE

David H. Bennett, *The Party of Fear: From Nativist Movements to the New Right in American History* (1988).

Kathleen M. Blee, *Women of the Klan: Racism and Gender in the 1920s* (1991).

Lyle W. Dorsett, *Billy Sunday and the Redemption of Urban America* (1991).

Ray Ginger, *Six Days or Forever? Tennessee v. John Thomas Scopes* (1958).

Nancy MacLean, *Behind the Mask of Chivalry: The Making of the Second Ku Klux Klan* (1994).

George M. Marsden, *Fundamentalism and American Culture* (1980).

Daniel Joseph Singal, *The War Within: From Victorian to Modernist Thought in the South, 1919–1945* (1982).

REFORM AND DISSENT

Daniel Aaron, *Writers on the Left* (1960).

Milton Cantor, *The Divided Left: American Radicalism, 1900–1975* (1978).

Clarke Chambers, *Seedtime of Reform, 1918–1933* (1956).

Nancy F. Cott, *The Grounding of Modern Feminism* (1977).

John P. Diggins, *The Rise and Fall of the American Left* (1992).

Donald J. Lisio, *The President and Protest: Hoover, MacArthur, and the Bonus Riot* (1994).

Nick Salvatore, *Eugene V. Debs: Citizen and Socialist* (1982).

David Thelen, *Robert M. La Follette and the Insurgent Spirit* (1976).

William Young and David E. Kaiser, *Postmortem: New Evidence in the Case of Sacco and Vanzetti* (1985).

RACE AND MINORITIES

Rodolfo Acuna, *Occupied America: A History of Chicanos* (1980).

Francisco E. Balderrama and Raymond Rodriguez, *Decade of Betrayal: Mexican Repatriation in the 1930s* (1995).

William B. Barlow, *"Looking Up at Down": The Emergence of Blues Culture* (1989).

Dan T. Carter, *Scottsboro: A Tragedy of the Modern South* (1969).

John Higham, *Strangers in the Land: Patterns of American Nativism, 1860–1925* (1955).

James de Jongh, *Vicious Modernism: Black Harlem and the Literary Imagination* (1990).

David Levering Lewis, *When Harlem Was in Vogue* (1989).

Manning Marable, *W. E. B. Du Bois: Black Radical Democrat* (1986).

Donald L. Parman, *Indians and the American West in the Twentieth Century* (1994).

Judith Stein, *The World of Marcus Garvey* (1986).

Ronald Takaki, *A Different Mirror: A History of Multicultural America* (1993).

Cheryl A. Wall, *Women of the Harlem Renaissance* (1995).

Raymond Wolters, *Negroes and the Great Depression* (1970).

THE CRASH AND RESPONSE

William J. Barber, *From New Era to New Deal: Herbert Hoover, the Economists, and American Economic Policy, 1921–1933* (1985).

Andrew Bergman, *We're in the Money: Depression America and Its Films* (1971).

Peter Fearon, *War, Prosperity, and Depression* (1987).

John Kenneth Galbraith, *The Great Crash: 1929* (1961).

Charles Hearn, *The American Dream in the Great Depression* (1973).

Charles Kindleberger, *The World in Depression* (1973).

Robert McElvaine, *The Great Depression: America 1929–1941* (1984).

David P. Peeler, *Hope among Us Yet: Social Criticism and Social Solace in the Depression Years* (1987).

Studs Terkel, *Hard Times: An Oral History of the Great Depression* (1979; reprint, 1986).

Tom Terrill and Jerrold Hirsch, *Such As Us* (1978).

T. H. Watkins, *The Great Depression: America in the 1930s* (1993).

SOUVENIR SEWING NEEDLE BOOK

Borrowing the current popular tune "Happy Days Are Here Again" as the theme song for Roosevelt's 1932 campaign was an inspired act of wishful thinking in those dark days. By 1936, conditions had improved enough that this souvenir needle book could celebrate "Happiness Restored" a bit more realistically. The major places where economic recovery was to be created — farm, factory, and office — are shown operating in full swing on the cover of this little container that held sewing needles. But in accord with the New Deal emphasis on security at home, the figure of domestic happiness looms largest in the center under the arch of prosperity.

Collection of Janice L. and David J. Frent.

THE NEW DEAL ERA
1932–1939

24

I N JULY 1932, A RAGGED, DUSTY CONTINGENT of some fifteen thousand World War I veterans marched into Washington, D.C. Calling themselves the Bonus Expeditionary Army, the men came to lobby Congress. Eight years earlier, Congress had voted to award veterans a bonus for their military service; the bonus was supposed to be paid in 1945. The Bonus Army had come to convince Congress that they needed the bonus now. Many of these unusual lobbyists came to Washington in boxcars, shipped free by sympathetic railway workers, sometimes under the label "Livestock." Unable to afford hotels, they camped in unfinished federal buildings just three blocks from the Capitol, and as their numbers swelled they spilled onto the mud flats along the Anacostia River.

The Bonus Army angered President Hoover. The Republican Party had recently nominated him for a second term as president, and he was eager to demonstrate his capacity for leadership and decisive action. The veterans were trespassing on official government property, Hoover said. They were an embarrassing eyesore that undercut his efforts to restore public confidence that prosperity was just around the corner. While the bonus marchers were setting up camp, Hoover prompted Congress to vote down immediate payment of the bonus because its $2.4 billion cost was too expensive.

Hoover also encouraged the press to spread a cloud of misinformation about the veterans. Hoover and other critics claimed that the bonus marchers were not veterans at all, although a careful Veterans Administration study showed that 94 percent had served in the armed forces. The *New York Times* called the marchers ingrates who should be satisfied with their regular service pensions. In fact, only career soldiers qualified for military pensions, not enlisted men like the bonus marchers. The most telling falsehood was that the marchers were led by Communists ("insurrectionists," Hoover said) who posed a revolutionary threat to the government. Everyone who came to know the Bonus Army discovered that almost all of its members believed in traditional values, although the depression had stripped them of jobs, homes, and hope. They came to Washington to regain their respectability, not to overthrow the government.

Isolated in the White House behind heavy drapes and tight security, Hoover became increasingly defensive and out of touch. A visiting reporter found him greatly changed. "He didn't look like the Hoover I had been seeing," the reporter recalled. "His hair was rumpled. He was almost crouching behind his desk." Hoover's military advisers, especially Army Chief of Staff Douglas MacArthur, argued that a show of force would quickly get rid of the Bonus Army and impress the nation with the government's authority. Feeling besieged, Hoover ordered the military to disperse the defenseless veterans and their families.

Late in the afternoon of July 28, commuters leaving their offices on Capitol Hill were surprised to see a thousand soldiers clogging Pennsylvania Avenue—cavalry with sabers drawn, infantry with bayonets ready, backed up by tanks. Hoover watched from the window of the Oval Office as the soldiers, under General MacArthur's command, headed for the Bonus Army's camp. They lobbed tear gas into the buildings occupied by the bonus marchers, forcing them to flee. In the gathering twilight, the troops paused as MacArthur surveyed the scene. Hoover had ordered MacArthur not to send his troops into the main camp on the Anacostia flats. MacArthur defied Hoover's order and commanded his troops to charge. The soldiers routed the Bonus Army, set the camp on fire, and sent the men and their families fleeing. Several marchers suffered bayonet wounds and one infant died of gas poisoning.

MacArthur was immensely pleased with the success of the attack. "Had [President Hoover] let it go on another week, I believe that the institutions of our government would have been severely threatened," he said. Privately, Hoover was bitter about MacArthur's insubordination, but he issued a public statement endorsing the dispersal of the bonus marchers, calling them "not veterans" but "Communists and persons with criminal records."

The beleaguered veterans fled into oblivion. As they traveled west, the police in each state hustled them to the next border. The remnants of the Bonus Army who made it across the Mississippi River were herded onto a special train that rumbled off to an unknown destination on the plains. There they scattered among the thousands of dispossessed Americans roaming the countryside in search of work and hope.

On the day after the Bonus Army was driven from Washington, Franklin D. Roosevelt, Hoover's Democratic rival in the 1932 presidential campaign, sat in bed surrounded by newspapers. Disabled by polio, he usually started his day immersed in the news of the world. As he read about the attack on the bonus marchers, he was overcome by "a feeling of horror," his wife, Eleanor, later recalled. Roosevelt summoned his campaign aide Rexford Tugwell to speak with him about the attack. Roosevelt wondered why Hoover hadn't just offered coffee and doughnuts to the protesters, rather than unleashing the army on them. The Bonus Army seemed to be desperate family men, he said, not dangerous subversives threatening the nation's capital. Were it up to him, Roosevelt declared, he would

have used the men for reforestation projects or found land where they could farm and regain their independence.

Roosevelt's instinctive response to news of MacArthur's attack on the Bonus Army echoed the slogan Roosevelt had announced when he accepted the Democratic nomination: "I pledge you, I pledge myself, to a new deal for the American people." Roosevelt's "new deal" did not include support for payments of the veterans' bonus; like Hoover, he thought the bonus was too expensive. But, unlike Hoover, Roosevelt declared repeatedly that if people desperately needed help, the government should try to help them.

Almost a year later—after Roosevelt had been elected president—a second group of about 3,000 veterans gathered in Washington to lobby again for payment of the bonus. Roosevelt arranged for the men to be fed and housed in military barracks at government expense while they petitioned Congress. Shortly after the men assembled, Eleanor Roosevelt strode into their camp to express her personal concern and to lead the men in singing favorite wartime songs. The occasion was so stirring that these bonus marchers elected Franklin Roosevelt an honorary member. He received a delegation at the White House and genially recalled how they had *all served together* in the war and reassured them that the government was prepared to rescue victims of the depression, although he could not support the bonus. In the end, 2,600 of the 3,000 marchers seized the chance to enroll in the government's Civilian Conservation Corps, designed to put people to work conserving the nation's natural resources, rather than accepting government transportation home.

The Second Bonus Army came to Washington as angry protesters and left with government-sponsored jobs, while Roosevelt's opposition to the bonus bill stayed in place. Roosevelt's deft response to the veterans stood in stark contrast to Hoover's refusal to meet with the first bonus marchers for fear that it would lend legitimacy to an invading mob. As the Second Bonus Army prepared to break camp, a reporter overheard remarks that brought into focus part of the meaning of Roosevelt's reform program that he called the New Deal. One rain-soaked veteran asked, "What is this bird Roosevelt up to?" Another shrugged and replied, "All I know is he's a hooman bein'."

The veteran caught the point that the New Deal would approach the downtrodden and the desperate with the simple proposition that they were peo-

WASHINGTON BONUS MARCH
This watercolor is one of a series executed by twenty-four-year-old Lewis Rubenstein in 1932
after traveling as an observer with the bonus marchers. Here he depicts the march in its early
stages as a hopeful, somewhat theatrical adventure. The figure on the runningboard of the car,
megaphone in hand, seems almost like a cheerleader encouraging the team as it advances on its
goal — in this case the steps of the United States Capitol.
Janet Marqusee Fine Arts Ltd.

ple in need of a helping hand to get back on their feet. The New Deal would prove to be remarkably free of concern about ideology. With a zest for experimentation, the Roosevelt administration set about to find work for the unemployed, to end chronic hard times in the countryside, and to stabilize business and financial practices so that the economy would be protected against future crashes. In the process, it created a coalition of supporters that gave the Democrats national power for twenty years.

How the American people were to be made productive and secure was the question. It was related most urgently to the millions of farmers and workers whose livelihood had been destroyed by the depression. But the issue involved Americans at all levels, since the depression left no one unscathed. At the center of these inclusive, progressive aims was the new president, Franklin Roosevelt, whose characteristics as a "hooman bein'" guided both the substance and the symbolism of the vast New Deal experiment. Roosevelt left the presidency and the nation fundamentally changed. The power of the president grew, the federal government assumed responsibility for the well-being of the nation, and citizens established a new relationship with Washington.

Franklin D. Roosevelt: A Patrician in Government

The man elected president in 1932 was very different from the people who elected him. To the manner born, he was every inch an aristocrat. Yet he managed to establish an extraordinary relationship with the American people, especially the poor and dispossessed. The explanation of his success lay partly in the circumstances in which he held office. In his twelve-year reign, he experienced two of the nation's greatest crises—the Great Depression and World War II. But simply presiding over economic catastrophe and war was no guarantee of popularity or greatness. The personality, the outreach, the actions, the times—all combined to make Franklin Roosevelt the dominant figure of his age. No other American politician in the twentieth century has had an impact as great as that of FDR.

The Growth of a Politician

Franklin Delano Roosevelt grew up in comfort and security on a beautiful Hudson River estate in New York. Born in 1882, the only child of a family with substantial inherited wealth, Roosevelt grew up in a safe and secure environment that steeped him in the values of Christian service. He absorbed early a belief, which never left him, that the privileged had a duty to look after the poor and weak. His education at Groton Academy and Harvard University prepared him to take his place within the leadership of his elite social class.

After a brief career as a reform member of the New York state legislature from 1910 to 1912, Roosevelt campaigned ardently for Woodrow Wilson, who appointed him assistant secretary of the navy in 1913. Roosevelt's bold and innovative efforts to modernize the navy during World War I and his attractive, crowd-pleasing ways moved the Democratic Party to nominate him for the vice presidency in the doomed campaign against Warren Harding in 1920. Roosevelt emerged from that campaign with a glowing reputation; a golden career in politics seemed to be ahead. He carried the name of a former president, was married to an earnest, public-spirited woman from his social class, and had strong state and national political connections.

Fate, however, had a grim detour in store for Roosevelt. In the summer of 1921, after a vigorous day of swimming in the icy water of the Bay of Fundy near his summer home on Campobello Island just over the Maine border in Canada and then fighting a ferocious brush fire, Roosevelt suffered a chill and collapsed. Within a few hours, he was paralyzed from the waist down, a victim of the polio virus. Though he battled the affliction with cheerful fortitude, Roosevelt would never again walk unassisted. With the help of his devoted wife, Eleanor, and his tireless aide Louis Howe, Roosevelt regained his intense desire for an active political career.

Roosevelt became a student of public life and gathered an encyclopedic knowledge of local conditions and political activities. Going places and getting to know people in their own setting had always been Roosevelt's personal and political style. After the polio attack, he reversed the tactic by finding ways to draw people to him. Maps, letters, phone calls, receptions, dinner parties, cruises, and the Warm Springs, Georgia, polio sanitarium that he founded all served that purpose. Roosevelt's uncomplaining adjustment to his disability convinced an uncle that he was "twice-born," that his ordeal had forced him to move beyond his shallow and spoiled youth to become a strong and compassionate person. Those closest to Roosevelt—Eleanor Roosevelt and Louis Howe among them—insisted that the illness did not transform him but merely shifted his focus. Tempered by constant suffering and no longer able to distract himself in physical activity, he concentrated on the art and practice of politics, including the persuasive uses of verbal and visual symbols.

Governor Roosevelt

Roosevelt's chance to return to political office came sooner than he expected. When New York Governor Al Smith prepared for his run at the presidency in 1928, he convinced Roosevelt to run for his vacated position and to help Smith capture the state's electoral votes. The tactic did not save Smith, who was defeated by Herbert Hoover, but Roosevelt managed a narrow upset victory. As the newly elected governor, he rejoiced at the opportunity to build New York's prosperity through a balanced program of conservation and scientific farming in the countryside combined with improved social services and working conditions in the cities.

The 1929 stock market crash forced him to confront a grim, unexpected reality. Unlike President Hoover, Governor Roosevelt was only momentarily at a loss. Because he believed that government's prime role was to respond to social need rather than to defend general principle, he was eager to act. He operated in the American tradition of the great patrician innovators, especially Thomas Jefferson, whose trust in the basic framework of American society was such that they felt free to try almost any approach that promised to answer particular needs. Unlike Hoover's fealty to a dogma of self-reliance, Roosevelt resisted ideology that would curb his ability to try out any new ideas that appealed to him. As the depression worsened, he urged experimentation to find more democratic and humane ways of dealing with the crisis.

Roosevelt accepted the progressive view that the genius of American government was the opportunity to use states as laboratories for national policy.

Roosevelt accepted the progressive view that the genius of American government was the opportunity to use states as laboratories for national policy. In that experimental spirit, he concluded that the severe economic crisis might require government to set aside conventional theories and customs in favor of whatever expedients would work to alleviate hardship and protect democracy. When a noted economist visited the State House in Albany to explain that a high level of human distress was inevitable while the laws of supply and demand permitted the free market system to recover its balance, Roosevelt cut him off and scolded, "People aren't cattle, you know."

Rather than rugged individualism or control by experts and economic law, Roosevelt preferred Abraham Lincoln's view that the government's duty was to step in when citizens were no longer able to help themselves. In an address to the New York legislature in August, 1931, Roosevelt declared:

> The duty of the State toward the citizen is the duty of the servant to its master. . . . One of these duties of the State is that of caring for those of its citizens who find themselves the victims of such adverse circumstances as make them unable to obtain even the necessities for mere existence without the aid of others. . . . To these unfortunate citizens aid must be extended by governments, not as a matter of charity but as a matter of social duty. . . . [No one should go] unfed, unclothed, or unsheltered.

On that basis of compelling necessity, Roosevelt set aside his budget-balancing orthodoxy and supported the largest state relief program in the nation's history. Yet he resisted even the appearance of radical change by naming the initiative the Temporary Emergency Relief Act (TERA). By labeling his innovations "temporary" and "emergency," Roosevelt sought to root new initiatives firmly within the established traditions of democracy and capitalism. He wanted to shore up the existing social and economic order, not subvert it. At the head of TERA, Roosevelt placed a social worker named Harry Hopkins, who was admired as an advocate of child welfare. Hopkins had grown up poor in Iowa, the son of a harness-maker. Nurtured in social gospel fervor at Iowa's Grinnell College, he set out for New York City, where he became a resident of the Christadora settlement house in the impoverished Lower East Side. Sallow and thin, with a hollow face, usually sucking on a cigarette, Hopkins resembled some of the neediest of those he sought to help. His empathy with the poor and their feelings of despair combined with his zestful energy to invigorate his leadership of New York's relief program.

The other mainstay of Roosevelt's relief effort was Frances Perkins, whom he named state labor commissioner. A veteran of hard-fought battles to reform industrial working conditions, Perkins was a tough-minded yet courtly woman with a com-

mitment to social service that had been ingrained during her student days at Mount Holyoke College. While serving in Al Smith's state administration, she had become acquainted with Eleanor Roosevelt and had helped in her personal struggle to escape the confines of her upper-class origins and to overcome her psychological wounds at having been considered an awkward and homely child. Perkins's plainspoken and witty remarks also helped Eleanor Roosevelt direct her husband's attention to the plight of industrial workers.

To coordinate New York's relief efforts, Roosevelt established in 1930 the Commission on Stabilization of Industry. The commission coordinated relief efforts in local communities and worked with industry to reduce unemployment. In a nation accustomed to letting the market take its course, it was the first state agency ever created to deal with problems of people who were out of work. Roosevelt sponsored another first in government cooperation by convening a conference of state governors at Salt Lake City in June 1930 to discuss the problems of the depression. There Roosevelt argued that the nation should follow the example of World War I by mobilizing national resources and enacting short-term emergency measures to win the war against economic collapse and hopelessness.

Roosevelt's highly visible efforts to do something constructive gained him the gratitude of constituents and the attention of national politicians. In 1930, New Yorkers reelected him governor by a margin of 750,000 votes and assured his position as the Democratic Party's leading candidate in the 1932 presidential election.

The Presidential Campaign of 1932

Roosevelt announced his candidacy for the presidency in January 1932, just a week before his fiftieth birthday. On the surface, he seemed to have everything going for him. Roosevelt's name, his earlier service in Washington, and his stature as a vice presidential candidate had made him a national figure. His smashing reelection and leading role among governors in combating the depression gave him stature as the most active champion of recovery. His record contrasted with Hoover's dismal image as a last-ditch defender of the old order. And Roosevelt was blessed with radiant personal charm, including a vibrant radio voice.

To supply him with fresh ideas, Roosevelt assembled a group of experts on national issues. Raymond Moley, a professor of government at Co-

ROOSEVELT CALLS FOR ACTION

*Franklin Roosevelt charged toward the presidential nomi-
nation in 1932, stressing the need for government action
against the depression. To dramatize his point, he broke
with custom by flying to the convention in Chicago. Once
at the podium to accept the call to launch a "New Deal,"
Roosevelt spoke with animated force to establish a contrast
with the stolid lecturing style of his opponent, Herbert
Hoover. As this and all other authorized pictures demonstrate, Roosevelt insisted that his activist image never be
undermined by any indication that without leg braces and
assistance, he could not walk.*

Franklin D. Roosevelt Library.

lumbia University, headed a team of advisers that
a journalist dubbed the "Brain Trust." The Brain
Trust's other leading figures were another Columbia professor, Rexford Tugwell, and a lawyer and
economist, Adolf Berle. Roosevelt's Brain Trust
equipped him with an arsenal of information and
the latest reform ideas. From his advisers, Roosevelt
heard passionate arguments in favor of government
planning to introduce stability and fair play into the
marketplace and a welfare state to aid the helpless
and end poverty.

Despite support from the Brain Trust and his
own personal and political strengths, Roosevelt still
had to overcome the old split in the Democratic
Party between rural strongholds in the South and
working-class enclaves in the cities, many of them
filled with recent immigrants. Moreover, he had to
devise a plan to attack the nation's woes that did
not alienate the Democratic Party faithful, who did
not agree among themselves. Roosevelt identified
himself with what he called "the forgotten man at
the bottom of the pyramid" and declared that helping that forgotten man called for "bold, persistent
experimentation." He tried to steer clear of divisive
issues and factional disputes within the party and
instead concentrated on building a victorious coalition by adding the West to his eastern and southern
base. He hoped to capture the party's nomination
with his support of direct cash subsidies to farmers
and with his commitment to the West's interest in
conservation of natural resources and water development.

Roosevelt needed all his impressive political
skills to overcome his rivals within the Democratic
Party. From the right, Al Smith, the party's 1928
presidential candidate, resented being overshadowed by Roosevelt and attacked him as a fomenter
of class conflict. On the left, progressives chided
Roosevelt for his unwillingness to offer bold plans
for redistributing wealth and regulating the economy,
steps considered class warfare by Smith's faction of
the party. Roosevelt's western strategy faltered
when the rival candidacy of John "Cactus Jack" Garner of Texas, Speaker of the House of Representatives, attracted so many supporters that Roosevelt
finally had to offer him the vice presidential nomination. At the end of the scramble for votes, Roosevelt
won the nomination at the head of a peculiar new
coalition. It lumped together his friends within the
Democratic Party's eastern establishment, big-city
machine bosses, old Wilsonian reformers, entrenched
southerners—many of them deeply conservative

and racist—along with angry farmers, labor unions, and urban ethnic communities. To galvanize that unwieldy coalition, Roosevelt realized that he needed to establish a personal, symbolic presence above the fray of political battle.

Roosevelt dramatized his candidacy by breaking with the precedent that the nominee should stay at home during the party's convention and await word of the party's choice. Instead, he flew to the Democratic convention in Chicago to deliver his acceptance speech in person. Roosevelt came before the delegates to restate his main case for innovation and experimentation. The flight, he declared, signified his intention to be bold and active. "Let it also be symbolic that in so doing I broke traditions. Let it be from now on the task of our Party to break foolish traditions and leave it to the Republican leadership, far more skilled in that art, to break promises." Roosevelt proposed to lead the party in the direction "of liberal thought, of planned action, of enlightened international outlook, and of the greatest good to the greatest number of our citizens." In conclusion, Roosevelt expressed his twin allegiance to the New Freedom of Woodrow Wilson and the Square Deal of Theodore Roosevelt by forging the label for his own program: the New Deal. As the delegates' applause died away, the band struck up "Happy Days Are Here Again," a bouncy new popular tune that became the anthem of Roosevelt's New Deal optimism.

During the presidential campaign, Roosevelt continued to make bold declarations of optimism and of the need for fresh initiatives in government, followed by careful hedging on specifics. In Topeka, Kansas, he promised wholesale reorganization of the Department of Agriculture to establish closer relationships between farmers and the government. In Seattle, he attacked high tariffs. In Portland, Oregon, he called for full disclosure of the financial activities of utility companies, where payoffs and corruption were rampant. In Detroit, where the slump in the automobile industry had created massive unemployment, Roosevelt declared his intention to eliminate the causes of poverty. The most thoroughgoing appeal to change came at the Commonwealth Club in San Francisco, where Roosevelt argued that the closing of the frontier meant that the days of boundless natural resources were over and that prosperity required careful public management of the nation's limited natural endowment.

President Hoover, the nominee of the Republican Party, attacked Roosevelt's proposed New Deal as un-American collectivism of the sort that Russian Communists used to subdue the masses. Exhausted and angry, Hoover declared that his opponent was a "chameleon on plaid" who threatened to undermine the foundation of American society by advocating handouts and bureaucratic controls instead of relying on the tried-and-true efforts of hardworking, self-disciplined individuals. During the campaign, Hoover's motorcade took him past somber, silent crowds. When he spoke, many in the audience sat on their hands. Hoover sensed the nation's desperation, but he had little idea what to do about it. "Perhaps what this country needs," he said just weeks before the voters went to the polls, "is a great poem. . . . We need something to raise our eyes beyond the immediate horizon . . . something simple enough for a child to put his hand on his chest and spout in school on Fridays."

The electorate, however, did not hunger for poetry. Many voters heard Hoover's appeals for individual effort and sacrifice as coldhearted, pompous rhetoric that ignored their suffering. While Roosevelt exuberantly thumped the tub for a New Deal for the "forgotten man," Hoover became the scapegoat for all ills. One Democratic slogan proclaimed, "A Vote for Roosevelt Is a Vote against Hoover." The

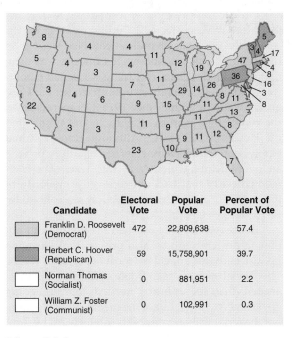

Candidate	Electoral Vote	Popular Vote	Percent of Popular Vote
Franklin D. Roosevelt (Democrat)	472	22,809,638	57.4
Herbert C. Hoover (Republican)	59	15,758,901	39.7
Norman Thomas (Socialist)	0	881,951	2.2
William Z. Foster (Communist)	0	102,991	0.3

MAP 24.1
The Election of 1932

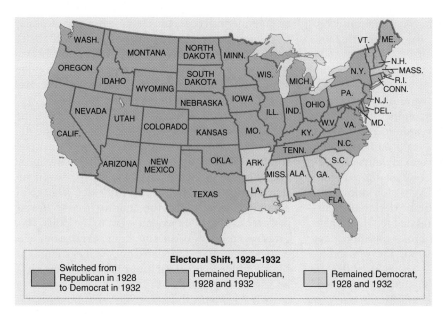

MAP 24.2
Electoral Shift, 1928–1932
Democratic victory in 1932 signaled the rise of a New Deal coalition within which women and minorities, many of them new voters, made the Democrats the majority party for the first time in the twentieth century.

Electoral Shift, 1928–1932

- Switched from Republican in 1928 to Democrat in 1932
- Remained Republican, 1928 and 1932
- Remained Democrat, 1928 and 1932

president's name became a label for poverty. New York City's Park Department officially designated as "Hoover Valley" a gully where derelicts huddled in Central Park. When home-run king Babe Ruth was criticized for requesting a salary higher than President Hoover's, the Babe shot back with indisputable accuracy, "So what? I had a better year."

On election day, Hoover went down to utter defeat. Roosevelt received 22.8 million votes, 57 percent of the total, to 15.8 million votes for Hoover. In the electoral college, Roosevelt's margin was even more lopsided, 472 to 59. Riding Roosevelt's political coattails, Democrats swept into control of Congress for the first time since 1916. Democrats ruled the Senate by a margin of 59 to 36 and dominated the House by 313 to 117. Although Roosevelt had barely secured the Democrats' nomination, he won an overwhelming victory at the head of a fragmented party that had not received a majority of the votes in a presidential election since Franklin Pierce was elected in 1852.

Roosevelt not only crushed his Republican opponent on the right; he also proved that left-wing politics had little appeal for most depression voters. The Socialist Party candidate, Norman Thomas, argued that the country needed thoroughgoing government ownership of the means of production, not the tepid welfare proposals put forward by Roosevelt. But the Socialist Party polled only 881,951 votes, leaving the party with no significant electoral future. The Communists did even worse. They gained

only 102,991 votes. Tiny, remote Crosby, Minnesota, an outpost of Finnish immigrant miners devastated by the industrial collapse, was the only place to give the Communists a majority. Even the Farm Laborites, with a Populist heritage nourished by a half-century of rural grievances, managed only to elect five members of Congress and a single senator.

The landslide for Roosevelt and the Democrats in 1932 was the greatest change in voter choice in the nation's history. A new coalition came together to repudiate Republican leadership and policy and place their faith in a man who promised change.

The electoral switch from a landslide for Hoover and the Republicans in the 1928 election to a landslide for Roosevelt and the Democrats in 1932 was the greatest change in voter choice in the nation's history. It began what political analysts have termed the "Roosevelt Revolution"—a fundamental realignment of voter allegiance that swept the New Deal into power. A new coalition of farmers, industrial laborers, white-collar workers, African Americans, immigrants, women, intellectuals, and others —came together to repudiate Republican leadership and policy and place their faith in a man who promised change.

The New Deal in Action: The Hundred Days

At noon on March 4, 1933, Americans anxiously gathered around their radios to listen to Franklin Delano Roosevelt deliver his first inaugural address. A frightened people heard a serene and confident new president declare that the "only thing we have to fear is fear itself." The United States was "a stricken nation in the midst of a stricken world," Roosevelt said, but the "people . . . have not failed." Rather than dealing with the depression by "talking about it," he promised "direct, vigorous action." He would even be willing to "ask the Congress for the one remaining instrument to meet the crisis— broad Executive power to wage a war against the emergency, as great as the power that would be given to me if we were in fact invaded by a foreign foe."

Roosevelt's confident optimism and his determination to do *something* offered Americans hope and the sense that at last someone in Washington was listening. Roosevelt had been too vague and contradictory in the campaign for the people to have a clear road map of his administration, but they knew to expect strong presidential leadership and bold action. The first months of his administration, called "the Hundred Days," were a blur of action. For the hurry-up new order, the most immediate task was to offer relief to the destitute, including the 25 percent of the workforce that was unemployed. Their plight pointed toward a second need: the recovery of business and farming so that jobs would be available to all workers. And that goal led in turn to the third challenge: how to reform the system to guard against any future economic collapse.

The New Dealers

Reformers looking for a chance to translate their ideas into action hurried to Washington in the spring of 1933, drawn by the combination of public desperation and the chance to serve under a president interested in active reform. "As for those first New Deal days," Gardiner C. Means, an economic adviser, recalled, "much of the excitement came from improvisation. Nothing was fully set in the minds of the people there. They were open to fresh ideas. Always." Means reveled in the "yeastiness of experimentation" and an atmosphere that was "highly personal and highly charged."

The New Deal was the only moment in American history when a president receptive to reforms took office in bad times rather than good. Roosevelt's reform heroes—Andrew Jackson, Theodore Roosevelt, and Woodrow Wilson—had the good fortune to serve during economic booms. Roosevelt confronted the more daunting task of reversing an economic depression without violating the nation's allegiance to democracy and capitalism. Rather than responding to bad times by blaming the victims, as Herbert Hoover had done, Roosevelt let it be known that he sympathized with the victims and that he was eager for new ideas to break the depression's merciless stranglehold.

In recognition of his sprawling party base, Roosevelt selected his cabinet and staff to represent important constituencies. He also chose advisers who would be loyal to him and who would be unlikely to become rivals for power. Vice President Garner was a source of pride to the Southwest and a shrewd negotiator with Congress. For secretary of state, Roosevelt chose an old Wilsonian southerner, Cordell Hull, a former senator from Tennessee and a longtime advocate of Wilsonian free trade. For secretary of the treasury, Roosevelt called upon Will Woodin, a former industrialist and lifelong Republican who was nonetheless eager to carry out Roosevelt's experimental approach. In these appointments, Roosevelt made clear his intention to establish a friendly, cooperative relationship with businessmen and bankers yet to proceed openly to test ways of rescuing the economic system.

For the heads of the Labor and Agriculture Departments, whose constituencies were more fully the forgotten and the hard-pressed, Roosevelt turned to reformers. Frances Perkins became the first female secretary of labor, much to the outrage of traditional labor leaders. Henry A. Wallace of Iowa, a voice for scientific experiment and government regulation of markets, was tapped to be secretary of agriculture. For secretary of the interior, Roosevelt also looked west when he selected the irascible progressive Republican lawyer from Chicago Harold A. Ickes. Roosevelt followed the principle of diversity in other, less central appointments and ended up with a cabinet and set of advisers that represented virtually all sections, both major parties, the three major religions, and both sexes. Roosevelt—happily responding to his new nickname, "the Chief"—took the responsibility to knit these disparate advisers into some semblance of cohesion.

Through it all, Roosevelt radiated good cheer and relished his task as the impresario of a great rescue operation and the restorer of public confidence. Lights burned late in the White House most nights. Roosevelt wore out his assistants, picking their brains, prodding them to find fresh solutions. To communicate with the public, he began his practice of frequent news conferences, which brought him face to face with the press thirty times during the Hundred Days and at least once a week thereafter. His wide grin and infectious optimism made him the personal symbol of recovery, the emblem of hope for millions.

Banking and Finance Reform

The new administration first targeted the disaster engulfing America's banking system. By March 4, 1933, when Roosevelt was inaugurated, the nation's governors had suspended almost all banking operations within their states. That was a desperate action, but since 1930, more than five thousand banks with $3.4 billion in assets had gone under. On March 5, 1933, Roosevelt made good his inaugural pledge for "action now" by announcing a four-day "bank holiday" that converted emergency state action into federal policy. Three days later, Roosevelt sent Congress the Emergency Banking Act, and four hours later a compliant Congress passed the administration's plan for rescue. Under the provisions of the

bill, the secretary of the treasury could decide which banks were stable enough to reopen and could authorize the Reconstruction Finance Corporation (RFC) to supply funds for immediate circulation. A few months later, Congress rounded out these regulatory changes by creating the Federal Deposit Insurance Corporation (FDIC) to insure bank customers against the loss of their deposits if their bank should fail.

The New Deal's more radical supporters were disappointed that Roosevelt had not nationalized the banks and made them a firm cornerstone for national planning. Instead, the private banking system was propped up with federal funds, banks were subjected to federal regulation and oversight, and individual deposits were secured with the full faith and credit of the United States government. Within a few days, most of the nation's major banks had reopened.

On March 12, Roosevelt broadcast his first "fireside chat" to the nation, explaining why the banking legislation was needed and how it gave good reason for confidence. That radio talk, suggesting a cozy gathering of the nation at the family hearth to discuss what was left in the sugar bowl, was a masterstroke. Roosevelt, speaking in cheerful, simple, fatherly terms, came through as a friendly savior echoing his inaugural address with his reassurance against fear. In the minds of a majority of Americans, the New Deal had established its competence

TABLE 24.1

MAJOR LEGISLATION OF THE NEW DEAL'S FIRST HUNDRED DAYS

Name of Act	Date Passed	Basic Provisions
Emergency Banking Act	March 9, 1933	Provided for reopening stable banks and authorizing RFC supply funds
Civilian Conservation Corps Act	March 31, 1933	Provided jobs for unemployed youth
Agricultural Adjustment Act	May 12, 1933	Provided funds to pay farmers for not growing surplus crops
Federal Emergency Relief Act	May 12, 1933	Provided relief funds for the destitute
Tennessee Valley Authority Act	May 18, 1933	Set up authority for development of electric power and conservation
National Industrial Recovery Act	June 16, 1933	Specified cooperation among business, government, and labor in setting fair prices and working conditions
Glass-Steagall Banking Act	June 16, 1933	Created Federal Deposit Insurance Corporation (FDIC) to insure bank deposits

LISTENING TO FDR'S FIRESIDE CHATS
Roosevelt's "fireside chat" radio talks enabled the president to address national problems in the intimate style of a family friend offering advice. In this photograph, one of the "common men" whom the New Deal would be expected to affect leans toward his radio in apparent recognition that he has much at stake in what is being said.
Franklin D. Roosevelt Library.

and humaneness, and a glimmer of the nation's old optimism returned. The banking panic ended, and the money that anxious Americans had stuffed in mattresses and buried in backyards began to flow back into the banks.

To provide a firm financial basis for economic recovery, the New Deal turned to the stock market, whose scandals so vividly symbolized the 1920s. While governor of New York, Roosevelt had frequently denounced shady dealings on Wall Street, and now as president he was eager to enact provisions that would end dubious practices such as the pyramiding of holding companies that created Samuel Insull's false fortune or profitable stock trading on the basis of insider information. At his insistence, Congress passed the Securities Act of 1933 and the Federal Securities and Exchange Act of 1934, which created the Securities and Exchange Commission (SEC). The new agency licensed investment dealers, monitored all stock transactions, restricted margin buying, and required corporate officers to make full disclosures of their stock offerings and be responsible for any claims they made about their companies.

Roosevelt named an abrasive and successful Wall Street trader, Joseph P. Kennedy, chairman of

the SEC. Critics opposed the choice of someone whose reputation had been clouded by shrewd stock manipulation, but Roosevelt replied wickedly, "Set a thief to catch a thief." Kennedy proved to be tough enough to face down threats by brokers, some of them with things to hide, to boycott the exchange or even move it out of the country. Soon the SEC won praise for its effectiveness, and Wall Street regained respect within business circles. In the end, the most spectacular casualty was not a brash upstart like Joe Kennedy but the impeccably well-bred stock exchange president, Richard Whitney, who went to jail for stealing from others' accounts to cover his own bad investments.

In addition to his efforts to save the financial structure at home, Roosevelt attempted to repair a sputtering international economy. He inherited a conference President Hoover had convened in London to find a way to stabilize the world's depressed monetary system and revive international trade. Hope for cooperation soon faded, however. When the conference deadlocked on the gold standard and trade policies, Roosevelt brought the conference to an abrupt end with a sharp rebuke of what he called "old-fashioned fetishes of so-called international bankers." Instead, he decided, the United States

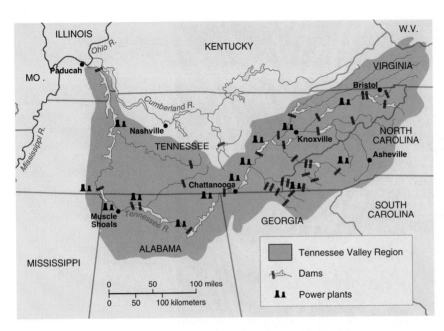

MAP 24.3
The Tennessee Valley Authority
The New Deal created the Tennessee Valley Authority to modernize a vast impoverished region with hydroelectric power dams and, at the same time, to reclaim eroded lands and preserve old folkways.

would take care of its own problems first and return to the international bargaining table when other nations learned to be more cooperative and balance their books. Though Roosevelt's decision to pull out of the conference left the rest of the world in a precarious state, it enabled his New Deal administration to concentrate on domestic problems.

Relief and Conservation Programs

Having rescued the banks, Roosevelt took on the plight of those with no means of support—the unemployed, the landless, the disabled, and those who were too old or too young to work. The Federal Emergency Relief Administration (FERA) Act made good on the president's promise that he would not abandon Americans to hunger and homelessness. The new initiative provided cash subsidies to bankrupt local relief agencies. Soon, the FERA supported from four to five million households each month and funded thousands of work projects for the unemployed. In Alabama, Dera Johnson, whose husband, a coal miner, had become too sick to work, got a teaching job with FERA. "That class was a lifesaver to my family," she remembered. "I taught it for a year, and his rest had improved Johnson so much that he went back to work." To publicize the terrible suffering that provoked this unprecedented federal initiative, FERA's director, Harry Hopkins, sent reporters out into the field to describe conditions. With support from an aroused public, FERA took the lead in providing vaccinations and immu-

nizations for millions of unprotected poor people, helped build desperately needed flood protection systems, and supported literacy classes for the most ill prepared citizens.

Having rescued the banks, Roosevelt took on the plight of those with no means of support— the unemployed, the landless, the disabled, and those who were too old or too young to work.

Agreeing with Hoover about the dangers of a federal "dole," the Roosevelt administration intended its efforts as temporary emergency measures to relieve suffering and jump-start the economy, without threatening individual self-reliance. Whenever possible, the administration favored aid in the form of a job that saved the recipient's dignity while accomplishing something useful. The New Deal's second major relief program, the Civil Works Administration (CWA), under Hopkin's direction, put more than four million Americans to work building schools and parks. But New Dealers perceived work relief as an emergency measure also, and within a year the Roosevelt administration began whittling back the CWA.

More enduring was Roosevelt's favorite work relief program, the Civilian Conservation Corps (CCC), which offered unemployed young men, mostly from the cities, a chance to perform useful outdoor work. The CCC reflected Roosevelt's long-standing enthusiasm for the outdoors and conservation. By the time the vigorous program ended in 1942, it had enrolled three million young people. From a big family, Blackie Gold had "to go out and beg for coal, buy bread that's two, three days old." In 1937, when he was seventeen, he joined the CCC at thirty dollars a month. "I really enjoyed it," he remembered. "I had three wonderful square meals a day." The CCC achieved significant results. Trees planted on the plains checked the disastrous dust storms that ravaged the Southwest in the early years of the decade. The CCC reversed the long-standing depletion of forest preserves by planting more than two billion new trees, fighting forest fires, and erecting more than five million dams to check soil erosion. It strung 83,000 miles of telephone wires, constructed 122,000 miles of minor roads and trails, and located 23,000 new water sources in the nation's wilderness. In the end, the CCC created magnificent outdoor recreation areas and made them accessible to millions of people.

The most spectacular accomplishment of the New Deal's conservation efforts was the Tennessee Valley Authority (TVA). The project fulfilled the long-frustrated aim of progressives to use government lands in Muscle Shoals, Alabama, along the Tennessee River for planned regional development, rather than selling them off to private developers. In April 1933, Roosevelt presented legislation to Congress designed to transform the Tennessee valley, one of the nation's most depressed areas and largely untouched by modern technology, into a model of cooperative development. The act creating the TVA set up a regional organization empowered to build hydroelectric power dams along the Tennessee River and to use the electricity generated to bring power and light to rural communities. To help guide the new prosperity, the TVA planned to build model towns for power station workers and provide new homes for farmers who would benefit from electricity and flood control. At the same time, the New Deal expressed its commitment to the con-

CIVILIAN CONSERVATION CORPS WORKERS
No New Deal program was more popular among its participants and the general public than the Civilian Conservation Corps. It offered healthy outdoor work for young men that got them out of the cities and eased their unemployment blues. To the public it showed that the New Deal would act against the depression in a way that would repair neglect of America's natural resources.
Forest Service Photo Collection.

servation of social custom, as well as natural re-sources, by including programs within the TVA to encourage local crafts and other folkways.

> *The most spectacular accomplishment of the New Deal's conservation efforts was the Tennessee Valley Authority (TVA).*

"It is time to extend planning to a wider field, in this instance comprehending in one great project many States directly concerned with the basin of one of our greatest rivers," Roosevelt declared when he signed the TVA bill. Crossing the state lines of Kentucky, Virginia, North Carolina, Tennessee, Georgia, Alabama, and Mississippi, the TVA set out to demonstrate that a partnership between the federal government and local residents could overcome traditional limitations of state boundaries and free enterprise to make efficient use of abundant resources and break an ancient cycle of poverty. The TVA became the most ambitious example of New Deal enthusiasm for planning. But hampered by bitter resistance from competing private power companies, the TVA never fully realized its utopian ends. It did, however, succeed in bringing electric power, flood protection, soil reclamation, and, therefore, sharply improved prosperity to the area it served.

Agricultural Initiatives

New Dealers formulated other plans to meet the crisis in agriculture that stretched far beyond the Tennessee valley. Farmers typically responded to low prices for their crops by increasing production, causing a self-defeating cycle of crop surpluses and still lower prices. At the same time, unemployment robbed consumers of the money to buy even low-priced farm products. Congress first considered the McNary-Haugen bill, which proposed dumping crop surpluses overseas at below market prices, with a subsidy from the government to make up the difference. That way, domestic supplies would not exceed demand and farmers would enjoy a good return. When the bill failed to pass, a farm economist named M. L. Wilson devised a new approach. His voluntary domestic allotment plan called for the federal government to pay farmers to leave some of their land idle, thus reducing crop surpluses and thereby boosting prices. Left for another day was the problem of feeding the hungry who could not afford the higher prices the plan was designed to set.

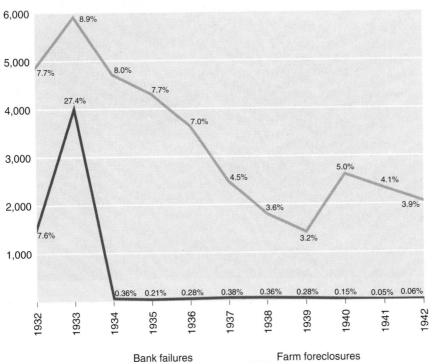

FIGURE **24.1**
Bank Failures and Farm Foreclosures, 1932–1942
New Deal legislation to stabilize the economy had its most immediate and striking effect in preventing banks, along with their depositors, from going under and farmers from losing their land.

SKETCH FOR A WPA MURAL

This sketch for a mural commissioned for Lenoir City, Tennessee, is typical of the Federal Arts Program's goal to memorialize significant moments of achievement in every region of the country. For rural folk, the sight of Rural Electrification Authority workers extending power lines was one of the more exciting symbols of the New Deal. When the REA came into existence in 1935, less than 10 percent of the nation outside the cities had electricity. By 1941, REA programs had increased that number to 40 percent; ten years later the figure had risen to 90 percent, and the gulf of silence and darkness between town and country was successfully bridged.
Public Buildings Service, General Services Administration.

The Agricultural Adjustment Act (AAA), which incorporated the domestic allotment plan and the Agricultural Adjustment Administration to apply it, sailed easily through Congress in May 1933. On the heels of the landmark AAA legislation, the Farm Credit Act eased another old farm grievance by providing credit to forestall foreclosures on mortgaged farm property and prevent debt-ridden farmers from being evicted from their land.

Once in place, these reforms dampened the urge for farm revolts and nudged prices upward. An Iowa farmer remembered, "People could now see daylight and hope. It was a whole transformation of attitude." Results, however, were mixed. New Dealers relied on grass-roots democracy to administer the programs fairly. In the corn, hog, and wheat region of the Midwest, farmers came together on a democratic basis, and a reasonably equitable distribution of benefits followed. In the South, however, local control meant that sharecroppers and tenant farmers on cotton plantations were denied a decent share of the benefits, while large growers reaped huge subsidies for putting land out of production—and tenant farmers out of work. Nonetheless, the AAA guided agriculture toward greater

overall prosperity. With almost all major crops limited, surpluses declined and gross farm income rose from $6.4 billion in 1932 to $8.5 billion in 1934.

Moreover, loans sponsored by the Farm Credit Administration (FCA) arrested farmers' steep slide into bankruptcy. The trickle of 7,800 federal loans in 1932 rose to a flood of 287,881 in less than a year after the FCA was enacted in 1933—a record 3,174 loans winning approval in a single day. By the end of the decade, the federal government had financed 40 percent of farm mortgage debt, and the shadow of foreclosure had receded from most farmers' doorsteps.

With both the TVA and AAA in place, the administration turned to fulfilling the old progressive dream that electricity and all its modern benefits be extended to rural America. When Roosevelt became president, about 90 percent of the country outside the cities and towns was without electricity. Power magnates like Samuel Insull saw little profit in sending expensive transmission lines into sparsely settled territory. Thus, the further cities moved into the electric age, the more rural America seemed backward, rather than the backbone of the country, as Jefferson had intended.

In May 1935, the New Deal finally overcame the resistance of the private power industry and created the Rural Electrification Administration (REA). Encouraged by the successes of the AAA and TVA in communal cooperation, the REA gave low-cost loans to farm cooperatives so that they could bring power into their communities. By 1941, the REA succeeded in raising to 40 percent the number of farms with electricity. One man recalled the lights coming on in his Arkansas farmhouse in 1940. "The lights just barely glowed," he said. But his mother was smiling, and "tears started to run down her cheeks." Others remembered their first radios and hearing Roosevelt's voice. By 1950, nine out of every ten American farms were electrified. With the possible exception of the automobile, nothing did as much to brighten the quality of rural life and close the gap between country and city.

Industrial Recovery

Industry was as devastated as any sector of the nation's economy. But the New Deal's National Recovery Administration (NRA), established in June 1933 under the National Industrial Recovery Act (NIRA), was a far less successful experiment than the agricultural programs. The NRA's objective was to coordinate management, labor, and the federal government through a network of industrial codes that governed industrial working conditions, prices, and trade practices. In exchange for the easing of antitrust regulations, business leaders agreed to allow the bill to guarantee labor's right to collective bargaining. The NRA hoped to set nationwide terms for how much each industry should produce, what it should charge consumers, and, subject to collective bargaining agreements, what pay and benefits workers should receive.

Under the energetic leadership of General Hugh Johnson, a veteran of the War Industries Board during World War I, the NRA captured public attention through speeches and gala parades with floats, movie stars, West Point cadets, and even a Miss NRA displayed in a shell-shaped float like Venus emerging from the sea. By the end of 1933, most industries were represented within the 541 NRA codes, and the Blue Eagle symbol displayed in store windows let the public know.

The stage seemed set for a major transformation of American industry, but opinions differed widely on the direction it would take. The New Dealers emphasized the possibilities for rational management and fair competition. They hoped that

NRA QUILT
The blue eagle of the National Recovery Administration, fiercely clutching a machine gear and lightning bolts, symbolized the government's determination to bring American industry around to a coordinated plan for recovery. The attempt to balance the interests of producers, workers, and consumers proved too much for the blue eagle however. Yet, as this backcountry quilt indicates, the blue eagle was sometimes able to carry the spirit of cooperation far from the centers of industrial turmoil.
Franklin D. Roosevelt Library.

coordination would produce a collective social conscience that would inhibit industry from cheating customers or destroying the environment and would make sure that workers were treated fairly. Critics, however, saw bureaucratic oppression. Because the NRA skirted antimonopoly laws and left industry subject to federal management, they claimed that the economy would become rigidly controlled from the top. The NRA scheme of linking business with government seemed to its critics an American version of Mussolini's corporate fascism in Italy, a means for controlling individuals by directing their economic lives.

In reality, neither prediction was accurate. The outcome was more an extension of conventional business practice than a radical change to either the right or the left. Johnson's sloppy management gave business leaders the opportunity to gain control of the code-writing mechanism, and they made sure the codes would first serve the interests of corporate profits rather than worker benefit or the general welfare. By the mid-1930s, prospects for a rationally coordinated business system had faded, and even New Dealers began to hope for some way to make a graceful escape from the NRA as it had developed.

The Hundred Days that initiated the First New Deal produced a blizzard of new agencies and programs.

The Hundred Days that initiated what became known as the First New Deal produced a blizzard of new agencies and programs. The central idea uniting the legislative onslaught was planning and coordination, in both industry and agriculture. The effort succeeded in reversing the economic decline and restoring the nation's confidence, but it did not produce full recovery. The magnitude and scope of the depression and the speed of the New Deal attack ensured that the Roosevelt administration would have as many failures as successes. Inevitably, resistance mounted.

Challenges to the New Deal

A majority of Americans supported the New Deal's initiatives and programs. After the early rush of excitement, however, discontent began to grow. Business expressed open hostility to the philosophy and practice of the First New Deal. Conservatives insisted that New Deal changes had been too radical, undermined economic stability, and threatened American democratic values. But the continuation of severe distress across much of the nation caused others to fault the administration for not having programs radical enough to meet the people's needs. Increasingly, opponents mounted political challenges to Roosevelt's initiatives.

Resistance to Business Reform

Backlash within the business community and among others opposed to government interference in the economy went beyond material self-interest.

Since the New Deal sought economic recovery, New Dealers expected business leaders to come around eventually and welcome cooperative economic planning. In that respect the administration was sorely disappointed. In the Tennessee valley, private power companies battled the TVA as "creeping socialism" and unfair competition. The NRA took even greater abuse. The alliance of the New Deal with urban labor and constant feuding between business representatives and NRA officials about how to devise codes of competition caused strain from the outset. Moreover, although business conditions improved steadily and the business failure rate declined to levels below those of the boom years of the 1920s, business leaders never reconciled themselves to the administration's planning concept. To one Republican senator, the creator of the NRA was "Frankenstein" Roosevelt and the Blue Eagle symbol was really "the Soviet duck" in disguise. The relentlessly anti-NRA Hearst newspapers chimed in with a poem that characterized the Roosevelt administration as

The Red New Deal with a Soviet seal
Endorsed by a Moscow hand;
The strange result of an alien cult
In a liberty-loving land.

Ironically, the business community kept up its criticism even though its situation improved more steadily during the depression than did that of most other social groups, including farmers and workers. The managerial elite remained mostly intact—despite some spectacular jailings, flights from prosecution, and suicides. So did the hierarchical corporate structure that had been developed during the boom years at the turn of the century. The greatest wounds had been to business leaders' confidence and pride. A desire by business leaders to ward off threats of government regulation, higher taxes, and union organization moved them to create public relations offices and—more ominously—a system of company spies and police forces to seek out disloyal workers. The rage of businessmen toward the New Deal fastened on Franklin Roosevelt as the source of their loss of public admiration and government favor. In the typical commuter line club car—otherwise known as the "assassination special"—rumors flew about that "traitor to his class," about "that man in the White House." Hostility among the well-to-do became so pervasive that when high society's leading party giver, Elsa Maxwell, planned a "Pet Hates" ball, she asked guests not to come dressed as the president or his wife to prevent everyone from wearing the same costume.

The most extreme example of anti–New Deal agitation was the American Liberty League, founded in 1934 as the NRA came under bitter attack. Prominent members of the league had once been leaders in the Democratic Party, but now they decried the New Deal as a betrayer of basic constitutional guarantees of freedom and individualism. These critics included the party's 1928 presidential candidate, Al Smith, his campaign chairman, John Jacob Raskob, and Jowett Shouse, a former chairman of the Democratic National Committee. The league furiously attacked almost every feature of the New Deal. The AAA was a "trend toward Fascist control of agriculture," relief programs marked "the end of democracy," and the NRA had plunged the nation into a "quicksand of visionary experimentation." Although the league's membership never exceeded 125,000 zealots, its well-financed publicity campaign inflamed the rift between Roosevelt and the business class. By 1935, the two major business organizations—the National Association of Manufacturers and the Chamber of Commerce—had become openly anti-New Deal.

Conservatives insisted that New Deal changes had been too radical, undermined economic stability, and threatened American democratic values.

Planners and labor leaders who favored more worker control attacked the New Deal from the other direction. In their view, the NRA had stifled enterprise by permitting monopolistic practices. They pointed out that industrial trade associations twisted codes to suit their aims, thwarted competition, and engaged in price gouging. Labor leaders especially resented the willingness of the NRA to allow companies to form their own unions, blocking the organization of genuine grass-roots unions that permitted workers to bargain on terms they chose for themselves.

In the midst of the cross fire of criticisms, the Supreme Court in May 1935 declared that the NRA unconstitutionally conferred legislative power on an administrative agency and overstepped the limits of federal power to regulate interstate commerce. The agency lingered briefly, but its codes evaporated, and business leaders rejected most proposals

for cooperation with government. The failure of the NRA demonstrated both historic American resistance to economic planning and the refusal of the business community to yield its autonomy unless it was forced to do so.

Reaction against the New Deal Farm Program

The AAA survived its battering by champions of the old order. Contentment among the majority of farmers was at a higher level than among the businessmen affected by the NRA. Even though farmers were reluctant to abandon their traditional practice of trying to increase production as a matter of pride and survival, the allotment checks for keeping land fallow and the higher prices for their produce created loyalty among those with enough acreage to participate.

Protest stirred, however, among those with smaller farms who were not fortunate enough to qualify for allotments. The Southern Farm Tenants Union, formed by tenant farmers themselves, argued passionately that the AAA was a device for enriching large farmers at the expense of the most vulnerable. By taking out of production the land on which tenants had lived, owners could simultaneously qualify for government subsidies and be relieved of the need to provide for those who had been dependent on them. Already at the bottom of the economic ladder, tenant farmers and sharecroppers faced a grave situation. One black sharecropper explained to an interviewer why only seventy-five dollars a year from the plantation cotton subsidies made its way down to her: "De landlord think he ought to have *all* the acre p'duction checks, cause it his land." Bypassing the intention of New Deal programs to benefit owners and tenants alike was simple enough in her part of Arkansas because "de landlord is landlord, de politicians is landlord, de judge is landlord, de shurf is landlord, ever'body is landlord, en we ain' got nothin'!" Stories like this convinced critics that the New Deal was fostering just the sort of inequality and misery—among both whites and blacks—that it had set out to eliminate.

The AAA's most potent critics, however, were not the dispossessed but agricultural processors and distributors. They were unhappy that the AAA reduced the volume of production—the source of their profits—while they were required to pay for the very program that disadvantaged them. In 1936, the Supreme Court agreed to their contention that they were the victims of an illegal attempt to regu-

BLACK SHARECROPPERS
A painful, unintended consequence of the New Deal plan to maintain farm prices by reducing acreage in production was the eviction of tenant farmers when the land they worked was unused. Champions of the tenant farmers, most notably the Southern Farm Tenants Union, protested that federal crop subsidies should be shared between owners and those who usually worked the land. Often, however, sharecroppers like these were simply cast adrift, and lobbies for farm owners thwarted any governmental challenge. The sad state of tenant farmers continued until World War II provided opportunities for displaced tenants to escape to the cities.
UPI/Bettmann Archives.

late agriculture and to tax one group (processors and distributors) to enrich another (farmers). The AAA rebounded from the Supreme Court ruling by redesigning its allotment provisions with legislation that focused more on conservation measures the Court found acceptable.

By establishing the principle of keeping prices up by keeping production down, the New Deal went far toward making American agriculture profitable. Success came, however, by favoring large-scale, capital-intensive agribusiness over the needs of small farmers. Those with large holdings could benefit most from crop subsidies; those with little land or on marginal land were the first to be displaced by plans to put surplus acreage out of production.

Politics on the Fringes

The New Deal also faced challenges from outside the bounds of organized politics or labor unions. These critics included a small but growing minority drawn to radical movements. The depression had given radicals many opportunities to use their talents for organizing discontent. Socialists and Communists accused the New Deal of mounting a feeble resistance

to business elites or, worse, rescuing capitalism from its self-inflicted crisis. Many intellectuals and artists moved left during the 1930s to embrace Marxist critiques of capitalism and ruling-class exploitation. They voiced powerful arguments for radical change. Socialist author Upton Sinclair ran for governor of California in 1934 on the EPIC (End Poverty in California) ticket. He lost a close race when a harsh smear campaign charging Sinclair with being a dangerous Communist caused Roosevelt to withdraw support for the EPIC plan to put the unemployed to work in idle factories.

With that one exception, the left was never able to mount a serious electoral challenge to the New Deal. And for all the doctrinaire talk of violent overthrow of the government by the proletariat or some other aggrieved group, there was no real chance of that happening after Roosevelt's election. The United States was a highly organized modern nation where legal means of exerting force were mostly in the hands of the authorities, and constitutional provisions for realizing individual and democratic values were already in place, although they were not always honored.

The poor and alienated largely shied away from radical change. Instead, as the Bonus Army demonstrations showed, they clung desperately to the belief that their status as loyal Americans entitled them to respect, material security, and the opportunity to improve their lot. With varying degrees of militancy, most Americans sought inclusion, not revolution, fundamental entitlements, not radical novelties. Accordingly, homespun populist agitators preaching old-style religion and harping on birthrights drew the biggest crowds looking for an alternative to the status quo.

The most formidable coalition of down-and-outers challenging the New Deal was led by a Catholic priest in Detroit named Charles Coughlin. Father Coughlin expressed his outrage at the depression in a series of radio broadcasts that gained him an unequaled nationwide audience of forty million by 1930. The "Radio Priest" found villains in all the conventional places. He began by denouncing Communists as traditional foes of the church but soon shifted to bankers and other "predatory capitalists," who, he increasingly insisted, were dominated by Jews. To his formula he added a touch of Midwest populism by calling for an expanded money supply backed by silver so that the poor could be rescued from the "cross of gold" that William Jennings Bryan had so famously associated with business domination of the economy.

In 1932, Father Coughlin, like most other urban, working-class Catholics, pinned his hopes on the Democratic Party and Roosevelt's election. But his pronouncements in favor of confiscating wealth for redistribution to the deserving poor and his growing insistence on his own importance set him at odds with the New Deal. After first welcoming Roosevelt as the nation's political savior, Coughlin soon turned against the administration for its failure to "drive the moneychangers from the temple." In 1935, Coughlin founded the National Union for Social Justice to promote legislation that would advance his cause. As the presidential election of 1936 neared, Coughlin converted his organization into the Union Party and called on other dissidents to join him in mounting an election challenge to Roosevelt.

One of those who answered Father Coughlin's call was a man of very different temperament and background. Dr. Francis Townsend was a sixty-six-year-old public health officer in Long Beach, California, when the New Deal began. Townsend's anger that his elderly patients existed in misery in the golden land roused him to action. As a remedy, he proposed the Old Age Revolving Pension in late 1933, which would pay all persons over age sixty

$200 a month on the condition that they spend the entire amount within thirty days and thereby stimulate the economy. Buoyed by 90 percent of all Long Beach voters who endorsed his petition to the federal government, Townsend organized pension clubs that soon sprouted across the country among older people looking for security. By the time Father Coughlin announced his National Union for Social Justice, there were between 2 and 3.5 million paying members of the Townsend movement looking for a political home. Townsend found the Coughlin organization attractive as another populist insurgency outside the status quo.

The most important of the rebellious populists came from another region ripe for protest. Huey Pierce Long, son of a backcountry farmer, had used his immense talents to become governor of Louisiana in 1928, the same year Roosevelt was elected governor of New York. Long, calling himself "the Kingfish" after a sly character in a radio comedy show, electrified the plain people of his state with brash rhetoric and country humor. With their support, he swept out of power a reactionary political machine that had kept Louisiana one of the poorest and most backward states. By delivering on his promises to build roads, schools, and hospitals and provide jobs, Long stood out as a beacon of hope among the desperate during the early depression years. The dark side, however, was that Long achieved his revolution in Louisiana by ruthlessly gathering power into his own hands.

Elected to the Senate in 1932, Long, like Coughlin, at first tried to tie his fortunes to the New Deal. But he too became disaffected when he could not bend Roosevelt to his will and simply use him to further his own ambition to become president. Long's national popularity rested on his Share Our Wealth plan for "making every man a king." Vaguely, the plan advocated steeply progressive income taxes to reduce large fortunes and to redistribute wealth through guaranteeing every family a "homestead" worth $5,000 and an annual income of $2,500. Like Townsend and Coughlin, Long scorned conventional economics, but his calculations sounded good to many poor people. A Chicago shoe salesman wrote Long: "I voted for President Roosevelt but it seems Wall St. has got him punch drunk. What we need is men with guts to go farther to the left as you advocate." Roosevelt called Long "one of the two most dangerous men in America"—the other was Douglas MacArthur, the general who had so offended him with his strong-arm tactics against the Bonus Army.

The populist threat mounted by Coughlin, Townsend, and Long stirred the New Deal administration to solidify its winning coalition. An early test came in the 1934 elections, normally a time when a seated president loses support as disillusion sets in among those who expected too much. Roosevelt approached the elections cautiously, wishing to keep himself within the reform center and at a safe distance from radical and crank causes on the right and left. In August, Roosevelt embarked on a national tour to express support for loyal Democratic candidates before large, friendly crowds who convinced him that the electorate would endorse his active efforts to jolt the country out of depression.

Roosevelt's keen appraisal of the situation was confirmed by the unusually high percentage of voters who turned out to give New Dealers a landslide victory. Democrats increased their numbers in the House of Representatives from 310 to 319 out of a total of 422; and in the Senate, the party gained 10 new seats to take a commanding two-thirds majority, the greatest margin ever achieved in that body.

The New Deal also escaped the threat of Huey Long's challenge in a way that some observers of his provocative career predicted. Long's ambitions reached the heights of bravado in 1935 when he published *My First Days in the White House*, which explained what he would do as president. But in September 1935 it all ended. While visiting the Louisiana State House to make sure his absolute power still prevailed, Long was fatally shot by one of the many Louisianans he had antagonized. With the disappearance of Long's brilliant personality, the followers he had whipped up scattered like dust in a whirlwind. Some of Long's admirers carried their alienation into the campaigns of Coughlin and Townsend. Most turned toward the New Deal. In the election to fill the Kingfish's seat, the candidate who pledged loyalty to the Roosevelt administration swept the field by a wide margin.

The Second New Deal and the Rise of the Welfare State

Following the congressional elections of 1934, newspaper editor William Allen White observed, "He has been all but crowned by the people." Roosevelt and the Democrats had triumphed, but New Dealers found the outlook troubling. While the First New Deal had made sweeping improvements in American life, halted the economic decline, and restored

hope, the nation was not restored to economic health. A glance at almost any economic index— employment, production, income—revealed how anemic the economy remained. The Hundred Days had spent itself, and major programs were faltering (AAA) or invalidated by the Supreme Court (NRA). Angry criticism was sprouting on the right and the left. "The air has been filled of late with the noise of things breaking up," reported the Washington *Star* in March 1935. Roosevelt decided that it was time for a departure.

Out of the welter of legislative and executive action that made up the Second New Deal emerged the first elements of an American welfare state.

In 1935, New Dealers surged ahead with a flurry of new policies that has been called the Second Hundred Days or the Second New Deal. The Second New Deal moved away from central economic planning, represented by the NRA and AAA, toward provision for the special needs of various social groups. By providing security for the downtrodden, Roosevelt sought to blunt the appeal of radicals on the left and the right. The keystone of the emerging coalition was labor. Workers had felt overlooked in the 1920s, and Roosevelt reached out with both legislation and his genuine concern and sympathy. Remarkably, the aristocratic president captured the hearts of working people across the country. In the opinion of a North Carolina mill worker, "Mr. Roosevelt is the only man we ever had in the White House who would understand that my boss is a sonofabitch." Out of the welter of legislative and executive action that made up the Second New Deal emerged the first elements of an American welfare state. An understanding that individual sufferers were more often victims of economic forces beyond their control, rather than failures who had only themselves to blame, moved reformers to look to the government as the legitimate, even sole, power able to improve the nation's economic health and guard its citizens' well-being.

Relief for the Unemployed

Roosevelt directed attention to the millions of Americans still out of work. Conditions had improved, but 20 percent of the nation's labor force

Huey Long: Demagogue or Champion of the Dispossessed?

FROM THE TIME HE HAD BEEN A SMALL CHILD, Huey P. Long was what one exasperated neighbor called a "pesterance." Defiant at school, artful at avoiding any disagreeable chores, ruthlessly driven to be the center of attention, Long had gotten ahead through the shrewdness of his extraordinary intelligence and brash willingness to flout conventional rules. Though he spent only brief periods at the University of Oklahoma and Tulane University, he cajoled a judge to convene a special bar examination, which he passed easily at the age of twenty-one. Declaring that he came out of that examination "running for office," Long rose swiftly from election as state railroad commissioner in 1918 to governor ten years later. Along the way, he dazzled the public with rhetorical gifts never before approached in the state and argued successfully before the Supreme Court with a skill that archconservative Chief Justice William Howard Taft—not a man to be taken in by a small-town southern lawyer—judged to be as keen as any he had ever encountered.

Circumstances and temperament dictated the political stance Long took all his life. The populist tradition of Winn Parish, where he grew up, instilled a basic loyalty to poor, rural folk. The small population of blacks in the parish and a history of blacks and whites forming a common front against rich sawmill and plantation owners meant that there never had been much race baiting in Winn. The rest of the state was very different, however. There, blacks and whites divided evenly, and the state's leaders made white supremacy the cornerstone of their rule. Out of step with majority opinion on race, Long could only hope to advance his fortunes by appealing to class division—rich against poor, rural against urban, the humble against the elite.

Long decided to focus his reform program on a more equitable distribution of income and opportunity. At St. Martinsville, deep in swampy Cajun country, he asked, "Where are the schools that you have waited for your children to have, that have never come? Where are the roads and the highways that you sent your money to build . . . ? Where are the institutions to care for the sick and disabled?" When Long assumed the governorship, Louisiana had only 331 miles of paved roads outside the cities. It was also the most illiterate state in the country. In 1893, when Long was born, 45 percent of those above the age of ten could not read; by 1920, the rate of illiteracy was still 22 percent, including 38 percent of all blacks.

Long articulated the grievances and hopes of the poor people of Louisiana; he also behaved utterly ruthlessly. After overcoming an impeachment effort in 1929, Long moved to consolidate his power. "I used to try to get things done by saying 'please,'" he said. "That didn't work and now I'm a dynamiter. I dynamite 'em out of my path." By 1930, Long completely dominated the state. Journalists around the country routinely referred to him as "the dictator of Louisiana." He made no effort to hide his power. Once, an angry opponent thrust a volume in his face and shouted, "Maybe you've heard of this book. It's the constitution of the state of Louisiana." Long shrugged and said, "I'm the constitution here now." He bullied and bribed the state legislature into a rubber-stamp body that passed a series of laws giving him the power to count ballots and thus determine the outcome of elections. He intimidated the courts and made them heel to his demands. Every state employee knew that his or her job depended on loyalty to the Kingfish.

His grasp on Louisiana firm, Long made his leap into the national limelight by winning election to the United States Senate in 1932. With none of the freshman senator's expected deference to senior members, his arms flailing, Long introduced a sweeping "soak-the-rich" tax bill that would outlaw annual personal incomes of more than $1 million and inheritances of more than $5 million. Swift rejection by the Senate, as Long expected, triggered his long-range strategy of becoming president by mobilizing the vast numbers of low-income Americans into a Share Our Wealth protest movement. Long's plan was to mount a presidential campaign in 1936 that would take enough votes from Roosevelt to tip the election to the Republican candidate. After four years of Republican failure to alleviate the depression with conservative policies, Long would sweep into the presidency in 1940, the savior of a suffering people.

HUEY LONG

Huey Long's ability to adapt his captivating stump speech style to the radio made him the one rival politician who gave Roosevelt serious concern in the mid-1930s. Here Long is shown in 1932 campaigning in Arkansas in support of Hattie Carraway's bid for election to the United States Senate. Carraway, stigmatized as both a women and a populist reformer, seemed a sure loser until Long crossed the border from Louisiana on her behalf. In a mere two weeks of speaking and pressing the flesh, Long brushed aside criticism that he was an interloper and boosted Carraway to victory as part of his crusade to share the wealth.

UPI/Bettmann Archive.

The electoral showdown never came, however. On September 8, 1935, a young physician named Carl Austin Weiss, enraged by the dishonor Long had visited on his family by removing his father from the Louisiana bench and suggesting black ancestry, fatally shot Long in a corridor of the Louisiana State House and was immediately gunned down by Long's bodyguards. The long lines of worn and ragged people passing by Long's coffin in the capitol and the smaller, better-dressed mourners at Weiss's funeral testified to the split in Louisiana along class lines. Some people at Weiss's funeral even proposed erecting a monument to Long's assassin.

Long always answered charges that he was a dictator, rather than a man of the people, by insisting that the polite ways of conventional democratic rules could never cure the nation's deepest ills. Only forceful means, he insisted, could finally break the hold of the privileged and extend opportunity to everyone. He could point to real achievements in Louisiana. As promised, he taxed the oil companies and utilities that had run Louisiana for decades and funneled the revenue into programs to benefit those who had been continuously left out. While he built monuments to his own vanity, like the thirty-four-story state capitol with his profile in bronze on the elevator doors, Long addressed some of the state's real social needs. At one time, Louisiana's road-building program was the biggest in the nation, and by 1935 the state had ten times more paved roads than when Long became governor. He made Louisiana State University a major university. He greatly expanded the state's pitiful public health facilities. For children, he provided free schoolbooks and new schools. For adults, he started night schools that attacked illiteracy.

Critics responded that Long was a homegrown fascist. They called him "the Messiah of the Rednecks," disdainful both of Long and those who turned to him. They compared him to Mussolini or Hitler and expressed relief that his life, and thus the damage he and the rabble who supported him could do, was cut short. The bitter controversy over Long related to vital American political issues. Roosevelt had recognized that the New Deal must reach out to the "forgotten man." Long reached farther to connect with dispossessed outsiders who could never be forgotten because they had never even been noticed. He offered Americans the only chance they ever had, for better or worse, to vote for a candidate with a broad national following who offered sweeping change comparable to parties on the radical right and left in other countries.

After Long's death, the hopes of the underclass to share the wealth lapsed into silent neglect. Mostly, they voted for Roosevelt, when they voted at all, but remained largely alienated from the prevailing system. They did achieve connection in memory, however. In 1974, a Louisiana newspaper asked citizens to name the greatest governor in the history of the state. Much to the paper's editorial dismay, the overwhelming choice was Huey Long.

had no jobs, which, Roosevelt said, was a devastating blow to "their self-respect, their self-confidence and courage and determination." As a remedy, he endorsed Harry Hopkins's innovative proposal to set up an independent agency that would employ people who lacked jobs and let them work for the public benefit. Roosevelt created the Works Progress Administration (WPA) by executive order in May 1935. The WPA imposed few limits as to the sort of work to be done. Instead, general guidelines specified that the projects be useful, be undertaken in places where unemployment was high, and produce results that would bring revenues back to the Treasury as soon as possible. The program was respectful of local initiative: State and municipal agencies had the responsibility to propose what needed to be done. By the time the WPA received its "honorable discharge" in 1943, it had generated jobs costing $10 billion that provided an average of a year's worth of work for each of the thirteen million unemployed put on the payroll.

Construction amounted to about three-fourths of the total WPA projects and left the mark of the New Deal broadly distributed over the countryside. By 1943, the WPA had built 572,000 miles of country roads, 40,000 buildings, 67,000 miles of city streets, 78,000 bridges, 8,000 parks, and 350 airports, along with a variety of smaller projects.

In a striking departure from the usual pick and shovel relief program, the WPA also allowed unemployed artists, musicians, and writers to make use of their talents for public benefit. When asked if artists should be included, Roosevelt replied, "Why not? They are human beings. They have to live. I guess the only thing they can do is paint and surely there must be some public place where paintings are wanted." Indeed, scores of artists painted murals on post office walls. At its peak, the WPA employed some six thousand artists, musicians, actors, journalists, Ph.D.'s, poets, and novelists. The roster included many unknowns but also towering figures such as novelist John Steinbeck and poet

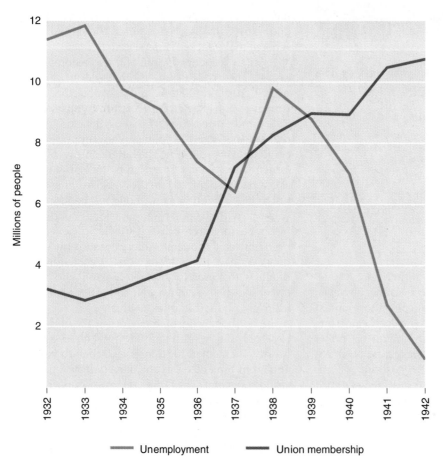

FIGURE 24.2
Unemployment and Union Membership, 1932–1942
The intersecting lines of this graph suggest a close relationship between prosperity, unemployment, and union membership. With New Deal support and economic recovery, unions gained strength until the number of unemployed dropped far below union membership in 1942. Only when the economy dipped during the recession of 1937–1938 did the trend reverse and unemployed workers again outnumber union members.

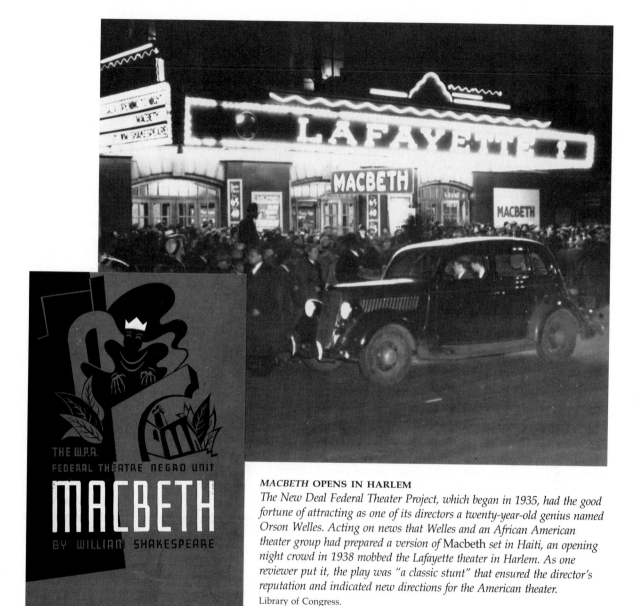

MACBETH OPENS IN HARLEM
The New Deal Federal Theater Project, which began in 1935, had the good fortune of attracting as one of its directors a twenty-year-old genius named Orson Welles. Acting on news that Welles and an African American theater group had prepared a version of Macbeth *set in Haiti, an opening night crowd in 1938 mobbed the Lafayette theater in Harlem. As one reviewer put it, the play was "a classic stunt" that ensured the director's reputation and indicated new directions for the American theater.*
Library of Congress.

Conrad Aiken. WPA Theater brought sixty million people into its performances. In the first fifteen months of the WPA Music Project, fifty million Americans heard concerts. The artist Robert Gwathmey recalled that the government imposed no restrictions: "You were a painter: Do your work. You were a sculptor: Do your work. You were a printmaker: Do your work. An artist could do anything he damn pleased." The entire cost of the WPA Arts Project was only $23 million, but the paintings, sculptures, and prints created continue to grace America's courthouses, public buildings, and museums.

Empowering Labor

Many workers desired more far-reaching change than that supported by the First New Deal or the old craft unions. In 1934, a series of local uprisings, mostly by unskilled workers who had no unions to join, set in motion a labor revolution. Striking workers in Toledo, Minneapolis, and San Francisco asserted their right to picket their employers. The pickets encountered ferocious opposition by police and the National Guard, who were deployed by state authorities sympathetic to employers to safeguard private property and to subdue strikers. Bloody battles erupted in the streets and on the docks. The uneasy stalemate that emerged roused militant labor leaders to seek new ways to break the dominance that industrial management had achieved over workers during the 1920s.

After the violence of 1934 subsided, the main focus of labor leaders settled on a bill to create federal supervision of labor disputes. The sponsor of the National Labor Relations Act (NLRA), Senator Robert Wagner of New York, was a veteran of progressive efforts to secure decent working conditions. Wagner's sympathy for working people reflected his own impoverished childhood after coming to the United States from Germany. The NLRA—justly termed a Magna Carta for labor—guaranteed workers the right to organize freely. It created a National Labor Relations Board to oversee elections for union representation. If the majority of workers voted for a union, the union became the sole bargaining agent for the entire workplace, and employers were required to negotiate with the duly elected union leaders. At first, Roosevelt was reluctant to see his NRA ideal of cooperative decision making replaced by adversarial collective bargaining. But he signed the Wagner Act into law in July 1935 as the best way available to protect the rights of workers and unions and attach them to the New Deal. At last, organized labor had a federal guarantee for collective bargaining and some legal protection against employers' power to fire labor organizers, suppress strikes, and stifle unions.

While the Wagner Act moved through Congress, unskilled workers who had been largely unrepresented within organized labor began to press for inclusion. Under the aggressive leadership of John L. Lewis, head of the United Mine Workers (UMW), and Sidney Hillman, head of the Amalgamated Clothing Workers, a coalition of unskilled workers gathered in 1935 to form the Committee for Industrial Organization (CIO; later the Congress of Industrial Organizations). The CIO struggled with the leadership of the American Federation of Labor (AFL) over who would take advantage of the New Deal's encouragement for union organization. After Lewis ended an argument on the main platform at the 1935 AFL convention in Atlantic City by dropping "Big Bill" Hutcheson of the Carpenters Union with a right cross to the jaw, the CIO went its own way. The following year, Lewis and Hillman broke with organized labor's apolitical tradition by forming the Non-Partisan League to support Roosevelt's reelection.

By mobilizing unskilled workers, who had always been scattered, the CIO greatly reduced the lordly power of industrialists and began to win significant concessions on wages and working conditions. Starting with a successful effort to organize rubber workers, the CIO began an embattled decade of triumph and disappointment. The CIO overcame fierce opposition to unionize the major steel and automobile companies. But fear and the habit of deference to authority were too great in textile manufacturing areas of the South to force unionization on that industry, despite the exploitation and misery that plagued its workers.

The achievements that flowed from the new militancy of labor and a sympathetic government were formidable. When Roosevelt took office in 1933, AFL membership stood at three million, down by half since the end of World War I. Cowed by business dominance, workers had shied away from the old unions. Work stoppages by demoralized union members actually decreased during the first years of the depression. Defeated workers tended to blame themselves for their plight. But after the Wagner Act took hold after 1935, unions expanded almost fivefold to fourteen million members by the time of Roosevelt's death in 1945. Thirty percent of the workforce was then unionized, the highest union representation ever reached.

Not only were more workers unionized, but different workers were unionized. Much of the union membership at the start of the 1930s, especially its leadership, was native-born, northern European in ancestry, and employed in the skilled trades. During the New Deal era, large numbers of unskilled assembly line workers, many of them African Americans or recently arrived immigrants, flocked to the unions.

CIO leaders admired the exceptional courage and organizing skill of Communists and other radicals, and they permitted committed leftists to help them take on the entrenched centers of resistance to unionism, the automobile and steel industries. The campaign by the United Auto Workers (UAW) to unionize workers at General Motors (GM) climaxed in January 1937 in a "sit-down" strike in the main assembly plant in Flint, Michigan. Workers simply sat down at their workstations, refusing either to work or to leave the premises. They were not completely inactive, however. When a police detachment charged the barricaded plant, strikers responded by throwing ball bearings at the fleeing lawmen in what the strikers jeeringly called the "battle of bulls run." The strikers reduced the plant's production of

15,000 cars a week to a mere 150. In desperation, General Motors gained court injunctions against the sit-down. But neither Roosevelt nor Michigan Governor Frank Murphy would act. Although they did not approve of the strikers' illegal occupation of the plant, they were unwilling to end the strike by force. Stymied, General Motors came to terms with the UAW. The agreement made the UAW the sole bargaining agent for all GM workers, prohibited the company from interfering with union activity, and arranged for contract negotiations to begin on February 15. Having beaten the automobile industry's leading producer, the UAW successfully organized throughout the auto industry, increasing its membership almost fourfold by the summer of 1937. In 1941, Henry Ford, who in 1937 had hired thugs to beat labor organizers, finally gave in and the UAW completed its campaign to unionize the entire automotive industry.

The CIO hoped to ride success in automobile plants to success in steel mills. But the steel industry managed to check the CIO short of full victory. A coalition of smaller steel firms, aided by the reaction of the courts and public opinion against the sit-down strike's infringement of property rights, impeded CIO efforts. In May 1937, a crowd of strikers gathered in a field outside Chicago to get ready for a march on Republic Steel, where they planned to set up a picket line. Without warning, police who had been sent there to keep order charged the crowd, firing their sidearms and wielding clubs, killing ten and injuring scores. The steelworkers halted their organizing campaign. They would finally succeed in 1941 when the war in Europe and the military buildup at home created a demand for steel and steelworkers.

In the same spirit of partnership, southern textile mills also received enough support from police and local officials to thwart an organizing drive. A steep recession in 1937 and 1938 threw thousands of textile workers out of work and further stalled the union campaign. The southern textile industry remained locked in uncertain battle until mobilization for war after 1940 revived the economy, gave laborers greater bargaining power, and brought unions into all major industries.

Despite setbacks, labor made enormous gains because of the Wagner Act. As Roosevelt hoped, labor remembered its benefactor and settled securely within Roosevelt's Democratic coalition. That attachment revealed itself most powerfully in the 1936 election.

Social Security and Tax Reform

Standing alongside the Wagner Act and the WPA as a major New Deal accomplishment in 1935 was the Social Security Act. Putting unemployed persons on relief was the most immediate priority of the New Deal, but taking care of hard-hit elderly people was a closely related goal. The population over the age of sixty-five doubled between 1870 and 1930 at the same time that work for the elderly declined. The tradition of self-reliance, boosted by the free enterprise spirit of the 1920s, inhibited government action to help poor, jobless older Americans. When the depression struck, only a third of the men and about 8 percent of the women over sixty-five had jobs. Of the tiny minority who worked, only 15 percent had pension plans. Insolvent corporations and banks often could not come up with funds during the depression to pay the meager pensions they had promised. Just eighteen states provided elderly assistance, which usually amounted to about a dollar a day for impoverished individuals.

These desperate circumstances lured millions to Dr. Townsend's pension scheme. Townsend's challenge, in turn, helped move Congress toward adopting a federal pension plan. Roosevelt became the first president to advocate protection for the elderly, describing it as "our plain duty to provide for that security upon which [the general] welfare depends." With the aggressive agitation of Townsend, Fr. Coughlin, and Huey Long rumbling ominously in the background, Roosevelt appointed Frances Perkins to chair a committee that readied the Social Security Act for his signature in August 1935.

The struggle for Social Security brought out class differences in their starkest form. Coming together in support of the measure was a coalition of advocate groups for the elderly and the poor, traditional progressives, leftists, social workers, labor unions, and educators. Arrayed against them were economic conservatives, including the Liberty League, the National Association of Manufacturers, the Chamber of Commerce, the American Medical Association, the conservative wing of the Republican Party, and assorted other defenders of wealth and privilege. Enact the Social Security system, these conservatives warned, and the government will gain a whip hand over private property, initiative will be destroyed, and proud individuals will be reduced to spineless loafers.

Obvious need and the large New Deal majority in Congress carried the day against the very well financed opposition. The strong objections to federal involvement in matters traditionally left to individual and local charity meant that Social Security had to strike a balance between federal, state, and personal responsibility. The Social Security program, therefore, required that pensions for the elderly be funded by tax contributions from workers and their employers. It also created unemployment insurance, paid for by employers' contributions. In a bow to traditional local responsibility for public assistance, Social Security also issued grants for the states to use to support dependent mothers and children, public health services, and the blind. A Supreme Court decision in 1937 upheld the right of Congress to require all citizens to pay for Social Security through their federal taxes and allowed the Social Security Act to be expanded to include benefits for dependent survivors of deceased recipients. Social Security raised the elderly out of the lowest economic status and established the principle that older Americans should be protected in their declining years from the crushing effects of poverty. As with the WPA and the Wagner Act, it helped secure the loyalty of the ordinary worker to the New Deal. At first, Social Security covered less than half of all workers, but over the years more and more workers were brought into the system.

The opposition to Social Security struck New Dealers as evidence that the rich and well-born had learned little from the depression. They apparently were still willing to clothe their opposition to federal insurance as a defense of a kind of individual opportunity that simply did not exist for most Americans. Roosevelt had long felt contempt for the moneyed elite, and he looked for a way to redistribute wealth that would, in a single stroke, weaken conservative opposition, advance the cause of social equity, and defuse populist challenges on the fringe. In June 1935, as the Social Security Act was being debated, Roosevelt delivered a message to Congress outlining comprehensive tax reform. He urged a graduated tax on corporations, a similar tax on holding company dividends used to shelter corporate income, an inheritance tax, and an increase in maximum personal income taxes from 63 to 79 percent. These measures aimed to pay for federal recovery and relief programs and balance the federal budget with a progressive tax that required those with the most money to pay the highest taxes.

Roosevelt promoted his plan by declaring that large fortunes put "great and undesirable concentration of control in [the hands of] relatively few individuals over the employment and welfare of

many, many others." He insisted that a more progressive tax structure would increase opportunity for the common people at the bottom of the economic ladder, "restrain the growth of unwholesome and sterile accumulations [of wealth], and . . . lay the burdens of Government where they can best be carried." Against charges that higher taxes on the rich would dampen their initiative, Roosevelt contended that the new measures would instead stimulate competition. If the idle rich were stripped of their unfair advantages of monopolies and inherited fortunes, there would be more opportunities for innovative enterprises and for the small businesses that employed so many Americans.

Roosevelt's tax package was more timid than Huey Long's "soak-the-rich" plan, and Congress was more timid still. But Congress endorsed Roosevelt's basic taxation principle by enacting a slightly progressive tax on undistributed corporate profits. From there, with the Revenue Act of 1937, Roosevelt moved to close loopholes that he considered outrageous. Threatening to name names of the wealthy who were not paying their fair share of taxes, Roosevelt persuaded Congress to eliminate a number of tax shelters, including such relics from the New Era as deductions for company yachts and country estates.

Broadening the New Deal Coalition

The largest groups that had been persistently excluded from economic and political benefits were women and African Americans. Their stories were strikingly parallel. Both received wages substantially lower than white men and owned only a tiny sliver of the nation's property. Though constitutionally entitled to vote since Reconstruction, most African Americans had been disfranchised by intimidation and legal subterfuge. Women, too, had the right to vote, which they won by 1920, but they were only starting to exercise their electoral power in numbers comparable to those of men. With relatively few voters in either group, women and African Americans had little influence within the political establishment and were largely unrepresented when the New Deal came into being. Although women and minorities had strong claims on the New Deal's commitments to assist those most in need, they had little political leverage to translate those commitments into action.

Eleanor Roosevelt was determined to use her position as First Lady to increase the political par-

ELEANOR ROOSEVELT MEETING WOMEN REPORTERS
Even though the editorial opinion of newspaper owners was about 80 percent opposed to the president and his wife, both Franklin and Eleanor Roosevelt had close rapport with the working press. Making the point that women had something important to contribute to public affairs and that the First Lady could be more than simply a White House hostess, Eleanor Roosevelt wrote a daily column, "My Day," and held regular news conferences to which only women reporters were admitted. She used the occasions to reinvigorate the commitment women had begun in the Progressive Era to education, equal rights, decent working conditions, and child welfare.
Stock Montage.

ticipation and influence of women and minorities. Her long-standing involvement in women's causes helped draw women into the New Deal and to mobilize them as a distinctive force for reform. In 1933, President Roosevelt allowed the Democratic National Committee to create a Women's Division to define women's issues and to screen candidates for administration positions. Molly Dewson, a former leader in the suffrage movement and the National Consumers League, became head of the Women's Division. Dewson created a talent pool of eighty thousand women from which the New Deal hired an unprecedented number for government positions.

Most remarkable was the entry of women into executive positions that had always been considered for men only. Frances Perkins became the first woman cabinet officer; Ruth Bryan Owen the first woman to hold an ambassadorial post as envoy to Denmark; Florence Allen the first woman judge on a district court of appeals; Nellie Tayloe Ross the first director of the Mint; and Marion Glass Banister the first assistant secretary of the treasury. Alongside these breakthroughs, women social workers and educators helped the New Deal to bring women into its programs of relief and welfare. Under the broad WPA umbrella, Ellen Woodward headed Women's and Professional Projects, Hallie Flanagan directed the Federal Theater Project, and Hilda Smith organized Workers' Education. Women also played key roles in the Division of Labor Standards, in the Children's Bureau, and in the administration of relief to the unemployed and destitute, both locally and in Washington.

These activities did not, however, result in equality between the sexes, either economically or politically. Attitudes that women should earn less and be subordinate in the public realm, if they chose to leave the home at all, were too pervasive. Indeed, the efforts women made within the New Deal were limited to improving particular social conditions; any service to the cause of equal opportunity and women's status was merely a by-product. In New Deal agencies, women devoted their energies to children, the infirm, the unemployed, and others who lacked the ability to take care of themselves. Nonetheless, the experience of women in community organization and the design of welfare legislation established a foundation of skill and influence that buttressed future efforts to attain equal rights.

Eleanor Roosevelt also helped link the causes of gender and racial discrimination through her identification with the underdog and her abhorrence of racism. One of her strongest allies among African American women was Mary McLeod Bethune, the founder of the Daytona Normal and Industrial Institute for Negro Women in Florida and a cofounder of the National Council on Negro Women in 1935. Her accomplishments brought Bethune to the attention of Eleanor Roosevelt and resulted in her appointment as the highest-ranking black official within the federal government, heading the office of minority affairs within the National Youth Administration. Like Molly Dewson and the women's network she created, Bethune used her New Deal post and the National Council to guide a core group of black professionals and civil rights activists to posts within the New Deal. This group, nicknamed the "Black Cabinet," was the first sizable African American presence within the federal government. Its members used their influence to inform the president of hardship and discrimination. Because of Eleanor Roosevelt, the Black Cabinet, and New Dealers, African Americans participated in some New Deal relief programs. By mid-decade, about one-quarter of all blacks received some sort of federal assistance.

The conditions with which the Black Cabinet grappled were bleak in the extreme. At the outset of the New Deal, about half of urban blacks were out of work, twice the unemployment rate among whites. The rural black majority had slim prospects of making a living or even retaining their place on the land, whether as owners or tenants. The racial atmosphere at mid-decade was ominous. During

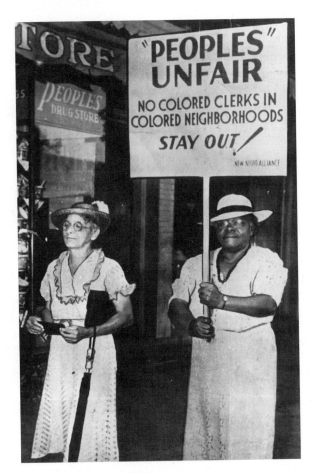

MARY MCLEOD BETHUNE
At the urging of Eleanor Roosevelt, Mary McLeod Bethune, a southern educational and civil rights leader, became director of the National Youth Administration's Division of Negro Affairs. The first black woman to head a federal agency, Bethune used her federal position to promote social change. Here Bethune takes her mission to the streets to protest the Peoples Drug Store chain's discriminatory hiring practices within the nation's capital.
Moorland Spingarn Research Center, Howard University.

the depression, lynching increased after years of decline. In Alabama, the "Scottsboro Boys" faced the death penalty for a rape they did not commit, and black radical Angelo Herndon toiled as a prisoner on a Georgia chain gang for trying to organize black workers. In 1935, a riot in Harlem, where the artistic Renaissance had once flourished, dramatized blacks' despair.

The New Deal response, despite sympathy for the plight of minorities, was cautious. Roosevelt believed that in order to enact ambitious New Deal reforms, he was obliged to appease conservative, segregationist, southern Democratic members of Congress. Reflecting these political pressures, landmark New Deal achievements—the NRA, WPA, and AAA—failed in large measure to serve African Americans. Because the NRA refused to require manufacturers to eliminate racial discrimination, the agency's initials were derided as "Negro Run Around" or "Negroes Ruined Again." Work gained through the WPA was also prejudicial. Only eleven of more than ten thousand WPA supervisors in the South were black. The AAA harmed blacks by rewarding white landowners for evicting their black tenants to get crop reduction bonuses for themselves.

Stymied administratively and legislatively, New Dealers turned to coalition building as a long-range way of overcoming entrenched opposition to improving the lot of blacks. Off the record, Roosevelt spoke of a time when politics would be realigned into opposing conservative and progressive parties, with the Republicans and southern Democrats making up the former and the New Deal coalition the latter. Blacks played a key role in Roosevelt's conception. At the time of Roosevelt's first presidential campaign, black journalist Robert Vann had called on African Americans to "turn Lincoln's picture to the wall. That debt has been paid in full." In 1934, the first significant electoral evidence surfaced that black voters were shifting from the Republican to the Democratic Party. Those who could cast ballots voted their hopes and helped elect New Deal Democrats in numerous congressional and gubernatorial races.

The new leverage of black voters lent weight to the efforts of Eleanor Roosevelt and the Black Cabinet for greater racial equity. During Roosevelt's first two terms, the numbers of blacks in federal service tripled, and white officials showed unprecedented willingness to hear what black leaders had to say. The frequent interviews Mary McLeod Bethune and Walter White, head of the National Association for the Advancement of Colored People (NAACP), held with the president, along with Eleanor Roosevelt's many visits to black institutions, led to an identification of black reform aims with the New Deal. The symbolic climax occurred in 1939 when the great black contralto Marian Anderson was refused permission by the Daughters of the American Revolution (DAR) to sing in the organization's Constitution Hall in Washington. Eleanor Roosevelt promptly resigned her membership in the DAR, and Interior Secretary Harold Ickes, himself a former president of an NAACP chapter in Chicago, arranged to have Anderson per-

form on the steps of the Lincoln Memorial. Anderson sang from the steps of the monument to an integrated throng of 75,000 in an electrifying demonstration of the tie between black aspirations and the spirit of the New Deal.

Concrete accomplishments were another matter, however. In 1940, the end of Roosevelt's second term, blacks still suffered severe handicaps. Most of the thirteen million black workers toiled at low-paying menial jobs. Infant mortality was half again as great as for whites, and life expectancy twelve years shorter. Segregation in the South was unmoved by the New Deal. Nor was the equal part of "separate but equal" much advanced. Black schools had less money and worse facilities than those of whites, and only 1 percent of black students earned college degrees. In southern states, where most blacks lived, there were no black police officers or judges and hardly any lawyers. Lynching of blacks went unpunished. By mid-decade, little had happened to refute the grim witticism that, for African Americans, America was "the land of the tree and the home of the grave."

Hispanic Americans and Asian Americans had even fewer voters than women and blacks and consequently less political clout. Without significant numbers and organizational strength, neither could lobby effectively with the New Deal coalition builders in Washington. Mexican Americans, already at the economic margins of American life, suffered greatly from the depression's effect on agriculture. Engaged throughout the West as farm laborers, they saw their wages in California's fields plummet to not much more than a dime an hour. Part of the explanation was new competition from other victims of the depression. When persistent drought raised huge dust storms and turned large areas of the plains into a "dust bowl," hundreds of thousands of ruined farmers—called "Okies" and "Arkies" because most of them came from Oklahoma and Arkansas—moved westward and competed with Mexican Americans for scarce agricultural work. In addition, local administration of many New Deal programs meant that the treatment of minorities rested in the hands of established leadership. In the West, when Hispanics and Indians were permitted to join government work projects, they often received lower pay than white Americans received. Relief programs also reflected local prejudice, with minorities receiving less aid.

Asian Americans fared no better than Mexican Americans. Asian immigrants to the United States were still excluded from citizenship, and in many

HISPANIC-AMERICAN ALLIANCE BANNER
Between 1910 and 1940, when refugees from the Mexican revolution poured across the American border, the Hispanic-American Alliance and other such organizations sought to protect Mexican American rights against nativist fears and hostility. In the years between the world wars, many alliance banners such as this one flew in opposition to the deportation of Mexican aliens, an attempt in 1926 to bar Mexican Americans from city jobs in Los Angeles, and the disproportionately high use of the death penalty against Mexicans convicted of crimes. Throughout these and other trials, the alliance steadfastly emphasized the desire of Mexican Americans to receive permanent status in the United States.
The Oakland Museum.

states they were not permitted to own land. But by 1930, more than half of the Japanese American population had been born in the United States. Still, no Japanese American was immune from discrimination, which the depression only reinforced. Even college-educated Japanese Americans worked at family shops, hotels, and fruit stands. As one frustrated young man said: "I am a fruitstand worker. I would much rather it were doctor or lawyer . . . but my aspirations of developing into such [were] frustrated

long ago by circumstances [and] I am only what I am, a professional carrot washer." Chinese Americans tended to remain in Chinatown sections of cities, where they labored in laundries and restaurants. The nation had always been a hard place for Asian Americans, and the depression offered no relief.

Native Americans, however, experienced a major change in their circumstances, especially in their relationship with the federal government. Ever since the Dawes Act of 1887, the government had tried to solve the "Indian problem" by encouraging assimilation, that is, an end to a separate Indian identity. Because of the remarkable commitment of John Collier, commissioner of Indian affairs, Congress adopted the Indian Reorganization Act of 1934, which ended the government's assault on the tribal structure that had undergirded Indian culture. The act restored to Native Americans the right to own land communally, a right they had lost in 1887. The change brought little immediate benefit, however. Indians remained the poorest of Americans. But it did provide a foundation for economic and cultural resurgence a generation later.

Throughout Roosevelt's first term, socialists and Communists had denounced the slow pace of change and charged the New Deal with failing to serve the interests of "the people"—the workers and farmers who produced the nation's wealth but kept only a meager portion of it. But in 1935, as the Second Hundred Days reached flood tide, the left made a surprising switch. The Soviet Union, which was worried about the threat of fascism in Europe, instructed Communists throughout the world to cease their attacks on moderates and to join hands in a "Popular Front" against fascism. Thus, even though one radical critic declared that Roosevelt reform was "about as exciting as near beer," most of those on the left joined the New Deal coalition.

In the summer of 1935, therefore, Roosevelt announced a new direction for the New Deal. He gave up trying to build a total coalition of all interests and instead focused on the growing antibusiness feeling among the public. The WPA had reached out to the unemployed, the Wagner Act to labor, and the Social Security Act to all working people; and his administration grew more sensitive to women and blacks. All bulwarks against radical challengers to the New Deal, these overtures established foundations for federal welfare policies for the next six decades. But Roosevelt's opponents never made peace with the New Deal's welfare state. It was clear that most of big business would remain stubbornly opposed to most New Deal programs. Roosevelt saw the situation as a struggle between a Hamiltonian faction of wealth and privilege and the heirs of Jeffersonians like himself who favored shared wealth and equal opportunity. The people would express their views in the presidential election of 1936.

The New Deal's Final Phase: From Victory to Deadlock

Neither the First nor the Second New Deal cured the depression. Economic recovery remained agonizingly slow. The tardy return to prosperity left the future of reform very much in doubt at the end of Roosevelt's first term in 1936. The Second New Deal's move to the left, however, had blunted the attack from that direction. Long was dead, and Townsend's and Coughlin's power was waning. Most radicals felt compelled to support the New Deal's welfare and labor reforms, even though the reforms stopped well short of revolutionary change. But forces on the right, especially conservative Republicans and southern Democrats, grew more unified and more powerful. Roosevelt's frustration led him into an ill-advised attack on the Supreme Court in an effort to defend and extend his programs. But even without judicial obstacles, reform was running out of steam. With one last flurry of legislation, the New Deal ended.

The Election of 1936

Roosevelt believed that the presidential election of 1936 would be a test of his leadership and New Deal policy. Republicans welcomed a national referendum and had reason to be hopeful. Public opinion

JOHN COLLIER MEETS WITH NAVAJO REPRESENTATIVES *Commissioner of Indian Affairs John Collier receives a Navajo delegation protesting restrictions set down by the Indian Reorganization Act of 1934. The Navajos display a blanket made from the wool of their own sheep to protest a limit set on the number of sheep they could raise. Collier had crafted the Act to revive Native American society by granting tribes an independent land base and many self-governing powers. However, his attempt to make the reservations economically viable through land conservation measures, including restrictions on grass-devouring sheep, roused resistance on the part of Indians who chose traditional ways of using resources. The tension between federal benevolence and Indian views of their own way of life has remained a painful issue.* Wide World Photos, Inc.

G.O.P. CONVENTION, CLEVELAND
This illustration of the 1936 Republican convention for an article in the progressive journal
Common Sense *displays artist Thomas Hart Benton's gift for energetic satire. Benton's aged*
and grotesque conventiongoers underscore the article's contention that the Republican old guard
is preparing "to join the Tyrannosaurus, the Pterodactyl and the Three-toed Horse." Unexpected
circumstances prevented Benton's illustration from being used, however, and the GOP survived
the article's prediction that "the Republican elephant [would become] as extinct as the dinosaurs,"
though the term "dinosaur" remained an epithet to be hurled at conservatives.

Thomas Hart Benton, American, 1889-1973. G.O.P. Convention, Cleveland, 1936. Black crayon, pen and black ink,
and black wash, over graphics, 37.4 x 53.4 cm. © The Cleveland Museum of Art, 1996. Leonard C. Hanna, Jr.,
1995. 70.

polls showed that Roosevelt's popularity had dipped. Between 8.5 million and 12.5 million workers were still unemployed, depending on which source one believed, and most farmers remained poor. The business community raged at any attempts to raise its taxes for fresh initiatives to cure the problems. A telephone poll by the magazine *Literary Digest*, which had always been very accurate, predicted that the Republican candidate would win handily. Republican Party leaders believed that the American people were poised to vote against power-mad politicians and bureaucrats in Washington who were undermining the traditional values that had made the country strong.

In their nostalgic appeal to the good old days, the Republicans turned to the Kansas heartland to select Governor Alfred Landon as their nominee for president. Henry Ford, in what he intended to be a compliment, dubbed Landon the "Kansas Coolidge." But Landon was a far cry from Coolidge. As governor, he had supported New Deal measures for conservation and farm relief. An independent oil producer, he endorsed Interior Secretary Ickes's efforts to better regulate the oil industry. He promised labor and independent unions a fair deal. He sought to keep blacks in their original party by speaking out strongly against racial prejudice. But Landon was not a Republican Roosevelt either. In traditional Republican language, he proposed to replace wasteful government spending with a balanced budget and businesslike efficiency and to ease the perils of illness and old age with old-fashioned neighborliness instead of Social Security.

Roosevelt put his faith in the growing coalition of New Deal supporters. He believed that they shared his conviction that the New Deal was the nation's liberator from a long period of privilege and wealth for a few and "economic slavery" for the rest. At the end of the campaign, Roosevelt struck a defiant pose before a thunderous crowd at Madison Square Garden. Assailing his "old enemies —monopoly, speculation, reckless banking, class antagonism"—he proclaimed, "Never before in all our history have these forces been so united against one candidate as they stand today. They are unanimous in their hate for me—and I welcome their hatred." When the crowd's roar subsided, Roosevelt concluded:

> I should like to have it said of my first Administration that in it the forces of selfishness and of lust for power met their match. I should like to have it said of my second Administration that in it these forces met their master.

Roosevelt did not let such intensity rob him of his light touch. Toward Alf Landon he took a relaxed, amused attitude, characterizing his opponent as a misguided throwback who fronted for sinister interests. He pointed out that while Landon and his supporters denounced the New Deal, Kansas drew 70 percent of its relief funds from New Deal programs. He cast doubt on Landon's status as a foe of big government by disclosing that, as governor, Landon had requested a federal grant of $35 million for a state-owned natural gas pipeline. Republican hypocrisy was accurately reflected, Roosevelt said, in the Kansas state flower that Landon had adopted as his symbol: The sunflower is yellow, has a black heart, is good only for parrot food, and dies before November.

Roosevelt triumphed in spectacular fashion. He received eleven million *more* votes than Landon. His 60.8 percent majority was the widest ever in a pres-

idential race and won him every state except the Republican strongholds of Maine and Vermont. Third parties on the right as well as the left—the Union of Social Justice Party, the Socialists, the Communists—attracted few supporters. Congressional results were equally lopsided, with Democrats outnumbering Republicans by more than three to one

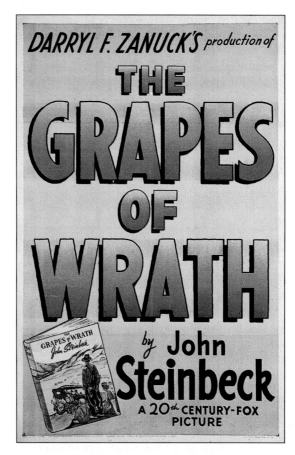

THE GRAPES OF WRATH
Movies had their greatest popularity in the depression when they offered momentary escape from the hard times outside. Through most of the 1930s, musicals like Top Hat, *with elegant dancers Fred Astaire and Ginger Rogers, set the pace, with comedies and costume dramas not far behind. By the end of the decade, however, years of labor strife, farm distress, and reform agitation had also created an audience for social problem films.* The Grapes of Wrath, *adapted in 1940 from John Steinbeck's novel of the flight of impoverished farmers from the midwestern Dust Bowl to California, made one of the most successful cinematic appeals to Americans' sympathy for the underdog and belief in social justice.*
The Oakland Museum.

in both houses. And in the states, Democrats won twenty-six of thirty-three gubernatorial races, including Landon's Kansas.

Roosevelt's triumph emerged from the New Deal's distinctive political coalition. Many Americans who had been alienated from politics during the 1920s rallied around Roosevelt's standard. Only about 45 percent of eligible voters actually voted in national elections during the 1920s; in 1936, in contrast, 57 percent of eligible voters turned out. New voters—women, blacks, young people, and especially laborers and ethnic minorities—boosted Roosevelt's margin of victory. Northern blacks gave Roosevelt 76 percent of their votes and provided the margins needed to swing the key states of Illinois, Michigan, and New Jersey away from the Republicans. In the nineteen northern cities where more than half the population was composed of first- and second-generation immigrants, the Democratic vote increased by 205 percent, Republican votes by only 29 percent. Roosevelt also managed to retain the support of every traditionally Democratic southern state, delaying Hoover's dream of bringing the South into the Republican Party.

Emphasizing his mandate from the voters, Roosevelt made it plain that he would try to ensure a decent standard of living for all citizens. In response to news that sixty million people had an income of less than $1,000 per year, he declared in his inaugural address: "In this nation I see tens of millions of its citizens—a substantial part of its whole population—who at this very moment are denied the greater part of what the very lowest standards of today call the necessities of life. . . . I see one third of a nation ill-housed, ill-clad, ill-nourished." With the voters' support, Roosevelt committed himself to do all that he could to help these disadvantaged citizens.

Court Packing

In the afterglow of his electoral triumph, Roosevelt went on a cruise to ponder how to remove the remaining obstacles to New Deal reforms. He returned intent on targeting the Supreme Court. Ladened with conservatives left over from the discredited Republican era, the Court had invalidated eleven New Deal measures as unwarranted interference with free enterprise; in more than 140 years before 1932, the Court had nullified only sixty laws. In Roosevelt's view, the Court's recent decisions had cast doubt "upon the ability of the Congress ever at any time to protect the Nation against catastrophe

by squarely meeting modern social and economic maladjustment." At that moment, Social Security, the Wagner Act, the Securities and Exchange Commission, and other New Deal innovations were moving toward an ominous rendezvous with the Court. Roosevelt concluded that he must do something to make sure the Court's "horse and buggy" notions did not nullify the popular will and demolish the New Deal.

A nationwide opinion poll showed that more than two-thirds of Americans believed that the Supreme Court should be free from political interference. Nevertheless, in 1937 Roosevelt moved toward a showdown with the Court and "judicial tyranny." He sent a bill to Congress proposing that one new justice be added to the Court for each existing judge who had already served for ten years and was over the age of seventy. It would give the president the power to overwhelm the elderly, conservative Republican justices by naming up to six New Dealers to the bench.

A nationwide opinion poll showed that more than two-thirds of Americans believed that the Supreme Court should be free from politician interference.

But the president had not reckoned with Americans' deeply rooted deference to the independent authority of the Supreme Court. Even Roosevelt's supporters were disturbed by the "court-packing" scheme. The implication that individuals over seventy had diminished mental capacity affronted many members of Congress who were past that age. Roosevelt's proposal also aroused the ire of the oldest Supreme Court justice, Louis Brandeis, the astute mentor of several able New Dealers and the Court's most liberal justice. Roosevelt deviously insisted that the bill was intended to improve the efficiency of an "overworked" Court, although it was plain to everyone that the real purpose was to make room for supporters of New Deal initiatives.

A storm of public protest, egged on by conservatives delighted that they had finally found a popular cause to use against the New Deal, sank the Court bill. Business spokesmen waxed indignant because Roosevelt's plan blatantly violated constitutional ideals and cleared the way, as the journalist Walter Lippmann claimed, "to establish the political framework for, and to destroy the safeguards against, a dictator."

Although the Court reform plan failed, it apparently sent a message to the Supreme Court justices. After the furor abated, Chief Justice Charles Evans Hughes and fellow moderate Owen Roberts reversed their views on certain New Deal cases. Their votes kept the Court from invalidating the Wagner Act and Social Security, inspiring a wit to point out that "a switch in time saves nine." Soon afterward, the most resistant of the elderly justices —the "four horsemen of reaction," as New Dealer and future Supreme Court Justice Felix Frankfurter called them—began to retire. After appointing no one to the Supreme Court during his first term, Roosevelt went on to name eight justices—more than any other president. His choice of liberals to fill the vacancies on the Court ultimately ensured safe passage of New Deal laws through the shoals of judicial review. But Roosevelt's error in proposing his court-packing scheme also did powerful damage to his administration. He had handed conservatives a popular issue to use against the New Deal.

Reaction and Recession

The court-packing fiasco stirred Republicans and southern Democrats to rally around their common conservatism and to jointly obstruct additional reform. Other factors also began to work against the extension of the New Deal. The progress made in reviving the economy and alleviating hardship tended to reduce the enthusiasm of many people for new efforts. Arguments over how to proceed and how far to go weakened the consensus among reformers and, as the Court fight showed, sparked antagonisms between Congress and the White House. The rise of belligerent regimes in Germany, Italy, Japan, and elsewhere in the 1930s also slowed reform; some Americans began to demand that the nation concentrate on defending what it had rather than striving for change. In a surprisingly short time, these impediments mounted and Roosevelt's 1936 landslide began to seem like a mirage.

No action by New Deal opponents was more damaging than the administration's self-inflicted wounds. Soon after his second term began, Roosevelt accepted the view that the steady, though incomplete, economic recovery since 1933 had largely eliminated the depression crisis. He was persuaded that additional deficit spending designed to pump up the economy was no longer necessary. He also worried that inflation would reduce the value of savings and new investments the New Deal had so earnestly tried to build up. Accordingly, Roosevelt moved cautiously toward a balanced budget by cutting funds for relief projects. At his urging, the Federal Reserve raised interest rates to discourage borrowing on easy terms for unwise speculation. *Time* magazine soothingly reported that in recent weeks, with the "Depression lapsing into memory, the portents of Boom drummed excitingly throughout the land."

Roosevelt's fiscal retrenchment soon backfired. Rather than preventing inflation, the reduction in deficit spending cooled down the economy too much. Roosevelt's anxiety about inflation had failed to take into full consideration how far the economy had to go before it would reach inflationary levels. Even at the high-water mark of recovery in the summer of 1937, unemployment remained at about 14 percent of the workforce, some seven million people in all. In the next few months, national income and production slipped backward so steeply that almost two-thirds of the economic gains since 1933 were lost by June 1938. The stock market followed suit with a sharper decline between August 1937 and May 1938 than in the Great Crash. Farm prices dropped 20 percent, and unemployment rose by more than two million.

This economic downturn hurt the New Deal politically. Conservatives argued that the recession proved that New Deal measures were fundamentally wrong and had produced only an illusion of progress. They maintained that the New Deal's progressive tax policy helped cause the recession by funneling money away from productive investment. Herbert Hoover had been right after all, they claimed. The way to weather the recession was to spend less, save more, and wait for the laws of the free enterprise system to restore prosperity.

Many New Dealers believed instead that the recession showed there was no going back to the orthodoxies of free enterprise. They insisted that the crash and the Great Depression had demonstrated the shortcomings of an unregulated economy. They demanded that the administration revive federal spending and redouble efforts to stimulate the economy. In 1938, Congress heeded Roosevelt's plea to enact a massive new program of spending to revitalize the economy.

The New Deal's methods received support from new economic ideas advanced by the brilliant British economist John Maynard Keynes. Keynes played a prominent role in shaping British economic policy, and he capped his career in 1936 with the publication of the most influential work on economics in the twentieth century, *The General Theory of Employment, Interest, and Money*. Keynes made a sophisticated, theoretical argument in favor of practices that New Deal relief agencies had developed in an ad hoc, commonsense way. A nation's economy, Keynes declared, could not automatically reach its full potential in the complex, interdependent modern world. The depression had painfully illustrated that economic activity could become stalled at a level far short of a society's true potential. When that happened, only government intervention could pump enough money into the system to revive production, boost consumption, and restore prosperity. In bad times, Keynes contended, government should provide paid jobs for unemployed workers in order to spread purchasing power throughout the economy. In good times, government should restrict the supply of money to prevent the economy from producing more goods and services than consumers can absorb.

Roosevelt never had the inclination or the time to follow his economic advisers into the thicket of Keynesian theory. But the recession scare of 1938 taught him the Keynesian lesson that economic growth had to be carefully nurtured. To clear the way for renewed government intervention in the economy, Roosevelt reemphasized the greed and irresponsibility of "economic royalists." In April 1938, as the economy reeled and conservatives gloated over the defeat of the Court bill, Roosevelt sent a message to Congress asking for "a thorough study of the concentration of economic power in American industry." The result was a congressional study that led to the establishment of the Temporary National Economic Committee (TNEC) in June 1938.

Debates within TNEC over economic reform revived the old argument that had divided progressives since the beginning of the century. As TNEC uncovered plentiful evidence of ruthless and corrupt business practices, some New Dealers argued in the spirit of Theodore Roosevelt for increased government planning to make the economy more rational and efficient. Another group echoed Wilsonian Democrats and urged the government to break up monopolies that restricted competition, reduced efficiency, and hindered the growth of new enterprises so vital for economic recovery. But an antimonopoly campaign lacked political support. Efforts to revive central planning also sputtered.

The Keynesian message, however, had great impact on New Deal policy. The notion of an active federal government freed from rigid economics and willing to engage in large-scale spending to alleviate distress appealed to the Roosevelt administration. Harry Hopkins's economics had always consisted largely of a desire to "feed the hungry, and Goddamn fast."

The Last of the New Deal Reforms

From the moment he entered office, Roosevelt had tinkered with the small and antiquated office of the presidency. He believed that the powers of the presidency were inadequate, especially during emergencies such as the depression. He also wanted more power over the federal bureaucracy. Arguing the need for "efficiency," Roosevelt submitted an ambitious plan of executive reorganization to Congress in 1937. The bill failed, but in September 1939, Congress passed the Administrative Reorganization Act, which gave Roosevelt part of what he desired and strengthened the office of the president. With a Democratic majority in Congress, a now friendly Supreme Court, the Keynesian fruits of the TNEC, and the revival of deficit spending, the newly empowered White House seemed to be in a strong position to move ahead with a third New Deal.

Resistance was also on the rise, however. Conservatives argued that the New Deal had pressed its centralization too far and was bent on creating what later came to be known as "the imperial presidency." Even the New Deal's friends became weary with one emergency program after another, especially while economic recession still shadowed New Deal achievements. By the midpoint of Roosevelt's second term, restive members of Congress balked at new initiatives. Clearly, the New Deal was winding down, but enough energy remained for one last burst of reform.

Desperate need among poor people in rural America still claimed federal attention. In 1937, the Agriculture Department created the Farm Security Administration (FSA) to provide housing and loans that would help tenant farmers become owners and give them the best possible chance to prosper. But the FSA was starved for funds and ran up against the major farm organizations, which were intent on serving the interests of the large farms. With only minor successes to show, the FSA petered out.

The New Deal completed its efforts to raise the farm sector to a secure plateau of prosperity with

NEW DEAL HOUSING GOALS

The eradication of slum housing (above) such as this in Atlanta in 1936 came to be a prime test of overcoming the depression. In his inaugural address for his second term, Roosevelt focused on the need to rescue the one-third of the nation still "ill-housed, ill clad, and ill-nourished." The most famous attempt to point the way was the greenbelt town program run by the Resettlement Administration of the Department of Agriculture to relocate people forced off the farms. The picture of Greendale, Wisconsin, (below) taken in 1939, offers an idea of the uniform utopia the Roosevelt administration favored but was prevented from continuing by the shifting of resources to fight World War II.
Library of Congress.

TECHNOLOGY IN AMERICA
Mechanized Cotton Picking

Here in 1935 two of the most important farm machines of the time, the Farmall tractor and the Rust cotton picker, cut through a sea of cotton, showing how mechanization could eliminate the backbreaking work of harvesting cotton by hand. Within ten years tractors would displace horses as the main means of doing heavy farm work, but success for mechanical cotton pickers was longer in coming. For a century and a half after the invention of the cotton gin in 1793 made cotton farming feasible, inventors tried to create a device that would make picking cotton as efficient as ginning it. The first patent for a crude mechanical picker was granted in 1850 and nearly 2,000 more followed before John Rust in 1931 demonstrated a machine that could pick more bales of cotton in a day than the average farmer in the deep South grew in a year.

Ironically, though Southerners had at last realized their dream of mechanizing cotton picking, the machine was so efficient that it was ill-suited to most southern cotton farms, whose yearly crop was relatively modest. Nor could most cotton growers afford the new machinery. In the midst of the Great Depression, when Rust demonstrated his invention in 1931, cotton prices had plunged from 35 cents a bale in 1919 to only 6 cents a bale.

In the next two decades, large farms using the new mechanical cotton picker became dominant and

that change shifted most cotton growing to the West, where vast agricultural holdings were the rule. Displaced by the decline of King Cotton in the South, field hands like the woman shown above migrated in thousands to the North in search of jobs.

Cotton picking machine: Mississippi State University Libraries; Cotton picker: Courtesy of the Harvard University Art Museums. Gift of Bernarda B. Shahn, Estate of Ben Shahn.

the Agricultural Adjustment Act (AAA) of February 1938. Secretary of Agriculture Henry Wallace centered the new act around the ancient Chinese tradition of an "ever normal granary." The plan combined production quotas on five staple crops—cotton, tobacco, wheat, corn, and rice—with storage loans through its Commodity Credit Corporation to moderate price swings by making sure that supply was at an "ever normal" level, sufficient to satisfy the market and prevent hunger. A grateful Iowa farmer remembered, "Henry Wallace and his ever-normal granary was the man who saved the farmer. The farmer would have passed clear out of the picture." The measure benefited well-endowed farmers but added an element of charity by providing surplus food for the poor through the act's Federal Surplus Commodities Corporation. Begun on a modest scale, the food stamp plan introduced a basic welfare role for agriculture in aiding the third of the nation that Roosevelt identified as ill fed. The AAA of 1938 brought stability to American agriculture for the next several years.

Advocates for the urban underclass also had modest luck gaining attention after decades of neglect. New York Senator Robert Wagner used a massive statistical study of suffering to convince Congress to pass the National Housing Act in September 1937. By 1941, some 160,000 residences had been made available at rates affordable for those below the poverty line. The project did not come close to meeting the need for affordable housing; but for the first time, the federal government took an active role in trying to replace the squalor of American cities with housing that met standards of decency and answered Roosevelt's inaugural pledge to aid the ill housed.

The last major piece of New Deal labor legislation, the Fair Labor Standards Act of June 1938, reiterated the original New Deal pledge to provide workers with a decent standard of living. After unprecedented haggling and compromise that revealed the waning strength of the New Deal, Congress finally agreed to intervene in the long sacrosanct free enterprise realm of contracts between employers and workers. The act set minimum-wage and maximum-hours standards and curbed the use of child labor. The minimum-wage level was modest —twenty-five cents an hour for a maximum of forty-four hours a week. And the act exempted merchant seamen, fishermen, domestic help, and farm laborers from these wage and hours standards in order to attract enough conservative votes to pass

the act. Nevertheless, the passage of minimum-wage and maximum-hours standards was an important step toward realization of the New Deal promise to work actively to eliminate poverty.

The final New Deal reform effort failed to make much headway against the hidebound system of racial segregation. Although Roosevelt was willing to denounce lynching as murder, he would not jeopardize his vital base of political support in the South by designating antilynching bills as "must" legislation. In 1934 and 1935, Congress voted down attempts to make lynching a federal crime, and in 1938 the last antilynching bill of the decade died in a Senate filibuster. Laws to eliminate the poll tax—used to deny blacks the opportunity to vote—encountered the same overwhelming resistance. African Americans received some meager benefit from employment opportunities in northern relief projects and federal agencies, but the New Deal refused even to confront the injustice of racial segregation.

The last major piece of New Deal labor legislation, the Fair Labor Standards Act of June 1938, set minimum-wage and maximum-hours standards and curbed the use of child labor.

By the end of 1938, the New Deal had run out of fresh ideas and into stiff opposition. As legislative initiative waned and programs played themselves out, the conservative tide rose. In the congressional elections of 1938, Republicans picked up seven seats in the Senate and eighty in the House, making them a power for the first time since 1932. New Dealers could claim unprecedented and resounding achievement since 1933 when Roosevelt entered the White House, but ten million unemployed five years later, about two-thirds as many as in 1932 under Hoover, were powerful reminders that the depression had not been whipped. In his annual message to Congress in January 1939, however, Roosevelt called a halt to the great reform movement of the Second New Deal. He spoke of preserving the reforms already achieved, not of extending them. The major theme of his address, in fact, was not domestic affairs at all. It was the enormity of the totalitarian threat overseas to international peace and American happiness.

Conclusion: A New Departure

"This election," Herbert Hoover announced in 1932, "is not a mere shift from the ins to the outs. It means deciding the direction our nation will take over a century to come." Franklin Roosevelt's election, he warned, would result in "a radical departure from the foundations of 150 years which have made this the greatest nation in the world." Hoover was right that Roosevelt's election would mean a significant departure, but like many conservatives, he misjudged his successor's radicalism.

Franklin Delano Roosevelt took the helm of a nation near collapse, starvation, and revolution. He confronted the unprecedented crisis head on, confident that vigorous government action could overcome the depression and its devastating human consequences. Roosevelt's constant improvisation, alleviation of suffering, and warmhearted sympathy restored hope and faith. The people agreed with the president that society should help those in need and that the federal government was an appropriate vehicle to deliver aid. In the process of fighting the blight of the depression, the Roosevelt administration vastly expanded the size and power of the federal government and changed the way the American people looked upon Washington. It won major successes such as Social Security, labor's right to organize, and measures to ensure that people could hold on to their savings, homes, and farms. The federal government assumed new responsibilities for the nation's economy and the people's welfare.

To Hoover and many of his contemporaries, Roosevelt appeared to be a dangerous radical who threatened the foundations of democracy and capitalism. But as Frances Perkins said, Franklin Roosevelt took capitalism as much for granted as he did his family. Rather than attack capitalism, he boldly sought to save it. The daring innovation and persistent experimentation took place within ideological boundaries that precluded radical and revolutionary transformation. Like his cousin Teddy, Franklin Roosevelt understood that things would have to change in order to remain the same. He left America greatly changed, but America also remained profoundly the same.

CHRONOLOGY

1932	The Bonus Army marches on Washington.
1933	Franklin D. Roosevelt assumes presidency.
	Roosevelt closes nation's banks for four-day "holiday" to allow time to stabilize the banking system.
	March–June. New Deal established through passage of reform legislation of the Hundred Days.
	The Civil Works Administration (CWA) begun under Harry Hopkins to provide relief for unemployed.
1934	Securities and Exchange Commission formed to license and regulate stock exchanges.
	Upton Sinclair loses bid to become governor of California and enact his EPIC work relief program.
	Wealthy conservatives of American Liberty League oppose New Deal.
	"Radio Priest" Father Charles Coughlin begins National Union for Social Justice.
	Dr. Francis Townsend devises Old Age Revolving Pension scheme to provide money to the impoverished elderly.
	Congress adopts Indian Reorganization Act.
1935	Louisiana Senator Huey Long assassinated.

As part of Second New Deal, legislation creates Works Progress Administration (WPA).

The Committee for Industrial Organization (CIO) founded to provide union representation for unskilled workers.

Congress passes Wagner Act to guarantee workers the right to organize unions and bargain collectively.

1936 John Maynard Keynes publishes *The General Theory of Employment, Interest, and Money*, providing theoretical justification for government deficit financing.

Franklin Roosevelt reelected by landslide over Republican Alfred Landon.

1937 CIO stages successful sit-down strike at the General Motors plant in Flint, Michigan.

Roosevelt's "court-packing" legislation defeated in Senate.

1937–1938 Economic recession slows recovery from depression.

1938 Second Agricultural Adjustment Act and Fair Labor Standards Act bring New Deal legislation to an end.

Congress fails to pass administration's antilynching bill.

1939 Administrative Reorganization Act enlarges scope and power of presidency.

African American contralto Marian Anderson gives concert at Lincoln Memorial.

BIBLIOGRAPHY

GENERAL WORKS

Anthony Badger, *The New Deal: The Depression Years, 1933–1940* (1989).

Alan Brinkley, *The End of Reform: New Deal Liberalism in Recession and War* (1995).

Paul Conkin, *The New Deal* (1967).

Kenneth S. Davis, *FDR*, 3 vols. (1972; reprint, 1985, 1986).

Steve Fraser and Gary Gerstle, eds., *The Rise and Fall of the New Deal Order* (1988).

William E. Leuchtenburg, *Franklin D. Roosevelt and the New Deal, 1932–1940* (1963).

William E. Leuchtenburg, *The FDR Years: On Roosevelt and His Legacy* (1995).

Katie Loucheim, ed., *The Making of the New Deal: The Insiders Speak* (1983).

Richard H. Pells, *Radical Visions and American Dreams: Culture and Social Thought in the Depression Years* (1973).

David Plotke, *Building a Democratic Political Order: Reshaping American Liberalism in the 1930s and 1940s* (1996).

Arthur M. Schlesinger Jr., *The Coming of the New Deal* (1959).

Arthur M. Schlesinger Jr., *The Politics of Upheaval* (1960).

Harvard Sitkoff, ed., *Fifty Years Later: The New Deal Evaluated* (1985).

THE ROOSEVELT LEADERSHIP

Philip Abbott, *The Exemplary Presidency: Franklin D. Roosevelt and the American Political Tradition* (1990).

John M. Allswang, *The New Deal and American Politics* (1978).

Kristi Andersen, *The Creation of a Democratic Majority, 1928–1936* (1979).

James MacGregor Burns, *Roosevelt: The Lion and the Fox* (1956).

Blanche Wiessen Cook, *Eleanor Roosevelt* (1992).

Joseph Lash, *Eleanor and Franklin* (1971).

Richard Polenberg, *Reorganizing Roosevelt's Government, 1936–1939* (1966).

Albert U. Romasco, *The Politics of Recovery: Roosevelt's New Deal* (1983).

Eleanor Roosevelt, *Autobiography* (1961).

Eliot A. Rosen, *Hoover, Roosevelt, and the Brains Trust: From Depression to New Deal* (1977).

Sean J. Savage, *Roosevelt: The Party Leader, 1932–1945* (1991).

Richard W. Steele, *Propaganda in an Open Society: The Roosevelt Administration and the Media, 1933–1941* (1985).

Geoffrey C. Ward, *A First-Class Temperament: The Emergence of Franklin Roosevelt* (1989).

Susan Ware, *Beyond Suffrage: Women in the New Deal* (1981).

Susan Ware, *Partner and I: Molly Dewson, Feminism, and New Deal Politics* (1987).

ECONOMICS AND PLANNING

William J. Barber, *From New Era to New Deal: Herbert Hoover, the Economists, and American Economic Policy, 1921–1933* (1985).

Donald R. Brand, *Corporatism and the Rule of Law: A Study of the National Recovery Administration* (1988).

Mark Gelfand, *A Nation of Cities: The Federal Government and Urban America, 1933–1945* (1975).

Otis L. Graham Jr., *Toward a Planned Society: From Roosevelt to Nixon* (1976).

Erwin C. Hargrove, *Prisoners of Myth: The Leadership of the Tennessee Valley Authority, 1933–1990* (1990).

Ellis Hawley, *The New Deal and the Problem of Monopoly: A Study in Economic Ambivalence* (1966).

Susan Estabrook Kennedy, *The Banking Crisis of 1933* (1973).

Mark Leff, *The Limits of Symbolic Reform: The New Deal and Taxation, 1933–1939* (1984).

Dean May, *From New Deal to New Economics* (1981).

Michael Parrish, *Securities Regulation and the New Deal* (1970).

Theodore Rosenof, *Patterns of Political Economy in America: The Failure to Develop a Democratic Left Synthesis, 1933–1950* (1983).

REFORM AND WELFARE

W. Andrew Achenbaum, *Shades of Gray: Old Age, American Values, and Federal Policies since 1920* (1983).

Edward D. Berkowitz, *America's Welfare State: From Roosevelt to Reagan* (1991).

William R. Brock, *Welfare, Democracy, and the New Deal* (1987).

John A. Clausen, *Looking Back at the Children of the Great Depression* (1993).

Phoebe Cutler, *The Public Landscape of the New Deal* (1986).

Linda Gordon, *Pitied but Not Entitled: Single Mothers and the History of Welfare* (1994).

William Graebner, *A History of Retirement: The Meaning and Function of an American Institution, 1885–1978* (1980).

Joseph Hutmacher, *Senator Robert Wagner and the Rise of American Liberalism* (1968).

Paul A. Kurzman, *Harry Hopkins and the New Deal* (1974).

Roy Lubove, *The Struggle for Social Security, 1900–1935* (1968).

Paul E. Mertz, *New Deal Policy and Southern Rural Poverty* (1978).

James T. Patterson, *America's Struggle against Poverty, 1900–1980* (1981).

John Salmond, *The Civilian Conservation Corps, 1933–1942* (1967).

Bonnie Fox Schwartz, *The Civil Works Administration, 1933–1934* (1984).

CHALLENGES TO THE NEW DEAL

Alan Brinkley, *Voices of Protest: Huey Long, Father Coughlin, and the Great Depression* (1983).

Otis L. Graham Jr., *An Encore for Reform: The Old Progressives and the New Deal* (1967).

William Ivy Hair, *The Kingfish and His Realm* (1991).

Harvey Klehr, *The Heyday of American Communism* (1984).

R. Alan Lawson, *The Failure of Independent Liberalism, 1930–1941* (1971).

Donald J. Lisio, *The President and Protest: Hoover, Conspiracy, and the Bonus Riot* (1974).

Huey Long, *Every Man a King: The Autobiography of Huey P. Long* (1933).

Huey Long, *My First Days in the White House* (1935).

James T. Patterson, *Congressional Conservatism and the New Deal* (1967).

Leo P. Ribuffo, *The Old Christian Right: The Protestant Far Right from the Great Depression to the Cold War* (1983).

Frank A. Warren, *Liberals and Communism: The "Red Decade" Revisited* (1966; reprint, 1993).

Clyde P. Weed, *The Nemesis of Reform: The Republican Party During the New Deal* (1994).

T. Harry Williams, *Huey Long* (1969).

George Wolfskill, *The Revolt of the Conservatives: A History of the American Liberty League, 1934–1940* (1962).

RURAL AMERICA, SOUTH AND WEST

David E. Conrad, *The Forgotten Farmers: The Story of the Share-Croppers in the New Deal* (1965).

Cletus E. Daniel, *Bitter Harvest: A History of California Farmworkers, 1870–1941* (1981).

David E. Hamilton, *From New Day to New Deal: American Farm Policy from Hoover to Roosevelt, 1928–1933* (1991).

Jack Temple Kirby, *Rural Worlds Lost: The American South, 1920–1960* (1987).

Richard Lowitt, *The New Deal and the West* (1984).

LABOR

John Barnard, *Walter Reuther and the Rise of the Auto Workers* (1983).

Irving Bernstein, *A Caring Society: The New Deal, the Worker, and the Great Depression* (1985).

Bert Cochran, *Labor and Communism* (1977).

Lizbeth Cohen, *Making a New Deal: Industrial Workers in Chicago, 1919–1939* (1990).

Sidney Fine, *Sitdown: The General Motors Strike of 1936–1937* (1969).

Steve Fraser, *Labor Will Rule: Sidney Hillman and the Rise of American Labor* (1991).

Gary Gerstle, *Working-Class Americanism: The Politics of Labor in a Textile City, 1914–1960* (1989).

Colin Gordon, *New Deals: Business, Labor, and Politics in America, 1920–1935* (1994).

James A. Hodges, *New Deal Labor Policy and the Southern Cotton Textile Industry, 1933–1941* (1986).

August Meier and Elliot Rudwick, *Black Detroit and the Rise of the UAW* (1979).

David Milton, *The Politics of United States Labor: From the Great Depression to the New Deal* (1980).

Judith Sealander, *As Minority Becomes Majority: Federal Reaction to the Phenomenon of Women in the Work Force, 1920–1963* (1983).

Robert H. Zieger, *John L. Lewis: Labor Leader* (1988).

RACE AND MINORITIES

Francisco E. Balderrama and Raymond Rodriguez, *Decade of Betrayal: Mexican Repatriation in the 1930s* (1995).

Christine Bolt, *American Indian Policy and American Reform* (1987).

Dan T. Carter, *Scottsboro* (1969).

Robin D. G. Kelley, *Hammer and Hoe: Alabama Communists during the Great Depression* (1990).

John B. Kirby, *Black Americans in the Roosevelt Era: Liberalism and Race* (1980).

Clifford Lytle, *American Indians, American Justice* (1983).

Doug McAdam, *Political Process and the Development of Black Insurgency, 1920–1970* (1982).

Harvard Sitkoff, *A New Deal for Blacks: The Emergence of Civil Rights as a National Issue: The Depression Decade* (1978).

Patricia Sullivan, *Days of Hope: Race and Democracy in the New Deal Era* (1996).

Graham D. Taylor, *The New Deal and American Indian Tribalism: The Administration of the Indian Reorganization Act, 1935–1945* (1980).

Nancy J. Weiss, *Farewell to the Party of Lincoln* (1983).

Robert L. Zangrando, *The NAACP Crusade against Lynching* (1980).

PUBLIC CULTURE

Kenneth J. Bindas, *All of This Music Belongs to the Nation: The WPA's Federal Music Project and American Society* (1996).

Jerre Mangione, *The Dream and the Deal* (1972).

Karal Ann Marling, *Wall-to-Wall America: A Cultural History of Post-Office Murals in the Great Depression* (1982).

Jane De Hart Mathews, *The Federal Theatre, 1935–1939: Plays, Relief, and Politics* (1967).

Richard McKinzie, *The New Deal for Artists* (1973).

Francis V. O'Connor, ed., *Art for the Millions: Essays from the 1930s by Artists and Administrators of the WPA Federal Art Project* (1973).

Geoffrey O'Gara, *A Long Road Home: In the Footsteps of the WPA Writers* (1989).

GOD BLESS AMERICA

MEMENTO OF WAR
To mark the seriousness of going to war, servicemen and their families often mounted photos in special settings, such as this painted-on-glass frame. Symbols of God and country sum up patriotic devotion to a just cause. And in the midst of these ritualized sentiments, as if looking back through a window draped in his honor, an unknown sailor seems about to tell us something more.
Private Collection.

THE UNITED STATES AND THE SECOND WORLD WAR

25

1939–1945

E XCITED AND UNCERTAIN ABOUT WHAT TO EXPECT, a noisy crowd of eight thousand jostled into the America First rally in Des Moines, Iowa, on the evening of September 1, 1941. They came to hear Charles Lindbergh, the first person to fly solo across the Atlantic, the nation's most famous hero. Lindbergh was speaking against President Franklin Roosevelt's order that would allow American warships to "shoot on sight" any German vessel that interfered with American shipping to Great Britain. A firestorm was the last thing Lindbergh wanted to ignite. A shy, private man, he resisted every effort by the media to make him a celebrity. Only a compelling sense of duty convinced him that he must suffer the spotlight again to take a stand against American involvement in another war.

Lindbergh's speech was sponsored by the America First Committee (AFC), organized in the fall of 1940 to keep the United States out of the war that had erupted in Europe the year before. The AFC's youthful organizers attracted a considerable following among those of draft age, including two future presidents, Gerald Ford and John Kennedy. But America Firsters, especially Lindbergh, had suffered harsh denunciation. Secretary of the Interior Harold Ickes labeled Lindbergh "America's No. 1 Nazi fellow traveler." "No one," Ickes pointed out in July 1941, "has ever heard Lindbergh utter a word of horror at, or even aversion to, the bloody career that the Nazis are following, nor a word of pity for the innocent men, women, and children who have been deliberately murdered by the Nazis." A year earlier, Roosevelt had gone even further. "I am absolutely convinced," he told Secretary of the Treasury Henry Morgenthau, "that Lindbergh is a Nazi."

Yet the man who had flown the Atlantic alone still had such a strong hold on the American imagination that the crowd in Des Moines settled down immediately when he stepped onto the stage, straight and tall, still at thirty-nine the godlike young aviator. In his clear, earnest voice Lindbergh declared that war would needlessly take the lives of the nation's best young men and bleed precious resources. He promised the "utmost frankness" in laying bare the forces behind the interventionist "subterfuge." Bluntly, he declared that "the three most important groups who have been pressing this country toward war are the British, the Jewish, and the Roosevelt administration." Lindbergh received a standing ovation when he identified the war "agitators." But elsewhere, accusations mounted that Lindbergh was anti-Semitic, if not pro-Nazi, and even close associates backed away. In the few months left before the United States entered the war, the "Lone Eagle" was alone again.

When the United States went to war in December 1941, the America First Committee shut its doors, and true to their insistence that they were patriots committed to the defense of their country, its members hurried to defend the flag. Lindbergh, however, had his way blocked by the implacable hostility of the Roosevelt administration. Denied a renewal of his commission in the air force, Lindbergh finally found work on the sidelines testing fighters and bombers for the Ford Motor Company. In 1944, Lindbergh seized the chance to continue flight testing in the Pacific war zone. His superb flying skills persuaded the fighter squadron on remote Biak Island to let him fly fifty combat missions. "Lucky Lindy" proved he had some luck left; in one firefight he barely escaped being shot down, and in another he finally destroyed an enemy plane just a few yards short of a head-on collision.

Even when the war ended in victory, however, Lindbergh believed that his dire predictions about the conflict had been correct. Although he had fought courageously, he steadfastly refused to draw sharp distinctions between the Allied and Axis sides, between "our" good and "their" evil. The brutality of war, he argued, "is not a thing confined to any nation or to any people. What the German has done to the Jew in Europe, we are doing to the Jap in the Pacific. . . . It is not the Germans alone, or the Japs, but the men of all nations to whom this war has brought shame and degradation."

In 1940–1941, millions of other Americans shared Lindbergh's concern that the nation would be drawn into war, but few resisted as hard or as long as he did. Haltingly at first, then boldly, the American people rallied behind Roosevelt and accepted his interpretation of the Nazi menace. When the nation entered the war, Americans threw themselves unreservedly into the struggle. They believed that they were engaged in a necessary war to preserve democracy, a righteous war to save civilization. Much more than during World War I, Americans said it was a "good war."

There was no specific moment when foreign affairs replaced domestic reform as Roosevelt's chief priority. Throughout the 1930s, as Roosevelt battled the depression, foreign problems gradually grew more insistent. The growth of fascism, the power of Germany and Japan, the Ethiopian War, the Spanish Civil War, and the war in China drew Roosevelt and the nation into a more active foreign policy.

After September 1939, when fighting erupted in Europe, an American president once again had to negotiate the treacherous waters of neutrality. Like Woodrow Wilson, Roosevelt promised to keep the nation out of the European conflict, but as he became convinced that a fascist victory would be catastrophic, he sought to educate the American people into a more aggressive defense of the Allied cause. Debate ended on December 7, 1941, when the Japanese attacked the American naval base at Pearl Harbor, Hawaii. The United States entered World War II, the most devastating and transforming conflict in history.

The American experience in World War II was unique. No bombs fell at home, no civilian starved, and no government toppled. Yet the nation engaged in a total war that influenced every American and almost every aspect of American life. The war put Americans to work again and ended the depression. It ended the New Deal's drive for reform and the nation's isolationism. American soldiers and sailors who had never been beyond their hometowns fought on distant continents and seas and came home changed. As one rifleman said of his experience abroad: "I went there a skinny, gaunt mama's boy, full of wonderment. I came back much more circumspect in my judgment of people. And of governments." Nearly four years of war also changed individuals and society at home. Women did "men's" work, minorities stepped out of their "places," and, as one woman remembered, people came out of the war "with more money than they'd had in years." But hundreds of thousands of families also lost fathers, husbands, and sons, wounds that would never heal. A victorious nation, grieving yet optimistic, emerged from World War II the most powerful industrial and military power in the world.

Peacetime Dilemmas

With the Japanese invasion of Manchuria in 1931, the arms buildup and talk of the glories of war in fascist Italy, and the swearing in of Adolf Hitler as chancellor of Germany in 1933, the world grew steadily more dangerous. The forces of aggression in Europe and in the Far East mocked the peace structure so hopefully put into place during the Versailles Peace Conference following World War I. The United States had rejected Woodrow Wilson's plea to join the League of Nations and commit to the principle of collective international security. The rising tide of violent nationalism throughout the world in the 1930s roused old fears of foreign entanglements and caused Americans to pull back behind their ocean shields. That recoil from international conflict paralleled the decision of New Dealers to concentrate on domestic policies first and not allow international complications to hinder the country's economic recovery from the depression. With few exceptions, American policy took on a peculiar polarity: In the face of crises, the nation's leaders took bold action at home but shrank from being involved abroad.

FDR and Reluctant Isolation

Nowhere was the contrast between domestic boldness and international caution more evident than in the change in Franklin Delano Roosevelt's public position on foreign policy. Roosevelt grew up within activist international circles. The Delano family had long been involved with China, and the family home in Hyde Park, New York, was filled with books, mementos, and talk about Asia. Moreover, his famous cousin Theodore had played a premier role in bringing the United States onto the world stage and had capped his achievements by winning the Nobel Peace Prize for negotiating an end to the Russo-Japanese War in 1905. In that heady atmosphere, when the twentieth century was young and the United States was beginning to flex its economic muscle, Franklin Roosevelt came to believe strongly that naval dominance determines the balance of power. When he joined the Wilson administration as assistant secretary of the navy in 1913, Roosevelt zestfully welcomed international action. He had urged American preparedness when World War I broke out in Europe and welcomed U.S. entry into the fray as an uplifting adventure.

True to Wilson's vision that the United States should take the lead in making the world "safe for democracy," Roosevelt went against the isolationist tide in the 1920s by arguing for American membership in the League of Nations. When he reentered politics in 1928 to run for governor of New York, he charged that the Republicans had undermined chances for a prosperous peace by setting high tariffs while also insisting that the exhausted Europeans pay off their loans and reparations.

The depression forced Roosevelt to retreat from his internationalism. Hard times made it easy for isolationists to persuade other Americans that ex-

pending effort and money on foreign ventures was a risky diversion from domestic recovery. During his 1932 run for the presidency against Herbert Hoover, Roosevelt was unnerved by charges that he was an international adventurer. He pulled back from his endorsement of the League of Nations and reversed his position on forgiving European war debts. With regret, Roosevelt concluded that the New Deal coalition he sought required him to curb his internationalism.

Once in office, Roosevelt wanted to join domestic economic recovery with a foreign policy that encouraged free trade and disarmament. He had always believed that peace, prosperity, and free trade were linked. "Foreign markets must be regained if America's producers are to rebuild a full and enduring domestic prosperity for our people," Roosevelt declared in 1935. "There is no other way if we would avoid painful economic dislocations, social readjustments, and unemployment." The concept of an interdependent and open world led to the most successful initiative of his first year in office—the recognition of the Soviet Union, which had been shunned as a revolutionary menace since the Bolshevik Revolution of 1917. After a careful survey of American public opinion convinced him that the nation supported bringing the USSR into the world community, Roosevelt pressed forward with negotiations that resulted in formal recognition on November 17, 1933.

The recoil from international conflict paralleled the decision of New Dealers to concentrate on domestic policies first and not allow international complications to hinder the country's economic recovery from the depression.

Despite this bold initiative, he also believed that until the American economy regained its balance, unhindered experimentation at home called for a safe distance from the world's troubles. He hoped that the United States would recover quickly and then be in a position to give active support to disarmament and removal of barriers to free trade. Instead, the depression dragged on and a series of crises abroad provoked wars and rivalries, rather than the spirit of cooperation that disarmament and free trade required.

Thus Roosevelt was hemmed in by circumstances. Because the New Deal needed support from isolationists in Congress, Roosevelt could not offer to help the League of Nations curb aggression. Nor could he agree to abide by decisions of the World Court, which was established by the League of Nations to settle international disputes. American endorsement of international cooperation could go no further than to express watery praise for the concept of collective security.

Almost as soon as Roosevelt entered office, the ability of the League of Nations to maintain peace declined when Japan withdrew from the league and rejected limitations on its naval strength imposed after World War I. In the fall of 1933, the new Nazi chancellor of Germany, Adolf Hitler, further dimmed the league's prospects by recalling Germany's representatives to the league and joining Japan in condemning the organization as an obstacle to Germany's national aspirations. Shocked by the ominous turn of events, Roosevelt reassured Americans that support of the league's objectives would not involve the United States in war. Under no circumstances, he declared, would the nation "use its armed forces for the settlement of any dispute anywhere."

Unable to launch foreign policy initiatives, Roosevelt turned to building U.S. defenses. In 1934, to counter the threatened Japanese naval buildup, Roosevelt authorized the largest expansion of the U.S. navy since 1916. At the same time, he instructed the State Department to play down Japan's expansion in China. Most citizens, absorbed in their domestic woes, paid little attention to foreign problems and were thankful for the oceans they thought could shelter them from involvement.

The Good Neighbor Policy

In his inaugural address in 1933, Franklin Roosevelt dedicated the United States to "the policy of the good neighbor" in foreign affairs. A few weeks later, he specifically applied the phrase to the nation's Latin American policy. Although the Hoover administration had moved away from the Roosevelt Corollary under which the nation had arrogantly claimed the right to intervene in the internal affairs of Latin American nations, the United States and other nations in the Western Hemisphere were hardly cordial neighbors when Roosevelt took office.

Roosevelt and Secretary of State Cordell Hull were committed to establishing a genuine Pan-American accord. By offering a "helping hand" and enjoying "the cooperation of others," Roosevelt declared, the United States could "have more order in this hemisphere and less dislike." In the Western Hemisphere, unlike elsewhere, isolationist Americans were willing to allow significant international cooperation. In December 1933, Hull traveled to Montevideo, Uruguay, to participate in the Inter-American Conference. The intense anti-American feeling he encountered abated when he signed the joint declaration that asserted that no nation has the right to intervene in the internal or external affairs of another.

The United States' commitment to nonintervention was quickly put to the test. When Mexico nationalized American oil holdings and when revolution boiled over in Nicaragua, Guatemala, and Cuba, Roosevelt refrained from his cousin Theodore's easy resort to sending in the marines to defend the interests of American corporations. In 1934, moreover, Roosevelt withdrew American marines from Haiti, where they had been since 1916. But nonintervention was a double-edged sword. While it honored the principle of national self-determination, it did not necessarily promote freedom. American business, emboldened by Roosevelt's policy, entered into lucrative arrangements with dictators like Anastasio Somoza in Nicaragua and Fulgencio Batista in Cuba that enabled those tyrants to become wealthy and powerful by exploiting and terrorizing the rest of the population.

Adoption of the "good neighbor policy," therefore, did not mean that Roosevelt had abandoned Woodrow Wilson's aim of achieving economic preeminence in the region. Roosevelt did not so much retreat from empire in Latin America as reject military force as a means of retaining it. With Roosevelt's blessing, Hull engineered passage of the Reciprocal Trade Agreements Act of 1934. The act gave the president power to reduce the nation's high tariffs on a nation-by-nation basis. By 1940, Hull's initiative persuaded twenty-two nations to sign reciprocal treaties and has broadened since to cover most of America's foreign trade. Trade reciprocity had significant results. Between 1929 and 1932, American exports to Latin America had fallen from $2 billion to $500 million. From 1933 to 1940, American exports doubled. Trade reciprocity, however, did not prevent a widening of the gap between American economic power and that of the rest of the Western Hemisphere. Still, Roosevelt's new departure in Latin America planted the seeds of friendship and solidarity, an achievement that grew in importance as events in Europe and Asia eroded the hope for peace.

The Price of Noninvolvement

Increasingly in the 1930s, international order broke down. Countries beset by economic hardship, ethnic rivalries, and historic grievances turned to aggressive nationalism as the way to end their troubles. Italian strongman Benito Mussolini set the pattern. Through harsh militarist means, Mussolini constructed an authoritarian state that created a semblance of order and efficiency. Even those who lamented the loss of democracy were likely to accept the myth that, in Italy, "at least the trains ran on time." But Mussolini's philosophy of aggression eroded European resolve to settle disputes peacefully. "War is to the man what maternity is to the woman," Mussolini proclaimed with a theatrical strut, eyes bulging and jaw thrust out. "I do not believe in perpetual peace; not only do I not believe in it, but I find it depressing and a negation of all the fundamental virtues of man."

In Germany, Hitler was feverishly rearming his nation in open defiance of the Versailles treaty. British, French, and Italian leaders had the power to compel German compliance, but they contented themselves with verbal protest. In 1935, Britain concluded a treaty with the Nazis that conceded Germany equality in submarines and the right to build a surface fleet one-third the size of the British navy. Still, Hitler ranted against the Jews as the enemies of the Aryan master race and threatened action to avenge humiliating defeat in World War I. His statements about restoring territories with German inhabitants to the "Fatherland" became harder to ignore.

Political and economic tensions in the Far East also gave rise to a militant movement in Japan that resembled European fascism in the way it subordinated the economy to a ruling caste and sought national advantage through conquest. After absorbing Manchuria in 1932, Japan's military rulers began a campaign to take the five northern provinces of China. What they believed would be a mere skirmish became a long and vicious war when Chinese Nationalist leader Chiang Kai-shek rallied his troops and courageously resisted the Japanese invasion.

At first, alarm in the United States over escalating hostility abroad played into the hands of the isolationists. Disillusionment over the failure of World War I to make the world safe for democracy convinced many Americans that the opponents of the war had been right all along. America's participation seemed useless and even foolish. And after 1933, it also seemed malicious. In that year, the Sen-

ate established a committee to conduct an investigation into the U.S. entry into the war. Chaired by Republican Gerald Nye of North Dakota, who became one of Lindbergh's most prominent allies in the fight against going to war again, the committee concluded that the greed of American munitions makers, bankers, and financiers was responsible for dragging the country into war. Although it had little evidence, the Nye committee nevertheless convinced thousands of Americans that such a tragic mistake must never happen again.

The Nye committee's report and the rapidly deteriorating international situation prodded Congress into action. Between 1935 and 1937, legislators passed a series of neutrality acts designed to prevent the recurrence of the circumstances that they now believed had dragged the country into World War I. One act forbade loans to nations at war. Another gave the president the power to warn Americans about traveling on ships of belligerent nations. A third prohibited arms sales to nations at war.

But by 1937, trade in nonmilitary goods had also become an issue. Some Americans argued that any trade, not just in munitions, could draw the nation into war and argued for a total embargo of all American products to warring countries. Most members of Congress, however, recognized that a total trade ban would devastate the shaky American economy. And yet, trade with nations at war might lead to American involvement. Was there a way out? Congress believed that it found a way with the Neutrality Act of 1937. Legislators decided to allow nonmilitary goods to continue to flow to nations at war *if* the foreign nations paid cash (thus avoiding American loans) and shipped the goods in their own vessels (thus avoiding the use of American ships in war zones). The so-called cash-and-carry policy seemed to promise that the United States could have both peace and prosperity.

Constrained by law and public opinion, the Roosevelt administration could do no more in the face of international aggression than express moral disapproval. Emboldened by democracy's presumed lack of military toughness and resolve to stand firm against pressure, Germany, Italy, and Japan went from one triumphant strike to the next. In March 1936, Nazi troops marched unopposed into the Rhineland on Germany's western border in blatant violation of the Treaty of Versailles, which had placed the area under French authority. One month later, Italian armies completed their conquest of Ethiopia, a cloud of bombers and poison gas preparing the way for their grand entry into the capital at Addis Ababa. Aggression in the Far East reached its climax in December 1937 when Japanese troops captured Nanking and celebrated their triumph with a murderous rampage that cost the lives of 200,000 Chinese civilians. Yet the rest of the world continued to stand aside, the League of Nations unable to mount sanctions and U.S. action limited to moral outrage and feeble warnings.

These brutal events occurred alongside a tragic drama in Spain that demonstrated the threat of fascist power to democracy. In 1936, Spain erupted in a civil war between the Loyalists, a coalition representing the existing republican government, and the Falangists, rebel fascists led by General Francisco Franco. In what became widely described as a rehearsal for the next world war, Germany and Italy sent troops and arms to Franco, and the Soviet Union, on a much smaller scale, came to the aid of the Loyalists. The American government and public opinion favored the Loyalists as the democratically elected government, but the United States, and European democracies as well, offered no assistance to either side. This neutrality meant that Loyalist forces were at a disadvantage against fascist forces amply supplied by allies that welcomed war. Rather than sit helplessly on the sidelines, however, more than three thousand Americans enlisted in the Lincoln Brigade and joined several thousand volunteers from other countries to fight with the Loyalists. Nevertheless, in 1939, the Loyalists went down to defeat. The Spanish Civil War dramatized the tragic consequences of neutrality legislation while offering a glimpse of what a war against fascism was apt to be like.

Increasingly convinced that the United States needed to play a stronger role in stopping fascist aggression in Europe and Asia, Roosevelt sought to break the hold of isolationists on American foreign policy. On October 5, 1937, in a speech in Chicago, the heartland of isolationist sentiment, the president attempted to persuade Americans to allow the government to take a more assertive international stance. He harked back to his internationalist sense of the link between intervention and peace. "America hates war," he said. "America hopes for peace. Therefore, America actively engages in the search for peace." Thinking particularly of the horrors of Japanese aggression in China, Roosevelt declared that aggressors must be "quarantined" by the international community. Otherwise, the "contagion" of war would spread to every shore.

The speech advocated no specific action, but just the hint of a desire for the United States to cross its ocean moat was enough to ignite a storm of protest. Peace groups unloosed a letter-writing campaign to newspapers and politicians. The *Chicago Tribune* charged that the president wanted to replace "Americanism" with "internationalism." Most ominously, leaders in Congress remained silent. Roosevelt, who already had his hands full with fighting the depression, pulled back. "It's a terrible thing," he remarked to an aide, "to look over your shoulder when you are trying to lead and find no one there."

The public's reaction was a sharp reminder that the American people had made Roosevelt president to wage war against domestic ills. To enlist support for the vigorous action he urged at home, Roosevelt had to be cautious in dealing with the rest of the world. Most Americans still preferred the isolationist policies of the previous decade, partly to protect the fragile American economy from foreign competition and disruption and partly because disillusionment over America's failed crusade in World War I still lingered.

The Onset of War

Events had not spiraled far enough into disaster by the start of Roosevelt's second term to convince the public that noninvolvement would have to give way to an active role in foreign affairs, backed up by expanded armed forces. To be sure, the saber-rattling rhetoric and actual aggression of fascist dictators had alerted some observers to the danger. But troubles in China, Ethiopia, and Spain seemed too remote and minor to bring most Americans around to the president's view that it was time to take a stand. While Americans strongly condemned ruthless aggression abroad, they even more strongly opposed any measure to halt aggression that might conceivably lead to war. By 1939, however, world events and Roosevelt's efforts to educate Americans to the dangers of isolationism were bringing about a profound change of attitude. When war finally came to America, the nation united to defeat the Axis powers.

Nazi Aggression and War in Europe

Under the spell of neutrality, Americans watched helplessly as Adolf Hitler continued his campaign to dominate Europe. In the name of Germany's "destiny" to unite all German peoples, Hitler in 1938 bullied his native land of Austria into accepting incor-

THE HARVEST
Cartoonist Daniel Robert Fitzpatrick of the St. Louis
Post-Dispatch *captures the rising impression of the
Nazis as ghoulish scavengers stripping dead victims of
their valuables. This cartoon appeared in 1938, soon after
Germany incorporated Austria and seized the Sudeten-
land from Czechoslovakia. Fitzpatrick is obviously skepti-
cal of British Prime Minister Neville Chamberlain's claim
that appeasing Hitler's appetite for other people's posses-
sions had achieved "peace in our time."*
Daniel Robert Fitzpatrick/St. Louis Post-Dispatch/John F. Kennedy
Library.

poration—"Anschluss"—into the Nazi Third
Reich. He then turned his attention to the German-
speaking Sudetenland, granted to Czechoslovakia
by the Versailles settlement. Although the Czechs
were prepared to fight rather than surrender territory, the British and French wanted peace and
sought to strike a deal with Hitler. British Prime
Minister Neville Chamberlain went to confer with
the German ruler in Munich. Chamberlain offered
terms of "appeasement," as he called it, that would
turn over the Sudetenland to Germany in exchange
for leaving the rest of Czechoslovakia alone. On
September 29, 1938, Hitler accepted the offer,
solemnly promising that he would make no more
territorial claims in Europe. Chamberlain returned
home convinced that he had obtained "peace in our
time." In March 1939, Hitler marched the German
army into weakened Czechoslovakia and took over
the entire country without a shot being fired.

Hardly pausing for breath, Hitler in April demanded that Poland return the German territory
that it had been awarded after World War I. At this
point, Britain and France finally recognized that the
policy of appeasement was a failure. They assured
Poland that they would go to its aid if Hitler attacked.
Intent on avoiding a two-front war, Hitler offered
Joseph Stalin concessions to prevent the Soviet
Union from joining Germany's adversaries in the
West. Despite deep enmity between Nazi Germany
and the Communist Soviet Union, the two powers
shocked the world by signing a Nazi-Soviet treaty
of nonaggression in August 1939. The agreement not
only provided that Germany and the Soviet Union
would not attack one another but stipulated that in
the event of territorial rearrangement in Eastern
Europe, the Soviet Union would profit.

Hitler mobilized his armies and prepared to
seize Poland. He fretted, "I am afraid some pig-dog
will make a proposal for mediation as at Munich."
To prevent any such interruption, he exhorted his
generals to be as ruthless as possible. "Close your
hearts to pity! Act brutally! . . . In starting and waging a war it is not Right that matters, but Victory."
At dawn on September 1, 1939, fully in accord with
Hitler's wishes and spirit, the German army crossed
the Polish border, mechanized to a swift and crushing degree never before conceived. France and
Britain kept their word by declaring war. The greatest conflict in history had begun.

From Neutrality to the Arsenal of Democracy

When war erupted, Roosevelt issued an official
proclamation of American neutrality. But unlike
Woodrow Wilson, he did not ask Americans to be
impartial in thought as well as deed. "This nation
will remain a neutral nation," he explained, "but I
cannot ask that every American remain neutral in
thought as well. Even a neutral has a right to take
account of facts. Even a neutral cannot be asked to
close his mind or his conscience." Roosevelt and the
vast majority of Americans were decidedly not neutral. They favored Britain, France, and the Allied
cause, but almost no one advocated going to war on
their behalf. An antifascist neutral, the nation debated
what it should do short of war to aid the Allies.

Roosevelt's immediate objective was to persuade Congress to repeal the arms embargo mandated by the neutrality legislation. He believed that
France and Britain could defeat Germany only if
they had access to weapons. The president's request

MAP 25.1
Axis Aggression to 1941
In a series of surprise military strikes, Hitler reclaimed German territories occupied by France
after World War I, annexed Austria, and then launched World War II to extend German
power over the "inferior" peoples across Germany's borders.

provoked frenzied debate across the nation. Charles Lindbergh said that the war was a European matter and that the United States should stay out of it. Senator William Borah of Idaho declared that Roosevelt's proposal was equivalent to taking sides and would drag the United States into war. But Congress finally consented to modify neutrality legislation so that selected belligerents could purchase armaments in the United States on a cash-and-carry basis. The narrow victory gained over vigorous isolationist

protest gave the Allies what Roosevelt hoped would be crucial assistance without involving the United States directly in the dangers of carrying war goods to Europe through the German submarine blockade.

After Hitler's armies overran Poland, they paused, but fighting resumed in the spring of 1940 with a series of Nazi hammer blows. In a lightning-fast attack called a "blitzkrieg," German dive-bombers and tanks smashed through Denmark, Norway, Belgium, and Holland and into northern

France. The French held out behind the Maginot Line, a massive concrete fortification that stretched from the Swiss border to the Ardennes forest on the edge of Belgium. But in early summer, Mussolini brought Italy into the war when his armies invaded France from the south, while Hitler's blitzkrieg flanked the Maginot Line in the north. British forces that had defended the north were cut off from their French allies by the swift German advance and retreated to the port of Dunkirk. By an extraordinary evacuation effort between May 26 and June 4, on every form of seagoing vessel available, 215,000 British troops, along with 120,000 French troops, were ferried safely back to Britain before the onrushing Germans could capture them. Less than three weeks later, reeling from a German sweep southward, the French surrendered the largest army in the world and signed an armistice that placed three-fifths of the country under German control. In the words of a British military expert, the French sword had turned out to be a broomstick.

The fall of France and the real possibility of British defeat shocked and frightened Americans. They watched breathlessly as Britain faced Germany alone. The British turned the appeaser Neville Chamberlain out of office and welcomed as prime minister the defiant Winston Churchill. With mounting fury, Churchill had watched from the sidelines as Chamberlain had kowtowed to Hitler. When the Germans attacked Britain itself, Churchill was ready with a vengeance to take over the last-ditch defense of the nation. Churchill's oratorical genius shone through the intensive bombing campaign the Germans inflicted on English cities in the summer and fall of 1940 in an attempt to break the nation's spirit. By the time the Royal Air Force won the Battle of Britain in November, ridding the skies of German bombers, Churchill (who even looked like an English bulldog) had become the symbol of indomitable British resistance.

Roosevelt strove for a comparable role as leader and symbol. His task was complicated, however, by

THE COUNTY OF LONDON ORCHESTRA
Gallant British resistance to the bombing of their cities captured American sympathy and helped to build support for U.S. entry into the war. Here in the Chelsea section of London in 1942, both the County of London Orchestra and an audience of mostly children demonstrate how to carry on in the ruins with poise and a stiff upper lip.
Hulton Deutsch Collection.

neutrality and distance from the conflict. In the spring of 1940, the president prevailed on Kansas journalist William Allen White to form the Committee to Defend America by Aiding the Allies. The committee mounted a nationwide campaign to combat isolationism and generate public support for Roosevelt's policy of providing all aid to the Allies short of war. Inevitably, isolationists (or noninterventionists, as they called themselves) organized in response. The America First Committee consisted of an odd assortment of pro-Nazi spokesmen, anti-British Irish Americans, and Italian Americans, socialists, Communists, pacifists, idealists, and thousands of patriotic Americans who genuinely thought the United States' safety depended on remaining in the Western Hemisphere and staying out of Europe's troubles.

In the midst of this hugely important debate about American foreign policy, the presidential election of 1940 unfolded. Having decided to run for an unprecedented third term rather than step aside in the midst of crisis, Roosevelt looked forward to a campaign pitting the reformist, internationalist thrust of the New Deal against Republican isolationism and business conservatism. Instead, progressive Republicans gained the nomination for Wendell Willkie, a former Democrat who supported most of the New Deal domestic program and generally agreed with Roosevelt's foreign policy. But realizing that he trailed Roosevelt badly, Willkie changed course and attacked Roosevelt as a warmonger, forcing the president to declare, "Your boys are not going to be sent into any foreign wars. . . . Your President says this country is not going to war." Although the margin of his victory was smaller than in 1936, Roosevelt won easily, 27.3 million votes to 22.3 million votes, and 449 electoral votes to 82.

The president interpreted his victory as a mandate to continue to support Britain in every way short of war. Indeed, Roosevelt's campaign to convince Americans that the United States could stay out of war with Germany only if Great Britain succeeded had won thousands of converts. But in the fall of 1940, Great Britain was in desperate straits. The British had exhausted their treasury and no longer could pay cash for weapons as required by the cash-and-carry policy. Rather than see American aid end, Roosevelt came up with a plan that he announced to the American people in a fireside chat.

On December 16, 1940, the president explained that only the British stood between the United States and Nazi aggression. To prevail, Britain needed war materiel. "We must be the great arsenal of democracy," he declared. As for how the British would pay,

he offered the homely example of a man who lent his neighbor a garden hose when his house caught on fire. "I don't say to him . . . 'you have to pay me $15 for it.' I don't want $15—I want my garden hose back after the fire is over."

The public response was overwhelmingly favorable, and the administration introduced the Lend-Lease Act to Congress in January 1941. In March, following sharp debate, Congress approved the measure, which allowed the British to obtain armaments from the United States and return them or their equivalent after the war was over. Lend-Lease was a transparent charade. As one observer noted, "Lending war materiel is a little like lending chewing gum. You don't want it back." With Lend-Lease, the United States dropped its pretense of neutrality. It engaged in full-fledged economic warfare against Germany. And since Britain could not sustain its shipping in the face of losses to German submarines, the United States would need inevitably to build and protect a vast merchant fleet. It was only a matter of time before an armed attack occurred of the sort that had precipitated World War I.

The predictable series of events began on June 11, 1941, when a German U-boat (submarine) sank the American freighter *Robin Moor* off the coast of Africa. Several months later, an American destroyer, the *Greer*, helped a British plane track a German submarine and then engaged it in a firefight. Roosevelt seized upon the incident as cause for issuing a "shoot on sight" policy for American escort vessels, and in September 1941 an "undeclared war" was under way. A month earlier, Roosevelt and Churchill had met on shipboard off the coast of Newfoundland to devise what became known as the Atlantic Charter. Although the United States was not officially at war, the joint statement of "certain common principles" looked forward to the destruction of the Nazis and the creation of a peaceful postwar world order.

As danger in the Atlantic mounted, Hitler took a terrible gamble by launching a massive invasion of the Soviet Union on June 22, 1941. Until that violent rupture of the Nazi-Soviet pact, Americans generally thought no better of the Communists than they did of the Nazis. But now things were different. Churchill bluntly welcomed his old archenemy Joseph Stalin to the cause, stating that he would not hesitate to deal with the devil if Hitler invaded hell. Roosevelt hailed the diversion of German forces away from the hard-pressed British and quickly persuaded Congress to extend Lend-Lease to the Russians.

MAP 25.2

Japanese Aggression through 1941

Beginning with the invasion of Manchuria in 1931, Japan sought to force its imperialist control over most of East Asia. Japanese aggression was driven by the need for raw materials for the country's expanding industries and by the military government's devotion to martial honor.

War Comes to America

Despite the United States' primary concern with Europe, the expansion of the Japanese empire made the danger of war most immediate in Asia. The rising tide of Japanese imperialism clashed with U.S. aspirations and commitments, especially in China. America's China policy had been set in 1899 when Secretary of State John Hay issued the Open Door notes demanding that the United States have equal access to the rich markets of China and that China maintain its territorial integrity. But the island-bound Japanese also wanted raw material and markets and their weak neighbor China was the natural place to turn. The military invasion of Manchuria in 1931 proved to be the opening salvo of continuing Japanese aggression in China. Each act of territorial conquest received a stern rebuke from the Roosevelt administration, but toothless proclamations caused the Japanese little concern. They dismissed American opinion and marched forward under the banner "Asia for the Asians," which really meant China for the Japanese.

In 1940, the crisis in Asia escalated. Japan signed the Tripartite Pact, a defensive alliance with Germany and Italy. It also obtained from the Vichy government, the German puppet regime in France, the right to build airfields and station troops in northern Indochina. In 1941, U.S. naval intelligence cracked the Japanese code and learned that Tokyo had set its sights on the resource-rich Dutch East Indies. In response, the Roosevelt administration announced a complete trade embargo, which denied Japan access to essential oil and scrap iron. Roosevelt understood that he had given Japan a choice. Japan would either have to knuckle under, halt its aggression, and restore relations and trade with the United States, or it would have to find new sources of vital supplies, most likely by seizing British, French, and Dutch possessions in the Far East.

Despite apprehensions, the American public generally supported Roosevelt's increasingly bold responses to Japanese imperialism. In part, public opinion rested on ill-informed prejudices that had grown strong over the decades. Like the Roosevelt administration, the American people believed that

Japan would shy away from war against the superior Americans. They felt secure, therefore, in using the economic boycott to force Japan out of China and reinstate the Open Door. Rather illogically, most Americans looked upon the Japanese as comically inferior, yet diabolically clever. "Made in Japan" was a term of derision for shoddy merchandise turned out by small, near-sighted people who lived in paper houses and substituted obedience to authority for creative thought. Throughout the 1930s, American newspapers and newsreels showed Japanese troops, sinister yet ludicrous in their baggy uniforms, swarming into wrecked Chinese cities.

Japanese nationalists were increasingly offended by American pressure against Japan's economic and territorial ambitions. In October 1941, a military clique took control from a more moderate group that believed Japan should avoid war with the United States. The new head of state, General Hideki Tojo, persuaded other leaders, including Emperor Hirohito, who originally called the idea "harebrained," that swift destruction of American bases in the Pacific would force a quick peace and leave Japan free to follow its destiny. Despite knowledge from decoded Japanese messages that an attack was imminent, the Roosevelt administration

PEARL HARBOR, DECEMBER 7, 1941
A rescue fireboat is hopelessly dwarfed by the enormous catastrophe of the battleship West Virginia *aflame and sinking at its mooring in Pearl Harbor. With the dramatic force of a vast seascape painting, this photograph was widely reproduced as a graphic indication of how great a crime the Japanese had committed.*
U.S. Army.

disastrously underestimated the reach of Japanese military power. Consequently, American forces were unprepared for the blow that struck the Pearl Harbor naval base in Hawaii on December 7, 1941. At dawn, a swarm of Japanese carrier-borne fighters, bombers, and torpedo planes found most of the American fleet at anchor and American planes neatly crowded together at Hickam Field. In two hours, the raiders sank or damaged all eight battleships of the fleet and disabled ten other ships. Three hundred and forty airplanes were wrecked and more than 3,500 Americans were killed or wounded.

Though the raid scored a stunning tactical success, in the larger sense it was a colossal blunder. Overnight, disagreement in the United States about foreign policy ended. Americans united in their commitment to war. Pearl Harbor also created a powerful rage for getting even. In his message to Congress declaring war, Roosevelt said:

> Yesterday, December 7, 1941—a date which will live in infamy—the United States of America was suddenly and deliberately attacked by naval and air forces of the Empire of Japan.... Always will we remember the character of the onslaught against us. No matter how long it may take us to overcome this premeditated invasion, the American people in their righteous might will win through to absolute victory.

Congress endorsed the message unanimously, except for Quaker pacifist Jeannette Rankin, who had also voted against U.S. entry into World War I. Although Hitler and Mussolini had not known about the Japanese attack in advance, Germany and Italy declared war against the United States on December 11.

Fighting Back: 1941–1943

Never had the United States faced such a desperate military situation or so staggering a task as it did in 1941. Hitler and his armies had conquered most of Europe, and the Japanese military machine was slicing through the Pacific with amazing speed. From the beginning, American concern had centered on the fascist menace in Europe. American policy held it necessary to save Britain and the Soviet Union from defeat so that the United States would not have to face Hitler alone. To that end, Roosevelt and his military commanders decided on a strategy that would concentrate on Germany first and then

bring the nation's full armed might to bear on the Japanese. But before turning to Hitler, the United States and its allies would have to stop the Japanese advance through the Pacific. By 1943, the Allies had checked their enemies and were pushing them back. But the Allies could claim victory in neither Europe nor Asia. The "good war" would also be a long one.

Turning the Tide in the Pacific

Following Pearl Harbor, Japan's leading military genius, Admiral Isoroku Yamamoto, ordered an all-out offensive in the Pacific on the belief that, if his forces did not win quickly, Japan would lose the war to America's far greater manpower and resources. With lightning speed, the Japanese attacked American airfields in Manila in the Philippines and captured the American outposts of Guam and Wake Island. Singapore, the great British naval base in Malaya, surrendered in February 1942. Most of Burma had fallen by March. All that stood in the way of Japan's total domination of the southwestern Pacific were the Philippine Islands.

Though the raid on Pearl Harbor scored a stunning tactical success, in the larger sense it was a colossal blunder. Overnight, disagreement in the United States about foreign policy ended. Americans united in their commitment to war.

Under intense attack, General Douglas MacArthur, who commanded the Philippine defenses, retreated to fortifications on the Bataan Peninsula across the harbor from Manila. In March, MacArthur escaped to Australian command headquarters, leaving General Jonathan Wainwright to hold out as long as possible. When Wainwright surrendered the Corregidor fortress in May, Japanese soldiers marched the starved and ill survivors sixty-five miles to a concentration camp. Hundreds of Americans and as many as ten thousand Filipinos died en route. Of those who survived the Bataan Death March, sixteen thousand died within weeks of disease and mistreatment in the brutal prison camp. By summer 1942, the Japanese war machine had also conquered the oil-rich Dutch East Indies and was poised to strike at Australia and New Zealand.

The dark events that followed Pearl Harbor struck hard at American confidence. Jukeboxes may have been blaring "Goodbye, Mama, I'm Off to Yokohama," but the nation had learned that the soldiers of the Rising Sun were tough and fearless. They were highly trained sharpshooters carrying better weapons and more ammunition than American infantrymen, and they were prepared to fight to the death for honor and the emperor. On sea, the Japanese had larger, faster, heavier armored ships with bigger guns and more accurate torpedoes. And the four different kinds of airplanes that descended on Pearl Harbor outperformed anything the Americans could send up against them.

The string of unbroken Japanese victories caused Americans at home to worry about their own safety. A false report that Japanese fighter planes had been spotted near Los Angeles set off an antiaircraft barrage and inspired the commander of West Coast defenses to announce that "death and destruction [from enemy planes] are likely to come at any moment." Antiaircraft guns sprouted up and down the Pacific coast. In Hawaii, still shaken from the attack on Pearl Harbor, one vigilant citizen advised the authorities that he had spotted a dog on the beach "barking in Morse code to Japanese subs offshore." Americans needed some sort of success to take the edge off panic.

By April 1942, the United States was ready to strike back. The new offensive began with a demonstration to the Japanese that they were not safe anywhere, even in the imperial capital. A squadron of sixteen B-25 bombers under the command of Lieutenant Colonel James H. Doolittle launched a bombing raid on Tokyo from the deck of the carrier *Hornet*. The raid did little material damage but created an authentic hero to cheer Americans at home.

Much more substantive was a mighty two-pronged offensive that the Americans hoped would stop and then reverse the Japanese advance. The plan called for forces under the command of General MacArthur to move north from Australia and recapture the Philippines, while forces under Admiral Chester W. Nimitz sailed west from Hawaii and retook the Japanese-held islands in the mid-Pacific. Both offensives scored immediate victories. On May 7, 1942, in the Coral Sea just north of Australia, planes from the *Lexington* and *Yorktown* stopped the Japanese fleet that was sailing around the coast of New Guinea.

The Battle of the Coral Sea was a prelude to an even more significant encounter. Learning that the Japanese were sending an invasion force against Midway Island, an outpost guarding the Hawaiian

Islands, Admiral Nimitz moved his carriers and cruisers into the Central Pacific. In a wild melee that raged from June 3 to June 6, American planes sank four Japanese carriers, a heavy cruiser, and two destroyers, while losing only one carrier and a destroyer. The Battle of the Coral Sea and the Battle of Midway marked the high tide of Japanese power in the Pacific. The Americans had stopped the Japanese advance. They began the long, bloody march to Tokyo.

For Admiral Yamamoto, the end came in April 1943 when he was on his way to one of his remaining air force units on the island of Bougainville in the Solomon Islands. Having intercepted a message describing Yamamoto's plan, Nimitz went after his nemesis. Swift P-38 fighters rushed out of ambush to send Yamamoto's plane down in flames. Deprived of its naval genius, the Japanese navy was even more vulnerable to American power.

The Campaign in Europe

Once the Japanese offensive in the Pacific was halted, American attention focused on defeating Germany. In the dark months after Pearl Harbor, the war news from Europe was as depressing as that from the Pacific. While imperial Japanese forces were spreading through Asia, Hitler's army smashed deep into the Soviet Union and prepared for an invasion of Britain. American efforts to come to the rescue had first to contend with the German attempt, as in World War I, to starve Britain into submission by destroying its seaborne lifeline. Advances in technology meant that the U-boats were far more effective than in World War I, and at first German submarines sank American ships faster than they could be built. The toll eventually reached 4,786 merchant ships, nearly double the number in World War I. Submarines also exacted a high military cost. Before the war ended, almost 200 warships became victims of torpedoes. The human toll reached 40,000 Allied seamen and almost as many Germans who perished in their 781 stricken U-boats.

The Germans profited from the fact that the Allies had done little to prepare for another battle on the Atlantic. The British had not laid down mines to defend coastal waters nor armed merchant vessels. Because Americans did not institute blackouts until the spring of 1942, shorelines brilliantly illuminated merchant targets. Using only 6 U-boats, the Germans sank 82 ships off the American East Coast and more than 200 additional ships in the waters around Bermuda and the Caribbean islands. Bathers at Virginia Beach in the bright sunshine of June 15, 1942, watched aghast as a U-boat on the surface sank two merchant vessels. Soon afterward the beach was awash with oily debris and bodies.

Until 1943, the war in the Atlantic remained in doubt and the British Isles hung by a precarious thread over the cruel sea. But with the use of newly invented effective radar detectors and production of sufficient destroyer escorts for merchant vessels, the United States gained the ability to move massive amounts of supplies to England and to the Soviet ports of Murmansk and Archangel. The battle of the Atlantic had been won.

While imperial Japanese forces were spreading through Asia, Hitler's army smashed deep into the Soviet Union and prepared for an invasion of Britain.

The big question was how to return to the European continent, which was dominated by the formidable German war machine. In the west, a buildup of Nazi military might threatened an invasion of Great Britain across the English Channel, and in the east two hundred Nazi armies devoured vast Soviet territory and millions of soldiers and citizens. Soviet Premier Joseph Stalin begged the Allies to open a second, western front against the Nazis to divert German divisions away from his bloody doorstep before they delivered a final, crushing blow. The issue was where the Allies should open a second front against Hitler. Stalin strongly urged an immediate and massive invasion of France across the English Channel, but Churchill favored something smaller, perhaps a Mediterranean target such as Europe's "soft underbelly," the Balkans. Roosevelt worried about a plan that would merely "peck on the periphery," but ultimately he backed an invasion of North Africa first. Since the United States' rapidly expanding military force was clearly the vital element in any western front, Roosevelt's wishes prevailed.

In October 1942, at El-Alamein in Egypt, the British halted General Erwin Rommel's Nazi soldiers who were driving on Egypt and the Suez Canal. In November, the Americans made their long-awaited landing in French Morocco under the leadership of the supreme commander of American forces in Europe, General Dwight D. Eisenhower. General George Patton, the ablest U.S. tank commander, joined with the British in pursuit of the Axis armies. In May

1943, Allied armies closed the jaws of a gigantic vice on the last German and Italian troops in North Africa. The North African campaign cost the Axis dearly—some 350,000 dead and captured—and re-opened the Mediterranean to Allied shipping. But in Stalin's view, North Africa was a miserable excuse for a second front, for it diverted only 15 German divisions from the Soviet Union, not the 40 Stalin wanted.

As the North African campaign unfolded, Roosevelt arrived at the Moroccan city of Casablanca in January 1943 to confer with his fellow Allied leaders. Joining him were Winston Churchill and General Charles de Gaulle, the leader of the Free French government in exile. Stalin, preoccupied with the desperate defense of Stalingrad at the easternmost penetration of the German advance, was an absent but watchful partner. Pledged to rid the world of the Axis menace, the Allied leaders announced that they would insist on "unconditional surrender." Of equal importance was their decision to postpone the cross-channel invasion of France. The decision meant that the Soviet Union would continue to absorb the brunt of the Nazi attack. Before the war ended, Soviet casualties would reach approximately 20 million, far more than those of any other nation. Instead of invading France, Roosevelt decided to strike Italy, while troop strength was building up in England for the crucial return to France. The plan was for Allied troops to invade Sicily first and then drive quickly up the boot of Italy, knocking the Axis's junior partner out of the war.

On July 10, 1943, a combined American and British amphibious operation, the largest in history, landed 160,000 troops in Sicily. The badly equipped Italian defenders, many of whom had lost their will to fight in the disastrous North African campaign, quickly withdrew to the mainland. The Allied capture of Sicily marked the end for Mussolini. The Fascist Grand Council expelled him from power. In September, the Allies invaded the Italian mainland. Five days later, the Italian government surrendered unconditionally. But the Germans rushed additional divisions into the country and seized Rome. The military campaign in Italy became a war of liberation against German occupation.

Success came hard against the Germans, who waited in sophisticated fortifications atop the mountainous Italian terrain. Not until June 1944, after a long and bloody campaign, did massive fire-power finally breach the German lines and enable Allied forces to liberate Rome. From then to the end of the war, the Allies struggled against German

AN ITALIAN TOWN SURRENDERS
In 1943 the Roosevelt administration authorized a special unit of "combat artists" to present an "integrated picture of war in all its phases." Edward Reep, a trained infantryman as well as an artist, achieved rare authenticity from his own combat experience. Contorted body postures and tilted buildings express the frenzied moment when Italian partisans celebrated the liberation of their town and terrified German soldiers ran to Reep's invading unit to escape revenge.
Courtesy U.S. Army Center of Military History.

mountain defenses in northern Italy. The Italian campaign was the costliest of the war to the American infantry. Eventually it diverted 25 German divisions that might otherwise have been thrown against the Russians or a second front in France. Still, it was not the all-out second front that an increasingly embittered Stalin demanded.

The War at Home

The experience of Americans during World War II was unlike that of other peoples around the world. For millions of French, German, Russian, Chinese, and Japanese, the war meant air raids, invasion, and occupation, devastation and terror, cities and countryside turned into battlefields. In the United States,

no physical destruction occurred, no territorial lines were redrawn, no governments fell, no one starved, and no civilians lost their lives in the fighting. Still, World War II changed the nation. Inevitably, a war as vast and as long as World War II disrupted the traditional social patterns it sought to defend. Total war meant that millions of troops went to unheard of places to face unimagined dangers. Total war also meant the mobilization of the entire home front to serve the nation's armed forces abroad.

Conversion of the economy to war purposes drew millions away from their roots to seize opportunities they never had before in places where they never expected to live. Women welding in the shipyards in California, men building tanks in the factories of Detroit, and children everywhere stripping scarce tinfoil from empty cigarette packs—all felt the impact of the war and were changed by it.

From Reform to Recovery

There is partial truth in the observation that Adolf Hitler was more responsible for ending the depression in the United States than was Franklin Roosevelt. The nation's military buildup of 1940–1941 did more to revive industry and reduce unemployment than had any New Deal program. But preparedness spending confirmed the Roosevelt administration's deficit-spending approach. It simply showed that Roosevelt's insistence on trying to balance the budget while defeating the depression was naive. In 1939, the federal budget was $9 billion. By 1945, it had grown to $100 billion. When Keynesian economics were allowed to work, the nation pulled out of the economic doldrums. But it did not do so overnight. In 1940, some 14.6 percent of the nation's workforce was unemployed. In 1941, when defense industries were starting to hum, unemployment still stood at nearly 10 percent. But after Pearl Harbor, war work at home and military service abroad virtually ended unemployment.

By 1941, there was no longer much talk about reform. The New Deal had run out of ideas and had been hampered by effective conservative opposition years before. Now the last thoughts of reform gave way to war. As Roosevelt said later, he had given up being "Dr. New Deal" in order to become "Dr. Win the War." The nation had entered World War I in the context of progressivism and its idealist expectations. But the U.S. entry into World War II came in the context of the depression and was less romantic than practical. The feeling was that there was a job to be done. Industry had to be converted to wartime production and an army and navy had to be raised. Preparedness campaigns before the war had put some men in uniform, but not enough. And the Lend-Lease program had begun to transform American industry, but industry remained far from a wartime footing.

The Roosevelt administration oversaw a miracle of production. The president brought to Washington businessmen from private industry to carry out the swiftest and fullest possible mobilization of the nation's productive capacity. These "dollar-a-year men" (so called because they served without pay) headed the rapidly multiplying war production agencies. The federal government invested billions in factories, military bases, power plants, and transportation facilities. The huge sums flowing into California shipyards and aircraft factories transformed the sleepy western state into one of the nation's most dynamic. Despite confusion and chaos, the country's economic achievement was staggering. The United States produced 275,000 airplanes during the war and by 1945 was launching a new ship every twenty-four hours. The United States not only produced what it needed to fight the Axis but also supplied the British, French, and Russians with a large part of what they required. By 1942, American production equaled that of Germany, Italy, and Japan combined. By 1944, it doubled Axis production.

Almost as impressive was the nation's mobilization of its armed forces. Draft boards registered 31 million men, of whom 10 million were inducted into service. In addition, more than 5 million men and women volunteered. When the war ended, 10,400,000 had served in the army, 3,900,000 in the navy, 600,000 in the marines, and 240,000 in the coast guard.

> *There is partial truth in the observation that Adolf Hitler was more responsible for ending the depression in the United States than was Franklin Roosevelt.*

The war boom favored large businesses and farms. In agriculture, family farms declined and tenant farmers virtually disappeared. The change was dramatically demonstrated by the migration of black farmworkers to urban centers, both North and South. By 1950, the census showed that only 115,000 African Americans remained on the land out of a total of 1,406,000 who had lived on farms when the war started. In general, however, agriculture prospered. To feed both Americans and Allies, American farmers increased production in 1942 by 25 percent and continued to increase it at that rate for the rest of the war. In business, large firms did better than small ones, but by 1943, business profits in general had soared well beyond those of 1929.

The war also restored prosperity to American workers. Rather than too little work for too many workers, as in the depression, the war years witnessed a booming economy and labor shortages. With more than 15 million adults in the military, new workers—the old, the young, and especially women—were brought into the labor force. The cost of living increased 30 percent from 1941 to 1945, while weekly earnings of workers employed in manufacturing increased 70 percent. But civilians

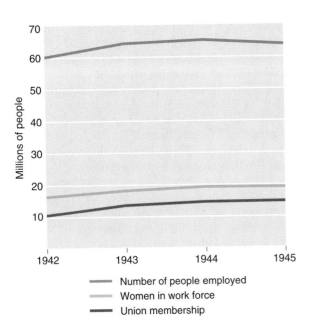

FIGURE 25.1
World War II and the Economy, 1942–1945
The end of the Depression followed by war mobilization
sent employment and union membership to high levels
that continued into peacetime. Women lost many jobs in
heavy industry after the war, but their increased numbers
in the total work force were sustained by the strong econ-
omy that followed.

on the home front also felt the pinch of war. Government management of the economy meant a system of wage and price controls that hurt some and aided others. Production for war meant that some items—automobiles, washing machines, refrigerators—were no longer being produced. The government also instituted a system of rationing of many basic items. Coffee was rationed because of the decline in ocean shipping, canned goods because of insufficient tin, and shoes because of the needs of soldiers and sailors. The government also rationed gasoline, which was plentiful, in order to save rubber tires, which were not. Americans were cautioned with the slogan "Hitler Smiles When You Waste Miles." Ration books were a tremendous bother, but they did not symbolize real privation.

Although the profits of war were not evenly distributed and rationing was a daily aggravation, Americans on the home front rallied around the war effort in unprecedented unity. Economic gains were broadly enough distributed so that the harsh rhetoric that characterized relations between rich and poor during the 1930s largely disappeared.

Moreover, after Pearl Harbor, Americans were convinced that they were engaged in a necessary war against evil regimes. With few dissenters, vigilantes rarely attacked other Americans in the name of patriotism. Wanting to avoid hysteria and hatred, Roosevelt opposed the creation of a high-powered propaganda campaign such as Wilson's during World War I. The government did not forgo control of news and opinion, however. It exercised censorship, especially of bad news from the war zone. But with one great and tragic exception, the nation survived the war without a wholesale violation of citizens' civil rights.

Political Crosscurrents

With the nation enjoying full employment and the need for New Deal programs waning, the Roosevelt administration had difficulty holding its governing coalition together. Resentment over price controls and shortages of rationed goods, white indignation over blacks leaving their subordinate place on southern farms, and dismay that the war was not going as well as it should provoked discontent with the Democratic administration. Moreover, in the congressional elections of 1942, Democrats were denied considerable support from soldiers and defense workers who were unable to cast their usual Democratic votes because the war had taken them away from the hometowns where they were registered. As a consequence, voter turnout was low in 1942, and Republicans gained forty-four seats in the House and nine in the Senate.

Republican opponents saw the war years as an opportunity to roll back New Deal reforms in favor of traditional American free enterprise values. The conservative coalition of Republicans and southern Democrats succeeded in abolishing several New Deal agencies in 1942 and 1943, including the Work Projects Administration and the Civilian Conservation Corps. But the Democratic administration did not sit idly by while Republicans dismantled their work of the 1930s. By persuading states to ease residency requirements and Congress to guarantee absentee ballots for servicemen, they arranged to bring scattered members of the New Deal coalition back into the fold.

Roosevelt also made strategic changes in preparation for the presidential election of 1944. Although exhausted and ill, he announced that he would run for an unprecedented fourth term. "All that is within me," he declared, "cries out to go back to my home on the Hudson River. . . . But as a good soldier . . . I will accept and serve." Convinced that many Americans had soured on liberal reform, Roosevelt replaced Vice President Henry Wallace, an outspoken progressive, with a more politically viable running mate, Senator Harry S. Truman of Missouri. A reliable party man from a border state, Truman seemed safe to urban Democratic leaders and to southerners nervous about challenges to segregation.

The Republicans, confident of riding the strong conservative upsurge to the White House, nominated the governor of New York, Thomas E. Dewey. Dewey was handicapped in the campaign by his general agreement with much of the New Deal and with Roosevelt's handling of the war. Dewey's chief advantage was Roosevelt's failing health, but the Republicans

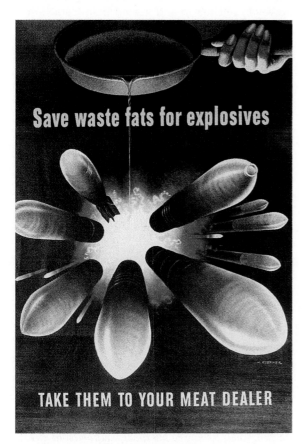

Save waste fats for explosives

TAKE THEM TO YOUR MEAT DEALER

OWI PROPAGANDA POSTER
The Office of War Information mobilized art and propaganda in many ways to connect the home front with the battlefield. Though little fat actually went from the frying pan into the firing line, this poster is a visually startling example of attempts to remind people that even the simplest acts could contribute to the war effort.
Library of Congress.

underestimated the unwillingness of the American people to change presidents at the height of a foreign war. Roosevelt's victory was his narrowest (53.5 percent of the popular vote), but it assured him of four more years in the White House, if he lived.

Women, Family, and the War

World War II meant astonishing changes in women's lives. Public attitudes about workingwomen changed overnight. During the depression, workingwomen were often accused of taking a husband's or father's job, but with the war, government and industry actively recruited women. Old ideas were not dead, of course. Women found themselves caught between the idealized role of the girl left behind to keep the home fires burning and the need to take up in the workplace where the warriors had left off. However uncomfortable their ambivalent situation, millions of women entered the workforce during the war, increasing by more than half the number of workingwomen. Three-fourths of the women entering were married and nearly four million had children. Women who were already working for wages often quit jobs as domestic servants and waitresses for war work at better pay.

The ambivalence for women between their place at home and in the factory showed in the fact that the average age for marriage went down to just over twenty and the birthrate rose, while at the same time women increased their presence in industry, especially in war production. By 1944, some 18 million women had jobs, 50 percent more than in 1939. The symbol for women performing what was traditionally men's work was "Rosie the Riveter," who according to a popular song was busy "making history working for victory." *Chicago Tribune* columnist Mike Royko remembered: "My sister became Rosie the Riveter. She put a bandanna on her head every day and went down to this organ company that had been converted to war work. There was my sister in slacks. It became more than work. There was a sense of mission about it. Her husband was Over There." The nation celebrated these women who loaded shells, packed parachutes, and built tanks, ships, and airplanes, and the women were rightfully proud of their accomplishments.

Women were often amazed at the salaries they earned. A mountain woman remembered her first job after the depression at a munitions plant in Viola, Kentucky. "We made the fabulous sum of thirty-two dollars a week," she said. "To us it was just an absolute miracle. Before that, we made nothing." A black woman from Clarksville, Tennessee, went to Los Angeles to work as a maid but ended up working in the aircraft industry at $40 a week. "When I left Tennessee," she remembered, "I was only makin' two-fifty a week, so that was quite a jump." Yet women's weekly wages averaged about $31, men made $54, a discrepancy reflecting women's more menial jobs and lower seniority.

World War II meant astonishing changes in women's lives. Public attitudes about working women changed overnight. By 1944, some 18 million women had jobs, 50 percent more than in 1939.

Alongside women in the civilian workforce stood 350,000 women who joined the Nurse's Corps and the newly created military units the army WACs, navy Waves, coast guard Spars, and the Women's Marine Corps. Women also served as pilots in the WASPs (Women Air Service Pilots). While barred from combat duty, women worked at nearly every noncombat assignment. Women in the military never achieved a secure place within the staunchly male system, but the Nurse's Corps, drawing on a respected tradition of service in America's wars, gained officer rank and attracted many recruits.

Despite the war's dynamic social changes, most women remained in the home and worked only part-time or not at all. The yearning in the midst of war for the peacetime joys of security and family, felt mutually by isolated women and fighting men, reinforced traditional attitudes. Those attitudes became more practical, too. With men no longer unemployed and wages up, family survival depended less on women earning money outside the home. The increase in consumer wealth also nurtured hopes for a comfortable home and the ability to raise children in vastly better circumstances than during the depression. While most women enjoyed the economic and social freedom that came with work outside the home, a substantial number saw work as necessary and temporary, something to set aside when the men came home.

Not all trends pointed in the direction of middle-class stability, however. The absence of millions of able-bodied young men left many families without a father in the house or traveling from one military base to the next. Drastic housing shortages near military installations and in cities where war work

boomed forced many families into poor living conditions. When one woman, who was fourteen years old in 1941, was asked about her wartime experience, she replied: "What I feel most about the war, it disrupted my family. That really chokes me up, makes me feel very sad that I lost that. On December 6, 1941, I was playing with paper dolls. . . . After Pearl Harbor, I never played dolls again."

The war took a toll on families. The number of marriages and the birthrate rose, but so too did illegitimacy and divorce. Teenagers encountered an unstable mix of opportunity and danger as they increasingly entered the workforce. The absence of older men also meant that young people had less guidance than usual. Juvenile delinquency, especially among girls, increased dramatically. Other children, however, pitched in and gained the satisfaction of

FEMALE DEFENSE WORKER
The war effort brought persons and activities together in unlikely ways, leading to unexpected outcomes. In this photo, for example, the Army magazine, Yank, *sought to boost morale by presenting a defense worker as pin-up girl. No one could know that the young propeller technician, nineteen year-old Norma Jean Baker Dougherty, would later remake herself as the most glamorous of movie stars, Marilyn Monroe.*
David Conover Images © Norma Jean Enterprises, a division of 733548 Ontario Limited.

being part of the war effort. Boy scouts, for example, sponsored scrap drives collecting iron, steel, brass, bronze, tin, and wastepaper. Wartime disruption redoubled the yearning for a stable, secure life when the war ended and the veterans came home.

Prejudice and the War

Fighting against Nazism and its ideology of Aryan racial supremacy under the banner of democracy forced Americans to examine prejudice in their own society. No one needed to instruct Asian Americans, Mexican Americans, African Americans, or Native Americans about the chasm between assertions of freedom and equality and the realities of prejudice and discrimination. War forced minority Americans to consider what they owed their country. On his way to the European front, a young Mexican American soldier reflected on his dilemma. "Why fight for America when you have not been treated as an American?" he asked. He answered that America was where he had been born, his home. "All we wanted," he decided, "was a chance to prove how loyal and American we were."

DOUBLE V BUTTON
The Double V became African Americans' special version of the official "V for victory" symbol. Thousands of these buttons were worn as a reminder that both the Axis powers and racial discrimination should surrender unconditionally. Private Collection.

African American leader W. E. B. Du Bois defined World War II as a War for Racial Equality and a struggle for "democracy not only for white folks but for yellow, brown, and black."

Minorities rallied to the war effort as Americans, but winning the war meant more than just defeating Hitler and Tojo. African American leader W. E. B. Du Bois defined World War II as a "war for racial equality" and a struggle for "democracy not only for white folks but for yellow, brown, and black." More than 13,000 Chinese Americans and more than 25,000 Native Americans fought in the armed forces. Mexican Americans feared that the war would mean deportation; instead, more than 200,000 laborers were imported from Mexico to cultivate American crops in the federal government's "*bracero*" program. Some 500,000 Mexican Americans served in the U.S. armed forces, but even while they were fighting for democracy abroad, they suffered racial violence at home. In 1943, "zoot suit" riots exploded in Los Angeles when hundreds of white servicemen

claiming they were punishing draft-dodgers, chased and beat young Chicano men who dressed in distinctive broad-shouldered, peg-legged suits. Racial prejudice, sometimes severe, remained in place to mock the nation's democratic war aims. Japanese Americans especially found their fellow Americans less accepting, not more. European Jews, who knew from experience that racism could become genocide, searched desperately for a haven from the horrors of the Holocaust but found small comfort in the United States.

African Americans and the Double V

As they had done in World War I, African Americans regarded the war as a chance to prove their patriotism and advance their condition. Such aspirations squared perfectly with official proclamations of the war as a fight for democracy. In a letter to the Southern Negro Youth Congress, Roosevelt declared that blacks were in the war "not only to defend America but . . . to establish a universal freedom under which a new basis of security and prosperity can be established for all—regardless of station, race, or creed." His opponent for the presidency in 1940,

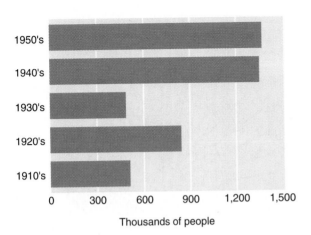

FIGURE 25.2
Black Migration from the South, 1910–1960
Spurred by desire for better economic and social conditions, African Americans after 1910 headed north in unprecedented numbers. The flow grew to a flood in the 1940s and 1950s, driven by the availability of defense work in the North and the decline of the sharecropping system in the South.

Wendell Willkie, pressed the issue even more insistently. The United States, Willkie stated, could not justly eliminate "the forces of imperialism abroad and maintain any form of imperialism at home." Encouraged by signs of sympathetic concern, the Pittsburgh *Courier*, a leading black newspaper, rejoiced that, though "war may be hell for some," it appeared ready to "open up the portals of heaven for us."

When the American defense industry moved into high gear in 1940–1941, however, African Americans learned that old discriminatory patterns pervaded the arsenal of democracy. Black organizations sent a barrage of petitions to Congress and the White House demanding that the federal government require companies receiving defense contracts to integrate their workforces. In the summer of 1941, black labor leader A. Philip Randolph, who had opposed World War I as a white man's cause, finally got Roosevelt's attention. As head of the Brotherhood of Sleeping Car Porters, a union made up overwhelmingly of blacks, he promised that 100,000 marchers would descend on Washington if the president did not eliminate discrimination in defense industries.

Alarmed at the prospect of such an embarrassment and persuaded by Eleanor Roosevelt's argument for justice, the president overcame his nervousness about offending old southern and union allies. He issued Executive Order 8802 directing defense contractors to hire blacks and whites on an equal basis and establishing a Committee on Fair Employment Practices to investigate violations of the order. Randolph called the march off, and civil rights champions hailed the historic significance of the first direct presidential intervention on behalf of black civil rights.

Actual progress developed slowly, however. Five and a half million blacks abandoned the rural South in the 1940s and flooded into industrial cities, making African Americans a predominantly urban population for the first time. Early black migrants discovered that industry policies barred them from many prospective jobs, skilled and unskilled. The rapidly expanding aircraft industry provided the most striking example of exclusion. Aircraft manufacture nationwide included only 240 black employees at the start of the war. Douglas Aircraft, a major supplier, had only 10 black workers. Much of organized labor, particularly the older AFL craft unions, defended exclusionary practices. Eighteen major unions, including such vital participants in the defense industry as the machinists, iron shipbuilders, and railway workers, had explicit bans against black membership.

In time, however, severe labor shortages and government pressure opened up defense plants to African American workers. Black unemployment dropped by about 80 percent during the war, and the percentage of blacks in the defense industry doubled to a level almost equal to the percentage of blacks in the general population. Earnings and union membership went up impressively. The end result, however, was not enough to wipe out centuries of discrimination. By the end of the war, the average income of black families was only half that of white families.

While migration into industrial cities improved African Americans' economic fortunes, it also led to racial friction. Racial antagonism boiled over in the hot summer of 1943. That year, there were 242 racial outbreaks in forty-seven different cities, far surpassing the total of 26 riots in the grim Red scare year of 1919. Worst of all were the two days of mayhem in Detroit. The city was coping with more than half a million newcomers, more than 50,000 of them black, who had come mostly to seek jobs at auto factories converted to war production and at the vast new Willow Run aircraft plant. Conflict between whites and blacks at a city park ignited a race war that saw whites smash their way with clubs through black neighborhoods and blacks retaliate by destroying and looting white-owned businesses in their neighborhoods. In the end, scores of persons suffered injury and thirty-four died, including twenty-five African Americans.

But race relations on the home front were not uniformly dismal. The National Association for the Advancement of Colored People (NAACP) launched the "Double V" campaign—victory at home and abroad—and attacked racism on a broad front. In 1942, civil rights activists who wanted to move more swiftly than the NAACP founded a new organization, the Congress of Racial Equality (CORE), that attacked segregation vigorously. CORE took direct action by organizing sit-ins against Jim Crow restaurants and theaters. By war's end, both the NAACP and CORE could point to large memberships and significant triumphs.

The military was no more free of discrimination than was the home front. Secretary of War Henry Stimson, who presided firmly over the war effort, opposed any change in the segregation of blacks and whites into separate units and declared that the military effort should not serve as a "sociological laboratory." In 1942, Stimson fumed in his diary about what he deemed the absurdly presumptuous claims of black reformers: "What these foolish leaders of the colored race are seeking is at bottom social equality." Top military brass echoed Stimson's sentiments and worked to keep African Americans in segregated units that were restricted to menial tasks. "Experiments to meet the wishes and demands of the champions of every race and creed for the solution of their problems," the army adjutant general's office warned, "are a danger to efficiency, discipline and morale, and would result in ultimate defeat."

Denied desegregated armed forces, blacks joined anyway, and by the end of the war nearly one million African American men and women had served. Segregated practices loosened as the war progressed. Blacks were trained as pilots for the first time, served on warships with white sailors, and saw extensive combat duty in the ground war in Europe and the Pacific. Yet military facilities remained segregated, and the Red Cross even segregated by race the blood it supplied to treat battlefield casualties.

In 1944, the Swedish sociologist Gunnar Myrdal in his classic report on race in America, *The American Dilemma*, concluded that "not since Reconstruction, has there been more reason to anticipate fundamental changes in American race relations." Indeed, World War II marked a watershed in the history of black Americans. Their wartime move upward inspired hope and shaped the tactics that blacks would use thereafter in the quest for rights and opportunity. But much of that battle lay ahead. Perhaps nothing more poignantly captured the reality of wartime race relations than the moment when Lloyd Brown, a black soldier caught in the dusty heat of a Kansas summer day, gazed past the restaurant owner denying him entry and saw a row of German prisoners of war enjoying their lunch at the counter.

The Plight of Japanese Americans

World War II did not witness a repetition of the madness, hysteria, and viciousness that had characterized the home front during World War I. Few questioned the war, and there was little to provoke repression. Americans were worried about espionage, however. Walls were plastered with slogans such as "Loose lips sink ships" and "Enemy agents are always near; if you don't talk, they won't hear." But the government engaged in no high-powered propaganda campaign to whip Americans into a frenzy against its enemies and mounted no wholesale attack on civil liberties.

There was one major exception—the drastic violation of the rights of Japanese Americans. Americans of Japanese ancestry were the only minority group to lose ground during the war. From the time of their first entry into the country in significant numbers in the 1890s, mainly to settle on the West Coast, the Japanese had encountered hostility as economic competitors and intruders in a "white man's country." Although they were law-abiding and successful in small businesses and farming, white prejudice prevailed. In 1907, the Japanese government was forced to accept a humiliating "gentleman's agreement" that reduced the numbers of new Japanese immigrants in exchange for the right of Asians to attend public schools in California.

In 1924, the federal government went even further by declaring that Japanese immigrants were "aliens ineligible to citizenship." In rejecting an appeal that the law violated the right of all citizens to equal protection, the Supreme Court declared that the Fourteenth Amendment conferring that right applied only to whites and ex-slaves. As intended, the ruling halted the influx of Japanese and left unnaturalized Japanese immigrants (called "Issei") permanently in limbo as residents who could never become citizens. The absurdity of the situation was heightened by the fact that the Issei's children ("Nisei") were automatically citizens by virtue of having been born in the United States.

Japanese Internment

Angrily determined that the bombing of Pearl Harbor would not be followed by more sneak attacks, military and political leaders on the West Coast targeted persons of Japanese descent—alien and citizen alike—as potential saboteurs. Early in 1942, General John DeWitt, commander of the Western Defense Command, persuaded President Franklin Roosevelt to issue an executive order authorizing the removal of the Japanese. Subsequently, some 110,000 Japanese Americans were confined to relocation camps in remote areas, surrounded by barbed wire and armed guards. DeWitt's recommendation expressed concern for military security within racist conceptions long used to curb Asian immigration.

DOCUMENT 1. Final Recommendations of the Commanding General, Western Defense Command and Fourth Army, Submitted to the Secretary of War

February 14, 1942

Memorandum for the Secretary of War.

Subject: Evacuation of Japanese and Other Subversive Persons from the Pacific Coast.

1. In presenting a recommendation for the evacuation of Japanese and other subversive persons from the Pacific Coast, the following facts have been considered:
    a. Mission of the Western Defense Command and Fourth Army.
        (1) Defense of the Pacific Coast of the Western Defense Command, as extended, against attacks by sea, land, or air;
        (2) Local protection of establishment and communications vital to the National Defense for which adequate defense cannot be provided by local civilian authorities.
    b. Brief Estimate of the Situation.
        (1) . . . The following are possible and probable enemy activities: . . .
            (a) Naval attack on shipping on coastal waters;
            (b) Naval attack on coastal cities and vital installations;
            (c) Air raids on vital installations, particularly within two hundred miles of the coast;
            (d) Sabotage of vital installations throughout the Western Defense Command.

Hostile Naval and air raids will be assisted by enemy agents signaling from the coastline and the vicinity thereof; and by supplying and otherwise assisting enemy vessels and by sabotage.

In the war in which we are now engaged racial affinities are severed by migration. The Japanese race is an enemy race and while many second and third generation Japanese born on United States soil, possessed of United States citizenship, have become "Americanized," the racial strains are undiluted. To conclude otherwise is to expect that children born of white parents on Japanese soil sever all racial affinity and become loyal Japanese subjects, ready to fight and, if necessary, to die for Japan in a war against the nation of their parents. . . .

It, therefore, follows that along the vital Pacific Coast over 112,000 potential enemies, of Japanese extraction, are at large today. There are indications that these are organized and ready for concerted action at a favorable opportunity. The very fact that no sabotage has taken place to date is a disturbing and confirming indication that such action will be taken. . . .

Imprisoned in bleak surroundings far from home, Japanese internees were prey to despair and bitterness. Looking back after forty years, Kazue Yamane recalled her confinement as a disturbing and baffling experience.

DOCUMENT 2. An Oral History of Life in the Japanese American Detention Camps

In April 1942, my husband and I and our two children left for camp, and my mother-in-law and father-in-law came about a month later. I wasn't afraid, but I kept asking in my mind, how could they? This is impossible. Even today I still think it was a nightmarish thing. I cannot reconcile myself to the fact that I had to go, that I was interned, that I was segregated, that I was taken away, even though it goes back forty years. . . .

I was separated from my husband; he went to the Santa Fe, New Mexico, camp. All our letters were censored; all our letters were cut in parts and all that. So we were not too sure what messages was getting through and not getting through, but I do know that I informed him many times of his mother's condition. He should have been allowed to come back to see her, because I thought she wouldn't live too long, but they never did allow him to come back, even for her funeral. They did not allow that. I learned that a lot of the messages didn't get to him; they were crossed out. I now have those letters with me.

In 1944 I was left with his parents and our kids. But I had no time to think of what was going to happen because my child was always sick and I had been quite sick. . . .

My son knew what was going on, and he too had many times asked me why . . . you know, why? why? Of course, I had no explanation why this was happening to us. . . .

*F*orcibly removed from the tension between his life as a student at the University of California at Berkeley and his unassimilated family, Charles Kikuchi sought in his prison camp diary to make sense of the internment and to judge where it would lead.

Document 3. The Kikuchi Diary

December 7, 1941, Berkeley, California
Pearl Harbor. We are at war! Jesus Christ, the Japs bombed Hawaii and the entire fleet has been sunk. I just can't believe it. I don't know what in the hell is going to happen to us, but we will all be called into the Army right away.

. . . The next five years will determine the future of the Nisei. They are now at the crossroads. Will they be able to take it or will they go under? If we are ever going to prove our Americanism, this is the time. The Anti-Jap feeling is bound to rise to hysterical heights, and it is most likely that the Nisei will be included as Japs. I wanted to go to San Francisco tonight, but Pierre says I am crazy. He says it's best we stick on campus. In any event, we can't remain on the fence, and a positive approach must be taken if we are to have a place in fulfilling the Promise of America. I think the U.S. is in danger of going Fascist too, or maybe Socialist. . . .

I don't know what to think or do. Everybody is in a daze.

April 30,1942, Berkeley
Today is the day that we are going to get kicked out of Berkeley. It certainly is degrading. . . .

I'm supposed to see my family at Tanforan as Jack told me to give the same family number. I wonder how it is going to be living with them as I haven't done this for years and years? I should have gone over to San Francisco and evacuated with them, but I had a last final to take. I understand that we are going to live in the horse stalls. I hope that the Army has the courtesy to remove the manure first. . . .

July 14, 1942
Marie, Ann, Mitch, Jimmy, Jack, and myself got into a long discussion about how much democracy meant to us as individuals. Mitch says that he would even go in the army and die for it, in spite of the fact that he knew he would be kept down. Marie said that although democracy was not perfect, it was the only system that offered any hope for a future, if we could fulfill its destinies. Jack was a little more skeptical. He even suggested that we [could] be in such grave danger that we would then realize that we were losing something. Where this point was he could not say. I said that this was what happened in France and they lost all. Jimmy suggested that the colored races of the world had reason to feel despair and mistrust the white man because of the past experiences. . . .

In reviewing the four months here, the chief value I got out of this forced evacuation was the strengthening of the family bonds. I never knew my family before this and this was the first chance that I have had to really get acquainted. . . .

Document 1. *Final Recommendations,* report by General John Lesesne Dewitt to the United States Secretary of War, February 14, 1942.

Document 2. John Tateishi, *And Justice for All.* Copyright ©1984 by John Tateishi. Reprinted by permission of Random House, Inc.

Document 3. John Modell, ed., *The Kikuchi Diary: Chronicle from an American Concentration Camp,* 43, 51, 183, 252. Copyright 1973 by the Board of Trustees of the University of Illinois. Used with the permission of the University of Illinois Press.

Hostility did not end with the cessation of immigration, however. In the 1930s, the *Los Angeles Times* led a fresh anti-Japanese campaign, arguing that Japanese Americans were still a threat because they would multiply endlessly and then, closed off within their sinister enclaves, conspire to outcompete "real" Americans. The argument made no demographic or economic sense. In 1940, there were only 127,000 Japanese Americans. They were concentrated in agriculture in California, and their role in the economy was to provide cheap food, exactly what white workers, managers, and homemakers should have hailed. What little tolerance there was evaporated in the storm of hatred that followed the attack on Pearl Harbor.

The idea that the Japanese were unassimilable, aliens who were forever loyal to the land of their ancestors, provided an excuse to regard them as a subversive threat. Even though a military survey concluded that Japanese Americans posed no danger, General John DeWitt, army commander for the West Coast, and California law officials decided to take them into custody. "A Jap's a Jap," DeWitt explained. "It makes no difference whether he's an American or not." On February 19, 1942, Roosevelt gave that racist premise the force of law in an executive order that authorized the roundup of all Americans of Japanese descent. Allowed little time to secure or sell their property, the victims lost most of their assets, their jobs, and their homes. Most were American citizens; no one was charged with a crime; and not a single case of subversion or sabotage was ever uncovered. Still, Japanese Americans were sent to "relocation centers"—makeshift prison camps—in remote areas of the Southwest and Great Plains—penned in by barbed wire and armed guards for more than three years. Remarkably, thousands of young Japanese American men went directly from these desert prisons to Europe, where they fought in the U.S. military against the Axis enemy. Only in 1988 did Congress award modest reparations to Japanese Americans for their wartime losses.

Gays in the Military

War posed challenges for homosexual Americans in some ways comparable to those faced by other marginalized groups. The view that gays were a threat to good order and were apt to crack under stress had long dominated military thinking. In World War I, that prejudice began to harden into a system of exclusion. The introduction of psychological testing prompted authorities to use traits associated with gays as a way of eliminating men they considered undesirable. Their efforts stalled, however, when a hunt for gay sailors at the naval training station in Newport, Rhode Island, created a sensation. Stung by revelations of entrapment tactics and the denial of rights of self-defense for the accused, the navy in 1921 established strict rules of fair courtroom procedure for trying homosexual acts as criminal conduct. That same year, the army, wanting to head off trouble at the outset, tightened its psychological screening process by issuing a set of standards that barred recruitment of sexual "perverts" and "psychopaths."

Despite their broad powers, authorities showed little inclination to act against gays in the period between the world wars when the military shrank into a small volunteer force. A few men did serve time in prison for sodomy, but psychological screening was seldom used, since officers were ill equipped to understand it. Essentially, those in charge ignored the issue of gays whenever they could conveniently do so.

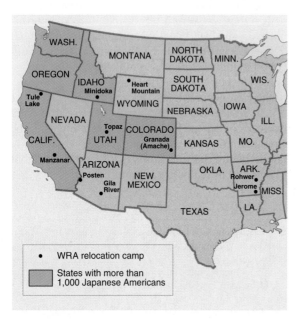

MAP 25.3
Western Relocation Authority Centers
Responding to prejudice and fear of sabotage, in 1942 President Roosevelt authorized the roundup and relocation of all Americans of Japanese descent. Taken from their homes in the cities and fertile farms of the far West, Japanese Americans were confined in desolate areas scattered as far east as the Mississippi River.

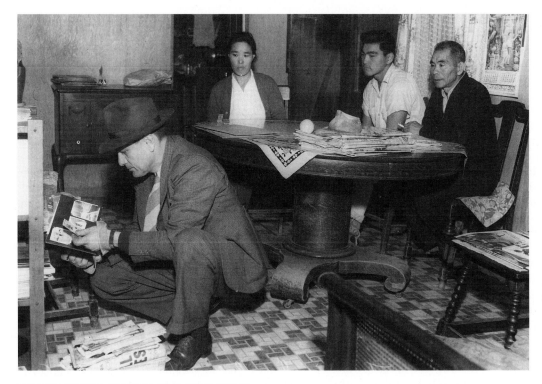

FBI SEARCHING JAPANESE AMERICAN HOME

When President Roosevelt informed military commanders that they might "from time to time" remove persons deemed dangerous, he had reason to suspect that virtually all Japanese Americans would be affected. An army "expert" on Asian culture had already advised the War Department that, "as you cannot . . . penetrate the Oriental thinking . . . the easiest course is to remove them all from the West Coast and place them . . . under guard." Intent on getting to the bottom of one Japanese American family's allegiance, an FBI agent in 1942 scrutinizes a picture album, while family members whose home has been invaded look on helplessly.

Los Angeles Daily News Morgue, Department of Special Collections, University Research Library, UCLA.

World War II aroused a new sense of crisis. Once the Selective Service Act of 1940 began bringing vast numbers of recruits into the armed forces, Secretary of War Henry Stimson reminded all commanding generals that they were expected to prosecute cases of sodomy. To screen effectively for persons who might commit such acts, the authorities turned to psychological experts in the latest theories of character disorders. Though many psychologists believed that homosexuality was a maladjustment that could be corrected, military authorities seized the experts' definition of homosexuality as a form of "disturbed sex development" and used it as grounds to purge gays from the ranks.

Stigmatized, gay Americans, like other disadvantaged minorities, found the war to be a special sort of transforming experience. Ironically, the very crisis that renewed prejudice also worked against enforcing it thoroughly. The need to build a huge fighting force made those in charge less able, or willing, to discriminate closely against potential recruits. During the course of the war, only four to five thousand men out of eighteen million examined for induction were excluded as homosexuals. And because screening procedures had been set up with only men in mind, lesbians volunteering for the newly formed women's branches of service had an even lower proportion of their numbers screened out.

Gays in the military thus served in about as many ways as other inductees, and studies made at the end of the war showed their records to be much the same. Like black and Japanese American service people, gays sought to demonstrate their worth under fire. "I was superpatriotic," explained a combat veteran. "And being a homosexual, I had that constant compelling need to prove how virile I was."

The brute experience of war put issues of sexual inclination into a blunt new perspective. In the midst of life or death realities, as one gay survivor of the Iwo Jima campaign put it, "who in the hell is going to worry about this shit?"

When peace came, gay veterans, both those who made it through the war undetected and those expelled without any veterans' benefits, tended to cluster in large cities where their sense of mutual interests and loyalty shaped their communities. Toughened by the military ordeal and angry that they had been part of a successful war against oppression while remaining oppressed themselves, veterans led the way in promoting the gay liberation movement. In 1950, a group of gay veterans formed the Mattachine Society to combat discrimination, and five years later lesbians in San Francisco followed their example by founding the Daughters of Bilitis. These efforts provided the impetus for gay activism to join in the broad front of civil rights insurgency that eventually arose in the 1960s.

Refugees from the Holocaust

As American resolve against totalitarian oppression stiffened, refugees from fascism and Nazism posed an increasingly difficult challenge to the national conscience. Throughout the 1930s, Spanish Loyalists fleeing Franco, opponents of Mussolini, and, most numerous, the targets of Hitler's maniacal racism clamored for asylum. As Hitler expanded his campaign to "purify" Germany and to clear conquered land for the Aryan master race, Jews, gypsies, religious dissenters, homosexuals, avant-garde artists, and other "degenerates" came under increasing pressure to flee or risk extermination. Within the United States, there arose a desperate contest between those who would rescue the victims of persecution and those who would bar the gate.

Roosevelt sympathized with the pleas for help, but only to an extent that did not jeopardize his foreign policy or his hold on the electorate. After the German army took over Austria in March 1938, crowds of Jews besieged the American embassy in Vienna, seeking immigration visas. Roosevelt tried to raise the annual quota, which allowed only 1,400 Austrians into the country, but Congress, trying to keep out of war and mindful of polls showing that 82 percent of Americans were against admitting Jewish exiles, refused the request. Roosevelt then sought to persuade countries in Latin America and Africa to accept refugees. None would agree. In a

last attempt before war broke out, friends of the refugees introduced legislation in Congress in 1939 that would grant asylum to 20,000 German refugee children, most of them Jewish. Anti-Semitism, as well as isolationism, was undoubtedly a factor in the defeat of the bill, for the following year refugee English children who were not predominantly Jewish gained entry without delay.

After fending off efforts to accept more refugees before the war, Congress maintained harsh terms of exclusion even after January 1942, when Hitler devised a comprehensive plan for the "final solution": Jews and other undesirables would be sent to concentration camps in remote areas. There, old people, children, and others deemed too weak to work would be gassed and cremated immediately; the able-bodied would be put to work until lack of food and harsh conditions killed them. The Nazis made the extermination of the Jews of Europe a top secret, but news leaked out. The World Jewish Congress then took the lead for a terrified, grieving Jewish community in seeking help from the Allies. But skeptical U.S. State Department officials stood firmly in the way. When the American consul in Geneva conveyed news of Hitler's concentration camps, he added a recommendation that the report be set aside because of "the fantastic nature of the allegation, and the impossibility of our being of any assistance if such action were taken."

After fending off efforts to accept more refugees before the war, Congress maintained harsh terms of exclusion even after January 1942, when Hitler devised a comprehensive plan for the "final solution."

The State Department's resistance to evidence reflected the way victims of Nazi persecution had long been cut off from adequate help. Most nations had repeatedly refused to admit many refugees from Nazi Germany, partly out of prejudice against Jews, partly to avoid additional new burdens during the economic hard times of the 1930s. In all, up to the start of war, only 152,000 Jews managed to gain entry into the United States. From there the numbers dropped steadily to a mere 2,400 in 1944. Those trapped in Europe could only wait for rescue by Allied armies, while their champions abroad vainly pleaded with the Allies to bomb the Nazi death camps and the railroad tracks leading to them to hamper the killing operation. (See Historical Question, page 1006).

When Russian troops arrived at Auschwitz in Poland in February 1945, they found only a handful of emaciated prisoners, some of them too weak to survive their liberation. Skeletal corpses, some half burned, lay around them; nearby were ponds and pits filled with the ashes of those who had perished. The Russians discovered sheds filled with loot stripped from the dead—clothing, gold fillings, false teeth, even cloth made from human hair. Two months later, the American Third Army came to Nordhausen, where they found 700 survivors and 3,000 bodies. At last, the truth about Nazi atrocities breached the wall of denial. But by then, Nazi extermination had reached its final toll of 9 million victims.

Military Victory: 1943–1945

By early 1943, the defensive phase of the war was over. Having halted the German and Japanese offenses in Europe and in Asia, the Allies faced the daunting task of driving the Axis back, retaking vast conquered areas, and finally defeating Germany and Japan on their home territory. The Allied alliance of the United States, Britain, and the Soviet Union suffered enormous stress over the matter of the "second front" in Europe to relieve the Soviet Union from the brunt of battle against Hitler. By June 1944, when a true second front was launched, the Soviet Union had already broken German power. In the Pacific, the United States, fighting with Australia and New Zealand, defeated the Japanese and ended World War II.

From Normandy to Berlin

In November 1943, as the Italian campaign ground on at its cold, muddy pace, Churchill, Roosevelt, and Stalin held meetings in Teheran, the capital of Iran, and Cairo to plan the final assault on Hitler. Stalin finally succeeded in getting Roosevelt and Churchill to commit to a definite time for the great invasion of Europe—May 1944. The Allies had been gathering an enormous army and navy in Great Britain for nearly two years in anticipation of a return to France. General Dwight D. Eisenhower, with his great tact and organizing skills, became Supreme

Commander of the Allied Forces—American, British, and Free French—while General Sir Bernard Montgomery, the hero of victory in North Africa, took charge of the landing itself.

Led by the master tactician General Erwin Rommel, the German forces strengthened the Atlantic wall by fortifying the cliffs and mining the beaches of northwestern France. Yet, as Rommel realized more clearly than Hitler, the huge deployment of German forces in the East trying to contain the massive Soviet offensive that began in the spring of 1943 left Rommel without adequate forces to stop the 3 million Allied soldiers waiting in England. Even more of a handicap was Rommel's inability to control the air. Hitler and his air marshall, Hermann Göring, thought of air power as support for assault troops and so concentrated on short-range fighters and dive bombers to cover ground offensives. The concept had served well in the blitzkriegs, but now the Luftwaffe had only 300 fighter planes to face 12,000 Allied aircraft of all types poised for massive bombardment.

The Germans expected the invasion to come in the Pas de Calais area, where the England Channel is narrowest. False radio signals, invented armies, and fake air sorties encouraged German suspicions, but the actual invasion took place miles to the south on the beaches of Normandy. First came raging air and naval attacks, then the landing of paratroopers behind the German lines, and then at 7:30 in the morning on June 6, 1944, referred to as "D Day," seaborne soldiers hit the beaches. For a perilous moment, rough seas and fortified machine guns stopped the assault in a chaos of overturned tanks, drowning men, and frantic attempts by those who made it ashore to find cover against the withering fire from the cliffs above. But paratroopers coming up behind the German line and rangers scaling the cliffs to knock out enemy gun emplacements finally secured the beachhead. As General Omar N. Bradley observed, the Allies prevailed only by "guts, valor, and extreme bravery."

Within a week, Allied forces had broken out of the Normandy pocket and had begun to drive toward the Rhine River. As the German army was being hammered badly on both its western and eastern fronts, some German military officers began to doubt the wisdom of the war. Hoping to replace the Nazis with a new government that would negotiate a peace, they made an unsuccessful bomb attempt against Hitler in July 1944. Suspicion mistakenly fell upon Rommel, who retired to his home and committed

Why Did the Allies Refuse to Bomb the Death Camps?

ONLY A FEW DAYS AFTER the German Blitzkrieg swept through Poland in September 1939, Adolf Hitler traveled to the front to exult over victory. He summoned military commanders to one of the cars of his special train and instructed them to begin, as swiftly as possible, making room for Germans by "housecleaning" the territory of its clergy, aristocracy, intelligentsia, and Jews. Soon afterward, Nazi soldiers began shooting clusters of men, women, and children standing in burial pits the victims had dug themselves. Seeking faster and more efficient means to annihilate millions of people that would also relieve reluctant army forces from the bloody horror of shooting them, Nazi engineers then designed airtight vans that roamed the countryside suffocating the condemned with carbon monoxide gas.

With the implementation of Hitler's "final solution," killing became quicker and more efficient. Though the Nazis endeavored to keep the final solution a secret, news of what was happening to Jews, gypsies, political prisoners, and others sent away in cattle cars for "resettlement" had surfaced by the summer of 1942. In July, a shaken German businessman with mines in Poland near Auschwitz, the main death camp, informed a Jewish associate in Switzerland of the plan he had discovered to exterminate 3.5 to 4 million Jews. The World Jewish Congress then led the horrified Jewish community in a campaign to get the Allies to take action.

Once the war started and the Nazis sealed the borders of their territories, opportunities for rescue narrowed considerably. With hope waning for the hundreds of thousands of European Jews not yet sent to their deaths, pleas mounted for the Allies to bomb the death camps and the railroad tracks leading to them in order to hamper the killing operation and block further shipments of victims. Insistence rose to frenzy in April 1944, after escapees from Auschwitz brought word to the outside world of the unimaginable horror of murder and starvation. The nightmare deepened on April 19, when Jews in the ghetto of Warsaw began an armed rebellion against slow death by attrition at the hands of the Nazis. For twenty-eight days, the Jewish defenders held and then suffered total annihilation.

The rising volume of proposals to bomb the railroads and camps got no farther than the desks of Assistant Secretary of War John J. McCloy in Washington and British Foreign Secretary Anthony Eden in London. Both men were seasoned members of foreign service elites, which Jews had never penetrated. Intent on achieving military victory as soon as possible without distraction, they routinely turned aside bombing requests by insisting that the air forces could not spare resources from their strictly military missions. There was an element of moral indifference, as well. Eden's Foreign Office was especially distant and patronizing, as if fending off the usual special-interest group looking for petty favors. An eloquent plea from Chaim Weizmann, one of the most imposing Jewish leaders, elicited a routine rejection letter that ended with tragic understatement: "I understand that this decision will be a disappointment to you, but be sure that the matter was considered exhaustively."

The value of bombing the death camps was not considered exhaustively, however. Tactically, there was no reason to hesitate. The German air force could offer little resistance after 1943, when the Allies gained full control of the air. The Allies had many extra planes that could have been assigned to bomb the death camps without any hindrance to the military advance into Germany. Worries expressed about loss of life were similarly hollow. Refusing to commit heavy bombers to the mission because they would kill *some* innocent people in the camps overlooked the fact that if nothing were done *all* the innocents would die. Testimony from Auschwitz survivors shows that inmates appreciated the distinction and strongly hoped the increasing number of Allied planes they saw overhead meant that their hell would soon be bombed into oblivion.

Cautious calculation of the public interest and doubt about what could be verified also prevented action. The Office of War Information (OWI) avoided the subject of death camps out of fear that charging the Germans with crimes against humanity would incite them to greater resistance that would prolong the war and cause more American casualties. Deprived of information to dispel widespread skepticism that death camps could really exist,

THE DEAD AT BUCHENWALD *In this stark moment, all distance between official Washington and the Holocaust is breached. Soldiers and civilians pause somberly in the background as Senator Alben Barkley of Kentucky, stooped in sadness, tries to comprehend the incomprehensible.* Pentagon, U.S. Army Signal Corps.

newspapers and journals relegated news of the Holocaust to the back pages. Better to wait until the victorious armed forces could prove or refute such charges than to risk giving fake propaganda the same prominence that had so discredited journalists in World War I.

In the midst of blackout and denial, the will to disbelieve grew so strong that, when verification of the true horror did finally filter through, it tended to induce numbness. Even Supreme Court Justice Felix Frankfurter, a Jew himself and a veteran of agonizing fights against bigotry and persecution, found the truth incomprehensible. After a member of the Polish underground gave him a detailed account of the mass murder in Poland, Frankfurter denied the information as beyond the realm of possibility. "I did not say this young man is lying," he explained. "I said I cannot believe him. There is a difference." McCloy clung to the same rationalization that the nightmare could not be real. At least once, though, the will to disbelieve wavered. Leon Kubowitzki of the World Jewish Congress, after repeatedly being rebuffed by false arguments masquerading as "technical reasons" for not intervening, remembered a tense meeting with the assistant

secretary in December 1944. McCloy took Kubowitzki aside and said anxiously, "We are alone. Tell me the truth. Do you really believe that all those horrible things happened?"

By then it was too late. The Nazis had shut down the killing operations in Poland in November and were about to flee to Germany. When Russian troops arrived at Auschwitz in February 1945, they found only a handful of emaciated prisoners, some of them too weak to survive their liberation.

We have since learned that, aside from the Nazis' hasty attempt just before they fled to hide what they had been doing by wrecking the gas chambers and crematoria, the only destruction of killing apparatus was carried out by the victims themselves. In the fall of 1944, when the debate over bombing the death camps reached its peak, four women prisoners smuggled dynamite from the munitions plant at Auschwitz to men assigned to take ashes from the furnaces. Realizing that their deed was suicidal, the ash men managed to blow up one of the four furnaces and kill several SS guards. Immediately, the women were hanged and the men shot, their heroic act unknown to those who dared not send bombers instead.

M A P 25.4
The European Theater of World War II, 1942–1945
*Russian reversal of the German offensive by breaking the sieges of Stalingrad and Leningrad,
combined with Allied landings in North Africa and Normandy, placed Germany in a closing vise
of armies from all sides.*

suicide to spare his family and himself the pain of Nazi retaliation. Hitler, who now doubted the loyalty of his officer corps, retreated more and more into directing the war on the basis of his own intuition.

On August 25, the Allies liberated Paris from four years of Nazi occupation. A month later, they succeeded in pushing the Germans out of most of France. In another month, they made their first foray into Germany to capture the city of Aachen. As the giant pincers of the Allied and Soviet armies closed on German headquarters in Berlin, Hitler took a mad gamble. In December 1944, he ordered

D DAY LANDING
Amid a dense thicket of landing craft, men and equipment lucky enough to have made it through rough seas and enemy fire struggle onto the beach at Normandy on June 6, 1944, to open a second front in Europe. An intrepid photographer caught this brief moment of safe passage just before the troops advanced into withering enemy fire from the high cliffs beyond the beach.
UPI/Bettmann Archive.

a counterattack through Belgium to recapture the port of Antwerp and deny the Allies their major supply port. Massive German forces drove fifty-five miles into Allied lines in what was known as the Battle of the Bulge before being stopped at Bastogne. German losses of 82,000 men and hundreds of tanks were disastrous. By committing so many of his reserves to the Bulge, Hitler left the part of his army facing the Russians close to collapse.

In February 1945, with the end in sight, Churchill, Roosevelt, and Stalin met secretly at the Russian Black Sea resort town of Yalta to discuss the structure of the postwar world. Discussions centered on three major topics: rearranging the political map of Europe; creating a new international organization; and achieving victory over Japan. Roosevelt arrived showing the ashen pallor and shaking hands of a man who was seriously ill. Although his stamina and mental alertness flickered, he still managed to secure a major share of what he sought. The Soviets

agreed to a declaration of self-determination for the countries their armies occupied in Eastern Europe. Chiang Kai-shek would receive Allied support as leader of China in the war against Japan. The Soviet Union would gain control over the Kuril and southern Sakhalin Islands near Japan and have a say in the governance of Korea and Manchuria in exchange for entering the war against Japan after the defeat of Germany.

The "Big Three" also agreed on the creation of a new international organization, the United Nations, the details of which had been decided the year before at a conference at Dumbarton Oaks estate outside Washington, D.C. All nations would have a place in the United Nations General Assembly, but the Security Council would wield decisive power. The Security Council would be composed of temporary members and of permanent representatives from China, France, Great Britain, the Soviet Union, and the United States, each of which would retain the veto. Delegates from fifty nations, inspired by the conviction that they must not fail a second time to secure the peace after a world war, met in San Francisco in April 1945 to approve the charter of the United Nations. The response of the United States was startlingly different than it had been to the League of Nations in 1919. Internationalism triumphed over isolationism when Republican Senator Arthur Vandenberg of Michigan declared that it was his mission to "end the miserable notion that the Republican Party will return to its foxhole when the last shot in this war has been fired and will blindly let the world rot in its own anarchy." The Senate ratified the charter in July by a vote of eighty-nine to two.

Following the Yalta agreement, the Allies began the final assault on Hitler. While American forces pounded Germany from the west, the Soviets,

having swept through Poland, arrived at the outskirts of Berlin in April 1945. Hitler, who had descended into his underground bunker on January 16, committed suicide on April 30. His body was burned amidst the din of Russian cannons and the remains hurriedly buried under what is now the median strip of a superhighway. A provisional German government surrendered on May 7, 1945, ending the Nazi nightmare in Europe.

Franklin Roosevelt did not live to witness the end of the Nazi horror. On April 12, while resting in Warm Springs, Georgia, the president suffered a fatal stroke. Americans grieved publicly for the man who had led them through more than twelve years of depression and world war. And they worried aloud about his successor, Vice President Harry S. Truman. The world stood at a fateful moment in its history, and Truman was largely unknown and

TECHNOLOGY IN AMERICA
Penicillin

National Archives.

The antibacterial drug, penicillin, shown being injected into a soldier, did more than any other medical advance to save lives on the battlefield during World War II. This success was the culmination of an intense period of discovery and debate that came

to fruition just in time to meet the desperate wartime need for drugs to fight infection. In 1928, the English biochemist, Alexander Fleming, accidentally discovered that mold left on laboratory culture plates could kill bacteria. Subsequent tests on mice using the organic form of arsenic extracted from the mold, which Fleming called penicillin, proved highly effective against a wide variety of bacterial infections. These experiments succeeded in 1940, just as the Battle of Britain against the German bombing blitz was reaching its climax. After the lifesaving use of penicillin on wounded airmen and later on soldiers in North Africa, a team of British researchers rushed to the United States in 1941 to urge mass production of the drug. The campaign came to a dramatic conclusion when the Pearl Harbor bombing ended a conference on battlefield medicine being held in Honolulu the day before the British team was to present its case for penicillin. American authorities moved cautiously to make use of the new wonder drug. By April 1943 fewer than 500 men had received penicillin, but word of its astonishingly successful results convinced U.S. authorities early in 1944 to urge all medical personnel to use penicillin "without hesitation." In the final tally of the war's damage, death rates in battle were half those of World War I, and largely because of penicillin, mortality rates for disease were 27 times lower.

YALTA CONFERENCE
In February 1945, President Roosevelt and British Prime Minister Winston Churchill met with Russian leader Joseph Stalin at the Black Sea resort of Yalta to plan the postwar reconstruction of Europe. Roosevelt, near the end of his life, and Churchill, soon to suffer reelection defeat, look weary next to the resolute "Man of Steel." Controversy would later arise over whether a stronger stand by the American and British leaders could have prevented the Soviet Union from imposing communist rule on Eastern Europe.
U.S. Army.

untested. He had been vice president less than three months, and Roosevelt had consistently left him out of discussions of the conduct of the war. Truman's colleagues in Congress generally agreed that he would preside over the end of the war as little more than a caretaker, another Harding perhaps. Truman seemed to agree. When a reporter called him "Mr. President," he replied uneasily, "I wish you didn't have to call me that." He said to other reporters, "Boys, if newspapermen pray, pray for me now." He soon showed himself to be tough-minded and a quick learner, with a knowledge of history deeper than that of almost any other president. He could be blunt and earthy, calling more than one opponent a "son of a bitch." But he had a clear sense of who he was, and it soon became clear that he did not hesitate to make hard decisions.

The Defeat of Japan

American victories at sea in early 1942 halted the Japanese advance in the Pacific. By mid-1942, the Americans had taken the offensive. Japan had intended to use its navy to shield a vast economic empire in China and Southeast Asia. Instead, it had to fend off a revived and aroused foe in the Pacific while also trying to quell renewed resistance on the Asian mainland. In China, the Japanese armies had scored many victories but were unable to finish off Chiang Kai-shek. Japanese forces had advanced westward almost to India, but in 1943 British and American forces, along with Indian and Chinese troops, were preparing for a counterthrust through Burma and into China. The most decisive action, however, came in the Pacific, where the Allies

MAP 25.5
The Pacific Theater of World War II, 1941–1945
To drive the Japanese from their far-flung empire, the Allies launched two combined naval and
military offensives — one to recapture the Philippines and then attack Japanese forces in China,
the other to hop from island to island in the central Pacific toward the Japanese mainland.

moved slowly and painfully, island by island, toward the Japanese homeland.

Victory at sea led to Allied success on land. In August 1942, the First Marine Division landed on Guadalcanal Island, where the Japanese were constructing an airfield. For the next six months, a savage battle raged for control of the strategic area. Both sides suffered terrible losses, but gradually the American navy won control of the seas, and the marines and army beat back the Japanese on land.

Japanese forces withdrew during the night of February 7, 1943. Guadalcanal was a significant victory, but it signaled just how costly the long march to Japan would be.

In mid-1943, American, Australian, and New Zealand forces under the naval and military commanders, Admiral Chester Nimitz and General Douglas MacArthur, launched new offensives that penetrated the outer perimeter of Japanese defenses. Bloody campaigns in New Guinea and the Solomon

GUADALCANAL: *GHOST TRAIL*
This painting, Ghost Trail *by combat artist Kerr Eby, captures the eerie, murky quality of jungle warfare first experienced fully in the campaign to capture the Pacific island of Guadalcanal. The troops blend into a dense maze of black and green that compounds the difficulties of detecting the hidden enemy.*
Navy Art Collection/Gift of Abbott Laboratories.

Islands gradually secured the South Pacific. In the central Pacific, amphibious forces, borne by the greatest fleet in history, took the Gilbert and Marshall Islands, which served eventually as forward positions for launching the decisive air and ground assaults on the Japanese home islands.

As the Allied offensive pressed on, resistance grew fiercer and more resourceful. Japanese soldiers were instructed to stand firm to the death to defend their homeland. The landing on Tarawa made plain the tenacity of the Japanese soldiers. Stymied by a tide that grounded their landing craft far from shore, the invading marines had to wade a half mile, waist-deep, through brutal enemy fire. Survivors of that barrage then faced concrete emplacements manned by well-armed troops who had no intention of retreating. Within three days, the marines had suffered 1,000 dead and another 2,000 wounded — all to take a barren coral island not three square miles. Only 17 of the 3,000 Japanese defenders were left alive to surrender. The island to island warfare took on an awful sameness of rooting the enemy

out of bunkers and caves with explosives and flamethrowers.

In October 1944, the Allies invaded the Philippines. In the battle for Leyte Gulf, the greatest naval battle in history, the Japanese lost practically their entire fleet — three battleships, four carriers, nine cruisers, and eight destroyers. Even before MacArthur had retaken the Philippines, Allied forces captured Iwo Jima, 750 miles from Japan, and Okinawa, only 370 miles from Tokyo. To defend Okinawa, the Japanese called on thousands of suicide pilots, known as "kamikaze" ("divine wind"). Their mission was to crash bomb-laden planes into Allied ships and thus, it was hoped, make the landing forces turn back. The kamikaze made life harrowing for the fleet but did not deter it. Rather, the suicide gesture destroyed the last vestige of the Japanese air force. By June 1945, the Japanese were virtually defenseless on sea and air. Thousands of B-29 Superfortresses bombed Japanese cities virtually unopposed, and the navy set up a total blockade of the Japanese homeland. The United States prepared to invade.

JAPANESE KAMIKAZE
In this painting by Sentaro Iwata, Japanese suicide pilots prepare to fly to the defense of Okinawa. The pilots, some wearing swords, look heavenward before going aloft as kamikaze, "divine wind," to deliberately crash their bomb-laden planes into enemy warships. In the fight for Okinawa, kamikaze caused over 4,000 U.S. casualties.
Painting by Sentaro Iwata, National Archives.

Atomic Warfare

Just as the island campaigns drew to an end, American scientists were completing work on a secret weapon. The race to develop an atomic bomb had been a long one. In 1942, warned by refugee scientists that the Nazis were working to convert nuclear energy into a superbomb, the Roosevelt administration had authorized the top-secret Manhattan Project —the largest organized scientific effort that had ever been undertaken—to develop the bomb before the Germans did. In thirty-seven locations across the country, coordinated by leading theorists at Los Alamos, New Mexico, 100,000 persons worked at top speed to win the race.

Germany surrendered before it produced a bomb and before the United States was ready to test its own. But just before dawn on July 16, 1945, a test explosion lit up the sky in an isolated corner of the Alamogordo Air Base near Los Alamos. Project

scientists had wagered in a betting pool that the blast, if the test device worked at all, would be equivalent to a few hundred tons of TNT. No one guessed the actual force of 20,000 tons. Nor was anyone prepared for a flash of multicolored light more brilliant than ever seen before—visible even to a blind woman miles away—or the vast fireball and mushroom-shaped cloud of dust and debris that rose eight miles into the upper atmosphere.

The small circle of scientists and officials who knew about the top-secret project had debated for months how atomic weapons should be used. Some scientists, troubled by the power they had unleashed, proposed a public demonstration of the bomb's doomsday force to persuade Japan to surrender. It seemed a prudent time for such a warning shot. With Japan's armed forces incapable of offensive action and Japan totally blockaded, test proponents argued that the United States could afford to wait until the point of the demonstration sank in. The

HIROSHIMA BOMBING
This rare shot taken by a news photographer in Hiroshima immediately after the atomic bomb exploded on August 6, 1945 suggests the shock and incomprehension that survivors would describe as their first reaction. Three days later another atomic bomb devastated Nagasaki.
U.N. photo.

Japanese government had already sent emissaries to see if a negotiated peace could be reached. The sticking point was that the Japanese wanted to retain their emperor, while the American government remained committed to unconditional surrender.

In the end, all reluctance to unleash the atomic monster on populated targets yielded to other urgent considerations. When President Harry Truman heard about the bomb test, he was involved in hard bargaining with the Soviets in Potsdam, Germany, about how to reorganize the postwar world. Truman showed his distrust of the Russians by keeping the news of the test secret. Then he adjusted his strategy to make use of the new weapon. Clearly, the bomb made it unnecessary to call on the Russian promise to hasten victory by declaring war on Japan. Rather, a surprise use of the new superweapon might have the advantage of ending the conflict before the Soviet Union could gain a foothold in Korea and Manchuria by attacking the Japanese armies

still there. Perhaps, also, the bomb's devastation would convince the Soviets that they could not safely challenge American leadership after the war.

A more basic motive was to save American lives. As Truman pondered his options, American troops and supplies were massing on the island of Saipan for Operation Downfall—the invasion of the Japanese home islands in the fall. Experience with Japanese who fought to the death filled American military and civilian leaders with dread. In the battle for Okinawa alone, which ended the island-hopping campaign just before the atomic bomb test, 7,000 American fighting men lost their lives. By resisting to the end, 70,000 Japanese soldiers and 80,000 Okinawans also died in the two-month-long battle. Intelligence reports indicated that an invasion of the Japanese homeland would be a bloodbath on a much vaster scale. More than 2 million Japanese army troops were available for a last-ditch defense of their homeland. Behind them were 28 million men, women, and boys of the civilian militia, armed with sharpened bamboo stakes and any other weapons they could muster.

Truman, who had been a commander of combat troops on the ground in World War I, was keenly sympathetic to the ordeal facing an invading army. He saw no reason not to use a weapon of war, even a terribly destructive one, if it would save American lives. But first he issued an ultimatum that Japan must surrender unconditionally or face utter destruction. When the Japanese failed to respond by the deadline, Truman turned to his advisory committee's recommendation that, to shock the Japanese into surrender, the bomb be dropped without warning on cities that had not already been heavily damaged. On August 6, a single B-29, the *Enola Gay*, droned over Hiroshima and released one of the three operational atomic bombs the Americans possessed. As the plane banked sharply away, crew members could see behind them the mushroom cloud that signified the obliteration of the city and the death of 78,000 inhabitants. Russia then declared war on Japan on August 8, and the next day a second atomic bomb obliterated Nagasaki, with more than 100,000 deaths.

According to one estimate, the death toll during World War II reached 35 million, evenly divided between military and civilian losses.

In the midst of ruin, a peace faction took control of the Japanese government from diehard military leaders, and with assurance that the emperor could retain his throne under Allied control, Japan surrendered on August 14. Whether allowing the Japanese to retain their emperor before using atomic bombs would have been enough to induce surrender can never be known. Emperor Hirohito's power to shift the Japanese spirit from war to peace became clear, however, when he informed his people in a radio broadcast—the first words that the public had ever heard the emperor utter—of his divine will that they cease fighting. Loyally, his subjects lay down their arms and stood quietly by as the giant battleship *Missouri* sailed into Tokyo harbor for the formal signing of surrender on September 2, 1945.

Conclusion: Victory and Uncertainty

For Americans, the attack on Pearl Harbor was just the first shock of a war whose scope and violence was unprecedented. World War I had meant ghastly destruction for parts of Europe, but never before had armies been flung across such vast stretches of the globe. And on the seas there were more battles, with more ships lost, than in all other modern wars combined. An accurate tally of the dead is impossible. According to one estimate, the death toll reached 35 million, evenly divided between military and civilian losses. Some countries suffered much more than others. Approximately 400,000 Americans lost their lives in military service; the Soviet Union lost more in the single battle of Stalingrad. Eventually, the Soviets suffered nearly 20 million civilian and military deaths. Despite its relatively light losses, the United States experienced far-reaching changes, none of which was more decisive than its rise to global power.

When World War II ended, the United States was unquestionably the most powerful nation on earth. Determined not to repeat the failure to secure a stable peace after World War I, the Roosevelt administration had begun to plan a postwar world even before the United States entered the conflict. But Roosevelt's hope for a peaceful and democratic postwar world was shadowed by wartime events and postwar developments. The Holocaust exposed humankind's capacity for unimaginable evil and raised indelible misgivings about postwar prospects. The annihilation of Hiroshima and Nagasaki by atomic bombs cast additional doubts about modern technology. Moreover, the United States and Western Europe soon found themselves at odds with dictatorial Communist countries led by the Soviet Union and soon to be joined by China. Efforts by Britain and France to maintain their colonial empires also violated democratic principles and met mounting resistance from national forces seeking liberation.

Nevertheless, most Americans emerged from World War II convinced that good had triumphed over evil. What purposes victory would ultimately serve, however, quickly became debatable, as the confidence bred of winning the "good war" gave way to the anxious uncertainties of the "cold war."

CHRONOLOGY

1933   Adolf Hitler becomes chancellor of Germany.
        United States recognizes Soviet Union.

1935–   Congress seeks to shield America from
1937   world conflicts with neutrality acts.

1936   Nazi Germany occupies the Rhineland.
        Mussolini's fascist Italian regime conquers Ethiopia.
        Civil war breaks out in Spain.

1937   Japanese troops capture Nanking.
        Roosevelt delivers speech urging "quarantine" against aggressor nations.

1938   Hitler annexes Austria.
        British Prime Minister Chamberlain meets with Hitler in Munich and agrees to German seizure of Sudetenland in Czechoslovakia.

1939   German troops occupy remainder of Czechoslovakia without resistance.
        Nazi Germany and Soviet Union sign nonaggression pact.
        September 1. Germany's attack on Poland begins World War II.
        United States and Great Britain conclude cash-and-carry agreement.

1940   **May–June.** British troops evacuated at Dunkirk.
        June. French sign armistice with Germany that puts most of France under direct German control.
        Isolationists, including Charles Lindbergh, create America First Committee.
        Roosevelt wins reelection against Wendell Willkie.

1941   Lend-Lease Act enables Britain to obtain war materials in United States on credit.
        June. Germany invades Soviet Union.
        August. Atlantic Charter devised by Roosevelt and Allies to guarantee human and international freedoms after war.

December 7. Japanese launch surprise attack on Pearl Harbor. United States declares war on Japan.

1942   Japan captures the Philippines.
        Civil rights activists found Congress of Racial Equality (CORE).
        U.S. navy scores its first major victories in Battle of Coral Sea and at Midway.
        Roosevelt authorizes top-secret Manhattan Project.
        November. U.S. forces invade North Africa.
        Roosevelt authorizes internment of Japanese Americans.

1943   Allied leaders agree that war will end only with unconditional surrender of Axis forces.
        "Zoot suit" riots explode in Los Angeles.
        U.S. forces invade Sicily.

1944   **June 6.** Combined Allied army stages successful D Day landing at Normandy.
        Roosevelt wins reelection against Thomas E. Dewey.

1945   The Allies meet to plan reconstruction of Europe after defeat of Germany.
        April 12. Franklin Roosevelt dies and Harry Truman becomes president.
        Delegates from fifty nations, meeting in San Francisco, approve charter of the United Nations.
        May 7. Germany surrenders.
        August 6. United States drops atomic bomb on Hiroshima.
        August 8. United States drops atomic bomb on Nagasaki.
        August 14. Japan surrenders and brings World War II to an end.

BIBLIOGRAPHY

GENERAL WORKS

Michael Adams, *The Best War Ever* (1994).

John Morton Blum, *V Was for Victory: Politics and American Culture during World War II* (1977).

Kenneth S. Davis, *FDR: Into the Storm, 1937–1940* (1993).

I. C. B. Dear and M. R. D. Foot, eds., *The Oxford Companion to World War II* (1995).

Paul Fussell, *Wartime* (1989).

Akira Iriye, *The Origins of the Second World War in Asia and the Pacific* (1987).

Richard Ketchum, *The Borrowed Years, 1938–1941: America on the Way to War* (1989).

Eric Larrabee, *Commander in Chief: Franklin Delano Roosevelt, His Lieutenants, and Their War* (1987).

Richard Polenberg, *War and Society: The United States, 1941–1945* (1972).

Michael S. Sherry, *In the Shadow of War: The United States since the 1930s* (1995).

Studs Terkel, *"The Good War": An Oral History of World War II* (1984).

Gerhard Weinberg, *World at Arms: A Global History of World War II* (1994).

FOREIGN POLICY

Robert Dallek, *Franklin D. Roosevelt and American Foreign Policy, 1932–1945* (1979).

Erwin F. Gellman, *Good Neighbor Diplomacy: United States Policies in Latin America, 1933–1945* (1979).

Waldo Heinrichs, *Threshold of War: Franklin D. Roosevelt and American Entry into World War II* (1988).

Robert Hilderbrand, *Dumbarton Oaks: The Origins of the United Nations and the Search for Postwar Security* (1990).

Akira Iriye, *The Globalizing of America, 1913–1945* (1995).

Walter LaFeber, *Inevitable Revolutions* (1983).

Frederick W. Marks, *Wind over Sand: The Diplomacy of Franklin Roosevelt* (1988).

Arnold Offner, *The Origins of the Second World War* (1975).

Robert Rosenstone, *Crusade of the Left: The Lincoln Battalion in the Spanish Civil War* (1969).

David F. Schmitz, *The United States and Fascist Italy, 1922–1944* (1988).

Gaddis Smith, *American Diplomacy during the Second World War, 1941–1945* (1985).

Jonathan Utley, *Going to War with Japan, 1937–1942* (1985).

PACIFISM AND ANTI-INTERVENTIONISM

Wayne S. Cole, *Roosevelt and the Isolationists, 1932–1945* (1983).

Robert A. Divine, *The Illusion of Neutrality* (1982).

Charles A. Lindbergh, *The Wartime Journals* (1970).

Charles A. Lindbergh, *Autobiography of Values* (1978).

Joyce Milton, *Loss of Eden: A Biography of Charles and Anne Morrow Lindbergh* (1994).

Geoffrey S. Smith, *To Save a Nation: American "Extremism," the New Deal, and the Coming of World War II* (1992).

John E. Wiltz, *In Search of Peace: The Senate Munitions Inquiry, 1934–1936* (1963).

MOBILIZATION AND THE HOME FRONT

Karen Anderson, *Wartime Women: Sex Roles, Family Relations, and the Status of Women during World War II* (1981).

D'Ann Campbell, *Women at War with America: Private Lives in a Patriotic Era* (1984).

Lewis A. Erenberg and Susan E. Hirsch, eds., *The War in American Culture: Society and Consciousness during World War II* (1996).

Mark Jonathan Harris, Franklin D. Mitchell, and Steve J. Schechter, *The Home Front: America during World War II* (1985).

Susan Hartmann, *The Homefront and Beyond: American Women in the 1940s* (1982).

Clayton R. Koppes and Gregory D. Black, *Hollywood Goes to War: How Politics, Profits, and Propaganda Shaped World War II Movies* (1987).

Nelson Lichtenstein, *Labor's War at Home: The CIO in World War II* (1983).

Gerald D. Nash, *The American West Transformed: The Impact of the Second World War* (1985).

William L. O'Neill, *A Democracy at War: America's Fight at Home and Abroad in World War II* (1993).

Geoffrey Perrett, *Days of Sadness, Years of Triumph: The American People, 1939–1945* (1985).

William Tuttle, *Daddy's Gone to War: The Second World War in the Lives of America's Children* (1993).

MILITARY ORGANIZATION AND CAMPAIGNS

Gar Alperovitz, *The Decision to Use the Atomic Bomb and the Architecture of an American Myth* (1995).

Stephen E. Ambrose, *D-Day, June 6, 1944* (1994).

Allan Berube, *Coming Out under Fire: The History of Gay Men and Women in World War Two* (1990).

Paul S. Boyer, *By the Bomb's Early Light: American Thought and Culture at the Dawn of the Atomic Age* (1985).

A. Russell Buchanan, *The United States and World War II*, 2 vols. (1964).

John Costello, *Virtue under Fire: How World War II Changed Our Social and Sexual Attitudes* (1986).

Albert E. Cowdrey, *Fighting for Life: American Military Medicine in World War II* (1994).

Gavan Daws, *Prisoners of the Japanese: POWs of World War II* (1992).

John Dower, *War without Mercy: Race and Power in the Pacific War* (1986).

Akira Iriye, *Power and Culture: The Japanese-American War, 1941–1945* (1982).

D. Clayton James, *A Time for Giants: The Politics of the American High Command in World War II* (1987).

Dan Kurzman, *Day of the Bomb: Countdown to Hiroshima* (1986).

William Manchester, *Goodbye, Darkness: A Memoir of the Pacific War* (1980).

Martin V. Melosi, *The Shadow of Pearl Harbor: Political Controversy over the Surprise Attack, 1941–1946* (1977).

Geoffrey Perrett, *Winged Victory: The Army Air Forces in World War II* (1993).

Gordon Prange, *At Dawn We Slept* (1981).

Richard Rhodes, *The Making of the Atomic Bomb* (1986).

Ronald Schaffer, *Wings of Judgment: American Bombing in World War II* (1988).

Michael Schaller, *Douglas MacArthur: The Far Eastern General* (1989).

Michael S. Sherry, *The Rise of American Air Power: The Creation of Armageddon* (1987).

E. B. Sledge, *With the Old Breed at Peleliu and Okinawa* (1990).

Ronald H. Spector, *Eagle against the Sun: The American War with Japan* (1985).

RACE AND MINORITIES

Alison R. Bernstein, *American Indians and World War II: Toward a New Era in Indian Affairs* (1991).

A. Russell Buchanan, *Black Americans in World War II* (1977).

Dominic Capeci, *The Harlem Race Riot of 1943* (1977).

Dominic Capeci, *Race Relations in Wartime Detroit* (1984).

Lyn Crost, *Honor by Fire: Japanese Americans at War in Europe and the Pacific* (1994).

Roger Daniels, *Concentration Camps: North American Japanese in the United States and Canada during World War II* (1971; reprint, 1989).

Peter H. Irons, *Justice at War: The Story of the Japanese Internment Cases* (1983).

Mauricio Mazon, *The Zoot-Suit Riots: The Psychology of Symbolic Annihilation* (1984).

Bernard C. Nalty, *Strength for the Fight: A History of Black Americans in the Military* (1989).

Lou Potter, with William Miles and Nina Rosenblum, *Liberators: Fighting on Two Fronts in World War II* (1992).

Page Smith, *Democracy on Trial: The Japanese American Evacuation and Relocation in World War II* (1995).

Ronald Takaki, *Strangers from a Different Shore: A History of Asian Americans* (1989).

Neil Wynn, *The Afro-American and the Second World War* (1976).

DEPICTING THE WAR

M. Joyce Baker, *Images of Women on Film: The War Years* (1981).

Thomas Doherty, *Projections of War: Hollywood, American Culture, and World War II* (1993).

Paul Fussell, *Wartime* (1989).

Library of America, *Reporting World War II*, 2 vols. (1995).

William Manchester, *Goodbye Darkness: A Memoir of the Pacific War* (1980).

Karal Ann Marling and John Wetenhall, *Iwo Jima: Monuments, Memories, and the American Hero* (1991).

Peter Maslowski, *Armed with Cameras: The American Military Photographers of World War II* (1993).

Mordecai Richler, *Writers on World War II* (1991).

George H. Roeder Jr., *The Censored War: American Visual Experience during World War II* (1993).

Vernon Scannell, *Not without Glory: Poets of the Second World War* (1976).

Holly Cowan Shulman, *The Voice of America: Propaganda and Democracy, 1941–1945* (1991).

E. B. Sledge, *With the Old Breed at Peleliu and Okinawa* (1990).

Frederick S. Voss, *Reporting the War: The Journalistic Coverage of World War II* (1994).

AMERICA AND THE HOLOCAUST

Robert Abzug, *Inside the Vicious Heart: Americans and the Liberation of Nazi Concentration Camps* (1987).

Richard Breitman and Alan Kraut, *American Refugee Policy and European Jewry* (1987).

Lucy Dawidowicz, *The War against the Jews, 1933–1945* (1986).

Leonard Dinnerstein, *America and the Survivors of the Holocaust* (1982).

Lawrence L. Langer, *Admitting the Holocaust: Collected Essays* (1995).

Deborah E. Lipstadt, *Beyond Belief: The American Press and the Coming of the Holocaust, 1933–1945* (1986).

Michael Marrus, *The Holocaust in History* (1987).

Verne W. Newton, ed., *FDR and the Holocaust* (1995).

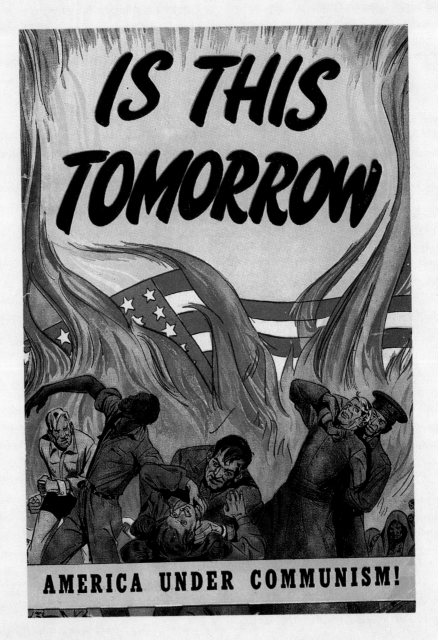

COLD WAR COMIC BOOK

Americans barely had time to celebrate the Allied victory in World War II when they per-ceived another threat, that posed by the Soviet Union. Fear of communism dominated much of postwar American life and politics, even invading the realm of popular culture. Four million copies of this comic book, published by a religious organization in 1947, painted a terrifying picture of what would happen to Americans when the Soviets took over the country. Such takeover stories appeared in movies, cartoons, and magazines as well as in other comic books.

Collection of Charles Christensen.

COLD WAR POLITICS IN THE TRUMAN YEARS

26

1945–1953

O N NOVEMBER 5, 1946, President Harry S. Truman, his wife, and his daughter boarded the train back to Washington from Truman's hometown, Independence, Missouri, where they had gone to vote. During the congressional campaigns, Republicans had blasted Truman as incapable of dealing with economic problems and with the threat of communism at home and abroad. The president's standing with the public had sunk to a mere 32 percent approval rate. Many Democratic candidates avoided mentioning his name, hoping to stir voters with recordings of the late Franklin Roosevelt's voice. Playing poker with reporters on the train as the returns came in, Truman appeared unconcerned. But the results were devastating: The Republicans had captured both the House and the Senate by substantial majorities.

When Truman stepped off the train in the capital at the lowest point of his presidency, only one member of his administration showed up to greet him, Undersecretary of State Dean Acheson. Acheson's gesture signaled a developing relationship of central importance to the two men as well as to postwar history. The fifty-three-year-old Acheson shared most of Truman's political principles, but their backgrounds could not have been more dissimilar. Acheson had enjoyed a typical upper-class education: prep school, Yale University, where classmates voted him "wittiest" and the "spiciest" dresser, and Harvard Law School. After clerking at the Supreme Court, Acheson earned a comfortable living as a lawyer specializing in work for international corporations. In contrast, Truman, the son of a Missouri farmer, had not attended college and had failed in a business venture before entering local politics in the 1920s.

Despite his wealth and privilege, Acheson supported most of the New Deal and staunchly defended organized labor. He spoke out against isolationism in the late 1930s, and in 1941 he accepted President Roosevelt's offer of a job at the State Department. Shortly after Truman became president, Acheson wrote his son that he observed shortcomings in Truman's "judgment and wisdom that the limitations of his experience produce," but he also found the fledgling president "straightforward, decisive, simple, entirely honest," a man who "will learn fast and will inspire confidence." In June 1947, Acheson left the State Department, but Truman lured him back eighteen months later, this time as secretary of state during the president's second term. Acheson appreciated the president's willingness to make tough decisions and respected the man whose "ego never came between him and his job." Truman cherished Acheson's abiding loyalty. Relying on him as secretary of state until they both left office in January 1953, Truman called Acheson "my good right hand."

Truman needed all the help he could get. The "accidental" president lacked the charisma, experience, and political skills with which Roosevelt had transformed both foreign and domestic policies, won four presidential elections, and forged a Democratic Party coalition that dominated national politics. Initially criticized and abandoned by many Roosevelt loyalists, Truman faced a resurgent Republican Party as well as revolts from within his own party.

Part of Truman's challenge lay in domestic problems left over from the New Deal. Without the war to fuel the economy, how could the nation achieve economic growth that would ensure a decent livelihood for its citizens and avoid another depression? Truman failed to achieve his goal of extending the New Deal with ambitious reforms in health care, education, housing, and civil rights, but his administration did consolidate and modestly expand the welfare state. Riding a postwar economic boom, Americans enjoyed an unparalleled standard of living. Still, at the end of the 1940s, about one-third of the population remained mired in poverty.

A watershed in foreign policy that required increasing expenditures for defense and foreign aid helped to stimulate prosperity during the Truman years. The nation's central goals—protecting the United States from foreign aggression, encouraging other countries to follow its political and economic system, and fostering U.S. economic interests abroad—were not new. What changed in the postwar period were the international context and the means used to pursue these goals.

World War II had left in its wake ruin, instability, and power vacuums in large parts of the globe. Restoring order would have been a challenge under any circumstances, but growing hostility between the two most powerful nations—the United States and the Soviet Union—made it infinitely more difficult. As early as 1946, Dean Acheson became convinced that the Soviet Union posed the major threat to U.S. security. With other officials, he helped to shape a containment policy, with the goal of thwarting Soviet power and influence wherever they threatened to spread. By 1947, a new term had been coined to describe the intense hostility and rivalry between the superpowers—the "cold war."

The containment policy worked enormously well in Western Europe, but foreign policy reverses elsewhere combined with partisan politics at home to produce a wave of hysteria about Communists within the United States. This anti-Communist frenzy produced a large-scale purge of individuals from public service and private employment. Free-

DEAN ACHESON
No individual had more to do with transforming America's role in the world after World War II than Dean Acheson, President Truman's closest foreign policy adviser. Acheson, seen here in 1945, criticized those who saw the cold war in black and white terms and communism as an evil that the United States could expel from the earth. Rather, he advocated that American leaders learn "to limit objectives, to get ourselves away from the search for the absolute, to find out what is within our powers." Library of Congress.

dom to express unpopular ideas or to criticize U.S. policies and institutions became a major casualty of the cold war.

Although Acheson kept his job, as the preeminent foreign policy official and defender of a former colleague accused of being a Soviet spy, he too reaped abuse from Republicans for being "soft on communism." At the height of the anti-Communist hysteria, Acheson received so much hate mail that guards were posted at his house. Yet he kept a sense of humor. When cab drivers asked him, "Aren't you Dean Acheson?" he would reply, "Yes. Do I have to get out?"

From the Grand Alliance to Containment

No sooner had Americans finished celebrating the victory over Japan in August 1945 than they began to besiege the government with demands to bring the troops home. Baby shoes and photos of children arrived at the White House and Congress with notes pleading for the return of fathers and husbands to civilian life. Throughout the world, servicemen themselves staged demonstrations demanding to be sent home, and they booed the secretary of war in Manila. Under pressure, Truman approved a more rapid demobilization than most of his advisers thought prudent, but no one expected the postwar world to require a large military establishment. Most Americans expected that the Allies, led by the United States and working within the United Nations, would cooperate to manage international peace and order.

These expectations vanished quickly. When the wartime alliance forged by the United States, Great Britain, and the Soviet Union crumbled, the United States began to develop the military and diplomatic means to contain the spread of Soviet power. By 1949, the nation had reestablished the military draft, embarked on a nuclear arms race, entered into its first peacetime alliance, and committed itself to a multibillion-dollar foreign aid program.

Conflicts in the Wartime Coalition

"The guys who came out of World War Two were idealistic," reported Harold Russell, a young paratrooper whose hands had been blown off in a training accident. The veterans believed they were "coming home to build a new world. . . . We felt the day had come when the wars were all over." Public opinion polls revealed that most Americans shared the veterans' confidence in the prospects for peace.

Political leaders were less optimistic. Winston Churchill had always distrusted the Soviets; in a moment of frustration during the war, he had remarked that the only thing worse than fighting with allies was fighting without them. Indeed, once the Allies had overcome the Axis powers and no longer fought a common enemy, the prewar mistrust and antagonism between the Soviet Union and the West resurfaced as they sought to implement very different plans for the postwar world.

The Soviets' deep suspicions of the United States had scarcely diminished during the war, es-

pecially when the Western allies resisted Stalin's repeated pleas for a speedy opening of a second front in Western Europe. Soviet leaders knew that their nation had made supreme wartime sacrifices, losing more than twenty million of its citizens and vast portions of its agricultural and industrial capacity. Soviet leader Joseph Stalin wanted to require Germany to pay for the rebuilding of the Soviet economy, to eliminate any future threats to Soviet security from neighboring countries, and to expand Soviet influence in the world. Above all, Stalin wanted governments friendly to the Soviet Union on its borders in Eastern Europe, especially in Poland, which had been the path of German aggression against the Soviet Union twice within twenty-five years.

When the wartime alliance forged by the United States, Great Britain, and the Soviet Union crumbled, the United States began to develop the military and diplomatic means to contain the spread of Soviet power.

In contrast, only in the United States had war and prosperity marched hand in hand. Its land was untouched by enemy fire, and its 405,000 dead amounted to 2 percent of the Soviet loss. With its vastly expanded productive capacity and its monopoly on atomic weapons, the United States emerged from the war as the most powerful nation on the planet, replacing Britain as the dominant power in the Western world. America's sheer possession of that power, its economic interests, its leaders' understanding of how the recent war might have been avoided, and supreme confidence in American institutions all induced Truman and his associates to grasp the unprecedented role of world leadership.

With the specter of the depression still haunting the nation, U.S. officials believed that the economy's health depended in large measure on what went on in the rest of the world. To avoid a return to the hard times of the 1930s, the United States needed access to raw materials, markets for its goods, and security for American investments abroad. These needs could most readily be met in countries with economic and political systems much like its own, not in countries whose governments might institute economic controls that would interfere with the free flow of products and dollars. As Truman put it in 1947, "The American system can survive in America only if it becomes a world system."

Truman's definition of American goals reflected many citizens' feelings of national superiority. Boasting of the best economic and political system in the world, American leaders encouraged other nations to copy the United States. Convinced of the superiority of their institutions and values, Americans viewed their foreign policy not as a self-interested campaign to meet economic needs, but as an idealistic crusade to bring freedom, democracy, and capitalism to the rest of the world.

Recent history also shaped American approaches to foreign policy. Americans believed that World War II might have been avoided had Britain, France, and the United States resisted rather than appeased Hitler's initial aggression. As early as September 1945, Secretary of the Navy James V. Forrestal doubted that the United States should attempt to "buy [the Soviets'] understanding and sympathy. We tried that once with Hitler." This "Munich analogy" (referring to the 1938 conference at which Britain and France agreed to Hitler's plan to annex part of Czechoslovakia) would be evoked time and again when new challenges to the international status quo arose.

Moving toward a Cold War

The man with the ultimate responsibility for U.S. policy came to the White House with little international experience but with strong anti-Communist sentiments. When Germany attacked the Soviet Union in 1941, then Senator Truman expressed publicly the wish that the two countries would bleed each other dry. Yet as president, he hoped to maintain Soviet-American cooperation, remarking in 1945 that the Russians "have always been our friends and I can't see any reason why they shouldn't always be." For that friendship to continue, Truman demanded that the Soviet Union agree with U.S. plans for the postwar world and restrain its expansionist impulses. Proud of his ability to make quick decisions and never look back, Truman was determined to be firm about Soviet expansionism, and he knew well that America's nuclear monopoly gave him the upper hand.

Soviet and American interests clashed first in Eastern Europe. Stalin interpreted the Allies' wartime agreements as giving him a free hand in the countries that the Red Army had defeated or liberated, just as the United States was unilaterally reconstructing governments in Italy and Japan. In Poland and Bulgaria, countries bordering the Soviet Union, Stalin used harsh methods to install Communist governments that followed Moscow's party line. Elsewhere, the Soviets displayed more restraint, tolerating non-Communist governments in Hungary and Czechoslovakia before Soviet-Western hostility became intense.

To Stalin, U.S. policy seemed hypocritical in demanding elections in Eastern Europe while supporting dictatorships friendly to U.S. interests in Cuba, Nicaragua, and other Latin American countries. The United States clung to its own sphere of influence while adamantly denying one to the Soviets. But the tough words of the Western allies were no match for the Soviet armies occupying Eastern Europe: The United States and Britain sharply protested Soviet actions but would not use military force against the puppet governments installed by Stalin.

In contrast to his insistence on controlling Eastern Europe, Stalin backed down when the Western allies opposed his actions in Iran, the Soviet Union's neighbor to the southwest. Hoping to take advantage of declining British power and to gain access to Iranian oil, Stalin delayed removing troops that had been dispatched there during the war until confronted by strong Western and Iranian demands in the spring of 1946. Once the Soviets had withdrawn, the door opened for the United States to supplant British influence in Iran and to gain important oil concessions.

The Soviet Union had much more at stake in central Europe, where in 1946 the future of Germany became a central point of contention among the Allies. Having suffered two invasions by Germany in twenty-five years, the Soviet Union resolved to keep that country weak and to exact heavy reparations that it could use to rebuild the Soviet economy. American policymakers agreed on stripping Germany of its military capacity, but they also wanted a rapid industrial revival there. An economically strong Germany would foster the economic recovery of Europe and thus America's own long-term prosperity.

Unable to resolve their different plans for Germany, the Allies divided it. The Soviet Union seized industrial equipment and installed a puppet Communist government in the eastern part of the country, occupied by the Red Army. In December 1946, Britain, France, and the United States unified their occupation zones into a single body, beginning a

MAP 26.1
The Division of Europe after World War II
The "Iron Curtain," a term coined by Winston Churchill to refer to the Soviet grip on Eastern and Central Europe, divided Europe for nearly fifty years. Communist governments controlled every country along the Soviet Union's western border, except Finland, which remained neutral.

process that led to creation of the Federal Republic of Germany (West Germany) in 1949.

Soviet and Western leaders faced off with hostile words in 1946. In February, Stalin called his former allies a more serious threat than Nazi Germany, a pronouncement that Supreme Court Justice William O. Douglas termed "the declaration of World War III." One month later, Truman traveled with Winston Churchill to Westminster College in Fulton, Missouri, where the former prime minister denounced Soviet suppression of the popular will in Eastern and central Europe. "From Stettin in the Baltic to Trieste in the Adriatic, an iron curtain has descended across the continent," Churchill said. Although Truman did not officially endorse

Churchill's words, his presence implied agreement with the call for the development of joint British-American strength to combat Soviet aggression. To Stalin, Churchill's "iron curtain speech" sounded a "call to war against the USSR."

As Soviet-Western conflict sharpened, in February 1946 career diplomat George F. Kennan sent a memo to the State Department that furnished a comprehensive rationale for the Truman administration's toughening stance. Kennan had spent years working in U.S. embassies in Eastern Europe and Moscow. Appalled at what he viewed as the "cynicism, shamelessness, [and] contempt for humanity" displayed by Soviet officials and convinced that optimistic assumptions about Soviet-American cooperation were "pipe dreams," Kennan urged a hard line. He explained that "the traditional and instinctive Russian sense of insecurity" combined with Soviet leaders' need to maintain their authority at home prompted Stalin to exaggerate dangers from the capitalist world abroad. These circumstances, Kennan argued, made it impossible to negotiate with the Soviets, a conclusion shared by Secretary of State James F. Byrnes, Undersecretary Dean Acheson, Navy Secretary Forrestal, and other key Truman advisers.

Although Kennan downplayed the role of Communist ideology in Soviet foreign policy, he predicted that the Soviet Union would try to "fill every nook and cranny available to it in the basin of world power." Yet he found Soviet leaders cautious and flexible, having "no compunction about retreating in the face of superior force." Therefore, the United States should respond with "unalterable counterforce" wherever the Soviets tried to expand their influence, an approach that came to be called "containment." Forcing Russia to "face frustration indefinitely," Kennan predicted, would eventually end in "either the breakup or the gradual mellowing of Soviet power."

Kennan's message received a larger audience when he published his views under the pseudonym "X" in *Foreign Affairs* magazine in July 1947. His analysis did not so much change U.S. policy as provide a rationale for resisting Soviet actions. Kennan later expressed dismay when others used his ideas to justify what he felt was an indiscriminate American response wherever communism seemed likely to succeed. But his analysis marked a critical moment in the development of the cold war, providing a powerful argument and an intellectual framework for using U.S. power to check the spread of Soviet influence.

Although the American people displayed no enthusiasm for taking on substantial new burdens in the world, popular sentiment seemed to echo Kennan's hard-line approach to the Soviet Union. A majority of respondents to a March 1946 poll viewed Soviet actions as attempts to become the ruling power in the world and favored a strong American response. Truman's political opponents at home, the Republicans, were no more eager than their fellow citizens to send dollars or soldiers abroad. In fact, the Republican Party contained a strong isolationist element led by Ohio Senator Robert Taft. However, that did not stop Republicans from seeking political gains by charging the Truman administration with being "soft on communism."

Administration officials promoting a more conciliatory policy toward the Soviets found themselves out of work. Secretary of Commerce Henry A. Wallace, Truman's predecessor as vice president, persistently urged Truman to be more sensitive to Soviets' fears and concerns about their nation's security. In a major speech in September 1946, Wallace insisted that " 'getting tough' never brought anything real and lasting—whether for schoolyard bullies or businessmen or world powers." He urged Americans to realize "that we have no more business in the political affairs of Eastern Europe than Russia has in the political affairs of Latin America, Western Europe, and the United States." Because Wallace's words challenged the hardening direction of U.S. policy toward the Soviet Union, State Department officials were furious. When Wallace refused to be muzzled on foreign policy topics, Truman fired him in September 1946.

Containment and the Truman Doctrine

In 1947, the United States moved from tough words to action, implementing the doctrine of containment that would guide foreign policy for the next four decades. It was not an easy transition; despite public approval of a verbal hard line, Americans had had enough of international challenges. They were eager to make up for the deprivations of the depression and the war and wanted to keep their soldiers and tax dollars at home. In addition to selling containment to the public, Truman had to persuade a Congress controlled by the Republicans after the 1946 elections.

Crises in two Mediterranean countries triggered the implementation of containment. In February 1947, Britain informed the United States that its crippled economy could no longer sustain military assistance to Greece and Turkey. Turkey was trying to resist Soviet pressures, and the monarchist government in Greece, propped up by British aid, faced a challenge from internal leftists. Truman promptly decided to ask Congress for authority to send military and economic missions along with $400 million in aid to the two countries.

To pave the way for approval of the aid, Truman and his aides first met privately with congressional leaders. Dismayed at their lack of enthusiasm, Acheson painted the issue in catastrophic terms, predicting that if Greece and Turkey fell, communism would soon consume three-fourths of the planet and threaten the United States itself. After a stunned silence, Michigan Senator Arthur Vandenberg, the Republican foreign policy leader and a recent convert from isolationism, said that to get congressional approval, Truman would have to "scare hell out of the country."

Truman did just that. Speaking before Congress, he echoed Acheson's grim predictions and summoned the United States to a global commitment. He presented what would later be called the "domino theory," warning that if Greece fell to the rebels, "confusion and disorder might well spread throughout the entire Middle East . . . and would have a profound effect upon . . . Europe." Failure to step in "may endanger the peace of the world— and . . . shall surely endanger the welfare of the nation."

The assumption that American security depended on rescuing any anti-Communist government from internal rebels or outside pressure became the cornerstone of U.S. foreign policy from 1947 until the end of the 1980s.

"I told my wife to dust off my uniform," one veteran studying under the GI bill at the University of Oklahoma said in response to Truman's words. The president's crisis rhetoric along with its staggering global implications evoked dismay from Kennan himself. According to what came to be called the "Truman Doctrine," it was not just Soviet military power that must be resisted. The United States must "support free peoples who are resisting attempted subjugation by armed minorities or by outside pressures." In agreeing to aid for Greece and Turkey, Congress did not formally accept the Truman Doctrine. Yet the assumption that American security depended on rescuing any anti-Communist government from internal rebels or outside pressure became the cornerstone of U.S. foreign policy from 1947 until the end of the 1980s.

The Marshall Plan

In May 1947, in a steamy gym at Delta State Teachers College in Cleveland, Mississippi, Dean Acheson rolled up his sleeves and began to prepare the public for the next application of containment. His speech concerned Western Europe, where the war had left "factories destroyed, fields impoverished and without fertilizer or machinery, . . . transporta-

tion systems wrecked, populations scattered and on the borderline of starvation, and long-established business and trading connections disrupted."

Most Americans knew about the desperate conditions, and millions had already opened their hearts and pocketbooks, sending CARE packages and money to provide food, shelter, and clothing to people overseas. A California couple adopted a French village that the Germans had left in ruin; and a Nebraska farmer who had been able to pay off his debt during the war sent the dollar equivalent of a thousand bushels of corn. In all, Americans sent two billion dollars to alleviate suffering abroad during the first six years after the war.

Yet private generosity was not enough. Europe needed even larger-scale aid that, Acheson asserted, the United States should provide "as a matter of national self-interest." European economic recovery, U.S. policymakers believed, would halt the growth of socialist and Communist parties in France and Italy and confine Soviet influence to Eastern Europe. And because the United States could not prosper without world markets, it needed an economically strong Europe for trade.

Retired General George C. Marshall, the new secretary of state, formally unveiled the administration's plan for European recovery in a speech at Harvard University in June 1947. He invited all the European nations and the Soviet Union to cooperate in preparing a request for aid. As administration officials expected, the Soviet Union refused to meet the American terms of free trade and financial disclosure and ordered its Eastern European satellites likewise to reject the offer. Sixteen nations outside the Soviet orbit then drew up a proposal outlining their economic plans and requesting contributions from the United States. In March 1948, Congress approved the Marshall Plan, officially known as the European Recovery Program, and over the next five years the United States allocated $13 billion to restore the economies of Western Europe.

A program of economic rather than military assistance, the Marshall Plan was one of the outstanding achievements of postwar foreign policy. It helped the nations of Western Europe rebuild their war-ravaged economies and move toward a united European economy. It was also good business for the United States. The European recipients spent most of the dollars to buy American products loaded by American workers onto American ships. The economic recovery of Europe expanded the realm of raw materials, markets, and investment opportunities available to American capitalists.

U.S. AID TO EUROPE
In addition to the $13 billion of Marshall Plan aid that the U.S. government provided to Europe, private citizens also pitched in to help rebuild countries devastated by World War II. Residents of Jersey City, New Jersey, donated this snowplow being unloaded in Rome and destined for the small village of Capracotta in the Italian mountains.
Corbis–Bettmann.

Moreover, the Truman administration could point to another victory for containment, since every Western European government remained non-Communist.

While Congress debated the Marshall Plan, in February 1948 the Soviets tightened their grip on Central Europe by staging a brutal coup against the elected government of Czechoslovakia and installing a Communist regime. Truman stepped up his cold war rhetoric, condemning Stalin's "ruthless course of action" in destroying "the independence and democratic character of a whole series of nations in Eastern and Central Europe."

The president matched words with actions when the Soviets threatened Western access to Berlin in the spring of 1948. The former capital of Germany lay within the Soviet occupation zone, but all four Allies—the United States, Britain, France, and the Soviet Union— jointly occupied Berlin, dividing it into separate administrative units. When the Western Allies moved forward with plans to organize West Germany as a separate nation, the Soviets retaliated by blocking access by road and rail from West Germany to the Western-held sections of Berlin. Thus the two million inhabitants of the Western sectors were cut off from food, fuel, and other essentials.

"We stay in Berlin, period," Truman responded to this effort to force the West out. Yet he also wanted to avoid an armed confrontation with So-

viet troops. So for fifteen months, U.S. and British pilots—landing a plane every eight minutes—airlifted 2.3 million tons of goods, enough to sustain the West Berliners. Stalin hesitated to shoot down these cargo planes, and in 1949 he lifted the Berlin blockade. The city was formally divided into East Berlin, under Soviet control, and West Berlin, which became part of West Germany. To U.S. officials, the Berlin airlift confirmed the wisdom of containment: When challenged, the Russians would back down, as Kennan had predicted.

The policy of containment reflected the dashed hopes that the major powers would cooperate through the United Nations. Instead, the new international organization served more as a propaganda body for its member nations. It provided a mechanism for nations to discuss disputes, and perhaps its moral authority and ability to claim world attention exercised restraints on nations. But it could not act without unanimity on the Security Council, where the Soviet-American split prevented any effective action.

Creating a National Security State

The new policy of containment demanded a military capacity to back it up. During the Truman years, the United States fashioned a five-pronged defense strategy: (1) development of atomic weapons, (2) strengthening of traditional military power,

THE BERLIN AIRLIFT
These German children standing on the rubble of war wave to planes carrying food and other ne-
cessities to Berlin during the Soviet blockade in 1948. Truman and his advisers were "prepared to
use any means that may be necessary to stay in Berlin." To reduce the risk of war, the president
decided on an airlift rather than attempting to send ground convoys through Soviet lines.
Corbis–Bettmann.

(3) military alliances with other nations, (4) programs of military and economic aid to friendly nations, and (5) an extensive espionage network and secret means to subvert Communist expansion.

When Truman's press secretary called reporters to his office and released a statement on September 23, 1949, they rushed so fast for the telephones that they destroyed a stuffed deer's head in the process. Sending them scrambling was Truman's announcement that the Soviets had detonated an atomic bomb. Even though U.S. policymakers had known that the Soviet Union was working on an A-bomb, its success came years ahead of most predictions and shocked the American public.

Losing its nuclear monopoly pushed the United States to build an even deadlier weapon. In January 1950, Truman approved development of the hydrogen bomb, a weapon based on a thermonuclear explosion equivalent to five hundred atomic bombs. At its first test explosion in March 1954, the hydrogen bomb—known as the "super bomb"—produced a force one thousand times greater than the atomic bomb used on Hiroshima. But America's

thermonuclear advantage was brief; in November 1955, the Soviet Union exploded its own super bomb.

From the 1950s through the 1980s, the United States conducted a nuclear defense strategy based on the concept of "deterrence": The Americans would strive to maintain a more powerful nuclear force than the Russians, thereby deterring the Soviets from attacking the United States. Because the Soviets pursued a similar policy, the superpowers became locked in an ever escalating race for nuclear dominance. Albert Einstein, whose mathematical discoveries had laid the foundations for nuclear weapons, commented grimly on the enormous destructive force now possessed by the superpowers. The war that came after World War III, he said, would be fought with stones.

Along with vastly increasing its nuclear arsenal, the United States beefed up its conventional military power to deter Soviet threats that might not warrant nuclear retaliation, such as the Berlin blockade. To curtail squabbling among the military branches and streamline defense strategy planning, Congress passed the National Security Act in 1947.

That law brought the military branches together under a single secretary of defense and created the National Security Council (NSC) to advise the president on defense policy.

As the Berlin crisis simmered in 1948, Congress stepped up appropriations for the air force and enacted a peacetime draft. Urged on by General Dwight D. Eisenhower and other military leaders, Congress also granted permanent status to the women's military branches, thereby allowing women to volunteer. With around 1.5 million men and women in uniform in 1950, the military strength of the United States stood at more than four times its prewar level, and in 1947, defense expenditures claimed one-third of the federal budget.

Collective security, the third arm of postwar military strategy and the sharpest break from America's past, also developed during the Berlin showdown of 1948. That June, the administration won Senate support for the general principle of regional alliances for collective security. One year later, the United States joined Canada and Western European nations in its first peacetime military alliance, the North Atlantic Treaty Organization (NATO), which was created to counter the Soviet threat to Western Europe. For the first time in its history the United States pledged to go to war should one of its allies be attacked.

The fourth part of postwar defense strategy operated foreign aid programs to strengthen friendly countries. Military and economic assistance to Greece and Turkey in 1947 was one example of this strategy. Another was the $13 billion Marshall Plan that helped Western European nations to revive their war-crippled economies. In addition, in 1949, Congress approved $1 billion of military aid to its NATO allies and began economic assistance to nations in other parts of the world.

Finally, the United States began to develop its espionage capacities and the means to subvert communism through secret activities, operations that would form a larger part of foreign policy after the Truman years. The National Security Act of 1947 created the Central Intelligence Agency (CIA) to gather information considered necessary to the national defense. Truman and his advisers assured legislators who were uneasy about a peacetime spying agency that the CIA's powers would be limited. Nonetheless, the legislation authorized the new agency to perform any "functions and duties related to intelligence affecting the national security" that the NSC might authorize. Eventually, CIA agents conducted secret operations that toppled legitimate foreign governments and violated the rights of U.S. citizens. In many respects, the CIA was unaccountable to Congress or the public.

By 1950, the United States had abandoned age-old tenets of foreign policy. In place of the isolationism and neutrality that had followed World War I, the country embarked on economic and military efforts to control events far beyond its borders. The new policy of containment worked reasonably well in Europe. Short of war, the United States could not stop the descent of the iron curtain, but it acted aggressively and successfully to promote economic recovery and a military shield for the rest of Europe, thereby diminishing the threat of any further extension of Communist power.

Superpower Rivalry around the Globe

Although Europe occupied the center of the Truman administration's attention, it was not the only place where the United States sought to implement containment. The defeat of Japan, Italy, and Germany and the declining power of Britain and France left immense power vacuums in parts of the world that these countries had controlled or colonized. Assuming that the Soviet Union would try to fill those vacuums, U.S. policymakers sought to promote stability in Asia and win friends among the nations casting off colonial domination throughout the world. These nations collectively came to be referred to as the "third world," a term denoting countries outside the Western and Soviet orbits (especially in Africa, the Middle East, and Asia) that had not developed industrial economies.

Assuming that the Soviet Union would try to fill power vacuums around the world, U.S. policymakers sought to promote stability in Asia and win friends among the nations casting off colonial domination.

The United States soon encountered enormous difficulties in attempting to extend containment beyond Western Europe. Political and economic conditions in the Middle East and Asia proved volatile and complex, and Truman failed to achieve the bipartisan consensus in Congress that had ensured approval of his European initiatives. The United States remained the most powerful nation in the world, but it could not manage events everywhere to suit its interests.

The Rise of National Liberation Movements

In Africa, the Middle East, and Asia, World War II furthered a tide of national liberation movements against war-weakened imperial powers. Between 1945 and 1960, forty countries containing more than one-quarter of the world's people won their independence. As these nations ousted their former colonial rulers, both the United States and the Soviet Union sought to foster governments that were friendly to their own interests and institutions.

Like Woodrow Wilson during World War I, Roosevelt and Truman promoted the ideal of national self-determination. The United States granted independence to its own dominion the Philippines on July 4, 1946. American officials applauded the British withdrawal from India, Burma, and Ceylon and the Dutch retreat from Indonesia in 1949, and they encouraged France to relinquish its empire in Indochina.

As the cold war intensified, however, the ideal of self-determination gave way to American leaders' worries about the nature of the new governments that had been established in the ruins of European and Japanese imperialism. Policymakers wanted to preserve opportunities for American trade, and U.S. corporations coveted the vast oil reserves in the Middle East. Access to that oil was also critical to the European nations.

Moreover, the United States viewed its own revolution as the best model for independence movements and expected newly emerging nations to create institutions in the American democratic and capitalist image. But many independence movements were more impressed with the Russian Revolution and the rapid economic growth it had spawned. Although they tended to have few or no direct ties with the Soviet Union, many newly independent nations adopted socialist or Communist ideas. American leaders insisted on viewing these movements as a threatening extension of Soviet power. And they increasingly demanded that new nations take sides in the cold war, forgetting the importance of neutrality in their own diplomatic tradition. The bipolar lens of United States–Soviet Union conflict colored the American and Soviet views of the entire world.

In 1949, the Truman administration initiated the Point IV program of technical aid to the third world. The program aimed to hold communism at bay by fostering economic development and political stability, but the dollars spent were few compared with those spent on European aid. For the most part, Africa and Latin America remained on the periphery of Truman's attention and did not become entangled in the global rivalry between the superpowers until the 1950s and 1960s. The Middle East and Asia were the third world hot spots of the Truman years.

Nationalist Turmoil in the Middle East

In 1943, when the U.S. government was doing little to save European Jews from the Nazi terror, then-Senator Harry Truman spoke passionately at a rally called to focus attention on the Holocaust. Urging the United States to do everything "humanly possible to provide a haven and a place of safety" for Hitler's victims, Truman maintained, "This is not a Jewish problem, it is an American problem—and we must . . . face it squarely and honorably."

As president, Truman grasped the opportunity to make good on his words when he confronted the establishment of a Jewish homeland in Palestine. Jews had been settling in Palestine since the nineteenth century, and Nazi persecution during World War II swelled the tide of Jewish migration. In 1917, Britain had promised the Jews a homeland in territory that Britain did not then control but that became a British protectorate with the defeat of the Turks in World War I.

After World War II, hundreds of thousands of European Jews sought refuge in Palestine. American immigration policy continued to allow relatively few Jewish refugees to settle in the United States, and Truman urged Britain to lift the limits it had set on Jewish immigrants to Palestine. Fighting between Palestinian Arabs and Jews raged into brutal terrorism on both sides, and the British were reluctant to do anything that might increase tensions or alienate Arabs in other parts of the Middle East who controlled oil resources.

Truman's support for a Jewish state in Palestine distressed nearly all of his foreign policy experts, who saw American-Arab friendship as a critical factor in blocking Soviet influence in the Middle East and securing U.S. interests in Arabian petroleum. The president was more sympathetic to the enormous pressure marshaled by Jewish organizations and to the resolutions from thirty-three state legislatures supporting a Jewish state in Palestine. His position reflected a moral commitment to the Holocaust survivors as well as his interest in keeping the American Jewish vote within the Democratic fold.

When Jews in Palestine declared the independent state of Israel in May 1948, Truman waited just eleven minutes after the declaration became official to recognize the new country. Arab forces immediately attacked Israel, and Truman pledged assistance, making the defense of Israel the cornerstone of U.S. Middle Eastern policy. In acting on his moral and political instincts, Truman uncharacteristically defied his foreign policy advisers. A national homeland was scant compensation for the horrors inflicted upon European Jews during World War II, yet its establishment drove thousands of Palestinians from their homes and left the Middle East in turmoil for decades to come.

Communism Triumphs in China

On the other side of the globe, a civil war raged in China, where the Communists, led by Mao Zedong (Mao Tse-tung), fought the official Nationalist government under Chiang Kai-shek. Eight years of war against the Japanese had taken a terrible toll, but the Communists gained increasing support among the peasants for their courageous stand against the Japanese and their land reforms. In contrast, Chiang's corrupt government and incompetent management of the war against Japan alienated much of the population.

The United States took a keen interest in China, dating back to the Open Door policy of the turn of the century. Although the Chinese Communists remained independent of Moscow and received very little Soviet aid, many U.S. officials feared the expansion of Soviet power should the Communists prevail in the civil war. Moreover, the Truman administration was under extreme pressure not to "lose" China to the Communists from the so-called China bloc, a lobby that included Republican members of Congress, religious groups with missionary ties to China, and Henry R. Luce, the son of missionaries and the publisher of the influential *Time* and *Life* magazines.

To Truman and his advisers, however, Europe remained the hub of U.S. interests. They believed that diversion of American resources from Europe to China would be not only unwise, but also futile, given the incompetence of Chiang's government. After a failed effort at negotiations in 1946, the United States provided some token aid to Chiang to mollify the China bloc and to signal its interest, but the Truman administration for the most part simply awaited the inevitable downfall of the Nationalists.

In December 1949, Mao established the People's Republic of China (PRC); the Nationalists fled to the island of Taiwan two months later. Some administration officials urged accommodation with Communist China, but the outbreak of war in Korea in June 1950 foreclosed that option. The United States refused to recognize the existence of the PRC, blocked its admission to the United Nations, and continued to provide aid to Chiang's government in Taiwan.

"We picked a bad horse," Truman remarked, explaining the Communist victory as the result of the corrupt Nationalist government. The State Department viewed Mao's victory as "the product of internal Chinese forces, forces which this country tried to influence but could not." Nothing less than a massive U.S. military commitment could have stopped the Chinese Communists. But some Americans blamed Truman and his advisers. Republicans

cried that Truman had "lost" China, and one critic assailed "the pro-Communists in the State Department who . . . aided in the Communist conquest of China."

Truman's political wounds over the "loss" of China were partially self-inflicted. He had warned repeatedly of the threat of Communist expansion, and he had implied that the United States could contain that threat. China tested the boundaries of U.S. power and found it to be limited, a situation that was difficult for Americans to accept. It was easier to believe the Republicans when they blamed subversives in the U.S. government for the Communist victory in China. China became a political albatross for the Democrats, who resolved never again to be in a position that would allow their opponents to accuse them of being soft on communism.

The Reverse Course in Japan

As it became clear that China could not fulfill American hopes for a stable ally in Asia, the administration reconsidered its plans for postwar Japan. Initially, it had aimed to prevent Japan from threatening peace again by reforming its political and economic institutions. The U.S. military occupation headed by General Douglas MacArthur purged Japanese militarists from official positions, pushed Japan to adopt a democratic constitution, and made plans to break up huge concentrations of economic power.

As the situation in China worsened, Truman's advisers began to reassess the occupation strategy, and by 1948 they had reversed their original plans for the economic decentralization of Japan. Now the United States promoted the swift economic recovery of its former enemy, just as it had done in Germany. The new goals were to rapidly reindustrialize and to secure Japanese access to markets and natural resources in Asia. The United States also moved to silence leftist groups and return to power many officials who had promoted wartime Japanese aggression. After a sluggish start, the Japanese economy flourished. Within three decades, Japan would challenge the industrial supremacy of the United States.

American soldiers remained on military bases in Japan, but the official occupation ended when the two nations signed a peace treaty and a mutual security pact in September 1951. As had been the case with Germany, Japan sat squarely within the American orbit, ready to serve as an economic hub for Asia.

CHIANG KAI-SHEK AND MAO ZEDONG
The leaders of the opposing sides in the Chinese civil war — the communist Mao Zedong (on the right) and the Nationalist Chiang Kai-shek — met in Chungking in 1945 to discuss forming a coalition government after driving out the Japanese. These negotiations failed. After four years of conflict, in 1949 the Communists established the People's Republic of China under Mao, while Chiang and his supporters fled to the island of Taiwan.
Jack Wilkes, *Life* Magazine © Time Inc.

Truman and the Fair Deal at Home

Referring to the Civil War general who coined the phrase "War is hell," Truman said in December 1945, "Sherman was wrong. I'm telling you I find peace is hell." Challenged by thorny problems abroad, Truman also had to deal with shortages, strikes, inflation, and other problems attending the reconversion of the economy to peacetime production. At the same time, he tried to expand New Deal reform, most notably into the areas of civil rights, housing, education, and health care.

> *Referring to the Civil War general who coined the phrase "War is hell," Truman said in December 1945, "Sherman was wrong. I'm telling you I find peace is hell."*

Yet obstacles abounded to Truman's domestic agenda, which came to be known as the Fair Deal. Four years of war had left most Americans weary of government intervention in the economy, eager to hold on to their wartime gains but not disposed to engage in more social and economic experiments. Business leaders' role in the wartime production miracle had greatly elevated their influence, which

they now directed against Truman's reform proposals. Not only did Truman battle Republicans in Congress, but even when the Democrats controlled Congress, he failed to win most of his legislative goals. For the most part, Truman had to settle for consolidation of reforms that were already in place.

Truman's Program and Postwar Politics

Despite the deprivations and inconveniences caused by World War II, most Americans had enjoyed a wartime standard of living that was higher than ever before. Economic experts and ordinary citizens alike worried about whether that standard could be sustained in peacetime and whether an economy no longer stimulated by massive government purchasing could provide jobs for millions of returning soldiers.

Truman wasted no time in unveiling his plan for converting the economy from military to peacetime production. Within days of the Japanese surrender, he went to Congress with a twenty-one-point program. Truman wanted to retain controls over the economy to ease the reconversion process and sought new authority to promote full employment. He proposed measures to assist minorities, low-income workers, farmers, and small businesses and called for long-range programs that would ensure decent housing, adequate medical care, and a good

TABLE 26.1
WORK STOPPAGES IN THE UNITED STATES, 1936–1947

Year	Number	Average Length of Stoppage (days)	Workers Involved (in thousands)
1936	2,172	23.3	789
1937	4,740	20.3	1,860
1938	2,772	23.6	688
1939	2,613	23.4	1,170
1940	2,508	20.9	577
1941	4,288	18.3	2,360
1942	2,968	11.7	840
1943	3,752	5.0	1,980
1944	4,956	5.6	2,120
1945	4,750	9.9	3,470
1946	4,985	24.2	4,600
1947	3,693	25.6	2,170

Source: U.S. Department of Labor, *Handbook of Labor Statistics,* 1974.

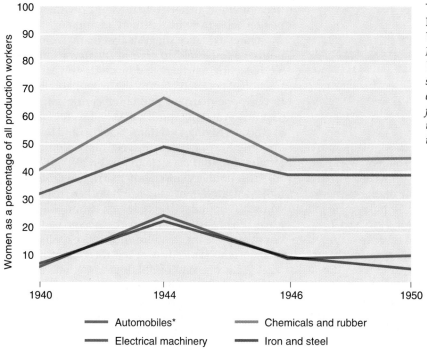

FIGURE 26.1
Women Workers in Selected Industries, 1940–1950
Women demolished the idea that some jobs were "men's work" during World War II, but they failed to maintain their gains in the manufacturing sector after the war.

*During World War II, this industry did not produce cars, but rather military transportation such as jeeps, tanks, aircraft, etc.

education for every citizen. "Not even President Roosevelt ever asked for as much at one sitting," exploded Republican leader Joseph W. Martin Jr.

Congress enacted Truman's proposal for full-employment legislation in a watered-down form. The Employment Act of 1946 declared it the "responsibility of the Federal Government . . . to promote maximum employment, production, and purchasing power," thereby formalizing what had been implicit in Roosevelt's actions to counter the depression—government's responsibility for maintaining a healthy economy. The law created a Council of Economic Advisers to assist the president in economic planning, but it authorized no new powers to translate the government's new obligation into effective action.

Inflation rather than unemployment turned out to be the most severe problem in the early postwar years. Unable to buy civilian goods during the war, in 1945 alone consumers had saved nearly $30 billion that they now itched to spend. But shortages of meat, automobiles, appliances, housing, and a host of other items persisted. Some six million people wanted new cars in 1946, but auto manufacturers managed to produce fewer than three million.

Housing was so scarce that returning veterans lived in basements, garages, and even automobiles.

Until industry could convert fully to civilian production, making more goods available, consumer demand could only drive up prices. Struggling with the problems of reconversion, Truman complained that the wartime unity had been replaced by greed. "The Congress [is] balking, labor has gone crazy, and management isn't far from insane in selfishness," he wrote his mother in October 1945.

Labor wanted to keep price controls but sought wage increases at the same time. Corporations, however, demanded that the government abandon price controls, and they found allies in Republicans and conservative Democrats. Truman took an inconsistent course until he scuttled the Office of Price Administration after the Republicans gained control of Congress in the 1946 elections. The consumer price index—an official measurement of the rate of inflation—shot up by 18 percent in 1946, but the shift to peacetime production occurred swiftly enough to save the United States from crippling inflation. However, it did not save the administration from taking the blame, during the 1946 elections, for rising prices.

What Happened to Rosie the Riveter?

ALTHOUGH STUDIES HAVE BEEN DONE of the postwar lives of World War II soldiers, we know much less about another group of "veterans," the women who helped fight the war on the domestic front. Statistics show that women's employment fell by more than two million between 1945 and 1947. But gross statistics don't reveal which women left the labor force and why, and they obscure the experiences of women who continued to work but in different jobs.

We do know what public officials and business and labor leaders expected of women who had taken up "men's" work during the war. With the shadow of the depression still hovering, Americans doubted that the economy could accommodate the six million new women workers along with millions of returning veterans once wartime production had ceased. A nearly universal response to anxieties about unemployment pushed a big part of the responsibility on women: In place of their wartime duty to produce the goods needed for victory came their postwar obligation to withdraw from the labor force.

The message that they should quit their jobs "for the sake of their homes as well as the labor situation" overwhelmed women. The company newspaper at Kaiser shipyards in the Pacific Northwest proclaimed in May 1945, "The Kitchen—Women's Big Post-War Goal." Putting words into the mouths of Kaiser's female employees, the article asserted, "Brothers, the tin hat and welder's torch will be yours! . . . The thing we want to do is take off these unfeminine garments and button ourselves into something starched and pretty." A General Electric ad predicted that women would welcome a return to "their old housekeeping routine" because GE intended to transform housework with new appliances. Some experts connected married women's employment to their obligations to help their husbands readjust to civilian life. A psychiatrist warned that women's economic independence might "raise problems in the future," urging women to realize that "reunion means relinquishing it [their independence]—to some extent at any rate."

Other evidence suggests that many women did not have to be told to give up their wartime jobs. Skyrocketing marriage and birthrates reveal the attraction of home and family life to people compelled to postpone marriage and childbearing during the depression and the war. Thanks to the accumulation of wartime savings, veterans' benefits, and favorable opportunities for men in the postwar economy, many families found it possible to rely on a single earner.

The double burdens of married women who took wartime jobs suggest another reason for women's voluntary withdrawal from the workforce. The wartime scarcity of goods had made housekeeping much more difficult, especially for women who typically worked forty-eight hours a week with one day off. Shopping became a problem because stores often sold out of goods early in the day, and few shops kept evening or Sunday hours. Washing machines, refrigerators, vacuum cleaners, and other appliances that might have lightened women's burdens were not produced at all during the war. Child care centers accommodated only about 10 percent of the children of employed mothers. Employed women with families to care for were simply worn out.

Yet surveys reported that 75 percent of women in wartime jobs wanted—and usually needed—to keep them. As two women employed at a Ford plant in Memphis put it, "Women didn't stop eating when the war stopped." Those who needed and wanted to remain in the workforce experienced the most wrenching changes. The vast majority were able to find jobs; in fact, women's workforce participation began growing again in 1947 and reached the wartime peak by 1950. But women lost the traditionally male, higher-paying jobs in durable goods industries (such as iron and steel and automobile and machinery production) and were pushed back into the lower-paying light manufacturing and service industries that had customarily welcomed them.

Statistics tell part of the story of this displacement. Women virtually disappeared from shipbuilding, and their share of jobs in the auto industry fell from 25 percent in 1944 to 10 percent in 1950. In the burgeoning Los Angeles aircraft industry, the proportion of women plunged from a wartime peak of 40 percent to 12 percent in 1948, rising to just 25 percent in the 1950s. Even in light manufacturing,

Sisters under the apron—Yesterday's war worker becomes today's housewife.

What's Become of Rosie the Riveter?

WOMEN'S POSTWAR FUTURE
This photograph headed an article in the New York Times Magazine *in June 1946. The article, written by the head of the Women's Bureau of the Department of Labor, discussed the needs of women workers, stressed their right to work and to equal pay, but also assumed that they would all but vanish from heavy manufacturing.*
Ellen Kaiper.

such as the electrical goods industry, where women had claimed one-third of the prewar jobs, women maintained their numbers but were bumped down to lower-paying work. During the war, women had narrowed the wage gap between men and women, but in 1950, women earned only 53 percent of what men did.

How women reacted to their displacement can be pieced together from what they were willing to say to reporters and oral history interviewers and what they wrote to government agencies and labor unions. "Women do not expect or want to hold jobs at the expense of returning soldiers," proclaimed a resolution passed by the Women's Trade Union League, expressing women's overwhelming support for veterans' claims to jobs based on seniority awarded for the years of their wartime service. According to Tina Hill, a black worker at North American Aircraft in Los Angeles, being laid off "didn't bother me much. I was just glad that the war was over . . . [and] my husband had a job." Nonetheless, after doing domestic work, when North American called her back, she recalled, "was I a happy soul!"

When management violated women's seniority rights by hiring nonveterans, some women protested bitterly. According to an automobile worker, "We have women laid off with seniority . . . and every day they hire in new men off the street. They hire men, they say, to do the heavy work. . . . During the war they didn't care what kind of work we did." When Ford laid off women with as many as twenty-seven years' seniority, 150 women picketed with signs that read, "The Hand That Rocks the Cradle Can Build Tractors, Too." A worker infuriated by her union's failure to protect women's seniority rights told a reporter, "We are making the bullets now, and we will give the [union executive] board members a blast that will blow them out of their shoes."

Protest from a minority of women workers could not save the jobs that "Rosies" had held during the war. Despite women's exemplary performance, most employers still saw women and men as different species fit for different roles and deserving of disparate rewards. Most labor unions paid lip service to representing all their members, but even the most progressive unions gave low priority to protecting women's seniority rights. In the absence of a feminist movement that could have given visibility and credibility to their claims for equal treatment, most Rosie the Riveters resigned themselves to the *status quo ante bellum*.

Labor Becomes More Militant

Labor relations constituted another thorn in Truman's side. Organized labor survived the war stronger than ever, its 14.5 million members making up 35 percent of the civilian workforce. Yet union members feared erosion of wartime gains. With wage controls in place throughout the war, the rising incomes enjoyed by working-class families had depended largely on the availability of new jobs and the chance to work longer hours. The end of overtime meant a 30 percent cut in take-home pay for most workers.

Women who had flocked into wartime jobs also saw their earnings decline. Many women were ready to return to their homes, but as many as 68 to 85 percent, according to some polls, wanted to keep their jobs. Most "Rosie the Riveters" (a nickname based on a wartime image of women factory workers popularized in a Norman Rockwell painting) who remained in the workforce did so only by accepting lower-paying jobs in light industry or the service sector. Displaced from her shipyard work, Marie Schreiber found work as a cashier. "You were back to women's wages, you know . . . practically in half," she recalled. Men replaced tens of thousands of women in iron, steel, and other heavy industries that paid relatively good wages. From a wartime high of 36 percent, in 1947 women held just 27 percent of all jobs.

Most unions paid scant attention to the problems of women workers as they struggled to defend labor's interests in the postwar economy. Using the power to strike, which unions had patriotically given up during the war, seemed the only way to avoid the hard times of the 1930s. As it had after World War I, labor militancy erupted soon after the surrender of Japan. From September 1945 to the end of 1946, five million workers stopped production in virtually every major industry. The nation lost more than twenty million worker-days in February 1946 alone, and more strikes took place in 1946 than at any other time in U.S. history.

Workers saw corporate owners and executives profiting at their expense. Shortly before his union took a strike vote, a twenty-four-year-old Pittsburgh steelworker and former marine read about a lavish party given by a company executive. He and his fellow carpoolers figured out that the party would cost more than their total earnings for a year's work in the steel mills. The veteran remembered, "That sort of stuff made us realize, hell, we *had* to bite the bullet . . . the bosses sure didn't give a damn for us."

Union members had reason to believe that Truman didn't give a damn for them either. Strikes interfered with rapid reconversion, and demands for higher wages threatened to thrust the economy into a spiral of inflation. Truman and his associates strong-armed both management and labor, but both sides frequently thumbed their noses at government recommendations. While the president vented his displeasure with labor and management alike, his efforts to curb strikes provoked angry attacks from labor leaders. When Truman tried to end the General Motors strike in December 1946, CIO President Philip Murray charged him with trying "to weaken and ultimately destroy labor union organization."

Although most Americans approved of unions in principle, they were fed up with labor stoppages, blamed unions for rising prices, and wanted more government restrictions on organized labor. Truman shared the public exasperation and resorted to drastic measures when strikes affected critical industries. In May 1946, after coal miners rejected government recommendations for a settlement, and their strike threatened the steel, auto, and railroad industries as well, Truman placed the mines under federal control.

Then, when the railroad workers walked out two days later, Truman decided to seek authority to draft into the armed services workers who struck in essential industries. Cautioned by his advisers who questioned the constitutionality of such a measure, Truman shot back, "We'll draft them and think about the law later." The plan to draft strikers infuriated labor and its liberal allies, and even conservative Republicans found his remedy too drastic. Settlement of the railroad strike just as Truman presented his proposal to Congress did little to quell the outrage against him.

Although strikes subsided by the end of 1946, antilabor sentiment lingered, and Truman faced the labor issue again in 1947. In general, labor's postwar militancy won wage increases of around 20 percent for unionized workers. But the loss of overtime combined with rising prices left labor's purchasing power only slightly higher than it had been in 1942, while real income in other sectors of the economy had risen.

Reconversion and the Economic Boom

By 1947, the nation had survived the strains of reconversion and avoided the nearly universally expected postwar depression. Wartime profits enabled businesses to invest in new plants and equipment.

Consumers used their billions of dollars in wartime savings to buy the houses, cars, and appliances that had been denied them during the depression and the war. Defense spending and the $38 billion in grants and loans that enabled war-torn countries to purchase American goods also stimulated the economy. A soaring birthrate, 25 percent higher in 1949 than in 1940, further sustained consumer demand.

The nation's gratitude to its returning warriors also boosted the economy. Under the Servicemen's Readjustment Act (the GI Bill), passed in 1944, sixteen million veterans could claim unemployment compensation while they looked for jobs; low-interest loans to purchase homes, farms, and small businesses; and funds for job training and educa-

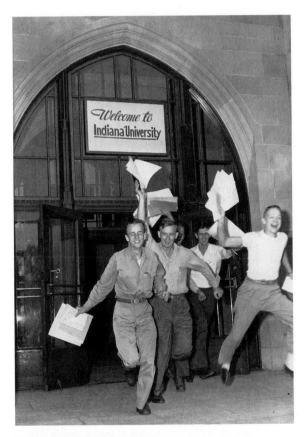

VETERANS GO TO COLLEGE
So many World War II veterans wanted to use their GI benefits for higher education that colleges were over-whelmed, and many had to turn away students. These veterans, sprinting out of the building where they have just registered, express their joy at having been admitted to Indiana University in 1947.
Indiana University Photographic Services.

tion. By 1948, some 1.3 million veterans had bought houses with government loans, and more than 7 million had received funds for tuition, books, and living expenses related to job training and education. Men who had dodged bullets at Normandy and Iwo Jima now poured into crowded college classrooms.

As a form of affirmative action program for veterans, the GI Bill inadvertently disadvantaged women, who filled just a tiny portion of military slots during the war. For example, women's enrollments grew after the war, but their share of college degrees dropped below the prewar level. Nor could the vast majority of women claim the preference in hiring that veterans enjoyed from private and public employers alike. As wives and daughters of veterans, women did benefit indirectly from the GI subsidies, which helped almost one of every four Americans.

Americans in the late 1940s went on a spending spree. Between 1946 and 1950, a population of about 150 million purchased more than 20 million automobiles and refrigerators, 5.5 million electric stoves, and 11.6 million television sets. The number of owner-occupied houses increased from 15.2 million in 1940 to 23.5 million in 1950; by the end of the decade, most families owned their own homes.

Yet economic prosperity was not universal. The real gains had been made during the war, and family income actually declined slightly between 1944 and 1950. Wages and salaries increased by 23 percent from 1945 to 1950, but prices went up by 36.2 percent. A recession in 1949 threw 7 percent of the labor force out of work; it abated only when the Korean War sparked economic recovery. Moreover, the one-third of all Americans who lived in poverty failed to receive any significant benefits from the return to peacetime production.

Black Protest and the Politics of Civil Rights

"I spent four years in the army to free a bunch of Frenchmen and Dutchmen," an African American corporal declared, "and I'm hanged if I'm going to let the Alabama version of the Germans kick me around when I get home." Black soldiers and civilians alike resolved that the return to peace would not be a return to the racial injustices of prewar America. Their political clout had grown with the migration of two million African Americans to northern and western cities, where they could vote and their ballots could make a difference. Even in the South, the proportion of blacks who cast ballots inched up from 2 percent to 12 percent in the 1940s. Pursuing civil rights through the courts and Congress, the National Association for the Advancement of Colored People (NAACP) counted half a million members.

> *"I spent four years in the army to free a bunch of Frenchmen and Dutchmen," an African American corporal declared, "and I'm hanged if I'm going to let the Alabama version of the Germans kick me around when I get home."*

In the postwar period, individual blacks broke through the color barrier, achieving several "firsts" for their race. Jackie Robinson integrated major league baseball when he took over second base for the Brooklyn Dodgers in 1947. Overcoming abuse from both fans and players, Robinson performed brilliantly and ended the season with the rookie of the year award. Two other African Americans toppled racial barriers in 1950: Ralph J. Bunche, who received the Nobel Peace Prize for his contributions to the United Nations, and Gwendolyn Brooks, who won the Pulitzer Prize for poetry.

However, in most respects, African Americans found that little had changed after the war, especially in the South, where a wave of violence erupted when they tried to assert their rights. White men with guns turned back Medgar Evers (who would become a key civil rights leader in the 1960s) and four other veterans who were trying to vote in Mississippi. Angry crowds flogged another Mississippi veteran who attempted to register. A mob lynched Isaac Nixon for voting in Georgia, and an all-white jury acquitted those accused of his murder. Governors, U.S. senators, and other southern politicians routinely intimidated potential voters with threats of economic retaliation and violence.

"My very stomach turned over when I learned that Negro soldiers just back from overseas were being dumped out of army trucks in Mississippi and beaten," wrote Truman. Shaken by the violence against blacks and pressured by civil rights leaders and their liberal allies, he believed that his responsibility as chief executive compelled action against blatant injustice. Truman grasped the importance of black and liberal votes to Democratic Party fortunes

in northern states, but he knew equally well how much the party relied on a solid bloc of white southern votes. Wrestling with these counterforces, Truman acted more boldly on civil rights than had any previous president.

In 1946, Truman created a Committee on Civil Rights. Not surprisingly, this committee of distinguished Americans found glaring and widespread racial discrimination, and it recommended measures to protect voting rights and eliminate segregation. In February 1948, Truman sent a special message to Congress calling for enactment of the committee's recommendations. The first president to address the NAACP, Truman announced to that group that all Americans should have equal rights to housing, education, employment, and the ballot.

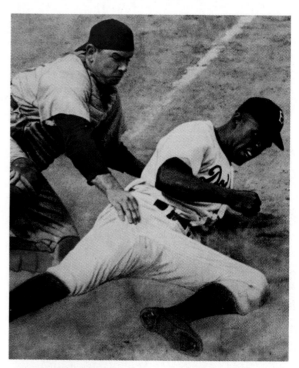

JACKIE ROBINSON
John Roosevelt Robinson slides into home in a game against the Philadelphia Phillies in 1952. Before he became, in 1947, the first African American to play major-league baseball, Robinson had excelled at track as well as baseball at UCLA and had been an Army officer in World War II. Even his brilliant play for the Brooklyn Dodgers did not save him from fans' and players' racial taunts or exclusion from restaurants and hotels that catered to his white teammates. Having paved the way for other black players, Robinson played until 1956.
The Michael Barson Collection/Past Perfect.

To the dismay of civil rights leaders, the president did not always match his words with equally forceful deeds. He failed to follow up on his messages by having specific bills introduced into Congress. In the throes of the 1948 election campaign, and under threat of civil disobedience action proposed by A. Philip Randolph (who had pressured Roosevelt by threatening an African American march on Washington in 1941), the president did issue an executive order to desegregate the armed services. But he allowed the order to go unimplemented until the need for military personnel during the Korean War forced the military's hand.

Though Truman continued to call for civil rights legislation, a combination of southern Democrats and Republicans killed every bill that was introduced. Nor was he able to rally much popular support for his program. Among those polled in a national survey in 1949, nearly half opposed federal action against job discrimination, while just 34 percent believed that the government should "go all the way" to ensure equal opportunity.

Nonetheless, Truman's Justice Department aligned the administration with the NAACP by filing *amicus curiae* ("friend of the court") briefs supporting legal challenges to segregation and discrimination. In 1948, the Supreme Court struck a blow at housing discrimination in *Shelley v. Kramer.* Two years later, it ruled that a state university could not segregate black students (*McLaurin v. Oklahoma State Regents*) and that an inferior school established to keep African Americans out of the University of Texas Law School violated their right to equal protection (*Sweatt v. Painter*).

Although the gap loomed large between what Truman said about civil rights and what his administration accomplished, the desegregation of the military and the support of civil rights cases in the Supreme Court kindled far-reaching changes. Breaking sharply with the past, Truman used the prestige and visibility of his office to educate the public and set a moral agenda, thereby encouraging the struggles of African Americans that would bring more substantial progress in years to come.

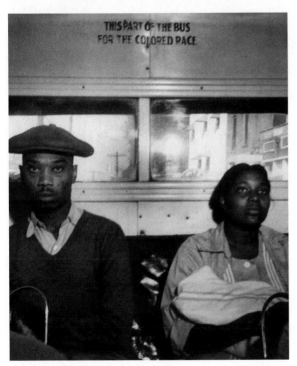

SEGREGATION
Signs like this were a normal feature of life in the South from the late nineteenth century until the 1960s. State and local laws mandated segregation in every aspect of life, literally from the cradle to the grave. African Americans could not use white hospitals, cemeteries, schools, libraries, swimming pools, playgrounds, restrooms, or drinking fountains. They were relegated to balconies in movie theaters and kept apart from whites in all public meetings.
Martin Magner/Courtesy, Center for Creative Photography, The University of Arizona.

The "Do-Nothing Congress" and the 1948 Election

Truman's difficulties with economic reconversion and strikes gave the Republicans an edge in the 1946 congressional elections. Portraying Truman as a little man in a big job that was way over his head, they accused his administration of "confusion, corruption, and communism" and jeered, "To Err Is Truman." Capturing Congress for the first time in fourteen years, the Republicans looked eagerly to the 1948 presidential campaign.

Although many Republicans campaigned against New Deal "regimentation," "bureaucracy," and "radicalism," their dominance of the 80th Congress, elected in 1946, failed to dismantle the reforms of the 1930s. Congress made slight assaults on reform programs with budget cuts and, overriding Truman's veto, favored higher income groups with tax cuts. Its most serious attack on the New Deal was the Taft-Hartley Act, passed in 1947.

Called a "slave labor" law and "Tuff-Heartless" by unions, Taft-Hartley imposed restrictions that

TRUMAN'S WHISTLE-STOP CAMPAIGN
Harry Truman rallies a crowd from his campaign train at a stop in Bridgeport, Pennsylvania, in October 1948. His campaign theme song, "I'm just wild about Harry," was borrowed, with the words slightly changed, from a musical written in 1921. This was the last election in which the pollsters predicted the wrong winner. They stopped taking polls in mid-October, after which many voters apparently changed their minds. One commentator praised the American citizenry, who "couldn't be ticketed by the polls, knew its own mind and had picked the rather unlikely but courageous figure of Truman to carry on its banner."
Photo: Truman Library; sheet music: Collection of Janice L. and David J. Frent.

limited the right to strike and made organizing workers more difficult. For example, it allowed states to pass "right to work" laws banning union shops, workplaces in which all workers were required to join a union once a majority had voted for it. The law also compelled union leaders to swear that they were not Communists and to report annually on their union's financial situation. From its role as supporter of unions, established in the Wagner Act of 1935, the federal government now

moved to a more neutral position between labor and management and between unions and individual workers. The New Deal principle of government protection for collective bargaining nonetheless remained intact.

Truman's impassioned attack on Taft-Hartley did not prevent Congress from overriding his veto, but it provided ammunition for his 1948 campaign. Planning to run as a strong liberal, he vetoed a number of bills that, he charged, favored the privileged.

Truman also took the offensive. Knowing that the Republican-controlled Congress would refuse his demands for liberal programs, he issued them anyway, constructing a case against what he called the "do-nothing Congress." Democratic Party leaders, unpersuaded that Truman could win, scurried around for an alternative candidate, but in the end they could not deny the president renomination.

Thomas E. Dewey, the Republican nominee who had lost to Roosevelt in 1944, was sure that his time had come, and so was nearly everyone else. In the 1948 elections, Truman faced not only a resurgent Republican Party, but also two revolts from within his own party. On the left, Henry Wallace, Roosevelt's vice president in the early 1940s and Truman's secretary of commerce, pushed out of the cabinet for his foreign policy views, led a new Progressive Party. On the right, South Carolina Governor J. Strom Thurmond headed the States' Rights Party—the Dixiecrats—formed by southern Democrats in opposition to the Democratic Party's growing support for civil rights.

Virtually alone in believing he could win, Truman crisscrossed the country by train, answering supporters' cries of "Give 'em hell, Harry," lambasting the 80th Congress, and warning voters against the return of "gluttons of privilege" to Washington. So bleak were Truman's prospects that the overconfident Dewey ran a low-key campaign and rarely went on the attack against Truman. Pollsters stopped polling, and on election night the *Chicago Tribune* printed its day-after-election issue with the banner headline "Dewey Defeats Truman."

But Truman surprised everyone, taking 303 electoral votes to Dewey's 189. The president's spirited campaign revitalized key segments of the Democratic coalition, including urban workers, farmers, and blacks. Not only did Truman hold on to his office, but his party also regained control of Congress. Even though Thurmond and Wallace collected more than a million votes each, mostly from Democrats, Truman finished more than two million votes ahead of Dewey. In addition to reflecting popular support for his foreign policy, Truman's win attested to his skills as a campaigner and to the enduring popularity of New Deal reform.

The Fair Deal Flounders

Truman viewed his victory as a mandate to enact the policies of his Fair Deal. But he found little support in Congress, where southern Democrats often joined the Republicans on domestic issues. Congress made modest improvements in Social Security and raised the minimum wage, but its only significant reform initiative was in housing. Sponsored by Ohio Republican Senator Robert Taft and passed in spite of strong opposition from the real estate industry, the Housing Act of 1949 furnished 350,000 units of government-constructed housing over the next fifteen years. Although it fell far short of actual need, and many projects were too cheaply built and poorly designed to provide a favorable environment for their inhabitants, the Housing Act represented a landmark commitment by the federal government to address the housing needs of the poor.

To the rest of the Fair Deal, Congress responded as it had to civil rights measures—with a resounding no. Congress rejected Truman's proposals for a federal health care program with national health insurance; for federal aid to education; and for a new agriculture program that would benefit small farmers, limit subsidies to giant commercial farmers, and keep prices low for consumers. Truman's proposals in civil rights, health, and education failed in the short run, but they laid foundations for enactment of similar programs in the 1960s.

Truman's efforts to revise immigration policy met a similar fate. In accord with the president's goals, the McCarran-Walter Act of 1952 ended

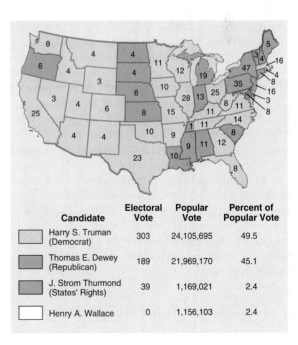

Candidate	Electoral Vote	Popular Vote	Percent of Popular Vote
Harry S. Truman (Democrat)	303	24,105,695	49.5
Thomas E. Dewey (Republican)	189	21,969,170	45.1
J. Strom Thurmond (States' Rights)	39	1,169,021	2.4
Henry A. Wallace	0	1,156,103	2.4

MAP 26.2
The Election of 1948

the outright ban on immigration and citizenship for Japanese and other Asians. But it authorized the government to bar suspected Communists and homosexuals. Most distressing to Truman, it maintained the quota system established in the 1920s, discriminating "deliberately and intentionally, against many of the peoples of the world," as Truman declared in his veto message. Overriding Truman's veto, Congress left the quota system intact for another fifteen years.

Although Truman blamed Republicans, conservative Democrats, and interest groups for defeating his Fair Deal, the reasons were much more complex, and some lay at his own doorstep. Truman devoted much more energy to foreign policy than to his domestic proposals. And he tended to throw many proposals at Congress without assigning priorities. Moreover, by late 1950 the Korean War embroiled Truman in controversy, diverted his attention from domestic affairs, and depleted his power as a legislative leader.

The Domestic Chill: A Second Red Scare

Truman's domestic program also suffered from a wave of anti-Communist hysteria that weakened leftist and liberal forces. "Red-baiting," the attempt to discredit individuals by accusing them of being Communists ("Reds") or sympathizers, was not new. Neither was official retaliation against leftist critics of government policies. Both had flourished during the Red scare at the end of World War I.

A second Red scare convulsed the United States after World War II. Born of partisan political maneuvering, collapse of the Soviet-American alliance, setbacks in U.S. foreign policy, and disclosures of Soviet espionage in the United States, Canada, and Britain, the postwar anti-Communist crusade swept through nearly every segment of American society. The new "witch-hunt" brought personal distress to thousands of citizens and created a climate of fear, stifling expression that did not conform to mainstream beliefs.

The Politics of Anticommunism

Republicans attacked New Deal programs by equating them with communism, and they jumped at the opportunities presented by the cold war to discredit

Democrats with the taint of communism. To Americans perplexed by the nation's inability to control events in Eastern Europe, China, and Korea, accusations of internal subversion offered simple explanations. As Wisconsin Republican Senator Joseph R. McCarthy, the leading anti-Communist, charged, "The Communists within our borders have been more responsible for the success of Communism abroad than Soviet Russia."

A second Red scare convulsed the United States after World War II. . . . The new "witch-hunt" brought personal distress to thousands of citizens and created a climate of fear, stifling expression that did not conform to mainstream beliefs.

Revelations of Soviet espionage and accusations made by former Communists furnished just enough credibility to such charges. In 1946, for example, the Canadian government discovered that several Canadian and British officials had passed military secrets to Russian agents. In the United States, a number of ex-Communists, including Whittaker Chambers and Elizabeth Bentley, testified that they and others had provided secret documents to the Soviets. In 1950, Klaus Fuchs, a British physicist attached to the atomic bomb project, confessed that he was a spy. He implicated several Americans, including a New York couple named Ethel and Julius Rosenberg. They pleaded innocent but were convicted of conspiracy to commit espionage; they were executed in the electric chair in 1953.

Most of the disloyalty charges against Americans involved allegations that they had connections to Communists long before the cold war had made the Soviet Union an enemy. At the peak of hysteria about internal subversives in the late 1940s, the U.S. Communist Party had only about twenty thousand members, some of them FBI agents. The party parroted the Soviet line on every issue and shrouded many activities in secrecy, but most members were open about their affiliation and acted within the law.

In addition to the twenty thousand party members, many more Americans had once been party members, had belonged to groups with Communist members, or had supported radical causes, but Red-hunters cared little for such distinctions. For more

THE RED SCARE
This map, entitled The Bear Grows and Grows, *appeared in the Sunday magazine section of the New York* News *in November 1947. What impact might such an image have on newspaper readers?*
The Michael Barson Collection/Past Perfect.

than ten years following World War II, the House Un-American Activities Committee (HUAC), the Senate Internal Security Subcommittee (SISS), and a host of other official bodies ordered citizens to testify about their past and present political associations.

Once witnesses admitted membership in a group that was deemed subversive, inquisitors asked them to name other members. If they tried to save their associates from a similar ordeal by refusing to identify them, they could be held in contempt of Congress. Consequently, many witnesses refused to answer any questions at all, claiming the Fifth Amendment protection from self-incrimination. Anti-Communists then charged that silence was tantamount to confession, and these "unfriendly witnesses" suffered the loss of jobs as well as public ostracism.

Nixon and McCarthy on the Attack

Richard Nixon was one of the Republicans who leaped at the chance to attack the Democrats for permitting subversives to operate in the United States. A member of HUAC during his first term in Congress in 1947–1948, Nixon took up the pursuit of Alger Hiss, a former New Dealer who had served in the wartime State Department. According to ex-Communist Whittaker Chambers, in the 1930s Hiss had belonged to a secret Communist cell that passed government documents to the Soviet Union.

Hiss denied the charges, but in 1950 a jury convicted him of lying to HUAC about his connections with Chambers, and Hiss spent four years in prison. The Hiss case became a hot spot of anti-Communist contention. Prominent Democrats such as Dean

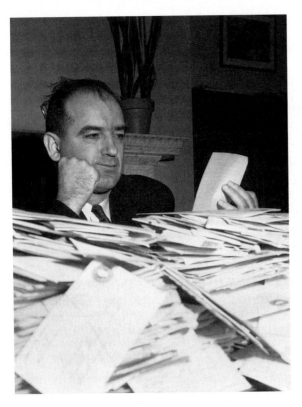

SENATOR JOSEPH R. McCARTHY
In March 1950, McCarthy reads letters responding to his claim to have a list of 205 Communists in the State Department. Although McCarthy made his reputation from anticommunism, he seized that issue more from the need to have a campaign platform in 1950 than from genuine concern grounded in real evidence. McCarthy loved politics from his high school days in Appleton, Wisconsin, and easily distorted the truth to promote his political ambitions. He died from alcoholism at the age of forty-eight, three years after the Senate condemned his conduct.
Corbis-Bettmann.

Acheson and Adlai Stevenson defended Hiss, while Republicans vilified him as a prime example of "twenty years of treason" under the Democrats. Nixon's pursuit of Alger Hiss won him national fame.

But Joseph McCarthy exceeded Nixon in his zeal to purge the United States of nonconformists. So great was his influence that "McCarthyism" became a term synonymous with the anti-Communist crusade, even though the hysteria ranged far beyond the senator's activities. McCarthy jumped into the national spotlight in 1950, when he claimed to have a list of 205 "known Communists" working in the State Department. He attacked individuals reck-

lessly, and even though many of his charges were absurd—such as his allegation that retired General George C. Marshall belonged to a Communist conspiracy—the press covered McCarthy avidly, and his photograph was featured on the covers of *Time* and *Newsweek*.

Although their party led it, not all Republicans joined McCarthyism. In 1950, Senator Margaret Chase Smith and six other Republicans issued a "declaration of conscience" condemning Republican efforts to gain power through "fear, ignorance, bigotry, and smear." Nor was McCarthyism confined to Republicans. Mississippi Democrat John E. Rankin led the effort to make HUAC a permanent committee, and he relentlessly hounded the witnesses who were called to testify. Other Democrats matched his Red-baiting, particularly southern politicians who labeled any efforts for racial justice Communist-inspired.

The Official Purge

Under increasing pressure from the Republicans and with public opinion strongly against the employment of Communists in government jobs, in March 1947 Truman issued Executive Order 9835 requiring investigation of every federal employee. Those found guilty of Communist affiliation or even of "sympathetic association" with Communists—often interpreted as membership in groups with radical leanings—lost their jobs without a hearing. Esther Brunauer, a State Department official, and her husband, Stephen, a noted chemist employed by the navy, lost their jobs in the anti-Communist hysteria. Attacked as subversives by McCarthy in 1950, the Brunauers quickly got caught up in Truman's loyalty-security program—"a nightmare from which there [was] no awakening," in Esther Brunauer's words.

Stephen Brunauer had belonged briefly to a Communist youth organization in the 1920s, and the Brunauers had associated with individuals or organizations that were allegedly sympathetic to communism. But there was no evidence of disloyalty or subversion, and the Brunauers' superiors affirmed the couple's loyalty in 1948. After McCarthy's charges, however, the government began new investigations. In 1951, the navy suspended Stephen Brunauer on security grounds. Rather than contesting the suspension, he resigned. Esther Brunauer endured two more hearings, in which she was accused of "close and habitual association" with her husband, before being ousted from the

State Department in 1952. She then found some editorial work, and her husband took a job with a cement association, their careers and reputations irreparably damaged.

The Brunauers and others accused of association with subversives had no opportunity to confront their informers, and they bore the burden of proving that they were not disloyal. In effect, Truman's loyalty program violated the principles of American justice by allowing anonymous informers to make charges and then demanding that the accused clear themselves. The program extended into the mid-1950s, as more than two thousand civil service employees lost their jobs and another ten thousand resigned from 1947 through 1956. Years later, Truman privately admitted that the loyalty program had been a mistake. "It was terrible," he said.

The Truman administration also went directly after the Communist Party. Just before the 1948 elections, the Justice Department began prosecuting eleven Communist Party leaders under the Smith Act, passed in 1940, which made it a crime to "advocate the overthrow and destruction of the Government of the United States by force and violence." A jury found the leaders guilty, convicting them

not for their actions but for their beliefs. They were sentenced to five years in prison. Although civil libertarians argued that the verdicts violated First Amendment rights to freedom of speech, press, and association, the Supreme Court ruled in 1951 (*Dennis v. United States*) that the severity of the Communist threat overrode the guarantees of the Constitution. Other prosecutions under the Smith Act followed, resulting in more than one hundred convictions through 1956.

Despite his own anti-Communist actions, Truman denounced the extremism of men like Nixon and McCarthy. He vetoed the McCarran Internal Security Act in 1950, rebuking Congress for putting the government in the "thought control business." The legislation denied passports and government or defense industry jobs to Communist sympathizers and authorized the government to build concentration camps to confine "subversives" in times of national emergency. Testifying to the strength of anti-Communist sentiment, Congress easily overrode the veto.

Although Republicans castigated Truman for being soft on communism, Truman himself contributed to McCarthyism. He had whipped up support for containment with words that intensified

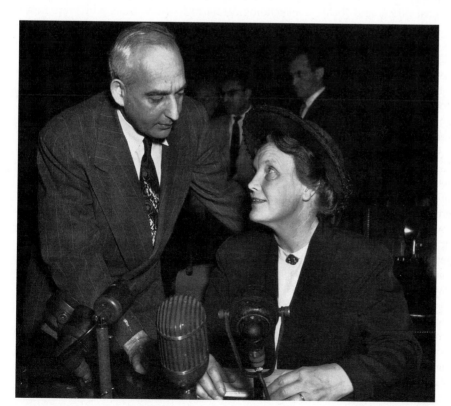

RED SCARE VICTIMS
Esther Brunauer speaks with her husband, Stephen, at the conclusion of her testimony in March 1950 before the Senate subcommittee investigating Senator Joseph McCarthy's charges that the State Department harbored Communist employees. As was true for thousands of government employees, McCarthyism terminated the Brunauers' professional careers.
Wide World.

fears of communism. The president and other Democrats engaged in Red-baiting against Henry Wallace in the presidential campaign of 1948. Moreover, the Truman administration's efforts to disarm the more rabid witch-hunters with the federal employee loyalty-security program actually fanned the flames.

The Pervasive Repression

The internal cold war spread beyond the nation's capital. State and local governments undertook their own investigations, demanded loyalty oaths from everyone from teachers to professional wrestlers, prosecuted Communist sympathizers, fired individuals suspected of disloyalty, banned books from public libraries, denied business licenses to alleged subversives, and more. Private organizations and businesses also purged dissidents and helped to create a climate of conformity.

McCarthyism drew sexual as well as political "deviants" into its web of victims. A 1950 Senate report claimed that homosexuals' "moral turpitude" and their susceptibility to blackmail made them unfit for government jobs. Purged from the civil service and drummed out of the military, gay men and women also suffered surveillance and harassment at the hands of the FBI, the post office, and local police forces.

Educational institutions grilled hundreds of teachers about their past and present political associations. When individuals refused to name associates, they often lost their jobs. Rutgers, Harvard, Michigan, Fisk, and a host of less prominent universities dismissed professors, and public school teachers lost their jobs in New York, Philadelphia, Los Angeles, and elsewhere. University of Chicago President Robert M. Hutchins decried the damage to freedom of inquiry: "The entire teaching profession of the U.S. is now intimidated." Teachers had every reason to fear the repercussions of expressing nonconformist political ideas.

Hollywood came under HUAC's scrutiny in 1947. Ronald Reagan, president of the Screen Actors Guild, and others in the movie industry cooperated with the committee, but ten writers and directors— who became known as the Hollywood Ten— refused to testify. After serving short prison terms, they found themselves barred from work in Hollywood, as did scores of others suspected of Communist associations. The entire entertainment industry blacklisted leftists, including the Weavers, Pete

Seeger's folksinging group whose "Goodnight Irene" had topped the record charts in 1950.

Labor unions, like other liberal organizations, were both victims and agents in the anti-Communist crusade. Although few workers were Communists, the party and its sympathizers had helped to reinvigorate the labor movement in the 1930s and continued to wield influence in several CIO unions. When employers used charges of communism to discredit unions, the CIO adopted a defensive strategy and expelled eleven unions whose leaders refused to take the anti-Communist line. Unions survived and continued to grow, but the labor movement wasted energy in internecine battles and lost many progressive activists who had placed the CIO on the cutting edge of reform in the 1930s.

Because the Communist Party championed racial justice, civil rights activists and organizations became the prey of McCarthyism. Again, one did not have to be a Communist Party member to be a target; it was enough simply to hold views that were shared by the party. As a chairperson of a government loyalty review board put it, "Of course the fact that a person believes in racial equality doesn't *prove* that he's a Communist, but it certainly makes you look twice, doesn't it?"

McCarthyism caused untold economic and psychological harm to individuals who were innocent of breaking any law. Thousands of people found themselves humiliated and discredited, hounded from their jobs, some put behind prison bars. The anti-Communist crusade violated fundamental constitutional rights of freedom of speech and association, stifled expression of dissenting ideas, and removed unpopular causes from public contemplation.

The Cold War Becomes Hot: Korea

The anti-Communist hysteria intensified after the cold war erupted into a shooting war in June 1950, when troops from Communist North Korea invaded South Korea. For the first time, Americans went into battle to implement containment. The United States in concert with the United Nations ultimately held the line in Korea but at great cost in lives, dollars, and domestic unity. Popular discontent with the Korean War helped sweep General Dwight D. Eisenhower into the White House. Confirming the global reach of the Truman Doctrine, U.S. involvement in Korea also marked the militarization of American foreign policy. Defense spending shot up sharply and remained high even after hostilities ended.

Korea and American Credibility

The war in Korea grew out of the artificial division of that country after World War II. Having expelled the Japanese, who had controlled Korea since the Russo-Japanese War of 1904, the United States and the Soviet Union divided Korea at the thirty-eighth parallel into two occupation zones. As various political factions vied for power, the Soviets supported the Korean Communist Party in the North. In the South, the United States backed the Korean Democratic Party, led by landowners, businessmen, and even former Japanese collaborators, and attempted to diminish the strength of the Communists and other forces on the left.

With Moscow and Washington unable to agree on a unification plan, in July 1948 the United Nations sponsored elections in South Korea. The American-favored candidate, a Korean nationalist named Syngman Rhee, who had spent most of his life in exile in the United States, was elected president, and the United States withdrew all but five hundred of its troops in July 1949. In the fall of 1948, the Soviets established a People's Republic of North Korea, and they too withdrew their occupation forces.

U.S. State and Defense Department officials did not consider Korea to be of vital strategic interest, and many officials doubted that Rhee's conservative government could sustain popular support. The Rhee government reacted with severe repression to economic problems and opposition from the left. What counted for the Truman administration, however, was Rhee's anticommunism, and Truman decided to supply a small amount of economic and military aid to the Rhee government.

Skirmishes between North and South Korean troops had occurred since 1948, with both sides crossing the thirty-eighth parallel. In June 1950, however, ninety thousand North Koreans swept into South Korea. Truman's advisers immediately assumed that the Soviet Union, China, or both had instigated the attack. Revelations by former Soviet

KOREA

During the winter of 1950–51, American soldiers in Korea faced bitter cold and bitter defeat as Chinese and North Korean troops pushed them back below the thirty-eighth parallel. Under the leadership of General Matthew Ridgway, American troops began to turn the tide again. When this photograph was taken, U.S. forces were close to regaining the thirty-eighth parallel in March 1951.

Corbis-Bettmann.

officials thirty years later indicated only that the Kremlin had acquiesced in North Korean plans.

Looking back on his presidency, Truman regarded his decision to defend South Korea as his most important one. As was his custom, he wasted no time in making it. On June 30, six days after learning of the attack, Truman decided to commit ground troops. In addition, the U.S. representative to the UN persuaded the Security Council to sponsor a collective effort to repel the attack. With the Soviet representative boycotting the meeting (in protest over the council's refusal to seat a representative from the People's Republic of China) and thus unable to exercise veto power, the Security Council authorized Truman to appoint a commander for the UN force. He named General Douglas MacArthur, hero of the American victory in the Pacific and head of the Allied postwar occupation in Japan.

> *Looking back on his presidency, Truman regarded his decision to defend South Korea as his most important one. As was his custom, he wasted no time in making it.*

Sixteen nations, including many of the NATO allies, sent troops to Korea, but the United States contributed most of the personnel and weapons. The United States deployed almost 1.8 million troops in Korea and essentially dictated military strategy. Yet Congress never declared war. Truman himself refused to call it a war. At first he said that it was simply the United States, as a member of the United Nations, "going to the relief of the Korean Republic to suppress a bandit raid." When pressed by a reporter, he agreed that it was a "police action under the United Nations," and "police action" became the official label for the war.

Truman acted within his legal powers in asking the United Nations to repel the aggression and in responding to the Security Council's call for troops. And Congress authorized the calling up of soldiers and the expenditures of funds to pursue the war. Yet some felt that fighting a war without an official declaration by Congress violated the spirit of the Constitution. Moreover, the president exposed himself to attacks by political opponents, who called it "Truman's war" when the military situation worsened.

The first American soldiers to reach Korea were woefully unprepared and ill equipped; some units rushed to the front without training. The North Koreans took the capital of Seoul and drove deeply

into the south between June and September, forcing UN troops to retreat south to Pusan. Then in September, MacArthur launched a bold counteroffensive, staging an amphibious landing at Inchon, 180 miles behind the North Korean lines. Overcoming tough resistance, these units joined up with forces that had broken out of the Pusan area and liberated Seoul. By mid-October, UN forces had pushed the North Koreans back to the thirty-eighth parallel. The brilliant strategy enhanced not only MacArthur's heroic stature but also his already overwhelming confidence in his own genius. Now Truman had to decide whether to authorize an invasion of North Korea and seek to unify Korea under UN supervision.

From Containment to Rollback to Containment

"Troops could not be expected . . . to march up to a surveyor's line and stop," remarked Dean Acheson, reflecting sentiment in Congress, the public, and the administration to transform the military objective from containment to elimination of the enemy and unification of North and South Korea. Only George Kennan and a few others in the State Department had doubts about expanding the war. Truman received UN approval and on September 27, 1950, ordered MacArthur to move beyond the thirty-eighth parallel if necessary to destroy North Korean forces. Concerned about possible intervention by China and the Soviet Union, Truman directed the general not to send UN troops close to the Chinese border. In October, he met with MacArthur on Wake Island and received his assurance that neither China nor the Soviets would intervene and that the unification of Korea could be accomplished by the end of the year. However, expansion of the war to North Korea sent UN troops on a march to disaster.

By November, MacArthur's assurances about Chinese neutrality proved to be worthless. As UN forces moved to within 40 miles of the Korean-Chinese border, more than 150,000 Chinese troops crossed the Yalu River to join the war. By December 1950, they had forced UN armies back below the thirty-eighth parallel and recaptured Seoul. It took three months of grueling battle for UN forces to work their way back to the thirty-eighth parallel. At that point, Truman decided to seek a negotiated settlement.

As the goal of the war reverted to containment, MacArthur vented his fury. All along, he had considered Asia more important to U.S. security than

MAP 26.3
The Korean War, 1950–1953
After each side had plunged deep into its enemy's terri-
tory, the Korean War ended in 1953 with the dividing line
between North and South Korea nearly the same as it had
been before the war.

Europe. To him, a holding action against communism represented defeat. "There is no substitute for
victory," he asserted. MacArthur was prepared to
carry the war to China, to bring in Chinese Nationalist troops, and even to use nuclear weapons.
Truman and his advisers, however, resolved to
avoid a wider war in Asia. In the words of General
Omar Bradley, chairman of the Joint Chiefs of Staff,
the war that MacArthur wanted to wage was "the
wrong war, at the wrong place, at the wrong time,
with the wrong enemy."

Despite administration efforts to restrain him,
MacArthur took his case public, in effect challeng-

ing the president's authority to make foreign policy
and violating the principle of civilian control over
the military. Fed up with MacArthur's insubordination, Truman relieved him of his command in
April 1951. "Quite an explosion . . . letters of abuse
by the dozens," Truman recorded in his diary. The
general came home to a hero's welcome, and when
he spoke to Congress, one legislator remarked that
there was not "a dry eye on the Republican side nor
a dry seat on the Democratic." Millions saw Mac-
Arthur's speech on television, and more than seven
million people turned out for his triumphant parade
in New York City. Three out of four Americans sided
with MacArthur rather than with Truman. Republicans castigated the administration unmercifully.

Americans' adulation of MacArthur reflected
their frustrations with containment. The general's
view of the war coincided with the entire military
history of the United States. In previous wars (except for the dimly remembered War of 1812), the
United States marshaled its total resources to win
all-out victory. Why should Americans die simply
to preserve the status quo rather than to wipe out
the enemy once and for all? To side with MacArthur
enabled Americans to hold on to their belief that the
United States was all-powerful and to pin the Korean stalemate on the government's ineptitude or
willingness to shelter subversives within its ranks.

Truman's success in "scaring the hell" out of
the American people came back to haunt him. If
communism was so threatening, so evil, why not
stamp it out as MacArthur wanted? When Congress
investigated MacArthur's firing, all of the top military leaders supported the president, yet he never
recovered from the political blows resulting from
MacArthur's dismissal. Nor was Truman able to
end the war. Cease-fire negotiations began in July
1951 as both sides held their ground roughly along
the thirty-eighth parallel. Peace talks dragged on for
two more years, while twelve thousand more U.S.
soldiers met their deaths.

Korea, Communism, and the 1952 Election

Popular discontent with "Truman's war" gave the
Republicans a decided edge in the election battles
of 1952. Their presidential candidate, General
Dwight D. Eisenhower, enjoyed immense stature as
the architect of victory in Europe. Reared in modest circumstances in Abilene, Kansas, Eisenhower
had attended West Point and had risen steadily
through the army ranks, serving under MacArthur

for a time in the 1930s. As supreme commander in Europe, he won widespread praise for his remarkable ability to forge the Allied armies into an effective coalition.

Reporters liked Eisenhower and portrayed him in the national media not only as a brilliant commander and vigorous leader but also as a sincere, decent, friendly individual. He quickly became a national hero, "Ike" to the general public as well as his friends. He spent his postwar years first in Washington as army chief of staff and then in New York City as president of Columbia University. In 1950, Truman appointed Eisenhower the first supreme commander of NATO forces.

As befitted a career soldier, Eisenhower had always refrained from public statements about political issues. His party preference was unknown, and both Republicans and Democrats had courted him for the presidency in 1948. Although he believed that civilian control over the military worked best when professional soldiers declined from office seeking, the political situation gave him compelling reasons to run for the presidency in 1952.

Eisenhower agreed with the broad scope of Democratic foreign policy—which he had helped to create and implement—while he deplored the Democrats' efforts to solve domestic problems with new federal programs and large expenditures. At the same time, he equally disliked the foreign policy views of the leading Republican presidential contender, Senator Robert A. Taft, who attacked containment, sought to cut defense spending, and opposed assigning U.S. troops to NATO bases. Eisenhower decided to run as much to stop Taft and the old guard (the conservative wing of the party) as to get the Democrats out of the White House.

Eisenhower defeated Taft for the nomination, but the old guard prevailed on the party platform. It damned the containment policy as "negative, futile, and immoral" and charged the Truman administration with shielding "traitors to the Nation in high places." Eisenhower's choice of thirty-nine-year-old Senator Richard M. Nixon as his running mate further appeased the Republican right wing and ensured that anticommunism would be a major theme of the campaign.

Nixon came from modest origins in southern California and had to work his way through college and law school. After navy service and a brief law career, he helped the Republicans capture Congress in 1946, defeating a liberal incumbent for a seat in the House of Representatives. Nixon quickly made a name for himself as a member of the House Un-American Activities Committee and a pursuer of Alger Hiss. Accusing the Democrats of being soft on communism, Nixon found an issue to boost his own career. In his 1950 bid for the Senate, he ran an effective smear campaign against Helen Gahagan

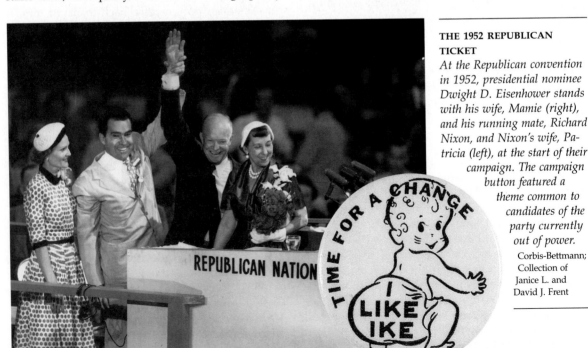

THE 1952 REPUBLICAN TICKET
At the Republican convention in 1952, presidential nominee Dwight D. Eisenhower stands with his wife, Mamie (right), and his running mate, Richard Nixon, and Nixon's wife, Patricia (left), at the start of their campaign. The campaign button featured a theme common to candidates of the party currently out of power.
Corbis-Bettmann; Collection of Janice L. and David J. Frent

TABLE **26.2**
THE ELECTION OF **1952**

Candidate	Electoral Vote	Popular Vote	Percent of Popular Vote
Dwight Eisenhower (Republican)	442	33,936,252	55.1
Adlai Stevenson (Democrat)	89	27,314,992	44.4

Douglas, charging her with being "pink [Communist] right down to her underwear."

Having decided not to run for another term, Truman persuaded Adlai E. Stevenson, governor of Illinois, to seek the Democratic nomination, which he easily won. Truman's unpopularity proved to be an unbearable burden for Stevenson, even though he was witty and eloquent and a popular governor, acceptable to both liberals and southern Democrats. Although Stevenson tried to distance himself from the president, he could not escape the domestic fallout from the Korean War.

The Republican campaign faltered just once, when the last item of its "Korea, Communism, and Corruption" campaign came back to haunt the party. A newspaper reported that Nixon had accepted $18,000 from supporters in California. Although such gifts were common in politics at that time, Democrats jumped on Nixon, hoping to divert attention from the scandals that involved several figures in the Truman administration and the Democratic Party. As newspapers printed editorials calling for Nixon to withdraw from the ticket, most of Eisenhower's advisers urged him to dump his running mate.

Nixon saved himself by exploiting the new medium of television. To a national audience, he made an emotional appeal, disclosing his financial affairs and documenting his modest standard of living. Referring to the family pet, Checkers, Nixon admitted that the cocker spaniel could be considered an illegal gift from supporters, but he vowed that he would not break his daughters' hearts by returning it. The overwhelming popular response to the "Checkers speech" turned the tide for Nixon. Eisenhower summoned his running mate and welcomed him with the words "You're my boy!" Despite these words, both men bore resentments about the incident, and their relationship was never easy or warm.

With the issue of corruption neutralized, the Republicans harped on communism at home and failure to end the Korean War. Eisenhower's most dramatic campaign statement came less than two weeks before the election. "I shall go to Korea," Eisenhower announced, and voters registered their confidence in his ability to end the war. Cutting sharply into traditional Democratic territory, Eisenhower won several southern states and 55 percent of the popular vote. His coattails carried a narrow Republican majority to Congress.

An Armistice and the War's Costs

Eisenhower made good on his pledge, flying to Korea a few weeks after the election. In July 1953, the two sides reached an armistice that left Korea divided as it had been three years earlier. The war took the lives of 54,000 and wounded more than 100,000 Americans. Total UN casualties included 118,515 killed, 264,591 wounded, and 92,987 captured, most of whom did not return alive.

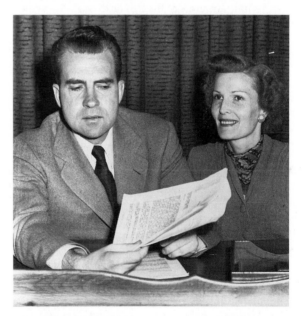

THE CHECKERS SPEECH
Republican vice presidential nominee Richard M. Nixon poses with his wife, Patricia, just before going on radio and TV to respond to charges of having received illegal campaign funds during the 1952 campaign. In an emotional speech that he finished in tears, Nixon saved his place on the ticket and probably his political career. Pat Nixon did not like the speech, asking her husband, "Why do we have to tell people how little we have and how much we owe?"
Corbis-Bettmann.

Korean and civilian casualties were heavier still. More than 1.6 million North Koreans and Chinese were killed or wounded, and 3 million South Koreans died of war-related causes. The nature of the war and the unpopularity of the Rhee government made it difficult for soldiers to distinguish between friends and enemies, since civilian populations sometimes harbored North Korean agents. Consequently, as one journalist reported, the situation "forced upon our men in the field, acts and attitudes of the utmost savagery . . . the blotting out of villages where the enemy *might* be hiding, the shooting and shelling of refugees who *may* be North Koreans."

Viewing Korea as a test of its credibility, the Truman administration judged the war a success. It had shown the world that it would help nations that were resisting communism even if they were not vital to U.S. security and were run by undemocratic, repressive governments. Not only was communism checked at the thirty-eighth parallel in Korea, but both Truman and Eisenhower managed to contain what amounted to a world war, in which twenty nations were involved on both sides, within a single country. Moreover, despite both presidents' threats to use nuclear bombs, they limited the Korean War to a conflict fought with conventional weapons.

In April 1950, two months before the Korean War began, the National Security Council had given Truman a top-secret document on the nation's military strength. NSC 68, as the report was called, painted the world in gravely threatening terms. The survival of the nation and the world, it said, required a massive military buildup. Truman read the report but took no action on recommendations that would perhaps triple the current defense budget.

Nearly all of the military buildup called for in NSC 68 came about in the context of the Korean War, which vastly increased U.S. capacity to act as a global power. Using the Korean crisis to expand the American presence elsewhere, Truman got Congress to approve the rearming of West Germany and the commitment of troops to NATO. Military spending shot up from $14 billion in 1950 to $50 billion in 1953, and it remained in the $34–40 billion range throughout the 1950s. By 1953, defense spending claimed 60 percent of the federal budget, and the size of the armed forces had tripled.

To General Matthew Ridgway, who succeeded MacArthur as commander of the UN forces, Korea taught the lesson that U.S. forces should never again fight a land war in Asia. Eisenhower concurred. Nevertheless, the Korean War induced the Truman administration to expand its influence in Asia by increasing aid to the French, who were fighting to hang on to their colonial empire in Indochina. As marines retreated from a battle against Chinese soldiers in 1950, they—prophetically—sang, "We're Harry's police force on call, / So put back your pack on, / The next step is Saigon, / Cheer up, me lads, bless 'em all."

Conclusion: Meeting the Challenges of the Postwar World

More than any development in the postwar world, the cold war defined American politics and society during the Truman administration and for years to come. Truman's decision to oppose communism throughout the world marked the most momentous foreign policy initiative in the nation's history. It transformed the federal government, shifting its attention from domestic to external affairs, greatly expanding its budget, and substantially increasing the power of the president. The nuclear arms race attending the cold war put the people of the world at risk, diverted resources that could have been used to improve living standards, and skewed the economy toward dependence on military projects. While Americans continued to debate who was responsible for the cold war and whether it could have been avoided, none could question its impact on American society or the world.

The boost to industry from cold war spending and the reconstruction of Western Europe and Japan contributed to an economic boom that provided nearly full employment during most of the Truman years and turned out an array of consumer goods that lifted the standard of living for a majority of Americans. Preoccupied with foreign policy, Truman failed to mobilize support for his ambition to assist the disadvantaged with new initiatives in education, health, agriculture, and civil rights, but he successfully defended most of the New Deal reforms. Thus, in sharp contrast to foreign policy, the domestic policies of the postwar years reflected continuity with the past.

The anti-Communist hysteria that grew out of the cold war also contributed to the domestic status quo by silencing the left, stifling debate, and narrowing the range of acceptable ideas. Partisan politics and the Truman administration's constant rhetoric about the Communist menace fueled McCarthyism, but the obsession with subversion also fed on popular frustrations over the new policy of containment and the failure of this policy to produce clear-cut victories. Convulsing the nation in bitter disunity, McCarthyism reflected a loss of confidence in American power. It would be a major challenge of the next administration to restore that unity and confidence.

CHRONOLOGY

1945 Harry Truman becomes president of United States upon death of Franklin D. Roosevelt.

Japan and Germany surrender to Allies, ending World War II.

1946 Severe labor unrest erupts throughout United States.

Truman creates Committee on Civil Rights.

United States grants independence to Philippines.

Congress passes Employment Act signifying government's responsibility for healthy economy.

Congressional elections result in Republican control of 80th Congress.

1947 George F. Kennan's article on policy of containment appears in *Foreign Affairs* magazine.

National Security Act of 1947 unifies military services under secretary of defense and creates National Security Council (NSC) and Central Intelligence Agency (CIA).

Truman asks Congress to appropriate aid to Greece and Turkey to counter communism and announces Truman Doctrine.

1948 Congress approves Marshall Plan, providing massive aid to help European countries recover from World War II.

Congress enacts law to make women permanent part of armed services.

Truman issues executive order to desegregate armed services.

United States recognizes state of Israel.

Truman defeats Republican Thomas E. Dewey to win full term as president.

1948– Soviets block access to West Berlin,
1949 setting off Berlin crisis and fifteen-month Western airlift of supplies to city.

1949 Communists under Mao Zedong win Chinese civil war and take over mainland China; Nationalists retreat to Taiwan.

NATO (North Atlantic Treaty Organization) organizes to counter Soviet threat to Western Europe.

Truman administration initiates Point IV technical aid program to third world nations.

Soviet Union explodes atomic bomb.

1950 Senator Joseph McCarthy begins campaign against alleged Communists in United States, giving his name to period of anti-Communist hysteria.

Truman approves development of hydrogen bomb.

United States sends troops to South Korea to repel North Korean assault.

1951 Truman relieves General MacArthur of command in Korea for insubordination.

United States ends postwar occupation of Japan; the two nations sign peace treaty and mutual security pact.

1952 Republican Dwight D. Eisenhower elected president of United States.

1953 Armistice signed in Korean War.

BIBLIOGRAPHY

GENERAL WORKS

John Patrick Diggins, *The Proud Decades: America in War and Peace, 1941–1950* (1988).

Robert J. Donovan, *Conflict and Crisis: The Presidency of Harry S. Truman, 1945–1948* (1977).

Robert J. Donovan, *Tumultuous Years: The Presidency of Harry S. Truman, 1949–1953* (1982).

Alonzo L. Hamby, *Man of the People: A Life of Harry S. Truman* (1995).

Michael J. Lacy, ed., *The Truman Presidency* (1989).

Melvyn Leffler, *A Preponderance of Power: National Security, the Truman Administration, and the Cold War* (1992).

Donald R. McCoy, *The Presidency of Harry S. Truman* (1984).

David McCullough, *Truman* (1992).

William L. O'Neill, *American High: The Years of Confidence, 1945–1950* (1986).

James T. Patterson, *Grand Expectations: The United States, 1945–1974* (1996).

William E. Pemberton, *Harry S. Truman: Fair Dealer and Cold Warrior* (1989).

Michael S. Sherry, *In the Shadow of War* (1995).

Harry S. Truman, *Year of Decisions* (1955).

Harry S. Truman, *Years of Trial and Hope* (1956).

DOMESTIC POLITICS AND POLICIES

William C. Berman, *The Politics of Civil Rights in the Truman Administration* (1970).

Bert Cochran, *Harry Truman and the Crisis Presidency* (1973).

Richard M. Dalfiume, *Desegregation of the U.S. Armed Forces: Fighting on Two Fronts* (1969).

Richard O. Davies, *Housing Reform during the Truman Administration* (1966).

Andrew J. Dunar, *The Truman Scandals and the Politics of Morality* (1984).

Robert H. Ferrell, *Harry S. Truman and the Modern American Presidency* (1983).

Susan M. Hartman, *Truman and the 80th Congress* (1971).

R. Alton Lee, *Truman and Taft-Hartley* (1966).

Nelson Lichtenstein, *The Most Dangerous Man in Detroit: Walter Reuther and the Fate of American Labor* (1996).

Norman D. Markowitz, *The Rise and Fall of the People's Century: Henry A. Wallace and American Liberalism, 1941–1948* (1973).

Allen J. Matusow, *Farm Policies and Politics in the Truman Years* (1967).

Donald R. McCoy and Richard T. Ruetten, *Quest and Response: Minority Rights and the Truman Administration* (1973).

Keith W. Olson, *The G.I. Bill, the Veterans, and the Colleges* (1974).

Monte M. Poen, *Harry S. Truman versus the Medical Lobby: The Genesis of Medicare* (1979).

David W. Reinhard, *The Republican Right since 1945* (1983).

Allen Yarnell, *Democrats and Progressives: The 1948 Presidential Election as a Test of Postwar Liberalism* (1974).

Robert Zieger, *The CIO, 1935–1955* (1995).

ORIGINS OF THE COLD WAR

Gar Alperovitz, *Atomic Diplomacy* (1985).

Lynn E. Davis, *The Cold War Begins: Soviet-American Conflict over Eastern Europe* (1974).

John L. Gaddis, *The United States and the Origins of the Cold War* (1972).

James L. Gormly, *The Collapse of the Grand Alliance, 1945–1948* (1987).

Fraser J. Harbut, *The Iron Curtain: Churchill, America, and the Origins of the Cold War* (1986).

Joyce Kolko and Gabriel Kolko, *The Limits of Power: The World and United States Foreign Policy* (1972).

Bruce R. Kuniholm, *The Origins of the Cold War in the Near East* (1980).

Deborah W. Larson, *Origins of Containment: A Psychological Explanation* (1985).

Ernest R. May, ed., *American Cold War Strategy: Interpreting NSC 68* (1993).

Wilson D. Miscamble, *George F. Kennan and the Making of Foreign Policy, 1947–1950* (1992).

Thomas G. Patterson, *Soviet-American Confrontation: Postwar Reconstruction and the Origins of the Cold War* (1973).

Thomas G. Patterson, *On Every Front: The Making of the Cold War* (1979).

Robert A. Pollard, *Economic Security and the Origins of the Cold War* (1985).

Michael Schaller, *The American Occupation of Japan: The Origins of the Cold War in Asia* (1985).

Hugh Thomas, *Armed Truce: The Beginnings of the Cold War, 1945–1946* (1987).

Randall B. Woods and Howard Jones, *Dawning of the Cold War: The United States' Quest for Order* (1994).

Daniel Yergin, *Shattered Peace: The Origins of the Cold War and the National Security State* (1977).

FOREIGN POLICY

Dean Acheson, *Present at the Creation* (1969).

William S. Borden, *The Pacific Alliance: United States Foreign Economic Policy and Japanese Trade Recovery, 1947–1955* (1984).

Gordon H. Chang, *Friends and Enemies: The United States, China, and the Soviet Union, 1948–1972* (1990).

Michael J. Cohen, *Truman and Israel* (1990).

Peter L. Hahn, *The United States, Great Britain, and Egypt: Strategy and Diplomacy in the Early Cold War* (1991).

Gary R. Hess, *The United States' Emergence as a Southeast Asian Power, 1940–1950* (1987).

Walter L. Hixon, *George F. Kennan: Cold War Iconoclast* (1989).

Michael J. Hogan, *The Marshall Plan: America, Britain, and the Reconstruction of Western Europe, 1947–1952* (1987).

Walter Isaacson and Evan Thomas, *The Wise Men: Six Friends and the World They Made: Acheson, Bohlen, Harriman, Kennan, Lovett, McCloy* (1986).

Lawrence S. Kaplan, *The United States and NATO: The Formative Years* (1984).

Stuart W. Leslie, *The Cold War and American Science* (1993).

Thomas J. McCormick, *America's Half-Century: United States Foreign Policy in the Cold War* (1989).

David S. McLellan, *Dean Acheson: The State Department Years* (1976).

Richard Rhodes, *Dark Sun: The Making of the Hydrogen Bomb* (1995).

John Snetsinger, *Truman, the Jewish Vote, and the Creation of Israel* (1974).

Nancy B. Tucker, *Patterns in the Dust: Chinese-American Relations and the Recognition Controversy, 1949–1950* (1983).

Imanuel Wexler, *The Marshall Plan Revisited* (1983).

Evan M. Wilson, *Decision on Palestine: How the U.S. Came to Recognize Israel* (1979).

Lawrence S. Wittner, *American Intervention in Greece, 1943–1949* (1982).

MCCARTHYISM

Michael R. Belknap, *Cold War Political Justice: The Smith Act, the Communist Party, and American Civil Liberties* (1977).

David Caute, *The Great Fear: The Anti-Communist Purge under Truman and Eisenhower* (1978).

Larry Ceplair and Steven Englund, *The Inquisition in Hollywood: Politics in the Film Community* (1980).

Sigmund Diamond, *Compromised Campus: The Collaboration of Universities with the Intelligence Community, 1945–1955* (1992).

Richard M. Freeland, *The Truman Doctrine and the Origins of McCarthyism: Foreign Policy, Domestic Politics, and International Security, 1946–1948* (1972).

Richard M. Fried, *Men against McCarthy* (1976).

Richard M. Fried, *Nightmare in Red: The McCarthy Era in Perspective* (1990).

Robert Griffith, *The Politics of Fear: Joseph R. McCarthy and the Senate* (1970).

Stanley I. Kutler, *The American Inquisition* (1982).

Harvey Levinstein, *Communism, Anticommunism, and the CIO* (1981).

David Oshinsky, *A Conspiracy So Immense: The World of Joe McCarthy* (1983).

Richard Gid Powers, *Not Without Honor: The History of American Anticommunism* (1995).

Ronald Radosh and Joyce Milton, *The Rosenberg File: A Search for the Truth* (1983).

Thomas C. Reeves, *The Life and Times of Joe McCarthy* (1983).

Ellen W. Schrecker, *No Ivory Tower: McCarthyism and the Universities* (1986).

Ellen W. Schrecker, *The Age of McCarthyism* (1994).

Peter L. Steinberg, *The Great "Red" Menace: United States Persecution of American Communists, 1947–1952* (1984).

Athan Theoharis, *Seeds of Repression: Harry S. Truman and the Origins of McCarthyism* (1971).

Allen Weinstein, *Perjury: The Hiss-Chambers Case* (1979).

KOREA

Bruce Cumings, *The Origins of the Korean War* (1981).

Rosemary Foot, *The Wrong War: American Policy and the Dimensions of the Korean Conflict, 1950–1953* (1984).

Gregory Henderson, *Korea: The Politics of the Vortex* (1968).

Burton I. Kaufman, *The Korean War: Challenges in Crisis, Credibility, and Command* (1986).

James I. Matray, *The Reluctant Crusade: American Foreign Policy in Korea* (1985).

Glenn D. Paige, *The Korean Decision: June 24–30, 1950* (1968).

David Rees, *Korea: The Limited War* (1964).

William Stueck, *The Road to Confrontation: American Policy toward China and Korea, 1947–1950* (1981).

William Stueck, *The Korean War: An International History* (1995).

John Toland, *In Mortal Combat: Korea, 1950–1953* (1992).

Richard Whelan, *Drawing the Line: The Korean War, 1950–1953* (1990).

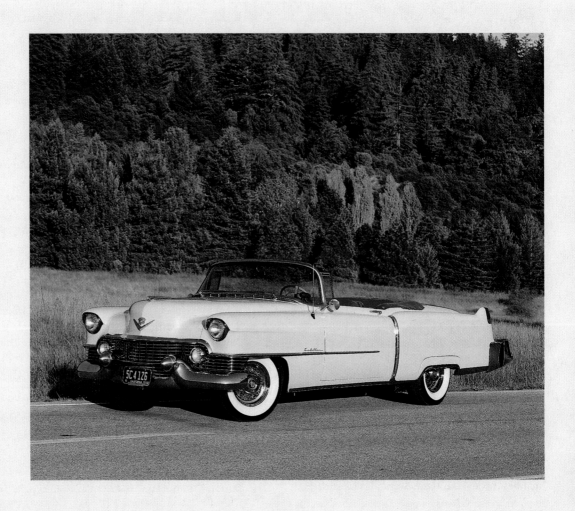

1954 CADILLAC

The automobile reflected both corporate and family prosperity in the 1950s. This car was a product of General Motors, the biggest and richest corporation in the world and the first to sell a billion dollars' worth of products. Costing about $5,000, the Cadillac was GM's top product, one of the first purchases the McDonald brothers made when they struck it rich with their hamburger stand in California. Even the cheaper models that average Americans could afford featured the gas-guzzling size and space-age-inspired style of this Cadillac.

Ron Kimball.

THE POLITICS AND CULTURE OF ABUNDANCE

27

1952–1960

TRAILED BY REPORTERS AND PHOTOGRAPHERS, Vice President Richard M. Nixon led Soviet Premier Nikita Khrushchev through the American National Exhibition in Moscow in July 1959. The display of American consumer goods followed an exhibit of Soviet products in New York, part of a cultural exchange between the two superpowers that reflected a slight thaw in the cold war. Both Khrushchev and Nixon seized on the propaganda potential of their encounter, and as they made their way through the display their verbal sparring turned into a slugfest of words and gestures that reporters dubbed "the kitchen debate."

Showing off a new color television set, Nixon conceded that the Soviet Union "may be ahead of us . . . in the thrust of your rockets for . . . outer space," but he bragged that the United States outstripped the Soviets in consumer goods. "Any steelworker could buy this house," Nixon boasted, as they walked through a model of a six-room ranch-style house. Costing about $14,000, such houses were within reach of working-class families, he insisted. Khrushchev responded that in the Soviet Union, "you are entitled to housing," whereas in the United States, "if you don't have a dollar," you are reduced to sleeping on the pavement.

While the two leaders inspected appliances in the model kitchen, Nixon declared, "These are designed to make things easier for our women." Khrushchev responded that his country did not have "the capitalist attitude toward women"; the Soviet Union appreciated women's contributions to the economy, not their domesticity.

Mocking American consumers' fondness for gadgetry, Khrushchev asked, "Don't you have a machine that puts food into the mouth and pushes it down?" The Soviet premier found many of the items on display "interesting but they are not needed in life. . . . They are merely gadgets." When Nixon insisted, "Isn't it far better to be talking about washing machines than machines of war?" Khrushchev agreed. Yet he affirmed the persistence of severe cold war tensions when he later blustered, "We too are giants. You want to threaten—we will answer threats with threats."

The Eisenhower administration had in fact begun with statements deeply threatening to the Soviet Union. Republican campaigners vowed to roll back communism and liberate "enslaved" peoples under Soviet rule. In practice, however, Eisenhower settled for a containment policy that differed from Truman's only in particulars. Eisenhower shifted the means of containment to a greater reliance on nuclear weapons and on combating communism secretly through the CIA. Yet, as

Nixon's visit to Moscow demonstrated, Eisenhower took advantage of changes in the government of the Soviet Union to reduce tensions in Soviet-American relations.

Continuity with the Truman administration also characterized Eisenhower's domestic policies. Eisenhower did slow the pace of domestic reform. He proposed no major initiatives to deal with growing problems in such areas as health care and housing, and he failed to support the rising aspirations of black Americans. The Eisenhower administration favored the business community with tax cuts and preferred state and private control rather than federal management of important resources and functions. Yet all the important reform programs of the New Deal and the Fair Deal remained in place. A majority of Americans enjoyed prosperity under the immensely popular president and seemed content with his "moderate Republicanism."

The American display in Moscow testified to the unheard-of material gains savored by many Americans in the postwar era. Weapons production spurred business prosperity and contributed especially to the burgeoning populations and economies of the West and Southwest. Rising incomes enabled millions of Americans to purchase homes, television sets, and a host of other new products. Suburban development transformed patterns of living, economic enterprise, and politics. To many, it seemed that the spectacular economic growth would enable the nation to transcend problems of poverty and race without cost to the "haves."

The 1950s also witnessed tremendous enthusiasm for marriage and family life, both in the media and in practice. The "baby boom" that had begun in the 1940s accelerated. In his "kitchen debate" comments about the American housewife, Nixon reflected the popular celebration of traditional gender roles. Yet in this respect the United States moved closer to the Soviet model, as more and more married women took jobs outside their homes.

African Americans struck a much stronger blow against the status quo. The Supreme Court ruled segregation in the public schools unconstitutional. More significantly, African American protest took a dramatic new direction when blacks in large numbers turned to direct action against the system of segregation and disenfranchisement. By the end of the decade, African Americans had developed the institutions, leadership, strategies, and will to mount a civil rights movement of unprecedented size and power.

Eisenhower and the Politics of the "Middle Way"

Eisenhower pronounced moderation the guiding principle of his domestic agenda and leadership style. His first State of the Union message pledged a "middle way between untrammeled freedom of the individual and the demands for the welfare of the whole Nation." His administration would "avoid government by bureaucracy as carefully as it avoids neglect of the helpless." Claiming that Democrats appealed to divisive class interests, Eisenhower presented himself as a leader who stood above partisan politics and selfish interest groups and would govern by compromise and consensus.

Eisenhower presided over an era of remarkable domestic stability and prosperity that enabled most Americans to ignore the existence of substantial poverty, urban decay, and a growing crisis in race relations.

Those qualities, along with Eisenhower's heroic military reputation, made him one of the most popular and beloved presidents. But he failed to translate his personal prominence into a mandate for Republican rule, and he did not use his popularity to seek new solutions to social and economic problems. Eisenhower presided over an era of remarkable domestic stability and prosperity that enabled most Americans to ignore the existence of substantial poverty, urban decay, and a growing crisis in race relations. Although liberals called the 1950s "years of flabbiness and self-satisfaction and gross materialism," a majority of citizens found the decade one of opportunity and fulfillment. They expressed their complacency in their affection and votes for Ike.

Moderate Republicanism and the "Hidden Hand"

For most of his two terms (1953–1961), Eisenhower presided over a divided government. His coattails carried a meager Republican majority into Congress in the 1952 elections, but in 1954 the Democrats regained control and maintained it for the rest of the decade. The "moderate Republicanism" of the Eisenhower years was shaped not just by Eisenhower's convictions but also by a Democratic majority in Congress that maintained the course charted by the New Deal and the Fair Deal.

Eisenhower claimed to be above interest-group politics, yet he turned for advice almost exclusively to leaders of the business community. He selected John Foster Dulles as secretary of state because of Dulles's extensive experience in foreign affairs, devotion to hard work, and willingness to take presidential orders; but like many foreign-policy makers under Truman, Dulles came to public service from a career in corporate law. Because most of Eisenhower's cabinet appointees were wealthy businessmen, when he appointed Martin Durkin, president of the AFL plumbers union, as secretary of labor, a liberal journal quipped that Eisenhower had "picked a cabinet of eight millionaires and one plumber." The "plumber" lasted less than a year and was replaced by a retail executive. Eisenhower became the second president to appoint a woman to his cabinet, choosing former WAC commander and Texas newspaper publisher Oveta Culp Hobby to head the newly created Department of Health, Education, and Welfare in 1953.

Eisenhower also garnered advice informally from a group of wealthy businessmen, whom he called his "gang." They went along on his vacations and discussed politics and economics while the president played golf or bridge. Eisenhower relied heavily on his advisers, but he remained firmly in charge, leading one scholar to characterize his administration as the "hidden-hand" presidency.

While Eisenhower's choice of businessmen as official and informal associates reflected his personal preferences, it was also compatible with his goal of unifying the Republican Party. This required winning over the conservative old guard Republicans, who wanted to repeal most of the New Deal and who attacked the containment policy, especially its focus on Europe. Eisenhower chose Richard Nixon for his running mate in 1952 in part because Nixon had close ties to the Republican right wing. Keeping Nixon on the ticket in 1956 underscored the president's commitment to party unity and his continuing attempts to swing the old guard toward moderate Republicanism.

The President and McCarthy

Eisenhower's desire to placate conservative Republicans influenced his approach to the anti-Communist fervor that had plagued the Truman adminis-

tration. Eisenhower shared Senator Joseph McCarthy's goal of eliminating communism from American life. He refused to commute the sentences of Ethel and Julius Rosenberg, who were convicted of treason and sentenced to death for passing atomic secrets to the Soviets during the war. Eisenhower resisted worldwide pressure to grant clemency to these parents of young children, and they were electrocuted in June 1953.

Although Eisenhower deplored McCarthy's method, he made little effort to silence him. Privately, Eisenhower explained that he would not demean the presidency by getting "into a pissing contest with that skunk," insisting that presidential attention would only give the senator greater publicity. Recognizing McCarthy's popularity, Eisenhower feared that to denounce him would alienate

THE PERSISTENCE OF MCCARTHYISM
This political cartoon, created in 1954, took a jab at both President Eisenhower and the U.S. Senate for allowing Senator Joseph McCarthy to destroy careers and reputations with his indiscriminate charges of communism.
Herblock © 1954/*The Washington Post.*

old guard Republicans who held powerful positions in Congress. Moreover, Republicans benefited from McCarthy's attacks on the Democrats. Republican Senator John Bricker of Ohio called McCarthy an "SOB" but continued, "Sometimes it's useful to have SOBs around to do the dirty work."

The changeover to a Republican administration failed to stop McCarthy's allegations that the government was rife with Communists; thousands of federal employees charged with disloyalty lost their jobs while Eisenhower was president. Drunk with power, the senator attacked several of Eisenhower's appointees and got the State Department to remove from overseas libraries books by such "subversive" authors as Mark Twain and John Dewey.

Eisenhower correctly predicted that McCarthy would ultimately destroy himself. With the conclusion of the Korean War, popular frustrations over containment abated, and the anti-Communist hysteria subsided. Because Eisenhower came across to most Americans as a staunch anti-Communist, when right-wing Republicans continued to cry Red after he was in charge of the government, they sounded like crackpots.

McCarthy tightened his own noose in 1954 when he went after alleged Communists in the army. As he hurled reckless charges during weeks of televised committee hearings, public opinion turned against McCarthy, who came across as a cruel, disruptive bully. "Have you left no sense of decency?" demanded the army's lawyer, Joseph Welch. The Senate, too, had had enough and in December 1954 voted to condemn him. After the vote, Eisenhower remarked that McCarthyism had become "McCarthywasism." But the president's inaction had allowed the senator to spread his poison longer than he might otherwise have done. Like Truman, Eisenhower lent the prestige and power of his office to the postwar Red scare and suppression of dissent.

The New Deal Confirmed

During the 1952 presidential campaign, Eisenhower warned that "four years more of Democratic, uninterrupted, government . . . will put us so far on the road to socialism that there will be no return to a free enterprise." Yet he knew that many of the social policies of the past two decades had fostered economic stability, and he understood their great popularity with voters. He wrote in his diary in 1954, "The Republican party must be known as a progressive organization or it is sunk."

Convinced that government was best left up to the states and economic decisions to private business, Eisenhower determined to limit the scope and size of the federal government. Nonetheless, in some cases, he was willing to expand the welfare state and to involve the federal government in new projects. His "middle way" applied the brakes, but it did not reverse the growing federal responsibility for economic development and for the welfare of Americans who were unable to survive in the free market.

In 1954, Eisenhower signed legislation that expanded improvements in Social Security by providing higher benefits and extending coverage to some ten million workers and self-employed individuals. Whereas Truman had failed to win congressional approval for a new Department of Health, Education, and Welfare, Eisenhower succeeded. Moreover, the Housing Act of 1954 continued the federal government's role in financing public housing, although the amount of construction fell far short of meeting the need.

Eisenhower supported massive federal public works projects, including the St. Lawrence Seaway, which connected the Great Lakes with the Atlantic Ocean. But his greatest initiative was the Interstate Highway Act of 1956, involving the federal government in road-building activities that previously had been conducted by states and localities. Promoted as an essential arm of the nation's cold war defense strategy and as a spur to economic growth, the law authorized construction of a national system of highways, with the federal government paying most of the costs through increased fuel and vehicle taxes.

Millions of Americans would benefit from the ease of travel and the improved transportation of goods on the interstate highway system, but the most direct and substantial gains went to the trucking, construction, and automobile industries, which had lobbied hard for the law. Greater than any previous public works project, the Interstate Highway Act created a larger federal government with subsidies for business interests, not for the poor. Unforeseen at the time, the monumental highway construction project eventually exacted severe costs in the form of air pollution, wasteful energy consumption, declining mass transportation, and the decay of central cities.

In other areas, Eisenhower restrained the federal government in favor of state governments and private enterprise. He achieved large tax cuts, for example, that favored business and the wealthy.

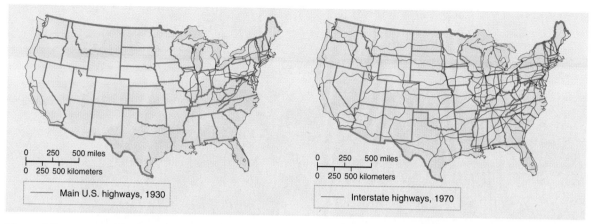

M A P 2 7 . 1

The Interstate Highway System, 1930 and 1970

Built with federal funds authorized in the Interstate Highway Act of 1956, superhighways soon criss-crossed the nation. Trucking, construction, and gasoline were among the industries that prospered, but railroads suffered from the subsidized competition.

Moreover, whereas Democrats sought to keep nuclear power in government hands, Eisenhower signed legislation authorizing the private manufacture and sale of nuclear power and directed the Atomic Energy Commission (AEC) to provide materials and services to private utilities at cost. Ground was broken at Shippingport, Pennsylvania, for the first commercial atomic power plant in the fall of 1954.

The president made only slight concessions to liberals who called for a larger federal role in the areas of health, education, and civil rights. Stubbornly resisting proposals that resembled Truman's national health insurance program, Eisenhower responded in very measured ways to the increasing difficulty Americans faced in securing adequate health care. For instance, the spread of polio, or infantile paralysis, the disease that had stricken Franklin D. Roosevelt in the 1920s, neared epidemic proportions in the 1950s. Terrified parents kept children away from swimming pools to protect them from the crippling disease. When Dr. Jonas Salk developed a vaccine, Eisenhower obtained funds from Congress for its distribution, even though conservatives preferred that states assume that responsibility.

The 1956 Election and the Second Term

Although Eisenhower retained his immense popularity, his health became a serious political issue in September 1955, when he suffered a heart attack that kept him away from the White House until the end of the year. After the heart attack, Eisenhower deliberated at length whether to run for a second term. When he announced his decision in February 1956, he knew that his health made the choice of running mate even more critical than it had been in 1952.

Eisenhower worried about placing Vice President Nixon a heartbeat away from the presidency. He admired Nixon's loyalty and dedication but doubted his maturity and ability to run the government. Eisenhower failed to lure Nixon off the ticket with an offer of a cabinet post but could not bring himself to dispose of Nixon forthrightly. He left the vice presidential choice up to the Republican national convention, where conservatives led a successful drive for Nixon's renomination.

Adlai Stevenson, chosen again by the Democrats, was hard-pressed to explain why voters should abandon Eisenhower in times of peace and prosperity. Stevenson's indirect references to Eisenhower's health helped little. He warned of the radioactive fallout from nuclear testing and called for a test ban, but most voters supported development of nuclear weapons and felt comfortable with Eisenhower's finger on the nuclear trigger. The president's experience in international affairs seemed even more important when crises erupted in Eastern Europe and the Middle East just before the election.

Losing only seven states, Eisenhower trounced Stevenson with 35.6 million to 26 million votes, doubling his 1952 margin. But even Ike's popularity could not break the Democrats' control of Congress.

POVERTY IN AN ERA OF ABUNDANCE
This photo of coal miner Orville Sturgill's family in front of their one-room shack on a country road near Mayking, Kentucky, in 1959 represents the hidden side of the affluent 1950s. The income from a very small truck mine that Sturgill worked with another man combined with the produce from a garden patch behind the house was not enough to lift this family out of poverty.
Wide World.

Two years later, the Democrats all but wiped out the Republican Party, gaining a 64–34 majority in the Senate and a 282–135 advantage in the House. Though Eisenhower captured voters' hearts, a majority of them remained wedded to the programs and policies of the Democrats.

In part because of the Democratic resurgence, Eisenhower's leadership faced more serious challenges in his second term. Illness struck again, in the form of a stroke in November 1957. The economy plunged into a recession in late 1957, and unemployment rose to 7 percent. Eisenhower fought with Congress over the budget and vetoed a number of Democrat-sponsored bills providing for expanded public works projects, a high level of price supports for farmers, and housing and urban development. The president and Congress did reach agreement in two important areas: enacting the first civil rights legislation in a century and establishing a new role for the government in education.

In the end, Eisenhower's middle way altered very little the relationship between the federal government and the individual that had been established under Roosevelt and Truman. The first Republican administration after the New Deal left the size and functions of the federal government intact, as it tipped federal policy somewhat more in favor of corporate interests. Unparalleled prosperity graced the Eisenhower years, and inflation was confined to an annual average of 1.5 percent. The nation experienced two recessions in the 1950s, but the economy recovered without putting to a test the president's aversion to substantial federal intervention.

Nevertheless, the prosperity of the 1950s blinded most Americans to the poverty endured by a substantial minority of the population. In 1960, some forty million people—more than 20 percent of the population—lived below the income levels that had been established by the government as the minimum necessary to provide a decent livelihood.

Another thirty-nine million who were above the poverty line survived only on stringent budgets, denied most of the consumer goods that symbolized the decade of affluence. Rural poverty was particularly pronounced, with farm families earning less than 50 percent of the income of the nonfarming population. The policies of the middle way sustained the postwar economic boom, but they failed to bring that prosperity, or even comfort, to a sizable minority of the nation.

Liberation Rhetoric and the Practice of Containment

Like Truman, Eisenhower saw communism as a threat not only to the nation's physical security but also to U.S. economic interests. As he wrote in 1951, the nation's foreign policy should seek "for the United States to obtain certain raw materials to sustain its economy, and, when possible, to preserve profitable foreign markets for our surpluses." What distinguished Eisenhower's foreign policy from Truman's was its rhetoric, its means, and—after Stalin's death in 1953—its overtures toward accommodation with the Soviet Union.

Republican rhetoric—voiced most prominently by Secretary of State John Foster Dulles—deplored containment as "negative, futile, and immoral" because it accepted the existing Soviet sphere of influence and control. Yet, despite promises to roll back Soviet power, the Eisenhower administration carried out a policy of containment. It directed anticommunism at the margins of Communist power in Asia, the Middle East, and Latin America, not at its core in Europe. Eisenhower assigned nuclear weapons and secret operations larger roles in defense strategy. He avoided involvement in new wars and took steps to ease tensions between the superpowers.

The "New Look" in Foreign Policy

Eisenhower's concern about federal spending governed defense strategy. To meet his goals of balancing the budget and cutting taxes, he had to reduce military expenditures. Moreover, he feared the domestic effects of massive defense spending. To Eisenhower, the internal economic strength and stability of the nation were as critical to its security as military power. A state based on warfare could de-

stroy the very society it was intended to protect. As he declared in 1953, "Every gun that is made, every warship launched, every rocket fired signifies, in the final sense, a theft from those who hunger and are not fed, those who are cold and not clothed."

Eisenhower's strategy concentrated U.S. military strength in nuclear weapons. After the Korean War, he and most other Americans rejected the possibility of large-scale involvement in conventional wars. The nation's allies could defend themselves with U.S. aid. Eisenhower pointed out that while "it cost $3,515 to maintain an American soldier each year, for a Pakistani the price was $485, for a Greek, $424." Instead of spending huge amounts for a large standing army, the United States would arm its allies and step up its nuclear capabilities. This was Eisenhower's "New Look" in foreign policy: Give friendly nations American weapons and back them up with an ominous nuclear arsenal.

Air power and nuclear weapons provided, in Dulles's words, "maximum deterrent at bearable cost," or, as Defense Secretary Charles Wilson put it, a "bigger bang for the buck." The New Look would enable the United States to deter Soviet expansion with the U.S. capacity for "massive retaliation." According to Dulles, America's willingness to "go to the brink" of war with its intimidating nuclear superiority would cause the Soviets to back down from any efforts to extend the territory under their control.

What distinguished Eisenhower's foreign policy from Truman's was its rhetoric, its means, and—after Stalin's death in 1953— its overtures toward accommodation with the Soviet Union.

The armed services, Democratic leaders, and some Republicans wanted to strengthen conventional military forces and maintain greater nonnuclear flexibility. Over their objections, Eisenhower stuck to his nuclear guns. He held the annual defense budget between $35 and $40 billion while maintaining U.S. nuclear superiority. The means for delivering weapons to their targets became more efficient, and bombs shrank in size even as they mushroomed in destructive force. By 1955, one U.S. bomber carried more force than all the explosives ever detonated in the entire history of humankind.

Although the Soviets quickly developed nuclear weapons, the United States retained its supe-

THE NUCLEAR ARMS RACE
This magazine-cover rendering of Soviet leader Nikita Khrushchev and President Dwight D. Eisenhower balanced on the head of a nuclear missile suggests the precarious world created by the nuclear arms race. The table on which the two men sit refers to the arms limitation negotiations under way when the magazine was published in 1959.

riority and deterrence capability. Nuclear bombs and missiles could not stop a Soviet attack, but they could inflict almost unimaginable destruction on the Soviet Union. Therefore, American bombers armed with nuclear weapons stayed airborne around the clock, ready to fly across the iron curtain and annihilate the enemy should it attack the United States. The certainty of that massive retaliation was meant to deter the Soviets from launching an attack on the United States. Because the Soviet Union could respond similarly to an American first strike, this delicately balanced nuclear standoff became known as "mutually assured destruction," or MAD. Winston Churchill called it a mutual balance of terror.

The balance of terror prevented the Eisenhower administration from fulfilling its promises to roll back the iron curtain and liberate peoples under Communist rule. The United States lacked the massive conventional forces necessary to pry the Soviets' grip from Eastern Europe. But the use of nuclear weapons would have destroyed the very people Eisenhower wanted to liberate. Thus, when an opportunity for liberation emerged, the administration's promises proved to be empty rhetoric.

In 1956, several Eastern European nations responded to Soviet leader Nikita Khrushchev's signals that the harsh policies of Stalin would be relaxed. Demonstrations in Poland won that nation a measure of independence from Soviet influence. In Hungary, students and workers massed in demonstrations against the Soviet puppet government and the Red Army. When Soviet tanks arrived to crush the revolt, the Hungarian Freedom Fighters sent a radio message that they were counting on American help: "SOS! They just brought us a rumor that the American troops will be here within one or two hours. . . . We are well and fighting." But no help came, and the Soviets suppressed the insurrection by killing thirty thousand Hungarians and executing the rebels' leader, Imre Nagy.

Eisenhower would not risk U.S. soldiers and a possible nuclear war to roll back the iron curtain. Talk of liberation had its partisan political uses, but it amounted to little more than grandstanding, since rollback lay outside the limits of American power.

From Korea to Vietnam

Accepting the status quo in Europe, the Eisenhower administration sought to contain communism in other parts of the world, just as the Truman administration had. Like Truman, Eisenhower assumed that the People's Republic of China (PRC) took its orders from Moscow. He continued the policy of nonrecognition—maintaining the fiction that the government of Chiang Kai-shek on Taiwan represented all the Chinese people—even though most nations had recognized the legitimacy of Mao Zedong's Communist government on the mainland. Twice the United States threatened to use nuclear bombs when the PRC made moves against the Nationalist-held islands Quemoy and Matsu, which lie close to mainland China. Continuing support of Nationalist China, Eisenhower and his advisers believed, provided a vital symbol of the nation's commitment to containment in Asia.

The major challenge to that commitment came in Southeast Asia, in Indochina, where a nationalist coalition called the Viet Minh, led by Ho Chi Minh, had declared the independence of Vietnam from France in 1945 after helping to defeat Japan. When France fought to maintain its colony, Ho fought back, plunging the area into war. U.S. officials found no direct connections between the Viet Minh and Soviet leaders. Nonetheless, because Ho declared himself a Communist, the Truman administration quietly began to provide aid to the French.

In 1950, after the Communist victory in China, the outbreak of the Korean War, and the Soviet recognition of the Viet Minh, the United States stepped up its support of the French. The United States recognized the puppet government of Bao Dai set up by the French in the south of Vietnam and began to supply it with economic aid and technical assistance. Soon the United States was paying 40 percent of the cost of the war against Ho Chi Minh.

Eisenhower fully agreed with Truman's Vietnam policy, viewing it as another domino about to topple from Communist aggression, much as Truman had regarded Greece and Turkey. "You have a row of dominoes set up," Eisenhower said, and "you knock over the first one, and what will happen to the last one is the certainty that it will go over very quickly." The president pointed to the "value of [Southeast Asia] in its production of materials that the world needs" and to "the possibility that many human beings [will] pass under a dictatorship that is inimical to the free world." He warned that the fall of Southeast Asia to communism could well be followed by the fall of Japan, Taiwan, and the Philippines. By 1954, the United States was contributing 75 percent of the cost of the war.

But the soldier-president also had a realistic view of American capabilities and interests. When in 1954 the French stood at the brink of defeat at Dien Bien Phu and demanded troops and airplanes from the United States, Eisenhower firmly said no. He was willing to pay for French combat but would not commit U.S. troops to another ground war in Asia. The British also turned down French appeals, and congressional leaders would not grant the president discretionary authority to dispatch U.S. forces without participation by allies. Dien Bien Phu fell in May 1954 and with it the French colony of Vietnam.

Two months later in Geneva, France signed a truce. The Geneva accords drew a temporary line across the seventeenth parallel of Vietnam and prohibited either the Viet Minh in the North or the government in the South from joining a military alliance or permitting foreign bases on their soil. Within two years, elections were to be held for the Vietnamese people to choose a unified government. The United States promised to support free elections, but it did not sign the accords.

The French defeat in Vietnam did not cause Eisenhower to abandon containment in Asia. Instead, he searched for allies. In September 1954, the United States organized the Southeast Asia Treaty Organization (SEATO), with Britain, France, Australia, New Zealand, Thailand, Pakistan, and the Philippines as members. A separate protocol to the SEATO pact committed the members to the defense of Cambodia, Laos, and South Vietnam. This was Eisenhower's attempt to prop up the dominoes of Southeast Asia after the French defeat.

The ink was barely dry on the SEATO alliance when the United States began to send weapons and military advisers to South Vietnam. Knowing that the election mandated by the Geneva accords would result in a victory for Ho Chi Minh, the United States supported South Vietnamese Prime Minister Ngo Dinh Diem in his refusal to hold the election, in effect violating the Geneva agreement. Diem did hold a referendum in the South: His government won 98 percent of the vote, including 605,000 votes from the city of Saigon, which had 405,000 registered voters. This fraudulent election marked but the first sign of the corruption and repression that characterized Diem's rule.

Seeking to make South Vietnam a bulwark against communism, the United States repeated most of the mistakes that had doomed the French. Between 1955 and 1961, the United States poured $1 billion into South Vietnam, 80 percent of which went to the South Vietnamese army (ARVN). However, Diem staffed the army with men known for their loyalty to him rather than for their military competence. Despite U.S. dollars, the ARVN proved to be grossly unprepared for the guerrilla warfare that the Vietminh began to mount in the late 1950s.

In 1959, Ho Chi Minh's government in Hanoi began sending military assistance to Vietminh rebels in the South, who stepped up their guerrilla attacks on the Diem government. The insurgents gained control over villages not only through sheer military power but also through support from peasants who were outraged by the Diem government's jailing of critics, failure to give peasants control over the land they worked, and relocation of peasants far from their homes. Unable to reverse the growing opposition to Diem in the South and unwilling to abandon his commitment to containment, Eisenhower would pass the deteriorating situation in Southeast Asia on to his successor, John F. Kennedy, in 1961.

Interventions in Latin America and the Middle East

While attempting to buttress friendly governments in Asia, the Eisenhower administration also worked to topple unfriendly ones in Latin America and elsewhere. Much more than Truman, Eisenhower relied on secret, behind-the-scenes efforts. His administration's covert activities against what it considered hostile governments justified the fears expressed in 1948 when Congress debated creation of the Central Intelligence Agency (CIA). Increasingly, the administration conducted foreign policy behind the back of Congress.

Taking extreme care not to leave a paper trail, Eisenhower authorized the CIA, headed by Allen Dulles, the brother of the secretary of state, to eliminate a threat to U.S. interests in oil-rich Iran. In 1951, Iran's left-leaning prime minister, Mohammed Mossadegh, nationalized oil fields and refineries, thereby upsetting the British monopoly of Iran's major national resource and setting a precedent that threatened Western oil interests throughout the Middle East. Mossadegh also challenged the power of the shah, Mohammad Reza Pahlavi, Iran's hereditary leader, who had favored foreign oil interests and the Iranian wealthy classes. Moreover, Mossadegh's acceptance of support from the Iranian Communist Party led U.S. officials to assume that he would draw closer to the Soviet Union.

With Eisenhower's approval, the CIA sent agents to Iran with funds to bribe Iranian army officers and to pay Iranians to demonstrate against Mossadegh's government. In August 1953, army officers took Mossadegh prisoner, and the shah's power was reestablished. Iran renegotiated oil concessions, giving U.S. companies a 40 percent share. Although the intervention worked in the short run, Americans in the 1970s and 1980s would harvest the full fury of Iranian opposition to the shah's repressive government that the United States had helped to reinstall.

FIDEL CASTRO TRIUMPHS IN CUBA
Castro came from a privileged family and attended law school at the University of Havana, but he spent his youth working for the overthrow of Cuban dictator Fulgencio Batista. After leading an assault on Batista's soldiers in 1953, he spent two years in prison and then slowly built up an army of guerrilla fighters. He is shown here during his triumphal entrance into Havana in January 1959.
Corbis-Bettmann.

Heady with the success in Iran, the Eisenhower administration soon turned to clandestine activities in Central America, where it perceived a Communist threat in Guatemala. As in Iran, the Guatemalan government was not Communist or Soviet-controlled, but it accepted support from the native Communist Party and threatened established economic interests. In both Guatemala and Iran, U.S. intervention thwarted the popular will, set up repressive dictatorships, and helped American corporations.

In 1951, Guatemalan voters elected Jacobo Arbenz as president. Arbenz sought to alleviate poverty through land reforms that nationalized the holdings of foreign companies, including the United Fruit Company, which was owned by U.S. investors. Eisenhower decided that Arbenz had to go and authorized the CIA to stage a coup in 1954.

The CIA organized a small army under its handpicked leader, Castillo Armas, supplied him with planes and bombs, and authorized CIA pilots to bomb Guatemalan targets. Unable to get support from the United Nations, Arbenz resigned, and a military dictatorship under Armas took over. The United Fruit Company got its land back, and Eisenhower achieved his primary objective: to prevent communism from gaining a foothold in Central America. He considered the Guatemalan coup among his proudest accomplishments.

"We're going to take care of Castro just like we took care of Arbenz," promised a CIA agent when Cubans' desire for political and economic autonomy erupted in 1959. An uprising led by Fidel Castro drove out dictator Fulgencio Batista, who had long been supported by the United States. American companies controlled a large portion of Cuba's critical resources, especially sugar and tobacco, and decisions made in Washington directly influenced the lives and livelihoods of the Cuban people. As a former ambassador to Cuba put it, "The American Ambassador was the second most important man in Cuba; sometimes even more important than the [Cuban] President."

CIA Director Allen Dulles warned Eisenhower that "Communists and other extreme radicals appear to have penetrated the Castro movement." When the United States denied Castro's requests for loans, he turned for help to the Soviet Union. After American companies refused Castro's offer to purchase them at their assessed value—which the Batista government had kept ridiculously low so that Americans could avoid heavy taxes—Castro began to nationalize their property. Eisenhower broke off diplomatic relations with Cuba and cast about for an alternative to Castro, authorizing the CIA to train Cuban exiles for an invasion of Cuba. Time ran out on the Eisenhower administration, and he bequeathed the Cuban situation, along with Vietnam, to the next administration.

Although Eisenhower expanded presidential power and conducted military operations that were kept secret from Congress and the public, he showed restraint when the risks of intervention seemed too high. He judged the risks of helping the French at Dien Bien Phu to be too great, and he reached similar conclusions when conflict erupted in the Middle East.

The Republican administration turned from Truman's all-out support for Israel and attempted to foster friendships with Arab nations. But these overtures to Arab states collapsed when the American insistence on complete loyalty to the United States conflicted with smaller nations' preference for nonalignment, which would allow them to seek aid from both the West and the Soviet Union and its allies. In 1955, Secretary of State John Foster Dulles began negotiating with Egypt about American support for building the Aswan Dam to control the Nile River. But in 1956, Egypt's leader, Gamal Abdel Nasser, declared his intention to obtain arms from Communist Czechoslovakia and negotiated a military alliance with other Arab nations. He also withdrew Egypt's recognition of the Nationalist Chinese government and recognized the People's Republic of China.

Unwilling to tolerate such independence, Dulles called off the deal for the Aswan Dam. On July 26, 1956, Nasser responded boldly by seizing the Suez Canal, then owned by Britain and France. Taking the canal advanced Nasser's prestige and power because it coincided with nationalist aspirations in the Arab world. Moreover, the revenue from the canal could provide capital for constructing the dam.

Britain and France immediately protested the canal seizure, but Eisenhower held back, announcing that the United States would not participate in military efforts to settle the Suez crisis. He recognized that the Egyptians, after all, had claimed their own territory, and he believed that Nasser "embodies the emotional demands of the people . . . for independence and for 'slapping the white Man down.'" To intervene against him, Eisenhower concluded, "might well array the world from Dakar to the Philippine Islands against us."

Ever since the establishment of Israel in 1948, Egyptian and Israeli forces had engaged in skirmishes along their common border. When Egypt seized the Suez Canal, Israel—with the knowledge of France and Britain—attacked Egypt. The two European nations then joined the military effort against Egypt. Shocked and angered by the Anglo-French intervention, Eisenhower declared an oil embargo on Britain and France while calling on the United Nations to arrange a truce. Without U.S. support, the French and British soon pulled back, and Israel was forced to retreat from territory it had captured in the Sinai Desert region of Egypt.

Although Eisenhower refused to intervene in the Suez crisis, he made clear that the United States would actively combat communism in the Middle East. In March 1957, Congress agreed to his request for a joint resolution approving economic and military aid to any Middle Eastern nation "requesting assistance against armed aggression from any country controlled by international communism." The president invoked this "Eisenhower Doctrine" to send aid to Jordan in 1957 and troops to Lebanon in 1958 to counter anti-Western pressures on those governments.

The Nuclear Arms Race

Although Eisenhower allowed his secretary of state to speak publicly of an "irreconcilable conflict" between the United States and the Soviet Union and to label the Soviet Union a nation of unmitigated evil, the president was determined to reduce superpower tensions. A number of events made accommodation with the Soviet Union a promising prospect. After Stalin's death in 1953, a more moderate leadership under Nikita Khrushchev emerged. For the first time, the Soviet Union withdrew troops from territory it had taken during World War II: After agreeing to a peace treaty with Austria that guaranteed Austrian neutrality, Soviet troops left that country. Like Eisenhower, Soviet Premier Khrushchev worried about the domestic costs of the cold war and wanted to reduce defense spending and check the arms race.

New developments in military technology and mounting evidence that radioactive fallout from nuclear testing produced horrible birth defects gave greater urgency to finding a way out of the nuclear arms race. By the mid-1950s, both superpowers had started to develop intercontinental ballistic missiles (ICBMs) armed with nuclear warheads. These new missiles, once launched, could not be recalled (as planes carrying conventional bombs could) and would strike their targets within minutes, thus ren-

dering them much more vulnerable to human miscalculation. The nuclear button had become a hair trigger.

Eisenhower and Khrushchev met in Geneva in 1955 at the first summit conference since the end of World War II. Though the summit produced no significant agreements, it nevertheless symbolized a lessening of tensions—as Eisenhower put it, "a new spirit of conciliation and cooperation." Thereafter, the two nations exchanged offers and counteroffers for limiting nuclear arms. In 1959, Khrushchev visited the United States, and Nixon went to the Soviet Union. By 1960, the two sides were within reach of a ban on nuclear testing, and Khrushchev and Eisenhower agreed to meet again in Paris in May.

To avoid jeopardizing the summit, Eisenhower canceled espionage flights over the Soviet Union, but his order came one day too late. On May 1, as the last U-2 spy plane flew over the Soviet Union, Soviet gunners shot it down. Assuming that the pilot, Francis Gary Powers, had not survived, the State Department denied that U.S. planes had been deliberately violating Soviet air space. When the Soviets produced not only Powers but also the photos taken on his flight, they caught the United States in a lie. Eisenhower assumed responsibility but refused to apologize. He met with Khrushchev briefly in Paris, but the U-2 incident dashed all prospects for a nuclear arms agreement and aborted Eisenhower's planned visit to Moscow. Both nations had suspended nuclear testing in the atmosphere in 1958 and continued to do so, but they could not agree on a permanent test ban.

Intercontinental ballistic missiles, once launched, could not be recalled and would strike their targets within minutes, thus rendering them much more vulnerable to human miscalculation. The nuclear button had become a hair trigger.

Eisenhower's "more bang for the buck" defense budget increased enormously the U.S. nuclear capacity. Between 1958 and 1960 alone, the stockpile of nuclear weapons grew from six thousand to eighteen thousand. Moreover, by the time Eisenhower left office in 1961, the United States had installed seventy-two ICBMs in the United States and Britain, was prepared to deploy additional missiles in Italy and Turkey, and had several hundred more under

CHILDREN IN THE AGE OF NUCLEAR ANXIETY
As schools routinely held drills to prepare for possible Soviet attacks, children directly experienced the anxiety and insecurity of the 1950s nuclear arms race. The Soviet launching of Sputnik *in 1957 intensified American fears and led to an even greater focus on civilian defense.*
Archive Photos.

contract. The first Polaris submarine carrying nuclear missiles was launched in November 1960.

The spectacular growth in nuclear defense capability, however, did not spare Eisenhower from charges that he had allowed the United States to fall behind the Soviet Union. Insisting that the United States needed a "flexible response" to Communist aggression, leading Democrats and military experts attacked the administration's emphasis on nuclear weapons to the neglect of conventional forces. Moreover, critics charged, the Eisenhower administration had not adequately pursued development of new delivery systems, thus contributing to a "missile gap" between the United States and the Soviet Union.

In August 1957, the Soviets test-fired the first intercontinental ballistic missile; two months later, they launched *Sputnik,* the first artificial satellite to circle the planet. To Senate majority leader Lyndon Johnson, these developments amounted to a scientific Pearl Harbor. *Sputnik* spread a sense of national humiliation as journalists, politicians, and others reported that the United States lagged behind not only in missile development and space exploration but also in science, education, economic growth, and national resolve. When the United States tried to launch a response to *Sputnik,* its satellite exploded. Newspapers expressed the humiliation by calling it

a "Stayputnik" or a "Flopnik." The United States finally launched its first satellite in January 1958.

Eisenhower correctly insisted that the United States possessed nuclear superiority, but in 1957 he was unable to disclose his strongest evidence, information about the Soviet arsenal obtained from the top-secret U-2 surveillance. He took steps to diminish public panic, supporting the formation of the National Aeronautics and Space Administration (NASA) in July 1958 and approving a gigantic increase in the budget for space research and development. Eisenhower also signed the National Defense Education Act in 1958, providing loans and scholarships for students in math, foreign languages, and science.

In the 1960 election campaign, the Democrats exploited the "missile gap" issue, which after the election was exposed as a partisan myth. Yet nuclear superiority did not guarantee security, and the United States was no safer when Eisenhower left office than when he became president. Though it lagged behind the United States in virtually every aspect of military technology, the Soviet Union nonetheless possessed sufficient nuclear weapons to devastate the United States. American schoolchildren regularly dove under their desks during drills in preparation for a nuclear attack, and the Civil Defense Administration recommended that families construct home bomb shelters. In 1959, *Life* magazine featured newlyweds who spent their fourteen-day honeymoon in their 8-by-11-foot shelter. Most American families did not build shelters, but they realized how precarious nuclear weapons had made their lives.

Just before he left office, Eisenhower emphasized another menace of the nuclear age: the growing influence of "the military-industrial complex" in American government and life. To keep the defense budget within reasonable limits, Eisenhower had struggled against unrelenting pressures from defense contractors who, in tandem with the military services, sought more dollars for newer, more powerful weapons systems. In his farewell address, he warned that the "conjunction of an immense military establishment and a large arms industry . . . exercised a total influence . . . in every city, every state house, every office of the federal government." The cold war had created a warfare state.

Winners and Losers in an Economy of Abundance

Military spending helped to stimulate domestic prosperity. Economic productivity increased enormously in the 1950s, a multitude of new products came on the market, consumption became the order of the day, and millions of Americans moved to the suburbs. Prosperity also provided the means for more young people to stay in school, and higher education became the norm for middle-class families. Although every section of the nation enjoyed the new prosperity, the West and Southwest especially boomed in production, commerce, and population.

As the economy surged, the nature of work itself changed: Farm labor continued to decline, white-collar employment overtook manufacturing jobs, and women constituted a growing share of the workforce. These economic shifts disadvantaged some segments of the population, but most Americans enjoyed a higher standard of living. In the 1950s, the United States became what economist John Kenneth Galbraith termed "the affluent society."

The Transformation of Agriculture

On October 2, 1944, on a plantation near Clarksdale, Mississippi, International Harvester demonstrated its first mechanical cotton picker. The machinery could replace fifty people and reduce the cost of picking a bale of cotton from forty dollars to five dollars. The mechanical cotton picker soon swept the South, transforming the sharecropping system that had been in place since Reconstruction and displacing hundreds of thousands of African Americans, who swelled an exodus to southern cities, the North, and the West.

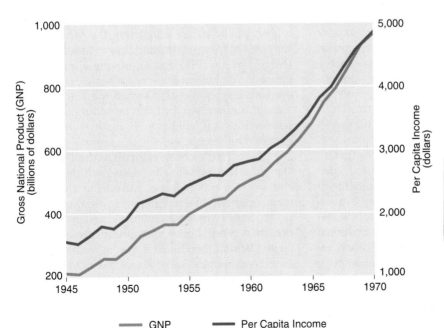

FIGURE 27.1
The Postwar Economic Boom: GNP and Per Capita Income, 1945–1970
American dominance of the worldwide market, innovative technologies that led to new industries such as computers and plastics, population growth, and increases in worker productivity all contributed to the enormous economic growth of the United States after World War II.

The cotton picker was just one element in a spectacular rise in agricultural production. Between 1940 and 1960, the output of American farms mushroomed, while the number of farmworkers declined by nearly one-third. In 1940, it took forty-four hours of work to yield one hundred bushels of wheat; by 1960, the same job took just eighteen hours. Farmers achieved nearly miraculous agricultural productivity through greater crop specialization, more intensive use of fertilizers, and, above all, mechanization. Tractors, mechanical corn and cotton pickers, and other forms of machinery increasingly replaced human labor and animal power.

Economic productivity increased enormously in the 1950s, a multitude of new products came on the market, consumption became the order of the day, and millions of Americans moved to the suburbs.

The decline of the family farm and the growth of large commercial farming, which came to be called "agribusiness," were both causes and consequences of mechanization. Larger farmers benefited handsomely from federal price support programs, and they more easily took advantage of technological improvements, while smaller producers lacked capital to invest in the machinery that was required to compete. Consequently, although the average farm size more than doubled between 1940 and 1964, the farm population declined from thirty million to thirteen million, and the number of farms decreased by more than 40 percent.

Many small farmers who hung on managed a bare subsistence standard of living and constituted a core of rural poverty that escaped the attention of those who celebrated the affluence of the 1950s. Southern sharecroppers were other victims of the transformation of agriculture, forced off the land when owners replaced them with machinery. Often they moved to cities, where a lack of jobs for which they could qualify and racial discrimination engendered growing urban poverty.

A Mississippi woman whose family had worked on a plantation since slavery confronted a difficult dilemma. She recalled that when her family got the news that "it was going to be machines now that harvest the crops, and there wasn't much we could do anymore," most of her relatives went to Chicago. Worrying that "it might be worse up

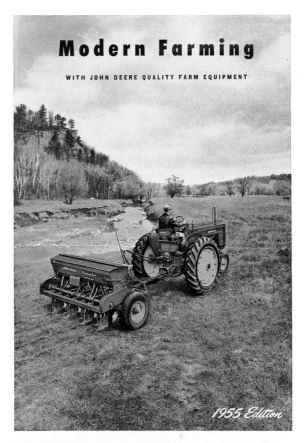

MECHANIZING AGRICULTURE
This farm equipment ad reflects the growing application of technology to agriculture. Ever more elaborate machinery created a long-term trend in which family farms were overtaken by agribusiness. Giant farms employed the latest technology and thus reduced the need for human labor. Between 1945 and 1960, the nation's population living on farms shrank from 17.5 to 8.7 percent.
John Deere Company.

---

there," she faced an agonizing choice: "I'm afraid to leave and I'm afraid to stay, and whichever I do, I think it might be real bad for my boys and girls."

New Jobs and New Workers

Tremendous gains in productivity were not confined to agriculture. Between 1945 and 1960, the gross national product (the value of all goods and services produced during the year) leaped by 250 percent, and per capita income rose by 35 percent. Although about one-fifth of the population continued to live below the poverty line, economists could claim that some 60 percent of the population en-

TECHNOLOGY IN AMERICA
Air Conditioning

Air conditioning developed primarily in response to the needs of industry. In 1902, Willis Haviland Carrier, an American engineer who formulated basic theories of air conditioning, designed the first system to control temperature and humidity and installed it in a Brooklyn printing plant. In 1915 he founded the Carrier Corporation to manufacture air-conditioning equipment. Because fibers are sensitive to moisture, the textile industry provided an early and important market for air conditioning. The process also helped to popularize movie theaters by making them a cool as well as entertaining retreat during hot summer months; and in the 1930s room air conditioners began to appear. This 1950 Carrier ad promoted the clean air in homes and offices that would come with purchase of a room air conditioner. Less than a million homes had room air conditioners in 1950, but nearly eight million did in 1960, and more than half of all homes had some form of air conditioning by 1975. Air conditioning was a mixed blessing: It improved air quality inside businesses, homes, and cars, but contributed to outdoor air pollution. Perhaps its greatest impact on the nation was to make possible the population explosion in the Sun Belt. One historian of the South, referring disparagingly to the impact of air conditioning on that region, proclaimed that "G.E. has proved a more devastating invader than even General Sherman."

Courtesy Carrier Corporation.

EXCUSE MY DUST

joyed middle-class incomes. By the late 1950s, when the nation's population stood at 175 million, there were seventy-four million cars on the road. Four of every five families owned television sets and washing machines, and nearly all had refrigerators.

A number of forces spurred this unparalleled abundance. Even with Eisenhower's conservative fiscal policies, government spending reached $80 billion annually and stimulated not only the creation of jobs but also research and development. A population explosion—from 140 million in 1945 to 176 million in 1960—expanded demand for products, and the rapidly growing youthful segment of the population stimulated industries ranging from baby goods to records. Consumer borrowing also fueled the boom, as more and more people purchased houses, cars, and appliances on installment plans.

American prosperity reflected the nation's dominance in the international economy. With U.S.

aid, the economies of Western Europe and Japan began to recover from the devastation of World War II, but American producers still found abundant markets for their products abroad and faced relatively little competition from foreign imports in the domestic economy. By the end of the 1950s, however, Western Europe and Japan became more competitive in world markets. Japanese-made products such as cameras, televisions, and automobiles began to compete with American manufactures. The first Volkswagen appeared in the United States in 1949. In 1958, Americans purchased nearly 400,000 imported automobiles.

As in agriculture, technological innovation increased industrial production. In the automobile industry, for example, new technology cut the number of labor-hours needed to manufacture a car by one-half between 1945 and 1960. Technology also transformed such industries as electronics, chemicals, and air transportation and promoted the growth of newer industries, such as television and computers. The first electronic computers were developed in the mid-1940s, and by the 1950s corporations had begun to use computers for processing data.

Labor unions enjoyed their greatest success during the 1950s as production workers saw their real earnings increase by 40 percent. The merger of the AFL and CIO in 1955 lessened jurisdictional conflicts and enabled labor to speak with one voice. The Eisenhower White House was generally unresponsive to organized labor, but unions helped to elect liberals to Congress and exercised considerable political clout.

Although labor lost much of its militancy in the postwar era, unions achieved gains for their members that went beyond wage increases. Fringe benefits—including pensions, health care, insurance, and paid vacations—became a staple of union contracts in most industries, though workers in steel, automobiles, and other heavy industries did much better than those employed in food processing, garment making, and other areas of light manufacturing. In addition, the United Auto Workers (UAW) pioneered in achieving a modified form of guaranteed income for its workers. Under this plan, laid-off workers could receive payments from a company fund to supplement their government unemployment benefits.

Unlike other industrial nations, where government provided most workers' benefits, the United States developed a mixed system in which company programs won by labor through collective bargaining played a much larger role. This system resulted in wide disparities among workers and put people who were not represented by unions at a severe disadvantage. Those nonunion workers began to constitute an increasing share of the workforce.

The absolute number of union members continued to increase, but union membership as a percentage of the labor force peaked at 27.1 percent in 1957. Automation and other forces chipped away at jobs in heavy industry, where most union workers were concentrated. Competing against the trucking industry and private automobiles, the railroads saw a 40 percent decline in jobs between 1947 and 1961; technological advances reduced the number of workers in the steel, copper, and aluminum industries by 17 percent. Moreover, the most rapidly growing economies of the South and Southwest were traditionally inhospitable to unions.

Above all, the economy as a whole was shifting from a production to a service orientation. The typical worker replaced a blue collar with a white one, which did not always mean a fatter paycheck. By 1960, blue-collar workers constituted just 40 percent of the workforce. Instead of manufacturing products, the typical worker now engaged in the distribution of goods, provision of services, record keeping, education, or government work. Although union organizing made headway in some of these fields, notably among retail clerks, communication workers, and public employees, most white-collar employees resisted unionization.

The growing clerical and service occupations swelled the demand for female workers, and women moved into the workforce during the 1950s at a rate four times that of men. By 1960, 35 percent of all women over age sixteen worked outside the home—twice as many as in 1940—and women held more than one-third of all jobs. Moreover, the largest increases in employment occurred for married women and women with children. Joining the women who had always entered the labor market simply to earn a living, increasing numbers of women sought a second family paycheck to allow their families to take advantage of the new commercial abundance. As one woman remarked, "My Joe can't put five kids through college, and then Sue needed braces . . . and the washer had to be replaced, and Ann was ashamed to bring friends home because the living room furniture was such a mess, so I went to work."

When women took jobs, they entered a sharply segregated workplace. The vast majority earned their paychecks as clerical and service workers, factory operatives in light manufacturing, domestic workers, teachers, and nurses. Union organizers neglected most of these areas, and because they were female occupations, wages were relatively low. In 1960, the average female worker, employed full-time all year, earned just 60 percent of the average wage for a male worker. At the bottom of the employment ladder, black women earned, on average, 42 percent of what white men earned.

Burgeoning Suburbs and Declining Cities

Nothing symbolized the prosperity of the 1950s more than the upsurge in suburban living. Suburbs were not new in the United States, but they entered a period of unparalleled growth in that decade. Of the thirteen million new homes built in the 1950s, eleven million appeared in the suburbs. While cities

AN AFRICAN AMERICAN SUBURB

The pioneer of mass-produced suburban housing, William J. Levitt, reflected the racism that kept blacks out of suburbia when he said, "We can solve a housing problem, or we can try and solve a racial problem but we cannot combine the two." These African Americans developed their own suburb, a planned community for middle-class blacks in Richmond, California, which welcomed the first families in 1950.

Courtesy Richmond Public Library.

failed to grow, the number of people living just outside cities increased by 45 percent, as more than one million Americans moved to suburban areas every year. By 1960, one in every four Americans lived in the suburbs.

A new feature of the suburban boom of the 1950s was its accessibility to families with modest incomes. William J. Levitt pioneered in constructing affordable housing with his 17,000-home development, called Levittown, on Long Island. Modifying the assembly line process developed for automobiles by Henry Ford, Levitt planned nearly identical houses so that each construction worker could move from house to house and perform the same single operation in each, such as caulking windows, hanging doors or cabinets, or installing bathtubs. Individuals could purchase these mass-produced houses for just under $8,000 in 1949. Developments similar to Levittown, as well as more luxurious ones, quickly went up around metropolitan areas throughout the country.

While private industry built the suburbs, the government made home ownership possible by guaranteeing long-term, low-interest mortgages through the Federal Housing Administration and the Veterans Administration. A veteran could move into Levittown with payments of just $58 per month for twenty-five years. Highway construction also indirectly subsidized suburban development. Cities constructed urban expressways linking suburbs to downtown areas, and the federal interstate system authorized 5,000 of its initial 41,000 miles to run through urban areas. Without the automobile and the freeway, the suburban explosion would not have been possible.

Suburban culture came in for its share of disapproval in the 1950s. Architecture critic Lewis Mumford blasted the suburbs as "a multitude of uniform, unidentifiable houses, lined up inflexibly, at uniform distances, on uniform roads, in a treeless communal wasteland, inhabited by people of the same class, the same income, the same age group." Suburban populations did tend to be homogeneous in terms of class, race, and age, but they sometimes brought together people of various ethnic ancestries. Moreover, within a few years, the initial sameness of the tract houses gave way to personal embellishments by individual home owners, and the barren land was softened by trees and shrubs. Regardless of what critics said, the new suburbanites enjoyed the convenience and spaciousness of their new homes and the social activities of their new neighborhoods.

Although suburbs fulfilled many of the dreams of their inhabitants, they contributed substantially to a more polarized society. The suburbs isolated women, many of whom spent their entire days with children and other mothers. Racial polarization was even more severe. Each family who purchased a house in Levittown signed a contract that "no dwelling shall be used or occupied by members of other than the Caucasian race." Although the Supreme Court declared such covenants unenforceable in 1948, and a few black families moved into Levittown in the 1950s, suburban America remained almost exclusively white.

Meanwhile, as white residents joined the suburban migration, blacks moved to cities in search of economic opportunity. As the white population declined by 13 percent in Chicago, the black population rose by 65 percent and constituted more than one-fifth of the total. In the 1950s, Washington, D.C., became the first major city with a black majority. In all cities of at least fifty thousand people, the number of black residents grew by 50 percent during the 1950s.

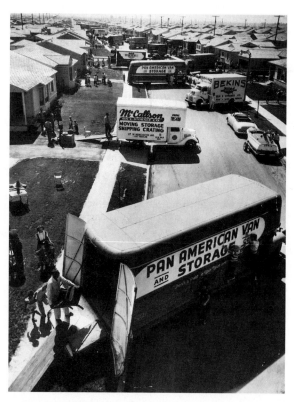

MOVING INTO THE SUBURBS

In the Los Angeles suburb of Lakewood, families gobbled up houses as fast as they could be built. Between 1946 and 1960, an average of 400 people moved into the Los Angeles area every day, and the population of Lakewood jumped from 2,000 to 100,000. What can you tell about the composition of the families moving into Lakewood?

J.B. Eyerman, Life Magazine © 1953 Time Inc.

TABLE 27.1

THE GROWING SUN BELT CITIES, 1920–1980

	1920	1940	1960	1980
Los Angeles	879	2,916	6,039	7,478
Houston	168	529	1,418	2,905
Dallas	185	527	1,084	2,430
Atlanta	249	559	1,017	2,030
San Diego	74	289	1,033	1,862
Miami	30	268	935	1,626
Phoenix	29	186	664	1,509
New Orleans	398	552	907	1,256
San Antonio	191	338	716	1,072
Tucson	20	37	266	531

(Population in thousands)

These newcomers came to cities that were already beginning to decline. Cities lost not only population to the suburbs, but also commerce and industry. New manufacturing and wholesaling facilities began to ring central cities, and shoppers gradually gave up downtown department stores in favor of suburban malls. Thus, many of the new jobs lay beyond the reach of new residents of the inner cities. Fewer people came downtown, and when they did, they preferred to drive their own automobiles along the new expressways, contributing to a decline in public transportation.

Urban governments faced falling tax revenues just as the poverty of their newer residents required greater services. With the move of manufacturing, retailing, entertainment, and transportation centers to the suburbs, downtown areas lost their diversity, becoming primarily office centers. When the workday ended, workers went home to the suburbs, leaving the downtown commercial areas dark and devoid of life.

The Democratization of Higher Education

The affluent postwar years spectacularly transformed higher education. Between 1940 and 1960, college and university enrollments leaped from 1.5 million to 3.6 million, vastly outstripping population growth. Whereas about 15 percent of college-age youths attended college in 1940, more than 40 percent did so by the mid-1960s. Higher education was no longer the domain of the privileged.

The general prosperity of the postwar years enabled many families to keep their children out of work and in school longer. Government policies, especially the GI Bill, also played a role in the democratization of higher education. Moreover, in waging the cold war, the federal government poured millions of dollars for defense-related research into universities and subsidized the education of more than 2 million World War II and Korean War veterans. In response to *Sputnik*, the National Defense Education Act of 1958 allocated $887 million for science, math, and foreign language education and $295 million in student loan funds.

Total tax dollars spent for higher education more than doubled from 1950 to 1960, as state and local governments also invested heavily. Municipalities began to build two-year junior or community colleges, and state governments vastly expanded the number of four-year colleges and universities. In 1960, California established a three-tier statewide system that made higher education accessible to all its inhabitants and that provided a model for other states to copy and adapt.

Initially, the democratization of higher education increased the gap in status between men and women. In absolute numbers, more women attended college than before, but their situation declined relative to that of men. In 1940, women constituted 40 percent of college graduating classes, but as veterans flocked to college campuses, women's proportion declined to just one-fourth in 1950. Even by 1960, women accounted for just 33 percent of college degrees, still below their 1940 share.

The large veteran enrollments did, however, bring a new group of women to college campuses and introduced a new feature of collegiate life: the married student. Colleges that had previously forbidden students to marry relaxed the rule to accommodate the mature, war-tempered population. The veterans' example made the combination of marriage and higher education an accepted pattern.

That pattern also encouraged women to drop out of college to marry. About half of the male students who started college received degrees, but only 37 percent of the women did so. Just as veterans' wives had taken jobs to make ends meet, female students often needed to find employment to enable their husbands to stay in school. These women talked of getting their Ph.T.'s, by "putting hubby through." Reflecting gender-role norms of the 1950s, most college women responding to a survey agreed that "it is natural for a woman to be satisfied with her husband's success and not crave personal achievement."

The GI Bill also made college possible for thousands of African Americans, the majority of whom attended black colleges. College enrollments of blacks surged from 37,000 in 1941 to 90,000 in 1961. Yet African Americans constituted only about 5 percent of all college students, less than half the percentage of African Americans in the general population. Unlike their white counterparts, black men and women attended college in nearly equal numbers.

Some observers of student life in the 1950s termed college students a "silent generation," complaining of their apparent passivity, caution, and conformity. Students seemed all too eager to suspend independent, critical thinking in favor of pleasing their professors and getting good grades to launch them on successful careers. In comparison to the "flaming youth" of the 1920s, *Time* mag-

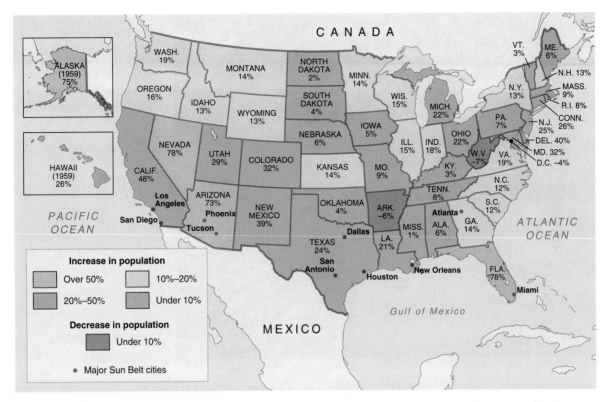

M AP 27.2
The Rise of the Sun Belt, 1940–1980
*The growth of defense industries, a nonunionized labor force, and the spread of air conditioning
all helped spur economic development and population growth, which made the Sun Belt the
fastest growing region of the nation between 1940 and 1980.*

azine called the 1950s generation "a still, small flame." Those who remembered favorably the activist student generation of the 1930s found students in the 1950s apolitical or safely conservative.

Regional Variations in the Economy of Abundance

The nation seemed to be tipped westward, quipped architect Frank Lloyd Wright: Everything not bolted down was sliding toward California. No region experienced the postwar economic and population boom more intensely than the West and Southwest. California's population more than doubled after World War II, reaching 19 million in 1960; California overtook New York as the most populous state in 1962. Low population density and a beautiful natural environment that promised a healthful and attractive lifestyle drew new residents to the West and

Southwest, but no magnet proved stronger than the promise of economic opportunity.

As railroads had spurred western growth in the nineteenth century, the automobile and airplane helped generate the post–World War II surge, providing efficient transportation for both people and products. The aerospace industry boomed in Los Angeles, Tucson, and Dallas-Fort Worth, and military bases helped underwrite prosperity in such cities as San Diego, San Antonio, and Seattle-Tacoma and throughout the so-called Sun Belt, which stretched from Florida to California.

Although defense dollars benefited regions such as New England, with its electronics and research and development operations, the West captured the lion's share of cold war spending for research and production of bombers, missiles, other weapons, and satellites. In California alone, the federal government spent more than $100 billion for

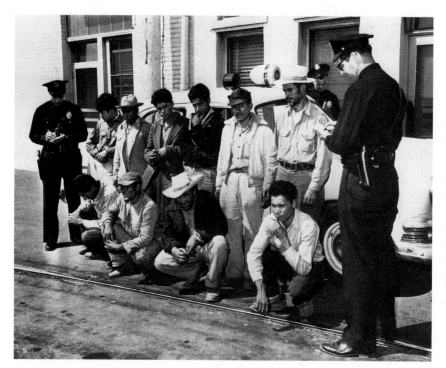

ROUNDING UP UNDOCUMENTED MIGRANTS
Not all Mexican Americans who wanted to work in the United States were accommodated by the bracero *program. In 1953, Los Angeles police arrested these men who did not have the legal documents and were hiding in a freight train. Americans used the crude term* wetback *to refer to illegal immigrants because many of them swam across the Rio Grande, on the border between the United States and Mexico.*
Corbis-Bettmann.

defense between 1945 and 1965. By 1960, California captured one-quarter of all defense dollars. Nearly one of every three California workers held a defense-related job.

The high-technology basis of postwar economic development drew well-educated and highly skilled workers to the West. But the economic promise also attracted the poor. "We see opportunity all around us here, whether we can grab hold of it or not. We smell freedom here, and maybe soon we can taste it," commented a black mother, one of the millions of Americans who flocked to California. Between 1945 and 1960, more than one-third of the African Americans who left the South moved to the West.

The Mexican American, or Chicano, population also grew, especially in California and Texas. To supply California's vast agribusiness industry, the government continued the *bracero* program begun during World War II. Until the program ended in 1964, more than 100,000 Mexicans entered the United States each year to labor in the fields, and many of them stayed, legally or illegally. But while the government encouraged the use of Mexican labor, it responded to white Americans' opposition to permanent Mexican immigration. In 1954, the government launched a series of raids called "Operation Wetback." Designed to ferret out and deport

illegal immigrants, the operation made U.S. citizens of Mexican descent feel unwelcome and threatened them with incidents of mistaken identity.

Native Americans increased their numbers but also suffered under new government policies. In 1953 with a policy called "termination," the Eisenhower administration sought to end the special status of American Indians, eliminate their reservations, and do away with tribal sovereignty. Termination and relocation of Indians to cities fit well with Eisenhower's preference for a limited federal government, but it proved devastating for Native Americans and was abandoned in the 1960s. Yet 170,000 Indians moved off their reservations, and, like most of the blacks who moved out of the rural South, they most typically exchanged rural poverty for urban poverty.

Free of the discrimination that denied economic opportunity to minority groups, white Americans reaped the fullest fruits of prosperity in the West. In April 1950, California developers advertised the opening of Lakewood, a new housing development in Los Angeles County that was larger even than Levittown. On the first day of sales, thirty thousand people lined up to purchase tract houses for eight to ten thousand dollars. Many of the new home owners were veterans, blue-collar and lower-level white-collar workers whose defense-based jobs at

McDonnell Douglas, Hughes, Rockwell, and other aerospace corporations or at the Long Beach naval station and shipyard enabled them to fulfill the American dream of the 1950s. They could purchase the products of abundance at a huge regional shopping mall, Lakewood Center. And as California's master plan for higher education went into effect, their children had access to several community colleges, four campuses of California State University, and two campuses of the University of California system—all within easy reach of Lakewood.

Society and Culture in an Era of Abundance

Economic growth underlay the cultural counterparts of Eisenhower's politics of consensus and moderation. With prosperity, more people married and the birthrate soared. Interest in religion quickened at the same time that Americans sought satisfaction in material possessions. Television entered the homes of most Americans, helping to promote a "consumer culture."

The dominant values, which favored family life and traditional gender roles, consumption, conformity, and "belongingness," drew their share of crit-

ics. Undercurrents of rebellion, especially among young people, defied some of the dominant norms. But these challenges to mainstream trends did not disrupt the complacency of the 1950s.

The Great Domestic Revival

The entrance of married women into the workforce in unprecedented numbers coexisted with the dominant ideology that celebrated traditional family life and conventional gender roles. Even though greater numbers of women left the home for work, including more than one-third of mothers with school-age children, the family ideal defined by popular culture and public figures persisted: a male breadwinner, a woman who devoted her life to wifehood and motherhood, and three or four children living a safe, comfortable life in a new suburban home. Americans were eager to realize a traditional norm that had been disrupted by economic depression in the 1930s and war in the 1940s.

Writer and feminist Betty Friedan gave a name to the idealization of women's domestic roles in her book *The Feminine Mystique,* published in 1963. Friedan claimed that advertisers, social scientists, educators, women's magazines, and public officials all encouraged women to seek their ultimate fulfillment in serving others through marriage and

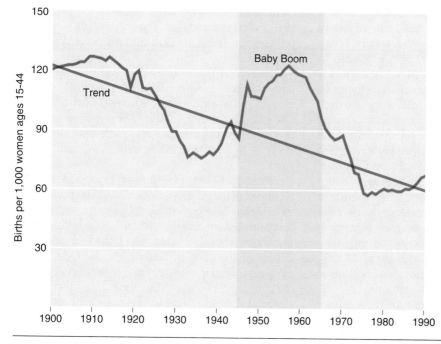

FIGURE 27.2
U.S. Birthrate, 1900–1990
Notice the long-term trend of decline in birthrate over the twentieth century. What helps to account for the unusual plunge in the 1930s and the steep but temporary ascent in the 1950s?

childrearing. The ideal woman, according to the feminine mystique, kept a spotless house, cooked creative meals, raised her children to be good citizens, served her husband's career, and provided him emotional and sexual satisfaction. In 1956, *Life* magazine had declared, "Of all the accomplishments of the American woman, the one she brings off with the most spectacular success is having babies."

The feminine mystique of the 1950s assumed that biological differences fitted men and women for entirely different roles in life. Women who sought independence or success in the masculine world were "neurotic," insisted one popular book. Another writer instructed women to realize that "just being a woman is her central task and her greatest honor. . . . Women must boldly announce that no job is more exacting, more necessary, or more rewarding than that of housewife and mother."

> *The entrance of married women into the workforce in unprecedented numbers coexisted with the dominant ideology that celebrated traditional family life and conventional gender roles.*

Although the glorification of domesticity clashed with the increasing participation in the labor force of married women, the lives of many Americans did in fact embody the family ideal. Postwar prosperity enabled more people to rush to the altar and to have more children. Both women and men married at younger ages than in the past. In 1960, some 68 percent of all adults were married, the largest percentage in the twentieth century. After declining for a century, especially during the depression, the birthrate soared after 1945, reaching a peak in 1957 with 4.3 million births and producing the "baby boom" generation. The baby boom occurred, however, at the very time when more and more couples used contraception. Americans were planning their families, but they wanted more children than had their parents. Whereas women who came of age in the 1930s had an average of 2.4 children, women in the more prosperous and optimistic 1950s produced an average of 3.2 children.

The millions of mothers who turned for advice to Dr. Benjamin Spock found the norms for childrearing more demanding than ever before. Magnifying the importance of maternal attention in the child's daily development, Spock's best-selling *Common Sense Book of Baby and Child Care* (1946) advocated a permissive approach in place of the more traditional emphasis on strictness and rigid schedules. Such an approach required that mothers devote their full time to childrearing, observe the child closely, and fine-tune their behavior to the needs of the child. Experts in the 1950s also urged fathers to cultivate family "togetherness" and spend more time with their children.

Although women had more children and faced more demanding standards for motherhood, they also enjoyed more child-free years. By spacing children closer together, the typical woman bore her last child by the time she was thirty-two. Having completed childbearing earlier, women looked forward to longer periods of decreasing domestic responsibilities. To the question of what women would do with those years, the feminine mystique offered no answer. One wife and mother, who wanted "more out of life," tried "large doses of everything from alcohol to religion, from a frenzy of sports activities to PTA. . . . Each served its purposes at the time, but . . . none had any real future."

The Rise of Religion

Along with a renewed emphasis on family life, the 1950s witnessed a surge of interest in religion. By 1960, about 63 percent of Americans belonged to churches and synagogues, up from 50 percent in 1940. Polls reported that 95 percent of all Americans professed a belief in God and 90 percent prayed. Evangelism took on new life, most notably in the nationwide crusades of Baptist minister Billy Graham, whose passionate and powerful oratory moved mass audiences to accept Christ. Roman Catholic Monsignor Fulton J. Sheen drew millions of Americans to his books and radio and TV shows; in 1954 he was named television's "man of the year."

President-elect Eisenhower expressed the enthusiasm of the religious revival when he proclaimed in 1952 that "our government makes no sense unless it is founded on a deeply felt religious faith—and I don't care what it is!" Congress linked religion more closely to the state by adding "under God" to the pledge of allegiance in 1954 and by requiring in 1955 that "In God We Trust" be printed on all currency. Eisenhower's indifference about exactly what religious faith should be practiced reflected a unifying trend among religions in the postwar era. Although religious conflict did not disappear, greater toler-

EVANGELIST BILLY GRAHAM
Crowds as large as this one in Times Square in New York City were usually New Year's Eve revelers, but in 1957 these people came to hear the Reverend Billy Graham, a young Baptist minister from North Carolina. He electrified mass audiences across the country, entreating them to find salvation in Jesus Christ and to uphold Christian moral standards. So large were his audiences that Graham extended this 1957 New York crusade from eight to sixteen weeks.
Billy Graham Center.

ance and cooperation was evident in ecumenical movements such as the World Council of Churches, which was organized in 1948. Eisenhower's pastor attributed the renewed interest in religion to economic progress, which "provided the leisure, the energy, and the means for a level of human and spiritual values never before reached." Others suggested that Americans sought reassurance and peace of mind from the anxieties of the cold war and the threat of nuclear annihilation. Perhaps the freedom to practice religion seemed all the more precious in contrast to the "godless communism" of the nation's enemy.

Social critics were skeptical about the depth of the religious revival, attributing the growth in church membership to a desire for conformity and a social outlet. One commentator, for example, noted that 53 percent of Americans could not name any book of the New Testament. The popularity of the Reverend Norman Vincent Peale, whose best-selling book *The Power of Positive Thinking* emphasized how to be successful and happy, suggested to critics the superficiality of Americans' attachment to religion.

Television Transforms Culture and Politics

Just as private family life and religion offered a respite from the anxieties of the cold war, so too did the new medium of television. In 1950, fewer than 10 percent of American homes boasted a television set, but by mid-decade, TV had entered a majority of households, and by 1960, an impressive 87 percent of all households owned a set. On the average, Americans spent more than five hours each day in front of the screen.

Television kept people at home more but did not necessarily enhance family relationships. Although parents and children gathered together, their attention focused on the TV screen and their conversation was limited. The new medium altered eating habits when, in 1954, the appearance of the frozen dinner, a complete meal in an easily portable tray, enabled families to spend the dinner hour in front of the TV set. Noticing that the heaviest water consumption took place on the hour and the half hour, civil engineers in Toledo, Ohio, recognized that television regulated even trips to the bathroom.

Variety shows and live drama became staples of early television. *Playhouse 90, Kraft Television Theatre,* and other programs aired plays by major dramatists performed by some of the most talented actors, including Humphrey Bogart, Henry Fonda, Laurence Olivier, and Joanne Woodward. Looking back on these ambitious productions, critics called the 1950s the "Golden Age of Television." *Ozzie and Harriet, Father Knows Best, The Honeymooners,* and other situation comedies were especially popular, but by the end of the 1950s, mystery, crime, and western series claimed a large share of the audience.

Situation comedies projected the family ideal and the feminine mystique into millions of homes. On TV, women with families did not work outside the home and ostensibly deferred to their husbands, though they often got the upper hand through subtle manipulation. In the most popular television show of the early 1950s, *I Love Lucy,* the husband-and-wife team of Lucille Ball and Desi Arnaz played the fictional couple Lucy and Ricky Ricardo. In step with the trends, they moved from an apartment to a house in suburbia. Ricky refused to allow his wife to work outside the home, and many of the plots revolved around Lucy's zany attempts to thwart his objections.

The show also reflected the childbearing mania of the 1950s. When Lucille Ball became pregnant, she wanted to continue working on the show and got the producers to write the pregnancy into the script. Although CBS would not allow the word "pregnant" to be spoken on the air, Americans followed the progress of Lucy's pregnancy, and forty-four million people watched the fictionalized birth, more than tuned in to Eisenhower's inauguration the next day. If Lucy Ricardo embodied the feminine mystique, Lucille Ball, who combined a career with motherhood, refused to let motherhood rule her life.

TV news, limited to just fifteen minutes a day on each network, did not become the public's main source of news until the 1960s. Yet television began to affect politics in the 1950s. Edward R. Murrow's documentaries on McCarthyism and the televised Army-McCarthy hearings helped to bring about the senator's downfall. Richard Nixon's televised "Checkers speech" enabled him to hang on to his place on the Republican ticket in 1952. The 1952 election campaign used TV advertising spots for the first time. Adlai Stevenson refused to participate in "selling the presidency like cereal," but Eisenhower succumbed to the new media and filmed forty ads.

THE MADE-FOR-TV FAMILY
This scene is from the popular television sitcom Father Knows Best, *which ran from 1954 to 1963 and which, along with other shows such as* Ozzie and Harriet *and* Leave It to Beaver, *idealized white family life. In these shows, no one got divorced or gravely ill, no one took drugs or seriously misbehaved, fathers held white-collar jobs, mothers did not work outside the home, and husbands and wives slept in twin beds.*
Culver Pictures/Rob Huntley, Lightstream/Picture Research Consultants, Inc.

But he was not happy about it, regretting that "an old soldier should come to this."

Television made political figures much more familiar to Americans and encouraged voters to place more emphasis on attractiveness and style than on experience and political wisdom. By 1960, television played a major role in candidates' chances for success. Reflecting on his narrow victory in 1960, President-elect John F. Kennedy remarked, "We wouldn't have had a prayer without that gadget."

Politics in turn affected television. Throughout the 1950s, networks boycotted writers and actors who were considered to be too closely linked with

Communist or radical causes. Murrow had to use his own funds to advertise his documentaries on McCarthyism because CBS refused to do so. That network and its sponsors found too controversial a script that portrayed neighborhood efforts to drive out an African American family. They persuaded the writer to make the unwelcome newcomer an ex-convict instead.

In little more than a decade, television came to dominate Americans' leisure time, influence their consumption patterns, and shape their perceptions of the nation's leadership and government.

Unlike government-financed television in Europe, private enterprise paid for American TV through advertising, and advertisers did not hesitate to interfere with shows that might jeopardize the sale of their products. On the *Camel News Caravan,* for example, the sponsor, producer of Camel cigarettes, insisted that any film clips showing "No Smoking" signs be cut. The American Gas Association, which sponsored *Judgment at Nuremberg,* censored the words "gas ovens" so as not to associate

the Nazi horrors with its product. Television became the major vehicle for selling the products of an affluent society; Procter and Gamble, for example, spent more than 90 percent of its advertising budget on TV.

In 1961, Newton Minow, chairman of the Federal Communications Commission, called television a "vast wasteland." Acknowledging some of TV's great achievements, particularly documentaries and drama, Minow depicted television programming as "a procession of game shows, violence . . . formula comedies about totally unbelievable families, blood and thunder, mayhem, violence, sadism, murder . . . and cartoons." Viewers disagreed—or at least they kept tuning in. In little more than a decade, television came to dominate Americans' leisure time, influence their consumption patterns, and shape their perceptions of the nation's leadership and government.

Countercurrents

Signals of unrest and dissent underlay the complacency of the 1950s. Some intellectuals took exception to the politics of consensus promoted by Eisenhower and to the materialism and conformity celebrated in popular culture. In *The Lonely Crowd*

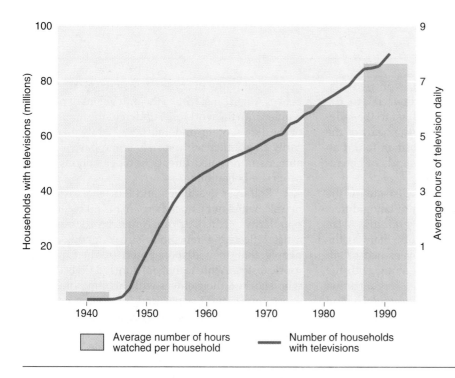

FIGURE 27.3
A Nation of Television Watchers
By the mid-1950s, television occupied a majority of U.S. homes. Set ownership and the number of hours Americans spent watching would continue to grow dramatically.

Average number of hours watched per household

Number of households with televisions

ELVIS PRESLEY
Young people seeking escape from white middle-class conformity thrilled to Elvis Presley's pulsating music, long sideburns and ducktail haircut, colorful clothing, and sensual movements. His gyrating hips illustrated in these 1956 photographs led to the appellation "Elvis the Pelvis," while adult reviewers complained about his "grunt and groin antics" and "unnecessary bump and grind routine."
Corbis-Bettmann.

(1950), sociologist David Riesman expressed dismay at a shift from the "inner-directed" to the "other-directed" individual. In contrast to the independent thinking that had been at the heart of the American character in the past, Riesman found an eagerness to adapt to external standards of behavior and belief.

Other critics shared Riesman's distaste for the importance of "belonging" and fear of being different. In his popular book *The Organization Man* (1956), William H. Whyte Jr. saw the villain as the modern corporation, whose employees had to tailor their behavior and ideas to get along with the group. According to Whyte, these "organization men" sacrificed the risk taking, individualism, and independence of the traditional American businessman, and they also displayed dull conformity in their suburban lives after work.

Less direct but more substantial challenges to the standards upheld in mainstream culture found

expression in the everyday behavior of large numbers of Americans. Just as the movement of married women into the workforce undercut the family ideal of the 1950s, other undercurrents, while not necessarily in conflict with society's emphasis on consumerism, revealed threats to older notions of appropriate behavior.

"Roll over Beethoven and tell Tchaikovsky the news!" belted out Chuck Berry in his hit record. The popularity of this African American rock-and-roll artist reflected a rebellious streak among young people that they demonstrated in their popular music tastes. White teenagers lionized Elvis Presley, who shocked their elders with his throbbing, sensuous music, tight pants, and hip-rolling gestures, considered by some TV producers so lewd that they would film him only from the waist up. Presley blended a country and western style with black rhythm and blues. In fact, rock and roll developed from the creativity of African American musicians such as Chuck Berry, Fats Domino, and Little Richard Penniman and Latino performers such as Ritchie Valens. Arthur Crudup, a black bluesman whose music Elvis exploited, noted, "I was makin' everybody rich and I was poor."

"Before there was Elvis . . . I started going crazy for 'race music,'" recalled a white man of his teenage years. "It had a beat. I loved it. . . . That got me into trouble with my parents and the schools." This man illustrated African Americans' contributions to rock and roll as well as the rebellion symbolized by white youths' attraction to black music. While some whites had been drawn to jazz for decades, white teenagers' infatuation with black music in the 1950s marked a turning point in cultural integration.

Just as rock and roll's sexual suggestiveness violated norms of middle-class respectability, the sexual behavior of many Americans departed from the family ideal of the 1950s. Two books published by Alfred Kinsey and a group of researchers at Indiana University, *Sexual Behavior in the Human Male* (1948) and *Sexual Behavior in the Human Female* (1953), uncovered a surprising range of sexual conduct. In a survey of eighteen thousand individuals, Kinsey found that 85 percent of the men and 50 percent of the women had had sex before marriage. Half of the husbands and one-fourth of the wives had engaged in extramarital sex. Although the vast majority considered themselves heterosexual, one-third of the men and one-seventh of the women reported homosexual experience. The books became best-sellers but also drew a firestorm of outrage. Evangelist Billy Graham protested "the damage this book will do to the already deteriorating morals of America," and the Rockefeller Foundation stopped funding Kinsey's work. Critics were most incensed by Kinsey's refusal to make moral judgments about his findings.

> *Just as rock and roll's sexual suggestiveness violated norms of middle-class respectability, the sexual behavior of many Americans departed from the family ideal of the 1950s.*

Playboy magazine, which began publication in 1953 and quickly gained a circulation of one million, offered another challenge to reigning standards of domesticity and respectability. With its photographs of naked young women, *Playboy* pro-

moted sexual freedom, at least for men. In contrast to most of the popular culture, the magazine idealized bachelorhood and pitied men who were "trapped" in marriages. Its publisher, Hugh Hefner, disparaged "foolish notions . . . about 'togetherness,' home, family, and all that jazz."

The most extreme rebellion against conventionality came from the self-proclaimed Beat generation, a small group of literary figures based in New York City's Greenwich Village and in San Francisco. Rejecting nearly everything in mainstream culture —patriotism, consumerism, technology, conventional family life, and discipline—they favored spontaneity and absolute personal freedom, which included drug consumption and freewheeling sex.

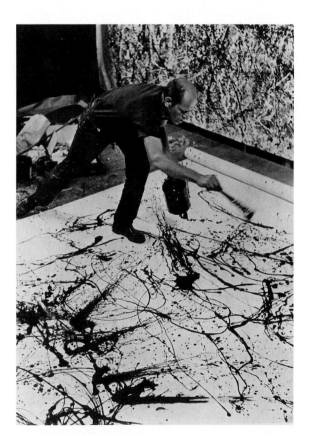

JACKSON POLLOCK
The leading artist in the post-World War II revolution in painting, Jackson Pollock here illustrates his technique of pouring and splattering paint onto the canvas. He worked with the canvas on the floor because, he said, "I feel nearer, more a part of the painting. . . . I can walk around it, work from the four sides and be literally 'in' the painting."
Jackson Pollock, 1950 photograph by Hans Namuth © 1991 Hans Namuth Estate. Courtesy, Center for Creative Photography, Tucson.

In his landmark poem *Howl* (1956), Allen Ginsberg inveighed against "Robot apartments! invisible suburbs! skeleton treasuries! blind capitals! demonic industries! . . . monstrous bombs!" and denounced the social forces that "frightened me out of my natural ecstasy!" Another leading member of the Beat generation, Jack Kerouac, wrote the best-selling novel *On the Road* (1957), but the Beats' shocking lifestyles affronted most "square" Americans. The Beats' rebelliousness would provide models for a much larger movement of youthful dissidents in the 1960s.

Developments in the visual arts also showed the 1950s to be more than a decade of bland conventionality. An artistic revolution that flowered in New York City redirected approaches to painting throughout the Western art world. Known as "action painting," "abstract expressionism," or the "New York school," this movement rejected the idea that painting should represent recognizable forms. Jackson Pollock and other abstract expressionists poured, dripped, and threw paint on canvases or substituted sticks and other implements for brushes. The work of the New York school emphasized energy and spontaneity, and it so captivated the art world that New York replaced Paris as its center.

Emergence of a Civil Rights Movement

African Americans challenged the status quo of the 1950s most dramatically as they sought to break the chains that had replaced the bonds of slavery. Every southern state mandated rigid segregation in public settings ranging from hospitals and schools to drinking fountains and rest rooms. Southern voting laws and practices disfranchised the vast majority of African Americans; employment discrimination kept them at the bottom of the economic ladder.

Although black protest was as old as American racism, in the 1950s that protest developed into a grassroots movement that attracted national attention and the support of white liberals. Pressed by civil rights groups and in the face of popular resistance and the will of elected officials, the Supreme Court initiated the most significant institutional reforms. But the most important changes of all occurred among blacks themselves. Ordinary African Americans in substantial numbers actively sought their own liberation, building a movement that would transform race relations in the United States.

A Sympathetic Court and a Reluctant President

A number of developments lay behind the rise of black protest in the 1950s. Between 1940 and 1960, more than three million African Americans moved out of the South into areas where they could vote and exert pressure on white politicians. White leaders also worried that the U.S.'s dismal record in race relations put the country at a disadvantage in cold war competition, as Soviet propaganda routinely exposed the gap between American ideals and practice.

Although black protest was as old as American racism, in the 1950s that protest developed into a grassroots movement that attracted national attention and the support of white liberals.

In the South, African Americans controlled resources that were essential to a mass movement. The very system of segregation encouraged the development of black institutions and kept black talents within the black community. In particular, black churches and colleges developed leadership skills within the African American community and provided a mass base and organizational network. Moreover, as African Americans moved into urban areas, their institutions grew in numbers and financial resources, and they shared in some economic benefits of the general postwar prosperity.

Growing even faster was the National Association for the Advancement of Colored People (NAACP), whose emphasis on litigation had begun to pay off in the late 1940s. Its crowning achievement came with the Supreme Court decision in *Brown v. Board of Education* in 1954. The *Brown* case resulted not just from the legal brilliance and financial resources of the NAACP, but also from the determination of black Americans to fight for their rights. One of the five suits consolidated into the *Brown* case began in 1951, when teenagers at Moton High School in Farmville, Virginia, initiated a strike to protest the inadequate schools set up for blacks.

NAACP lawyers, led by Thurgood Marshall, who would later be appointed to the Supreme Court, urged the Court to overturn the fifty-eight-year-old precedent established in *Plessy v. Ferguson*, which had enshrined "separate but equal" as the law of the land. A unanimous court, headed by Chief Justice Earl Warren, declared, "Separate edu-

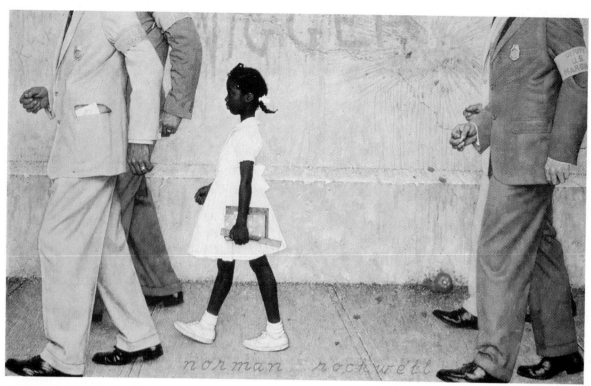

SCHOOL INTEGRATION

In 1964, the popular artist Norman Rockwell painted The Problem We All Live With, *based on the experience of Ruby Bridges during the 1962 integration of the New Orleans public schools. He hoped through this painting to get people to realize what America was doing to its children. How effective is this painting in stirring emotions? What about the structure of the scene and the characteristics of the people indicate Rockwell's intentions?*

Norman Rockwell Family Trust and Curtis Archives.

cational facilities are inherently unequal" and thus violated the Fourteenth Amendment. In 1955, after waiting a year to deal with implementation, the Court called for desegregation "with all deliberate speed" but established no deadline.

As chief executive, President Eisenhower bore the ultimate responsibility for enforcement of *Brown,* but he refused to use his enormous popularity to win acceptance of the decision from Americans. Officially, Eisenhower announced his intention to obey the decision. But before the Supreme Court ruling, he had privately expressed to Chief Justice Warren his sympathy for white southerners. All they wanted, Eisenhower said, was that "their sweet little girls" not have to "sit in schools alongside some big black bucks." Asked if he had any advice to give the South in responding to *Brown,* he replied, "Not in the slightest." The president's failure to endorse the decision or to urge the South to comply reflected his own racial prejudice, insensitivity to the aspirations of blacks, preference for a limited fed-

eral role in the nation's affairs, and leadership style that favored consensus and gradual progress.

In some cases, Eisenhower used his executive powers against segregation, ordering the integration of public facilities in the District of Columbia and at army and navy bases, for example. More often, he remained aloof. In 1955, when whites lynched a fourteen-year-old black boy named Emmett Till for whistling at a white woman in Mississippi, Eisenhower rejected advice that he speak out against the atrocity. Nor would he act in March 1956, when the University of Alabama violated a federal court order to admit its first black student.

Eisenhower's inaction fueled southern officials' determined resistance to school desegregation and contributed to the gravest constitutional crisis since the Civil War. The crisis came in Little Rock, Arkansas, in September 1957. Local officials dutifully prepared for the integration of Central High School, but on the first day of school, Governor Orval Faubus sent National Guard troops to block

The Brown Decision

The Brown decision along with a second Supreme Court ruling in 1955 about implementing desegregation outraged many southern whites. In 1956, more than one hundred members of Congress signed a manifesto pledging resistance to the decision.

In 1954, Chief Justice Earl Warren delivered the unanimous opinion of the Supreme Court in Brown v. Board of Education of Topeka, *declaring racial segregation in public education unconstitutional and explaining why.*

DOCUMENT 1. *Brown v. Board of Education of Topeka*

In these days, it is doubtful that any child may reasonably be expected to succeed in life if he is denied the opportunity of an education. Such an opportunity, if the state has undertaken to provide it, is a right that must be made available to all on equal terms. . . .

We come then to the question presented: Does segregation of children in public schools solely on the basis of race, even though the physical facilities and other "tangible" factors may be equal, deprive the children of the minority group of equal educational opportunities? We believe that it does. . . .

In *McLaurin* [a 1950 case], the Court, in requiring that a Negro admitted to a white graduate school be treated like all other students, again resorted to intangible considerations: ". . . his ability to study, to engage in discussions and exchange views with other students, and, in general, to learn his profession." Such considerations apply with added force to children in grade and high schools. To separate them from others of similar age and qualifications solely because of their race generates a feeling of inferiority as to their status in the community that may affect their hearts and minds in a way unlikely ever to be undone.

We conclude that in the field of public education the doctrine of "separate but equal" has no place. Separate educational facilities are inherently unequal. . . .

DOCUMENT 2. Southern Manifesto on Integration

We regard the decision of the Supreme Court in the school cases as a clear abuse of judicial power. It climaxes a trend in the Federal judiciary undertaking to legislate . . . and to encroach upon the reserved rights of the states and the people.

The original Constitution does not mention education. Neither does the Fourteenth Amendment nor any amendment. . . . The Supreme Court of the United States, with no legal basis for such action, undertook to exercise their naked judicial power and substituted their personal political and social ideas for the established law of the land.

This unwarranted exercise of power by the court, contrary to the Constitution, is creating chaos and confusion in the states principally affected. It is destroying the amicable relations between the white and negro races that have been created through ninety years of patient effort by the good people of both races. It has planted hatred and suspicion where there has been heretofore friendship and understanding. . . .

We pledge ourselves to use all lawful means to bring about a reversal of this decision which is contrary to the Constitution and to prevent the use of force in its implementation.

In the face of white hostility, black children carried the burden of implementing the Brown *decision. The following accounts by black students reflect varied experiences, but even those who entered white schools fairly easily found obstacles to their full participation in school activities. Nonetheless, they cherished the new opportunities, favoring integration for reasons different from those given by the Supreme Court.*

Document 3. A High School Girl in the Deep South

The first day a news reporter rode the bus with us. All around us were state troopers. In front of them were federal marshals. When we got to town there were lines of people and cars all along the road. A man without a badge or anything got on the bus and started beating up the newspaper reporter. . . . He was crying and bleeding. When we got to the school the students were all around looking through the windows. The mayor said we couldn't come there because the school was already filled to capacity [and] if six of us came in it would be a fire hazard. He told us to turn around and go back. We turned around and the students started yelling and clapping. When we went back [after obtaining a court order] there were no students there at all. There were only two teachers left so they had to bring a couple of teachers from other places. [The white students did not return, so the six black students finished the year by themselves.] The shocking thing was during the graduation ceremonies. All six of the students got together to make a speech. After we finished, I looked around and saw three teachers crying. The principal had tears in his eyes and he got up to make a little speech about us. He said at first he didn't think he would enjoy being around us. You could see in his face that he was really touched. We said something like we really enjoyed school together and that we were glad they stuck it out and all that kind of stuff.

Document 4. A High School Boy in Oak Ridge, Tennessee

I like it a whole lot better than the colored school. You have a chance to learn more and you have more sports. I play forward or guard on the basketball team, only I don't get to participate in all games. Some teams don't mind my playing. Some teams object not because of the fellows on the team, but because of the people in their community. Mostly it's the fans or the board of education that decides against me. . . . The same situation occurs in baseball. I'm catcher, but the first game I didn't get to participate in. A farm club of the major league wrote the coach that they were interested in seeing me play so maybe I'll get to play the next time.

Document 5. A High School Girl in the Deep South

I chose to go because I felt that I could get a better education here. I knew that the [black] school that I was then attending wasn't giving me exactly what I should have had. As far as the Science Department was concerned, it just didn't have the chemicals we needed and I just decided to change. When I went over the students there weren't very friendly and when I graduated they still weren't. They didn't want us there and they made that plain, but we went there anyway and we stuck it out. The lessons there were harder, lots harder, but I studied and I managed to pass all my subjects.

Document 6. A High School Girl in Louisville, Kentucky

I'm accepted now as an individual rather than as a person belonging to the Negro race. People say to me, "I'm glad I met you because if I met someone else I might not have liked them." I don't think it's fair, this individual acceptance. I feel like I was some ambassador from some foreign country.

I couldn't go out for any extracurricular activities. Cheerleading, band, drum majorettes, the people who are members of these organizations, they go to camps in the summer which are segregated. Well, what can you do? It just leaves me out. It's not the school, it's the community.

Document 1. *Brown*, 347 U.S. 483 (1954).

Document 2. "Southern Manifesto on Integration" (1956).

Document 3. *In Their Own Words: A Student Appraisal of What Happened after School Desegregation* (Washington, D.C.: Department of Health, Education, and Welfare, Office of Education, 1966), 17–18.

Document 4. Dorothy Sterling, *Tender Warriors* (New York: Hill and Wang, 1958), 83.

Document 5. *In Their Own Words: A Student Appraisal of What Happened after School Desegregation* (Washington, D.C.: Department of Health, Education, and Welfare, Office of Education, 1966), 44.

Document 6. Dorothy Sterling, *Tender Warriors* (New York: Hill and Wang, 1958), 83.

MONTGOMERY CIVIL RIGHTS LEADERS
During the Montgomery, Alabama, bus boycott of 1955–1956, local white officials harassed African Americans with arrests and lawsuits. Here Rosa Parks, catalyst of the boycott and one of ninety-two defendants, ascends the steps of the Montgomery County courthouse in March 1956. She is accompanied by E.D. Nixon, a forceful civil rights leader and her longtime friend and associate in the Montgomery NAACP.
Wide World.

the enrollment of nine black students, claiming that it would cause public disorder.

Reluctant to intervene, Eisenhower waited nearly three weeks, until Faubus agreed to allow the black students to enter. But Faubus also withdrew the National Guard, leaving the nine students to face an angry mob of whites. As television cameras transmitted the ugly scene across the nation, the president was forced into action. He sent in one thousand regular army troops and took federal control of the Arkansas National Guard. In this first federal military intervention in the South since Reconstruction, Eisenhower took pains to point out that he acted not to achieve integration, but to enforce the law. Escorted by paratroopers, the black students stayed in school, and Eisenhower withdrew the army in November.

Other southern cities closed public schools to avoid integration and used tax dollars to support private, white-only schools. During the first three years after the *Brown* decision, 750 school districts, primarily in border states, began desegregation, but only 49 new efforts came between 1957 and 1960. When Eisenhower left office in 1961—nearly seven years after the Supreme Court had outlawed segregation—only 6.4 percent of southern black students attended integrated schools. (See Texts in Historical Context, page 1090.)

Eisenhower did support the first federal civil rights legislation since Reconstruction, the Civil Rights Acts of 1957 and 1960. Both laws focused on voting rights, and the 1957 legislation established the U.S. Commission on Civil Rights and a Civil Rights Division in the Justice Department. But the legislation lacked strong enforcement provisions and represented only marginal progress toward the enfranchisement of blacks. Baseball star Jackie Robinson spoke for many African Americans when he wired Eisenhower, "We disagree that half a loaf is better than none. Have waited this long for bill with meaning—can wait a little longer."

The Eisenhower years represented a retreat in presidential leadership on civil rights. Forceful and decisive in foreign affairs, the president saw no moral imperative in civil rights and moved in that arena only with the greatest reluctance. Eisenhower appointed the first black professional to the White House staff, but E. Frederick Morrow confided to his diary, "I feel ridiculous . . . trying to defend the administration's record on civil rights." Morrow later remembered Eisenhower as "a great, gentle, and noble man . . . but neither intellectually nor emotionally disposed to combat segregation in general."

Montgomery and Mass Protest

From individual acts of defiance and slave revolts through the legal and lobbying efforts of the NAACP, black protest enjoyed a long tradition in

American society. What set the civil rights movement of the 1950s and 1960s apart from earlier
protests were the great numbers of people involved,
blacks' willingness to confront white institutions directly, and the use of nonviolence and passive resistance to bring about change. The Congress of
Racial Equality (CORE) and other groups had experimented with these innovations in the 1940s, but
the first sustained protest to claim national attention occurred in Montgomery, Alabama, in 1955 and
1956.

On December 1, 1955, Montgomery police arrested a black woman, Rosa Parks, for violating a
local segregation ordinance by refusing to give up
her seat on a city bus to a white man. Parks had
long been active in the local NAACP, and this was
not the first time that she had rebelled against segregation. Montgomery blacks who had been considering a challenge to segregation prepared to
move. Three groups helped to orchestrate the challenge: a women's organization, the NAACP chapter, and community ministers. In 1946, black professional women had founded the Women's
Political Council (WPC) to work on voter registration, desegregation of public facilities, and employment of blacks in municipal services. Its leader was
Jo Ann Robinson, an English professor at Alabama
State College in Montgomery, who had been humiliated by a bus driver when she inadvertently sat
in the white section. The WPC had already dis-

cussed plans for a boycott of the city bus system.
After Parks's arrest, the group consulted with E. D.
Nixon, head of the Montgomery NAACP and the
local Brotherhood of Sleeping Car Porters. Nixon
too had been looking for an opportunity to mount
a boycott, and he sought support from ministers.

In the early morning hours after Parks's arrest,
WPC members and Alabama State students and faculty blanketed the black community with leaflets
urging support of a bus boycott. On December 5,
leaders of local organizations founded the Montgomery Improvement Association (MIA) to organize and maintain the boycott. The MIA ran an alternative transportation system, marshaled more
than 90 percent of the black community to sustain
the year-long boycott, and mounted a legal challenge that persuaded the Supreme Court to strike
down the bus segregation ordinance in November
1956.

Elected to head the MIA was Martin Luther
King Jr., a newcomer to Montgomery. Born in 1929,
King was the son of a minister who had risen from
sharecropper origins and married the daughter of a
prominent pastor of Ebenezer Baptist Church in Atlanta. The younger King attended Morehouse College and preached his first sermon at Ebenezer at
the age of eighteen. He went on to Crozer Theological Seminary in Pennsylvania and then to
Boston University, where he earned his doctorate in
theology. In 1954, he answered the call to be pastor

at the Dexter Avenue Baptist Church in Montgomery.

Only twenty-six years old, King rose to the challenge of the boycott. As a minister, he held a prominent place in the institution that became the focal point of black protest, providing the movement with a mass base, talented leadership, a financial foundation, and meeting places. Day after day, Montgomery blacks gathered at their churches to plan strategy and receive instructions and inspiration. A captivating speaker, King summoned their courage and inspired commitment by linking racial justice to the redeeming power of Christian love. He asked his people to abandon "that patience that makes us patient with anything less than freedom and justice." He promised, "If you will protest courageously and yet with dignity and Christian love . . . historians will have to pause and say, 'There lived a great people—a black people—who injected a new meaning and dignity into the veins of civilization.' This is our challenge and our overwhelming responsibility."

Montgomery blacks summoned up their courage and determination in abundance. They walked miles when the carpool was unavailable, contributed their meager financial resources, and stood up with dignity and discipline to legal, economic, and physical intimidation. King himself endured arrest and the firebombing of his house. Montgomery blacks demonstrated that even without the ballot, African Americans could struggle successfully against their oppression.

In January 1957, black churchmen from across the South met to coordinate local protests against segregation and to secure the ballot for blacks. They founded the Southern Christian Leadership Conference (SCLC) and chose King to head it. Although ministers dominated the SCLC, its success owed much to Ella Baker, a seasoned NAACP activist who came from New York to set up the SCLC office and handle its organizational affairs.

King's face on the cover of *Time* magazine in February 1957 marked his rapid rise to national and international fame. He crisscrossed the nation and the world, speaking to large audiences, raising funds, and meeting with other activists. In June 1958, Eisenhower extended his first invitation to black leaders, and King and three others met with the president. Meanwhile, in the late 1950s, the SCLC, NAACP, and CORE developed centers in several southern cities, paving the way for a mass movement that would revolutionize the racial system of the South.

Conclusion: Assessing the "Ike Age"

By most measures, the Eisenhower years represented a time of tranquility, stability, and prosperity. The 1950s saw tremendous economic growth, a rising standard of living for most Americans, and low inflation rates. Cold war spending drove up the federal budget, which now played a permanent and significant role in the economy as a whole. One of every ten American jobs depended directly on defense spending. The Eisenhower administration restrained spending for domestic purposes and tipped the balance between the federal government and private enterprise in favor of big business, but it maintained the basic foundations of the welfare state.

The president's insistence on moderation, consensus, and a limited role for the federal government seemed to fit the mood of the 1950s well, but it also meant an accumulation of problems for the future. Although economic productivity reached a level sufficient to meet the material needs of all Americans, twenty percent of the U.S. population lived in poverty. Eisenhower refused to use his enormous popularity to rally the nation behind efforts to promote racial justice, and he launched no major programs to deal with urban slums or the growing inadequacies in health care and public education.

In large matters, Eisenhower's foreign policy demonstrated restraint and a recognition of the limits of U.S. power. He promoted development of more destructive atomic weapons, which held Americans under the threat of nuclear obliteration, but he kept the defense budget from skyrocketing, and the superpowers avoided war. Even though the United States and the Soviet Union made no substantive progress in solving cold war issues, Eisenhower began negotiations and helped to lessen tensions between the superpowers.

Eisenhower took from Truman the assumption that the United States must fight communism everywhere, reinforced it in his public utterances, and passed it on to the next administration. The president realized that the "protection of our own interests and our own system demands [understanding of] the spirit of nationalism, coupled with a deep hunger for some betterment in physical conditions and living standards." Yet when movements for such conditions in Iran, Guatemala, and Vietnam seemed to him too radical, too friendly to communism, or too inimical to American economic interests, he did not hesitate to oppose them, often deploying American power in operations kept hidden from congressional and public scrutiny.

Thus, although Eisenhower presided over eight years of peace, his foreign policy inspired anti-Americanism, established dangerous precedents for the expansion of executive power, and forged commitments that future generations would deem unwise. As Eisenhower's successors took on the struggle against communism and grappled with the domestic problems that he had avoided, the tranquility and consensus of the 1950s would give way to the turbulence and conflict of the 1960s.

CHRONOLOGY

1952 Dwight D. Eisenhower elected president of United States.

I Love Lucy becomes number one television show.

1953 The government begins policy of termination of special status of American Indians and relocates thousands off reservations.

CIA engineers coup against government of Prime Minister Mohammed Mossadegh in Iran.

Julius and Ethel Rosenberg executed for passing atomic secrets to Soviet Union.

Playboy magazine begins publication.

1954 CIA stages coup against government of Jacobo Arbenz in Guatemala.

Eisenhower administration continues many New Deal and Fair Deal initiatives, including expansion of Social Security.

Eisenhower administration begins aid program to government of South Vietnam.

Government launches "Operation Wetback," series of raids designed to seek out and deport illegal immigrants.

Ground broken in Pennsylvania for first commercial nuclear power plant.

U.S. Supreme Court declares segregation in public schools unconstitutional in *Brown v. Board of Education*.

United States organizes Southeast Asia Treaty Organization (SEATO) in wake of French defeat in Vietnam.

1955 Eisenhower and Khrushchev meet in Geneva for first superpower summit since end of World War II.

1955–1956 Montgomery, Alabama, bus boycott by African Americans focuses national attention on civil rights.

1956 Interstate Highway Act involves federal government in road-building activities previously done by state and local governments.

President Eisenhower reelected by landslide to second term.

Allen Ginsberg publishes poem *Howl*, expressing rebelliousness of Beat generation.

1957 Southern Christian Leadership Conference (SCLC) organizes and elects Martin Luther King Jr. its president.

Soviets launch *Sputnik*, first satellite to orbit earth.

Labor union membership peaks at 27.1 percent of labor force.

1958 United States and Soviet Union suspend nuclear testing in atmosphere.

1958–1960 U.S. nuclear weapons stockpile triples in size.

1960 Soviets shoot down U.S. U-2 spy plane, causing rift in U.S.-Soviet relations.

Women represent one-third of labor force; 35 percent of women work outside the home.

One-quarter of Americans live in suburbs.

BIBLIOGRAPHY

GENERAL WORKS

John Patrick Diggins, *The Proud Decades: America in War and Peace, 1941–1960* (1988).

Alan Ehrenhalt, *The Lost City: Discovering the Forgotten Virtues of Community in the Chicago of the 1950s* (1995).

David Halberstam, *The Fifties* (1993).

Douglas T. Miller and Marion Nowak, *The Fifties: The Way We Really Were* (1977).

J. Ronald Oakley, *God's Country: America in the Fifties* (1986).

William L. O'Neill, *American High: The Years of Confidence, 1945–1960* (1986).

DOMESTIC POLITICS AND POLICIES

Charles C. Alexander, *Holding the Line: The Eisenhower Era, 1952–1961* (1975).

Craig Allen, *Eisenhower and the Mass Media: Peace, Prosperity, and Prime-Time TV* (1993).

Stephen E. Ambrose, *Eisenhower*, vol. 2, *The President* (1984).

Jeff Broadwater, *Eisenhower and the Anti-Communist Crusade* (1992).

Robert F. Burk, *Dwight D. Eisenhower: Hero and Politician* (1986).

Fred I. Greenstein, *The Hidden Hand Presidency: Eisenhower as Leader* (1982).

R. Alton Lee, *Dwight D. Eisenhower: Soldier and Statesman* (1981).

Chester J. Pach Jr. and Elmo Richardson, *The Presidency of Dwight D. Eisenhower* (rev. ed., 1991).

Herbert S. Parmet, *Eisenhower and the American Crusades* (1972).

Gary W. Reichard, *The Reaffirmation of Republicanism* (1975).

Mark H. Rose, *Interstate: Express Highway Politics, 1941–1956* (1979).

FOREIGN POLICY

Stephen E. Ambrose, *Ike's Spies: Eisenhower and the Espionage Establishment* (1981).

Michael R. Beschloss, *Mayday: Eisenhower, Khrushchev, and the U-2 Affair* (1986).

Blanche Weisen Cook, *The Declassified Eisenhower: A Divided Legacy of Peace and Political Warfare* (1981).

Robert A. Divine, *Eisenhower and the Cold War* (1981).

Robert A. Divine, *The Sputnik Challenge* (1993).

Steven Z. Freiberger, *Dawn over Suez: The Rise of American Power in the Middle East, 1953–1957* (1992).

George C. Herring, *America's Longest War: The United States and Vietnam, 1950–1975* (2nd rev. ed., 1986).

Richard H. Immerman, *The CIA in Guatemala* (1982).

Richard H. Immerman, *John Foster Dulles and the Diplomacy of the Cold War* (1990).

Stanley Karnow, *Vietnam: A History* (rev. ed., 1991).

Walter LaFeber, *Inevitable Revolutions: The United States in Central America* (1983).

Donald Neff, *Warriors at Suez: Eisenhower Takes America into the Middle East* (1981).

Stephen G. Rabe, *Eisenhower and Latin America: The Foreign Policy of Anticommunism* (1988).

Andrew J. Rotter, *The Path to Vietnam: Origins of the American Commitment to Southeast Asia* (1987).

Robert W. Stookey, *America and the Arab States* (1975).

WOMEN, GENDER ROLES, AND THE FAMILY

Wini Breines, *Young, White, and Miserable: Growing Up Female in the Fifties* (1992).

Stephanie Coontz, *The Way We Never Were: American Families and the Nostalgia Trip* (1992).

Barbara Ehrenreich, *The Hearts of Men: American Dreams and the Flight from Commitment* (1983).

Peter Filene, *Him/Her/Self: Sex Roles in Modern America* (2nd ed., 1986).

Betty Friedan, *The Feminine Mystique* (1963).

Eugenia Kaledin, *Mothers and More: American Women in the 1950s* (1984).

Elaine Tyler May, *Homeward Bound: American Families in the Cold War Era* (1988).

Joanne Meyerowitz, ed., *Not June Cleaver: Women and Gender in Postwar America, 1945–1960* (1994).

Steven Mintz and Susan Kellogg, *Domestic Revolutions: A Social History of American Family Life* (1988).

Arlene Skolnick, *Embattled Paradise: The American Family in an Age of Uncertainty* (1991).

Rickie Solinger, *Wake Up Little Susie: Single Pregnancy and Race before Roe v. Wade* (1992).

ECONOMIC, SOCIAL, AND CULTURAL TRENDS

Erik Barnouw, *Tube of Plenty: The Evolution of American Television* (rev. ed., 1982).

William Boddy, *Fifties Television: The Industry and Its Critics* (1994).

Paul Boyer, *By the Dawn's Early Light: American Thought and Culture at the Dawn of the Atomic Age* (1985).

Richard O. Davies, *The Age of Asphalt: The Automobile, the Freeway, and the Condition of Metropolitan America* (1975).

Scott Donaldson, *The Suburban Myth* (1969).

Simon Frith, *Sound Effects: Youth, Leisure, and the Politics of Rock and Roll* (1981).

Herbert Gans, *The Levittowners: Ways of Life and Politics in a New Suburban Community* (2nd ed., 1982).

Serge Guilbaut, *How New York Stole the Idea of Modern Art: Abstract Expressionism, Freedom, and the Cold War* (1983).

Peter Guralnick, *Last Train to Memphis: The Rise of Elvis Presley* (1994).

Kenneth T. Jackson, *Crabgrass Frontier: The Suburbanization of the United States* (1985).

Barbara Kelly, *Expanding the American Dream: Building and Rebuilding Levittown* (1993).

Michael P. Malone and Richard W. Etulain, *The American West: A Twentieth Century History* (1989).

David Mark, *Democratic Vistas: Television in American Culture* (1984).

Karal Ann Marling, *As Seen on TV: The Visual Culture of Everyday Life in the 1950s* (1994).

Larry May, ed., *Recasting America: Culture and Politics in the Age of the Cold War* (1989).

Gerald D. Nash, *The American West in the Twentieth Century* (1973).

Lynn Spigel, *Make Room for TV: Television and the Family Ideal in Postwar America* (1992).

Jon C. Teaford, *The Twentieth-Century American City* (1993).

Cecelia Tichi, *Electronic Hearth: Creating an American Television Culture* (1991).

Stephen J. Whitfield, *The Culture of the Cold War* (1991).

Robert Wuthnow, *The Restructuring of American Religion: Society and Faith since World War II* (1988).

CIVIL RIGHTS

Taylor Branch, *Parting the Waters: America in the King Years, 1954–63* (1988).

Robert Fredrick Burk, *The Eisenhower Administration and Black Civil Rights* (1984).

Adam Fairclough, *To Redeem the Soul of America: The Southern Christian Leadership Conference and Martin Luther King, Jr.* (1987).

David J. Garrow, *Bearing the Cross: Martin Luther King, Jr., and the Southern Christian Leadership Conference* (1986).

David J. Garrow, ed., *The Montgomery Boycott and the Women Who Started It: The Memoir of Jo Ann Gibson Robinson* (1987).

Richard Kluger, *Simple Justice: The History of* Brown v. Board of Education *and Black America's Struggle for Equality* (1976).

Doug McAdam, *Political Process and the Development of Black Insurgency, 1930–1970* (1982).

Aldon D. Morris, *The Origins of the Civil Rights Movement: Black Communities Organizing for Change* (1984).

E. Frederick Morrow, *Black Man in the White House* (1963).

Mark V. Tushnet, *Making Civil Rights Law: Thurgood Marshall and the Supreme Court, 1936–1961* (1995).

"COUNTRY JOE" MCDONALD'S GUITAR

Music was an omnipresent element of protest movements in the 1960s. Civil rights demonstrators sang, "We Shall Overcome," anti-war rallies featured folk singers, and hippies turned on to acid rock. The guitar was the central musical instrument for each kind of music: traditional African American, folk, and rock. This wood acoustic guitar belonged to "Country Joe" McDonald who started his band, Country Joe and the Fish, at a draft protest in Oakland in 1965. The band was one of many that originated in the San Francisco Bay area, but its popularity soon spread across the country.

The Oakland Museum of California.

A DECADE OF REBELLION AND REFORM 28

1960–1968

I N THE SUMMER OF 1960, twenty-year-old white college student Tom Hayden went to Los Angeles to cover the Democratic National Convention for the University of Michigan *Daily*. He heard presidential candidate John F. Kennedy declare, "We stand on the edge of a New Frontier . . . of unfulfilled hopes and threats." The speech, Hayden reported, "stirred me deeply," but his encounter with Martin Luther King Jr. inspired him even more. By the time the Democrats met in Chicago eight years later, both Kennedy and King had been murdered. Hayden and thousands of other protesters were there in open rebellion against much of what the Democrats and the government stood for. Hayden's personal political journey through the 1960s—the fading of his initial hopes into anger and frustration—mirrored a more general shift among Americans from optimism and consensus to disillusionment and divisiveness.

In contrast to Kennedy's vague call for Americans to attack unsolved problems with idealistic service, King was specific. "Ultimately, you have to take a stand with your life," he told Hayden in 1960. In 1961, Hayden went south to work with black activists. There he joined a civil rights movement that shook the national conscience, raised hopes for the possibility of change, and provided a model of protest that inspired other marginalized groups.

The prosperity of the 1960s contributed to the nation's buoyant confidence and belief that the federal government should advance social welfare. Voters elected two Democratic presidents, John F. Kennedy and Lyndon B. Johnson, who favored an activist government and wanted to replace the complacency of the 1950s with a vigorous attack on social and economic problems. Nonetheless, grassroots movements representing people far from the centers of power built the strongest engine driving domestic reform and pushed official leaders beyond their original intentions.

Although foreign policy was Kennedy's supreme concern, as grassroots pressures mounted he began to push for innovative domestic programs in 1963. After Kennedy's assassination in November 1963, Johnson took up domestic reform with a passion, launching a multitude of programs aimed at promoting general economic growth and improving the conditions of racial minorities and the impoverished. These, along with education, health care, urban development, and environmental reforms, came to be known as the Great Society and constituted the most far-reaching innovations in U.S. domestic policy since the New Deal.

The Supreme Court also contributed substantially to this domestic revolution. Beginning in the 1950s, with pathbreaking decisions relating to civil rights, criminal justice, political representation, and the treatment of dissenters, the Court forcefully promoted the realization of equality in the United States. Many of its decisions were hotly contested, but most withstood challenge and contributed notably to the egalitarian thrust of public policy in the 1960s.

Underlying the transformation in domestic policy was the black freedom struggle, which took on new form and urgency in 1960 when African Americans in massive numbers began to apply the tactics of civil disobedience in demonstrations throughout the South. White repression and violence made the costs of progress high for the protesters, who endured brutality, saw their homes and churches burned, and sometimes lost their lives, but by the end of the decade, law had caught up with the American ideal of equality.

Yet it did not catch up fast enough. Legal guarantees of civil rights left untouched the deplorable economic conditions resulting from three centuries of poverty and oppression. By 1966, a minority of African American activists had discarded the original tenets of integration and nonviolence and demanded black power. Simultaneously, urban riots erupted in black neighborhoods throughout the nation. The second half of the decade saw a splintering among those who supported civil rights and a sharp decline in white support for its goals. Yet the black freedom struggle stimulated a multitude of new social movements. Other racial and ethnic minorities, students, and women benefited from the visibility of African American protest as well as from the civil rights movement's ideas, tactics, and policy precedents.

Tom Hayden went from civil rights activism to student organizing to protest against the U.S. role in the war in Vietnam. Hayden and other student radicals who formed what came to be called the New Left, scorned Kennedy's New Frontier and Johnson's Great Society for failing to strike at the roots of America's unjust political and economic system. Conservatives cried that the Great Society went too far and expressed outrage at the wholesale challenge to American values and institutions mounted by blacks, students, and others. Even before the decade's end, the optimism and idealism with which it had begun had given way to disillusionment and polarization.

Kennedy and the New Frontier

In his New Frontier speech that stirred Tom Hayden at the Democratic nominating convention in 1960, John F. Kennedy promised to confront "unsolved problems of peace and war, unconquered pockets of ignorance and prejudice, unanswered questions of poverty and surplus." Once in office, Kennedy instituted an aggressive foreign policy. Believing that most domestic problems could be solved by promoting economic growth, he asked Congress for a broad range of reform legislation, but he failed to back up his requests with effective leadership. Not until his final months did massive grassroots pressures spur Kennedy to launch a substantial assault on the problems of racism and poverty. Before these efforts reached fruition, an assassin ended his life.

The Election of 1960

John F. Kennedy grew up in privilege, the son of a wealthy Irish Catholic businessman who served in Franklin D. Roosevelt's administration and nourished his son's political career. With the aid of a distinguished World War II navy record, John Kennedy won election to the House of Representatives in 1946 and to the Senate in 1952. The Massachusetts senator set his sights on the White House for 1960, using his family's fortunes to build a superb political machine directed by his brother Robert. A major challenge was to woo Democratic liberals who were put off by Kennedy's undistinguished record in Congress and his failure to take a strong stand against McCarthyism.

Kennedy's opponents included Adlai E. Stevenson, Senate Majority Leader Lyndon B. Johnson of Texas, and Hubert H. Humphrey, the liberal senator from Minnesota. With his overwhelming financial advantage, his handsome appearance, and his dynamic style, Kennedy triumphed in a series of state primaries. A critical victory over Humphrey in West Virginia eliminated the question of his Catholicism, an issue that had doomed Al Smith's candidacy in 1928. Kennedy's impressive margin in that heavily Protestant state demonstrated that religious intolerance no longer raised an insuperable barrier between a Catholic and the presidency.

At the Democratic convention, after winning the nomination on the first ballot, Kennedy stunned nearly everyone by choosing Lyndon Johnson as his running mate. Although ticket balancing was a time-honored tradition, liberals detested the choice of a man whom they viewed as a typical southern conservative. The party platform, however, embodied liberal priorities, including the strongest civil rights plank the Democrats had ever endorsed. It also called for increased defense spending to bolster the nation's position in the cold war.

On the Republican side, Vice President Richard M. Nixon deflected challenges from liberal New York Governor Nelson Rockefeller and from Arizona Senator Barry Goldwater on the right. Support for Goldwater, who urged his party to "quit copying the New Deal," indicated that Eisenhower had not won over Republican conservatives to moderation. But the convention nominated Nixon on the first ballot.

While Nixon based his campaign on his experience as vice president, Kennedy took the initiative on issues. Kennedy called for a stronger defense system and a more vigorous approach to the cold war, and he promised to expand the welfare state and increase the rate of economic growth to "get this country moving again." Nixon, stuck with defending the policies of the Eisenhower administration, seemed less dynamic, though the two candidates actually differed little on defense and foreign policy questions.

Unmoved by any sense of moral urgency and concerned about the votes of southern whites, both candidates stepped gingerly around the issue of race. Yet Kennedy's advisers pushed him to seize an opportunity for attracting black support when Martin Luther King Jr. was arrested at a demonstration in Atlanta on October 19, 1960. Kennedy called King's wife to offer his sympathy, Robert Kennedy made a phone call to the judge, and the campaign circulated two million flyers about the incident in African American churches the Sunday before the election.

In the excruciatingly close election, Kennedy depended on black voters. Nixon won 52 percent of the white vote, but the black preference for Kennedy enabled him to outpoll Nixon by about 120,000 votes. African Americans provided essential margins in Illinois, Michigan, South Carolina, and other states vital to Kennedy's 303–219 majority in the electoral college. Of course, Kennedy needed more than black votes. Lyndon Johnson took credit for capturing most of the South for the Democratic ticket, but a third Eisenhower recession, which

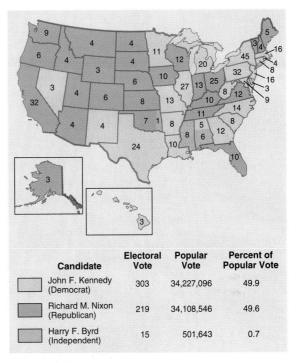

Candidate	Electoral Vote	Popular Vote	Percent of Popular Vote
John F. Kennedy (Democrat)	303	34,227,096	49.9
Richard M. Nixon (Republican)	219	34,108,546	49.6
Harry F. Byrd (Independent)	15	501,643	0.7

MAP 28.1
The Election of 1960

pushed unemployment above 6 percent in 1960, also contributed to the incumbent party's defeat. Kennedy's religion won him extra votes from Catholics in the North but caused him losses elsewhere.

Kennedy benefited from the first televised debates between presidential candidates. He came across as cool, experienced, handsome, and in command of the issues. Nixon appeared nervous, sweaty, and pale. Radio listeners declared the debate a draw, but television viewers came away more impressed with Kennedy. Television also helped to increase interest in the campaign: At 64 percent, voter turnout for this election was the highest in the twentieth century.

The Style and Promise of the New Frontier

The Kennedy administration projected an aura of dynamism, idealism, and glamour, reflecting the president's personal style as well as the tone of the government. He charmed the press corps with his grace, vigor, and self-mocking wit and was the first president to hold press conferences for a live TV au-

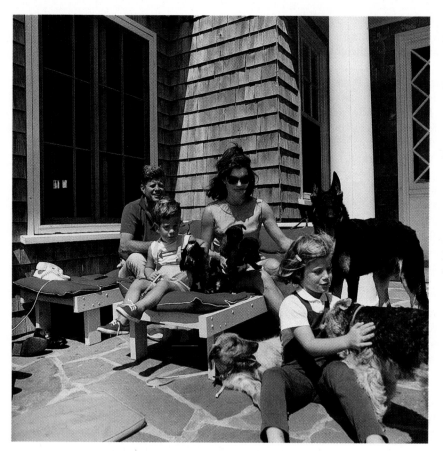

THE KENNEDY FAMILY
John F. Kennedy's youthful good looks, glamorous background, and attractive family added to his appeal and continue to fascinate many Americans decades after his death. Here he relaxes with his wife, Jacqueline, and their children, Caroline and John, at their vacation home in Hyannisport on Cape Cod. This photograph was taken in July 1963, a few months before Kennedy's assassination.
John F. Kennedy Library.

dience. The nation warmed to images of a young president competing in touch football, sailing with his chic and cultured wife, Jacqueline, and playing in the executive office with his toddler daughter and infant son. The Kennedys transformed the White House into a national showcase of culture and the arts, inviting prominent writers, artists, and musicians to visit and perform.

Kennedy surrounded himself with diverse advisers, including men from the Republican Party and Wall Street as well as liberal Democrats. Wanting to control foreign policy himself, Kennedy chose for secretary of state Dean Rusk, who was known for his loyalty in Truman's State Department. Most controversial was the appointment of Robert Kennedy as attorney general. Questioned about his brother's youth and lack of experience, Kennedy fell back on his wit, responding that he saw nothing wrong with "giving Robert some legal experience before he goes out to practice law."

The appointment of Robert S. McNamara as secretary of defense most reflected the style of the administration. Known for his keen analytic ability

and decisiveness, the hard-driving McNamara had risen to the top of the Ford Motor Company. A number of Kennedy's appointments to lower-level posts and the White House staff shared McNamara's youth, brilliance, and eagerness to apply technology and engineering to problem solving. Many were intellectuals from Ivy League schools, including fifteen Rhodes scholars; they exuded confidence, enjoyed competition, and welcomed crisis and risk. However, they were not especially well schooled in practical politics. When Lyndon Johnson told Speaker of the House Sam Rayburn how impressed he was with the brilliance of the Kennedy men, the older Texan replied, "I'd feel a whole lot better . . . if just one of them had run for sheriff once."

Kennedy's inaugural address called on all Americans to serve the common good. As the youngest elected president took the reins of government from the oldest president up to that time, Kennedy noted that he was the first president born in the twentieth century and that a "new generation" was assuming leadership. He asked Americans to cast off the complacency and self-indulgence of the 1950s, to "ask not what your country can do for you—ask what you can do for your country."

To what ends would this service be put? The brief, eloquent inaugural address described the cold war in a tone of crisis, emphasizing the United States' "role of defending freedom in its hour of maximum danger." Kennedy insisted, "If a free society cannot help the many who are poor, it cannot save the few who are rich"; yet his address gave domestic problems short shrift and delineated no specific programs. Nonetheless, the idealism of his speech touched many, especially the young, inspiring them to strive for the common good and to replace self-interest with service to a larger cause.

The Substance of the New Frontier at Home

Commenting on Kennedy's actions on civil rights, Martin Luther King Jr. described the president as "committed but . . . feeling his way," a characterization that King could easily have applied to Kennedy's domestic achievements in general. After campaigning on a party platform that promised to expand the welfare state, particularly in the areas of health care and education, Kennedy failed to achieve any major legislation. Nor did he assume leadership on behalf of racial justice until near the end of his life, when pressures from civil rights activists gave him no choice.

A number of factors account for the large gap between what Kennedy said he stood for and his achievements. Even though his party controlled Congress, a combination of southern Democrats and Republicans constituted a force that was large enough to block reform. Having been elected by a slim margin, Kennedy saw no reason to go out on a limb for social justice. He displayed much more zeal for foreign policy and consigned domestic reform to a back burner.

Kennedy did win support for several items that congressional Democrats had been pushing in the 1950s. New legislation included a two-billion-dollar slum clearance and urban renewal program; the Area Redevelopment Act of 1961, which aided depressed areas through incentives for companies to locate in them; and the Manpower Development and Training Act of 1962, which provided training for the unemployed. But two key items on the Democratic agenda, federal aid to education and health care for the elderly, got nowhere. Referring to a book Kennedy had written, *Profiles in Courage,* liberals

jokingly expressed their dissatisfaction with his leadership by asking that he show "less profile and more courage."

Two initiatives of the Kennedy administration —a presidential commission on women and equal pay legislation—received relatively little attention but had important ramifications. Although Kennedy had no particular interest in women's rights, he heeded the advice of Esther Peterson, head of the Women's Bureau in the Department of Labor. In 1961, she persuaded Kennedy that he could strengthen his support among women by appointing a President's Commission on the Status of Women.

Chaired by Eleanor Roosevelt and composed of leaders from the government and private organizations, the commission reported its findings in October 1963, eight months after Betty Friedan had attacked sex discrimination in her best-selling book *The Feminine Mystique.* The commission report, *American Women,* identified widespread discrimination against women, insisted that such discrimination harmed the country as well as individuals, and made recommendations for action. Spawning counterparts at the state level, the president's commission helped to create networks of women aware of sex discrimination and eager for action, providing an impetus for the launching of a grassroots women's movement a few years later.

Having been elected by a slim margin, Kennedy saw no reason to go out on a limb for social justice. He displayed much more zeal for foreign policy and consigned domestic reform to a back burner.

The president's commission addressed the age-old custom of paying women less than men for doing the same work. Although Kennedy's domestic agenda did not list sex discrimination among even the minor issues, he allowed Peterson to spearhead a drive for equal pay legislation, a goal that women's organizations and labor unions had been pushing for two decades. After Kennedy signed the Equal Pay Act in June 1963, wage disparities based solely on gender became illegal. Within a few years, women began to win wage increases and back pay worth millions of dollars.

The phrase "a rising tide lifts all boats" expressed Kennedy's belief that economic growth could solve most problems, that increased production provided the best means to eradicate poverty. In addition to meeting domestic needs, greater productivity would make the nation more competitive with the Soviet Union, whose rate of economic growth exceeded that of the United States throughout the 1950s. Consequently, Kennedy sought to increase the government's role in restraining inflation, eliminating recessions, and promoting economic growth.

Restraining inflation depended on cooperation from organized labor and corporations. When U.S. Steel and other big companies announced price increases in excess of rising labor costs in 1962, the president marshaled all of his resources to bring them back into line. He publicly criticized the steel executives, had the Justice Department begin investigations of price-fixing, and canceled government orders from the offending companies. "I'm beginning to sound like Harry Truman," he remarked, referring to Truman's lambasting of business. His vigorous action, unparalleled on other domestic fronts, ultimately forced the steel industry to retreat.

Although Kennedy called big businessmen "sons of bitches" in a widely reported comment during the steel controversy, he was also prepared to treat business kindly to further his goal of economic growth. Through new tax guidelines and legislation granting credits for new investment, corporations won a 10 percent tax cut in 1962.

Kennedy's biggest innovation in "getting the country moving again" came with his call for an enormous tax cut in 1963. Key economic advisers persuaded him that infusing money into the economy by reducing taxes would increase demand, boost production, and decrease unemployment. This use of fiscal policy to stimulate the economy even when there was no recession gained the name "the new economics." Kennedy, however, failed to sell his tax bill to Congress even after modifying it to make it more advantageous to the rich. Legislators worried that the tax cut would result in a budget deficit. Organized labor opposed the bill because the largest share of the reduction would go to the wealthy.

Kennedy did not live to see approval of his bill. Passed in February 1964, the law provided $10 billion in tax cuts over 1964 and 1965, and it received major credit for the greatest economic boom since World War II. Unemployment dropped to 4.1 percent, and the gross national product shot up by 7 to 9 percent annually between 1964 and 1966.

Questioning the wisdom of the tax cut, critics disputed its economic impact, pointing out that the surge was already under way before the law went into effect. Conservatives warned that cutting taxes would spark inflation. John Kenneth Galbraith and other liberals maintained that economic growth alone would not eliminate poverty, arguing instead for increased spending on schools, hospitals, urban renewal, and other public programs and facilities directed at the needs of ordinary citizens.

Some of these needs had gained the Senate's attention in 1960, when a subcommittee reported "a growing and intense problem," the poverty of eight million older Americans, whose "declining years are without dignity. . . . They are sick . . . they are without money." That same year Kennedy came face to face with the rural poor of Appalachia when he asked for their votes in his 1960 campaign in West Virginia. In 1962, he read *The Other America*, Michael Harrington's devastating account of the hopelessness and wretched conditions in the lives of more than one in every five Americans. And by 1963, Kennedy's key economic advisers recognized that economic growth in itself would not eradicate poverty.

The summer of 1963 marked a turning point in Kennedy's attitude toward domestic reform. In addition to asking aides to plan an attack on poverty, he issued a dramatic call for passage of a comprehensive civil rights bill. Whether he could have achieved these breakthroughs in domestic policy was left unanswered by his assassination on November 22, 1963.

Assassination of a President

The murder of the president in Dallas, Texas, seared the consciousness of Americans as had no other event since the end of World War II. Within minutes of the shooting, radio and television broadcast the unfolding horror to the nation. Millions watched the return of *Air Force One* to Washington bearing the president's coffin, his widow in her bloodstained suit, and the new president, Lyndon Baines Johnson, who had taken the oath of office aboard the jet.

From Friday afternoon until the burial on Monday, Americans shared in the tragedy through television, which abandoned regular programming. They saw newsreels of President Kennedy in life, experts assessing his career, somber-faced world leaders arriving to pay their respects, and thousands of tearful Americans filing past his coffin in

JOHN F. KENNEDY'S FUNERAL
For the few days following November 22, 1963, normal life stopped in the United States. Schools
and businesses were closed, while tens of thousands of Americans traveled to Washington, D.C.,
to file past Kennedy's coffin in the rotunda of the Capitol. The relatively new medium of television
unified the nation, as it allowed millions of viewers to experience every moment of that long, terrible
weekend, culminating in the funeral procession, shown here. The president's widow, Jacqueline
Kennedy, is escorted in the procession by the president's brothers Robert (left) and Edward.
© Henri Dauman NYC.

the Capitol. Even many of Kennedy's opponents and critics expressed their shock and personal grief.

Stunned Americans struggled to determine what had happened and why. As Kennedy had ridden with his wife and Texas Governor John B. Connally in a motorcade in an open car, three shots were fired, killing Kennedy and injuring Connally. The police quickly arrested Lee Harvey Oswald, a loner with an irregular past, and concluded that he had fired the shots from a nearby building. Two days later, as a television audience watched Oswald being transferred from one jail to another, a local nightclub operator and gambler, Jack Ruby, killed him.

Suspicions arose that Ruby had killed Oswald to cover up a conspiracy. Some people believed there had been a plot among ultraconservative Texans who hated Kennedy. Others, pointing to Oswald's Russian wife, his three-year residence in the Soviet Union, and his activities on behalf of Cuba's Castro, suspected a Communist plot. To get at the truth and calm public fears, President Johnson ap-

pointed a commission headed by Chief Justice Earl Warren, which concluded in September 1964 that both Oswald and Ruby had acted alone. Several experts pointed to errors and omissions in the report, and later investigations both supported and contested the lone-killer explanation. As with Lincoln's assassination, the controversy persisted for decades. The weight of opinion favored the original Warren report but never became conclusive enough to satisfy skeptics.

Debate also continued over how to assess Kennedy's domestic record. It had been unremarkable in his first two years, but his initiatives on taxes, civil rights, and poverty in 1963 suggested an important turning point. Whether Kennedy could have persuaded Congress to translate his proposals into legislation cannot be known. In the words of journalist James Reston, "What was killed was not only the president but the promise. . . . He never reached his meridian: We saw him only as a rising sun."

Johnson and the Great Society

Within six months after becoming president, Lyndon Johnson had a theme for his administration. In May 1964, he announced the goal of a "Great Society, [which] rests on abundance and liberty for all. It demands an end to poverty and racial injustice, to which we are totally committed." In pursuing that Great Society, Johnson not only signed a host of measures that had lain beyond Kennedy's grasp —the tax cut, a civil rights law, federal aid to education, and medical care for the aged and poor. He also got Congress to approve two more civil rights acts, an antipoverty program, a massive housing program, and legislation to protect consumers, control pollution, and preserve the environment.

In pursuing the Great Society, Johnson got Congress to approve three civil rights acts, an antipoverty program, a massive housing program, and legislation to protect consumers, control air and water pollution, and preserve the environment.

The legislation of the 1960s constituted a remarkable record of reform yet fell short of achieving the Great Society. A backlash arose to thwart African Americans' aspirations before equality became a reality for all. The number of Americans living in poverty was cut in half, but inadequately funded and hastily designed programs achieved only partial success. Above all, the Great Society fell victim to an escalating war in Vietnam, which depleted federal revenues, diverted the president's attention from domestic affairs, and damaged the credibility of his leadership.

Fulfilling the Kennedy Promise

Johnson assumed the presidency with a wealth of political experience. A self-made man from the poor Texas hill country, he won election to the House of Representatives in 1937 and to the Senate in 1948. Although his Texas base required caution on civil rights and attention to the needs of the oil industry and other business interests, Johnson's growing ambitions for national leadership led him to take more liberal stands. By 1955, he had secured the top post of Senate majority leader, which he used brilliantly to forge a Democratic consensus on the Civil Rights Acts of 1957 and 1960 and other liberal programs.

Johnson's coarse wit, excessive vanity, intense ambition, and Texas accent put off many who were accustomed to the sophisticated Kennedy style. His extreme need to dominate reached the point of humiliating aides and friends. Lacking Kennedy's eloquent and dynamic speaking style, Johnson excelled at behind-the-scenes planning, maneuvering, and persuading. Legislators found themselves enticed, cajoled, or threatened into support of his objectives. The famous "Johnson treatment" became legendary. In his ability to achieve his overriding goal of consensus—and in the means to which he was willing to resort—he had few peers in American history.

Johnson masterfully led the nation through the trauma of Kennedy's murder, stressing above all continuity and consensus. Mobilizing emotions aroused by the assassination, he asked Congress to act so that "John Fitzgerald Kennedy did not live or die in vain." He quickly applied his political skills to the slain president's tax proposal. By trimming the federal budget and promising government frugality, he won over fiscal conservatives and signed the tax cut in February 1964.

Still more revolutionary was the Civil Rights Act of 1964. Although Johnson gave responsibility for managing the bill to Robert Kennedy, who stayed on as attorney general until the fall of 1964, the president also worked mightily to line up enough Republicans and southern Democrats to ensure passage. "No memorial oration or eulogy could more eloquently honor President Kennedy's memory," he asserted. Referring to the "Johnson treatment" applied to Senate Republican leader Everett Dirksen, an aide reported that the president "never left him alone for thirty minutes." Enacted in July 1964, this act was the strongest civil rights measure since Reconstruction.

Antipoverty legislation followed fast on the heels of the Civil Rights Act. Still in an embryonic stage when Kennedy died, the poverty program captured Johnson's immediate attention. While Kennedy's body still lay in state, Johnson instructed an aide, "Give it the highest priority. Push ahead full tilt." In his first State of the Union message, Johnson called for "an unconditional war on poverty." Just two months later, the administration sent a draft bill to Congress, and in August Johnson signed the Economic Opportunity Act of 1964.

The new measure authorized ten programs to be administered by an Office of Economic Opportunity, allocating $800 million dollars for the first

THE "JOHNSON TREATMENT"
Abe Fortas was a distinguished lawyer who had argued one of the major criminal rights cases, Gideon v. Wainwright *(1963), before the Supreme Court and who was a close friend and adviser to President Lyndon Johnson. When Johnson asked him to serve on the Supreme Court, he was reluctant to leave his lucrative law practice, and Johnson had to use his famous persuasive powers to secure his assent. This photograph of the president and Fortas taken in July 1965 illustrates how Johnson used his body as well as his voice to bend people to his will.*
Yoichi R. Okamoto/LBJ Library Collection.

year (around 1 percent of the federal budget). Many provisions were targeted at youth, from Head Start, a preschool program for poor children, to the Upward Bound program and work-study grants for college students. There were also job training programs for youth (the Job Corps) and adult heads of families; loans to businesses willing to hire the long-term unemployed; aid to small farmers and rural businesses; and the VISTA program, which funded modest subsidies for volunteers to work on behalf of the disadvantaged. A legal services program that provided lawyers for the poor resulted in lawsuits that expanded and enforced impoverished Americans' rights to welfare programs.

The most novel and controversial part of the law, the Community Action Program (CAP), required "maximum feasible participation" of poor people themselves in coordinating poverty programs. Unlike other aspects of the poverty program, which sought to equip the poor to succeed in the existing system, this provision offered potential challenges to the system itself and a redistribution of power. In cities that took maximum feasible participation seriously, poor people began to organize community action programs to take control of their neighborhoods and to reform the welfare agencies, school boards, police departments, housing authorities, and other agencies on which they relied for services. Within months, mayors complained to the White House that activists were using federal funds to attack local governments and to "foster class struggle."

The last thing Johnson wanted was conflict, and he expressed his irritation at the "kooks and sociologists" involved in administering CAPs who caused him problems with Democratic mayors. Under his direction, federal poverty officials became less insistent on genuine representation for the poor, and local leaders found means to obtain federal funds without empowering people likely to challenge their control. Although the CAP failed to live up to its promise, for the first time in many cities those who were routinely excluded from the governmental process gained a voice, an incentive to act on their own behalf, and the opportunity to develop leadership skills.

A young black antipoverty worker in Mississippi reported that his Head Start project could offer poor people "doctors for their kids and good food," as well as employ "poor people who never had seen a check in their lives" to work as aides at the centers. "They're learning how to spell right and speak right," reported a mother with children in Head Start, but even more important to her, they were "learning about . . . us the colored people and what we've gone through . . . and what we've done for the country."

The 1964 Landslide

With the tax cut, civil rights, and antipoverty measures behind him, Johnson prepared to claim the presidency in his own right. He faced only one significant problem as the Democrats gathered for their

TABLE 28.1
REFORMS OF THE GREAT SOCIETY, 1964–1968

1964

24th Amendment	Abolished poll tax as prerequisite for voting.
Tax Reduction Act	Provided $10 billion in tax cuts over 1964–1965.
Civil Rights Act	Banned discrimination in public accommodations, public education, and employment.
Economic Opportunity Act	Created programs for the disadvantaged, including Head Start, VISTA, Job Corps, and CAP.
Wilderness Preservation Act	Set aside 9.1 million acres of national forest for protection.

1965

Elementary and Secondary Education Act	Provided $1.3 billion in aid to elementary and secondary schools.
Medical Care Act	Provided health insurance (Medicare) for all citizens age 65 and over. Extended federal health benefits to welfare recipients. (Medicaid)
Voting Rights Act	Banned literacy tests and other voting tests and authorized the federal government to act directly to enable African Americans to register and vote.
Executive Order 11246	Banned discrimination on the basis of race, religion, and national origin by employers awarded government contracts and required them to "take affirmative action to ensure equal opportunity."
Department of Housing and Urban Development (HUD)	New government department created to provide programs to address housing and community issues.
National Arts and Humanities Act	Created National Endowment for the Humanities (NEH) and National Endowment for the Arts (NEA) to support the work of artists, musicians, writers, and scholars.
Water Quality Act	Required states to set and enforce water quality standards.
Immigration and Nationality Act	Abolished fifty-year old quotas based on national origins, increasing the number of non-Western and Northern European immigrants.
Air Quality Act	Imposed air pollution standards for motor vehicles.
Higher Education Act	Expanded federal assistance to colleges and universities.

1966

National Traffic and Motor Vehicle Safety Act	Established federal safety standards.
Highway Safety Act	Required federally approved safety programs at the state level.
Department of Transportation	New government department created to administer transportation programs and policies.
Model Cities Act	Authorized more than $1 billion to ameliorate nation's slums.

1967

Executive Order 11246	Order extended to allow discrimination ban and requirement of affirmative action to cover women.

1968

Civil Rights Act of 1968	Banned discrimination in housing and in jury service.
National Housing Act	Subsidized the private construction of 1.7 million units of low-income housing.

MISSISSIPPI FREEDOM DEMOCRATIC PARTY RALLY
*These activists are singing at a rally outside the Democratic National Convention hall in 1964,
supporting the Mississippi Freedom Democratic Party (MFDP) in its challenge to the all-white
delegation sent by the regular Mississippi Democratic Party. In the foreground are Fannie Lou
Hamer, one of the MFDP delegates; Eleanor Holmes Norton, a civil rights lawyer; and Ella
Baker, who helped organize the Southern Christian Leadership Conference (SCLC) and later
managed MFDP headquarters in Washington, D.C.*
Matt Herron.

national convention in the summer of 1964. In Mississippi, blacks and their supporters had organized a delegation to challenge the all-white state contingent chosen by party regulars. Determined that consensus would reign over his convention, Johnson instructed Minnesota Senator Hubert H. Humphrey to arrange a settlement that would avoid a fight on the convention floor. The resulting "compromise" allotting them just two at-large seats while leaving the forty-four-member all-white delegation intact outraged black Mississippians, but Humphrey received his reward when Johnson chose him for his running mate.

The Democrats' refusal to guarantee racial justice within the party did not cost their ticket much support from civil rights advocates. They had nowhere else to go. At a bitterly divided Republican national convention, Arizona Senator Barry M. Goldwater won the nomination, defeating the liberal and moderate wing that had dominated the party since the 1940s.

Republican Phyllis Schlafly wrote a book to promote Goldwater's candidacy, calling it *A Choice Not an Echo* and aptly capturing right-wing Republicans' frustration with what they considered the "me-tooism" of their party. Goldwater told the convention that "extremism in defense of liberty is no vice" and embarked on a campaign that indeed put him near the extreme right of U.S. politics. He attacked the entire framework of the welfare state and called for the government to leave the economy to "free enterprise." Criticizing the Democrats' failure to use every means available to crush communism in Vietnam, he suggested that he would use nuclear weapons if necessary.

Goldwater proved an easy mark for Johnson. Having safely steered the nation through the assassination trauma and established his capacity for national leadership, Johnson projected stability and security. With the economy booming, only a minority of voters proved willing to risk a change as dramatic as Goldwater promised. Although Goldwater captured five states in the Deep South, Johnson accomplished a record-breaking landslide of 61 percent of the popular vote. On his coattails came resounding Democratic majorities in the House (295–140) and Senate (68–32).

Completing the Great Society Agenda

"I want to see a whole bunch of coonskins on the wall," Johnson told his aides, using a hunting analogy to stress his determination to make the most of his mandate. He wanted to surpass even the domestic achievements of his mentor, Franklin Roosevelt. In the sheer amount and breadth of new legislation, Johnson succeeded extraordinarily, and public opinion polls gave impressively high marks to both the president and Congress. Reporters called the legislation of the 89th Congress (1965–1966) "unprecedented" and "a political miracle"; organized labor lauded that Congress as "the most productive congressional session ever held."

The Economic Opportunity Act of 1964 had been just the opening shot in the War on Poverty. Congress increased the program's funding in 1965 to $2 billion and initiated two new assaults on poverty. The Appalachian Regional Development Act and the Public Works and Economic Development Act attacked poverty in depressed regions that the general economic boom had bypassed. Rather than combatting poverty directly, these programs—like the tax cut of 1964—sought to help the poor indirectly by stimulating economic growth and providing jobs through road building and other public works projects.

A second approach, one that was new to the 1960s, promised to equip the poor with the training and skills necessary to find jobs. The 1964 antipoverty legislation included the Head Start and Job Corps programs for just this purpose. But the largest assault on poverty through education was the Elementary and Secondary Education Act of 1965.

Ever since establishing the land-grant college system in the nineteenth century, the federal government had promoted education, but only in the form of funds for a specific purpose, such as science education in the National Defense Education Act of 1957. Legislators who opposed federal involvement in what had always been the preserve of state and local governments had stalled Truman's proposal for general aid to public education for two decades. Other conflicts concerned whether aid to parochial schools violated the constitutional separation of church and state.

To sidestep the religious issue, Johnson proposed aid for "the educational needs of educationally deprived children" rather than to schools per se. Thus private and parochial schools could receive aid for equipment and supplies to be used for poor children, and public school districts would be granted funds on the basis of the number of poor children in their schools. When Congress passed the Elementary and Secondary Education Act in April 1965, Johnson flew to the little school in Texas where he had begun his education to sign the bill with his first teacher at his side.

With the Higher Education Act of 1965, Congress also vastly expanded federal assistance to colleges and universities, providing not only funds for buildings and programs but also scholarships and low-interest loans for students. In 1966, Congress renewed its commitment to education, appropriating nearly $4 billion for higher education for the next three years and $6.1 billion for a two-year extension of the elementary and secondary education program.

The administration broke a second congressional deadlock in the area of health care. Trimming down the plan for universal care that Truman had first proposed, Johnson focused his proposal on the elderly, who constituted a large portion of the nation's poor. Congress responded with the Medicare program, which provided the elderly with universal compulsory hospital insurance financed largely through Social Security taxes and a voluntary insurance program for doctors' bills and other costs funded by the government and individual contributions. Congress took the initiative in authorizing the Medicaid program, a system of federal grants to supplement state programs paying for medical care for poor people below the age of sixty-five. Demonstrating again his flair for the dramatic, Johnson flew to Independence, Missouri, to sign the Medicare-Medicaid bill under the gaze of former

President Truman, who had first called for a national commitment to adequate health care.

The whirlwind of legislation from the 89th Congress included additional efforts to assist the impoverished. A food stamp program, begun as a demonstration project in 1961, replaced the distribution of surplus commodities, giving poor people greater choice in obtaining food. Rent supplements allowed some poor families to acquire another basic necessity without resort to public housing. Congress attacked the environment of poverty with the Model Cities Act, authorizing more than $1 billion to improve conditions in the nation's slums.

In response to the growing force of the civil rights movement, Johnson persuaded Congress to pass the Voting Rights Act of 1965. The Immigration and Nationality Act of 1965 eliminated a different form of discrimination. The new law continued to restrict the numbers of immigrants and for the first time placed limits on immigration from the Western Hemisphere. But it also did away with the fifty-year-old quotas based on national origins, thereby ending discrimination against immigrants from areas outside northern and western Europe.

The benefits of the Great Society reached well beyond the poverty-stricken. Pressures from a growing consumer movement led by liberal activist Ralph Nader and others produced legislation to make automobiles safer and to raise standards for the food, drug, and cosmetics industries. In 1965, Johnson became the first president to send Congress a special message on the environment, and Congress responded with measures to control water and air pollution and to preserve the natural beauty of the American landscape. Another law, the National Arts and Humanities Act of 1965, created programs to support artists, musicians, writers, and scholars and to bring their work to public audiences.

The flood of reform legislation dwindled to a trickle after 1966, when midterm elections reduced the overwhelming majorities that the Democrats previously enjoyed. Even though a sizable majority of the poor were whites, who benefited proportionately from the war on poverty, the public tended to associate antipoverty programs with African Americans. White support for black aspirations withered, and a wave of urban riots between 1964 and 1968 caused many voters and legislators to contend that the poor needed "law and order," not more government assistance. The appearance of buttons reading "I fight poverty—I work" indicated a growing backlash against the disadvantaged.

The Vietnam War dealt the largest blow to domestic reform, for at the same time that Johnson pursued his Great Society at home he rapidly escalated the U.S. presence in Vietnam. Growing opposition to the war diverted the president's attention from domestic affairs and put his entire leadership in jeopardy. Even more damaging was the war's cost, which rose to more than $2 billion a month by 1966 and increased the federal deficit. Moreover, rising military expenditures began to exert inflationary pressures on the economy.

The Vietnam War dealt the largest blow to domestic reform, for at the same time that Johnson pursued his Great Society at home he rapidly escalated the U.S. presence in Vietnam.

In August 1967, Johnson called for a temporary tax increase to control the deficit and check inflation. While Congress hesitated, the president reduced spending, cutting especially deeply into social welfare programs. Congress finally enacted an income tax surcharge, but not until July 1968. By then, consumer prices were increasing at what was considered a high annual rate of 5 percent, and inflation continued despite the tax increase.

The declining years of the Johnson administration were not completely lacking in significant reforms. The president pried one more civil rights law out of Congress in 1968, and he also secured a new housing program. Construction of public housing over the previous two decades had lagged behind need, and millions of people continued to live in substandard dwellings. Moreover, public housing often took the form of massive high-rise buildings that afforded a poor environment for children. In addition, projects tended to be located in areas that offered minimal employment opportunities and inadequate public transportation and services.

Johnson proposed both an enormous increase in construction of low-income housing and a new way of providing it. The National Housing Act of 1968 authorized construction of 1.7 million units in the next three years but left construction and ownership in private hands. Poor people could purchase houses with low-interest loans guaranteed by the government, and developers could obtain low-interest loans to construct housing for the needy.

Assessing the War on Poverty

Measured by statistics, the reduction in poverty in the 1960s was significant. The number of impoverished Americans fell from forty million in 1959 to twenty-five million in 1968, reducing the poor from 22 percent of the population to around 13 percent. Certain groups fared much better than others. Large numbers of the aged and members of male-headed families rose out of poverty, while the economic circumstances of female-headed families actually worsened. Moreover, although African American family income grew from 54 percent of white family income to 61 percent, whites escaped poverty at a faster rate than blacks, and blacks constituted one-third of the poor population at the end of the decade.

Intangible changes flowed from the War on Poverty in the form of shifting attitudes. In the 1960s, a substantial part of the population expressed a concern about poverty, located its causes in economic and social circumstances rather than in individuals' shortcomings, and assumed a national responsibility for alleviating it. Especially through the Community Action Programs, poor people themselves gained more control of their circumstances and a sense of their right to a fairer share of America's bounty.

The rising tide of the economy played a large role in the reduction in poverty. Yet government programs that transferred funds and services to the poor also contributed. Whereas the distribution of surplus food benefited about fifty thousand participants at the cost of $1 million in 1961, by the 1970s, twelve million people received more than $2 billion in food stamps. Within ten years after their inauguration, Medicare and Medicaid provided $32 billion worth of health care for the elderly and the poor. In addition, the War on Poverty helped to make the needy aware of their eligibility for aid programs and to remove restrictions that discouraged them from applying for aid. Between 1960 and 1970, the number of recipients of Aid to Families with Dependent Children (AFDC), a program launched by the New Deal, grew from three million to ten million.

The heart of the antipoverty program, the Office of Economic Opportunity (OEO), remained underfunded throughout its life. Poverty experts projected expenditures of $6.5 billion for OEO by 1968, but they never rose above $2 billion. Moreover, despite the large increases in direct subsidies for

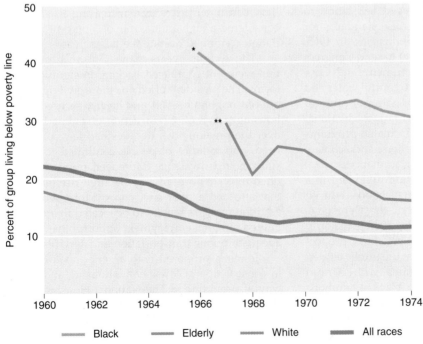

Figure 28.1
Poverty in the U.S., 1960–1974
The short-term effects of economic growth and the Great Society's attack on poverty are seen here. Which groups experienced the sharpest decline in poverty and what might account for the differences?

—— Black   —— Elderly   ····· White   ▬▬ All races

*Statistics on blacks for years 1960–1965 not available.
**Statistics on the elderly for years 1960–1966 not available.

AFDC, food stamps, housing, and medical care, no significant redistribution of income resulted. The poorest 20 percent of the population received 5.1 percent of total national income in 1964 and 5.4 percent in 1974.

Conservatives charged that the Great Society programs discouraged initiative among the poor by giving them "handouts." Critics on the left claimed that the emphasis on training and education placed the responsibility for poverty on the poor themselves rather than on the economic system. Most job training programs prepared graduates for low-level occupations and could not guarantee that jobs would be available on the completion of training. Surveys in 1966 and 1967, for example, found 28 percent of Job Corps graduates unemployed six months after completing their training.

Who reaped the greatest benefits from the Great Society programs? Critics pointed out that most of the funds for Appalachia and other depressed areas went to highway building and thus to the construction industry. Real estate developers, investors, and moderate-income families reaped the lion's share of benefits from the mortgage subsidies under the National Housing Act of 1968. Noting that in slum clearance programs, commercial development and high-income housing often displaced poor families, blacks called urban renewal "Negro removal." Physicians' fees and hospital costs soared after enactment of Medicare and Medicaid. Other beneficiaries of the Great Society programs were middle-class professionals who staffed the growing bureaucracy that was needed to run them.

Some critics of the War on Poverty suggested that the solution to poverty lay in a major redistribution of income, through raising taxes and using those funds in the public sector to create jobs, overhaul social welfare systems, and rebuild slums. The Johnson administration programs did invest more heavily in the public sector, but they had little effect on the existing distribution of resources. Determined above all to promote consensus and avoid conflict, Johnson would not take from the advantaged to provide for the poor. Funds for the poverty programs had to come from increasing revenues generated by economic growth, not from new taxes on the rich or middle class. Economic prosperity allowed spending for the poor to rise and significantly improved the lives of millions, but that spending never approached the amounts that would have been required to declare a victory in the war on poverty.

The Second Reconstruction

Unlike many of the Great Society reforms, which failed to live up to their promise and evoked widespread criticism, the civil rights movement effected a revolution in the legal status of African Americans and won widespread acceptance. The first Reconstruction in the aftermath of the Civil War had ended slavery and written racial equality into the Constitution; the second Reconstruction a century later made the guarantee of equal status under the law a reality. That accomplishment depended heavily on the courage, resourcefulness, and determination of black people themselves. In the words of Sheyann Webb, one of the thousands of marchers in the Selma, Alabama, campaign for voting rights, "We were just people, ordinary people, and we did it."

Unlike many of the Great Society reforms, which failed to live up to their promise and evoked widespread criticism, the civil rights movement effected a revolution in the legal status of African Americans and won widespread acceptance.

Begun as an effort to end legal segregation and discrimination in the South, the civil rights movement in the mid-1960s expanded its purpose in two ways. It extended its concern to racial injustice throughout the country, and it attacked the deplorable economic conditions of African Americans that equal rights left untouched. The movement to extend legal equality to blacks initially won broad support from white Americans. But when the movement began to seek equality through systematic change in the economic system, white support declined, and a strong backlash developed. By the end of the 1960s, the revolution in the legal status of blacks was complete, but the black freedom struggle had lost much of its momentum, and African Americans remained at the bottom of the economic ladder.

The Flowering of the Black Freedom Struggle

The Montgomery bus boycott in the mid-1950s had given national visibility to the plight of southern blacks, produced a national leader in Martin Luther

LUNCH COUNTER SIT-IN
John Salter Jr., a professor at Tougaloo College, and students Joan Trumpauer and Anne Moody take part in 1963 in a sit-in at the Woolworth lunch counter in Jackson, Mississippi. Shortly before this photograph was taken, whites had thrown two students to the floor, and police had arrested one student. Salter was spattered with mustard and ketchup. Moody would write a popular book in 1968 about her experiences in the black freedom struggle, Coming of Age in Mississippi.
State Historical Society of Wisconsin.

King Jr., and demonstrated the effectiveness of mass mobilization. Nevertheless, although it took enormous energy and determination, the boycott remained in a way a passive action—Montgomery blacks avoided riding the buses. In the 1960s, the form of protest underwent a major change, mobilizing blacks into direct and personal confrontation with the people and institutions that segregated them or discriminated against them: lunch counters, department stores, public parks and libraries, buses and depots, municipal service providers, and voting registrars.

Direct action as a mass movement began in February 1960, when four African American freshmen at North Carolina A&T College in Greensboro sat at the whites-only Woolworth's lunch counter and asked for service. Within days, hundreds of young people joined their demonstration. By the end of February, blacks had launched sit-ins in thirty-one cities in eight southern states. These local movements received encouragement from the NAACP, the Congress of Racial Equality (CORE), and the Southern Christian Leadership Conference (SCLC). At the SCLC, executive secretary Ella Baker picked up the phone and challenged her contacts at various colleges: "What are you going to do? It's time to move."

In April, Baker got student activists together at Raleigh, North Carolina. With her support they decided to remain independent from the older generation and its established civil rights organizations. They founded the Student Nonviolent Coordinating Committee (SNCC, pronounced "snick"), creating a decentralized, nonhierarchical structure that encouraged the development of leadership and decision making at the grassroots level.

Although SNCC rejected the organizational patterns of the older groups, it embraced the strategy of civil disobedience and the nonviolent principles of Martin Luther King Jr. and others in the SCLC and CORE. Directly confronting the agents of oppression, students would stand up for their rights, but they would not practice self-defense against their enemies. At SNCC's founding conference, minister James Lawson defined a strategy for blacks that he believed could change the hearts of their oppressors: "We affirm . . . nonviolence as a foundation of our purpose, the presupposition of our faith, and the manner of our action." Love was at the heart of nonviolence, he pointed out: "It matches the capacity of evil to inflict suffering with an even more enduring capacity to absorb evil, all the while persisting in love." With its appeal to human conscience, "nonviolence nurtures the atmosphere in which reconciliation and justice become actual possibilities."

When students returned to the field, their optimism and commitment to nonviolence met severe testing. Although some local leaders managed to negotiate quiet accommodations to student demands, in most cases authorities and local citizens reacted with violence. Hostile whites poured food over demonstrators, burned them with cigarettes, called them "nigger," and pelted them with rocks. Local police went after protesters with clubs, fire hoses, and tear gas; they arrested more than 3,600 civil rights demonstrators in the year following the Greensboro sit-in. Spurning complicity with an unjust system, demonstrators frequently refused to pay fines, choosing jail instead.

Another wave of protest arose in 1961, when CORE organized Freedom Rides to integrate interstate transportation. On May 4, six whites and seven blacks boarded two buses in Washington, D.C., for a thirteen-day ride to New Orleans. The riders crossed the color line without harm in bus stations in Virginia and North Carolina, but in Alabama, white hoodlums bombed a bus and beat the riders with baseball bats. When the brutality turned some Freedom Riders back, SNCC members rushed in to take their places.

A mob of more than a thousand people attacked the Freedom Riders when they arrived in Montgomery. Angry whites knocked unconscious a federal government observer who tried to help the protesters. After failing to get the activists to call off the rides, Attorney General Robert Kennedy dispatched

federal marshals to restore order. Alabama and Mississippi authorities agreed to protect the buses, but when they reached Jackson, Mississippi, the Freedom Riders were promptly arrested. Refusing to post bail, several hundred spent parts of the summer in Mississippi jails.

Encouraged in part by Kennedy administration officials who viewed voting rights as less controversial than civil disobedience (and more likely to benefit the Democratic Party), SNCC and other groups began a Voter Education Project in the summer of 1961. Yet as activists sought to register black voters in the Deep South, they met no less violence than had the Freedom Riders. Whites beat Robert Moses, an African American and the first SNCC activist in Mississippi, and police arrested him as he worked to get blacks registered to vote. When a Mississippi legislator killed Herbert Lee, one of the first blacks to attempt to register, no charges were brought against the murderer.

When African Americans mobilized, whites bombed their churches, threw tenant farmers out of their homes, and beat and jailed the activists. Plantation worker Fannie Lou Hamer, for example, lost her job and home when she attempted to register to vote in Mississippi in 1962. Undeterred, she continued her efforts, and one year later police arrested and battered her so savagely that she would not show her face to her family for a month. In June 1963, a white man gunned down Mississippi NAACP leader Medgar Evers in front of his house in Jackson.

Television brought home to the entire world the brutality of southern resistance to racial equality in May 1963, when Martin Luther King Jr. and the SCLC launched a campaign in Birmingham, Alabama, to integrate public facilities and open jobs to blacks. As blacks massed in demonstrations, the city's police chief, Eugene "Bull" Connor, responded with police dogs, electric cattle prods, and high-pressure hoses. Hundreds of demonstrators, including school-age children, went to jail, and firebombs exploded at King's motel and his brother's house. Four months later, a bomb killed four black children attending Sunday school in a Birmingham church.

The largest demonstration took place in Washington, D.C., in August 1963. Civil rights leaders revived the march on Washington strategy used by A. Philip Randolph in 1941 to get President Roosevelt to ban discrimination in defense jobs. Sponsored by the major civil rights organizations and coordinated by Bayard Rustin, a pacifist, socialist, and civil

BIRMINGHAM DEMONSTRATORS
In April 1963, Martin Luther King Jr. and the Southern Christian Leadership Conference (SCLC) initiated a campaign to integrate Birmingham, Alabama, known as the most segregated city in the nation. City officials filled the jails with demonstrators, including King himself, and nine hundred children, like these young people being attacked with powerful hoses. One police officer remarked to a colleague, "Ten or fifteen years from now, we will look back on all this and we will say, 'How stupid can you be?'" Photographs like this one evoked outrage around the country.
Charles Moore/Black Star.

rights activist, the march drew 250,000 blacks and whites to the nation's capital. Gathered below the Lincoln Memorial, they heard from many singers and speakers, but it was King who put his indelible stamp on the day.

Moved by the intense emotions of the crowd, King departed from his formal speech, using all the passion and skills that made him the greatest orator of his day. His words came from the Bible, from Negro spirituals, and from the nation's patriotic anthems. "I have a dream," he repeated again and again, spelling out a future when "the sons of former slaves and the sons of former slave owners will be able to sit down together at the table of brotherhood." With the crowd roaring in support, he looked toward the day "when all of God's children . . . will be able to join hands and sing . . . 'Free at last, free at last; thank God Almighty, we are free at last.'"

Media and public response to the March on Washington was overwhelmingly positive, but the buoyant euphoria of that day quickly faded as activists returned to continued resistance throughout the South. The movement next launched the Mississippi Freedom Summer Project in 1964. Organized primarily by SNCC, the project mobilized more than one thousand northern college students, who paid their own expenses to conduct voter ed-

ucation classes and help blacks register to vote in Mississippi. Resistance was fierce. By the end of the summer, only twelve hundred new voters had been placed on the rolls, several people had been killed, eighty had been beaten, more than a thousand had been arrested, and thirty-five black churches had been burned.

Still the movement persisted. In January 1965, the SCLC and SNCC launched a voting drive in Selma, Alabama, where for two months local authorities met demonstrators with clubs, whips, cattle prods, and arrests. In March, Alabama troopers used such brutal force to turn back a fifty-mile march from Selma to the state capitol in Montgomery that the incident earned the name "Bloody Sunday." Hundreds of representatives from religious groups and other organizations then poured into Selma to support the demonstrators. Finally, President Johnson called up the Alabama National Guard, and the march proceeded under the guard's protection to the capitol. Before the Selma campaign was over, whites had shot or beaten to death three demonstrators.

John Lewis, chairman of SNCC and a leader of the march on Bloody Sunday, was beaten and hospitalized but managed to make the final march. Looking back on that demonstration, he recalled it as one of the most meaningful events in his life: "In

THE MARCH ON WASHINGTON
*More than a quarter of a million Americans, including fifty thousand whites, gathered on the
Mall in the nation's capital on August 28, 1963, to pressure the government to support the civil
rights of African Americans. After Martin Luther King Jr. gave his "I have a dream" speech,
Malcom X said to march organizer Bayard Rustin, "You know this dream of King's is going to
be a nightmare before it's over."*
James P. Blair/National Geographic Society Image Collection.

October of that year the Voting Rights bill was
passed and we all felt we'd had a part of it." The
black freedom struggle brought untold changes in
the dignity and self-confidence of southern blacks,
but for Lewis and other activists the nation's capital
was the site of the first major fruits of their struggle.

The Response in Washington

Civil rights leaders would have to wear sneakers,
Lyndon Johnson said, if they were going to keep up
with him. But he misrepresented cause and effect in
the history of civil rights. Indeed, although both
Kennedy and Johnson went further than any previous president, and although Johnson's civil rights
leadership far surpassed Kennedy's, both presidents
acted more in response to events created by the black
freedom struggle than on their own initiative.

During his first two years in office, Kennedy
used the Civil Rights Act of 1957 to file voting rights

suits in southern counties, and he appointed black
justices to federal courts, including NAACP lawyer
Thurgood Marshall to the U.S. circuit court of appeals. Yet he also appointed several segregationist
justices, who would hamper civil rights enforcement in the South. Moreover, Kennedy hesitated
when it came to executive action and legislation.
During the campaign, Kennedy had promised to
end discrimination in housing with "a stroke of the
presidential pen." Not until late in 1962, after activists had sent thousands of pens to the White
House, did Kennedy issue an executive order to ban
discrimination in federally insured housing.

The president moved most forcefully when
events in the South gave him little choice. He sent
federal marshals to Montgomery to protect the Freedom Riders. In 1962, he dispatched federal troops
to enable James H. Meredith, a black air force veteran, to enroll in the all-white University of Mississippi. And he called up the Alabama National

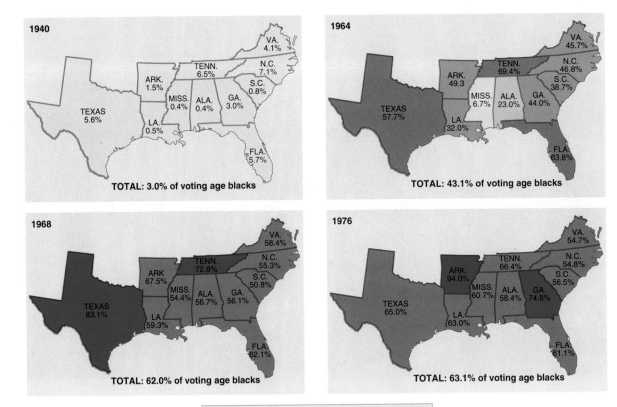

M A P 2 8 . 2
The Rise of the African American Vote, 1940–1976
*Voting rates of Southern blacks increased gradually in the 1940s and 1950s, but shot up dramat-
ically in the Deep South after the Voting Rights Act of 1965 provided for federal agents to enforce African Americans' right to vote.*

Guard during the Birmingham demonstrations in May 1963. But to activists who wanted more federal protection, Kennedy replied that law enforcement was a local matter. Well aware of the political costs of deploying federal force against fellow Democrats who headed state and local governments, the president and attorney general made it clear that when they intervened it was to enforce the law, not to support the demonstrators.

Seeking to contain civil rights activism, the Kennedys frequently proposed cooling-off periods and even tried to get black leaders to call off the March on Washington, though the president did in-

vite them to the White House after the march. In response to one of these appeals, CORE leader James Farmer pointed out that blacks had been "cooling" for a hundred years. "If we got any cooler we'd be in a deep freeze," he said.

In June 1963, the president finally made good on his campaign promise to seek legislation. In a nationally televised speech, he called civil rights "a moral issue . . . as old as the scriptures and . . . as clear as the American Constitution" and specifically supported voting rights and equal access to public schools and accommodations. Pointing to the discrimination and humiliations experienced by blacks, Kennedy asked white Americans, "Who among us would then be content with the counsels of patience and delay?"

Johnson took up Kennedy's commitment with zeal, and a number of factors assisted his efforts. Television captured the dignity and courage of African Americans and the brutal repression of southern officials. Many whites were appalled at the violence against peaceful black demonstrators, who were often on their knees in prayer. The growing public support for civil rights, the "Johnson treatment," and the president's ability to turn the measure into a memorial to the martyred Kennedy produced the Civil Rights Act of 1964.

Passed in July 1964, the Civil Rights Act guaranteed access for all Americans to public accommodations, public education, employment, and voting, thus sounding the death knell for the South's system of segregation and discrimination. Title VII of the measure, which banned discrimination in employment, also attacked racial inequality outside the South. The ability of a massive civil rights movement to sway a majority of the white population secured passage of the law. At the same time, it spotlighted Johnson's political capabilities and enabled him to cast off his sectional identity and become a genuinely national leader. Many southern whites called the first southerner in the White House since Woodrow Wilson a traitor to his race and region.

Title VII of the Civil Rights Act also prohibited sex discrimination in employment, although this provision came not from the administration but from a conservative southern representative, Howard W. Smith, an opponent of civil rights. Its adoption resulted from the efforts of Representative Martha Griffiths, a Democrat from Michigan and a women's rights advocate, intense lobbying by a tiny band of feminists, and support from southerners who hoped that including the sex provision would defeat the entire bill. Because Title VII applied not just to wages but to every aspect of employment, including hiring and promotion, it represented a giant step toward equal employment opportunity for women as well as racial minorities.

Within months after passage of the Civil Rights Act of 1964, Johnson ordered his aides to draft a new law, one that would remove "every remaining obstacle to the right and the opportunity to vote." A week after the violent Bloody Sunday in Selma, Johnson went to Congress to plead for its passage. In his televised speech, he insisted, "Should we defeat every enemy, should we double our wealth and conquer the stars" without achieving racial equality, "we will have failed as a people and as a nation." Invoking the freedom song of the movement, he concluded, "We shall overcome." The Voting Rights Act, which empowered the federal government to act directly and immediately to enable African Americans to register and vote, was signed by Johnson in August 1965. A major transformation began in southern politics. (See Historical Question, page 1120.)

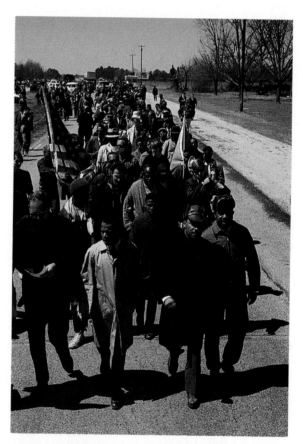

THE SELMA MARCH
In 1963, the Student Nonviolent Coordinating Committee (SNCC) began a campaign for voting rights in Selma, Alabama, where white officials had registered only 335 of the 15,000 African Americans old enough to vote. As often happened, after younger activists had gotten things started, Martin Luther King Jr. came to Selma in January 1965 and made the city his primary focus. Here King leads the third — and successful — effort, begun March 21, 1965, to walk the fifty-four miles from Selma to Montgomery, the state capital. On the right is Ralph Abernathy, King's close associate.
Bob Adelman/Magnum Photos, Inc.

What Difference Did Black Voting Rights Make?

BORN TO POOR BLACK SHARECROPPERS in the Mississippi Delta, Unita Blackwell hearkened in church one Sunday in 1964 when a SNCC worker talked about voter registration. The very next day she went to the courthouse where, predictably, officials refused her application. Undeterred, she succeeded on the third try, threw herself into activism as a SNCC organizer, and saw her share of jail cells. In fact, she and her husband planned their protest activities so that only one would risk arrest and the other would remain free to care for their child. A founder of the Mississippi Freedom Democratic Party, which was established to challenge the all-white state organization, Blackwell saw the challenge compromised away at the 1964 Democratic national convention. But four years later, she participated in the national convention with Mississippi's reconfigured biracial delegation. Subsequently, she served as vice chair of the state Democratic Party and on the Democratic National Committee. When her small town of Mayersville incorporated in 1976, Blackwell won election as its first mayor and the first black female mayor in Mississippi.

Blackwell's career is but one measure of the transformations generated by African Americans' struggle for the most basic right of citizenship. Their determination to register to vote and the resulting resistance and violence of southern whites created a crisis that the federal government could not ignore. Its response, the Voting Rights Act of 1965 and subsequent extensions, suspended the literacy tests that had been used to disqualify blacks but not whites, and brought electoral operations in most southern states under federal supervision. The law required the Justice Department to approve in advance any changes in state procedures that might disadvantage black voters, and it empowered the attorney general to send federal agents to observe registration and election processes and even to register voters in areas of continued white resistance.

"Legislation is not self-implementing," noted NAACP leader Roy Wilkins. "There is work to be done." As was the case with its passage, implementation of the Voting Rights Act depended on the efforts of African Americans themselves. More than two hundred voter registration drives between 1966 and 1968 paid off in dramatic increases in the numbers of blacks registered. Throughout the South, the proportion of African Americans on voter rolls jumped from 43 percent in 1964 to 62 percent in 1968. In Mississippi, the percentage leaped from just 6.7 in 1964 to 68 percent in 1968.

African Americans also gained political offices in unprecedented numbers. Fewer than two dozen blacks held elective office in the South in 1964. In 1970, they claimed almost five hundred elected government posts, and two years later the number reached nearly twelve hundred. Just seven years after whites bludgeoned civil rights activists during the Selma voting drive, black candidates won half of the ten seats on Selma's city council. With the victories of Barbara Jordan from Houston, Texas, and Andrew Young from Atlanta, Georgia, in 1972, the former Confederacy sent its first African Americans to the House of Representatives since Reconstruction. Black electoral success was not limited to the South. Across the nation, African Americans held fifteen hundred elected positions in 1970, and by 1990 that number exceeded seven thousand. The total of black representatives in Congress inched up from ten in 1970 to twenty-five in 1990 and then soared to thirty-eight in the 1992 elections.

The greatest progress came at the local level. The number of black mayors grew sixfold to more than 300 in the 1990s; the number of black city council members vaulted from 552 in 1970 to nearly 3,000 in 1989. Electoral success translated into tangible benefits. When black officials took office, their constituents saw improvements in public facilities, police protection, roads, trash collection, and other basic services. Referring to Unita Blackwell's accomplishments as mayor, a Mayersville resident noted, "She brought in the water tower. Mostly it was pumps then. . . . Sewage, too. There wasn't nothing but those little old outdoor houses." Another constituent pointed to "old folks' houses. And paved streets. I grew up here when they wasn't paved." Black local officials also awarded more government jobs to African Americans and contracts to minority businesses. Elected mayor of Atlanta in 1973, Maynard Jackson appointed a black police chief and increased blacks' share of city jobs from 42 percent to 51 percent.

Most black officials had far less power than Jackson, but even when they were outnumbered by whites, their mere presence on local governing bodies paid dividends. They could at least introduce issues of concern to blacks that whites had ignored, and they gained access to information about behind-the-scenes government. An African American serving on a city council in Florida pointed out that "no matter what happened," his white colleagues "knew I was listening to everything that went on." Activist Fannie Lou Hamer noted the psychological benefits of electoral progress. When blacks had no political voice, she recalled, "some white folks would drive past your house in a pickup truck with guns hanging up on the back and give you hate stares. . . . Those same people now call me Mrs. Hamer."

Yet political power did not readily guarantee African Americans economic equality or even ma-

terial security. Their minority status in the population and residential dispersion, combined with many whites' disinclination to vote for blacks, meant that even by the 1990s, African Americans occupied fewer than 2 percent of all elected positions in the nation. As African Americans looked to increase their political force and shape policy to meet their needs, they recognized that they would have to revive grassroots activism and seek coalitions with nonblacks. In addition they considered a number of electoral strategies to solidify black and minority strength in a majoritarian system: reducing the number of at-large elections, which dilute minorities' power, and increasing the number of single-member district systems; monitoring electoral redistricting to ensure as many black-majority districts as possible; and proportionate or cumulative voting.

Despite the limited reach of black enfranchisement, most experts nonetheless view the voting rights revolution as the most successful of all civil rights initiatives. As Unita Blackwell put it, "We didn't have nothing, and we changed the whole world with nothing. We changed a whole outlook."

Johnson had also pronounced the need "to move beyond opportunity to achievement," to achieve "not just equality as a right and theory, but equality as fact and as result." To this end, he used his authority as president to issue Executive Order 11246 in September 1965. Not only did that order ban discrimination by employers holding government contracts (affecting about one-third of the labor force), but it also required them to take affirmative action to ensure equal opportunity.

Extended to cover women in 1967, the affirmative action program provoked more controversy than any of the civil rights measures. Calling it "reverse discrimination," many people thought—incorrectly—that affirmative action required absolute quotas for hiring minorities and women or that it required hiring or promoting unqualified candidates. In fact, the order sought to overcome the effects of centuries of discrimination by requiring employers not just to stop discriminating but to act forcefully to bring the composition of their labor force into line with the available pool of qualified candidates. Despite its controversial nature, affirmative action withstood attacks until the 1990s and came to be seen as a good employment practice by most large businesses.

Johnson's final effort to reconcile the actuality of race relations with the nation's vision of itself was the Civil Rights Act of 1968. That measure banned racial discrimination in housing—the most controversial provision—and in jury selection, and it empowered the federal government to intervene to protect civil rights workers from violence.

Like Kennedy, Johnson tried, unsuccessfully, to keep the movement from getting ahead of him. Johnson sided with Democratic mayors, such as Richard J. Daley in Chicago, when Martin Luther King Jr. and others began to attack discrimination in housing, education, and employment outside the South. Moreover, under Johnson the FBI continued the wiretapping and electronic surveillance of King that had begun under Kennedy and expanded its activities to "expose, disrupt, misdirect, discredit, or otherwise neutralize" the activities of militant black protest organizations.

The three civil rights measures of the 1960s formed the most important legal gains for African Americans since Reconstruction and constituted Johnson's most far-reaching contributions to domestic reform. Yet the progress failed to match the rising aspirations of African Americans or to satisfy the needs of blacks that antidiscrimination measures in themselves could not address. As the cry

for racial equality moved outside the South and intensified in militancy, the president most committed to promoting civil rights became the object of bitter criticism from a large segment of the black freedom movement.

Black Nationalism and the End of the Civil Rights Coalition

By 1966, the black freedom struggle had undergone dramatic changes. Initially focused on the South, the movement sought integration and legal equality, and activists assumed that blacks and whites could work together through nonviolent direct action to change the hearts and behavior of white oppressors. By 1966, movement leaders' attention encompassed racial oppression throughout the nation; their goals had broadened to eliminate the poverty and miserable living conditions that defined the lives of millions of African Americans; and many activists had given up both on white allies and the tactics of nonviolence.

In part the new emphases resulted from the very success of civil rights legislation, as one layer of oppression receded only to reveal others more subtle but just as pervasive. Civil rights leaders knew that equal access to public facilities and institutions did little to improve the material conditions of blacks throughout the country. What did it matter that African Americans had the freedom to patronize a restaurant if they could not afford the price of a meal?

King himself realized that racism reached beyond the South, even though northern whites liked to think otherwise. In 1965, he moved his campaign north, and the SCLC mounted a drive for better jobs, schools, and housing in Chicago. King also pressed the government for more adequate funding of the antipoverty program and initiated plans for a Poor People's March to the nation's capital in 1968. Yet even as his goals changed, King clung to the principle of nonviolence and attempted to work with white supporters and government officials. For this he came increasingly under criticism from activists in CORE and SNCC.

African Americans suffering the daily terror associated with civil rights activism in southern communities deplored the federal government's failure to protect them from violence. Their disillusionment with white allies increased even as hundreds of white students came to organize in Mississippi in 1964. Black organizers felt that white students too often tried to run things, and they doubted the commitment of students who would return to lives of ease and security at the end of the summer. The Democratic Party's rejection of the black-based Mississippi Freedom Democratic Party at the 1964 convention intensified skepticism about playing by the rules. Expressing the black delegates' bitter disillusionment over the sellout by white liberals, Fannie Lou Hamer declared, "We didn't come all this way for no two votes."

In the North, a powerful voice rose to challenge the dominant ethos of the civil rights movement. Malcolm Little had grown up in poverty, first in Nebraska and then in Michigan. His father, a supporter of Marcus Garvey's pan-Africanism, was harassed

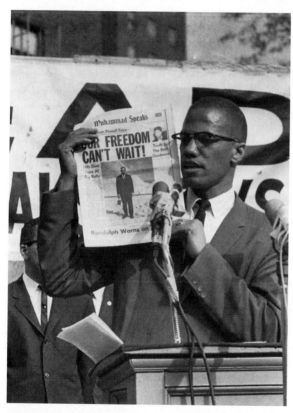

MALCOLM X

Malcolm X addresses a Black Muslim rally in New York City on July 1963. The name of the newspaper he displays refers to the organization's leader, Elijah Muhammad, who had headed the Nation of Islam since 1934. In 1964, Malcolm broke with the leader. He did not abandon black nationalism and continued to urge radical change, but he no longer equated whites with the devil. "The white man is not inherently evil," he said, "but America's racist society influences him to act evilly."
Wide World.

by the Ku Klux Klan and died after whites pushed him under a streetcar. Convicted of attempted burglary at the age of twenty-one, Malcolm Little went to prison, where he educated himself and converted to the Nation of Islam, whose adherents were called Black Muslims. The Nation drew on a long African American tradition of nationalism and separatism.

Released from jail in 1952, Malcolm Little changed his name to Malcolm X, to symbolize the African identity stripped from his ancestors, and went to work for the Nation of Islam. He attracted a large following, especially in urban ghettos, to his doctrine of separation from the "corrupt [white] society," black pride and autonomy, and self-defense against white violence. In 1964, Malcolm broke from the Black Muslims, began to cultivate a wider constituency, and expressed an openness to working with whites. At a Harlem rally in February 1965, three members of the Nation of Islam shot and killed him. Yet his ideas outlived his death and began to resonate in CORE and SNCC.

Black rage and impatience with legal changes erupted into a wave of riots that ignited cities in the North, Midwest, and West every summer from 1964 to 1968. Usually sparked by an incident between white police and local blacks, the most intense of these riots involved thousands of people who battled with the police, burned buildings, and looted stores. The Watts district of Los Angeles in 1965, Newark and Detroit in 1967, and the nation's capital in 1968 saw the most destruction and violence, but hundreds of other eruptions occurred across the country. In Detroit, rioters swept through fourteen square miles of the black ghetto; the result was 43 deaths, 7,000 arrests, 1,300 destroyed buildings, and 2,700 shops looted. Surveying the carnage, Detroit's mayor remarked, "It looks like Berlin in 1945."

Rioters exhibited pride and exhilaration in their new defiance and sense of power, however fleeting. They generally remained in African American neighborhoods and tried to avoid damaging black-owned and public buildings, saving their rage for white businesses and local police. "Our nation is moving toward two societies, one black, one white —separate and unequal," warned an investigating commission appointed by President Johnson in 1967. But Johnson ignored the commission's recommendations for a more vigorous campaign against racism and poverty, and little was done to ameliorate the basic conditions from which the riots sprang.

Revealing the intensity of black discontent, the rebellions suggested to some activists the potential for a more militant assault on racism. At a rally in Greenwood, Mississippi, in June 1966, SNCC chairman Stokely Carmichael gave that new approach a name. Using slang that belied his university education, Carmichael asserted, "This is the twenty-seventh time I have been arrested—I ain't going to jail no more." Then he shouted, "We want black power!" again and again as the audience cheered and called back the words. "Black power" quickly became the rallying cry in SNCC and CORE. Though embraced by only a minority of African Americans, the black power movement claimed the lion's share of national attention in the late 1960s.

Activists issued no single systematic definition of black power, but the words and deeds of Carmichael and other leading exponents delineated its major elements. Black power meant separation from whites. Carmichael called integration "a subterfuge for the maintenance of white supremacy." Working with white liberals perpetuated "a paternalistic, colonial relationship."

The black power movement rejected assimilation into the dominant society because that implied the superiority of white institutions and values. The phrase "Black is beautiful" emphasized the authenticity and worth of African American culture and racial pride. African Americans were encouraged to develop independent businesses and control their own schools and other community institutions. They were also encouraged to form their own all-black political organizations, such as the Black Panther Party, founded in Oakland, California, in 1966 to combat police brutality.

To black power advocates, nonviolence only brought more beatings and killings. Malcolm X had said, "If someone puts a hand on you, send him to the cemetery." Carmichael agreed: "Black people should and must fight back." The press paid an inordinate amount of attention to black radicals, and the black power movement sparked a severe white backlash. Some black power advocates, including Carmichael, H. Rap Brown, and Eldridge Cleaver, carried guns and openly called for black insurrection. Although the urban riots erupted spontaneously, triggered by specific incidents, horrified whites blamed them on black power militants. By 1966, a full 85 percent of the white population thought that blacks were pressing for too much too quickly; two years earlier, only 34 percent had thought so.

King agreed with black power advocates about the need for "a radical reconstruction of society" but clung to nonviolence and integration as the means

to this end. In March 1968, the thirty-nine-year-old leader took his movement to Memphis to support a strike of municipal garbage workers, most of whom were black. There, on April 4, King was shot and killed while standing on the balcony of his motel. James Earl Ray, an escaped white convict, was arrested and confessed to the murder but later denied that he had killed King and insisted that he was a scapegoat for a wider conspiracy.

Black power advocates receded from national visibility by the end of the decade. Never able to command substantial support in the African American community, which revered King and his philosophy, black militants were harassed by the FBI, jailed, and sometimes killed by the police, whom they also sometimes killed. Black nationalism's emphasis on black pride and black culture and its critique of American institutions, however, resonated broadly and helped to shape the protest of other groups.

Demands for Power to the People

Beyond its impact on the lives and status of African Americans, the black freedom struggle encouraged a multitude of movements that fueled social change in the 1960s. With its incontrovertible moral claims, the civil rights movement helped to make protest respectable, and its ability to capture national attention and move the federal government suggested possibilities for other groups with grievances. College students, opponents of the war in Vietnam, women, Native Americans, Mexican Americans, and other minority groups all drew in some measure on the black freedom struggle for inspiration, models of protest, and critiques of American institutions. These groups became more militant, engaging in direct action protests, expressing their own cultural nationalism, and challenging existing institutions and values.

Native American Protest

Protest was not new to the group with the oldest grievances, but Native American activism took on new militancy and goals in the 1960s. The cry "red power" reflected the influence of black radicalism on Native Americans who rejected the goal of assimilation into the mainstream. As one Indian put

**THE AMERICAN
INDIAN MOVEMENT**
*Dennis Banks (right), a Chip-
pewa who had served in the
U.S. air force, was a founder
and leader of the American
Indian Movement (AIM). Russell Means, a Sioux born on the
Pine Ridge reservation, joined
AIM in 1969. This photo was
taken in 1973 when Banks and
Means led an occupation of
Wounded Knee, a part of the
Pine Ridge reservation where
the army had massacred the
Sioux in 1890. The two-month
stand by two hundred occu-
piers, during which the Indians
and federal agents exchanged
gunfire that killed two Indians,
produced no substantive reforms but called attention to
the plight of Native Americans.*
Wide World.

it, the civil rights struggle led by King "was within
the System, and the System had nothing to do with
Indians." Rather, American Indians sought tribal sovereignty and just treatment as independent nations.

*College students, opponents of the war in
Vietnam, women, Native Americans, Mexican
Americans, and other minority groups all
drew in some measure on the black freedom
struggle for inspiration.*

In 1963, Northwest Indians mounted "fish-ins"
to enforce fishing rights that were guaranteed by
century-old treaties. Elsewhere, Native Americans
demonstrated and occupied territory and public
buildings, claiming rights to natural resources and
lands that they had owned collectively before European settlement. A new, more militant generation
participated in these demonstrations through the
National Indian Youth Council, founded in 1961. In
the most dramatic action, Indians seized Alcatraz
Island in San Francisco Bay and used it as a cultural
and educational center from 1969 until the federal
government ran them out in 1971.

"The American Indian Movement hit our
[Lakota Sioux] reservation like a tornado," recalled
Mary Crow Dog. Two Chippewa, Russell Banks and
George Mitchell, founded the American Indian
Movement (AIM) in 1968 in Minneapolis initially to
deal with problems in cities, where about 300,000
Indians lived. AIM focused on Native Americans
encouraged or forced by the relocation and termination programs of the 1950s to migrate to urban
areas only to find unemployment, poverty, and
alienation from their traditions. In addition to
protecting Indians from police harassment and
securing antipoverty program funds for Indian-
controlled organizations, AIM chapters established
"survival schools" where children were educated in
the history and values of their own culture.

The appeal of AIM spread beyond urban areas,
electrifying Native Americans like Mary Crow Dog.
When AIM members first visited her reservation in
South Dakota, it "loosened a sort of earthquake inside me," she later wrote. The AIM people "had a
new look about them, not that hangdog reservation
look I was used to." The militant tactics of AIM and
other radical groups rarely achieved their goals,
but—in addition to stirring Native American self-
respect—they helped sensitize Americans to Indian
grievances and fostered more moderate aims.

CHICANO POWER
This mural in Los Angeles with symbols used by Chicano activists illustrates Mexican American pride.
Craig Aurness/Woodfin Camp.

Native American protest won more responsiveness from the Bureau of Indian Affairs, legislation to meet educational and health needs of Indians, and government decisions recognizing Indian rights to ancestral lands. Taos Indians, for example, regained sacred lands in New Mexico, and the government paid the Sioux more than $100 million for lands that were taken when gold was discovered there in the nineteenth century. Native Americans recovered a measure of identity and pride, a greater respect for and protection of their culture, and, in the words of President Johnson's special message to Congress in 1968, a recognition of "the right of the First Americans to remain Indians while exercising their rights as Americans."

Hispanic American Struggles for Justice

The fastest-growing minority group in the 1960s was Hispanic Americans, people of Mexican, Puerto Rican, Caribbean, and other Spanish-speaking origins. Hispanics of Puerto Rican and Caribbean descent tended to live in urban areas on the East Coast. But the largest group, comprising more than half of the Hispanic population of the United States, was some six million Mexican Americans, who were concentrated in California, Texas, Arizona, New Mexico, and Colorado. In addition, thousands of immigrants illegally crossed the unguarded two-thousand-mile border between Mexico and the United States in search of economic betterment.

Throughout the twentieth century, Mexican Americans had formed local and national organizations to push for political power and economic rights. But, as was true among African Americans and Native Americans in the 1960s, young Hispanics increasingly rejected the traditional politics practiced by their elders in favor of militant strategies of direct action. One symbol of this generational challenge was the adoption of the name "Chicano" by young Mexican American activists.

The first organizing among Chicanos that gained national attention occurred in California, where migrant workers endured wretched living and working conditions as they followed the harvests of fruits and vegetables around the state. In 1963, Cesar Chavez organized the United Farm Workers Association (UFW) to improve conditions for Chicanos through union representation. UFW marches and strikes gained widespread support, and a national boycott of California grapes helped the UFW to win union recognition and a wage increase in 1970.

Chicanos mobilized elsewhere to end employment and educational discrimination, win their share of antipoverty funds, and combat police brutality. Starting in East Los Angeles in 1968 and spreading through the Southwest, a series of strikes, called "Blow Outs," among thousands of high school students protested the racism experienced by Mexican Americans in the public schools. In Denver, Rodolfo "Corky" Gonzales organized the Crusade for Justice, setting up "freedom schools," where Chicano children learned Spanish and studied Mexican American history and culture and marched down the halls chanting, "Chicano power." The separatist and nationalist strains of Chicano protest were evident in La Raza Unida (the United Race), a third party founded by José Angel Gutierrez in Texas and based on cultural pride and brotherhood.

Mexican Americans gradually won greater representation in government and more effective enforcement of antidiscrimination legislation. With blacks and Native Americans, they continued to be overrepresented among the poor but gained a sense of their potential power and respect for their culture through such programs as bilingual education in the schools and Chicano studies programs.

Student Rebellion and the New Left

Connections between civil rights and other protest movements appeared direct and immediate, as white activists returned from civil rights projects in the South to organize student protests, the antiwar movement, and the new feminist movement. Their confrontation with extreme racism and their disillusionment with the federal government radicalized and sensitized them more deeply to injustice. They also developed greater self-confidence and learned new tactics.

Tom Hayden's first meeting with SNCC activists in the fall of 1960 "was a key turning point, the moment my political identity began to take shape." He became involved with Students for a

Democratic Society (SDS), a small group of whites formed in 1960 from the remains of an older socialist-oriented student organization. In 1961, Hayden went south, where he was beaten and jailed while working with SNCC in Georgia. In 1962, he played a key role in defining the purpose and structure of SDS, which soon became the organizational focus of white student protest in the 1960s.

Idealistic students criticized the complacency of their elders, the remoteness of decision makers from the will of the people, and the powerlessness and alienation that people experienced in a society run by large, impersonal bureaucratic institutions.

The Port Huron Statement, named for the site in Michigan where about sixty student leaders and a few older activists met, articulated SDS's principles. "We are people of this generation, bred in at least modest comfort, housed now in universities, looking uncomfortably at the world we inherit," the statement began. The idealistic students criticized the complacency of their elders, the remoteness of decision makers from the will of the people, and the powerlessness and alienation that people experienced in a society run by large, impersonal bureaucratic institutions.

SDS aimed to mobilize a new social movement, called the New Left, with civil rights, peace, and universal economic security as its major targets. Both the means and ends of change were to be a "participatory democracy" in which each individual would "share in those social decisions determining the quality and direction of his life." SDS remained small until 1965, but other forms of student activism soon followed in its wake.

The first large-scale white student protest arose in the Free Speech movement at the University of California at Berkeley in the fall of 1964, when university officials banned student organizations from a campus site where they had set up tables to recruit support for civil rights and other causes. Led by Mario Savio and other whites who had worked for civil rights in the South, the students claimed the right to freedom of expression and political action. They occupied the administration building and confronted police in their attempts to disobey the ban. More than seven hundred students were arrested before they got the California Board of Regents to overturn the new restrictions.

Hundreds of student rebellions followed. Opposition to the Vietnam War activated the largest number of students, who marched, rallied, and occupied buildings in protest against universities' activities linked to the war. But they did not stop there. Attacking the impersonality of universities and their unresponsiveness to students' needs, protesters issued a broad range of demands, including curricular reforms, more financial aid for minority and poor students, independence from paternalistic rules over their lives outside the classroom, the freedom to hear controversial speakers on campus, and a larger voice in campus decision making.

Student protest spread from large universities and elite institutions to small colleges and religious schools. It ranged far beyond SDS, which exercised virtually no control over its local chapters. According to surveys taken in 1967 and 1968, more than 140,000 students (about 2 percent of the college population) were affiliated with SDS, and nearly 13 percent identified themselves as radicals. In addition to its contributions to the antiwar movement, student insurgency also brought about changes ranging from new black, Chicano, and women's studies programs to coed dormitories.

Student rebels came from the "baby boom" generation that swelled enrollments in higher education in the 1960s and gave young people a sense of power and generational solidarity. Most white students came from middle- and upper-class families. Materially secure and free of the immediate need to provide for themselves, they enjoyed the luxury of attacking the very system that made their rebellion possible. Such conduct bewildered and angered older Americans, who were equally shocked by a growing revolt against nearly every conventional standard of behavior.

The Counterculture

By 1967, national media had begun to take notice of another revolution that was under way. Growing up alongside the New Left and student movements and often overlapping them, the counterculture drew on the ideas and behavior of the Beats of the 1950s. Although many young people were both cultural and political rebels, the cultural revolution focused on personal rather than political and institutional change.

Cultural radicals, or "hippies," as they were called, scorned mainstream norms that valued the work ethic, material possessions, rationality, order, and sexual control. The phrase "Do your own thing" expressed their belief in spontaneity, living for the moment, and distrust of all authority. Hippies stood out with their long hair and unusual, wildly colorful and often ragged clothing, including tie-dyed and Indian fabrics, jeans, beads, and sandals, when they wore shoes at all. The Haight-Ashbury district of San Francisco harbored the most widely known hippy community, but thousands of cultural radicals established communes in cities or on farms, where they renounced the concept of private property and shared everything, often including sex partners. Seeking heightened perceptions and freedom from all inhibitions, they replaced the alcohol, nicotine, and tranquilizers of their elders with illegal drugs such as marijuana and experimental drugs like the new hallucinogenic drug LSD (lysergic acid diethylamide), unaware of its harmful effects.

Rock music played a central role in both the counterculture and the political left. English groups such as the Beatles and the Rolling Stones and homegrown products including Bob Dylan, Janis Joplin, the Jefferson Airplane, and Jerry Garcia's Grateful Dead took American youth by storm. Rock music shared with rock and roll the sensual, pulsating beat that had thrilled young people in the 1950s. Lyrics encouraged drugs—"I'd love to turn you on"—and spontaneous sex—"Why don't we do it in the road."

But the 1960s music often carried insurgent political and social messages. "Eve of Destruction," a top hit of 1965, despaired of the violence around the world and the threat of nuclear annihilation—"There'll be no one to save with the world in a grave" —and reminded young men, "You're old enough to kill but not for votin'." Other popular songs derided authority, touted the mind-expanding thrills of marijuana and LSD, celebrated sexual freedom, and called for peace, love, and revolution.

Although cultural rebels remained a small minority, many elements of the counterculture—from rock music to jeans and long hair—filtered into the mainstream. Sexual relations outside marriage and tolerant attitudes about sexual morality increased to such an extent that experts proclaimed a "sexual revolution." Self-fulfillment became a dominant concern of many Americans, and questioning of government and other authority became much more widespread. Even though the counterculture was just one of several forces promoting changes in American society, it continued to influence American society after the hippies faded away in the early 1970s.

WOODSTOCK

The Woodstock Music Festival, held on a farm near Bethel, New York, in August 1969, featured the greatest rock and folk musicians of the era and epitomized the values and hopes of the counterculture. Despite terrible conditions created by bad weather and the failure of festival organizers to plan for so many people, the youthful crowd of 400,000 created a loving, peaceful community for three days filled with music, sex, and drugs.
Image Works.

Beginnings of a Feminist Movement

Both the civil rights struggle and the New Left served as inspiration and models for a new women's movement. The ban against sex discrimination in the Civil Rights Act of 1964 and President Johnson's executive order extending affirmative action to women reflected feminists' efforts to "piggyback" onto civil rights measures. The new laws raised women's expectations, and feminists grew impatient when the government moved slowly against sex discrimination in employment. Deciding that they needed a "civil rights organization for women," Betty Friedan and others founded the National Organization for Women (NOW) in 1966.

A more radical wing of the new feminism grew out of young women's activism in civil rights and the New Left. In SNCC and SDS, women absorbed the values of self-determination and individual

worth but faced significant barriers to the full use of their talents, quickly grasping a contradiction between the ideal of equality and the actual status of women. Two white women, Mary King and Casey Hayden, first raised the issue in SNCC in 1964, and in 1965 they began circulating their ideas to women who were active in SDS and other New Left groups.

King and Hayden pointed out that, like blacks, women "seem[ed] to be caught up in a common-law caste system . . . forcing them to work around or outside hierarchical structures of power which may exclude them." Women, they contended, were also exploited and subordinated in personal relations. The 1965 memo struck a responsive chord among white activist women, but the chief response from male radicals was indifference or ridicule. Consequently, feminists moved to form an independent women's liberation movement.

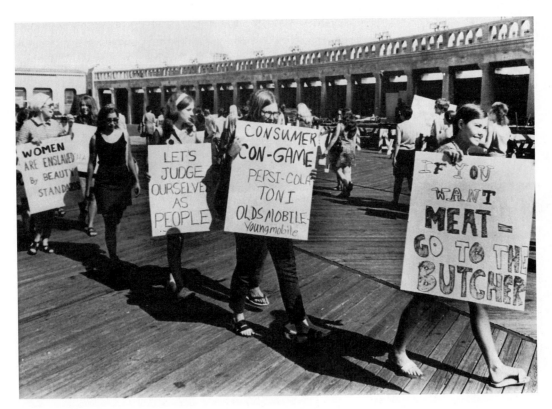

FEMINISTS PICKET THE MISS AMERICA PAGEANT
These picketers were among the feminists who demonstrated at the Miss America pageant at
Atlantic City, New Jersey, in 1968. They protested society's conditioning of women "to compete
for male approval, enslaved by ludicrous 'beauty' standards." They set up a "freedom trash can"
and invited women to throw away their "bras, girdles, curlers, false eyelashes, wigs, and
Cosmopolitan." And they decorated a live sheep with ribbons and crowned it Miss America.
Wide World.

By the end of the 1960s, radical women had established women's liberation groups in Chicago, New York, Boston, New Orleans, and elsewhere across the nation. They translated black pride into pride of womanhood, and they implemented the "participatory democracy" of SDS in all their activities. Staging marches, sit-ins, and other demonstrations, they began to gain public attention, especially when in 1968, one hundred demonstrators picketed the Miss America beauty pageant, throwing girdles, bras, and hair curlers into a "freedom trash can" in protest against being forced "to compete for male approval, enslaved by ludicrous 'beauty' standards." Activism by radicals and more moderate feminists surged into a mass movement that dramatically changed public policy and popular attitudes in the 1970s.

The Judicial Revolution

For more than a decade, beginning with the *Brown* school desegregation decision in 1954, the Supreme Court under Chief Justice Earl Warren (presiding from 1953 to 1969) spearheaded another form of change. During the 1960s, Eisenhower referred to the appointment of Warren as "the biggest damn-fool mistake I ever made." Eisenhower was especially upset with Court decisions on the rights of Communists and criminals. Other critics charged the Warren Court with usurping power from the states, the president, and Congress. Liberal supporters praised the Court for infusing new life into the Bill of Rights and serving as the nation's conscience.

In articulating the rights of disadvantaged groups, Supreme Court decisions in the 1950s and 1960s departed from judicial tradition and often got out ahead of legislators' sentiment and public opinion. Upsetting customary practices in race relations, personal liberty and privacy, criminal justice, political representation, and religion, the Warren Court's rulings protected the constitutional rights of marginal and powerless Americans—minorities, the poor and uneducated, and political dissenters.

Civil Rights and Voting Rights

Following the pathbreaking *Brown* decision, the Warren Court ruled against all-white public facilities in a number of cities and states and struck down educational plans devised by southern states to avoid integrating their schools. Moreover, by upholding the constitutional rights of African Americans to freedom of assembly and freedom of speech, the Court enabled the black freedom struggle to continue sit-ins, mass marches, and other civil disobedience tactics that were so critical to its success.

> *Upsetting customary practices in race relations, personal liberty and privacy, criminal justice, political representation, and religion, the Warren Court's rulings protected the constitutional rights of marginal and powerless Americans.*

Chief Justice Earl Warren considered *Baker v. Carr* (1963) the most important decision of his sixteen-year tenure. This case grew out of a complaint that Tennessee electoral districts were so inequitably drawn that sparsely populated rural districts had far more representatives in the state legislature than did densely populated metropolitan areas. Other states had also failed to redraw voting districts to reflect growing urban populations, thereby exaggerating the influence of rural interests. Congressional districts were less badly apportioned, but in some states they too diluted the power of urban and suburban voters in favor of rural constituents.

Grounding its decisions on the Fourteenth Amendment guarantee of "equal protection of the laws" in *Baker* and companion cases, the Court established the principle of "one person, one vote" for both houses of state legislatures and for the House of Representatives. Requiring most states to redraw electoral districts, the "one person, one vote" rulings helped to revitalize state legislatures and make them more responsive to metropolitan interests and problems. The decisions struck at entrenched power bases, and many politicians denounced them as unwarranted judicial intervention in political matters.

Criminal Justice

The egalitarian thrust of the Warren Court also touched the criminal justice system. Between 1957 and 1967, the Court overturned a series of convictions on the grounds that the accused individuals had been deprived of "life, liberty, or property, without due process of law" and thus had been denied their rights under the Fourteenth Amendment. Furthermore, the Court interpreted that amendment to prevent the states as well as the federal government from violations of the Bill of Rights. These rulings dramatically reformed law enforcement practices and the treatment of individuals accused of crime. As one plaintiff, Clarence Gideon, remarked, "I didn't start out to do anything for anybody but myself, but this decision has done a helluva lot of good."

In the case he initiated, *Gideon v. Wainright* (1963), the Court ruled that states must provide lawyers to poor people accused of serious crime who cannot afford to pay lawyers themselves. In *Escobedo v. Illinois* (1964), the justices extended the right to counsel to the period when suspects are being questioned by police officers. Two years later, in *Miranda v. Arizona*, the Court issued general guidelines requiring officers to inform suspects that they may remain silent, that anything they say can be used against them, and that they are entitled to a lawyer.

The Court established additional guidelines that law enforcement officials must follow in obtaining evidence. In a series of cases, it overturned convictions resulting from evidence obtained by unlawful arrest, by wiretapping and other kinds of electronic surveillance, and by entering property without a search warrant. These decisions pressured police officials to pay careful attention to suspects' rights, since evidence that was obtained illegally could not be used in court.

Critics accused the Supreme Court of letting criminals go free (Escobedo, in fact, ran afoul of the law soon after his release) and obstructing law enforcement. Liberals, however, argued that these rulings promoted equal treatment in the criminal justice system: The wealthy always had access to legal counsel, and practiced criminals were well aware of their right to remain silent. The beneficiaries of the decisions were the poor, the ignorant, and the weak as well as the general population whose right to privacy was strengthened by the Court's stricter guidelines for admissible evidence.

Dissent and Religious Issues

The Warren Court also strengthened protections for individuals suspected of being Communists or subversives. For example, it set limits on the states and federal government in investigating and prosecuting suspected subversives and prevented state bar associations from denying membership to those suspected of having Communist associations. Like the criminal justice cases, these rulings guaranteed the rights of people on the margins of American society and reaped their share of criticism.

The Warren Court's decisions on prayer and Bible reading in the public schools provoked even greater outrage. In *Abington School District v. Schempp* (1963), the Court overturned a Pennsylvania law requiring Bible reading and recitation of the Lord's Prayer at the beginning of the schoolday. Such a law, it ruled, violated the First Amendment principle of separation of church and state. Later decisions ruled out prayer in public schools even if students were not required to participate. An outraged Alabama legislator fumed, "They put Negroes in the schools and now they've driven God out." The Court's supporters, however, declared that the religion cases protected the rights of non-Christians and atheists.

Two or three justices, who believed that the Court was overstepping its authority, often issued sharp dissents in decisions on voting rights, criminal rights, and other cases. Outside the Court, opponents worked to pass laws or constitutional amendments that would upset despised decisions, legal experts pleaded for the Court to exercise judicial restraint, and billboards demanded, "Impeach Earl Warren." Nonetheless, the Court's major decisions withstood Warren's retirement in 1969 and the test of time.

The innovations of the Supreme Court in the 1950s and 1960s constituted a watershed in domestic policymaking. In expanding the Constitution's promise of equality and protection of individual rights, the Court shifted power from the states to the judicial branch of the federal government. The

Warren Court recast the Constitution from a document concerned primarily with restricting injustices by government to one requiring the government to act to prevent injustice and discrimination.

Conclusion: Achievements and Limitations of 1960s Liberalism

Surveying the record of the Johnson administration, Senate majority leader Mike Mansfield concluded that the president "has outstripped Roosevelt. . . . He has done more than FDR ever did, or ever thought of doing." Yet opposition to his leadership grew so strong by 1968 that Johnson abandoned hopes for reelection. As his liberal vision lay in ruins, he asked, "How was it possible that all these people could be so ungrateful to me after I have given them so much?"

The egomania reflected in that question was but one of several factors that contributed to Johnson's demise and the waning of Democratic liberalism. Inadequately planned and funded, many of the antipoverty programs ended up benefiting particular industries and the nonpoor as much as or more than they helped the impoverished. Because Johnson refused to ask for sacrifices from prosperous Americans, the Great Society never approached the redistribution of wealth and resources that would have been necessary for the elimination of poverty.

Black aspirations exceeded white Americans' commitment to genuine equality. It was easy for nonsoutherners to be sympathetic (and self-righteous) when a civil rights movement focused on crude and blatant forms of racism in the South. But when the movement attacked the subtler forms of racism that existed throughout the nation and sought equality in fact as well as in rights, the black freedom struggle confronted a powerful backlash.

Most surprising was the opposition to liberalism from the left. Radicalized by the black freedom struggle, a small but vocal minority of whites and blacks emphasized the shortcomings of the Great Society and questioned whether real reform could be achieved within the framework of traditional American institutions and values. Young radicals engaged in direct confrontations with the government and the universities that, together with racial conflict, escalated into political discord and social disorder not seen since the union wars of the 1930s.

The war in Vietnam polarized American society as much as did the question of race or the behavior of young people. Johnson's conduct of the war undermined faith in his leadership, as his darker side—his arrogance, vindictiveness, secrecy, and carelessness with the truth—manifested itself apace with the growing opposition to the war. The war starved the Great Society, devouring revenues that might have been used for social reform. Vietnam not only cut short the promise of reform; it also eclipsed the substantial progress that had actually been achieved.

CHRONOLOGY

1960 African American college students in Greensboro, North Carolina, stage sit-in at whites-only lunch counter.

John F. Kennedy elected president of United States.

Student Nonviolent Coordinating Committee (SNCC) established to mobilize young people for direct action for civil rights.

Students for a Democratic Society (SDS) founded.

1961 Congress of Racial Equality (CORE) sponsors Freedom Rides to desegregate interstate transportation in South.

President Kennedy establishes President's Commission on the Status of Women.

1963 *Baker v. Carr* mandates electoral redistricting to enforce "one-person, one-vote" principle.

Betty Friedan's best-selling book *The Feminine Mystique* published.

Equal Pay Act makes wage disparities based solely on gender illegal.

Mississippi NAACP leader Medgar Evers assassinated in Jackson.

Bayard Rustin organizes March on Washington, largest civil rights demonstration in U.S. history.

President's Commission on the Status of Women issues report detailing widespread discrimination against women.

President Kennedy assassinated in Dallas, Texas; Vice President Lyndon B. Johnson becomes president.

Cesar Chavez founds United Farm Workers Association (UFW).

1964 Congress enacts Civil Rights Act of 1964, the strongest such measure since Reconstruction.

Economic Opportunity Act passed.

Free Speech movement, first large-scale white student protest of 1960s, organized at University of California at Berkeley.

Malcolm X breaks from Nation of Islam and attracts wide following with his message of black pride and autonomy.

President Johnson elected to a full term in landslide over Republican Senator Barry Goldwater.

Tax cut bill proposed by Kennedy administration passed.

1965 Malcolm X assassinated in New York City.

Selma-to-Montgomery march for voting rights takes place; Johnson orders federal protection for marchers after they are attacked.

Congress passes Voting Rights Act.

1965– 89th Congress passes most of Johnson's
1966 Great Society domestic programs, including antipoverty measures, public works acts, aid to education, and Medicare-Medicaid.

1966 Black Panther Party founded, advocating African American economic and political autonomy.

In *Miranda v. Arizona*, Supreme Court requires police to inform suspects of their rights.

National Organization for Women (NOW) founded.

1968 The American Indian Movement (AIM) founded.

BIBLIOGRAPHY

GENERAL WORKS

John Morton Blum, *Years of Discord: American Politics and Society, 1961–1974* (1991).

David Farber, *The Age of Great Dreams: America in the 1960s* (1994).

Hugh Davis Graham, *The Civil Rights Era: Origins and Development of National Policy, 1960–1972* (1990).

Jim F. Heath, *Decade of Disillusionment: The Kennedy-Johnson Years* (1975).

Allen J. Matusow, *The Unraveling of America: A History of Liberalism in the 1960s* (1984).

Douglas T. Miller, *On Our Own: Americans in the Sixties* (1996).

Edward P. Morgan, *The Sixties Experience: Hard Lessons about Modern America* (1991).

William L. O'Neill, *Coming Apart: An Informal History of America in the 1960s* (1971).

Barbara L. Tischler, ed., *Sights on the Sixties* (1992).

Irwin Unger, *The Best of Intentions: The Triumph and Failure of the Great Society* (1996).

THE BLACK FREEDOM STRUGGLE

Peter J. Albert and Ronald Hoffman, eds., *We Shall Overcome: Martin Luther King, Jr., and the Black Freedom Struggle* (1990).

Jervis Anderson, *Bayard Rustin: Troubles I've Seen* (1997).

Taylor Branch, *Parting the Waters: America in the King Years, 1954–63* (1988).

Carl M. Brauer, *John F. Kennedy and the Second Reconstruction* (1977).

James W. Button, *Black Violence: Political Impact of the 1960s Riots* (1978).

Clayborne Carson, *In Struggle: SNCC and the Black Awakening of the 1960s* (1981).

David J. Garrow, *Protest at Selma: Martin Luther King, Jr., and the Voting Rights Act of 1965* (1978).

David J. Garrow, *Bearing the Cross: Martin Luther King, Jr., and the Southern Christian Leadership Conference* (1986).

Peter L. Goldman, *The Death and Life of Malcolm X* (1979).

Ralph G. Gomes and Linda Faye Williams, eds., *From Exclusion to Inclusion: The Long Struggle for African American Political Power* (1992).

James C. Harvey, *Black Civil Rights during the Johnson Administration* (1973).

Steven F. Lawson, *Black Ballots: Voting Rights in the South, 1944–1969* (1976).

Steven F. Lawson, *Running for Freedom: Civil Rights and Black Politics in America since 1941* (1991).

Doug McAdam, *Freedom Summer* (1989).

August Meier and Elliott M. Rudwick, *CORE: A Study in the Civil Rights Movement, 1942–1968* (1973).

Stephen B. Oates, *Let the Trumpet Sound: The Life of Martin Luther King, Jr.* (1982).

Charles Payne, *I've Got the Light of Freedom: The Organizing Tradition and the Mississippi Freedom Stuggle* (1995).

Kenneth O'Reilly, *"Racial Matters": The FBI's Secret File on Black America, 1960–1972* (1989).

Frank R. Parker, *Black Votes Count: Political Empowerment in Mississippi after 1965* (1990).

Bruce Perry, *Malcolm: The Life of a Man Who Changed Black America* (1991).

James R. Ralph Jr., *Northern Protest: Martin Luther King, Jr., Chicago, and the Civil Rights Movement* (1993).

William L. Van Deburg, *New Day in Babylon: The Black Power Movement and American Culture, 1965–1975* (1993).

POLITICS AND POLICIES OF THE NEW FRONTIER AND GREAT SOCIETY

Henry J. Aaron, *Politics and the Professors: The Great Society in Perspective* (1978).

Vaughn Davis Bornet, *The Presidency of Lyndon B. Johnson* (1983).

David Burner, *John F. Kennedy and a New Generation* (1988).

Robert Caro, *The Years of Lyndon Johnson*, vols. 1 and 2 (1982, 1990).

Paul K. Conkin, *Big Daddy from the Pedernales: Lyndon Baines Johnson* (1986).

Robert A. Divine, ed., *Exploring the Johnson Years* (1981).

Robert Alan Goldberg, *Barry Goldwater* (1995).

Eric Goldman, *The Tragedy of Lyndon Johnson* (1969).

Doris Kearns, *Lyndon Johnson and the American Dream* (1976).

Sar Levitan and Robert Taggart, *The Promise of Greatness* (1976).

Robert Mann, *The Walls of Jericho: Lyndon Johnson, Hubert Humphrey, Richard Russell, and the Struggle for Civil Rights* (1996).

Gerald Posner, *Case Closed: Lee Harvey Oswald and the Assassination of JFK* (1993).

Jill Quadagno, *The Color of Welfare: How Racism Undermined the War on Poverty* (1994).

Richard Reeves, *President Kennedy: Profile of Power* (1993).

Mark Stern, *Calculating Visions: Kennedy, Johnson, and Civil Rights* (1992).

James L. Sundquist, *Politics and Policy: The Eisenhower, Kennedy, and Johnson Years* (1968).

PROTEST MOVEMENTS

Terry H. Anderson, *The Movement and the Sixties* (1995).

Stewart Burns, *Social Movements of the 1960s: Searching for Democracy* (1990).

David Chalmers, *And the Crooked Places Made Straight: The Struggle for Social Change in the 1960s* (1991).

Martha F. Davis, *Brutal Need: Lawyers and the Welfare Rights Movement, 1960–1973* (1993).

Vine Deloria Jr., *Behind the Trail of Broken Treaties* (1974).

Alice Echols, *Daring to Be Bad: Radical Feminism in America, 1967–1975* (1989).

Sara Evans, *Personal Liberation: The Roots of Women's Liberation in the Civil Rights Movement and the New Left* (1978).

Jo Freeman, *The Politics of Liberation* (1975).

Ignacio M. Garcia, *United We Win: The Rise and Fall of La Raza Unida Party* (1989).

Todd Gitlin, *The Sixties: Years of Hope, Days of Rage* (1987).

Juan Gómez-Quiñones, *Chicano Politics: Reality and Promise, 1940–1990* (1990).

Richard Griswold del Castillo and Richard A. Garcia, *Cesar Chavez: A Triumph of Spirit* (1995).

Cynthia Harrison, *On Account of Sex: The Politics of Women's Issues, 1945–1968* (1988).

Laurence M. Hauptman, *The Iroquois Struggle for Survival: World War II to Red Power* (1986).

Maurice Isserman, *If I Had a Hammer . . . : The Death of the Old Left and the Birth of the New Left* (1987).

George Katsiaficas, *The Imagination of the New Left: A Global Analysis of 1968* (1987).

Cyril Levitt, *Children of Privilege: Student Revolt in the Sixties* (1984).

Peter B. Levy, *The New Left and Labor in the 1960s* (1994).

Peter Matthiessen, *In the Spirit of Crazy Horse* (1983).

James Miller, *"Democracy Is in the Streets": From Port Huron to the Siege of Chicago* (1987).

Joan Moore and Harry Pachon, *Hispanics in the United States* (1985).

Donald L. Parman, *Indians and the American West in the Twentieth Century* (1994).

Manuel P. Servin, *An Awakened Minority: The Mexican Americans* (2nd ed., 1974).

William Wei, *The Asian American Movement* (1993).

THE SUPREME COURT

Archibald Cox, *The Warren Court: Constitutional Decision as an Instrument of Reform* (1968).

Richard Y. Funston, *Constitutional Counterrevolution? The Warren Court and the Burger Court: Judicial Policy Making in Modern America* (1977).

Philip B. Kurland, *Politics and the Warren Court* (1970).

Paul L. Murphy, *The Constitution in Crisis Times, 1918–1969* (1972).

Bernard Schwartz, *Super Chief: Earl Warren and His Supreme Court, a Judicial Biography* (1983).

Melvin I. Urofsky, *The Continuity of Change: The Supreme Court and Individual Liberties, 1953–1986* (1991).

FATIGUE HAT WITH PROTEST BUTTONS
The button on this fatigue hat of a veteran who had served two tours of duty evinces veterans' response to the many Americans who just wanted to forget the war that the United States had failed to win. Because their war was so different from other American wars, Vietnam veterans often came home to hostility or indifference. The POW-MIA pin referred to prisoners of war and those missing in action.

Nancy Gewitz/Antique Textile Resource/Picture Resource Consultants, Inc.

VIETNAM AND THE LIMITS OF POWER

29

1961–1975

A s CHARLES ANDERSON'S PLANE PREPARED TO LAND, the pilot announced, "Gentlemen, we'll be touching down in Da Nang, Vietnam, in about ten minutes. . . . Fasten your seat belts, please. On behalf of the entire crew and staff, I'd like to say we've enjoyed having you with us . . . and we hope to see all of you again next year on your way home. Goodbye and good luck." As did most soldiers after 1966, Charles Anderson went to war on a commercial jetliner, complete with stewardesses (as they were called then) in miniskirts.

Military personnel traveling to battle as if they were businessmen or tourists was not the only thing that made the Vietnam War so different from America's previous wars. Marine infantry officer Philip Caputo landed at Da Nang in March 1965 confident that the enemy "would be quickly beaten and that we were doing something altogether noble and good." But in just a few months, "what had begun as an adventurous expedition had turned into an exhausting, indecisive war of attrition in which we fought for no other cause than our own survival."

Another soldier discovered even more quickly that "something was wrong." Wondering why the bus taking him from the air base to the compound had wire mesh over the windows, he was told, "It's the gooks man. . . . The gooks will throw grenades through the windows." Looking out, he saw "shriveled, little old men squatting beside the road. . . . They looked up at me with real contempt on their faces. Here we are at one of the largest military installations in the world and we have to cover the windows to protect ourselves from little old men."

Soldiers in Vietnam initially used the racist word *gook* to refer to the enemy— the North Vietnamese or their supporters in the South—but it quickly became a term used for any Vietnamese. "From one day to the next, you could see for yourself changes coming over guys on our side—decent fellows, who wouldn't dream of calling an Oriental a 'gook' back home," reported one American. The problem was that in this civil war, "they couldn't tell who was their friend and who wasn't. Day after day, out on patrol we'd come to . . . a shabby village, and the elders would welcome us and the children come running with smiles on their faces, waiting for the candy we'd give them. But . . . just as we were leaving the village behind, the enemy would open up on us, and there was bitterness among us that the villagers hadn't given us warning."

Americans' horrifying and bewildering experiences in Vietnam grew out of cold war commitments made in the 1940s and 1950s by presidents Harry S. Truman and Dwight D. Eisenhower. John F. Kennedy wholeheartedly took on those commitments, promising more innovative, flexible, and vigorous efforts to thwart communism. In the most memorable words of his inaugural address he declared, "Let every nation know, whether it wishes us well or ill, that we shall pay any price, bear any burden, meet any hardship, support any friend, oppose any foe to assure the survival and the success of liberty."

Kennedy asked the American people to pay a steep price. It included enormous increases in spending to bolster U.S. nuclear superiority and arm the country for both conventional and guerrilla warfare. Moreover, when the Soviet Union attempted to install nuclear missiles in Cuba in 1962, Kennedy asked Americans to risk nuclear war to stand up to the Soviets.

The conflict in Vietnam became the foremost test of what the United States would or could do to "assure the survival and the success of liberty." Kennedy sent increasing amounts of American arms and personnel to help sustain the South Vietnamese government, and Johnson dramatically escalated that commitment. By 1965, the civil war in Vietnam had become America's war.

The Americanization of the war increased the number of U.S. military personnel in Vietnam to 540,000 at peak strength in 1968 and to more than three million total throughout the war's duration. Yet not only did this massive intervention fail to defeat the North Vietnamese and their allies in South Vietnam, but it added a new burden to the costs of fighting the cold war—intense discord among the people at home. Believing that the war was immoral or futile, hundreds of thousands of Americans protested it.

The Vietnam War cost President Johnson another term in office and contributed to the political demise of his Republican successor, Richard M. Nixon. Nixon gradually withdrew ground troops, but neither efforts to strengthen the South Vietnamese nor ferocious bombing campaigns daunted the enemy. The peace treaty signed in 1973 did little more than provide a short interval between American withdrawal and victory for the North Vietnamese.

Lieutenant David Donovan, sent to Vietnam as a counterinsurgency expert, gave a bitter twist to Kennedy's rousing inaugural words. In Vietnam, according to Donovan, the United States found "a price too high, a burden too heavy, a friend too incompetent, a foe too intractable for us to continue to hold high the cause of liberty." Those who agreed with Donovan lauded the American goal in Vietnam and damned only the nation's unwillingness

to pursue it effectively. Others believed that preserving a non-Communist South Vietnam was neither in the best interests of the United States nor within its capacity to achieve.

But none could deny the war's enormous costs. "The promises of the Great Society have been shot down on the battlefield of Vietnam," said Martin Luther King Jr. In addition to derailing domestic reform, the Vietnam War inflicted a heavy cost in American lives and dollars, kindled internal conflict and disorder, and led to the violation of the rights of antiwar protesters. With the exception of the African American freedom struggle, no post-World War II event affected Americans so intensely.

New Frontiers in Foreign Policy

John F. Kennedy moved quickly to fulfill his campaign promises of a tougher, more aggressive, more flexible foreign policy. He embraced the goal of containment and believed that the United States could pursue it much more effectively than his predecessors had done. With his like-minded secretary of defense, Robert S. McNamara, Kennedy expanded the nation's nuclear arsenal, increased its ability to fight conventional battles, and developed its capability for combating guerrilla warfare. To ensure U.S. superiority over the Soviet Union in every area, Kennedy accelerated the nation's space exploration program and increased American attention to the third world, with new programs to promote economic development, political stability, and friendly governments.

Believing that Eisenhower's caution and passivity had encouraged Soviet and Chinese expansion, and mindful of charges that he was too young and inexperienced, Kennedy resolved to present a tough posture. To demonstrate his unflinching determination to halt communism, he took the United States to the brink of nuclear war during the 1962 Cuban missile crisis. Less dramatically, but no less tenaciously, Kennedy stepped up American contributions of arms, aid, and personnel to save the government of South Vietnam from Communist insurgents. During his last months in office, Kennedy moved to decrease Soviet-American tensions, but he did not waver from his commitment to South Vietnam.

Meeting the "Hour of Maximum Danger"

Kennedy and other Democrats criticized the Eisenhower administration for placing too much reliance on nuclear weapons, thereby denying the nation a "flexible response" to Communist expansion. Moreover, Kennedy charged, Eisenhower's desire to limit defense spending had allowed the United States to fall behind even in nuclear capability, thereby creating a "missile gap" with the Soviet Union. In January 1961, Kennedy warned that the nation faced a grave peril: "Each day the crises multiply. . . . Each day we draw nearer the hour of maximum danger."

Although Kennedy exaggerated the actual threat to national security, several developments in 1961 heightened the sense of crisis and provided rationalization for a military buildup. In a speech made shortly before Kennedy's inauguration, Soviet Premier Nikita Khrushchev had encouraged "wars of national liberation," thereby aligning the Soviet Union with independence (usually anti-Western) movements in the third world. Khrushchev wanted to bolster Soviet leadership of the Communist world, which was then being challenged by the People's Republic of China; and he needed to shore up his political position at home by projecting forcefulness abroad. U.S. officials, however, interpreted Khrushchev's words as signaling new efforts to upset the status quo of containment.

The status quo had already shifted in 1959, when Fidel Castro's revolution moved Cuba—only ninety miles from the United States—into the Soviet orbit. Under Eisenhower, the CIA had been planning an invasion by anti-Castro exiles. Kennedy ordered the invasion to proceed even though his military advisers gave it only a "fair" chance of success. To do otherwise, the president

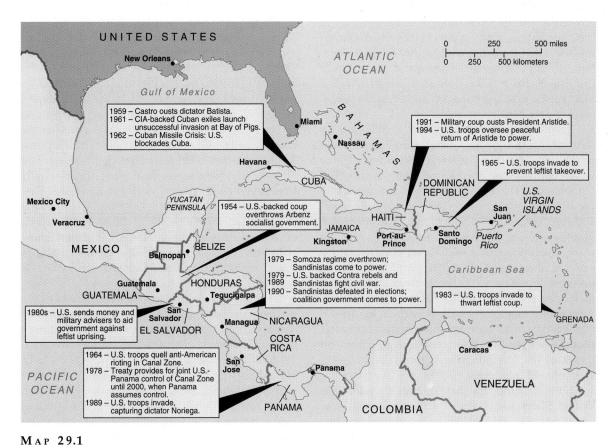

M AP 29.1
U.S. Involvement in Latin America and the Caribbean, 1954–1996
During the Cold War, the U.S. frequently intervened in Central American and Caribbean countries to suppress Communist or leftist movements.

felt, would create an appearance of weakness. Kennedy believed that to deal effectively with the Soviets, the United States had to do more than simply possess superior power. The nation also had to demonstrate the will to exercise that power and to project an image of strength.

To demonstrate his unflinching determination to halt communism, Kennedy took the United States to the brink of nuclear war during the 1962 Cuban missile crisis.

Kennedy's efforts to hide the American role in the Cuban invasion resulted in an operation that was poorly planned, inadequately manned, and without sufficient air and naval support. On April 17, 1961, about 1,300 anti-Castro exiles, who had been trained and armed by the CIA, landed at the Bay of Pigs on the south shore of Cuba. Contrary to the anticipation of the planners, who had gravely miscalculated the sentiments of the Cuban population, no popular uprising materialized to support the anti-Castro brigade. Kennedy would not provide direct military support, and Castro's forces quickly defeated the invaders.

The Bay of Pigs disaster was humiliating for Kennedy and the United States. Although Kennedy refused direct military intervention, no one in the world doubted that the United States was behind the invasion. The attempted armed interference in the affairs of another nation compromised the moral authority of the United States, and its failure raised questions about the wisdom and effectiveness of U.S. foreign policy and military strategy. The invasion also increased Cubans' support for Castro, reinforced Cuba's ties to the Soviet Union, and evoked memories of Yankee imperialism among Latin American nations. The sorry debacle at the Bay of Pigs posed a stark contrast to Kennedy's inaugural promise of a new, more effective foreign policy and increased his determination to project an image of strength and toughness.

Shortly before the Bay of Pigs invasion, the United States had suffered a psychological blow when Soviet astronaut Yuri Gagarin orbited the earth, the first human to do so. In the late 1950s, the Eisenhower administration had stepped up American research on space exploration in response to *Sputnik*, the Soviet satellite that had orbited the earth. But the United States still lagged behind in "manned" spaceflight competition, having sent

only monkeys into space on suborbital missiles. The first American entered the new frontier in space on May 5, 1961, when Alan B. Shepard Jr. made a three-hundred-mile flight.

That same month, Kennedy called for a huge new commitment to the space race, which he clearly viewed as one element of U.S.-Soviet competition. "If we are to win the battle that is now going on around the world between freedom and tyranny," he told Congress, the United States must "take a clearly leading role in space achievement." His goal: an American on the moon within six to eight years. Congress authorized the Apollo program and substantially boosted appropriations for space exploration. In 1962, John H. Glenn orbited the earth, less than a year behind the Soviets. And in 1969, the United States surpassed the Soviet Union in the space race when two Americans, Neil A. Armstrong and Edwin E. ("Buzz") Aldrin Jr., became the first humans to set foot on the moon.

In the early months of his presidency, Kennedy sought a meeting with Khrushchev. "I have to show him that we can be as tough as he is," Kennedy said. "I'll have to sit down with him and let him see who he's dealing with." Their meeting took place in Vienna, Austria, in June 1961. Contrary to his expectations, Kennedy met a strident, belligerent, and threatening Khrushchev, and the president left the meeting with his confidence shaken. British Prime Minister Harold Macmillan noted that Kennedy had "for the first time in his life . . . met a man wholly impervious to his charm." To journalist James Reston, the shocked president reported, "He just beat [the] hell out of me. . . . If he thinks I'm inexperienced and have no guts . . . we won't get anywhere with him. . . . Now we have a problem in trying to make our power credible, and Vietnam looks like the place."

The immediate problem was Berlin, one of the earliest points of conflict in the cold war. Khrushchev demanded an agreement recognizing the existence of two Germanys; otherwise, he warned, the Soviets would sign a separate treaty with East Germany. Should this happen, the Soviet Union would no longer recognize American occupation rights in and access to West Berlin, which lay some one hundred miles within East Germany. Kennedy held his ground. Returning home, he ordered more troops to Europe and a large increase in military forces. West Berlin, he declared, was "the great testing place of Western courage and will."

A major embarrassment for the Communists was the massive exodus of East Germans into West

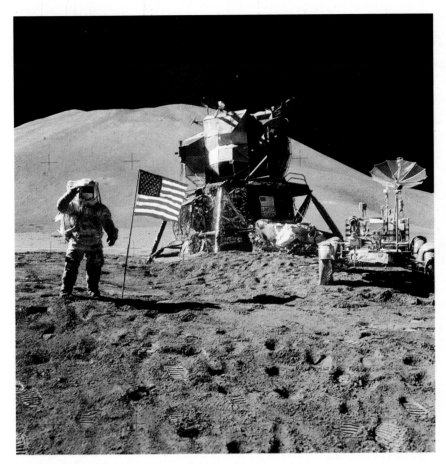

HUMANS REACH THE MOON
In July 1969, less than a decade after President John F. Kennedy announced the goal of "landing a man on the moon and returning him safely to the earth," the space capsule Apollo 11 *carried astronauts Edwin E. Aldrin Jr. and Neil A. Armstrong to the moon. As millions of people watched on television, Armstrong became the first human to step on the moon's surface, saying, "That's one small step for a man, one giant leap for mankind." Armstrong and Aldrin collected rock samples and conducted scientific experiments. Other missions to the moon followed. In this 1971 photograph of the* Apollo 15 *mission, astronaut James B. Irwin salutes near the lunar module and lunar roving vehicle.*
NASA/Johnson Space Center.

Berlin. To stop the flow of escapees from behind the iron curtain, on August 13, 1961, East Germany stunned the world by erecting a wall between East and West Berlin. To Kennedy, the wall was "a hell of a lot better than a war," and the United States did not interfere, although at one point in the crisis, armed American tanks faced off with Soviet tanks less than a football field away. With the Berlin Wall stemming the tide of East German migration, Khrushchev backed off from his threats. But not until 1972 did the superpowers settle the issue of the two Germanys with recognition of East and West Germany as separate nations and a guarantee of Western access to West Berlin.

Kennedy used the Berlin crisis to diversify and fortify the nation's military establishment. In the summer of 1961, he got Congress to add $3.2 billion to the defense budget. By increasing draft calls and mobilizing the reserves and National Guard, he expanded the size of the military by 300,000. This buildup in conventional forces met Kennedy's demand for "a wider choice than humiliation or all-out nuclear action" by providing a "flexible re-

sponse" strategy. When the Soviet Union terminated its three-year moratorium on nuclear testing, the United States followed suit, and Kennedy pushed the development of new nuclear weapons and delivery systems.

New Approaches to the Third World

Kennedy administration officials believed that they had found new ways to deal with the wave of nationalism, reform, and revolutionary movements that had convulsed the world since the end of World War II. Much more than his predecessors had, the president publicly supported third world democratic and nationalist aspirations. He proposed that foreign aid be based on the recipient country's willingness to undertake democratic reform. By helping to fulfill hopes for independence and democracy, he asserted, the United States could win the hearts and minds of people in the developing nations.

To that end, Kennedy created the Alliance for Progress, promising $20 billion in aid for Latin America over the next decade. Like the Marshall

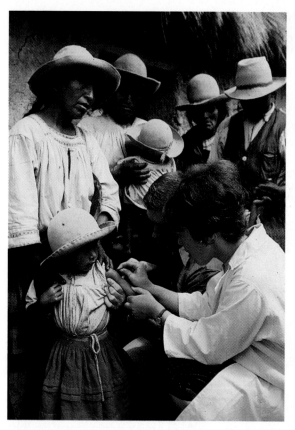

PEACE CORPS VOLUNTEERS IN BOLIVIA

The majority of Peace Corps volunteers worked on educational projects in developing countries. Others helped to increase food production, build public works, and curb diseases, as did these volunteers vaccinating a young Bolivian girl. President John F. Kennedy saw the Peace Corps volunteers, with their dedication to freedom, "overcoming the efforts of Mr. Khrushchev's missionaries who are dedicated to undermining that freedom." In the course of their missions, however, some volunteers came to question the single-minded focus of U.S. policy on anticommunism. David S. Boyer©National Geographic Society.

Plan, the Alliance for Progress was a cold war measure designed to thwart communism and hold nations within the American sphere by fostering economic development. Kennedy also brought foreign assistance programs together in a new Agency for International Development (AID) and reversed the emphasis from military to economic aid. With an idea borrowed from Senator Hubert H. Humphrey, Kennedy launched his most dramatic third world initiative. He established the Peace Corps in 1961, under the direction of his brother-in-law R. Sargent Shriver.

The Peace Corps exemplified the idealism and sacrifice that Kennedy had called for in his inaugural address. One volunteer spoke of easing his conscience "that I and my peers were born between clean sheets when others were issued into the dust with a birthright of hunger." Peace Corps volunteers studied a country's language and culture before going to work directly with its people. Some seven thousand of them by the end of Kennedy's presidency and more than sixty thousand by the mid-1970s fanned out around the globe, serving two-year stints in villages in Latin America, Africa, and Asia, where they opened schools, provided basic health care, assisted with agriculture and nutrition projects, and helped develop small economic enterprises.

Nonetheless, Kennedy's foreign aid initiatives fell far short of their objectives. Though almost universally welcomed, Peace Corps projects numbered too few to make a dent in the poverty and suffering in third world countries struggling to develop their economies. By 1969, the United States had provided only half of the $20 billion promised to the Alliance for Progress. Much of the aid was military, and ruling elites in the receiving countries skimmed off a large part while failing to initiate meaningful social and economic reforms. In addition, a soaring birthrate in Latin America counteracted most of the gains made in economic productivity, and these nations increasingly bore burdens of foreign indebtedness.

Kennedy did not neglect more direct, military means to bring political stability to the third world. Although his speeches aligned the United States with popular movements seeking independence and better living conditions, he drew the line at uprisings that appeared to have Communist connections or goals. Thus his actions frequently contradicted his words. Even when increasing hostility between the Soviet Union and Communist China presented an opportunity for improving U.S. relations with China, Kennedy continued to adhere to the basic tenet of the cold war: that communism was a monolithic force and had to be contained, no matter what form it took. To that end, he promoted counterinsurgency forces to put down revolutions or insurrections that smacked of communism.

The showcase of the administration's counterinsurgency strategy was an elite corps from the army, air force, navy, and coast guard that was trained to wage unconventional warfare. Called "special forces," the corps had been established under the Eisenhower administration to aid groups that were sympathetic to the United States in their fight against Communist-leaning national liberation movements. Kennedy rapidly expanded the special forces and authorized their new name and official headgear, the green beret, which he called "a mark of distinction in the fight for freedom." He sought to recruit the best officers and enlisted men for the Green Berets and to make them a highly disciplined, daring force, equipped with the latest technology and trained for guerrilla warfare.

The Arms Race and the Nuclear Brink

The final piece of the Kennedy-McNamara defense strategy involved U.S. nuclear strength. Kennedy realized quickly that the "missile gap" he had warned about during the 1960 campaign was a myth, but that knowledge did not lessen his determination to make the United States even stronger. Because the Soviets had the ability to expand their own nuclear arsenal, Kennedy and McNamara reasoned that the United States should push ahead to enlarge its superiority. The drive for nuclear dominance continued into the Johnson administration. By then, the United States had increased the number of nuclear weapons based in Europe from 2,500 to 7,200, and it had multiplied fivefold its supply of intercontinental ballistic missiles (ICBMs).

To the Soviets, the American nuclear buildup suggested that the United States wanted not just superiority, but the capacity to launch a first strike, wiping out the Soviet missile sites before the Soviets could respond. The Kremlin therefore stepped up its own ICBM program, and the most intense arms race ever ensued. McNamara would later conclude that the U.S. superiority was "in fact more than we require[d]." Despite the enormous American buildup, the Soviets were closer to parity with the United States when McNamara resigned in 1967 than they had been in 1961.

In October 1962, the superpowers came perilously close to using those weapons of terror, when Cuba once again took center stage. During the summer of 1962, Khrushchev made his biggest gamble of all: He decided to install nuclear missiles in Cuba. When American U-2 spy planes spotted defensive, surface-to-air missiles in Cuba, Kennedy warned the Soviets not to attempt to install offensive, ground-to-ground missiles.

The Soviet ambassador to the United States conveyed assurances from Khrushchev that they had no such intentions. But on October 16, 1962, the CIA showed Kennedy new surveillance pho-

tographs that exposed Khrushchev's lie. Launching sites in Cuba were being constructed for missiles that had ranges of one thousand and twenty-two hundred miles. The ensuing thirteen-day Cuban missile crisis brought the world closer to nuclear annihilation than ever before or since.

Working with a small group of top advisers meeting secretly and daily during the crisis, Kennedy developed the American position. Though determined to keep offensive missiles out of Cuba, he rejected suggestions for nuclear or conventional strikes against the sites or an invasion of the island. On October 22, the president told a television audience that he had placed the military on full alert and was imposing a "strict quarantine on all offensive military equipment" headed from the Soviet Union to Cuba. The U.S. navy would stop, search, and, if necessary, turn back any Soviet vessel suspected of carrying offensive missiles to Cuba. (Only later did the United States find out that offensive missiles were already in Cuba.) Kennedy warned Khrushchev that any attack launched from Cuba would trigger a full nuclear attack against the Soviet Union.

The president called the missiles an "unjustified change in the status quo which cannot be accepted . . . if our courage and our commitments are ever to be trusted again either by friend or foe." Kennedy's aides later conceded that the missiles would not in reality have shifted the balance of power. As McNamara put it, "It makes no great difference whether you're killed by a missile fired from the Soviet Union or from Cuba." But to Kennedy, projecting the appearance of toughness was paramount. According to his speechwriter, Theodore Sorensen, although the missiles did not "alter the strategic balance in fact . . . that balance would have been substantially altered in appearance; and in matters of national will and world leadership . . . such appearances contribute to reality."

Although Kennedy was willing to risk nuclear war for appearances, he also exercised considerable caution. To avoid a confrontation, which neither side wanted, he refused advice from the military to bomb the missile sites and instead called for the quarantine to allow time for negotiations. On October 24, Russian ships carrying nuclear warheads suddenly stopped or turned back. Secretary of State Dean Rusk then remarked, "We are eyeball to eyeball, and I think the other fellow just blinked." Kennedy matched Khrushchev's restraint. When one ship crossed the blockade line, he ordered the navy to follow it rather than to attempt to stop it.

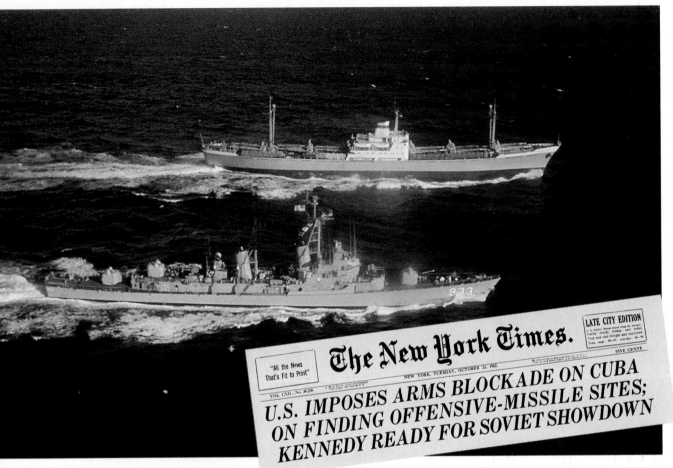

THE CUBAN MISSILE CRISIS
In October 1962, President John F. Kennedy dispatched more than one hundred U.S. ships to
quarantine Cuba and prevent the importation of Soviet offensive nuclear missiles. After Soviet
leader Nikita Khrushchev agreed to remove the missiles already in Cuba, the U.S. navy continued
to monitor the movement of Soviet ships. Here the U.S.S. Barry steams alongside a Soviet
freighter, outbound from Cuba and carrying military equipment.
Corbis-Bettmann.

"We don't want to push him [Khrushchev] to a pre-cipitous action," he said. But a small number of Americans believed that Kennedy helped create a crisis, playing "chicken, with mankind on the bumpers."

While Americans experienced the most fearful days of the cold war, Kennedy and Khrushchev exchanged offers and counteroffers. Finally, the Soviets removed the missiles and pledged not to introduce new offensive weapons into Cuba. In exchange, the United States promised not to invade the island. Secretly, the United States also agreed to remove its own missiles based in Turkey and aimed at the Soviet Union, a decision that Kennedy had made months before but had not implemented.

Although the United States' no-invasion promise was face-saving for Khrushchev, in miscalculating the resolution of Kennedy he lost badly. As a result, the Soviets suffered in their contest with China for the allegiance of third world countries, and Khrushchev himself was so weakened that he was deposed two years later. Kennedy emerged triumphant. The image of a new, inexperienced president fumbling the Bay of Pigs invasion and being bullied by Khrushchev in Vienna gave way to that of a brilliant leader combining firmness with restraint and bearing the United States through its "hour of maximum danger."

Having proved his toughness, Kennedy could afford to be conciliatory. After the Cuban missile crisis, the president acted to reduce the danger of future confrontations. He and Khrushchev agreed to install a special telephone "hot line" to speed top-level communication in moments of crisis. In a major speech at American University in June 1963, Kennedy called for a reexamination of the assumptions of the cold war. Appealing for a greater understanding of the Soviet Union, he asked Americans "not to see only a distorted and desperate view of the other side, not to see conflict as inevitable." Acknowledging that the superpowers could not quickly resolve all their differences, Kennedy pointed to what they had in common: "We all inhabit this small planet. We all breathe the same air. We all cherish our children's future and we are all mortal."

Responding in part to pressures from scientists and other Americans alarmed by the dangers of nuclear testing and the threat of nuclear war, Kennedy called for an end to "a vicious cycle" in which "new weapons beget counterweapons." The United States would stop testing nuclear weapons aboveground and begin negotiations with the Soviet Union for a permanent ban on nuclear testing, he announced. In August 1963, the United States, the Soviet Union, and Great Britain signed a limited test-ban treaty, a goal that had eluded Eisenhower. Because France and China refused to sign, the agreement failed to stop the proliferation of nuclear weapons, and it did not apply to underground testing. The limited test ban did, however, reduce the threat of radioactive fallout from nuclear testing, and it raised hopes for accommodation between the superpowers on other issues.

Venturing into a Quagmire in Vietnam

Whether the new approach to the cold war that Kennedy outlined at American University could have been realized was left forever unanswered by his assassination. It was clear, however, that the new approach did not mean abandoning efforts to save the South Vietnamese government from its Communist foes and their supporters. Kennedy had criticized the idea of "a Pax Americana enforced on the world by American weapons of war," but he continued to increase the flow of those weapons into South Vietnam.

The foreign policy setbacks during Kennedy's first six months in office suggested the need to make a strong stand somewhere. As he remarked to an associate, "There are just so many concessions that one can make to the Communists in one year and survive politically." Kennedy also remembered the political blows to the Democratic Party when in 1949 "China was lost....We don't want that." Moreover, the pro-United States government in Laos, which bordered Vietnam, also confronted insurrection, and Kennedy subscribed to the falling domino theory enunciated by Eisenhower.

Kennedy's strong anticommunism, his interpretation of "the lessons of history," and his commitment to a tough, activist foreign policy prepared him to take a stand in Vietnam. The new counterinsurgency program provided the means. Kennedy's key military adviser, General Maxwell Taylor, thought that Vietnam would be a good testing ground for the Green Berets. Author of the "flexible response" strategy, Taylor believed that holding firm in Vietnam would show the Soviets that wars of national liberation were not "cheap, safe, and disavowable [but] costly, dangerous, and doomed to failure."

> *Kennedy's strong anticommunism, his interpretation of "the lessons of history," and his commitment to a tough, activist foreign policy prepared him to take a stand in Vietnam.*

Two major problems, however, undercut Taylor's analysis. First, the South Vietnamese insurgents—called Vietcong, short for Viet Nam Cong-san ("Vietnamese Communists"), by the Americans—were a genuine indigenous force, whose initiative came from within, not from the Soviet Union or China. Even Ho Chi Minh's Communist government in North Vietnam did not begin to supply the rebels in the South with weapons or soldiers until 1959, after local insurgents had initiated guerrilla activities against the South Vietnamese government on their own. Because the government in South Vietnam had failed to hold the elections promised in the Geneva accords and, in fact, was doing everything possible to exterminate its opponents, the rebels saw no choice but to take up arms.

The second problem lay in the South Vietnamese government and army (the Armed Forces of the Republic of Vietnam, or ARVN), which proved to be ineffective vehicles for the American goal of suppressing wars of liberation. The government in Saigon consistently avoided economic reforms that could have gained popular support. In fact, its corruption and repression of opponents of all stripes alienated growing portions of the South Vietnamese population, not just the Communists. Ngo Dinh Diem, South Vietnamese premier from 1954 to 1963, chose military leaders for their personal loyalty, and they, in turn, made decisions to protect their own positions rather than to defeat the enemy.

The growing intervention by North Vietnam made matters worse. In 1960, the Hanoi government established the National Liberation Front (NLF), composed of South Vietnamese rebels but directed by the North. Although the NLF recruited most of its forces from among the South Vietnamese and fought largely with American weapons captured from ARVN, Hanoi constructed a network of infiltration routes (called the "Ho Chi Minh Trail") in neighboring Laos through which it sent people and supplies to help liberate the South. Violence escalated between 1960 and 1963, and the Saigon government seemed close to collapse.

When Kennedy took office, more than $1 billion of aid and about seven hundred military advisers from the United States had failed to stabilize the South Vietnamese government. Some Kennedy aides urged applying any force necessary to save South Vietnam from communism. Opposing views came from two advisers who believed that the Saigon government was unsalvageable. W. Averell Harriman, former diplomat and foreign policy adviser under Roosevelt and Truman, thought that the United States should not "stake its prestige in Vietnam," and Undersecretary of State Chester Bowles warned that the country was "headed full blast up a dead end street."

Kennedy resisted pressure for an all-out effort, but beginning in the spring of 1961, he gradually escalated the American commitment. He remained skeptical about the prospects for victory and suspicious of the continuing pressure for additional forces. "It's like taking a drink," he said. "The effect wears off, and you have to take another." Yet he would not bring himself to abandon the commitment. Between 1961 and 1962, Kennedy doubled the amount of military aid and increased to nine thousand the number of American military advisers, whose activities expanded from training and advice to occasional participation in the fighting. Although

the United States extracted new promises of reform from Diem with every increase of aid, the South Vietnamese government never made good on them.

Kennedy and most of his advisers assumed that the latest military technology and sheer vastness of U.S. power would eventually stem the Communist tide in South Vietnam. Yet that power and technology was ill suited to a guerrilla-type war, and it hurt the very people it meant to save. Military personnel had trouble distinguishing the Vietcong and their supporters from the general population. Thousands of peasants were uprooted from their land and villages (which in Vietnamese culture are sacred) and resettled in new "strategic hamlets," where they were supposed to be out of the reach of the Communists. Those left in the countryside suffered bombing and strafing by South Vietnamese forces, which used bombs containing the highly flammable substance napalm. In January 1962, United States planes began to spray leaf and plant killers such as Agent Orange in efforts to wipe out the Vietcong's jungle hideouts and devastate their food supply.

A new threat to the South Vietnamese government developed in 1963, as Buddhist monks protested the repressive and unrepresentative nature of Diem's Catholic-dominated government. ARVN troops shot at Buddhist demonstrators, triggering more protests and extreme actions by individual monks, who committed suicide by dousing themselves with gasoline and setting themselves on fire. Diem resisted U.S. demands that he stop persecuting the Buddhists, and in August 1963, U.S. officials signaled ARVN officers that Diem's overthrow would not be unwelcome.

South Vietnamese military leaders effected a coup on November 2, 1963, brutally executing Diem and his brother Ngo Dinh Nhu, who headed the secret police. The killings shocked Kennedy, but in the three weeks he had left to live, he gave no indication of any change in policy. In a speech scheduled to be given in Dallas on the very day he was assassinated, Kennedy would have called Americans to their responsibilities as "the watchmen on the walls of world freedom." Referring specifically to Southeast Asia, his undelivered speech warned, "We dare not weary of the task."

Though never going as far or as fast as his military advisers advocated, Kennedy radically raised the U.S. stakes in Vietnam. At his death, sixteen thousand Americans served in Vietnam, and one hundred of them had died there. He bequeathed to

Lyndon Johnson a vastly expanded commitment to a South Vietnamese government that was no more in control than it had been before the infusion of American power.

Lyndon Johnson's War against Communism

Following the basic outlines of Kennedy's foreign policy, Johnson retained his predecessor's key foreign policy and military officials. Secretary of Defense McNamara continued the massive buildup of nuclear weapons and conventional and counterinsurgency forces that had begun in the early 1960s. At the same time, Johnson built on the less hostile climate between the United States and the Soviet Union that had followed the Cuban missile crisis. In 1968, he signed a nuclear nonproliferation agreement with the Soviet Union, Britain, and fifty-eight nonnuclear nations, and he initiated plans for Soviet-American negotiations to control the arms race.

Johnson's adherence to the basic assumptions of the cold war was manifested in his approach to Latin America and Southeast Asia, two major trouble spots that had consumed Kennedy's attention. In 1965, when the South Vietnamese government approached collapse, Johnson took the fateful steps of ordering U.S. troops into combat and initiating sustained bombing of the North. Yet even this enormous intervention did not break the enemy's capability. That same year, closer to home, Johnson sent U.S. marines to the Dominican Republic to crush a leftist rebellion.

Toward an All-Out Commitment in Vietnam

During the first year of his presidency, Lyndon Johnson stuck to the course laid out by Kennedy in Vietnam, deciding "to do more of the same and do it more efficiently." He expanded secret raids on North Vietnam, boosted military and economic aid to the South Vietnamese, and increased the number of American advisers to twenty-three thousand by the end of 1964. Johnson appointed General William Westmoreland, a World War II and Korean War veteran, to command the U.S. military effort. Westmoreland confronted a South Vietnam in which the Vietcong controlled more than 50 percent of the population and more than 40 percent of its land.

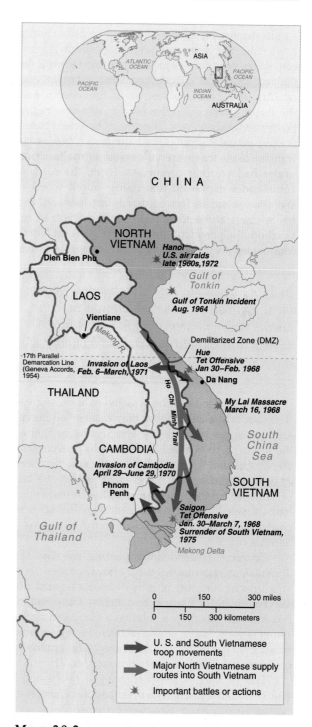

MAP 29.2
The Vietnam War, 1964–1975
The United States sent more than two million soldiers to Vietnam and spent more than $150 billion on the longest war in American history; but it was unable to prevent the unification of Vietnam under a Communist government.

In August 1964, Johnson seized an opportunity to increase the pressure on North Vietnam. American ships routinely engaged in espionage in the Gulf of Tonkin off the coast of North Vietnam, and on August 4, two U.S. destroyers, the *Maddox* and the *Turner Joy,* reported that North Vietnamese gunboats had fired on them. The reports had been based not on actual sightings, but on sonar and radar transmissions that were vulnerable to malfunction under bad weather conditions. Later, the *Maddox* commander expressed uncertainty about whether the attacks had in fact occurred, but Johnson and his advisers chose to believe that they had. In retaliation, the president ordered air strikes on North Vietnamese torpedo bases and oil storage facilities.

In 1965, when the South Vietnamese government approached collapse, Johnson took the fateful steps of ordering U.S. troops into combat and initiating sustained bombing of the North.

Johnson also used the occasion to ask Congress for a resolution authorizing him to take "all necessary measures to repel any armed attacks against the forces of the United States and to prevent further aggression." His portrayal of the situation was at best misleading, for he revealed neither the uncertainty about the attacks nor that the United States had engaged in provocative actions in staging covert raids and operating close to the North Vietnamese coast.

Congress responded by passing the Gulf of Tonkin Resolution on August 7, 1964. The House vote was unanimous, and only two senators voted no, Wayne Morse of Oregon and Ernest Gruening of Alaska, who called the resolution a "predated declaration of war." Public opinion mirrored congressional sentiment. The percent of Americans who approved U.S. policy in Vietnam shot up from 52 to 71.

The president's tough stance just two months before the 1964 elections helped counter charges of his opponent, Barry Goldwater, that Johnson was "soft on communism." Yet Johnson also presented himself as the peace candidate when Goldwater proposed massive bombing of North Vietnam and even entertained the possible use of atomic weapons. Johnson countered that bombing would expand the war and send American forces into battle. "We are not going to send American boys nine or ten thousand miles away from home to do what

Asian boys ought to be doing for themselves," Johnson insisted. Again and again, he claimed, "We seek no wider war."

Within months, however, Johnson did widen the war. He rejected peace feelers from North Vietnam, which insisted on American withdrawal and establishment of a coalition government in South Vietnam as steps toward the ultimate unification of the country. McNamara and most advisers urged Johnson to begin a bombing campaign against the North. Bombing North Vietnam, they said, would boost South Vietnamese morale, reduce Hanoi's ability to infiltrate personnel and equipment into the South, and thereby break the will of what Johnson called a "raggedy-ass little fourth-rate country" to continue the war.

In February 1965, Johnson initiated Operation Rolling Thunder, a strategy of gradually intensified bombing of North Vietnam. The administration did not reveal that strategy to the public but instead justified the initial strikes as a reprisal for recent Vietcong attacks on U.S. military quarters. Less than a month later, two battalions of marines landed near Da Nang, South Vietnam, the first U.S. combat troops to serve in Vietnam. In July, Johnson shifted the previously defensive mission of U.S. troops to that of offensive operations and authorized the dispatch of fifty thousand more soldiers.

Johnson took pains to obscure the significance of those two decisions, ordering aides to "minimize any appearance of sudden changes of policy." He told reporters, "I know of no far-reaching strategy that is being suggested or promulgated." Yet those decisions, whose import was kept from Congress and the public, marked a critical turning point in the war. Now it was genuinely America's war.

Preventing Another Castro in Latin America

Closer to home, Johnson faced perpetual problems, despite the efforts of the Alliance for Progress, in Latin America. Thirteen times during the 1960s, military coups replaced Latin American governments, and local insurgencies grew apace. The administration's response to such turmoil varied from case to case but centered on the determination to prevent any more Castro-type revolutions.

In 1964, riots erupted in the Panama Canal Zone, which the United States had seized early in the century and made a U.S. territory. Instigated by Panamanian nationalists who viewed the United States as a colonial power and wanted sovereignty

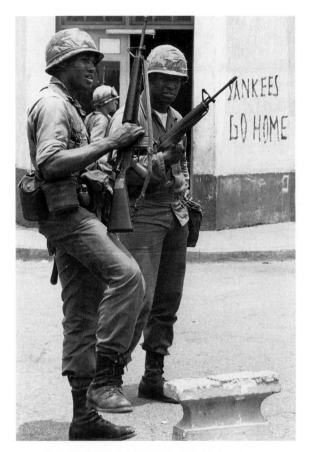

U.S. TROOPS IN THE DOMINICAN REPUBLIC
These United States paratroopers were among the twenty thousand troops sent to the Dominican Republic in April and May 1965. The American invasion helped restore peace, but it also kept the popularly elected government of Juan Bosch from regaining office. Dominicans expressed their outrage in anti-American slogans that greeted troops throughout the capital, Santo Domingo. Bosch himself said, "This was a democratic revolution smashed by the leading democracy in the world."
Corbis-Bettmann.

over all Panamanian territory, the riots resulted in the death of four U.S. soldiers and more than twenty Panamanians. Johnson authorized U.S. troops to quell the rioting, but he also initiated negotiations with Panamanian leaders. These talks dragged on until 1978 when they produced treaties providing for Panama to assume full authority over operation of the canal and for neutrality of the Canal Zone territory by the year 2000.

In 1965, Johnson's Latin American policy generated a new surge of anti-Americanism and cries of "Yankee imperialism." Voters in the Dominican

Republic had ousted the decades-old dictatorship of Rafael Trujillo and elected a constitutional government headed by Juan Bosch in 1961. After a military coup in 1963 overthrew Bosch, his supporters rallied in an uprising against the military government in April 1965. When the revolt was just four days old, Johnson ordered marines to the island and eventually sent more than twenty thousand soldiers to take control.

The president defended the intervention as necessary because the Boschist rebels included Communists who were likely to take over the Dominican Republic, a view that was never substantiated. Along with the marines, Johnson also sent a special ambassador, who arranged a truce between the opposing sides and installed an interim government. When Dominican elections in 1966 established a constitutional government under a moderate rightist, it appeared that Johnson's policy had worked.

Yet as the first outright show of Yankee force in Latin America in forty years, the Dominican intervention damaged the Johnson administration's credibility both at home and abroad. It quickly became clear that Communists had played no significant role in the revolt, and U.S. intervention kept the reform-oriented Boschists from returning to power. Moreover, the president had acted without the consent of the Dominicans or the Organization of American States (OAS), to which the United States had pledged to respect national sovereignty in Latin America. Once the troops landed in the Dominican Republic, Johnson did ask for approval and joint occupation from the OAS members, but several nations, including Mexico, Chile, Peru, and Venezuela, refused to support the United States.

Fear of being compared unfavorably with Kennedy obsessed Johnson throughout his presidency. The Texan's lowly origins and lack of an Ivy League education left a sense of insecurity that appeared in his efforts to show that he was just as smart and tough as Kennedy. Johnson also believed that demonstrating strength in the Caribbean would help convince the enemy in Vietnam of the depth of American resolve. In turn, the apparent success in the Dominican Republic no doubt encouraged the president to press on in Vietnam.

The Americanized War

From Operation Rolling Thunder in 1965 to early 1968, the United States employed a strategy of gradually escalating attacks against the North Vietnamese and their Vietcong allies, with the goal of

HELICOPTERS IN VIETNAM
This helicopter has just delivered soldiers on a mission near the Ho Chi Minh Trail in April 1968. Because the enemy in Vietnam was widely dispersed, the helicopter became a key implement of war and an example of American reliance on technology. The United States used helicopters to evacuate wounded, or drop napalm and defoliants. The helicopter's mobility enabled efficient placement of troops, and as gunships, they combined built-in weapons with the fire of soldiers on board.
Philip Jones Griffith/Magnum Photos, Inc.

breaking the will of the North Vietnamese while avoiding massive intervention by the Chinese. Johnson crudely explained the strategy to reporters as one of "seduction," from which the United States might ease off, rather than one of "rape," which might provoke China to respond as it had done in Korea. Intensely concerned with the bombing of the North, Johnson liked to boast, "They can't even bomb an outhouse without my approval."

Bombing intensified in both the North and the South, and over the course of the war U.S. pilots eventually dropped 3.2 million tons of explosives, more than the United States had launched in all of World War II. By 1967, the war was costing more than $2 billion a month, and nearly 500,000 Americans were fighting in Vietnam. By 1968, American GIs were dying at the rate of more than 1,000 a month.

The intensive bombing claimed monthly death tolls of more than 2,000 North Vietnamese civilians and military personnel but failed to dampen the North's commitment. The Hanoi government dispersed and concealed industrial and military facilities, taught its citizens how to protect themselves from bombing, and relied on human labor to rebuild transportation routes. Both the Soviet Union and China helped North Vietnam replace what the bombing destroyed, supplying an estimated $2 billion worth of materials between 1965 and 1968.

In South Vietnam, General Westmoreland conducted a strategy of attrition designed to search out and kill the Vietcong and North Vietnamese regular army. Military officials calculated the progress of the war not in territory gained or strategic positions seized, as they had in previous wars. Instead, they computed "body counts" and "kill ratios," the number of enemies killed in relation to the cost in American and ARVN lives. Under these circumstances, GIs did not always take care to distinguish between the enemy and noncombatants. Lieutenant Philip Caputo reported that the operating rule was "If it's dead and Vietnamese, it's VC [Vietcong]."

To carry out the strategy of attrition, Westmoreland could count on the best-equipped army in history. In addition to massive firepower and highly maneuverable helicopters that could move troops and artillery at a rapid pace, American forces used sophisticated computers and enemy-detecting systems as well as herbicides to destroy millions of acres of forests where the enemy hid. The United States relied even more heavily on airpower in the South, raining down more than twice the tonnage of bombs dropped on North Vietnam.

In contrast to World War II, when the average soldier was twenty-six years old, teenagers fought the Vietnam War. Until a constitutional amendment reduced the voting age from twenty-one to eighteen in 1971, most U.S. soldiers, whose average age was nineteen, could not even vote for the officials who sent them to Vietnam. As Americanization of the war progressed, the ratio of draftees to enlisted men increased, and the war's dependence on the draft added to its unique character.

Mike Clodfelter, sent to Vietnam in 1965, noticed that working-class youth did most of the fight-ing. "From my own small hometown [Plainville, Kansas] all but two of a dozen high school buddies would eventually serve in Vietnam and all were of working-class families," he observed. "I know of not a single middle-class son of the town's businessmen, lawyers, doctors, or ranchers from my high school graduating class who experienced the Armageddon of our generation."

Unlike World War II, which distributed the fighting among young men of various economic levels, the Vietnam War was the war of the poor and working class, who constituted about 80 percent of the troops.

Unlike World War II, which distributed the fighting among young men of various economic levels, the Vietnam War was the war of the poor and working class, who constituted about 80 percent of the troops. More privileged youth enjoyed greater ability to avoid the draft, usually through college deferments. Others evaded service in Vietnam by using family connections to get into the National Guard. Whereas 21 percent of high school graduates served in Vietnam, only 12 percent of college graduates did so, and these were half as likely to see combat as were soldiers with less education. In

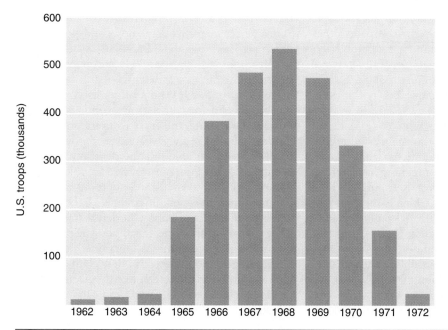

FIGURE **29.1**
U.S. Troops in Vietnam, 1962–1972
The steepest increases in the American military presence in Vietnam came in 1965 and 1966. Although troop levels declined in 1971 and 1972, the U.S. continued massive bombing attacks.

Why Couldn't the United States Bomb Its Way to Victory in Vietnam?

WORLD WAR II DEMONSTRATED the critical importance of airpower in modern war. According to the official U.S. study of strategic bombing during World War II, "No nation can long survive the free exploitation of air weapons over its homeland." In the Vietnam War, U.S. planes delivered even more explosives than they had in World War II. Why, then, did strategic bombing not bring victory in Vietnam?

"Our airpower did not fail us; it was the decision makers," asserted Admiral U. S. Grant Sharp, World War II veteran and commander in chief of the Pacific Command during the Vietnam War. Military officials welcomed President Johnson's order to begin bombing North Vietnam in February 1965 as a means to destroy the North's capacity and will to support the Communist insurgents in South Vietnam. But they chafed at Johnson's strategy of gradual escalation and the restrictions he imposed on Operation Rolling Thunder, the three-and-a-half-year bombing campaign. Military officials believed that the United States should have begun Operation Rolling Thunder with all-out massive bombing and continued until the devastation brought North Vietnam to its knees. Instead, they charged, civilian decision makers compelled the military to fight with one hand tied behind its back. Their arguments echoed General Douglas MacArthur's criticism of Truman's policy during the Korean War—though they did not repeat MacArthur's insubordination.

Unlike military officials, who could single-mindedly focus on defeating the enemy, the president balanced political considerations against military objectives and found compelling reasons to limit the application of airpower. Recalling the Korean War, Johnson noted that "China is there on the [North Vietnamese] border with 700 million men," and he studiously avoided action that might provoke intervention by the Chinese, who now possessed nuclear weapons. Johnson's strategy also aimed to keep the Soviet Union out of the war, to avoid inflaming antiwar sentiment at home, and to avert international criticism of the United States.

Consequently, the president would not permit bombing of areas where high civilian casualties might result and areas near the Chinese border. He banned strikes on airfields and missile sites that were under construction and thus likely to contain Chinese or Soviet advisers, and he refused to mine North Vietnam's harbors, through which Soviet ships imported goods to North Vietnam. But Johnson did escalate the pressure, increasing the intensity of the bombing fourfold by 1968. In all, Operation Rolling Thunder rained 643,000 tons of bombs on North Vietnam between 1965 and 1968.

Military leaders agreed with Johnson's desire to spare civilians. The Joint Chiefs of Staff never proposed, for example, strikes against a system of dikes and dams that could have disrupted food production and flooded Hanoi under twenty feet of water. Rather, they focused on destroying North Vietnam's industry and transportation system. Even after the Tet Offensive in early 1968, military advisers did not suggest direct attacks on civilians. Noncombatant casualties in North Vietnam contrasted sharply with those in World War II, when Anglo-American bombing of Dresden, Germany, alone took more than 35,000 civilian lives and the firebombing of Japan caused 330,000 civilian deaths. Operation Rolling Thunder's three and a half years of bombing claimed an estimated 52,000 civilian lives.

The relatively low level of economic development in North Vietnam and the North Vietnamese government's ability to mobilize its citizens counteracted the military superiority of the United States. Sheer man-, woman-, and child-power compensated for the demolition of transportation sources, industry sites, and electric power plants. When bombs struck a rail line, civilians rushed with bicycles to unload a train's cargo, carry it beyond the break, and load it onto a second train. Three hundred thousand full-time workers and 200,000 farmers labored in their spare time to keep the Ho Chi Minh Trail usable in spite of heavy bombing. When bridges were destroyed, the North Vietnamese resorted to ferries and pontoons made from bamboo, and they rebuilt bridges slightly underwater to make them harder to detect from the air. They dispersed oil storage facilities and production centers throughout the countryside, and when bombs knocked out electric power plants, the Vietnamese turned to more than two thousand portable generators and used oil lamps and candles in their homes.

THE B-52 BOMBER
After 1965, B-52 bombers constantly filled the skies over Vietnam, and at times over Laos and Cambodia. Designed originally to deliver nuclear bombs, a single B-52 carried thirty tons of explosives. A mission of six planes could destroy an area one-half mile wide by three miles long. The B-52 flew too high to be heard on the ground, and a single payload hit with such force that it could kill people in underground shelters.
Co Rentmeester, Life Magazine
© 1972 Time Magazine.

North Vietnam's needs were relatively small, and officials found ample means to meet them. In 1967, North Vietnam had only about 55,000 soldiers in South Vietnam, and because they waged a guerrilla war with only sporadic fighting, the insurgents in the South did not require huge amounts of supplies. What U.S. bombs destroyed, the North Vietnamese replaced with Chinese and Soviet imports. In 1967 alone, China provided 600,000 tons of rice, and it supplied small arms and ammunition, vehicles, and other goods throughout the war. Competing with China for influence in North Vietnam and favor in the third world, the Soviets contributed tanks, fighter planes, surface-to-air missiles, and other sophisticated weapons. Foreign aid substantially curtailed the effect of Operation Rolling Thunder, and the Soviet-installed modern defense systems made the bombing more difficult and dangerous for U.S. pilots.

In July 1969, Seventh Air Force commander General William W. Momyer commented on Operation Rolling Thunder to the retiring air force chief of staff, "We had the force, skill, and intelligence, but our civilian betters wouldn't turn us loose." Johnson refused to turn the military loose because in addition to the goal he shared with the military —breaking Hanoi's ability to support insurgency in the South—he also wanted to keep China and the Soviet Union—and nuclear weapons—out of the war and to contain domestic and international criticism of U.S. policy. Whether a more devastating air war would have provoked Chinese or Soviet intervention, of course, can never be known.

Nor can we know whether all-out bombing of the North could have guaranteed an independent non-Communist government in the South. We do know that Johnson's military advisers imposed their own restraints, never recommending the wholesale attacks on civilians that took place in World War II. Short of decimating the civilian population, it is questionable whether more intense bombing could have completely halted North Vietnamese support for the Vietcong, given the nature of the North Vietnamese economy, the determination and ingenuity of its people, and the plentiful assistance from China and the Soviet Union. Whether the strategic bombing that worked so well in a world war against major industrial powers could be effective in a third world guerrilla war remained in doubt after the Vietnam War.

the early years of the war, African Americans constituted 31 percent of all combat troops, often having enlisted in the military because their opportunities were so meager in the civilian economy. Death rates among black soldiers were twice as great as the proportion of black to white soldiers in Vietnam until 1966, when the military adjusted assignments of personnel to produce a more racially balanced distribution of sacrifice.

American troops faced extremely difficult conditions. This was a war whose purpose was unclear, a war without established battle lines. "There were no Normandies or Gettysburgs for us," wrote infantry officer Philip Caputo. For most combat troops, the war meant "weeks of expectant waiting and, at random intervals, of conducting vicious manhunts through jungles and swamps where snipers harassed us constantly and booby traps cut us down one by one."

Soldiers fought in thick jungles and swamps filled with leeches and in oppressive heat, rain, and humidity that rotted their feet and legs. Search-and-destroy missions sent platoons out into the darkness where ambushes, traps, and snipers could spring up at any moment. A harmless-looking civilian might be a deadly enemy. In the war of attrition, the U.S. military inflicted great losses on the enemy, estimated at more than 200,000 by the end of 1967. Yet the United States could claim no more than a stalemate.

After a series of coups and short-lived regimes, in 1965 the South Vietnamese government settled into a period of stability, if only in terms of personnel. Air Marshal Nguyen Cao Ky became prime minister, and General Nguyen Van Thieu took over as commmander in chief of the military. In 1967, in elections boycotted by the Buddhists, the South Vietnamese selected a constitutional assembly. It produced a document that was modeled after the U.S. and French constitutions, but with numerous provisions designed to enable the current leaders to remain in power. In subsequent elections, Thieu won the presidency, with Ky as his vice president. However, the Thieu-Ky ticket could muster only 35 percent of the vote, while an opponent who called for negotiations with the Vietcong won 17 percent.

The Thieu-Ky government was no more able than Diem had been to rally popular support for the war. Graft and corruption continued to flourish, and the massive American presence often made things worse. In the intensified fighting and inability to distinguish friend from foe, thousands of South Vietnamese civilians were killed and wounded, and

FIGHTING THE CLIMATE AND GEOGRAPHY
Steamy tropical conditions and an inhospitable terrain were among the nonhuman enemies U.S. troops faced in Vietnam. Soldiers like these men making their way through rice paddies in 1968 were soaked for weeks on end. Veteran Philip Caputo wrote about "being pounded numb by ceaseless rain" during the monsoon; "at night we squatted in muddy holes, picked off the leeches that sucked on our veins."
C. Simon Pietri/Sygma.

South Vietnamese farms and villages were bombed and burned. By 1968, five million people, nearly 30 percent of the population, had become refugees; many were forced into camps or urban centers. Massive infusions of American dollars and goods produced rampant inflation, more opportunities for graft, the demise of local industries, and an increased dependence on foreign aid.

Americanization of the war also strained relations between the United States and its key allies. Australia, New Zealand, the Philippines, South Korea, and Thailand supported the U.S. effort by sending small military contingents to Vietnam. But no help came from the United States' most important allies. In fact, French President Charles de Gaulle openly criticized U.S. policy in Vietnam, while Canadian, British, and West German leaders more quietly sought an end to the war. Some of the allies had moral or practical reservations about U.S. intervention, and all wanted the United States to concentrate its attention and resources in areas that they deemed more critical to the West.

Johnson's Americanization of the war resulted from decisions that were carefully considered and cautiously reached, and they flowed logically from the commitments made by three presidents before him. All the same, 1965 marked a critical turning point because Americanization of the war shifted the rationale for involvement from the need to contain communism in Southeast Asia to the need to prove to the world the will and ability of the United States to make good on its commitments. As George F. Kennan, a chief architect of the containment policy, insisted in 1966, American withdrawal from Vietnam would result in damage to U.S. interests that would be "greater than any that might have been involved by our failure to engage ourselves in the first place."

A Nation Polarized

By 1968, President Johnson was fighting a war on two fronts. Unable to secure a non-Communist government in South Vietnam, yet unwilling to withdraw and admit American defeat, the United States entered into a period of internal conflict and violence unparalleled since the Civil War. Domestic opposition to the war grew rapidly after 1965, and radical groups became more vocal and visible, challenging not just the war but the most basic values and institutions of American society.

In response to his critics, President Johnson presented optimistic appraisals of the war and engaged the CIA and FBI in illegal operations to destroy the antiwar movement. In 1968, however, Johnson realized that he must find a way out of Vietnam. Torn between his domestic critics and the military's clamor for more and more troops, in March 1968 the president announced restrictions on the bombing, a new effort at negotiations, and his decision not to pursue reelection.

Those announcements did not quell the domestic unrest. Throughout 1968, demonstrations, violence, and assassinations convulsed the nation.

Vietnam took center stage in the election, and voters chose by a narrow margin the Republican candidate, former Vice President Richard Nixon, who promised to "bring Americans together again" and to achieve "peace with honor."

The Widening War at Home

Before 1965, American actions in Vietnam evoked little criticism in the United States. Small groups of pacifists and radicals had objected to the sending of American advisers and arms since the early 1960s. There were also a few military and civilian officials whose experiences in Vietnam gave them second thoughts. Accepting the basic assumption that the United States must preserve a non-Communist South Vietnam, such critics argued that success depended on transforming the South Vietnamese government and army into institutions that could win popular support.

Domestic opposition to the war grew rapidly after 1965, and radical groups became more vocal and visible, challenging not just the war but the most basic values and institutions of American society.

Johnson's decision to launch Operation Rolling Thunder in the spring of 1965 sparked a mass movement against the war. In April 1965, Students for a Democratic Society (SDS) launched the first major protest and surprised everyone by recruiting 20,000 people for a rally in Washington, D.C. Thereafter, SDS chapters multiplied rapidly across the country, springing up on more than three hundred college campuses and enrolling more than 100,000 members. Although the vast majority of students did not join SDS, thousands of young people joined campus protests against Reserve Officers Training Corps (ROTC) programs, recruiters from the CIA, companies that manufactured war materials, and university departments that conducted research for the Defense Department. A new draft policy in 1967, which ended deferments for postgraduate education, gave students a greater stake in seeing the war end. In the spring of 1968, as many as one million college and high school students participated in a nationwide strike.

Though a critical element, students constituted just one part of the antiwar movement, which entered society's mainstream. The *New York Times*

FIGURE 29.2

Public Opinion about the Vietnam War, 1965–1974
This chart reflects the percent of people answering yes to a Gallup poll question, "In view of the developments since we entered the fighting in Vietnam, do you think the United States made a mistake in sending troops to fight in Vietnam?"

AFRICAN AMERICAN ANTIWAR PROTEST

The first expression of African American opposition to the war in Vietnam occurred in Mississippi in July 1965 when a group of civil rights workers called for draft resistance. Blacks should not fight for freedom in Vietnam "until all the Negro People are free in Mississippi," they said, nor should they "risk our lives and kill other Colored People in Santo Domingo and Viet Nam." This protester on the West Coast in April 1967 expresses similar sentiments.
Robert LeBeck/Black Star.

began to question the administration's policy in 1965, and by 1968 media critics included the *Wall Street Journal*, *Life* magazine, and popular TV journalist Walter Cronkite. The organization Clergy and Laymen Concerned about Viet Nam, founded in 1965, attracted primarily Protestants but also Catholics and Jews who opposed the war. Businesspeople, scientists, and physicians formed their own groups to pressure Johnson to stop the bombing and start negotiations. Although most of organized labor supported the president, some unions and their leaders joined the peace movement. In-

creasing numbers of prominent Democratic senators, including J. William Fulbright, George McGovern, and majority leader Mike Mansfield, urged Johnson to substitute negotiation for force. Popular dissatisfaction brought out some 200,000 people who protested in New York City in April 1967.

Opposition to the war took diverse forms: letter-writing campaigns to officials; teach-ins on college campuses; mass marches in Washington, D.C., and cities throughout the nation; student strikes; withholding of federal taxes; and draft card burnings. Protests also included shouting down officials attempting to defend the war in public forums, civil disobedience against military centers and manufacturers of war materials, efforts to stop trains carrying troops, and burnings of ROTC facilities.

Prominent writers Arthur Miller and Robert Lowell turned down invitations to the White House. Singer Eartha Kitt attended a White House luncheon hosted by Lady Bird Johnson, the president's wife, and used the occasion to condemn the war. Father Philip Berrigan and three other Catholics poured pig blood on draft records. Army doctor

Howard Levy refused to train special forces, announcing that training "murderers of women and children" violated the Hippocratic Oath that all doctors must uphold. Although the peace movement never claimed a majority of the population, it brought the war to the center of media attention and severely limited the administration's options. Above all, it revealed that the twenty-year-old consensus about cold war foreign policy had been broken.

Substantial numbers of young men refused to fight in the war. The World Boxing Association stripped Muhammad Ali, heavyweight champion of the world, of his title when he refused to serve in what he called a "white man's war." More than 170,000 young men who opposed the war on moral grounds became conscientious objectors and performed nonmilitary duties at home or in Vietnam. Whether for moral or other reasons, others avoided military service in different ways. About 60,000 young men fled the country to escape the draft, more than 200,000 were accused of failing to register for the draft or other draft offenses, and 25,000 were indicted.

Opponents of the war held far from unanimous views. Some condemned the war on moral grounds, challenging the right of the United States to inter-fere in the affairs of another country. To them, U.S. intervention had only propped up a corrupt, repressive government, magnified the suffering of the North and South Vietnamese people, and damaged the moral authority of the United States throughout the world. Their goal was total withdrawal from the war and major reorientation of U.S. foreign policy.

The largest segment of antiwar sentiment reflected practical considerations. As draft calls increased, young men and their families wondered whether American interests in Southeast Asia were worth their lives. Liberals recoiled at the mounting costs of the war in American lives, dollars, and the sacrifice of domestic reform. As American intervention escalated with no tangible results, many concluded that the war could not be won or, if it could, that the cost would be too great to bear. Not demanding withdrawal, they wanted Johnson to stop bombing North Vietnam and seek a negotiated settlement.

The antiwar movement outraged millions of Americans who supported the war. The domestic conflict sometimes cut through families; the older generation that had fought against Hitler could not understand a younger generation that failed to stand one hundred percent behind the government. Most repellent to many Americans were antiwar

THE ACCIDENTS OF WAR
As this Vietnamese boy walked to church in Saigon in 1968, he was struck by a rocket and later died. A U.S. helicopter, aiming at Vietcong three hundred yards away, overshot its mark. In a war without a defined front and with the enemy hiding potentially anywhere, such mistakes were not uncommon. Images like this one, showing the human devastation of war, appeared regularly on American TV and helped to stir antiwar sentiment.
Philip Jones Griffith/Magnum Photos, Inc.

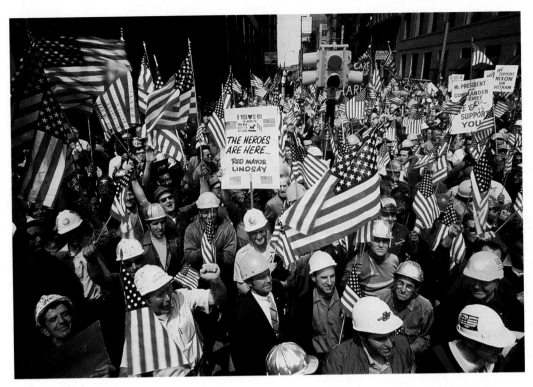

PRO-WAR DEMONSTRATORS
*Supporters as well as opponents of the war in Vietnam took to the streets, as these New Yorkers did
in support of the U.S. invasion of Cambodia in May 1970. Construction workers — called "hard
hats" — and other union members marched with American flags and posters supporting President
Nixon's policies and blasting New York Mayor John Lindsay for his antiwar position. Following the
demonstration, supportive union leaders presented Nixon with an honorary hard hat.*
Paul Fusco/Magnum Photos, Inc.

leaders like Tom Hayden, who went to North Vietnam and praised its people, and thousands of peace advocates who expressed support for the enemy. "How can Americans take sides against their own young men sent to Vietnam to fight and perhaps die?" asked supporters of government policy, who demonstrated with banners declaring, "Support our boys in Vietnam." A firefighter whose son had died in Vietnam expressed his hatred for the peace advocates: "They don't really love this country. Some of them almost seem glad to have a chance to criticize us. . . . To hell with them! Let them get out, leave, if they don't like it here. My son didn't die so they can look filthy and talk filthy and insult everything we believe in."

This man reflected the views of many working-class people. While they expressed doubts about the war as often as middle-class Americans, working-class people were conscious of the class dimensions of both the war and the public opposition to it. The

firefighter maintained, "It's people like us who give up our sons for the country. The businesspeople, they run the country and make money from it. The college types . . . go to Washington and tell the government what to do. . . . But their sons don't end up in the swamps over there, in Vietnam." His wife added her view that antiwar protesters' "hearts are with other people, not their own American people, the ordinary kind of person in this country."

In his domestic economic policies, Johnson tried to contain opposition to the war by avoiding actions that would focus attention on its burdens. Therefore, he escalated the war without asking Americans to pay higher taxes. In 1967, however, the growing costs of the war and resulting budget deficits began to stimulate a rise in the cost of living. The president refused to ask for price and wage controls, which had been employed in other wars to control inflation, but at the end of 1967 he did ask for a tax increase. In June 1968, Congress agreed to a 10 percent surcharge on federal income taxes only after Johnson pledged to trim the budget deficit by reducing domestic spending. Johnson's Great Society programs suffered, but the surcharge failed to reverse the inflationary surge.

The rising cost of living and diversion of funds from reform programs broadened antiwar sentiment, to which Johnson reacted harshly. He agonized over casualty reports and was personally hurt by protesters who chanted outside the White House, "Hey, hey, LBJ, how many kids have you killed today?" The president also recognized public opinion as a critical weapon in the war effort. He told a reporter in 1967 that the enemy was not the major problem; rather, it was opposition at home, which was "leading the enemy to believe that we might quit." In addition to undertaking a public relations campaign that cast the war's progress in a deceptively optimistic light, Johnson sought to discredit opponents by labeling them "nervous Nellies," Communists, or unwitting dupes of the enemy.

The administration also employed direct means to silence its critics. On Johnson's orders, the CIA spied on peace advocates, compiling secret files on more than seven thousand citizens. Law enforcement officials indicted not just draft resisters but also those like Dr. Benjamin Spock, the famous baby care expert, who counseled them. Without the president's specific authorization, the FBI launched COINTELPRO (for "counterintelligence programs"), infiltrating the peace movement and disrupting its work. FBI agents schemed to discredit antiwar leaders' reputations by, for example, sending anonymous letters to the press suggesting that a peace activist was a homosexual. However, even the resort to illegal measures failed to subdue the opposition.

The Tet Offensive and the Decision to Deescalate

Although the majority of Americans remained detached from the peace movement and many opposed it vigorously, by late 1967 public impatience and frustration had intensified. Television brought the carnage of the Vietnam War into American homes day after day, making it the first "living room war." The public also watched leading members of Congress question administration officials about the war. Major newspapers around the country editorialized for a change in policy, and in October 1967, public opinion polls found that a mere 28 per-

cent of Americans approved of Johnson's conduct of the war.

Among those dissatisfied with the president's leadership, the "hawks" charged that the United States was fighting with one hand tied behind its back and wanted to apply more power against North Vietnam. The "doves" wanted deescalation or withdrawal. Most Americans were torn between their weariness of the war and their worry about abandoning the American commitment. As one woman said to a pollster, "I want to get out but I don't want to give up."

By the spring of 1967, grave doubts about the war had penetrated the administration itself. The most important defector was Secretary of Defense McNamara, a principal architect of U.S. involvement who now doubted that the war was winnable. Ho Chi Minh, he believed, "won't quit no matter how much bombing we do." McNamara also feared for the image of the United States, "the world's greatest superpower killing or seriously injuring 1,000 noncombatants a week, while trying to pound a tiny, backward nation into submission on an issue whose merits are hotly disputed." Although Johnson shared some of his adviser's concerns, he rejected McNamara's suggestions for deescalation. McNamara did not disclose his views to the public until thirty years later, but in early 1968 he left the administration to head the World Bank.

The critical turning point for Johnson came with the Tet Offensive, which began on January 30, 1968. Just a few weeks after General Westmoreland had reported to Washington that "the enemy has been driven away from the population centers [and] has been compelled to disperse and evade contact," the North Vietnamese and Vietcong attacked key cities and towns and every major American base in South Vietnam. The enemy even invaded the grounds of the U.S. embassy in Saigon, killing two American MPs and holding the compound for six hours. Meanwhile, marines hustled the U.S. ambassador, in pajamas, from his residence to safety.

The Tet Offensive, named for its occurrence during the Vietnamese lunar new year celebration, Tet, was the biggest surprise of the war—and not simply because it violated a truce that both sides had generally observed during the holiday. More important, Tet displayed the enemy's vitality and refusal to let the presence of half a million American soldiers deter it from launching its most daring offensive. Militarily, the Vietcong and North Vietnamese suffered a defeat, losing more than 30,000 men, ten times the casualty rate of ARVN and U.S.

forces. The ARVN fought unusually well, and within a few weeks the enemy had been routed.

Psychologically, however, the Tet Offensive was a devastating blow. It highlighted the credibility gap between official statements and the actual progress of the war, in part because the press emphasized the magnitude of the attacks rather than how quickly they had been repelled. The Tet Offensive created one million more South Vietnamese refugees along with widespread destruction, especially in the ancient city of Hue, whose archaeological treasures were left in rubble after three weeks of intense fighting. Referring to a village that he had helped to defend, a U.S. army official said, "We had to destroy the town to save it." This statement epitomized for more and more Americans the contradiction between means and ends in Vietnam and the brutality and senselessness of the war.

In the aftermath of the Tet Offensive, Johnson reversed the direction the war had taken since the spring of 1965. When Westmoreland requested 200,000 additional troops in Vietnam by the end of the year, the president conferred with his civilian advisers in the Department of Defense, now headed by Clark Clifford, a Washington lawyer and former aide to Harry Truman. He also sought advice from an unofficial group of foreign policy experts who had played key roles in designing cold war policies under successive presidents since World War II. Dubbed the "Wise Men," they met with Johnson in March. Dean Acheson, one of Truman's secretaries of state, summarized their conclusion: "We can no longer do the job we set out to do in the time we have left and we must begin to take steps to disengage."

On March 31, 1968, Lyndon Johnson addressed the nation on television. He announced that the United States would henceforth cut back its bombing of North Vietnam to a small area north of the South Vietnamese border and that he was prepared to begin peace talks with North Vietnam. Then he stunned his audience by concluding, "I shall not seek, and I will not accept, the nomination of my party for another term as your president."

Johnson's decision marked the end of the gradual escalation that had begun in 1965. It signaled the beginning of a shift from "Americanization" to "Vietnamization" of the war, but it was a shift in strategy rather than policy. The United States did not abandon the goal of a non-Communist South Vietnam; it simply hoped to reach that goal by relying more heavily on the South Vietnamese. In that sense, Johnson's announcement represented a return to the pre-1965 policy.

Johnson's explanation for withdrawing from the presidential campaign stressed his need to devote full attention to ending the war and reducing the bitter discord at home. He also hoped that the dramatic step would convince North Vietnam of his sincere desire for a negotiated settlement. Concerns about his health and the possibility of losing the election also motivated his decision. Before Johnson announced his withdrawal, Senator Eugene McCarthy of Minnesota had already begun a race for the Democratic nomination on an antiwar platform and had nearly defeated the president in the New Hampshire primary. Shortly thereafter, Senator Robert F. Kennedy, the late president's brother, began his own campaign.

North Vietnam quickly seized on Johnson's overture, and on May 10, 1968, the two sides began negotiations in Paris. But the United States would not agree to recognition of the NLF, a coalition government, and an American withdrawal. The North Vietnamese would agree to nothing less. Although the talks continued, so did the fighting. The American presence neared its peak at 540,000 in mid-1968, but the cost in American lives was nearly as high after peace talks began as before.

1968: Year of Upheaval

Violence escalated at home. Two months after the murder of Martin Luther King Jr. and the riots that erupted in its wake, another assassination stunned the nation. Senator Robert F. Kennedy had just celebrated his triumph in the California Democratic primary when he was shot in the head by a Palestinian Arab refugee, Sirhan Sirhan, who was outraged by Kennedy's recent statement of support for Israel. Heroic efforts to save Kennedy failed, and he died twenty-six hours later on June 6. For millions of Americans, his death seemed to foreclose the possibility of peace in Vietnam and the renewal of attention to the needs of society's least privileged members.

The spring of 1968 also saw campus violence escalate, as students in France, Britain, Germany, and elsewhere took to the streets and barricades. Of some two hundred campus protests in the United States in the first half of the year, the bloodiest occurred at Columbia University. There, students took over five buildings, demanding that the university stop uprooting African Americans as it sought to expand into the neighboring community and do more to meet the needs of black students. The students also wanted the university to stop sponsoring research for the Department of Defense and grant amnesty to past and current student demonstrators. When negotiations failed, university officials called in the New York City police, who cleared the buildings, sent more than one hundred demonstrators to the hospital, and arrested more than seven hundred students. An ensuing student strike brought the academic year to a premature end.

In August, protesters battled the police in Chicago, where the Democratic Party convened to nominate its presidential ticket. Several thousand demonstrators came to Chicago, some to show their support for Eugene McCarthy's peace candidacy, others mobilized by the Youth International Party (Yippies), a splinter group of SDS. Its leaders, Abbie Hoffman and Jerry Rubin, urged students to demonstrate their hatred of the establishment by creating chaos and disorder in the backyard of the Democratic convention and provoking the police to violence.

Chicago's mayor and leading Democrat, Richard J. Daley, had already made clear his intention to brook no civil disorder when he ordered police to "shoot to kill" arsonists and "shoot to maim" looters during the riots following King's assassination. Now he forbade demonstrators to hold rallies or marches, insisted that the parks be cleared after 11 P.M., and mobilized thousands of police to carry out his will. When police ordered demonstrators in Lincoln Park to disperse on August 25, only to be met with taunts and jeers, they attacked the protesters with tear gas and clubs.

Street battles between police and protesters continued for three days, culminating in what an

PROTEST IN THE STREETS
The worst violence surrounding the 1968 Democratic National Convention in Chicago came on August 28 when protesters attempted to march to the convention site. Near the Hilton Hotel, where most of the delegates stayed, some three thousand protesters came up against a line of police. The police attacked the demonstrators, as well as reporters, hotel guests, and bystanders, with nightsticks and mace, driving a crowd through the plateglass window of the Hilton's cocktail lounge. What other police confrontation in Chicago does the name of the bar in the background recall?
Corbis-Bettmann.

official commission later termed a "police riot" on the night of August 28. Taunted by cries of "Gestapo pigs" and pelted with rocks and bottles, the police attacked with mace and nightsticks, clubbing not only those who had come in hopes of provoking violence, but also reporters, peaceful demonstrators, convention delegates and workers, and bystanders.

The bloodshed in the streets had little effect on the outcome of the convention. Peace Democrats lost their battle for a platform plank offering some concessions to North Vietnam that might break the deadlock in the peace talks. They also lost the presidential nomination, as Vice President Hubert H. Humphrey trounced Eugene McCarthy by nearly three to one. McCarthy's refusal to share the podium with Humphrey on the final night of the convention provided a stark illustration of the bitter split within the party.

In contrast, the Republican convention, which had occurred three weeks earlier, provided little drama. Referring to the lack of excitement and Miami's heat and humidity, one columnist wrote that the convention had been "planned in advance by six bores and a sadist." Former Vice President Richard Nixon won on the first ballot. For his running mate, Nixon chose Maryland Governor Spiro T. Agnew, hoping to gather southern support while not alienating northern and western voters.

For the first time in nearly fifty years, a strong third party entered the electoral scene. Former Alabama Governor George C. Wallace, who had gained national attention for his all-out efforts to maintain "segregation forever" in Alabama schools, ran on the ticket of the American Independent Party. Although his support was strongest in the Deep South, Wallace appealed to Americans throughout the country who were alarmed and disgusted by the changes that were sweeping their society and frustrated by the nation's inability to work its will in Vietnam.

Wallace supporters included considerable numbers of lower-class and working-class whites, who believed that civil rights initiatives and antipoverty programs benefited the undeserving at their expense. And he appealed to citizens outraged by the assault on traditional values that had reverberated through the 1960s. Privileged students attacking their universities, antiwar protesters resorting to civil disobedience and sometimes violence, young people experimenting with drugs and flouting sexual mores—all seemed to threaten the very foundations of American society. Wallace promised to restore law and order, respect for authority, disci-

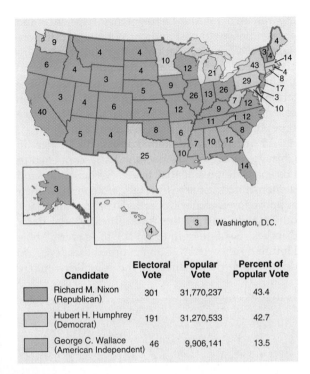

Candidate	Electoral Vote	Popular Vote	Percent of Popular Vote
Richard M. Nixon (Republican)	301	31,770,237	43.4
Hubert H. Humphrey (Democrat)	191	31,270,533	42.7
George C. Wallace (American Independent)	46	9,906,141	13.5

MAP 29.3
The Election of 1968

pline, and patriotism. Striking a chord with those Americans who could not accept the limitations of U.S. power in the world, he called for stronger measures against America's enemies, both at home and in Vietnam.

Voters could discern very little difference between the two major party candidates on the central issue of Vietnam. Nixon had the advantage because he could criticize the incumbent party for "four years in Vietnam with no end in sight." He promised "to bring an honorable end" to the war but gave no indication of how he would do it. Attacking the Great Society for "pouring billions of dollars into programs that have failed" and appealing to "the forgotten Americans, the non-shouters, the non-demonstrators," Nixon more guardedly played on the resentments that fueled the Wallace campaign.

Humphrey had strong reservations about U.S. policy in Vietnam, yet as vice president he wanted to avoid a break with Johnson. In late September, Humphrey distanced himself marginally from official policy by expressing willingness to "stop the bombing of the North as an acceptable risk for peace." At the end of October, Johnson gave

Humphrey's campaign a further boost when he announced a halt to the bombing of North Vietnam. By election eve, Nixon and Humphrey were in a neck-and-neck race.

With nearly ten million votes (13 percent of the total), the American Independent Party produced the strongest third-party finish since 1924. Nixon squeaked by Humphrey with a popular vote of 31.8 million to Humphrey's 31.3 million, prevailing more strongly in electoral college votes, with 301 to Humphrey's 191 and Wallace's 46. The Democrats lost a few seats in Congress but maintained control of both the House and the Senate.

The 1968 elections revealed deep cracks in the coalition that had, with the exception of the Eisenhower years, kept the Democrats in power for thirty years. Opposition to the Democrats' policies on race moved most of the South behind Nixon or Wallace, as that region decidedly broke a century of Democratic Party ascendency. Although union leaders rallied strongly behind Humphrey, significant numbers of the rank and file and unorganized blue-collar workers demonstrated their displeasure with recent tumultuous changes and frustration over the Vietnam War by voting for Wallace or Nixon. Voters aimed grievances concerning civil rights policies, Great Society reforms, inflation, antiwar protesters, campus rebels, changing sexual mores, drug use, urban riots, and America's impotence in Vietnam at the Democratic Party. These resentments continued to simmer, later to be mobilized into a resurging right in American politics.

Nixon's Failed Search for Peace with Honor

"I'm not going to end up like LBJ, holed up in the White House afraid to show my face on the street," the new president asserted. "I'm going to stop that war. Fast." Yet, having promised "peace with honor," Nixon was no more willing than Johnson had been to allow South Vietnam to fall to the Communists and no more able to find a way to prevent it. Like Johnson, he faced two obstacles: A majority of Americans did not want to see the war drag on, and North Vietnam and the National Liberation Front would settle for nothing less than an independent, united nation.

To quiet domestic opposition to the war, in 1969 Nixon began a gradual withdrawal of U.S. ground troops combined with attempts to strengthen the South Vietnamese military. He pursued peace through negotiations while expanding military operations into neighboring Cambodia and Laos and engaging in sporadic but ferocious bombing of North Vietnam, thereby intensifying opposition to the war. The Nixon administration further polarized the nation and outdid its predecessor in deceiving Congress and the public and in harassing dissenters.

Having promised "peace with honor," Nixon was no more willing than Johnson had been to allow South Vietnam to fall to the Communists and no more able to find a way to prevent it.

Unable to marshal support at home or to defeat the enemy abroad, in January 1973 the administration concluded a truce that ended the direct involvement of the United States. Far from achieving peace with honor, the United States accepted conditions that led to total victory for the North Vietnamese in April 1975. By then, public disclosure of the illegal means Nixon had applied to silence his critics and defeat the political opposition at home had driven the president from office.

Vietnamization and Negotiations

"No secretary of state is really important," Nixon remarked in 1967. "The president makes foreign policy." Both his secretary of state and his secretary of defense found themselves overshadowed in the making of foreign policy and often left in the dark on important initiatives. Nixon's most important adviser was Henry A. Kissinger, a German-born refugee from Hitler's Holocaust and a Harvard professor of international relations. During the 1968 campaign, Kissinger had manuevered himself into the favor of both Humphrey and Nixon by offering advice to each. In the new administration he became the president's assistant for national security.

Nixon and Kissinger embraced the goal of the three preceding administrations: a non-Communist South Vietnam. By 1969, however, that goal had become almost incidental to the larger objective of maintaining American credibility. According to Kissinger, regardless of the wisdom of the initial intervention, "the commitment of five hundred thousand Americans has settled the importance of Vietnam. For what is involved now is confidence in American promises."

From 1969 to 1972, Nixon and Kissinger pursued a four-pronged approach. First, they aimed to strengthen the South Vietnamese military and government. Second, they negotiated with both North Vietnam and the Soviet Union. Third, they agreed to apply sufficient force to make Hanoi amenable to American terms at the bargaining table. Fourth, to disarm the antiwar movement at home, Nixon gradually withdrew U.S. soldiers from combat. Serving in their place would be South Vietnamese soldiers and American technology and bombs.

U.S. military officials carried out an ambitious program to strengthen South Vietnam. ARVN forces grew to more than one million, supplied with the latest American equipment and supported with improved training, increased pay scales, and added benefits. The South Vietnamese air force became the fourth largest in the world. U.S. advisers and funds also assisted "pacification" efforts in the countryside, which involved land reform, holding village elections, and building schools, hospitals, and transportation facilities. Despite these improvements, whether South Vietnam could stand on its own remained doubtful.

The other side of Vietnamization was the withdrawal of U.S. forces. The number of GIs peaked at 543,000 in June 1969 and thereafter decreased to 334,600 in 1970 and 140,000 by the end of 1971. Casualties likewise declined, the average monthly death rate of American soldiers falling from nearly 800 in 1969 to 352 in 1970. Decreasing draft calls and casualties helped undercut the strength of the antiwar movement, yet more than 20,000 Americans perished in Vietnam during the last four years of the war.

Morale fell among the Americans left in Vietnam. Having been exposed to the antiwar movement at home, many of these soldiers had less faith in the purpose or value of the war than their predecessors had. In addition to mounting racial tensions among soldiers, more incidents of "fragging" (attacks on officers by enlisted men) occurred than in any previous wars. A government study in 1971 reported that half of the U.S. army personnel sought escape from boredom and horror by smoking marijuana, and one-fourth used heroin, opium, and other drugs.

While reducing the U.S. presence in Vietnam, Nixon and Kissinger also endeavored to capitalize on Soviet interest in expanded trade and arms reductions by linking U.S. desires in Vietnam with Soviet concerns elsewhere. However, their breakthroughs in summit diplomacy with the Soviet Union and China (discussed in chapter 30) failed to change the course of the war. The Communist leaders in Vietnam zealously pursued their goal of unification and national independence, and little that either the Soviet Union or China could or would do deterred them from the objective to which they had dedicated twenty or more years of their lives.

Nor did intensification of force against the enemy achieve its objective. While maintaining the general halt in the bombing of North Vietnam, Nixon approved several ferocious assaults throughout Vietnam and ordered secret attacks on enemy strongholds in neighboring Cambodia and Laos. Kissinger believed that a "fourth-rate power like North Vietnam" had to have a "breaking point," but the hundreds of thousands of tons of bombs delivered by U.S. pilots failed to find it. Fierce application of American power bought time, but little else. (See Historical Question, page 1152.)

The bombing inflamed passions at home, and the antiwar movement plagued the Nixon administration through 1971. Some protesters devised new and extravagant methods. A small group called Women against Daddy Warbucks invaded a draft board in New York City in July 1969, removed draft files, and stripped typewriters of the 1 and the A keys, which were used to type the code 1-A, designating those who were eligible for the draft. Other protests were legal and peaceful and involved massive numbers of people. On October 15, 1969, two million citizens across the nation took part in marches, rallies, and readings of the names of dead soldiers. One month later, tens of thousands of people marched from Arlington National Cemetery to Capitol Hill, wearing black armbands, each bearing a card with the name of a dead American or a destroyed village. Passing the White House, each marcher called out a victim's name. More than half a million people gathered the next day at the Washington Monument.

Vietnam Becomes Nixon's War

In the spring of 1969, Nixon began a fierce air war in Cambodia. Pilots were commanded to destroy their orders after every mission, and Nixon kept the bombing hidden from Congress and the public for more than a year. Designed to knock out North Vietnamese sanctuaries in Cambodia, from which the enemy launched attacks on South Vietnam, the campaign, dropping more than 100,000 tons of bombs, resulted only in sending the North Vietnamese to other hiding places. To support a new, pro-Western

KENT STATE
Mary Ann Vecchio, who was not a student but happened to be at Kent State University in Ohio on May 4, 1970, expresses grief and horror just after National Guardsmen's bullets killed Jeff Miller and three other Kent State students. Shock and outrage spread across the United States. After the Kent State killings, about 1.5 million students boycotted classes; one of every five campuses shut down for at least a day, and some closed for the rest of the academic year.
John Filo.

Cambodian government that came to power in 1970 through a military coup and "to show the enemy that we were still serious about our commitment in Vietnam," in April 1970 Nixon ordered a joint U.S.-ARVN invasion of Cambodia.

With that order, the president made Vietnam "Nixon's war" and provoked immediate outrage at home. Aware that he was "going to get unshirted hell" for the attack, Nixon made a belligerent speech announcing his move, which he called an "incursion" because the Cambodian government acquiesced in it. He concluded by emphasizing the importance of American credibility: "If when the chips are down, the world's most powerful nation acts like a pitiful helpless giant, the forces of totalitarianism and anarchy will threaten free nations . . . throughout the world."

"This will make the students puke," a cabinet member said when he read Nixon's speech. They did more. A protest in Washington drew upward of 100,000 people, and students demonstrated and boycotted classes on hundreds of campuses. At Kent State University in Ohio, where protesters had burned an ROTC building, the governor called out National Guard troops. At a peaceful rally on May 4, 1970, nervous troops fired at students, killing four, two of whom were bystanders, crippling another for life, and wounding ten others. "They're

starting to treat their own children like they treat us," commented a black woman in Harlem. In a confrontation at Jackson State College in Mississippi on May 14, police shot into a dormitory, killing two black students. In August, a national Chicano antiwar rally held in Los Angeles erupted in violence when police used clubs and tear gas against the protesters.

Furious at the secret bombing and invasion of Cambodia, legislators attempted to rein in the president. The Senate voted to terminate the Gulf of Tonkin Resolution, which had been passed in 1964 and gave the president virtually a blank check in Vietnam, and to cut off all funds for the Cambodian operation by the end of June. The House of Representatives refused to go along, but Congress was clearly becoming an obstacle to the Nixon administration's plans. By the end of June, Nixon pulled out all U.S. soldiers from Cambodia. But he also authorized an intensified assault on his domestic opponents, one that ultimately drove him from the White House.

The Cambodian invasion inflicted heavy blows on the North Vietnamese but failed to break their will. Instead, it set in motion a terrible tragedy for the Cambodian people. The North Vietnamese moved farther into Cambodia and increased their support of the Khmer Rouge, Communist insurgents attempting to overthrow the U.S.-supported government of Lon Nol. Cambodians endured heavy bombing until Congress forced its end in 1973. A brutal civil war lasted until 1975, when the Khmer Rouge triumphed and quickly imposed a savage genocidal rule over the Cambodian population. The Khmer Rouge slaughter and the murderous effects of the war took millions of lives, giving the name "killing fields" to the land of this historically peaceful people.

After the spring of 1971, there were fewer massive antiwar demonstrations, but vehement protest continued in other forms. Public attention focused on the horrors of U.S. intervention in Vietnam at the court-martial of Lieutenant William Calley, which began in November 1970 and resulted in his conviction. During the trial, Americans learned that Calley's company had massacred more than two hundred civilians in the hamlet of My Lai in March 1968. Among those murdered were children and women, some of whom were raped first. The military had covered up the atrocity for more than a year.

In 1971, Vietnam veterans themselves became a visible part of the peace movement, the first men in United States history to oppose a war in which they had fought. Veterans held a public investigation of U.S. "war crimes" in Vietnam, rallied in front of the U.S. Capitol and cast away their war medals, and occupied the Statue of Liberty. In May 1971, veterans numbered among 40,000 protesters who engaged in civil disobedience in an effort to shut down Washington. Officials made more than 12,000 arrests, which courts later ruled violations of protesters' rights.

Administration policy suffered a greater blow in June 1971 with publication of the *Pentagon Papers,* a secret, critical government study of U.S. policy in Vietnam. While working as an aide to Henry Kissinger, Daniel Ellsberg, who had previously served as a civilian adviser in Vietnam, came across the documents. Convinced that the war was futile and frustrated in his attempts to persuade officials of his view, Ellsberg copied the papers and gave them to the *New York Times.*

The Nixon administration quickly obtained a court injunction against further publication of the papers, only to have the injunction overturned by the Supreme Court as a violation of freedom of the press. Ellsberg then became another victim of Nixon's obsession with punishing his enemies. Instructed by the president to do anything necessary to discredit Ellsberg, a group of men hired by Nixon

aides broke into the office of Ellsberg's psychiatrist, stole confidential records, and leaked them to the press. Although these actions escaped public notice until 1973, the *Pentagon Papers* episode spurred disillusionment with the war by casting doubts on the government's credibility. Seventy-one percent of respondents to public opinion polls in 1971 thought that it had been a mistake to send American troops to Vietnam; 58 percent considered the war to be immoral.

The Peace Accords and the Fall of Saigon

In 1972, Nixon and Kissinger continued to pursue a combined strategy of military force and negotiations. In March, responding to the heaviest offensive by the North Vietnamese since the Tet Offensive of 1968, the United States resumed sustained bombing of the North, mined Haiphong and other harbors for the first time, and announced a naval blockade. Nixon boasted, "The bastards have never been bombed like they're going to be bombed this time."

The escalation of the war probably heightened North Vietnam's interest in a settlement, and by October, secret negotiations between Kissinger and North Vietnamese envoy Le Duc Tho brought the two sides close to agreement. But when the talks sputtered to a new deadlock in December 1972, Nixon turned once again to intimidation. Over the Christmas holiday, he ordered the most devastating bombing of North Vietnam yet: In twelve days, U.S. planes dropped more bombs than they had in all of 1969–1971. On January 27, 1973, representatives of the United States, North Vietnam, the South Vietnamese government, and the Vietcong (now called the People's Revolutionary Government) signed a formal accord in Paris.

The agreement required removal of all U.S. troops and military advisers within sixty days but allowed North Vietnamese forces to remain in place. Both sides agreed to return prisoners of war, including hundreds of Americans, some of whom had been held since the mid-1960s. The Thieu government continued in power, but the People's Revolutionary Government won a role in determining the political future of South Vietnam. The peace treaty allowed the United States a face-saving withdrawal but fell far short of the goal for which the United States had intervened in the first place, since it was doubtful that South Vietnam would remain non-Communist for long.

EVACUATING SOUTH VIETNAM
As Communist troops rolled south toward Saigon in the spring of 1975, desperate South Viet-
namese attempted to flee along with the departing Americans. Here an American official punches
a man trying to get on an already overloaded plane leaving Nha Trang on April 1. Thousands of
Vietnamese who wanted to be evacuated were left behind. But not South Vietnamese President
Nguyen Van Thieu, who escaped with fifteen tons of baggage on a U.S. plane to Taiwan.
Corbis-Bettmann.

Though the Paris agreement had established a cease-fire, fighting resumed immediately among the Vietnamese, and the United States continued to bomb Cambodia. Nixon found his efforts to support the South Vietnamese government, and indeed his ability to govern at all, increasingly eroded by a series of revelations of administration wrongdoing that came to be known as the Watergate scandals (discussed in chapter 30). In June 1973, Congress enacted legislation that ended all military operations in Laos and Cambodia. The House upheld Nixon's veto, but public opposition compelled the president to stop the bombing.

In 1975, North Vietnam launched a new offensive in South Vietnam, calculating that it would take two more years to achieve victory. It took just five months. As South Vietnam neared collapse, Congress approved funds to evacuate Americans and to serve "humanitarian" purposes but refused to authorize any more military aid. On May 1, 1975, Vietcong troops occupied Saigon and renamed it Ho Chi Minh City in honor of the Communist leader, who had died before seeing his goal of Vietnamese unification and independence achieved.

Confusion, humiliation, and tragedy marked the hasty evacuation of Americans and their South Vietnamese allies. The United States got its own citizens out, as well as 150,000 Vietnamese. But there were not enough aircraft and ships and not enough time to evacuate all those who wanted to leave. U.S. marines beat back some of the desperate Vietnamese who tried to escape through the U.S. embassy. Some South Vietnamese troops, frightened and angry at being left behind, even fired on departing Americans.

The Legacy of Defeat

It took Nixon four years to end the war; twenty thousand additional Americans lost their lives, the conflict expanded into Laos and Cambodia, and Southeast Asia endured massive bombing campaigns. During that time, the Vietnam War became a genuinely bipartisan war. And it was not only the president's war. Although increasing numbers of legislators criticized the war, Congress never denied the funds to fight it. "This chamber reeks of blood," George McGovern had declared on the Senate floor in 1970, castigating his colleagues for "our pitiful willingness to let the Executive carry the burden that the Constitution places on us." Congress moved slowly to assert itself, not repealing the Gulf of Tonkin Resolution until the end of 1970.

Only after the U.S. military withdrawal from Vietnam in 1973 did the legislative branch stiffen its constitutional authority over the making of war. In November 1973, Congress enacted the War Powers Act over Nixon's veto. The law required the president to report to Congress within forty-eight hours when he deployed military forces in places where hostilities existed or were likely to occur. If Congress failed to endorse his action within sixty days, the troops would have to be withdrawn.

Because both Democrats and Republicans bore responsibility for America's involvement in Vietnam, the defeat did not become a subject of partisan debate. In fact, most Americans wanted simply to forget the war. Moreover, the dire predictions of three presidents did not materialize. The failure to preserve a non-Communist South Vietnam did not open the floodgates to Communist expansion, the original premise of U.S. intervention. Although

---

TABLE 29.1

VIETNAM WAR CASUALTIES

United States	
Killed in action	47,382
Wounded	153,303
Died, non-combat	1,811
Missing, captured	10,753

South Vietnam	
Killed in action	110,357
Military wounded	499,026
Civilians killed	415,000
Civilians wounded	913,000

Communist regulars and guerrillas	
Killed in action	666,000

Source: U.S. Department of Defense.

Vietnam, Laos, and Cambodia all fell within the Communist camp in the spring of 1975, Thailand, Burma, Malaysia, and the rest of Southeast Asia did not. When China and Vietnam soon reverted to their historical relationship of hostility, the myth of a monolithic Communist power overrunning Asia evaporated.

Three features of the war denied Vietnam veterans the traditional homecoming: its lack of strong support at home, its character as a guerrilla war, and its ultimate failure.

The Americans most directly affected by the nation's first military defeat were the veterans and those who had lost loved ones to the war. The nation had always honored soldiers' sacrifices for a noble and victorious cause. However, three features of the war denied Vietnam veterans the traditional homecoming: its lack of strong support at home, its character as a guerrilla war, and its ultimate failure. As one veteran remarked, "The left hated us for killing, and the right hated us for not killing enough."

Because the Vietnam War was in large part a civil war without easily identifiable enemies, combat was especially brutal. As antiwar opposition grew, more and more GIs could find no purpose in the war beyond staying alive, no redeeming quality beyond comradeship and loyalty to their fellow soldiers. For combat soldiers, the terrors of conventional warfare were multiplied, and so were the opportunities and motivations to commit atrocities. The massacre of civilians by U.S. troops in My Lai was the most publicized war crime, but 9 percent of a sample of veterans in a government study reported that they had committed abusive violence against civilians or prisoners of war, and 30 percent had witnessed such acts.

To demonstrate the immorality of the war, peace advocates stressed the atrocities, to which the media also gave substantial coverage in the later stages of the war. This emphasis on the war's cruelties contributed to an image of the Vietnam War veteran as dehumanized and violent and thus deserving of public hostility or indifference. Veterans themselves who had committed or witnessed atrocities carried a severe burden of guilt.

Veterans expressed two kinds of reactions to the defeat. Many regarded the commitment as an honorable one and castigated the government for betraying them and their dead comrades by not letting them win the war. Others, sometimes expressing shame or guilt, blamed the government for sacrificing its youth in an immoral or useless war. The soldiers themselves best expressed the sense of the war's futility in the slang term they used in referring to a comrade's death: He was "wasted."

No parades or other heroes' welcomes greeted the returning soldiers. Some were treated to first-class seats by sympathetic airline attendants, but the common advice was to get out of uniform as quickly as possible. Returning veterans sometimes faced harassment from antiwar activists who did not distinguish the war from the warriors. A veteran who had stepped on a mine in Vietnam reported that being spit on "hurt as much as the wounds I sustained." Another veteran remembered the "feelings of rejection and scorn that a bunch of depressed and confused young men experienced when they re-

turned home from doing what their country told them to do."

Most military personnel came home to public indifference. Government benefits were less generous to Vietnam War veterans than they had been to World War II and Korean War soldiers. Many felt unwelcome even by veterans of earlier wars, who could not relate to soldiers who had failed to win their war. The 11,500 women who had served in Vietnam felt even more isolated and ignored by the government, the public, and veterans' groups.

Two-thirds of Vietnam veterans said that they would serve again, and most veterans readjusted well to civilian life under difficult conditions. Yet a substantial minority endured the aftereffects of war for decades. The Veterans Administration (VA) estimated that nearly one-sixth of the three million veterans suffered from posttraumatic stress disorder, with its symptoms of fear, recurring nightmares, feelings of guilt and shame, violence, drug

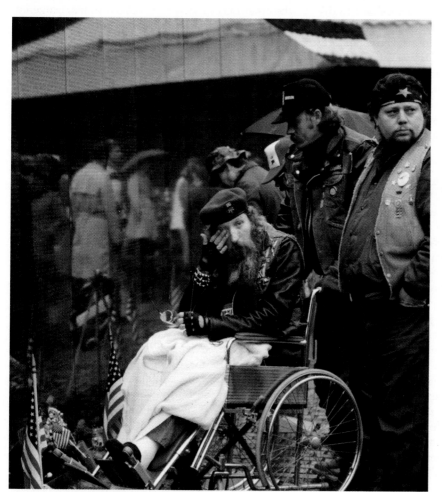

THE VIETNAM VETERANS MEMORIAL
These Vietnam veterans honor their dead comrades at the memorial in the nation's capital. Many veterans found a healing moment in standing before the wall. As one explained at the memorial's dedication in 1982, they came "to find the names of those we lost in the war, as if by tracing the letters cut into the granite we could find what was left of ourselves."
Peter Marbottom/Magnum Photos, Inc.

and alcohol abuse, and suicidal tendencies. More than fifteen years after the war's end, veterans remained on long waiting lists for treatment.

Symptoms of another kind of war casualty began to appear among veterans in the late 1970s. In greater proportions than the general population, those who had served in Vietnam bore deformed children and fell ill themselves with cancer, severe skin disorders, and other ailments. Veterans claimed a link between these illnesses and Agent Orange, an herbicide that contained the deadly poison dioxin. The military had sprayed twenty million gallons of Agent Orange and similar herbicides over five million acres in Vietnam.

For a decade the Veterans Administration insisted that no direct link could be proved, and it rejected virtually all veterans' applications for benefits based on claims that Agent Orange had caused their diseases. In response to a suit filed by 15,000 veterans, manufacturers of the chemical refused to admit fault but settled the suit by agreeing to pay $180 million in claims. Scientists continued to disagree about the chemical's effects on veterans, but in 1989 the VA began to use less severe standards in evaluating veterans' claims. In 1991, Congress enacted legislation extending benefits to veterans with diseases linked to Agent Orange and mandating further research.

Reversal of the government's position on Agent Orange coincided with a shift in the climate surrounding Vietnam War veterans. "It wasn't until the early 1980s," one veteran observed, "that it became 'all right' to be a combat veteran." Before then, he had never seen crowds cheer Vietnam War veterans who marched in Fourth of July parades. The Vietnam War began to enter the realm of popular culture with novels, TV shows, and hit movies depicting a broad range of military experience—from soldiers reduced to brutality to men and women serving with courage and integrity.

The incorporation of the Vietnam War into the collective experience was symbolized most dramatically in the Vietnam Veterans Memorial, designed by Maya Lin and unveiled in Washington, D.C., in November 1982. The black, V-shaped wall inscribed with the names of 58,000 men and women lost to the war became the second most visited site in the capital. It evoked emotional responses from visitors, many of whom adorned it with flowers, flags, messages, and mementos. In an article describing its dedication, a Vietnam combat veteran spoke to and for his former comrades: "Welcome home. The war is over."

Conclusion: The Limits of American Power

The Vietnam War was America's longest war. The United States spent $150 billion and sent more than 3 million of its young men and women to Southeast Asia. Fifty-eight thousand never returned, and 300,000 suffered wounds. The war shattered consensus at home and contributed to the most severe internal disorder in a century. It created opportunities for the aggrandizement of presidential power at the expense of congressional authority and public accountability and led to the downfall of two presidents.

The Vietnam War was a logical extension of the United States' post–World War II commitment to contain communism everywhere on the planet. Truman had begun that commitment when the United States had enjoyed an extraordinary margin of power, largely because World War II had so ravaged the other major nations. As other nations recovered, the United States lost its artificial and temporary advantage. Defeat in Vietnam did not make the United States the "pitiful helpless giant" predicted by Nixon, but it did suggest the relative decline of U.S. power and the impossibility of containment on a global scale.

One of the constraints on U.S. power was the tenacity of revolutionary movements that were determined to achieve national independence and autonomy. Failing to learn from the French experience in Vietnam, U.S. officials badly underestimated the sacrifices that the North Vietnamese and Vietcong were willing to make for the goal of national liberation. Policymakers overestimated the effectiveness of American technological superiority, and they failed to realize how easily the United States could be perceived as a colonial intruder, no more welcome than the French had been.

A second constraint on Eisenhower, Kennedy, Johnson, and Nixon in their decisions about Vietnam was their resolve to avoid a major confrontation with the Soviet Union or China. Johnson, who conducted the largest escalation of the war, especially needed to be cautious to avoid provoking direct intervention by the Communist superpowers. After China exploded its first atomic bomb in 1964, the potential heightened for the Vietnam conflict to escalate into worldwide disaster.

Third, in Vietnam the United States faced the problem of containment by means of an extremely weak ally. The South Vietnamese government never won the support of a majority of its population, and the intense devastation and suffering the war brought to the civilian population only made things worse. Short of taking over the South Vietnamese government and military, the United States could do little to strengthen South Vietnam's ability to resist communism.

Finally, domestic opposition to the war constrained the options of Johnson and Nixon. Although the antiwar movement never claimed a majority of the population, by 1968 it counted significant portions of mainstream America and the voices of prominent religious, media, business, and political

leaders. Moreover, as the war dragged on, with increasing American casualties and no signs of victory and with growing evidence of the damage being inflicted on the Vietnamese, more and more Americans simply became weary of the war.

By 1968, distinguished experts who had fashioned and implemented the containment policy recognized that erosion of support for the war made its continuation untenable. Yet the United States fought on for five more years before Nixon and Kissinger bowed to the resolution of the enemy and the limitations of U.S. power.

CHRONOLOGY

1961 CIA-backed Cuban exiles launch unsuccessful invasion of Cuba at Bay of Pigs.

Berlin Wall erected, dividing East and West Berlin.

Kennedy administration increases military aid and military advisors in South Vietnam.

Kennedy administration creates the Alliance for Progress and the Peace Corps.

1962 Cuban missile crisis.

1963 Limited nuclear test-ban treaty signed by United States and Soviet Union.

South Vietnamese military overthrows President Ngo Dinh Diem.

1964 U.S. troops quell anti-American rioting in Panama Canal Zone.

President Johnson uses Gulf of Tonkin incident to get congressional resolution of support for escalating the war.

1965 First major protest demonstration in Washington, D.C., against the Vietnam War attracts 20,000 people.

Johnson administration initiates Operation Rolling Thunder, intensified bombing of North Vietnam.

Johnson orders increase in the number of U.S. troops in Vietnam, which rises to 543,000 by 1969.

U.S. troops invade Dominican Republic to prevent leftist government from taking power.

1968 Hundreds of thousands of Americans demonstrate against war.

Vietnamese Communists' Tet Offensive leads Johnson administration to reverse its policy in Vietnam and seek negotiated settlement.

In wake of Tet Offensive, President Johnson decides not to seek second term.

Richard Nixon elected president.

1969 Nixon orders secret bombing of Cambodia.

1970 Nixon orders joint U.S.–South Vietnamese invasion of Cambodia.

1971 *New York Times* publishes *Pentagon Papers,* a secret, critical government study of U.S. policy in Vietnam.

1973 The Paris accords between United States, North and South Vietnam, and Vietcong bring formal end to U.S. role in Vietnam.

Congress enacts War Powers Act, limiting president's ability to send Amercans to war without congressional consent.

1975 North Vietnam launches final offensive and takes over all of South Vietnam, ending war in Vietnam.

BIBLIOGRAPHY

GENERAL WORKS

David Halberstam, *The Best and the Brightest* (1972).

George C. Herring, *America's Longest War: The United States and Vietnam, 1950–1975* (1986).

Walter A. McDougall, *The Heavens and the Earth: A Political History of the Space Age* (1985).

Kim McQuaid, *The Anxious Years: America in the Vietnam and Watergate Era* (1989).

James S. Olson and Randy Roberts, *Where the Domino Fell: America and Vietnam, 1945–1990* (1996).

Irwin Unger and Debi Unger, *Turning Point: 1968* (1988).

Marilyn B. Young, *The Vietnam Wars, 1945–1990* (1991).

FOREIGN POLICY IN THE 1960S

Graham T. Allison, *Essence of Decision: Explaining the Cuban Crisis* (1971).

Trumbull Higgins, *The Perfect Failure: Kennedy, Eisenhower, and the CIA at the Bay of Pigs* (1987).

Walter Isaacson, *Kissinger: A Biography* (1992).

Jerome Levinson and Juan de Onis, *The Alliance That Lost Its Way* (1970).

Abraham Lowenthal, *The Dominican Intervention* (1972).

Charles Murray and Catherine Bly Cox, *Apollo: The Race to the Moon* (1989).

James A. Nathan, ed., *The Cuban Missile Crisis Revisited* (1992).

Thomas G. Paterson, *Contesting Castro: The United States and the Triumph of the Cuban Revolution* (1994).

Thomas G. Paterson, ed., *Kennedy's Quest for Victory: American Foreign Policy, 1961–1963* (1989).

Gerald T. Rice, *The Bold Experiment: JFK's Peace Corps* (1986).

Robert D. Schulzinger, *Henry Kissinger: Doctor of Diplomacy* (1989).

D. Michael Shafe, *Deadly Paradigms: The Failure of U.S. Counterinsurgency Policy* (1988).

Deborah Shapley, *Promise and Power: The Life and Times of Robert McNamara* (1993).

Robert Smith Thompson, *The Missiles of October: The Declassified Story of John F. Kennedy and the Cuban Missile Crisis* (1992).

THE WAR IN VIETNAM

David L. Anderson, *Shadow on the White House: Presidents and the Vietnam War* (1993).

Loren Baritz, *Backfire: A History of How American Culture Led Us into Vietnam and Made Us Fight the Way We Did* (1985).

Larry Berman, *Lyndon Johnson's War: The Road to Stalemate in Vietnam* (1989).

Robert Buzzanco, *Masters of War: Military Dissent and Politics in the Vietnam Era* (1996).

Mark Clodfelter, *The Limits of Air Power: The American Bombing of North Vietnam* (1989).

Bernard Fall, *The Two Vietnams: A Political and Military Analysis* (1967).

Frances FitzGerald, *Fire in the Lake: The Vietnamese and the Americans in Vietnam* (1972).

Lloyd C. Gardner, *Lyndon Johnson and the Wars for Vietnam* (1995).

James William Gibson, *The Perfect War: Technowar in Vietnam* (1986).

Allan E. Goodman, *The Lost Peace: America's Search for a Negotiated Settlement of the Vietnam War* (1978).

Ellen J. Hammer, *A Death in November: America in Vietnam, 1973* (1987).

Arnold Isaacs, *Without Honor: Defeat in Vietnam and Cambodia* (1983).

Stanley Karnow, *Vietnam: A History* (1983; rev. ed., 1991).

Gabriel Kolko, *Anatomy of a War: Vietnam, the United States, and the Modern Historical Experience* (1985).

Guenter Lewy, *America in Vietnam* (1978).

Robert S. McNamara, *In Retrospect: The Tragedy and Lessons of Vietnam* (1995).

Harold G. Moore, *We Were Soldiers Once—and Young: Ia Drang, the Battle That Changed the War in Vietnam* (1992).

John M. Newman, *JFK and Vietnam: Deception, Intrigue, and the Struggle for Power* (1992).

David Rudenstine, *The Day the Presses Stopped: A History of the Pentagon Papers Case* (1996).

Ronald H. Spector, *After Tet: The Bloodiest Year in Vietnam* (1993).

Roger Warner, *Shooting at the Moon: The Story of America's Clandestine War in Laos* (1997).

THOSE WHO FOUGHT

Christian G. Appy, *Working-Class War: American Combat Soldiers and Vietnam* (1993).

Lawrence M. Baskir and William A. Strauss, *Chance and Circumstance: The Draft, the War, and the Vietnam Generation* (1978).

Philip Caputo, *A Rumor of War* (1977).

David Donovan, *Once a Warrior King: Memories of an Officer in Vietnam* (1985).

Bernard Edelman, ed., *Dear America: Letters Home from Vietnam* (1985).

Peter Goldman, *Charlie Company: What Vietnam Did to Us* (1983).

Bob Greene, *Homecoming: When the Soldiers Returned from Vietnam* (1989).

Ron Kovic, *Born on the Fourth of July* (1976).

Myra MacPherson, *Long Time Passing: Vietnam and the Haunted Generation* (1984).

Kathryn Marshall, *In the Combat Zone: Vivid Personal Recollections of the Vietnam War from the Women Who Served There* (1987).

Harry Maurer, *Strange Ground: Americans in Vietnam, 1945–1975, an Oral History* (1989).

Al Santoli, *Everything We Had: An Oral History of the Vietnam War* (1981).

Neil Sheehan, *A Bright Shining Lie: John Paul Vann and America in Vietnam* (1988).

John Wheeler, *Touched with Fire: The Future of the Vietnam Generation* (1984).

THE ANTIWAR MOVEMENT

Charles DeBenedetti, with Charles Chatfield, *An American Ordeal: The Antiwar Movement of the Vietnam Era* (1990).

Adam Garfinkle, *Telltale Hearts: The Origins and Impact of the Vietnam Antiwar Movement* (1995).

Todd Gitlin, *The Whole World Is Watching* (1980).

Thomas Powers, *Vietnam: The War at Home* (1973).

Melvin Small, *Johnson, Nixon, and the Doves* (1988).

Melvin Small and William D. Hoover, eds., *Give Peace a Chance: Exploring the Vietnam Antiwar Movement* (1992).

Amy Swerdlow, *Women Strike for Peace: Traditional Motherhood and Radical Politics in the 1960s* (1993).

Michael Useem, *Conscription, Protest, and Social Conflict: The Life and Death of a Draft Resistance Movement* (1983).

Nancy Zaroulis and Gerald Sullivan, *Who Spoke Up? American Protest against the War in Vietnam* (1984).

DOMESTIC POLITICS

Dan T. Carter, *The Politics of Race: George Wallace, the Origins of the New Conservatism, and the Transformation of American Politics* (1995).

David Halberstam, *The Unfinished Odyssey of Robert Kennedy* (1969).

Stephan Lesher, *George Wallace: American Populist* (1994).

Jonathan Schell, *The Time of Illusion* (1976).

Theodore H. White, *The Making of the President, 1968* (1970).

Jules Witcover, *85 Days: The Last Campaign of Robert Kennedy* (1969).

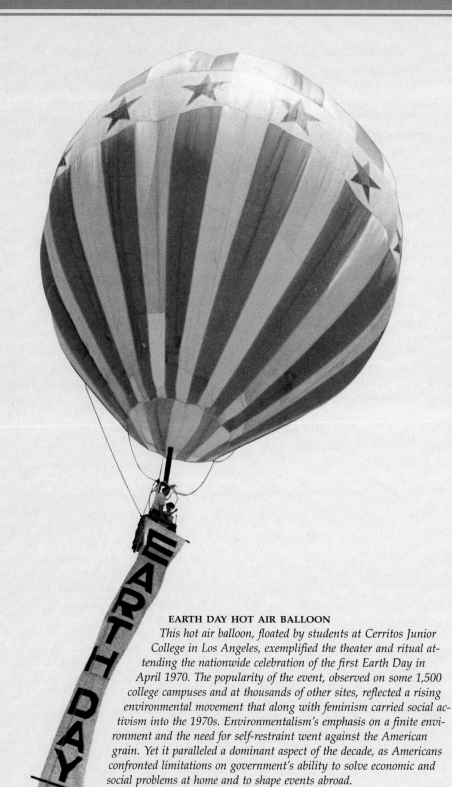

EARTH DAY HOT AIR BALLOON
This hot air balloon, floated by students at Cerritos Junior College in Los Angeles, exemplified the theater and ritual attending the nationwide celebration of the first Earth Day in April 1970. The popularity of the event, observed on some 1,500 college campuses and at thousands of other sites, reflected a rising environmental movement that along with feminism carried social activism into the 1970s. Environmentalism's emphasis on a finite environment and the need for self-restraint went against the American grain. Yet it paralleled a dominant aspect of the decade, as Americans confronted limitations on government's ability to solve economic and social problems at home and to shape events abroad.
Julian Wasser/Time Magazine.

THE DECLINE OF TRUST AND CONFIDENCE

30

1968–1980

O N THE EVENING OF JULY 25, 1974, Representative Barbara Jordan gazed solemnly into the television cameras. Not since the 1954 McCarthy hearings on charges of alleged Communists in the army had the activities of a congressional committee so riveted Americans to their TV screens. In a deep, commanding voice, Jordan said, "I am not going to sit here and be an idle spectator to the diminution, the subversion, the destruction of the Constitution." Thus began Jordan's argument for the impeachment of Richard M. Nixon, president of the United States.

That an African American woman from the South could influence the fate of the presidency indicated the significance of the civil rights struggles of the preceding decade. Born in 1936, Jordan grew up in an all-black neighborhood in Houston, Texas, living with her grandparents, parents, and two sisters in a two-bedroom house. Her father's income as a warehouse clerk and part-time minister provided a modest standard of living but few extras. Instilled with discipline and ambition by her parents, Jordan attended a segregated high school and then went to the all-black Texas Southern University. Riding at the back of the bus, drinking out of water fountains marked "colored," and attending segregated, underfunded schools were routine for Jordan and her friends in the 1950s.

In high school and college, Jordan discovered and honed her skills as an orator and debater. When she decided to attend law school at Boston University, her entire family scrimped to pay her expenses. After earning her degree in 1960, she returned home and set up a law practice. Local Democrats recognized her remarkable speaking skills, sent her out campaigning, and supported her candidacy for the Texas House of Representatives in 1962 and 1964. Running in countywide at-large elections, she lost both times to white candidates.

But the U.S. Supreme Court's "one person, one vote" decisions in the 1960s forced Texas to reapportion its legislative districts and opened political doors for Jordan. In 1966, she won election to the Texas Senate from her district, now heavily populated by African Americans, Chicanos, and white labor unionists, and became one of the first two African Americans to serve as Texas senators since 1882. In 1972, voters sent her to the U.S. House of Representatives, where she was appointed to the House Judiciary Committee.

Jordan's argument for impeachment reflected lifelong habits of painstaking research and careful deliberation, as she measured the illegal activities of President

Nixon against historical and legal standards. If Nixon's offenses did not add up to impeachment, Jordan concluded, "then perhaps that eighteenth-century Constitution should be abandoned to a twentieth-century paper shredder." The next day, billboards sprang up in Houston reading, "Thank you, Barbara Jordan, for explaining the Constitution to us."

Before the House could act on impeachment, Nixon resigned the presidency in disgrace. His successor, Gerald R. Ford, occupied the Oval Office for little more than two years, losing his bid for a full term when Jimmy Carter led the Democrats back into the White House in the 1976 election. After a single term, Carter, too, was voted out of office.

This rapid turnover in the presidency reflected in part a widespread loss of trust and confidence in government in the 1970s, expressed cynically by some Americans whose bumper stickers exhorted, "Don't vote...It only encourages them." Public opinion polls reported a drop from 56 percent to 29 percent in citizens' belief that government would "do what is right most of the time." Those who thought that "the people running the country don't really care what happens to you" shot up from 26 percent to 60 percent. And voter turnout continued to decline, reaching only 52.3 percent in 1980.

Nixon's moral failings and Ford's and Carter's weak leadership contributed to the demise of all three. Yet Ford and Carter also confronted problems that might well have defeated more talented politicians. Changes in the institutions of politics and government made effective leadership more difficult just when new domestic and foreign challenges demanded great vision and heroic efforts at persuasion and consensus building.

Barbara Jordan came to a Congress determined to reassert its authority in reaction to the expansion of presidential power under Johnson and Nixon. Yet at the same time, the House and Senate instituted reforms that dispersed power more broadly throughout Congress and undercut the traditionally strong position of congressional party leaders. Moreover, political parties lost influence as primary elections replaced party conventions as the vehicle for nominating candidates. Elected officials depended less on party support and relied more on campaign funds from special interest groups. They used these contributions to appeal directly to voters, largely through television. Consequently, while the legislature set limitations on presidential power, the decline of party influence undermined the ability of Congress itself to provide coherent leadership.

BARBARA JORDAN
After gaining national attention for her role in the Nixon impeachment hearings, Barbara Jordan served in the House of Representatives until she retired in 1978. The representative from Texas supported women's rights as well as civil rights; here she addresses the government-sponsored National Women's Conference in Dallas, Texas, in 1977.
Owen Franken/Sygma.

This fragmented leadership confronted critical challenges during the 1970s, including shifting relations between the superpowers and new shock waves in the Middle East that threatened Western access to oil. Economic problems further shook national confidence as the United States suffered simultaneous galloping inflation and rising unemployment and as a sluggish economy and declining productivity replaced the rapid economic growth of the 1960s.

An increasingly vocal minority of Americans joined right-wing political groups in the 1970s, yet the reforming impulse of the 1960s did not come to a complete halt. Even though the black freedom struggle had been devastated by government harassment, assassination of its leaders, internal conflicts, and white backlash, civil rights advocates retained some influence in Washington, and a few

African Americans, such as Barbara Jordan, slowly edged into the margins of the power structure. Key elements of Lyndon Johnson's Great Society actually expanded in the early 1970s, and a reconstituted Supreme Court under Chief Justice Warren Burger maintained most of the Warren Court's protections of individual rights. Two social movements that had begun late in the 1960s—environmentalism and feminism—achieved their greatest strength during the decade.

Yet a more prevalent pessimism overshadowed these signs of faith that the government could still tackle social problems and promote the general welfare. By the end of the 1970s, a majority of Americans saw their standard of living slipping and the global position of their nation in decline. The heady optimism of the post–World War II era, badly shaken by defeat in Vietnam, shattered with the economic crises and foreign policy setbacks of the 1970s. Limitations rather than possibilities characterized both the popular mood and the state of the nation.

Politics and the Persistence of Reform

Richard Nixon took his victory in 1968 and the strong showing made by George Wallace as evidence that most Americans were fed up with social protest and government efforts to expand individual rights and opportunities. As president, Nixon continued to appeal to those frustrations, and the pace of reform slackened considerably during his administration. Yet in defeating Ronald Reagan on the right and Nelson Rockefeller on the left, Nixon had won the Republican nomination as a centrist. Like Eisenhower, he did not try to turn the clock back a decade, nor did his presidency bring reform efforts to a screeching halt.

Congress remained in the hands of a Democratic majority, and the government faced pressures from popular movements that survived the 1960s. Supporters of the black freedom struggle retained some clout in Congress and the courts, which compelled the Nixon administration to accept civil rights advances that were at odds with the president's antireform rhetoric. Two newer movements prompted Congress and the president to enact reforms in women's rights and environmental protection.

Nixon's "Southern Strategy" and Race Relations

Nixon's 1968 campaign had exploited southern antipathy to black protest and new civil rights policies to woo white southerners away from the Democratic Party. This "southern strategy" delivered the electoral votes of the Upper South to Nixon, yet George Wallace ran strongly in the South and made inroads into traditional white voting blocs in northern and western cities. The prospect of another Wallace campaign in 1972 encouraged Republicans to write off the black vote and appeal to whites who thought racial progress had gone far enough.

Nixon himself believed that "the laws have caught up with our consciences" and that legal solutions had done about as much as they could to improve the status of African Americans. His key adviser, Daniel Patrick Moynihan, a Democrat who had worked in the Johnson White House, claimed that the issue of race had been "taken over by hysterics, paranoids, and boodlers" and called for a period of "benign neglect" in which "Negro progress continues and racial rhetoric fades." Although blacks made some advances during the Nixon administration, the president's public rhetoric and policies sought to slow the momentum of racial change and reap the political benefits of the white backlash.

Richard Nixon took his victory in 1968 as evidence that most Americans were fed up with social protest and government efforts to expand individual rights and opportunities.

In 1968, fourteen years after the *Brown* decision, school desegregation had barely touched the South: Two-thirds of African American children did not have a single white schoolmate. Nixon wanted a freedom-of-choice approach that forbade discrimination but did not use federal power to compel integration. Nonetheless, when the Supreme Court overruled efforts by the Justice Department to delay court-ordered desegregation, in 1969 the administration agreed to enforce the law. By the time Nixon left office, fewer than one in ten black children attended totally segregated schools in the South.

In fact, school segregation was more extreme in northern and western cities, where segregated residential patterns left half of all African American

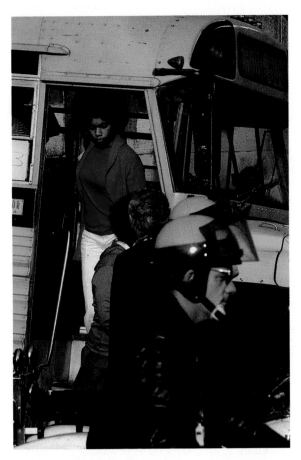

SCHOOL BUSING
Controversy over busing as a means to integrate public schools erupted in Boston when the school year started in autumn 1974. Opposition was especially high in white ethnic neighborhoods like South Boston, whose residents resented liberal judges from the suburbs assigning them the burden of integration. Clashes between blacks and whites in South Boston prompted authorities to dispatch police to protect black students.
Ira Wyman.

children attending virtually all-black schools. By 1971, busing students from white to black neighborhoods to achieve desegregation had become one of the most inflammatory civil rights issues. That year, in *Swann v. Charlotte-Mecklenburg Board of Education,* the Supreme Court ruled unanimously that busing in Charlotte, North Carolina, and the surrounding county was an appropriate remedy to overcome segregation previously sanctioned by the city. Subsequently, federal courts approved busing plans in cities outside the South that had not offi-

cially maintained segregated schools but that had residential patterns resulting in de facto segregation.

Although children had been riding buses to school for decades, especially in rural areas, busing for racial integration provoked outrage. When busing began at the formerly all-white South Boston High School in 1974, virtually all of the white students boycotted classes while angry opponents of busing threw rocks at black students. The whites most likely to be bused came from working-class families, who remained in cities that more affluent whites had fled and who already felt their status eroding while the government attended to the needs of minorities and the poor. Moreover, white children rode buses to predominantly black schools where overcrowding and deficient facilities often meant inferior education. African Americans themselves were divided over the desirability of busing children across district lines.

Nixon attacked "forced integration" but failed to persuade Congress to end court-ordered busing. But with four new justices appointed by Nixon, the Supreme Court moved in the president's direction in 1974. In a five-to-four decision concerning the Detroit public schools (*Milliken v. Bradley*), the Court imposed strict limits on the use of busing to achieve racial balance.

Despite Nixon's conservative rhetoric and practice, his administration did take some initiatives against discrimination. Secretary of Labor George Shultz implemented the so-called Philadelphia plan, later extended to other cities, which required contractors and unions to increase the number of minority members employed on construction projects funded by the federal government. The Nixon administration also gave a modest boost to African American entrepreneurs by increasing the number of government contracts and loans awarded to minority businesses.

Congress took the initiative in other areas. Overcoming administration opposition, in 1970 Congress extended for five more years the Voting Rights Act of 1965, one of the most important instruments for the empowerment of African Americans. Pressured by feminists and civil rights activists, in March 1972 Congress strengthened the Civil Rights Act of 1964. It enlarged the jurisdiction of the Equal Employment Opportunity Commission, the act's enforcement agency, and granted it authority to initiate lawsuits against employers who were suspected of discrimination.

The Supreme Court after Earl Warren

To Nixon, the Warren Court had been "unprecedentedly politically active . . . too often using their interpretation of the law to remake American society according to their own social, political, and ideological precepts." Through his judicial appointments, Nixon planned both to reverse the Court's directions and to implement his "southern strategy." When Chief Justice Earl Warren resigned in June 1969, Nixon replaced him with Warren E. Burger, a federal appeals court judge, who was seen as a more conservative strict constructionist. Burger easily won Senate confirmation, but Nixon's next nominations provoked bitter fights.

Unions and civil rights groups mounted strong campaigns against Nixon's next two nominees, southern federal judges known for their conservative positions, especially on civil rights. The Senate defied Nixon on both nominations, forcing him to settle on a candidate acceptable to the Senate, federal judge Harry A. Blackmun from Minnesota, who over the years turned out to be a moderate in his rulings. Two more vacancies enabled Nixon to appoint Lewis F. Powell and William H. Rehnquist, both of whom Nixon hoped would be more sympathetic to his political agenda.

Even with Nixon's more conservative justices, the Supreme Court in the 1970s maintained considerable continuity with the 1960s Court, carrying on social reform through judicial rulings. Several decisions of the Burger Court, for example, expanded the rights of welfare recipients. The Court narrowed somewhat the protections that the Warren Court had extended to accused criminals, but it also nullified all state death penalty laws in 1972, primarily on the grounds that the death penalty was arbitrarily applied. Four years later, the Court upheld the rights of states to impose capital punishment if they established specific procedural safeguards.

Although the Court restricted busing to achieve school integration, overall its decisions favored victims of discrimination based on race and sex. A unanimous court, for example, established the rule of "disparate impact," deciding in *Griggs v. Duke Power Company* (1971) that under the Civil Rights Act of 1964 a company's employment practices, even when established in good faith, could be found illegal if the result was to discriminate against women and minorities.

The issue of affirmative action, however, sharply divided the Court. In *Regents of the University of California v. Bakke* (1978), the Court ruled in favor of a white man who had been denied admission to a University of California medical school even though his test scores were higher than those of some minority applicants who were admitted. Yet the Court sanctioned affirmative action programs to attack the results of past discrimination as long as strict quotas or racial classifications were not involved. The Court also took giant steps in protecting women's rights and minimizing sex discrimination.

The New Feminism

On August 26, 1970, fifty years after women won the right to vote, tens of thousands of women took to the streets. In nationwide protests, called Women Strike for Peace and Equality, they carried signs reading "Sisterhood Is Powerful," "Don't Cook Dinner—Starve a Rat Today," and "Don't Iron While the Strike Is Hot." Some of the banners proclaimed, "The Women of Vietnam Are Our Sisters," and others demanded racial justice. But this time, women placed their own liberation at the forefront.

Conceived by Betty Friedan and organized largely by chapters of the National Organization for Women (NOW), the strike reflected the diverse strands that constituted the new feminism of the 1970s: radical women in jeans and conservatively dressed former suffragists, peace activists and politicians, teenagers and older women, and a sprinkling of women of color. The strike centered on NOW's three main demands: equality for women in employment and education; child care centers throughout the nation; and women's control over reproduction, including the right to abortion.

Feminism came into its own in the 1970s, spawning hundreds of new organizations, radical changes in how women perceived themselves and their interests, and policy changes that amounted to a revolution in women's status under the law. Women's liberation, the radical wing of feminism, erupted from women's experiences in the civil rights and antiwar movements of the 1960s. Representing feminism's mainstream was NOW, founded in 1966, an outgrowth of the publication of Friedan's *The Feminine Mystique,* the work of the President's Commission on the Status of Women, and federal attention to sex discrimination in the Equal Pay Act of 1963 and the Civil Rights Act of 1964.

Although NOW elected a black president, Aileen Hernandez, in 1970, white middle-class

TECHNOLOGY IN AMERICA

The Pill

Two reform-minded women and three male scientists played prominent roles in the development of the birth control pill. Margaret Sanger had fought for women's control over reproduction since the 1910s. In the 1950s her main priority was the development of an oral contraceptive and she persuaded wealthy heiress Katharine Dexter McCormick, the second woman to graduate from MIT, to bankroll research on the pill with a portion of her enormous fortune. McCormick supported the work of biologists Gregory Goodwin Pincus and M.C. Chang, who then brought physician John Rock into their research on hormones. They began testing the pill in 1956, and the Food and Drug Administration approved it in 1960.

"Modern woman is at last free as man is free," declared Clare Boothe Luce, playwright and former congresswoman. Separating contraception from the act of intercourse for the first time, the pill afforded greater spontaneity in sexual relations. It also was more reliable than other forms of birth control since it was nearly one hundred percent effective in preventing pregnancy. Within three years more than two million women were "on the pill" and their numbers continued to increase as doses were adjusted to reduce side effects and risk of stroke, cancer, and other ailments. In the 1990s, nearly twenty million women relied on the pill, the most widespread form of contraception aside from sterilization.

Wyeth-Ayerst Laboratories.

women in the political mainstream provided most of the national leadership and much of the constituency for the new feminism. They were justifiably criticized for their frequent indifference to the concerns of women who were unlike themselves. Yet support for feminism was exceedingly multifaceted. Although most black women, for example, remained cool to NOW and other mainstream groups, polls showed that their support for feminist goals exceeded that of white women.

Like other women of color, most African American women worked through their own groups such as the older National Council of Negro Women and the National Black Feminist Organization, founded in 1973. Similarly, women from forty-three Indian nations established the Native American Women's Association in 1970, Mexican American women held the first national Chicana conference in 1971, and Asian American women formed their own local movements. Blue-collar women organized the National Coalition of Labor Union Women in 1974, clerical workers founded Nine-to-Five, and women

over forty founded the Older Women's League. Lesbians established collectives in communities throughout the country as well as their own caucuses in organizations such as NOW. Women formed a host of other groups that focused on single issues such as health, abortion rights, education, and violence against women.

Feminist activism produced the most sweeping changes in laws and policies concerning women since the Nineteenth Amendment in 1920 guaranteed women's right to vote.

The range of feminist activism ran the gamut from lobbying Congress to direct action. In 1970, nine San Francisco women upset a meeting of CBS stockholders, protesting against "derogatory images of women in programming and commercials." (Later that year, CBS executives circulated a memo calling for "a new image of a woman as a doer, as an educated, serious-minded individual person.") Women began to speak out publicly about personal experiences, such as rape and abortion, that had always been shrouded in secrecy. Tens of thousands marched throughout the country to demand an Equal Rights Amendment to the Constitution, and a handful of women illegally occupied state capital buildings and went on hunger strikes. In 1972, journalist Gloria Steinem and other women founded *Ms.*, a feminist magazine that sold 300,000 copies in a week and became the popular voice of feminism. Throughout the nation, women joined consciousness-raising groups where they discovered that what they had considered "personal" problems reflected a well-entrenched system of discrimination against and devaluation of women.

Common threads underlay the great diversity of organizations, issues, and activities. Above all, feminism represented the belief that women were barred from, unequally treated in, or poorly served by the entire male-dominated public arena, whether the political system, the medical establishment, the law enforcement bureaucracy, the educational system, or organized religion. Feminists challenged traditional norms that identified women primarily as wives and mothers, and they sought equality in both the private and public spheres.

The women's movement was an effect rather than a cause of women's rising employment, but feminism lifted female aspirations and helped lower barriers to jobs historically monopolized by men. Women made some inroads into skilled crafts and management positions. During the 1970s, their share of law degrees shot up from 5.4 percent to nearly 30 percent, and their proportion of medical degrees from 8.4 percent to 23 percent. In political office-holding at all levels of government, women started from a near-zero base, and their gains came at an excruciatingly slow pace. Yet by the late 1980s, women served as mayors in ten large cities and held 15 percent of municipal offices and state legislative seats.

Feminist activism produced the most sweeping changes in laws and policies concerning women since the Nineteenth Amendment in 1920 guaranteed women's right to vote. In 1972, Congress passed Title IX of the Education Amendments Act, banning sex discrimination in education. Covering athletics as well as admissions, hiring, and student services, the law evoked outrage from the male sports establishment, which did not want to share its subsidies. Nonetheless, women's participation in high school and college athletics grew enormously over the next two decades. Congress outlawed sex

discrimination in granting credit in 1974 and in 1978 prohibited discrimination against pregnant women. It opened the military academies to women and gave an official stamp to the women's movement by appropriating funds for the first National Women's Conference. This conference, attended by a cross section of American women, met in Houston, Texas, in 1977 and established a national policy agenda for women.

Changes in other areas came largely at the state and local levels and often resulted from the efforts of radical feminists. They spoke out about rape, forced law enforcement agencies to treat rape victims more humanely, and won new state laws that banned cross-examination of rape victims about

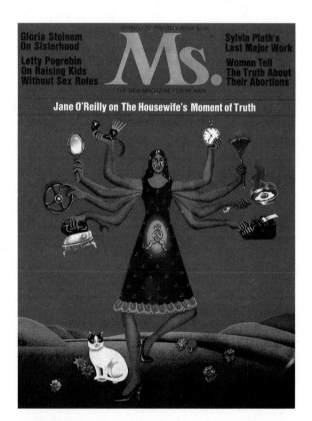

MS. MAGAZINE
In 1972, Gloria Steinem and other journalists and writers published the premier issue of the first mass-circulation magazine to be controlled for and by women. Ms.: The New Magazine for Women *ignored the recipes and fashion tips of typical women's magazines. It featured literature by women writers and articles on a broad range of feminist issues. What concerns are suggested by the cover of this premier issue?*
Courtesy, Lang Communications.

past sexual history and eliminated the traditional requirement that victims produce either a witness or proof of resistance. Domestic violence was another issue made visible by feminists. Throughout the country, groups of women set up shelters to provide safety for battered women and their children. Nearly every state passed laws affording greater protection for victims of domestic violence and more effective prosecution of offenders. A number of states used revenues from marriage license fee increases for domestic violence programs.

Women's demand for reproductive freedom focused on the right to abortion. Feminists pressured state legislatures to reform or repeal restrictions on abortion, and many testified publicly about their own illegal abortions. They also filed lawsuits, and in 1973 the Supreme Court issued the landmark *Roe v. Wade* decision. Upholding the individual rights of both women and physicians, the Court ruled that the Constitution protects the right to abortion and that states could not prohibit abortions in the early

stages of pregnancy. However, later decisions allowed state governments to refuse to pay for abortions under Medicaid and other government-financed health programs.

The Court also struck down laws that treated men and women differently, for example, in granting Social Security and welfare benefits, workers' compensation, and access to military programs; in establishing the age of adulthood; in forming juries; and in determining alimony. Although the Court refused to adopt the same strict standard for laws differentiating on the basis of sex as it did for those involving race, these and other rulings overturned centuries of law based on women's dependency as daughters, wives, and mothers.

Public opinion polls registered majorities in favor of most feminist goals, yet by the mid-1970s, feminism faced a strong countermovement. The movement was led by Phyllis Schlafly, who had built her political career in the right-wing politics of fervent anticommunism, demands for a stronger defense establishment, and opposition to big government and social welfare programs. In the 1970s, Schlafly and other conservatives broadened their program to include a defense of conventional sex roles and the traditional family. For example, an organization called the Moral Majority, led by fundamentalist minister Jerry Falwell, combined long-standing conservative positions with opposition to nearly every goal of the women's movement.

Antifeminism achieved its greatest victory in blocking ratification of the Equal Rights Amendment (ERA). Stating simply that "equality of rights under law shall not be denied or abridged by the United States or by any State on account of sex," the ERA would outlaw any differential treatment of men and women under all state and federal laws. Initially proposed by a small band of feminists in 1923, the ERA rode through Congress in 1972 on the wave of the new feminism. Most states rushed to ratify the amendment, but by 1973, Schlafly and others had begun to organize massive resistance. When the time limit on ratification ran out in 1982, after Congress had extended it in 1978, only thirty-five states had ratified the amendment, three short of the necessary three-fourths majority.

A handful of male votes in a few state legislatures made the difference, yet conservative women played prominent roles in defeating the amendment. Arguing that the ERA would deprive women of important privileges, including their right to stay home and be supported by their husbands and their exemption from military service, and that it would

TABLE 30.1
WOMEN ENTER THE PROFESSIONS, 1975 AND 1988

Occupation	Percent of women of total employed	
	1975	1988
Airplane pilot, navigator	—	3.1
Architect	4.3	14.6
Bus driver	37.7	48.5
Carpenter	0.6	1.5
Child care worker	93.8	97.3
Computer programmer	25.6	32.2
Computer systems analyst	14.8	29.5
Data entry keyer	92.8	88.2
Dentist	1.8	9.3
Economist	13.1	35.5
Elementary school teacher	85.4	84.8
College, university teacher	31.1	38.5
Lawyer, judge	7.1	19.5
Mail carrier	8.7	22.0
Physician	13.0	20.0
Police officer	2.7	13.4
Registered nurse	97.0	94.6
Secretary	99.1	99.1
Telephone installer, repairer	4.8	12.1
Telephone operator	93.3	89.8

Source: U.S. Bureau of Labor Statistics.

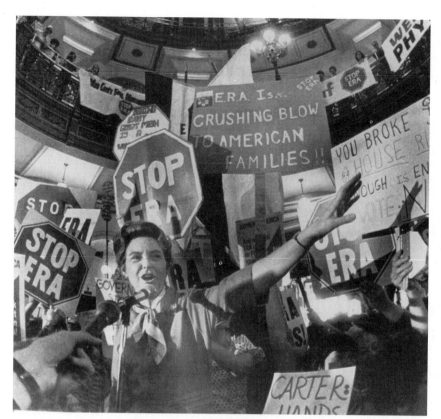

PHYLLIS SCHLAFLY
As one of the few nonsouthern states that rejected ratification of the proposed Equal Rights Amendment, Illinois was the scene of feverish activity by supporters and opponents. Here STOP ERA leader Phyllis Schlafly rallies her followers in the rotunda of the Illinois capitol in Springfield in June 1978. STOP ERA women handed legislators apple pies bearing the words "For the sake of the family please vote no."
Corbis-Bettmann.

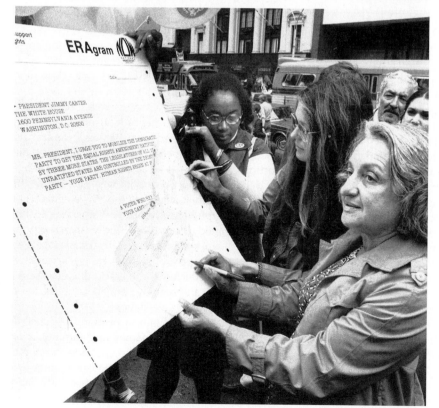

BETTY FRIEDAN AND GLORIA STEINEM
Two prominent feminists, Betty Friedan (foreground) and Gloria Steinem (to her right), sign telegrams in July 1977 entreating President Jimmy Carter to help get three more states to ratify the proposed Equal Rights Amendment. The appeal to Carter urged him to translate his commitment to human rights abroad into vigorous support of human rights at home.
Corbis-Bettmann.

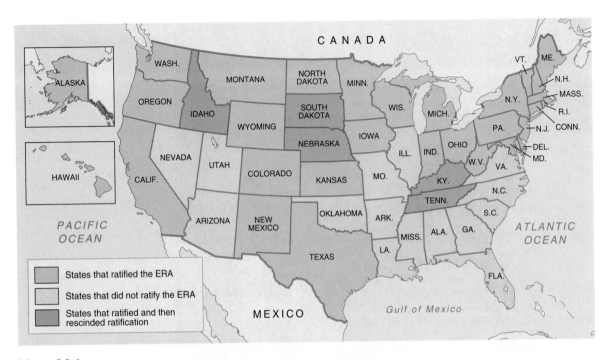

MAP 30.1
The Fight for the Equal Rights Amendment
Many states that failed to ratify the Equal Rights Amendment had previously refused to ratify the women suffrage amendment (or ratified it decades later, as did North Carolina in 1971). Why do you think so many nonratifying states were in the South?

destroy the traditional family, grassroots antifeminists wrote letters, lobbied, and demonstrated. These women had invested a lot in their traditional roles, which they saw as God-given, and feared a breakdown of gender differences. The antifeminists defeated the major goal of the women's movement, even though public opinion polls showed that a majority of both men and women favored the ERA.

Opposition to a second major goal of the women's movement, the right to abortion, was more complex. Many Americans believed that human life begins with conception, and they equated abortion with murder. The Catholic Church and other religious organizations provided institutional support for their protest. Right-wing politicians and their supporters, who identified abortion with the emancipation of women and the destruction of conventional sex roles and the family, constituted another segment of the right-to-life movement. As did opponents of the ERA, the right-to-life movement mobilized thousands of women who believed that abortion devalued motherhood and saw feminism as a threat to their traditional roles.

Although the right-to-life movement failed to achieve a constitutional amendment banning abortion, it helped defeat pro-choice politicians and achieved restrictions on abortion at the state and federal levels. In 1977, Congress began to deny the use of Medicaid and other federal funds for abortions. States also enacted laws that made it more difficult for women, especially poor women, to obtain abortions.

Defense of abortion rights was just one of the challenges feminists faced as the 1970s ended. For all the highly publicized inroads women made into male-dominated occupations, the vast majority of women still worked in traditionally female jobs. Pay scales in such occupations as clerical work, nursing, and teaching reflected the historic devaluation of women's worth and seemingly lay beyond the reach of antidiscrimination legislation.

Women continued to bear primary responsibility for the care of their homes and families even while they increasingly worked outside the home. Most husbands of women in the labor force expanded their share of domestic duties only marginally, while women worked a "double day"—one at the workplace and one at home. As the number of female-headed families grew from 10 percent to 20 percent of all families between 1970 and 1990, the situation of employed mothers became even more critical. Congress's only significant effort to ease the problems of employed mothers—the passage of a comprehensive child care bill—fell to President Nixon's veto in 1971. At the end of the 1970s, feminists needed stamina not only to preserve the gains of the past decade, but also to address the problems that were untouched by the legal revolution of the 1970s.

A Movement to Save the Environment

Mass demonstrations in the 1960s and early 1970s were not confined to the civil rights, antiwar, and feminist movements. In April 1970, millions of Americans observed the first Earth Day to register their concern over the ravaging effects of industrial development on the environment. In Wisconsin, students distributed flyers encouraging recycling, and a group of Detroit women picketed a steel plant that discharged industrial waste into a river. Girl scouts cleaned garbage from the Potomac River, Berkeley citizens attended an environmental teach-in, and African Americans in St. Louis dramatized the effects of poisons in lead paint. Some students in Michigan shattered a Ford to protest automobile emissions, and people planted trees all over the country.

Inheriting their concern for the natural world from the decades-old conservation movement, the new environmentalists had a far broader agenda. Even more important than preserving portions of the natural world for aesthetic and recreational purposes was protecting human beings from the devastating side effects of industrial development and economic growth—polluted air and water and the spread of deadly chemicals. This pollution threatened wildlife, plants, and a delicate ecological balance and had the potential to imperil human life itself.

Biologist Rachel Carson had drawn the first national attention to environmental concerns in 1962 with her best-seller *Silent Spring,* which stressed the harmful effects of toxic chemicals, particularly the pesticide DDT. Older conservation organizations like the Sierra Club and the Wilderness Society expanded the scope of their concerns, and they were

joined by a host of new organizations. The Environmental Defense Fund, for example, specialized in litigation. In 1971, environmentalists founded Greenpeace, an organization that protested nuclear testing around the world and campaigned to save whales, other ocean animals, and tropical rain forests. Even more militant was Earth First!, created in 1980 and committed to direct action and sabotage of projects injurious to the environment.

President Nixon asserted that the nation must begin "reclaiming the purity of its air, its waters, our living environment" and urged legislation to "end the plunder of America's natural heritage." Yet he obstructed several objectives of the environmental movement and forced Congress to override his veto to continue the anti–water pollution measures begun in the 1960s. Nixon gave priority to economic growth and increasing the nation's energy supply over environmental considerations. Against objections from environmentalists, he pushed Congress to authorize construction of a 789-mile-long pipeline to carry oil across Alaska.

Inheriting their concern for the natural world from the decades-old conservation movement, the new environmentalists had a far broader agenda: protecting human beings from the devastating side effects of industrial development and economic growth.

In other respects, the Nixon administration proved a friend—or at least not an enemy—of the environmental movement. In 1970, he established the Environmental Protection Agency (EPA). Charged with enforcing clean air and water policies and regulating pesticides, the EPA soon became the largest federal regulatory agency. Nixon also signed the Occupational Safety and Health Act (OSHA), which safeguarded workers against workplace accidents and disease. For example, it set limits on worker exposure to cotton dust, which caused devastating brown lung disease among textile workers, and imposed restrictions on the use of cancer-causing asbestos.

The strongest measure supported by the Nixon administration was the Clean Air Act of 1970. It established national standards for air quality, imposed restrictions on factory and automobile emissions, and included penalties of jail sentences as well as

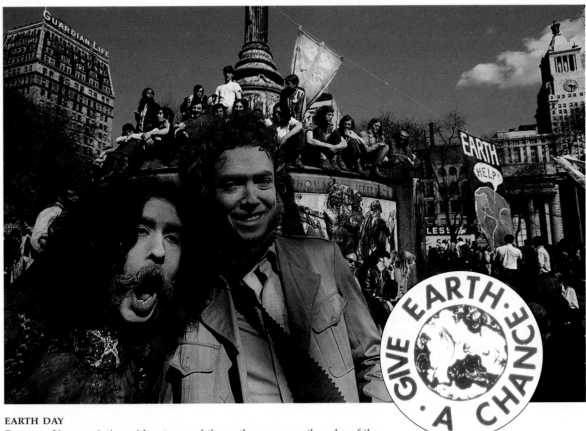

EARTH DAY

*Because of its association with nature and the earth, green was the color of the
environmental movement, and environmentalists called themselves "greens." These
activists leave no doubt about their affiliation at an Earth Day celebration in New York City
in April 1970. The button, a takeoff on the antiwar slogan "Give Peace a Chance," reflects the continuing impact of the antiwar movement.*

Dennis Stock/Magnum Photos, Inc.; button: private collection.

fines. Twenty years after enactment, no major city
met the new health standards, and more than half
the population lived in areas that defied the law's
promise that "air . . . shall have no adverse effects
on any American's health." But even with lenient
enforcement, the Clean Air Act cut the amount of
air pollutants by one-third, despite population and
economic growth. Denver residents could see the
mountains more clearly after pollution was cut in
half, and even Los Angeles experienced less smog
after the controls.

The environmental movement made further
progress during the Carter administration (1977–
1981). With the president's sponsorship, Congress
passed legislation to improve clean air and water
programs; to preserve vast areas of Alaska; to control strip mining, which left ugly scars along moun-
tainsides; and to provide $1.6 billion for cleanup of
hazardous wastes left by the chemical industry.

Nuclear energy posed an even greater threat.
When Carter took office in 1977, nuclear power
plants produced about 11 percent of the country's
electricity. A growing antinuclear movement
warned of the hazards of radiation leakage, the potential for accidents, and the problem of disposing
of nuclear wastes. The perils of nuclear energy came
into dramatic focus in March 1979, when an accident occurred at the Three Mile Island nuclear facility in Pennsylvania. Technicians worked for days
to prevent a meltdown of the reactor core, while
thousands of people who lived in the vicinity of the
plant fled their homes and the threat of fatal radiation. A combination of economic factors (mainly the
staggering costs of building nuclear plants) and

popular opposition stalled further development of the nuclear power industry, but antinuclear activism remained on the environmental movement's agenda. The environmental movement persisted into the 1980s as it sought to preserve the advances of the past two decades against attempts to relax or repeal environmental laws.

Domestic and Foreign Initiatives of the Nixon Era

Not all of the reforms of the 1970s originated outside the White House. Much of Richard Nixon's public rhetoric appealed to Americans unhappy with the expanding federal programs of the 1960s and frustrated by the nation's seeming inability to deter its great enemy, communism. Yet in practice, the Nixon administration not only moved the United States toward cooperation with China and the Soviet Union but also pursued a domestic agenda that bore marks of the very government activism that Nixon decried in his speeches.

The Nixon administration not only moved the United States toward cooperation with China and the Soviet Union but also pursued a domestic agenda that bore marks of the very government activism that Nixon decried in his speeches.

Nixon's domestic policies grew out of political expediency, a Congress controlled by the Democrats, a body of advisers representing a broad spectrum of political positions, the president's desire for history's approving gaze, and serious economic problems. Thus his administration sustained many of the reforms of the 1960s and advanced the government's role in some areas. While transferring some power from the federal government to the states through a revenue-sharing program, the Nixon administration also enlarged the federal government's role in the economy with expanded aid to the poor, new environmental regulations, deficit spending, devaluation of the dollar, and price and wage controls—all heretical deviations from traditional Republican economics.

Nixon's foreign policy also deviated from Republican orthodoxy, most markedly in its moves toward accommodation with the Soviet Union and China. Yet at the same time, in Vietnam, the Middle East, and Latin America, the administration pursued policies straight out of the cold war book of unrelenting opposition to communism.

Extending the Welfare State

Richard Nixon's second inaugural address in 1973 encapsulated his objections to much of Lyndon Johnson's Great Society: "In trusting too much to government, we have asked more of it than it can deliver. . . . Government must learn to take less from people so people can do more for themselves." The Great Society's efforts to solve every social problem, Nixon argued, both overextended federal power and proved ineffective in practice. Nixon's words also played to "middle America," which resented government's apparent disregard for its interests while favoring individuals who lacked the discipline and willingness to help themselves: "America was built not by government, but by people—not by welfare, but by work."

Congress successfully resisted many of Nixon's attacks on programs that had been initiated with the War on Poverty, refusing, for example, to eliminate the Office of Economic Opportunity. Skirmishes between the president and Congress resulted in some changes in antipoverty programs but left intact key programs such as Head Start, Legal Services, and job training. At the same time, Nixon blocked congressional efforts at reform. Although he supported day care programs for welfare recipients, the president vetoed the child care bill passed by Congress in 1971. He objected not only to the program's $2 billion cost but also to "communal approaches to child rearing," which he believed had "family-weakening implications."

Nixon also reached beyond his veto powers to undermine congressional initiatives. Concerned about the budget deficit and angry at Congress for appropriating more funds than he wanted for social welfare, environmental protection, and other programs, in 1972 Nixon simply refused to spend nearly $9 billion of appropriations. Federal courts later found this "impoundment" of appropriations to be a violation of presidential powers.

More significant than the Nixon administration's battle against federal programs was its extension of government assistance to the disadvantaged. Budgets for social services during Nixon's presidency exceeded defense spending for the first time since World War II. Social Security benefits went up and for the first time were legally required to rise with the cost of living. Subsidies for low-income housing, which totaled less than $1 million in 1969, reached nearly $3 billion in 1973. A new program, the Basic Opportunity Grant program, provided $1 billion in so-called Pell grants (named for Democratic Congressman Clayborne Pell, who sponsored the law) for low-income students to attend college.

Much of the expansion of the welfare state during the Nixon years was simply maintenance of existing programs or acquiescence to congressional initiatives. However, the Nixon administration itself proposed a major reform, a Family Assistance Plan (FAP) that would provide a guaranteed minimum income for all families. With this bold proposal, Nixon hoped to eliminate problems in the welfare system, reduce the welfare bureaucracy, aid the working poor, and secure his place in history. Unlike existing policy, established in the 1930s and administered through the Aid to Families with Dependent Children (AFDC) program, Nixon's proposal established a national standard for benefits and provided income supplements to the working poor. As Nixon expected when he presented the FAP in August 1969, conservatives immediately objected to the cost and to increasing the number of welfare recipients. White southerners especially feared its impact on the ability to hire poor blacks at low wages: "There's not going to be anybody left to roll these wheelbarrows and press these shirts. They're all going to be on welfare," commented one southern representative.

Liberals and grassroots movements representing the poor attacked the low level of the income guarantee—even after the administration increased it from $1,600 to $2,400 a year. Groups such as the National Welfare Rights Organization decried a work requirement that would force mothers of young children into substandard jobs. Organized labor, too, deplored a work requirement that would compel recipients to work at jobs below the minimum wage and, in effect, "subsidize the employers of cheap labor."

The FAP foundered over the dilemma inherent in an economy that failed to provide sufficient jobs at adequate wages: how to provide satisfactory support for those who cannot earn a decent livelihood while at the same time containing welfare expenditures and retaining incentives to work. Conservatives believed that Nixon's FAP would weigh too heavily on taxpayers, reduce work incentives, and encourage a reliance on welfare; liberals argued that its level of support was woefully inadequate.

WELFARE
Beginning in the 1960s, Congress repeatedly attempted to reform welfare (the program's official name was Aid to Families with Dependent Children, or AFDC), usually with requirements to encourage or force welfare recipients to take jobs. This mother of three children who was separated from her husband was trying to become self-supporting by attending college, but officials in Schenectady, New York, removed her from the welfare rolls when she refused to take a job.
Wide World.

Although Congress refused to pass the FAP and establish a guaranteed annual income for poor families, it did so for the aged, blind, and disabled by enacting Supplementary Security Income in 1972. Moreover, in response to growing public attention to undernourishment and indications that the Democrats were going to capitalize on the issue of hunger, Nixon proposed a huge expansion of the food stamp program. The new guidelines mandated a nutritionally adequate diet for everyone, including the working poor, and the number of recipients of food stamps grew from 2.5 to 15 million between 1969 and 1974. By 1975, the value of food stamps available to a family of four had risen to almost $2,000 a year.

The New Federalism

Nixon called his domestic agenda the New Federalism, expressing traditional Republican distaste for federal control and preference for state and local autonomy and responsibility. To this end, he made revenue sharing, the transfer of federal funds to state and local governments, a cornerstone of his domestic program, even though he thought it didn't have much political "sex appeal." Revenue sharing gave states and localities considerable discretion in spending decisions and strengthened their financial foundations. State and local governments, many of which faced budget crises, provided a powerful lobby, and Congress enacted the measure in October 1972. The law transferred more than $5 billion of federal funds annually to state and local governments. Not designated for specific programs, these funds supplemented existing federal transfers for education, urban development, and the like.

When it came to transferring funds for and authority over existing programs, Congress balked. That approach would have constituted a more substantial attack on the national bureaucracy while increasing decision making at lower levels of government. In later years, the administration moved in this direction by consolidating several funding programs into broad block grants, as with the Comprehensive Employment and Training Act (CETA), which was designed to provide jobs and training for the poor. Although still targeted for a specific purpose such as community development or job training, block grants allowed local governments greater discretion in their use. Both general revenue sharing and block grants continued after the Nixon administration, but represented only a small step in the decentralization of government power.

Indeed, the expansion of federal controls in other areas overshadowed the New Federalism's revenue sharing. Despite Nixon's aversion to a growing federal bureaucracy, certain problems eluded solution on the state level or posed economic or political threats that were too great to risk inaction. Thus, in addition to approving new environmental controls, Nixon expanded the government's role in dealing with energy shortages, inflation, and unemployment.

In the 1970s, Americans confronted two costs of the post–World War II economic boom that had amply enriched their standard of living: environmental damage and an insatiable demand for energy that left the nation increasingly dependent on foreign sources of oil. The nation's own abundant oil deposits along with access to huge, cheap supplies of Middle Eastern oil had encouraged entrepreneurs to build large cars, suburban housing developments, and glass-enclosed skyscrapers and houses with no concern for fuel efficiency. The traditional American assumption that energy resources were boundless and the resulting wasteful practices meant that by the 1970s, the United States, with just 6 percent of the world's population, consumed one-third of its fuel resources.

In the fall of 1973, the United States faced its first energy crisis. Furious at the Nixon administration's support of Israel during the Yom Kippur War, Arab nations cut off oil shipments to the United States, and nations that did not join the embargo raised prices nearly tenfold. As supplies of oil fell in the winter of 1973–74, long lines formed at gas stations, where prices had nearly doubled. Shortages of heating oil meant that many homes were cold and some schools had to close. A traveling salesman complained, "I can't get gas to go on the road," while a laid-off airline pilot said, "We've never had a crunch like this before."

In response to the energy crisis, Nixon relaxed deadlines on environmental regulations, pressed for the Alaska pipeline bill, and pushed ahead on the production of nuclear energy. He signed legislation authorizing temporary emergency powers to allocate petroleum and establishing a national 55-mile-per-hour speed limit to save gasoline. But Nixon opposed rationing gasoline and vetoed a bill that, in an effort to prevent oil companies from unduly profiting from the crisis, set ceilings on domestic crude oil prices. By the spring of 1974, the energy crisis had eased, thanks largely to voluntary conservation, a relatively mild winter, and cessation of the Arab oil embargo. But the United States had yet to come to grips with its seemingly unquenchable demand for fuel and its dependence on foreign oil.

Soaring energy prices contributed to the second serious economic problem: a rising cost of living. From the Johnson administration, Nixon inherited an economy under strong inflationary pressures. In 1969, the inflation rate rose to 7 percent, an enormous increase to Americans used to inflation rates of about 2 percent. By 1970, unemployment had joined inflation as a serious problem. This unprecedented combination of a stagnant economy and inflation soon received the name "stagflation."

Domestic troubles were compounded by the decline of American dominance in the international economic system. Having fully recovered from World War II with U.S. aid, the economies of Japan and Western Europe grew faster than the economy of the United States. Cars, electronic equipment, and other foreign products competed favorably with American goods throughout the world. In 1971, for the first time in decades, the United States imported more than it exported, which meant that more dollars were flowing out of the country than were coming in. As the United States spent billions of dollars abroad for defense purposes, the amount of dollars in foreign hands exceeded U.S. gold reserves. The nation could no longer back up its dollars with gold.

Political considerations helped to shape the president's response to these economic problems, a response that deviated considerably from conventional Republican doctrine. With an eye to the 1972 election and believing that Eisenhower's recession had ensured his defeat by Kennedy in 1960, Nixon announced a "New Economic Policy" in August 1971. He abandoned the convertibility of dollars into gold, devalued the dollar to make American goods cheaper in foreign markets and thus increase exports, and imposed a 10 percent surcharge on most imports. Nixon also froze wages and prices, thus enabling the government to stimulate the economy without fueling more inflation.

In the short run, these policies worked. Exports surged ahead of imports, inflation subsided, unemployment fell below 5 percent, and Nixon was resoundingly reelected in 1972. Yet the New Economic Policy treated only the superficial wounds of the economy. The lifting of price and wage controls in 1973, the Arab oil embargo, and rising food prices (the result of a drought in the Midwest and huge Soviet purchases of American grain) sent the consumer price index soaring again. In 1974, inflation reached 11 percent, while unemployment edged back up. Nixon's bold intervention in the economy proved only a temporary respite, and his successor inherited the most severe economic crisis since the depression of the 1930s.

New Opportunities and Dangers in a Multipolar World

The challenges and opportunities of foreign policy captured Nixon's greatest enthusiasm, and his highest hopes to make his mark on history lay in the international arena. He possessed a broad understanding of international relations and the ability to analyze how changing world patterns would affect national interests. The discord between the Soviet Union and China and the growing power of Europe and Japan, Nixon believed, indicated that the "rigid and bipolar world of the 1940s and 1950s" was giving way to "the fluidity of a new era of multilateral diplomacy." With his chief foreign policy adviser, Henry Kissinger, Nixon prepared to grasp a "historic opportunity to turn the transformations of the last twenty-five years into new avenues for peace."

New approaches to China and the Soviet Union formed the keystone of Nixon's foreign policy, and his most important innovation was to deflate ideology as the driving force. As Kissinger put it in 1969, "We will judge other countries, including Communist countries, ... on the basis of their actions and not on the basis of their domestic ideology." Nixon repeated that premise in 1972: "What is important is not a nation's internal political philosophy. What is important is its policy toward the rest of the world and toward us."

Nixon and Kissinger moved to exploit the deterioration in Soviet-Chinese relations that had begun in the early 1960s and escalated into military clashes along their common border in 1969. If these two nations balanced and checked each other's power, the threat of either of them to the United States would lessen. As Nixon later recalled, "The hostility between China and the Soviet Union served our purposes best if we maintained closer relations with each side than they did with each other."

U.S. overtures through intermediaries, followed by Kissinger's secret visit to China in July 1971, set the stage for Nixon's most dramatic act as president. With his arrival carefully orchestrated to take advantage of prime-time television, in Febru-

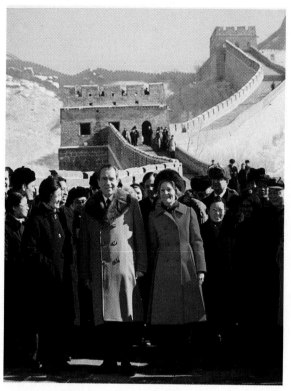

NIXON IN CHINA

"This was the week that changed the world," proclaimed President Richard M. Nixon in February 1972, emphasizing the dramatic turnaround in relations with America's former enemy the People's Republic of China. The Great Wall of China forms the setting for this photograph of Nixon and his wife, Pat.

Nixon Presidential Materials Project.

ary 1972 Nixon became the nation's first president to set foot on Chinese soil—an astonishing act by a man who had climbed the political ladder as an all-out anti-Communist. Indeed, it was Nixon's irreproachable anti-Communist credentials that enabled him to conduct this shift in U.S.-Chinese relations with no significant objections at home. As he remarked to the Chinese leader, Mao Zedong, "Those on the right can do what those on the left only talk about."

Neither side expected concrete, immediate results from Nixon's historic but largely symbolic visit. Plans proceeded for cultural and scientific exchanges, and American producers began to find markets in China. The United States did not abandon the Nationalist Chinese government on Taiwan, but Nixon acknowledged that Taiwan was a part of

China, its fate to be settled by the Chinese themselves. By ending the isolation of China, Nixon's visit brought U.S. policy more into conformity with the actual world and paved the way for normal diplomatic relations by the end of the decade.

As Nixon and Kissinger hoped, the warming of U.S.-Chinese relations increased Soviet responsiveness to the Nixon-Kissinger strategy of détente, the term given to efforts to ease conflicts with the Soviet Union. In pursuing détente, Nixon and Kissinger did not abandon the principle of containment but instead concentrated on issues of common concern to the two superpowers. Containment would be achieved not only by military threat, but also by ensuring that Russia and China had stakes in a stable international order and would therefore refrain from precipitating crises. The goal, as Nixon defined it in 1972, was "a stronger, healthy United States, Europe, Soviet Union, China, Japan, each balancing the other."

Arms control, trade, and stability in Europe were three areas of common interest. In November 1969, the United States and the Soviet Union resumed the Strategic Arms Limitation Talks (SALT), and in 1971 they moved to defuse potential crises by improving the hot line between Moscow and Washington. Conflict over Berlin eased through an agreement in August 1971, when the Soviet Union guaranteed access routes to West Berlin and in turn won permission to open a consulate there.

Nixon turned the spotlight on détente in May 1972, when—three months after his trip to China—he made another historic visit. Meeting with Soviet leaders in Moscow, Nixon came away with several agreements regarding trade and cooperation in science and space. Most significantly, Soviet and U.S. leaders signed arms limitation treaties that had grown out of SALT. Both sides gave up the pursuit of a defense against nuclear weapons, agreeing to restrict antiballistic missile systems (ABMs) to two each. Curbing offensive weapons proved more difficult, but the superpowers reached an interim five-year agreement limiting the number of strategic missile launchers each could build.

The SALT agreement left the Soviets ahead in absolute numbers of missiles, but U.S. weapons were more accurate, and the United States retained the lead in bombers, which were not covered by the treaty. The agreement deterred neither side from weapons research and development, so both the Soviet Union and the United States pursued qualitative improvements in strategic arms. Kissinger him-

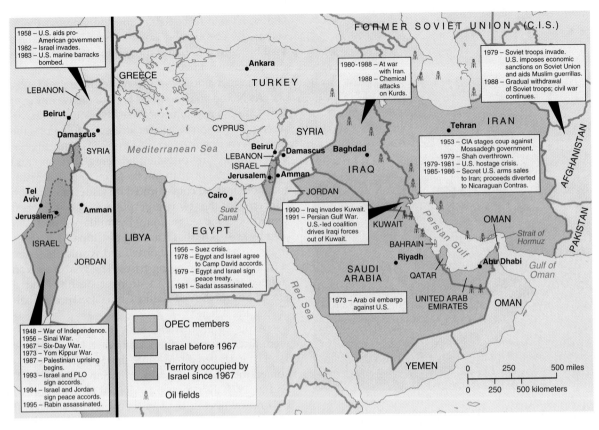

1958 – U.S. aids pro-
       American government.
1982 – Israel invades.
1983 – U.S. marine barracks
       bombed.

1980-1988 – At war
            with Iran.
1988 – Chemical
       attacks
       on Kurds.

1979 – Soviet troops invade.
       U.S. imposes economic
       sanctions on Soviet Union
       and aids Muslim guerrillas.
1988 – Gradual withdrawal
       of Soviet troops; civil war
       continues.

1953 – CIA stages coup against
       Mossadegh government.
1979 – Shah overthrown.
1979-1981 – U.S. hostage crisis.
1985-1986 – Secret U.S. arms sales
       to Iran; proceeds diverted
       to Nicaraguan Contras.

1990 – Iraq invades Kuwait.
1991 – Persian Gulf War.
       U.S.-led coalition
       drives Iraqi forces
       out of Kuwait.

1956 – Suez crisis.
1978 – Egypt and Israel agree
       to Camp David accords.
1979 – Egypt and Israel sign
       peace treaty.
1981 – Sadat assassinated.

1973 – Arab oil embargo
       against U.S.

1948 – War of Independence.
1956 – Sinai War.
1967 – Six-Day War.
1973 – Yom Kippur War.
1987 – Palestinian uprising
       begins.
1993 – Israel and PLO
       sign accords.
1994 – Israel and Jordan
       sign peace accords.
1995 – Rabin assassinated.

OPEC members

Israel before 1967

Territory occupied by
Israel since 1967

Oil fields

MAP 30.2
The Middle East, 1948–1996
U.S. determination to preserve access to the rich oil reserves of the Middle East and its commit-
ment to the security of Israel were the fundamental — and sometimes conflicting — principles of
U.S. foreign policy in that region.

self suggested the limited nature of détente: "The way to use this freeze is for us to catch up."

In his second inaugural address, Nixon said, "The time has passed when America will make every other nation's conflict our own... or presume to tell the people of other nations how to manage their own affairs." Yet even while Nixon and Kissinger dealt with China and the Soviet Union on the basis of practical politics rather than ideology, in Vietnam and elsewhere they continued to equate the ideology of Marxism with a threat to U.S. interests and actively resisted social revolutions that might lead to communism.

In Chile, the Nixon administration found that threat in Salvador Allende, a self-proclaimed Marxist. Since 1964, the CIA and U.S. corporations concerned about nationalization of their Chilean properties had provided funds to Allende's opponents.

When Allende won the 1970 presidential election, Nixon announced that the United States "accepted that decision." Yet the CIA had taken covert action, including plans for a military coup, to overthrow Allende. Thereafter the United States continued to exert political and economic pressure to destabilize the Allende government. "I don't see why we have to let a country go Marxist just because its people are irresponsible," Kissinger remarked privately. In 1973, the Chilean military engineered a coup, killed Allende, and established a dictatorship under General Augusto Pinochet.

The Nixon administration moved closer to repressive governments in other parts of the world. It eased pressures on ruling white minorities in southern Africa, believing that the "whites are here to stay.... There is no hope for the blacks to gain the political rights they seek through violence, which will lead only to chaos and increased opportunities for Communists." In the Middle East, the United States found in Iran a stable anti-Communist ally—one with enormous petroleum reserves. In 1972, the Nixon administration began secretly to provide massive amounts of arms to the shah of Iran, cementing a relationship that would ignite a new crisis for the United States when the shah was overthrown in 1979.

Like its predecessors and successors, the Nixon administration pursued a delicate balance between honoring its commitments to Israel's security and seeking the goodwill of Arab nations that were strategically and economically important to the United States. Conflict between Israel and the Arab nations had escalated into all-out war (the Six Day War) in 1967, in which Israel won a stunning victory over Egyptian, Syrian, and Jordanian forces. The Six Day War ended with Israel occupying the Sinai Peninsula and Gaza Strip (Egyptian territory), the Golan Heights of Syria, and the West Bank of Jordan, which included the Arab sector of Jerusalem—territory that amounted to twice the original size of Israel.

After Israel's decisive victory in the Six Day War, Palestinian refugees stepped up guerrilla attacks against the Israelis, and the Soviet Union expanded military aid to Arab countries. American diplomats' efforts to reduce tensions in the Middle East had little success in the late 1960s and early 1970s. The Arab countries refused to recognize Israel's right to exist; Israel would not withdraw from the territories occupied during the Six Day War; and no solution could be found for the Palestinian refugees who had been displaced by the creation of Israel in the late 1940s.

In October 1973, on Yom Kippur, the holiest day in the Jewish calendar, Egypt and Syria surprised Israel by launching a full-scale attack. After the Nixon administration sided with the Israelis, the Arab nations imposed an oil embargo. Although the Soviets threatened to intervene, the United States held its ground, and Israel repulsed the attack. Shortly after the war, the United States adopted the role of mediator as Kissinger embarked on "shuttle diplomacy," moving back and forth across the Middle East. Although unable to resolve the underlying conflicts, he achieved some limited disengagements between Israeli forces and their enemies. As a result, the Arab nations lifted the oil embargo, and Soviet influence in the area declined as U.S. credibility among Arabs increased.

Constitutional Crisis and Restoration

In the 1972 presidential election, Richard Nixon turned his narrow victory of 1968 into a massive landslide. At year's end, he and Henry Kissinger graced the cover of *Time* as the magazine's Men of the Year, and the president's approval ratings in the polls neared 70 percent. Less than two years later, Nixon abandoned the presidency in disgrace. He was not turned out of office by voters dissatisfied with his domestic or foreign policies. Rather, Nixon's abuse of presidential power and his efforts to cover up crimes that had been committed by subordinates betrayed the public trust and forced the first presidential resignation in history.

Nixon's handpicked successor, Gerald Ford, brought to the White House a reputation for decency and openness that helped to restore confidence in the presidency. Ford maintained the basic policy directions set by the Nixon administration, but he faced economic problems even more severe. In 1976, Ford lost the presidency to Democrat Jimmy Carter in an election that failed to stir much excitement for either candidate.

The Landslide Election of 1972

Nixon's most spectacular foreign policy initiatives, détente with the Soviet Union and the opening of relations with China, heightened his prospects for reelection in 1972. Although the war in Vietnam continued, antiwar protests diminished with the decrease in American casualties and the continuing withdrawal of U.S. ground forces. Nixon's New Economic Policy had temporarily checked both inflation and unemployment, and his attacks on busing and antiwar protesters had solidified his support on the right. At their convention in Miami Beach in August 1972, the Republicans resoundingly renominated Nixon and his vice president, Spiro Agnew.

A large field of contenders vied for the Democratic nomination, including Hubert Humphrey, back for a third effort, and New York Representative Shirley Chisholm, the first African American politician to make a serious bid for the presidency. Senator George S. McGovern of South Dakota chalked up primary victories in key states, while on the right, Governor George Wallace of Alabama won a series of southern primaries as well as those in Michigan and Maryland. Wallace's campaign was cut short, however, when a deranged man shot him, leaving him paralyzed below the waist.

McGovern's primary victories established him as the clear leader by the time the Democrats convened in Miami Beach in July, and the composition of the convention delegates made his position even stronger. After the bitter 1968 convention, the party had initiated major reforms requiring delegations to represent the relative proportions of minorities, women, and youth in their states. These newcomers displaced many regular Democrats—officeholders, labor leaders, and representatives of urban political machines and traditional ethnic groups. Some party regulars such as Representative Edith Green thought that "the Democratic Party was taken over by kooks" and stayed home. Referring to the significant numbers of young people and women, a labor leader remarked that there was "too much hair, and not enough cigars at this convention."

Nixon's abuse of presidential power and his efforts to cover up crimes that had been committed by subordinates betrayed the public trust and forced the first presidential resignation in history.

McGovern won the nomination easily, and his supporters pushed through platform planks calling for an immediate end to the Vietnam War, support for busing, and other controversial issues. Women constituted 40 percent of the delegates, and feminists organized at the convention for the first time. McGovern's handpicked running mate, Senator Thomas F. Eagleton of Missouri, won nomination easily, but women rallied 13 percent of the vice presidential vote behind Texas politician Frances Farenthold and wrote fifteen women's rights planks into the platform.

The Democratic campaign floundered almost immediately when the press reported that Eagleton had undergone psychiatric treatment for nervous exhaustion and depression during the 1960s. Refusing to bow to prejudice concerning mental illness, McGovern declared, "I am one thousand percent behind Tom Eagleton." But he soon changed his mind and replaced Eagleton with R. Sargent Shriver, former head of the Peace Corps and Johnson's antipoverty program. The incident hurt McGovern by casting doubt on his judgment, decisiveness, and sincerity.

Moreover, the Democratic nominee failed to capture the middle ground of his party. Many Democrats objected to his call for immediate withdrawal from Vietnam, his pledge to cut $30 billion from the Pentagon's budget, and his waffling on welfare reform. Republicans portrayed McGovern as an extremist on the left. Capitalizing on many of his early statements, they construed them as demands for legalizing marijuana and liberalizing abortion laws. Labor leader George Meany called McGovern "the candidate of amnesty, acid, and appeasement." Traditional Democrats defected from the party in massive numbers.

Nixon received 60.7 percent of the popular vote and carried every state except Massachusetts in a landslide victory second only to that of Johnson in 1964. Although the Democrats maintained control of the House, the Senate, and thirty-one governorships, Nixon won a majority of votes among southerners, Catholics, urbanites, and blue-collar workers, all traditionally strong supporters of the Democratic Party. But the president had little time to savor his triumph or consolidate his support, as a series of revelations began to emerge about crimes and misdemeanors that had been committed to ensure the victory.

Watergate

During the early morning hours of June 17, 1972, five men working for Nixon's reelection campaign crept into Democratic Party headquarters housed in the Watergate apartment and office complex near the Potomac River, just a mile from the White House. Wearing surgical gloves, they carried Mace, lock-picking equipment, cameras, and telephone-bugging devices to repair a bugging device installed in an earlier break-in. Their arrest on the scene and the subsequent efforts of Nixon and his aides to cover up their connections to administration officials set in motion the most serious constitutional crisis since the Civil War. The crisis took its name, "Watergate," from the scene of the burglary.

As the events of Watergate unfolded over the next two years, Americans learned that Nixon and his associates had engaged in a host of other abuses. These included accepting illegal campaign contributions, using "dirty tricks" to sabotage Democratic candidates, and unlawfully attempting to silence critics of the Vietnam War.

Nixon was by no means the first president to lie to the public or to misuse presidential power. On the eve of World War II, Franklin Roosevelt misled

WATERGATE SHOOTOUT
This political cartoon by Edward Sorel portrays a besieged President Richard Nixon and his associates who were involved in Watergate and other scandals. Some, such as Vice President Spiro Agnew, in the center of the floor, and Attorney General John Mitchell, to his right, are already down. What could be the artist's intention in putting a picture of Eisenhower on the wall?
Collection of Byron Dobell.

the public about U.S. naval operations in the Atlantic Ocean that violated congressional intentions to keep the nation out of war. Every president after Roosevelt had enlarged the powers of the presidency, justifying his actions as necessary to protect national security in the cold war. This expansion of executive powers, often called the growth of the "imperial presidency," weakened some of the traditional checks and balances on the executive branch and opened the door to abuses.

Some of Nixon's activities followed patterns set by his predecessor. Lyndon Johnson deceived Congress about the Gulf of Tonkin attacks, for example, and allowed CIA and FBI interference in the affairs of civil rights and antiwar activists. Moreover, Nixon and Johnson shared certain personality traits —the self-righteousness of self-made men, a sense of insecurity, exhilaration over presidential power, suspiciousness, and a tendency to see opposition as a conspiracy against them. All of these traits encouraged both men to employ the vast powers of the executive against their enemies.

Johnson, however, enjoyed more self-confidence as well as an openness to advice. He abandoned the opportunity for reelection rather than intensifying his efforts to silence the opposition. Nixon, introverted and socially ill at ease, had few intimate friends. His relationships with most of his

closest aides rested on political calculations rather than on trust and loyalty. These aides tried above all to protect themselves, and few would confront him with the truth and the opportunity to save his presidency. Unable to distinguish his real enemies from those who simply disagreed with him, Nixon saw opposition to his policies not only as a personal attack but also as an attack on the presidency and the country.

Watergate began when White House adviser Charles Colson established a secret unit nicknamed the "plumbers" to stop the kind of "leaks" that had led to publication of the *Pentagon Papers* in 1971. Former CIA agent E. Howard Hunt and former FBI employee G. Gordon Liddy led the plumbers, some of whom soon turned to projects to disrupt the Democratic presidential nomination process and discredit potential candidates. They went to work for the Committee to Re-elect the President (CRP, called "CREEP" by its critics), a group that was independent of the Republican Party and directed by Nixon's former attorney general John Mitchell. The CRP funneled money, including illegal campaign contributions, into the campaign, and in 1972 CRP officials authorized the Watergate break-in to bug the Democratic Party's phones and find out whether the Democrats had any information that they could use against the Republicans.

When police arrested the five men found in the Watergate—four Cuban Americans and James Mc-Cord, a former CIA agent and current security director for CRP—they discovered papers linking them to Hunt and Liddy. The Nixon administration immediately denied any connection with the break-in. A grand jury indicted Hunt, Liddy, and the five alleged burglars, but Democratic charges of a cover-up during the 1972 elections fell on deaf ears in the media and among the public.

Brought to trial in early 1973 in the federal district court of John J. Sirica, all seven men either pleaded guilty or were convicted of theft and illegal electronic surveillance. McCord then broke ranks with the cover-up. In March 1973, he told Judge Sirica that perjury had been committed at the trial and suggested that administration officials had been involved in the break-in. A grand jury began to investigate these charges, and the Senate soon began its own inquiry. As press reports began to implicate Mitchell, John W. Dean, counsel to the president, and presidential aides John Ehrlichman and H. R. Haldeman, Nixon decided that it was time to act.

In a television address at the end of April 1973, Nixon accepted official responsibility for Watergate but denied any personal knowledge of the break-in or of a cover-up. He also cleaned house, announcing the resignations of Dean, Ehrlichman, Haldeman, and Attorney General Richard Kleindienst. In May, he authorized the appointment of an independent special prosecutor, Archibald Cox, to conduct an investigation.

Meanwhile, sensational revelations exploded in the Senate investigating committee, headed by Sam J. Ervin of North Carolina. TV audiences watched as John Dean described White House projects to harass "enemies" through income tax audits and other illegal means and asserted that the president had long known of efforts to cover up the Watergate burglary. White House aide Alexander Butterfield struck the most damaging blow when he disclosed that the Oval Office in the White House had a voice-activated taping system that automatically recorded conversations.

Both Cox and the Ervin committee immediately asked for tapes on which Nixon discussed Watergate with his aides. When Nixon refused to give them up, citing executive privilege and separation of powers, Cox and Ervin took their case to Judge Sirica's federal district court. Sirica ruled that the tapes should be turned over to him for review so that he could decide whether they should be released to the special prosecutor.

In the midst of the battle for the tapes, Nixon had to deal with more disclosures that expanded the scandal to include the suggestion of personal gain through public office. The General Services Administration reported that Nixon had spent $10 million of federal funds on his personal homes. Later, the IRS disclosed that Nixon owed a half million dollars in back taxes and in 1970 and 1971 had paid federal income taxes of less than $1,000, an amount usually paid by individuals earning $10,000.

In August 1973, the Justice Department announced that Vice President Agnew was under investigation for taking bribes when he was governor of Maryland. Maintaining his innocence and claiming he was a victim of politics, Agnew struck a deal, pleading no contest to a lesser charge of income tax evasion in exchange for a suspended sentence and his resignation. Although Nixon's choice of House minority leader Gerald Ford of Michigan to succeed Agnew won widespread approval, the vice president's resignation further tarnished the administration and led some to think that the president, too, might be replaceable.

Nixon continued to hold on to the tapes. On October 19, 1973, he ordered special prosecutor Cox to cease his efforts to get them. When Cox refused, Nixon ordered Attorney General Elliot Richardson to fire Cox. Richardson balked and resigned instead, as did William D. Ruckelshaus, second in line at the Justice Department. Finally, the solicitor general, Robert Bork, agreed to carry out the president's order. The press called the series of dismissals and resignations the "Saturday night massacre." Nixon's defiance outraged the public, who fired off 250,000 telegrams condemning his action. Stunned by the reaction, Nixon appointed a new special prosecutor, Leon Jaworski, but failed to quell editorials in major newspapers demanding that he resign and serious talk about impeachment in Congress. The president's support in public opinion polls plummeted to 27 percent.

In February 1974, the House of Representatives voted to begin an impeachment investigation. In April, Nixon began to release transcripts of the tapes that he himself had edited. As the public read passages sprinkled with "expletive deleted," House Republican leader John Rhodes abandoned his support of the president, calling the transcripts a "deplorable, shabby, disgusting, and immoral performance by all." The transcripts included Nixon's orders to Mitchell and Dean in March 1973: "I don't give a shit what happens. I want you all to stonewall it, let them plead the Fifth Amendment, cover up or anything else, if it'll save it—save the plan."

In July 1974, the House Judiciary Committee began its nationally televised debate over specific charges for impeachment: (1) obstruction of justice, (2) abuse of power, (3) contempt of Congress, (4) unconstitutional waging of war by the secret bombing of Cambodia, and (5) tax evasion and the selling of political favors. The committee approved the first three charges, with two to six Republicans joining the Democrats on each vote. The last two counts failed to get a majority, but the committee had enough to take its three charges to the House, where a vote of impeachment seemed certain.

On July 24, a unanimous Supreme Court ordered Nixon to comply with Judge Sirica's request for the tapes. When the president released transcripts of three previously unheard tapes on August 5, he sealed his fate. Conversations between Nixon and Haldeman just six days after the break-in revealed that Nixon had tried to manipulate the CIA to hinder the FBI investigation of the burglary. This was the "smoking gun," evidence sufficient to persuade even his staunchest supporters. An angry Senator Barry Goldwater told a Nixon aide, "The president has only twelve votes in the Senate. He has lied to me . . . [and] to my colleagues for the last time."

On August 8, 1974, Nixon announced his resignation to a television audience. Acknowledging that he had made some incorrect judgments, he insisted that he had always tried to do what was best for the nation. The next morning, Nixon ended a rambling, emotional farewell to his staff with some advice: "Always give your best, never get discouraged, never get petty; always remember, others may hate you, but those who hate you don't win unless you hate them, and then you destroy yourself." Had he but practiced that advice, he might have saved his presidency.

The Ford Interregnum

As Nixon's jet sped him back to private life in California, Gerald Ford took the presidential oath of office. "Our Constitution works," he declared. "Our great Republic is a government of laws and not of men." The new leader of that Republic had represented Michigan in the House of Representatives since 1948. He was elected minority leader in 1965,

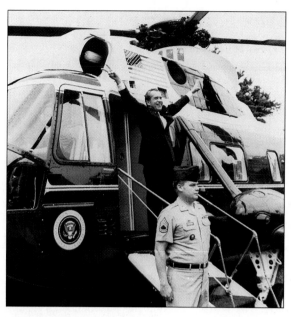

NIXON RESIGNS
President Richard M. Nixon, just before his resignation took effect on August 9, 1974, waves good-bye to his staff from a helicopter on the White House lawn.
Nixon Presidential Materials Project.

having built a reputation as a conservative, solid party loyalist who treated opponents with openness and cordiality. Neither a brilliant thinker nor an eloquent speaker, Ford was known for his integrity, humility, and dedication to the responsibilities of public office. "I'm a Ford, not a Lincoln," he acknowledged. Most of official Washington and the American public looked favorably on his succession.

Upon taking office, Ford announced, "Our long nightmare is over," but he shocked many Americans one month later when he ended the particular nightmare of the former president. On September 8, 1974, Ford granted Nixon a pardon "for all offenses against the United States which he . . . has committed or may have committed or taken part in" during his presidency. In its universality and its promulgation even before any charges were filed, the pardon was the most extravagant one ever issued, and it saved Nixon from nearly certain indictment and trial. It also provoked a tremendous outcry from Congress and the public. A majority of Americans opposed the pardon, and many suspected that Nixon had made a deal with Ford when he appointed him vice president. (See Historical Question, page 1198.) Capitalizing on the revulsion

Was Ford Right in Pardoning Nixon?

I N NOVEMBER 1973, during Gerald R. Ford's confirmation hearings for the vice presidency, a senator asked Ford whether he believed that a new president could stop criminal proceedings against the president he replaced. Ford replied, "I do not think the public would stand for it." Yet less than a year later, Ford did exactly that when he gave a blanket pardon to Richard M. Nixon just one month after Nixon had resigned the presidency to escape impeachment.

After returning from church on Sunday morning, September 8, 1974, President Ford called reporters to the White House, where he read a statement and signed a proclamation granting Nixon a "full, free, and absolute pardon" for all crimes that he "committed or may have committed or taken part in" while president. When Ford called congressional leaders just before announcing the pardon, Democratic leader Tip O'Neill had said, "You're crazy." And so thought a large segment of the public. White House switchboards lit up immediately, with opinion running strongly against the pardon. Ford's approval rating in public opinion polls plunged by twenty percentage points.

There were immediate charges that Ford had made a deal to pardon Nixon. Certainly, some of Nixon's aides—and no doubt Nixon himself— gave thought to a pardon even before he resigned. J. Fred Buzhardt, one of Nixon's lawyers, drafted a pardon in Ford's name while Nixon was still president. When Nixon's chief of staff, Alexander Haig, met with Ford to brief him on the release of tapes that would probably lead to Nixon's resignation, Haig outlined various strategies, one of which was that Nixon could be pardoned even be-

fore any indictment had taken place. When Ford reported the conversation to his own advisers, they insisted that he call Haig and tell him that nothing he had discussed with Haig should figure in Nixon's decision about whether to resign. Scholars have found no evidence of a deal, and Ford steadfastly denied any such thing. Nonetheless, Haig impressed on Ford the notion that a president had the power to issue a pardon even without an indictment.

If there was no deal, why did Ford pardon Nixon? First of all, the question of a possible pardon hovered over the White House throughout Ford's first weeks in office. Some of Nixon's aides whom Ford had kept on—including Haig, Henry Kissinger, and special counsel Leonard Garment— lobbied the new president to pardon their former boss. In addition, staff members at Nixon's home in San Clemente sent reports emphasizing the former president's serious health problems. The press hammered administration officials about a possible pardon, and reporters opened Ford's first televised press conference by asking whether Nixon should have immunity from prosecution. Ford later remarked, "I thought they had wasted my time," distracting him and the nation from important issues concerning the economy and foreign policy.

In the pardon proclamation and the statement accompanying it, Ford gave a number of reasons for his decision. He said that the "serious allegations and accusations hang[ing] like a sword" over the former president threatened his health. He insisted that "Nixon and his loved ones have suffered enough, and will continue to suffer no matter what I do." Drawing on private opinions that he had sought from special prosecutor Leon Jaworski (along with the understanding that Jaworski would not oppose a pardon), the president suggested that pretrial publicity and lengthy delays would prevent Nixon from getting a fair trial and "equal justice." Ford questioned whether having "already paid the unprecedented penalty of relinquishing the highest office in the United States," Nixon should be exposed "to further punishment and degradation."

Although moved by compassion for Nixon, Ford insisted that "it is not the ultimate fate of

GERALD FORD'S MOMENTOUS DECISION
On September 8, 1974, President Gerald Ford granted former president Richard Nixon a "full, free, and absolute pardon" for whatever crimes he may have committed in the Watergate affair. The pardon enabled Nixon to build a post-Watergate career as elder statesman, while it clouded the remainder of Ford's presidency and contributed to his defeat at the polls in 1976.
©1974 Time Inc. Reprinted by permission.

Richard Nixon that most concerns me." Most of all, he said, the pardon was necessary to get rid of Watergate, the "ugly passions" that it aroused and the "polarization" that it engendered. During the debate over the proposed Constitution, Alexander Hamilton had envisioned the pardon provision being used at "critical moments, when a well-timed offer of pardon . . . may restore the tranquility of the commonwealth." Ford did not refer to the Founders, but he declared it his duty "to shut and seal this book" to ensure "domestic tranquility."

In the long run, the pardon probably furthered Ford's goal of getting the political establishment to put Watergate behind it and focus on what Ford considered the real issues confronting the nation. In the short run, however, it reopened the wounds, because many people believed that the pardon violated the principle that all Americans are equal under the law. Upon learning that Ford was going to issue the pardon, his press secretary, Jerald F. terHorst, submitted his resignation. It was "ethically wrong," he said, to "put just one man above the law," especially when all of Nixon's aides "were left to run the gauntlet of our judicial system."

TerHorst lamented that "Ford could throw away the new national mood of trust . . . without getting in return a signed confession." Adding fuel to the firestorm of protest was Nixon's response to the pardon. He failed to acknowledge guilt or express contrition for the abuses of power and obstruction of justice that were charged against him in the articles of impeachment and supported by the tapes. In Nixon's statement, which had been negotiated by Ford and Nixon's aides before the pardon was issued, he expressed only "regret" that he had made "mistakes and misjudgments" and acknowledged merely that he was "wrong in not acting more decisively and more forthrightly in dealing with Watergate."

Although we cannot measure the degree to which the pardon turned voters against the president and the Republican Party, Ford did pay a political price for it. Two months after the pardon, Republicans lost an exceedingly high number of seats in the congressional elections, and the pardon undoubtedly played a role in Ford's painfully close defeat for reelection in 1976. For Nixon, the pardon meant a new political life. His ability over the next two decades to rebuild his image into that of an elder statesman rested in large part on having gained a pardon without having to admit that he had broken the law, violated his oath of office, and betrayed his constituents' trust.

over Watergate, Democrats made impressive gains in the congressional elections in November.

To defend the pardon, Ford testified before Congress, the only president since Lincoln to do so. Although the president has absolute authority to issue pardons, Congress did prevent Ford from turning presidential papers and tapes over to Nixon. In addition to escaping criminal prosecution, the former president also avoided testifying in trials of other Watergate defendants because he was ill with phlebitis and had to undergo surgery. Thirty Nixon associates ultimately were convicted or pleaded guilty, though none served very long sentences; the longest was the nineteen-month imprisonment of former Attorney General John Mitchell.

The grilling of President Ford about the pardon reflected Congress's determination to reassert its authority. Legislators also subjected Ford's choice for vice president, former New York governor Nelson Rockefeller, to long, hard questioning before permitting him to take office in December. To prevent future abuses in election campaigns, Congress enacted the Federal Election Campaign Act of 1974, which established public financing of presidential campaigns.

Having set limits on presidential power in foreign policy by enacting the War Powers Act over Nixon's veto, Congress now moved to check abuses by intelligence agencies both at home and abroad. Special committees in the House and Senate undertook investigations that implicated the FBI and the CIA in a host of illegal activities stretching back to the 1950s. Both agencies had operated programs to harass and discredit political dissenters, and the CIA had even intercepted mail from the Senate Intelligence Committee's chair, Frank Church, to his mother-in-law. The CIA not only had harassed administration critics at home, but also had taken part in plans to assassinate Fidel Castro and other foreign leaders. In response to these revelations, Ford established new controls on covert operations and brought George Bush, head of the U.S. Liaison Office in China, home to head the CIA. Congress established permanent committees to oversee the intelligence agencies.

These measures did little to diminish the public cynicism and lack of trust in government that had been developing since the Johnson years. The Democrats had had their own share of scandals. Wilbur Mills, chair of the House Ways and Means Committee and erstwhile presidential candidate, turned up one night drunk and in the company of a stripper known as "the Argentine Firecracker." In

1976, an employee of Wayne Hays, another prominent Democratic representative, reported that she was on the congressional payroll purely for sexual services: "I can't type, I can't file, I can't even answer the phone." And a cloud continued to hover over Massachusetts Senator Edward M. Kennedy, who in 1969 was driving a car involved in an accident in which a young woman drowned. The accident took place after a party on Chappaquiddick Island, off Martha's Vineyard; Kennedy never managed to give satisfactory explanations of how the accident happened or why he delayed in reporting it.

Public confidence in the federal government's ability to solve critical economic problems also slumped. Both joblessness and inflation intensified in 1974 and 1975 as the president and Congress quarreled over appropriate remedies. Lacking Nixon's flexibility and boldness, Ford reverted to traditional Republican policy, proposing to fight inflation by tightening the money supply and by cutting spending and increasing taxes to balance the federal budget. This set him on a collision course with the heavily Democratic Congress, which pursued a tax cut and increased spending to stimulate the economy and create jobs.

Dubbed by Democratic opponents "the most veto-prone Republican president in the twentieth century," Ford curtailed some federal programs over the objections of Congress. Yet Congress prevailed with a tax cut, increased Social Security benefits, a higher minimum wage, and a $4 billion public works program. Unemployment and inflation abated somewhat, but underlying weaknesses in the U.S. economy remained: a low rate of growth, higher than normal unemployment, a deficit in foreign trade, and high energy prices tied to dependence on oil from abroad.

Keeping Nixon's key foreign policy adviser, Henry Kissinger, as secretary of state, Ford pursued foreign policy goals set by his predecessor. Just two weeks after South Vietnam's collapse in April 1975, the Ford administration seized upon an incident to reassert U.S. power when Cambodian patrol boats captured an American cargo ship, the *Mayagüez*, which was sailing along the Cambodian coast. Ford quickly ordered U.S. forces to bomb Cambodian boats and authorized a plan to rescue the crew of the *Mayagüez*. The president and the U.S. military were unaware that Cambodia had already released the crew, and the attack was carried out, costing forty-one American lives. Although it was unnecessary, the attack produced a burst of approval and pride at home. Senator Barry Goldwater exulted, "It was wonderful. It shows we've still got balls in this country."

Ford and Kissinger, however, failed to sustain widespread support of détente. The secrecy and failure to consult with Congress during the Nixon-Kissinger initiatives had alienated some legislators, and members of both parties worried that Soviet strength was overtaking that of the United States. Some Democrats charged that détente ignored Soviet violations of human rights. In response, Congress derailed trade agreements with the Soviet Union, refusing economic favors unless the Soviets stopped their harsh treatment of internal dissidents and gave Jews who wanted to leave the country permission to emigrate.

Although negotiations continued, the superpowers achieved no further agreements to limit strategic arms during Ford's presidency. The administration's most notable international agreement took place in 1975 in Helsinki, Finland, where Ford, Soviet leader Leonid Brezhnev, and European leaders formally recognized the existing post-World War II boundaries in Europe. In signing the Helsinki accords, the United States accepted the Soviets' domination over their satellite countries in Eastern Europe—a condition to which it had objected so bitterly thirty years earlier as the cold war began.

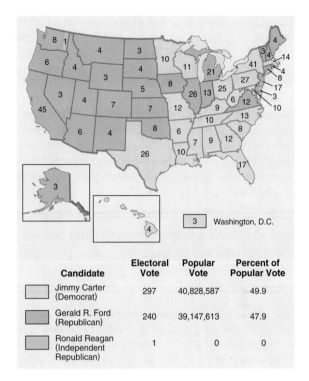

Candidate	Electoral Vote	Popular Vote	Percent of Popular Vote
Jimmy Carter (Democrat)	297	40,828,587	49.9
Gerald R. Ford (Republican)	240	39,147,613	47.9
Ronald Reagan (Independent Republican)	1	0	0

MAP 30.3
The Election of 1976

The Election of 1976

Opposition to détente fueled the biggest challenge to Ford's nomination for a full term in 1976, a challenge that came from the Republican right. The president's leading opponent in the Republican primaries, former California Governor Ronald Reagan, deplored the "collapse of the American will and the retreat of American power," charging that Nixon and Ford had allowed the United States to become "number two in a world where it is dangerous—if not fatal—to be second best." Taking a position to the right of Ford on domestic issues as well, Reagan came close to snatching the nomination from Ford. But in an attempt to unify the party, Ford bowed to conservative Republicans on key platform planks that criticized his own foreign policy and selected conservative Senator Robert Dole of Kansas as his running mate.

Smelling victory, Democratic contenders came out in abundance. Former Georgia Governor James Earl (Jimmy) Carter Jr. began early, traveling across the country campaigning for congressional candidates in 1974 and for himself by early 1975. A graduate of the U.S. Naval Academy, Carter spent seven

years in the navy before his father's death called him back to Plains, Georgia, in 1953 to take over the family peanut farming business. In 1962, he won election to the Georgia state senate, where he served for four years. After a failed bid for the governorship in 1966, he won election in 1970 and served a successful four-year term. As soon as he left office in early 1975, he threw himself into the presidential campaign.

Well financed by businessmen, Carter at first ran a lonely yet sophisticated and grueling campaign that took him into every state's contest for convention delegates and gained extensive media coverage. Highly intelligent and well prepared on the issues, the soft-spoken Carter stressed his small-town roots, deep religious commitment, unpretentiousness, and distance from the popularly suspect national government. Although not a riveting speaker, after the revelations of corruption in the Nixon administration, the candidate who carried his own bags, lived modestly, and went home almost every week to teach a Bible class at his Baptist church had considerable appeal.

"I will never tell a lie to the American people," Carter promised, stressing his campaign theme of morality in government. Pledging vaguely to "re-store to our country what has been lost," he avoided stands on controversial issues. The Georgian won endorsements from black religious leaders, but black politicians remained wary, especially after Carter approved of neighborhoods maintaining "ethnic purity" against "intrusion of alien groups," remarks for which he was compelled to apologize. Liberal Democrats questioned Carter's commitment to the New Deal-Great Society reform tradition, but they failed to rally around an alternative candidate.

"I will never tell a lie to the American people,"
Carter promised, stressing his campaign theme
of morality in government.

Winning the Democratic nomination on the first ballot, Carter sought to unify the party by selecting liberal Senator Walter F. Mondale of Minnesota as his running mate and by accepting a platform that affirmed broad goals compatible with traditional Democratic principles. His nomination nonetheless represented a decided rightward turn in the party, reflected in Carter's campaign promises to eliminate the budget deficit and reduce federal controls and regulations on business.

Carter benefited from the Watergate backlash, the economic problems that plagued the Ford administration, the damage that the Reagan challenge had done to Ford, and his own ability to attract sufficient votes from the traditional Democratic coalition of blacks, southerners, organized labor, and ethnic groups. Yet his victory over Ford was narrow. Democrats retained substantial margins in the House and Senate, but Carter received just 50.1 percent of the popular vote to Ford's 48 percent.

The "Outsider" Presidency of Jimmy Carter

In his campaign autobiography, *Why Not the Best?*, Jimmy Carter (the name he used even when signing state documents) held out the ideal of a government that was "competent," as well as "honest, decent, open, fair, and compassionate." Carter was extremely well informed and hardworking, a kind and decent individual who was uninterested in personal or political aggrandizement. Yet while Carter

refrained from abusing the power of his position, he seemed unable to wield his legitimate authority effectively and failed to win a second term.

Carter's undoing stemmed from his style of leadership and from a configuration of domestic and foreign crises that culminated during his last year in office. Prone to attempt too many initiatives at once, Carter worked poorly with Congress, even though it remained under Democratic control. He faced at more intense levels the energy shortages and stagflation that had confounded his predecessors. Carter also reaped the blame for deteriorating Soviet-American relations and for the rise of an intensely anti-American government in Iran, which held fifty-two Americans hostage through his last year in office.

The disastrous final year of Carter's presidency overshadowed some significant accomplishments of his administration, most notably in environmental and energy policies. In foreign affairs, Carter obtained ratification of treaties ending U.S. control over the Panama Canal—the most blatant symbol of Yankee imperialism—and, following up on Nixon's initiatives, he established normal diplomatic relations with China. His most brilliant achievement was securing a peace treaty between Israel and Egypt.

Retreat from Liberalism

Jimmy Carter promised "to help the poor and aged, to improve education, and to provide jobs" but at the same time "not to waste money." He wanted a humane government that would help those in need, but one that also was efficiently managed and prudent in its spending. When these two aims conflicted, especially when inflation threatened economic stability, Carter's commitment to reform assumed second place. Liberal Democrats accused him of deserting the Democratic reform tradition that stretched back to Franklin Roosevelt.

Symbolizing his desire to be known as a "man of the people," Carter substituted a business suit for the traditional formal dress at his inauguration and with his wife, Rosalynn, led the inaugural parade on foot rather than riding in a car. Carter stressed his status as an "outsider" to the deals, bargaining, and inefficiency that characterized national politics. Believing that congressional action was unduly shaped by powerful special interests and legislators' concerns for the next election, Carter saw his job as countering those special interests by acting as the trustee of all the people.

PRESIDENT CARTER'S INAUGURAL DAY
After his inauguration in January 1977, Jimmy Carter eschewed the customary presidential limousine and instead walked with his family down Pennsylvania Avenue from the Capitol to the White House. He wanted to emphasize his opposition to some of the trappings of office that separated the government from the people. Ordering cabinet heads to drive their own cars, he said, "Government officials can't be sensitive to your problems if we are living like royalty here."
Jimmy Carter Presidential Library.

Although Carter's outsider status helped him into office, it left him without strong ties either to party insiders or to prominent legislators. He lacked experience in the horse trading and compromise that got things done in Washington and opposed them in principle. His desire to propose comprehensive solutions to national problems went against the congressional tendency to take a piecemeal, incremental approach. Legislators complained of inadequate consultation with the White House during policy formulation, and they grew exasperated when Carter flooded them with a large number of unprioritized proposals.

Even a president within the mainstream of the Democratic Party and an expert in the art of congressional persuasion might not have done much better than Carter. Congress was flexing its muscles in response to Watergate and the aggrandizement of presidential power under Johnson and Nixon. In addition to reasserting its authority vis-à-vis the executive branch, in the 1970s Congress reduced the power of its own committee chairs and instituted reforms that weakened party control over legislators and decentralized the decision-making process.

Carter worked poorly with Congress and faced energy shortages and stagflation. He also reaped the blame for deteriorating Soviet-American relations and for the rise of an intensely anti-American government in Iran.

For his White House staff, Carter relied heavily on associates from Georgia—who, like him, lacked experience in national politics—but his cab-

AN ACTIVE FIRST LADY

Rosalynn Carter was the most active First Lady in public affairs since Eleanor Roosevelt. Various members of Congress and diplomats criticized President Jimmy Carter for sending her on an official mission to Latin America to emphasize his administration's commitment to human rights and democracy there. Though critics said Latin American leaders wouldn't take her seriously, the seven-country visit in June 1977 proved successful. Here she meets with President Carlos Andrés Pérez of Venezuela.

Walter Bennett/Sygma.

inet appointments included several men from the Kennedy and Johnson administrations. Continuing their relationship as business and political partners, the president discussed nearly everything with his wife, who played a larger role in affairs of state than any First Lady since Eleanor Roosevelt. Carter involved other women in policymaking (including three at cabinet-level rank), far surpassing his predecessors in appointing women as well as members of minority groups to federal judgeships and high government positions. He also undertook a reorganization of the executive branch and won congressional approval for the creation of two new departments, the Department of Education and the Department of Energy.

Carter began his presidency confident that he could solve the unusually formidable set of prob-

lems that had eluded the efforts of the Nixon and Ford administrations—unemployment, inflation, a slow rate of economic growth, and energy shortages. Though some critics complained that his program didn't do enough, Carter signed bills pumping $14 billion into the economy through public works and public service jobs programs and cutting taxes by $34 billion over a three-year period. Unemployment, which had hovered near 8 percent in late 1976, fell below 6 percent in 1978.

However, rising inflation quickly overshadowed the creation of new jobs. Carter refused the mandatory controls on prices and wages that Nixon had implemented briefly in 1971. Instead, while the Federal Reserve system tightened the money supply by increasing interest rates, Carter tried to curtail federal spending. These policies not only failed to halt inflation, which surpassed 13 percent in 1980, but also contributed to rising unemployment, reversing the progress that had been made in Carter's first two years.

The Carter administration achieved little progress on issues traditionally central to the Democratic Party. The president's commitment to holding down the federal budget frustrated Democratic legislators pushing for comprehensive welfare reform and a national health insurance program. To ensure solvency in the Social Security system, Carter and Congress agreed on measures to increase employer and employee contributions. Although these measures shored up the Social Security fund, they also increased the tax burden of lower- and middle-income Americans.

Carter, however, won approval for several proposals that favored business. As Social Security taxes went up, a sharp cut in the maximum rate on capital gains reduced the tax burden on the wealthy. When the Chrysler Corporation approached bankruptcy in 1979, Congress responded with $1.5 billion worth of loan guarantees to ensure the survival of the tenth largest corporation in the country. The government also reduced federal controls in several industries. Congress approved Carter's proposals to deregulate airlines in 1978 and the banking, trucking, and railroad industries in 1980. Airline deregulation at first stimulated lower fares and the rise of new companies, but the 1980s saw reduced

service to smaller communities, increasing concerns about safety, and the dominance of a few large conglomerates because of the demise of financially insecure airlines and a series of mergers.

Response to the Energy Crisis

Designating the energy issue "the moral equivalent of war," Carter fought for a comprehensive energy program. But his goal to limit consumption and to reduce U.S. dependence on foreign oil fell victim to his uneasy relationship with Congress and to competing demands among energy producers and consumers. In 1978, Congress passed the National Energy Act of 1978, a compromise measure that included penalties on gas-guzzling automobiles and other incentives to conserve energy. The legislation also provided measures to promote alternative fuel sources and changes in natural gas policies to increase supplies and achieve more equitable distribution.

In 1979, before even this limited program could have an effect, declines in oil production abroad, linked in part to a revolution in Iran, created the most severe energy shortage yet. Hundreds of cars lined up at gas stations in some areas, and motorists' tempers rose even higher when prices at the pumps began to reflect enormous price hikes by the Organization of Petroleum Exporting Countries (OPEC). Carter appealed to the public for support

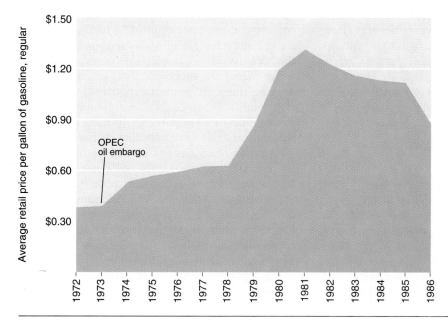

FIGURE 30.1
The Price of Gasoline, 1972–1986
The sharp increase in gasoline prices in 1973 and the even sharper one beginning in 1978 reflected price increases by the Organization of Petroleum Exporting Countries (OPEC) and contributed to inflation in the United States.

of new energy measures, and Congress eventually authorized programs to stimulate alternative fuel sources at the same time that it reduced controls on oil and gas and imposed a windfall profits tax on producers to redistribute some of the profits that would accrue with deregulation. Still falling short of Carter's initial proposal, the energy measures represented the nation's first comprehensive efforts to limit consumption and decrease its dependency on foreign oil.

In July 1979, Carter told a national TV audience that the country faced a "crisis of confidence." Along with losing their faith in progress, too many Americans had sacrificed their pride in "hard work, strong families, close knit communities and our faith in God" to the "worship of self-indulgence and consumption."

In July 1979, Carter told a national TV audience that the nation's problems went far beyond the energy crisis. The country, he said, faced a "crisis of confidence." Along with losing their faith in progress, too many Americans had sacrificed their pride in "hard work, strong families, close-knit communities and our faith in God" to the "worship of self-indulgence and consumption." To many listeners, Carter's speech seemed to blame the American people for his own failure to lead the way to solutions for national problems. Perceptions of flawed leadership multiplied when, two days later, Carter announced sweeping changes in his cabinet. By the end of the month, pollsters reported Carter's approval rating at just 25 percent. Developments abroad would undermine even further the nation's confidence in Carter's ability to govern effectively.

Idealism and Human Rights in Carter's Foreign Policy

Moral principles, Jimmy Carter promised, would guide his approach to America's relationships with the rest of the world. His predecessors' obsession with protecting and expanding U.S. power by any means, Carter believed, had violated the nation's principles of freedom and human dignity. "We've seen a loss of morality . . . and we're ashamed of what our government is as we deal with other nations around the world," he said. The cynical support of dictators, the

secret diplomacy, the interference in the internal affairs of other countries, the excessive reliance on military solutions—Carter promised to reverse them all.

Human rights formed the cornerstone of Carter's approach. Led by the president, U.S. officials took every opportunity to focus attention on governments that denied their citizens basic political and civil rights or freedom of religion and expression. The administration also used economic sanctions, denying aid or trading privileges to nations that oppressed their citizens. It applied economic pressure against a number of countries, including Argentina, Chile, El Salvador, and the white minority governments of Rhodesia and South Africa, which blatantly violated the rights of their black majorities.

Yet the administration implemented the human rights policy with glaring inconsistencies. In 1979, the United States established formal diplomatic relations with the People's Republic of China, concluding the process that Nixon and Kissinger had begun. In this case, improved relations with China took priority over attempts to secure democratic rights for the Chinese people. Moreover, in dealing with staunch, anti-Communist U.S. allies, Carter sacrificed human rights to strategic and security considerations. The administration invoked no sanctions against Iran, South Korea, and the Philippines, even though official oppression was obvious in those countries.

Cold war considerations dominated concern for human rights in the administration's approach to Nicaragua, which had been ruled since 1936 by the corrupt and viciously oppressive regime of the Somoza family. The administration complained about the Nicaraguan dictatorship's excesses and invoked some economic sanctions, but when civil war erupted there, its greatest concern was to contain Communist influence in the anti-Somoza movement. Officials were particularly uneasy about the Sandinistas, who were a leading element in the opposition and had ties to Cuba. Nonetheless, when the Somoza regime fell in 1979 and Sandinista leader Daniel Ortega assumed power, the United States extended recognition and economic aid to the new government. Critics on the right attacked Carter for pressuring Anastásio Somoza on human rights and thus helping to undermine his regime. These critics demanded the more typical test for U.S. support during the cold war years: whether a country was anti-Communist and friendly to U.S. interests, not how it treated its citizens.

THE CAMP DAVID ACCORDS
*President Jimmy Carter over-
sees the meeting of Egyptian
President Anwar Sadat, left,
and Israeli Prime Minister
Menachem Begin at Camp
David, Maryland, in September 1978. Carter's passionate
commitment to promoting
peace helped produce the first
easing of hostility between
Arabs and Israelis in thirty
years.*
Corbis-Bettmann.

The president took on even greater political burdens in applying moral principles to relations with Panama. Carter sped up the negotiations over control of the Panama Canal that had been under way since the Johnson administration. In 1977, the United States and Panama reached agreement on the terms of two treaties, one providing for joint control of the canal until the end of the century and the second defining U.S. rights after Panama assumed control.

The treaties evoked intense opposition. Although Carter and his supporters viewed them as recompense for the blatant use of U.S. power in obtaining the canal in 1903, others insisted on maintaining control of this vital waterway. "We bought it, we paid for it, it's ours, and we're going to keep it," claimed Ronald Reagan in his 1976 campaign for the Republican nomination. Behind the opposition lay anxieties about the decline of U.S. power. After the Carter administration undertook a massive campaign to rally popular and congressional support, the Senate ratified the treaties by the narrowest margins. Opponents continued to use the Panamanian accords as a political weapon: Several pro-treaty senators lost reelection bids, and Carter

saw the issue as an important factor in his own defeat in 1980.

In applying his moral authority toward peace in the Middle East, Carter achieved his most brilliant victory, one that was not tarnished by acrimony at home. He took advantage of the courage and foresight of Egyptian President Anwar Sadat, the first Arab leader to risk his political future by talking directly with Israeli officials. When initial discussions between Sadat and Israeli Prime Minister Menachem Begin faltered, Carter invited the two leaders to the presidential retreat at Camp David, Maryland, in September 1978. Carter studied all the issues down to the smallest details and then spent thirteen days at Camp David mediating between Begin and Sadat, carrying proposals and counterproposals from one cabin to the other. His enormous investment paid off in the form of a tentative agreement known popularly as the Camp David accords.

When subsequent negotiations for an official treaty bogged down, Carter flew to Jerusalem and Cairo and applied his tenacious diplomacy once more, obtaining a treaty that Begin and Sadat signed on the White House lawn in March 1979. Under the terms of the treaty, Egypt recognized Israel, and Israel agreed to gradual withdrawal from the Sinai Peninsula, territory that it had seized in the 1967 war. The issues of Palestinian self-determination in other Israeli-occupied territories (the West Bank and Gaza) and the plight of Palestinian refugees remained unresolved. Nonetheless, the first real steps toward peace in the Middle East had been taken, and Jimmy Carter had earned much of the credit.

Foreign Policy in Disarray

The last two years of the Carter administration saw both a shift in policies and severe setbacks to Carter's original goals. Relations between the United States and the Soviet Union deteriorated, and the administration began a sizable military buildup. Although external events in 1979, particularly the Soviet invasion of Afghanistan and the Iranian revolution, stimulated the turn toward militarism, it also reflected currents that had existed within the administration from the beginning.

For counsel on foreign policy issues, Carter leaned most heavily on his secretary of state, Cyrus Vance, and his national security adviser, Zbigniew Brzezinski. Even though the two had recommended each other for their respective posts, once in office they discovered acute differences in their approaches to policy. Polish-born Brzezinski, an international relations professor at Columbia University, held traditional cold war views, emphasizing the Soviet and Communist threat and urging the maximization of U.S. power. Vance, a New York lawyer who had served in the Kennedy and Johnson administrations, had come to see the limitations of American power and the need to work with the Soviet Union to reduce the threat of nuclear war.

Preferring to pursue national security through nonmilitary means, Carter initially approached the Soviet Union with an air of accommodation and reassurance. Although the president never ceased to speak out about Soviet suppression of Jews and dissidents, he set Vance to work on a new strategic arms limitation agreement to replace SALT I, which was due to expire in 1977. He also cast a cautious eye on new weapons systems and canceled production of the neutron bomb, a high-radiation weapon designed to be used on the battlefield. Carter also halted production of the new B-1 bomber, thereby infuriating a large number of its supporters in Congress.

Two years of negotiations with the Soviet Union produced a SALT II treaty in 1979, but by then

Carter had accepted Brzezinski's warnings about the need to counter a Soviet military buildup. The president authorized development of new intermediate-range missiles to be deployed in Western Europe as well as an enormous new missile system (known as MX) to be built in the United States. However, this new emphasis on military strength did not defuse criticism of SALT II and arms control, opposition that had grown with Carter's cancellation of the B-1.

With Senate ratification of SALT II becoming increasingly unlikely, Carter withdrew the treaty in December 1979. He acted shortly after the Soviet Union invaded its neighbor Afghanistan, whose recently installed pro-Soviet government was threatened by Muslim opposition. Carter asserted that the invasion "could pose the greatest threat to peace since the Second World War." In response, he imposed economic sanctions on the Soviet Union, canceled U.S. participation in the 1980 Olympic Games in Moscow, and persuaded Congress to approve legislation requiring all nineteen-year-old men to register for the draft.

The president claimed that Soviet actions posed a threat to oil supplies from the Middle East and announced his own "Carter Doctrine," stating that the United States would intervene with any means necessary should an outside force try to gain control of the Persian Gulf. The human rights policy fell by the wayside as the United States stepped up aid to Pakistan, Afghanistan's neighbor, controlled by a military regime that had overthrown and executed the popularly elected head of state. Finally, Carter called for hefty increases in defense spending over the next five years.

On November 4, 1979, a crowd broke into the U.S. embassy in Teheran and held more than sixty Americans captive there, demanding that the United States return the shah for trial.

Events in Iran fueled this reversion to a hard-line, militaristic approach. All the U.S. arms and support had not enabled the shah to suppress growing opposition to his regime. Iranian dissidents still resented the CIA's role in the overthrow of the Mossadegh government in 1953, and they deplored the Westernization of their country that accompanied the shah's rule as well as his savage attempts to silence opposition. On New Year's Eve 1977, Carter toasted the shah's "great leadership" at a banquet in Teheran. But in little more than a year, a revolution forced the shah to abandon his throne and country. By March 1979, the Iranian government was in the hands of the Ayatollah Ruholla Khomeini and other Shiite Islamic fundamentalists who were intensely hostile to the United States, which they blamed for supporting the shah's brutalities and undermining the religious foundations of their country.

When Carter permitted the shah to enter the United States for medical treatment, anti-American demonstrations escalated in Teheran. On November 4, 1979, a crowd broke into the U.S. embassy and held more than sixty Americans captive there, demanding that the United States return the shah for trial. When Khomeini supported the captors and refused to negotiate, Carter froze Iranian assets in U.S. banks and placed an embargo on Iranian oil. The only Iranian concessions were to free thirteen blacks and women and later a seriously ill hostage. For the next year, the hostage crisis received an inordinate amount of television coverage and vast amounts of the administration's time and energies.

Every attempt to negotiate was frustrated, and in April 1980, Carter resorted to force to rescue the hostages. But the small military operation ran into

AMERICAN HOSTAGES IN IRAN
Iranian militants display one of the hostages they took when they occupied the American embassy in Teheran on November 4, 1979. Until the hostages were released in January 1981, Americans regularly watched TV images of the American captives being paraded before angry Iranian crowds. The bound, blindfolded hostages served as humiliating symbols of the limitations of American power.
Ph. Ledru/Sygma.

difficulties landing in the Iranian desert and had to abort the mission. Eight Americans died when a U.S. plane and helicopter collided during the evacuation. Secretary of State Vance, who had opposed a rescue attempt and had been kept out of the plans, resigned in protest. Failure of the rescue mission further embarrassed the president, and the hostage crisis burdened Carter's campaign for reelection. Continuing efforts to reach an agreement with Iran finally produced release of the hostages on the day Carter left office.

Conclusion: The Loss of American Ascendency

Public confidence and trust in government declined in the 1970s, partially in response to Watergate and other revelations of deception and corruption among public officials. Presidents Ford and Carter restored morality to the White House, but both were deficient in political skills. The 1970s saw continuation of key domestic reforms of the 1960s as well as new legislation in response to movements for women's rights and environmental protection. Yet the government seemed unable to deal with the gravest economic problems since the Great Depression—a low rate of economic growth, inflation combined with unemployment, and an increasing trade deficit.

Nor could Americans take much comfort in their country's relationships with the rest of the world. They applauded Carter's success in inching the Middle East slightly in the direction of stability, but the Israeli-Egyptian accord failed to resolve the larger Middle East problems that affected Americans directly by disrupting energy supplies. And even though the Panama Canal treaties moved the United States toward more equitable relations with Latin American countries, they provoked strong opposition.

Normalization of relations with the People's Republic of China won widespread support, but critics of strategic arms limitation and Soviet-American détente gained the upper hand. This opposition, combined with the Soviet invasion of Afghanistan, nullified the thaw in Soviet-American relations that Nixon and Kissinger had begun. By 1980, the hostile tone of the United States toward the Soviet Union and the growing emphasis on military expansion resembled the early years of the cold war.

Officials in both parties who supported a more militaristic approach to foreign policy found support in a public perplexed by the nation's apparent inability to influence global events. Four years after the fall of South Vietnam, another humiliation rocked the nation when Iran erupted into a burst of anti-Americanism and the United States proved unable to rescue its citizens who were held hostage there.

Americans' feeling of impotence in the face of the hostage crisis did reflect a decline in U.S. power, but it was a relative descent from an artificially high base. The global political and economic ascendancy of the United States existed only as long as it took for other countries to recover from the ravages of World War II. The growing power of the Soviet Union and China set limits on the ability of the United States to intervene throughout the world without risking superpower confrontation. And the rise of nationalism in the third world posed further constraints on American power.

The recovery of Europe and Japan challenged U.S. economic supremacy and contributed to the domestic problems that plagued each administration in the 1970s, particularly the loss of foreign and domestic markets; the decline in electronics, steel, automobile, and other major industries; and the accompanying rising unemployment and sluggish economy. Whether and how the United States could regain its economic and political power provided the script for the 1980 elections.

CHRONOLOGY

1968 Richard Nixon elected thirty-seventh president of the United States.

1969 Warren E. Burger appointed chief justice of United States by Nixon.

1970 Earth Day demonstrations held to support environmental goals.

Congress passes Occupational Safety and Health Act.

Environmental Protection Agency established by Nixon.

Native American Women's Association founded.

Women Strike for Peace and Equality demonstrations take place nationwide.

1971 First national Mexican American women's conference held.

In *Swann*, Supreme Court upholds legality of busing to achieve integration.

Nixon announces abandonment of gold standard in his New Economic Policy.

Nixon vetoes comprehensive child care bill.

1972 Congress passes federal revenue-sharing laws.

Congress passes Title IX of Education Amendments Act, banning sex discrimination in education.

Ms. magazine founded by Gloria Steinem and other feminists.

Nixon becomes first U.S. president to visit China.

Nixon visits Moscow to sign arms limitation treaties with Soviets.

Nixon campaign aides apprehended breaking into Democratic Party headquarters in Watergate apartment complex in Washington, D.C.

Richard Nixon reelected president in landslide.

1973 Arab oil embargo in retaliation for U.S. support of Israel creates energy crisis in United States.

National Black Feminist Organization founded.

Senate Watergate hearings reveal widespread abuses of power in Nixon administration.

In *Roe v. Wade*, Supreme Court rules that abortion is constitutionally protected.

1974 Nixon resigns as president in face of certain impeachment by House of Representatives over his role in Watergate affair; Gerald Ford becomes thirty-eighth president of United States.

Ford pardons Nixon of any crimes he may have committed while president.

Supreme Court imposes some limitations on use of busing to achieve racial integration in schools.

1976 Jimmy Carter, former Democratic governor of Georgia, elected thirty-ninth president of United States, defeating Ford.

1978 Carter helps negotiate peace agreement between Israel and Egypt (Camp David accords).

Congress passes National Energy Act.

In *Bakke*, Supreme Court rules against racial quotas and "reverse" discrimination.

Congress passes law banning discrimination against pregnant women.

1979 **November 4.** Beginning of hostage crisis in Iran.

1980 Attempt to free U.S. hostages in Iran fails.

BIBLIOGRAPHY

GENERAL WORKS

Peter N. Carroll, *It Seemed Like Nothing Happened: America in the 1970s* (1982).

Thomas Ferguson and Joel Rogers, *Right Turn: The Decline of the Democrats and the Future of American Politics* (1986).

Raymond Garthoff, *Détente and Confrontation: American-Soviet Relations from Nixon to Reagan* (1985).

Kim McQuaid, *The Anxious Years: America in the Vietnam-Watergate Era* (1989).

DOMESTIC ISSUES

Barry Bluestone and Bennett Harrison, *The Deindustrialization of America: Plant Closings, Community Abandonment, and the Dismantling of Basic Industry* (1982).

Vincent J. Burke and Vee Burke, *Nixon's Good Deed: Welfare Reform* (1974).

Paul R. Dommel, *The Politics of Revenue Sharing* (1974).

Daniel Patrick Moynihan, *The Politics of a Guaranteed National Income: The Nixon Administration and the Family Assistance Plan* (1973).

Herman Schwartz, ed., *The Burger Years: Rights and Wrongs in the Supreme Court* (1987).

Melvin Urofsky, *A Conflict of Rights: The Supreme Court and Affirmative Action* (1991).

ENERGY AND THE ENVIRONMENT

S. David Aviel, *The Politics of Nuclear Energy* (1982).

Thomas R. Dunlap, *DDT: Scientists, Citizens, and Public Policy* (1981).

Samuel P. Hays, *Beauty, Health, and Permanence: Environmental Politics in the United States, 1955–1985* (1987).

Michael J. Lacey, ed., *Government and Environmental Politics* (1991).

Martin V. Melosi, *Coping with Abundance: Energy and Environment in Industrial America* (1985).

Philip Shabecoff, *A Fierce Green Fire: The American Environmental Movement* (1993).

Franklin Tugwell, *The Energy Crisis and the American Political Economy: Politics and Markets in the Management of Natural Resources* (1988).

John C. Whitaker, *Striking a Balance: Environment and Natural Resources Policy in the Nixon-Ford Years* (1976).

Daniel Yergin, *The Prize: The Epic Quest for Oil, Money, and Power* (1990).

THE NIXON AND FORD ADMINISTRATIONS

Stephen E. Ambrose, *Nixon: The Triumph of a Politician, 1962–1972* (1989).

Gerald R. Ford, *A Time to Heal: The Autobiography of Gerald R. Ford* (1979).

Michael A. Genovese, *The Nixon Presidency: Power and Politics in Turbulent Times* (1990).

John Robert Greene, *The Limits of Power: The Nixon and Ford Administrations* (1992).

Joan Hoff, *Nixon Reconsidered* (1994).

Richard M. Nixon, *RN: The Memoirs of Richard Nixon* (1978).

Herbert S. Parmet, *Nixon and His America* (1989).

A. James Reichley, *Conservatives in an Age of Change: The Nixon and Ford Administrations* (1981).

Edward L. and Frederick H. Schapsmeier, *Gerald R. Ford's Date with Destiny: A Political Biography* (1989).

Tom Wicker, *One of Us: Richard Nixon and the American Dream* (1991).

WATERGATE

Carl Bernstein and Bob Woodward, *All the President's Men* (1974).

Fred J. Cook, *The Crimes of Watergate* (1981).

Leon Jaworski, *The Right and the Power: The Prosecution of Watergate* (1976).

Stanley I. Kutler, *The Wars of Watergate: The Last Crisis of Richard Nixon* (1990).

Gladys Engel Lang and Kurt Lang, *The Battle for Public Opinion: The President, the Press, and the Polls during Watergate* (1983).

Kathryn S. Olmsted, *Challenging the Secret Government: The Post-Watergate Investigations of the CIA and FBI* (1996).

Arthur M. Schlesinger, *The Imperial Presidency* (1973).

Michael Schudson, *Watergate in American Memory* (1992).

John J. Sirica, with John F. Stacks, *To Set the Record Straight: The Break-in, the Tapes, the Conspirators, the Pardon* (1979).

WOMEN'S MOVEMENTS

Mary Frances Berry, *Why ERA Failed* (1986).

Anne N. Costain, *Inviting Women's Rebellion* (1992).

Barbara Hinkson Craig and David M. O'Brien, *Abortion and American Politics* (1993).

Alice Echols, *Daring to Be Bad: Radical Feminism in America, 1967–1975* (1989).

Myra Marx Ferree and Beth B. Hess, *Controversy and Coalition: The New Feminist Movement* (1985).

Jo Freeman, *The Politics of Women's Liberation* (1985).

Joyce Gelb and Marion Lief Palley, *Women and Public Policies* (1987).

Susan M. Hartmann, *From Margin to Mainstream: American Women and Politics since 1960* (1989).

Jane J. Mansbridge, *Why We Lost the ERA* (1986).

Donald G. Mathews and Jane Sherron De Hart, *Sex, Gender, and the Politics of ERA* (1990).

Rosalind Pollack Petchesky, *Abortion and Woman's Choice: Private Morality and Public Policy* (1981).

Winifred D. Wandersee, *On the Move: American Women in the 1970s* (1988).

Guida West, *The National Welfare Rights Movement: The Social Protest of Poor Women* (1981).

Joan Hoff Wilson, *Rites of Passage: The Past and Future of the ERA* (1986).

THE CARTER ADMINISTRATION

M. Glenn Abernathy, Dilys M. Hill, and Phil Williams, eds., *The Carter Years: The President and Policymaking* (1984).

Peter G. Bourne, *Jimmy Carter: A Comprehensive Biography from Plains to Post-Presidency* (1997).

Jimmy Carter, *Keeping Faith: Memoirs of a President* (1982).

John Dumbrell, *The Carter Presidency: A Reevaluation* (1995).

Betty Glad, *Jimmy Carter: In Search of the Great White House* (1980).

Erwin C. Hargrove, *Jimmy Carter as President: Leadership and the Politics of the Public Good* (1988).

Charles O. Jones, *The Trusteeship Presidency: Jimmy Carter and the United States Congress* (1988).

Burton I. Kaufmann, *The Presidency of James Earl Carter* (1993).

Kenneth Earl Morris, *Jimmy Carter, American Moralist* (1996).

Herbert D. Rosenbaum and Alexej Ugrinsky, eds., *The Presidency and Domestic Policies of Jimmy Carter* (1993).

FOREIGN POLICY

James A. Bill, *The Eagle and the Lion: The Tragedy of American-Iranian Relations* (1988).

Seyom Brown, *The Crisis of Power: Foreign Policy in the Kissinger Years* (1979).

Zbigniew Brzezinski, *Power and Principle: Memoirs of the National Security Adviser, 1977–1981* (1983).

Raymond I. Garthoff, *Détente and Confrontation: American-Soviet Relations from Nixon to Reagan* (1994).

Mark J. Gasiorowski, *U.S. Foreign Policy and the Shah: Building a Client State in Iran* (1991).

Seymour Hersh, *The Price of Power: Kissinger in the Nixon White House* (1983).

J. Michael Hogan, *The Panama Canal in American Politics* (1986).

Keith I. Nelson, *The Making of Détente: Soviet-American Relations in the Shadow of Vietnam* (1995).

Gaddis Smith, *Morality, Reason, and Power: American Diplomacy in the Carter Years* (1986).

Terry Terriff, *The Nixon Administration and the Making of U.S. Nuclear Strategy* (1995).

Cyrus Vance, *Hard Choices: Critical Years in America's Foreign Policy* (1983).

WALL STREET VIDEO

The popular 1987 movie Wall Street *captured elements of the economy and society that led some observers to talk about the "money culture" and call the 1980s the decade of "greed." Wealth accumulation and lavish consumption were more visible than usual. One indication of the prosperity enjoyed by some was the growing presence of technology in the home, including computers, microwave ovens, compact disc players, and, especially, video cassette recorders. As the number of households with VCRs jumped from one million in 1980 to nearly 70 million in 1990, more and more people saw movies like "Wall Street" by renting videotapes for home viewing.*

THE REAGAN-BUSH COUNTERREVOLUTION

31

1980–1991

"FRANKLIN DELANO REAGAN," headlined the *New York Times* editorial on Ronald Wilson Reagan's acceptance speech at the Republican convention in 1980. The presidential nominee had repeatedly quoted Roosevelt, all the while promising to reduce drastically the federal government's role in American life. Once in the White House, Reagan promptly rehung a portrait of President Calvin Coolidge—that staunch Republican believer in the virtues of big business—but he continued to grasp the mantle of Roosevelt even as his policies formed the antithesis of New Deal liberalism.

Reagan's invocation of Franklin Roosevelt made good politics, bolstering his appeal to traditional Democrats. It also served to reconcile Reagan's own history —he had once been an active Democrat and ardent Roosevelt supporter—with his present conservative Republicanism. He pulled off his identification with Roosevelt by quoting selectively and by emphasizing Roosevelt's early advocacy of government retrenchment and frugality. Reagan genuinely admired Roosevelt's dynamism and confidence in the nation's ability to rise to new challenges. He intended to exercise that same spirited leadership and to restore the United States to a global role as powerful as the one it held at the time of Roosevelt's death. He also aimed for a revolution in domestic policy as striking as Roosevelt's in extent, though not in kind, and a new national political alignment that would be as impressive as Roosevelt's New Deal coalition.

The frequent appeal by the most conservative president since Calvin Coolidge to the example of Franklin Roosevelt was not the only contradiction of the Reagan presidency. Reagan promised fiscal stringency and a balanced budget, but when he left office, the government owed the largest debt in the nation's history. He limited the role of the federal government through tax cuts and relaxation of regulations on business, but federal spending increased and the federal bureaucracy expanded during his eight years as president. Reagan appealed to Americans uncomfortable with the sexual permissiveness, new family structures, and other social changes of the 1960s and 1970s. Social conservatives liked his emphasis on "family values," but Reagan himself was divorced and estranged from some of his children. The darling of religious fundamentalists, the president rarely attended church.

Reagan set out to restore confidence in government, and he contributed mightily to a revival of national pride. Yet dozens of his aides were linked to government scandals, and many of his statements clouded the line between fact and fantasy. Although Reagan voiced the most hawkish rhetoric since the days of John Foster Dulles and promoted the largest military buildup in peacetime, when he left office the United States and the Soviet Union had moved closer together than at any time since World War II.

Unlike the era of Roosevelt, which had focused on the disadvantaged, the spotlight of the 1980s turned on the affluent. The Reagan administration conquered the inflation and unemployment that had bedeviled presidents in the 1970s, and the economy entered its longest boom in the nation's history. Better-off Americans enjoyed the greatest benefits. Resembling the 1920s rather than the 1930s in economic terms, the Reagan era saw wealth redistributed upward while prosperity bypassed large segments of the population.

Reagan's successor, George Bush, deviated only slightly from Reagan's antigovernment philosophy. He proposed few domestic policy initiatives and vetoed many passed by the Democrat-controlled Congress. Aside from new laws dealing with civil rights and environmental protection, domestic policy changed little from the Reagan years. With the president and Congress caught in gridlock, the economy slid into a recession in 1990.

In contrast to the domestic arena, which appeared stagnant, massive changes swept through the world, surprising even the most astute foreign policy observers. Eastern Europe broke free of Communist control in 1989, and the Soviet Union disintegrated in 1991. With the end of the cold war, which had been the obsession of U.S. foreign policy for forty-five years, Bush heralded a "new world order." Freed from having to worry about the Soviet Union's response to U.S. intervention, Bush responded quickly to a new crisis in the Middle East. When Iraq invaded Kuwait in 1990, the United States led an international coalition that expelled the invaders.

When Bush left the presidency in 1993, the United States had yet to articulate an overall strategy for a post-cold war era no longer defined by containment of communism. On the home front, Bush left the Reagan antigovernment legacy intact along with a continuing federal deficit and a declining economy.

The Rising Tide of Conservatism

Ronald Reagan's landslide election to the presidency in 1980 marked the most important turning point in politics since Franklin D. Roosevelt's victory in 1932. Eisenhower and Nixon had campaigned as middle-of-the-road Republicans, but Reagan's victory established conservatism's dominance in the Republican Party and enabled the right to shape the national political agenda during the decade to come. Since the 1930s, the Democratic Party had defined the major issues; in the 1980s, the Republicans assumed that initiative, while the Democrats moved toward the right in their search for an effective response.

Reagan's victory established conservatism's dominance in the Republican Party and enabled the right to shape the national political agenda during the decade to come.

An extraordinarily adept politician, Reagan appealed to a wide spectrum of conservative groups and sentiments. He won the allegiance of free-market conservatives, militant anti-Communists, fundamentalist and evangelical Christians, and white working-class Democrats who were disenchanted with Great Society programs. Above all, Reagan benefited from the economic disarray that had caused both inflation and unemployment rates to soar in the last years of the Carter administration. These conditions enabled Reagan to win votes from people who suffered economically but who otherwise would not have supported a conservative.

The Election of 1980

Ronald Reagan captured the 1980 Republican nomination from a large field of contenders, and his success was remarkable in several respects. The oldest candidate ever nominated for the presidency, Reagan was born in 1911 to a staunchly Democratic father who served as administrator of work relief in Dixon, Illinois, during the New Deal. After attending a small religious college in Illinois, Reagan worked as a sportscaster before becoming a movie actor.

In the 1940s, he became active in the Screen Actors Guild, a performers' union, ultimately becoming its president. When the Red scare reached Hollywood, Reagan worked energetically to rid the movie industry of alleged Communists and sympathizers. His conservatism developed further in the 1950s, when, after his acting career faded, General Electric Corporation (GE) hired him for public relations work. Speaking for GE all over the country, Reagan harped on the evils of big government.

In 1964, he campaigned for Barry Goldwater, his shift to conservatism complete.

Reagan's own political career took off when he was elected to the first of two terms as governor of California in 1966. Although he ran a conservative campaign, denouncing excessive government, welfare giveaways, and student protests at the state's universities, as governor he displayed considerable flexibility. He approved a major tax increase (blaming the need for it on the extravagance of the previous Democratic administration), a strong measure to control water pollution, and a liberal abortion bill.

Reagan displayed similar flexibility in his 1980 presidential campaign, softening, for example, his earlier attacks on the Panama Canal treaties and Social Security. As his running mate, he chose George Bush, a representative of the Republican center, who had attacked central features of the Reagan agenda when they were rivals in the primary races. (Once he became a member of Reagan's team, however, Bush displayed unswerving loyalty to the Reagan program.) Reagan's amiable personality helped him to avoid being cast as a rigid right winger, and his energetic campaign assuaged doubts that he was too old for the presidency.

Despite Reagan's move toward the center, some liberal Republicans balked at his nomination and at the party platform, which reflected the domination of the right wing. When the party adopted a plank reversing its forty-year support for the Equal Rights Amendment, moderate and liberal Republican women marched outside the convention hall to show their dismay. Some of these women, along with other liberal Republicans, found a more acceptable standard-bearer in John B. Anderson, representative of Illinois, who deserted his party to run as an independent candidate.

The poor state of the economy and the country's declining international stature provided ample weapons for Reagan's campaign. He kept reminding voters of the "misery index"—the combined rates of unemployment and inflation—and asked, "Are you better off now than you were four years ago?" Reagan also capitalized on the Soviet invasion of Afghanistan and the Iranian hostage crisis, accusing Jimmy Carter of weakening U.S. military strength and losing the confidence of the nation's allies and the respect of its enemies. "They say that the United States has had its day in the sun, that our nation has passed its zenith," Reagan scoffed. Staunchly rejecting that view, he insisted that more effective leadership and a determination to "take

THE REAGAN PRESIDENCY BEGINS
Ronald Reagan, one of the most popular presidents of the twentieth century, takes the oath of office in 1981 from Chief Justice Warren Burger. His wife, Nancy, looks on.
Dick Halstead/Time.

government off the backs of the people" would restore Americans' morale and other nations' respect.

Having lost confidence in Carter and his ability to contain inflation and unemployment, a narrow majority of voters responded to Reagan's upbeat message. Fifty-one percent of the electorate cast their votes for Reagan, while 41 percent favored Carter, 7 percent Anderson. Though his popular majority was slim, Reagan overwhelmed Carter 489 to 49 in electoral college votes. The Republicans also picked up thirty-three new seats in the House and won control of the Senate.

The returns appeared to reflect a rejection of Carter rather than an affirmation of Reagan. Only 52.3 percent of those eligible bothered to vote. One eighteen-year-old remarked, "I didn't want to be responsible for electing either one." Of those who did vote, more supported Reagan because "it was time for a change" than because they found his conservative principles compelling. Some analysts read the election results as signifying a major shift in popular attitudes, but others found persistent public support for a substantial government role in solving social and economic problems.

Reagan and the Spectrum of Conservatism

Whatever the election results signified, conservatism had gained greater ascendancy in American political culture than at any time since the 1920s. Reagan clearly benefited from a lingering backlash against the upheavals associated with the 1960s—the civil rights revolution, the reforms of the Johnson era, the antiwar movement, feminism, the new sexual permissiveness, and the liberalism of the Supreme Court.

Much of Reagan's support came from religious conservatives with an avid interest in social issues, who constituted a relatively new phenomenon known as the New Right. During the 1970s, evangelical Christianity not only claimed thousands of new adherents but also abandoned the customary political neutrality of fundamentalist religion. The New Right made adept use of powerful new techniques for mobilizing support, notably sophisticated mass-mailing techniques and the "electronic ministry." Evangelical ministers such as Jerry Falwell, Jim Bakker, and Pat Robertson preached to huge television audiences. Attacking feminism, abortion, homosexuality, and pornography, they called for restoration of old-fashioned "family values." They wanted prayer back in and sex education out of the schools.

Conservatives created or revitalized a raft of political organizations and journals. The religious right sought a specific Christian voice in government through the Moral Majority founded by Jerry Falwell in 1979 and subsequently through the Christian Coalition, which Pat Robertson created in 1989. Within a few years, the Christian Coalition claimed 1.6 million members and control of the Republican Party in more than a dozen states. The instruments of more traditional conservatives—those who advocated limited government at home and militant anticommunism abroad—likewise flourished. These included publications such as the *National Review*, edited by William Buckley, and think tanks (research foundations) such as the American Enterprise Institute and the Heritage Foundation, which supported experts who developed and publicized new policy approaches.

Reagan embraced the full spectrum of conservatism and avowed his agreement with the New

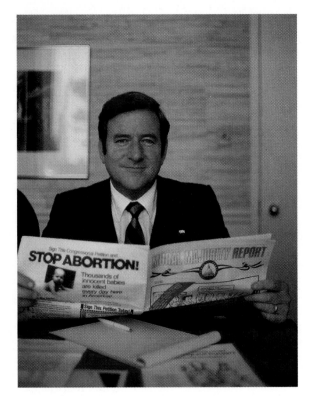

EVANGELIST JERRY FALWELL
One of the most popular televangelists, Baptist minister Jerry Falwell of Lynchburg, Virginia holds up the newsletter of the Moral Majority, the organization he founded in 1979. Established to promote "pro-God, pro-family policies in government," the Moral Majority and other groups of conservative Christians in the 1980s began to play a significant role in the Republican Party.
Eve Arnold/Magnum Photos, Inc.

Right on abortion, school prayer, and other social and moral issues. While these positions heartened social conservatives, they were not wholeheartedly embraced by the more traditional right, and few major policy changes came to fruition in these areas. Rather, Reagan's greatest success in promoting the conservative agenda lay in strengthening the nation's anti-Communist posture and reducing government restraints on free enterprise.

"In the present crisis," Reagan argued, "government is not the solution to our problem, government *is* the problem." Excessive government regulation and burdensome taxation crippled productivity, he claimed, while unbridled government spending was "mortgaging our future . . . for the temporary convenience of the present." Reagan asserted that the nation had prospered historically because "we unleashed the energy and individual genius of man to a greater extent than has ever been done before." A return to individualism would produce a booming economy once again.

Reagan also pledged to restore the nation's global power. Using the most bellicose rhetoric since the early years of the cold war, Reagan called the Soviet Union an "evil empire," one whose leaders "reserve unto themselves the right to commit any crime, to lie, to cheat." The United States, he insisted, must vastly increase its military might and demonstrate its resolve to confront communism anywhere in the world.

Enacting the Conservative Agenda

The United States underwent a huge military buildup during Reagan's first term. Yet despite the new aggressiveness—or, as some argued, because of it—throughout the 1980s, superpower conflict was confined to public rhetoric and the bargaining table. On the periphery of the cold war, however, the United States pursued a more activist role, intervening in the Middle East and the Caribbean.

While enlarging the nation's power and presence abroad, Reagan intended to cut back the government's power at home. On the domestic front, the Reagan administration left its most important mark on economic policies: victory over inflation, continued deregulation of industry, a moratorium on social spending, enormous tax cuts, and a staggering budget deficit. The deficit resulted in part from huge increases in military spending, which formed the basis of Reagan's efforts to reassert U.S. dominance abroad.

Militarization and Interventions Abroad

Reagan moved quickly to accelerate the arms buildup that Carter had begun, overseeing plans for new bombers and missiles, an enhanced nuclear force in Europe, an expanded navy, and a rapid-deployment force. The objectives were to enable the nation to fight three Vietnam-type wars at the same time and to close what the president claimed was a "window of vulnerability," through which U.S. missiles were exposed to a Soviet attack.

Despite the implications for the growing budget deficit, Congress approved most of the presi-

dent's defense programs, and military expenditures shot up by one-third in the first half of the 1980s. Throughout Reagan's presidency, defense spending averaged $216 billion a year, up from $158 billion in the Carter years and higher even than in the Vietnam era.

One justification for the arms buildup was to enable the United States to negotiate with the Soviets from a position of strength. Its unintended effect was to provoke an outburst of calls for a halt to the arms race. A rally demanding a freeze on nuclear weapons at current levels drew 700,000 people in New York City in 1982. Hundreds of thousands of Europeans demonstrated across the continent, stimulated by fears of new U.S. missiles that were scheduled for deployment in NATO countries in 1983.

Reagan startled many of his own advisers in March 1983 by announcing plans for research on a Strategic Defense Initiative (SDI). Immediately dubbed "Star Wars" by its critics, the project envisioned deploying lasers in space to destroy enemy missiles before they could reach their targets. Though SDI had a certain popular appeal because it was defensive and promised ultimate protection from nuclear weapons, most scientists scoffed at it as unrealistic.

While enlarging the nation's power and presence abroad, Reagan intended to cut back the government's power at home.

Star Wars represented a dramatic abandonment of the old system of mutual deterrence based on the threat of retaliation. Reagan conceded that it could be seen as "fostering an aggressive policy." Possessing an exclusive defense, the United States could fire first and not fear retaliation. The Soviets reacted angrily because SDI development violated the 1972 treaty restricting antiballistic missile systems and would require the Soviets to invest huge sums in their own Star Wars technology. For several years, Reagan's passionate attachment to SDI impeded superpower agreement on strategic arms control.

The U.S. military buildup placed the Soviets on the defensive, but it did not guarantee American dominance in the world. Iran released the American hostages at almost the exact hour of Reagan's inauguration, thanks to negotiations conducted during the Carter administration, but terrorism con-

THE NUCLEAR FREEZE CAMPAIGN
An active movement in the United States and Europe worked to limit nuclear weapons and diminish the threat of nuclear destruction in the early 1980s. In 1982, half a million antinuclear protesters marched and rallied in New York City.
Corbis-Bettmann.

tinued to plague the United States. When its military personnel and civilians became victims of murder, kidnapping, and hijacking by various Middle Eastern extremist groups, the United States responded with toughness. To bargain with terrorists, Reagan insisted, would only encourage more assaults, and he pledged never to do so.

In 1982, Lebanon became the major crisis spot in the Middle East. Ravaged by civil war between Christians and Muslims, Lebanon was invaded by Israeli troops, sent to crush Palestine Liberation Organization (PLO) forces that had settled there. Hoping to counter Soviet influence in the Middle East, the United States sent 800 marines to Lebanon to join a peacekeeping force with France and Italy. But some Muslim factions saw the American presence as an attempt to bolster their Christian enemies, and in October 1983 an Islamic extremist drove a bomb-filled truck into a marine barracks, killing 241 Americans. Although Middle Eastern hostilities continued to simmer, Reagan withdrew the marines early the following year.

Closer to home, the U.S. military flexed its muscles. Just two days after the marine disaster, U.S. troops invaded Grenada, a small British Commonwealth island nation in the Caribbean, in response to a coup by left-wing forces. Ostensibly undertaken to protect U.S. medical students on the island, the intervention reflected administration fears that Grenada would fall into the Cuban-Soviet orbit. Margaret Thatcher, the conservative prime minister of Great Britain, called the invasion a violation of international law, but a majority of Americans exulted in the display of national power.

Elsewhere, the United States sought to contain leftist movements privately and less aggressively. In Asia, Afghan rebels fighting to dislodge the Soviet-backed government received U.S. aid. In the African nation of Angola, the United States armed rebel forces against the Soviet- and Cuban-backed government. Siding with the racist South African government in the Angolan crisis did not trouble the president. In one of his more colossal misrepresentations, he told reporters—at a time when the South

African government was brutally suppressing black protest against apartheid—that South Africa had eliminated "the segregation that we once had in our own country." Congress had to force the administration to apply economic sanctions against South Africa, as most U.S. allies had already done, by overriding Reagan's veto of a sanctions bill in 1985.

Left-wing movements in Central America created the most alarm among administration officials. These movements, Reagan charged, were led by "professional guerrillas dedicated to the same philosophy that prevails in Nicaragua, Cuba, and . . . the Soviet Union." They threatened to "destabilize the entire region from the Panama Canal to Mexico." In response, the United States sent money and military advisers to prop up the conservative government of El Salvador that was threatened by a leftist uprising, even though that government had committed murderous human rights violations and opposed social reform.

In neighboring Nicaragua, Reagan aimed to unseat the Sandinistas, who had overthrown the repressive Somoza dictatorship and assumed power in 1979. Jimmy Carter had recognized and extended aid to the Sandinista government. But the Reagan administration threw itself into efforts to undercut the Nicaraguan government by aiding the Contras, a coalition of armed opposition to the Sandinistas that included many individuals from the ousted regime. Many Americans feared being drawn into another Vietnam and opposed aligning the United States with reactionary forces not supported by the majority of Nicaraguans. Holding its own against unrelenting administration efforts, Congress repeatedly instructed the president to cut off aid to the Contras or to limit it to nonmilitary purposes.

Deliberately violating congressional will, the administration secretly used economic pressure to destabilize the Sandinista government and provided weapons and training to the Contras, called "freedom fighters" by Reagan. The CIA itself directed assaults on economic targets and was involved in the covert mining of Nicaraguan harbors in 1984. Through legal and illegal means, the Reagan administration helped sustain the Contra opposition and wreck the Nicaraguan economy, thereby undermining support for the government. After nine years of civil war, Daniel Ortega, the Sandinista president, agreed to a political settlement that had been negotiated among the leaders of the five Central American states. When elections were held in 1990, a coalition of all the opposition groups defeated the Sandinistas, and Ortega stepped aside.

Unleashing Free Enterprise

Reagan's plan to reduce taxes in the face of inflation and huge budget deficits contradicted orthodox economics and traditional Republican doctrine, which stressed a balanced budget. His plan came from a few conservative economists who argued that tax cuts were compatible with deficit reduction and would actually increase federal revenues. Reagan made this thesis a key point in his campaign (a stand that drew from another Republican contender, his eventual vice president, George Bush, the derisive charge of "voodoo economics").

The new theory was called "supply-side economics," because it emphasized boosting production, or supply, which would in turn raise demand. In this view, high taxes had discouraged investment and weakened the economy; lower levies would enable businesses to expand and encourage individuals to work harder because they would keep more of their earnings. Savings, investment, and production all would rise. According to supply-siders, tax reduction would increase the amount of goods and services produced so dramatically that even with lower rates, more revenue would flow to the federal government.

Supply-side economics fit neatly with Reagan's emphasis on optimism and possibilities. In sharp contrast to Carter's talk of limitations and sacrifice, Reagan's agenda appeared to be pain-free. It fed on a popular resistance to the increasing tax load (though not to reduction of government services), exaggerated by inflation's tendency to push individual incomes into higher tax brackets. To sell his tax cut, however, Reagan had to allay worries about the budget deficit. So in addition to predicting an increase in revenues, he promised to cut federal expenditures, a position fully compatible with his antigovernment views.

In the summer of 1981, Congress passed the Economic Recovery Tax Act, the largest tax reduction in history. Individual income taxes were cut, the lowest rate falling from 14 percent to 11 percent and the highest from 70 percent to 50 percent. (The largest previous tax cut, in 1964, had reduced the lowest rate from 20 percent to 14 percent, and the highest from 91 percent to 70 percent.) Corporations also received tax breaks, and taxes on capital gains, gifts, and inheritances dropped. In contrast, Social Security contributions and other taxes that affected Americans across the board increased during the 1980s. The net effect was to make the entire tax structure more regressive—that is, affluent Americans saved far more on their tax bills than did the average taxpayer, further skewing the distribution of wealth in favor of the rich.

"Hack, chop, crunch!" was how *Time* magazine characterized the administration's efforts to liberate private enterprise from government restraints. Carter had initiated deregulation, but he had confined it to particular industries such as finance and transportation while promoting more regulation in areas such as health, safety, equal employment opportunity, and environmental protection. The Reagan administration, by contrast, pursued across-the-board deregulation.

Reagan presided over the most lax enforcement of the Sherman Antitrust Act—the law designed to reduce monopoly and promote competition—since its early history in the 1890s. The government's enforcement staff shrank by 40 percent, and in a decade of unprecedented business mergers and takeovers, the government opposed not a single one. The Reagan administration also loosened restraints on business imposed by employee health and safety measures and helped to weaken organized labor. When 13,000 members of the Professional Air Traffic Controllers Organization (PATCO) went on strike in 1981, in part to protest working conditions that compromised air traffic safety, Reagan fired them and destroyed their union.

Environmental regulatory laws were another target of deregulation. Blaming such laws for the nation's sluggish economic growth, Reagan set about reversing the tide. James Watt, his first secre-

TECHNOLOGY IN AMERICA
The Computer

Among the new technologies that profoundly shaped American society in the last half of the twentieth century, the computer was perhaps the most pervasive. With the ability to rapidly process enormous amounts of information and to control systems, computers have transformed work, medicine, communications, warfare, and even leisure. Computers have became so ubiquitous that few people even notice their use in such common activities as buying groceries, getting cash from a bank machine, making a telephone call, or riding in an airplane.

Engineers and scientists during World War II developed the first digital computers for the military. Later, Cold War military needs drove most computer research; computers were used in the design of the hydrogen bomb. By the late 1950s, most large corporations relied on computers. An important medical application was the invention of the computerized brain scanner in 1972. During the 1980s, personal computers, or PCs, became commonplace in offices, schools, and homes, with some 50 million installed by 1990. The 1990s also ushered in a communication revolution as the Internet and World Wide Web provided immediate access to immense amounts of information and put people in instant contact across the globe.

The chip, a thin piece of silicon or other semiconducting material, is the heart of the contemporary computer. It enables a tiny computer to perform vastly more functions than the 1945 MIT computer prototype, which required 200 miles of circuitry and rows of vacuum tubes.

1945 prototype: Eric Schaal/*Life* Magazine © Time, Inc.; Chip: © Chuck O'Rear/Westlight.

tary of the interior, declared, "We will mine more, drill more, cut more timber," and released federal lands to private exploitation. Similarly, the head of the Environmental Protection Agency reduced her staff and eased enforcement of air and water pollution measures. Environmental organizations experienced increasing membership rolls and fundraising as popular support for environmental protection blocked complete realization of the Reagan administration's deregulatory goals. Congress overrode vetoes of clean water legislation and a bill to promote cleanup of hazardous waste sites (the Superfund). Thus, the Reagan administration slowed environmental protections but failed to reverse either public sentiment or national policy on the environment.

Deregulation of the banking industry, begun under Carter and supported by Democrats and Republicans alike, created a crisis in the savings and loan industry and, ultimately, a burden for taxpayers. When deregulatory laws lifted interest rate ceilings and permitted savings and loan institutions (S&Ls) to lend money more freely, some S&Ls extended enormous loans to real estate developers and invested in other high-yield but risky ventures. The Reagan administration simultaneously slashed the number of federal regulators, and some officials yielded to pressure from both Republican and Democratic legislators to relax investigations. S&L owners reaped lavish profits during the early 1980s, and their depositors enjoyed high interest rates.

But when real estate values began to plunge in the mid-1980s, especially in California and the Southwest, hundreds of S&Ls went bankrupt. Depositors in bankrupt institutions were protected by federal insurance up to a limit of $100,000, and many institutional and wealthy depositors had covered their risks by investing in $100,000 units in multiple S&Ls. After Congress voted to bail out the S&L industry in 1989, the burden of the largest financial scandal in American history fell on American taxpayers, few of whom had profited from deregulation.

Budget Deficits, Inflation, and Unemployment

The S&L crisis deepened the federal budget deficit, which soared during the 1980s despite Reagan's pledge to pare federal spending. Although Reagan's budget director, David Stockman, doubted the rosy predictions of the supply-siders and urged draconian cuts in spending, cabinet officers were loath to

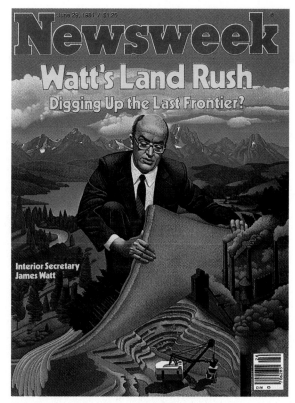

CONTROVERSY OVER THE ENVIRONMENT
Secretary of the Interior James Watt joined the Reagan cabinet committed to dismantling much of the environmental regulation of the previous two decades. His efforts drew considerable opposition. He failed to turn back the clock substantially, and in 1983 President Reagan appointed a more moderate replacement.
Illustration by Wilson McLean. Reprinted with permission of the artist and *Newsweek* Magazine.

see their own budgets slashed. Reagan himself drew back from politically risky cutbacks in entitlement programs such as Social Security and federal and military pensions. Since these consumed a substantial share of the budget, little room remained in which to make significant cuts.

The administration achieved some savings in entitlement programs under Social Security and Aid to Families with Dependent Children. But these programs were not gutted; the Reagan program represented an attack on the Great Society rather than the New Deal. Congress agreed to cut food stamps (14 percent), job training (39 percent), aid to low-income students (16 percent), and health services (33 percent). Hundreds of thousands of people lost eligibility or some of their benefits. Those with in-

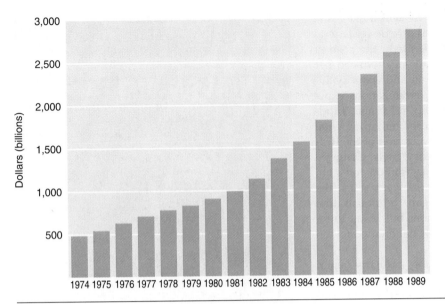

FIGURE 31.1
Rise in the National Debt, 1974–1989
Heavy military spending and large tax cuts contributed to the great leap in the national debt during the 1980s.

comes just around the poverty line took the hardest hits.

Even these cuts occupied too small a share of the total budget to make significant inroads in the deficit. Furthermore, they were counterbalanced by increases in defense spending, which overtook expenditures for human resources (excluding Social Security and Medicare). After a recession in 1981–1982, the economy entered an unprecedented period of growth. But the promises of the supply-siders proved empty. The budget deficit soared from $74 billion when Carter left office to a high of $220 billion in 1986, when interest on the national debt consumed one-seventh of all federal expenditures.

The problems of inflation and unemployment proved easier to control. Luck helped the administration's efforts to restrain inflation when a worldwide decline in the cost of oil pulled down domestic prices. Meanwhile, the Federal Reserve Board, with Reagan's support, tightened growth of the money supply. By 1983, the inflation rate was under 4 percent, down from a high of 12 percent in 1980. Control of inflation remained an enduring mark of the Reagan years.

It took the severest recession since the 1930s, however, to squeeze inflation out of the U.S. economy. Beginning in 1981, unemployment rose sharply, approaching 11 percent late in 1982. Record numbers of banks and businesses closed, thousands of families lost their farms, and twelve million workers could not find jobs. The threat of unemployment further undermined organized labor,

forcing unions to make concessions that management insisted were necessary for industry's survival. The economy recovered in 1983, and the number of jobs increased substantially, although unemployment never fell below 5 percent.

Liberalism on the Defensive

The recession hurt Republicans in the 1982 congressional elections, but by 1984 the economy was booming, with inflation and unemployment at their lowest points in a decade. Reagan delivered a humiliating defeat to the Democratic ticket in his 1984 reelection, although the Democrats retained control of the House of Representatives and picked up two Senate seats.

Liberal movements survived the Reagan triumph, but their accomplishments during the 1980s were largely defensive.

Liberal movements survived the Reagan triumph, but their accomplishments during the 1980s were largely defensive. Civil rights advocates fought off administration attacks in the courts, and, when that failed, they managed to find some help in Congress. Feminists discovered a few issues on which they could gain White House support and looked to the states and to electoral politics to advance other items on their agenda. The gay rights movement acquired members and visibility, making small inroads against intolerance of and discrimination against homosexuals.

Most alarming to many liberals was President Reagan's opportunity to reconstitute the federal courts, which had been a critical ally in their pursuit of social reform. With one notable exception, liberals found themselves helpless to block the nominations of conservative justices. By the end of his second term, Reagan had appointed half of the entire federal judiciary and three new Supreme Court justices.

The "Teflon President" and the Landslide of 1984

Even a candidate with considerably less ingrained optimism than Reagan would have approached the 1984 election with confidence. No serious international crises loomed, and the economy was booming. Since the easing of the 1981–1982 recession, public opinion stood strongly in the president's favor.

Political observers marveled at Reagan's popularity. He was liked even by Americans who opposed his policies and even when he made glaring mistakes. At one meeting, he failed to recognize his own secretary of housing and urban development, calling him "Mr. Mayor." On another occasion he proclaimed that vegetation caused 90 percent of all air pollution. He made so many misstatements to reporters that aides severely limited his press conferences and shielded him from reporters.

The Reagan administration also witnessed a striking number of scandals, and many insiders spoke of a president who was passive, incurious, and largely detached from policy formation. Reagan kept his cabinet officials at a distance, and he did not devote long hours to his duties. According to his first secretary of state, Alexander Haig, the White House was "as mysterious as a ghost ship; you heard the creak of the rigging . . . and sometimes even glimpsed the crew on deck. But which of the crew had the helm?"

Reagan associates and his wife, Nancy, managed the presidency of the former movie actor as if it were a Hollywood production. One aide reported that "every moment . . . was scheduled, every word was scripted, every place where Reagan was expected to stand was chalked with toe marks." Donald Regan, secretary of the treasury during Reagan's

first term and White House chief of staff during his second, even used an acting analogy to describe how Reagan formulated policy: "He listened, acquiesced, played his role, and waited for the next act to be written." Reagan's press secretary, Larry Speakes, admitted that he made up statements and then fed them to the press as Reagan's words.

Democratic Representative Patricia Schroeder tagged Reagan the "Teflon President" because none of his administration's mistakes, or even his own errors and falsehoods, seemed to stick to him. Reagan gave his own explanation when he was asked during the 1980 campaign what people saw in him: "Would you laugh if I told you that I think, maybe, they see themselves and that I'm one of them?" he replied. Near the end of his second term, he elaborated: "Well, I genuinely like people, and I think, perhaps, people can tell."

Reagan was at ease with himself—unlike Nixon—and supremely self-confident. He possessed an easygoing ability to laugh at himself that was unmatched by any president since Kennedy. Referring to reports of his leisurely business hours, Reagan remarked, "It's true that hard work never killed anybody, but I figure why take a chance at this late age." He also gained public sympathy after being shot by a would-be assassin in March 1981. Just before surgery for removal of a bullet in his chest, Reagan joked to physicians, "I hope you're Republicans." His rapid recovery calmed doubts about the health of the oldest president in history.

Democratic Representative Patricia Schroeder tagged Reagan the "Teflon President" because none of his administration's mistakes, or even his own errors and falsehoods, seemed to stick to him.

Even when he substituted fantasy for fact, Reagan came across as sincere. He often confused the facts of his own past with what he wanted to believe, talking, for example, about a role he had played in a World War II movie as if he had had genuine combat experience. Part of his popular appeal was his ability to ignore or recast the darker aspects of the nation's past and present a version of history that Americans could feel good about—just as he did with the facts of his own past.

"America is standing tall," the president exulted. In response his audience at the 1984 Repub-

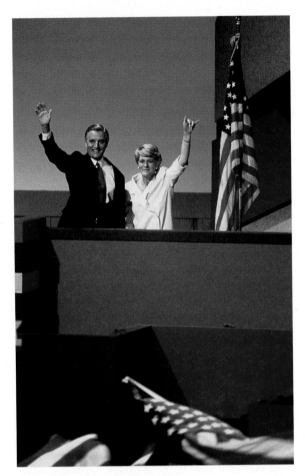

THE DEMOCRATIC TICKET, 1984
Responding in part to feminist pressure, presidential nom-
inee Walter F. Mondale electrified the Democratic Party
convention when he announced his choice of Geraldine
Ferraro for his running mate. An Italian-American
Catholic mother of three, Ferraro represented Queens,
New York, in the House of Representatives. Although
Reagan's landslide swept away Mondale and Ferraro, her
candidacy was an important breakthrough for women in
politics.
Randy Taylor/Sygma.

ocrats. Among the eight candidates for the 1984 presidential nomination was the Reverend Jesse Jackson, who had fought civil rights battles with Martin Luther King Jr. and who ran a vigorous campaign that concentrated on the needs of the disadvantaged. After a rocky start, however, Walter F. Mondale, who had been Carter's vice president, emerged as the Democratic nominee. Mondale electrified the Democratic National Convention by naming as his running mate New York Representative Geraldine A. Ferraro, the first woman nominated on a major party ticket.

The Mondale-Ferraro campaign emphasized the hardships that the unemployed, the poor, and victims of discrimination suffered under the Reagan presidency. Attacking the budget deficit, Mondale insisted that taxes would have to be raised and suggested that Reagan knew that to be true. Reagan simply turned that challenge around: Democrats, he claimed, "see an America where every day is April 15th [the due date for income tax returns] . . . we see an America where every day is the Fourth of July."

Voters responded to the president's vision and to the economic comeback. With 59 percent of the vote, Reagan's landslide was only slightly less over-

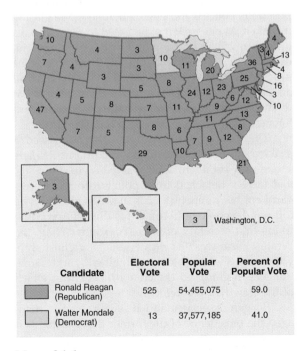

Candidate	Electoral Vote	Popular Vote	Percent of Popular Vote
Ronald Reagan (Republican)	525	54,455,075	59.0
Walter Mondale (Democrat)	13	37,577,185	41.0

M A P   31.1
The Election of 1984

lican National Convention chanted, "USA! USA!" Reagan's ability to revive national pride and confidence, to revitalize the myth of American superiority, reached beyond Republican loyalists. He defined the choice in the 1984 election as "two different versions of the future." The Democrats, he insisted, stressed America's limits and failures; his vision emphasized success and possibility.

Reagan's popular appeal and the prospering economy posed a formidable challenge for the Demwhelming than those of Roosevelt in 1936, Johnson in 1964, and Nixon in 1972. Both the elderly and youth gave Reagan a healthy majority of their votes. And even though the president was not seen as a friend of labor, nearly half of all union members chose the Republican ticket.

What the president would do with his mandate was not clear. In contrast to his first campaign, he had said little about programmatic plans for a second term. The Democrats, for their part, pondered what it would take to stem the exodus of longtime loyalists—particularly southern white males—to the Republican Party. Stung by Republican charges that the Democratic Party was captive to "special interests" such as labor, women, and minorities, many Democratic leaders read the election results as a signal to shift further toward the right. Others urged rededication to the issues that had produced Democratic victories in the past.

Civil Rights on the Defensive

In keeping with its antigovernment philosophy, the Reagan administration made vigorous efforts to reverse federal protections of civil rights. Nixon's rhetoric had played upon the fears and prejudices of whites, but overall the Nixon administration had sustained and in some cases even advanced mechanisms for attacking discrimination. Reagan, however, was the first president to break sharply with the national commitment to equal opportunity undertaken in the 1960s.

Busing to achieve school integration and affirmative action were particularly repellent to the administration. Reagan's special counsel (and later attorney general) Edwin Meese, along with William Bradford Reynolds of the Justice Department's Civil Rights Division, worked to overturn busing and affirmative action agreements, even those that had been entered into voluntarily by school districts and public and private employers. When the Civil Rights Commission challenged administration positions, Reagan fired three of the commission's Carter appointees. A court ruled that action illegal, but Reagan eventually secured a majority on the commission, rendering it ineffective.

The administration also tried to overturn an Internal Revenue Service policy that denied tax-exempt status to segregationist private schools. In this instance, the Supreme Court sided with equal opportunity, holding that private schools practicing racial discrimination could not maintain their tax-exempt status. But the Court was more responsive to the administration regarding the use of federal funding decisions to promote equal opportunity. Agreeing with a Justice Department brief, the Court ruled in *Grove City College v. Bell* (1984) that an institution could practice discrimination in one of its programs, such as athletics, and still receive federal funds for scholarships and other programs that did not discriminate. This decision gutted Title IX of the Education Amendments Act of 1972, one of two major laws promoting equal opportunity in education.

Grove City allowed the Justice Department to abandon dozens of civil rights cases against schools and colleges. It also galvanized a coalition of civil rights organizations and groups representing women, the aged and disabled, and their allies. After four years of struggle and compromise, Congress passed the Civil Rights Restoration Act of 1988 and subsequently overturned a presidential veto. Not only was the administration's victory in *Grove City* reversed; the new law went even further. Not just schools and colleges but any organization that practiced discrimination on the basis of race, color, national origin, sex, handicap, or age was banned from receiving government funds.

Congress also renewed the Voting Rights Act for twenty-five more years, despite administration objections to provisions strengthening the measure and threats of a veto. After both houses passed the improved bill by overwhelming margins in 1982, Reagan not only signed it but took credit for enactment of "the crown jewel of American liberties." It was another example of the president's facility at adjusting facts to what he wanted to believe.

Reagan argued that minorities should look to his economic policies and their positive effects on inflation and employment as evidence of his commitment to equal opportunity. To be sure, his administration ended high inflation and high unemployment, which hit the poorest the hardest. Even so, the material status of most minority groups declined during the 1980s.

Congress and the courts deflected the administration's drive to shrink the government's support for civil rights, but the cause of equal opportunity languished in the absence of presidential leadership. Critics claimed that the administration established a national climate that made it no longer unfashionable to express prejudice and thus contributed to new outbreaks of racial violence in the late 1980s.

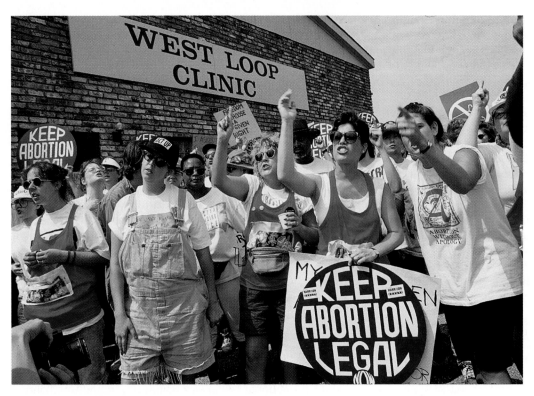

CONFRONTATIONS OVER ABORTION
Failing to win a constitutional amendment banning abortion, in the late 1970s and 1980s some
groups in the right-to-life movement adopted more militant tactics, picketing abortion clinics,
yelling at patients and employees, and trying to block entrance into clinics. In response, prochoice
activists shown here, defend clinic access and the right to abortion.
Paul S. Howell/Gamma Liaison.

Shifting Strategies of the Women's Movement

Women, too, suffered from the Reagan administration's efforts to weaken antidiscrimination enforcement. In 1980, for the first time, the Republican Party took an explicitly antifeminist tone. Reversing previous positions, it opposed both the Equal Rights Amendment (ERA) and a woman's right to abortion, two principal goals of women's rights activists.

In the face of a hostile political environment, the women's movement in the 1980s shifted its strategies and goals. A renewed fight for the ERA occupied a low place on most feminists' agendas. Defense of abortion rights, antidiscrimination measures, and affirmative action remained high priorities. But activists increased their attention to women's economic and family problems, which eluded the grasp of antidiscrimination policies.

The new agenda reflected the increasing diversity of the women's movement and greater recognition of the needs of women of color, poor women, and working-class women. It also acknowledged the disproportionate representation of women and children among the poor, a development that some termed "the feminization of poverty." In addition, the shift in priorities evinced feminists' efforts to recapture the initiative from the New Right, which claimed to be the sole voice for the homemaker and the family.

The Reagan administration had its own concerns about women. Republican leaders worried about the "gender gap"—women's tendency, manifested in elections throughout the 1980s, to vote for liberal and Democratic candidates in larger numbers than men did, large enough in some cases to provide the margin of victory. Reagan appointed three women to cabinet posts and the first woman, Sandra Day O'Connor, to the Supreme Court. But these "showcase" actions accompanied a general decline in the number of women and minorities in high-level administrative and judicial posts. Moreover, the administration's assaults on antidiscrimination and affirmative action policies hurt women as they did racial minorities. And because poverty rates were higher among women than among men, women were hit hardest by budget cuts in social programs.

Feminists did find some common ground with the Reagan administration, however, producing two measures that addressed women's economic distress. The Child Support Enforcement Amendments made it easier to collect court-ordered child support payments from absent fathers, affording some relief to single and divorced mothers. The Retirement Equity Act of 1984 benefited older women by strengthening the claims of divorced and widowed women to their husbands' pensions and by enabling women to qualify more easily for private pensions. Feminists generally held their ground on the abortion issue, but they ran into a stone wall in their efforts to strengthen day care services, aid displaced homemakers, end discrimination in insurance, and promote pay equity—that is, equal pay for traditionally female jobs that were found to be comparable in worth to jobs performed primarily by men.

The Reagan administration's assaults on antidiscrimination and affirmative action policies hurt women as well as racial minorities. And because poverty rates were higher among women than among men, women were hit hardest by budget cuts in social programs.

Like other pressure groups, the women's movement pursued locally what it failed to achieve at the federal level. The pay equity movement took hold in several states, where new legislation mandated job evaluation studies that resulted in higher wages for jobs held primarily by women. Many states strengthened their laws against rape, and most passed legislation making it a crime for a man to force his wife to have sexual relations. States also increased funding for domestic violence programs and stepped up efforts to protect victims and prosecute abusers.

Using sophisticated fundraising and electioneering techniques, feminists made incremental

gains in their efforts to elect more women to political office. By the end of the 1980s, women had made their marks as governors of Kentucky, Vermont, and Nebraska; and women served as mayors of several large cities, including Jane Byrne of Chicago, Dianne Feinstein of San Francisco, and Kathryn Whitmire of Houston. Women won three U.S. Senate races, and their share of congressional seats inched up to 5.6 percent from 2.8 percent in 1971. By the end of the decade, women claimed 17.2 percent of seats in state legislatures. Although Geraldine Ferraro had to endure media scrutiny of her appearance, her husband's business dealings, and other matters unrelated to her qualifications, she broke an important political barrier for women. When Democrat Patricia Schroeder and Republican Jeanne J. Kirkpatrick considered presidential races in 1988, the media took them seriously.

The Gay and Lesbian Rights Movement

An American organization for homosexual rights had existed as early as 1924, but not until the 1980s did a national mass movement play a significant role in U.S. politics. The contemporary movement emerged out of the social upheaval of the 1960s, its beginnings symbolized by the Stonewall riot of 1969, when gay men and lesbians fought back against a police raid on a gay bar in New York City's Greenwich Village. Influenced by the black freedom struggle, the New Left, the counterculture, and feminism, gays and lesbians began to claim equal rights for homosexuals and to express pride in their sexual identities.

In the 1970s, the gay and lesbian rights movement persuaded professional organizations of psychiatrists and social workers to stop considering homosexuality a disease. Although the Supreme Court in 1986 upheld the right of states to enforce sodomy laws, most states had repealed their laws against homosexuality by the end of the decade. The federal government lifted its ban against homosexuals in all areas except the military and intelligence agencies. Beginning with the election of Elaine Noble to the Massachusetts legislature in 1974, several openly gay politicians won election and reelection to offices from mayor to member of Congress. The Democrats began to include gay rights planks in their party platforms.

The acquired immune deficiency syndrome (AIDS) epidemic further mobilized the gay and lesbian rights movement in the 1980s, because at first male homosexuals accounted for the majority of AIDS cases. As the disease swept through and devastated communities of gay men in New York, San Francisco, and elsewhere, society responded with indifference—or worse: assertions by some right-wing politicians and religious leaders that AIDS represented just punishment for immoral behavior. Gay men and lesbians pressed for public education about AIDS and public funding for its treatment and prevention.

The gay and lesbian rights movement helped thousands of homosexuals experience the relief of being able to live openly. By "coming out" in great numbers, gay men and lesbians helped to make homosexuality more visible and somewhat more accepted in the larger population. Activists organized gay rights and gay pride marches throughout the country, bringing 500,000 demonstrators to Washington, D.C., in 1987. Gradually, the movement began to win local victories, gaining for lesbians and gay men protections that were enjoyed by heterosexual citizens. By the early 1990s, more than eighty-five cities banned job discrimination against homosexuals, and, beginning with Wisconsin in 1982, seven states expanded their civil rights laws to include sexual orientation as a protected category. (See Texts in Historical Context, page 1232.)

Yet these piecemeal victories left the majority of gay men and lesbians still vulnerable to discrimination. The New Right targeted gays and lesbians as symbols of national immorality and organized campaigns to overturn homosexual rights measures. In 1992, Cincinnati voters nullified an equal rights ordinance that the city council had enacted, and Colorado voters approved a measure prohibiting any laws that banned discrimination against homosexuals. Heartened by Oregon voters' defeat of a similar referendum, the gay and lesbian rights movement and its allies mounted a challenge to the Colorado measure. They achieved victory in 1996, when the Supreme Court declared the Colorado law unconstitutional (*Romer v. Evans*).

The Conservative Shift in the Federal Courts

Since the 1950s, proponents of reform had grown accustomed to counting on the federal judiciary as a powerful ally in their struggles for minority rights and social justice. Yet in the 1980s, liberals saw their critical allies slipping away as the Supreme Court and the lower federal courts became increasingly populated with conservative justices.

THE AIDS CRISIS
American pop artist Keith Haring made this AIDS awareness drawing before the disease killed him in 1990, citing the "growing burden that each of us carries as the AIDS crisis continues to escalate around the world." During the 1990s scientists made important advances in treatment, but the disease continued to elude a vaccine or a cure.
© The Estate of Keith Haring.

The changing composition of the federal judiciary reflected a determined strategy on the part of the Reagan administration. Given the opportunity to appoint half of the 761 federal court judges and three new Supreme Court justices, administration aides carefully selected candidates. They wanted to appoint individuals with strongly conservative views who would help reverse the liberal direction taken by the Supreme Court since the days of Earl Warren. Just 2 percent of Reagan appointees were black, in contrast to 14.3 percent under Carter. Women constituted 15.5 percent of Carter's appointments but only 8.2 percent of Reagan's.

The Supreme Court did not execute an abrupt about-face. It upheld important affirmative action and antidiscrimination policies (such as denying tax-exempt status to segregated private schools) and ruled that sexual harassment in the workplace constituted sex discrimination. But with Reagan's appointees, the tide began to turn in favor of the doctrine of strict construction—that is, strict interpretation of the original aims of the Constitution's authors, an approach that limits judicial power to protect individual rights.

After appointing the moderate conservative Sandra Day O'Connor in 1981, Reagan strengthened the strict constructionists by elevating William J. Rehnquist, a Nixon appointee, to chief justice when Warren Burger retired in 1986. His next nominee, Antonin Scalia, tipped the balance further to the right. But in 1987, when Reagan attempted to repeat that achievement by nominating Robert H. Bork, a court of appeals judge and former Yale law professor, he provoked a bitter national controversy over the role of the Supreme Court.

Opponents of Bork's nomination organized a diverse coalition of civil rights advocates, trade unionists, feminists, environmentalists, and senior citizens. They feared that Bork's passionate adherence to a strict interpretation of the Constitution would undermine civil rights and affirmative action, abortion rights, criminal rights, and a host of other reform initiatives. Bork's opponents testified before the Senate Judiciary Committee, took out newspaper ads, lobbied their senators, and mounted an unprecedented media assault on the nominee. Despite the president's steadfast support, the Senate rejected Bork. In the end, however, it was an empty victory for liberals. Anthony M. Kennedy, who was confirmed by the Senate, seemed more moderate than Bork, but subsequent decisions made clear that conservatives now constituted a slim majority on the highest court (Reagan's three appointees plus Rehnquist and Byron White).

The full impact of Reagan's appointments continued after he left office. The Court stopped short of overturning *Roe v. Wade*, which gave constitutional protection to the right to abortion, but it allowed states to impose severe restrictions that limited access to abortion for poor and uneducated women and those living in rural areas. Other rulings further weakened affirmative action efforts, limited the use of statistics to prove discrimination, and in some employment discrimination cases shifted the burden of proof from employers to plaintiffs. The Court also whittled away at legal protections for individuals who were under sentence of death and upheld the right to execute convicted murderers who were mentally retarded or as young as sixteen.

Disasters and Triumphs of Reagan's Second Term

In Reagan's second term (1985–1989) the costs of the administration's economic achievements became starkly clear. The federal budget deficit worsened through 1986 and then improved only slightly. The decline in the nation's global economic competitiveness continued, and the government, corporations, and individuals became ever more dependent on borrowing.

Reagan had achieved his counterrevolution in domestic affairs during his first term. Thereafter, Congress took control of the domestic agenda, reaching accord with the administration on major changes in the tax and welfare systems. Though hamstrung by the budget deficit, Congress enacted over presidential objections reforms in such areas as civil rights and the environment.

In Reagan's second term the costs of the administration's economic achievements became starkly clear.

Reagan's second term saw his worst disaster and his most impressive triumph in the realm of foreign policy. The Iran-Contra affair, which involved revelations of confused policy and illegal activities, seriously damaged the president's credibility. Yet he also responded favorably to new initiatives from the Soviet Union and presided over the most impressive improvement in superpower relations since the shattering of the World War II alliance.

The Debt-Based Economy

The gross national product increased by 25 percent during the Reagan years, and inflation remained in check. But along with this growth, evidence mounted of deep economic flaws. As it had in the nineteenth century, when it was still a developing country, the United States once again was importing more than it exported and depending heavily on foreign credit. The steel, automobile, and electronics industries failed to maintain a competitive edge over those of such countries as Germany and Japan, as Americans bought more and more Toyotas and Hondas and fewer Fords and Chevrolets. Because Americans purchased more foreign-made goods than domestic producers sold abroad, the

Protecting Gay and Lesbian Rights

Paul Moore, Episcopal bishop of New York, made a religious argument for gay rights in his letter to the editor of the New York Times.

DOCUMENT 2. Letter to the Editor from Paul Moore, November 23, 1981

Since the 1970s, the gay and lesbian rights movement has worked for passage of laws and ordinances to protect homosexuals from discrimination. In 1982, Wisconsin became the first state to ban discrimination on the basis of sexual orientation, following the lead of several cities that passed gay rights ordinances in the 1970s. By the mid-1990s, nine states and more than eighty cities had such legislation on the books. These measures ignited controversy that continued to surround the issue through the 1990s.

In 1974, the city council of Minneapolis amended its civil rights ordinance to cover discrimination based on sexual preference. The law provided a rationale for banning discrimination and, unlike some laws focusing exclusively on employment, encompassed a broad range of activities.

DOCUMENT 1. Ordinance of the City of Minneapolis, 1974

It is determined that discriminatory practices based on race, color, creed, religion, national origin, sex or affectional or sexual preference, with respect to employment, labor union membership, housing accommodations, property rights, education, public accommodations, and public services, or any of them, tend to create and intensify conditions of poverty, ill health, unrest, civil disobedience, lawlessness, and vice and adversely affect the public health, safety, order, convenience, and general welfare; such discriminatory practices threaten the rights, privileges and opportunities of all inhabitants of the city and such rights, privileges and opportunities are hereby to be declared civil rights, and the adoption of this Chapter is deemed to be an exercise of the policy power of the City to protect such rights.

I quote our diocesan resolution: "Whereas this Convention, without making any judgment on the morality of homosexuality, agrees that homosexuals are entitled to full civil rights. Now therefore be it resolved this Convention supports laws guaranteeing homosexuals all civil rights guaranteed to other citizens."

The Bible stands for justice and compassion for all of God's children. To deny civil rights to anyone for something he or she cannot help is against the clear commandment of justice and love, which is the message of the word of God.

As a New Yorker I find it incredible that this great city, populated by more gay persons than any other city in the world, still denies them basic human rights. They make an enormous contribution to the commercial, artistic, and religious life of our city.

This statement from the Roman Catholic Church reflects the views of many religious groups that take positions against gay rights.

DOCUMENT 3. Vatican Congregation for the Doctrine of the Faith, August 6, 1992

"Sexual orientation" does not constitute a quality comparable to race, ethnic background, etc., in respect to nondiscrimination. Unlike these, homosexual orientation is an objective disorder and evokes moral concern.

There are areas in which it is not unjust discrimination to take sexual orientation into account, for example, in the placement of children for adoption or foster care, in employment of teachers or athletic coaches, and in military recruitment.

Although the U.S. Congress has never enacted legislation banning discrimination on the basis of sexual orientation, it has considered a number of bills for that purpose. Charles Cochrane Jr., an army veteran and police sergeant, testified on behalf of such a bill in 1982.

Document 4. Testimony of Charles Cochrane Jr. before the House Subcommittee on Employment Opportunities of the Committee on Education and Labor, January 27, 1982

I am very proud of being a New York City policeman. And I am equally proud of being gay. I have always been gay.

I have been out of the closet for 4 years. November 6 was my anniversary. It took me 34 years to muster enough courage to declare myself openly.

We gays are loathed by some, pitied by others, and misunderstood by most. We are not cruel, wicked, cursed, sick, or possessed by demons. We are artists, business people, police officers, and clergymen. We are scientists, truck drivers, politicians; we work in every field. We are loving human beings who are in some ways different. . . .

During the early years of my association with the New York City Police Department a great deal of energy did go into guarding and concealing my innermost feelings. I believed that I would be subjected to ridicule and harassment were my colleagues to learn of my sexual orientation. Happily, when I actually began to integrate the various aspects of my total self, those who knew me did not reject me.

Then what need is there for such legislation as H.R. 1454? The crying need of others, still trapped in their closets, who must be protected, who must be reassured that honesty about themselves and their lives will not cost them their homes or their jobs. . . .

The bill before you will not act as a proselytizing agent in matters of sexual orientation or preference. It will not include affirmative action provisions. Passage of this bill will protect the inherent human rights of all people of the United States, while in no way diminishing the rights of those who do not see the need for such legislation. Finally, it will signify, quite clearly, recognition and compassion for a group which is often maligned without justification.

Carl Horowitz, a policy analyst at a conservative think tank, the Heritage Foundation, expresses arguments of those opposed to measures banning discrimination against homosexuals.

Document 5. Carl F. Horowitz, "Homosexuality's Legal Revolution," May 1991

Homosexual activists have all but completed their campaign to persuade the nation's educational establishment that homosexuality is normal "alternative" behavior, and thus any adverse reaction to it is akin to a phobia, such as fear of heights, or an ethnic prejudice, such as anti-Semitism.

The movement now stands on the verge of fully realizing its use of law to . . . intimidate heterosexuals uncomfortable about coming into contact with it. . . .

The movement seeks to win sinecures through the state, and over any objections by "homophobic" opposition. With a cloud of a heavy fine or even a jail sentence hanging over a mortgage lender, a rental agent, or a job interviewer who might be discomforted by them, homosexuals under these laws can win employment, credit, housing, and other economic entitlements. Heterosexuals would have no right to discriminate against homosexuals, but apparently, not vice versa. . . .

These laws will create market bottlenecks. Heterosexuals and even "closeted" homosexuals will be at a competitive disadvantage for jobs and housing. . . .

The new legalism will increase heterosexual anger — and even violence — toward homosexuals.

Document 1. Norman Dorsen and Aryeh Neier, eds., *The Rights of Gay People: The Basic ACLU Guide to a Gay Person's Rights* (New York: E. P. Dutton, 1992), 251.

Document 2. Paul Moore, letter to the editor, *New York Times,* December 8, 1981.

Document 3. Vatican Congregation for the Doctrine of the Faith, *Origins,* August 6, 1992.

Document 4. Hearing on H.R. 1454, House Subcommittee on Employment Opportunities of the Committee on Education and Labor, 97th Cong., 2nd sess., 1982, 54–56.

Document 5. Carl F. Horowitz, "Homosexuality's Legal Revolution," *Freeman,* May 1991.

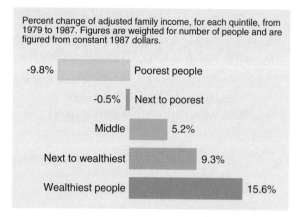

Percent change of adjusted family income, for each quintile, from 1979 to 1987. Figures are weighted for number of people and are figured from constant 1987 dollars.

-9.8%   Poorest people

-0.5%   Next to poorest

Middle   5.2%

Next to wealthiest   9.3%

Wealthiest people   15.6%

FIGURE 31.2

The Growth of Inequality: Changes in Family Income, 1979–1987

For most of the post-World War II period, income increased for all groups on the economic ladder; but after 1979, income of the poorest families actually declined, while it grew substantially for the richest 20 percent of the population.

nation's trade deficit (the difference between imports and exports) soared to $126 billion in 1988.

In response to heightened international competition, some older companies collapsed. Others moved their factories (and jobs) abroad to position themselves better to penetrate foreign markets or to benefit from the low wage standards of countries such as Mexico, the Philippines, and Korea. The growth of service industries created new jobs at home, but former blue-collar workers who were forced to make the shift found their wages substantially lower. David Ramos earned $12.75 an hour as a machine operator in a steel plant before being laid off in 1982. His new job as a security guard paid only $5 an hour, and his family of six had to rely on food stamps. Overall, the number of full-time workers earning wages below the poverty level ($12,195 for a family of four in 1990) rose sharply from 12 percent to 18 percent of all workers in the 1980s.

Labor unions called for the government to raise tariffs to protect American producers from foreign competition. One group of Detroit autoworkers summoned reporters and then demonstrated their frustration by taking sledgehammers to a Japanese-produced car. Committed to free trade and opposed to tariffs, the Reagan administration sought to make other countries more receptive to U.S. exports. It imposed some restrictions on imports but resisted extreme measures to keep out foreign products.

The trade gap necessitated a vast increase in borrowing from foreign investors. Once the largest creditor nation, the United States became the largest debtor nation in the space of a decade. Foreign investors from Japan, Western Europe, and the Middle East purchased American stocks and bonds, real estate, and corporations. Time-honored companies such as Firestone, Ralston Purina, Brooks Brothers, Sohio, 20th Century-Fox, and Capitol Records passed into foreign ownership. Local communities welcomed infusions of foreign capital, and several states went to great lengths to encourage Japanese companies to establish automobile plants within their boundaries.

Foreign investment in the U.S. economy helped compensate for a decline in domestic investment in the 1980s. Instead of putting their tax savings into new business enterprise or machinery that would boost productivity and create new jobs, as supply-siders had promised, entrepreneurs used them to take over other companies or to support lavish lifestyles. As savings and investment declined, indebtedness soared among the wealthy as well as ordinary Americans. Household debt, especially credit card spending, surpassed $3 trillion, and corporate debt reached $2 trillion, double the level of 1980.

The federal government made its own contribution to national indebtedness with an annual deficit that reached $220 billion in 1986. The president clung to his panacea—a constitutional amendment requiring a balanced budget. But he disclosed no new means for implementing such a requirement. Congress rejected Reagan's other solution—empowering the president to veto individual items in the budget, called the "line-item veto." In 1985, the president and Congress agreed to the Gramm-Rudman-Hollings deficit reduction law; it set deficit limits to be reached by certain dates in the near future and required automatic across-the-board cuts should the government fail to reach the targets. By the time Reagan left office, the deficit had fallen to $160 billion, but prospects for further reduction were poor. With the accumulating annual budget deficits, in eight years the government had increased the national debt from $834 billion to $2.3 trillion.

Reagan refused to rethink the wisdom of the 1981 tax cuts, but his willingness to undertake tax reform made it the most important domestic initiative of his second term. The Tax Reform Act of 1986 included both tax cuts and tax reforms. Conservatives won reductions in the maximum rate on individual incomes from 50 percent to 28 percent and on businesses from 48 percent to 34 percent. The law also eliminated income taxes for millions of low-income people, raised the capital gains tax, and reduced deductions and loopholes that overwhelmingly favored corporations and the wealthy.

The Initiative Shifts to Congress and the States

The Reagan administration exercised scant leadership in setting a domestic agenda after 1986. Having largely achieved the president's goal—getting the government off the back of free enterprise—Reagan was not about to reverse that trend with new programs. While his rhetoric continued to preach the aims of social conservatives, issues such as abortion were too politically charged to risk an all-out presidential effort.

Moreover, several developments crippled Reagan's domestic leadership. Disclosures of fraud and corruption among Reagan officials mounted. By the end of 1987, more than one hundred senior officials had been forced to resign, had been indicted, or had been accused of illegal or unethical conduct. Beset by internal conflicts, the administration also faced a more independent Congress after the Democrats recaptured the Senate in 1986.

In addition to defeating Bork's nomination, Congress overrode presidential vetoes of environmental protection legislation and highway and mass-transit programs and forced compromises with the executive branch on other issues. In 1987, Reagan reluctantly signed bills to aid the homeless. And in 1988, the two branches hammered out a $2.7 billion antidrug law, which included treatment programs for drug users and more severe penalties for dealers, including the death penalty for certain drug traffickers.

An overhaul of the welfare system in 1988 reflected give-and-take between those who believed that aid to the poor was inadequate and those who insisted that government handouts encouraged chronic "welfare dependency." The Family Support Act required all states to provide welfare benefits to impoverished families even when both parents were present. It also contained "workfare" provisions, which required at least one unemployed parent to work sixteen hours a week in unpaid community service jobs to remain eligible for welfare.

The Family Support Act sought to end welfare dependency by compelling single parents with children over the age of three to get jobs or to enroll in a new Job Opportunities and Basic Skills Program (JOBS). During a transitional period, they would receive Medicaid and help with transportation and day care costs. Critics argued that workfare ignored the fact that not enough jobs at decent wages existed for relatively untrained welfare recipients. The jobs that did exist would pay at or around the minimum wage, and losing access to Medicaid and other services would render people worse off than they had been on welfare.

Even the law's sponsors considered the five-year appropriation of $3.34 billion inadequate for the training and education that would be required to escape poverty. Efforts to alleviate poverty were held hostage—like many other initiatives—to the federal deficit. The revival of Democratic strength in Congress tempered the president's efforts to minimize federal activity, but advocates of new programs were stymied by the lack of resources to fund them.

"Our federal politics are gridlocked, and governors have become the ones who have to have the courage to put their necks out," said a spokesperson for state governors. In trying to compensate for the federal government's inaction and the paralyzing effect of the deficit, for the first time in decades state legislatures became more innovative than Washington. States passed legislation to block corporate takeovers, raise the minimum wage, establish parental leave policies, require equal pay for jobs of comparable worth in state and local governments, improve food labeling, protect the environment, and promote foreign trade. But by the end of the decade, the shifting of funding burdens from Washington to the states left state governments with their own financial crises.

The Iran-Contra Scandal

The most serious revelations of executive branch misconduct since Watergate surfaced during Reagan's second term. In the events that became known as the Iran-Contra scandal, administration officials engaged in secret and illegal activities, destroyed evidence of their undertakings, and lied to Congress. The president himself escaped criminal charges. But evidence that he had said one thing and done another and that he had failed to exercise control over his staff and policy shattered confidence in his leadership.

The Iran-Contra affair began in 1985 as a scheme invented by Robert C. McFarlane, head of the National Security Council (NSC), his successor

John Poindexter, NSC aide marine Lieutenant Colonel Oliver North, and CIA Director William Casey. They planned to sell arms to Iran, which was then at war with neighboring Iraq, in exchange for the Iranians' exertion of pressure on Muslim terrorists to bring about the release of seven American hostages who were being held in Lebanon. Funds from the arms sales were then diverted from the U.S. Treasury and channeled through Swiss bank accounts to aid the Nicaraguan Contras in their efforts to overthrow that country's leftist government. Over the objections of Secretary of State George Shultz and Defense Secretary Caspar Weinberger, Reagan approved the arms sales. He subsequently disclaimed knowledge of the diversion of funds to the Contras, as did his cabinet secretaries.

When news of the affair surfaced in November 1986, the administration faced a number of serious charges. First, the president had consistently pledged never to bargain with terrorists. Now it was revealed that the administration had in fact bargained with terrorists, aiding the virulently anti-American Iranian government of Ayatollah Khomeini and violating the United States' stated neutrality in the Iran-Iraq war. Even worse, the administration had defied Congress's express ban on military aid for the Contras.

Although North and others destroyed incriminating documents, enough evidence remained to demonstrate the culpability of seven individuals. Brought to trial by an independent prosecutor appointed by Reagan, all pleaded guilty or were convicted of lying to Congress and/or destroying evidence. North's felony conviction was later overturned on a technicality, and President George Bush pardoned six officials in December 1992. A joint congressional committee investigation found no evidence that Reagan knew of the diversion of funds to the Contras but criticized the president's lax management: He simply was not in charge.

Reagan's public statements confirmed the impression of a detached, fumbling leader who could not remember key events. He at first denied that the arms deal represented an exchange of weapons for hostages. Confronted with an official report to the contrary, Reagan responded that "my heart and my best intentions still tell me that is true [that he did not trade arms for hostages], but the facts and evidence tell me it is not." Public opinion polls reported that a substantial majority did not trust Reagan's assertions about his knowledge of the Iran-Contra affair. The independent prosecutor's

final report, issued in 1994, found no evidence that Reagan had broken the law but concluded that both Reagan and Vice President Bush had known about the diversion of funds to the Contras and that Reagan had "knowingly participated or at least acquiesced" in covering up the scandal.

The United States delivered five shipments of arms to Iran, primarily antitank missiles. Two hostages were released, but terrorists killed a CIA official and took more hostages. By 1987, terrorists

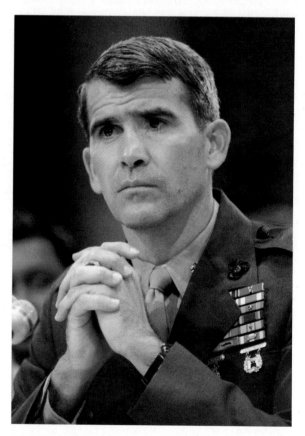

OLIVER NORTH

The central figure in the Iran-Contra affair, Lieutenant Colonel Oliver North, in his U.S. marine uniform, testified in July 1987 for six days before a congressional investigating committee. To many television viewers, North came across as a handsome young patriot whose lying to Congress, destroying public records, and other illegal actions were justified in the fight against Communism. In spite of his later conviction for a felony, which was overturned on a technicality, North maintained a strong following, especially among the right wing of the Republican Party, and nearly secured a Virginia Senate seat in 1994.
Corbis-Bettmann.

held two more Americans than they had when the dealing began. The president ultimately accepted responsibility for what happened during his watch but never articulated his understanding of exactly what went wrong. Nor did he express outrage at the criminal acts of his aides. North remained for him "a hero" and Poindexter "an honorable man."

In the events that became known as the Iran-Contra scandal, administration officials engaged in secret and illegal activities, destroyed evidence of their undertakings, and lied to Congress.

The Iran-Contra scandal left the Reagan administration in disarray. Reagan ended his term with relatively high approval ratings, but his image as a confident leader was tarnished. More ominous for the nation, the Iran-Contra affair revealed that, despite all the efforts begun during the Nixon years to make the executive branch accountable to Congress and the public, abundant room remained for it to conduct a secret foreign policy outside the law.

A Thaw in Soviet-American Relations

Reagan weathered the Iran-Contra storm in part because he presided over a momentous thaw in the cold war, one all the more surprising because it occurred under an administration whose militant anti-communism exceeded that of any previous administration. Reagan's flexibility contributed to the Soviet-American accord, but it would not have happened without the innovative Soviet head of state who recognized that his country's domestic problems demanded a relaxation of cold war antagonism.

Mikhail Gorbachev assumed power in 1985 determined to revitalize a Soviet economy plagued with bureaucratic inefficiencies, a massive military budget, and an inability to deliver basic consumer goods and services. Hoping to stimulate production and streamline distribution, Gorbachev called for *perestroika* (economic restructuring), including the introduction of elements of free enterprise. He proclaimed a new era of *glasnost* (greater freedom of expression), eventually allowing such challenges to Communist rule as new political parties and contested elections.

Gorbachev recognized that economic revival depended on cutting the enormous costs of military production. Reagan, meanwhile, faced increasing congressional resistance to funding the arms race and popular support for arms reductions. Prodded too by Nancy Reagan, who had substantial influence on her husband, the president made disarmament a major goal in his last years in office. When Gorbachev took the initiative, Reagan was ready to respond.

A positive personal chemistry developed between Reagan and Gorbachev when the two met for the first time in Geneva in November 1985 and again at Reykjavik, Iceland, in 1986. Negotiations stalemated when Reagan refused to stop research and development on Star Wars, but eventually Gorbachev gave up that demand. By December 1987, negotiators had completed an intermediate-range nuclear weapons (INF) agreement, which eliminated all short- and medium-range missiles from Europe. These weapons amounted to a small portion of the entire nuclear arsenal, and other weapons would cover their targets. Nonetheless, the agreement provided for on-site inspection for the first time and raised expectations for strategic arms reduction talks (START).

When Gorbachev arrived in Washington in December 1987 to sign the INF treaty, Americans responded with a burst of "Gorbymania." Here was a new breed of Soviet leader—dynamic, witty, and sophisticated; he and his wife, Raisa, a professor of philosophy, made an engaging couple. Above all, here was a leader who could fulfill Americans' hopes for eliminating the anxieties of the cold war and stemming the flow of national resources into the war machine.

Reagan and Gorbachev did not realize their hopes to crown their accomplishments with a START treaty, but they enjoyed a fourth cordial meeting in Moscow in June 1988. When pressed by American reporters about the "evil empire," Reagan finally said, "I was talking about another empire." His remark articulated a major shift in his foreign policy. It also acknowledged genuine changes in Soviet internal affairs and global relations.

In 1988, Gorbachev announced a gradual withdrawal from Afghanistan, which had become the Soviet equivalent of America's Vietnam. In Africa, the Soviet Union, Cuba, and the United States agreed on a political settlement for the civil war in Angola. And in the Middle East, both superpowers supported a cease-fire and peace talks in the eight-

GORBYMANIA

Soviet leader Mikhail Gorbachev enjoyed great popularity with the American people on his trip to the United States in December 1987. Bystanders on a street in Washington, D.C., press around him to shake his hand. When President Reagan saw his appeal, he bantered, "I don't resent his popularity. Good Lord, I co-starred with Errol Flynn once."
Wide World Photos, Inc.

year-old war between Iran and Iraq. Although the Soviet Union had seized the initiative, Reagan could justifiably claim a share of the credit for what he called "a satisfying new closeness with the Soviet Union"—a détente that far surpassed what Nixon and Kissinger had accomplished.

American Society in the 1980s

"More prosperous, more secure and happier than it was eight years ago." So Ronald Reagan described American society as he left the presidency in January 1989. And so it was for a majority of Americans, especially for those who had already been poised to profit from the economic revolution created by the Reagan administration. Great fortunes were made during the 1980s, and making money and displaying wealth were celebrated in popular culture.

At the same time, however, American society became more polarized along class lines. Increasing homelessness and growing poverty reversed the post–World War II trend toward greater economic equality. New immigration made the nation more culturally diverse, but African Americans, Hispanic Americans, and other minority groups fell disproportionately among those passed over by the surge of prosperity.

The Money Culture

Not since the 1920s had American culture so venerated free enterprise and the entrepreneur, and not since the Gilded Age had wealth been so extravagantly displayed. Books by businesspeople climbed onto best-seller lists. The press described lavish parties costing millions of dollars. Popular magazines featured articles entitled "High Life Afloat: Superduper Yachts" and "They're Like Us, Except

They're Rich." Evidence of immense fortunes and conspicuous consumption ranged from multimillion-dollar price tags on Manhattan apartments to specific area codes assigned to coastal waters to accommodate the proliferation of yachts.

Fascination with wealth and consumption drew vast audiences to prime-time TV serials such as *Dallas* and *Dynasty*. College students told poll takers that their primary ambition was to make money. Even fundamentalist ministers enjoyed homes with swimming pools and travel on private jets, though none lived as extravagantly as TV evangelist Jim Bakker, whose doghouses were air-conditioned and whose wife Tammy's shopping sprees were legendary.

Most Americans profited from the economic boom of the 1980s, but those already well off enjoyed the greatest gains. Family income for the richest one-fifth of the population increased by 11.1 percent between 1979 and 1987. The number of millionaires doubled during the decade, and the number of billionaires grew from thirteen to fifty-one. Greater concentration of wealth in fewer hands had been developing since the 1970s, but Reagan's tax and spending policies intensified the trend.

Participating conspicuously in the affluence of the 1980s were some members of the baby boom generation known popularly as "yuppies," short for "young urban professionals." These mostly white, well-educated young men and women tended to live in urban condominiums and to pursue fast-track careers; in their leisure time, they consumed lavishly—BMWs and other fancy sports cars, gourmet food, travel, electronic gadgets, and health clubs. Though constituting just a minority of their generation, they established consumption standards that were highly popularized and that others tried to emulate.

A striking feature of the new wealth of the 1980s was the extent to which it came from moving assets around rather than from producing goods. There were notable exceptions, of course, such as Steven Jobs, who invented the Apple computer in his garage, and Liz Claiborne, who in thirteen years turned a $250,000 investment into a billion-dollar fashion enterprise. But many others got rich—or richer—by manipulating debt and restructuring corporations. Called "paper entrepreneurs" by one expert, these were the investment bankers, bond brokers, and their lawyers and accountants who arranged corporate mergers and takeovers.

Large fortunes were made by "corporate raiders." These men generated the capital to take over a corporation by issuing junk bonds, so called because they were high-risk and high-yield. Once in control, the raiders reaped huge profits by selling off some of the corporation's valuable divisions. Corporate restructuring sometimes resulted in greater efficiency and productivity, but all too often the result was to line the financiers' pockets and leave the corporation deeply in debt.

Great fortunes were made during the 1980s. At the same time, however, American society became more polarized along class lines and increasing homelessness and growing poverty reversed the post–World War II trend toward greater economic equality.

"To say these guys are entrepreneurs is like saying Jesse James was an entrepreneur," opined Texas businessman Ross Perot, who defined entrepreneurship as making things rather than making money. While most financial entrepreneurs operated within the law, in some notable cases greed led to criminal convictions. The pioneer of junk bonds, Michael Milken, took home well over $50 million a year. But he and others ended up in jail for using insider information to maximize their financial manipulations.

The Other Side of the 1980s

Even yuppies and financiers had to be aware that the economic boom passed many Americans by. Affluent urbanites could see men and women sleeping in subway stations and on grates over steam vents, some within a mile of the White House. Experts debated the number of homeless Americans —estimates ranged from 350,000 upwards—but no one doubted that homelessness had increased. Women and children constituted the fastest-growing population without shelter: One-fourth of the homeless were families with children.

What accounted for the increasing numbers of homeless? The Reagan administration slashed new federal commitments for low-income housing from $33 billion to $8 billion, yet because of previous authorizations and congressional determination, federal spending on low-income housing actually increased during the 1980s, and the number of government-subsidized units grew as well. Nonetheless, hundreds of thousands still lacked affordable

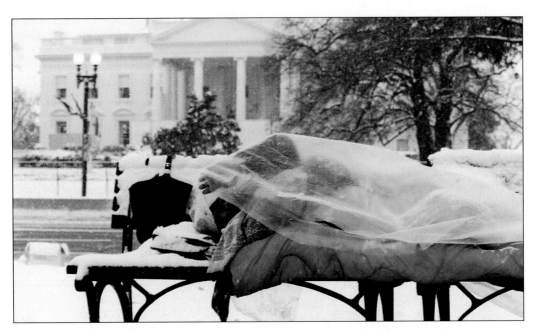

HOMELESSNESS
The increased presence of homeless people in cities across the nation challenged the view of the 1980s as a decade of prosperity. Hundreds of homeless people could be found on the sidewalks of the nation's capital every night. In November 1987, during the first snow of the season, a homeless man sleeps in Lafayette Square across from the White House.
Corbis-Bettmann.

shelter. These included the victims of long-term unemployment, erosion of welfare benefits, and slum clearance as well as individuals suffering from mental illness, drug abuse, and alcoholism.

Homelessness was just one measure of the limited reach of economic expansion. Infant mortality was another. The United States fell behind other countries on this commonly used indicator of the general health of a nation. In fact, the United States ranked twentieth, below such countries as East Germany and Singapore.

Reagan insisted that a booming economy would benefit everyone. Average personal income did rise during his tenure, but the trend of income polarization that had begun in the 1970s sharpened in the 1980s, in part because of the new tax policies. The rich got richer, a portion of the middle class did well, and the poor got poorer. Personal income shot up sharply for the wealthiest 20 percent of Americans while it fell for the poorest by 9.8 percent between 1979 and 1987.

Poverty statistics, too, revealed a reversal of the trend toward greater equality. Between 1980 and 1988, poor people increased from 11.7 percent to 13.5 percent of the total U.S. population—the highest poverty rate in the industrialized world. A relatively low poverty rate among the elderly testified to the lasting success of New Deal and Great Society programs, especially Social Security and Medicare. Less fortunate were large segments of other groups that the economic boom had bypassed: racial minorities, female-headed families, and children. At the end of the decade, one in every five children lived in a household with income below the official poverty line.

Many nonpoor Americans struggled not to lose ground. The decline in manufacturing jobs and the weakening of organized labor eroded the position of blue-collar men with only high school educations. A second income was needed to stave off economic decline; in fact, families occupying the broad middle of the economic ladder achieved income gains only through female earnings. By 1990, nearly 60 percent of married women with young children worked outside the home, and women contributed nearly one-third of total family income. Yet even with the growth of two-income families, fewer young families could purchase their first home.

By 1990, employed women had narrowed the wage gap to the point that their median earnings were 72 percent those of men. However, this apparent achievement reflected a decline in male earnings as much as it did progress for women. It also mirrored the overall income redistribution in that the poorest women's income crept up scarcely at all while that of the top fifth grew by 35 percent. Moreover, the disparity between male and female earnings still amounted to an average of $10,000 a year, a vast difference to the nearly 20 percent of families that were headed by women. One mother of two, divorced from an abusive husband, found employment, but reported, "Jobs just don't pay good money." She managed to make ends meet by selling her blood and accepting help from her church.

Minorities' Struggles and Successes

Five million new immigrants sought to realize the American dream in the 1980s, surpassing the totals for every decade in the twentieth century but the first. The new wave of immigration was distinguished by a striking difference in country of origin. While 85 percent of the previous immigrants had come from Europe, almost half of the recent arrivals were Asians, and nearly 40 percent migrated from Latin America and the Caribbean.

The racial composition of the new immigration revived the century-old wariness of the native-born toward recent arrivals. Arguments for more restrictive policies included beliefs (generally unfounded) that immigrants took jobs from the native-born; anxiety about the tendency of highly motivated, hardworking immigrants to edge out U.S.-born students at prestigious universities; fears that immigrants would erode the dominant culture and language; and concern about population pressures on the environment. Many of the new immigrants "do not assimilate satisfactorily into our society," wrote Republican Senator Alan Simpson in 1985, worried about "the unity and political stability of our nation."

Americans expressed particular concern about immigrants who entered the country illegally. Primarily Latin Americans fleeing civil war and economic deprivation, they were estimated to number at least three million. To stem this tide, Congress passed the Immigration Reform and Control Act of 1986, which penalized employers who hired undocumented aliens, a step that critics feared would

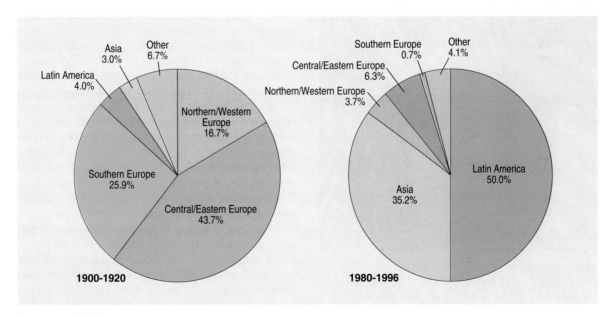

FIGURE 31.3
The Changing Profile of Immigration, 1900–1920 and 1980–1996
The United States received its largest number of immigrants during the opening and closing decades of the twentieth century, but the cultures and countries of origin of the new arrivals shifted dramatically between the two periods.

encourage discrimination against foreign-looking workers. One of the law's more benevolent provisions granted amnesty to undocumented immigrants who could prove residence before 1982. Around two million people took advantage of this provision.

The Immigration Reform and Control Act embodied both the generous and restrictive traditions in American policy, but two other laws were unequivocally open-hearted. In response to the plight of Vietnamese children fathered by U.S. servicemen and often treated as outcasts in Vietnam, the Amerasian Homecoming Act opened the door to these children and their immediate families.

Efforts to make amends for the past also extended to Japanese Americans. In 1983, a special

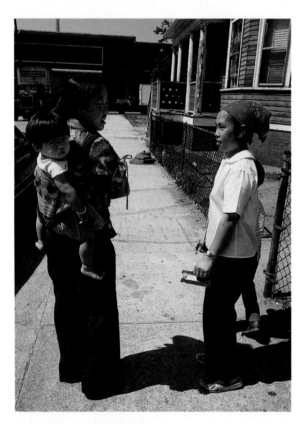

THE NEW IMMIGRATION
Among Asian immigrants in the 1980s, the largest number came from southeast Asia, where the Vietnam War and its aftermath created hundreds of thousands of refugees. Most of these refugees had little money and found adjustment difficult. Many like these Laotian Hmong immigrants in Providence, Rhode Island, came from rural, premodern societies.
Ira Wyman/Sygma.

commission declared the World War II internment of Japanese Americans to have been "a grave injustice," the result of "race prejudice, war hysteria, and a failure of political leadership." In 1988, Congress issued an official apology and granted $20,000 in reparations to each of the approximately 70,000 surviving internees.

Higher fertility rates among Hispanic Americans, Asian Americans, and African Americans, in combination with migration patterns, increased the racial and ethnic diversity in American society. While the total population increased by around 9 percent in the 1980s, the black population grew by 13 percent, the Hispanic population by 39 percent, and the Asian American population by nearly 50 percent. By 2010, the Census Bureau projected, people of color would account for nearly 30 percent of the nation's residents. In California and several other states, they would constitute a majority.

Minorities continued to occupy the lower rungs of the economic ladder, and their situation worsened with the upward flow of wealth. Median income for white families surpassed $32,000 in 1988, in contrast to $18,000 for African Americans and $20,300 for Hispanic Americans. Poverty afflicted one in three African Americans and 28 percent of all Hispanic Americans. With higher than average rates of drug use, these groups accounted for a disproportionate number of AIDS cases, often generated through sharing of intravenous drug needles.

The general sharpening of class differences in the 1980s also affected minorities. African Americans were barely present among the very rich, but substantial numbers improved their economic position, enlarging the black middle class. The most prosperous African Americans were members of two-parent families in which both parents had jobs; their median income reached 82 percent of that of comparable whites. But women headed half of all black families, whose average income was less than one-third that of the typical American family.

The media hailed Asian Americans as "America's Super Minority" but failed to note vast differences among Asian Americans or their overall economic disadvantage. Median family income for Asian Americans surpassed that of whites, but only because Asian families had more wage earners. Despite the greater educational achievement of Asian Americans (39 percent had completed college, in contrast to 22 percent of whites), they lagged behind whites in per capita income, and their poverty rates surpassed those of whites. Poor Chinese American women employed in the New York gar-

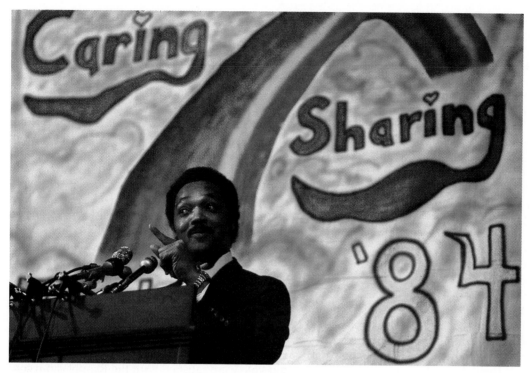

A NEW VOICE IN POLITICS
Jesse Jackson was among the civil rights activists who turned to electoral politics. A Baptist minister and dynamic speaker, Jackson mounted campaigns for the Democratic presidential nomination in 1984 and 1988, appealing to what he called a "Rainbow Coalition" of disadvantaged groups. Here he addresses students at Dartmouth College in January 1984.
Ira Wyman/Sygma.

ment industry endured wages, hours, and working conditions resembling those of the early-twentieth-century sweatshops.

Minorities edged slowly into the corridors of political power. At the end of the 1980s, more than seven thousand blacks held public office, an increase of nearly 50 percent from 1980. The most impressive gains occurred in city government, where black mayors presided over Atlanta, Chicago, Los Angeles, New Haven, Philadelphia, Seattle, and other large cities. The election of David Dinkins as mayor of New York City in 1989 epitomized the rise of black leaders even in cities with predominantly white electorates.

Jesse Jackson's campaigns for the presidency in 1984 and 1988 inspired African Americans and demonstrated that many whites were willing to support a minority candidate. In 1989, Democrat L. Douglas Wilder of Virginia became the first black governor since Reconstruction, joining the only Hispanic governor, Republican Bob Martinez of Florida. Access to the highest offices in the land

came slowly. In the 1992 elections, African Americans captured 38 seats in the 435-member House of Representatives, while Hispanics won 17 and Asian Americans 5. African American Carol Moseley Braun and Native American Ben Nighthorse Campbell won election to the Senate.

Domestic Gridlock and a New World Order

When Vice President George Bush announced his bid for the presidency in 1987, he declared, "We don't need radical new directions." Generally satisfied with the agenda set by Ronald Reagan, Bush displayed little interest in domestic affairs, and he faced a strong Democratic majority in Congress. Although the president and Congress reached agreement on a few important measures, overall stalemate marked the domestic record of the Bush presidency.

In foreign policy, too, Bush tended to react to events rather than to try to shape them. He acted aggressively in sending troops to overthrow the corrupt dictator of Panama. And the United States entered a full-scale war when Iraq threatened Middle Eastern stability by invading Kuwait in 1990. But the United States stood on the sidelines of the most momentous world events, which took place in Europe as one by one the Eastern bloc nations threw out their Communist rulers. After allowing the breakup of the system that had anchored its security since 1945, the Soviet Union itself disintegrated in 1991.

The Issueless Campaign of 1988

Explaining George Bush's campaign for the presidency in 1988, one of his aides remembered, "The biggest single factor was whether Ronald Reagan would turn the nation over in good shape. If he did that, Bush was home free." The vice president's campaign benefited from the country's continuing economic expansion and the warming relationship with the Soviet Union.

George Bush's election to the presidency capped a long career in politics and government. The son of a wealthy investment banker who had represented Connecticut in the U.S. Senate, George Herbert Walker Bush grew up in a privileged milieu that put a premium on public service. Bush interrupted his education to serve as a navy combat pilot in World War II; after earning his Yale degree, he settled in Texas to make his own way in the oil industry and politics.

Bush represented Texas in Congress during the 1960s and later served as head of the U.S. Liaison Office in China and director of the CIA during the Nixon-Ford years. When Ronald Reagan achieved a commanding lead in the 1980 primaries, Bush put his own aspirations on hold and accepted second place on the Republican ticket. His vice presidency was distinguished above all by absolute loyalty to Reagan. That, however, was not enough to secure his succession, and he won the Republican nomination only after bruising battles in the primaries.

The Democratic race was even more crowded. Jesse Jackson, whose Rainbow Coalition campaign centered on the needs of people who had been ignored by the political mainstream—blacks and other minorities, women, working-class families, and the poor—won several state primaries, gathering seven million votes, almost one-third of them from white voters. In the end, however, his race,

lack of experience in public office, and position on the left wing of the Democratic Party proved to be insuperable obstacles. Michael Dukakis, then serving his third term as governor of Massachusetts, won the nomination.

"The Trivial Pursuit of the Presidency," the subtitle of one account of the 1988 campaign, expressed the general view of political commentators. Neither Bush nor Dukakis presented a clear vision of how he wanted to use the power of the presidency, and the campaign was unprecedentedly issueless and vitriolic. Proving more adept at negative campaigning, Bush's staff distorted Dukakis's record and portrayed him as a dangerous liberal, soft on criminals, and out of step with traditional American values. Dukakis tried to present himself as a moderate, competent administrator, but he came across as arrogant and passionless, and his early lead slipped away.

Half of the eligible voters stayed home on election day. The lowest voter turnout since 1924 suggested the electorate's general disgust with an ugly, issueless campaign. Fifty-four percent of those who did vote were satisfied with the Republican record on peace and prosperity. But the Democrats gained seats in the House and Senate; for the first time since 1960, the strength of the presidential ticket did not translate into congressional gains for the party.

Domestic Stalemate

President Bush saw himself primarily as steward and guardian of the Reagan legacy. He promised "a kinder, gentler nation" and was more inclined than Reagan to approve government activity in the private sphere. But his most famous campaign pledge was "Read my lips: No new taxes." Boxed in by the budget deficit and his adamant refusal to seek new tax revenues, Bush opposed most proposals requiring federal funds to make the nation kinder and gentler for the poor, racial minorities, employed women, and other needy groups.

The president's aversion to new federal spending could not withstand the crisis in the savings and loan industry. In 1989, Bush signed legislation for the biggest federal bailout in history. The law authorized the government to sell off failing S&Ls at an estimated $159 billion cost to taxpayers over the next ten years. Bush also approved environmental protection legislation, the costs of which would be borne by industry and consumers. The Clean Air Act of 1990 was the strongest, most comprehensive environmental law in history, requiring power

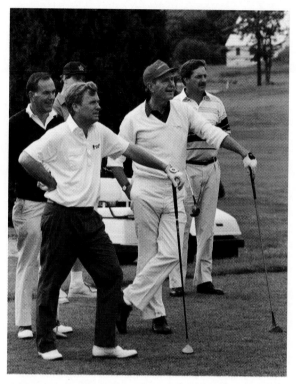

PRESIDENTIAL RECREATION
President George Bush and Vice President Dan Quayle play golf near the Bush summer home in Kennebunkport, Maine. Although Bush was a hardworking president, after the economy slipped into recession in 1990, photos such as these contributed to his image as uncaring and unwilling to act to relieve ordinary Americans' economic distress.
Corbis-Bettmann.

Richard Gephardt in 1991. Bush blocked congressional initiatives thirty-six times, vetoing bills that lifted abortion restrictions, extended unemployment benefits, raised taxes, mandated family and medical leave for workers, and reformed campaign financing. By the end of his term, press reports were filled with the words *stalemate, gridlock,* and *divided government.* To a Republican who preferred a more activist president, the Bush domestic policy was "all stop and no go."

The deadlock between president and Congress crippled the government's ability to deal with the budget deficit and the economic downswing that began in 1990. In June 1990, the worsening budget situation forced Bush to concede the fantasy of his "no new taxes" pledge. The next year's deficit was projected at a minimum of $160 billion, far above the Gramm-Rudman-Hollings limit of $64 billion. Failure to meet the target would trigger automatic cuts of 25 percent in military spending and 37 percent in most domestic programs.

The administration and Congress hammered out a compromise that set spending limits, increased taxes modestly for high-income Americans, and raised taxes on gasoline, cigarettes, alcoholic beverages, and luxury items. Although the budget agreement brought in new revenues and Congress stuck to the spending limits, three years later the deficit was even higher, boosted by rising costs in entitlement programs such as Social Security and Medicare-Medicaid as well as by spending on unforeseen emergencies of war and natural disasters. Conservative Republicans expressed so much outrage at Bush for going against his "no new taxes" pledge that in 1992 he conceded that the budget agreement had been a "mistake."

> "If you're looking for George Bush's domestic program, and many people are, this is it: the veto pen," charged Democratic House majority leader Richard Gephardt in 1991.

Failure to control the deficit also resulted from an economic downswing that began in 1990. With higher unemployment and a drop in the economy's growth rate, federal revenues declined. Congress and the president found it even harder to agree on antirecession measures than they had on curbing the deficit. Bush signed a measure that would create jobs by funding $151 billion worth of highway

plants to cut sulphur dioxide emissions by more than half by the year 2000 and oil companies to develop cleaner-burning gasoline.

Some 35 million to 43 million disabled Americans reaped the benefits of other regulatory legislation. Reflecting the growing power of the disability rights movement, the 1991 Americans with Disabilities Act banned job discrimination against the handicapped and required that private businesses, public accommodations, and transportation be made accessible to the disabled. Under pressure from legislators of both parties, Bush also signed the Civil Rights Act of 1991, which overcame Supreme Court rulings that made it harder for women and minorities to prove employment discrimination.

"If you're looking for George Bush's domestic program, and many people are, this is it: the veto pen," charged Democratic House majority leader and mass-transit construction over a six-year period. But Congress flatly refused to pass a capital gains tax cut that Bush claimed would stimulate economic growth; and Bush vetoed the Democrats' bill to cut taxes for the middle class. After vetoing aid to workers who had been thrown out of jobs by the recession in 1991, Bush reversed himself and approved legislation extending unemployment benefits in 1992.

Although the recession (as defined technically by economists) ended in 1991, the economy grew at a snail's pace. General Motors, Time Warner, Xerox, and other major corporations announced permanent reductions in their workforces. Economists characterized the sluggish economy as "jobless recovery" from the recession. As he faced his reelection campaign, Bush had to answer for an unemployment rate above 7 percent.

The president's greatest opportunity to influence policy in a lasting way came through Supreme Court appointments. Justice William Brennan's decision to retire in 1990 meant the departure of a justice who, even more than Earl Warren, had shaped the liberal direction of the Court. In selecting a successor, Bush avoided the turmoil and humiliation of the Bork nomination by naming David Souter, a federal court of appeals judge from New Hampshire who had left a scant written record and few clues about his views on judicial restraint or on specific issues. The Senate confirmed him easily.

In 1991, when Bush had to replace Justice Thurgood Marshall, the only African American on the Court, he set off a national controversy by nominating Clarence Thomas, a conservative black court of appeals judge. Thomas had opposed most affirmative action programs and busing as head of the Equal Employment Opportunity Commission under Reagan. Charging that Thomas would not protect minority rights, the NAACP and other civil rights organizations opposed the nomination. In spite of this opposition and Thomas's low rating by the American Bar Association, confirmation seemed certain until the media reported charges that Thomas had sexually harassed Anita Hill, a law professor, when she worked for him in the early 1980s. The Senate Judiciary Committee held three days of nationally televised hearings to investigate the charges. Thomas angrily and steadfastly denied the alleged incidents, and Hill's testimony failed to sway the Senate, which voted fifty-two to forty-eight to confirm him.

The hearings sensitized the public to sexual harassment and gave the women's movement a boost.

Many women, including a dozen Congresswomen, expressed outrage at the shabby treatment that Hill received from senators who tried to discredit her. Feminists complained that men "still don't get it" and began preparing to put more women into office in the 1992 elections.

Toward a New World Order

"All the action is in Moscow and Berlin, not here," complained a former Reagan aide, referring to the Bush administration's distance from events unfolding in Europe. The administration possessed no grand strategies, and Bush articulated no commanding goal like Carter's emphasis on human rights or Reagan's drive to return the United States to global ascendency. Rather, the president and his secretary of state, James Baker, responded cautiously to initiatives produced by Gorbachev and European leaders.

In the most dramatic moment in the collapse of the postwar order, East Germany opened the border with West Germany. On November 12, 1989, ecstatic Germans danced on the Berlin Wall, using whatever was at hand to begin demolishing that dominant symbol of the cold war.

The forces of change that Gorbachev had helped to unleash in the Soviet Union spread in 1989 to Eastern Europe, where popular uprisings demanded an end to state repression, official corruption, and economic bureaucracies that failed to deliver an acceptable standard of living. Communist governments fell like dominoes, in most cases with little bloodshed. In Czechoslovakia, East Germany, Hungary, Poland, and Yugoslavia, citizens voted in multiparty elections for the first time since World War II. Non-Communist governments took office everywhere but in Albania and Bulgaria, and even those countries instituted reforms. In the most dramatic moment in the collapse of the postwar order, East Germany opened the border with West Germany. On November 12, 1989, ecstatic Germans danced on the Berlin Wall, using whatever was at hand to begin demolishing that dominant symbol of the cold war.

West German Chancellor Helmut Kohl's call for a united Germany immediately after the fall of the Berlin Wall shocked U.S. leaders. Nevertheless,

FALL OF THE BERLIN WALL
*After 1961, the Berlin Wall symbolized the cold war and the iron grip of Communism over Eastern
Europe and the Soviet Union; more than four hundred easterners were killed trying to flee. After
Communist authorities opened the wall on November 9, 1989, permitting free travel between east
and west, Berliners from both sides gathered at the wall to celebrate.*
Eric Bouvet/Gamma Liaison.

President Bush helped to persuade Gorbachev that
the Soviet Union had nothing to fear from the unification of East and West Germany, a move that sped
to completion in 1990. Germany would become a
member of NATO, and though U.S. military forces
would remain in Europe, the commanding role of
the United States had been eclipsed. The same was
true of its economic clout: Western Europe, including a unified Germany, would become a united
economy in 1992. The destiny of Europe, to which
the United States and the Soviet Union had held the
key for forty-five years, now lay in European hands.

The superpowers continued to attune their relationship to the realities of a post-cold war world
as well as to domestic economic needs. Gorbachev
came to Washington in June 1990 and took home
another breakthrough in arms reductions. More far-
reaching than earlier accords, which had merely
limited production of additional weapons, the
strategic arms reduction treaty (START) actually
eliminated existing nuclear weapons—about 30

percent of each superpower's nuclear arsenal. Bush
and Gorbachev also pledged to scrap most of their
poison gas weapons and to work to eliminate chemical weapons from the planet.

The Bush administration's approach to problems closer to home developed in distinct contrast
to its cautious response to European developments.
In fact, while the Soviet Union moved along a non-
interventionist path, the United States sent military
forces into Panama in 1989 to overthrow its dictator, General Manuel Noriega. Noriega had long fed
off the CIA payroll, delivering information about
Communist activities in Cuba and Central America
and aiding the government's secret war against the
Sandinistas. But he also passed information to
Cuba's Castro while amassing a fortune through
dealing in illegal drugs, torturing and killing his domestic opposition, and wrecking the Panamanian
economy. In 1988, a Miami grand jury indicted Noriega for drug trafficking, and administration officials decided that he had to go.

MAP 31.2
Events in Eastern Europe, 1989–1992
The overthrow of Communist governments throughout Eastern and Central Europe and the splinter-
ing of the Soviet Union into more than a dozen separate nations were the most momentous changes
in the world since World War II.

In December 1989, President Bush ordered 25,000 troops into Panama to capture the dictator. The invasion forces quickly overcame Noriega's troops, at the cost of 23 American lives and hundreds of Panamanian lives, many of them civilians. The administration called the invasion Operation Just Cause. But although most Panamanians and their Central American neighbors rejoiced to see the corrupt tyrant go, they were not sure that the end justified the means. "Good causes don't justify breaking good principles," insisted one Latin American diplomat. The resort to military intervention revived the image of "Yankee imperialism," a stark contrast to the principles of self-determination and nonintervention that held sway in Eastern Europe.

The administration deployed much greater force and it acted with allies when Iraq's army invaded and quickly took over the small, oil-rich country of Kuwait in August 1990. Iraqi President Saddam Hussein cited long-standing boundary disputes as grounds for the invasion, but his primary target was the Kuwaiti oil fields. Struggling with an enormous debt from the ten-year war against Iran, Hussein desperately needed revenues, and control of Kuwaiti oil would give him powerful leverage over prices. Within days of invading Kuwait, Iraqi troops moved toward the Saudi Arabian border, threatening the world's largest oil reserves.

In reacting to the invasion, President Bush invoked principles of national self-determination and international law, but oil primarily determined the U.S. response. As the largest oil importer, the United States consumed one-fourth of the world's supply. With the consent of Saudi Arabia, Bush ordered Operation Desert Shield, a massive mobilization of land, air, and naval forces to counter the Iraqi threat. At the same time, the administration began to assemble an international coalition—ultimately involving more than thirty nations—to repel the aggression.

Reflecting the end of superpower conflict in the Middle East, the Soviet Union and the United States issued a joint condemnation of Iraq, and the Soviets cut off Iraq's supply of arms. The United Nations instituted economic sanctions, and most of the world joined an embargo on oil from Iraq and Kuwait. In November, the United Nations authorized the use of force against Iraq if it did not withdraw from Kuwait by January 15, 1991. By early January, the United States had deployed 400,000 soldiers to Saudi Arabia, where 265,000 troops from European nations, Egypt, Syria, and several other Arab states joined them. Meanwhile, Bush asked Congress for authorization to use military force against Iraq. Considerable public and legislative sentiment favored waiting to see whether the embargo would force Hussein to back down. But after three days of solemn debate, Congress approved what amounted to a declaration of war by a margin of five votes in the Senate and sixty-seven in the House. Unlike Johnson in Vietnam, Bush would go to war with clear congressional authorization.

On January 17, 1991, Operation Desert Shield became Operation Desert Storm, when the U.S.-led coalition began a forty-day air war against Iraq. Bombs and missiles smashed not only military targets but also power plants, oil refineries, and transportation networks. Having severely crippled Iraq through air bombardment, the coalition launched an all-out ground assault against Iraqi troops on February 23. "These people threw down their arms and ran," said an American artillery officer. Allied forces quickly routed the Iraqi soldiers, and within one hundred hours, Hussein announced that he would withdraw from Kuwait.

"By God, we've kicked the Vietnam syndrome once and for all," said President Bush on March 1. Most Americans found no moral ambiguity in the Persian Gulf War and took pride in the display of military competence. The war's costs were relatively cheap: Germany and Japan (who sent no troops) and other coalition allies paid a substantial part of the bill, while 146 U.S. servicemen and -women were killed in action, and 124 died outside of combat. The United States stood at the apex of global leadership, steering a massive coalition in which, for the first time, Arab nations fought beside their former colonial rulers.

Yet victory did not bring stability to the Middle East. The position of Israel, which had endured

Iraqi missile attacks, was more secure, but the Israeli-Palestinian conflict continued to simmer. Despite considerable military losses, Saddam Hussein remained in power and turned the remains of his war machine on Iraqi Kurds and Shiite Muslims, whom the United States had encouraged to rebel. Two million rebels became refugees; other Iraqi citizens suffered malnutrition, disease, and death caused by the destruction of the nation's fuel, communications, and transportation systems.

After the Gulf War, the Bush administration reverted to a bystander role as the world continued to remake itself. By the end of 1991, changes initiated by Gorbachev had brought about his own demise. Inspired by the liberation of Eastern Europe, Soviet republics sought their own indepen-

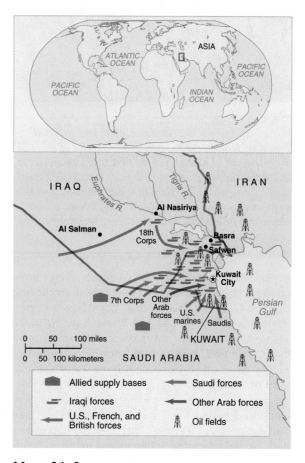

MAP 31.3
The Gulf War, February 1991
The heavy forty-day bombing of Iraq and the massive international mobilization on its borders enabled the U.S.-led United Nations force to defeat Iraq in just four days of ground war.

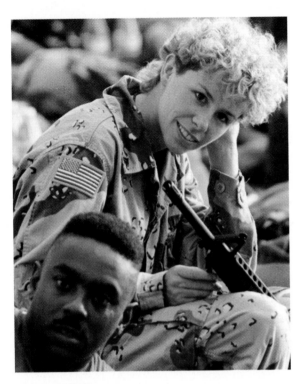

THE GULF WAR
These soldiers from the 24th Infantry arrived in Saudi Arabia in August 1990 as part of the U.S.-led effort to drive Iraq out of Kuwait. For the first time women served in combat-support positions with more than 33,000 stationed throughout the Gulf; eleven died and two were held as prisoners of war. Among their duties, women piloted planes and helicopters, directed artillery, and fought fires.
Corbis-Bettmann.

dence, while the Soviet Union's efforts at economic change brought widespread destitution. According to one Muscovite, "Gorbachev knew how to bring us freedom but he did not know how to make sausage." Gorbachev survived an attempted coup in August 1991, but he could not hold the Soviet Union together. In December, Boris Yeltsin, president of the Russian Republic, announced that Russia and eleven other republics had joined a new Commonwealth of Independent States. The three Baltic republics—Estonia, Latvia, and Lithuania—and Georgia became independent nations. With nothing left to govern, Gorbachev resigned.

The United States officially recognized Russia, but the breakup of the Soviet Union seemed as ominous as its existence had once appeared. "During the cold war, the threat was deliberate Soviet attack," declared Democratic Representative Les Aspin. "Now the bigger threat seems to be chaos in a nation with 30,000 nuclear weapons." Russia and the three other republics possessing nuclear weapons—Ukraine, Belarus, and Kazakhstan—pledged to implement START, and Congress provided $400 million to help these nations store or destroy their nuclear weapons; but that process would take years. Meanwhile, the Russian economy deteriorated further, causing widespread destitution and despair, and Yeltsin maintained a precarious hold on the government. Civil wars broke out in several former Soviet republics, and power struggles among republics with nuclear weapons created a powderkeg.

Conclusion: Watersheds at Home and Abroad

During the Reagan-Bush years, the United States turned explicitly away from the assumptions that had shaped domestic policy since the New Deal of Franklin Roosevelt. To be sure, Republican Presidents Eisenhower and Nixon had attempted to curb the role of the federal government in addressing national problems. Moreover, since the late 1960s, growing numbers of Americans had questioned both the appropriateness and the effectiveness of government activism on behalf of economic stability and social justice. But no president before Ronald Reagan had applied the brakes so sharply to liberal reform or enjoyed such widespread popular support for those efforts.

The Reagan-Bush counterrevolution appealed to Americans whose real incomes declined in the 1970s as their tax bills increased and who believed that the federal government was sacrificing their well-being to the interests of poor and minority groups. Reagan cultivated these sentiments by winning enormous tax reductions and by portraying civil rights initiatives as favoritism or "reverse discrimination." The tax cuts, combined with hefty increases in defense spending, created a federal deficit crisis that justified cuts in spending for social welfare programs and made new federal initiatives unthinkable. Many Americans continued to look favorably on specific federal programs at the end of the Reagan-Bush years, but public sentiment about the government in general had undergone a U-turn from the Roosevelt era. To a large segment of the population, not only was the federal government ineffective at solving national problems, but government intervention often made things worse.

If Reagan and Bush could take credit for domestic change, the roots of global change were much more complex. Reagan and Bush claimed that the massive arms buildup they had undertaken in the 1980s had brought the Soviets to their knees and accounted for the worldwide fall of communism. Others pointed to the internal weaknesses of the Soviet economic system and the courageous risk taking of Mikhail Gorbachev. None could deny, however, that between 1988 and 1992 the world had experienced the most cataclysmic changes since the 1940s.

Containment of communism had shaped the American economy and politics for nearly fifty years and formed the linchpin of U.S. foreign policy. Its sudden collapse left policymakers unprepared to forge a new global strategy. When Iraq invaded Kuwait, the Bush administration reacted decisively. In its first substantial military engagement in forty-five years that was not directed against communism, the United States demonstrated that the end of the cold war did not mean a diminution of U.S. leadership in world affairs.

However, its leaders had yet to articulate what overarching vision would replace the containment of communism as the major foreign policy goal and define the American purpose in the world.

By 1992, however, domestic problems seemed most urgent. Part of the Reagan-Bush legacy was a host of economic problems that had been accumulating for more than a decade: the decline of industrial production and loss of good jobs, business instability and dependence on foreign investment, a worsening budget deficit, the end of the American dream of upward mobility for much of the middle class, and increasing poverty and growing economic disparity between the rich and poor and between whites and people of color. While public officials and the media trumpeted U.S. victory in the cold war, the nation had yet to come to grips with the economic casualties of that struggle. How the United States dealt with one part of the Reagan-Bush legacy—the economic problems—would depend on the strength and depth of the other part of that legacy—the turn against government as the guarantor of social and economic well-being.

CHRONOLOGY

1980 Ronald Reagan elected fortieth president of United States, defeating incumbent Jimmy Carter.

1981 Researchers identify cause of AIDS epidemic as virus.

Would-be assassin wounds Reagan in Washington, D.C.

Congress passes Economic Recovery Tax Act advocated by Reagan, largest tax cut in U.S. history.

Reagan appoints Sandra Day O'Connor, first female justice to sit on U.S. Supreme Court.

1982 Congress extends Voting Rights Act over Reagan administration's objections.

Banking industry deregulated.

United States invades Grenada and topples its Marxist government.

1983 U.S. involvement in Lebanon terminated after bombing of marine barracks and deaths of 241 U.S. troops.

Reagan announces plans for Strategic Defense Initiative ("Star Wars").

1984 Democrats nominate Walter F. Mondale for president and Geraldine Ferraro for vice president.

Ronald Reagan reelected president.

U.S. Supreme Court rules that schools can continue to receive federal funds even if they practice discrimination in some programs (*Grove City College v. Bell*).

1985 Congress passes Gramm-Rudman-Hollings deficit reduction law.

1986 Iran-Contra scandal shakes Reagan administration.

1987 Soviet leader Mikhail Gorbachev visits Washington to sign INF agreement.

Senate defeats nomination of Robert H. Bork for seat on U.S. Supreme Court.

1988 Reverend Jesse Jackson mounts strong campaign for Democratic presidential nomination.

Democrats nominate Michael Dukakis for president and Lloyd Bentsen for vice president.

Vice President George Bush elected forty-first president of United States.

1989 Communism collapses in Eastern Europe, and Berlin Wall falls.

United States invades Panama and ousts dictator Manuel Noriega, who is jailed in United States.

1990 Bush and Congress agree to tax increase because of mounting federal deficit.

1991 Bush's nominee Clarence Thomas becomes second African American to sit on U.S. Supreme Court.

United States commits more than 400,000 troops to oust Iraqi army from neighboring Kuwait in Persian Gulf War.

BIBLIOGRAPHY

GENERAL WORKS

Sidney Blumenthal and Thomas Byrne Edsall, eds., *The Reagan Legacy* (1988).

Kevin Phillips, *The Politics of Rich and Poor: Wealth and the American Electorate in the Reagan Aftermath* (1990).

Michael Schaller, *Reckoning with Reagan: America and Its President in the 1980s* (1992).

Gary Wills, *Reagan's America: Innocents at Home* (1987).

THE REAGAN WHITE HOUSE

Martin Anderson, *Revolution* (1988).

Lou Cannon, *President Reagan: The Role of a Lifetime* (1991).

Robert Dallek, *Ronald Reagan: The Politics of Symbolism* (1984).

Michael Deaver, *Behind the Scenes* (1987).

David C. Martin and John Walcott, *Best Laid Plans* (1988).

Donald Regan, *For the Record: From Wall Street to Washington* (1988).

Larry Speakes, with Robert Pack, *Speaking Out: Inside the Reagan White House* (1988).

DOMESTIC POLICIES

Jeffrey H. Birnbaum and Alan S. Murray, *Showdown at Gucci Gulch: Lawmakers, Lobbyists, and the Unlikely Triumph of Tax Reform* (1987).

Kathleen Day, *S&L Hell: The People and the Politics behind the $1 Trillion Savings and Loan Scandal* (1993).

Martha Derthick and Paul J. Quirk, *The Politics of Deregulation* (1985).

Benjamin Friedman, *Day of Reckoning: The Consequences of American Economic Policy under Reagan and After* (1988).

Lawrence Lindsey, *The Growth Experiment: How the New Tax Policy Is Transforming the U.S. Economy* (1990).

Martin Lowy, *High Rollers: Inside the Savings and Loan Debacle* (1994).

Richard P. Nathan and Fred C. Doolittle, *Reagan and the States* (1987).

Paul Craig Roberts, *The Supply-Side Revolution* (1984).

Murray Weidenbaum, *Rendezvous with Reality: The American Economy after Reagan* (1988).

POLITICS

Sidney Blumenthal, *The Rise of the Counter-Establishment: From Conservative Ideology to Political Power* (1986).

Steve Bruce, *The Rise and Fall of the New Christian Right: Conservative Protestant Politics in America, 1978–1988* (1988).

Thomas Byrd Edsall, with Mary D. Edsall, *Chain Reaction: The Impact of Race, Rights, and Taxes on American Politics* (1992).

Thomas Ferguson and Joel Rogers, *Right Turn: The Decline of the Democrats and the Future of American Politics* (1986).

Jack W. Germond and Jules Witcover, *Wake Us When It's Over: Presidential Politics of 1984* (1985).

Jack W. Germond and Jules Witcover, *Whose Broad Stripes and Bright Stars? The Trivial Pursuit of the Presidency, 1988* (1989).

Paul Gottfried and Thomas Fleming, *The Conservative Movement* (1988).

David Stockman, *The Triumph of Politics: How the Reagan Revolution Failed* (1986).

INDIVIDUAL RIGHTS AND THE SUPREME COURT

Barry D. Adam, *The Rise of a Gay and Lesbian Movement* (1987).

Norman C. Amaker, *Civil Rights and the Reagan Administration* (1988).

Robert H. Bork, *The Tempting of America: The Political Seduction of the Law* (1989).

Gerald David Jaynes and Robin M. Williams Jr., eds., *A Common Destiny: Blacks and American Society* (1989).

Michael Pertschuk and Wendy Schaetzel, *The People Rising: The Campaign against the Bork Nomination* (1989).

Herman Schwartz, *Packing the Courts: The Conservative Campaign to Rewrite the Constitution* (1988).

James F. Simon, *The Center Holds: The Power Struggle inside the Rehnquist Court* (1995).

FOREIGN POLICY AND ARMS CONTROL

Cynthia J. Arnson, *Crossroads: Congress, the Reagan Administration, and Central America* (1989).

Michael R. Beschloss and Strobe Talbott, *At the Highest Levels: The Inside Story of the End of the Cold War* (1993).

Thomas Carothers, *In the Name of Democracy: U.S. Policy toward Latin America in the Reagan Years* (1991).

John Dinges, *Our Man in Panama: How General Noriega Used the United States—and Made Millions in Drugs and Arms* (1990).

Theodore Draper, *A Very Thin Line: The Iran-Contra Affair* (1991).

Lawrence Freedman and Efraim Karsh, *The Gulf Conflict, 1990–1991: Diplomacy and War in the New World Order* (1993).

Raymond I. Garthoff, *The Great Transition: American-Soviet Relations and the End of the Cold War* (1994).

Michael J. Hogan, ed., *The End of the Cold War: Its Meanings and Implications* (1992).

Robert Kagan, *A Twilight Struggle: American Power and Nicaragua, 1977–1990* (1996).

Frederick Kempe, *Divorcing the Dictator: America's Bungled Affair with Noriega* (1990).

David E. Kyvig, ed., *Reagan and the World* (1990).

Sanford Lakoff and Herbert F. York, *A Shield in Space?* (1989).

Richard Ned Lebow and Janice Gross Stein, *We All Lost the Cold War* (1994).

William Pfaff, *Barbarian Sentiments: How the American Century Ends* (1989).

Peter Schweizer, *Victory: The Reagan Administration's Secret Strategy That Hastened the Collapse of the Soviet Union* (1995).

Elaine Sciolino, *The Outlaw State: Saddam Hussein's Quest for Power and the Gulf Crisis* (1991).

George P. Shultz, *Turmoil and Triumph: My Years as Secretary of State* (1993).

Strobe Talbott, *The Master of the Game: Paul Nitze and the Nuclear Peace* (1988).

Daniel Wirls, *Buildup: The Politics of Defense in the Reagan Era* (1992).

THE ECONOMY AND SOCIETY

Michael Bernstein, David E. Adler, and Robert Heilbroner, *Understanding American Economic Decline* (1994).

Joel Blau, *Homelessness in the United States* (1992).

George J. Borjas, *Friends and Strangers: The Impact of Immigrants on the U.S. Economy* (1990).

Kathryn Marie Dudley, *The End of the Line: Lost Jobs, New Lives in Postindustrial America* (1994).

L. H. Gann and Peter J. Duignan, *The Hispanics in the United States: A History* (1986).

David Gelsanliter, *Jump Start: Japan Comes to the Heartland* (1990).

Andrew Hacker, *Two Nations: Black and White, Separate, Hostile, Unequal* (1992).

Bennett Harrison and Barry Bluestone, *The Great U-Turn: Corporate Restructuring and the Polarizing of America* (1988).

Christopher Jencks, *The Homeless* (1994).

Sarah J. Mahler, *American Dreaming: Immigrant Life on the Margins* (1995).

David M. Reimers, *Still the Golden Door: The Third World Comes to America* (rev. ed., 1992).

Al Santoli, *New Americans: An Oral History* (1988).

John E. Schwarz and Thomas J. Volgy, *The Forgotten Americans* (1993).

Randy Shilts, *And the Band Played On: Politics, People, and the AIDS Epidemic* (1987).

David E. Simcox, *U.S. Immigration in the 1980s* (1988).

Peter Skerry, *Mexican Americans: The Ambivalent Minority* (1993).

Adam Smith, *The Roaring '80s* (1988).

Ronald Takaki, *Strangers from a Different Shore: A History of Asian Americans* (1989).

Sanford J. Ungar, *Fresh Blood: The New American Immigrants* (1995).

William Wei, *The Asian American Movement* (1993).

THE BUSH ADMINISTRATION

Ryan J. Barilleaux and Mary E. Stuckey, *Leadership and the Bush Presidency: Prudence or Drift in an Era of Change?* (1992).

Colin Campbell and Bert Rockman, *The Bush Presidency: First Appraisals* (1991).

Michael Duffy and Dan Goodgame, *Marching in Place: The Status Quo Presidency of George Bush* (1992).

David Mervin, *George Bush and the Guardianship Presidency* (1996).

**STATUE OF PRESIDENT
AS SAXOPHONIST**

*At a low point in his 1992 presidential
campaign, Bill Clinton went on the Arsenio
Hall television talk show, donned sunglasses, and
played the saxophone, prompting the African American
host to comment, "I'm glad to see a Democrat blow something besides an election." Clinton's
appearance on Arsenio Hall's show as well as on the cable Music Television channel, were efforts to appeal to younger voters. The instrument became Clinton's symbol, and after his victory saxophone pins were the hottest selling inaugural items. Bill Potts of Denver, Colorado
made this carving and presented it to the president in 1993.*

National Archives.

THE CLINTON ADMINISTRATION AND THE SEARCH FOR A POPULAR CENTER

32

1992–1997

I N 1992, THE DEMOCRATIC PARTY concluded its nominating convention as it had in years past, with the candidates, their families, and supporters celebrating on a massive podium above the cheering delegates. This year, however, the candidates represented something new. William Jefferson "Bill" Clinton and Albert Gore were both in their mid-forties, the first baby boomers to run on a major party ticket, the first candidates not to have experienced World War II. And the music, too, symbolized a new era. Instead of the traditional "Happy Days Are Here Again," the Democratic theme song since the 1930s, the band blared Fleetwood Mac's rock music. "Don't stop thinking about tomorrow," the lyrics sang. "Yesterday's gone."

Clinton and Gore symbolized the change that most voters seemed to want. "I was ready for a change," explained a Michigan grade school teacher who voted for Clinton that November. "I'm eager to see a fresh young face, and I'm eager to see new ideas. . . . What have we got to lose?" On the eve of Clinton's inauguration in January 1993, three of every four Americans responding to a poll expressed the need for "major changes in the way the federal government works."

Whether the new Clinton administration could deliver on its promise of change was another matter. "I think he promised a lot, and he may have promised too much," said a twenty-five-year-old voter just before Clinton's inauguration. Clinton voters had great expectations of the new administration but no consensus about what kinds of changes should occur. Some Americans worried about the growing federal debt, but most opposed higher taxes and did not want to give up the government benefits they enjoyed. As businesses tried to trim budgets and become more competitive, victims of corporate downsizing worried about finding new jobs while others were anxious about keeping theirs. Access to good health care and reducing crime constituted other major concerns, but seriously attacking those problems depended on more federal spending or more federal intrusion than most Americans seemed willing to accept.

The Clinton administration sought to reverse the disdain for government that Ronald Reagan had so successfully cultivated. Clinton wanted to restore confidence in government as a positive force for good. But he also inherited a national debt that had grown from less than $1 trillion in 1981 to $4.4 trillion in 1993—and the interest on that debt consumed one-fifth of the federal budget. Just as Clinton was

CLINTON THE CAMPAIGNER
Bill Clinton loved campaigning and was remarkably good at creating a rapport with audiences.
Here he dives into the crowd at Jackson, Mississippi as his presidential campaign entered the
homestretch in October 1992.
Ira Wyman/Sygma.

short on cash for using government in positive ways, he was also short on political capital. During his first two years in office, he had a slim Democratic majority in Congress, but thereafter he faced a legislature controlled by Republicans.

The end of the cold war also made governing more difficult. For decades the United States–Soviet rivalry had helped to unify the nation with a clear enemy against which Americans could rally. The cold war had given Americans a sense of national purpose and had encouraged domestic reform to strengthen the nation at home in order to combat communism abroad. Moreover, for better or worse, the cold war had provided a rationale by which officials made decisions about the international role of the nation. After the cold war no clear standards emerged to determine where and under what conditions the United States should act beyond its borders.

Clinton's personal qualities also complicated his presidency. Very smart, dedicated, and extraordinarily hardworking, Clinton suffered, particularly in his first years in office, from disorganization, failure to focus, overextending himself and his agenda, and indecisiveness. Moreover, his administration was distracted by a number of allegations

and scandals involving himself, his wife, and close aides. These problems and the president's inability to deliver on many of his promises helped the Republicans capture both the House and the Senate in 1994, the first time they had done so since the 1950s. Running against a weak candidate in 1996, Clinton hung on to the presidency, but voters evinced a lack of trust in either party, when they elected a Republican Congress.

A Mandate for Change: The 1992 Election

In March 1991, President Bush's chances for reelection in 1992 looked golden. Successful completion of the Gulf War sent his approval rating up to 88 percent, causing the most prominent Democrats to opt out of the presidential race. That, however, did not deter Bill Clinton, who at age forty-five had served as governor of Arkansas for twelve years. Clinton's childhood was far from the American dream: His father was killed in an auto accident before he was born, and his stepfather was an alco-

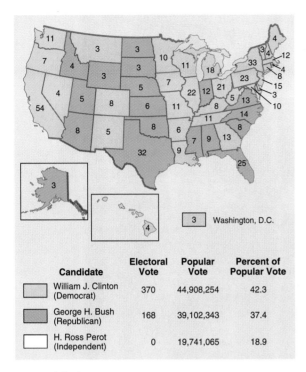

Candidate	Electoral Vote	Popular Vote	Percent of Popular Vote
William J. Clinton (Democrat)	370	44,908,254	42.3
George H. Bush (Republican)	168	39,102,343	37.4
H. Ross Perot (Independent)	0	19,741,065	18.9

M A P 32.1
The Election of 1992

holic. But Clinton's mother, who worked as a nurse most of her life, had endless faith in her son and nourished his political ambitions.

Clinton had attended Georgetown University and had won a prestigious Rhodes scholarship to Oxford University in England. He earned his law degree from Yale University, where he met his wife, Hillary Rodham, whose intelligence and ambition equaled his. While Clinton was governor of Arkansas, she pursued her own career in a prominent Little Rock law firm and at the same time served as one of her husband's most important advisers. The extent of her participation in her husband's career drew heavy criticism and was reflected in the derisive name Clinton-haters gave to the couple—"Billary."

Rejecting the traditional pattern of ticket balancing, Clinton chose Senator Albert Gore Jr. for his running mate. At forty-four, even younger than Clinton, Gore too hailed from the South. The son of a prominent U.S. senator, Gore had represented Tennessee in the House and Senate for a total of sixteen years. The youthfulness of the Democratic ticket reinforced Clinton's campaign theme of change.

Like Jimmy Carter in 1976 and Michael Dukakis in 1988, Clinton and Gore presented themselves as

"new Democrats." Both belonged to the Democratic Leadership Council, which Clinton had helped found in 1985 to rid the party of its liberal image. Clinton deliberately distanced himself from Jesse Jackson and his Rainbow Coalition and appealed to voters who believed that some Americans were getting a free ride at their expense. "We're going to put an end to welfare as we know it," Clinton claimed. Disavowing the "tax and spend" label that Republicans pinned on his party, Clinton promised a tax cut for the middle class.

Yet Clinton also advocated an active, positive role for the federal government, urging voters to put a Democrat in the White House to break the legislative-executive gridlock that had thwarted efforts to promote economic growth and deal with health care, crime, and other problems. Portraying President Bush as a do-nothing official even while unemployment neared 8 percent, Clinton promised to reinvigorate government and the economy.

The popularity of a third candidate revealed Americans' frustrations with government and thirst for change. In announcing his candidacy for president on a popular talk show, self-made Texas billionaire H. Ross Perot set the tone of his entire unconventional campaign. He used television extensively but gave no press conferences; he dropped out of the campaign in July, then dropped back in again in October; he chose an inexperienced running mate; and his promises were short on detail. But he had plenty of money and managed to attract a sizable grassroots movement with his down-to-earth personality and appeals to voters' disgust with Washington politics and politicians. Perot's candidacy hurt Bush more than it hurt Clinton, and it established the federal budget deficit as a key campaign issue.

In casting two-thirds of their votes for Clinton or Perot, voters in the 1992 election demonstrated a clear mandate for change but formed no majority around a particular direction that change should take.

The Bush campaign capitalized on revelations about Clinton's past and private life. Clinton had opposed the war in Vietnam and pulled strings to avoid being drafted; he confessed to having smoked marijuana; and, faced with allegations of extramarital affairs, he admitted "troubled" times in his marriage. Attempting to focus the election on personal

WOMEN SENATORS
The elections of 1996 sent nine women to the Senate, the greatest number in U.S. history. As the 105th Congress opened in January 1997, eight of them met to celebrate and to discuss opportunities to cooperate across party lines. Democrat Barbara Mikulski of Maryland, sixth from left, had served in Congress for twenty years; and Democrat Carol Moseley-Braun of Illinois was the first African American woman to serve in the U.S. Senate.
Joe Marquette/Wide World.

qualities rather than issues, Bush asked voters to choose experience, integrity, and character. But he failed to distract voters from their primary concerns —the economy and jobs, health care, and the deficit.

Americans reversed the thirty-year decline in voter turnout as 55 percent of those eligible went to the polls. They gave Clinton 43 percent of their votes, Bush 38 percent, and Perot 19 percent—the strongest third-party finish since Theodore Roosevelt's Progressive Party candidacy in 1912. In casting two-thirds of their votes for Clinton or Perot, voters demonstrated a clear mandate for change but formed no majority around a particular direction that change should take.

The Democrats barely maintained their majority in Congress, but the presence of women and minorities jumped significantly. Four Democratic women's victories in Senate races raised the female presence to six, while in the House the number of

seats held by women increased from twenty-eight to forty-seven. African Americans gained twelve seats in the House, bringing their total to thirty-eight, while the number of Hispanic representatives increased from ten to seventeen. Although the numbers did not jump so dramatically, the diversification of Congress continued through the 1990s.

Domestic Change and the Politics of Incrementalism

Clinton ran as a moderate, but he came to the White House with ambitious plans to spur economic growth, reform the health care system, improve public education, reduce taxes on the middle class, and more. Although he made good on many of his promises, the changes effected during his administration tended to be incremental rather than sweeping. Halfway through his first term, Clinton remarked, "Most everybody is for change in general and then against it in particular." Limiting what he accomplished were the budget deficit, Republican strength in Congress, lack of consensus among Democrats, and Clinton's desire to avoid the label of "liberal." Especially after the Republican victory in the 1994 congressional elections, Clinton forswore significant reforms in order to present himself as a centrist.

Right after the 1992 election, president-elect Clinton began to put together a cabinet "that looked like America." In keeping with his promise, he selected the most diverse group of department heads ever assembled.

After the election, president-elect Clinton began to put together a cabinet "that looked like America." In keeping with his promise, he selected the most diverse group of department heads ever assembled. Of twenty-three key appointments, six were women, three African Americans, and two Latinos. Janet Reno became the first female attorney general, and in his second term in office Clinton appointed the first female secretary of state, Madeleine K. Albright.

Clinton's judicial appointments had a similar cast. Of his first 129 appointments to federal courts, nearly one-third were women, 31 were black, and 11 were Hispanic. In June 1993, he appointed the second woman to the Supreme Court, Ruth Bader Ginsburg. Unlike the woman she joined, Reagan appointee Sandra Day O'Connor, Ginsburg was a self-identified feminist who had planned legal strategy and won key women's rights rulings from the Supreme Court before President Carter made her a federal appeals court judge in 1980.

Upon taking office in 1993, Clinton quickly used his executive powers to reverse policies of Presidents Reagan and Bush. He issued a series of executive orders easing restrictions on abortion counseling, allowing U.S. military hospitals abroad to perform privately funded abortions, and paving the way for importation of the French abortion pill, RU-486. But he failed to implement his campaign promise for an executive order to lift the ban on homosexuals in the military. Vehement opposition to allowing gays and lesbians openly to serve in the military from military leaders, enlisted men, and key legislators forced Clinton to back away from his promise. In June 1993, Clinton announced a compromise, called the "don't ask, don't tell" policy. It forbade officials from asking military personnel about their sexuality, but those who said they were gay or engaged in homosexual behavior could be dismissed.

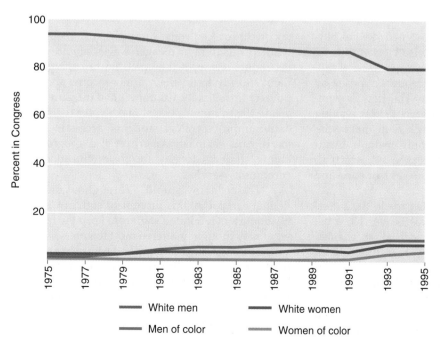

FIGURE **32.1**
Towards a More Diverse Congress
In the last quarter of the twentieth century, women and minorities began to make their presence felt in the 535-member national legislature. White men continued to hold an overwhelming majority in Congress, but now some one hundred legislators were either white women or members of a minority group. Of the 57 women serving in the 105th Congress (1997–1998), more than one-fourth were women of color, including 12 African Americans, 3 Latinas, and an Asian American.

GAYS IN THE MILITARY
When Chairman of the Joint Chiefs of Staff Colin Powell spoke at Harvard University's commencement in June 1993, gay rights advocates protested the government's ban on homosexuals in the military. Many found it ironic that Powell, an African American, did not support President Clinton's effort to end discrimination against gay men and lesbians in military service.
Wide World.

More successfully, Clinton signed several bills that had been vetoed or otherwise blocked during the past twelve years. One was a gun control bill, first introduced in 1987 but vigorously opposed by the National Rifle Association. The new law required gun purchasers to undergo a short waiting period while records were checked to make sure they were not criminals or mentally unstable. In addition Clinton won a huge anticrime bill, which allocated $30 billion to prevention and prisons and banned assault weapons.

A Democratic president also made the difference for the Family and Medical Leave Act, a bill that Bush had vetoed. That legislation enabled workers in larger companies to take time off for childbirth, adoption, caring for aging parents, or medical emergencies affecting family members. To fulfill his campaign promise that no full-time worker should live in poverty, Clinton pushed through a substantial increase in the earned income

tax credit for low wage earners. Thus, people who worked full time at meager wages would receive tax reductions or, if they paid no taxes, a government subsidy to lift their family income above the poverty line. Finally, Clinton signed measures to increase the minimum wage, make voter registration easier, improve college students' access to federal loans, and establish Americorps, a program enabling students to pay for their education with community service.

"The economy, stupid." Throughout the presidential campaign, this prominent sign at Clinton's headquarters reminded staffers to keep the focus on what they thought mattered most to voters. Already by the election, the economy had begun to grow out of recession, but Clinton was as concerned with long-term growth as with short-term recovery. His economic program rested on the assumption that Americans could enjoy a higher standard of living only with substantial gains in productivity. Increasing an average of 2.9 percent a year during the 1950s and 1960s, rising productivity underwrote the tremendous material gains Americans had enjoyed in that era, but since 1974 productivity growth slumped to only about 1 percent a year. Clinton sought to boost output with greater public and private investment. He wanted government to invest more heavily in "infrastructure"—roads, harbors, communications systems, and the like—and in people, through education and training. And he wanted tax incentives to encourage private investment in new technology and equipment.

Clinton's investment program fell victim to the huge federal deficit, which Perot had spotlighted in his campaign and which gave legislators an excuse for rejecting new federal spending. Upon finding the projected deficit even larger than anticipated, Clinton abandoned his middle-class tax cut. Both Republicans and Democrats wanted to reduce the deficit, but Republicans wanted deeper cuts, their determination symbolized by a Republican member of the House Appropriations Committee who brought a machete and two knives to the first committee meeting of 1995.

Clinton and Congress battled so fiercely over budget bills that the Republicans shut down government twice near the end of 1995; but they did make a dent in the deficit. Between 1992 and 1996, the combination of budget cuts, tax increases that fell primarily on the wealthy, declining unemploy-

ment, and economic expansion reduced the deficit by about half. The government still operated at an annual deficit of about $150 billion; the national debt continued to rise, although more slowly; and no solution appeared to a fiscal crisis predicted for around 2010, when the baby boomers would begin to turn sixty-five and claim Social Security payments and Medicare. Nonetheless, the seemingly inexorable trend of increasing government debt had turned around.

In contrast, Clinton stumbled badly over health care reform. His plan had two key objectives: to help the 39 million Americans who lacked health insurance by providing universal coverage and to curb the steeply rising costs of medical care—an objective necessary for continued progress on deficit reduction. The goals in themselves stirred little opposition, but how to implement them stirred much.

The administration dealt its own blows to health care reform by presenting an extraordinarily complex bill that raised the specter of higher taxes and government interference in health care decisions. Elements of the health care industry ran TV ads encouraging such fears, and partisan Republicans ferociously attacked the Clinton plan. Concerns about cost and government interference also found expression among Democrats, whose disagreements among themselves helped to derail health reform. Yet, although comprehensive reform failed, private industry made significant progress in

"DILBERT" AND DOWNSIZING
This 1992 cartoon captures a prevalent feature of the economy of the 1990s, as corporations fired employees, or downsized, in order to reduce costs and become more competitive. Abandoning his own middle-management job to earn a fortune as a cartoonist, Scott Adams created the enormously popular strip "Dilbert" exposing idiocies in the workplace by poking fun at bosses, management fads, and other aspects of the business world.
Reprinted by permission of United Feature Syndicate.

**THE FIGHT OVER
HEALTH CARE REFORM**
Featured in a series of TV commercials, the middle-class couple "Harry and Louise" criticize President Clinton's health-care plan. The Health Insurance Association of America paid $10 million for the ads, which helped to defeat the bill and cause the biggest failure of Clinton's first term.
Goddard-Clausen/First Tuesday.

curtailing costs, at patients' expense, some argued. And Congress enacted incremental reform by making it easier for workers who changed jobs to retain health insurance.

The 1996 Election and the Battle for Center Ground

When voters swept away the Democratic majorities in both houses of Congress in 1994, Republicans assumed that control of the White House would follow in 1996. Democrats took the heat for voters' disgust with congressional infighting and stonewalling and their disillusionment with the president. Clinton had delivered on some of his promises—an expanding economy, progress on deficit reduction, an attack on crime—but had failed to achieve health care reform, welfare reform, and a middle-class tax cut. Moreover, scandals surrounding the Clintons' financial dealings in Arkansas and charges of sexual harassment against the president while he was governor shook the administration, contributing to the image of a president with character and leadership defects.

Led by Representative Newt Gingrich of Georgia, Republicans considered the 1994 elections a mandate for their "contract with America," a conservative platform that included drastic contraction of the federal government, deep tax cuts, constitutional amendments to ban abortions and to require a balanced federal budget, and term limits on members of Congress. Although Gingrich succeeded in moving the debate to the right, Clinton vetoes and opposition from Democrats and more moderate Republicans stymied most of the contract pledges.

A more extreme antigovernment movement operated far from Washington, in grassroots armed militias claiming patriotism and the need to defend themselves from government tyranny. Anticipating government repression, they stockpiled, in the words of one militia leader, "the four Bs: Bibles, bullets, beans, and bandages." The militias embraced a wide variety of sentiments, including opposition to taxes and the United Nations, anti-Semitism, and white supremacy. Recruitment for militias rose after gun control legislation passed and after government agents stormed the headquarters of an armed religious cult in Waco, Texas, resulting in more than eighty deaths. On the second anniversary of that event, April 19, 1995, a bomb leveled a federal building in Oklahoma City, taking 169 lives—including 19 children—and constituting the worst terrorist attack in the nation's history. Authorities arrested two militia members as prime suspects.

Clinton's reassuring handling of the Oklahoma City bombing helped restore his presidential stature. In addition, he began, on the one hand, to stand up to the Republican Congress and, on the other, to compromise on certain measures. Looking toward the 1996 election, Clinton used his veto power and threats of vetoes against what he labeled "extreme" Republican measures. As he forced the shaping of legislation along more moderate lines, he himself moved toward the center and approved it. For example, he stood firm against deep Republican cuts in education, environment, and welfare programs, but he cooperated with Republicans to fashion a plan that would balance the budget in seven years.

Clinton's determination to cast himself as a centrist was nowhere more apparent than in his han-

dling of welfare reform. Since Lyndon Johnson's war on poverty in the 1960s, public sentiment had shifted. Instead of viewing poverty as the result of a shortage of adequate jobs and child care, poor education, and other circumstances beyond an individual's control, more people were inclined to blame the poor themselves and the government welfare program, Aid to Families with Dependent Children (AFDC), that, it was argued, kept poor people in cycles of dependency. Nearly everyone considered work better than welfare but disagreed about whether the nation's economy could provide sufficient jobs and how much government assistance poor people needed in the transition from work to welfare. Most estimates showed that it was cheaper to support a family on welfare than to provide the job training, child care, and other supports necessary for that transition.

Clinton allowed the Republicans to take the initiative in welfare reform. He vetoed two measures,

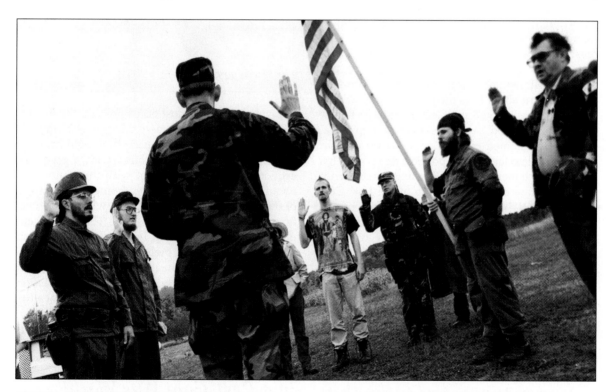

ARMING AGAINST THE GOVERNMENT
Organizing against what they called government tyranny, paramilitary groups, or militias, arose in more than twenty states in the 1990s. These groups stockpiled weapons and prepared to defend themselves against government efforts to take away their guns or otherwise encroach on what they considered their rights. Pictured here are members of the Michigan Militia at a training session in Wolverine, Michigan in 1995.
Valica Boudryl/*Detroit Free Press*/Corbis-Bettmann.

and then, having forced a less punitive bill, he signed the third as the 1996 election approached. The Personal Responsibility and Work Opportunity Reconciliation Act represented a dramatic reversal of social policy that had provided a safety net since the 1930s. It abolished AFDC and with it society's pledge to provide a minimum level of subsistence for all its children. In place of AFDC, the law established a system of grants to the states, with the requirement that most recipients be cut off welfare in two years whether they could find a job or not. The law set a lifetime limit of aid at five years; barred legal immigrants who had not become citizens from food stamps and supplemental security income for the elderly and disabled; and gave states the authority to stop Medicaid to legal immigrants.

A "moment of shame," cried Marian White Edelman, president of the Children's Defense Fund, when Clinton signed the bill. Liberal Senator Paul Simon called the measure "welfare denial," not welfare reform. State and local officials across the country scrambled to understand the law and then to figure out how to implement it while sustaining the most disadvantaged part of the population. "We certainly endorse the overall direction toward work," a Minnesota official said, while expressing grave concern about how the particular law would operate. "A child could very well have to go to foster care," predicted a social worker in Louisiana.

Clinton claimed that the new law meant that "welfare will no longer be a political issue," and his signature on it meant that the Republicans could not use the welfare issue against him in the 1996 election campaign. In an election distinguished by the electorate's lack of interest, the president ran as a moderate who would save the country from extremist Republicans.

In an election distinguished by the electorate's lack of interest, Clinton ran in 1996 as a moderate who would save the country from extremist Republicans.

In fact, the Republican Party also moved to the center, passing over a field of conservatives to nominate Kansan Robert Dole, former Senate majority leader who had served in Washington for more than two decades. The last candidate of the World War II generation and admired for his struggle to overcome grievous war wounds, the seventy-two-year-

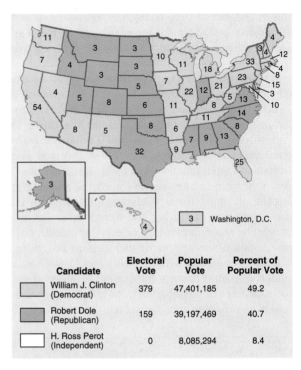

Candidate	Electoral Vote	Popular Vote	Percent of Popular Vote
William J. Clinton (Democrat)	379	47,401,185	49.2
Robert Dole (Republican)	159	39,197,469	40.7
H. Ross Perot (Independent)	0	8,085,294	8.4

Map 32.2
The Election of 1996

---

old Dole had spent most of his political life brokering compromises and was unable to articulate his own vision of what his presidency would bring.

Whether out of satisfaction with a favorable economy or out of boredom with the candidates, about half of all voters stayed home. Fifty percent of those who voted chose Clinton, while 41 percent favored Dole, and 9 percent Perot. The largest gender gap to date appeared in the election: Women awarded 54 percent of their votes to Clinton and 38 percent to Dole, while men split their votes between Dole and Clinton nearly evenly. Although Clinton won reelection with room to spare, voters sent a Republican majority back to Congress.

Creating Foreign Policy in a Post-Cold War World

With the cold war no longer monopolizing the foreign-policy agenda, global economic issues assumed a much larger place. Clinton built on progress made in the Reagan and Bush administrations and won bipartisan support for easing restrictions on international trade. In November 1993, Congress approved the North American Free Trade Agreement (NAFTA), a pact eliminating all tariffs and trade barriers among the United States, Canada, and Mexico. NAFTA ran into stiff opposition from organized labor and other groups—including Perot and his supporters—that feared loss of jobs and industries to Mexico where wages were substantially lower. Proponents argued that the United States would benefit from greater export opportunities, creation of more jobs in the long run, and the global clout the three trading partners would enjoy. With 360 million people and a $6 billion economy, the NAFTA trio constituted the largest trading bloc in the world.

A year later, the Senate took another step toward the elimination of trade barriers by ratifying the General Agreement on Tariffs and Trade (GATT), a treaty involving more than one hundred nations. GATT established a World Trade Organization to enforce provisions of the treaty, which included substantial tariff reductions and elimination of quotas on imports. Unlike NAFTA, GATT did not come close to achieving free trade, but the debates were similar in reflecting two visions of America's place in the world economy. Opponents of the agreements tied the nation's economic health to nurturing its established industries, keeping its traditional jobs at home, and maintaining labor and environmental standards. Those who ultimately prevailed envisioned American prosperity flowing from the greater export opportunities that would come with freer trade.

Clinton also inherited from the Bush administration the task of defining a clear and consistent role for the nation in a post-cold war world. Bush had acted decisively when Iraq invaded Kuwait in 1990, threatening the world's oil supply, and he rallied the nation behind him. But while the oil reserves in the Middle East made stability in that region of great concern to the United States, crises elsewhere in the world seemed less directly related to American self-interest. Both the Bush and Clinton administrations wrestled with decisions about whether and where to deploy American power in the world of some 190 nations.

In the case of the small African country of Somalia, where a famine was exacerbated by warring factions who disrupted the food supply, President Bush bowed to humanitarian pressures in December 1992 and dispatched U.S. troops to join a United Nations operation there. But in the summer of 1993,

Clinton allowed the humanitarian mission to turn into "nation building," an effort to restore national stability. Eighteen U.S. soldiers were killed, and an outcry at home suggested that most Americans were not prepared to sacrifice lives when they perceived no vital interests at stake.

As a consequence, the Clinton administration moved slowly in deciding to risk U.S. troops in Haiti, where the United States had maintained a military presence from 1915 to 1934. After American withdrawal, Haitians suffered under harsh dictatorships until December 1990, when the Reverend Jean-Bertrand Aristide won the Haitian presidency in the country's first free election. Nine months later, a military coup led by General Raoul Cedras overthrew the government.

The United States joined a United Nations embargo of oil and arms to Haiti, but Cedras maintained an iron grip, presiding over the killing of more than three thousand Haitians. Thousands of Haitians tried to escape the poverty and violence of the military dictatorship, many of them building flimsy boats and heading for Florida. With anti-immigrant sentiment already high in Florida and in the country as a whole, Clinton was pressed hard to stop the refugee flow. At the same time, the Black Congressional Caucus and others insisted that the nation had a moral responsibility to end the suffering and restore democracy in Haiti.

After winning UN authorization for the use of force, in September 1994 Clinton announced the dispatch of twenty thousand troops but also sent a last-minute mission to negotiate with Cedras. Hours before the U.S. invasion was to begin, the team led by former President Jimmy Carter reached an agreement under which the military leaders promised to step down. Consequently, when U.S. forces began landing on September 19 and then disarming Haitian troops, they did so peacefully and with tremendous gratitude from the Haitian people. Cedras resigned on October 10, and President Aristide returned to cheering crowds on October 15. Initially a huge success, U.S. Haitian policy would continue to be tested until the Aristide government met the grave challenges of economic and political reconstruction.

The situation in Yugoslavia appeared even more risky to officials in both the Bush and Clinton administrations. During the cold war, the Communist government in Yugoslavia had held ethnic tensions in check. But after the Communists were swept out, Yugoslavia disintegrated into the three

Still a Promised Land?

"THE UNITED STATES IS OUR LAND. . . . We intend to maintain it so. The day of unalloyed welcome to all peoples, the day of indiscriminate acceptance of all races, has definitely ended." So spoke Washington Senator Albert Johnson in 1924, just after Congress severely limited immigration with passage of the National Origins Act, which Johnson had sponsored. Thereafter immigration, which had forcefully shaped American society since its beginning, ebbed for several decades as the restrictive law combined with the Great Depression and World War II to discourage potential newcomers. In fact, during the worst years of the depression, more people left than migrated to the United States. Yet the immigration question had not been settled once and for all. By the 1980s, large numbers of immigrants once more entered the United States, reigniting old debates about whether Americans should share their political freedoms and economic opportunities with people from other lands.

What reopened the door to immigration after World War II? Economic considerations always loomed large in prompting migration to the United States and in determining how welcome immigrants would be: The twenty-five-year economic boom that followed World War II exerted a positive force on both ends. In fact, until 1964 the U.S. government actively encouraged the temporary migration of Mexicans by continuing the so-called *bracero* program that was begun during World War II to fill a shortage of agricultural workers. Hundreds of thousands of Mexicans established social networks in the United States and grew accustomed to crossing the border for jobs, even when the jobs were backbreaking and low-paying by U.S. standards. When the *bracero* program ended, many Mexicans continued to come north for work whether they could obtain legal authorization or not.

In addition to a prosperous economy, the United States also manifested a growing tolerance toward people of different races and ethnic groups in the decades following World War II. Like the key civil rights laws passed around the same time, the Immigration Act of 1965 reflected a more broad-minded climate of opinion based on the belief that people should be treated as human beings rather than as members of a particular group. The new immigration law ended the national quotas that were so insulting to non-Western European groups. It made possible a tremendous rise in the volume of immigration and facilitated a huge increase in newcomers from Asia and Latin America.

The new immigration law set an annual ceiling of 270,000, but the actual volume was much higher. Besides those who came illegally, hundreds of thousands of people fell into special categories that gained them legal admission above and beyond the ceiling. In 1986, for example, the United States admitted 335,000 immigrants over and above those entering under the ceiling: About two-thirds of these were children, spouses, or parents of U.S. citizens, and the rest were refugees and asylum seekers. Migration chains were thus established by which, once newcomers became citizens, their sisters, brothers, and adult children received special preference, while even closer relatives gained entry without regard to the limit.

The new waves of immigration also grew directly from U.S. foreign policy after World War II. The cold war spread U.S. military and other personnel throughout the world, enabling foreigners to learn about the United States and make personal contacts with Americans. Once the cold war identified communism as an unmitigated evil, the United States could hardly refuse asylum to its enemy's victims. In the twenty-five years following Fidel Castro's revolution, for example, more than 800,000 Cubans fled to the United States. The Vietnam War and its aftermath brought more than 600,000 Vietnamese, Laotians, and Cambodians to the United States in the decade following 1974.

Not all refugees entered the United States so easily, for American refugee policy bore a distinct anti-Communist bias. Haitians, Salvadorans, and others fleeing right-wing dictatorships were frequently turned back or, having reached the United States, were denied asylum and deported. "Why let Poles stay but not Salvadorans?" demanded one advocate for these refugees, pointing out the more favorable treatment given to immigrants from Communist countries.

Even though U.S. policy failed to accommodate all who wanted to immigrate, by the 1980s immigration was once more a major force in American society. During that decade the six million legal and an estimated two million undocumented immigrants

CUBAN REFUGEES
These Cubans are being towed by the U.S. Coast Guard into port at Miami, Florida. Their desire for
the expected economic opportunity and political freedom of the United States is evinced in their willing-
ness to flee Cuba on a crowded, makeshift vessel. Some "boat people" drowned in these risky ventures.
John Kral/*Miami Herald.*

accounted for more than one-third of total population growth. Seventy-five percent of the immigrants settled in just seven states, with California, New York, Texas, and Florida receiving the most. After the 1990 census, California won five additional seats in the House of Representatives solely on the basis of immigrant additions to the population. A 1983 *Time* magazine article called Los Angeles "the new Ellis Island" because of its large Asian and Hispanic populations. A decade later, one-third of Los Angeles area residents were foreign-born.

The higher volume of immigration, its third world sources, and the economy's recession combined to increase nativist sentiment in the 1980s. Increasingly, Americans saw immigrants as taking jobs from the native-born and acting as a drain on schools, health care, police, and other services. In the 1990s, anti-immigrant sentiment grew especially strong in California, then reeling from an economic slump owing to the downsizing of defense produc-

tion. That state took in more than one-third of the nation's immigrants in the 1980s and an estimated one-half of the undocumented ones.

Like people in the rest of the nation, Californians focused hostility on immigrants who entered without legal documentation, a phenomenon that the 1986 law penalizing employers of such people had not significantly curtailed. Some states, including California, Florida, and New Jersey, filed lawsuits charging the federal government with failure to stop the flow of illegal immigration and suing for the costs it added to state budgets.

Economic and political crises elsewhere and the continuing appeal of the U.S. meant that high levels of immigration—legal and illegal—persisted into the 1990s, as did the debate about how open U.S. policy should be. Even as anti-immigrant sentiment increased, however, the United States remained—as sociologist Nathan Glazer put it—a "permanently unfinished country."

THE FIRST WOMAN SECRETARY OF STATE
Madeleine K. Albright is sworn in as Secretary of State by Vice President Albert Gore, as her
three daughters and President Bill Clinton look on. Formerly a professor of international affairs
at Georgetown University, Albright served in the first Clinton cabinet as U.S. representative to
the United Nations.
Greg Gibson/Wide World.

states of Serbia, Croatia, and Bosnia and then fell into a brutal civil war. The Serbs' ruthless aggression against the Bosnian Muslims horrified much of the world, and people remembered how an event in Sarajevo had sparked World War I. For several years, the United States joined with its European allies in NATO and the United Nations in peace efforts, but both the United States and the European nations studiously avoided direct intervention.

As the terror, rape, and torture in Bosnia worsened, American leaders worried about the image of the most powerful nation unwilling to use its power to stop the violence. In November 1995, the United States brought the leaders of Serbia, Croatia, and Bosnia to Dayton, Ohio, where they hammered out a peace treaty. President Clinton then agreed to send twenty thousand American troops to Bosnia as part

of a NATO peacekeeping mission. The peace held through 1996, but Anthony Lake, the president's national security adviser, said, "We won't know for some years" whether the mission would succeed.

Promoting stability in the Middle East continued to be a goal of American foreign policy. Although the Clinton administration played a far less critical role than President Jimmy Carter had in the Egypt-Israel accord of 1979, U.S. officials encouraged negotiations that led to two dramatic breakthroughs. In September 1993, with President Clinton presiding over a ceremony on the White House lawn, Yasir Arafat, head of the Palestine Liberation Organization, and Yitzhak Rabin, Israeli prime minister, took a momentous step toward peace in the Middle East. They signed a declaration recognizing each other's existence for the first time and providing for Israeli withdrawal and self-government for Palestinians in the Gaza Strip and Jericho. Less than a year later, in July 1994, Clinton presided over another turning point as King Hussein of Jordan and Prime Minister Rabin of Israel signed a declaration of peace. Progress toward peace, however, suffered a severe setback when a right-wing Israeli murdered Rabin in November 1995, and a government came to power less trusting of Arab willingness to respect Israel's security.

"The post-cold war world is decidedly not postnuclear," said Clinton's first secretary of defense. Perhaps the biggest threat to American security lay in the proliferation of governments in possession of nuclear weapons.

"The post-cold war world is decidedly not postnuclear," said Clinton's first secretary of defense, Les Aspin. Perhaps the biggest threat to American security lay in the proliferation of governments in possession of nuclear weapons. The breakdown of the Soviet Union meant that four countries with nuclear weapons now stood in place of one—Russia, Ukraine, Belarus, and Kazakhstan—in addition to Britain, France, China, India, Israel, Pakistan, and possibly North Korea, still under a Communist dictatorship. Yet in 1996, the world took a small step away from the nuclear brink when the leaders of the nuclear powers signed a comprehensive test ban treaty at United Nations headquarters. Using the same pen with which John F. Kennedy had signed the limited test ban treaty in 1963, Clinton insisted, "Our children deserve to walk the earth in safety." He pledged continuing support for the UN "because our world is more interdependent than ever before."

Conclusion: Approaching the Twenty-First Century

With the largest economy in the world, the United States remained deeply embedded in the global economy as products and people crossed international borders with ever greater frequency. U.S. of-

ficials monitored developments across the globe and tried through diplomacy to promote order and democracy, expand economic opportunities for American business, reduce population growth, and curtail environmental destruction. But, in contrast to their counterparts at the end of the nineteenth century, Americans displayed little taste for foreign adventures as the twentieth century drew to a close. Nor did a majority want to see their tax dollars used for international purposes.

Instead, most Americans saw the main challenge as coming from within, and that challenge involved issues of economic justice, violence, and diversity that had engaged the nation for much of its history. A declining standard of living for a large portion of the middle class, a growing chasm between the educated and the unskilled, a rising income gap between the rich and the poor, and a poverty rate of 20 percent among children threatened the American promise of opportunity and security. Moreover, the persistent poverty in urban ghettos contributed to a stream of violence that undermined Americans' physical security. As the United States became even more heterogeneous, American identity and the extent to which the American promise should extend to diverse groups such as new immigrants, racial minorities, and homosexuals remained contested ground. (See Historical Question, page 1266.)

How to respond to the challenges of economic justice, physical security, and diversity often involved the question of the appropriate role of government. With a population derived to a great extent from people fleeing overweening governments, the United States had for more than two centuries experienced debates over what the government could or should do about the nation's aspirations and troubles and what was best left to private enterprise, churches, families, and other voluntary institutions. Far more than other democracies, the United States had taken the path of private rather than public obligation, individual rather than collective solutions. In the twentieth century especially, Americans had entrusted the federal government with significantly greater powers and responsibilities. But as the century wound down, the debate grew particularly intense again as Americans and their representatives struggled over both how to define and how to approach fulfillment of the American promise for the next century.

CHRONOLOGY

1992 Bill Clinton elected forty-second president of the United States.

1993 Janet Reno appointed first female attorney general in U.S. history.

Ruth Bader Ginsburg appointed second woman to U.S. Supreme Court.

Clinton announces "don't ask, don't tell" policy for gays in military.

Israeli Prime Minister Yitzhak Rabin and PLO leader Yasir Arafat sign peace accords.

Gun control and anticrime bills passed.

Eighteen U.S. soldiers killed on humanitarian mission in Somalia.

Congress approves North American Free Trade Agreement (NAFTA).

Clinton signs Family and Medical Leave Act, enabling many workers to take time off for childbirth, adoption, or family medical emergencies.

1994 U.S. troops oversee peaceful return of Haitian President Aristide to power.

Senate ratifies General Agreement on Tariffs and Trade (GATT).

Republicans recapture both House and Senate in congressional elections.

Representative Newt Gingrich declares 1994 elections a mandate for Republicans' conservative "contract with America."

1995 Bomb destroys federal building in Oklahoma City on April 19, claiming 169 lives; two militia members arrested as prime suspects.

U.S. leaders broker peace accords among Serbia, Croatia, and Bosnia in Dayton, Ohio, temporarily ending civil war in former Yugoslavia.

1996 Clinton signs Personal Responsibility and Work Opportunity Reconciliation Act, ending the federal welfare program begun in 1930s.

Clinton reelected president.

Leaders of nuclear powers sign comprehensive test ban treaty at United Nations.

BIBLIOGRAPHY

Dan Balz and Ronald Brownstein, *Storming the Gates: Protest Politics and the Republican Revival*, 1996.

Jennifer L. Hochschild, *Facing Up to the American Dream: Race, Class, and the Soul of the Nation*, 1995.

Haynes Johnson and David S. Broder, *The System: The American Way of Politics at the Breaking Point*, 1996.

Jacob S. Hacker, *The Road to Nowhere: The Genesis of President's Clinton's Plan for Health Security*, 1997.

David Maraniss, *First in His Class: A Biography of Bill Clinton*, 1995.

David Mixner, *Stranger among Friends*, 1996.

Roger Morris, *Partners in Power: The Clintons and Their America*, 1996.

Kevin Phillips, *Boiling Point: Democrats, Republicans and the Decline of Middle-Class Prosperity*, 1993.

Gerald Posner, *Citizen Perot: His Life and Times*, 1996.

Ralph Reed, *Active Faith: How Christians Are Changing the Soul of American Politics*, 1996.

Robert J. Samuelson, *The American Dream in the Age of Entitlement, 1945–1995*, 1996.

Martin Walker, *The President We Deserve: Bill Clinton, His Rise, Falls, and Comebacks*, 1996.

APPENDIX I. DOCUMENTS

THE DECLARATION OF INDEPENDENCE

In Congress, July 4, 1776,

THE UNANIMOUS DECLARATION OF THE
THIRTEEN UNITED STATES OF AMERICA

When in the course of human events, it becomes necessary for one people to dissolve the political bands which have connected them with another, and to assume, among the powers of the earth, the separate and equal station to which the laws of nature and of nature's God entitle them, a decent respect to the opinions of mankind requires that they should declare the causes which impel them to the separation.

We hold these truths to be self-evident, that all men are created equal; that they are endowed by their Creator with certain unalienable rights; that among these, are life, liberty, and the pursuit of happiness. That, to secure these rights, governments are instituted among men, deriving their just powers from the consent of the governed; that, whenever any form of government becomes destructive of these ends, it is the right of the people to alter or to abolish it, and to institute a new government, laying its foundation on such principles, and organizing its powers in such form, as to them shall seem most likely to effect their safety and happiness. Prudence, indeed, will dictate that governments long established, should not be changed for light and transient causes; and, accordingly, all experience hath shown, that mankind are more disposed to suffer, while evils are sufferable, than to right themselves by abolishing the forms to which they are accustomed. But, when a long train of abuses and usurpations, pursuing invariably the same object, evinces a design to reduce them under absolute despotism, it is their right, it is their duty, to throw off such government and to provide new guards for their future security. Such has been the patient sufferance of these colonies, and such is now the necessity which constrains them to alter their former systems of government. The history of the present King of Great Britain is a history of repeated injuries and usurpations, all having, in direct object, the estab-

lishment of an absolute tyranny over these States. To prove this, let facts be submitted to a candid world:

He has refused his assent to laws the most wholesome and necessary for the public good.

He has forbidden his governors to pass laws of immediate and pressing importance, unless suspended in their operation till his assent should be obtained; and, when so suspended, he has utterly neglected to attend to them.

He has refused to pass other laws for the accommodation of large districts of people, unless those people would relinquish the right of representation in the legislature; a right inestimable to them, and formidable to tyrants only.

He has called together legislative bodies at places unusual, uncomfortable, and distant from the depository of their public records, for the sole purpose of fatiguing them into compliance with his measures.

He has dissolved representative houses repeatedly for opposing, with manly firmness, his invasions on the rights of the people.

He has refused, for a long time after such dissolutions, to cause others to be elected; whereby the legislative powers, incapable of annihilation, have returned to the people at large for their exercise; the state remaining in the mean-time exposed to all the danger of invasion from without, and convulsions within.

He has endeavoured to prevent the population of these States; for that purpose, obstructing the laws for naturalization of foreigners, refusing to pass others to encourage their migration hither, and raising the conditions of new appropriations of lands.

He has obstructed the administration of justice, by refusing his assent to laws for establishing judiciary powers.

He has made judges dependent on his will alone, for the tenure of their offices, and the amount and payment of their salaries.

He has erected a multitude of new offices, and sent hither swarms of officers to harass our people, and eat out their substance.

He has kept among us, in times of peace, standing armies, without the consent of our legislature.

He has affected to render the military independent of, and superior to, the civil power.

He has combined, with others, to subject us to a jurisdiction foreign to our Constitution, and unacknowledged by our laws; giving his assent to their acts of pretended legislation:

For quartering large bodies of armed troops among us:

For protecting them by a mock trial, from punishment, for any murders which they should commit on the inhabitants of these States:

For cutting off our trade with all parts of the world:

For imposing taxes on us without our consent:

For depriving us, in many cases, of the benefit of trial by jury:

For transporting us beyond seas to be tried for pretended offences:

For abolishing the free system of English laws in a neighboring province, establishing therein an arbitrary government, and enlarging its boundaries, so as to render it at once an example and fit instrument for introducing the same absolute rule into these colonies:

For taking away our charters, abolishing our most valuable laws, and altering, fundamentally, the powers of our governments:

For suspending our own legislatures, and declaring themselves invested with power to legislate for us in all cases whatsoever.

He has abdicated government here, by declaring us out of his protection, and waging war against us.

He has plundered our seas, ravaged our coasts, burnt our towns, and destroyed the lives of our people.

He is, at this time, transporting large armies of foreign mercenaries to complete the works of death, desolation, and tyranny, already begun, with circumstances of cruelty and perfidy scarcely paralleled in the most barbarous ages, and totally unworthy the head of a civilized nation.

He has constrained our fellow citizens, taken captive on the high seas, to bear arms against their country, to become the executioners of their friends, and brethren, or to fall themselves by their hands.

He has excited domestic insurrections amongst us, and has endeavored to bring on the inhabitants of our frontiers, the merciless Indian savages, whose known rule of warfare is an undistinguished destruction of all ages, sexes, and conditions.

In every stage of these oppressions, we have petitioned for redress; in the most humble terms; our repeated petitions have been answered only by repeated injury. A prince, whose character is thus marked by every act which may define a tyrant, is unfit to be the ruler of a free people.

Nor have we been wanting in attention to our British brethren. We have warned them, from time to time, of attempts made by their legislature to extend an unwarrantable jurisdiction over us. We have reminded them of the circumstances of our emigration and settlement here. We have appealed to their native justice and magnanimity, and we have conjured them, by the ties of our common kindred, to disavow these usurpations, which would inevitably interrupt our connections and correspondence. They, too, have been deaf to the voice of justice and consanguinity. We must, therefore, acquiesce in the necessity which denounces our separation, and hold them as we hold the rest of mankind, enemies in war, in peace, friends.

We, therefore, the representatives of the United States of America, in general Congress assembled, appealing to the Supreme Judge of the world for the rectitude of our intentions, do, in the name, and by authority of the good people of these colonies, solemnly publish and declare, that these united colonies are, and of right ought to be, free and independent states: that they are absolved from all allegiance to the British Crown, and that all political connection between them and the state of Great Britain is, and ought to be, totally dissolved; and that, as free and independent states, they have full power to levy war, conclude peace, contract alliances, establish commerce, and to do all other acts and things which independent states may of right do. And, for the support of this declaration, with a firm reliance on the protection of Divine Providence, we mutually pledge to each other our lives, our fortunes, and our sacred honor.

The foregoing Declaration was, by order of Congress, engrossed, and signed by the following members:

JOHN HANCOCK

New Hampshire
Josiah Bartlett
William Whipple
Matthew Thornton

Massachusetts Bay
Samuel Adams
John Adams
Robert Treat Paine
Elbridge Gerry

New York
William Floyd
Phillip Livingston
Francis Lewis
Lewis Morris

New Jersey
Richard Stockton
John Witherspoon
Francis Hopkinson
John Hart
Abraham Clark

Rhode Island
Stephen Hopkins
William Ellery

Connecticut
Roger Sherman
Samuel Huntington
William Williams
Oliver Wolcott

Delaware
Caesar Rodney
George Read
Thomas M'Kean

Pennsylvania
Robert Morris
Benjamin Rush
Benjamin Franklin
John Morton
George Clymer
James Smith
George Taylor
James Wilson
George Ross

North Carolina
William Hooper
Joseph Hewes
John Penn

Maryland
Samuel Chase
William Paca
Thomas Stone
Charles Carroll,
    of Carrollton

Virginia
George Wythe
Richard Henry Lee
Thomas Jefferson
Benjamin Harrison
Thomas Nelson, Jr.
Francis Lightfoot Lee
Carter Braxton

South Carolina
Edward Rutledge
Thomas Heyward, Jr.
Thomas Lynch, Jr.
Arthur Middleton

Georgia
Button Gwinnett
Lyman Hall
George Walton

Resolved, That copies of the Declaration be sent to the several assemblies, conventions, and committees, or councils of safety, and to the several commanding officers of the continental troops; that it be proclaimed in each of the United States, at the head of the army.

THE CONSTITUTION OF THE UNITED STATES*

Preamble

We the people of the United States, in order to form a more perfect union, establish justice, insure domestic tranquility, provide for the common defense, promote the general welfare, and secure the blessings of liberty to ourselves and our posterity, do ordain and establish this Constitution for the United States of America.

Article I

Section 1 All legislative powers herein granted shall be vested in a Congress of the United States, which shall consist of a Senate and a House of Representatives.

Section 2 The House of Representatives shall be composed of members chosen every second year by the people of the several States, and the electors in each State shall have the qualifications requisite for electors of the most numerous branch of the State Legislature.

No person shall be a Representative who shall not have attained to the age of twenty-five years, and been seven years a citizen of the United States, and who shall not, when elected, be an inhabitant of that State in which he shall be chosen.

Representatives and direct taxes shall be apportioned among the several States which may be included within this Union, according to their respective numbers, *which shall be determined by adding to the whole number of free persons, including those bound to service for a term of years and excluding Indians not taxed, three-fifths of all other persons.* The actual enumeration shall be made within three years after the first meeting of the Congress of the United States, and within every subsequent term of ten years, in such manner as they shall by law direct. The number of Representatives shall not exceed one for every thirty thousand, but each State shall have at least one Representative; *and until such enumeration shall be made, the State of New Hampshire shall be entitled to choose three, Massachusetts eight, Rhode Island and Providence Plantations one, Connecticut five, New York six, New Jersey four, Pennsylvania eight, Delaware one, Maryland six, Virginia ten, North Carolina five, South Carolina five, and Georgia three.*

When vacancies happen in the representation from any State, the Executive authority thereof shall issue writs of election to fill such vacancies.

The House of Representatives shall choose their Speaker and other officers; and shall have the sole power of impeachment.

Section 3 The Senate of the United States shall be composed of two Senators from each State, *chosen by the legislature thereof,* for six years; and each Senator shall have one vote.

Immediately after they shall be assembled in consequence of the first election, they shall be divided as equally as may be into three classes. The seats of the Senators of the first class shall be vacated at the expiration of the second year, of the second class at the expiration of the fourth year, and of the third class at the expiration of the sixth year, so that one-third may be chosen every second year; *and if vacancies happen by resignation or otherwise, during the recess of the legislature of any State, the Executive thereof may make temporary appointments until the next meeting of the legislature, which shall then fill such vacancies.*

No person shall be a Senator who shall not have attained to the age of thirty years, and been nine years a citizen of the United States, and who shall not, when elected, be an inhabitant of that State for which he shall be chosen.

The Vice-President of the United States shall be President of the Senate, but shall have no vote, unless they be equally divided.

The Senate shall choose their other officers, and also a President *pro tempore*, in the absence of the Vice-President, or when he shall exercise the office of President of the United States.

The Senate shall have the sole power to try all impeachments. When sitting for that purpose, they shall be on oath or affirmation. When the President of the United States is tried, the Chief Justice shall preside: and no person shall be convicted without the concurrence of two-thirds of the members present.

Judgment in cases of impeachment shall not extend further than to removal from the office, and disqualification to hold and enjoy any office of honor, trust or profit under the United States: but the party convicted shall nevertheless be liable and subject to indictment, trial, judgment and punishment, according to law.

Section 4 The times, places and manner of holding elections for Senators and Representatives shall be prescribed in each State by the legislature thereof; but the Congress may at any time by law make or alter such regulations, except as to the places of choosing Senators.

---

*Passages no longer in effect are in italic type.

The Congress shall assemble at least once in every year, and such meeting *shall be on the first Monday in December, unless they shall by law appoint a different day.*

Section 5 Each house shall be the judge of the elections, returns and qualifications of its own members, and a majority of each shall constitute a quorum to do business; but a smaller number may adjourn from day to day, and may be authorized to compel the attendance of absent members, in such manner, and under such penalties, as each house may provide.

Each house may determine the rules of its proceedings, punish its members for disorderly behavior, and with the concurrence of two-thirds, expel a member.

Each house shall keep a journal of its proceedings, and from time to time publish the same, excepting such parts as may in their judgment require secrecy; and the yeas and nays of the members of either house on any question shall, at the desire of one-fifth of those present, be entered on the journal.

Neither house, during the session of Congress, shall, without the consent of the other, adjourn for more than three days, nor to any other place than that in which the two houses shall be sitting.

Section 6 The Senators and Representatives shall receive a compensation for their services, to be ascertained by law and paid out of the treasury of the United States. They shall in all cases except treason, felony and breach of the peace, be privileged from arrest during their attendance at the session of their respective houses, and in going to and returning from the same; and for any speech or debate in either house, they shall not be questioned in any other place.

No Senator or Representative shall, during the time for which he was elected, be appointed to any civil office under the authority of the United States, which shall have been created, or the emoluments whereof shall have been increased, during such time; and no person holding any office under the United States shall be a member of either house during his continuance in office.

Section 7 All bills for raising revenue shall originate in the House of Representatives; but the Senate may propose or concur with amendments as on other bills.

Every bill which shall have passed the House of Representatives and the Senate, shall, before it become a law, be presented to the President of the United States; if he approve he shall sign it, but if not he shall return it with objections to that house in which it shall have originated, who shall enter the objections at large on their journal, and proceed to reconsider it. If after such reconsideration two-thirds of that house shall agree to pass the bill, it shall be sent, together with the objections, to the other house, by which it shall likewise be reconsidered, and, if approved by two-thirds of that house, it shall become a law. But in all such cases the votes of both houses shall be determined by yeas and nays, and the names of the persons voting for and against the bill shall be entered on the journal of each house respectively. If any bill shall not be returned by the President within ten days (Sundays excepted) after it shall have been presented to him, the same shall be a law, in like manner as if he had signed it, unless the Congress by their adjournment prevent its return, in which case it shall not be a law.

Every order, resolution, or vote to which the concurrence of the Senate and House of Representatives may be necessary (except on a question of adjournment) shall be presented to the President of the United States; and before the same shall take effect, shall be approved by him, or being disapproved by him, shall be repassed by two-thirds of the Senate and House of Representatives, according to the rules and limitations prescribed in the case of a bill.

Section 8 The Congress shall have power

To lay and collect taxes, duties, imposts, and excises, to pay the debts and provide for the common defense and general welfare of the United States; but all duties, imposts and excises shall be uniform throughout the United States;

To borrow money on the credit of the United States;

To regulate commerce with foreign nations, and among the several States, and with the Indian tribes;

To establish an uniform rule of naturalization, and uniform laws on the subject of bankruptcies throughout the United States;

To coin money, regulate the value thereof, and of foreign coin, and fix the standard of weights and measures;

To provide for the punishment of counterfeiting the securities and current coin of the United States;

To establish post offices and post roads;

To promote the progress of science and useful arts by securing for limited times to authors and inventors the exclusive right to their respective writings and discoveries;

To constitute tribunals inferior to the Supreme Court;

To define and punish piracies and felonies committed on the high seas and offences against the law of nations;

To declare war, grant letters of marque and reprisal, and make rules concerning captures on land and water;

To raise and support armies, but no appropriation of money to that use shall be for a longer term than two years;

To provide and maintain a navy;

To make rules for the government and regulation of the land and naval forces;

To provide for calling forth the militia to execute the laws of the Union, suppress insurrections and repel invasions;

To provide for organizing, arming, and disciplining the militia, and for governing such part of them as may be employed in the service of the United States, reserving to the States respectively the appointment of the officers, and the authority of training the militia according to the discipline prescribed by Congress;

To exercise exclusive legislation in all cases whatsoever, over such district (not exceeding ten miles square) as may, by cession of particular States, and the acceptance of Congress, become the seat of the government of the United States, and to exercise like authority over all places purchased by the consent of the legislature of the State, in which the same shall be, for erection of forts, magazines, arsenals, dock-yards, and other needful buildings;—and

To make all laws which shall be necessary and proper for carrying into execution the foregoing powers, and all other powers vested by this Constitution in the government of the United States, or in any department or officer thereof.

Section 9 *The migration or importation of such persons as any of the States now existing shall think proper to admit shall not be prohibited by the Congress prior to the year one thousand eight hundred and eight; but a tax or duty may be imposed on such importation, not exceeding ten dollars for each person.*

The privilege of the writ of habeas corpus shall not be suspended, unless when in cases of rebellion or invasion the public safety may require it.

No bill of attainder or ex post facto law shall be passed.

No capitation, or other direct, tax shall be laid, unless in proportion to the census or enumeration herein before directed to be taken.

No tax or duty shall be laid on articles exported from any State.

No preference shall be given by any regulation of commerce or revenue to the ports of one State over those of another; nor shall vessels bound to, or from, one State be obliged to enter, clear, or pay duties in another.

No money shall be drawn from the treasury, but in consequence of appropriations made by law; and a regular statement and account of the receipts and expenditures of all public money shall be published from time to time.

No title of nobility shall be granted by the United States: and no person holding any office of profit or trust under them, shall, without the consent of the Congress, accept of any present, emolument, office, or title, of any kind whatever, from any king, prince, or foreign state.

Section 10 No State shall enter into any treaty, alliance, or confederation; grant letters of marque and reprisal; coin money; emit bills of credit; make anything but gold and silver coin a tender in payment of debts; pass any bill of attainder, ex post facto law, or law impairing the obligation of contracts, or grant any title of nobility.

No State shall, without the consent of Congress, lay any imposts or duties on imports or exports, except what may be absolutely necessary for executing its inspection laws: and the net produce of all duties and imposts, laid by any State on imports or exports, shall be for the use of the treasury of the United States; and all such laws shall be subject to the revision and control of the Congress.

No State shall, without the consent of Congress, lay any duty of tonnage, keep troops, or ships of war in time of peace, enter into any agreement or compact with another State, or with a foreign power, or engage in war, unless actually invaded, or in such imminent danger as will not admit of delay.

Article II

Section 1 The executive power shall be vested in a President of the United States of America. He shall hold his office during the term of four years, and, together with the Vice-President, chosen for the same term, be elected as follows:

Each State shall appoint, in such manner as the legislature thereof may direct, a number of electors, equal to the whole number of Senators and Representatives to which the State may be entitled in the Congress; but no Senator or Representative, or person holding an office of trust or profit under the United States, shall be appointed an elector.

The electors shall meet in their respective States, and vote by ballot for two persons, of whom one at least shall not be an inhabitant of the same State with themselves. And they shall make a list of all the persons voted for, and of the number of votes for each; which list they shall sign and certify, and transmit sealed to the seat of government of the United States, directed to the President of the Senate. The President of the Senate shall, in the presence of the Senate and House of Representatives, open all the certificates, and the votes shall then be counted. The person having the greatest number of votes shall be the President, if such number be a majority of the whole number of electors appointed; and if there be more than one who have such majority, and have an equal number of votes, then the House of Representatives shall immediately choose by ballot one of them for President; and if no person have a majority, then from the five highest on the list said house shall in like manner choose the President. But in choosing the President the votes shall be taken by States, the representation from each State having one vote; a quorum for this purpose shall consist of a member or members from two-thirds of the States, and a majority of all the States shall be necessary to a choice. In every case, after the choice of the President, the person having the greatest number of votes of the electors shall be the Vice-President. But if there should remain two or more who have equal votes, the Senate shall choose from them by ballot the Vice-President.

The Congress may determine the time of choosing the electors, and the day on which they shall give their votes; which day shall be the same throughout the United States.

No person except a natural-born citizen, *or a citizen of the United States at the time of the adoption of this Constitution*, shall be eligible to the office of President; neither shall any person be eligible to that office who shall not have attained to the age of thirty-five years, and been fourteen years a resident within the United States.

In cases of the removal of the President from office or of his death, resignation, or inability to discharge the powers and duties of the said office, the same shall devolve on the Vice-President, and the Congress may by law provide for the case of removal, death, resignation, or inability, both of the President and Vice-President, declaring what officer shall then act as President, and such officer shall act accordingly, until the disability be removed, or a President shall be elected.

The President shall, at stated times, receive for his services a compensation, which shall neither be increased nor diminished during the period for which he shall have been elected, and he shall not receive within that period any other emolument from the United States, or any of them.

Before he enter on the execution of his office, he shall take the following oath or affirmation:—"I do solemnly swear (or affirm) that I will faithfully execute the office of the President of the United States, and will to the best of my ability preserve, protect and defend the Constitution of the United States."

Section 2   The President shall be commander in chief of the army and navy of the United States, and of the militia of the several States, when called into the actual service of the United States; he may require the opinion, in writing, of the principal officer in each of the executive departments, upon any subject relating to the duties of their respective offices, and he shall have power to grant reprieves and pardons for offenses against the United States, except in cases of impeachment.

He shall have power, by and with the advice and consent of the Senate, to make treaties, provided two-thirds of the Senators present concur; and he shall nominate, and by and with the advice and consent of the Senate, shall appoint ambassadors, other public ministers and consuls, judges of the Supreme Court, and all other officers of the United States, whose appointments are not herein otherwise provided for, and which shall be established by law: but Congress may by law vest the appointment of such inferior officers, as they think proper, in the President alone, in the courts of law, or in the heads of departments.

The President shall have power to fill up all vacancies that may happen during the recess of the Senate, by granting commissions which shall expire at the end of their next session.

Section 3   He shall from time to time give to the Congress information of the state of the Union, and recommend to their consideration such measures as he shall judge necessary and expedient; he may, on extraordinary occasions, convene both houses, or either of them, and in case of disagreement between them, with respect to the time of adjournment, he may adjourn them to such time as he shall think proper; he shall receive ambassadors and other public ministers; he shall take care that the laws be faithfully executed, and shall commission all the officers of the United States.

Section 4   The President, Vice-President and all civil officers of the United States shall be removed from office on impeachment for, and on conviction of, treason, bribery, or other high crimes and misdemeanors.

Article III

Section 1   The judicial power of the United States shall be vested in one Supreme Court, and in such inferior courts as the Congress may from time to time ordain and establish. The judges, both of the Supreme and inferior courts, shall hold their offices during good behavior, and shall, at stated times, receive for their services a compensation which shall not be diminished during their continuance in office.

Section 2   The judicial power shall extend to all cases, in law and equity, arising under this Constitution, the laws of the United States, and treaties made, or which shall be made, under their authority;—to all cases affecting ambassadors, other public ministers and consuls;—to all cases of admiralty and maritime jurisdiction;—to controversies to which the United States shall be a party;—to controversies between two or more States;—*between a State and citizens of another*

State;—between citizens of different States;—between citizens of the same State claiming lands under grants of different States, and between a State, or the citizens thereof, and foreign states, citizens or subjects.

In all cases affecting ambassadors, other public ministers and consuls, and those in which a State shall be party, the Supreme Court shall have original jurisdiction. In all the other cases before mentioned, the Supreme Court shall have appellate jurisdiction, both as to law and fact, with such exceptions, and under such regulations, as the Congress shall make.

The trial of all crimes, except in cases of impeachment, shall be by jury; and such trial shall be held in the State where said crimes shall have been committed; but when not committed within any State, the trial shall be at such place or places as the Congress may by Law have directed.

Section 3   Treason against the United States shall consist only in levying war against them, or in adhering to their enemies, giving them aid and comfort. No person shall be convicted of treason unless on the testimony of two witnesses to the same overt act, or on confession in open court.

The Congress shall have power to declare the punishment of treason, but no attainder of treason shall work corruption of blood, or forfeiture except during the life of the person attainted.

Article IV

Section 1   Full faith and credit shall be given in each State to the public acts, records, and judicial proceedings of every other State. And the Congress may by general laws prescribe the manner in which such acts, records, and proceedings shall be proved, and the effect thereof.

Section 2   The citizens of each State shall be entitled to all privileges and immunities of citizens in the several States.

A person charged in any State with treason, felony, or other crime, who shall flee from justice, and be found in another State, shall on demand of the executive authority of the State from which he fled, be delivered up, to be removed to the State having jurisdiction of the crime.

No Person held to service or labor in one State, under the laws thereof, escaping into another, shall, in consequence of any law or regulation therein, be discharged from such service or labor, but shall be delivered up on claim of the party to whom such service or labor may be due.

Section 3   New States may be admitted by the Congress into this Union; but no new State shall be formed or erected within the jurisdiction of any other State; nor any State be formed by the junction of two or more States, or parts of States, without the consent of the legislatures of the States concerned as well as of the Congress.

The Congress shall have power to dispose of and make all needful rules and regulations respecting the territory or other property belonging to the United States; and nothing in this Constitution shall be so construed as to prejudice any claims of the United States, or of any particular State.

Section 4   The United States shall guarantee to every State in this Union a republican form of government, and shall protect each of them against invasion; and on application of the legislature, or of the executive (when the legislature cannot be convened), against domestic violence.

Article V

The Congress, whenever two-thirds of both houses shall deem it necessary, shall propose amendments to this Constitution, or, on the application of the legislatures of two-thirds of the several States, shall call a convention for proposing amendments, which, in either case, shall be valid to all intents and purposes, as part of this Constitution, when ratified by the legislatures of three-fourths of the several States, or by conventions in three-fourths thereof, as the one or the other mode of ratification may be proposed by the Congress; provided *that no amendments which may be made prior to the year one thousand eight hundred and eight shall in any manner affect the first and fourth clauses in the ninth section of the first article*; and that no State, without its consent, shall be deprived of its equal suffrage in the Senate.

Article VI

All debts contracted and engagements entered into, before the adoption of this Constitution, shall be as valid against the United States under this Constitution, as under the Confederation.

This Constitution, and the laws of the United States which shall be made in pursuance thereof; and all treaties made, or which shall be made, under the authority of the United States, shall be the supreme law of the land; and the judges in every State shall be bound thereby, anything in the Constitution or laws of any State to the contrary notwithstanding.

The Senators and Representatives before mentioned, and the members of the several State legislatures, and all executive and judicial officers, both of the United States and of the several States, shall be bound by oath or affirmation to support this Constitution; but no religious test shall ever be required as a qualification to any office or public trust under the United States.

Article VII

The ratification of the conventions of nine States shall be sufficient for the establishment of this Constitution between the States so ratifying the same.

Done in convention by the unanimous consent of the States present, the seventeenth day of September in the year of our Lord one thousand seven hundred and eighty-seven and of the Independence of the United States of America the twelfth. In witness whereof we have hereunto subscribed our names.

GEORGE WASHINGTON
PRESIDENT AND DEPUTY FROM VIRGINIA

New Hampshire
John Langdon
Nicholas Gilman

Massachusetts
Nathaniel Gorham
Rufus King

Connecticut
William Samuel
    Johnson
Roger Sherman

New York
Alexander Hamilton

New Jersey
William Livingston
David Brearley
William Paterson
Jonathan Dayton

Pennsylvania
Benjamin Franklin
Thomas Mifflin
Robert Morris
George Clymer
Thomas FitzSimons
Jared Ingersoll
James Wilson
Gouverneur Morris

Delaware
George Read
Gunning Bedford, Jr.
John Dickinson
Richard Bassett
Jacob Broom

Maryland
James McHenry
Daniel of
    St. Thomas Jenifer
Daniel Carroll

Virginia
John Blair
James Madison, Jr.

North Carolina
William Blount
Richard Dobbs
    Spaight
Hugh Williamson

South Carolina
John Rutledge
Charles Cotesworth
    Pinckney
Charles Pinckney
Pierce Butler

Georgia
William Few
Abraham Baldwin

AMENDMENTS TO THE CONSTITUTION WITH ANNOTATIONS
(Including the six unratified amendments)

In their effort to gain Antifederalists' support for the Constitution, Federalists frequently pointed to the inclusion of Article 5, which provides an orderly method of amending the Constitution. In contrast, the Articles of Confederation, which were universally recognized as seriously flawed, offered no means of amendment. For their part, Antifederalists argued that the amendment process was so "intricate" that one might as easily roll "sixes an hundred times in succession" as change the Constitution.

The system for amendment laid out in the Constitution requires that two-thirds of both houses of Congress agree to a proposed amendment, which must then be ratified by three-quarters of the legislatures of the states. Alternatively, an amendment may be proposed by a convention called by the legislatures of two-thirds of the states. Since 1789, members of Congress have proposed thousands of amendments. Besides the seventeen amendments added since 1789, only the six "unratified" ones included here were approved by two-thirds of both houses and sent to the states for ratification, however.

Among the many amendments that never made it out of Congress have been proposals to declare dueling, divorce, and interracial marriage unconstitutional as well as proposals to establish a national university, to acknowledge the sovereignty of Jesus Christ, and to prohibit any person from possessing wealth in excess of ten million dollars.[1]

Among the issues facing Americans today that might lead to constitutional amendment are efforts to balance the federal budget, to limit the number of terms elected officials may serve, to limit access to or prohibit abortion, to establish English as the official language of the United States, and to prohibit flag burning. None of these proposed amendments has yet garnered enough support in Congress to be sent to the states for ratification.

Although the first ten amendments to the Constitution are commonly known as the Bill of Rights, only Amendments 1–8 actually provide guarantees of individual rights. Amendments 9 and 10 deal with the structure of power within the constitutional system. The Bill of Rights was promised to appease Antifederalists who refused to ratify the Constitution without guarantees of

individual liberties and limitations to federal power. After studying more than two hundred amendments recommended by the ratifying conventions of the states, Federalist James Madison presented a list of seventeen to Congress, which used Madison's list as the foundation for the twelve amendments that were sent to the states for ratification. Ten of the twelve were adopted in 1791. The first on the list of twelve, known as the Reapportionment Amendment, was never adopted (see p. A-13). The second proposed amendment was adopted in 1992 as Amendment 27 (see p. A-23).

Amendment I

Congress shall make no law respecting an establishment of religion, or prohibiting the free exercise thereof; or abridging the freedom of speech, or of the press; or the right of the people peaceably to assemble, and to petition the government for a redress of grievances.

The First Amendment is a potent symbol for many Americans. Most are well aware of their rights to free speech, freedom of the press, and freedom of religion and their rights to assemble and to petition, even if they cannot cite the exact words of this amendment.

The First Amendment guarantee of freedom of religion has two clauses: the "free exercise clause," which allows individuals to practice or not practice any religion, and the "establishment clause," which prevents the federal government from discriminating against or favoring any particular religion. This clause was designed to create what Thomas Jefferson referred to as "a wall of separation between church and state." In the 1960s, the Supreme Court ruled that the First Amendment prohibits prayer (see Engel v. Vitale, *p. A-46) and Bible reading in public schools.*

Although the rights to free speech and freedom of the press are established in the First Amendment, it was not until the twentieth century that the Supreme Court began to explore the full meaning of these guarantees. In 1919, the Court ruled in Schenck v. United States *(see p. A-45) that the government could suppress free expression only where it could cite a "clear and present danger." In a decision that continues to raise controversies, the Court ruled in 1990, in* Texas v. Johnson, *that flag burning is a form of symbolic speech protected by the First Amendment.*

---

[1]Richard B. Bernstein, *Amending America*, (New York: Times Books, 1993), 177–81.

Amendment II

A well-regulated militia being necessary to the security of a free State, the right of the people to keep and bear arms shall not be infringed.

Fear of a standing army under the control of a hostile government made the Second Amendment an important part of the Bill of Rights. Advocates of gun ownership claim that the amendment prevents the government from regulating firearms. Proponents of gun control argue that the amendment is designed only to protect the right of the states to maintain militia units.

    In 1939, the Supreme Court ruled in United States v. Miller *that the Second Amendment did not protect the right of an individual to own a sawed-off shotgun, which it argued was not ordinary militia equipment. Since then, the Supreme Court has refused to hear Second Amendment cases, while lower courts have upheld firearms regulations. Several justices currently on the bench seem to favor a narrow interpretation of the Second Amendment, which would allow gun control legislation. The controversy over the impact of the Second Amendment on gun owners and gun control legislation will certainly continue.*

Amendment III

No soldier shall, in time of peace, be quartered in any house without the consent of the owner, nor in time of war, but in a manner to be prescribed by law.

The Third Amendment was extremely important to the framers of the Constitution, but today it is nearly forgotten. American colonists were especially outraged that they were forced to quarter British troops in the years before and during the American Revolution. The philosophy of the Third Amendment has been viewed by some justices and scholars as the foundation of the modern constitutional right to privacy. One example of this can be found in Justice William O. Douglas's opinion in Griswold v. Connecticut *(see p. A-47).*

Amendment IV

The right of the people to be secure in their persons, houses, papers, and effects, against unreasonable searches and seizures, shall not be violated, and no warrants shall issue but upon probable cause, supported by oath or affirmation, and particularly describing the place to be searched, and the persons or things to be seized.

In the years before the Revolution, the houses, barns, stores, and warehouses of American colonists were ransacked by British authorities under "writs of assistance" or general warrants. The British, thus empowered, searched for seditious material or smuggled goods that could then be used as evidence against colonists who were charged with a crime only after the items were found.

    The first part of the Fourth Amendment protects citizens from "unreasonable" searches and seizures. The Supreme Court has interpreted this protection as well as the words search *and* seizure *in different ways at different times. At one time, the Court did not recognize electronic eavesdropping as a form of search and seizure, though it does today. At times, an "unreasonable" search has been almost any search carried out without a warrant, but in the two decades before 1969 the Court sometimes sanctioned warrantless searches that it considered reasonable based on "the total atmosphere of the case."*

    The second part of the Fourth Amendment defines the procedure for issuing a search warrant and states the requirement of "Probable cause," which is generally viewed as evidence indicating that a suspect has committed an offense.

    The Fourth Amendment has been controversial because the Court has sometimes excluded evidence that has been seized in violation of constitutional standards. The justification is that excluding such evidence deters violations of the amendment, but doing so may allow a guilty person to escape punishment.

Amendment V

No person shall be held to answer for a capital, or otherwise infamous crime, unless on a presentment or indictment of a grand jury, except in cases arising in the land or naval forces, or in the militia, when in actual service in time of war or public danger; nor shall any person be subject for the same offence to be twice put in jeopardy of life or limb; nor shall be compelled in any criminal case to be a witness against himself, nor be deprived of life, liberty, or property, without due process of law; nor shall private property be taken for public use without just compensation.

The Fifth Amendment protects people against government authority in the prosecution of criminal offenses. It prohibits the state, first, from charging a person with a serious crime without a grand jury hearing to decide whether there is sufficient evidence to support the charge and, second, from charging a person with the same crime twice. The best-known aspect of the Fifth Amendment is that it

prevents a person from being "compelled . . . to be a witness against himself." The last clause, the "takings clause," limits the power of the government to seize property.

Although invoking the Fifth Amendment is popularly viewed as a confession of guilt, a person may be innocent yet still fear prosecution. For example, during the Red-baiting era of the late 1940s and 1950s, many people who had participated in legal activities that were associated with the Communist Party claimed the Fifth Amendment privilege rather than testify before the House Un-American Activities Committee because the mood of the times cast those activities in a negative light. Since "taking the Fifth" was viewed as an admission of guilt, those people often lost their jobs or became unemployable. (See chapter 26.) Nonetheless, the right to protect oneself against self-incrimination plays an important role in guarding against the collective power of the state.

Amendment VI

In all criminal prosecutions, the accused shall enjoy the right to a speedy and public trial, by an impartial jury of the State and district wherein the crime shall have been committed, which district shall have been previously ascertained by law, and to be informed of the nature and cause of the accusation; to be confronted with the witnesses against him; to have compulsory process for obtaining witnesses in his favor, and to have the assistance of counsel for his defence.

The original Constitution put few limits on the government's power to investigate, prosecute, and punish crime. This process was of great concern to the early Americans, however, and of the twenty-eight rights specified in the first eight amendments, fifteen have to do with it. Seven rights are specified in the Sixth Amendment. These include the right to a speedy trial, a public trial, a jury trial, a notice of accusation, confrontation by opposing witnesses, testimony by favorable witnesses, and the assistance of counsel.

Although this amendment originally guaranteed these rights only in cases involving the federal government, the adoption of the Fourteenth Amendment began a process of applying the protections of the Bill of Rights to the states through court cases such as Gideon v. Wainwright *(see p. A-46).*

Amendment VII

In suits at common law, where the value in controversy shall exceed twenty dollars, the right of trial by jury shall be preserved, and no fact tried by a jury shall be otherwise reexamined in any court of the United States, than according to the rules of the common law.

This amendment guarantees people the same right to a trial by jury as was guaranteed by English common law in 1791. Under common law, in civil trials (those involving money damages) the role of the judge was to settle questions of law and that of the jury was to settle questions of fact. The amendment does not specify the size of the jury or its role in a trial, however. The Supreme Court has generally held that those issues be determined by English common law of 1791, which stated that a jury consists of twelve people, that a trial must be conducted before a judge who instructs the jury on the law and advises it on facts, and that a verdict must be unanimous.

Amendment VIII

Excessive bail shall not be required, nor excessive fines imposed, nor cruel and unusual punishments inflicted.

The language used to guarantee the three rights in this amendment was inspired by the English Bill of Rights of 1689. The Supreme Court has not had a lot to say about "excessive fines." In recent years it has agreed that despite the provision against "excessive bail," persons who are believed to be dangerous to others can be held without bail even before they have been convicted.

Although opponents of the death penalty have not succeeded in using the Eighth Amendment to achieve the end of capital punishment, the clause regarding "cruel and unusual punishments" has been used to prohibit capital punishment in certain cases (see Furman v. Georgia, *p. A-47) and to require improved conditions in prisons.*

Amendment IX

The enumeration in the Constitution, of certain rights, shall not be construed to deny or disparage others retained by the people.

Some Federalists feared that inclusion of the Bill of Rights in the Constitution would allow later generations of interpreters to claim that the people had surrendered any rights not specifically enumerated there. To guard against this, Madison added language that became the Ninth Amendment. Interest in this heretofore largely ignored amendment revived in 1965 when it was used in a concurring opinion in Griswold v. Connecticut *(see p. A-47). While Justice William O. Douglas called on the Third Amendment to support the right to privacy in deciding that case, Justice Arthur Goldberg, in the concurring opinion, argued that the right to privacy regarding contraception was an*

unenumerated right that was protected by the Ninth Amendment.

In 1980, the Court ruled that the right of the press to attend a public trial was protected by the Ninth Amendment. While some scholars argue that modern judges cannot identify the unenumerated rights that the framers were trying to protect, others argue that the Ninth Amendment should be read as providing a constitutional "presumption of liberty" that allows people to act in any way that does not violate the rights of others.

Amendment X

The powers not delegated to the United States by the Constitution, nor prohibited by it to the States, are reserved to the States respectively, or to the people.

◆ ◆ ◆

The Antifederalists were especially eager to see a "reserved powers clause" explicitly guaranteeing the states control over their internal affairs. Not surprisingly, the Tenth Amendment has been a frequent battleground in the struggle over states' rights and federal supremacy. Prior to the Civil War, the Democratic Republican Party and Jacksonian Democrats invoked the Tenth Amendment to prohibit the federal government from making decisions about whether people in individual states could own slaves. The Tenth Amendment was virtually suspended during Reconstruction following the Civil War. In 1883, however, the Supreme Court declared the Civil Rights Act of 1875 unconstitutional on the grounds that it violated the Tenth Amendment. Business interests also called on the amendment to block efforts at federal regulation.

The Court was inconsistent over the next several decades as it attempted to resolve the tension between the restrictions of the Tenth Amendment and the powers the Constitution granted to Congress to regulate interstate commerce and levy taxes. The Court upheld the Pure Food and Drug Act (1906), the Meat Inspection Acts (1906 and 1907), and the White Slave Traffic Act (1910), all of which affected the states, but struck down an act prohibiting interstate shipment of goods produced through child labor. Between 1934 and 1935, a number of New Deal programs created by Franklin D. Roosevelt were declared unconstitutional on the grounds that they violated the Tenth Amendment. (See chapter 24.) As Roosevelt appointees changed the composition of the Court, the Tenth Amendment was declared to have no substantive meaning. Generally, the amendment is held to protect the rights of states to regulate internal matters such as local government, education, commerce, labor, and business, as well as matters involving families such as marriage, divorce, and inheritance within the state.

Unratified Amendment
Reapportionment Amendment (proposed by Congress September 25, 1789, along with the Bill of Rights)

After the first enumeration required by the first article of the Constitution, there shall be one Representative for every thirty thousand, until the number shall amount to one hundred, after which the proportion shall be so regulated by Congress, that there shall be not less than one hundred Representatives, nor less than one Representative for every forty thousand persons, until the number of Representatives shall amount to two hundred; after which the proportion shall be so regulated by Congress, that there shall not be less than two hundred Representatives, nor more than one Representative for every fifty thousand persons.

◆ ◆ ◆

If the Reapportionment Amendment had passed and remained in effect, the House of Representatives today would have more than 5,000 members rather than 435.

Amendment XI
[Adopted 1798]

The judicial power of the United States shall not be construed to extend to any suit in law or equity, commenced or prosecuted against one of the United States by citizens of another State, or by citizens or subjects of any foreign state.

◆ ◆ ◆

In 1793, the Supreme Court ruled in favor of Alexander Chisholm, executor of the estate of a deceased South Carolina merchant. Chisholm was suing the state of Georgia because the merchant had never been paid for provisions he had supplied during the Revolution. Many regarded this Court decision as an error that violated the intent of the Constitution.

Antifederalists had long feared a federal court system with the power to overrule a state court. When the Constitution was being drafted, Federalists had assured worried Antifederalists that section 2 of Article 3, which allows federal courts to hear cases "between a State and citizens of another State," did not mean that the federal courts were authorized to hear suits against a state by citizens of another state or a foreign country. Antifederalists and many other Americans feared a powerful federal court system because they worried that it would become like the British courts of this period, which were accountable only to the monarch. Furthermore, Chisholm v. Georgia prompted a *series of suits against state governments by creditors and suppliers who had made loans during the war.*

In addition, State legislators and Congress feared that the shaky economies of the new states, as well as the country as a whole, would be destroyed, especially if Loyalists who had fled to other countries sought reimbursement for land and property that had been seized. The day after the Supreme Court announced its decision, a resolution proposing the Eleventh Amendment, which overturned the decision in Chisholm v. Georgia, *was introduced in the U.S. Senate.*

Amendment XII
[Adopted 1804]

The electors shall meet in their respective States, and vote by ballot for President and Vice-President, one of whom, at least, shall not be an inhabitant of the same State with themselves; they shall name in their ballots the person voted for as President, and in distinct ballots the person voted for as Vice-President, and they shall make distinct lists of all persons voted for as President, and of all persons voted for as Vice-President, and of the number of votes for each, which lists they shall sign and certify, and transmit sealed to the seat of government of the United States, directed to the President of the Senate;—the President of the Senate shall, in the presence of the Senate and House of Representatives, open all the certificates and the votes shall then be counted;—the person having the greatest number of votes for President shall be the President, if such number be a majority of the whole number of electors appointed; and if no person have such majority, then from the persons having the highest numbers not exceeding three on the list of those voted for as President, the House of Representatives shall choose immediately, by ballot, the President. But in choosing the President, the votes shall be taken by States, the representation from each State having one vote; a quorum for this purpose shall consist of a member or members from two-thirds of the States, and a majority of all the States shall be necessary to a choice. And if the House of Representatives shall not choose a President whenever the right of choice shall devolve upon them, before *the fourth day of March* next following, then the Vice-President shall act as President, as in the case of the death or other constitutional disability of the President.

The person having the greatest number of votes as Vice-President shall be the Vice-President, if such number be a majority of the whole number of electors appointed; and if no person have a majority, then from the two highest numbers on the list the Senate shall choose the Vice-President; a quorum for the purpose shall consist of two-thirds of the whole number of Senators, and a majority of the whole number shall be necessary to a choice. But no person constitutionally inel-

igible to the office of President shall be eligible to that of Vice-President of the United States.

The framers of the Constitution disliked political parties and assumed that none would ever form. Under the original system, electors chosen by the states would each vote for two candidates. The candidate who won the most votes would become president, while the person who won the second-highest number of votes would become vice president. Rivalries between Federalists and Antifederalists led to the formation of political parties, however, even before George Washington had left office. Though Washington was elected unanimously in 1789 and 1792, the elections of 1796 and 1800 were procedural disasters because of party maneuvering (see chapters 9 and 10). In 1796, Federalist John Adams was chosen as president, and his great rival, the Antifederalist Thomas Jefferson (whose party was called the Republican Party), became his vice president. In 1800, all the electors cast their two votes as one of two party blocs. Jefferson and his fellow Republican nominee, Aaron Burr, were tied with seventy-three votes each. The contest went to the House of Representatives, which finally elected Jefferson after thirty-six ballots. The Twelfth Amendment prevents these problems by requiring electors to vote separately for the president and vice president.

Unratified Amendment
Titles of Nobility Amendment (proposed by Congress May 1, 1810)

If any citizen of the United States shall accept, claim, receive or retain any title of nobility or honor or shall, without the consent of Congress, accept and retain any present, pension, office or emolument of any kind whatever, from any emperor, king, prince or foreign power, such person shall cease to be a citizen of the United States, and shall be incapable of holding any office of trust or profit under them, or either of them.

This amendment would have extended Article 1, section 9, clause 8 of the Constitution, which prevents the awarding of titles by the United States and the acceptance of such awards from foreign powers without congressional consent. Historians speculate that general nervousness about the power of the Emperor Napoleon, who was at that time extending France's empire throughout Europe, may have prompted the proposal. Though it fell one vote short of ratification, Congress and the American people thought the proposal had been

ratified and it was included in many nineteenth-century editions of the Constitution.

The Civil War and Reconstruction Amendments (Thirteenth, Fourteenth, and Fifteenth Amendments)

In the four months between the election of Abraham Lincoln and his inauguration, more than two hundred proposed constitutional amendments were presented to Congress as part of a desperate attempt to hold the rapidly dissolving Union together. Most of these were efforts to appease the southern states by protecting the right to own slaves or by disfranchising African Americans through constitutional amendment. None were able to win the votes required from Congress to send them to the states. The relatively innocuous Corwin Amendment seemed to be the only hope for preserving the Union by amending the Constitution.

The northern victors in the Civil War tried to restructure the Constitution just as the war had restructured the nation. Yet they were often divided in their goals. Some wanted to end slavery; others hoped for social and economic equality regardless of race; others hoped that extending the power of the ballot box to former slaves would help create a new political order. The debates over the Thirteenth, Fourteenth, and Fifteenth Amendments were bitter. Few of those who fought for these changes were satisfied with the amendments themselves; fewer still were satisfied with their interpretation. Although the amendments put an end to the legal status of slavery, it took nearly a hundred years after the amendments' passage before most of the descendants of former slaves could begin to experience the economic, social, and political equality the amendments had been intended to provide.

Unratified Amendment

Corwin Amendment (proposed by Congress March 2, 1861)

No amendment shall be made to the Constitution which will authorize or give to Congress the power to abolish or interfere, within any State, with the domestic institutions thereof, including that of persons held to labor or service by the laws of said State.

Following the election of Abraham Lincoln, Congress scrambled to try to prevent the secession of the slaveholding states. House member Thomas Corwin of Ohio proposed the "unamendable" amendment in the hope that by protecting slavery where it existed, Congress would keep

the southern states in the Union. Lincoln indicated his support for the proposed amendment in his first inaugural address. Only Ohio and Maryland ratified the Corwin Amendment before it was forgotten.

Amendment XIII

[Adopted 1865]

Section 1   Neither slavery nor involuntary servitude, except as a punishment for crime whereof the party shall have been duly convicted, shall exist within the United States, or any place subject to their jurisdiction.

Section 2   Congress shall have power to enforce this article by appropriate legislation.

Although President Lincoln had abolished slavery in the Confederacy with the Emancipation Proclamation of 1863, abolitionists wanted to rid the entire country of slavery. The Thirteenth Amendment did this in a clear and straightforward manner. In February 1865, when the proposal was approved by the House, the gallery of the House was newly opened to black Americans who had a chance at last to see their government at work. Passage of the proposal was greeted by wild cheers from the gallery as well as tears on the House floor, where congressional representatives openly embraced one another.

The problem of ratification remained, however. The Union position was that the Confederate states were part of the country of thirty-six states. Therefore, twenty-seven states were needed to ratify the amendment. When Kentucky and Delaware rejected it, backers realized that without approval from at least four former Confederate states, the amendment would fail. Lincoln's successor, President Andrew Johnson, made ratification of the Thirteenth Amendment a condition for southern states to rejoin the Union. Under those terms, all the former Confederate states except Mississippi accepted the Thirteenth Amendment, and by the end of 1865 the amendment had become part of the Constitution and slavery had been prohibited in the United States.

Amendment XIV

[Adopted 1868]

Section 1   All persons born or naturalized in the United States, and subject to the jurisdiction thereof, are citizens of the United States and of the State wherein they reside. No State shall make or enforce any law which shall abridge the privileges or immunities of citizens of the United States; nor shall any State deprive any person of life, liberty, or property, without due process of law; nor deny to any person within its jurisdiction the equal protection of the laws.

Section 2   Representatives shall be appointed among the several States according to their respective numbers, counting the whole number of persons in each State, excluding Indians not taxed. But when the right to vote at any election for the choice of Electors for President and Vice-President of the United States, Representatives in Congress, the executive and judicial officers of a State, or the members of the legislature thereof, is denied to any of the male inhabitants of such State, being twenty-one years of age and citizens of the United States, or in any way abridged, except for participation in rebellion, or other crime, the basis of representation therein shall be reduced in the proportion which the number of such male citizens shall bear to the whole number of male citizens twenty-one years of age in such State.

Section 3   No person shall be a Senator or Representative in Congress, or Elector of President and Vice-President, or hold any office, civil or military, under the United States, or under any State, who, having previously taken an oath, as a member of Congress, or as an officer of the United States, or as a member of any State legislature, or as an executive or judicial officer of any State, to support the Constitution of the United States, shall have engaged in insurrection or rebellion against the same, or given aid or comfort to the enemies thereof. Congress may, by a vote of two-thirds of each house, remove such disability.

Section 4   The validity of the public debt of the United States, authorized by law, including debts incurred for payment of pensions and bounties for services in suppressing insurrection or rebellion, shall not be questioned. But neither the United States nor any State shall assume or pay any debt or obligation incurred in aid of insurrection or rebellion against the United States, or any claim for the loss or emancipation of any slave; but all such debts, obligations, and claims shall be held illegal and void.

Section 5   The Congress shall have power to enforce, by appropriate legislation, the provisions of this article.

◆ ◆ ◆

Without Lincoln's leadership in the reconstruction of the nation following the Civil War, it soon became clear that the Thirteenth Amendment needed additional constitutional support. Less than a year after Lincoln's assassination, Andrew Johnson was ready to bring the former Confederate states back into the Union with few changes in their governments or politics. Anxious Republicans drafted the

Fourteenth Amendment to prevent that from happening. The most important provisions of this complex amendment made all native-born or naturalized persons American citizens and prohibited states from abridging the "privileges or immunities" of citizens; depriving them of "life, liberty, or property, without due process of law"; and denying them "equal protection of the laws." In essence, it made all ex-slaves citizens and protected the rights of all citizens against violation by their own state governments.

As occurred in the case of the Thirteenth Amendment, former Confederate states were forced to ratify the amendment as a condition of representation in the House and the Senate. The intentions of the Fourteenth Amendment, and how those intentions should be enforced, have been the most debated point of constitutional history. The terms due process *and* equal protection *have been especially troublesome. Was the amendment designed to outlaw racial segregation? Or was the goal simply to prevent the leaders of the rebellious South from gaining political power?*

The framers of the Fourteenth Amendment hoped Article 2 would produce black voters who would increase the power of the Republican Party. The federal government, however, never used its power to punish states for denying blacks their right to vote. Although the Fourteenth Amendment had an immediate impact in giving black Americans citizenship, it did nothing to protect blacks from the vengeance of whites once Reconstruction ended. In the late nineteenth and early twentieth centuries, section 1 of the Fourteenth Amendment was often used to protect business interests and strike down laws protecting workers on the grounds that the rights of "persons," that is, corporations, were protected by "due process." More recently, the Fourteenth Amendment has been used to justify school desegregation and affirmative action programs, as well as to dismantle such programs.

Amendment XV

[Adopted 1870]

Section 1   The right of citizens of the United States to vote shall not be denied or abridged by the United States or by any State on account of race, color, or previous condition of servitude.

Section 2   The Congress shall have power to enforce this article by appropriate legislation.

◆ ◆ ◆

The Fifteenth Amendment was the last major piece of Reconstruction legislation. While earlier Reconstruction acts had already required black suffrage in the South, the Fifteenth Amendment extended black voting rights to the entire nation. Some Republicans felt morally obligated to do away with the double standard between North and South since many northern states had stubbornly refused to enfranchise blacks. Others believed that the freedman's ballot required the extra protection of a constitutional amendment to shield it from white counterattack. But partisan advantage also played an important role in the amendment's passage, since Republicans hoped that by giving the ballot to northern blacks, they could lessen their political vulnerability.

Many women's rights advocates had fought for the amendment. They had felt betrayed by the inclusion of the word male in section 2 of the Fourteenth Amendment and were further angered when the proposed Fifteenth Amendment failed to prohibit denial of the right to vote on the grounds of sex as well as "race, color, or previous condition of servitude." In this amendment, for the first time, the federal government claimed the power to regulate the franchise, or vote. It was also the first time the Constitution placed limits on the power of the states to regulate access to the franchise. Although ratified in 1870, however, the amendment was not enforced until the twentieth century.

The Progressive Amendments (Sixteenth–Nineteenth Amendments)

No amendments were added to the Constitution between the Civil War and the Progressive Era. America was changing, however, in fundamental ways. The rapid industrialization of the United States after the Civil War led to many social and economic problems. Hundreds of amendments were proposed, but none received enough support in Congress to be sent to the states. Some scholars believe that regional differences and rivalries were so strong during this period that it was almost impossible to gain a consensus on a constitutional amendment. During the Progressive Era, however, the Constitution was amended four times in seven years.

Amendment XVI

[Adopted 1913]

The Congress shall have power to lay and collect taxes on incomes, from whatever source derived, without apportionment among the several States, and without regard to any census or enumeration.

Until passage of the Sixteenth Amendment, most of the money used to run the federal government came from customs duties and taxes on specific items, such as liquor. During the Civil War, the federal government taxed incomes as an emergency measure. Pressure to enact an in-

come tax came from those who were concerned about the growing gap between rich and poor in the United States. The Populist Party began campaigning for a graduated income tax in 1892, and support continued to grow. By 1909, thirty-three proposed income tax amendments had been presented in Congress, but lobbying by corporate and other special interests had defeated them all. In June 1909, the growing pressure for an income tax, which had been endorsed by Presidents Roosevelt and Taft, finally pushed an amendment through the Senate. The required thirty-six states had ratified the amendment by February 1913.

Amendment XVII

[Adopted 1913]

Section 1 The Senate of the United States shall be composed of two Senators from each State, elected by the people thereof, for six years; and each Senator shall have one vote. The electors in each State shall have the qualifications requisite for electors of [voters for] the most numerous branch of the State legislatures.

Section 2 When vacancies happen in the representation of any State in the Senate, the executive authority of such State shall issue writs of election to fill such vacancies: Provided, that the Legislature of any State may empower the executive thereof to make temporary appointments until the people fill the vacancies by election as the Legislature may direct.

Section 3 This amendment shall not be so construed as to affect the election or term of any Senator chosen before it becomes valid as part of the Constitution.

The framers of the Constitution saw the members of the House as the representatives of the people and the members of the Senate as the representatives of the states. Originally senators were to be chosen by the state legislators. According to reform advocates, however, the growth of private industry and transportation conglomerates during the Gilded Age had created a network of corruption in which wealth and power were exchanged for influence and votes in the Senate. Senator Nelson Aldrich, who represented Rhode Island in the late nineteenth and early twentieth centuries, for example, was known as "the senator from Standard Oil" because of his open support of special business interests.

Efforts to amend the Constitution to allow direct election of senators had begun in 1826, but since any proposal had to be approved by the Senate, reform seemed impossible. Progressives tried to gain influence in the Senate by instituting party caucuses and primary elections, which gave citizens the chance to express their choice of a senator who could then be officially elected by the state legislature. By 1910, fourteen of the country's thirty senators received popular votes through a state primary before the state legislature made its selection. Despairing of getting a proposal through the Senate, supporters of a direct-election amendment had begun in 1893 to seek a convention of representatives from two-thirds of the states to propose an amendment that could then be ratified. By 1905, thirty-one of forty-five states had endorsed such an amendment. Finally, in 1911, despite extraordinary opposition, a proposed amendment passed the Senate; by 1913, it had been ratified.

Amendment XVIII

[Adopted 1919; Repealed 1933 by Amendment XXI]

Section 1   After one year from the ratification of this article the manufacture, sale, or transportation of intoxicating liquors within, the importation thereof into, or the exportation thereof from the United States and all territory subject to the jurisdiction thereof, for beverage purposes, is hereby prohibited.

Section 2   The Congress and the several States shall have concurrent power to enforce this article by appropriate legislation.

Section 3   This article shall be inoperative unless it shall have been ratified as an amendment to the Constitution by the legislatures of the several States, as provided in the Constitution, within seven years from the date of the submission thereof to the States by the Congress.

◆ ◆ ◆

The Prohibition Party, formed in 1869, began calling for a constitutional amendment to outlaw alcoholic beverages in 1872. A prohibition amendment was first proposed in the Senate in 1876 and was revived eighteen times before 1913. Between 1913 and 1919, another thirty-nine attempts were made to prohibit liquor in the United States through a constitutional amendment. Prohibition became a key element of the Progressive agenda as reformers linked alcohol and drunkenness to numerous social problems, including the corruption of immigrant voters. While opponents of such an amendment argued that it was undemocratic, supporters claimed that their efforts had widespread public support. The admission of twelve "dry" western states to the Union in the early twentieth century and the spirit of sacrifice during World War I laid the groundwork for passage and ratification of the Eighteenth Amendment in 1919. Opponents added a time limit to the

amendment in the hope that they could thus block ratification, but this effort failed. (See also Amendment XXI.)

Amendment XIX

[Adopted 1920]

Section 1   The right of citizens of the United States to vote shall not be denied or abridged by the United States or by any State on account of sex.

Section 2   Congress shall have the power to enforce this article by appropriate legislation.

Advocates of women's rights tried and failed to link woman suffrage to the Fourteenth and Fifteenth Amendments. Nonetheless, the effort for woman suffrage continued. Between 1878 and 1912, at least one and sometimes as many as four proposed amendments were introduced in Congress each year to grant women the right to vote. While over time women won very limited voting rights in some states, at both the state and federal levels opposition to an amendment for woman suffrage remained very strong. President Woodrow Wilson and other officials felt that the federal government should not interfere with the power of the states in this matter. Others worried that granting suffrage to women would encourage ethnic minorities to exercise their own right to vote. And many were concerned that giving women the vote would result in their abandoning traditional gender roles. In 1919, following a protracted and often bitter campaign of protest in which women went on hunger strikes and chained themselves to fences, an amendment was introduced with the backing of President Wilson. It narrowly passed the Senate (after efforts to limit the suffrage to white women failed) and was adopted in 1920 after Tennessee became the thirty-sixth state to ratify it.

Unratified Amendment

Child Labor Amendment (proposed by Congress June 2, 1924)

Section 1   The Congress shall have power to limit, regulate, and prohibit the labor of persons under eighteen years of age.

Section 2   The power of the several States is unimpaired by this article except that the operation of State laws shall be suspended to the extent necessary to give effect to legislation enacted by Congress.

Throughout the late nineteenth and early twentieth centuries, alarm over the condition of child workers grew.

Opponents of child labor argued that children worked in dangerous and unhealthy conditions, that they took jobs from adult workers, that they depressed wages in certain industries, and that states that allowed child labor had an economic advantage over those that did not. Defenders of child labor claimed that children provided needed income in many families, that working at a young age developed character, and that the effort to prohibit the practice constituted an invasion of family privacy.

In 1916, Congress passed a law that made it illegal to sell goods made by children through interstate commerce. The Supreme Court, however, ruled that the law violated the limits on the power of Congress to regulate interstate commerce. Congress then tried to penalize industries that used child labor by taxing such goods. This measure was also thrown out by the courts. In response, reformers set out to amend the Constitution. The proposed amendment was ratified by twenty-eight states, but by 1925, thirteen states had rejected it. Passage of the Fair Labor Standards Act in 1938, which was upheld by the Supreme Court in 1941, made the amendment irrelevant.

Amendment XX

[Adopted 1933]

Section 1   The terms of the President and Vice President shall end at noon on the 20th day of January, and the terms of Senators and Representatives at noon on the 3rd day of January, of the years in which such terms would have ended if this article had not been ratified; and the terms of their successors shall then begin.

Section 2   The Congress shall assemble at least once in every year, and such meeting shall begin at noon on the 3d day of January, unless they shall by law appoint a different day.

Section 3   If, at the time fixed for the beginning of the term of the President, the President-elect shall have died, the Vice-President-elect shall become President. If a President shall not have been chosen before the time fixed for the beginning of his term, or if the President-elect shall have failed to qualify, then the Vice-President-elect shall act as President until a President shall have qualified; and the Congress may by law provide for the case wherein neither a President-elect nor a Vice-President-elect shall have qualified, declaring who shall then act as President, or the manner in which one who is to act shall be selected, and such person shall act accordingly until a President or Vice-President shall have qualified.

Section 4   The Congress may by law provide for the case of the death of any of the persons from whom the House of Representatives may choose a President whenever the right of choice shall have devolved upon them, and for the case of the death of any of the persons from whom the Senate may choose a Vice-President whenever the right of choice shall have devolved upon them.

Section 5   Sections 1 and 2 shall take effect on the 15th day of October following the ratification of this article.

Section 6   This article shall be inoperative unless it shall have been ratified as an amendment to the Constitution by the Legislatures of three- fourths of the several States within seven years from the date of its submission.

Until 1933, presidents took office on March 4. Since elections are held in early November and electoral votes are counted in mid-December, this meant that more than three months passed between the time a new president was elected and when he took office. Moving the inauguration to January shortened the transition period and allowed Congress to begin its term closer to the time of the president's inauguration. Although this seems like a minor change, an amendment was required because the Constitution specifies terms of office. This amendment also deals with questions of succession in the event that a president- or vice president-elect dies before assuming office. Section 3 also clarifies a method for resolving a deadlock in the electoral college.

Amendment XXI

[Adopted 1933]

Section 1   The eighteenth article of amendment to the Constitution of the United States is hereby repealed.

Section 2   The transportation or importation into any State, Territory, or Possession of the United States for delivery or use therein of intoxicating liquors, in violation of the laws thereof, is hereby prohibited.

Section 3   This article shall be inoperative unless it shall have been ratified as an amendment to the Constitution by conventions in the several States, as provided in the Constitution, within seven years from the date of the submission thereof to the States by the Congress.

Widespread violation of the Volstead Act, the law enacted to enforce prohibition, made the United States a nation of lawbreakers. Prohibition caused more problems than it solved by encouraging crime, bribery, and corruption.

Further, a coalition of liquor and beer manufacturers, personal liberty advocates, and constitutional scholars joined forces to challenge the amendment. By 1929, thirty proposed repeal amendments had been introduced in Congress, and the Democratic Party made repeal part of its platform in the 1932 presidential campaign. The Twenty-First Amendment was proposed in February 1933 and ratified less than a year later. The failure of the effort to enforce prohibition through a constitutional amendment has often been cited by opponents to subsequent efforts to shape public virtue and private morality.

Amendment XXII

[Adopted 1951]

Section 1 No person shall be elected to the office of the President more than twice, and no person who has held the office of President, or acted as President, for more than two years of a term to which some other person was elected President shall be elected to the office of President more than once. But this article shall not apply to any person holding the office of President when this Article was proposed by the Congress, and shall not prevent any person who may be holding the office of President, or acting as President, during the term within which this Article becomes operative from holding the office of President or acting as President during the remainder of such term.

Section 2 This article shall be inoperative unless it shall have been ratified as an amendment to the Constitution by the legislatures of three-fourths of the several States within seven years from the date of its submission to the States by the Congress.

George Washington's refusal to seek a third term of office set a precedent that stood until 1912, when former President Theodore Roosevelt sought, without success, another term as an independent candidate. Democrat Franklin Roosevelt was the only president to seek and win a fourth term, though he did so amid great controversy. Roosevelt died in April 1945, a few months after the beginning of his fourth term. In 1946, Republicans won control of the House and the Senate, and early in 1947 a proposal for an amendment to limit future presidents to two four-year terms was offered to the states for ratification. Democratic critics of the Twenty-Second Amendment charged that it was a partisan posthumous jab at Roosevelt.

    Since the Twenty-Second Amendment was adopted, however, the only presidents who might have been able to seek a third term, had it not existed, were Republicans Dwight Eisenhower and Ronald Reagan. Since 1826, Congress has entertained 160 proposed amendments to

limit the president to one six-year term. Such amendments have been backed by fifteen presidents, including Gerald Ford and Jimmy Carter.

Amendment XXIII

[Adopted 1961]

Section 1 The District constituting the seat of Government of the United States shall appoint in such manner as the Congress may direct: A number of electors of President and Vice-President equal to the whole number of Senators and Representatives in Congress to which the District would be entitled if it were a State, but in no event more than the least populous State; they shall be in addition to those appointed by the States, but they shall be considered for the purposes of the election of President and Vice-President, to be electors appointed by a State; and they shall meet in the District and perform such duties as provided by the twelfth article of amendment.

Section 2 The Congress shall have the power to enforce this article by appropriate legislation.

When Washington, D.C., was established as a federal district, no one expected that a significant number of people would make it their permanent and primary residence. A proposal to allow citizens of the district to vote in presidential elections was approved by Congress in June 1960 and was ratified on March 29, 1961.

Amendment XXIV

[Adopted 1964]

Section 1 The right of citizens of the United States to vote in any primary or other election for President or Vice-President, for electors for President or Vice-President, or for Senator or Representative in Congress, shall not be denied or abridged by the United States or any State by reason of failure to pay any poll tax or other tax.

Section 2 The Congress shall have the power to enforce this article by appropriate legislation.

In the colonial and Revolutionary eras, financial independence was seen as necessary to political independence, and the poll tax was used as a requirement for voting. By the twentieth century, however, the poll tax was used mostly

to bar poor people, especially southern blacks, from voting. While conservatives complained that the amendment interfered with states' rights, liberals thought that the amendment did not go far enough because it barred the poll tax only in national elections and not in state or local elections. The amendment was ratified in 1964, however, and two years later, the Supreme Court ruled that poll taxes in state and local elections also violated the equal protection clause of the Fourteenth Amendment.

Amendment XXV

[Adopted 1967]

Section 1 In case of the removal of the President from office or of his death or resignation, the Vice-President shall become President.

Section 2 Whenever there is a vacancy in the office of the Vice-President, the President shall nominate a Vice-President who shall take office upon confirmation by a majority vote of both Houses of Congress.

Section 3 Whenever the President transmits to the President pro tempore of the Senate and the Speaker of the House of Representatives his written declaration that he is unable to discharge the powers and duties of his office, and until he transmits to them a written declaration to the contrary, such powers and duties shall be discharged by the Vice-President as Acting President.

Section 4 Whenever the Vice-President and a majority of either the principal officers of the executive departments or of such other body as Congress may by law provide, transmit to the President pro tempore of the Senate and the Speaker of the House of Representatives their written declaration that the President is unable to discharge the powers and duties of his office, the Vice-President shall immediately assume the powers and duties of the office as Acting President.

Thereafter, when the President transmits to the President pro tempore of the Senate and the Speaker of the House of Representatives his written declaration that no inability exists, he shall resume the powers and duties of his office unless the Vice-President and a majority of either the principal officers of the executive department[s] or of such other body as Congress may by law provide, transmit within four days to the President pro tempore of the Senate and the Speaker of the House of Representatives their written declaration that the President is unable to discharge the powers and duties of his office. Thereupon Congress shall decide the issue, assembling within forty-eight hours for that purpose if not in session. If the Congress, within twenty-one days after receipt of the latter written declaration, or, if Congress is not in session, within twenty-one days after Congress is required to assemble, determines by two-thirds vote of both Houses that the President is unable to discharge the powers and duties of his office, the Vice-President shall continue to discharge the same as Acting President; otherwise, the President shall resume the powers and duties of his office.

◆ ◆ ◆

The framers of the Constitution established the office of vice president because someone was needed to preside over the Senate. The first president to die in office was William Henry Harrison, in 1841. Vice President John Tyler had himself sworn in as president, setting a precedent that was followed when seven later presidents died in office. The assassination of President James A. Garfield in 1881 posed a new problem, however. After he was shot, the president was incapacitated for two months before he died; he was unable to lead the country, while his vice president, Chester A. Arthur, was unable to assume leadership. Efforts to resolve questions of succession in the event of a presidential disability thus began with the death of Garfield.

In 1963, the assassination of President John F. Kennedy galvanized Congress to action. Vice President Lyndon Johnson was a chain smoker with a history of heart trouble. According to the 1947 Presidential Succession Act, the two men who stood in line to succeed him were the seventy-two-year-old Speaker of the House and the eighty-six-year-old president of the Senate. There were serious concerns that any of these men might become incapacitated while serving as chief executive. The first time the Twenty-Fifth Amendment was used, however, was not in the case of presidential death or illness, but during the Watergate crisis. When Vice President Spiro T. Agnew was forced to resign following allegations of bribery and tax violations, President Richard M. Nixon appointed House Minority Leader Gerald R. Ford vice president. Ford became president following Nixon's resignation eight months later and named Nelson A. Rockefeller as his vice president. Thus, for more than two years, the two highest offices in the country were held by people who had not been elected to them.

Amendment XXVI

[Adopted 1971]

Section 1 The right of citizens of the United States, who are eighteen years of age or older, to vote shall not be denied or abridged by the United States or by any State on account of age.

Section 2 The Congress shall have power to enforce this article by appropriate legislation.

◆ ◆ ◆

Efforts to lower the voting age from twenty-one to eighteen began during World War II. Recognizing that those who were old enough to fight a war should have some say in the government policies that involved them in the war, Presidents Eisenhower, Johnson, and Nixon endorsed the idea. In 1970, the combined pressure of the antiwar movement and the demographic pressure of the baby boom generation led to a Voting Rights Act lowering the voting age in federal, state, and local elections.

In Oregon v. Mitchell (1970), *the state of Oregon challenged the right of Congress to determine the age at which people could vote in state or local elections. The Supreme Court agreed with Oregon. Since the Voting Rights Act was ruled unconstitutional, the Constitution had to be amended to allow passage of a law that would lower the voting age. The amendment was ratified in a little more than three months, making it the most rapidly ratified amendment in U.S. history.*

Unratified Amendment

Equal Rights Amendment (proposed by Congress March 22, 1972; seven-year deadline for ratification extended, June 30, 1982)

Section 1   Equality of rights under the law shall not be denied or abridged by the United States or by any State on account of sex.

Section 2   The Congress shall have the power to enforce, by appropriate legislation, the provisions of this article.

Section 3   This amendment shall take effect two years after the date of ratification.

◆ ◆ ◆

In 1923, soon after women had won the right to vote, Alice Paul, a leading activist in the woman suffrage movement, proposed an amendment requiring equal treatment of men and women. Opponents of the proposal argued that such an amendment would invalidate laws that protected women and would make women subject to the military draft. After the 1964 Civil Rights Act was adopted, protective workplace legislation was removed anyway.

The renewal of the women's movement, as a by-product of the civil rights and antiwar movements, led to a revival of the Equal Rights Amendment (ERA) in Congress. Disagreements over language held up congressional passage of the proposed amendment, but on March 22, 1972, the Senate approved the ERA by a vote of eighty-four to eight, and it was sent to the states. Six states ratified the

amendment within two days, and by the middle of 1973 the amendment seemed well on its way to adoption, with thirty of the needed thirty-eight states having ratified it. In the mid-1970s, however, a powerful "Stop ERA" campaign developed. The campaign portrayed the ERA as a threat to "family values" and traditional relationships between men and women. Although thirty-five states ultimately ratified the ERA, five of those state legislatures voted to rescind ratification, and the amendment was never adopted.

Unratified Amendment

D.C. Statehood Amendment (proposed by Congress August 22, 1978)

Section 1   For purposes of representation in the Congress, election of the President and Vice President, and article V of this Constitution, the District constituting the seat of government of the United States shall be treated as though it were a State.

Section 2   The exercise of the rights and powers conferred under this article shall be by the people of the District constituting the seat of government, and as shall be provided by Congress.

Section 3   The twenty-third article of amendment to the Constitution of the United States is hereby repealed.

Section 4   This article shall be inoperative, unless it shall have been ratified as an amendment to the Constitution by the legislatures of three-fourths of the several states within seven years from the date of its submission.

◆ ◆ ◆

The 1961 ratification of the Twenty-Third Amendment, giving residents of the District of Columbia the right to vote for a president and vice president, inspired an effort to give residents of the district full voting rights. In 1966, President Lyndon Johnson appointed a mayor and city council; in 1971, D.C. residents were allowed to name a nonvoting delegate to the House; and in 1981, residents were allowed to elect the mayor and city council. Congress retained the right to overrule laws that might affect commuters, the height of federal buildings, and selection of judges and prosecutors. The district's nonvoting delegate to Congress, Walter Fauntroy, lobbied fiercely for a congressional amendment granting statehood to the district. In 1978, a proposed amendment was approved and sent to the states. A number of states quickly ratified the amendment, but, like the ERA, the D.C. Statehood Amendment ran into trouble. Opponents argued that section 2 created a separate category of "nominal" statehood. They argued that the federal district should be eliminated and that the territory should be reabsorbed into the state of Maryland. Although these theoretical arguments were strong, some scholars believe that racist attitudes toward the predominantly black population of the city was also a factor leading to the defeat of the amendment.

AMENDMENT XXVII

[Adopted 1992]

No law, varying the compensation for the services of the Senators and Representatives, shall take effect, until an election of Representatives shall have intervened.

While the Twenty-Sixth Amendment was the most rapidly ratified amendment in U.S. history, the Twenty-Seventh Amendment had the longest journey to ratification. First proposed by James Madison in 1789 as part of the package that included the Bill of Rights, this amendment had been ratified by only six states by 1791. In 1873, however, it was ratified by Ohio to protest a massive retroactive salary increase by the federal government. Unlike later proposed amendments, this one came with no time limit on ratification. In the early 1980s, Gregory D. Watson, a University of Texas economics major, discovered the "lost" amendment and began a single-handed campaign to get state legislators to introduce it for ratification. In 1983, it was accepted by Maine. In 1984, it passed the Colorado legislature. Ratifications trickled in slowly until May 1992, when Michigan and New Jersey became the thirty-eighth and thirty-ninth states, respectively, to ratify. This amendment prevents members of Congress from raising their own salaries without giving voters a chance to vote them out of office before they can benefit from the raises.

U.S. POLITICS AND GOVERNMENT

PRESIDENTIAL ELECTIONS

Year	Candidates	Parties	Popular Vote	Percentage of Popular Vote	Electoral Vote	Percentage of Voter Participation
1789	**GEORGE WASHINGTON (Va.)***				69	
	John Adams				34	
	Others				35	
1792	**GEORGE WASHINGTON (Va.)**				132	
	John Adams				77	
	George Clinton				50	
	Others				5	
1796	**JOHN ADAMS (Mass.)**	Federalist			71	
	Thomas Jefferson	Democratic-Republican			68	
	Thomas Pinckney	Federalist			59	
	Aaron Burr	Dem.-Rep.			30	
	Others				48	
1800	**THOMAS JEFFERSON (Va.)**	Dem.-Rep.			73	
	Aaron Burr	Dem.-Rep.			73	
	John Adams	Federalist			65	
	C.C. Pinckney	Federalist			64	
	John Jay	Federalist			1	
1804	**THOMAS JEFFERSON (Va.)**	Dem.-Rep.			162	
	C. C. Pinckney	Federalist			14	
1808	**JAMES MADISON (Va.)**	Dem.-Rep.			122	
	C. C. Pinckney	Federalist			47	
	George Clinton	Dem.-Rep.			6	
1812	**JAMES MADISON (Va.)**	Dem.-Rep.			128	
	De Witt Clinton	Federalist			89	
1816	**JAMES MONROE (Va.)**	Dem.-Rep.			183	
	Rufus King	Federalist			34	
1820	**JAMES MONROE (Va.)**	Dem.-Rep.			231	
	John Quincy Adams	Dem.-Rep.			1	
1824	**JOHN Q. ADAMS (Mass.)**	Dem.-Rep.	108,740	30.5	84	26.9
	Andrew Jackson	Dem.-Rep.	153,544	43.1	99	
	William H. Crawford	Dem.-Rep.	46,618	13.1	41	
	Henry Clay	Dem.-Rep.	47,136	13.2	37	
1828	**ANDREW JACKSON (Tenn.)**	Democratic	647,286	56.0	178	57.6
	John Quincy Adams	National Republican	508,064	44.0	83	

*State of residence when elected president.

Year	Candidates	Parties	Popular Vote	Percentage of Popular Vote	Electoral Vote	Percentage of Voter Participation
1832	**ANDREW JACKSON (Tenn.)**	Democratic	687,502	55.0	219	55.4
	Henry Clay	National Republican	530,189	42.4	49	
	John Floyd	Independent			11	
	William Wirt	Anti-Mason	33,108	2.6	7	
1836	**MARTIN VAN BUREN (N.Y.)**	Democratic	765,483	50.9	170	57.8
	W. H. Harrison	Whig			73	
	Hugh L. White	Whig	739,795	49.1	26	
	Daniel Webster	Whig			14	
	W. P. Magnum	Independent			11	
1840	**WILLIAM H. HARRISON (Ohio)**	Whig	1,274,624	53.1	234	80.2
	Martin Van Buren	Democratic	1,127,781	46.9	60	
	J. G. Birney	Liberty	7,069		—	
1844	**JAMES K. POLK (Tenn.)**	Democratic	1,338,464	49.6	170	78.9
	Henry Clay	Whig	1,300,097	48.1	105	
	J. G. Birney	Liberty	62,300	2.3	—	
1848	**ZACHARY TAYLOR (La.)**	Whig	1,360,967	47.4	163	72.7
	Lewis Cass	Democratic	1,222,342	42.5	127	
	Martin Van Buren	Free-Soil	291,263	10.1	—	
1852	**FRANKLIN PIERCE (N.H.)**	Democratic	1,601,117	50.9	254	69.6
	Winfield Scott	Whig	1,385,453	44.1	42	
	John P. Hale	Free-Soil	155,825	5.0	—	
1856	**JAMES BUCHANAN (Pa.)**	Democratic	1,832,995	45.3	174	78.9
	John C. Frémont	Republican	1,339,932	33.1	114	
	Millard Fillmore	American	871,731	21.6	8	
1860	**ABRAHAM LINCOLN (Ill.)**	Republican	1,865,593	39.8	180	81.2
	Stephen A. Douglas	Democratic	1,382,713	29.5	12	
	John C. Breckinridge	Democratic	848,356	18.1	72	
	John Bell	Union	592,906	12.6	39	
1864	**ABRAHAM LINCOLN (Ill.)**	Republican	2,206,938	55.0	212	73.8
	George B. McClellan	Democratic	1,803,787	45.0	21	
1868	**ULYSSES S. GRANT (Ill)**	Republican	3,012,833	52.7	214	78.1
	Horatio Seymour	Democratic	2,703,249	47.3	80	
1872	**ULYSSES S. GRANT (Ill.)**	Republican	3,597,132	55.6	286	71.3
	Horace Greeley	Democratic; Liberal Republican	2,834,125	43.9	66	
1876	**RUTHERFORD B. HAYES (Ohio)**	Republican	4,036,572	48.0	185	81.8
	Samuel J. Tilden	Democratic	4,284,020	51.0	184	
1880	**JAMES A. GARFIELD (Ohio)**	Republican	4,454,416	48.5	214	79.4
	Winfield S. Hancock	Democratic	4,444,952	48.1	155	
1884	**GROVER CLEVELAND (N.Y.)**	Democratic	4,879,507	48.5	219	77.5
	James G. Blaine	Republican	4,850,293	48.2	182	
1888	**BENJAMIN HARRISON (Ind.)**	Republican	5,439,853	47.9	233	79.3
	Grover Cleveland	Democratic	5,540,309	48.6	168	
1892	**GROVER CLEVELAND (N.Y.)**	Democratic	5,555,426	46.1	277	74.7
	Benjamin Harrison	Republican	5,182,690	43.0	145	
	James B. Weaver	People's	1,029,846	8.5	22	

Year	Candidates	Parties	Popular Vote	Percentage of Popular Vote	Electoral Vote	Percentage of Voter Participation
1896	WILLIAM McKINLEY (Ohio)	Republican	7,104,779	51.1	271	79.3
	William J. Bryan	Democratic-People's	6,502,925	47.7	176	
1900	WILLIAM McKINLEY (Ohio)	Republican	7,207,923	51.7	292	73.2
	William J. Bryan	Dem.-Populist	6,358,133	45.5	155	
1904	THEODORE ROOSEVELT (N.Y.)	Republican	7,623,486	57.9	336	65.2
	Alton B. Parker	Democratic	5,077,911	37.6	140	
	Eugene V. Debs	Socialist	402,283	3.0	—	
1908	WILLIAM H. TAFT (Ohio)	Republican	7,678,908	51.6	321	65.4
	William J. Bryan	Democratic	6,409,104	43.1	162	
	Eugene V. Debs	Socialist	420,793	2.8	—	
1912	WOODROW WILSON (N.J.)	Democratic	6,293,454	41.9	435	58.8
	Theodore Roosevelt	Progressive	4,119,538	27.4	88	
	William H. Taft	Republican	3,484,980	23.2	8	
	Eugene V. Debs	Socialist	900,672	6.1	—	
1916	WOODROW WILSON (N.J.)	Democratic	9,129,606	49.4	277	61.6
	Charles E. Hughes	Republican	8,538,221	46.2	254	
	A. L. Benson	Socialist	585,113	3.2	—	
1920	WARREN G. HARDING (Ohio)	Republican	16,143,407	60.5	404	49.2
	James M. Cox	Democratic	9,130,328	34.2	127	
	Eugene V. Debs	Socialist	919,799	3.4	—	
1924	CALVIN COOLIDGE (Mass.)	Republican	15,725,016	54.0	382	48.9
	John W. Davis	Democratic	8,386,503	28.8	136	
	Robert M. LaFollette	Progressive	4,822,856	16.6	13	
1928	HERBERT HOOVER (Calif.)	Republican	21,391,381	58.2	444	56.9
	Alfred E. Smith	Democratic	15,016,443	40.9	87	
	Norman Thomas	Socialist	267,835	0.7	—	
1932	FRANKLIN D. ROOSEVELT (N.Y.)	Democratic	22,809,638	57.4	472	56.9
	Herbert Hoover	Republican	15,758,901	39.7	59	
	Norman Thomas	Socialist	881,951	2.2	—	
1936	FRANKLIN D. ROOSEVELT (N.Y.)	Democratic	27,751,597	60.8	523	61.0
	Alfred M. Landon	Republican	16,679,583	36.5	8	
	William Lemke	Union	882,479	1.9	—	
1940	FRANKLIN D. ROOSEVELT (N.Y.)	Democratic	27,244,160	54.8	449	62.5
	Wendell Willkie	Republican	22,305,198	44.8	82	
1944	FRANKLIN D. ROOSEVELT (N.Y.)	Democratic	25,602,504	53.5	432	55.9
	Thomas E. Dewey	Republican	22,006,285	46.0	99	
1948	HARRY S. TRUMAN (Mo.)	Democratic	24,105,695	49.5	303	53.0
	Thomas E. Dewey	Republican	21,969,170	45.1	189	
	J. Strom Thurmond	State-Rights Democratic	1,169,021	2.4	38	
	Henry A. Wallace	Progressive	1,156,103	2.4	—	
1952	DWIGHT D. EISENHOWER (N.Y.)	Republican	33,936,252	55.1	442	63.3
	Adlai Stevenson	Democratic	27,314,992	44.4	89	
1956	DWIGHT D. EISENHOWER (N.Y.)	Republican	35,575,420	57.6	457	60.6
	Adlai Stevenson	Democratic	26,033,066	42.1	73	
	Other	—	—		1	

Year	Candidates	Parties	Popular Vote	Percentage of Popular Vote	Electoral Vote	Percentage of Voter Participation
1960	**JOHN F. KENNEDY (Mass.)**	Democratic	34,227,096	49.9	303	62.8
	Richard M. Nixon	Republican	34,108,546	49.6	219	
	Other	—			15	
1964	**LYNDON B. JOHNSON (Tex.)**	Democratic	43,126,506	61.1	486	61.7
	Barry M. Goldwater	Republican	27,176,799	38.5	52	
1968	**RICHARD M. NIXON (N.Y.)**	Republican	31,770,237	43.4	301	60.6
	Hubert H. Humphrey	Democratic	31,270,533	42.7	191	
	George Wallace	American Indep.	9,906,141	13.5	46	
1972	**RICHARD M. NIXON (N.Y.)**	Republican	47,169,911	60.7	520	55.2
	George S. McGovern	Democratic	29,170,383	37.5	17	
	Other	—	—		1	
1976	**JIMMY CARTER (Ga.)**	Democratic	40,828,587	50.0	297	53.5
	Gerald R. Ford	Republican	39,147,613	47.9	241	
	Other	—	1,575,459	2.1	—	
1980	**RONALD REAGAN (Calif.)**	Republican	43,901,812	50.7	489	52.6
	Jimmy Carter	Democratic	35,483,820	41.0	49	
	John B. Anderson	Independent	5,719,722	6.6	—	
	Ed Clark	Libertarian	921,188	1.1	—	
1984	**RONALD REAGAN (Calif.)**	Republican	54,455,075	59.0	525	53.3
	Walter Mondale	Democratic	37,577,185	41.0	13	
1988	**GEORGE BUSH (Texas)**	Republican	47,946,422	54.0	426	50.2
	Michael S. Dukakis	Democratic	41,016,429	46.0	112	
1992	**WILLIAM J. CLINTON (Ark.)**	Democratic	44,908,254	42.3	370	55.2
	George Bush	Republican	39,102,282	37.4	168	
	H. Ross Perot	Independent	19,721,433	18.9	—	
1996	**WILLIAM J. CLINTON (Ark.)**	Democratic	47,401,185	49.2	379	49
	Robert Dole	Republican	39,197,469	40.7	159	
	H. Ross Perot	Independent	8,085,294	8.4	—	

PRESIDENTS, VICE PRESIDENTS, AND CABINETS

The Washington Administration (1789–1797)

Vice President	John Adams	1789–1797
Secretary of State	Thomas Jefferson	1789–1793
	Edmund Randolph	1794–1795
	Timothy Pickering	1795–1797
Secretary of Treasury	Alexander Hamilton	1789–1795
	Oliver Wolcott	1795–1797
Secretary of War	Henry Knox	1789–1794
	Timothy Pickering	1795–1796
	James McHenry	1796–1797
Attorney General	Edmund Randolph	1789–1793
	William Bradford	1794–1795
	Charles Lee	1795–1797
Postmaster General	Samuel Osgood	1789–1791
	Timothy Pickering	1791–1794
	Joseph Habersham	1795–1797

The John Adams Administration (1797–1801)

Vice President	Thomas Jefferson	1797–1801
Secretary of State	Timothy Pickering	1797–1800
	John Marshall	1800–1801
Secretary of Treasury	Oliver Wolcott	1797–1800
	Samuel Dexter	1800–1801
Secretary of War	James McHenry	1797–1800
	Samuel Dexter	1800–1801
Attorney General	Charles Lee	1797–1801
Postmaster General	Joseph Habersham	1797–1801
Secretary of Navy	Benjamin Stoddert	1798–1801

The Jefferson Administration (1801–1809)

Vice President	Aaron Burr	1801–1805
	George Clinton	1805–1809
Secretary of State	James Madison	1801–1809
Secretary of Treasury	Samuel Dexter	1801
	Albert Gallatin	1801–1809
Secretary of War	Henry Dearborn	1801–1809
Attorney General	Levi Lincoln	1801–1805
	Robert Smith	1805
	John Breckinridge	1805–1806
	Caesar Rodney	1807–1809
Postmaster General	Joseph Habersham	1801
	Gideon Granger	1801–1809
Secretary of Navy	Robert Smith	1801–1809

The Madison Administration (1809–1817)

Vice President	George Clinton	1809–1813
	Elbridge Gerry	1813–1817
Secretary of State	Robert Smith	1809–1811
	James Monroe	1811–1817
Secretary of Treasury	Albert Gallatin	1809–1813
	George Campbell	1814
	Alexander Dallas	1814–1816
	William Crawford	1816–1817
Secretary of War	William Eustis	1809–1812
	John Armstrong	1813–1814
	James Monroe	1814–1815
	William Crawford	1815–1817
Attorney General	Caesar Rodney	1809–1811
	William Pinkney	1811–1814
	Richard Rush	1814–1817
Postmaster General	Gideon Granger	1809–1814
	Return Meigs	1814–1817
Secretary of Navy	Paul Hamilton	1809–1813
	William Jones	1813–1814
	Benjamin Crowninshield	1814–1817

The Monroe Administration (1817–1825)

Vice President	Daniel Tompkins	1817–1825
Secretary of State	John Quincy Adams	1817–1825
Secretary of Treasury	William Crawford	1817–1825
Secretary of War	George Graham	1817
	John C. Calhoun	1817–1825
Attorney General	Richard Rush	1817
	William Wirt	1817–1825
Postmaster General	Return Meigs	1817–1823
	John McLean	1823–1825

Secretary of Navy	Benjamin Crowninshield	1817–1818
	Smith Thompson	1818–1823
	Samuel Southard	1823–1825

The John Quincy Adams Administration (1825–1829)

Vice President	John C. Calhoun	1825–1829
Secretary of State	Henry Clay	1825–1829
Secretary of Treasury	Richard Rush	1825–1829
Secretary of War	James Barbour	1825–1828
	Peter Porter	1828–1829
Attorney General	William Wirt	1825–1829
Postmaster General	John McLean	1825–1829
Secretary of Navy	Samuel Southard	1825–1829

The Jackson Administration (1829–1837)

Vice President	John C. Calhoun	1829–1833
	Martin Van Buren	1833–1837
Secretary of State	Martin Van Buren	1829–1831
	Edward Livingston	1831–1833
	Louis McLane	1833–1834
	John Forsyth	1834–1837
Secretary of Treasury	Samuel Ingham	1829–1831
	Louis McLane	1831–1833
	William Duane	1833
	Roger B. Taney	1833–1834
	Levi Woodbury	1834–1837
Secretary of War	John H. Eaton	1829–1831
	Lewis Cass	1831–1837
	Benjamin Butler	1837
Attorney General	John M. Berrien	1829–1831
	Roger B. Taney	1831–1833
	Benjamin Butler	1833–1837
Postmaster General	William Barry	1829–1835
	Amos Kendall	1835–1837
Secretary of Navy	John Branch	1829–1831
	Levi Woodbury	1831–1834
	Mahlon Dickerson	1834–1837

The Van Buren Administration (1837–1841)

Vice President	Richard M. Johnson	1837–1841
Secretary of State	John Forsyth	1837–1841
Secretary of Treasury	Levi Woodbury	1837–1841
Secretary of War	Joel Poinsett	1837–1841
Attorney General	Benjamin Butler	1837–1838
	Felix Grundy	1838–1840
	Henry D. Gilpin	1840–1841
Postmaster General	Amos Kendall	1837–1840
	John M. Niles	1840–1841
Secretary of Navy	Mahlon Dickerson	1837–1838
	James Paulding	1838–1841

The William Harrison Administration (1841)

Vice President	John Tyler	1841
Secretary of State	Daniel Webster	1841
Secretary of Treasury	Thomas Ewing	1841
Secretary of War	John Bell	1841
Attorney General	John J. Crittenden	1841
Postmaster General	Francis Granger	1841
Secretary of Navy	George Badger	1841

The Tyler Administration (1841–1845)

Vice President	None	
Secretary of State	Daniel Webster	1841–1843
	Hugh S. Legaré	1843
	Abel P. Upshur	1843–1844
	John C. Calhoun	1844–1845
Secretary of Treasury	Thomas Ewing	1841
	Walter Forward	1841–1843
	John C. Spencer	1843–1844
	George Bibb	1844–1845

Secretary of War	John Bell	1841
	John C. Spencer	1841–1843
	James M. Porter	1843–1844
	William Wilkins	1844–1845
Attorney General	John J. Crittenden	1841
	Hugh S. Legaré	1841–1843
	John Nelson	1843–1845
Postmaster General	Francis Granger	1841
	Charles Wickliffe	1841
Secretary of Navy	George Badger	1841
	Abel P. Upshur	1841
	David Henshaw	1843–1844
	Thomas Gilmer	1844
	John Y. Mason	1844–1845

The Polk Administration (1845–1849)

Vice President	George M. Dallas	1845–1849
Secretary of State	James Buchanan	1845–1849
Secretary of Treasury	Robert J. Walker	1845–1849
Secretary of War	William L. Marcy	1845–1849
Attorney General	John Y. Mason	1845–1846
	Nathan Clifford	1846–1848
	Isaac Toucey	1848–1849
Postmaster General	Cave Johnson	1845–1849
Secretary of Navy	George Bancroft	1845–1846
	John Y. Mason	1846–1849

The Taylor Administration (1849–1850)

Vice President	Millard Fillmore	1849–1850
Secretary of State	John M. Clayton	1849–1850
Secretary of Treasury	William Meredith	1849–1850
Secretary of War	George Crawford	1849–1850
Attorney General	Reverdy Johnson	1849–1850
Postmaster General	Jacob Collamer	1849–1850
Secretary of Navy	William Preston	1849–1850

Secretary of Interior	Thomas Ewing	1849–1850

The Fillmore Administration (1850–1853)

Vice President	None	
Secretary of State	Daniel Webster	1850–1852
	Edward Everett	1852–1853
Secretary of Treasury	Thomas Corwin	1850–1853
Secretary of War	Charles Conrad	1850–1853
Attorney General	John J. Crittenden	1850–1853
Postmaster General	Nathan Hall	1850–1852
	Sam D. Hubbard	1852–1853
Secretary of Navy	William A. Graham	1850–1852
	John P. Kennedy	1852–1853
Secretary of Interior	Thomas McKennan	1850
	Alexander Stuart	1850–1853

The Pierce Administration (1853–1857)

Vice President	William R. King	1853–1857
Secretary of State	William L. Marcy	1853–1857
Secretary of Treasury	James Guthrie	1853–1857
Secretary of War	Jefferson Davis	1853–1857
Attorney General	Caleb Cushing	1853–1857
Postmaster General	James Campbell	1853–1857
Secretary of Navy	James C. Dobbin	1853–1857
Secretary of Interior	Robert McClelland	1853–1857

The Buchanan Administration (1857–1861)

Vice President	John C. Breckinridge	1857–1861
Secretary of State	Lewis Cass	1857–1860
	Jeremiah S. Black	1860–1861

Secretary of Treasury	Howell Cobb	1857–1860
	Philip Thomas	1860–1861
	John A. Dix	1861
Secretary of War	John B. Floyd	1857–1861
	Joseph Holt	1861
Attorney General	Jeremiah S. Black	1857–1860
	Edwin M. Stanton	1860–1861
Postmaster General	Aaron V. Brown	1857–1859
	Joseph Holt	1859–1861
	Horatio King	1861
Secretary of Navy	Isaac Toucey	1857–1861
Secretary of Interior	Jacob Thompson	1857–1861

The Lincoln Administration (1861–1865)

Vice President	Hannibal Hamlin	1861–1865
	Andrew Johnson	1865
Secretary of State	William H. Seward	1861–1865
Secretary of Treasury	Samuel P. Chase	1861–1864
	William P. Fessenden	1864–1865
	Hugh McCulloch	1865
Secretary of War	Simon Cameron	1861–1862
	Edwin M. Stanton	1862–1865
Attorney General	Edward Bates	1861–1864
	James Speed	1864–1865
Postmaster General	Horatio King	1861
	Montgomery Blair	1861–1864
	William Dennison	1864–1865
Secretary of Navy	Gideon Welles	1861–1865
Secretary of Interior	Caleb B. Smith	1861–1863
	John P. Usher	1863–1865

The Andrew Johnson Administration (1865–1869)

Vice President	None	
Secretary of State	William H. Seward	1865–1869
Secretary of Treasury	Hugh McCulloch	1865–1869
Secretary of War	Edwin M. Stanton	1865–1867
	Ulysses S. Grant	1867–1868
	Lorenzo Thomas	1868
	John M. Schofield	1868–1869

Attorney General	James Speed	1865–1866
	Henry Stanbery	1866–1868
	William M. Evarts	1868–1869
Postmaster General	William Dennison	1865–1866
	Alexander Randall	1866–1869
Secretary of Navy	Gideon Welles	1865–1869
Secretary of Interior	John P. Usher	1865
	James Harlan	1865–1866
	Orville H. Browning	1866–1869

The Grant Administration (1869–1877)

Vice President	Schuyler Colfax	1869–1873
	Henry Wilson	1873–1877
Secretary of State	Elihu B. Washburne	1869
	Hamilton Fish	1869–1877
Secretary of Treasury	George S. Boutwell	1869–1873
	William Richardson	1873–1874
	Benjamin Bristow	1874–1876
	Lot M. Morrill	1876–1877
Secretary of War	John A. Rawlins	1869
	William T. Sherman	1869
	William W. Belknap	1869–1876
	Alphonso Taft	1876
	James D. Cameron	1876–1877
Attorney General	Ebenezer Hoar	1869–1870
	Amos T. Ackerman	1870–1871
	G. H. Williams	1871–1875
	Edwards Pierrepont	1875–1876
	Alphonso Taft	1876–1877
Postmaster General	John A. J. Creswell	1869–1874
	James W. Marshall	1874
	Marshall Jewell	1874–1876
	James N. Tyner	1876–1877
Secretary of Navy	Adolph E. Borie	1869
	George M. Robeson	1869–1877
Secretary of Interior	Jacob D. Cox	1869–1870
	Columbus Delano	1870–1875
	Zachariah Chandler	1875–1877

The Hayes Administration (1877–1881)

Vice President	William A. Wheeler	1877–1881
Secretary of State	William M. Evarts	1877–1881
Secretary of Treasury	John Sherman	1877–1881
Secretary of War	George W. McCrary	1877–1879
	Alex Ramsey	1879–1881
Attorney General	Charles Devens	1877–1881
Postmaster General	David M. Key	1877–1880
	Horace Maynard	1880–1881
Secretary of Navy	Richard W. Thompson	1877–1880
	Nathan Goff, Jr.	1881
Secretary of Interior	Carl Schurz	1877–1881

The Garfield Administration (1881)

Vice President	Chester A. Arthur	1881
Secretary of State	James G. Blaine	1881
Secretary of Treasury	William Windom	1881
Secretary of War	Robert T. Lincoln	1881
Attorney General	Wayne MacVeagh	1881
Postmaster General	Thomas L. James	1881
Secretary of Navy	William H. Hunt	1881
Secretary of Interior	Samuel J. Kirkwood	1881

The Arthur Administration (1881–1885)

Vice President	None	
Secretary of State	F. T. Frelinghuysen	1881–1885
Secretary of Treasury	Charles J. Folger	1881–1884
	Walter Q. Gresham	1884
	Hugh McCulloch	1884–1885

Secretary of War	Robert T. Lincoln	1881–1885
Attorney General	Benjamin H. Brewster	1881–1885
Postmaster General	Timothy O. Howe	1881–1883
	Walter Q. Gresham	1883–1884
	Frank Hatton	1884–1885
Secretary of Navy	William H. Hunt	1881–1882
	William E. Chandler	1882–1885
Secretary of Interior	Samuel J. Kirkwood	1881–1882
	Henry M. Teller	1882–1885

The Cleveland Administration (1885–1889)

Vice President	Thomas A. Hendricks	1885–1889
Secretary of State	Thomas F. Bayard	1885–1889
Secretary of Treasury	Daniel Manning	1885–1887
	Charles S. Fairchild	1887–1889
Secretary of War	William C. Endicott	1885–1889
Attorney General	Augustus H. Garland	1885–1889
Postmaster General	William F. Vilas	1885–1888
	Don M. Dickinson	1888–1889
Secretary of Navy	William C. Whitney	1885–1889
Secretary of Interior	Lucius Q. C. Lamar	1885–1888
	William F. Vilas	1888–1889
Secretary of Agriculture	Norman J. Colman	1889

The Benjamin Harrison Administration (1889–1893)

Vice President	Levi P. Morton	1889–1893
Secretary of State	James G. Blaine	1889–1892
	John W. Foster	1892–1893
Secretary of Treasury	William Windom	1889–1891
	Charles Foster	1891–1893
Secretary of War	Redfield Proctor	1889–1891
	Stephen B. Elkins	1891–1893

Attorney General	William H. H. Miller	1889–1893
Postmaster General	John Wanamaker	1889–1893
Secretary of Navy	Benjamin F. Tracy	1889–1893
Secretary of Interior	John W. Noble	1889–1893
Secretary of Agriculture	Jeremiah M. Rusk	1889–1893

The Cleveland Administration (1893–1897)

Vice President	Adlai E. Stevenson	1893–1897
Secretary of State	Walter Q. Gresham	1893–1895
	Richard Olney	1895–1897
Secretary of Treasury	John G. Carlisle	1893–1897
Secretary of War	Daniel S. Lamont	1893–1897
Attorney General	Richard Olney	1893–1895
	James Harmon	1895–1897
Postmaster General	Wilson S. Bissell	1893–1895
	William L. Wilson	1895–1897
Secretary of Navy	Hilary A. Herbert	1893–1897
Secretary of Interior	Hoke Smith	1893–1896
	David R. Francis	1896–1897
Secretary of Agriculture	Julius S. Morton	1893–1897

The McKinley Administration (1897–1901)

Vice President	Garret A. Hobart	1897–1901
	Theodore Roosevelt	1901
Secretary of State	John Sherman	1897–1898
	William R. Day	1898
	John Hay	1898–1901
Secretary of Treasury	Lyman J. Gage	1897–1901
Secretary of War	Russell A. Alger	1897–1899
	Elihu Root	1899–1901
Attorney General	Joseph McKenna	1897–1898
	John W. Griggs	1898–1901
	Philander C. Knox	1901
Postmaster General	James A. Gary	1897–1898
	Charles E. Smith	1898–1901
Secretary of Navy	John D. Long	1897–1901
Secretary of Interior	Cornelius N. Bliss	1897–1899
	Ethan A. Hitchcock	1899–1901
Secretary of Agriculture	James Wilson	1897–1901

The Theodore Roosevelt Administration (1901–1909)

Vice President	Charles Fairbanks	1905–1909
Secretary of State	John Hay	1901–1905
	Elihu Root	1905–1909
	Robert Bacon	1909
Secretary of Treasury	Lyman J. Gage	1901–1902
	Leslie M. Shaw	1902–1907
	George B. Cortelyou	1907–1909
Secretary of War	Elihu Root	1901–1904
	William H. Taft	1904–1908
	Luke E. Wright	1908–1909
Attorney General	Philander C. Knox	1901–1904
	William H. Moody	1904–1906
	Charles J. Bonaparte	1906–1909
Postmaster General	Charles E. Smith	1901–1902
	Henry C. Payne	1902–1904
	Robert J. Wynne	1904–1905
	George B. Cortelyou	1905–1907
	George von L. Meyer	1907–1909
Secretary of Navy	John D. Long	1901–1902
	William H. Moody	1902–1904
	Paul Morton	1904–1905
	Charles J. Bonaparte	1905–1906
	Victor H. Metcalf	1906–1908
	Truman H. Newberry	1908–1909
Secretary of Interior	Ethan A. Hitchcock	1901–1907
	James R. Garfield	1907–1909
Secretary of Agriculture	James Wilson	1901–1909
Secretary of Labor and Commerce	George B. Cortelyou	1903–1904
	Victor H. Metcalf	1904–1906
	Oscar S. Straus	1906–1909
	Charles Nagel	1909

The Taft Administration (1909–1913)

Vice President	James S. Sherman	1909–1913
Secretary of State	Philander C. Knox	1909–1913
Secretary of Treasury	Franklin MacVeagh	1909–1913
Secretary of War	Jacob M. Dickinson	1909–1911
	Henry L. Stimson	1911–1913
Attorney General	George W. Wickersham	1909–1913
Postmaster General	Frank H. Hitchcock	1909–1913
Secretary of Navy	George von L. Meyer	1909–1913
Secretary of Interior	Richard A. Ballinger	1909–1911
	Walter L. Fisher	1911–1913
Secretary of Agriculture	James Wilson	1909–1913
Secretary of Labor and Commerce	Charles Nagel	1909–1913

The Wilson Administration (1913–1921)

Vice President	Thomas R. Marshall	1913–1921
Secretary of State	William J. Bryan	1913–1915
	Robert Lansing	1915–1920
	Bainbridge Colby	1920–1921
Secretary of Treasury	William G. McAdoo	1913–1918
	Carter Glass	1918–1920
	David F. Houston	1920–1921
Secretary of War	Lindley M. Garrison	1913–1916
	Newton D. Baker	1916–1921
Attorney General	James C. McReynolds	1913–1914
	Thomas W. Gregory	1914–1919
	A. Mitchell Palmer	1919–1921
Postmaster General	Albert S. Burleson	1913–1921
Secretary of Navy	Josephus Daniels	1913–1921
Secretary of Interior	Franklin K. Lane	1913–1920
	John B. Payne	1920–1921
Secretary of Agriculture	David F. Houston	1913–1920
	Edwin T. Meredith	1920–1921
Secretary of Commerce	William C. Redfield	1913–1919
	Joshua W. Alexander	1919–1921
Secretary of Labor	William B. Wilson	1913–1921

The Harding Administration (1921–1923)

Vice President	Calvin Coolidge	1921–1923
Secretary of State	Charles E. Hughes	1921–1923
Secretary of Treasury	Andrew Mellon	1921–1923
Secretary of War	John W. Weeks	1921–1923
Attorney General	Harry M. Daugherty	1921–1923
Postmaster General	Will H. Hays	1921–1922
	Hubert Work	1922–1923
	Harry S. New	1923
Secretary of Navy	Edwin Denby	1921–1923
Secretary of Interior	Albert B. Fall	1921–1923
	Hubert Work	1923
Secretary of Agriculture	Henry C. Wallace	1921–1923
Secretary of Commerce	Herbert C. Hoover	1921–1923
Secretary of Labor	James J. Davis	1921–1923

The Coolidge Administration (1923–1929)

Vice President	Charles G. Dawes	1925–1929
Secretary of State	Charles E. Hughes	1923–1925
	Frank B. Kellogg	1925–1929
Secretary of Treasury	Andrew Mellon	1923–1929

Secretary of War	John W. Weeks	1923–1925
	Dwight F. Davis	1925–1929
Attorney General	Henry M. Daugherty	1923–1924
	Harlan F. Stone	1924–1925
	John G. Sargent	1925–1929
Postmaster General	Harry S. New	1923–1929
Secretary of Navy	Edwin Denby	1923–1924
	Curtis D. Wilbur	1924–1929
Secretary of Interior	Hubert Work	1923–1928
	Roy O. West	1928–1929
Secretary of Agriculture	Henry C. Wallace	1923–1924
	Howard M. Gore	1924–1925
	William M. Jardine	1925–1929
Secretary of Commerce	Herbert C. Hoover	1923–1928
	William F. Whiting	1928–1929
Secretary of Labor	James J. Davis	1923–1929

The Hoover Administration (1929–1933)

Vice President	Charles Curtis	1929–1933
Secretary of State	Henry L. Stimson	1929–1933
Secretary of Treasury	Andrew Mellon	1929–1932
	Ogden L. Mills	1932–1933
Secretary of War	James W. Good	1929
	Patrick J. Hurley	1929–1933
Attorney General	William D. Mitchell	1929–1933
Postmaster General	Walter F. Brown	1929–1933
Secretary of Navy	Charles F. Adams	1929–1933
Secretary of Interior	Ray L. Wilbur	1929–1933
Secretary of Agriculture	Arthur M. Hyde	1929–1933
Secretary of Commerce	Robert P. Lamont	1929–1932
	Roy D. Chapin	1932–1933
Secretary of Labor	James J. Davis	1929–1930
	William M. Doak	1930–1933

The Franklin D. Roosevelt Administration (1933–1945)

Vice President	John Nance Garner	1933–1941
	Henry A. Wallace	1941–1945
	Harry S. Truman	1945
Secretary of State	Cordell Hull	1933–1944
	Edward R. Stettinius, Jr.	1944–1945
Secretary of Treasury	William H. Woodin	1933–1934
	Henry Morgenthau, Jr.	1934–1945
Secretary of War	George H. Dern	1933–1936
	Henry A. Woodring	1936–1940
	Henry L. Stimson	1940–1945
Attorney General	Homer S. Cummings	1933–1939
	Frank Murphy	1939–1940
	Robert H. Jackson	1940–1941
	Francis Biddle	1941–1945
Postmaster General	James A. Farley	1933–1940
	Frank C. Walker	1940–1945
Secretary of Navy	Claude A. Swanson	1933–1940
	Charles Edison	1940
	Frank Knox	1940–1944
	James V. Forrestal	1944–1945
Secretary of Interior	Harold L. Ickes	1933–1945
Secretary of Agriculture	Henry A. Wallace	1933–1940
	Claude R. Wickard	1940–1945
Secretary of Commerce	Daniel C. Roper	1933–1939
	Harry L. Hopkins	1939–1940
	Jesse Jones	1940–1945
	Henry A. Wallace	1945
Secretary of Labor	Frances Perkins	1933–1945

The Truman Administration (1945–1953)

Vice President	Alben W. Barkley	1949–1953
Secretary of State	Edward R. Stettinius, Jr.	1945
	James F. Byrnes	1945–1947
	George C. Marshall	1947–1949
	Dean G. Acheson	1949–1953

Secretary of Treasury	Fred M. Vinson	1945–1946
	John W. Snyder	1946–1953
Secretary of War	Robert P. Patterson	1945–1947
	Kenneth C. Royall	1947
Attorney General	Tom C. Clark	1945–1949
	J. Howard McGrath	1949–1952
	James P. McGranery	1952–1953
Postmaster General	Frank C. Walker	1945
	Robert E. Hannegan	1945–1947
	Jesse M. Donaldson	1947–1953
Secretary of Navy	James V. Forrestal	1945–1947
Secretary of Interior	Harold L. Ickes	1945–1946
	Julius A. Krug	1946–1949
	Oscar L. Chapman	1949–1953
Secretary of Agriculture	Clinton P. Anderson	1945–1948
	Charles F. Brannan	1948–1953
Secretary of Commerce	Henry A. Wallace	1945–1946
	W. Averell Harriman	1946–1948
	Charles W. Sawyer	1948–1953
Secretary of Labor	Lewis B. Schwellenbach	1945–1948
	Maurice J. Tobin	1948–1953
Secretary of Defense	James V. Forrestal	1947–1949
	Louis A. Johnson	1949–1950
	George C. Marshall	1950–1951
	Robert A. Lovett	1951–1953

The Eisenhower Administration (1953 – 1961)

Vice President	Richard M. Nixon	1953–1961
Secretary of State	John Foster Dulles	1953–1959
	Christian A. Herter	1959–1961
Secretary of Treasury	George M. Humphrey	1953–1957
	Robert B. Anderson	1957–1961
Attorney General	Herbert Brownell, Jr.	1953–1958
	William P. Rogers	1958–1961

Postmaster General	Arthur E. Summerfield	1953–1961
Secretary of Interior	Douglas McKay	1953–1956
	Fred A. Seaton	1956–1961
Secretary of Agriculture	Ezra T. Benson	1953–1961
Secretary of Commerce	Sinclair Weeks	1953–1958
	Lewis L. Strauss	1958–1959
	Frederick H. Mueller	1959–1961
Secretary of Labor	Martin P. Durkin	1953
	James P. Mitchell	1953–1961
Secretary of Defense	Charles E. Wilson	1953–1957
	Neil H. McElroy	1957–1959
	Thomas S. Gates, Jr.	1959–1961
Secretary of Health, Education and Welfare	Oveta Culp Hobby	1953–1955
	Marion B. Folsom	1955–1958
	Arthur S. Flemming	1958–1961

The Kennedy Administration (1961–1963)

Vice President	Lyndon B. Johnson	1961–1963
Secretary of State	Dean Rusk	1961–1963
Secretary of Treasury	C. Douglas Dillon	1961–1963
Attorney General	Robert F. Kennedy	1961–1963
Postmaster General	J. Edward Day	1961–1963
	John A. Gronouski	1963
Secretary of Interior	Stewart L. Udall	1961–1963
Secretary of Agriculture	Orville L. Freeman	1961–1963
Secretary of Commerce	Luther H. Hodges	1961–1963
Secretary of Labor	Arthur J. Goldberg	1961–1962
	W. Willard Wirtz	1962–1963
Secretary of Defense	Robert S. McNamara	1961–1963
Secretary of Health, Education and Welfare	Abraham A. Ribicoff	1961–1962
	Anthony J. Celebrezze	1962–1963

The Lyndon Johnson Administration (1963 – 1969)

Vice President	Hubert H. Humphrey	1965–1969
Secretary of State	Dean Rusk	1963–1969
Secretary of Treasury	C. Douglas Dillon	1963–1965
	Henry H. Fowler	1965–1969
Attorney General	Robert F. Kennedy	1963–1964
	Nicholas Katzenbach	1965–1966
	Ramsey Clark	1967–1969
Postmaster General	John A. Gronouski	1963–1965
	Lawrence F. O'Brien	1965–1968
	Marvin Watson	1968–1969
Secretary of Interior	Stewart L. Udall	1963–1969
Secretary of Agriculture	Orville L. Freeman	1963–1969
Secretary of Commerce	Luther H. Hodges	1963–1964
	John T. Connor	1964–1967
	Alexander B. Trowbridge	1967–1968
	Cyrus R. Smith	1968–1969
Secretary of Labor	W. Willard Wirtz	1963–1969
Secretary of Defense	Robert F. McNamara	1963–1968
	Clark Clifford	1968–1969
Secretary of Health, Education and Welfare	Anthony J. Celebrezze	1963–1965
	John W. Gardner	1965–1968
	Wilbur J. Cohen	1968–1969
Secretary of Housing and Urban Development	Robert C. Weaver	1966–1969
	Robert C. Wood	1969
Secretary of Transportation	Alan S. Boyd	1967–1969

The Nixon Administration (1969 – 1974)

Vice President	Spiro T. Agnew	1969–1973
	Gerald R. Ford	1973–1974
Secretary of State	William P. Rogers	1969–1973
	Henry A. Kissinger	1973–1974
Secretary of Treasury	David M. Kennedy	1969–1970
	John B. Connally	1971–1972
	George P. Shultz	1972–1974
	William E. Simon	1974
Attorney General	John N. Mitchell	1969–1972
	Richard G. Kleindienst	1972–1973
	Elliot L. Richardson	1973
	William B. Saxbe	1973–1974
Postmaster General	Winton M. Blount	1969–1971
Secretary of Interior	Walter J. Hickel	1969–1970
	Rogers Morton	1971–1974
Secretary of Agriculture	Clifford M. Hardin	1969–1971
	Earl L. Butz	1971–1974
Secretary of Commerce	Maurice H. Stans	1969–1972
	Peter G. Peterson	1972–1973
	Frederick B. Dent	1973–1974
Secretary of Labor	George P. Shultz	1969–1970
	James D. Hodgson	1970–1973
	Peter J. Brennan	1973–1974
Secretary of Defense	Melvin R. Laird	1969–1973
	Elliot L. Richardson	1973
	James R. Schlesinger	1973–1974
Secretary of Health, Education and Welfare	Robert H. Finch	1969–1970
	Elliot L. Richardson	1970–1973
	Caspar W. Weinberger	1973–1974
Secretary of Housing and Urban Development	George Romney	1969–1973
	James T. Lynn	1973–1974
Secretary of Transportation	John A. Volpe	1969–1973
	Claude S. Brinegar	1973–1974

The Ford Administration (1974 – 1977)

Vice President	Nelson A. Rockefeller	1974–1977
Secretary of State	Henry A. Kissinger	1974–1977
Secretary of Treasury	William E. Simon	1974–1977

Attorney General	William Saxbe	1974–1975
	Edward Levi	1975–1977
Secretary of Interior	Rogers Morton	1974–1975
	Stanley K. Hathaway	1975
	Thomas Kleppe	1975–1977
Secretary of Agriculture	Earl L. Butz	1974–1976
	John A. Knebel	1976–1977
Secretary of Commerce	Frederick B. Dent	1974–1975
	Rogers Morton	1975–1976
	Elliot L. Richardson	1976–1977
Secretary of Labor	Peter J. Brennan	1974–1975
	John T. Dunlop	1975–1976
	W. J. Usery	1976–1977
Secretary of Defense	James R. Schlesinger	1974–1975
	Donald Rumsfeld	1975–1977
Secretary of Health, Education and Welfare	Caspar Weinberger	1974–1975
	Forrest D. Mathews	1975–1977
Secretary of Housing and Urban Development	James T. Lynn	1974–1975
	Carla A. Hills	1975–1977
Secretary of Transportation	Claude Brinegar	1974–1975
	William T. Coleman	1975–1977

The Carter Administration (1977 – 1981)

Vice President	Walter F. Mondale	1977–1981
Secretary of State	Cyrus R. Vance	1977–1980
	Edmund Muskie	1980–1981
Secretary of Treasury	W. Michael Blumenthal	1977–1979
	G. William Miller	1979–1981
Attorney General	Griffin Bell	1977–1979
	Benjamin R. Civiletti	1979–1981
Secretary of Interior	Cecil D. Andrus	1977–1981
Secretary of Agriculture	Robert Bergland	1977–1981
Secretary of Commerce	Juanita M. Kreps	1977–1979
	Philip M. Klutznick	1979–1981
Secretary of Labor	F. Ray Marshall	1977–1981
Secretary of Defense	Harold Brown	1977–1981

Secretary of Health, Education and Welfare	Joseph A. Califano	1977–1979
	Patricia R. Harris	1979
Secretary of Health and Human Services	Patricia R. Harris	1979–1981
Secretary of Education	Shirley M. Hufstedler	1979–1981
Secretary of Housing and Urban Development	Patricia R. Harris	1977–1979
	Moon Landrieu	1979–1981
Secretary of Transportation	Brock Adams	1977–1979
	Neil E. Goldschmidt	1979–1981
Secretary of Energy	James R. Schlesinger	1977–1979
	Charles W. Duncan	1979–1981

The Reagan Administration (1981 – 1989)

Vice President	George W. Bush	1981–1989
Secretary of State	Alexander M. Haig	1981–1982
	George P. Shultz	1982–1989
Secretary of Treasury	Donald Regan	1981–1985
	James A. Baker, III	1985–1988
	Nicholas Brady	1988–1989
Attorney General	William F. Smith	1981–1985
	Edwin A. Meese, III	1985–1988
	Richard Thornburgh	1988–1989
Secretary of Interior	James Watt	1981–1983
	William P. Clark, Jr.	1983–1985
	Donald P. Hodel	1985–1989
Secretary of Agriculture	John Block	1981–1986
	Richard E. Lyng	1986–1989
Secretary of Commerce	Malcolm Baldridge	1981–1987
	C. William Verity, Jr.	1987–1989
Secretary of Labor	Raymond Donovan	1981–1985
	William E. Brock	1985–1987
	Ann D. McLaughlin	1987–1989
Secretary of Defense	Caspar Weinberger	1981–1987
	Frank Carlucci	1987–1989

Secretary of Health and Human Services	Richard Schweiker	1981–1983
	Margaret Heckler	1983–1985
	Otis R. Bowen	1985–1989
Secretary of Education	Terrel H. Bell	1981–1985
	William J. Bennett	1985–1988
	Lauro F. Cavazos	1988–1989
Secretary of Housing and Urban Development	Samuel Pierce	1981–1989
Secretary of Transportation	Drew Lewis	1981–1983
	Elizabeth Dole	1983–1987
	James H. Burnley	1987–1989
Secretary of Energy	James Edwards	1981–1982
	Donald P. Hodel	1982–1985
	John S. Herrington	1985–1989

The Bush Administration (1989 – 1993)

Vice President	J. Danforth Quayle	1989–1993
Secretary of State	James A. Baker, III	1989–1992
Secretary of Treasury	Nicholas Brady	1989–1993
Attorney General	Richard Thornburgh	1989–1991
	William P. Barr	1991–1993
Secretary of Interior	Manuel Lujan	1989–1993
Secretary of Agriculture	Clayton K. Yeutter	1989–1991
	Edward Madigan	1991–1993
Secretary of Commerce	Robert Mosbacher	1989–1992
	Barbara Franklin	1992–1993
Secretary of Labor	Elizabeth Hanford Dole	1989–1991
	Lynn Martin	1991–1993
Secretary of Defense	Richard Cheney	1989–1993
Secretary of Health and Human Services	Louis W. Sullivan	1989–1993
Secretary of Education	Lauro F. Cavazos	1989–1991
	Lamar Alexander	1991–1993
Secretary of Housing and Urban Development	Jack F. Kemp	1989–1993

Secretary of Transportation	Samuel K. Skinner	1989–1992
	Andrew H. Card, Jr.	1992–1993
Secretary of Energy	James D. Watkins	1989–1993
Secretary of Veterans Affairs	Edward J. Derwinski	1989–1993

The Clinton Administration (1993 –   )

Vice President	Albert Gore	1993–
Secretary of State	Warren M. Christopher	1993–1997
	Madeleine K. Albright	1997–
Secretary of Treasury	Lloyd Bentsen	1993–1995
	Robert E. Rubin	1995–
Attorney General	Janet Reno	1993–
Secretary of Interior	Bruce Babbitt	1993–
Secretary of Agriculture	Mike Espy	1993–1995
	Dan Glickman	1995–
Secretary of Commerce	Ronald H. Brown	1993–1996
	Mickey Kantor	1996–1997
	William Daley	1997–
Secretary of Labor	Robert B. Reich	1993–1997
	Alexis Herman	1997–
Secretary of Defense	Les Aspin	1993–1994
	William J. Perry	1994–1997
	William Cohen	1997–
Secretary of Health and Human Services	Donna Shalala	1993–
Secretary of Housing and Urban Development	Henry G. Cisneros	1993–1997
	Andrew Cuomo	1997–
Secretary of Education	Richard W. Riley	1993–
Secretary of Transportation	Federico F. Peña	1993–1997
	Rodney Slater	1997–
Secretary of Energy	Hazel R. O'Leary	1993–1997
	Federico F. Peña	1997–
Secretary of Veterans Affairs	Jesse Brown	1993–

ADMISSION OF STATES TO THE UNION

State	Date of Admission
Delaware	December 7, 1787
Pennsylvania	December 12, 1787
New Jersey	December 18, 1787
Georgia	January 2, 1788
Connecticut	January 9, 1788
Massachusetts	February 6, 1788
Maryland	April 28, 1788
South Carolina	May 23, 1788
New Hampshire	June 21, 1788
Virginia	June 25, 1788
New York	July 26, 1788
North Carolina	November 21, 1789
Rhode Island	May 29, 1790
Vermont	March 4, 1791
Kentucky	June 1, 1792
Tennessee	June 1, 1796
Ohio	March 1, 1803
Louisiana	April 30, 1812
Indiana	December 11, 1816
Mississippi	December 10, 1817
Illinois	December 3, 1818
Alabama	December 14, 1819
Maine	March 15, 1820
Missouri	August 10, 1821
Arkansas	June 15, 1836

State	Date of Admission
Michigan	January 16, 1837
Florida	March 3, 1845
Texas	December 29, 1845
Iowa	December 28, 1846
Wisconsin	May 29, 1848
California	September 9, 1850
Minnesota	May 11, 1858
Oregon	February 14, 1859
Kansas	January 29, 1861
West Virginia	June 19, 1863
Nevada	October 31, 1864
Nebraska	March 1, 1867
Colorado	August 1, 1876
North Dakota	November 2, 1889
South Dakota	November 2, 1889
Montana	November 8, 1889
Washington	November 11, 1889
Idaho	July 3, 1890
Wyoming	July 10, 1890
Utah	January 4, 1896
Oklahoma	November 16, 1907
New Mexico	January 6, 1912
Arizona	February 14, 1912
Alaska	January 3, 1959
Hawaii	August 21, 1959

SUPREME COURT JUSTICES

Name	Service	Appointed by
John Jay*	1789–1795	Washington
James Wilson	1789–1798	Washington
John Blair	1789–1796	Washington
John Rutledge	1790–1791	Washington
William Cushing	1790–1810	Washington
James Iredell	1790–1799	Washington
Thomas Johnson	1791–1793	Washington
William Paterson	1793–1806	Washington
John Rutledge†	1795	Washington
Samuel Chase	1796–1811	Washington
Oliver Ellsworth	1796–1799	Washington
Bushrod Washington	1798–1829	J. Adams
Alfred Moore	1799–1804	J. Adams
John Marshall	1801–1835	J. Adams
William Johnson	1804–1834	Jefferson
Henry B. Livingston	1806–1823	Jefferson
Thomas Todd	1807–1826	Jefferson
Gabriel Duval	1811–1836	Madison
Joseph Story	1811–1845	Madison
Smith Thompson	1823–1843	Monroe
Robert Trimble	1826–1828	J. Q. Adams
John McLean	1829–1861	Jackson
Henry Baldwin	1830–1844	Jackson
James M. Wayne	1835–1867	Jackson
Roger B. Taney	1836–1864	Jackson
Philip P. Barbour	1836–1841	Jackson
John Catron	1837–1865	Van Buren
John McKinley	1837–1852	Van Buren
Peter V. Daniel	1841–1860	Van Buren
Samuel Nelson	1845–1872	Tyler
Levi Woodbury	1845–1851	Polk
Robert C. Grier	1846–1870	Polk
Benjamin R. Curtis	1851–1857	Fillmore
John A. Campbell	1853–1861	Pierce
Nathan Clifford	1858–1881	Buchanan
Noah H. Swayne	1862–1881	Lincoln
Samuel F. Miller	1862–1890	Lincoln

*Chief Justices appear in bold type.
†Acting Chief Justice; Senate refused to confirm appointment.

Name	Service	Appointed by
David Davis	1862–1877	Lincoln
Stephen J. Field	1863–1897	Lincoln
Salmon P. Chase	1864–1873	Lincoln
William Strong	1870–1880	Grant
Joseph P. Bradley	1870–1892	Grant
Ward Hunt	1873–1882	Grant
Morrison R. Waite	1874–1888	Grant
John M. Harlan	1877–1911	Hayes
William B. Woods	1880–1887	Hayes
Stanley Matthews	1881–1889	Garfield
Horace Gray	1882–1902	Arthur
Samuel Blatchford	1882–1893	Arthur
Lucious Q. C. Lamar	1888–1893	Cleveland
Melville W. Fuller	1888–1910	Cleveland
David J. Brewer	1889–1910	B. Harrison
Henry B. Brown	1890–1906	B. Harrison
George Shiras	1892–1903	B. Harrison
Howell E. Jackson	1893–1895	B. Harrison
Edward D. White	1894–1910	Cleveland
Rufus W. Peckham	1896–1909	Cleveland
Joseph McKenna	1898–1925	McKinley
Oliver W. Holmes	1902–1932	T. Roosevelt
William R. Day	1903–1922	T. Roosevelt
William H. Moody	1906–1910	T. Roosevelt
Horace H. Lurton	1910–1914	Taft
Charles E. Hughes	1910–1916	Taft
Willis Van Devanter	1910–1937	Taft
Joseph R. Lamar	1911–1916	Taft
Edward D. White	1910–1921	Taft
Mahlon Pitney	1912–1922	Taft
James C. McReynolds	1914–1941	Wilson
Louis D. Brandeis	1916–1939	Wilson
John H. Clarke	1916–1922	Wilson
William H. Taft	1921–1930	Harding
George Sutherland	1922–1938	Harding

Name	Service	Appointed by
Pierce Butler	1923–1939	Harding
Edward T. Sanford	1923–1930	Harding
Harlan F. Stone	1925–1941	Coolidge
Charles E. Hughes	1930–1941	Hoover
Owen J. Roberts	1930–1945	Hoover
Benjamin N. Cardozo	1932–1938	Hoover
Hugo L. Black	1937–1971	F. Roosevelt
Stanley F. Reed	1938–1957	F. Roosevelt
Felix Frankfurter	1939–1962	F. Roosevelt
William O. Douglas	1939–1975	F. Roosevelt
Frank Murphy	1940–1949	F. Roosevelt
Harlan F. Stone	1941–1946	F. Roosevelt
James F. Byrnes	1941–1942	F. Roosevelt
Robert H. Jackson	1941–1954	F. Roosevelt
Wiley B. Rutledge	1943–1949	F. Roosevelt
Harold H. Burton	1945–1958	Truman
Frederick M. Vinson	1946–1953	Truman
Tom C. Clark	1949–1967	Truman
Sherman Minton	1949–1956	Truman
Earl Warren	1953–1969	Eisenhower
John Marshall Harlan	1955–1971	Eisenhower
William J. Brennan Jr.	1956–1990	Eisenhower
Charles E. Whittaker	1957–1962	Eisenhower
Potter Stewart	1958–1981	Eisenhower
Byron R. White	1962–1993	Kennedy
Arthur J. Goldberg	1962–1965	Kennedy
Abe Fortas	1965–1969	Johnson
Thurgood Marshall	1967–1991	Johnson
Warren E. Burger	1969–1986	Nixon
Harry A. Blackmun	1970–1994	Nixon
Lewis F. Powell Jr.	1972–1988	Nixon
William H. Rehnquist	1972–1986	Nixon
John Paul Stevens	1975–	Ford
Sandra Day O'Connor	1981–	Reagan
William H. Rehnquist	1986–	Reagan
Antonin Scalia	1986–	Reagan
Anthony M. Kennedy	1988–	Reagan
David H. Souter	1990–	Bush
Clarence Thomas	1991–	Bush
Ruth Bader Ginsburg	1993–	Clinton
Stephen Breyer	1994–	Clinton

SIGNIFICANT SUPREME COURT CASES

Marbury v. Madison (1803)

This case established the right of the Supreme Court to review the constitutionality of laws. The decision involved judicial appointments made during the last hours of the administration of President John Adams. Some commissions, including that of William Marbury, had not yet been delivered when President Thomas Jefferson took office. Infuriated by the last-minute nature of Adams's Federalist appointments, Jefferson refused to send the undelivered commissions out, and Marbury decided to sue. The Supreme Court, presided over by John Marshall, a Federalist who had assisted Adams in the judicial appointments, ruled that although Marbury's commission was valid and the new president should have delivered it, the Court could not compel him to do so. The Court based its reasoning on a finding that the grounds of Marbury's suit, resting in the Judiciary Act of 1789, were in conflict with the Constitution.

For the first time, the Court had overturned a national law on the grounds that it was unconstitutional. John Marshall had quietly established the concept of judicial review: The Supreme Court had given itself the authority to nullify acts of the other branches of the federal government. Although the Constitution provides for judicial review, the Court had not exercised this power before and did not use it again until 1857. It seems likely that if the Court had waited until 1857 to use this power, it would have been difficult to establish.

McCulloch v. Maryland (1819)

In 1816, Congress authorized the creation of a national bank. To protect its own banks from competition with a branch of the national bank in Baltimore, the state legislature of Maryland placed a tax of 2 percent on all notes issued by any bank operating in Maryland that was not chartered by the state. McCulloch, cashier of the Baltimore branch of the Bank of the United States, was convicted for refusing to pay the tax. Under the leadership of Chief Justice John Marshall, the Court ruled that the federal government had the power to establish a bank, even though that specific authority was not mentioned in the Constitution.

Marshall maintained that the authority could be reasonably implied from Article 1, section 8, which gives Congress the power to make all laws that are nec-

essary and proper to execute the enumerated powers. Marshall also held that Maryland could not tax the national bank because in a conflict between federal and state laws, the federal law must take precedence. Thus he established the principles of implied powers and federal supremacy, both of which set a precedent for subsequent expansion of federal power at the expense of the states.

Scott v. Sanford (1857)

Dred Scott was a slave who sued for his own and his family's freedom on the grounds, that, with his master, he had traveled to and lived in free territory that did not allow slavery. When his case reached the Supreme Court, the justices saw an opportunity to settle once and for all the vexing question of slavery in the territories. The Court's decision in this case proved that it enjoyed no special immunity from the sectional and partisan passions of the time. Five of the nine justices were from the South and seven were Democrats.

Chief Justice Roger B. Taney hated Republicans and detested racial equality; his decision reflects those prejudices. He wrote an opinion not only declaring that Scott was still a slave but also claiming that the Constitution denied citizenship or rights to blacks, that Congress had no right to exclude slavery from the territories, and that the Missouri Compromise was unconstitutional. While southern Democrats gloated over this seven-to-two decision, sectional tensions were further inflamed and the young Republican Party's claim that a hostile "slave power" was conspiring to destroy northern liberties was given further credence. The decision brought the nation closer to civil war and is generally regarded as the worst decision ever rendered by the Supreme Court.

Butchers' Benevolent Association of New Orleans v. Crescent City Livestock Landing and Slaughterhouse Co. (1873)

The *Slaughterhouse* cases, as the cases docketed under the *Butchers'* title were known, were the first legal test of the Fourteenth Amendment. To cut down on cases of cholera believed to be caused by contaminated water, the state of Louisiana prohibited the slaughter of livestock in New Orleans except in one slaughterhouse, effectively giving that slaughterhouse a monopoly. Other New Orleans butchers claimed that the state had deprived them of their occupation without due process of law, thus violating the Fourteenth Amendment.

In a five-to-four decision, the Court upheld the Louisiana law, declaring that the Fourteenth Amendment protected only the rights of federal citizenship, like voting in federal elections and interstate travel. The federal government thus was not obliged to protect basic civil rights from violation by state governments. This decison would have significant implications for African Americans and their struggle for civil rights in the twentieth century.

United States v. E. C. Knight Co. (1895)

Also known as the *Sugar Trust* case, this was among the first cases to reveal the weakness of the Sherman Antitrust Act in the hands of a pro-business Supreme Court. In 1895, American Sugar Refining Company purchased four other sugar producers, including the E. C. Knight Company, and thus took control of more than 98 percent of the sugar refining in the United States. In an effort to limit monopoly, the government brought suit against all five of the companies for violating the Sherman Antitrust Act, which outlawed trusts and other business combinations in restraint of trade. The Court dismissed the suit, however, arguing that the law applied only to commerce and not to manufacturing, defining the latter as a local concern and not part of the interstate commerce that the government could regulate.

Plessy v. Ferguson (1896)

African American Homer Plessy challenged a Louisiana law that required segregation on trains passing through the state. After ensuring that the railroad and the conductor knew that he was of mixed race (Plessy appeared to be white but under the racial code of Louisiana was classified as "colored" because he was one-eighth black), he refused to move to the "colored only" section of the coach. The Court ruled against Plessy by a vote of seven to one, declaring that "separate but equal" facilities were permissible according to section 1 of the Fourteenth Amendment, which calls upon the states to provide "equal protection of the laws" to anyone within their jurisdiction. Although the case was viewed as relatively insignificant at the time, it cast a long shadow over several decades.

Initially, the decision was viewed as a victory for segregationists, but in the 1930s and 1940s civil rights advocates referred to the doctrine of "separate but equal" in their efforts to end segregation. They argued that segregated institutions and accommodations were often *not* equal to those available to whites, and finally succeeded in overturning *Plessy* in *Brown v. Board of Education* in 1954 (see p. A-46).

Lochner v. New York (1905)

In this case, the Court ruled against a New York state law that prohibited employees from working in bakeries more than ten hours a day or sixty hours a week. The purpose of the law was to protect the health of workers, but the Court ruled that it was unconstitutional because it violated "freedom of contract" implicitly protected by the due process clause of the Fourteenth Amendment. Most of the justices believed strongly in a laissez-faire economic system that favored survival of the fittest. They felt that government protection of workers interfered with this system. In a dissenting opinion, Justice Oliver Wendell Holmes accused the majority of distorting the Constitution and of deciding the case on "an economic theory which a large part of the country does not entertain."

Muller v. Oregon (1908)

In 1905, Curt Muller, owner of a Portland, Oregon, laundry, demanded that one of his employees, Mrs. Elmer Gotcher, work more than the ten hours allowed as a maximum workday for women under Oregon law. Muller argued that the law violated his "freedom of contract" as established in prior Supreme Court decisions.

Progressive lawyer Louis D. Brandeis defended the Oregon law by arguing that a state could be justified in abridging freedom of contract when the health, safety, and welfare of workers was at issue. His innovative strategy drew on ninety-five pages of excerpts from factory and medical reports to substantiate his argument that there was a direct connection between long hours and the health of women and thus the health of the nation. In a unanimous decision, the Court upheld the Oregon law, but later generations of women fighting for equality would question the strategy of arguing that women's reproductive role entitled them to special treatment.

Schenck v. United States (1919)

During World War I, Charles Schenck and other members of the Socialist Party printed and mailed out flyers urging young men who were subject to the draft to oppose the war in Europe. In upholding the conviction of Schenck for publishing a pamphlet urging draft resistance, Justice Oliver Wendell Holmes established the "clear and present danger" test for freedom of speech. Such utterances as Schenck's during a time of national peril, Holmes wrote, could be considered the equivalent of shouting "Fire!" in a crowded theater. Congress had the right to protect the public against such an incitement to panic, the Court ruled in a unanimous decision. But the analogy was a false one. Schenck's pamphlet had little power to provoke a public firmly opposed to its message. Although Holmes later modified his position to state that the danger must relate to an immediate evil and a specific action, the "clear and present danger" test laid the groundwork for those who later sought to limit First Amendment freedoms.

Schechter Poultry Corp. v. United States (1935)

During the Great Depression, the National Industrial Recovery Act (NIRA), which was passed under President Franklin D. Roosevelt, established fair competition codes that were designed to help businesses. The Schechter brothers of New York City, who sold chickens, were convicted of violating the codes. The Supreme Court ruled that the NIRA unconstitutionally conferred legislative power on an administrative agency and overstepped the limits of federal power to regulate interstate commerce. The decision was a significant blow to the New Deal recovery program, demonstrating both historic American resistance to economic planning and the refusal of the business community to yield its autonomy unless it was forced to do so.

Brown v. Board of Education (1954)

In 1950, the families of eight Topeka, Kansas, children sued the Topeka Board of Education. The children were blacks who lived within walking distance of a whites-only school. The segregated school system required them to take a time-consuming, inconvenient, and dangerous route to get to a black school, and their parents argued that there was no reason their children should not be allowed to attend the nearest school. By the time the case reached the Supreme Court, it had been joined with similar cases regarding segregated schools in other states and the District of Columbia. A team of lawyers from the National Association for the Advancement of Colored People (NAACP), led by Thurgood Marshall (who would later be appointed to the Supreme Court), urged the Court to overturn the fifty-eight-year-old precedent established in *Plessy v. Ferguson*, which had enshrined "separate but equal" as the law of the land. A unanimous Court, led by Chief Justice Earl Warren, declared that "Separate educa-

tional facilities are inherently unequal" and thus violate the Fourteenth Amendment. In 1955, the Court called for desegregation "with all deliberate speed" but established no deadline.

Roth v. United States (1957)

In 1957, New Yorker Samuel Roth was convicted of sending obscene materials through the mail in a case that ultimately reached the Supreme Court. With a six-to-three vote, the Court reaffirmed the historical view that obscenity is not protected by the First Amendment. Yet it broke new ground by declaring that a work could be judged obscene only if, "taken as a whole," it appealed to the "prurient interest" of "the average person."

Prior to this case, work could be judged obscene if portions were thought able to "deprave and corrupt" the most susceptible part of an audience (such as children). Thus, serious works of literature such as Theodore Dreiser's *An American Tragedy*, which was banned in Boston when first published, received no protection. Although this decision continued to pose problems of definition, it did help to protect most works that attempt to convey ideas, even if those ideas have to do with sex, from the threat of obscenity laws.

Engel v. Vitale (1962)

In 1959, five parents with ten children in the New Hyde Park, New York, school system sued the school board. The parents argued that the so-called Regents' Prayer that public school students in New York recited at the start of every school day violated the doctrine of separation of church and state outlined in the First Amendment. In 1962, the Supreme Court voted six to one in favor of banning the Regents' Prayer.

The decision threw the religious community into an uproar. Many religious leaders expressed dismay and even shock; others welcomed the decision. Several efforts to introduce an amendment allowing school prayer have failed. Subsequent Supreme Court decisions have banned reading of the Bible in public schools. The Court has also declared mandatory flag saluting to be an infringement of religious and personal freedoms.

Gideon v. Wainwright (1963)

When Clarence Earl Gideon was tried for breaking into a poolroom, the state of Florida rejected his demand for a court-appointed lawyer as guaranteed by the Sixth Amendment. In 1963, the Court upheld his demand in a unanimous decision that established the obligation of states to provide attorneys for indigent defendants in felony cases. Prior to this decision, the right to an attorney had applied only to federal cases, not state cases. In its ruling in *Gideon v. Wainwright*, the Supreme Court applied the Sixth through the Fourteenth Amendments to the states. In 1972, the Supreme Court extended the right to legal representation to all cases, not just felony cases, in its decision in *Argersinger v. Hamlin*.

Griswold v. Connecticut (1965)

With a vote of seven to two, the Supreme Court reversed an "uncommonly silly law" (in the words of Justice Potter Stewart) that made it a crime for anyone in the state of Connecticut to use any drug, article, or instrument to prevent conception. *Griswold* became a landmark case because here, for the first time, the Court explicitly invested with full constitutional status "fundamental personal rights," such as the right to privacy, that were not expressly enumerated in the Bill of Rights. The majority opinion in the case held that the law infringed on the constitutionally protected right to privacy of married persons.

Although the Court had previously recognized fundamental rights not expressly enumerated in the Bill of Rights (such as the right to procreate in *Skinner v. Oklahoma* in 1942), *Griswold* was a landmark case because it was the first time the Court had justified, at length, the practice of investing such unenumerated rights with full constitutional status. Writing for the majority, Justice William O. Douglas explained that the First, Third, Fourth, Fifth, and Ninth Amendments imply "zones of privacy" that are the foundation for the general right to privacy affirmed in this case.

Miranda v. Arizona (1966)

In 1966, the Supreme Court, by a vote of five to four, upheld the case of Ernesto Miranda, who appealed a murder conviction on the grounds that police had gotten him to confess without giving him access to an attorney. The *Miranda* case was the culmination of the Court's efforts to find a meaningful way of determining whether police had used due process in extracting confessions from people accused of crimes. The *Miranda* decision upholds the Fifth Amendment protection against self-incrimination outside the courtroom and requires that suspects be given what came to be known as the Miranda warning, which advises them of their right to remain silent and warns them that anything they say might be used against them in a court of law. Suspects must also be told that they have a right to counsel.

New York Times Co. v. United States (1971)

With a six-to-three vote, the Court upheld the right of the *New York Times* and the *Washington Post* to print materials from the so-called *Pentagon Papers*, a secret government study of U.S. policy in Vietnam, leaked by dissident Pentagon official Daniel Ellsberg. Since the papers revealed deception and secrecy in the conduct of the Vietnam War, the Nixon administration had quickly obtained a court injunction against their further publication, claiming that suppression was in the interests of national security. The Supreme Court's decision overturning the injunction strengthened the First Amendment protection of freedom of the press.

Furman v. Georgia (1972)

In this case, the Supreme Court ruled five to four that the death penalty for murder or rape violated the cruel and unusual punishment clause of the Eighth Amendment because the manner in which the death penalty was meted out was irregular, "arbitrary," and "cruel." In response, most states enacted new statutes that allow the death penalty to be imposed only after a postconviction hearing at which evidence must be presented to show that "aggravating" or "mitigating" circumstances were factors in the crime. If the postconviction hearing hands down a death sentence, the case is automatically reviewed by an appellate court.

In 1976, the Court ruled in *Gregg v. Georgia* that these statutes were not unconstitutional. In 1977, the Court ruled in *Coker v. Georgia* that the death penalty for rape was "disproportionate and excessive," thus allowing the death penalty only in murder cases. Between 1977 and 1991, some 150 people were executed in the United States. Public opinion polls indicate that about 70 percent of Americans favor the death penalty for murder. Capital punishment continues to generate controversy, however, as opponents argue that there is no evidence that the death penalty deters crime and that its use reflects racial and economic bias.

Roe v. Wade (1973)

In 1973, the Court found, by a vote of seven to two, that state laws restricting access to abortion violated a woman's right to privacy guaranteed by the due process clause of the Fourteenth Amendment. The decision was based on the cases of two women living in Texas and Georgia, both states with stringent anti-abortion laws. Upholding the individual rights of both women and physicians, the Court ruled that the Constitution protects the right to abortion and that states cannot prohibit abortions in the early stages of pregnancy.

The decision stimulated great debate among legal scholars as well as the general public. Critics argued that since abortion was never addressed in the Constitution, the Court could not claim that legislation violated fundamental values of the Constitution. They also argued that since abortion was a medical procedure with an acknowledged impact on a fetus, it was inappropriate to invoke the kind of "privacy" argument that was used in *Griswold v. Connecticut* (see p. A-47), which was about contraception. Defenders suggested that the case should be argued as a case of gender discrimination, which did violate the equal protection clause of the Fourteenth Amendment. Others said that the right to privacy in sexual matters was indeed a fundamental right.

Regents of the University of California v. Bakke (1978)

When Allan Bakke, a white man, was not accepted by the University of California Medical School at Davis, he filed a lawsuit alleging that the admissions program, which set up different standards for test scores and grades for members of certain minority groups, violated the Civil Rights Act of 1964, which outlawed racial or ethnic preferences in programs supported by federal funds. Bakke further argued that the university's practice of setting aside spaces for minority applicants denied him equal protection as guaranteed by the Fourteenth Amendment. In a five-to-four decision, the Court ordered that Bakke be admitted to the medical school, yet it sanctioned affirmative action programs to attack the results of past discrimination as long as strict quotas or racial classifications were not involved.

Webster v. Reproductive Health Services (1989)

By a vote of five to four, the Court upheld several restrictions on the availability of abortions as imposed by Missouri state law. It upheld restrictions on the use of state property, including public hospitals, for abortions. It also upheld a provision requiring physicians to perform tests to determine the viability of a fetus that a doctor judged to be twenty weeks of age or older. Although the justices did not go so far as to overturn the decision in *Roe v. Wade* (see p. A-47), the ruling galvanized interest groups on both sides of the abortion issue. Opponents of abortion pressured state legislatures to place greater restrictions on abortions; those who favored availability of abortions tried to mobilize public action by presenting the decision as a major threat to the right to choose abortion.

Cipollone v. Liggett (1992)

In a seven-to-two decision, the Court ruled in favor of the family of Rose Cipollone, a woman who died of lung cancer after smoking for forty-two years. The Court rejected arguments that health warnings on cigarette packages protected tobacco manufacturers from personal injury suits filed by smokers who contract cancer and other serious illnesses.

Miller v. Johnson (1995)

In a five-to-four decision, the Supreme Court ruled that voting districts created to increase the voting power of racial minorities were unconstitutional. The decision threatens dozens of congressional, state, and local voting districts that were drawn to give minorities more representation as had been required by the Justice Department under the Voting Rights Act. If states are required to redraw voting districts, the number of black members of Congress could be sharply reduced.

Romer v. Evans (1996)

In a six-to-three decision, the Court struck down a Colorado amendment that forbade local governments from banning discrimination against homosexuals. Writing for the majority, Justice Anthony Kennedy said that forbidding communities from taking action to protect the rights of homosexuals and not of other groups unlawfully deprived gays and lesbians of opportunities that were available to others. Kennedy based the decision on the guarantee of equal protection under the law as provided by the Fourteenth Amendment.

THE AMERICAN ECONOMY

THESE FOUR "SNAPSHOTS" of the U.S. economy show significant changes over the past century and a half. In 1849, the agricultural sector was by far the largest contributor to the economy. By the turn of the century, with advances in technology and an abundance of cheap labor and raw materials, the country had experienced remarkable industrial expansion and the manufacturing industries dominated. By 1950, the service sector had increased significantly, fueled by the consumerism of the 1920s and the post-World War II years, and the economy was becoming more diversified. Note that by 1990, government's share in the economy was more than 10 percent and activity in both the trade and manufacturing sectors had declined, partly as a result of competition from Western Europe and Asia.

Main Sectors of the U.S. Economy: 1849, 1899, 1950, 1990

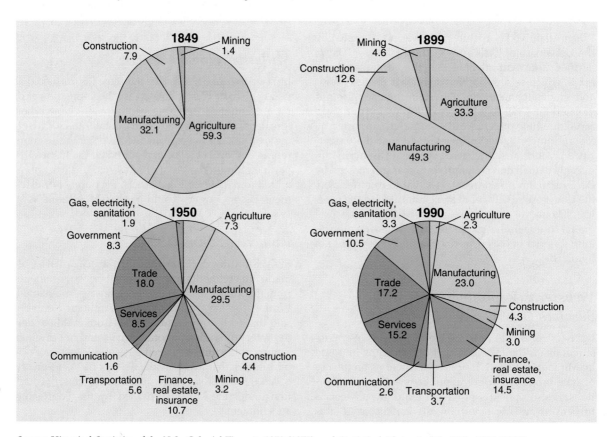

Source: *Historical Statistics of the U.S., Colonial Times to 1970* (1975) and *Statistical Abstract of the U.S., 1996* (1996).

Federal Spending and the Economy, 1790 – 1995

Year	Gross National Product (in billions)	Foreign Trade (in millions)		Federal Budget (in billions)	Federal Surplus/Deficit (in billions)	Federal Debt (in billions)
		Exports	Imports			
1790	NA	20	23	0.004	0.00015	0.076
1800	NA	71	91	0.011	0.0006	0.083
1810	NA	67	85	0.008	0.0012	0.053
1820	NA	70	74	0.018	−0.0004	0.091
1830	NA	74	71	0.015	0.100	0.049
1840	NA	132	107	0.024	−0.005	0.004
1850	NA	152	178	0.040	0.004	0.064
1860	NA	400	362	0.063	−0.01	0.065
1870	7.4	451	462	0.310	0.10	2.4
1880	11.2	853	761	0.268	0.07	2.1
1890	13.1	910	823	0.318	0.09	1.2
1900	18.7	1,499	930	0.521	0.05	1.2
1910	35.3	1,919	1,646	0.694	−0.02	1.1
1920	91.5	8,664	5,784	6.357	0.3	24.3
1930	90.4	4,013	3,500	3.320	0.7	16.3
1940	99.7	4,030	7,433	9.6	−2.7	43.0
1950	284.8	10,816	9,125	43.1	−2.2	257.4
1960	503.7	19,600	15,046	92.2	0.3	286.3
1970	977.1	42,700	40,189	195.6	−2.8	371.0
1980	2,631.7	220,600	244,871	590.9	−73.8	907.7
1990	5,524.5	393,600	495,300	1,252.15	−221.1	3,233.3
1995	7,237.5	583,900	743,400	1,519.1	−163.9	4,921.0

Source: *Historical Statistics of the U.S., Colonial Times to 1970* (1975) and *Statistical Abstract of the U.S., 1996* (1996).

WHEN THE FEDERAL GOVERNMENT BEGAN OPERATING IN 1790, its size and expenditures were limited. Over time its functions increased, but its budget remained fairly small relative to the country's gross national product. The second half of the twentieth century witnessed a dramatic expansion in federal budget outlays. As the government's role increased and receipts could no longer offset growing expenditures, budget deficits mounted. In 1976, the federal deficit reached $65.6 billion and continued to rise, soaring as high as $290 billion in 1992, during the last year of George Bush's presidency. During the first Clinton administration, a combination of budget cuts, tax increases, declining unemployment, and economic expansion reduced the deficit by about half to approximately $145 billion.

The Federal Budget: Receipts, Outlays, and the Deficit, 1945 – 1995

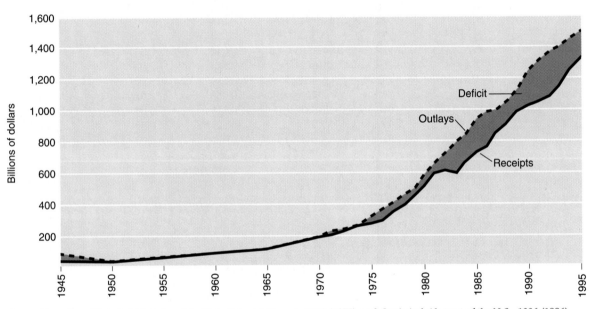

Source: Data from *Historical Statistics of the U.S., Colonial Times to 1970* (1975) and *Statistical Abstract of the U.S., 1996* (1996).

A DEMOGRAPHIC PROFILE OF THE UNITED STATES AND ITS PEOPLE

POPULATION

FROM AN ESTIMATED 4600 WHITE INHABITANTS IN 1630, the country's population grew to a total of just under 250 million in 1990. It is important to note that the U.S. census, first conducted in 1790 and the source of these figures, counted blacks, both free and slave, but did not include American Indians until 1860. The years 1790 to 1900 saw the most rapid population growth, with an average increase of 25 to 35 percent per decade. In addition to "natural" growth—birth rate exceeding death rate—immigration was also a factor in that rise, especially between 1840 and 1860, 1880 to 1890, and 1900 to 1910 (see table on page A-59). The twentieth century witnessed slower growth, partly a result of 1920s immigration restrictions, and a decline in the birth rate, especially during the Depression era and the 1960s and 1970s. The U.S. population is expected to reach almost 300 million by the year 2010.

Population Growth, 1630 – 2000

Year	Population	Percent Increase
1630	4,600	————
1640	26,600	473.3
1650	50,400	89.1
1660	75,100	49.0
1670	111,900	49.1
1680	151,500	35.4
1690	210,400	38.9
1700	250,900	19.3
1710	331,700	32.2
1720	466,200	40.5
1730	629,400	35.0
1740	905,600	43.9
1750	1,170,800	30.0
1760	1,593,600	36.1
1770	2,148,100	34.8
1780	2,780,400	29.4
1790	3,929,214	41.3
1800	5,308,483	35.1
1810	7,239,881	36.4
1820	9,638,453	33.1
1830	12,866,020	33.5
1840	17,069,453	32.7
1850	23,191,876	35.9
1860	31,443,321	35.6
1870	39,818,449	26.6
1880	50,155,783	26.0
1890	62,947,714	25.5
1900	75,994,575	20.7
1910	91,972,266	21.0
1920	105,710,620	14.9
1930	122,775,046	16.1
1940	131,669,275	7.2
1950	150,697,361	14.5
1960	179,323,175	19.0
1970	203,302,031	13.4
1980	226,542,199	11.4
1990	248,718,301	9.8
2000	274,634,000*	11.0

*Projected

Source: Historical Statistics of the U.S. (1960), Historical Statistics of the U.S. from Colonial Times to 1970 (1975), and Statistical Abstract of the U.S., 1996 (1996).

The Ten Most Populous Cities, 1700–1994

Year	City	Population	Year	City	Population
1700	Boston	6,700	1910	New York	4,767,000
	New York	4,900		Chicago	2,185,000
	Philadelphia	4,400		Philadelphia	1,549,000
				St. Louis	687,000
1790	Philadelphia	42,500		Boston	670,600
	New York	33,100		Cleveland, Ohio	560,700
	Boston	18,000		Baltimore	558,500
	Charleston, S.C.	16,400		Pittsburgh	533,900
	Baltimore, Md.	13,500		Detroit, Mich.	465,800
	Salem, Mass.	7,900		Buffalo, N.Y.	423,700
	Newport, R.I.	6,700			
	Providence, R.I.	6,380	1930	New York	6,930,000
	Marblehead, Mass.	5,700		Chicago	3,376,000
	Portsmouth, N.H.	4,700		Philadelphia	1,951,000
				Detroit	1,569,000
1830	New York	197,100		Los Angeles	1,238,000
	Philadelphia	161,400		Cleveland	900,400
	Baltimore	80,600		St. Louis	822,000
	Boston	61,400		Baltimore	804,900
	Charleston	30,300		Boston	781,200
	New Orleans, La.	29,700		Pittsburgh	669,800
	Cincinnati, Oh.	24,800			
	Albany, N.Y.	24,200	1950	New York	7,892,000
	Brooklyn, N.Y.	20,500		Chicago	3,621,000
	Washington, D.C.	18,800		Philadelphia	2,072,000
				Los Angeles	1,970,000
1850	New York	515,500		Detroit	1,850,000
	Philadelphia	340,000		Baltimore	949,700
	Baltimore	169,000		Cleveland	914,800
	Boston	136,800		St. Louis	856,800
	New Orleans	116,400		Washington	802,200
	Cincinnati	115,400		Boston	801,500
	Brooklyn, N.Y.	96,800			
	St. Louis, Mo.	77,900	1970	New York	7,896,000
	Albany	50,800		Chicago	3,369,000
	Pittsburgh, Pa.	46,600		Los Angeles	2,812,000
				Philadelphia	1,950,000
1870	New York	942,300		Detroit	1,514,000
	Philadelphia	674,000		Houston	1,234,000
	Brooklyn	419,900		Baltimore	905,800
	St. Louis	310,900		Dallas	844,400
	Chicago, Il.	298,900		Washington	756,700
	Baltimore	267,300		Cleveland	750,900
	Boston	250,500			
	Cincinnati	216,200			
	New Orleans	191,400			
	San Francisco, Calif.	149,500			(continues)

The Ten Most Populous Cities, 1700 – 1994 (continued)

Year	City	Population	Year	City	Population
1990	New York	7,323,000	**1994**	New York	7,333,000
	Los Angeles	3,485,000		Los Angeles	3,449,000
	Chicago	2,784,000		Chicago	2,732,000
	Houston	1,631,000		Houston	1,702,000
	Philadelphia	1,586,000		Philadelphia	1,524,000
	San Diego	1,111,000		San Diego	1,152,000
	Detroit	1,028,000		Phoenix	1,049,000
	Dallas	1,007,000		Dallas	1,023,000
	Phoenix	983,400		San Antonio	999,000
	San Antonio, Tex.	935,900		Detroit	992,000

U.S. Population, 1790 – 2010

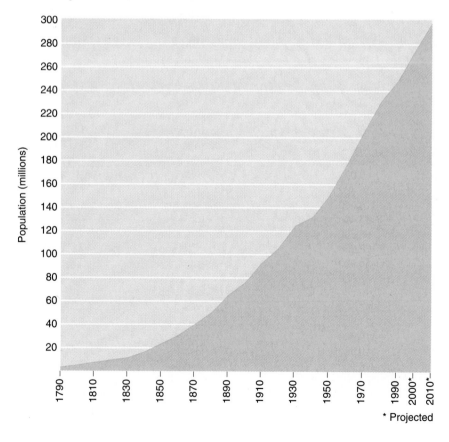

* Projected

Appendix II • Facts and Figures

A DEMOGRAPHIC PROFILE OF THE UNITED STATES AND ITS PEOPLE

VITAL STATISTICS

WITH SOME MINOR FLUCTUATIONS, the birth rate has been trending downward throughout the past century and a half, dipping especially low during the 1930s Depression
years, when many economically hard-hit Americans postponed having children. A
major exception to this decline was the steep but temporary rise nicknamed the "Baby
Boom," which occurred during the relatively affluent post-World War II period. Improvements in health care and lifestyles have contributed to a decline in the death
rate over the past century, which, in turn has increased life expectancy figures. Over
time, as people lived longer and the birth rate declined, the median age of Americans
has increased from approximately seventeen in 1820 to thirty-three in 1990, and continues to rise.

Birth Rate, 1820 – 2000

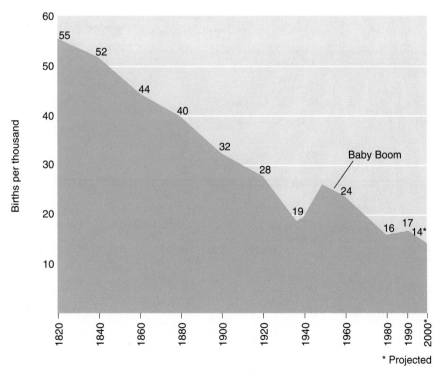

Source: Data from *Historical Statistics of the U.S., Colonial Times to 1970* (1975) and *Statistical Abstract of the U.S., 1996* (1996).

Death Rate, 1900 – 2000

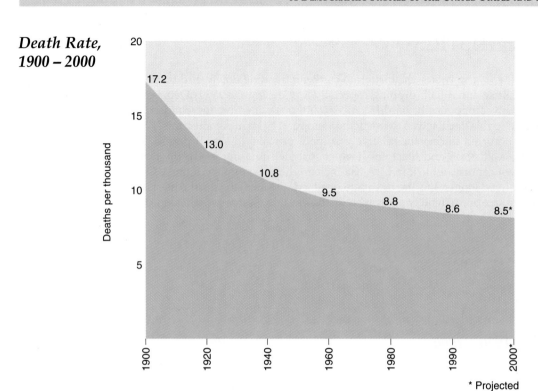

* Projected

*Source: Historical Statistics of the U.S., Colonial Times to 1970 (1975) and
Statistical Abstract of the U.S., 1996 (1996).*

Life Expectancy, 1900 – 2000

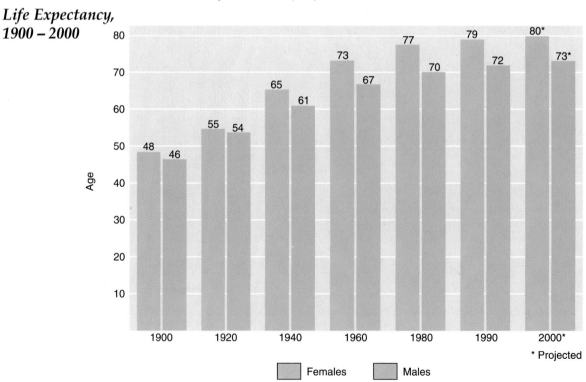

Females   Males

* Projected

*Source: Historical Statistics of the U.S., Colonial Times to 1970 (1975) and
Statistical Abstract of the U.S., 1996 (1996).*

MIGRATION AND IMMIGRATION

WE TEND TO ASSOCIATE INTERNAL MIGRATION with movement westward, yet equally significant has been the movement of the nation's population from the country to the city. In 1790, the first U.S. census recorded that approximately 95 percent of the population lived in rural areas. By 1990, that figure had fallen to less than 25 percent. The decline of the agricultural way of life, late nineteenth-century industrialization, and immigration have all contributed to increased urbanization. A more recent trend has been the migration, especially since the 1970s, of people to the "Sun Belt" states of the South and West, lured by factors as various as economic opportunities in the defense and high-tech industries and good weather. This migration has swelled the size of Sun Belt cities like Houston, Dallas, Tucson, Phoenix, and San Diego, all of which in recent years ranked among the top ten most populous U.S. cities (see the table on page A-53).

Rural and Urban Population, 1750 – 2000

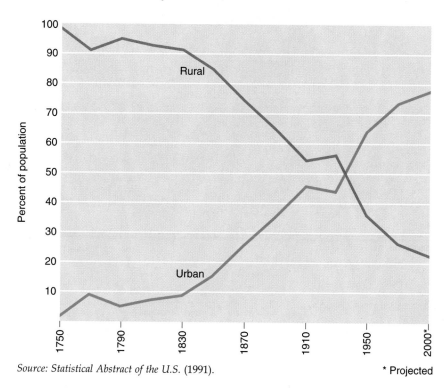

Source: Statistical Abstract of the U.S. (1991).   * Projected

Projected Change in State Populations by Percent, 1995 – 2010

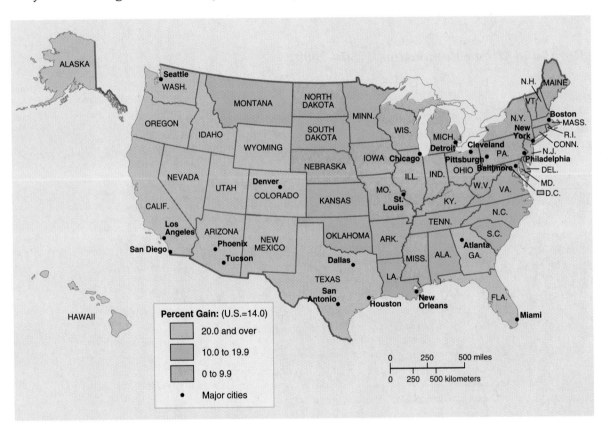

Source: Statistical Abstract of the U.S., 1996. (1996).

THE QUANTITY AND CHARACTER OF IMMIGRATION to the U.S. has varied greatly over time. During the first major influx, between 1840 and 1860, newcomers hailed primarily from Northern and Western Europe. From 1880 to 1915, when rates soared even more dramatically, the profile changed, with 80 percent of the so-called "new immigration" coming from Central, Eastern, and Southern Europe. Following World War I, strict quotas reduced the flow considerably. Note, also, the significant fall-off during the years of the Great Depression and World War II. The sources of immigration during the last half century have changed significantly, with the majority of people coming from Latin America, the Caribbean, and Asia. The latest surge during the 1980s brought more immigrants to the U.S. than in any decade except 1901–1910.

Rates of Immigration, 1820 – 1994

Year	Number	Percent of Total Population
1821–1830	151,824	1.6
1831–1840	599,125	4.6
1841–1850	1,713,521	10.0
1851–1860	2,598,214	11.2
1861–1870	2,314,824	7.4
1871–1880	2,812,191	7.1
1881–1890	5,246,613	10.5
1891–1900	3,687,546	5.8
1901–1910	8,795,386	11.6
1911–1920	5,735,811	6.2
1921–1930	4,107,209	3.9
1931–1940	528,431	0.4
1941–1950	1,035,039	0.7
1951–1960	2,515,479	1.6
1961–1970	3,321,677	1.8
1971–1980	4,493,300	2.2
1981–1990	7,338,100	3.0
1991	1,827,167	7.2
1992	973,977	3.8
1993	904,292	3.5
1994	804,416	3.0

Source: Historical Statistics of the U.S., Colonial Times to 1970 (1975), Statistical Abstract of the U.S., 1996 (1996).

Major Trends in Immigration, 1820 – 1990

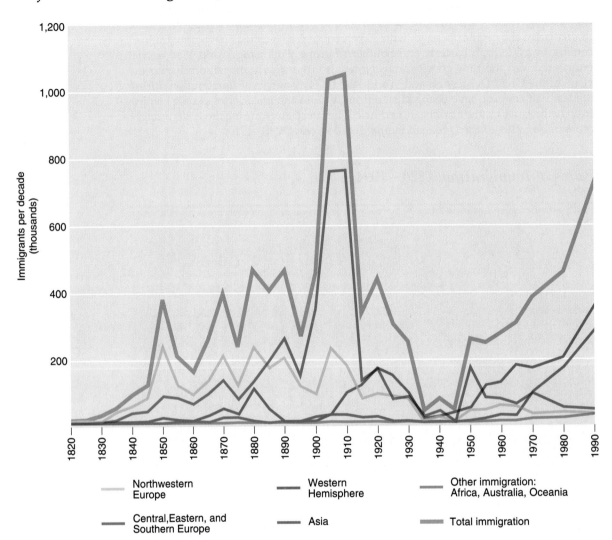

Source: Historical Statistics of the U.S., Colonial Times to 1970 (1975) and *Statistical Abstract of the U.S., 1996* (1996).

LABOR

FOR MUCH OF THE NINETEENTH CENTURY, the United States was a nation of small farmers, with over half the population employed in agriculture. With the rise of industrialization, movement to the cities, and increasing takeover of farming by agribusiness (large-scale mechanized farming requiring little manpower), Americans increasingly moved from farming to work in manufacturing and other industries. In the twentieth century the number of people employed in services has increased; membership in labor unions peaked around 1970. Perhaps the most significant change in labor patterns has been the increase in the number of working women from approximately one sixth of the work force in 1890 to close to one half by 1994.

The Changing Nature of Work, 1810 – 1994

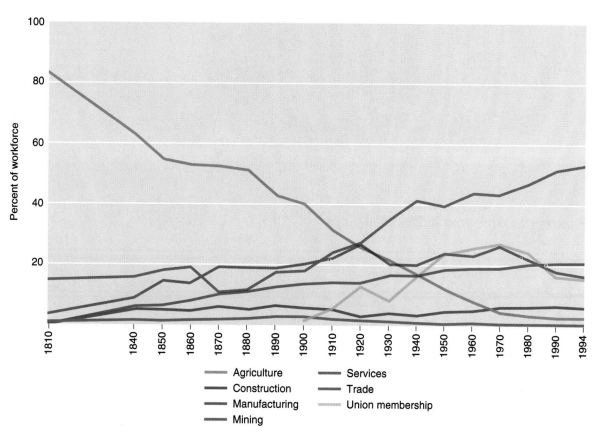

Source: *Historical Statistics of the U.S., Colonial Times to 1970* (1975) and *Statistical Abstract of the U.S., 1996* (1996).

Women in the Work Force, 1820 – 1994

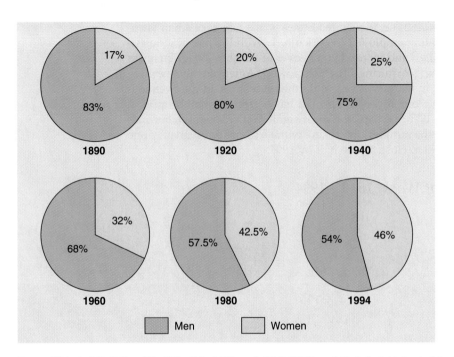

Source: Historical Statistics of the U.S., Colonial Times to 1970 (1975) and *Statistical Abstract of the U.S., 1996* (1996).

Farming in America, 1850 – 1990

Year	Farm Population (in thousands)	Percent of Total Population	Number of Farms (in thousands)	Total Acres (in thousands)	Average Acreage Per Farm
1850	NA	NA	1,449	293,561	203
1860	NA	NA	2,044	407,213	199
1870	NA	NA	2,660	407,735	153
1880	21,973	43.8	4,009	536,082	134
1890	24,771	42.3	4,565	623,219	137
1900	29,875	41.9	5,740	841,202	147
1910	32,077	34.9	6,366	881,431	139
1920	31,974	30.1	6,454	958,677	149
1930	30,529	24.9	6,295	990,112	157
1940	30,547	23.2	6,102	1,065,114	175
1950	23,048	15.3	5,388	1,161,420	216
1960	15,635	8.7	3,962	1,176,946	297
1970	9,712	4.8	2,949	1,102,769	374
1980	6,051	2.7	2,440	1,039,000	426
1990	4,591	1.9	2,140	987,000	461

NA = Not available

Source: Historical Statistics of the U.S., Colonial Times to 1970 (1975) and *Statistical Abstract of the U.S., 1996* (1996).

COMMUNICATIONS

THE TWENTIETH CENTURY WITNESSED the growing presence of communications technology in American homes. Especially revolutionary were radio and telephone, which connected people with the outside world in ways previously unimaginable. By 1994, telephones, radios, and televisions were standard in more than 90 percent of American homes, while more and more households had acquired cable television and video cassette recorders. The 1980s also saw the rise of the personal computer, which by 1993 could be found in nearly a quarter of American homes. As the graph shows, kids under seventeen make up a substantial percentage of computer users.

Households with Telephones, 1920 – 1994

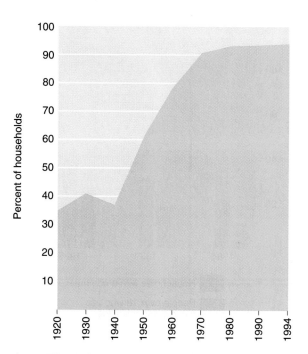

Source: *Historical Statistics of the U.S., Colonial Times to 1970* (1975) and *Statistical Abstract of the U.S., 1996* (1996).

Households with Radios and Television Sets, 1920 – 1970

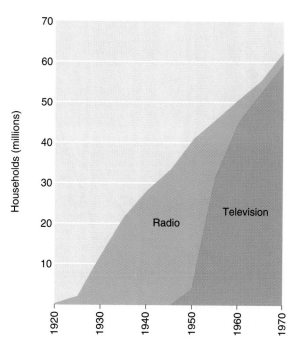

Source: *Historical Statistics of the U.S., Colonial Times to 1970* (1975) and *Statistical Abstract of the U.S., 1996* (1996).

Percent of Households with Radio, Television, Cable, and VCR, 1970 – 1994

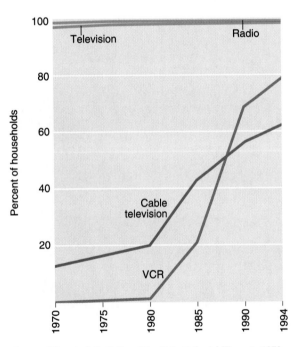

Source: Historical Statistics of the U.S., Colonial Times to 1970 (1975) and Statistical Abstract of the U.S., 1996 (1996).

Computer Use and Access, 1984 – 1993

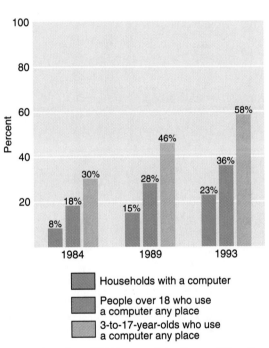

Source: Data from U.S. Bureau of the Census, Education and Social Stratification Branch, Population Division.

A DEMOGRAPHIC PROFILE OF THE UNITED STATES AND ITS PEOPLE

EDUCATION

DURING THE TWENTIETH CENTURY, there have been substantial increases in enrollments in secondary education and slower but still steady progress in degrees granted in higher education. In 1910, less than 14 percent of the population obtained high school diplomas; by 1995, that figure had risen to more than 80 percent. The number of people completing bachelor's degrees has grown steadily, from 400,000 in 1960 to just under 1.2 million in 1994, while the increasing professionalization of the workforce is reflected in the number of advanced degrees granted since 1960: Between 1960 and 1994, master's degrees awarded rose from almost 75,000 to almost 400,000, while doctoral degrees earned increased from 10,000 to 42,000.

Years of Schooling Completed, Ages 25 and Over, 1910 – 1995

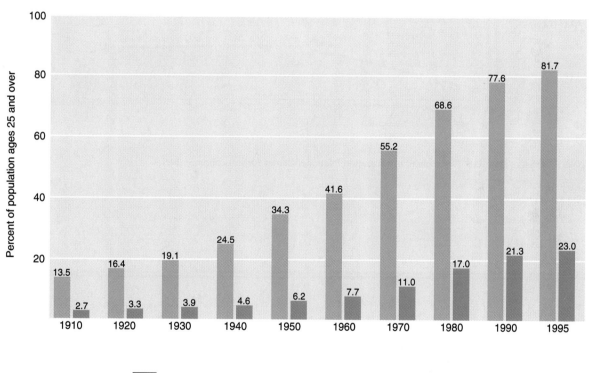

People ages 25 and over who completed 4 or more years of high school

People ages 25 and over who completed 4 or more years of college

Source: Statistics from U.S. Department of Commerce, Bureau of the Census.

Higher Education: Degrees Conferred, 1960 – 1994

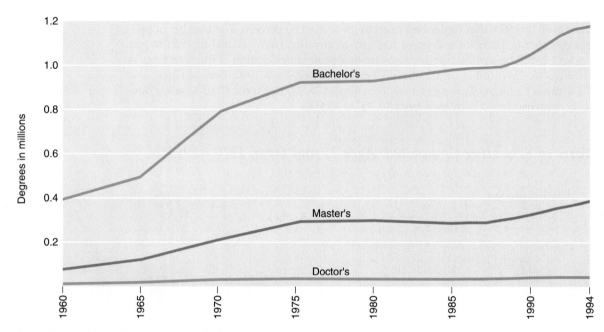

Source: Statistics from U.S. Department of Education, National Center for Education Statistics.

APPENDIX III. RESEARCH RESOURCES IN U.S. HISTORY

While doing research in history, you will use the library to track down primary and secondary sources and to answer questions that arise as you learn more about your topic. This appendix suggests helpful indexes, references, periodicals, and sources of primary documents. It also offers an overview of electronic resources available through the Internet. The materials listed here are not all carried at all libraries, but they will give you an idea of the range of sources available. Remember, too, that librarians are an extremely helpful resource. They can direct you to useful materials throughout your research process.

Bibliographies and Indexes

American Historical Association Guide to Historical Literature. 3rd ed. New York: Oxford University Press, 1995. Offers 27,000 citations to important historical literature, arranged in forty-eight sections covering theory, international history, and regional history. An indispensable guide recently updated to include current trends in historical research.

America History and Life. Santa Barbara: ABC-Clio, 1964–. Covers publications of all sorts on U.S. and Canadian history and culture in a chronological/regional format, with abstracts and alphabetical indexes. Available in computerized format. The most complete ongoing bibliography for American history.

Freidel, Frank Burt. *Harvard Guide to American History.* Cambridge: Harvard University Press, Belknap Press, 1974. Provides citations to books and articles on American history published before 1970. The first volume is arranged topically, the second chronologically. Though it does not cover current scholarship, it is a classic and remains useful for tracing older publications.

Prucha, Francis Paul. *Handbook for Research in American History: A Guide to Bibliographies and Other Reference Works.* 2nd rev. ed. Lincoln: University of Nebraska Press, 1994. Introduces a variety of research tools, including electronic ones. A good source to consult when planning an in-depth research project.

General Overviews

Dictionary of American Biography. New York: Scribner's, 1928–1937, with supplements. Gives substantial biographies of prominent Americans in history.

Dictionary of American History. New York: Scribner's, 1976. An encyclopedia of terms, places, and concepts in U.S. history; other more specialized sets include the *Encyclopedia of North American Colonies* and the *Encyclopedia of the Confederacy.*

Dictionary of Concepts in History. New York: Greenwood, 1986. Contains essays defining concepts in historiography and describing how the concepts were formed; excellent bibliographies.

Encyclopedia of American Social History. New York: Scribner's, 1993. Surveys topics such as religion, class, gender, race, popular culture, regionalism, and everyday life from pre-Columbian to modern times.

Encyclopedia of the United States in the Twentieth Century. New York: Scribner's, 1996. An ambitious overview of American cultural, social, and intellectual history in broad articles arranged topically. Each article is followed by a thorough and very useful bibliography for further research.

Specialized Information

Black Women in America: An Historical Encyclopedia. Brooklyn: Carlson, 1993. A scholarly compilation of biographical and topical articles that constitute a definitive history of African American women.

Carruth, Gordon. *The Encyclopedia of American Facts and Dates.* 9th ed. New York: HarperCollins, 1993. Covers American history chronologically from 986 to the present, offering information on treaties, battles, explorations, popular culture, philosophy, literature, and so on, mixing significant events with telling trivia. Tables allow for reviewing a year from a variety of angles. A thorough index helps pinpoint specific facts in time.

Cook, Chris. *Dictionary of Historical Terms.* 2nd ed. New York: Peter Bendrick, 1990. Covers a wide variety of terms—events, places, institutions, and topics—in history for all periods and places in a remarkably small package. A good place for quick identification of terms in the field.

Dictionary of Afro-American Slavery. New York: Greenwood, 1985. Surveys important people, events, and topics, with useful bibliographies; similar works include *Dictionary of the Vietnam War*, *Historical Dictionary of the New Deal*, and *Historical Dictionary of the Progressive Era*.

Knappman-Frost, Elizabeth. *The ABC-Clio Companion to Women's Progress in America*. Santa Barbara: ABC-Clio, 1994. Covers American women who were notable for their time as well as topics and organizations that have been significant in women's quest for equality. Each article is brief; there are a chronology and a bibliography at the back of the book.

United States. Bureau of the Census. *Historical Statistics of the United States, Colonial Times to 1970*. Washington, D.C.: Government Printing Office, 1975. Offers vital statistics, economic figures, and social data for the United States in time series. An index at the back helps locate tables by subject. For statistics since 1970, consult the annual *Statistical Abstract of the United States*.

Primary Sources

There are many routes to finding contemporary material for historical research. You may search your library catalog using the name of a prominent historical figure as an author; you may also find anthologies covering particular themes or periods in history. Consider also the following special materials for your research.

The Press

American Periodical Series, 1741–1900. Ann Arbor: University Microfilms, 1946–1979. Microfilm collection of periodicals from the colonial period to the turn of the century. An index identifies periodicals that focused on particular topics.

Herstory Microfilm Collection. Berkeley: Women's History Research Center, 1973. A microfilm collection of alternative feminist periodicals published between 1960 and 1980. Offers an interesting documentary history of the women's movement.

New York Times. New York: New York Times, 1851–. Many libraries have this newspaper on microfilm going back to its beginning in 1851. An index is available to locate specific dates and pages of news stories; it also provides detailed chronologies of events as they were reported in the news.

Readers' Guide to Periodical Literature. New York: Wilson, 1900–. This index to popular magazines started in 1900; an earlier index, *Poole's Index to Periodical Literature*, covers 1802–1906, though it does not provide such thorough indexing.

Diaries, Pamphlets, Books

The American Culture Series. Ann Arbor: University Microfilms, 1941–1974. A microfilm set, with a useful index, featuring books and pamphlets published between 1493 and 1875.

American Women's Diaries. New Canaan: Readex, 1984–. A collection of reproductions of women's diaries. There are different series for different regions of the country.

The March of America Facsimile Series. Ann Arbor: University Microfilms, 1966. A collection of more than ninety facsimiles of travel accounts to the New World published in English or English translation from the fifteenth through the nineteenth century.

Women in America from Colonial Times to the 20th Century. New York: Arno, 1974. A collection of reprints of dozens of books written by women describing women's lives and experiences in their own words.

Government Documents

Congressional Record. Washington D.C.: Government Printing Office, 1874–. Covers daily debates and proceedings of Congress. Earlier series were called *Debates and Proceedings in the Congress of the United States* and *The Congressional Globe*.

Foreign Relations of the United States. Washington D.C.: Department of State, 1861–. A collection of documents from 1861, including diplomatic papers, correspondence, and memoranda, that provides a documentary record of U.S. foreign policy.

Public Papers of the Presidents. Washington D.C.: Office of the Federal Register, 1957–. Includes major documents issued by the executive branch from the Hoover administration to the present.

Serial Set. Washington, D.C.: Government Printing Office, 1789–1969. A huge collection of congressional documents, available in many libraries on microfiche, with a useful index.

Local History Collections

State and county historical societies often house a wealth of historical documents; consider their resources when planning your research—you may find yourself working with material that no one else has analyzed before.

Internet Resources

The Internet has been a useful place for scholars to communicate and publish information in recent years. Electronic discussion lists, electronic journals, and primary texts are among the resources available for historians on the Internet. The following sources are good places to find historical information. You can also search for information on the World Wide Web using any of a number of search engines. However, bear in mind that there is no board of editors screening Internet sites for accuracy or usefulness, and the search engines generally rely on free-text searches rather than subject headings. Be critical of all of your sources, particularly those found on the Internet.

American Memory: Historical Collection from the National Digital Library Program. <http://rs6.loc.gov/amhome. html> An Internet site that features digitized primary source materials from the Library of Congress, among them African American pamphlets, civil war photographs, documents from the Continental Congress and the Constitutional Convention of 1774–1790, materials on woman suffrage, and oral histories.

Directory of Scholarly and Professional Electronic Conferences. <http://n2h2.com/KOVAKS/>. A good place to find out what electronic conversations are going on in a scholarly discipline. Includes a good search facility and instructions on how to connect to e-mail discussion lists, newsgroups, and interactive chat sites with academic content. Once identified, these conferences are good places to raise questions, find out what controversies are currently stirring the profession, and even find out about grants and jobs.

Historical Text Archive. <http://www.msstate.edu/Archives/History>. A Web interface for the oldest and largest Internet site for historical documents. Includes sections on Native American, African American, and U.S. history, in which can be found texts of the Declaration of Independence, the U.S. Constitution, the Constitution of Iroquois Nations, World War II surrender documents, photograph collections, and a great deal more. These can be used online or saved as files.

Index of Resources for Historians. <http://kuhttp.cc. ukans.edu/history/index.html>. A vast list of more than 1700 links to sites of interest to historians, arranged alphabetically by general topic. Some links are to sources for general reference information, but most are on historical topics. A good place to start an exploration of Internet resources.

MAPS, CHARTS, AND TABLES

Maps

Charts and Tables

ABOUT THE AUTHORS

James L. Roark

Born in Eunice, Louisiana, and raised in the West, James L. Roark received his B.A. from the University of California, Davis, in 1963 and his Ph.D. from Stanford University in 1973. His dissertation won the Allan Nevins Prize. He has taught at the University of Nigeria, Nsukka; the University of Nairobi, Kenya; the University of Missouri, St. Louis; and, since 1983, Emory University, where he is Samuel Candler Dobbs Professor of American History. In 1993, he received the Emory Williams Distinguished Teaching Award. He has written *Masters without Slaves: Southern Planters in the Civil War and Reconstruction* (1977). With Michael P. Johnson, he is author of *Black Masters: A Free Family of Color in the Old South* (1984) and editor of *No Chariot Let Down: Charleston's Free People of Color on the Eve of the Civil War* (1984). He has received research assistance from the American Philosophical Society and the National Endowment for the Humanities. Active in the Organization of American Historians and the Southern Historical Association, he is also a fellow of the Society of American Historians.

Michael P. Johnson

Born and raised in Ponca City, Oklahoma, Michael P. Johnson studied at Knox College, Illinois, where he received a B.A. in 1963, and at Stanford University, where he earned a Ph.D. in 1973. He is now professor of history at the Johns Hopkins University in Baltimore. His publications include *Toward a Patriarchal Republic: The Secession of Georgia* (1977); with James L. Roark *Black Masters: A Free Family of Color in the Old South* (1984) and *No Chariot Let Down: Charlestown's Free People of Color on the Eve of the Civil War* (1984); *Reading the American Past: Selected Historical Documents,* the documents reader for *The American Promise;* and articles that have appeared in the *William and Mary Quarterly,* the *Journal of Southern History, Labor History,* the *New York Review of Books,* the *New Republic,* the *Nation,* and other journals. Johnson has been awarded research fellowships by the American Council of Learned Societies and the National Endowment for the Humanities. He

has directed a National Endowment for the Humanities Summer Seminar for College Teachers and has been honored with university awards for outstanding teaching. He is an active member of the American Historical Association, the Organization of American Historians, and the Southern Historical Association.

Patricia Cline Cohen

Born in Ann Arbor, Michigan, and raised in Palo Alto, California, Patricia Cline Cohen earned a B.A. at the University of Chicago in 1968 and a Ph.D. at the University of California, Berkeley in 1977. In 1976, she joined the history faculty at the University of California at Santa Barbara. Cohen has written *A Calculating People: The Spread of Numeracy in Early America* (1982) and has published articles on numeracy, prostitution, sexual crime, and murder in journals including the *Journal of Women's History, Radical History Review,* the *William and Mary Quarterly,* and the *NWSA Journal.* Her scholarly work has received assistance from the National Endowment for the Humanities, the National Humanities Center, the American Antiquarian Society, the Schlesinger Library, and the Newberry Library. In the mid-1980s, she helped establish the Women's Studies Program on her campus, and she has been chair of the program since 1991.

Sarah Stage

Sarah Stage was born in Davenport, Iowa, and received a B.A. from the University of Iowa in 1966 and a Ph.D. in American studies from Yale University in 1975. She has taught twentieth-century U.S. history for more than twenty-five years at Williams College and the University of California, Riverside. Currently she is professor and chair of Women's Studies at Arizona State University West in Phoenix. Her books include *Female Complaints: Lydia Pinkham and the Business of Women's Medicine* (1979) and the forthcoming *Rethinking Women and Home Economics in the Twentieth Century.* Among the fellowships she has received are the Rockefeller Foundation Humanities Fellowship, the American Association of University Women dissertation fellowship, a fellowship from the Charles Warren Center for the Study of History at Harvard University, and the University of California President's Fellowship in the Humanities. She is at work on a book entitled *Women and the Progressive Impulse in American Politics, 1890–1914.*

Alan Lawson

Born in Providence, Rhode Island, Alan Lawson received his B.A. from Brown University in 1955 and his Ph.D. from the University of Michigan in 1967. Since winning the Allan Nevins Prize for his dissertation, Lawson has served on the faculties of the University of California, Irvine, Smith College, and, currently, Boston College. He has written *The Failure of Independent Liberalism* (1971) and coedited *From Revolution to Republic* (1976). While completing the forthcoming *The New Deal and the Mobilization of Progressive Experience,* he has published book chapters and essays on political economy and the cultural legacy of the New Deal. He has served as editor of the *Review of Education* and the *Intellectual History Newsletter* and contributed articles to those journals as well as to the *History Education Quarterly.* He has been active in the field of American studies as director of the Boston College American studies program and as a contributor to the *American Quarterly.* Under the auspices of the United States Information Agency, Lawson has been coordinator and lecturer for programs to instruct faculty from foreign nations in the state of American historical scholarship and teaching.

Susan M. Hartmann

Professor of history and women's studies at Ohio State University, Susan M. Hartmann grew up in St. Louis and received her B.A. from Washington University in 1961 and her Ph.D. from the University of Missouri in 1966. After specializing in the political economy of the post–World War II period and publishing *Truman and the 80th Congress* (1971), she expanded her interests to the field of women's history, publishing many articles and two books, *The Home Front and Beyond: American Women in the 1940s* (1982) and *From Margin to Mainstream: American Women and Politics since 1960* (1989). She has won research fellowships and grants from the Truman Library Institute, the Rockefeller Foundation, the National Endowment for the Humanities, and the American Council of Learned Societies. Hartmann has taught at the University of Missouri, St. Louis, and Boston University, and she has lectured on American history in Greece, France, Austria, Germany, Australia, and New Zealand. She has served on book and article award committees of the American Historical Association, the Organization of American Historians, the American Studies Association, and the National Women's Studies Association. At Ohio State she has served as director of women's studies, and in 1995 she won the Exemplary Faculty Award in the College of Humanities.

A note about the index:

Pages containing main coverage or description of a topic or person are set in bold-face for easy reference. Entries also include dates for important events and major figures.

Letters in parentheses following pages refer to:
- (i) for illustrations, including photographs and artifacts, as well as information contained in picture captions
- (f) for figures, including charts and graphs
- (m) for maps
- (t) for tables

establishment of, 1031
Nixon presidency and, 1192–1193
Italian immigrants, 801, 805
in the nineteenth century, 669, 670,
671, 672, 672(f), 673, 676
work and, 727, 728, 729, 731, 754,
755
Italy, 38–39
conquest of Ethiopia by, 981–982
U.S. acceptance of Mussolini in, 980
World War I and, 849, 850(m)
World War II and, 991–992, 992(i)

Jackson, Andrew (1767–1845), 167, 378,
379, 384(i), **385–386**, 396, 402, 406,
453, 503, 506, 711, 939
Adams and, in the election of 1828,
398–401
background of, 385, 446
Battle of New Orleans (1815) and,
366, 367, 385
Biddle and the Bank of the United
States and, 418–419, 422(i)
California settlement and, 502
Democratic Party and, 414
election of 1824 and, 377–378, 377(i),
386
election of 1828 and, 398–401,
399(m), 400(i)
election of 1832 and, 418–419
inauguration of (1829), 387–388, 401
Indian policy of, **414–417**, 416(m)
invasion of Florida by, 374–375, 385
presidency of, 386, 401–402
slavery and, 385–386
War of 1812 and, 365, 366, 367
Jackson, Jesse, 1226, 1243
Jackson, Maynard, 1121
Jackson, Thomas J. ("Stonewall"), 572
James I, king of England (1566–1625),
116–117
James II, king of England (1633–1688),
146–147
James, William (1842–1910), 811
Jamestown, Virginia, 78(i), **79–80**, 94,
96(m), 100–101
Japan, 823
bombing of Hiroshima and Nagasaki
in, 1015(i), 1016
cold war years and, 1033
invasion of Manchuria (1931) by,
823, 978, 980
Pearl Harbor attack (1941) by, 978,
988(i), 989, 1002
World War I and, 875
World War II and, 987(m), 1011–1013
Japanese Americans
New Deal programs and, 962
World War II and, 999–1002, 1003(i)
Japanese immigrants, 652, 658, 669,
727, 729, 823, 1044

Jay, John (1745–1829), 271, 296, 307,
316, 335
Jay Treaty (1795), 335–336, 337
Jazz, in the 1920s, 906–907
Jazz Age, 888
Jefferson, Thomas (1743–1826), 225,
231, 269, 291(i), 319, 338, 379, 711,
934
African influence in chess set of,
176(i)
appearance of, 351, 351(i)
Chesapeake incident and, **357–360**
Continental Congress and, 243, 246,
282
creation of a national bank and,
328, 351
debates over Alien and Sedition
Acts and, 339(i), 341
Declaration of Independence and,
247, 284
diplomatic relations with France
and, 316
economic policy of, 351–352
election of 1796 and, 336, 337
election of 1800 and, 342, 349, 350,
473
inaugural address of, 342, 346(i)
independent farmer envisioned by,
352, 353(i), 657, 945
John Adams's judicial appointments
canceled by, 354–355
John Adams's presidency and, 337,
349, 351
land ordinances proposal of, 291–
293, 292(i), 294
Lewis and Clark Expedition and,
347–348, 349
location of the nation's capital and,
324–325
Louisiana Purchase and, **355–356**
monetary system design and, 320
presidency of, **349–360**
religious liberty and, 302–303
republicanism of, 350–352
"Revolution of 1800" and, **349–
350**
road projects sponsored by, 388
on slavery, **176**, 181, 374, 443
Washington's presidency and, 316,
351
westward migration and, 493
Jesuit missionaries, 146(i), 147
Jews, 303(i)
colonial immigration by, 138
Father Coughlin's broadcasts on,
950
Holocaust and, 1004–1005
immigration in the nineteenth
century by, 669, 670, 671–672,
676, 736, 754
party politics and, 712

progressive reform and, 801, 805
ratification of the Constitution and,
302
Jim Crow laws, 668, 836–837
Jingoism, 789
Job Corps, 1107, 1110
Jobs. *See* Employment; Work
Johnson, Andrew (1808–1875), 597,
605, 622(i)
background of, 614
black codes during reconstruction
and, **615–617**
impeachment of, 622–623
Lincoln's death and, 614
reconstruction program of, **614–615**
slavery and, 615
Johnson, Hugh, 946, 947
Johnson, James Weldon (1871–1938),
908
Johnson, Lyndon B. (1908–1973), 1099,
1126
civil rights movement and, 1119–
1122
election of 1964 and, 1107–1110
election of 1968 and, 1161–1163,
1161(i)
Great Society programs of, **1106–
1113**, 1108(t)
Kennedy presidency and, 1100, 1101
rise in politics by, 1106, 1107(i)
Vietnam and, 1138, 1147–1155
Johnson, Richard M., 422
Johnson, Thomas Lofton, 678, 812,
812(i)
Johnson, William, 202, 204
Johnston, Albert Sidney, 574
Johnston, Joseph E., 572, 593
Jones, Thomas Catesby, 502
Jones, William ("Billy"), 728, 738
Jordan, Barbara, 1120, **1175–1176**,
1176(i), 1177
Judicial review, 355
Judiciary, John Adams's appointments
to, 352–354
Judiciary Act of 1789, 353, 354–355
Judiciary Act of 1801, 353, 355
Jungle, The (Sinclair), 817

Kamikaze pilots, 1013, 1014(i)
Kansas, 776–777, 965
farmers' protests in, 766, 767, 768,
769(i)
homesteading in, 644(i), 647, 648,
649, 650(m)
slavery issues and, 540–543
Kansas City, 677, 725
Kansas-Nebraska Act (1854), 532–534,
534(m), 546
Kaskaskia Indians, 331(i)
Kearney, Stephen Watts, 511
Keaton, Buster (1895–1966), 904

Louisiana *(Cont.)*:
slavery in, 434, 444
sugar cultivation in, 437–438
Louisiana Purchase, 347, 354(m), **355–356**, 535
Lowell, Massachusetts, mill workers, 392, 393, 393(i)
Lower East Side, New York City, 671–672, 673, 676
Loyalists, 246, 256, 257(m), 270, 288
British strategy and, 253, 257–259, 272
in southern states, 258, 259, 266, 268
Luce, Henry R. (1898–1967), 1032
Lumber production, in the South, 438(m), 440, 654
Lusitania (passenger liner), sinking of, 851–852, 851(i)
Luther, Martin (1483–1546), 66, 116, 185
Lutheran Church, 138, 163, 408
Lyceum, 406
Lynching, 971
of African Americans, 911(i), 1040, 1089
of gold miners, 504
Wells's campaign against, 764–766
Lynd, Robert and Helen, 900–901
Lyon, Mary, 404
Lyons, Maritcha, 766

MacArthur, Douglas (1880–1964), 950, 1033, 1152
Bonus Army marchers and, 931, 932
Korean War and United Nations, 1051
World War II and, 989, 990, 1012, 1013
Macmillan, Harold, 1140
Macune, C. W., 770, 779
Macy's department store, 739, 740
Madden, Willis, 457(i)
Madison, James (1751–1836), 232, 314, 319, 336, 349, 352, 379, 395
background of, 296
Continental Congress and, 241, 282
debates over Alien and Sedition Acts and, 339(i), 341
drafting and ratification of the Constitution and, **296–297**, 297(i), 299, 300, 301
election of 1808 and, 360–361
embargoes of British trade and, 360, 361, 363
Hamilton's plan for the public debt and, 327
location of the nation's capital and, **324–325**
passage of the Bill of Rights and, 316, 317

religious liberty and, 302–303
road projects sponsored by, 388
War of 1812 and, 365(i)
Magdalen Societies, 411
Magellan, Ferdinand, 45–46
Maginot Line, 985
Mail service, 422
growth of (1790–1820), 323(t)
transportation improvement in the nineteenth century and, 387
Maine
alcoholic beverage legislation in, 486
cession of western lands (1782–1802) and, 281(m)
colonial settlement of, 119, 123(m)
ratification of the Constitution and, 306(m)
Maine (battleship), sinking of (1898), 791
Malcolm, John, 222(i), 223
Malinali (Marina), 48, 49(i)
Mallory, Stephen R., 570
Management, and cult of efficiency, 811–812
Managers, 737
ethnic prejudices and, 728
in the nineteenth century, 738
scientific management principles and, 811–812, 898–900
Manassas (Bull Run), battles of
first, 571–572
second, 572
Manchuria, Japanese invasion of (1931), 823, 978, 980, 987(m)
Manhattan Island, purchase of, 135
Manhattan Project, 1014
Manifest Destiny, 493–495, 502, 532
Manila
capture of (1898), 791–794, 791(m)
in World War II, 989
Mann-Elkins Act (1910), 804
Manpower Development and Training Act (1962), 1103
Manufacturing
assembly line and mass production in, 897, 898, 1076
Civil War and, 587(i)
Clay's plan for, 388, 503
in the eighteenth century, 182
Hamilton's plan for, 328, 392
introduction of steam in, 474
mechanization in, 477–478, 588
natural resources and products manufactured (1865–1900), 726(m)
production of consumer goods (1920–1930) and, 899(f)
shift in the country after the Civil War and, 690
tariffs of 1828 and, 397–398
women workers in, 392–394, 731, 732(f)

Manumission of slaves, in the South, 289
Mao Zedong (1893–1976), 1032–1033, 1033(i)
Mapmaking, exploration and changes in, 44–47
Maps
American colonies at the end of the seventeenth century, 143(m)
American Expeditionary Force (1917–1918), 867(m)
American Revolution, war in the North (1775–1778), 254–255(m)
American Revolution, war in the South, 265(m)
Atlantic slave trade, 175(m)
Atlantic trade in the eighteenth century, 168(m)
auto manufacturing, 897(m)
Axis aggression to 1941, 984(m)
Battle of Bunker Hill (1775), 244(m)
Carolina and the West Indies in the seventeenth century, 104(m)
cession of western lands (1782–1802), 281(m)
Chesapeake colonies in the seventeenth century, 96(m)
Civil War, 1861–1862, 573(m)
Civil War, 1863–1865, 591(m)
Compromise of 1850, 527(m)
continental drift, 6(m)
cotton in the South (1820–1860), 431(m)
division of Europe after World War II, 1025(m)
Eastern Europe (1989–1992), 1248(m)
economic regions of the world, 728(m)
election of 1800, 350(m)
election of 1824, 376(m)
election of 1828, 399(m)
election of 1848, 523(m)
election of 1860, 552(m)
election of 1864, 598(m)
election of 1876, 639(m)
election of 1884, 715(m)
election of 1892, 780(m)
election of 1896, 783(m)
election of 1912, 827(m)
election of 1920, 890(m)
election of 1932, 937(m)
election of 1948, 1043(m)
election of 1960, 1101(m)
election of 1968, 1162(m)
election of 1976, 1201(m)
election of 1984, 1226(m)
election of 1996, 1264(m)
electoral shift (1928–1932), 938(m)
Europe after World War I, 875(m)
European alliances after the outbreak of World War I, 850(m)